WORLD FILM DIRECTORS
Volume I
1890–1945

Biographical Reference Books from
The H. W. Wilson Company

American Reformers

Greek and Latin Authors 800 B.C.–A.D. 1000
European Authors 1000–1900
British Authors Before 1800
British Authors of the Nineteenth Century
American Authors 1600–1900
Twentieth Century Authors
Twentieth Century Authors: First Supplement
World Authors 1950–1970
World Authors 1970–1975
World Authors 1975–1980

The Junior Book of Authors
More Junior Authors
Third Book of Junior Authors
Fourth Book of Junior Authors and Illustrators
Fifth Book of Junior Authors and Illustrators

Great Composers: 1300–1900
Composers Since 1900
Composers Since 1900: First Supplement
Musicians Since 1900
American Songwriters

Nobel Prize Winners

World Artists 1950–1980

World Film Directors: Volumes I, II

WORLD FILM DIRECTORS
Volume I
1890–1945

Editor
JOHN WAKEMAN

THE H. W. WILSON COMPANY

NEW YORK

1987

PRINTED IN THE UNITED STATES OF AMERICA

Library of Congress Cataloging-in-Publication Data

World film directors.

    Contents: v. 1. 1890–1945.
    1. Moving-picture producers and directors—
Biography—Dictionaries. I. Wakeman, John.
PN1998.2.W67   1987   791.43'0233'0922 [B]   87–29569
ISBN 0–8242–0757–2 (v. 1)

CONTENTS

DIRECTORS

DIRECTORS INCLUDED IN VOLUME II

Chantal Akerman
Robert Aldrich
Tomás Gutiérrez Alea
Woody Allen
Robert Altman
Santiago Alvarez
Lindsay Anderson
Theodoros Angelopoulos
Michelangelo Antonioni
Hal Ashby
Alexandre Astruc
Richard Attenborough
Marco Bellocchio
Shyam Benegal
Robert Benton
Bruce Beresford
Ingmar Bergman
Luis García Berlanga
Bernardo Bertolucci
Bertrand Blier
Peter Bogdanovich
Sergei Bondarchuk
John Boorman
Walerian Borowczyk
Stan Brakhage
Philippe De Broca
Mel Brooks
Richard Brooks
Kevin Brownlow
Michael Cacoyannis
Henning Carlsen
John Carpenter
John Cassavetes
Claude Chabrol
Youssef Chahine
Grigori Chukrai
Věra Chytilová
Michael Cimino
Shirley Clarke
Jack Clayton
Francis Coppola
Roger Corman
Constantin Costa-Gavras
Michael Crichton
André Delvaux
Jonathan Demme
Jacques Demy
Brian De Palma
Michel Deville
Stanley Donen
Clive Donner
Jörn Donner
Marguerite Duras
Clint Eastwood

Blake Edwards
Jean Eustache
Zoltán Fábri
R. W. Fassbinder
Federico Fellini
Marco Ferreri
Bryan Forbes
Milos Forman
Bill Forsyth
Georges Franju
John Frankenheimer
William Friedkin
Sam Fuller
István Gaál
Ritwik Ghatak
Jean-Luc Godard
Claude Goretta
Yilmaz Güney
Bert Haanstra
Wojciech Has
Monte Hellman
Werner Herzog
George Roy Hill
Walter Hill
King Hu
Kon Ichikawa
Shohei Imamura
James Ivory
Miklós Jancsó
Vojtěch Jasný
Norman Jewison
Claude Jutra
Jan Kadár
Philip Kaufman
Mani Kaul
Jerzy Kawalerowicz
Elia Kazan
Gene Kelly
Burt Kennedy
Irvin Kershner
Elmar Klos
Alexander Kluge
Masaki Kobayashi
András Kovács
Stanley Kramer
Stanley Kubrick
Albert Lamorisse
John Landis
Richard Leacock
Jean-Pierre Lefebvre
Claude Lelouch
Sergio Leone
Richard Lester
Jerry Lewis
Ken Loach

Joseph Losey
George Lucas
Sidney Lumet
Ida Lupino
David K. Lynch
Alexander Mackendrick
Dušan Makavejev
Terrence Malick
Louis Malle
Delbert Mann
Chris Marker
Albert Maysles
David Maysles
Paul Mazursky
Dariush Mehrjui
Jean-Pierre Melville
Jiří Menzel
Márta Mészáros
Nikita Mikhalkov
Mario Monicelli
Robert Mulligan
Andrzej Munk
Jan Němec
Mike Nichols
Ermanno Olmi
Marcel Ophuls
Nagisa Oshima
Alan J. Pakula
Gleb Panfilov
Sergei Paradjanov
Alan Parker
Pier Paolo Pasolini
Ivan Passer
Sam Peckinpah
Arthur Penn
Nelson Pereira dos Santos
Lester James Peries
Elio Petri
Maurice Pialat
Roman Polanski
Sydney Pollack
Abraham Polonsky
Gillo Pontecorvo
Richard Quine
Bob Rafelson
Nicholas Ray
Satyajit Ray
Karel Reisz
Edgar Reitz
Alain Resnais
Tony Richardson
Dino Risi
Michael Ritchie
Martin Ritt
Jacques Rivette

Glauber Rocha
Nicolas Roeg
Lionel Rogosin
Eric Rohmer
Francesco Rosi
Jean Rouch
Raúl Ruiz
Ken Russell
Helma Sanders-Brahms
Jorge Sanjinés
Carlos Saura
Claude Sautet
John Sayles
John Schlesinger
Volker Schlöndorff
Evald Schorm
Paul Schrader
Martin Scorsese
Ousmane Sembène
Mrinal Sen
Larissa Shepitko
Kaneto Shindo
Masahiro Shinoda
Vasili Shuksin
Joan Micklin Silver
Jerzy Skolimowski
Michael Snow
Steven Spielberg
Jean-Marie Straub
Joseph Strick
Hans Jürgen Syberberg
István Szabó
Alain Tanner
Andrei Tarkovsky
Frank Tashlin
Jacques Tati
Bertrand Tavernier
Paolo Taviani
Leopoldo Torre Nilsson
Jan Troell
Margarethe Von Trotta
François Truffaut
Roger Vadim
Agnès Varda
Andrzej Wajda
Andy Warhol
Peter Weir
Wim Wenders
Lina Wertmüller
Bo Widerberg
Frederick Wiseman
Peter Yates
Krzysztof Zanussi
Mai Zetterling

PREFACE

This book provides introductions to the work and lives of about four hundred of the world's best-known film directors, from the beginning of cinema to the present. It is arranged in two volumes: directors born before 1920 and well launched on their careers before 1945 are treated in the first volume; more recent figures appear in Volume II. A list of all the directors covered in Volume II may be found on page ix.

World Film Directors is an attempt to do for filmmakers what *Twentieth Century Authors, World Authors,* and other works in the Wilson Company's Authors Series do for writers. Except for a few signed articles, the book makes no claims to original research, simply bringing together in one place information previously scattered through many reference books, monographs, histories, biographies, critical essays, reviews, and interviews.

Assembling the information in these articles was difficult—especially because films, unlike books, involve their directors in crucial collaborations with other artists and technicians. Providing what *Twentieth Century Authors* called "a fair summation of representative critical response" proved, in the case of filmmakers, to be even more difficult. Since (at least) the advent of the *Cahiers* critics, reputations have soared or plummeted with sobering abruptness, and almost every director of note is currently being scrutinized and reappraised from a great variety of critical positions. We have charted this dizzying flux as comprehensively and objectively as time, space, and patience allowed.

Most of the directors in this book did not expect their films to be analyzed frame by frame, but to stand or fall on the basis of single viewing by a congregation of tired or amorous or otherwise distracted individuals in a darkened movie theatre; this is one reason why we have recorded not only the deliberations of academic critics but the spontaneous responses of good reviewers.

World Film Directors is intended primarily for students and moviegoers, though scholars may find it useful to have so much information about so many directors available in a single book (in a single *volume* was the intention; during eight years of preparation, *World Film Directors* imposed its own dimensions). To keep this project to a manageable size, we have interpreted "directors" rather strictly and excluded figures who are best known as animators or producers.

In selecting directors for inclusion from the whole history of world cinema, we have favored those films that can be seen in the United States (where the book was published), in Britain (where it was edited), and in other English-speaking countries. This has meant that the emerging or flourishing cinemas of the Third World have perhaps received less attention than they deserve. It is the absence of Chinese directors that we most regret, since Chinese films are now becoming accessible to Western viewers and have been a revelation. Our plans to include at least a few of the most admired Chinese directors were undone by lack of reliable information, but this omission will be remedied as soon as possible in *WFD*'s first revision or supplement.

A few of the articles that follow are preceded by first-person statements contributed by the directors themselves. Each article is accompanied by a filmography and a brief bibliography of books and essays. The filmographies, except in a few specified cases, are complete—or as complete as present scholarship allows. Titles are given in the original languages, and generally in English as well. These translated titles are normally those that were adopted on release in English-speaking countries, but in some cases, failing to find any such, we have supplied a direct translation of the original title. The date given for each film is the year of first release, except where otherwise specified.

Film scholarship is still in its infancy, and the existing literature bristles with dubious and contradictory information. Our attempts to resolve such conflicts and to correct errors that have become part of cinema mythology have added years to the book's gestation period. Even so, it would be foolish to claim it as any more than a preliminary mapping of what solid ground can be discerned. Most of the research was done at the library of the British Film Institute in London, to whose able, agreeable, and often inspired staff we owe an immense debt of gratitude. Thanks are also due to the staffs of the film libraries at Lincoln Center and the Museum of Modern Art in New York, at Syracuse University, and at the Cinémathèque Française and the Centre André Malraux in Paris, for invaluable assistance in the later stages of the project.

J.W.
August 1987

CONTRIBUTORS

M.A.	Michael Adams	An.L.	Alan Lovell
S.A.	Steven Anzovin	D.McV.	Douglas McVay
P.A.	Patricia Aufderheide	S.A.MacQ.	Scott A. MacQueen
B.B.	Brian Baxter	G.M.	Gerald Mast
K.B.	Konstantin Bazarov	J.J.M.	John J. Michalczyk
W.L.B.	William L. Bischoff	J.M.	James Monaco
S.B.	Stephen Bottomore	C.M.	Charles Musser
K.C.	Kingsley Canham	R.P.	Richard Peña
S.C.	Sumita Chakravarty	J.P.	Jim Pines
V.C.	Valerie Cossey	D.P.	Derek Prouse
D.DeN.	Dennis DeNitto	H.A.R.	Howard A. Rodman
P.D.	Patricia Dowell	M.R.	Miriam Rosen
T.E.	Thomas Elsaesser	P.R.	Patrizio Rossi
S.F.	Simon Field	L.R.	Lenny Rubenstein
J.A.G.	John A. Gallagher	R.S.	Roy Sherwood
T.G.	Teresa Grimes	A.E.S.	Amy E. Slaton
G.H.	Gillian Hartnoll	Mk.S.	Mike Steer
L.H.	Liz Heron	M.S.	Michael Szporer
K.J.	Karen Jaehne	F.T.	Frank Thompson
P.K.	Philip Kemp	D.T.	Doris Toumarkine
R.K.	Richard Koszarski	A.T.	Andrew Tudor
C.L.	Christopher Lambert	Ad.T.	Adrian Turner
S.L.	Stuart Liebman	D.W.	David Williams
A.L.	Albert Lindauer		

KEY TO PRONUNCIATION

ā āle

â câre

a add

ä ärm

ē ēve

e end

g go

î ice

i ill

κ German *ch* as in *ich* (iκ)

N Not pronounced, but in-
dicates the nasal tone of
the preceding vowel, as
in the French *bon* (bôN)

ō ōld

ô ôrb

o odd

oi oil

o̅o̅ ooze

o͝o fo͝ot

ou out

th then

th thin

ū cūbe

û ûrn; French eu, as in *jeu*
(zhû), German ö, *oe*, as
in *schön* (shûn),
Goethe (gû´te)

u tub

ü Pronounced approxi-
mately as ē, with
rounded lips: French

u, as in *menu*
(me-nü); German ü,
as in *grün*

ə the schwa, an un-
stressed vowel rep-
resenting the sound
that is spelled
a as in sofa
e as in fitted
i as in edible
o as in melon
u as in circus

zh azure

´ = main accent

˝ = secondary accent

WORLD FILM DIRECTORS
Volume I
1890–1945

ARZNER, DOROTHY (January 3, 1897–October 1, 1979), American director, editor, and scenarist, was born in San Francisco and grew up in Los Angeles, where her father, Louis Arzner, owned a well-known Hollywood restaurant, the Hoffman Café. Dark-paneled, gently lighted, and intimate, the Hoffman featured a round table at which gathered stage celebrities from the theatre next door and filmmakers and actors of the caliber of D. W. Griffith, William S. Hart, James Cruze, Mack Sennett, Charlie Chaplin, Erich von Stroheim, Hal Roach, and Douglas Fairbanks. Arzner has said that her friends always predicted a movie career for her because she apparently loved actors, but that she "didn't love them. I was afraid of them. They were always tossing me up in the air."

Growing up in this environment and unimpressed by it, Dorothy Arzner was drawn by contrast to a career in medicine. When she left the Westlake School she began pre-med studies at the University of Southern California, taking courses also in history of art and architecture. A summer spent working in a surgeon's office raised doubts about her medical vocation. World War I had begun and Arzner signed up as an ambulance driver. Though she never left the United States, the experience was exciting and unsettling enough to turn her conclusively away from further studies. She began to look for other work and even to consider the movie career that had been predicted for her.

With the war over, Hollywood was moving into high gear, and the flu pandemic increased the demand for workers of all kinds. Sometime in 1919, Dorothy Arzner secured an appointment to meet William DeMille, Cecil's older brother, at the Famous Players–Lasky Corporation studios—soon to become Paramount. DeMille gave her a week to familiarize herself with the workings of the studios. "I watched the four companies that were working," she said, "particularly that of Cecil B. DeMille. And I remember making the observation, 'If one was going to be in this movie business, one should be

DOROTHY ARZNER

a director because he was the one who told everyone what to do.'"

However, by the end of the week Arzner had come to the conclusion that everything was "grounded in the script"; she told William DeMille that she wanted to start at the bottom as a typist in the script department. She was taken on at $15 a week, showing so much ability that within months she was promoted to script supervisor. Arzner said years later that it was as a typist and script girl that she learned most about film structure—a basic education that stood her in good stead when, soon afterwards, she began to train as an assistant cutter.

"In those days," Arzner said, "there were no Moviolas or machinery. Everything was done by hand. The film was read and cut over an eight-by-ten-inch box set in the table, covered by frosted glass and a light bulb underneath. The film pieces were placed over a small sprocketed plate, overlapped, and scraped about 1/16th of an inch, dabbed with glue, and pressed by hand."

Arzner rapidly mastered these techniques and in 1921 was assigned to Realart Studios, a Paramount subsidiary, as chief editor. In the course of a year she cut and edited fifty-two pictures—one a week—at the same time training and supervising negative cutters and splicers. In 1922 she was recalled to Paramount to earn her first credit as editor of Fred Niblo's *Blood and Sand*. She is said to have saved $50,000 (and possibly Rudolph Valentino's health) by creating the brilliant bullfight scenes out of stock footage, with matching shots of Valentino in action.

James Cruze was so impressed that he took her on as editor of his epic Western *The Covered Wagon* (1923), shot on location in the deserts of the Great Basin. She shared the extraordinary rigors and dangers of the filming and (benefiting from the advice of her grandfather, a former miner who told her never to drink desert water) was almost the only member of the crew to escape dysentery. By the mid-1920s Arzner was established as "the best cutter in the business"—indeed, the historian Kevin Brownlow writes that she was "the only editor from the entire silent period to be officially remembered." At about the same time, she wrote or coauthored her first scenarios for movies like *The Breed of the Border* (1924), *Inez From Hollywood* (1924), *The No-Gun Man* (1924), Walter Lang's *Red Kimono* (1925), William Wellman's *When Husbands Flirt* (1925), and Cruze's *Old Ironsides* (1926).

By this time Arzner was impatient to embark on her own career as a director but saw no hope of this at Paramount. Harry Cohn at Columbia—then a "poverty row" company—offered her a chance, and she told B. P. Schulberg that she was leaving Paramount. The production chief was so eager to retain her services that he capitulated. He handed her a French stage farce by Armond and Marchand, telling her to turn it into a movie "and get yourself on the set in two weeks." With Percy Heath, Jules Furthman, and Herman J. Mankiewicz as scenarists and adaptors, she met this deadline, shot thirty set-ups on her first day, and brought the film in well ahead of schedule as *Fashions for Women* (1927). It was only years later that Arzner confessed the panic she felt when she first faced a crowd of extras. For ten days she was so nervous that she couldn't eat, but then a friend forced her to sit through the rushes shot the previous day by all the Paramount directors, and she lost her fear in the realization that her own work was as good as the others'. At this crucial stage in her career, she later maintained, "no one gave me trouble because I was a woman. Men were more helpful than women."

Fashions for Women stars Esther Ralston as an enterprising cigarette girl who makes her way to the top of the Parisian fashion world by masquerading as a famous *modiste*—a bogus empress in new clothes who successfully dupes the foolish men around her. It was described as a triumph for its "star and woman director," and was followed by two more lightweight comedies, *Ten Modern Commandments* (1927), again starring Esther Ralston, and *Get Your Man* (1927), based on another *boulevard* stage piece, in which the man that Clara Bow gets is a French aristocrat (Charles Rogers) with whom she spends a night locked in a wax museum.

A story by Ernest Vajda provided the basis for *Manhattan Cocktail* (1928) which, though it had no dialogue, introduced music and sound effects. With Nancy Carroll and Richard Arlen in the lead, this movie, according to Francine Parker, turns "the entire island of Manhattan into the Isle of Crete, replete with impresario Paul Lukas as predatory Minotaur." In 1928 the Swiss publication *Close-Up* commented that "Dorothy Arzner, in her so-far brief career as a director, has already won an established reputation and a following of discriminating admirers . . . and promises to become an increasingly important factor in the evolution of cinema technique."

Arzner's first talkie followed in 1929: *The Wild Party*, a sound remake of a silent that she had edited in 1923. Adapted from Warner Fabian's *Unforbidden Fruit* and photographed by Victor Milner, it has Clara Bow as a headstrong college girl who forms a scandalous society of "hard-boiled maidens" to make nighttime visits to men's colleges and speakeasies. Arzner took Fredric March from the stage to play the maidens' professor and is also credited by some historians with another significant innovation in this picture—finding her actors' movements restricted by the stationary microphones, she told her sound man to attach them to fishing rods, thus casually inventing the "fish-pole mike."

"From her first feature," according to Gerald Peary, "Arzner sides time and again with her dashing, flashy, women-on-the-go characters against the shallow, conceited male characters who try to run women's lives." But, Peary goes on, Arzner also expands "her horizons to equal support for all manifestations of womanhood," including the "'womanly women' who also populate her movies." One such is Sarah Storm in *Sarah and Son* (1930), a German immigrant whose child has been stolen from her, who eventually finds him again, and then has to struggle to recover him from his wealthy foster parents. Adapted from a novel by Timothy Shea, this was the first of several Arzner movies scripted by Zoe

Akins. It made an international star of Ruth Chatterton, formerly a stage actress, and was a smash hit, putting Dorothy Arzner in the forefront of Paramount directors.

In 1930 Arzner made uncredited contributions to two films attributed to Robert Milton, *Behind the Makeup* and *Charming Sinners* (called *The Constant Wife* in Britain, and based on Somerset Maugham's play). She explained that Milton, a fine theatre director, knew nothing about film technique: "He directed the performances. I blocked the scenes for camera and editing." The same year Arzner filmed "The Gallows Song" as her contribution to *Paramount on Parade,* designed as a showcase for the stars, directors, and technical resources of what was then indeed the paramount studio. *Anybody's Woman* (1930), with Ruth Chatterton, Clive Brook, and Paul Lukas, centers on a chorus girl who marries an alcoholic lawyer when he is drunk and then finds herself spurned by his snobbish small-town friends. Admired for its witty and experimental use of sound effects, it was another box-office hit. After that, Arzner said, "Paramount gave me about everything I wanted."

There is evidence of this in *Honor Among Lovers* (1931), which introduced Ginger Rogers in her first small screen role—a dumb blonde in pursuit of a millionaire. Rogers had been starring on Broadway in *Girl Crazy,* but Arzner "saw her and liked her" and Paramount hired her: "I imagine they offered her much money." Austin Parker's script is about a secretary (Claudette Colbert) with a playboy boss (Fredric March). She effectively runs his business for him but refuses his offer of marriage and winds up with another man, who gambles everything on the stockmarket and loses. The happy ending has the heroine reconciled with her boss and setting off with him on an ocean voyage—still married to the other man.

Asked if there had been resistance to such a risqué outcome, Arzner explained that she "had very little interference with her pictures and when there was she usually had her way: 'You see, I was not dependent on the movies for my living, so I was always ready to give the picture over to another director if I couldn't make it the way I saw it.'" John Gillett has said that the film's early scenes "benefit from excellent scripting and the neatly-turned, relaxed playing of both Colbert and March, and it is interesting to see how Arzner sketches in their motivations and shows how the heroine wavers between the obvious charms yet uncertain qualities of the March character and the rather ordinary, even boorish, character of the man she eventually mar-

ries. . . . The fact that the film somehow fails to convince and cohere towards the end is due to some awkwardly placed melodramatics and the inadequate playing of Monroe Owsley as the husband."

The least successful of the movies Arzner made during the 1930s was *Working Girls* (1931), from another script by Zoe Akins (based on a play by Vera Caspary and Winifred Lenihan). It follows and contrasts the fortunes of two young women trying to make their way in New York: Mae (Dorothy Hall), a natural victim who is forced to make a hasty marriage after she is seduced and made pregnant, and Judith (June Thorpe), who deliberately exploits her sexuality to "get her man." A comedy with tragic overtones, it was called "preposterous and unreal" by contemporary reviewers. Arzner herself thought it ahead of its time, and a recent critic, Francine Parker, calling it a "real sleeper of a movie," praises its deep-focus photography by Harry Fishbeck and says (of this film and its successor) that "one cannot but be impressed by Arzner's innovative use of sound; the juxtaposition of sound and image; her eloquent overlappings and segues; her remarkable early use also of continuously running theme music." It has been seen as a sketch for the later *Dance, Girl, Dance.*

Another sad comedy followed, the Lubitschian *Merrily We Go to Hell* (1932), wittily scripted by Edwin Justin Mayer from a story by Cleo Lucas. Joan Prentice (Sylvia Sidney), an insecure young heiress, falls in love with Gerry Corbett (Fredric March), an alcoholic journalist and would-be dramatist. Over her father's resistance they marry, but Gerry leaves Joan for another woman. Joan takes to drink herself and looks around for another man, but in the end, after she has lost Gerry's baby in childbirth, they are reconciled.

The revival of interest in Arzner's work that began in the 1970s has been mainly along feminist lines, and *Merrily We Go to Hell* is one of the pictures discussed at some length in two essays by Claire Johnston and Pam Cook in *The Work of Dorothy Arzner: Towards a Feminist Cinema.* As an immensely successful woman director in the male stronghold of Hollywood, Arzner's own career belongs of course on any feminist role of honor, and many (but not all) of her films can be seen as celebrations of the courage, independence, ingenuity, or initiative of her heroines. Arzner herself disclaimed any feminist intentions, however, and those who attribute such qualities to her work have tended to find their evidence in semiological analyses of the form and structure of her films, as much as in their content. "I want my work to be judged on its merits," she insisted, "Why should I be pointed out as a strange creature because I happen to be the only woman director? Intelligence has no sex."

Thus, *Merrily We Go to Hell* is described by Johnston and Cook as episodic—"a series of tableaux"—and Pam Cook in particular examines some of these "tableaux" to show how Arzner, "through a displacement of identification, through discontinuity and a process of play," generates "a set of contradictions" which call in question "the patriarchal ideology of classic Hollywood cinema." Both essayists refer to the marriage sequence, in which Gerry hands Joan a corkscrew in place of a wedding ring; it is, as Claire Johnston writes, "a token of Gerry's inebriated past and an omen for the future," as well as an example of the way in which "the universe of the male . . . is rendered strange" so that "the discourse of the male can no longer function as the dominant one." Later, when Joan, having lost her baby, takes Gerry in her arms and calls *him* "my baby," Pam Cook sees "an example of the use of ironic reversal to open up contradictions rather than present a closure. . . . The image of reconciliation, unity, plenitude is shot through with connotations of death, loss, and absence."

In 1932, Arzner left Paramount to widen her horizons as a freelance. Her first assignment was *Christopher Strong* (1933), made for David Selznick at RKO. Another Zoe Akins script, adapted from a novel by Gilbert Frankau, it was planned as an Ann Harding vehicle. She was taken out because of contract problems, and Arzner substituted Katherine Hepburn, rescuing her from "a Tarzan-type picture" (and literally from its set, where Arzner found her "up a tree with a leopard skin on"). Hepburn plays Lady Cynthia Darrington, a famous British flyer who falls in love with a married man, Sir Christopher Strong (Colin Clive). He urges her to give up her dangerous vocation, and in a brilliantly suggestive bedroom scene, undone by love, she agrees. But her hunger to fly again grows and at last, finding herself pregnant and realizing that the relationship is socially impossible, she makes one more flight—a successful bid for the world altitude record—before ending her life.

Claire Johnston sees this tragic ending as a typical "refusal of unification and closure, and a resolution instead to play out the discourse of the woman to the bitter end," while Martyn Auty calls the film "a fascinatingly compromised work . . . within a narrative that functions as a fortuitous metaphor" for the movie industry (male-dominated, like flying). Arzner herself said that her main interest was in her hero; dis-

missed by feminists as an "all-consuming chauvinist," he seemed to the director "a man 'on the cross.' He loved his wife, and he fell in love with the aviatrix. He was on a rack. I was really more sympathetic with him, but no one seemed to pick that up. Of course, not too many women are sympathetic about the torture the situation might give to a man of upright character."

Earlier critics were full of praise for *Christopher Strong*. Gilbert Frankau came away delighted by the authenticity of the atmosphere, "feeling the picture had been made in England," and another writer commended the way Hepburn had been "directed to a terrific quietness and intensity which I think she has never since reached." There was also much admiration for Arzner's direction of Billie Burke, who gave what some considered her best performance as Strong's priggish, cruelly inhibited wife.

Sam Goldwyn thought *Christopher Strong* "the best picture of the year" and on the strength of it hired Arzner to direct *Nana* (1934), an adaptation of Zola's novel about the Paris demimonde in the 1880s. Goldwyn wanted a prestigious vehicle in which to launch his discovery and protegée Anna Sten, the Russian actress who he hoped would rival Garbo. The film had Gregg Toland as cinematographer and songs by Rodgers and Hart, but Anna Sten showed no proclivity for greatness and Arzner said "the only thing I could do was not let her talk so much."

The director discovered a more satisfactory star for her next picture, *Craig's Wife* (1936), made for Columbia and based on George Kelly's stage play. Rosalind Russell, until then a bit player, was reportedly so terrified that she offered to surrender a year's salary if she could be spared the assignment, but took it in the end and earned an Oscar nomination. The film is a study of a middle-class housewife who takes "the cult of domesticity to its logical conclusion . . . sacrificing everything and everyone for material security, order, and cleanliness." With a cast that included John Boles, Billie Burke, Jane Darwell, and Thomas Mitchell, this was one of the most successful of all Arzner's movies.

Claire Johnston regards *Craig's Wife* as a sort of early *Jeanne Dielman*, subverting and dislocating the male-established conventions of plot and development: "Here, the rituals of housework and the obsession with order acquire, as the film progresses, a definite validity, and it is evidence of people living and breathing in the house which is rendered strange. The marks of a trunk having been pulled along the floor or someone having sat on a bed acquire a sinister meaning within the text of the film."

Joan Crawford, who greatly admired *Craig's Wife*, subsequently starred in a remake, *Harriet Craig* (1950). And it was she (perhaps at her own request) who took the lead role in Arzner's next movie, *The Bride Wore Red* (1937). This derived from a Molnar play about a prostitute who is taken up by a Pygmalion-like aristocrat to prove that anyone, appropriately dressed and groomed, can enter high society. The film was to have starred Luise Rainer, but MGM substituted Crawford and presented Arzner with a lightweight adaptation of the text (by Tess Slesinger and Bradbury Foote) and with lavish sets that she used only reluctantly. She herself considered the result synthetic and unsatisfactory. The same year Arzner made an uncredited contribution to Richard Boleslawsky's version of Lonsdale's *The Last of Mrs. Cheyney*, also starring Crawford (who became a close friend).

None of Arzner's films has been so thoroughly discussed and analyzed as *Dance, Girl, Dance* (1940), adapted by Tess Slesinger and Frank Davis from the novel by Vicki Baum. The picture was the pet project of Eric Pommer, then a producer at RKO. Finding after a week's shooting that his conception was being destroyed by the original director, he brought in Arzner, who extensively reworked the script. As completed, the film tells the story of two young dancers in a troupe managed by the dedicated Madame Basilova (Maria Ouspenskaya); Bubbles (Lucille Ball) is a vamp, primarily interested in men as the source of money and power, while Judy (Maureen O'Hara) is an aspiring ballet dancer seeking artistic self-fulfillment. Bubbles gets a job as a burlesque dancer and takes Judy on as her stooge—the first in a series of humiliations from which Judy is finally rescued by an impresario (Ralph Bellamy) who has recognized her talent and will train her to be a great dancer.

Ann Laemmle sees the film as the story of Judy's progress to humanity and maturity, even though she reaches maturity "only to end up in the arms of a man who cradles her like a child." Pam Cook, however, maintains that "it would be a mistake to read the film in 'positive' terms as representing the progress of its heroine to 'maturity' or 'self-awareness.' The value of the film lies not in its creation of a culture-heroine with whom we can finally and fully identify, but in the ways in which it *displaces* identification with the characters and focuses our attention on the problematic position they occupy in their world."

By way of illustration, Cook describes the scene in the burlesque house when Judy turns on her audience of voyeurs and in a furious speech "fixes them in relation to *her* critical look," reversing "the ideology of woman as spectacle, ob-

ject of their desire." But the standing ovation she receives redefines "Judy's speech *as* a performance" and is followed by a sexually exciting catfight between Judy and Bubbles. And in the "final ironic reversal Judy 'gets what she wants' at the expense of any pretensions to 'independence.'" In Cook's view, Arzner has set forth the story in a way that emphasizes "the contradiction between women's desire for self-expression and culture, and the cultural processes which articulate a place for woman as spectacle." The Johnston and Cook essays have themselves been discussed in *Jump Cut* (12/13 1976) by another feminist writer, E. Ann Kaplan. She applauds their work but disagrees with some of their conclusions, suggesting that they make "rather extravagant claims for Arzner as a revolutionary filmmaker."

During World War II Dorothy Arzner made a number of training films for the Women's Army Corps and in 1943 returned to Columbia to direct *First Comes Courage*, an unexceptional war film about the Norwegian underground starring Merle Oberon and Brian Aherne. The final scenes were filmed by another director after Arzner contracted pneumonia. She was seriously ill for almost a year and decided when she recovered that she would make no more movies: "I had had enough—twenty years of directing, I think, is about enough." She sold her Hollywood estate and retired to the desert to cultivate her garden.

Dorothy Arzner was not entirely lost to the cinema during the thirty-six years of her retirement. She began the first filmmaking course at the Pasadena Playhouse on a nonexistent budget, working with a single camera and a tape recorder. She made over fifty Pepsi commercials for her friend Joan Crawford. And she returned to teaching for four years during the 1960s at UCLA, where Francis Coppola was her "most promising" student, if "rather eccentric." At the 1975 Directors Guild of America tribute to Arzner (its first woman member), Coppola recalled her impact on him: "Everywhere you went was this negative thing. . . . this was the first time in my life someone had said something encouraging." In her last years she was at work on an ambitious historical novel about the settling of Los Angeles. She died at the age of eighty-two at La Quinta, near Palm Springs, where she had spent the last part of her life.

Ann Laemmle writes that "feminist ideology is not a cause which Arzner sought to champion, but a way of seeing the world which is implicit throughout her work as a natural extension of it since she is the only notably successful woman director of the thirties and forties in the dominantly male world of Hollywood. It is interesting to speculate on why Arzner never married and dressed constantly in male attire when directing her films, thereby skirting two social indexes which would have served to isolate her femininity in a male-oriented industry. Had the image she chose to project been more characteristically female, her presence on the Paramount lots might have generated more deference and less freedom in her treatment as a director."

FILMS: Fashions for Women, 1927; Ten Modern Commandments, 1927; Get Your Man, 1927; Manhattan Cocktail, 1928; The Wild Party, 1929; Sarah and Son, 1930; (with Robert Milton) Behind the Makeup, 1930; (with Robert Milton) Charming Sinners (U.K., The Constant Wife), 1930; The Gallows Song episode in Paramount on Parade, 1930; Anybody's Woman, 1930; Honor Among Lovers, 1931; Working Girls, 1931; Merrily We Go to Hell, 1932; Christopher Strong, 1933; Nana (Lady of the Boulevard), 1934; Craig's Wife, 1936; The Bride Wore Red, 1937; Dance, Girl, Dance, 1940; First Comes Courage, 1943.

ABOUT: Johnston, C. (ed.) The Work of Dorothy Arzner: Towards a Feminist Cinema, 1975; Kay, K. and Peary, G. (eds.) Women and the Cinema, 1977; Williamson, A. M. Alice in Movieland, 1927. Periodicals —Action July–August 1973, March–April 1975; Cinema (USA) Fall 1974; Independent Woman November 1953; Jump Cut 12/13 1976; Los Angeles Times October 8, 1979; New York Times October 12, 1979; Silver Screen December 1933; Time October 12, 1936; Variety October 10, 1979; Velvet Light Trap Fall 1973.

ASQUITH, The Hon. ANTHONY (November 9, 1902–February 21, 1968), British director and scenarist, was the son of Herbert Asquith, first Earl of Oxford and Asquith, and Prime Minister of Britain (1908–1915), and his second wife, Margot Tennant. Anthony Asquith, nicknamed "Puffin," was born in London and educated at Winchester and Balliol College, Oxford University, where in 1925 he became one of the founder members of the Film Society. Graduating the same year, he studied filmmaking in Hollywood for six months before joining British Instructional Films under H. Bruce Woolfe, who had been impressed by a script submitted by Asquith (and by the representations of the formidable Lady Oxford, his mother).

Asquith served his apprenticeship at British Instructional on Sinclair Hill's Ancient British epic Boadicea (1926), working as property master, assistant make-up man, assistant editor, and general dogsbody. In a long blonde wig and flowing robes, he also stood in for the star, Phyllis Neilson-Terry, in the more hazardous chariot scenes. Asquith put what he learned from this

ANTHONY ASQUITH

experience into a script called Shooting Stars and submitted it to H. Bruce Woolfe. British Instructional, then venturing into studio-made features after some years of successful documentary production, had adopted a policy of recruiting bright young graduates and letting them try out their ideas under the restraining influence of older hands. Woolfe liked Asquith's script and set him to work on it, with the veteran A. V. Bramble—who was credited as director—in fact serving as codirector and supervisor.

Shooting Stars (1928) has Annette Benson as a movie star who sets out to murder her husband (Brian Aherne) when he discovers that she is having an affair; her plan literally misfires, killing her lover instead. This melodramatic story is set against a subtly satirical account of the film industry and studio life that has retained its "elegance and charm." The "elaborate and varied" lighting effects, the dramatic use of crane-shots and of "rapid and impressionistic cutting" were (as Rachael Low wrote) "calculated to electrify the plodding British film industry, accustomed as it is to find glitter only in the work of the prodigious young Hitchcock." These experimental touches were generally attributed to Asquith rather than his codirector, and the picture was greeted as a triumphant vindication of British Instructional's enlightened policy.

Asquith's first solo assignment followed the same year—a thriller centering on the London Underground, again scripted by the director, and starring Brian Aherne and Elissa Landi. Like its predecessor, it made sparing use of titles, relying on the images to make its point. Critics had seen the influence of Eisenstein in some of the shots in *Shooting Stars,* but German Expressionism seemed to be the model for the chiaroscuro lighting and "weird effects" in *Underground,* which had a more mixed reception. One contemporary reviewer wrote that "Asquith is well soaked in German technique. What he has to learn is how to use it." All the same, a more recent critic thought that the film's "best parts have a likeable bravura, especially the tautly shot and edited chases through the Underground and the climactic fight in the power station."

The Runaway Princess (1929), also known as *Princess Priscilla's Fortnight,* was the result of an arrangement between H. Bruce Woolfe and a German production company—a "charmingly quirky" romantic comedy that gave Asquith scope to indulge his fondness for location shooting when the princess (Mady Christians), escaping from an arranged marriage, runs away to London. Asquith's growing reputation was confirmed by *A Cottage on Dartmoor* (1930), adapted by the director from a story by Herbert Price. It is a study in jealousy, about an escaped convict who seeks out the woman he has lost. The last, best, and most successful of Asquith's silent films, *A Cottage on Dartmoor* in fact includes one dialogue sequence—a clip from a wittily parodied American talkie that the heroine and her future husband go to see on their first date. This is only one example of the film's inventiveness: it also makes masterly use of crosscutting, experiments effectively with the subjective camera, and at one point cuts straight to a flashback without the use of explanatory titles.

Asquith's first sound film was *Tell England* (1931), which he adapted from Ernest Raymond's novel and codirected with Geoffrey Barkas. Filmed largely on location in Malta and Britain, it is an indictment of the pointless Dardanelles campaign of World War I, contrasting the idyllic upper-class home life of its two young heroes with the insane slaughter of the Battle of Gallipoli. Asquith does not always escape the class-consciousness and sentimentality of the novel, but the film was universally praised for its imagination and power, and called "one of the two or three outstanding British talkies made so far." Paul Rotha thought its battle scenes the equal of those in Pudovkin's *End of St. Petersburg* and Milestone's *All Quiet on the Western Front.*

That Asquith should switch from the horrors of war to a ballet film called *Dance Pretty Lady* is not as surprising at it seems, since his intense interest in the integration of movement and music is evident in all his sound films. *Dance Pretty*

Lady (1932), based on Compton Mackenzie's novel *Carnival,* tells the "rather insipid" story of an Edwardian ballet dancer (Ann Casson) who loves but almost loses a rich young artist (Carl Harbord). A gaslit London is attractively evoked by Ian Campbell-Gray, Asquith's usual art director at this time, and the ballet sequences were unsurpassed for many years. In this film, wrote John Grierson, "movement is laced together with the feeling for movement which only half a dozen directors in the world could match."

At this time, Asquith and Hitchcock were generally regarded as the two best directors in Britain, and they were endlessly compared. Grierson suggested that Hitchcock had the experience of life and the gusto that Asquith lacked, while Asquith had knowledge and taste—"he knows more in his head and less in his solar plexus. . . . He has no feeling for people except as they can be observed from the outside. He is born and bred a spectator, capable only of drawing people as puppets. That is to the good; puppeteering is as great a trade as any, if you take it seriously for the satire, fantasy and poetry that is in it." C. A. Lejeune decided that "Asquith lags behind Hitchcock in craftsmanship, comes very close to him in picture sense and passes him in fervency and conviction of thought. If he fails, as I sometimes fear he will fail, to get beyond the lyricism of his recent films, it will be because of a strong individualist strain his work, a cultured uncommunal ideology that has little contact with the urgencies of the age and too fine a fibre for the method of the machine."

In fact, with the absorption of British Instructional by British International Pictures and the departure of his friend and mentor Bruce Woolfe, Asquith entered upon an unsettled and relatively barren phase of his career, making only three films in six years. *The Lucky Number* (1933), the first of Asquith's movies not scripted by himself, is a comedy about a footballer and a French lottery ticket, produced by Michael Balcon for Gainsborough Pictures. The story is weak, but Basil Wright found "a firmness of touch about the main sequences" that Asquith's earlier films had lacked, and an "extremely witty" use of music to comment on the action.

Unfinished Symphony (1934), the English version of an Austrian picture about Schubert, was followed by a similar bilingual venture, the anglicization of a French spy thriller, *Moscow Nights* (1935), with Harry Baur as a war profiteer and Laurence Olivier as an embittered soldier. Asquith was inactive for two years after that, until in 1937 he began preparatory work as coauthor and codirector (with Leslie Howard) on George Bernard Shaw's *Pygmalion.* The producer Gabriel Pascal had persuaded Shaw to give him the film rights to all his plays, but it was not until May 1938 that Pascal had found the necessary backing and production could begin.

Asquith had David Lean as editor, Laurence Irving as production designer, and Arthur Honegger as composer, as well as a splendid cast headed by Leslie Howard as Professor Higgins. The virtually unknown Wendy Hiller became a star overnight with her portrayal of Eliza Doolittle, and there is a marvelous performance from Wilfrid Lawson as Eliza's father. "The most important thing about *Pygmalion*," wrote Basil Wright, "is that it represents a triumph for Anthony Asquith, whose sincere cinematic sensitivity has been all too neglected by producers in recent years. . . . He brings to the film that warm sense of the humanities, and that feeling for composition which never descends to the artistic, which still make his early silent films . . . a vivid and abiding memory. To this he adds an almost incredible ingenuity of movement and editing which turns what might so easily have been a photographed stage play into something essentially filmic."

A popular as well as a critical success, *Pygmalion* reestablished Asquith among the leading British directors. He had another hit with his next film—another adaptation of a stage play, Terence Rattigan's *French Without Tears*. Ray Milland stars in this likable farce about young English gentlemen at a cram school in the south of France, all lolloping like hypnotized rabbits around a flirtatious sex-object (Ellen Drew). "The shadow of World War II looms over them," wrote John Gillett in his notes for a 1981 Asquith retrospective, "and adds a touch of poignancy to the laughter. Roland Culver, as the only adult among them, is a wonderfully funny example of naval rectitude, and Asquith's fluent and witty direction makes all the right points about the curious behavior of the pre-war Englishman abroad."

The war had begun by the time Asquith made his next film, and *Freedom Radio* (1940) was his first response to it—a dramatic and well-characterized story about a Viennese doctor (Clive Brook) who broadcasts warnings about the Nazi threat on a hidden radio. The same year, Asquith confirmed his reputation as an affectionate satirist of the British way of life—a kind of English René Clair—with *Quiet Wedding*, adapted from Esther McCracken's play by Terence Rattigan and Anatole de Grunwald (who had also collaborated on the script of *French Without Tears*). A slight tale about a young couple (Derek Farr and Margaret Lockwood) whose romance is almost ruined by their parents' elaborate plans for their wedding, it seemed to Bosley Crowther a "completely unpretentious and charming film, the component parts of which are as delicately balanced as the mechanism of a watch."

Asquith made four short semi-documentary films for the Ministry of Information during the war, beginning with *Channel Incident* (1940), an unconvincing drama about a woman (Peggy Ashcroft) searching the Channel for her husband after the evacuation of Dunkirk. *Rush Hour* (1941) was more successful—a comedy short about workers trying to cope with the British transport system that effectively illustrated the desirability of staggered working hours. In between came *Cottage to Let* (1941), a workmanlike but uninspired thriller about an inventor (Leslie Banks) working on a new bombsight on a Scottish estate that has been infiltrated by a Nazi agent. That paragon of British patriotism, John Mills, is shrewdly cast as the Nazi, and there is a memorable performance from the youthful George Cole as the Cockney evacuee who unmasks him.

Another routine war drama, *Uncensored* (1942), was followed by *We Dive at Dawn* (1943), a tense story in the documentary style about a British submarine assigned to pursue and sink a German battleship. The scenes of working-class home life when the crew are on leave are painfully inept, but the brilliantly handled action sequences more than compensate for this weakness, and there are fine performances from John Mills and Eric Portman in what has been claimed as "one of the best submarine pictures ever made."

There was a generally warm reception also for *The Demi-Paradise* (1943), scripted and produced by Anatole de Grunwald. Laurence Olivier stars as a young Soviet marine engineer who, visiting England just before the war, is chilled by the reserve and apparent chauvinism of the British, but learns to love them when he sees them girded for war on a second visit in 1941. The movie established Olivier "in the top flight of British film actors," but now seems smug and patronizing. There is more charm and tact in *Welcome to Britain* (1943), an hour-long introduction to British people and institutions made as a guide for GIs stationed in England, with Burgess Meredith as codirector and interpreter, and guest appearances by Beatrice Lillie and Bob Hope, among others.

After the fatuous but highly profitable Victorian melodrama *Fanny by Gaslight* (1944), with James Mason as the evil Lord Manderstoke and Phyllis Calvert as the ill-used heroine, came another short semi-documentary, *Two Fathers*

(1944), and then the last and best of Asquith's wartime features, *The Way to the Stars* (1945), called *Johnny in the Clouds* in the United States. Scripted by Terence Rattigan with Anatole de Grunwald (who also produced), it makes moving use of poems by John Pudney and a fine score by Nicholas Brodsky to tell the story of an RAF bomber station and the lives, loves, and sometimes deaths of its British and American personnel, whose initial distrust of each other grows into understanding and affection.

As Peter Noble wrote, "nothing set the nostalgic mood of the film as skilfully as Asquith's opening scenes, the camera wandering through the dead and deserted airfield, with its quick observation of the various living quarters, the faded inscriptions on the walls of wash-houses, the tattered remnants of security posters flapping on the sides of empty buildings." The cast is headed by Michael Redgrave as the poet-flyer killed in action, Douglass Montgomery as the American who comforts Redgrave's widow before he too dies, and John Mills as a young pilot who comes to believe that flyers should not marry. Trevor Howard and Jean Simmons, both in relatively small parts, soon afterward rose to stardom. The picture won the *Daily Mail* National Film Award.

David Thomson has described Asquith as "a dull journeyman supervisor of the transfer to the screen of proven theatrical properties." This is evidently unjust as an account of his work as a whole, less so if it is applied only to his postwar films, beginning with competent but unexceptional adaptations of two Terence Rattigan plays, *While the Sun Shines* and *The Winslow Boy*. These were the only products of International Screenplays, the company formed in 1945 by Asquith, Rattigan, and Anatole de Grunwald, and neither was much more than "canned theatre."

After two years in which the director worked on various aborted projects, he returned to the screen with *The Woman in Question* (1950), a modest thriller from an original script by John Cresswell. As Paul Dehn put it, "it shows Jean Kent (a garrotted corpse) as she variously appeared, in life, to five material witnesses and, in death, to two police officers. Fair acting and good direction redeem the mediocre script which falls a shade gracelessly between the twin stools of psychology and detection."

Another Rattigan adaptation followed in 1951, *The Browning Version,* with a magisterial performance by Michael Redgrave as the crushed and dried-up classics teacher brought alive by a small gift from one of his pupils. Asquith's last major success was *The Importance of Being Earnest,* "an elegant and sparkling" version of Oscar Wilde's play scripted by himself. Edith Evans' reading of the role of Lady Bracknell is said to have left the rest of the cast "fighting for their lives," even though they included players of the caliber of Michael Redgrave, Joan Greenwood, Dorothy Tutin, and Margaret Rutherford. This was, surprisingly, Asquith's first film in color.

His own favorite among his later pictures was *Orders to Kill* (1958), scripted by Paul Dehn, and centering on a young ex-pilot (Paul Massie) sent to France in 1944 to kill an enemy agent who turns out to be an apparently harmless old man. One critic wrote that "Asquith evades none of the implications (the actual killing is hideously difficult) and uses all his cinematic skills to convey the killer's agony of conscience."

The majority of Asquith's other postwar movies were adaptations of plays, including two by George Bernard Shaw, *The Doctor's Dilemma* (1959) and *The Millionairess* (1960). The latter, called a "fairly radical version" enploying "a whole battery of technical tricks to drive the romp along at a lively pace," has Sophia Loren as the formidable Epifania, who meets her match in a gently idealistic Indian doctor (Peter Sellers). Asquith also made two more films from Rattigan scripts, *The VIPs* (1963) and *The Yellow Rolls Royce* (1964), said to possess "a faded elegance which recalled the appeal of his best films but which was out of key with audiences of the sixties." The latter was the last picture he made before his death in 1968.

As John Gillett has said, the "lively experimental sense" that distinguished Asquith's earliest films soon evaporated and he moved into "safer, more conventional territory" from which he "viewed the various strata of English society with a kind of bemused affection which eschewed both malice and real analysis. In fact, he belonged to the long tradition of 'liberal' artists which is part of Britain's cultural legacy." And Asquith's obituarist in the London *Times* suggested that perhaps he "always remained a straightforward and old-fashioned romantic, with a romanticism which underlay his essentially kindly and good-natured comedy and came unashamedly to the surface in his dramas. His control over his medium was complete, to such an extent that his unusual skill and stylistic polish were . . . too often called in to produce workmanlike versions of stage plays which allowed him little freedom for personal creations."

"Puffin" Asquith was a shy and self-effacing man who avoided publicity of any kind. He was devoted to music and the theatre arts, especially ballet, and his later work included documentaries about the Glyndebourne Opera and the Royal Ballet. After his death, the Society of Film and Television Arts established an annual Anthony Asquith Memorial Award for the year's best film score. His other great passion was the well-being of his fellow-workers in the film industry. He was first president of the Association of Cinematograph, Television, and Allied Technicians, and gave much of his time to trade union work and related political and social activities.

—R.S.

FILMS: (with A.V. Bramble) Shooting Stars, 1928 (uncredited); Underground, 1928; The Runaway Princess (English version of Anglo-German coproduction, also known as Princess Priscilla's Fortnight and, in Germany, as Priscillas Fahrt ins Glück), 1929; A Cottage on Dartmoor (U.S., Escaped From Dartmoor), 1930; (with Geoffrey Barkas) Tell England (U.S., Battle of Gallipoli), 1931; Dance Pretty Lady, 1932; The Lucky Number, 1933; Unfinished Symphony (English version of film by Willi Forst), 1934; Moscow Nights (U.S., I Stand Condemned; English version of French film, Les Nuits de Moscou), 1935; (with Leslie Howard) Pygmalion, 1938; French Without Tears, 1939; Freedom Radio (U.S., The Voice in the Night), 1940; Quiet Wedding, 1941; Cottage to Let (U.S., Bombsight Stolen), 1941; Uncensored, 1942; We Dive at Dawn, 1943; The Demi-Paradise (U.S., Adventure for Two), 1943; Fanny by Gaslight (U.S., Man of Evil), 1944; The Way to the Stars (U.S., Johnny in the Clouds), 1945; While the Sun Shines, 1947; The Winslow Boy, 1948; The Woman in Question (U.S., Five Angles on Murder), 1950; The Browning Version, 1951; The Importance of Being Earnest, 1952; The Net (U.S., Project M7), 1953; The Final Test, 1953; The Young Lovers (U.S., Chance Meeting), 1954; Carrington VC (U.S., Court Martial), 1954; Orders to Kill, 1958; The Doctor's Dilemma, 1959; Libel, 1959; The Millionairess, 1960; Two Living, One Dead, 1962; Guns of Darkness, 1962; The VIPs, 1963; The Yellow Rolls-Royce, 1964. Documentaries and semi-documentaries—Channel Incident, 1940; Rush Hour, 1941; (with Burgess Meredith) Welcome to Britain, 1943; Two Fathers, 1944; On Such a Night, 1955; An Evening With the Royal Ballet, 1963.

ABOUT: Belmans, J. Anthony Asquith, 1902–1968, 1972 (in French); Elvin, G. and others. Anthony Asquith, 1968; Frewin, L. Puffin Asquith, 1973; Minney, R. J. The Films of Anthony Asquith, 1976; Noble, P. (ed.) Anthony Asquith, 1951; Thomson, D. A Biographical Dictionary of the Cinema, 1975. Periodicals—Cine Technician August 1937, May 1939, May–June 1947, July–August 1951, September–October 1951, November–December 1952; Cinema Studio October-November 1950; Film and TV Technician April 1968; Film Dope December 1972, March 1974; Films and Filming February 1958, February 1959, October 1963; National Film Theatre Booklet July 1981; Sight and Sound Spring 1938, Autumn 1958, Spring 1968; Theatre Arts April 1953; Thousand Eyes November 1975; Times (London) February 22, 1968.

*AUTANT-LARA, CLAUDE (August 5, 1903–), French director and designer, was born at Luzarches, near Paris, the son of a successful architect and stage designer, Edouard Autant, and the former Larapidie de L'Isle, an actress and member of the Comédie Française whose stage name was Louise Lara. An outspoken pacifist, Louise Lara became so unpopular during World War I that she had to leave France, taking the young Claude, then a student at the Lycée Janson de Sailly, with her to London, where he was enrolled in the Mill Hill School. He returned to Paris a few years later to study at the École Nationale Supérieure des Arts Decoratifs and the École des Beaux Arts.

Autant-Lara began his movie career as a designer before he was out of his teens. He worked for Marcel L'Herbier on such "impressionist" films as Le Carnaval des vérités (1919), Don Juan et Faust (1922), L'Inhumaine (1923), and Le Diable au coeur (1927), and also designed Jacque Catelain's Le Marchand de plaisir (1923) and the costumes for Renoir's Nana (1926). During this period he served as René Clair's assistant on Paris qui dort (1923) and Le Voyage imaginaire (1925) and directed his own first short films. These included an avant-garde piece called Fait divers (1923), the documentary Vittel (1926), and Construire un feu (1927–1928), an early experiment in the use of the anamorphic lens and wide screen based on Jack London's story "To Build a Fire."

This varied apprenticeship made Autant-Lara a versatile craftsman of the cinema but led to no immediate success. In 1930–1932 he worked in Hollywood, dubbing American films into French, and in 1932–1933 he made a few more shorts before receiving his first feature assignment, Ciboulette (1933), an adaptation by Autant-Lara and Jacques Prévert of a Reynaldo Hahn operetta. Unfortunately, it was a box-office disaster, and the director made his next film in England: My Partner Master Davis (1936), adapted by Prévert from a novel by Jeraro Prieto, and starring Alastair Sim.

Autant-Lara then worked on three films for Maurice Lehmann: L'Affaire du courrier de Lyon (1937), Le Ruisseau (with Françoise Rosay and Michel Simon), and Fric-Frac (1939). Lehmann credited himself as director of these films, Autant-Lara only as "technical collaborator"—in fact, according to Georges Sadoul and others, all three were directed by Autant-Lara with Lehmann as producer. The best of them was Fric-Frac, a comedy in which Fernandel, as an innocent jeweler's assistant, becomes involved with a gangland moll (splendidly played by Arletty) and her companion (Michel Simon), an inept burglar. Michel Duran's script

°ō tän´´ lä rä´

CLAUDE AUTANT-LARA

was based on a play by Edouard Bourdet and is rich in untranslatable thieves' argot, but this did not prevent foreign as well as French critics from delighting in the film's "mixture of irony and mischievous observation" and its "spirit of common sense and flesh-and-blood humanity."

During the German occupation Autant-Lara finally established himself as an important director in his own right with four graceful period entertainments starring the young Odette Joyeux: *Le Mariage de Chiffon* (1942); *Lettres d'amour* (1942); *Douce* (*Love Story,* 1943)—a romantic tragedy set in Paris in the 1880s, astringent in its treatment both of arrogant aristocrats and grasping servants—and *Sylvie et le fantôme* (*Sylvia and the Phantom,* 1945). In the last Joyeux plays a beautiful young heiress who falls in love with the castle ghost (Jacques Tati making a rare and tenebrous appearance in another director's film). The castle is soon full of eager suitors masquerading as phantoms, and the unhappy spirit is rejected in favor of François Périer.

Autant-Lara's next film was more in the manner of *Douce,* though it excelled it in almost every way. *Le Diable au corps* (*The Devil in the Flesh,* 1947), based on Raymond Radiguet's novel and set during World War I, is a harshly poetic account of an affair between a seventeen-year-old student (Gérard Philipe) and a married woman (Micheline Presle) whose husband is away at the front. The film opens with the Armistice celebrations of 1918. Marthe has died giving birth to her lover's child, and François, desolate amid the rejoicing, cannot even attend her funeral. As he listens to the service from outside the church, the bell tolls him back to the days of their happiness.

The poignant ambivalence of François's character, teetering between boyhood and manhood, is conveyed by Gérard Philipe with a force and subtlety that established him at once both as a serious actor and an idolized romantic lead. There was much praise also for the sensitive adaptation written by Jean Aurenche and Pierre Bost and for Max Douy's richly atmospheric sets. These three worked with Autant-Lara on virtually all of his subsequent pictures, as did the film's composer René Cloërec and its editor Madeleine Gug. (Autant-Lara has been slightly less consistent in his choice of cameramen, but the majority of his films have been photographed by Michel Kelber or Jacques Natteau.)

Le Diable au corps, Autant-Lara's first completely personal feature film and arguably his best, was as controversial as it was financially successful. Lo Duca called it one of the most beautiful films of a productive year and wrote that it "achieves true greatness in the rhythm of its scenes. . . . This is perhaps the first time that Autant-Lara has succeeded in expressing pure emotion. . . . It is his most expressive and balanced work, his best achievement, and one of the most important achievements of the French cinema." It received the International Critics' Prize at the Brussels Film Festival, where Philipe was voted best male actor of the year. Moralists were shocked, however, not only by the explicitness of the love scenes—wholly convincing in their evocation of physical passion—but by Autant-Lara's tender and often humorous treatment of his theme—his unqualified celebration of an adulterous wartime liaison. The director is a militant atheist and a radical socialist, and *Le Diable au corps* was the first of a number of films in which his open contempt for bourgeois myths and assumptions brought him into conflict with their defenders.

Autant-Lara scored another international success with *Occupe-toi d'Amélie* (*Oh Amelia!,* 1949), perhaps the best of all the many screen adaptations of Feydeau farces. This play within a play within a film is distinguished by its breakneck pace and flawless timing, and features an irresistible performance by Danielle Darrieux. Autant-Lara transfers Feydeau's own dissection of bourgeois hypocrisy to the screen with evident relish, and he carried the process a good deal further in his next film, *L'Auberge rouge* (*The Red Inn,* 1951). An almost Voltairean black comedy, this is a period piece set in a lonely inn whose owners (Carette and Françoise Rosay) make a living by murdering their guests and stealing their belongings.

Overtaken by a storm, a coachload of travelers take refuge at the inn. Fernandel gives one of his best performances as a monk who learns in a makeshift confessional of the fate that awaits his fellow guests. Improvising frantically, he manages to save them without betraying his oath of secrecy, only to see them drive off the next morning over a precipice, victims of another, less scrupulous, murderer (or possibly an Act of God). The monk is a mixture of avarice, cowardice, and low cunning, and the "respectable" travelers are no better—a despicable collection of mean and callous hypocrites who fully deserve their fate. The film seemed to some Catholic critics nothing short of blasphemous, and it was savagely attacked in France and elsewhere (including Britain, where it was denied release for six years). Alain Tanner thought it too literary and too bitter, with "too little scope for spontaneity or sensitivity"; on the other hand "the narrative, as one would expect from Aurenche and Bost, is flawlessly developed; the dialogue as sharp and blasphemous as anyone could wish." Tanner concluded that this was "an important film, in that it represents an aspect of French thought which has rarely been so freely expressed on the screen."

Autant-Lara contributed the episode on pride to Les Sept Péchés capitaux (The Seven Deadly Sins) and then, after a minor film called Le Bon Dieu sans confession, returned to the theme of sexual love between an adolescent and an older woman in his sensitive adaptation of Colette's novel Le Blé en herbe (Ripening Seed, 1954). Here the vacation romance between the young Pierre-Michel Beck and Edwige Feuillère is ultimately painful and destructive for the woman, but for the boy a stage in his growth towards maturity and a deeper relationship with a girl of his own age (Nicole Berger).

The theme recurs yet again in Le Rouge et le noir (1954), in the love between the ambitious young Julien Sorel (Gérard Philipe) and Madame de Rênal (Danielle Darrieux), whose children he is tutoring. Many critics found these early scenes the most satisfactory in a long film that almost inevitably fails to do justice to the complex characterizations of Stendhal's novel. However, the picture had its admirers and brought Autant-Lara the Grand Prix du Cinéma Français. There was also much praise for the handsome color photography of Michel Kelber, "many of whose shots looked like well-composed paintings." The film provoked fresh charges of anticlericalism, and some took its references to Napoleon as covert criticism of De Gaulle. (This mixed reception did not deter Autant-Lara, later in his career, from making a television serial of another Stendhal novel, Lucien Leuwen.)

Autant-Lara turned to more recent history in La Traversée de Paris (Pig Across Paris, 1956),

set in 1942 during the German Occupation and loosely based by Aurenche and Bost on a Marcel Aymé short story. It is an extremely funny but fundamentally very sour account of the adventures and misadventures of two men as they carry four cases of blackmarket pork across wartime Paris. Martin (Bourvil) is a petty criminal; his temporary accomplice Grandgil (Jean Gabin) is a painter—not a house painter as Martin at first supposes but a well-known artist who takes on the job for the sake of a little excitement. The difference becomes important when they are caught and questioned by an art-conscious SS officer. Grandgil, who can quote Heine, goes free; Martin goes to jail. Years later when they meet by chance at a railroad station, Grandgil is prosperous, Martin still carrying bags for other people. The film gives a picture of the Occupation far removed from the Resistance heroics of other movies on the period. It was generally admired as an excellent satirical farce, and for some critics it was more than that. François Truffaut wrote that in it Autant-Lara had "found the subject of his life, a script that really suited him," and Richard Roud has called it "one of the few films about the Occupation that still seems to ring true . . . a high point in the otherwise bleak French cinema of the '50s."

En cas de malheur (1958) contrasts the world and mores of a wealthy lawyer and his wife (Gabin and Edwige Feuillère) with those of a young prostitute and her student lover (Brigitte Bardot and Franco Interlenghi). Roy Armes was reminded of Clouzot's La Verité but thought this adaptation of a Simenon story lacking in conviction, especially in its treatment of the younger couple. Le Joueur (1958), based on Dostoevsky's The Gambler, was also found inadequate in spite of Gérard Philipe's fine performance in the lead. Nor did Autant-Lara earn much critical favor with Les Régates de San Francisco (1959), one of his frankest treatments of the theme of adolescent love, much cut by its producers and the censors, or with the two minor films that followed.

At this point, with his reputation in decline, Autant-Lara found an Italian backer for a film that he had wanted to make for over ten years, Tu ne tueras point (Thou Shalt Not Kill, 1961). It is an attack on militarism centering on the failure of French law to recognize conscientious objection, which can or could be punished by indefinite imprisonment, meted out one year at a time. Autant-Lara collaborated with Aurenche and Bost on the script, which contrasts two cases that actually came before a postwar military tribunal on the same day in 1949. Adler (Horst Frank), a German priest who under orders had killed a French Resistance fighter, is acquitted by the court; Cordier (Laurent Terzieff), a young Frenchman who had refused to fight on religious grounds, is jailed.

Forbidden to shoot the film in either France or Italy (in both of which countries it was subsequently banned), Autant-Lara made it in Yugoslavia, with a Yugoslavian cast (apart from the principals) and crew. Critics recognized that this accounted for a certain lack of sophistication in photography, sets, and supporting performances, but differed as to film's overall quality and impact. For Robert Russell, "its powerful originality, its impeccable logic, its universal simplicity, place it in a class by itself," and Wendy Michener, who thought that Autant-Lara had loaded the dice in favor of his pacifist hero, agreed that "the film still has considerable emotional impact by virtue of its courage, sincerity, and storytelling skill." However, many other critics concluded that the movie was more verbal than visual—a well-intentioned but rather ponderous tract, in spite of excellent performances from the principal actors, especially Suzanne Flon, who received the Volpi Cup at the Venice Film Festival for her portrayal of Cordier's mother. Disappointed and in financial straits, Autant-Lara concentrated for some years on strictly commercial projects. There have been a few more personally committed films since then, like *Journal d'une femme en blanc* (*Woman in White,* 1965), which deals courageously if somewhat predictably with questions of abortion and contraception.

According to Roy Armes, "Autant-Lara's style is as bare and unemphatic as that of Luis Buñuel, totally lacking in technical flourish or visual exuberance. . . . That Autant-Lara has a forceful personality cannot be doubted by anyone who has read any of his contributions to the numerous controversies aroused by his films, but his work shows little originality of construction." For Armes, "the most interesting aspect of Autant-Lara's work is the consistency with which he expounds his idiosyncratic views." Having been attacked by conservatives in his heyday as a social rebel, a blasphemer, and an amoral champion of sexual love, he has since been excoriated by Truffaut and other *nouvelle vague* critics as a pillar of the despised "tradition of quality" in filmmaking. The courage, skill, and versatility of his best work will presumably be forgotten until the critical climate changes.

Autant-Lara is a widower. His wife, the former Ghislaine Auboin, served as assistant director of *Tu ne tueras point* and was coauthor with Gabriel Arout of another of her husband's films, *Marguerite de la nuit* (1955), a version of the Faust story updated to the 1920s and starring Michèle Morgan and Yves Montand. In technique it is the most unorthodox of the director's feature films, with deliberately stylized sets and color changes keyed to changes in mood. Autant-Lara was president (1948–1955) of the Syndicat des Technicians du Cinéma Français and president (1957–1963) of the Fédération Nationale du Spectacle, subsequently serving as honorary president of both organizations. He is a Chevalier de la Légion d'honneur and a Commandeur des Arts et des Lettres. In 1956 he received the Prix Femina Belge du Cinéma. The only leisure activity he lists in *Who's Who in France* is tennis.

FILMS: *Shorts*—Fait divers, 1923; Vittel, 1926; Construire un feu, 1928; Le Gendarme est sans pitié, 1932; Un Client sérieux, 1932; Monsieur le duc, 1932; La Peur des coups, 1933; Invite Monsieur à dîner, 1933. *Features*—Ciboulette, 1933; My Partner Master Davis/The Mysterious Mr. Davis, 1936 (Britain); L'Affair du Courrier de Lyon, 1937; Le Ruisseau, 1938; Fric-Frac, 1939; Le Mariage de Chiffon, 1942; Lettres d'amour, 1942; Douce (Love Story), 1943; Sylvie et le fantôme (U.S., Sylvia and the Phantom/ U.K., Sylvia and the Ghost), 1945; Le Diable au corps (Devil in the Flesh), 1947; Occupe-toi d'Amélie (U.S., Oh Amelia!/ U.K., Keep an Eye on Amelia), 1949; L'Auberge rouge (The Red Inn), 1951; L'Orgueil (Pride) *episode in* Les Sept Péchés capitaux (The Seven Deadly Sins), 1952; Le Bon Dieu sans confession, 1953; Le Blé en herbe (Ripening Seed), 1954; Le Rouge et le noir (U.S., Rouge et Noir/ U.K., Scarlet and Black), 1954; Marguerite de la nuit, 1955; La Traversée de Paris (Pig Across Paris), 1956; En cas de malheur, 1958; Le Joueur, 1958; Les Régates de San Francisco, 1959; La Jument verte, 1959; Le Bois des amants, 1960; Tu ne tueras point (Thou Shalt Not Kill/Non Uccidere), 1961 (Yugoslavia); Vive Henri IV, Vive l'amour, 1961; Le Compte de Monte Cristo, 1961; Le Meurtrier, 1963; Le Magot de Joséfa, 1963; Journal d'une femme en blanc (Woman in White), 1965; Le Nouveau Journal d'une femme en blanc/ Une Femme en blanc se révolte, 1966; Aujourd'hui *episode in* Le Plus Vieux Métier du monde, 1967; Le Franciscain de Bourges, 1968; Les Patates, 1969; Lucien Leuwen, 1973 (for television); Gloria, 1977. *Published scripts*—La Traversée de Paris *in* L'Avant-Scène du Cinéma January 1967.

ABOUT: Armes, R. French Cinema Since 1946: 1, 1970; International Who's Who, 1979–80; Leprohon, P. Présences contemporaines, cinéma, 1957; Roud, R. (ed.) Cinema: A Critical Dictionary, 1980; Who's Who in France, 1979–1980. *Periodicals*—Cahiers du Cinéma March 1967; Cahiers de la Cinémathèque Spring 1973 (Autant-Lara issue), Autumn 1973; Cinématographe April 1978; Films and Filming January 1955, October and November 1960; Positif September 1961.

BARNET, BORIS VASILIEVICH (June 18,
1902–January 1965), Soviet director, scenarist,
and actor, was born in Moscow. He owed his un-
Slavic name to his grandfather, an Englishman
who settled in Russia in the nineteenth century
and opened a printing business on the outskirts
of Moscow. Boris Barnet studied painting at the
Moscow School of Art and Architecture but left
in 1919 to join the Red Army, serving as a medic.
He was an athletic young man, and after the civil war he served for a time as an army physical
training instructor before drifting into professional boxing. Spotted by the director Lev
Kuleshov, he was given the role of Jeddy, the
cowboy bodyguard, in *The Extraordinary Adventures of Mr. West in the Land of the
Bolsheviks* (1924), a slapstick satire modeled on
American silent comedies, full of chases and visual trickery.

Kuleshov, the Russian cinema's pioneer and
first theorist of montage, had established his
enormously influential film workshop in Moscow in 1920. There he put his students through
a rigorous physical training program and with
them sought "a firm theoretic basis for the training of film [as distinct from theatre] actors." After *Mr. West*—a huge success—Barnet joined
the Kuleshov workshop as a student, propman,
and general handyman, and soon showed a flair
for inventing visuals. In the mid-1920s he had
minor acting roles in several movies, including
Pudovkin's *Chess Fever* and Dmitriev's *On the
Right Track*.

It was Mezhrabpom, the studio then responsible for films for young people, that gave Barnet
his chance as a director. In collaboration with
Theodore Otsep, he made *Miss Mend* (1926), a
twenty-one-reel thriller serial based on a novel
by Marietta Shaginyan ("Jim Dollar"). The heroine is Vivian Mend (Natalie Glan), an American
girl reporter, and the film is an action-packed
account of the running battle between Vivian
and her three intrepid colleagues and a fascistic
gang led by the archvillain Komarov. There are
poisoned apples, deadly gases, kidnappings, and
coffins, and the story culminates in a hectic pursuit involving cars and horses.

John Gillett, who assembled a major Barnet
retrospective at the British National Film Theatre in 1980, praised the serial for its prolific visual invention and amusingly convoluted
plotting, and wrote that it fused elements of
Fairbanks, Feuillade, and Lang: "Like Feuillade, Barnet and Otsep realized the value of
shooting dark and desperate deeds on real locations (busy streets, snowy country landscapes,
etc.). . . . At times, the film has a darker tone
than the Feuillade subjects (the death of the little
boy). . . . But Barnet and Otsep have their own

BORIS BARNET

distinctive style in building up a climax (a very
mobile camera, tense crosscutting) which is best
demonstrated in the concluding passages involving the villain and the elevator, and there is a
particularly charming, even poetic, coda. . . .
It is difficult to discover which director did what
in the film. On the evidence of their later work,
it would seem probable that Barnet contributed
much of the light comedy business and Otsep
perhaps exerted technical control over the staging of the dramatic business."

The "very assured film sense" revealed in *Miss
Mend* is even more polished in Barnet's first solo
picture, *Devushka s korobkoi* (*Girl With the
Hatbox*, 1927), a comedy with a triangular love
story developed from a prosaic assignment to
publicize a state lottery. Like several other contemporary movies, it tells the story of a country
girl who comes to the big city just after the civil
war—a chaotic period marked by profiteering
and crime. Natasha (Anna Sten) gets a job in a
hat factory, resists financial temptation, and
achieves well-deserved happiness.

Again there is some rewarding location work
(especially in the opening scenes in a snowy
countryside) and a good deal of excellent comedy business (like the sequence elaborating on the
problems of sleeping in an overcrowded apartment). Much influenced by American comedies
of the period, the film combines humor, social
satire, and touches of sadness in a way that reminded some critics of Chaplin, and which came
to be recognized as characteristic of Barnet's
work. "Personally," he said once, "I like the droll
aspects of a drama and the tragic elements of
comedy. It is a question of proportions, not always easy to find."

In 1927 all the Soviet studios were dutifully turning out films celebrating the tenth anniversary of the October Revolution. Mezhrabpom assigned Barnet to direct *Moskva v Octyabr* (*Moscow in October,* 1927), a not particularly inspired recreation of the beginnings of the Revolution in Moscow, chiefly distinguished by a cast that included Stalin, Rykov, and Bukharin, among others, all playing themselves. Barnet also took a small part in the film, but his lack of enthusiasm for the project is reflected in some carelessly edited sequences, and it was not a success. He turned with obvious relief to his next movie, *Dom na Trubnoi* (*The House on Trubnaya Square,* 1928), another comedy about a country girl in the wicked city. Parasha (Vera Maretskaya) is taken on as a servant in the household of a new-rich hairdresser (Vladimir Fogel) in a Moscow tenement. Full of warm-hearted curiosity, she is soon involved in the lives of the people around her, and has her first taste of municipal politics. When her exploitative employer tries to throw her out, she stands up for her rights, inspired in part by a comical amateur production of a play about Joan of Arc.

Gillett wrote that the film begins "with the camera craning down a marvellous composite tenement set. Barnet continues to surprise with freewheeling shooting in crowded streets and a lovely gag involving a freeze frame. . . . [The film] also takes in some sharp antibureaucratic satire, but its main qualities lie in the loving character sketches of a community always on the go, for good or bad." This picture gave Maretskaya her first big role and Vladimir Fogel his last—that versatile actor, who appeared in most of Barnet's early films, died in 1929.

Popular as it was, *The House on Trubnaya Square* had a mixed critical reception, some reviewers evidently finding its affectionate satire of Soviet life overly harsh. Perhaps for this reason, it was three years before Barnet completed his next feature. Meanwhile he took small acting roles in Pudovkin's *Storm Over Asia* and Otsep's *The Living Corpse,* and made a brace of documentaries about the manufacture of musical instruments. When he did direct his next feature, *Lyodolom* (*The Thaw,* 1931), it was a total departure from his earlier work, a dark and violent story about conflict between poor and rich peasants (*kulaks*) in the early 1920s. Similar in theme and tone to Ermler's *Peasants* (1935), it apparently had an extremely controversial reception. According to Gillett, this film opens "with a series of pellucid lyrical images which haunt the memory long after the subsequent turgid conflict . . . has faded. Barnet seems to have realized that this kind of politicking was not his forte, since he never again entered this territory

quite so explicitly. Some time during this period, he seems to have consciously decided to vary his style as much as possible, setting himself little formal problems which could be worked out without running counter to the outward demands of Socialist Realism."

Returning once more to comedy, Barnet made his first sound film, and one of the most universally admired of all his pictures. *Okraina* (*Patriots/Outskirts,* 1933) was adapted by Barnet and Konstantin Finn from the latter's story about divided loyalties in a small Russian town during World War I. An adroit and characteristic blend of comic, ironic, and tragic elements, it forms a distinctly equivocal study of the results of fraternization with the enemy. *Okraina* has been much praised for the skill with which it evokes a whole community and its frequently eccentric inhabitants and for the unobtrusive naturalism of its use of sound, especially offscreen effects.

Jay Leyda—no great admirer of Barnet—wrote that the story "does that extraordinary thing so rare and valuable in films—it seems to tell itself without anyone pushing it. You can't be sure whether the next scene will be funny or pathetic, gentle or violent," and "the performances are given the same spontaneity by Barnet and an excellent cast." That cast includes Yelena Kuzmina, showing hitherto unexpected gifts as a comedienne, Nikolai Bogolyubov, and Nikolai Kryuchkov (just beginning his distinguished career). "The ensemble playing of this varied cast remains a great credit to Barnet," Leyda concluded; "his admirers from the days of his farces and satires, weathering the crisis of his *Moscow in October,* had at last a film to justify their patience." The Soviet critic O. Borisov thought that "in the pictorial structure of *Okraina* there is something of Chekhov's plays, with an action of interior development as well as an outer action. In it an important role is played by everything that goes on *beneath* the words—the concealed and repressed emotions of its characters, the pauses and hints, the circumstances and atmosphere of events, the combination of comic and dramatic elements, all building a profound inner rhythm."

Okraina is now widely regarded by Soviet as well as Western critics as Barnet's masterpiece. Nevertheless, according to A. S. Birkos, Barnet had "apparently missed the subtle shifts in Party ideology at the time because he was criticized for inaccurately portraying Russian life" —perhaps the film was too clearly pacifist in its sympathies. After *Adin i dysach* (*One and Ten,* 1934), an obscure work apparently made in collaboration with another director, Barnet made his next picture on location, well away from the Moscow hot seat. This was *U samovo sinyevo morya* (*By the Bluest of Seas,* 1936), codirected by S. Mardanov. One of the earliest Soviet color films, it is a lighthearted comedy in which two Caspian Sea fishermen (Lev Sverdlin and Kryuchkov) compete for the hand of Yelena Kuzmina.

However, it was becoming increasingly clear that the dourly political cinema of Socialist Realism held no place for such *jeux d'esprit. Noch v Sentyabr* (*A Night in September*), released after a three-year silence in 1939, was a quite uncharacteristic drama about Stakhanovites and saboteurs in the Donbas mines. And Barnet's next film, *Stari nayezdnik* (*The Old Jockey*), completed in 1940, was banned. A comedy about a veteran rider (I. Skuratov) trying to make a comeback, it seems on the face of it politically inoffensive, but was not released until nearly twenty years later.

The Soviet Union's *Fighting Film Albums*—each comprising two or three short pieces on wartime themes—went into production in 1941, the year the German invasion began. Barnet contributed to the third and tenth albums, but his war film *Novgorodnii* (*The Novgorodians,* 1943) was banned like *The Old Jockey* for reasons that have never been explained. Another war drama followed, *Odnazhdi noch* (*One Night,* 1945). Made at the Erevan studios in Soviet Armenia, it was based on Fyodor Knorr's play about peasants hiding wounded Soviet flyers from the Nazis, and has been described by Jay Leyda as almost expressionist in style.

Barnet took a part in this film, as he did in the more notable one that followed, *Podvig razvedchika* (*Exploit of an Intelligence Agent,* 1947). The agent of the title (Pavel Kadochnikov) is sent into Germany towards the end of World War II and confronts the wicked Nazi general (played with gusto by Barnet) in his own headquarters. It is an extraordinary film, combining expressionist or *film noir* elements that reminded reviewers of Fritz Lang's American war films with tongue-in-cheek touches almost in the spirit of Barnet's early comedies. Much admired abroad, it was also very well received in the Soviet Union, where one critic praised Barnet for transcending the genre by concentrating on the disorienting effect of the hero's sudden immersion in a society with a totally alien political structure and psychological make-up.

After this striking comeback, Barnet collaborated with Alexander Macharet on *Stranitsy zhizn* (*Pages of Life,* 1948), about a woman worker who becomes director of a factory, and then made *Schedroye lito* (*Generous Summer,* 1951), an agreeable entertainment set on a Ukrainian collective farm just after the war and starring Kryuchkov. Another *kolkhoz,* this time in Moldavia, was the setting for *Liana* (1955), a musical comedy. Kryuchkov starred again in *Poet* (1957), which recounts the adventures of a revolutionary poet in a southern port during the Russian civil war. This is one of a number of Barnet films showing his taste for cyclical construction, with the opening and closing scenes either identical or similar.

One of the most likable of Barnet's late films followed, *Boryets i kloun* (*The Wrestler and the Clown,* 1957), directed in collaboration with Konstantin Yudin. Set in Russia at the turn of the century, it is based on the real-life friendship between the wrestling champion Poddubny (played by S. Chekan) and the clown and animal trainer Durov (A. Mihailov). John Gillett called this one of Barnet's "most personal works, with an exquisite re-creation of little Czarist towns *en fête* for the arrival of the circus, and a gently poetic subplot concerning the wrestler's love for a doomed lady trapezist, caught by the camera in midair as she practices and traced in gliding crane-shots before the fatal fall. Equally memorable are the scenes of the wrestler roaming a countryside shimmering in a summer haze as memories of the old circus days flood in."

Barnet made only three more films. *Annushka* (1959) deals with the heartbreaks and joys of a peasant woman (Irene Skobtseva) struggling to raise her children after her husband is killed in the war; *Alionka* (1962) is based on Serge Antonov's stories about a little girl in school; and *Polustanok* (*Whistle Stop,* 1963) is an anecdotal comedy about an important city official who goes off to the country to paint and there discovers unexpected friendships and new loyalties. Western critics have found *Whistle Stop* a lyrical and engaging movie but it apparently had a cool reception in the Soviet Union, and this presumably contributed to Barnet's decision to take his own life in 1965. He left a note saying that he seemed to have lost the ability to make good films, and with it the desire to live.

"I am not a theoretical man," Barnet told Georges Sadoul in 1959. "I take the material for my films from life." This, together with the fact that he was never a member of the "montage school" so influential in the heroic age of the Soviet cinema, may account for the fact that Barnet has until recently been regarded by most critics as a relatively minor figure in the Soviet pantheon. There have always been a few who recognized his real worth, however—especially in France. Sadoul called him "the best Soviet director of comedies, gentle and lyrical in his approach, full of warmth in his perceptive observation of behavior." It is a view likely to be more widely held after the British retrospective of 1980, which showed eleven of his best films (including some unavailable for many years). Indeed, there were signs of an immediate reassessment of Barnet's work—Tony Rayns called him "one of the greatest 'undiscovered' directors ever," and said that "his feeling for locations and characters is completely modern, and his use of studio sets is wonderfully inventive."

John Gillett has described Barnet as "a narrative director possessing some affinities with American filmmakers like Hawks, McCarey, and La Cava." In the best of his films, "we find very distinctive qualities: a love for eccentric, way-out characters, a skill in staging physical action . . . and an ability to use specific locations as vivid backdrops to his stories. . . . The main connecting link can be found in his women, most of whom avoid the coy and clichéd stereotypes which often disfigure Soviet films . . . [and are] usually perky, punchy and confident. . . . Barnet's best films, ranging over nearly forty years of work, can still give pleasure because they possess a lasting exuberance and lyricism, allied to a feeling for film language which is at least as potent as some of his more publicised contemporaries."

The actress Yelena Kuzmina, in a memoir written shortly after Barnet's death, recalled his unorthodox way with a script: "With huge scissors he cut and clipped the text, tearing it apart into individual pieces, sequences and shots. These pieces he rearranged, reinserted, wrote something on, threw something out, and finally glued them together in an infinitely long scroll. If he had to find a certain place, he would spread the scroll out on the floor and crawl along it on all fours." And very often after all this "when shooting started, the scroll was calmly left at home. Something completely different was shot." When he was immersed in filming, he sometimes worked day and night for long periods without leaving the studio. Then he might go out; drink, talk, and be "the life of the party," and afterwards "dunk his head in cold water" and go back to work. Barnet was "a strange, surprising man," Kuzmina says, and "infinitely kind"—in very cold weather "he could rip off his scarf and gloves to wrap up some child who happened along the way. He could turn his pockets inside out and give away everything, down to his last coin." He was "a wonderful talker, a wonderful drinking companion" but basically a lonely man, with "no true friends."

FILMS: (with Theodore Otsep) Miss Mend, 1926 (serial); Devushka s korobkoi (Girl With the Hatbox/When Moscow Laughs), 1927; Moskva v Octyabr (Moscow in October), 1927; Dom na Trubnoi (The House on Trubnaya Square), 1928; Production of Musical Instruments, 1930 (documentary); The Piano, 1930 (documentary); Lyodolom (The Thaw/Anka), 1931; Okraina (Patriots/Borderland/Outskirts), 1933; (as codirector) Adin i dysach (One and Ten), 1934; (with S. Mardanov) U samova sinevo morya (By the Bluest of Seas), 1936; Noch v Sentyabr (A Night in September), 1939; Stari nayezdnik (The Old Jockey), 1940 (released 1959); Muzestvo (Manhood/Courage) in Fighting Film Album No. 3, 1941; Bescennaja golova (A Priceless Head) in Fighting Film Album No. 10, 1942; Novgorodnii (The Novgorodians), 1943 (not released); Odnazhdi noch (One Night/Dark Is the Night), 1945; Podvig razvedchika (Exploit of an Intelligence Agent), 1947; (with Alexander Macharet) Stranitsy zhizn (Pages of Life), 1948; Schedroye lito (Generous Summer), 1951; Kontsert maystriv Ukrainskogo mystetstva (Concert of Masters of Ukrainian Art), 1952 (documentary); Liana, 1955; Poet (The Poet), 1957; (with Konstantin Yudin) Boryets i kloun (The Wrestler and the Clown), 1957; Annushka, 1959; Alionka, 1962; Polustanok (Whistle Stop), 1963.

ABOUT: Birkos, A. S. Soviet Cinema, 1976; Leyda, J. Kino, 1960; Who's Who in the USSR, 1961–1962. Periodicals—Film Comment Fall 1968; Film Culture Fall 1965; Film Dope March 1973; Morning Star (Britain) July 8, 1980; Sight and Sound Autumn 1980; Time Out July 11–17, 1980.

BECKER, JACQUES (September 15, 1906–February 20, 1960), French director, was born in Paris, the son of a wealthy French industrialist and a Scotswoman who later directed a Paris fashion house. He had his formal schooling at the Lycée Condorcet, Schola Cantorum, and Breguet College but, according to Jean Quéval, received a no less important part of his education in movie theatres and through phonograph records of the great jazz musicians of his youth. His father wanted him to train as an engineer and put him to work in a factory manufacturing electric storage cells. Becker had other ideas and at the age of eighteen got himself a job in charge of the baggage service of a shipping line operating between Le Havre and New York, in this way meeting or at least hearing live such heroes as Duke Ellington.

The Beckers were friends of the family of the painter Paul Cézanne. It was while vacationing at Marlotte with the Cézannes that Jacques Becker first met Jean Renoir, son of another great Impressionist. Renoir, who was just beginning his career as a film director, was not much impressed. The twenty-year-old Becker seemed "the perfect embodiment of everything that I

JACQUES BECKER

most dislike—a member of the French upper class, well acquainted with bars and nightclubs and given to the pursuit of elegant sports." Moreover, Becker "possessed a talent for elegance. He understood fashion and knew how to adapt it to his own personality. I am not thinking only of clothes but of the modes of thought and action, of seating oneself, of paying the waiter who serves the drink in a café, which were current among the small group of people who were 'in the know.' In all the ritual gestures of life he was ten years ahead of his time."

However, Renoir goes on, "when I had got past that veneer I found myself confronted by someone who was both lovable and ardent. His enthusiasm for the films which I also liked, notably Stroheim's *Greed,* and above all his approach to his fellow men definitely rid me of the idea that he was a snob. He loved mankind not in any generalized, theoretical way but directly and in terms of the individual." For Becker's part, the meeting with Renoir turned him definitely towards filmmaking as a career. Over the next few years he made various attempts to enter the industry, on one occasion almost talking himself into a job as assistant to King Vidor. He met Renoir again by chance in 1931 and worked with him from 1932 until 1939. Becker was Renoir's assistant on some of his finest films, including *Boudu sauvé des eaux* (in which he also played a minor role), *Madame Bovary* (in which he contributed to the script), *Le Crime de Monsieur Lange, Les Bas-fonds, Une Partie de campagne, La Grande Illusion* (in which he played an English officer), *La Bête humaine,* and *La Règle du jeu.* For part of this period he lived as a member

of the Renoir family—Renoir called him "my brother and my son."

In 1934 Becker was codirector with Pierre Prévert of a delightful short comedy called *Le Commissaire est bon enfant,* based on two Courteline farces. About the same time, according to Georges Sadoul, he made the five-reel *Tête de turc* (1935), but later refused to acknowledge it as his work. He also repudiated his first feature, *L'Or du Christobal* (*The Gold of Christobal*). Becker started this film in 1939 but had to abandon it when he was inducted into the army at the outbreak of World War II.

Becker's career as a director began in earnest in 1941, when he returned to France after two years in a German prisoner-of-war camp. The first of the three films he made during the Occupation was *Dernier Atout* (*The Last Trump,* 1942), an expert but conventional thriller that was intended as a substitute for the American films denied to French audiences by the war. *Goupi Mains Rouges* (*It Happened at the Inn,* 1943), adapted from a Pierre Véry novel by Becker and the author, is also a detective mystery but with a peasant setting, shot on location in the Charente. Four generations of the quarrelsome Goupi family dominate their village, and when one of the family is killed and another suspected of the murder they close ranks to present a united front. Fernand Ledoux gives a memorable performance as the peasant poacher Goupi Mains Rouges (Goupi Red-hands). The action centers around a country inn, and the authenticity and warm humor of this carefully detailed portrait of French rural life made it a highly successful film in the bleak years of the Occupation. *Falbalas* (*Paris Frills,* 1945) is a tragicomedy about intrigues behind the scenes in a large Parisian fashion house.

While making the picture, Becker and his crew managed to hide film stock and equipment at various points around the city; these materials were used for a Resistance documentary on the street fighting that preceded the Liberation.

In his wartime works Becker had clearly developed a personal style, realistic in a manner that showed the extent of his debt to Renoir but marked by an almost obsessive concern with detailed authenticity and an "entomological" interest in human psychology and relationships. His first three postwar films were all psychological comedies with Paris settings, gently humorous explorations of the changing relationships within a carefully observed section of French society. Though *Antoine et Antoinette* (1947) involves a search for a lost lottery ticket, the plot is no more than an excuse for an affectionate study of the misunderstandings, quarrels, and reconciliations of the young couple of the title, and the everyday details of their lives in a working-class suburb. The film was called a "minor revelation," and warmly praised by Peter Ericsson for the "intriguing mixture of detachment and sympathy" Becker brings to the portrayal of his characters and their relationships—their "scarcely perceptible reactions, the interplay of suspicions and allegiances, of sudden switches of atmosphere or tension." In *Rendez-vous de juillet* (*Rendezvous in July,* 1949), the group under study is made up of five young people in postwar Paris whose lives revolve around college and Left Bank jazz clubs and whose love affairs, enthusiasms, and ambitions are recorded with sympathetic curiosity. In this film, as in its predecessor, Becker shot on location and used a great number of individual camera set-ups, cutting rapidly from one to another to convey a vigorous and richly detailed sense of the city and its people. It is an example of Becker's exceptional skill in achieving an appropriate rhythm for each of his extremely varied films.

The most successful of Becker's Parisian comedies was *Édouard et Caroline* (1951). Its slender plot concerns a young couple—beautifully played by Anne Vernon and Daniel Gélin—whose marriage almost founders in the course of an attempt to launch Édouard in high society at a reception where he is to make his name as a concert pianist. The film has been compared to Renoir's *La Règle du jeu* and has the same kind of charm and lightness of touch, ironically exploring the emptiness and hypocrisy of fashionable society without ever descending to caricature or denying the humanity of its characters.

Casque d'Or (*Golden Helmet/Golden Marie*), the very different film that followed in 1952, is regarded by many critics as Becker's masterpiece. Written mostly by the director himself, it is set at the turn of the century and based on the true story of a young workingman who was drawn into the Paris underworld by his love for the beautiful prostitute Casque d'Or, killed for her, and died on the guillotine. Becker marvellously evokes the Paris of the 1890s, beginning with the carefree scene on the river—like a Renoir painting—where Manda (Serge Reggiana) first sees Casque d'Or, played with powerful sensuality by the young Simone Signoret. There is no attempt to romanticize the brutality of the underworld, with its knife fights and treacheries, but these ugly scenes are balanced by the poignant lyricism of moments like the unforgettable one when the two lovers wake up to their first breakfast together in the sunlit tranquility of a country cottage. And the film ends not with the obscene haste and squalor of Manda's execution—watched by the desolate Casque d'Or from a rented attic—but with a flashback to the two lovers dancing together in their time of happiness. In this film, as Roy Armes wrote, "the scenes are unfolded with a fine sense of rhythm and the action moves easily from the studio sets out into the open air and back again. . . . All Becker's usual attributes are present; a concern with love and friendship, exactitude in the handling of details of background, an ability to sustain transitions of mood and atmosphere; but here . . . there is the added dimension of death, for the love is of a kind that drives a man to murder and the friendship of a degree that demands self-sacrifice."

In *Rue de l'Estrapade* (*Françoise Steps Out,* 1953), Becker tried to repeat the success of *Édouard et Caroline* with another Parisian comedy. The result seemed to most critics weak and predictable. Becker turned to the gangster movie with *Touchez pas au Grisbi* (*Grisbi/Honor Among Thieves,* 1954), adapted from a novel by Albert Simonin (who also wrote the book on which Jules Dassin's 1955 *Rififi* was based. These two pictures began the vogue for *film noir* which became such a feature of French cinema in the late 1950s.) Though the story is a fairly standard one about gang warfare after a big gold bullion robbery, Becker's interest is focused on the paradoxes of the criminal character, rather than on violence for its own sake. He is fascinated by the contrast between the luxurious apartments and fastidious manners of his gangsters and their methodical violence and casual treachery. Jean Gabin has one of his finest roles as Max-le-Menteur, a rich, powerful, but aging gangster who, behind the inscrutable face he presents to the world, is tiring of the life he has chosen, and who in the end sacrifices a fortune out of loyalty to an old friend.

Ali Baba et les quarante voleurs (*Ali Baba and the Forty Thieves,* 1954) is a lavish adaptation of the Arabian Nights story, with Fernandel as a naive servant who outwits the forty thieves to win the love of a beautiful dancer. It was followed by *Les Aventures d'Arsène Lupin* (*The Adventures of Arsène Lupin,* 1956), in which Robert Lamoureux plays Maurice Leblanc's gentleman thief (and part-time detective). With its period settings beautifully created in color, this was a sophisticated and highly enjoyable comedy-thriller. There was a mixed critical reception for *Montparnasse 19* (*The Lovers of Montparnasse,* 1957), in which Gérard Philipe gave a superb performance as the Italian-born painter and sculptor Modigliani, who settled in Paris in 1906 and became the archetypal bohemian artist.

Even more than Toulouse-Lautrec, Gauguin, or Van Gogh, Modigliani led a life that seems almost custom-made for romantic film treatment. The handsome young artist was addicted not only to women but to drink and drugs, and was obliged to sell his wonderfully expressive drawings for a few *sous* at café tables. "I am going to drink myself dead," he said, and he achieved that aim at thirty-five, despite the efforts of numerous devoted women (including his pregnant mistress, who committed suicide two days after his death). The film gained pre-release notoriety because of a controversy over its script. Max Ophuls had at the time of his death been working on it with Henri Jeanson; when Becker took over he rewrote it completely, provoking a violent quarrel with Jeanson. Becker pursued historical accuracy even more rigorously here than in *Casque d'Or,* but Tom Milne thought that "despite moments of brilliance . . . and despite Godard's brilliant defense of it as a film about the fear of making a film," *Montparnasse 19* was one of Becker's weakest films, "partly because the script founders in notions of Art, Suffering, and Romance, but more particularly because Becker was obviously inhibited by the need to stick to so-called facts."

Becker's last film, *Le Trou* (*The Night Watch/The Hole,* 1960), deals with an escape from prison. Its use of nonprofessional actors and austere, almost documentary style brought inevitable comparisons with Bresson, whose own great film on a similar theme, *Un Condamné à mort s'est échappé,* had been made three years earlier. But where Bresson's interest is in the spiritual effects of isolation and confinement and the exultation of freedom, Becker's is characteristically a much more humanistic interest—a psychological exploration in depth of the characters of his prisoners. The story is simple: Four men are sharing a cell into which a fifth prisoner is sent, a young car salesman who has tried to murder his rich wife. They draw him into their plan to dig a hole and tunnel their way out, using improvised tools ingeniously created out of anything that comes to hand. There is no music, only natural sounds, as we watch the prisoners working together to overcome obstacles, with suspense and tension mounting until the final agonizing betrayal.

Tom Milne wrote that *Le Trou* was the most perfectly crafted of Becker's films "in its spare, classical simplicity," but "also his least memorable. . . . it is not really *moving* because it obstinately refuses to yield the resonance that comes from the quality of memory inherent in Becker's images elsewhere." However, some Anglo-Saxon critics and many French ones consider *Le Trou* to be Becker's best film, preferring it to *Casque*

d'Or, which was not much admired in France. (André Bazin said of the latter that it was only Lindsay Anderson's high regard for it "that led me to reconsider my own view and to see virtues in the film which had escaped me.")

Becker died when he was only fifty-three and at the height of his powers. Roy Armes called him "one of the most talented and certainly the most versatile of his generation, for his unfeigned liking of people allowed him to be equally at home in domestic comedy and period tragedy, with peasants and with gangsters. Despite this diversity of subject matter virtually all of Becker's work bears his distinctive signature." All the same, Armes believes that Becker "lacked the genuine creative impulse" and points out that he relied mostly on scripts written by others (though "his preference for thin plots was perhaps a way of ensuring the predominance of his own contribution, the visual element"). Penelope Houston received from Becker's work "a sense of talent never employed for long at full stretch"—"of a sympathetic voice muffled by hesitancies about precisely what was to be said." On the other hand, Armes allows that "the remarkable thing about his work is the frequency with which he succeeded despite his script."

There is a growing feeling in some quarters that Becker's films have been underestimated, partly because of the contemporary critical emphasis on social criticism. Becker was too fond of people to present any of them as absolute villains (except perhaps the *apache* Leca in *Casque d'Or*) and less inclined to attack or satirize social groups than to explore them. The imaginative sympathy with which he did this gives even the most lighthearted of his comedies value as social documents and has put some critics in mind of Balzac. Becker's admirers believe that this, together with his technical mastery, his warm humanity and poetic power, and his great skill as a director of actors, should earn him a higher place among postwar French directors than he has so far been allowed.

Becker was married to the actress Françoise Fabian and had four children, one of whom, Jean, is also a film director. Jacques Becker was president of the Fédération Française des Ciné-Clubs.

—*K.B.*

FILMS: (with Pierre Prévert) Le Commissaire est bon enfant (The Superintendent Is a Good Sort), 1935 (short); L'Or du Christobal (The Gold of Christobal), 1939 (completed by Jean Stelli); Dernier Atout (The Last Trump, 1942); Goupi-Mains-Rouges (It Happened at the Inn/It Happened in the Inn), 1943; Falbalas (Paris Frills), 1945; Antoine et Antoinette (Antoine and Antoinette), 1947; Rendez-vous de juillet

(Rendezvous in July), 1949; Édouard et Caroline (Edward and Caroline), 1951; Casque d'Or (Golden Helmet/Golden Marie), 1952; Rue de L'Estrapade (Françoise Steps Out), 1953; Touchez pas au Grisbi (U.S., Grisbi/U.K., Honour Among Thieves), 1954; Ali Baba et les quarante voleurs (Ali Baba and the Forty Thieves), 1954; Les Aventures d'Arsène Lupin (The Adventures of Arsène Lupin), 1956; Montparnasse 19 (The Lovers of Montparnasse), 1957; Le Trou (U.S., The Night Watch/U.K., The Hole), 1960. *Published scripts*—Rendez-vous de juillet, by Raymond Queneau and Jean Quéval, 1949 (France); Le Trou *in* L'Avant-Scène du Cinéma March 1962; Casque d'Or *in* L'Avant-Scène du Cinéma December 1964.

ABOUT: Armes, R. French Cinema Since 1946: 1, 1966; Ehrlich, E. Cinema of Paradox, 1985; Gilson, R. Becker, 1966 (France); Jeanne, R. and Ford, C. Paris vu par le cinéma, 1969 (France); Leprohon, P. Présences contemporaines, cinéma, 1957 (France); Quéval, J. Jacques Becker, 1962 (France); Renoir, J. My Life and My Films, 1974; Roud, R. (ed.) Cinema: A Critical Dictionary, 1980; Sadoul, G. French Film, 1953. *Periodicals*—L'Avant-Scène du Cinéma 13 1962; Bianco e Nero July 1964; Cahiers du Cinéma November 1953, February 1954, April 1960; Cinéma (France) May 1958, May, June, and July 1960; Films and Filming March 1955; Films in Review April 1960; Image et Son October 1960, November 1969; New York Times February 22, 1960; Sight and Sound Spring 1960, Summer 1969.

"BERKELEY, BUSBY" (William Berkeley Enos) (November 29, 1895–March 14, 1976), American director and choreographer, was born in Los Angeles, the second son of Francis Enos and the former Gertrude Berkeley. Both parents acted and toured with the Tim Frawley Repertory Company, the father also serving on occasion as director. Busby (nicknamed after another Frawley actress, Amy Busby) traveled all over the United States with the company and made an unremarked debut at the age of five, when his brother George, then appearing as an Arab in *Under Two Flags,* smuggled him on stage under his burnoose.

Berkeley's parents, who had wanted a better career for their sons than the theatre, frowned on this development and in due course packed Busby off to the Mohegan Lake Military Academy in New York State. Graduating in 1914, he found a job as a management trainee in a Massachusetts shoe factory. It was not what he wanted, and in 1917, the day before the United States entered World War I, he enlisted in the army.

It was in France, as a second lieutenant in the artillery, that Berkeley had his first experience of conducting large numbers of people through complex movements. Bored with routine parade

BUSBY BERKELEY

drills, he "worked out a trick drill for the twelve hundred men. I explained the movements by numbers and gave the section leaders instructions for their companies and had them do the whole thing without any audible orders. . . . It was quite something to see a parade square full of squads and companies of men marching in patterns, in total silence."

After a stint in occupied Germany as an assistant entertainment officer, Berkeley returned jobless to civilian life. His show business career began around 1920 when the theatre (and later screen) director John Cromwell, a family friend, overcame his parents' resistance and gave him a role in a stock company production of *The Man Who Came Back.* That lasted a year and was followed by a long period of unemployment, then by an assortment of jobs as actor, assistant stage manager, and director with stock companies, and three years (1923–1926) playing the fashion designer Madame Lucy in a Broadway revival of *Irene.* Soon afterwards Berkeley received his first assignments as a dance director, and he had his first success in 1927 with Rodgers and Hammerstein's *A Connecticut Yankee.*

"I don't know one note of music from another and I never took a dancing lesson in my life," Berkeley told an interviewer many years later. What he lacked in expertise he made up for in gall. In *A Connecticut Yankee,* for example, he decided that in a scene featuring Guinevere's dancing class the queen should teach the first five positions of the dance. Unfortunately Berkeley didn't know what these were, so he bluffed the dancers on stage into demonstrating them. Further assignments followed in quick succession, and in 1928 he was producer and director as well as choreographer of *The Street Singer.*

By 1930 Berkeley was one of the most sought-after dance directors on Broadway, with a reputation for devising complex dance numbers featuring flamboyant groupings on staircases or tiered revolves, with swirling drapes and brilliant lighting. At that point Sam Goldwyn brought Berkeley to Hollywood to direct the production numbers for *Whoopee* (1930), starring Eddie Cantor as a hypochondriac on a western dude ranch. This sort of importation was common enough at the time. The Hollywood studios were still grappling with the transition to sound and looked to Broadway for its experts on the proper uses of words and music. The initial result was a series of musicals and semi-musicals in which the performers sang, spoke, and danced while the camera sat front-row center, a motionless spectator.

Whoopee did not depart radically from this formula except during one otherwise routine dance number set in an Indian reservation. "Suddenly," wrote Arthur Knight, "the camera . . . leaped aloft and the dancers began to form geometric patterns designed solely for its benefit. . . . For a brief, exhilarating moment, the movies had been liberated from the literal limitations of a stage. For a brief, exhilarating moment, we were permitted to soar into the realm of pure cinema." Berkeley, who had accepted the assignment without much enthusiasm, found the new medium unexpectedly challenging and stayed on as dance director of other Goldwyn musicals—*Kiki,* with Mary Pickford (1931), *Palmy Days* (1931), *Flying High* (1931), *Night World* (1932), King Vidor's *Bird of Paradise* (1932), and Leo McCarey's *The Kid From Spain* (1932).

Though some of these movies were said to be "more fluid" than the average Hollywood musical of the period, none of them showed the capacity to astonish that had flared briefly in *Whoopee.* It was not until Berkeley moved to Warner Brothers in 1933 that his talents flowered. By this time he had "realized that in the theatre your eyes can go any place you want, but in pictures the only way I could entertain an audience was through the single eye of the camera. But with that single eye, I could go anywhere I wanted to."

He showed what he meant in his first Warners musical, *42nd Street,* Lloyd Bacon's 1933 remake of a film called *On With the Show* (1929), with Warner Baxter as a Broadway producer ordered into retirement by his doctor but determined to stage one last spectacular hit. It starred the new singing team of Dick Powell and Ruby

Keeler and gave Ginger Rogers her first major role as a tough, wisecracking blonde with a heart of gold. (It also features the archetypal and prophetic line, delivered by Baxter to Ruby Keeler: "You're going out there a kid, but you're coming back a star.") Such riches notwithstanding, *42nd Street* owed its immense success above all to Busby Berkeley, who here emerged as the pioneer of a revolution in screen choreography, single-handedly and at a stroke reversing a sharp decline in the production and consumption of Hollywood musicals.

Berkeley never tired of proclaiming his ignorance of the elements of dance, and Arthur Knight has said that "the interesting thing about the best of the Busby Berkeley routines . . . is that dancing *per se* really had very little to do with it. The people in his movies really weren't dancers. . . . In Berkeley's beloved serpentine movements, it was enough that each dancer merely extended her leg in the proper succession, or remove a hat. . . . Well before abstractionism had become established as a basic principle of modern art, Berkeley was using it in his films. The last thing I should want to do, however, would be to claim any conscious link between Berkeley as an avant garde film artist and any of the other avant garde artists of the day. I think such a link exists, mind you; but as something evolving from all art forms simultaneously, not as a preconceived notion on Berkeley's part. . . . And yet it's all there—the concern with image above sense, the concern with style above content, the concern with form above communication."

The great set pieces in *42nd Street* include Berkeley's staging of "Shuffle Off to Buffalo" inside a Pullman car, and the title song itself, which opens with Ruby Keeler dancing on the roof of a taxicab and soon has Manhattan itself dancing, each chorus girl carrying a section of skyscrapered skyline. For Arthur Knight, the Berkeley magic first showed itself "when the camera began to move restlessly between the shapely legs of the chorines in *42nd Street,* all of them performing feats of erotic athleticism to the tune of 'I'm Young and Healthy.' Certainly, by the show's finale, a sharply visual interpretation of the film's catchy title song, most of us were aware that something new and exciting had happened to movie musicals. Although framed in a proscenium arch, the curtain had barely risen on the stylized Times Square setting before Berkeley's camera . . . [was] in motion, building a whirlwind kaleidoscope of a young hick's first impression of the Big City, complete with thieves, prostitutes, and an abundant array of showgirls."

Warner Brothers had just built their splendid new studios at Burbank—a vast, hangar-like construction housing one of the largest sound stages in the world—and were prepared to gamble on their brilliant young crowd-pleaser. *Gold Diggers of 1933,* directed by Mervyn LeRoy and choreographed by Busby Berkeley, opens with "We're in the Money," a gorgeously vulgar number featuring Ginger Rogers garbed in gold dollars, and goes on to the sexually suggestive "Pettin' in the Park" and an elaborate show-stopper called "The Shadow Waltz," in which sixty illuminated violins, slung around the necks of as many chorines in transparent skirts, build into a single enormous violin shape. And lest these glittering fantasies should seem escapist in the gloom of the Depression, there is "My Forgotten Man," sung by Joan Blondell and Etta Moten—a direct if sentimental reminder of the fate of the jobless veterans of World War I.

Footlight Parade, directed by Lloyd Bacon the same year, features three major production numbers purporting to be movie theatre "prologues"—brief stage shows offered as *aperitifs* to major feature films. Those in *Footlight Parade* are in fact far too elaborate to fit on any movie house stage—the prurient "Honeymoon Hotel" with its enormous set; "Shanghai Lil," in which Ruby Keeler impersonates a Chinese prostitute and James Cagney her sailor lover; and "By a Waterfall," the quintessential Berkeley production number.

"By a Waterfall" begins in a Hollywood dell, where Dick Powell croons to an ecstatic Ruby Keeler. The camera then pulls back to reveal the waterfall itself with Berkeley girls sliding down it like half-naked nymphs. The camera retreats still further to disclose an immense pool where the girls dive, swim, and float to form geometric patterns that fold and unfold like flowers, separate and rejoin in new shapes, and finally assemble themselves into a multitiered human fountain from which water cascades into the pool. Through all this, as Arthur Knight points out, the principals are virtually forgotten, while "the dance itself is fragmented almost beyond belief—shots from out front, from above, from below, under water, shots from a mobile camera as it swoops past the girls, shots from an immobile camera placed at wildly askew angles. It is the camera that is doing the dancing, not the chorines!"

Berkeley's delight in the extravagant and bizarre extended increasingly to costumes as well as sets, and "Those Beautiful Dames" in *Dames* (1934) is virtually a fashion parade. "I Only Have Eyes for You" in the same movie achieves a new level of surreal play. Here, according to

Arlene Croce, Berkeley "plays not only with human geometry but with optical mazes and illogical transitions in scale, reaching the Nirvana of pure abstraction. The end of the number is a pull-back from a giant scaffold on the several levels of which girls recline. When the screen becomes a grid filled with tiny figures, Dick Powell's head bursts through it in close-up."

Though he was without formal training, Berkeley had an extraordinary instinct for what the camera could achieve and a lively erotic imagination—he is said to have conceived many of his numbers while soaking himself for hours in a hot bath. He knew exactly what he wanted and Warner Brothers, riding high on the profits from his extravaganzas, were prepared to let him have it. Berkeley spent as much as $10,000 a minute on his production numbers—a staggering sum in those days—and Warners grinned and bore it as his demands for new equipment grew ever more ambitious and outlandish.

With the sometimes skeptical assistance of the studio's brilliant technical team, he installed a monorail for overhead tracking shots and marshalled the most awesome array of cranes, hoists, and aerial platforms ever seen. He is said to have spent much of his time sixty feet in the air, descending god-like on an enormous boom to address his disciples, whisking himself out of reach if interfering executives appeared on set. As John Gillett says, "if there is a single stylistic device always associated with Berkeley, it is the overhead shot with objects moving up to the lens, or simply a vertical top shot looking down on dancers who suddenly splay out into flower formations or shimmer like a kaleidoscope. Berkeley recalled that in order to get high enough he bored several holes in the roofs of Warners' sound stages. He certainly did not originate the device . . . but he used it as a graphic 'show stopper.'" Berkeley's achievements are all the more remarkable in that he always worked with a single camera, instead of the three or four used in similar production numbers by others (thus achieving a voyeuristic single viewpoint on the gyrations of his chorines).

None of his triumphs would have been possible without the handpicked "Berkeley Girls." He had a dozen of them under personal contract "and these would be the pearls against which the other girls, needed for each new film, would be matched." Fed and exercised like athletes, these wretched young women would dance and smile their way through long days of rehearsal under the lights, wearing aluminum brassieres or thirty-pound dollar motifs; they would stand for hours up to their necks in tepid water or slide, still smiling, over abrasive waterfalls. The bait, of course, was the possibility of stardom, but only a few escaped the chorus line, the most famous of these being Lucille Ball, Paulette Goddard, and Betty Grable. There were those in the 1930s who called Berkeley's choreography fascistic, saying that he used human beings as mere components in abstract designs (just as Leni Riefenstahl did in *Triumph of the Will*). Others denied this, pointing out that Berkeley's routines were studded with close-ups of his dancers—itself an innovation in this kind of choreography.

Berkeley's success seems to have been equally compounded of his grandiose visions and his dogged, detailed perfectionism in bringing them to life—the insistence on planning and rehearsing every human and every camera movement until all the problems were ironed away and a scene could be wrapped up in one long take. Berkeley said that he "never needed retakes. I would plan it all so carefully in my mind, I knew *exactly* what I wanted hours before I got to the studio. . . . I had the best talent, the best designers, the best writers. But I worked out every single camera set-up. I cut in the camera. If an editor had to trim more than three or four feet off the end of a take then I knew I had overshot the mark. . . . I asked nothing that wasn't possible; it was simply a matter of getting cooperation."

The first movie that Berkeley directed as well as choreographed was *Gold Diggers of 1935,* which contained two of his most spectacular production numbers. In "The Words Are in My Heart," fifty-six white grand pianos, each "played" by its own chorus girl, gyrate around the enormous sound stage in waltz time (maneuvered by stage hands dressed in black for invisibility). The brilliant "Lullaby of Broadway" (which earned Berkeley an Oscar nomination) opens with a white dot on a black screen. The dot enlarges to become the face of Wini Shaw, filling the screen as she sings her lullaby. After a montage of New York nightlife, Wini Shaw returns to her squalid tenement in the early morning while the rest of the city starts its day, and in the evening resumes her febrile pursuit of pleasure with top-hatted Dick Powell. This reaches a crescendo in a great ballroom with a hundred dancers tapping out the rhythm, and ends with Wini Shaw's suicidal fall from the balcony of a skyscraper and a quiet rendering of "Good Night, Baby."

Later the same year the high life nearly killed Berkeley himself. He was driving home from a party when a tire blew out and he crashed into another car. Berkeley was pulled from his burning roadster and charged with drunk driving and second-degree murder. After three trials,

Berkeley was cleared, but the scandal damaged his reputation. Moreover, the heyday of the musical extravaganza was passing—the public was losing its taste for this kind of entertainment and the studios were beginning to find it prohibitively expensive. The last three big Warner Brothers musicals choreographed by Berkeley were *Varsity Show* (1937), *Hollywood Hotel* (1937), and *Gold Diggers in Paris* (1938). None of them was a hit.

Berkeley was perfectly prepared to try his hand at other genres and in 1938 made *Garden of the Moon,* starring Pat O'Brien as a night club owner, John Payne as a band leader, and Margaret Lindsay as the girl they both want. A musical, but one without major production numbers, it was moderately well received as "a delightful satire on Los Angeles manners." A more unexpected departure was *They Made Me a Criminal* (1939), a gritty thriller with John Garfield as a boxer who flees west because he believes that he has killed a man, is pursued by a relentless detective (Claude Rains), but is eventually saved by a gang of golden-hearted young toughs (played by Billy Halop, Leo Gorcey, Huntz Hall, and other Dead End Kids). Most critics have found it uneven in tone and overly sentimental.

Denied a promised salary increase, Berkeley left Warner Brothers and went to MGM. His first film as director there was *Babes in Arms* (1939), a Rodgers and Hart musical starring Judy Garland and Mickey Rooney. A likable backstage piece about young troupers driving out discredited old vaudevillians, it was a hit, and MGM exploited this successful new formula (with the same stars) in *Strike Up the Band* (1940), about a high school band, and *Babes on Broadway* (1941), in which Garland and Rooney stage a show for charity. All three movies were liberally spiced with spectacular production numbers, though some critics thought that Berkeley's work by now showed an almost obsessive interest in the purely mechanical aspects and a comparative paucity of invention. At the same time Berkeley was continuing to work as choreographer on MGM movies by other directors, including Robert Z. Leonard's *Ziegfeld Girl* (1941), Norman Z. McLeod's *Lady Be Good* (1941), and Norman Taurog's *Girl Crazy* (1943).

On loan to Twentieth Century-Fox in 1943, Berkeley recovered his form with *The Gang's All Here,* in which Phil Baker plays a rich boy posing as a poor GI to woo a dancer (Alice Faye). For a number of critics, this surreal extravaganza remains Berkeley's masterpiece. There is a manic (and phallic) piece of lunacy involving Carmen Miranda and a number of giant bananas, but it was the finale, the "Polka-Dot

Ballet," that astonished the reviewers. Berkeley later explained that he had built "a great kaleidoscope, two mirrors fifty feet high and fifteen feet wide which together formed a V design. In the center of this I had a revolving platform eighteen feet in diameter, and as I took the camera high up between these two mirrors, the girls on the revolving platform below formed an endless design of symmetrical forms. In another shot, I dropped from above sixty neon-lighted hoops which the girls caught and used in their dance maneuvers." The number ends, according to another account, "with the tiny disembodied heads of the entire cast bobbing about the screen in full-throated song."

In 1946 Berkeley's beloved mother died, after a prolonged and expensive illness that left him penniless and in debt, and his fifth marriage collapsed. Berkeley attempted suicide and, though he survived, began to speak of himself as a "has-been." Two years later, tired of that role, he found himself one or two modest assignments and then was taken on by MGM as director of *Take Me Out to the Ball Game* (1949), a period piece starring Frank Sinatra and Gene Kelly as ball players who double as vaudeville entertainers and find one day that their team has been taken over by a woman (Esther Williams). Warm-hearted, funny, and effervescent, it was choreographed not by Berkeley but by Gene Kelly and Stanley Donen, and it has been seen as a forerunner of *On the Town* and of a new kind of movie musical. It brought Berkeley *Photoplay*'s Blue Ribbon Award and the industry's Laurel Award, but had a mixed reception from the critics.

Take Me Out to the Ball Game was the last movie directed by Busby Berkeley, though he was choreographer or second unit director on seven more films during the early 1950s, and in 1962 came out of retirement to devise the elaborate circus numbers for MGM's ambitious screen version of Rodgers and Hart's *Jumbo*. Otherwise, Berkeley spent the last two decades of his life with his sixth wife, Etta Dunn, in a modest villa at Palm Desert, California. He directed plays at a local theatre and "waited for the phone to ring." It began to do so with increasing frequency after a National Film Theatre retrospective in 1965. A compilation film called *An Evening With Busby Berkeley* began to circulate at festivals, and revivals of his musicals on late-night television turned him into a cult figure. In 1971 he played a cameo role in a movie called *The Phynx*, and in 1971 he returned to Broadway as "supervisor" of a revival of *No, No, Nanette,* with his old star Ruby Keeler. During his last years he traveled all over the world to accept awards and deliver lectures.

Arlene Croce wrote that by the late 1970s, Berkeley had "moved from being a semi-fatuous enthusiasm of the avant-garde to a staple of the '30s-memorabilia addicts and the subject of something like a popular cult." In her opinion, "he was probably the greatest choreographer who has ever worked directly with the processed effects possible only in the movies." Another writer has called him "a real artist of the absurd."

Berkeley himself would have rejected the word "choreographer"—"Me, I was always a dance director." His philosophy, he said, "was purely—call it gigantic entertainment." According to Ruby Keeler, "he was a forceful, positive man bursting with ideas. He was into everything and seemed to know everything. He would argue with cameramen and composers and producers who would tell him what he wanted couldn't be done. But it would be done, and done exactly as he wanted it. He was energetic, tireless, tough, and sometimes rough, but look at his pictures and tell me how any other kind of man could have achieved what he did." The filmography below lists the films he choreographed as well as those he directed since, as Georges Sadoul says, he was "far more the author" of many of these than their credited directors.

FILMS: *As choreographer*—Whoopee, 1930; Kiki, 1931; Palmy Days, 1931; Flying High, 1931; Night World, 1932; Bird of Paradise, 1932; The Kid From Spain, 1932; 42nd Street, 1933; Gold Diggers of 1933, 1933; Footlight Parade, 1933; Roman Scandals, 1933; Wonder Bar, 1934; Fashions of 1934, 1934; Twenty Million Sweethearts, 1934; Dames, 1934; Go Into Your Dance, 1935; In Caliente, 1935; Stars Over Broadway, 1935; Gold Diggers of 1937, 1936; The Singing Marine, 1937; Varsity Show, 1937; Gold Diggers in Paris, 1938; Broadway Serenade (Serenade), 1939; Ziegfield Girl, 1941; Lady Be Good, 1941; Born to Sing, 1941; Girl Crazy, 1943; Two Weeks With Love, 1950; Call Me Mister, 1951; Two Tickets to Broadway, 1951; Million Dollar Mermaid (The One-Piece Bathing Suit), 1952; Small Town Girl, 1953; Easy to Love, 1953; Rose Marie, 1954; Jumbo (Billy Rose's Jumbo), 1962. *As director*—(with George Amy) She Had to Say Yes (Beautiful But Dangerous), 1933; Gold Diggers of 1935, 1935; Bright Lights (Funny Face), 1935; I Live for Love (I Live for You), 1935; Stage Struck, 1936; The Go-Getter, 1937; Hollywood Hotel, 1937; Men Are Such Fools, 1938; Garden of the Moon, 1938; Comet Over Broadway, 1938; They Made Me a Criminal, 1939; Babes in Arms, 1939; Fast and Furious, 1939; Forty Little Mothers, 1940; Strike Up the Band, 1940; Blonde Inspiration, 1941; Babes on Broadway, 1941; For Me and My Gal, 1942; The Gang's All Here (The Girls He Left Behind), 1943; Cinderella Jones, 1946; Take Me Out to the Ball Game (Everybody's Cheering), 1949.

ABOUT: Current Biography, 1971; Dunn, D. The Mak-

ing of No, No, Nanette, 1972; Meyer, W. R. Warner
Brothers Directors, 1979; Pike, B. and Martin, D. The
Genius of Busby Berkeley, 1973; Roud, R. (ed.) Cine-
ma: A Critical Dictionary, 1980; Thomas, T. and Ter-
ry, J. The Busby Berkeley Book, 1973.
Periodicals—Action May–June 1974; Avant Scène du
Cinéma April 1978; Cahiers in English 2 1966; Cinéma
(France) January 1966; Écran May 1976; Film Dope
August 1973; Film Quarterly Fall 1976; Guardian De-
cember 27, 1972; New York Times Magazine March
2, 1969; Positif September 1975; Velvet Light Trap
Spring 1971 (reprinted Winter 1977); Wide Angle
Spring 1976.

BLASETTI, ALESSANDRO (July 3, 1900–
February 1, 1987), Italian director, scenarist,
critic, and teacher, was born in Rome, the son of
Giulio Cesare and Augusta Lulani Blasetti. He
began law studies but, infatuated with the cinema, left the university in 1919 to try his hand as
an actor. He began his new career with a bit part
in a thriller by Mario Caserini and other small
parts followed, but after three months he was
fired ("my sacred flame," he explained ironically, "burnt too fiercely for the trade of bit player,
in whom enthusiasm, élan, and unrequested initiative are inappropriate"). He went back to the
university and completed his law degree.

When Blasetti reentered the movie world, it
was as a film critic on *L'Impero*. The year was
1925, and the Italian film industry, formerly one
of the most productive and successful in the
world, had been almost wiped out by foreign
competition and the economic effects of the war.
It was turning out barely a dozen films a year—
spineless formula movies aiming for the lowest
common denominator. In *L'Impero*, Blasetti
launched a violent and remorseless campaign
against the commercial production and movie
magazines, with such effect that his column, "Lo
Schermo" (The Screen), soon outgrew its parent
newspaper and became an independent journal
whose aim was "to give Italy back its own
cinema." In 1926, "after our eventful, battle-
filled first year," the magazine was renamed
Cinematografo.

Like its predecessor, *Cinematografo* campaigned vigorously and noisily for a cinema that
would eschew costume epics and melodrama
and address itself to contemporary Italian life
and problems. Among those who joined Blasetti
as contributors to that famous journal were
many who contributed in important ways to the
subsequent renaissance of the Italian cinema, including Libero Solaroli, Mario Serandrei, Aldo
Vergano, Goffredo Alessandrini, Francesco Pasi-
netti, Ferdinando Poggiolo, and Massimo Bon-
tempelli. After three years of public controversy

ALESSANDRO BLASETTI

and private planning, Blasetti and his associates
launched their own cooperative production
company, Augustus, and in December 1928 began shooting their first film. This was *Sole* (*Sun,*
1929), directed by Blasetti and written by him
with Vergano "but with the consultation of
everyone."

Putting their theories into practice and setting
their faces against the whole direction of a cinema designed for "the amusement of idiots," the
Augustus group tackled a contemporary Italian
social issue, showing idealistic young peasants
overcoming conservatism and vested interests in
the name of progress. The subject they chose was
the draining of the Pontine marshes—one of the
undoubted achievements of Mussolini's regime.
"Without deliberately setting out to produce
Fascist propaganda," wrote Carlo Lizzani,
"Blasetti happened to be in agreement with the
slogans of the regime," and the film has suffered
from the fact that it was touted as the first adequate cinematic expression of the Fascist spirit.

Sole was controversial also in its preoccupation with form. Lizzani wrote that "the tight editing, the audacious framings, and . . .
[Blasetti's] tendency to consider bodies and faces
as a form of still life, as beautiful objects rather
than as centers of emotion, passion, and suffering, shifted the center of interest to the form, to
the composition, and away from the scrutiny
and discovery of human nature." While some
have seen in these tendencies the influence of
the great directors of the "heroic age" of Soviet
cinema, the picture has been attacked by anti-
Fascist critics for its formalism—as the first example of what was later labeled "calligraphy."

Because of its theme, on the other hand, *Sole* has been claimed as a forerunner of neorealism. Moreover, the picture was immensely successful, heralding a modest revival in the Italian cinema at the very end of the silent era. A technically uneven, sometimes beautiful, rather ponderously dogmatic film, it is nevertheless of lasting historical interest and importance. Blasetti said, "Its success was so great that it plunged me into bitter passivity, because I realized right away that the best time of my life was over, forever."

Emerging from this sad state with reasonable alacrity, Blasetti made his second feature (in order of filming, not release), *Resurrectio* (*Resurrection*), a sentimental drama of the kind he had spent the previous years denouncing. Attempting to explain this development, a writer in the symposium volume *The Fabulous Thirties* said that Blasetti is more than a director—he is "a total man of the cinema interested in all aspects of this industry-art. . . . Blasetti's great merit lay in not separating the art of film from the industry of cinema, but of always linking the living spirit of experimentation with professionalism. It should not therefore be surprising if one finds in his filmography both innovative films . . . and formula films. . . . These are the two faces of Blasetti, who always strained to make his own individual aims coincide with the evolution of the industry in all its complexity, who always worried lest he became an intellectual cut off from the structures in which films are concretely made. . . . Blasetti has . . . always had the ambition of making films that would influence the Italian cinema, that would constitute models for it." Nino Frank no doubt meant something similar when he called Blasetti "the Don Quixote of the Italian cinema, the least naive and the canniest Don Quixote of them all."

All this makes it at least slightly easier to understand why Blasetti, for long a vehement opponent of the coming of sound, should have been one of the first Italian directors to use it. This was in *Nerone* (*Nero*, 1930), a parody starring the great Roman comic actor Ettore Petrolini. *Terra madre* (1930), another peasant drama, marred by sentimentality but giving further evidence of Blasetti's sense of composition, was followed by *Palio* (1932), starring Guido Celano and Leda Gloria and set in Siena during the traditional horserace around the city square. According to Vernon Jarratt, "Blasetti was at great pains to recapture the characteristic feverish atmosphere of the place during this period, sketching it in with many little touches and subtleties which were sometimes at odds with the rather stolid comedy [of the musical on which it was based]. But although uneven, it has some magnificent moments."

La tavola dei poveri (*The Table of the Poor,* 1932) was a mediocre vehicle for the Neapolitan dialect comedian Raffaele Viviani. The year was more notable for Blasetti's founding of Italy's first film school—initially a department of the Rome Academy of Music but reestablished a few years later as a separate institution, the Centro Sperimentale di Cinematografia. Blasetti taught directing there and served on the board of governors. Beginning in 1937 the CSC published the influential journal *Bianco e Nero* and, though founded under the Fascists, did much to foster the eclectic spirit that permitted the evolution of neorealism. Meanwhile, Blasetti made another important contribution to the development of that movement with *1860* (1933), still regarded by some critics as his masterpiece.

Taken from a story by Gino Mazzucchi, *1860* deals with the adventures of a Sicilian mountaineer who leaves his new bride to fight with Garibaldi. There are some powerful scenes, like the young wife's frantic search for her husband among the dead and dying on the battlefield, and her encounter with a blind, dying soldier who takes her for his mother. According to Ettore Margadonna, *1860* "was the first of the Italian films to use actors taken from real life, and it was one of the best examples of the new cinema style. It was shot largely in Sicily among the actual scenes of Garibaldi's adventurous activities. *1860* is distinguished from contemporary productions by its unusual freshness, by its mass movements which were far different from the 'colossal' formulae of the silent screen, and for an excellence of photography and lighting hitherto unknown."

Carlo Lizzani has drawn attention to the fact that "Garibaldi appears only incidentally and that the main thread is provided by the humble doings of a Sicilian mountain peasant and his young wife." Pierre Leprohon suggests that "this distortion of the usual historical perspective served Blasetti's artistic and perhaps even his political aims. It shifted the center of interest from historical facts to the aspirations of the people, to the point of eclipsing the national hero with a couple played by genuine peasants. His firm adoption of a popular standpoint and a humble authenticity indicate an equivocal attitude towards the imperatives of the regime. The film prudently went no further than Garibaldi's first victory at Calatafimi, thereby avoiding the delicate problems of the hero's struggle against the Papacy. Thus, consciously or unconsciously, Blasetti sidestepped the more or less avowed direction of the dictatorship in order to express what most people felt."

In fact, as *Sole* made clear, Blasetti enthusiastically supported the idealism of the early days of Italian Fascism. According to Lizzani, however, he "was continually on the point of going out on a limb. The more seriously he took Fascism in the years that followed, the further his warm and generous nature took him from the path of conformism." This is very evident in *Vecchia guardia* (*The Old Guard,* 1934), an account of the 1922 March on Rome which led to Mussolini's appointment as Prime Minister. John Gillett has called this one of the key works of the 1930s and "one of Blasetti's most brilliant filmic essays," which "brings us right into the centre of a family caught up in the fever of the new régime by means of a naturalism which takes in sweeping location shooting, natural sound, and the feeling of a lived-in community." However, Blasetti's interest in the people he depicts with such "tenderness and irony" seems greater than his enthusiasm for the March itself, and the film apparently displeased the authorities.

Perhaps for this reason, Blasetti then turned away from contemporary themes and after *Aldebaran* (1935), a conventional tribute to the Italian navy, launched into a series of historical spectaculars. *La Contessa di Parma* (*The Countess of Parma,* 1937), a lively fantasy, was followed by *Ettore Fieramosca* (1938), the story of a medieval condottiere, "full of sweeping movement, picturesque scenes and some fine handling of masses of men," with a memorable duel scene. *Un'avventura di Salvator Rosa,* the swashbuckler that followed in 1939, was the first of several films written by Blasetti in collaboration with Renato Castellani, soon to become a notable director in his own right. Recent critics have discovered a strong element of irony in this movie, one suggesting that "Gino Cervi *acts* the part of the hero, imitating the gestures of Douglas Fairbanks or Errol Flynn, almost as though to tell us that in Italy a hero can exist only as a joke."

Similarly ambivalent intentions have been attributed to *La corona di ferro* (*The Iron Crown,* 1941), which at the time of its release had a critical reception that might have qualified it as one of "the best worst films" ever made. It is a complicated fable with "a timid antiwar theme" about the journey of a great crown sent as a gift by the Byzantine emperor to the pontiff in Rome, and stars Massimo Girotti as a cross between Hercules and Superman. This "Byzantine horse opera" cost forty million lire and employed an army of extras, seven thousand horses, and an entire zoo. It won the Grand Prix in 1941 at the Venice Biennale (then not much more than the festival of the Rome-Berlin axis), but in France it was received with delighted derision. Some critics maintained that Blasetti must have made it tongue in cheek, but the director has

said that he was bitterly disappointed by the critical response to a film he had intended as "a damning accusation against a violent king [Mussolini?] and a condemnation of war." Revived in the 1960s, it was, according to Leprohon, "received with some warmth by younger critics, who found its mad nightmare world in keeping with the pace of their period." *La cena delle beffe* (*The Jester's Supper,* 1941) was another "incredibly ambiguous" costume drama, based on a famous Florentine play full of elaborate hoaxes, bloody revenges, and (according to recent critics) dire Freudian implications.

By this time, the Italian cinema was once more moribund—the Fascists had poured money into the industry but had created a society in which individual creativity was virtually stifled. Then in 1942, the year the Italian opposition parties came back to life, Blasetti—for the second time in his career—completed a movie that heralded a renaissance. This was *Quattro passi fra le nuvole* (*Four Steps in the Clouds*), a film which could scarcely have been more remote from the themes and styles that had engaged him for the previous seven years. Scripted by the director in collaboration with several other writers (most notably Cesare Zavattini), it tells the story of Paolo (Gino Cervi), a harassed salesman on a business trip who meets a girl named Maria (Adriani Benetti) on the train. It turns out that she is going home to confess to her dour peasant family that she is pregnant. Very reluctantly the man agrees to go with her, masquerading as her husband; later, when the deception is discovered, he persuades the puritanical parents to forgive their erring daughter. The interlude is over, and he returns to the city—to his squalid apartment and his sour wife.

"Easily as this could have descended into sentimentality," wrote Joan Lester, "it never does. One of the secrets of its success is its penetrating, affectionate understanding of humanity. Even while you laugh at the bus driver who turns a journey into a riot because of the birth of his son, your heart warms towards him. . . . The contrast between the cheerful, noisy, superficial rush and tumble of town and overcrowded train is sharply contrasted with the slow solid prejudices of the country and the people who still have their roots in it. Gino Cervi acts with magnificent restraint as the 'commercial' whose fundamental kindness and love of life reluctantly and spasmodically penetrate the armour with which his conventional life has surrounded him." C. A. Lejeune found it "impossible to convey the delicacy, the sense of taste that springs from a clear eye and a good heart, with which this tale is told." And Georges Sadoul said that "here, after being obliged for so long to watch himself parading up and down on the screen disguised as a soldier, the man in the street could at last recognize himself in the overworked employee who is the hero of the film. . . . Everything in this charming film was falling into ruins, and this comedy thereby bore witness to the age when the cracks in the regime's grandiloquent façade had begun to foretell the imminent collapse of Fascism."

Four Steps in the Clouds was another important step in the direction of neorealism, which in fact made its first unequivocal appearance the same year in Visconti's *Ossessione*. But *Ossessione* was banned immediately after its premiere, and the revelation of neorealism had to wait until 1945–1946—for Rossellini's *Open City*, Lattuada's *The Bandit*, and Blasetti's *Un giorno nella vita* (*A Day in the Life*), a powerful and brutal account of the massacre by the Nazis of a convent of nuns who had aided the partisans. Unpredictable as ever, Blasetti then threw himself into the most elaborate super-spectacle of his career, *Fabiola* (1948), a French-Italian remake of Nicholas Wiseman's story of ancient Rome, with an unheard-of budget of eight hundred million lire and cast that included Michèle Morgan, Michel Simon, Gino Cervi, and Massimo Girotti, among others. This box-office blockbuster was followed by a return to the territory of *Four Steps* in *Prima communione* (*First Communion,* 1951), a rather sour satirical comedy about the tribulations of a self-important pastry cook trying to track down the white dress in which his daughter is to celebrate her first communion.

In his subsequent films Blasetti has continued to show a sure instinct for box-office values. He contributed notably to the Italian vogue for episode or anthology films, beginning with *Altri tempi* (*Times Gone By,* 1952), starring Vittorio de Sica, Gina Lollobrigida, Aldo Fabrizi, and others in a string of short pieces drawn from various nineteenth-century stories. In a companion movie, *Tempi nostri* (*Our Times,* 1953), he was the first to pair Sophia Loren and Marcello Mastroianni, and he repeated this highly successful combination in *Peccato che sia una canaglia* (*Too Bad She's Bad,* 1954) and *La fortuna di essere donna* (*Lucky To Be a Woman,* 1956). And in *Europa di notte* (*European Nights,* 1959) he pioneered another profitable formula—the "erotic documentary," reporting on night life in various cities. Blasetti's last film of any note was *Io io io . . . e gli altri* (*Me, Me, Me . . . and the Others,* 1966), a star-studded and very disillusioned film about a journalist who undertakes an investigation into human selfishness and discovers that he himself has this disease in an acute and chronic form. Since then the director has devoted himself mostly to television.

When Blasetti appeared as Blasetti in Visconti's *Bellissima* (1951), he portrayed himself as a cynical purveyor of pap for the masses—of films devised for "the amusement of idiots." It was no doubt a sad commentary on a career that began with the ringing idealism of *Cinematografò* and *Sole,* but Blasetti's achievements are not to be dismissed. Ettore Margadonna maintains that as a director Blasetti is somewhat deficient in a sense of construction and rhythm, but that he is "excellent and sometimes even magnificent in directing actors and crowd scenes, and is a master of settings and lighting." Mario Gromo wrote that he carried into the twentieth century "the echoes of a nineteenth-century tradition of 'civilization' and 'progress.' He is animated by a warmth that springs straight from the people, free of cultural patterns, faithful to good craftsmanship." Blasetti and Mario Camerini are generally recognized to be the best Italian directors of the 1930s and Vinicio Marinucci goes further—speaking of his work as a critic, a teacher, a pioneer of styles and themes, he writes that "Alessandro Blasetti *is* the Italian cinema."

FILMS: *Features*—Sole (Sun), 1929; Nerone (Nero), 1930; Terre madre, 1930; Resurrectio (Resurrection), 1931; Palio, 1932; La tavola dei poveri (The Table of the Poor), 1932; 1860/I Mille di Garibaldi, 1933; Il caso Haller, 1933; L'impiegata di papà, 1933; Vecchia guardia (The Old Guard), 1934; Aldebaran, 1935; La Contessa di Parma (The Countess of Parma), 1937; Ettore Fieramosca, 1938; Retroscena, 1939; Un'avventura di Salvator Rosa, 1939; La corona di ferro (The Iron Crown), 1941; La cena delle beffe (The Joker's Banquet), 1941; Quattro passi fra le nuvole (Four Steps in the Clouds), 1942; Nessuno torna indietro (No One Turns Back), 1943; Un giorno nella vita (A Day in the Life), 1946; Fabiola, 1948; Prima communione (First Communion/Father's Dilemma/His Majesty Mr. Jones), 1951; Altri tempi (Times Gone By/In Olden Days/Infidelity), 1952; La Fiammata (The Blaze/Pride, Love and Suspicion), 1952; Tempi nostri (Our Times/Anatomy of Love), 1953; Peccato che sia una canaglia (Too Bad She's Bad), 1954; La fortuna di essere donna (Lucky To Be a Woman), 1956; Amore e chiacchiero (Love and Chatter), 1957; Io amo, tu ami (I Love, You Love), 1961; La lepre e la tartaruga (The Hare and the Tortoise) *in* Le 4 Verità (Les Quatres Vérités/The Four Truths), 1963; Liolà (A Very Handy Man), 1965; Io, io, io . . . e gli altri (Me, Me, Me . . . and the Others), 1966; La ragazza del Bersagliere (The Girl of the Bersagliere), 1967; Simon Bolivar, 1969. *Documentaries*—Assisi, 1932; Caccia alla Volpe, 1938; Abuna Messias, 1939; Napoli e le terre d'oltremare, 1940 (unfinished); Sulla cupola di San Pietro, 1946; Il duomo di Milano, 1946; Castel Sant'Angelo, 1947; La gemma orientale dei Papi, 1947; Ippodromi all'alba, 1950; Quelli che soffrono per voi, 1951; Miracolo a Ferrara, 1953; Europa di notte (European Nights), 1959; Venezia, una mostra per il cinema, 1969. *For television*—La lunga strada del ritorno (The Long Road Home), 1942 (three programs); Gli italiani del cinema italiano, 1964; I Borboni del regno di Napoli, 1970; Dov'eravate? *in* 10 giugno 1940 (June 10, 1940), 1970; Storie dell'emigrazione, 1972 (five programs); L'arte di far ridere, 1978 (five programs); Racconti di fantascienza, 1978 (three programs).

ABOUT: Apra, A. and Pistagnesi, P. (eds.) The Fabulous Thirties, 1979; Armes, R. Patterns of Realism, 1971; Jarratt, V. The Italian Cinema, 1951; Leprohon, P. The Italian Cinema, 1972; Malerba, L. and Siniscalco, C. (eds.) Fifty Years of Italian Cinema, 1954. *Periodicals*—Bianco e Nero April 1939; Cinema Nuovo July–August 1964, September–October 1964, May–June 1978, November–December 1978; Film Dope March 1974.

*BOETTICHER, "BUDD" (Oscar Boetticher Jr.) (July 29, 1916–   ), American director, producer, and scenarist, was born in Chicago and studied at Ohio State University, where he was a star boxer and football player. After one violent football season he was sent to Mexico to convalesce from his injuries. Like Ernest Hemingway, whose love of action and adventure and stoic notion of manliness he shares, Boetticher fell in love with the art and mystique of bullfighting. He studied under the matador Lorenzo Garza and himself fought in Mexico as a professional matador.

In 1941, on account of this experience, Boetticher was invited to serve as technical adviser on the bullfight sequences in Rouben Mamoulian's remake of *Blood and Sand,* starring Tyrone Power. Fascinated by the movie world, he stayed on in Hollywood, working for a time as messenger-boy at Hal Roach's studios. In 1942 or 1943 he was taken on as assistant director of William A. Seiter's *Destroyer* (1943), and he served in the same capacity on George Stevens' *The More the Merrier* (1943), Charles Vidor's *The Desperadoes* (1943) and *Cover Girl* (1944), and William Berke's *Girl in the Case* (*The Silver Key,* 1944).

Boetticher says that he "gave up that job quite soon, because it really had nothing to do with directing. In the USA an assistant is more on the production, not the direction, side. Usually it's a young man whose job is to spy on the director and report his findings to the producer—the mistakes his director makes, whether he's getting behind schedule. I was no good; I always took his side." (This quotation and many others in this note are from an interview conducted by Bertrand Tavernier for *Cahiers du Cinéma* July 1964 and quoted in Jim Kitses' BFI dossier *Budd Boetticher: The Western,* in a translation by Susan Bennett.)

In 1944 Boetticher directed his own first mov-

BUDD BOETTICHER

ies as Oscar Boetticher Jr.—*One Mysterious Night, The Missing Juror,* and *Youth on Trial.* One reviewer wrote of the first of these, a Chester Morris thriller, that it "wasn't released; it escaped"—a comment that Boetticher says he "will die remembering." The other two were apparently not much better, nor were the seven B features Boetticher made between 1945 and 1950. Most of them were cut-rate thrillers, but one was a Western, *Black Midnight* (1949), starring Roddy McDowell and Damian O'Flynn in a story about the rivalry between a ranch foreman and a crooked saloon owner. During this period Boetticher also directed a number of propaganda films for the United States armed forces and one of these, *The Fleet That Came to Stay,* achieved commercial distribution.

According to Boetticher, "the less said about [these early movies] . . . the better. . . . I was really working in the dark. I had no idea where I was going . . . but I couldn't show people what a mess I was in. I simply didn't know what I was doing. Those films only took eight, ten, twelve days, and there isn't a bit of directing in them. None of them is any good, but I did meet a lot of interesting people who have since become famous in Hollywood, like Burt Kennedy, my favorite scriptwriter."

Boetticher's first significant film—and the first credited to "Budd" rather than to Oscar Boetticher—was *The Bullfighter and the Lady* (1951). The director wrote the script himself (and received an Oscar nomination for it). Drawing on Boetticher's own experiences, it tells the story of a young American, Chuck Regan (Robert Stack), who is drawn to bullfighting and

*be´ ti sher

is taken under the wing of a great Mexican matador (Gilbert Roland). Immature and arrogant, the boy insists on fighting before he is sufficiently experienced, and his mentor saves his life at the cost of his own. At the climax, Regan has to return to the ring and prove himself in the face of a hostile crowd who hold him responsible for the death of their idol.

Herbert J. Yates, head of Republic Pictures and producer of the movie, was away in Europe when Boetticher completed the shooting. One day he plucked up his courage and showed the footage to John Ford, then working in the same studios. Boetticher says he lost twenty pounds while waiting for Ford's reaction, but when it came it was enthusiastic. Ford "took charge of almost all the editing of *The Bullfighter and the Lady*," Boetticher says. "I had one or two disappointments, because he cut passages I liked, especially bits with the horses . . . but just the fact of having been helped by John Ford did me a lot of good." Moderately well received by the critics and "a great success on its second run," *The Bullfighter and the Lady* brought Boetticher a contract with Universal-International. There he made eleven films, most of them hurried, low-budget affairs, but not without interest.

Boetticher's first picture for Universal was an Audie Murphy Western, *The Cimarron Kid* (1951), which opens with the Kid leaving jail and ends with his arrest on new charges—a circular structure that recurs in many of Boetticher's films. Boetticher considerably rewrote Louis Stevens' script (and history) in portraying a raid by the James and Dalton brothers, explaining that "I'm not faithful to history if it might spoil the film." After *Bronco Buster* (1952) came one of Boetticher's few war films, *Red Ball Express*, starring Jeff Chandler. Boetticher believes passionately in the individual's right to choose his own destiny and therefore dislikes war films: "I prefer my films to be based on heroes who want to do what they are doing, despite the danger and the risk of death. . . . In war, nobody wants to die and I hate making films about people who are forced to do such-and-such a thing."

For this reason Boetticher is much happier with Westerns, like *Horizons West* (1952), whose remarkable cast included Robert Ryan, Julia Adams, Rock Hudson, John McIntyre, Raymond Burr, and Dennis Weaver. Boetticher himself says of this otherwise undistinguished movie: "There were some very good actors . . . who began their careers in that film, which is a fact I'm quite proud of. . . . That's my only vivid memory of that film, except Julia Adams, who was really radiant and beautiful and who I was

madly in love with. She had just got divorced at that time, and we went off together. That's all I can say about that film."

One of the worst of Boetticher's Universal movies was *City Beneath the Sea* (1953)—he himself calls it "a joke," but makes it clear that it might have been even more dire if he and his cast had not rewritten the appalling script "as we went along." At least, Boetticher says, he had the consolation of working with his friends Robert Ryan and Anthony Quinn, and a certain amount of fun with special effects—he shot the "underwater" sequences by having Ryan and Quinn walk (in slow motion) on foam rubber, and superimposed the water and fish. At this time Boetticher was churning out movies at a killing pace: "I'd finish a film on Thursday or Friday and begin on another the next Tuesday or Wednesday. I had the weekend to read the script."

Seminole (1953), also made with Quinn (as well as Rock Hudson, Barbara Hale, and Lee Marvin), was also very harshly reviewed, but Boetticher defends the film. He had studied the Seminole, finding that they had never surrendered in their war with the United States and "gave the West Point boys a good thrashing. . . . That was what I wanted to show." There was a somewhat better press for *The Man From the Alamo* (1953), a relatively ambitious and expensive picture starring Glenn Ford and Julia Adams in a story about a man who escaped from the besieged fortress to go to the rescue of his family, and was branded a coward. In fact, as Peter Wollen points out, "he risked his life—and his repute—for a precise personal goal rather than stay, under the pressure of mass feeling, to fight for a collective cause. He is a typical Boetticher hero."

Julia Adams starred again, opposite Van Heflin, in *Wings of the Hawk* (1953), in which Heflin plays an American mining engineer who becomes involved in a Mexican revolution. The movie was shot in 3-D (against Boetticher's wishes) and suffers from "having that 3-D camera dead in front of the actors all the time." Some reviewers praised it as an anti-dictatorship tract, but Boetticher says that "in this film, as in all my other work, I'm much more interested in my characters than the ideas they stand up for. . . . It's the *ways* in which people defend their beliefs which interest me, not the beliefs themselves."

East of Sumatra (1953), "a very bad film" which Boetticher made only because it provided a part for his friend Anthony Quinn, was followed by his second bullfighting movie, *The Magnificent Matador* (1955). Scripted by the director, it is a melodrama in which Quinn plays a famous matador who abandons his career in an attempt to prevent his illegitimate son from taking up the same dangerous trade. The critics found it a highly uneven work, and preferred *The Killer Is Loose* (1955), a taut thriller in which Joseph Cotten is rather oddly cast as an underpaid cop and Rhonda Fleming as his wife, threatened by a psychopathic killer (Wendell Corey).

Between 1955 and 1960 Boetticher also did a certain amount of work for television—the pilot show for *Maverick,* four episodes of *The Dick Powell Show,* the sixty-minute *Count of Monte Cristo,* and one episode of *Hong Kong.* More important, working for John Wayne's Batjac company, he made a Randolph Scott Western called *Seven Men From Now* (1956), scripted by Burt Kennedy. Scott plays Ben Stride, who is ruthlessly hunting down the seven men who murdered his wife in a raid on a Wells Fargo station. In the desert Stride encounters an Eastern couple, the Greers (Gail Russell and Walter Reed), and two outlaws (Lee Marvin and Donald Barry). It is with the brutal but almost irresistibly amusing and engaging Marvin character that the hero's final confrontation must come, while a growing involvement with Annie Greer is responsible for softening his initial implacable coldness.

A commercial success, *Seven Men From Now* also brought Boetticher his first serious critical recognition, especially in France, where André Bazin gave it a long review in *Cahiers du Cinéma* (August–September 1957). Bazin (as translated by Susan Bennett in Jim Kitses' BFI dossier), called it "possibly the best Western that I have seen since the war" and "very superior to *Shane.*" He went on: "The first thing to be admired about *Seven Men From Now* is the script, which effects the *tour de force* of constantly surprising us, despite its rigorously classical plot. . . . Even more than the inventiveness which thought up the exciting twists in the plot, I admire the humor with which they are treated. . . . But the remarkable thing is that the humor does not get in the way of the film's emotional impact. . . . It is only when the director loves the characters and the situations that he invents to such a degree, that he is able to stand back and look at them with a humorous eye. . . . That kind of irony does not diminish the characters, but it allows their naiveté and the director's intelligence to coexist without tension. For it is indeed the most intelligent Western I know, while being at the same time the least intellectual, the most subtle and the least aestheticizing, the simplest and finest example of the form. . . . Boetticher has made remarkable use of the landscape, and the varying textures of the soil and the rocks. I think the photogenic quali-ties of horses have never been made better use of. . . . Lastly there is Randolph Scott, whose face bears an unmistakable resemblance to William Hart, even down to the sublimely inexpressive blue eyes."

Recognizing in this unexpected success a chance to revive his declining career, Randolph Scott embarked on a series of Westerns directed by Boetticher, starring himself, and produced by his business partner Harry Joe Brown for Scott-Brown Productions, later Ranown. These Westerns (including *Seven Men From Now*) have come to be known, for the sake of convenience, as the Ranown cycle. Four of them were written by Burt Kennedy with Boetticher's collaboration. (Boetticher has explained that his usual approach to any movie is "to read the best script I can find" and then to decide on the cast. "Then after that I get together with the author and we rewrite the script to suit the actors." Kennedy has said that the Ranown scripts were as much Boetticher's as his, though only Kennedy is credited.)

Robin Wood, writing in Richard Roud's *Cinema,* suggests that the Ranown films "can best be explained in terms of one of those happy collaborations that occur occasionally in the Hollywood cinema—Kelly/Donen is the most obvious example—in which the best is brought out of talents noticeably less distinguished in isolation. . . . The films take the most traditional genre elements—the hero/villain conflict, the revenge motif, the gang, the Indians—on which Boetticher and Kennedy perform subtle and idiosyncratic variations. The tone is always unassuming, and the genre is always respected: we never feel a self-conscious straining after 'significance,' or any sense that the artists feel superior to their raw material and are bent on transforming it. . . . our delight arises from our simultaneous recognition of the convention and the variation."

Jim Kitses, to whose work on Boetticher Robin Wood pays tribute, finds in the Ranown films "the deepest commitment to a highly romantic individualism: life is seen as a solitary quest for meaning, an odyssey; action as a definition and expression of the self which is its own reward; compromise of personal integrity as indefensible. . . . In general, the Boetticher hero as created by Scott can be said to possess (or to be moving towards) a great serenity, the knowledge that we are fundamentally alone, that nothing lasts, that what matters in the face of all this is 'living the way a man should.'" He is often a man who has lost everything except his stoic sense of honor, and "this makes the figure oddly anachronistic, a man who continues to assert values out of an image of himself that has its roots in the past."

Our second view of this figure (if Ben Stride is taken as the first) comes in *The Tall T* (1957) in the character Pat Brennan. He is introduced in terms of broad comedy—he bets that he can ride a bull to a standstill and winds up in a watering trough. Having forfeited his horse, Brennan hitches a ride on the stage driven by his old friend Rintoon (Arthur Hunnicutt) and carrying a boy and the newly-married Doretta Mims (Maureen O'Hara) and her husband. The mood darkens abruptly when the stage is held up by Usher (Richard Boone) and his companions (Henry Silva and Skip Homeier). Rintoon, the boy, and the cowardly Willard Mims are murdered; Brennan and Doretta are held for ransom. Brennan sets out to undermine the outlaws' trust in one another.

Usher is the most attractive of the Boetticher villains whose prototype was the Marvin character (Masters) in *Seven Men From Now*. Brutalized as he is, Usher is a character of great charm, wit, and intelligence, and as his admiration for Brennan's iron rectitude deepens into something very close to love, we recognize his dissatisfaction with himself, his impulse towards redemption, although we also recognize that his sins are too great to escape punishment. And indeed, as Kitses points out, "the basic deception in the films in the Ranown cycle, the key to their dramatic structure, is that the Randolph Scott figure is the hero only in a technical sense; it is, of course, the villain who is our true hero. . . . We understand him in a way we cannot the hero—and the films stand finally as celebrations of this character who attempts to *create* action in a way that Scott cannot."

The next two pictures in the cycle were scripted by Charles Lang Jr. rather than Kennedy. *Decision at Sundown* (1957) is another revenge Western and a bitter one. It begins with Bart Allison (Scott) riding with his friend Sam (Noah Beery Jr.) into a corrupt and frightened town ruled by the man (John Carroll) he holds responsible for his wife's suicide; it ends with him riding out alone, unavenged and aware that his wife had been less sinned against than sinning. *Buchanan Rides Alone* is set in and around another corrupt community but is much lighter in tone. Arrested together with a young Mexican (Manuel Rojas) who has killed in defense of his sister's honor, Buchanan teams up with him and rids the town of the dreadful Agry family in a tremendous shoot-out, control of the town then passing to another of Boetticher's charming rogues, Abe Carbo (Craig Stevens). Boetticher himself found this "a very amusing, very mathe-matical Western," and Kitses points out that the Agrys are "*humours* in the medieval sense, farcical expressions of ignorance and greed."

In *Ride Lonesome* (1959), written by Kennedy, Scott is again a numbed engine of revenge—former sheriff Ben Brigade, searching for a man named Frank (Lee Van Cleef) who hanged Brigade's wife. Brigade captures Frank's brother Billy John and travels slowly back to town, using Billy John as bait for Frank. Along the way he is joined by two outlaws (Pernell Roberts and James Coburn) and by Carrie Lane (Karen Steele), whose husband has been killed by Indians. Frank duly shows up and is killed by Brigade, who then rides away, leaving Carrie and the likable, redeemable Pernell Roberts character to attempt a life together. Some critics tried to attach a religious significance to Brigade's burning of the crosslike tree on which his wife had died, but Boetticher says that the tree was "a symbol for the things . . . [Brigade] hated" and that "at the same time this gesture was an attempt to destroy his own past; he didn't want people to be hanged anymore."

Jim Kitses writes that "the meaning in a Boetticher movie resides less in its bright moments of good humour, its dark moments of violence, than in the continuum, a seasonal movement, a perpetual interplay of light and shade, success and decline, life and death. . . . Thus *Ride Lonesome* moves through three days and nights, the company pushing on over dangerous open vistas of arid country each morning and afternoon to cluster in the dappled dark of an evening camp. If dusk is often a kind, contemplative time for talk of the future, danger rides in bright and early at sun-up to temper hope and throttle dreams."

Kitses goes on to describe a brief but resonant image from the film—a water vase that hangs from the roof of a swing station, swaying gently as the group rides out in single file and we follow each character across the frame: the image has a narrative function "but the composition and lighting are so delicate that they finally are a pleasure in themselves. The tension between static black border and bright rhythmic play within is so fine that ultimately the image has the quality, the essence of Boetticher, of an animated still-life. At moments like these Boetticher achieves a formal rigour and philosophical nuance that recalls the most unlikely of parallels, the Japanese master Yasujiro Ozu."

Westbound (1959) is not part of the Ranown cycle, though it stars Randolph Scott. It is a routine, big-budget Western made for Warner Brothers, of no particular interest. *Comanche Station,* scripted by Kennedy and the last in the

Ranown cycle, followed in 1960. Here the perennially widowed Randolph Scott plays Jefferson Cody, whose wife was stolen by Indians ten years earlier. Hearing of a white woman offered for ransom by the Comanches he goes to trade for her. It is not his wife—it never is—but another man's, and Cody sets out to reunite her with her husband. The husband is blind and has offered a reward for her return. The money attracts other adventurers (Claude Akins, Skip Homeier, Richard Rush) and the dangers multiply.

Speaking of the Ranown movies, Boetticher has said that most of them were made on a twelve-day shooting schedule, but "I did try, each time, to make a better film than the one before, a deeper film." Kitses writes that in *Ride Lonesome* and *Comanche Station* "the construction and pace are tightly controlled, the action unwinding with spell-binding formal rigour, the films finally resembling pure ritual. Seizing on the cyclical pattern of the journey Western, the alternation of drama and lyricism, tension and release, intimacy and space, Boetticher gradually refines it to arrive at the remarkable balance of an ambiguous world poised between tragedy and pastoral comedy." And Ian Cameron said of *Comanche Station* that Boetticher "observes landscapes and the people moving about in them with a sensitivity rivaling Renoir's in *Le Déjeuner sur l'herbe*. . . . The first shot of the film shows Scott riding along the top of a ridge in silhouette, and ends with a camera movement as the rider disappears behind an outcrop of rock and emerges below the level of the camera—a linked movement of actor and camera which is genuinely beautiful. . . . And the picture of man as a part of nature persists and strengthens throughout the film until at the end when the hero returns to his search he is back in the landscape in which we discovered him at the beginning of the film and is almost absorbed into it."

"Boetticher's West is quite simply *the world*," Kitses writes, "a philosophical ground over which his pilgrims move to be confronted with existential choices wholly abstracted from social contexts. . . . The moral of Boetticher's films is . . . [that] everyone loses. Life defeats charm, innocence is blasted. The world is finally a sad and funny place, life a tough, amusing game which can never be won but must be played."

The message is much the same in *The Rise and Fall of Legs Diamond* (1960), another ironic morality play, set this time in New York during Prohibition. The character played by Ray Danton only faintly resembles the historical Jack "Legs" Diamond—he is any small-time hoodlum with a blind itch for power and no idea what to do with it. His charm, style, and ruthlessness take him to the top so rapidly that he comes to believe himself invulnerable; he comes down even faster because his old-style individualism is overtaken by the new "corporate capitalism of the underworld boardroom" and because, having discarded friends, family, and lovers on the way up, he finally has to face the Syndicate quite alone.

For Boetticher himself, the message of the movie is that "you can stay alive as long as somebody loves you." Nobody loves Legs Diamond in the end, not even his dim, boozy, despised wife-mistress Alice (Karen Steele). Boetticher thinks Alice his only "successful study of a woman," apart from those in his two early bullfighting pictures—generally in his films the heroine is only important for what she has "caused to happen" to the hero. The director has described how he and his cameraman Lucien Ballard set out to make the film in the style of the 1920s, outraging the front office by slightly preexposing the filmstock, dispensing with such modern camera movements as dolly shots and most traveling shots, and going "back to the old flat lighting."

At first dismissed by most reviewers as just another gangster B-movie, *Legs Diamond* rose rapidly in critical esteem as its pace, economy, and style began to be recognized. Anna Yates noted how the cold brutality of Legs's world is conveyed "by means of harsh lighting and stiff geometrical patterns in the decor; by a constant use of sharp contrasts between black and white." Andrew Sarris called it "a minor classic in the perverse *Scarface* tradition," and wondered "where directors like Boetticher find the energy and the inspiration to do such fine work, when native critics are so fantastically indifferent."

In 1960, when critical recognition and financial security seemed at last assured, Boetticher left Hollywood in his Rolls Royce, accompanied by his latest wife (Debra Paget), and went to Mexico to complete his documentary about his friend Carlos Arruza, the greatest Mexican matador of recent times. Boetticher had been shooting footage for this movie for years, in the intervals between other projects, and expected to complete it in a few months. In fact it cost him eight years, his marriage, everything he owned, and almost his sanity and his life—an ordeal beyond anything imagined by Burt Kennedy for any of Boetticher's stoical heroes.

In his book *When in Disgrace* (1969), Boetticher gives a fictionalized account of those years in Mexico, during which he was financially ruined, divorced, jailed, committed to an insane asylum, and nearly killed, first by hunger, then by a lung disease. Carlos Arruza died in a freak automobile accident and so did most of Boetticher's film crew, but the director, living on three tamales a day, turned down fat offers from Hollywood and completed the picture, sustained by his absolute faith in what he was trying to do and his belief in "living the way a man should." In Arruza, Boetticher explained later, "I had my own private genius for eight years, who did what I wanted, stood where I asked him to, walked out in the sun to be in the light, and fought the bulls to the best of his ability"—"Wouldn't it have been a wonderful thing if the director of *The Agony and the Ecstasy* had Michelangelo instead of Charlton Heston?"

Arruza (1968) begins with the matador in retirement and traces his two comebacks—first as a *rejoneador* (fighting on horseback) and in a triumphant last appearance in Plaza Mexico a few months before his pointless death. The film has had a mixed reception, some critics praising it as an exemplary and moving documentary, others finding it boring, or "nauseating" in its cruelty. Boetticher himself has no doubt that it is his masterpiece, a pure film, in which he "did not compromise on *any* shot"—"if people don't like it, they're wrong."

Returning to Hollywood, Boetticher began a new business association with his friend Audie Murphy. It produced only one film before Murphy was killed in a plane crash in 1971. *A Time for Dying* (1969), scripted by Boetticher, photographed by Lucien Ballard, and produced by Murphy, follows the brief career of an aspiring young gunfighter (Richard Lapp) in Arizona, and his love affair with the girl he rescues from a brothel (Anne Randall). Audie Murphy appears as Jesse James and Victor Jory as the monstrous old clown Judge Roy Bean. Boetticher called the movie "a Western about all the unmarked graves, about all the kids who had everything but just didn't win." Kitses has pointed out that "the film describes a perfect circle for all its principals" and Robin Wood writes of the "black futility" of the hero's meaningless death, "a bitter nihilism which might be found appropriate to a last word." In fact, Boetticher has so far made no more films. His script, *Two Mules for Sister Sara,* was directed by Don Siegel.

Like John Ford, Boetticher is said to be "a man of the outdoor life most at ease in good male company"; he has nevertheless been married four times. He has something of a reputation for being "violent and quarrelsome," but his friend Burt Kennedy would "simply say that he was *alive.*" The Ranown cycle is said to have provided the model for Sam Peckinpah's *Ride the High Country,* and Georges Sadoul has called Boetti-

cher "with Peckinpah . . . the best modern director of Westerns."

FILMS: *As Oscar Boetticher Jr.*—One Mysterious Night, 1944; The Missing Juror, 1944; Youth on Trial, 1944; A Guy, a Gal, and a Pal, 1945; Escape in the Fog, 1945; The Fleet That Came to Stay, 1946 (short); Assigned to Danger, 1948; Behind Locked Doors, 1948; Black Midnight, 1949; Wolf Hunters, 1949; Killer Shark, 1950. *As Budd Boetticher*—The Bullfighter and the Lady, 1951; The Sword of D'Artagnan, 1951; The Cimarron Kid, 1951; Bronco Buster, 1952; Red Ball Express, 1952; Horizons West, 1952; City Beneath the Sea, 1953; Seminole, 1953; The Man From the Alamo, 1953; Wings of the Hawk, 1953; East of Sumatra, 1953; The Magnificent Matador, 1955; The Killer Is Loose, 1955; Seven Men From Now, 1956; The Tall T, 1957; Decision at Sundown, 1957; Buchanan Rides Alone, 1958; Ride Lonesome, 1959; Westbound, 1959; Comanche Station, 1960; The Rise and Fall of Legs Diamond, 1960; Arruza, 1968 (documentary; released 1971); A Time for Dying, 1969 (released 1971).

ABOUT: Boetticher, B. When in Disgrace, 1969; Kitses, J. (ed.) Budd Boetticher: The Western, 1969; Kitses, J. Horizons West, 1969; Roud, R. (ed.) Cinema: A Critical Dictionary, 1980; Sherman, E. and Rubin, M. The Director's Event, 1970. *Periodicals*—Cahiers du Cinéma July 1964; Cinema (USA) December 1968, Fall 1970; Cinestudio May and June 1971; Film Dope March 1974; New Left Review 32 1965; Positif November 1969; Screen July–October 1969.

BOLESLAWSKI or **BOLESLAVSKY, RICHARD** (February 4, 1889–January 17, 1937), American director, was born Ryszard Srzednicki Boleslawski in Warsaw, Poland. He became a stage actor at the age of sixteen and went to Russia, where he studied and performed under Stanislavsky at the Moscow Art Theatre. According to some accounts he became director of the Art Theatre's Second Studio. He began to appear in Russian films in 1914 and the following year made his debut as a movie director with *Tri Vstrechi* (*Three Meetings*).

After the Revolution, in 1918, Boleslawski codirected with Boris Suskevich the Bolshevik propaganda feature *Khleb* (*Bread*), with a distinguished cast that included Leonid Leonidov, Olga Baklanova, Yevgeni Vakhtangov, and Boleslawski himself. But by 1919 he was back in Poland, fighting against the Bolsheviks as a cavalry officer under Pilsudski. He was put in charge of film coverage of the Polish army and in 1920 combined newsreel footage and acted sequences into a semidocumentary about the Soviet defeat of August 21st, *The Miracle of the Vistula.*

By this time, the growth of the German film industry was attracting talent from all over Eu-

RICHARD BOLESLAWSKI

rope. Boleslawski went to Berlin in 1921 and was one of the distinguished cosmopolitan cast of Carl Dreyer's denunciation of anti-Semitism, *Die Gezeichneten* (*Love One Another,* 1922). After that, and a brief stay in France, Boleslawski sailed for the United States. Beginning as an actor and acting coach, he was soon established as a successful director, both of Broadway plays and musicals and of experimental works at Laboratory Theatre.

In 1929, with the advent of the talkies, Boleslawski joined the Broadway exodus to Hollywood, quickly moving up from dialogue coach to director of minor programmers for RKO and Columbia. During this period he became a regular contributor to *Theatre Arts Monthly,* where he published the articles on Stanislavsky's method eventually collected in *Acting: The First Six Lessons.* He also wrote *The Way of a Lancer,* an account of his adventurous early life that became a bestseller and made him something of a celebrity.

It was MGM's spectacularly controversial *Rasputin and the Empress* (1933) that established Boleslawski as a major director. The movie provided rich pickings for the gossip columnists almost from its inception, when someone at MGM hit on the gimmick of casting the three famous Barrymores in the same film. Ethel Barrymore was to play the Empress, Lionel the libertine "monk" who became the power behind the Romanov throne, and John the leader of a group of jealous aristocrats who eventually and laboriously assassinated Rasputin.

All three Barrymores were notoriously temperamental and self-serving actors, and now they turned their talents against each other in what has been described as "one of the greatest all-out battles of scene-stealing, mugging [and] posturing" in film history. Numerous scriptwriters were hired and fired in the attempt to arrive at a scenario that would satisfy their conflicting demands, and the original director, Charles Brabin, was dismissed a few weeks into shooting at the insistence of Ethel Barrymore. It was reportedly she who suggested as his replacement the relatively unknown Richard Boleslawski, but not even he could persuade her to stay in Hollywood once she had worked out her contract, even though shooting was incomplete. New scenes had to be devised to conceal her absence, Boleslawski combining acted material and newsreel footage as he had in *Miracle of the Vistula.*

Rasputin and the Empress was eventually completed at a cost of about $1 million but was received with such enthusiasm that it soon recovered most of MGM's huge investment. It was praised above all for its acting—not only the Barrymores', but Ralph Morgan's as the Czar and Diana Wynyard's as Natasha, who is raped or seduced by Rasputin and subsequently marries his principal assassin. But soon after the film's release, MGM was sued and brought to trial in a famous and precedent-setting libel case by Princess Youssoupoff, wife of the Russian aristocrat who had actually played the principal role in Rasputin's murder. She and her counsel (Sir Patrick Hastings) maintained that although fictitious names were used in the film, it identified her by implication with the besmirched Natasha. She won her case, and MGM was forced to withdraw the film and to pay an estimated $750,000 in costs.

Boleslawski survived this colorful and expensive episode with his own reputation intact and indeed enhanced. His next picture was *Storm at Daybreak* (1933), with Walter Huston, Kay Francis, and Nils Asther. A triangular love story set in Hungary during World War I, it began with a much-praised reconstruction of the event that precipitated the war—the Sarajevo assassination of 1914. In the opinion of Eric Rideout, the film "presented the most convincing European scenes to come from an American studio. By no other means could the inevitability of the Sarajevo assassination be made so vivid."

After *Beauty for Sale* (1933), an unexceptional adaptation of Faith Baldwin's novel *Beauty,* Boleslawski had a major and much discussed success in *Men in White* (1934), based on Sidney Kingsley's Group Theatre hit. Described by a contemporary critic as "a courageous exposure of the defects of the modern voluntary hospital at the mercy of pompous donors," it starred

Clark Gable as the dedicated Dr. Fergusson, Myrna Loy as his spoiled and demanding fiancée, and Jean Hersholt as "the great Dr. Hochberg, lover of beer and science."

C. A. Lejeune wrote that the picture opens "with a fatal accident to a workman on a girder and ends with an emergency call, between which sequences there are deaths and major operations, x-ray diagnoses and blood transfusions, the whole thing taking place within the whitewashed walls of the hospital, with loudspeakers calling out the names of the doctors and their cases like a chorus of doom." She found "the total effect not at all depressing," however, and praised Boleslawski's management of "the emotional mechanics" of the film and his "studied use of black and white, bearing out the suggestion of the title—shadows of retorts on a wall, slats of light from a venetian blind across a face."

Two slighter entertainments followed—a thriller called *Fugitive Lovers* (1934) and, the same year, *Operator 13*. The latter was a Civil War romance and something of a collector's item for connoisseurs of the bizarre in that it has Marion Davies, as an actress spying for the North, passing as a black girl the better to overhear the secrets of her employers. Complications ensue when she falls in love with a white Confederate spy (Gary Cooper). "The period has been very conscientiously reconstructed," wrote Eric Rideout, "in manners and in dress and architecture—the place of the Negro in the domestic life of the South being particularly well observed."

Boleslawski's last film for MGM was *The Painted Veil* (1934), adapted from the play by Somerset Maugham. Herbert Marshall plays Dr. Walter Fane, working himself to death for the numberless poor of China, and Greta Garbo his wife Katrin. Neglected and bored, she has an affair with a diplomat (George Brent) who promptly drops her when Fane finds out. The latter goes up-country to a city in the grip of a cholera epidemic and Katrin accompanies him, healing the breach in their marriage when she insists on working with him against the epidemic. To prevent the spread of the disease, Fane orders the destruction of part of the city and is shot by an irate Chinese householder.

In the film (unlike the play), it seems probable that Fane will recover. Some critics objected to this more or less happy ending and to a general dilution of Maugham's bitterness, but most were content to enjoy the film's splendid set pieces—"The Chinese festival is quite lovely, and the scenes of panic in the stricken city are full of . . . urgency and electric tension." Under Boleslawski's direction Garbo was thought to move and speak faster and with more vitality than in the past, surrendering some of her "inner austerity"—a development that some reviewers welcomed and others did not.

Boleslawski moved to Darryl F. Zanuck's Twentieth Century for *Clive of India* (1935), in which for the first time he had full scope to employ his talent for spectacle. The film traces the rise of a natural military genius from underpaid East India Company clerk to the virtual mastery of India, encompassing on the way the horrors of the Black Hole of Calcutta and a succession of battle scenes of which the most extraordinary features the armored battle elephants used by Suraj Ud Dowlah at Plassey. Quieter interludes explore the strains placed on Clive's marriage by his devotion to India, with excellent performances from Ronald Colman and Loretta Young. Enthusiastically received almost everywhere, it reminded one angry British reviewer of an American gangster movie in that "the hero is shown as a liar, a trickster, a forger, and a ruthless deserter of wife and children in the cause of Empire, and is surrounded by a . . . mist of romantic humbug calculated to deceive and gratify ninety-nine percent of any ordinary audience."

There had already been six screen adaptations of Victor Hugo's novel *Les Misérables* before Boleslawski's 1935 version, and there have been several since. Boleslawski's, scripted by W. P. Lipscomb and photographed by Gregg Toland, is widely regarded as the best of them all. Fredric March plays Jean Valjean, who as a young man is condemned to the galleys for a trivial crime. He emerges brutalized by this experience but is redeemed by the generosity of Bishop Bienvenu (Cedric Hardwicke). Valjean becomes a prosperous businessman and respected citizen. However, he had broken his parole when he was freed from the galleys, and for this he is hounded implacably by the fanatical police detective Javert (Charles Laughton).

Otis Ferguson thought the early scenes in the galleys "too artificial to be powerful" and found "a certain sweet irreality" in the relationship between Valjean and his "rather insipid" niece, but "the action scenes in general—mobs, carriage rides, challenges, armed turbulence, movement in the streets—are carried off boldly and well. . . . Richard Boleslawski's genius as a director lies more in the coordination of complex matters than in attention to character." André Sennwald described Laughton's reading of Javert as "one of the great screen portraits," and the picture was immensely successful.

Metropolitan (1935) has Alice Brady as a temperamental prima donna who turns down a role at the Metropolitan and forms her own opera company, taking with her a young singer from the Metropolitan's chorus (Lawrence Tibbett) as her principal tenor. When her temperament threatens to wreck the new company, he takes charge, hustles funds from a beautiful heiress (Virginia Bruce), and raises the curtain on *I Pagliacci*. The movie was another hit, both commercially and critically, praised for Richard Day's sets, the photography of Rudolph Maté (with its "welcome depth in the long shots"), and for its spirited satire on the opera establishment. A British critic found it full of "genuine drama and natural humour," and wrote that "the quiet, unexpected ending of the film, after the prologue to *I Pagliacci,* is typical of the restraint and economy of the film as a whole."

O'Shaughnessy's Boy (1935), with Wallace Beery and Jackie Cooper, followed the successful formula of *The Champ* in a story about a circus animal trainer and his beloved small son; its sentimentality was somewhat ameliorated by spectacular circus scenes and a performance of "magnificent vindictiveness" by Sara Haden as the boy's mother. This was followed in 1936 by one of the most memorable of Boleslawski's films, a lavish remake of *The Garden of Allah* for Selznick International Pictures. W. P. Lipscomb and Lynn Riggs scripted the movie from Robert Hichens' novel, Max Steiner provided the score, and the film was shot in the new "three-strip" Technicolor process, with Lansing C. Holden as color designer.

The Arizona desert stood in for the Sahara and an Arab town was built just outside Yuma. During the three weeks on location, filming took place from 3 a.m. to 11 a.m., when the temperature reached 148 degrees. Charles Boyer was cast as Boris Androvsky, the tormented Trappist monk who breaks his vows and runs away to the Sahara, and Marlene Dietrich as Domini Enfilden, who has also gone to the desert in search of spiritual peace. They fall desperately in love, but in the end she renounces him because her rival is "not of the flesh but of the spirit." The cast also included Basil Rathbone, Joseph Schildkraut, John Carradine, C. Aubrey Smith, and Tilly Losch as the desert temptress whose wonderfully sensual dance provided what was for some the most arresting sequence in the movie.

Even in 1936 the plot seemed dated, and by contemporary standards it is hokum, but magnificent hokum. T. J. Fitzmorris thought that this version of the story even contrived to make the final renunciation "both logical and emotionally satisfying." Boyer was said to have given the finest performance of his career and Dietrich—"hauntingly lovely" in the new color

process—"loosed talents heretofore kept in reserve." Howard Barnes wrote that the film "makes magnificent use of color photography, mixing rich blues, browns and reds in a succession of lovely compositions," and Ronald Haver in a more recent discussion of the picture said that it was "probably the most sumptuously beautiful of all '30s color films." However, this "folly de Selznick" had cost $2.2 million, and though well received and popular, it failed to recover its costs.

Though Boleslawski is thought of primarily as a director of action and spectacle, there is evidence in the few comedies he made that he had an equal talent for that mode. In *Theodora Goes Wild,* made for Columbia in 1936, Irene Dunne plays a New England girl primly raised by two maiden aunts who outrages her prudish small town when her "daring" romantic novel is serialized in the local newspaper. It becomes a bestseller, and Theodora, visiting her New York publisher and teased by her book's illustrator (Melvyn Douglas), casts away her remaining inhibitions in a spectacular spree. Admired for its "subtle satire on a small New England town, its people, its church, and literary club," it earned comparison with *Mr. Deeds Goes to Town* and established Irene Dunne as "a comedienne of superlative charm and ability."

Boleslawski's version of Peter B. Kyne's much-filmed Western *Three Godfathers* (1936) starred Chester Morris, Lewis Stone, and Walter Brennan as the three desperadoes who are regenerated when they accept responsibility for a baby they find abandoned in the desert. The New York *Times'* reviewer thought that the movie "succeeds in catching the spirit of the Westerns of two decades back, when bad men could be heroes too," but for Richard Watts the sentiment was "laid on too thick for comfort." Boleslawski was at work on a remake of *The Last of Mrs. Cheyney* when he died suddenly of a heart attack. He was not quite forty-eight years old.

From 1933 until his death, Boleslawski was regarded as a major director and even, by some, as a "great" one. It is difficult to account for this now, but in the course of his brief Hollywood career he made a handful of intelligent entertainments that will always be worth citing as evidence in defense of the studio system.

FILMS: Tri Vstrechi (Three Meetings), 1915; (with Boris Sushkevich) Khleb (Bread), 1918; Bohaterstwo Polskiego Skavto, 1919; Cud Nad Wisla (The Miracle of the Vistula), 1920; Treasure Girl, 1930 (short); The Last of the Lone Wolf, 1930; The Gay Diplomat, 1931; Woman Pursued, 1931; Rasputin and the Empress (U.K., Rasputin—The Mad Monk), 1933; Storm at Daybreak, 1933; Beauty for Sale, 1933; Men in White, 1934; Fugitive Lovers, 1934; Operator 13 (U.K., Spy 13), 1934; The Painted Veil, 1934; Clive of India, 1935; Les Misérables, 1935; Metropolitan, 1935; O'Shaughnessy's Boy, 1935; The Garden of Allah, 1936; Theodora Goes Wild, 1936; Three Godfathers, 1936; The Last of Mrs. Cheyney, 1937 (completed by George Fitzmaurice).

ABOUT: Rideout, E. H. The American Film, 1937; Thomson, D. A Biographical Dictionary of the Cinema, 1980. *Periodicals*—Kino (Poland) June and July 1980.

BORZAGE, FRANK (April 23, 1893–June 19, 1962), American director and producer, was born in Salt Lake City, Utah, into a large, musical, and noisy family that has been variously identified as Irish, Swedish, and Italian in origin. It seems most probable that his father, Lewis Borzage, was an immigrant from the Italian Tyrol and "an expert stonemason."

At the age of thirteen Borzage worked in a silver mine to pay for a correspondence course in acting. The same year he joined a group of traveling players as a prop boy, subsequently acting with a variety of such companies. It was as an actor that he arrived in Hollywood in 1912, working with Thomas Ince's company as an extra and bit player. He soon graduated to larger parts, playing stock villains and sometimes lead roles in Ince Westerns and some Mutual comedies. The filmography in John Belton's *Howard Hawks, Frank Borzage, Edgar G. Ulmer* lists fifty-eight films in which Borzage appeared between 1912 and 1916, and suggests that he probably acted in even more, though *Film Dope* researchers were able to confirm only thirty-four.

Like many actors at that time, Borzage also turned his hand to scriptwriting and, in 1915 or 1916, became a director. Some sources say that his directorial career began with *That Gal of Burke's* (1916) but Frederick Lamster, in his monograph on Borzage, maintains that his first film was *The Pitch o' Chance* (1915), only part of which survives. Lamster describes this Western in some detail, concluding that it "plays upon melodramatic conventions . . . [but extends them], especially through the inclusion of the idea of spiritual growth. . . . Throughout, the film camera movement and visual setup undercut as well as reinforce the drama in a planned manner, and character placement, in particular, is never random."

Borzage directed fifteen films during 1916, all or most of them distributed by American Mutual. He scripted some of these himself and starred or acted in all of them, often opposite Anna Little. In 1917 he joined the Triangle Film Corpo-

FRANK BORZAGE

ration, which had become the most prestigious studio in Hollywood. He made three films there in 1917 and nine in 1918, most of them produced by Allan Dwan. When Triangle collapsed in 1918, Borzage moved on to William Randolph Hearst's Cosmopolitan and then to First National before joining William Fox for a fruitful seven years (1925–1932). He often acted in his Triangle pictures, though seldom in lead roles; thereafter he stayed behind the camera.

Although Borzage is credited with the direction of over fifty silent films, only a handful seem to have survived. Judging by these, and contemporary reviews of others, the loss is a major one for cinema. Borzage's silents included contributions to most of the genres then popular—Westerns, melodramas, society dramas, comedies, and at least one gangster movie. The lost films include the melodrama *Humoresque* (Cosmopolitan, 1920), which won the *Photoplay* Gold Medal as best picture of the year and has been cited as Borzage's first significant film. A celebration of mother love scripted by Frances Marion from a Fannie Hurst story, it starred Alma Rubens. A reviewer in the New York *Times* wrote: "The power of the motion picture thus to create atmosphere, more vividly, more convincingly, than is possible in written words, except those of rare masters, is not often so emphatically and delightfully demonstrated."

One of the earliest surviving silents is *Lazybones* (Fox, 1925), another Frances Marion script and a film of great tenderness, charm, and humor about a lazy man (Buck Jones) who rouses himself to rescue a woman from drowning. He raises her daughter, falls in love with her, but lets her slip away from him. For William Thomaier the movie has "an almost Chekhovian awareness of the lost opportunities of life." Another modern critic, Andrew Sarris, remarks that "the long dolly shot of the little girl . . . walking home from school and from one layer of consciousness to another, marks Borzage as a master of transcendent cinematic forms very early in his career." *The First Year* (1926), about a disastrous dinner party given by a pair of newlyweds, impressed Paul Willemen on account of "the delightful comic atmosphere which pervades the basically tender relationship of the young couple."

The film that made Borzage famous appeared in 1927. *Seventh Heaven,* adapted from a successful play by Austin Strong, was the first of his great melodramas. It tells the story of Chico (Charles Farrell), a young Parisian sewer worker who gives a home to a destitute waif, Diane (Janet Gaynor). They fall in love but before they can marry are separated by World War I. Away at the front, Chico remains telepathically in touch with Diane. He is killed and the daily communication ceases. Nevertheless, in the final sequence, a blinded Chico fights his way through the crowds celebrating the Armistice and climbs to their seventh-story garret, their "seventh heaven."

"If metaphor is the essence of poetry," writes Jean-Pierre Coursodon in his *American Directors* (1983), Borzage "was one of the screen's natural poets, for his peculiar talent was the revitalizing of moral stereotypes through metaphorical imagery." For Borzage, "the real world was more sign than substance, the external form of a concealed spiritual truth which it is the artist's role to probe and make manifest. Thus, an infinite attention to detail can go hand in hand, in his films, with a blithe disregard for verisimilitude."

John Belton compares Borzage with D. W. Griffith, who shared his "wholehearted commitment to a melodramatic worldview. . . . What distinguishes Borzage's melodramas from Griffiths' is their spirituality. . . . His concern is not with external but with internal order," and his characters "possess a strange, fascinating mixture of spiritual purity and physical attractiveness." Typically, Borzage's lovers "go beyond their initial mutual sexual desire to a more spiritual, quasi-religious awareness of and dependence on one another." And indeed, as Belton says, in *Seventh Heaven* "Chico and Diane's love defies not only time and space but also mortality. The ending . . . destroys narrative logic and physical reality to reveal the strength of the spirit behind that reality."

Seventh Heaven was released both silent and with the addition of a synchronized score and some sound effects. It was a huge critical and commercial success. Borzage received an Academy Award as best director (the first ever awarded), and there were Oscars also for Janet Gaynor as best actress and Benjamin Glazer for his adaptation. The film brought Gaynor immediate stardom, launching her and Charles Farrell as a romantic team in a dozen pictures beginning with Borzage's *Street Angel* (1928), which many place even above *Seventh Heaven* as the director's greatest silent film.

Street Angel, another play adaptation, resembles *Seventh Heaven* in plot but is set in Naples. Needing medicine for her dying mother, Angela (Janet Gaynor) is driven to theft and even essays prostitution. Sought by the police, she escapes with a traveling circus where she is joined by the young artist (Farrell) who has fallen in love with her. His painting of her, as Frederick Lamster says, "becomes the spiritual guardian of their relationship." Separated by her imprisonment, they are reunited in a church where Angela's portrait hangs, transformed into a painting of the Madonna. (Lamster's book takes its title from the famous first intertitle of this movie: "Everywhere . . . in every town . . . in every street . . . we pass, unknowing, human souls made great through love and adversity.")

In visual terms, *Street Angel* seems to Jean-Pierre Coursodon "possibly Borzage's finest achievement. The most elaborate and most successful instance—with Murnau's *Sunrise*—of the Fox style of large-scale, stylized art direction, it is also, like *Sunrise,* remarkable for the extreme fluidity of its camerawork [Ernest Palmer and Paul Ivano]. The two elements combine to best effect in the opening sequence, in which a constantly moving camera roams the streets of an immense Neapolitan set, picking up a dazzling range of street activities. . . . A particularly impressive set piece is the trial and prison sequence, which, in design, staging, and photography, is as startlingly expressionistic as anything in American cinema. There is nothing gratuitous about the virtuosity of such scenes."

Street Angel was released in both silent and sound versions (including some talking sequences), as was *The River* (1928), this time starring Charles Farrell with Mary Duncan. Banned in some states but rapturously received in France, *The River*'s merits were obscured by the furor over a scene in which the heroine warms the half-drowned (and half-naked) Farrell with her own body. After the unexceptional Gaynor-Farrell melodrama *Lucky Star* (1929) came Borzage's first Fox talkie, *They Had to See Paris*

(1929), starring Will Rogers, and the John Mc-
Cormack musical *Song o' My Heart* (1930).

Borzage made the transition to sound with no
apparent difficulty. His first talkie of real merit
was *Bad Girl* (1931), which won him his second
Oscar. It turns on the fears and financial worries
of an impoverished young couple (James Dunn
and Sally Eiler) expecting their first baby. In the
end the man faces a beating in the boxing ring
to pay the woman's hospital bills. The story is the
very stuff of melodrama, but Edwin Burke's
wisecracking script and the pace and humor of
the direction made this one of Borzage's sunniest
movies. Paul Willemen wrote that it showed him
"to be stunningly skillful when interweaving
comedy and melodrama as well as in his original
dialogue directing."

After two more pictures for Fox in 1932, Borzage went freelance, not signing another long-
term contract until he joined MGM in 1937. *A
Farewell to Arms,* made for Paramount in 1932,
was adapted by Benjamin Glazer from Hemingway's novel set in Italy during World War I, and
splendidly photographed by Charles Lang. Gary
Cooper plays the embittered Lieutenant Henry
and Helen Hayes the nurse, Catherine, that he
allows himself to love and then loses to death. (In
fact the film was released in two versions: one
with this conclusion and another for American
distribution—abominated by Hemingway—in
which Catherine recovers.)

The Lacanian Paul Willemen, in his notes for
the 1975 Borzage season at the British National
Film Theatre, sees his dramas as revolving
around a double contradiction: "on the one hand
between the real (economic hardship, political
persecution) and the imaginary (the special
world where lovers unite); and on the other hand
between the imaginary (fantasy of total fusion
with love object) and the symbolic (the insurmountable barrier which simultaneously sets desire in motion and bars its way to total
satisfaction)."

If *Street Angel* is one of the clearest examples
of the first contradiction, *A Farewell to Arms,*
Willemen suggests, exemplifies [in the "tragic"
version] the second. The barrier to the lovers' desire is the war; they are finally reunited at the
point at which the war ends and Catherine dies:
"His loved one once more escapes him: his desire
created her and was kept going and intensified
by virtue of their enforced separation. When the
distance between desire and the object is abolished—a dynamic inherent in the very concept
of desire itself—both the object and desire cease
to exist: what remains is death and release."

John Belton reads the Borzagian paradox rather differently. He points out that the film's ending is as much celebratory as tragic. Lieutenant
Henry carries his dead beloved to the window
and looks down on the jubilant crowds celebrating the Armistice below. "Peace," he mutters;
and the film ends with a shot of pigeons flying
free. For Belton, the "paradox that reappears
throughout the director's work" is that "his characters achieve spiritual gain only through physical loss."

Yet another interpretation of this aspect of
Borzage's work is offered by Jean-Pierre Coursodon, who maintains that "much of his creative
energy was channeled toward devising ways of
making sexual fulfillment difficult, impossible,
or unthinkable for his protagonists. . . . It is not
suprising that Borzage, as the screen's ultimate
romantic idealist, should have developed his entire dramatic system on the basis of maximum
sexual denial. . . . One suspects . . . that what
some critics assume to be a deep religious feeling
was little more than another of Borzage's devices
to hold Eros at bay while still keeping him sufficiently stimulated."

Secrets (1933) was Borzage's sound remake of
his 1924 silent melodrama, starring Mary Pickford (in her last film) as the selfless wife originally played by Norma Talmadge. Much more
notable was *Man's Castle* (1933), characteristically finding transcendent love among the insulted and injured of the American Depression.
Bill (Spencer Tracy), apparently affluent, picks
up the starving Trina (Loretta Young) in Central
Park and treats her to an expensive meal. In fact
he is as penniless as she; when he takes her home
with him, it is to a shantytown by the East River.

Restless and hard-boiled, Bill resists Trina's efforts to turn the shack into a "safety zone" for the
two of them, but progressively surrenders his immature cynicism as he falls in love. At the end,
with Trina pregnant in her wedding dress, they
hop a freight train. "Borzage's camera," writes
John Belton, "in a movement that echoes their
final spiritualisation and freedom, cranes up and
away from them, as they lie together on the
straw-covered floor of a boxcar. Detached from
their restricting environment, they seem to float
freely in space, triumphant and eternal in their
love."

Borzage found a perfect instrument for his ro-
mantic transcendentalism in Margaret Sullavan.
In her four films with him (three of them set in
Germany), she achieved a heartbreakingly elu-
sive radiance that no other director could draw
from her. Their first picture together was *Little
Man, What Now?* (1934), from Hans Fallada's
novel about a young married couple during the
Depression in Germany. For her husband Hans
(Douglass Montgomery), beset by the unemploy-

ment, disillusionment, and decadence of post-war Germany, Sullavan's Lämmchen is a redemptive icon whose luminous spiritual beauty is magnified in soft-focus shots, such as the one where she sits before a triptych mirror in a fantastic dress of white lace, shining with sequins.

Not all of Borzage's films achieved or attempted this level of intensity. In the mid-1930s he made two Ruby Keeler–Dick Powell musicals for Warner Brothers, *Flirtation Walk* and *Shipmates Forever*, both scripted by Delmer Daves, as well as several routine romances. *Desire* (1936), a wonderfully polished comedy with Marlene Dietrich as a high-class jewel thief redeemed by a homespun American engineer (Gary Cooper), was produced for Paramount by Ernst Lubitsch; it has struck many critics as more Lubitsch than Borzage in its total eschewal of spiritual depths. Spirituality reappeared and indeed toppled over into a somewhat morbid religiosity in two adaptations of novels by Lloyd C. Douglas, *Green Light* (1937) and *Disputed Passage* (1939).

In between came Borzage's second film with Margaret Sullavan, *Three Comrades* (1938), one of the eleven movies he made for MGM between 1937 and 1942. Based on the novel by E. M. Remarque and set in Germany just after World War I, it stars Robert Taylor, Robert Young, and Franchot Tone as three devoted army buddies who set up a small auto-repair shop. Into their closed circle comes a consumptive and impoverished aristocrat (Sullavan) who contributes something to the life of each of them and marries Taylor before she sacrifices her own life for them.

Knowing that she is so ill that to leave her bed is suicide, she rises and goes to the balcony, in this way freeing the two surviving comrades to make a new life unhandicapped by her illness. This scene, as Robert E. Smith wrote, was "photographed (by Joseph Ruttenberg) in a stunning ascending crane shot" as "the emotional and thematic apogee of the film." Afterwards comes a sequence in a cemetery where the two survivors are reunited with the ethereal images of their dead loved ones before all four set off together into the future. This heavy-handed fancy was not in Scott Fitzgerald's first draft of the script but was among the changes made by E. E. Paramore and the producer Joseph L. Mankiewicz in a rewrite that elicited Fitzgerald's *cri de coeur*: "Oh Joe, can't producers ever be wrong? I'm a good writer, honest."

Little Man, What Now? and *Three Comrades* have been much praised as prophetic exposures of the roots of Nazism in Germany, but Jean-Pierre Coursodon questions this. He suggests that in *Little Man* the only specifically political content is anticommunist, and says the movie is in essence not political at all, but "a perfect example of Borzage's romantic individualism." And *Three Comrades*, Coursodon argues, is set too early (1920) to even adumbrate the rise of Nazism. One of the comrades (Robert Young) is indeed politically engaged, but the group he supports is unidentified: "They might be right-wing fanatics just as soon as dedicated Marxists."

The Mortal Storm (1940), the last of Borzage's German trilogy, opens on the eve of Hitler's accession to power and is undeniably anti-Nazi. Margaret Sullavan plays Freya, daughter of a Jewish professor who dies in a concentration camp. Her two brothers and her fiancé join the Nazis and Freya herself dies in an attempt to escape with her new love (James Stewart).

However, as Robert E. Smith wrote in *Bright Lights* (Spring 1975), "the final sequence of the film reverses the downward spiral when Sullavan's younger half-brother renounces Nazism. As he walks through the empty house the camera travels with him, slowly picking up speed as it progresses. Voices from the past are heard. . . . The camera then leaves the house following the brother and focuses on his footsteps as they slowly fill in with snow. When they are filled in, the camera cranes up and the film ends. Borzage has put his characters to the greatest moral test imaginable and they triumph. The human spirit can surmount even the aberration of Nazism. As the screen goes white with the snow-filled footsteps, the ultimate unimportance of physical events is demonstrated." What the film demonstrated to Basil Wright, on the other hand, was "the purely sentimental approach to Nazism"; nevertheless, "with all its bogus trappings it almost comes near to genuine tragedy. This is largely due to Frank Borzage's brilliance. . . . To the most hackneyed scenes he brings a freshness of eye and a great mastery of technique."

During the same period Borzage made three films with Joan Crawford. The series began with *Mannequin* (1938), in which Crawford escapes poverty by marrying a con man, then meets a shipping magnate (Spencer Tracy) who falls in love with her. An entertainment of some charm, it was followed the same year by *The Shining Hour*, about a New York showgirl who marries into a Wisconsin farm family, releasing a positive explosion of self-sacrificial gestures that, as Belton writes, "changes its characters' petty, superficial, self-indulgent romantic longings into a more genuine, deeply-felt, quasi-religious awareness."

The religiosity that had first become overt in

Borzage's Lloyd C. Douglas adaptations reached its most extreme level in *Strange Cargo* (1940), his third Crawford movie. Adapted from a novel by Richard Sale, it concerns a group of convicts who escape from a Devil's Island penal colony. There is, as Paul Willemen noted, a "torrid love relationship between Verne (Clark Gable) and Julie (Joan Crawford). In fact, the erotic scenes are so powerful and unmistakably physical that the Legion of Decency condemned this allegedly religious film because of its "irreverent use of Sacred Scriptures" and "lustful implications in dialogue and situation."

Lust is however transformed into something much deeper, and the desperate journey through jungle and swamp and across windless seas becomes a pilgrims' progress. The agent of this apotheosis is Cambreau (Ian Hunter), a redemptive figure of Christlike omniscience, who disappears at the end of the film as mysteriously as he had appeared in the penal colony. "Borzage's demand that his characters attain a spiritual awareness that goes beyond an immediate love relationship to a sympathy with and need for the world around them," wrote Belton, "marks a significant expansion of the director's concerns and a deepening of the beauty of his art." Not so Coursodon, who complained that Belton "seems quite impervious to the leaden pretentiousness of the script and the plodding clumsiness of the direction" in this "stupefyingly boring" film.

None of Borzage's remaining films for MGM were of much interest. He left that studio in 1942 and freelanced again for the next three years. *His Butler's Sister* (1943), an entertaining Deanna Durbin comedy for Universal, was followed by *Till We Meet Again* (Paramount, 1944), in which French nun Barbara Britton conducts American flyer Ray Milland to freedom through occupied France, achieving enlightenment and martyrdom in the process. *The Spanish Main* (RKO, 1945) is a conventional swashbuckler enlivened by the ebullient presence of Walter Slezak (as the villain), while *Magnificent Doll* (Universal, 1946) miscasts Ginger Rogers as Dolley Madison in a ponderous biopic.

In 1946 Borzage signed a remarkable contract with Republic, a studio best known for low-budget action movies; it gave him complete artistic control over his films there, though he had to work without the first-class players and studio facilities he had been accustomed to. Denying that Borzage "made the same film" over and over again throughout his career, Robert E. Smith maintains that "we see a subtle but clear development in themes, character and style as

his career progresses. The evenly-lit never-never-land decor utilized from his late Fox silents through *Man's Castle* gives way to the more naturalistic design and lighting in the Warner Brothers and MGM films. . . . By the time of his Republic contract (1946–1949) the lighting of his films has become predominantly dark" and "in the later films we see a departure from classical, serene, though sorely tested, protagonists, to characters who are psychologically troubled."

This is certainly true of Borzage's first Republic picture (and Republic's first in Technicolor), *I've Always Loved You* (1946), a Borden Chase script. A young pianist (Catherine McLeod) falls in love with her egotistical teacher (Philip Dorn). When he grows jealous of her talent, she marries her childhood sweetheart. In the end, in spite of the telepathic communication she shares with the maestro through their music, she realizes that her real love is her devoted husband. Luc Moullet commented enigmatically that the movie's "mawkishness and sentimentality are so excessive as to annihilate critical judgment and reach pure beauty." Coursodon also admires this film, saying that it was prevented from joining the ranks of Borzage's masterpieces only by "its uncharacteristic humorlessness."

After *That's My Man*, a horse-racing melodrama, came the best of Borzage's late films, *Moonrise* (1949), set in a Virginia of swamps and swirling mists. Danny Hawkins (Dane Clark) is the son of a murderer whose hanging opens the film in a brilliantly stylized post-credit sequence of nightmarish power. Taunted all his life by his peers, Danny finally kills his chief tormentor in a drunken fight and then tries to conceal the crime. Obsessed by guilt and sure that he will follow his father to the scaffold, Danny (as Belton puts it) "locks himself up in the prison of his own fear and hatred." But at last, supported by the love of Gilly (Gail Russell), he comes to terms with the past and gives himself up, "rejoining the human race."

Photographed by John L. Russell and evidently influenced by *film noir, Moonrise* differs even from Borzage's other late films in the predominance of oppressive low-key lighting and unusually dynamic compositions. Moreover, although in typical Borzageian style the alienated hero is redeemed by a woman's love, *Moonrise* struck David Kehr (*Focus*, Spring–Summer 1973) as the director's "only completely subjective film. The spiritual growth of Danny Hawkins is shown from the inside, the *mise-en-scène* gradually developing over the course of the film as a reflection of the changing state of the mind of the single character." Gavin Lambert praised the "sardonic humour" in Borzage's "portrait of a little town, lethargic and turned in on itself."

Critically well received as it was, *Moonrise* was not successful at the box office. At that point, although he had completed only three of his contracted five films for Republic, Borzage quit. He made a comeback ten years later to direct two more movies, *China Doll* (1958), an interesting and touching love story, and the three-hour biblical epic *The Big Fisherman* (1959), based on yet another ponderous novel by Lloyd C. Douglas but distinguished by Lee Garmes' magnificent photography.

Borzage died three years later, survived by his third wife, Juanita. Shortly before his death he received the D. W. Griffith Award for "outstanding contributions in the field of film directing." Two of Borzage's brothers also worked in the movies, Lew as producer of some of Frank's most successful pictures and Danny as a member of John Ford's production staff. Borzage had been one of Hollywood's best all-round athletes, a polo and squash player, yachtsman, star golfer, and handball champion.

As far as it is possible to judge from what survives, Borzage did his best work between 1927 and 1940. After that, with the exception of *Moonrise,* his films are either studio assignments allowing only occasional personal touches or (worse) virtual parodies of his own best work. In his best films, however, as Georges Sadoul wrote, he was "the equal of his contemporaries, John Ford, Howard Hawks, or King Vidor."

For John Belton, "what makes the religious-romantic content of Borzage's films so powerful is the transcendent nature of his visual style. . . . His sets and characters often seem to glow with an otherworldly luminescence. Part of this has to do with the way Borzage lights them—the tones of his backgrounds, often as light as or lighter than his characters' faces, give his frames a weightless quality. Borzage's lighting is consistent throughout the frame; each part of the frame seems equally and evenly lit" and this "unifies his frame into a single level of depth and into a single *tonal* unity of foreground and background. In other words, characters do not derive their spirituality from specific objects in the frame or from specific parts of the frame, as in Griffith, but from the tonal quality of the whole frame and the succession of frames around it, by editing rhythms imposed upon characters from a logic that exists outside the frame itself."

Borzage himself was most vocal on the subject of characterization, which he believed "is what makes pictures attractive, sincere, true characterization. . . . I believe in developing every character, no matter how small." Gary Cooper was one of a number of actors who paid tribute to Borzage, saying in 1936 that he "directs with less effort and more effect than any other director in Hollywood. It is significant that he directs a picture without reading the script during production. Whenever he has occasion to read the script, he calls upon the script clerk to read it to him aloud. . . . I am sure that he does so primarily because reading is a mental process, and that interferes with the free play of his imagination and emotions. . . . It was he who taught me that the best acting was not acting at all, but a perfect naturalness." Borzage disliked retakes "as much as the average actor does. In case of accidents, it is always necessary to take a scene two or three times. But I don't suppose I shoot more than one scene out of every hundred more than four times."

Andrew Sarris, writing in Richard Roud's *Cinema,* summed Borzage up as "an elusive figure" who at the time of his death "had been almost completely submerged in the stream of film history. . . . His resurrection as a resonant director depends less on the ideological implications of his images than on the force of his feelings. And the new generations of the '60s and '70s seem to be attuned more to emotional intensity than to intellectual irony." As early as 1922 Borzage defended his fondness for melodramas, telling an interviewer that "critics are inclined to belittle them and call them cheap. But they don't seem to sense the idea that life is made up largely of melodrama."

—*G.H.*

FILMS: The Pitch o' Chance, 1915; That Gal of Burke's, 1916; (with James Douglass) Mammy's Rose, 1916; (with Lorimer Johnston) Life's Harmony, 1916; The Silken Spider, 1916; The Code of Honor, 1916; Nell Dale's Men Folks, 1916; The Forgotten Prayer, 1916; The Courtin' of Calliope Clew, 1916; Nugget Jim's Pardner, 1916; The Demon of Fear, 1916; Land o' Lizards, 1916; Immediate Lee, 1916; Enchantment, 1916; The Pride and the Man, 1916; Dollars of Dross, 1916; (with Charles Miller) Wee Lady Betty, 1917; Flying Colors, 1917; Until They Get Me, 1917; The Atom, 1918; The Gun Woman, 1918; Shoes That Danced, 1918; Innocent's Progress, 1918; An Honest Man, 1918; Society for Sale, 1918; Who Is to Blame?, 1918; The Ghost Flower, 1918; The Curse of Iku, 1918; Toton, 1919; Prudence of Broadway, 1919; Whom the Gods Destroy, 1919; Ashes of Desire, 1919; Humoresque, 1920; The Duke of Chimney Butte, 1921; Get-Rich-Quick Wallingford, 1921; Back Pay, 1922; Billy Jim, 1922; Hair Trigger Casey (reedited version of Immediate Lee, 1916), 1922; Silent Shelby (reedited version of Land o' Lizards, 1916), 1922; The Good Provider, 1922; The Valley of Silent Men, 1922; The Pride of Palomar, 1922; The Nth Commandment (U.K., The Higher Law), 1923; Children of Dust, 1923; The Age of Desire, 1923; Secrets, 1924; The Lady, 1925; Daddy's Gone a-Hunting, 1925; Lazybones, 1925; The Circle, 1925; Wages for Wives, 1925; The First Year, 1926; The Dixie Merchant, 1926; Early to Wed, 1926; "Marriage License" (U.K., The Pelican), 1926; Seventh Heaven, 1927; Street Angel, 1928; The River, 1928; Lucky Star, 1929; They Had to See Paris, 1929; Song o' My Heart, 1930; Liliom, 1930; Doctors' Wives, 1931; As Young As You Feel, 1931; Bad Girl, 1931; After Tomorrow, 1932; Young America (U.K., We Humans), 1932; A Farewell to Arms, 1932; Secrets, 1933 (remake); Man's Castle, 1933; No Greater Glory, 1934; Little Man, What Now?, 1934; Flirtation Walk, 1934; Living on Velvet, 1935; Stranded, 1935; Shipmates Forever, 1935; Desire, 1936; Hearts Divided, 1936; Green Light, 1937; History Is Made at Night, 1937; Big City (rereleased as The Skyscraper Wilderness), 1937; Mannequin, 1938; Three Comrades, 1938; The Shining Hour, 1938; Disputed Passage, 1939; Strange Cargo, 1940; The Mortal Storm, 1940; Flight Command, 1941; Smilin' Through, 1941; The Vanishing Virginian, 1942; Seven Sweethearts, 1942; Stage Door Canteen, 1943; His Butler's Sister, 1943; Till We Meet Again, 1944; The Spanish Main, 1945; I've Always Loved You (U.K., Concerto), 1946; The Magnificent Doll, 1946; That's My Man (U.K., Will Tomorrow Ever Come?), 1947; Moonrise, 1949; China Doll, 1958; The Big Fisherman, 1959.

ABOUT: Agel, H. and Henry, M. Frank Borzage, 1893–1961, 1971 (in French); Belton, J. Howard Hawks, Frank Borzage, Edgar G. Ulmer (The Hollywood Professionals, Vol. 3), 1974; Coursodon, J.-P. American Directors, vol. 1, 1983; Lamster, F. Souls Made Great Through Love and Adversity: The Film Work of Frank Borzage, 1981; Latham, A. Crazy Sundays: F. Scott Fitzgerald in Hollywood, 1971; Milne, P. Motion Picture Directing, 1922; Roud, R. (ed.) Cinema: A Critical Dictionary, 1980. *Periodicals*—Bright Lights Spring and Summer 1975; Film Dope March 1974; Film Journal (Australia) April 1963; Focus Spring–Summer 1973; Motion Picture Classic September 1920; National Film Theatre (Britain) Booklet May–August 1975; Positif July–August 1976.

BOULTING, JOHN (November 21, 1913–June 17, 1985) and **BOULTING, ROY** (November 21, 1913–   ), British directors and producers, were born at Bray, Berkshire, the identical twin sons of Arthur Boulting and the former Rose Bennett. At the age of seven or eight they were taken by their nanny, four times in one week, to see Rudolph Valentino in *The Four Horsemen of the Apocalypse*. "We were absolutely hooked," John Boulting said. "One of us was so excited that he actually wee-ed himself. I say it was Roy, he says it was me. But from that week on we never wanted to work in any other business." Both of them, meanwhile, attended Reading School, where Roy launched the first film club ever formed at an English

ROY BOULTING

"public" school and John was captain of the rugby team.

When Roy left school he went off to Canada, where he bummed around, sampling a variety of jobs, until he met an Englishman working there for a Hollywood production company. This led to his first film job, writing dialogue for a movie made at the Trenton Studios in Ontario. In 1933 he worked his way home on a cattle boat. After a spell as a film salesman he joined a small London firm, Marylebone Studios, as assistant assistant director and tea boy.

John followed a slightly different route, starting his career in 1933 as office boy for a London film distributor at a salary of fifteen shillings a week and working his way up to salesman. In 1935, tiring of this, he joined Roy at Marylebone Studios in an equally menial capacity, serving a "hard but educative apprenticeship." Early in 1937 he volunteered to drive an ambulance for the government forces in the Spanish Civil War. He arrived before the end of the battle of Guadalajara and was in the thick of the Brunete and Belchite offensives, narrowly escaping capture on two occasions.

When John Boulting returned to Britain at the end of 1937, he and his brother decided to make their own films and with the backing of three friends formed Charter Film Productions. Their first short and medium-length movies were directed by Roy. *The Landlady* (1937) was a comedy, but *Consider Your Verdict* (1937) raised some serious questions about the British jury system. Their first full-length feature, *Trunk Crime* (Roy Boulting, 1939), starring Manning Whiley and Barbara Everest, was equally serious, showing how a sensitive university student is driven by bullying and persecution to breakdown and almost to murder.

These movies and the courtroom drama *Inquest* (1939) were all "quota quickies," though far more interesting than most. *Pastor Hall* (Roy Boulting, 1940), with a cast that included Wilfrid Lawson, Sir Seymour Hicks, Nova Pilbeam, and Barbara Mullen, was more ambitious. Adapted from Ernst Toller's play—a fictionalized account of the arrest and confinement in a concentration camp of the anti-Nazi pastor Martin Niemöller—it was the first British film to expose the horrors of the German camps, and was widely shown in Allied and neutral countries.

At that point, Charter Films suspended operations, the Boultings having been inducted into the armed forces—Roy as a trooper in the Royal Armoured Corps, John as an equally lowly flight mechanic in the Royal Air Force. In 1941 they were temporarily released to make *Thunder Rock* (Roy Boulting, 1942), adapted by Jeffrey Dell and Bernard Miles from Robert Ardrey's play. The setting is a lonely lighthouse on the Great Lakes in the late 1930s. The keeper (Michael Redgrave) is a former political journalist who has retired there in bitter disillusionment at the world's failure to heed his warnings about the rise of fascism.

A ship carrying immigrant settlers had foundered on Thunder Rock in 1849, and the misanthropic keeper is visited by the spirits of those who died (Barbara Mullen, Lilli Palmer, Frederick Valk). In the end, moved by the courage with which they had faced their own fears and hardships, the keeper decides to involve himself once more in the struggle for a better world. Intelligently written and extremely well acted, this unusually thoughtful piece of propaganda had an even greater international success than *Pastor Hall*.

Back in uniform, and commissioned now as Captain Roy and Flight Lieutenant John Boulting, the brothers were assigned to the Army and the Royal Air Force film units respectively. Roy played a leading role in the filming of the immensely hazardous commando raid on Vaagso in occupied Norway on Christmas Day 1941 and subsequently made three excellent compilation documentaries about the war—*Desert Victory* (1943), *Tunisian Victory* (1944, made in collaboration with Frank Capra), and *Burma Victory* (1945). The most memorable of these is *Desert Victory*, a vivid, moving, firsthand record of the Eighth Army's campaign against Rommel in the North African deserts, with music by William Alwyn.

John Boulting's first film as director, made for the RAF in 1945, was *Journey Together*, a fictionalized documentary of the type pioneered by the British filmmaker *Harry Watt*. Scripted by Terence Rattigan, it is an account of the training of RAF bomber crews in England, Canada, and the United States, centering on two young men. One of them (Jack Watling) shows natural aptitude as a pilot; the other, a working-class youth splendidly played by Richard Attenborough, fails as a pilot but finally makes the grade as a navigator. Bessie Love and Edward G. Robinson appear briefly in the American sequences. The picture was very warmly praised as "one of the few really fine and exciting films to come out of the war" (which, however, was over before the Ministry of Information managed to organize its release).

The Boultings' first postwar film, directed by Roy, produced by John, was an adaptation by Nigel Balchin of Howard Spring's novel *Fame Is the Spur* (1947). Obviously modeled on the career of Ramsay MacDonald, it has Michael Redgrave as a revolutionary young socialist politician subtly corrupted by success, ending up with a title and a post in the cabinet, the fire in his belly quite gone out. It was called a "dignified, if rather dull" adaptation.

Two more adaptations followed, the first scripted by Graham Greene and Terence Rattigan from Greene's novel *Brighton Rock* and directed by John Boulting. Set in the most elegant of British seaside resorts, it is a study of a sadistic seventeen-year-old gang leader, Pinkie (Richard Attenborough). The twisted Catholicism that produced this young monster is largely omitted from the film, but it was generally admired all the same as an exciting thriller, notable for its portrait of Brighton in vacation time, and for the excellence of its minor characterizations—especially the blowzy, promiscuous but warmly human Ida (Hermione Baddeley).

There are faint echoes of the Boultings' 1939 movie *Trunk Crime* in *The Guinea Pig* (1948), based on a play by Warren Chetham Strode. Attenborough again plays a teenager—this time a fifteen-year-old working-class boy who, in a postwar educational experiment, is admitted to an elite public school. Bullied and despised, he learns from a kind old teacher that he must hold on and work within the snobbish system to change it. By now the Boultings had settled into a policy of alternating the roles of director and producer, so it was Roy who signed this rather "stodgy and depressed" picture.

John Boulting followed this with *Seven Days to Noon* (1950), written by Roy Boulting and Frank Harvey from an original idea by Paul Dehn and made for Alexander Korda's London

Films. An idealistic scientist (Barry Jones) steals an atomic device and threatens to destroy himself and London unless the government promises to renounce atomic weapons. The metropolis is evacuated while he holes up with his unwilling companion, a middle-aged prostitute (Olive Sloan) who has something in common with the Ida of *Brighton Rock*. David Thomson called it "a brilliant idea that exerts every half screw of tension," and it was the Boultings' first real postwar success.

The same scenarists were responsible for *High Treason* (Roy Boulting, 1951), somewhat similar in plot but, as Raymond Durgnat pointed out, showing a decreasing sympathy for dissidence and an increasing regard for authority. The conspirators who plan to hamstring the country by seizing vital power stations are a sorry mixture of confused idealists and left-wing trendies, and it is the police who save the day. After that, the Boultings took a five-year rest from social and political issues.

The Magic Box (John Boulting, 1951), the film industry's contribution to the Festival of Britain, is a star-studded but uninspired tribute to William Friese-Greene (Robert Donat), sometimes claimed, with little justification, as the inventor of cinematography. *Singlehanded* (Roy Boulting, 1952), adapted from C. S. Forester's novel *Brown on Resolution*, for some reason has the American Jeffrey Hunter as a British sailor conducting a one-man war against a German battleship. The brothers codirected *Seagulls Over Sorrento* (1954), a comedy best forgotten, and this was followed by two films directed by Roy Boulting, *Josephine and Men* (1955), based on Nigel Balchin's romantic comedy, and *Run for the Sun* (1956), an "energetic and violent reworking" of the much-filmed *The Hounds of Zaroff*, with Trevor Howard as the mad sportsman hunting Richard Widmark and Jane Greer with savage dogs.

In January 1955, both brothers joined the board of British Lion Films Ltd., formed out of the ruins of Sir Alexander Korda's bankrupt British Lion and devoted mainly to the provision of financial and distribution guarantees for independent producers. The majority of the Boultings' subsequent films were made by the revived Charter Film Productions Ltd. and distributed by British Lion. And over the following decade, most of their pictures were satirical comedies that, as Durgnat says, were aimed at "the depressing selfishness of absolutely everybody, from the highest to the lowest in the land. In other words, both the high expectations of their earlier films and the mild paranoia of *High Treason* have been surmounted, and replaced by a still pained, but a humourous, acceptance that idealism is neither here nor there."

The series began with *Private's Progress* (1956), directed by John Boulting and scripted by him and Frank Harvey. The cast included Richard Attenborough, Dennis Price, Terry-Thomas, and Ian Carmichael, many of whom reappeared in later works in the series. Price plays the heroic officer who rescues art treasures in a daring commando raid and then steals them; Carmichael is the earnest middle-class innocent who is left holding the bag. While laying about with cheerful gusto at the expense of officers, gentlemen, and aesthetes, the movie is also an extremely convincing sketch of the idiocies of army life.

Private's Progress was a success and *Brothers in Law* (Roy Boulting, 1957) was a bigger one. This time Carmichael plays a naive young barrister whose ignorance and idealism alienate large sections of the legal profession; he is only rescued from bankruptcy by success in his home town. Adapted from Henry Cecil's novel, and relatively gentle in its satire, it seemed to Arthur Knight to have "a feel of good technique, a sense of communication that is both personal and appealing." Less effective satires followed, of university life (John Boulting's *Lucky Jim*, a disappointingly broad adaptation of Kingsley Amis's novel) and of British diplomacy (Roy Boulting's *Carlton-Browne of the F.O.*, called *Man in a Cocked Hat* in the United States).

The most controversial and passionately debated of the Boulting's satires was *I'm Alright Jack* (John Boulting, 1959), scripted by the director, Frank Harvey, and Alan Hackney from the latter's novel. Carmichael (the middle-class Candide) is this time an Oxford graduate who takes a job in his uncle's missile plant and starts at the bottom. From that position he observes with mounting horror the exploitative greed and dishonesty of management (Dennis Price, Richard Attenborough) and the suicidal lethargy and cynicism of the workers. Finally driven to speak his mind on television, Carmichael is sent for psychiatric treatment as a disturbed troublemaker.

Peter Sellers received the British Film Academy's best actor award for his marvelously judged and oddly touching portrayal of an ignorant but doggedly idealistic fanatic of a shop steward, and the movie was extremely popular and successful. But David Robinson found it a "defeatist and destructive" film, echoing "the popular audience's narrowest and meanest fears and prejudices," and the Left resented it bitterly. As late as 1979 it was denied a showing on British television for fear that it might damage the Labour Party's chances in the general election.

There are no pretensions to social criticism in Roy Boulting's *The French Mistress* (1960), a straightforward farce in which a pretty French teacher (Agnès Laurent) innocently disrupts a British public school. *Suspect* (*The Risk*), codirected by John and Roy Boulting, is a drama reminiscent of *High Treason*, with an embittered concert pianist tempting a young scientist to betray the secret of a potentially dangerous vaccine to a high-sounding front organization.

Realizing perhaps that their anthology of satires of British institutions did not include an attack on organized religion, the Boultings remedied the omission in *Heavens Above!* (John Boulting, 1963), based on an idea conceived by Malcolm Muggeridge. Peter Sellers stars (in a role that would formerly have gone to Ian Carmichael) as an innocent young clergyman who simply tries to put Christian precepts into practice. He appoints a black churchwarden, opens the vicarage to a homeless family, and turns the church hall into a free supermarket. The result, of course, is social and economic disaster, and ends with Sellers being dispatched by space capsule to a place where he may do less harm.

Penelope Gilliatt wrote that "the Boultings have a basilisk eye for self-righteous platitudes and empty pomp," but found "a disconcerting mixture of sophistication and simple-mindedness" in the film. Others were considerably harsher, the *New Statesman* complaining of "a splenetic dislike . . . of pretty well everything and everyone," and Derek Hill attributing to the brothers "the courage and humour of a small boy whispering a dirty word for the first time." But it seemed to Raymond Durgnat that "only disappointed idealism would dare, and know how, to parody the obstinate illusions of idealism with such sober inventiveness."

Rotten to the Core (1965), a satire on things in general and the upper classes in particular, was not a success. This was John Boulting's last film as a director. Thereafter, though he continued to produce his brother's films, he was increasingly immersed in the affairs of British Lion, whose managing director he became in 1969. Roy Boulting, who was always more prolific, has continued to work as a director, though the intervals between his films have grown longer.

In *The Family Way* (1966), written by Nigel Balchin and based on a novel by Howard Spring, he brought off a convincing, nonsatirical working-class drama of a rather old-fashioned kind, with a cast that included Hayley Mills, John Mills, and Hywel Bennett. Bennett and Hayley Mills (who was later for a time Roy Boulting's wife) also star in *Twisted Nerve* (1968), a study

of a psychopathic killer that "set out to out-Psycho *Psycho*" by intensifying its everyday realism." The critics greatly disliked this film, and Roy Boulting has not returned to the genre, devoting himself instead to comedies like *Soft Beds and Hard Battles* (*Undercover Hero*, 1974), in which the staff of a French brothel foil Hitler's plan to destroy Paris (and Peter Sellers plays Hitler and five other parts).

John and Roy Boulting both left the board of British Lion in 1973. They both had large families (Roy having been married five times) and a passion for cricket. Once the *enfants terribles* of the British cinema and always "utterly opposed to censorship," they nevertheless found themselves worried and depressed by the tendency of films in recent years to "tell of life in grim and aberrated terms." Looking back over their own careers, John Boulting said that "our chief source of pride is that we've managed to aggravate, provoke, irritate, annoy, and perhaps stimulate practically every side of the [film] business."

FILMS: *Directed by Roy Boulting*—The Landlady, 1937 (short); Consider Your Verdict, 1937; Ripe Earth, 1938 (short); Seeing Stars, 1938 (short); Trunk Crime (Design for Murder), 1939; Inquest, 1939; Pastor Hall, 1940; Dawn Guard, 1941 (short); Thunder Rock, 1942; They Serve Abroad, 1942 (short); Desert Victory, 1943 (documentary); (with Frank Capra) Tunisian Victory, 1944 (documentary); Burma Victory, 1945 (documentary); Fame Is the Spur, 1947; The Guinea Pig (The Outsider), 1948; High Treason, 1951; Singlehanded (Sailor of the King), 1952; Josephine and Men, 1955; Run for the Sun, 1956; Brothers in Law, 1957; Happy Is the Bride, 1958; Carlton-Browne of the F.O. (Man in a Cocked Hat), 1959; The French Mistress, 1960; The Family Way, 1966; Twisted Nerve, 1968; There's a Girl in My Soup, 1970; Soft Beds and Hard Battles (Undercover Hero), 1974; Danny Travis, 1978; The Last Word, 1979; The Moving Finger, 1985 (for television). *Directed by John Boulting*—Journey Together, 1945; Brighton Rock (Young Scarface), 1947; Seven Days to Noon, 1950; The Magic Box, 1951; Private's Progress, 1956; Lucky Jim, 1957; I'm Alright Jack, 1959; Heavens Above!, 1963; Rotten to the Core, 1965. *Directed by Roy and John Boulting*—Seagulls Over Sorrento (Crest of the Wave), 1954; Suspect (The Risk), 1960.

ABOUT: Armes, R. A Critical History of British Cinema, 1978; Durgnat, R. A Mirror for England, 1970; Warman, E. Preview 1960, 1959; Who's Who, 1981. *Periodicals*—Commonweal July 5, 1963; Film Dope March 1974; Films and Filming February 1959, February 1974; Sight and Sound Autumn 1958.

BRENON, HERBERT (January 13, 1880– June 21, 1958), American director, scenarist, actor, and producer, was born in Dublin, Ireland,

HERBERT BRENON

the son of Edward St. John Brenon, an editor and drama critic, and the former Frances Harris, a writer who was herself a native of Dublin. He grew up in London, where his father at that time worked, attending a prestigious "public" school, St. Paul's, and King's College in the Strand.

At the age of sixteen, for reasons that are not specified in the available material, Brenon left home and emigrated to the United States. His first job was as a messenger boy for Joseph Vion, a New York vaudeville agent, who paid him $4 a week. This gave him a taste of the theatrical life and, after or during stints as a store clerk and real estate salesman, he secured a walk-on part in a spectacle called *Sporting Life* at the old Academy of Music, subsequently talking himself into the job of call boy at Daly's Theatre. He stayed there for three seasons, occasionally playing small roles.

Brenon's first real chance came when he joined Walker Whiteside's stock company as assistant stage manager. He toured with Whiteside for a year, learning his craft as an actor as he went along. At twenty-three he moved to the Ferris Stock Company in Minneapolis, and the following year, in 1904, married a Minneapolis girl named Helen Oberg. She had no stage experience but, when the Ferris company fell on hard times, it was Helen Brenon who suggested that she and her husband might try vaudeville. She proved to be a talented natural actress and, as Brenon and Dowling, they toured for about a year, playing dramatic sketches on the Orpheum and other circuits before settling down in Johnstown, Pennsylvania, as the leading figures in the town's Auditorium Stock Company. Their son Cyril was born there in 1906.

It was not long before Brenon had assumed complete directorial control of the theatre. As an extra attraction he began to screen movies between the acts of the plays he staged, showing old Biograph and Vitagraph releases. The idea was so popular that, after about two years, a rival built a full-fledged movie theatre in Johnstown. Brenon found his audiences dwindling and eventually, in desperation, abandoned theatricals altogether and turned the Auditorium into a roller-skating rink, with films as an additional drawing card. The gamble failed and Brenon began casting around for more lucrative and stable employment. He had painful experience of the immense and growing popularity of the cinema, and he decided that, if he could not lick the new medium, he would join it.

In 1909 Brenon went to New York and secured an interview with Carl Laemmle, head of IMP—the Independent Motion Picture Company, precursor of Universal. Laemmle passed him along to Julius Stern, IMP's general manager, who took him on as a scenario writer and trainee editor. After three years of this, with additional experience as an actor and stuntman, Brenon was given his chance as a director with *All for Her* (1912). A one-reeler about the love and sacrifice of two old musicians for a little girl, it starred George Ober and was said to be distinguished by "delicate sentimental touches." Four or five other short features followed the same year (including *The Long Strike,* in which Brenon himself performed a particularly dangerous stunt, leaping from a liner into the sea).

As a director, Brenon was an immediate success. Within months he was being hailed by the critics as a brilliant new talent. In 1913 Laemmle sent him to Europe to make a series of pictures in foreign locations. The first—though it was not released until 1914—was *Across the Atlantic,* a flying film starring the future director King Baggot and the pioneer aviator Claude Graham White, with Brenon himself as a Japanese spy. This was filmed in Britain, as was Brenon's ambitious version of *Ivanhoe,* shot on location at Chepstow Castle. One of the first four-reelers, this cast King Baggot in the title role, Brenon as Isaac of York, and his wife as Elgitha. *Ivanhoe* was a great success, and was followed by *Absinthe,* made in Paris with King Baggot, and one or more films (including *Time Is Money*) made in Germany.

Returning in triumph from Europe, Brenon was soon on location again, this time in Bermuda, where he made a picture even more lavish and spectacular than *Ivanhoe.* This was the seven-reel fantasy *Neptune's Daughter* (1914), in which inhabitants of the earthly realm of King William (William E. Shay) accidentally became embroiled with those of the magical domain of King Neptune (William Welsh). The whole elaborate mélange was built around the charms and talents of Annette Kellerman or Kellermann, an Australian swimming star who was the Esther Williams of her day. She had the title role and Brenon himself played the principal heavy, Roador the Wolf. The movie set new attendance records, but Brenon paid for his success; he was wrestling with the heroine in an underwater scene when their glass tank burst, injuring him so badly that he was hospitalized for a month.

Soon after this, leaving IMP, Brenon launched his own company, Tiffany Films. It failed after producing only one film, a screen version of David Belasco's stage hit *The Heart of Maryland,* released in 1915. Meanwhile, Brenon had joined William Fox. In 1915 he directed the screen's first vamp, Theda Bara, in four pictures, among them *The Kreutzer Sonata, The Clemenceau Case,* and *The Two Orphans,* himself appearing in the last as a crippled but heroic scissorsgrinder. Brenon placed great emphasis on his scenarios, demanding "real artistic merit," and at this early stage of his career wrote many of his screenplays himself, as well as acting in his films and frequently producing them as well.

By 1915 Brenon was becoming a celebrity in the movie industry, and the following year he achieved a fame (and notoriety) that elevated him to the Hollywood pantheon alongside D. W. Griffith and Cecil B. DeMille, where he remained throughout most of the silent era. Brenon had persuaded William Fox to underwrite a new "mermaid" extravaganza that would outdo even *Neptune's Daughter.* He sailed for the West Indies with Annette Kellerman and a vast retinue of technicians and actors, and there "remodeled one end of Jamaica." He altered the course of a river, restored an old Spanish fortification (at a reported cost of $100,000), built an enormous tower for Kellerman's spectacular dives, and constructed a colossal Moorish city (mainly of plaster of Paris).

William Fox became increasingly enraged, both by Brenon's extravagance and by the immense amount of personal publicity the director was receiving. When Brenon finally returned, after months on location, Fox announced that the film was a disaster, that it was to be completely reedited, and that Brenon's name was to be removed from the credits. (In fact, a contemporary program for *A Daughter of the Gods* lists J. Gordon Edwards as "supervising director" and elsewhere describes the picture as "Mr. Fox's screen fantasy"; Brenon's name does not appear at all.)

Brenon responded with a series of lawsuits,

and the conflict rose to new heights of lunacy, all avidly reported. Fox ordained that Brenon should be excluded from the premiere and, hearing that he had gatecrashed, had the theatre systematically searched. The director was eventually discovered, disguised in false whiskers, watching the movie "from the best seat in the house." Many such anecdotes have gathered around the name of Herbert Brenon. He was described by Terry Ramsaye as "one of the motion pictures' most spectacular and volatile personalities," and by others in stronger terms. A fellow director recalled him arriving on set one morning, borne aloft by his assistants on a huge Chinese throne, like "an Eastern potentate reviewing his army."

Billed as a "$1,000,000 film spectacle," *A Daughter of the Gods* was a sumptuous farrago of nonsense about a fairy prince and princess in "the land of a mighty sultan," replete with vast and exciting battle sequences, magical happenings, and "startling nude scenes"—something for everyone, and the very stuff of the silver screen. Having filled the gossip columns for months, it was an enormous success. Flushed with success (in spite of Fox's efforts to claim the credit for the film), Brenon in 1916 launched the Herbert Brenon Film Corporation in Hudson Heights, New Jersey.

The new corporation's first product seems to have been *War Brides* (1916)—the provenance of the eight other Brenon movies released in that year is not clear. Described by George Geltzer as "perhaps the best film of Brenon's early period," *War Brides* marked the screen debuts of both Richard Barthelmess and Alla Nazimova (who had starred in the stage version). A trenchant attack on war and conscription, it was enthusiastically received at its premiere but denied release by the US government, then about to join the Allies in World War I.

Other products of the Herbert Brenon Film Corporation included Bert Lytell's first film, a melodrama called *The Lone Wolf* (1917); *The Fall of the Romanoffs* (described as "a minor masterpiece," but a failure at the box office); and *The Passing of the Third Floor Back* (1918). The latter, based on Jerome K. Jerome's sentimental moral fable, was made with the cast of the very successful stage version, headed by Sir Johnston Forbes-Robertson. It flopped, and Brenon's production company died with it.

The same year, the director was commissioned by the British War Office to make an ambitious propaganda film called *The Invasion of Britain*—a warning of what might happen if the Allies lost the war. According to Kevin Brownlow, the movie "was the worst-kept secret of the war. Everyone knew that it was extremely expensive, that Hall Caine had written the story, and that Matheson Lang, Marie Lohr, and Ellen Terry had donated their services. But the production dragged on and on, through the spring and summer of 1918, with no end in sight. A studio fire in June destroyed some of the negative and reshooting added weeks to the schedule."

Brownlow quotes a vivid contemporary record of Brenon's handling of a crowd scene in this film—"how this solitary figure with a megaphone, dwarfed by the massive Town Hall at Chester, coaxed and cajoled emotion from an embarrassed and shy crowd of women"—forcing them to consider what an invasion would mean to them and their families, and turning a giggling assembly into a fervent army that "might have stepped out of the French Revolution." Along with Brenon's authority and conviction went an arrogance and self-regard that aroused much hostility in Britain, and some ridicule. George Pearson recalled the shock he received from a large notice in the maestro's studio: "Silence—As the Church is to the Devout Worshipper, so is the Studio to the Sincere Artist."

The 1918 Armistice made *The Invasion of Britain* an irrelevance and, with some £70,000 already spent, production was halted—having had his pacifist film upstaged by the war, Brenon had now had his war film throttled by the peace. He sailed for the United States in December 1918 to file his final papers as an American citizen, and then returned to Britain to make *Twelve-Ten* (1919), a "heavy mystery drama" starring Marie Doro. This led to several other films made in Italy with the same actress, including *La Principessa misteriosa* (*The Mysterious Princess*, 1919), *Beatrice* (1920), and *Sorella contro sorella* (*Sister Against Sister*, 1920).

As Richard Koszarski says, Brenon's "directorial success with the widest range of silent stars remained unparalleled," and he was admired particularly as a director of women. Annette Kellerman, Theda Bara, Alla Nazimova, and Marie Doro had all flourished under his guidance, and in 1921, returning to the United States under the patronage of Joseph M. Schenck, he directed three Norma Talmadge vehicles: *The Sign on the Door,* with Lew Cody, and *The Passion Flower* and *The Wonderful Thing,* both costarring Harrison Ford. By now reconciled with William Fox, he made two movies for him and then signed with Jesse L. Lasky.

After a dazzling beginning, Brenon had encountered during the war years a succession of failures and misfortunes that might have ended the career of a lesser man. He had struggled back to popularity, however, and the films he made for Famous Players–Lasky between 1923 and 1927 returned him to his former position as one of the three or four most "bankable" directors in Hollywood. His first big Lasky assignment was *The Spanish Dancer* (1923), an elaborately staged costume romance about the tragic love affair between an impoverished Spanish nobleman (Antonio Moreno) and a gypsy dancer (Pola Negri). It was photographed by James Wong Howe, who worked with Brenon on eight subsequent pictures as well.

Somewhat overshadowed by *Rosita*, Lubitsch's treatment of the same story, *The Spanish Dancer* nevertheless did reasonably well, and Brenon directed Pola Negri again in *Shadows of Paris*, an *apache* melodrama. She was supposed to be so temperamental and unstable as to be almost impossible to work with, but Brenon called her "the greatest actress on either stage or screen today," and said that "when you understand her she is the easiest person in the world to direct."

Brenon created a new star when he cast the seventeen-year-old Betty Bronson in the title role of *Peter Pan* (1924). She was called "the find of years," and Bronson fan clubs sprang up overnight. The verve and charm of her performance was supported by a brilliant cast—Esther Ralston as Mrs. Darling, Anna May Wong as Tiger Lily, Mary Brian as Wendy, George Ali recreating his famous stage performance as Nana the nurse-dog, and the scene-stealing Ernest Torrence mugging furiously as Captain Hook. Brenon and his scenarist Willis Goldbeck worked closely with J. M. Barrie on the script, and the adaptation is said to surpass all subsequent versions in "capturing the delicate essence of . . . Barrie's highly personal mixture of whimsy, magic, and old-fashioned moralizing."

"Despite a few dull patches," wrote John Gillett fifty years later, "*Peter Pan* confirms that Brenon was a genuinely creative director . . . [it] has yet to be fully reevaluated." The film, Gillett says, "mixes studio interiors, simulated exteriors, and real locations without causing a jarring note. Mention should be made of the exquisite design sense which permeates the whole film: the delicate decorations of the Darlings' home, the cavernous forests, the shimmering seashore (with those marvellous high shots of the mermaids swimming away), and the pirate ship itself, fully rigged and placed squarely in the ocean, and all shot with a painter's eye for light and shade by the great James Wong Howe. . . . Depite a few fleeting glimpses of wires, the magical elements are extremely well contrived [by Roy Pomeroy]. . . . Brenon also exploits to the full both the wit and the heavily applied pathos of the original and somehow makes it work."

Brenon released only two minor movies in 1925, but 1926 was an *annus mirabilis* for him, beginning with the phenomenal success of his version of P. C. Wren's novel of the French Foreign Legion, *Beau Geste*. It opens with the extraordinary scene in which a relief force arrives at a remote desert outpost, Fort Zinderneuf, and finds it garrisoned by dead Legionnaires, propped in the embrasures as if they were still defending the fort. Among the dead is the aristocratic young Englishman Beau Geste (Ronald Colman), and from the desert charnel house of Fort Zinderneuf we flash back to the golden childhood of the Geste brothers, their young manhood, and the quixotic act of self-sacrifice that had brought all three brothers into the Legion. In the end Beau's brothers set fire to Zinderneuf, giving him the "Viking's funeral" they had promised him as children.

Called "one of the classic action-spectacles of the silent screen," and "one of the most elaborate location pictures in movie history," *Beau Geste* also shows a sensitivity in Brenon's handling of his cast that adds weight to John Gillett's call for a reappraisal of the director's work. It was generally agreed that Ronald Colman was acted off the screen by the "wonderful villainy" of Noah Beery as the brutal, fearless Sergeant Lejaune and William Powell as Boldini, and there was much praise for J. Roy Hunt's "exquisite photography of spectacular desert scenery." According to George Geltzer, William Wellman's 1939 remake of *Beau Geste* duplicated Brenon's "almost frame by frame."

Brenon's adaptation of Scott Fitzgerald's *The Great Gatsby* was apparently no more successful than the later attempts to film that unfilmable novel, but he had another hit with *A Kiss for Cinderella*, his second picture with Betty Bronson. A fable about an ill-used servant girl, it has retained its "charm, humor, and fairy-tale magic." *Dancing Mothers*, also released in 1926, gave Clara Bow one of her best roles as "a flapper . . . sky-rocketed to stardom," and was described by George Geltzer as "a curious film" that "had dramatic power despite static camerawork, large-scale but imaginative sets, and an off-beat ending." Brenon's two other films of the year, *The Song and Dance Man* (with Tom Moore and Bessie Love) and *God Gave Me Twenty Cents* (starring Lois Moran), seem to have made less impact.

At that point Brenon left Famous Players–Lasky in a dispute over *Sorrell and Son*, the popular novel by Warwick Deeping. The studio saw no box-office potential in the book, so Brenon, as intransigent as ever, bought the rights himself and made the movie as an independent production under the auspices of United Artists and his friend Joseph M. Schenck. It stars H. B. Warner as a British officer who loses everything in World War I except his little son. An effective tearjerker, the film justified Brenon's faith in the story and was the director's own favorite among his works.

Thereafter, until 1933, Brenon worked for various Hollywood studios—primarily RKO—usually producing the films he directed. *Laugh, Clown, Laugh* (1928), with Lon Chaney and Loretta Young, was his last completely silent picture. The same year he declared his opposition to the sound film which, he said, "violates the pantomimic art" and "cannot compete with the flesh-and-blood theatre." Less than a year later he retracted this statement and added music and synchronized sound effects to *The Rescue*. His first talkie, and adaptation of Fannie Hurst's novel *Lummox*, followed in 1930.

Brenon made six more talkies in Hollywood—most notably *The Case of Sergeant Grischa*, with Chester Morris—but in fact his sound films never equaled the best of his silents. In 1935 Brenon returned to England, where he directed about a dozen pictures for Associated British and other companies. The best of these was *The Housemaster*, adapted from Ian Hay's play and starring Otto Kruger, and *Yellow Sands*, notable for its excellent location work in the west of England. His last picture was an Edgar Wallace thriller, *Flying Squad* (1940). After that, Brenon returned to the United States, spending his long retirement in Los Angeles.

FILMS: All for Her, 1912; The Clown's Triumph, 1912; The Long Strike, 1912; Leah the Forsaken, 1912; The Nurse, 1912; Ivanhoe, 1913; Absinthe, 1913; Time Is Money, 1913; The Anarchist, 1913; The Angel of Death, 1913; Kathleen Mavourneen, 1913; Across the Atlantic (U.K., The Secret of the Air), 1914; (with Otis Turner) Neptune's Daughter, 1914; Sin, 1915; The Soul of Broadway, 1915; The Heart of Maryland, 1915; The Kreutzer Sonata, 1915; The Two Orphans, 1915; The Clemenceau Case, 1915; A Daughter of the Gods, 1916; The Bigamist, 1916; The Governor's Decision, 1916; Whom the Gods Would Destroy, 1916; Bubbles, 1916; Love or an Empire, 1916; The Marble Heart, 1916; The Missing Witness, 1916; The Ruling Passion, 1916; The Voice Upstairs, 1916; War Brides, 1916; The Lone Wolf, 1917; The Eternal Sin (Lucretia Borgia), 1917; The Fall of the Romanoffs, 1917; Empty Pockets, 1918; The Passing of the Third Floor Back, 1918; The Invasion of Britain (Victory and Peace), 1918; A Sinless Sinner, 1919; Twelve-Ten, 1919; La Principessa misteriosa (The Mysterious Princess), 1919; Beatrice, 1920; Sorella contro sorella (Sister Against Sister), 1920; Chains of Evidence, 1920; The Sign on the Door, 1921; The Passion Flower, 1921; The Wonderful Thing, 1921; A Stage Romance, 1922; Shackles of Gold, 1922; Any Wife, 1922; Moonshine Valley, 1922; The Custard Cup, 1922; The Spanish Dancer, 1923;

The Rustle of Silk, 1923; The Woman With Four Faces, 1923; The Alaskan, 1924; The Side Show of Life, 1924; Shadows of Paris, 1924; The Breaking Point, 1924; Peter Pan, 1924; The Little French Girl, 1925; The Street of Forgotten Men, 1925; Beau Geste, 1926; The Great Gatsby, 1926; A Kiss for Cinderella, 1926; Dancing Mothers, 1926; The Song and Dance Man, 1926; God Gave Me Twenty Cents, 1926; Sorrell and Son, 1927; The Telephone Girl, 1927; Laugh, Clown, Laugh, 1928; The Rescue, 1929; Lummox, 1930; The Case of Sergeant Grischa, 1930; Beau Ideal, 1931; Transgression, 1931; Girl of the Rio, 1932; Wine, Women and Song, 1933; Honors Easy, 1935; Royal Cavalcade/Regal Cavalcade, 1935 (documentary); Living Dangerously, 1936; Someone at the Door, 1936; The Dominant Sex, 1937; Spring Handicap, 1937; The Live Wire, 1937; The Housemaster, 1938; Yellow Sands, 1938; Black Eyes, 1939; Flying Squad, 1940.

ABOUT: Dictionary of American Biography Supplement 6 (1956–1960); Koszarski, R. Hollywood Directors: 1914–1940, 1976. *Periodicals*—Films Illustrated August 1975; Films in Review March 1955; Photoplay March 1918; Picturegoer November 1923; Times (London) June 24, 1958.

*BRESSON, ROBERT (September 25, 1907 –), French director and scenarist, was born in the mountainous Auvergne region of France at Bromont Lamothe (Puy-de-Dôme), the son of Léon Bresson and the former Marie Elizabeth Clausels. He spent his formative years in the countryside until his family moved to Paris, when he was eight. Between thirteen and seventeen he studied classics and philosophy at the Lycée Lakanal in Sceaux, intending later to become a painter. In 1926 he married Leidia Van der Zee. Although Bresson abandoned painting around 1930 because it made him "too agitated," he remains a "painter" to this day. For many years he played the piano and despite "having lost the nimbleness in my fingers" he is still passionately devoted to music, attending concerts weekly and listening to records. Bresson lives in Paris on the top floors of a seventeenth-century house on the Isle St. Louis, near Nôtre Dame. This, with a country retreat, has been his home for over thirty years.

These biographical notes are crucial to an understanding of this extraordinary director's work. He rejects the term "director" and uses "cinematographer." He believes that cinema is a fusion of music and painting, not the theatre and photography, and defines "cinematography" as "a new way of writing, therefore of feeling." His theories are precisely given in his book, *Notes on the Cinematographer*. His films have resolutely followed these beliefs, and are dominated by his Catholicism.

°bres son´

ROBERT BRESSON

When Bresson decided to abandon painting he moved towards cinema. During the following decade he was on the fringes of cinema and "saw everything." Of this period nothing of importance exists. His work was mainly as a "script consultant," first on *C'était un musicien* (1933), directed by Frédéric Zelnick and Maurice Gleize, then on Claude Heymann's comedy *Jumeaux de Brighton* (1936) and Pierre Billon's *Courrier Sud* (1937), and fleetingly with René Clair. His only significant work was a short film, financed by the art historian Roland Penrose, made in 1934. Called *Les Affaires publiques*, this comedy has long been lost and little is known of it.

Of this film Bresson remarks: "It's often said that I don't wish it to be rediscovered but that's not true. There is something in it which exists outside my other work. The star of the film, which I wrote, edited, and directed, was a droll comedian named Beby. It was in three episodes based around a grotesque dictator in a legendary country. All of the events are without logic and derived from magic and the circus." Bresson admits to liking the work of Charles Chaplin— especially *The Circus* and *City Lights*—and he was earlier linked with the surrealist movement in Paris. Since few people have seen *Les Affaires publiques* we can only speculate on the quality and nature of this youthful work. One contemporary review by Roger Leenhardt describes it as "hesitant," and Osvaldo Campassi in *Ten Years of French Cinema* (1949) writes about it at length, summing it up as a "frenetic caprice." Unless it is rediscovered by the Cinémathèque Française, which is now doing restoration work on Bresson's earliest films, we are left with only those two accounts and Bresson's own comments.

In 1939 Bresson joined the French army and was a prisoner of war between June 1940 and April 1941. His imprisonment profoundly affected him, even though he was not confined like many of his protagonists (notably Fontaine, in *A Man Escaped*). Instead, "I was set to work in a forest, for local peasants who—luckily—fed us. After a year or so I simulated a fever and with other prisoners who were sick I was released. I returned to Paris."

In occupied France, at the height of the war, Bresson began preparing his first feature, *Les Anges du péché* (1943), based on an idea by a friend, the Reverend Raymond Brückberger, and inspired by a novel. Bresson wanted to call the film "Bethanie"—the name of the convent where the action is centered. He wrote the screenplay and then asked the playwright Jean Giraudoux to supply the dialogue.

Although Bresson regards his debut film and the two works that followed as incomplete and spoiled by the intrusion of conventional music and actors, rather than the "models" (in the sense of artists' models) he subsequently used, *Les Anges du péché* remains one of the most astonishing first features in world cinema. It not only displays complete mastery of the medium, but puts into practice many of the theories Bresson later refined and distilled. He says: "I knew at this stage what I wanted, but had to accept the actresses. I warned them immediately to stop what they were doing in front of the camera, or they—or I—would leave. Luckily they were in nun's habits so they could not gesticulate."

Les Anges du péché proved a great commercial success and won the Grand Prix du Cinéma Français. It tells a basically melodramatic story set in a convent devoted to the rehabilitation of young women. An eager young novice, Anne-Marie (Renée Faure), is regarded as proud by the nuns. During a prison visit she meets her destiny, a hardened criminal named Thérèse (Jany Holt). Upon her release from prison, Thérèse shoots her lover dead and takes refuge in the convent, where Anne-Marie overwhelms her with her attempts to save her soul. Eventually Anne-Marie is expelled but returns each night to the grounds, exposing herself to the elements. She is discovered, weak and ill, and brought back into the convent. Meanwhile the police have established Thérèse's guilt for her lover's murder. Anne-Marie, near death, tries to take her final vows, but is too weak to speak. Thérèse—at last understanding the love and self-sacrifice of her savior—speaks them for her and then surrenders

to the waiting police, leaving the way clear to expiation and grace. Anne-Marie, for her part, has moved at great cost from pride to humility. Both transformations are inspired by love, which is God.

By Bresson's later standards the film is flamboyant, with stylized dialogue and specially composed music by Jean-Jacques Grünenwald that simply underlines the action in a way Bresson later rejected: "Music takes up all the room and gives no increased value to the image to which it is added." The film is also more dramatically photographed (by Philippe Agostini) than all but Bresson's second picture, with greater contrast between blacks and whites. There is, as Amedée Ayfre remarks, "some psychology of character"—another element later eschewed. Even so, in Raymond Durgnat's words, Bresson's vision "is almost mature in his first feature." It already shows his preference for a narrative composed of many short scenes, as well as his fascination with human skills and processes, observing in detail the nuns' work and rituals. On the other hand, we also see his characteristic use of ellipsis, as when Thérèse, buying a gun, is simply shown receiving it over a counter.

Bresson resolutely proclaims himself a painter, not a writer, the task he finds most difficult of all. For his second film, *Les Dames du Bois de Boulogne*, he sought more literary inspiration, a novel by Diderot, *Jacques le fataliste*. Actually he used only one chapter and for the second and last time sought help with the dialogue—from his friend Jean Cocteau, who nonetheless stuck closely to the original. It was Cocteau who later said of Bresson, "He is one apart from this terrible world."

Bresson's films are unique. Most of them deal with the religious themes of predestination and redemption, but in terms of tightly constructed dramatic narratives. However, Bresson scorns the easy pleasures and illusions of the storyteller's art, and is quite likely to leave out what others would regard as a dramatic high point. We may simply be told that the event has taken place, or shown only a part of it, while being treated to all the associated activities that mere storytellers take for granted—people coming in and out, opening and closing doors, going up and down stairs. Recognizing the great persuasive power of the film image, its ability to make us believe what we see and feel what the image suggests, Bresson deliberately subverts this power by directing our attention to a world beyond that of his narrative. What is left is not the illusion of "realism," but what he calls the "crude real" of the cinematic image itself, which for Bresson carries us "far away from the intelligence that complicates everything"; that is why he calls the camera "divine."

For *Les Dames du Bois de Boulogne* (1945) Bresson was again obliged to use professional actors and the same composer and cameraman. Because the film was made under wartime conditions, many of the interiors were shot within a studio, though Bresson prefers to work on location and if possible in the actual settings prescribed by the script. He has transposed the incident within the book into a timeless story of passion and revenge—what John Russell Taylor describes as "one of the most remarkable of *films maudits.*"

The setting here is Paris. Hélène (Maria Casarès) believes that her lover Jean (feebly played by Paul Bernard) no longer cares for her. She tells him that their affair is over and is dismayed at his relief. Vowing revenge, she institutes an elaborate plan. She introduces him to Agnès (Elina Labourdette), a young prostitute, and when he subsequently falls in love with her, she announces—at their grand wedding—"You have married a slut." Jean goes off but returns to find his new wife seriously ill. He begs her to stay with him and she says that she will. As in the previous film, two souls are united by the purity of love, despite the jealous and evil powers that have sought to destroy then.

With its intensely stylized costumes, formal dialogue (characters never use the familiar), and perfunctory motivations, the film was a critical and financial failure in postwar Paris, and only later achieved the recognition it deserved. One contemporary champion was the director Jacques Becker. He noted the complaints about characters "who come and go, look, sit, rise, go up and down stairs, take the elevator, and exchange laconic words in a strange language," but insisted that all this "strangeness" was an element in an entirely original "new style." Bresson himself says "I knew what I wanted from the beginning, but I waited too long to achieve it."

His third film, and the one that established his international reputation, came six years later and can be seen now as a transitional work. Based on the famous novel by the Catholic writer Georges Bernanos, *Le Journal d'un curé de campagne* (*Diary of a Country Priest*, 1951), this is a first-person account by a young priest (Claude Laydu) who is given a rural parish in the village of Ambricourt, in northern France. The young man—innocent, awkward, and unworldly—is treated with scorn and ridicule. He is drawn into a drama that is unfolding at the local château and takes upon himself the almost impossible task of reconciling the countess to her God. He succeeds, but the cost to him—as it was

to Anne-Marie—is his life. The young priest, existing on a diet of bread and too much cheap wine, grows more and more ill and weak, and is finally diagnosed as having cancer of the stomach. He dies at the home of friends, and his last words are "What does it matter? All is grace." The image on the screen fades into one of a dark gray cross. In a contemporary review, Gavin Lambert commented on the "inner exaltation" of the film, and in a famous essay André Bazin, describing it as a masterpiece, adds that it impresses "because of its power to stir the emotions, rather than the intelligence," which is exactly Bresson's avowed aim in all his films.

The film was praised by critics and awarded numerous international prizes, including the Prix Louis Delluc and the 1951 Grand Prize at the Venice Festival. It also achieved considerable success at the box office. In it, Bresson moved towards the use of nonprofessional actors and, although Grünenwald once again supplied the score, the soundtrack is infinitely more complex than in the earlier films and may be seen as the beginning of Bresson's use of sound and image as complementary elements. Thus we see the priest writing his journal and hear him reading his words in voice-over, then we see the remembered scene, with the voice-over commentary continuing until finally the dialogue takes over. Bresson later remarked in his notes, "An ice-cold commentary can warm, by contrast, tepid dialogues in a film. Phenomenon analogous to that of hot and cold in painting." Another characteristic use of sound occurs during the climatic conversion scene, whose drama is counterpointed by the mundane sound of the gardener raking the path outside.

Several years elapsed before the emergence of the first uncompromised and definitive Bresson masterpiece, a work that remains among his most highly regarded and best-known films. *Un condamné à mort s'est échappé* (*A Man Escaped*, 1956) was inspired by an article in *Figaro Littéraire*. It was written by a former prisoner of war, Commandant André Devigny, and described his astonishing escape from Montluc Prison in Lyons while awaiting execution by the Germans. Bresson wrote the screenplay, the sparse dialogue, and the commentary that counterpoints and illuminates the action. He eschewed a conventional score and used—sparingly—excerpts from Mozart's Mass in C Minor (K427). With this film Bresson achieved the complete control he sought by the use of "models"—nonprofessionals with no dramatic training who are taught to speak their lines and move their bodies without conscious interpretation or motivation, precisely as Bresson instructs them—in effect, as one critic wrote, Bresson plays all the parts. The hostility this often provokes in the hapless models creates a tension of its own, without destroying the director's conception of a shot.

Bresson prefaces the film with two sentences. The first—an alternative title—is Christ's admonition to Nicodemus: "The wind bloweth where it listeth." Then comes the comment: "This is a true story. I have told it with no embellishments." It is true that by shooting at the actual prison, by painstaking reconstruction of the methods and instruments of Devigny's escape, Bresson brings an absorbing verisimilitude to the surface of a story whose outcome we already know. This surface, said Amedée Ayfre, stems from "the precise choice of details, objects and accessories, through gestures charged with an extreme solid reality"—what Eric Rohmer called "the miracle of objects." Bresson himself said: "I was hoping to make a film about objects that would at the same time have a soul. That is to say, to reach the latter through the former."

Devigny (called Fontaine in the film) is utterly determined to escape. He does so by endless perseverance, self-help, and a degree of divine intervention. Jane Sloan, in her book on Bresson, points out that this is a central theme in his work—the need to help oneself by making the right choices and doing things "lovingly," while remaining open to the possibilities of improvisation and God-given grace. Nowhere is this more manifest than in the arrival of the boy Jost, who is put into Fontaine's cell just before the escape. At first Fontaine contemplates killing the youngster. He relents and takes him along, to find that without him he could never have made it. The film ends with the two fugitives setting out into the night to the accompaniment of Mozart and the boy's simple comment: "If only my mother could see me now"; the image of a snake; and the noise of a passing train. The juxtaposition of the extraordinary and the everyday gives the film its quality and its resonance.

Bresson gives us an almost documentary portrait of a prison, its relationships, its routine: the clanging pails, the clinking keys. From these bare bones, he builds one of the most profound interior examinations of a human being ever shown. This work, which brought Bresson the award as best director at Cannes and several other honors, established him internationally and confirmed his stature as, in Jean-Luc Godard's words, "to French cinema what Mozart is to German music and Dostoevsky is to Russian literature." No higher accolade could be given to Bresson, who regards Dostoevky as "the greatest novelist," to whom he is indebted in no less than three of his thirteen films. This debt is explicit in Bresson's next work, *Pickpocket* (1959), which derives from *Crime and Punishment*. Michel, a lonely and arrogant young man, is an expert pickpocket who feels himself above the law and normal human emotions. Eventually, thanks to the relentless pursuit of a detective, he is caught and sent to prison—something "predestined." In the final moments of the film he is redeemed by the love of Jeanne, whose help he has previously refused. (Paul Schrader's *American Gigolo* is not only indebted to the same source and to the work of the director he most admires, but the final minutes of his film are a direct "copy" of and *hommage* to Bresson's film.)

Like its predecessor, *Pickpocket* has a convincingly "documentary" feel to it and a delight in human skills (here those of a criminal), using locations and—importantly—a professional pickpocket to help achieve this verisimilitude and the moments of suspense that are so much part of the film. Inevitably there is a spiritual dimension to Bresson's study of an isolated, antisocial man almost willing himself to be caught. Amedeé Ayfre suggests that Michel is freedom without grace, unconsciously seeking it. We witness a kind of miracle, as in the case of Fontaine and Jost's escape or Thérèse's redemption. In Schrader's words, this is "the transference of . . . [Michel's] passion from pickpocketing to Jeanne"; in the prison he is "faced with an explicitly spiritual act within a cold environment . . . it is a 'miracle' which must be accepted or rejected."

As usual, Bresson used nonprofessional "models" and collaborated only with trusted associates (his most frequent collaborators have been Pierre Charbonnier as art director, Raymond Lamy as editor, and until 1961, Léonce-Henry Burel as cameraman). Bresson believes that in cinematography "an image must be transformed by contact with other images," that there is "no art without transformation." He therefore favors a relatively inexpressive or "neutral" image, of maximum versatility in combination with other images. Hence his preference for the medium shot, with the camera straight on its subject to produce a "flattened image." The music, used sparsely for its "spiritual" qualities, comes from the work of the seventeenth-century composer Jean-Baptiste Lully.

Characteristically, the film is short (under 75 minutes), reflecting Bresson's compression of narrative and his desire to make one image "suffice where a novelist would take ten pages." As Godard noted, he was now "the master of the ellipsis," which he uses for a variety of purposes—for economy, to avoid the titillation of violence, often to unsettle the viewer by denying his narrative expectations. For some critics, however, Bresson had gone too far in this direction; Robert Vas even accused him of self-parody.

Unmoved, Bresson carried compression even further in *Procès de Jeanne d'Arc* (*The Trial of Joan of Arc,* 1962), the effect of which, as Derek Prouse simply but effectively noted, was "like being hit over the head by a sledgehammer." In little over sixty minutes Bresson shows us the imprisonment, trial, and the execution of Joan, splendidly "modeled" by Florence Carrez.

Bresson's entire screenplay is based on contemporary written accounts, including the transcript of the trial. As with Devigny's escape we know the outcome, but the trial and its immediate consequences are not important. Bresson is concerned with Joan's inner struggle. She is questioned and tortured, her virginity is tested, and only once does she despair. But the road to salvation is certain and the last sequence when she is burned is astounding: the devastating image of the charred stake, the birds flying upwards, the dog running around in confusion, and the use of a single drum roll (the only music in the film apart from a brief fanfare) conclude a sequence—and a work—of the utmost purity.

Importantly the film is not an historical "reconstruction" (Bresson deplores such films), but it uses the costumes (for the English), documents, and artifacts of the period to convey the sense of "another time." We see Joan on the rack but Bresson characteristically spares (or denies) us any explicit scenes of torture. The use of models, the startling compression, the lack of ornamentation and the continued striking of exactly the "right note," give the film a timeless strength. Again the images are "flattened," a 50mm lens providing a constant physical perspective, with few traveling shots. (Bresson has used a 50mm lens since his second film.) This rigorousness seemed to demand a change. Bresson had gone as far in the direction of pure cinematography as he could. The linear quality of the prison films could be likened to the path of an arrow. For his next work, one of several Franco-Swedish coproductions undertaken on the initiative of the Swedish Film Institute, he moved to an altogether more complex form.

The result was described by Tom Milne as "perhaps his greatest film to date, certainly his most complex." Bresson had been thinking about the film for years, deriving the initial inspiration from Dostoevsky's *The Idiot. Au hasard, Balthazar* (*Balthazar,* 1966) is, says Bresson, "made up of many lines that intersect one another." The picaresque and episodic story links two souls—the girl Marie and the donkey Balthazar. Balthazar passes through a series of encounters, each representing one of the deadly sins of humanity. The donkey, naturally, cannot choose his fate. That is determined by the will of others, and he suffers at the hands of those who are avaricious, proud, lustful, and so on. Marie is a human being, yet her victimization is as appalling as that of the little creature she adopts at the beginning of the film. At the conclusion she has been raped and beaten up by a gang of *blousons noirs* and their leader—Gérard—uses Balthazar to carry smuggled goods across the Franco-Swiss border.

Balthazar is shot by customs men and dies amidst a flock of sheep on the hillside where he was born, a victim but also a symbol of Christian faith. Despite the use of a nonhuman protagonist, Bresson achieves his most complex and saintly portrait within a film without sentimentality or a false note. By choosing a commentary on the deadly sins, set over an extended period in a varied social milieu, he moves on from the rarified atmosphere of the two previous works. His examination of such basic failings as gluttony—through the character of the drunken Arnold—allows us to relate unequivocally to the work, while never losing sight of the spiritual significance of the film. It has great immediacy *and* resonance. However, his next film proved even more accessible.

Mouchette (1966) followed with unprecedented rapidity, thanks to money from French television—the first time that ORTF had collaborated with cinema. Based like *Diary of a Country Priest* on a novel by Georges Bernanos, and exhibiting an uncharacteristic degree of naturalism, it tells of a fourteen-year-old schoolgirl, isolated from her schoolmates and from her family. Mouchette (Nadine Nortier) is spirited, stubborn, and resilient, and yet is finally unable to resist the pressures of the grinding poverty—material and spiritual—of her pathetic existence. Her father and brother are drunkards, her desperately ill mother is on her deathbed.

Brief instances show Mouchette's strength, and in a scene on the Dodg'em cars at a fairground (something unlike any other sequence in Bresson's work) she experiences a sense of exhilaration and excitement that is cut short by her father's heavy hand. In a darker sequence she is raped by a drunken poacher whom she has tried to help and only half-resists, almost welcoming the attack as an acknowledgment of her existence.

After her mother's death, Mouchette finds herself even more isolated. She rejects the false charity of a shopkeeper but accepts clothes given her by an old woman. Mouchette carries them to a nearby field where she waves to a passing tractor driver. He ignores her, and in a spontaneous response she wraps a white dress around her like a shroud and rolls down an embankment towards a stream. She stops at the edge, rolls down again, and falls unresisting into the stream. The accompaniment to this act of despair and loneliness is Monteverdi's "Magnificat." The effect is another sledgehammer blow, as one sits transfixed by the devastation of a life and the implied belief that Mouchette has at last achieved peace.

The paradox presented here has troubled many viewers, especially Catholics. Bresson denies that he is a pessimist, yet the more obvious optimism of, say, the escape of Fontaine and Jost, has been lost by the time of these films of rural life. Bresson continues to affirm the dignity of the human spirit while seeming to admit that earthly forces—increasingly immediate and powerful in his films—can erode that spirit. More and more his work acknowledges the bleakness of the human condition, and he uses that knowledge and awareness as the jumping-off point for his "miracles."

Bresson's next film is noteworthy as his first in color—something of which he has always been wary. *Une Femme douce (A Gentle Creature,* 1969) was his first direct (albeit updated) adaptation of Dostoevsky: something he felt permissible since the original was a short story, not a major novel. The setting is no longer the harsh countryside, but modern Paris. The film *begins* with the suicide of a young woman—suicide, or unwillingness to save one's life where it might be be possible, features in about half of Bresson's works. The story is told in a series of flashbacks, narrated by the bereft young husband to the maid. He is a pawnbroker and had met the heroine as an impoverished customer. He had fallen in love, and she had agreed to marry him to escape dependence on relatives. A free spirit, eager to grow, she had found herself shackled to a gross materialist, crushed by his jealousy and poverty of spirit. He does his best to change, to be what she wants, and she promises to be his "faithful wife." And then she jumps. The suicide is repeated at the end of the film, the heroine's white scarf, floating down in slow motion, signifying the soul's survival.

Unusually for Bresson, we are able to study and contrast the two protagonists in a variety of environments. There are visits to the movies (to see Michel Deville's *Benjamin,* photographed by Ghislain Cloquet, who also shot *A Gentle Creature*); to the theatre to see *Hamlet;* to art galleries and museums. Jane Sloan points out that there are also persistent but unacknowl-

edged references to an early feminist film, Germaine Dulac's *La souriante Madame Beudet* (1922), also dealing with economic domination. Each episode serves to underline the couple's differences and lack of communication, but this is hardly a portrait of a marriage that doesn't work out. That is simply the surface to the spiritual examination of the central character. Jan Dawson suggests that for this martyred heroine, as for Mouchette, "self-destruction is the only possible affirmation of a state of purity otherwise missing from their lives."

The film had a relatively cool reception. The use of color, however elegantly muted, seemed to some reviewers to soften its impact, and Dominique Sanda, who played the heroine and went on to become a professional actress, gives more of a "performance" than Bresson usually allows his "models." However, Paul Joannides, one of those who greatly admired the picture, praised its "precise control . . . maintained throughout the film, the linking between shot and shot combining formal consistency and emotional profundity," and the real "purified to such an extent that there is no longer a separation between it and the symbolic."

Quatre nuits d'un rêveur (Four Nights of a Dreamer, 1971), was adapted from a more famous Dostoevsky story, *White Nights,* already filmed by Ivan Pyriev in Russia and by Visconti in Italy. Bresson moves the novella's setting to Paris. A young woman, Marthe, waits on the Pont Neuf for her lover, exactly a year after they have parted. When he does not appear, she comes close to suicide, but is befriended by a young artist, Jacques, who falls in love with her. She keeps him dallying, waiting each night for the other's return, while Jacques pours his dreams and hopes into his tape recorder. On the fourth night she sees the man, kisses him, and leaves Jacques alone. He makes one more interminable recording of his love for her.

An accessible love story then, and one that could easily fall into the lush romanticism of Visconti's theatrical rendition. But Bresson was attracted to what Carlos Clarens describes as "the idea of love being stronger than the love story itself." The result is an altogether more secular work than any which had preceded it. All the same, it seemed to Gavin Miller that "the intensity and tranquility with which the themes have been pursued gives the film a unique flavour, an atmosphere of mysticism which is almost oriental . . . No greater effort has been made in cinema to forbid the froth of naturalism from distracting us from the moment that may or may not be revealed."

Even Bresson's admirers worried about his

preoccupation with young love and his use of "popular" music in the film, although no one could be other than ravished by the breathtaking scene of the *bateau-mouche* floating down the Seine (filmed near his Paris home) and the gentle, somber use of color throughout. By some standards a "minor" film, it was yet of a stature to receive the British Film Institute award as "the most original film" of its year.

In 1974 Bresson returned to grander things and—after twenty years planning—achieved his dream of filming "The Grail" or, as it came to be called, *Lancelot du Lac* (*Lancelot*). This was his most elaborate and costly work and, although he could not film it in separate English and French versions as he had hoped, it was otherwise made without compromise.

The film opens in a dark forest with a close-up of two swords wielded in combat. There are glimpses of other scattered conflicts and of groups of riderless horses galloping through. Titles describe how the Knights of the Round Table had failed in their quest for the Holy Grail. Lancelot and the other survivors return, and he begs Queen Guinevere to release him from their adulterous bond so that he may be reconciled with God. Mordred lurks, fomenting dissension. There is a tournament and the victorious Lancelot is wounded and goes into hiding. He abducts Guinevere, who is under suspicion, but in the end restores her to King Arthur. Mordred stirs up rebellion and Lancelot fights on the King's side. Arthur and all his knights, encumbered by their obsolete armor and idealism, fall before Mordred's disciplined bowmen—a great junk heap of chivalry. Lancelot dies last, whispering the name of Guinevere.

Some critics saw a moral triumph in Lancelot's renunciation of Guinevere; others, like Jane Sloan, thought Guinevere "the only one who is grounded, willing to take life for what it is," and Lancelot a prideful dreamer, foolish to deny her love. Most agreed that the film was deeply fatalistic and pessimistic, with none of the certainty of grace that inspired the earlier films, and "darker than any Bresson film to date, both morally and literally" (Tom Milne).

There are numerous deliberate anachronisms because Bresson maintains that "you must put the past into the present if you want it to be believable." For Jane Sloan, *Lancelot du Lac* "is a film about the end of things and the illusory heights of idealism. . . . The reliance on individual series of repeated images as set-pieces also presents the clearest instance of the approximation of musical form in Bresson's work. The riderless horses galloping through the dark woods are a particularly haunting melody in this re-

spect, but there are many other instances: the opening and closing of the visors that punctuate a conversation between the knights; Gawain's repeated utterance of 'Lancelot' during the tournament; and the several series of multicolored horse trappings. The elegance and coldness of this aesthetic search for the 'purely abstract' has its parallel in the search for the Grail, the impossible search for the spiritual in the living world."

"Think about the surface of the work," Bresson says (with Leonardo da Vinci). "Above all think about the surface." Various critics have fastened on various different aspects of the surface in *Lancelot*. Jonathan Rosenbaum found his "manner of infusing naturalistic detail with formal significance . . . particularly masterful in the marvellous use he makes of armour. . . . It functions as an additional layer of non-expressiveness, increasing neutrality and uniformity in separate images and cloaking identities in many crucial scenes. . . . The concentration on hands and feet that is a constant in Bresson's work becomes all the more affecting here when it is set against the shiny metal in other shots. Or consider the overall effect of contrast achieved between the suits of armour and the image of Guinevere standing in her bath, which makes flesh seem at once more rarified and vulnerable, more soft and graceful, more palpable and precious. The on- and off-screen rattle of the armour throughout the film reinforces this impression."

Bresson's use of animals in this film (as elsewhere) was also much discussed. Tom Milne wrote that "the mysterious, poetic precision of the film springs from . . . images invested with Bresson's belief that animals are more sensitive, more perceptive perhaps, than humans" —images like those of "the birds flying graceful and free above the knights, the horses toiling through the mud and dying with their riders."

From the haunted medieval forests of *Lancelot du Lac*, Bresson returned to modern Paris for a story arguably even darker. *Le Diable, probablement* (*The Devil, Probably*, 1977), photographed like its predecessor by Pasqualino de Santis, was based on a newspaper story. It centers on four disaffected young intellectuals— two men and two women—completely disillusioned with the world created by their elders. The quartet pad through Paris, witnesses to a world that is insanely materialistic, inhuman, and exploitative of its natural resources. This is a work far more overtly political than anything that preceded it; Bresson called it "a film about money, a source of great evil in the world whether for unnecessary armaments or the senseless pollution of the environment." These evils are shown in brilliantly orchestrated newsreel and other footage of despoliation and waste.

The quartet is dominated by the clever, amusing, androgynous Charles, who has some of the moral arrogance of the protagonist in *Pickpocket*. He promises marriage to both girls, but contemplates suicide. Charles' problem, as he explains to a psychiatrist, is that "I hate life. I hate death. . . . My sickness is that I see things clearly." He finds his solution in a "Roman" suicide, bribing a drug addict whom he has lovingly tended to shoot him dead in the Père-Lachaise cemetery.

The film's title is a reply to a question asked by one of the characters: "Who is responsible for this mockery of mankind?" If the possibility of grace seemed remote in *Lancelot du Lac*, it is almost inconceivable here. Jan Dawson called this "Bresson's most daring and uncompromsing film to date," partly because "Charles appears, to us if not to his girlfriends, as the most antipathetic of Bresson's protagonists to date. In rejecting all forms of twentieth-century society, he is rejecting us, the audience, for our complicity in that society: his behaviour, like his eventual death, is an affront to our own survival. . . . And the film's ending is a doubly cold one because at the moment of Charles' final, Pascalian wager, the sense of doubt seems uppermost. There is no triumphant music to trumpet his spiritual ascent. And if, cut off in mid-sentence, he has achieved a state of grace, it is a nihilistic grace: the death of a sacrificed victim rather than of a redeemer."

L'Argent (*Money*, 1982; first drafted in 1977) is loosely based on Tolstoy's story "The False Note." Jean Sémolué points out the "brutality" of this title—the first time Bresson had used an object for this purpose—and the film shows a bleak, appalled rigor of content and means, proving an uncomfortable experience for many of those at the Cannes premiere and later.

A hard-up schoolboy passes a forged note in a photographer's shop, whose furious owner foists it off on Yvon, who delivers the kerosene. Yvon innocently tenders the note in a café, is arrested, and loses his job. Desperate, he takes part in an abortive robbery and is jailed. His child dies while he is inside. Yvon attempts suicide and his wife abandons him.

Meanwhile the photographer has bribed his assistant Lucien to keep his mouth shut. Imitating this dishonesty, Lucien cheats his employer, is fired, and becomes a sort of Robin Hood, stealing from the rich to aid the poor. He goes to prison as Yvon is released. Yvon goes to a small hotel and murders and robs the owners. He is taken in by a widow who is unmoved by the news that he is a murderer. Observing this wretched woman drudging for her parasitic family, and failing to find any money in the house, Yvon slaughters them all with an ax and then confesses to the police.

With the stark ineluctability of a Victorian moral fable, the greed for money leads from a childish misdemeanor to mass murder. And yet, as Tom Milne says, "there is something more intangible here, something which leads to the extraordinary apotheosis of the final sequence, which Bresson has casually described as a routing of the forces of evil. A startling interpretation, on the face of it, for brutal murder and abrupt confession, yet one confirmed rather than denied by the sense of tranquil finality in the image of Yvon watching as the ripples close over his bloody ax in the pond, and of breathless wonderment in the last shot of onlookers frozen as they gaze into the empty room from which all evidence of crime has gone."

Milne finds "familiar difficulties in trying to pin down the emotional resonance of Bresson's images: where a shot of a gardening fork left stuck in a potato patch can evoke aeons of toil and suffering; where a tiny orchard strung with washing lines can suggest paradise lost; where a woman slapped as she is carrying a bowl of coffee, yet still preserving most of its contents from spilling, can recall the humble penitence of Mary Magdalene. It isn't as if there were any overt religious dimension. . . . Yet the meaning of Yvon's final suite of murders is inescapable: deliverance for the woman, retribution for society, expiation for his own membership of that society. Even bleaker than *Le Diable, probablement*, *L'Argent* is even more unmistakably a masterpiece. And even here, finally, 'All is Grace.'"

Bresson himself describes *L'Argent* as the film "with which I am most satisfied—or at least it is the one where I found the most surprises when it was complete—things I had not expected." For him, the making of a film comprises "three births and two deaths": the birth of the idea is followed by its "death" in the agony of writing; it comes alive again in the period of preparation and improvisation, only to die again during the actual filming; and then there is rebirth in a new form during the editing, where the "surprises" come. At Cannes in 1983 it shared the "Grand Prize for Creation" with Andrei Tarkovsky's *Nostalghia*.

For the time being, Bresson has abandoned his long-cherished plan to base a film, "Genesis," on the first chapters of the Old Testament, finding the logistical problems insuperable. In 1987, almost eighty, he was planning a "lighter film" derived from a modern novel about two girls who leave their dreary jobs and head for Monte Carlo and then Italy, gambling and stealing as they go, and knowing that their inevitable destiny is prison. The director is also finishing a major book to supplement and amplify his *Notes on the Cinematographer.*

In his long career, Bresson has made just thirteen feature films and earned the right to two clichés. He is a genius of the cinema, and he remains unique. Since his 1943 debut, he has steadily refined and perfected a form of expression that places him apart from and above the world of commercial movie-making. He has preferred to remain inactive rather than compromise and has chosen never to work in the theatre or in television (a medium he dislikes). He is the cinema's true *auteur* in that his films are completely and immediately recognizable and he has controlled every aspect of their creation. He has built a pyramidic, densely interwoven body of work of great purity and austerity of expression, in which, as Jonathan Rosenbaum has written, "nothing is permitted to detract from the overall narrative complex, and everything present is used." Bresson has often been called the Jansen of the cinema, because of his moral rigor and his concern with predestination; but his films often seem to embody a passionate struggle between that bleak creed and a Pascalian gamble on the possibility of redemption.

Too singular a creator to lead a "school" of filmmakers, Bresson has nevertheless influenced many directors and has been intensely admired by Jacques Becker, Louis Malle, Paul Schrader, François Truffaut, and Jean-Luc Godard, among others. He remains resolutely attracted to the idea of youth, "its suppleness and potential," and has become increasingly hardened in his dislike of the commercial cinema, maintaining that he has not seen a film through to the end for twenty-five years. Yet nothing could be further from the truth than the suggestion of a hermetic, cynical, or bitter man. Late in 1986, in a conversation with this writer he said simply: "I love life."

—B.B.

FILMS: Les Affaires publiques, 1934 (short); Les Anges du péché, 1943; Les Dames du Bois de Boulogne, 1945; Le Journal d'un curé de campagne (Diary of a Country Priest), 1951; Un condamné à mort s'est échappé (A Man Escaped), 1956; Pickpocket, 1959; Procès de Jeanne d'Arc (The Trial of Joan of Arc), 1962; Au hasard, Balthazar (Balthazar), 1966; Mouchette, 1967; Une Femme douce (A Gentle Creature), 1969; Quatre nuits d'un rêveur (Four Nights of a Dreamer), 1971; Lancelot du Lac (Lancelot), 1974; Le Diable, probablement (The Devil, Probably), 1977; L'Argent (Money), 1982. *Published scripts*—Le Film de Béthanie: texte de Les Anges du péché, Gallimard,

1944; Procès de Jeanne d'Arc, Julliard, 1962; Les Dames du Bois de Boulogne *in* L'Avant-Scène du Cinéma November 1976; Mouchette *in* L'Avant-Scène du Cinéma April 1968.

ABOUT: Armes, R. French Cinema Since 1946, Vol. 1, 1966; Ayfre, A. L'Univers de Robert Bresson, 1963; Bazin, A. What Is Cinema?, 1967; Bresson, R. Notes on the Cinematographer, 1975; Briot, R. Robert Bresson, 1957 (in French); Buchka, P. and others. Robert Bresson, 1978 (in German); Burch, N. Theory of Film Practice, 1973; Cameron, I. (ed.) The Films of Robert Bresson, 1969; Drouget, R. Robert Bresson, 1966 (in French); Estève, M. Robert Bresson, 1974 (in French); Ferrero, A. Bresson, 1976 (in Italian); Roud, R. (ed.) Cinema; A Critical Dictionary, 1980; Schrader, P. Transcendental Style in Film: Ozu, Bresson, Dreyer, 1972; Sémolué, J. Robert Bresson, 1959 (in French); Sloan, J. Robert Bresson: A Guide to References and Resources, 1983; Sitney, P.A. (ed.) The Essential Cinema, 1975; Sontag, S. Against Interpretation, 1966; Taylor, J.R. Cinema Eye, Cinema Ear, 1964. *Periodicals*—Cahiers du Cinéma October 1957, May 1963, April 1969, July–August 1975, August–September 1977; Cahiers in English February 1967; Cinéma (France) February 1963; Cinématographe November–December 1974, May 1977; L'Écran Français October 17, 1945; November 12, 1946; Études Cinématographiques 18–19 1962; Film Culture 20 1959; Film Dope July 1974; Film Quarterly Spring 1960, Fall 1977; Image et Son 269 1973, 291 1974; Téléciné 25 1950; Velvet Light Trap Summer 1973; Yale French Studies 60 1980.

BROWN, CLARENCE (May 10, 1890–August 17, 1987), American director, was born in Clinton, Massachusetts, the son of Larkin H. Brown, a loom-repairer. His mother was a weaver. When Brown was eleven the family moved to Knoxville, Tennessee, where his parents worked in the Brookside Mills. Graduating at fifteen from Knoxville High School, Brown went on to the University of Tennessee, where he obtained degrees in both electrical and mechanical engineering. Cars were his first love, and he began his career in 1909 in the engineering department of an automobile manufacturer—the Moline Company—working his way up to a position on the sales staff and then moving on to the Stevens Duryea Company in Massachusetts. Later he opened his own car agency in Birmingham, Alabama.

Brown's interest in filmmaking was aroused when he saw a location unit shooting in Fort Lee, New Jersey. In 1914 he quit the Brown Motor Company and talked his way into a job with "the man I consider the greatest of them all —Maurice Tourneur," who was then at the Peerless Studios in New Jersey. During this apprenticeship, Brown worked with Tourneur as

CLARENCE BROWN

general assistant, editor, title writer, assistant director, and second unit director. His career was interrupted in 1917 by World War I, in which Brown learned to fly and served for a time as a flying instructor. After the war he returned to Tourneur, working with him until 1920.

Brown often says that his engineering experience helped him to master the technical intricacies of filmmaking, especially when sound came and "the Western Electric people tried to blind us with science." But he insisted that everything he knew about the film as art he learned from Maurice Tourneur, "my god." Certainly the influence of Tourneur's picturesque style, with its emphasis on atmosphere, lighting, and composition, is very evident in Brown's own fondness for intimate, low-lit scenes—"scenes with a shadowy, hushed texture; illuminated only partially, and mysteriously, by a flickering candle, a crackling log fire, or a nocturnal stream of light from the stars." Brown retained this highly pictorial style throughout his career, and spoke of the cinema screen as "a broader canvas on which to paint."

He was still with Tourneur when the latter started work on *The Last of the Mohicans* (1920). Tourneur became ill during the filming, and Brown is said to be responsible for the greater part of this excellent version of the story. However, the first film Brown claimed as his own is *The Great Redeemer* (1920). The script, based on a newspaper story, was written by Brown himself in collaboration with John Gilbert, who was then working as an assistant to Tourneur as well as an actor. It is a highly romantic story about a convict whose jail paintings

inspire religious conversions, and the picture was a hit. It was followed by *The Light in the Dark* (1922) and then by *Don't Marry for Money* (1923), which brought Brown a contract with Universal.

During his three years with Universal, Brown made five movies. They included *Smoldering Fires* (1925), a powerful drama about a woman of forty (Pauline Frederick) who falls in love with a much younger man, and *The Goose Woman* (1925), inspired partly by the New Jersey "Pig Woman" trial. In this film—a popular and critical success—a once famous opera singer (Louise Dresser) is scratching an alcoholic living as a goose farmer when a murder is committed nearby; she invents a story that restores her name to the headlines. Its melodramatic second half notwithstanding, the picture is outstanding in its command of atmosphere and naturalistic detail (like the very convincing squalor in which the Goose Woman lives). There was also much praise for the skill with which Brown develops a triangular love story alongside the murder mystery. In fact, the romantic triangle is a theme much favored by this director, and because the formula involves the use of three stars in principal roles, some of Brown's silent movies anticipated the multi-star blockbusters that were to emerge in Hollywood in the early 1930s.

In 1924 Brown left Universal and went to United Artists to direct Rudolph Valentino in *The Eagle* (1925), a tongue-in-cheek romantic comedy of great charm. After completing a Norma Talmadge vehicle (*Kiki*, 1926) for the same studio, he moved on to Metro-Goldwyn-Mayer, where he remained for the rest of his career. This move to the most opulent of the Hollywood studios had its effect on Brown's work. The "discreet directorial style" of his early films gave way to the extravagant sets, the glossy and star-studded productions that were the MGM "house style." All the same, as David Robinson has remarked, he "remained supremely a 'commercial' director without ever compromising his great talent and very personal, romantic vision."

Clarence Brown was never a tyrannical or dogmatic director. When he started work on a picture, he liked his actors to approach their roles in their own way, only suggesting amendments if their own readings seemed to him inadequate. This patient and democratic method worked well for him, establishing him as a director with a special flair for getting the best out of his stars. Thus his first assignment at MGM was to direct Louis B. Mayer's new screen goddess Greta Garbo in her third American film, *Flesh and the Devil* (1926). With a scenario by Benjamin Glazer based on a Hermann Sudermann novel, it is a romantic melodrama, set in Prussia, about the deadly rivalry that develops between two friends for the love of the beautiful Felicitas (who dies in an attempt to avert a duel between them). The Prussian atmosphere is "beautifully recreated," and Georges Sadoul has drawn attention to the "extraordinary communion service scene in which Garbo turns the chalice so that her lips will touch the spot from which her lover drank."

Flesh and the Devil, which attracted a great deal of publicity because of the passionate love scenes between Garbo and her costar John Gilbert, was a major success. Brown was dubbed "Garbo's Man Friday" and made six more films with her, including *A Woman of Affairs* (1928), one of the last of her silents, and five sound pictures. The first of these ("Garbo Talks!") was Brown's version of Eugene O'Neill's play *Anna Christie,* about a waterfront prostitute and her love for a young seaman. Set against "a background of sea fog and coal-barge squalor," it seemed to some critics richly visual, and artful in its use of dialogue and sound effects, though the National Board of Review found it "a very talkie, uncinematic affair," only salvaged by fine acting.

On ten of Brown's films, including all those with Garbo but the last, he had William Daniels as his lighting cameraman, and the evenness of visual texture between the films must be attributed to this partnership. Daniels would follow the director through the rehearsals and the two would work out their camera set-ups in collaboration, with Brown often depending on Daniels to evoke cinematically a dramatic effect that seemed to him inherent in a scene or a location (like the silhouette effect in the duel scene in *Flesh and the Devil*). Brown worked no less closely with his writers, although he always gave priority to the visual, sometimes rewriting a scene himself in order to exploit the cinematic possibilities of a particular location. Having learned his business in the silent era, Brown always maintained that "silent pictures were more of an art than talkies ever have been." All the same, and although he approached his first sound film (*Navy Blues,* 1929) "with trepidation," he seems to have made the transition more easily than many of his contemporaries.

Eyman Scott has suggested that Brown "specialized in capturing primal fears— disorientation and the elemental anguish of loss." His principal characters tend to be motivated by complex emotions that drive them towards unconventional modes of behavior, and often it is the strong-willed women in his films

who provide the catalyst for drama—Garbo in all her films with him, Norma Shearer in *A Free Soul* (1931), Joan Crawford in *Possessed* (1931), *Letty Lynton* (1932), and *Sadie McKee* (1934). Notable among Brown's films of the 1930s are *Anna Karenina* (1935), starring Garbo, Fredric March, and Basil Rathbone; an excellent and very successful adaptation of Eugene O'Neill's *Ah, Wilderness!* (from which developed the Andy Hardy series); and *The Gorgeous Hussy* (1936), a bowdlerized biography of Peggy O'Neale, the tavern-keeper's daughter who cut a wide swath through President Jackson's administration. *Gorgeous Hussy* was impressive mainly for a cast-list including Joan Crawford, Lionel Barrymore, Franchot Tone, Melvyn Douglas, Robert Taylor, and James Stewart.

Conquest (1937, called *Marie Walewska* in Britain) was Brown's last picture with Garbo—a "measured, dignified, and often rather dull historical fiction, lightened by excellent performances and production." Two years later, MGM loaned Brown to 20th Century–Fox to direct *The Rains Came* (1939), in which some high-class parasites in India during the Raj redeem themselves when a flood disaster strikes. Starring Myrna Loy, Tyrone Power, and George Brent, this was one of the most accomplished and memorable of Brown's films. Many years later Charles Higham described the outbreak of the monsoon—"a curtain billowing in the breeze, a lamp casting a shadow of latticework against white silk, servants scattering for cover"—and concluded that "it would be difficult to improve on the [film's] direction" (a statement born out when the film was remade as *The Rains of Ranchipur* in 1955).

Back at MGM, Brown made *Edison, the Man* (1940), a scrupulous biography starring Spencer Tracy; *Come Live With Me* (1941), which has Hedy Lamarr as a Viennese refugee seeking citizenship and finding love in the arms of James Stewart; and *They Met in Bombay* (1941), in which not the rains but love comes to two jewel thieves on the run in India (Clark Gable, Rosalind Russell). *The Human Comedy* (1943), based on Saroyan's novel about small-town heartbreak in World War II, was more popular with its wet-eyed audiences than with the critics, many of whom found it appallingly sentimental. There was a similar response to the "tearful flagwaver" *The White Cliffs of Dover* (1944).

National Velvet (1944), about an English schoolgirl who rides her own horse to victory in the Grand National, is now chiefly remembered as the movie that gave Elizabeth Taylor to the world, but it also brought Anne Revere an Oscar as best supporting actress for her performance as

Velvet's mother. It was followed by *The Yearling* (1947), based on Marjorie Kinnan Rawlings' novel exploring a Florida boy's relationship with nature and especially his love for a foundling deer. Brown had traveled incognito through the South looking for a boy to play the lead. He found Claude Jarman Jr., a Nashville fifth-grader with no movie experience, and extracted from him a performance that earned the boy a special Academy Award. "The only thing I know about directing children," Brown says, "is the performance I got from Claude. Every word, every action, every gesture was manipulated. The boy was smart enough to do just what I told him. For the hysterics when he has to shoot the deer, I asked him to imagine his mother was dying."

In 1906 Clarence Brown had witnessed the Atlanta race riots: "I saw fifteen Negroes murdered by a goddamned mob of white men." That is why he chose to film William Faulkner's *Intruder in the Dust,* about an aging and dignified black man (Juan Hernandez) who is falsely accused of murdering a white and almost lynched before his innocence is proved by his lawyer and a few others of good will. The film focuses on the relationship between the old man and the lawyer's young nephew (played by Jarman), whom we see growing in humanity and compassion as a result. Adapted by Ben Maddow (the poet David Wolff), *Intruder* was photographed by Robert Surtees on location in Oxford, Mississippi—Faulkner's home town. Made at a time when most Hollywood directors were carefully avoiding controversial subjects, it is the angriest of Brown's films and strikingly free both of the glossy MGM house style and of the cheap emotive devices that often mar "mob violence" pictures. Georges Sadoul called it a "harsh, sensitive film" which "superbly recreates the atmosphere and bigotry of small-town life and is one of the best adaptations of a Faulkner novel."

In 1952 Brown directed his last film, *Plymouth Adventure.* He says he quit when he found making movies no longer any fun—"besides, I was making too much money in real estate and investments to want to work that hard anymore." All the same, he rarely went to the movies because when he saw a good film, "the old instincts start working and I want to go racing off and get back to work." He also raced in more literal ways: he was a member of the Quiet Birdmen, an organization for World War I aviators, and first flew a jet faster than the speed of sound when he was seventy-one. He also retained his lifelong passion for automobiles and owned several Mercedes Benzes: "I tinker with cars. That's my weakness. I still open up to 140mph in the desert." The director is said to

have "an incisive, occasionally querulous, biting temperament."

Andrew Sarris has suggested that Brown's career shows an evolution from films influenced by German Expressionism to the "American Gothic" of *Intruder in the Dust,* but the director himself—apart from the great debt he acknowledged to Maurice Tourneur—showed no interest in identifying his work with cinematic trends and styles. "I only knew what was human and what I saw in real life," he said, and "I can't make anything unless it's the best I can do."

—J.P.

FILMS: (with Maurice Tourneur) The Last of the Mohicans, 1920; The Great Redeemer, 1920; (with Tourneur) The Foolish Matrons, 1922; The Light in the Dark, 1922; Don't Marry for Money, 1923; The Acquittal, 1923; (as "Clarence Bricker") Robin Hood Junior, 1923; The Signal Tower, 1924; Butterfly, 1924; Smoldering Fires, 1925; The Goose Woman, 1925; The Eagle, 1925; Kiki, 1926; Flesh and the Devil, 1926; The Trail of '98, 1928; A Woman of Affairs, 1928; Wonder of Women, 1929; Navy Blues, 1929; Anna Christie, 1930; Romance, 1930; Inspiration, 1931; A Free Soul, 1931; Possessed, 1931; Emma, 1932; Letty Lynton, 1932; The Son-Daughter, 1932; Looking Forward (U.K., Service), 1933; Night Flight, 1933; Sadie McKee, 1934; Chained, 1934; Anna Karenina, 1935; Ah, Wilderness!, 1935; Wife Versus Secretary, 1936; The Gorgeous Hussy, 1936; Conquest (U.K., Marie Walewska), 1937; Of Human Hearts, 1938; Idiot's Delight, 1939; The Rains Came, 1939; Edison, the Man, 1940; Come Live With Me, 1941; They Met in Bombay, 1941; The Human Comedy, 1943; The White Cliffs of Dover, 1944; National Velvet, 1944; The Yearling, 1947; Song of Love, 1947; Intruder in the Dust, 1949; To Please a Lady, 1950; Angels in the Outfield (U.K., The Angels and the Pirates), 1951; When in Rome, 1951; Plymouth Adventure, 1952.

ABOUT: Brownlow, K. The Parade's Gone By, 1969; Koszarski, R. Hollywood Directors 1941–1976, 1977; Oxford Companion to Film, 1976. *Periodicals*—Action January–February 1974; Bright Lights 8 1979; Écran June, July 1979; Film Dope July 1974; Filme Cultura November–December 1969; Films in Review February 1951, December 1973; Focus on Film Winter 1975–1976; Picturegoer May 5, 1939; May 13, 1939; May 20, 1939; March 3, 1945; La Revue de Cinéma 6 1930; The Velvet Light Trap 8 1979.

BROWNING, "TOD" (Charles Albert Browning) (July 12, 1880 or 1882–October 6, 1962), American director, scenarist, and producer, was born in Louisville, Kentucky. He ran away from home when he was sixteen and joined a circus. After a season as a roustabout and barker, he was taken on as a clown by the Ringling Brothers Circus. A few years later he was ap-

TOD BROWNING

pearing the river-boat shows as "The Living Hypnotic Corpse." Turning to vaudeville, he worked up a successful double act with a black-face minstrel called Roy or Ray C. Jones and toured with it for years, subsequently joining a well-known vaudeville troupe as a contortionist and clown. Browning never lost his love of the circus and the carnival, and drew on these ancient forms of entertainment in many of his films.

In 1913, a former vaudeville partner named Charles Murray introduced Browning to D. W. Griffith, then at the Biograph Studios in the Bronx. The director tried him out in a bit part as an undertaker, liked what he did, and coopted him into the Griffith "family." Later the same year, when Griffith went to Hollywood to join Harry Aitken's Reliance-Majestic production company, Browning went with him.

Thanks to his experience in the circus and vaudeville, Browning was able to play anything from a heavy to a slapstick comedian, and he is said to have been a daring and accomplished stuntman as well. Much in demand as a performer, he was soon trying his hand as a scenarist and director also. Browning directed his first films in 1915 and 1916—two-reelers with titles like *The Living Death, The Burned Hand, Puppets,* and *The Deadly Glass of Beer.* He was an assistant director (along with Erich von Stroheim and W. S. Van Dyke) of Griffith's *Intolerance* and also has a small part in the film. Browning's first feature was *Jim Bludso* (1917), a Civil War romance based on a poem by Lincoln's secretary John Milton Hay, directed in collaboration with its star, Wilfred Lucas. Lucas was also codirector

of *A Love Sublime* (1917), starring Alice Rae, whom Browning had recently married.

In 1917–1918 Browning made half-a-dozen movies for Metro, most of them starring Edith Storey, like *The Eyes of Mystery* (1918), in which she plays the inheritor of an eerie Southern mansion. Before the end of 1918, he had directed five more pictures for Bluebird Photoplays, all of them with Priscilla Dean or Edith Roberts and one of them, *Set Free,* scripted by Browning himself. At the end of the year he joined Universal, for whom he directed more than a dozen routine programmers over the next five years, beginning with *The Wicked Darling* (1919).

The Wicked Darling was the first in a long series of routine melodramas starring Priscilla Dean, often as a girl criminal redeemed in the last reel. The film is chiefly notable as being the first in which Browning worked with Lon Chaney. Chaney also appeared (in two roles) in *Outside the Law* (1921), but other Priscilla Dean movies of the period had Wallace Beery as the heavy—a libidinous potentate in *The Virgin of Stamboul* (1920), an opium dealer in *Drifting* (1923), and a gangster in *White Tiger* (1923).

White Tiger was Browning's last picture for Universal and in 1924 he made only two films. The reason was that Browning was in the throes of a two-year attempt, as he put it, to drink up "all the bad liquor in the world." Then Irving Thalberg of MGM offered Browning a script by Waldemar Young called *The Unholy Three,* based on a story by Tod Robbins. No one else was prepared to tackle the script, but Browning was enthusiastic about its possibilities. With Thalberg's unwavering support and encouragement, he pulled himself back from the brink of chronic alcoholism and made his first important movie.

The "unholy three" of the title are carnival performers who have turned to crime—Echo the ventriloquist (Lon Chaney), the strongman Hercules (Victor McLaglen), and Tweedledee (Harry Earles), a malevolent midget who hates "all the big people." Their front is a pet shop run by dear old Granny O'Grady. She is actually Echo in drag, and the ventriloquist uses his skills to make star talkers out of his mute parrots. The parrots naturally fall silent when the customers get them home, and then Granny calls to investigate the problem, bringing the light-fingered Tweedledee disguised as a baby. One thing leads to another, including murder. This is too much for Echo, who is altogether less unholy than his companions; when an innocent man is charged with the crime, Echo saves him by ventriloquial trickery in court (even though he is his rival in love) and thereafter goes straight. Hercules murders Tweedledee and is himself dispatched by a gorilla.

"The tempers and tensions of the disparate criminals are set in motion with wild relish," wrote Elliott Stein. "Harry Earles is brilliant as Tweedledee. . . . an unsentimentalized malignant midget who kicks a child's teeth out in the very first scene. . . . Several passages are introduced by huge contrasting shadows of the trio, the actors themselves offscreen. During his marinated semi-retirement, Browning apparently had some time for movie-going. His natural penchant for murkiness responded favourably to the wave of horror-fantasy films made in Germany (*The Golem, The Cabinet of Dr. Caligari*, etc.) which were then being distributed in the United States. From *The Unholy Three* on, his own films were increasingly filled with Germanic warning shadows, chiaroscuro effects, miasmas and tenebrous compositions. . . . Browning's camera, during most of the silent stage of his career, was leaden. But here, alert editing often supplies a kinesis of its own, and what goes on within the frame is so fascinating, so finely composed, that the result is never static and makes for tense and tough grotesque drama. The picture approaches greatness in the ease and mastery with which cruelty and laughter are combined."

The Unholy Three was a nationwide hit. After *The Mystic* (MGM, 1925), another story with a crime and carnival background, and *Dollar Down* (Truart, 1925), about crooked financiers, came the nine MGM films, several of them produced by Browning himself, which established him as an important and "bankable" director. Almost all of them starred Lon Chaney and indeed were built around that masochistic genius's capacity for transformational makeup and creative self-mutilation. "When I am working on a story for Chaney," Browning said, "I never think of the plot. That follows of itself after you have conceived a characterization."

The series began with *The Black Bird* (1926), set in a dark and claustrophobic Limehouse haunted by the arrogant and ruthless gangster known as the Blackbird and by his brother, a misshapen but compassionate and much-loved mission-house keeper. In fact both are the same man, the virtuous cripple being only a disguise assumed by the Blackbird to throw the law off his track. Chaney apparently effected the extraordinary transformation scenes purely by contorting his body, without altering his makeup and without the use of trick photography. The atmospheric sets were the work of MGM's supervising art director Cedric Gibbons, who designed many of Browning's films.

The Black Bird, somewhat weakened by Waldemar Young's poorly constructed script, was followed by *The Road to Mandalay* (1926), in which Chaney plays Singapore Joe, a gangster so ugly that he conceals his identity from his own daughter, fearing her horrified rejection. *London After Midnight* (1927), also scripted by Young from an original idea by Browning, was the director's first tentative approach to the Dracula theme—a story about a hypnotist who masquerades as a vampire to wring a confession from a murderer.

Waldemar Young, Browning's regular scenarist at this period, also wrote *The Show* (1927), adapted from a novel by Charles Tenny Jackson. Made without Chaney, it is set in a Hungarian carnival where Salome (Renée Adorée) nightly decapitates her beloved (John Gilbert). Lionel Barrymore also adores Adorée and sets a poisonous gila monster on his rival, only to be bitten himself. Discussing Browning's technique in this and other films, Stuart Rosenthal notes that "the audience (which has already been put on edge by the film's intrinsic tension) is disconcerted by an unexpected change in camera angle or perspective. These alterations come as a jolt in contrast to the simple three-shot narrative style used for the rest of the film. One reacts not only to the action when Barrymore and John Gilbert are trapped inside a closet with a poisonous iguana . . . , but also to the unexpected shift from a succession of head-on shots to a high angle one."

One of Browning's most disturbing horror stories followed in *The Unknown* (1927). Chaney plays Alonzo the Armless Wonder, a circus knife-thrower who hurls his deadly weapons in the direction of his frigid but beloved Estrellita (Joan Crawford) with his feet. In fact Alonzo is less armless than he appears, those members (one equipped with two thumbs) being strapped out of sight for the sake of the act. Thrashed by Estrellita's father Zanzi (Nick de Ruiz), Alonzo throttles him, and then finds it expedient to have the telltale thumbs (and both arms) amputated to escape detection. But if Alonzo had been only apparently armless, Estrellita had been only temporarily frigid, and Alonzo returns after his operation to find that he has a formidable rival in Malabar the strongman. An ingenious scheme to have Malabar's arms torn from their sockets by his own horses goes wrong, and Alonzo is trampled to death.

Elliott Stein wrote that this "truly memorable" movie "had nearly every ingredient for a great film. . . . Chaney's rendition of corporal distortion surpasses his feats in other films—after years of practice, his body here attains a sort of baroque state of grace as he uses his feet as hands while drinking, smoking, clutching knives, gesturing emotions. . . . In her eleventh film, the young Crawford is exquisite as the seductive, neurotic Estrellita. . . . At sixty-five minutes, *The Unknown* is bursting at the seams with extraordinary events and images" and "would have gained from another reel of characterization and plausible fleshing out of the shock sequences, especially near the hasty, somewhat botched climax." Freudian critics read the film as a series of variations on the theme of castration and sexual fear, quoting the title which tells us that "Estrellita wishes God had taken the arms from all men."

The Big City (1928), about a gangster who eventually reforms, stars Chaney for once without distorting makeup. This lapse into physical normality was promptly remedied in *West of Zanzibar* (1928), in which he appears as a circus performer who is turned into a slithering horror when his wife's lover (Lionel Barrymore) adds injury to insult by pushing him off a balcony. Dead Legs follows his enemy to Africa planning a diabolical revenge, but as usual in a Browning movie, is hoist by his own plot—he winds up sacrificing his life to save the girl he thought was Barrymore's daughter but turns out to be his. (Stuart Rosenthal has pointed out how often in Browning's movies the physical mutilation of the protagonist induces a mental or spiritual mutilation—he becomes a rabidly vengeful animal that must be destroyed, though our sympathy for him may be reenlisted when he receives his final comeuppance.)

Browning's last silent film was *Where East Is East* (1929), in which Chaney is sound of body but facially disfigured by the claws of the wild beasts he captures for circuses. This was also Browning's last collaboration with Chaney, who died in August 1930. The conventional wisdom has been that Browning did most of his best work in the silent era, never successfully adapting to sound, but Elliott Stein disputes this: "With the exception of *The Unholy Three*, those of Browning's silents available today indicate that much of his earlier work, based on his own stories . . . was plodding, contrived and repetitive, seriously hampered by narrative flaws."

Stein acknowledges that "Chaney's masochistic drive to impersonate all kinds of cripples provided a perfect objective correlative for Browning's aversion to open spaces," and that the resulting "claustral melodramas" are the best known products of Browning's silent period. But, Stein maintains, Chaney "had become Browning's crutch"—"their last films together suggest that the formula they had adopted with

such psychological ease was, through its very facility, paralysing their own creativity. . . . Although the sound films continued to be enriched by his struggles with personal demons, his later work, when taken as a whole, benefits from a wider range of interest, each picture marked by greater individuality than the repetitive silent thrillers."

The Thirteenth Chair (1929), based on a popular play about a fatal seance, was released in both sound and silent versions. Leaving MGM for a while, Browning then made *Outside the Law* for Universal. Starring Edward G. Robinson and Mary Nolan, it is generally described as a remake of Browning's 1921 silent, though it has a very different cast of characters. But Browning's first important talkie was his version of *Dracula* (1931), intended by Universal as a vehicle for Chaney and made instead with Bela Lugosi playing the evil Count, as he already had with great success on the stage.

Browning's *Dracula* is arguably inferior to *Nosferatu* (1922), F. W. Murnau's interpretation of Bram Stoker's story. It nevertheless has some brilliant moments, especially during the first two reels, when Renfield (Dwight Frye), leaving the frightened Transylvanian village, is driven by coach through mountains reminiscent of a Doré etching, the horses guided by a bat, and brought into the massive castle (designed by Charles Hall) where Dracula's women emerge from their coffins, ravenous for Renfield's blood, and are driven back by the courteous Count. Elsewhere there are passages justifying criticisms that the picture is theatrical rather than cinematic, with too much of the vital action taking place offscreen. Even the unusually mobile and elegant camerawork has been attributed less to Browning than to his cameraman on this film, the great cinematographer of German Expressionism, Karl Freund. The absence of a musical score, powerfully effective at certain horrific moments, otherwise strikes most modern viewers as an impoverishment.

Such criticisms weighed little with contemporary audiences. *Dracula* was an immense commercial success, made an international star of Bela Lugosi, and launched Universal's great cycle of horror classics. After *The Iron Man* (Universal, 1931), an adaptation of a W. R. Burnett novel starring Lew Ayres and Jean Harlow, Browning returned to MGM to make *Freaks* (1932), the most famous and controversial of all his films, scripted by Willis Goldbeck and Leon Gordon from a story by Tod Robbins.

Freaks reverses the pattern of Browning's movies with Chaney, in which a "normal" man, mutilated, becomes a horrifying monster. The bizarrely malformed "circus attractions" in *Freaks* are really so—Siamese twins, midgets, a Human Skeleton, a Bearded Lady, a Half-Man, a Living Torso. They are introduced to us as objects of horror when, hopping and crawling in a forest clearing, they frighten the wits out of a gamekeeper. We begin to warm to them when we see their own fear of the gamekeeper and his employer, and learn that they are only enjoying the sun on a day off from the circus. And in the more or less documentary sequences that follow, as we study the courage and ingenuity with which they have adjusted to their appalling handicaps, our admiration for them grows.

There are whole and well-formed people in the circus also, and, we learn, it is they who are the monsters. One of them is the beautiful trapeze artist Cleopatra (Olga Baclanova), who finds it amusing to flirt with the midget Hans (Harry Earles). When she learns that he has inherited money, she takes him more seriously. Hans breaks his engagement to his fellow midget Frieda and is married to Cleopatra at a fantastic, Buñuelian wedding feast, at the end of which he is carried off to his honeymoon night on his wife's back. But even at the feast, when the freaks generously announce their willingness to make Cleopatra "one of us," she cannot conceal her revulsion. After it, aiming to share Hans's money with her lover, the strongman Hercules, she begins to poison her husband. But for the freaks, "the hurt of one is the hurt of all"; they discover Cleopatra's plot and, in the midst of a terrible storm, they pursue her and her lover into the woods and literally make her one of them, transforming her into a legless, clucking monstrosity like a plucked chicken.

In 1932, many exhibitors refused to show *Freaks,* though it was reasonably well reviewed, and such audiences as it had tended to be affronted or outraged. MGM called in all prints, and it was scarcely seen again for thirty years. This rejection has generally been attributed to the fact that Browning used real freaks in the picture, but Elliott Stein suggests that the real problem is the way our acceptance of and sympathy for the freaks are so violently erased in the chase sequence, when they slither and crawl through mud and lightning after their normally proportioned victims—a morally complex reversal of the conventional horror movie chase sequence in which a mob of "normal" people hunt down a monster and provide a "facile and pleasurable crypto-fascist audience identification."

Freaks was not much more than an alarming myth when, in 1962, it was shown and acclaimed at the Venice Festival. Release followed in Britain and the United States, and it has since become a cult film. Richard Roud has suggested that Browning, like Velasquez in his portraits of dwarfs and buffoons, makes us realize "that Man is still Man, however monstrously he may be deformed," and this has become the general view. It should be noted, however, that the professional freak Montague Addison, a dwarf who reviewed the picture in *Film Quarterly* (Spring 1964), found it objectionable and exploitative: "We hate cavalier assumptions about us and attempts to show us as objects of pity to be drooled over with pious teachings."

Browning steered well clear of controversial material in *Fast Workers* (1933), or tried to—in fact, its sexist attitudes have greatly irritated more recent critics. It has Robert Armstrong as a gullible construction worker who relies on his cynical buddy (John Gilbert) to rescue him from the attentions of "gold diggers" by seducing his various fiancées. Mae Clarke plays the woman who interests them both and threatens this perhaps covertly homosexual arrangement. *Mark of the Vampire* (1935) was a clumsy remake of *London After Midnight* that failed in spite of a cast which included Lionel Barrymore, Elizabeth Allan, Bela Lugosi, Lionel Atwill, Jean Hersholt, and Donald Meek.

Browning returned to form with *The Devil Doll* (1936), scripted by the director with Garrett Fort, Guy Endore, and Erich von Stroheim from a novel by Abraham Merritt. Lionel Barrymore stars as Paul Lavond, a French banker sent to Devil's Island for crimes perpetrated by his associates. Lavond escapes with a friend who has perfected a technique for miniaturising human beings, and goes to Paris. Disguised as an old woman, Lavond opens a toy shop where he sells to his former associates the exquisitely detailed little "dolls" that, telepathically controlled, will destroy them. Particularly memorable is the sequence in which one of the miniature people (Grace Ford) creeps by night from the arms of a sleeping child, scales a chest of drawers to steal a necklace for her master, and then, ascending her victim's bed with infinite difficulty, runs a poisoned stiletto into his arm. Brilliantly photographed by Leonard Smith, *The Devil Doll* makes wonderfully convincing used of outsized furniture and is full of imaginative touches (like the vengeful doll that hangs by a ribbon from a Christmas tree, awaiting his moment to strike).

But Browning's reputation never really recovered after the failure of *Freaks.* After *The Devil Doll,* three years passed before his next movie appeared and that, a moderately interesting thriller called *Miracles for Sale,* was his last picture. For two years he tried to interest MGM in an assortment of projects (including *They Shoot*

Horses, Don't They?) but without success. He and his wife Alice retired to Malibu in 1941 and Browning died there in 1962 (in spite of the fact that *Variety* had published his obituary in 1944).

"The Edgar Allan Poe of the cinema," as he was sometimes called, was a businesslike filmmaker, as untemperamental on set as if he were running "an office of book-keepers." Elliott Stein writes that "the natural residence of Browning's psyche was an attic, a crypt, a closet, a coffin, a shadow, a staircase, a trunk; it was terrorized by sunlight, fields, deserts, woods, and open spaces. That terror became his style and strength. In succeeding films, his anxieties drove him further into the shadows. Tod Browning: the agoraphobic director *par excellence*." Much admired by the Surrealists, Browning has always found his most enthusiastic admirers in France. Louis Seguin wrote in 1956 that "only a contempt as stupid as it is ineradicable has kept Browning, one of the greatest directors that ever lived, an unknown and shadowy figure: actually, he is by far superior to man like John Ford or Hitchcock." The British critic Iris Barry, more moderately, concluded that "Browning had whatever it was that made Stevenson a notable writer in spite of his being a very second-rate mind."

FILMS: *Shorts*—The Lucky Transfer, 1915; The Highbinders, 1915; The Living Death, 1915; The Burned Hand, 1915; The Woman From Warren's, 1915; Little Marie, 1915; Puppets, 1916; Everybody's Doing It, 1916; The Deadly Glass of Beer/The Fatal Glass of Beer, 1916. *Features*—(with Wilfred Lucas) Jim Bludso, 1917; (with Wilfred Lucas) A Love Sublime, 1917; (with Wilfred Lucas) Hands Up!, 1917; Peggy, the Will o' the Wisp, 1917; The Jury of Fate, 1917; The Unpainted Woman, 1917; The Eyes of Mystery, 1918; The Legion of Death, 1918; Revenge, 1918; Which Woman, 1918; The Deciding Kiss, 1918; The Brazen Beauty, 1918; Set Free, 1918; The Wicked Darling, 1919; The Exquisite Thief, 1919; A Petal on the Current, 1919; Bonnie, Bonnie Lassie, 1919; The Virgin of Stamboul, 1920; Outside the Law, 1921; No Woman Knows, 1921; The Wide Kid, 1922; Under Two Flags, 1922; Man Under Cover, 1922; Drifting, 1923; White Tiger, 1923; Day of Faith, 1923; The Dangerous Flirt (A Dangerous Flirtation), 1924; Silk Stocking Sal, 1924; The Unholy Three, 1925; The Mystic, 1925; Dollar Down, 1925; The Black Bird, 1926; The Road to Mandalay, 1926; London After Midnight (The Hypnotist), 1927; The Show, 1927; The Unknown, 1927; The Big City, 1928; West of Zanzibar, 1928; Where East Is East, 1929; The Thirteenth Chair, 1929; Outside the Law, 1930; Dracula, 1931; The Iron Man, 1931; Freaks, 1932; Fast Workers, 1933; Mask of the Vampire, 1935; The Devil Doll, 1936; Miracles for Sale, 1939.

ABOUT: Clarens, C. Illustrated History of the Horror Film, 1972; Rosenthal, S. Tod Browning (The Holly-wood Professionals 4), 1975; Roud, R. (ed.) Cinema: A Critical Dictionary, 1980. *Periodicals*—Avant-Scène du Cinéma July–September 1975; Cinema (USA) June–July 1963; Film Dope July 1974, October 1975; Films in Review October 1953; Midi-Minuit Fantastique January 1963 (special issue on Dracula); Motion Picture Classic March 1928; New York Times October 10, 1962; Positif July–August 1978.

*BUÑUEL, LUIS (February 22, 1900–July 29, 1983), Spanish director, scenarist, and producer, was born in the village of Calanda in Aragon. His father, Leonardo, a native of the province, had gone to Cuba in his youth with the Spanish military and stayed on to make his fortune as a hardware merchant. Returning home in 1898, at the age of forty-two, he met and married Maria Portoles, a seventeen-year-old girl from a wealthy aristocratic family. Luis was the first of their three sons and four daughters; four months after his birth, the family moved to the town of Saragossa but retained a country house in Calanda, and the atmosphere of this "completely feudal village," as Buñuel referred to it, is often reflected in his films. (In later years, Buñuel liked to point out that although he had been born in Calanda, he had been conceived in Paris.)

Buñuel's education, thoroughly religious until he reached the age of fifteen, included a year with the French order of the Sacred Heart followed by seven years at the Jesuit Colegio del Salvador; an excellent student, he willingly immersed himself in scripture and other religious writings, but his greatest interest was the study of insects and animals. Around the age of fourteen or fifteen, he began to have serious doubts about the faith, and during two years of study at the secular Instituto Nacional de Enseñanza Media, read Spencer, Rousseau, Marx, and above all, Darwin, whose *Origin of the Species* particularly affected his thinking.

In 1917, eager to break away from the closed environment of Saragossa, he went off to Madrid to enter the university. His own inclination was to study music, but his father set him on the more practical course of agricultural engineering; when it became clear that he was not good enough in math for such a program, he switched to the natural sciences and pursued his longstanding interest in entomology by working as an assistant to a distinguished insect specialist at the Museum of Natural History. But the decisive education that Buñuel received during his first stay in Madrid came not so much from the university as from the circle of writers and artists that he encountered at the Residencia de Estudiantes (student residence), including Ramón Gómez de la Cerna, Rafael Albertini, Federico

*boon nyoo el´

LUIS BUÑUEL

García Lorca, Juan Ramón Jimenez (the founder of the 1927 group of Surrealist poets), and his future collaborator Salvador Dali. In their company he contributed to the review *La Gaceta literaria*, became a supporter of the anarchist movement, and definitively switched from science to the Faculty of Philosophy and Letters, with a concentration in history.

In 1925, after completing his degree and fourteen months of military service, Buñuel seized an opportunity to go to Paris as secretary to a Spanish diplomat. As was to be the case over the next few years, his path was smoothed by financial assistance from his mother (his father had died two years earlier), and he made his way into the city's café culture, already a home for Spanish intellectuals and artists. Two major developments followed in short order: he met his future wife, Jeanne Rucar (an Olympic gymnast ten years his junior), and he realized that he wanted to become a filmmaker.

As Buñuel recalls in *My Last Breath,* the memoirs he dictated at the end of his life, he saw his first film at the age of eight—an animated cartoon featuring a singing pig, whose song came from a phonograph behind the screen. In the years that followed, he saw the comedies and adventures of Max Linder and Georges Méliès imported from France, romantic melodramas from Italy, and his favorites, the American comedies of Mack Sennett, Ben Turpin, Harold Lloyd, Buster Keaton, and Charlie Chaplin. Once in Paris, he immersed himself in the city's rich cinematic offerings. On the basis of articles he wrote for the *Cahiers d'art,* he obtained a movie pass and began spending entire days and nights at the cinema—attending private projections of American films in the morning, neighborhood theatres in the afternoon, art theatres at night. It was Fritz Lang's *Der mude Tod (Weary Death,* 1921) that finally jarred him into the realization of what film could do: "I came out of the Vieux-Colombier [theatre] completely transformed. Images could and did become for me the true means of expression. I decided to devote myself to the cinema."

Making his way to the avant-garde filmmaker Jean Epstein's academy of cinema (where he found himself in a class of nineteen, with eighteen White Russians), he convinced Epstein to let him work as an assistant on *Mauprat* (1926). Around the same time he also served as an assistant to Henri Etiévant and Marius Nalpa on *La Sirène des tropiques,* starring Josephine Baker, and played a small role as a smuggler in Jacques Feyder's *Carmen.* In 1927 he had a brief go at a theatrical career, first as scriptwriter for a Spanish *Hamlet,* performed in the cellar of the Select Cafe, and then as director of a production in Amsterdam of Manuel de Falla's *El Retablo de Maese Pedro.*

Buñuel's inroads into cinema continued apace when he became Epstein's first assistant for *La Chute de la Maison Usher (The Fall of the House of Usher),* but he wound up quitting the production after an argument with the director over Abel Gance (to whom Buñuel refused to be civil, dismissing him as a hack [*pompier*]). The incident, which reflected basic differences in orientation between Epstein and Buñuel, was not without repercussions: as Maurice Drouzy points out, Buñuel was now not only out of work but labeled as a troublemaker in Epstein's avant-garde circles. In any case, it was at this point that he once again involved himself with the Residencia de Estudientes in Madrid, organizing the first series of avant-garde films ever presented in Spain. The screenings—of Rene Clair's dadaist *Entre'acte* (1924), Alberto Cavalcanti's "city symphony" *Rien que les heures* (1926), and Alan Crosland's pioneering talkie *The Jazz Singer,* among other films—were a tremendous success and gave rise to the establishment of the first Spanish cine-club.

By this time, Buñuel was also thinking about films of his own: he wrote a scenario on the Spanish painter Goya (whose imagery later turns up in his films) and worked with his friend Ramón Gómez de la Cerna to adapt one of the latter's short stories. Neither of these projects got very far, and in January 1928, while visiting Salvador Dali at his home in Figueras, Buñuel suggested that they do a film together. They started talking about their dreams, and decided that they would use these and other images in a film that would be constructed by free association. According to Buñuel they wrote the scenario in eight days: "We identified with each other so much that there was no discussion. We put together the first images that came into our heads, and conversely, we systematically rejected everything that came to us from culture or education."

The money for the production came from Buñuel's mother; it was, he explains, the equivalent in intention, though not amount, of the dowries she'd given to two of his sisters. He promptly went off to Paris and squandered half of it on soirées with friends, but realized he'd better get on with the film "because I was a responsible man and didn't want to cheat my mother." In March he gathered together a cast and crew, mainly friends (including Epstein's cameraman Albert Duverger), rented space at the Billancourt Studios, bought the film stock, and shot the script in ten days; Dali arrived from Spain in time for the final scenes only. Neither the cast nor the crew knew quite what they were working on, although Buñuel himself followed the scenario quite closely, a practice he continued throughout his career.

The result of this venture was *Un Chien andalou* (*An Andalusian Dog,* 1929), the archetype of surrealist cinema. The film was originally to be called *Es peligroso arsomarse al interio* (*Danger: Do Not Lean Inside*)—a play on the warning posted next to the windows of European trains—but the two authors decided this was too literary and, at Dali's suggestion, adopted the title Buñuel had selected, equally at random, for a collection of his own poems: *Un perro andaluz,* which became in French *Un Chien andalou.*

The seventeen-minute film begins with the famous prologue where a man standing on a balcony slits a young girl's eye as a cloud passes over the full moon. This was Buñuel's dream image, and it is Buñuel who wields the razor, thus opening both the film and his filmmaking career with one shocking gesture. (The woman was Simone Mareuil; the eye, filmed in closeup, was actually that of a dead calf.) After this gruesome introduction—"I filmed it," Buñuel declared, "because I had seen it in a dream and because I knew it would disgust people"—the scene switches to a rainy street, "eight years later," according to the intertitle. A man incongruously dressed in frills and carrying a small striped box around his neck (Pierre Batcheff) arrives on a bicycle and tumbles to a halt. The woman of the prologue (eye intact), watching from upstairs, runs down to him, then returns upstairs to engage in a kind of ritualistic display of the con-

tents of the box. The man reappears in the room for the second well-known segment of the film (Dali's dream): he stares at his hand as ants pour out of a hole in his palm. After a brief cut to the beach and then back to the street, where an androgynous-looking figure is seen poking at a severed hand with a long stick, there is a sequence of sexual pursuit. The man (of the bicycle) grabs the woman's clothed breasts; these fade to naked breasts, then to buttocks. The man's face becomes ghoulish, corpselike; he tugs at two ropes lying on the floor and hauls in two bizarre but identical linkages—cork floats, calabashes, Marist brothers, and finally two grand pianos, each propped open to reveal the rotting carcass of a donkey.

Another intertitle indicates that it is "around 3 a.m.": the same woman in the same room receives another man at the door; the newcomer—the double of the cyclist—orders the latter to leave. "Sixteen years earlier" (intertitle) the cyclist shoots the newcomer with two books that become revolvers in his hands. As he falls, the victim touches the bare shoulder of a woman seen to be sitting in a park. After a few more abrupt cuts from one setting to another, the man and the woman appear on a beach, buried in sand up to their chests; a burning sun beats down on them, and they are attacked by a swarm of insects while the incongruously idyllic words *au printemps* ("in the springtime") appear in the sky above.

In its evocation of dream states, its forceful expressions of sexuality and sexual frustration, and the resulting affront to bourgeois morality, *Un Chien andalou* exemplifies surrealist cinema. In fact, Buñuel's personal connection with the surrealists came only after the film was completed. But both he and Dali were intrigued by the movement from what they had read and heard about it from a distance. The poems of Benjamin Peret in particular, Buñuel recalled, "made us die laughing." As a number of researchers have pointed out, it is probable that the two aspiring filmmakers were also aware of a previous venture in the domain of surrealist cinema, *La Coquille et le clergyman* (*The Seashell and the Clergyman*), directed by Germaine Dulac from a scenario by Antonin Artaud, and first shown publicly at the Studio des Ursulines on February 9, 1928. Like *Un Chien andalou, La Coquille* was intended to shatter the conventions of narrative and bridge the gap between the conscious and the unconscious, with a mix of eroticism and violence. If of nothing else, Buñuel and Dali would certainly have heard of the film's uproarious screening at the Studio des Ursulines, where a band of surrealists, believing that Dulac had betrayed the scenario, caused a near-riot.

At any rate, having created a surrealist film, Buñuel and Dali were themselves ready to become surrealists. The connection was made when Buñuel was introduced to Man Ray at La Coupole, a Montparnasse café; Man Ray's own film, *Les Mystères du château du Dé* was scheduled to be screened at the Studio des Ursulines, and he invited Buñuel to bring *Un Chien andalou* along to show to André Breton and the other surrealists who were expected to attend. Unsure of how the audience would react—and doubtless aware of the pandemonium created by the same crowd at the screening of *La Coquille* the year before—Buñuel came armed with a pocketful of rocks and stood behind the screen ready to launch a counterattack. As it turned out, the film was a grand success, and the surrealists immediately welcomed him into the fold.

Le Chien andalou soon reached a wider audience as well: when the Studio des Ursulines declined to project it publicly for fear of a ban by the censors, it was purchased by Studio 28, where it enjoyed an eight-month run. Jean Vigo, in his remarks before the first projection of *À propos de Nice* in June 1930, hailed *Un Chien andalou* as "a capital work, from every point of view: sureness of the *mise-en-scène*, skill in the lighting, perfect knowledge of visual and ideological associations, solid logic of the dream, admirable confrontation of the subconscious and the rational." Ironically, even the bourgeois public that Buñuel and Dali sought to affront "appropriated" the film for themselves.

Likewise, *Un Chien andalou* has been subjected to precisely the kind of rational analysis that Buñuel sought to discourage. As Buñuel told José de la Colina and Thomas Perez-Turrent in the late 1970s, "a cavalry captain from Saragossa, a German professor, and a bunch of others have reached the same conclusions. 'The man going towards the woman represents the sexual drive; the ropes are moral constraints; the two corks, the frivolousness of life; the two dry gourds, testicles; the priests, religion; the piano, the lyricism of love; and the two donkeys, death.'" But for Buñuel, the significance of these images lay outside of narrow symbolism: "They should accept them such as they are, [asking] do they move me? disgust me? attract me? They should leave it at that."

In the wake of *Un Chien andalou* Buñuel threw himself into the surrealist movement and its guerrilla campaign against the conventional and the repressive. "I had put all my activity at the service of surrealism, and it represented all my hopes," he told Colina and Perez-Turrent. When he was taken to task by his new colleagues for agreeing to publish the film's scenario in *La Revue du cinéma*, he gave it to *La Révolution surréaliste* as well, adding a note: "This is the only publication I authorize. I affirm, with no qualifications, my complete adhesion to Surrealist thought and action. If Surrealism didn't exist, there would be no *Chien andalou*."

As for filmmaking, Buñuel apparently considered abandoning his career altogether: the commercial cinema, he explains in *My Last Breath*, was not an option, and he couldn't continue asking his mother for money. But on this score too, surrealism saved the day. His friends put him in touch with a wealthy patron, the Vicomte de Noailles, who had taken to commissioning a film for his wife's birthday every year—this was also the origin of Man Ray's *Les Mystères du château du Dé* (1929) and Jean Cocteau's *Le Sang d'un poète* (1930–1932). In short order, Buñuel had a million old francs to make his second film. He and Dali had originally planned to incorporate some of the leftover images from *Un Chien andalou* in a sequel called *La Bête andalouse*, but after a brief attempt at working together in Spain, it became clear that the two men were moving in different directions, and the collaboration (along with their friendship) came to an end. Buñuel returned to France to write the scenario on the estate of his patron, de Noailles. At one point Dali wrote to him with additional suggestions (and is credited as coscenarist), but the making of *L'Age d'or* was Buñuel's work and his great achievement.

The repertoire of themes in *L'Age d'or* is much the same as that of *Un Chien andalou*—frustrated love and sexuality, physical violence, attacks on clergy and state—and there is even some repetition of imagery, not to mention the overriding intent to shock the bourgeoisie. But *L'Age d'or* is at once much more complex (and almost four times as long) and much more deliberately structured. As Buñuel himself remarked, "In *Un Chien andalou* there is no conducting thread, while in *L'Age d'or*, yes, [there is] a line . . . that runs from one thing to another via a certain detail."

The central "narrative," such as it is, concerns a pair of frustrated lovers (Gaston Modot and Lya Lys), but they make their appearance through precisely the kind of incidental detail that Buñuel describes. The film begins with documentary footage on scorpions; this leads into a series of incidents on a rocky seashore, where a gang of bandits (led by surrealist painter Max Ernst) is invaded first by a group of chanting bishops and then by a flotilla of dignitaries who have come to found the Roman Empire. It is in the midst of the foundation ceremony that sounds of passionate lovemaking draw attention to the two lovers, who are off to the side reveling in the mud. The woman is quickly dragged away, while the man continues to fantasize. After another round of ceremonies and another short documentary sequence on urban life, the man reappears in the company of two policemen, while the woman retires to her room to find a huge cow on her bed. The man finally extricates himself from the police—he is a dignitary representing the International Assembly of Good Works—and phones his beloved from the gala reception following the foundation ceremony. They are briefly reunited, then interrupted by a phone call; on his return, she leaves him to go off with the orchestra conductor. To the sound of beating drums, the rejected lover starts hurling objects out of the window—a flaming Christmas tree, a huge plow, an archbishop, a giraffe, feathers from a pillow he has slashed in his rage. And meanwhile, according to a lengthy intertitle, at the faraway chateau of Selligny (an allusion to de Sade's *120 Days of Sodom,* which Buñuel had read just before the filming began) a procession of debauchees appears, led by the Compte de Blangis (Lionel Salem) in the guise of Jesus Christ. A final sequence shows a cross in the snow, covered with tresses blowing in the wind to the tune of a *paso doble.*

In his autobiography, *The Secret Life of Salvador Dali* (1942), Buñuel's former collaborator claimed that his conception of *L'Age d'or* had been a thoroughly religious one, expressing the violence of love and passion "imbued with the splendor of the Catholic church." As a result he was "terribly disappointed" with Buñuel's film, which, he insisted after the fact, was "a caricature of my ideas." Dali was not the only one to attack the film. After a premiere on their estate and a second private screening at the Pantheon cinema, the Noailles found themselves thrown out of the exclusive Jockey Club, and the vicount's mother was apparently obliged to travel to the Vatican to dissuade the Pope from excommunicating the couple.

On December 3, 1930, the day after the film opened at Studio 28, two right-wing vigilante groups, the Patriot's League and the Anti-Jewish League, stormed the theatre, hurling ink and rotten eggs at the movie screen, setting off teargas and stink bombs, and clubbing members of the audience to cries of "Death to the Jews!" and "You'll see that there are still Christians in France!" Two days later, the police instructed the theatre director to cut "the two scenes with the bishops," and although the film had already been cleared by the censor, this was done. The conservative press began its campaign: citing "scenes of the lowest and most disgusting pornography," *L'Echo de Paris,* for example,

dismissed *L'Age d'or* as "a pretentious and dreary burden that has nothing to do with art." *Le Figaro,* meanwhile, decrying the film as "an exercise in Bolshevism of a very special kind . . . which is intended to rot us away," called on police commissioner Chiappe to intervene. And indeed on December 10 Chiappe banned the film and ordered all copies confiscated.

For the next fifty years, *L'Age d'or* remained largely a tantalizing memory. To the surrealist Ado Kyrou, it represented "perfection in free cinematographic expression. . . . In describing love, Buñuel dealt the police, the family, the army the most vigorous blows they have ever received." For Georges Sadoul, also a member of the movement for a time, it was "a masterpiece in its violence, its purity, its lyric frenzy, its absolute sincerity." And for Buñuel's biographer Freddy Buache it was a "film-cry and a film-blasphemy" which "joins the most flagrant provocation to vehement subversion and unleashes cyclones of mad love across the screen." When the film was finally re-released (in New York in 1980 and in Paris in 1981) its shock value had worn off—in Marcel Oms' words, "the perfume had evaporated"—but in other respects it seemed hardly to have suffered from the passage of time. As Oms points out, in *L'Age d'or* "Buñuel established his entire personal problematic and initiated a veritable revolution in cinematographic language that he would never cease to amplify right up to his last film."

In its form and in its themes and motifs, *L'Age d'or* is significant as the harbinger of Buñuel's subsequent work. Raymond Lefèvre notes, for example, how the juxtaposition of documentary and drama prefigures Buñuel's constant play on the continuum between reality and fiction. Similarly, in terms of themes, the repressive "friends of darkness"—the clergy, the bourgeoisie, the army, and police—were to appear again and again, as were the frustrated lovers, the domineering mothers, the unsympathetic blind man, all manner of animals, and the literary creations of the Marquis de Sade. In Lefèvre's words, *L'Age d'or* is the "storehouse film" of an entire oeuvre faithful to its origins: "Luis Buñuel always went back to its real treasures to develop them on the level of a sequence or a film. He updated them and brought them to the peak of their effectiveness."

In fact, now that the content of *L'Age d'or* is not so overwhelming, the truly revolutionary nature of its cinematographic form can be more fully appreciated. "The assault on the viewer," writes Joël Magny, "is here less in what is represented . . . than in the mode of representation." The film does not invent another cinematographic language, he explains, but "employs the most classic narrative procedures independently of their habitual use. All the points of reference of the spectator's imagination slip away."

When *L'Age d'or* came under attack in 1930, the surrealists published a manifesto condemning the incident, and the leftist press came to Buñuel's defense as vigorously as their rightist counterparts denounced him. One of the film's more unlikely fans, though, was the European agent of MGM, who indicated that although he didn't understand it, he was impressed. As a result, he offered Buñuel a six-month contract in Hollywood: for $250 a week, the budding director was to sit on the sets and learn how American movies were made. Buñuel accepted immediately and left for the United States in December 1930 (which meant that he missed the *L'Age d'or* controversy entirely and, by his own account, never saw the film again).

Once in Hollywood, he quickly made contact with a group of illustrious expatriates—Chaplin, Eisenstein, Sternberg, Feyder, Brecht—but the visit ended abruptly after he flatly refused to screen a film that starred Lili Damita as a Spanish-speaking courtesan, declaring he didn't want to "hear the whores." He was back in France by March 1931 and in Madrid just days before the end of the Spanish monarchy and the proclamation of the Second Republic. He began working on an adaptation of André Gide's *Les Caves du Vatican,* which was to be filmed in the Soviet Union, but this fell through, and he turned to a less costly project, a documentary. The idea for the film came from a 1927 study by Maurice Legendre on the human geography of Las Hurdes, an extremely isolated and backward region of western Spain. With no producer in sight, Buñuel's friend Ramón Acin, a militant anarchist, promised to finance the film if he won the lottery—which he did—and despite objections from fellow anarchists, turned over twenty thousand pesos for the project. Borrowing a camera from Yves Allegret, Buñuel set off for Las Hurdes in April 1932 with his friends Pierre Unik (a fellow surrealist and communist) and Eli Lotar and spent just over a month filming. By the time they got back, there was no more money, and Buñuel edited the footage on his kitchen table with a magnifying glass. ("Undoubtedly," he writes in his memoirs, "I threw out some interesting images that I couldn't see very well.") At the first screening, the commentary, written by Unik and Julio Acin, was spoken by Buñuel; it was only two years later that a grant from the Spanish embassy in Paris enabled him to record the soundtrack.

Notwithstanding these constraints, *Las Hurdes* (*Tierra sin pan, Land Without Bread,* 1932) became the most famous documentary of the Second Republic. It was conceived, according to the intertitle at the beginning, as "a cinematographic essay in human geography," but the result is shockingly consistent with the surrealist vision of *Un Chien andalou* and *L'Age d'or.* The camera traces the increasingly desolate route to Las Hurdes by way of one church after another, while the commentary explains that until 1922 there was no road, and the area was unknown even to most Spaniards. A "curious detail" is noted when the film crew finally arrive: "In the villages of Las Hurdes we never heard a song." Grotesque images of a malnourished, mentally retarded, and physically deformed population are accompanied by a chillingly dispassionate account of their afflictions—goiter, snakebite, malaria, cretinism. Death is everywhere: a donkey is attacked by a swarm of insects and eaten alive; a little girl bitten by a snake dies on camera; an infant is buried. There is only one image of well-being—the interior of a church. "The only thing of luxury we encountered in Las Hurdes were the churches. This one is located in one of the most miserable villages."

Las Hurdes was the most explicitly militant of Buñuel's films. Unlike the study that inspired it, which took the misery of Las Hurdes as a given and proposed charity as the only solution, Buñuel's film sought to expose the underlying causes of the situation—indifference and exploitation at the hands of the same old "friends of darkness," the state and the church. Indeed, in an epilogue added to the film after the election of the Popular Front in 1936, he cited the example of other Spanish peasants, mountain-dwellers, and workers who had succeeded in improving their lot by uniting to demand their rights. Noting the menace of Franco's royalist forces, he expressed the belief that "with the aid of anti-fascists throughout the world, tranquility, work, and happiness will supersede the Civil War and dispel forever the centers of misery you have seen in this film."

The implications of *Las Hurdes* had not been lost on the Second Republic, which had banned the film at home and tried to prevent its being shown outside the country as well; only in the upheaval of the Civil War was Buñuel able to find a European distributor. During the war, according to Buñuel, a friend in the Republican government came across his police file, which described him "as a dangerous libertine, an abject morphine addict, and above all as the director of this abominable film, a veritable crime against the homeland."

As André Bazin pointed out in a 1951 article, *Las Hurdes*, despite its documentary form and politicized content, hardly constituted a repudiation by Buñuel of his earlier films: "On the contrary, the objectivity, the impassiveness of the reportage surpassed the horrors and the powers of the dream. The donkey devoured by bees attains the nobility of a brutal Mediterranean myth that equals the marvels of the dead donkey on the piano." And Buñuel himself clearly shared this view; a few years later he told *Cahiers du cinéma*, "I made *Las Hurdes* because I had a Surrealist vision and because I was interested in the problem of humankind. I saw the reality in a different way than I would have seen it before Surrealism."

The years that followed the filming of *Las Hurdes* and its release in France were difficult ones for Buñuel. In 1932 he broke with the surrealists: "I left the group as simply as I joined it," he recalls in his memoirs. He also decided to give up directing and took a job dubbing films in Spanish for Paramount Pictures in Paris and Madrid. In 1934 he had a serious bout with sciatica and nearly quit filmmaking altogether, but he wound up accepting an offer from Warner Brothers to supervise the dubbing of their films in Spain. He and Jeanne Rucar were married that year, and their first child, Juan-Luis, was born shortly afterwards.

At this point Buñuel joined his long-time friend Ricardo Urgoïti in a commercial production venture known as Filmofono Films. Urgoïti had started out distributing foreign films, but decided to launch his own productions and turned to Buñuel for help. Over the next two years Buñuel was involved with four Filmofono productions: *Don Quintin el Amargado* (*Don Quintin the Bitter,* 1935) and *La hija de Juan Simon* (*Juan Simon's Daughter,* 1936), both of which were quite successful; *Quien me quiere à mi?* (*Who Loves Me?,* 1936), not well received, despite the publicity generated by a search for the "Spanish Shirley Temple," and *Centinela alerta!* (*On Alert, Sentinel!,* 1936), a military vaudeville starring Jean Gremillon that got lost in the outbreak of the Civil War. Because of Buñuel's political notoriety after *L'Age d'or* and *Las Hurdes*—and probably because of the crass commercialism of the Filmofono productions as well—his name appears on the credits as executive producer, but as was determined years later through interviews with his co-workers, in each case Buñuel actually directed the film as well. In the lagging Spanish film industry, his knowledge of modern production techniques and his insistence on disciplined work habits were very welcome. But as Marcel Oms points out, the experience was equally important for Buñuel as

his first exposure to the demands of commercial production.

Filmofono came to an end with the fascist coup in July 1936, and as Buñuel writes in *My Last Breath,* "Although I had ardently hoped for subversion, for the reversal of the established order, when I was suddenly placed in the center of the volcano, I was afraid." He accepted a post as cultural attaché for the Republican government at their embassy in Paris, where he was responsible for preparing propaganda materials. In 1939 he was once again invited to Hollywood, this time to work as historical and technical advisor on *Cargo of Innocents,* a film about the Spanish Civil War, but after he got there, the Association of American Producers, yielding to pressure from the US government, suspended all productions dealing with the current situation in Spain.

Stranded in Hollywood with his wife and son, Buñuel was rescued by Iris Barry, head of the film department at the Museum of Modern Art in New York, who found work for him on various war-related projects at the Museum. The first of these involved reediting two Nazi films recently smuggled out of Germany (Leni Riefenstahl's 1935 *Triumph des Willens* and Hans Bertram's 1939 *Feldzug in Polen*) to show their impact as propaganda. Buñuel then began supervising the dubbing of anti-Nazi films for distribution in Latin America. But his already precarious existence in exile was totally disrupted in 1942 with the publication of Salvador Dali's autobiography, in which Dali characterized his former friend as a communist who had perverted the original idea for *L'Age d'or* to suit Marxist ideology. This accusation was picked up by the right-wing *Motion Picture Herald,* and the Museum of Modern Art was soon under pressure to get rid of Buñuel. Although Barry and others stood behind him, Buñuel opted to quit his job and once again headed west with his family (now including a second child, Rafael, born in 1940).

Another two years went into working on the Spanish versions of English-language films for Warner Brothers; he wrote an uncredited sequence for Robert Florey's *The Beast With Five Fingers* (1945) and saw various projects come to nothing, but the main fruit of this third Hollywood stint was enough money to allow him to take a year off. At the invitation of Denise Tual, the former wife of Pierre Batcheff (the man in *Un Chien andalou*), he went to Mexico to work on an adaptation of García Lorca's last play, *La Casa de Bernarda Alba.* Once again the plan fell through, but the trip turned out to be decisive: Buñuel renewed his acquaintance with producer

Oscar Dancigers and signed up to make a film for him in Mexico. After a decade of inactivity—and fifteen years since he had made a film under his own name—he entered the most prolific phase of his career.

The beginning of this Mexican period was inauspicious at best. *Gran Casino* (1947) was a musical melodrama rather inappropriately adapted from a novel about the oil industry in Tampico. Buñuel inherited the two stars (Jorge Negrete and Libertad Lamarque) with his contract, and as he later explained, "I had there the two greatest Mexican and Argentinian singers, so I had to make them sing as much as possible." Another melodrama followed, this time without the music and with somewhat more of Buñuel's own antibourgeois and anticlerical humor. *El gran calavera* (*The Great Profligate*, 1949) is the story of a wealthy widower (Fernando Soler) who takes to drowning his sorrows in drink and debauchery. In hopes of curing him, his relatives stage an elaborate ruse to convince him that the family fortune is lost. The widower eventually discovers the deception, but deciding that poverty has salutory effects, declares bankruptcy. For Buñuel, *El gran calavera* was "a decent film but without a scene worthy of interest," and when it was shown in France in 1966 along with the director's other unknown Mexican films, critics tended to agree. All the same, it was a commercial success in Mexico in 1949, and as a result, with Oscar Danciger's backing now assured, Buñuel was able to make a film of his own conception.

Los olvidados (*The Forgotten/The Young and the Damned*, 1950) shows the impact of Italian neorealism on a surrealist imagination. The film opens with a bunch of street kids playing toreador. The word is out that their old friend Jaïbo (Roberto Cobo) has escaped from reform school and come back to settle a score with Julien (Javier Amezcua), the one who betrayed him to the police. Jaïbo duly makes his appearance to lead an attack on a blind beggar; when this fails, the gang await their prey a second time at a construction site and break his musical instruments and beat him up before running away. Julien is next. Jaïbo seeks him out at his workplace and beats him to death in front of another horrified member of their crowd, Pedro (Alfonso Mejia). From that moment on, the fates of the two youths are intertwined. Jaïbo haunts Pedro in his dreams and in his life; he turns up at the cutlery shop where Pedro is working, talks about the investigation of Julien's death, and then makes off with a knife. Pedro, blamed for the theft, winds up in a farm-school for youthful offenders. Sent on an errand with fifty pesos, he has the misfortune to run into Jaïbo, who steals the money.

This time Pedro pursues him; after a violent brawl, Pedro blurts out the story of Julien's murder. Not long after, Jaïbo exacts another revenge, killing Pedro with a metal rod. The blind beggar alerts the police, who apprehend Jaïbo in an alley and shoot him to death. A young girl and her grandfather load the body on the back of a mule and carry it off to the garbage dump.

In the words of J. Hoberman, "no film has ever been less equivocal than *Los olvidados* in suggesting that suffering does not ennoble." It was directly inspired by Vittorio de Sica's *Sciuscia* (*Shoeshine,* 1946), the pathbreaking treatment of poverty and crime among young shoeshine boys in Rome; in the neorealist tradition, Buñuel developed his story among the people who lived it, spending four or five months in the slums around Mexico City, sometimes alone, sometimes with his coscenarist Luis Alcoriza or his set designer Edward Fitzgerald. "My film is entirely based on real cases," he said. "I tried to expose the wretched conditions of the poor in real terms because I loathe films that make the poor romantic and sweet." But at the same time, he insisted that "I absolutely didn't want to make a propaganda film. . . . I saw things that moved me, and I wanted to bring them to the screen, but always with the sort of love I have for the instinctive and the irrational, which can turn up anywhere." Indeed, Buñuel tempered his semi-documentary approach with surrealist devices: dreams and hallucinations loaded with images of sex and violence. And as he indicates in his memoirs, he intended to disrupt some of the most realistic scenes with totally unrelated elements "which would have made the viewers say, 'Did I really see what I saw?'"

This approach was ruled out by the producer, but even without the hundred-piece orchestra Buñuel had envisioned in the background of the scene where Jaïbo murders Pedro, *Los olvidados* managed to shock its viewers. Even the production crew was hostile, he recalled, and one of the writers refused to allow his name to appear on the credits. The reaction was even more negative after the film was released: it was attacked by the Mexican public, the press, and the labor unions for its brutal portrayal of the underclass; it closed after only four days, and there were demands that Buñuel be expelled from the country.

This groundswell of negative opinion was abruptly reversed after *Los olvidados* was shown at Cannes in 1951 and received both the award for best direction and the International Critics Prize. Buñuel was effectively rediscovered on the international scene, and the film was recognized in all its dimensions. André Bazin, for example, wrote of *Los olvidados* that "at a distance of eighteen years and five thousand kilometers, it's the same inimitable Buñuel, a message faithful to *L'Age d'or* and *Las Hurdes*, a film that lashes the spirit like a red-hot iron and leaves the conscience no possibility of rest." Comparing the film to Jean Gênet's *Miracle de la Rose* in its eschewal of moral categories or Manichaean characters, Bazin linked it not only to Buñuel's surrealist past but to Spanish traditions in the visual arts: "This taste for the horrible, this sense of cruelty, this search for the extreme aspects of the human being, all of this is also the heritage of Goya, Zurbarán, Ribera" (and as Marcel Oms was to point out later, there is also no small measure of Spain's picaresque literary heritage in the film, notably from *Lazarillo de Tormes*). *Los olvidados* was always one of Buñuel's favorite films, and its place in the history of cinema is still unchallenged. "Three decades after its jolting appearance at the 1951 Cannes Film Festival," J. Hoberman wrote in 1983, "the film remains absolutely contemporary; if anything, it is a prototype whose full impact has yet to be felt."

Buñuel followed *Los olvidados* with three commercial melodramas. *Susana (Demonio y carne, Susana/Devil and Flesh*, 1950) plays on the conventions of the *comedia rustica* (rural comedy) in the story of a young girl (Rosita Quintana) who escapes from a reform school and wreaks havoc in a proper landowning family. According to Ado Kyrou, Buñuel himself had little good to say about the film (although at the end of his life he indicated he'd like to do a remake with "more sophisticated, less conventional eroticism"), but various critics have singled it out as a masterful subversion of commercial genres as well as a key prefiguration of the central role women play in his later works. The other two films in this group have had no defenders at all. *La hija del engaño (Don Quintin el Amargado/Don Quintin the Bitter*, 1951), a remake of the 1935 Filmofono production about a betrayed husband who disowns his daughter has been described as an "incredible commercial stew," while *Una mujer sin amor (Cuando los hijos nos juzgan/Pierre and Jean*, 1951), a remake of André Cayatte's 1943 *Pierre et Jean* about a sacrificing mother, was in Buñuel's opinion "undoubtedly my worst film."

After these rapid-fire money-making ventures, Buñuel was approached by an old friend from Madrid, the writer Manuel Altolaguirre, who wanted to produce an adaptation of one of his own short stories. The result of this temporary break with Oscar Dancigers was a freewheeling and much more successful social comedy, *Subida al cielo (Climbing to the Sky*, released in 1953). On the day of his marriage, Oliverio

(Estaban Marquez) is summoned by his dying mother who wants him to go to the city and change her will. Adventures abound en route: a woman gives birth, a politician gets stoned, the bus driver makes a detour to celebrate his own mother's birthday. After a night of reveling, most of the passengers have forgotten about their travel plans, and Oliverio seizes the opportunity to make off with the bus. He soon discovers he's not alone: Raquel (Lilia Prado), the flirtatious woman he's been dancing with at the party, has stowed away aboard, and soon provides him with his first opportunity for adultery. He finally arrives in the city and collects the necessary papers from the notary; he then embarks on a return trip that takes him through a funeral procession (for a young girl bitten by a snake, as in *Las Hurdes*) and a rejection from Raquel ("I got what I wanted"), before he discovers that Mama is already dead. Faithful to the spirit of the law—and his mother—he takes a thumbprint from the corpse and returns to his wedding celebration.

Subida al cielo brought Buñuel back to Cannes in 1952 and earned him the avant-garde film award, but those who expected more of the harsh violence of *Los olvidados* were surprised at this revelation of the director's lighter side. Nonetheless, as Marcel Oms suggests, the film was not without a serious message: "Under the guise of a pleasant comedy, Buñuel talks about freedom of love and desire: conscious of the ambiguity of each, he makes every effort to do away with guilt in demystifying the original sin."

Returning to Oscar Dancigers in 1952, Buñuel turned out three more films in the course of the year: *El bruto (L'Enjôleuse/The Brute), The Adventures of Robinson Crusoe,* and *El (Him/Torments)*. As the title suggests, *El bruto* moves back into the realm of violence with the story of a strongman, Pedro the Brute (Pedro Armendariz) who is called in by a wealthy slumlord, Don Andrès (Andrès Soler) to bring a group of tenants into line. He beats one of them to death and is forced to flee, but not before he has been seduced by Don Andrès' wife, Paloma (Katy Jurado). He takes refuge with the dead man's daughter, Meche (Rosita Arenas), who innocently falls in love with him, but Paloma, jealous of the younger woman, reveals his identity. When this fails to bring Pedro back to her, she tells her husband that he raped her. Don Andrès goes after his hireling and a quarrel ensues, in the course of which it becomes clear that they're father and son. Pedro stabs the older man to death and takes flight for a second time; he seeks out Meche, but as he begs her forgiveness, the police, alerted by Paloma, shoot him down.

Although *El Bruto* was a studio production, shot in eighteen days, it is often cited as an example of how much Buñuel was able to do within the commercial cinema and the extent to which he challenged its limitations. For Antonio Rodrig, it is even one of the director's most personal films, while Gérard Talon suggests that in its reflection on cinematographic form, it is even more important for the evolution of Mexican cinema: "It is from the standpoint of using the image to denounce the taboos that shackle freedom of speech that *El Bruto* is important. One finds [in the film] that sublime shot where a man and woman get into bed, and a modest camera wisely starts to pan and films the other side of the room. . . . In this voluntary absence of image practiced by Buñuel, in this breach where the presence of taboos is unveiled, lies the task that Mexican filmmakers must accomplish: to say the non-said."

The Adventures of Robinson Crusoe was an American-Mexican coproduction and Buñuel's first film in color. It was also made in the relatively luxurious period of three months. According to Buñuel, he was not very enthusiastic about the Defoe novel to begin with, but "in the course of the production I started to get interested in the story and introduced some elements of sexual life (dream and reality) and the scene of madness where Robinson sees his father again." Buñuel's Robinson Crusoe (Dan O'Herlihy) is no longer an exemplar of righteous individualism and free enterprise, but a man who can't stand being alone, whose faith in God proves useless, and whose master-slave relationship with Friday (Jaime Fernandez) evolves into a mutual friendship.

The film is divided into two parts: the period of solitude following Robinson's shipwreck and the encounter with Friday. The first part in particular is laced with Buñuel's personal imagery—in *My Last Breath*, for example, he describes how his own father appeared to him in a hallucination the night of the father's death. The second part, as Marcel Oms points out, is recast in the framework of one of Buñuel's favorite authors, the Jesuit priest Baltasar Gracián, whose *Criticón* describes how a "critical thinker" joins a "savage" on an island and then goes off to discover the world with him. (Quotations from Diderot and de Sade also make their way into this section.)

In his 1954 interview with *Cahiers du cinéma*, Buñuel explained that "I wanted to show man's solitude, man's anguish in human society." And this message, with all of its contemporary implications, was clearly and approvingly received by the critics. As Tony Richardson wrote in *Sight and Sound*, "Buñuel has created out of a character motivated with strict psychological accuracy an immense and powerful symbol of our own times." For Paule Sengissen, who compared Buñuel's tone to that of Voltaire, "*Robinson Crusoe* is without a doubt the first great atheist film of value that the cinema has given us."

With the last film of 1952, *El*, this fairly benign atheism yields once again to a violent attack on established religion. Based on a novel by Mercedes Pinto, *El* is the story of a forty-five-year-old bachelor, Francisco (Arturo de Cordova), whose primary attribute, besides his landholdings, is his Catholic piety. Quite appropriately, then, it is at the Good Friday service that he falls in love with the comely foot of a female worshiper. The woman, Gloria (Delia Garcés), turns out to be engaged to someone else, but Francisco pursues her relentlessly until she becomes his wife. After a lapse of several years, she runs into her old fiancé, Raoul (Luis Beristain), and reluctantly discloses the horrors that the marriage has entailed—above all, Francisco's unimaginable jealousy; on the very night of their wedding, she tells him, the presence of an old friend of hers in their hotel sent him into a fit of impotent rage.

When she returns home and is forced to disclose the chance meeting with Raoul, another crisis is precipitated. This time the jealous husband waits until his wife is asleep and then goes to her bedroom with a sinister assortment of instruments—ropes, razor blade, surgical needle and thread, cotton. He is at the point of tying her hands when she wakes up and drives him away with her screams (an episode taken directly from the conclusion of de Sade's *La Philosophie dans le boudoir*). The next day Gloria is gone; Francisco, armed with a pistol, seeks her in the church. In a state of paranoid delusion (expressed through the reeling angles of a subjective camera), he thinks he sees her with Raoul, mocking him, and he rushes to the altar and tries to strangle the priest.

Another lapse of time finds Francisco retired to a monastery, where, dressed in a monk's robe, he watches the arrival of Gloria and Raoul and their son, Francisco, at a distance. After they leave, he confides to a priest that his madness had abated, then lurches toward the void at the end of the corridor.

According to Buñuel, *El*, like the rest of his Mexican productions, was the result of a conscious grappling with the dictates of the producers on the one hand and his own inclinations on the other: "They propose a film to me, but instead of accepting it such as it is, I try to make a counterproposal that, even though it's still commercial, seems more appropriate for expressing some of the things that interest me." In this case, his solution was not particularly well received: when the film was shown at Cannes in 1953, the jury and most of the public apparently found it too commonplace, and in Mexico, only the prestige of Arturo de Cordova kept it playing for two or three weeks. Nonetheless, it remained one of Buñuel's favorite films, exemplifying the challenge of the Mexican period. And his view was upheld early on by critic Georges Sadoul, who insisted that *El* was "typically Buñuelian for anyone who understands that it is a film with more than one false bottom to it." Underlying the conventional story, the commercial sets, the Hollywood dialogue, he argued, were Buñuel's subversive black humor and obsessive themes, serving up continual affronts to good taste. In fact, Sadoul considered *El* in this respect a remake of *L'Age d'or*, although the director himself denied the association, insisting that consciously, at least, he "wanted to make a film about love and jealousy."

Buñuel continued along much the same line with *Abismos de pasión* (*Wuthering Heights*, 1953), a fairly daring adaptation of Emily Brontë's romantic novel. This was a project that went back to 1932, when he first undertook the adaptation with Sadoul and Pierre Unik but was unable to find a producer. After twenty years, he had lost interest in the project, but two weeks into filming a comedy, an offer was made and he took it.

Buñuel's *Wuthering Heights* drastically truncates the original, eliminating twenty-eight of Brontë's thirty-four chapters to focus on the middle of the narrative. The action begins after Catarina (Iraseme Dilian) has married her wealthy neighbor, Eduardo (Ernesto Alonso) and joined him and his sister, Isabel, in the easy life of the landed aristocracy. With the return of her former servant, Alejandro (Jorge Mistral), a long-suppressed passion flares up, but Alejandro, victimized and humiliated by Catarina's brother Ricardo (Luis Aceves Castañeda) during their youth, now seeks to exact his revenge. Not content with foreclosing the brother's gambling debts and seizing his property, he forces his way into the family by marrying Isabel. But when the long-suffering Catarina dies, Alejandro cannot live without her: he goes to her tomb and throws himself onto her corpse, at which point Ricardo shoots him, reuniting the two lovers in death.

When Buñuel abandoned his comedy to make *Wuthering Heights*, he was not able to abandon the actors already under contract, with the result that the film was gravely miscast. As Buñuel recalled in *My Last Breath*, "Unfortunately I had to accept the actors engaged by Oscar [Dancigers] . . . Jorge Mistral, Ernesto Alonso, a singer and rumba dancer Lilia Prado—a *rumbera* to play a romantic young woman—and a Polish actress, Irasema Dilian, who, in spite of her Slavic features, was supposed to be the sister of a Mexican mestizo." Likewise, the director claimed that an overbearing fifty minutes of *Tristan and Iseult* was imposed on the soundtrack after he requested a little Wagner for the epilogue. With these very noticeable defects, *Wuthering Heights* made its way into the Hispanic melodrama circuit and was not picked up for distribution in France. But when it surfaced at the Swiss Cinématheque in 1960 and opened in Paris three years later—after Buñuel had returned to Europe to work—the film came to be seen in a different light. Although the casting and the music hardly improved with age, critics were generally moved to overlook these flaws because of the emotional intensity Buñuel achieved (particularly in comparison with William Wyler's academic adaptation of 1939): "The great and utterly demented beauty of the finale takes away any reservations," wrote Marcel Martin. "Breaking all its moorings with realism and verisimilitude, the work spills into fantasy and madness when the two lovers are reunited in death against the background of a raging storm. If Buñuel seemed to be momentarily absent, at that point we find him totally there once again."

Buñuel followed *Wuthering Heights* with *La ilusion viaja en tranvia* (*Illusion Travels by Streetcar*, 1953), a social comedy about two transit workers who learn their streetcar is about to be retired from service and decide to make one last junket about the city. Picking up the fantastic journey theme of *Subida al cielo* (along with Lilia Prado in the role of the coquette), Buñuel again plays on the juxtaposition of the real and the surreal, with a mixture of fine-tuned portraits of daily life and vivid excursions into the world of dreams and fantasies. A similarly folkloric treatment occurs in *El rio y la muerte* (*The River and Death*, 1953), but this melodrama about a family vendetta ("seven deaths, four burials, and I don't know how many . . . wakes," according to Buñuel) apparently failed to get beyond local interest. When it was shown at Venice in 1954, the audience reacted with howls of laughter, greeting each murder with cries of "More, more!" Buñuel himself felt that the film was not easily accessible to Europeans because of the underlying notion of *machismo*, the brute sense of male honor "characteristic of the Hispano-Indian crossbreeding."

After this commercial quickie (made in fourteen days), the director was back on the track with *Ensayo de un crimen* (*La vida criminal d'Archibaldo de la Cruz/ The Criminal Life of Archibald de la Cruz*, 1955), generally considered one of the most important works of his Mexican period. Like the protagonist of *El*, Archibald de la Cruz is a bourgeois antihero whose piety is equaled only by his perversity— in this case, an irrepressible desire to control women by killing them. As the film's prologue shows, this urge goes back to childhood, when Archibald's governess catches him dressing up in his mother's corset and bra. He has just been given a music box that is supposed to make all his wishes come true, and now he directs an evil thought at this intrusive female. Immediately a stray bullet from the Mexican Revolution flies through the window and leaves her dead on the carpet, her skirt hiked over her knees—a voluptuous thrill for young Archibald, but also a terrible secret. This sequence sets the pattern for all that ensues years later, when Archibald the adult (Ernesto Alonso) comes upon the fateful music box in an antique shop and nearly swoons at the memory it evokes. Now a quiet, respectable bachelor, he never thinks of wishing for mundane advantage; he wishes to kill again, and he proceeds to focus his dire attentions on one woman after another—a nun, a pretty casino patron, even his own insufficiently virginal fiancée. And with the alarming logic of dreams, each of his "victims" promptly dies—but never according to plan: events, in their haste to serve him, rob him of the pleasures of murder, while slyly confirming his religious ethic of intent. Archibald becomes increasingly distraught until, overcome by frustration and guilt, he confesses all to the police. His confession is what we have seen, and when it is finished, he is dismissed as a harmless crackpot. Thinking it over, Archibald decides to throw the music box away, and goes off hand in hand with the only woman who has so far escaped his powers.

For Buñuel, Archibald represented an "erotic gourmet," someone who sought to achieve his dream of violent conquest "like others want to climb the Alps or cultivate an exotic plant." And this normalization, or banalization, of the abnormal (a kind of surrealism in reverse) is implicit in all of Buñuel's Mexican films, imposed in part by the demands of commercial production but at the same time, a means of subverting that system. "In each of his films," writes Antonio Rodrig, "he introduces in varying degrees those surreptitious doses of poison that totally change the anticipated result." As Rodrig and many others have pointed out, the Mexican films are replete with Buñuel's "fixations"—fetishism, anticlericalism, woman as temptress, the "bestiary" of the animal kingdom. What is per-

haps most notable about *La vida criminel* is the way that all of these elements come to be integrated within a perfectly classical narrative— the antithesis of Buñuel's initial attempts to express very similar concerns by means of disjuncture. Buñuel himself was clearly aware of this evolution and its positive effects on his conceptions of filmmaking; in a 1963 interview with Wilfred Berghahn he explained that in Mexico, "I became a cinema professional. Until then I made a film the way a writer writes a book, and with money from friends. I'm very grateful and very happy to have lived in Mexico and to have been able to make each of my films as it would not have been possible in any other country. It's true that in the beginning, limited by necessity, I had to make films cheaply. But I didn't make one film that contradicted the dictates of my conscience and my convictions; films that were artificial and without interest I didn't make."

From the international perspective, Buñuel's activity in Mexico more or less faded into the earlier period of oblivion when he was in Spain and the United States. *Los olvidados* had been recognized at Cannes, and *La vida criminel* made an impression when it arrived in France in 1957, but the intervening works were largely unseen outside of Mexico. It was only in 1966, with a retrospective of five previously unknown films in Paris, that a "Mexican oeuvre" began to be perceived and taken seriously, and by that time, Buñuel himself was in the thick of the international scene.

After *La vida criminel* he accepted an offer to go to France and collaborate with an old friend from the surrealist circle, Jean Ferry, on an adaptation of Emmanuel Roblès' 1952 novel, *Cela s'appelle l'aurore* (*That's Called the Dawn*, 1955). In at least three respects, this film marks a striking departure from his earlier works: it offers a positive hero, a positive romance, and an overtly political context. But at the same time (and not surprisingly), the underlying values and overriding themes remain Buñuelian.

The story revolves around the personal commitments—in love, marriage, and friendship— of a factory doctor, Valerio (Georges Marechal), living in Corsica with his wealthy and disgruntled wife, Angela (Nelly Borgeaud). While his wife is visiting her family in Nice, Valerio goes to look after Magda Galli, the wife of an old friend, Sandro (Gianni Esposito), who works as a caretaker for the factory owner. Soon after, the doctor is called in by the local police chief to examine a young girl raped by her grandfather, and it is at this point that he meets and falls in love with an attractive Italian widow, Clara (Lucia Bosé). Sandro, meanwhile, has been forced to leave his job because he refuses to put his wife in the hospital and return to work; in spite of Valerio's intervention, the factory owner insists that the couple vacate their home, and Magda does not survive the move. The grief-stricken Sandro kills the factory owner and takes refuge with Clara and Valerio, but unable to go on without Magda and unwilling to compromise his friends with the police, Sandro commits suicide. Valerio has seen the friendship through to the end ("If you're a man, there are things you have to do," he declares), and the departure of his wife frees him of his marriage obligation, with the result that he and Clara can begin a new life together: "That's called the dawn."

Although Buñuel failed to enlist Yves Montand and Simone Signoret for the main roles as he had intended, *Cela s'appelle l'aurore* was generally well received. Buñuel himself liked it because of the basic statement it made: "Love yes, police no." For their part, the critics seem to have been more intrigued by the way the director once again integrated his own worldview into a story written by someone else. "He has given us very few films as Buñuelian as *Cela s'appelle l'aurore*," wrote Georges Sadoul in 1956, citing images of children shooting each other in the streets, a cigar-smoking violinist on a bicycle, a turtle on its back during a love scene, and the vitriolic still-life on the police chief's desk: the complete plays of Paul Claudel, a pair of handcuffs, and a reproduction of Salvador Dali's *Crucifixion*.

Cela s'appelle l'aurore (which was a Franco-Italian coproduction) brought Buñuel back onto the European scene, but the path was by no means smooth. There were several more unsuccessful projects before he was able to put together a Franco-Mexican coproduction with his old friend Oscar Dancigers for *La Muerte en este jardin* (*Death in This Garden/Evil Eden*, 1956). A jungle adventure adapted with great effort from an undistinguished novel, this was Buñuel's first color film since *Robinson Crusoe*, and although the images themselves were highly acclaimed, neither Buñuel nor the critics much liked the film as a whole.

After a year went by, Buñuel returned to black and white, to a strictly Mexican production, and to his most explicitly religious subject to date: *Nazarin* (1958). The title character (played by Francisco Rabal) is an idealistic neighborhood priest with a flock of less-than-canonical parishioners. After a local prostitute, Andara (Rita Macedo), kills one of her sisters in a brawl and takes refuge with Nazarin, he is accused of unchastity. Disillusioned with the church establishment, he decides to shed his clerical garb and set out on a personal mission. He soon meets up with Andara, as well as the disconsolate Beatriz (Marga Lopez), who has already tried to hang herself because her boyfriend Pinto has left her. In Christlike fashion (but without the miracles), Nazarin and his companions make their way from village to village, encountering plague, deformity, and the wrath of Beatriz' lover, who sets the police on their trail. Nazarin and Andara are arrested; Beatriz, now in love with the priest, is taken away by Pinto. In prison, Nazarin is beaten by a murderer and saved by a church-robber who tells him, "You only do good, I only do bad, and we're just as useless, one another. We're good for nothing." And indeed, this judgment of utter failure is underscored in epilogue form: Nazarin's bishop, concerned about the image of a former priest on a road gang, manages to get him separated from the other prisoners. As Nazarin and his guard are making their way along the road, Pinto speeds by in his car with Beatriz asleep at his side. Nazarin himself is such a pitiful sight that a poor woman selling fruits by the roadside offers him a pineapple. He tries to say no, but winds up taking it for his long trek to nowhere.

Nazarin was based on an 1895 novel by Benito Pérez Galdós, and Buñuel's adaptation remained faithful enough to the positive image of Pérez Galdós' crusader priest that many people thought the director had finally made his peace with religion. Awarded the jury prize at Cannes in 1959, the film came very close to receiving the Catholic Film Office prize as well. But Buñuel hardly encouraged such overtures: "People are free to find whatever they want in my film," he told *Le Monde* in an often-quoted interview. "Personally I was astounded to read certain commentaries. Where do these people dig up what they write? I like *Nazarin* because it's a film that lets me express certain things I care about. But I don't think I've renounced or foresworn anything at all: thank God, I'm still an atheist."

In fact, Buñuel had made significant changes in his adaptation, notably replacing Pérez Galdós' ending, where a typhoid-stricken Nazarin has a vision of Christ, with his own defeat-ridden epilogue. (He also drew portions of the dialogue from de Sade's *Dialogue d'un prêtre et un moribond*.) From a novel expressing faith in the renewal of religion outside the church, Buñuel created a parable of the Christ who failed. And notwithstanding the shock value of the narrative, no small part of the film's strength lay in its visual form: Guy Gauthier went so far as to call it "one of the most striking films in the history of the cinema, where the vigor of its thought is thrown into relief by a style that is at once rigorous, sparse, and dazzling."

The two films that followed marked another round of commercial productions for Buñuel, although their subject matter remained hotly topical. *Los Ambiciosos* (*La Fièvre monte à El Pao/The Republic of Sin*, 1959), a Franco-Mexican coproduction, traced the fortunes of a kind of secular Nazarin, a liberal politician (played by Gérard Philippe) trying to reform a dictatorship from within. As Freddy Buache and others have suggested, the film had obvious implications for Franco's Spain, but ultimately it remained on the level of melodrama. Buñuel himself considered it the worst of his French films and recalled several years later that "during the shooting Gérard Philippe and I kept asking ourselves why we were making such a piece of rubbish; neither he nor I knew why."

The Young One (1960), which was an American-Mexican coproduction and Buñuel's only film in English, took on the unnerving issues of racism and youthful sexuality through the encounters of a black fugitive (Bernie Hamilton) and a teenage orphan (Kay Meersman) with their respective pursuers. For Luc Mollet, *The Young One* ranked among one of Buñuel's most important films in terms of the social problems it explored, but the *mise-en-scène* fell solidly among the director's most commercial productions. "The work is as relaxed as can be," he wrote, "and gives the delightful impression of a genius working solely for his own pleasure." But while this mix was well received at Cannes, the response in the United States was only lukewarm. In part, Buñuel blamed the distributor, Columbia Pictures, whom he accused of "buying intelligence in order to destroy it," but he sensed a more profound problem with the North American public: the need for simple—and simplistic—approaches to social issues. "In order for people to like that kind of film," he told interviewers in 1967, "the black man must be a hero who saves the white, or vice versa, at the end. But in my film there aren't any heroes."

When Buñuel completed *The Young One* he was sixty years old, and he had spent nearly twenty-five years in exile because of the Franco dictatorship in his native Spain. While the time spent in Mexico had reinforced the political break with geographical distance, his international coproductions—and his reputation—brought him back in contact with Europe. The 1960 Cannes film festival, in particular, allowed him to meet a new generation of Spanish filmmakers, and in the course of extended discussions with Carlos Saura, Buñuel was persuaded to embark on a Spanish-Mexican coproduction to be shot in Spain. The decision had tremendous repercussions—along with Pablo Picasso and Pablo Casals, he had been one of the three symbols of cultural opposition to the Franco regime, and his apparent concession was strongly condemned by his fellow exiles in Mexico. But as might have been expected, the real shock was to come with the film he went on to make. *Viridiana* (1961) was a direct assault on the pillars of the Spanish dictatorship. Significantly, Buñuel himself wrote the story upon which the screenplay was based; his dual point of departure, he recalled, was the name of a fourteenth-century Spanish saint (Viridiana), and the image of a girl drugged by an old man. "I proceeded from there," he explained, "and the work flowed out like a fountain." As Marcel Oms points out, *Viridiana* is "essentially a film of return. It is in effect a work in which characters come back to places they've left, others come back to places they've been chased from, events return to the memory of those who lived them, and finally, the trap closes in on everyone."

The first return is that of Viridiana (Silvia Pinal, the wife of the film's Mexican producer, Gustavo Alatriste), a young novice sent to visit her uncle before she takes her vows. Upon her arrival, the uncle, Don Jaime (Fernando Rey), is shocked by the resemblance she bears to his wife, who died on their wedding night. During her stay, Viridiana goes along with his request to try on the dead woman's wedding gown, but when her uncle asks her to marry him, she insists on returning to the convent the next day. Aided by his servant, Ramona, Don Jaime drugs her, with the idea of making love to her while she sleeps. Though he fails to go through with the rape, he tells Viridiana that he did, in hopes that she'll abandon her plans. But she flees his house, and the remorseful Don Jaime hangs himself.

The second cycle of return begins when Viridiana decides not to reenter the convent but to pursue her religious vocation out in the world—she will convert her uncle's estate into a hospice for beggars. Along with a crew of undesirables worthy of Goya, she is joined by Don Jaime's natural son, Jorge (Francisco Rabal), a practical man who comes back, with his mistress, to superintend the farming operation. Like Nazarin, Viridiana soon learns the futility of her mission: while she and Jorge are away, the beggars invade the house and revel their way into an orgy. In the film's most notorious sequence, a dirty old woman "photographs" the banqueting beggars, and the frame obligingly freezes on a travesty of Leonardo da Vinci's "Last Supper" (accompanied by "The Hallelujah Chorus"). The reappearance of the two would-be benefactors only channels the violence of the event: one of the beggars attacks Jorge while another tries to rape Viridiana. Saved by her half-cousin at the last minute, she undergoes a second profound transformation, discovering her own sexuality and deciding to give herself to Jorge. When she enters his room, he is playing cards with Ramona, who has now replaced his previous mistress. Confident of his impending conquest, Jorge invites her to join the game: "I'm sure you'll like it," he tells her. "You won't believe this, but the first time I saw you, I told myself, 'My cousin Viridiana will wind up playing cards with me.'"

When Buñuel decided to return to Spain with *Viridiana* (he had been planning to film it in Mexico), he made his political position clear by choosing to coproduce with the anti-Franco UNINCI. From there on, he played by the rules of the game, submitting his scenario to the censors and following their directive to change the ending (originally Viridiana was to have entered Jorge's room to find Ramona in his bed—he later acknowledged that the card game was a great improvement). Apart from the main roles, he selected his cast from a pool of old friends and unemployed actors, mostly on the basis of appearance. The shooting was done with great speed—Carlos Saura recalled that Buñuel generally did each scene in one take, with two or three linking shots to be edited in. Leaving a work print with the censors, the director quickly went off to Paris to complete the editing and mixing. The film was to be premiered at Cannes, but was not in the official competition because the Spanish producers did not want it connected with the government. But once the film was screened (on the last day, because of a delay in the printing), the jury insisted on awarding the first prize jointly to *Viridiana* and Henri Colpi's *Une Aussi Longue Absence*. At this point the director-general of the Spanish cinema claimed the film as his government's official entry, but Madrid soon overrode his enthusiasm, not simply banning *Viridiana*, but retroactively revoking the authorization to make the picture and destroying the out-takes Buñuel had left behind. *Viridiana* was not shown in Spain until 1977; it was reclaimed as a Spanish production in 1983 with its inclusion among the best films of that year.

Outside of Spain—and the Vatican, where *Osservatore romano* denounced *Viridiana* as blasphemy and sacrilege—the film was recognized as a masterpiece, "one of the gems in Buñuel's oeuvre," according to Marcel Martin, who also considered it one of his craziest works, one of the most surrealist, and "one of the most brilliantly revealing with regard to his morals and his humanism." Like many other critics, Martin expressed appreciation for the film's visual character, including Buñuel's "treasury" of symbols, the formal beauty of the picture, and the simplicity and "necessity" of the

mise-en-scène. At the same time, Martin elaborated on the two dominant themes of religion and violence. "He's a great *social* moralist who has no illusions about human nature but who understands and makes us understand (like Brecht) that people are too often corrupted by the conditions of their lives and that you have to reform society before you can hope to transform human beings."

Buñuel's next film, *El angel exterminador* (*Exterminating Angel*, 1962) deals with very similar social preoccupations, but pointedly rejects the surface narrative of *Viridiana* and the Mexican films in a manner that recalls his first surrealist ventures and at the same time marks the direction he was to follow for the remainder of his career. Another Spanish-Mexican coproduction, this time shot in Mexico, *Exterminating Angel* was adapted by Buñuel from *Los Naufragos de la calle de la Providencia (The Castaways of Providence Street)*, a cinedrama he had written with Luis Alcoriza in the early 1950s. It is basically a desert island story set in the home of a wealthy, gracious couple named Nobile (played by Enrique Rambal and Lucy Gallardo). Some twenty guests have been invited to dinner after the opera, but the elaborate meal is long over and no one seems able to leave (except the servants). Over the next few days and nights, the orgy of the beggars in *Viridiana* plays itself out among the liberal bourgeoisie with drugs, sex, and violence: a sheep is slaughtered for food, a water pipe broken for drink, one man dies of a heart attack, and two lovers carry out a suicide pact. A crowd gathers outside, behind police lines, but there is no movement in either direction. The impasse is broken only when Letitia the Valkyrie (Silvia Pinal) decides to give up her virginity to the Christlike host, Edmund Nobile. On Letitia's instructions, the surviving guests go back to their original places and repeat whatever they were saying before the ordeal began. Abruptly the spell is broken, and the guests, released from the Nobile mansion, pile into the cathedral for a service of thanksgiving—only to find themselves immobilized anew. More demonstrators gather outside; this time the police fire on them. A whole flock of sheep press into the church.

When he presented *Exterminating Angel* in Paris, Buñuel prefaced the film with an explicit warning: "If the film you are going to see strikes you as enigmatic or incongruous, life is that way too. . . . Perhaps the best explanation for *Exterminating Angel* is that, 'reasonably, there isn't one.'" Like his Mexican producer, Gustavo Alatriste, who told him, "I didn't understand anything; it's marvelous," critics were quick to declare the stunningly inexplicable film a masterpiece. Shown at Cannes in 1962, it received the International Critics Prize and the prize of the Society of Writers and Television Artists as well as the André Bazin Prize at Acapulco and the grand prize at Sestri-Levanti.

Over the years, various ingenious, if not necessarily illuminating interpretations have been advanced. In a 1966 lecture series on surrealism, for example, Maurice de Gandillac offered a biblical reading, whereby the gathering in the Nobiles' house represents the Hebrews in the desert released from the curse of God by Letitia's entry into womanhood. For Fernando Cesarman, the whole story might well be Letitia's fantasy, while Marcel Oms would emphasize the allegorical implications for Franco's Spain. Notwithstanding his own warning, Buñuel himself was to offer his own remarks in *My Last Breath* (where he indicates that it was one of the rare films he saw after it was completed); the underlying idea, he said, was the same one that runs throughout his films: "the inexplicable impossibility of satisfying a simple desire."

Exterminating Angel takes place in an unspecified locale—most likely Mexico, possibly Madrid, and yet, according to Buñuel, he "imagined it in Paris or London instead." The time period also remains ambiguous, for the characters as well as the audience, and the spoken references to "yesterday evening" or "three or four days ago" are somewhat akin to the fictive intertitles of *Un Chien andalou*. In any case, Buñuel seemingly went to the opposite extreme with his next film, a detailed period piece set in the French countryside of the late 1920s. *Le Journal d'une femme de chambre* (*Diary of a Chambermaid*, 1964), the first of Buñuel's six French productions, marked the beginning of his collaboration with producer Serge Silberman and scenarist Jean-Claude Carrière. The story was based on Octave Mirbeau's famous novel about the landed gentry of Normandy seen through the eyes (and the diary) of the title character. While Mirbeau had sketched a portrait of the late nineteenth century, Buñuel chose to move the action forward to the period that corresponded to his own arrival in France, which was also the period of the rise of fascism in Europe.

In Buñuel's adaptation, Célestine (Jeanne Moreau) arrives at the estate of Monsieur and Madame Monteil (Michel Piccoli and Françoise Lugagne) in 1928. She is not slow to observe the peculiarities of the landed gentry—Monteil's lust; his wife's frigidity; the foot fetish of the father-in-law, Rabour (Jean Ozenne); along with the pronounced racism of the gardener, Joseph (Georges Geret), and the fierce antiroyalist pride of the neighbor, Captain Mauger (Daniel Ivernel). Affronted and abused by all of them, she finds her sole ally in the free-spirited servant-girl Claire (Dominique Sauvage). After Rabour is found dead in his bed (clutching a woman's boot in his hand), Célestine decides to return to Paris, but on the same day, Claire is raped and murdered in the woods. Célestine, suspecting the gardener of the crime, stays on and embarks on a bizarre course of her own, promising to marry Joseph in order to trap him. Once he is under arrest, she marries Captain Maugar and retires to a comfortable life. But the larger menace of fascism is already on the horizon: Joseph is freed for lack of evidence and opens a bistro in Cherbourg. In the street, the Right is demonstrating with cries of "Down with foreigners!" and "Long live Chiappe!"

As was generally the case with Buñuel's adaptations, *The Diary of a Chambermaid* greatly condensed the literary source, focusing on characters far more than narratives. According to his sister Conchita, the film contains many elements from their childhood at the country house in Calanda, and quite obviously, with the "Viva Chiappe!" at the end of the film, Buñuel was finally getting his revenge against the Paris police chief who suppressed *L'Age d'or* in 1930. But at the same time—and this is also common for Buñuel—much of the "Buñuelian" detail in the film comes directly from the novel; citing the example of the foot fetishist, Robert Benayoun commented, "Buñuel has chosen his characters so well that he will undoubtedly be accused of having 'Buñuelized' to the utmost episodes that are quite consistent with the original."

Despite a certain enthusiasm for Jean-Claude Carrière's dialogue and Jeanne Moreau's acting, *The Diary of a Chambermaid* was not a great success in France, and Buñuel retreated somewhat from the Parisian scene. He had an offer from David O. Selznick to do a Hollywood film starring Jennifer Jones, but he turned this down and rejoined Gustavo Alatriste for a final Mexican production. *Simon del Deserto* (*Simon of the Desert*, 1965), a thoroughly Buñuelian evocation of an early Christian ascetic who spends thirty-seven years sitting on top of a column, took up an idea from the director's student days, when García Lorca had drawn Buñuel's attention to the life of Simeon Stylites. The film was intended to be feature length, but it was cut off at forty-five minutes when the money ran out; abruptly abandoning the remaining sequences, Buñuel ended the story by showing Simon (Claudio Brook) on a junket to New York City in the company of a woman devil (Silvia Pinal) who condemns him to remain in this "hell on earth" (echoing García Lorca's observation, "Hell is a city much like New York"). Notwithstanding the production problems, *Simon* was an immediate success and received a special jury prize at the Venice Film Festival in 1965. "Traditional conception, classic filming technique, [cameraman Gabriel] Figueroa's typically beautiful photography," noted Michel Cournot at the time. "The grandeur is in the idea."

After *Simon*, Buñuel resumed the collaboration with Jean-Claude Carrière that was to last, in work and friendship, to the very end of his life. They developed a scenario for Matthew Gregory Lewis' *The Monk*, but the production fell through and Buñuel lost interest. (The scenario was finally passed along to Ado Kyrou, who filmed it in 1973.) He was then approached by the Hakim brothers in Paris to do an adaptation of Joseph Kessel's 1923 novel, *Belle de Jour*, the story of a doctor's wife who decides to deal with her boredom, as well as her masochistic tendencies, by working in a brothel during the afternoons. Buñuel frankly admitted that he didn't like the novel, "but I found it interesting to try and turn something I didn't like into something I did." This was largely accomplished by the interpolation of the woman's fantasies and flashbacks into the narrative episodes, suspending linear chronology and replacing it once again with an ambiguous dream state. The film opens with Pierre de Sérizy (Jean Sorel) and his wife, Séverine (Catherine Deneuve), in a horse-drawn carriage; on the husband's orders, Séverine is tied to a tree and whipped by the coachman. After this graphic introduction to Séverine's state of mind—the episode is revealed to be a fantasy when her husband breaks in to ask, "What are you thinking about?"—the story advances through the dual realms of action and thought. Séverine hears of a friend who works as a call girl. A flashback reveals that she was molested as a child. She seeks out the brothel of Madame Anaïs (Geneviève Page). A second flashback reminds her that she refused first communion. She begins working as "Belle de Jour" ("Daytime Beauty," an allusion to her schedule), welcoming the abuse of a succession of clients. She is beset by nightmares and fantasies of infidelity. A young hoodlum, Marcel (Pierre Clementi), becomes attached to her; soon after, her husband's friend Husson (Michel Piccoli) discovers her at the brothel and she leaves, but Marcel pursues her to her home. He shoots her husband and is killed by the police as he flees. Some time later, Husson visits the now-paralyzed Pierre to reveal the secret of Séverine's other life. Following his friend's departure, Séverine sees (in one state of mind or another) Pierre get up from his wheelchair. He asks her again what she's thinking about, and an empty carriage passes through the park below.

Buñuel had another bout with the censors before *Belle de Jour* was released—he wound up cutting a scene of necrophilia from one of Séverine's fantasies—but when the film was shown at Venice in 1967, it received the grand prize. Among those who enthusiastically praised it was Joseph Kessel: "Buñuel's genius," he declared, "went far beyond anything I could have hoped for. It's the book and it's not the book. We're in another dimension, that of the subconscious, of dreams, of secret instincts suddenly bared." Film critics in France, England, and the United States followed suit, hailing it (in the words of Elliot Stein) as "a masterpiece, technically Buñuel's most accomplished, free-flowing work." Nonetheless, there were some reservations. Marcel Martin, for example, asked whether *Belle de Jour* was really a "great Buñuel" and concluded that "myself, I'm not entirely convinced." Something of the "carnality" of *Nazarin* or *Viridiana* was missing, he wrote, and this suggested to him that "Buñuel is uncomfortable filming in a strange environment, not being at home."

In fact, Buñuel had made *Belle de Jour* with the idea that it was to be his last film: he was sixty-six years old and had been suffering from deafness and dizzy spells for a number of years. But after the success at Venice, he turned to Jean-Claude Carrière with an idea he'd been thinking about since he first went to Mexico twenty years earlier—a film on Christian heresies. The two men spent six weeks in Spain piecing together a scenario, which Buñuel then took back to Mexico and reworked in the same hotel where he had written all his scenarios since 1948. The resulting film, *La Voie lactée* (*The Milky Way*, 1969), invites what Raymond Lefèvre calls "a Surrealistic promenade in the Christian zoo of heresies."

Peter (Paul Frankeur) and John (Laurent Terzieff), two scruffy 1960s wanderers, take the medieval pilgrimage route known as the Milky Way to the cathedral shrine of Santiago de Compostella. Once they set foot on the path, however, they enter a world in which everyone—from the waiter at a roadside inn to a band of lisping schoolgirls—is utterly engrossed in excited (and sometimes murderous) theological debate. Escaping from one time warp only to fall into another, the pilgrims blunder through church history as reflected in the looking-glass of suppressed Christian heresies. Some of these are enacted: the denial of Christ's divine nature, for instance, occasions a parodic New Testament scene, in which an all-too-human mama's boy performs "miraculous" tricks. Others are represented by historical or symbolic figures, including orgiasts and ascetics, the fourth-century

Spanish mage Priscillian (Carrière), the devil himself (Pierre Clementi), and that most compulsive of libertines, the Marquis de Sade (Michel Piccoli). Orthodox Christianity is trounced at every turn: a priest who defends the dogma of transubstantiation is hauled off by men in white coats, while a bland Mariolater glosses over a possibly authentic vision.

Hungry and tired, the pilgrims find it difficult to get a bed or a bite to eat in the general furor. It is with some relief, then, that they learn from a prostitute (Delphine Seyrig) that their trip has no point—the saint's tomb at the cathedral was long ago preempted by Priscillian. Gratefully, Peter and John leave the Milky Way for the pleasures of the flesh; in the background, Christ reappears, restoring the sight of the faithful. With the exception of a single line toward the end of the film, all the dialogue dealing with the heresies is drawn from religious literature.

The Milky Way was released in France on a double bill with *Simon of the Desert*, which was recognized in retrospect as a kind of introductory sketch. The response was quite favorable, although, according to Buñuel, interpretations varied greatly: citing two celebrated Latin American writers, he notes in *My Last Breath* that Carlos Fuentes considered *The Milky Way* a militantly antireligious film, while Julio Cortazar alleged that it could have been financed by the Vatican. Among the critics, there was above all a sense of awe at the cumulative effect of Buñuel's forty-year career. For Jean de Baroncelli, for example, *The Milky Way* was "above all the film of a poet who, on a theme that has never ceased to haunt him, recounts in his [characteristic] manner his dreams, his fantasies, his childhood memories, his uncertainties, and his adult revolts."

Still declaring that *The Milky Way* was his last film, Buñuel proceeded to take up another project that had been on his mind—and in the works—for a number of years. This was an adaptation of Benito Pérez Galdós' *Tristana*, which Buñuel had first undertaken in 1961, after *Viridiana*. At that time, he had hoped to continue making films for Spanish audiences, and Galdos' novel offered a Spanish subject that was not overly complex and, more important, was acceptable to the government. "*Tristana* is Galdós' worst book," Buñuel said, "but it allows me to observe some aspects of Spanish life and customs that interest me." As it turned out, in 1963, after he had completed all the preparations, the government denied him permission to film, but in 1969 he was invited back by his Spanish producers, and after several refusals, the government approved the project.

As the film was originally conceived, Silvia Pinal and Fernando Rey were to have played opposite each other as they did in *Viridiana*, but in the final Franco-Italian-Spanish coproduction, Catherine Deneuve appears in the title role. At the outset, she is yet another innocent young woman who comes under the tutelage of an older man, Don Lope (Rey). This time, though, she becomes his mistress, and with her loss of innocence comes a will to dominate. Her contempt for Don Lope is such that she pursues an affair with a young painter, Horacio (Franco Nero) and finally runs away with him to Madrid (although she, like Don Lope, rejects marriage as a constraint on passion). But when she falls ill two years later, she makes her way back, with Horacio, to seek help. A tumor on her leg necessitates amputation. Horacio leaves and Don Lope welcomes her back. In the absence of any passion at all, they marry. One night, Tristana is awakened by a recurring nightmare: the head of Don Lope is swinging in a bell-tower. She hears her husband cry out for help in the next room but only pretends to call the doctor, letting him die.

According to Buñuel's assistant, Pierre Lary, the director made *Tristana* to "exorcise" his old age in the character of Don Lope. Once again, he personalized an adaptation with details from his own past on the one hand—the story is set in the key year of 1929, for example—and with his repertoire of themes on the other—the female seductress, decadent priests, foot fetishism via an artificial limb, necrophilia, dream states, chance encounter. On this level, as some critics acknowledged, the film was probably less forceful than *Viridiana*, but at the same time, the figure of Don Lope (the liberal bourgeois) injected a dimension of political and social commentary that was quite striking in the Spanish context. As Miguel Bilbatua wrote, "*Tristana* is the x-ray of a failure that concerns us all, because we're still paying the consequences . . . the failure of the liberal Spanish bourgeoisie whose superficial disdain for religion is nothing but a glossy facade. . . . Nor is *Tristana* uniquely the failure of Don Lope, it's also that of Horacio, of the intellectuals who are incapable of relationships, personal or otherwise, at the level demanded by the times; and it's also the failure of the Tristanas who are incapable of overcoming the traumas society has created in them."

Declaring *Tristana* in its turn his last film, Buñuel duly geared up for another round with the status quo, this time in the form of an original scenario that he wrote with Jean-Claude Carrière. *Le Charme discret de la bourgeoisie (The Discreet Charm of the Bourgeoisie*, 1972) brings *L'Age d'or* into the 1970s, in terms of its social preoccupations as well as its cinematic form. The title characters, in the main, are two couples, the Sénéchals (Jean-Pierre Cassel and Stéphane Audran) and the Thévenots (Paul Frankeur and Delphine Seyrig), along with Mme. Thévenot's lover (Raphael Acosta), her sister (Bulle Ogier), and the ambassador of Miranda (Fernando Rey). As in *L'Age d'or*, their common plight is frustration, but this now takes a thoroughly banal form: they cannot seem to get through a meal together. The first failure occurs when the Thévenot entourage arrives for dinner at the Sénéchals', only to discover that they are a day early. Thévenot's proposal to adjourn to an inn is no more successful, owing to the recent demise of the innkeeper, whose corpse is laid out in the next room. When the Thévenots return to the Sénéchals' a day later, their hosts are too engrossed in lovemaking to answer the door; subsequent gatherings are interrupted by the army, the police, and a band of gangsters, as well as the revelation that each episode is only a dream. This narrative, such as it is, is interpolated with scenes suggesting that the bourgeoisie is neither discreet nor charming: the ambassador (a Nazi war criminal) deals drugs; a police chief tortures a detainee; a gardener-priest shoots a dying man who was responsible for the murder of the priest's parents (this episode was cut in Spain). And every once in a while, the scene switches to a country road, where the same bourgeoisie is shown marching determinedly to nowhere.

It was Buñuel's producer, Serge Silberman, who provided the starting point for *The Discreet Charm* in the form of a personal anecdote he told about a forgotten dinner invitation—the first sequence—and Silberman had a hand in the film's technical evolution of the film as well, convincing Buñuel to experiment with video monitors during the shooting. As Robert Benayoun notes, the effect was tremendous: Buñuel's signature style of minimal camera movements and monumental close-ups gives way to bold zooms and traveling shots. The result, in Benayoun's view, is "perhaps his most direct and most 'public' film," but at the same time, one that "keeps its secrets." Indeed, critics were once again able to extract the truths of their preference, whether psychological, sociological, political, or religious, while the public flocked to see the bourgeoisie lambasted, and even the American movie industry honored Buñuel with an Oscar, for best foreign film of 1972.

For Buñuel, *The Discreet Charm* involved an element of search on more than one level. Like *The Milky Way*, it was one of his rare original scenarios, and one that, he took pains to point out, had been reworked five times. But thematically as well, Buñuel conceived of *The Discreet Charm* as a continuation of the "search for the truth" that he had attempted to explore in *The Milky Way*, and after it was done and well received, he decided to develop the theme further in yet a third film. Disappointed as always with the way the exegetes had dissected *The Discreet Charm*, he consciously sought to make the next film more resistant to critical analysis: "It's a film that will lend itself less, in any case, with greater difficulty, to symbolism," he declared.

Le Fantôme de la liberté (*Phantom of Liberty*, 1974), another original scenario coscripted with Jean-Claude Carrière, had as its starting point a story by the Spanish poet Gustavo Adolfo Bécquer about the French army's desecration of tombs and churches during the Napoleonic wars. The film opens with a tableau based on Goya's famous painting, *May 3, 1808*, showing Napoleon's soldiers executing a group of prisoners, among them Buñuel (playing a monk), Serge Silberman, and two non-actor friends. Their dying cry is "Vivan las cadenas!" (Long live the chains!)—a declaration that the Spanish monarchy is preferable to the French Revolution. The sequence that follows (inspired by Bécquer's story) plunges into necrophilia as a French army captain, impassioned by a female tomb statue in the church of Toledo, orders his soldiers to open the tomb and transport the corpse to his bed. This episode in turn is revealed to be a story that a family maid is reading aloud in the park while she is supposed to be watching two young girls, Valérie and Véronique. The children, meanwhile, seize the opportunity to make the acquaintance of a dirty old man, who gives them a packet of postcards with the admonition that they are not for adult eyes. This episode leads back to the Foucaud household, where the parents (Monica Vitti and Jean-Claude Brialy) are scandalized by the obscenity of the cards—shown to be views of Paris—and the maid is fired. A perplexing dream that M. Foucaud has that night carries the action to a doctor's office, but before any interpretation can be offered, the nurse becomes the focus of attention, requesting a leave to visit her sick father in the provinces. Taking to the road (which turns out to be closed), she winds up in an inn with a group of monks playing poker, a young man in amorous pursuit of his aunt, a masochistic hatter (Michel Lonsdale) and his obliging female business partner, among others. When a professor asks the nurse for a ride in the morning, the story veers through the police academy where he teaches to follow two young policemen chasing a speeding driver. The speeder (Jean Rochfort) is soon revealed to have other problems: cancer and a missing daughter. But the cancer disappears and the daughter reappears, and while everyone continues to search for her, the focus shifts to a sniper who guns down eighteen people and becomes a celebrity. In the final turn of events, the police chief in charge of the case of the not-missing daughter (Julien Bertheau) makes his way to the cemetery for yet another act of necrophilia—this time tinged with incest—and gets arrested for desecrating his sister's tomb. At the police station, he encounters his double—a second police chief (Michel Piccoli)—and the two of them go off to direct a crackdown at the zoo. As the camera comes to rest on an ostrich, the cry is again "Vivan las cadenas!"

In retrospect, Buñuel explained, *Phantom of Liberty* was the third part of a trilogy, "or rather a triptych, as in the Middle Ages," along with *The Milky Way* and *The Discreet Charm of the Bourgeoisie.* "They talk about the indispensable search, about chance, about personal morality, about the mystery that must be respected." Buñuel himself recognized that *Phantom of Liberty* was structured according to the same principle as *L'Age d'or*, the "conducting thread of seemingly inconsequential detail," and as he might have declared thirty-five years earlier, he told interviewers, "I wanted to make a film based on chance, on the importance of chance." But he also acknowledged that his tone had changed with time: "Today I say with humor what I said before with violence. . . . Today scandal and violence are everywhere . . . so [they] no longer serve for anything, they've become useless for us, the artists."

After *Phantom of Liberty*, Buñuel, now approaching his middle seventies and completely deaf, again renounced filmmaking, but three years later he was back at work on a project he'd begun twenty years earlier, an adaptation of Pierre Louÿs' *La Femme et le pantin* (*The Woman and the Puppet*), which he titled *Cet obscur objet du désir* (*That Obscure Object of Desire*, 1977). Louÿs' story of two men's obsessive love for a chambermaid had already served as the basis for four or five films, including Josef von Sternberg's *The Devil Is a Woman* (1935). According to Buñuel, he remained "rather close to the book" but introduced "a certain number of interpolations that changed the tone completely." Among other things, the two suitors are reduced to a single aging bachelor, Mathieu Faber (played by Buñuel's alter ego, Fernando Rey), and the setting, originally confined to Seville, is spread all over Europe, which is not only a locus of love and desire but also one of political agitation and ideological confrontation.

In a 1956 interview, Buñuel made it clear that he couldn't identify with the "surface eroticism" of the novel—"I'm modest," he said. "I blush." What he wanted to express, he went on to explain, was "a sensuality that is otherwise more profound, more consuming, more terrible. I'd like to make the portrait of feminine perversity." But he indicated at the time that he would have to find the right actress, "a sensual, virginal, demonic little girl." In 1977, Maria Schneider was cast as the chambermaid, Conchita, but she quit after three days, unable to play the part as Buñuel wanted. Two replacements were proposed—the French actress Carole Bouquet and the Spanish actress Angelina Moline—and Buñuel, in pursuit of his virginal demon, decided to use both of them, playing on the differences in their appearances and personalities to intensify the irrationality of desire.

The story begins with a double departure: Mathieu is leaving for Paris, and Conchita is leaving the household. Mathieu makes his way to the railroad station—encountering a booby-trapped car along the way—and installs himself in a compartment with three other passengers, who soon observe him pouring a bucket of water on the head of a young woman outside. In Archibald de la Cruz fashion, Mathieu recounts his story in flashback to the other passengers. He becomes enamored of the young and seemingly virginal Conchita on their first meeting, but she rebuffs his advances and disappears the next day. Their paths cross again on the road to Lausanne, and he obtains her Paris address. Unsuccessful at buying her favors, he tries to negotiate with her mother, a pious woman nonetheless eager for worldly gain. Conchita disappears again; two months later she and Mathieu meet in a Paris cafe where she works as a hat-check girl. This time she volunteers her virginity but turns up in bed wearing a modern-day iron maiden. The game of pursuit continues until the night that Mathieu discovers her with her guitarist lover; this time he opts for revenge and gets Conchita and her mother expelled from France. They meet again in Seville where she says she's working in a nightclub and turns out to be dancing nude for tourists. Ever hopeful, Mathieu buys her a house, but she locks him out and makes love with her guitarist before his eyes. Another round of revenge—the beating that precipitated the departures that opened the film. The flashback comes to a close with the train ride, but the epilogue continues in Paris, where Conchita welcomes Mathieu with her own bucket of water. The couple is last seen arm-in-arm at a shopping mall, when a terrorist bomb goes off, putting a fiery end to the mall, the story, and the film.

Although Buñuel went on to complete two

more scenarios with Jean-Claude Carrière—an adaptation of Huysmans' *Là-bas* and an original script dealing with terrorism—*That Obscure Object of Desire* turned out to be his last film. It is, in Raymond Lefèvre's words, "a sort of anthology of the principal themes and forceful images of the Buñuelian universe"—the ravages of love, the liberating force of desire, the hatred of repressive elements, the mocking of taboos, reality as dream-state, the surrealist incongruity of chance, along with the character types of the youthful temptress, liberal bourgeois gentleman, and conniving mother. But at the same time, and at the time of Buñuel's life when he had "seen the progressive and ultimately total disappearance of my sexual instinct, even in dreams," he mustered all of his imaginative and cinematic resources to create a new image of desire, one that hinges on the ever-present paradoxes of seeing and knowing. That two Conchitas are seen on the screen negates the reality of the narrative, but at the same time establishes a conceptual reality: the nature of desire. "Desire born of need," writes Marcel Oms, "still does not know its true object, and from scene to scene, Mathieu sees the two images of his desire follow each other without discerning Conchita's true identity." The spectators too are drawn into the trap, Oms argues, by their "own participation in the phenomenon of projection/identification," and in the end (as in the very beginning of Buñuel's career, when he appeared on the balcony, razor blade in hand), "the filmmaker remains the sole master of the game, and he conducts it as he pleases."

Buñuel was back in Paris again the year after he completed *That Obscure Object* with the intention of making another film, but he ultimately decided against it for fear of falling ill while he was there alone, and returned to Mexico. He died, of benign old age, in the English Hospital of Mexico City five years later, and following his last wishes, his body was cremated.

The mental world of Luis Buñuel—the turbulent unconscious given to eroticism, violence, the ways of chance—is well documented in the thirty-six films that he directed over nearly half a century. But in a body of work that is nothing if not ironic, perhaps the greatest irony of all is the fact that Buñuel's personal life was so remote from the inner world of eroticism, violence, and chance that he brought to the screen. In the words of his friend Michel Piccoli, "He was like a monk!" He remained married to one woman for all of his life; he preferred reading a book to going to the movies, and the only indulgence he seems to have allowed himself was alcohol, which he consumed for one hour a day (with his watch on the table, according to Piccoli) late in the afternoon, and never to the point of drunkenness. Disciplined in his work as well, he wrote and rewrote his scenarios and then filmed them with care and precision: "He only shot what was in the scenario and would do a single take if it was possible," Piccoli recalled, adding "After that, all the editor had to do was a simple end-to-end." And while he was always very considerate of the people he worked with, as well as the people who lived in the places where he was filming, he demanded what his assistant Pierre Lary called "terrifying exactitude."

Wherever the juncture of the private man and his public oeuvre lay (and according to his collaborator Jean-Claude Carrière, Buñuel himself had little interest in finding out, rejecting psychological analysis as "arbitrary, useless"), his legacy of themes, forms, and inspirations has been enormous: "This supposed filmmaker," wrote Carrière, "was in reality a personality of a greater stature, monumental for some." The records of Cannes or Venice speak clearly of his European trajectory, but his impact in the Third World, and particularly Latin America, is probably even greater. As Glauber Rocha observed even in 1966, with the first stirrings of Brazil's *cinema novo*, "In the absurd framework of the reality of the Third World, Buñuel is the *possible consciousness*: in the face of oppression, the police, obscurantism, and institutional hypocrisy, Buñuel represents a liberating morality, a breaking of new ground, a constant process of enlightening revolt."

—*M.R.*

FILMS: Un Chien andalou (An Andalusian Dog), 1929; L'Age d'or (The Golden Age), 1930; Las Hurdes (Tierra sin pan, Land without Bread), 1932 (documentary); (credited as assistant director and executive producer) Don Quintin el Amargado (Don Quintin the Bitter), 1935; (credited as assistant director and executive producer) La hija de Juan Simon (Juan Simon's Daughter), 1936; (credited as coscenarist and executive producer) Quien me quiere à mi? (Who Loves Me?), 1936; Centinela alerta! (On Alert, Sentinel!), 1936; España leal en armas/Espagne 37 (Spain Loyal in Arms/Spain '37), 1937 (documentary); Gran Casino, 1947; El gran calavara (The Great Profligate), 1949; Los olvidados (The Forgotten/The Young and the Damned), 1950; Susana (Demonio y carne, Susana/Devil and Flesh), 1950; La hija del engaño (Don Quintin el Amargado, Don Quintin the Bitter), 1951; Una mujer sin amor (Cuando los hijos nos juzgan/Pierre and Jean), 1951; Subida al cielo (Climbing to the Sky), 1953 (filmed in 1951); El Bruto (L'Enjôleuse/The Brute), 1952; Las aventuras de Robinson Crusoe/The Adventures of Robinson Crusoe, 1952; El (Him/Torments), 1952; Abismos de pasión (Wuthering Heights), 1953; La ilusion viaja en tranvia (Illusion Travels by Streetcar), 1953; El rio y la muerte (The River and Death), 1954; Ensayo de un crimen (La Vida criminal de Archibaldo de la Cruz/The Criminal

Life of Archibald de la Cruz), 1955; Cela s'appelle
l'aurore/Amanti di domani (That's Called the Dawn),
1955; La Muerte en este jardin (Death in This Garden/
Evil Eden), 1956; Nazarin, 1958; Los ambiciosos (La
Fièvre monte à El Pao/The Republic of Sin), 1959;
The Young One, 1960; Viridiana, 1961; El angel exterminador (Exterminating Angel), 1962; Le Journal
d'une femme de chambre (Diary of a Chambermaid),
1964; Simon del desierto (Simon of the Desert), 1965;
Belle de Jour, 1966; La Voie lactée (The Milky Way),
1969; Tristana, 1971; Le Charme discret de la bourgeoisie (The Discreet Charm of the Bourgeoisie), 1972;
Le Fantôme de la liberté (Phantom of Liberty), 1974;
Cet obscur objet du désir (That Obscure Object of Desire), 1978. *Published scripts*—Un Chien andalou *in*
L'Avant-scène du cinéma June 1963, (English) 1968;
L'Age d'or *in* L'Avant-scène du cinéma June 1963, No-
vember 1983, (English) 1968; Las Hurdes *in*
L'Avant-scène du cinéma April 15, 1964; Los olivida-
dos *in* L'Avant-scène du cinéma June 1973, (English)
1972, (Spanish) 1980; Nazarin *in* L'Avant-scène du
cinéma February 1969, (English) 1972; Viridiana
(French) 1962, 1984, (Spanish) 1963, (English) 1969;
El Angel exterminador *in* L'Avant-scène du cinéma
June–July 1963, (Spanish) 1964, (English) 1969, 1972;
Journal d'une femme de chambre *in* L'Avant-scène du
cinéma 1964 (Seuil) 1971; Simon del desierto *in*
L'Avant-scène du cinéma July–September 1969, (En-
glish) 1969; Belle de Jour *in* L´Avant-scène du cinéma
April 15, 1978, (English) 1971; La Voie lactée *in*
L'Avant-scène du cinéma July–September 1969; Tri-
stana *in* L'Avant-scène du cinéma January 1971, (En-
glish) 1971; Le Moine (with Jean-Claude Carrière)
1971; Le Charme discret de la bourgeoisie *in*
L'Avant-scène du cinéma April 1973; Le Fantôme de
la liberté *in* L'Avant-scène du cinéma October 1974;
Cet obscur objet du désir *in* L'Avant-scène du cinéma
November 1985, (Italian) 1981.

ABOUT: Abel, R. French Cinema, The First Wave 1915–
1919, 1984; Abruzzese A. and Masi, S. I film di Luis
Buñuel, 1981; Agel, H. Le Visage du Christ à l'écran,
1985; Alcala, M. Buñuel, Cine e ideologia, 1973; Aranda, J. F. Luis Buñuel: A Critical Biography, 1975; Bazin, A. Qu'est-ce que la cinéma? vol 3, 1961; Buache,
F. Luis Buñuel, 1970 (in English: The Cinema of Luis
Buñuel, 1973); Buñuel, L. Mon dernier soupir, 1982
(My Last Breath, 1983); Buñuel, L. Obra literaria,
1982; Cameron, I. Luis Buñuel, 1979; Cesarman, F. El
ojo de Buñuel, 1976; Drouzy, M. Luis Buñuel architec-
te du rêve, 1978; Durgnat, R. Luis Buñuel, 1968 (in
English: Luis Buñuel, 1978); Goetz, A. and Banz, H.
Buñuel: eine Dokumentation, 1965; Grange, F. and
Rebolledo, C. Luis Buñuel, 1964 (in French); Higgen-
botham, V. Luis Buñuel, 1979; International Film
Guide 1965; Kyrou, A. Luis Buñuel, 1962 (in English:
Luis Buñuel, 1963); Kyrou, A. Le Surrealisme au
cinéma, 1963; Larraz, E. Le Cinema espagnol des ori-
gines à nos jours, 1986; Lefèvre, R. Luis Buñuel, 1984;
Lizalde, E. Luis Bũnuel 1962 (in Spanish); Matthews,
J. H. Surrealism and Film, 1971; Mellen, J. (ed.) The
World of Luis Buñuel, 1978; Mora, C. J. Mexican Cin-
ema: Reflections of a Society 1896–1980, 1982; Oms,
M. Don Luis Buñuel, 1985 (in French); Passek, J.-L.
(ed.) Dictionnaire du cinéma, 1986; Rubenstein, E. in
Lyon, C. (ed.) International Dictionary of Films and
Filmmakers, 1984; Sadoul, G. Rencontres, 1984; Wil-
liams, L. Figures of Desire: A Theory and Analysis of
Surrealist Film, 1981. *Periodicals*—American Film
September 1982, June 1983; Cahiers du cinéma De-
cember 1951, February 1953, June 1954, August–
September 1954, June 1956, October 1956, November
1957, September 1961, March 1966, June 1967; Cahiers de la Cinémathèque (Toulouse) Summer–
Autumn 1980, Winter 1984; Cineaste 1976; Cine Cu-
bano 1973; Cinéma (France) November 1954,
November 1957, June 1959, January 1961, April 1962,
June 1963, September–October 1963, March 1965,
April 1966, July–August 1967, May 1971, November
1973, July–August 1981, September 1983, July–August
1984, September 18, 1985; Cinema Papers (Mel-
bourne) July 1974; Cinématographe September 1977,
July–August 1981, September–October 1983; Contracampo (Madrid) October–November 1980; Etudes
cinématographiques 20–23 1962/1963; Film Culture
Summer 1960, Spring 1962, Summer 1966; Film Quarterly Winter 1958, April 1960, Fall 1979; Film und
Fernsehen February 1980; Films and Filming October
1961, November 1961; Image et son/Revue du cinéma
November 1954, Summer 1962, November 1962, December 1962, October 1965, April 1966, May 1971,
November 1977; Jeune cinéma February 1966, April
1969; New York Times Magazine March 11, 1973; Positif November 1961, March 1962, March 1963, November 1963, May 1966, September ˙1967, January
1973, February 1973, October 1974, January 1981,
October 1981, October 1983, March 1984; Sight and
Sound January–March 1954, Summer 1962, Winter
1965/66, Autumn 1967, Summer 1974, Summer 1975;
Yale French Studies 17 1965. *Films about*—Andre La-
barth (dir.) Luis Buñuel, 1967; Petite Confession
filmée de Luis Buñuel, 1981 (interview with Jean-
Claude Carrière).

*CAMERINI, MARIO (February 6, 1895–
February 6, 1981), Italian director and scenarist,
was born in Rome. His legal studies were interrupted by World War I, during which he served
as an infantry officer, spending the last part of
the war in prison camps in Austria and Germany. He entered the cinema in 1920 as a scriptwriter and assistant to his cousin, the prolific
director Augusto Genina.

Camerini directed his own first movie in
1923, *Jolly, clown da circo,* and during the 1920s
made five more commercial films including
Maciste contro lo sceicco (Maciste Versus the
Sheik, 1925), one of the popular series of pictures
about the virtuous superman Maciste—a hero in
the Tarzan mold—played by Bartolomeo Pa-
gano. None of them was of any particular interest except *Kiff Tebbi* (*Desert Lovers,* 1927),
which was shot partly on location in North Africa and used a special device for moving the camera over sand dunes so as to give a vertiginous
impression of the terrain's undulations.

°kä mə rē´ nē

MARIO CAMERINI

His first serious film was *Rotaie* (*Rails,* 1929, released 1931), which shares the social and realist concerns (but not the Fascist ideology) of Blasetti's *Sole,* made the same year. Starring Maurizio D'Ancora and Kathë von Nagy, *Rotaie* tells the story of two young people and their long but eventually successful search for work. It was shot silent by Ubaldo Arata with a minimum of titles—only two in the whole first half; music, sound effects, and some snatches of dialogue were added later. "The recurring contrast between the lives of the poor and the rich is done with comprehension, sympathy, and adequate subtlety," wrote Vernon Jarratt. "Typical are the railway scenes, alternating between the first class carriages, with their luxury but their reserved and frigid atmosphere, and the warm humanity and crowded discomfort of the third class carriages. . . . Memorable, too, [are] . . . the face of the young man when he is losing at roulette, the atmosphere of the railway stations, especially at night, and . . . the rush of the train through the countryside."

La riva dei bruti (1930), the Italian version of William Wellman's *Dangerous Paradise,* was directed by Camerini at the Joinville studios near Paris, where Paramount at that time was shooting talkies scene by scene in a succession of languages, using the same actors, the same sets, and stationary cameras. After this "half-baked" experiment, Camerini returned to Rome and made his first original sound film, *Figaro e la sua gran'giornata* (*Figaro's Big Day,* 1931), which was partly dubbed and partly recorded live. Set in the Veneto in the nineteenth century, it is based on a play by Fraccaroli about the arrival

in a small town of a touring production of *The Barber of Seville* and the attempt to put a local girl into the cast in the face of her father's objections. A movie of unfading charm and good humor, it shows that Camerini had already developed his ability to capture the atmosphere of a particular time and place with wit and sympathy.

It was the director's next picture that established his international reputation. *Gli uomini, che mascalzoni* (*Men Are Such Rascals,* 1932), based on a short story by Cesare Zavattini, was scripted by Camerini with Aldo De Benedetti and a newcomer to the cinema, Mario Soldati. No more happens than that a chauffeur and a salesgirl fall in love, quarrel, try to make each other jealous, and wind up reconciled, but the sentimentality of this comedy is balanced by a freshness and lightness of touch that reminded reviewers of René Clair. Moreover, the film has attracted a great deal of attention because all the exterior scenes were shot with a mobile camera on location in Milan and at the Milan Trade Fair grounds. (Some critics have gone so far as to claim *Gli uomini* as a forerunner of neorealism, but Roy Armes suggests that "this is to underestimate the director's degree of a stylisation in treatment and the script's undoubted theatrical contrivance.") The film made not only Camerini's reputation but that of the rising young romantic actor who brought such charm and polish to the role of the chauffeur-hero, Vittorio De Sica.

Another factor in the movie's success was "Parlami d'amore Mariù," the immensely popular song written by Cesare Bixio. Camerini himself, with his usual down-to-earth modesty, said, "The film has two main virtues: the song, and the fact that basically it is a silent film. Technically—for instance in the car chase scene and the accident—the film was made by editing in little pieces of soundtrack that were sometimes no longer than a few frames. It's a method I myself invented. It's like in the days of the silents. You don't have the long tracking shots they used to use so as not to cut the soundtrack. Indeed, I remember I gave up three thousand lire of my own salary in order to get the soundtrack printed separately, so I could make tests. I believe the film's success was due entirely to technique: the fast pacing, plus Bixio's music."

A string of hits followed. *T'amerò sempre* (*I'll Always Love You,* 1933), including scenes shot in a real hospital maternity ward, combined documentary, melodrama, and sentimental comedy in a story about a poor girl (Elsa De Giorgi) who is left pregnant by a feckless aristocrat and eventually finds happiness with a better man (Nino

Besozzi); Camerini directed an unsatisfactory re-make ten years later with Alida Valli and Gino Cervi. *Il cappello a tre punte* (*The Three-Cornered Hat,* 1934) transplanted Alarcón's fa-mous novel to seventeenth-century Naples un-der Spanish domination and cast the brilliant Neapolitan dialect actors Eduardo and Peppino de Filippo in leading roles.

An amiable farce (also later remade by Camerini), it describes what happens when the beautiful wife of an ambitious young miller catches the roving eye of the governor. Comedy though it is, it has a number of episodes showing peasants ill-used by soldiers and officials, and this so angered Mussolini that he knocked over a chair; as Camerini says, "it talked about work-ers, about poor people, while what they wanted was films about bravery, about the army, about Scipio Africanus." Two scenes were cut by the government censors, and in *Anno 13,* a journal edited by the Duce's son Vittorio, Camerini was called "anti-Fascist and anti-Italian." (The direc-tor objected to the latter charge but not the for-mer, saying, "I didn't like Fascism and I did like to make movies with stories that were a bit ro-mantic, a bit sentimental, and a bit human."

One of Camerini's greatest successes during this period was *Darò un milione* (*I'll Give a Million,* 1935), another in the series of comedies he made with De Sica. It is a rather Capra-esque film about a disillusioned millionaire who mas-querades as a poor man, planning to give a mil-lion lire to the first person who treats him with unselfish good will. Vernon Jarratt wrote that "the story is in the episodic form natural to this sort of film, but there is a very lively invention of incident, and the feeling is very well maintained." It was this picture that first brought together De Sica and the scenarist Ce-sare Zavattini—a combination that was to prove extremely fruitful when De Sica turned to di-recting.

By then, however—as Camerini said—the Fascist regime was becoming increasingly insis-tent on a very different kind of cinema, one that was as swaggeringly nationalistic as Fascism it-self. Camerini responded with *Il grande appello* (*The Last Roll-Call,* 1936), which he confessed years later was "the only thing I really regret in my whole career in film. Because Soldati and I started out with the idea of striking a blow against Fascism—by having a character smash the record of 'Giovinezza' [the Fascist song]—but we ended up making a colonialist film." (Perhaps Camerini was too hard on the movie; an Italian critic recently praised it as "an antici-pation of neorealism" in "its extraordinary Re-noir-esque acting by Camillo Pilotto, the

mixture of languages in the scenes in Gibuti, the frankness with which a non-Fascist Italian is shown.")

After that, returning to familiar territory, Camerini made *Il signor Max* (*Max the Gentleman,* 1937)—also co-scripted by Solda-ti—a satire in which De Sica plays a newsdealer trying to break into high society. It has been found notable for the "dialectic between what is said and what is left unsaid in this game of identities"—a dialectic believed to underlie all of Camerini's work. Assia Noris provides the ro-mantic interest in this film, as she does in *I'll Give a Million* and in *Batticuore* (*Heartbeat,* 1938), where she plays a diplomat's daughter in Paris who acquires the socially disturbing art of picking pockets. *Grandi magazzini* (1939), again starring De Sica and examining life behind the scenes in a great department store, further dis-tressed the Fascist regime—one of Mussolini's ministers is said to have threatened that "if Camerini keeps on making these movies . . . about two young people who don't have much to eat, we won't let him make any at all." In fact, what Camerini did—following the example of many of his colleagues—was to turn away from the contemporary scene and its hazards and to immerse himself in literary adaptations and films with historical themes, like *Una romantica avventura* (1940), scripted by the future director Renato Castellani, and his ambitious but rather stodgy version of Manzoni's *I promessi sposi* (*The Betrothed,* 1941).

The first film Camerini made after the end of the dictatorship was *Due lettere anonime* (*Two Anonymous Letters,* 1945). As an Italian critic wrote, it "has the courage to show Rome under the Nazi occupation with all the paltry conniv-ances that linked inhabitants and occupiers—something which, a few months after the Libera-tion, could not be a very pleasing memory for the public, who preferred the heroic image of the city offered by *Open City.* Only today, per-haps, is it possible to give full value to the sincere pain that permeates the film, where Camerini reveals himself without holding back."

After *La figlia del capitano* (*The Captain's Daughter,* 1947), a workmanlike adaptation of a story by Pushkin, came *Molti sogni per le strade* (*Woman Trouble,* 1948), about an Italian veteran driven by his nagging wife to steal a car. Camerini here seemed to be trying to gain a foothold in the neorealist movement but without much success. Jarratt found his handling of Mas-simo Girotti "rather wooden, while Anna Magnani's performance was, one felt, perhaps unjustly, exactly what she would have done had there been no director there at all."

Il brigante Musolino (*Musolino the Bandit*, 1950) stars Amedeo Nazzari and Silvana Mangano in an exciting story about a young man who takes to banditry after being wrongfully imprisoned. It was highly successful, and so was *Ulisse* (*Ulysses*, 1954), a stylish spectacle with a cast that included Kirk Douglas, Anthony Quinn, and Silvana Mangano. None of Camerini's other late films was of any real distinction, though he seems to have enjoyed himself with *Kali Yug la dea della vendetta* (*Goddess of Vengeance*, 1963), a cheerfully improbable thriller about the battle against the murderous devotees of Kali in nineteenth-century India; a sequel, *Il misterio del tempio Indiano*, appeared the following year. After *Don Camillo e i giovani d'oggi* (1972), Camerini went into retirement, pursuing his interest in modern literature and travel and enjoying his status as a grand old man of Italian cinema. He died on his eighty-sixth birthday, survived by his second wife and two daughters.

Seeking to explain the rather perfunctory nature of much of Camerini's postwar work, one critic maintained that "filmmaking was amusing for him only in a climate—like that of Fascism—in which it made sense to speak metaphorically or, in other words, in which it made sense to work inside the conventions of a genre. In postwar Italy working within a genre became a choice more than a necessity, given that within certain limits one could say certain things openly. But then, according to Camerini, it was no longer necessary to make films, and if one did, it was out of habit, because the cinema was by then a profession, in whose function one perhaps no longer believed."

After the rise of neorealism, the films made under the Fascists were generally dismissed—with a few exceptions—as trivial or pernicious. They remained unseen and forgotten until, in the late 1970s, retrospectives of the work of this period were arranged in Pesaro, New York, and London. As Ken Wlaschin wrote, the 1930s were then seen to have been "a rich and lively development ground for the postwar Italian cinema, a veritable greenhouse for new ideas and techniques." It became clear that the foundations of neorealism were laid in the work of Camerini and Blasetti, who emerged as the ablest and most influential directors of the period.

Not that Camerini would ever have made large claims for himself—Carlo Lizzani once described him as "the confessor of the middle classes, scrutinizing with an always most prudent art the hearts of the faithful in order to find there any small sins; he never concerned himself with recounting their secret passions or with making

them face the major problems of existence." And Camerini would probably have agreed. "All of my work is, let's say, escapist," he confessed cheerfully, going on to assert that "film is a craft, it's not an art, because it's created by so many people working together. . . . There are some conditions—the wrong actor or cameraman—that don't depend on the director but on the situation. . . . Once, the only time I ever wrote an article . . . I compared cinema to a lottery."

A writer in *The Fabulous Thirties* concedes "that in the delicate balance between reality and cinema, for him the cinema always comes first; that his connection with reality is always mediated and, most often, metaphoric; that what counts for him more than anything else is a 'discretion' which manifests itself through purely filmic elements: rhythm, lighting, acting. It is the rhythm above all that strikes one in Camerini, the speed with which his shots follow one another, creating the 'evanescence' of his films, where everything exists on the screen alone." His touch is "very, very light but quite unmistakeable" and has "caused Camerini to be compared to Clair and Lubitsch. . . . What is enchanting in the films of Camerini is their presence on the screen and the pleasure one derives from watching them; they are, in Italy, the conclusion of a cinema of artifice that no longer exists."

FILMS: Jolly, clown da circo, 1923; La casa dei pulcini, 1924; Voglio tradire mio marito, 1925; Maciste contro lo sceicco, 1925; Saetta: Principe per un giorno, 1925; Kiff Tebbi (Desert Lovers/As You Please), 1927; Rotaie (Rails), 1929 (released 1931); La riva dei bruti, 1930; Figaro e la sua gran'giornata (Figaro's Big Day), 1931; L'ultima avventura, 1931; Gli uomini, che mascalzoni (Men Are Such Rascals), 1932; T'amerò sempre (I'll Always Love You), 1933 (remade in 1943); (with Augusto Camerini) Cento di questi giorni, 1933; Giallo (Mystery), 1934; Il cappello a tre punte (The Three-Cornered Hat), 1934 (remade in 1955 as La bella mugnaia—The Miller's Beautiful Wife); Come le foglie, 1934; Darò un milione (I'll Give a Million), 1935; Ma non è una cosa seria (But It's Nothing Serious), 1936 (German version released as Der Mann der nicht nein sagen kann, 1937); Il grande appello (The Last Roll-Call), 1936; Il signor Max (Max the Gentleman), 1937; Batticuore (Heartbeat), 1938; Grandi magazzini, 1939; Il documento, 1939; Centomila dollari, 1940; Una romantica avventura, 1940; I promessi sposi (The Betrothed/The Spirit and the Flesh), 1941; Una storia d'amore, 1942; Due lettere anonime (Two Anonymous Letters), 1945; L'angelo e il diavolo, 1946; La figlia del capitano (The Captain's Daughter), 1947; Molti sogni per le strada (Woman Trouble), 1948; Il brigante Musolino (Musolino the Bandit/Fugitive), 1950; Due mogli sono troppe, 1951; Moglie per una notte (Wife for a Night), 1952; Gli eroi della domenica (Sunday Heroes), 1953; Ulisse (Ulysses), 1954; Suor Letizia (The Last Temptation/The Awakening), 1956; Vacanze a Ischia (Holiday Island/ Holiday on Ischia/One Week

With Love), 1957; Prima amore (First Love), 1959;
Via Margutta (Run With the Devil), 1960; Crimen
(Killing at Monte Carlo/Suddenly It's Murder), 1960
(remade in 1971 as Io non vedo tu non parli lui non
sente); I briganti Italiani (Seduction in the South),
1961; Kali Yug la dea della vendetta (Goddess of Vengeance), 1963; Il misterio del tempio Indiano, 1964;
Delitto quasi perfetto (Imperfect Murder/The Almost
Perfect Crime), 1966; Don Camillo e i giovani d'oggi,
1972.

ABOUT: Apra, A. and Pistagnesi, P. (eds.) The Fabulous
Thirties, 1979; Armes, R. Patterns of Realism, 1971;
Jarratt, V. The Italian Cinema, 1951; Leprohon, P.
The Italian Cinema, 1972. *Periodicals*—Bianco e Nero
December 1959; Positif October 1976; Times (Lon-
don) February 26, 1981.

FRANK CAPRA

CAPRA, FRANK (May 18, 1897–   ), American director, scenarist, and producer, was born
in Bisaquono, a village near Palermo in Sicily.
He is the youngest of the seven children of Salvatore Capra, a fruitgrower, and the former Sarah
Nicolas. Capra spent his first six years in an "old
cracked house of stone and mortar, clinging by
its toenails to the rocks in the village." He celebrated his sixth birthday "in a howling Atlantic
storm, in the *Germania*'s black steerage hold,
crammed with retching, praying, terrorized
immigrants."

That first journey ended on Castelar Street, a
Sicilian ghetto in Los Angeles. His father worked
as a fruitpicker and Frank Capra sold newspapers after school. He "hated being poor" and to
his parents' dismay refused to end his education
with high school. Money earned as a banjo player in Los Angeles nightclubs covered his admission fee at the California Institute of Technology
in 1915. Capra studied chemical engineering for
three years, paying his way by running the student laundry, waiting tables, and wiping engines
at the Pasadena power plant. He wrote later that
Cal Tech "changed his whole viewpoint on life
from the viewpoint of an alley rat to the viewpoint of a cultured person."

Graduating in the spring of 1918, Capra enlisted in the army. Having served in the ROTC,
he was assigned as a second lieutenant to teach
mathematics to artillerymen at Fort Scott, San
Francisco. His father died in 1919 and after the
war Capra went home to live with his mother.
His two brothers and four sisters all had jobs (or
husbands with jobs), but Frank Capra, the family's only college graduate, remained chronically
unemployed. Around 1920, taunted by his siblings and convinced that he was a failure, he became depressed and ill, suffering from acute
abdominal pains. He was bedridden for two

months and did not fully recover for a year.
(Much later it was established that he had suffered a burst appendix.)

As soon as he was well enough, Capra left
home. During the next few years he lived in
flophouses in San Francisco or else hopped
freight trains and wandered the West, working
on farms or as a movie extra, or hustling a living
as a poker player or salesman of wildcat oil stock.
In 1922 he achieved a degree of respectability
as a book salesman, peddling Elbert Hubbard's
Little Journeys in a fourteen-volume deluxe edition. All the same, Capra reportedly possessed
only twelve cents when he read in the newspaper that Walter Montague was launching a new
movie studio in an abandoned gymnasium in
San Francisco.

Montague, an old Shakespearean actor, wanted to make screen versions of famous poems. Capra called on him and intimated that he was
"from Hollywood." Montague was impressed
and hired him (for a total fee of $75) to direct
his first project, a one-reeler based on Kipling's
ballad "Fultah Fisher's Boarding House." Having taken in a few movies by way of learning his
new trade, Capra enlisted the services of a cameraman he happened to know and set about casting his film with amateurs–"bellhops and so on."
His motives for insisting on a nonprofessional
cast were not those of the neorealists: "I didn't
want real actors . . . [because they] might show
me up." Capra made his first movie in two days.
It cost $1,700 and was sold to Pathé for $3,500.
According to Alva Johnston, "critics noted that
it was free from stunts, mannerisms, camera angles, and Hollywood tricks. It had to be free

from them as Capra had never had time to learn anything of them."

Capra left Montague when the old man decided that the poems on which he would base his future productions would be his own. Capra was already hooked on the movies, however, and got himself a job with another minor San Francisco producer, Paul Gerson; then one with Harry Cohn in Los Angeles. Having worked as property man, film cutter, title writer, and assistant director, he became a gag writer for Hal Roach's *Our Gang* series before incarcerating himself in Mack Sennett's notorious "writers' tower." There he wrote a number of movies for the comedian Harry Langdon; according to Capra (though not to Langdon) it was Capra who invented a distinct and consistent character for Langdon—a saintlike fool in a naughty world. When Langdon left Sennett to make feature-length movies for First National, Capra went with him as his writer and director.

Capra made three films with Langdon —*Tramp, Tramp, Tramp* (1926), *The Strong Man* (1926), and *Long Pants* (1927). All of them, and especially *The Strong Man*, were immensely successful with the critics and the public, establishing Langdon as a comedian of the caliber of Chaplin or Keaton. After he fired Capra and began to direct his own movies, his career declined. Capra made one more picture for First National, *For the Love of Mike* (1927), a routine comedy about a waif raised by three bickering godfathers, a German, a Jew, and an Irishman. It was such a resounding failure that Claudette Colbert, who played the lead, returned to the stage for two years. Capra himself nearly abandoned the movies but in the end rejoined Harry Cohn.

Cohn, his brother Jack, and Joseph Brandt had founded their film production company in 1920, calling it the CBC Sales Corporation. CBC, soon known in the industry as "Cornbeef and Cabbage," produced mostly shorts and two-reel comedies. It was one of the many small studios on "Poverty Row" in Los Angeles. Denied access to the first-run houses, they churned out low-budget quickies for provincial exhibitors. This tough business became steadily tougher as the major studios carved up among themselves the means of production, distribution, and exhibition. Most of the independent producers went to the wall; the vulgar and egregious Harry Cohn survived because he was tougher and shrewder than his competitors. In 1924 CBC became Columbia Pictures, with a new policy of producing feature films. They were still quickies, generally made in two weeks or less, but they included a sprinkling of stars (often actors just dropped by the major studios). Costs were kept down by "bunching" the scenes in which these expensive assets appeared, so that all those scenes could be shot in a few days.

It was Capra who made a success of Cohn's new policy. During his first year at Columbia he directed nine films. They included *The Way of the Strong* (1928), a melodrama about a criminal who loves and loses a blind girl, and *The Power of the Press* (1928), starring Douglas Fairbanks Jr. as a gangbusting reporter—the first of many Capra movies with a newspaper background. Cohn's first attempt at something more ambitious than a routine quickie was an all-action naval adventure story called *Submarine* (1928). It starred Jack Holt and Ralph Graves and used some relatively expensive sets and effects. Capra, who took over from Irvin Willet when Cohn became dissatisfied with his efforts, filmed his tough-guy stars without makeup and in unpressed uniforms and added other touches of realism, as well as some comedy. The result was highly successful, establishing Holt and Graves as a popular starring team and Capra as a "bankable" director. Cohn, who had started Capra at $1,000 per movie, now gave him a contract at $25,000 a year.

Submarine, which had sound effects and snatches of dialogue, was followed by Capra's first real talkie, *The Younger Generation* (1929), a rags-to-riches-and-back-again romance based on a Fannie Hurst bestseller. Capra welcomed the transition to sound. "I wasn't at home in silent films," he told an interviewer. "I thought it was very strange to stop and put a title on the screen and them come back to the action . . . When I got to working with sound, I thought, my, what a wonderful tool has been added." He used direct sound in the location shooting for *Flight* (1929), his second Holt-Graves armed services drama.

Capra wrote as well as directed *Flight* and, encouraged by its success, wrote a show business story called "Ladies of the Evening." Cohn was enthusiastic and so were all of Cohn's yesmen, but Jo Swerling, a New York newspaperman on a short contract with Columbia, said the story was preposterous and explained why at a meeting attended by "a little dark guy" he thought was Cohn's secretary. In fact it was Capra, who after the meeting insisted that Swerling be hired as his collaborator. Capra's script was rewritten as *Ladies of Leisure* (1930), which by the standards of the industry at that time—and of Columbia in particular—is a film of some sophistication. Under Capra's direction, Barbara Stanwyck acted with a sincerity and naturalness that launched her as a star. The picture was Columbia's first important critical success and the first of several Capra films written by Swerling.

After an engaging circus comedy called *Rain or Shine* (1930) came *The Miracle Woman* (1931), an early example of the exposé film. This one was aimed at the revival racket and starred Barbara Stanwyck as an evangelist clearly modeled on the notorious Aimée Semple Macpherson (though Stanwyck is redeemed by love at the last). It combines tough realism and romantic hokum in a way that even the New York critics found palatable. *Platinum Blonde* (1932), a Jean Harlow vehicle, introduced in the newspaper woman Gallagher (Loretta Young) a prototype of the Capra heroine—a wisecracking working girl whose cynicism masks a tender heart. The sharp dialogue was written by Robert Riskin, and he and Capra went on to become Hollywood's most admired writer-director team.

It was Riskin who wrote *American Madness* (1932), in which Capra's social concerns quite suddenly emerged. This Depression movie tells the story of an idealistic bank president, Tom Dickson (Walter Huston), who terrifies his greedy board of directors by lending money to people whose only collateral is honesty and an appetite for hard work. Bedeviled by a crooked cashier and murderous gangsters, and uncertain of his wife's fidelity, Dickson nearly loses heart. A run on the bank begins, but in the nick of time, the small businessmen who owe their survival to Dickson crowd in to deposit their money and demonstrate their confidence in his bank.

"Capra's mastery of the medium is obvious in *American Madness*," wrote John Raeburn, "as it would be in most of his later films. Form and content are inextricably linked, and meaning derives from the fusion of the two. The tempo of the film, for example, is perfectly synchronized with the action," building from the long and leisurely tracking shots of the opening to the increasingly jerky and staccato camera movements when the run on the bank begins: "As the intensity of the panic increases, Capra reduces the duration of each shot and uses more and more crosscutting and jump cuts to emphasize the 'madness' of what is happening." Riskin's dialogue is vivid and colloquial, and "Capra added to the naturalistic quality of the dialogue by having speakers overlap one another, as they often do in ordinary life; this was an innovation that helped to move the talkies away from the example of the legitimate stage . . . Capra also used sound as an important element for creating mood and for underscoring what was being seen on the screen . . . *American Madness* was not a film with sound added, but . . . truly a sound film." This is especially evident during the run on the bank, when "the camera and the microphone work together organically" to register the growing panic and hysteria of the mob. Raeburn

considers Capra second only to Griffith as a director of crowds. The message of *American Madness* is in effect the one Roosevelt offered soon afterwards as the rallying cry of the New Deal—"The only thing we have to fear is fear itself." However, this film, the first of Capra's "fantasies of goodwill," has been treated with great hostility by Marxist critics, who regard it as propaganda for a paternalistic capitalism.

Denied an Oscar for *American Madness,* Capra tried again with *The Bitter Tea of General Yen* (1933). This was adapted from a novel by Grace Zaring Stone, not by Riskin but by Edward Paramore. Barbara Stanwyck plays a prim New Englander who goes to China during the Revolution to marry her missionary fiancé. Instead she falls into the clutches of a much-feared warlord (Nils Asther). While she tries to convert him to Christianity, he introduces her to art and the senses. Her sexual awakening comes in a dream that does not occur in the novel, a brilliant sequence that has reminded some critics of Cocteau. When the war turns against Yen, the heroine stays with him until his suicide.

The photography in this extraordinary film was the work of Joe Walker, cameraman on a score of Capra movies. Elliott Stein, who considers it Capra's masterpiece, called it "a work of exquisite textures . . . It is the only film the director ever made in which an interesting and credible narrative is given serious support from the writer—significantly not Riskin—down to the final reel." It did not bring Capra an Oscar, but it demonstrated his victory in his struggle with Cohn to gain complete artistic control over his films, from choice of subject to final cut. "One man—one film" was Capra's watchword; in his opinion, though moviemaking involves much consultation and collaboration, in the end "one man has to make the decisions, one man says yes or no. That man should be the director."

Lady for a Day (1933) features May Robson as an old New York apple seller who has to pass as high society to impress her daughter's titled fiancé and who is abetted by assorted golden-hearted gangsters, gamblers, and molls (and ultimately by the mayor and the governor). This sentimental Runyon comedy was sentimentally adapted by Robert Riskin, and critics for whom Capra's early movies were his best tend to blame Riskin for all that is saccharine and simplistic in the more famous works that followed. There is much disagreement on this issue, however, and it was Riskin who wrote the perfectly judged triumph that established Capra as a major director in 1934, *It Happened One Night*.

The first of the "screwball comedies" was based on a story called "Night Bus" by Samuel

Hopkins Adams and featured two second-rank stars that Capra borrowed from other studios. Claudette Colbert (taking another chance on Capra) plays Ellie Andrews, escaping from her tycoon father in Miami to join her playboy fiancé in New York. Broke, she has to take a handout from Peter Warne (Clark Gable), a tough but fundamentally decent reporter also heading for New York. He has just lost his job and sees in this spoiled brat the makings of a scoop. When their bus is halted by torrential rain, they share a single motel room (a blanket hung between their beds: "The Walls of Jericho"). They bamboozle her father's detectives and hitchhike on together (Ellie showing her gumption and her legs to stop a car when Peter can't). Their class-rooted hostility gives way to love, encouraged in the end by Ellie's father (Walter Connolly) who, having made his millions by the sweat of his brow, knows a good man when he sees one.

Some contemporary critics (and many since) were appalled by the "wish-fulfillment" involved in this transformation of a bullying tycoon into a good fairy, a trick that recurs in other Capra comedies. In fact, Capra was by no means the only 1930s director guilty of this particular fantasy. As Andrew Bergman writes, the "cold-eyed, suspicious and edgy" comedy of 1930–1933 gave way in the mid-1930s to "a comedy at once warm and healing" which sought to reconcile the irreconcilable, creating "an America of perfect unity" in which "all classes are one." The "screwball comedies" of the Depression were escapist variations on the American Dream, but they probably meant well and were certainly well-received, proving, as Bergman says, "a bonanza" for Hollywood.

It Happened One Night won Oscars for best film, screenplay, director, actor, and actress— the first movie to be so comprehensively honored. It was the great hit of 1934, making the names and the fortunes of Capra, Columbia, Colbert, and Gable, and inspiring countless imitations. It owed its success to its pace and invention, its good-humored wit, its amiable eroticism, and its kindly observation of a great gallery of American types and characters encountered between Florida and New York. The picture has been called a picaresque, an early road movie, and (by Robert Stebbins) "the classic genteel romantic story" in which "the rich girl gives up her rebellious freedom for the pleasure of the hero's wit and imagination" and the hero, in exchange for the girl, "weds his vitality and vision to the dominant social class." But, Stebbins says, "Capra and Riskin brought as much to the genteel formula story as they took from it. Above all they took it out of the drawing rooms of the rich and filled it with the settings and people of everyday life."

Broadway Bill, another screwball comedy, this time about horse players, was also released in 1934 and was also a hit. But at this stage in his career Capra arrived at a new conception of his role. No longer content simply to entertain, he decided that he must use his mastery of the Hollywood entertainment machine to convey a message to the American public: "My films must let every man, woman, and child know that God loves them, that I love them, and that peace and salvation will become a reality only when they all learn to love each other." This revelation Capra attributes in a much-quoted anecdote to a "faceless little man" introduced to him during a period of illness by a Christian Scientist friend. His visitor, whose name he never learned, pointed out that he was able to "talk to hundreds of millions, for two hours—and in the dark. The talents you have, Mr. Capra, are not your own, not self-acquired. God gave you those talents; they are His gifts to you, to use for His purpose."

Capra embodied his message in a series of films, all but one of them written by Riskin, which Richard Griffith has labeled "fantasies of goodwill," and which in fact bear a strong resemblance in mood and structure to an earlier Capra-Riskin collaboration, *American Madness.* The first (and for many the best) of the series was *Mr. Deeds Goes to Town* (1936). Longfellow Deeds (Gary Cooper) lives in a small town called Mandrake Falls and is happy. He writes greeting card verses, plays the tuba in the town band, and is captain of the volunteer fire department. Then an eccentric uncle dies and leaves him a vast fortune, and he goes off reluctantly to live in his mansion in New York. There Deeds demonstrates his moral and intellectual superiority to the city slickers and phony intellectuals who try to shake him down. But Babe Bennett (Jean Arthur), star reporter of the *Gazette,* masquerading as an out-of-work stenographer, cheats her way into his household and writes a series of inside stories that present him as a dim-witted yokel. This does not prevent her from falling in love with him, and he reciprocates until he discovers her real identity.

Deeds is about to go home to the sanity and decency of Mandrake Falls when a dispossessed farmer forces his way into the mansion and tries to shoot him, enraged because he is sitting on millions while others starve. Much moved, Deeds decides to spend his fortune on small farms for the landless. He is promptly taken into custody, indicted by his rapacious lawyers as a lunatic. In a brilliantly contrived trial scene he establishes his sanity, gets the girl, and secures the farmers their land.

Longfellow Deeds is a character of real originality (as well as what one critic calls "the

Wasp's idealized image of himself"). The film contains some love scenes of great freshness and charm; it also provides (in Jean Arthur) a telling example of the "reactive character"—-in Stephen Handzo's opinion "a · key to Capra's cinema." As Handzo says, "for a director who walks a slack tightrope between the ridiculous and the sublime, the reactive character anticipates audience skepticism and enables Capra to undercut his own sentimentality (and perhaps express his own qualms) . . . What William S. Pechter calls the quality of 'irreducible foolishness' in Capra's heroes necessitates someone else with whom the audience can identify—like experienced, commonsensical Jean Arthur, the hero's simultaneous confidante and betrayer. If a sophisticated newspaperwoman can be 'converted,' the audience must succumb to the suspension of disbelief." Capra's "*Saturday Evening Post* socialism" was decried by intellectuals, but the "little people" beloved of Mr. Deeds loved the movie and so did most of its reviewers. It bought Capra a second Oscar and was another box-office smash. Only Alistair Cooke observed that the director was "starting to make movies about themes instead of people." *Lost Horizon* (1937), based on James Hilton's sentimental utopian fantasy, was not about anything worth discussing but cost two million dollars and added "Shangri-La" to the language as the quintessential escapist haven.

The American mythology created by Capra and Riskin was even more explicit in *You Can't Take It With You* (1938), a whimsical celebration of creative eccentricity derived from the Kaufman-Hart stage play. Grandpa Vanderhof (Lionel Barrymore) talks to God man-to-man while his son-in-law makes fireworks in the cellar with the iceman (who called seven years earlier and couldn't tear himself away). A daughter happily writes unpublishable novels and a granddaughter practices ballet as she sets the table. This American Shangri-La is threatened by the monstrous King Kirby (Edward Arnold), who wants the site for a munitions factory, much to the shame of his son (James Stewart) who loves one of the Vanderhof granddaughters (Jean Arthur). Love and pacifism triumph when the fearsome Kirby is converted by the irresistible Vanderhofs to harmonica-playing euphoria. "It sounds awful," wrote Graham Greene, "but it isn't as awful as all that, for Capra has a touch of genius . . . We may groan and blush as he cuts his way remorselessly through all finer values to the fallible human heart, but infallibly he makes his appeal." The movie took two Oscars and, according to some accounts, was the most profitable of all Capra's films.

Mr. Smith Goes to Washington (1939) centers on another of Capra's embodiments of small-town idealism and naive eccentricity. Jefferson Smith (James Stewart) is head of the Boy Rangers, and when crooked politicians send him to the Senate he communicates with his mother by carrier pigeon. The grafters want him up front in Washington because they assume he will be too dumb to rock their crooked boat, but he is not and does, with the help of his enchanting and disenchanted secretary (Jean Arthur). The villains manipulate the press to discredit Smith, but he fights back with a twenty-three hour filibuster that is the equivalent of the trial scene in *Mr. Deeds,* and just as brilliantly managed. Its Lincolnesque echoes so move a corrupted Senator (Claude Rains) that he attempts suicide and then publicly confesses his betrayal of the people's trust. Euphoria is general, but as carping critics pointed out, nothing has happened to end the political and press corruption that the movie so vividly illustrates. For many, nevertheless, it is "a great film," perfectly paced and magnificently acted by a cast that includes Edward Arnold, Eugene Pallette, Guy Kibbee, Thomas Mitchell, and Harry Carey (unforgettable as the Vice President).

Mr. Smith was Capra's last movie for Columbia; for his next he set up his own production company, Frank Capra Productions, with Riskin as his partner. *Meet John Doe* (1941) has been the most controversial of the Capra-Riskin movies. Its hero, Long John Willoughby, is not a small-town idealist but a former baseball player on the bum. He is selected as a representative common man in a cynical stunt dreamed up by a newspaperwoman (Barbara Stanwyck), but then discovers that he really is "John Doe"—a common denominator able to capture the imagination of ordinary Americans. When John Doe Clubs start springing up all over the country a fascistic publisher (Edward Arnold) recognizes in the movement a road to power. Willoughby, finding himself caught up in this scheme and aware that he is leading millions of John Does to disaster, decides on suicide. Having got this far, Capra and Riskin could find no satisfactory way to end the movie: "You can't kill Gary Cooper." In the version they wound up with, Willoughby is talked out of martyrdom by Barbara Stanwyck and a deputation of his followers to become an American Christ uncrucified and live happily ever after.

Meet John Doe, made at the end of the isolationist period when war with the Axis seemed imminent, has been taken as a deliberate reaffirmation of American values, but one that reveals a surprising uncertainty about their survival and perhaps even about their nature. Andrew Sarris has gone further than most to make the last point, saying that Capra here "crossed the line between populist sentimentality and populist demagoguery," embodying in Gary Cooper "a barefoot fascist, suspicious of all ideas and all doctrines, but believing in the innate conformism of the common man." For Richard Glazer, the film is an autobiographical one, reflecting Capra's own uncertainties: "Long John's accidental transformation from drifter to national figure parallels Capra's own early drifting experience and subsequent involvement in moviemaking . . . *Meet John Doe,* then, was an attempt to work out his own fears and questions." These arguments have drawn attention away from the picture's stylistic achievements, but Stephen Handzo has discussed the crowd scenes like the John Doe Rally, in which "the camera tracks through row upon row of singing, rain-soaked conventioneers, and provides a 'set piece' of political spectacle equaling *Potemkin* or *Triumph of the Will.* As the convention turns into a riot, a wet newspaper thrown at Cooper streaks the headline 'John Doe a Fake' across his face . . . One wonders if Capra isn't too perfect and deliberate for modern taste."

During World War II Capra made a number of propaganda films for the War Department. Admired to the point of adulation at the time, some of them (like *The Negro Soldier*) have since been condemned as stereotyped or even racist. Capra's own "Why We Fight" series is on the whole better balanced, and the effectiveness of these documentaries as hard-hitting propaganda has been widely recognized: Churchill called them the most powerful "statement of our cause" that he had ever encountered. Capra, who began the war as a major, ended it as a colonel, earning a DSM and the Legion of Merit, and becoming an officer of the Order of the British Empire.

After the war Capra set up a new production company, Liberty Films Incorporated, which as it turned out made only one movie, *It's a Wonderful Life* (1946). George Bailey (James Stewart), who wants to get out in the world and do great things, instead steps aside for others, passes up his chances, and winds up no more than a good man in a small town. The time comes when it seems to him that he has failed even here and that his family and the world in general would be better off without him. At that point, James Agee wrote, "an angel named Clarence shows him what his family, friends, and town would have been like if he hadn't been [born] . . . The story is somewhere near as effective, of its kind, as *A Christmas Carol.* In particular, the hero is extravagantly well played by James Stewart." However, Agee had his misgivings, which cen-

tered on the film's refusal to face the fact that "evil is intrinsic in each individual." Richard Griffith agreed, writing that the movie's "study of dog-eat-dog methods in business is so carefully rendered, so grimly accurate . . . that one demands a solution, or an ending, equally realistic." Nevertheless, Griffith thought that "Capra's way with incident and situation has never been more brilliant, his understanding and mastery of the film medium is more complete than ever." This is Capra's own favorite among his films and Griffith called it "one of the most personal visions ever realized in commercial cinema."

There was much less enthusiasm for *State of the Union* (1948), adapted from a Pulitzer Prize–winning drama by Howard Lindsay and Russel Crouse. Spencer Tracy plays a wealthy politician who accepts nomination for the Presidency, then realizes that he is being used as a front by corrupt industrialists and makes a public confession to the people in a radio broadcast before leaving politics. The film was released by MGM, Capra having by then sold Liberty Films to Paramount. Stephen Handzo found it "tempting to connect Spencer Tracy's fall from grace . . . with Capra's sell-out of his figurative and literal Liberty to a major studio," and indeed Capra mde his own public confession in his autobiography, *The Name Above the Title* (1971): "I fell never to rise to be the same man again either as a person or a talent . . . I lost my nerve . . . for fear of losing a few bucks."

In fact, none of Capra's subsequent movies had much success. They included two remakes of earlier hits: *Riding High* (1950), a new version of *Broadway Bill,* and *A Pocketful of Miracles* (1961), the most interesting of Capra's late films, and the last of them. A remake of *Lady for a Day,* it was a multiple corporation venture that Capra produced as well as directed, though with little of his former freedom. It failed at the box office and had a generally poor press, Andrew Sarris finding it "disastrously but touchingly dated." All the same, it had its admirers, like William S. Pechter, who pointed out that it had "the greatest array of character actors assembled since the thirties" and a bravura performance by Bette Davis as Apple Annie. Pechter called it "a truly subversive work" that "defies criticism; almost, one might say, defies art. It is one of the funniest and one of the bleakest, as well as being one of the most technically adroit films ever made." He says that the audience he saw it with "laughed at the comedy and cried at the pathos as at no other film of my recent experience . . . How one aches for the simple innocence of the world on the screen."

In the typical Capra movie, as Richard Griffith has pointed out, "a messianic innocent . . . pits himself against the forces of entrenched greed. His inexperience defeats him strategically, but his gallant integrity in the face of temptation calls forth the goodwill of the 'little people,' and through their combined protest, he triumphs." During the golden age of Hollywood, Capra's "fantasies of goodwill" made him one of the two or three most famous and successful directors in the world. However, beginning in the late 1950s, when the *Cahiers du Cinéma* critics in France launched an *auteurist* reassessment of the American film, his reputation declined sharply. It seems surprising that the *Cahiers* critics had so little regard for a director who was so completely the "author" of his films—one of the few to have his "name above the title" in the credits and advertising and to win complete artistic control over his work. John Raeburn suggests that Capra's best films were unknown to the French—too quintessentially American to be exportable. The *Cahiers* disciples in the United States were more aggressively negative, however, mostly on political grounds. Capra was accused of grossly oversimplifying and sentimentalizing serious political and social issues, and of a belief in "the tyranny of the majority."

Ten years later, it was clear that this trend had reversed itself. Post-*auteurist* critics once more acclaimed Capra as a cinematic master, and perhaps more surprisingly, young people packed Capra festivals and revivals on campuses all over the United States. As John Raeburn writes, it was once more recognized that "for all their devotion to middle-class life, Capra's films are saved from emotional thinness and vapid sentimentality by, on the one hand, a limited but omnipresent vein of social criticism and, on the other, by the director's skill in animating and making credible an ideal conception of American national character . . . There is a strong libertarian streak in Capra's films, a distrust of power wherever it occurs and in whomever it is invested." Young people are won over by the fact that his heroes "are uninterested in wealth" and "are characterized by a vigorous . . . individualism, a zest for experience, and a keen sense of political and social justice . . . Capra's heroes, in short, are ideal types, created in the image of a powerful national myth."

There is always a degree of improvisation in Capra's work. He went onto the set with a script written in master scenes only: "What you need is what the scene is about, who does what to whom, and who cares about whom . . . All I want is a master scene and I'll take care of the rest—how to shoot it, how to keep the machinery out of the way, and how to focus attention on the actors at all times." In this almost casual way, Capra produced movies of great but unobtrusive craftsmanship—unobtrusive because he thought it was bad directing to distract the audience with fancy technical gimmicks. William S. Pechter describes Capra's style as one "of almost classical purity; and it seems somehow appropriate to the American ethos of casual abundance that the director of quite possibly the greatest technical genius in the Hollywood film, post-Griffith, pre-Hitchcock—a genius, as Richard Griffith has suggested, on the order of those of the silent Russian cinema at its zenith—should have placed his great gifts at the service of an apparently frivolous kind of comedy."

Pechter maintains that Capra's style is based on editing, "since it depends for its effect on a sustained sequence of rhythmic motion . . . But whereas Eisenstein's complex and intricate editing seems, finally, to attempt to impose movement on material which is essentially static, Capra's has the effect of imposing order on images constantly in motion, imposing order on chaos. The end of all this is indeed a kind of beauty, a beauty of controlled motion, more like dancing than painting, but more like the movies than like anything else . . . There is always a gap between what Capra wishes to say and what he actually succeeds in saying. He seems obsessed with certain American social myths but he observes that society itself as a realist . . . His films move at a breathtaking clip: dynamic, driving, taut, at their extreme even hysterical; the unrelenting, frantic acceleration of pace seems to spring from the release of some tremendous accumulation of pressure. The sheer speed and energy seem, finally, less calculated than desperate, as though Capra were aware, on some level, of the tension established between his material and what he attempts to make of it."

Frank Capra was married in 1923 to Helen Howell, an actress. They were divorced in 1928, and in 1933 Capra married Lucille Warner, by whom he has had a daughter and three sons, one of whom died in infancy. Capra has been four times president of the Academy of Motion Picture Arts and Sciences and three times president of the Screen Directors' Guild, which he helped to found and which, under his presidency, did much to secure a degree of artistic control for Hollywood directors. Capra once nursed an ambition to teach science and in a sense fulfilled that ambition during the late 1950s, when he made some educational TV films for the Bell System Science Series. A short, stocky, vigorous man, formerly devoted to hunting, fishing, and mountain climbing, he now contents himself with strumming his guitar and "collecting rejection slips" for his songs and short stories. He won a reputation for fierce independence in his dealings with Harry Cohn and other front-office tyrants, but on set was said to be gentle and considerate, "a director who displays absolutely no exhibitionism."

FILMS: Fultah Fisher's Boarding House, 1922 (short); (with Harry Edwards) Tramp, Tramp, Tramp, 1926; The Strong Man, 1926; Long Pants, 1927; For the Love of Mike, 1927; That Certain Thing, 1928; So This Is Love, 1928; The Matinee Idol, 1928; The Way of the Strong, 1928; Say It With Sables, 1928; Submarine, 1928; The Power of the Press, 1928; The Donovan Affair, 1929; The Younger Generation, 1929; Flight, 1929; Ladies of Leisure, 1930; Rain or Shine, 1930; Dirigible, 1931; The Miracle Woman, 1931; Platinum Blonde, 1932; Forbidden, 1932; American Madness, 1932; The Bitter Tea of General Yen, 1933; Lady for a Day, 1933; It Happened One Night, 1934; Broadway Bill, 1934; Mr. Deeds Goes to Town, 1936; Lost Horizon, 1937; You Can't Take It With You, 1938; Mr. Smith Goes to Washington, 1939; Meet John Doe, 1941; Arsenic and Old Lace, 1944; It's a Wonderful Life, 1946; State of the Union (U.K., The World and His Wife), 1948; Riding High, 1950; Here Comes the Groom, 1951; A Hole in the Head, 1959; A Pocketful of Miracles, 1961. *Wartime Propaganda Films: The "Why We Fight" Series*—Prelude to War, 1942; The Nazis Strike, 1943; Divide and Conquer, 1943; The Battle of Britain, 1943; The Battle of Russia, 1944; The Battle of China, 1944; War Comes to America, 1945. *Other Wartime Propaganda Films*—Know Your Ally: Britain, 1944; The Negro Soldier, 1944; Tunisian Victory, 1944; Know Your Enemy: Japan, 1945; Know Your Enemy: Germany, 1945; Two Down—One to Go, 1945. *TV Educational Films*—Our Mr. Sun, 1956; Hemo the Magnificent, 1957; The Strange Case of the Cosmic Rays, 1957. *Published Scripts*: You Can't Take It with You *and* Lady for a Day *in* Noble, L. (ed.) Four Star Scripts, 1936; Mr. Smith Goes to Washington *in* Wald, J. and Macauley, R. (eds.) The Best Pictures: 1939–1940, 1940; Meet John Doe *in* Thomas, S. (ed.) Best American Screenplays, 1987.

ABOUT: Capra, F. The Name Above the Title: An Autobiography, 1971; Carney, R. American Vision: The Films of Frank Capra, 1986; Current Biography, 1948; Glatzer, R. and Raeburn, J. (eds.) Frank Capra: The Man and His Films, 1975; Griffith, R. Frank Capra, 1950; Hovland, C. I. (and others) Experiments on Mass Communication: 3, 1949; MacCann, R. D. The People's Films, 1973; Mast, G. The Comic Mind, 1973; Poague, L. The Cinema of Frank Capra: An Approach to Film Comedy, 1975; Shales, T. American Film Heritage, 1972; Who's Who in America, 1978–1979; Willis, D. C. The Films of Frank Capra, 1974. American Film October 1978; Cinéaste Summer 1977; Film Comment November–December 1972 (Capra issue); Film Society Review February 1972; Films and Filming September 1960, September 1962; Focus on Film 27 1977; Journal of Popular Film Summer 1974; New York Times June 24, 1971; Penguin Film Review September 1948; Saturday Evening Post May 14, 1938; Sight and Sound Summer 1972; Take One September 1975.

*CARNÉ, MARCEL (ALBERT) (August 18, 1909–), French director and critic, was born in Paris—in Montmartre, where he grew up. He is the son of Paul Carné, a cabinetmaker, and Marie Racouët. His father got him a job with an insurance company, but Carné was intent on a career in the cinema and went to evening classes in cinematography given by the Association Philomatique, an institution sponsored by the Paris city council. In 1928, without telling his father, he left the insurance company to work as assistant cameraman on Jacques Feyder's *Les Nouveaux Messieurs* (1928) and Richard Oswald's *Cagliostro* (1929). Carné made his own first film in collaboration with a well-known amateur named Michel Sanvoisin. This was *Nogent, Eldorado du Dimanche* (*Nogent, the Sunday Eldorado*, 1929), a lyrical little silent documentary about Parisian working people enjoying their Sunday afternoon in the country. The following year Carné worked as one of René Clair's two assistant directors on *Sous les toits de Paris*.

Meanwhile Carné had entered a competition organized by *Cinémagazine* for the best film criticism written by an amateur. He won the competition and from 1929 to 1933 was a regular contributor to *Cinémagazine*, also writing for *Cinémonde* (edited by his friend and roommate Maurice Bessy) and other journals, sometimes under the pseudonym "Albert Cranche." During this period Carné made a number of short advertising films in collaboration with the writer Jean Aurenche and the animator Paul Grimault. He also served briefly as editor of the weekly *Hebdo-film* but resigned when the proprietor made him publish a negative article about Chaplin's *City Lights*.

In any case, Carné was more interested in making films than reviewing them, and in 1933 he became permanent assistant director to Jacques Feyder (Carné says "I owe him everything"). He worked with Feyder on three of the director's best films—*Le Grand Jeu* (1934), *Pension Mimosas* (1935), and *La Kermesse héroïque* (1935). When Feyder went to England to make *Knight Without Armor* for Korda, he arranged for Carné to direct a film he was to have made, *Jenny* (1936). It stars Feyder's wife Françoise Rosay as the manager of a shady nightclub whose lover, the reluctant gangster Lucien (Albert Préjean), falls in love with her daughter (Lisette Lanvin).

In spite of its melodramatic plot, Carné's first feature is of great interest, showing that he already possessed an exceptional talent for visual narrative and characterization, and a predilection for misty and tenebrous backgrounds. His great ability as a director of actors was apparent in his handling of a cast that also included Jean-

°kär´nā

MARCEL CARNÉ

Louis Barrault, Roger Blin, and Charles Vanel. *Jenny* began Carné's fertile partnership with the poet and scenarist Jacques Prévert, coauthor of the script (from a novel by Pierre Rocher) and author of the skillful dialogue.

It was followed by *Drôle de drame* (*Bizarre, Bizarre*, 1937), a fantastic farce set in London and played by another brilliant cast. The hectic plot involves an impoverished bourgeois couple (Michel Simon and Françoise Rosay), a bishop who secretly writes the thrillers he attacks in his sermons (Louis Jouvet), a lunatic who murders butchers (Jean-Louis Barrault), and a young milkman (Jean-Pierre Aumont) falsely accused of murder. Some critics have detected a prophetically Absurdist note in Prévert's insolently implausible script, and the film has been revived in recent years with great success. The witty sets, representing a shamelessly bogus London, were by Alexander Trauner, who became Carné's regular designer, and the score was by Maurice Jaubert, who provided music for some of the director's best films.

However, it is as a master of the melancholy tradition of poetic realism that Carné is (or was) revered—poignant stories about decent people ill-used by fate (and its human instruments) who find a brief interlude of happiness through love before destiny sweeps them apart forever. The emergence of this despairing mode in France in the late 1930s has been attributed to the growing threat of war, coupled with the failure of the Popular Front. Certainly there is a strong populist elements in these films—Carné asserted his preference for stories about "the simple life of ordinary people" rather than "the overheated ambience of dance parties."

The first of the Prévert-Carné films in this manner was *Quai des brumes* (*Port of Shadows,* 1938), which stars Jean Gabin as a deserter from a French colonial regiment who finds refuge in a squalid inn on the mist-shrouded harbor at Le Havre. There he meets a girl (Michèle Morgan) who has run away from her evil guardian Zabel (Michel Simon). They fall in love and spend a single night together. The next day the soldier kills Zabel in a fight. He is preparing to leave on a ship bound for Brazil when he is shot dead by the gangster Lucien (Pierre Brasseur). The ship sails without Gabin, just as it does in Duvivier's *Pépé-le-Moko*: in the films of poetic realism, the dream of escape to a happier life in a better place is always only a dream. Jean Quéval wrote that "unity of action, space, and time contrives to give this film a classical finish, found for the first time in Carné's work. The images have as much narrative weight as the dialogue, the editing reveals a close, effective relationship (not at first perceptible) between words and images. The atmosphere is strangely unreal and fascinating, and the personalities of Jean Gabin and Michèle Morgan convey a kind of supplementary fascination to their actual portrayals."

The "strangely unreal and fascinating" atmosphere owes a great deal to Trauner's sets—this film, like almost all of Carné's pictures apart from his first documentary, was shot entirely in the studio. And yet at the beginning of his career he had been one of the most vocal advocates of location shooting, writing in 1932 that he could not see "without irritation the current cinema shutting itself away, fleeing from life in order to delight in sets and artificiality." It was evidently the desire for complete artistic control that won Carné over to filming in the studio, where he could plan his camera movements and lighting effects with absolute confidence. Speaking perhaps of *Quai des Brumes* he said, "Before shooting a film I prepare my palette. Then I see to it that everything is done in the same shade, always bearing in mind the main idea of the work. . . . One must compose images as the old masters did their canvases, with the same preoccupation with effect and expression. Cinema images have the same needs."

There is actually a happy ending for the young lovers Pierre and Renée in *Hôtel du Nord* (1938), though the film begins with their botched attempt at suicide in a cheap hotel by the Canal Saint-Martin. It is Edmond, a middle-aged man with a dubious past, who dies when his hope of happiness with Renée evaporates. Once again Carné showed his gift for assembling a cast of extraordinary ability—Louis Jouvet, Arletty, Annabella, Jean-Pierre Aumont, Bernard Blier, François Perier. The picture was admired for its acting, for the naturalistic photography of the canal and its surroundings (reconstructed by Trauner), and for such notable set-pieces as the dancing in the street at the end, but most critics thought it seriously weakened by its shapeless plot and anecdotal structure. The script, based on a populist novel by Eugène Dabit, was written not by Prévert but by Henri Jeanson and Jean Aurenche.

Le Jour se lève (*Daybreak*), which followed in 1939, is the quintessential achievement of "poetic realism." It begins with the fatal shooting of a man on the fourth floor of a workers' tenement in an industrial suburb of Paris. His killer, François, barricades himself in his room, the police surround the house, and a siege begins. François (Jean Gabin), trapped in a room intermittently raked by police bullets, spends the long night remembering the circumstances that brought him there. A steelworker, he had fallen in love with a flower-seller (Jacqueline Laurent), and for a while they had been happy. Then the girl becomes infatuated with Valentin, a music-hall dog-trainer, and François himself has a casual affair with Valentin's assistant Clara (Arletty). The half-mad sadomasochist Valentin, portrayed by Jules Berry as one of the most obscenely despicable villains in all cinema, visits François and taunts him with hints about the flower girl's sexual dependence on him. François, goaded beyond endurance, shoots him. These recollections have brought us back to the hopeless present. François smokes his last cigarette and then shoots himself. The room fills with police teargas. Day breaks and light floods in through the fumes, over broken glass, a teddy bear, a brooch, a cigarette packet, some photographs—a few objects summarizing a life in which no sun will rise again. The dead man's cheap alarm clock begins insistently to ring.

It has been said that Carné has the talents of a producer as well as a director, in that his best films owe much to his genius for selecting and harnessing exceptional talents. This is nowhere more true than in *Le Jour se lève*. The film's unsurpassed use of flashback, brilliantly executed by Carné, was first structured by Prévert, who is also responsible for what Quéval calls the "almost Jansenist division of the world into good and bad people." And the charged, poetic simplicity of Prévert's dialogue would seem incongruous if Trauner's splendid expressionistic sets had not already removed this ostensibly naturalistic film some way from realism. (Presumably Trauner was also partly responsible for the way the sets, and individual objects within the sets, are used again and again to reveal aspects of their owners' characters and social backgrounds.) Jaubert's inventive score, the perfectly

calculated rhythms of the camera movements, the exact balancing of character against character—Carné welds all of the elements of the film into a seamlessly coherent and powerfully persuasive vision of a world in which human love is inevitably defeated by the blind forces of evil, though the sun also rises.

Arletty was as warmly praised for her "superbly casual" performance as Jules Berry was for the disgusting brilliance of his, but it was Gabin's contribution that has been most widely discussed. André Bazin described him as "the tragic hero of the contemporary cinema. With every new Gabin film the cinema rewinds the infernal machine of his destiny—just as in *Le Jour se lève*, that night, as on every night, he winds up the alarm clock whose ironic and cruel ringing will sound at daybreak the hour of his death."

Le Jour se lève was almost universally recognized as a great film, and it established Carné as a dominant figure—along with René Clair and Jean Renoir—in the French cinema. There was an international outcry when RKO attempted to buy and destroy all prints of the picture to make way for Anatole Litvak's mediocre postwar remake, *The Long Night*. However, during the German occupation of France a school of thought emerged in Vichy circles that blamed Carné's fatalistic films, together with the works of Gide, Cocteau, Proust, and others, for encouraging "defeatism" and thus hastening or even causing the fall of France. Carné replied that the artist must be the barometer of his times, and it was not the barometer's fault if it foretold the coming storm. Nevertheless, these criticisms no doubt contributed to the fact that Carné made only two films during the Occupation, both of them set in the past to avoid the need for any overt comment on ugly contemporary realities.

Les Visiteurs du soir (*The Devil's Envoys*, 1942) deals with the basic Carné-Prévert theme—the struggle between good and evil—in terms of a medieval morality play. The devil's envoys (Alain Cuny and Arletty) arrive at a baronial banquet intent on creating emotional anarchy. They succeed until one of them falls genuinely in love, but after that the devil himself (Jules Berry) is powerless to separate the two lovers; he changes them into statues, but their hearts continue to beat. Some critics have seen in this elegant, soberly designed, rather static film a covert attack on the evils of the Occupation itself, and a promise that France would survive.

It was followed by a picture that some place above even *Le Jour se lève* in Carné's oeuvre, *Les Enfants du paradis* (*The Children of Paradise*). It is set in Paris in the 1840s, when melodrama and pantomime were the most popular forms of entertainment, and the Boulevard de Crime—the theatre district—lived up to its name. The plot centers on the beautiful Garance (Arletty), who in the course of the film is loved by the witty and dandified murderer Lacenaire (Marcel Herrand), the rising young mime Baptiste Deburau (Jean-Louis Barrault), and the great tragedian Frédéric Lemaître (Pierre Brasseur)—all historical figures—as well as the wealthy Compte de Montray (Louis Salou). The action takes place mostly in the theatres of the Boulevard or in the crowded streets outside, among the tumblers and jugglers and vendors. The story is too complicated to describe in detail, but it emerges in the end that Garance, who loves only Baptiste, will not separate him from his family or his métier, and they lose each other among the carnival crowds on the Boulevard de Crime.

Work began on this ambitious and expensive film in August 1943 and continued, with interruptions, for nearly two years. There were armies of extras, and Trauner's magnificent reconstruction of the Boulevard de Crime alone cost more than five million francs. (Trauner's contribution to the film had to be clandestine, as did that of Joseph Kosma, who provided the brilliantly evocative score: both were of Jewish descent, and Kosma later paid tribute to Carné courage in employing him during this period.) Arletty's performance as Garance—intelligent, passionate, but with a mysterious underlying melancholy—was the finest of her career; Richard Roud calls it "one of the greatest portraits of a woman in all cinema. . . . a performance for the ages."

Few historical films so convincingly evoke a period and a milieu. It was immediately recognized as a masterpiece, but to many critics it seemed a flawed one. Jean Mitry said that it was "a very great film as much in its scope as in its ambitions, but it is a very great film that has misfired." It had done so, he thought, because of a radical change in the relationship between Carné and Prévert (who provided the witty and poetic dialogue, and also the rather sprawling and shapeless plot): "In the past . . . Carné had the upper hand in the breakdown into the shooting script and in the cinematographic construction of the film. . . . [Now] it is Prévert who conceives the subject of the film, who develops it, writes the continuity and often breaks it down into an extremely detailed form. . . . They are no longer Carné's films with dialogue by Prévert, but Prévert's films directed by Carné" and "the visuals serve only to illustrate a story whose development is never indicated except in words." There is truth in this, but, imperfect and

uneven as it is, *Les Enfants du paradis* has a vigor and humanity that continue to earn it a place on any list of the classics of the cinema.

None of Carné's postwar fims equaled the best of his earlier work, and the first of them was a disaster. *Les Portes de la nuit* (*Gates of the Night*, 1946), conceived as a vehicle for Gabin and Dietrich, had to make do with the inexperienced Yves Montand and Nathalie Nattier in a Prévert story (based on a ballet) about collaborators and black marketeers in postwar Paris, with Destiny intervening in the shape of a battered vagabond (Jean Vilar). Impatient reactions to the picture made it clear that the public mood had changed. As Penelope Houston wrote, "fatalism began to look like affectation. We had been there once too often." What is more, the movie had been made with a staggering and pointless extravagance that damaged Carné's reputation within the industry. His next film, *La Fleur de l'âge,* begun in 1946, had to be abandoned when it overran its budget. This abortive project was Carné's last collaboration with Jacques Prévert.

After that, Carné made no more pictures for three years. His fortunes began to revive a little with *La Marie du Port* (1950), based on a Simenon story and adapted (like most of his later films) by Carné himself in collaboration with another scenarist. It starred Jean Gabin in a new kind of role, as a wealthy Cherbourg *hotelier* trapped by a calculating woman. A polished and atmospheric piece, financially very modest and with none of the fatalistic overtones of poetic realism, it is a good film but a minor one. *Juliette ou La Clef des songes* (1951) was closer to Carné's old style—a fantasy in which a young convict dreams of escape to a magical world in search of his beloved. Released from prison, he loses his girl and elects to return as a suicide to the dream world. The film has sets by Trauner and music by Kosma—both working for Carné for the last time—but neither these nor Gérard Philipe's attractive performance in the lead could rescue it from banality.

One of the most admired of Carné's postwar films was *Thérèse Raquin* (1953), adapted from Zola's novel by Carné and Charles Spaak and set in present-day Lyons. In Carné's version of the story it is not social forces but a malevolent destiny that controls the lives of Thérèse (Simone Signoret) and her lover (Raf Vallone). Roy Armes wrote that "Carné's handling of composition and editing is assured as always and nowhere more strikingly displayed than in the death of the blackmailer which forms the film's ironic climax." There was an excellent performance as the blackmailer from Roland Lesaffre, who had become a regular member of Carné's team. He appeared again as a young boxer in *L'Air de Paris* (1954), which starred Gabin and Arletty in an undistinguished piece about a retired fighter and the young hopeful he trains for the championship. *Les Tricheurs* (1958), an old-fashioned "exposé" of the sins of modern youth, also had a notable cast (including Jean-Paul Belmondo, Laurent Terzieff, and Jacques Charrier) and enjoyed a considerable financial success. Carné's later films have been routine, perhaps the best of them being *Trois Chambres à Manhattan* (1965), another modest and convincing Simenon adaptation.

It was fashionable for a time to attribute the abrupt decline in Carné's immense reputation to the end of his collaboration with Prévert, but this seems implausible. As Richard Roud points out, it was Prévert who wrote *Les Portes de la nuit*, the first and most spectacular of Carné's failures, while there were only a few successes among the films Prévert wrote for other directors. A more obvious explanation is that in the age of neorealism, improvisation, and political engagement, there was simply no place on the screen for Carné's sad vision of a world at the mercy of fate. He turned to other themes, but his heart was not in them.

Carné, who is unmarried, is an officer of the Légion d'honneur. He received the Prix Louis Delluc for his work as a whole in 1966 and the Grand Prix Oecuménique at Cannes in 1977.

FILMS: Nogent, Eldorado du Dimanche (Nogent, the Sunday Eldorado), 1929; Jenny, 1936; Drôle de drame (Bizarre, Bizarre), 1937; Quai des brumes (Port of Shadows), 1938; Hôtel du Nord, 1938; Le Jour se lève (Daybreak), 1939; Les Visiteurs du soir (The Devil's Envoys), 1942; Les Enfants du paradis (The Children of Paradise), 1945; Les Portes de la nuit (Gates of the Night), 1946; La Fleur de l'âge (The Flower of the Age), 1947 (unfinished); La Marie du Port, 1950; Juliette ou La Clef des songes (Juliet, or the Key to Dreams), 1951; Thérèse Raquin (The Adultress), 1953; L'Air de Paris (The Song of Paris), 1954; Le Pays d'où je viens (The Country Whence I Come), 1956; Les Tricheurs (The Cheats), 1958; Terrain vague (Wasteland), 1960; Du mouron pour les petits oiseaux (Some Chickweed for the Little Birds), 1963; Trois Chambres à Manhattan (Three Rooms in Manhattan), 1965; Les Jeunes Loups (The Young Wolves), 1968; La Force et le droit (Might and Right), 1970; Les Assassins de l'ordre (The Assassins of Order), 1971; La Merveilleuse Visite (The Wonderful Visit), 1974; Le Bible (The Bible), 1977.

ABOUT: Brunius, J. B. En marge du cinéma français, 1954 (France); Carné, M. La vie à belles dents: souvenirs, 1957 (France); Chazal, R. Marcel Carné, 1965 (France); Chiarette, T. (ed.) Clair, Carné, Duvivier, 1967 (France); Jeanne, R. and Ford, C. Paris vu par le cinéma, 1961 (France); Landry, B.-G. Marcel Carné, 1952 (France); Lapierre, M. Aux portes de la nuit, 1946 (France); Leprohon, P. Présences contemporaines, cinéma, 1957 (France); Morandini, M. and Amico, G. Personale di Marcel Carné, 1960 (Italy); Quéval, J. Marcel Carné, 1950 (Britain); Who's Who in France, 1979–1980. *Periodicals*—Bianco e Nero December 1948; Cahiers de la Cinémathèque Winter 1972 (Carné issue); Film November–December 1959; Film Quarterly Summer 1959; Image et Son July 1952; Lettres Françaises March 1956.

CAVALCANTI, ALBERTO (Alberto de Almeida-Cavalcanti) (February 6, 1897–), Brazilian director, producer, scenarist, and art director, was born in Rio de Janeiro, the son of a distinguished mathematician of Italian descent. A precocious youth, he began law studies at the age of fifteen in Rio, where he was the youngest member of the university, but was soon expelled "because of a quarrel with an old professor." His father sent him to study architecture in Geneva, Switzerland, instructing him to stay away from politics and the law. When he was eighteen Cavalcanti moved on to Paris, where he at first worked as an architect's draftsman. Finding his income inadequate, he switched to interior decoration and then entered the film industry as a designer.

It was a time of productive ferment in the French cinema, the beginning of the "impressionist school" or "first avant-garde." Cavalcanti first attracted attention with his designs for three films by Marcel L'Herbier—the uncompleted *Résurrection* (1922); the extraordinary experiment *L'Inhumaine* (1923), which also employed the talents of Fernand Léger, Claude Autant-Lara, and Robert Mallet-Stevens; and *Feu Mathias Pascal* (1925), on which Cavalcanti worked with Lazare Meerson. He also served as art director of Louis Delluc's *L'Inondation* (1924), Jaque-Catelain's *La Galerie des monstres* (1924), and George Pearson's *The Little People* (1925), a British film made in France.

Interviewed by Elizabeth Sussex for *Sight and Sound* (Autumn 1975), Cavalcanti described the first avant-garde as a movement torn (and enlivened) by violent dispute: "We hated ourselves. . . . We couldn't bear any of the others. We had one thing in common and one only—we were in disagreement with our masters' art, the art of the people we were working for. I thought L'Herbier didn't face films to try to make them speak their own language. He tried to make films speak literature, and all our masters used films as kind of novels or plays. They weren't concerned in finding a language for films. We

ALBERTO CAVALCANTI

all had that in common: we thought there was a language, and that it must be searched for, it must be found." In retrospect, Cavalcanti suspects that this mutual disapproval was a healthy thing, and he goes on: "We had a trump card in our hands. We were friendly with all the great artists of our time in Paris—all the painters, sculptors, writers. They liked us and they helped us."

Cavalcanti made his own first films in 1926—*Le Train sans yeux,* which he adapted from a 1919 novel by Louis Delluc, and *Rien que les heures.* It was the latter that made his name, an impressionistic documentary shot on the streets of Paris and evoking a day and a night in the life of the city in a manner similar to Walter Ruttmann's more famous *Berlin,* which it preceded. *Rien que les heures* opens with a shot of elegant ladies descending a staircase. This action freezes, and then a pair of hands picks up the frozen frame and tears it into pieces, which become garbage on a street. There we first encounter the derelict old woman whose hobbling figure recurs throughout the film. The picture is full of such ingenious devices and employs superimpositions, split screen, wipes, and an assortment of other special effects, as well as a few dramatized scenes.

The film has been found inferior to *Berlin* in its technique—lacking the symphonic structure of Ruttmann's great documentary, utilizing less rich material, and marred by some heavy and unsuccessful attempts at social irony. Some critics prefer it all the same on account of its unsentimental feeling for the poor of Paris, who are observed with real sympathy (if not without a

certain surreal humor). Cavalcanti himself calls it "a social document about the lack of work, about the lives in miserable places," and it is still regarded as one of the more important achievements of the French avant-garde.

En rade (Sea Fever, 1927), in which a poor boy dreams of eloping over the seas to a happier life, is less well known than *Rien que les heures* but no less admired by those who have seen it, in spite of the slowness of its action. Produced by Pierre Braunberger, it was photographed (like all of Cavalcanti's early films) by Jimmy Rogers, and praised less for its slight story line than for the beauty of the compositions evoking the sea and the quays and ships of Marseilles.

Like some other members of the avant-garde (including René Clair and Jean Renoir), Cavalcanti during the late 1920s alternated privately sponsored experimental shorts with more accessible and commercial films, many of them literary adaptations. An excellent example of the latter sort was *Yvette* (1927), based on Maupassant's story and (like most of Cavalcanti's films at that time) starring Renoir's wife, Catherine Hessling. A notable by-product of this movie was *La P'tite Lili* (1927), shot during a three-day period when bad weather halted the filming of *Yvette.* It is a largely improvised and entirely delightful burlesque of a traditional song, with Catherine Hessling as a prostitute and Jean Renoir himself as her pimp. The camera lens was draped with coarse gauze to give the film something of the effect of an old sampler, or of a painting on rough canvas. Sound was added later, including a score contributed by Darius Milhaud.

After respectable adaptations of Molière (*La Jalousie du barbouillé*) and Gautier (*Le Capitaine Fracasse*) came Cavalcanti's first real talkie, *Le Petit Chaperon rouge* (1929). In this version of Little Red Riding Hood, Maurice Jaubert provided the music, Hessling was the heroine, and the wolf was played by her husband. Jacques Rivette has said that the film's "aesthetic" was that of "an orgy done *à la* Mack Sennett," but it seems possible that he was referring here to a parodic trailer for the picture made at the same time and called *Vous verrez la semaine prochaine.*

In the best of Cavalcanti's early films, like *Rien que les heures, En Rade,* and *Yvette,* Georges Sadoul found "descriptions of ordinary life allied to a somewhat melancholy poetic fantasy and the suggestion of an unattainable 'elsewhere'" which make him "an obvious forerunner of French poetic realism of the 1930s." Because of the constraints imposed by synchronized and single-track sound, his later French movies were on the whole more conventional. They included a series of French-language versions of Hollywood movies made for Paramount in 1930–1931—George Abbott's *Halfway to Heaven* (*À mi-chemin du ciel*), Edmund Goulding's *The Devil's Holiday* (*Les Vacances du diable*), Dorothy Arzner's *Sarah and Son* (*Toute sa vie*), and William Wellman's *Dangerous Paradise* (*Dans une île perdue*). A series of adaptations followed of French stage comedies like *Le Truc du Brésilien* (1932), *Le Mari garçon* (1933), and *Coralie et Cie* (1933).

These latter, Cavalcanti says, were "terrifically successful commercially" but "very primitive" in their use of sound. Sound greatly interested him, and in 1934, when John Grierson's General Post Office Film Unit in Britain acquired its own sound studios, he joined the Unit "to experiment with sound" and to pass on his expertise to Grierson's young disciples. Meaning to stay for a few weeks, he remained for seven years, as teacher, producer, and director.

The GPO Film Unit was established in 1933 as a successor to Grierson's Empire Marketing Board Film Unit. It was intended to publicize the GPO's services but made a number of films that had no perceptible connection with the work of the post office, as well as many that did. In the process it trained a talented generation of young filmmakers and established a documentary tradition of international influence and importance—a movement that revitalized the British film industry, in particular demonstrating that the working class was a fit subject for serious cinematic consideration (rather than for mere comic relief, as in the past).

There is a good deal of uncertainty about who actually did what in the great days of the GPO Film Unit, not least because the selfless enthusiasm engendered by Grierson made his followers careless about such trivia as credits. "We kept on putting on the names of the young people, not the names of the people who were concerned," Grierson said. "There were years when Cavalcanti's name never went on a picture. We weren't concerned with that aspect of things, with credits." The situation is further complicated by the fact that Grierson and Cavalcanti were somewhat at loggerheads, the austere and rather puritanical Grierson not altogether approving of Cavalcanti's delight in technical experiment and his surreal sense of poetry and humor.

Some of Grierson's disciples shared his attitude—John Taylor, for example, once declared that Cavalcanti "didn't understand what documentary was supposed to be doing." But it seems clear that the majority of Grierson's young men were full of admiration for "Cav," who had already acquired a world reputation as an avant-garde filmmaker and who became their self-effacing mentor and teacher, endlessly sympathetic to both their technical and their personal problems. Basil Wright says that Cavalcanti's "ideas about the use of sound were so liberating that they would liberate in you about a thousand other ideas," and Harry Watt believes that "the arrival of Cavalcanti in the GPO Film Unit was the turning point of British documentary. If I've had any success in films I put it down to my training from Cavalcanti, and I think a lot of other people should say the same thing." Elsewhere, Watt concludes that "while the ideas and inspiration of the British documentary movement came from Grierson, its style and quality came from Cavalcanti."

One of Cavalcanti's first experiments at the GPO was a fantasy called *Pett and Pott* (1934), designed to accustom the Unit to the use of its new sound-recording equipment. In fact the soundtrack was recorded first, the visuals being added afterwards. A great deal of talent was deployed in this surreal comedy—Basil Wright and Stuart Legg were assistant directors, John Taylor was cinematographer, Humphrey Jennings designed the sets, and the cast was made up of Wright, Jennings, and the German dancer and singer Valeska Gert (b. 1900), whose name runs like a colorful thread through the history of the cinema from 1925 to the late 1970s. The result was more of a curiosity that a work of art (and far from Grierson's notion of documentary).

Cavalcanti helped Basil Wright with the soundtrack of his poetic documentary *Song of Ceylon* (1934), though he maintains that his contribution to that fine film was slight; made a workmanlike short called *New Rates* (1934); and in 1935–1936 produced Norman McLaren's *Book Bargain*, Harry Watt's *Big Money*, Len Lye's *Rainbow Dance*, and Evelyn Spice's *Calendar of the Year*. The Film Unit (like the first avant-garde) often called on the talents of major artists from outside the cinema, and Cavalcanti's short documentary *Coalface* (1936) presented its facts and statistics in verse by W. H. Auden and to music by Benjamin Britten. The experiment was not satisfactory, uneasily combining a straightforward account of the processing and distribution of coal with bitter protest against the exploitation of the miners. R. M. Barsam found the film strident, and wrote that the "attempt to integrate choral singing, chanting, narration, and music do not reach . . . successful symphonic fusion."

The real importance of *Coalface* was as a trial

run for *Night Mail* (1936), arguably the most brilliant of all the products of the Film Unit. Directed by Basil Wright and Harry Watt, it follows an express mail train on a night run from London to Scotland. Learning from his earlier experiments, Cavalcanti (who is credited as sound director) here combined the rhythm of the locomotive's wheels, Auden's verse, and Britten's music to brilliant effect. Barsam writes that "there is power in *Night Mail*, the power of sight and sound, and there is also charm. . . . it is a technical landmark in its use of sound and integration of image, music, and narrative." Another critic has said that "the film visuals of *Night Mail* were conceived at the same time as their sound accompaniment. . . . The preoccupation with sound perspective, the selection of the dominant sounds, and the study of punctuation obtained results which opened wide possibilities for the use of sound in the dramatic film."

In 1937 Cavalcanti directed a series of short documentaries made by the GPO Film Unit in collaboration with the Swiss government. They included *We Live in Two Worlds,* a sadly uncinematic illustrated lecture by J. B. Priestley on the supposed political benefits of electronic communication, and *The Line to Tcherva Hut.* The latter, showing how telephone services are extended to a remote mountaineering post in the Swiss Alps, is a much more concrete and specific film, making imaginative and effective use of sound (and Britten's music). Barsam calls it "a model of subtle conception, shooting, and editing."

The same year John Grierson left the Film Unit for other challenges, and Cavalcanti replaced him as head of production. Cavalcanti is said to have lacked some of Grierson's talent for wringing money from civil servants for Film Unit projects, but to have increased the Unit's involvement in technical experiment and the use of dramatization (especially in its wartime documentaries) and to have inspired a wider and livelier scrutiny of British society. Certainly the Unit's output seems to have continued unabated. Between 1937 and 1940 Cavalcanti himself produced about fifteen films by Harry Watt, Stuart Legg, Len Lye, Norman McLaren, Pat Jackson, Ralph Elton, and Humphrey Jennings, among others.

With the outbreak of war in September 1939, the GPO Film Unit was taken over by the Ministry of Information; in April 1940 it was renamed the Crown Film Unit. With the Unit given over mainly to wartime propaganda films, it was considered unsuitable to have a foreigner in charge. Cavalcanti refused to abandon his Brazilian nationality, and in 1940 he left the Unit to join Michael Balcon's Ealing Studios. His role at Ealing seems to have been very similar to the one he fulfilled at the GPO, and Balcon has acknowledged the importance of his contribution to the characteristic flavor of the Ealing films, especially through his guidance of such young directors as Charles Frend, Charles Crichton, and Robert Hamer. In particular he has been held responsible for the introduction of documentary realism into the feature film (thus balancing out what he had done to encourage the use of dramatization in the GPO documentaries).

However talented the young Ealing directors were, Balcon says, "they were still short of experience in dealing with visual images on the screen. And this is what Cavalcanti could do for them. He was a vastly experienced man as to how to transfer images to the screen—a curious man, you know, in some respects, until he got going. By virtue of the fact that he didn't know English very well, he could sometimes be completely inarticulate, especially when he got excited. But somehow when he was on the floor, near the camera, talking to these people, just some little things he could do would make all the difference. . . . Men like Charles Frend, good as they were, made better films with Cavalcanti by their side. Apart from anything else, he was a man of infinite taste. He knew about settings. He knew about music. He knew about European literature. He was a highly civilized man."

The first film Cavalcanti directed at Ealing was a short called *Yellow Caesar* (*The Heel of Italy* in the United States). This was a frequently witty compilation of newsreel footage of Mussolini, opening with a famous cut from the hand of a street entertainer, winding the crank of his barrel organ, to the rotating hand of the Italian dictator in full oratorical flight. Its scenarists were Frank Launder and Michael Foot. The following year saw the release of *Film and Reality,* Cavalcanti's anthology of excerpts from documentary and factual films of all kinds and all countries, commissioned by the British Film Institute in 1939. This work was received with considerable bitterness by some British filmmakers who, like Paul Rotha, thought it "did less than justice to the social aims of the British documentary group." Other critics greatly admire the film as "a classic reference work," and it has been widely used in film education.

Cavalcanti's own favorite among the films he directed at Ealing was his first feature there, *Went the Day Well?*, called *Forty-Eight Hours* in the United States. Based on a story by Graham Greene, it imagines what might happen if a party of German paratroopers, masquerading as British soldiers, were to occupy a British village.

Once they have been unmasked, the Germans show their true natures, imprisoning the villagers who had so trustingly welcomed them and ruthlessly putting down opposition. Then the villagers gain the upper hand and turn on their oppressors with a cold-blooded ferocity exceeding that of the Germans themselves.

Went the Day Well? was an extraordinary movie to come out of a British studio in wartime—a deeply pacifist film which, as Cavalcanti himself said, showed that "people of the kindest character, such as the people in that small English village, as soon as war touches them, become absolute monsters." Elizabeth Sussex writes that this picture "pulls together most of the threads that run through Cavalcanti's work: the documentary authenticity, the drama, the surrealism [in certain scenes of grim humor]. A remarkable thing about him is that, despite being a Brazilian with a European background, or perhaps because of it, he could put his finger precisely on the essential Britishness of the British and make it a special point of interest."

Cavalcanti's next feature was *Champagne Charlie* (1944), starring the comedian Tommy Trinder in a comedy-drama about the great days of British music hall. It was liked for its characteristic sense of social realism, though some thought that this "well-washed, cheerful, determinedly innocent film" missed some of the music hall's vulgarity and gusto. *Dead of Night* followed in 1945—an eerie framing story tying together strange anecdotes directed by Robert Hamer, Basil Dearden, Charles Crichton, and Cavalcanti. It was almost universally recognized that the most accomplished and memorable of these stories was Cavalcanti's, in which Michael Redgrave plays a ventriloquist whose personality is gradually taken over by his murderous dummy. Cavalcanti's version of *Nicholas Nickleby* (1946), adapted by John Dighton and giving employment to a number of Britain's best-known character actors, was a disappointment—conscientious, but lacking in drive or sparkle.

It was followed by what some critics regard as the best of Cavalcanti's British feature films, *They Made Me a Fugitive* (U.S., *I Became A Criminal*, 1947). Adapted by Noel Langley from a novel by Jackson Dudd, it tells the story of a RAF flyer (Trevor Howard), bored after the war, who is drawn into the black market, then betrayed by his degenerate boss (Griffith Jones) when he refuses to deal in drugs. Jailed, he escapes and goes looking for revenge. Contemporary reviewers were disturbed by the violence and morbidity of this picture, but it has been increasingly recognized as "one of the most darkly poetic of all crime films." Brian Baxter has called it a "masterly social drama," using its Soho background to brilliant documentary effect and benefiting greatly from Otto Heller's atmospheric photography and, above all, from Cavalcanti's deep sympathy for his characters. Arthur Vesselo was reminded of the German cinema of the 1920s.

The First Gentleman (U.S., *Affairs of a Rogue*, 1947), a "pointedly irreverent" portrait of George IV (Cecil Parker) was a less personal work (and reportedly offended some of the guests when it was unwisely selected for a Royal Command Performance). Cavalcanti's last Ealing film was *For Them That Trespass* (1948), based on Ernest Raymond's novel, with Richard Todd wrongly imprisoned because of another man's moral cowardice. The script (by Jack Lee-Thompson) is unconvincing in its attempt to capture working-class speech but, in Raymond Durgnat's opinion, "the film remains notable for its mood of diffuse guilt and for Cavalcanti's sense, quite worthy of Carné, of the sad poetry of squalid, smoky streets."

Michael Balcon has said that Cavalcanti helped him, "probably more than anybody else," to create the Ealing image. Nevertheless, in the late 1940s, Cavalcanti left Ealing to freelance, apparently in pursuit of a higher income, and in 1950 he left England altogether. His plan to film Charles Morgan's *Sparkenbroke* for Rank had fallen through and his mother (a central influence on him) had died. He accepted an invitation to lecture on film at the Museum of Modern Art in São Paulo, and returned to Brazil.

In São Paulo what seemed like an exciting new opportunity presented itself, and Cavalcanti became production chief of the Vera Cruz film company. He hoped to create there a truly Brazilian movie industry but encountered every kind of obstacle and resistance, not least from American interests intent on retaining their grip on the Brazilian market. He was starved of film stock and called a communist but nevertheless produced three films before he lost his job, including Lima Barreto's prizewinning documentary *Painel* (1951). Cavalcanti stayed on in Brazil for three more years after that and himself directed three pictures: *Samão, o caôlho* ("Cross-Eyed Simon," 1952), based on a story by Galeão Coutinho; *O Canto do mar* ("Song of the Sea," 1954); and a comedy called *Mulher de verdade* ("A Real Woman," 1954).

The best of these films was *O Canto do mar,* about the suffering of a peasant family in the parched northeast of Brazil and the decision of the son of the family to set out for the south. It was in effect a remake in a Brazilian setting of *En rade*. It took first prize at Karlovy Vary and is said to be "marked by its bleak pictorial symbolism and its use of folklore, dominant characteristics of many later Brazilian films." During his stay in Brazil, Cavalcanti also published a collection of essays on the cinema, *Filme e realidade*, and helped to found the Brazilian Film Institute. Cavalcanti has described his expedition to his native country as a mistake that cost him everything he had, "an unhappy adventure," but Georges Sadoul has said that he created a movement there which had an impact "whose ripples have still not subsided."

In 1955 Cavalcanti was called back to Europe to direct in Austria a screen version of Berthold Brecht's satirical comedy *Herr Puntila und sein knecht Matti*. Cavalcanti says that before he met Brecht he was terrified of him, remembering that he had brought legal actions against both Pabst and Lang for their treatment of his writings; in fact, they got on very well, delivering a film that one critic called a "slightly stagey work directed with grace and wit."

It was Cavalcanti's old friend Joris Ivens who arranged this assignment, and Ivens was the producer of *Die Windrose* (1956), an anthology of politically oriented stories about women, with episodes by five different directors from as many countries. Cavalcanti helped Ivens to assemble these contributions and directed the Brazilian episode himself. He next worked in Romania on *Castle in the Carpathians*, a film—based on a Jules Verne novel—that was never completed, and then in Italy made *La prima notte* (1958), starring Martine Carol, Vittorio De Sica, and Claudia Cardinale, and photographed by Gianni Di Venanzo. Cavalcanti returned to Britain in 1960 to make a children's film, *The Monster of Highgate Pond,* and in 1967 went to Israel to direct an hour-long documentary called *Thus Spake Theodor Herzl* (*The Story of Israel*).

In recent years Cavalcanti has lived mostly in France, where he has directed a number of stage productions as well as two plays for television—a comedy called *Les Empailles* and Dürrenmatt's *Der Besuch der alten Dame*. He taught at UCLA in the 1960s, characteristically becoming involved in all aspects of student filmmaking, and in 1975 lectured at the Film Study Center in Cambridge, Massachusetts.

Cavalcanti has named Méliès as his master, saying that "the filmmakers of my generation had to go back to Méliès to find the poetry of cinema." Michael Balcon once remarked that "if there is a British cinema, I would put Cavalcanti's contribution pretty well as high as any," and George Sadoul called him "one of the most important filmmakers in the history of the cinema," though "largely unsung." Sadoul writes that Cavalcanti made "significant and often basic contributions to the French *avant-garde* 1925–1930, to the English documentary and the 'Ealing' style 1934–1948, and to the renaissance of the Brazilian cinema 1949–1952. He was not always able to direct the films as he intended, but those he created in complete freedom are characterized by their sensitivity, their sense of human and social realities, their understanding, their visual refinement, and their reflection of his delight in the cinema."

FILMS: Le Train sans yeux, 1926; Rien que les heures, 1926; Yvette, 1927; En rade (Sea Fever), 1927; La P'tite Lili, 1927 (short); La Jalousie de barbouillé, 1927; Le Capitaine Fracasse, 1928; Le Petit Chaperon rouge, 1929; Vous verrez la semaine prochaine, 1929 (short); À mi-chemin du ciel, 1930; Les Vacances du diable, 1930; Toute sa vie, 1930; Dans une île perdue, 1931; En lisant le journal, 1932; Le Jour du frotteur, 1932 (short); Revue Montmartroise, 1932; Nous ne ferons jamais de cinéma, 1932 (short); Le Truc du Brésilien, 1932; Le Mari garçon, 1933; Coralie et Cie., 1933; Plaisirs défendus, 1933 (short); Le Tour de chant, 1933 (short); Pett and Pott, 1934 (medium-length); New Rates, 1934 (short); Coalface, 1936 (short); We Live in Two Worlds, 1937 (short); The Line to Tcherva Hut, 1937 (short); Who Writes to Switzerland?, 1937 (short); Message From Geneva, 1937 (short); Four Barriers, 1937 (short); Men of the Alps, 1939 (short); A Midsummer Day's Work, 1939 (short); Yellow Caesar (U.S., The Heel of Italy), 1941 (short); Film and Reality, 1942; Went the Day Well? (U.S., Forty-Eight Hours), 1942; Alice in Switzerland, 1942 (medium-length); Watertight, 1943 (military instruction film); Champagne Charlie, 1944; (with others) Dead of Night, 1945; The Life and Adventures of Nicholas Nickleby, 1946; They Made Me a Fugitive (U.S., I Became a Criminal), 1947; The First Gentleman (U.S., Affairs of a Rogue), 1947; For Them That Trespass, 1948; Simão, o caôlho, 1952; O Canto do mar, 1954; Mulher de verdade, 1954; Herr Puntila und sein knecht Matti, 1955; (with others) Die Windrose, 1956; La prima notte, 1958; The Monster of Highgate Pond, 1960 (short); Thus Spake Theodor Herzl (The Story of Israel), 1967.

ABOUT: Armes, R. A Critical History of the British Cinema, 1978; Barsam, R. M. Nonfiction Film, 1974; Beveridge, J. John Grierson, 1978; Klaue, W. Alberto Cavalcanti, 1962 (in German); Rocha, G. Revisión critíca del cine brasilero, 1965. *Periodicals*— Écran November 1974; Film Dope November 1974, October 1975; Filme Cultura November 1978; Film Ideal December 15, 1960; Films November 1939; Literature Film Quarterly Winter 1978; Quarterly of Film, Radio, Television Summer 1955; Screen Summer 1972; Sight and Sound January–March 1955, Summer 1970, Autumn 1975.

*CAYATTE, ANDRÉ (JEAN) (February 3, 1909–   ), French director, scenarist, novelist, poet, and journalist, was born in the ancient walled city of Carcassonne in southern France, the son of a manufacturer, Louis Cayatte. He was educated at the Carcassonne *lycée* and published a first collection of verse when he was only seventeen. Another volume of poems followed a year later and then his first novel, *Artaban* (1929). By that time Cayatte was studying at the Sorbonne in Paris, where he earned degrees in both literature and law. He worked during the 1930s as a journalist with *L'Oeuvre* and *L'Intransigeant* and for a time practiced as an advocate at the Paris bar. It was his involvement in a lawsuit between a film producer and a star that first aroused in him an interest in the cinema, and in the late 1930s he began to make a place for himself in the industry as a scriptwriter. Meanwhile he continued to write fiction, and with some success. *Les Aventures de Julien Cazalis*, a two-volume novel written in collaboration with Robert de Ribon, appeared in 1932 and was followed by a trilogy, *Vie d'un monstre*, written with Philippe Lamour. The first volume of this, *Un Dur*, received the Prix Rabelais in 1933, and a later novel, *Le Traquenard* (1939), brought Cayatte the Prix Cazes.

Cayatte served with the French army at the beginning of World War II and was awarded the Croix de Guerre. Having written scripts for Marc Allegret's *Entrée des artistes* and Grémillon's *Remorques* among other films, he embarked in 1942 on a new career as a director, turning out a succession of unremarkable but increasingly competent films until he had his first international success with *Les Amants de Vérone* (*The Lovers of Verona*, 1948). A modern version of the Romeo and Juliet story, this tender, fatalistic picture had the benefit of a script by Jacques Prévert and a cast that included Serge Reggiani, Pierre Brasseur, and (in her film debut) Anouk Aimée.

It was followed in 1950 by *Justice est faite* (*Justice Is Done*), the first in a series of films attacking various aspects of the French legal system. Drawing on Cayatte's firsthand knowledge of the law and written by him in collaboration with the distinguished scenarist Charles Spaak, these films established the director's international reputation. *Justice est faite* sets out to illustrate fallacies in the jury system. Based on an actual "mercy killing" trial, it probes the lives of the jurors to show how their own temperaments and backgrounds interact to predetermine their verdict. The picture received the Golden Laurels at Venice, but there was some feeling that Cayatte's sense of outrage was not matched by his technical skill and control, and a few critics accused him of preaching.

ANDRÉ CAYATTE

There were no such reservations about the film that followed, *Nous sommes tous des assassins* (1952), released in the United States as *We Are All Murderers* and in Britain as *Are We All Murderers?* It begins with the execution of a French Resistance fighter by German troops for whom this patriot is no more than a terrorist. We then move to the postwar period and see the arrest of René le Guen (Marcel Mouloudji), an ignorant and pathetic young drifter who had also served in the Resistance. Having learned to kill he has unfortunately done so *after* the Liberation, when such conduct has become criminal rather than heroic. Convicted of murder, René is sent to La Santé prison to await execution, sharing his cell with a changing selection of fellow *condamnés* including a Corsican who has killed in the name of family honor, an impoverished father who has murdered his baby in a drunken rage, and a physician found guilty of poisoning his wife (this man insists on his innocence to the end). Their conversations and arguments take place in a terrible atmosphere of suspense, since, under French law at the time, a condemned person was not informed in advance of the date of his execution; none of the characters knows when it will be his turn to die.

The blind stupidity of imposing the same punishment for different kinds of offense is evident. And the film asks how these various kinds of murder are more abominable than the method of "legal murder" then current in France. We are shown how the warders at La Santé remove their boots, creep to the cell, and suddenly burst in to seize their chosen victim, who is dragged screaming to the guillotine, attended by a ghoulish priest hoping for a last-minute confession.

°ka yät´

Cayatte draws a number of fine performances from his large cast (which includes no stars) and achieves an almost documentary realism. The film caused a furor in France and an even greater one in Britain, where it was shown at a time when capital punishment was being urgently debated following the report of a Royal Commission. "With none of the murderers," wrote Dilys Powell, "is there any attempt to gloss over the hatefulness of his crime. . . . and characters are introduced throughout to put the case in favour of capital punishment. . . . But each time Cayatte has an answer. . . . A ferocity which is intellectual as well as physical gives the film" its conviction and quality. The London *Times's* critic agreed that the picture is "saved from the basely sensational by the passion of [Cayatte's] sincerity."

Avant le déluge (*Before the Flood,* 1954) centers on three youths and a girl (played by Marina Vlady) who form a gang and are led into serious crime and then to murder. It is a study of delinquency produced not by poverty but by the failure of bourgeois values in the postwar world. *Le Passage du Rhin* (*The Crossing of the Rhine,* 1960), starring Charles Aznavour and Georges Rivière in a suspense story about French prisoners of war escaping from Germany, won the Golden Lion at the Venice Film Festival. It was followed by *Le Glaive et la balance* (*Two Are Guilty,* 1963), another collaboration with Charles Spaak, with an ingenious plot and a cast that includes Anthony Perkins, Fernand Ledoux, and Jean-Claude Brialy. Filmed on location on the French Riviera, it begins with the kidnapping and murder of a child by two men who are later trapped by the police in a lighthouse. However, not two but three men emerge from the lighthouse, each claiming to be innocent, each with an unsavory past. All three are acquitted but die as a result of mob action after the trial, so that the audience never learns which were the guilty ones.

Equally original, though in a very different mode, is *La Vie conjugale* (*Anatomy of a Marriage,* 1963), written by the director. It consists of two full-length films examining the breakdown of a marriage first from the point of view of the husband (Jacques Charrier), then from that of the wife (Marie-José Nat). In the first movie the husband is seen as a man selflessly devoted to his family and profession, while his wife is apparently uncommitted to the marriage, determined to further her own career, and flagrantly unfaithful. However, in the wife's account of the same events, it appears that she—though much cleverer and more able than her husband—has loyally stifled her own ambitions to further his, valiantly resisted the advances of

various attractive men, and given up on the marriage only when her husband's pettiness and suspicion became intolerable. Hollis Alpert called the result "a veritable tour de force" but thought it "rather a pity that it is all done so slickly." *Newsweek's* reviewer was more impressed: "Cayatte shows us two separate worlds which merely touch. It is very sad, and in its quiet way, very moving."

Piège pour Cendrillon (*Trap for Cinderella,* 1965) is a thriller that earned comparisons with Hitchcock, and there was a good deal of praise also for *Les Chemins de Khatmandou* (*The Roads to Katmandu,* 1969), about a young idealist losing his illusions but perhaps finding love on the way to Nepal. However, the most successful of Cayatte's later films was *Mourir d'aimer* (*To Die of Love,* 1970), a fictionalized version of the immensely controversial Russier case. Gabrielle Russier was a divorced teacher in her early thirties whose love affair with a precocious student half her age led to her imprisonment, disgrace, and eventual suicide, while the boy was subjected to "sleep cures" and other psychiatric torments by his politically progressive parents. The film, starring Annie Girardot, ignores the ironies and complexities of the case (including Russier's rather bizarre image of herself as a literary heroine and her draconian treatment of her own two children) and is simply a polemic against hypocrisy and the double standard. Pauline Kael found the film inept, and Molly Haskell called it "slick and glossy in the best French bourgeois tradition . . . incompletely factual and insufficiently romantic. . . . an insult to Gabrielle Russier's memory." For Rex Reed on the other hand it is a "great film . . . a piercing, powerful and provocative film that raises serious questions no thinking person can afford to dodge." And whatever the critics may have thought, it received the Grand Prix du Cinéma and was immensely successful in France and throughout Europe, outgrossing even *Love Story.*

Family tragedies baffle and defeat the law in Cayatte's next two films. In *Verdict* (1974), an impassioned Italian mother (Sophia Loren) takes hostage the wife of Judge Jean Gabin in the hope of extorting an acquittal for her son, accused of rape and murder. The judge invokes a peculiar codicil that allows a jury to ignore evidence, and so frees the boy—a mistake, for during the ride home this teenage monster casually admits to both crimes, and his mother steers the car into a wall. *À chacun son enfer* (*To Each His Hell,* 1977) has Annie Girardot as an equally distraught French mother pleading on television for the life of her ten-year-old daughter, kidnapped by persons unknown. A ransom is paid, and then (in an allusion to several actual cases) the child's body is discovered; the villain of the film is the woman's stepson, whose smoldering jealousy—evident to the audience all along—has been exacerbated by her frantic appeals. Like the Loren character, the woman executes her own judgment.

Neither of these rather sensational tales received very good reviews, but both profited from the presence of major stars, as did *La Raison d'état* (*Reasons of State*, 1977), a polemical exercise in which Monica Vitti stumbles on a dirty little secret pertaining to government arms trafficking. *L'Amour in question* (*The Love in Question*, 1978), however, was recognized as vintage Cayatte. An intellectually provocative courtroom drama, it follows a magistrate investigating the murder of an architect. Suspicion falls on the man's wife and her English lover, and they are brought to trial separately, allowing Cayatte to draw incisive contrasts between the theatrics of the British trial, verging at times on blood sport, and the non-adversarial and ultimately collusive proceedings in France. Neither legal system, it is implied, can insure against a wrongful verdict, and this is borne out by an ironic denouement. There were excellent performances by Girardot as the magistrate and Bibi Andersson as the wife, their scenes together having a psychological acuteness not always discernible in this director's work.

David Thomson has said that Cayatte's films are "mundane because their messages are unequivocal," and Basil Wright, similarly, concludes that they are "unequal in quality though not in sincerity; their value tends to lessen in proportion to the more obvious intrusion of propaganda messages. But when the filmic, dramatic and propagandist balance is achieved, the result can be terrific." According to one interviewer, Cayatte is "a handsome, jarringly cheerful man whose seriousness is all but masked by his polish and charm." Cayatte was married in 1945 to Hélène Mercier and has a son. His recreations include tennis and book collecting.

—*K.B.*

FILMS: La Fausse Maîtresse, 1942; Au bonheur des dames, 1943; Pierre et Jean, 1944; Le Dernier Sou, 1944; Sérénade aux nuages, 1945; Roger-la-Honte, 1945; Le Revanche de Roger-la-Honte, 1946; Le Chanteur inconnu, 1946; Le Dessous des cartes, 1948; Les Amants de Vérone (The Lovers of Verona), 1948; Tante Emma, *episode in* Retour à la vie, 1949; Justice est faite (Justice Is Done/Let Justice Be Done), 1950; Nous sommes tous des assassins (We Are All Murderers/Are We All Murderers?), 1952; Avant le déluge (Before the Flood), 1954; Le Dossier noir (The Black Dossier), 1955; Oeil pour oeil (Eye for Eye), 1956; Le Miroir à deux faces (The Mirror With Two Faces), 1958; Le Passage du Rhin (The Crossing of the Rhine), 1960; Le Glaive et la balance (Two Are Guilty), 1963; La Vie conjugale (Anatomy of a Marriage): My Nights With Françoise; My Days With Jean-Marc, 1963; Piège pour Cendrillon (Trap for Cinderella), 1965; Les Risques du métier (Occupational Hazards), 1967; Les Chemins de Khatmandou (The Roads to Katmandu), 1969; Mourir d'aimer (To Die of Love), 1970; The Verdict, 1974; À chacun son enfer (To Each His Hell), 1977; La Raison d'état (Reasons of State), 1978; L'Amour en question (Love in Question), 1978. *Published scripts*—(with Jacques Prévert) Les Amants de Vérone, 1949.

ABOUT: Bazin, A. Qu'est-ce que le cinéma?, 1961 (France); Braucourt, G. André Cayatte, 1969 (France); Wright, B. The Long View, 1974; Who's Who in France 1979–1980. *Periodicals*—Continental Film Review October 1953; Film Dope November 1974.

CHAPLIN, Sir CHARLES (SPENCER) (April 16, 1889–December 25, 1977), Anglo-American clown, star, director, producer, writer, and composer, was born and raised in the working-class London districts of Walworth, Lambeth, and Kennington. His parents, both music-hall entertainers, had fallen on hard times. Chaplin's baritone father, also named Charles, had taken to the bottle and to beating his fragile soubrette wife, Hannah. Before Chaplin was three, his father deserted the family for another woman, leaving Hannah to sink into the insanity that marked the rest of her life. The young Chaplin and his older half-brother, Sydney, lived for a while with Chaplin senior and his mistress, and in 1898 Chaplin was briefly reunited with his mother, whom he adored. However, he spent his childhood mostly in public charity homes and on the streets, where he quickly learned the power of money and propriety, while carefully observing the little jobs and stratagems that allowed the least fortunate members of society to survive.

According to Chaplin, he made his music hall debut at the age of five, taking his mother's place on stage one evening when she lost her voice. His career began in earnest in the summer of 1898. Though he was not from Lancashire, he became one of the Eight Lancashire Lads, a children's musical troupe that toured England's provincial music halls. The featured role of Billy in *Sherlock Holmes*, first with H. A. Saintsbury in a 1903 tour of the provinces, then with its original American author and star, William Gillette, brought Chaplin in 1905 to London's West End. In 1907 he joined Fred Karno's Pantomime Troupe. England's most accomplished company of physical farceurs (whose alumni also included Stan Laurel). By 1908 Chaplin had risen to be Karno's star attraction, specializing in his dexter-

CHARLES CHAPLIN

ous portrayal of a comic drunk—a routine he would recreate in films over the next forty years. Between 1909 and 1913 Chaplin accompanied the Karno troupe on tours to Paris and the United States. On the second American tour he received an offer to join Mack Sennett's Keystone Company in Hollywood. Mabel Normand, Sennett's leading comedienne, Adam Kessel, co-owner of the Keystone Company, and Sennett himself all take credit for discovering Chaplin in the Karno act.

Chaplin arrived on the Sennett lot in December 1913 with a contract for a year's work at $150 per week. He had been making only $50 weekly as a star of the music hall stage. His first reaction to the movie business was a combination of shock and dismay. Accustomed to the temporal continuity of stage comedy, Chaplin couldn't understand how a scene or routine could be cut into non-chronological pieces. Compared with the careful comic craftsmanship of the Karno crew, he found Sennett's method careless, sloppy, and crude. Working frantically to produce at least two comic reels a week, Sennett never invested time in deepening the texture or complicating the structure of gags. The Sennett style showed less interest in comic observations of human behavior than in run, bash, smash, and crash. "Chaplin was used to a slower, subtler, and more individual pantomime," according to Thodore Huff, his first major biographer. Chaplin's first Keystone comedy, *Making a Living* (1914), dressed him in a stereotypic English music hall outfit, then kept him racing across the frame for an entire reel. But his second Keystone film, *Kid Auto Races at Venice,*

was the comic revelation in which Chaplin assembled his trademark Tramp costume for the first time—bowler hat, reedy cane, baggy pants (borrowed from Fatty Arbuckle), floppy shoes (borrowed from Ford Sterling).

Like many Keystone films, *Kid Auto Races* was improvised around an actual event—the racing of homemade cars on a weekend afternoon. The Tramp arrives to watch the races but meets an unexpected challenge—a movie camera and crew recording the event, presumably for a newsreel. In an unstructured half-reel of improvised clowning, Chaplin plays two comic games with the supposed newsreel camera: he makes himself the star of the newsreel and he resists any attempt of the camera crew to boot him out of its frame.

Chaplin's remaining Keystone films of 1914 come directly from *Kid Auto Races.* They demonstrate the Tramp's plucky refusal to be pushed around by anyone: any kick you can give me I can give back harder. And they demonstrate the way Chaplin can convert an inanimate object, like a movie camera, into a living opponent. Very early in his Keystone year Chaplin realized that movies could animate the inanimate. In *His Favorite Pastime*, the drunken Tramp does battle with a saloon door. In *Mabel's Married Life*, the swinging door bashes the drunken Charlie every time he pushes it away. In *His Trysting Places* Chaplin transforms a plate of beans into a musical instrument, basing a comic routine on the juicy slurps of eating: with facial reactions and gestures alone, Chaplin allows us to "hear" the noises and "feel" the liquids emanating from his fellow diner (played by Mack Swain). In this, the longest single take in a Keystone film, Chaplin declared both his technique (using the uninterrupted take to develop an intricate comic routine) and his style (supplying missing senses—sounds, touch, smells—by visual means).

Most of his Keystones stick with familiar Sennett material—aggressive physical objects; a kick in the butt and a romp around the park, propelled by three states of inebriation: drunk, drunker, and drunkest. It was a period when, as Chaplin later observed, you made a movie by taking Mabel Normand, a bucket of whitewash, and a camera to a park and improvising. After four months of apprentice work, Chaplin began to direct his films. Among the most interesting, pointing toward later work, was *The New Janitor.* Charlie, the lowly janitor of an office building, saves a pretty secretary from attack by a thief. In a deliberate irony, the thief turns out to be a "respectable" employee of the firm, the handsome gent to whom the secretary was previously attracted. By protecting her from this apparent pillar of rectitude, Chaplin demonstrates both that he is the worthier man and that society's conceptions of worth based on good looks and social graces are themselves askew. In many later films Chaplin's Tramp would demonstrate his moral worth by protecting a fragile, idealized woman against foes bigger, stronger, richer than himself.

By the end of his Keystone year, Chaplin had become so popular in America's nickelodeons that merely displaying the Tramp's wooden effigy with the words "I'm here today" would attract long lines of loyal fans. Sennett offered Chaplin five times his 1914 salary, $750 per week, for another year at Keystone, but the Essanay Company of Chicago offered Chaplin $1250 per week, plus a $10,000 bonus upon signing. Chaplin left Hollywood for Chicago. After two films he transferred to the Essanay lot in California, where he could escape both the winter chill and a hostile management.

Chaplin's year at Essanay was a transitional period between the knockabout Sennett farces and the more subtle comedies of psychological observation and moral debate that mark the mature Chaplin. Many of the Essanay films look backward to films at Keystone: miscellaneous confrontations and confusions in parks, beaches, movie studios, hotels, and restaurants (*His New Job, A Night Out, In the Park, By the Sea*). Some of these films are only a single reel (about ten minutes), like many of his Keystones, rather than the two-reelers that became his norm until 1918.

His sixth film at Essanay, *The Tramp*, pointed in the opposite direction. It was the first film in which Chaplin was fully conscious of both his Tramp persona and the relationship of that persona to the respectable social world. As in *The New Janitor*, Chaplin's Tramp protects a frail woman from physical harm—this time from fellow tramps, members of his own "class." (The actress, Edna Purviance, joined Chaplin's troupe early in his Essanay year. She was to play the idealized woman in every Chaplin film for the next eight years, and she remained on the Chaplin payroll until her death in 1958.) Rewarded with a job on Edna's father's farm, the Tramp finds himself unable to master the regular routines of farm life—the familiar Chaplin motif that he can mimic the activities of others but never fit into any regular social pattern. When the tramps who attacked Edna return to rob her father, Charlie defeats them again. He is wounded in the battle—moral commitment is always costly and painful for the Tramp—and Edna nurses him back to health. At first mistaking her kindness for another kind of love, Charlie learns that the pretty, respectable Ednas of the world

are not for tramps like him when her handsome boyfriend comes home from the city. The Tramp returns to the road and, in the film's final image, takes his leave, back to the camera, moving slowly at first, only to pick up his heels and walk briskly toward his future. This ending—the Tramp's disappointment and return to the road—would dominate Chaplin films for two decades, a recognition that the Tramp's life *was* the road, that singularity meant solitude.

Other films in the Essanay group develop unique qualities of the Chaplin Tramp or unique devices of the Chaplin style. In *A Night in the Show* Chaplin recreates the drunk routines of his Karno days, for the first time playing two roles in one film—the rich upper-crust drunk and the rowdy working-class heckler. In *Work* Chaplin extends his play with comic objects to a statue of a female nude in a respectable middle-class home. His routine with this statue reduces it simultaneously to a useless piece of bourgeois junk and a fashionable form of pornography. In *The Bank* Charlie, again a humble janitor in an institution of high finance, saves his employer from attack by robbers—only to awaken from a dream. This first Chaplin film-dream implies that the Tramp can manage heroic accomplishment only in dreams, not in the waking world. He ends by embracing not Edna—who has rejected his gift of flowers—but his smelly mop, the mortal reminder of his lowly trade and social position. In *Police*, the final film of his Essanay year, every character who offers to help Charlie "go straight" wants to swindle him, so that when Edna offers Charlie a place in her bourgeois home after he has rescued her from attack, he decides he'd rather remain free. Charlie ends the Essanay series with a return to the road, racing away from the camera, a pursuing cop at his heels.

In his Essanay films Chaplin defined the central conflict for the Tramp as between the world of the "straight" and his own personal system of morality and value. The Tramp could resist (and implicitly criticize) the "straight" obsession with property because his needs were more elemental—survival, shelter, food, and love. And the Tramp could either flout or poignantly refine upon the niceties that meant so much to the respectable world. Chaplin's cinema style also gradually abandoned Sennett's mechanical reliance on editing—building scenes quickly and cheaply from small snippets. Instead, Chaplin drew on the lesson of the musical soup in *His Trysting Places*, seeking the precise camera position to convey the essential view, tone, and meaning of an intricately choreographed routine: "With more experience I found that the placing of a camera was not only psychological but articulated a scene; in fact, it was the basis of cinematic style." Chaplin's technique would always depend on framing rather than cutting—the precise organization of persons, objects, and their movements within a stable, psychologically defined space. Chaplin met a key collaborator at Essanay, the cameraman Rollie Totheroh, who would shoot every Chaplin film—and only Chaplin films—until his death in 1946.

As Chaplin's comic theme and cinema style matured at Essanay, his popularity grew at an astonishing rate. Essanay offered $500,000 for another year of two-reel films. It wasn't enough. In late 1915 he signed a contract with the Mutual Film Corporation for $10,000 per week and a bonus of $150,000 upon signing. In return, Chaplin was to supply a dozen two-reel films which he would write, direct, and perform as he pleased. The contract for only twelve films—one a month—allowed Chaplin to slow his pace of production so as to invest more time in comic detail, structure, and observation (compared to thirty-five Keystone films in 1914 and fourteen at Essanay in 1915). The twelve Mutual films actually required eighteen months of work. Chaplin had begun to exercise his mania for perfection in the conception and complication of comic routines—rehearsing, shooting, and reshooting them until extended sequences were perfectly executed by camera, cast, and star. By 1917, Chaplin was exposing 50,000 feet of film for a two-reel (2000 feet) Mutual comedy, an astonishing shooting ratio of 25 to 1, which would later swell to 100 to 1. (In comparison, major feature films today expect a shooting ratio of, perhaps, 9 to 1, with the shooting ratio for television films about half that.)

The twelve Mutual films in 1916–1917 represent the fruit of Chaplin's experience with the twenty-minute comedy: comic gems of social commentary and psychological observation, of balletic chases and transmutations of inanimate objects into almost sentient beings—all built on an exact understanding of who the Tramp was, how he saw the respectable social world, and how it saw him. In The Floorwalker Charlie is entangled in mistakes, thefts, and chases in a department store, a modern emporium of mercantile materialism. Chaplin here introduces his first lookalike, a thief who resembles the Tramp—Chaplin's derisive comment on his many imitators in competing films: you can imitate the Tramp's look and walk but only Chaplin can imitate Chaplin. The Fireman was the first of Chaplin's Mutuals to feature Eric Campbell, a comic behemoth imported from England's D'Oyly Carte company to portray Charlie's physical, social, and psychological opposite.

The Vagabond represented an enormous departure for Chaplin, pushing his comic style and Tramp character into regions where farce comedy had never been. The Vagabond used a familiar motif from Victorian melodramas and novels—the long-lost daughter, stolen by gypsies, finally reunited with her family. It also wrung more pathos than any previous film from the Tramp's loneliness and despair after the Edna he had protected returns to her proper family and handsome suitor. As opposed to the ending of The Tramp, Charlie is emotionally unable to kick up his heels when Edna deserts him. His only salvation is her abrupt return after a change of heart. The questions this evokes—can the Tramp mate with the pretty, proper young girl? And if not, how will he endure her rejection?—become central to Chaplin's later films.

After the pathos of The Vagabond, Chaplin's next Mutual film, One A.M., was a contrasting tour de force. Except for a taxi driver in the opening scene (played by fellow British comedian Albert Austin), Chaplin was the only human player in this film, surrounded and attacked by a house full of menacing objects. Chaplin again tailored his Karno drunk for the movie camera, in a setting where the ugly artifacts of bourgeois propriety become not possessions but enemies, culminating in a five-minute duel with a Murphy bed that refuses to let its drunken master master it. In The Count Chaplin explored the contrast between the social graces of the haut monde and the inadequacies of poor pretenders, a motif that goes back to such Keystone films as Caught in a Cabaret. The Pawnshop, another comedy of objects, took the Tramp into a world where objects are the essential commodity of existence; Behind the Screen glimpsed life inside a movie studio (like The Masquerader at Keystone and His New Job at Essanay); The Rink put Chaplin on roller skates for the first time. Skating seemed like a visual expression of his ethereal spirit, lifting him—like a tragedian in buskins—to new heights of physical grace and wit.

Easy Street, the ninth of the Mutual series, represented another Chaplin departure—a satire of the Christian ideal that faith, hope, and charity can eradicate the blight of human misery. For the first (and last) time in his career Charlie played a cop, the Tramp's natural enemy. After being inspired in a charity mission, Charlie joins the force, only to discover that the police have no force in the slums where crime, poverty, hunger, and might are the sole realities. Easy Street converted the most sordid social subjects—wife-beating, drug addiction, gang warfare, rape, police brutality, the stench of overcrowded slum rooms—into surprisingly funny material for comic routines.

After a brief vacation in *The Cure*, where the drunken Charlie brought drunken chaos to an entire health spa, Chaplin's Mutual series ended with two remarkable films. In *The Immigrant* the solitary Tramp was identified with the plight of a whole class—the unlettered, unemployed, and propertyless strangers who have yet to find opportunity in "the Land of Opportunity." In *The Adventurer*, Chaplin paid another brief visit to the world of the rich in a film that was a virtual perpetual-motion machine. This non-stop race to escape his police pursuers was Chaplin's ultimate tribute to the kind of chase that his former boss, Mack Sennett, had made intrinsic to film comedy.

With the close of the Mutual cycle in mid-1917, both Chaplin's life and career reached a turning point. For four years he had done little but make films, steadily increasing his artistic control, confidence in his medium, understanding of his Tramp character, and popularity with his public. The new contract he signed in 1918 looked no different from previous ones but was to prove so: a $1 million agreement with the First National Exhibitors Circuit. This alliance of theater owners, battling the growing power of film production companies, contracted directly with stars like Chaplin for films. Chaplin built his own film studio in 1918 at the corner of Sunset Boulevard and La Brea Avenue in Hollywood. Like his previous Mutual contract, the First National agreement called for a dozen two-reel comedies in a year. In point of fact, it took Chaplin five years, during which he made just eight films, only three of which were two-reelers (*A Day's Pleasure*, 1919; *The Idle Class*, 1921; *Pay Day*, 1922)—the least remarkable of the group. Three First Nationals were three-reelers (*A Dog's Life*, 1918; *Shoulder Arms*, 1918; *Sunnyside*, 1919), one was four (*The Pilgrim*, 1923), and one was six (*The Kid*, 1921). Chaplin was both slowing the pace of his work and extending the length of his comic explorations.

The public notoriety that became as much a Chaplin trademark as his bowler hat also reached him in 1918. Chaplin both benefited and suffered from the avid public interest in movies and movie stars during the decade following 1910, as Hollywood grew into the world's most powerful producer of cultural messages and images. With the single exception of Mary Pickford, no movie star was as well known and well loved as Chaplin, the first twentieth-century "superstar" created by the century's global media. Even a Chaplin sneeze was news, and Chaplin did more than sneeze. In 1918 he toured the country with his friend Douglas Fairbanks, raising money for war bonds, a response to those who asked why Chaplin was not fighting for King and Country in the trenches. He was also married for the first time in 1918—to Mildred Harris, thirteen years his junior and "no intellectual heavyweight," in Chaplin's own words. The marriage established a new Chaplin pattern—the surprise marriage to a very young bride (rumored to be pregnant), ending quickly in rancorous and highly publicized divorce—in this case in 1920.

In 1919 Chaplin and three other famous figures of the day, D.W. Griffith, Mary Pickford, and Douglas Fairbanks, formed the United Artists Corporation to finance and distribute their own films—the first concerted exercise of Hollywood artists on their own commercial behalf. Chaplin took a trip abroad in 1921, visiting England for the first time in eight years. He was amazed at the enormous crowds who sought a glimpse of him at docks and railway stations. Even the most distinguished men of the age—Churchill, Gandhi, H. G. Wells, Bernard Shaw—wanted to meet him. For a rising younger generation of European artists and thinkers, no one combined the popular appeal and the artistic insight of Chaplin, the ultimate artist of the people in an increasingly democratic century. The cultural critic Robert Warshow found it no hyperbole to call Chaplin "surely one of the few comic geniuses who have appeared so far in history."

Between travels through America, Europe, the marriage bureau, and the divorce court Chaplin worked with both intensity and brilliance. *A Dog's Life*, which opened the First National series in 1918, was longer and richer than any film he had previously attempted. Demonstrating his ever-deepening understanding of the Tramp's moral values and social limits, Chaplin created his first tramp-surrogate, the mongrel Scraps—an outcast who must fight to survive in a world of tougher, bigger dogs. As opposed to the lookalike in *The Floorwalker*, Scraps is a think- and actalike for the Tramp; the film's extended comic sequences show Tramp and mongrel working either separately or together toward the same end—usually something to eat. *Shoulder Arms* moved from the metaphoric to the topical—transporting the Tramp to the battlefield trenches of Europe. As he had done in *Easy Street*, Chaplin converted the serious and sordid into hilarious comedy—the daily struggle to survive against not only bullets but fleas, rats, and mud. As in *The Bank*, the Tramp's heroic triumph, capturing a German general, is followed by a rude awakening that reveals his heroism "over there" as mere dream.

After these two triumphs Chaplin suffered a major disappointment and his career seemed to mark time for two years. *Sunnyside* was the first Chaplin film not to find favor with his public, a sarcastic look at the Tramp in rural America. As he had done in *Easy Street* and *Shoulder Arms*, Chaplin exposed the uglier, dirtier side of life. *Sunnyside* is not at all sunny, a debunking of the rural idyll's claims to moral purity and Christian charity. Despite its failure, several sequences rate among Chaplin's most memorable: his dreaming himself into the role of an allegorical Pan, cavorting across meadows with classical nymphs; his comic failure to duplicate the style and manner of the handsome city slicker whom he sees as a rival for Edna's affections.

More than eighteen months elapsed before *The Kid* appeared, his longest and most ambitious film, a response to his crumbling marriage and the death of a stillborn child that, according to Mildred Harris, ended it. *The Kid* combined the Victorian melodrama and pathos of *The Vagabond*, the tramp-surrogate of *A Dog's Life*, the vicious urban struggle to survive of *Easy Street*, and the allegorical dream of *Sunnyside*. In the film's opening sequence, Edna, an unwed mother, rejected by a callous artist-lover, gives birth to a child that she abandons, hoping it will find a legitimate, richer life with an adopted family. Although she considers suicide, Edna stays alive to become a successful actress and enjoy a reunion with the long-lost child. Chaplin makes explicit use of Christian symbolism, comparing the burden of the unwed mother to Christ's carrying the heavy cross.

The child's adoptive parent turns out to be the wandering Tramp, who finds the infant bundle in a garbage-filled alley. Although he tries to rid himself of the responsibility that he knows the child will become, he finally responds to the infant's need. Five years later we see Tramp-father and waif-child in their poor but happy home. The boy has become a little mirror of the man; they react identically to enemies, whether police, bullies, thieves, or bureaucratic representatives of the legitimate social order. They walk, move, work, and think alike—an accomplishment of both child actor, Jackie Coogan, and patient director Chaplin, who carefully shaped the boy into his own mirror. In the film's final sequence, when a desolate Charlie fears that Jackie has gone forever, Chaplin offers a parodic dream-allegory of the Fall of Man, a pastiche of *Paradise Lost* that contrasts human aspirations toward the Good with the overwhelming realities and temptations of mortal existence. The lascivious temptress in this dream was played by twelve-year-old Lita Grey, who would become Chaplin's real-life temptress—both his second girl-wife (in 1924) and his second ex-wife (in 1926). The ending in *The Kid* was much more

felicitous. Edna alleviates the Tramp's despair, just as she had in *The Vagabond*, by returning for him and inviting him into her comfortable home for a joyous reunion with Jackie. The question that this ending avoids is whether the Tramp could in fact ever inhabit such a house.

The final film of the First National group, *The Pilgrim*, returns to this question. Like *Sunnyside*, *The Pilgrim* transports the citified Tramp to the open countryside, suggesting a contrast between its claims to moral health and the hypocrisies of urban civilization. As an escaped convict who has adopted clerical garb to avoid the pursuing police, Chaplin wears the enemy's uniform—just as he did as a cop in *Easy Street*. The costume allowed Chaplin to mime an ironic sermon on David and Goliath, an acknowledgement of the Tramp's underlying myth, and he proceeds to reveal his own personal moral code, protecting Edna and her family against a former cellmate. *The Pilgrim* ends the First National cycle with one of Chaplin's most memorable images of self-definition. As he walks away from the camera in his familiar manner, his legs straddle the border between Mexico (defined as a land with no law except might) and the United States (defined as a land of laws that persecute Tramps). Condemned under either system, the Tramp can only straddle the border between them. He simply belongs nowhere.

Chaplin's first United Artists production was another daring departure. *A Woman of Paris* (1923) was not a slapstick farce but a witty comedy of manners set in the demimonde of Paris. The Tramp does not exist in such a milieu, and Chaplin himself appears only briefly as a railway porter. Instead, this directorial showpiece exhibited Chaplin's ability to coach actors into subtle comic portrayals and to coax inanimate objects into ironic revelations of human behavior. The film was also Chaplin's farewell gift to Edna Purviance, her final starring role in a Chaplin film. Growing both stouter and older than the Tramp's fragile ideal, Edna once more plays a woman led astray by men. When Marie St. Clair (Edna) believes herself abandoned by her artist lover, she becomes the most famous courtesan of Paris, kept by its most elegant bachelor, Pierre Revel (Adolphe Menjou appearing for the first time in a role that was to become his specialty). Even without the Tramp, Chaplin's cinema style depended on the dexterous manipulation of physical objects to reveal the slyly sexual intentions of their human handlers. This first elegantly stylish comedy of manners in the American cinema, reflecting Jazz Age interest in the rich and decadent, became a powerful influence on Ernst Lubitsch, the eventual grand master of the genre.

Chaplin's next four features for United Artists, his entire artistic output for the next decade, return to the Tramp and his conflict with "normal" American social expectations. The four films—*The Gold Rush* (1925), *The Circus* (1927), *City Lights* (1931), and *Modern Times* (1936)—form a distinct unit, which might be called Chaplin's "marriage group." All four return to the question posed by the ending of *The Kid*: under what circumstances might the Tramp marry and settle down with a woman in ordinary bourgeois society? The films suggest four different answers under four different circumstances. Having struck it rich in *The Gold Rush*, the Tramp becomes an acceptable mate for Georgia (Hale), who has learned the worthlessness of good-looking suitors who exploit her sexually. But in *The Circus*, Charlie fails to fulfill Merna Kennedy's vision of romance, embodied for her by the tightrope walker, Rex. After bringing the two lovers together, the Tramp takes his lonely leave, returning to the road once more. *City Lights* cannot supply an answer. Having fallen in love with a blind flower-seller (Virginia Cherrill) who loved him for his kindness but imagined him as handsome and rich, Charlie fears that he will disappoint her once she recovers her sight. Though Charlie was her social equal when she was blind, how can the two share a life when she is able to see him, a lowly tramp? The film's poignant ending—"The greatest piece of acting and the highest moment in movies," according to the critic James Agee—closes on this unanswered question. In *Modern Times*, however, Charlie finds his female equal in the Gamin (Paulette Goddard), a homeless child of nature who, like Charlie (and Scraps and Jackie) belongs nowhere in organized society. Charlie and Paulette flee to the road—traveling together, away from the camera, toward some place beyond the horizon.

Chaplin extended the length and complexity of his comic routines at the same time that he deepened the conflict between the ethereal Tramp and the material world. *The Gold Rush*, identified by Huff as Chaplin's "most celebrated picture," is also the film Chaplin called "the picture I want to be remembered by." In its most famous comic sequence, Charlie roasts his trademark shoe and carves it for dinner, twirling its laces like spaghetti, sucking the meat off its nails, even offering a bent nail to his dinner companion (Mack Swain) as a wishbone. The sequence demonstrated the familiar magic of Chaplin's mime: transforming one kind of object into another. It also demonstrated the familiar Chaplin method of turning the most desperate human suffering—here two starving men—into a source of comedy. The film's most poignant sequence is another dinner party, an elegant New Year's Eve supper Charlie has planned for Georgia and her friends (this time he roasts a real joint of beef). While Charlie dreams of social success—entertaining his guests with the dancing of two bread rolls on the end of two forks, parodies of his own gigantic shoes—he awakens to discover that midnight has passed, Georgia has not come, and he is alone as always. Charlie can only succeed in his dreams—until Georgia finally accepts him at the film's end, itself more than a little dreamlike.

Although *The Circus*—for Huff at least—"missed the poetry, brilliance, and feeling of *The Gold Rush*," the film has risen steadily in esteem since its return to circulation in 1970. A circus is one institution where the Tramp ought to find a place for himself—a society of the road, devoted solely to entertaining others. But even here the Tramp is an oddity, finding it impossible to master the traditional routines of circus clowns. He can amuse audiences only by spontaneous confrontations with life itself. Locked in a lion's cage, running from a savage donkey, maintaining his balance on the high wire while monkeys tug at his trouser cuffs, Chaplin comedy is based on survival, on being a mortal animal in an animal world. The film's conclusion, perhaps the saddest of any Chaplin film, deposits the Tramp in an empty field where the shape of a circus ring remains imprinted in the dust. Memories of the laughter and excitement that this ring once contained suggest the ephemerality of all human experience. Recently divorced for the second time, Chaplin here also perhaps offers a personal confession: the richness of his comic career and the emptiness of his life outside the circus ring called a movie screen.

Between *The Circus* and *City Lights*, the arrival of synchronized sound overthrew silent film production in Hollywood. Silence was not something imposed on Chaplin; it was the medium in which the Tramp lived. A speaking Tramp was simply not the Tramp—he had never even mouthed words. Chaplin made what seemed a radical decision in 1931 and a sensible decision ever after: to make *City Lights* as a silent mimed comedy with musical scoring and sound effects. A skilled though self-taught musician on the violin and cello, Chaplin himself composed the score for the film, as he did for all his sound films, as well as adding musical tracks to silent classics. Chaplin is the only film director to win an Oscar for composing, and one of two directors (Victor Schertzinger is the other) to write hit songs: "Smile," the theme of *Modern Times*, and "Eternally," that of *Limelight*.

In *City Lights*, Chaplin's music established

and emphasized the film's variations in tone—the farcical adventures of the Tramp with a drunken millionaire, set to bouncy brass; the touching scenes of the Tramp with the blind flower-seller, set to sentimental strings. In the musical contrast was the thematic contrast. The millionaire, who enjoyed every material advantage, was spiritually barren—a loveless, suicidal drunk. The flower-seller, enjoying no material advantages whatever, not even sight, was spiritually rich (flowers had been a consistent Chaplin symbol of spiritual beauty since the 1915 Essanay, *A Night Out*). The Tramp could travel between the two extremes because the drunk millionaire was as blind as the girl to external appearances. The Tramp's journey between them represented the spirit of absolute selflessness, the Christ figure toward which this character's entire development had tended. He undergoes baptism (with the suicidal millionaire in a river), raises the dead (convincing the millionaire not to take his life), cures the blind, is denied three times (whenever the millionaire is sober enough to see), suffers crucifixion (prison), and resurrection (when he finds that the girl can see). Perhaps the film cannot end with a marriage because the vow of chastity accompanies that of poverty.

Modern Times can end with a marriage because the Tramp returns from the spiritual realm to the physical world of human survival—in modern, urban, Depression America. Again critics were disappointed: "Fuzziness in the form, drag in the pace, breaks in the continuity, and lack of climax" (Huff). Again the years have proven otherwise. Chaplin always constructed his films the way he had learned to do it in his Keystone days, as a string of vignettes. Here each incident engages the Tramp in an elemental battle to survive: his comic routines are built around keeping a job, making a home, and finding a meal. When Tramp and Gamin take to the road at the film's end, it was also the end of the Tramp's road: the first time he had walked it with another and the last time he would ever appear in a Chaplin film. For Chaplin it was both an end and a beginning: he could no longer resist synchronized sound. *Modern Times* used not only a musical score but three talking sequences, in the last of which Chaplin himself spoke for the first time in a film. Ironically, his speech is a song and the language is gibberish, a jumble of nonsense sounds comprehensible only because of physical mime and musical tone, the way he always communicated with an audience. He had also secretly married Paulette Goddard in 1936 after a four-year romance. Perhaps the ending of *Modern Times* announced Chaplin's intention to resign the battle and retire to domestic com-

fort. He would not do so until after another marriage and another stormy decade.

Chaplin's final three American films were conventional dialogue films with unconventional twists: *The Great Dictator* (1940), *Monsieur Verdoux* (1947), and *Limelight* (1952). In *The Great Dictator* Chaplin played two contrasting social roles (as he did in *A Night in the Show* and *The Idle Class*): a Jewish barber in the ghetto, resembling the Tramp in manner and appearance; and Adenoid Hynkel, dictator of Tomania, a burlesque of Hitler whose toothbrush moustache infringed upon another Chaplin trademark. The film was made before the facts were known about the Nazi death camps, and Chaplin claims he would never have made it if he had known. His burlesque reflects general American opinion in 1940, treating Hitler as maniacal clown. In its most memorable sequence, Hynkel becomes a cooch dancer, performing a hypnotic bubble dance with a globe of the earth, the ethereal balloon of his imperial desires. For two decades Chaplin had depicted the Tramp's dreaming that collapses in the cold light of day. Here the Tramp's illusion becomes a dictator's delusion of grandeur, burst by a cathartic pin.

Monsieur Verdoux is another political fable. Having relinquished the unity and universality of the Tramp, Chaplin continued to play multiple roles in a single film—sea captain, antique dealer, loving husband. Verdoux is a man with many lives and many wives, whose business is marrying and murdering for money. Having lost his job as a bank teller during the Depression, Verdoux marries rich, repellent, elderly ladies and kills them to support his beloved wife and child on an idyllic farm. The film draws explicit parallels between Verdoux's murderous trade and more acceptable professions—munitions manufacture, stock trading, banking—which have brought death and social chaos on a much grander scale. The motif of prostitution had always remained just below the surface of earlier Chaplin films (the dance-hall euphemism of *The Gold Rush*, for example), but an unequivocal prostitute becomes Chaplin's metaphor for all business enterprise in *Monsieur Verdoux*. If the film's moral argument was overly insistent, its blackly comic proceedings (particularly Verdoux's unsuccessful plots to dispose of big-mouth comedienne Martha Raye) and the cast of grotesques who represent the normal bourgeois citizenry were as savagely funny as anything in comedy since Ben Jonson's *Volpone*. For Robert Warshow, "Probably the closest thing to *Monsieur Verdoux* is Swift's *Modest Proposal*."

American audiences began to connect Chaplin's savage political positions on screen with his perceived political stance offscreen. For Chaplin it was a decade of continuous legal and public turmoil. Having appeared at 1942 rallies supporting a Russian counterattack on Germany (the Second Front), Chaplin became a target of right-wing suspicion and FBI investigation. Most items in J. Edgar Hoover's Chaplin file turned out to be morsels from the gossip columns of Louella Parsons in the right-wing Hearst press, many planted by Hoover himself. Conservative pressure groups asked why Chaplin should be permitted to make so many American dollars without becoming an American citizen. He even owed the Internal Revenue Service a significant amount in unpaid taxes on those profits. Chaplin was divorced from Paulette Goddard in 1942 and in 1943 married Oona O'Neill, the playwright's youngest daughter—the fourth time Chaplin (now 54) had married a much younger woman (she was 18). The marriage was almost simultaneous with Chaplin's most scandalously publicized legal battle: Joan Barry's 1943 paternity suit naming Chaplin as her lover of two years and the father of her child. Although Chaplin denied her claims and genetic evidence refuted them, the court ruled for Barry. *Monsieur Verdoux* was Chaplin's first box-office failure since *Sunnyside*.

Even amid public hostility in the 1952 America of Joseph McCarthy, the House Un-American Activities Committee, and Hollywood blacklisting, Chaplin made a final affectionate tribute to his art and its traditions. *Limelight* was another film in which Chaplin played multiple roles—or rather the same character at different times of his life. He is Calvero, now an old, drunken has-been, rejected by his audience (as Chaplin has himself suffered rejection), but once, forty years earlier, a star music-hall comedian. The old man's dream sequences evoke memories and recreate routines of Chaplin's youth, classic music-hall sketches that suggest not only the Tramp but the entire tradition of comic mime from which the Tramp grew. Not accidentally, Chaplin's final routine in the film is what Warshow called an "unendurably funny" comic duet with Buster Keaton, another silent clown-star with roots in the same stage tradition. The death of Calvero at the end of *Limelight* is also the death of that clown tradition, which began on the stages of Europe, traveled (like Chaplin himself) to the playhouses of America, culminated in the American silent cinema, and barely survived as an aging anachronism (again like Chaplin himself) in the sound cinema. But in the death of Calvero and his tradition there is also continuity and renewal. The union Chaplin forged between the physical and the musical continues in ballet: the union of the young dancer, Terry (Claire Bloom) and the young composer (played in a twist of generational irony by Sydney Chaplin, the younger of Chaplin's two sons by Lita Grey). At the end of *Limelight*, the old clown dies but the dance itself continues.

After completing *Limelight* Chaplin and Oona took the usual trip abroad for the film's European release. Not being a citizen, Chaplin needed advance permission to return to the United States. After a series of interrogations about his political beliefs, the State Department finally issued a reentry permit—only to revoke it as soon as the *Queen Elizabeth* left the dock in New York. Chaplin received a shipboard cable informing him that he would be required "to answer charges of a political nature and moral turpitude." While politely pretending to answer these charges in London, Chaplin quietly sent Oona back to America to liquidate his assets—from the Beverly Hills mansion to the United Artists company to the Sunset Boulevard studio. The Chaplin family moved to Switzerland, where they lived comfortably for twenty-five years. The family eventually included eight children, the oldest—Geraldine—now an actress.

Chaplin refused to return to America for two decades—long after the State Department had relented—but in 1972 the Motion Picture Academy awarded him a conciliatory Oscar, and he made a triumphal visit to receive it. His feature films, which had also been withdrawn from American circulation for two decades (an exception was a brief New York retrospective in 1963), were released to a generation that had never seen them. In 1975 Chaplin, the former London street urchin and eternal Tramp, was knighted by Queen Elizabeth II.

Chaplin made two last films in exile, *A King in New York* (1957), a bitterly clumsy satire of contemporary American culture, and *A Countess From Hong Kong* (1967), a sweetly clumsy return to *A Woman of Paris*, in color and Cinemascope, with Sophia Loren and Marlon Brando. Inhibited by low budgets, tight schedules, and a production team of strangers, both films unintentionally revealed Chaplin's dependence on the unique way he had made films for forty years—in his own studio, at his own pace, as his own boss, with his own family of players and technicians.

Chaplin's ultimate accomplishment was not merely a long list of masterful comic films over a career of four decades but the creation of a cultural archetype who embodied the contradictions within twentieth-century industrial society—the battle between the material and the spiritual, the individual and the community, the natural and the artificial, the institutional and the spontaneous, the respectable and the moral. It is no small irony that the Tramp, this archetype of vital chaos, the elemental foe of social machinery and institutions, has been used in the 1980s to advertise the wares of an immense industrial corporation. That the Tramp would become a salesman for IBM computers was simply inconceivable in the 1916 of *Easy Street*, the 1936 of *Modern Times*, or the 1952 of his virtual deportation. Reflecting on Chaplin's achievement, James Agee observed that "of all comedians, he worked most deeply and most shrewdly within a realization of what a human being is, and is up against. The Tramp is as centrally representative of humanity, as manysided and as mysterious, as Hamlet, and it seems unlikely that any dancer or actor can ever have excelled him in eloquence, variety, or poignancy of motion."

—*G.M.*

FILMS: Making a Living, Kid Auto Races at Venice, Mabel's Strange Predicament, Between Showers, A Film Johnnie, Tango Tangles, His Favorite Pastime, Cruel Cruel Love, The Star Boarder, Mable at the Wheel, Twenty Minutes of Love, Caught in a Cabaret, Caught in the Rain, A Busy Day, The Fatal Mallet, Her Friend the Bandit, The Knockout, Mabel's Busy Day, Mabel's Married Life, Laughing Gas, The Property Man, The Face on the Barroom Floor, Recreation, The Masquerader, His New Profession, The Rounders, The New Janitor, Those Love Pangs, Dough and Dynamite, Gentlemen of Nerve, His Musical Career, His Trysting Place, Tillie's Punctured Romance, Getting Acquainted, His Prehistoric Past, 1914; His New Job, A Night Out, The Champion, In the Park, A Jitney Elopement, The Tramp, By the Sea, Work, A Woman, The Bank, Shanghaied, A Night in the Show, 1915; Carmen, Police, The Floorwalker, The Fireman, The Vagabond, One A.M., The Count, The Pawnshop, Behind the Screen, The Rink, 1916; Easy Street, The Cure, The Immigrant, The Adventurer, 1917; A Dog's Life, Triple Trouble, The Bond, Shoulder Arms, 1918; Sunnyside, A Day's Pleasure, 1919; The Kid, The Idle Class, 1921; Pay Day, 1922; The Pilgrim, A Woman of Paris, 1923; The Gold Rush, 1925; The Circus, 1928; City Lights, 1931; Modern Times, 1936; The Great Dictator, 1940; Monsieur Verdoux, 1947; Limelight, 1952; A King in New York, 1957; A Countess From Hong Kong, 1967.

ABOUT: Asplund, U. Chaplin's Films, 1971; Bazin, A. What Is Cinema? Vol. II, 1971; Brownlow, K. The Parade's Gone By, 1968; Chaplin, C. Charlie Chaplin's Own Story, ed. by Harry Geduld, 1986; Chaplin, C. My Autobiography, 1964; Chaplin, C. My Life in Pictures, 1974; Chaplin, C. My Trip Abroad (U.K., My Wonderful Visit), 1922; Chaplin, C., Jr. My Father, Charlie Chaplin, 1960; Chaplin, L. G. My Life With Chaplin, 1965; Chaplin, M. I Couldn't Smoke the Grass on My Father's Lawn, 1966; Delluc, L. Charlot, 1921 (in French); Francis, D. and Sobel, R. Chaplin: Genesis of a Clown, 1977; Huff, T. Charlie Chaplin, 1951; Kerr, W. The Silent Clowns, 1975; Lyons, T. J.

(ed.) Charlie Chaplin: A Guide to References and Resources, 1977; Maland, C. J. American Visions: The Films of Chaplin, Ford, Capra, and Welles, 1977; McCabe, J. Charlie Chaplin, 1978; McCaffrey, D. Focus on Chaplin, 1971; McCaffrey, D. Four Great Comedians, 1968; Manvell, R. Chaplin, 1974; Mast, G. The Comic Mind, 1979 (rev. ed.); Mast, G. and Cohen, M. (eds.) Film Theory and Criticism, 1985 (rev. ed.); Mitry, J. Tout Chaplin: Tous les films, par le texte, par le gag et par l'image, 1972; Payne, R. The Great God Pan, 1952; Robinson, D. Chaplin: A Mirror of Opinion, 1983; Ross, L. Moments With Chaplin, 1980; Roud, R. (ed.) Cinema: A Critical Dictionary, 1980; Sadoul, G. Vie de Charlot, 1978; Sennett, M. and Shipp, C. King of Comedy, 1954; Smith, J. Chaplin, 1984; Tyler, P. Chaplin: Last of the Clowns, 1947; Warshow, R. The Immediate Experience, 1962. *Periodicals*—Atlantic Monthly August 1939; Colliers October 26, 1935; Écran March 1978; Film Comment Winter 1969, September–October 1972, March–April 1978; Film Culture Spring 1972; Films in Review November 1981; Image et Son November 1972, January 1977; Life March 10, 1957; Partisan Review November–December 1940; Positif July–August 1973; Quarterly Review of Film Studies Fall 1977; Screen Writer July 1947; Sight and Sound Spring 1946, Summer 1946, Autumn 1957, Autumn 1980; Wide Angles 1979. *Films about*—Brownlow, K. and Gill, D. The Unknown Chaplin, 1983.

CHRISTENSEN, BENJAMIN (called **CHRISTIANSON** in the United States) (September 28, 1879–April 3, 1959), Danish director, scenarist, and actor, was born in Viborg. Accounts of his early career vary a great deal, but it seems clear that he studied medicine for a time at the University of Copenhagen and then dropped out, probably in 1902, to become an opera singer and, later, a stage actor. According to some sources he secured one of the coveted scholarships to the Royal Theatre Academy in Copenhagen and was involved as an actor and/or director in Danish, German, and French plays at the Royal Theatre and the Aarhus Theatre. There are also indications that he may have acted in Danish films as early as 1906.

Though Christensen is reputed to have shown great promise as a stage actor, he quit the theatre in 1907 for reasons that so far remain obscure. After working for a time as a wine merchant, he entered the booming Danish film industry, in or around 1912, as an actor and scenarist. Movies in which he appeared include Sven Rindom's *Skaebnebaeltet* (*Destiny*, 1912) and Elith Reumert's *Lille Klaus og Store Klaus* (*Little Klaus and Big Klaus*, 1913). As a scenarist he is said to have worked for August Blom, a pioneer Danish director of extraordinary ability and originality whose possible influence on Christensen deserves investigation.

BENJAMIN CHRISTENSEN

The latter's first film as a director was *Det Hemmelighedsfulde X* (*The Mysterious X,* 1913), a rambling thriller about a malevolent master spy who compromises the virtuous wife of a loyal naval officer but is outsmarted by their determined young son. Made for the Dansk Biograf Kompagni, the movie was scripted by Laurids Skands. Christensen, who appears in it as the naval officer—a fairly large role—and had as his assistant director A. W. Sandberg, later a distinguished filmmaker himself.

When sections of this picture were screened at the 1964 Venice Film Festival, the critics greeted it as a revelation. Tom Milne wrote that, in the subtlety of its chiaroscuro interior lighting and the sophistication of its camera movement, it was far in advance of both Griffith and Feuillade. John Gillett was equally astonished, saying that "the photographic texture was immensely rich . . . the camera panned easily . . . each shot cut perfectly with the next. When the lights went up we checked the programme book warily for the date: 1913."

For his second film, *Haevnens Nat* (*The Night of Revenge,* 1915), also for Dansk Biograf, Christensen was his own scenarist and also played the lead as a circus performer who receives a long jail sentence for stealing food to save his starving child. By the time he is released, he is a deranged old man intent on revenge. John Gillett found this as advanced as its predecessor in its "sophisticated lighting . . . , forward-looking panning and dolly shots, and . . . acute awareness of how decor can be integrated into narrative" (as in "the comings-and-goings in the strange house, with lights being switched on and off and shadowy faces peering into windows and mirrors"). The camera style seemed to Gillett "most startling of all . . . with its stressing of detail in close-up and gradual revelation of what the characters are doing. . . . The story, in fact, is seen *through* the camera and not merely recorded by it, not least in the climax with its veritable flurry of cross-cutting as the avenging convict stalks the mistress of the house from room to room."

The same year, Christensen started a third film for Dansk Biograf, *Manden uden Ansigt* (*Man Without a Face*), but work on this was halted by World War I. His next picture—though it used a number of Danish actors and technicians—was made in Sweden, which by the end of the war was outstripping Denmark as a film producer, both in technical development and output. In 1919, the two major Swedish companies merged to form Svensk Filmindustri, and the new company invited Christensen to write and direct a documentary on the subject of witchcraft.

Most Swedish films at that time were adaptations of literary works, but Christensen, intent on creating something wholly original and cinematic, devoted two years to an obsessive study of his theme in medieval documents, esoteric books, and judicial manuscripts. Svensk Filmindustri must have been aware of his reputation as a meticulous perfectionist who took as long as six months to make a movie—then an almost unheard-of investment of resources—but they could not have bargained for this. Begun in 1919, it was not until 1922 that the result was released as *Häxan* (*Witchcraft Through the Ages*).

Inclined by temperament and training to give his material fictional form but constrained by the production company's demand for a documentary, Christensen wrote and discarded several scripts before arriving at a compromise—a highly personal illustrated history of medieval witchcraft. The film begins with an introduction consisting of photographs of medieval drawings (tinted in some prints), interspersed with explanatory subtitles. This is followed by dramatized reconstructions of typical episodes in the grim story. The explanatory titles are written in the first person throughout. They make no pretense of impartiality, presenting Christensen's own opinion that the witches were harmless hysterics monstrously victimized by a superstitious and repressive Church.

The longest of the dramatized episodes, taking up the lion's share of the film's 110 minutes, is a witchcraft trial that is used to illustrate the medieval attitude to the phenomenon as a whole. There is also a "modern" section in which

Christensen draws on his medical training to show various examples of hysterical behavior and then—by the use of flashbacks—to suggest how such behavior could have given rise to medieval fears and superstitions about demonic possession. This last section has been described as "a remarkable example of filmic 'composition,' resembling an exact visual counterpart to the musical device . . . in which the final movement [of a symphony] recapitulates and reworks the themes introduced in the earlier sections."

The cast is a mixture of professional and nonprofessional actors. Christensen himself appears as a "hairy, jovial Satan" and two well-known Scandinavian actresses, Clara Pontoppidan and Tora Teje, play a medieval nun and a twentieth-century kleptomaniac war-widow respectively. The Danish comedian Oscar Stribolt impersonates a monk who is seduced by his housekeeper. But the desiccated old women who play a witch and a suspected witch (in the trial scene) are said to have been discovered in a Copenhagen hospice, the painter Alice Fredrikson appears as a blasphemous hysteric, and a well-known Danish critic is pointedly cast as the torturer. Denmark's "most beautiful model" is seen briefly in the nude at a witches' sabbath. The acting is generally considerably more naturalistic than was then common.

Christensen worked closely with his cinematographer, Johan Ankerstjerne, and is said to have been much influenced by the work of another Danish cameraman named Folkman, whose lighting style was inspired by German painting. These methods, applied to scenes of torture and gross hysteria, and the fantastic images achieved by exaggerated make-up and papier-maché masks and props, created effects that have reminded many critics of the work of Hieronymus Bosch. According to one anonymous critic, "technical devices such as reverse action, double-printing, back projection, iris effects, framing devices, etc., are much used, not as effects, but to solve the problem of presenting fantasy on the screen with a truly fantastic mood."

Released in Sweden in 1922 and elsewhere in Europe the following year, *Häxan's* scenes of torture and nudity provoked an assortment of censorship problems. Moreover, though it was a *succes d'estime,* it failed at the box office—perhaps for the reason suggested by *Film Daily* when the movie finally reached New York in 1929: "The subject matter is too grim for most picture houses." Svensk Filmindustri at the same time entered a period of severe financial difficulty, and with so much stacked against it,

Häxan disappeared from view for nearly thirty years, during which time it acquired an almost legendary status.

It finally reemerged in 1956, when a print from the Belgian Cinémathèque was screened at the National Film Theatre in London. On that occasion *Häxan* was "roared through as a farce," presumably on account of the unfashionable earnestness of its tone and subtitles. Even then, however, many recognized its quality, and further screenings have had a very different reception. Ado Kyrou paid homage to it in his *Amour-Érotisme et Cinéma* (1957) and then in *Le Surréalisme au Cinéma* (1963), calling it "sublimely nightmarish . . . a film of disconcerting liberty," and "one of the great masterpieces of world cinema." And in 1968 R. R. Anger described *Häxan* as "a movie of vaulting imagination, one of the great landmarks of the fantasy film, yet . . . deeply rooted in truth and reality. It has a terrible poetry and demands much from the audience. Christensen remains true to the almost unbelievable reality his researches had revealed to him, and does not flinch from anything, no matter how distasteful, erotic, or shocking. Yet there is not the slightest hint of the merely sensational anywhere in the movie. Most strongly, it gives the impression of being a personal vision. . . . I think it . . . likely that he sought to explore that in human nature which leads men to do terrible things in the names of causes or beliefs. The tone of *Häxan* is one of barely suppressed fury and outrage, the testament of a profoundly humanistic man. A man, perhaps, who realized that even in his modern world, that inhuman dedication still lurked."

"One is struck immediately by the extraordinary cinematic presentation of the images," wrote Gideon Bachmann. "And this was a film shot for the editing board: no other film before, and none until Dreyer's *Passion of Joan of Arc,* was so effectively mounted and rhythmically constructed in relation to the content of its frame-images." One critic after another has made the connection between *Häxan* and Dreyer, "in its creation of an atmosphere of fanaticism, in its intense suffering images of human faces riven by bewilderment and pain, in its obsession with the mystique of cruelty and depravity." And Dreyer made no secret of his admiration for Christensen's work: he called him a man "who did not fabricate his films but *created* them out of love and an infinite care for detail. He was thought mad. But time has showed that it was he who made a pact with the future." It seems to R. R. Anger "inescapably apparent that Benjamin Christensen was the major influence on Carl Theodor Dreyer, not D. W. Griffith as any film history will tell you."

Another myth—that *Häxan* was Christensen's only important achievement—was exploded when his two earlier movies were screened during the 1960s, with an impact that has already been described. As John Gillett says, the rediscovery of all the films he made subsequently in Germany, Hollywood, and Denmark has become "a matter of urgency." Christensen went to Berlin in 1923, when Germany was replacing Sweden as the principal European film producer. He joined Erich Pommer's Decla division of UFA, making his debut there with *Seine Frau, die Unbekannte* (*His Mysterious Adventure*, 1923), tragicomedy about a blind war veteran. The lead roles were played by Lil Dagover and (against Christensen's wishes) a newcomer named Willi Fritsch, soon to become one of the most popular of German stars.

It was in 1923 also that Christensen—at the director's request—played a major role as the painter in Dreyer's *Mikaël* (*Chained*), another Decla production. In the course of the same busy year Christensen is said to have written scripts for other Decla directors and to have himself directed a film called *Unter Juden* (*Among Jews*), again starring Willi Fritsch. His last German move was *Die Frau mit den Schlechten Ruf* (*The Woman Who Did*, 1925), an international production starring Lionel Barrymore and Gustav Frohlich.

In 1925 Christensen joined the exodus of German filmmakers to Hollywood, where he began with two assignments for MGM. Both of these pictures were scripted by the director, and both have survived. *The Devil's Circus* (1926) tells a wildly romantic story about a petty criminal redeemed by his love for a circus performer (Norma Shearer) who is crippled in the line of duty while he is away paying his debt to society—setbacks that are resolved by love when the sufferers are reunited. William D. Routt wrote that this melodrama was transformed by Christensen's *mise-en-scène* into "something of conviction and substance"—a "slow and deliberate use of the middle-distance forces concentration on the action and, like Hawks' or Boetticher's work, produces a kinetic involvement, the experience of the image as ritual."

It seemed to Routt that, though there are religious elements in this movie, the principal motivating force is sex. He came to much the same conclusion about Christensen's second MGM picture, *Mockery* (1927), in which "sex acts as a pivotal, revolutionary force." The unfortunate thus acted upon is Lon Chaney, here portraying a moronic and near-animal Russian serf given to robbing the dead. He nevertheless saves the life of a beautiful aristocrat and is taken into her service, thereafter alternating between masochistic servility to her and bestial lust. The former tendency wins out, unfortunately, and in the end, having rescued his mistress from the Bolsheviks, he dies in her arms. Routt thought this a "potential masterpiece" that had been marred by "studio/producer interference," though he adduces no evidence of such interference. He warmly praises the "magnificent restraint" of Chaney's performance, and goes on: "Underlying everything is such a hearty contempt for leaders, for their pitiless exploitation of man, for their selfishness and inhumanity, as I have seldom seen in any motion picture."

After *Mockery*, Christensen moved on to First National, where he made four pictures: *The Hawk's Nest* (1928), starring Milton Sills; *The Haunted House* (1928); *The House of Horror* (1929), with Chester Conklin, Thelma Todd, and Louise Fazenda; and *Seven Footprints to Satan* (1929), with Creighton Hale, Thelma Todd, and Sheldon Lewis. All or most of these movies seem to have been thrillers or horror films with a touch of comedy, but only the last has come to light since the revival of interest in Christensen's work. *Seven Footprints to Satan* was based on A. Merritt's eerie adventure serial and has titles by William Irish, himself an excellent writer of thrillers. Reviewers were reminded of Feuillade by this inventive and "very funny" horror picture, with its "typically mobile camerawork" and bizarre gallery of monsters and ghouls in a vintage "old dark house." While he was in Hollywood, Christensen also appeared as an actor in an adaptation of Jules Verne's novel *The Mysterious Island* that is credited to Lucien Hubbard but includes footage directed by two other filmmakers who had previously tackled the assignment—Maurice Tourneur and Christensen himself.

With the coming of sound, Christensen left Hollywood and returned to Denmark, where after ten years' silence he resumed his career with four pictures for Nordisk Film Kompagni. Though Nordisk is said to have prints of these films, they are not known abroad, but are evidently very different from his earlier work, dealing not with haunted houses and satanism but with contemporary social problems like divorce, abortion, and rebellious adolescents. These films are said to be as serious in manner as in content and generally unremarkable. After them, Christensen made no more movies, reportedly spending the last part of his long life as the manager of a Copenhagen movie theatre.

The rediscovery of Feuillade and then of Christensen has set in motion a radical revision of earlier accounts of the development of the cinema as an art form, showing that the unique importance attached to the achievements of D. W. Griffith did an injustice to the less available work of some of his rivals. "A pioneer Griffith certainly was," wrote one critic, "but we now see that while he was turning out mushy one- and two-reelers for the nickelodeon, Feuillade and Christensen were making long story films with an assured grasp of film technique far in advance of his." Indeed, some critics regard Christensen as the equal of Dreyer in his mastery of film technique, while acknowledging that his writing lacked the depth and subtlety of Dreyer's. His place in the pantheon is assured, though precisely what it is will not be established until his missing films are rediscovered.

FILMS: Det Hemmelighedsfulde X (The Mysterious X), 1913; Haevnens Nat (The Night of Revenge), 1915; Häxan (Witchcraft Through the Ages), 1922; Unter Juden, 1923; Seine Frau, die Unbekannte (His Mysterious Adventure), 1923; Die Frau mit den Schlechten Ruf (The Woman Who Did), 1925; The Devil's Circus, 1926; Mockery, 1927; The Hawk's Nest, 1928; The Haunted House, 1928; The House of Horror, 1929; Seven Footprints to Satan, 1929; Skilsmissen Born (Children of Divorce), 1939; Barnet (The Child), 1940; Gaa med Mig Hjem (Return With Me), 1941; Damen med de Lyse Handsker (The Lady With the Colored Gloves), 1942.

ABOUT: Ernst, J. Benjamin Christensen, 1967 (in Danish), 1967; Roud, R. (ed.) Cinema: A Critical Dictionary, 1980. Periodicals—Cinema-TV Digest Fall 1964; Film Dope April 1975; Focus (Chicago) Spring 1972; National Film Theatre Booklet (Britain) October 1977; Sight and Sound Spring 1966; Toronto Film Society Program Notes March 18, 1968.

*"CHRISTIAN-JAQUE" (Christian Maudet) (September 4, 1904–), French director, was born in Paris, the son of Edouard Maudet, manager of a smelting works, and the former Joséphine Baumet. He attended the Collège Rollin in Paris and went on to study architecture at the École Nationale des Beaux Arts and the École des Arts Decoratifs. In 1924, while still a student, he began to supplement his income by designing movie posters and film sets for Gaumont and First National. His collaborator was a fellow student whose given name was Jaque and they adopted the joint pseudonym Christian-Jaque, agreeing that it should become the sole property of whichever of them first achieved celebrity.

After service with the army in Morocco, Christian-Jaque resumed his architectural studies for a time but soon decided that his future lay in the movie industry. He served as a

CHRISTIAN-JAQUE

film critic on Le Gaulois and in 1926 was cofounder of a new monthly review, Cinégraph. In 1927–1931 he worked as art director on more than a dozen pictures by Henri Roussel, André Hugon, and Jules Duvivier, including the latter's La Vie miraculeuse de Thérèse Martin, Au Bonheur des dames, and Maman Colibri.

Christian-Jaque directed his own first movie in 1931, and no less than twenty-six others followed during the next six years, most of them made for Paramount in a matter of ten days or so. He came to specialize in vaudeville comedies—unpretentious fantasies that are mostly forgotten but which taught the young director his craft. These early films included Rigolboche (1936), starring the great Mistinguett; François 1er (Francis the First, 1937), with Fernandel; and Les Pirates du rail (1937). The latter, much more ambitious than its predecessors, stars Charles Vanel as a French railroad engineer in China and Erich von Stroheim as the cruel warlord Tchou-King, whose marauders threaten the survival of the new line. With its fine performances and spectacular action sequences, the movie was widely praised as an exciting entertainment in the Hollywood manner.

This strictly commercial success in no way prepared the critics for the extraordinary quality and atmosphere of Les Disparus de Saint Agil (Boys' School, 1938), adapted by J.-H. Blanchon from a novel by Pierre Véry. Combining mystery and satirical comedy, it is set in a dreadful French boarding school whose staff includes Michel Simon as a drunken art teacher and Erich von Stroheim as a German-born teacher of English whose Teutonic manner conceals a tender

° krēs´´tyăn´ zhäk´

heart. It is on the latter that suspicion falls when two of the pupils disappear.

Graham Greene wrote that it would be possible "to praise and dismiss *Les Disparus de Saint Agil* as a skilful, exciting, rather absurd 'story for boys'. . . . There is a headmaster who commits murder, and is tracked down and denounced by one of his pupils. There is an art master who forges bank notes, a kidnapping, a secret passage behind the blackboard, but strange though it may seem in such a plot, there is also a sense of reality; a child's dream of what Alain-Fournier called 'this wild life, full of risks, games and adventures,' is expressed through an adult imagination. One is reminded again and again, in the elusive poetry of the story of escape, of Fournier's great novel *Le Grand Meaulnes*: the small contained dormitory cells, the school play with its daggers and doublets, the master padding by at night on insomniac feet, the classroom after dark by candlelight with the white phosphorescent chalk marks on the board, these are like vivid inexplicable symbols in a surrealist painting." Others were reminded of the early versions of *Emil and the Detectives* and of Jean Vigo's *Zéro de conduit.*

After *L'Enfer des anges* (1939), a competent shocker about juvenile delinquency and drug peddling, came another oddly poetic and dreamlike movie, *L'Assassinat du Père Noël* (*Who Killed Santa Claus?*, 1941). It gave Harry Baur his last screen role as Cornusse, an old mapmaker who, though he has never left his native village in the Savoy, spins wonderful stories for the children about his imaginary travels and adventures. He has a strange daughter (Renée Faure) married to a mysterious aristocrat, and an annual assignment as the village's Santa Claus. One year things go wrong: the village church's precious St. Nicholas ring is stolen, Cornusse disappears, and an imposter is found dead in Père Noël's costume. With the village snowbound, the schoolmaster and the mayor become amateur detectives.

Like *Les Disparus de Saint Agil*, the picture was adapted from a novel by Pierre Véry, who worked as a scenarist on a number of Christian-Jaque's movies, but in *L'Assassinat du Père Noël* the dreamlike quality whirls at times "towards the borderline of nightmare." Some reviewers seemed disturbed by the darker elements in this extraordinary movie, but as many were delighted by Baur's performance as the ramshackle Santa Claus, the heady atmosphere, "the clear sound of boys' voices singing at midnight Mass, the ring of winter in the mountains."

Returning to more orthodox assignments, Christian-Jaque made *La Symphonie*

fantastique (1942), a romanticized biography of Hector Berlioz marred by a weak script but ameliorated by magnificent music and an impassioned performance by Jean-Louis Barrault. Notable among Christian-Jaque's other wartime productions was "a very hot-blooded and sensuous" version of *Carmen* (1943), using Bizet's music as background and adhering closely to Mérimée's original story, with Viviane Romance as a Carmen who could well drive strong men to ruin.

Something of the nightmarish quality of *L'Assassinat du Père Noël* reappeared in *Sortilèges* (*The Bellman*/*The Sorcerer*, 1944), a drama starring Fernand Ledoux, Renée Faure, and Madeleine Robinson about a bellringer in the Auvergne who becomes the object of superstitious fears that lead to murder. There was a good deal of praise for the mist and snow scenes shot on location by Louis Page, as there was for Christian Matras' very different landscape photography for *Boule de suif* (*Angel and Sinner*, 1945). The latter, based on Guy de Maupassant's much-filmed story about a prostitute (Micheline Presle) and her impact on a party of travelers, was wittily and imaginatively updated by Henri Jeanson from the Franco-Prussian War to World War II.

Christian-Jaque's first postwar film, and one of his best, was *Un Revenant* (*A Lover's Return*, 1946). A famous ballet impresario (Louis Jouvet) returns after twenty years to the provincial city he had left as a penniless and desperate youth. His intention is to revenge himself on the woman he had loved (Gaby Morlay), her brother (who had tried to murder him), and her mean-spirited bourgeois husband. He winds up as a sardonic *deus ex machina*, rescuing the brother's talented and likable son from a living death of provincial respectability.

Un Revenant seemed to some purists an excessively prolix and literary movie, but most critics warmed to it nevertheless, praising the wonderfully witty dialogue, the nice observation of the provincial *milieu*, and above all the gallery of portraits created by the brilliant cast—the aged Marguerite Moréno as "a magnificent old woman," François Périer as the endearing boy, Ludmilla Tcherina as the gorgeous ballerina who becomes his mistress, and above all Jouvet as the *revenant* himself, a "living, breathing, contradictory, likable, exasperating human creature."

Jean-Louis Barrault, Christian-Jaque's Berlioz, provided him with another notable impersonation in *D'Homme à hommes* (*Man to Men*, 1948), a biography of Henri Dunand, founder of the Red Cross, and the same year saw the release of *La Chartreuse de Parme,* a superficial but sumptuous adaptation of Stendhal's novel with fine performances from Gérard Philipe and Maria Casarès. *Singoalla* (1950), variously translated as *The Wind Is My Lover* and *The Mask and the Sword,* is a costume melodrama about the love affair between a beautiful gypsy (Viveca Lindfors) and a nobleman (Michel Auclair) in fourteenth century Sweden. It was shot in that country in French, English, and Swedish versions, and followed by *Souvenirs perdus* (1950), in which four objects that turn up in a Paris lost-and-found lead into as many sketches. Excellent entertainment, *Souvenirs perdus* employs a formidable array of talents—Edwige Feuillère, Pierre Brasseur, François Périer, Bernard Blier, Yves Montand, Suzy Delair, Gérard Philipe, and Danièle Delorme among them.

Two years later came the best known and financially most successful of Christian-Jaque's films, *Fanfan-la-Tulipe* (*Fanfan the Tulip*), which brought him the director's prize at Cannes. Set during the Seven Years War, it traces the career of the dashing young hero (Gérard Philipe) from the day he is signed up by a villainous recruiting sergeant (Noël Roquevert) to the glorious moment when he captures the enemy's general staff and wins the war singlehanded, having in the meantime courted a beautiful gypsy (Gina Lollobrigida) and Louis XV's daughter, rescued the Marquise de Pompadour from bandits, and narrowly escaped hanging.

An amiable spoof on swashbuckling movies (and on militaristic heroics in general), *Fanfan-la-Tulipe* has a frequently caustic script by Henri Jeanson, breakneck pace, and some fine color photography by Christian Matras. It was filmed in Provence, reportedly in an atmosphere of "great good humor and merriment." As Georges Sadoul wrote, Gérard Philipe "gives a very striking performance that endeared him to millions of admirers, while Gina Lollobrigida's appearance in the film made her an international star."

Christian-Jaque was married three times between 1931 and 1947, twice to actresses (Simone Renant and Renée Faure). His fourth marriage, to Martine Carol, lasted from 1954 to 1959, before and during which time she appeared in a number of his films, including *Adorable Créatures* (*Night Beauties,* 1952); *Lucrèce Borgia* (*Sins of the Borgias,* 1953); *Madame Du Barry* (1954); *Nana* (1955); and *Nathalie* (1957). In 1956 Christian-Jaque and his wife went on a three-month world tour, promoting French films on behalf of Unifrance Film and the Ministry for Foreign Affairs.

After a string of costume movies whose principal justification was Martine Carol's *poitrine,* the director's next film was a notable departure. *Si tous les gars du monde* (*If All the Guys in the World/ Race for Life,* 1955) was adapted by Christian-Jaque and Henri-Georges Clouzot from a story by Jacques Remy that was itself based on an actual incident. The crew of a Breton trawler, far from land in the North Sea, are struck by a mysterious illness. The ship's radio is out of action and the only hope is the captain's own amateur short-wave transmitter. His distress signals are picked up by a buff in Togoland, who passes the message to a boy in Paris. By this time the disease has been diagnosed as botulism, and a human chain of helpers begins to form across Europe to carry the necessary serum to the stricken trawler before it is too late.

C. A. Lejeune called this "a noble film" whose subject "is quite simply human brotherhood. . . . There is nothing preachy, politic, or sentimental about the treatment. The film is exciting; enormously exciting. I remember no work finer of its kind since Pabst's *Kameradschaft.*" Dilys Powell was almost equally enthusiastic, concluding that "it is a humane film, based on positive goodness. . . . It is extremely well directed. And it is finely played by a cast, without great names, which wins sympathy and makes the final sequence deeply moving." The picture won the main prizes at Karlovy Vary and Edinburgh and other awards from Belgium, Venice, and the Soviet Union.

Thereafter Christian-Jaque contented himself with routine assignments in a variety of genres—comedies like *La Loi c'est la loi* (with Fernandel and Toto) and the sprightly *Babette s'en va-t'en guerre* (*Babette Goes to War,* with Brigitte Bardot); satires like *Nathalie* (*The Foxiest Girl in Paris*) and *Le Repas des fauves;* adventure stories like *Le Gentleman de Cocody* (*Ivory Coast Adventure,* emulating the successful formula of *L'Homme de Rio*) and *La Tulipe Noire* (*The Black Tulip,* with Alain Delon); and *policiers* like *Le Saint prend l'affût* and *Deux Billets pour Mexico* (*Dead Run*).

One of the best of these later movies was *Les Bonnes Causes* (*Don't Tempt the Devil,* 1963), with Marina Vlady as a beautiful husband-killer, Pierre Brasseur as her lawyer and lover, and Bourvil as an examining magistrate who "upholds the law's integrity as though he would like to drop it and run." Beautifully played, it almost comes off as an elegant spoof on French justice but is flawed by an uncertainty of tone that leaves it dangling between suspense and satire. The worst of the bunch was almost certainly *Lady Hamilton* (*The Making of a Lady,* 1969), which reduces the story of Horatio Nelson and Emma Hamilton to a vehicle for Michèle Mercier, star of the "Angélique" series. Somewhat better was *Les Pétroleuses* (*The Legend of Frenchie King*, 1971), starring Brigitte Bardot and Claudia Cardinale in a comedy Western about women outlaws that has traces of the charm and pace of *Fanfan-la-Tulipe*. Since then, Christian-Jaque has concentrated mainly on television, though he did make two movies in the mid-1970s.

Georges Sadoul described the director as "a complete professional" who "has a sense of conviction and often of liberality." He is an excellent director of actors, and though he has always been dependent on the quality of his scenarists, he has honorably interpreted enough good scripts to earn more gratitude from cinephiles than he often receives. An elegant man of confident charm, he made his fifth marriage in 1961 to Laurence Christol. His recreations include swimming and book collecting. Christian-Jaque is a chevalier de la Légion d'Honneur and holds the Croix de Guerre for his services to the wartime Resistance.

FILMS: Bidon d'or, 1931 (medium-length); Le Tendron d'Achile, 1932; (with Paul Mesnier) Adhémar Lampiot, 1932; Ça colle, 1933; Le Boeuf sur la langue, 1933; La Montre, 1933 (medium-length); Atroce Menace, 1934 (medium-length); Vilaine Histoire, 1934 (medium-length); L'Hôtel du Libre-Échange, 1934; Le Père Lampion, 1934; Compartiment des dames seules, 1934; La Sonnette d'alarme, 1935; Voyage d'agrément, 1935; La Famille Pont-Biquet, 1935; Sacré Léonce, 1935; Sous la griffe, 1935; On ne roule pas Antoinette, 1936; L'École des journalistes, 1936; Un de la Légion, 1936; Rigolboche, 1936; Monsieur Personne, 1936; Josette, 1936; La Maison d'en face, 1936; Les Dégourdis de la onzième, 1937; (with Sacha Guitry) Les Perles de la couronne (The Pearls of the Crown), 1937; À Venise, une nuit, 1937; Les Pirates du rail, 1937; François 1er (Francis the First), 1937; Les Disparus de Saint Agil (Boys' School), 1938; Ernest le rebelle/C'était moi, 1938; Raphaël le tatoué, 1938; Le Grand Élan, 1938; L'Enfer des anges, 1939; L'Assassinat du Père Noël (Who Killed Santa Claus?/ The Murder of Father Christmas), 1941; Premier Bal, 1941; La Symphonie fantastique, 1942; Carmen, 1943; Voyage sans espoir, 1943; Sortilèges (The Sorcerer/ The Bellman), 1944; Boule de suif (Angel and Sinner), 1945; Un Revenant (A Lover's Return), 1946; La Chartreuse de Parme, 1948; D'Homme à hommes (Man to Men), 1948; Barrières, 1949 (short); Singoalla (The Wind Is My Lover/The Mask and the Sword), 1950; Souvenirs perdus (Lost Property), 1950; Barbe-Bleue (Bluebeard), 1951; Fanfan-la-Tulipe (Fanfan the Tulip), 1952; Adorables Créatures (Night Beauties), 1952; Lucrèce Borgia (Sins of the Borgias), 1953; Lysistrata *episode in* Destinées (Daughters of Destiny), 1954; Madame Du Barry, 1954; Nana, 1955; Si tous les gars du monde (If All the Guys in the World/Race for Life),

1955; Nathalie (The Foxiest Girl in Paris), 1957; La Loi c'est la loi (The Law Is the Law), 1959; Babette s'en va-t'en guerre (Babette Goes to War), 1960; Le Divorce *episode in* La Française et l'amour (Love and the Frenchwoman), 1961; Madame Sans-Gêne (Madame), 1962; Les Bonnes Causes (Don't Tempt the Devil), 1963; La Tulipe noire (The Black Tulip), 1964; Le Repas des fauves, 1964; Le Gentleman de Cocody (Ivory Coast Adventure), 1965; La Guerre secrète (The Dirty Game), 1965; (with others) Marco Polo, 1965; La Seconde Vérité, 1966; La Saint prend l'affût, 1966; Deux Billets pour Mexico (Dead Run), 1967; Lady Hamilton (The Making of a Lady), 1969; Les Pétroleuses (The Legend of Frenchie King), 1971; Docteur Justice (Doctor Justice), 1975; La Vie Parisienne, 1977.

ABOUT: Leprohon, P. Présences contemporaines, 1957; Who's Who in France, 1979–1980. *Periodicals*—Film Dope April 1975; Travelling (Switzerland) Autumn 1976.

"CLAIR," RENÉ (René Chomette) (November 11, 1898–March 15, 1981), French director, scenarist, actor, and critic, was born in Paris, the second son of Marius Chomette, a soap merchant, and the former Marie Senet. He grew up in his parents' apartment above their shop on the Rue des Halles, overlooking the city's principal market. When he was seven he was given a puppet theatre and began writing his own plays for it, or restaging with his brother Henri the plays and operas their parents took them to see. Encouraged by his father, he decided before he was in his teens that he wanted to be a writer.

René Chomette was educated at the Lycée Montaigne and the Lycée Louis-le-Grand in Paris. He is said to have been a brilliant student of the classics and exceptionally able at most other nonmathematical subjects, though he failed his philosophy finals. A high-spirited youth, fond of fencing and boxing, he gave the school authorities a certain amount of trouble. In 1917, near the end of World War I, he joined an ambulance corps as a volunteer and went to the front. He was invalided out a few months later in a state of physical and emotional collapse following a spinal injury. An intense religious crisis followed, and he retreated for a time to a Dominican monastery. His anguish and bitterness at what he had seen of the war were expressed in the moving poems of *Terre* (1919).

In 1919 Chomette began his career as a journalist on *L'Intransigeant*, where he remained until 1922. He had many friends in Parisian literary, musical, and artistic circles, and recalls "uncomfortable" meetings with Marcel Proust, then in his last illness and inclined to converse with "a curious detachment." At this point Chomette had no interest in the cinema, but one day

RENÉ CLAIR

he joined some friends who thought it might be amusing to perform in a film as extras. Very soon afterwards he was playing lead roles, first in Loïe Fuller's *Le Lys de la vie* (1920) and Protozanov's *Le Sens de la mort* (1921), then in two Feuillade serials, *L'Orpheline* (1921) and *Parisette* (1921).

It was because he thought his involvement with the cinema would be no more than a brief flirtation that Chomette adopted a pseudonym: René Clair. Indeed, he is said to have been only a mediocre actor. His interest in the medium grew nevertheless, and he began seeing films as well as acting in them, studying in particular the Mack Sennett comedies and above all the films of Chaplin, whom he idolized. In 1922, when his brother Henri went to Brussels to study the work of the director Jacques de Baroncelli, Clair left *L'Intransigeant* and followed him, winding up as Baroncelli's assistant director on *Carillon de Minuit* and *La Légende de soeur Béatrix*, both made in 1922. This experience completed his conversion, and he returned to Paris an enthusiast and champion of the cinema, taking a post as film editor of *Le Théâtre et Comœdia Illustré*.

René Clair made his first film as a director in 1923: *Paris qui dort* (*The Crazy Ray*, 1924). It begins with the nightwatchman of the Eiffel Tower descending to the streets one morning to find himself alone in a dormant city: a taxi driver has gone to sleep in the act of changing gears; a gendarme has dozed off with his hand outstretched to nab a pickpocket; a suicide is poised to dive into the Seine. The nightwatchman Albert is able to make useful adjustments to some of these situations before the mad scientist who

put Paris to sleep is persuaded to reverse the process. "The bones of the best comic cinema in Europe were in that early picture," wrote C. A. Lejeune a few years later, and it is true that *Paris qui dort* illustrates many of the most characteristic elements of a Clair movie—his love of Paris and its people, his strong and simple moral sense, his distrust of science and the corrupting power of money, as well as his fastidious wit and his immaculate sense of comic timing.

In his review of *Paris qui dort* René Bizet wrote that Clair "has succeeded in getting some amazing effects out of this study of movement: comic effects, dramatic ones, effects of surprise—that is cinema. It is all images and nothing but images, without useless intellectualism. The psychology is not born before the images, but of them." That must have pleased Clair, because he had set out in this film to point out the contrast between movement and immobility in cinematic terms. In the manifesto he wrote for its premiere, he said: "If cinema has any aesthetics of its own, they were discovered at the same time as the camera and the film, in France, by the Lumière brothers. They are summed up in one word: movement. The external movement of objects perceived by the eye, to which we will now add the internal movement of the action. The union of these two movements can produce what one speaks about so often and sees so rarely—rhythm."

In all the essays and reviews he published at this time, Clair was campaigning against the art films of the period—the static adaptations of literary classics—and calling for a return to the visual concerns and robust popular traditions of the pioneers of the cinema. His second film, *Entr'acte*, was a homage to such early masters of screen comedy as Méliès, the Lumières, and Ferdinand Zecca, made with the connivance of an important section of the Paris avant-garde. Clair had by this time added ballet to his list of enthusiasms, and *Entr'acte* was made to fill the fifteen-minute interval between the two acts of Francis Picabia's dadaist ballet *Relâche* (No Performance, 1924). Full of visual trickery, chases, and magic, this exuberant entertainment features such luminaries as Man Ray, Marcel Duchamp, Georges Auric, Picabia, and Erik Satie (who also provided a carefully irrelevant accompanying score). The ballet itself provoked a riot and the film was scarcely less controversial, though to Roger Régent it seemed that "in everything that makes it preposterous and explosive, charming and light, *Entr'acte* remains the French masterpiece of pure cinema."

At about this time Clair was associated for a while with Jean Epstein, Marcel L'Herbier, and other leaders of the cinema's "first avant-garde," though he was never really a member of this or any other movement. He continued his explorations of the medium's resources in two engaging fantasies—*Le Fantôme du Moulin-Rouge* (*The Phantom of the Moulin Rouge,* 1925), which makes great use of superimposition in a story about the pranks of a disembodied spirit, and *Le Voyage imaginaire* (*The Imaginary Journey,* 1925), a silent forerunner of *Les Belles-de-Nuit.* These were followed by one of Clair's few lapses into mere commercialism, *La Proie du vent* (*Prey of the Wind*), an efficient screen adaptation of a novel by Armand Mercier. Unremarkable in itself, it marked the beginning of Clair's association with the designer Lazare Meerson, who worked thereafter on all of Clair's films through *Quatorze juillet,* influencing the development of the director's work and the whole course of film design.

The picture that established Clair's international reputation was *Un Chapeau de paille d'Italie* (*The Italian Straw Hat,* 1927). It was based on the Labiche-Michel farce about a young bridegroom's frantic search for a hat exactly like the one consumed by his horse while its owner was preoccupied with her lover, a vengeful officer who demands a replacement. The characters are not individuals but types, brilliantly "placed" by Meerson's costumes and sets of the 1890s and Clair's translation of verbal tics into visual traits. The search theme itself is full of cinematic possibilities, inventively exploited, and the film's satire on bourgeois mores and affectations was sufficiently telling to alienate large sections of its audience. *Un Chapeau de paille d'Italie* was not a commercial success but it was a critical one, praised for its originality, wit, and polish, and found reminiscent of the Russian ballet and the Greek drama in its presentation of puppetlike human types at odds with destiny. Roger Manvell found it "without equal, except for the best work of Chaplin, Lubitsch, and Stroheim," and thought it would "remain one of the permanent 'classics' of the silent cinema."

Georges Périnal, the great cinematographer who contributed as much as Meerson to some of the best of Clair's early films, first collaborated with him on *Le Tour* (1928), a lyrical little film poem about the Eiffel Tower. This was followed by Clair's last silent picture, *Les Deux Timides* (*Two Timid Souls,* 1928), another Labiche-Michel adaptation. Not very highly regarded on release, it has since been increasingly admired for its technical inventiveness—its magisterial use of a split screen, and the famous sequence in which a halting speech by a nervous young lawyer is represented not by the scene in court but

by the ludicrous events he is trying to describe, the action stopping when he loses the thread, accelerating when he picks it up again.

"What is basic to the cinema is that which cannot be told," Clair said. With such an opinion, it is not surprising that he was full of forebodings about the arrival of the talkies, unsure if it meant "rebirth or death" for the cinema. He inclined to the latter view but, after seeing Harry Beaumont's *Broadway Melody* (1929), conceded that "it is not impossible that a real art of talking films should emerge." He proved his point with *Sous les toits de Paris* (*Under the Roofs of Paris,* 1930), "the first French talkie of importance." The story is slight, and it is in effect a series of genre pictures of the "little people" of Paris—shopkeepers, streetsingers, petty thieves—viewed with a mixture of irony and affection.

Clair knew that the cinema is concerned with showing, not telling, and in *Sous les toits,* at a time when most talkies were nothing *but* talk, he reduced dialogue to an absolute minimum, using it to convey only information that could not be supplied visually or in other ways; as Lewis Jacobs wrote, he overcame "the immobility of dialogue by relying on the mobility of the camera." And as if to point up the insignificance of mere speech, he introduced the astonishingly sophisticated device of filming conversations that could not be heard (because the actors were arguing behind a glass door, or their words were drowned by background noise): "It is not important that the sound of applause be *heard,* if one can *see* the hands clapping," he said.

It was not only the immobilizing effect of dialogue that worried Clair, but also the fact that it radically reduced his audience, tending to limit it to those who understood French. Music, however, is as universally comprehensible as the visual image, and in *Sous les toits* he made his first attempts to eke out the sparse dialogue by using songs and background music to further the plot and to establish mood. The film was an immense success, and its innovations were emulated by directors in Hollywood as well as in Europe. Mark Van Doren wrote that *Sous les toits* "came as near to perfection as any conceivable film of its kind," and Theodore Huff noted how "reality and its characters are interpreted by Clair's mood and fancy; taking all the ingredients of real life, he transformed them into a Clair world, as distinctive as the Chaplin world."

The "Clair world" is delineated even more fully in *Le Million* (*The Million,* 1931), in which a pair of young lovers pursue an old coat containing a winning lottery ticket, others join in the hunt, and there is a final *débâcle* on the stage of the opera house, with everyone snatching up some sort of costume and turning the opera into a riot. The chase leads all over a Paris built by Meerson and photographed by Périnal—a city recognizable but stylized, made softer and more mysterious than the real one. The people are also stylized—typical lovers, policemen, creditors, crooks—chasing through their imaginary city or decoratively grouped in a way that again suggested comparisons with ballet, and also with opera.

Catherine de la Roche has called *Le Million,* based on a vaudeville comedy, "Clair's greatest pioneering achievement. Wishing to preserve the movement and the irreality of the original vaudeville, he replaced most of its dialogue with lyrics written by himself and new music composed to fit the action, so creating a musical film style." Music and sound are used throughout this immensely influential movie with the greatest wit and ingenuity, both to further the action and to comment on it. Thus, while two fat singers deliver a sentimental duet, we see the young lovers hiding in the wings enact the words in earnest. And the *mêlée* on stage, with everyone fighting for possession of the famous coat, is turned to play by the use of whistles and other sound effects of a soccer game. Alexandre Arnoux, at the time of the film's release, wrote: "We have just witnessed the birth of an eminently French masterpiece," and James Agate called it "one of the two best films I have ever seen" (he had "no notion" what the other one was). For William Whitebait it was "the *Beggar's Opera* of our time. . . . the first screen opera."

Le Million was both a critical and commercial success but it did not please everyone—Clair was attacked as a communist by the extreme Right and as a fascist by the extreme Left. He himself said: "I have no political opinion. I am just French." That he nevertheless did have a social point of view was demonstrated in *À nous la liberté* (*Freedom for Us,* 1932), another picture in which music plays a vital role. A former convict established a large phonograph factory, where a fellow-inmate comes to work.

The film graphically illustrates the parallels between assembly-line methods in the prison and those in the factory, and in the end both boss and worker escape to happy vagabondage. The film is a celebration of friendship, one of Clair's favorite themes, and a mild and witty attack on capitalist hypocrisy and greed and the notion of the "sanctity of labor" (on this account arousing a surprising amount of controversy). Catherine de la Roche thought the film had "qualities more important than its rather superficial social criticism. The virtuosity with which Clair combined images and sounds in flowing rhythmic patterns . . . is striking. He also introduced a rich vein of kindliness and geniality into the coldly fantastic backgrounds of mechanical and financial power." Chaplin borrowed so heavily from *À nous la liberté* in *Modern Times* that the producers of the Clair film sued; Clair put an end to the case by announcing that he himself was pleased by this tribute from his idol.

The last of the magnificent group of films-with-music that Clair made with Périnal and Meerson was *Quatorze juillet* (*July the Fourteenth,* 1932), a series of vignettes of life in a Paris suburb on the eve of Bastille Day. Like *Sous les toits,* it is a poetic celebration of life and love and of Paris itself, with touches of sadness and even of bitterness, and characters more fully individuated than in Clair's other early films. Perhaps because it broke no new ground it has not been much discussed, but Gavin Lambert found it "a film of almost miraculous slightness, perfectly sustained in mood and atmosphere" and "in many ways Clair's most intimate and attractive work."

Clair's early sound films were all produced by Films Sonores Tobis, a Germany company. This arrangement ended when Hitler came to power, and his next picture, *Le Dernier Milliardaire* (*The Last Multimillionaire,* 1934), was eventually made for Pathé. It is a nonmusical and rather grim satire about a megalomaniac banker who becomes dictator of a country (like Monaco) that depends for its revenue on gambling. Released at a time of political turmoil following the assassination of King Alexander of Yugoslavia, it provoked fascist riots and had to be withdrawn. Though it later won prizes abroad, Clair regarded it as a failure and partly for this reason accepted Alexander Korda's invitation to work in Britain.

The film he made for Korda was *The Ghost Goes West* (1935), adapted by Robert Sherwood from a *Punch* story about an American millionaire (Eugene Pallette) who buys a Scottish castle and rebuilds it in Florida, complete with its resident ghost. Robert Donat played both the ghost and his descendant, the present laird, and Jean Parker the millionaire's pretty daughter. It was the first of Clair's films that he had not written himself (though it is said that he always collaborated with his writers, even when uncredited). He was, moreover, working in a foreign country with an unfamiliar crew. The result was found more static, verbal, and technically conventional than its predecessors but an expert and entertaining comedy nevertheless, full of nice satirical touches. It was commercially successful and over the years has risen in critical esteem.

Clair's other British film had less to recommend it. This was *Break the News* (1938), a moderately amusing remake with Jack Buchanan and Maurice Chevalier of a French comedy called *La Mort en fuite*. Returning to France, Clair embarked on *Air pur* (*Fresh Air*), a film about poor children on vacation at a summer camp near Nice. It would have been a considerable departure for Clair—a realist picture in the documentary tradition, filmed mostly on location—but it was never completed. The war intervened, and in 1940 Clair left France with his wife and son and went to the United States, where he was received with adulation.

His first Hollywood film was the romantic comedy *The Flame of New Orleans* (Universal, 1941). Marlene Dietrich gives a captivating performance as a European adventuress who poses as a countess to capture a rich banker (Roland Young) but finds herself inconveniently attracted by a tough young sailor (Bruce Cabot). Clair collaborated with Norman Krasna on the witty script and had Rudolph Maté, an old friend, as his cameraman. This elegant and ironic picture was not a success in the United States but was much admired when it was shown in France after the war. In 1942 Clair contributed one episode to the portmanteau film *Forever and a Day*, replacing Alfred Hitchcock at the last minute; this was reportedly the only piece he ever directed without making any contribution to the scenario, and he has excluded it from his filmography.

I Married a Witch (Paramount, 1942) was the movie that launched Veronica Lake, in the role of a young witch burned by the Puritans who is reborn in modern New York. She sets out to revenge herself on a descendant of her persecutors (Fredric March), but discovers that love is stronger than witchcraft. Catherine de la Roche wrote that "Veronica Lake's witchery often seems essentially natural and the machinery of modern society absurdly artificial—hence the logic, credibility and humour of a screenplay in which reality and fantasy are neatly balanced."

A more serious and dramatic fantasy followed, *It Happened Tomorrow* (United Artists, 1944), working out on the screen a notion that has attracted a number of writers: the benefits that might accrue if someone were given a copy of tomorrow's newspaper—and the anguish if it contained a report of his own death. With a cast that includes Dick Powell, Linda Darnell, and Jack Oakie, it is the director's favorite among the films he made in Hollywood. The last of these, *And Then There Were None* (Twentieth Century-Fox, 1945), was based on Agatha Christie's classic detective story. The least original of Clair's Hollywood films, it was nevertheless financially very successful. The director's English-language pictures, formerly regarded as potboilers remote from his real concerns, have recently been reassessed and are now studied seriously as integral and creditable contributions to his *oeuvre*.

Clair's first postwar film was *le Silence est d'or* (*Man About Town,* 1947), nostalgically evoking the early days of the French film industry—the golden days of the silents. Starring Maurice Chevalier as a director of the old school and François Perier as his shy young assistant (who eventually wins the girl his master loves), it is a perfectly judged mixture of irony and pathos. It won the Grand Prix at both the Brussels and the Locarno festivals and for many critics, as for Georges Charensol, "was more than a success"—a "revival of our youth" and a "tender, bantering homage to the first artisans of the cinema, to whom René Clair owes so much." Charensol called this "the most French" of all Clair's films—clear evidence that his long absence abroad had not separated him from his roots. It is notable also as the first picture the director made with the designer Léon Barsacq, who contributed almost as much to his late films as Meerson had to the early ones.

La Beauté du diable (*Beauty and the Devil,* 1950), written in collaboration with Armand Salacrou, is a tragicomic version of the Faust legend. Mephisto (Michael Simon) gives Faust youth, love, and power, asking nothing in return, then reduces him to poverty and insignificance. Faust (Gérard Philipe) signs away his soul to regain his former status, but renounces it when he is shown a horrific vision of himself as a director corrupted by power in a world made hideous by scientific "progress." Set in Italy (where it was filmed) in the seventeenth century, the picture had a mixed reception, some critics finding in it a new richness and maturity, others calling it pretentious and unconvincing, its happy ending banal.

That Clair had found in Gérard Philipe an actor perfectly equipped to interpret his wryly romantic vision was confirmed by *Les Belles-de-nuit* (*Beauties of the Night,* 1952), which was conceived as a comic version of *Intolerance*. It stars Philipe as a discontented music teacher in a noisy provincial town who dreams about brave deeds and sexual triumphs in the glamorous past. The dreams change to nightmares, obliging him to stay awake long enough to notice the real-life charms of the girl at the garage. The music (by Georges Van Parys) is more fully integrated into the action than in any of Clair's films since those of the early 1930s, and the picture provided ample evidence that he had not lost the "Clair touch." Though some reviewers thought it escapist and frivolous, many warmly praised its lyrical charm and elegant construction.

Gérard Philipe appeared again in *Les Grandes Manoeuvres* (*The Grand Maneuver*, 1955), a variation on the Don Juan theme and Clair's first film in color. Set in a provincial garrison town just before World War I, it stars Philipe as a feckless young cavalry officer who wagers that he can seduce any lady in town, to be chosen by lot. In fact he falls deeply in love with his victim (Michèle Morgan), only to find that his reputation as a lecher makes it impossible for her to believe his protestations, made for the first time in total sincerity. Beginning as a comedy of small-town manners and mores, the film modulates into a gentle tragedy of love irredeemably lost. Catherine de la Roche thought it perhaps "the most complete expression of Clair's artistic personality. Scene after scene is built on fascinating associations of ideas in word and image. . . . The colour composition . . . assumes poetic or symbolic value. The film is also remarkable for its characters, who are in fact more interesting than their story."

In *Le Silence est d'or* and *Les Grandes Manoeuvres* critics found "more heart and warmth" than Clair displays in any of his earlier work. His view of life is nevertheless fundamentally pessimistic. "Comedy," he wrote in 1953, "can have only provisional endings, for it tends to leave an impression of happiness; only in tragedy can *dénouements* be real. But this might involve us in a discussion of the human condition, which would be inappropriate and lacking in originality at a time when fashionable authors are discovering in their various ways—albeit somewhat later than Ecclesiastes—the disadvantages of this condition."

This pessimism is evident in *Porte des Lilas* (*Gates of Paris*, 1957). Juju (Pierre Brasseur) is a middle-aged drunkard who has nothing in life but his friendship with a street musician (Georges Brassens). He acquires a new sense of self-respect when he shelters a wanted criminal (Henri Vidal) from the police, but the gangster exploits both Juju and the girl he hopelessly loves (Dany Carrel), and Juju, trying to prevent him from stealing the girl's money, accidentally kills him. His attempt to do something useful in the world thus ends in disaster. This "dramatic comedy" seemed to some critics Clair's definitive treatment of the themes of friendship and loyalty which recur throughout his work, and a characteristically bittersweet study of the "little people" of Paris. To some younger writers, however, it seemed empty and artificial—a faultless

technical achievement with nothing to say of the slightest contemporary relevance.

It was followed by *Tout l'or du monde* (*All the Gold in the World*, 1961), starring Bourvil in a comedy about a peasant family's stubborn resistance to the blandishments and pressures of city tycoons hungry for their land. Shot, for once, on location, it has some agreeable and witty touches, but is a minor piece. Apart from episodes in two portmanteau films, Clair made only one more picture, *Les Fêtes galantes* (*Gallant Festivals*, 1965), a polished, witty, but somewhat laborious chronicle of war's absurdities filmed in Romania.

For some thirty years, beginning in the early 1930s, Clair's status was secure as one of the world's great filmmakers and as the most famous of all French directors. In 1960 he became the first director ever elected to the Académie Française on the strength of his films alone. But the world Clair shows us is always partly an imaginary one, conceived on paper, constructed in the studio, and inhabited by characters who perform symbolic roles in a predestined history. What he says about society and the terms in which he says it are alien to the influential critics associated with *Les Cahiers du Cinéma*, and though Clair's work has not been excoriated as harshly as that of some of his contemporaries, it is not at present much discussed.

"At once a conservative and a revolutionary," writes Catherine de la Roche, "René Clair has created a style which belongs to no school and no movement, only to himself. The ideology in his films is often conventional; the satire superficial; the women's roles usually subordinate to the men's. . . . But, in pioneering cinema as an art form, he has also extended its scope in other directions. His enthusiastic explorations of the possibilities of movement, imagery, sound and colour, have led him also to find or invent new subjects for the screen. And his place in film history is assured not only on account of his discoveries and influence: the world of dancing lovers and shadowless spirits, of camaraderie in the Paris streets and erring heroes brought to book—this world of his, in which violence, vulgarity and cant have no place, has delighted the millions of people for whom it was created."

Clair never entirely abandoned his literary interests. His episodic first novel *Adams* (1926; translated by John Marks as *Star Turn*, 1936), dedicated to Chaplin, is a satirical fantasy about the commercialization of the American cinema. *La Princesse de Chine* and *De fil en aiguille*, two novellas, were published together in 1951, and there was a volume of short stories, *Jeux de hasard*, in 1976. A play, *L'Étrange ouvrage des cieux* (1971), was staged in 1974 at the Paris Odéon as *La Catin aux lèvres douces*. Clair's articles and essays on the cinema have been collected in two volumes, *Réflexion Faite* (1951, translated by Vera Traill as *Reflections on the Cinema*, 1953) and *Cinéma hier, Cinéma d'aujourd'hui* (1970).

In 1967 an interviewer described René Clair as "a sharp-featured, alert man, slight and athletic," with gray hair "severely brushed." He was married in 1928 to Bronia Perlmutter and has one son. Apart from his membership of the Académie Française, Clair is a Grand Officer de la Légion d'honneur and a Commandeur des Arts et des Lettres. He holds the Grand Cross of the French Order of Merit and has an honorary doctorate from Cambridge University.

FILMS: Paris qui dort (The Crazy Ray), 1924; Entr'acte, 1924; Le Fantôme du Moulin-Rouge (The Phantom of the Moulin Rouge), 1925; Le Voyage imaginaire (The Imaginary Journey), 1925; La Proie du vent (Prey of the Wind), 1926; Un Chapeau de paille d' Italie (The Italian Straw Hat), 1927; La Tour (The Tower), 1928; Les Deux Timides (Two Timid Souls), 1928; Sous les toits de Paris (Under the Roofs of Paris), 1930; Le Million (The Million), 1931; À nous la liberté (Freedom for Us), 1932; Quatorze juillet (July the Fourteenth), 1932; Le Dernier Milliardaire (The Last Multimillionaire), 1934; The Ghost Goes West, 1935; Break the News, 1937; The Flame of New Orleans, 1941; *episode in* Forever and a Day, 1942; I Married a Witch, 1942; It Happened Tomorrow, 1944; And Then There Were None/Ten Little Niggers/Ten Little Indians, 1945; Le Silence est d'or (Man About Town), 1947; La Beauté du diable (Beauty and the Devil), 1950; Les Belles-denuit (Beauties of the Night/Night Beauties), 1952; Les Grandes Manoeuvres (The Grand Maneuver/Summer Maneuvers), 1955; Porte des Lilas (Gate of Lilacs/ Gates of Paris), 1957; Le Mariage (Marriage) *episode in* La Française et l' amour, 1960; Tout l' or du monde (All the Gold in the World), 1961; Les Deux Pigeons (The Two Pigeons), *episode in* Les Quatre Vérités, 1962; Les Fêtes galantes (Gallant Festivals), 1965. *Published scripts*: The Ghost Goes West *in* Successful Film Writing, by Seton Margrave, 1938; Entr' acte, edited by Glauco Viazzi, 1945 (Italy); Le Million, edited by Bianca Lattuada, 1945 (Italy); Le Silence est d'or, 1946; Comédies et Commentaires (contains Le Silence est d'or, La Beauté du diable, Les Belles-de-nuit, Les Grandes Manoeuvres, Porte des Lilas), 1959; Entr'acte and À nous la liberté *in* L'Avant-Scène du Cinéma November 1968.

ABOUT: Amenguel, B. René Clair, 1963 (France); Blumer, R. H. The Critic's View of René Clair, 1965; Bourgeois, J. René Clair, 1949 (France); Charensol, G. and Régent, R. Un Maître du Cinéma: René Clair, 1952 (France); Charensol, G. René Clair et Les Belles-de-nuit, 1953 (France); Chiaretti, T. René Clair, 1967; Clair, R. Reflections on the Cinema, translated by Vera Traill, 1953; Clair, R. Cinéma d'hier, cinéma d'aujourd'hui, 1970; Current Biography, 1941; De la

Roche, C. René Clair: An Index, 1958; Leprohon, P. Présences contemporaines, cinéma, 1957 (France); Mast, G. The Comic Mind, 1973; Mitry, J. René Clair, 1960 (France); Samuels, C. T. Encountering Directors, 1972; Viazzi, G. René Clair, 1946 (Italy). *Periodicals*—American Scholar Spring 1971; Bianco e nero August–September 1951, February 1962, March–April 1968, September–October 1968; Bookman (London) April 1932; Cahiers du Cinéma May 1957; Cinema Journal Spring 1977; Film Culture Spring 1963; Film Quarterly Winter 1970–1971; Films and Filming June 1957; Films in Review November 1960; Focus on Film Winter 1972; Image et Son October–November 1956; Nation June 8, 1932; November 1, 1933; January 29, 1936; New Republic June 12, 1944; New Yorker September 14, 1940; November 29, 1958; Sight and Sound January–March 1952.

*CLÉMENT, RENÉ (March 18, 1913–), French director and scenarist, was born in Bordeaux, first of the three children of Jean Clément, an interior decorator, and the former Marguerite Bayle. His father gave him a magic lantern when he was six and he delighted in that toy, soon graduating to the even greater satisfactions of moving pictures. The cinema became both his favorite pastime and a refuge from the problems of childhood. His own first "films" were drawn or painted on miniature "screens"—squares of white paper carefully edged in black.

From the Bordeaux *lycée*, Clément went on to the École National Supérieure des Beaux Arts as a student of architecture. It was then that he bought his first movie camera and (at the age of eighteen) made his first film, an animated cartoon in which statues of Julius Caesar and Vercingetorix descend from their plinths and discuss the past. Two years later the death of Clément's father obliged him to abandon his architectural studies. In 1934 Clément met Jacques Tati, then making his debut as a music-hall pantomimist, and helped him to work up his act. Clément became a devotee of the music hall, from which he learned an acute sense of gesture and timing and an extreme concern for precision.

Accounts of the early part of Clément's career vary somewhat in their details, but he probably made his first film in 1936—*Soigne ton gauche* (*Remember Your Left*), a two-reel comedy written by and starring Jacques Tati as a country boy who wants to become a champion boxer. Several more short films followed, including *L'Arabie interdite* (*Forbidden Arabia*, 1937), a color documentary made on an archeological expedition which later won a prize in a competition at Biarritz. Clément developed the characteristic realism of his style in the short documentaries he

RENÉ CLÉMENT

directed at this time, when he also worked as cameraman on shorts directed by J.-K. Raymond-Millet and others. During the German occupation Clément studied at the Nice film school, where he made a propaganda short called *Chefs de demain* (*Leaders of Tomorrow,* 1943).

In 1943 Clément returned to Paris and started work on his first feature film, *La Bataille du rail* (*Battle of the Rails,* 1946). Based on actual events and written by Clément in collaboration with the novelist Colette Audry, it is a moving and exciting tribute to the part played in the wartime Resistance by French railroad workers. The film was shot on location and performed mostly by nonprofessionals (many of them railroad workers reenacting their own exploits). "Its story of ingenious heroism is admirably told in cinematic terms," wrote Dilys Powell. "The modesty of the acting . . . gives a kind of depth to the simple realism; and . . . I can find no flaw in the confident and often beautiful handling of the train sequences." *La Bataille du rail* received the international jury prize at Cannes and the Grand Prix du Cinéma Français. It earned favorable comparison with the best products of Italian neorealism and to many critics seemed a promise of a French realist movement that in fact never developed.

As a result of this success, Jean Cocteau sought Clément's services as technical director for *La Belle et la Bête* (1946), though Clément's contribution to that masterpiece is said to have been slight. The same is probably true of *Le Père tranquille* (1946), a minor piece about the Resistance which credits Clément as director but which is said to be largely the creation of its author and star, Noël-Noël. Another film with a wartime setting followed, *Les Maudits* (*The Damned,* 1947), about a party of defeated Nazis who try to escape by submarine to Latin America but end by destroying each other. Conventional characterization and a wordy script (by Clément and Jacques Rémy) weakened a movie of great technical skill and assurance, brilliantly photographed by Henri Alekan, whose collaboration with Clément began when the latter was making his first documentaries before the war.

Au delà des grilles (*The Walls of Malapaga,* 1949) was the first of a number of Italian-French coproductions that Clément has filmed in Italy. It stars Jean Gabin in a role strongly reminiscent of the ones that made him famous in the late 1930s, as a fugitive from justice hiding out in Genoa and enjoying a brief interlude of love and happiness before the police close in. This rather dated and melodramatic situation contrasts oddly with the neorealistic elements contributed by the original scriptwriters (Cesare Zavattini and Suso Cecchi d'Amico) and the documentary realism of Clément's location work in the streets and tenements of Genoa. In the United States, nevertheless, the movie carried off an Oscar as the best foreign film of the year. There are also some strikingly inventive visual touches in *Le Château de Verre* (*The Glass Castle,* 1950), an otherwise unexceptional piece based on a Vicki Baum bestseller and starring Michèle Morgan and Jean Marais.

One of the most uneven of major directors, Clément recovered and enhanced his fading reputation with *Jeux interdits* (*Forbidden Games,* 1952), adapted by Jean Aurenche, Pierre Bost, and Clément from a story by François Boyer. It is set early in World War II and begins with a German air attack on a column of refugees—a sequence given terrifying immediacy by inspired camerawork and editing. A little Parisian girl whose parents die in the raid is taken in by a peasant family. She makes friends with the family's youngest son and they begin their secret game, searching for dead animals to which they give elaborate funerals. Surrounded by incomprehensible carnage, the children tame death by turning it into an innocent but compulsive ritual. Clément had shown his great talent as a director of nonprofessional actors in *La Bataille du rail,* and in *Jeux interdits* he drew from the five-year-old Brigitte Fossey and the slightly older Georges Poujouly performances of almost documentary naturalness and simplicity. The result has been called "one of the most striking films ever made on the subject of war." Unaccountably refused a festival showing at Cannes, it won an independent Grand Prix there, the Lion d'Or (the highest award) at the 1952 Venice Biennale, and an American Oscar as the best foreign film of the year.

It was followed by a picture that a few critics place even above *Jeux interdits* and which won a special jury prize at Cannes in 1954, *Monsieur Ripois* (*Lovers, Happy Lovers* in the United States; *Knave of Hearts* in Britain). It stars Gérard Philipe as a young Frenchman on the make in London, living by his wits and his talents as a Don Juan. We see in flashback Ripois' ingenious seductions of a career woman (Margaret Johnston), a middle-class innocent (Joan Greenwood), a prostitute (Germaine Montero), and a rich snob (Valerie Hobson), but his skills desert him when he falls genuinely in love with a fifth girl (Natasha Parry). Wooing in earnest, he is rejected, and injures himself seriously in a feigned suicide attempt, winding up crippled by love.

Monsieur Ripois was almost universally praised for its wit and irony, for the charm and delicacy of Philipe's performance, and for the startling—even revolutionary—realism of its "lived-in, everyday London," shot on location by Oswald Morris, frequently with a concealed camera. Karel Reisz thought this "dry, sardonic comedy" the equal of the best work of Preston Sturges and essentially more serious in its moral concerns. Reisz went on: "Clément's invention and effortless command of all the camera's tricks keep the story full of surprises and galloping at an extraordinary pace; it is a pleasure to see so wittily controlled a piece of craftsmanship. Ripois' affairs are quickly and boldly sketched in, with sure characterization and an awareness of English social life that is astonishing in a French director. . . . The script, by Raymond Queneau, Hugh Mills, and Clément, is economical, sharp and dextrous with casual dialogue; the musical score by Roman Vlad, giving each mistress an ironical theme tune of her own, is ingeniously witty; and Clément's picture of London is extraordinarily vivid and real. . . . No British feature director has used London so well."

Clément's first period film was *Gervaise* (1956), adapted by Aurenche and Bost from *L'Assommoir*, Zola's savage study of alcoholism. Its theme, Clément said, "is not limited to its period. I can take you to a Coupeau house in about ten different parts of Paris and you will find all the characters. This relevancy attracted me." This did not prevent him from striving for absolute fidelity in his studio reconstruction of nineteenth-century Paris and in the unblinking realism with which he portrays the squalor and degradation of the Coupeau family. "Exactness must be a mania," Clément believes. "One must not accept a hairstyle or a wallpaper that was not in existence at that time. The public does not always realize this but knows subconsciously that it has not been cheated." In pursuit of this exactness Clément and the actor François Périer, who plays the drunkard Coupeau, visited mental institutions and alcoholic wards to study the effects of the disease. As a result, Périer gave one of the finest performances of his career in a film of great power (though opinions differed about the merits of Maria Schell's handling of the title role). *Gervaise* won the critics' prize at Venice and other awards in Britain, New York, Japan, and elsewhere.

Barrage contre le Pacifique (*The Sea Wall*, 1958), an international coproduction shot on location in Thailand, boasts a cast that includes Silvana Mangano, Alida Valli, Anthony Perkins, Jo Van Fleet, and Richard Conte, but seemed to many reviewers a trivialization of the novel (by Marguerite Duras) on which it was based. *Plein Soleil* (*Purple Noon*, 1959) is another adaptation, this time of Patricia Highsmith's *The Talented Mr. Ripley*. The movie had its admirers, but some of those who had read the original thought that Clément had turned an ingenious and controversial thriller into a queasy Mediterranean travelogue short on both characterization and suspense. Garbicz and Klinowski have remarked on the film's "deceptive and repulsive opalescence."

Another period piece followed, *Quelle joie de vivre* (1961), set in Rome in 1922 and mixing hectic comedy with violence in a story about the conflict of that time between anarchists and fascists. Roy Armes was reminded of René Clair's *À nous la liberté* and wrote that the film "is handled with verve and technical brilliance and the period detail is skilfully caught, though it is doubtful whether Clément has sufficient real comic talent to control a plot that veers from burlesque to near tragedy." *Quelle joie de vivre* was an Italian-French coproduction and so was *Le Jour et l'heure* (*The Day and the Hour*, 1963), about a rich *bourgeoise* (Simone Signoret) who becomes involved in the Resistance, and the American airman (Stuart Whitman) she tries to smuggle to safety. The film scrupulously reconstructs the wartime atmosphere but is otherwise interesting mainly for the virtuoso camera work of Henri Decaë. *Les Félins* (*The Love Cage*, 1963), starring Jane Fonda, Lola Albright, and Alain Delon in another story about a man on the run, is also more remarkable for the technical skills of director and crew than for its content.

The most ambitious of Clément's international coproductions was *Paris brûle-t-il?* (*Is Paris Burning?*, 1966), an account of the liberation of

Paris by the Allied forces with a cast that includes (among many others) Orson Welles, Charles Boyer, Kirk Douglas, Gert Fröbe, Yves Montand, Simone Signoret, Jean-Paul Belmondo, Leslie Caron, Alain Delon, Glenn Ford, and Anthony Perkins. It was adapted by Gore Vidal and the young Francis Coppola from the book by Dominique Lapierre and Larry Collins. Technically excellent and often exciting, the film nevertheless seemed to many reviewers to have been capsized by its enormous freight of stars, all hamming vigorously to fill out their "cameo" roles.

None of Clément's subsequent pictures has done much to salvage his reputation. The most successful has been *Le Passager de la pluie* (*Rider on the Rain,* 1969), a thriller scripted by the mystery writer Sébastien Japrisot, with many Hitchcockian grace notes. Marlene Jobert plays a young housewife who shoots a rapist and then does her best to insure that no one, least of all her possessive husband, will ever find out. Soon, of course, a mysterious stranger (Charles Bronson) appears, asking pointed questions and alternately menacing and protecting the heroine. This film was very popular at the box office but not with the critics, who generally felt that the sequences devoted to the psychology of the heroine were not well integrated with the fast-paced genre material.

Roy Armes believes that Clément's work reflects very exactly the "various complex and contradictory tendencies of the French cinema" since the war—from the realism of *La Bataille du rail,* through the pioneering location work of *Monsieur Ripois,* to big-budget international coproductions like *Paris brûte-t-il?* In several of his later pictures, Armes says, he "has pursued with Henri Decaë his own experiments in camera flexibility in a manner that parallels the approach of many of the newer directors. There is hardly a trend, old or new, to which he has not made a notable contribution." His work has been highly uneven, but even the least of his pictures have been admired by other filmmakers for their technical mastery and superb visual sense—he is above all, perhaps, a director's director.

Clément was married in 1940 to Bella Guritch, who is of Russian birth. They divide their time between houses in Paris and Monte Carlo. Clément is a collector of books, paintings, and model boats. He enjoys listening to music and retains from his days as a student of architecture an interest in design. A founder member of the Institute of Advanced Studies in Cinematography, he is a Chevalier de la Légion d'honneur and a Commandeur des Arts et des Lettres.

FILMS: Soigne ton gauche (Remember Your Left), 1936 (short); La Grand Chartreuse (The Great Chartreuse), 1937 (short); Arabie interdite (Forbidden Arabia), 1937 (short); La Bièvre, fille perdue (La Bièvre, Lost Girl), 1939 (short); Le Tirage (The Draught), 1942 (short); Ceux du rail (Those of the Railroad), 1942 (short); Toulouse, 1943 (short); La Grande Pastorale (The Great Pastorale), 1943 (short); Chefs de demain (Leaders of Tomorrow), 1943 (short); Mountain, 1943 (short); La Bataille du rail (Battle of the Rails), 1946; Le Père tranquille (The Tranquil Father), 1946; Les Maudits (The Damned), 1947; Au delà des grilles (The Walls of Malapaga/Le Mure di Malapurga), 1949 (Italian-French); Le Chateau de verre (The Glass Castle), 1950; Jeux interdits (U.S., Forbidden Games/ U.K., Secret Games), 1952; Monsieur Ripois (U.S., Lovers, Happy Lovers/U.K., Knave of Hearts), 1954; Gervaise, 1956; Barrage contre le Pacifique (The Sea Wall/This Angry Age/La diga sul pacifico), 1958 (Italian); Plein Soleil (Purple Noon), 1959 (Italian); Quelle joie de vivre! (What Joie de Vivre!/Che gìoia vivere!, 1961 (Italian-French); Le Jour et l'heure (The Day and the Hour), 1963 (Italian-French); Les Félins (The Love Cage/Joy House), 1963; Paris brûle-t-il? (Is Paris Burning?), 1966; Écrit sur le sable (Written in the Sand), 1966; Le Passager de la pluie (Rider on the Rain), 1969 (Italian-French); La Maison sous les arbres (The Deadly Trap), 1971 (American-French); La Course du lièvre à travers les champs (And Hope to Die), 1972 (American-French); La Baby-sitter, 1975 (Italian-German-French). *Published scripts*—(with Colette Audry) La Bataille du rail, 1947; Jeux interdits *in* L'Avant-Scène du Cinéma May 1962; Monsieur Ripois *in* L'Avant-Scène du Cinéma January 1966.

ABOUT: Bazin, A. Qu'est-ce que le cinéma?, 1958–1962; Farwagi, A. René Clément, 1967 (France); Garbicz, A. and Klinowski, J. Cinema: The Magic Vehicle, 1983; International Who's Who, 1979–80; Leprohon, P. Présences contemporaines, cinéma, 1958 (France); Who's Who, 1979; Who's Who in France, 1979–1980. *Periodicals*—Film Culture September and October 1957; Film Dope April 1975; Film Journal October 1961; Films and Filming October 1960, December 1966; Image et Son July 1965; Positif November 1956; Sight and Sound June 1950.

*CLOUZOT, HENRI-GEORGES (November 20, 1907–January 1, 1977), French director, scenarist, and dramatist, was born in Niort (Deux-Sevrès) in the west of France. In his teens he entered the naval academy at Brest, but on graduation he was rejected by the navy itself because of poor sight. He then began the study of law with a view to entering the French diplomatic service, abandoning this plan at the age of twenty to become a journalist. From 1927 to 1930 he worked for the daily newspaper *Paris-Midi.*

Clouzot began his film career in 1931 as a scriptwriter. That same year he directed a short picture, *Le Terreur des Batignolles,* and soon af-

°kloo zō´

HENRI-GEORGES CLOUZOT

ter he served as assistant director to Anatole Litvak and the German director E. A. Dupont. In 1932–1933 he worked in Berlin, preparing French versions of German movies. Clouzot was plagued all his life by ill health and in his late twenties spent four years in a Swiss sanatorium—an experience, it has been suggested, that contributed a great deal to the profound pessimism that characterizes his work. Apart from this interruption, he spent most of the ten years from 1931 to 1941 as a scenarist, writing or collaborating on scripts for films directed by Carmine Gallone, Pierre Fresnay, and Georges Lacombe, among others. During the same period Clouzot wrote a number of plays, two or three of which have been staged, and an opera libretto.

Fresnay starred in the first feature Clouzot directed, *L'Assassin habite au 21* (*The Killer Lives at 21,* 1942), based on a thriller by S. A. Steeman. Clouzot wrote his own scenario (as he generally did, often in collaboration with Jean Ferry or Jérôme Géronimi), and the result was found competent but unexceptional. It was followed by *Le Corbeau* (*The Crow,* 1943), which remains one of Clouzot's finest films, though it almost ended his career. An absorbing mystery story about a poison-pen campaign, it is also a brilliant if malicious study of life in a small provincial town. Every one of the principal characters is shown to be tainted in some way by evil or corruption, and any one of them might be the dreaded Crow—a fact that is powerfully dramatized in the famous scene in which a swinging lamp alternately illuminates and darkens the faces of the suspects. In an interview with Paul

Schrader Clouzot said that his films were always inspired by an image and cited *Le Corbeau* as an example. Years before, having fallen while skiing, he became aware of the way the shadows were moving back and forth over the snow and searched thereafter for a story in which he could use this strange visual effect.

Since *Le Corbeau* was made during the German occupation, it was produced perforce by the Nazi stooge company Continental. Goebbels thought he saw propaganda value in its savage portrait of French decadence and distributed it widely in occupied Europe (where it was much admired). It fact the script—for once not by Clouzot but by Louis Chavance—had been written before the war and was based on well-publicized events that had actually taken place in Tulle. After the Liberation, nevertheless, the military censors banned the film, and Clouzot was unable to work again until 1947.

He reestablished his reputation with *Quai des Orfèvres,* based on another Steeman detective novel—the title refers to the French equivalent of Scotland Yard. The story centers on an unscrupulous young singer (Suzy Delair) and her devoted husband Maurice (Bernard Blier) who find themselves implicated in the murder of a rich old lecher. There is a Maigret-like detective, brilliantly played by Louis Jouvet at his most sardonic, and a script (by Clouzot and Jean Ferry) that is both witty and subtle (as in the scene where a statement given at the Quai des Orfèvres by the sensitive young husband seems quite false when it is translated into police jargon). The background of shabby police offices and seedy music-halls is captured with a haunting realism that owes a great deal to the skill of Clouzot's favorite cameraman, Armand Thirard. Some critics were disturbed by the brutality of the film's unblinking portrayal of the young husband's suicide attempt, but *Quai des Orfèvres* received the Director's Prize at the 1947 Venice Film Festival. Two years later Clouzot collected the Grand Prix for his next picture, *Manon.*

Clouzot based *Manon* on the Abbé Prévost's classic novel *Manon Lescaut,* but updated it as a harsh indictment of moral chaos in the aftermath of World War II. Manon, played by the sixteen-year-old Cécile Aubry, prostitutes herself and corrupts Robert, her young lover (Michel Auclair), turning a Resistance fighter into a black marketeer. She tells him that "nothing is disgusting when two people love each other" and their strange love is evidently real; when Robert, on the run for murder, joins the illegal Jewish emigration to Palestine, she unhesitatingly accompanies him and they go to their deaths in the desert. It seemd to Roy Armes that the "multiplicity of settings does in some ways detract from the impact of the film, which is more diffuse and less gripping than most of Clouzot's work."

Miquette et sa mère (*Miquette and Her Mother,* 1949), adapted from a vaudeville farce, is a minor and unsatisfactory piece, in spite of a cast that includes Jouvet, Bourvil, and Danièle Delorme. Clouzot was married in 1950 and turned down several attractive assignments to go off with his young wife Véra to her native Brazil. They hoped to make a film—"La Voyage au Brésil"—which was to be an account of Clouzot's discovery of that country. The project was never realized because of production difficulties, but Clouzot's stay in Brazil was not wasted: he wrote a book about the country (*Le Cheval des Dieux*), and his two years there stood him in good stead when he came to build the sets and to create an appropriate atmosphere for his next picture.

This was *Le Salaire de la peur* (*The Wages of Fear,* 1953), the most admired and profitable of all his films. It opens in a squalid little town in Central America, and the first half of the film introduces us to the European criminals, failures, and assorted riffraff who remain in this hellhole because they lack the means to move on. They are unexpectedly offered a chance of escape when the exploitative American oil company that owns the town discovers that it contains the nitroglycerin needed to extinguish an oil-well fire three hundred miles away. The only way that this highly volatile cargo can be transported is over the terrible local roads, and the oil company is prepared to pay four men two thousand dollars a head to attempt the journey in two trucks. Competition for this suicidal assignment is keen and indeed murderous, but the four are eventually selected and the journey begins.

This ordeal occupies the film's remorselessly suspenseful second half. The nitroglycerin is liable to explode at the slightest jolt, and the road leads through swamps and jungles, over mountains and rotting bridges. The fearless ex-Nazi Bimba (Peter Van Eyck) and the amiable Italian Luigi, apparently the most efficient team, are blown up when their success seems assured. The other two are both Frenchmen: Mario (Yves Montand) and Jo (Charles Vanel). Jo, the older man, is at first the dominant member of the team, but he cracks under the strains of the journey; roles are finally reversed when Mario (to save his own skin) drives the great truck over Jo's leg. One of the film's rare glimpses of human warmth follows in the camaraderie that unexpectedly develops between the dying Jo and his murderer. Mario delivers the explosive, wins the reward and a hero's welcome, but dies on the ju-

bilant return journey when his truck crashes over a precipice, its siren screaming in the wilderness over the end titles.

Clouzot disliked the uncertainty of location work, and *The Wages of Fear* was filmed mostly on sets constructed near Nîmes, cunningly photographed by Thirard. It received the Grand Prix at Cannes in 1953, but not before one French critic had called it "an atheistic film" and another had described it as a piece of communist propaganda—an attack on American capitalism disguised as an adventure film. What was almost universally agreed was that in its mastery of the techniques of suspense, the picture was unsurpassed. John Weightman wrote that it depicted "a world of material necessity and pure appetites, roughly organized according to virile codes. But what are these codes but a futile gesturing in the face of the unknown? . . . And it is a particularly fine touch, I think, to make the exhausted Mario, a temporary hero, stagger out of the lorry into the glare of the burning oil-well. The blaze represents the senseless energy of the universe, which man can harness in little ways—Mario's achievement will allow the engineers to put out this particular fire—but which will reassert itself against man in the long run." To Adam Garbicz and Jacek Klinowski, the film is the acme of French *film noir,* "a brilliant adventure thriller which combines Existentialist contexts with social criticism."

The Wages of Fear represents the high point in Clouzot's work. *Les Diaboliques* (*The Fiends,* 1955), was admired for the almost contemptuous skill with which the director manipulates, terrifies, and shocks his audience, but it provoked none of the serious philosophical and political discussion that greeted its predecessor (except that some critics angrily rejected the film's unrelievedly pessimistic view of human nature). It is set in a shabby provincial private school run by a sadistic bully (Paul Meurisse). Véra Clouzot, who had played a small part in *The Wages of Fear,* appears as the headmaster's ailing wife, who is persuaded by his mistress (Simone Signoret) to join in a plot to murder him. The plan works, but the headmaster's body disappears from the school swimming pool, and the mystery deepens after a boy claims to have seen the man alive. The twist at the end is truly shocking— both as a *coup de théâtre* and as a revelation of human perfidy.

A very different kind of film followed. In *Le Mystère Picasso* (*The Mystery of Picasso,* 1956) we are allowed to watch Pablo Picasso in the act of creation, sketching and painting on a translucent screen, mugging amiably for the camera, exploring an idea, dropping it in favor of some new inspiration, retracing his steps, pressing forward to completion. This unique, technically adventurous, and life-affirming movie owes a great deal to the color photography of Claude Renoir and to Georges Auric's expressive music. *Les Espions* (*The Spies,* 1957) is by contrast a perfunctory thriller, uneasily mixing brutality and farce in an adaptation of a novel by Egon Hostovsky. Such interest as it has derives from Clouzot's careful realization of the provincial town in which it is set and an international cast that includes Peter Ustinov, Curt Jurgens, Sam Jaffe, Martita Hunt, and Véra Clouzot.

Véra Clouzot was one of her husband's several collaborators on the script of *La Vérité* (*Truth,* 1960), which, like *Manon,* is a not unsympathetic study of youthful amorality. Dominique (Brigitte Bardot) is on trial for the murder of her lover, but the truth comes out not in the professional histrionics of the rival advocates but in flashbacks that pointedly contrast their ringing moral certainties with Dominique's shiftless world of Latin Quarter coffee bars. There are echoes here of the incomprehension with which Maurice's statement was received by the police in *Quai des Orfèvres,* and the gulf between the establishment and its victims and rebels evidently engaged Clouzot deeply. All the same, his handling of the theme in *La Vérité* struck some critics as pedestrian and at times clumsy. The filming moreover was attended by scandal and eventually by tragedy. Both Véra Clouzot and Brigitte Bardot's husband became ill, and gossips attributed this to a liaison between the star and the director (who denied that his influence over Bardot was anything other than professional and aesthetic). After a public brawl between her husband and her costar (Sami Frey), Bardot attempted suicide. Véra Clouzot died the same year, at the age of thirty-nine. Soon after Clouzot married Inez de Gonzales, an Argentinian thirty years his junior.

La Vérité was to be Clouzot's last feature film for eight years. Ill health had already forced him to relinquish an earlier script, *Si tous les gars du monde,* to another director, Christian-Jaque. In 1964, after many months of preparation, Clouzot began filming "L'Enfer" (Hell), an ambitious study of jealousy which had to be abandoned a few days after shooting began when the director suffered a heart attack. Apart from some television films recording notable performances of such works as Verdi's Requiem and Beethoven's Fifth Symphony, he made no more pictures until *La Prisonnière* (*The Prisoner*) in 1967–1968. A story about a painter's wife (Elisabeth Wiener) corrupted by a perverted photographer (Laurent Terzieff), it has been dubbed into English

as *Woman in Chains.* The film had a moderately respectful reception, especially for the long nightmare sequence at the end, in which Clouzot experiments with a surreal montage of pop art and sexual symbols.

Clouzot was one of the New Wave's principal targets in their campaign against their predecessors, and he made no more movies. Indeed he was everything the New Wave opposed—a meticulous director who prepared his work very carefully in advance and insisted on complete control of every phase of its development. He is said to have been quite ruthless in his handling of actors, for example bullying one young actor to the verge of breakdown and then amiably informing him that this was exactly the effect that was wanted on the screen. Simone Signoret said, "He is concerned with every detail, almost to an obsession. He cannot work in peace. He has to work in a constant *ambiance* of crisis. . . . He does not ask you to do things, he demands that you do things. . . . Clouzot does not really respect actors. He claims he could make anyone act." Rather surprisingly, perhaps, the high standard of performance he extracted from his actors tends to bear out this claim.

Clouzot said that for him "the great rule is to push the contrasts as far as they will go, the dramatic highlights being separated by 'neutral zones.' To move the spectator I always aim at emphasizing the chiaroscuro, opposing light and shade. It is for this reason that my films have been criticized as oversimplifications." That criticism has indeed been made of his work, not only for the reason he gives but because of his willingness, especially in his later work, to go to any lengths to build up tension and suspense, even at the cost of distorting character. As Roy Armes has written, Clouzot's work is characterized by "an extremely pessimistic view of the world, a ruthlessness and significant lack of humour. It is this latter that differentiates him most strongly from his only serious rival as master of the thriller genre—Alfred Hitchcock."

—*K.B.*

FILMS: L'Assassin habite au 21 (The Killer Lives at 21), 1942; Le Corbeau (The Crow/The Raven), 1943; Quai des Orfèvres, 1947; Manon, 1949; Le Retour de Jean, *episode in* Retour à la vie (Return to Life), 1949; Miquette et sa mère (Miquette and Her Mother), 1949; Le Salaire de la peur (The Wages of Fear), 1953; Les Diaboliques (The Fiends), 1955; Le Mystère Picasso (The Mystery of Picasso), 1956; Les Espions (The Spies), 1957; La Vérité (Truth), 1960; La Prisonnière (The Prisoner/Woman in Chains), 1968. *Published scripts*—(with Louis Chavance) Le Corbeau, 1948; (with Jean Ferry) Retour à la vie, 1949; (with Jérôme Géronimi) La Salaire de la Peur *in* L'Avant-Scène du Cinéma July 1962; (with Jean Ferry) Quai des

Orfèvres *in* L'Avant-Scène du Cinéma September 1963.

ABOUT: Armes, R. French Cinema Since 1946: 1, 1968; Bianchi, P. Henri-Georges Clouzot, 1951 (Italy); Chalais, F. Henri-Georges Clouzot, 1950 (France); Cournot, M. Le Premier Spectateur, 1957 (France); Evans, P. Bardot, 1972; Garbicz, A. and Klinowski, J. Cinema: The Magic Vehicle, 1983; Lacassin, F. and Bellour, R. Le Procés Clouzot, 1964 (France); Leprohon, P. Présences Contemporaines, Cinéma, 1957 (France); Mauriac, C. L'Amour du Cinéma, 1954 (France); Pilard, P. Henri-Georges Clouzot, 1969 (France); Sadoul, G. French Film, 1953; Winnington, R. Film Criticism and Caricatures, 1975; World Encyclopedia of the Film, 1972. *Periodicals*—L'Avant-Scène du Cinéma April 15, 1977; Cinema (U.S.A.) Winter 1969; Écran February 1977; Film March–April 1956; Films and Filming July 1955, December 1958; New York Times January 14, 1977; New Yorker February 12, 1955; Sight and Sound Spring 1958; Times (London) January 14, 1977; Yale French Studies Summer 1956.

JEAN COCTEAU

*COCTEAU, JEAN (July 5, 1889–October 11, 1963), French director and scenarist, poet, novelist, dramatist, and illustrator—one of the most diversely talented creators of the twentieth century—was born into a rich middle-class family in Maisons-Laffitte, near Paris. He was brought up mainly in Paris, where his maternal grandfather owned a house in the vicinity of Pigalle, on the Rue la Bruyère. He thus belonged to Montmartre, though to the bourgeois rather than to the artistic part of it. His father, Georges Cocteau, spent all his life working as a stockbroker, though his only real passion was painting. Cocteau's mother Eugènie was the daughter of Eugène Lecomte, who owned the brokerage where Georges worked, the family houses, and a rich collection of art objects, including several Stradivarius violins that were regularly used by visiting virtuosi at the Lecomtes' weekly chamber music concerts.

Jean Cocteau was educated at the Lycée Condorcet and later insisted (characteristically) that he was *le cancre par excellence* there—the prize booby of his class. His school reports contradict this. He was undeniably an *enfant terrible* (and was expelled from the school in the spring of 1904), but one who showed signs of a lively mind and a precocious talent for sketching and versifying. It was at Condorcet that Cocteau had his first homosexual infatuation, with a boy called Pierre Dargelos whose haunting reincarnations appear throughout Cocteau's work—the shameless untutored faun whose mouth and eyes can kill.

Frederick Brown argues from this "that Cocteau was already at odds with the ideal double he would spend his life pursuing. Dargelos is a real name—it may be found on yellowing rosters—but it is equally Cocteau's pseudonym for his primal malediction, for the angelic offspring of his catastrophe. A decade after leaving Condorcet he wrote: 'At an age when gender does not yet influence decisions of the flesh, my desire was not to reach, not to touch, nor to embrace the elected person, but to *be* him. . . . What loneliness!' This original forfeiture, placing the locus of Being outside himself, would make solitude intolerable and anonymity a form of death. He was fated to crave love in order to be." This hunger for love and recognition accounts well enough for Cocteau's constant striving to be in the forefront of the social, artistic, and literary avant-garde, and his ardent pursuit of friendship with all the other leaders of artistic Paris.

It was fitting that one who played such a vital role in the cult of the new and the youthful should make his own debut as a teenage prodigy, declaiming his poems to Parisian celebrities at the Théâtre Fémina as protégé of the middle-aged homosexual actor Edouard de Max, who loved sponsoring new young talents who might enhance his own reputation. By the middle of World War I, Cocteau was writing for the Ballets Russes, obeying Diaghilev's famous injunction "Astonish me" with the ballet *Parade* (décor by Picasso, music by Erik Satie), the great *succès de scandale* of 1917. Cocteau was exempted by ill health from military service but made his way to the battlefront with an ambulance unit, met and flew with the aviator Roland Garros, and en-

°kok tō´

countered the problems and adventures imaginatively recalled in his novel *Thomas l'imposteur* (1923).

Cocteau's star rose rapidly after the war. *Le Potomak*, a fantastic medley of prose, verse, and cartoons, appeared in 1919. His pantomime-ballet *Le Boeuf sur le toit* (with music by Milhaud) was staged in 1920 and the poetic spectacle *Les Mariés de la Tour Eiffel* in 1921. A collected poems was published in 1924 and a volume of critical essays in 1926. There were modernistic adaptations of Sophocles' *Antigone* (1922, with scenery by Picasso) and of Shakespeare's *Romeo and Juliet* (1924), and an original one-act play, *Orphée* (1926). Not content to seem merely a universal man of letters, Cocteau painted and drew, designed tapestries, tinkered with typography, wrote program notes for avant-garde composers, and championed American jazz and Charlie Chaplin. His enemies said that the serious artists of Paris tolerated Cocteau only because he was useful to them as a publicist. However that may be, he knew everyone of interest or social importance, from Picasso to the Prince of Wales. He also formed a close emotional and creative liaison with the younger writer Raymond Radiguet, whose death at the age of twenty-three temporarily shattered Cocteau. He sought solace in opium, then in religion, but before long thumbed his nose at Jacques Maritain, his spiritual counselor, and resumed his old life.

The most persistent criticism of Cocteau's multifarious works has been that they are without weight or depth, the glittering confections of a brilliant showman, concerned above all to "astonish." Some critics have tried to attribute this "awful vacuity" to Cocteau's homosexuality, which is supposed to have prevented him from establishing a solid emotional foundation for either his life or his work. His admirers, on the other hand, maintain that his work is far from empty—that it adumbrates a hermetic world of personal symbolism and private association to which one surrenders totally or not at all. This argument is nowhere more tenable than in Cocteau's films, which have been called dramas of self-examination.

For Cocteau, poetry was the supreme art and the poet the supreme being, uniquely in touch with ultimate realities, especially death, which in his work is not the end but a gateway to self-realization. This is the theme of virtually all of his films, including the first, *Le Sang d'un poète* (*The Blood of a Poet*, 1930–1932). In this silent allegory the poet recognizes and tries to escape his muse, wrestles with his past, dies and is resurrected. These incidents, recounted in narcissistic images of mirrors and self-portraits that speak, are framed by a shot of a collapsing building to show that they take place in only a moment of "real" time.

With its dreamlike atmosphere and mysterious imagery, this autobiographical film-poem resembles such surrealist pictures as Buñuel's *L'Age d'or,* made at the same time and for the same patron, the Vicomte de Noailles. (Cocteau, who regarded the surrealists as rivals, denied the resemblance.) *Le Sang d'un poète* greatly impressed Chaplin and others but now seems rather static, and confusing in its dream imagery. It is interesting nevertheless as an introduction to the symbols and motifs Cocteau later used to much greater effect in *Orphée*—including the central theme of the poet's struggle to choose between the attractions of the everyday world and the unknowable.

The golden days when gifted amateurs could make movies under private patronage ended with the advent of sound, and Cocteau directed no more films for fifteen years. His best novel, *Les Enfants terribles,* was published in 1929, and the 1930s brought him several notable successes as a dramatist. During the German occupation his reputation was damaged by charges of collaboration, but it now seems that though "he associated with all the smart collaborationists . . . he was far from being one himself." He did not abandon the cinema altogether during this period but wrote scenarios, dialogue, and adaptations for a number of movies by other directors. These ranged from relatively unimportant entertainments like Marcel L'Herbier's *La Comédie du bonheur* (1940) and Serge de Poligny's *Le Baron fantôme* (1943) to more personal and significant works. The most notable of these was his modernization of the Tristan and Isolde legend in *L'Eternel Retour* (1943), directed by Jean Delannoy but full of Cocteau's characteristic themes and symbols. He also wrote the dialogue for Bresson's brilliant study of passion and revenge, *Les Dames du bois de Boulogne* (1944).

Cocteau's second film as director was *La Belle et la Bête* (*Beauty and the Beast,* 1946). To save her father from the Beast's wrath, Beauty (Josette Day) allows herself to be incarcerated in the monster's magic castle, which is lit by candelabra held by disembodied arms and decorated with living statues. Gradually she comes to recognize the Beast's essential gentleness and melancholy, and warms to him when he allows her to visit her sick father. But she stays too long, and when she returns the heartbroken Beast is dying. Her dissolute admirer Avenant arrives to rescue her and to steal the Beast's treasure. He fails, and dies at the same moment as the Beast. Avenant becomes the dead monster and the Beast, transfigured by Beauty's look of love, is reborn as a more princely Avenant.

In Cocteau's hands the story becomes an illustration of his central theme: "To live you must die." To this paradox he adds thought-provoking ambiguity by casting Jean Marais as both Avenant and the Beast. There was great praise for Cocteau's handling of tone and pace in the film, from the broad humor of Beauty's rustic home-life to the dreamlike slow motion of her entry into the castle. He and his designer Christian Bérard rigorously eschewed the kind of misty effects usually employed to suggest magic and the supernatural—Cocteau said of Bérard that "he was the only one to understand that vagueness is unsuitable to the world of the fairy tale and that mystery exists only in precise things." Bérard's gorgeous costumes and Henri Alekan's camera style are both said to have been inspired by Dutch paintings, especially the works of Vermeer. The score was by Georges Auric, who provided the music for all of Cocteau's films except the last. *La Belle et la Bête*, "one of the great works of poetic cinema," was made in the face of a daunting succession of difficulties and afflictions, described in Cocteau's *Diary of a Film* (1950).

There followed two pictures which Cocteau adapted from his own plays. *L'Aigle à deux têtes* (*The Eagle Has Two Heads*, 1947) is about a tragic queen (Edwige Feuillère) who welcomes with open arms her would-be assassin (Jean Marais). This being a Cocteau story, they fall in love and die together. Most critics thought that Cocteau had failed to turn this stagey piece into a work of cinema. He had much more success with *Les Parents terribles* (1948), which he made no attempt to "open up," instead deliberately emphasizing its claustrophobic theatricality. The most admired of his plays, it is a savage farce about emotional cannibalism in a bourgeois family. The sacred monster of a mother (Yvonne de Bray) refuses to accept the fact that her son (Jean Marais) is no longer a child, and kills herself when reality intrudes. (The reality is that her husband and her son are both in love with another woman—Josette Day.) This film was praised above all for the quality of the performances Cocteau extracted from his cast. *Les Enfants terribles* (1950) is a companion piece—another claustrophobic study of bourgeois life centering this time on two young people, a brother and sister who live in a hermetic fantasy world from which there is only one escape. The picture was directed by Jean-Pierre Melville, reportedly in close association with Cocteau, who is credited only as scenarist and adapter (of his own novel).

Central to Cocteau's work in the cinema are the three intensely personal films in which he explores through the figure of Orpheus his obsession with the role of the poet, torn between the familiar and the unknown. This trilogy, which began with *Le Sang d'un poète*, continued with *Orphée* (*Orpheus*, 1950), developed from his 1925 play, and universally recognized to be his masterpiece. Orpheus (Jean Marais) is a celebrated poet living in Paris, where one day he sees a younger poet, Cégeste, run down and killed by two motorcyclists. They are the emissaries of a beautiful Princess (Maria Casarès), who is Death. The Princess drives with Orpheus out of the city into an unfamiliar countryside, where her radio announces a strange poetry that Orpheus finds obsessively fascinating: "L'oiseau chante avec ses doigts. Je repète. Deux fois. L'oiseau chante avec ses doigts." It is the dead Cégeste, we learn later, who is broadcasting this surreal litany.

Eurydice, Orpheus's wife, is the next to die. Orpheus follows her into the Underworld, partly in an attempt to save her, partly because he is fascinated by the Princess—by death itself. He saves Eurydice, who journeys back to daylight in an oddly farcical scene but then voluntarily returns to the Underworld, believing that her husband no longer loves her. Orpheus is attacked by the Bacchantes—militant feminist poets who believe him responsible for Cégeste's death. He is killed, but the Princess, who loves him, returns him to life and reunites him with Eurydice before going off to face some unthinkable punishment. Through death the poet is reborn, renouncing the influence of Cégeste's poetry (which is the poetry of death) and recovering his own vision.

Gavin Lambert wrote that *Orphée* is first of all "an unmatched achievement in the telling of a magical adventure. The balance of the real and the magical is marvellously sustained . . . [and] the narrative is so full of invention that it never ceases to be dramatic." The film "reasserts wonder, ritual, the power of illusion and magic, reinterpreting them in a contemporary setting which brings the myth closer, gives it a disturbing edge of reality." Many of the images and devices introduced in *Le Sang d'un poète* are used here with a new delight in the cinema's capacity for illusion. The way into the Zone—the limbo between this world and the next, filmed in the bombed-out ruins of the Saint-Cyr military academy—is through a mirror; a vat of mercury was used to make it appear that Orpheus's hands are passing through glass. Other astonishing effects were obtained by substituting plain glass for mirrors, and by the use of duplicate rooms, doubles, reverse projection, and false perspective. The theme is the autobiographical one of *Le Sang d'un poète* but, Cocteau said, "then I strummed it with one finger, now I orchestrate it." *Orphée* won the Grand Prix at the Venice Film Festival.

It was nine years before Cocteau completed his Orphic trilogy with *Le Testament d'Orphée,* which he clearly intended as his own testament as well as Orpheus'. It is a fable in which the director himself (then seventy) appears as a time-traveler. He enters our world and is led by a centaur to a cave. There he finds Cégeste (played as in *Orphée* by Cocteau's adopted son Edouard Dermit), who gives him a flower. Cocteau tries to draw the flower but succeeds only in producing his own likeness. He is ordered to take the flower to the goddess Minerva and, after various ordeals and encounters, he finds her. She scorns his gift and strikes him dead. Resurrected, the poet continues his wanderings, finally vanishing together with Cégeste. The film is in effect an account of Cocteau's life as an artist and a manifesto of his theories and beliefs, crowded with his lovers and friends, including Marais, Dermit, Picasso, Yul Brynner, the bullfighter Dominguin, and Brigitte Bardot. Serene and often witty, it has been dismissed by some critics as a facetious coda to his work and hailed by others as one of the cinema's greatest confessional documents.

In 1955 the *enfant terrible* Cocteau became one of the "Immortals" of the Académie Française. "It is not up to us to obey the public, which does not know what it wants," he said once, "but to compel the public to follow us. If it refuses we must use tricks: images, stars, decors, and other magic lanterns, suitable to intrigue children and make them swallow the spectacle."

— *K.B.*

FILMS: Le Sang d'un poète (Blood of a Poet), 1932; La Belle et la Bête (Beauty and the Beast), 1946; L'Aigle à deux têtes (The Eagle Has Two Heads), 1947; Les Parents terribles (Intimate Relations), 1948; Orphée (Orpheus), 1950; Le Testament d'Orphée (The Testament of Orpheus), 1959. *Published scripts in English*—Two Screenplays (The Blood of a Poet, The Testament of Orpheus), 1968; Three Screenplays (The Eternal Return, Orpheus, Beauty and the Beast), 1972.

ABOUT: Armes, R. French Cinema Since 1946: 1, 1966; Ashton, D. and others Jean Cocteau and the French Scene, 1984; Brown, F. An Impersonation of Angels: A Biography of Jean Cocteau, 1968; Cocteau, J. Cocteau on the Film, 1972; Cocteau, J. Diary of a Film, 1950; Cocteau, J. Journals, edited by Wallace Fowlie, 1964; Cocteau, J. Professional Secrets, edited by Robert Phelps, 1972; Crosland, M. Jean Cocteau, 1955; Evans, A. B. Jean Cocteau and His Films of Orphic Identity, 1977; Fraigneau, A. Cocteau (translated by

D. Lehmkuhl), 1961; Gilson, R. Jean Cocteau (translated by Ciba Vaughan), 1969; Pillaudin, R. Jean Cocteau Tourne Son Dernier Film, 1960 (France); Sadoul, G. French Film, 1953; Simon, K. G. Jean Cocteau, 1958 (Germany); Steegmuller, F. Cocteau, 1970; Tyler, P. Classics of the Foreign Film, 1967; Who Was Who 1961–1970. *Periodicals*—Cahiers du Cinéma February 1964; Cinema Journal Spring 1972; Film Quarterly Fall 1964; Films and Filming July 1960, January and February 1978; Image et Son June–July 1972; Listener May 1, 1952; Observer (London) November 30, 1952; Sight and Sound July–September 1952, Winter 1959–1960; World Theatre Spring 1959; Yale French Studies Summer 1956.

COOPER, MERIAN C(OLDWELL) (October 24, 1893–April 21, 1973), American director and producer, was born in Jacksonville, Florida, the youngest of the three children of John C. Cooper and the former Mary Coldwell. His father, a lawyer who became chairman of the Federal Reserve Board in Florida, was descended from Scotch-English cotton planters, and Merian Cooper was raised in the traditions of Southern chivalry, patriotism, and religious certainty.

At the age of six, according to Ron Haver, Cooper was given Paul Du Chaillu's *Explorations and Adventures in Equatorial Africa,* finding the seeds of *King Kong* in the book's highly imaginative account of giant apes that were supposed to terrorize the jungle villages—including one that carried off a screaming woman. He decided that he, like Du Chaillu, would find fame as an explorer, and later, when he was sent north to the Lawrenceville School near Princeton, he trained himself for the rigors of this career as a boxer, wrestler, and swimmer.

In 1911, still dreaming of travel and adventure, Cooper entered Annapolis Naval Academy. A high-spirited young man, he "took chances and got caught too many times"; in 1915—his graduating year—he resigned from Annapolis (presumably upon request) and joined the merchant marine. When the Germans sank the *Lusitania*, Cooper recognized that war was coming and decided that he wanted a part in it. Ron Haver says that he "literally jumped ship in London," injuring himself in the process.

Shipped back to the United States, Cooper worked as a journalist in Minneapolis, Des Moines, and St. Louis. In 1916, desperate for his piece of the Great War, he joined the Georgia National Guard, believing that it would be sent to Europe. Instead he found himself skirmishing against Pancho Villa on the Mexican border. He volunteered for flight training with the Signal Corps and at last, in September 1918, was sent to France. The war was almost over, but Cooper

MERIAN C. COOPER

was in time to be shot down and severely burned. He greeted the Armistice in a German prison hospital.

Released, Cooper was assigned to an American relief office in Poland. His interviews there with refugees from the Russian Civil War confirmed his belief that communism posed an international threat. He left the American army to fight with the Poles against the Bolsheviks, flying with the Kosciuszco Squadron—some sources, indeed, claim that he both founded and commanded the squadron, though this does not seem likely. In July 1920 he was shot down once more and sent to a prison camp near Moscow. After ten months he escaped with two others and made his way to Latvia. There he was imprisoned again as a suspected Communist until an American relief mission bailed him out.

Cooper returned to New York in 1921, laden with medals. He worked for the New York *Daily News* and the New York *Times* as a reporter and feature writer, also contributing to the *Times* articles about his own adventures that he signed "A Fortunate Soldier." Still intent on becoming an explorer, he spent hours every day at the American Geographical Society, studying mapmaking and survival techniques. His chance came when he learned that Captain Edward A. Salisbury was planning an exploratory world cruise, hoping to gather material for articles, films, and a book. Salisbury needed someone with writing and navigational experience, and Cooper was accepted. When the expedition's cameraman absconded after a particularly ferocious typhoon, Cooper suggested as his replacement a young combat photographer he had met on the

way to Poland—Ernest B. Schoedsack, who had trained at Mack Sennett's Keystone studios.

Cooper and Schoedsack first worked together on a film when the expedition reached North Africa. They planned a documentary about Ethiopia and Haile Selassie and shot a great deal of film. This burned a few weeks later in a fire that also destroyed the expedition's ship. Cooper and Schoedsack decided to continue their globetrotting collaboration by other means. Inspired no doubt by the worldwide success of Flaherty's *Nanook of the North,* they conceived the idea of a documentary about the Bakhtiari, a fiercely independent nomad people who every year drove their flocks over the mountains of central Persia to the grazing lands beyond. Back in the United States, Cooper borrowed $5,000 from his family and $5,000 more from a new partner, Marguerite Harrison, an adventurous journalist who had supplied him with food, books, and blankets when he was a prisoner in Russia.

The three Americans went via Turkey to Persia and then on horseback and on foot to Shustar, capital of Arabistan. There they met the Bakhtiari khans and secured permission to join the migration of 50,000 tribesmen and half a million animals. For twenty-six days they shared all the hardships of the journey over the Zagros mountains—fording rivers on goatskin rafts, scaling trackless and snow-covered peaks—until they reached the grassy valleys on the other side. Cooper and Schoedsack photographed it all with Schoedsack's heavy Debrie camera, and Marguerite Harrison noted that Cooper had "a flair for the bizarre"—"was for ever striving for startling climaxes and sharp contrasts." He was also "disdainful of all the refinements of life. . . . Stubborn as a mule, moody, quick-tempered but generous, loyal to the point of fanaticism."

The journey over, Cooper and Schoedsack took their film to Paris. Arriving there practically penniless, they developed and edited it themselves into a feature-length documentary they called *Grass*. Schoedsack went off to the Galapagos Islands on an expedition led by William Beebe, and Cooper took *Grass* on the lecture circuit. Its success was so great that Jesse Lasky offered to release it through Paramount. It created a sensation, grossing many times its miniscule cost (and incidentally promoting the sales of Cooper's diary of the journey, published under the same title as the film).

Though Cooper and Schoedsack are credited as codirectors, Cooper in his diary gives most of the credit for the film to his friend. A modern critic, Elliott Stein, writes that "Schoedsack's camera captured some of the most remarkable and strikingly framed outdoor footage of the 20s. . . . Unhappily, Terry Ramsaye, Paramount's title writer, churned out an endless string of inanities ('Gosh, it's another day!'). And since *Grass* is a collective odyssey, it never deals with families or individuals—the Bakhtiaris are seen from a distance like some race of rugged compulsive insects—the concentration on panoramic visions eventually fatigues."

Cooper and Schoedsack were well aware of this weakness and, before their money ran out, had hoped to repeat the journey, viewing it from the point of view of a single family. This was the approach they adopted in their second documentary, *Chang* (1927). Amply financed by Jesse Lasky (to the tune of about $60,000), it was the product of almost two years' filming in the jungles of northern Siam (Thailand). This heavily fictionalized documentary centers on a Lao tribesman, Kru. With his family he leaves the village, clears a patch of land in the jungle, battles against tigers, leopards, and the encroaching vegetation, and tames a wild *chang* (elephant) as a work animal—a triumph of private enterprise over an inimical environment.

In assembling their material, the filmmakers faced nearly as many dangers as their hero. Schoedsack, perched in a tree, almost paid with his life for his shot of a tiger leaping up at the lens. Cooper, a man of uncontrollable rages, publicly slapped a Lao chieftain during an argument and that evening was served a chicken stew laced with minute bamboo barbs; only the accidental presence of a missionary doctor saved him from an agonizing slow death. But there was also a good deal of comic relief—in the filming as in the film—much of it provided by Bimbo, an eccentric gibbon.

Chang opened in April 1927 at the Criterion Theatre in New York, with a score composed and conducted by Hugo Riesenfeld. The orchestra included a percussion section of twenty men pounding six-foot jungle drums during the climactic elephant stampede. This spectacular sequence (footage from which was later used in at least a dozen other films) was projected at the Criterion through a magnifying lens onto a screen about three times the normal size, in a process, known as Magnascope, that had a brief vogue during the mid-1920s. *Chang* (which was also one of the first films shot on panchromatic stock) was a critical success and the top-grossing movie of the year. It launched a whole cycle of jungle thrillers like *Trader Horn* and *King of the Jungle*. All the same—enjoyed as it was for its showmanlike mingling of comedy and drama— there are many who prefer the "stark, heart-breaking" simplicity of *Grass*.

In a natural progression, Cooper and Schoedsack went from *Chang* to their first wholly fictional feature—the second silent version of A. E.W. Mason's novel *The Four Feathers* (1929). Richard Arlen plays Harry Faversham, the gentle, introspective young officer who resigns his commission just as his regiment is leaving for the Sudan to avenge the death of General Gordon. He receives white feathers—symbols of cowardice—from four of his nearest and dearest. One of these is his fiancée (Fay Wray) and another is a brother officer (Clive Brook). After being blinded in the desert, the Brook character led to safety by a mute heroic tribesman; much later he learns that this was the despised Harry Faversham. David O. Selznick was assigned by Paramount as production supervisor.

The Four Feathers matched exterior footage (shot mostly in the Sudan and Tanganyika, sometimes with doubles) and scenes filmed in the studio, with a care and precision that had not previously been attained. Like *Chang* (but with less justification), it included many fine documentary studies of wildlife. One of the last major silent films, it was released with synchronized music and sound effects but, though it was well received by the critics, seems to have been rather overlooked by audiences clamoring for talkies.

Perhaps for this reason Cooper left the film industry for two years and turned to his other passion, the airplane. Investing the profits from *Grass* and *Chang*, he became one of the founding stockholders and first directors of both Western Airlines and Pan American Airways. In his spare time he wrote a book (never published) about baboons, a species whose behavior had caught his interest when he was filming *The Four Feathers*. His researches reminded him of the stories about giant apes that he had read as a boy, and the idea for a film began to take shape. Further inspiration came from his friend Douglas Burden, an explorer who told him fascinating stories about the "prehistoric" island of Komodo in the Dutch East Indies, inhabited by lizards twelve feet long.

Cooper settled down to write the first of several treatments for what was to become *King Kong*, working out in detail what could be achieved with the special effects then possible. He was forced to discard the idea of using a real (but magnified) gorilla in his film, and to investigate instead ways in which models of monsters, filmed on miniature sets, could be combined with live action scenes projected on the same miniature scale. It was at this point that David O. Selznick, by then head of production at RKO, invited Cooper to become his executive assistant, evaluating the commercial prospects of current and proposed RKO productions. In this way he met Willis O'Brien.

O'Brien was a cartoonist and animator of genius who, in *The Lost World* (1925) and other films, had perfected the technique of "stop-motion animation." In this process, small models are given the appearance of life by photographing them, one frame at a time, in successive stages of a movement. In O'Brien and his team of model-makers and matte artists, Cooper saw the solution to his remaining technical problems in *King Kong*. Selznick was excited by Cooper's proposals, and so was Schoedsack when he returned to Hollywood from another project. Cooper prepared an elaborate case for his film, including detailed sketches of some of its most spectacular scenes, and eventually RKO—cautious in that Depression year—authorized an expenditure of $5,000 on a test reel.

Cooper added another $5,000 of his own money, and work began. After one false start, Willis O'Brien and his crew constructed three eighteen-inch model gorillas, each weighing ten pounds. For each, a skeleton of articulated steel was equipped with a latex rubber muscular system and padded out to shape with cotton. The whole was painted with liquid latex and, after this had dried into a "skin," a final covering of animal fur was applied. For close-ups, O'Brien's team also built a gigantic bust and head of Kong, with movable eyes and mouth, as well as a giant-sized leg and arm. Models of the principal locations—"Skull Island" and Manhattan—were built on tables on a closed stage. The jungle sets were copied from Doré's engravings for *Paradise Lost*—a favorite of Cooper's and a work highly relevant to his theme. These sets were painted on sheets of glass, each nine feet by twelve, placed one behind the other to give an extraordinary impression of mysterious depths. Live action scenes were shot on the swampy jungle set constructed for another Cooper-Schoedsack project, *The Most Dangerous Game*.

Meanwhile, Cooper was developing a full shooting script. He worked with several collaborators, including Edgar Wallace, but it was reportedly Schoedsack's wife Ruth Rose who contributed most to Cooper's script, giving the dialogue the "fairy-tale simplicity" he wanted in this, his first talkie. Fay Wray was cast as the heroine, the movie star Ann Darrow; Robert Armstrong was to play Carl Denham, an intrepid filmmaker obviously modeled on Cooper himself; and the part of Jack Driscoll, the sailor who becomes Ann Darrow's lover, went to a young Canadian, Bruce Cabot. Impressed by the test reel, RKO came up with a budget of $500,000 (which Selznick boosted to $650,000 by squeezing other projects).

Shooting began in the spring of 1932. It is believed that Schoedsack directed the quiet but tense scenes at the beginning of *King Kong,* Cooper the violent action that follows. The latter was a tyrant on the set: for the scene in which Kong fights the allosaurus—the first back-projection sequence ever filmed at RKO—he worked Fay Wray for a full twenty-four hours. There are also many anecdotes about the conflicts between Cooper and his collaborators, with Schoedsack and Willis O'Brien constantly but unsuccessfully opposing Cooper's insistence on the monstrous violence he attributes to the film's real hero, Kong. And it was Cooper who ordained that Kong's apparent height should change, in the course of the picture, from eighteen feet to about sixty feet—he "felt confident that if the scenes moved with excitement and beauty, the audience would accept any height that fit into the scene." By and large, he was right.

The score for *King Kong* was the work of Max Steiner, head of RKO's music department. It was as extraordinary as everything else about the film, often dissonant and using leitmotifs for characters in the manner of Wagner. As Ron Haver says, Steiner "wrote a score for an eighty-five-piece orchestra that heaves, rumbles, and shrieks its way through the film, underlining emotions, adding suspense, terror, and a kind of epic aural accompaniment. A grunt from an animal was immediately picked up with a corresponding growl from the orchestra, while Wray's screams were echoed and intensified constantly by the strings. Nobody had ever heard music like this before in a film, or so much of it. Steiner's music for *King Kong* was, and is, a landmark in film scoring."

King Kong opens in New York with preparations for a film to be made on location on Skull Island, reputed to be inhabited by prehistoric beasts. Led by Carl Denham, the filmmakers sail for the remote island. The long voyage is uneventful, but full of "carefully orchestrated hints of what lies ahead." On the island, the filmmakers find that the inhabitants live within a huge palisade as protection from the island's monsters. But Kong, the most fearsome of them all, is only placated by sacrificial offerings of young girls. Ann Darrow is kidnapped and offered to Kong. Instead of killing her, he is infatuated, fighting in her defense against the other monsters. Jack Driscoll and the others rescue Ann and capture Kong, who is taken to New York for exhibition. He breaks loose and searches for Ann, terrorizing the city. In the end, he climbs with his beloved to the top of the Empire State Building, where he is machine-gunned to death by two flyers (Cooper and Schoedsack).

The film was previewed in San Bernadino in

January 1933. A scene in which Kong shakes some sailors from a log and they fall into a ravine full of huge, slimy (and carnivorous) insects caused so much screaming in the theatre that it was removed. Otherwise, the film opened intact on March 2, 1933 at two new theatres, the RKO Roxy and Radio City Music Hall, which had a combined capacity of 10,000. Heralded by a massive publicity campaign, including the first use of radio plugs, it played to over 50,000 people on its first day and went on to become one of the greatest box-office successes there has ever been. Three sequences were cut when the film was reissued in 1938 and not restored until 1969—one of Kong curiously picking off Fay Wray's clothes, and two of exceptional violence.

As Ron Haver says, *King Kong* is a "twentieth-century version of the myth of the Beauty and the Beast and the destructive powers of both love and civilization." Elliott Stein, who has seen the picture more than two hundred times, calls it "the greatest adventure film ever made," and Carlos Clarens wrote that "one questions, or marvels at, or wonders at the first sight of the monster, but thereafter one is caught in nothing but the sheer flow of events, each thrill surpassing the previous one in splendid outrageousness. The film's art is to make the technical tour de force seem effortless."

Since then, as Stein says, Kong has "emerged . . . as one of our great culture heroes, an absorbed and central personage of the American mythos." He is "a major leitmotiv in Thomas Pynchon's novel *Gravity's Rainbow* and an incarnation of the hero's fantasies in Karel Reisz's film *Morgan*," as well as a familiar reference point in ads, cartoons, and comedy shows. During the button craze of the 1960s, one of the most popular read "King Kong Died for Our Sins." And for one British critic, "it is the principal triumph of the film that our sympathy is always with Kong. . . . man is directly culpable, man with his movie cameras, gas bombs, and aeroplanes. Man as Faust, unable to let things be. It is because, for all its limited technical means and strict conventions, this film succeeds in finding the perfect form and content to transmit this truth that *King Kong* will remain a triumph of cinema." The $24 million remake by Dino De Laurentiis in 1976 seemed by comparison "knowing, full of nudging Freudian jokes."

During the filming of *King Kong,* Selznick resigned from RKO in a dispute, and Cooper succeeded him as vice-president in charge of production. Among the films he produced or supervised were George Cukor's *Little Women* (1933) and several directed by Schoedsack, including *The Most Dangerous Game* (1933,

called *The Hounds of Zaroff* in Britain), *Son of Kong* (1933), and *The Last Days of Pompeii* (1935). In *Flying Down to Rio* (1933) he teamed Fred Astaire and Ginger Rogers for the first time. Cooper was one of the first to see the possibilities of the new Technicolor three-color process, and with John Hay Whitney formed Pioneer Pictures to exploit the process in films like Rouben Mamoulian's *Becky Sharp* (1935). He also persuaded Whitney to invest in Selznick International Pictures, founded in 1935, of which Cooper served as vice-president.

During World War II Cooper returned to active service with the air force, becoming chief of staff to General Chennault in China. He participated in the 1942 air attacks on Japan and the New Guinea invasion and afterwards served as deputy chief of staff to General MacArthur, finally achieving the rank of brigadier general in the air force reserve.

In 1946 Cooper formed an independent production company with John Ford, Argosy Pictures. He had already produced one Ford film, *The Lost Patrol* (1934), and now he supervised some of the finest of the director's postwar picture, among them *The Fugitive* (1947), *Fort Apache* (1948), *She Wore a Yellow Ribbon* (1949), *Wagonmaster* (1950), *Rio Grande* (1950), and *The Searchers* (1956). He also produced one more film of Schoedsack's, *Mighty Joe Young* (1949), an extremely interesting variation on the *Kong* theme. In 1952, as always in the forefront of technical advances, he coproduced *This Is Cinerama*, the first movie made in the new three-strip process. It grossed over $30 million in the United States alone. The same year Cooper was honored by the Academy of Motion Picture Arts and Sciences for "his many innovations and contributions to the art of the motion picture."

"Cooper was no faceless studio executive or colorless technical innovator," wrote Ron Haver. "His personality was distinct, a blend of the culture and traditions of the South, where he was born and raised; the more aggressive and pragmatic North, where he was educated; his reading of romantic writers such as Kipling, Harte, London, and Haggard; and the works of Shakespeare and the Bible, a book he read every day. Muscular, short, with sparse, sandy hair, and an outthrust jaw, he had a blunt, forthright manner. He would size up a person through crackling brown eyes which could freeze to ice when he was displeased or angry." Cooper was quite often very angry indeed: in 1932, when his first car stalled and he could not restart it, he pushed it off a cliff.

He died in 1973, survived by his wife, the actress Dorothy Jordan; two daughters; and a son, a major in the air force.

FILMS: (all with Ernest B. Schoedsack)—Grass (Grass; A Nation's Battle for Life/Grass: The Epic of a Lost Tribe), 1925; Chang, 1927; The Four Feathers, 1929; King Kong, 1933.

ABOUT: Brownlow, K. The War, the West, and the Wilderness, 1979; Chateau, R. King Kong Story, 1976; Goldner, O. and Turner, G. E. The Making of King Kong, 1975; Roud, R. (ed.) Cinema: A Critical Dictionary, 1980. *Periodicals*—American Film December 1976–January 1977; L'Avant-Scène du Cinéma November 15, 1982; Film Dope October 1975; Films in Review January 1966; New York Times April 22, 1973; Variety April 25, 1973.

CHARLES CRICHTON

*CRICHTON, CHARLES (August 6, 1910–), British director, producer, and editor, was born in Wallasey, Cheshire. On leaving Oundle School he tried his hand at gold prospecting in Canada but at the insistence of his parents returned home and completed his education, studying history at New College, Oxford University. It was while he was at Oxford that he became seriously interested in the cinema. When Leontine Sagan and Zoltan Korda visited the university to film sequences for their *Men of Tomorrow*, he approached them for a job, and in 1931 he joined London Film Productions as an assistant in the cutting rooms. By 1935 he had progressed to film editor, in which capacity he worked on such well-known London Film Productions movies as *Sanders of the River, Things to Come, Elephant Boy, Prison Without Bars,* and *The Thief of Baghdad.*

In 1940 Crichton moved to Michael Balcon's Ealing Studios as an editor and the following year directed his first film, a documentary short called *Young Veterans,* produced by Alberto Cavalcanti. According to an Ealing press release, "his promotion to the sphere of directing was held up by one thing and one thing only. He became one of the best editors in the British film industry." Crichton's first feature film was *For Those in Peril* (1944), a drama about the wartime Air-Sea Rescue service starring David Farrar and Ralph Michael. There is a strong documentary element in this "absolutely orthodox" movie, and there was a good deal of praise for the opening montage of boats, gulls, and roofscapes in the early morning, before the patrol sets out. *Painted Boats* (1945), about the life of English canal workers, is even closer to documentary, and has a voice-over commentary written by Louis MacNeice. In the same year

Crichton directed one of the five episodes comprising *Dead of Night,* an anthology of ghost stories involving Ealing Studios' finest talents. It is significant that Crichton was assigned to direct a humorous piece—a "Golfing Story" featuring Basil Radford and Naunton Wayne.

Although during his long sojourn at Ealing Crichton's work was to be divided fairly equally between light comedy and drama, his greatest successes were to be in the former mode. And it was a comedy that in 1947 established Crichton as a director of exceptional promise. *Hue and Cry,* the first of the postwar cycle of Ealing comedies, was written by T.E.B. Clarke and involves the detection and apprehension, by a gang of Cockney kids, of fur thieves who send coded messages to one another through a boys' magazine. The film is essentially an amiable fantasy but, as Crichton explained, "we had to emphasise the absurdity of our story through the realism with which we stated it, to enrich our fantasy by the conviction of its telling."

Hue and Cry demonstrates Crichton's talent for extracting first-rate performances from actors, especially child actors like Harry Fowler, who plays the fifteen-year-old sleuth Joe. Alastair Sim contributes a marvelously baroque and eccentric performance as a writer of boys' stories, and the cast also includes such Ealing stalwarts as Jack Warner, Valerie White, and Jack Lambert. Crichton showed a natural talent for location work, especially in the climactic chase in which three hundred boys scramble over the blitzed ruins of London in hot pursuit of the villains.

"The director, Charles Crichton, has given

°krī´t'n

proof of great talent," wrote one reviewer, and another in the London *Times* thought that the director had given his simple story "all the painstaking and lively detail that a good adventure story should have. Scene after scene is brilliantly composed, with the dialogue always giving bite to what is merely conventional in the situation." Richard Winnington welcomed the film as "one of the most refreshing, blood-tingling and disarming pictures of its kind that the British, or in fact any filmmakers, have produced so far—*Emil and the Detectives* and *Nous Les Gosses* not excepted." It was an instant hit, though it was to be some time before the Ealing team realized that they had invented a new comedy genre.

Crichton followed *Hue and Cry* with *Against the Wind* and *Another Shore*, both released in 1948. The former stars Robert Beatty, Jack Warner, and Simone Signoret in a wartime drama about Allied saboteurs in occupied Belgium. Beatty plays the lead in *Another Shore* also, somewhat miscast as an Irishman who dreams of adventure in the South Seas but is sidetracked into marriage (to Moira Lister) and a steady job. Neither film made much impact, nor did *Train of Events* (1949), which in separate episodes (directed by Sidney Cole, Basil Dearden, and Crichton) explores the lives of four victims of a train crash. *Dance Hall* (1950) also tells several stories but this time weaves them into a single narrative about four London factory girls, their soul-destroying jobs, and their pursuit of something more exciting at the local "Palais de Danse." It is a solid piece of work, interesting as a more or less serious study of working-class life (still rare in British cinema) and with an excellent cast including, among others, Natasha Parry, Jane Hylton, Diana Dors, Petula Clark, Donald Houston, Kay Kendall, and Harry Fowler.

In his study of Ealing Studios, Charles Barr points out that the essential element in an Ealing comedy is fantasy: "Given the 'fantasy' premise, the story proceeds in a naturalistic style, in real or at least realistic settings . . . within this framework, Ealing can play out at leisure the daydream of a benevolent community and can partly evade, partly confront in a more manageable form, those awkward 'postwar' issues, social and personal, with which it has hitherto been somewhat glumly trying to deal." Barr locates "the mainstream of Ealing production after the war" in the work of the scriptwriter T.E.B. Clarke and of the directors Basil Dearden and Charles Crichton. The latter's second film with Clarke was *The Lavender Hill Mob* (1951), in which a meek Bank of England clerk sets out to steal a million pounds in gold bullion from his employers by casting it into souvenir models of the Eiffel Tower which can then be "exported" out of the country. Alec Guinness gives a brilliantly observed performance as the genteel criminal, while the excellent camerawork is by Crichton's usual cinematographer, Douglas Slocombe.

The film was received as warmly as *Hue and Cry* had been four years earlier and according to the *Times* critic showed the same "great skill in the handling of the crowd scenes and in the exploitation of character. . . . There is also a great fertility of invention in minor details and in the incidents of the chase which such a film as this demands and which is handled by Mr. Charles Crichton with all the skill that he has shown in his earlier films." The traveling matte was used with great effect in the "riotous, rapid sequences" in which Guinness and his accomplice (Stanley Holloway) chase down the Eiffel Tower. *The Lavender Hill Mob* received an Oscar for the best screenplay of 1951, the British Film Academy's award as the best British film of 1951, and the best scenario award at the Venice Film Festival.

Hunted (1952), in which a runaway boy joins forces with a fugitive murderer (Dirk Bogarde), was made for GFD/Independent Artists and was followed by another Crichton-Clarke comedy, *The Titfield Thunderbolt* (1953). This, Ealing's first comedy in Technicolor, starred Stanley Holloway, George Relph, Naunton Wayne, John Gregson, and Hugh Griffith in a story about the inhabitants of a small country town and their campaign to save a railroad branch line from closure through the machinations of an evil bus company and heartless bureaucrats. It is an archetypal Ealing comedy theme, but there were signs that the genre was losing its freshness and declining into self-conscious quaintness and a sentimental and conservative celebration of tradition for its own sake. As Charles Barr points out, the sense of community involvement, so important in earlier Ealing comedies like *Hue and Cry* and *Passport to Pimlico*, is here entirely spurious: "There is no grasp of a *living* community in the film, or of the relevance of the train to people's daily needs. It's the hobby of a few eccentric amateurs." And there were other complaints. One critic wrote that "somebody must give back to director Charles Crichton that sense of comic timing which *Hue and Cry* and *The Lavender Hill Mob* showed him to possess. . . . Mr. Crichton has allowed too many incidents to continue on the screen longer than we are quite prepared to laugh at them." And C. A. Lejeune agreed that the movie "might have done with crisper cutting" and "more direct direction."

The Love Lottery (1954), a feeble comedy starring David Niven as a film star offered as a prize in a lottery, was followed the same year by the most successful of Crichton's serious movies, *The Divided Heart*. It is about a Yugoslav woman (Yvonne Mitchell)—a survivor of Auschwitz who had been separated from her baby—and of her struggle ten years later to win her child back from the loving German couple who had subsequently adopted him. The theme was topical in that postwar Europe still contained many such displaced children, and the story (by Jack Whittingham and Richard Hughes) was based on a case heard before the United States Control Commission in Germany two years earlier.

A reviewer in the *Daily Sketch* decided that "a story unexampled in its human, heartbreaking quality has been screened with dignity and art. . . . But above all this is a director's picture, and Charles Crichton's greatest success is in his handling of ten-year-old Michael Ray," who played the wretched child. C. A. Lejeune also thought that "Charles Crichton's direction is good direction in that it guides but never checks good players in the course they are naturally inclined to take." *The Divided Heart* won the British Academy award for the best performance by a British actress in 1954 (Yvonne Mitchell) and that for the best performance by a foreign actress (Cornell Borchers, who played the German mother). The film also received the United Nations award as best film of 1954 and the Golden Laurel at the Edinburgh Festival.

Crichton made only one more film for Ealing, a flying drama called *The Man in the Sky* (*Decision Against Time* in the U.S.), released in 1957. *Floods of Fear* (Rank, 1958) was followed by *Law and Disorder* (British Lion, 1958), a T. E.B. Clarke comedy begun by Henry Cornelius and completed by Crichton. Two more comedies followed—*The Battle of the Sexes* (1959), based on the James Thurber story "The Catbird Seat" and starring Peter Sellers, and *The Boy Who Stole a Million* (1961), for which Crichton was also coauthor—both made for Bryanston Films.

In 1961 Crichton went to the United States to direct what was to have been his first Hollywood picture, *The Birdman of Alcatraz*. It is hard to imagine why he was ever considered for such an assignment, and in fact he left the production soon after shooting had begun, the film being completed by John Frankenheimer. Some fourteen years later Crichton told an interviewer what had happened: "Had I known that Burt Lancaster was to be *de facto* producer," he said, "I do not think I would have accepted the assignment as he had a reputation for quarreling with

better directors than I. But Harold Hecht, the credited producer, had assured me that there would be no interference from Lancaster. This did not prove to be the case."

Back in England, Crichton made *The Third Secret* (1964), an intelligent psychological thriller with an impressive cast (it includes Jack Hawkins, Richard Attenborough, Patricia Neal, Diane Cilento, and Steve McQueen). His last feature film, *He Who Rides a Tiger* (1965), is a drama about a criminal (Tom Bell) who tries to go straight when he falls in love (with Judi Dench). Since then Crichton has made two documentaries, *Tomorrow's Island* (1968), about the island of Dominica, and *London—Through My Eyes* (1970), a tongue-in-cheek portrait of London as seen by a young Swedish singer. In 1956 Crichton had made a television version of Ibsen's *Wild Duck,* and after 1965 he became increasingly involved in that medium, directing episodes in several popular British series including *The Avengers* and *Danger Man* (both 1965), *Man in a Suitcase* (1967), and *The Adventures of Black Beauty* (1972 and 1973).

Charles Crichton is an untemperamental and self-effacing craftsman—an immensely skillful interpreter of scripts rather than an original creator. According to *Film Dope,* "the sad thing for Crichton was that following the golden days at Ealing the available scripts got steadily more puerile and more vulgar and as a result—though one can only conjecture on what might have happened if *Birdman* had gone well—his decline was slow but inexorable. The more interesting of Crichton's later films, like the comedies *Law and Disorder* and *Battle of the Sexes* which (from memory) were funny enough to look really good in today's barren comedy climate, only underline the shameful waste of his skills."

—*R.S.*

FILMS: Young Veterans, 1941 (short); For Those in Peril, 1944; Painted Boats (U.S., The Girl on the Canal), 1945; (with others) Dead of Night, 1945; Hue and Cry, 1947; Against the Wind, 1948; Another Shore, 1948; (with others) Train of Events, 1949; Dance Hall, 1950; The Lavender Hill Mob, 1951; Hunted (U.S., The Stranger in Between), 1952; The Titfield Thunderbolt, 1953; The Love Lottery, 1954; The Divided Heart, 1954; The Man in the Sky (U.S., Decision Against Time), 1957; Floods of Fear, 1958; Law and Disorder, 1958; Battle of the Sexes, 1959; The Boy Who Stole a Million, 1961; The Third Secret, 1964; He Who Rides a Tiger, 1965; Tomorrow's Island, 1968 (documentary); London—Through My Eyes, 1970 (documentary for television).

ABOUT: Barr, C. Ealing Studios, 1977; International Who's Who, 1980–81; Marner, T. S. Directing Motion Pictures, 1972. *Periodicals*—Film Dope October 1975; Penguin Film Review 7 1948.

"CROMWELL, JOHN" (Elwood Dager)
(December 23, 1886 or 1887–September 26,
1979), American stage and film director and actor, was born in Toledo, Ohio. "For some
reason," he said, "they got into a horrible mess
over me and I was never able to determine
whether I was born in 1886 or 1887." Cromwell
studied English literature and acted in school
plays at the Howe School in Howe, Indiana, then
worked for a short time in his father's iron and
steel business in Cleveland before joining a
Cleveland stock company. After one season he
went to New York and for the next three years
toured from there with various stock companies.
He made his first significant Broadway appearance in 1912 as John Brook in *Little Women,*
billing himself for the first time as John Cromwell. The following year he directed his first
production, *The Painted Women,* for William
Brady, his mentor in the theatre.

As an actor Cromwell appeared in the first
American productions of Shaw's *Major Barbara*
(1915) and *Captain Brassbound's Conversion*
(1916), and after a brief wartime stint in the U.S.
Army, his stage career went from strength to
strength. He had his first hit in 1923 with
Tarnish and notable successes with productions
of two Sidney Howard plays, *Lucky Sam
McCarger* and *The Silver Cord.* He also directed
and acted in plays in various regional theatres
and in London.

In 1928 Cromwell directed and played the
lead role as Captain McQuigg in a Los Angeles
production of a gangster drama called *The
Racket,* also starring Edward G. Robinson.
Cromwell was "spotted" and offered a contract
by Ben Schulberg of Paramount. The talkies had
just arrived, and directors with stage experience
were being sought after eagerly in Hollywood.
Cromwell said "the first thing that struck me was
the absolute paralysis of fear that the talkies had
cast over all of Hollywood."

Joining Paramount in the summer of 1928,
Cromwell methodically set about learning his
new profession. He spent three months in the
cutting room, then took a small acting role—as
the detective in *The Dummy* (1929)—to find
out how it felt to work in front of the cameras.
He directed his first two films in collaboration
with an experienced director, Eddie Sutherland:
Close Harmony (1929), a romance with a jazzband background, and a show-business comedy
called *The Dance of Life* (1929). Cromwell's
first solo effort was *The Mighty* (1929), starring
George Bancroft in a melodrama about the battlefield regeneration of a crook.

David O. Selznick had joined Paramount
shortly before Cromwell did, and in 1930, when

JOHN CROMWELL

he was preparing his first movie as producer
there, he asked Cromwell to direct it. This was
The Street of Chance, starring William Powell
as a gambler who sacrifices his life in a successful
attempt to cure his kid brother (Regis Toomey)
of gambling fever. At the end, shot down by
gangsters, "Natural" Davis dies making bets
with the ambulance men. The Oscar-winning
script was by Howard Estabrook and the terse
dialogue by Lenore Coffee. As Cromwell remarked, "it created quite a stir," partly because
it was obviously based on the career of Arnold
Rothstein, the "King of the Roaring Twenties."
The cast also included Kay Francis, Jean Arthur,
and Cromwell himself, who often took small
parts in his movies.

Cromwell and Selznick "hit it off very well
together," and Selznick also produced *The
Texan* (1930), starring Gary Cooper in an O.
Henry story about another outlaw salvaged by
conscience. Cromwell maintained that he had
very little to do with *Seven Days' Leave* (1930),
usually credited to him, and is, in fact, less than
enthusiastic about most of the movies he made
for Paramount. These included *For the Defense*
(1930); one of the numerous versions of *Tom
Sawyer* (1930); *Scandal Sheet* (1931), a George
Bancroft vehicle; *Unfaithful* (1931), based on a
story by John Van Druten; and *Vice Squad*
(1931). Trained in the theatre, Cromwell believed strongly in the value of rehearsals and at
first had his way. In 1930, when he was preparing *For the Defense,* Schulberg told him there
would be no more rehearsals, since the other
Paramount directors considered them a waste of
time. Cromwell insisted, and proved his point by

cutting two days off the movie's shooting schedule of seventeen days with the help of four days' rehearsal without cameras.

However, Cromwell became increasingly frustrated with the trivial assignments he was given at Paramount and particularly disliked working with George Bancroft, then the studio's biggest star. *Rich Man's Folly* (1931), a modern dress version of *Dombey and Son,* seemed to Cromwell full of possibilities: "It should have been absolutely splendid for Bancroft except that it required in the actor a consciousness of the material—of which he had none." Cromwell was then assigned to direct Bancroft again in *The World and the Flesh* (1932), about a soldier of fortune in the Russian Revolution. He accepted the task reluctantly, on the understanding that his next assignment would be the screen version of Hemingway's *A Farewell to Arms. The World and the Flesh* "was the high point of degradation" for him; he had "taken a great interest in the Russian Revolution" and was disgusted by the "asinine, concocted story" he was given to film. Then Ben Schulberg was fired, *A Farewell to Arms* went to Frank Borzage, and Cromwell "walked off the lot." On the advice of his agent, Myron Selznick, he followed Myron's brother David to RKO.

"RKO was always an endearing place to me," Cromwell said. "It had a distinct feeling of independence and individuality it never lost. It was always short of good writers, good directors and actors, but it would never admit it." Cromwell treated his writers with a respect that was rare in Hollywood in those days; he said once "I liken a director of a picture or a play to the director of a symphony orchestra . . . his job is merely his interpretation of the author's idea through which he [the director] makes his personal comment on the story." All the same, by the time he got to RKO he had grasped the fact that films— even the talkies—were primarily visual artifacts. At RKO he found writers who understood this, like Jane Murfin, who wrote many of his movies there. The studio allowed him to take a hand in the development of his scripts and to rehearse his actors. Between 1933 and 1935 he turned out a string of pictures which, although most of them were made very cheaply and many were melodramatic in their plots, were considerably more complex and sophisticated in characterization than his Paramount movies, and notably well acted.

In *Sweepings,* for example, a sort of modern *Lear* about a businessman embittered by his family's ingratitude, he drew an unusually restrained performance from Lionel Barrymore. Jane Murfin's adaptation of Sidney Howard's play *The Silver Cord* is extraordinarily frank in showing what "smother love" does to the sex lives of the matriarch's two sons. Laura Hope Crews, who had starred in Cromwell's stage production, repeats her brilliant and appalling performance as the mother, Joel McCrea and Eric Linden are the hapless sons, and Irene Dunne is formidable as the daughter-in-law who wrenches McCrea away from his mother's apron strings. According to Brenda Davies, Cromwell rehearsed this cast so thoroughly that they could have given a stage performance and deliberately refrained from "opening up" the play. By confining the action almost entirely to the mother's house (and mostly to one room), he powerfully reinforced the impression of near-incestuous claustrophobia.

Ann Vickers (1933), based on Sinclair Lewis' novel, was followed by *Spitfire* (1934), in which Katharine Hepburn plays a wild and illiterate mountain girl whose independent spirit and ability to heal through prayer bring her ostracism as a witch. The film was shot mostly on location, and its striking composition, soft-key lighting, and mobile camerawork (by Edward Cronjagen) are much admired. Cromwell felt that Hepburn was miscast in this picture, but she nevertheless conveys very convincingly the eccentricity, spiritual intensity, and physical exuberance of the character.

After *This Man Is Mine* (1934), a comedy-drama in which Irene Dunne disentangles her erring husband (Ralph Bellamy) from the seductive arms of Constance Cummings, came the film that established Cromwell's critical reputation, an adaptation by Lester Cohen of Somerset Maugham's novel *Of Human Bondage.* The bondage is that of a naive young medical student (Leslie Howard) to a vulgar and predatory waitress. Cromwell picked Bette Davis for the part, and her performance established her as an actress rather than an ingenue. The movie confirmed Cromwell's growing reputation as a filmmaker with a special gift for what used to be called "women's pictures" and as a director of actresses. Cromwell himself, with his usual modesty, said that "handling women was governed mostly by the nature of the parts. I never made any point, as Cukor has at times, of developing their feminine aspects; I was always governed by the nature of the part so I was never conscious of developing skills or handling personalities."

Kingsley Canham, whose essay on Cromwell is subtitled "Memories of Love, Elegance and Style," finds all of these considerations embodied in *The Fountain* (1934), which he regards as a key film in Cromwell's career. Derived by Jane Murfin from a rather pretentious Charles Morgan novel and rigorously pruned, it centers on a British officer (Brian Aherne) who is interned during World War I in neutral Holland. He is seeking spiritual peace through contemplation but is distracted from this search when he is billeted with Julie (Ann Harding), an old college friend with whom he falls passionately in love. Paul Lukas plays Julie's German husband, who returns from the war seriously wounded and gives the lovers his blessing before he dies. The film's restraint and maturity were widely praised, and Canham has drawn attention to the skill with which Cromwell used camera movements to reflect the spiritual restlessness of the two principals. Brenda Davies called the early scenes in the P.O.W. camp "splendidly authentic," but thought that the rest of the film suffered from "some overemphatic art direction and an insistent Max Steiner score."

Cromwell himself had a high regard for *The Fountain* and also for *Village Tale,* the drama of small-town life that followed in 1935. After a not very successful version of Mazo de la Roche's *Jalna* came *I Dream Too Much* (1935), a vehicle for the diminutive singer Lily Pons. At that point Cromwell left RKO to direct a remake of *Little Lord Fauntleroy,* David Selznick's first independent production (released through United Artists). Selznick was a perfectionist with a reputation for interfering in his directors' films, but Cromwell shared his high standards and in spite of occasional battles they worked well together. Having left RKO Cromwell found that he enjoyed his freedom and thereafter worked on individual projects or short contracts for a number of different studios.

"Everything about it seemed the best I'd had yet," Cromwell said of *Little Lord Fauntleroy*; "the story preparation, the cast; everything about it was done in such an orderly, professional, highly artistic way. The shooting was fairly easy, and it all came out very well." The critics agreed, noting how this much-filmed story about an American boy who inherits a British peerage is saved from sentimentality by thoughtful characterization and restrained performances. Freddie Bartholomew makes a marvelously natural and humorous character out of Fauntleroy and the film, which was adapted by the novelist Hugh Walpole, was called "a just above perfect piece of interpretation."

Banjo on My Knee, starring Barbara Stanwyck and Walter Brennan in an off-beat yarn about Mississippi riverboat people, was followed by *The Prisoner of Zenda* (1937). Like *Fauntleroy,* it was a remake of a silent movie (and one that Cromwell was warned was hopelessly dated). The swashbuckling story (from Anthony Hope's novel) involves an Englishman (Ronald Colman) standing in for a threatened Ruritanian king, and becoming involved in palace plots and a romance with the queen (Madeleine Carroll). It was not the easiest movie in Cromwell's career. The shooting script had to take account of the fact that one of Colman's profiles was inferior to the other, and Madeleine Carroll then claimed a similar problem with the same profile. Furthermore, without consulting Cromwell, Selznick brought in George Cukor and W. S. Van Dyke to direct specific scenes that he thought them specially qualified to handle. (In fact, the scene in which the queen renounces the hero, directed by Cukor, has been thought the least satisfactory in the movie.) However, Cromwell's loyalty to Selznick survived even this, and on the credit side were the contributions of James Wong Howe as cameraman, Lyle Wheeler as art director, and a cast that included Raymond Massey, Douglas Fairbanks Jr., Mary Astor, David Niven, and C. Aubrey Smith. The result was a work of great charm, elegance, and panache, perhaps the best-remembered of all Cromwell's films.

Algiers (1938) was a remake for Walter Wanger of Duvivier's *Pépé le Moko,* which had been released only two years earlier, with Charles Boyer and Hedy Lamarr in the roles created by Jean Gabin and Mireille Ballin. Cromwell, who had admired Duvivier's film, decided that "the right and only thing to do [was] . . . to come as close as I could to a replica." Most critics thought Cromwell's version a reasonable if somewhat less poetic copy of the original, and it was highly profitable. Hired by Sam Goldwyn to direct *The Adventures of Marco Polo* and fired a week later, Cromwell returned briefly to the theatre before accepting an offer from Selznick to film *Made for Each Other* (1939), with Carole Lombard and James Stewart. A beautifully played romantic comedy about the joys and sorrows of a newly married couple, it is both funny and touching, its more fanciful moments perfectly balanced by sharp touches of realism, its sentimentalities undermined by hints of parody. The melodramatic final sequence, in which the Masons' baby becomes dangerously ill and is only saved when a rare drug is flown at great risk through a storm, was imposed by Selznick—his brother Myron had been cured of a grave illness under similar circumstances shortly before, and Selznick could not bear to waste the incident's cinematic possibilities.

In Name Only, a romantic "triangle" with Lombard as the "other woman" in Cary Grant's life, was followed by *Abe Lincoln in Illinois* (1940). Adapted by Robert Sherwood and Grover Jones from Sherwood's play, it had to face the competition of John Ford's *Young Mr. Lincoln,* covering much the same period in the President's life. Ruth Gordon, in her film debut, gives a perfectly judged performance as the ambitious Mary Todd, and Raymond Massey had the part of his life in the lead. "The early pastoral scenes have a beautiful feeling for the rural life of the period," wrote Brenda Davies, "and fluent camera movements follow a series of engaging incidents: logging on a rapid river, chasing stray pigs ('My name's Lincoln, ma'am. I don't know the name of the pig'), drilling volunteers, wooing Ann Rutledge. The strength of Massey's performance is that while he gets full value out of the pawky rustic humor of these early scenes, one always feels in the character a deep core of strength and high seriousness."

Cromwell's version of Joseph Conrad's *Victory* was ruined by a poor script, and *So Ends Our Night* (1941), based on Remarque's novel about the rise of Nazism, was also commercially unsuccessful, in spite of a starry cast (and Cromwell's own conviction that this was one of his best pictures). After *Son of Fury* (1942), an uneven Tyrone Power swashbuckler, Cromwell rejoined Selznick for *Since You Went Away* (1944), about the problems that face a Midwestern family whose menfolk are away fighting World War II. An ambitious, expensive, and very long film (nearly three hours), it has an enormous cast headed by Claudette Colbert, Jennifer Jones, Shirley Temple, Joseph Cotten, Monty Woolley, Robert Walker, and Lionel Barrymore. Jennifer Jones was Selznick's latest *protégée* (later his wife), and filming was complicated by the fact that Robert Walker, who plays her fiancé, was in real life her estranged husband. Nevertheless, the movie—Cromwell's last with Selznick—is a typically polished product of their collaboration, a "ten handkerchief weepie" and excellent wartime propaganda for "the unconquerable fortress of 1943—the American family."

The Enchanted Cottage, from Pinero's play, is a romantic fantasy in which a disfigured war hero (Robert Young) and a shy, plain woman (Dorothy Maguire) find happiness through the good offices of a blind composer (Herbert Marshall). Once again, Cromwell's fastidious professionalism turned a potentially cloying story into a delicate and moving one, and the director was particularly fond of this picture, as he was of its successor, *Anna and the King of Siam* (1946), an opulent and intelligent nonmusical version of the now familiar story, marred only by the miscasting of Rex Harrison as the King. Irene Dunne is excellent as the bossy heroine, and the film won Oscars for black-and-white photography (Arthur Miller) and art direction (Lyle Wheeler).

Cromwell agreed to direct *Dead Reckoning* for Columbia because Humphrey Bogart asked for him. Bogart, to whom Cromwell had given his first stage part, plays a tough veteran out to avenge a murdered buddy and a double-crossing by Lizabeth Scott, whose woodenness is a liability in this very violent but highly effective *film noir.* After that, Cromwell signed a contract to make one movie a year for RKO—"the best contract I had in Hollywood." At that promising point in his career, the director was cited by Adolph Menjou at hearings of the House Committee on Un-American Activities. "I was nothing but what I called a 'liberal' Democrat with no interest in what we call popular politics until we came to the advent of Roosevelt's third term," Cromwell said, "and then I got concerned because I felt it was essential that he was re-elected. I joined and worked pretty consistently for, a small organization called the Hollywood Democratic Committee, eventually finding myself the head of the thing." His involvement with this innocent body was enough to place him under suspicion, and Howard Hughes, who had just bought RKO, did his best to make Cromwell break his contract. He quietly resisted and was then loaned to Warner Brothers to direct *Caged.*

All of the personal bitterness Cromwell felt at this time comes through in the film, an exposé of brutality and sadism in a women's prison and of official indifference and political corruption outside, showing how these conditions virtually guarantee the corruption of a first offender (Eleanor Parker). The claustrophobia and violence of the world she enters at the beginning of the film are evoked with great force and economy, and the story proceeds with an almost classical sense of inevitability to a climactic riot scene. The film ends with the heroine's release and the resigned comment of the sympathetic head warden (Agnes Moorehead, interestingly cast against type): "She'll be back."

In 1951 Cromwell filmed *The Racket,* the play that had first brought him to Hollywood, with Robert Mitchum as McQuigg, the honest cop in a crooked city, and Robert Ryan as the psychotic gangster played on stage by Edward G. Robinson. After this chillingly pessimistic film, which completed his RKO contract, Cromwell returned once more to the theatre, where among other things he directed and acted in Samuel Taylor's *Sabrina Fair* and won a Tony award for his performance in *Point of No Return.* He was lured back to Hollywood to direct *The Goddess* (1958), if anything an even more savagely disillusioned film than *Caged.* Adapted by Paddy Chayefsky from his own play, it studies the rise and fall of a great star, modeled according to some accounts on Ava

Gardner but often reminiscent of Marilyn Monroe. The wretched heroine seeks fulfillment in sex, in fame, in a string of husbands, in religion, in various addictions and enthusiasms, but never finds a substitute for the love she had been denied as an unwanted child. Cromwell drew an astonishing performance from Kim Stanley, and the film contains some of his best work, but it was vandalized in the editing, apparently by Chayefsky himself. In the end Cromwell walked out on the project. He never directed another film in the Hollywood he anatomized so bitterly in *The Goddess.*

Cromwell did make two more movies, one in the Philippines and one in Sweden, both doomed by impossible scripts. He devoted the latter part of his long life mostly to the theatre. He wrote three plays, all of them staged in New York, starred opposite Helen Hayes in a revival of *What Every Woman Knows,* directed the original company of *Desk Set,* and appeared in *Mary, Mary.* For some years, impatient with Broadway commercialism, he worked in regional theatres, including four seasons at the Tyrone Guthrie Theatre in Minnesota. When he did return to Hollywood it was as an actor, and he gave his last performance in Robert Altman's *A Wedding* (1978), appearing (at the age of ninety) as Bishop Martin.

A tall, dignified, and genial man, Cromwell was married four times, always to actresses and finally, for thirty years, to Ruth Gordon, who often worked with him. He had one son, James. In 1944–1945 he served as president of the Screen Directors' Guild. A man of extraordinary humility, he said in 1973: "I never got accustomed to the terrific range of the camera, and what the choice of shot can do to a scene. . . . I was always very aware of composition. I had to rely enormously on my cameramen, especially at first. . . . I would talk, mostly about how I felt about a scene, what it meant to me in terms of lighting, as near as I could tell, and rely entirely upon them."

"To Cromwell," wrote Richard Koszarski, "the work of the director was not to throw off individual sparks of creativity but to fuse the efforts of the entire creative team for the best interests of the finished work. Such selflessness has always been rare in filmmaking, and Cromwell has long been overlooked by critics and historians alike. But recent reassessments of his work have established him as a director of substance as well as style." Brenda Davies finds no unity of style among Cromwell's films but writes that "each has a style of its own which expresses, not the filmmaker's own ideas and obsessions, but his response to his subject. From the choice

of these subjects and the quality of that response it is possible to discern a civilised, compassionate and liberal man behind the camera."

—K.C.

FILMS: (with Edward Sutherland) Close Harmony, 1929: (with Edward Sutherland) The Dance of Life, 1929; The Mighty, 1929; The Street of Chance, 1930; The Texan, 1930; (with Richard Wallace) Seven Days' Leave (U.K., Medals), 1930; For the Defense, 1930; Tom Sawyer, 1930; Scandal Sheet, 1931; Unfaithful, 1931; Vice Squad, 1931; Rich Man's Folly, 1931; The World and the Flesh, 1932; Sweepings, 1933; The Silver Cord, 1933; Double Harness, 1933; Ann Vickers, 1933; Spitfire, 1934; This Man Is Mine, 1934; Of Human Bondage, 1934; The Fountain, 1934; Village Tale, 1935; Jalna, 1935; I Dream Too Much, 1935; Little Lord Fauntleroy, 1936; To Mary—With Love, 1936; Banjo on My Knee, 1936; The Prisoner of Zenda, 1937; Algiers, 1938; Made for Each Other, 1939; In Name Only, 1939; Abe Lincoln in Illinois (U.K., Spirit of the People), 1940; Victory, 1940; So Ends Our Night, 1941; Son of Fury, 1942; Since You Went Away, 1944; The Enchanted Cottage, 1945; Anna and the King of Siam, 1946; Dead Reckoning, 1947; Night Song, 1947; Caged, 1950; The Company She Keeps, 1951; The Racket, 1951; The Goddess, 1958; The Scavengers, 1959 (U.S.-Philippines); De Sista Stegen (U.S., A Matter of Morals), 1960 (Sweden).

ABOUT: Canham, K. John Cromwell *in* The Hollywood Professionals: 5, 1976; Davies, B. John Cromwell, 1974; Koszarski, R. Hollywood Directors: 1914–1940, 1976; Naumburg, N. (ed.) We Make the Movies, 1937; Thomson, D. A Biographical Dictionary of the Cinema, 1975. *Periodicals*—Action May–June 1973; Cinema (Los Angeles) Spring 1968; Film Dope October 1975; Films and Filming March 1971; Films Illustrated November 1974; Interview February 1972; New York Times September 28, 1979; Picturegoer October 27, 1934; Positif March 1979; Sight and Sound Autumn 1972; Velvet Light Trap Fall 1973.

"CRUZE, JAMES" (Jens Cruz Bosen) (March 27, 1884–August 4, 1942), American director, was born at Five Points, near Ogden, Utah, the only boy among the eighteen children of a Danish immigrant couple. His parents were Mormons who had crossed the plains in a covered wagon and settled in Utah as farmers. The door was never locked, and Cruze could remember coming downstairs on cold winter mornings to find two or three Indian women sitting on the kitchen floor, waiting patiently for breakfast. The boy was set to work on the farm at the age of seven and according to one account had only two years of formal education. "The only thing I knew of the outside world," he said, "was when covered wagons would draw up under our cottonwoods for the night, and I'd talk with the kids, and sometimes tent shows would come by.

JAMES CRUZE

I suppose they were poor trash, but they seemed wonderful to me."

They certainly seemed more wonderful to him than what he was doing at fifteen, which was weeding his father's onions at twenty-five cents a day. He said that "every day, a freight train would crawl up alongside the onion patch . . . and I'd wish each time that I was on it going away from there. And one day I got my nerve together and without saying a word to anyone, climbed into a box car. . . . Eventually I landed in San Francisco, and my first position there was as a dishwasher in a café that could hardly be called first class. Of course my ambition was to be an actor even before I left home, and washing dishes was only a means to an end. But the emoluments could hardly have been termed generous so I shipped to Alaska. I came back with $1100 . . . worked hard for, in a fishery. Fish and onions are in the same category for me."

Cruze used the money to pay his way through "Colonel" F. Cooke Caldwell's drama school. He seems to have begun his theatrical career as a barker with Billy Banks's traveling stock company, hawking patent medicine during the intermission, before graduating to more respectable roles, including the title part in David Garrick. He is said to have organized a theatre troupe of his own in 1903, when he was only nineteen, and from 1906 to 1911 he played in vaudeville and repertory in New York, for a time as the male lead in David Belasco's much-loved The Heart of Maryland.

Though some sources say that Cruze acted in movies as early as 1908, it seems more likely that he entered the industry in 1911. In that year he joined the Thanhouser Company and starred in one of the numerous silent versions of Rider Haggard's She. A tall and powerfully built man whose black eyes were supposed to be evidence of Indian blood, Cruze became well known as the hero of such Thanhouser serials as The Million Dollar Mystery (1914) and Zudora (1914–1915). His co-star in the former, Marguerite Show, became his first wife—they were married before the cameras on a stage at the Thanhouser studio in Boyle Heights, Los Angeles. Incapacitated for a while by a broken leg sustained in stunt work, Cruze returned to acting with Lasky–Famous Players, making his directorial debut in 1918 with the same company.

Cruze's first picture was a comedy called Too Many Millions, and this was followed by a series of films starring Wallace Reid, among them The Roaring Road, Valley of the Giants, and The Lottery Man (all 1919). In The Roaring Road, Reid plays a hot-tempered young auto racer in love with his boss's daughter (Ann Little). A race between a car and a train was "well handled," according to Hazel Simpson Naylor: "Every ounce of suspense, interest and thrill is maintained until the very end, while all the comedy possible is extracted" from the conflict between Reid and his equally irascible employer.

It was as a director of comedies that Cruze made his name, beginning in 1921 with a string of movies starring the former Keystone comic actor Roscoe "Fatty" Arbuckle. Notable among them were The Dollar-a-Year Man, Gasoline Gus, and Crazy to Marry. Then in September 1921 Arbuckle was charged with the rape and murder of a young actress who had died at a drunken party, and though he was acquitted, his career was finished. Cruze had another success with a very different sort of comedian, the cowboy philosopher Will Rogers, in One Glorious Day (1922), and then, after three or four insignificant programmers, began work on what remains the best known of all his films, The Covered Wagon.

Adapted by Jack Cunningham from the novel by Emerson Hough, The Covered Wagon introduced a now familiar theme that, according to Kevin Brownlow, had for years attracted Cruze, himself the son of pioneer parents. The story begins at Westport Landing (now Kansas City), where a huge train of wagons assembles to begin a two-thousand-mile journey across the plains to Oregon. Melodrama is introduced in the romance between Molly Wingate (Lois Wilson) and Will Banion (J. Warren Kerrigan) and the machinations of Banion's rival, Sam Woodhull (Alan Hale). But the real drama grows out of the epic journey itself—the rigors of desert and snow, the hazardous crossing of the Platte River, a prairie fire, Indian attacks, and a buffalo hunt. An army courier brings news that gold has been discovered in California, and the wagon train divides, some settlers pushing on to Oregon, others joining the gold rush. Banion goes to California, finds gold, and (the villainous Woodhull having been disposed of) is reunited with his Molly in Oregon.

Cruze chose as his principal location a ranch in the Snake River Valley, on the border of Utah and Nevada, where an army-style camp was created. Conditions were almost as rough as they had been for the original pioneers. Dorothy Arzner, who went with Cruze as his editor, told an interviewer that virtually everyone except herself had dysentery (a condition she avoided by drinking milk instead of water, as advised by her own pioneering grandfather). But, she says, "there was a wonderful spirit in those days," and Cruze commanded great loyalty. When shooting was delayed by snow and "even Paramount wanted us to come back and finish the picture on the Lasky lot," Cruze refused and won the enthusiastic support of everyone involved in the film.

Intent on authenticity, Cruze employed a team of researchers and claimed that "there wasn't a false whisker in the picture." He recruited local Indians from a variety of tribes, with the future Western star Colonel Tim McCoy as their supervisor and interpreter. His cowboys and pioneers included a former sheriff, Ed "Pardner" Jones, and Yakima Jim, a halfbreed and reputed killer who subsequently died in a gunfight. Oxen were broken to the yoke, and many of the wagons were real Conestogas, preserved as heirlooms by descendants of the pioneers. The spectacular crossing of the Platte River (actually a local lake) was done just as the pioneers did it—by caulking the wagons and floating them across, with the stock swimming. Animals were used—and several were killed— with the callousness of the time, and the crew and cast faced almost equal dangers. The photographer Karl Brown was nearly killed by a charging buffalo and only saved by the almost incredible speed and accuracy of "Pardner" Jones' shooting.

Released in 1923, The Covered Wagon ran for two and a half hours. Robert E. Sherwood hailed it as "the one great American epic the screen has produced," and most contemporary critics agreed. Its enormous financial success doubled the output of Westerns within a year. Nevertheless—and in spite of Cruze's research—there were complaints of anachronisms in the film,

like the great size of the wagon train. Tully Marshall's portrayal of Jim Bridger, the Mormons' leader, as a drunk with two Indian wives brought an unsuccessful suit for damages from Bridger's daughter.

Later writers have tended to criticize The Covered Wagon less on historical grounds than for the intrusion of a foolish and irrelevant romance into what is otherwise a magnificent documentary reconstruction of an era. J. Warren Kerrigan, in his tight-fitting costume and obvious make-up, looks ludicrously out of place among the extras, with their old workclothes and "rough, tanned faces." But it seemed to C. A. Lejeune that "the American cinema came of age when it produced The Covered Wagon, a film not in itself a major bit of work . . . but of immense historical interest as the first commercial picture to play straight for the ideals and loyalties of the public and build them into the structure on the screen. . . . what mattered was the idea behind the story, the courage of that trek westwards to open out new country for a young race."

Iris Barry wrote that "in translating the novel into visual terms, Cruze had profited by the technical discoveries of D. W. Griffith, particularly as displayed in the cutting of the open-air sequences of The Birth of a Nation. . . . Photographically, The Covered Wagon is remarkable, for this was taken before the days of panchromatic stock. Especially rich are the night scenes at the fort before the Indian attack, and the shots of the livestock and wagons crossing the river. In both, photographic brilliance is combined with considerable editorial skill—the shots are timed and assembled most excitingly." More recently Cruze has been called "the founder of an 'odyssey' tradition in the American Western."

After this triumph, Cruze returned to the satires and domestic comedies that many of his contemporaries regarded as his real forte. Hollywood (1923), based on Frank Condon's story about a girl who goes to the movie capital in search of fame, is said to have been remarkable for its expressionistic dream sequences (and its bold references to the Arbuckle scandal). The heroine can't get a job, but her ailing grandfather is hired and so are her pants-presser boyfriend and most of her family. "It was utter insanity," wrote Robert E. Sherwood admiringly. "The various stars, garbed as sheikhs, licentious club-men, aristocratic roués, bathing-girls, apaches, and the like, moved about in weird confusion through a distorted nightmare. There was slow motion photography, reverse action, and double exposure; no sense was made at any given point."

This was followed by Cruze's version of *Ruggles of Red Gap*, Harry Leon Wilson's comedy about an English butler (Edward Everett Horton) exported to America, and in 1924 came *Merton of the Movies*. A companion piece to Cruze's *Hollywood*, it centers on a screen-struck Illinois store clerk (Glenn Hunter), his Walter Mitty–like fantasies of cinematic glory, and his initially disastrous "collision with the world of celluloid make-believe." Based on another Harry Leon Wilson play, it seemed to one reviewer to have emphasized pathos at the expense of the original's "biting satire," but it was another critical and financial success.

Two more notable comedies appeared in 1925. *The Goose Hangs High* was a popular if relatively sentimental piece about a family of selfish children brought to recognize the sacrifices their parents have made for them at Christmas. Much more interesting was *Beggar on Horseback*, starring Edward Everett Horton as a serious young composer forced to earn his living by playing jazz. Containing some sharp satire on the *nouveaux riches* of the period, it carried Cruze's "quasi-expressionistic" visual experiments almost to the point of surrealism. A failure at the box office, this was the director's own favorite among his films. The same year Cruze demonstrated his "splendid feeling for Western locations" in *Pony Express*, otherwise a rather dull big-budget melodrama in which a scheming empire-builder is thwarted by some democratic Westerners.

Cruze's most expensive project was *Old Ironsides* (1927), about the U.S. frigate *Constitution* and her attack on Tripoli harbor to avenge the loss of the *Philadelphia*. A National Board of Review critic praised the film for its correct nautical detail and wrote that the sea "has never been shot with a motion picture camera in a way to equal the cinematics of *Old Ironsides*; nor has the motion of the hull under sail . . . been at any previous time put upon the screen in a comparable way. Through a special camera device, it would appear, the horizon stands steady while the ship rises and plunges . . . giving us . . . the almost perfect sensation of one who actually stands upon a heaving deck." The "special camera device" was a tripod devised by Leigh M. Griffith in the Lasky camera shop that compensated hydraulically for the movement of the ship. And this was not the only innovation unveiled in *Old Ironsides*.

When the film had its premiere at the Rivoli Theatre in December 1927, Mordaunt Hall wrote that "the scene that ended the first half of the picture was a startling surprise, for the stan-

dard screen disappeared and the whole stage, from the proscenium arch to the boards, was filled with a moving picture of . . . Old Ironsides. This brought every man and woman in the audience to their feet and Dr. Hugo Riesenfeld's orchestra and a chorus of voices further stirred the spectators with 'Ship of State.'" The Rivoli's ordinary screen was about twelve by eighteen feet; the screen used for the spectacular battle scenes in the last half of *Old Ironsides* was thirty by forty feet. The image was enlarged to fill this screen by attaching a magnifying lens to the projector. This early wide-screen technique, known as Magnascope, was the work of another Lasky inventor, Glen Allvine. Several other films were projected in this way in first-run houses before the innovation was abandoned for financial reasons.

In spite of some evidence to the contrary, Cruze's friend Jim Tully wrote that *Old Ironsides* was the director's "first great failure . . . severely handled by the critics." The "word went around that he had slipped" and the same year, when Famous Players–Lasky amalgamated with the Paramount distribution company under the latter name, Cruze's "option was dropped." He formed his own production company and in 1930 made his first important sound film, *The Great Gabbo*, which was also Erich von Stroheim's first talkie as an actor. According to Jonathan Rosenbaum, Stroheim, as the megalomaniacal ventriloquist, gave a performance of "sublime and all but hallucinatory tedium," speaking each line "at roughly half the speed of everyone else in the cast."

In general, Cruze—like many of his contemporaries—seems to have found it difficult to come to terms with the new sound medium. As John Gillett says, he made a "few sharp, slick dramas like the political satire *Washington Merry-Go-Round* (1932)," but most of his work during the early 1930s was "on a B-picture level, enjoyable yet unexceptional." He attempted a comeback with *Sutter's Gold* (1936), a mammoth production about the California goldrush that had originally been suggested to Paramount by Sergei Eisenstein. Its financial failure ended Cruze's career as a major director, though he made a few more competent programmers. John Gillett writes that Cruze "belongs to that group of relatively unknown directors whose work is seriously in need of reappraisal today," and this is perhaps especially true of his comedies.

Cruze was married to Marguerite Snow from 1913 to 1924, to Betty Compson from 1924–1930, and for the last part of his life to a woman who, unlike her predecessors, was not an actress. He had a daughter, Julie. Cruze is known to have carried his own supply of gin when he went abroad, and Louise Brooks, who worked under his direction in *The City's Gone Wild* (1927), said he was "the strangest man I ever knew. . . . He almost never talked and he drank from morning to night"—albeit without apparent effect. As far as Dorothy Arzner was concerned, Cruze "saved Paramount from bankruptcy, and . . . was one of the finest, most generous men I knew in the motion picture business. He had no prejudices." Jim Tully recalls that visitors to Cruze's house were requested not to make racist jokes that might offend his black servants, since "it's bad enough to have to work for me."

FILMS: Too Many Millions, 1918; The Dub, 1918; The Roaring Road, 1919; Alias Mike Moran, 1919; You're Fired, 1919; The Love Burglar, 1919; Valley of the Giants, 1919; Hawthorne of the U.S.A., 1919; The Lottery Man, 1919; An Adventure in Hearts, 1919; Mrs. Temple's Telegram, 1920; The Sin of St. Anthony, 1920; Terror Island, 1920; What Happened to Jones?, 1920; Always Audacious, 1920; A Full House, 1920; The Dollar-a-Year Man, 1921; Food for Scandal, 1921; The Charm School, 1921; Gasoline Gus, 1921; Crazy to Marry, 1921; One Glorious Day, 1922; Is Matrimony a Failure?, 1922; The Dictator, 1922; The Old Homestead, 1922; Thirty Days, 1922; The Covered Wagon, 1923; Hollywood, 1923; Ruggles of Red Gap, 1923; To the Ladies, 1923; The Garden of Weeds, 1924; The Fighting Coward, 1924; The City That Never Sleeps, 1924; The Enemy Sex, 1924; Merton of the Movies, 1924; The Goose Hangs High, 1925; Beggar on Horseback, 1925; Welcome Home, 1925; Marry Me, 1925; The Pony Express, 1925; Waking Up the Town, 1925; Mannequin, 1926; The Waiter From the Ritz, 1926; Marriage, 1926; Old Ironsides, 1927 (U.K., Sons of the Sea); We're All Gamblers, 1927; On to Reno, 1927; The City's Gone Wild, 1927; The Red Mark, 1928; Excess Baggage, 1928; The Mating Call, 1928; A Man's Man, 1929; The Duke Steps Out, 1929; The Great Gabbo, 1929; Once a Gentleman, 1930; She Got What She Wanted, 1930; Salvation Nell, 1931; Washington Merry-Go-Round, 1932 (U.K., Invisible Power); (with others) If I Had a Million, 1932; Sailor Be Good, 1933; Racetrack, 1933; I Cover the Waterfront, 1933; Mr. Skitch, 1933; David Harum, 1934; Their Big Moment, 1934 (U.K., Afterwards); Helldorado, 1935; Two-Fisted, 1935; Sutter's Gold, 1936; The Wrong Road, 1937; Prison Nurse, 1938; Gangs of New York, 1938; Come On, Leathernecks!, 1938.

ABOUT: Brownlow, K. The War, the West, and the Wilderness, 1978; Tully, J. A Dozen and One, 1943. *Periodicals*—Film Dope April 1976; Films in Review June–July 1954.

*CUKOR, GEORGE (DEWEY) (July 7, 1899–January 24, 1983), American director, was born in New York City. He was the son of Victor Cukor, who worked in the office of the Manhat-

GEORGE CUKOR

tan District Attorney, and the former Helen Gross. Cukor grew up at 222 East 68th Street, along with his sister Elsie, his parents, and his grandparents. It was his Hungarian-Jewish grandfather who chose his forenames, in an access of patriotic fervor over Admiral George Dewey's victory at Manila Bay.

Cukor attended Public School 82 and De Witt Clinton High School. A "stagestruck kid," he often cut school to watch Broadway matinees from the top balcony but "had a very snobbish attitude towards movies." He joined the Students' Army Training Corps in 1917 and a year later the "postwar army of job seekers." Determined to work in the theatre, he answered newspaper advertisements and was eventually hired as assistant stage manager of the Chicago company of *The Better 'Ole.* In 1920, after further experience in Toronto, Cukor organized a stock company for the Lyceum Theatre in Rochester, New York. He directed it for seven years and then returned to New York City as manager of the old Empire Theatre. It was at that time, working with the likes of Ethel Barrymore, Jeanne Engels, and Laurette Taylor, that he began to build his reputation as a "woman's director."

In Hollywood, meanwhile, technology had overtaken technique, and the filmmakers found themselves embarked on the sound era with no experience of writing or speaking dialogue. They turned for help to the theatre, importing actors, dramatists, and directors wholesale from Broadway and the London stage. Cukor joined the exodus in 1929, when he went to Paramount as dialogue director of *River of Romance,* based on Booth Tarkington's play *Magnolia.* He

°koo kər

worked in the same capacity on Lewis Milestone's *All Quiet on the Western Front* for Universal, and then Paramount assigned him as director of the Maurice Chevalier–Jeanette MacDonald romantic comedy *One Hour With You.*

"It was very early in the game" for Cukor, and though he did the best he could, "it really wasn't very good." In the end the film's producer, Ernst Lubitsch, took over and reshot virtually everything he had done. For *Grumpy* (1930)—the first film for which Cukor received directorial credit—Paramount teamed him with a veteran of the silents, Cyril Gardner. Cukor said that he learned a lot from Gardner, but there is no evidence of this in *Grumpy,* a stagey and old-fashioned trifle about a lovably irascible lawyer.

After *The Virtuous Sin* (1930), a "ghastly picture" made in collaboration with Louis Gasnier, Cukor had Gardner as his codirector again on *The Royal Family of Broadway,* a thinly veiled portrait of the Barrymores adapted from the Ferber-Kaufman play. Like its two predecessors, this was essentially a piece of "canned theatre," but according to Gary Carey there were signs that here, for the first time, Cukor was beginning "to work out the difference between staging action before the camera and before the proscenium arch," and he secured some lively performances from a cast headed by Ina Claire and Fredric March.

Cukor's first solo film for Paramount was also the talkie debut of Tallulah Bankhead, *Tarnished Lady* (1931). It was adapted by Cukor's favorite scenarist, Donald Ogden Stewart, from Stewart's own short story about the sentimental education of a spoiled socialite. This spasmodically witty drama pleased neither the critics nor Cukor himself, and the director expressed scarcely more commitment to his next movie, *Girls About Town* (1931), a "low-brow farce" with Kay Francis and Lilyan Tashman as two gold diggers on the make. Cukor had meanwhile been engaged in a legal dispute with Paramount over his removal from *One Hour With You,* and at that point he quit the studio and joined RKO, where his friend David O. Selznick had taken over as head of production.

At RKO, Cukor enjoyed far more creative freedom than he had been allowed at Paramount, and his work benefited. His first film there, produced by Selznick, was *What Price Hollywood?* (1932), about the mutually destructive relationship between an alcoholic movie director (Lowell Sherman) and the pretty waitress (Constance Bennett) whom he guides to stardom. Carlos Clarens called it "the first sound picture to deal with some seriousness with the ethics of the star system . . . There are biting little truths about the film industry stated with detachment and precision," while Constance Bennett's performance "was Cukor's first unmistakable success on the screen." As Clarens says, this picture "serves as a blueprint for the two subsequent versions of *A Star Is Born.*"

Cukor had a greater success against larger odds when he directed Katharine Hepburn in her debut film, *A Bill of Divorcement* (1932), from a play by Clemence Dane. No one else at RKO knew what to make of Hepburn's screen test, but Cukor was impressed by her "freshness [and] spirit, and also because she was one of the oddest-looking girls I had ever seen." He insisted on casting her, and she rewarded him with a performance of star quality.

Hepburn plays Sydney, whose father Hilary (John Barrymore) is supposed to have died in World War I and whose mother (Billie Burke) is about to remarry. In fact, Hilary has spent fifteen years in a mental hospital as a shell-shock victim, and at the beginning of the film he returns. The growing sympathy and tenderness between father and daughter is movingly recorded, and at the end, when Hilary fakes a relapse in order to set his wife free, Sydney sees through the deception and breaks off her own engagement to care for her father.

As Gary Carey says, Cukor had by this time "begun to perfect his technique. He broke the continuous stage action into its separate elements but maintained the feeling of flow. Analyzing exactly which part of the action would be in focus moment by moment—the whole stage, a conversation between two people, a private action—he concentrated his camera upon it and then linked it to the next moment by the most functional editing or graceful camera movement." The Cukor style was already emerging—an elusive entity defined by Henri Langlois as "knowledge of the world, elegance, distinction of actors chosen, everything in half-tone, suggested and never overstressed."

Cukor was next called in to rescue *Rockabye,* a "confession film" by George Fitzmaurice, after its disastrous previews. He reshot this "trashy story" in less than three weeks and concluded, "It was still trashy but it seemed all right." Nor did he express much enthusiasm for his next RKO movie, an adaptation of Somerset Maugham's brittle satire on Mayfair mores, *Our Betters.* As Cukor said, "it dealt with a world that they didn't know about in pictures, that of English high society," and indeed Joel Greenberg complained of "a jarring air of unreality." Carlos Clarens defends the film on other grounds, however. In Pearl (Constance Bennett), the American heiress who marries a penniless peer and follows his example of infidelity, Clarens sees "the New American Woman asserting her sexual rights. . . . Even for the permissive pre-Code period, a philandering leading lady who goes unpunished *and* unremorseful must stand as one of the great emancipated heroines."

In 1933, Cukor followed Selznick to MGM, where they scored an immediate and sensational success with *Dinner at Eight,* scripted by Herman J. Mankiewicz and Frances Marion from the Ferber-Kaufman play. A comedy-drama of the events leading up to a society dinner, it tells several interlocking stories in a way reminiscent of the previous year's hit, *Grand Hotel.* Lionel Barrymore, Billie Burke, and Madge Evans play the upper-class Jordans, Wallace Beery and Jean Harlow the *nouveaux riches* Packards. Marie Dressler is a fierce society dragon, and John Barrymore, who under Cukor's direction in *A Bill of Divorcement* had shown unaccustomed restraint and control, here achieved "an authentic poignancy" in his portrayal of a character much like himself—an alcoholic movie star on the skids.

Cukor was equally successful in his direction of Jean Harlow, who established herself in this "superb ensemble production" as a natural comedienne. Cukor revealed part of the secret of his success as a director of actors in a comment he made about Marie Dressler; he said he at first tried to mold her into "the Ethel Barrymore type," then came to his senses and gave her her head: "That's what one must do in pictures. Don't stand in the way. In films, it's what you *are* rather than what you act."

This hit was followed by an even greater one, Cukor's version of Louisa May Alcott's *Little Women* (1933), with an Oscar-winning script by Sarah Y. Mason and Victor Heerman, and splendid sets and costumes by Hobe Erwin and Walter Plunkett respectively. Katharine Hepburn played Jo March, the headstrong Concord girl in Civil War Massachusetts, growing up through good times and bad with her three sisters (Joan Bennett, Frances Dee, and Jean Parker). Gary Carey has called the result "a total triumph of charm and genuine naiveté, perhaps the director's finest achievement." Though other recent critics seem to doubt that naiveté is Cukor's forte, in 1933 this film confirmed his position as a director of the first rank.

Little Women was Cukor's most successful picture up to that time, and as he said, it typed him as a "literary director." A whole string of adaptations followed—a mode that was in any case an attractive option in 1933 for studios inclined to avert their eyes from what was happening in the contemporary world. The series began with *David Copperfield* (1935), produced by Selznick and preceded by a trip to England, where Selznick and Cukor shot some background footage and took hundreds of stills for the MGM art department. The distinguished novelist Hugh Walpole was called in to write the adaptation.

Cukor decided that "performances were everything" in *David Copperfield,* and he engineered some memorable ones—W. C. Fields' "vaudevillian" reading of Mr. Micawber, Freddie Bartholomew as a likable young David, Edna May Oliver a formidable Aunt Betsey Trotwood, and Lennox Pawle touching as Mr. Dick. The trouble was that, in reducing Dickens' enormous novel to 133 minutes of screen time, the characters were left as nothing much more than the sum of their eccentricities. Sydney Carrol wrote that the picture "repeats without stint all . . . [Dickens'] habits of exaggeration, caricature and journalese dialogue. Superbly photographed, magnificently mounted . . . it enjoys a lot of brilliant acting and suffers from a continuous overemphasis. . . . Never have I been so repelled by goodness in a film or so unattracted by badness."

All the same, most critics agree that *David Copperfield* was an honorable attempt at an impossible task, and it was another popular success for Cukor, unlike his next movie. *Sylvia Scarlett* (1936), produced by Pandro S. Berman for RKO, was drawn from a trilogy of novels by Compton Mackenzie and concentrates on an episode in the first of them. Sylvia Scarlett (Katharine Hepburn) masquerades as a boy to escape with her father (Edmund Gwenn), an embezzling bookkeeper, from France to his native England. With an amiable rogue named Jimmy Monkley (Cary Grant) they join a pierrot troupe in Cornwall. In the end, Sylvia's father dies in pursuit of a woman, Jimmy takes up with another, and Sylvia herself, sadder and wiser, is reconciled to respectability (and femininity) by her love for a handsome artist (Brian Aherne).

Cukor said once that *Sylvia Scarlett* was his favorite picture, "perhaps because we were all so happy while making it." He didn't know why it flopped so totally, but recent critics have suggested that contemporary audiences were disturbed by the heroine's sexual ambiguity and the responses it drew from both male and female characters in the film, which was "edgy and not always pleasant, full of shifts of mood and implications that would have startled [Compton] Mackenzie." But even contemporary writers conceded that Cary Grant, previously a conventional romantic lead, had given the performance of his life as the Cockney immoralist Jimmy

Monkley, and Cukor lived to see this premature black comedy adopted as a cult movie.

There has been no such resurrection for Cukor's *Romeo and Juliet* (1936), an MGM prestige production on which Irving Thalberg lavished all of the studio's resources of money and talent. Cedric Gibbons was the art director, with Oliver Messel imported from Britain as artistic consultant. The photography was by William Daniels and the choreography by Agnes De Mille, but nothing could prevent the film from turning into what one critic called an "empty pageant"—least of all its aging lovers, Leslie Howard and Norma Shearer. The director remarked that *"Romeo and Juliet* was Thalberg's project and it lost one million dollars for the studio."

According to Cukor, *Camille* (1937) "was also Thalberg's picture, though his name did not appear on the credits." Cukor's respect for Greta Garbo as a fellow professional shines through all he has said about her—she "always knew what she was doing, what the camera was doing . . . she was all there on the screen." Many critics maintain that as an actress Garbo achieved her apotheosis in what Pauline Kael called her "sublime, ironic performance" as Marguerite Gauthier, the *grande courtesan* who renounces her one true love (Robert Taylor) for the sake of his career but is reunited with him for one of the cinema's most glorious death scenes.

"I never allow myself to be called an *auteur*," Cukor said once. "I have too much respect for writers to presume to such a title." And elsewhere he insisted that "a director must never overwhelm a picture, he must serve it." Because of this generous humility, the great distinction and elegance of Cukor's style were not recognized until late in his career. Thus we find Otis Ferguson, a distinguished contemporary reviewer of *Camille*, expressing his surprise that the ancient melodrama should have come "to such insistent life on the day's screen." Ferguson acknowledged that "the life of the times grows up unobtrusively around the people as they take their dramatic position in the story, so that the complexities of an unfamiliar code of living and way of life become the simple background." But it seems not to have occurred to him that this unobtrusive miracle was the achievement of a master; Cukor is commended for no more than "a firm and straight-out piece of film work."

Returning to the sophisticated comedy of his earlier films, Cukor made what some regard as the most accomplished of all his movies of the 1930s, *Holiday* (1938). He had the services of Donald Ogden Stewart, adapting a play by Philip Barry, and two stars with whom he was wholly in sympathy—Katharine Hepburn as Linda Seton, bored and frustrated daughter of despotic snobs, and Cary Grant as the exuberantly anarchic Johnny Case, who comes to the Seton mansion as suitor to Linda's spoiled young sister. Lew Ayres plays Linda's brother Ned, who escapes from his parents' domination into alcoholism just as Linda does into her old playroom. The heart of the film is the long, lyrical, funny scene in which Johnny, a truant from his own engagement party, greets the new year with Linda and a few friends at an alternative celebration in the playroom, waltzing by candlelight to a music-box tune.

"In Cukor's hands," wrote Carlos Clarens, *Holiday* becomes "a modern American fable, full of social and moral implications, delicate choices and unspoken kinships, a most Rohmerian film . . . Cukor's favorite situation—the outsider breaking into an alien closed circle, and the heroine stirring into awareness . . . are conveyed in *Holiday* with grace and subtlety by means of twin, complementary courses through the Seton mansion, each floor defining a moment of moral development of the characters . . . *Holiday* may be the talkiest picture of its year. But talk never dislocates the image, still a shade too neutral for partisans of eye cinema at all costs."

As David Thomson succinctly puts it, Cukor's "abiding preoccupation is theatricality and the various human postures between acting and lying." A great many of his films, from *The Royal Family of Broadway* on, deal directly with the theatre or the movie industry, and *Zaza* (1939) has been called "a stylish memoir of French music-halls at the turn of the century." Its heroine (Claudette Colbert) is a music-hall star whose talent, deepened by suffering when she renounces her married lover (Herbert Marshall), wins her a revered place in the legitimate theatre. The film has earned comparisons with Jean Renoir's *French Cancan,* both on account of its theme and because Cukor shares Renoir's delight in the interaction of illusion and reality.

Cukor spent over a year on pre-production work for *Gone With the Wind,* scouting locations and testing scores of actresses for the role of Scarlett, as well as shooting half-a-dozen scenes. Why Selznick then fired Cukor and replaced him with Victor Fleming is still a matter of speculation, but it now seems clear that, even after Cukor had left the film, he secretly continued to coach Vivien Leigh and Olivia de Havilland in their roles, and that virtually all the sequences he had shot were retained in the final cut. It was characteristic of Cukor that for years he denied these claims, too proud or too professional to scrabble for a little glory.

Instead Cukor went back to MGM and scored a success of his own with *The Women* (1940), adapted by Anita Loos, Jane Murfin, and Scott Fitzgerald (uncredited) from Clare Boothe's bitchy play about a woman (Norma Shearer) maneuvered by her "friends" into a divorce she doesn't want. This misogynistic comedy was not one of Cukor's own favorites, but its craftsmanship is impeccable. A curiosity of the piece is that the erring husband is never seen, and neither is any other male, even on the street. There are nevertheless over a hundred speaking parts in the film, each sharply differentiated, and Cukor drew a memorable performance from Joan Crawford as the "other woman."

Joan Crawford starred in Cukor's next picture, *Susan and God* (1940), an "uneasy satire" that is one of the director's weakest films. His fortunes temporarily revived with the phenomenal success of *The Philadelphia Story* (1940), like *Holiday* based on a Philip Barry play, adapted by Donald Ogden Stewart, and starring Katharine Hepburn and Cary Grant. Hepburn (for whom Barry had written the part) plays Tracy Lord, a vulnerable but arrogant socialite who rejects her playboy husband Dexter (Grant) and becomes engaged to a priggish social climber. Dexter retaliates by introducing into her household a reporter (James Stewart) from a gossip magazine who contrives to melt Tracy's icy exterior before quixotically surrendering her to her first husband.

Cukor elected to gamble everything on his splendid cast and witty script, effacing himself in a *mise-en-scène* so discreet as to be virtually invisible. John Howard Reid complained that the "breezy opening, with its swift editing and rapid tracking, is built upon the same formula as *The Women*," but "thereafter both pace and camera bog down in a welter of overlong dialogue." The film nevertheless earned Oscars for its script and for James Stewart's performance, as well as a sheaf of nominations, several lesser awards, and a great deal of money. Its sophisticated excellence was underlined by comparison with Charles Walters' plodding musical remake *High Society* (1956), and it remains a model of the high comedy style.

"The prettiest sight in this pretty world of ours is that of the privileged classes enjoying their privileges," says a character in *The Philadelphia Story*. However ironically spoken, the line reflects an insouciance that was unacceptable in the crisis atmosphere of the 1940s, a decade in which Cukor seemed on the whole ill at ease. It began for him with *A Woman's Face* (1941), a remake of Gustaf Molander's *En kvinnas ansikte*, about a disfigured woman criminal rehabilitated by plastic surgery. Joan Crawford

played Anna Holm, the role created by Ingrid Bergman, and there is a magnificently malign performance from Conrad Veidt as the heroine's decadent lover Barring.

It seems that Cukor, faced with a banal script, decided to indulge himself for once in a bravura display of technique. Inspired perhaps by the presence of Conrad Veidt, he and his cameraman Robert Planck plunged into Expressionist chiaroscuro, low camera angles, and semi-abstraction. From the opening courtroom scene (where witnesses give differing accounts of the events leading up to Anna's murder of Barring), the flashbacks to the events described are, as Joel Greenberg wrote, "slow dissolves of one image over another—a silently closing door, a hotel glimpsed through the trees, an elaborate birthday cake." Greenberg goes on: "The famous sequence of the removal of . . . [Anna's] bandages after the operation is completely in silence; no dialogue at all is used in the cablecar scene in which Crawford is tempted to hurl Barring's nephew over the side, the whole emotional conflict being conveyed by cutting, natural sound, and facial expression."

This intermittently powerful curiosity was followed by the disastrous *Two-Faced Woman* (1941), with Greta Garbo as a newly married wife who, discovering her husband's adultery, masquerades as her own libidinous twin to seduce him into fidelity. The Catholic Church was outraged by the moral implications of this old story, and MGM timidly inserted ameliorating scenes that made nonsense of the plot. The picture flopped, and Garbo, already disenchanted with the movies, quit them forever.

Cukor's unsought reputation as a "woman's director" was further damaged when a "rehashed farce" called *Her Cardboard Lover* (1942), another failure, put paid to the already fading career of Norma Shearer. At that point Cukor was inducted as a private in the Army Signal Corps and posted to the studio in Astoria, New York, where he had begun his career thirteen years earlier. He reportedly billeted himself in a Manhattan hotel, rising at 5 A.M. to arrive in good time at the studio, where he made a training film—incomprehensible to its director—called *Resistance and Ohm's Law* (1943).

Honorably discharged from the army on account of his age, Cukor directed the first, most serious (and least successful) of his series of films teaming Katharine Hepburn and Spencer Tracy. *Keeper of the Flame* (1943), scripted by Donald Ogden Stewart from the novel by I.A.R. Wylie, is about a celebrated journalist (Tracy) investigating the mysterious death of a great American patriot. He becomes suspicious of the dead man's widow (Hepburn) but falls in love with her anyway, learning that she had indeed allowed her husband to die in an accident that she could have averted, but only to prevent him from leading a fascist coup d'état and to preserve his legend for the faithful. Gene D. Phillips has noted the subtlety of the visual metaphors of obfuscation and concealment in this somberly lit *film noir,* but Louis B. Mayer walked out on its Radio City premiere, infuriated by its leftish political implications. The screenplay was later used in evidence against Donald Ogden Stewart by the House Un-American Activities Committee, which blacklisted him, but Cukor himself seems to have regarded the film as no more than a psychological thriller.

And his next picture was an exercise in what he defined as "Victorian melodrama pure and simple." This was *Gaslight* (1948), a second screen version of Patrick Hamilton's play made only four years after the first—Thorold Dickinson's taut and stylish adaptation was bought up and suppressed by MGM to make way for its own big-budget movie, a fact that brought a sour note into many of the British reviews. Cukor, of course, had no hand in this transaction, and it subsequently emerged that some prints of the Dickinson version had survived MGM's vandalism.

Gaslight (tactfully retitled *Murder in Thornton Square* for British release) tells the story of a murderer (Charles Boyer) in Victorian London who marries an innocent young woman (Ingrid Bergman), settles into the dark house on Thornton Square, and with cold, systematic efficiency sets out to drive her insane. "Instead of shock and surprise," wrote Carlos Clarens, "Cukor works insidiously through detail and mood, usually ahead of the script . . . The house is no mere element of decor but a third protagonist, upholstered, stifling, a closed world. Cukor's master touch is in the way he assigns various charges of tension to each level, and the vertical suspense this generates is uniquely filmic and disturbing." Such qualities, and the excellent performances of Boyer and Bergman, mollified those who resented the suppression of the Dickinson version, though James Agee criticized the movie's perverse hint of complicity between tormentor and tormented, finding it morally questionable in a melodrama.

After *Winged Victory* (1944), a patriotic war drama whose banality Cukor acknowledged, came *A Double Life* (1947), the first of his collaborations with the scenarists Ruth Gordon and Garson Kanin. Their only melodrama, it features a deranged matinee idol (Ronald Colman) who is so carried away by his roles that he commits

a real murder during an extended run of *Othello.* Cukor enjoyed filming the New York theatrical background, showing that he was by now as much at home on location as in the studio, but the movie is scarcely to be taken seriously (even though it brought Colman his only Oscar). And *Edward My Son* (1949), from the play by Robert Morley and Noel Langley, interesting for Cukor's highly theatrical use of long takes, was ruined by the miscasting of both of its principals, Spencer Tracy and Deborah Kerr.

Cukor used Tracy again in *Adam's Rib* (1949), along with Katharine Hepburn, and he also continued to use very long takes (one of over seven minutes without a cut), having decided that this technique "was better to build the intensity of a scene." The film is the second of the seven scripted for Cukor by Ruth Gordon and/or her husband Garson Kanin, most of them comedies and all but *A Double Life* centering on a woman who in one way or another oversteps the bounds of the existing social system.

Adam's Rib has Tracy as a male chauvinist district attorney and Hepburn as his wife, a defense lawyer with whom he clashes in and out of court over the case of Doris Attinger (played by Judy Holliday with such charm that she almost stole the film). Doris is a deceived wife who has taken a few shots at her husband (Tom Ewell), and Hepburn wins her acquittal (and almost loses her own husband) by turning the court into a theatre and demonstrating through role-reversal that accepted morality depends on sexual bias. The theatrical motif is carried through the film in such devices as the use of stage curtains to separate the scenes in court from those in the lawyers' home. Witty and entertaining as it is, this is not the best of the Tracy-Hepburn comedies, being weakened by some domestic passages that are only rescued from whimsy by the tough and acerbic style of its perfectly matched stars.

Not even Cukor could do much to enliven Lana Turner's numb performance in *A Life of Her Own* (1950), about the rise and fall of a cover girl, but in *Born Yesterday,* released the same year, he launched a new star in Judy Holliday, who had played the female lead in Garson Kanin's original play. She is Billie Dawn, a near-illiterate ex-chorine and mistress of a crooked millionaire (Broderick Crawford) who hires a liberal journalist (William Holden) to teach her a little class and gets his comeuppance when she learns to think for herself. Asked about his long takes and sometimes immobile camera, Cukor replied simply that "if the scenes are funny in themselves, you don't need to play about with them."

Judy Holliday earned an Oscar for her funny and touching performance in *Born Yesterday*. Cukor next made an agreeable but slighter comedy called *The Model and the Marriage Broker*, and then used Holliday again in *The Marrying Kind* (1952), also a comedy but one that sometimes approaches tragedy. Regarded by some as the Kanins' best script, it closely resembles King Vidor's silent populist classic *The Crowd* in its account of an "achingly commonplace" couple who meet on an outing, marry, wrestle with financial worries (and a near-win in a radio quiz), and lose a child in a tragic accident.

Demoralized, ready to accept the failure of their marriage, they give their often conflicting versions of the facts to a sympathetic divorce judge in flashbacks that reveal with brilliant economy how many of their problems arise from their own bemused lack of self-knowledge. In the end, a little better equipped to separate reality from fantasy, they agree to try again. Cukor shot most of the film either on location in and around New York or in the couple's cluttered, claustrophobic apartment, offsetting all this naturalism with an excellent dream sequence reflecting both the husband's sense of inferiority to his strong-willed wife and the dehumanizing effects of his post office job. And from the unknown Aldo Ray Cukor drew a performance as disarming and moving as Holliday's—the best of his short career. The film nevertheless failed at the box office, perhaps because the Kanins' wonderfully funny games with the failures and subterfuges of the language could not in the end conceal the disturbing seriousness of their social criticism.

The last and most likable of the Kanins' Tracy-Hepburn comedies followed. *Pat and Mike* (1952) has Hepburn as an upper-class sportswoman and Tracy as the rough and slightly shady promoter-manager who sets out to make a champion of her. Richard Winnington called it "suave, pungent and genuine entertainment," whose principals uphold "a comedy style beyond the powers of younger stars." Tracy also stars in *The Actress* (1953), this time as a landlocked and cantankerous ex-seaman at odds with his stagestruck daughter (Jean Simmons). Adapted from Ruth Gordon from her autobiographical play *Years Ago*, the film presents an "emotionally accurate portrait" of a claustrophobic small town in New England around the time of World War I, and as V. F. Perkins wrote, "observes its backstage setting with a sardonic romanticism."

An original script by Garson Kanin took Cukor back to New York for *It Should Happen to You* (1954), with Judy Holliday playing Gladys Glover, a girdle model who loses her job and, hungry to recover her sense of identity, blows her savings on a huge billboard bearing the simple legend "Gladys Glover." New York is intrigued, the celebrity manufacturers go into action, and Gladys becomes "a household name that stands for nothing at all" until, recognizing the emptiness of her fame, she gives it all up and returns to her dumb but honest boyfriend Pete (Jack Lemmon).

Carlos Clarens called this manic fable "the first and best of the media comedies," in which "every detail of dialogue, situation and characterization is concerned with anomie and identity, privacy and exposure, name and image." This was Jack Lemmon's first movie, and he has recalled how enraged he became when Cukor repeatedly asked him to tone down his performance. "Are you trying to tell me not to *act?*," he demanded finally, and Cukor replied, "Oh, God, yes!" Lemmon says that he has learned his craft from that advice.

Cukor's *What Price Hollywood?* (1932) had been remade five years later by William Wellman as *A Star Is Born*, in which the protagonists are both movie stars whose marriage goes on the rocks because one of them (Janet Gaynor) is on the way up and the other (Fredric March) is on the way down. In 1954 Cukor, who was normally "wary of doing remakes," made the second, musical version of *A Star Is Born* with a new script by Moss Hart and songs by Harold Arlen and Ira Gershwin. James Mason played Norman Maine, the screen idol who declines through drink to suicide, and the role of his wife Vicki went to Judy Garland, making a comeback (in her first dramatic part) after being replaced by Betty Hutton in *Annie Get Your Gun* (1950). Nervous as she understandably was, and overweight, she gave with Cukor's patient encouragement one of the truest and most moving performances in the history of the screen musical.

A Star Is Born was Cukor's first film in color, and here, as in many of his later pictures, he had the assistance of the photographer George Hoyningen-Huene, who was responsible for the subtle coordination of color in sets, costumes, and photography. Cukor was also working for the first time with Cinemascope, for in which, he was told, he must keep the action at the center of the screen and "line up the actors right in front of the camera at all times." He ignored this advice, moving the action all over the wide screen—Cukor said later that he was inspired by reproductions in art books in which only one detail of a broad panorama was highlighted. The result, as Gary Carey wrote, "was that much of the intimacy, fluidity, and selectivity which had been lost in the first wide-screen films was here recaptured." And when Garland sings "The Man Who Got Away" in a small nightclub after hours, and Cukor follows her in what Douglas McVay called "overwhelming hand-held camera plunges," they created what has been claimed as the best song number ever filmed.

The long "Born in a Trunk" production number was directed not by Cukor but by his choreographer Richard Barstow, and it brought the film's running time to some three hours. After Cukor had left for Pakistan to direct *Bhowani Junction,* Warners cut important scenes without consulting him. "Mangled" as it was, *A Star Is Born* is regarded by many as "one of the greatest flawed movies ever made," and Cukor's masterpiece.

Bhowani Junction (1956), from the novel by John Masters, is set in 1947 during the British withdrawal from India and stars Ava Gardner in one of her best performances as an Anglo-Indian nurse who has to decide where her racial (and sexual) loyalties belong. It is Cukor's only epic, but so expert in its handling of crowd scenes, riots, and train wrecks that it earned comparison with the work of Cecil B. DeMille. It was followed by an agreeable but relatively conventional backstage musical, *Les Girls* (1957), with songs by Cole Porter. Kay Kendall plays a former showgirl whose memoirs of a European tour with Gene Kelly are disputed by another member of the troupe (Taina Elg); the pair bring their conflicting recollections before a judge in a way reminiscent of *The Marrying Kind.*

The gap between fact and fantasy is also the theme of *Wild Is the Wind* (1957), in which Nevada rancher Anthony Quinn imports his dead wife's sister (Anna Magnani) from Italy as a replacement spouse, but fails to value her for herself until she has an affair with his adopted son (Anthony Franciosa). Most critics thought that Cukor had failed to suppress Magnani's habit of overacting in this "tearful tirade," but he had no problems at all with another Italian star, Sophia Loren, in *Heller in Pink Tights* (1960). Again costarring Anthony Quinn and set in the American West, it reexamines the legends and conventions of that magical region along with those of his beloved theatre in an extremely funny and inventive film about an intrepid touring company hamming the likes of *Mazeppa* and *La Belle Hélène* before audiences of cowboys, gamblers, and gunfighters.

Let's Make Love (1960) also centers on the theatre and its illusions. Yves Montand plays a billionaire who, hearing that he is being lampooned in a Greenwich Village revue, attends incognito and falls in love with one of the performers (Marilyn Monroe). Taking him for a starving actor, she gets him a job in the show, where he is required to impersonate himself, gets singing lessons from Bing Crosby, and is reprimanded for failing to carry conviction in his entirely heartfelt love-song—a neat comment on the relationship between emotion and artifice. Praising Cukor's "brilliant use of small areas of the wide screen," V. F. Perkins concluded that "the best sequences—which are superb—are achieved at the expense of overall stucture." At about this time Cukor completed, without credit, an indifferent biopic of Franz Liszt called *Song Without End,* taking over when his friend Charles Vidor died three weeks into shooting. Another uneven film, *The Chapman Report* (1962), adapted from Irving Wallace's bestseller about American sexual mores, was monstrously recut by the studio and the censors, but remains notable for Claire Bloom's "subtle, tormented rendering of erotic obsession."

Warner Brothers spent $17 million on its screen version of *My Fair Lady* (1964), the triumphant Lerner and Loewe musical based on Shaw's *Pygmalion.* "I didn't try to tamper with *My Fair Lady,*" Cukor said. "It was perfect on stage. It had cinema effects, like dissolves. On the contrary, I tried to preserve the theatrical aspect of certain scenes, like the Ascot number." Rex Harrison played Professor Higgins, and Audrey Hepburn was a magical and radiant Eliza Doolittle. As Carlos Clarens wrote, Cukor was "hamstrung from all sides by the play's success and by the sheer opulence of the undertaking," and there were some who thought the film more stolid and less filmic than the stage version. The movie was nevertheless Cukor's most honored and financially successful film, bringing him his first and only Oscar as best director, and garnering seven other Academy Awards as well (including best film), among numerous other honors.

Cukor was less at home with *Justine* (1969), a mélange of sexual ambiguity and labyrinthine deception set in the hothouse world of Lawrence Durrell's Alexandria, and featuring Anouk Aimée, Dirk Bogarde, Anna Karina, and Philippe Noiret, among others. The film had its admirers but Cukor, who inherited the cast and several scenes from an earlier director, Joseph Strick, admitted that he never had "the greatest conviction about it." Three years later, when he had become (with Hitchcock) the oldest working director in the American cinema, Cukor adapted another distinguished English novel for the screen, Graham Greene's *Travels With My Aunt.* Alec McCowen played the middle-aged virgin Henry Pulling and Maggie Smith his Aunt

Augusta, an ancient libertine who in the course of a journey half way round the world (and into her shady past) rescues him from sterility. Greene was unhappy with the adaptation, but Jay Cocks praised "the easefully luxurious style of its director, whose sense of subdued but splendid theatricality is everywhere in evidence, from the meticulous *mise en scène* and the unobtrusive movement of the camera to the careful, practiced composition of every scene."

In 1975 Cukor turned his attention to television in *Love Among the Ruins,* set in Edwardian London and starring Katharine Hepburn and Laurence Olivier as aging former lovers in whom the long-dormant spark is happily rekindled. It carried off Emmy awards for best direction, best actor and actress, best script (James Costigan), and best production design (Carmen Dillon). *The Bluebird* (1976) was a less satisfactory departure—a musical version of Maeterlinck's fable made in Leningrad as a Russian-American coproduction. Cukor liked the Russians but not their ancient equipment, their inadequate technicians, their food, or their weather. And in spite of a cast that included Elizabeth Taylor, Jane Fonda, and Ava Gardner, the film was a failure.

Cukor made another television film with Hepburn, an unexceptional version of Emlyn Williams' *The Corn Is Green* (1979) and then, at the age of eighty-one, went before the cameras for the last time as the director of *Rich and Famous,* a $10 million updating of Vincent Sherman's Bette Davis–Miriam Hopkins vehicle *Old Acquaintance.* Cukor's film opens in 1959, with Jacqueline Bisset and Candice Bergen as Liz and Merry, the college roommates whose careers we then follow through the years. Liz becomes a serious writer who lives in a tasteful Connecticut farmhouse, Merry an immensely successful scribbler of sexy bestsellers with a mansion in Beverly Hills and no qualms about stealing her old friend's lovers. One critic remarked that Cukor had "gift-wrapped this item with such hermetic skill that no contaminating trace of honest emotion . . . has crept in," but most reviewers nevertheless enjoyed the package, in which Candice Bergen emerged under Cukor's direction as "one of the screen's most arresting comedians."

Thus to the very end of his career Cukor continued to be admired above all as a director of actresses, in spite of the debts owed to his sympathetic guidance by John Barrymore, Cary Grant, James Stewart, Ronald Colman, Aldo Ray, and Jack Lemmon, among other male stars. It is probably true to say (as Carlos Clarens has) that "the Cukor values are best embodied in women" and that (to quote Gary Carey) "the women in Cukor's films are always superior to the men" and are seen "less from a man's point of view than from the view of the women themselves."

Because the "man's point of view" prevailed unchallenged in the cinema for the first thirty years of Cukor's very long career, he was undervalued by serious critics, who deplored the "frivolity" of his subjects, his refusal to espouse populist causes, his "steady rejection of the tragic." The situation was exacerbated by his own modest insistence that he was an interpretative rather than a "creative" director, and especially by his lack of interest in montage, which was for so long held to be the essence of cinema. As Richard Roud wrote at the time of Cukor's death in 1983, his rehabilitation, "his access to his rightful place in the history of the cinema had to await these two post-war developments: the first the realisation that *mise-en-scène* was at least as important as montage and the second that women and their problems are as important as men and theirs." Roud concluded that it was "only in the past two decades that George Cukor came to be recognised as one of our greatest directors."

A plump and stocky man for most of his life and an "elfin wisp" in his last years, Cukor was bouyant and witty, a lover of "food, comfort, and opulence" who never married. He lived throughout most of his movie career in a Hollywood mansion whose famous oval drawing room was the scene of many equally famous parties (including the legendary tête-à-tête he contrived for two of his favorite women, Mae West and Greta Garbo). He continued to see every new film of promise up to the time of his death, though he seemed increasingly impatient of the "amateurism" of the modern cinema as opposed to the solid craftsmanship provided—for all its limitations—by the studio system. But he never ceased to believe that "anyone who looks at something special in a very original way makes you see it that way forever." He received the D. W. Griffith Award in 1981 and a Golden Lion (for life achievement) at Venice in 1982.

FILMS: (with Cyril Gardner) Grumpy, 1930; (with Louis Gasnier) The Virtuous Sin/ Cast Iron, 1930; (with Cyril Gardner) The Royal Family of Broadway/ The Royal Family, 1930; Tarnished Lady, 1931; Girls about Town, 1931; What Price Hollywood?, 1932; A Bill of Divorcement, 1932; Rockabye, 1932; Our Betters, 1933; Dinner at Eight, 1933; Little Women, 1933; David Copperfield, 1935; Sylvia Scarlett, 1936; Romeo and Juliet, 1936; Camille, 1937; Holiday/Free to Live/ Unconventional Linda, 1938; Zaza, 1939; The Women, 1939; Susan and God/The Gay Mrs. Trexel, 1940; The Philadelphia Story, 1940; A Woman's Face, 1941; Two-Faced Woman, 1941; Her Cardboard Lover, 1942; Keeper of the Flame, 1943; Gaslight/ Murder in

Thornton Square, 1944; Winged Victory, 1944; A Double Life, 1947; Edward My Son, 1949; Adam's Rib, 1949; A Life of Her Own, 1950; Born Yesterday, 1950; The Model and the Marriage Broker, 1951; The Marrying Kind, 1952; Pat and Mike, 1952; The Actress, 1953; It Should Happen to You, 1954; A Star Is Born, 1954; Bhowani Junction, 1956; Les Girls, 1957; Wild Is the Wind, 1957; Heller in Pink Tights, 1960; Let's Make Love, 1960; Song Without End, 1960 (uncredited); The Chapman Report, 1962; My Fair Lady, 1964; Justine, 1969; Travels With My Aunt, 1972; Love Among the Ruins, 1975 (for television); The Blue Bird, 1976; The Corn Is Green, 1979 (for television); Rich and Famous, 1981. *Published scripts*—Adam's Rib (Viking, 1972).

ABOUT: Carey, G. Cukor and Company, 1971; Clarens, C. Cukor, 1976; Comizio, E. Cukor, 1977 (in Italian); Current Biography, 1943; Domarchi, J. George Cukor, 1965 (in French); Estrin, A. Capra, Cukor, Brown (The Hollywood Professionals), 1980; Higham, C. and Greenberg, J. The Celluloid Muse, 1969; Kantor, B. R. and others (eds.) Directors at Work, 1970; International Film Guide, 1977; Phillips, G. D. George Cukor, 1982; Roud, R. (ed.) Cinema: A Critical Dictionary, 1980; Sarris, A. Interviews With Film Directors, 1967; Selznick, D. O. Memo From David O. Selznick, 1972; Thomson, D. A Biographical Dictionary of the Cinema, 1980. *Periodicals*—American Film February 1978; Bright Lights Fall 1974; Cahiers du Cinéma 115 1961; Cinema (USA) 35 1976; Cinéma (France) February 1974; March 1983; Cinématographe February 1983; Écran October and November 1976; Film Comment March–April 1978; Film Dope April 1976; Film Ideal June 15, 1964 (Cukor issue); Film Journal (Australia) July 1957; Films and Filming August and September 1960; Films in Review January 1982; Screen Autumn 1973; Sight and Sound Spring 1955, Autumn 1964; Thousand Eyes Magazine January 1977.

"CURTIZ, MICHAEL" (MIHÁLY KERTÉSZ) (December 24, 1888–April 11, 1962), American director and producer, was born in Budapest, Hungary, of Jewish parentage, the eldest of three sons. Later in life, Curtiz enjoyed creating mystery about his origins and upbringing and sometimes maintained that his father was "a poor carpenter." The generally accepted account, though, is that his family was comfortably off, his father being an architect and his mother an opera singer. Curtiz himself is said to have made his stage debut, aged eleven, in an opera in which his mother was starring. At seventeen, he ran away to join a traveling circus, performing with them as strongman, acrobat, juggler, and mime. He is also reported to have been a member of the Hungarian fencing team at the 1912 Stockholm Olympics.

It seems certain, at any rate, that Curtiz studied at Markoszy University in Budapest and then at the Royal Academy of Theatre and Art. Hav-

MICHAEL CURTIZ

ing completed his studies, he joined the National Hungarian Theatre, whose repertoire consisted mostly of "boulevard comedies" like those of Molnár, several of which Curtiz would later film. He began his theatrical career in traditional style, taking on all the dogsbody jobs from candyseller to cashier. Curtiz soon graduated to acting roles and before long was also established as one of the company's most promising young directors.

Ma és holnap (*Today and Tomorrow*, 1912) was proudly announced as "The First Hungarian Dramatic Art Film." Curtiz took one of the leading roles and is generally believed to have directed as well, although no director was credited. He was certainly named as the director of *Az utolsó bohém* (*The Last Bohemian*, 1912), and he made at least two more pictures before setting out for the Nordisk studios in Copenhagen, at that time the preeminent center of film production in Europe. Curtiz spent six months at Nordisk, learning all he could about filmmaking and working with leading Scandinavian directors like Mauritz Stiller and Victor Sjöstrom. He assisted August Blom in the direction of a big-budget epic, *Atlantis* (1913) and is also supposed to have directed a film of his own for Nordisk, although no record of it has survived.

Back in Hungary, adorned with the prestige of his Danish experience, Curtiz found himself much in demand. From 1914 to 1919 he directed at least thirty-seven films, many of which—following the contemporary Scandinavian example—showed a preference for naturalistic outdoor locations. *Bánk bán* (1914), based on a popular Hungarian folk story, was the first of several major successes. On the outbreak of war, Curtiz was drafted into the Austro-Hungarian artillery, but through shrewd use of personal connections got himself first transferred to the Army film unit and then in 1915 discharged. Soon after resuming civilian life, he married a seventeen-year-old aspiring actress, Lucy Doraine, despite her family's opposition to her choice of both husband and career.

Early in 1917, Curtiz was appointed director of production at Phoenix Films, the leading studios in Budapest. He worked exclusively for them until he left Hungary. None of his Hungarian films has survived intact, and most are completely lost; but the fragments that remain suggest that Curtiz's talent for fluent narrative and vivid composition was already well developed. So, too, was his notoriously autocratic attitude to filmmaking: in a 1917 article for the periodical *Mozhihét* he stated, "An actor's success is no more than the success of the director whose concept of the whole brings into harmony the performance of each character on the screen."

In April 1919, Béla Kun's short-lived socialist Republic of Councils announced the nationalization of the film industry. This was little to Curtiz's taste. Abandoning his current project, a version of Molnár's *Liliom*, he left Hungary for good. According to some sources, he visited Sweden, where a persistent but improbable legend has him directing a film featuring the fourteen-year-old Greta Gustafsson (Garbo) as Marie Antoinette. No trace of any such work has survived, nor of an early episode of Fritz Lang's serial *Die Spinnen* (*The Spiders*, 1919), which Curtiz is said to have directed in Germany. With or without detours, he ended up in Vienna, where he and Lucy Doraine were signed up by Count Alexander Kolowrat, owner of Sascha Films.

While working for Sascha, Curtiz later wrote, he "learned the basic laws of film art, which, in those days, had progressed further in Vienna than anywhere else" (thus apparently dismissing as negligible the experience gained on his forty or so Hungarian films). The pictures that he directed for Sascha—twenty-one at least—fall mainly into two categories: sophisticated light comedies and historical (in the loosest sense) spectaculars. The comedies, such as *Die Dame mit den schwarzen Handschuhen* (*The Lady With the Black Gloves*, 1919), or *Cherchez la Femme* (1921), were designed as vehicles for Lucy Doraine, whom Curtiz succeeded in launching as an international star. (Their personal relationship was less successful; they were divorced in 1923. There was one child—a daughter, Katherine.) His own reputation,

though, was established by his De Mille–style biblical spectaculars, notably *Sodom und Gomorrha* (1922) and *Die Sklavenkönigin* (*Moon of Israel,* 1924), with their cannily commercial mixture of sexual display and moral deprecation. *Sodom und Gomorrha,* though at the time the most expensive film ever made in Austria, more than recouped its cost; thanks largely to Curtiz, Sascha was fast becoming the leading Austrian studio and establishing lucrative connections with the mighty UFA company of Berlin.

Moon of Israel, produced by a fellow Hungarian exile, Sándor (later Sir Alexander) Korda, achieved wide international distribution. Jack Warner, scouting for talent in Europe with his brother Harry, saw it in Paris and was "laid in the aisles by Curtiz's camera work . . . [by] shots and angles that were pure genius." Warners, lean and ambitious, had already snapped up Lubitsch, and now decided to sign Curtiz for their planned superproduction, *Noah's Ark*—a film intended to beat De Mille at his own game. Curtiz readily accepted their offer but before leaving Europe completed a last assignment for Sascha: three German-international coproductions aimed at launching the French revue star Lily Damita (later briefly, and stormily, married to Errol Flynn).

In 1926, when Curtiz arrived in Hollywood, Warner Brothers was still a small and financially shaky studio; the jackpot of Vitaphone and *The Jazz Singer* was a year in the future. Kertész now became Curtiz; but before letting their newly-christened director loose on *Noah's Ark,* the studio cautiously assigned him to a batch of programmers, beginning with a melodrama, *The Third Degree* (1926). Curtiz, with some sixty films already to his credit and obsessively dedicated to his work, slid effortlessly into the Hollywood system, rapidly proving himself capable of making a smooth, professional job out of even the least promising material. He was to stay with Warners for the next twenty-eight years and direct eighty-six films for them, including all his best work.

The Third Degree, according to John Davis and Tom Flinn in *The American Film Heritage,* "is literally a showcase of the major characteristics that form the Curtiz style. . . . As Curtiz later admitted, he realized that his entire career depended upon how strongly he could depict this rather tired story. . . . Never again would Curtiz so blatantly reveal his directorial hand as in the film's flamboyant, expressionistic sequences and tricky subjective shots; at one point the camera even plays the role of a lethal bullet." Like many of his early Warners films, the picture starred Dolores Costello, at that time one of the studio's few female stars. She was also featured in his first part-talkie, *Tenderloin* (1928), and in the long-awaited *Noah's Ark* (1929), which achieved a substantial box-office success, even if it failed to eclipse De Mille. Davis and Flinn considered it "conclusive proof of Curtiz's ability to create stunning spectacle with great visual style."

During his first few days in Hollywood Curtiz had met Bess Meredyth, a screenwriter, and they were married a year or two later. Despite Curtiz's imperious behavior, persistent neglect of his wife, and frequent affairs with young actresses, the marriage lasted until 1961, when they divorced a year before his death. Some sources mention a son, David, who also worked in the film industry, though this may well have been the director's youngest brother.

Curtiz scored another commercial hit with *Mammy* (1930), a backstage murder vehicle for Al Jolson with songs by Irving Berlin, set in a heavily romanticized Old South. His first commercial failure, *The Mad Genius* (1931), starred John Barrymore as a megalomaniac dance impresario; the film, which marks an early appearance of Curtiz's recurrent theme of cynicism versus idealism, was probably too similar to the recent *Svengali* (also with Barrymore) to impress the public. *The Strange Love of Molly Louvain* (1932), a social drama, rates in John Baxter's opinion as "among the earliest of his masterpieces. . . . The milieu of slum streets and hotel rooms is recreated with chilling detail, the story told with a pitiless intensity."

Warners were now the fastest-growing studio in Hollywood, and Curtiz's stock rose with them. *Cabin in the Cotton* (1932) was an early example of a Warners speciality—hard-hitting social (near-) realism, in this case enlivened by the first of Bette Davis's rich gallery of malicious Southern belles. She appeared in a more sympathetic light in another "message picture," *20,000 Years in Sing Sing* (1933), playing the girlfriend of Spencer Tracy; in a wildly romantic gesture of self-sacrifice, Tracy goes to the chair for the murder she has committed. Curtiz's realistic portrayal of the dreariness and squalor of prison life may now seem commonplace, but was found fresh and revelatory at the time.

Around this time Curtiz also directed two of Warners' rare excursions into the horror genre. John Baxter found *Doctor X* (1932) "one of the greatest of the classic horror films, incorporating most of the key Germanic elements"; if few other critics have been quite so enthusiastic, the movie certainly includes some vividly atmospheric scenes, quite clearly influenced by Lang

and Murnau. *Doctor X* was shot in two-color Technicolor, although only monochrome prints seem now to be extant, but a color print of *The Mystery of the Wax Museum* (1933) has luckily survived. The process, noted Tom Shales, "adds the ideal eerie glow to the story of dark doings. . . . The film does not suffer under the restriction [of the limited color options] but, in fact, benefits from it." As the demented sculptor, Lionel Atwill raves splendidly, and Fay Wray reprises a scream or two from *King Kong*.

Curtiz, perhaps surprisingly, directed few of the tough, pacy gangster movies for which Warners was by now famous; but he did an efficient job on a couple of production-line series thrillers: *The Kennel Murder Case* (1933), with William Powell playing Philo Vance, and *The Case of the Curious Bride* (1935), with Warren William as Perry Mason. Between these two he took on—among other things—a steamy, sub-Maugham tropical melodrama, *Mandalay* (1934), featuring Kay Francis bumping off unwanted lovers; and *British Agent* (1934), a richly implausible affair supposedly set in 1917 revolutionary Moscow, with Leslie Howard in the title role and Kay Francis as Lenin's stenographer.

All through the 1930s, Curtiz tirelessly hammered out four or five movies a year, seemingly as ready to take on low-budget programmers as more prestigious assignments. By the middle of the decade, though, he was established as Warners' top director, increasingly assigned to the studio's major stars (Davis, Cagney, Muni, William Powell) and more expensive productions—at least by Warners' notoriously parsimonious standards. The studio's financial stability was now assured, but old habits died hard—especially those of Hal Wallis, Warners' formidable and tight-fisted production chief. Curtiz, versatile, industrious, and supremely adept at creating lavish results on minimal budgets, fitted the studio philosophy perfectly. "Curtiz never gave second-hand treatment to an assignment once it was accepted," commented William Meyer; "he went ahead and graced plot and character with fluid camera movement, exquisite lighting, and a lightning-fast pace. Even if a script was truly poor and the leading players were real amateurs, Curtiz glossed over inadequacies so well that an audience often failed to recognise a shallow substance until it was hungry for another film a half-hour later."

Equally well established by this time was Curtiz's reputation as one of the most detested directors in Hollywood, second only perhaps to Josef von Sternberg. Jack Edmund Nolan (*Films in Review*, November 1970) described him as "a manic-depressive sort of man, up one day and down the next. In the euphoric phase he would appear on set splendidly accoutred, even flamboyantly (scarf, costume jewelry), and be full of extroverted, self-confident assertiveness. In the depressed phase he would be unkempt and would refuse to talk even about things that were of concern to him. In both states he was mindful of the feelings of others only occasionally."

Autocratic and overbearing on set, Curtiz clashed constantly with his actors; thriving under pressure, he expected them to do the same. Many actors, including Errol Flynn, eventually refused to work with Curtiz. Bette Davis, never one to be dominated, fought with him ceaselessly. (Curtiz is said to have referred to her, in her presence, as a "goddamned nothing nogood sexless son of a bitch.") Joan Blondell described him as "a cruel man, with animals and actors, and he swung that whip around pretty good. He overworked everyone. But he was also amusing, and he turned out some good pictures."

All his life Curtiz retained a strong Hungarian accent, and his creative mishandlings of the English language deserve to be as famous as those of Sam Goldwyn. He once stormed at a confused propman: "Next time I send a damn fool, I go myself!" He expressed dissatisfaction with a child actor by remarking scathingly: "By the time I was your age, I was fifteen." A scene in one of his films, he predicted, would "make your blood curl."

For all his unsympathetic treatment of actors, Curtiz showed a knack for detecting and fostering unknown talent. Among the players who achieved stardom under his direction were Walter Slezak, John Garfield and—rather unexpectedly—Doris Day. His most famous discovery, though, was undoubtedly Errol Flynn, who in Curtiz's hands rose from minor bit parts to become one of the great romantic heroes of the cinema, the first (and perhaps only) true successor to Douglas Fairbanks. The first of their dozen collaborations, *Captain Blood* (1935), defined the most enduring aspect of Flynn's screen persona: the dashing, devil-may-care swashbuckler, sword in hand and heart on sleeve.

Adapted from a ripe piece of period tushery by Rafael Sabatini, *Captain Blood* assembled all the right ingredients—piracy, swordplay, wrongful imprisonment, flowery sentiments, a fine score (his first) from Erich Korngold, plus Olivia de Havilland as the sweet, spirited heroine and Basil Rathbone sneering impeccably as the villain. Robert Donat was originally to play the title role; when he dropped out through illness, Curtiz cast the inexperienced Flynn in spite of the studio's misgivings. As it turned out, both Curtiz *and* Warners were right: Flynn couldn't act, but it didn't matter in the least.

Captain Blood displays most of the characteristics of Curtiz's cinematic style at this period, as enumerated by Sidney Rosenzweig: "High crane shots to establish a story's environment; unusual camera angles and complex compositions in which characters are often framed by physical objects; much camera movement; subjective shots . . . ; and high contrast lighting, with pools of shadow." The same expressionistic style was employed in *Black Fury* (1935), about a strike in the mining industry. It was received with adulation in some quarters, and seemed to Otis Ferguson better than Pudovkin. Thirty-five years later, Andrew Bergman called it "one of the real frauds of the thirties." Paul Muni plays a Polish miner manipulated by a shyster detective agency into leading a wildcat strike. The result, Bergman says, "was simply a fairy story, weighed down by shyster motifs and sure of the intrinsic solidarity between benevolent capitalism and conservative unionism."

Following the success of *Captain Blood*, Curtiz and Flynn were reunited for *The Charge of the Light Brigade* (1936), a blatantly unhistoric account of the famous Crimean débacle (most of the action takes place in India). Flynn was once again cast as the social rebel, this time fighting against the incompetence and indecision of his senior officers, and Curtiz directed with all his inherent sense of rhythm and timing. The film builds inexorably to the final, climactic charge, which an unsigned article in *Classic Images* (January 1983) summed up as "a myriad of sweeping long shots, low tracking shots, close-ups, and dynamic editing merged together in one of the most exciting panoramic pieces of cinema ever filmed." It was also, by all accounts, one of the most dangerous. One man died and several more were badly injured in the filming of it; so many horses were killed that the SPCA raised a public protest.

Curtiz returned to Warners' urban realist mode with *Kid Galahad* (1937), a boxing melodrama in which, wrote Davis and Flinn, he "detailed the sordid aspects of the fight scene, the raucous hotel parties, the gambling and gangsterism, with the same care he lavished on the brutal fight scenes." As the ruthless manager who turns a bellhop into a world champion, Edward G. Robinson gave a bravura performance—tough, sardonic, and ultimately (of course) soft-hearted. The same could be said, allowing for their different acting styles, of Cagney as gangster Rocky Sullivan in *Angels With Dirty Faces* (1938). Idolized by the young hooligans of his neighborhood, Sullivan is finally persuaded by the local priest (Pat O'Brien) to "die yellow" when he goes to the chair; the kids, disgusted by their hero's apparent cowardice, are thus deterred from a life of crime. The ending perhaps says more for Warners' social conscience (or eye to the Hays Office) than for their regard for narrative credibility.

Curtiz, wrote Nick Roddick, "could be relied upon to deliver the goods in terms of action, but not always in terms of schedule." He quotes a revealing series of harassed memos from Frank Mattison, unit production manager on *Angels*: "Company is now four days behind schedule. You can tell from yesterday's report that Mike spent the day adding shots that were not in the script. . . . Mr. Curtiz is yelling for iron doors and bars along the prison set. . . . While the shots he has added are no doubt building up the sequence, there is no mind reader on the lot that can keep ahead of Mike when you turn him loose with machine guns, revolvers, bullets and gas bombs. I think he would rather play cops and robbers than eat."

So long as Curtiz's films did well at the box office, though—and, almost invariably, they did—the studio was happy to overlook minor idiosyncrasies of this kind. Curtiz and Flynn were now reckoned a foolproof winning combination, and in spite of Flynn's complaints of Curtiz's "bloodthirstiness," they were regularly teamed together. Two lesser efforts, *The Perfect Specimen* (1937), a social comedy, and *Gold Is Where You Find It* (1938), a Western, were followed by the best of all their films together and perhaps the finest swashbuckler of all time, *The Adventures of Robin Hood* (1938).

Curtiz, William Meyer maintained, "is to the swashbuckler what John Ford is to the Western." *Robin Hood* alone might well serve to substantiate such a claim. Filmed in glowing Technicolor, it easily surpassed the earlier Dwan-Fairbanks version, which seems slow and ponderous by comparison. The film had originally been assigned to William Keighley, who was replaced after some six weeks shooting—mainly of the Sherwood forest sequences—supposedly for adopting too "light-hearted" an approach. If so, the joins scarcely showed; the whole film has an irresistible, almost operatic, sweep and panache, climaxing in the superb final duel, all lunging shadows on torchlit stone walls. Flynn's sheer vitality made up for his indifferent acting; Rathbone and de Havilland were once more villain and heroine, and there was the delectable bonus of Claude Rains as a silkily malevolent Prince John. Korngold contributed a rousing score, for which he won an Oscar, as did Carl Jules Weyl for his majestic Nottingham Castle sets, and Ralph Dawson for his editing.

Swapping genres with unfailing insouciance, Curtiz next directed a sentimental small-town

soap opera, *Four Daughters* (1938), which was saved from utter mawkishness by a wryly ironic performance from Claude Rains and by the bitter intensity of John Garfield, making his screen debut. The film was hugely successful, and Curtiz made two sequels, *Daughters Courageous* (1939) and *Four Wives* (1939).

Despite increasing tension between director and star, the Flynn-Curtiz partnership continued with *Four's a Crowd* (1938), a dull comedy, and *Dodge City* (1939), the first of three big-budget Westerns. In an article in *Monogram* (October 1975), David Morse pointed out that *Dodge City* presents, in its sprawling narrative, a virtual compendium of Western iconography: "We are shown the stagecoach, the steam locomotive, buffalo hunters, a cattle drive, lynchings, saloons and gambling halls, the temperance league, a children's picnic, the covered wagons, a barber's shop, a cattle auction, a funeral at Boot Hill, a pioneer newspaper, a cattle stampede, a barroom brawl." Curtiz took all the clichés in his stride: the film opens with a race between stagecoach and railroad, and continues at much the same breakneck pace throughout the action.

Curtiz won the first of his two Oscars for a patriotic short, *Sons of Liberty* (1939). It starred Claude Rains, exceptional among actors in that he generally got on well with Curtiz and enjoyed working for him. There followed *The Private Lives of Elizabeth and Essex* (1939). A lavish costume drama complete with Korngold score and the faithful Olivia de Havilland, this was no swashbuckler but a sumptuous vehicle for the Queen of the Warners lot, Bette Davis. It was originally to be called *Elizabeth the Queen*; Davis, furious at the title change and even more so at getting Flynn as Essex when she had demanded Laurence Olivier, played the entire film in an towering rage, clashing incessantly with Curtiz. Flynn, trapped between two roaring egos, was visibly cowed; the film turned out grandiose, static, and—apart from Davis's impressive histrionics—dead.

Both Curtiz and Flynn were far more in their element in another Elizabethan drama, *The Sea Hawk* (1940), an exhilaratingly paced swashbuckler which, as Whitemore and Cecchettini put it, "does for the ocean what *Robin Hood* died for the forest." The Queen this time was Flora Robson, a less intimidating figure, and her scenes with Flynn convey an enjoyable sense of mutual amusement. *Virginia City* (1940) was perhaps the best of the Curtiz-Flynn Westerns, although the director never seemed as fully at home in this genre as he did with swashbucklers. Set during the Civil War, it uses the clash between Flynn (a Northern agent) and Randolph Scott (a noble Southern leader) to explore Curtiz's favorite theme of divided loyalties. Humphrey Bogart, who disliked Flynn and detested Westerns, was improbably cast as a villainous bandit, complete with Mexican moustache.

The last of the Western trilogy, *Santa Fe Trail* (1940), presented a recklessly fictionalized account of the pursuit of the abolitionist leader John Brown by Jeb Stuart (Flynn) and George Armstrong Custer (Ronald Reagan). Brown, in an intensely high-voltage performance from Raymond Massey, is depicted throughout as a crazed fanatic; Curtiz consistently shoots him from a low angle, harshly lit, eyes glittering wildly as he rants in bloodthirsty prophecy. "Although dealing with a liberal subject," wrote Kingsley Canham, "it is totally anti-liberal; and it makes very little concession to the historical importance of its subject matter . . . ; concentrating instead on perpetuating the Flynn character as . . . the invincible American hero." Within this ideologically outrageous framework, the film contained some fine set pieces of action, most notably the final battle at Harpers Ferry. Relations between Curtiz and Flynn were now near the breaking point. They made one more film together—the mediocre *Dive Bomber* (1941)—during which they were reportedly scarcely on speaking terms. Thereafter Flynn refused to work with Curtiz again.

With the start of the 1940s and the ending of the ebullient Flynn cycle, a darker, more pessimistic tone gradually seemed to suffuse Curtiz's output—although many critics would argue that in this, as throughout his career, Curtiz the archetypal studio workhorse was merely reflecting an overall shift in Hollywood's—and America's—mood. Whatever the cause, *The Sea Wolf* (1941) marked a dramatic departure from the yo-ho-ho athleticism of his earlier sea pictures. Easily the best version of Jack London's much-filmed novel, it gave Edward G. Robinson one of his richest roles as the tormented Nietzschean captain, Wolf Larsen, who tyrannizes all those unlucky enough to board his ship. Curtiz also elicited fine performances from the rest of the cast, especially John Garfield, Ida Lupino, and Alexander Knox.

"The film hauntingly captured an eerie, malevolent atmosphere, brooding and full of terror," wrote Higham and Greenberg. Sidney Rosenzweig thought it "one of Curtiz's strongest, richest movies." Nick Roddick, though, found it less successful: "it tries to introduce the moral despair of the *film noir* into a novel to which it was reasonably suited, but into a genre of film into which it fitted much less happily." Indifferently

received on its release, *The Sea Wolf* has since gained in reputation, and many critics now class it among Curtiz's finest films.

Moral despair, at any rate, was conspicuously absent from the first of Curtiz's wartime hits, *Yankee Doodle Dandy* (1942). Davis and Flinn considered it "the finest musical biography ever filmed"; it was without any doubt the most energetic. As George M. Cohan, composer, showman, and superpatriot, James Cagney strutted superlatively, earning himself an Oscar; his performance, and that of Walter Huston as his father, did much to ensure the film's lasting appeal, despite the deafening blare of nationalistic bombast.

A year later, Curtiz directed a further exercise in national propaganda, of a rather different kind: *Mission to Moscow* (1943), an amazingly overt Stalinist apologia, based on the memoirs of Joseph E. Davies, ex–US Ambassador to the USSR. In it, Russia was depicted, as James Agee put it, as "a great glad two-million-dollar bowl of canned borscht, eminently approvable by the Institute of Good Housekeeping." The film, which went so far as to endorse the 1937 show trials, caused much embarrassment a few years later when the wind changed: a twitchy Jack Warner informed HUAC that it had been made at the express request of President Roosevelt. *Mission to Moscow* was suppressed for some years, becoming available again during the 1960s. Higham and Greenberg, commending "its epic sweep, its magnificently lavish studio pastiche recreation of Russia, its brilliant, well-nigh irresistible propagandist verve," classed it "with *Triumph of the Will* and *Ten Days That Shook the World,* as one of the great propaganda pieces of the screen."

Also in 1943, Curtiz was assigned to what had originally been planned as a low-budget melodramatic programmer, to star Ronald Reagan and Ann Sheridan. For some reason, the project was upgraded to major-budget status, Bogart and Ingrid Bergman were brought in to play the leads, a new scriptwriter was drafted (Howard Koch, who also scripted *Mission to Moscow*), and one of the great cult movies was born. *Casablanca* (1943) is undoubtedly Curtiz's best-known film, more written about than any of his others (quite possibly more than all his others put together); it won him his only Best Director Oscar; and it established, more decisively even than *The Maltese Falcon* or *The Big Sleep,* the iconographic Bogart persona. Its low-key, nostalgically romantic appeal has not diminished; in August 1983 a British Film Institute Members' poll voted it, by a wide margin, top of a list of all-time favorite films.

As Rick, jaded and world-weary proprietor of a night spot in Vichy Casablanca, Bogart embodies perfectly the moral choice that lies at the heart of so many of Curtiz's films: public versus private morality, cynical detachment versus commitment. In the easy-going 1930s, the choice had been largely a formality; Errol Flynn's reluctance to become sheriff and clean up Dodge City had been little more than a momentary hesitation. In *Casablanca*, though we sense that ultimately Bogart will do the right thing, the choice is more drawn-out, more agonized: not until the very last moments of the film does he relinquish Bergman to resistance leader Victor Laszlo (Paul Henreid) and ally himself irreversibly to the cause of freedom and democracy. This ambiguity no doubt stems partly from the uncertainty of the actors (and even of the director) as to how the film would end; most of the script was apparently written while shooting progressed. "That picture was made good on set," Curtiz remarked later. "I have three writers working on set every day as we shoot."

Besides the principal actors, Warners assembled an exceptionally fine supporting cast: Sydney Greenstreet, Peter Lorre, Conrad Veidt, Dooley Wilson (as Sam, playing it again), and "the ambiguous emotional center of the film, the human embodiment of Casablanca's mystery and corruption," as Richard Schickel put it— Claude Rains as the Vichy police chief, Louis Renault. Together with Max Steiner's score (incorporating, of course, "As Time Goes By"), Weyl's sets, and Arthur Edeson's evocative camerawork, they enabled Curtiz to create, Kingsley Canham suggested, "one of the most outstanding works ever to emerge from a Hollywood studio," a distillation of the style and aspirations of wartime America.

Bogart's Rick, wrote Sidney Rosenzweig, "is an irresistible identification figure for that urge in all of us for a splendid and noble martyrdom." "Isolationism is no longer a practical policy, my dear Rick," remarks Sydney Greenstreet blandly, underlining the political parallel between the man and his country (the film is set in 1941); a hero for his time, Rick somberly but inexorably heads towards the foggy nocturnal airfield where he shoots the Nazi Colonel Strasser, hands over Bergman to Henreid, and strolls off arm-in-arm with Rains to join the Free French over the next hill. The film was enthusiastically acclaimed, barring a grumpy dissenting note from James Agee ("The camera should move for purposes other than those of a nautch dancer"), and showered with Oscars; over the years, its stature as a cinematic classic has become unassailable.

Yet, as Richard Schickel admitted, "ob-jectively speaking, the film . . . remains what it always was—a somewhat better-than-average example of what the American studio system could do when it was at its most stable and powerful." The plot is often shaky and implausible. Though much of the dialogue is witty and memorable (Rains, inviting an increased kickback: "I'm only a *poor* corrupt official . . ."), much more is unadulterated schmaltz. Bergman to Bogart, in mid-tryst as the Germans invade Paris: "Was that cannon fire, or was it my heart pounding?" Bogart to Bergman, recalling the same events: "I remember every detail—the Germans wore gray, you wore blue." Several fine actors, notably Lorre and Greenstreet, are largely wasted. *Casablanca*, by any standards, is not great art. But it is, beyond all doubt, superb cinema.

It was also a hard act to follow. *Passage to Marseille* (1944) reunited Curtiz with several of the same stars (Bogart, Rains, Greenstreet, and Lorre) but utterly lacked the earlier film's resonance. Still, it had its own bizarre charm, padding out a minimal plot with a lunatic Chinese-box structure of multiple flashbacks.

By this stage in his career, Curtiz had to some extent modified his cinematic style and toned down the vividly dramatic expressionism of his earlier years. His camera remained fluid, but the angles were becoming less startling, the compositions less crowded and complex, though he retained his taste for stark contrasts in lighting. "I have progressed, too," he remarked around this time. "I was too European, too stagey, too sentimental. Now at fifty-six I do better work." Most critics would say that, on the contrary, at fifty-six Curtiz had almost all his best work behind him and was about to direct his last major film.

Mildred Pierce (1945), adapted from a novel by James M. Cain, was intended as a vehicle for Joan Crawford, recently ousted from MGM and badly in need of a boost for her flagging career. She got it; the film won her an Academy Award (her first and only) for her performance as the drivingly ambitious housewife who works her way up from waitress to owner of a chain of restaurants, and in doing so destroys her life and her family. But *Mildred Pierce* transcends its origins as a Crawford vehicle; a model *film noir*, it presents an icily graphic picture of the souring of the American dream of success. "The family and mother love are both undermined," observed David Thomson. "Suburbia inextricably confuses happiness and the dollar."

Michael Wood cited *Mildred Pierce* as one of the few *films noirs* in which the action of the movie lives up (or perhaps down) to the lowering menace of the atmosphere: "The unrequited love of Joan Crawford for her stuck-up daughter dominates even the film's murky, compelling mood, converting that mood into a metaphor for the stormy, tortured confusion of her feelings." The opening has become deservedly famous: in a remote, night-bound beach house shots are fired, shattering a mirror; a man slumps to the lamplit floor, gasping a woman's name with his last breath; a car revs off into the night. "The film," wrote Higham and Greenberg, "conveys Curtiz's love of the American night world, of piers shining under rain, dark beaches, the Pacific moonlight seen through a bar's windows; and the tough direction of the players at all times pays dividends."

By way of total contrast, Curtiz's next two films offered optimistic, upbeat Americana. *Night and Day* (1946) purported, without much justification, to be a biography of Cole Porter, represented by Cary Grant at his most debonair, casually scribbling snatches of the title song in the World War I trenches. *Life With Father* (1947) was a sunlit period piece, set in 1880s New York, with William Powell perfectly cast as the irascible but finally soft-hearted paterfamilias; the film made up in charm for what it lacked in pace.

In 1946 Frank Capra, George Stevens, and William Wyler had formed Liberty Pictures, a directors' cooperative aimed at achieving freedom from studio tyranny, and had invited Curtiz to join them. Alarmed, Jack Warner offered his star director a nominally autonomous unit within the studio, Michael Curtiz Productions. Considerably hampered by having to seek the studio's final script approval on all projects, the fledgling company finally produced *The Unsuspected* (1947), a stylishly Gothic murder story which handed Claude Rains a bravura role as a megalomaniac, and eventually homicidal, radio personality. Perhaps encouraged by the frank improbability of the plot, Curtiz pulled out some of his best UFA-style camera tricks, and one sequence (according to Higham and Greenberg) "remains the quintessence of Forties *film noir*. The camera moves out of a train window, across a narrow street filled with neon signs, and up to a room where a killer lies smoking, terrified in the dark, listening to the story of his crimes related by Victor Grandison [Rains] on the radio."

After a couple of vapid musicals, notable only for giving Doris Day her start in movies, Curtiz's outfit produced its final film, *Flamingo Road* (1949). This was in many ways a companion piece to *Mildred Pierce,* substituting steamy Southern locations for rain-washed California, with Joan Crawford as a cabaret singer encountering small-town political corruption. As the venal sheriff, Sydney Greenstreet in his penultimate role exuded soft-spoken evil with practiced skill. Curtiz now sold his company back to Warners, tired of exercising an independence that was barely more than nominal.

Those critics who regard Curtiz purely as a creature of the studio system have pointed out that the two flourished and declined together, and that by the end of the 1940s both were evidently past their best. Of his remaining films for Warners, few have attracted much critical attention, although Yves Boisset (*Cinéma,* June 1962) somewhat perversely rated *The Breaking Point* (1950) Curtiz's best film. This was a remake, starring John Garfield, of Hemingway's *To Have and Have Not,* considerably more faithful to the original than Hawks's enjoyable romp (1944) with Bogart and Bacall—but also far less entertaining.

As Warner Brothers' top director, Curtiz had been earning $5,000 a week. In 1954 Warners, along with the rest of Hollywood, was running into financial difficulties, and Jack Warner asked all the studio's highest-paid personnel to accept a fifty percent cut in salary. Curtiz refused, and quit the studio where he had worked for twenty-eight years. His decision may not have resulted entirely from wounded pride; that same year he was cited by a young actress in a paternity suit, and the judgment went expensively against him.

During the remaining eight years of his life, Curtiz freelanced for all the major studios (especially Paramount), directing a further fifteen films. They were a mixed and largely mediocre bunch, though Curtiz could still command big budgets and top box-office acting talent, and his technical competence remained impressive. Ironically, one of these late films, *White Christmas* (1954), a saccharine musical with Bing Crosby and Danny Kaye, proved the biggest commercial hit of his career. It would be difficult to imagine a less typical Curtiz movie— if such a thing exists.

The general critical consensus on Michael Curtiz has been that he was a studio director par excellence, bringing a high degree of technical mastery to whatever Warners threw at him, undoubtedly at his best with fast-paced action dramas, but lacking any overall personal vision or directorial signature. In other words, Curtiz was not an *auteur,* unlike the almost equally versatile if less prolific Howard Hawks. "Perhaps more than any other director, Curtiz reflected the strengths and weaknesses of the studio system in Hollywood," Andrew Sarris wrote, going on to describe *Casablanca* as "the happiest of happy accidents, and the most decisive exception to the *auteur* theory." Still more dismissively, Richard Roud suggested that "perhaps there is little to say, except that his films have given much mindless pleasure."

Ephraim Katz, though, observed that "his forceful personality frequently broke through the most routine material, and it was often difficult to tell who was subservient to whom, Curtiz to the studio system or the studio system to Curtiz." Describing Curtiz as "the ultimate professional," John Baxter commented that such an attribute "has seldom been regarded as more than a poor second best to the most sporadic pursuit of the feeblest personal vision." Despite the implication that Curtiz wholly lacked any such vision, Baxter added that he brought to all his films "a sly and high sexual Viennese humour," and elsewhere remarked that he "lays a substantial claim to being the best director of the Thirties. . . . Curtiz seems the embodiment of a European tradition totally opposed to the elegance and sly wit of a Lubitsch. . . . His films are among the most pitiless, grotesque and erotic in the history of the cinema."

Curtiz certainly displayed a "personal vision" in the purely physical sense, in that the bulk of his films share a distinctive and identifiable "look," a deliberate visual approach. John Davis, writing in *Velvet Light Trap* (June 1917), remarked that "Curtiz always knew exactly how far from the action, and at what angle, to place the camera to achieve maximum emotional identification from his audience." Paul Henreid, whom Curtiz directed in *Casablanca*, also noted his "instinctual visual sense. . . . Every now and again he would stop the camera and say 'There's something wrong here, I don't know what it is.' By and by he'd realize what it was and we'd begin the scene again." Sidney Rosenzweig identified Curtiz's visual style as the key aspect of his directorial signature, with "its unusual camera angles and carefully detailed, crowded, complex compositions, full of mirrors and reflections, smoke and fog, and physical objects, furniture, foliage, bars, and windows, that stand between the camera and the human characters and seem to surround and entrap them."

Rosenzweig further suggested that Curtiz's personal attitude to his material can be deduced from this visual approach: "Curtiz seems to define his characters by their environment, often suggesting they are trapped by that environment. In fact, environment becomes a form of fate, and Curtiz's characters often struggle against fate, trying to mold their own lives, shape their own destinies. The typical Curtiz hero is a morally divided figure, forced . . . to make a serious moral decision." Paul Leggatt (*Focus on Film,* Winter 1975–76) identified similar thematic preoccupations: "Time and again Curtiz presented a cynical yet idealistic hero in conflict with the society around him. . . . No matter how absurd and degenerate the world . . . , there still existed a moral base that could be appealed to and could even be made effective in a hostile world—if a man were willing to pay the price for taking a moral stand."

Curtiz himself tended to deflect with irony any attempt to delve beneath the polished surface of his films. "I put all the art into my pictures I think the audience can stand," he once remarked; and, again, "I don't see black-and-white words in a script when I read it. I see action." If he hardly qualifies, as John Baxter conceded, as "an artist of ideas," the bittersweet romanticism that suffuses all his best films would still make him something more than the impersonally efficient studio filmsmith he has sometimes been taken for. "One must allow Curtiz the credit," wrote David Thomson, "for making melodrama and sentimentality so searingly effective and such glowing causes for nostalgia. . . . *Yankee Doodle Dandy, Casablanca* and *Mildred Pierce* are an unrivalled trinity of inventiveness transforming soppiness to such an extent that reason and taste begin to waver at the conviction of genre in full flow."

Michael Curtiz never retired. Indefatigable to the last, he continued to direct a regular two films a year well into his seventies. Almost his last movie, bringing him full circle to his starting-point, was an adaptation of a play by Molnár, *Olympia* (filmed as *A Breath of Scandal,* 1960). Curtiz died of cancer in a Hollywood hospital a few months after completing *The Comancheros* (1961), a John Wayne Western.

—P.K.

FILMS: Ma és holnap (Today and Tomorrow), 1912; Az utolsó bohém (The Last Bohemian), 1912; Hazasodik az uram (My Husband Lies), 1913; Rablélek (Captive Soul), 1913; A hercegnö Pongyolában (Princess Pongyola), 1914; Az éjszaka rabjai (Slaves of the Night), 1914; Aranyáso (The Golden Shovel), 1914; A kölcsönkért csecsemök (Borrowed Babies), 1914; A tolonc (The Vagrant), 1914; Bánk bán, 1914; Akit ketten szeretnek (Loved by Two), 1915; Doktor ur (The Doctor), 1916; A fekete szivarvany (The Black Rainbow), 1916; A Magyar föld ereje (The Force of the Hungarian Soil), 1916; Az ezust kecske (The Silver Goat), 1916; Farkas (The Wolf), 1916; Karthausi (The Carthusian), 1916; A medikus (The Apothecary), 1916; Makkhetes (Seven of Clubs), 1916; A föld embere (The Man of the Soil), 1917; A kuruzslo (The Charlatan), 1917; A béke utja (The Road to Peace), 1917; A senki fia (Nobody's Son), 1917; A Szentjóbi erdö titka (The

Secret of St. Job Forest), 1917; A vörös Sámson (The Red Samson), 1917; Arendás zsidó (John, The Tenant), 1917; Az utolsó hajnal (The Last Dawn), 1917; Az ezredes (The Colonel), 1917; Halálcsengö (The Death Bell), 1917; Zoárd Mester (Master Zoard), 1917; Egy krajcár története (The Story of a Penny), 1917; Tatárjáras (Invasion), 1917; Tavasz a télben (Spring in Wintertime), 1917; Szamárbör (The Donkey Skin), 1918; (with Fritz Ödön) Alraune, 1918; A csunya fiu (The Ugly Boy), 1918; A napraforgós hölgy (The Lady With Sunflowers), 1918; A skorpió (The Scorpion), 1918; A Wellingtoni rejtély (The Wellington Mystery), 1918; Az ördög (The Devil), 1918; Judás, 1918; Kilencvenkilenc (Ninety-nine), 1918; Lu, a kokott (Lu, the Cocotte), 1918; Lulu, 1918; Varázskeringö (Magic Waltz), 1918; Vig özvegy (The Merry Widow), 1918; Jön az öcsem (John the Younger Brother), 1919; Die Dame mit den schwarzen Handschuhen (The Lady With the Black Gloves), 1919; Die Gottesgeisel (The Scourge of God), 1919; Der Stern von Damaskus (The Star of Damascus), 1920; Die Dame mit den Sonnenblumen (The Lady With Sunflowers), 1920; Herzogin Satanella (Duchess Satanella), 1920; Boccaccio, 1920; Mrs. Tutti Frutti, 1920; Cherchez la Femme, 1921; Frau Dorothys Bekenntnis (Frau Dorothy's Confession), 1921; Wage des Schreckens/Labyrinth des Grauens (Labyrinth of Horror), 1921; Sodom und Gomorrha (part 1), 1922; Sodom und Gomorrha (part 2), 1922; Die Lawine (Avalanche), 1923; Der junge Medardus (Young Medardus), 1923; Namenlos (Nameless), 1923; Ein Spiel ums Leben (A Deadly Game), 1924; Harun al Raschid, 1924; Die Sklavenkönigin (Moon of Israel), 1924; Célimène, Poupée de Montmartre (Das Spielzeug von Paris/Red Heels), 1925; Der goldene Schmetterling (The Road to Happiness), 1926; Fiaker Nr. 13 (Cab No. 13), 1926; The Third Degree, 1926; A Million Bid, 1927; Good Time Charley, 1927; The Desired Woman, 1927; Tenderloin, 1928; Noah's Ark, 1929; The Glad Rag Doll, 1929; Madonna of Avenue A, 1929; Hearts in Exile, 1929; The Gamblers, 1929; Mammy, 1930; Under a Texas Moon, 1930; The Matrimonial Bed (U.K., A Matrimonial Problem), 1930; Bright Lights, 1930; A Soldier's Plaything, 1930; River's End, 1930; Dämon des Meeres (German version of Moby Dick, directed by Lloyd Bacon), 1931; God's Gift to Women (U.K., Too Many Women), 1931; The Mad Genius, 1931; The Woman From Monte Carlo, 1932; (with Lloyd Bacon) Alias the Doctor, 1932; The Strange Love of Molly Louvain, 1932; Doctor X, 1932; Cabin in the Cotton, 1932; 20,000 Years in Sing Sing, 1933; The Mystery of the Wax Museum, 1933; The Keyhole, 1933; Private Detective 62, 1933; Goodbye Again, 1933; The Kennel Murder Case, 1933; Female, 1933; Mandalay, 1934; British Agent, 1934; Jimmy the Gent, 1934; The Key/High Peril, 1934; Black Fury, 1935; The Case of the Curious Bride, 1935; Front Page Woman, 1935; Little Big Shot, 1935; Captain Blood, 1935; The Walking Dead, 1936; Stolen Holiday, 1936; The Charge of the Light Brigade, 1936; Kid Galahad, 1937; Mountain Justice, 1937; The Perfect Specimen, 1937; Gold Is Where You Find It, 1938; (with William Keighley) The Adventures of Robin Hood, 1938; Four Daughters, 1938; Four's a Crowd, 1938; Angels With Dirty Faces, 1938; Dodge City, 1939; Sons of Liberty, 1939 (short); Daughters Courageous, 1939; The Private Lives of Elizabeth and Essex, 1939; Four Wives, 1939; Virginia City, 1940; The Sea Hawk, 1940; Santa Fe Trail, 1940; The Sea Wolf, 1941; Dive Bomber, 1941; Captains of the Clouds, 1942; Yankee Doodle Dandy, 1942; Casablanca, 1943; Mission to Moscow, 1943; This Is the Army, 1943; Passage to Marseille, 1944; Janie, 1944; Roughly Speaking, 1945; Mildred Pierce, 1945; Night and Day, 1946; Life With Father, 1947; The Unsuspected, 1947; Romance on the High Seas, 1948; My Dream Is Yours, 1949; Flamingo Road, 1949; The Lady Takes a Sailor, 1949; Young Man With a Horn, 1950; Bright Leaf, 1950; The Breaking Point, 1950; Jim Thorpe—All-American, 1951; Force of Arms, 1951; I'll See You in My Dreams, 1952; The Story of Will Rogers, 1952; The Jazz Singer, 1953; Trouble Along the Way, 1953; The Boy From Oklahoma, 1954; The Egyptian, 1954; White Christmas, 1954; We're No Angels, 1955; The Scarlet Hour, 1956; The Vagabond King, 1956; The Best Things in Life Are Free, 1956; The Helen Morgan Story, 1957; The Proud Rebel, 1958; King Creole, 1958; The Hangman, 1959; The Man in the Net, 1959; The Adventures of Huckleberry Finn, 1960; A Breath of Scandal, 1960; Francis of Assisi, 1961; The Comancheros, 1961. Published scripts—The Adventures of Robin Hood (University of Wisconsin), 1979; Casablanca (Overlook), 1973, also in Best Film Plays of 1943–44 (Crown), 1945, also (ed. Anobile), Film Classics Library, 1974; Mildred Pierce (University of Wisconsin), 1980; Mission to Moscow (University of Wisconsin), 1980; Mystery of the Wax Museum (University of Wisconsin), 1979; The Sea Hawk (University of Wisconsin), 1982; Yankee Doodle Dandy (University of Wisconsin), 1981.

ABOUT: Baxter, J. Hollywood in the Thirties, 1968; Canham, K. The Hollywood Professionals, vol. 1, 1973; Higham, C. and Greenberg, J. Hollywood in the Forties, 1968; Meyer, W. R. Warner Brothers Directors, 1978; Nemeskürty, I. Word and Image: History of the Hungarian Cinema, 1968; Roddick, N. A New Deal in Entertainment: Warner Brothers in the 1930's, 1983; Rosenzweig, S. Casablanca and Other Major Films of Michael Curtiz, 1982; Sarris, A. The American Cinema, 1968; Shales, T. (and others) The American Film Heritage: Impressions From the American Film Institute Archives, 1972; Thomson, D. A Biographical Dictionary of the Cinema, 1980; Thomson, D. America in the Dark, 1977; Viviani, C. Michael Curtiz, 1973 (in French); Whittemore, D. and Cecchettini, P. A. Passport to Hollywood, 1976; Wood, M. America in the Movies, 1975. Periodicals—Cinema (UK) Summer 1971; Cinéma June 1962; Classic Images January 1983; Film Dope April 1976; Filme Cultura May–June 1972 (in Portuguese); Films and Filming June 1956; Films in Review November 1970; Filmvilag 9 1966 (in Hungarian); Focus on Film Winter 1975–6; Image et Son/Écran February 1982; National Film Theatre Booklet (Britain) April–May 1971; Sunset Boulevard Winter 1971 (In Danish).

*DAQUIN, LOUIS (May 30, 1908–October 2, 1980), French director and scenarist. The following note was compiled just before Daquin's death by his friend Jean-Pierre Berthomé from material provided for that purpose by Daquin, supplemented by excerpts from his books:

"The critics enjoy tracing in new directors the influences of those who were their teachers, but they are mistaken in interesting themselves only in the purely formal questions of style. I certainly learnt my craft with Jean Grémillon, who taught me, among other things, the science of actor direction, but the most important lesson I learnt from him was about people. Now I can thank him for saying to me one day: 'Stop, breathe deeply, open your eyes and choose'.

"I did choose the day that I decided to put myself at the service of the cinema and gave up putting the cinema at my service.

"People of my generation are the first to have been marked by the cinema from a very early age. Without either regrets or nostalgia I saw the mutation from silent to talking pictures. For reasons that I only realized later I decided to become a film director. At that time it was disreputable to want to direct films; it was not considered serious. Those who criticized us made the mistake of not foreseeing the extraordinary possibilities of an art form that was still developing. Aware of the necessity for an apprenticeship which should not be limited to one speciality—and also by necessity—I became assistant director, assistant editor, prop man, bit actor, production manager. Our apprenticeship was chaotic but very rich in arduous personal research, difficult and painful experiences that those following us will never know. We were condemned to discovering haphazardly the essence of an art that was in the making.

"Confronted with the contradictions of an art enslaved by money and the degrading consequences of this situation, Grémillon managed to make me conscious of the responsibility weighing on us, the filmmakers: responsibility to ourselves, responsibility to the audience. Thanks to him I realized much more quickly than most what my choice would be the day I became a film director.

"Through its multiplicity of expression a film enables you to reveal not only someone's personality but also the nature of the social surroundings, cultural environment, and national community to which he belongs. Numerous French films give a true image of France, for example those by Jean Renoir or Marcel Pagnol or—more recently—René Allio and René Feret. Mine as well, I think, and it is this authenticity of the social, political, and cultural environment

LOUIS DAQUIN

that I have tried to bring to the screen. And within this environment the awakening of conscience, which is the main theme of three of my films and appears in several others to throw a light on the central theme.

"In one of my first films, *Le Voyageur de la Toussaint,* you find everything I wanted to do in embryo. It is an attack against the bourgeoisie whose decadence and cruelty I describe—what Luis Buñuel expressed so well later on with his own particular genius—and at the same time the description of the birth of a social conscience.

"In another one, *Bel Ami,* I was able to tackle the problem of the French colonial wars. It is one of the cinema's roles to treat certain social or national problems which traumatize a nation, and so force it to ask itself questions. That is what Francis Ford Coppola had done for America with *Apocalypse Now.*

"But we have to use more energy to have a film project accepted than to actually make the film. The greater part of our time is spent elaborating projects that will never see the light of day. One can dream about an imaginary Cinémathèque, made up of all the films that we have been forbidden to make. But it is not on those films that we are judged. There is no other way but to make concessions. Without ever repudiating youself, however. Keeping your self-respect is an difficult as fighting your own intransigence." (*Summer 1980*)

Louis Daquin was born in Calais, the son of Auguste Daquin, a wine merchant, and the for-

mer Claire Langelier. Daquin originally qualified as a lawyer but seems never to have
practiced and was more attracted to the theatre
until "through *Potemkin* and the Russian cinema
I realized I must be a filmmaker." This was easier said than done, and he began his career as a
publicity writer for Renault (1931–1932) and
then as publicity director for a stationery company (1932–1933), meanwhile trying his hand
without much success as a playwright.

In 1933 Daquin entered the film industry as
script boy on Pierre Chenal's *La Rue sans nom.*
He worked for a year as a journalist, and then rejoined Chenal as assistant on *Crime et châtiment*
(1935), *L'Homme de nulle part* (in which he also
played a minor role), and *Les Mutinés de
l'Elseneur* (1936)—heavily stylized films much
admired at the time. Other assistant director-
ships followed on Abel Gance's *Un Grand
Amour de Beethoven* (1936) and Fedor Ozep's
La Dame de pique (1937) before Daquin joined
Jean Grémillon as assistant on *Hercule.*
Grémillon was unhappy with this film and
walked out, Daquin following soon after (incidentally being replaced as assistant by France
Gourdji, later better known in French politics as
Françoise Giraud).

Daquin made three more films with his mentor Grémillon, beginning with *Gueule d'amour*
(1937), in which he also had a small acting role.
It was shot in Berlin for a French subsidiary of
UFA, and the left-wing Daquin later described
the doubts he felt about working in Hitler's Germany: "I thought to myself . . . as long as they
don't ask me to do anything contrary to my
ideas. . . . And it's true, I never felt there were
any problems." He then assisted Grémillon on
L'Étrange Monsieur Victor (1938), also serving
as second-unit director—shooting some material
in Toulon needed for an introductory sequence.

In an extremely useful interview in *Film
Dope* (April 1976), Daquin said that his
"intellectual and political awakening" both date
from his association with Grémillon, "a man who
should be judged by the films he was not able to
make, rather than those he made." With
Grémillon, Daquin "never took part in the writing of the script . . . but each day he gave me
what he had written and I had to work out what
was needed to shoot it. . . . I never left the set
and it was through watching Grémillon that I
learned how to direct actors. . . . If you like, I
did a rough draft which he corrected and gave
a final form, corresponding with his own vision;
at that time you could allow yourself all that. In
fact it wasn't just a collaboration on the films, it
was also a permanent exchange of ideas between
us. Grémillon was to me what Renoir was to

Becker; we were in a way 'in the master's
workshop.'"

After assisting Albert Valentin on
L'Entraîneuse (1938), Daquin codirected with
Gerhard Lamprecht the French-language version of Lamprecht's *Der Spieler,* and then started work with Grémillon on *Remorques.* This was
interrupted in September 1939 by the outbreak
of World War II. Daquin found himself in a fortress in Alsace, where he was ordered to defend
the route to Paris with an 1895 cannon. This plan
was soon abandoned, and the Franco-German
Armistice followed. Before the end of 1940
Daquin was back in Paris, where he was chosen
to head a newsreel unit; soon realizing that "my
only alternative was to become a collaborator or
go to jail," he withdrew, clandestinely worked
with the French workers' union (CGT), and in
1941, joined the Communist Party.

Remorques was completed in 1941, when film
production resumed under German supervision,
and the same year Daquin directed his own first
movie, *Nous les gosses (Us Kids/Portrait of
Innocence),* from an original screenplay by Gaston Modot and Maurice Hiléro, adapted by Marcel Aymé and Daquin himself (who worked on
the scripts of all of his films). It was shot by Jean
Bachelet with a cast of children picked from the
streets of the impoverished Paris suburb where
it was set. The plot could scarcely be simpler, although it had obvious allegorical implications
for France under German occupation: a boy
kicks a football through a vast school window
and is told by the authoritarian headmaster that
he must replace it, at a cost of 1,800 francs. It is
an impossibly huge sum and his parents are poor,
but his schoolmates rally around him and decide
to spent the Easter vacation raising the money.

The children sing in the streets, sell flowers,
and do odd jobs. One team operates a shoeshine
business, ably supported by a unit of shoe dirti-
ers. Three children hire themselves out as the
pitiful offspring of a professional beggar. In
these and other ingenious ways, they assemble
the necessary money, which is then stolen by a
petty thief. The children put their new-found
solidarity to work to hunt down the malefactor
and recover the cash, only to find that the window has already been replaced by "the
administration" with one embodying a hideous
symbolic design showing a wolf and a lamb. The
day it is to be unveiled, another unfortunate kick
sends a football through the new window.

Daquin said that it was the solidarity theme
that had attracted him to the film. He "thought
the Germans would reject some scenes, but no,
they did not say anything. My problem with this
film was that I had to prove I was a good techni-

cian but if I used too much technique . . . I would not get the spontaneity of the kids. So I kept it simple, and I was right. The awful thing was this love story that . . . [none of us] wanted, but which the producer imposed on us. . . . And that's what makes it seem a bit old-fashioned now."

Released in France in 1941, *Nous les gosses* was a smash hit. As Daquin said, life then "was very hard and grim . . . [and here] suddenly was a film that made you laugh, an optimistic film. . . . Producers are wrong to remake successful films, because a big success always corresponds with a particular atmosphere at a given time. They should do remakes of unsuccessful films, the ones that were released before their time." But even after the war, when the movie was given international distribution, it was just as popular with foreign audiences, praised everywhere for its robust wit and charm, the absolute naturalness of the child actors, its integrity and "poetic realism." There were many comparisons with *Emil and the Detectives,* but it was agreed that here "the moral is more clearly pointed: friendship, it says, is strength."

For his second film, Daquin chose to make a thriller, *Madame et le mort* (1942), adapted by himself, Marcel Aymé, and Pierre Bost from a novel by Pierre Véry, with a cast headed by Renée Saint-Cyr and Pierre Renoir. According to Daquin, "the film is a bit crazy, more of a parody of a thriller than a classic thriller, full of strange scenes, a bit surrealist." The same year Daquin published a thriller of his own, *L'Enigme de Pelham,* using the pseudonym "Lewis MacDackin."

Le Voyageur de la Toussaint (1943), the film that contained "everything I wanted to do in embryo," weaves together the mystery of a detective story with a biting critique of the bourgeoisie. Based on a Simenon novel the story begins on the eve of All Saints' Day, when Gilles Mauvoisin (Jean Desailly) returns to La Rochelle, the home town of his recently deceased parents. His arrival provokes immediate hostility from a shadowy group known as "the syndicate"—two ship owners, the town notary, and the newspaper editor, as well as his own mother's sister. He then learns that he has inherited a large sum of money from a wealthy uncle, but with it comes the stipulation that he move into his uncle's home and look after his widow, Colette (Assia Noris). The plot is further complicated by a strongbox for which Gilles has no combination and then a murder charge brought against Colette, who is equally disliked by "the syndicate." In the end, corruption is unmasked, justice served, and Gilles leaves La Rochelle with Colette.

Scripted by Marcel Aymé, the film featured a musical score by Jean Wiener, who became Daquin's regular composer (but who in this case appears in the credits under a non-Jewish pseudonym, a ruse commonly adapted by French filmmakers during the Nazi occupation). Simone Signoret puts in a small uncredited appearance, while Desailly, Noris, and other stage actors made their film debuts. Jacques Siclier felt that *La Voyage de la Toussaint* was perhaps Daquin's best film, recreating "the muted, secret life of the provinces" with a poetic realism that was "half-way between Carné's *Quai des brumes* and Clouzot's *Le Corbeau.*" Andre Bazin, by contrast, thought that Daquin had "partially missed the boat."

Bazin was also disappointed by *Premier de cordée* (1944), scripted by Daquin and Alexandre Arnoux from one of the mountaineering novels of Frison-Roche and photographed by Philippe Agostini. For Daquin, the main objective was "to get out of the studios . . . I wanted to approach the cinema in another way. From the outside." But, he explained, political circumstances were also at work: "From the moment that censorship limited the content of films, one was quite naturally led to pay attention to form." Nonetheless it seemed to Bazin that even though the film was shot on location "in unbelievably difficult conditions," "at no time is the presence of the mountain really felt. . . . It is perhaps also true, and this is more serious, that Daquin, whose taste is so sure when it comes to the details of a sequence, lacks vigor when it comes to overall film design." The movie nevertheless had very considerable commercial success.

During the German occupation Daquin was active in the left-wing Resistance organization Front National. In 1944 the Comité de Libération du Cinéma was formed, with Daquin as secretary-general. He also served on the editorial committee of their clandestine publication, *Les Lettres française.* "We were not heroes," Daquin said, "but it could be said that it was thanks to us there was no collaboration [in the film industry]. . . . But what was most important for us was to seize the newsreel resources at the Liberation. A team of Resistance technicians . . . prepared for this six months in advance. Thanks to this preparation, within twenty-four hours we had everything we needed and were able to make a film [*Le Journal de la Résistance*] on the Liberation of Paris that would have been impossible otherwise." Just after the Liberation Daquin was elected secretary-general of the filmworkers' union (the Syndicat des Techniciens du Film), serving in that capacity until 1962. He was also named president of the Coopérative Générale du Cinéma, which produced a number of films after the war, including René Clément's *La Bataille du rail*.

The Comité and the union occupied Daquin full-time from the end of 1943 until 1946. By that time, he said, "I was broke; I needed to make a film straightaway." He chose a play by Victorien Sardou, set in the sixteenth century and dealing with themes of occupation, resistance, and treason—the conflict between public duty and private life. With Pierre Bost and Charles Spaak, Daquin adapted the play to bring out the contemporary parallels, so that the Prince of Orange, for example, is given lines very similar to those spoken by the contemporary liberator, General de Gaulle. With a cast headed by Pierre Blanchar, Jean Desailly, and Maria Mauban, and using sets originally constructed for Jacques Feyder's 1935 film *La Kermesse heroïque,* Daquin in *Patrie* at times achieved "a nobility of tone, a poetry, and an authentically epic grandeur," but did not always manage to escape melodrama. The same year, 1946, he made a medium-length documentary for the French Communist Party, *Nous continuons la France.*

Daquin's adaptation of Jean Prévost's novel *Les Frères Bouquinquant* (1947) was dominated by Madeleine Robinson's full-blooded performance as a woman loved by two brothers and responsible for the death of one of them. She suffers imprisonment and remorse and is finally freed when she promises her confessor (Jean Vilar) that she will never again see the surviving brother, the man she loves. Daquin said in his *Film Dope* interview that the story contained "some of my personal contradictions of the time. This conflict between religious and secular ethics and . . . the fact that the plot concerned a kid—it corresponded with something very subjective and profound in me at the time, the desire to have a kid." Asked why he had chosen the novelist Roger Vailland to write the adaptation, he said it was "because I always look for a collaborator who will fight me. . . . The good thing about us—he always said this—was that we were so completely different."

The film that followed, *Le Point du jour* (1948), is regarded by many critics as Daquin's masterpiece. He said he made it because he came from northern France and "wanted to show that there were poetry in the North too," and also "because my political evolution led me to want to make a film about the working class." He and his coauthor Vladimir Pozner spent two months in the coal-mining country of the North, researching, interviewing workers, and every night writing up the notes from which they drew their script.

Le Point du jour is set among the grim-faced houses of the mining villages in the Pas-de-Calais. It was shot on location by André Bac and two cameramen and uses nonprofessionals drawn from the region together with such professionals as Jean Desailly, René Lefevre, Jean-Pierre Grenier, Loleh Bellon, and Michel Piccoli. Weaving together a number of stories to create a panorama of different social groups, the film focuses primarily on three characters: the engineer Larzac (Desailly), who comes from a comfortable background but does his best to adapt to life among the miners; Marles (Grenier), the miners' delegate, who is portrayed as the heroic "new man" of the times; and Marie (Bellon), the miner's daughter who refuses to exchange her job at the mines for the post of housewife. What most impressed the critics, however, was not the film's narrative content but the documentary realism with which it portrayed daily life—the miners' shanties coming to life at dawn, the descent into the mines, romances, generational conflicts, the rich legacy of strikes.

Georges Sadoul, who thought it the best French film of the year, wrote that *Point du jour* was "one of the rare films that has gotten beyond the facile travesties of populism to show [genuinely] popular reality. For that reason it ranks at the forefront of the avant-garde in every sense of this word." One of the very few French films to show the clear influence of Italian neorealism, it was too grimly naturalistic to have much popular success (and poorly distributed in any case), and its commercial failure ended any hope there might have been for a neorealist movement in France.

In Louis Marcorelles' words, "Louis Daquin was to pay dearly for his political commitment." He encountered a good deal of official obstruction in the filming of *Le Point du jour*, partly on account of documentary about a coal miners' strike that he made at the same time. According to Daquin, when he took on this film, *La Grande lutte des mineurs* (1948) for the CGT, "it wasn't the director who went there but the militant. It was because of militancy that I turned to documentary." In fact, the resulting film was so militant that the Ministry of the Interior confiscated all the prints at the laboratory. The following year Daquin made another *engagé* short, *La Bataille de la vie*, for the Mouvement de la Paix, together with a wildly different commercial assignment, an undistinguished remake of Marcel L'Herbier's exotic 1931 thriller *Le Parfum de la dame en noir*, based on a Gaston Leroux novel. This was followed by *Maître après Dieu* (*Skipper Next to God*, 1951), adapted by Daquin and Jan de Hartog (with uncredited help from Jorge Semprun) from the latter's play about a cynical and truculent ship's captain (Pierre Brasseur) who discovers respect for humanity in the course of a desperate journey from Hamburg to Egypt in 1938 with a cargo of Jewish refugees.

In 1951–1954 Daquin made French versions of several films by Polish directors, most of them shorts. The Cold War had begun, and because of Daquin's Communist allegiance, none of the French studios would employ him. During the same period he wrote a screenplay on the Paris Commune with Jorge Semprun that was never used, and directed a play by Roger Vailland that was banned after two showings. He also adapted and directed a radio production of Abel Bonnard's *Agamemnon,* with Madeleine Robinson as Clytemnestra.

It was not until 1954 that Daquin directed his next feature film, and he had to go to Austria to do that. It was an adaptation of Maupassant's novel *Bel Ami,* scripted by Daquin, Vailland, and Vladimir Pozner, with music by Hans Eisler. The film was made simultaneously in French and German versions, the former starring Jean Danet, Anne Vernon, and Renée Faure. In his adaptation, Daquin is said to have stressed social and political motives more than the psychological determinism on which the novel is based. The result was generally admired as "a ruthless, uncompromising, completely fascinating study of a man who owes his money and his power entirely to the women" he has seduced and discarded, set against a background of corruption in nineteenth-century French society and politics. In France, however, the picture was banned for two years and even then released only after extensive cuts.

In 1955 Daquin wrote another scenario with Vailland, an adaptation of a Victor Hugo novel, but that also failed to find a producer. Daquin made his next picture in Romania, *Ciulinii Baraganului* (*The Thistles of the Baragan,* 1957), based on a novel by Panait Istrati. It views the Romanian peasant revolution of 1907 through the eyes of a boy from the Baragan plain. He sees his father starve to death and eventually joins the uprising, surviving the brutal repression that followed to fight again. Still unable to find work in France, Daquin then went to East Germany to make *Trübe Wasser* (*Les Arrivistes,* 1959), adapted from Balzac's novel *La Rabouilleuse* and starring Madeleine Robinson. His last feature followed a few years later in 1963. Another literary adaptation, based on a novel by Jean Charles, *La Foire aux cancres* is a comedy of disasters in a suburban school strongly reminiscent of *Nous les gosses.*

The same year Daquin made a French version of a long documentary by the Soviet director Ro-

man Karmen, and in 1964 a documentary of his own, *Naissance d'une cité,* for the municipality of Gennevilliers. None of the scripts he wrote thereafter were realized, but he served as production director on several films by others, accepted a number of acting roles, and conceived and coauthored the twelve-part television series *Café du Square* (1968). In 1970 he joined the faculty of IDHEC (Institut des Hautes Études Cinématographiques) and in 1970 became director of studies, a post he retained until 1977. In 1960 he had published a book on the film, *Le Cinéma, notre métier,* and in 1980, shortly before his death, came his autobiographical novel *On ne tait pas ses silences* (roughly, "Nothing Speaks Louder Than Silence").

Daquin made an auspicious beginning that seemed to promise achievements comparable to those of Becker and Clouzot, who began their careers at about the same time. As *Film Dope* says, "his refusal to compromise made him the main victim of the Cold War in the French cinema." It was the same quality that accounted for the integrity of his best films, *Nous les gosses* and *Le Point du jour.* Daquin was married in 1953 to the actress Clara Gancarska and had two sons.

FILMS: (with Gerhard Lamprecht) Le Joueur (French-language version of Lamprecht's Der Spieler), 1938; Nous les gosses (Us Kids/ Portrait of Innocence), 1941; Madame et le mort, 1942; Le Voyageur de la Toussaint, 1943; Premier de cordée, 1944; Patrie, 1946; Nous continuons la France, 1946 (short); Les Frères Bouquinquant, 1947; La Grande Lutte des mineurs, 1948 (short); Le Point du jour, 1948; Le Parfum de la dame en noir, 1949; La Bataille de la vie/L'Oiseau blanc, 1949 (short); Maître après Dieu (Skipper Next to God), 1951; Bel Ami, 1954; Ciulinii Baraganului (Les Chardons du Baragan/The Thistles of Baragan), 1957; Trübe Wasser (Les Arrivistes), 1959; Machine Mon Ami, 1960 (short); Parallèles, 1962 (short); La Foire aux cancres, 1963; Naissance d'une cité, 1964 (short); Café du Square (TV), 1968.

ABOUT: Bazin, A. French Cinema of the Occupation and Resistance, 1981; Daquin, L. Le Cinéma, notre métier, 1960; Daquin, L. On ne tait pas ses silences, 1980 (autobiographical novel). *Periodicals*—L'Avant Scène du Cinéma April 1 1978; Cinéma (France) January 1979, November 1980; Cinématographe May 1978; Film Dope April 1976; Image et Son May 1970, November 1980; Télérama January 31, 1971; La Vie ouvrière November 6, 1980.

D'ARRAST, HARRY (Henri d'Abbadie d'Arrast) (1893 or 1897–March 16, 1968), American director, was born in Argentina into an aristocratic French family which held the château of Échaux in the Basque region of the Basses-Pyrénées.

Why d'Arrast's parents were in Argentina at the time of his birth, or when they returned to France, has not so far been recorded. According to Herman G. Weinberg's article about him in *Film Comment* (Fall 1969)—the only source of detailed information about the director—d'Arrast was educated at the Lycée de Sailly in Paris and at an extremely unsmart British university, Bradford, adding English to the two languages he already spoke perfectly, French and Spanish.

D'Arrast served with the French army as a second lieutenant during World War I and was decorated after an action in which he was badly wounded. In Paris after the war, he met the French-born director George Fitzmaurice, who urged him to come to Hollywood. D'Arrast arrived there in the spring of 1922.

According to Weinberg, d'Arrast was "a charming young fellow, handsome, debonair, very 'high society,' a Count [?], clubman, who had already met many famous Americans in Deauville, Monte Carlo and such places," and in Hollywood was "received everywhere." In 1922 he played a bit part in Sam Wood's *My American Wife* and instructed the cast in the mysteries of the tango—perhaps the first tango in Hollywood. Chaplin was charmed by him, employing him as technical adviser on *A Woman of Paris* (1923) and as his assistant on *The Gold Rush* (1925).

Through Chaplin, d'Arrast met William Randolph Hearst and Marion Davies, becoming a regular visitor of Xanadu, their palatial mansion at San Simeon. Nothing came of plans for him to direct a film for Hearst's Cosmopolitan Pictures, but in 1927, in spite of his inexperience, d'Arrast was signed by Paramount to direct four silent features.

It seems that he owed this break to his friend Adolphe Menjou, whom he had met while working on *A Woman of Paris* and who starred also in d'Arrast's first Paramount assignment, *Service for Ladies* (1927). In this story by Ernest Vajda and Benjamin Glazer, Menjou plays Albert, a Parisian *maître d'hôtel*—a genius whose skills as a blender of sauces and fondler of egos make him the confidant of millionaires and kings. Infatuated by an American debutante (Kathryn Carver), Albert follows her incognito to Switzerland, where she is entranced by his apparent intimacy with visiting royalty. A happy ending seems imminent but, in a denouement of Molnaresque bittersweet irony, the couple part, each supposing the other to be of unapproachable social eminence.

Weinberg saw the influence of both Chaplin and Lubitsch in this picture, citing scenes like the one in which Albert "embarks on a description of the house specialty, *canard bigarade flambée*, so rhapsodically . . . that both he and the guest are almost moved to tears. But a minute later, when Albert instructs the waiter what to bring the party, it is summed up briefly and perfunctorily in the simple word 'Duck.' And the carving of a duck by Albert is an artistic proceeding wherein he reveals his thorough knowledge of the bird's anatomy, and, for performing this task, he is wont to stick a monocle in his eye."

"There are a thousand little touches throughout," wrote Mordaunt Hall, "which may be attributed in part to the scenarists . . . and certainly in even greater part to the director." Richard Watts agreed that this was "a deft and engaging light comedy, skillfully directed by Harry d'Arrast and brilliantly acted. It stands in the high and select company of [Mal St. Clair's] *The Grand Duchess and the Waiter* and the Lubitsch comedies. . . . Throughout the mood of deft high comedy has been . . . maintained, and to this has been added just a touch of half-ironic sentimentality that is delightful." The film was remade in 1932 by Alexander Korda, with Leslie Howard in the lead.

D'Arrast's highly successful debut was followed the same year by two more comedies. *A Gentleman of Paris* (the title obviously promising a companion piece to Chaplin's *A Woman of Paris*) was a Charles Sprague screenplay, with titles by Herman Mankiewicz. Menjou starred again, this time as a philandering marquis constantly extricating himself with a mixture of cunning and audacity from dangerous confrontations with cuckolded husbands and irate fathers. He almost receives his just deserts when his faithful valet (Nicholas Soussanin) learns that his master's conquests include his own former wife. The marquis is sent off to a card game unaware that a spare ace lurks up his sleeve. When it is discovered, another "gentleman" hands the marquis a pistol so that he may do the "right thing." A shot is in due course heard, but it emerges that the marquis has his own notion of what the right thing is.

André Sennwald of the New York *Times* thought that the movie "fell far short of *Service for Ladies*, a work as close to perfection as any . . . audience has a right to expect." Other contemporary reviewers disagreed, finding *A Gentleman of Paris* "a work of sophisticated allure, of imaginative direction and intelligent fun."

Fifty years later, in his notes for a season of vintage Paramount pictures, John Gillett saw in this one "not only a total mastery of silent techniques, but a remarkable range of tone and attitudes. Beginning in a somewhat Lubitsch-like style with a neatly sketched-in portrait of the Marquis as an eternal philanderer, the characterization slowly becomes more complex and blacker with the valet's discovery . . . and the subsequent portrait of a ritual-bound high society. . . . The ending is extremely bleak and cynical, with everyone doing what is expected of them and yet, at the same time, destroying their outward veneer of respectability."

Gillett thought the climactic card game "marvelously conveyed without titles, and staged with an unerring eye for meaningful setups with the two opposing figures surrounded by the curious guests forming a claustrophobic circle around them. Like Lubitsch in his silent period, d'Arrast was clearly a master at conveying witty nuances through a brief close-up, or simply a direct cut from one scene to another. . . . This kind of subtle by-play cannot be achieved without a perfect rapport between director and players. . . . A final nod of praise to Harold Rosson's impeccably shaded lighting . . . and to the uncredited art director (could it have been Hans Dreier?) who brings to the interiors just the right tone of well-upholstered, decadent, easy living which is really what the film is all about."

D'Arrast's third film with Menjou was *Serenade,* another Ernest Vajda screenplay, set this time in Vienna. Menjou is a married composer of operettas whose music, though successful, lacks feeling until he falls in love with a passionate singer. That therapy accomplished, the errant hero is returned to the straight and narrow by his benevolently scheming wife. This "silken production" persuaded John S. Cohen of the New York *Sun* that d'Arrast was "clearly the most intelligent and the cleverest director in the jungles of Hollywood. Taste, charm, a flair for romance and exquisite humor . . . . Moreover, photography, lighting, camera placement and tempo [are all] of the highest order. . . . A graduate of Chaplin's studios in Hollywood, an obviously cultivated and talented man, he brings a new note to movieland. One feels that, for the first time, an adult intelligence, an adult sense of humor . . . have at last been discovered in a director who is also a practical technician."

The last of d'Arrast's silent comedies for Paramount was *The Magnificent Flirt* (1928), adapted by the director and Jean de Limur from a minor French stage comedy called *Maman.* Florence Vidor starred as a coquettish lady of Paris whose flirtations embarrass her daughter (Loretta Young) and eventually threaten the girl's marriage plans. At this point, *maman* recalls her maternal duty and settles down, marry-

ing her future son-in-law's uncle (Albert Conti). This frothy entertainment was as warmly received as its predecessors, praised for the freshness and originality of the director's eye, the "artistic highlights and shadows," and "soft, velvety photography" that "catches up the sheen of exquisite gowns, the steely surfaces of modernistic settings and furnishings, and turns them into eye-filling spectacles." Cohen declared that "the director can actually photograph a telephone in close-up and make it a thing of beauty."

D'Arrast moved on to Fox for *Dry Martini* (1928), about a middle-aged American (Albert Gran), a refugee from Prohibition, who is happily ensconced at Harry's American Bar when his daughter (Mary Astor) shows up to disturb his single-minded pursuit of self-indulgence. The girl promptly becomes involved with a villainous French artist (Albert Conti) but is retrieved for married virtue by a decent if dim-witted young American (Matt Moore), allowing Papa to resume his stool at Harry's with an untroubled conscience.

For André Sennwald, the movie was "rendered cheerful by the happy faculty of refusing to take seriously such worthy items as the Younger Generation, the Divorce Question and the Kept Woman. It should be stated at once that the greater attributes of the picture are those given by the deft directorial touch of Harry d'Arrast." The director also refused to take seriously the cinematic convention that the hero gets the girl by beating up the villain; his all-American hero is clobbered by the villain (and a *foreign* villain, at that) and in this unorthodox manner wins the heroine's sympathetic heart, an innovation that Richard Watts found "not only pleasant, but unparalleled."

D'Arrast's friend Monta Bell, then a producer at Paramount's Long Island studio, invited him back to Paramount for his first credited talkie, *Laughter* (1930). The flimsy story was concocted by d'Arrast and Douglas Doty, the excellent dialogue by Donald Ogden Stewart. Nancy Carroll plays a former chorine married to a rich financier (Frank Morgan). She runs into an old flame, a struggling composer (Fredric March), and begins to regret her choice. The story then takes an unexpectedly dark turn with the suicide of another character (Glenn Anders) who has been dallying with Carroll's stepdaughter; as one surprised modern critic wrote, "this is shot realistically and convincingly, with no last-real cop-out." After this, the heroine abandons the high life and runs off to Paris with the composer.

"Out of the smallest things d'Arrast made delight," wrote Herman G. Weinberg; "when Nancy Carroll puts out her hands to receive several diamond bracelets from her maid, she places her wrists together with a tired smile as if she were about to be handcuffed, for that's what her jeweled bracelets are." And at the end, sitting with March at a café table, Carroll is eyeing an elegant woman climbing into her chauffeured limousine: "March watches her wistfully watching the woman. Then Carroll turns back to him and breaking out into an innocent smile says, 'I didn't say anything.' And they both laugh. End. It was one of the most delicious moments in the cinema."

John Gillett was equally impressed. "Nowhere is there any forced moral judgment," he wrote; "the heroine is basically a gold-digger, the hero feels no scruples in breaking up the marriage, but behind all the larking lurk the pressures of class and the lure of rich respectability. The overall tone has the veneer of Lubitsch without the nudging visual juxtapositions; the direction of the players is unobtrusively precise and pointed. A totally adult entertainment, in fact, with the camera constantly catching the characters in little gestures of surprise and pleasure, as in the scene when March barges into the house, cadges some food from the hostile butler, sits down at the piano, and finally persuades the butler to reveal hidden musical talent by joining him in a duet." Gillett found much in this movie that prefigured the comedies of Cukor, Hawks, and McCarey, and thought d'Arrast "particularly forward-looking in what could now be called 'spatial relationships.' He invariably composes in depth, starting from the rear of a room and moving forward to catch two or three figures in midclose shot, as in the tense conversation just before the hapless lover's suicide when he and the two girls are framed before a window in a half-circle and the scene is played entirely with backs to the camera."

At about this time—whether before or after *Laughter* is not clear—Samuel Goldwyn hired d'Arrast to direct *Raffles* (1930), an adaptation by the dramatist Sidney Howard of E. W. Hornung's stories about an upper-crust jewel thief. The cast was headed by Ronald Colman and Kay Francis, and d'Arrast had both George Barnes and Gregg Toland as cinematographers. After a row with Goldwyn, d'Arrast was fired and the movie was credited to George Fitzmaurice, who completed it. The result was "a film of taste and charm," but it is not known how much of it can be attributed to d'Arrast.

In 1932, after a couple of idle years, d'Arrast was taken on by Joseph Schenck to direct *Hallelujah, I'm a Bum* (1933) for 20th Century. He quit during rehearsals, when the studio refused to replace Al Jolson with his own choice for

the lead, Fred Astaire. Thus, for the second time within three years, d'Arrast lost a commission on account of what his friend Robert Florey called his "sensitivity"—his aristocratic refusal to be dictated to (least of all, perhaps, by a former errand boy like Schenck).

Almost at once, however, d'Arrast was offered a much more congenial assignment by David Selznick at RKO, an adaptation by Ben Hecht of *Topaze,* the hugely successful stage comedy by Marcel Pagnol. John Barrymore starred as the naive professor at a French boys' school who teaches his students that honesty is the best policy, and believes it, until his scrupulousness costs him his job. Topaze's disillusionment is completed when he goes to work for a corrupt businessman and he winds up a more ruthless and successful tycoon than his employer, aided by the latter's beautiful mistress (Myrna Loy).

Photographed by Lucien Andriot and with a score by Max Steiner, *Topaze* seemed to William K. Everson "one of the most successful Hollywood translations of a French play or film . . . both top Barrymore and top d'Arrast. . . . Barrymore, admirably subdued, playing with both charm and poignancy, seems a perfect teammate for the light-as-a-feather d'Arrast. . . . Stage-derived it may be, but it is always subtly visual."

D'Arrast made his last film in Spain, a version of Pedro de Alarcón's long short story *The Three-Cornered Hat,* itself derived from an old ballad. The film was produced by a company set up by d'Arrast in conjunction with his codirector, Ricardo Soriano. D'Arrast's wife Eleanor Boardman played the miller's beautiful and virtuous wife, Allan Jeayes the licentious mayor who gets his comeuppance when he tries to seduce her. Made in English, Spanish, and French versions, the picture was a critical success but a box-office flop.

A contemporary reviewer predicted as much, praising the film in *Cinema News* for its "rare humorous savour achieved by brilliant and sensitive handling of simple and hearty comic situations. . . . Pervasive lyric quality mingled with rich and delicious touches of humour and characterizations, enhanced by superb pictorial compositions of authentic Spanish sun-drowsy village and pastoral scenes. . . . Excellent leading portrayals and sure minor characterizations; clever dramatic use of spontaneous rhythmic dances; sparing use of well-written English dialogue" and concluding that "it is so much above the heads of the average patrons as to be definitely out of the popular box-office class."

Back in Hollywood, d'Arrast was engaged by Pickford-Lasky Productions but never employed by the newly formed company. He next interested 20th Century–Fox in a version of Rostand's *Cyrano de Bergerac,* but that proposal also came to nothing. D'Arrast returned to France but left again with the outbreak of World War II, which he spent in idleness in Hollywood. In 1946 he went back to Europe, trying without success to put together various deals in England, France, and Spain. His friend Donald Ogden Stewart had said in 1930 that d'Arrast directed *Laughter* "as he directed his life . . . with wit, understanding, control, compassion, and great whole-hearted laughter." By 1946, according to another friend, "he seemed to have lost his ambition, he was not the same 'old Harry.'"

Divorced from Eleanor Boardman, he spent his last years living alone in a Monte Carlo hotel, scraping a precarious living at the roulette tables. He died there at the age of seventy-one and was buried at his family's tumbledown château.

John Gillett called Harry d'Arrast "one of the cinema's most mordant (and entertaining) dissectors of moral codes," while William K. Everson found it "incredible that a director with such superb talkies as . . . [*Topaze,*] *Raffles,* and *Laughter* behind him, should suddenly find himself unwanted in Hollywood." Part of the reason for this was no doubt the aristocratic intransigence that went along with d'Arrast's famous charm and style.

Another (and related) reason for his eventual failure in Hollywood is implicit in Herman G. Weinberg's admiring assessment of his work. Weinberg calls him "a master (I would say, an instinctive one) of pace and cutting, with never a frame too much, in which the slightest gesture counted and the human face—most important of all—reflected that joy of living that seems today to have gone out of the world. . . . His films were comedies . . . of manners . . . done in high comic style—as if the cinema were not a mass medium but a patrician one, an aristocratic and cerebral one."

FILMS: Service for Ladies, 1927; A Gentleman of Paris, 1927; Serenade, 1927; The Magnificent Flirt, 1928; Dry Martini, 1928; Laughter, 1930; (uncredited; completed by George Fitzmaurice) Raffles, 1930; Topaze, 1933; (with Ricardo Soriano) The Three-Cornered Hat/It Happened in Spain, 1934 (also made in Spanish as La Traviesa molinera and in French as Le Tricorne/ La meunière débauchée).

ABOUT: Thomson, D. A Biographical Dictionary of the Cinema, 1980. *Periodicals*—Film Comment Fall 1969; Film Dope April 1976; Films and Filming October 1982.

*DASSIN, JULES (December 18, 1911–), American director, scenarist, and producer, was born Julius Dassin in Middletown, Connecticut. He is one of the eight children of Samuel Dassin, a barber, and the former Berthe Vogel, both Russian Jewish immigrants. The family moved to New York City when Dassin was still a small child and settled in Harlem. "We were so poor it was ridiculous," he says. "At that time Harlem wasn't entirely black. There were about three or four minority groups living in the ghetto, at each other's throats all the time: Jewish, Negro, Irish, and some Italian, divided among themselves and taking out their wrath and their poverty upon each other. I was conscious of this, and of the daily problem of eating. And it was cold . . . it was always so cold."

Dassin was educated at Morris High School in the Bronx. It is clear that he was already interested in the theatre and show business—a passion apparently inherited from his grandfather, who dabbled in local productions while working as the village wigmaker in Russia. Upon graduation he spent two years traveling throughout Europe to study theatre while supporting himself with odd jobs. His "most beautiful memory" of this vast tour was "a King Lear heard in Yiddish in Moscow, from the mouth of Michoels, an actor who was almost a dwarf but who was thirty feet tall dramatically." Returning to New York in 1936, he learned Yiddish in order to act with the Yiddish theatre companies that flourished at the time. He also joined the Artef Players, a Jewish socialist collective, and appeared in their productions of *The Good Soldier Schweik* (1937) and *Clinton Street* (1939). In 1937 he played the lead in *Revolt of the Beavers,* a Marxist musical for children staged by the WPA Federal Theater Project. For five summers during this period Dassin worked as entertainment director of a Jewish camp in the Catskills, where, among other things, he engaged the young campers in productions of Shakespeare. At this time he was briefly a member of the Communist party but, according to his own account, left it in 1939.

By 1940, Dassin was writing for Kate Smith's radio show and adapting literary classics for fifteen-minute radio broadcasts. His adaptation of Gogol's story "The Overcoat" drew the attention of Broadway producer Martin Gabel, who then gave him his first assignment as a director with *Medicine Show,* a plea for socialized medicine staged as a "living newspaper." John Mason Brown wrote that the piece was "directed with uncommon felicity," and although it was not particularly successful, it brought Dassin to the attention of the RKO talent scouts.

In 1941 he was invited to Hollywood by RKO as an apprentice director. For six months he did

°das´ in

JULES DASSIN

nothing but "sit and observe" the shooting of Alfred Hitchcock's *Mr. and Mrs. Smith* and Garson
Kanin's *They Knew What They Wanted*, receiving $200 a week for the privilege. Not surpris-
ingly, he learned most from Hitchcock, though
he felt greater rapport with Kanin. Hitchcock
liked "to amuse himself at the expense of innocents. He would never print a take without
shouting in my direction, 'Is that all right for
you?'—and I would blush and hide. But he invited me to lunch very often and with great patience and kindness he would draw all over the
tablecloth the different technical details he was
explaining to me."

At the end of this well-paid period of high
quality instruction, Dassin was unaccountably
fired by RKO. He hung around Hollywood for
six months, looking for work, and was about to
give up "when an extraordinary circumstance
presented itself. I still don't know why . . . but
suddenly I was on the MGM lot and everybody
seemed to think I was a nephew of Louis B.
Mayer." Dassin had never met Louis B. Mayer
but, offered a chance to show his paces as a director, saw no reason to argue and made three
short films—one each about Artur Rubenstein
and Pablo Casals, and an adaptation of Edgar
Allan Poe's story "The Tell-Tale Heart."

Directing the latter, Dassin says, "was a blind
experience. . . . I didn't know what the hell I
was doing." He was not yet on the MGM payroll
and would not be until the film had been seen
and approved. But "it was the racetrack season. . . . Three months went by and nobody
saw it and I was *starving*." But Dassin's extraordinary luck held: one day the movie theatre next

to the MGM lot lost a newsreel and, to fill out the
program, borrowed a print of *The Tell-Tale
Heart*. It was an immediate success, was widely
released, and won a number of prizes.

Dassin's *Tell-Tale Heart*, starring Joseph
Schildkraut, is regarded by some critics as the
best of the several screen versions of the story.
Gordon Gow, in his two-part article about Dassin in *Films and Filming* (February and March
1970), called it "a small masterpiece of accelerating tension: emphasis upon the dead eye which
seemed to stare at the non-hero and drive him
madder and madder until he made it dead for
real—and then was assaulted by the throbbing
heart in his head, the pulse of conscience."

Dassin was promptly given a seven-year contract by MGM and promoted to feature director.
He was put to work on a string of routine comedies (*The Affairs of Martha, Young Ideas*) and
war films (*Nazi Agent*, in which Conrad Veidt
played a Nazi consul and also his twin brother,
and *Reunion*, with Joan Crawford and John
Wayne as heroes of the French Resistance). The
latter was a popular success, and so was *The
Canterville Ghost* (1944), an amiable if rather
ponderous comedy based on the story by Oscar
Wilde but updated to World War II. Robert
Young leads the platoon of American Rangers
quartered at Canterville Castle, Margaret
O'Brien is the six-year-old Lady Jessica, and
Charles Laughton the ghost. Dissatisfied with
MGM's scenario, Dassin had sought to revise it,
but had run into resistance from the studio. In
hopes of getting out of his contract, he staged a
one-man strike for fourteen months, but MGM
refused to give in. When Dassin was finally
forced to resume work, he quickly turned out
the sentimental comedy *A Letter for Evie*
(1945), about a correspondence between a soldier and a girl who have never met, and *Two
Smart People* (1946), in which Lucille Ball and
John Hodiak star as government bond thieves.

At that point Dassin left MGM and joined the
producer-scenarist Mark Hellinger at Universal.
It was this partnership that led to Dassin's first
feature of real quality, *Brute Force* (1947).
Scripted by another Hellinger protégé, Richard
Brooks, and photographed by William Daniels,
it is set in a jail ruled by a sadistic chief guard
(Hume Cronyn) who carries out his beatings to
the music of Wagner. The audience's sympathy
is with the prisoners, led by Burt Lancaster. In
spite of cuts imposed by Universal, *Brute Force*
remains an extremely violent film, the brutality
of the guards breeding such simmering hatred
among the inmates that their bloody vengeance
in the climactic attempted break-out seems inevitable. Even critics who were shocked by the

film were impressed by its grim realism and un-remitting pace—one called it "harrowingly exciting," and there was much praise for the per-formances Dassin had extracted from Lancaster and Hume Cronyn.

Dassin's next picture, *Naked City* (1948), was the last produced by Mark Hellinger, who re-corded the narration but died of a heart attack just after the shooting began. Set in New York City, it opens in the early hours of a summer morning. We watch the city come slowly to life, streetcleaners and milkmen going about their business, and then a cleaning woman finds her young employer murdered. A police lieutenant (Barry Fitzgerald) and his assistant (Don Taylor) go to work on the case, using neither deductive genius nor violence, but simply plodding around the hot streets asking questions until, little by lit-tle, the truth begins to emerge.

The real star of the film, as the French critic Georges Sadoul remarked at the time, is the city itself, lovingly photographed with a concealed camera by William Daniels. *Naked City* was not the first Hollywood thriller to be shot on location and in the documentary style, but it was the first movie made in this way to become a major hit. However, *Naked City*, which had been coscript-ed by Albert Maltz, one of the Hollywood Ten, had also been censored by the studio in the final edit: "I wouldn't say that they cut it," Dassin told *Cahiers du cinéma* in 1955, "but that they tore out the heart of the film." He walked out of the New York premiere to protest the studio's inter-ference, but the film itself was a tremendous suc-cess, warmly and almost universally praised for its authenticity and pace, its detailed sketches of minor characters, and its "vivid and realistic por-trayal of ordinary American people . . . going about their daily life." It inspired a long-running television series and, more important, overcame the studios' resistance to location shooting, end-ing the reign of the studio-made *film noir* and launching the vogue for semi-documentary thrillers.

How much credit for *Brute Force* and *Naked City* belongs to Dassin, how much to Mark Hel-linger, is not clear. Certainly Dassin's next two thrillers, made for other producers, were inferi-or, but this may also have reflected his growing contempt for the movie industry. The better of the two was *Thieves' Highway* (20th Century–Fox, 1949). Richard Conte stars as a World War II vet who invests everything he has in a truck and a load of early-season apples and sets off on the two-day journey to San Francisco. He has two aims—to get his apples to market and to avenge his father, who has been robbed and maimed by a produce racketeer (Lee J. Cobb).

The film is a violent and exciting account of his journey but lacks the warmth and humanity of *Naked City*.

By this time Dassin was feeling the pressures of the blacklist. "There was a studio head who had the courage to buy the rights to an Albert Maltz novel, *The Journey of Simon McIver*, for me. He had no doubts about the scandal that would create. . . . I spoke on the radio . . . I fought back. . . . Then the studio head told me, 'Beat it. Get yourself to London fast. There's a film to make there.' That's how I made *Night and the City*." Based on Gerald Kersh's novel about wrestling racketeers, *Night and the City* (Fox, 1950) starred Gene Tierney and Richard Widmark; it met with little enthusiasm in En-gland (although it was well received in France) and became a film that Dassin has "chosen to forget." He spent the rest of the year in Europe, writing plays, scenarios, and short stories.

It was not the failure of *Night and the City* that ended Dassin's Hollywood career, but the fact that in 1952 Edward Dmytryk and Frank Tuttle named him as a Communist in testimony before the House Committee on Un-American Activities. With the studios closed to him, Dassin made one 16mm documentary for the "Meet the Masters" series on great musicians, then turned to Broadway (where he had staged two produc-tions in 1948), starting work on the unsuccessful revue *Two's Company* (1952), starring Bette Da-vis in her first song-and-dance role. He was still at work on the revue when he was subpoenaed by the committee to testify, on those grounds se-curing a postponement. According to Dassin, he was eventually informed that his testimony had been "postponed indefinitely." This did not alter the fact that he was unemployable in the United States, and in 1953 he set off for France with his wife (the former Beatrice Launer) and their three children.

Things were at first not much better in Eu-rope. Dassin had been invited to France to direct a Fernandel comedy called *Public Enemy No. One*; he was fired two days before shooting was to begin, apparently because the female lead, Zsa-Zsa Gabor, had questioned Dassin's alleged Communist ties, and when the producer started making inquiries in the United States, it became clear that American distributors would blacklist the movie if Dassin's name appeared on the credits. He wrote some plays and some poetry and got into debt, but says that his years on the blacklist were not wasted: "I had time to think and feel. I began those years as a technician. I came out of them an artist." And in the end Das-sin found a French producer willing to back a low-budget movie based on an Auguste le Breton thriller. The result was *Du Rififi chez les hommes* (*Rififi*, 1955).

Rififi is the prototypical caper movie, showing how a well-characterized and likable gang of jewel thieves execute a carefully planned robbery, thus attracting the attention of a ruthless syndicate. Photographed by Philippe Agostini and with music by Georges Auric, the film stars Jean Servais, Carl Möhner, and Robert Manuel. Dassin himself collaborated on the script and appears (under the pseudonym Perlo Vita) as a dapper safecracker with a weakness for women.

One critic found *Rififi* inferior to *The Asphalt Jungle* in that "its relationships are not so densely structured and it lacks the formal economy of the Huston picture. But it is still an intensely exciting film, and the long sequence of the robbery, with the criminals silently engrossed in the carrying out of their meticulously detailed plan, is masterly. The recognisable pattern of natural reactions to a normal working day creates a wonderful irony in view of the nature of the work. . . . It is this absorbed dedication in the plan's brilliant detail which creates such a strong sense of personal involvement." Virginia Graham agreed that the half-hour robbery sequence, which is entirely without dialogue or music, "builds up so potent an atmosphere of excitement that it becomes difficult to breathe." Others were reminded of the documentary technique of *Naked City* by the film's view of what Gavin Lambert called "a grey, busy, ordinary Paris, full of anonymous figures hurrying along streets nearly always glistening with rain."

Rififi brought Dassin the prize as best director at Cannes and became the most profitable French film ever made up to that time; it is also said to have inspired several imitative robberies. Dassin has said that making the picture was very difficult because he was still learning French: "I sometimes ask myself whether so much of the film was silent because of my own lack of French." However, Gordon Gow has pointed out that the "silent" robbery, though devoid of dialogue and music, was in fact "alive with a cunning orchestration of small sounds—falling plaster and so forth—denoting danger for the thieves." (And in fact the atmosphere of tense apprehension has already been established in a preceding sequence by Auric's brilliant score, with its suggestion of hammers tapping and burglar alarms shrilling.)

At the 1956 Cannes Festival, Dassin met the Greek actress Melina Mercouri, who had just made her movie debut in Cacoyannis' *Stella*. She became Dassin's companion, his star, and in due course his wife. With the help of her father, a member of the Greek parliament, Dassin made his next film on the island of Crete. *Celui qui doit mourir* (He Who Must Die, 1958) was adapted by Dassin and Ben Barzman from Nikos Kazantzakis' novel *The Greek Passion*. It is set in 1921 in a Greek village under Turkish rule. One day the village is approached by a horde of emaciated refugees from a rebel village that has been burned by the Turks. The local priest Grigoris (Fernand Ledoux) refuses assistance for fear of angering the Tuirks, so the refugees camp on the hillside, there to starve. Slowly and almost unconsciously, the townspeople who have been chosen for parts in the annual village Passion Play begin to enact their roles in real life. Manolios (Pierre Vaneck), the timid, stuttering shepherd who has been chosen to play Christ, decides to smuggle food to the refugees. He is joined by some of his "disciples" and by the whore Katerina (Melina Mercouri)—Mary Magdalene in the play. The situation rapidly gets out of hand, both Greek and Turkish authorities become alarmed, and Manolios is eventually murdered in the church by the man cast as Judas in the play. But his death inflames the little town and inspires the people to rebellion: the film (unlike the book) ends with refugees and villagers massed behind homemade barricades, awaiting the onslaught of the Turkish army.

The film has political as well as religious implications, and at least one American hate group alleged that it was an "anti-Christian filthy film" filled with Communist and Jewish propaganda. But Isabel Quigly found *Celui qui doit mourir* "a brave film and an exciting one, intellectually as well as emotionally," and for Bosley Crowther it was "one of the most powerful films of recent years . . . one that should shock, excite and foment a lot of thinking about humanity." Another critic thought that it was too wide-ranging and unfocused in its concerns, though "a film of such rare, uncompromising honesty and uprightness that one longs to be completely won to it."

Where the Hot Wind Blows (1958), based on Roger Vailland's Goncourt novel *La Loi,* about the injustices wrought by obsolete laws in the Italian south, was made with an international cast that included Melina Mercouri, Gina Lollobrigida, Marcello Mastroianni, Yves Montand, and Pierre Brasseur. Lollobrigida and Mastroianni were foisted onto Dassin at the last moment by a producer who would have lost his backing without them. Dassin had to write them into what he thinks was originally "the best screenplay I'd ever written" or let down the actors and crew he had already assembled. The result, as he says, was "a mess . . . just sheer nightmare."

Returning to Greece, Dassin and Mercouri set up their own production company (Melinafilm) to make what became the most famous of Dassin's pictures, *Pote Tin Kyriaki* (*Never on Sunday,* 1959), scripted and produced by himself, and made on a miniscule budget of $150,000. It was to save money that Dassin cast himself in a lead role as Homer Thrace, an idealistic American academic in love with the glory that was Greece. In the Athens port of Piraeus he encounters Ilya (Mercouri), a prostitute who is nevertheless her own woman—she goes to bed only with men she likes, for whatever they can pay, and never never works on Sunday. The film is an account of Homer's fortunately unsuccessful attempt to improve and educate this exuberantly loving and carefree child of nature.

Time's reviewer wrote that "Dassin's satire is obviously directed at the United States, but his touch is light and his affection for the object of his satire unmistakable. . . . The idea is scarcely original, but Dassin expresses it in a wonderful rush of animal spirits and earthy humor." C. A. Lejeune was reminded of Restoration comedy, and Tony Crawley thought that "for all its rough-hewn faults, cinematic and artistic, it remains one of the most *zestful* of movies." *Never on Sunday* established the mercurial Mercouri as an international star, its bouzouki theme tune by Manos Hadjidakis became a major hit, and the title (of film and song) passed into many of the world's languages. The development of the Greek film industry that followed has been attributed to this vast international success.

Jacques Natteau, Dassin's photographer on *Celui qui doit mourir* and *Never on Sunday,* excelled himself in Dassin's modernized version of *Phaedra,* which has Mercouri as the libidinous wife of a shipping tycoon (Raf Vallone), in love with her stepson (Anthony Perkins). Full of decorative scenes of international high life, it seemed to most critics a well-meaning but rather foolish and forgettable movie (though several admired the impressionistic lighting of a passionate love scene in which the couple seem to be literally on fire).

There was a better press for *Topkapi* (1964), based on an Eric Ambler novel about an eccentric gang of jewel thieves and how they go about stealing an unstealable treasure from the Topkapi Palace in Istanbul. Combining a witty script, extravagant color photography (Dassin's first), and equally extravagant playing by Peter Ustinov, Robert Morley, Mercouri, and Akim Tamiroff, it also cheerfully parodies the famous caper in *Rififi* without surrendering suspense. Less successful were the next two films, a rather pretentious adaptation of Marguerite Duras' novel *10.30 p.m. Summer,* with Mercouri as an alcoholic losing her husband (Peter Finch) to a

younger woman (Romy Schneider), followed by *Survival 1967* (1968), a pro-Israeli documentary about the Arab-Israeli war made in collaboration with Irwin Shaw.

By this time it had become possible for Dassin to work again in the United States. He had done so in 1962, staging an unsuccessful play called *Isle of Children,* and five years later he and Mercouri returned with their triumphantly successful musical version of *Never on Sunday.* They were still in New York with *Illya Darling* when, in April 1967, a junta of senior army officers turned Greece into a police state. Mercouri and her husband are both intensely political people and, Dassin says, "we decided to give our lives to Greece, which seemed more important than anything else." They threw themselves wholeheartedly into propaganda and fund-raising work against the new regime, with such effect that the Colonels stripped Mercouri of her citizenship and confiscated her Greek properties. There were reported threats on her life.

Dassin's hatred of repression is visible, in a different context, in *Uptight* (1968). This was based on Liam O'Flaherty's novel of the Irish Troubles, *The Informer,* which had already inspired two films, but which is here, in the wake of Martin Luther King's assassination, translated into a drama of the black liberation movement. Dassin wrote the screenplay in collaboration with Julian Mayfield, who also plays the tormented informer Tank, and with Ruby Dee, who appears as Tank's girlfriend. A number of other parts were taken by residents of Cleveland's black ghetto, where the film was shot. The result was admired for its attempt to deal honestly with the conflict between black militants and moderates, but found sadly old-fashioned in its dialogue and clumsy in execution.

Melina Mercouri starred again in *La Promesse de l'aube* (*Promise at Dawn,* 1970), playing the indomitable mother in this adaptation of Romain Gary's autobiographical novel, set in Russia, Poland, and France. Despite various production difficulties—Polish authorities refused permission to shoot in Krakow, and Dassin broke both his legs in a fall at the French studios—the film was well received.

Around this time, Dassin and Mercouri were formally charged, along with fifty-five others, with conspiring against the Greek junta, and Dassin was summoned to stand trial in Athens (which he did not do). Three years later, following the massacre by the Greek colonels of fifteen students at Athens Polytechnic University in November 1973, Dassin undertook *The Rehearsal* (1974), a powerful reenactment of the event presented in the form of a play rehearsal. Mercouri produced the film on a minimal budget, and a number of international theatre celebrities participated without charge, among them Laurence Olivier, Maximilian Schell, Arthur Miller, and Lillian Hellman. A few days before *The Rehearsal* was to premiere in New York, the colonels were ousted from power, and the film was never released commercially.

With the fall of the junta, Dassin and Mercouri were able to return to Greece, where they divided their time between theatre and filmmaking. After staging Brecht and Weill's *Threepenny Opera* in Greek in 1975, they began working on *A Dream of Passion*, inspired by Mercouri's theatre performance in *Medea*. The film stars Mercouri as a fading actress, in Greece to play Medea, who, as a publicity stunt, visits a pathetic American woman (Ellen Burstyn) jailed for infanticide. A complex relationship develops between the two women. "Finally," wrote Richard Schickel, "the modern Medea's story gets told, the play opens, and the picture ends, leaving the audience no wiser . . . unless, of course, one is interested in some 'personal statements' about the state of the movie business, contemporary issues, and the star and director themselves that they manage to tuck in along the way. It perhaps need not be added that these are of a piece with the rest of *A Dream of Passion*—awkward, pretentious, and empty."

A Dream of Passion had its admirers, however, and so did Dassin's last film, *Circle of Two* (1980), shot in Toronto and New York, with Richard Burton as a blocked artist unblocked by his wintry fling with a teen-aged girl (Tatum O'Neal). But here again the general response was dismissive—Paul Taylor called it "an utterly redundant romance" incorporating "the sad spectacle of the veteran Dassin attempting to pass judgement on a film culture that has evidently passed him by." According to Dassin, neither the scenario nor the two stars were of his own choosing, and after this unhappy experience, he concentrated on directing plays in Greece and on writing a novel.

Dassin is not the first film director whose career has ended in a minor key. It is necessary to remember that he has made at least two innovative and extremely influential movies (*Naked City* and *Rififi*), at least one picture of intellectual weight and real emotional power (*Celui qui doit mourir*), and a whole string of superlative and humane entertainments in a variety of genres. A few hours of inflated emotion and intellectual pretension is not a great deal to set on the debit side of this record.

Dassin was divorced from Beatrice Launer in 1962 and married Melina Mercouri in 1966. His daughters Julie and Richelle are both actresses, and his son Joe Dassin was a popular singer in France until his death of heart attack at the age of forty-two. Hearing the news of Joe's death, Dassin himself suffered a heart attack, and he has not undertaken any large-scale projects since. He is said to be a mild, quiet, and unobtrusive man, white-haired and slight, with the face of "a Medici cardinal." Summing up his long career, Siclier and Levy write, "Realist poet if there is one, he views the world with a lucid eye that never lacks tenderness. . . . Dassin wouldn't know how to define himself within one film genre. . . . His talent manages to unfold equally well in the detective story (*La Cite sans voiles*), the biography (*Promesse de l'aube*), the epic fresco (*Celui qui doit mourir*), or the humorous parable (*Never on Sunday*). . . . Dassin's art has one merit above all: sincerity. If it is necessary to single out one word that defines the whole of his development and his work, that would be it."

FILMS: Artur Rubenstein, 1941 (short); Pablo Casals, 1941 (short); The Tell-Tale Heart, 1941 (short); Nazi Agent (originally called Salute to Courage), 1942; The Affairs of Martha (U.K., Once Upon a Thursday), 1942; Reunion/Reunion in France (U.K., Mademoiselle France), 1942; Young Ideas, 1943; The Canterville Ghost, 1944; A Letter for Evie, 1945; Two Smart People, 1946; Brute Force, 1947; Naked City, 1948; Thieves' Highway, 1949; Night and the City, 1950; Trio/Million Dollar Trio, 1952 (short); Du Rififi chez les hommes (Rififi), 1955; Celui qui doit mourir (He Who Must Die), 1957; La Loi (Where the Hot Wind Blows), 1958; Pote Tin Kyriaki (Never on Sunday), 1959; Phaedra, 1961; Topkapi/The Light of Day, 1964; 10:30 p.m. Summer, 1966; Survival 1967, 1968 (documentary); Uptight, 1968; La Promesse de l'aube (Promise at Dawn), 1970; The Rehearsal, 1974; A Dream of Passion, 1978; Circle of Two, 1980.

ABOUT: Arnold, F. and Esser, M. Hommage für Melina Mercouri und Jules Dassin, 1984; Current Biography, 1971; Jacob, G. Le cinéma moderne, 1964; McArthur, C. Underworld U.S.A., 1972; Mercouri, M. I Was Born Greek, 1971; Siclier, F. and Levy, J. Jules Dassin (in French), 1986. *Periodicals*—Cahiers du Cinéma April and May 1955; Cineaste Autumn 1978; Cinéma (France) January 1964, November 1964; Film Criticism Spring 1984; Film Dope April 1976; Films Illustrated May 1981; Films and Filming February and March 1970; Variety December 2, 1970.

*DAVES, DELMER (LAWRENCE) (July 24, 1904–August 17, 1977), American director, scenarist, actor, and producer, was born in San Francisco, the son of Arthur Lawrence Daves, a businessman, and the former Nan Funge. Daves' grandfather had emigrated from Ireland during

°dā´ vēz

DELMER DAVES

the American Civil War, in which he fought for the Union. After the war he made two wagon treks with the Mormons and at their invitation settled in Salt Lake City. There he went into the wagon freight business, transporting army supplies from Utah and Colorado to Sante Fe, New Mexico. He also rode with the Pony Express and had his heel shot away by Ute Indians. Daves' grandmother was born in California in 1854, two months after *her* mother had crossed by covered wagon.

The family's intimate involvement with Western history continued into Delmer Daves' generation—before he was a year old he and his parents were evacuated from San Francisco by refugee train after the great earthquake of 1905. The family settled in Los Angeles, where Daves made his movie debut at the age of ten in a film starring the future director Robert Z. Leonard. Occasional bit parts followed during his years at Los Angeles public schools and at Polytechnic High School, but at that period Daves planned a career in civil engineering. By the time he left the Polytechnic he had changed his mind, and went north to Stanford University to study law.

Daves worked his way through Stanford as a draftsman (for the City of Palo Alto), illustrator, and poster designer, and as a teacher of drawing and lettering. He also somehow found time to act in many student productions and to serve as director and business manager of the drama society and manager of the glee club. In his graduate year he was a much-praised Macbeth. By the time he left Stanford in 1926 or 1927 he had a degree in law but very little interest in it. He took a three-month vacation, wandering among

the Hopi and Navajo Indians of the South-West, and then joined the Pasadena Playhouse, along with his fellow Stanford alumnus Lloyd Nolan. Soon afterwards, deciding that his heart was after all in the movies, he left his friend behind and joined the director James Cruze as an assistant property boy.

A husky young man, six feet two inches tall, Daves made himself exceptionally useful around the old Metropolitan lot. He first attracted notice by helping out the ailing property man by lifting a piano singlehanded, and soon showed such varied talents as bit-part actor, stuntman, poster designer, and deviser of special effects that Cruze began to take an interest in him. When Daves said that his ambition was to direct, Cruze started him on his way by letting him help out in the cutting room under Mildred Johnson.

In 1928, when Cruze went to MGM, he took Daves along with him. Daves was promoted to technical director on the college movie *The Duke Steps Out* (1929) because he (unlike Cruze) had actually been to college. The same film brought him his first important acting assignment. Dissatisfied with the puny physique of the actor cast as campus boxing champion (and as Joan Crawford's temporary boyfriend), Cruze gave the role to Daves.

Daves also had Cruze to thank for his first assignment as scenarist. Campus movies were then much in vogue, and the MGM director Sam Wood wanted to make the first college talkie. Cruze sent his young protégé to Wood, who asked him for a story idea. Daves had no idea how to submit his material and handed Wood a twenty-page scenario scribbled in pencil on yellow paper. The director read it anyway, and liked it so well that he put Daves on the payroll of the MGM script department. *So This Is College* (1930), which introduced Robert Montgomery and Elliott Nugent, was a hit, and Daves subsequently worked on the scripts of Harry Pollard's *Shipmates* (1931) and George Hill's *Clear All Wires* (1932). Daves also acted in *So This Is College* and *Shipmates* but thereafter confined himself to writing—reportedly at the earnest request of Ward Bond, who complained that Daves always got the roles that would otherwise have been his.

In 1933 Daves quit MGM and took a vacation—a bicycle tour of Europe. He returned to Hollywood the following year and joined Warner Brothers, working as scenarist or coscenarist of a string of Dick Powell musicals directed by Lloyd Bacon, Frank Borzage, and Mervyn LeRoy, and also on Archie Mayo's excellent thriller *The Petrified Forest* (1936). After that Daves turned free-lance, earning credits on two more Dick Powell vehicles and on an assortment of other movies, including Leo McCarey's comedy-drama *Love Affair* (1939) and Borzage's *Stage Door Canteen* (1943). None of these pictures was particularly distinguished, but Daves was enjoying life—he worked nine months a year, traveled for the other three, and (until he married the actress Mary Lou Lender in 1938) was a much sought-after Hollywood bachelor. When the chance to direct came his way in 1943, he was far from eager to accept the challenge.

The opportunity presented itself when Daves went back to Warner Brothers to write (in collaboration with Albert Maltz) a submarine drama called *Destination Tokyo*. The film was to be made with the cooperation of the navy, and, in the interests of authenticity, the writers were asked to spend some time in a submarine at sea. By the time the scenario was completed, Jack Warner realized that Daves knew more about submarine warfare than anyone else on the lot, and asked him to direct the picture. Daves demurred, pointing out that as a writer he didn't get ulcers, but Warner and the producer Jerry Wald finally prevailed.

Destination Tokyo (1943) stars Cary Grant as commander of the submarine *Copperfin,* struggling to cope not only with the hazards of war, but with the presence on board of a womanizing troublemaker (John Garfield). The result was praised for some well-handled moments of tension and a generally "firm control of character and situation," but some reviewers thought it too long (at 135 minutes) and marred by sentimentality and intrusive patriotic rhetoric. James Agee wrote that it "combines a good deal of fairly exciting submarine warfare with at least as much human interest, which I found neither very human nor . . . very interesting." Others were more impressed, however, and the picture did well enough at the box office to establish Daves in his new role as a director.

There is a good deal of sentimentality also in *The Very Thought of You* (1944), in which Eleanor Parker's wartime marriage to Dennis Morgan, stifled by her possessive family, is rescued by the arrival of a baby. However, in his two-part article about Daves in *Films and Filming* (April and May 1963), Richard Whitehall wrote that this movie's "long searching look" at the American family was refreshingly free from the clichés of the genre: "Daves portrays the family unit as a trap from which the young should endeavour to escape. . . . The idea of the family as an octopus with tenacious tentacles strangling the initiative of the young is a recurrent theme in the early Daves films."

Hollywood Canteen (1944), a star-stuffed wartime musical, was followed by *The Pride of the Marines* (1945), written by Albert Maltz. It tells the story of Al Schmid (John Garfield), a young Philadelphian who joins the Marines, fights heroically at Guadalcanal, is blinded by a grenade, and then has to fight even more bravely to come to terms with his disability. As in *Destination Tokyo,* there is a certain amount of embarrassing rhetoric about the American way of life, but there are also some pointed attacks on racial and religious bigotry (involving Schmid's Jewish buddy, played by Dane Clark).

The movie received a good deal of praise, especially for the family scenes at the beginning and the action sequences. William R. Meyer wrote that Daves had "used the technique of double printing with a sixty percent positive and forty percent negative image to evoke the horror of a grenade exploding in Schmid's face," and called the night battle "agonizingly real." James Agee remained relatively unmoved, finding the picture "long-drawn-out and never inspired, but very respectably honest and dogged, thanks considerably, it appears, to Albert Maltz's script."

Daves wrote *The Red House* himself, introducing in his murderous farmer (Edward G. Robinson) a figure that has recurred in his films—one whose consuming egocentricity makes him a force for evil and destruction. This "powerful mood-piece" was followed by *Dark Passage* (1947), also scripted by Daves. It stars Humphrey Bogart as Vincent Parry, a San Quentin lifer wrongly convicted of murdering his wife. He escapes, and, aided by Irene (Lauren Bacall), a San Francisco socialite who believes in him, undergoes plastic surgery to alter his appearance. After trying but failing to bring the real killer to justice, Parry escapes with Irene to South America. The first part of the film—until Parry emerges from the surgeon's bandages looking like Bogart—was shot "subjectively" with a hand-held camera (a captured German Arriflex).

William R. Meyer called Daves' script "a winding, often hysterical narrative, offering weak motivations," but admired the supporting performances of Clifton Young (a blackmailer), Tom D'Andrea (a taxi driver), and Agnes Moorehead. For Richard Whitehall, however, this was a "minor masterpiece" reminiscent of early Fritz Lang, and "one of the most extraordinary American films of the late forties," distinguished by "meticulous observation of background detail" and of minor characters: "All the people Parry meets, whether friend or enemy, are beautifully realised, and the whole work has an exhilarating compactness and freedom."

To the Victor (1948), set mainly in Paris just after the war, is a bleak love story involving an embittered blackmarketeer (Dennis Morgan) and a woman (Viveca Lindfors) whose life is in danger because she has undertaken to testify against her husband, a wartime collaborator. It is a dark and cynical movie, softened by some touching love scenes and benefiting from a good script by Richard Brooks. *Task Force* (1949), a dutiful dramatized history of the U.S. Naval Air Arm, and the banal comedy *A Kiss in the Dark* (1949), were Daves' last films as a contract director for Warner Brothers.

Moving on to Twentieth Century–Fox, Daves made his first Western, *Broken Arrow* (1950), adapted by Michael Blankfort from Elliott Arnold's novel *Blood Brother*. Sickened by the United States' pointless and bloody war with the Apaches, the liberal ex-soldier Tom Jeffords (James Stewart) takes his life in his hands and opens peace negotiations with the chief Cochise (Jeff Chandler). The attempt is at least temporarily successful, and when the treaty is broken, it is not by the Indians. In the interim, Jeffords is briefly and idyllically married to the Apache maiden Sonseeahray (Debra Paget).

Broken Arrow was one of the first Westerns to show the American Indian in a sympathetic light and to portray love between an Indian and a white. Drawing on his own family connections with the Southwest and his wanderings as a young man among the Indians of that region, Daves made a film in which his respect for the Apaches shines through, as Richard Whitehall wrote, "in his sympathetic treatment of Cochise and his understanding and poetic treatment of Indian ceremonials and customs, particularly the wedding ceremony with its beautiful marriage poem" and in "the lovely low-angled shots as Tom Jeffords and Sonseeahray enter their marriage wickiup. . . . Although it is not a great Western, it is one of the loveliest, with its beautiful color photography by Ernest Palmer."

The picture brought Chandler an Oscar nomination for his performance and Daves a Directors Guild prize. It was a commercial success and ushered in an era of "adult" and "socially significant" Westerns. William K. Everson has written that *Broken Arrow*, "whicle it may have been prompted by the controversial but commercially successful race problem . . . films of the 1940s, managed the rare movie trick of making a social comment without overloading the scales. The side issues of *Broken Arrow* were rapidly commercialized to the hilt. . . . [and] its controlled documentary qualities were also copied shamelessly by many lesser Westerns. But the original film was good enough to survive

even this subsequent exploitation; it was and is a warm, poignant, and often poetic film."

A succession of bad or mediocre studio assignments followed, including two remakes, a "pleasantly atmospheric" contemporary Western called *Return of the Texan*, a drama called *Never Let Me Go*, and the early Cinemascope epic *Demetrius and the Gladiators*. It was not until 1954 that Daves was able to make a more personal movie, the Warner Brothers Western *Drum Beat*, scripted by the director and based on contemporary accounts of the United States' war with the Modoc Indians of the California-Oregon border in the 1870s.

Up to a point, *Drum Beat* reverses the argument of *Broken Arrow*, taking the point of view of the white settlers. A "bleeding-heart" liberal persuades President Grant to negotiate with the Modoc renegade Captain Jack (Charles Bronson); the experienced Indian fighter John MacKay (Alan Ladd) warns against this course and, when his advice is ignored, has to pick up the pieces. The drift of the film is not against the Modocs as a whole—they are shown to be generally peaceable and honorable—but against the appeasement of a treacherous renegade. Some commentators saw analogies between events in the film and the Cold War, though Daves said that he had not intended this connection.

Daves was also the scenarist (with Russell Hughes) of *Jubal*, adapted from Paul Wellman's novel *Jubal Troop* and made for Columbia in 1956. Its publicity described it as "virtually a Greek tragedy, but with a happy ending, laid in the setting of a Wyoming cattle ranch." Others were reminded of Melville's *Billy Budd* by this story of the conflict between Jubal Troop (Glenn Ford), a Shane-like drifter hired by rancher Ernest Borgnine, and the psychotically destructive cowhand Pinky (Rod Steiger). It was generally admired, both for its unusually sophisticated characterization and for its portrayal of everyday work and play on the ranch.

A less reflective but more exciting film followed, *The Last Wagon* (1956)—a "revenge Western" that becomes a "journey Western" as an embittered loner (Richard Widmark) leads the survivors of an Apache raid back to civilization. And *3.10 to Yuma* (1957) has been classified as yet another species of the genre—a "chamber Western," in which much of the action takes place indoors. Holed up together in a hotel bedroom are Ben Wade (Glenn Ford), a much-feared outlaw, and a decent farmer named Dan Evans (Van Heflin) who has undertaken to deliver Wade to Yuma Penitentiary and who knows that Wade's gang is gathering outside.

Evans accepts the assignment because it will earn him the money he needs to save his farm, but he gradually comes to realize that he is fighting also for such imponderables as peace and decency. He pursues his apparently suicidal but morally correct course out of an almost fatalistic sense of necessity, and in this resembles the heroes of other "adult" Westerns of the 1950s, like *High Noon, The Gunfighter,* and Budd Boetticher's "Ranown" cycle. *3.10 to Yuma* was shot by Charles Lawton Jr. in black and white, red filters being used in the outdoor sequences to intensify the impression of a parched and hostile terrain. It was much admired for its photography, its "wonderfully visual use of shadows for dramatic effect," and its adroit balance of action, irony, and allegory.

Cowboy (1958), based on Frank Harris' account of his disillusioning experiences as a young easterner in the Old West, was a more ambitious but less satisfying film, shot by Lawton in color and cinemascope and starring Jack Lemmon and Glenn Ford. Daves made two more Westerns after that—*The Badlanders* (1958), a translation to Arizona of W. R. Burnett's *The Asphalt Jungle,* and *The Hanging Tree* (1959), with Gary Cooper, Maria Schell, and Karl Malden. The ulcers that Daves regarded as the director's lot finally got him during the filming of the latter, and the shooting was completed from his sketches by Karl Malden.

None of Daves' later pictures was of much merit. Most of them were rather turgid romances that he wrote and produced as well as directed. He made his last picture in 1965 and, until his death twelve years later, went on trying to generate new projects through his Diamond D Production Company. He was survived by his wife and three children. Daves was described as "one of the happiest men in Hollywood" and "one of the best-liked directors," open and easygoing. He was a Republican and an Episcopalian, and once listed twenty-eight hobbies, including minerology, etymology, painting, etching, calligraphy, photography, enameling, woodcarving, the construction of miniature furniture, and "forgery detection." He had a cabin in the San Bernadino mountains which he designed and partly built himself in the Tyrolean style, with the motto "Know Thyself" over the hearth.

Richard Whitehall called Daves "the documentarist of the Western film" and wrote that "few directors have caught so exactly the flavour of bleak, wooden constructions and sterile dust of the shack-town of the desert or have tried to set their characters so firmly as part of a *working community.*"

FILMS: Destination Tokyo, 1943; The Very Thought of You, 1944; Hollywood Canteen, 1944; Pride of the Marines, 1945; The Red House, 1947; Dark Passage, 1947; To the Victor, 1948; Task Force, 1949; A Kiss in the Dark, 1949; Broken Arrow, 1950; Bird of Paradise, 1951; Return of the Texan, 1952; Treasure of the Golden Condor, 1953; Never Let Me Go, 1953; Demetrius and the Gladiators, 1954; Drum Beat, 1954; Jubal, 1956; The Last Wagon, 1956; 3.10 to Yuma, 1957; Cowboy, 1958; Kings Go Forth, 1958; The Badlanders, 1958; The Hanging Tree, 1959; A Summer Place, 1960; Susan Slade, 1961; Parrish, 1961; Rome Adventure (Lovers Must Learn), 1962; Spencer's Mountain, 1963; Youngblood Hawke, 1964; The Battle of the Villa Fiorita, 1965.

ABOUT: Agel, H. Le Western, 1966 (in French); Everson, W. K. A Pictorial History of the Western Film, 1969; Kreck, J. Delmer Daves: Dokumentation, 1972 (in German); Meyer, W. R. Warner Brothers Directors, 1979. *Periodicals*—Cinema (UK) October 1969; Film Dope April 1976; Filmkritik January 1975 (special issue); Films and Filming April and May 1963; Screen July–October 1969.

*DELANNOY, JEAN (January 12, 1908–   ), French director and scenarist, writes (in French): "I was born at Noisy-le-Sec, near Paris. My mother was headteacher of a kindergarten, and my father worked as a civil servant for the city of Paris. My brother was a sculptor, my sister an actress. They are all deceased.

"After studying at the Lycée Montaigne and the Lycée Louis-le-Grand in Paris, I entered the Faculty of Letters. In order to earn a living I became, in turn, bank agent, journalist, and scenery designer. I tried my luck in the cinema as an actor. This was still in the era of silent films. I interrupted my studies to get married. I was nineteen years old. Military service in the Cinematographic Section of the Armed Forces, which I left to become a cutter at Paramount studios at St. Maurice. It was here that my real career began. In three years, I put together about forty films and finally made my debut as a director at the age of twenty-six.

"Since then I have never stopped filming. Forty films, one a year, and five television productions.

"In 1938 I divorced in order to marry my present wife, who occupies the most important place in my life, together with my daughter, her husband, who is also a film director, and their three children.

"My work has often baffled the critics, as it is eclectic. For me a film, if it invokes a poetic vision of the world, remains above all a beautiful object to be created, destined for a vast public. This is the greatness and the obligation of this

°də lan nwä´

JEAN DELANNOY

craft. The diversity of subjects I have handled reflects very exactly the diversity of my preoccupations and involvements. I have never attempted, even after the greatest success, to take the same path twice. I have always felt the need to change subject and style. This is the price of my concern for personal development. Indeed, how can one progress if one does not change one's *genre?* Hence the diversity, as with William Wyler, of chosen themes: detective films, films on childhood, on the drama of the couple, on faith, historical or spy films. My inner world demanded this constant variety, without which creating would have become, for me, insipid and sterile.

"For the last four years I have devoted myself to television because I find it gives me the possibility of handling subjects that I like and that French cinema is no longer capable of producing.

"With the collaboration of Jean Anouilh I have made a film on Charlemagne for TFI, and one six hours long on Manon Lescaut, based on the Abbé Prévost novel. I recounted the accession of Napoleon III in *Le Coup du 2 Décembre,* and the story of a modern couple in *L'Eté indien,* based on a personal scenario. I am now finishing *Frère Martin,* a film on Martin Luther.

"Together with my professional activities, I hold the chairmanship of IDHEC (Institut des Hautes Études Cinématographiques), that of SNAC (Syndicat National des Auteurs et Compositeurs), and the vice-chairmanship of SACD (Société des Auteurs et Compositeurs Dramatiques)."

_____

As he says, Delannoy supported himself as a literature student at the Sorbonne by working at an assortment of jobs and taking bit parts in films, in this following the example of his sister Henriette, who achieved some success as an actress in the silents. He learned something of his craft during his stint (1930–1932) with the Service Cinématographique de l'Armée and more during his three years as an editor with Paramount. Delannoy's own first films were shorts, of which the most notable was *Une Vocation irrésistible* (1934), about a barber who aspires to an acting career; these were followed by a string of low-budget comedies—*Paris-Deauville* (1935), *Ne tirez pas Dolly!* (1937), and *La Vénus de l'or* (1938). He had his first commercial success with *Le Diamant noir* (1940), adapted from a novel by Jean Aicart and starring Gaby Morlay and Charles Vanel.

Macao, l'enfer du jeu (*Gambling Hell*), an ambitious thriller about gunrunning and other skulduggery in the mysterious East, was completed in 1939 with a cast that included Erich von Stroheim, Sessue Hayakawa, and Mireille Balin. By the time it was due for release, France was in the hands of the Germans, who would not countenance the distribution of a film featuring the anti-Nazi Stroheim. All the scenes in which he appeared were reshot with Pierre Renoir, and the movie was released in this version in 1942, in the Stroheim version in 1945.

During the German occupation, Delannoy remained in the free zone, avoiding any collaboration with Continentale, the German production company that had engaged Marcel Carné and others. Among his wartime output, *Fièvres* (1942), with Tino Rossi, was followed by *L'Assassin a peur la nuit,* based on a novel by Pierre Véry, and then by *Pontcarral, colonel d'empire* (1942), starring Pierre Blanchar and Annie Ducaux in an expensive epic about an impoverished aristocrat who soldiers for Napoleon, marries a woman who doesn't love him, and dies gallantly in Africa. It was the first of a number of films shot for Delannoy by Christian Matras, and the camerawork, an exciting story, and an excellent performance by Blanchar made it a box-office hit. There was also a less obvious factor in the movie's success—the scene in which Pontcarral, interrogated about his hostility to the July Monarchy, replies, "Under such a regime, sir, it is an honor to be condemned." Roger Régent reported that audiences during the German occupation regularly applauded that line, and, according to James Reid Paris, one resistance leader adopted "Pontcarral" as his *nom de guerre.*

All the same, Delannoy, like many of his colleagues during the occupation, found it expedient to concentrate on uncontroversial historical stories or on fantastic or mythological ones like *L'Éternel retour* (*Love Eternal*/ *The Eternal Return*, 1943). In Delannoy's words, "*Pontcarral* and *L'Eternel retour* are the two poles of what one could do during the war and the occupation and give a good indication, in such a troubled time, of the two attitudes of the filmmaker: to distract the public, in the sense of a certain beauty, a certain escape, or, by contrast, with *Pontcarral*, to try to communicate the spirit of the Resistance to them by means of a character still endowed with grandeur and steadfastness." It was this film, a modernized version of the legend of Tristan and Isolde starring Jean Marais and Madeleine Sologne, that established Delannoy as a major director. The screenplay was the work of Jean Cocteau, and reflects his preoccupation with death as the only proper apotheosis for a great love, as well as his fondness for *dei ex machina* (here the malevolent dwarf Achille).

John Russell Taylor goes so far as to call *L'Éternel retour* "in every respect a Cocteau original except that Cocteau himself did not direct it. . . . Cocteau himself was in constant attendance during the film's shooting, though strictly, he insisted, as an observer and a learner. The film has stylistically some of the stiffness, the immaculate, dead finish one associates with the work of the director Jean Delannoy. . . . But the spirit is very typically Cocteau, and the look of the film also recalls Cocteau so strongly that it is probably not too imaginative to see in it at least his designing hand."

On the other hand, André Bazin, who saw the film when it was first released, had "the strongest reservations about the scenario, because implicit in it are all the weaknesses of the film," while "the art of Delannoy and his cameraman, Roger Hubert. . . . surpasses anything that the French cinema has given us since the war. . . . If our first sight of the dwarf has so much dramatic power, it is because it has been prepared for at length by a dolly shot; and reciprocally, the face of the dwarf, despite the extraordinary acting of Piéral, would never have achieved that expressive intensity without the lighting and angles of Roger Hubert. . . . With *L'Éternel retour* we decidedly take another step on the road opened by [Carné's] *Les Visiteurs du Soir*. . . . an entire conception of the relationship of cinema and poetry is defined by these works, though it is no longer a question of borrowing untransmittable prestige from other arts, but of conquering an autonomous poetic language, in which Delannoy's film, after Carné's film, will mark a date in our cinematic history."

L'Éternel retour had enormous financial success in France in 1943, though when it was first shown abroad after the war some critics were disquieted by "the pervading mood of defeatism sublimating itself in death." Delannoy followed it with a melodrama, *Le Bossu* (1944), and then the prestigious *La Part de l'ombre* (*Blind Desire*, 1945), a psychological drama starring Edwige Feuillère and Jean-Louis Barrault, scripted by Charles Spaak, photographed by Matras, and with music by Georges Auric, who at this time scored most of Delannoy's films.

Delannoy's first postwar picture, *La Symphonie pastorale* (1946), was an even bigger success than *L'Éternel retour*. The movie is based on the novel by André Gide, adapted for the screen by the distinguished scenarists Jean Aurenche and Pierre Bost, along with Delannoy himself (who is said to have had a hand in all his scripts, whether he is credited or not). Magnificently photographed by Armand Thirard, it is set in a Swiss village where the austere Protestant pastor (Pierre Blanchar) adopts a half-wild blind waif. She grows up to be beautiful, and the pastor, though he cannot admit this to himself, falls in love with her, as does his son. An operation cures her and the jealous passions from which she has been insulated by her blindness blaze up into tragedy.

The film won the grand prix at Cannes in 1946, where Michèle Morgan was also chosen as best actress for her performance as Gertrude and Georges Auric won the award for the best score. "The whole thing is bounded by the snow," wrote C. A. Lejeune. "Snow presses against the doors; the rooms are filled with the white light of snow; voices are muffled by the snow; footprints lead to the river's edge and vanish in the snow. The film is played with a kind of bleak stillness . . . and it is by the smallest movements of the hands and eyes, the hint of strain in a voice, the fleeting expression of wonder or suffering on a face . . . that Jean Delannoy, the director, has brought home his tragedy. *Symphonie pastorale* is full of intimate moments so exactly noted that you feel it is almost indecent to be observing them. . . . It is not quite a great film, for it lacks proportion . . . but it is the work of an artist of plainly individual temper, and in its wintry way it is a very strong film indeed."

Jean-Paul Sartre himself—in collaboration with Pierre Bost and Delannoy—adapted his story *Les Jeux sont faits* (*The Die Is Cast*/ *The Chips Are Down*) for Delannoy's next film. This fable opens in the afterworld with a meeting between a man and a woman who have died simultaneously—Pierre (Marcel Pagliero) is a worker who was killed leading an insurrection; Eve (Micheline Presle) is a rich woman poisoned by her husband, who covets her younger sister. This ill-assorted couple fall in love and are given a second chance—twenty-four hours of life in which to test their new passion against the conflicting demands of old loyalties and ideologies. The picture had a mixed reception, critics tending to be depressed by Sartre's bleak view of human foolishness but impressed by Delannoy's eschewal of "celestial gimcrackery" in suggesting "the transition . . . from flesh to spirit." Delannoy himself acknowledged that "The story undoubtedly went a little beyond the public's comprehension. But I still insist on the ambition behind Les Jeux sont faits. These are simple, human sentiments: love, the difficulty of loving each other, and then, through the relationship of a woman from the bourgeoisie and a foreman, the notion of class solidarity and the presence of the system on the socio-philosophical level. . . . "

Two much less serious movies followed (demonstrating the eclecticism Delannoy speaks of above). Jean Marais achieves a happy ending with Michèle Morgan in the romantic Aux yeux du souvenir (Souvenir, 1949) and an unhappy one with Dominique Blanchar in the even more romantic Le Secret de Mayerling (1949), one of several cinematic attempts to explain why the heir to the Austrian empire committed suicide with his beloved in the Mayerling hunting lodge. Dieu a besoin des hommes (God Needs Men/ Isle of Sinners, 1950) was a different matter again. Adapted by Aurenche and Bost from a novel by Henri Queffélec, it is set in the last century on a bleak island off the coast of Brittany, where the primitive islanders are in the habit of luring ships onto their rocks and looting them. The curé leaves in disgust, but the local sacristan, a simple fisherman who believes that sinners need God no less than the virtuous, slips gradually into the role of priest until a doctrinaire cleric arrives to point out the enormity of his offense. And even after that the sacristan has to make one more choice between the laws of the Church and those of compassion.

Some critics found the film lacking in emotional conviction—oddly detached—but most were impressed by the harsh beauty of the Breton landscapes and seascapes photographed by Robert Lefebvre, and by Pierre Fresnay's performance in the lead as a "devout unlettered man, torn between vanity and a genuine sense of spiritual responsibility and terror of his own (blasphemous) masquerade." The film received the grand prix at Venice and another from the Office Catholique International du Cinéma (in spite of its condemnation of the Church's worldliness and lack of compassion).

After Le Garçon sauvage (1951), a Madeleine Robinson vehicle, came La Minute de vérité (The Moment of Truth, 1952), with Jean Gabin as a Paris doctor, Michèle Morgan as his actress wife, and Walter Chiari as the impetuous and violent young artist who draws the latter into an affair before he takes his own life. Patrick Gibbs thought that the subtlety of the characterization gave freshness and distinction to "the old situation," and went on: "The milestones of the affair are shown in a series of flashbacks . . . a sequence in which comment and illustration, past and present, are combined with great technical brilliance."

Delannoy's output continued unabated throughout the 1950s, and if he achieved no major international hits, he crafted many polished and successful vehicles for the major stars of the day—Michèle Morgan in the psychological drama Obsession (1954) and Marie Antoinette (1956), Jean Gabin as an enlightened judge in Chiens perdus sans collier (1955) and as a definitive Inspector Maigret in two Simenon adaptations. Delannoy's version of The Hunchback of Notre Dame (1957), starring Anthony Quinn and Gina Lollobrigida, had the benefit of a script by Jean Aurenche and Jacques Prévert, but was disappointing.

It was a film scripted by Jean Cocteau that established Delannoy as an important director, and Cocteau also wrote his last really ambitious picture, La Princesse de Clèves (1960), based on the novel written in 1678 by Madame de la Fayette. It is a story of star-crossed lovers at the French court, not unlike the Tristan and Isolde legend of L'Éternel retour—there is even a malignant dwarf (played by Piéral again) to symbolize the intrigues of the court. In fact, Cocteau had written the script immediately after L'Éternel retour, intending it for the same stars. In the later film, however, the young lovers are played by Jean-François Poron and Marina Vlady rather than by Marais and Solange (though Marais gets a part as the heroine's husband, the Prince de Clèves). The result struck most critics as an interesting anachronism, "put at a further remove from the present by the glacial formality of M. Delannoy's direction, the beautiful but somehow rather embalmed colour, and the evident failure of . . . the young principals . . . to feel any great involvement."

As an "academic" studio director of the old school, Delannoy suffered greatly in the late 1950s at the hands of the nouvelle vague critics. "I've seen Chiens perdus sans collier three times so as to learn exactly what not to do!" François Truffaut announced in 1957. His reputation has not yet recovered, although opinion is beginning to come around again: "Jean Delannoy is 'classic,'" Charles Ford wrote in a 1986 homage, "in the sense that he avoids all the excesses, all the extremes." He has never ceased to work, moreover, turning out routine comedies, thrillers, and costume pieces into the 1970s, and then undertaking, as he says, various television projects. Almost all of his works for TV have been multi-episode series, such as the six-part *Histoire du Chevalier des Grieux et de Manon Lescaut* (1978) or the two-part *Crime de Pierre Lacaze* (1983), adapted from a Jean Laborde novel. According to Delannoy, he finds himself stimulated by the mini-series format, which is "drawn out, like real life." Television, he says, "isn't so different from film. The way of telling a story is the same, but you simply have a much larger audience, which makes me feel a little more responsible." If a certain emotional frigidity has kept even his best films from greatness, Delannoy remains a meticulous craftsman and a total professional who has never exploited or betrayed the medium.

FILMS: Franches lippées, 1922 (short); L'École des détectives, 1934 (short); Une Vocation irrésistible, 1934 (short); Paris-Deauville, 1933; La Moule, 1934 (medium-length); Ne tirez pas Dolly!, 1935 (some sources give this title as Ne tuez pas Dolly!); Tamara la complaisante (1937, collaboration with Félix Gandéra); Le paradis de Satan (1938, collaboration with Félix Gandéra); La Vénus de l'or, 1938; Le Diamant noir, 1941; Macao, l'enfer de jeu (Gambling Hell), 1942 (re-released in original version, 1945); Fièvres, 1942; L'Assassin a peur la nuit, 1942; Pontcarral, colonel d'empire, 1942; L'Éternel Retour (Love Eternal/The Eternal Return), 1943; Le Bossu, 1944; La Part de l'ombre (Blind Desire), 1945; La Symphonie Pastorale, 1946; Les Jeux sont faits (The Chips Are Down/The Die Is Cast), 1947; Aux yeux du souvenir (Souvenir), 1948; Le Secret de Mayerling, 1949; Dieu a besoin des hommes (God Needs Men/Isle of Sinners), 1950; Le Garçon sauvage (Wild Boy/Savage Triangle), 1951; La Minute de vérité (The Moment of Truth), 1952; Jeanne d'Arc episode in Destinées (Daughters of Destiny), 1953; Pompadour episode in Secrets d'alcôve (Il Letto/The Bed), 1954; La Route Napoléon, 1953; Obsession, 1954; Chiens perdus sans collier, 1955; Marie Antoinette (Shadow of the Guillotine), 1956; Notre Dame de Paris (The Hunchback of Notre Dame), 1956; Maigret tend un piège (Maigret Sets a Trap/ Inspector Maigret), 1958; Guinguette, 1959; Maigret et l'affaire Saint-Fiacre, 1959; Le Baron de l'Écluse, 1959; Adolescence episode in La Française et l'amour (Love and the Frenchwoman), 1960; La Princesse de Clèves, 1961; Le Rendez-Vous, 1961; Venere imperiale, 1962; Les Amitiés particulières (This Special Friendship), 1964; (as codirector) Le Lit à deux places (The Double Bed), 1965; Le Majordôme, 1965; Les Sultans, 1966; Le Soleil des voyous (The Action Man), 1967; La Peau de torpédo, 1970; Pas folle la guêpe, 1972; Le Jeune homme et le lion, 1976 (TV); Histoire du Chevalier des Grieux et de Manon Lescaut, 1978

(TV); Le coup d'état du 2 Decembre, 1979 (TV); L'Été indien, 1980 (TV); Frère Martin, 1981 (TV); Le Crime de Pierre Lacaze, 1983 (TV); La Messagère, 1984.

ABOUT: Guiget, C., Papillon, E., and Piniturault, J. Jean Delannoy, 1985; Leprohon, P. Présences contemporains, 1957; Marion, D. (ed.) Le Cinéma français par ceux qui le font, 1948; Siclier, J. La France de Petain et son cinéma, 1981. *Periodicals*—L'Avant-Scène du Cinéma April 15 1961; Film Dope September 1976; Film Français March 17, 1978.

*DELLUC, LOUIS (-JEAN-RENÉ) (October 14, 1890–March 22, 1924), French theorist and critic of the film, director, scenarist, dramatist, novelist and poet, was born in Cadouin, in the Dordogne. His father kept a pharmacy in the village and was deputy mayor. Within a few years of his birth the family moved to Bordeaux and then, in 1903, to Paris, where Delluc attended the Lycée Charlemagne. There he met Léon Moussinac, beginning a life-long friendship that developed into a collaboration in the field of cinema. Delluc's first interests, however, were literature and the theatre and by the time he was fourteen he had written a number of plays. Ill health interrupted his studies but allowed him time to write, and he was barely fifteen when he won a prize with his first published poem. He was soon regularly publishing verse and drama criticism and his first poetry collection, *Chansons du jeune temps,* appeared in 1908.

Between 1907 and 1909 Delluc contributed poetry and criticism to the *Petit Poète de Nice, Le Courrier de Paris-Province* and *La Revue Française.* During the same period he was studying for the entrance exam to the École Normale Supérieure, but he abandoned this aim in 1909 to devote himself to journalism, joining the staff of the prestigious theatre journal *Comoedia illustré* the following year. His work there made him many friends in the theatre world, among them the director Irénée Mauget, who in 1911 staged Delluc's first play, *Francesca,* and the actor Eduoard de Max, whose conversations with Delluc on the theatre and the art of acting formed the basis for Delluc's study, *Chez de Max* (1918).

Delluc was twenty-three when he met the Belgian actress Eva François, known professionally as Eve Francis, whom he was later to marry. Both delighted in the Ballet Russe, Ida Rubenstein, *Parsifal,* the music of Debussy, and the plays of Paul Claudel, in which Eve Francis often played leading roles. These influences and the symbolist aesthetic shaped Delluc's critical perspective. Initially he was hostile to the cinema, seeing it as a poor mechanical substitute for

°də lük´

LOUIS DELLUC

the kind of beauty that the theatre had to offer. Even Francis took him to many films for which he had nothing but contempt until his introduction to American cinema. According to her memoirs, the moment of conversion came with Cecil B. DeMille's 1915 film *The Cheat:* "Delluc, sitting beside me, was trembling. For the first time ever on the screen, objects bore witness." Though he dedicated himself thereafter increasingly to film criticism and filmmaking, Delluc never entirely abandoned his earlier interests. His first novel, *Monsieur de Berlin,* was published in 1916, and another, *La Guerre est morte,* followed in 1917.

Only a few days after his marriage to Eve Francis in January 1918, Delluc was mobilized. He served in the army until July 1919 but managed to continue his work as a film critic, journalist and novelist. Between 1917 and 1919 he edited the magazine *Le Film* and in 1918–1922 contributed a weekly film column to the daily *Paris-Midi.* There had until then been very little serious and independent film criticism in France—only the enthusiastic outpourings of hacks paid by the producers to publicize their films. Riciotto Canudo and others had done some pioneer work in the field, but the volume and significance of Delluc's writings gives him primacy as "the creator of film criticism." His regular articles had an almost immediate influence in intellectual and literary circles: the essays of Jean Cocteau, Blaise Cendrars, Max Jacob, Louis Aragon, and others bear witness to a new-found respect and enthusiasm for the cinema. Journalism also was affected as more and more publications opened their columns to film reviewers.

Delluc published two more novels in 1919 (and one of these, *Le Train sans yeux,* was filmed by Cavalcanti in 1926, after Delluc's death). A collection of Delluc's weekly *Paris-Midi* articles also appeared in 1919 as *Cinéma et cie* and was followed in 1920 by another volume of critical and theoretical essays, *Photogénie.* Delluc's study of Chaplin, whom he described as "a unique instrument of expression," appeared in 1921 as *Charlot* (and was translated by Hamish Miles as *Charlie Chaplin,* 1922).

Roger Manvell has suggested that Delluc's writings on film theory are important chiefly because he gave "elegant and elliptical" expression to principles that the French "had unwittingly discovered . . . when the cinema was invented" but which had been "allowed to sink into oblivion." Not everyone would dismiss so lightly Delluc's contributions towards an aesthetic of the film, and Eugene C. McCreary has analyzed his writings at some length in *Cinema Journal* (Fall 1976), stressing the breadth and depth of his interests and knowledge, which extended to virtually every aspect of filmmaking.

According to McCreary, Delluc always acknowledged that the cinema was an industry as well as an art, but thought the commercial producers underestimated their audiences—he believed that "beauty earns money." He also prized the silent film—this "mute and sure means of eloquence"—as a unique and universal medium of communication. "The cinema is marvelous in that it speaks to the entire world," he wrote, and he insisted that—like the bullfight and the Greek theatre—it appeals not to the masses but to "the crowd. And the crowd includes everybody." For the same reason Delluc valued (and feared) the cinema's power as a propaganda instrument. But above all he saw it as "the only truly modern art"—"the child of technology and human ideals."

Delluc valued sincerity, simplicity, and authenticity, defining an ideal cinema close to that achieved many years later in the best products of neorealism. He wanted filmmakers to take their stories from everyday life—to eschew the self-conscious and the elaborately artificial and to let workers be played by workers, peasants by peasants. Alternatively filmmakers should seek to reveal the deep and universal truths embodied in myths, legends, and "the marvelous." He admired the American Western—and especially the films of Thomas Ince—because in this genre the hero is stylized into a type, his life into a myth. The director should not strive for beautiful effects but should seek truth; then beauty would inevitably result. Truth was best revealed through the selection of significant details, coordinated with a precise sense of appropriate rhythm and presented for our contemplation in such a way that, thanks to the mysterious and revelatory power of the movie camera, we are "obliged to see." And the film must be shaped into the harmonious unity that is achieved when all of its elements are subordinated to a single dominating idea, since "film is not photography. Film is an animated painting."

Through Eve Francis, Delluc met Germaine Dulac, whose work as a filmmaker he already admired, and it was she who directed his first script, *La Fête espagnole* (*The Spanish Fiesta,* 1919). The film gives clear evidence of Delluc's admiration for the American cinema: set in Spain, its plot is strongly reminiscent of an Ince Western. Jean Mitry described the film as a memorable moment in the history of French cinema—the first example of a script conceived cinematically, "thought out in images." Eve Francis, who has a leading role in all but one of Delluc's films, plays the part of the beautiful Soledad, loved by two rich landowners. The rivals fight to the death, while Soledad is carried off to the fiesta by another young man, dancing past the corpses without even noticing them. The film's interest and its modernity lay not in this flimsy plot but in its creation of atmosphere, its presentation of the madness and passion of the fiesta. Delluc said that he saw the characters and the plot as subordinate to these considerations, but he felt that the film would have more truly captured the authenticity of atmosphere he desired if it had been filmed on location in Spain. His friend Léon Moussinac considered that Germaine Dulac's execution did not match the cinematic excellence of Delluc's conception.

Delluc and Dulac have been described by some film historians as respectively the "head" and the "heart" of a group of filmmakers that included Marcel L'Herbier, Abel Gance, and Jean Epstein—the "impressionist school" or "first avant-garde." This view is not shared by Delluc's biographer, Marcel Tariol, who sees him not exactly as the leader of this group but rather as an *éveilleur,* encouraging and "awakening" others to the potential of film and the need for a truly French cinema. Tariol and some other critics like Richard Abel maintain that Delluc's work was influential but individual, and in a 1968 issue of *Cahiers du Cinéma* Noël Burch and Jean-André Fieschi separate Delluc radically from Epstein, L'Herbier and the other "impressionists": "Despite his intellectual closeness, historical distance makes it difficult to see him as their contemporary. He is more of a refined heir to the Americans." Personal reminiscences of Delluc tend to confirm this picture of him as an isolated, melancholy figure, some-

times hiding his feverish dedication to work behind an air of nonchalance and gaiety: "This great sad man," Abel Gance called him, "with the eyes of a wounded gazelle."

The first film directed by Delluc was *Fumée noire* (*Black Smoke,* 1920), in which a woman and her husband visit an uncle who has returned from a long trip to the Orient. His stories, and the hypnotic effect of the exotic objects he has brought back with him, evoke dreams that for a time appear to have become reality. More ambitious than skillful, this apprentice film introduced themes that recur in Delluc's work—the confrontation between the present and the past, the real and the imagined, and the uncertainty of memory. These preoccupations are central in *Le Silence* (*Silence,* 1920), which Jean Mitry regards as Delluc's first true film as a *metteur-en-scène.* Pierre (played by Gabriel Signoret), awaits the arrival of his mistress Suzie (Eve Francis), but a letter arrives saying that she will be late. Something about it sets off a chain of images—memories and imaginings: an anonymous letter telling him of his wife's infidelity, her illness, her death at his hands. And the anonymous note is in the same hand as Suzie's. Suzie arrives to find Pierre at his desk, a bitter smile on his face, a bullet hole in his head. It is the film's structure that takes it beyond melodrama. Brief and concise—only twenty minutes long—it alternates between past and present, memory and fantasy, in sequences that become progressively shorter. This accelerating tempo gives the film great tension, and the dramatic juxtaposition of images achieves something close to real tragedy.

Silence uses a stream of consciousness technique, in which the sequence of events is not chronological but determined by the characters' mental associations or states of mind; in this it is a precursor of films like Resnais' *Last Year at Marienbad.* Jean Epstein described *Silence* as "true cinema" and wrote: "The lens, as if by itself, discovered in the most trivial and unyielding things a new aspect of depth, of symbolic truth, of dramatic complicity with the event." In this remark Epstein echoed an important element in Delluc's aesthetic—his perception of the "transparency" of cinema, its ability to reveal a beauty and truth unrecognized by the eye (a notion later developed by the prophet of the *nouvelle vague* André Bazin).

The first issue of *Le Journal du Ciné-club* (soon retitled *Ciné-club*) appeared in January 1920. Founded by Delluc and a group of friends including Léon Moussinac, its aim was to establish a nationwide association of movie enthusiasts. The attempt was premature and the magazine expired in 1921, but the Ciné-club movement survived and grew. Delluc, Moussinac, and Riciotto Canudo organized film programs that people flocked to in the same spirit as they would to a concert or an exhibition. Delluc and Moussinac were responsible for the first French screening of *The Cabinet of Doctor Caligari*, and introduced the Swedish school and a wide range of American films to France. In 1921 Delluc's search for backing for his own films bore fruit in another direction. A patron of the arts, Arkady Romanoff, reluctant to risk capital on a movie, instead financed another project: *Cinéa*, a journal intended to "be to the cinema what *Comœdia illustré* was to the theatre." *Cinéa* was launched in May 1921 and Delluc edited it until 1923, making it a forum for the critical and theoretical writing of the avant-garde.

Fièvre (*Fever*, 1921), another story of passion and jealousy ending in murder, is considered by Georges Sadoul to be Delluc's best film. As usual with Delluc, plot is secondary to the creation of atmosphere. The drama takes place in a Marseilles sailors' tavern—the French equivalent of an Ince saloon—and the sets, rather than the characters, have the leading role. Sadoul wrote: "The 'populism' of the subject, the creation of an 'atmosphere,' the pursuit of the unities of time and place bring *Fièvre* close to the German school being developed at that time by Carl Mayer, with *Scherben* and *Hintertreppe*. Their concerns coincide, rather than exert reciprocal influences." Mitry praised it for its naturalism, its vivid and atmospheric portrayal of a low-life milieu, pointing the way for many films in the coming decade that explored similar concerns.

After *Fièvre*, Delluc made two less successful films. *Le Chemin d'Ernoa* (*The Road to Ernoa*, 1921) was his first attempt to exploit the visual possibilities of landscape; by all accounts that was skillfully done, but the film as a whole was a failure, even in Delluc's eyes, while *Le Tonnerre* (*Thunder*, 1921) appears to have been an unmitigated disaster. *La Femme de nulle part* (*The Woman From Nowhere*, 1922) renewed his reputation. Here again Delluc explores time and memory, past and present. Eve Francis is the mysterious woman who revisits the house she left in her youth, abandoning her husband for a lover and a rootless future. She finds there a young woman facing a similar choice. The narrative interest depends on what the girl will decide to do, but this is almost incidental to the film's concern with the relationship between past and present. "For the first time in the cinema," Mitry wrote, "memory became the psychological medium of the plot. The relationship between present and past, maintained throughout, developed the action on two levels which constantly interacted in counterpoint, with the couple from the past representing the imaginary projection of the couple in the present, and memory acting as the link."

Mitry preferred this film even to *Fièvre*, and considered it to be Delluc's masterpiece: "The *mise-en-scène* was more meticulous, more refined than in any of his earlier films. . . . Yet if *The Woman From Nowhere* prefigures a whole future cinema it is through its theme and its treatment even more than through its *mise-en-scène*." The film is generally regarded as the finest example of Delluc's ability to create mood and atmosphere through landscape, and to achieve a harmony between acting, characters, and setting on film. There was also much praise for the sensitivity and poetry of such images as the final shot, in which Eve Francis gradually fades and disappears into the distance at the end of a long road.

Overwork and persistent financial difficulties aggravated Delluc's chronically delicate health, and *L'Inondation* (*The Flood*, 1923) was to be his last film. Influenced by the Swedish school of directors, it also uses landscape—and especially the River Rhône—to create a kind of visual poem. It tells the story of a woman who returns to her native village in the Rhône valley, falls in love with another woman's fiancé, and is drowned under mysterious circumstances when the river floods its banks. The picture was criticized on the grounds that the flood was superfluous to the plot and had only a poetic function, but Tariol and others have recognized its role as metaphor—as nature echoing human tragedy—and admire the film as another superb example of Delluc's "photogenia."

Delluc died of tuberculosis at the age of thirty-three. The consensus is that he died before he had fully realized his theories in his work, and that he is important less for what he achieved in his own films than as a pioneer who showed his contemporaries and successors the way forward. Henri Langlois called him a prophet. Later French directors have taken up and developed both of his central concerns as a filmmaker—naturalism and the nonnaturalistic representation of mental states—just as later critics have continued to explore the problems and insights first stated in his writings. He was the earliest critic-*auteur* in what was to be a French tradition, and he himself coined the term *cinéaste*. For Léon Moussinac he was "one of the heroes of the heroic epoch of the cinema."

—L.H.

FILMS: (with Rene Coiffart) Fumée noire (Black Smoke), 1920; Le Silence (Silence), 1920; Fièvre (Fever), 1921; Le Chemin d'Ernoa (The Road to Ernoa;

also known as L'Américain), 1921; Le Tonnerre (Thunder; also known as Evangeline et le tonnerre), 1921; Le Femme de nulle part (The Woman From Nowhere), 1922; L'Inondation (The Flood), 1923. *Published scripts*—Drames de cinéma, 1923 (contains La Fête espagnole, Le Silence, Fièvre, La Femme de nulle part).

ABOUT: Abel, R. French Cinema: The First Wave, 1915–1929, 1984; Bardèche, M. and Brasillach, R. L'Histoire du cinéma, 1953; Fescourt, H. La Foi et les montagnes, 1959; Francis, E. Temps Héroïques, 1949; Jeanne, R. and Ford, C. L'Histoire encyclopédique du cinéma, 1947–1968; Lapierre, M. Les cent visages du cinéma, 1948; Manvell, R. Experiment in the Film, 1949; Moussinac, L. L'Âge ingrat du cinéma, 1967; Tariol, M. Louis Delluc, 1965; Vincent, C. Histoire de l'art cinématographique, 1939; World Encyclopedia of the Film, 1972. *Periodicals*—L'Avant-Scène du Cinéma January 1971; Bianco e Nero 8–9 1953; Cahiers du Cinéma June–July 1968; Ciné-club March 1949 (Delluc issue); Cinema Journal Spring 1970, Fall 1976; L'Écran Français July 24, 1950; Film Dope September 1976; Film Form February 1959; Image et Son July 1957; Quarterly Review of Film Studies May 1976.

CECIL B. DeMILLE

DeMILLE, CECIL B(LOUNT) (August 12, 1881–January 21, 1959), American director and producer, was born in Ashfield, Massachusetts, the second of three children. His father, Henry Churchill de Mille, was descended from a Dutch family that had settled in America in 1658. His mother, formerly Beatrice Samuel, was English of Jewish stock, and had been a professional actress until her marriage. Henry de Mille had also wanted to be an actor, but in deference to his parents' wishes became a schoolteacher, writing plays in his spare time. He was an enthusiastic lay preacher in the Episcopalian church and for a time considered taking holy orders.

DeMille and his elder brother William (their younger sister Agnes died in infancy) were brought up at Echo Lake, New Jersey, in an atmosphere of strict piety and theatrical romanticism. Each evening Henry de Mille would read to his sons, with "a beautifully modulated voice and a fine sense of the dramatic values," one chapter from the Old Testament, one from the New, plus an episode from history or from such novelists as Thackeray or Victor Hugo. Encouraged by his wife, he became a collaborator of David Belasco, the most successful American playwright of his day, and the plays they wrote together did so well that de Mille was able to give up teaching and become a full-time author. In 1892 he moved with his family into a fine new house in Pompton Lakes, New Jersey. In February of the following year he died suddenly, of typhus.

Beatrice de Mille, a resolute woman, turned the family house into a girls' school, which provided the funds to send William to Columbia University and Cecil, in 1896, to Pennsylvania Military College. With the outbreak of the Spanish-American War, Cecil ran away from college and tried to enlist, but was turned down because he was too young. Both brothers had inherited their parents' love of theatre. William wrote plays at Columbia, and in 1898 Cecil enrolled at the Academy of Dramatic Arts in New York, to study acting. He graduated in 1900 and soon after made his Broadway debut in *Hearts Are Trumps* at the Garden Theatre. "I wanted to be an actor and I think I was fairly good. There is, however, some lingering difference of opinion upon that point."

DeMille continued to earn his living as an actor for the next ten years. (Professionally, he always spelled his name 'DeMille,' though privately he used the family spelling of "de Mille'.) In 1902 he married a fellow player, Constance Adams, the daughter of a Massachusetts judge. Their only child, Cecilia, was born in 1908; they later adopted three more children, John, Katherine, and Richard. Whatever his abilities, DeMille had no great success as an actor, endlessly touring small towns, often out of work for months at a time, sometimes hungry. The height of his stage career came in 1907, with a lead role in *The Warrens of Virginia*; but since the play was based on the adventures of DeMille's grandfather, written by his brother, and staged by David Belasco, the casting may not have been decided solely on merit. He also collaborated with his brother on several plays, none of them as successful as William's solo efforts, and provided a piece for Belasco, *The Return of Peter Grimm*, about an industrialist who comes back from the afterlife to right the wrongs he committed on earth. To DeMille's chagrin, Belasco extensively rewrote the play and put it out under his own name.

In 1910 Beatrice de Mille formed a theatrical agency, the DeMille Play Company, and made her younger son general manager. Among the impresarios DeMille met through his mother's agency was a former cornettist and vaudevillian, Jesse L. Lasky. Charming and convivial, Lasky soon became a close friend, and the two men worked together on three musicals, all moderately well received. DeMille, though, was becoming disillusioned with show business. After twelve years of hand-to-mouth existence in dingy lodgings, he dreamed of escaping to the South Seas or the Australian goldfields, and was even making serious plans to join Pancho Villa's revolutionary army in Mexico when Lasky offered an alternative suggestion.

Together with his brother-in-law, a glove salesman named Sam Goldfish (later changed to the less risible Goldwyn), Lasky had decided to go into motion pictures. Needing a director, the two approached D. W. Griffith, who turned them down, justifiably questioning their financial solvency. In blithe optimism, or perhaps desperation, Lasky proposed DeMille as a substitute. By way of training, the newly appointed Director-General of the Jesse L. Lasky Feature Play Company was sent to spend a day at the Edison Studios in the Bronx, where he watched the director point a camera at a girl while she climbed over a wall, ran down the road in simulated terror, and encountered a man to whom she talked with much vigorous gesticulation. "I went back to Jesse and Sam and reported, 'If that's pictures, we can make the best pictures ever made!'"

The infant company had acquired the rights to an old Broadway hit, *The Squaw Man*, by Edwin Milton Royle. This was a melodrama set largely in Wyoming, but DeMille set out for Flagstaff, Arizona. He took with him a leading Broadway actor, Dustin Farnum; a cameraman, Alfredo Gandolfi; and Oscar Apfel, an experienced movie director from Edison. En route, DeMille and Apfel roughed out a shooting script. Flagstaff, though, proved disappointing. Some accounts mention torrential rain; DeMille's version was that the area—hardly surprisingly—failed to look much like Wyoming. Whatever the reason, he made a snap decision: the party got back on the train and continued to the end of the line—Los Angeles. Once there, they looked around for a suitable location.

DeMille is often credited with having "founded" Hollywood, though he was not the first to film there; a short-lived outfit called the Nestor Company had built a studio there in 1911. But no other filmmakers, it seems, were in evidence in late December 1913, when the Lasky party arrived in a small, straggling township ten miles north of Los Angeles and established, in two-thirds of a barn on the corner of Selma Avenue and Vine Street, what was to become Paramount Studios. The rest of the barn was retained by the owner, Jacob Stern, to stable his horses and carriage, and DeMille kept a large wastebasket as "a very convenient refuge for my feet whenever Mr. Stern washed his carriage and the water ran under my desk."

To direct his first movie, DeMille adopted a distinctive costume which he retained largely unaltered throughout his working career and which came to represent the publicly accepted image of an old-style movie director: open-necked shirt, riding breeches, boots and puttees, along with a riding-crop, a large megaphone, and a whistle on a neck-cord. Charges of theatricality were met with pained denial from DeMille, who always insisted that his garb was strictly functional: the boots and puttees afforded support to his weak ankle and protection against snakes. But his costume also undoubtedly reflected his favorite self-image—the movie director as bold and masterful adventurer, intrepid pioneer and empire-builder.

Certainly *The Squaw Man* (1914), on which DeMille and Apfel shared directorial credit, was in several ways a pioneering work. At six reels, it was the first feature-length film to be made in the United States. It was also, as far as is known, the first film to have been adapted from a Broadway play, the first to utilize indoor lighting, and the first to carry a list of acting credits. Filming was dogged by the usual picturesque hazards attendant on early movie-making, including attempted sabotage by agents of the Patents Company, always eager to discourage independent filmmakers. Twice DeMille was shot at while riding to work, and once several hundred feet of negative were found torn from the reel and trampled underfoot. Fortunately, DeMille had taken the precaution of shooting a duplicate.

The film's plot derives from the well-tried conventions of nineteenth-century melodrama. An English aristocrat, nobly assuming responsibility for an embezzlement committed by his cousin the earl, exiles himself to the Wild West and marries an Indian girl. The earl, wounded in a hunting accident, confesses on his deathbed, the Indian girl obligingly kills herself, and the hero returns home to inherit the earldom and his cousin's wife, whom he has always secretly (but honorably) loved. DeMille threw in a storm at sea and plenty of gunplay, and completed the film for nearly twice what Lasky and Goldfish had anticipated.

The producers' alarm was compounded at the initial screening. The picture jumped, skittered, and jerked; actors' heads vanished off the top of the screen and reappeared below their feet. In despair, DeMille and Lasky appealed for help to a leading Philadelphia exhibitor, Sigmund Lubin, known as an expert on film stock. A founder member of the Patents Company, Lubin had little enough incentive to help these incompetent upstarts. Nonetheless, with remarkable generosity, he diagnosed the problem—DeMille, using a cheap second-hand machine, had sprocketed his film at 65 holes per foot instead of 64—and had the film reperforated to run impeccably.

Its teething troubles over, *The Squaw Man* proved a triumphant success, taking in over $250,000 at the box office. Contemporary reviewers praised its narrative fluency. "In point of sustained interest it gives place to none," commented the *New York Dramatic Mirror*; "best of all, there is a real story told in photographed action, not in lengthy subtitles illustrated by fragmentary scenes." Reviews of DeMille's first solo film, *The Call of the North* (1914), were even more laudatory. "A lofty ambition to attain the highest ideals in the motion picture art gave birth to this feature," W. Stephen Bush enthused in *The Moving Picture World*, "which I am tempted to describe as one of the greatest classics ever produced on American soil." A revenge story set amid the Canadian snows (and largely filmed at 100° temperatures at Big Bear Lake, California), it starred two prominent stage actors: Robert Edeson, who had played the lead in the stage version, and Theodore Roberts, a stately veteran who was to feature in twenty-three DeMille films, culminating in his performance as Moses in *The Ten Commandments*. The cameraman, Alvin Wyckoff, was a former actor who combined seemingly instinctive command of natural light with tireless ingenuity in devising new techniques of artificial lighting. With characteristic authorial arrogance, DeMille himself appears during the credits to introduce the actors.

Lasky, eagerly buying up likely literary properties, now offered DeMille a classic Western novel, Owen Wister's *The Virginian*, which was to become the source of several movies and a long-running television series. DeMille's was the first screen version (1914), and included the much-loved line "When you say that—smile!" Dramatic use of lighting effects, highly sophisti-

cated for the period, lent weight to the undemanding story of an easygoing cowboy impelled to action after seeing his best friend hanged for involvement with a gang of rustlers. The hanging itself was shown only obliquely, via a pattern of shadows—a device suggested by Wyckoff, who also developed lenses allowing DeMille to shoot straight into the sun, or to show a darkened room lit by a single match. Charles Wolfe, in Coursodon's *American Directors,* noted that "DeMille's mise-en-scène in these early films is never casual. Each scene has its own texture and dramatic weight: high-contrast lighting for strange or threatening situations; soft, dapple-lit backgrounds for the romantic outdoors; an authentic sense of dust and gloom amid tenements; heavily draped domestic interiors for the aristocracy."

In a matter of months, and with only three films, DeMille had established himself as one of the foremost new directors, and the Lasky Company as a major force in the industry. Along with the remaining third of Jacob Stern's barn, the company had now acquired the adjoining land for the construction of a hundred-foot stage, plus workshops and prop rooms, and Lasky had leased twenty thousand acres of mountain, forest, and desert for location shooting. DeMille moved into a house in Cahuenga Pass and brought his wife and daughter from New York to join him. His brother William also arrived, having lost his initial skepticism about the movies in the face of the vast sums being made by Cecil and his partners, and was appointed head of the scenario department. By the end of 1914 four units were shooting simultaneously on the Lasky lot: one headed by DeMille himself, and three others, directed by Oscar Apfel, Frederick Thompson, and George Melford respectively, under his supervision.

During the next two years, DeMille directed (and often scripted and edited) twenty feature-length films, besides supervising, and directing occasional sequences in, the films assigned to other directors. At one point in 1915 he directed two movies, *The Cheat* and *The Golden Chance,* back-to-back in twelve days. He continued to favor filmed versions of middlebrow stage hits, adapting such writers as Booth Tarkington (*The Man From Home,* 1914), Belasco (*Rose of the Rancho,* 1914; *The Girl of the Golden West,* 1915), and William de Mille (*The Warrens of Virginia,* 1915; *The Wild Goose Chase,* 1915). These were for the most part traditional melodramas with period or Wild West settings, though DeMille also turned his hand to exotic adventures (*The Captive,* 1915; *The Arab,* 1915) and even a couple of knockabout comedies (*Chimmie Fadden,* 1915; *Chimmie Fadden Out*

West, 1915) featuring the vaudeville comedian Victor Moore as a well-meaning lad from the Bowery.

Not all of DeMille and Wyckoff's technical innovations were accepted without protest. Some dramatic chiaroscuro lighting for *The Unafraid* (1915) elicited a worried telegram from Sam Goldfish. He feared that, since only half of each actor's face was visible, exhibitors would pay only half-price for the film. DeMille wired back: "If you and the exhibitors don't know Rembrandt lighting when you see it, it's no fault of mine." "For Rembrandt lighting," Goldfish responded happily, "the exhibitors will pay double."

Perhaps the finest of DeMille's early pictures—for some critics, indeed, the best film he ever made—was *The Cheat* (1915). In *Du Muet au Parlant* Alexandre Arnoux wrote that "*The Cheat* covertly determined the whole subsequent development of cinema. . . . it opened the door to technique, anticipated the creative role of the camera, accustomed us to changing camera angles, elliptical cutting and the rhythms and resources of montage, and laid the foundations of terse, uncluttered screen narrative." A melodrama, though for once set in modern urban surroundings, the film conveys a vivid atmosphere of moral and emotional hysteria. A spoiled socialite gambles away charity funds and panic-stricken, borrows $10,000 from a rich oriental admirer in return for a promise of sexual favors. When she tries to renege on the deal, he brands her on the shoulder, and she shoots him. Her husband takes the blame, but at the trial she confesses, displaying her branded flesh.

The Cheat may well have been the first film to make use of psychological, rather than spatial or temporal, editing. The principle of cutting between two simultaneous, though separate, events (heroine awaits death on railroad track while faithful dog races for help) was already well established. DeMille, though, interrupts a conversation between husband and wife with repeated shots of the wife's admirer, who is miles away—not to show us what the man is doing, but simply to indicate that he, not the nearby husband, is the focus of her thoughts. Commonplace enough today, such editing at the time contributed a valuable new resource to cinematic narrative.

For a modern audience, the film's main weakness—as so often with early movies—lies in the acting. Fannie Ward's "baby vamp" mannerisms as the heroine (she was forty-three at the time of shooting) are especially hard to take. By way of contrast, Sessue Hayakawa gives a superbly controlled portrayal of cool, sensual malice, all the more telling, in its restraint, alongside the mugging and posturing of his fellow-players.

The Cheat was widely admired, particularly in France—where it influenced a whole generation of directors, including L'Herbier, Delluc, and Charensol—and was later twice remade. DeMille was now rated among the finest American directors, the equal of Thomas Ince and second only to D. W. Griffith, to whose supremacy and influence he always paid tribute. "Griffith had no rivals," he observed many years later. "He was the teacher of us all. . . . Griffith was the first to photograph thought." It may, all the same, have been in the hope of rivaling the older man, who had just made *Birth of a Nation*, that DeMille began to yearn for grander, more elaborate projects—an ambition certainly encouraged, and possibly instigated, by his collaborator Jeanie Macpherson. Having joined the company as an actress, in *Rose of the Rancho*, she became in rapid succession DeMille's stenographer, co-screenwriter, and mistress. She was to stay with him, with the fidelity that marked many of his closest associates, until her death in 1947.

Jesse Lasky had achieved a notable coup in securing the services—if not the voice—of the leading operatic star Geraldine Farrar, whom he had signed to play the title role in a silent *Carmen* (1915): "a Stradivarius without its strings," observed *Photoplay* scornfully. DeMille directed her in this, with some success, though a rushed-out rival version from Raoul Walsh took the lion's share of the box-office. Two more Farrar vehicles, *Temptation* (1916) and *Maria Rosa* (1916), were well received, and DeMille announced, despite Lasky's misgivings, a ten-reel version of the life of Joan of Arc, with Farrar as Joan.

Joan the Woman (1917) launched the long line of grand historical spectaculars of which DeMille became the supreme exponent. Carlos Clarens (in Richard Roud's *Cinema*) wrote that DeMille "assimilated within the film romanticism, emphasis, *verismo*, truculence, overacting, aestheticism . . . in short, opera." Vast sets were constructed for *Joan the Woman*, including painstaking replicas of medieval buildings photographed in France by emissaries. Genuine fifteenth-century weapons and other artifacts were purchased from museums, with the obsessive mania for authenticity in trivial details that characterized all of DeMille's period films. With Wyckoff's eager cooperation, DeMille experimented with double exposure, color photography, and night-for-night shooting.

Possibly in order to lend relevance to these remote historical events, the main story was framed within a contrived prologue and epilogue set in the trenches of the Somme. Chronological sandwiches of this kind were served up regularly in DeMille's pictures, especially those scripted by Macpherson, throughout the silent period; a modern story would abruptly transpose its characters to supposed previous existences, or an ancient story be yoked to a modern "parallel." It was probably this quirk, rather than any blatant anachronism, that inspired Nicholas Bentley's famous clerihew (much resented by its subject):

> Cecil B. DeMille,
> Rather against his will,
> Was persuaded to leave Moses
> Out of *The Wars of the Roses*.

The problems of shooting *Joan the Woman* were exacerbated not only by Farrar—always temperamental, and now overweight as well—but also by the power struggle going on within the Lasky Company. Lasky had negotiated a merger with Adolph Zukor's Famous Players. Zukor, a cold, calculating man known to his subordinates as "Creepy," soon refused to work with Sam Goldfish, who tactfully resigned. With Goldfish out of the way, Zukor readily established his ascendancy over the easygoing Lasky and began exerting pressure on DeMille, whom he considered wantonly extravagant.

Joan the Woman was respectfully received by the critics. "If anything . . . were needed to convince the photoplay-going public that Cecil B. DeMille belongs in the front rank of the day, his direction of *Joan the Woman* should supply it in full measure," wrote George Blaisdell in *Motion Picture World*. Convinced or not, the public showed little inclination to go to this particular photoplay. *Joan* flopped badly on release, and Lasky, pushed by Zukor, insisted on cutting two whole reels. DeMille reluctantly acquiesced, but the shortened version did no better.

Mary Pickford, whose career was at an awkward juncture, had signed a short-term contract with Lasky and, as the first top movie star ever to join the company, was naturally assigned to DeMille. Director and star took an immediate dislike to each other; he found her mannered and conceited, and she objected to his autocratic style of working. They made only two films together: *Romance of the Redwoods* (1917), a sentimental Western, and *The Little American* (1917). The latter, an opportunistic flagwaver, ended with a shot of Pickford kissing her German suitor, whom love has redeemed from his Hunnish beastliness, through the wire of a POW camp. The sight of America's Sweetheart kissing a German (even a redeemed one) proved more than the public could take, and DeMille hastily

shot a substitute ending, in which the German was killed and Pickford wound up with her other lover, a foppish Frenchman.

After two last, indifferent pictures with Farrar—*The Woman God Forgot* (1917), a historical drama set in Aztec Mexico, and *The Devil Stone* (1917)—DeMille made perhaps the strangest, most somber film of his career, *The Whispering Chorus* (1918). Anticipating in mood, and in Wyckoff's shadowy lighting, something of the *noir* style of thirty years later, the project was one "in which DeMille," according to Kevin Brownlow, "sunk not only a large sum of money but also his heart." A young husband, desperate for cash, steals from his boss and then, finding a corpse in the river, disguises it to look like himself. Years later he is arrested for his own murder; his wife, meanwhile, has remarried and is pregnant. To save her from scandal, he makes a false confession and goes to his death. The chorus of the title are the voices of his own impulses, some good, some evil, who appear round him as ghostly, disembodied faces.

Reactions to *The Whispering Chorus* were puzzled and mostly hostile. Reviewers complained of "abnormal morbidity," and audiences shunned the picture. From this disappointment some critics have dated a decline in the quality of DeMille's work. "DeMille changed his attitude towards his audience," Kevin Brownlow maintained. "As he lowered his sights to meet the lowest common denominator, so the standard of his films plummeted." Undoubtedly at this time DeMille's career was faltering. He needed to find a new direction, and a limp remake of *The Squaw Man* (1918) was certainly not the answer.

Other interests were occupying his attention. He had elected himself captain of the Lasky Home Guard, which would march down Hollywood Boulevard with prop rifles and wardrobe uniforms, but to his lasting regret was turned down for active service. However, he was told that the army was eager for pilots, regardless of age. He promptly started to take flying lessons and, fascinated and delighted by the experience, soon bought his own plane. He had also recently embarked on a long-term liaison with the actress Julia Faye, who had a small role in *The Woman God Forgot*. Constance DeMille reacted as usual with serene tolerance, but Jeanie Macpherson was furiously jealous, rather to DeMille's amusement. Eventually he persuaded Fay and Macpherson to accept joint billing, as mistress-in-chief. Quite how he reconciled these relationships, and various more transitory affairs, with his strict Episcopalian creed and frequently stated belief in the sanctity of marriage, remains a mystery, since no one ever dared ask him.

Once again Jesse Lasky provided the impetus for a fresh departure. For some months he had been pressing on DeMille the script of a social comedy about the marital behavior of the newly rich. Based on a popular novel, *Old Wives for New* (1918) concerned a man who divorces one woman for another, leaves her for a third, only to end up, chastened, with the one he has really loved all along. When DeMille reluctantly got around to filming it, it proved a smash hit with the public and most of the critics. Those reviewers who dissented tended to condemn the picture for "disgusting debauchery" and "most immoral episodes," thus further boosting box-office receipts.

Lasky and DeMille had hit on a formula perfectly attuned to the times. *Old Wives for New* set the style for a whole series of DeMille social comedies, besides paving the way for more openly cynical variations on the theme by Stroheim and Lubitsch. The "new morality" of sexual liberation and easy divorce could be presented in all its alluring glamour, amid scenes of glittering affluence and fast living; but in the final reel the eternal verities, slightly shopworn but still serviceable, were comfortingly reaffirmed. The erring spouse, almost invariably, returned sadder but wiser to the forgiving arms of the original partner. DeMille found himself at once reviled as a purveyor of sexual titillation and praised for his defence of marital virtue. *Motion Picture Magazine* hailed him as "the apostle of domesticity. Surely no married couple would come to grief who heeded his lessons."

"Divorce . . . fails to provide the satisfactions it at first promises, and contrition leads to a reformed marriage," noted Charles Wolfe, encapsulating the theme of *We Can't Have Everything* (1918). "The reassertion of monogamous moral values consequently does not ignore the desires that first motivate the drama—it encompasses them." Part of the film's action was set in a movie studio (which allowed Tully Marshall, playing a temperamental director, to give a neat impersonation of DeMille), and William de Mille's script originally called for it to burn down; in order to cut costs, he and Cecil agreed that this scene should be omitted. While shooting was still in progress, though, the Lasky Studios—presumably by fortunate chance—caught fire. Cameras were hastily set up, and the studio blaze was shot as written.

We Can't Have Everything was the first DeMille film to credit Anne Bauchens as editor. Bauchens, who was to edit all his remaining films, never thereafter worked for any other director, thus joining the small band of women, including Macpherson, Faye, and his secretary Gladys Rosson, who dedicated virtually their entire lives to DeMille. "His effect on the womenfolk," his niece Agnes de Mille observed, "was always that of a cock in a barnyard."

Don't Change Your Husband (1919)—the overt sermonizing of DeMille's pictures was starting to infiltrate even the titles—gave former comedienne Gloria Swanson her first major starring role, as a wife who tires of her slobbish, nouveau-riche husband. She divorces him for a suave playboy who of course proves to be a two-timing cad—by which time her first husband, conveniently, has mended his ways and is happy to welcome her back. Reviews were still generally appreciative—"clean and wholesome, sustained in interest . . . it touches home both man and woman," commented *Variety*—but here and there, as in Julian Johnson's notice in *Photoplay*, a hint of amused condescension could be detected: "Here is life—just as life springs up and grows in gardens fertilized with gold."

James Barrie's stage hit, *The Admirable Crichton*, extensively adapted by Macpherson, was transformed into *Male and Female* (1919). (Barrie's straight-faced reaction to the change of title, "Capital—why didn't I think of it myself?", was accepted as high praise by DeMille, on whom irony was wasted.) The picture adhered broadly to Barrie's plot—when a group of pampered socialites are shipwrecked, the butler, a natural leader, comes to dominate the group but "the emphasis of the story," as David Robinson pointed out, "was altered so that its message was now essentially the supremacy of sex over class barriers." Macpherson also dragged in, on the flimsiest of pretexts, one of her beloved historical flashbacks; back in Babylon, the butler (Thomas Meighan) was king and his snooty employer (Swanson) a slave. The costumes were designed by Mitchell Leisen, just starting out on his Hollywood career; he went on to act as designer on most of DeMille's pictures through *Cleopatra*, before turning director on his own account.

Why Change Your Wife? (1920) presented the mixture as before but with the triangle reversed: Thomas Meighan being fought over (literally at one point) by Swanson and Bebe Daniels. The surroundings were lusher than ever; affluence in DeMille's pictures was acquiring its own moral value. "In *Why Change Your Wife?*," Sumiko Higashi wrote, "sexual frigidity or incompatibility is solved by a trip to the boutique to purchase a precariously constructed swimsuit. Commodities invested with extraordinary powers could effect magical transformations on screen and thus acquired allure for the spectator." Burns Mantle, writing in *Photoplay*, described it as "the most gorgeously sensual film of the month; in decoration the most costly, in physical allure the most fascinating, in effect the most immoral."

Perhaps hoping to recoup his reputation, DeMille reverted to pious melodrama with *Something to Think About* (1920), in which Swanson's selfless love transfigures an embittered cripple but neither critics nor public were impressed. *Forbidden Fruit* (1921) rehashed the earlier *The Golden Chance*, with the addition of a staggeringly elaborate interpolation of *Cinderella*, for which Mitchell Leisen crossed kitsch with Hieronymus Bosch. Schnitzler's 1893 play *Anatol* furnished the basis for *The Affairs of Anatol* (1921)—an enjoyable enough comedy that wholly missed the bittersweet cynicism of the original. "It should be enormously popular," remarked Robert E. Sherwood in *Life*, "especially with those who think Schnitzler is a cheese."

The note of contempt in Sherwood's review was by now typical, particularly among the more sophisticated; DeMille's critical standing was in what turned out to be permanent decline. As each successive picture strove to outdo its predecessors in salaciousness and visual sumptuousness ("The Most Gorgeous Gowns of any DeMille Picture!" gushed the publicity for *Saturday Night*), his reputation slipped from that of a major director to "the hokum merchant par excellence" (Tamar Lane), or a "mentor of erotica and display" (Lewis Jacobs). The widely accepted view of Hollywood as gilded peepshow, where the toiling masses could gawp in envy or derision at the opulence of the idle rich, finds its origin in DeMille's films of this period. The director himself asserted that "your poor person wants to see wealth, colorful, interesting, exotic—he has an idea of it many times more brightly colored than the reality. How do I know? Because, when doing twenty weeks solid of one-night stands, without baths . . . my dreams of wealth . . . [had] color, lights, fun."

The theme of cross-class attraction had been cautiously broached in *Male and Female*; it was taken a step further in *Saturday Night* (1922), where a society heiress elopes with her chauffeur, while her millionaire fiancé marries his laundress's daughter. Social distinctions, though, are not to be flouted. Both couples are shown to be hopelessly mismatched, and by the final reel have split and reformed along class lines. This simple anecdote was expanded to nine reels by some spectacular disaster sequences and the usual lavish production design. "When it comes to the creation of a bizarre bed or a fantastic negligée or a rococo bathroom," Arthur Denison wrote in *Filmplay Journal*, "no one can touch Mr. DeMille, not even the police, apparently."

If DeMille resented these critical jibes ("Every time I make a picture," he once remarked, "the critics' estimation of the American public goes down ten percent"), he could take comfort from his box-office returns and his reputation as a shaper—for better or worse—of public taste. Sumiko Higashi calls his Jazz Age films "textbooks for consumption" in the new era of mass production, and says that "his impact upon the consumption of such commodities as fashion apparel and furnishings, as well as a preoccupation with social etiquette, was well-noted at the time."

DeMille's own growing affluence by no means derived solely from his movie work. As early as 1916 he had built himself a palatial house in Laughlin Park, on what later was named DeMille Drive, and had acquired a 600-acre ranch in the Sierra Madres. Though aviation had failed to get him into the war, it remained a passion. He bought eight more planes, and in May 1919 formalized his operations into the Mercury Aviation Company, California's first commercial airline. The venture prospered, soon occupying so much of DeMille's attention that the studio finally persuaded him, in September 1921, to sell out to a rival airline. He had also—partly for protection against Zukor, with whom relations continued strained—formed Cecil B. DeMille Productions, which diversified into real estate, oil, securities, and banking.

Manslaughter (1922) found him back in didactic vein, with a moral tale of a social butterfly who finds regeneration through a prison sojourn and the love of a reforming District Attorney (Thomas Meighan). "Is the Modern World Racing to Ruin on a Wave of Jazz and Cocktails?" demanded the posters. As a parallel to such modern decadence, DeMille introduced a flashback to ancient Rome, complete with gladiators, wild animals, and orgiastic near-naked extras who are trampled by the DA as Attila the Hun. He delved yet deeper into the past for *Adam's Rib* (1923); a modern love affair between two employees of a natural-history museum leads back to the stone age for a prehistoric courtship.

Reviewers had by now declared open season on his movies. (A favored ploy was to compare them adversely with those of William de Mille, now well established as a director, whose pictures—few of which have survived —were said to be far more subtle and perceptive.) *Adam's Rib* was slammed unmercifully. *Variety* called it "a silly, piffling screenplay," and in the *News*

Sentinel Mabel Oppenheimer dismissed it as "a star example of the kind of thing which makes intelligent people laugh at the motion pictures." It was also condemned for salacity, like many of its predecessors, to DeMille's indignation. "I am not prudish in matters of either life or art. You cannot have drama without conflict, and the age-old conflict of good and evil demands that the evil should be shown clearly for what it is." Censorship, he maintained, was "the most pernicious influence in America today." Despite this, he was instrumental in having Will H. Hays installed as prime guardian of screen morality—no doubt preferring that Hollywood should censor itself rather than have someone else do it. He also helped frame the notorious Hays Code, whose basic principles, he announced, "have been valid since they were revealed on Mount Sinai."

The *ex cathedra* tone was characteristic, De-Mille never being loath to pronounce on the ethical role of the cinema in general and his own films in particular. "We hold great power," he once told his fellow filmmakers. "Make it a power for good—for truth, for beauty, and for freedom." He always denied, however, that he made films with any didactic purpose. "My pictures do not preach. I shoot for the drama and let the sermons fall where they may."

The silent social-comedy cycle, of which *Adam's Rib* was the final installment, have been overshadowed in DeMille's output by his later series of epics. Yet these comedies, for all their ludicrous aspects—the self-conscious ostentation, the smug moralizing, the glib recourse to trite historical parallels—seem today in many ways the most interesting of his films, exemplifying as they do the central ambiguity of his work and of his personality. As many writers have observed, DeMille's values, both moral and aesthetic, remained all his life essentially those of the nineteenth century. His dramatic approach derived straight from Belasco, himself the heir of a long, thunderous tradition of Victorian melodrama; and his morality rested on the old bourgeois belief in material success based upon—and thus justifying—the certainty of one's own Christian rectitude.

These brassbound, slightly preposterous values DeMille brought to bear, in his comedies, on the fluid, self-questioning, iconoclastic America of the Jazz Age; hence their central dichotomy. Many critics, then and since, have accused De-Mille of cynicism or hypocrisy. Others have located the schizophrenia within DeMille himself, or in the West Coast culture of the period, torn between two ages, two incompatible value systems. For the first fifty years of its existence,

Hollywood struggled to contain the emotional overdrive of the world's greatest dream factory within the morality of a nineteenth century middle-class nursery. DeMille's films are perhaps only the most conspicuous manifestation of that struggle. Carlos Clarens has suggested that he was really "a sociologist, hence his attention to fashion and manners, his delight in props, décor, utensils."

The failure of *Adam's Rib*—financial as well as critical—prompted DeMille to consider a change of course. Despite the poor reception accorded *Joan the Woman,* he still longed to make historical spectaculars; the persistent flashbacks embedded in so many of his modern films could well be seen as half-submerged chunks of unmade epics. Inspired, or so he claimed, by the results of a poll held by the Los Angeles *Times,* he announced that his next picture would be a biblical blockbuster, *The Ten Commandments* (1923). The studio heads reacted with notable lack of enthusiasm—"Nobody wants to see a picture about people running around wearing bedsheets"—and the press were scarcely more encouraging. *Screen Classics* suggested that he might film the telephone directory for an encore.

Doggedly, DeMille pressed ahead, amassing vast quantities of ancient artifacts and reams of background research. His original plan to shoot on location in Egypt and Palestine was vetoed by Zukor, and he had to settle for a desert area in central California. Twenty-five hundred actors and forty-five hundred animals were assembled, along with a small army of technicians; and a whole city, complete with streets, schools, hospitals, and a detachment of the Eleventh Cavalry, was constructed to house them. DeMille's own police corps patrolled the streets, with instructions to crack down on gambling, bootlegging, or fraternization between the rigorously segregated male and female sections of the camp. Sets of unprecedented magnitude were erected in the desert, and the logistics of shooting were worked out, if not invariably effected, with military precision.

DeMille had always enjoyed—quite possibly in both senses—a reputation as an exceptionally autocratic dictator, exacting total loyalty and unquestioning obedience. From this production, though, can be dated the enduring legend, source of innumerable anecdotes and jokes, of the megalomaniac Boss, bullying and terrorizing actors and crew alike, bending thousands to his will: a stocky, balding figure pacing furiously about the set, riding crop slapping against jackboots, followed by an obsequious entourage, as reported by *Time* magazine: "Wherever he goes on the set, one man follows to whip a chair under him, another to shove a megaphone in front of him, while a secretary devotedly notes down every word he says."

Though DeMille in his autobiography deprecated this image, his on-set behavior by all accounts did little to discourage it. "If he wasted zeal in self-questioning, he couldn't keep up the pace," wrote Agnes de Mille, who had observed him in action. "This is the unflagging zeal, the undivided strength of the prophet, the fanatic— or . . . the absolute monarch." This absolutist stance, Sumiko Higashi suggested, extended even to his public: "His brand of spectacle demanded hierarchical relations with him at the apex, a staff that deferred to him as God, and a childlike audience." "In later years," Carlos Clarens says, "it was customary for DeMille to announce his forthcoming productions personally, in trailers much longer than usual; and his voice is often heard on the soundtrack, dubbing for History or God."

The Ten Commandments was initially budgeted at $700,000, with Zukor's grudging agreement, and soon ran over budget. When costs reached $1,000,000, Zukor demanded that shooting be abandoned. DeMille responded by offering to buy the picture for a million dollars, and Zukor, unsure of his ground, backed down. The film was finally brought in for $1,475,000. (Zukor's own recollection of these events, recorded in 1967 when he was ninety-four and DeMille safely dead, was somewhat different. "My most successful film was *The Ten Commandments* made in 1923. . . . I always believed that anything to do with religion would be good. There was no precedent for it. But fortunately I found a man who agreed with me. . . . That was Cecil DeMille.")

DeMille's persistence was vindicated. The film was a roaring success, recouping its massive costs several times over. Even the critics were enthusiastic; James R. Quirk hailed it in *Photoplay* as "the best photoplay ever made. The greatest theatrical spectacle in history. . . . It wipes the slate clean of charges of immoral influence." The first half of the picture, filmed in early Technicolor, in which Moses frees the Children of Israel from bondage, leads them through the desert, and receives the Tablets of the Law, still looks imposing today. "Theatricality is on the grandest scale," wrote Eric Rhode, "with masterly lighting and art direction sustaining large gestures; . . . while some of the miracles, such as the parting of the Red Sea, remain among the most impressive ever filmed."

On to all this is grafted a modern story, about two brothers who both fall in love with a waif brought home by their pious mother. One brother is a sad degenerate who indulges in such debauchery as playing his phonograph on Sunday—and this despite the exhortations of his mother, who pursues him around the house brandishing the largest family Bible in the history of bookbinding. She dies when a church built by the bad brother falls on her, after which he goes into rapid decline, takes a Eurasian mistress, and dies in a motorboat crash. The good brother collects the love of both God and the waif.

DeMille had clearly found his true metier, but it would be a few years before he was able to practice it regularly. Meanwhile he reverted to melodramas, interspersed with the occasional comedy. *Triumph* (1924) managed to be neither one nor the other, merely dull; its successor, *Feet of Clay* (1924), in Charles Higham's estimation "arguably the most peculiar film DeMille ever made," offered a bizarre cocktail of social melodrama and spiritualism. A young athlete, having lost his toes to a shark, subsequently gasses himself along with his wife; in the afterworld the young couple are given a second chance by a portentous being called the Keeper of the Book, and restored to life.

With *The Golden Bed* (1925) DeMille's cinema of conspicuous consumption achieved its most literal expression. A spoiled Southern belle, having disposed of one husband and various lovers, marries a candy manufacturer and pushes him into throwing a ruinously extravagant Candy Ball to upstage the local gentry. Amid gigantic candy boxes filled with brown satin chocolates, musicians arrayed as candy sticks played to dancers dressed in lollipops and barley sugar. The sequence culminated in young men licking the chocolate off living, female chocolate bars.

In January 1925, shortly before *The Golden Bed* was released, DeMille quit Paramount (as, through various mergers and takeovers, the studio had become). Despite efforts at mediation by the unhappy Lasky, the feud with Zukor had come to a head. At the final showdown, to DeMille's lasting resentment, Zukor stated coldly, "Cecil, you have never been one of us."

With the help of a banking associate, Jeremiah Milbank, DeMille set up as his own producer, buying the old Ince Studios and the ailing Producers' Distribution Corporation to form the Cinema Corporation of America. Those stars who proved amenable to bribery or flattery were enticed away from Paramount. An ambitious program of films was announced, to include an epic treatment of the life of Christ. DeMille's first two independent productions, though, hardly augured well for the new company. *The Road to Yesterday* (1925) featured a spectacular train crash, four of whose victims are then transported back to previous lives in medieval England where their destinies were fatally intertwined. The public was not taken with this, nor with *The Volga Boatman* (1926), a large-scale drama of the Russian Revolution. (In spite of his right-wing views, DeMille treated the revolutionary cause with more sympathy than it usually got from Hollywood.) Reviews were good, but the picture fared badly at the box office.

"One thing I have always admired about my younger brother," William de Mille wrote with gentle irony, "is his ability to bite off more than he can chew, and then chew it." The company, dangerously underfunded from the first, was now in serious financial trouble. None of its productions—there were several other directors working at the studios, William de Mille among them—had scored a major success, and DeMille's own films so far had been disastrous. The directors of the Keith Cinema chain, with whom CCA had merged, were implacably hostile to DeMille and all he stood for. Undeterred, he pushed ahead with one of the most ambitious projects of the silent period, with a final budget in excess of two and a half million.

King of Kings (1927), in David Robinson's view, "remains a direct and honourable piece of craftsmanship." For once, DeMille resisted Jeanie Macpherson's attempt to tack on a modern story; the film deals with the ministry, trial, and death of Christ, though coming at it from a highly DeMillean angle. "I decided to jolt them all out of their preconceptions with an opening scene that none of them would be expecting: a lavish party in the luxurious home of . . . [Mary Magdalene, whose] admirers taunt her because one of their number, young Judas, has evidently found the company of some wandering carpenter more interesting. . . ." H. B. Warner made a gentle, dignified Christ. The film was shot in monochrome and Technicolor; J. Peverell Marley, DeMille's regular cinematographer since Alvin Wyckoff had quit after a row during *The Ten Commandments*, deployed seventy-five different lenses to achieve some striking lighting effects, notably in the swirling, Doré-esque crucifixion sequence.

As shooting proceeded and costs rose, DeMille came under renewed attack in the boardroom of CCA, with Milbank, who shared his evangelical instincts, often his sole defender. To solve the pressing financial problems, a merger with Pathé was proposed, much to DeMille's disgust.

He shot off a desperate cable: "Pathé has stood for the cheapest brand of motion pictures for so long and the name DeMille has stood for the best brand it would be a little like combining Tiffany and Woolworth." But the merger went ahead. Once again, DeMille's single-minded determination was vindicated at the box office. Reviews were mixed, but commercially *King of Kings* was an overwhelming worldwide success. Letters poured in testifying to the picture's inspirational impact, and prints were still in circulation forty years later.

DeMille's last film as an independent producer was *The Godless Girl* (1929), a tirade against the atheistic propaganda which, so he claimed, "is secretly distributed among students in high schools and which tends to subvert American ideals." Although DeMille at this time dismissed talking pictures as a passing fad, sound was added to the final reels; it did little to help "this hack yarn with religious undercurrents," as *Variety* caustically described it.

These talking sequences were directed by the German actor Fritz Feld, not by DeMille, who had already moved on. By 1928 the rickety, self-lacerating CCA had fallen into the unmerciful hands of the Boston financier Joseph Kennedy, who began molding it into what would become RKO. DeMille, who had little liking for Kennedy (a feeling that was reciprocated), signed a three-picture deal with Louis B. Mayer and in August 1928 moved with his entire staff across to MGM.

"My three years at MGM," he later recalled, "were not particularly happy ones." After fifteen years of near-autonomy, it was hard for him to relinquish control over both content and casting; but independence was never something that any director—even one so eminent—could expect much of at Metro. Nor were religious epics likely to fit in with the house style. Still, his three MGM talkies, if hardly his best work, can each be seen as summing up in its own way one aspect of his silent oeuvre: melodrama, comedy, and Western.

Dynamite (1929), his first sound picture, centered on yet another spoiled socialite, this time one who marries a tough miner about to hang, only to see him reprieved at the last moment. DeMille threw in some social dazzle and a mining disaster, and the picture—which gave Charles Bickford his starring debut as the miner—was moderately well received. Not so *Madame Satan* (1930), DeMille's one and only musical, which flopped badly. A zany postscript to the earlier cycle of social comedies, it starts by reworking the plot of *Why Change Your Wife?* (neglected wife transforms into sexy siren to lure back errant husband) and climaxes in a song-and-dance extravaganza on board a Zeppelin moored to the Empire State Building. Richard Roud found it "one of his most peculiarly engaging films . . . it has to be seen to be believed."

Both director and studio were by now eager to see the back of each other. To complete his contract, DeMille fell back on an old maxim: when in doubt, remake *The Squaw Man* (1931). This third version of the creaky old Western drama looked even feebler than its 1918 predecessor and met with a predictable response from the public. Labeled "box-office poison," and with no base for future operations, DeMille quit MGM. A plan to set up an independent creative venture, the Directors' Guild, with Lewis Milestone, King Vidor, and Frank Borzage, came to nothing, and he and his wife left for an extended European vacation. The trip took in Russia, where DeMille was cordially received and found that *The Godless Girl,* its titles rewritten and most of the last reel excised, was playing to packed houses as a eulogy of atheism.

Back in Hollywood at the end of 1931, DeMille found himself, like many other filmmakers at that time, an outdated, unwanted figure, a failed leftover from the primeval silent era. Swallowing his pride, he approached Lasky and asked to be taken back at his old studio. With the help of Ben Schulberg, the head of production, Lasky succeeded in talking round the hostile Zukor, though only at a price: DeMille must accept a fraction of his former salary, guarantee to stick exactly to budget, and furthermore put up half the money on his own security. It was also made clear that he had only one chance; anything less than a smash hit and he was through.

The Sign of the Cross (1932) shrewdly combined the formulas of DeMille's two most successful types of picture to date, the sex comedy and the religious epic: lurid displays of sexual debauchery in opulent surroundings, lavish historical spectacle, and a sentimentally devout message to tie up the final reel. Set in Nero's Rome, the plot hinges on the efforts of Marcus Superbus, Prefect of Rome (Fredric March), to seduce a virtuous Christian maiden (Elissa Landi). Eventually, of course, love and faith win out, and the two go up together to death in the arena and, no doubt, to life everlasting. The film also featured torture, the burning of Rome, an attempted lesbian seduction, a richly over-the-top performance from Charles Laughton (playing Nero with more than a hint of Mussolini), and the most elaborately baroque of all DeMille bathroom scenes, with Claudette Colbert's Poppaea splashing in a poolful of asses' milk, attend-ed by eunuchs, scantily clad handmaidens, and a couple of appreciatively lapping black kittens.

"However contemptible one may find DeMille's moralising," John Baxter wrote, "it is impossible not to be impressed by *The Sign of the Cross*. . . . There are few films of the Thirties more rich in sexuality than this exotic masterpiece." Charles Wolfe finds the movie "more tightly structured" than DeMille's other biblical epics, and with "a greater intimacy, a concern for dramatic effects within smaller spaces. The furtive life of the Christians is richly expressed through the chiaroscuro lighting of Karl Struss's cinematography." DeMille got the hit he needed, his first since *King of Kings*; just as well, since both Lasky and Schulberg had meantime been ousted and he had few friends left on the Paramount board. "From now on," Charles Higham asserted, "he would completely cease to have the artistic aspirations which had driven him as a young man. He would simply set out to be a supremely successful filmmaker."

If this was so, he miscalculated badly with his next two pictures. Neither *This Day and Age* (1933), a morality piece with unsavory fascist undertones, nor *Four Frightened People* (1934), a jungle adventure that veered uneasily between comedy and melodrama, found much favor. "Better do another historical epic, Cecil, with plenty of sex," Zukor suggested. DeMille took the advice, and stuck to it. For the rest of his career—with two marginal exceptions—all his films followed the broad historical path, steering safely clear of modern ambiguities.

Cleopatra (1934) fulfilled Zukor's precept to the letter. It packed in even more sex and spectacle than *Sign of the Cross*, while for once dispensing with any evangelical message. Drawing on Shakespeare, Shaw, Plutarch, and popular mythology, the action covered Cleopatra's liaisons with Caesar and Mark Antony, her defeat by Octavius, and her death. Colbert made a suitably sensuous and self-amused Cleopatra, compensating to a large degree for the woodenness of her male protagonists, Warren William as Caesar and Henry Wilcoxon, a DeMille discovery, as Antony. Dialogue, in DeMille's films rarely better than serviceable and frequently a lot worse, in *Cleopatra* verged occasionally on the witty.

Visual highpoints included a powerful montage sequence, worthy of Eisenstein, depicting the Battle of Actium, and of course the barge scene, in which Cleopatra seduces the bemused Antony with the help of an inexhaustible supply of undulating, provocatively clad slavegirls. John Coleman singled out the moment when the Roman, helplessly succumbing, is drawn "into a bedded alcove, silk curtains swishing across, a lone girl dancing amid flung petals, the camera steadily, implacably withdrawing to take in the toiling hands of galley-slaves." Contemporary notices poked fun as usual, but a tinge of reluctant admiration could be sensed. "It holds the attention stupendously," conceded Derek Drabble in *Film Weekly,* adding, "Its pomposity is appalling. Dignity it has none." Any such lack evidently failed to trouble the public, since the picture was highly successful.

"Mr. Cecil de Mille's evangelical films are the nearest equivalent today to the glossy German colour prints which sometimes decorated mid-Victorian Bibles," observed Graham Greene, reviewing *The Crusades* (1935) for the *Spectator.* "There is the same complete lack of a period sense, the same stuffy horsehair atmosphere of beards and whiskers, and, their best quality, a childlike eye for details." Wilcoxon again starred, as Richard I, opposite Ian Keith's cultured Saladin, and DeMille's daughter Katharine pouted effectively ("an agreeably medieval face," Greene noted) as Alice of France. There was plenty of massive spectacle; the storming of Acre and the clash before Jerusalem were rated by John Baxter "some of the most striking battles ever filmed." By previous standards, though, there was relatively little sex—"It contains no baths," reported *Time* in some surprise—which may explain the lukewarm public response.

"The King is dead!" Zukor exulted, when *The Crusades* showed a loss of $700,000. His triumph was premature. DeMille's position at Paramount had become far more secure, especially since the appointment of Ernst Lubitsch as head of production, and could withstand the effect of a single flop, albeit a major one. As it turned out, *The Crusades* was to be DeMille's last box-office failure. All his ten remaining films made money, and most of them made colossal amounts. The legend of the Great Showman, Barnum and Bailey of Hollywood, the man with his finger positioned infallibly on (or, as Joe Mankiewicz preferred, up) the national pulse, holds good only for this final stage of his career. It was a legend that DeMille himself, as might be expected, readily fostered. "I believe that in my make-up as a film producer, the showman and the artist are most happily combined and reconciled," he once modestly affirmed.

Abandoning for the time being ancient and Old World history, DeMille turned to a cycle of early Americana, in which the evangelical theme was overlaid by that of Manifest Destiny, the radiant future of God's own country. *The Plainsman* (1937) presented, as even the film's prologue acknowledged, a heavily fictionalized

account of the career of Wild Bill Hickok, played by Gary Cooper at his most gravely fatalistic. Some critics have considered it DeMille's best film; Graham Greene, writing shortly before the great age of Westerns, thought it "perhaps . . . the finest Western in the history of the film." The minimal plot—Hickok is forced to turn outlaw to defeat a renegade gunrunner—is archetypal in its simplicity, and at moments the mood approaches the mythic quality of Ford or Hawks. John Baxter cited the sequence that closes the film: "As Cooper's body lies on the ground after his murder, DeMille dissolves so that it seems to melt into the earth. Hickok has become part of the land and its mythology. This is the image of a genuine cinematic poet."

While preparing *The Plainsman,* DeMille was invited by Lever Brothers to act as presenter of their sponsored radio program, the *Lux Radio Theater,* at a salary of $2,000 a week. The series, broadcast over the Columbia network on Monday evenings, featured summary versions of Hollywood movies, often with the original stars, and was said to attract forty million listeners. DeMille hosted and directed nearly four hundred shows before resigning from the series in 1945.

History again took a considerable battering in *The Buccaneer* (1938), a period swashbuckler with Fredric March as Jean Lafitte, the Louisiana pirate who helped US forces against the British in the War of 1812. A supporting role was taken by Anthony Quinn, who shortly afterwards married the director's daughter Katharine. *Union Pacific* (1939), borrowing a sizeable chunk of plot from Ford's 1924 *The Iron Horse,* recounted the laying of the eponymous railroad through the Rockies in 1869, aided by Joel McCrea and Barbara Stanwyck—the latter emoting valiantly through a studied Irish brogue—and hindered by assorted villains, Quinn and Brian Donlevy among them. Cataclysmic train crashes of course figured largely, and DeMille, recuperating from a prostate operation, directed much of the film lying prone on a stretcher.

North West Mounted Police (1940), set against the historical backdrop of the 1885 Riel rebellion in Saskatchewan, was DeMille's first film in full color; he made the most of it with some majestic location shooting (Oregon standing in for Canada, due to wartime problems). Gary Cooper played the Texas Ranger pursuing a killer (George Bancroft) beyond the Forty-ninth Parallel, and Paulette Goddard made a spirited halfbreed. Anne Bauchens was awarded an Oscar for her editing—the first woman editor ever to win one. *Reap the Wild Wind* (1942) was a Technicolor sea adventure set on the 1840 Florida coast, with evil wreckers threatening America's sea lanes and the nation's commerce. The cast included John Wayne, Ray Milland, Paulette Goddard, Raymond Massey, and a thirty-foot, bright red, electrically operated sponge-rubber squid. "Like the rest of DeMille's sagas," wrote Sumiko Higashi, "the picture was calculated not only to entertain but to reaffirm audience belief in the nation's future, especially its destiny as a great commercial power."

By this stage DeMille was virtually running his own studio, an independent unit within Paramount with its own staff, technical crew, and production facilities—and even its own entrance, the "DeMille gate." Choice of subject lay wholly within his control. After *Reap the Wild Wind* he was considering *Queen of Queens,* a long-standing project on the Virgin Mary, or *Rurales,* a remake of *The Volga Boatman* with a Mexican setting, when he heard Roosevelt, in a radio broadcast, mention a heroic doctor, Corydon M. Wassell. Wassell, a former missionary with a Navy commission, had taken nine wounded men through Japanese-occupied Java and brought them safely to Australia. DeMille instantly rounded up the bewildered doctor and set James Hilton to work concocting an outline from his narrative.

Gary Cooper, obligatory casting, played the lead. *The Story of Dr. Wassell* (1944), though suiting the mood of the times, makes embarrassing viewing today; the real Wassell, it seems, was fairly thoroughly embarrassed even at the time. James Agee, writing in *The Nation,* declared that "Cecil DeMille's screen version . . . is to be regretted beyond qualification. It whips the story . . . into a nacreous foam of lies whose speciousness is only the more painful because Mr. DeMille is so obviously free from any desire to alter the truth except for what he considers to be its own advantage."

As a regular broadcaster, DeMille was a member of the American Federation of Radio Artists, which in August 1944 requested $1 from each member to help combat a state proposition aimed at ending the closed shop. DeMille loudly and publicly refused to support the union, resigned from the *Lux Radio Theater* in January 1945, and soon afterwards set up the DeMille Foundation for Political Freedom. Always conservative (in 1938 he had been offered the nomination as Republican senator for California), DeMille now turned virulently anticommunist, and the Foundation became one of Hollywood's earliest "witch-hunting" organizations.

Unconquered (1947) rounded off his Americana cycle with an episodic adventure tale set in pre-Revolutionary Pennsylvania. Paulette Goddard and Gary Cooper, in their last roles for DeMille, played respectively a transported convict and the army officer who rescues her from servitude and various other perils. "Just about as subtle as a juvenile comic strip and cut on a comparable pattern," snorted Bosley Crowther in the *New York Times.* James Agee, in *Time,* was more indulgent. "It is, to be sure, a huge, high-colored chunk of hokum; but the most old-fashioned thing about it is its exuberance, a quality which . . . DeMille preserves almost single-handed from the days when even the people who laughed at movies couldn't help liking them."

Old-fashioned by now DeMille clearly was. Throughout his career his cinematic style hardly changed. Though he took on board the main technical advances as they occurred—color, sound, wide screen, sophisticated lenses, and special effects—he was still framing and constructing his movies in the mid-1950s much as he had done in 1915. Several writers have pointed out that his style was never in any case essentially cinematic. "DeMille introduced 'style' into films," Lewis Jacobs observed, "but so far as direction was concerned his style was largely theatrical. . . . He conceived of a film not as a moving and changing medium but as a series of separate pictures." Sumiko Higashi similarly related his style to the static tradition of didactic painting: "DeMille characteristically employed a camera that was stationary and eschewed excessive panning and tracking. . . . Camera placement emphasized perpendicularity with respect to framing of the shot and resulted in a rigorous frontality and shallow organization of space. Compositions were symmetrically balanced and carefully lit to produce a sculptured effect. . . . DeMille's editing style . . . rendered film as a series of tableaux that expressed his painterly vision."

So inextricably has DeMille's name become associated with biblical epics that it comes as a surprise to realize that only four of his seventy movies fall into this category. He returned to the genre after an interval of over twenty years to make *Samson and Delilah* (1949), by far the worst of the four. The title roles were taken woodenly by Victor Mature and Hedy Lamarr, inspiring Groucho Marx's immortal comment that it was "the only movie I ever saw where the male lead's tits were bigger than the female's." Mature's heroic victory over a patently stuffed lion aroused further derision. "Perhaps De Mille's survival," the *New Yorker* speculated, "is due to the fact that he decided in his nonage to ally himself with God as his co-maker and to get his major scripts from the Bible, which he has always handled with the proprietory air of a gentleman fondling old love letters. . . . This time I'm not at all sure that he has produced a work that enhances the glory of him or his Associate." Sex and spectacle were, as ever, stirred liberally into the mix, which climaxed with an undeniably impressive destruction of the temple by the blinded Samson. "In its way," *Time* wrote tolerantly, "it is as much fun as a robust, well-organized circus."

It had always irked DeMille that he had so far been denied an Academy Award. Honors had been heaped on him by a wide assortment of bodies, such as the US Treasury Department, the National School Boards Association, the Cine Fans of South India (as 'Darshaka Brahma', or Father of Cinematic Art), the National Association of Plumbers ("for giving the industry professional status in the eyes of the world"), and, rather oddly, by the Al Malaikah Temple, Los Angeles, "for bringing honor and pride to the nobility." There was also a clutch of decorations and honorary degrees—but no Oscar. The omission was partially rectified in 1949 with a Special Academy Award "for thirty-seven years of brilliant showmanship," and in 1950 he appeared as the archetypal Hollywood director in Billy Wilder's *Sunset Boulevard.* But his own Best Picture Oscar came only with his next, penultimate movie.

The Greatest Show on Earth (1952) found DeMille venturing back into the modern era, though only as far as the enclosed, timeless world of the circus. The all-human-life-is-there plot followed the lives and loves of a varied band of artistes, played by—among others—Cornel Wilde, Betty Hutton, Dorothy Lamour, Gloria Grahame, Charlton Heston (in his first major role as the ringmaster), and James Stewart (fulfilling a lifelong ambition to play a clown). Thrills, spills, spangles, and yet another massive train crash filled up enough of the 153 minutes to keep audiences happy, and even the critics were mostly kind. "Here it's right for DeMille to be vulgar, obvious, gaudy. For what else is a circus?" asked the *Saturday Review.*

Charles Wolfe suggested that *"The Greatest Show on Earth* may be DeMille's most personal film. The merger of pioneerism and show business which hovered over his first journey to Hollywood . . . comes full circle here in the figure of the circus manager. . . . Field marshal and father figure, commanding and cajoling his performers, he resembles the mythic movie director who . . . sacrifices his personal desires on behalf of the perfect creation of DeMille's universe—the colossal show." DeMille was incensed by the Catholic League of Decency which, find-

ing some of the circus costumes overly revealing, slapped a B rating (Morally Objectionable in Part for All) on the film. He consoled himself, though, with his Oscar and a Thalberg Award. He was nominated for Best Director, but lost out to John Ford.

Ford had also figured in one of the most discreditable episodes of DeMille's career. The Screen Directors Guild, in which DeMille's influence was strong, had in 1950 elected Joseph Mankiewicz president. DeMille for some reason decided that Mankiewicz, a middle-of-the-road liberal, was a "pinko" and a 'fellow traveler," and initiated an underhand campaign to have him ousted. Mankiewicz's supporters fought back, calling a special meeting of the Guild at which DeMille, to his incredulous fury, found himself heavily under attack. When Ford, whom not even McCarthy could have accused of leftist tendencies, demanded that he apologize or resign, the fight was over; DeMille and his supporters were forced to resign from the committee. In his autobiography he passed over the whole sorry affair in silence.

"I can make a picture out of any fifty pages of the Bible—except possibly the Book of Numbers," DeMille once boasted. For his last film he returned to his favorite book with a no-expense-spared remake of his first epic success, *The Ten Commandments* (1956). After thirty years, Hollywood had caught up with (or perhaps regressed to) DeMille. Epics were all the rage, as the studios met the upstart threat of television by hurling color, wide screens, colossal casts, and monumental sets at their dwindling audiences. The blockbuster mentality—a vast investment to secure an even vaster return—had yet to receive its first serious jolt with the *Cleopatra* debacle of 1963, and not even Zukor objected when DeMille announced that this time he would shoot the exteriors in Egypt.

Wisely jettisoning the modern story from his 1923 version, he devoted the whole three and a half hours' running time to Moses, from his discovery in the bulrushes to his death within sight of the promised land. Heston, again keeping the show on the road, played the adult Moses, with Yul Brynner as his adversary Rameses II, Edward G. Robinson as the apostate Dathan, and a long, starry roster of supporting players including, for old times' sake, Henry Wilcoxon and Julia Faye. Much of the film dragged ponderously; the clarity of Vistavision showed up such special effects as the parting of the Red Sea as painfully maladroit; and the overall impression, as *Time* put it, was "roughly comparable to an eight-foot chorus girl—pretty well put together, but much too big and much too flashy." Most reviewers, though, had realized by now that attacking a DeMille film made as much sense as throwing darts at Mount Rushmore. It was big, it was vulgar, and no matter what anyone said a lot of people would come to stare—and go away happy.

Probably no other major director has been the subject of so little serious critical discussion as Cecil B. DeMille. There seem to be three main reasons why most writers have backed off from his films: distaste, embarrassment, or the feeling that, in the end, not much can really be said about them. Even in France, few attempts have been made to rehabilitate his reputation, although Kevin Brownlow quoted one unidentified French critic to the effect that DeMille's talent was "marginally greater than that of Eisenstein." In an article in *Films in Review* (December 1950) Joseph and Harry Feldman challengingly described him as "one of the greatest masters of the screen . . . one of the few men in the industry who understand the difference between the theatre and the cinema," but took the argument no further than bare assertion. Otherwise, praise of DeMille has generally been reluctant, hedged about with qualifying clauses. In *Sight and Sound* (February 1951) Simon Harcourt-Smith allowed that "grudgingly . . . one recognises a mastery—repellent, monstrous, blatant perhaps, but a mastery, not to be denied. Here is no fumbling, nor ineptitude. We may not like what Cecil B. DeMille sets out to achieve; but we must grant that he achieves it with absolute precision."

Not all critics, perhaps, would agree about the precision, nor about the lack of ineptitude; but many have found in DeMille's films at their best a compensating gusto, an uncomplicated narrative vigor. For Andrew Sarris, DeMille "may have been the last American director who enjoyed telling a story for its own sake." He himself would have heartily concurred: "A 'spectacle' isn't what makes a picture. It isn't a star. It isn't a director. It is just one thing—story."

The focal point, for anyone trying seriously to engage with the DeMille phenomenon, must be the period around 1920 when the quality of his films, and his reputation, went into rapid and irreversible decline. Some writers have diagnosed a desire, stemming perhaps from his years as an indigent actor, for financial success at any cost. Adela Rogers St. John, who worked with him, saw it as sheer calculation. "He could always fool the public and he knew it. He was one hundred percent cynical." In Agnes de Mille's view, far less conscious processes were at work. "I think he got seduced by his own sexual dreams. I think he just went soft and became corrupted by them. He was driven by thoughts of power—power

and sex. He even combined sex and religion because that seemed to be the magic box-office formula . . . and along with that went a degree of sadism."

Whatever his motivation, the fact remains that DeMille, especially in the latter part of his career, became the most consistently and massively successful director, in purely financial terms, in the history of the cinema; by the time of his death in 1959, his seventy pictures had grossed $750 million. Hokey, stagey, vulgar, and sanctimonious as he may have been, he had something that the public wanted. "DeMille succeeded," Sumiko Higashi wrote, "because he realized and disseminated his own fantasies on an extravagant enough scale." In the face of such a vast popular impact, normal critical criteria hardly apply. Lewis Jacobs commented: "If in the artistic perspective of American film history Cecil B. DeMille is valueless, in the social history of films it is impossible to ignore him."

Perhaps the best case that can be made for DeMille is Carlos Clarens'. He says that "DeMille has not left us with a profound body of works; everything in his films is given to us on the surface; the metaphor, if any, is circular and explicit and does not refer the viewer to any secret . . . a wide-open filmmaking, beyond all decoding." And yet Clarens names DeMille as one of the three seminal influences of the early American film, along with D. W. Griffith and Thomas Ince: "By 1915, Griffith had almost mastered the image; it remained for DeMille to perfect film narrative."

While filming *The Ten Commandments* in Egypt, DeMille had suffered a heart attack. Defying his doctor's advice, he completed the picture, and after the triumphal premiere began planning further projects. *Queen of Queens* was mooted again, and a history of the Boy Scout movement, to be entitled *Be Prepared*. His last film work, though, was as executive producer on an unspeakably bad remake of *The Buccaneer* (1958), directed by his son-in-law, Anthony Quinn. Gritting his teeth, the old man embarked on a publicity tour of New Orleans and New York to promote this calamity and suffered another heart attack on his return. He died at his home in Laughlin Park about a month later, aged seventy-seven. His *Autobiography* was published posthumously, later that year.

—*P.K.*

FILMS: (with Oscar Apfel) The Squaw Man (U.K., The White Man), 1914; The Call of the North, 1914; The Virginian, 1914; What's His Name, 1914; The Man From Home, 1914; Rose of the Rancho, 1914; The Girl of the Golden West, 1915; The Warrens of Virginia, 1915; The Unafraid, 1915; The Captive, 1915; The

Wild Goose Chase, 1915; The Arab, 1915; Chimmie Fadden, 1915; Kindling, 1915; Carmen, 1915; Chimmie Fadden Out West, 1915; The Cheat, 1915; The Golden Chance, 1915; Temptation, 1916; The Trail of the Lonesome Pine, 1916; The Heart of Nora Flynn, 1916; Maria Rosa, 1916; The Dream Girl, 1916; Joan the Woman, 1917; Romance of the Redwoods, 1917; The Little American, 1917; The Woman God Forgot, 1917; The Devil Stone, 1917; The Whispering Chorus, 1918; Old Wives for New, 1918; We Can't Have Everything, 1918; Till I Come Back to You, 1918; The Squaw Man, 1918; Don't Change Your Husband, 1919; For Better, for Worse, 1919; Male and Female (U.K., The Admirable Crichton), 1919; Why Change Your Wife?, 1920; Something to Think About, 1920; Forbidden Fruit, 1921; The Affairs of Anatol, 1921; Fool's Paradise, 1921; Saturday Night, 1922; Manslaughter, 1922; Adam's Rib, 1923; The Ten Commandments, 1923; Triumph, 1924; Feet of Clay, 1924; The Golden Bed, 1925; The Road to Yesterday, 1925; The Volga Boatman, 1926; The King of Kings, 1927; The Godless Girl, 1929; Dynamite, 1929; Madame Satan, 1930; The Squaw Man, 1931; The Sign of the Cross, 1932; This Day and Age, 1933; Four Frightened People, 1934; Cleopatra, 1934; The Crusades, 1935; The Plainsman, 1937; The Buccaneer, 1938; Union Pacific, 1939; North West Mounted Police, 1940; Reap the Wild Wind, 1942; The Story of Dr. Wassell, 1944; Unconquered, 1947; Samson and Delilah, 1949; The Greatest Show on Earth, 1952; The Ten Commandments, 1956.

ABOUT: Baxter, J. Hollywood in the Thirties, 1968; Brownlow, K. The Parade's Gone By, 1969; Brownlow, K. Hollywood: The Pioneers, 1979; Coursodon, J.-P. American Directors, vol. I, 1983; De Mille, A. Speak to Me, Dance with Me, 1973; DeMille, C. B. Autobiography, 1959; De Mille, W. C. Hollywood Saga, 1939; Dictionary of American Biography, supplement 6 (1956–1960); Essoe, G. and Lee, R. DeMille: The Man and his Pictures, 1970; Ford, C. Cecil B. DeMille, 1967 (in French); French, P. The Movie Moguls, 1969; Higashi, S. Cecil B. DeMille: A Guide to References and Resources, 1985; Higham, C. Cecil B. DeMille, 1973; Koury, P. Yes, Mr. DeMille, 1959; Mourley, M. Cecil B. DeMille, 1968 (in French); Norman, B. The Hollywood Greats, 1985; Pratt, G. C. (ed.) Spellbound in Darkness, 1966; Ringgold, G. and Bodeen, DeW. The Films of Cecil B. DeMille, 1969; Robinson, D. Hollywood in the Twenties, 1968; Rotha, P. and Griffith, R. The Film Till Now, 1960; Roud, R. (ed.) Cinema: A Critical Dictionary, 1980; Sarris, A. The American Cinema, 1968; Thomson, D. A Biographical Dictionary of the Cinema, 1980. *Periodicals*—American Classic Screen January–February 1983; Bianco e Nero August 1955, April 1959; Cahiers du Cinéma September 1951; Cinéma February 1958; Dirigido June–September 1976; Esquire January 1964; Film Comment January–February 1976; Films and Filming October 1956; Films in Review December 1950, August–September 1981; Image November 1956; Picturegoer September 7, 1935; November 1, 1950; December 2, 1950; Présence du Cinéma Autumn 1967; Sight and Sound February 1951.

DEREN, MAYA (1917–October 13, 1961), American avant-garde director, producer, actress, and aesthetician, was born in Kiev, Russia, the daughter of a Russian-Jewish psychiatrist, Dr. Alexander Deren. A few years after the Revolution—in 1927 according to some sources but in 1922 according to P. Adams Sitney—the family migrated to the United States. Dr. Deren joined the staff of the State Institute for the Feeble-Minded in Syracuse, New York, and eventually became its director.

Maya Deren was sent for her high school education to the League of Nations School in Geneva, Switzerland. Rejoining her family after graduation, she studied journalism at Syracuse University—a training whose benefits are evident in her unusually articulate writings on the cinema. She made an early marriage and moved with her husband to Greenwich Village in New York, where both of them were active in the American Socialist Party. Deren took her B.A. degree at New York University and soon after that was divorced. She went on to do graduate work in literature at Smith College, writing her master's thesis on the influence of the French symbolists on the imagist poets.

Immersing herself in the heady atmosphere of Greenwich Village in the late 1930s, Deren devoted herself to experimental poetry and the modern dance. Though not herself a trained dancer, she began a book on modern dance theory in collaboration with the black dancer-choreographer Catherine Dunham. Through Dunham she met other black dancers, sharing their developing interest in African and Haitian tribal dance, mythology, and ritual. These discoveries gained exciting new levels of significance from the importance attached to "primitive" art and mythology both by Surrealism and by Jungian psychology. Deren found herself increasingly drawn to Jungian concepts of the "collective unconscious" and the archetypal symbol, and away from the Freudian psychoanalysis absorbed from her father.

In late 1941 Maya Deren left New York and accompanied Catherine Dunham and her dance company on tour. In Los Angeles she met the Czech documentary filmmaker Alexander Hammid, accomplished as a director, cameraman, and editor. They were married in 1942 and Hammid taught Deren, as she put it, "the mechanics of film expression, and, more than that, the principle of infinite pains." She wrote: "I had been a poet up until then, and the reason that I had not been a very good poet was because my mind worked in images which I had been trying to translate or describe in words; therefore, when I undertook cinema, I was relieved of the false step of translating images into words, and could

MAYA DEREN

work directly so that it was not like discovering a new medium so much as finally coming home into a world whose vocabulary, syntax, grammar, was my mother tongue; which I understood, and thought in, but, like a mute, had never spoken."

Hammid was Deren's codirector on her first film, *Meshes of the Afternoon* (18 minutes, 1943). With borrowed 16mm equipment, themselves as actors, their Los Angeles house as set, and Hammid as the principal photographer, they shot the film in two and a half weeks. Like most of her films, it is silent, and has no plot in the conventional sense.

P. Adams Sitney, writing in Richard Roud's *Cinema: A Critical Dictionary* (1980), described *Meshes of the Afternoon* as "an intricately structured cyclic dream. . . . In the initial sequence a woman returns to her home after glimpsing a mysterious black-veiled figure before her. She observes the dislocation of several objects which will eventually assume symbolic dimensions: a key, a knife, a telephone, a record-player. She settles into an armchair before a window and falls asleep. That pattern of action is repeated three times as the objects become progressively more menacing. At the climax of the third repetition, three versions of herself perform a ritual around the dining-room table which ends in the election of one to attack the sleeping figure with a knife. But just at the point of stabbing, the dream apparently ends: her lover's kiss wakes her from the dream. Together they climb to the upper bedroom as she notices that all the previously displaced objects are where they should be."

But, Sitney goes on, "when they lie down together she suddenly grabs the knife and jabs it into his face. Yet at the moment of contact . . . [the target] is revealed to have been an illusion. She has stabbed and shattered a mirror in which his face had been reflected. The pieces of the mirror fall mysteriously to the edge of a sea. . . . In the final cycle of the film a man approaches and enters the house again in the same pattern as her previous entrances only to find her dead, her throat apparently cut, with seaweed clinging to her, and the fragments of the shattered mirror about her."

Parker Tyler understood *Meshes of the Afternoon* as Deren's account in symbolic terms of "the death of her narcissistic youth." A number of other critics place the film in the tradition of European surrealism, and its use of such familiar symbols as the mirror, the knife, and the key within a dream experience does seem to invite such an interpretation. Deren herself, however, always denied that *Meshes* was a surrealist film, and rejected any psychoanalytic reading of it. She wanted it to be seen as a film "concerned with the relationship between the imaginative and the objective reality. The film begins in actuality and, eventually, ends there. But in the meantime the imagination, here given as a dream, intervenes. It seizes upon a casual incident and, elaborating it into critical proportions, thrusts back into reality the product of its convolutions. The protagonist does not suffer some subjective delusion, of which the world outside remains independent, if not oblivious; on the contrary, she is, in actuality, destroyed by an imaginative action. Such a development is, obviously, not a function of some 'realistic' logic; it is a . . . destiny established as a logic of the film itself. Thus the formal whole is, itself, the reality and the meaning of the film."

Deren's interpretation suggests an attempt to authenticate the imaginative life, and to demonstrate its power to alter "reality." But Sitney, in his magisterial *Visionary Film*, points out that *Meshes* was not Deren's film alone: "The general fluidity of the camera style, the free movements and the surrealistic effects, from slow motion to the simultaneous appearance of three Maya Derens in the same shot, are . . . [Hammid's] contribution" to a film that is also his "portrait of his young wife. . . . As psychodrama, *Meshes of the Afternoon* is the inward exploration of both Deren and Hammid. The central theme of all the psychodramas that marked the first stage of the American avant-garde cinema is the quest for sexual identity; in their film, unlike those that follow . . . , it is two people, the makers of the film, who participate in this quest."

Meshes of the Afternoon, however it is interpreted (and setting aside some isolated but interesting experiments of the 1930s), is widely regarded as the first film of the American avant-garde, introducing in the United States what Sitney calls the "trance film"—"the dominant avant-garde film genre of the late 40s and early 50s," in which "a somnambulistic protagonist wanders through a forbidding landscape or a mysterious house in quest of a revelation of his own sexuality."

If *Meshes* is not to be seen as a Surrealist film, Maya Deren's next project, *The Witch's Cradle,* was planned as a vehicle for her impressions of surrealist artifacts as "the cabalistic symbols of the twentieth century," and of surrealist artists as modern magicians in their defiance of "rational" notions of time, space, and logical causality. Filmed in the Surrealist "Art of This Century" gallery, with the artists Marcel Duchamp and Pajarito Matta as actors, it was never completed (though it was released in its incomplete form in 1961). Perhaps, as has been suggested, Deren found no creative potential in the surrealist-psychoanalytic approach. Certainly her subsequent films lend themselves more readily to a Jungian interpretation.

In a letter to her friend James Card, Deren drew attention to a very short but very important sequence in *Meshes of the Afternoon,* "when the girl with the knife rises from the table to go towards the self which is sleeping in the chair. As the girl . . . rises, there is a close-up of her foot as she begins striding. The first step is in sand (with suggestion of sea behind), the second stride (cut in) is in grass, the third is on pavement, and the fourth is on the rug, and then the camera cuts up to her head with the knife descending towards the sleeping girl. What I meant when I planned that four-stride sequence was that you have to come a long way—from the very beginning of time—to kill yourself, like the first life emerging from the primeval waters. These four strides, in my intention, span all time."

The concept of movement spanning and transcending time and space is central in *At Land* (1944, 15 minutes), made with the technical assistance of Hella Heyman and Alexander Hammid. Waves (moving in reverse) deposit on a lonely beach a sleeping girl (Deren). She awakens and climbs a dead tree trunk until her head disappears out of shot at the top of the frame. When the girl's head appears at the bottom of the next frame, it confronts not a tree top but a banqueting table. Ignored by the diners, she crawls along the table to the end, where a chess game is laid out. She snatches a chess piece,

drops it, and pursues it through various landscapes. For a time, she finds herself talking to a man who is repeatedly replaced by other men. Finding another chess game in progress, she again steals and flees, watches by images of herself, until she disappears among the dunes.

It seemed to Lewis Jacobs that "the film's major cinematic value lay in its fresh contiguities of shot relationships achieved through the technique of beginning a movement in one place and concluding it in another. Thus real time and space were destroyed. In its place was created a cinematic time and place." The effect was of a relativistic universe in which, Deren said, "the problem of the individual as the sole continuous element, is to relate itself to a fluid, apparently incoherent, universe. It is in a sense a mythological voyage of the twentieth century."

The illusion of spatial continuity created by smoothly matched cuts during the subject's movements suggested to Deren the possibility of a new, cinematic choreography, freed from the limitations of real space and time. Working with the dancer Talley Beatty, she next made *A Study in Choreography for the Camera* (1945), a very short film (three minutes) exploring the cinematic possibilities of a deliberately restricted sequence of ballet movements: a run, a pirouette, and a leap.

The film begins, in Sitney's account, "with a circular pan in a clearing in the woods. In making the one circle the camera periodically passes the dancer; at each encounter he is further along in his slow, up-stretching movement. At the end of this camera movement, he extends his foot out of the frame and brings it down in a different place; this time, inside a room. The dance continues through rooms, woods, and the courtyard of a museum until he begins a pirouette, which changes, without a stopping of the camera, from very slow motion to very fast. Then he leaps, slowly, very slowly, floating through the air, in several rising, then several descending shots, to land in a speculative pose back in the wood clearing."

John Martin, ballet critic of the New York *Times,* found in this film "the beginnings of a virtually new art of 'choreo-cinema,' in which the dancer and the camera collaborate on the creation of a single new work of art." Sitney pointed out in *Visionary Film* that "the dance movement provides a continuity through a space that is severely telescoped and a time that is elongated." He went on: "The film has a perfection which none of Maya Deren's other films has ever achieved. . . . [She] introduced the possibility of isolating a single gesture as a complete film form. In its concentrated distillation of both the narrative and the thematic principles, this form comes to resemble the movement in poetry called Imagism, and for this reason I have . . . called a film using this device an imagist film."

A Study in Choreography was followed by the longer and more ambitious dance film that is generally regarded as Deren's fullest realization of her theories, *Ritual in Transfigured Time* (1946, 16 minutes). "A ritual," she wrote, "is an action distinguished from all others in that it seeks the realization of its purpose through the exercise of form. . . . In ritual, the form is the meaning. More specifically, the quality of movement is not a merely decorative factor; it is the meaning itself of the movement. . . . The quality of individual movements, and, above all, the choreography of the whole, is mainly conferred and created by filmic means—the varying camera speeds, the relating of gestures which were, in reality, unrelated, the repetition of patterns. . . . Being a film ritual, it is achieved not in spatial terms alone, but in terms of a Time created by the camera."

This film ritual illustrates "a critical metamorphosis, the changing of a widow into a bride." The widow in black dances through the stages of the ritual, looking to another female figure (Deren) for guidance. At the climax of the film the widow is frightened by a figure that changes from a man into a statue and, when she flees, back into a man who pursues her. She is finally transformed—by a specifically cinematic device, negative processing—from a widow in black to a bride in white.

Only two of the film's performers were actually dancers (Rita Christiani and Frank Westbrook) but as Deren said, "the film confers dance upon non-dancers"—notably in a party scene that is treated as "a choreographic pattern of movements. . . . a constantly moving group of smiling, socially anxious people, striving to reach one another, to embrace one another, to avoid one another in a continuous ebb and flow of motion." Moreover, to quote a CinemaTexas program note (February 27, 1978), Deren here "develops her dance movement-gesture by combining the motions among several people in the same way she joined movements in *Choreography*. In the two woman winding yarn, at the party and in the statue-making sequence, one person begins a movement while another continues it and another completes it."

Ritual has been seen as completing an autobiographical trilogy begun in *Meshes of the Afternoon* and *At Land*, and exploring a quest for sexual and personal identity. Not everyone agrees about the outcome of that quest, however. Near the end of the film the widow, pursued, runs into the sea. "As she sinks," writes P. Adams Sitney, "we see her in negative, her black gown now white . . . prepared as a bride for the young man who has not followed her into the water." Not so Lauren Rabinovitz and Marjorie Baumgarten in the CinemaTexas program notes; they claim this as a woman's film and conclude that the widow "ultimately weds, not the present male figure, but the sea, the Freudian and Jungian symbol for the eternal female principle."

At this point in her career, Maya Deren was also lecturing and writing extensively on her conception of the "personal film," visiting colleges, art schools, and museums all over the United States. She set out her theories in *An Anagram of Ideas on Art, Form and Film* (1946), described by David Curtis as "one of the most complete statements by any film artist of their total position until the publication of Brakhage's *Metaphors on Vision* in 1963."

"Agony and experience" was how Deren defined her films: "subjective films concerned with personal feelings and problems in which the people are not individuals but symbols, abstractions or generalizations." However, the subjectivity of her cinema did not permit the distortion of the image itself by anamorphosis or other means; she always insisted that the cinema should be grounded in photographic realism. Subjectivity entered for her in the *choice* of image and camera position, the length and juxtaposition of shots, the use of slow or reverse motion. For her, as Sitney succinctly explains, the camera becomes an instrument of "invention" when it "records imaginative constructs in reality and reconstructs them through the illusions of editing." Her intention, she said, was to "experiment with filmic time and space and through this new time and space to stir and disturb, evoke feelings and emotions."

As Kay and Peary note in *Women and the Cinema,* for Deren "personal filmmaking meant personal film distribution." In 1946 she rented the Provincetown Playhouse on MacDougal Street in New York for the first public screenings in the United States of privately-made 16mm films, attracting large audiences. The success of this venture led in time to other experiments in noncommercial distribution, including Frank Stauffacher's "Art in Cinema" series at the San Francisco Museum of Art, launched in 1947, and Amos Vogel's Cinema 16, a showcase for avantgarde films and, beginning in 1950, a distribution center also.

Also in 1946 Deren shared the distinction—with the Whitney brothers—of being awarded the first Guggenheim fellowship ever given for creative filmmaking, and this initiated a departure from her earlier work. She went to Haiti to prepare a film that would explore new aspects of her interest in myth and ritual. The film was never completed, though some years later she published a book about Haitian cults, *The Divine Horseman* (1953). She said that she had gone to Haiti "as an artist, as one who would manipulate the elements of a reality into a work of art," but had been undone by "the irrefutable reality and impact of Voudoun mythology. . . . I end by recording, as humbly and accurately as I can, the logics of a reality which had forced me to recognize its integrity and to abandon my manipulations."

When Deren resumed filmmaking in 1948 with *Meditation on Violence*, it was evident that her Haitian experiences had altered her motivations. Rabinovitz and Baumgarten suggest that, whereas *Ritual in Transfigured Time* represented a culmination of Deren's "interest in the manipulation of time and space through purely cinematic means," *Meditation on Violence* intellectualized this process "so completely that the artistic effort becomes a somewhat sterile application of her theories."

The film is a dance poem employing movements used in training by two ancient schools of Chinese boxing, Wu-tang and Shao-Lin. The camera first watches the dancer and then becomes the opponent seeking to evade his blows. The first of Deren's films to employ a soundtrack, it has a score played on Chinese flute and Haitian drums. Her aim was to "abstract the principle of ongoing metamorphosis and change," and to this end she drew up charts showing in precise detail how time and movement were to be related in the film. She herself was dissatisfied with the result, however, and often spoke of reediting and shortening this twelve-minute film—an intention that was never realized.

Music also featured in Deren's last film, *The Very Eye of Night* (1959, 15 minutes), the score being provided by her third husband, Teijo Ito. Another dance film that also used a good deal of optical printing, it took Deren "out in space about as far as I can go." In her letter to James Card, she wrote that the film was inspired mostly by an operation in which she almost died: "I came out of it with a rapidity that dazzled. . . . Then I actually realized that I was overwhelmed with the most wondrous gratitude for the marvelous persistence of the life force. . . . And then I had a sudden image: a dog lying somewhere very still, and a child, first looking at it, and then, compulsively, nudging it. Why? to see whether it was still alive. . . . to make it move

to make it live. So I had been doing with my camera."

Maya Deren died in 1961 at the age of forty-four, after a series of cerebral hemorrhages. As her films show, she was an extremely beautiful woman, with thick dark hair and sensual features. Her "dramatic appearance and charismatic personality" made her a central figure in the Greenwich Village artistic community in the 1940s. However, according to Rabinovitz and Baumgarten, her qualities alienated as many as they attracted: "Rudolf Arnheim, Anais Nin, and James Agee have labeled her everything from strong-willed, commanding, seductive and hypnotic to dogmatic, obstinate, restless, unsatisfied, and energetic to the point of violence."

Deren had been called the "mother of the underground film," and this tag is not far from the truth. Beyond that, as Rabinovitz and Baumgarten have said, "her theories on the structural aspects of the creative process and cinematic form anticipated Structuralist theories and trends in painting, sculpture and film, while the rich heritage of her film *oeuvre* has provided a model and inspiration for American independent filmmakers and for the further development of poetic film form. Her promotional and organizational efforts helped make widescale American independent filmmaking a reality."

—V.C.

FILMS: (with Alexander Hammid) Meshes of the Afternoon, 1943; At Land, 1944; A Study in Choreography for Camera, 1945; Ritual in Transfigured Time, 1946; Meditation on Violence, 1948; The Very Eye of Night, 1959; The Witch's Cradle, 1961 (released incomplete).

ABOUT: Agee, J. Agee on Film, Vol. 1, 1969; Curtis, D. Experimental Cinema, 1971; Deren, M. An Anagram of Ideas on Art, Form and Film, 1946; Deren, M. The Art of the Cinema: Selected Essays, edited by George Amberg, 1972; Erens, P. Sexual Stratagems: The World of Women in Film, 1979; Kay, K. and Peary, G. (eds.) Women and the Cinema: A Critical Anthology, 1977; Manvell, R. (ed.) Experiment in the Film, 1949; Nin, A. The Diary of Anais Nin, Vol. 4, edited by Gunther Stuhlmann, 1971; Renan, S. The Underground Film, 1967; Roud, R. (ed.) Cinema: A Critical Dictionary, 1980; Sitney, P. A. Visionary Film, 1974; Tyler, P. Underground Film, 1969. *Periodicals*—Camera Obscura Fall 1977, Summer 1979; CinemaTexas Program Notes February 27, 1978; Daedalus Winter 1960; Écran February 1977; Film critica September 1975; Film Culture Summer 1961, Spring 1962, Summer 1963, Winter 1965, 67–69 1979; Film Library Quarterly Winter 1971–1972; Film wise 2 1961; Frauen & Film December 1976; New Directions IX 1946; October Fall 1980; Theatre Arts May 1947.

GIUSEPPE DE SANTIS

*DE SANTIS, GIUSEPPE (February 11, 1917–), Italian director, scenarist, and critic, was born in Fondi, an ancient town between Rome and Naples. He studied literature and philosophy at university and then entered the Italian film school, the Centro Sperimentale in Rome. De Santis first made his name as a film critic—as a prominent and rigorously severe contributor to *Cinema*.

This magazine, under the nominal editorship of Vittorio Mussolini, the Duce's son, and Luciano De Feo, provided a rallying point for a group of leftist young critics who prepared the way for the coming of neorealism—among them Visconti, Lizzani, and Antonioni. In 1941 De Santis wrote: "We are fighting for the dawn of an awareness that will lead towards realism. We have learned to scan the horizons of an imagination that is forever opposed to the miserable conditions of man, his solitude, his difficulty in escaping, and which finds, even in escapism, the imposing strength of reciprocal human communication. Our sympathies are joined always with a cinema that breathes the intimate essence of reality through historical education. The level of civilization cannot be separated from the land that gave birth to it."

The Italian neorealists, influenced by French cinema, could find no worthy models in their own contemporary culture and instead looked back to the novels of the great nineteenth-century Sicilian realist Giovanni Verga, who had already inspired a brief flowering of *verismo* in the early days of the Italian cinema, around the beginning of World War I. De Santis' short stories were modeled on Verga's, and his criticism was permeated with his admiration for a writer who offered "the strongest and most human, the most marvelously virgin and authentic ambience that can inspire the imagination of a cinema seeking things and facts in a time and space dominated by reality so as to detach itself from facile suggestions and decadent bourgeois taste."

Luchino Visconti shared this enthusiasm for Verga, and De Santis became his assistant director and one of the scenarists on *Ossessione* (*Obsession*, 1942), based on James M. Cain's brutally naturalistic thriller *The Postman Always Rings Twice*. Transposing this story of passion and murder to a bleakly authentic Italian landscape, the film provided a brilliant introduction to many of the preoccupations of the neorealists. De Santis also worked on the script of Rossellini's *Desiderio* (completed by Pagliero) and collaborated with Mario Serandrei, Pagliero, and Visconti on *Giorni di gloria* (Days of Glory, 1945), a documentary compiled from newsreels about the contribution of the Italian Resistance to the Liberation. The following year De Santis

was coscenarist and assistant director of Aldo Vergano's *Il sole sorge ancora* (1946), a feature about the political education of a young partisan.

Il sole sorge ancora was one of two postwar films financed by the ANPI, the left-wing organization of former partisans; the other was De Santis's own first film, *Caccia tragica* (*Tragic Hunt*, 1947). This examination of the postwar fate of the partisan spirit is set in the Romagna just after the Liberation and—like many of De Santis's films—is based on a newspaper story. Putting his theories into practice, the director shot the picture entirely on location, indoors and out, and—along with a professional cast that included Silvana Pampanini, Amedeo Nazzari, and Massimo Girotti—used local peasants as extras and bit-players.

The film opens with the newly married Michele and Giovanna, former partisans, on their way to join in the creation of a collective farm; traveling in the same truck is an official carrying the government subsidy on which the farm depends. They are ambushed by bandits (including Alberto, a former comrade) who murder the farm official, steal the money, and kidnap Giovanna. The rest of the film deals with the pursuit of the bandits by Michele and members of the collective. Cutting from one group to the other, the picture explores the motives of both—the social idealism of the peasants; the tragic passion that binds Alberto to the woman gangleader Daniela. In the end, Alberto redeems himself by shooting Daniela, and Giovanna (and the money) are recovered.

Some contemporary reviewers found *Caccia*

°dā sän´ tēs

tragica vulgar, sensational, and confused, but for others the director's passionate sincerity was "more compelling than the novelettish detail," and there was praise for his fluid camerawork (with a striking and at that time uncommon use of crane shots) and his attractive composition within the frame. Roy Armes in *Patterns of Realism* (1971) called it "a remarkable first work which, despite its unevenness, strikingly emphasises the vitality of the director. . . . The many crowd scenes . . . are handled by De Santis with a sincerity and force which recall . . . the early Soviet film. In a very real sense the enemies of the peasants are not the bandits themselves but the rich, whose agents are explicitly presented as being in league with the gang. . . . The specific political issues treated in *Caccia tragica* have lost some of their relevance . . . but the film retains its power because . . . the human beings never cease to come alive. As an example of this one might cite the complicity that springs up between the two women despite their roles of kidnapper and victim and the genuine and in no way contrived sensuality with which they are endowed."

Riso amaro (*Bitter Rice*, 1949) was scripted by De Santis with two other *Cinema* critics, Carlo Lizzani and Gianni Puccini, and was based on careful research among workers in the Po valley, where every year thousands of city girls went to the flooded fields to harvest rice under appalling conditions. From this documentary base, however, there somehow emerged a melodramatic tale about the relationship that develops between Silvana (Silvana Mangano), whose moral standards have been eroded by a diet of pulp fiction and trashy Hollywood movies, and the small-time crook Walter (Vittorio Gassman). Silvana sees the light, shoots her deceitful lover, and throws herself off the camp watchtower. Whereupon (in a scene that many found embarrassingly unconvincing), her fellow-workers file past her body, sprinkling it with rice in forgiveness and benediction. Having set out "to express man, woman and society in their . . . natural primitive integrity," De Santis wound up with a movie whose worldwide commercial success was clearly attributable to its violent eroticism and a generous display of Mangano's exceptional physique."

De Santis set his next film in his own native region of Ciociara: "I made it in Fondi, the village where I was born. I signed on all my childhood friends, not to mention my nurse. I myself tell the story in the commentary." *Non c'è pace tra gli ulivi* (*No Peace Under the Olives*, 1950) is about Francesco (Raf Vallone) a young peasant who comes home from the war to find that both his flock and his girl (Lucia Bosè) have been stolen by a local landowner, Bonfiglio (Folco Lulli). When Francesco tries to take the law into his own hands, Bonfiglio has him imprisoned on false charges and rapes his sister, knowing that no one will dare to bring charges against him. But Francisco escapes from jail, rallies the peasants against Bonfiglio's power and greed, and kills him in a final confrontation.

Charged with melodrama, De Santis explained that he had done no more than "respect local custom. The peasants of the region are proud and distant; they have a natural tendency to pose; they don't like to look each other straight in the eye, and that is why in the film they sometimes deliver their dialogue while facing the camera." Some critics remained unconvinced, but many admired this uneven but uncompromising, visually beautiful, and intermittently powerful film and applauded De Santis's message—that only through solidarity can the workers defeat their exploiters.

De Santis planned another film of peasant life that was to consider the problem of land distribution in Calabria, but nothing came of it, and in his next picture he turned his attention to the city and postwar unemployment. *Roma, ore undici* (*Rome, Eleven O'Clock*, 1952), based on a book by Elio Petri, who also worked on the script, shows us two hundred girls lining up on a rickety staircase to apply for a single poorly paid typing job. The staircase collapses, injuring many of the girls and killing one of them. De Santis had interviewed a number of the women involved in the actual tragedy, and the film sketches in the stories of some of them—from a prostitute trying to go straight to a rich girl who had run away from home.

"Sometimes the film lacks restraint," wrote Mario Gromo, "as in the long sequence in which the radio reporter interviews some of the injured girls in the hospital," but on the whole the movie seemed to Gromo "more clean-cut and incisive" than its predecessors: "alternately bitter and sardonic, the episodes flash by like scenes in a kaleidoscope." Some critics regard this as the most moving and accomplished of De Santis's films, thanks partly to the fine performances he drew from a cast that includes Eva Vanicek, Carla Del Poggio, Massimo Girotti, Lucia Bosè, Raf Vallone, and Lea Padovani.

Unfortunately, none of the director's later films have equaled this standard, though his next movie is of some interest as a feminist document. *Un marito per Anna Zaccheo* (*A Husband for Anna*, 1953) centers on a beautiful girl who rejects her arranged marriage and gets herself a job; when an affair with a sailor ends unhappily, she goes off alone. *Giorni d'amore* (*Days of*

Love, 1954), starring Marcello Mastroianni and Marina Vlady in a story of village life and young love triumphant, picked up an award at San Sebastian but is dismissed by most critics as "novelettish," and so is *Uomini e lupi* (*Men and Wolves,* 1956), in which Yves Montand and Silvana Mangano battle against animals and the elements in the Abruzzi. *Una strada lunga un anno* (*The Road a Year Long,* 1958), made in Yugoslavia, was followed by *La garçonnière* (1960), a cautionary tale starring Raf Vallone as a middle-aged man who leaves his wife for a young mistress and winds up abandoned by both women. *Italiani brava gente* (*Attack and Retreat,* 1964), a Russian-Italian coproduction about World War II, was called "a film whose high-minded intentions are spoiled by a farfetched and heavy-handed treatment."

Jean Quéval once described De Santis as "a primitive and vaguely Christian Communist, and perhaps more superstitious than Christian," while Pierre Leprohon suggests that "the need to sugar his [ideological] pill for general consumption accounts for the uneven quality of almost all of De Santis's films. One is tempted to criticize him also for the exuberance of his style and technique. In his search for effect and mass he is forever jostling his script from one theme to another. He makes his cast act at full stretch, occasionally hitting upon the perfectly appropriate tone and attitude and crowning his feverish quest with success." But Georges Sadoul remembers that "as a young critic . . . he defined the basic tenets of what was to become neorealism" and calls De Santis "the best filmmaker of the second neorealist period, with a forceful, baroque style, dedicated and deeply concerned with social and human realities."

FILMS: (with others) Giorni di gloria, 1945; Caccia tragica (Tragic Hunt/Pursuit), 1947; Riso amaro (Bitter Rice), 1949; Non c'è pace tra gli ulivi (No Peace Under the Olives/Under the Olive Tree/Blood on Easter Sunday), 1950; Roma, ora undici (Rome, Eleven O'Clock/It Happened in Rome), 1952; Un marito per Anna Zaccheo (A Husband for Anna), 1953; Giorni d'amore (Days of Love), 1954; Uomini e lupi (Men and Wolves), 1956; Una strada lunga un anno (The Road a Year Long/Cesta duga godinu dana), 1958; La garçonnière, 1960; Italiani brava gente (Attack and Retreat), 1964; Un apprezzato professionista di sicuro avvenire, 1972. Published screenplays—Riso amaro: un film diretto da Giuseppe de Santis, 1978.

ABOUT: Armes, R. Patterns of Realism, 1971; Jarratt, V. The Italian Cinema, 1951; Landy, M. Fascism in Film, 1986; Leprohon, P. The Italian Cinema, 1972; Liehm, M. Passion and Defiance: Film in Italy from 1942 to the Present, 1984; Malerba, L. and Siniscalco, C. (eds.) Fifty Years of Italian Cinema, 1954; Masi, S. Giuseppe De Santis; Parisi, A. Cinema di Giuseppe De Santis,

1983. *Periodicals*—Cinéma (France) April 1959; Cinema e Cinema January/March 1977, January/March 1982; Cinema Nuovo September–October 1969; Positif April 1957, May 1980; Sight and Sound August 1950.

*DE SICA, VITTORIO (July 7, 1902–November 13, 1974), Italian director, producer, and actor, was born in Sora, a small market town midway between Rome and Naples. He was the third child of Umberto De Sica and the former Teresa Manfredi. Italian sources variously give six days and three years as the time he actually stayed in Sora before his father, a clerk in the Banca D'Italia, was transferred to Naples—a city to which De Sica proudly asserted his spiritual allegiance throughout his life, although the family also resided in Florence and Rome during his formative years. But the ebullience of Naples cast a lasting spell. He recalled that as a child in Naples he was well-known to the ladies of the local bordello, to whom he prattled from the family balcony.

Umberto De Sica, a former journalist, always admired show business people and sought such a career for his handsome son. Thanks to his contacts, Vittorio De Sica made his screen debut in his teens, playing the young Clemenceau in a biopic about the French statesman. He was also popular as a singer of Neapolitan songs in amateur entertainments. In spite of these early successes, however, De Sica himself craved a secure occupation, studying accountancy at a Rome technical college. After completing his military service in the elite Grenadiers, he was ready to embark on a career in accountancy. But the finances of the De Sica family were at a low ebb, and when a friend told him of a vacancy in the Rome theatre company where he worked, De Sica, diffident but encouraged by his father, applied for the job. The company was that of Tatiana Pavlova, a popular Russian actress. Madame Pavlova, clearly impressed by the young man's attractive and striking good looks, engaged him. The die was cast.

During the next years, De Sica played everything from clowns to old men, and soon graduated to lead roles in romantic comedies. By 1930 he was a matinee idol. Early on he had appeared briefly in one or two silent films and he had his first speaking part in Amleto Palermi's *Le vecchia signora* (1931). It starred the great Emma Gramatica who, years later, was to find her best screen role in De Sica's *Miracolo a Milano.* But it was in the popular films of Mario Camerini that De Sica became a star of the screen. Adored by his fans (mainly women), he became known

*dâ sē´ kä

VITTORIO DE SICA

as the Italian Maurice Chevalier; then, as his debonair appeal matured, as the Italian Cary Grant. "Brides left their husbands on their wedding nights to pursue me," he declared with characteristic Neapolitan brio. He himself was married in 1937 to the actress Giuditta Rissone. One of the early Camerini successes, *Darò un millione* (*I'll Give a Million*), was scripted by the journalist and critic, Cesare Zavattini, who was later to forge with De Sica one of the most fruitful writer-director partnerships in the history of the Italian cinema.

De Sica's first assignment as film director (partial: he directed only the actors) was *Rose scarlatte* (*Twenty-Four Red Roses,* 1940), an adaptation by Aldo De Benedetti of his 1936 play, a comedy-romance that De Sica had directed and starred in on the stage. As a filmed stage piece, with little cinematic merit apart from the sure direction of the actors, it enjoyed a mild success. De Sica also acted in this movie, as he did in the three that followed. The next, *Maddelena, zero in condotta* (*Maddelena, Zero for Conduct,* 1941), was another somewhat sentimental minor work but already showed a developing screen technique. *Teresa Venerdì* (*Doctor Beware,* 1941), about a young doctor working in an orphanage for girls, revealed a surer sense of rhythm and narrative timing, in spite of its undistinguished plot.

De Sica's fourth film was a miscalculation. *Un garabaldino al convento* (*A Garibaldian in the Convent,* 1942) is an old lady's reminiscence, told in flashback, about a soldier of the Risorgimento who seeks refuge in a convent. The film's point of view seems uncertain; and it was per-

haps because of its facile romantic mood that the fascist censor of the time took no exception to it. In fact, all sympathy in the film is directed toward the rebel against the opportunistic authorities, the movie's true patriots are on the side of the opposition. But De Sica was still far from the penetrating humanist works he was to create a few years later.

It was in his next film, *I bambini ciguardano* (*The Children are Watching Us,* 1943), that a vital aspect of his creative genius became apparent; his remarkable perception of the feelings of children. Based on Cesare Giulio Viola's 1928 novel, *Pricò,* and scripted by the author Zavattini and De Sica, the film examines the impact on a young boy's life of his mother's extramarital affair with a family friend. Pricò (from the Italian word for precocious) becomes agonizingly aware of the rift in his family life, and his sense of loss is made even more acute when he is placed in a Jesuit boarding school. The affair leads to the father's suicide. At the end, when Pricò's mother comes to the school to reclaim him, he rejects her and walks away alone, a small figure dwarfed in the impersonal school lobby. (This was the first of several final scenes that reflect the influence on De Sica of the director he most revered, Charles Chaplin.) The cause of the marital rift leading to the wife's infidelity is never revealed; the concern of the authors is purely with the effect of the rupture on the child—and it is this that gives a basically banal, even melodramatic tale a profounder aspect. The film owes much to the remarkable performance by the boy, Luciano De Ambrosis, himself orphaned just before work on the film began, whom De Sica spotted in a crowd of children acting in a Pirandello play. *I bambini* proved to be a key work, both thematically and stylistically, in the De Sica–Zavattini collaboration.

La porta del cielo (*The Gate of Heaven,* 1944) followed and had a chequered career. De Sica had received an invitation (or command) from Hitler's Propaganda Minister, Dr. Goebbels, to make a film in Prague. A simultaneous commission from the Catholic Cinema Center supplied a fortuitous alternative to serving under the fascist banner. *La porta del cielo* recounted a train journey to the shrine of the Blessed Virgin at Loreto, famous for curing the afflicted. In various interwoven vignettes, Zavattini, De Sica, and Diego Fabbri investigated the stories of some of the travelers, among them a young worker blinded in a factory accident and a concert pianist with a paralyzed hand, who is making the pilgrimage in spite of his atheism.

De Sica's account seems to have lacked the mystical fervor the Vatican had hoped for, and the completed film was mysteriously "lost." Nevertheless, it resurfaced in Paris some four years later, amplified by archival shots intended to give the impression that it concerned a pilgrimage to Lourdes, in a bid to increase its appeal to French cinema-goers. It was also briefly shown in Rome in November 1944, but today, as far as known, no complete copies of the original film remain. Years later, De Sica said that he considered it one of his best works. A report in *Écran Français* (October 1948) suggests the work was firmly in the neorealist mode: "It had a lot of haphazard lighting and framing; the images, often grey, recalled news events taken in the worst conditions. But much of the film's strength stemmed from this . . . rich in marvelously observed details, tender, cruel, or ironic."

The film that followed, *Sciuscià* (*Shoeshine*, 1948) was a landmark in the work of the De Sica-Zavattini partnership. Reviewing the film in *Sequence*, Lindsay Anderson wrote: "What is it about these Italian pictures which makes the impression they create so overwhelming? First, their tremendous actuality; second, their honesty; and third, their passionate pleading for what we have come to term human values."

The "*sciuscià*" were the vagrant war orphans of southern Italy who organized their enterprises (many of them illegal) in the wake of the Allied invasion. One source of income was cleaning the shoes of the occupying troops, and the call *Siuscià, Gio?*" was the boys' rendering of "Shoeshine, Joe?" The dream of two of these shoeshine boys is to own a horse, but in their efforts to drum up money for this they become party, albeit innocently, to a robbery. They are apprehended by the police and, when they refuse to implicate their friends, are sent to prison as juvenile delinquents.

What is sometimes overlooked in the growth of the neorealist tradition in Italy is the fact that some of its most admired aspects sprang from the dictates of postwar adversity: a shortage of money made the real locations an imperative choice over expensive studio sets, and against such locations any introduction of the phony or the fake would appear glaringly obvious, whether in the appearance of the actors or the style of the acting. De Sica therefore chose to work with unknowns who, under his sympathetic direction, could retain their naturalness and would bring with them no aura of personal legend or glamour.

In *Sciuscià*, the grainy newsreel quality of Anchise Brizzi's photography, the sharp cutting, and the seemingly spontaneous naturalism of the acting (particularly of Rinaldi Smordoni and Franco Interlenghi as the two boys, Giuseppe

and Pasquale) all sustain the almost tangible feel of the exhausted city, bereft of its pride. This same weariness infects the prison authorities; the prison scenes have an almost documentary air of squalor, physical and moral.

In his review, Lindsay Anderson analyzes the friendship of Giuseppe and Pasquale, calling it "an affair of innocence—the boys are never sentimentalised, but they are shown, for all their acuteness, as innocents, with innocent love, candour and trust. By contact with the world we see these qualities perverted and finally destroyed. When the casual brutality of a warder separates them, when one hand gropes vainly for another, then we perceive the inevitability of disaster. At this point *Sciuscià* becomes a tragedy." Another tribute to the sensitive depiction of the adolescent world comes from Pierre Leprohon: "Beyond its sense of actuality, *Sciuscià* ranks among the most pathetic evocations of that lost time of youth; it delves into the whole secret complexity, into the most mysterious of zones of influence—domination and submission—which leads one to suspect that between Giuseppe and Pasquale there exists, in spirit if not in the act, what adults (who can no longer apprehend it in its juvenile purity) call a 'very special friendship' [*une amitié articulière*]."

When the two boys acquire their horse, no conditions or ownership claims need to be defined: the horse belongs to both of them and involves them totally. The symbolic climax, in which Giuseppe dies by his friend's hand, realizing too late that Pasquale has not betrayed him, seems to arise, unforced, from the events, as their beloved horse gallops off into the dark. However, De Sica at the 1947 Cannes Festival declared that "the end of *Sciuscià* was dictated by the producer. If it had been left to me, it would not have ended on a note of such dark hopelessness. It is the last time I will accept the impositions of producers." He was also opposed to shooting the final bridge scene in the studio, but there was not enough money to wait for good weather.

In official Italian circles, the film aroused great antagonism. Nicola Chiaromonte wrote: "After *Sciusciá*, De Sica's name was anathema within the walls of the Ministry of Justice and even more so among the officials of the Department of Correction. De Sica had dared to show life inside a prison." Abroad, things were different, and *Sciuscià* won a "Special Award" at the 1947 Oscar presentations, the beginning of De Sica's international recognition as a major director. His next work would establish that position beyond any doubt.

With the passage of time and the recovery of

the Italian economy, some of the original impact of, *Ladri di bicyclette* (*Bicycle Thieves/ The Bicycle Thief,* 1948) has been obscured. The film can only be fully appreciated when it is related to the traumatic, chaotic postwar years when a defeated Italy was occupied by Allied forces. It is this failure to assess the film in its social-historical context that has ousted it from the place it occupied for many years in leading critics' lists of best films. To describe this picture, as Antonioni once did, as a story of a man whose bicycle has been stolen, is deliberately to miss the point. Here we have a man who has been deprived of a rare chance to earn tomorrow's bread; it is as urgent as that. The long Sunday the film describes becomes for him a kind of nightmare that betrays him into conduct which is fundamentally alien to him. *Ladri di biciclette,* loosely based on Luigi Bartolini's novel, was scripted primarily by Zavattini and De Sica. The latter, unable to find studio backing, produced it himself with financial help from friends.

In postwar Rome unemployment is rife; transport is limited mainly to overcrowded trams. An unemployed workman, Ricci, gets the chance of a job as a bill-poster on condition that he provide his own bicycle, which he retrieves from the pawnshop by pledging his bed sheets. But while he is pasting up a glamorous poster of an American pin-up girl, his bicycle is stolen: disaster! He spends the entire day scouring the city with his little son, Bruno, hunting for the thief of whom he catches only tantalizing glimpses. When at last he finds him, he can prove nothing and is attacked by a street gang, intent on protecting one of their number. At that point he spots an unattended bicycle outside a house. He tries to steal it but is immediately caught and shamed. In that climactic moment of frustration he strikes his son, who runs away from him. They are temporarily alienated, but nightfall finds the two of them reunited but powerless against the bleak threat that tomorrow holds. The camera traces them as they walk away into a crowd, in an ending that once more has Chaplinesque overtones.

Pierre Leprohon in his admirable study of De Sica in the *Cinéma D'Aujourd'hui* series, writes "What must not be ignored on the social level is that the character is shown not at the beginning of a crisis but at its outcome. One need only to look at his face, his uncertain gait, his hesitant or fearful attitudes to understand that Ricci is already a victim, a diminished man who has lost his confidence." Another perceptive film critic and biographer, Lotte Eisner, sets the scene: "No famous monument shows that the action takes place in Rome. Here are drab suburban streets, ugly houses, instead of ancient or contemporary ruins. The Tiber flows sluggishly, its embankments are dusty and deserted. This could be anywhere in the world where people are poor, where dawn brings the dustmen emptying the bins, the workmen going to the factories, the crowded tramcars. Nothing of the picturesque South: there are not even any beggars to be seen. They are to be found herded like a flock of sheep into an enclosure, where the lady members of a religious organization, with tight smiles, and a hurried charity which sacrifices one hour a day to the verminous, call the poor starvelings to their knees for a mechanical prayer in return for a bowl of thin soup."

For Lotte Eisner, *The Bicycle Thief* was the best Italian film made since the war. Others made higher claims: in 1952, a poll of 100 international filmmakers voted their choices of the best ten films of all time. The list was headed by *Potemkin,* followed by *The Gold Rush* and *The Bicycle Thief.* But, once again, the film received far greater acclaim in France, America, and England than it did in Italy. It won a special Academy Award as best foreign film, the awards of the New York Film Critics and of the British Film Academy, and the grand prix at the Belgian film festival; Richard Winnington noted that it most likely holds "the most successful record of any foreign film in British cinemas." At home, *Bicycle Thief* exacerbated the hostility De Sica had aroused with *Sciuscià* for propagating an unflattering view of his country, though it received the Silver Ribbon there—the Italian Oscar.

Guido Aristarco was one Italian critic who praised *The Bicycle Thief* highly, though pointing out the risk for De Sica "that sentimentalism might at times take the place of artistic emotion." Luchino Visconti, the precursor of Italian neorealism with his 1942 *Ossessione,* considered that De Sica had made a mistake in using a professional actor to dub the part of Ricci, finding the voice at variance with Lamberto Maggiorani's performance; others thought this a sophisticated criticism which would occur to few apart from the Italian cinema's arch-perfectionist. De Sica chose Maggiorani, a factory worker from Breda, when he brought his son to an audition for the part of the young Bruno. The role of Bruno in fact went to Enzo Staiola, the eight-year-old son of a flower-seller whom De Sica noticed in the crowd gathered to watch the shooting of a street scene for *The Bicycle Thief.*

For his second film as producer-director, De Sica turned to a subject which Zavattini had long held dear. The idea had gone through many stages: a story outline in 1940, a novel called *Totò the Good* in 1943, a working script entitled

The Poor Disturb, and eventually the final version, *Miracolo a Milano* (*Miracle in Milan*, 1951), which Zavattini prepared in collaboration with other notable scriptwriters including Suso Cecchi D'Amico and Mario Chiari.

Perphaps in anticipation of the varied interpretations his "philosophical tale" would be subjected to, De Sica declared at the outset that "it is a fable, and my sole intention is to tackle a twentieth-century fairy tale". And in fact the film opens on a painting by Pieter Brueghel over which, as it comes to life, the words "Once upon a time" are superimposed, followed shortly after by the discovery by an old woman (Emma Gramatica) of a naked child in a cabbage in her garden. This is Totò, and we follow his adventures as he grows up, becoming, through his natural optimism and ability to locate a glimmer of poetry in the harshest reality, a prop to all and sundry. He is living in a shantytown on the outskirts of Milan when oil is discovered on the squatters' patch of land. The rich move in to exploit it, and Totò sees a vision of the old woman who makes him a gift of her magic dove, by whose aid he can perform miracles—even make the sun appear. But the squatters are finally no match in this world for the industrialist Mobbi, abetted by regiments of police, and they take off on broomsticks "towards a kingdom where 'good morning' really means good morning."

"The film," says De Sica, "is a fable for young and old alike. Even the special effects are childish tricks. Very simple, almost puerile, born out of a child's imagination. I wanted to bring to the screen, apart from any political considerations professed and shared by all of us, the Christian, human sense of solidarity." As for the film's meaning, he added, "it's simply the triumph of goodness; that men should learn to be good to one another. That is my film's only politics."

Not everyone was content to see the film in such simple terms: the Vatican condemned it for materialism, because a child is seen to be born from a cabbage, while some right-wing critics, assessing the angle of the squatters' flight over the Cathedral of Milan, figured that they were heading east, that is, towards Moscow! "Part social satire, part fantasy," wrote Pauline Kael, "this . . . film suggests a childlike view of Dostoevsky's *The Idiot*. . . . the failure of innocence as in *The Bicycle Thief* and *Umberto D* is tragic, but here the failure of innocence is touchingly absurd—stylized poetry." This blend of fantasy and reality was not, after all, such a thematic departure from the earlier films as it might first seem: the familiar concern for the underprivileged was strongly there, and so were the harsh social realities seen through the eyes of a child.

The film shared the 1951 Grand Prix at Cannes and also won the New York film critics' award for the best foreign film of the year. De Sica once stated that he was "obsessed by two monsters: Charlie Chaplin and René Clair. Working on the scenario for *Miracle in Milan*, it would happen that some days we were quite satisfied with our work and our discoveries. Not for long! Next day, I'd hit my head and say to myself: Chaplin thought of that twenty-five years ago! Or: René Clair did that in such-and-such a film!" It must have given De Sica great pleasure when Clair proclaimed *The Bicycle Thief* to be the best film that he had seen for thirty years.

About his preference for nonprofessional actors, De Sica said: "The man in the street, in the hands of a director who is at the same time an actor, represents malleable material that you can mold according to your wishes." All his colorful down-and-outs for *Miracle in Milan* he discovered on the streets of Milan's suburbs. "It was sufficient to explain something about the métier, show them a few actors' tricks, in the best sense of the word, for them to reveal themselves as incomparable actors."

For *Umberto D* (which many critics consider to be his finest work), De Sica encountered his main protagonist walking along a Roman street on his way to a lecture. He was Professor Carlo Battisti, a celebrated philologist from the University of Florence. He plays a retired government clerk, whose struggle against loneliness, destitution, and humiliation is the film's subject. The only other human character of importance is the housemaid (Maria Pia Casilio), pregnant, defeated, but for a while a companion in misery. *Umberto D* was De Sica's favorite among his works, and the film is dedicated to his own father, another Umberto.

Here the director-writer team carried their neorealistic approach to its most concessionless expression, coming closest to Zavattini's avowed ambition: to insert into a film ninety minutes of a man's life wherein nothing happened. The lonely old man, subsisting on his meager pension, is seen shuffling around his shabby room where an entire reel is devoted to his preparations for bed. The servant girl is observed preparing, in like detail, for yet another eventless day. The minutiae of drab, everyday lives are penetratingly observed, and they exert a powerful fascination. And then there is the old man's closest companion—his dog. Although the film's tone is decidedly more austere than in *The Bicycle Thief*, there are many parallels to be drawn in the depiction of the central friendship: Ricci loses and refinds his son Bruno; Umberto loses his dog and eventually discovers it in the pound, destined for the gas chamber; Bruno hits his son and is temporarily estranged from him; Umberto loses his dog's trust when, having failed to find it a better home, he contemplates their double suicide under a passing train. All the incidents are seamlessly woven into a beautifully observed texture of simple lives which is never guilty of a calculated, sentimental onslaught on the senses.

After the film's opening performance, Giulio Adreotti, State Undersecretary, published an article deploring the neorealist trend in current Italian movies and, in particular, calling for a "more constructive" optimism from De Sica. De Sica later stated that if he had to do the film again he would change nothing except for the "uplifting" and rather weak final shots of children playing. When the film was eventually released in America some three years later, it won once again an award for De Sica from the New York film critics. In the meantime the director had been approached by Hollywood to make his first English-language film. Howard Hughes, it seemed, was prepared to back him in a film of his own choice. De Sica was installed in a luxurious hotel in Bel Air, where, deprived of his habitual contact with the life of the streets, he fretted and waited in vain for a summons to meet the mysterious and elusive Hughes. Eventually, David Selznick made an offer for him to produce and direct an English-language film in Italy. An original story by Zavattini was decided upon, dealing with the parlous nature of divorce in Italy. Truman Capote was hired for the English dialogue. The result was *Stazione Termini* (1953, *Indiscretion of an American Wife* in the US, *Indiscretion* in Britain).

It was an ill-fated venture; a kind of Italian-American *Brief Encounter*, with an American woman obliged to return to her husband and child and her Italian lover desperate to keep her in Italy. The entire ninety-minute drama of separation was set inside and just outside of Rome's magnificent railway terminal but the plight of the principal characters (Jennifer Jones, costumed and be-tippetted by Christian Dior, and an uneasy Montgomery Clift) failed to merge with the interspersed cameos of the swirling life around them. Almost one-third of the film was cut for American distribution, including a festive marriage scene featuring Maria Pia Casilio, who gave such an effective performance as the servant girl in *Umberto D*.

After his American debacle, De Sica seems to have felt the need to return to his origins: the result was *L'oro de Napoli* (*The Gold of Naples*, 1954), made up of six sketches of Neapolitan life drawn from stories by Giuseppe Marotta. The fi-

nal episode, depicting a religious procession for a dead child, was deleted, and the remaining five episodes have seldom been shown in their entirety; under the title *Every Day's a Holiday*, the film was released in Britain with only three episodes. The film nevertheless enjoyed a considerable box-office success, although the Italian critic, Guido Aristarco, considered that both Marotta and De Sica were guilty of perpetuating Neapolitan stereotypes, living out their lives in a ferment of sun and merriment.

In this same period De Sica was also cementing his reputation as a film actor of distinction in roles ranging from the suave baron of Max Ophüls' *The Earrings of Madame de . . .* to the rural policeman of Luigi Comencini's *Pane, amore e fantasia* (*Bread, Love and Dreams*, 1954). In this latter role he played opposite Gina Lollobrigida; they were such a hit as a team that a sequel to this comedy was made the following year.

Back in Rome, De Sica embarked on what many regard as the last strictly neorealist film: *Il tetto* (*The Roof*, 1956). This time, he chose for his leading characters Gabriella Pallotta, a seventeen-year-old salesgirl from a children's clothing store in Rome, and Giorgio Listuzzi, a former soccer player from Trieste. In the film they appear as impoverished newlyweds who, to escape from the two-room apartment they share with a swarm of relatives, make a desperate bid to erect overnight four walls and a roof on a patch of wasteland—the Roman police being empowered to demolish any such mushroom dwellings they find uncompleted by dawn.

There are some memorable sequences, as genuinely compassionate and moving as any in the earlier works; an example is the sequence in which the couple have to share a bedroom with the husband's parents and young sister. But the plight of this attractive couple lacks a consistent intensity. As Arlene Croce pointed out, in spite of its honorable intentions, "the script's descent from poetry to journalism proves almost fatal; he [De Sica] is unable to lift the level of *The Roof* above that of a human interest editorial. . . . the human beings are never seen in their uniqueness, only in their generality." Jean-Paul Sartre found that "the force of social criticism in *The Bicycle Thief* is lost in *The Roof*. It is a well-made film but a conventional one"; while Lindsay Anderson, writing after the film's first showing at the Cannes Festival, felt that De Sica and Zavattini had "reached a point in their works in which they are exploiting rather than exploring the effects of poverty." But Gordon Gow expressed the overall reaction to the film: "Quite possibly neorealism has had its heyday, but it can still warm the heart when practised by a master." *The Roof* marked the end of De Sica's most personal contribution to Italian cinema history.

La Ciociara (Two Women; 1960) followed from Alberto Moravia's story of a mother and her daughter in wartime Italy who, while making their way back to their native village, are raped by marauding Moroccan troops. The mother's role was originally intended for Anna Magnani, with Sophia Loren as her daughter—a casting that Magnani adamantly refused. Finally the roles were adapted to allow Loren to play the mother, with a much younger daughter (Eleonora Brown). Under De Sica's sensitive direction, Loren rose superbly to the dramatic challenge (as fellow Neapolitans they had an exceptionally strong rapport) and won an Oscar for her performance—the first time one was ever awarded for a performance in a foreign-language film. But apart from Loren's compelling interpretation and certain scenes of an undeniable dramatic violence, De Sica's tact and sobriety, paramount in his earlier films, are not in evidence.

Several slight and/or unsuccessful ventures followed. *Il giudizio universale (The Last Judgment,* 1961), a project that De Sica had worked on for four years and interrupted to make *La Ciociara,* was a satirical fable with an international cast about the behavior of people upon the announcement of the Last Judgment, and their reactions to its postponement. It aimed at the spirit of *Miracolo a Milano* but woefully misfired. An episode in a four-part film, *Boccaccio '70* (1962)—the other three were directed by Fellini, Visconti, and Monicelli—provided Sophia Loren with a bravura role as the prize in a country fair lottery. This was followed by an adaptation by Abby Mann of Jean-Paul Sartre's play *Les Séquestrés D'Altona (The Condemned of Altona,* 1962), about the Nazi past of Hamburg ship barons; in the ponderous treatment of this theme it is virtually impossible to detect the hand of De Sica. Finally, a forgotten film, *Il Boom,* set in the period of Italy's economic revival, concerns a rich man who has lost an eye in an accident and the bankrupt building contractor (Alberto Sordi) who, in his desperation, sells him one of his.

This period of professional doldrums was revitalized by yet another return to the Neapolitan scene for two films with Sophia Loren and Marcello Mastroianni: *Ieri, oggi, domani (Yesterday, Today and Tomorrow* 1963), a three-episode film providing Loren with three separate roles: Adelina of Naples, Anna of Milan, and Mara of Rome; and *Matrimonio all'Italiana (Marriage Italian Style,* 1964), adapted by Eduardo De Filippo from his stage success, *Filumena Marturano.* Although some foreign critics found the films too brash and salacious for comfort, the director and his stars ebulliently evoked the Neapolitan spirit—raffish, warm, and defiant—that was so essentially a part of them all. The films found an appreciative world market and can be considered as a small crest of the wave in De Sica's career—this time of solidly commercial nature.

Despite very mixed critical responses to both these commercial hits, *Yesterday, Today and Tomorrow* won yet another Academy Award for the best foreign film while *Marriage Italian Style* brought Loren the best actress award (in Moscow, surprisingly) for her performance as Filumena.

De Sica and Zavattini, now both in their sixties, moved on to France and made their first French-language film, *Un monde nouveau (A New World,* 1966). This story of a young unmarried couple, pursuing separate careers and coping with an unwanted pregnancy, emerged as curiously old-fashioned, out of touch with the times; it was generally seen as a failed attempt to measure up to the fresh approach of the new generation of French filmmakers.

Caccia alla volpe (After the Fox, 1966), starring Peter Sellers and scripted by Neil Simon and Zavattini from a story by Simon, fared no better. For Enzo Nalta, writing in *Cineforum,* this was "the lowest level that De Sica had reached. *A New World,* which is conventional and ambiguous, is just a little better." The main point of interest in De Sica's episode in *Le Streghe (The Witches,* 1967) is the appearance of a somewhat bemused Clint Eastwood as the husband of Silvana Mangano, with "nothing much to do but look patient" (Vincent Canby). *Woman Times Seven (Sept fois femme,* 1967) filmed in Paris, afforded Shirley MacLaine the chance to romp through seven roles and caused Bosley Crowther in the New York *Times* to express his bewilderment at De Sica's treatment of women here, after his sensitive depiction of them in past films.

In 1968 De Sica became a French citizen in order to obtain a divorce from his first wife; he was married the same year to the actress Maria Merceder, with whom he had lived since 1942. Manuel, the elder of their two sons, composed the music for some of De Sica's films.

Amanti (A Place for Lovers, 1968), starring Faye Dunaway and Mastroianni, found few defenders: Ermanno Comuzio in *Cineforum* dismissed it as "an attempt to revive romanticism in these times of protest against the pornographic and erotic." The same reviewer found *I Gira-soli (Sunflower,* 1970) (filmed mainly in Moscow and reuniting Loren and Mastroianni), although marginally better than *Amanti,* "a melodrama realized with a lot of money . . . to move large audiences." These audiences did not appear, and it seemed as if the rot irretrievably had set in. An episode in a three-part film, *Le coppie (The Couples,* 1970), did little to restore confidence.

But De Sica, temporarily estranged from Zavattini, was to enjoy one more triumph and be lauded by critics who had written him off as a spent force. *Il giardino dei Finzi-Contini (The Garden of the Finzi-Continis,* 1971), though not a great film, was still a densely textured work and a refined evocation of a tragic society. Adapted from Giorgio Bassani's basically autobiographical novel and shot mainly on location in Ferrara, it is set in the years just before and during World War II. Its theme is the fate of the Italian Jews under the Fascists; in particular the Finzi-Continis, a rich aristocratic family from Ferrara. Locked in their false Eden—the garden is almost never sullied by the eyes of strangers—the children of the family indulge in their amorous intrigues, almost wantonly unaware of the threat mounting outside to their decorous, fastidious way of life, ultimately to be shattered brutally by the family's arrest prior to deportation. "How does De Sica's garden grow? Beautifully," commented David Denby in a glowing account of the film in the New York *Times.* And Pauline Kael called it "a major film artist's" account of "a minor novel." The director's sure guidance of his actors is once more in evidence, with Dominique Sanda particularly effective as the aristocratic girl whose relationship with the son of a middle-class Jewish family is spoiled by her jealously incestuous feelings for her brother. The film won the first prize at the Berlin Festival and, once again, an Oscar for the best foreign-language film.

It was to be De Sica's last work of distinction. There followed a modest assignment, once more with Zavattini, *Lo chiameremo Andrea (We'll Call Him Andrew,* 1972), about the tensions within a marriage caused by the couple's inability to have a child. *Una breve vacanza (A Brief Vacation,* 1973) showed De Sica and Zavattini harking back to their neorealist vein and concerned once more with the plight of the poor in a lachrymose drama about a downtrodden, consumptive Milanese housewife.

De Sica's last film, *Il viaggio (The Voyage* 1974), was a melodramatic saga based on a Pirandello novella. Starting in a Sicilian village in the early 1900s, it spanned the years until the declaration of the 1914 war. Adriana (Sophia Loren), an impoverished young woman of the upper middle class, is constrained to marry a son of an aristocratic family (out of deference to his dying father's last wishes) while in love with his brother (Richard Burton). When the husband dies, the brother takes charge of the now ailing Adriana and her son, thereby offending Sicilian susceptibilities regarding widowhood. He also becomes her lover, and the journey of the title is one undertaken by the couple to Naples and eventually Venice where Adriana, stricken with an incurable heart disease, dies. This death scene was actually shot in the Hotel Milan in the room where Giuseppe Verdi died. In spite of its lavish settings and distinguished cast the film was not a success. Vincent Canby in the New York *Times* saw it as anachronistic, with Burton and Ian Bannen ill-suited to their roles as the brothers, and Loren with no real part to play.

In a French interview, given at the time of the successful presentation of *The Garden of the Finzi-Continis,* De Sica agreed with Guy Braucourt that this was his best work since *The Roof* and went on to clarify his position during recent years: "It's true that I've often worked both as director and actor (I haven't done anything worthwhile as the latter since *Il generale Della Rovere* [directed by Rossellini in 1959] without really being able to choose my films, the real head of the undertakings being the producer, and, through him, the money source. Italian filmmakers no longer enjoy the liberty they did in the neorealist time, of which *The Roof* was the last manifestation. Also, as far as I'm concerned, it's always in taxing conditions and with the most difficult subjects that I manage to give of my best, whereas when I get trapped into easy projects, I fail. That's why, having dreamed for over fifteen years of adapting Flaubert's *Un Coeur simple,* and knowing that it is a very delicate task, I've high hopes of achieving, one day, at least one more successful film."

High hopes which were never to be realized. In 1974, this elegant, unfailingly courteous man, a voracious reader and compulsive gambler who also loved to play the piano and tell Neapolitan jokes, died in Paris on the day that *The Voyage* was scheduled for its French premiere.

Ted Perry, writing in Richard Roud's *Cinema,* said that De Sica's "greatest films as a director . . . all share an ability to present situations as if the feelings and thoughts arose spontaneously from within the people. Upon examination, however, each script is seen to be a highly structured artifact, and is, in fact, the result of great organization and skill. What . . . makes them texts for definitions of neorealism, is that the scriptwriter . . . felt it absolutely necessary to convey his own strong ideological positions in and through episodes which had the feeling of life being experienced, and De Sica was able through direction and editing to accomplish this sense of unstructured reality." André Bazin thought that "to explain De Sica, we must go back to the source of his art, namely his tenderness, his love. The quality shared in common by *Miracle in Milan* and *The Bicycle Thief* is the author's inexhaustible love of his characters."

—D.P.

FILMS: Rose Scarlatte (Red Roses), 1940; Maddelena, zero in condotta (Maddelena, Zero for Conduct), 1941; Teresa Venerdì (Doctor Beware), 1941; Un Garibaldino al convento (A Garibaldian in the Convent), 1942; I bambini ci guardano (The Children are Watching Us/The Little Martyr), 1943; La porta del cielo (The Gate of Heaven), 1944; Sciuscià (Shoeshine), 1946; Ladri di biciclette (Bicycle Thieves/The Bicycle Thief), 1948; Miracolo a Milano (Miracle in Milan), 1951; Umberto D, 1952; Stazione termini (Indiscretion/Indiscretion of an American Wife), 1953; L'oro di Napoli (The Gold of Naples, 1954); Il tetto (The Roof), 1956; La Ciociara (Two Women), 1960; Il giudizio universale (The Last Judgment), 1961; La riffa (The Raffle) *episode in* Boccaccio '70, 1962; I sequestrati di Altona (The Condemned of Altona) 1962; Il Boom, 1963; Ieri, oggi, domani (Yesterday, Today, and Tomorrow) 1963; Matrimonio all'Italiana (Marriage Italian Style) 1964; Un monde nouveau (A New World) 1966; Caccia alla volpe (After the Fox) 1966; Una Sera come le altre (A Night Like Any Other), *episode in* Le Streghe (The Witches), 1967; Woman Times Seven/Sept fois femme, 1967; Amanti (A Place for Lovers), 1968; I girasoli (Sunflower), 1970; Si leone (The Lion) *episode in* Le Coppie (The Couples), 1970; Il giardino dei Finzi-Continis (The Garden of the Finzi-Continis), 1971; Lo chiameremo Andrea (We'll Call Him Andrew), 1972; Una breve vacanza (A Brief Vacation/The Holiday), 1973; Il viaggio (The Voyage), 1974. *Published scripts*: in English—The Bicycle Thief, Simon & Schuster, 1968 (published in England by Lorrimer as Bicycle Thieves); Miracle in Milan, Orion Press, 1969; Sciuscià (seven episodes) *in* Hollywood Quarterly Fall 1949. *In Italian*—Il giudizio universale, Salvatore Sciascia Editore, 1961; Il tetto, Cappelli Editore, 1956; Umberto D: Dal soggetto alla sceneggiatura, Fratelli Bocca Editore, 1953.

ABOUT: Agel, H. Vittorio De Sica (Anthologie du Cinéma series), 1978; Armes, R. Patterns of Realism, 1971; Baldelli, P. Cinema dell'ambiguità, 1969; Bazin, A. What Is Cinema? (Vol. 2), 1971; Canziani, A. Gli anni del neorealismo, 1977; Darretta, J. Vittorio De Sica: A Guide to References and Resources, 1983; Hotchner, A. E. Sophia, Living and Loving, 1980; Jarratt, V. The Italian Cinema, 1951; Leprohon, P. Vittorio De Sica, 1966 (in French); Marcorelles, L. Living Cinema, 1973; Mercader, M. La mia vita con Vittorio De Sica, 1978; Pecori, F. Vittorio De Sica, 1980 (in Italian); Zavattini, C. Sequences From a Cinematic Life, 1970. *Periodicals*—Bianco e Nero July 1951, September–December 1975 (De Sica issue); Cahiers du Cinéma December 1951; Cineforum January 1975; Filmcritica February 1951; Film Dope January 1977; Filmkritik 7 1962; Films and Filming September 1955, December 1955, January, February and March 1956, October and November 1964; Hollywood Quarterly Fall 1949, Spring 1951; New Yorker December 18, 1971; Sight and Sound April 1950, October–December 1952, February 1955.

"DE TOTH, ANDRÉ" (Sásvrái Farkasfawi Tóthfalusi Tóth Endre Antai Mihaly) (May 15, 1913–), American director, scenarist, and producer, was born in Mako, Hungary. He writes: "My birthdate changes between 1900 and 1920 according to the different publications but the fact remains that I was born. The truth is, I don't remember the event. I was told by reliable sources it was 1913, May 15, in Hungary.

"I suffered through the first four years of my education in one school. During the subsequent eight years I was obliged to leave six different establishments. That the last two years were spent in one school may create some kind of a record. The reason for this lengthy stay was the fact that my class principal was the copublisher and editor-in-chief of the most important, the only, newspaper in the county, the Nogradi Hirlap; he made me cub reporter, typesetter and delivery boy all at once. I was the staff of one. Added to this, I was writing, directing and playing in school plays. I have never felt more important in my life. And to everybody's—including my own—shocked surprise, I graduated among the top.

"Now I had to face life.

"During a three-day celebration of my birth, my father, an ex-Hussar officer, and his first cousin, Colonel Szirmay of the Hussars, had decided my future. I had not seen this distinguished warrior since I wet on his mirror-shiny boots during that three days' celebration. A general is a big man in any army; a Hussar general in Hungary, without being blasphemous, equals God. In addition, he was the commanding general of the Ludovica Academia, Hungary's answer to West Point, Annapolis, and Sandhurst. I walked into his palatial office and was duly impressed by the statue of bronzed silver-haired strength. He praised me for my right decision in wanting to be a Hussar officer. An instant green patina covered his bronzed face when I announced I did not want to be a Hussar, I wanted to be in the air force, a pilot. I was curtly dismissed and enjoyed my first free flight down the magnificent broad marble staircase.

"My father was heartbroken when he found out I did not even want to be a pilot, I wanted

ANDRÉ DE TOTH

to be in films. My mother shrugged, smiled and asked me to get a diploma of law and political science just in case my film career fizzled out. Just to please her, I graduated with unanimous honors in law from the University of Budapest. Strangely, two "artistic" disasters honed me for motion pictures. Barely fourteen, I had an exhibition of paintings and sculptures. I was not aware then of the German Expressionists, nor were the viewers of that hick town. They laughed at my work and ridiculed me. I slashed my paintings and smashed my statues. The next disaster was my first play. It was a one-act play. A five-act play could not do the job better or more cruelly. It was taken off after the dress rehearsal, not even a first night. It was raining. The lights sparkled through the wet air. The black letters stood out harsh on the painfully white marquee of the theatre, like mourners at a funeral. I watched the man across the street on a stepladder taking off my name. I kept telling myself it didn't matter, what mattered was that I enjoyed what I was doing, writing, and since then credits have meant little or nothing to me. Some say I am wrong. Could be. A white-haired man in a grey flannel suit with a monocle dangling from the lapel came up to me. I knew he was not going to ask for my autograph, I ignored him. He spoke up, 'It is the worst play I have ever seen but it has a bitter integrity, an unusual approach.' Before I could swing at him, he continued, 'My name is Ferenc Molnar. I know how you must feel.' Yes, he was *the* Ferenc Molnar.

"I always think of Molnar as the best man at my marriage to motion pictures, to images and words.

"While attending the university, through Molnar I started to patch up scripts in Budapest, then, through the Hungarian connections, worked all over Europe as assistant director, actor, in the cutting rooms in Vienna, Berlin, and of course with the Kordas in London.

"I was convinced that Hollywood was waiting for me. I found no red carpet treatment when I arrived. I knew how to fly a plane, drive a racecar, play polo, and of course then I thought I knew how to make pictures. Thank God I know now how little I do know and what a pleasure it is to learn.

"I never had any respect for money of my own, it is only to spend, and I like to live well so I soon ran out of what little I had stashed away. Nobody offered me a job to fly a plane, to drive a racecar nor of course to play a chukka. What upset me most, nobody offered me a job in pictures. Any job. Instead of a racecar I drove an orange truck from Pomona to the market, earned my living as a rangehand riding the herd on the rough slopes of the High Sierras and what I earned was enough to have one lunch and one dinner in the best places once a week in town and a couple of cocktails in the Garden of Allah. Everybody thought I was a millionaire and I was approached to produce pictures independently. I met everybody important in town. They were the nicest warmest people but I couldn't get the job I wanted, to write and direct motion pictures.

"I went back to London to the womb of the Kordas. I was associated in various capacities with most of the Korda projects that got off the ground during the early/mid thirties. My most invaluable experience was watching Alex Korda building sandcastles with Winston Churchill.

"I must have inherited the wanderlust from one of my ancestors who went on the Crusades and still did not return. I moved on to Vienna, landed an assignment with Geza von Bolvary on the script of *Ernte*, second unit on its Hungarian locations. A short stay in Paris, then to Rome for a film for the Scuola Nazionale di Sci in Cortina d'Ampezzo. The snow-capped peaks rekindled my homesickness for the Sierras.

"Back to Hollywood in 1937, scripts with Geza Herceg including *Zola* (no credit) which won an Academy Award. Returned to Budapest at the end of 1938, and started working as a director in January 1939."

———

De Toth made his first film as a director under the name Endre Tóth. This was *Toprini nász* (*Wedding in Toprin*, 1939), coscripted by himself. At that time many Hungarian pictures were exported to the United States, largely for the Hungarian immigrant population, and De Toth's debut movie was selected by the American critics as one of the three best foreign films of the year. Four more films followed the same year, including *Semmelweiss,* about the doctor who helped to end the scourge of puerperal fever, and *Hat hét boldogság* (*Six Weeks of Happiness*). The latter, scripted by Zoltan Varkonyi, is said to be a good-humored social satire, reminiscent of Capra, about an old convict who educates his daughter as a lady.

With the outbreak of World War II, the Hungarian film industry came under increasingly rigid control by the right-wing and anti-Semitic National Film Committee. Bitterly opposed to the Horthy regime, De Toth one day drove his car to the Budapest railroad station, locked it, and threw away the keys, thus symbolically severing his links with his native country. Accounts differ as to precisely what happened next. According to one version De Toth was briefly involved in filming the Nazi invasion of Poland before slipping away to rejoin Korda in England as production assistant on *The Four Feathers* (1939) and *Thief of Bagdad* (1940).

Moving on again, De Toth made another brief visit to America in 1940. Hollywood, however, remained closed to him. In 1941–1942 he was back in England working uncredited as coscenarist and production assistant on Julien Duvivier's British film *Lydia,* and then in India as second-unit director on Korda's *The Jungle Book.* His long-planned Hollywood career finally began in 1943 with *Passport to Suez,* and between then and 1960 he directed a total of twenty-four features, almost all of them action films.

In 1944 De Toth began his eight-year marriage to the actress Veronica Lake, famous for the long blonde hair that fell provocatively over one eye. She starred in *Ramrod,* the first of his films to earn serious discussion. Made in 1947 for United Artists, it was also De Toth's first Western, based on a novel by Luke Short. Veronica Lake plays the willful daughter of a cattle baron (Charlie Ruggles). Her feud with her father stirs up a range war in which Ruggles' foreman (Joel McCrea) has to choose sides. Admired for Russell Harlan's "gorgeous" black-and-white photography and a good score by Adolph Deutsch, this "lean and individualistic" Western exhibited a quality soon to be recognized as the hallmark of De Toth's films—what Andrew Sarris called "an understanding of the instability and outright treachery of human relationships."

Alert critics found similar qualities in *Pitfall* (1948), which has Dick Powell as an insurance adjuster bored with his suburban life and wife (Jane Wyatt). Tempted into a single lapse from virtue with a criminal's girlfriend (Lizabeth Scott), he suddenly finds himself fighting for his life—"an Awful Warning," as one reviewer remarked, "to married men who have similar urges." Some critics resented *Pitfall*'s unrelenting glumness, but many admired this "sharp, observant little film" for its "wry insight" and for Raymond Burr's performance as a vengeful private eye.

De Toth and William Bowers received an Oscar nomination for their original story for *The Gunfighter,* made by Henry King in 1950, and said to be "probably the first Western to enlist the audience's sympathies in the cause of an anti-hero." De Toth reportedly turned down a chance to direct the film because Twentieth Century–Fox refused to cast his friend Gary Cooper in the lead. Instead, working for Columbia, De Toth made *Man in the Saddle* (1951), with Randolph Scott as the object of a manhunt ordered by an insanely jealous range baron (Alexander Knox). "Next to [Jacques Tourneur's] *Canyon Passage,*" wrote Brian Garfield, "this may be the best cinematic adaptation of an Ernest Haycox novel."

Four more De Toth Westerns appeared in 1952. *Carson City* and *Thunder Over the Plains* were both vehicles for the leathery charms of Randolph Scott, but in *Springfield Rifle* De Toth had the services of Gary Cooper as a Union officer assigned to discover who is stealing Yankee horses, and how. A subplot examines the murderous effectiveness against the Indians of the new breech-loading Springfield. The picture was found "without flair" in either direction or acting, but there was a warmer reception for *Last of the Comanches,* about a hardbitten cavalry sergeant (Broderick Crawford) who finds himself responsible for a stagecoach and its well-assorted passengers after a brutal Indian attack. Again reviewers were struck by De Toth's "curious detachment and casual attitude toward violence and treachery."

In his next film De Toth turned from these wide-open if bloody spaces to the horrors of turn-of-the-century New York. *House of Wax* was made in 3-D for Warner Brothers in 1953, when a new stereoscopic process was enjoying a brief vogue. De Toth was an odd choice for such an assignment since, having only one eye, he is himself unable to perceive the stereoscopic illusion. Nevertheless, he took the device more seriously than most of his colleagues, insisting that 3-D is "not a gimmick. It's an art form which combines the best possibilities of motion pictures and the theatre. 3-D for me is like music; you have to orchestrate it."

A remake of Michael Curtiz's *The Mystery of the Wax Museum* (1935), *House of Wax* was scripted by Crane Wilbur and starred Vincent Price in his first horror role as a sculptor of wax figures whose museum is destroyed in a fire in which he himself is presumed to have died. But after a while a new museum opens displaying wax figures of an astonishing realism. A crazed and hideously deformed figure in a black cape stalks the streets, corpses disappear from the city morgue, suspicious deaths follow, and the police are considerably more baffled than the audience.

House of Wax was the most successful of all the 3-D movies made in the early 1950s, and for most critics also the best. De Toth, wrote Jay Cocks, "comes up with several chilling images— for instance, the faces of the wax images being put to flame and melting into mush—and keeps the action moving briskly along its hopelessly illogical course." William Paul called it "the granddaddy of all 3-D horror films" and, "because of its ruthlessly elaborate manipulation of the emergence effect. . . . , the ultimate 3-D film," with elements that recall Grand Guignol and foreshadow the Theatre of Cruelty.

The Stranger Wore a Gun (1953), a "confused but interesting" Randolph Scott Western, was also originally released in 3-D. Five more action movies followed in 1953–1954, among them *Crime Wave,* an excellent and fast-paced low-budget thriller with Gene Nelson as a parolee trying to go straight whose home is invaded by hoodlums on the run. Phyllis Kirk plays his wife and fellow hostage, and Sterling Hayden is a tough but honest cop.

In 1955 came what many regard as the best of De Toth's Westerns, *The Indian Fighter,* the first film made by Kirk Douglas' independent production company Bryna. Douglas stars as an army scout who falls in love with a Sioux woman (Elsa Martinelli) and is inspired to strive for peace between Indians and whites. There is a spectacular siege of a wooden fort by tribesmen equipped with fireballs and an improvised land torpedo, and unusually generous rations of both humor and sex. Praising Wilfred Cline's spectacular color photography of the Oregon locations, Franz Waxman's score, and Walter Matthau's performance as the villain, Brian Garfield also noted that "the Indians are given more depth than was usual at the time."

Monkey on My Back (1957) was De Toth's stark (and early) contribution to the Hollywood vogue for movies about drug addiction. It is based loosely on the life story of Barney Ross (Cameron Mitchell), welterweight champion of the world in 1934–1938, whose weakness for

gambling and high living cost him his championship and his fortune. A hero at Guadalcanal, he comes home wounded and ill, is given morphine to relieve his malarial headaches, and becomes abjectly addicted. In the end, encouraged by his wife (Dianne Foster), he fights his way back to health at the drug addiction hospital in Lexington, Kentucky. There was a mixed reception for this grim movie in which, wrote *Time's* reviewer, "the camera dotes on scenes of degradation with such lickerish delight that the rolled sleeve becomes a more important symbol of sensuality than the lifted skirt."

The best of the films De Toth made over the next three years was *Day of the Outlaw* (1959). Robert Ryan plays a tough rancher who is brought to recognize his responsibilities to the community when the town is taken over by a brutal gang of outlaws (led by Burl Ives). The picture is by no means free of clichés, but it seemed to Brian Garfield that the "conflict cranks up tight and the climax, involving a long trek into blizzard-slashed mountains, is harrowing."

De Toth directed one more film in Hollywood, the mediocre *Man on a String* (1960), then accepted an invitation in Italy. He made three pictures there, none of them of any merit, and in 1962 served uncredited as consultant on David Lean's *Lawrence of Arabia.* His career almost ended in 1964, when he was seriously injured in a skiing accident, but by 1967 he was working for Albert Broccoli as a scriptwriter and then as producer of Ken Russell's *Billion Dollar Brain* (1967).

A year later De Toth took over from René Clément as director of *Play Dirty,* scripted by Lotte Colin and the novelist Melvyn Bragg and set during World War II in the North African desert (though actually filmed in Spain). It stars Michael Caine as a decent British officer who is detailed to blow up Rommel's gasoline dump and learns something about the morality of war when he acquires the services of Nigel Davenport's band of mercenaries. "They wear the enemy's own uniform," wrote Alexander Walker, "shoot the innocent, gun down Red Cross personnel and have to be paid . . . to make sure their own officers get back alive. The film has several surprise twists, but really the big surprise is finding how uncompromising it is in its disillusioned view of life and death."

In 1970 De Toth produced John Guillermin's *El Condor.* Since then he has worked in less exalted capacities, mostly overseas and generally uncredited, on an assortment of projects. He spent a year as flying unit director on the first two *Superman* movies, based at Pinewood Studios in London but traveling the world shooting background plates against which Christopher Reeve would later be seen flying. He subsequently served as script doctor and action director on Moustapha Akkad's epic *Lion of the Desert,* working out of the unit's lavish "concentration camp" in the Libyan desert. In 1981 he was back in Hollywood preparing a new 3-D film, *Fool's Gold*—a Western about a teenager who takes up with outlaws.

At that time, when De Toth was sixty-eight (or older, according to some accounts), he was said to be still lean and "incredibly fit-looking." An athletic man, he was liable in his younger days to throw himself personally into a fight sequence rehearsal to show his actors how it should be done. One writer described him as a "do-it-yourself" director, and a perfectionist who rehearsed every scene exhaustively but in shooting would still demand take after take until he was wholly satisfied. Scarcely an *auteur,* he is, as David Thomson wrote, "an entertaining director, especially when dealing with violence, treachery, and the psychological cruelty beneath them. His films are economical and sardonic."

FILMS: Toprini nász (Wedding in Toprin), 1938; Öt óra 40 (At 5.40), 1938; Két lány az utcán (Two Girls of the Street), 1938; Hat hét boldogság (Six Weeks of Happiness), 1938; Semmelweiss, 1938; Passport to Suez, 1943; None Shall Escape, 1944; Dark Waters, 1944; Ramrod, 1947; The Other Love, 1947; Pitfall, 1948; Slattery's Hurricane, 1949; Man in the Saddle (U.K., The Outcast), 1951; Carson City, 1952; Springfield Rifle, 1952; Last of the Comanches (U.K., The Sabre and the Arrow), 1952; Thunder Over the Plains, 1952; House of Wax, 1953; The Stranger Wore a Gun, 1953; Riding Shotgun, 1954; Crime Wave (U.K., The City Is Dark), 1954; The Bounty Hunter, 1954; Tanganyika, 1954; The Indian Fighter, 1955; Monkey on My Back, 1957; Hidden Fear, 1957; The Two-Headed Spy, 1958; Day of the Outlaw, 1959; Man on a String (U.K., Confessions of a Counterspy), 1960; (with Primo Zeglio) Morgan il pirata (Morgan the Pirate), 1960; (with Leopoldo Savona) I Mongoli (The Mongols), 1961; (with Sabatino Ciuffini) Oro per i Cesari (Gold for the Caesars), 1962; Play Dirty, 1968.

ABOUT: Garfield, B. Western Films, 1982; Thomson, D. A Biographical Dictionary of the Cinema, 1980. *Periodicals*—Film Dope January 1977; Monthly Film Bulletin (Britain) May 1973; Variety June 3, 1981.

DICKINSON, THOROLD (BARRON) (November 16, 1903–), British film director, author, administrator, and teacher, writes: "It all began with my learning French at Clifton College, Bristol, under the admirable teacher Otto Siepmann who made it very enjoyable. When I

THOROLD DICKINSON

left school in 1921, an aunt gave me £50 to go to live with a French family for three months in the Dordogne. At Oxford University I made friends with the son of the leading filmmaker George Pearson, who needed a French interpreter; it was 1925 and no film studios were open in Britain. The Film Quota Act was not passed until 1926 and almost every available film was American; Alfred Hitchcock spoke German and was making his first films silent in Berlin. Pearson wanted to work in Paris but did not speak the language. There were no film schools. I wanted to learn about cinema and, as interpreter to the film unit, I would have to ask each member of the unit who wanted something in Paris to explain precisely what he wanted me to ask for. It was enormously exciting working in the Abel Gance Studio, which was entirely staffed by White Russian refugees who also used interpreters all the time. Working night and day on two British films about London, I learnt more about cinema than I could have thought possible, and more about life too.

"In 1926, with the Film Quota in operation, money began to flow into film production, and directors no longer had time to write scripts or edit their films. I became one of the first British film editors, under the guidance of George Pearson. I was so busy that I never had time to learn how to join two strips of film together. Within two years the sound track was introduced, first as accompaniment and then more and more shot in synchronisation. There was no time to make experiments; we had to complete each job on the spot. To deliver on time Gracie Field's *Sing As We Go,* I had to work 140 hours a week, sleeping four hours a night in the projection room and eating meals in the cutting room with no day off for five weeks, which eventually earned me promotion to my first production, *The High Command*, 1937.

"The Film Quota Act ceased after ten years and another slump began through indifference in the Tory Government, who were equally indifferent to the Spanish Civil War, regarding the Nazis and Fascists as no menace at all. So I tried my hand at documentary work in Spain, risking my reputation by being labelled by the Ministry of Information in the 1939 War as a 'premature anti-Fascist.' But instead of being interned in the Isle of Man, I was set to work for the War Office creating *The Next of Kin* and finished up as a Major producing military training films. The last two reels of *The Next of Kin* consisted entirely of military action which had to convince every leading soldier in the Allied Armies, and it was this experience which carried me through *Hill 24 Doesn't Answer* (1952–4) and led to this Israeli war film being snapped up by the Dutch Army as containing the only accurate demonstration of streetfighting they had ever found on film. The secret was that military action on film cannot be scripted first: it has to be staged on the chosen spot in front of the cameras, a much more costly business in manhours.

"Another of my innovations was to make, early in 1940, the film version of Patrick Hamilton's melodrama *Gaslight* in story sequence, all the principal sets having been built beforehand. The film was too successful: after two years on release the rights were bought by MGM and the film withdrawn, to be remade in Hollywood by George Cukor with Ingrid Bergman (1944). The fury in the British press did not prevent my work being forgotten just as I came back from the war. In Britain this piratical venture was renamed *The Murder in Thornton Square*.

"Having visited the Soviet Union as an ardent trade-unionist, I was mad enough to tackle Alexander Pushkin's costume story *The Queen of Spades* five days after first reading it. That classic actress Dame Edith Evans made it her first feature film, and my old friend from *Gaslight*, Anton Walbrook, played opposite her. In a small inadequate old studio we didn't do too badly in 1948. But I was losing my touch for conventional subjects, and after making my own story, *Secret People*, for Sir Michael Balcon, I went off to Israel and was persuaded to tackle their war film, which led Dag Hammarskjöld to bring my wife—the architect—Joanna Macfadyen and myself to the United Nations in New York. Thus came the privilege of working for a genius. War films had been hard enough to tackle, but peace films were almost impossible: no member government would submit to being criticised in a UN film. Only long film was *Power Among Men* in colour and black-and-white. Best film was the short *Overture*, wordless, with Beethoven's 'Egmont' Overture on the sound track. By then I had discovered that civil servants are trained to censor words and never to object to pictures. The government of India accepted this German music by making four hundred prints for circulation in villages.

"After four years I left the UN in 1960 to introduce film studies in British higher education at the Slade School of Fine Art in University College London, where I stayed for twelve years."

———

Dickinson was born in Bristol, England, the son of Charles Dickinson and the former Beatrice (Thorold) Vindhya. His father, an Anglican clergyman, was at one time Archdeacon of Bristol. Dickinson was educated at Clifton College, in Bristol and at Keble College, Oxford University. At Oxford, where Dickinson showed more interest in directing college dramatic productions than in his examinations, he met the son of the prolific British film producer and director George Pearson, as he says above. Dickinson seized the chance to meet Pearson himself, and in 1925, when he should have been taking examinations, went off to Paris to work as an interpreter and general assistant on Pearson's film *Mr. Preedy and the Countess*. The following year he worked on another Pearson silent, *The Little People*.

After graduating from Oxford in 1926 Dickinson worked as a stage director with Lena Ashwell's repertory company in Notting Hill Gate, London, and then as a film editor for Pearson's company, Welsh-Pearson. In 1929, the year in which he married Joanna Macfadyen, Dickinson visited the United States to study sound techniques. On his return to Britain he became sound editor successively for British and Dominion, Gainsborough, and Stoll Films. Thus Dickinson's early career spanned the dying years of the silent era and the birth of the sound film (and led him to the conclusion that "the silent film was much closer to ballet and the music hall than to literature and the theatre").

Dickinson edited Cyril Gardner's *Perfect Understanding*, made in Britain by Gloria Swanson's short-lived film company and released in 1933 through United Artists. And he edited and coproduced (with Basil Dean) Carol Reed's first feature film *Midshipman Easy* (1935) for Associated Talking Pictures at Ealing Studios.

The first picture that Dickinson directed, *The*

High Command (1936), was produced by G. W. Wellesley for Fanfare Films. (This film was also known by the name of the Lewis Robinson novel on which it was based, *The General Goes Too Far*.) Set in West Africa, it tells of a general's successful attempt to trap a blackmailer's murderer in order to protect his own daughter from scandal. The film enjoyed a modest success and, though it has dated, is said to have been "rather interestingly performed and directed." Dickinson then went to the USSR as a delegate of the Association of Cine Technicians, of which he was vice president (he served in this office from 1936 to 1953). The Spanish Civil War began the same year, and in January 1938 Dickinson went to Spain with the Progressive Film Unit. In collaboration with Sidney Cole he made two pro-Republican documentaries, *Spanish A.B.C.* (1938), about the Republicans' educational program, and *Behind the Spanish Lines* (1938).

After a stint as second unit director on Victor Schertzinger's *The Mikado* (1939), Dickinson directed *The Arsenal Stadium Mystery* (1940), a crime story about the poisoning of a star soccer player before a crucial match. It was still being edited when World War II began in September 1939. Dickinson turned his attention to propaganda, directing the pilot picture in the Ministry of Information's series of "five-minute films." This was *Westward Ho!* (1940), made in fourteen days for £450. It was designed to encourage public acceptance of the need for children to be evacuated from urban centers to escape the German blitz. Later the same year Dickinson made another film in the series, *Yesterday Is Over Your Shoulder*. Starring Robertson Hare, it is a comedy about an unlikely group of individuals learning to become craftsmen at a Government Training Center. Lighthearted as it is, the movie nevertheless has serious overtones as a post-Dunkirk call to the nation for a united response to the war effort.

By this time Dickinson was embarked on his first major feature film, *Gaslight* (*Angel Street* in the United States), based on Patrick Hamilton's stage thriller and produced by John Corfield for British National Pictures. Adapted by A. R. Rawlinson and Bridget Boland, and with photography by Bernard Knowles, art direction by Duncan Sutherland, and music by Richard Addinsell, it displayed for the first time all the meticulous attention to technical detail and visual polish that distinguish the best of Dickinson's films. It tells the story of a homicidal schizophrenic (Anton Walbrook) who sets out to drive his wife insane when she seems likely to stumble on his guilty past. Diana Wynyard plays the hapless wife and Frank Pettingell the detective Rough. The film loses nothing of the play's suspense and brilliantly recreates the airless claustrophobia of the Victorian setting largely, according to one critic, "through fluid camerawork: the opening scene, which is silent, has an interplay of moving camera, moving actors, and (it almost seems) moving sets, worthy of the best French cinema of the 1930s." A writer in *Sequence* agreed that "the electric sense of tension and mid-Victorian atmosphere are entirely cinematic."

In 1944 MGM bought the rights to remake *Gaslight* and was thought to have destroyed all copies of Dickinson's version, including the negative. For a number of years thereafter, the Dickinson film existed only in the realms of legend, until some prints were found to have survived. Dickinson's *Gaslight* is generally preferred to George Cukor's more opulent but less taut version, in spite of Ingrid Bergman's Oscar-winning performance in the latter. Dickinson followed it with *The Prime Minister* (Warner Brothers, 1941), a modestly budgeted but star-studded life of Benjamin Disraeli, with John Gielgud as the Victorian premier and Diana Wynyard as his wife.

The Next of Kin, produced by Michael Balcon and made at Ealing Studios for the Directorate of Army Kinematography, was planned as a feature-length military training film on the subject of counterespionage, its message being "careless talk costs lives." The story was written by Dickinson and Basil Bartlett, and a cast was assembled that included Mervyn Johns, Reginald Tate, Stephen Murray, Jack Hawkins, and Nova Pilbeam, among others. It is an account of a British commando raid on the French coast and how the operation was jeopardized by an insufficient regard for secrecy. The movie makes its point so powerfully and in such exciting terms that it was generally released in 1942 for civilian propaganda and was still being revived as an entertainment thriller twenty years later. "Credit was due to Thorold Dickinson for creating the atmosphere of actuality and suspense that drove home . . . the propaganda message of the film," wrote Roger Manvell in *Films of the Second World War*. And William Whitebait found that "the detail everywhere is curious and surprising, with something of the fascination of a Simenon crime being unraveled." It has been seen as a forerunner of Louis de Rochemont's "semi-documentary" films in the United States.

In 1942 Thorold Dickinson, as a major in the Royal Army Ordnance Corps, was assigned to organize the Army Kinematograph Service Production Group, established at Wembley Film Studios in London with a staff of one hundred and fifty service men and women, including directors Carol Reed and Jay Lewis and a pool of talented writers, among Peter Ustinov and Eric Ambler. After a year with the Group, during which it produced seventeen military training films, Dickinson was released to make a picture for Filippo Del Giudice's Two Cities Films on behalf of the Colonial Office—a semi-documentary on the then fashionable theme of "colonial development." During 1943–1944 Dickinson and his crew spent months in Tanganyika searching for locations, clearing land, shooting exteriors, and recording native music (some of which was incorporated by Arthur Bliss into his score). *Men of Two Worlds* (1946), written by the novelist Joyce Cary, centers on an educated African (Robert Adams) who helps the district commissioner (Eric Porter) to persuade villagers to quit an area infested by the tsetse fly. It was regarded as a thoughtful study of Africa in transition, though one that perhaps did not fully justify the nearly three years that went into its making.

There followed two frustrating years of illness and aborted projects, during which Dickinson nevertheless managed to write (with Catherine De La Roche) a book on a subject that had long interested him—*Soviet Cinema* (1948). He then began work on *The Queen of Spades*. Pushkin's story, set in czarist St. Petersburg, is about a young army officer, an inveterate gambler, who learns that the ancient Countess Ranevskaya, through a devilish pact, has acquired the secret of winning at faro. The impoverished officer embarks on an affair with the Countess's young ward Lisaveta, gains entry to the old lady's bedroom, and surprises her there when she returns from a ball. He demands to know her secret, but the terrified Countess dies of fear. Later her ghost visits him and reveals the secret on condition that he marry Lisaveta. He does so and begins to win enormously at faro, but on the last play his triumphant ace changes to a Queen of Spades, which smiles mockingly at him with the Countess' own features as he faces the loss of all his winnings and descends into madness.

Discussing the making of the film in the 1950 edition of the Penguin annual *Cinema*, Dickinson says that "the subject itself is of a type unfamiliar in British films. And first attempts to bend the manner of the film to the British convention of the 'stiff upper lip' produced results which were quite meaningless. . . . After the first day I cast convention overboard and aimed in every scene at colourful, conscious contrast. . . . In this epoch of neorealism, *The Queen of Spades* must have come as something of a visual shock." There was a mixed response to Anton Walbrook's bravura performance in the lead, some critics finding it uncomfortably melodramatic,

others considering it wholly appropriate to the baroque mood of the film. And Edith Evans' terrifying interpretation of the role of the old Countess, "the embodiment of a mischievous evil," was universally admired. There was also much praise for Oliver Messel's designs (executed by the art director William Kellner) and for Otto Heller's photography, which cleverly conceals the fact that the film was shot on ludicrously small sets. Though some reviewers found the movie rather slow, it was generally acclaimed for its visual richness, its "fluid and creative" camerawork, and its "brilliantly atmospheric" recreation of Pushkin's story. Most critics regard it as Dickinson's best picture.

From 1949 to 1950 Dickinson worked as a scriptwriter for Associated British Films and then began work on *Secret People* (1952). An original story, written by Dickinson in collaboration with Wolfgang Wilhelm, it was produced by Sidney Cole for Ealing Studios Ltd. Louis Balan (Serge Reggiani), a young revolutionary, is sent to England to assassinate General Galbern, the roving ambassador of his country's totalitarian government. In London he meets Maria (Valentina Cortese), who had been his mistress in their homeland, and her sister Nora (Audrey Hepburn in her first important film role). Louis arranges for Nora, a dancer, to perform at a garden party given in honor of General Galbern. With Maria's help, a bomb is planted at the General's table, but when it goes off it is not the General but a young waitress who receives the force of the blast. Maria is left to resolve a terrible conflict between loyalty and conscience.

Lindsay Anderson's account of the filming of *Secret People*, published in 1952 as *Making a Film*, includes the movie's shooting script and is of great interest to cinephiles. The picture itself divided the critics. Penelope Houston thought that "the tension and power of the film make it one of the most remarkable British productions for some time," while Raymond Durgnat has suggested that it shared with *The Queen of Spades* much of the visual flow of the silent classics of the Russian cinema, carrying this fluidity "at moments, to the point of the handheld rapidity associated with Godard and the New Wave. The interplay in *Secret People* between the dancing of Audrey Hepburn and the camera yields an aesthetic pleasure of its own, in its lively conjunction of two mercurial, dynamic sensibilities. Dickinson, like an English Visconti, blends the chameleonic and the leonine." Many critics were less impressed, however, and Richard Winnington wrote: "That *Secret People*, despite the creative agonies recorded by Mr. Lindsay Anderson, should turn out to be a confused, uncoordinated spy thriller concealing a tentative message deep down below some strained efforts of style is another tragedy of British film hopes."

In 1953 Dickinson went to Israel to advise on the production of a film about the emergence of the new state. Israel captured his imagination, and he stayed on to coauthor and direct *The Red Ground*, a short propaganda film for the Israeli Defence Forces. In 1954–1955 he returned to make *Hill 24 Doesn't Answer* (1955), a passionate account of an incident in the Arab-Israeli War of 1948 based on stories by Zwi Kolitz. The adaptation was made by Dickinson in collaboration with his wife, who also worked with Dickinson on the editing. Haya Hararit, who starred in the film, received the homage of the jury at the 1955 Cannes Festival. Raymond Durgnat wrote that Dickinson "shares Israel's military struggle in a spirit, and a style, not dissimilar from Renoir's *La Marseillaise*."

Hill 24 Doesn't Answer was Dickinson's last feature film. In 1956 he went to New York as chief of Film Services at the United Nations. The documentaries made during his years there included Lionel Rogosin's *Out* (1957), and Ian MacNeill's controversial *Blue Vanguard* (1957), which dealt with the activities of the United Nations Emergency Force in the Middle East and was banned in Britain, France, and Israel. Dickinson himself served as producer of *Power Among Men* (1959), a full-length documentary about technological and other developments in various parts of the world, written by Dickinson and J. C. Sheers, with music by Virgil Thomson. It won prizes at the Moscow and Venice Documentary Film Festivals, and a Selznick Golden Laurel in the United States. In 1960 Dickinson left the United Nations to establish a film department at the Slade School of Fine Arts, London University, where in 1967 he became Britain's first Professor of Film. He retired as professor emeritus in 1971 and the same year published his second book, *A Discovery of Cinema*.

Dickinson was chairman of the British Film Academy in 1952–1953 and has served on the committees of the National Film Archive (1950–1956) and the British Film Institute's Experimental Fund (1952–1956). In 1958–1966 he was president of the International Federation of Film Societies and in 1968 acted as consultant to the American Film Institute. Dickinson received a CBE in 1973 and has honorary doctorates from the universities of London and Surrey.

Comparing Dickinson with his contemporary Anthony Asquith, Raymond Durgnat writes: "If Asquith typifies English liberalism at its most open, Dickinson's liberalism impels itself towards the radical pole. Whereas Asquith remains within the ambit of Home Counties gentlemanliness, Dickinson, of not dissimilar generation and background, arrives at an international perspective. This spiritual breadth is matched by a stylistic range which, in a small oeuvre, nevertheless runs the gamut from documentary through reconstructed documentary like *The Next of Kin* through to the claustrophobic period melodrama of *Gaslight* and the supernatural fantasy of *The Queen of Spades*." Dickinson's contributions to the cinema, as filmmaker, administrator, and teacher, have all been pragmatic in style rather than ideological. He himself says that, as a director he has approached each of his films on its own terms, endeavoring to reach "a paraphrase of reality which will contain the essence of the real." An interviewer has described him as "a tall man of commanding appearance with an academic manner, which has an engaging way of dissolving into frequent and unexpected laughter at life's little incongruities." Dickinson lists his hobbies as politics, the theatre, film, walking, reading, and travel.

—R.S.

FILMS: The High Command/The General Goes Too Far, 1937; Spanish A.B.C., 1938 (documentary); Behind the Spanish Lines, 1938 (documentary); The Arsenal Stadium Mystery, 1940; Westward Ho!, 1940 (short); Yesterday Is Over Your Shoulder, 1940 (short); Gaslight (U.S., Angel Street), 1940; The Prime Minister, 1941; The Next of Kin, 1942; Men of Two Worlds, 1946; The Queen of Spades, 1949; Secret People, 1952; The Red Ground/Border Incident, 1953 (short); Hill 24 Doesn't Answer, 1955. *Published scripts*—Secret People *in* Anderson, L. Making a Film: The Story of Secret People, 1952.

ABOUT: Anderson, L. Making a Film: The Story of Secret People, 1952; Durgnat, R. Films and Feeling, 1967; Durgnat, R. A Mirror for England: British Movies from Austerity to Affluence, 1970; Manvell, R. (ed.) The Cinema 1950; The Cinema 1951; The Cinema 1952; Manvell, R. Films of the Second World War, 1974; Who's Who, 1980. *Periodicals*—Film Culture October 1957; Film Dope January 1977; Times (London) January 13, 1961; May 27, 1967.

*DIETERLE, WILLIAM (July 15, 1893– December 9, 1972), American director, was born Wilhelm Dieterle at Ludwigshafen, a city in western Germany just across the Rhine from Mannheim. He was the ninth and youngest child of Jacob and Berthe Dieterle and grew up in considerable poverty, learning to shift for himself at an early age as a juvenile scrap dealer and in an assortment of other enterprises. His father

°dē´ tər lē

WILLIAM DIETERLE

envisaged a future for him as a carpenter and glazier, but at the age of thirteen Dieterle fell in love with the theatre. He improvised a stage in the family barn, where he performed for the benefit of relatives and friends, and at sixteen joined a traveling theatre company as a handyman, scene shifter, and apprentice actor.

At some point, according to one account, Dieterle attended a theatre school in Mannheim. Extremely tall, well-built, and striking, he soon established himself as a talented romantic actor. In 1911–1913 he appeared at theatres in Arnsberg, Heilbronn, and Plauen, and in the latter year earned his first movie credit in a short film called *Fiesco*, possibly directed by Carl Hoffman. He was at that time not interested in the cinema, however, and continued his theatrical career.

In 1914–1916 Dieterle worked at the Mainz Stadttheater and the following year at theatres in Zurich, achieving his first major success there in a production of *Wilhelm Tell*. This brought him to the attention of Max Reinhardt, architect of a new, nonnaturalistic German theatre. Dieterle was cast as Brutus in Reinhardt's production of *Julius Caesar* in Munich (1919) and from 1920 to 1923 worked with Reinhardt at his Deutsches Theater in Berlin and at the Salzburg Festival.

It was during his years with Reinhardt that Dieterle became a movie actor. His heart was still in the theatre but, as he later explained, "this was during the inflation and you had to work like the devil to make your living. . . . Since the stage didn't pay enough, I was forced into film work." He began in 1921 in E. A. Dupont's *Die*

Gier-Wally, a Henny Porten vehicle made on location in the Bavarian Alps, and the same year appeared in Leopold Jessner's Expressionist film *Hintertreppe,* which had Paul Leni as art director, and in Felix Basch's *Fraülein Julie.* It was in 1921 also that Dieterle was married to Charlotte Hagenbruch, the actress and later scenarist with whom he spent his life.

In 1922–1923 Dieterle appeared in ten movies by the likes of Karl Grune, Richard Oswald, Dupont, and Murnau. According to Francis Koval he became typecast "in parts of country yokels and simpletons, which he played with great gusto and to the public's enormous delight." He was anxious to direct, but had become such a box-office attraction that producers were reluctant to lose his services as a character actor. In the end, tired of clowning through the "kitschy, schmaltzy" movies that were beginning to dominate the German cinema, Dieterle scraped together some money and made his first film as director, *Der Mensch am Wege* (*Man by the Roadside,* 1923).

Dieterle scripted the picture himself from a story by Tolstoy and also played the lead (as he did in most of his German films, primarily to save money). His costar was a young actress later to find fame as Marlene Dietrich. Dieterle told an interviewer many years later that "we were just four or five very young, enthusiastic, and revolutionary people who wanted to do something different. We brought it out; it didn't make any money, but was shown, and it was a very interesting experiment." In the same spirit, Dieterle in 1924 left Reinhardt to form his own short-lived theatre company in Berlin, Das Dramatische Theater.

Though he directed no more pictures for several years, Dieterle acted in many—more than thirty between 1924 and the end of 1927. Notable among them was Paul Leni's *Das Wachsfigurenkabinett* (*Waxworks,* 1924), one of the last true Expressionist films, and P. W. Murnau's *Faust* (1926). Dieterle said of Murnau, "I loved him, and I think he was the finest German director—in spite of all the rest. . . . He was a great poet, a wonderful man first, and a great artist. He was very serious. . . . You could not buy him for anything."

In 1927 Dieterle and his wife formed their own production company, Charrha-Film. Their first picture was *Das Geheimnis des Abbé X* (*The Secret of Abbé X,* 1927), a drama about a tormented priest that Dieterle scripted, produced, directed, and starred in, as well as serving as scenery shifter, handyman, and props master. It was under these conditions that he took to wearing the white cotton gloves that became his

trademark on set—not out of neurotic fastidiousness or for other, darker reasons, as was sometimes averred, but because they kept his hands
clean and enabled him to switch from manual
labor to acting at the drop of a glove.

Charrha-Film's second (and last) production
was *Die Heilige und ihr Narr* (*The Saint and Her
Fool*, 1928), in which Dieterle scored a great
personal success as a "deeply human fool." He
had no great opinion of the movie but acknowledged that it helped his career, bringing him
half-a-dozen directorial assignments for established production companies, including the German subsidiaries of two American companies,
First National and Universal.

As political and economic conditions in Germany worsened and the Hollywood legend grew
ever more fabulous, emigration seemed an increasingly attractive proposition to German
filmmakers. With the arrival of sound it also became increasingly feasible, especially for those
with experience in directing spoken dialogue in
the theatre. According to Dieterle, "in Berlin it
was a running joke . . . if the phone rang at a
restaurant: they said 'It must be Hollywood.'
Well, one night my wife and I were out dining
and it really happened."

Dieterle was called to the Berlin office of First
National and hired to make synchronizations:
"Sound had just come in, and Hollywood was
afraid of losing foreign markets. So they hired
German, French, and Spanish units to make foreign versions of important features. I got four
scripts and was able to hire about five actors, just
for the leads. We got passports and off we went."
When he and his wife arrived in Hollywood in
July 1930, "the four films we were to make had
already been completed. All the sets were still
standing and dressed—we used the same costumes and everything. The big difference was
that we had just ten days to make each picture."

The films of which Dieterle made German
versions were Lloyd Bacon's *Moby Dick*
(*Dämon des Meeres*), William Beaudine's *Those
Who Dance* (*Der Tanz geht weiter*), Frank
Lloyd's *The Way of All Men* (*Die Maske fällt*),
and John Francis Dillon's *Kismet*. *Dämon des
Meeres*, in which Dieterle also played Captain
Ahab, was credited not to him but to Michael
Curtiz, who also worked on the film. It was nev-
ertheless Dieterle's favorite among the
four—"the only story I did that I had known
since childhood. . . . It had never been done in
Germany. They didn't have the means, the big
sailing ship, the whale. It was a sensation."

In those early days of sound, the Hollywood
studios used a camera for each of the principal
actors in a scene and another for the master shot.

Dieterle found this "crazy and wasteful" but
agreed to "shoot it . . . [their] way first and then
my way with one camera. They said they'd never be able to cut it, but I told them to just go
ahead and try. The next day when the rushes
came back everyone was amazed. Three days
later the boss, Hal Wallis, came down and asked
if I wanted to stay." Dieterle accepted and settled in Hollywood, in 1937 becoming an American citizen.

The Last Flight (1931), his first original
American film, was based on a story by John
Monk Saunders about four American flyers in
Europe after World War I, and the girl they
meet in Paris. Dieterle, whose English was still
poor, found the story in the *Saturday Evening
Post* and liked it enough to have it translated into
German for himself. As he described it to an interviewer, "it starts in hospital as the war ends:
'Boys, *la guerre est fini*. Now what?' 'Get tight.'
'Then what?' 'Stay tight.' That's . . . exactly
how we started the picture. The flyers refuse to
return home and be heroes. They each have a little tic, each one has been wounded physically or
psychologically by the war. They want to live
life as they find it from day to day, train station
to train station."

In fact, according to a review by Tom Shales,
The Last Flight "begins with furious air battle
footage borrowed from *The Dawn Patrol* (1930).
The frenzy of it is in sharp contrast to the rest
of the film, though director William Dieterle
never lets things get lazy. The characters may be
lost, but the director isn't. . . . One of Dieterle's
neatest touches is a slow dissolve after the battle
footage, from a propellor gradually winding
down to a meandering clock. . . . The director
so cleverly avoids the static and theatrical that
an overwritten script fails to slow the movie. . . . It moves."

Excellently played by Richard Barthelmess
and Helen Chandler, *The Last Flight* was hailed
as a "forgotten masterpiece" when it was
screened in 1970, and in 1977 a critic in *Film
Dope* wrote that it "manages to be a splendid
comedy-drama whilst at the same time quintessentially suggesting the spirit of Scott Fitzgerald's novels." Dieterle himself once went so far
as to call it "the best picture I ever made."

Recent screenings have also elicited a great
deal of critical enthusiasm for *Her Majesty, Love*
(1931), a musical of very considerable charm
starring W. C. Fields, Marilyn Miller, and Ben
Lyon. But neither of Dieterle's first two American movies made much impact in 1931, and over
the next three years he churned out a dozen programmers in a variety of genres for First National and then for Warner Brothers, which took

over First National in 1932. He established himself as a dependable workhorse neither cursed
wth "temperament" nor blessed with genius—
"extremely scrupulous, not fussy at all on the
floor, and always dead on time within the
schedule."

Discussing his years at Warners, Dieterle said
that his problem was always "how to get a good
story, because a director is only as good as his story. . . . At Warners there were ten directors
ahead of me—two top directors, LeRoy and
Curtiz. . . . A further problem I had was that
I knew nothing about cards, and if you don't
play poker in Hollywood, well, poor fellow, because that's where the pictures are cast and the
deals made."

All the same, some of the movies Dieterle
made during this period were far from negligible. *Jewel Robbery* (1932) was a stylish comedy-
thriller set in Vienna and starring William Powell—an actor, according to Dieterle, of such
charm that "with him you could steal horses."
Powell also starred opposite Bette Davis in *Fog
Over Frisco* (1934), a mystery melodrama
which, as one contemporary reviewer conde-
scendingly wrote, "reveals those qualities of pace
and velocity and sharpness which make the Hollywood product acceptable." *Madame Du Barry*
(1934), with Dolores Del Rio in the lead, was an
interesting and rather blackly comic historical
movie that upset reviewers who expected a more
reverent treatment of its heroine and her grisly
end.

In 1934, Dieterle's old patron Max Reinhardt
was in Los Angeles, staging his extravagant version of *A Midsummer Night's Dream* at the Hollywood Bowl. Dieterle managed to convince
Warners that a screen version of so prestigious
a work would "raise Warner Brothers from a second-rate studio right into the ranks of the
aristocrats." An extraordinary cast was assembled that included Olivia de Havilland as Her-
mia, Dick Powell as Lysander, Victor Jory as
Oberon, James Cagney as Bottom, Joe E. Brown
as Flute, and the eleven-year-old Mickey
Rooney as Puck. The fantastic settings were designed by Anton Grot and photographed by Hal
Mohr (replacing Ernest Haller, who "couldn't
get the mood right"). Reinhardt knew very little
about filmmaking and, Dieterle says, "was very
shy about it. He would rehearse the actors.
When he thought it was right, he would sit down
and I would arrange it for the cameras."

A Midsummer Night's Dream had an extremely mixed reception on release. A reviewer
in the London *Times* complained that "the play
is cut to ribbons, all the more important passages
of poetry omitted, scenery is substituted for de-

scriptions, and action for speeches." The acting,
according to another purist, lacked "proper
Shakespearian diction and bearing." Even then,
however, a few critics applauded these very
qualities, and over the years the freshness and vitality of this "frolic in a magic wood" have established it as a minor masterpiece.

Handed a "really terrible" script about a
small-town doctor who becomes a gangbuster,
Dr. Socrates, Dieterle accepted the assignment
on condition that he and the movie's star, Paul
Muni, could work together on a projected Warner Brothers biopic, *The Story of Louis Pasteur.*
Jack Warner agreed, but grudgingly, providing
a minute budget of $330,000 and ordering that
only contract players and old sets should be used.
Under these inauspicious circumstances, Dieterle began what he recognized as the second phase
of his American career, when a string of immensely successful and prestigious biographical
films established him as "the Plutarch of
Hollywood."

The Story of Louis Pasteur (1935) is a dramatic account of the life of the great French chemist
who among many other things discovered the
principles of vaccination, and of his fight for recognition against the skepticism of the medical
establishment. It was warmly and almost universally praised for its passion and humanity and for
"something almost approaching to reverence for
its subject," though one reviewer acknowledged
that "no one will go to it for the sake of dazzling
spectacle, daring fantasy, or exceptional lighting
and rhythm." Paul Muni received an Oscar for
what many thought the best film of the year.

As Dieterle said, *Pasteur* "raised the prestige
of Warners considerably, but at Warners the
moment you had a success they gave you something terrible to keep you from getting a swelled
head." What Dieterle got was *Satan Met a Lady*
(1936), the second screen adaptation of Dashiell
Hammett's *The Maltese Falcon,* ruined by a
script so awful that Bette Davis walked out on
the film. *The White Angel* (1936), another
biopic with Kay Francis as Florence Nightin-
gale, was also seriously marred by its scenario,
but Dieterle had a certain amount of fun with
The Great O'Malley (1937), a sentimental comedy-drama starring Pat O'Brien as an overenthu-
siastic young cop and Humphrey Bogart as the
man he unwittingly drives to crime.

After the fatuous *Another Dawn,* Dieterle was
at last given a chance at another solid biopic,
The Life of Emile Zola (1937), again with Muni
in the lead. The film emphasizes the latter part
of the novelist's life, when he committed himself
at great personal cost to the cause of Dreyfus (Joseph Schildkraut), the Jewish officer falsely

convicted of treason. Numerous historical inaccuracies were generally forgiven as "necessary adjustments . . . which in no way obscure the fundamental truths which the film so successfully presents," and other inadequacies were overlooked out of admiration for Zola's "passionate speeches in praise of Justice and Tolerance and Truth." It seemed to Basil Wright that Dieterle had "more than an ability for period reconstruction; he can convey in nearly every scene an authenticity of atmosphere which virtually enables one to step back through time and participate in the actual event," while Frank S. Nugent called *Zola* "the finest historical film ever made and the greatest screen biography." It earned Oscars as best film and for best screenplay and best supporting actor (Schildkraut).

Blockade (1938), made not for Warners but for United Artists and produced by Walter Wanger, is set during the Spanish Civil War. It has Madeleine Carroll working (against her will) as a spy for Franco's forces and falling in love with Henry Fonda, a dedicated Loyalist. William R. Meyer thought that John Howard Lawson's script (or studio interference?) "made it difficult to tell the good guys from the bad guys," but Peter Ellis called it "a modern miracle. . . . Against a conventional spy melodrama plot Lawson and Dieterle have given us a powerful indictment of totalitarian war. . . . It cries out against the inhumanity of our so-called democratic nations which stand by and allow Italian and Nazi pirates to torpedo relief and food ships. . . . Although *Blockade* does not take sides openly, Lawson and Dieterle make their sympathies for the Spanish people, the Loyalists, very clear. The united forces of reaction, therefore, are determined to sabotage the film." And indeed there is evidence that pressures were exerted against *Blockade*, most obviously in the abrupt and unexplained cancelation of its gala premiere at Grauman's Chinese Theatre.

Nevertheless, after an automobile accident that incapacitated him for five months, Dieterle made another of the films that established him as "the quintessential 'liberal' director of the 1930s." *Juarez* (1939), based on a play by Franz Werfel, starred Muni as the Indian lawyer who became president of Mexico and ousted the Emperor Maximilian. Designed by Anton Grot, it was photographed by Tony Gaudio, partly on-location, partly in the studio (where he achieved some dramatic effects by discarding the glaring floodlights of the period in favor of spotlights with dimmers).

Robert Stebbins noted in his review of *Juarez* that, apart from some spectacular set pieces, "the visual material is completely subsidiary, com-

pletely the handmaiden of the spoken and written word," but defended the result as "an extraordinarily political film" very little of which "does not pertain to the immediate problems and plight of today's world." A later critic, David Thomson, preferred this to Dieterle's other biopics "because it goes further into exaggeration and because Bette Davis [as Maximilian's wife] gives a truly hysterical performance that relieves Muni's Aztec impassivity in the title role." Interviewed in 1972, Dieterle said that he could not understand why *Juarez* was no longer shown: "It should be the biggest kind of picture right now—a big modern army worn down by guerrilla fighters. The parallel with Vietnam is so obvious."

Dieterle had another huge success with *The Hunchback of Notre Dame* (1939), in which Charles Laughton hams magnificently as Quasimodo in a cast that also includes Maureen O'Hara, Cedric Hardwicke, and Thomas Mitchell. It is generally regarded as the best of the several screen versions of Hugo's novel and "a masterpiece of studio technique." Expressionist influences have been seen in the crowd scenes and "also in the treatment of light and shade, so perfectly achieved by Joseph H. August's photography, as well as the settings (both winding and distorted)." Hervé Dumont, in an article about Dieterle in the Swiss journal *Travelling* (September–October 1973), pointed out how Dieterle had used the film to comment on authoritarianism and brutality at a time when all Europe was falling to the Nazis.

Two more Dieterle biopics appeared in 1940, both starring not Muni but Edward G. Robinson. *Dr. Erlich's Magic Bullet* tells the story of Paul Erlich's discovery of Salvarsan, which made syphilis a curable disease, and does so with a notable absence of prudery, prurience, or histrionics. *A Dispatch From Reuter's*, somewhat lighter in mood than its predecessors, deals with the man who established the world's first news agency. It was Dieterle's last picture for Warner Brothers.

His next, which he also produced, was made for RKO. This was *All That Money Can Buy* (1941), based on Stephen Vincent Benét's fantasy *The Devil and Daniel Webster*, which translated the Faust legend to nineteenth-century New Hampshire. Edward Arnold plays the lawyer Webster and Walter Huston the amiable devil Mr. Scratch. Dieterle again had the services of Joe August, whom he called "perhaps the best cameraman I ever worked with," and there is a splendid score by Bernard Herrman.

A contemporary reviewer, Cecilia Ager, wrote with relief that Dieterle "has now cast off the weighty meanings [of his biopics]. No long pauses, no pregnant angles, no grave responsibilities to history now shackle him. He has a rollicking yarn to tell and he tells it, fantasy laid lightly upon reality, a wondrous fable against a background of it-does-so-happen-here." Not a commercial success, *All That Money Can Buy* remains one of the most zestful and likable of Dieterle's films.

In 1942 Dieterle established a company of his own, William Dieterle Productions. It made only one film, *Syncopation,* a romantic drama about the early days of jazz that failed at the box office. Joining MGM, Dieterle directed another biopic, *Tennessee Johnson* (1943), with Van Heflin as the man who succeeded Lincoln and Lionel Barrymore as his antagonist Thaddeus Stevens, and then a Technicolor remake of *Kismet,* starring Ronald Colman and Marlene Dietrich.

For many years, the conventional view of Dieterle's career was that it had reached its peak in his biographical films of the 1930s, afterwards "descending into routine, facile melodramas." Critical attitudes have changed radically since then, and David Thomson for one regards the biopics as "ponderous, Germanic works, suffering from staginess and the unrestrained histrionics of Paul Muni." Thomson is not alone in preferring the later films, like *Love Letters* and *Portrait of Jennie,* which reveal a previously submerged talent for "the lavish romantic."

Love Letters (1945), made for Paramount, has a wildly complicated and improbable plot about a British officer (Joseph Cotten) who writes love letters on behalf of a dissolute friend and falls in love with the girl (Jennifer Jones) himself. Moved by the letters, she marries the friend; by the time Cotten catches up with her, she has lost the letters and her memory and, apparently, murdered her husband. Many complained of the implausibility of the film's British settings, but *Time*'s reviewer wrote that "this complicated fantasy is so elegantly presented tht it becomes not only exciting but almost believable. Director William Dieterle wrings the last dramatic drop out of scene after scene. Photographer Lee Garmes, aided by some new painted canvas reflectors of his own designing, turns out a mellow masterpiece of lights and textures."

After two uninspired studio films, *This Love of Ours* (1945) and *The Searching Wind* (1946), Dieterle worked (uncredited) on David O. Selznick's *Duel in the Sun* (1947) and is said to have been responsible for the flamboyant opening in the saloon. A suspense film, *The Accused* (1949), was followed by *Portrait of Jennie* (1949), adapted from the novel by Robert Na-

than about a hungry young artist (Joseph Cotten) who falls in love with a mysteriously elusive and protean girl whom he meets in Central Park. He paints a portrait of her that brings him fame, loses her again, and is finally reunited with her on a storm-swept beach in New England where, as Paul Hammond wrote, "these two wage an epic battle, not only against the devouring menace of a gigantic tidal wave, but also with the darker, cosmic forces of time and reality."

Portrait of Jennie was another Selznick project, selected as a vehicle for his beloved Jennifer Jones, and made with an almost insane disregard for cost. Shooting began with an incomplete and inadequate script, and when the film was finished, Selznick started again with a revised script, shooting much new footage and using wide screen and stereo sound for the climactic storm scene. In the end, he managed to spend $4 million on what was essentially a small-scale ghost story. The result, though it could not hope to recoup its costs, was a beautiful and sensitive film. Joe August used a "texturing" process filter which contributed to the haunting strangeness of many sequences, as did Dmitri Tiomkin's arrangement of the music of Debussy (never before used in the cinema).

In deep financial difficulty, Selznick sold Dieterle's contract to Paramount, where he made most of his subsequent American films. He was "not very happy" there, feeling that Hal Wallis "used me to try to make something out of very second-rate material." And in fact, none of his late films were of much originality, though they included several good thrillers and a pleasantly wistful romance, *September Affair* (1951). Dieterle's problems at Paramount were compounded by the McCarthy witchhunts. He came under suspicion partly because of his connection with such libertarian films as *Blockade,* whose scenarist John Howard Lawson was one of the blacklisted "Hollywood Ten," partly because he and his wife had worked throughout the 1930s to get people out of Nazi Germany and had given aid and comfort to Bertolt Brecht and other left-wing refugees. Dieterle said that he was branded a "premature antifascist," and "though I was never to my knowledge on any blacklist, I must have been on some kind of gray list because I couldn't get any work."

In 1954, when Dieterle was ready to go to Ceylon to make *Elephant Walk,* the State Department held up production for three months before allowing him a passport. After that, he made only two more films in Hollywood, neither of any merit—the Wagner biopic *Magic Fire* (1956) and *Omar Khayyam* (1957). In 1958 Dieterle returned to Germany and to the theatre, working in Stuttgart, Essen, Bremen, and Berlin, and at the Bad Hersfield Festival. He also made a handful of films in Europe before his retirement.

Dieterle's work, as a critic wrote in *Film Dope,* shows a "rather disquieting unevenness," but "the peaks manifestly demonstrate that his career is long overdue for reassessment in the form of a major retrospective. . . . Hopefully, such a retrospective would . . . concentrate on two areas: the unknown quantities (both sets of German films, the 1930–1935 Hollywood period) and those films that have already indicated Dieterle to be an extremely gifted director and, on occasion, an unrestrained romanticist. Of the latter, *All That Money Can Buy, Love Letters,* and particularly *Portrait of Jennie* all share an eccentric and arresting style eminently suited to their romantic flavour."

FILMS: Der Mensch am Wege, 1923; Das Geheimnis des Abbé X/Der Mann, der nicht lieben darf, 1927; Die Heilige und ihr Narr, 1928; Geschlecht in Fesseln: die Sexualnot der Gefangenen, 1928; Ich lebe für Dich/Triumph des Lebens, 1929; Frühlingsrauschen/Tränen, die ich Dir geweint, 1929; Das Schweigen in Walde, 1929; Ludwig der Zweite, König von Bayern, 1929; Eine Stunde Glück, 1930; Der Tanz geht weiter, 1930; Die Maske fällt, 1930; Kismet (German version only), 1930; The Last Flight, 1931; Her Majesty, Love, 1931; Man Wanted, 1932; Jewel Robbery, 1932; The Crash, 1932; Six Hours to Live, 1932; Scarlet Dawn, 1932; Lawyer Man, 1933; Grand Slam, 1933; Adorable, 1933; The Devil's in Love, 1933; From Headquarters, 1933; Fashions of 1934 (U.K., Fashion Follies of 1934), 1934; Fog Over Frisco, 1934; Madame Du Barry, 1934; The Firebird, 1934; The Secret Bride (U.K., Concealment), 1934; (with Max Reinhardt) A Midsummer Night's Dream, 1935; Dr. Socrates, 1935; The Story of Louis Pasteur, 1935; Satan Met a Lady, 1936; The White Angel, 1936; The Great O'Malley, 1937; Another Dawn, 1937; The Life of Emile Zola, 1937; Blockade, 1938; Juarez, 1939; The Hunchback of Notre Dame, 1939; Dr. Erlich's Magic Bullet, 1940; A Dispatch From Reuter's (U.K., This Man Reuter), 1940; All That Money Can Buy/The Devil and Daniel Webster, 1941; Syncopation, 1942; Tennessee Johnson (U.K., The Man on America's Conscience), 1943; Kismet, 1944; I'll Be Seeing You, 1945; Love Letters, 1945; This Love of Ours, 1945; The Searching Wind, 1946; The Accused, 1949; Portrait of Jennie (U.K., Jennie), 1949; Rope of Sand, 1949; Vulcano/Volcano, 1949; Paid in Full, 1950; Dark City, 1950; September Affair, 1951; Peking Express, 1951; Boots Malone, 1952; Red Mountain, 1952; The Turning Point, 1952; Salome, 1953; Elephant Walk, 1954; Magic Fire, 1956; Omar Khayyam/The Loves of Omar Khayyam, 1957; Herrin der Welt (in two parts), 1959; Il Vendicatore/Dubrowsky, 1959; Die Fastnachts beichte, 1960; The Confession/Quick, Let's Get Married/Seven Different Ways, 1964.

ABOUT: Meyer, W. D. Warner Brothers Directors, 1978;

Thomson, D. A Biographical Dictionary of the Cinema, 1980; Tuska, J. (ed.) Close Up: The Contract Director, 1976. *Periodicals*—L'Avant-Scène du Cinéma November 15, 1977; Cinema Quarterly Winter 1935; Film Dope January 1977; Films in Review April 1957; Travelling (Switzerland) September–October 1973; Velvet Light Trap Fall 1975.

*DMYTRYK, EDWARD (September 4, 1908–), American director and producer, was born in Grand Forks, a small town in British Columbia, Canada. He is the second of the four sons of Ukrainian immigrants, Michael and Frances Dmytryk, and during the first few years of his life was taken several times to the Ukraine, where his parents still owned a farm. They had another—a small truck farm—at Grand Forks, and his father also worked winters at the local copper smeltery.

Dmytryk's devout Catholic mother died when he was five or six, and his religious education ended then. His father sold the farm and moved the family to San Francisco, where he found a job as a streetcar motorman and married a Protestant, Clara Mertz, before settling finally in Los Angeles. Dmytryk says that "I had carried my weight with the family budget since I was six years old. I had peddled papers on street corners, delivered them morning and evening, [and] caddied at the Los Angeles Country Club (where I learned that the richer the player, the smaller the tip)."

When Dmytryk was twelve, a psychologist identified him and his brother Arthur as gifted children, with IQs of 140 or more. Two years later Dmytryk "realized that the beatings I was getting at home were counterproductive. So I split, a sweater on my back and 35¢ in my pocket." He was picked up by the juvenile authorities who, after investigating his home conditions, agreed with him that he would be better off living in a rented room while working his way through Hollywood High. Through a boys' organization that he belonged to, a job was found for him at the Famous Players–Lasky studios. He was to work evenings and weekends as a messenger and office boy in the "sample-copy" room, where a team of cutters assembled each day's rushes for screening.

In this way, Dmytryk entered the movie industry in March 1923 at a salary of $6 a week. Ill-paid as it was, he needed the job and, seeking to make himself indispensable, taught himself the art of hand-splicing film, at sixteen becoming also a part-time projectionist. Working in the viewing room, he was able to study the rushes of a great variety of films and to eavesdrop on the

°də mē´ trik

EDWARD DMYTRYK

comments of their directors, among them Stroheim, De Mille, James Cruze, Raoul Walsh, and William Wellman. He also took every chance he could to observe these heroes at work on the lot.

It was an excellent education for a future director, but at that time Dmytryk was more interested in physics and mathematics. He graduated from high school with straight A's and went on to the California Institute of Technology, his path eased by a gift of $1,000 from a studio executive who had taken an interest in his exceptional school record. At Cal Tech, for the first time in his life, Dmytryk was able to indulge his passion for sports, earning his freshman numeral in football, basketball, baseball, tracks, and wrestling. During vacations he drove to Hollywood in his own $15 Model T and worked as a relief projectionist.

By the end of his freshman year, Dmytryk knew that the academic ivory tower was not for him. He dropped out of Cal Tech and, after an anxious period of unemployment, found a full-time job as projectionist with his old studio, just reestablished as the Paramount Pictures Corporation. That was in 1927, when Dmytryk was nineteen. Early in 1929, in the turmoil caused by the arrival of sound, Dmytryk switched to the cutting room, where he was soon working on Spanish-language versions of Paramount films, then on new features, beginning in 1930 with Cyril Gardner and Edwin Knopf's *Only Saps Work.*

Regarded as something of a boy wonder, Dmytryk worked as a Paramount editor throughout the 1930s on films like Gardner's and George Cukor's *The Royal Family of Broadway,*

Duck Soup, Eddie Cline's *Million Dollar Legs,* Leo McCarey's *Belle of the Nineties* and *Ruggles of Red Gap,* and Cukor's *Zaza.* In 1932 he was married to Madeleine Robinson. Dmytryk directed his first movie in 1935, a Western called *The Hawk.* It was not a Paramount production, however, but an independent one, made in five days for $5,000 as a favor to a friend who had written the script and had a little money. Dmytryk did not take the exercise very seriously, saying that he "just took a few days off from editing" and "didn't really consider it my start as a director."

In his autobiography, *It's a Hell of a Life But Not a Bad Living,* Dmytryk says that "it was in the cutting rooms that I learned the rudiments of filmmaking." Throughout his career, he has asserted his belief in the importance of editing as "the only film craft that is entirely indigenous to the cinema," and one that "has some bearing on every other facet of the art."

Dmytryk finally left the cutting room in 1939. By that time he had already staged a few sequences in B pictures made by other directors, and when a new Paramount director displeased the front office with his first assignment, Dmytryk was assigned as codirector of his second, finally being asked to take over as uncredited director. He says: "The film was *Million Dollar Legs.* Not the broad comedy made some years earlier, but a light college musical starring Betty Grable. . . . I finished on schedule. The film was probably no worse—and certainly no better—than if the original director had finished it. But the front office felt vindicated. . . . [and] I was offered a contract to direct, at $250 a week."

In 1939–1940 Dmytryk directed four low-budget programmers for Paramount—thrillers and melodramas using young contract players like William Henry, Richard Denning, and Anthony Quinn. Along with other B-picture directors, he lost his job when Sol Siegel took over as production chief at Paramount and decided to start from scratch. In 1940 Dmytryk made a musical for Monogram, and then joined Columbia for half a dozen more low-budget entertainments, including contributions to the "Lone Wolf" and "Boston Blackie" series, a Boris Karloff horror film, and *Under Age,* an "exposé" movie about teenage prostitutes that Dmytryk thinks is the worst picture he ever made.

Things began to pick up when he moved to RKO, where his first film was *Seven Miles From Alcatraz* (1942). It was a taut thriller about two convicts who escape from Alcatraz and hole up in a lonely lighthouse, making prisoners of the keeper and his daughter. Discovering that the lighthouse radio operator is a Nazi agent, they forfeit their freedom to smash a spy ring. The "more than competent" cast was headed by James Craig and Bonita Granville, and the movie was enjoyed as a "well-built melodrama."

This new promise was confirmed by *Hitler's Children* (1943). Bonita Granville stars again as an American girl born in Germany but raised in the United States. Returning to visit her grandparents in Germany, she meets a young German (Tim Holt) who has been indoctrinated with the Nazi ideology. She is conscripted into a women's labor camp, resists, and is killed, but her devotion to her ideals of freedom and democracy converts the young Nazi, who also dies a martyr. The cast includes Otto Kruger as a Gestapo colonel and H. B. Warner as an anti-Nazi bishop.

A reviewer in the London *Times* praised the film for its intelligent analysis "of the methods by which the Nazi party captured the minds and loyalties of the children" in the years between 1933 and 1939. One of the first Hollywood movies to deal with life inside Nazi Germany, it was among the sleepers of the year. It grossed $7.5 million and earned Dmytryk a seven-year contract with RKO.

By this time the director was already at work on *The Falcon Strikes Back* (1943), a competent but routine wartime thriller in the series based on Michael Arlen's character. In this movie, Tom Conway took over as the Falcon, previously played by his brother, George Sanders. *Captive Wild Woman*, released by Universal in 1943 but apparently made a year or two earlier, was a horror film similar in theme to Jacques Tourneur's *Cat People* (1943). A mad scientist (John Carradine) turns an ape into a beautiful woman. The transformation fools humans but not the animals that "Paula" works with in a circus. In the end, deranged by sexual jealousy, she reverts to animal form. The picture has something of a following among horror buffs.

Seeking to repeat the success of *Hitler's Children*, RKO next assigned Dmytryk to direct an anti-Japanese companion piece, *Behind the Rising Sun* (1943). It employs a similar plot about a young Japanese aristocrat (Tom Neal), educated in the United States, who goes home and is indoctrinated with the new nationalism and militarism. He realizes his mistake too late and dies for it. Described as the "first all-out atrocity film of World War II," it was nevertheless well received by the reviewers and made even more money than *Hitler's Children*. It was followed by Dmytryk's first A picture, a wartime weepie called *Tender Comrade* (1944) starring Ginger Rogers as a young wife who, soon after the birth of her first baby, learns that her soldier-husband has been killed.

It was Dmytryk's next film that established him as something more than a journeyman studio director. *Murder, My Sweet* (1945) teamed him for the first time with the producer Adrian Scott and the scenarist John Paxton, who wrote this "tight, tense" screen version of Raymond Chandler's novel *Farewell My Lovely* (the movie's British title). Dick Powell, the cherubic crooner of 1930s Warner Brothers musicals, was cast as Chandler's tough, disenchanted private eye Philip Marlowe, giving a performance in that unlikely role that revitalized his fading career.

Marlowe is hired by a dim-witted ex-con (Mike Mazurki) who wants to locate a former girlfriend. He soon finds that he has become a link in a chain of double-crossings and killings involving an assortment of powerful interests. He is beaten almost to death, pumped full of dope, and importuned by a bad woman (Claire Trevor) and a good one (Anne Shirley). Made for less than $500,000, the film was praised for its convincing "atmosphere of toughness, hard drink, insomnia, and sour cracks" and for the "lurid nightmares" experienced by the hero under the influence of drugs and blows. It has been called "the most Chandleresque of all the Marlowe films," and a *film noir* in which Richard Winnington recognized the influence of Fritz Lang "and other masters of macabre melodrama." There were several comparisons with John Huston's *The Maltese Falcon*.

After *Back to Bataan* (1945), a routine John Wayne war film, Dmytryk collaborated again with Scott, Paxton, and Dick Powell on *Cornered* (1945). Powell plays a Canadian flyer tracking down his wife's killer, a French collaborationist, in Switzerland and Buenos Aires. David Badder called it "a strange thriller . . . which has a distinctive, disjointed style enhanced by an edgy, unnerving ambience." Romano Tozzi, in his article about Dmytryk in *Films in Review* (February 1962), wrote that "the showdown was brilliantly executed by Dmytryk" with a "shock power [that] has rarely been surpassed"—the director believes that the last reel-and-a-half of this film contains some of his best work.

Till the End of Time (1946) starred Dorothy McGuire as a war widow courted by an embittered young ex-Marine (Guy Madison). He eventually overcomes his self-pity and gets a job and the heroine. Dmytryk himself thinks the film maudlin and most reviewers thought so too, although there was a great deal of praise for Robert Mitchum's performance as the hero's sardonic buddy. Working with Scott and Paxton again, Dmytryk next went to Britain to make *So Well Remembered* from James Hilton's novel about an idealistic newspaper editor (John Mills) in the strike-torn North of England between the wars. A success in Britain in 1947, it was not released until years later in the United States because Howard Hughes, who had acquired control of RKO, detected communistic attitudes in the film and insisted on cuts.

The most admired of all Dmytryk's films followed. *Crossfire*, produced by Adrian Scott, was based on Richard Brook's novel *The Brick Foxhole*, about the murder of a homosexual. In John Paxton's adaptation, the victim is not a homosexual but a Jew, killed by a rabidly anti-Semitic soldier (Robert Ryan) at a drunken party where the other GIs present conspire to cover up the crime. It is the absence of a conventional motive for the murder that leads the investigating detective (Robert Young) to suspect a racist one.

Careful planning made it possible to film *Crossfire* in twenty days on a budget of $550,000. According to Louis Black, "there were few sets, no mob scenes and several extended takes. Dmytryk shot roughly seven setups per six-and-a-half-hour work day, for a total of only 140 setups in the entire film." Black wrote that "the film is classic *noir* in its lighting, its camerawork and even its pacing. It is a starkly beautiful film, a slow-building pursuit, with the tension mounting throughout the film." All the same, *Crossfire* avoided the "paranoia and malevolence of the traditional *noir* film . . . there is definitely a confusion and a sense of being lost [in the society it portrays], but the film is also very much about people trying to work out their lives and caring very much about the people around them." James Agee called it "the best Hollywood movie in a long time."

The picture was a huge financial success and received five Oscar nominations—best film, best director, best supporting actor (Ryan), best supporting actress (Gloria Grahame), and best screenplay, as well as several other awards. These were accepted on behalf of RKO by Dore Schary, soon after he had fired the film's director and producer. In October 1947, Sam Wood had testified before the House Committee on Un-American Activities that several members of the Screen Directors' Guild, including Dmytryk, had tried to take over the Guild in the interests of the American Communist Party. Brought before the Committee a week later, Dmytryk refused to say whether or not he had ever been a member of the Party. He was cited for contempt of Congress and became one of the blacklisted "Hollywood Ten," along with his producer Adrian Scott and eight screenwriters.

The same year, Dmytryk was divorced from his first wife. In May 1948 he made a second and

lasting marriage to the actress Jean Peters. And in October 1948, unable to find work in the United States, he signed a contract with Independent Sovereign Films to direct a picture in England, for distribution through Eagle-Lion. *The Hidden Room* (U.K., *Obsession*, 1949), described by Alton Cook as "a little masterpiece of horror and suspense," has Robert Newton as a husband who, discovering his wife's infidelity, plans the "perfect murder" of her lover. Naunton Wayne plays the deceptively chatty detective.

Dmytryk's second film for Eagle-Lion was a much more personal work. *Salt to the Devil* (1949), in Britain called *Give Us This Day*, was scripted by Ben Barzman from Pietro Di Donato's novel *Christ in Concrete*. The story is set during the 1920s in the New York slums. Geromio (Sam Wanamaker) is a poor Italian-American bricklayer whose immigrant wife (Lea Padovani) has set her heart on owning a home of her own. Through thrift and hard work, they save almost enough before the slump of 1929 throws them back into poverty. Geromio takes a job on a construction site where he knows the safety precautions are inadequate and is killed on Good Friday, drowned in setting concrete, his arms outstretched like Christ on the cross. His insurance is enough to buy his widow her house.

Salt to the Devil, much honored in Britain but long blacklisted in the United States, is said to be Dmytryk's own favorite among his films. The studio sets of Lower East Side streets and tenements were found exceptionally and surprisingly convincing, and Lea Padovani's performance, in particular, was warmly praised. But though one British reviewer thought the film "far superior to anything . . . [Dmytryk] had done in Hollywood," most critics had some reservations about the picture. It seemed to Dilys Powell that the script "frequently uses artificial and cadenced language against a realistic background," so that the viewer can "neither accept the realism nor submit himself to the rhythms of the speech."

In 1950, with further work awaiting him in England, Dmytryk was ordered back to the United States to renew his passport. He expected only a brief visit, but in June 1950 he was tried and sentenced to six months' imprisonment for contempt of Congress. When he was released from Mill Point Prison Camp in November 1950, he could again find no producer willing to employ him. He came to the conclusion, as he put it in his autobiography, that "I was being forced to sacrifice my family and my career in defense of the Communist Party, from which I had long been separated and which I had grown to dislike and distrust." He decided to testify before HUAC and did so in April 1951, giving the names of more than a score of people he knew to be Party members (most of them already known to HUAC).

Even after this "purging," bitterly attacked by his former comrades, Dmytryk found it difficult to secure work. Before his blacklisting he had been earning $2,500 a week at RKO; when a new assignment finally did come along, for a minor independent studio, he was paid a total of $5,000 to direct a low-budget potboiler called *Mutiny* (1952). Set aboard an American privateer during the War of 1812 and starring Mark Stevens and Angela Lansbury, it was found "minor but interesting."

Then Stanley Kramer, at that time working as an independent producer under the aegis of Columbia, approached him with a four-picture contract that began his rehabilitation. His first film for Kramer was the best of the four, *The Sniper* (1952), scripted by Harry Brown from a story by Edward and Edna Anhalt and made on location in San Francisco. Arthur Franz gives a sympathetic portrayal of a young psychopath who tries but fails to overcome his compulsion to pick off random representatives of the female sex that so frightens him. Adolphe Menjou is equally convincing as a police lieutenant who is slowly converted by a city psychiatrist (Richard Kiley) from his faith in conventional police methods to a belief in preventive social action. Superbly photographed in black and white by Burnett Guffey, the dark settings and expressionistic lighting were very much in the *film noir* style of some of Dmytryk's finest pictures. A critic in *Saturday Review* called *The Sniper* both "a beautifully executed melodrama" and "the drama of the policeman becoming a citizen."

Eight Iron Men (1952), an off-beat war film, had a more mixed reception, and *The Juggler* (1953) was also received without much enthusiasm. The first Hollywood film shot in Israel, it stars Kirk Douglas as a survivor of the Nazi death camps newly arrived in that country. In paranoid panic he attacks a policeman who asks for his papers and, thinking that he has killed that man, goes on the run. The film ends on the promise that he will eventually find happiness with the girl (Milly Vitale) who had given him succor during his flight and persuaded him to accept psychological help.

If *The Sniper* was the most admired of Dmytryk's films for Kramer, the most successful of them was *The Caine Mutiny* (1954). This was a $2 million adaptation of Herman Wouk's bestselling novel about a paranoid naval commander

(Humphrey Bogart) who, cracking up during a typhoon, is relieved of his authority by his second-in-command (Van Johnson). Much of the film concentrates on the court-martial that follows, with José Ferrer as the Navy lawyer who drives Captain Queeg to reveal his madness in court but later rounds on the officers he has successfully defended and berates them for their disloyalty to a man destroyed by his wartime sufferings.

One of the major hits of the year (thanks partly to a massive promotional campaign), *The Caine Mutiny* earned several Oscar nominations. C. A. Lejeune complained of "a lack of imaginative courage" in the direction, but most reviewers thought that Dmytryk's technique in transferring an immensely popular book to the screen was quite properly self-effacing. Virginia Graham called it "a finely rounded, compact piece of work, intelligently written, admirably acted and directed with the minimum of fuss."

An excellent Western followed, *Broken Lance*, made for Twentieth Century-Fox in 1954. The film was a remake of an earlier Fox movie (based on a novel by Jerome Weidman) called *House of Strangers*, about a New York banking dynasty; the same plot was used yet again with a circus setting in *The Big Show* (1961). Richard Murphy and Philip Yordan's fine script for *Broken Lance* centers on a willful cattle baron (Spencer Tracy) and his battles with his Comanche wife (Katy Jurado) and his sons by an earlier marriage (played by Robert Wagner, Richard Widmark, Earl Holliman, and Hugh O'Brian).

Brian Garfield called *Broken Lance* "a big and rewarding movie" and "by far the best of the domineering father versus sibling-sons Westerns," owing as much to *The Brothers Karamazov* as to Jerome Weidman. "The complicated rich story builds to a harrowing cliff-top climax," Garfield went on, and there is a "towering performance" from Tracy. Philip Yordan won an Oscar for his story, and Katy Jurado a nomination as best supporting actress.

After this came a string of less interesting films, beginning in 1954 with a "lackluster" adaptation of Graham Greene's novel *The End of the Affair*. The following year brought *Soldier of Fortune*, a Clark Gable action-adventure made on location in Hong Kong; and *The Left Hand of God*, which has Humphrey Bogart as an American flyer in pre-Communist China, putting on grace along with a cassock when, to escape a ruthless warlord, he masquerades as a priest in a remote village. *The Mountain* (1956) improbably teams Spencer Tracy and Robert Wagner as mountaineering brothers who make a suicidal ascent in the French Alps to search for survivors of an air crash. There were mixed reviews again for *Raintree County* (1957), a three-hour, $6 million adaptation of Ross Lockridge's mammoth novel of American life before and after the Civil War. Whatever the critical reservations about this sprawling movie, it was a box-office hit and brought Elizabeth Taylor her first Oscar nomination.

Another expensive literary adaptation followed, a $3 million screen version of Irwin Shaw's World War II novel, *The Young Lions.* In Edward Anhalt's adaptation, the narrative centers on two soldiers, one American and one German, cutting from one story to the other until the two converge fatefully in the last days of the war. Montgomery Clift, whose car accident and self-destructive habits had greatly complicated the filming of *Raintree County,* was cast as Noah, the young Jewish GI who is appallingly bullied by his comrades but who eventually masters his fears. Marlon Brando plays Christian, a blond Bavarian who (like the young hero in *Hitler's Children*), acquiesces in Nazism, learning gradually and tragically that he has sold his soul to the devil. Most critics thought *The Young Lions* (1958) one of the best films to have come out of World War II, although "after a while both heroes, German and American, cease to grow for us and the tension slackens off fatally before the climax."

The "uneven but fascinating" Western *Warlock* (1959) casts Henry Fonda as a gunfighter hired as marshall to protect the frontier town of Warlock against "regulators" employed as strikebreakers by local mineowners. Anthony Quinn plays Fonda's unstable sidekick, and Richard Widmark a bad guy who reforms. Dmytryk thought that Robert Alan Aurthur's script showed "the development of a society in microcosm," and Brian Garfield found in it "aspects of everything from homosexuality to Greek classicism."

The decline in Dmytryk's reputation continued after that. A remake of Sternberg's *The Blue Angel,* with Mai Britt attempting the Marlene Dietrich role, failed completely. Nor—apart from the debut of Jane Fonda—was there much to commend *A Walk on the Wild Side* (1962), a screen version of Nelson Algren's novel of New Orleans low-life. *The Reluctant Saint* (1962), a likable biopic of the levitating peasant saint Joseph of Cupertino, flopped at the box-office. More profitable but considerably less likable were two adaptations of Harold Robbins' bestsellers, *The Carpetbaggers* and *Where Love Has Gone,* both full of "feisty smut."

Dmytryk made a temporary recovery with *Mirage* (1965), showing that he was still capable of inventiveness and "displayed craftsmanship" when he had a script that stimulated his imagination. This was an adaptation by Peter Stone of a novel by Howard Fast—a suspense thriller set in New York, with Gregory Peck as a scientist suffering from shock amnesia. His efforts to assemble the jigsaw puzzle of his former life are dangerously complicated by the involvement of people prepared to go to any lengths to secure a formula locked in his unconscious. Walter Matthau scored a personal success as a tyro private eye, and there was much praise for what David Robinson called the "tidy narrative style and classical use of intercut images of scenes momentarily remembered by the hero." *Life's* reviewer went so far as to call the film a minor masterpiece.

Since then Dmytryk has made a couple of Westerns, a war film, a dreadful Richard Burton vehicle called *Bluebeard,* and a distasteful revenge drama, *The Human Factor.* A later movie, *He Is My Brother* (1976), seems not to have been released, and the director has now become a teacher at the University of Texas. David Badder has described Dmytryk as "an outstanding conveyor of mood and atmosphere" who reached the peak of his career in the years between 1943 and 1947, subsequently suffering from "his bad luck with scripts of great vapidity."

Short and muscular, Dmytryk was for many years a weightlifter and a boxer. His principal hobby is the study of Chinese, which he has learned to write as well as read. *It's a Hell of a Life But Not a Bad Living,* his unusually lucid and intelligent autobiography, appeared in 1979.

FILMS: The Hawk, 1935; Television Spy, 1939; Emergency Squad, 1940; Golden Gloves, 1940; Mystery Sea Raider, 1940; Her First Romance, 1940; The Devil Commands, 1941; Under Age, 1941; Sweetheart of the Campus, 1941; The Blonde From Singapore, 1941; Secrets of the Lone Wolf, 1941; Confessions of Boston Blackie, 1941; Counter-Espionage, 1942; Seven Miles From Alcatraz, 1942; Hitler's Children, 1943; The Falcon Strikes Back, 1943; Captive Wild Woman, 1943; Behind the Rising Sun, 1943; Tender Comrade, 1944; Murder, My Sweet (U.K., Farewell My Lovely), 1945; Back to Bataan, 1945; Cornered, 1945; Till the End of Time, 1946; Crossfire, 1947; So Well Remembered, 1947; The Hidden Room (U.K., Obsession), 1949; Salt to the Devil (U.K., Give Us This Day), 1949; Mutiny, 1952; The Sniper, 1952; Eight Iron Men, 1952; The Juggler, 1953; The Caine Mutiny, 1954; Broken Lance, 1954; The End of the Affair, 1954; Soldier of Fortune, 1955; The Left Hand of God, 1955; The Mountain, 1956; Raintree County, 1957; The Young Lions, 1958; Warlock, 1959; The Blue Angel, 1959; The Reluctant Saint (Cronache di un Convento), 1962; Walk on the

Wild Side, 1962; The Carpetbaggers, 1964; Where Love Has Gone, 1964; Mirage, 1965; Alvarez Kelly, 1966; Anzio (Lo Sbarco di Anzio/The Battle for Anzio), 1968; Shalako, 1968; Bluebeard, 1972; The Human Factor, 1975; He Is My Brother, 1976.

ABOUT: Bentley, F. Are You Now Or Have You Ever Been?, 1972; Dmytryk, E. It's a Hell of a Life But Not a Bad Living, 1979; Kahn, G. Hollywood on Trial, 1948; Tuska, J. Close-Up: The Contract Director, 1976. *Periodicals*—Cahiers du Cinéma April 1951; Film Dope June 1977; Filmmakers Monthly January 1979; Films Illustrated October 1971; Films in Review February 1962; Guardian August 9, 1975; Saturday Evening Post May 19, 1951.

DONSKOI, MARK (SEMENOVICH)

(March 6, 1901–March 1981), Soviet director, was born in the great cosmopolitan Ukrainian port of Odessa. The son of a boiler-maker, he seized eagerly on the educational opportunities opened up for his generation by the Revolution: "Our country was giving birth to a new intelligentsia," he says. "We felt we had to go through at least two colleges. We wanted to reach out for everything—to know everything." Donskoi himself reached out quite widely, studying psychiatry, law, piano, and musical composition before he finally graduated from the faculty of law of Simferopol University, in the Crimea. Before he could begin his career as a lawyer, though, he was caught up in the post-Revolutionary Civil War, fighting on the Red side and being taken prisoner by the Whites.

In 1925, while working as a lawyer and as a private detective for the Ukrainian police, Donskoi published a volume of short stories based on his experiences as a prisoner of war. A talented amateur boxer, he then considered turning professional. Instead, encouraged by the acceptance of his first filmscript (*The Last Stronghold*, 1925), he turned decisively to a career in the cinema. In 1926 he entered the Moscow Film School, where he studied under Eisenstein, at the same time gaining experience as an actor, writer, assistant director, and editor (of Grigori Roshal's *His Excellency*, 1927).

Donskoi's own first full-length film was *V bolshoi gorode (In the Big City,* 1927). Written and directed in collaboration with Mikhail Auerbach, it is a lighthearted piece about the urban adventures of a dissipated peasant poet strongly reminiscent of the "hooligan" poet Sergei Esenin (1895–1925). The best known of Donskoi's early films is his first sound film, *Pesnya o shchastye* (*Song of Happiness,* 1934), made under the supervision of Sergei Yutkevich, and with Vladimir Legoshin as codirector. It gives a relaxed,

MARK DONSKOI

good-humored portrayal of the life of the Mari people of the Volga, a Finno-Ugrian group related to the Hungarians, who have preserved the earliest sorts of Hungarian pentatonic folk songs. The film anticipates Donskoi's famous Gorky trilogy both in its Volga settings and in its theme of a boy growing up and acquiring an education—in this instance an education in music. It provided the experience on which Donskoi based his theories about the successful direction of child actors.

Donskoi's adaptation of his friend Gorky's autobiographical trilogy has become one of the best-loved works of all Russian cinema. Although Maxim Gorky is often thought of as a proletarian writer, he was actually born into the provincial middle class. His grandfather was the owner of a dye-works which during Gorky's childhood declined into ruin. The first film in the trilogy, *Detstvo Gorkovo (The Childhood of Gorky,* 1938), traces the gradual impoverishment and destruction of the once prosperous family, showing how it was held together as long as possible by the women and above all by the indomitable grandmother—a person of great goodness, simplicity, and intuitive understanding, unforgettably portrayed by Varvara Massalitinova. The film has an almost equally memorable performance by Mark Troyanovsky as the mean, stupid, brutal old grandfather. As their fortunes decline, the family moves to smaller and smaller houses, and the break-up begins. The quarreling sons take their share of the inheritance and leave home, and the orphaned Gorky sets out on what is to become a romantic quest for education.

The Russian title of the second part of the trilogy, *V lyudyakh* (1939), generally translated as *My Apprenticeship* or *In the World,* actually means *Among People.* Turned out at the age of eleven to fend for himself, Gorky plunges into the lower depths of society, scraping a living by drudgery on boats and in bakeries and icon-painters' shops along the Volga. The huge river itself, with its constant traffic of steamers and barges, is not just a background but a leading character throughout the trilogy. Despite misery and privation, the young Gorky is determined to educate himself. We see him, during a stint as dishwasher on a Volga steamer, reading Gogol's *Taras Bulba* aloud to the fat and sentimental cook—both so entranced that neither notices when a vicious waiter sabotages all the boy's work by throwing his newly washed glasses back into the dirty water. People persist in falling short of Gorky's expectations, as when the captivating demimondaine he meets and idealizes while staying with some hypocritical relatives turns out to be all too human.

At the age of sixteen Gorky arrived in the Volga city of Kazan feeling that "for the bliss of studying at the University even torture might be endured." This is the beginning of the third part of the trilogy, *Moi universiteti* (*My Universities,* 1940). In fact, as the boy slowly comes to see, the only university he needs is life itself—especially such instructive episodes as the famous one in an underground bakery. The baker, marvelously played by Stephen Kayukov, is one of the great characters of the trilogy, ful of peasant cunning, and constantly involved in a battle of wits with the rebellious Gorky. In this third film, however, Gorky is no longer portrayed by the boy actor Alexei Lyarsky, but by a young man who is neither so accomplished nor so appealing. Moreover, Donskoi and his coscriptwriter Gruzdev chose to end the trilogy with a scene from another of Gorky's reminiscences, in which he encounters a peasant girl in labor beside the sea and helps her to deliver her baby. Not all of the film's critics approved of this substitution, and Basil Wright concluded that "the immense images of the ocean smashing itself against the rocks, with which Donskoi intercuts the woman's labour, are magnificent to look at but too pompously symbolic. They are no substitute for the superabundant permeations of love and life with which the Volga inundated the earlier parts of this magnificent trilogy."

As Jay Leyda says, the Gorky trilogy is Donskoi's masterpiece: "All that was brightest and most hopeful in his own unsimple character responded fully to Gorky's belief in people and his anger at their waste." Dilys Powell described the films as having "to an extraordinary degree the ability to communicate the poetic quality in human relationships," and William Whitebait wrote: "It is the triumph of the Trilogy as of the books that inspired it, that it involves us as it does across years, distances, classes, upbringings. Let me urge everyone to go and enjoy this great work."

Donskoi's last prewar film was a semidocumentary which like *Song of Happiness* deals with one of the smaller national groups in the Soviet Union, the Chukchi, a Palaeoarctic people living in the frozen northeast on the Bering Strait, related to the American Indians who crossed that strait thousands of years ago. Donskoi's film *Romantiki* (1941) centers on the pioneers who set up the first school for the Chukchi children; a half-hour version called *Children of the Soviet Arctic* was shown in all British factories during World War II.

Donskoi directed some of the best Soviet feature films made during the war. The first of these was *Kak zakalyalas stal* (*How the Steel Was Tempered,* 1942), based on Nikolai Ostrovsky's best-selling fictionalized autobiography. It tells the moving story of a young man, paralyzed and blind as a result of his wounds in the Civil War, who sets out to make himself a new life as an author (in fact this was Ostrovsky's only completed book; he died at the age of thirty-two). Donskoi's script concentrates on those chapters dealing with Ukrainian resistance to the German invaders in 1918, filmed so as to emphasize the obvious parallels with the latest German invasion. And Donskoi also gave this rather uneven film a structure resembling the Gorky trilogy, showing a boy accumulating lessons in his encounters with life.

The terrible holocaust of the Ukraine under Nazi occupation was the theme of Vanda Vasilevskaya's novel *Raduga* (*The Rainbow*), which the author herself adapted for Donskoi's film version. A group of notable actresses portrayed the Ukrainian women's heroic resistance to the invaders, and there was a powerful performance also by Hans Klering as the German garrison commander. Donskoi interviewed a number of captured German officers and soldiers so as to give more depth to his portrayal of the enemy (though in evoking the hardships of a terrible Ukrainian winter the cast were obliged to forget they were sweltering in evacuation in Turkestan). Basil Wright has called it "one of the most searing and horrible war films ever made": it was directed, as Jay Leyda says, "with all the anger Donskoi was capable of expressing."

Donskoi's next film, *Nepokorenniye* (*The Unvanquished,* 1945), also set in the occupied Ukraine, was based on the novel by Boris Gorba-

tov about an ordinary Kiev family and its participation in the underground resistance
movement. The actors themselves were all too
familiar with the reality they were depicting:
Dunaisky, the actor who played the old beekeep-
er, and who had played the grandfather in *The
Rainbow,* had himself lost all his family when
they were driven off to slavery by the Nazis. And
Donskoi recalls that "the day we shot the most
important scene of the film the actress Elena
Tyapkina (Fedosya in *The Rainbow*) received
notification of the death of her son." War crimes
shown in the film include the slaughter of Jews
at Babi Yar.

In his first postwar film Donskoi returned to
his favorite theme with *Selskaya uchitelnitsa* (*A
Village Schoolteacher,* 1947), a sympathetic portrait of a girl who goes to teach in a remote part
of pre-Revolutionary Siberia and stays to educate generations of children until the end of
World War II. As Nina Hibbin says, this immensely successful film "embodies many of
Donskoi's qualities—highly individual characterisations (and a superb central performance
from Vera Maretskaya), splendid handling of
children, rhythmic, lyrical evocation of the
countryside (in association with Urussevski's fine
camerawork) and vivid reconstruction of the
past."

Donskoi's later films include screen versions of
two of Gorky's best-known novels. *Mat* (*Mother,*
1956), which again stars Vera Maretskaya, tells
the story of how a peasant mother, in spite of her
fears, is gradually drawn into the revolutionary
underground in the wake of her activist son.
Donskoi's adaptation is much more faithful to
the original than the silent version made by Pudovkin in 1926. Another Gorky novel, *Foma
Gordeyev,* was filmed by Donskoi in 1959.
Foma's father is one of those strong, self-made
Volga merchants who had become a flourishing
class in Gorky's own time, but Foma, born to
wealth, rebels against the values his father has so
eagerly been creating. Once more the River Volga itself has a role in the drama, as a symbol of
elemental strength which properly channeled
can be marvelously creative, but frustrated can
cause destruction and havoc. Unlike his father,
Foma can find no productive outlet for his dynamic energy, turning instead to self-destructive
debauchery. Foma's rebellion, inspired by a
search for a higher truth than his father's, leads
ironically to his ruin. *Dorogoi tsenoi* (*At a High
Price,* 1957) is a tragic love story which has
something of the quality of a fairy tale.

Soviet directors have made many films about
Lenin. It is characteristic of Donskoi that when
he turned to the subject in two of his later films

the focus in both of them was on Lenin's youth,
and above all on his relationship with his mother,
movingly played by Elena Fadeyeva. The first
of them, *Serdtse materi* (*A Mother's Heart,*
1966), studies the emotional turmoil of a middle-
class mother when she finds her sons rejecting
the respectable professional futures she has
planned for them. Nina Hibbin wrote: "Here is
another rich recreation of provincial life at the
end of the nineteenth century—the comfort of
the prosperous and affectionate home; the intimacy of the streets in which all the people are
on nodding terms with each other; the lively,
bustling riverside scenes that are a constantly recurring theme in Donskoi's works." It seemed to
John Gillett that "it is the small, personal details
of [the family's] relationships which give the film
its unmistakable Donskoy flavour," and that
here, as in the Gorky trilogy, "Donskoy's most
personal set-pieces fuse together those particularly Russian qualities of anguish and faith in the
future." In the later sections of the film and in
Vernost materi (*A Mother's Devotion,* 1966), socialist orthodoxies intrude, and there are passages of banality and bathos.

Nina Hibbin described Donskoi as "small,
stocky, warmhearted and emotional, with a live,
lined, and slightly pugnacious face, a gusty sense
of humour, and an expressive flow of words
punctuated by dramatic gesticulations. He has
the energy and vitality of a man half his
age. . . . It is no accident that the first big peak
of Donskoi's career should have sprung from the
personal memoirs of Gorky; for in some ways
Donskoi is the Gorki of the screen. Like Gorki he
is disturbed, yet fascinated, by human degradation, angered by injustice and suffering, and inspired by man's capacity for heroism and self-
sacrifice and by his eternal quest for truth. With
his gift for visual lyricism, for the creation of
character and for the evocation of period atmosphere and mood, he is a master of poetic
realism." Others have praised his skill in depicting "the relation of characters to landscape," and
his "eloquent use of cinematic space."

Donskoi was married in 1936 to Irina Sprink,
and had two sons. His many awards included the
Order of the Red Banner of Labor, People's Artist of the USSR (1966), Hero of Socialist Labor
(1971), and two Orders of Lenin (1972). His
obituary was signed by Leonid Brezhnev and
other Kremlin officials.

—*K.B.*

FILMS: (with Mikhail Auerbach) Zhizn (Life), 1927
(short); (with Mikhail Auerbach) V bolshoi gorode (In
the Big City), 1927; (with Mikhail Auerbach) Tsena
cheloveka (The Value of Man), 1928; Pizhon (The
Fop), 1929 (short); Chuzhoi bereg (Alien Shore/The

Other Shore), 1930; Ogon (Fire), 1930; (with Vladimir Legoshin) Pesnya o shchastye (Song of Happiness), 1934; Detstvo Gorkovo (The Childhood of Maxim Gorky), 1938; V lyudyakh (My Apprenticeship/Among People/Out in the World), 1939; Moi universiteti (My Universities), 1940; Romantiki (Children of the Soviet Arctic), 1941; Fighting Film Album No. 9: Beacon, 1941 (short); Kak zakalyalas stal (How the Steel Was Tempered), 1942; Mayak (The Lighthouse), 1942 (*episode in* The Diary of a Nazi); Raduga (The Rainbow), 1944; Nepokorenniye (The Unvanquished), 1945; Seklskaya uchitelnitsa (A Village Schoolteacher/ Varvara/The Emotional Education), 1947; Alitet ukhodit v gory (Alitet Leaves for the Hills), 1949; Nashi chempiony (Our Champions/Sporting Fame), 1950 (short); Mat' (Mother), 1956; Dorogoi tsenoi (At Great Cost/At a High Price), 1957; Foma Gordeyev, 1959; Zdrastvyite deti (Hello, Children), 1962; Serdtse materi (A Mother's Heart), 1966; Vernost materi (A Mother's Devotion), 1966; Chaliapin, 1970; Nadezhda, 1973.

ABOUT: Cervani, A. Mark Donskoi, 1966 (France); Edelman, R. *in* Lyon, C. International Dictionary of Films and Filmmakers, 1984; International Film Guide, 1971; International Who's Who, 1978–79; Kak ya stal rezhisserom (*chapter in* How I Became a Director), 1946 (USSR); Leyda, J. Kino, 1960; Oxford Companion to Film, 1976; World Encyclopedia of Film, 1972; Wright, B. The Long View, 1974. *Periodicals*—Cinéma 59 November–December 1959; Film Dope June 1971; Films and Filming January 1955, July 1970; Focus on Film March–April 1970; Image et Son November 1964.

*DOVZHENKO, ALEXANDER PETRO-VICH (September 12, 1894–November 25, 1956), Ukrainian film director, writer, and artist, was born in the town of Sosnitsa, on the River Desna, near the ancient cathedral city of Chernigov. Of Ukrainian Cossack descent, he and his films were nourished by the sad songs, the folklore and fantastic legends that were still part of an ancient, patriarchal way of life. His father, Petro Dovzhenko, was an illiterate farmer whose few sandy meadows could not support the family and who therefore worked also as a driver and as a pitch-burner. There were fourteen children of whom only two survived, Alexander and his sister Polina, who became a doctor. He writes in his autobiography: "The other children died at different times, hardly any of them reaching working age. Now, whenever I think of my childhood and of my home, in my mind I see crying and funerals. . . . I still cannot bear to look at funerals, and yet they pass through all my scripts and all my pictures, for the question of life and death affected my imagination when I was still a child and left its imprint on all my work."

*dov zhen´ ko

ALEXANDER DOVZHENKO

Dovzhenko's childhood was not all unhappiness: "The second thing in my childhood that was decisive for my work was love of nature and a true appreciation of its beauty. We had a fairytale-like meadow by the Desna River. To the end of my days it will stay in my memory as the most beautiful spot on earth. With that meadow I associate my first fishing trip, and berries and mushrooms. . . . Now that meadow lives on in my work."

He was a dreamy but intelligent child, and from the Sosnitsa secondary school, encouraged by his parents, he went on before he was sixteen to the Teachers' Institute in Glukhov. Younger by far than most of the students there, Dovzhenko was lonely and disoriented at the Institute, which set out to train "well-behaved [and] politically illiterate" teachers. He failed to win a scholarship and had to work as a tutor to support himself. Even that was not enough, and his father in the end sold part of his small farm: "he cut it off from his heart."

Forced to attend the Institute chapel, Dovzhenko ceased to believe in God but began to develop an interest in politics. The Ukraine at that time was divided between Russia and Poland. Books and magazines in the Ukrainian language were prohibited, and the upper classes had attached themselves to foreign cultures. Only the peasants, in their folklore and legends and songs, preserved Ukrainian culture and the Ukrainian spirit. Student teachers at the Glukhov Institute were forbidden to speak Ukrainian: "They were making us into Russifiers of our country." Nevertheless, a Ukrainian nationalist movement was growing, and Dovzhenko was introduced by another student to its clandestine publications.

Graduating in 1914, Dovzhenko went to work as a science teacher in Zhitomir. He enjoyed teaching and liked his pupils but was soon in trouble for speaking Ukrainian to them and for disseminating "anti-state propaganda" and "peasant democratism." He and his colleagues greeted the Russian Revolution of 1917 as if it were the millennium. He "called out phrases at meetings and was as happy as a dog let off a chain, sincerely believing that now all men were brothers, that everything was completely clear, that the peasants had the land, the workers had the factories . . . the Ukrainians had Ukraine, the Russians had Russia; that the next day the whole world would find out about this and, struck with our vision, would do likewise."

The same year Dovzhenko was transferred to a teaching post at Kiev, where he studied at the Commercial Institute and for a time at the Academy of Fine Arts, meanwhile becoming increasingly involved in nationalist political activism as a propagandist and organizer of student rallies. During the Civil War, Dovzhenko joined the Red Army as a volunteer, serving as a staff school instructor with the division led by the partisan commander Mykola Shchors. In 1920 he joined the communist-nationalist Borotbist Party and then the Communist Party itself. It is not entirely clear when or how fully he transferred his commitment from the dream of a truly independent Ukraine to the ideals of international communism. In any case, at the deepest level his remained "a Ukrainian consciousness, made in [the] Ukraine."

Towards the end of the Civil War, working underground in the Korovynetsk region during the Polish occupation, Dovzhenko was captured by a Polish cavalry patrol and treated "very roughly." He was about to be shot when he was rescued by a Red Army unit. After the liberation he was appointed secretary of the education department in the Kiev region. He worked prodigiously in this post, serving also as director of the local art department and commissar of the Shevchenko Theatre and traveling all over the region to organize educational facilities and local governments. In June 1920 he married Barbara Krylova, a village school teacher, from whom he was divorced six years later. In 1921 Dovzhenko was sent as a diplomat of the Ukrainian Republic to Warsaw. After a year there he was transferred to the embassy in Berlin, where he was able to pursue his art studies. In 1923 Dovzhenko returned to the Ukraine, then in the midst of a short-lived national cultural revival. For the next three years he worked in Kharkov as an illustrator and political cartoonist for the local party newspaper.

During this period Dovzhenko eked out his income by illustrating books and designing film posters, and in this way he met people in the Ukrainian film industry. His interest in the movies grew, encouraged by party enthusiasm for the cinema as the most popular and democratic of mediums and the one that would supplant the elitist arts of the past. "In June 1926," Dovzhenko wrote, "I sat up all night at my studio, assessed my thirty-two unsuccessful years of life, and in the morning picked up cane and suitcase, leaving behind my canvases and painting materials, and departed from the house, never to return. I went to Odessa and got a job at the film studio as a director. You could say that I stood a naked man on the Black Sea coast. In the thirty-third year of my life I had to start learning all over again: I had not been an actor or a stage director, did not go to see films very often, and was not familiar with film theory. But there was no time to study, and in Odessa probably no one to study with."

It is surprising now to find that Dovzhenko (who prided himself on his resemblance to Charlie Chaplin) at first wanted to write and direct only comedies. His first script was a story about a small-town boy who tries to put the world to rights single-handedly, *Vasya-reformator* (*Vasya the Reformer*). It was filmed quickly by another director and released in July 1926 only a few weeks after Dovzhenko's arrival in Odessa. A total flop, it was soon followed by his first film as both writer and director, a short slapstick comedy called *Yagodki lyubvi* (*The Little Fruits of Love*). Written in three days and filmed in eight, this was to remain his only completed comedy, though he wrote scripts for others, including one in which Charlie Chaplin is shipwrecked on a desert island. His characteristic visual style began to emerge in *Sumka dipkur'era* (*The Diplomatic Pouch*, 1927), a political thriller in which, after two Soviet couriers have been waylaid and murdered by the British secret police, the vital documents are delivered to their destination by British sailors and workers. Dovzhenko himself appears as a stoker in the movie, which was highly successful. On March 22, 1927, the day of its premiere, Dovzhenko was married to Julia Solntseva, an actress who became his assistant and then a director in her own right.

Dovzhenko's unique vision was first fully revealed in *Zvenigora* (1928), an extraordinary mixture of legend and history evoking a thousand years of Ukrainian peasant life. The recurrent theme concerns a legendary treasure buried in the magic mountain Zvenigora. In the central story, an old man regales his two grandsons with such exciting stories about this treasure that, while the worthy Tymish stays at home to join in the revolutionary struggle, his brother Pavlo runs off to seek his fortune. Pavlo becomes an adventurer whose career reaches its climax in the famous scene in which he swindles a Prague theatre audience that has paid to see him commit suicide (a sly comment on the sensation-mongering of the time). Pavlo goes home to join the Ukrainian nationalists and wickedly persuades his grandfather (representing the past) to try to derail a train (the future). When the attempt fails, Pavlo kills himself and the old man joins forces with Tymish, who explains that the real buried treasure is the mineral wealth of the Ukraine.

This eccentric film worried the studio bosses at Odessa. Eisenstein described how he was begged for his opinion and how he and Pudovkin sat enthralled through this lyrical fantasy, in which wizard monks emerge from the earth and black horses are painted white. They found it a poetic mixture of the contemporary and the legendary, the comic and the pathetic, in some ways reminiscent of Gogol. "The show was over," Eisenstein wrote. "The audience rose silently. But the atmosphere was tense with a feeling that a new talent had appeared in film art." Nevertheless, the general public found the picture and its flashbacks and experiments confusing, and the authors of the original scenario (heavily rewritten by Dovzhenko) removed their names from the credits.

After this, Dovzhenko always wrote his own scripts, a procedure he disliked because it "overburdens the director, forces him to perform the creative act twice, and shortens his life." The scenario for his next film, *Arsenal* (1929), was written in two weeks. Almost as personal and idiosyncratic as its predecessor, it gives a synoptic view of the misery and heroism of the revolution in the Ukraine, siding with the Bolsheviks against "reactionary Ukrainian nationalism." In the struggle for a Kiev munitions factory, the heroic young Tymish (Semen Svashenko, who also played the Tymish of *Zvenigora*), receives quite unharmed several volleys of rifle fire at point-blank range from the nationalists. (As Marco Carynnyk writes, "Dovzhenko is never afraid of artistic exaggeration" and his work is full of "abrupt changes of mood and . . . humorous or fantastic incidents.") Dovzhenko was "oppressed" but not surprised when Ukrainian nationalist intellectuals, his former friends, reviled the film and himself. The communist establishment just as predictably approved of the picture, and it was otherwise and deservedly a great critical and popular success. Eisenstein called it *the* example of a "liberation of the whole action from the definition of time and space," of "a dramaturgy of the visual film-form."

Danylo Demutsky, Dovzhenko's cameraman on *Yagodki lyubvi* and *Arsenal,* also worked with him in creating the lovely images of his masterpiece *Zemlya* (*Earth,* 1930), the first picture he made at the Kiev Studio. The story is slight, and the film is simply and beautifully an affirmation of man's oneness with the earth, relating his life and death with irresistible directness to the flowering and beneficent decay of the fruits of the soil. The theme is introduced in a prologue, in which an old man, peacefully dying, bites joyfully into an apple. A collective buys a tractor, but before it reaches the village its radiator boils over. The resourceful peasants solve the problem by urinating into the radiator. The collective's young chairman Vasyl (Semen Svashenko) uses the tractor to smash down the fence separating their land from that of an uncooperative kulak.

There follows the marvelous central sequence expressing what Dovzhenko himself called a "biological, pantheistic conception." Marco Carynnyk has described how, "in the moonlight of a warm summer night, after scenes of plentiful harvest, cattle ruminate, storks nest for the night, and young couples gaze at the dark sky in motionless ecstasy, the hands of the boys on the girls' breasts. Among them are Vasyl and his betrothed Natalka. They part." Drunk with love and happiness, Vasyl begins to dance all alone in the moonlight. He is nearing home, still dancing, when a shot rings out and Vasyl falls dead. His grief-stricken father, formerly opposed to all change, now drives away the priest and calls for a Soviet funeral. As Vasyl's body is carried to the grave, to the accompaniment of joyous songs, his mother goes into labor with a new life. No one hears the hysterical confession of the wretched kulak.

It seemed to C. A. Lejeune that the great central section "contains perhaps more understanding of pure beauty in cinema, more validity of relation in moving image, than any ten minutes of production yet known to the screen. . . . We long to pick this sequence out of the storyframe . . . to run it through again and again until we have mastered its secret speeds and transitions, and yet we are conscious, all the while, that no one moment of *Earth* is completely valid without the moments that precede and follow it. . . . *Earth* is so far the best of the films of the soil because it works in the track of a philosophy . . . the philosophy of a pregnant world brought to labour in an endless cycle of beauty."

Carynnyk speaks of the film's "passionate simplicity . . . which has made it a masterpiece of world cinema"—one that has twice been placed by critics among the dozen best films—and points out that, though it ends with a funeral, the effect is of a "powerful lyric affirmation of live."

Lewis Jacobs, discussing both *Arsenal* and *Earth,* wrote that to the structural innovations of Eisenstein and Pudovkin, Dovzhenko "had added a deep personal and poetic insight. . . . [The films] are laconic in style, with a strange, wonderfully imaginative quality difficult to describe. Says Dovzhenko, 'Excitement runs like a red thread through all my films.' Neither of these works has a story; both spring from moods, concepts, and images of Ukrainian legends. Both contain some of the most sensitive pictorial compositions the screen has ever known, superbly related in angle, tone, and movement. So personalized are these pictures that they achieve the emotional intensity of great lyrical poems." For Ivor Montague, "the key to all the poignancy in Dovzhenko's films is death. Just that, the simplest thing of all. Death apprehended never as an end . . . But death as a sacrifice, the essential one, a part of the unending process of reviving life. . . . No empty cycle, but the hope and certainty, because the inescapable method, in fact the *ritual* of process. A poet of death as part and parcel of eternal life."

Meanwhile, however, Stalin's lethal grip on the Ukraine was tightening, and the great flowering of the arts that had followed the revolution was ending. *Zemlya* was described by the party hack Demyan Bedny as "counterrevolutionary" and "defeatist" and was brutally abridged. This attack so distressed Dovzhenko that he "literally aged and turned gray overnight." He went to Europe for a few months, showing his films and lecturing. When he returned to the Ukraine he was instructed to make his first sound film, *Ivan* (1932). Still in a state of shock, near breakdown, and working with inadequate sound equipment, Dovzhenko had been given an impossible deadline: "Nevertheless I did manage to turn the film in on time," he wrote, "although at the end I had to work at the cutting table without sleep or rest for eighty-five hours."

All the same, *Ivan* shows that Dovzhenko could handle dialogue and sound with the same masterly fluidity as his visual images, and that he could impart a passionate lyricism to the most unlikely subject—in this case the construction of the Dnieper Dam. The story centers on a simple young peasant who, like millions of others at that time, leaves the countryside to work on a construction site. Strong, confident, but untrained, he refuses an offer of further education but soon learns that strength without skill is not enough and goes back to school. Dovzhenko wrote that "the film is completely lacking in dramatic conflict. I am deliberately discarding the entire arsenal of effects used to insure the audience's attention and enthusiasm. I am making a clear and simple picture that will resemble its clear and simple heroes. Hence the simplicity of the formal composition."

This simplicity confounded the critics, who accused Dovzhenko of fascism, pantheism, "biologism," and "Spinozaism." He was dismissed from the Kiev Studio and treated as "an unreliable fellow traveler." About the same time he learned that his father, then seventy-three, had been driven out from the collective farm where he was living, presumably as a further punishment for Dovzhenko. As Stalin's "war against the Ukraine" continued and the persecution of artists and intellectuals gathered momentum, Dovzhenko decided that he would try to head trouble off at its source. He went to Moscow and wrote directly to Stalin, asking him to "protect me and help me develop as an artist." The dictator graciously agreed, and Dovzhenko was assigned to the Mosfilm studios in Moscow.

Aerograd (1935), shown in the United States as *Frontier,* is set in the Siberian Far East, where a new "air city" is being built, and has a melodramatic plot about the attempt of Japanese agents to sabotage it. Dovzhenko had fallen in love with the Far East, and the film conveys his delight in the beauty of the Siberian *taiga* and of planes in flight. Western critics greatly admired the picture for its originality and its confident use of music and speech, but the Soviet reviewers found it difficult and "paradoxical." Dovzhenko, who had received the Order of Lenin early in the year and was still in favor with Stalin, defended himself vigorously before the Moscow Writers' Union in November 1935.

Jay Leyda met Dovzhenko at about this time, attending a reading of the script of *Aerograd*: "His voice, as powerful and convincing as I imagined Mayakovsky's must have been, filled his hotel room to the bursting point. His dynamic person exactly fitted my imagined maker of *Arsenal* and *Earth.* When I later watched him work at Mosfilm I saw that his relation to actors was to infect them with his immense enthusiasm in the same way that he swept me off my feet with his reading. It was an exhilarating experience."

It was Stalin himself who suggested Dovzhenko's next subject, and the director returned to the Kiev studio to make a film biography of his old commander, the Ukrainian partisan leader Mykola Shchors. But Stalin's interest meant that the production was hampered by every kind of political and bureaucratic interference, and Shchors emerges as a god-like hero of impossible rectitude. There is far more life in the earthy, emotional old peasant Vasyl Bozhenko (modeled, like all of Dovzhenko's "grandads," on his own beloved grandfather). Dovzhenko has been personally involved in many of the film's political and military actions, and even in this made-to-order product his visual genius shines through. "*Shchors,*" wrote Jay Leyda, "leaves in the memory burning images of death and passionate life. To move from the pitiless ferocity of the opening to the tragic dirge of the close—both set in the same shattered fields—gives the film a wide form that can absorb any amount of speechifying. But all the rhetoric of the film is outweighed by *moving pictures*—riderless horses, smoking ruins of destroyed homes and lives, a boisterous wedding procession that jingles through a bombardment, cavalry through snowy meadows and icy avenues . . . pictures that pour across the screen."

In the fall of 1939, when the Soviet Union annexed the Western Ukraine and Bucovina, Dovzhenko was sent to film these regions, which contained large Ukrainian populations. He returned to Kiev in 1940 with twenty thousand meters of film—the raw material of his documentaries *Liberation* and *Bucovina—Ukrainian Land*. In 1941 he was appointed artistic supervisor of the Kiev Studio, which later that year was evacuated to Central Asia. Dovzhenko's parents remained behind in Kiev throughout the German occupation, during which his apartment was sacked and mined and his father was robbed, beaten, and thrown down the stairs. The old man died soon afterwards, but Dovzhenko's mother survived. When the Russian Army reentered Kiev she asked the soldiers about her famous son and word of this reached Khrushchev, who told Dovzhenko that his mother was still alive. He found her living in a cellar with a dozen other old women, "like animals." She stayed with him after that until her death at the age of eighty-six.

Dovzhenko himself served during World War II as a war correspondent, expressing his anguish at the destruction of the Ukraine in articles for *Red Army* and *Izvestia* and in the fictional works that increasingly engaged him, including stories, a novel, and a play. He also wrote scenarios for two features, *Ukraine in Flames* and *Chronicle of Flaming Years*. Both were filmed after his death by his wife, but in 1944–1945 their passionate concern for the Ukraine was considered a threat to the integrity of the Soviet Union. Dovzhenko was summoned before Stalin and Beria at the Kremlin, where he was verbally "hacked to pieces." He was fired from the Kiev Studio, reassigned to Mosfilm, and forbidden to return to the Ukraine.

The only films Dovzhenko was allowed to make during the war were documentaries, and with *The Battle for Our Soviet Ukraine* (1943) he achieved a powerful film poem which is clearly his work (though his wife is credited as director, Dovzhenko only as scenarist and supervisor). The material was shot at different parts of the front by twenty-four cameramen to whom Dovzhenko gave detailed instructions and even drawings of what he wanted. David Robinson thinks this one of the most exciting of all his films: "The images roar along, each sweeping in the next with the inevitability of a musical structure. Thrillingly these factual, often harrowing images refer back to the feature films: the struggling horses from *Arsenal,* a dead soldier whose comrades mourn him like the peasants in *Earth.* People, like the earth and its fruits, tend to survive. Alongside the war and its devastations, the peasants still work the land and the corn still grows." The same group later made another documentary, *Pobeda na pravoberezhnoi Ukraine* (1945), which was shown abroad as *Ukraine in Flames*, though it has no connection with the feature film of that title.

Dovzhenko "squeezed, groaned, and suffered" for three years over *Michurin* (1949), a film biography of the famous agronomist who developed hundreds of new fruit species. There is something of Dovzhenko himself in his portrait of Michurin, who has "the troubles of Job on his face" and "encounters every conceivable obstacle, frustration, and disappointment," though the film's ending, typically, is all blossom, children, and triumph. This picture was Dovzhenko's first in color and has a score by Shostakovich. It failed to satisfy Stalin, and a second version was made largely without Dovzhenko's involvement.

Heart attacks interrupted Dovzhenko's long-cherished plans to film Gogol's Ukrainian epic *Taras Bulba,* and his last years were devoted mostly to literature, including the unfinished epic novel *The Golden Gate.* The censorship eased with Stalin's death in 1953, and Dovzhenko began work on an ambitious film trilogy about a Ukrainian village like his own. It was to begin with *Zacharovannaya Desna (The Enchanted Desna),* the story of Dovzhenko's own childhood. This was to be followed by *Povest plammennykh let (Chronicle of Flaming Years),* about the village during the war years, using the 1944 script that had been rejected by Stalin. The trilogy was to end with *Poema o morye (Poem of a Sea),* in which the village is drowned beneath the waters of a great lake when a hydroelectric dam is built.

Dovzhenko decided to film the last part of the trilogy first. For two years he and his cameramen recorded the building of a hydroelectric dam at the town of Kakhovka, Southern

Ukraine. Meanwhile, Dovzhenko worked on the script, and as was his practice, made detailed drawings of how the story was to be visualized. His scenario, originally written in the form of a play, reflects a characteristic ambivalence—pride at man's ability to transform his environment, regret for the resulting destruction of natural beauty and an ancient way of life. Dovzhenko (who had by this time recovered his religious faith) wrote in his diary: "This must be a titanic film. To create a film worthy of my people's greatness: that is the only goal, the only significance of my life. Lord, bless my infirm hands."

Dovzhenko died the night before studio shooting was to begin on *Poem of a Sea*. After his death his widow, using his notes and the existing documentary footage, completed the film, and went on to make the rest of the trilogy as well as other projects planned by Dovzhenko. Most critics share the view of David Robinson, that "Dovzhenko's was a talent that could not, ultimately, outlive him; but the will of his widow to perpetuate this artist . . . is a touching and brave tribute to Dovzhenko's own conviction of life's continuity."

In *Alexander Dovzhenko: The Poet As Filmmaker* (1973) Marco Carynnyk has provided an excellent English translation of the director's autobiography and a selection from his notebooks, together with an illuminating introduction to his life and work. There are two collected editions of Dovzhenko's writings: *Tvory v pyaty tomakh* (Works in Five Volumes), published in Kiev in 1964–1966; and *Sobraniye sochineniy* (Collected Works), published in Moscow in 1966–1969. Carynnyk warns, however, that these two collections "differ radically not only because they print the Ukrainian or the Russian variants, but also because the respective editors delete, usually without indication, different 'undesirable' passages. . . . there is, as yet, no reliable edition of Dovzhenko's writings. Many of his treatments, scenarios, diaries, drafts, and especially notebooks, are still inaccessible."

"Taking the whole of Alexander Dovzhenko's output, writings as well as films, one realizes quickly that he was a stubbornly single-minded man," Carynnyk writes. "Possessed of a strongly mythopoeic imagination, he had the ambition to create a vast synthesis, both literary and cinematic, into which he could fold history, mythology, and personal beliefs. Few film directors have produced so unified a body of work as Dovzhenko. . . . And it is this unity—coupled with his enormous cinematic skill—that is responsible for the number of Dovzhenko's masterpieces." Jay Leyda considered that Dovzhenko and Eisenstein were "the two greatest Soviet film artists," and many think Dovzhenko "the cinema's greatest epic poet."

FILMS: Yagodki lyubvi (The Little Fruits of Love/Love's Berrry), 1926; Sumka dipkur'era (The Diplomatic Pouch), 1927; Zvenigora, 1928; Arsenal, 1929; Zemlya (Earth), 1930; Ivan, 1932; Aerograd (Frontier/Air City), 1935; Shchors, 1939; (With Julia Solntseva) Liberation, 1940 (documentary); Bucovina—Ukrainian Land, 1940 (documentary; direction credited to Julia Solntseva, with Dovzhenko as "artistic supervisor"); Bytva za nashu Radyansku Ukrayinu (The Battle for Our Soviet Ukraine), 1943 (documentary; direction credited to Julia Solntseva and Yakiv Avdiyenko, with Dovzhenko as artistic supervisor and author of narration); (with Julia Solntseva) Pobeda na Pravoberezhnoi Ukraine (Victory in Right-Bank Ukraine/Ukraine in Flames), 1945 (documentary); Michurin (original version called Life in Blossom), 1949. *Films completed by Julia Solntseva*—Poema o morye (Poem of a Sea/Poem of an Inland Sea), 1958; Povest plammennykh let (Chronicle of Flaming Years), 1961; Zacharovannaya Desna (The Enchanted Desna), 1965; Ukraine in Flames/The Unforgettable, 1968; Zolotye vorota (The Golden Gate), 1969 (based on Dovzhenko's writings). *Published screenplays in English*—Earth, translated by Diana Makas *in* Two Russian Screen Classics, 1973.

ABOUT: Amengual, B. Alexandre Dovjenko, 1970 (France); Bazhan, M. Oleksondr Dovzhenko, 1930 (Ukraine); Dovzhenko, A. The Poet As Filmmaker, edited and translated by Marco Carynnyk, 1973; Leyda, J. Kino, 1960; Maryamov, A. Dovzhenko, 1968 (Russia); Oms, M. Alexandre Dovjenko, 1968 (France); Schnitzer, L. and J. Dovjenko, 1965 (France); Schnitzer, L. and J. (eds.) Cinema in Revolution, 1973; Wright, B. The Long View, 1974; Yurenev, R. N. Aleksandr Dovzhenko, 1959 (Russia). *Periodicals*—Film Comment Fall 1971; New York Times November 27, 1956; Sight and Sound November 1947, Summer 1957, Fall 1971; Take One August 1976.

DREYER, CARL THEODOR (February 3, 1889–March 20, 1968), Danish director and scenarist, was born in Copenhagen. According to recent research by Maurice Drouzy, he was the illegitimate son of a Swedish woman, Josefin Bernhardin Nilsson. His father, Jens Christian Torp, owned a farm near Kristianstad in southern Sweden, where Josefin Nilsson worked as housekeeper. To avoid scandal, she went to Copenhagen to have her baby in anonymous seclusion. For the first two years of his life, the child lived in a succession of foster homes, before his mother succeeded in having him adopted early in 1891. A few weeks later she died, poisoned by phosphorus, which she had taken in a misinformed attempt to abort a second pregnancy.

The boy's adoptive parents were a young

CARL THEODOR DREYER

Danish couple, Carl Theodor and Inger Marie Dreyer. Carl Dreyer senior worked as a typographer for the progressive newspaper *Aftenbladet*. The family was not well off and often had to move in search of cheaper lodging. Perhaps partly as a result of this poverty, Dreyer's childhood, as he described it to his friend Ebbe Neergaard, was unhappy and emotionally deprived; his adopted family "never ceased to let him feel that he ought to be grateful for the food he was given, and that he really had no claim to anything, considering that his mother had managed to escape paying for him by departing this world." As soon as possible, he was encouraged to start earning his keep. His brother-in-law, a talented musician, had given him piano lessons, and for his first job Dreyer was sent to provide background music in a fashionable café on the Store Kongensgade. At the end of his first evening's playing, the management suggested that he need not bother to return.

Hoping for a chance to travel, Dreyer applied for a post with the Great Northern Telegraph Company and was accepted—but only for the Copenhagen accounts department. The work was well-paid, enabling him to leave home for good in 1906, but stultifyingly dull. He persevered for nearly a year and a half, until one day a senior accountant took him down into the vaults and, pointing to the long, dusty rows of files, remarked proudly: "There you see my whole life." Appalled by this vision of the future, Dreyer resigned the next day and took up instead the more exciting and precarious occupation of journalism.

Beginning with theatre reviews for the pro-

vincial press, Dreyer soon graduated to the more prestigious Copenhagen dailies and in 1909 started to write regularly for both *Riget* and *Berlingske Tidende*. As the latter paper's air correspondent, he trained as a balloon pilot, making several flights, and in 1910 became the first passenger to be carried by plane between Denmark and Sweden. In 1912 he joined *Ekstrabladet* and began writing a regular series of articles entitled "Heroes of Our Time," under the pseudonym "Tommen" ("Inch"), in which he satirized the pretensions of various well-known literary and artistic figures. The previous year, 1911, he had married Ebba Larsen. Dreyer, always a reserved and reticent man, rarely discussed his personal life, but his marriage was to all appearances a happy one, lasting until his death fifty-seven years later. The couple had two children: a daughter, Gunni, born in 1913, and a son, Erik, born in 1923.

While still working for *Ekstrabladet,* Dreyer began writing film scripts, and received his first writing credit on *Bryggerens Datter* (*The Brewer's Daughter,* 1912). In 1913 he joined Nordisk Films Kompagni as a part-time screenwriter, becoming a full-time employee two years later. At that time the Danish film industry was at the height of its brief Golden Age, producing a spate of movies that rivaled those of Hollywood for international popularity. Between 1910 and 1916 Nordisk alone turned out over a hundred films a year. Dreyer's first task was to devise dialogue for intertitles, but soon he was writing complete scripts, editing films, and acting as literary consultant on potential properties. From 1913 to 1918 he was credited with scripts for more than twenty films and worked uncredited on many more. It served him, he later said, as "a marvelous school."

In 1918, having worked a five-year apprenticeship, Dreyer suggested that Nordisk should let him direct. The studio agreed readily enough, and Dreyer began work on *Praesidenten* (*The President,* 1919), to his own script from a novel by Karl Franzos. The film proved a creaky, old-fashioned melodrama, full of seductions, illegitimacies, improbable coincidences, and impossibly stagy acting, all strung around a complicated flashback structure that betrayed the ill-digested influence of D. W. Griffith. Dreyer subsequently attributed the hammy gesticulations to his directorial inexperience: "I let the actors do what they liked. Later I saw my mistakes on the screen."

More characteristic of Dreyer's later work was his handling of some of the smaller roles, where he cast nonprofessionals in the interests of authenticity, and his treatment of the décor, which was clean and uncluttered, contrasting black and white in starkly dramatic compositions. *Praesidenten* also marks the first appearance of Dreyer's perennial theme: an isolated, suffering woman victimized by intolerant society. The plot and the acting now make the film almost unwatchable, but at the time it did well at the box office, and Nordisk were happy to let Dreyer direct another film for them.

The influence of Griffith was again evident in *Blade af Satans Bog* (*Leaves From Satan's Book,* 1919), derived from a typically gushy novel by Marie Corelli. Clearly inspired by *Intolerance,* this was a four-episode story in which Satan adopts various guises through the ages to tempt people to betray each other. Unlike Griffith, though, Dreyer wisely chose to tell his four tales—the Betrayal of Christ, the Inquisition, the French Revolution, and the Russo-Finnish War of 1918—in chronological sequence, rather than risk any complex interweaving. Once again, much of the acting was heavily overdone by modern standards, but Dreyer's flair for décor and milieu was increasingly apparent, and George Schnéevoigt contributed some luminous exterior photography.

Dreyer's perfectionist approach to details of set-design and casting on *Leaves* had led to clashes with Nordisk even before shooting started. At one point the director attempted to have his budget doubled, then grudgingly settled for a twenty-five percent increase. Further problems arose during filming. In the final Finnish episode (the first to be shot), Dreyer aimed to build up tension by means of exceptionally rapid cutting, with some six hundred shots averaging about three seconds each. This disconcerted the actors, who claimed their performances would be ruined, and the studio, alarmed, demanded that Dreyer complete and screen the episode before proceeding with the rest of the film. In the screening the fast, rhythmic editing manifestly made perfect sense, and Dreyer was permitted to continue.

Irritated by these disputes and by the film being drastically cut for its Oslo premiere, Dreyer quit Nordisk and embarked on a resolutely independent international career. His remaining seven silent movies were made for seven different production companies in five different countries. The first of them, *Prästänkan* (*The Parson's Widow,* 1920), marked a complete break with his previous films in every way. Made for Svensk Filmindustri, it was shot entirely on location in Norway, and in its lyrical use of pastoral settings suggests the influence of Stiller and Sjöström. Dreyer scripted from a novel by Kristofer Janson, based on the true seventeenth-century story of a young curate who is forced, in order to obtain a living, to marry the aged widow of the previous incumbent. "This film of delicately shifting moods and sympathies," wrote Derek Malcolm, "entirely belies ideas of Dreyer's work as being all weight and gloom." The transition from the broad comedy of the opening scenes to the elegiac tenderness of the final sequence, in which the old woman takes a final leave of her farm before lying down to die, is deftly handled, and Dreyer elicits fine, natural performances from his cast—most notably from Hildur Carlberg as the widow. (The actress, who was mortally ill when she accepted the role, died a few weeks after filming was over.)

Most of the smaller roles were taken by members of the local farming community, and their weathered faces, along with the old farmhouse interiors, contributed powerfully to the overall sense of authenticity, aided by Schnéevoigt's sensitive photography. For his next two films, though, Dreyer reverted to studio-bound artificiality. *Die Gezeichneten* (*Love One Another,* 1921), made for the small Berlin company Primusfilm, was a turgid melodrama about anti-Semitism, set in prerevolutionary Russia, and bogged down by simplistic characterization and a hopelessly convoluted plot. *Der Var Engang* (*Once Upon a Time,* 1922) found Dreyer back in Denmark, adapting a popular fairy-tale play for a Copenhagen theatre-owner, Sophus Madsen. Only fragments of this film have survived: it seems to have been pleasant but lightweight, Dreyer's slightest work. He himself rated it "a complete failure," adding that "it taught me . . . that you cannot build a film on atmosphere alone. . . . People are primarily interested in people."

The German film industry, led by the mighty UFA studios in Berlin, was now at the height of its influence and prestige, and it was for Decla-Bioscop, the "artistic" wing of UFA, that Dreyer directed *Mikael* (1924), with Erich Pommer producing. The plot, from a novel by Hermann Bang, concerned the triangular relationship between an eminent painter, his handsome young male model, and an emigrée Russian princess. As the young man's affection turns towards the woman, the painter finds himself drained of vitality, creative talent, and finally even of life. Despite the heavily expressionist symbolism favored by the studio, Dreyer succeeded in making his characters both credible and sympathetic, helped by an outstanding cast that included the Danish director Benjamin Christensen as Zoret, the painter; the young Walter Slezak in the title role of his protégé; and Nora Gregor (later to star in Renoir's *La Règle du jeu*) as the princess. Hugo Häring, an architect with no previous film experience, contributed some extravagantly fantastic sets—in particular Zoret's cavernous, *fin-de-siècle* salon, dominated by a huge sculpted head with blind, staring eyes.

"*Mikael*," in Tom Milne's opinion, "is perhaps Dreyer's first masterpiece, assured, reticent, and radiant with subtle inner connections." Certainly it enabled Dreyer to explore, more fully than in any of his previous films, his technique of expressing his characters' inner moral condition through the décor that surrounds them. Ebbe Neergaard, defending *Mikael* against charges of pretension and ponderousness, described it as "a completely genuine representation of a completely false milieu, which contained wretched human beings buried in all . . . pomposity." The film was enthusiastically received, especially by the German critics, who hailed it (to Dreyer's gratification) as "the first *Kammerspiel* film"—the first film in the style of an intimate "chamber" drama.

It had originally been planned that Dreyer would make another film for UFA. However, after a disagreement with Pommer, who had apparently changed the ending of *Mikael* without his consent, Dreyer left Berlin and returned to Denmark for his next film, *Du Skal Aere Din Hustru* (*Master of the House*, 1925). Although utterly different in tone, this can also be classified as a *Kammerspiel*. Paul Schrader summed up the term in relation to Dreyer's films as "a simplicity of scenic means, a refusal to use declamatory effects, a systematic realism, rigorous action, and a measured symbolism." This is a fair summary of *Master of the House*, though omitting the sly humor which makes it perhaps the most thoroughly enjoyable of all Dreyer's silent films. Adapted by Dreyer and Svend Rindom from the latter's play *Tyrännens Fald* (*The Fall of a Tyrant*), the film recounts the downfall of a spoilt, domineering husband who terrorizes his wife and children. The old family nanny persuades the wife to pretend to leave him and in her absence takes over the household, instituting a stern new regime that takes not the least account of the husband's hitherto sacrosanct comfort. By the time his wife returns, he has learned to appreciate her.

Dreyer at first intended to shoot inside a typical two-room Copenhagen apartment. This proved impractical, so instead he had a complete replica constructed in the studio, with all the walls and doors in position and the gas, water, and electricity hooked up. Filming in this deliberately confined space, he achieved a wealth of intimate domestic detail and drew from his players performances of appealingly unforced naturalism. *Master of the House* also displays Dreyer's increasingly assured use of facial close-ups as a key element in the construction of his films. "Nothing in the world," he once wrote, "can be compared to the human face. It is a land one can never tire of exploring. There is no greater experience in a studio than to witness the expression of a sensitive face under the mysterious power of inspiration. To see it animated from inside, and turning into poetry."

Master of the House enjoyed considerable success, especially in France, prompting the Société Générale des Films to offer Dreyer a contract for the film that would soon make him famous. First, though, he went back to Norway to direct *Glomdalsbruden* (*The Bride of Glomdal*, 1925), a simple and lyrical love story that made poetic use of the sweeping Norwegian landscape. Since most of his cast were stage actors on their summer vacation, Dreyer had no time to prepare a written script but worked from an outline, improvising with the actors from day to day. The film has great charm, if little depth.

Dreyer had now directed eight films in seven years. In the remaining forty-two years of his life he was to make only six more features—although they include all the five films on which his reputation now rests. Had he stopped directing after *The Bride of Glomdal*, he would almost certainly today be rated merely an obscure early figure in Scandinavian cinema, not so well-known as Christensen or Stiller. Yet these initial films, for all their limitations, display most of the thematic preoccupations and stylistic traits of his later masterpieces. The harsh intolerance of society is a constant theme, generally presented through the predicament of an isolated woman (though sometimes, as in *The Parson's Widow* and *Master of the House*, presented in a relatively lighthearted vein). Throughout these films, too, Dreyer can be seen striving for truth and sincerity on the screen, pressing for naturalistic settings and performances in the hope of achieving emotional truth. "What interests me," he explained, "—and this comes before technique—is to reproduce the feelings of the characters in my films: to reproduce as sincerely as possible feelings which are as sincere as possible. For me, the important thing is not only to seize the words they say, but also the thoughts behind those words." Also increasingly evident is what Tom Milne described as "Dreyer's preoccupation with texture, with the way the material world impinges on the human beings who live apparently detached from it, and with the tangibility of a gesture or a glance and with the equal tangibility of objects."

All these elements coalesce in Dreyer's next, and still his most famous, film. Invited to Paris, he proposed a choice of three subjects to the Société Générale—Marie Antoinette, Catherine de Medici, and Joan of Arc—and finally (by drawing matches, Dreyer later claimed) settled on Joan. Given ample time and a generous budget of seven million francs, he spent several months in research and preparation before starting production on an unhurried schedule. To represent Rouen Castle, a huge concrete complex was constructed of interconnecting walls, towers, houses, a drawbridge, and a church, designed by Hermann Warm (set designer on *Caligari*) and Jean Hugo. Warm drew his inspiration from medieval miniatures, with their disconcerting angles and naive perspective. Dreyer's script was based largely on the original transcripts of Joan's trial, though the twenty-nine separate interrogations were telescoped into one single, harrowing sequence.

It is virtually impossible today, even on a first viewing, to come to *La Passion de Jeanne d'Arc* (*The Passion of Joan of Arc,* 1927) with a wholly fresh eye, so familiar have stills from it become. This may partly explain why some critics have tended to dismiss the film as no more than "an extension of still photography." Certainly few films, before or since, can have contained such a high proportion of facial close-ups—dictated, according to Dreyer, by the inherent nature of the material. "There were the questions, there were the answers—very short, very crisp. . . . Each question, each answer, quite naturally called for a close-up. . . . In addition, the result of the close-ups was that the spectator was as shocked as Joan was, receiving the questions, tortured by them." There is also a notable lack of establishing situation-shots: deprived of any clear sense of the geographical layout of the various settings, we are left as helplessly disoriented as Joan herself.

Jeanne d'Arc comes across, in Jean Sémolué's term, as "a film of confrontation"—a sustained assault on the heroine (and the viewer) full of unsettling camera angles and off-center framings. "The architecture of Joan's world," wrote Paul Schrader, "literally conspires against her; like the faces of her inquisitors, the halls, doorways, furniture are on the offensive, striking, swooping at her with oblique angles, attacking her with hard-edged chunks of black and white." In the title role, Maria Falconetti gave one of the most intense performances of mental and physical anguish in the history of cinema. (Astonishingly, it was the first and only film she ever made.) Her suffering face has achieved iconographic status as the classic cinematic depiction of martyrdom. "That shaven head," observed Jean Renoir, "was and remains the abstraction of the whole epic of Joan of Arc."

Along with the rest of the cast, Falconetti acted completely without make-up; Rudolph Maté's high-contrast lighting brought out every detail of the actors' features with stark clarity. Antonin Artaud was at his most gauntly beautiful as the sympathetic Massieu, while the faces of Joan's accusers, all lumps and warts and fleshy pouches, frequently recall the onlookers in crucifixions by Breughel or Bosch. These hostile figures are repeatedly shot from ground-level, to make them appear huge and intimidating; to this end, Dreyer had numerous holes dug all over the set, causing the film crew to nickname him "Carl Gruyère."

From this film, and especially from his allegedly harsh treatment of Falconetti, dates Dreyer's reputation as an exacting and tyrannical director. He himself, while conceding that he made considerable demands on his actors, rejected any suggestions of tyranny, stressing instead the importance of mutual cooperation. A director, he maintained, must be "careful never to force his own interpretation on an actor, because an actor cannot create truth and pure emotions on command. One cannot push feelings out. They have to arise from themselves, and it is the director's and actor's work in unison to bring them to that point."

Jeanne d'Arc was a huge world-wide critical success but a commercial flop. Almost instantly hailed as a classic, it has consistently maintained its position as one of the enshrined masterpieces of the cinema. Godard paid homage to it when, in *Vivre sa vie,* he showed Anna Karina watching it in a movie theatre, moved to tears. Some critics, though, have expressed reservations. "It was one of the most remarkable productions ever realised in the history and development of the cinema," stated Paul Rotha, "*but it was not a full exposition of real filmic properties*" (his italics). Tom Milne argued that "somehow the style Dreyer found for the film seems irremediably false. Instead of flowing naturally from his chosen materials . . . it seems imposed upon them. . . . Throughout the film there is a constant stylistic uncertainty, an impurity, which jars heavily today." Despite this, Milne conceded that "*Jeanne d'Arc* has a majestic power which steamrollers its way through all its faults and excesses."

The Société Générale had intended Dreyer to make a second film for them, but the financial failure of *Jeanne d'Arc* and of the even more catastrophic *Napoléon* of Abel Gance (which the Société had also backed) made this impossible. Dreyer, already irritated because his film—or so he claimed—had been mutilated to avoid offending Catholic susceptibilities, sued for breach of contract. The lawsuit dragged on, and not until the autumn of 1931 was Dreyer, having won his case, at last free to make another film.

A wealthy young film enthusiast, Baron Nicholas de Gunzburg, now approached Dreyer with a proposal that they form an independent production company. The film they produced was *Vampyr* (1932)—one of the strangest, most idiosyncratic horror films ever made. Shot largely in a derelict chateau, with a cast composed almost entirely of nonprofessionals, it conjures up a pale, drifting, drowned world, in which events glide with the hallucinatory slowness of dreams, and menace resides in the intangible reverberations of sights and sounds that seem to hover just beyond the reach of consciousness. Without gore or Grand Guignol, or the harsh gothic chiaroscuro of Murnau or James Whale, *Vampyr* creates an uncannily convincing universe of fantastic unreality.

Dreyer's script was adapted, very freely, from two stories by the nineteenth-century Irish writer, Sheridan Le Fanu. The plot, such as it is, tells of a young man, David Gray, who comes to a remote village where a vampire, the un-dead Marguerite Chopin, preys on the living bodies of young women, abetted by the village doctor. Eventually Gray succeeds in destroying the vampire, and the curse is lifted. But plot in *Vampyr* is totally subordinated to mood and atmosphere. A grey, floating mist, as if everything were in a state of dissolution, pervades the film—an effect that Dreyer and his photographer, Rudolph Maté, hit on by lucky accident when a light shone on the camera lens during the first day's shooting. The general incompetence of the acting also contributes to the dissociated mood: the film's producer, Baron de Gunzburg, himself playing the hero under the pseudonym of Julian West, shambles somnambulistically through the action, seeming (in Paul Schrader's words) "not an individual personality, but the fluid, human component of a distorted, expressionistic universe." The film was post-dubbed by the actors themselves into English, French, and German versions, thus further heightening the sense of unreality, since few of them were fluent in all three languages.

Vampyr, wrote Robin Wood in *Film Comment* (March 1974), "is one of the most dreamlike movies ever made, and one of the few to capture successfully the *elusiveness* of dream. . . . Dreyer has here created a visual style unlike that of any other film, including any of his own." David Thomson, though, pointed out that "its intensity reflects back on all Dreyer's other films, showing how entirely they are creations of light, shade, and camera

position." Most critics would now agree with Tom Milne in seeing *Vampyr* as "one of the key works in his career . . . quintessentially Dreyer"; but when released it was a critical—as well as a financial—disaster, and for years afterwards could be dismissed as "a puerile story about phantoms" (Georges Sadoul).

Dreyer had now acquired the reputation of being a difficult and demanding director, averse to compromise, given to disputes and recriminations, and one moreover whose films lost money. Refusing to submit himself to the discipline of any of the major studios, Dreyer found himself unemployable. For the next ten years, at the height of his powers, he made no films. Various projects came to nothing: discussions in Britain with John Grierson; a version of *Madame Bovary* which eventually went to Renoir (1934); an idea for a film about Mary Queen of Scots. In 1936 he traveled to Somalia to make a semidocumentary film, *Mudundu,* with French and Italian backing. Several thousand meters of film were shot before Dreyer clashed with the producers and eventually withdrew, leaving the picture to be completed by Ernesto Quadrone.

After this fiasco, Dreyer returned to Denmark and once more took up journalism under his old pseudonym of "Tommen," writing film reviews and law reports. His chance to direct again came in 1942. With imported films blocked under the German occupation, the Danish film industry had regained a greater share of the market and needed products. To prove that he could work on commission and within a budget, Dreyer directed a government documentary short, *Modrehjaelpen (Good Mothers,* 1942), about social care for unmarried mothers. On the strength of this, Palladium (for whom he had made *Master of the House*) offered him a contract for a feature film.

Vredens Dag (Day of Wrath, 1943) is, according to Robin Wood, "Dreyer's richest work . . . because it expresses most fully the ambiguities inherent in his vision of the world." It also unites all those elements that are held, perhaps unfairly, to be most typical of Dreyer's films. Its prevailing mood is somber, lowering, intense; the narrative pace is steady and deliberate, presenting horrific events with chilling restraint; and it deals with religious faith, the supernatural, social intolerance, innocence and guilt, and the suffering of women. In its visual texture *Day of Wrath* arguably presents, even more than *Jeanne d'Arc,* the most complete example of Dreyer's use of light and darkness to express moral and emotional concerns.

The story is set in the early seventeenth century. An old woman is hunted down and burned as a witch, despite an attempt by the parson's young wife, Anne, to save her. Anne falls in love with her own grown-up stepson; when her elderly husband dies, she is accused of having caused his death through witchcraft. Deserted by her lover, she admits the accusation and is condemned. "The interest in Dreyer's films," suggested Jean Sémolué, "resides not in the depiction of events, nor of predetermined characters, but in the depiction of the changes wrought on characters by events." This clearly applies to *Day of Wrath*, where the narrative focuses on Anne's transformation from an innocent, somewhat naive girl into a woman conscious of her own sexual and psychological powers, and half-believing that they may be those of a witch.

Day of Wrath, as Dreyer conceived it, presented "possibilities for great monumental visual effects—four or five figures as sharply defined as medieval wood sculptures." In total contrast to *Vampyr*, the film constantly confronts us with clean-edged visual compositions: severe, black-garbed figures against white walls, opposing lines of force creating tension within the frame. Dreyer himself (in an interview in *Cahiers du Cinéma*, September 1965) commented on the dramatic effect of a strong vertical, emphasizing the horror of the moment when the old, white-haired woman is tied to a long ladder before being toppled into the flames. Anna Svierkier's moving performance as the pathetic old victim is surpassed only by that of Lisbeth Movin as Anne, incarnating with total conviction the character's troubling ambiguity.

On its release *Day of Wrath* aroused no great enthusiasm among Danish reviewers, who found it labored and slow-moving. Since the end of the war, when the film received wider circulation, its reputation has steadily grown, and most critics now rank it with *Jeanne d'Arc* as one of Dreyer's greatest works. At the time, though, many Danes saw in it a topical significance: religious oppression and witch-hunting were taken as hinting at the Nazi occupation and the persecution of the Jews. Dreyer protested, apparently in all sincerity, that no such parallel had occurred to him, but was persuaded by friends that he might be wise to withdraw to Sweden for the duration of the war.

In Stockholm he was offered the opportunity to direct a film for Svensk Filmindustri, *Två Människor* (*Two People*, 1944). Dreyer so disliked the result—"a film that was doomed from the start, completely"—that he refused, after its dismal Stockholm premiere, to let it be shown publicly in his lifetime. He attributed its failure to the disastrous casting insisted upon by the pro-ducer. Even given ideal casting, though, it would be difficult to imagine how Dreyer could have made much of the convoluted plot which, nudged along by creaking coincidences and fatal letters that arrive at opportune moments, is oddly reminiscent of his first film, *The President*. Back in Denmark after the war, he once again could find no one to back him and kept his hand in with some more short films for government agencies. Between 1946 and 1954 he directed seven of these, to his own scripts; the best-known of them, *De Naede Faergen* (*They Caught the Ferry*, 1948), conveyed a safety message through the story of a young couple on a motorcycle who literally race with Death—and of course lose.

In 1952 Dreyer's immediate financial problems were eased by the Danish government, which has a custom of honoring its eminent cinematic figures by awarding them, for life, the lease of one of the major Copenhagen cinemas. Dreyer received the managership of the Dagmar, a prestigious art-house, and was thus enabled to start planning a feature film, again to be produced by Palladium.

Ordet (*The Word*, 1954) is based on a play by Kaj Munk, a Lutheran pastor who was killed by the Germans in 1944. Much of the film was shot at Vedersö, the village in Jutland where he had been pastor. The action involves a religious feud between two families, the Borgens and the Skraedders, adherents of different sects, which is complicated by an attraction between a son of one family and a daughter of the other, and by the death of Inger Borgen in childbirth. At the film's climax, Inger is raised from the dead by a miracle, and the families are reconciled.

Despite its intensely emotional subject matter, the keynote of *Ordet* is cool simplicity. Dreyer filmed in very long takes, his camera moving steadily and deliberately around sets that he had carefully reduced to a significant minimum of detail. Ib Monty relates how Dreyer "made the film crew equip the kitchen with everything he considered right for a country kitchen. Then . . . he set about removing the objects. Finally only ten–fifteen remained, but they were just what were wanted to create the right psychological illusion." He followed a similar process in the script, cutting dialogue and removing what he thought inessential from the play, while remaining faithful to Munk's central message of the inseparability of all forms of love, human or religious. When Inger has supposedly died, her husband Mikkel responds to well-meant assurances that her soul is now safe in heaven with the desolate cry: "But I loved her body too!"

"The interior scenes," Tom Milne wrote, "are luminous with a sense of expansive affection arising from the rich, warmly observed detail of the relationships. . . . Throughout the film, Dreyer's emphasis is on the density of emotion allied to gesture which he first explored in *Master of the House.*" Robin Wood agreed that "our sense of the interdependence of the characters and their actions is communicated visually. . . . One cannot but admire the total command and the elimination of everything but essentials, a process that certainly imbues those essentials with expressive intensity. At the same time, I find it difficult not to react against the style as repressive and deadening." Similarly, Ib Monty felt that *Ordet* "failed to avoid a certain formal rigidity." Nonetheless, it was Dreyer's first film since *Jeanne d'Arc* to enjoy immediate acclaim, being enthusiastically received in Denmark by both audiences and reviewers. Foreign critics were equally favorable, and *Ordet* won the Golden Lion at the 1955 Venice Festival.

During the next ten years, Dreyer worked on a number of film projects: an adaptation of Euripides' *Medea,* a version of Faulkner's *Light in August,* treatments of Ibsen's *Brand,* Strindberg's *Damascus,* and O'Neill's *Mourning Becomes Electra*—as well as his most cherished project, a life of Christ to be filmed in Israel. But he completed only one more film: *Gertrud* (1964), based on the play by Hjalmar Söderberg.

In *Gertrud* can be seen the culmination of a process of increasing simplification and austerity in Dreyer's shooting style. From the multiple cutting and dramatized angles of *Jeanne d'Arc,* the endlessly fluid, gliding tracking shots of *Vampyr,* Dreyer progressively, through *Day of Wrath* and *Ordet,* slowed down his camera, restricted his angles, and increased the length of his takes until he arrived, with *Gertrud,* at something perilously close to stasis. The film consists of a relatively small number of mostly long takes, generally two-shots during which both camera and actors often remain still for minutes at a time. Almost deliberately, it seems, in thus taking the principles of *Kammerspiel* to the extreme, Dreyer invited charges of visual monotony.

Gertrud is about a woman who demands love on her own unconditional terms or not at all, and the three men—one husband, two lovers—who fail to live up to her exacting standards. Finally she leaves all three, for a solitary life in Paris; in an epilogue, grown old and still alone, she speaks her epitaph: "I have known love." "Of all Dreyer's works," Jean Sémolué wrote, "it is the most inward, and thus the culmination, if not the crown, of his aesthetic." Penelope Houston thought it "an enigmatically modern film with the deceptive air of a staidly old-fashioned one. . . . It is a kind of distillation, at once contemplative and compulsive." The consensus of critical opinion has come to regard *Gertrud* as Dreyer's final, tranquil testament—"the kind of majestic, necromantic masterpiece," as Tom Milne put it, "that few artists achieve even once in their lifetimes."

On its first appearance, though, *Gertrud* aroused an extraordinary degree of anger and hostility. Premiered in Paris, as part of an elaborate homage to Dreyer, it was greeted with catcalls by the audience and uncomprehending vituperation by the French press. In a typical review, *Cinéma 65* commented: "Dreyer has gone from serenity to senility. . . . Not a film, but a two-hour study of sofas and pianos." The film was booed at Cannes, and in America the critics were equally unappreciative. In *Esquire* (December 1965) Dwight Macdonald wrote: "*Gertrud* is a further reach, beyond mannerism into cinematic poverty and straightforward tedium. He just sets up his camera and photographs people talking to each other." Dreyer reacted with dignity in the face of these attacks, calmly explaining: "What I seek in my films . . . is a penetration to my actors' profound thoughts by means of their most subtle expressions. . . . This is what interests me above all, not the technique of the cinema. *Gertrud* is a film that I made with my heart."

In considering Dreyer's work as a whole, most critics, without disparaging his considerable skills as a screenwriter, have stressed the visual aspect of the films as his most distinctive achievement. "Dreyer's style is wholly pictorial," asserted Richard Rowland (*Hollywood Quarterly* Fall 1950), "it is visual images that we remember . . . faces, lights and shadows." Equally remarkable, though, is how utterly different one Dreyer film can look from another, while still remaining unmistakably his in theme and style. Dreyer himself, when this was once suggested to him, was delighted, "for that is something I really tried to do: to find a style that has value for only a single film, for *this* milieu, *this* action, *this* character, *this* subject." "The characteristic of a good style," he remarked on another occasion, "must be that it enters into such intimate contact with the material that it forms a synthesis."

"There is nothing decorative about Dreyer's work," André Bazin stated. "Each nuance contributes to the organization of a mental universe whose rigor and necessity dazzle one's mind." Most writers would concur that Dreyer's films, especially the latter ones, are characterized by an intense deliberateness, pared of inessential detail, and some have found this oppressive.

Robin Wood, contrasting Dreyer's work with Renoir's "sense of superfluous life . . . a world existing beyond the confines of the frame," found in Dreyer "a progressive stylistic tightening and rigidifying, a movement away from freedom and fluency . . . into an increasingly arid world where it becomes harder and harder to breathe." Certainly those films for which Dreyer is best known—*Jeanne d'Arc, Day of Wrath, Ordet*—have tended to reinforce his image as a purveyor of metaphysical gloom and anguish, a daunting Great Director better written about than seen.

This accepted view of Dreyer was fairly accurately summarized by Eileen Bowser: "His martyrs, his vampires, his witches and his holy madmen are different facets of the same theme: the power of evil, the suffering of the innocent, the inevitability of fate, the certainty of death." But this doomladen resumé is not all of Dreyer; and with his earlier silent films—especially *The Parson's Widow, Mikael,* and *Master of the House*—gaining wider circulation and with *Vampyr* growing steadily in critical regard, there are signs that the conventional picture of this director may be changing, and that the lighter, often even cheerful, aspects of his work are achieving recognition.

After *Gertrud,* Dreyer continued to work on preparations for *Jesus,* completing the script (which was later published), learning Hebrew, and visiting Israel to hunt for locations. His age and exacting reputation, though, made potential backers wary. Finally, in November 1967, the Danish government offered three million kroner. In February 1968 the Italian state television company, RAI, announced that it was also prepared to back the film. Dreyer's dream of twenty years seemed at last about to be realized. The next month he died, of heart failure, aged seventy-nine.

—*P.K.*

FILMS: *Features*—Praesidenten (The President), 1919; Blade af Satans Bog (Leaves From Satan's Book), 1919; Prästänkan (The Parson's Widow/The Fourth Marriage of Dame Margaret), 1920; Die Gezeichneten (Love One Another), 1921; Der Var Engang (Once Upon a Time), 1922; Mikael, 1924; Du Skal Aere din Hustru (Master of the House/Thou Shalt Honor Thy Wife), 1925; Glomdalsbruden (The Bride of Glomdal), 1925; La Passion de Jeanne d'Arc (The Passion of Joan of Arc), 1927; Vampyr, 1932; Vredens Dag (Day of Wrath), 1943; Två Människor (Two People), 1944; Ordet (The Word), 1954; Gertrud, 1964. *Shorts*—Modrehjaelpen (Good Mothers), 1942; Vandet på Landet (Water From the Land), 1946; Landsbrkirken (The Danish Village Church), 1947; Kampen mod Kraeften (The Struggle Against Cancer), 1947; De Naede Faergen (They Caught the Ferry), 1948;

Thorvaldsen, 1949; Storstromsbroen (The Bridge of Storstrom), 1950; Et Slot i et Slot (Castle Within a Castle), 1954. *Published scripts*—The Passion of Joan of Arc, Vampyr, Day of Wrath, Ordet (in English) *in* Four Screenplays (Indiana University Press), 1970; Jesus (Dial Press), 1972.

ABOUT: Agel, H. Les Grands Cinéastes, 1960; Bazin, A. (and others) La Politique des Auteurs, 1972; Bordwell, D. The Films of Carl-Theodor Dreyer, 1981; Bowser, E. The Films of Carl Dreyer, 1964; Brakhage, S. The Brakhage Lectures, 1972; Cuenca, C. F. Carl Theodor Dreyer, 1964 (in Spanish); Dreyer, C. Th. Dreyer in Double Reflection (edited by D. Skoller), 1973; Drouzy, M. Carl Th. Dreyer né Nilsson, 1982; Milne, T. The Cinema of Carl Dreyer, 1971; Monty, I. Carl Th. Dreyer: Danish Film Director, 1968; Nash, M. Dreyer, 1972; Neergaard, E. En Filminstruktors Arbejde: Carl Theodor Dreyer og hans ti film, 1940; Neergaard, E. Carl Dreyer: A Film Director's Work, 1950; Parrain, P. (and others) Dreyer: Cadres et Mouvements, 1967; Passek, J.-L. (ed.) Le Cinéma Danois, 1979; Perrin, C. Carl Th. Dreyer, 1969 (in French); Roud, R. (ed.) Cinema: A Critical Dictionary, 1980; Sarris, A. (ed.) Interviews With Film Directors, 1967; Schrader, P. Transcendental Style in Film: Ozu, Bresson, Dreyer, 1972; Sémolué, J. Dreyer, 1962; Sémolué, J. Carl Th. Dreyer, 1970; Thomson, D. A Biographical Dictionary of the Cinema, 1975; Tone, P. G. Carl Theodor Dreyer, 1978 (in Italian); Trolle, B. The Art of Carl Dreyer: An Analysis, 1955. *Periodicals*—Avant-Scène du Cinéma February 1970; Bianco e Nero September 1948, June 1955, July–August 1968, January–February 1979; Cahiers du Cinéma June 1955, December 1956, October 1961, January 1962, July 1962, August 1962, October 1964, September 1965, December 1968; Celulóide 59 1962; Cineforum January 1964, May 1964, May 1965, November 1965, June 1968; Cinéma (France) November 1955, March 1956, January 1980; Cinema (USA) Fall 1970; Cinema (Switzerland) 43 1965; Cinema Nuovo January–February 1965; Cinestudio February 1971; Film (Germany) February 1968; Film Comment March–April 1974; Film Culture Winter 1964–1965; Film Dope January 1978; Film Ideal July 15, 1964; Film Quarterly Fall 1965; Filmcritica April 1968, May 1968, June 1968; Filme Cultura November 1968; Filmkritik May 1968; Films and Filming November 1955, March 1964, February 1968; Films in Review January 1952; Filmstudio 40 1963; Hollywood Quarterly Fall 1950; Image et Son July 1953; Kino (Finland) 2 1964; Kosmorama 44 1959, 56 1962; National Film Theatre Booklet October 1977; Revue du Cinéma Autumn 1947; Rivista del Cine January 1967, April 1968; Scen og Salong November 1963; Sight and Sound Winter 1955–1956, Spring 1965, Autumn 1965, Summer 1974, Spring 1975; Telecine 118 1964; Theatre Arts April 1951.

*DUDOW, SLATAN (January 30, 1903– August 12, 1963), German film and theatre director, scenarist, and dramatist, was born in Zaribrod, Bulgaria, the son of Theodor Dudow,

°dōō´dou

SLATAN DUDOW

a railroad engineer and committed socialist. In his teens, Slatan Dudow was equally active in politics and the theatre, directing a production of Gogol's *Marriage* while still at school. In 1917 he participated in the demonstrations in Bulgaria that greeted the news of Russia's October Revolution and joined a revolutionary organization. He was still only seventeen when he became involved in street fighting against the Bulgarian police, who put a violent end to the transport strike of 1920. These experiences prompted him, when he left school, to embark on a systematic study of mass communication methods as a means of increasing worker solidarity.

Dudow's father died in 1919 and his mother remarried. In 1922, with his stepfather's financial help, Dudow went to Berlin, ostensibly to study architecture. In fact, his ambitions centered on the stage, and once in Berlin he settled down to learn German, to immerse himself in Marxist and cultural studies, and to prepare for a career in the theatre. After a year as a student at Emanuel Reicher's drama school, he enrolled in the winter of 1925–1926 in Max Hermann's institute of theatre studies at the University of Berlin, at the same time gaining practical experience as an amateur actor at the National Theatre and as a member of a choir under the direction of Erwin Piscator.

By this time, Dudow's interests had extended to the cinema, and in 1925 he managed to talk his way into the UFA studios and to persuade Fritz Lang to let him observe the filming of *Metropolis*. This was an important if negative experience for Dudow, convincing him that expressionism did not lend itself to the sort of polit-

ical films he wanted to make. Four years later, in April 1929, he went to Moscow to pursue his research for a thesis on the Soviet theatre, observing (and sometimes participating in) productions by Meyerhold, Tairoff, Wachtangov, and Stanislavski, among others. He also met Eisenstein, whose *Battleship Potemkin* he had already seen and admired, and came away deeply impressed by the director's views on ideological cinema and montage.

Back in Berlin in the fall of 1929, Dudow had his first meeting with Bertolt Brecht—an encounter that was later to have important consequences. The same year he met the documentarist Victor Blum and in 1929–1930, while pursuing his study of montage, had his first experience of filmmaking as Blum's assistant on several documentaries made for Weltfilm, a German Communist Party production company. He made his own first film under the same auspices: *Wie der Berliner arbeiter wohnt?* (*How Does the Berlin Worker Live?*, 1930), a documentary about the city's housing crisis. Serving as scenarist, director, and cameraman, and influenced by Dziga Vertov, Dudow employed the technique now known as *cinéma-vérité*, often using a hidden camera. He filmed the workers and the unemployed on the streets and in employment bureaus and also showed them being dispossessed of their homes. Blum's films had all been banned and Dudow's was also, so alarming the authorities that they forbade the making of any more Communist documentaries.

Dudow had meanwhile begun his theatre career, in 1929 staging a drama by Anna Gmeyner. Beginning in 1930 he was coauthor and/or codirector of several plays by Brecht. In return, the latter served as coscenarist with Ernst Ottwalt of Dudow's first and best-known feature film, *Kühle Wampe* (1932). Produced by Georg Höllering and Robert Scharfenberg and with a score by Hanns Eisler, the film was made in the face of immense difficulties, financial and political. It uses only a few professional actors, along with thousands of extras recruited from an assortment of left-wing organizations.

Kühle Wampe begins by introducing us to a typical working-class family of the period. The jobless, hopeless father takes refuge in drink, the mother clings to a blind faith in the system, and only the daughter Anni (Hertha Thiele) has a job. The son, learning that his dole is to be cut, commits suicide. The second part of the film is set in Kuhle Wampe, the tent colony that grew up during the Depression on the outskirts of the capital. The family has been taken there by Anni's lover Fritz (Ernst Busch), a mechanic.

Finding that Anni is pregnant, Fritz urges her to have an abortion but is persuaded by a socialist fellow-worker to accept his responsibilities. An engagement party follows at which the older people, obviously defeated by life, eat and drink themselves senseless. Anni is not defeated, however, and, discovering Fritz's reluctance to marry, goes off alone to Berlin.

In the last section, at a socialist sports festival, Anni and Fritz meet again. We see that Fritz (now unemployed) has matured, politically and emotionally, and is better able to cope with the realities of their situation. Their encounter takes place against a *cinéma-vérité*-style record of vigorous athletic contests and open-air agitprop performances, ringing with optimistic socialist songs. A final sequence on the train back to the capital features discussions between the young Communists and the middle-class commuters, stressing the economic realism of the former, the hopeless conformity and conservatism of the latter.

Initially banned by the censors, *Kühle Wampe* was released after protests, albeit in a mutilated version. Siegfried Kracauer wrote that Dudow "had learned from the Russians to characterize social situations through well-chosen faces and suggestive camera angles" and cites the opening sequence, in which a group of the unemployed (including the son) search for work. When the newsboy arrives with the day's papers, the young men skim through the ads and hurry off. "They bicycle past 'No Help Wanted' signboards, enter a factory gateway without alighting and re-emerge instantly, repeat this vain attempt several times, and wheel on and on, never separating and always increasing in speed. It is rare that the intangible spirit of a whole epoch is crystallized in such clearcut images. This sequence with its telling details and rotating wheels and noncommittal house facades gives a concise idea of what German life was like during the crucial pre-Hitler days."

Elsewhere, however, the film shows signs of Dudow's inexperience, though some of its deficiencies must be attributed to the intervention of the censors. In particular Kracauer criticizes the film for glorifying youth at the expense of the older workers, who are shown as greedy and demoralized. Lotte Eisner pointed out that the sports meeting "unwittingly anticipates the Nazi parades" soon to be celebrated in Leni Riefenstahl's *Triumph of the Will.* There has been a good deal of praise for Eisler's score, but the interspersed ballads (with lyrics by Brecht's wife Helen Wiegel) were thought to weaken the movie's overall effect. *Kühle Wampe* remains important for its courageous rejection of the

studio—its often brilliant use of real locations and real workers—and its equally courageous (if sadly misguided) affirmation of faith in the future.

Seifenblasen (*Soap Bubbles*), ascribed by some historians to the years 1928–1929, was actually begun in 1933 from a script written some time earlier. It is very different from its predecessor in style, a visually inventive and witty satire about a bourgeois employee who loses his job and descends into poverty without being able to let go of his middle-class values—his dreams of wealth and power. He ends up in jail. Dudow made the movie more or less clandestinely and smuggled the negative to Paris, leaving it in the care of the critic Heinz Lüdecke. Soon afterwards, when Hitler's accession to power forced Dudow to leave Germany, he retrieved the negative and completed the film with postsynchronized dialogue written by Jacques Prévert.

In Paris, Dudow directed stage productions of Brecht's plays *Die Gewehre der Frau Carrar* (1937) and *Furcht und Elend des Dritten Reiches* (1938). He spent the war years mostly in Switzerland, writing a number of satirical plays. In 1946 he went to East Germany where, after a period of research and reorientation, he joined DEFA (Deutsche Film Aktien Gesellschaft), the state-owned production company. His comic play *The Coward* was produced at the Deutsches Theatre in East Berlin in 1948.

Dudow's first postwar film—and his first for fifteen years—was *Unser täglich Brot* (*Our Daily Bread,* 1949), written by the director (who coauthored all his postwar movies) in collaboration with Hans Joachim Beyer and Ludwig Turek. It deals with the reconstruction of East Berlin in the aftermath of the war, focusing on the problems of a single family and contrasting the inflexibility of the father with the forward-looking attitudes of one of his sons. Once again, Dudow had the benefit of a score by Hanns Eisler, but the film is marred by melodrama and oversimplification.

There was an even cooler reception for *Familie Benthin* (*The Benthin Family,* 1950), a cold war exercise which Dudow codirected with Kurt Maetzig, but *Frauenschicksale* (*A Woman's Destiny,* 1952), Dudow's first film in color, attracted more attention. Episodic in style and showing something of the influence of neorealism, it deals with a group of women from various milieux just after World War II who have in common only the fact that they are all seduced by the same man (Hanns Groth). Carefully adhering to the official Party line on both of its themes—the division of Germany and the status of women—it brought Dudow the award as best director at Karlovy Vary, but seemed to most Western critics hopelessly old-fashioned in its attitudes.

There was much less unanimity, even among non-Communist reviewers, about *Stärker als die Nacht* (*Stronger Than the Night*, 1954). This drama about the German resistance centers on Hans Löning (Wilhelm Koch-Hooge), a Hamburg factory worker and Communist activist, and his wife Gerda (Helga Göring). It was admired by some as "a powerful film, made with great technical skill and a sure sense of dramatic values," and several critics referred to a "moving sequence showing the husband being beaten up by the Gestapo, intercut with shots of his wife, who at that moment is giving birth to their son." However, even the *Daily Worker*'s reviewer found the movie marred at times "by the tendency of leading characters to make speeches instead of talking" and there were a number of objections to the "smooth evasions and suppressions of fact" that contributed to an impression that the Communists (with the generous backing of the Soviet Union) were "the only repository of true German idealism" under the Third Reich.

Der Hauptmann von Köln (*The Captain From Cologne*, 1956) had less impact abroad but was much preferred by some of those who had dismissed *Stärker als die Nacht* as "facile propaganda" and "a little monster of prevarication." An attack on neomilitarism in West Germany, the later film obviously invites comparison with Helmut Käutner's amiable satire on Prussian militarism, *The Captain From Köpenick*, but is a far more virulent work. A harmless unemployed waiter (Rolf Ludwig) calls at a hotel in search of work and finds himself in the midst of a reunion meeting of former Nazis. He is mistaken for a war criminal who has fled to the Argentine and welcomed with enthusiasm. A job is found for him, and he is elected to Parliament before the real captain returns under an amnesty and denounces him. He is brought to trial but, unable to produce even the smallest war crime, cannot claim protection under the amnesty; he is sent to jail as an imposter.

This mordantly witty satire remains the best of Dudow's later films. *Verwirrung der Liebe* (*Love's Confusion*, 1959), a romantic comedy about the misunderstandings and temptations that temporarily disturb the love affairs of two young couples, was a complete failure. Dudow had begun work on another movie, *Christine*, said to be a return to the theme of women's liberation, when he was killed in an automobile accident. He was a member of the German Academy of Arts and had been awarded the GDR's National Prize.

FILMS: Wie der Berliner arbeiter wohnt?, 1930 (documentary); Kühle Wampe (To Whom Does the World Belong/Whither Germany?), 1932; Seifenblasen (Soap Bubbles/Bulles de savon), 1934; Unser täglich Brot (Our Daily Bread), 1949; Familie Benthin, 1950; Frauenschicksale (A Woman's Destiny), 1952; Stärker als die Nacht (Stronger Than the Night), 1954; Der Hauptmann von Köln (The Captain From Cologne), 1956; Verwirrung der Liebe (Love's Confusion), 1959. *Published scripts*—Kuhle Wampe in *Junge Weld*, March 1, 1958.

ABOUT: Aubry, Y. Slatan Dudow, 1970 (in French); Dudow, S. La responsabilité sociale du cinéaste, 1945; Eisner, L. The Haunted Screen, 1969; Herlinghaus, H. Slatan Dudow, 1965 (in German); Kracauer, S. From Caligari to Hitler, 1947; Kuhn, G. Tümmler, K., and Wimmer, W. (eds), Film und revolutionäre Arbeiterbewegung in Deutschland, 1975. *Periodicals* —Film Dope January 1978; Film und Fernsehen September 1973, March 1976; Image et Son December 1975.

*DULAC, (CHARLOTTE ELISABETH) GERMAINE (November 17, 1882–July 1942), French director, scenarist, and theorist, was born in Amiens in the Somme valley in northern France. Her father, Pierre Maurice Saisset-Schneider, was a cavalry officer (eventually a general), and her childhood years were divided between Paris and Compiègne or St. Etienne, where her father was stationed. Later she went to live at the home of her grandmother in Paris, finding there both stability and intellectual stimulation. She studied music and became interested in photography.

She married in 1905. Her husband, whom she divorced fifteen years later, was Albert Dulac, an agricultural engineer (and/or a novelist, according to one source). Germaine Dulac was a militant feminist and, having no wish to be confined to domesticity, set out to make a career for herself as a dramatist and then, more successfully, as a journalist. In 1909 she joined the staff of *La Française*, a feminist journal. For four years she wrote articles on and interviews with prominent and successful women, afterwards serving as the journal's drama critic. Her first visit to a film studio was in 1914 when a friend, the actress Stacia de Napierkowska (who later appeared in two of her early films) took her onto the set of *Caligula*. She was soon convinced that film offered her the most fitting medium for artistic expression. Shortly after her initiation into filmmaking she said: "Of all the arts, not one has been able to sum up my feelings like the cinema. Only through the image have I been able to express all my thoughts." In 1915 she set up an independent production company, Delia Film, in

°dŭ lak´

GERMAINE DULAC

association with the poet and novelist Irene Hillel-Erlanger. Dulac's husband was the financial manager.

Dulac's first film was *Soeurs ennemies* (*Enemy Sisters,* 1916), scripted by Hillel-Erlanger, who also wrote her next two films, *Géo le mysterieux* (*Géo the Mysterious,* 1916) and *Vénus Victrix* (1917). These early films are apprentice works. It was not until *Âmes de fous* (*Mad Souls,* 1917), written by herself, that she achieved much critical recognition. Edmond Floury voiced feelings that were apparently shared by a number of critics: "The mise-en-scène was the work of Madame Albert-Dulac who is no longer just a beginner and deserves all our praise. . . . I will just make one little criticism: the *contre-jour* technique has been a bit overdone, and with the actors sadly plunged into shadow we cannot see their features any longer, they are moving silhouettes; in the end this business becomes wearisome. As Scribe said, the audience that pays wants to see something, not just characters passing through a thick shadow."

For Dulac herself, *Âmes de fous* marked her discovery of the true nature of cinema: it "made me understand that beyond specific facts and events, atmosphere is an element of emotion, that the emotional value of a film lies less in the action than in the nuances that come out of it, and that if the expression of an actor is obviously of value in itself, it can only attain its fullest intensity by a complementary play of images that emerge in reaction to it. Lighting, camera placement and editing all appeared to me as more essential elements than the production of a scene

that is played solely according to dramatic conventions." This assertion of the profoundly visual nature of film was to be echoed by the new generation of experimental filmmakers in France.

The leading role in *Âmes de fous* was played by the well-known actress Eve Francis, whose husband was Louis Delluc, a young theorist and critic of cinema. Around him gathered the "first avant-garde." This impressionist school, as it was called, included Dulac, Marcel L'Herbier, Abel Gance, and later Jean Epstein. While aiming to create a national French cinema, it looked to the American cinema for inspiration, finding it in Chaplin and Griffith, and in the Westerns of Tom Ince, and learning also from the German expressionists and the Swedish school.

Delluc had high praise for the beauty of Dulac's work in *Le Bonheur des autres* (*The Happiness of Others,* 1918) and wrote his first film script for her. The result was *La Fête espagnole* (*The Spanish Fiesta,* 1919), in which two men vie for the love of a woman (Eve Francis) who in the end chooses a third. The film is set in an exotic Spain, but the plot recalls an Ince Western. Leon Moussinac said that "nothing has been written in our country that is more cinematic than this tale of blood, voluptuousness, and death," but thought that the director had not done justice to the writer's conception. Others agreed, though there was praise for Dulac's semidocumentary treatment of the fiesta itself. The film remains one of great interest as the only direct collaboration between Dulac and Delluc, who have been called respectively the "head" and the "heart" of the first avant-garde.

After *La Fête espagnole* Dulac made several films that added to her reputation as a *metteur-en-scène* and apostle of the film as art: *La Cigarette* (1919), *Malencontre* (*Misadventure,* 1920), and *La Belle Dame sans merci* (1920), another film scripted by Hillel-Erlanger, which Delluc singled out for its brilliance. In *La Mort du Soleil* (*The Death of the Sun,* 1921), about a scientific genius, Dulac's innovatory attempts to represent the psychological irritated audiences as pointless deviations from the plot (itself mediocre), and the film suffered cuts at the hands of the exhibitors. Sadoul has suggested that many of Dulac's films were marred by "grandiloquent, improbable stories." In 1921 she visited Hollywood, where she met Griffith and was greatly impressed by the technical resources of the studios and the cooperative character of the film crews.

In 1923 Dulac made the film that is generally regarded as her masterpiece: *La Souriante Madame Beudet* (*The Smiling Madame Beudet,*

1923), an adaptation by André Obey of a play he had written with Denys Amiel. Sadoul compared it to a Maupassant short story for its tautness and economy and said that in it "the psychology was precise and more developed than anything current in silent cinema." The film also constitutes an exceptional example of innovation within the commercial cinema, and recent criticism has identified it as the first feminist film ever made.

In *Madame Beudet* Dulac exemplified in visual terms Obey's "theory of silence"—the notion that silences are dramatically more significant than words. The main character, sensitively played by Germaine Dermoz, is a kind of Madame Bovary, a provincial *bourgeoise* married to a dull and insensitive shopkeeper. The film depicts her various mental states during the course of a single day. Years of bored subservience have reduced Madame Beudet to a listless, melancholic woman who comes to life only in her romantic daydreams of streams, ponds, and young lovers. Even in fantasy, an attempt to kill her husband fails, and her life returns to conjugal monotony. The woman's subtle psychological shifts are represented through the use of a number of experimental techniques, including distortions, superimpositions, and slow motion. Thus we see the enraged Beudet through her eyes, transformed into an ogre, and share her fantasy about the handsome young tennis player who leaps off the page of a magazine to take a swipe at her husband. Objects are used with telling effect, like the vase that is constantly being shifted, first by the husband, then by the wife, like a piece in an endless chess game.

La Souriante Madame Beudet had a resonance that confirmed Dulac's stature as a *metteur-en-scène* and established her as a respected figure in the studios, admired for her formidable intellect and her mastery of craft. André Daven described her at about this time as an urbane, self-possessed woman with frenetic energy—"Fingers a mass of rings, wrists sculpted in bracelets, one ankle encircled with gold. A cane. Smoking and smoking." Charles Ford's impression is of a woman who inspired enormous affection and transmitted her own passionate interest in the cinema to everyone she met. It is in fact not Dulac's work as a filmmaker that has earned her most recognition, but her role as a film theorist and evangelist. Between 1920 and 1928 she published many pioneering theoretical essays in the cinema journals. In 1922 she was elected secretary-general of the Ciné-Club de France, in the founding of which she had played a major role, and she was instrumental in the importation of many influential foreign films. While she strove to elevate film to an art form with a coherent aesthetic of its own, she was no less concerned with accessibility, believing that the cinema was not an elitist medium but had a "universal vocation."

Dulac's desire to reach a popular audience caused variations of style in the films she made after *Madame Beudet*. She saw in *Gossette* (1922–1923)—a film in six episodes made for the Société des Ciné-Romans (serial films)—a chance to achieve a compromise between art and commercialism, but she was disappointed with the result. Her next film, *Le Diable dans la ville* (*The Devil in the Streets*, 1924), although well received by the critics, reinforced her dissatisfaction. Still in pursuit of the same goal, she made *Âme d'artiste* (*Soul of an Artist*, 1925) in collaboration with the Russian director Alexander Volkoff. This was a film aimed deliberately at an international audience, and Charles Ford regards it as one of her major works, successfully combining art and dazzling spectacle. *La Folie des vaillants* (*The Folly of the Brave*, 1925) was a return to a more abstract form of expression, but *Antoinette Sabrier* (1926) was another attempt at a popular film for the Société des Ciné-Romans.

The work that followed, *La Coquille et le clergyman* (*The Seashell and the Clergyman*, 1927), was of an altogether different order, marking Dulac's final break with the commercial cinema and her decision to pursue her ideal of "pure cinema." Indeed, *La Coquille* has become a landmark in cinema history—the first surrealist film. An attempt to represent in visual terms the dream world of a repressed priest, it was made from a script by the poet and prophet of "total theatre," Antonin Artaud. The collaboration was a difficult one, and the film's opening at the Studio des Ursulines—one of the temples of the avant-garde—provoked a violent demonstration, the surrealists denouncing Dulac for her betrayal of the script, and others in the audience attacking the apparent incoherence of the Freudian images and the absence of any real plot. (Artaud is reputed to have shouted, "Germaine Dulac is a cow!") One accusation was that she had "feminized" the script—an interesting reflection, as later critics have remarked, on the surrealists' view of women. On the other hand, the critic Alain Virmaux went so far as to say that "*The Seashell and the Clergyman* is not only the first surrealist film, but the greatest film of the decade." Film historians like Sadoul and Brassillach have been less wholehearted in their enthusiasm, and critics unenamored of the avant-garde have found in the picture's dreamlike sequences, with their split-screen effects and superimpositions, "an excess of trick effects." In Britain it was rejected by the Board of Film Censors on the grounds that it was "so cryptic as to be almost meaningless. If there is a meaning it is doubtless objectionable."

Regina Cornwell, writing in *Film Library Quarterly,* acknowledges the importance of Dulac's attempts to reconcile art and commercialism but concludes: "Eventually, with later films, she had moved from a position supporting an intelligent cinema within the domain of the French film industry to one in which she realised the impossible hiatus between the commercial and the avant-garde film. She felt the avant-garde of today could only, over time, affect the commercial film of tomorrow." Having come to this decision, Dulac intensified her efforts as a theoretician and propagandist. In 1927 she founded the journal *Schémas* (which failed to survive beyond the first issue), taught at the École Technique de Photographie et de Cinématographie, and became president of the federation of Ciné-Clubs. In 1930 she was named an officer of the Legion of Honor in recognition of her contribution to the development of film as a unique art form. Henri Fescourt said: "The good that this woman has done for the seventh art is enormous, and hardly credible."

Dulac continued making films. *L'Invitation au voyage (Invitation to the Voyage,* 1927), based on Baudelaire's poem, was an attempt to create "the pure film we all dream of making . . . a visual symphony, composed of rhythmic images which the artist's feelings alone organize and project on the screen." *Disque 927 (Disc 927,* 1928), *Thèmes et variations* (1928), and *Étude cinégraphique sur une arabesque (Film Study of an Arabesque,* 1929) are all visual evocations of music, while *Germination d'un haricot (Germination of a Bean,* 1928) is a botanical documentary which she often used in her lectures. A temporary departure from this experimental work was *Le Cinéma au service de l'histoire (The Cinema in the Service of History,* 1927), a kind of newsreel montage, followed by her "swan song as a *metteur-en-scène," La Princesse Mandane* (1928). Two further films were made under her supervision: *Mon Paris* (1928), directed by Albert Guyot, and *Le Picador* (1932), by Jaquelux.

Little is known about the last twelve years of Dulac's life. With the advent of sound she declared herself theoretically against the talking film but saw cinematic possibilities in the use of sound in terms of her conception of the "visual symphony." For a short time she was adjunct director at Gaumont, and then, feeling that the newsreel was a form full of hope for the future, she founded France-Actualités-Gaumont, where she was head of production. This work came to

an end with the occupation of Paris in 1940. Dulac died in July 1942 after an illness that had lasted several years.

It is Charles Ford's opinion that Dulac's work as a filmmaker has been unduly neglected and that her importance as a theorist is also undervalued. He claims that Dulac should be regarded as the foremost theorist in French cinema of the silent period, thereby ranking her above even Delluc. He locates her superiority in "having at times reconciled what seemed irreconcilable—aesthetic exigencies and commercial imperatives—and having expressed in clear and accessible language what the others articulated in formulas that were often hermetic." Apart from Ford's interest, Dulac has received comparatively little attention from cinema historians, though feminist critics have now embarked on a reassessment of her work and its relevance to the avant-garde of the 1970s, which shares her belief that theory and practice must develop in tandem.

The regard in which Germaine Dulac was held by her contemporaries in the "first avant-garde" is clear from these words, written by Marcel L'Herbier in 1946: "It is around her thought and her work that are crystallized in large part the principles on which an intelligence of the cinema can be founded in order to grow."

—*L.H.*

FILMS: Les soeurs ennemies (Enemy Sisters), 1916; Géo, le mystérieux (Geo the Mysterious), 1916; Vénus Victrix, ou Dans l'Ouragan de la vie (Venus Victrix, or In the Whirlwind of Life), 1917; Âmes de fous (Mad Souls), 1917; Le Bonheur des autres (The Happiness of Others), 1918; La Fête espagnole (The Spanish Fiesta), 1919; La Cigarette (The Cigarette), 1919; Malencontre (Misadventure), 1920; La Belle Dame sans merci (The Beautiful Lady Without Pity), 1920; La Mort du Soleil (The Death of the Sun), 1921; Werther, 1922 (unfinished); La Souriante Madame Beudet (The Smiling Madame Beudet), 1923; Gossette, 1922–1923 (six episodes); Le Diable dans la ville (The Devil in the Streets), 1924; Âme d'artiste (Soul of an Artist), 1925; La Folie des vaillants (The Folly of the Brave), 1925; Antoinette Sabrier, 1926; Le Coquille et le clergyman (The Seashell and the Clergyman), 1927; L'Invitation au voyage (Invitation to the Voyage), 1927; Le Cinéma au service de l'histoire (The Cinema in the Service of History), 1927 (documentary); La Princesse Mandane, 1928; (as supervisor) Mon Paris (My Paris), 1928; Disque 927 (Disc 927), 1928; Thèmes et Variations (Themes and Variations), 1928; Germination d'un Haricot (Germination of a Bean), 1928 (documentary); Étude Cinégraphique sur une arabesque (Film Study of an Arabesque), 1929; (as supervisor) Le Picador, 1932. *Published screenplays*—La Fête espagnole, by Louis Delluc, 1919 (France); La Souriante Madame Beudet, by André Obey, 1923 (France); La Coquille et le clergyman, by Antonin Artaud, 1927 (France).

ABOUT: Abel, R. French Cinema: The First Wave, 1919–1929, 1984; Bardèche, M. and Brasillach, R. Histoire du cinéma, 1953; Brunius, J. B. En marge du cinéma français, 1954; Dictionnaire de biographie française, 1970; Fescourt, H. La Foi et les montagnes, 1959; Ford, C. Germaine Dulac, 1968 (France; originally published as supplement to L'Avant-Scène du Cinéma January 1968); Ford, C. Les Femmes cinéastes, 1972; Lawder, S. D. The Cubist Cinema, 1975; Manvell, R. (ed.) Experiment in the Film, 1949; Smith, S. Women Who Make Movies, 1975; Van Wert, W. Women and the Cinema, 1977. *Periodicals*—Chaplin December 1968; Cinema Journal Spring 1970; Close Up June 1928; Film Comment November–December 1972; Film Library Quarterly Winter 1971–1972; Films in Review November 1950; New York Times July 23, 1942; Take One November–December 1970; Wide Angle 1 1979; Woman and Film 5–6 1974.

JULIEN DUVIVIER

*DUVIVIER, JULIEN (October 8, 1896–October 29, 1967), French director and scenarist, was born in Lille, in northern France. He attended schools in the city and enrolled at Lille University, but left when he decided that he wanted to become an actor. After study at a Paris drama school he returned to Lille and began his career at the local theatre, in time moving on to the Paris Odéon, where he played a variety of roles in the classical repertoire. Duvivier turned from acting to directing when he was given the opportunity to become an assistant to André Antoine, prophet of naturalism in the French theatre and founder of the Théâtre Libre, which staged experimental plays of all kinds.

After a few seasons with Antoine, Duvivier found himself increasingly interested in the budding art of the cinema, which seemed to him to offer richer possibilities as a mode of expression than the theatre. With Antoine's encouragement, he began searching for a way into the film world and finally accepted work as an extra. His first picture, *Haceldama,* was made in 1919 under the niggardly sponsorship of a rich mustard manufacturer. To keep down the costs, Duvivier served as scenery builder, messenger, and costume designer as well as director, but just before shooting was to begin, the scenery was destroyed by fire. According to Duvivier, his sponsor "screamed when he heard the news, and continued screaming even after psychiatrists took the necessary steps and locked him away." After this discouraging beginning, Duvivier served his apprenticeship at Gaumont as writer, assistant director, and/or editor to such masters as Louis Feuillade and Marcel L'Herbier, and was soon a full-fledged director himself.

During the 1920s Duvivier made more than twenty silent films, ranging from family melodramas to religious epics, from comedy to documentary. He first attracted attention with *La Tragédie de Lourdes* (*The Tragedy of Lourdes,* 1924), a controversial if superficial drama about the conflict between science and religion. It had its premiere before an audience of three thousand in Duvivier's native Lille and was successful enough to warrant a sequel, *L'Agonie de Jérusalem* (*The Agony in Jerusalem,* 1926). *La Machine à refaire la vie* (*The Machine for Recreating Life,* 1925), made in collaboration with Henri Lepage, is a three-hour history and anthology of the cinema (including excerpts from *Caligari*). These early films were capable but on the whole undistinguished, the best of them being *Poil de Carotte* (1925), an adaptation of Jules Renard's autobiographical novel, and Duvivier's last silent film, a screen version of Zola's *Au bonheur des dames* (1929).

Duvivier's true talent emerged with the coming of sound. He showed his grasp of the new medium in his first talkie, *David Golder* (1930), based on Irène Nemirovsky's novel about an old Jewish financier abandoned by his friends and family, a sort of contemporary King Lear. Harry Baur gave a memorable performance in the title role, and the film enjoyed an international critical success.

There was an even warmer reception for Duvivier's remake in sound of *Poil de Carotte* (*Carrot-Top/The Red Head,* 1932), in which the child actor Robert Lynen brilliantly portrayed the sullen, sensitive, country boy, bullied by his monstrous mother, unbearably frustrated and misunderstood until his attempted suicide at last awakens his father's concern. Contrasting with

°dŏŏ vē vyā´

the misery of his home life is the famous episode of Poil de Carotte's "wedding" to his small girl-friend—a lyrical celebration of innocence amid blowing blossom and sparkling streams, the wedding march led by a cavorting old man with a hurdy gurdy. "All this might easily have slipped into sentimentality," wrote Dilys Powell. "The rhythm, the delicate use of detail, the reticent allusions of the camera have given it instead something of the innocence of a fragment of Blake." William Whitebait regards this small masterpiece as the best of all the director's films.

Duvivier followed it with a string of successes during the 1930s. *Maria Chapdelaine* (1934), from Louis Hémon's novel of French-Canadian life, was filmed on location in Canada. Rescued from melodrama by polished direction and a notable cast that included Madeleine Renaud, Jean-Pierre Aumont, and Jean Gabin, it won the Grand Prix du Cinéma Français and in the United States was voted one of the ten best films of 1935. Gabin, who was unknown until Duvivier recognized his potential, was to create some of his most famous roles under Duvivier's direction. He appeared again as Pontius Pilate in *Golgotha* (1935), a straight-forward and impressive account of the Crucifixion, and as a criminal seeking oblivion in *La Bandera* (1935), a story of Franco's Spanish Foreign Legion notable for exciting action scenes and (to quote Alistair Cooke) for Duvivier's "practically unique power . . . of looking generously at beautiful scenery without bursting into sobs." *La Bandera*, a great commercial and critical success, was the first of Duvivier's films to be scripted by Charles Spaak, the best of his writers and the scenarist also of some of the finest films of Jacques Feyder and Jean Renoir.

Gabin's screen persona as the tough, defiant, but sensitive working man was first clearly defined in *La Belle Équipe* (*The Good Bunch*, 1936), another Spaak script. The *"équipe"* is a group of workless men who sleep in a wretched flop-house and daily tramp the streets in a fruitless search for jobs. They win some money in a lottery and decide to buy a broken-down vaudeville theatre and run it themselves as a pleasure-garden and restaurant, working together for the common good in the spirit of the Popular Front. Duvivier filmed two endings to this story—an upbeat one for the regular audience and a tragical one for the elite. Although some critics have condemned the director for thus catering to the market, they have found little to dislike in either version of this admirable picture. *La Belle Équipe* was followed by Duvivier's unremarkable treatment of the Golem story and then (as if to demonstrate his versatility) by *L'Homme du jour* (*The Man of the Day*, 1936), starring Maurice Chevalier, a charming comedy reminiscent of René Clair.

Pépé-le-Moko (1936) is one of Duvivier's major contributions to the elegiac, fatalistic style of "poetic realism" that dominated the French cinema in the years leading up to World War II. It tells the romantic story of a notorious French outlaw drawn by love out of the safety of the Algiers Casbah, and was such an enormous box-office success that MGM immediately remade it as *Algiers* (1938), with Charles Boyer (whom Duvivier had originally wanted for the part) playing the role created by Gabin. The Hollywood version was also a great success, though Bosley Crowther had no doubt that Duvivier's was better in its "raw-edged, realistic, and utterly frank exposition of a basically evil story."

It was followed by the picture that confirmed Duvivier's international reputation as a major director, and with which his name has ever since been most intimately connected, *Un Carnet de bal* (*A Dance Program*, 1937). Made from the director's own script, it begins in a mood of sentimental nostalgia as a young widow decides to seek out the men she danced with at her first ball; it becomes increasingly bleak as she learns what the years have done to their hopes and ambitions. Reviewers vied with each other in their praise of the sensitivity and inventiveness of Duvivier's direction, and the brilliance of a pantheon of stars that includes Harry Baur, Raimu, Louis Jouvet, Fernandel, Françoise Rosay, and Pierre Blanchar.

Most critics singled out for special commendation the two most harrowing episodes in the film—the story that features Françoise Rosay as a woman, crazed by grief, who refuses to believe that her son is dead by suicide, and one in which Blanchar plays an epileptic abortionist in Marseilles, with winches and cranes shrieking from the docks outside and every shot taken at an angle: "the [abortionist's] dreadful cataracted eye," wrote Graham Greene, "the ingrained dirt upon his hands, the shrewish wife. . . . Nostalgia, sentiment, regret: the padded and opulent emotions wither before the evil detail: the camera shoots at a slant so that the dingy flat rears like a sinking ship. . . . There has been nothing to equal this episode on the screen since *Pépé*." Widely regarded by contemporary critics as Duvivier's masterpiece and "one of the great films of all time," *Un Carnet de bal* set the pattern for several of the director's subsequent pictures in which some unifying plot device holds together a number of star-studded vignettes.

In 1938 Duvivier directed his first Hollywood film, *The Great Waltz*, about the life and career of Johann Strauss the younger (played by Fernand Gravet). It had a mixed reception, Franz Hoellering describing it as "phony, awkwardly written, and with the exception of the [Vienna Woods] sequence, as unoriginal as it is crudely directed." Duvivier himself was unhappy with the film—he felt that he had been hamstrung by a bad script—but it had its admirers, and in an assessment of Duvivier's work written thirty years later, it was called "one of the great masterpieces of the romantic cinema, pervaded by the heady rhythms of the waltz, a symphony in soft focus." Duvivier made three more films in France before the outbreak of World War II— most notably *La Fin du jour* (*The End of the Day,* 1939). Written by Charles Spaak, it is another elegiac piece, set in a home for retired actors who attempt a comeback in the face of the ultimately insurmountable obstacles of infirmity and approaching death.

Duvivier left France in 1940 with his wife and young son and went to the United States. His first film as an expatriate was *Lydia* (1941), made for Alexander Korda. Starring Merle Oberon, it is virtually a remake of *Un Carnet de bal.* During the war years the director formed a company with Charles Boyer to make two more episodic films on the same pattern, *Tales of Manhattan* (1942) and the whimsical *Flesh and Fantasy* (1943). He returned to France in 1945 and for a time continued to make pictures in the style of poetic realism associated with Marcel Carné and his own prewar work, among them *Panique* (*Panic,* 1946), distinguished by Michel Simon's virtuoso performance as an eccentric persecuted by a mean-spirited community, *Au royaume des cieux* (*Woman Hunt,* 1949), and *Sous le ciel de Paris* (*Under the Paris Sky,* 1951).

However, the romantic melancholy of these films seemed inappropriate to the postwar mood, and in fact none of Duvivier's later work matched his highest achievements of the 1930s, though it was far from negligible. His adaptation of *Anna Karenina,* written by Jean Anouilh and starring Vivien Leigh and Ralph Richardson, was called an "exquisitely elegant and romantic version" even though purists complained that it misrepresented Tolstoy. Financially it fared poorly, but Duvivier's fortunes revived with the international success of *The Little World of Don Camillo* (1951) and *The Return of Don Camillo* (1953)—amiable entertainments based on the books by Giovanni Guareschi about a wily parish priest (Fernandel) and his running war with the town's communist mayor.

These successes allowed Duvivier to experiment a little in some of his last films. *La Fête à Henriette* (1952), in which two scriptwriters quarrel about how the story should develop, includes a sophisticated burlesque of film clichés, while *Marianne de ma jeunesse* (1955) is a subtle and stylish evocation of German romanticism made, Duvivier said, simply to please himself. In 1957 he scored another success with his bittersweet comedy *Pot-Bouille* (*The House of Lovers*), adapted from Zola. *La Femme et le pantin* (*A Woman Like Satan,* 1959) starred Brigitte Bardot in a story—rather in his old style of poetic fatalism—about a man progressively destroyed by his love for a young dancer.

Roy Armes has suggested that Duvivier, "who had for a while in the thirties given the illusion of being a great director, returned to purely commercial production after 1945, and his numerous films, though reaching a wide audience, have little lasting value." This harsh and sweeping judgment is the fashionable one, but it is not universally held. It is true that Duvivier was not one of those great masters of the "cinema eye" who impose their singular visions on whatever material comes to hand; he could not make good films from bad scripts. But he had a real talent for the creation of atmosphere and the imaginative sympathy to draw fine performances from his actors. Moreover, as his obituarist wrote in the London *Times,* there is in his work "a persistent strain of romantic nostalgia . . . and in his best and most lasting films this comes to the surface, either to be happily elaborated, or analysed and rejected (as in *Carnet de bal*). . . . His other films could have been made by many another skilled craftsman, but in these he created something memorable and quite individual."

Duvivier was a "shy and slender man," affable and unassuming in private life though a martinet on the set, impatient of delays and incompetence. Many of his films have urban settings, but in fact he disliked crowds, cities, and noise, and in *Poil de Carotte* and a few other pictures gives lyrical proof of his feeling for the countryside.

—*K.B.*

FILMS: Haceldama/Le Prix du sang, 1919; (with Bernard Deschamps) L'Agonie des aigles, 1921; Les Roquevillard, 1922; L'Ouragan sur la montagne, 1922; Der Unheimliche Gast/Le Logis de l'horreur, 1922 (Germany); Le Reflet de Claude Mercoeur, 1923; Coeurs farouches, 1923; L'Oeuvre immortelle, 1924 (Belgium); La Tragédie de Lourdes (The Tragedy of Lourdes)/Credo, 1924; (with Henri Lepage) La Machine à refaire la vie (The Machine for Recreating Life), 1925 (remade with sound 1933); L'Abbé Constantin, 1925; Poil de Carotte (The Red Head/Carrot-Top), 1925 (remade with sound 1932); L'Agonie de Jérusalem (The Agony in Jerusalem), 1926; L'Homme à l'Hispano, 1926; Le Mariage de Mademoiselle Beulemans, 1927; Les Mystères de la Tour Eiffel, 1927; Le Tourbillon de Paris, 1928; La Vie miraculeuse de Thérèse Martin, 1929; La Divine croisière, 1929; Maman Colibri, 1929; Au Bonheur des dames, 1929; David Golder, 1930; Les Cinq Gentlemen maudits, 1931; Allo Berlin? Ici Paris!, 1932; La Vénus du collège, 1932; Le Petit roi, 1933; La Tête d'un homme, 1933; Le Paquebot Tenacity, 1934; Maria Chapdelaine (The Naked Heart), 1934; Golgotha, 1935; La Bandera, 1935; La Belle Équipe (The Good Bunch/They Were Five), 1935; Le Golem (The Legend of Prague), 1935 (Czechoslovakia); L'Homme du jour (The Man of the Day), 1936; Pépé-le-Moko, 1936; Un Carnet de bal (A Dance Program/Life Dances On/Christine), 1937; The Great Waltz, 1938 (USA); La Fin du jour (The End of the Day), 1939; La Charrette fantôme, 1939; Untel père et fils (The Heart of a Nation), 1940; Lydia, 1941 (Britain); Tales of Manhattan, 1942 (USA); Flesh and Fantasy/Obsessions, 1943 (USA); The Imposter, 1943 (USA); Panique (Panic), 1946; Anna Karenina, 1947 (Britain); Au royaume des cieux (Woman Hunt), 1949; Black Jack, 1950 (Spain); Sous le ciel de Paris (Under the Paris Sky), 1951; Il piccolo mondo di Don Camillo/Le Petit Monde de Don Camillo (The Little World of Don Camillo), 1951 (Italy); La Fête à Henriette (Henriette), 1952; Il ritorno di Don Camillo/Le Retour de Don Camillo (The Return of Don Camillo), 1953; L'Affaire Maurizius (On Trial), 1953; Voici le temps des assassins (Murder à la carte), 1955; Marianne de ma jeunesse, 1955; Pot-Bouille (The House of Lovers), 1957; L'Homme à l'imperméable, 1957; Das Kunstseidene Mädchen/La Grand Vie, 1959 (GFR); Marie-Octobre, 1959; La Femme et le pantin (A Woman Like Satan), 1959; Boulevard, 1960; Le Diable et les dix commandements (The Devil and the Ten Commandments), 1962; La Chambre ardente (The Burning Court/The Curse of the Coffin), 1962; Chair de poule (Highway Pick-Up), 1963; Diaboliquement votre (Diabolically Yours), 1967.

ABOUT: Current Biography, 1943; Chirat, R. Julien Duvivier, 1968 (France); Jeanne, R. and Ford, C. Paris vue par le cinéma, 1969; Leprohon, P. Julien Duvivier, 1968 (France); Leprohon, P. Présences contemporaines, Cinéma, 1957 (France); Robinson, D. World Cinema, 1973; Sadoul, G. French Film, 1953. Periodicals—Bianco e nero January 1956; Cahiers de la Cinémathèque Spring, Summer 1975; New York Times October 30, 1967; Times November 10, 1967; Times (London) October 30, 1967.

ALLAN DWAN

DWAN, "ALLAN" (JOSEPH ALOYSIUS) (April 3, 1885–December 21, 1981), American director, scenarist, and producer, was born in Toronto, Canada, the younger son of Joseph Michael Dwan, a clothing merchant, and the former Mary Hunt. While Dwan was still young his family moved first to Detroit, and then in 1893 to Chicago. From North Division High School he entered Notre Dame University to study electrical engineering. He also became a football star "in a small way" and an enthusiastic member of the dramatic society.

After graduating in 1907, Dwan was invited to stay on for a year, coaching football and teaching math and physics. By now, tired of the teasing, he had changed his given name from Aloysius to the more robust "Allan." His postgraduate year over, he joined a local engineering firm, the Peter Cooper Hewitt Company, as a lighting engineer, and helped develop the mercury vapor arc, forerunner of the neon tube. While Dwan was supervising the installation of these lamps in the Chicago Post Office, a passerby came in to ask if their light would be good for photography. Certainly, said Dwan; whereupon the stranger, George K. Spoor of the Essanay Film Company, ordered a consignment for his studio.

During the installation of the arcs at Essanay, Dwan took the opportunity of studying the movie business in action: "It kind of fascinated me— the silly pictures they were making under the lights." Finding that the studio bought their stories "from anybody" and paid up to $25, he dug out fifteen he had written for the Notre Dame college magazine. Essanay bought the lot, and furthermore offered Dwan the job of scenario editor at $300 a week—far more than he could earn as an engineer.

Soon after Dwan joined Essanay, a group of executives broke away to form their own company, the American Film Company, and invited him to come in with them at twice his current salary. Dwan readily accepted, working in Tucson, Arizona, as a combined scenarist and unit manager with the director Frank Beal. Early in 1911, he was sent out to California, where Beal had been transferred, to find out why no films were emanating from the unit. Dwan finally tracked it down in San Juan Capistrano. What happened then was amusingly dramatized by Peter Bogdanovich in his movie about the pioneering days of the industry, *Nickelodeon* (1976).

According to Dwan, "There were about eight actors, a lot of cowboys, some horses, and everyone was sitting there doing nothing. I said, 'Why aren't you working?' They said, 'Well, our director has been away on a binge for two weeks in Los Angeles, and we don't see him very often, so we haven't made any pictures.' It looked like a pretty sad situation and I wired the Chicago office, 'I suggest you disband the company. You have no director.' They wired back, 'You direct.' So I got the actors together and said, 'Now, either I'm a director or you're out of work.' And they said, 'You're the best damn director we ever saw. You're great.' I said, 'What do I do? What does a director do?' So they took me out and showed me. And it worked."

Evidently, so it did. Between May 1911 and June 1913, working on a succession of California locations, Dwan turned out some 250 one-reelers or half-reelers, scripting, directing, and editing two or three films a week, and taking the weekend off. "We could have made five or six films [a week], but the producers didn't need them, so we just shot three." The great majority were Westerns (not surprisingly, given the ready-made locations), but Dwan happily threw in the occasional documentary—*Santa Catalina, Magic Isle of the Pacific* (1911) or *A Midwinter Trip to Los Angeles* (1912). American seemed delighted to take whatever he sent them. "We'd just send the negatives in and they'd print them and write back their congratulations. They didn't make any comment except 'Fine, keep them coming.' . . . I never asked anybody's permission for anything." Even the Patents' Company, bane of early filmmakers, left the outfit alone after Dwan treated a Company heavy to a display of fancy tin-can shooting.

Towards the end of 1912 he set up a second unit under Wallace Reid, which produced an equally copious flow of one-reelers, with Dwan acting as supervisor. Among his team at this time were two other future directors, Victor Fleming and Marshall Neilan, both Dwan discoveries, as well as Eugene Pallette, still relatively slim and usually cast as a villain. Little of the work that Dwan directed under American's Flying A logo has survived; but what there is, Peter Bogdanovich suggested, shows how rapidly he was learning and developing his technique. "*Three Million Dollars* (1911), shot in his fifth month as a director (and already close to his fortieth one-reeler), reflects the primitive beginnings. . . .

The camera records the entire action of each scene from one set-up—usually a medium long-shot—without cutting it up. . . . A year and a half—and almost two hundred shorts—later, *Calamity Anne's Trust* (1913) reveals [D. W. Griffith's] impact. The camera is much closer to the action now, there is cutting within scenes, greater flexibility, the compositions are no longer merely functional, and the acting has some charm."

Dwan was by now recognized to be a thoroughly capable and professional director, and in mid-1913 Carl Laemmle offered him an astonishing $1,500-a-week contract at Universal. He moved over, taking both his Flying A units with him, and graduated to the relatively leisurely business of making two-reelers—two or three a month. The more relaxed schedule allowed Dwan to show he could be imaginative and versatile as well as prolific: his output for Universal included melodramas, comedies, several Civil War pictures, and a film based on Gray's "Elegy," *The Restless Spirit* (1913), incorporating twenty-four dissolves—an unheard-of number at that time, when each dissolve had to be done in the camera, and one slip could ruin the whole reel. He was also chosen to direct a promotional film, *The Great Universal Mystery* (1914), featuring the entire studio payroll, Laemmle included. (Dwan's own unit included two notable prop men: Jack—later John—Ford, and Lon Chaney, whose eagerness to act was so evident that Dwan soon gave him his first role in *Back to Life*, made in 1913.) His final film for Universal was also his first feature-length movie, the six-reel costume drama *Richelieu* (1914).

In 1914 Dwan accepted an offer from Famous Players, which had been set up in New York by Adolph Zukor to raise the tone of the movie industry by bringing in noted stage actors. "That intrigued me. . . . But the theatre actors were terrible. They couldn't work our way." Undeterred, Dwan continued to extend and improve his technique, bringing to his films inherent dramatic and visual skills, and an engineer's knack for solving technical problems. For *David Harum* (1915) he invented the dolly shot, mounting the camera on a specially-prepared Ford car to follow an actor down the street. Exhibitors protested that these antics made their audiences feel seasick, but Dwan went on to devise the first crane shot, by attaching his camera to a construction derrick. Later, Dwan tended to deprecate his own innovations, paying tribute to Griffith as the great pioneer. "I watched everything he did, and then I'd do it, in some form or another. I'd try to do it in another way—I'd try to do it better. And I'd try to invent something that *he'd* see. . . . We did lots of things Griffith didn't do. But his achievements are the real, vivid things."

Dwan stayed a year with Famous Players, directing over a dozen features for them (including two starring Mary Pickford), before Griffith "finally sent for me and said he was sick of competing, and would I join him at Triangle?" Dwan would and did, relishing the chance of working alongside the great man. That same year, 1915, he married Pauline Bush, who had starred in virtually all of his films at Universal.

While Dwan drew inspiration from Griffith's creative flair, Griffith in his turn benefited from Dwan's technical ingenuity. In *Intolerance* (1916) Griffith wanted the camera to soar to the top of his colossal Babylonian set and descend again, but could see no way of achieving it. He consulted Dwan, who devised a contraption consisting of an elevator on railroad tracks—rock steady, and minutely controllable. The resulting sequence, in Kevin Brownlow's opinion, "is still the most gasp-producing shot in film-history."

At Triangle, Dwan directed vehicles for Norma Talmadge, Lillian Gish, and Dorothy Gish, and began a highly successful association with Douglas Fairbanks. Starting with *The Habit of Happiness* (1916), the two men together made eleven films that constitute some of the best work either of them ever did. Dwan, who shared much of Fairbanks' cheerfully extrovert character, was the ideal collaborator in establishing the star's persona as the genial, all-American hero, gracefully athletic. Peter Bogdanovich described their fourth film together, *Manhattan Madness* (1916), as "fast-paced . . . , cleverly written, even boisterously witty in its look at western and eastern lifestyles (a cowboy comes to New York to sell his cattle) . . . it is evocatively photographed on location in the city, features unusual and impressive lighting and confirms beyond question that by this time Dwan already had complete mastery of his medium."

From 1917 onwards, while continuing to supervise productions at Triangle, Dwan began to direct for a number of independent outfits, including Mary Pickford's Artcraft Company, where several of his Fairbanks pictures were made. His first independent film was made for a company that Dwan himself set up with Joe Schenck and Norma Talmadge. This was *Panthea* (1917), a Russian drama, in which Dwan demonstrated a skill that would later stand him in good stead: the ability to create opulent effects out of minimal resources, as Kenneth MacGowan noted in *New Republic* of September 15, 1917. "He builds up amazingly effective prisons with nothing but inky shadows,

and constructs a palatial dining room out of a great space of floor and table and a very large chandelier above. . . . When he gets to the swiftest part of his story, he drives us through it unerringly and irresistibly by following physical actions to the minutest details."

Writers on Dwan's films have often singled out his characteristically effective use of visual space. "From his earliest silent films to his last films in color," observed Jean-Claude Biette in *Cahiers du Cinéma* (February 1982), "one finds a constant exaltation of space, like that of Keaton." The comparison is apt: both men were fascinated by machinery and enthusiastic creators of intricate devices; both came to filmmaking by sheer accident, without any previous training; and both seem to have been endowed with an innate sense of narrative pacing and cinematic composition. To this instinct, Dwan added a relaxed sense of humor, an evident joy in dramatic motion, and a knack for eliciting natural, unforced playing from his actors. A stocky, congenial man, he was known as a good-humored and considerate director, who never took himself seriously enough to become dictatorial. He was also popular with his crews, who appreciated his practical ability and lack of pretension.

In 1920 Dwan and a number of other directors—among them Maurice Tourneur, Thomas Ince, Clarence Brown and Mack Sennett—formed an independent company called Associated Producers. Dwan directed three pictures for Associated—one of which, *A Perfect Crime* (1921), featured the first screen role of the twelve-year-old Carole Lombard—but the company never achieved financial viability, and lasted only a couple of years.

The climax of Dwan's association with Fairbanks came with *Robin Hood* (1922), at that time the most expensive film ever made. Fairbanks, initially reluctant to play "a flat-footed Englishman walking through the woods" and worried that he might be upstaged by the gigantic castle set, became increasingly enthusiastic as Dwan demonstrated how the towering walls, battlements, and staircases would become a spectacular backdrop for his exuberant stunts.

Dwan's confidence proved justified. *Robin Hood* was hugely successful, both at the box office and with the critics. Robert Sherwood acclaimed it as "the highwater mark of film production—the farthest step that the silent drama has ever taken along the high road to art." More recently, Kevin Brownlow asserted that "purely on the level of art direction, *Robin Hood* is an unsurpassed and unsurpassable achievement. . . . Nobody connected with it ever achieved anything quite like it again." Dwan himself rated it among his favorite pictures, and it remains the film for which he is best remembered. For all its visual grandeur, though, much of the picture now seems ponderous, especially by comparison with the spirited Flynn-Curtiz version of 1938. Crucial roles are poorly cast—Paul Dickey, as the villainous Guy of Gisbourne, hams outrageously (a rare fault in Dwan's films), and Enid Bennett makes an insipid Marian. In the first half of the movie at least, Eileen Bowser thought, even Fairbanks seemed "a little subdued by it all."

Dwan's marriage to Pauline Bush ended in divorce in the early '20s. His second marriage, to Marie Shelton, a former Ziegfeld Follies girl, took place not long afterwards. With the success of *Robin Hood,* Dwan now ranked as one of Hollywood's leading directors, a status confirmed by *Big Brother* (1923), a romantic gangland movie in which a hood adopts a homeless orphan. Several scenes were shot on location in Harlem, using real gangsters as extras; Dwan described it as "one of those that just jelled and meshed—everybody loved it. A nothing that turned into something big." *Big Brother* was made for Dwan's old outfit Famous Players—now aggrandized into Famous Players–Lasky–Paramount—which he had just rejoined. For them he also directed seven films with Gloria Swanson, beginning with *Zaza* (1923), in which she played a music-hall artiste in love with a married diplomat. As with Fairbanks, Dwan established an exceptional rapport with Swanson, and their films together, in David Robinson's opinion, represent "Dwan's most appealing work . . . which dealt good humouredly with recognisable human situations."

Manhandled (1924), Dwan's own favorite, is generally reckoned the best of the series. Swanson plays a shopgirl who, neglected by her inventor boyfriend, decides to sample high society in the guise of a Russian princess. The film includes a startlingly realistic subway sequence, in which Swanson as a humble commuter gets ruthlessly battered by the rush-hour crowds. Since the actress had never traveled by subway, Dwan stood her to a trip on the 42nd Street shuttle: "I waited for a real pack, shoved her aboard, and left her in there. . . . When we did the subway scene she was terrific. She got howls of laughter. She knew what she was doing." Dwan exploited Swanson's comic talents equally effectively in *Stage Struck* (1925), where she plays a small-town waitress aspiring to become a great actress. For her dream sequence Dwan, intrigued as ever by technical innovation, broke into Technicolor—one of the earliest uses of the process in a feature film.

In 1926 Dwan signed with Fox, for whom he was to work on and off for the next fifteen years. It may have been a bad move. From this point, insofar as one can be fixed, seems to date the decline in his career; the remaining silent films that he made for Fox (not all of which have survived) were an unremarkable bunch. Dwan always regretted the passing of the relaxed, unregulated era in which he had learned his craft: "When we had control of our pictures, we had no trouble. Our trouble has happened when others have control." He also regretted the passing of silent movies ("It was the end of a fine art") but with his habitual technical fluency took effortlessly to sound. His first sound film was in fact a short newsreel: *West Point* (1927), where he filmed a troop review to show the nervous studio executives that sound filming on location presented no great problems.

Dwan still had one good silent movie to direct: *The Iron Mask* (1929), his last film with Douglas Fairbanks, made for United Artists. A sequel to *The Three Musketeers,* the picture has an elegiac feel to it; it was not only Dwan's last silent film, but effectively the end of Fairbanks' career. At the end of the film he died on-screen—for the first and only time—and then appeared in a spoken epilogue to take his leave of the audience.

The assignments were becoming noticeably less prestigious, but Dwan continued to explore the potential of his medium, experimenting with the newly invented zoom lens in *Tide of Empire* (1929) and attaching the supposedly static microphone to a traveling boom for *Frozen Justice* (1929). ("It terrified the sound people: 'You can't do it—impossible!' But we did.") By way of a coda to his silent years, he directed one last film with Gloria Swanson, whose fortunes were also in decline. *What a Widow!* (1930) was her last successful picture, until Billy Wilder coaxed her into *Sunset Boulevard* twenty years later.

Throughout his career, Dwan could be relied on to make a workmanlike job—and often something more—out of the least inspiring material. Despite a rickety plot, *While Paris Sleeps* (1932) is "his best early talkie, and . . . one of his most interesting films," according to Peter Bogdanovich, who thought that its "gloomy, dank and shadowy atmosphere" foreshadowed Marcel Carné's fatalistic classics of the late 1930s. After this, Dwan spent a year and a half in Britain, where he directed three films—one of them (*Her First Affaire,* 1933) starring Ida Lupino, then fifteen.

Memories in Hollywood, always short, were never shorter than during the early years of sound. Dwan returned after his eighteen months' absence to find himself one of the forgotten people, an outmoded primitive from the archaic silent era. Patiently he started again from scratch, writing a script which he then offered to Fox on condition they let him direct. This was *Black Sheep* (1935), a lightly amusing shipboard comedy with Claire Trevor; it looked like a masterpiece by comparison with the string of wretched B-movies to which the studio now assigned him. Dwan tackled them with his customary professionalism and good humor, and gradually fought his way back to slightly better projects, beginning with two Shirley Temple vehicles. Dwan's children's movies, wrote William Routt in *American Film* (September 1976), "ring with sincerity and are never condescending." Certainly *Heidi* (1937) and *Rebecca of Sunnybrook Farm* (1938) are far less mawkish and cutesy than most of Temple's films. Dwan aimed to temper the sentimentality with a good deal of humor, "because it can get awfully sticky if you really make those kind of stories seriously."

Having proved himself, Dwan was entrusted with a big-budget assignment: the historical spectacular *Suez* (1938), starring Tyrone Power as de Lesseps, builder of the Canal. What the picture lacks in dramatic interest it makes up for with impressive special effects, in particular a terrifying sandstorm that threatens to destroy the half-finished canal—a sequence whose technical challenges Dwan took up with evident relish. After a couple of spoofs—*The Three Musketeers* (1939), which managed to be funny despite the unappealing presence of the Ritz Brothers, and *The Gorilla* (1939), which didn't—Dwan rounded off the decade with a good Western: *Frontier Marshal* (1939), starring Randolph Scott as Wyatt Earp cleaning up Tombstone, Arizona.

Despite good box-office returns, Dwan found himself back on the B-movie treadmill; he seems, for some reason, to have been unpopular with Darryl Zanuck, Fox's chief of production. Whenever possible, he worked for other studios, directing for Universal an enjoyable comedy-Western, *Trail of the Vigilantes* (1940), and for RKO *Look Who's Laughing* (1941), the first of three amiably inane comedies showcasing various radio personalities.

When his contract expired in 1941 Dwan quit Fox and signed with Edward Small, an independent producer. Their first film together was *Friendly Enemies* (1942), an adaptation of a Broadway hit which Dwan, to fill a hiatus in Small's schedule, prepared and shot in sixteen days "on a set we inherited from Paramount." He then spent some months working with the Army's Photographic Division, helping to train camera units, before returning to Small to make a run of fast-paced, farcical comedies: *Up in Mabel's Room* (1944), *Abroad with Two Yanks* (1944), *Brewster's Millions* (1945), and *Getting Gertie's Garter* (1946).

These films, warmly received at the time, have since aroused oddly diverse critical opinions. William Routt saw them as a "lecherous bunch of comedies . . . full of extroverted tastelessness and vulgarly elemental humor." By contrast, Donald Phelps admired the way that Dwan "reduced the conventions of second-rate stage humor to pure speed: these comedies are fantasies of speed and maneuver, all prurience (except what serves to clock the players) boiled away: seamless, translucent, and not so much funny as exhilarating." Jeff Wise, though, writing in *Bright Lights* (Summer 1976), detected in them, as in Dwan's later Westerns, "an ugly and undeniable fatalism," and John M. Smith (*Brighton Film Review,* February 1970) found the comedy of *Brewster's Millions*—where a man must spend a million dollars with nothing to show for it, in order to inherit seven million more—"nightmarish and on the point of despair." The director's own uncomplicated rationale was that "I knew they'd be seen by a lot of kids at war and in army camps—and they'd cheer them up."

In 1945 Dwan signed a long-term contract with Republic Pictures, a B-movie factory run by Herbert J. Yates—"a fine man, a good businessman and a *lousy* producer" (Dwan's italics). "I had all the freedom in the world, except that the final decision as to whether a story would be made or not, and what the cast would be, was up to Herbert Yates." Further occupational handicaps at Republic were the boss's obsessive stinginess over budgets and frequent obligatory casting of his wife, the glacially untalented Vera Hruba Ralston. Nonetheless, during his eight years with the studio, Dwan managed to make a few passable films and one outstanding war movie, while having quiet fun sending up the rest of the material.

His first film for Republic was one of the better ones: *Rendezvous With Annie* (1946), another lively sex comedy, in which a serviceman sneaks home AWOL to see his wife and then has to account for the subsequent pregnancy. There followed a brace of trivial musicals, *Calendar Girl* (1947) and *Northwest Outpost* (1947), which Dwan made with his tongue lodged firmly in his cheek: "Nelson Eddy riding . . . into town with a lot of Cossacks singing 'hallabaloo'"; *Driftwood* (1947), a rural drama engagingly acted by Walter Brennan and the nine-year-old Natalie Wood; *The Inside Story* (1948), an economic parable; *Angel in Exile* (1948), the first of Dwan's late Westerns; and his last big picture, *Sands of Iwo Jima* (1949).

For *Iwo Jima,* a highly patriotic war movie, Dwan talked Yates into allowing him a workable budget and stretched it with skillful use of wartime actuality footage; the resulting battle sequences still carry a startlingly powerful impact. John Wayne starred; his performance as the tough, emotionally scarred Sergeant Stryker gained him his first Oscar nomination. The film was a considerable success, Dwan's only postwar box-office hit; on the strength of it, he tried to persuade Yates to think big a second time, but to no avail. "He had heart failure when he had that much money tied up in one picture." The rest of Dwan's time at Republic was spent on largely undistinguished programmers. He visited RKO for a Western, *Montana Belle* (1952), and moved to that studio in 1954.

Dwan's own view of his career, broadly accepted by such writers as Brownlow and Bogdanovich, placed his finest work firmly in the silent era, and dismissed most of his subsequent films (barring perhaps *Suez* and *Iwo Jima*) as little more than negligible hackwork. In more recent years, though, a different perspective has been suggested, and several critics would concur with Gary Morris's assessment (*Bright Lights,* 1979) that "his richest period is the fifties." In particular, these writers have singled out the string of low-budget Westerns and dramas that Dwan made with Benedict Bogeaus at RKO.

As an independent producer, Bogeaus had gained a reputation for extravagance; the studio accordingly assigned Dwan to him as a practically-minded restraining influence. "We had a very good relationship. . . . I went in as a policeman and ended up friendly with him." Their first film together was a Western, *Silver Lode* (1954), in which a rancher on his wedding day is falsely accused of murder and hunted down. In this, as in much of Dwan's late work, Jacques Lourcelles (*Présence du Cinéma,* Autumn 1966) perceived "the idea of a place of refuge . . . found and threatened and lost, and which must therefore be recaptured." Jean Coursodon admired it as "a violently anti-McCarthy political Western with fine dialogue by Karen de Wolfe."

On *Passion* (1954), a revenge drama set in old California, Dwan was able to make good use of his favourite magpie approach to set-building: "We rented magnificent Spanish sets Warner Bros had built for some big picture, and then we moved over to Universal and used a lot of their sets. . . . And we were thieves too. We'd rent a certain section of a set on the lot, and if there was no one else working nearby, we'd pretty soon ex-

pand to a dozen sets instead of one little one. So we really got a picture that looked expensive and it wasn't."

Sometime during 1954, Dwan's wife Marie Shelton died. His next Western, *Tennessee's Partner* (1955), was rated by Bogdanovich "Dwan's most personal and sensitive work of the fifties," with "a melancholy glow that is most affecting and memorable." The plot, of the director's own choosing, was adapted from a Bret Harte story about two raffish frontier characters, a gambler and a saloon madam, caught up in a fatal double cross. Donald Phelps named the film, along with *Passion* and *The Most Dangerous Man Alive,* as "my favourite Dwans . . . with their coruscations of plot, their picaresque chains of incident, through which Dwan traces a skein of narrative logic."

In *Slightly Scarlet* (1956), taken from a novel by James M. Cain, Dwan vividly captured the grubby, sexually overheated atmosphere of Cain's world, although he felt himself "handcuffed" by the prevailing censorship. With Bogeaus, he moved over to Fox to make *The River's Edge* (1957), another offbeat Western, with interesting casting—Ray Milland and Anthony Quinn—weakened by the addition of Debra Paget ("she came with the rent"). Dwan stayed at Fox for the last of all his Westerns, the bizarre *The Restless Breed* (1957), in which the whole cast spend their time spying on each other. "The artificiality of the film is continually reinforced by ostentatious double-framing," wrote William Routt; "almost every scene takes place within the confines of an arch, a doorway, a window. . . . When violence finally erupts, its impact is doubled as battling figures literally burst through the visual restraints that have held them in check."

Dwan's last film, and his only science-fiction movie, was *The Most Dangerous Man Alive,* about a convict who starts to mutate after surviving a nuclear explosion. (In backhanded homage, Wim Wenders based his 1982 *The State of Things* on the vicissitudes of a film crew trying to shoot a remake of Dwan's movie.) Though completed in 1958, the film was not released until 1961, due to some unsuccessful sharp practice by Bogeaus. Dwan later worked on a project for Warners, to be called *Marine!,* but it fell through in 1967 when Jack Warner sold the studio.

Dwan's unpretentiously straightforward attitude to filmmaking has attracted relatively little critical attention. Apart from the invaluable book-length interview by Peter Bogdanovich and a chapter in Kevin Brownlow's *The Parade's Gone By,* "the quietest of directors" (as John M. Smith termed him) has been the subject of only a handful of articles. Writers largely agree that more than at first appears lies beneath the limpid surface of his films. "Dwan's economy," wrote Donald Phelps, "is not simple mechanical expediency, but something closer to courtly austerity. . . . Not simply the will to deny, but to deny in order to assert—even indulge—himself; wherein he is an artist." "His frankness, intimacy and gentleness are among the most moving qualities possessed by any director," John M. Smith stated, adding: "He conceals his art to what is probably a unique extent, and a great deal of his ingenuity goes into this concealment." John Dorr (*Take One,* May–June 1972), calling Dwan "a director without pretensions," remarked that "the rhythms of his editing, the clear, precise economical succession of shots, the detached, uncritical observation, suggest an abstract, meditative involvement more on the order of classical music—an art untouched by time." Less dauntingly, Jean-Claude Biette commented that Dwan "left us films which never raise their voices."

On the question of just what does lurk beneath the surface of Dwan's work, there is less unanimity. Jeff Wise, as mentioned above, detected an "undeniable fatalism"; in similar vein, Jacques Lourcelles spoke of "this tragic view of life, which one finds all through Dwan's work." John M. Smith suggested a less wholly pessimistic philosophy: "One of the central threads in Dwan's career is the overcoming of despair . . . by an appreciation of the potentially permanent value of relationships which are less than ideal." Dwan himself never conceded any thematic preoccupations beyond an interest in "any human story. Adventure, movement and romance. I deplored tragedy. . . . I don't mean you can't make unhappiness occasionally, but I just don't like to aim at a downbeat end."

"Dwan's best films," wrote Donald Phelps, "seem to me triumphs of brisk, clear intelligence which can extract the essential of narrative and character from a shaggy screenplay; an economy which fuses expediency and elegance (so that a high-budgeter like *Suez* and a cheapie like *Silver Lode* share the same urbane fluidity); and a quiet intensity of storytelling which follows even clichés which their screenwriters have stopped believing in, to their natural conclusions." Or, as Bogdanovich put it, "the feeling persists that Dwan could effectively do *something* with anything." Had he been less good-natured, less tolerantly ready to take whatever was offered, rather than hold out for worthwhile material, his reputation would most likely stand higher than it does. But then, his work might not have conveyed the sheer uninhibited delight in filmmaking that shines through all his movies, good and indifferent alike. As he told Kevin Brownlow, "It isn't a job, it's a disease. . . . Directing movies—I'd do it free, I like it that well."

Though nostalgic for the silent era, Dwan never expressed resentment or bitterness over the loss of his erstwhile preeminence in the film world. "If you get your head above the mob," he once remarked, "they try to knock it off. If you stay down you last for ever." In 1963, asked his ambition by *Cahiers du Cinéma,* he responded "to keep making films till I die," and though he directed nothing for the last twenty years of his life, he was still writing scripts in his mid-nineties. In November 1981 he suffered a stroke at his home in California; he died at the Motion Picture Country House, Woodland Hills, some six weeks later, aged ninety-six. He had no children by either of his marriages.

—*P.K.*

FILMS: *Shorts*—1911: Brandishing a Bad Man, A Western Dreamer; A Daughter of Liberty; A Trouper's Heart; Rattlesnakes and Gunpowder; The Ranch Tenor/The Foreman's Fixup; The Sheepman's Daughter; The Sagebrush Phrenologist; The Elopements on Double L Ranch; $5000 Reward—Dead or Alive; The Witch of the Range; The Cowboy's Ruse; Law and Order on Bar L Ranch; The Yiddisher Cowboy; The Broncho Buster's Bride; The Hermit's Gold; The Actress and the Cowboys; The Sky Pilot's Intemperance; A Western Waif; The Call of the Open Range; The Schoolma'am of Snake; The Ranch Chicken; Cupid in Chaps; The Outlaw's Trail; The Ranchman's Nerve; When East Comes West; The Cowboy's Deliverance; The Cattle Thief's Brand; The Parting Trails; The Cattle Rustler's End; Cattle, Gold and Oil; The Ranch Girl/The Ranch Girl's Rustler; The Poisoned Flume; The Brand of Fear; The Blotted Brand; Auntie and the Cowboys; The Western Doctor's Peril; The Smuggler and the Girl/The Diamond Smugglers; The Cowboy and the Artist; Three Million Dollars; The Stage Robbers of San Juan; The Mother of the Ranch; The Gunman; The Claim Jumpers/The Range Squatter; The Circular Fence; The Rustler Sheriff; The Love of the West; The Trained Nurse at Bar Z; The Miner's Wife; The Land Thieves; The Cowboy and the Outlaw; Three Daughters of the West; Caves of La Jolla (documentary); The Lonely Range; The Horse Thief's Bigamy; The Trail of the Eucalyptus; The Stronger Man; The Water War; The Three Shell Game; The Mexican; The Eastern Cowboy; The Way of the West; The Test; The Master of the Vineyard; Sloppy Bill of the Rollicking R; The Sheriff's Sisters; The Angel of Paradise Ranch/The Girl of the Ranch; The Smoke of the Forty-Five; The Man Hunt; Santa Catalina, Magic Isle of the Pacific (documentary); The Last Notch; The Gold Lust; The Duel of the Candles; Bonita of El Cajon;

1912: A Midwinter Trip to Los Angeles (documentary); The Misadventures of a Claim Agent; Broncho Busting for Flying A Pictures/Bucking Horses; The Winning of La Mesa; The Locket; The Relentless Outlaw; Justice of the Sage; Objections Overruled; The

Mormon; Love and Lemons; The Best Policy; The Real Estate Fraud; The Grubstake Mortgage; Where Broadway Meets the Mountains; An Innocent Grafter; Society and Chaps; The Leap Year Cowboy/February 29; The Land Baron of San Tee; An Assisted Elopement; From the Four Hundred to the Herd; The Broken Ties; After School; A Bad Investment; The Full Value; The Tramp's Gratitude; Fidelity; Winter Sports and Pastimes of Coronado Beach (documentary); The Maid and the Man; The Cowboy Socialist/The Agitator; Checkmate; The Ranchman's Marathon; The Coward; The Distant Relative; The Range Detective; Driftwood; The Eastern Girl/Her Mountain Home; The Pensioners; The End of the Feud; The Wedding Dress; The Mystical Maid of Jamasha Pass; The Other Wise Man; The Haters; The Thread of Life; The Wandering Gypsy; The Reward of Valor; The Brand; The Green Eyed Monster; Cupid Through Padlocks; For the Good of Her Men; The Simple Love; The Weaker Brother; Fifty Mile Auto Contest/Auto Race-Lakeside; The Wordless Message; The Evil Inheritance; The Marauders; The Girl Back Home; Under False Pretenses; Where There's a Heart; The Vanishing Race/The Vanishing Tribe; The Fatal Mirror; Point Loma, Old Town (documentary); The Tell-Tale Shells; Indian Jealousy; San Diego (documentary); The Canyon Dweller; It Pays to Wait; A Life for a Kiss; The Meddlers; The Girl and the Gun; The Battleground; The Bad Man and the Ranger; The Outlaw Colony; The Land of Death; The Bandit of Point Loma; The Jealous Rage; The Will of James Waldron; The Greaser and the Weakling; The Stranger at Coyote; The Dawn of Passion; The Vengeance that Failed; The Fear; The Foreclosure; White Treachery; Their Hero Son; Calamity Anne's Ward; Father's Favorite/The Favored Son; Jack of Diamonds/Queen of Hearts; The Reformation of Sierra Smith/The Lost Watch; The Promise; The New Cowpuncher; The Best Man Wins; The Wooers of Mountain Kate; One, Two, Three; The Wanderer; Maiden and Men; God's Unfortunate; Man's Calling; The Intrusion at Lompoc; The Thief's Wife; The Would-Be Heir; Jack's Word/A Man's Word; Her Own Country; Pals; The Animal Within; The Law of God; Nell of the Pampas; The Daughters of Señor Lopez; The Power of Love; The Recognition; Blackened Hills; Loneliness of Neglect;

1913: The Fraud that Failed; Another Man's Wife; Calamity Anne's Inheritance; Their Masterpiece; His Old-Fashioned Mother; Where Destiny Guides; The Silver-Plated Gun; A Rose of Old Mexico; Building the Great Los Angeles Aqueduct (documentary); Women Left Alone; Andrew Jackson; Calamity Anne's Vanity; The Fugitive; The Romance; The Finer Things; Love Is Blind; When the Light Fades; High and Low; The Greater Love; The Jocular Winds; The Transgression of Manuel; Calamity Anne, Detective; The Orphan's Mine; When a Woman Won't; An Eastern Flower; Cupid Never Ages; Calamity Anne's Beauty; The Renegade's Heart; Matches; The Mute Witness; Cupid Throws a Brick; Woman's Honor; Suspended Sentence; In Another's Nest; The Ways of Fate; Boobs and Bricks; Calamity Anne's Trust; Oil on Troubled Waters; The Road to Ruin; The Brothers; Human Kindness; Youth and Jealousy; Angel of the Canyons; The

Great Harmony; Her Innocent Marriage; Calamity Anne Parcel Post; Ashes of Three; On the Border; Her Big Story; When Luck Changes; The Wishing Seat; Hearts and Horses; The Reward of Courage; The Soul of a Thief; The Marine Law; The Road to Success; The Spirit of the Flag; The Call to Arms/In Love and War; Women and War; The Powder Flash of Death; The Picket Guard; Mental Suicide; Man's Duty; The Animal; The Wall of Money; The Echo of a Song; Criminals; The Restless Spirit; Jewels of Sacrifice; Back to Life; Red Margaret, Moonshiner; Bloodhounds of the North; He Called Her In; The Menace; The Chase; The Battle of Wills;

1914: The Lie; Honor of the Mounted; Remember Mary Magdalene; Discord and Harmony; The Menace to Carlotta; The Embezzler; The Lamb, the Woman, the Wolf; The End of the Feud; Tragedy of Whispering Creek; The Unlawful Trade; The Forbidden Room; The Hopes of Blind Alley; The Great Universal Mystery; The Small Town Girl; The Man on the Case. 1927: West Point (newsreel short).

Features—Richelieu, 1914; Wildflower, 1914; The County Chairman, 1914; The Straight Road, 1914; The Conspiracy, 1914; The Unwelcome Mrs Hatch, 1914; The Dancing Girl, 1915; David Harum, 1915; The Love Route, 1915; The Commanding Officer, 1915; May Blossom, 1915; The Pretty Sister of Jose, 1915; A Girl of Yesterday, 1915; The Foundling, 1915; Jordan is a Hard Road, 1915; Betty of Greystone, 1916; The Habit of Happiness/Laugh and the World Laughs, 1916; The Good Bad Man/Passing Through, 1916; An Innocent Magdalene, 1916; The Half-Breed, 1916; Manhattan Madness, 1916; Fifty-Fifty, 1916; Panthea, 1917; The Fighting Odds, 1917; A Modern Musketeer, 1917; Mr Fix-It, 1918; Bound in Morocco, 1918; He Comes Up Smiling, 1918; Cheating Cheaters, 1919; Getting Mary Married, 1919; The Dark Star, 1919; Soldiers of Fortune, 1919; The Luck of the Irish, 1920; The Forbidden Thing, 1920; A Perfect Crime, 1921; A Broken Doll, 1921; The Scoffer, 1921; The Sin of Martha Queed, 1921; In the Heart of a Fool, 1921; The Hidden Woman, 1922; Superstition, 1922; Robin Hood, 1922; The Glimpses of the Moon, 1923; Lawful Larceny, 1923; Zaza, 1923; Big Brother, 1923; A Society Scandal, 1924; Manhandled, 1924; Her Love Story, 1924; Wages of Virtue, 1924; Argentine Love, 1924; Night Life of New York, 1925; Coast of Folly, 1925; Stage Struck, 1925; Sea Horses, 1926; Padlocked, 1926; Tin Gods, 1926; Summer Bachelors, 1926; The Music Master, 1927; The Joy Girl, 1927; East Side, West Side, 1927; French Dressing, 1927; The Big Noise, 1928; The Iron Mask, 1929; Tide of Empire, 1929; The Far Call, 1929; Frozen Justice, 1929; South Sea Rose, 1929; What a Widow!, 1930; Man to Man, 1930; Chances, 1931; Wicked, 1931; While Paris Sleeps, 1932; Her First Affaire, 1933; Counsel's Opinion, 1933; The Morning After/I Spy, 1934; (with Richard Boleslawski and Roy Rowland) Hollywood Party, 1934; Black Sheep, 1935; Navy Wife, 1935; Song and Dance Man, 1936; Human Cargo, 1936; High Tension, 1936; 15 Maiden Lane, 1936; Woman-Wise, 1937; That I May Live, 1937; One Mile From Heaven, 1937; Heidi, 1937; Rebecca of Sunnybrook Farm, 1938; Josette,

1938; Suez, 1938; The Three Musketeers, 1939; The Gorilla, 1939; Frontier Marshal, 1939; Sailor's Lady, 1940; Young People, 1940; Trail of the Vigilantes, 1940; Look Who's Laughing, 1941; Rise and Shine, 1941; Friendly Enemies, 1942; Here We Go Again, 1942; Around the World, 1943; Up in Mabel's Room, 1944; Abroad with Two Yanks, 1944; Brewster's Millions, 1945; Getting Gertie's Garter, 1945; Rendezvous With Annie, 1946; Calendar Girl, 1947; Northwest Outpost, 1947; Driftwood, 1947; The Inside Story, 1948; (with Philip Ford) Angel in Exile, 1948; Sands of Iwo Jima, 1949; Surrender, 1950; Belle Le Grand, 1951; The Wild Blue Yonder, 1951; I Dream of Jeanie, 1952; Montana Belle, 1952; The Woman They Almost Lynched, 1953; Sweethearts on Parade, 1953; Flight Nurse, 1954; Silver Lode, 1954; Passion, 1954; Cattle Queen of Montana, 1954; Escape to Burma, 1955; Pearl of the South Pacific, 1955; Tennessee's Partner, 1955; Slightly Scarlet, 1956; Hold Back the Night, 1956; The River's Edge, 1957; The Restless Breed, 1957; Enchanted Island, 1958; The Most Dangerous Man Alive, 1958 (rel. 1961).

ABOUT: Bogdanovich, P. Allan Dwan: The Last Pioneer, 1971; Brownlow, K. Hollywood: The Pioneers, 1979; Brownlow, K. The Parade's Gone By, 1968; Coursodon, J. P. American Film Directors, 1983; Phelps, D. Covering Ground: Essays for Now, 1969; Robinson, D. Hollywood in the Twenties, 1968; Roud, R. Cinema: a Critical Dictionary, 1980; Sarris, A. The American Cinema, 1968; Thomson, D. A Biographical Dictionary of the Cinema, 1980. *Periodicals*—American Film September 1976; Bright Lights Summer 1976, 2–4 1979; Brighton Film Review February 1970; Cahiers du Cinéma February 1982; Cinéma (France) February 1982; Présence du Cinéma Autumn 1966; Take One May/June 1972.

EISENSTEIN, SERGEI MIKHAILOVICH (January 23, 1898–February 10, 1948), Soviet director, scenarist, and theoretician, was born in Latvia. He was the son of Mikhail Eisenstein, an engineer of German-Jewish descent who worked for the city of Riga, rising to become its chief architect, and of a Russian mother, Julia. Mikhail Eisenstein was a robust, vain, and jovial man but a domestic tyrant, with a neurotic passion for order. His wife, the daughter of a successful haulage contractor, was of a very different type— elegant, pretty, and wholly absorbed with the trivia of bourgeois life. The family was prosperous and cosmopolitan, conversing as freely in French or German as in Russian.

As a child, Sergei Eisenstein was docile and hypersensitive, and a voracious reader. He admired his father and hungered for the love and attention of his frivolous mother, receiving both in fuller measure from his illiterate nurse, Totya Pasha, a warm and motherly woman who provided the most stable relationship of Eisenstein's

SERGEI EISENSTEIN

childhood but also instilled in him the peasant superstitions he so nervously observed all his life. He had a Christian upbringing, his father (or grandparents) having renounced Judaism, and was profoundly impressed by the drama of the Russian Orthodox ritual, passing through "a period of hysterical, puerile religiosity and juvenile sentiments of mysticism" before he lost his faith.

Yon Barna, whose biography is the principal source of this note (together with Marie Seton's more detailed and more subjective account) singles out several formative experiences in Eisenstein's childhood. His "conscious awareness" was first aroused by a branch of white lilac hanging against his bedroom window—a "close-up" almost exactly repeated some years later on a Japanese screen placed in his room, but this time with a painted landscape behind, through which, Eisenstein said, he "became familiarized with the beauty of composition in depth." A much darker memory was of his mother on an occasion when she terrified him by denying their relationship, moving towards him with set face. Referring to the images of inexorable fate that recur in his films, Eisenstein wrote that "there you have all the characteristic elements: a fixed, stony expression; a mask with ice-cold eyes." And the "ocean of cruelty" in his own films he traces partly to a branding scene in an otherwise forgotten movie—a scene that haunted his dreams.

That could not have been the first film Eisenstein saw—his introduction to the cinema was a Méliès comedy, seen during a visit to Paris in 1906 with one or the other of his parents. By that time the family had broken up, his mother having used the upheavals of the 1905 Revolution as an excuse to leave her husband, with whom her relations had become increasingly strained. She had an income of her own and used it to furnish an elegant apartment in St. Petersburg. For a time Eisenstein divided his time between Riga and the imperial capital, where he began his education under an English governess.

In due course, his father found a post in St. Petersburg and the family was reunited. But one day Eisenstein came home from school to find that his mother had stripped the apartment and gone off alone to Paris. Bitterly hurt, he turned increasingly to his nurse for love and reassurance. It was she who took him regularly to the movies and introduced him to the circus, an entertainment that profoundly excited him. According to Marie Seton, he identified in particular with a clown—small like himself, and with a similarly large head—whose concealing makeup and costume he greatly envied.

Eisenstein's parents divorced in 1909, and for some years after that he lived mostly with relatives in Riga. There he began his lifelong friendship with Maxim Strauch, attended a *lycée,* and developed the precocious talent for sketching that won him a place at the School of Fine Arts. His father had other plans for him, however, and in 1914 Eisenstein returned to St. Petersburg (by then Petrograd) and entered the Institute of Civil Engineering, picking a course that "led not to mechanical, technical fields but . . . to architecture." He later acknowledged that it was the pursuit of "exact knowledge" begun at the Institute that led him to delve "deeper and deeper into the fundamentals of creative art."

In the capital, Eisenstein immersed himself in the theatre, the opera, and vaudeville, spending much spare time planning stage settings for imaginary productions. Early in 1917, a series of *avant-garde* productions by Vsevolod Meyerhold clinched his "unexpressed resolve to give up engineering" and devote himself to art. He seems to have been scarcely aware that Russia was hurrying towards revolution, being far more interested in his latest hero, Leonardo da Vinci. Reading Freud's psychoanalytical study of Leonardo confirmed his sense of a profound connection between himself and that aloof and multifaceted genius, at the same time awakening his interest in Freud and his work.

With the abdication of the Czar in March 1917 and the installation of Kerensky's Provisional Government, Eisenstein was at last drawn into the enormous events taking place around him, some of which formed the subjects of his first published newspaper cartoons. In November 1917 the Provisional Government was re-

placed by the revolutionary Council of People's Commissars and the following year the civil war began. Along with the other students at the Institute of Civil Engineering, Eisenstein joined the Red Army, for the next two years playing his part very consciously in the making of history. His father supported the Whites and later fled to Germany.

At first Eisenstein's engineering training was put to work in the building of defenses at Petrograd, Kholm, and Veliky Luky. During all the trials and horrors of his army service, he is said to have been "unfailingly good-humoured and full of life and energy," though he characteristically extended his day with long hours of reading, devouring the works of Maeterlinck, Ibsen, and Schopenhauer, among others. Marie Seton suggests that his blasphemous and foulmouthed wit developed at this time to disguise his acute physical modesty and "mortifying sensitivity" from coarser companions.

At Veliky Luky there was a lively theatrical company led by a painter named Eliseyev, and Eisenstein drew on its resources in organizing a drama group with soldiers from his unit, in February 1920 staging his first amateur productions. Eliseyev was impressed and soon afterwards secured Eisenstein's transfer to his theatre company as a designer. Various productions were planned and abandoned as the company was shuttled from place to place. At Minsk Eisenstein worked for a time on the decoration of an agitprop train, and soon after he was released from his duties to enter the Oriental Languages Department of the General Staff Academy in Moscow.

By this time Eisenstein had already learned several hundred words of Japanese. Accounts differ as to what had drawn him to these studies, but there is no doubt that he was fascinated by the language, by Japanese art and culture, and especially by the Kabuki theatre. And the impulse towards the development of Eisenstein's conception of cinematic montage is said to have grown out of his study of the written Japanese language, with its frequent combination of two stylized pictures or ideograms to convey a third idea (the notion of weeping, for example, being conveyed by representations of water and an eye).

In fact, Eisenstein never did pursue his Japanese studies. Arriving in starving, freezing Moscow in the autumn of 1920, with no ration book and nowhere to stay, he by chance encountered his boyhood friend Maxim Strauch, already intent on an acting career. They wandered the streets all night, talking about the past, the future, and their eagerness to share in the theatrical revolution that had already begun. Eisenstein moved into his friend's cramped flat on Chysti Prudi—his home for many years—and they began their search for jobs. The Moscow theatre was then in a state of creative and intellectual ferment, struggling to replace the bourgeois and academic conventions of the past with a truly revolutionary art and boiling with theories as to how this should be achieved. Many of the theorists came to lecture at the Moscow Proletkult—a discussion center as well as a workers' theatre—and it was there that Eisenstein and Strauch were eventually taken on.

Eisenstein's first assignment was to design the sets and costumes for *The Mexican,* an agitprop adaptation of a Jack London boxing story. His designs were highly stylized, contrasting spherical and square shapes in both costumes and sets, and he suggested that this stylization should be further contrasted with a totally naturalistic presentation of the key scene, a boxing match. This idea proved strikingly effective and brought Eisenstein promotion to codirector. The lead role in *The Mexican* was played by a young actor named Grigori Alexandrov, who became one of Eisenstein's closest collaborators. It is an indication of contemporary conditions that their long friendship began with a fight over a hunk of black bread, surrendered by Eisenstein when he discovered that Alexandrov had not eaten for two days.

In fact, these young artists seemed scarcely to notice their hardships. Eisenstein was then twenty-two and totally immersed in his new medium, but already troubled by doubts about it. It was, he was beginning to realize, a "poisonous" art which could so involve a spectator that he might find its fantasies a substitute for real experience and action. He decided that he must master the secrets of the medium, if only to "tear off its mask." In the fall of 1921, with this in mind, he entered Vsevolod Meyerhold's new State School for Stage Direction.

Meyerhold's directorial method combined improvisations with precise planning, a contradictory mixture very much in line with Eisenstein's own instincts. Meyerhold later claimed that "all Eisenstein's work has its origins in the laboratory where we once worked together as teacher and pupil. But our relationship was not so much the relationship of teacher and pupil as of two artists in revolt." Eisenstein acknowledged that he had never "loved, revered, and respected" anyone as much as Meyerhold.

During this period of study, Eisenstein subsisted partly on meals provided by the mother of another future film director, his friend and fellow student Sergei Yutkevich. There were no scholarships, and Eisenstein and Yutkevich supported themselves by designing sets and costumes for a great variety of Moscow productions, from Foregger's contemporary satires to Tikhonovich's production of *Macbeth.* In the summer of 1922 Eisenstein accompanied Foregger's troupe to Petrograd. There he met Grigori Kozintsev and Leonid Trauberg, leaders of the FEKS company (the Factory of the Eccentric Actor), which delighted him with its incorporation of circus and vaudeville techniques into dramatic productions.

Returning to Moscow in the fall of 1922, Eisenstein tried to interest Meyerhold in mounting a production in the FEKs manner, but failed. Soon after, following another disagreement, he left Meyerhold's school (though they were eventually reconciled). Eisenstein then accepted an invitation to become manager and artistic director of Pere Tru, a new and independent company based at the Moscow Proletkult. There, in emulation of FEKs, he established a rigorous training program that included circus skills, acrobatics, fencing, boxing, and other sports and games as well as more orthodox studies.

It was at this time that Eisenstein published his first important theoretical article, which appeared in *Lef* (3 1923), the influential magazine edited by the poet Vladimir Mayakovsky. The former engineer Eisenstein, seeking a "unit for measuring the force of art," believed he had found it in the "montage" (or assembling) of what he called "attractions." And "attractions" he defined as "every element that can be verified and mathematically calculated to produce certain emotional shocks"—like, for example, the gouging out of an eye in Grand Guignol. These attractions and excitements, "arbitrarily selected," should be organized into a "free montage" with "the aim of establishing certain final thematic effects."

Eisenstein was to carry these ideas very much further, but they played a crucial role in Pere Tru's first production, *Even a Wise Man Stumbles* (1923). Very loosely based on Ostrovsky's comedy of family intrigue, it became in Eisenstein's hands a rapid montage of political and religious satire, clown acts, and slapstick, set in a circus arena, and enlivened by acrobatic stunts, music-hall songs, and Grigori Alexandrov's death-defying traverse of the arena on the high wire. Another "attraction" was the screening of a short film in which Glumov (Alexandrov) mutates into a series of other characters and objects before driving off to the Proletkult Theatre (where Alexandrov would burst in person through the screen, waving the reel of film). And this film—Eisenstein's first—was itself a parody of Dziga Vertov's *Kino-Pravda* newsreels.

Even a Wise Man Stumbles was the hit of the 1923 season in Moscow, and Eisenstein continued his experiments in the "montage of attractions" with two propaganda plays by Sergei Tretyakov, *Listen Moscow* (1923) and *Gas Masks* (1924). In an attempt to make his "poisonous" art serve the purposes of revolutionary realism, Eisenstein staged the latter in an actual gas factory. The play closed after four performances, partly because it disrupted operations at the gasworks, partly because the reality of the setting only emphasized the play's artificiality. This was the final proof for Eisenstein that the theatre, "as an independent unit within a revolutionary framework . . . is out of the question. It is absurd to perfect a wooden plough; you must order a tractor." And that, for him, meant the cinema.

By this time, Eisenstein was familiar with D. W. Griffith's use of montage and the experiments of the German Expressionists, and had attended Lev Kuleshov's cinema workshop in the attic of Meyerhold's theatre. Even more valuable, he had studied the work of his friend, the editor-filmmaker Esther Shub, and in March 1924 actually assisted her in cutting Fritz Lang's *Dr. Mabuse* for Soviet audiences, for the first time fully realizing, as Yon Barna says, "that a piece of celluloid is a neutral thing as long as it remains in isolation, taking on meaning and the power to communicate only when it is united with a second piece."

Eisenstein's chance to apply his swarming ideas to the cinema came in 1924, when he was invited to collaborate on the script of a film to be coproduced by Proletkult and the Goskino studios. This was *Stachka* (*Strike*), planned as one of a series on the history of communism. Eisenstein researched the subject for months, working day and night, before he settled to the script. Apart from his Proletkult coscenarists, he drew on the skills and experience of Esther Shub and of the cameraman assigned to the film, Eduard Tisse or Tissé, thus beginning one of the most richly fruitful partnerships in cinema history. Eisenstein knew precisely what effects he wanted to achieve in *Strike,* but it was Tisse who showed him how they could be realized and who helped him secure confirmation as the film's director.

It had been agreed from the outset that the picture should deal with a typical rather than a specific strike, seeking to convey the very essence of revolutionary struggle. And this revolutionary theme was to be expressed in revolutionary terms. There was to be no "bourgeois" story line and no detailed characterization—only exemplary figures such as a "worker," "foreman," "spy," etc. The hero was to be the working class itself, not some Hollywood-style superman. Proletkult provided the actors, including Strauch and Alexandrov, who were joined by thousands of young factory workers for the crowd scenes. As soon as shooting began, it was clear that Eisenstein had visualized every scene in infinite detail and that he would accept no compromise.

At the basis of Eisenstein's conception of *Strike* were the ideas he had already evolved during his years in the theatre. The documentary realism attempted in *Gas Mask* is achieved in the opening shots of smokestacks and the huge machine shop, but these are juxtaposed with grotesque images of the bloated factory manager and his scurrying office staff reminiscent of the propaganda poster exaggerations of *Even a Wise Man Stumbles.* In the factory the workers are planning action, their discussions spied on by the manager's minions, until the suicide of a worker accused of theft sparks off the strike. There follows an almost idyllic interlude when the workers explore their unaccustomed leisure, but then hardship bites, treasured possessions are pawned, and the police use bribery, provocation, and force in an attempt to smash the workers' solidarity. When these techniques fail, the Cossacks invade the workers' tenements and an appalling massacre follows.

All of these scenes, in accordance with Eisenstein's theory of the "montage of attractions," are packed with visual shock effects and eccentric images (like the bizarre tangoing midgets in the bribery scene). The most discussed shock effect of all was achieved by editing—the final sequence in which Eisenstein cuts between the massacre of the workers and scenes in an abbatoir showing the slaughter of a bull. The director himself came to regard this device as clumsy and mistaken, in that the abbatoir scenes had no connection with the film as a whole—were simply dragged in to make a point. The sequence remains an immensely powerful demonstration of the dialectical function of montage—the juxtaposition of two disparate images to convey a third and richer visual message.

Strike had its premiere in February 1925 and was released the following April. Reviewers tended to be puzzled by the jolting disparity between the seriousness of the film's content and the circus-style eccentricities of its form, but the consensus seems to have been overwhelmingly favorable. Mikhail Koltsov called it "the first revolutionary creation of our cinema," *Izvestia* acclaimed it, and it was endlessly debated by other Soviet filmmakers. Kozintsev reported to his FEKS group—by then also working in the cinema—that by comparison with *Strike* "everything we've been doing up till now is mere childish nonsense." Dziga Vertov saw the film as an application of his "cinema-eye" methods, though Eisenstein, who admired Vertov, denied his influence on *Strike.*

The ordinary public was less enthusiastic and Eisenstein seems to have been depressed by this. Though he defended the film vigorously at the time, he later wrote that it "floundered about in the flotsam of a rank theatricality." He was also forced to adjust his conception of the "montage of attractions," recognizing that the effect on an audience of such a powerful but clumsy tool was harder to control than he had supposed. Flawed as it is, *Strike* nevertheless contains in embryo most of the concepts that Eisenstein developed in his mature work. According to Marie Seton, the director's sense of failure over the film was compounded by the fact that Grigori Alexandrov had casually begun an affair with Meyerhold's actress daughter, then a member of Proletkult, for whom Eisenstein nursed a romantic passion that he was too shy to express.

Eisenstein's next project was assigned to him by the committee set up to coordinate celebrations for the twentieth anniversary of the 1905 Revolution. Filming began in March 1925 of a carefully researched cinematic history of the fateful year, written by Eisenstein in collaboration with Nina Agadzhanova-Shutko, with episodes set in many parts of the country. Poor light in Moscow and Leningrad drove the unit south to Odessa in pursuit of the sun. And there Eisenstein decided to jettison the footage already shot and to devote his film to a series of events that seemed to him to symbolize the entire revolution—the mutiny on the armored cruiser *Potemkin* and the scenes that followed in Odessa.

Eisenstein was himself largely responsible for the impression that he was a cold theoretician who obtained his miraculous effects by the rigid application of carefully calculated techniques. His films were indeed planned in accordance with his theories, but they grew and changed in the heat of creativity. New theories were then evolved to ratify the products of artistic intuition. When Vsevolod Vishnevsky read Eisenstein's *post facto* analysis of an episode in *Potemkin,* he wrote that it had made him "sick with its mathematical and other calculations. But the sequence itself was made with spontaneity, fire and passion." Yon Barna's careful study of Eisenstein's montage notes for *Potemkin* and other relevant materials bears this out: the film was very precisely planned, but many of its most famous and memorable scenes are departures from that plan.

By 1925 the *Potemkin* itself no longer existed, but its sister ship, *The Twelve Apostles,* was discovered—minus its superstructure—moored in the Gulf of Sevastopol and converted to a mine store. The superstructure was rebuilt in plywood and most of the film was shot aboard (alongside the mines, which prohibited violent action and smoking), though some scenes were filmed on a working cruiser or with a model. Making his headquarters in Odessa, Eisenstein gave Strauch the job of scouring the city for faces that fitted his conception of the film's characters—an approach to casting that he later developed into his "typage" theory. Performers selected in this way, he explained, "do not act roles. They simply are their natural selves." Thus, though Strauch, Alexandrov, and a few other well-tried professionals appear in the film, Eisenstein found the "type" he wanted for the ship's doctor shoveling coal in his hotel, while the *Potemkin's* priest usually worked as a gardener.

The filming of *Potemkin,* including editing, was completed in three months. The massacre on the Odessa steps—perhaps the most famous single sequence in the entire history of the cinema—was written in three days and filmed in a further seven. This extraordinary speed and efficiency was the product of Eisenstein's powers of organization, the complete understanding between him and Tisse, and the latter's endless ingenuity. Dolly shots were then almost unknown in Russian films, but a camera-trolley was built the whole length of the Odessa steps. Other effects in the same sequence were achieved by strapping a camera to the waist of a circus-trained assistant able to tumble down the steps.

Potemkin opens in the ship's sleeping quarters, with hammocks slung close together at conflicting angles, conveying a sense of tension increased by frequent shot changes and the restlessness of the sleeping sailors. A spying quartermaster moves among them and insults a young sailor, provoking the rebellious Vakulinchuk to an angry outburst. In the morning the men gather around a joint of meat hanging on a hook. A close-up shows that it is crawling with maggots. The ship's doctor examines it through his pince-nez and pronounces it fit to eat. The meat is cooked but the men refuse to eat it. Resentment rises and a plate is smashed.

The entire crew is paraded on the quarterdeck. The captain orders those who are satisfied with the food to step forward and says that the rest will die. The small group with the courage to resist are now frighteningly isolated from their comrades. A tarpaulin is draped over them, reducing them to a grotesque, amorphous mass on which the marines train their rifles. A priest raises his crucifix and the order to fire is given. "Brothers!" cries Vakulinchuk, "Do you realize whom you are shooting?" The marines lower their rifles. The mutiny has begun and in wild excitement the sailors hunt down the officers and pitch them overboard, the doctor among them. His pince-nez catch in the rigging and swing there. One sailor has died in the struggle—Vakulinchuk. The crew sail the *Potemkin* into Odessa harbor, preceded by a tender bearing Vakulinchuk's body. It is laid to rest in a tent near the pier.

Fog over the harbor. Vakulinchuk's mother weeps over his body in the tent. A few Odessans come down from the town to pay their respects to the dead hero, and the trickle of people becomes a stream and the stream becomes a torrent. The crowd turns to the *Potemkin* and cheers its red flag. Mourning becomes celebration.

Little sailing boats swarm around the *Potemkin,* carrying food to the mutineers. In the town, the great marble steps that lead down to the harbor are packed with people on their way to join the celebration. Suddenly, a long line of Cossacks appears at the top of the steps. The crowd wavers; then a stampede begins. Steadily, inexorably, the soldiers march down the steps, their boots enormous, smoke puffing from their rifles. Now some of the people are not running but falling. A woman turns on the soldiers, her dead child in her arms, but she too is shot down. An ownerless baby carriage bounces down step after step. At the bottom wait more Cossacks, mounted, and armed with sabres and whips. A marble statue of a lion appears to rise rampant against the slaughter, and from the harbor the *Potemkin* opens fire on the town's government buildings.

But at sea, massive forces are gathering against the *Potemkin.* Soon it is encircled by a whole squadron of battleships. The *Potemkin* moves against them, guns manned, dials flickering, engines gathering speed, although the odds are hopeless. And then tiny signal flags flower from the *Potemkin*: "Don't fire, brothers." The unbreakable steel line lets the *Potemkin* pass without a shot fired, and the ship comes on, straight into the camera, until its bows black out the screen.

Eisenstein edited *Potemkin* in less than three weeks, working day and night with a single assistant to complete the film in time for its gala opening at the Bolshoi Theatre on December 21, 1925. He was still cutting the final reels (and still experimenting) when the gala showing began. As each reel was completed, Alexandrov rushed it to the Bolshoi on his motorcycle (and, when that broke down, on foot). The last reel was still held together with spit when it was screened. *Bronenosets Potemkin* (*Battleship Potemkin*) was received at its premiere with thunderous applause but was released in Russia to second-rate theatres only and coolly treated by Party critics—called "a glorified documentary" and "a poor presentation of the subject," above the heads of ordinary filmgoers. As a propagandist work, it was not expected to do well abroad and was only very reluctantly released for foreign distribution. But it was shown in Berlin in 1926 with an exciting score by Edmund Meisel, and then all over the world (in the United States in a version edited by a young Scot named John Grierson).

Battleship Potemkin brought Russia its "first victory in the foreign film-market." It encountered official hostility in a number of countries, but it was everywhere acclaimed by the critics and the general public. Alberto Cavalcanti said that it marked "the beginning of a new period in film history, and a period of truth and realism," and it convinced Max Reinhardt that "the stage will have to give way to the cinema." For Douglas Fairbanks it was "the most intense and profoundest experience of my life," and for Chaplin it was "the best film in the world." It was re-released in Russia in the best movie theatres, and went on to become the most minutely and exhaustively analyzed motion picture ever made in the Soviet Union or anywhere else, widely regarded as the ultimate model of film structure. As late as 1958 it was voted by an international jury of a hundred and seventeen film historians "the best film of all time."

In planning and editing *Potemkin,* Eisenstein extended the technique of montage into a coherent and versatile language. D. W. Griffith had already demonstrated some of the uses of montage, notably the juxtaposition of two parallel lines of action to build tension. Eisenstein showed how two images could be juxtaposed to create a new *concept,* extending montage "from the sphere of action to that of significance." The new concept arises "from the collision of independent shots—shots even opposite to one another," in a way strongly reminiscent of the principle of Marxist dialectics. Thus, in the mutiny sequence, a shot of the priest tapping his crucifix against his palm is followed by one of an officer fingering the hilt of his sword—a juxtaposition which gives rise to the thought that the Church supports the military in the oppression of the people.

Along with this "dialectic" or "intellectual" montage, *Potemkin* is full of examples of Eisenstein's virtuoso use of "rhythmic montage," in which (he wrote) "formal tension by acceleration is obtained . . . by shortening the pieces not only in accordance with the fundamental plan, but also by violating this plan." In the massacre sequence, for example, "the rhythmic drum of the soldiers' feet as they descend the steps violates all *metrical* demands. Unsynchronized with the beat of the cutting, this drumming comes in *off beat* each time. . . . The final pull of tension is supplied by the transfer from the rhythms of the descending feet to another rhythm—a new kind of downward movement—the next intensity level of the same activity—the baby-carriage rolling down the steps." The film also contains Eisenstein's first experiments in what he called "tonal" montage—a form of "polyphonic" composition illustrated in the sequence in the misty harbor, where mist, water, rocking boats, and settling gulls are counterpointed in complex fugal patterns.

Another part of the filmmaker's vocabulary acquires new functions in *Potemkin*—the close-up. Formerly used mostly for expressive and emotive purposes, it is here employed also "to *signify*, to *give meaning*, to *designate*." A famous example is the shot of the doctor's pince-nez dangling from the rigging after the mutiny, symbolizing the fate of an individual and of his whole discredited class. And Noël Burch suggests that "the extraordinary shock effect" of the Odessa steps sequence derives partly from the fact that the camera never pulls back to "establish" the steps as a whole. Instead we are given a "profusion of 'nonsituated' close-ups"—the runaway baby-carriage, for example, "falls not so much down a flight of stone steps as from one image to the next." Burch considers this "an absolutely decisive step," leading to the cinema's "final emancipation from the theatrical space of the nineteenth century."

At this stage in his career, in the midst of the enormous worldwide success of *Potemkin*, Eisenstein gave an impression of arrogance that was intensified by his physical appearance—especially the massive head with its domelike forehead. Kurt London spoke of "the thickset, choleric Eisenstein, with a face like a clever ape, behind which one feels the brain of an almost corporeal power." His manner, and his undisguised contempt for the hacks and timeservers who thronged the profession, made him many enemies. On the other hand he frequently showed a fondness for childlike buffoonery and fun, in that resembling his father. And when he chose, he could exert an almost hypnotic charm.

He was unstinting in his praise and encouragement of those he recognized as fellow artists (with the notable exception of his great rival Pudovkin), and no less generous with his always limited time and money. Sometime during 1926 he met Pera Fogelman, a filmworker whose professional name was Pera Attasheva. At first repelled by his Olympian manner, she became his nurse when he contracted influenza, and then his devoted secretary.

After *Potemkin*, Eisenstein began work on a major three-part film about China that was dropped for technical and political reasons, then on one about Soviet agriculture. With Tisse and Alexandrov he spent some gloriously happy months in the country, studying collectivization and mechanization. Shooting of *The General Line* had already begun when this project also was set aside. Pudovkin had begun work on a film to mark the tenth anniversary of the October Revolution—*The End of Saint Petersburg*—assigned to him by the Mezhrapom studios. The Sovkino studios responded with *Oktiabr* (*October*/*Ten Days That Shook the World*), naming Eisenstein as director, with Alexandrov as his coauthor and assistant director.

As usual, Eisenstein devoted months to research before he began work on his much-revised script. Originally planned to cover the whole history of the Revolution, the film (like *Potemkin*) was finally whittled down to a few key events including the attack on the Winter Palace, the rise and fall of Kerensky, and the victory of Lenin. An important source, but by no means the only one, was John Reed's *Ten Days That Shook the World*. Eisenstein's prestige at this time was so great that he was denied nothing. In Leningrad/St. Petersburg, the streets, the Winter Palace, and thousands of workers and soldiers were at his disposal. He had two film units shooting simultaneously at night, even during city power cuts. Pudovkin, working at the same time on *The End of St. Petersburg*, reported that Eisenstein's "bombardment" of the Winter Palace one night "broke two hundred windows in private bedrooms."

Just as he had once soaked himself in the "feel" and sweep of the Odessa steps, Eisenstein now immersed himself in the atmosphere of the Winter Palace (where he had himself photographed lolling on the Czar's throne). His ambitions were always absolute, and he now set out to discover nothing less than "the key to pure cinema." *Potemkin* he described as a "poster"; *October* was to be its "dialectical opposite" —subjective, abstract, and "intellectual." In it, he continued his exploration of rhythmic and "tonal" montage, and carried much further his use of the kind of "symbolic" montage demonstrated in *Potemkin* in the rearing up of the stone lion.

In one much-quoted example, Kerensky's rise to power (and his essential nonentity) is satirized in shots of him steadily climbing the palace steps, while titles indicate the increasingly powerful ranks he achieves as he plods upwards. There is a whole history of (and commentary upon) religion in a series of shots of icons and idols. And a similar technique is at work in the opening sequence, where the people of St. Petersburg, as they attach ropes to the statue of Czar Alexander III and topple it to the ground, are joined in spirit by other revolutionary crowds, witnessing and applauding the dead.

The same opening sequence makes use of another addition to the filmmaker's vocabulary, the replacement of "real" time with a subjective or cinematic notion of time. The device had been used rather clumsily in *Strike* and much more successfully in *Potemkin*, where the Odessa steps massacre occupied more time on screen than it did in fact (but not longer than it must have seemed to those involved). In *October*, when the great statue falls, we witness its collapse not once but half-a-dozen times, from different angles and distances. There is an even more complex and sophisticated use of this "stretching" technique in the famous sequence where the Dvortsovy Bridge, bearing a shattered carriage and the bodies of a girl and a white horse, splits at the center and slowly raises its two arms, toppling its tragic load down.

As Noël Burch points out, "the opening of the bridge is filmed and edited from contradictory points of view, so that even the continuity of direction . . . is constantly challenged on the surface of the screen itself," just as "the continuity of the temporal flow" is destroyed by the repeated overlapping. "To this structure is added a further complexity," Burch says, "for the sequence as a whole in fact operates on two distinct temporal levels. . . . on the one hand there is the level of 'logical' progression, which includes the bourgeois citizens mockingly watching the scene, and on the other the level of sloweddown, splintered progression, arbitrary and basically unreal, as the bridge is opened. The way in which this second temporal stream flows from the first, eddying away in an oneiric maelstrom, then blending again with normal time as the dead horse and the carriage fall, makes this sequence a truly exceptional moment in cinematographic art."

But the bridge sequence had to be shot little by little—twenty minutes or so every morning before the traffic took over. Such problems were exacerbated by Sovkino's "crude, recalcitrant, treacherous machinery" and by Eisenstein's own perfectionism and passion for experiment. Soon he was under such pressure to complete the film that he and his assistants resorted to "pep pills" to keep them alert through the long hours of shooting. Meanwhile, Stalin was mounting an increasingly virulent campaign against Trotsky, and one day Eisenstein was confronted with the realization that all the scenes in which that fallen idol figured would have to be cut—as much as a third of the total, according to some accounts. Only a few reels of *October* were completed in time for the anniversary celebrations, when Pudovkin's *The End of St. Petersburg* was acclaimed.

Finally shown in March 1928, *October* was very harshly reviewed in the Soviet Union. Nikolai Lebedev called it a conspicuous failure in which Eisenstein had, by his own admission, presented not the facts of the October Revolution but the associations and "visual puns" these facts inspired in his own mind. There was a kinder reception abroad, but even there some of the film's admirers found it lacking in narrative coherence. Alexander Bakshy acknowledged that it "may add to the resources of the cinema. It may bring about a new, essentially descriptive genre of the screen art. But it is fundamentally antidynamic and antidramatic, and as such lies off the main road of artistic progress in the medium. . . . It remains to be added that in spite of its rococo discursiveness and its lack of organized dramatic development . . . [it] is replete with magnificent scenes of mass movement." On the other hand, some later critics, including Noël Burch, regard it as one of Eisenstein's two masterpieces (with *Potemkin*), and as "one of the first examples in cinema of an open form, which seems to determine its own shape even as it unfolds with the untrammeled ease of an exercise in free association."

For Eisenstein himself, the montage techniques he had developed in *October* came to seem inadequate—purely "literary parallelism." Eager to explore more dynamic ways in which the "intellectual film" could express abstract ideas, he devoted months to the idea of filming Marx's *Das Kapital*, concluding in the end that the project demanded sound. At Stalin's "suggestion," he and his team went back to work on their film about collectivization, *The General Line*. This time he was determined to make a popular and accessible picture. He settled on the familiar story of a backward and impoverished peasant community that develops into a thriving collective, guided and inspired by the district agronomist and one peasant woman with the vision to see what the collectivized future might hold.

But it was, of course, impossible for Eisenstein to tell his simple propagandist story in simple propagandist terms. At the center of his conception are three crucial symbols—a tractor, a cream-separator, and a bull. There is a strong folkloric element in *The General Line,* as well as a good deal of Freudian symbolism. When the peasant Marfa rescues from the feckless men the money saved to buy the bull, she goes to sleep with it clutched in her hand and dreams of a bull that fills the sky and causes a deluge of milk to rain on the earth. Then we see the village preparing for a wedding (in scenes in which the black-and-white film is interspersed with lengths of leader hand-painted with splashes of color). The wedding turns out to be the ceremonial mating of bull and cow, during which the earth trembles and the screen explodes in fireworks that dissolve into numberless cattle.

The cream-separator also becomes a symbol of supernatural fertility and abundance, pointedly compared with the religious procession that tries but fails to invoke rain. In this scene, according to Jean Mitry, Eisenstein attempted to achieve something like hypnosis from the screen, "a sort of beatific state through which the spectator—his consciousness as it were suspended—enters into a state of immediate receptiveness." Contrasting with these metaphoric visions are ironic fables like the one, sardonically emphasizing the wastefulness of individual ownership, in which two dimwitted peasant brothers divide their inheritance so literally that even the house is sawn in half.

The General Line was made under immensely difficult conditions, the unit constantly having to move on in pursuit of the sun. Pera Attasheva described the two-month search for a woman of the right "type" to play the heroine (and who could also milk and plough). Thousands of faces were considered before they found what they wanted in an illiterate peasant woman named Marfa Lapkina (who was only with great difficulty cajoled away from her farm work). As usual, time was running out and towards the end Eisenstein was filming twelve hours a day with as many as five cameras, at the same time giving much time to the vast theoretical writings that increasingly occupied him.

Exhausted, Eisenstein edited the film in an almost religious "creative ecstasy." The Kabuki theatre had visited Moscow, and this art in which "we actually 'hear movement' and 'see sound'" blended with his study of Einstein's "space-time continuum," sending Eisenstein in pursuit of a "filmic fourth dimension." The path to this was through "overtonal montage"—an extreme development of the "tonal montage" introduced in *Potemkin,* counterpointing over-

tones and undertones in a complex polyphony reminiscent of the music of Debussy and Scriabin. Thus, he said, the extraordinary montage for the religious procession was linked "not merely through one indication—movement, or light values, or stage in the exposition of the plot, or the like—but through a *simultaneous advance* of a multiple series of lines." At the same time Eisenstein and Tisse were giving new attention to composition in depth, since "overtonal montage" was only possible if both background and foreground action were clearly in focus and fully coordinated.

The General Line was completed in April 1929, but Stalin was dissatisfied with the ending and two more months of filming went into meeting his requirements. Even so, the picture was severely criticized for "formalism" and for its sardonic treatment of the peasants. It was finally released under a less significant title as *Staroye i novoye* (*Old and New*) and was fairly successful, thanks largely to the warmth of Marfa Lapkina's performance. Yon Barna wrote that, for all its flaws, it "represented the culmination of a succession of works of art and theoretical deductions. With it, in short, Eisenstein had reached the ultimate point to which the silent film could be developed."

By August 1929, when *The General Line* had its premiere, Eisenstein was abroad, beginning a tour that in the end lasted for nearly three years. Pera Attasheva was left behind, but Tisse and Alexandrov went along, each supplied with $25 in spending money. Their first stop was the First International Congress of Independent Cinematography, held in a château near Lausanne, where Eisenstein collaborated with Hans Richter on a lighthearted short film that seems to have been lost. They went on to Berlin, where Eisenstein was feted as a celebrity, meeting everyone from Murnau, Pabst, and Lang to Brecht, George Grosz, and Freud's disciple Hanns Sachs. Marie Seton says that he also spent much time at the Max Hirschfeld Institute studying homosexuality. Eisenstein was often called a homosexual, and though he denied that he ever had been, he was much troubled by fear of a phenomenon that he believed could lead only to creative death. He studied it so that he could recognize its indications and if necessary suppress them.

Eisenstein was delighted by Paris, where the party went next, exploring the city endlessly and meeting another gallery of cultural heroes, gaining most from his many long discussions with James Joyce. In Paris he and his colleagues made a short (and apparently quite orthodox) sound film showing off the talents of a singer named

Mira Giry, which financed their stay there. In November 1929 they went to England, where Eisenstein's lectures at the London Film Society are said to have had much influence on British filmmakers. Eisenstein met Richter again and appeared (as a London policeman!) in Richter's short film *Everyday,* not edited until 1966. Further lectures and other engagements took Eisenstein back to the Continent, where in France he began an investigation into religion and mystical experience, a long-suppressed interest. And in France he received and accepted an invitation from Paramount to make a film in Hollywood.

Arriving in New York in the spring of 1930, Eisenstein found himself expected to behave with the decorum of a major celebrity, and responded by turning up for an important luncheon unshaven and wearing a worker's cap. He met Griffith and Rin-Tin-Tin, lectured to black audiences in the Deep South, and arrived at last in Hollywood. He and his party (which now included the British filmmaker and critic Ivor Montague) moved into a Spanish-style house in Beverly Hills. Eisenstein met everyone, committed a whole series of social *gaffes* (many of them no doubt deliberate), and formed a close friendship with Chaplin. He also became the target of a virulent anti-Semitic and anti-communist campaign led by one Major Frank Pease, but nevertheless worked with his usual devotion and concentration on two scripts, an allegory called "The Glass House" and *Sutter's Gold,* a Gold Rush film based on a novel by Blaise Cendrars. Both were rejected by Paramount, and both were later filmed by others.

At the suggestion of Jesse Lasky, Eisenstein then turned his attention to Theodore Dreiser's greatest novel, *An American Tragedy.* His fourteen-reel adaptation of the enormous book, embodying his ideas about the cinematic representation of interior monologue, found the young hero morally innocent of murder and fixed the blame ultimately on the capitalist ethic. This was too much for the Paramount chiefs, and in October 1930 they terminated Eisenstein's contract. Various other projects were mooted, including the notion of a documentary about Mexico. Encouraged by Robert Flaherty, whom he met at this time, Eisenstein became intensely excited by this idea. The socialist novelist Upton Sinclair found him backers (including Sinclair's own wife), and in December 1930 Eisenstein, Alexandrov, and Tisse left Hollywood for Mexico and disaster.

Their Mexican adventure began badly—in jail—but after that ludicrous *contretemps* was sorted out, Eisenstein set out to discover the country, soaking himself in its landscape and colors while studying its history, economy, religion, art, and violent pastimes. In love with the linear purity of what he saw and the shocking contrasts between violence and beauty, dazzling light and pious black, he resumed his childhood passion for sketching. Like other travelers before him, he found his inhibited nature released by this extreme and primeval country. In thousands of abstract, sensual, and bizarre line drawings he began to explore the submerged connections between religion and sexual ecstasy, martyrdom and the orgasmic release of blood in the bullring, and the endless cycle of death and rebirth that seemed to him the essence of Mexico.

Eisenstein's original conception—a kind of travelogue with each episode an act of homage to a Mexican artist—now seemed quite irrelevant. *Que Viva Mexico!* was to be unlike anything he had conceived before—a passionate, sensual epic poem about the country's bloody history, from the Aztec death cult through conquest, feudalism, and revolution, to the contemporary Day-of-the-Dead festival, which begins with obeisances to the dead and ends in an orgiastic affirmation of life. This history was to be unfolded in separate stories, set in different periods with different characters—stories as "violently contrasting" as the colors of a serape, but held together by "the unity of the weave." In some versions of the scenario there were to be six of these stories, in others four, seven, or five, but the basic plan was consistent.

Filming began in December 1930, long before Upton Sinclair was shown any version of the scenario. Eisenstein made his headquarters at Tetlapayac, in a hacienda that seemed to him "the place I had been looking for all my life." Having reached the end of his experiments in montage, he was now concentrating on the problems of composition within the frame and in depth, devoting infinite time and patience, according to Yon Barna, to such "arrestingly bizarre" compositions as "the close-up of a skull dominating a background scene of penitents on pilgrimage, or the profile of a young Mexican girl set against the distant silhouette of a pyramid." Marie Seton has described the mystical and indeed religious importance Eisenstein ascribed to the pyramid and the triangle in the compositional scheme of *Que Viva Mexico!* Between shooting sessions, he studied physics and philosophy and worked on his own book on film aesthetics.

Thanks to Eisenstein's constantly changing conception of the film, murderous heat, obstructionist authorities, and the language barrier, the original deadline and budget were soon exceeded (though the total spent on the film seems to have been only $53,000). Sinclair's brother-in-law Hunter Kimbrough was sent to check on the situation at Tetlapayac and clashed with Eisenstein, and in November 1931 Sinclair received a cable from Stalin saying that Eisenstein had lost the confidence of his Soviet colleagues. A slanderous campaign began against Eisenstein, and in January 1932 Sinclair announced that there would be no further funds for *Que Viva Mexico!* (although another seven or eight thousand dollars would have permitted its completion).

Eisenstein and his friends returned via the United States to Moscow, arriving in March 1932. During their absence, the Soviet cinema's "golden age" of freewheeling experiment had given way to the rigid conventions of "socialist realism," and direction of the industry had passed to Boris Shumyatsky, a mediocrity profoundly jealous of Eisenstein's brilliance, who now lost no opportunity to discipline and humiliate this darling of the intellectuals. Tisse and Alexandrov were soon involved in projects of their own and Eisenstein found himself facing, almost alone, a campaign of villification in which he was portrayed as a renegade corrupted at foreign flesh-pots and a "formalist" out of touch with the new Russia and the new Soviet cinema.

Meanwhile, the wrangle with Upton Sinclair continued. Artists and intellectuals all over the world joined in the controversy and at times it seemed that Sinclair was about to bow to Eisenstein's requests and send him the *Que Viva Mexico!* footage for editing. Then he would change his mind, and there would be a further spate of accusations and slanders. In August 1932, Eisenstein learned that Sinclair, "to recover our investment," had assigned Sol Lesser to cut some of the material into the film eventually released as *Thunder Over Mexico*; the same month Eisenstein broke down and went into a sanatorium with "a serious nervous disorder." More negative was mutilated in the creation of *Death Day, Eisenstein in Mexico,* Marie Seton's well-intentioned *Time in the Sun,* and various shorts. Eisenstein eventually saw some of these "cinematographic discordances cobbled together by the filthy hands of moneymakers" and found in them nothing but ineradicably bitter memories of "the death of my own child on whom I lavished so much love, work, and passionate inspiration."

The only good news for Eisenstein during this grim period was his appointment as head of the directors' course at GIK, the Institute of Cinematography. He threw himself into the project with his customary thoroughness and vigor, evolving a complete four-year course and proving to be a splendid teacher. At the same time he contin-ued with his own researches and writings and worked on a number of film projects. He wrote a script for a grotesque satire to be called "M.M.M." (plunging at the same time into a thorough investigation of the nature and theory of comedy) and, when this was rejected by Shumyatsky, planned a panoramic history of Moscow somewhat resembling *Que Viva Mexico!* This also was rejected, as was a proposed adaptation of A. K. Vinogradov's novel *The Black Consul,* in which Paul Robeson was to have starred as Haitian revolutionary Toussaint l'Ouverture.

Then came the infamous All Union Conference of Cinematographic Workers of January 1935, when Eisenstein (though he chaired the conference) was pilloried by such friends and protegés as Dovzhenko, Sergei Vasiliev, and Sergei Yutkevich, and defended only by Lev Kuleshov and Nikolai Lebedev. Eisenstein accepted a humiliatingly minor award, swallowed the insults, and soon afterwards was allowed to begin work on his first sound film, *Bezhin Lug* (*Bezhin Meadow*).

Adapted and updated by Alexander Rzheshevsky from a story by Turgenev, *Bezhin Meadow* centers on Stepok, a communist Young Pioneer who organizes his comrades to defend the harvest of a collective farm against sabotage and is murdered on that account by his enraged kulak father, becoming a martyr and hero of the revolution. Tisse, as usual, led the crew, and Eisenstein had a useful new assistant in Elisabeta Teleshova. A theatre director cast in the film as president of the collective farm, she soon showed herself adept at smoothing tempers ruffled by Eisenstein's impatient brusqueness in dealing with actors. She became his casting adviser, his mistress, and apparently his wife. (The facts are blurred by the rather casual Soviet attitude to marriage at that time; Pera Attasheva, who survived Teleshova, seems also to have been registered as Eisenstein's spouse, and was certainly his heir.)

As early as 1928, Eisenstein, in collaboration with Pudovkin and Alexandrov, had published a seminal manifesto on the future of the sound film, distinguishing between the purely naturalistic use of sound in commercial films, and its creative use, which would be *"directed along the line of its distinct non-synchronization with the visual images,"* leading to "the creation of an *orchestral counterpoint* of visual and aural images. . . . Sound, treated as a new montage element." With *Bezhin Meadow,* at last, Eisenstein was able to put his theories to work in a sound film that was to be "expressive of a specific artistic form and of a psychological interpretation of reality."

Temperamentally and by conviction hostile to socialist realism, Eisenstein sought a renewal of "film poetry." The sets and make-up for the film reflect the impressionism of Turgenev's style, and there is a distinctly subjective intensity in Eisenstein's treatment of the father-son relationship in the story, as well as a mystical element in scenes like the one in which Stepok's head is haloed with light. Jay Leyda, who worked on the film as one of Eisenstein's assistants, wrote that "there are places in the film where an encyclopedic culture has been so integrally welded into cinematography that they remind you of nothing but Eisenstein."

The director's health was at a low ebb, and during the filming of *Bezhin Meadow* he was more or less seriously ill with ptomaine poisoning, smallpox, and two bouts of influenza. Progress was painfully slow even before Shumyatsky demanded radical changes. Isaac Babel was called in to help with the revision, which was found no more acceptable. In March 1937 Shumyatsky called a halt, giving his reasons in an article in *Pravda*. The characters, he complained, were "not images of collective farmers, but biblical and mythological types," and the film's conception was based on a "struggle between 'good' and 'evil.'" At a conference set up to discuss *Bezhin Meadow*, Eisenstein accepted the criticisms and repudiated his film, which is said to have been destroyed by water during World War II. In 1966 Sergei Yutkevich assembled stills from it into a work that gives some idea of what it might have been.

After this *débacle*, it is perhaps surprising that Eisenstein did not share the fate of so many other artists lost in Stalin's purges. Perhaps, as Yon Barna suggests, he was saved by Stalin's fondness for the cinema and his special sympathy for Eisenstein himself, with whom he had many meetings. At any rate, later in 1937, after he had issued an abject confession of his political and artistic errors, Eisenstein was entrusted with an important new assignment. He was to make a patriotic epic about the marauding Teutonic knights who in the thirteenth century were destroyed at Novgorod by a Russian army under Alexander Nevsky—a theme that reflected Soviet alarm about the threat of aggression from Nazi Germany. Eisenstein was provided with a coscenarist (Piotr Pavlenko) and a codirector (Dmitri Vasiliev) who were to give him no scope for formalist overelaboration or ideological deviation.

The high point of the film was to be the climactic battle on a frozen lake, in which the Teutons are driven back across ice that eventually cracks under their weight—a scene whose conception Eisenstein is said to have derived from a passage in Milton's *Paradise Lost* (a source he would presumably have kept from his new collaborators). To avoid a long delay, the ice battle and other winter scenes had to be shot in high summer, using artificial snow, white-painted trees, and a lake covered with tons of "ice" supported on pontoons. Tisse devised a filter that gave a wintry look to the intense summer light. Eisenstein supervised every detail himself, from make-up to costume fittings, though he delegated much of the actual shooting to Vasiliev.

Eisenstein worked very closely and in complete accord with Sergei Prokofiev, who composed the score. As a result, he believed that he had discovered the "key to the measured matching of a strip of music and a strip of picture," subsequently analyzing what he had done to produce minutely detailed theoretical principles for the use of sound. He also applied what he had learned in his two aborted films about composition in depth, balancing foreground and background images with geometrical precision. Jean Mitry has pointed out other elements in the compositional structure, like the fact that the white-garbed Teutons always appear in rigid geometrical formation, the Russians in black and in irregular waves. Their alternate appearances create, as Mitry puts it, "plastic rhymes incorporated in a symphony of lines, forms, and colors which unfold a single symphony of movement."

Determined to prove his efficiency, Eisenstein (with Vasiliev's help) completed *Alexander Nevsky* five months ahead of schedule. By the time it had its premiere in November 1938, Eisenstein's principal enemy Shumyatsky had been removed from power. The film was an immense critical and popular success in Russia, returning Eisenstein to his former eminence. Early in 1939 he was awarded the Order of Lenin (as was Nikolai Cherkasov, who played Nevsky). Some foreign critics were equally enthusiastic, but others saw in the film an abandoning of Eisenstein's "typage" principle and of dialectical montage in favor of the "positive heroes" and stiff tableaux of socialist realism. The "operatic" quality of the work, intensified by the close matching of music and image, delighted some critics and appalled others. With the signing of the Nazi-Soviet pact in August 1939, *Nevsky*'s anti-German message became an embarrassment, and it was temporarily withdrawn.

Exhausted by his efforts on *Nevsky*, Eisenstein nevertheless went to work on a new script about the Civil War, "Perekop," in collaboration with Alexander Fadeyev, and then put this aside to write a historical panorama of Central Asia, "Ferghana Canal." Filming of the latter was about to begin when it was abruptly canceled—a blow so bitter that Eisenstein reportedly came close to suicide. In 1939 or 1940 he was named artistic director of Mosfilm and, refusing to treat the appointment as a mere formality, plunged into script conferences and filming sessions. He was also drawn into the cultural programs celebrating the Russian-German accord, notably in his grandiose production of Wagner's *Die Walküre* at the Bolshoi in November 1940. Other film projects came and went, notably a movie about the life of Pushkin that was to have explored the dramatic uses of color.

Early in 1941, Eisenstein was released from his Mosfilm duties to begin work on the script of *Ivan Grozni* (*Ivan the Terrible*), intended to reassess the life and achievements of the sixteenth-century Czar, infamous for his barbaric cruelty, who nevertheless achieved the unification of Russia. Eisenstein acknowledged that "the scenario for *Ivan the Terrible* in certain respects contains the author's own apologia," and Marie Seton says that he "fought the battles of his own soul in Ivan."

In the autumn of 1941, with the German army approaching Moscow, Mosfilm was evacuated to Alma Alta in Kazakhstan, where Eisenstein continued his work on the script and where Prokofiev joined him in the spring of 1942. *Ivan* was to have begun with a prologue showing the murder of the future Czar's mother when he was eight, and his first intimations of high destiny when his nurse sings him an old song about Russia's lost might. This material was later transferred to another part of the film which, as released, opens with Ivan's crowning at seventeen. In this scene he is already surrounded by the principal actors in the drama—his evil aunt Euphrosinia, his beloved first wife Anastasia, and the two powerful friends who became his bitterest enemies.

Bending historical fact when he thought it necessary, Eisenstein elevated drama into myth as the adult Ivan (played by Cherkasov) begins his struggle to unite Russia, and Euphrosinia plots with the Boyar nobles to install her own son as Czar. She poisons Anastasia, and there follows the famous scene of Anastasia's funeral service in the Uspensky Cathedral where Ivan's anguish at his loss and uncertainty about his course are reflected in the words of the Sixty-ninth Psalm, interwoven with news of ever more damaging treacheries. Gathering his will, Ivan announces his intention to abdicate until the people recall him to "burn out treason with fire." And Anastasia's dead features seem to soften in approval. Ivan goes into exile, surrounded by his incorruptible "iron ring" of guards, the Oprichniks, until an endless pilgrimage of people comes to him across the snowy wastes, begging him to rule them again.

Filming began in April 1943 during a Kazakhstan heat wave, in which Eisenstein showed his customary ruthlessness to actors suffering in heavy armor and painful make-up, and his customary perfectionism—one headdress was sent back for alterations forty times. He was nevertheless in high good humor, though he was driving himself, as usual, "at a madman's pace." The Institute of Cinematography had also been evacuated to Alma Alta, and Eisenstein was teaching there as well as continuing his theoretical work. His first book, edited and translated by Jay Leyda, had appeared in 1942 as *The Film Sense,* an extremely important and influential collection of four essays.

In the fall of 1944 Mosfilm returned to Moscow and Eisenstein began the montage and sound synchronization of Part I of *Ivan.* It was released in January 1945 and acclaimed in Russia but, like *Alexander Nevsky,* had a mixed reception abroad. Again there were complaints about the operatic style and the academic montage, though many were entranced by the richness of the images and a deliberately exaggerated acting style reminiscent of the Kabuki theatre or of "frescos come to life." Yon Barna has praised the "complex polyphonic composition" of the scene in the Uspensky Cathedral, where Ivan's agonized postures around Anastasia's coffin are reproduced abruptly, one after the other, without transition between them, almost (as Eisenstein wrote) "as if a series of separate, self-contained characters were being presented, selected by the camera, not according to criteria of physical or spatial presence but according to the degree of emotion as it mounts in intensity with the action." Many were struck by the resemblances between Stalin's monstrous career and Ivan's, and wondered if the film was intended as an apologia for the dictator.

Throughout 1945 and into 1946 Eisenstein worked on Part II of *Ivan,* much of it already filmed, and on the scenario for a proposed Part III, never completed. In Part II, Ivan's struggle continues against the Boyars and Euphrosinia, and against her allies in the Orthodox Church. As Ivan's sense of divine mission grows, his cruelties become ever more appalling. The scene of Anastasia's funeral is reinvoked in another great sequence in the Uspensky Cathedral when Ivan, once more frantic to justify his crimes but with no Anastasia to give him her silent blessing, finds himself, as it were, eye to eye with the Czar of Heaven. One sequence in Part II—the Oprichnik's dance—was filmed in color, giving Eisenstein his only opportunity to work out in practice his theories about the "dramaturgy of color."

One day in February 1946, Eisenstein completed the editing of Part II of *Ivan the Terrible* and went off to a party to celebrate his receipt of the Stalin Prize for Part I. He was dancing with the actress Vera Maretskaya when he suffered a serious heart attack. Humiliated, he rose to his feet and walked unaided from the room before allowing himself to be driven to hospital. There he hovered between life and death for weeks, but gradually made a partial recovery. Meanwhile, Stalin and the Central Committee of the Communist Party saw Part II of *Ivan* and disliked it, though this was kept from Eisenstein while his condition was critical. In June 1946 he moved to his dacha in the country. Teleshova had died of typhoid in 1943 and his old nurse Totya Pasha, who had become his housekeeper, was also gone. He was joined for a time by his mother, who had returned to Russia years previously, but she too soon died. In September 1946 the Central Committee published its resolution censuring Part II of *Ivan,* among other films, as "unsuccessful" and "erroneous." Eisenstein publicly bowed to this "stern and timely warning" and acknowledged his "misrepresentation of historical facts."

In September 1946 Eisenstein began making notes for a film conceived as an epic poem in color about Moscow's eight hundred years of history. Towards the end of the same year he at last saw prints of *Thunder Over Mexico* and *Time in the Sun* and was seized by a passionate desire to remake them into something closer to his conception of *Que Viva Mexico!,* the "child" whose loss was the bitterest of all his losses. He was too weak for any such effort, though he sometimes taught a little and continued to write and plan his books (including a second collection of essays edited and translated by Jay Leyda, *Film Form*). The massive series of theoretical works he had worked on for so long remained uncompleted. He died at the age of fifty, as a fortune teller had told him he would, and received a state funeral.

Yon Barna describes Eisenstein as "a giant—the supreme exponent of the seventh art. The creator of so many legends, he was himself the hero of one, the embodiment of tragic myth and of the invincibility of the human spirit." Many critics nowadays quarrel with such claims, especially in the West, where the "totalitarian conception of composition" in *Nevsky* and *Ivan* is increasingly condemned. But, writes Noël Burch, "the young Eisenstein who wanted the cinema to reveal its artifices, and who consequently pushed them to their ethical and aesthetic extremes, helped to lay the foundations for all the constructions which are now permitting the cinema to rediscover *its* reality. Although the compositional style may be outdated today and the 'dramatics' on occasion a little simplistic, Eisenstein's *attitudes* towards his art,

and his rigorous scientific dialectic, offer an inexhaustible source of inspiration for the young filmmakers of today and tomorrow."

FILMS: Stachka (Strike), 1925; Bronenosets Potemkin (Battleship Potemkin), 1925; Oktiabr (October/Ten Days That Shook the World), 1928; Staroye i novoye (Old and New; also known as Generalnaya linya—The General Line), 1929; Que Viva Mexico!, 1930–1932 (unfinished; portions later edited by others and released under various titles); Bezhin Lug (Bezhin Meadow), 1935–1937 (unfinished; stills version made by Sergei Yutkevich in 1966); (with Dmitri Vasiliev) Alexander Nevsky, 1938; Ivan Grozni (Ivan the Terrible), Part I, 1945; Part II, 1946 (released 1958). *Published scripts in English*—Three Films (Battleship Potemkin, October, Alexander Nevsky), 1974; An American Tragedy *in* Montagu, I. With Eisenstein in Hollywood, 1969; Battleship Potemkin, 1969; Ferghana Canal *excerpts in* Eisenstein, S. M. The Film Sense, 1957; Ivan the Terrible, 1962 and 1970; Old and New (The General Line) in Jacobs, L. Film Writing Forms, 1934; Que Viva Mexico!, 1952; Strike *excerpts in* Eisenstein, S. M. The Film Sense, 1957; Sutter's Gold *in* Montagu, I. With Eisenstein in Hollywood, 1969.

ABOUT: Agel, H. Esthétique du cinéma, 1962; Albera, F. Notes sur l'esthétique d'Eisenstein, 1973; Amengual, B. Que Viva Eisenstein!, 1980; Aumont, J. Montage Eisenstein, 1979; Barna, Y. Eisenstein, 1973; Brakhage, S. The Brakhage Lectures, 1972; Carasco, R. Hors-cadre Eisenstein, 1979; Eisenstein, S. M. Film Essays, edited and translated by Jay Leyda, 1968; Eisenstein, S. M. Film Form, edited and translated by Jay Leyda, 1957; Eisenstein, S. M. The Film Sense, edited and translated by Jay Leyda, 1957; Eisenstein, S. M. Immoral Memories, 1983; Eisenstein, S. M. Notes of a Film Director, edited and translated by X. Danko, 1959; Geduld, H. M. and Gottesman, R. Sergei Eisenstein and Upton Sinclair: The Making and Unmaking of Que Viva Mexico!, 1970; Harcourt, P. Six European Directors, 1974; Leyda, J. Kino, 1960; Mitry, J. S. M. Eisenstein, 1978 (in French; third edition); Montagu, I. With Eisenstein in Hollywood, 1969; Moussinac, L. Sergei Eisenstein, translated by D. Sandy Petrey, 1970; Nizhny, V. Lessons With Eisenstein, edited and translated by Ivor Montagu and Jay Leyda, 1968; Rotha, P. and others. Eisenstein 1898–1948, 1948; Roud, R. (ed.) Cinema: A Critical Dictionary, 1980; Schlegel, H. J. Sergei M. Eisenstein (three volumes), 1973–1975 (in German); Shklovsky, V. Once Upon a Time, 1966; Shub, E. In Close-Up, 1969; Seton, M. Sergei M. Eisenstein, 1978 (revised edition); Swallow, N. Eisenstein: A Documentary Portrait, 1976; Wollen, P. Signs and Meaning in the Cinema, 1972; Yutkevich, S. The Director's Counterpoint, 1960. *Periodicals*—Bianco e Nero January–February 1973, July–August 1978; Cahiers du Cinéma January 1971; Cinéma (France) March 1974, February 1975, October 1976; Cinema Journal Fall 1977, Spring 1978; Commentary March 1949; Écran September–October 1973; Educational Theatre Journal December 1961; Film Journal Fall–Winter 1972; Filmkritik December 1974; Film und Fernsehen 1 1978; Image et Son June 1965; Jump Cut March 1977; Millennium Winter–Spring 1979; Quarterly Review of Film Studies Spring 1978; Screen Winter 1974–1975; Sight and Sound June 1951, Winter 1973–1974.

JEAN EPSTEIN

EPSTEIN, JEAN (March 25, 1897–April 3, 1953), French director, scenarist, producer, theorist, poet, and novelist, was born in Warsaw, Poland, of a French father and a Polish mother, and registered as a French citizen. He spent his earliest years in Warsaw, but from 1900 to 1906 lived at Zakopane, in the Tatra mountains, and at Soczewka, near Kutno. His father was deeply involved in business affairs, but as a child Epstein traveled widely with his mother and his sister Marie, always his confidante and friend and later his collaborator.

In 1908, after the early death of Epstein's father, the family moved to Switzerland. Epstein attended a French school in Fribourg in 1910–1914, then went to Lyons with his family to continue his studies. Enrolled in the Faculty of Medicine, he also served as an intern at the local hospital. There he met the biochemist Auguste Lumière, who had worked with his brother Louis to invent the cinematographe, the combined film camera and projector that paved the way for the cinema.

Epstein's principal extracurricular interest had been literature. A poet and critic, he founded the literary review Le Promenoir in 1920, publishing texts by Fernand Léger, Blaise Cendrars, and Apollinaire, among others. The same year he watched the filming of Abel Gance's La Roue at Nice. The cinema increasingly absorbed him, as it did many of his literary friends. At that time of intellectual and aesthetic ferment, as Jean-André Fieschi writes in Richard Roud's Cinema, the film seemed "a sort of incarnation of . . . [the] modernist spirit . . . , a celluloid muse, a scientific instrument, and an instrument of the emotions."

In 1920 Epstein sent his first book-length manuscript to Paul Lafitte's publishing house, La Sirène. Lafitte not only accepted it but invited Epstein to Paris to work with him. Abandoning his medical studies, Epstein accepted. La Sirène published his La Poésie d'aujourd'hui in 1921 and, the same year, Bonjour Cinéma.

Bonjour Cinéma is a collection of essays and poems in celebration of the film. Fieschi calls it "the record of a fever, a craving," in which "the whimsical typography, the alternation of blank verse with short prose sections . . . , the illustrations with overlapping perspectives in the Cubist manner, all betoken a certain contemporary cultural ambience and a kinship with Apollinaire, Cendrars and Dada." And the tone and nature of Epstein's enthusiasms identified him as an adherent—soon to become an admired member—of the cinema's "first avant-garde," the group of "impressionist" filmmakers whose leaders included Abel Gance, Louis Delluc, Germaine Dulac, and Marcel L'Herbier.

Fieschi says that Bonjour Cinéma "is a dream of cinema, but a very precise dream" compared to those of Gance and L'Herbier: "Epstein's verbal lyricism, even his enthusiasm, is more technical, and constitutes an overall grasp of cinema with each of its constituent elements considered in formal terms in relation to the others. Epstein is attempting, intuitively at first, to formulate his method." And "the inaugural sign" of this method is the close-up, the device that so conclusively separates cinema from theatre.

A few years later, in another collection of essays published as Le Cinématographe vu du l'Etna (1926), Epstein writes: "Cinema is a language [and one that attributes] a semblance of life to the objects it defines. . . . The almost godlike importance assumed in close-ups by parts of the human body or by the most frigid elements in nature, has often been noticed. Through the cinema, a revolver in a drawer, a broken bottle on the ground, an eye isolated by an iris, are elevated to the status of characters in the drama. . . . a close-up of a revolver is no longer a revolver, it is the revolver character, in other words the impulse towards, or remorse for, crime, failure, suicide. It is as dark as the temptations of the night, bright as the gleam of gold lusted after, taciturn as passion, squat, brutal, heavy, cold, wary, menacing. It has a temperament, habits, memories, a will, a soul."

By this time, Epstein's "intuitions" had been put to the test in his own first films. He began as assistant to Louis Delluc on *Le Tonnerre* (1921). Soon afterwards he met the producer-director Jean Benoit-Levy, who invited him to direct a centennial tribute to Louis Pasteur. The film, made under the supervision of Benoit-Levy and much of it shot on location in the places where the scientist lived and worked, was released in April 1923, with Henri Monnier in the title role.

Pasteur was an apprentice work but was said to exhibit "an impressive maturity of vision and an original, experimental use of variable camera angles." Epstein himself recalled that "during the making of *Pasteur,* I contrived all sorts of ways of seeing how things could be made to look from all sorts of different angles. I had taken many shots looking down, and my greatest worry during the editing was to see all those downward shots where the spectator seemed to be walking on the ceiling. . . . My main recollection of *Pasteur* is trying to make the film come down off the ceiling. . . . In that movie I wanted to see how a camera was used, how it was loaded. There were alembics, retorts, all sorts of laboratory material, but photographed in such a way that they are concrete objects and, at the same time, a transfiguration, a dream."

In 1922, before *Pasteur* was released, Epstein had joined Pathé with a ten-year contract as a director. His first film there was *L'Auberge rouge* (*The Red Inn,* 1923), scripted by himself from Balzac's story "Une ténébreuse affaire." Léon Mathot starred as Prosper Magnan, with Gina Manès as the innkeeper's daughter. A group of travelers sit around a table listening to a story set in the previous century, during the Directorate, culminating in the heroine's unsuccessful race to prevent the execution of an innocent man.

In this climactic scene, the preparations for the execution are intercut with shots recording the girl's desperate run—a technique Epstein had learned from D. W. Griffith, just as elsewhere in the film he profits from the experiments of L'Herbier. As Garbicz and Klinowski write in *Cinema: The Magic Vehicle,* "The multitude of originally composed shots, frequent changes of narrative rhythm, slowed-down sequences, dissolves, multiple exposures, unusual camera movements—all these elements of the film director's craft were blended to form a coherent whole. The famous tracking shot around the circular table in the inn, or the very convincing attempts at subjective narrative, are Epstein's own successful contribution." And Henri Langlois, in an article translated in *Cinemages* (2 1955), wrote that "in this film, objects (play-

ing cards, jewels) suddenly take over the screen and become characters . . . like the objects in Picasso's, Léger's, or Gris' still-lifes."

L'Auberge rouge, enthusiastically welcomed by the avant-garde, was attacked by others for its deliberate artificiality and formalism—especially the slow rhythms Epstein had used to create "an atmosphere of expectancy, mystery and unease" at the beginning of the picture. His next film caused a sensation.

Coeur fidèle (*The Faithful Heart,* 1923), from Epstein's own original script, tells a melodramatic tale about the rivalry of an honest worker (Léon Mathot) and an ingratiating scoundrel (Edmond van Daële) for the love of a waitress (Gina Manès) in a Marseilles waterfront café. She chooses the villain; the worker wounds his rival in a fight and is jailed. There is another struggle after the hero's release, but the villain is killed by a crippled girl.

This naive story was transfigured by the film's style, or rather, as Fieschi says, "by the contrast of different styles—a first intuition of the serial and contrapuntal possibilities later pushed much further" by the director. Most of the controversy the film created centered on a fairground sequence shot with the camera fixed to a carousel. Epstein had written his script in only one night, but several years earlier had noted in *Bonjour Cinéma:* "I envisage a drama on board a carousel of wooden horses. . . . The fairground below would gradually become less and less distinct. Centrifugalized in this way, the drama would be greatly enhanced visually by the photogenic qualities of giddiness and whirling."

Henri Langlois, in his *Cinemages* article, called *Coeur fidèle* "the high point of impressionism of movement" and "also the triumph of the modern spirit. . . . Its images were seemingly in relief; they literally burst through the screen to such an extent that in theatres audiences suffered physically from dizziness attacks, or nausea, as they watched the carousel whirl around." But, as Garbicz and Klinowski say, "although *Coeur fidèle* was shot on location and its photography is clinically precise, the overall impression of the film is dreamlike. It was not the external realism of the décor that mattered to the director—who achieves here a rare psychological precision, using each frame of the film as a key to a state of mind; from his moody drama of overcast skies and pools glistening in the light of dawn a fatalism emanated which in the next decade was to impress deep marks upon the French cinema."

After *La Montagne infidèle* (1923), a documentary about the eruption of Mount Etna in June 1923, came *La Belle nivernaise* (*The Beau-*

ty of Nivers, 1923), based on the novella by Alphonse Daudet and adapted by Epstein, who also edited the film. His principal cameraman on this work, as on its two predecessors, was Paul Guichard.

Jean-André Fieschi has pointed out that Epstein's work developed "along two major axes: an axis of sophistication, artifice, fantasy, spectacle, and an axis of simplicity, spontaneity, documentary, everyday reality." After the hectic experiments of Coeur fidèle, he turned to the opposite pole in La Belle Nivernaise, a slow, simple story about a girl (Blanche Montel) adopted by a family of barge workers and drifting happily across France on La Belle Nivernaise. She is found by rich relations and taken to the city, but pines for her lost idyll and in the end returns to it. Foreshadowing Jean Vigo's L'Atalante in its theme and mood, this has been called "one of the purest works of French silent cinema," while Guichard's misty shots of bridges and river banks were found reminiscent of the paintings of Corot and Renoir.

Epstein then began work on La Goutte de sang (A Drop of Blood, 1924), from a story by J. Mary. As a result of difficulties with the Société des Cinéromans, he abandoned the film halfway. It was completed by (and attributed to) Maurice Mariaud, and Epstein left Pathé and joined Alexander Kamenka's Albatros Films, staffed almost entirely by Russian emigrés and devoted to extravagant spectaculars in the manner of the old tsarist studios.

Le Lion des Mogols (The Lion of the Moguls, 1924) was written by its star, Ivan Mozhukhin. His script was contemptuously dismissed by Henri Langlois as "a fairy tale for shop girls . . . everything was artificial, the characters' motivations and their country. It harked back to the Russian ballet and was soaked through with bourgeois conformity and sanctimoniousness and imbecile naiveté."

Langlois nevertheless defends Epstein's involvement in the project because Albatros gave him his first chance to work with large resources—"to see just how far the [movie] machine would take him." In spite of the "shallow and stupid script," Langlois insists, "Le Lion des Mogols can be criticized on only one basis: that it is not entirely a fantastic film; that it is not, from first to last, totally impregnated with that surreal realism that Epstein was able to create in the scenes at the Jockey Club, the taxi race, the lights of Paris, the dance at the masked ball, without ever leaving realism. For instance, in the scene at the Jockey Club, where the scenery of the Montparnasse cabaret was perfectly recreated . . . everything is transfigured, not by

external impressionistic means or by a transformation of the actors' playing, but simply through montage effects and the rhythm that gives the scene a supernatural overtone."

Epstein's initiation into the problems of commercial filmmaking continued in his next two movies for Albatros. In L'Affiche (The Poster, 1924), scripted by his sister Marie, he had to contend with the studio's fashionably expressionistic sets and a fifty-five-year-old star, Nathalie Lissenko, cast as a young woman. Lissenko was cast closer to her real age in Le Double Amour (Double Love, 1928), another Marie Epstein script, in which the director was said to have successfully mastered his well-known impatience with professional actors ("when they do act they are false and when they don't they are stiff. Actually, the more an actor is an actor the more I dislike him, the more difficult it is to handle him so he doesn't seem like an actor").

The five-episode serial, Les Aventures de Robert Macaire (1925), was Epstein's last project for Albatros. Largely ignored in 1925, it seemed to Henri Langlois a classic of the form, with "not one boring moment, not one mistake. . . . If we are comparing and looking for a present-day equivalent of The Adventures of Robert Macaire, we should talk about High Noon, and even then what a difference in perfection!"

Nevertheless, after Albatros, Epstein's Photogénies (1925), a short experimental film that seems never to have been released, sounds like a reaffirmation of his central concerns. The term photogénie, a key concept of the "first avant-garde," is defined by Paul Willemen in the Epstein issue of Afterimage (Autumn 1981) as "that mysterious, indefinable something present in the image which differentiated cinema from all other arts and therefore constituted the very foundation of cinematic art." Like his colleagues, Epstein wrote of photogénie in mystical and idealistic terms, saying that when this quality is present "all volumes are displaced and reach flashpoint. Life recruits atoms, molecular movement is as sensual as the hips of a woman or a young man. The hills harden like muscles. The universe is on edge. The philosopher's light. The atmosphere is heavy with love. I am looking." Noting that Epstein and his friends insisted on the indefinability of photogénie, Willemen in 1981 suggests that it is actually "a term marking the fetishistic aspect of cinematic looking."

Mauprat (1926), from the novel by George Sand, was the first production of the director's own company, Les Films Jean Epstein. In spite of some "extraordinary moments of cinematic poetry"—and the services of Luis Buñuel as assistant director—it was not a success, artistically or commercially. Nor was *Six et demi onze (un kodak)* (*Six and a Half by Eleven: A Kodak,* 1927), scripted by Marie Epstein and making complex use of flashbacks in a story about a man trying to understand his brother's suicide.

Much more interesting was *La Glace à trois faces* (*The Three-Sided Mirror,* 1927), from a story by Paul Morand. Epstein gave this summary of the story: "Ignoring three . . . assignations made with or by three different women, a young man, happy to be on holiday as it were, alone and free, takes his sports car out of the garage and speeds away . . . until he smashes himself up on the road to Deauville." His friend, obliged to notify the man's three mistresses of his death, finds that each had had a totally different impression of him, so that they seem to be describing three different men.

Fieschi finds this film "still astonishing for its accomplished polyphonic experiments. . . . The non-chronological assembly of sequences, the overlapping of documentary and 'sophisticated' scenes (corresponding to the various social milieux involved), the meticulous polish given to each shot (framing, lighting, content), often heightened by purple patches, as well as the complexity of the formal links connecting them, the modernity of the actors . . . , the effectiveness of the rhythmic experiments (on speed and its sudden checks, as in the final car journey intercut with graphic signals), the intense economy of the visual signs punctuating the narrative, the violently dreamlike quality of the close-ups of objects (rings, watches, glasses, telephones), or of faces . . . , the constant inventiveness of the linking shots (from scene to scene and sequence to sequence)—all this bears witness to the close attention paid to the elements of meaning in their totality, as the product and not merely the sum of their parts."

"Before thinking of expressing ideas," Epstein said, "one must prepare the means that will enable them to be expressed." For Fieschi, this is the key to Epstein's formalism: "Epstein does not rely on the subject alone. His attention is directed to preparing his means—all his means: decor, actors, framing, composition, movements, ellipses, process work, editing—and above all their ability to combine. As Jean Mitry notes, he marks a definite point of rupture between the literary idea of cinema (Canudo, Delluc) and the first film aestheticians; but also the point of rupture which gave birth to modern cinema, if one understands by that a cinema *conscious of its own means.*"

The last picture made by Les Films Jean Epstein was one of the most admired of his works,

La Chute de la maison Usher (*The Fall of the House of Usher,* 1928), which draws not only on Poe's story of that title but on his "The Oval Mirror." Roderick Usher (Jean Debucourt), painting his wife's portrait, finds that as the work progresses, life drains from the woman herself (played by Abel Gance's wife Marguerite). But family tradition demands that the portrait be finished. . . .

Garbicz and Klinowski have called this "a poetic horror film—the most outstanding achievement of this genre in cinema history," and "a sort of anthology of the language of the pre-sound French school." It achieves its atmosphere "by an exemplary employment of both natural means and technical expertise. Epstein shot the location sequences of the film in the gloomy autumn landscape of the marshy Sologne country. He consistently stresses such elements of design as the candles in the huge, empty rooms of the castle. The camerawork employed mostly lazy panning and tracking shots, and introduced a magnificent scale of variable lighting. The key role rests with multiple exposure and trick and slow-motion photography: the whirling leaves, the pendulum of a clock, books falling out of shelves by themselves, phanton candles accompanying the funeral cortège. These elements have combined to produce an unrepeatable, elegiac film."

Langlois was equally enthusiastic about this "perfect work," in which "everything contributes to . . . [its] unity. . . . Since the French impressionist school has always considered the cinema to be like a visual symphony, we might call this film by Epstein the cinematic equivalent of Debussy's works." Catherine Wunscher agrees that "Edgar Allan Poe was not betrayed." According to Ian Christie, Epstein was "inadvertently responsible for launching Buñuel's career as a director, after sacking him as assistant on *La Chute* for his intemperate criticism of Gance"—at loose ends, Buñuel proceeded to make *Un Chien Andalou* with Salvador Dali.

"Read in conjunction," Christie wrote in *Afterimage* (Autumn 1981), "the texts and films of 1921–8 represent a dynamic exploration of the *potential* of cinema which is scarcely less radical than contemporary Soviet work. Yet lacking a theory and a discipline, Epstein's phenomenology of cinema contained the seeds of its own destruction. At the end of the decade he suffered a double eclipse. The restructuring of French cinema brought about by sound technology finished off low-budget experimental production and drove Epstein to a self-appointed exile making Breton subjects and sponsored shorts. Simultaneously there is a gradual change in his writing, which becomes more diffuse and rhetorical, finally retreating to a utopian mysticism, tinged with personalism and theosophy."

Many critics share Christie's view of the growing imprecision of Epstein's writing, but by no means everyone has been so dismissive about his "self-appointed exile making Breton subjects." There had always been "an axis of simplicity, spontaneity, documentary" in Epstein's work, and he turned to it conclusively under the influence of contemporary Soviet achievements— Eisenstein's *October* and Pudovkin's *The End of St. Petersburg.*

The first of Epstein's Breton films was *Finis Terrae* (1929), shot on location in the Ouessant archipelago between May 1928 and January 1929. Epstein fell in love with Brittany and the islanders, and was happy to work without sets or décor or professional actors or makeup: "No décor and no costume will have the look, the hang of the real thing. No pseudo-professional will have the marvelously technical gestures of the seaman or fisherman."

Epstein's script was based on a true story that he heard from the islanders. During the seaweed harvest, two young men quarrel over a trifle, but when one of them becomes ill with an infected wound, the other performs prodigious feats to get a doctor to him, and there is a successful operation at sea during a storm. Langlois thought that Epstein was still unsure of his new "documentary" style in this film, and found an "aestheticism of image" that was purged from subsequent works in the same mode. But in general the film was received with great enthusiasm and inspired many imitations.

Some critics indeed prefer Epstein's Breton films to his earlier experiments. Catherine Wunscher, writing in *Sight and Sound* (October–December 1953), called the early works "curiously démodé," and said that "the 'modernistic' and historical styles of décor appear restrictive now. . . . the real revelation comes with *Finis Terrae* . . . and continues up to *Le Tempestaire* (1947). . . . Before writing of Rossellini and the birth of neorealism, critics should look at these films by Epstein. All the beauty of the austere images in the final scene of *Paisa* is already there in 1929, in Epstein's figures stretched out on a white sandy beach, scarcely distinguishable from the surrounding rocks. . . . Unlike the Flaherty of *Man of Aran,* Epstein does not describe exceptional circumstances, but a people whom he watched living day by day, his eyes opened wide by love."

A commerical feature, *Sa tête* (1929), and a commissioned documentary, *Le Pas de la mule*

(1930), were followed by *Mor'Vran* (*La Mer des corbeaux/The Sea of Ravens,* 1931), set on the Ile de Sein, near Brest, and postsynchronized with music based on Breton folk songs. Langlois called it "one of the most beautiful documentaries of the French cinema . . . a veritable poem on Brittany and the sea."

In 1931–1932 came a series of postsynchronized short films made for Synchro-Ciné, most of them "cinematic poems" in which the images complement well-known songs like "La Chanson des peupliers" or "Les Berceaux." Returning to Brittany—this time to the island of Hoedik— Epstein made one of the finest of his "neorealist" films, *L'Or des mers* (*Gold From the Sea,* 1932). It is about what happens when an old outcast finds a chest washed up by the tide. The islanders conclude that it must be full of gold and become so generous to the old reprobate the he soon dies of drink. Before long his daughter is being courted by the handsomest man on the island.

Epstein wrote the script himself, saying afterwards that he "would have liked to limit speech to the role once played by intertitles . . . , but I was induced to extend the dialogue a little." By now he had discovered that "in slow motion any scene is good, even a bad actor is good in slow motion," and he make excellent (but perhaps excessive) use of this perception.

L'Homme à l'Hispano (1932) and *La Chatelaine du Liban* (1933) were both adapted by Epstein from contemporary novels and both failed, arguably because Epstein continued to concern himself with visual experiment at a time when audiences were only interested in "filmed theatre." Another feature, *Marius et Olive à Paris* (1935), was so mangled by its producers that Epstein withdrew his name from the credits. Now his career really was in eclipse. Epstein made only one or two commercial features and some commissioned documentaries from 1935 until 1939, when he stopped making films altogether for the duration of World War II. He worked for the Red Cross and wrote the essays published in 1947 as *L'Intelligence d'une machine* and *Le Cinéma du diable.*

By this time a forgotten figure, Epstein returned to Brittany in 1947 and made *Le Tempestaire* (*The Storm*), filmed on the island of Belle-Ile-en-Mer. This "legend of the sea" is about a girl whose lover, a fisherman, is at sea when a storm comes up. Her mother tells her about an old man with the power to quell tempests. She searches for him and finds him. As he blows softly on his witch-ball, the waves subside, the clouds disperse. Langlois tells a story about the making of this film that illustrates Epstein's great technical accomplishment. They were filming in the middle of a storm when the cameraman, "clinging to the camera to prevent it from flying away, cried, 'There won't be anything on the film.' 'Don't worry about that,' said Epstein, 'use such and such a lens, open to such and such, do this, do that,' and the cameraman, on his return to Paris, discovered to his amazement that not only did the film have impressions, but that the images were marvelously beautiful."

In *Le Tempestaire* Epstein uses not only visual slow motion but slowed-down sound. As he explained in *Le Cinéma du diable*, this technique has a "surrealizing force similar to that of slow motion. . . . Drawing out the duration of a sound . . . augments the distinguishing power of the sense of hearing, which acquires the ability to analyze more accurately the complex of sounds. . . . That which for the human ear is only the monotonous and confused roar of the sea during a storm . . . we hear as a polyphony of sounds so strange, so new, that many of them still have no name in any language. With each passing second, the sea utters another cry."

Henri Langlois considered *Le Tempestaire* Epstein's "last masterpiece . . . the most masterly, the richest, and the simplest." A few contemporary critics agreed, like J. B. Jeener, who wrote that "the Dantesque dialogue of the wind, of the sea, and of the rocks resembles nothing else." But for the most part the film was ignored until Langlois showed it at the Cannes festival in 1953, when "so many people of good faith looked dumbfounded at one another wondering why they had never seen *Le Tempestaire*. . . . It was not madness, they were all victims—and Epstein the first—of a conspiracy: a conspiracy of stupidity, ignorance, cinematic illiteracy, prejudices of a business that never looks backward, only ahead."

Epstein made only one more film, a United Nations documentary about the Brittany lighthouse keepers called *Les Feux de la mer* (*The Fires of the Sea,* 1948). Langlois said that "he died gagged, without being able to express himself," and Abel Gance that he "preferred to die as a victim rather than live by prostituting his art." Another volume of essays, *Esprit de cinéma*, was published posthumously in 1955, and his writings on film, including the previously unpublished *Alcool et cinéma*, were collected in the two-volume *Écrits sur le cinéma* (1974).

Fieschi says that Epstein created "one of the most experimental *oeuvres* of the entire silent cinema"—that he was a precursor of the "poetic realism" of the 1930s, of neorealism, and even of the temporal experiments of Resnais, while his theoretical work was "the germ even behind the semiological analyses of Christian Metz." Ian Christie writes that "Epstein's obsessive discourse on the power and 'mystery' of cinema played a vital part in the first era of reflection on the nature of cinema, and if it later declined into an arid mysticism, it also . . . identified the problems which later film theory would tackle."

FILMS: Pasteur, 1922; Les Vendages, 1922 (documentary); L'Auberge rouge (The Red Inn), 1923; Coeur fidèle (The Faithful Heart), 1923; La Montagne infidèle, 1923 (documentary); La Belle nivernaise (The Beauty of Nivers), 1923; Le Lion des mogols (The Lion of the Moguls), 1924; L'Affiche (The Poster), 1924; Le Double Amour (Double Love), 1925; Les Aventures de Robert Macaire (in five episodes), 1925; Mauprat, 1926; Au Pays de George Sand, 1926 (documentary); Six et demi-onze: un Kodak (Six and a Half by Eleven: A Kodak), 1927; La Glace à trois faces (The Three-Sided Mirror), 1927; La Chute de la maison Usher (The Fall of the House of Usher), 1928; Finis Terrae, 1929; Sa tête (His Head), 1929; Mor'Vran (La Mer des corbeaux/The Sea of Ravens), 1930; Notre-Dame de Paris, 1931 (documentary); La Chanson des peupliers, 1931 (filmed song); Le Cor, 1931 (filmed song); L'Or des mers (Gold From the Sea), 1932; Les Berceaux, 1932 (filmed song); La Villanelle des rubans, 1932 (filmed song); Le Vieux Chaland, 1932 (filmed song); L'Homme a l'Hispano (The Man With the Hispano), 1933; La Châtelaine du Liban, 1933; Chanson d'Armor, 1934 (documentary); La Vie d'un grand journal, 1934 (documentary); Cuor di vagabondo (Coeur de gueux), 1936; La Bretagne, 1936 (documentary); La Bourgogne, 1936 (documentary); Vive la vie, 1937 (documentary); La Femme du bout du monde, 1937; Les Bâtisseurs, 1938 (documentary); Eau-vive, 1938 (documentary); (with René Lucot) Artères de France, 1939 (documentary); Le Tempestaire (The Storm), 1947; Les Feux de la mer, 1948 (documentary).

ABOUT: Abel, R. French Cinema, The First Wave 1915–1929, 1984; Centrofilm Jean Epstein, 1963 (in Italian); Garbicz, A. and Klinowski, J. Cinema: The Magic Vehicle Vol. 1, 1983; Haudiquet, P. Epstein, 1966 (in French); Leprohon, P. Jean Epstein, 1964 (in French); Manvell, R. Experiment in the Film, 1949; Roud, R. (ed.) Cinema: A Critical Dictionary, 1980. *Periodicals*—Afterimage Autumn 1981 (Epstein issue); L'Avant-Scène du Cinéma October 1983 (Epstein issue); Cahiers du Cinéma June 1953; Cinemages 2 1955 (Epstein issue); Film Dope March 1978; Sight and Sound October–December 1953.

ERMLER, FRIEDRICH MARKOVICH

(May 13, 1898–1967), Soviet director, scenarist, and administrator, was born in Lettonie, Latvia, more or less at the same time that the cinema was born in France. He grew up with the movies and, while still a child, would organize his

FRIEDRICH ERMLER

friends to act out his own scenarios in his back yard. Ermler at first planned a career in pharmacy and during his adolescence was apprenticed to a pharmacist in the Latvian town of Rechitsa. However, in 1919 he joined the Communist Party and fought with the Red Army during the civil war. He was captured by the Whites on the northern front and severely tortured. Recovering, he served for a time in the anti-smuggling section of the Cheka before deciding to pursue his childhood passion for the cinema. In 1922 he played a bit part in Vyacheslav Viskovsky's *Red Partisans* and the following year entered the Leningrad Technicum of Screen Arts. Originally an acting student, he soon became more interested in directing.

Grigori Kozintsev met Ermler in 1924 when the latter, while studying at the Technicum, was also serving as secretary of Sevkapino (North-Western Cinema). Kozintsev and Leonid Trauberg were then making their names as the youthful directors of FEKS, an intensely anti-academic Leningrad theatre company committed to formal experiment and mixed-media productions drawing on the circus, vaudeville, and cinema. They visited Sevkapino with their first scenario and Kozintsev has described how Ermler, "a young man with long hair and a leather jacket . . . welcomed us in a friendly way: within minutes we were on familiar terms of address, at the end of half an hour we were friends." (Their script was accepted at Sevkapino and filmed as the outrageous comedy *Adventures of Octyabrina*.)

Ermler was the only Party member among the Technicum students, and his commitment was total and militant—there is a story that he showed up for his first class with his army Mauser on his hip. He was appalled to find that students were addressed as "gentlemen" instead of "comrades" and promptly recruited two other Komsomols (Young Communists) to form a three-man "Communist Assembly" at the Technicum. He also organized an experimental workshop there, known as KEM (which acted out its screenplays on stage for lack of film stock to shoot them on). The group's objective, as explained in Ermler's manifesto, was the creation of a new revolutionary cinema based on material derived from the study of society and its problems—a concern that was always central in his own work. In spite of Ermler's friendship with Kozintsev and Trauberg, KEM was to some extent a reaction against FEKS—an insistence on the need for "revolutionary content" rather than "revolutionary form." Ermler mistrusted formal experiment and preferred realism partly because he had an innate "taste for reality" and partly because he considered it the director's duty to make his films as clear and comprehensible as possible to ordinary moviegoers.

He was still a student when he persuaded the state health authorities to sponsor his first film, a competent educational short about scarlet fever and public health. Graduating from the Technicum in 1925 he made his first feature for Leningradkino in collaboration with another young graduate, Eduard Johanson. *Deti Buri* (*Children of the Storm*, 1926), set in Petrograd (later Leningrad) during the Civil War, deals with the detective work of a group of Komsomols trying to rescue a party of their comrades who have been captured by White Guards. It tells an exciting story very simply and directly, and successfully launched Ermler's career.

His second film is much more typical of his mature work, both in style and content, though it is not altogether clear whether it was a solo effort or a second collaboration with Johanson. *Katka—bumazhnyr anyot* (*Katka's Reinette Apples*, 1926) is about a country girl (Veronica Buzhinskaya) who comes to Petrograd in search of work just after the civil war—a period marked by profiteering and gangsterism. Reduced to selling apples on the street, she falls into the clutches of the underworld, is cheated, seduced, and abandoned, but rescued by the gentle, eccentric Fyodor. This offbeat character, with his battered hat and crumpled tie, is played with great charm by Fyodor Nikitin, whom Ermler used in all his subsequent silent films.

Katka introduced a characteristic Ermler theme—the moral regeneration of Soviet society after the cynicism of the NEP period. It was greatly admired as a portrait of urban life during that time of transition and greatly liked for its warmth and humanity. Designed by Yevgeni Enei and photographed by Yevgeni Mikhailov and Andrei Moskvin, the film is fundamentally realistic but shows signs of the influence of German expressionism, especially in the haunting street scenes at the opening. According to A. S. Birkos it also reflects "the lessons of montage" that Ermler had learned from seeing Eisenstein's *Strike*.

Parizhsky sapozhnik (*The Parisian Cobbler*, 1928) caused something of a sensation. It stars Nikitin as the deaf-mute cobbler Kirik, who comes to the aid of a young woman (Buzhinskaya again) left pregnant by a Komsomol. It was extremely daring to suggest that a non-Party man like Kirik might behave better than a Young Communist, but the film coincided with an official campaign to clean up the Komsomol organization, whose arrogant amorality was becoming a scandal. Released with Party blessing, it was received with popular and critical enthusiasm. It was followed a month later by another hit, *Dom v sugrobakh* (*The House in the Snow Drifts*), a film that tells three stories, each set on a different floor of a house in Petrograd during the civil war.

Ermler's last silent feature—his fifth in three years—confirmed his standing as a major new director. *Oblomok imperii* (*Fragment of an Empire*, 1929) written by Ermler and Katerina Vinogradskaya, begins with a prologue in which we see the hero, Filimonov (Nikitin), working at a provincial railroad depot during the civil war and saving a wounded Red Army soldier from execution by the advancing Whites. The film proper opens a decade later at the same depot, and we learn that Filimonov has spent the intervening years as an amnesiac. In an extraordinary montage sequence the hero recovers his memory. He hurries home to the city he still remembers as Petrograd to find everything strangely altered. The old master no longer owns the factory where Filimonov used to work—everyone is "master" now. Filimonov is won over to this exciting new society and in due course rediscovers his wife. She has failed to adjust to changing conditions and, still clinging to outworn conventions, has married a cultural worker (whose cowardice and bourgeois hypocrisy are revealed with broad and rather cruel humor). Filimonov returns to his new friends and the new challenges they will face together.

As Jay Leyda wrote, there are elements of stylization in the picture but "because they are controlled within the clear propaganda aim of the film, they never obtrude or take over" its style. The story, Leyda points out, deals acutely and in some depth (albeit often humorously) with "the most serious problems of the period—the human aspects of socialist construction, questions of new working relationships, of mass culture (and its misuses), and of marriage and modern family life. . . . The treatment of this material is a model of realism, presented without any sophistication—almost as if Filimonov were telling a parable in the terms of Rip Van Winkle or Enoch Arden—although its technique recalls both Eisenstein [whom Ermler consulted about the editing of this film] and Dovzhenko, and even Pabst."

Ermler's concern for realism was such that he sent Nikitin to study amnesia victims at a psychiatric clinic and also made him walk around in public in costume and makeup until he felt totally in character as Filimonov. Leyda says that "it was Ermler's sharp observation of both mental disease and of war that makes the fantastic sequence of the return of memory so compelling. An accidental juxtaposition of objects and movements brings back scraps of images, dimly remembered sounds, swinging a kaleidoscopic cluster of images into a recognizable pattern of the past—and Filimonov is himself again."

At this point in his career, Ermler's future seemed bright. With the coming of sound, he began work on a scenario for a film tentatively called "Song." Then, for reasons that have never been fully explained, he lost confidence in his ability to cope with the new medium and decided to make no more films. Lev Arnshtam and Jay Leyda were among those "who always believed in the great power of his talent" and begged him to persevere, but it was Sergei Yutkevich who gave Ermler back his confidence, by involving him as codirector in *Vstrechnyi* (*Counterplan*, 1932), an ambitious and important sound film designed to celebrate the fifteenth anniversary of the October Revolution. Dealing with conflict in a Leningrad factory between dedicated Komsomols and old guard workers resisting revolutionary change, *Counterplan* was based on scrupulous study of actual conditions and workers in similar factories, and has been recognized as a precursor of "socialist realism." Yutkevich and Ermler divided the directorial work between them, Ermler concentrating on the older workers (and earning praise for his sympathy and understanding from Vladimir Gardin, who gave a memorable performance as the old foreman Babchenko).

With his confidence restored, Ermler then spent a year on various collective farms with V. Portnov and Mikhail Bolshintov, the coauthors of his next film, *Krestyaniye* (*Peasants*, 1935).

The most naturalistic of Ermler's films and the most intense, it is set on a hog-raising *kolkhov* where Gerasim, a member of a *kulak* (rich peasant) family, plots to sabotage collectivization by every means up to and including murder. The story is told with a raw brutality of style that some have found repellent but that peasant audiences called "absolutely true to life." At an award-giving ceremony in January 1935 (when Eisenstein was ostentatiously passed over), Ermler was one of ten or eleven filmmakers to receive the Soviet Union's highest cultural award, the Order of Lenin. The same year he was a member of the official delegation that visited New York and Hollywood to publicize Soviet films.

During the making of *Counterplan*, Ermler had met Sergei Kirov, the able and influential Communist Party head of the Leningrad district, subsequently murdered under mysterious circumstances. Because of this connection and his proven dedication to the Party, Ermler was chosen to direct *Veliki grazhdanin* (*The Great Citizen*), an account of Kirov's career and death. Written by Ermler in collaboration with Mikhail Bleiman and Mikhail Bolshintov, and with a score by Shostakovich, it explores conflicts within the Party hierarchy to show Kirov (here called Shakhov and played by Nikolai Bogolyubov) struggling against his "Trotskyite" enemies and their foreign allies to such effect that they find it necessary to eliminate him. The film thus follows the official Party explanation of the assassination; in fact, it is now clear that Stalin himself ordered the murder of this alarmingly popular "favorite of the Party" and then set about finding scapegoats. The result was the Moscow "show trials" and the purges that followed.

The trials were only just finishing as work began on the film, and it is difficult to imagine a less attractive or more frighteningly delicate assignment. Actors were reluctant to appear in the picture, especially in negative roles, and it was blocked and delayed in every possible way by Lenfilm executives and Party officials who had good reason to dispute its version of the facts. Production went ahead only after the arrest and execution of obstructionist "enemies of the people." The film was finally released in twenty-six reels and two parts in February 1938 and November 1939, and shown all over the world as an apologia for the Moscow trials and the purges.

Discussing the film in *Sight and Sound*, Robert Vas wrote that it was "the biggest of all the prestige propaganda films; a psychological portrait of a real Bolshevik, his tragic moral victory and the breakdown of his neurotic enemies; a seemingly sober and accurate account of what had allegedly happened. But this is used by Ermler as basis for a film of contained passions: a typical case of anti-*mise en scène* turned into something no less authentically cinematic. 'Because much of the theme was developed through philosophical and ideological dialogue,' wrote Catherine de la Roche, 'Ermler wanted uninterrupted continuity in each scene . . . and wanted both camerawork and cutting to remain unnoticeable. The camera angles were from the audience's viewpoint.'

"Clearly," Vas goes on, "Ermler had the courage to look his most difficult subject straight in the eye and to present it in the sharpest way in the sharpest political circumstances. . . . And in its seriousness and determination *The Great Citizen* compares only with Bresson's . . . [*Diary of a Country Priest*], however different the concepts. This is perhaps the utmost limit of conviction, restraint and assurance that a propaganda film can achieve. For many viewers it may be the biggest bore of them all—but as a tragic manifestation of an artist's dedication, his attempt to follow a cause and serve it to the utmost of his power, the film remains a uniquely moving document. . . . we are dealing with the work of an artist who had faith—and who was fatally, villainously cheated."

In 1940, Ermler was appointed head of the Lenfilm studio and a year later supervised its evacuation to Alma-Ata in Kazakhstan. It was not until 1943 that his own first wartime film was completed. *Ona zashchishchayet rodinu* (*She Defends Her Country*) is about a peasant woman whose husband is killed at the front and whose family is murdered by the invading Germans. Half-crazed by grief, she recovers to become leader of a partisan group. The heroine is played by Vera Maretskaya, whose own husband was killed in action just before the film's preview and who was made a People's Artist for her performance. *She Defends Her Country* was extremely popular in the Soviet Union and abroad—a dubbed version was shown in Britain and the United States as *No Greater Love*. According to A. S. Birkos, however, the movie now seems badly dated and does not compare with Ermler's second war film, *Veliki perelom* (*The Great Turning Point,* 1946).

The notion of making a film about a Soviet general had been in Ermler's mind since early in 1942, but he and his coscenarist Boris Chirskov could devise no satisfactory structure until "the great finale of the Battle of Stalingrad" provided one. Serious problems remained, as the scenarists recalled: "How could we portray the drama of personal human passions through the medium of the professional conversations of generals? . . . The vision of a map, as a symbol of boredom, dogged us." They showed their scenario to soldiers and officers at the front and, after being told by General Vatutin that it was naive, scrapped it and started again: "The really surprising thing was that front-line life revealed to us the secret of the film's genre. At the front we came to understand that we were not planning a battle film but a psychological film."

Lenfilm had returned to its own badly damaged studios by the time filming began on *The Great Turning Point.* "All the machinery had been wrecked," Ermler said, "and in filming we had to use old, antiquated lighting equipment. Wednesdays were off-days for filming, as this was rehabilitation day, when everyone—directors, actors, technical staff—from studio head to commissionaire—rolled up their sleeves and lent a hand in rebuilding the wrecked studio." The battle scenes were shot in the ruins of Leningrad but as the scenarists explained, the film's emphasis was not on them. The central character, Muravyev (Mikhail Derzhavin), is a composite of the several generals interviewed by the scenarists. As commander of the Stalingrad forces, his problem is to hold the town without drawing on his strategic reserves, who must be held for the final encirclement of the German divisions in accordance with the inviolable plan of the Commander-in-Chief (Stalin). Not even Muravyev's closest associates can be told of this plan, and many of his decisions therefore seem to them inexplicable. And the strain and loneliness of Muravyev's situation is compounded by the death of his wife. This grim, powerful, and dramatic film won the National Prize at Cannes.

Great Force (1950), a highly patriotic film about Soviet scientists ending their misguided allegiance to foreign theories, was to have been followed by a piece of Cold War propaganda called "Guarding the Peace." This project was abandoned when Ermler became seriously ill. It was not until 1955 that his next film appeared—*Neokonchennaya povest* (*An Unfinished Story*), a romantic tale about the self-sacrificing love between a doctor (Yelena Bystritskaya) and her crippled patient (Sergei Bondarchuk) which showed little of Ermler's usual concern for the social and political implications of his material. After *Pervi den* (*The First Day*, 1958), he worked in television until, shortly before his death, he made one more extraordinary film.

Pered sudom istorii (*Before the Judgement of History*) centers on Vassili Shulgin, born a wealthy landowner in czarist Russia and a member of the last Imperial Duma (parliament). Exiled after the Revolution, Shulgin was arrested in Prague and spent years in Stalin's labor camps. After his release in 1956 he remained in Russia, occasionally writing letters to the papers and forming a sort of loyal opposition to the Soviet government. In the film the old man is shown visiting the historic sites of Leningrad, reminiscing about the past and the Revolution, and arguing with the anonymous historian who is his companion, especially on the theme of freedom and justice under the Soviets. Flashbacks and old newsreels are used to illustrate these discussions, and as one reviewer wrote, "the emphasis throughout is one of respect for an old man who is still misguided on many points, but understands that in the main the Soviet regime is right."

It was generally accepted by Western commentators that this extremely unorthodox film was a response to the growing complaints of young Soviet citizens about the crudeness and crassness of Party propaganda. According to a Moscow reporter in the London *Times,* the film "is particularly interesting because of the subtlety with which its message is conveyed [and] the sophistication of its dialogue"—"judging from the scramble outside the cinema this afternoon for any spare tickets and the rapt attention and whispered arguments of the audience, it is achieving its purpose."

"The basis of my films generally comes from me," Ermler said, "but to develop it, I have always used a scriptwriter. I never adapt a script during filming. I don't have enough talent to improvise. I study it carefully then use it like a conductor uses a music score, knowing what I must draw from the actors and the sets. It is men who matter the most to me and, with actors, their faces." Even critics who do not share his political beliefs admire his passionate revolutionary idealism, for which he underwent physical torture at the hands of the White Guards and (it may be surmised) emotional torment in the making of *The Great Citizen.* He is generally recognized as one of the major realist filmmakers, whose absolute commitment to his country's political system was almost never allowed to suppress his equally deep concern for psychological truth.

FILMS: Scarlet Fever, 1924 (documentary); (with Eduard Johanson) Deti buri (Children of the Storm), 1926; (with Eduard Johanson?) Katka—bumazhnyr anyot (Katka's Reinette Apples/Katka, the Apple Girl), 1926; Parizhsky sapozhnik (The Parisian Cobbler), 1928; Dom v sugrobakh (The House in the Snow Drifts), 1928; Oblomok imperii (Fragment of an Empire), 1929; (with Sergei Yutketvitch) Vstrechnyi (Counterplan/The Challenge), 1932; Krestyaniye (Peasants), 1935; Veliki grazhdanin (The Great Citizen): Part I, 1938, Part 2, 1939; Ona zashchishchayet rodinu (She Defends Her Country/No Greater Love),

1943; Veliki perelom (The Great Turning Point/ The Turning Point), 1946; Great Force/Great Power, 1950; Neokonchennaya povest (An Unfinished Story), 1955; Pervi den (The First Day), 1958; Pered sudom istorii (Before the Judgement of History), 1967.

ABOUT: Biographical Dictionary of the USSR, 1958; Birkos, A. S. Soviet Cinema, 1976; Kovarsky, N. Fridrikh Ermler, 1941 (in Russian); Leyda, J. Kino, 1960; Who's Who in the USSR, 1961–1962. *Periodicals*—Cahiers du Cinéma 1 1960, November 1967; Films and Filming October 1967; Iskusstvo Kino 7 1969, September 1973; Sight and Sound Summer 1962.

PAUL FEJOS

*FEJOS, PAUL (January 24, 1897–April 23, 1963), Hungarian-born filmmaker and ethnologist, was born Pal Fejös in Budapest, one of the two children of Desiré Fejös and the former Aurora Novelly. Many published accounts have it that his father was a captain in the Hussars, his mother a lady-in-waiting to the Empress, and Fejos himself later an official of the Imperial Court. Such tales are apparently a reflection of his refusal to be contained by anything so prosaic as facts, especially such unromantic facts as those of his own family background. It does seem to be true that his mother's family, originally Italian, had some kind of aristocratic lineage, but his father was a pharmacist in Dunaföldvar, a small town near Budapest. Shortly before Paul was born, Desiré Fejös sold his business and moved to the capital, intending to buy a shop there, but died of a heart attack before the deal was completed.

Paul and his older sister Olga were raised by their mother in her parents' home. The boy attended a school at Veszprem run by the Piarist Fathers and another at Kecskemet. He was a lively child with a phenomenal memory, early addicted to the cinema. He went on to study medicine. During World War I Paul Fejos served as a medical orderly with the Imperial Austrian Army on the Italian front, where he also ran a theatre for the troops. Claims that he was an officer in the Hussars, that he was three times wounded, and that he was one of the first to pilot a combat airplane, all seem to be more interesting than accurate.

After the war Fejos returned to Budapest, where he earned his living as a set painter, first for the opera, then for the Orient-Film production company. In 1919 or 1920 he made his own first films for the Mobil Studio. These included a mythological piece, *Pán* (1920); an adaptation of Oscar Wilde's *The Crime of Lord Arthur Saville* (1920); a film about police corruption in New York called *The Black Captain* (1921); *The*

Last Adventure of Arsène Lupin (1921), modeled on the American serials then popular; and *The Queen of Spades* (1922), adapted from Pushkin.

Even in these early days, according to the actor Lajos Balint, Fejos regarded the cinema as a matter of "moving images," closer to painting than the theatre. Like artists from Rembrandt to the Impressionists, Fejos said, the filmmaker must concern himself with the problems of light and shadow. He believed that the cinema could expect no proper solution to these problems until films could be made in color, but that black, white, and gray meanwhile provided sufficient resources to insure the primacy of the image over playacting. Balint said that Fejos struggled hard to apply his principles, handicapped though he was by primitive studios and equipment.

The combined effects of postwar economic crisis and the repressions of the Horthy regime made this a grim era for the Hungarian cinema and for the country as a whole. Filmmakers like Alexander Korda and Michael Curtiz began to leave Hungary, and in 1923 Fejos joined the exodus. A personal factor in his decision to make a new start was his separation from his first wife, Mara Jankowsky. They were married in 1914 and divorced in 1921, reportedly on account of his irrational jealousy. When Fejos left Hungary he went first to Vienna, where he worked for a time with Max Reinhardt. After a stint with Fritz Lang in Berlin, apparently as an extra, he moved on to Paris, where he staged Walter Hasenclever's avant-garde play *L'Homme*. This production was not particularly successful, and Fejos decided to try his luck in the United States.

°fā´ yōsh

Fejos arrived penniless in New York in October 1923, and at first took whatever jobs he could, working in a funeral parlor, a piano factory, and elsewhere. By the spring of 1924 his English had improved greatly, and he secured a job as laboratory technician with the Rockefeller Institute for Medical Research, earning $80 a month. He worked there for two years and in 1925 made a second marriage, to a fellow-employee named Mimosa Pfalz, which apparently lasted only thirty days. His artistic ambitions seem to have been reawakened by a part-time stint with the Theatre Guild, helping to establish the correct Hungarian atmosphere for a production of Molnar's *The Glass Slipper*. In the spring of 1926, having spent all his savings ($45) on an ancient Buick, Fejos set off for Los Angeles.

Further privations followed in Hollywood, though Fejos did secure one or two assignments as a scenarist. (It is possible that *Stronger Than Death* and *Square Shooting*, sometimes included in Fejos filmographies, were in fact unused scenarios.) At any rate, there were times during his first two years in California when Fejos only survived by hitchhiking down to Pasadena and stealing fruit from the orange groves there. On one of these foraging expeditions he was picked up by a sumptuous automobile containing Edward Spitz, a rich young New Yorker whose ambition was to produce movies. Spitz was impressed by what he heard of his passenger's brilliant career in filmmaking but not entirely carried away: "He gave me five thousand dollars to make a film," Fejos said. "In those days the average cost of a film was five hundred thousand dollars."

Fejos accepted the assignment and in October 1927 began work on *The Last Moment*, completing it twenty-eight days later. He acquired the services of actor friends with time to spare, promising payment if the film succeeded, and made a similar arrangement with Chaplin's leading lady Georgia Hale (who normally earned five thousand dollars a week but found the young director's effrontery irresistible). He employed a completely untried cameraman, Leon Shamroy, hired a studio not by the day but by the minute, and used sets built for other films, if necessary adapting his scenario. Filmstock was obtained free from DuPont, then attempting to challenge the domination of Kodak and Agfa. During periods when sets or actors were unavailable, Fejos kept his crew busy shooting closeups of hands, feet, cars, and anything else that took his fancy, incorporating these images into his montage with great effect.

The Last Moment, in which a suicide (Otto Matiesen) reviews in flashback as he drowns the events of his life, is a seven-reel silent, eschewing captions. No copies seem to have survived, but contemporary accounts suggest that Fejos had not changed his ideas about the nature of cinema—the film is much more effective visually than it is dramatically, full of "dizzying wipes, multiple superimpositions, and vertiginous camera movements." Released in 1928, it received adulatory notices. Chaplin praised it, Tamar Lane called it "one of the most remarkable films that has ever been presented on the screen," and others hailed it as a work of genius, rivaling Murnau. The major studios vied for the director's services, and he finally signed with Universal, which promised him absolute control over the films he would make, from choice of subject to final editing.

His first movie for Universal was *Lonesome* (1928), the most admired and best-known of all his films. Inspired by an article about the loneliness of city life, it was written by Edward T. Lowe Jr. and Tom Reed, and produced by Carl Laemmle Jr. Glenn Tryon and Barbara Kent play two young people who, unknown to each other, live in adjoining rooms in the same New York boardinghouse. Separately they go off to work, come home, and drift off to Coney Island. They meet there by chance, are instantly attracted, but lose each other in the confusion when the wheel of the Big Dipper catches fire. Returning miserably home, they rediscover each other as neighbors. There are some hand-tinted sequences, and some "talkie" passages were added after the film was completed.

Andrew Sarris has described *Lonesome* as "a tender love story in its silent passages" but "crude, clumsy, and tediously tongue-tied in its 'talkie' passages." Charles Higham thought that "its visual style, initially attractive, becomes a monotonous succession of busy shots, dissolving over each other in a perpetual flurry," though he allowed that "the film's charm is real." For Jonathan Rosenbaum, "the brilliant opening of *Lonesome*, with its lightning-sharp notations of city life set against the morning behaviour, rituals and jobs of hero and heroine . . . suggests a potentially major talent fusing some of the metaphysical grandiosity of a Lang or Murnau with some of the social and gestural sensitivity of an Eisenstein or Pudovkin. And if the rest of the film fails to live up to this promise, it is at once rigorous and likeable enough to sustain dramatically its formal conceit of parallel construction. The wonderfully natural performances of the couple are contained and contrasted throughout within this pattern as they pursue their day separately and together." Georges Sadoul and others have seen *Lonesome* as an important precursor of neorealism.

The Last Performance (1929), also a part-sound film, starred Conrad Veidt in a visually striking but rather foolish drama about a stage magician in love with his young assistant. It was another box-office success and Fejos, who had made *The Last Moment* for five thousand dollars, was given a million to spend on *Broadway* (1929), an all-sound adaptation of a successful musical by Jed Harris, George Abbott, and Philip Dunning. Fejos assigned most of his enormous budget to the construction of equally enormous sets—including a spectacular cubistic nightclub—and on the most versatile camera crane in the world, a monster weighing twenty-eight tons. The plot, involving Glenn Tryon and Evelyn Brent among others, was considerably less impressive, and Fejos himself regarded the movie as a failure, though in *Manuscript of the American Musical Film,* Miles Kreuger wrote that "the images of the Paradise Club and the huge musical number ('Finale in Technicolor') have become basic screen literature." There was a remake in 1942 by William A. Seiter.

Captain of the Guard (1930, originally called *Marsellaise*) was equally lavish. In a single sequence of this French Revolution drama—the storming of the Bastille—Fejos employed three thousand extras. While shooting this scene the director fell from a scaffold and sustained a concussion that put him out of action for six weeks. John Stuart Robinson completed the film and was credited as director. Fejos was further aggrieved when John Murray Anderson was listed as sole director of *King of Jazz* (1930), a Paul Whiteman vehicle on which Fejos had done some work (though probably less than he claimed). The last straw came the same year, when Fejos was passed over for the directorship of *All Quiet on the Western Front,* which he had coveted. He broke his contract with Universal and switched to Metro-Goldwyn-Mayer, for whom he made French and German versions of George Hill's prison drama *The Big House*—versions which are said to be different from the original in many ways, and notable films in their own right.

In 1931 Fejos accepted an invitation from Pierre Braunberger to film in France, where his experience as a director of talkies was much needed. He left Hollywood in some bitterness, complaining of its commercialism and asserting that the American film was a drug, offering fantasy happy endings to blind the workers to the hopelessness of their lives: "In fact, if the movie theatres were suddenly closed in America, there would be revolution." He had returned to Europe, he said, in the belief that there he might find a public for "films made in the name of art." In France Fejos supervised the comedy

L'Amour à l'Americaine (1931), the first film by a young director named Claude Heyman, and himself directed *Fantômas* (1931), a remake of the Feuillade serial, forerunner of such fantasies as *Superman.*

In 1932 Fejos returned to Hungary and the same year made a film which some critics place even above *Lonesome.* This was *Tavaszi Zápor* (*Marie, a Hungarian Legend,* also known as *Spring Shower* and *A Story of Love*). It stars Annabella as Marie, a teenage servant girl who is seduced and abandoned, and who dies in poverty and disgrace after giving birth to a child. Scrubbing floors in Heaven, she sees her daughter facing a similar seduction sixteen years later, and causes a shower of rain to avert a repetition of her own tragedy. Jonathan Rosenbaum regards the picture as a slighter film than *Lonesome,* though one "with some magical moments of its own. Much as *Lonesome* seems indebted to the city and amusement park scenes in [Marnau's] *Sunrise,* the nocturnal lighting and sensuality of Marie's seduction and its mysterious musical aftermath recall certain rustic night scenes in the same film. But unlike the determinism of Murnau's compositions and camera movements, Fejos' anthropological distance and fairy-tale encapsulations imply a different sort of relationship to his characters: the rapid cutting between details in a brothel parlour to convey Marie's confusion before fainting encourages an identification with sensations, not thoughts or feelings. And the beauty of Annabella's performance and a violin-and-clarinet theme may help one overlook some of the more reductive aspects of the folk legend that define the film's dimensions."

It is reported of Fejos (and would be characteristic of him) than when Annabella was on her way home to France after filming *Tavaszi Zapor,* he piloted a plane over her train and showered it with roses. He was extremely gallant and romantic in all his dealings with women, and John W. Dodds goes so far as to say that every time Fejos moved from one country to another at this stage of his itinerant career, it was on account of the ending of a love affair.

Fejos made one more film in Hungary, *Ítél a Balaton* (*The Verdict of Lake Balaton*), notable for its beautiful water photography and its almost documentary treatment of the fishermen and peasants of the region. This film and its predecessor were fiercely attacked in Hungary for what they revealed of the narrow mindedness and bigotry of village life, and in 1933 Fejos moved on again to Austria to film *Sonnenstrahl* (*The Golden Smile*), again starring Annabella. Haudiquet describes this little-known study of unemployment and poverty in Vienna as a masterpiece, "the summit of Fejos' art in Europe . . . too often ignored by the critics." *Frühlingstimmen* (*The Voice of Spring*), a light comedy, followed in the same year. With his friends Lothar Wolff (assistant director) and Ferenc Farkas (composer), who had worked on all his films since *Tavaszi Zápor*, Fejos then went to Denmark, where in 1934 and 1935 they made three movies for Nordisk Films. These were *Flugten fra millionerne*, a comedy; *Fange Nr. 1* (*Prisoner Number One*), a farce set in a world where prisons and policemen have become unnecessary; and *Det Gyldne Smil* (*The Golden Smile*). The latter, starring the distinguished Danish actress Bodil Ipsen, is an exploration of the relationship between art and life, adapted by Fejos from a play by Kaj Munk.

Fejos was becoming increasingly frustrated by the artificialities of studio shooting, and at this point he went to Madagascar for Nordisk with a view to using the island as a setting for a feature film that would be shot on location. The director fell in love with Madagascar and its people and spent nine months there, recording on film the island's plant and animal life and the tribal societies and customs of its people. Unfortunately, the thirty thousand metres of film he shot there included nothing that could be used in the fictional film that had been intended. With the help of Gunnar Skoglund of Svensk Filmindustri, this material was instead edited into a number of short documentaries. Fejos also collected on Madagascar a number of artifacts which he presented to the Royal Geographic Society of Denmark. Encouraged by Dr. Thompsen of the Copenhagen Museum, he embarked on the study of cultural anthropology, beginning a completely new chapter in his life.

Further journeys followed under the auspices of Svensk Filmindustri. Over the next few years Fejos made ethnological documentaries in Indonesia, the Philippines, Ceylon, New Guinea, and elsewhere, including Thailand, where he filmed the notable long documentary *En Handfull Ris* (*A Handful of Rice*, 1938), also known as *Man och Kvinna* (*Man and Woman*). Returning from Thailand, Fejos by chance met the Swedish industrialist and philanthropist Axel Wenner-Gren, then sailing the southern seas in his yacht. It was an encounter uncannily like Fejos's first accidental meeting with Edward Spitz, and its effects were no less productive. The two men became friends, and Wenner-Gren financed Fejos's expedition to Peru at the end of 1939. In Cuzco Fejos discovered an account by a Franciscan friar of lost cities in the Peruvian jungle, and with Wenner-Gren's backing went in search of them, eventually discovering the remains of eighteen Incaic cities. Fejos went on to the headwaters of the Amazon, where he spent a year studying and filming the Yagua Indians. His *Ethnology of the Yagua* (1943) launched the Viking Fund Series of Publications in Anthropology.

In 1941 Fejos settled in New York as research director (and effective head) of the Viking Fund, later the Wenner-Gren Foundation for Anthropological Research. He became a much respected administrator, ahead of his time in his urgent awareness of the need for communication between the various branches of anthropology and its related disciplines. He taught at Stanford, Yale, and Columbia, and was the recipient of many honors.

According to David Bidney, his obituarist in the *American Anthropologist*, "Paul Fejos had the temperament of an artist rather than that of a scholar or research scientist. . . . He supported not only research projects but also, and primarily, individuals whom he trusted and considered worthy of support. . . . His personal support of Pierre Teilhard de Chardin during the last years of the life of this eccentric genius is but one outstanding example. . . . He leaves behind him the Wenner-Gren Foundation for Anthropological Research which he built, an international host of friends whom he has helped, and a wife whom he cherished and appreciated." And, it might be added, a few brilliant films.

His last wife, the former Lita Binns, whom he married in 1958, succeeded him as research director of the Wenner-Gren Foundation. Fejos became an American citizen in 1930.

—*Mk.S.*

FILMS: *Hungary*—Pán, 1920; Lidércnyomás (The Crime of Lord Arthur Saville/Hallucination/Nightmare), 1920; Ujraélők (The Resurrected), 1920; Fekete Kapitaný (The Black Captain), 1921; Arsèn Lupin Utolsó Kalandja (The Last Adventure of Arsène Lupin), 1922; Pique Dame (The Queen of Spades), 1922; Szenzació (Sensation), 1922 (some scholars believe this to be an alternative title for Pique Dame). *United States*—The Last Moment, 1928; Lonesome, 1928; The Last Performance (Erik the Great/Erik the Great Illusionist), 1929; Broadway, 1929; Captain of the Guard, 1930; The Big House (French and German versions only), 1930. *France*—Fantômas, 1931. *Hungary*—Tavaszi Zápor (Marie, a Hungarian Legend/Spring Shower/A Story of Love/Marie, légende hongroise), 1932; Ítél a Balaton (The Verdict of Lake Balaton/Storm at Balaton), 1932. *Austria*—Sonnenstrahl (The Golden Smile/Gardez le sourire), 1933; Frühlingstimmen (The Voice of Spring), 1933. *Denmark*—Flugten fra millionerne (Flight From the Millions), 1934; Fange Nr. 1 (Prisoner Number One), 1935; Det Gyldne Smil (The Golden Smile), 1935. *Madagascar*—Svarta Horisonter (Black Horizons), series of six documentaries: The Dances of Esira, Beauty Salon in the Jungle, The Most Useful Tree in the World, The Dance of the Jungle, Sea Devil, The Graves of Our Fathers, 1935–1936. *Indonesia, Philippines and New Guinea*—Unknown number of documentaries, including The Tribe Still Lives, The Bamboo Age of Mentawei, The Chief's Son Is Dead, The Komodo Dragon, The Village Near the Pleasant Fountain, 1937–1938. *Siam (Thailand)*—En Handfull Ris (A Handful of Rice/Man och Kvinna/Man and Woman), 1938. *Peru*—Yagua, 1940–1941.

ABOUT: Dodds, J. W. The Several Lives of Paul Fejos, 1973; Haudiquet, P. Paul Fejos, 1968 (France); Koszarski, R. Hollywood Directors, 1914–1940, 1976; Petrie, G. Hollywood Destinies: European Directors in America 1922–1931, 1986; Roud, R. (ed.) Cinema: A Critical Dictionary, 1980; Whittemore, D. and Cecchettini, A. Passport to Hollywood, 1976; Who Was Who in America, 1961–1968. *Periodicals*—American Anthropologist February 1964; Film Dope September 1978; Filmkritik August 1979; Filmkultura 4 1960; Film Quarterly Winter 1978; Film, Szinhaz, Muzsika August 17, 1968; Filmvilag July 15, 1966; New York Times April 24, 1963; Pour Vous January 31, 1929; September 10, 1931; Sight and Sound Summer 1978.

LOUIS FEUILLADE

*FEUILLADE, LOUIS (JEAN) (February 19, 1873–February 25, 1925), French director, scenarist, and producer, was born in the vineyard town of Lunel, in the south of France, near Montpellier. He was the fifth child of Barthélemy Feuillade, a well-to-do landowner and wine broker, and the former Marie Avesque. According to Henri Fescourt, he was "a diligent student at Lunel, the modest and sunny town where he was born, and already revealed a gift as a comic actor. No entertainment was arranged in the district without calling on his services. He recited monologues, sang comic songs, and by the age of ten was quite a local celebrity."

When Feuillade was twelve, his devotedly religious parents, seeking to protect him from the contaminations of a secular and Republican education, sent him off to a Catholic seminary in Carcassonne. He was deeply affected by the sense of history that infuses that medieval walled city and the drama and mystery of the Catholic liturgy. Some have attributed to those cloistered years the bizarre world of Feuillade's films—a realm of fiercely retributive justice meted out by terrifying black-robed figures. His biographer Francis Lacassin suggested that "the strange, surrealist flashes of anarchy which spark through the work of this pillar of society can only be explained as some sort of unconscious revolt to which he gave rein in his dreams—that is to say, in his films."

Leaving the seminary in 1891, he enlisted forthwith for his compulsory military service, wanting to have done with it "so as to be able to get married more quickly." He spent four years in the cavalry, ending as a sergeant with the Fourth Dragoons. Within weeks of returning to civilian life, on Halloween of 1895, he married Jeanne-Léontine Jaujou, daughter of a Lunel fruit merchant.

If Feuillade had been scarred by his years in the seminary, there was no evidence of it in his manner. Fescourt says that he was "frank, openhearted, gay and energetic" and "a robust, hearty man, broad-shouldered, with a rugged face, and strong *méridional* [southern] accent, a broad forehead, penetrating eyes behind his glasses, and a stiff, clipped mustache."

Back in Lunel, in Lacassin's words, Feuillade "devoted himself a little to the wine trade, much to poetry, and passionately to the art of the bullfight." Writing for the Montpellier *Éclair* and other regional newspapers, he soon acquired a considerable local reputation as a bullfight critic and, in his spare time, as an amateur actor. However, Feuillade wanted more than local renown. In 1902, after his parents' early deaths, he went off to Paris to seek his fortune, accompanied by his wife and her father.

Starting out as a correspondent for the *Éclair de Montpellier*, Feuillade was soon working also for La Maison de la Bonne Presse, publishers of numerous Catholic and right-wing journals and pamphlets. The pay was abysmal and the family went through some difficult times, although Feuillade was a tireless worker, endlessly embarking on hopeful new projects. He founded a short-lived satirical weekly, *La Tomate* (1903),

°fû yăd´

scribbled poems on every conceivable subject (as he did all his life), and made repeated attempts to break into the theatre as a dramatist. *Le Clos*, a one-act play in verse written in collaboration with his old friend Étienne Arnaud, was staged in Béziers in 1905, but the dramas, comedies, and operettas he wrote with André Heuzé all remained unproduced. Meanwhile, in 1904, he at last secured a moderately well-paid post with the *Revue mondiale*.

One day Heuzé showed up in an ostentatiously expensive new suit; he had been engaged as a scriptwriter by Pathé. Taken with his friend's newfound wealth and occupation, Feuillade wrote some scenarios of his own and, in the fall of 1905, sent them through a colleague to Pathé's arch-competitor Gaumont. They were read by Léon Gaumont's artistic director, the remarkable Alice Guy-Blaché, who not only accepted them but invited Feuillade to direct them. He had just become a father and was reluctant to give up his secure job with the *Revue mondiale*. At his suggestion, Guy-Blaché hired his friend Étienne Arnaud to direct Feuillade's scripts.

The first of these productions, released in January 1906, was *Attrapez mon chapeau! ou Le Coup de vent* (*Catch My Hat! or The Gust of Wind*). It was a 45-meter chase comedy in which a hat, blown away by the wind, leads its owner on from place to place and catastrophe to catastrophe. Guy-Blaché was pleased, and Feuillade became Gaumont's principal writer, turning in three scenarios a week for some months until he was persuaded to abandon his journalistic career to become a film director. Even then, according to Lacassin, "his invention was so prolific that for the next year or so he continued to provide plots for most of the films made for his colleagues" (as he always did for his own pictures).

Feuillade directed his first films in 1906. Years later, recalling these apprentice efforts for his assistant Robert Florey, he spoke of "*L'Homme aimanté* (*The Magnetized Man*), *Le Coup de vent*, *Le Thé chez la concierge*, and a whole lot more of so little importance that I can't even remember their titles. Nothing but chases, endless pursuits by ever-growing tides of people charging after a flying pumpkin or a postage stamp blown away by the wind. The public went into ecstasies over these burlesque fantasies. How far the cinema has come since those days."

Most of Feuillade's earliest films were comedies. "With the systematic use of trick effects in open-air settings . . . ," wrote Georges Sadoul, "he combined a sound, if somewhat pedestrian, sense of comic observation. He understood how, launching out from some absurd situation, it was possible to draw from it, with meticulous logic, a thousand lunatic consequences. In one of the best films he made at that time, *L'Homme aimanté*, the hero buys himself a coat of mail as a protection against nocturnal attackers. Two young scamps magnetize the coat—whereupon coffeepots, plates, iron tables, shop-signs, draincovers, all attach themselves to the unhappy wearer. Escorted to the police station, he is the cause of a burlesque dance of greeting performed by the swords of the police officers."

Feuillade's energy and good humor infected everyone who worked with him. Alice Guy-Blaché left for the United States in 1907, and, at her recommendation, Feuillade succeeded her as Gaumont's artistic director, in charge of all programing and production. He nevertheless continued to write and direct films of his own at breakneck speed, working with an assortment of cameramen—Manichoux, Klausse, Glattei, and Guérin among them.

His output was soon as varied as it was bountiful, including comedies, dramas, and brief costume pieces like *Judith et Holopherne* and *La Mort de Mozart* (both 1909). One of the most admired of these was the 1908 *Prométhée* (*Prometheus*; 125 meters). Feuillade later confessed of this film that "I have on my conscience the death by gunfire of three lions, five lionesses, a boa-constrictor, and the eagle which devoured Prometheus' liver. . . . It was the heroic age of the cinema."

In 1910 Feuillade launched a series called *Le Film esthétique*, designed to attract a more highbrow audience to the cinema and, not incidentally, to rival Pathé's up-market subsidiary, the *Société Cinématographique des Auteurs et Gens de Lettres*, which produced adaptations of literary classics, and Charles Delac's *Film d'art* series, scripted and performed by luminaries of the Comédie Française. According to Feuillade's manifesto for the new series, "The *film esthétique*, whether allegorical, poetical, or symbolical, whether drawing its inspiration from Christianity or from the Gods of Olympus, will be visual first and foremost, not theatrical." Though the diatribe was directed primarily against Gaumont's competitors, Feuillade's belief in cinema as something different from and more than a kind of filmed theatre was something he adhered to all his life.

The series comprised fifteen films, most of them extravagant biblical or mythological epics, notably *Les Sept Péchés capitaux* (*The Seven Deadly Sins*) and *La Nativité* (both 1910). The latter caused Feuillade to be brought to court by the painter Luc Olivier Merson, accused of plagiarizing the latter's tableau "Le Repos en Egypte." The series as a whole flopped at the box office, bringing Gaumont to the brink of insolvency.

To recoup its losses, Gaumont turned to the production of contemporary subjects that did not require elaborate sets or large casts. "Making a virtue of a necessity," wrote David Robinson, "Feuillade issued an ambitious manifesto in defence of cinematic realism, to launch a series of films with the general title *La Vie telle qu'elle est* [*Life as It Is*]." Feuillade spoke of these films as "slices of life" which "eschew any fantasy and represent men and things as they are, not as they should be."

In the opinion of Richard Roud, "one of the earliest and most beautiful" films in the series was *La Tare* (1911). Its heroine (Renée Carl), seeking redemption through drudgery in an orphanage, is thrown out when her sinful past is discovered and attempts suicide. "In an extraordinary shot, Feuillade shows her in her attic room, with a bright shaft of light cutting the room in two; she goes to the window, climbs onto the sill and is poised there ready to jump when her despairing face is illuminated by the bright sunshine. She hesitates, then falls back into the semi-dark room. The film leaves her there, her head bowed in misery. Although the plot is melodramatic, the treatment is restrained, and one can already see in this early work that extraordinary combination of realistic treatment and melodramatic subject that was to be the hallmark of Feuillade's *oeuvre*."

Other pictures in the series, often co-starring Renée Carl and René Navarre, offer slices of less humble lives. *Le Trust* (1911) deals with an American inventor kidnapped by foreign agents; *L'Accident* (1912) has Navarre, en route to an assignation with his mistress, involved in an auto accident that teaches him the value of marital fidelity. In *Le Pont sur l'abîme* (*The Bridge Over the Abyss*, 1912) Navarre, in jail and on the brink of suicide after being ruined in the stock market, is saved by a last-minute reconciliation with a forgiving Renée Carl. As Lacassin has pointed out, despite Feuillade's references to Zola and Maupassant, most of these "slices of life" were actually violent melodramas. Generally well-received at that time, the series is nowadays considered dull.

Closer to Feuillade's heart were the unpretentious short comedies starring the five-year-old Anatole Clément Mary, known as Bébé. The Bébé series—seventy-six films between 1910 and 1912—was hugely successful. When Mary's parents and Gaumont became involved in a dispute, the series abruptly ended, to be instantly replaced by Feuillade's equally successful series about the exploits of Bout-de-Zan (René Poyen),

who had appeared in some of the Bébé films. An *enfant* truly *terrible*, he terrorized everyone who came within range, and not least Paul Manson, Renée Carl, and Madame Saint-Bonnet, who played Bout-de-Zan's parents and nurse just as they had Bébé's. Feuillade went on to direct some forty other comedies, including the series *La Vie drôle*, starring Marcel Levesque, and *Belle Humeur*, built around the vaudeville actor Georges Biscot.

For thirty-two consecutive months in 1911–1913, all France breathlessly awaited the next book-length installment of *Fantômas*, the cliff-hanger exploits of the eponymous archvillain, the "Emperor of Crime." Fantômas' serial adventures, conjured up by Pierre Souvestre and Marcel Allain, were all-time bestsellers; and in each bulky monthly volume Fantômas, master of disguise and intrigue, would once again thwart his would-be nemeses Inspector Juve and the journalist Fandor. Gaumont acquired the film rights and in May 1913 the terrible Fantômas, played by René Navarre, strode for the first time across the screen in a series "in three parts and thirty tableaux."

Paris was possessed anew by Fantômas fever. Navarre became a star of the first magnitude, unable to leave his house without being mobbed, and Feuillade plunged into a series of sequels. The first *Fantômas* concerns Juve's arrest of Fantômas after a theft at the Excelsior Palace, and the villain's escape by substituting the actor Valgrand for himself at the guillotine. *Juve contre Fantômas* (September 1913) involves the theft of 150,000 francs by Fantômas and his stunning accomplice, Josephine, on the Simplon express. *Le Mort qui tue* (November 1913) has Fantômas wearing "gloves" fashioned from the skin of one of his victims in order to leave behind fingerprints not his own. In *Fantômas contre Fantômas* (February 1914), Scotland Yard summons Juve to aid in apprehending Fantômas, and *Le Faux Magistrat* (April 1914) finds Fantômas disguised as a judge who has died while serving as the clapper of a church bell. Completing five Fantômas serials within a year, Feuillade also found time during the same period to direct forty-seven other films, mostly in the Bout-de-Zan series.

"With his menacing black hood and hundred disguises," wrote Tom Milne, Navarre's Fantômas is "always leaving the hopeful police doggedly a pace or two behind, and as likely to cut somebody's throat or blow him into little pieces as look at him." Milne invokes the melodramatic plots of "prolific and frenzied inventiveness, freely dispensing corpses, poisons, perambulating pythons, mysterious death-dealing pens and guns, and any number of hooded figures." But, he maintains, what matters is the way Feuillade uses his material." Lacassin agrees, saying that "before Antonioni, Feuillade had discovered the secret of *grisaille*. He understood that there is nothing more beautiful than that urban poetry which springs from uneven streets, bleak, crumbling districts, silent and deserted, stretches of wasteland with strange buildings silhouetted in the distance."

David Robinson found piquancy as well as beauty in the fact that Feuillade's fantasy "finds its setting in a familiar world. The thrill is all the greater when corpses sit in the elegant chairs of fashionable 1914 salons, and assassins, kidnappers and mesmerists lurk around the corner of the most innocent-looking Parisian street. . . . Feuillade liked cellars and caves and subterranean places; but his most characteristic arena is a gray Paris *banlieu* [residential district] or the sun-drenched avenues of the Riviera. . . . Years later Alfred Hitchcock was to rediscover what Feuillade knew so well, that the greatest terror stalks at noon, lurking in familiar places and under unobtrusively plain disguises." And for David Thomson *Fantômas* is simply "the first great movie experience; Feuillade the first director for whom no historical allowances need to be made. . . . All the roots of the thriller and suspense genres are in Feuillade's sense that evil, anarchy and destructiveness speak to the frustrations banked up in modern society."

In mid-1914 Feuillade retreated to Lunel to rest. That winter, Gaumont summoned him to Marseilles where, in addition to short burlesques and the seemingly infinite Bout-de-Zan series, he made several patriotic war films. Unlike the works of many of his contemporaries, Feuillade's war movies concentrated on the home front, depicting the lot of broken families, bankrupted businesses. In 1915 the director was called briefly to active duty. Upon his discharge four months later he commenced work on *Les Vampires*, with which Gaumont hoped to capture the audience garnered by Pathé's *Les Mystères de New York*, a compendium of American melodramas starring *Perils of Pauline* heroine Pearl White.

Les Vampires, an adventure in the Fantômas tradition, follows the exploits of a gang of black-suited arch-criminals led by the anagrammatic Irma Vep (played with high allure by the actress Musidora). Released in ten episodes from November 1915 to June 1916, *Les Vampires* revived the old charges that Feuillade was glorifying criminality—the Vampire crew was seen to resemble the *bande à Bonnot*, a gang of anarchists whose depredations had dominated the headlines a few years before. The Paris police banned the series until a visit by Musidora to the Prefect smoothed things over.

Unlike *Fantômas*, which had been based fairly closely on the original novels, *Les Vampires* was conceived by Feuillade himself, and a good deal of it was improvised. According to Lacassin, Feuillade would take his whole company out "to the new avenues being built at Montmartre, to the forest of Fontainebleau, or to some quiet, deserted street picked at random. The hazards of fate would play an important part in the improvisation of whatever scene was on hand. The dismissal of an actor, or the director's dissatisfaction with him; someone's illness or unavailability; the need to find use for footage shot for another purpose; these were the factors that governed the development of the film" and accounted for its "epileptic, whirlwind rhythm. . . . Big vampires and little vampires, lusting for love and fighting over the archdevil in her black tights, ships which explode, hopeful ladies lassoed as they peer out of a window . . . all this makes *Les Vampires* a dazzling surrealist poem and triumph of black comedy." For many critics the series is Feuillade's masterpiece.

His next major film was *Judex* (1916). At Gaumont's insistence, it featured a black-cloaked hero (René Cresté) whose vengeful activities were clearly on the side of the law; while the villainess (Musidora again) was made considerably less enticing. At the end of *Judex*'s twelve episodes she is killed off and Judex marries the virtuous Jacqueline. The 1917 sequel, *La Nouvelle Mission de Judex*, featured a happily married avenger, and was considerably less interesting.

A straightforward drama followed in *Vendémiaire* (1918). It starred two of Feuillade's principal serial actors, Cresté and Edouard Mathé, in a contemporary story about refugees (with two German spies among them) displaced from the war zone to the vineyards of the south. According to Richard Abel in his *French Cinema: The First Wave*, "the film stresses the allegorical, almost Biblical elements of the narrative and operates according to an alternation of sequences that obsessively juxtapose war and peace. Yet, at times, it is surprisingly realistic, even lyrical—perhaps, as Francis Lacassin suggests, because Feuillade chose to set the film in the landscape of his own childhood. Particularly moving are the prologue that follows a boat of refugees down the Rhône river and a documentary-like sequence on the sense of community that develops among the peasants during the grape harvest." Now regarded as an early masterpiece of French realism, it was indifferently receive in 1918 (perhaps because the French public was then eager to forget the war).

Feuillade then returned to his beloved serials with *Tih Minh* (1918) and *Barrabas* (1919), both filmed in and around Gaumont's Nice studio and both shamelessly in the *Fantômas* tradition. In the twelve-episode *Tih Minh*, René Cresté stars as a French explorer in search of war treasure, Mary Harald as Tih Minh, the Indochinese princess he falls in love with; the opposing gang includes a German agent, a Hindu fakir, and the resurrected remnants of the Vampires, seeking revenge for the death of Irma Vep. As Lacassin says, "scenes like the fight on the roof of the Hotel Negresco possess that dreamlike evil magnificence which no one was ever able to achieve so completely as Louis Feuillade." *Barrabas*, also much admired by some critics, deals with another international gang of criminals operating behind the front of a prestigious banking corporation.

Neither of these films equaled the success of their predecessors, and Gaumont decided that the crime serial had had its day. *Les Deux Gamines* (1920) was the first of three twelve-part serials starring the Russian emigré actress Sandra Milowanoff in intensely sentimental stories about orphaned innocents; the other two, *L'Orpheline* (1921) and *Parisette* (1921), both featured the future director René Clair.

In these serials, writes Richard Abel, "the narrative became less an accumulation of bizarre and baffling intrigues and more a character-oriented, dramatic structuring of separation, adventure/misfortune, and reunion. The former exotic or urban settings were replaced by family dwellings, villages, and convents in the provinces. . . . And in the end, the long-suffering characters realized their undying hopes in marriage. . . . In their frankly romantic and sentimental appeal, Feuillade's serials had become lengthy bourgeois melodramas. Although the few film critics and historians who have seen these melodramatic serials find them much less interesting than *Les Vampires*, *Tih Minh*, and *Barrabas*, the French public of the early 1920s, most film reviewers, and Feuillade's own friends were delighted."

How delighted Feuillade himself was is less clear. By the summer of 1923, he was admitting to complete physical and artistic exhaustion. His last film, a "drama in six chapters" called *Le Stigmate* (1925), was codirected by his cameraman (and son-in-law) Maurice Champreux. It was released the month after his death, of complications following peritonitis, at the age of fifty-two.

In the 1920s, Feuillade's thrillers were held in contempt by the critical establishment. The *cinéaste* and theorist Louis Delluc denounced these "serialistic abominations" and proclaimed: "Friends took me to see *The New Mission of Judex*. I'll never again step inside a movie theatre, never, never, never." It was left to the Surrealists to champion this subversive bourgeois. "There is nothing more realistic and, at the same time, more poetic than the serial," wrote Louis Aragon and André Breton in their play *The Treasure of the Jesuits*. "It is to *Les Vampires* that one must look for the great reality of this century. Beyond fashion, beyond taste." And the young Luis Buñuel, scorning the self-conscious artiness of Delluc and his followers, said that his models were *Fantômas* and *Les Vampires*, direct transcriptions of "an unwonted reality."

A reassessment of Feuillade's work began in the 1940s and gathered pace in the 1960s, led by Francis Lacassin and taken up by André Bazin and the *nouvelle vague* critics. There had been several inferior remakes of *Fantômas* over the years, and in 1963 Georges Franju directed a version of *Judex*, scripted by Lacassin. Feuillade's influence has been seen in the work of Franju, Jacques Rivette, and Alain Resnais; in the development of the serial, of German expressionism, and of the thriller genre as a whole. Resnais remarked that "people say there is a Méliès tradition in the cinema, and a Lumière tradition. I believe there is also a Feuillade current, one which marvelously links the fantastic side of Méliès with the realism of Lumière, a current which creates mystery and evokes dreams by the use of the most banal elements of daily life." Many now regard Feuillade as the most important French director of the period from 1910 to 1920—the superior of those who despised him.

"Please believe me," Feuillade wrote, "when I tell you that it's not the experimenters who will finally obtain for film its proper recognition, but rather the makers of melodrama—and I count myself among the most devoted of their number. . . . I believe I come closer to the truth than they do."

—*H.A.R.*

FILMS (partial list; abbreviations in parentheses designate film series, as identified by Francis Lacassin: LFE—Le Film esthétique; LVT—La Vie telle qu'elle est; DD—Le Détective Dervieux; LVD—La Vie drôle; BH—Belle Humeur.)

Le Billet de banque, C'est Papa qui prend la purge, Les Deux Gosses, La Porteuse de Pain, (with Alice Guy Blaché) Mireille, N'te promène donc pas toute nue, 1906;

La Course des belles-mères, Un Facteur trop ferré, La Légende de la fileuse, Un Pacquet embarrassant, La sirène, La Thé chez la concierge, Vive le sabotage, 1907;

La Grève des Apaches, Nettoyage par le vide, Une Nuit agitée, Un Tic, Les Agents tels qu'on nous le présente, Une Dame vraiment bien, Prométhée, Le Roman de Soeur Louise, Le Récit du colonel, 1908;

Les Heures (4 episodes), Histoire de puce, L'Aveugle de Jérusalem, Judith et Holopherne, La Mère du moine, Le Printemps, La Mort de Mozart, La Possession de l'enfant, La Savatier et le financier, Vainqueur de la course pédestre, Le Collier de la reine, La Légende des phares, La Chatte métamorphosée en femme, Fra Vincenti, Le Huguenot, Le Mort, Les Filles du cantonnier, La Cigale et la fourmi, 1909;

Le Festin de Balthazar, Esther, Maudite soit la guerre, Le Pater (LFE), La Fille de Jephté, Benvenuto Cellini, L'Exode, Le Roi de Thulé, Les Sept Péchés capitaux (3 episodes), Mater Dolorosa, La Nativité, Bébé fume, Bébé apache, Bébé pêcheur (and 73 other Bébé films, 1910–1912), Mil huit cent quatorze, Le Christ en croix, L'An 1000, 1910;

Dans la vie, Les Doigts qui voient, Le Fils de Locuste, La fille du juge d'instruction, Sous le joug, Les Vipères (LVT), Le Mariage de l'aînée (LVT), La Roi Lear au village, Le fils de Sunamite, En grève (LVT), Le Bracelet de la marquise, Les Petites Apprenties, L'Aventurière, dame de compagnie, Fidélité Romaine, Le Trafiquant, Le Bas de laine/La Trésor (LVT), La Vierge d'Argos, La tare (LVT), Le Poison (LVT), La "Souris Blanche" (LVT), Aux lions les Chrétiens, Le Trust/Les Batailles de l'argent (LVT), Le Chef-lieu de canton (LVT), Le Destin des mères (LVT), Quand les feuilles tombent, Tant que vous serez heureux (LVT), Charles VI, 1911;

L'Aventurière, La Demoiselle du notaire, La Fille du Margrave, Le Mort vivant, Les Cloches de paques, La Maison des lions, La Prison sur le gouffre, L'Accident, Androclès, Les Braves Gens (LVT), Château de la peur, Dans la brousse, La Cassette de l'émigrée, Le proscrit (DD), Préméditation, Le Témoin, Le Tourment, Au Pays des lions, Le Coeur et l'argent, Le Nain (LVT), Napoléon, Amour d'automne, L'anneau fatal, Le Pont sur l'abîme (LVT), Tyrtée, L'Attrait du bouge, La Hantise, L'Oubliette (DD), Le Petit Poucet, Bout-de-Zan revient du cirque (followed by 59 other Bout-de-Zan comedies), La Course aux millions, Haut les mains!, L'Homme de proie, La Vertu de Lucette (LVT), La Vie ou la mort, Le Maléfice, Le Noël de Francesca, Les Noces siciliennes, Les Yeux qui meurent, 1912;

Les Audaces du coeur, La Conversion d'Irma, Erreur tragique, L'Intruse, La Mort de Lucrèce, La Vengeance du sergent de la ville, Le Bon Propriétaire, Le Guet-apens (DD), Le Mariage de Miss Nelly, Le Revenant, Le Secret du Forçat, Les Yeux ouverts, L'Écrin du rajah (DD), L'Angoisse, Le Browning, Fantômas (3 parts), Les Chasseurs de lions, L'Effroi, Le Ménestrel de la reine Anne, La Petite Danseuse, L'Agonie de Byzance, S'Affranchir (LVT), Juve contre Fantômas (Fantômas II, in 4 parts), La Gardienne du feu (3 parts), La Rose blanche, Un Drame au pays basque,

Les Millions de la bonne (LVD), Le Mort qui tue (Fantômas III, in 6 parts), Au gré des flots, La Marche des rois, La Momie (LVD), Bonne Année, Un Scandale au village, 1913; L'Hôtel de la gare (LVD), L'Illustre Machefer (LVD), La Rencontre, Les Somnambules (3 parts), Fantômas contre Fantômas (Fantômas IV, in 4 parts), La Jocond (LVD), Les Lettres, Manon de Montmartre, L'Enfant de la roulotte (in 5 parts), Paques rouges, Le Faux Magistrat (Fantômas V), Le Gendarme est sans culotte (LVD), Le Calvaire, Severo Torelli (in 5 parts), Tu n'épouseras jamais un avocat (LVD, in 3 parts), Les Fiancés de Séville, Le Coffret de Tolède, Les fiancés de 1914, Le Diamant du Sénéchal, L'Épreuve, La Gitanella, La Neuvaine, La Petite andalouse, 1914;

Le Furoncle, L'Expiation, Le Colonel Bontemps, Celui qui reste, Le Coup de fakir, Deux françaises, L'Escapade de Filoche, Fifi tambour, Union sacrée, Les Noces d'argent, La Sosie (LVD), L'Angoisse au foyer, La Barrière, Le Collier de perles, Le Fer à cheval, Les Vampires (first 3 episodes), Le Noël de poilu, Le Blason, La Course à l'abîme, 1915;

Les Vampires (episodes 4–10), Les Mariés d'un jour (LVD), Les Fourberies de Pingouin (LVD), C'est le printemps, Le Double Jeu, Les Fiançailles d'Agénor, Le Malheur qui passe, L'Aventure des millions, Le Poète et sa folle amante (LVD), Un Mariage de raison, Notre pauvre coeur, Le Retour de Manivel, Judex (12-episode serial), Lagourdette, gentleman cambrioleur (LVD), La Peine du talion (LVD), Si vous ne m'aimez pas (LVD), 1916;

La Déserteuse, Débrouille-toi (LVD), La Passe de Monique (in 3 parts), Mon oncle (LVD), La Femme fatale (LVD), Herr Doktor (in 3 parts), L'Autre (in 3 parts), Le Bandeau sur les yeux (in 3 parts), La Nouvelle mission de Judex (12-episode serial), La Fugue de Lily (in 3 parts), 1917;

Aide-toi (LVD), Les Petites Marionettes (in 3 parts), Vendémiaire, Tih Minh (12-episode serial), 1918;

L'Homme sans visage (in 4 parts), L'engrenage (in 4 parts), Le Nocturne (in 4 parts), L'énigme/Le Mot de l'énigme (in 4 parts), Barrabas (12-episode serial), 1919;

Les Deux Gamines (12-episode serial), 1920; Zidore ou Les métamorphoses (BH), Séraphin ou Les Jambes nues (BH), Saturnin ou Le bon allumeur (BH), L'Orpheline (12-episode serial), Gustave est médium (BH), Marjolin ou La fille manquée (BH), Parisette (12-episode serial), 1921; Lahire ou Le valet de coeur (BH), Gaétan ou Le commis audacieux (BH), Le Fils de flibustier (12-episode serial), 1922. Vindicta (in 5 parts), La Gosseline, Le Gamin de Paris, L'Orphelin de Paris (6-episode serial), 1923; La Fille bien gardée, Pierrot Pierrette, (with Maurice Champreux) Lucette, (with Maurice Champreux) Le stigmate (in 6 parts), 1924.

Published scripts—Fantômas, Juve contre Fantômas,

Le Mort qui tue, Fantômas contre Fantômas, Le Faux Magistrat *in* L'Avant-Scène du Cinéma 271 (in French); Vindicta *in* Cahiers de la Cinématheque Fall 1981 (in French).

ABOUT: Abel, R. French Cinema: The First Wave, 1915–1929, 1984; Delluc, L. Cinema & Cie, 1919; Fescourt, H. La Foi et les montagnes, 1959; Lacassin, F. Louis Feuillade, 1964 (in French); Roud, R. (ed.) Cinema: A Critical Dictionary, 1980; Thomson, D. A Biographical Dictionary of the Cinema, 1980. *Periodicals*—L'Avant-Scène du Cinéma May 1966, July 1–15, 1981 (Feuillade issue); Cahiers de la Cinémathèque Winter 1979; Cinéma (France) April and June 1961, 95 1965; Écran October 1978; Film Dope September 1978; Filme July–August 1981; Filméchange Winter 1983; Revue du Cinéma August 1931; Sight and Sound Summer 1963, Winter 1964–1965; Velvet Light Trap Summer 1973; Village Voice April 19, 1983.

JACQUES FEYDER

*"FEYDER," JACQUES (Jacques Frédérix)** (July 21, 1885–May 25, 1948), French director and scenarist, was born in Ixelles, Belgium, the son of Alfred Frédérix and the former Angèle Piérard. The family had both literary and military connections, and the boy was encouraged to follow the latter profession, in 1905 enrolling as an officer cadet at the Nivelles academy. A natural bohemian, he hated the life, and his father used family influence to secure him instead an administrative post at a cannon foundry in Liège. This was no more to his taste, and around 1909, shortly after his mother's death, he appalled his father by announcing his intention to become an actor. Eventually accepting the inevitable, Alfred Frédérix ordained that his son should never carry the family name onto the boards. Jacques Frédérix became Jacques Feyder, adopting the name of a street he passed as he left the family home, valise in hand.

A handsome young man, Feyder soon found roles in theatres in Paris (1910–1912) and Lyons (1913–1914). Meanwhile, in 1912, he had begun to act in films also. Painfully shy on the stage, he found screen acting less daunting and appeared in minor roles in films by Méliès, Feuillade, and other pioneers of the silent cinema. Before long, Feyder found himself more interested in filmmaking than in acting, and set out to learn all he could by studying the methods of the directors and technicians he worked with.

The moment of opportunity came in 1915 when Ravel was drafted and Feyder completed the film they were working on, *Monsieur Pinson policier*; he went on to direct a series of shorts for Gaumont, many of which he scripted himself. The first of these, *Têtes de femmes, femme de tête* (1916), introduced a young actress named Françoise Rosay, whom Feyder had met when he was working in Lyons. Married the next year, they shared personal and professional lives for more than three decades. Rosay's acting versatility enabled her to assume a variety of roles from film to film (and even within a single film), and when necessary she also took over directing responsibilities for her husband.

In 1917 Feyder was mobilized in the Belgian army and spent the rest of the war as an actor with an army troupe directed by Victor Francen. After that he returned to make one more film for Gaumont and then quit to embark on his first major work. This was *L'Atlantide*, scripted by himself from the novel by Pierre Benoit. It tells the intensely romantic story of two French officers (Jean Angelo and Georges Melchior) who discover in the African desert the lost city of Atlantis and its queen Antinea (Stacia Napierkowska), an irresistible seductress. One of the intruders does resist her hypnotic charms, however, with disastrous results. Feyder worked for two years on the film. Having explored North Africa for suitable locations, he shot the exteriors in the summer of 1920. The interiors were filmed in an improvised studio in Algiers, where Feyder's cameraman Georges Specht combined natural and artificial light to match the exterior footage.

L'Atlantide (*Woman of Atlantis*, 1921) runs for three and a half hours. It is marred by some faintly ludicrous naiveties, by a sometimes clumsy script, and more seriously by the miscasting of Napierkowska. As Richard Roud has explained, "she was Feyder's choice, but between the time he first saw her as a sylphlike dancer and the day she arrived for the shooting, her volume had increased to a degree that makes it difficult for us to see her as a great seductress." In fact, as Louis Delluc remarked, the best actor in the film was the sand. Feyder's gift for handling space was already apparent, and "the vast plains of shimmering sand" at the beginning and end of the picture are made to seem infinitely remote and mysterious. "For the first time," wrote Roger Régent, "one felt the real heat and drought of the desert come over on the screen."

To the moviegoing public of the day, this desert fantasy was a wholly fresh experience. In spite of its great length, L'Atlantide was an immense financial success and placed Feyder at once in the front rank of French directors. It continued to attract an audience even after Pabst made a sound version with Brigitta Helm in 1932. Another but very different literary adaptation followed: Crainquebille (1923), based on a story by Anatole France and again scripted by the director, who was also his own designer. Crainquebille (Maurice de Féraudy), an old vegetable-seller, is falsely accused of insulting a policeman and jailed. Crushed and embittered, upon his release he drives away his customers and is almost ruined, but in the end recovers his faith in humanity thanks to the sympathy and kindness of a tough little street urchin, La Souris (Jean Forest).

The upbeat ending was added by Feyder, but the harsh social satire of the original story is not ignored in the film where, as Roger Régent said, Feyder "let himself go on technical virtuosity" for the only time in his career, using "slow-motion photography and perspective distortion in order to show the overwhelming disproportion between an accused man and his judges." The trial scene, indeed, is perceived as a kind of fantastic nightmare, with robed judges flapping about like great birds, the court a sea of eyeballs staring at the bewildered Crainquebille, and a vast policeman towering over the minute witness for the defense.

For many critics, however, the abiding merit of the film was not in its avant-garde technique or its social message, but in its patient, scrupulous pursuit of psychological truth. Ephraim Katz has said that it "echoed German expressionism and at the same time heralded the poetic realism that was to take firm hold of the French cinema of the 30s." Greatly admired by D. W. Griffith, this admirable but sometimes rather dull film proved too "difficult" for contemporary audiences: it was a critical but not a popular success.

Feyder's script for Visages d'enfants (Faces of Children, 1925) was, for once, not based on a literary work but of his own invention, and some consider this the most personal of his pictures. Jean Forest—the mischievous but good-hearted La Souris of Crainquebille—here plays a sensitive, introspective small boy growing up in the beautiful Haut Valais region of Switzerland, alienated because his mother has died and his father has remarried, resentful of his new stepmother and stepsister, but happily reconciled in a somewhat melodramatic dénouement involving a spectacular avalanche.

Liam O'Leary, who calls this film "a little masterpiece," writes that "Feyder has a keen appreciation of the relation of character to environment. From the first shots of the funeral we are introduced to the life of the locality and the sense of reality is at once created. . . . Never, perhaps, have children appeared so unselfconsciously themselves as in this film and, moreover, reflected the adult character which with time they would assume. . . . It is his concern with human behaviour which makes Feyder such a great director. He seldom allows the sentimentality in him to swamp his judgement."

In the form of Visages d'enfants, O'Leary goes on, "there is a vivid directness of imagery always precisely observed. . . . The movement of the film is leisurely and unforced and events control the rhythm, but when expressing intense moments, Feyder knows how to make his cut in the action. Considering the date of the film, it is rather remarkable to find a cutting sequence of such rapid movement as that leading up to the point where Jean faints at the graveside. Here the images progress from measurements of nine frames to as little as two, and each image is a precise observation of intensified awareness." Another critic pointed out that "the turbulent events, and the grandiose mountain scenery against which they take place, are never allowed to take over from the intimate recording of experience."

In 1925 Feyder accepted the post of artistic director at the new Vita Films studio in Vienna, together with a contract to direct three films of his own. The first of these (and the last, as it turned out) was L'Image (1925), made in color, and scripted by no less a literary personage than the novelist and prophet of Unanimism Jules Romains. The film is a fable about four men in love with the same woman (Arlette Marchal) but unaware that they are rivals because they know her only from her photograph, which conveys something quite different to each of them.

Apart from what it says about the human capacity for self-delusion, and about the illusory nature of art, this story is a very direct expression of a theme that, as Tom Milne says, is a recurrent preoccupation in Feyder's work—the woman who means different things to different men. Mutilated by its uncomprehending distributors, *L'Image* failed commercially, but remained Feyder's own favorite among his works and was extravagantly admired by some critics (like Jean Mitry, who called Feyder one of the greatest "musicians of silence of the cinematographic art").

Quitting Vita Films, Feyder returned to Paris, where he wrote the script for Julien Duvivier's study of impoverished rural childhood, *Poil de Carotte*, based on the novel by Jules Renard, and himself made a film about an affluent urban boyhood, *Gribiche* (1925). Also adapted from a novel (by Frédéric Boutet), it was Feyder's third film with Jean Forest and the first full-length feature in which he directed his wife, Françoise Rosay. Forest here plays a poor boy adopted by a rich American (Rosay) but desperately homesick for his own family. Feyder extracted another remarkable performance from Forest, and the movie was generally enjoyed for this and for some notable location photography of Paris.

Gribiche was also the first of the numerous films designed for Feyder by the Russian emigré art director Lazare Meerson, who made telling contributions to Feyder's version of *Carmen* (1926). There was much praise for Feyder's use of the dramatic chiaroscuro provided by the strong light of Spain, where the film was shot, and Raquel Meller made a splendidly fiery Carmen. Heavy shadows are used in a more claustrophobic and expressionist manner in Feyder's next picture, *Thérèse Raquin* (1928), made in German studios and with German actors for DEFU.

Feyder collaborated with Fanny Carlson and Willy Haas in writing this adaptation of Zola's grim novel about two lovers who murder the woman's husband and are then driven by fear and guilt to mutual hatred and eventual suicide. Gina Manès gave the performance of her life as Thérèse, and Paul Rotha wrote that "Feyder's treatment of Thérèse, her inner mind, her unsatisfied sex, her viciousness and her sensuality was an amazing example of dramatic direction. By the smallest movement, by the flicker of an eyelash, by a sudden glance at Laurent (Hans-Adalbert von Schlettow), by her partly opened mouth, by her calm composure at the Raquin home, and by her passion in the studio of her lover, the spectator was forced to share the mind of this remarkable woman. In the handling of Wolfgang Zeller, as Camille the husband . . . , Feyder was equally brilliant, bringing to the surface the pitiful desolation of the little man's life. . . . Feyder built his film by the use of se-lected detail, by indirect suggestion, and by symbolism into a strong emotional realisation of a dramatic theme."

And it seemed to C. A. Lejeune that Feyder, in this film, "gives the impression of a complete preparation to the most minute detail of the shortest scene: before one foot of scene is shot, we feel that, once started, nothing could stop him, nothing could be changed, nothing need be changed. . . . Every shot, every angle, every inanimate object in the film is chosen to play a part in the drama, to explain a character, to clarify a motive, to define a change. . . . *Thérèse Raquin* is a superb director's film. There is nobody, in Europe or America, who cannot learn something from its methods and its invention . . . and it should be remembered as one of the cinema's genuine achievements, none the less because it has made no extravagant claims of its own virtue and effected no revolution on the screen." An earlier version of *Thérèse Raquin* had been made in Italy in 1915, and Marcel Carné directed the first sound version in 1953. According to Richard Roud, writing in 1980, Feyder's *Thérèse Raquin*, widely regarded as his masterpiece, had not been seen for decades, and all prints appeared to have been lost.

Thérèse Raquin was followed by another demonstration of Feyder's "astonishing versatility"—an almost equally brilliant picture in a totally different mode. This was *Les Nouveaux Messieurs* (1928), a satirical comedy about politics adapted by Charles Spaak and Feyder from a contemporary play.

It was made for Albatros, the company that produced René Clair's *An Italian Straw Hat* (1927), and used several of the same technicians—including the photographer Maurice Desfassiaux and the designer Lazare Meerson—as well as the actors Albert Préjean, Gaby Morlay, and Henry Roussell. "The foibles of the rival politicians were mercilessly exploited," wrote Paul Rotha, "as a silent protest against the childishness of party political strife. Technically, it was interesting for some competent camerawork, with frequent use of low-level angles and clever composite photography."

At this point Feyder was invited to Hollywood to direct Greta Garbo in *The Kiss* (1929), made for MGM—a courtroom melodrama of no particular interest (except as Garbo's last silent picture). Feyder stayed with MGM to make a German version of Clarence Brown's *Anna Christie* (1930), again starring Garbo; a French version of Ben Hecht's *The Unholy Night* (*Le Spectre vert*, 1930); and French and German versions of Lionel Barrymore's *His Glorious*

Night (*Si l'Empereur savait ça* and *Olympia,* 1930). The most notable of these was the German *Anna Christie* which, according to Richard Roud, was "longer than the Clarence Brown version, with a different cast (except, of course, for Garbo)" and also "more realistic and therefore more convincing." Feyder also made two American talkies for the same company: *Daybreak* (1931), adapted from Arthur Schnitzler's *Aube*; and *Son of India* (1931), from a novel by F. Marion Crawford: both were vehicles for Ramon Novarro.

Wearying of such unrewarding chores, Feyder returned to France (where he had become a citizen in 1928). A lover of literature and language, who believed that the silent film had exhausted its possibilities, Feyder welcomed the coming of sound. He worked for nearly two years on his first important sound film, *Le Grand Jeu* (1934), for which he assembled a formidable team of collaborators—Charles Spaak as coscenarist, Harry Stradling as photographer, Meerson as designer, and Hanns Eisler as composer of the score. Even Feyder's assistant directors were of star quality—Marcel Carné and Henri Chomette.

Le Grand Jeu is set in the Sahara, like *L'Atlantide* and, though more polished, is scarcely less romantic. Pierre (Pierre Richard-Willm), his heart broken by a Parisian society beauty, joins the Foreign Legion to forget but instead finds his beloved's double singing in a desert bar. Indeed, both women are played by the same star, Marie Bell, though in the role of the singer her voice is dubbed by another actress, thus (as Richard Roud puts it), "concretely conveying to us Pierre's Pirandellian puzzlement." Françoise Rosay is on hand as a fortune-teller knowledgeable about the mysterious workings of destiny, and the film, according to Basil Wright, achieved "a sense of genuine and abiding tragedy."

Always tempted to melodramatic excess, Feyder was in fact at his best in films that gave scope to his gift for careful psychological observation, like *Pension Mimosas* (1935). Made with much the same team as *Le Grand Jeu*, the film is dominated by Françoise Rosay's tour-de-force performance as a Riviera boardinghouse owner whose excessive devotion to her playboy adopted son (Paul Bernard) he ruthlessly exploits. One of the most admired of Feyder's films, it is preferred by some critics even to *Thérèse Raquin*, though in its own time it was eclipsed by his next film, *La Kermesse Héroïque* (*Carnival in Flanders,* 1935).

This, made in both French and German versions, was adapted by Spaak and Feyder from Spaak's novel. It is set in 1916 in a small town in Flanders. On the eve of the annual carnival, the town council learns that a detachment of Spanish troops—dreaded as rapists and butchers—are to be quartered on the town for the night. The pompous burgomaster (Alerme) finds it expedient to fake his own death, and the aldermen similarly decide to lie low, leaving their wives to deal with the Spaniards as best they may.

A brilliant triumvirate of designers—Lazare Meerson, Alex Trauner, and Georges Wakhevich—created a magnificent reconstruction of a seventeenth-century Flemish town. As Liam O'Leary wrote, these sets, "peopled with actors dressed in the costumes designed by J. K. Benda . . . literally brought the pictures of the Flemish masters of painting to the service of the cinema. . . . This comedy of the war of the sexes, and the conflict of the prosaic and the poetic, and the real and the imagined, is played with verve and style by a brilliant cast": it included Françoise Rosay as the burgomaster's resourceful wife, Jean Murat as the gallant Spanish duke, and Louis Jouvet as his sly and worldly chaplain.

O'Leary called this "a great living human comedy." He and other contemporary reviewers were reminded variously of Breughel and Chaucer by its gusto and its gallery of ironic character studies. Howard Barnes wrote that "with this work, Feyder takes his place with René Clair and Charlie Chaplin as one of the most distinguished comic artists of the cinema." It received the Grand Prix of the Cinéma Français, the prize for best direction at the Venice Biennale, and other awards in America and Japan. Banned in Belgium for showing the Flemish people in a less than heroic light and condemned in the United States by the Legion of Decency, it was nevertheless an enormous international success.

Its reputation has dimmed over the years, however. When it was revived in London in 1967, Penelope Houston found that this "optimistic antimilitary anecdote" now seemed "overburdened rather than sustained by its style," while John Coleman disliked the sequence (cut in some prints) in which the aldermen envisage scenes of rape and slaughter—a "very nasty" passage that turned "the high farce which surrounds it into something off-key and uneasy." For David Thomson, the film looked like "an intolerably pretty Dutch interior, proof that as fine a photographer as Harry Stradling could be reduced to inertia if asked simply to produce exquisite shots."

The following year, Feyder went to England to film James Hilton's novel *Knight Without Armor* (1937) for Alexander Korda, taking Stradling with him as his photographer (assisted by

Jack Cardiff) and Meerson as his designer. Set during the Russian Revolution, this film has an engaging performance from Robert Donat as a revolutionary spy, and Marlene Dietrich in what seemed to many a rather bored caricature of her familiar role as seductress.

Made at a reputed cost of a quarter of a million pounds, *Knight Without Armor* was marked, according to Basil Wright, by "the lavish longueurs and overelaboration which are becoming the hallmark of British superproductions," but achieved all the same "a real sense of atmosphere" and "the verisimilitude of a newsreel" in some of "the scenes of railway stations and roads crowded with miserable refugees." It seemed to Wright that "Feyder's genius has always been in his attention to detail. He is one of those rare creatures who can produce a single emotion out of a collection of bric-à-brac carefully and painstakingly arranged and rearranged."

Les Gens du voyage (1938), made simultaneously in a German version as *Fahrendes Volk,* was a complicated circus film that seems to have been moderately well received, but *La Loi du Nord* was "maudlin and mawkish," with Michèle Morgan expiring elegantly amid the Canadian snows after completing touching private farewells to no less than three manly admirers.

With the fall of France, Feyder and Françoise Rosay fled to Switzerland, where they made one more film together, *Une Femme disparaît (A Woman Disappeared,* 1942), scripted by Feyder with Jacques Viot. It is a variation on the theme of *L'Image.* The body of a woman is found in a Swiss lake, and after a photograph is published, four people come forward to claim the body, each giving his or her own account of the departed. Rosay plays each of the missing women—an aging stage star unwanted by her married daughter, an obstinate old peasant, a gentle amnesiac schoolteacher, and the rowdily passionate wife of an Italian tugboat skipper. The critics vied with one another in their praise of Rosay's virtuosity, but most shared C. A. Lejeune's opinion that "the different incidents are not very well integrated; the story is too long in coming to the point; and there are marks of some drastic and apparently hasty cutting."

After this string of failures or near-failures, Feyder made no more films although he did several works for the theatre and assumed the artistic direction of Marcel Blistène's Macadam. By that time he was seriously ill, and he died two years later. "I am a craftsman in the true sense of the word," he declared, "limited but worthy of respect." Indeed, as Richard Roud says, "if

Jacques Feyder was overrated during his lifetime, the pendulum has certainly swung too far the other way since his death." Many of his films are lost or "ridiculously difficult to see," and the conventional view of him is that stated by Nino Frank when he said: "I consider Feyder to be an artisan rather than an artist, a technician rather than an *auteur,* in the sense that he uses "raw materials borrowed from somebody else and which, no matter how much he adapts, alters or shapes them, remain fundamentally alien to him."

But Abel Gance said that Feyder's career, with its dismal end, put him among the cinema's martyrs, and Georges Sadoul saw him as "one of the major creators of poetic realism in the Thirties." Another critic has written admiringly of his determination—at a time when the French cinema was divided between commercialism and a too rarified aestheticism—"to keep the cinema in touch with life and some social truth." It is true that (as Paul Rotha said) his style "appears to change with each of his . . . productions," but as the cult of the *auteur* fades, and it seems once more permissible to admire the skills of the creative interpreter, the recognition grows that Feyder has been condemned as unjustly as his own Crainquebille.

FILMS: *Short features*—Monsieur Pinson, policier, 1916 (begun by Gaston Ravel, completed by Feyder); Têtes de femmes, femmes de tête, 1916; Le Pied qui étreint, 1916 (four episodes); Le Bluff, 1916; Un Conseil d'ami, 1916; L'Homme de compagnie, 1916; Tiens, vous êtes à Poitiers?, 1916; Le Frère de lait, 1916; L'Instinct est maître, 1917; Le Billard cassé, 1917; Abrégeons les formalités, 1917; La Trouvaille de Buchu, 1917; Le Pardessus de demi-saison, 1917; Les Vieilles Femmes de l'hospice, 1917; (with Raymond Bernard) Le Ravin sans fond, 1917; La Faute d'orthographe, 1919. *Features*—L'Atlantide (Woman of Atlantis/Missing Husbands), 1921; Crainquebille (U.K., Coster Bill of Paris), 1923; Visages d'enfants (Faces of Children), 1925; L'Image, 1925; Gribiche, 1925; Carmen, 1926; Au Pays du roi lepreux, 1927 (not released); Thérèse Raquin (Thou Shalt Not/Shadows of Fear), 1928; Du sollst nicht ehe brechen! (German version of Thérèse Raquin), 1928; Les Nouveaux Messieurs (The New Gentlemen), 1928; The Kiss, 1929; Anna Christie (German version of film by Clarence Brown), 1930; Le Spectre vert (French version of Ben Hecht's The Unholy Night), 1930; Si l'Empereur savait ça (French version of Lionel Barrymore's His Glorious Night), 1930; Olympia (German version of above), 1930; Daybreak, 1931; Son of India, 1931; Le Grand Jeu, 1934; Pension Mimosas, 1935; La Kermesse héroïque (Carnival in Flanders), 1935; Die klugen Frauen (German version of above), 1935; Knight Without Armor, 1937; Les Gens du voyage, 1938; Fahrendes Volk (German version of above), 1938; La Loi du Nord, 1945 (abridged version of above released in 1942 as La Piste du Nord); Une Femme disparaît (A Woman Disappeared/

Portrait of a Woman), 1942. *Published scripts*—La Kermesse heroique in L'Avant-Scène du cinéma May 15, 1963.

ABOUT: Bachy, V. Jacques Feyder: Artisan du cinéma, 1968; Boulanger, P. Le Cinéma colonial, 1975; Comité National Jacques Feyder Jacques Feyder ou le cinéma concret, 1949; Feyder, J. and Rosay, F. Le Cinema: notre métier, 1944; Ford, C. Jacques Feyder, 1973 (in French); Hunter, W. Scrutiny of Cinema, 1932; Lejeune, C. A. Cinema, 1931; Roud, R. (ed.) Cinema: A Critical Dictionary, 1980; Thomson, D. A Biographical Dictionary of the Cinema, 1980. *Periodicals*— Ciné-Club November 1948; Écran Français June 8, 1948 (Feyder issue); May 30, 1951; June 13, 1951; Film Dope September 1978; Revue du cinéma July 1, 1930.

ROBERT J. FLAHERTY

FLAHERTY, ROBERT J(OSEPH) (February 16, 1884–July 23, 1951), American director, scenarist, cinematographer, and producer, often called the "father of the documentary," was born on Iron Mountain, Michigan, the eldest of the seven children of Robert Henry Flaherty and the former Susan Klöckner. His father was the son of an Irish Protestant immigrant; his mother was of German Catholic descent. She was an intensely devout woman, and Flaherty's brother David said of her that though she "didn't know about music and such things, as my father did . . . , she loved people dearly and had a great and deep compassion."

According to Arthur Calder-Marshall in his biography of Flaherty, *The Innocent Eye*, the director's father was the owner of an iron-ore mine, and Flaherty had a relatively privileged childhood as the boss's son in "the poverty-stricken country in which . . . [they] lived." Robert Lewis Taylor, in an entertaining if somewhat fanciful *New Yorker* profile of Flaherty, says that at school he "learned with ease, far outstripping his tractable colleagues, but he refused to observe the rules. When the humor was upon him, he would turn up every day for a week or so, but he was likely to lounge in around eleven o'clock smoking a cigar," leaving in time "for the mid-afternoon fishing."

The Flaherty mine was closed down by the slump of 1893 and the family fortunes declined. Flaherty's father went off prospecting into Canada, returning after a year with exciting stories of his adventures and, for his romantic firstborn, "real Indian moccasins . . . of smoked buckskin." Flaherty never wore them: "I slept with them under my pillow at night and dreamed of Indians in a land of gold."

In 1896 the older Flaherty returned to Canada as manager of the Golden Star Mine in the Rainy Lake region of Ontario. Bob Flaherty, then twelve years old, went with him. The only child in a rowdy community of miners, prospectors, prostitutes, and assorted adventurers, he was spoiled by everyone, including the bands of Indian who drifted into camp. They brought him gifts, taught him to hunt and track, and sometimes allowed him into their tipis, introducing him to a way of life remote from that of the gold-hungry whites. There was no formal education to be had, but Flaherty devoured the works of Francis Parkman, James Fenimore Cooper, and R. M. Ballantyne, and somehow—perhaps from his father—learned to play the violin, a source of satisfaction to him all his life.

The ore ran out at Rainy Lake in 1898, and the Flahertys went on to another Canadian mine in the Lake of the Woods country, where the whole family was reunited. Mrs. Flaherty was distressed by her son's lack of learning and it was decided that he should go to Upper Canada College in Toronto, an institution modeled on such English public schools as Harrow. Bob Flaherty was remembered there as "a tousle-headed boy who had little idea of the ways of civilization." He ate with his knife and "smoked like a stove"; not surprisingly, perhaps, he was popular with the other boys. He lasted about a year at the college, then rejoined his father in the wilderness. Still in his teens, he went on prospecting expeditions "often for months at a time, traveling by canoe in summer and by snowshoe in winter."

In 1900 Flaherty's father joined the US Steel Corporation in Port Arthur (now Thunder Bay, Ontario), the family home for the next several years. The parents made one more attempt to educate Bob Flaherty, sending him to the Michigan College of Mines. According to Robert Lewis Taylor, he took to sleeping in the woods and answered questions, "when at all, in Chippewa." He was expelled after seven months and received a letter from his father wishing him the best of luck but indicating that he was henceforth on his own.

The College of Mines did indeed bring Flaherty good luck. It was there that he met his future wife and collaborator Frances L. Hubbard, a Bostonian and Bryn Mawr graduate who nevertheless shared his passion for the wilderness. Her father was the mineralogist, geologist, ornithologist, and bibliophile Lucius L. Hubbard. As a child she had accompanied him on journeys into the forests of Maine, and she never lost her wanderlust. Bob Flaherty lacked her formal education, but was already living the life she wanted for herself. She assumed that "when we were married, we would go and live in the woods."

Flaherty had other plans, however: to travel light and keep moving north. After a stint in a Michigan copper mine, he was allowed to rejoin his father on prospecting trips for US Steel, learning properly now how to map and prospect. Further northern explorations followed, with an English mining engineer, the remarkable H. E. Knobel. In 1906 Flaherty traveled up the west coast of Vancouver Island, searching for marble deposits. He was visited there by Frances Hubbard and they became formally engaged. The same year he spent some time in and around the Vancouver city of Victoria, where he and his violin were much in demand at musical soirées. An acquaintance described him then as "a most likeable soul, kind-hearted, generous, but improvident," who spent most of the allowance he received from his mother on books and fancy neckties.

Arthur Calder Marshall said of Flaherty at this point that "he was not articulate. He did not propound an aim and then proceed to fulfil it. He flowed to his end, like a stream, finding its way by a careful exploration of possibilities; and the end was purely and simply to get north and stay north. . . . His quest for the North was spiritual, a sort of humanist Pilgrim's Progress, provoked perhaps by his father but inspired by the sort of religious feeling which his mother satisfied in the Mass."

Over the next three years Flaherty prospected for a mining syndicate above Lake Huron and for another company along the Mattagami River in Eastern Ontario. His father was by then working as a consultant engineer for Sir William Mackenzie, "the Cecil Rhodes of Canada," whom Flaherty met in 1910. It was a momentous encounter. Recognizing the young man's quality, Mackenzie sent him prospecting to the little-known Nastapoka Islands on Gulf Hazard, on the sub-Arctic east coast of Hudson Bay. Flaherty traveled by canoe and sailing boat until winter set in, then went on by sledge, first with a party of Indians, then with a solitary Eskimo, a celebrated hunter known as Nero. He found no important mineral deposits on the Nastapokas, but learned from the Eskimos of another and more promising group of islands, virtually uncharted, called the Belcher Islands.

Again sponsored by Mackenzie, Flaherty spent nineteen months trying to reach the Belchers but (he said in a radio talk) "got wrecked. . . . Instead, I made a survey of the Ungava Peninsula by sledge with an Eskimo. Also during this next summer (1912), I made two equidistant cross-sections of an area about the size of Germany in the Barren Lands." As Paul Rotha wrote in his biography of Flaherty, "this modest statement gives no indication of the hazards of these journeys or the degree of his achievement. Two previous attempts had been made to cross the barren of Ungava. . . . Both had failed." Indeed, Flaherty's diaries of these journeys show that even his Eskimo guides repeatedly lost their way and succumbed to snow-blindness and near-despair.

In August 1913 Flaherty set out again for the Belchers, this time provided by Mackenzie with an 83-ton topsail schooner, The Laddie, and a crew of nine. "Just as I was leaving," Flaherty said, "Sir William said to me casually, 'Why don't you get one of these new-fangled things called a motion picture camera?'" Flaherty liked the idea of thus 'taking notes' on the expedition. He bought a primitive Bell and Howell camera and portable developing and printing equipment, and took a three-week course in cinematography.

The Laddie took Flaherty and his party a thousand miles to Baffin Land, where they settled in for the winter. In the calm weather of February, Flaherty started filming scenes from Eskimo life—igloo building, dances, conjuring, sledging, and seal-hunting. His proposed climax, the record of a great deer hunt, was lost when a sledge went through the ice and the remaining material proved "too crude to be interesting." When the weather permitted, the party went on to the Belcher Islands, discovering that they were indeed as considerable as the Eskimos had reported, though with only minor mineral deposits. The largest of the islands Flaherty mapped is named for him.

Flaherty returned to civilization in October 1914. The following month he and Frances Hubbard were at last married. He was hard up, as usual, and the bride reportedly paid for both ring and license. A few months later, in the summer of 1915, they were separated again when Flaherty rejoined *The Laddie* and returned to the Belcher Islands for further exploration and mapping. There he "completed a series of motion pictures showing the primitive life, crafts, and methods of hunting and traveling of the islanders."

Back in Toronto, Flaherty put this footage and his earlier film into some sort of continuity. The entire negative—70,000 feet—went up in flames when he dropped a cigarette on it. Flaherty was badly burned and hospitalized. Fortunately, he had already sent a positive print to an acquaintance at Harvard and this, the only copy of his first film, was screened at various gatherings for a time. Eventually lost or discarded, this film seemed to Flaherty "utterly inept, simply a scene of this and a scene of that, no relation, no thread of a story or continuity whatever."

Never one to give up easily, he became increasingly obsessed by his failure in what was still a peripheral aspect of his real vocation as an explorer. From endless discussions with his wife grew the idea of filming a year in the life of a typical Eskimo family, but in the midst of World War I this intriguing project had to be postponed. Meanwhile the Flahertys lived first in Michigan, then in Connecticut, and Flaherty began a new career as a writer, describing his earlier adventures in two articles for the *Geographical Review*.

All the same, by 1920, when he was thirty-six, Flaherty was by material standards a failure, dependent mostly on his wife's private income to support their family, which by then included three small girls. In that year, at a cocktail party, Flaherty met Captain Thierry Mallet of Revillon Frères' fur-traders and the principal rivals of the Hudson Bay Company. A man of infectious enthusiasm and great eloquence, Flaherty persuaded Mallet to underwrite his dreamed-of Eskimo film.

In August 1920 Flaherty arrived by schooner at Revillon Frères' Port Harrison post on the northeast coast of Hudson Bay. He had with him all he needed to light, shoot, develop, print, and project his film. After careful consideration he had chosen two Akeley cameras, partly because they were lubricated with graphite, not likely to freeze, partly because they incorporated a newly developed gyro motion in the tripod-head. This permitted the camera to be panned horizontally or tilted vertically "without the slightest distracting jar or jerk or vibration."

"Of the Eskimos who were known to the [Port Harrison] post," Flaherty recalled, "a dozen all told were selected for the film. Of these Nanook (The Bear), a character famous in the country, I chose as my chief man." Flaherty first filmed a walrus hunt, three days later showing the rushes to the bewildered and excited hunters and their families. Processing the rushes turned out to be no easy matter. The light from Flaherty's small generator was too uneven for printing, so he made ingenious use of natural light. He covered the window of his hut completely, except for an aperture the size of a motion picture frame, controlling the amount of light admitted with layers of muslin. The drying room was hazardously heated by a coal-burning stove, and water for washing the film was hauled up in barrels filled by the Eskimos from a hole chiseled through six feet of ice.

"It has always been important for me to see my rushes—it is the only way I can make a film," Flaherty said. "But another reason for developing the film in the north was to project it to the Eskimos so that they would accept it and understand what I was doing and work together with me as partners." The Eskimos at first found it difficult to "read" even a still photograph of themselves, failing to perceive the relationship between the two-dimensional image and the three-dimensional reality. Before Flaherty left them, they were working with him not only as actors and laborers but as technicians. One of them successfully reassembled a complicated still camera that had defeated Flaherty himself. His hut, with a constant supply of hot tea, was always full of visitors from miles around. Flaherty had taken along his violin and an old phonograph, and the Eskimos greatly enjoyed both, Nanook indeed even trying to eat one of the phonograph records.

As Arthur Calder-Marshall wrote, "the white man who wants to show what Eskimo life is like normally has to manipulate it on film." Flaherty, finding that Nanook and his companions were wearing manufactured clothing, dressed them traditionally so that they would "appear on the screen as genuinely Inuit [Eskimo] as they were." The average Eskimo igloo was too small for filming the interior scenes so, at Flaherty's behest, Nanook built a giant igloo, twenty-five feet in diameter, and then removed half the roof to admit sufficient light. Much criticized for these and other manipulations, Flaherty maintained that "one often has to distort a thing to catch its true spirit."

He filmed for a year around Port Harrison, making one fruitless and almost fatal 600-mile journey to Cape Sir Thomas Smith in search of bear. By August 1921, when the yearly ship returned to Port Harrison, Flaherty's film stock was exhausted and, ready or not, shooting was over. During the winter of 1921–1922, aided by Charles Gelb, Flaherty edited *Nanook of the North* down to a five-reel film of about 70 minutes, with titles by himself and Carl Stearns Clancy. He offered it to Paramount, then to First-National; neither company was interested in so unorthodox a picture, but Pathé took it on, and after some dickering it opened in the summer of 1922 at the Capitol Theatre in New York.

The film begins with the slightly slapstick arrival of Nanook and his family at Hopewell Sound, Northern Ungava—six of them spilling out of a smallish kayak. At a trading post, Nanook barters his furs for beads and knives. Inside, he plays an old phonograph and bites the record. He goes off on floating ice, spears salmon with a trident and kills them with his teeth. There is news of walrus and a small fleet of kayaks join the hunt. Nanook harpoons a two-ton bull walrus. Its mate locks her tusks with his in an attempt to pull him to safety, but after a tremendous struggle the hunters haul the stricken beast to shore. They butcher it with ivory knives and begin eating on the spot.

Winter sets in, bringing blizzards. Nanook stalks and kills a white fox and then builds an igloo, carving blocks of frozen snow and skillfully inserting a window of ice. He teaches his son to hunt with a bow and arrow, using a snow model of a small bear. The family wake up in their igloo; Nanook's wife Nyla chews his leather boots to soften them and washes the smallest child with saliva.

They set off for the seal-grounds, glazing the runners of their sledge with ice and whipping the half-wild huskies into obedience. Nanook finds a breathing hole in the ice. He thrusts his spear down it and begins a long tussle with whatever is under the ice. It almost defeats him, but the family arrive in the nick of time to help and a seal is hauled up (all too obviously long dead). The dogs fight for scraps of the meat, tangling their traces. This delays the departure and the family take refuge that night in an abandoned igloo. The snow falls so heavily that the dogs are covered and hardly visible, but a small igloo is provided for the pups. Outside the blizzard rages, but Nanook and his family, naked in their fur sleeping bags, sleep soundly.

Nanook had a cautious reception from most contemporary reviewers, who had no idea what to make of it. However, Frances Taylor Patterson, writing in the *New Republic*, observed that "it may be said to be the first photoplay of the natural school of cinematography." And Robert E. Sherwood, in *The Best Moving Pictures of 1922–1923*, said it "was entirely original in form. . . . There have been many fine travel pictures, many gorgeous 'scenics,' but there is only one that deserves to be called great. That one is *Nanook of the North*. It stands alone, literally in a class by itself. . . . Here was drama rendered far more vital than any trumped-up drama could ever be by the fact that it was all *real*." According to Kevin Brownlow, the Hollywood professionals, with a few exceptions, responded with envious hostility. One exception was the director Rex Ingram, who said: "*Nanook* is one of the most vital, dramatic and human films that has ever flashed across the screen. Because its drama is made tremendous by its naturalness and sincerity. Because its story is the first and most dramatic of all stories—man's fight for his daily bread. And vitally important, its director was unhampered by studio methods, traditions and equipment."

The film fared better at the box office in Britain and Europe than it did on its first release in the United States, and was received by many foreign critics as a revelation. However, in 1926 the British critic Iris Barry called it "an enchanting romance" which "was actually taken in the latitude of Edinburgh and acted by extremely sophisticated Eskimos." (It might be remarked that Nanook himself was apparently not "sophisticated" enough; he starved to death in the Ungava two years after the film was made.) Hostility towards the film mounted, and in 1947, when a sound version was released with music and voice-over narration, one critic went so far as to call it "a phoney" and its director an "imposter." Flaherty's own defense of his methods was that he was "not going to make films about what the white man has made of primitive peoples. What I want to show is the former majesty and character of these people, while it is still possible."

Paul Rotha, in his 1983 biography of Flaherty, had this to say about *Nanook*. "Its continuity is rough and there are many unexplained interruptions. The passing of time is either clumsily handled or deliberately ignored. Technically, it is almost an amateur's work. These, however, are minor flaws when compared with the overall conception. . . . Some sequences . . . will always be memorable in the history of the cinema," and more important than the technical weaknesses "is the fact that the film conveys the sheer struggle for existence of these people and their carefree acceptance of their fight for survival." For Rotha, it remained "one of the first masterpieces in a new medium."

Nanook has been claimed as the first feature-length documentary, which it was not—Captain F. E. Kleinschmidt's record of the Carnegie Museum's Alaska-Siberian expedition of 1911 preceded it by a decade. Unlike other early "scenics," however, *Nanook* demonstrated "the creative treatment of actuality"—John Grierson's definition of the documentary style. Grierson himself wrote in 1938 that "here the sketch came to life and the journalistic survey turned to drama. Flaherty's theory that the camera has an affection for the spontaneous and the traditional . . . stands the test of twenty years, and *Nanook*, of all the films that I have ever seen . . . is least dated today." And another filmmaker, Sergei Eisenstein, said that "we Russians learned more from *Nanook* than from any other foreign film. We wore it out, studying it. That was in a way our beginning."

None of these comments entirely conveys the unique quality of *Nanook* and Flaherty's other films. Paul Rotha attributed this quality to the influence on Flaherty of Eskimo life and art. He quotes from a book by Edmund Carpenter which explains that an Eskimo artist does not set out with a specific artifact in mind "but picks up the ivory, examines it to find its hidden form and, if that's not immediately apparent, carves aimlessly until he sees is, humming or chanting as he works. . . . What emerges from the ivory, or more accurately from the artistic act, isn't simply a carving of a seal, but an act which explicates, with beauty and simplicity, the meaning of life to the Eskimo. . . . Eskimo are interested in the artistic act, not in the product of that activity." Rotha believed that two Eskimo qualities—"the acute power of observation and the letting of material shape its own meaning—form an integral part of Flaherty's art as a filmmaker." In 1976 *Nanook* was restored to its original silent form with titles, and a new score was composed by Stanley Silverman; the 1947 sound version was then withdrawn.

After *Nanook*, Flaherty in collaboration with his wife wrote an account of the making of the film, published in 1924 as *My Eskimo Friends*. Meanwhile he received an astonishing offer from Jesse Lasky, head of Famous Players–Lasky. "I want you to go off somewhere and make me another *Nanook*," Lasky said. "Go where you will, do what you like. I'll foot the bills. The world is your oyster." Paramount, then the distribution wing of Famous Players–Lasky, had turned *Nanook* down and seen this shoestring movie blossom into a great international success, financial and critical. Lasky was ready to learn from previous mistakes and was besides an enthusiastic amateur of exploration himself.

Elated, Flaherty contacted Frederick O'Brien, author of the best-selling *White Shadows in the South Seas*, about the disastrous impact of white traders and missionaries on the Marquesas. They met in New York at Flaherty's favorite haunt, the Coffee House Club near Times Square. Flaherty left convinced that, after so many years in the frozen north, it was time to sample the opposite extreme, the fortunate islands of Samoa. O'Brien told him: "Go to the village of Safune on the island of Savaii and you may still be in time to catch some of that beautiful old culture before it passes away."

Frances Flaherty, who had believed that she was marrying into a life of travel and exploration, had spent ten years at home while her husband did the adventuring. This time, it was agreed, she would go along. So would their three daughters, aged six, four, and two, and Flaherty's younger brother David, who was to serve as production manager. The party sailed for Tahiti in April 1923, after a splendid farewell dinner at the Waldorf-Astoria attended by luminaries of the arts, sciences, and big business.

According to Frances Flaherty, "Bob had no illusions whatever as to what Paramount expected of him in the way of thrills and sensations for the box office," including fights with "the sea-monsters there doubtless were down around those islands." What they found on Savaii were beautiful people on a beautiful island so blessed by nature that, Frances wrote, "life was a game, a dance, a frieze on a Grecian urn." This was not entirely true: the island, mandated to New Zealand, was said to have been scandalously maladministered, but this was not the sort of drama the Flahertys were looking for. Indeed, their most useful contact, at least initially, was a blatant example of maladministration—a German trader named Felix David who called himself the king of the island. A promising baritone in his youth, he had been denied an operatic career by his Junker father and had exiled himself to this island paradise, where every evening he regaled his "subjects" with Wagnerian recitals.

Months passed in the search for violent adventures of the sort the Flahertys had envisaged. Meanwhile they tested village beauties for star quality, becoming involved in all sorts of local rivalries. Gradually they were forced to the realization that there simply were no sea-monsters to be had—not so much as a tiger shark. Flaherty's growing despondency was deepened by his disappointment over the quality of the black-and-white film he was shooting with his Akeley camera. The orthochromatic stock he was using, being insensitive to red, entirely failed to suggest the luminous colors of the island, the flesh tones of the islanders.

Flaherty had also brought along a Prizma color camera and a supply of the new panchromatic film. One day, apparently on a whim, he loaded his Akeley with panchromatic film. The results were naturally in black and white but, Frances Flaherty wrote, "the figures jumped right out of the screen. They had a roundness and modelling and looked alive and, because of the color correction, retained their full beauty and texture." Ignoring warnings that the new stock was unreliable, Flaherty scrapped the 40,000 feet of film he had already shot and cabled home for more panchromatic.

It has been generally held that the beauty of Flaherty's film revolutionized cinematography, leading directly to the general adoption of panchromatic film. However, in *The War, the West, and the Wilderness*, the historian Kevin Brownlow flatly contradicts this received wisdom, saying that "panchromatic had been used by Hollywood cameramen for years" and that "Flaherty planned *Moana* as a panchromatic picture from the beginning." It is hard to see how these radically disparate accounts can be reconciled, especially since, according to Frances Flaherty, the discovery provided the theme for which they had sought in vain for months: "The drama of our picture should lie in its sheer beauty, the beauty of *fa'a* Samoa, rendered by panchromatic film."

Fa'a Samoa was the elaborate structure of custom and ritual that ruled the lives of the islanders, contributing a rigor and discipline otherwise absent from their idyllic circumstances. Flaherty settled down to this theme but, after about a year's work, found that dark flashes were marring the developed print, making it unusable. The two young islanders whom Flaherty had trained to develop and print his rushes worked in a cave fitted out as a laboratory. Eventually it was found that the water in the cave was fouled by chemicals washed off the film and deposited back onto subsequent footage. When the film was washed in rainwater instead, the results were perfect, but the whole of the film had to be reshot. This discovery also explained the mysterious illness that had afflicted Flaherty the previous year; it was silver nitrate poisoning, the result of his habit of drinking the water in the cave laboratory.

The Flahertys' stay on the island ended in a series of dramas that might well have made a film in themselves (or a Conradian novel). One of the laboratory assistants, Imo, killed a young man from another village who had offended against *fa'a* Samoa by making advances to a married woman of Safune. A revenge party from the dead man's village was expected and

the Flahertys guarded their film all night, armed with shotguns. No attack came but Imo and his colleague were arrested. When the Flahertys wrote a letter on their behalf to the authorities, the trader Felix David reported to the resident commissioner that they were "obstructing the course of justice."

David's initial enthusiasm for the filmmakers had changed to hatred as the visitors usurped his influence with the islanders, and his operatic performances were deserted for their film shows. He would appear drunk at the screenings, shaking his fist in the projector beam. Soon after the arrest of Imo, David and the resident commissioner, both homosexuals, were charged with corrupting island youths. The commissioner shot himself and David was banished from his island paradise, whereupon he "withered away and died." The murder charge against Imo was reduced to manslaughter and he received a five-year jail sentence.

The Flahertys left Samoa in December 1924, more than a year and a half after they arrived. Including the wasted material, Flaherty had shot 240,000 feet of film, eventually reduced to a twelve-reel rough cut. Editing and titles were credited to a Lasky writer named Julian Johnson, though David Flaherty insists that Robert and Frances Flaherty were actually responsible for both. Lasky and the studio top brass were initially enthusiastic, but told Flaherty to reduce the film to six reels. In the interim, studio interest waned. Eventually Paramount agreed to test *Moana* in six notoriously hard-boiled towns around the country where, with the support and promotional efforts of the National Board of Review, it did better than average business.

Billed as "The Love-Life of a South Sea Siren," *Moana* was finally premiered at the Rialto on Broadway in February 1926. General release followed. Like *Nanook*, but in much more detail and with many more individual shots, *Moana* begins by introducing the principal participants. The young heroine Fa'angase, the hero Moana (Ta'avale), and his small brother Pe'a are first seen gathering the food that grows everywhere in luxuriant abundance. A wild boar is trapped and tied up, and everyone returns to the beautiful village of Safune. The scene shifts to the sea for a sequence showing fish being speared for food in the crystal-clear water. Meanwhile, back in the village, Moana's mother Tu'ungaita is making bark-cloth, a complex and fascinating process requiring great skill. The boy Pe'a climbs a huge coconut tree with a rope twisted around his feet and throws down the fruit.

More "scenes from island life" follow—Moana

and his friends in an outrigger canoe, Pe'a catching a giant crab, a turtle hunt. There is another domestic sequence, showing Tu'ungaita preparing an elaborate meal. Moana is anointed with oil and elaborately dressed for the *siva* (dance) performed by him and his betrothed Fa'angase. There follows the film's climax, the tatooing of Moana's body from hips to knees—the traditional rite of passage into manhood.

The tatooing process, which takes six weeks and is extremely painful, was by then already obsolescent; Ta'avale submitted to this ordeal very reluctantly, and only because Flaherty challenged him to do so for the honor of the island. Frances Flaherty wrote that "tatooing is the beautification of the body by a race who, without metals, without clay, express their feeling for beauty in the perfection of their own glorious bodies. Deeper than that, however, is its spring in a common human need, the need for some test of endurance, some supreme mark of individual worth and proof of the quality of the man." The film ends with a great *siva* and, as the sun goes down behind the mountains, the betrothal dance of Moana and Fa'angase.

"In *Moana*," wrote Arthur Calder-Marshall, "Flaherty for the first time used close-ups, sometimes very large indeed, in a succession of shots, not in isolation but in continuity—usually, in order to show a process. . . . The way these sequences were shot could not be bettered today and Flaherty himself never surpassed this choice of camera set-ups and camera-movement in his later work. *Moana* also showed increased use of camera-movement, panning and tilting to follow or anticipate action. . . . Long-focus lenses were also used more daringly than before. . . . The visual quality of *Moana* is very lovely. Seeing the film today on copies taken from dupe-negatives, we still feel no need for colour, even though some of the original quality has been lost. The film has a wonderful organic unity. Every incident is an integral part of the family's everyday life. It is a lyric of calm and peace. . . . For all its human feeling and warmth of approach, *Nanook* had a detachment, as if the characters were being watched from outside. The triumph of *Moana* was its intimacy."

The New York reviewers gave the film a generally good reception. The most interesting and significant review appeared in the New York *Sun* and was written by a visitor from England, John Grierson. "The film is unquestionably a great one," he wrote, "a poetic record of Polynesian tribal life, its ease and beauty and its salvation through a painful rite. *Moana* . . . reveals a far greater mastery of cinematic techniques than Mr. Flaherty's previous photoplay, *Nanook*

of the North. . . . Its camera angles, its composition, the design of almost every scene, are superb. The new panchromatic film used gives tonal values, lights and shading that have not been equaled." And all this, Grierson said, was in addition to its "documentary value." He borrowed the term "documentary" from *documentaire*, applied by French critics to "serious" travel films; this was the first recorded use of a crucial and endlessly controversial term.

Paul Rotha in Britain also thought that of Flaherty's first two films, "*Moana* was perhaps the finer." The French and Swedish critics were equally enthusiastic, and the chiefs of Safune allowed that it was suitably *fa'a* Samoa, and therefore sacred. But, unlike *Nanook*, it was not chosen as one of the ten best films of the year in the United States, and Terry Ramsaye guessed that it grossed no more than $150,000 (as against an estimated $510,000 for *Nanook*).

Moana was thus a critical but not a financial success, enhancing Flaherty's reputation with lovers of film art but not in Hollywood, where the money was. Apart from completing this film, the only work he found in 1925–1927 was directing two sponsored shorts. The first was *The Pottery Maker* (14 minutes), underwritten by the actress Maude Adams, a fervent admirer of Flaherty's work. Shot in the basement of the Metropolitan Museum in New York, it used the new Mazda incandescent lamps but was interesting primarily as a sketch for the famous pottery-making sequence in a later film, *Industrial Britain*.

After that, Maude Adams tried to raise backing for a version of Kipling's *Kim*, and when that failed Flaherty made *Twenty-Four Dollar Island* (1927), a two-reel documentary about Manhattan financed by "a wealthy socialite." Shot largely from the tops of skyscrapers, this "curious, flat, foreshortened" view of the city greatly impressed some critics with its poetic quality, which reminded some of Walter Ruttmann's *Berlin* (1927) and subsequent city "symphonies"; reduced in length, it was used as a backdrop for the stage ballet *The Sidewalks of New York*.

Flaherty was next engaged by MGM to collaborate with W. S. Van Dyke on *White Shadows*, to be based on Frederick O'Brien's *White Shadows in the South Seas*—the book that had sent him to Polynesia in the first place. With Raquel Torres as the island heroine, an army of MGM technicians, and producer Hunt Stromberg eager to "fill the screen with tits," Flaherty decided that he had no contribution to make and resigned. It should be said, however, that the resulting movie, released in 1928, was by no means as bad as it could have been and had many illustrious champions, among them D. W. Griffith and Luis Buñuel.

More abortive projects followed. In 1928 Flaherty started work on a film for Fox about the Pueblo Indians of New Mexico. David Flaherty had meanwhile gone to Hollywood to discuss a story outline he had written with his brother based on the strange life of trader Felix David. There he met the great German emigré director F. W. Murnau, whose last two pictures for Fox had flopped. Murnau had bought a yacht and was about to set off for the south Pacific to make films on his own. He admired Robert Flaherty's work and suggested a collaboration, reporting that Fox was in any case about to call off Flaherty's Indian film because he refused to insert a conventional love story.

Murnau-Flaherty Productions Inc. was launched with funding from an ambitious new company, Colorart. In April 1929 Murnau and David Flaherty sailed in Murnau's yacht for Tahiti, Robert Flaherty leaving later but arriving before them by mail steamer. He met them at Papeete with the news that Colorart had failed to come up with any money. Murnau decided to finance the film himself on a tight budget. The American technicians were sent home and Flaherty set about training a crew of Tahitians.

For all their mutual respect, Murnau and Flaherty were radically different in temperament and, it soon became clear, had opposing notions of the film they were supposed to be making, *Tabu*. Both took as their starting point an anecdote told by Flaherty about a pearl fisher. Murnau came up with a romantic story about a young man who falls in love with a sacred virgin dedicated to the Polynesian gods, and is consumed by the sea. Flaherty on the other hand wanted to make a film about the exploitation and corruption of Polynesia by white traders— the film he had failed to make in *Moana* and had been prevented from making in *White Shadows*. Murnau held the purse strings and there was nothing Flaherty could do but withdraw into the background. *Tabu* (1931) was a critical and financial success, but it was Murnau's film, although he died a week before its release.

In December 1930 Flaherty joined his wife and daughters in Germany, where the girls were being educated. It was to be ten years before he returned to the United States. He had been as impressed by Eisenstein's *Potemkin* as Eisenstein was with *Nanook*, and in Berlin he saw Dovzhenko's *Earth*, which he regarded as "the greatest of all films." He also met Pudovkin in Berlin, and the Dutch documentarist Joris D. Ivens. When his hopes of finding German back-

ing dwindled, he considered working in the Soviet Union. His idea for a film about the nomads of Central Asia was turned down because Flaherty envisioned a lament for dying cultures, while the Russians wanted to celebrate their sovietization.

The Flahertys then appealed to John Grierson, "father" of the British documentary movement, who was at that time production chief of the Film Unit of the Empire Marketing Board. Grierson had already demonstrated his admiration for Flaherty as a pioneer and artist, and at once saw the advantages of adding so prestigious a name to his dedicated team of young documentarists. In 1931 the Flahertys went to London. Soon after their arrival, to give Flaherty a chance to acclimatize himself, Grierson sent him to Devonshire in the company of Basil Wright, a young protégé then making his first film there.

Wright has given an illuminating account of his drive to Devon in the company of the great man, who was intent on tasting all the pleasures of English pub life, gently disregarding Wright's mounting anxiety over his tight shooting schedule. Wright's ordeal was not for nothing, however. What he remembered most vividly "is the soft, careful and tactful manner in which, over a number of days shooting, he (as it were) lent me his wonderful eyes. . . . Almost as in passing, he commented on the play of light on fields and woods and distant landscape, or on certain movements of horses or cattle. . . . It's almost impossible to explain his way of seeing things in this manner. . . . I certainly would say that in those few days he enriched my understanding of looking at things and people in terms of movie in a way that ten million dollars would not buy."

Flaherty's lack of interest in budgets and shooting schedules, his mild but absolute refusal to provide himself with a script, reportedly led to stormy scenes between him and Grierson. But somehow, with a great deal of "additional direction" by Grierson, Wright, and Arthur Elton, a two-reel film about craftsmanship in British industry was completed. It dealt with such traditional crafts as basketry and weaving, then moved on to coal mining, pottery making, glass blowing, lens manufacture, and the making and testing of steel.

Industrial Britain was finally released, with a voice-over narration, in November 1933. Grierson wrote of it: "I saw the material a hundred times and . . . should have been bored by it. But there is this same quality of great craftsmanship in it which makes one see it always with a certain new surprise. A man is making a pot, say. Your ordinary director will describe it; your good director will describe it well. . . . But what will you say if the director beats the potter to his own movements, anticipating each puckering of the brows, each extended gesture of the hands in contemplation, and moves his camera about as though it were the mind and spirit of the man himself? I cannot tell you how it is done, nor could Flaherty."

Paul Rotha added: "The wonderful faces of these craftsmen . . . caught in deep concentration on the job in hand, linger in one's memory. If *Industrial Britain* was significant for no other reason, it put the true faces of British workmen on the public screens in a way not seen before. The British worker—for so long portrayed in films as a comic stock figure—was at last given his rightful dignity." And Arthur Calder-Marshall wrote that *Industrial Britain*, "a stopgap job" for Flaherty, was "a landmark in British documentary."

On the ship from New York to London, amid gloomy talk of the Wall Street crash, Flaherty had listened to a young Irishman who had spoken lyrically about the Aran Islands off the west coast of Ireland. Life there, he said, was so poor and primitive that the islanders had to create their own soil out of seaweed and sand; in the face of realities like that, worries about slumps and booms became irrelevant. This was Flaherty talk, and while he worked on *Industrial Britain* he was reading and thinking about a project closer to his heart. Grierson put him in touch with Michael Balcon, production head of Gaumont-British, then under attack for churning out vacuous entertainments that ignored the realities of British life. Partly to appease the critics, Balcon agreed to put £10,000 into a sound film about Aran—less than the cost of *Nanook*, made silent ten years earlier.

The Flahertys went to Ireland in the fall of 1931. They stayed for a time in Dublin, where Flaherty found congenial drinking companions, then settled down in a fishing hotel on Achill Island off the Mayo coast. J.N.G. Davidson of the EMB Film Unit, assigned to ride herd on Flaherty, tried without success to move him on to the Aran Islands. Flaherty refused to budge, perhaps because he was aware of how much was at stake for him—how much he needed a major success; he declared that he had "a sort of mental hookworm." Eventually, fortified by great quantities of Irish whisky, he agreed to proceed. He found the Aran Islands as barren and dramatic as he had been told, and returned to London to prepare *Man of Aran*.

In January 1932 the Flahertys settled into a rented house on Inishmore, largest of the three Aran Islands and the best supplied with fresh water. Flaherty was accompanied by his wife and daughters and the seventeen-year-old John Taylor, who had worked as production assistant on *Industrial Britain*. Flaherty was to be his own cameraman; Taylor was in charge of film processing and extra camerawork. An old wharfhouse was converted into a laboratory and a cottage was built by local craftsmen for interior scenes. Meanwhile Flaherty began his usual procedure of searching for suitably photogenic local people to appear in his film. Always a lengthy procedure, this was complicated on Inishmore by fears that Flaherty was in league with the devil and intended to convert the island's children to Protestantism or even Socialism.

Flaherty had to enlist the aid of the island's priest before the penniless but deeply suspicious Dillane family gave permission for their young son Mikeleen to "star" in the picture. Maggie Dirrane, who played Mikeleen's mother, was won over when Flaherty gave her a cow so that her own children could have milk. "Tiger" King, the blacksmith and part-time fisherman cast as Maggie's husband, was "discovered" by one of Flaherty's daughters.

One day in April 1932 Flaherty saw a huge fish, some twenty-five or thirty feet long, swimming in the cove near his house. It was identified as a basking shark, a vast but harmless creature that had once been hunted for its liver, rich in oil for lamps. Flaherty had intended to shape his film around a story by Liam O'Flaherty, a native of Aran, but now decided that he must have a spectacular shark hunt; he had found the "sea-monster" that had eluded him in Samoa. Undeterred by the fact that no one on the island had hunted these creatures for sixty years, Flaherty unearthed some rusty old harpoons, had them copied, and set his cast to relearn this lost skill. The film had been scheduled for completion by the end of 1932 but the shark season was over before the hunting sequence had been shot. Flaherty asked for and got a year's extension. Meanwhile John Goldman, one of Michael Balcon's bright young men, joined the unit at his own request and began the editing of the mountain of film that had already accumulated.

Notoriously profligate in his use of film, Flaherty shot 200,000 feet of it for *Man of Aran*, eventually less than 7,000 feet long (76 minutes). It should be noted, however, that the stock supplied by Gaumont-British consisted of "short ends" left over from studio productions, while processing on the island was immeasurably cheaper than in a London laboratory. John Goldman said of Flaherty that "his feeling was always for the camera. This wanting to do it all in and *through* the camera was one of the main causes of his great expenditure of film—so often he was

trying to do what could *not* in fact be done."
Frances Flaherty wrote that "he simply went out
with his camera and shot and shot and shot, exploring every angle, every vantage, every location, every light, delving as far as imagination
could take him into his subject, photographing
exhaustively everything about it that the camera's eye could possibly see." And Pat Mullen,
their chauffeur and liaison man on Inishmore,
recalled: "He'd see some spot in the distance
where he would figure he should put up his camera. Well, nothing could stop him getting there.
He made a direct line, and he'd bolt through a
field of briars, you know, that would hold a
bull—that sort of way. He had that fire in him,
you see—say nothing, but do it if it costs you
your life."

Goldman has also testified graphically to the
intensity of Flaherty's concentration when he
was working: "Nothing else existed or had meaning for him. The result was an atmosphere difficult to describe if not experienced. It was heavy,
thick and charged. There was a tension everywhere, an unbearable tension, thunderous black
tension, a tension you could feel with your
hand . . . , all-pervading, contagious and paralytic. It would swell and inflate and grow thicker
and darker; emptiness and frustration and failure . . . , life slowed down into profound depression, compressed, explosive, dangerous. The
subsequent explosion was like a volcano blowing
its top. It had to be. The atmosphere then lightened, work started anew and grew into a furious
pace until the tide ebbed again and the fog gathered round and the tension again grew and
stretched and brooded. And there was no relief. . . . It was temperament, real temperament, the tremendous power of a force of
nature. . . . There was nothing rational about
it. There was nothing rational about making a
film with Flaherty from the beginning to the
end."

Along with Flaherty's "temperament" went
his legendary generosity and immense conge-
niality. The future director Harry Watt joined
the unit as an assistant and wrote that he "got
fat" on Guinness. John Grierson visited and was
reportedly nearly harpooned by Tiger King after a lengthy poteen session. Other visitors included the Irish playwright Denis Johnston, who
based his play *Storm Song* on the experience,
Jack Yeats, and Geraldine Fitzgerald. Grierson
remarked that Flaherty among his admirers was
"like a feudal baron among his retainers." An insomniac, he would keep the party going until
three or four in the morning, then while away
the rest of the night reading through his set of
Everyman's Encyclopaedia.

The shooting of *Man of Aran* was finally
wound up in August 1933 after twenty months.
It was edited in London by John Goldman, an
adherent of Soviet montage principles, in often
difficult collaboration with Flaherty, who insisted that he "photographed what the camera
wanted to photograph," not what continuity demanded. As Arthur Calder-Marshall wrote, his
was the "Eskimo way of filmmaking, fumbling,
intuitive and exploratory, treating the material
as if it contained some inner nature which needed to be understood."

This is fully borne out by Goldman's account
of Flaherty's editing, which took place "in the
projection-room. Here he would sit, running
through reel after reel over and over again, cutting, sorting, eliminating the dross [any shot that
'was dead and lifeless, meaningless in its own
terms'] and joining up what remained. . . . Imperceptibly during this sorting process, the shots
would start to sort themselves, migrating from
film can to film can and gathering like mole-
cules round a nucleus. . . . One day a mere collection of shots joined together; the next, a
perceptible semblance of a sequence, seemingly
self-generated, organic, belonging. . . . Flaherty in my mind . . . did not work by inspiration
but by revelation."

Like its predecessors, *Man of Aran* begins by
introducing the central family in typical pursuits. The boy Mikeleen is discovered searching
a rock pool. Maggie is at home. She and Mikeleen go to the cliff top and watch Tiger King and
his crew battling towards the shore in their curragh (a primitive boat of tarred canvas stretched
over ribs of thin wood). After a terrific struggle
against heavy seas, the men get ashore, though
the curragh is damaged.

Though this is a sound film, Flaherty insisted
on retaining some titles. One explains how the islanders mix seaweed and broken rocks with their
scant soil to make a kind of compost for potato-
growing. We see this done, then Tiger repairs his
battered boat. Mikeleen, fishing from the cliff
top, sees something in the sea and scrambles excitedly down the cliff. What he has seen is the
first basking shark of the season. A sequence follows showing men harpooning the great creatures from their curraghs.

The hunting continues for two days, the sea
growing rougher. A big iron cauldron is rolled
along the cliff, a peat fire lit under it, and the
sharks cut up. Maggie stirs the cauldron as night
falls. Next morning, with Maggie carrying a
heavy load of seaweed along the cliffs, we see
that the Atlantic is ferocious. As at the beginning, Tiger King's curragh is fighting its way towards the shore, but this time the waves are

gigantic. The men win their battle against the elements, but the curragh is lost. The film ends with the little family staring out at the wrath of the sea.

Man of Aran was premiered in London in April 1934, with the audience in evening dress and Irish folk music played by the band of the Irish Guards. Flaherty exerted all his great natural talent as a publicist, and "the journalists ate out of his hand." But this film, so different from its usual offerings, was something of an embarrassment to Gaumont-British. After test screenings in six British cities, it was given conventional release, booked most often as a second feature. Even so, it grossed £50,000—double its costs—within six months, though Flaherty never received a penny from it apart from his salary of £40 a week during its making. In September 1934 it was invited to Mussolini's Italy for the Venice Film Festival and chosen as the best film of the year, as it was by the National Board of Review in the United States.

The critical reaction, however, was stormy, reopening the debate about the integrity of Flaherty's work. The hostile view was summed up by the Marxist filmmaker Ralph Bond in *Cinema Quarterly* (2 4 1934): "There is no doubting Flaherty's genius for dramatising the conflict between man and nature. The storm scenes in the opening and closing sequences reveal Flaherty cutting at its best. But two storms and a shark-hunt do not make a picture and we are more concerned with what Flaherty has left out. . . . *Man of Aran* is escapist in tendency. . . . Flaherty would have us believe that there is no class-struggle on Aran, despite ample evidence to the contrary. There is . . . no mention of the absentee landlords who sent men to tear down their huts and scatter their soil. . . . Why does he merely present us with the spectacle of a handful of islanders (out of a population of 1200) waging incessant war against the fury of the sea? We must assume that he is a romantic idealist striving to escape the stern and brutal realities of life, seeking ever to discover some backwater of civilisation untouched by the problems and evils affecting the greater world outside. . . . Very little is seen of the life of the island itself and nothing of the island customs, traditions and ceremonies."

John Grierson did his best to defend the film, writing in *Cinema Quarterly* (3 1 1934) that "one may not—whatever one's difference in theory—be disrespectful of a great artist and a great teacher. Flaherty taught documentary to create a theme out of natural observation. . . . It is of course reasonable for a later generation of filmmakers to want a documentary tougher, more

complex, colder and more classical than the romantic documentary of Flaherty. . . . [But] it would be foolish . . . to complain of a pear that it lacked the virtue of a pomegranate. . . . I wonder that so much was done within commercial limitations. No English film has done so much. Not half-a-dozen commercial films in the year can compare with *Man of Aran* in simple feeling and splendid movement." But even Grierson, in an earlier essay in *Cinema Quarterly* (1 1 1932), had expressed the hope that "the neo-Rousseauism implicit in Flaherty's work dies with his exceptional self."

The American critic Richard Griffith, who in 1935 had been among the film's harshest critics, saw it again in 1940 and recanted completely. In *The World of Robert Flaherty*, Griffith recalled how the British documentarists had first welcomed Flaherty "as the inventor and master of the technique of camera observation which they meant to make their own," turning against him as the European social and political scene darkened. American documentarists had joined in the denunciation of *Man of Aran* "as a vehicle of reaction. . . . They even minimized it as a work of art, though none comparable with it emerged from anyone's camera anywhere in the world in the years of its making. . . . Hindsight is easy, but it is necessary to suggest that the . . . snubbing or ostracism of Flaherty's films was a major error for the documentary movement, the more so because it took place in public. . . . the world public responds to the humanism of Flaherty's films as they have to the work of no other documentary director."

More technical criticisms centered on the editing, which remained "curiously disjointed," and on the quality of the film's sound effects and snatches of speech, obviously recorded indoors. There were also complaints about John Greenwood's pedestrian score. Many critics found the film's three central characters wooden and unconvincing, and the famous shark hunting sequence seemed to Rotha "tame and confused." Most critics agreed that the film's strength was in its photography, and especially the photography of the storms at sea. According to John Goldman, "it took us two-thirds of the whole time we took to make *Man of Aran* to make this one sequence"; for him, it had "a grandeur of conception that I have not seen equalled on the screen, Lear-like in its force. . . . I believe that in this sequence the whole pent-up fury of Flaherty's genius flared up and expended itself."

Richard Griffith reports that Flaherty was "chilled" by the critical reception of *Man of Aran*, and a misunderstanding led to a long silence between him and John Grierson, interrupting a friendship that Grierson once described as "a dialectical pub-crawl across half the world." The "pub-crawl" continued in London without Grierson. Flaherty's favorite haunt there was the brasserie of the Café Royal in Regent Street, where the company often included such luminaries as Augustus John, Jacob Epstein, Graham Greene, A. P. Herbert, and Cavalcanti.

At the Café Royal, Rotha wrote, "as all through his life, he was overgenerous in buying rounds of drinks. . . . Flaherty had only to spot you through the smoke among the crowd and he would wave you across to his table. As the evening wore on, the circle around him grew wider. More chairs were dragged up. More drinks appeared. Flaherty loved an audience, especially one that would listen to his fabulous tales. . . . Flaherty's tales from the Arctic, the South Seas, and other places he had been have become legendary. He could tell a story that lasted a full half-hour and hold his listeners for every minute of it."

In terms of charm and persuasiveness, Flaherty met his match in Alexander Korda, creator of the thriving London Film Productions. Korda was eager to add Flaherty to his stable of illustrious names and, appealing to him as a fellow artist, talked him into a contract that gave Korda overriding supervisory powers. The film was to be one that the Flahertys had been gestating for years. It grew out of a story Flaherty had written about a Mexican (or Spanish) boy and a fighting bull. At some point this was transmuted into a similar narrative about an Indian boy and an elephant. At Korda's suggestion, the script was to be underpinned by Kipling's story "Toomai of the Elephants."

The Flahertys, including their daughter Barbara and David Flaherty, assembled in Bombay early in 1935. What was by Flaherty standards an army of technicians soon joined them, with an arsenal of equipment. It was decided to film *Elephant Boy* in Mysore in southern India, whose maharajah had offered his terrain, his elephants, and the use of a spare palace. The usual hunt began for a boy to play the lead and, after much searching, Flaherty's director of photography Osmond Borrodaile chanced upon a real "elephant boy" at the royal stables—the orphaned son of a *mahout*, and a splendid natural actor, named Sabu.

Flaherty being Flaherty, the months passed and the budget rose with very little material coming out of Mysore. Accounts differ radically, but it is clear that Korda grew increasingly worried, sending first Monta Bell and then his own brother Zoltan to hurry things along. "In the final weeks," according to David Flaherty, "three separate units were frantically shooting three different stories."

When shooting ended in June 1936, about 300,000 feet of film had been exposed—a record even for Flaherty. When this material was screened, it was found to contain a few good sequences and some "marvelous backgrounds," but nothing approaching a coherent story. The novelist John Collier was called in to devise a simple plot and the new material was directed in the studio by Zoltan Korda. The gigantic task of editing the Indian material was entrusted to the future director Charles Crichton.

As finally released in April 1937, *Elephant Boy* centered on Sabu as Toomai, son of a *mahout* who is killed by a tiger. His elephant Kala Nag is ill-treated by another *mahout* and runs amok. Toomai calms the maddened beast and rides him away to safety in the jungle, where he witnesses the legendary dance of the wild elephants (shot in the studio with zoo elephants and models of elephant feet). The white hunter Petersen Sahib (Walter Hudd) organizes a great drive to capture the wild elephants in a stockade and, with Toomai's help, succeeds.

The "studio scenes shot at Denham are obvious for their gaucherie," wrote Paul Rotha. "These include all the ingenuous dialogue sequences, the white hunter interlude, the unbelievable elephant dance, and the revolting ending sequence. If these are discarded as the crude and astoundingly bad pieces of filmmaking that they are, what remains is worth looking at." But "of all Flaherty's films seen in retrospect, it is the most outdated and lacking in living essence."

In spite of these and other criticisms, *Elephant Boy* won an award for best direction at Venice and, if nothing else, launched the career of Sabu, though it did nothing to advance Flaherty's. For the next two and a half years he was offered no film work apart from a commission from the British Commercial Gas Association. He came up with a story about a young stowaway, and this was developed into a script by Cecil Day Lewis and Basil Wright, but never filmed. Flaherty also wrote two novels based on his Hudson Bay experiences, *The Captain's Chair* (1938) and *White Master* (1939). Otherwise he mooched around his favorite London bars, perfected his skill at shove ha'penny, and continued to entertain his friends like a *grand seigneur* of infinite wealth.

In September 1938, with World War II brewing, Frances Flaherty returned to the United States. Her husband stayed behind, still hoping for work. In January 1939 he met and formed a close friendship with Jean Renoir. That summer, increasingly worried about the threat of war, Frances Flaherty asked John Grierson to get her husband home. The Machiavellian Grierson (whose friendship with Flaherty had meanwhile been mended) managed this by suggesting to Pare Lorentz, head of the New Deal's short-lived US Film Service, that Flaherty might be invited to direct a film about American agriculture.

Flaherty, delighted, returned to the United States in July 1939 and went to Washington to meet Lorentz. *The Land* was intended to show the state of agriculture throughout the United States, and to argue the case for parity payments to farmers. According to Russell Lord, who with Flaherty wrote the voice-over narration, "Flaherty never even tried to get the functions of the varying farm-relief agencies straightened out," let alone to understand "that sacred word *parity.*" But, having spent most of his life in Canada or abroad, Flaherty now discovered his own country and with a sense of revelation.

The US Film Service was shut down in 1940, but filming continued under the auspices of the Department of Agriculture. In all, Flaherty traveled 20,000 miles over a period of two years to shoot *The Land*. He was exhilarated by the richness of the Iowa corn country, appalled and outraged by the other effects of farm mechanization. There was no longer any question of celebrating the Noble Savage. For the first time, perhaps, Flaherty fully confronted the costs of greed and exploitation—the terrible harvest of unemployment, poverty, and homelessness, the erosion of the soil and of the human spirit.

When shooting ended in the early summer of 1941, Flaherty had shot a great quantity of film but had little idea what to do with it. Roosevelt's lend-lease program of aid to Britain had changed everything; American agriculture was booming, unemployment was dwindling, and the film's original theme was no longer relevant. Flaherty turned to Helen van Dongen, a very talented editor of documentaries and the wife of Joris Ivens. She was at first bewildered by the apparent absence of any unifying theme in the material but, watching it again and again with Flaherty, listening to his apparently unconnected talk about the war, agricultural industrialization, and the situation of the Okies, she slowly came to see the film "through Flaherty's eyes." *The Land* was completed by the end of 1941. It ran 43 minutes, with a voice-over narration read by Flaherty himself—Helen van Dongen insisted that no one else could speak his words correctly—and an interesting score by a young British composer, Richard Arnell.

Richard Corliss, in Richard Roud's *Cinema,* writes that "instead of a single, simple vision,

The Land projects a series of eloquent images. A dozen men crowd round a foreman; one stays outside the group, sitting hopelessly. A dying cow, a dead house, dead-eyed children—all are still standing. . . . An old Negro, oblivious to the camera, emerges from a rat-infested, death-corroded house, looks around, sees nothing, polishes and rings an old carillon, surveys the land again, says 'Where they all gone?' and returns to his home, closing the door on his unseen voyeurs to converse at peace with his demons. A boy sleeps, his hands moving; his mother says, 'He thinks he's picking peas'; she strokes his hair and the hands stop; as the scene fades out, the hands start moving again. *The Land* is a film without heroes or villains—only victims. . . . And the closest . . . [Flaherty] comes to an optimistic conclusion . . . is his camera's infatuation with contour farming. . . . one can see his eye take in the rolling man-made designs of earth, and feel his hand caress this huge, gorgeous, *functional* sculpture."

Paul Rotha commended the American government for sponsoring a film that revealed not only the triumphs but the "seamy human side of a headlong emergency government program." As it happened, however, *The Land* was never released or exported. After Pearl Harbor, it was decided that the film could be screened only for domestic audiences involved in agriculture; in alien hands, wrote Arthur Calder-Marshall, "it could have caused incalculable damage to the Allies." *The Land* was withdrawn in 1944, but a print was donated to the Robert Flaherty Foundation and this has been screened in recent years by film societies and in Flaherty retrospectives.

After that, the fifty-eight-year-old director made an attempt to settle down, as his wife wished, in the old farmhouse she had bought on Black Mountain, Vermont. His retirement was interrupted for a while in 1942, when he joined Frank Capra's War Department Film Division to make newsreels about the home front. Flaherty did not see eye to eye with either Capra or the army and soon retreated to Vermont, where he spent two bored and frustrated years, endlessly scheming to get back to work. In 1944 he supervised three educational shorts directed by his brother David for the Sugar Research Foundation, and in 1945 he was commissioned to make a film about the John Howard Benson system of calligraphy, a picture never completed because of disagreements between Flaherty and Benson.

Meanwhile, a much more considerable project was taking shape. A friend at the Standard Oil Company had written to him in the spring of 1944, asking if he would be interested in making a film that would illustrate the difficulties and dangers of getting oil out of the ground—"one that would have enough story and entertainment value to play in standard motion picture houses." He and his wife drove down to the oil country of the southwest and fell in love with Louisiana and its Acadian people. One day they saw an oil derrick "moving up the bayou, towed by a launch. In motion, this familiar structure suddenly became poetry, its slim lines rising clear and taut above the unending flatness of the marshes. . . . We knew then that we had our picture. Almost immediately a story began to take shape in our minds."

The Flahertys established their unit in Abbeville, Louisiana, in an old rented house where they set up a darkroom, cutting room, and projector. For their principal location they were given the use of Avery Island, "a magnificent preserve teeming with wildlife, including alligators." A Standard Oil affiliate put an oil derrick and crew at Flaherty's disposal, and he began his usual search for photogenic local people. He found his lead in Joseph Boudreaux, a boy of about twelve. "From that time on," wrote Frances Flaherty, "Bob was insistent that no one should show any affection for the boy except himself. He wanted sole control over him, as he had done with Sabu and Mikeleen." A trapper named Lionel LeBlanc was cast as the father, and Frank Hardy, one of the oil crew, as the driller on the derrick. Helen van Dongen was brought in as editor, and the future documentarist Richard Leacock as cameraman, both doubling as associate producers.

Flaherty's contract with Standard Oil was uniquely enlightened and generous. The company advanced to him the sum of $175,000, the estimated total cost of the film. Flaherty was to retain the distribution rights, with no obligation to refund costs out of the eventual revenues. The film was to be a Robert J. Flaherty production, and need make no reference whatever to Standard Oil.

The filming of Louisiana Story began in May 1946. Helen van Dongen's diary records all the familiar and manifold problems of a Flaherty film, including the many arising from the lack of a detailed shooting script. Flaherty as usual insisted on shooting anything that interested him, and then was faced with the problem of squeezing it into the film. "The big problem," van Dongen wrote, "will be to begin a discussion . . . with Flaherty. . . . He has a tendency to take every point that is brought up as a criticism. . . . It is hardly possible to have an exchange of ideas with him. . . . A curious one-track mind." She nevertheless concluded that

"Flaherty inspires the skill and creative ability of his fellow-workers; that is why working with him is such an experience."

By the time shooting ended in March 1947, the entire budget of $175,000 had been spent. Standard Oil agreed to further expenditure, bringing the total cost to $258,000. This included the score by Virgil Thomson, who worked closely with Helen van Dongen to produce what Paul Rotha described as "one of the most successful scores ever to be written for a motion picture; not only musically but in its integration with the film and the rest of its sound track."

Louisiana Story opens in a dark swamp rich in fantastic foliage. The narrator (Flaherty) tells us where we are: in the Petite Anse bayou country. A slender pirogue (dugout canoe) glides into view. Standing upright in it as he paddles is the young hero, Alexander Napoleon Ulysses Latour. We learn that he believes firmly in werewolves and mermaids, and protects himself against them by carrying a bag of salt at his waist and a mysterious something else—in fact a live frog—under his shirt.

We see a huge water snake and an alligator. The boy goes ashore with his rusty old rifle, but his hunting is interrupted by an explosion and the appearance of an amphibious "swamp-buggy" on caterpillar tracks that climbs up out of the water near where he is hiding. Scared, he goes home. He finds his father signing an agreement to allow an oil company to drill on his land. The oil crew arrives and one day their derrick arrives by water, moving majestically up the bayou. The boy is fascinated by their work and little by little overcomes his shyness and makes friends with them.

Back in the swamp the boy digs up some alligator eggs and watches the emergence of a baby alligator. He is so fascinated that he does not notice the arrival of the mother, and barely escapes. When he returns to his canoe he finds that his pet racoon has disappeared, and decides that an alligator has taken him. Bent on revenge, he sets out to capture an alligator. One takes his bait and hook. There is a desperate tug o' war, reminiscent of the walrus hunt in Nanook, but the alligator escapes.

There is a blow-out at the oil rig and it seems that drilling will be abandoned. The boy pours his magic salt into the borehole and spits into it for good measure, but is jeered at by the oil men and goes off deeply hurt. The magic works, however. Drilling is resumed and oil is found. The boy's father buys him a new rifle, and his pet racoon finds its way home as well. The bore is capped and the derrick is towed away down the lagoon. The boy waves goodbye to his friends, and spits to remind them that it was his magic, not theirs, that succeeded.

Louisiana Story was premiered in August 1948 at the Edinburgh Film Festival. It was enthusiastically received there and at its New York premiere, and Virgil Thomson received the first Pulitzer Prize for film music. All in all, the film earned more critical acclaim than any of its predecessors. In box-office terms it fared less well, being screened mostly in art houses, though it continues to be revived and televised.

David Thomson called the film "uselessly beautiful," banal in its symbolism, and flatulent in conception, but this is very much a minority response. More characteristic was Ian Hamilton's review in the Manchester *Guardian* (August 28, 1948). "This is elegy," he wrote. "Its theme is the wonder of childhood. . . . There is no comment, no propaganda, no uplift. There is scarcely any dialogue. . . . In every sequence where human beings are under the lens love is evoked. . . . Here, from a remote corner of a remote state, is Flaherty showing us the true world, the source—and it is bathed, like the work of any true poet, in "the master light of our seeing."

Arthur Calder-Marshall saw the film as a fable, "in the sense that the people, the animals and the actions have a fabulous significance transcending the particular." The boy's "childhood is . . . on another level, the childhood of the human race. The snakes and alligators which live in the swamp are the symbols of the predators which threaten the life of primitive man; and the mermaids and werewolves are the local spirits of good and evil. . . . It is a world of terror and magic and danger. But it is also a world of beauty and love and achievement. . . . For me, part of the emotional impact of that magnificent final scene with Alexander Napoleon Ulysses Latour astride the 'Christmas tree' is that through the pipe up which the oil is welling, he is linked with prehistory. This is a fact and it doesn't matter whether or not Flaherty consciously planned this. The greatest symbolism is unconscious."

Flaherty was deeply moved by Picasso's great mural *Guernica* and in 1948 made a series of studies for a film examining the work. The exploratory footage he shot was subsequently assembled by David Flaherty into a 12-minute film—"a remarkable microcosm of what is already a microcosm of the bloody tragedy of the Spanish Civil War." In 1950 Flaherty was sent by the State Department on a goodwill mission to occupied Germany. It was hoped that he and his films might provide an antidote to European notions of American vulgarity and materialism,

and by all accounts his tour of the American zone was an unqualified success. Back in the United States, he received an honorary doctorate from the University of Michigan. There was talk of a Flaherty film about Hawaii for the State Department's "American Way of Life" series, but nothing came of this.

In January 1951, the Screen Directors Guild honored Flaherty with a festival of his films at the Museum of Modern Art; he was hailed by numerous critics and fellow artists as "the father of documentary." It was a splendid tribute but, as Flaherty was fond of saying, "all the reputation in the world won't buy anyone a ham sandwich." The same year Flaherty was invited by Mike Todd and Lowell Thomas to lend his prestige to their new toy, Cinerama. He needed the money and accepted, apparently half horrified and half fascinated by the device.

Flaherty made one Cinerama film—a record of General MacArthur's triumphal return from Korea. After that, he was supposed to set off with a battery of three-dimensional color cameras to make a world-wide "film symphony." At that point he was stricken with pneumonia, then with arthritis, then with shingles. He threw off each of these afflictions and went home to Black Mountain. But, Richard Griffith wrote, "his heart, always sound before, just couldn't stand the strain." He died at the age of sixty-seven.

Paul Rotha said of Flaherty that "you noticed, before anything else, his eyes. They were a limpid, brilliant blue, lying like lakes in the broad and rugged landscape of his face. . . . Flaherty stood five feet nine inches tall. He was bulky and sensitive about it. He was immensely strong, especially in his youth. . . . When he sat down, he squared himself into an area sufficient for two lesser men and put his broad hands on his knees. His voice was musical and . . . captured your entire attention. We remember him as a monolithic figure."

It seemed to Rotha that Flaherty "was not a complex character. . . . In many respects he was like a child—perpetually inquisitive, perpetually surprised or delighted by new and usually simple discoveries, prone to tantrums or temper which lasted only a short time. . . . Inside Flaherty there lived a lonely man." Grierson agreed, saying that "I never saw a man so worried about being alone. That's why he poured out the best of his creative power in conversation."

Rotha suggests that Flaherty's influence "has been and will continue to be significant. It can be seen in the work of Sucksdorff, Haanstra, Rouquier, Satyajit Ray, and others. John Huston has gone on record as saying that directors such as John Ford, William Wyler, Billy Wilder, and certainly himself were all profoundly influenced by Flaherty." But, Jean Renoir said, "Flaherty was not the type of artist we can consider as the teacher. There will be no Flaherty School. Many people will try to imitate him, but they won't succeed because he has no system. His system was just to love the world, to love humanity, to love animals, and love is something you cannot teach."

In the end, Rotha concluded, Flaherty "defies critical scrutiny. This explorer, always roaming with a hungry heart, traversed the world without charts—proud perhaps to take no more than a penny atlas with him into the mysterious regions of creative expression; and this perhaps is one of the grand gestures of genius. He traveled alone, for even those who went with him could not be told whether the destination would be paradise or a barren landfall. As handsome in style as he was handsome as a man, he fought his way to a result with an immense, an almost terrifying simplicity of purpose. If the result was a failure, the rest of us can airily explain why; if a success, we can only guess at the reason for it."

FILMS: Nanook of the North, 1922; The Pottery Maker, 1925 (short); Moana: A Romance of the Golden Age, 1926; Twenty-Four Dollar Island, 1927 (short); Industrial Britain, 1933 (short); Man of Aran, 1934; (with Zoltan Korda) Elephant Boy, 1937; The Land, 1942 (medium-length); Louisiana Story, 1948; Guernica, 1949 (short).

ABOUT: Agel, H. Robert J. Flaherty, 1965 (in French); Barnouw, E. Documentary, 1976; Barsam, R. M. Nonfiction Film, 1973; Brownlow, K. The War, the West, and the Wilderness, 1979; Calder-Marshall, A. The Innocent Eye: The Life of Robert J. Flaherty, 1963; Clementé, J. L. Robert Flaherty, 1963 (in Spanish); Flaherty, F. H. Elephant Dance, 1937; Flaherty, F. H. The Odyssey of a Filmmaker: Robert Flaherty's Story, 1960; Flaherty, R. J. My Eskimo Friends: Nanook of the North, 1924; Grierson, J. Grierson on Documentary, 1946; Griffith, R. The World of Robert Flaherty, 1953; Gromo, M. Robert Flaherty, 1952 (in Italian); Lord, R. Forever the Land, 1950; Mullen, P. Man of Aran, 1934; Murphy, W. T. Robert Flaherty: A Guide to References and Resources, 1978; Rotha, P. Robert J. Flaherty: A Biography, edited by Jay Ruby, 1983; Roud, R. (ed.) Cinema: A Critical Dictionary, 1980; Thomson, D. A Biographical Dictionary of the Cinema, 1980; Williams, C. Realism in the Cinema, 1980. Periodicals—Cinéma (France) 9 and 10, 1956; Film Comment November–December 1953; Film Culture 20 1959, Spring 1972; Film Dope February 1979; Film Quarterly Summer 1965; Hollywood Quarterly Fall 1950; Image et Son April 1965; New Yorker June 11, 18, and 25, 1949; Quarterly Review of Film Studies Fall 1980; Sight and Sound October–December 1951.

FLEISCHER, RICHARD (December 8, 1916–), American director, was born in Brooklyn, New York, the son of the animator Max Fleischer and his wife Essie. With his brother Dave, Max Fleischer created Betty Boop and Popeye the Sailor and in the 1930s was Walt Disney's chief rival.

Fleischer says that his father "tried to discourage me for a while from having anything to do with Hollywood, so I studied psychology at Brown University [B.A.] which is, I guess, what eventually led me to Compulsion, the story of the Leopold-Loeb murder. But I also somehow got myself involved in directing musical comedies and that led me to the Yale Drama School [M.F.A.]." It was there that Fleischer met and married a fellow student, Mary Dickson.

At Yale, Fleischer founded the Arena Players, experimenting with theatre-in-the-round at a time when it was virtually unknown. He took the company on a tour of five New England hotels, including the Lake Tarleton Club, where his production of George S. Kaufman's Butter and Egg Man was seen and admired by Arthur Willi, an RKO talent scout. Hired by that studio, Fleischer operated a theatre café in Providence, Rhode Island, and directed plays at the Hilltop Theatre in Baltimore, before beginning work at RKO's New York office in 1942.

At first Fleischer wrote commentaries for RKO Pathé newsreels. Before long he graduated to writing and directing two-reel wartime documentaries in the "This Is America" series, as well as writing and producing a series he apparently devised himself—of reedited excerpts from silent movies called "Flicker Flashbacks."

These chores, as Fleischer has said, were "of inestimable value" in teaching him the basic techniques of filmmaking. At the end of the war, returning to RKO from a seven-month stint in the army, he went not to the New York office but to Hollywood. There is some confusion in accounts of Fleischer's first assignments as a feature director. He himself has been quoted as saying that he began with the Oscar-winning Design for Death, but this appears to have been released after two B movies written and produced by Lillie Hayward, both starring the child actor Sharyn Moffatt: Child of Divorce (1946) and Banjo (1947). Neither made much impact.

Design for Death (1947) was a feature-length documentary compiled from captured Japanese newsreel footage and tracing the growth in nationalism and militarism that led to Pearl Harbor and its aftermath. No director was credited, Fleischer being named as coproducer of the film with Theron Warth. When it received an Oscar as best feature-length documentary of 1947,

RICHARD FLEISCHER

Fleischer's father sent him a telegram reading "What took you so long?"

Fleischer made his next film not for RKO but for Stanley Kramer, just beginning his career as an independent producer. *So This Is New York* (1948), adapted by Carl Foreman and Herbert Baker from Ring Lardner's *The Big Town,* is a comedy set in the 1920s. Dealing with the impact of New York on a visiting small-town family, it features Henry Morgan, Rudy Vallee, Hugh Herbert, and Virginia Grey. Raymond Durgnat found it "agreeably caustic" but thought it "never quite defines a purpose for itself and comes to seem a little too brittle." It failed at the box office.

Kramer was nevertheless so impressed by Fleischer's work on the film that he tried to buy out his RKO contract. The studio refused and Fleischer reluctantly worked out the contract— much of the time, according to his own account, on suspension. He says that "in those seven years RKO had fourteen different studio heads and I quarrelled with every one of them; what I really wanted to do was to go off and work with Stanley Kramer . . . , but RKO kept assigning me B pictures instead, and I kept refusing to make them, and that's how seven years went by."

In fact, between 1946 and 1952, Fleischer directed seven movies for RKO, as well as *Trapped,* made for Eagle-Lion in 1949. Though the director is dismissive of these early B pictures, several of them attracted an unusual amount of attention, especially the last, *The Narrow Margin* (1952), scripted by Earl Felton. Described by C. A. Lejeune as "a short, crisp, really businesslike little thriller," it has Charles

McGraw as a cop trying to deliver a key witness by train from Chicago to Los Angeles. "After an hour of plot and counterplot," Lejeune wrote, "the picture ends with a sudden surprise twist, which I could have kicked myself for not having anticipated."

Wrapping up his RKO contract, Fleischer promptly joined Stanley Kramer, now operating his own unit at Columbia. Fleischer made only one film there, *The Happy Time* (1952), a rather coy study of a quaintly eccentric French-Canadian family in the 1920s, starring Charles Boyer as papa, Marsha Hunt as *maman,* and Bobby Driscoll as the pubescent Bibi. After that Fleischer moved over to MGM to make *Arena* (1953), a predictable 3-D spectacle with Gig Young as a rodeo rider who nearly loses his wife (Polly Bergen) before the death of his buddy Henry Morgan convinces him that it's time to quit his dangerous trade.

Meanwhile, Fleischer had been approached by Walt Disney to direct a wide-screen version of Jules Verne's *Twenty Thousand Leagues Under the Sea.* Fleischer's problem, as he explained to Sheridan Morley (London *Times,* January 1, 1976) was that his father viewed Disney with deep hostility, as the usurper of his own preeminence as an animator. Fleischer "phoned him and told him about it, but said that I wouldn't work for Disney if it would offend him. Happily my father felt that my career had to come first, and while we were doing the picture Disney gave him a celebration lunch to which he invited all the cartoonists who'd worked with him in the early days of animation—most of whom were by then on Disney's payroll." As a result, the old rivals became good friends.

Earl Felton's adaptation of Verne's nineteenth-century story opens with scientist Paul Lukas and his two companions (Kirk Douglas and Peter Lorre) investigating stories of a mysterious sea monster that has been sinking warships. Before long they are in the belly of the monster, which turns out to be a submarine built by the Byronic Captain Nemo (James Mason). A brilliant scientist deranged by the murder of his wife and child, he is seeking to abolish war by destroying the armaments manufacturers through their clients.

It seemed to Kenneth Coyte that "Disney has at last succeeded in making a good movie with human beings . . . instead of animals or animations. When Jules Verne wrote the novel . . . much of what he predicted was sheer fantasy to the contemporary world. . . . The submarine *Nautilus,* although sufficiently aberrant not to resemble a modern submarine, is not the whale-like creature Verne described. . . . And yet, despite this, the awe and the interest which such a vessel would have aroused when submarines were almost unheard of is recreated here, partly by judicious use of Verne's dialogue and description—the stateroom in *Nautilus* with its pipe-organ and red-velvet Victorianism is a masterpiece—partly by Till Gabbani's excellent underwater photography, and partly by some fine acting."

A later critic, John Brosnan in his *Future Tense* (1978), agreed that "considered purely as a science-fiction adventure story . . . , *Twenty Thousand Leagues Under the Sea* is an almost perfect film, possessing that intangible sense of wonder that sf fans maintain is the most important ingredient of the genre." The movie won Oscars for its art direction (John Meehan and Emile Kuri) and for its special effects, and grossed over $25 million.

Fleischer directed his next film for Twentieth Century-Fox, the studio for which he has made the majority of his subsequent pictures. *Violent Saturday* (1955), written by Sydney Boehm, renovates a familiar theme—the effects on ordinary peaceable citizens, of an encounter with violent outlaws. Stephen McNally, J. Carroll Naish, and Lee Marvin are a trio of smoothly professional but very dangerous hoods who rob a small-town bank and take the proceeds to an Amish farm, where they know there will be no telephone to tip off the police.

Threaded through the details of the heist, as Virginia Graham wrote, "are snippets of their victims' lives, troubled, of course, as are all lives. There is the drunk tycoon and his unfaithful wife, the nurse who loves him, the peeping-Tom bank manager, the librarian who steals money to pay her debts, and the father whose boy despises him for not winning a war medal. All are excellent, in particular Richard Egan as the tippler and Victor Mature as the soon-to-be-heroic father. . . . What might have been a patchy business has been skilfully conjoined, good dialogue, characterisation and editing working together to make a wonderfully refreshing version of a by no means original tale."

There was also a generally favorable reception for *The Girl in the Red Velvet Swing* (1955), an account (scripted by Walter Reisch) of the events surrounding the sensational murder in 1906 of the prominent architect Stanford White (Ray Milland), shot dead in his own Madison Square Garden by millionaire playboy Harry K. Thaw (Farley Granger), husband of White's former mistress Evelyn Nesbit (Joan Collins). The title refers to one of the features of a bizarre secret apartment White had "fitted up for the enticement of young women." Patrick Gibbs found the movie disappointingly shapeless, but others called it "erotic and stylish" and "an excellent study of turn-of-the-century New York high society."

Bandido, a rather perfunctory Earl Felton script that involved *gringo* Robert Mitchum in Mexican revolution, was followed by *Between Heaven and Hell* (1956), a violent but antimilitaristic war movie whose attractions include Broderick Crawford as the half-mad commander of an American army unit resembling a cross between Robert Aldrich's Dirty Dozen and a bandit encampment.

Taking a break from Twentieth Century-Fox (and switching from Cinemascope to Technirama), Fleischer went off to Norway to film *The Vikings* (1958). This was made by Kirk Douglas's own production company with a United Artists budget of around $4 million that paid for real Viking longships and some real American stars. Douglas is Einar, son and heir of King Ernest Borgnine; Tony Curtis is Einar's half-brother and rival Eric; and Janet Leigh is a Welsh princess lusted after by both. After much rape and pillage, blinding and hand-lopping, most of the principals still have enough limbs left to fight their way into Valhalla. This bloody romp reminded Hollis Alpert of "a handsomely animated comic strip" and was one of the year's top earners.

After an unexceptional Western, *These Thousand Hills* (1959), Fleischer directed the first of several movies reflecting his interest in criminal psychology. *Compulsion* (like *The Girl in the Red Velvet Swing*) deals with an actual and sensational crime—the Leopold-Loeb case of 1924. In that year a child was murdered in cold blood by two rich Chicago teenagers—Nietzschean intellectuals exploring "the beauty of evil." Defended by Clarence Darrow, they escaped execution and spent most of their lives in jail.

Richard Murphy's script, based on Meyer Levin's fictionalized account of the case, changes the names of the principals. The young killers are played by Dean Stockwell and Bradford Dillman, the defense lawyer by Orson Welles (and these three shared the top acting award at the Cannes film festival). Arthur Knight called the film "a taut, pointed, eloquent drama" and praised its restraint. Pauline Kael liked its "stylish, jazz-age format" but thought that "the script can't make up its little bit of mind—is it an exploitation of thrills and decadence, a piece of crime research, or an attack on capital punishment?"

Fleischer had Welles and Dillman again in *Crack in the Mirror* (1960), produced by Darryl F. Zanuck and almost universally condemned for its intellectual pretentiousness. As William Whitebait put it, the filmmakers had "had the stupendously cracked idea of employing three actors in six parts. One trio is in high society, the other in low. . . . Murder in the *bas-fonds* brings out the law's big guns among the high and mighty; and so the triangles intersect. That brilliant young barrister Bradford Dillman kisses goodbye to his mistress (Juliette Greco) and goes straight to a prison cell where the accused woman turns round—Juliette Greco! But does he even notice the resemblance? Of course not, because this kind of thing goes on all the time."

The Big Gamble (1961), also produced by Darryl F. Zanuck, was a moderately entertaining variation on the theme of Clouzot's *The Wages of Fear,* with tyro haulers Stephen Boyd and Juliette Greco trucking through desperate terrain in the African interior. It was followed in 1962 by a Technirama spectacular for Dino De Laurentiis—an adaptation by Christopher Fry of Par Lagerkvist's Nobel Prize-winning novel *Barabbas.* Overwhelmed perhaps by a huge budget and Anthony Quinn's excesses in the title role, Fleischer turned out a movie that was generally dismissed as solemn, tiresome, and "religiose" (though Richard Roud praised it as "the best of the Roman epics").

Three years passed before Fleischer got back into harness at Twentieth Century-Fox with *Fantastic Voyage* (1966), his second venture into science fiction. An important scientist is dying of a blood clot on the brain, inaccessible to ordinary surgery. But what if a medical team could be packed into a submarine, miniaturized, and injected into his bloodstream to begin a life-saving dash up through his body to the precious brain? The movie shows how with $6.5 million worth of special effects, including a heart forty feet wide. Stephen Boyd leads the heroic team, with Raquel Welch at his side and Donald Pleasence out to sabotage the mission.

For Pauline Kael, the idea "promised poetry, mystery, excitement. . . . But Richard Fleischer and his crew have managed to make a standard, stereotyped adventure of it," full of "uncharacters" mouthing "moldy platitudes about man and the universe"; even "the interior of the body looks new and pretty and expensive, like a colored refrigerator." Tom Milne was also disappointed but found "occasional touches of genuine imagination," like "the cyclonic winds which toss . . . [the team] to and fro as the lungs breathe in and out; the sudden tidal waves created in the canals of the inner ear when a nurse drops a pair of scissors in the operating theatre." There were Oscars for the art direction and the special effects, and the movie—always popular

with audiences—seems to have grown in critical esteem over the years.

Not so *Doctor Dolittle* (1967), a "lavish flop." Based on Hugh Lofting's children's books about a man (played by Rex Harrison) who can talk to animals, it seemed to most critics much too long: "152 minutes plus interval is quite a stretch to hold a child's attention, or even an adult's," wrote one. "It is too lacking in incident, its wonders are not wonderful enough—even the pushmi pullyu and the giant pink sea-snail are a bit unexciting in the flesh, and the songs—which stop the show in all the wrong scenes—and the ineffectual romantic interest will probably bore children stiff."

Returning to the concerns of *Compulsion,* Fleischer next made *The Boston Strangler,* adapted by Edward Anhalt from Gerold Frank's book about Albert DeSalvo (Tony Curtis), a happily married maintenance man who confessed that it was he who had terrorized Boston in 1962–1964, murdering thirteen women. The first half of the film concentrates on the muddled and desperate police efforts to track down the killer, the second half on DeSalvo himself, presented as a bewildered schizophrenic—a Jekyll who has no idea that he is capable of being a Hyde.

The reviewers praised Curtis's performance as DeSalvo and Henry Fonda's as the chief investigator. There were mixed opinions of Fleischer's repeated use of the split screen (a device then in vogue), though it was generally recognized to be chillingly effective in scenes "showing us the faces of victim and strangler on either side of an intervening door). A few have claimed this as Fleischer's best film, but there was a fairly widespread feeling, well expressed by Derek Malcolm, that it was "not easy to give full approval" to this "money-spinning" movie, "an object lesson in how to make a patently sincere but palpably dishonest film. Sincere, because Fleischer had made no attempt to sensationalize his grisly material and indeed every attempt to point an unhysterical moral—that DeSalvo, if he really was the strangler, was the product of a society intrinsically as violent and schizoid as he. Dishonest, because the director is constantly upended by the necessity to make a commercial film with the usual entertainment values."

There was something close to critical unanimity about *Che!* (1969), a biopic about Che Guevara (Omar Sharif, with Jack Palance as Fidel Castro), and a "bloated flop." The movie, as Fleischer acknowledged, tried "to tell all the truth about him we could find on both sides, the good and the bad. It was a big mistake. A film has to have a point of view." *Tora! Tora! Tora!*

(1970) was equally impartial and even more "bloated"—it cost $23 million. This account of Pearl Harbor was made half by Fleischer, half by the Japanese directors Toshio Masuda and Kinji Fukasaku, who were given a free hand to film the facts as they saw them. Nigel Andrews found the result "refreshingly impartial" but "critically short of any unifying style."

10 Rillington Place (1970) examines the case of Reginald Christie (Richard Attenborough), a British murderer who killed almost as many people as the Boston Strangler. Clive Exton's script (from a book by Ludovic Kennedy) focuses a good deal of attention on Timothy Evans (John Hurt), who has hanged for crimes actually committed by Christie. Fleischer himself regards "criminality as an illness, capital punishment as barbarity," and the film emerges as a powerful indictment of the latter.

The principal criticism of the film, voiced by several reviewers, was its "tasteful" suppression of the numerous blackly farcical aspects of the horrific story (like Christie's incompetence at burying his victims, leaving thigh-bones thrusting up through the garden soil when police called). However, as John Russell Taylor wrote, "we should doubtless be grateful for a film as good, truthful and thoroughly decent as we have been given. . . . the central story is soundly dramatized, using as much as possible of the recorded dialogue and reconstructing where necessary with a fine sense of period and character."

Turning from actual to fictional horror, Fleischer in *Blind Terror* (1971) submits the unfortunate Mia Farrow first to the loss of her sight (in a riding accident) and then to a nightmare experience groping through a house that—as she only gradually comes to realize—is littered with corpses. The movies was widely condemned for its inept and distasteful script, and seemed to many equally weak in its direction, showing no trace of "Fleischer's sporadic talent."

The latter reemerged for *The Last Run* (1971), one of Fleischer's best-liked pictures. George C. Scott stars as an aging wheelman hauled out of retirement in a Portuguese village to drive a fugitive and his girlfriend across the French border to safety. Praising Scott's handling of Alan Sharp's "spiky dialogue," Michael Billington called the movie "a conscious act of homage to the Bogart tradition. . . . It's not perhaps an important film, but it makes one nostalgic for the forties." Scott also dominates *The New Centurions* (1972), scripted by Stirling Silliphant. David Thomson called it "a routine endorsement of the police, illuminated only by the brooding sequence in which George C. Scott kills himself."

Opinions differ about Fleischer's abilities as a director of science fiction. John Brosnan, who had so admired *Fantastic Voyage,* described *Soylent Green* (1973) as "the best film to date dealing with overpopulation." In this adaptation of Harry Harrison's novel *Make Room! Make Room!,* Charlton Heston plays Thorn, a police detective in the New York of 2022 a.d.—a wholly corrupt city of rationing and riots where the most abundant food supply is a mysterious artificial project called "soylent green." Investigating a murder, Thorn discovers the horrid truth about this commodity—that it is manufactured from human corpses.

The movie, made for MGM and photographed by Richard Kline, has Edward G. Robinson as Sol, Thorn's seventy-year-old roommate—a human repository of forgotten values who in the end rejects the new ones in a "suicide parlor." Robinson's performance (his last) was one of the "occasional delights" Richard Combs found in a film that seemed to him otherwise an exercise in Fleischer's "most lacklustre, social document style," characterized by "a bland insistence on predictable detail." Other reviewers were kinder, and this financially successful movie, like *Fantastic Voyage,* has developed something of a cult following.

An extremely violent Mafia movie, *The Don Is Dead* (1973), was followed in 1974 by two "pleasant" (and slightly less violent) films: *Mr. Majestyk,* with Charles Bronson peacefully growing melons in Colorado, then forced to take arms against a Mafia hitman; and a Western called *The Spikes Gang,* with Lee Marvin as an aging bank robber who inveigles three innocent Texas farmboys into lives—and deaths—of crime.

Fleischer said of his next picture, *Mandingo* (1975), that it "got the worst notices of the year. The American critics really savaged it. But it's doing fantastic business." Both responses can be explained by the fact that this Dino De Laurentiis production offers "two full hours of racist brutality"—along with large helpings of nonracist brutality, rape, murder, and miscegenation. Scripted by Norman Wexler from a fat bestseller by Kyle Onstott and photographed by Richard Kline, it stars James Mason as a monstrous antebellum slave breeder. This was Andy Warhol's "favorite bad film of the year."

Perturbed perhaps by the critical hostility to *Mandingo,* Fleischer followed it with a *Reader's Digest* production of stultifying decorum, *The Incredible Sarah,* a biopic of Sarah Bernhardt (Glenda Jackson). Pauline Kael called it "an aberration, stuffier and more anachronistic than the Warners bios of the thirties." Fleischer's remake of *The Prince and the Pauper* (1977), made for Ilya and Alexander Salkind, boasted a script by George MacDonald Fraser, photography by Jack Cardiff, and a cast that included Oliver Reed, Raquel Welch, George C. Scott, and Charlton Heston, with Mark Lester in the dual role of Prince Edward and Tom Canby. Mildly entertaining, it brought Fleischer another poor press for "lackluster direction." *Ashanti* (1979), with Dr. Michael Caine trying to retrieve his wife from Arab slaver Peter Ustinov, was called "a trivially implausible adventure yarn."

Fleischer's $15 million dollar remake of Al Jolson's *The Jazz Singer*, which ushered in talking films in 1927, received overwhelmingly unfavorable reviews. A musical vehicle for Neil Diamond, *The Jazz Singer* (1981) told the story of a young Orthodox cantor, Yussel Rabinovitch, who wants to become a singing star. Changing his name to Jess Robin, he sings rock songs with some black friends at a honky tonk, goes to Hollywood and achieves fame, while all the time yearning for a reconciliation with his tradition-bound father, played by Laurence Olivier. Richard Corliss observed that the movie is "schmaltz in three-quarter time," and "plods along earnestly, endlessly." David Ansen remarked that "one look at Laurence Olivier giving his vampy sideways glances and pursing his lips in patriarchal grief and you know you're in for another of his sad, take-the-money-and-run performances."

The Jazz Singer was followed by a series of negligible films that include *Amityville 3-D* (1983), *Conan the Destroyer* (1984), and *Red Sonja* (1985). In *Amityville 3-D*, the third installment of a cycle of supernatural thrillers, Tony Roberts plays a writer who, following his breakup with his wife, moves into the famous haunted house, refusing to believe that terrible things happen there. The film was roasted in reviews. In *Conan the Destroyer*, a sequel to *Conan the Barbarian*, Arnold Schwarzenegger sets off in pursuit of a magical horn, accompanied by a band of others that includes the disco queen Grace Jones. Vincent Canby wrote that "Fleischer seems to want this film to be funnier than the first one, directed by John Milius, but Mr. Schwarzenegger . . . can't easily get his tongue in his cheek"; and David Ansen thought the movie nonsense that was "not hard to watch, but it would be a lot more fun if someone had bothered to give Conan a personality." Schwarzenegger appears again in *Red Sonja*—as Kalidor, a kind of clone of Conan, who becomes involved in the quest of a female warrior, Sonja, played by Brigette Nielsen, for a mysterious green gem. Janet Maslin remarked of the film that "Mr. Fleischer brings absolutely no playfulness to what might, at least, have been enjoyably light.

And he brings out the worst in a cast that was ill-chosen to begin with." Critics generally felt that the performances of both Schwarzenegger and Nielsen were uncomfortably wooden.

Leslie Halliwell says of Fleischer that "his films usually sound more interesting than they turn out to be." Pauline Kael calls him "a glorified mechanic" who "pleases movie executives because he has no particular interests and no discernible style," while Richard Combs complains of his "inability to find a style which illuminates his subject rather than imprisoning it." David Robinson claims that "in recent years, Fleischer has aimed at being the most prolific and least identifiable director in America." Fleischer has described himself as a "mercenary."

On the other hand, Georges Sadoul praised Fleischer's "virtuosity and skill" and thought him underrated, and Ephraim Katz finds "a sure-handed technical flair even in his failures." Michael Billington sees him as "the epitome of the Hollywood professional: the man capable of turning his hand to all manner of subjects and reserving his personal statements [about the psychological basis of crime and perniciousness of capital punishment] for a few jealously guarded works."

Perhaps the most illuminating comment on Fleischer's work is *Film Dope*'s (February 1979). Agreeing with hostile critics that the director is "too much at the mercy of his collaborators to qualify as any sort of *auteur*," the writer maintains that he is not at his best on his favorite subject, "the reconstructed case histories of deranged criminal minds at odds with society." In fact, *Film Dope* suggests, "what Fleischer does supremely well is stage action sequences. . . . The best way to appreciate Fleischer is to forget the sociological pretensions and concentrate instead on the vigorous strip-cartoon imagery of *Twenty Thousand Leagues, The Vikings,* or *Fantastic Voyage.*"

Fleischer and his wife, Mary Dickson, have two sons and a daughter. He has been described as a "small, soft-spoken, quietly articulate man," who is "extremely courteous" and "patient, workmanlike, and persistent." Bart Mills calls him "a very reserved man who controls his work and himself with equal care."

FILMS: Child of Divorce, 1946; Banjo, 1947; Design for Death, 1947 (documentary); So This Is New York, 1948; Bodyguard, 1948; The Clay Pigeon, 1949; Follow Me Quietly, 1949; Make Mine Laughs, 1949; Trapped, 1949; Armored Car Robbery, 1950; The Narrow Margin, 1952; The Happy Time, 1952; Arena, 1953; Twenty Thousand Leagues Under the Sea, 1954; Violent Saturday, 1955; The Girl in the Red Velvet Swing, 1955; Bandido, 1956; Between Heaven and

Hell, 1956; The Vikings, 1958; These Thousand Hills, 1959; Compulsion, 1959; Crack in the Mirror, 1960; The Big Gamble, 1961; Barabba/Barabbas, 1962; Fantastic Voyage, 1966; Doctor Dolittle, 1967; The Boston Strangler, 1968; Che!, 1969; (with Toshio Masuda and Kinji Fukasaku) Tora! Tora! Tora!, 1970; Ten Rillington Place, 1970; Blind Terror (U.K., See No Evil), 1971; The Last Run, 1971; The New Centurions (U.K., Precinct 45, Los Angeles Police), 1972; Soylent Green, 1973; The Don Is Dead, 1973; Mr. Majestyk, 1974; The Spikes Gang, 1974; Mandingo, 1975; The Incredible Sarah, 1976; The Prince and the Pauper/Crossed Swords, 1977; Ashanti, 1979; The Jazz Singer, 1981; Amityville 3-D, 1983; Conan the Destroyer, 1984; Red Sonja, 1985.

ABOUT: Brosnan, J. Future Tense, 1978; Thomson, D. A Biographical Dictionary of the Cinema, 1980. *Periodicals*—Cinéma (France) April and May 1979; Film Dope February 1979; Film Ideal 1 1964 (Fleischer issue); Films and Filming December 1970; Guardian April 20, 1970; August 23, 1975; New York Times June 29, 1984, July 3, 1985; Newsweek January 5, 1981; Photoplay March 1971; Times (London) October 10, 1970, January 17, 1976; Washington Post November 25, 1983.

FLEMING, VICTOR (February 23, 1883–January 6, 1949), American director and producer, was born in Pasadena, California. Not much has been published about his childhood, except that his family was poor and he is said to have had some American Indian blood. Educated in Los Angeles public schools, he showed exceptional mechanical aptitude. He became an automobile mechanic when cars were still a novelty and was also an excellent still photographer. Years later his favorite cameraman Harold Rosson said that Fleming "knew as much about the making of pictures as any man I've ever known—all departments. He was a craftsman of the first order, he was a machinist, he did the mechanics. I doubt very much if he lacked the knowledge to answer any [mechanical] problem."

By 1910 Fleming was working as a chauffeur for a family in Los Angeles. Some accounts suggest that by then he was already interested in the movies and had done some photographic laboratory work. In 1911 he met the director-producer Allan Dwan when he was asked to repair his car. Dwan discovered that Fleming knew as much about cameras as he did about automobiles. An engineer himself, Dwan took to this able and self-assured young man and offered him a job at the American Film Manufacturing Company's studios near Santa Barbara. Fleming joined the "Flying A" studio as assistant to Dwan's cameraman Roy Overbaugh.

VICTOR FLEMING

At that time Dwan was grinding out one-reel movies at the rate of two or more a week, most of them Westerns starring J. Warren Kerrigan and/or Marshall Neilan. In mid-1913 Dwan moved his unit to Universal, where Neilan began directing his own comedy shorts. Fleming worked on these as well, gaining an immense amount of extremely varied experience. In 1915 he followed Dwan to Triangle, where he often worked under the supervision of D. W. Griffith and, beginning in 1916, was director of photography on a number of films starring Douglas Fairbanks, among them *His Picture in the Papers, The Habit of Happiness, The Good Bad Man, The Americano, Wild and Woolly, Down to Earth,* and *The Man From Painted Post.* Fleming is said to have been an innovative cameraman, especially talented at devising trick effects.

When the United States entered World War I, Fleming joined the photographic section of the Army Signal Corps. He shot combat footage in France and after the war—by then a first lieutenant—accompanied President Wilson to the Versailles Conference as his personal cameraman.

By the time Fleming returned to Hollywood in 1919, Douglas Fairbanks was the undisputed "king" of the movie colony. Fleming promptly joined his court. He photographed one more Fairbanks movie, *His Majesty, the American* (1919), and then the Douglas Fairbanks Film Corporation gave him the chance to make his first film, assigning the more experienced Theodore Reed as his codirector. *When the Clouds Roll By* (1919), costarring Fairbanks and Kathleen Clifford, was a mixture of action and effervescent comedy, described by Kevin Brownlow as "unalloyed delight." Another Fairbanks vehicle followed, *The Mollycoddle* (1920), this time directed by Fleming alone. Shot partly on Navajo reservations in Arizona, it featured a spectacular fistfight between Fairbanks and Wallace Beery and, like its predecessor, was a box-office hit.

Successfully launched on his new career, Fleming moved on with Fairbanks' blessing to First National, where he directed three comedies scripted by Anita Loos and John Emerson. At the end of 1921, he signed a seven-year contract with Famous Players–Lasky, which released through the Paramount distribution company and in 1927 became the Paramount Pictures Corporation. Fleming made nearly twenty pictures there, and though few of them have survived, it is clear that they completed his education as a filmmaker competent in most cinematic genres but especially well-equipped as an action director.

In fact, his first four pictures for Lasky were routine melodramas. Then in 1923 Fleming directed two Westerns, *To the Last Man* and *Call of the Canyon,* both adapted by Doris Schroeder from novels by Zane Grey, both photographed by James Wong Howe, and both starring Richard Dix, Lois Wilson, and Noah Beery. They were extremely successful, launching the studio on an almost endless series of Zane Grey Westerns, most of them inferior to their prototypes.

His first film as producer and director was *Empty Hands* (1924), a romantic adventure story set in the Canadian wilderness and introducing a new star in Norma Shearer. Not much can be said in favor of Fleming's next four assignments. The best of them was *Adventure* (1925), a lively South Seas action movie adapted from the Jack London novel and starring Pauline Starke and Tom Moore, with Wallace Beery as the heavy. The worst of the four was an excruciating melodrama called *A Son of His Father*, derived from a contemporary bestseller by Harold Bell Wright. Bessie Love, who starred in it with Warner Baxter and Raymond Hatton, said that she had "asked . . . [Fleming] frankly why he had agreed to make such a bad film and he asked me, frankly, if I knew how much the picture had made."

A much more memorable picture followed, an adaptation of Joseph Conrad's novel *Lord Jim,* scripted by John Russell. According to John Howard Reid's article about Fleming in *Films and Filming* (January 1968), six men scoured the West Coast from north to south to assemble the small flotilla of boats the picture called for—two steamships (one of them raised from a watery grave for the film), a three-masted schooner, two mine-sweepers, a Chinese junk, eight sampans, two tugs, and twenty-five other vessels.

Percy Marmont gave a thoughtful performance as the outcast hero, and Nick de Ruiz was suitably beady-eyed as the villainous Rajah Doramin. John Howard Reid thought the "scenic effects . . . so good that one might almost believe that this production, filmed in Hollywood, was really pictured on the far-flung shores of the Indian Ocean." *Lord Jim* secured Fleming's reputation as a director of importance; on this film also he served as his own producer.

A highly popular melodrama, *The Blind Goddess* (1926), was followed the same year by *Mantrap,* based on a novel by Sinclair Lewis about the havoc wrought in a community of strong, silent woodsmen when the local storekeeper (Ernest Torrence) marries a libidinous flapper from Minneapolis. The liberated heroine was played with boundless vivacity and shameless charm by Clara Bow, then on the verge of fame as the "It" girl. Percy Marmont is the divorce lawyer from New York who is Alverna's first victim. This cheerfully amoral movie was a smash hit, and can still be enjoyed for Clara Bow's performance and for James Wong Howe's beautiful location photography; a modern critic, Kevin Brownlow, found it "a slight but bewitching little picture."

Fleming's much-publicized affair with Clara Bow added to his reputation as a womanizer. He was also, according to Allan Dwan, "a guy who loved to drink and fight." Fleming offered his male stars a rough, jokey camaraderie but tended to deal with difficult actresses by publicly slapping their faces—Judy Garland, Lana Turner, and Ingrid Bergman all received this treatment. Fleming flew his own plane, raced cars and motorcycles, and in general conformed to or exceeded the standards of what John Gallagher, in an article about the director in *Films in Review* (March 1983), called "the man's man school of Hollywood director."

Fleming had James Wong Howe as his photographer again in the lavish prestige production *The Rough Riders* (1927). A celebration of the part played in the Spanish-American War by Theodore Roosevelt's cavalry regiment, it was also an indictment of the bureaucratic red tape that apparently cost the Rough Riders much hardship and peril. It was shot on location in San Antonio, Texas, and featured an early crab dolly invented by Howe to follow the action scenes. Reviewers praised Frank Hopper's "unexpectedly restrained performance" as Teddy

Roosevelt, and "a quite remarkable evocation of period atmosphere."

It was further evidence of Fleming's growing standing when he was assigned to direct the adulated German actor Emil Jannings in his first American feature, *The Way of All Flesh* (1927). This was adapted by Jajos Biro and Jules Furthman not from Samuel Butler's novel but from one considerably less distinguished by Perley Poore Sheean. Jannings had a custom-tailored role as a God-fearing German-American family man who works in a Milwaukee bank until he is undone by a young hustler on a train. Robbed, he accidentally kills the girl's partner, and ends up selling chestnuts on windy corners and watching his family's Christmas celebration through the window before turning away into a snowstorm.

The first part of the movie, establishing Jannings as an apparently solid pillar of society, seemed to John Howard Reid "the most brilliant sequence I have ever seen him do." But the melodramatic remainder, he said, we watch "with the peculiar uneasiness which afflicts us when we are forced to follow the detailed development of a situation which has begun by revolting our sense of probability. . . . The film has been admirably directed . . . but the producers . . . have so systematically attempted to reproduce . . . the surest-fire tragic effects of certain other pictures that they have wasted much first-rate ability on what is essentially a maudlin film." Nevertheless, in 1929, when the first Oscars were presented, Jannings received a retroactive Academy Award as best actor for his performance.

The studio system being what it was, Fleming was then recalled from these sentimental heights to direct *Hula* (1927), a particularly mindless vehicle for Clara Bow, by then Paramount's greatest box-office asset. A screen version followed of Anne Nichols' hit play *Abie's Irish Rose,* released silent and then withdrawn to be reissued with some sound sequences, and then Fleming was loaned to Sam Goldwyn to make *The Awakening* (1928), a Vilma Banky melodrama. Fatuous as it frequently is, it was innovatory in that its hero (Walter Byron), a young officer who falls in love with a country girl, is a German—until then the postwar cinema's German soldiers had almost invariably been portrayed as subhuman monsters.

Back at Paramount, Fleming made "the World's First Musical Film Romance," *Wolf Song* (1929). It teamed the rising young star Gary Cooper and Lupe Velez, and their off-screen romance was soon filling the gossip columns. Set in California in the 1830s, it casts Cooper as a trapper who comes down from the mountains to woo the "Mexican Spitfire." Fleming was evidently nervous of the new medium, overburdening the film with endless close-ups and painfully slow movement. When Velez sings, the action stops altogether until she has finished.

Fleming's second talkie showed that he had learned from his mistakes. *The Virginian* (1929)—the third and best screen version of Owen Wister's novel—was shot mostly on location in the High Sierras near Sonora, and the realism this brought to the film was enhanced by the naturalness of the movement and of the sound. One contemporary critic wrote that "the sounds, whether footfalls, horses' hoofs, rumbling wheels or voices, are remarkably well recorded and reproduced. The voices are so natural that one has to listen keenly to hear them, which is as it should be." The shy honesty conveyed by Cooper's performance delighted audiences, and the film was a personal triumph for him and a great financial success. Paul Rotha wrote that "the use of American natural landscapes and types in this picture was highly creditable, and, despite the limitations imposed by dialogue, I have no hesitation in saying that it was amongst the best (if not the best) pictures to come from Hollywood since the opening of the dialogue period. . . . It lifts Victor Fleming in my estimation out of the ruck of second-rate directors, although credit must also be given to J. Roy Hunt for his superb exterior photography."

The Virginian was Fleming's last film for Paramount. Its great success brought him a short contract with Fox, for whom he made two unremarkable movies, and this was followed by a world tour with the restless Douglas Fairbanks, shooting footage that was edited down into an engaging travelogue, *Around the World in Eighty Minutes* (1931). Back home, Fleming was signed to a lucrative "permanent" contract with MGM, by then Hollywood's leading studio.

His first film for MGM was *The Wet Parade* (1932), based on Upton Sinclair's novel about the demon drink, and adapted by John Lee Mahin, who became Fleming's favorite scenarist. The dire effects of alcohol are illustrated in a series of vignettes—a Southern aristocrat commits suicide in a pigsty, a drunk kills his wife, a young man is blinded by poisoned alcohol, and a Prohibition agent dies in the war against the bootleggers. The distinguished cast included Walter Huston, Lewis Stone, Myrna Loy, and Dorothy Jordan—some of whom at least shared the director's lack of commitment to the film's temperance theme—and the Prohibition agent and his partner were improbably played in the style of

Izzy and Moe by Jimmy Durante and Robert Young. This peculiar two-hour movie includes documentary sequences about the manufacture of bootleg whiskey and the political background to Prohibition.

Red Dust (1932) was an assignment much more to Fleming's taste. A romantic melodrama set on a rubber plantation in French Indochina, it electrified audiences with the interplay between Clark Gable's arrogant machismo and Jean Harlow's uninhibited sexuality as the golden-hearted prostitute Vantine. The wise-cracking script was written by John Lee Mahin, with uncredited contributions from Howard Hawks and Donald Ogden Stewart, and the steaming jungle sets and incessant rain, photographed on the Metro sound stages by Harold Rosson, perfectly matched the steamy eroticism of Harlow and Gable. "Given *Red Dust's* brazen moral values," wrote a reviewer in *Time*, "Gable and Harlow have full play for their curiously similar sort of good-natured toughness. The best lines go to Harlow. . . . Her effortless vulgarity, humor, and slovenliness make a noteworthy characterization as good in the genre as the late Jeanne Eagels' Sadie Thompson." Gable later recreated his part in *Mogambo* (1953), John Ford's remake of *Red Dust*.

Henry Hathaway, who began his career as Fleming's assistant, thought that the director's personality provided the model on which Gable based his screen persona. They were close friends and worked together with great empathy. Their second collaboration was very different from the first—a remake of *The White Sister*, with Helen Hayes as the ill-used orphan who becomes a nun, and Gable as her long-lost lover, who inopportunely shows up after she has taken the veil. It was called "a reverent and spiritual picture," but had little of the impact of Henry King's silent version, with Lillian Gish and Ronald Colman.

Fleming directed Jean Harlow again in *Bombshell* (1933), an excellent Hollywood satire on Hollywood, scripted by Mahin and Jules Furthman. Harlow plays Lola Burns, a sexy superstar tired of the Hollywood goldfish bowl and pining for marriage and/or children. Her hopes of adopting a child are dashed by the antics of her con-man father (Frank Morgan)—a character reportedly based on Harlow's own stepfather—and her marital plans are scuttled by the machinations of her ruthless, fast-talking press agent, played with wonderful relish by Lee Tracy.

The picture features clips of Gable and Harlow in Sam Wood's *Hold Your Man* and of Harlow filming retakes for *Red Dust*, with Pat

O'Brien masquerading as the tough director. *Photoplay* called this "one of the fastest and funniest Hollywood pictures ever made," and the New York *Herald-Tribune* raved about Harlow's "increasingly impressive acting talents," saying that she "reveals again that gift for an amalgamation of sophisticated sex comedy with curiously honest innocence that is the secret of her individuality."

An excellent and generally faithful version of *Treasure Island* followed, filmed on location on Catalina Island, with Jackie Cooper as Jim Hawkins and Wallace Beery as Long John Silver. The ending was somewhat marred by the studio's insistence that the pair should invoke again "the tear-stained sentiment of their previous triumph in *The Champ*," but the film shows Fleming's flair for atmosphere and detailed authenticity, the fights are brilliantly staged, and if Lionel Barrymore hams too self-indulgently as Billy Bones, there are fine supporting performances from Nigel Bruce, Lewis Stone, and Otto Kruger.

Reckless (1935) has Jean Harlow as a Broadway musical comedy star, William Powell as a cantankerous promoter, and Franchot Tone as a young millionaire who sweeps Harlow off her feet when he buys up all the seats in the theatre so that he can enjoy her performance in solitary splendor. Fleming made this rather uneven movie on loan to David Selznick and then went to Fox under a similar arrangement to direct *The Farmer Takes a Wife* (1935), a comedy-drama set in the mid-nineteenth century about life along the Erie Canal. Henry Fonda, whose movie debut this was, credited Fleming with teaching him the difference between screen and stage acting, and the film consolidated the director's reputation as "a master of atmosphere." In 1936, back at MGM, Fleming took over as director of *The Good Earth* after George Hill's suicide, but himself became ill before shooting began. The following year, again uncredited, he completed the shooting of *The Great Waltz* after Julien Duvivier quit.

In 1937 Fleming had another immense critical and commercial success with *Captains Courageous*, adapted from Kipling's novel. Spencer Tracy starred as the simple, brave, and honorable Portuguese fisherman Manuel, who teaches the manly virtues to Freddie Bartholomew, a spoiled rich kid fished from the sea after he had fallen overboard from a liner. The supporting cast includes Melvyn Douglas, Lionel Barrymore, and Mickey Rooney, and the script was by Mahin, Marc Connelly, and Dale Van Every.

Fleming bought a two-masted schooner in

Gloucester, Massachusetts, sailed to Newfoundland and Novia Scotia for background shooting, then through the Panama Canal to California, where Long Beach Harbor doubled for Gloucester. There the schooner was converted into the fishing boat captained by Lionel Barrymore, and the fishing scenes were shot in Catalina Channel with live cod shipped down from Washington in tanks. *Variety* found the result "one of the best pictures of the sea ever made," and Howard Barnes placed it among "the screen's few masterpieces." John Howard Reid credits Fleming with the film's technical innovations—an "iron egg" camera swinging like a gyroscope to give a stable picture in high seas, and a sprayproof lens consisting of a disc of plate glass rotated by a motor in front of the lens. Wonderfully photographed by Hal Rosson, *Captains Courageous* came in third in *Film Daily*'s annual poll and brought Spencer Tracy his first Oscar.

Gratefully discarding his curly wig and Portuguese accent, Tracy was himself again in *Test Pilot* (1938), playing mechanic and best buddy to fearless flyer Clark Gable, with Myrna Loy as the girl they both love. Gable gets the girl and Tracy, in the second movie running, dies heroically. In spite of some friction between Tracy and Gable off the set, they and Loy worked together splendidly under Fleming's direction, and their "chemistry" and the superb aerial sequences made this MGM's biggest hit of the year. James Shelley Hamilton found it uneven, "often probing with extraordinary keenness . . . , sometimes slipping into a wordy bathos," as in the "pseudo-poetic talk about a girl in blue in the sky—the Lorelei of the clouds." Tracy, he thought, managed to subvert such excesses by "kidding" them, "casually but cuttingly." The film was nominated for an Oscar.

When MGM decided to make the first Technicolor version of Frank L. Baum's fantasy *The Wizard of Oz*, with Mervyn LeRoy as producer, the project was at first assigned to Richard Thorpe. He was replaced after two weeks by George Cukor, who in turn left only three days later to direct Selznick's *Gone With the Wind*. LeRoy called in Fleming. As David Thomson says, the film was "far outside Fleming's territory," but the result was nevertheless "by turns a moving and dark fantasy, beautifully played by an adventurous cast."

As all the world knows, Judy Garland landed the role of Dorothy, the wide-eyed Kansas farm girl who, after being knocked unconscious by a tornado, is transported to Munchkinland and, unable to get home again, sets off along the Yellow Brick Road to seek the help of the Wizard of Oz. Her companions, each with one equally desperate need, are the Scarecrow (Ray Bolger), the Tin Man (Jack Haley), and the Cowardly Lion (Bert Lahr), and their fearsome enemy is the Wicked Witch of the West (Margaret Hamilton). The Wizard (Frank Morgan) turns out to be something of a disappointment, but in the end all the wishes are granted anyway and Dorothy gets safely home again. This much-loved classic, which has been shown on television once a year since 1965, owes much of its enormous popularity to the songs by E. Y. Harburg and Harold Arlen—especially "Over the Rainbow," which won an Oscar for best original song. The Technicolor photography, an important factor in the film's original success, now seems garish.

And an even greater blockbuster followed for Fleming when, with *The Wizard of Oz* still ten days from completion, Selznick asked him to replace George Cukor as director of *Gone With the Wind*, his epic screen version of Margaret Mitchell's bestselling romance of the American Civil War. Fleming had little faith in the project, which he told Selznick would be "one of the biggest white elephants of all time," but accepted anyway as a favor to its star, Clark Gable. Five books have been written about the making of *GWTW*, detailing Fleming's battles with Vivien Leigh, whom he detested, and his arguments with Selznick. These became so intolerable that at one point Fleming walked off the picture and had (or faked) a nervous breakdown. He was replaced by Sam Wood, but eventually returned to complete the movie.

Gavin Lambert estimates that Fleming directed about forty-five percent of the film's 220 minutes, with important contributions from Sam Wood, George Cukor, and the production designer William Cameron Menzies. But though Fleming was the only credited director (and in that capacity received one of the picture's eight Oscars), it is generally recognized that *GWTW* was above all a "producer's picture"—much more the creation of David Selznick than of any of the directors he hired. Often too self-consciously aesthetic in its Technicolor photography, it remains powerfully dramatic in its larger-than-life emotions and sometimes magnificent in its spectacle. It grossed more money than any other film in the history of the cinema until it was finally topped twenty-five years later by *The Sound of Music*. The quintessential and crowning product of the Hollywood studio system in its heyday, an American myth and a great vulgar poem, its negative is appropriately housed in a golden canister.

Fleming's *Dr. Jekyll and Mr. Hyde* (1941),

scripted by Mahin, relied less than other versions of Stevenson's novel on special effects and horrific makeup, attempting a Freudian interpretation of this fable of schizophrenia and repression. A dream montage replete with phallic steeple and the rape of Leda was expurgated out of deference to the Hays Office, but Hyde's vision of himself as a charioteer exultantly lashing the bare shoulders of Ingrid Bergman and Lana Turner was retained, and the movie is full of symbols of his sadism and lust (like the giant eye focused on Bergman through the slow-running sand of an hourglass). As the good doctor periodically transformed into a sexually voracious killer, Spencer Tracy was handicapped by the struggle to conceal his natural decency, but Ingrid Bergman scored a triumph as Hyde's pathetic victim, Ivy.

There was a mixed response to *Tortilla Flat* (1942), adapted by Mahin and Benjamin Glazer from Steinbeck's sentimental novella about a community of boozy, good-hearted riff-raff in a Southern California fishing village. The cast was headed by Tracy, Hedy Lamarr (in one of her best performances), and John Garfield, with Frank Morgan, Akim Tamiroff, and Donald Meek in support. The atmosphere was appropriately leisurely, with the emphasis on character, and Karl Freund contributed some fine exterior photography. Rather apathetically received by most critics, it has been claimed by John Howard Reid as Fleming's best picture.

Tracy starred yet again in *A Guy Named Joe* (1943), a fantasy scripted by Dalton Trumbo about a World War II fighter pilot who is killed in action and assigned by a celestial general to be the guardian angel of a young flyer (Van Johnson). When the latter cops a suicide mission, the dead hero and his former girlfriend (Irene Dunne), who is by now attached to Johnson, fly the mission on his behalf. The story is a variation on a theme so popular in the 1940s as to comprise a subgenre, seen for example in films like *Heaven Can Wait*, the Topper series, *Here Comes Mr. Jordan*, and *Stairway to Heaven*. John Howard Reid found it "strong and exciting, despite such weaknesses as verbosity and a climax that is almost pure serialese. Its strength lies in the restraint of its acting and its flying sequences."

Beset by problems, including an auto accident that incapacitated Van Johnson for months, the film took almost a year to shoot. After the preview, the MGM producer Everett Riskin decreed that the ending should be changed so that Johnson could get the girl. Fleming walked out and stayed out for over a year, only returning because Clark Gable asked him to direct *Adventure* (1945). This was unrelated to Fleming's earlier film of that title. Based on a novel by Clyde Brion Davis, it concerns the brief encounter between a tough sailor and a lady librarian (Greer Garson). "Gable's back and Garson's got him," went the famous advertising slogan for a movie that failed both critically and commercially.

At this low point in his career, Fleming saw Ingrid Bergman in Maxwell Anderson's play *Joan of Lorraine* and decided that he must capture her performance in a screen version. To do so he went into partnership with Walter Wanger and Bergman herself to form Sierra Pictures. These three contributed nearly $5 million of their own money. They leased an entire studio for two years and spent lavishly on cast, technicians, costumes, and props. Bergman wrote in her memoirs that "Vic Fleming wore himself out on the picture. He was here and there and everywhere. . . . Nobody thought there was any box office in a young girl saving her country, especially with no love story. I think the pressures got to Victor Fleming."

Released in 1948 as *Joan of Arc*, the film earned Oscars for best color photography and color costume design, and there was a special Oscar for Wanger as producer. But the public stayed away and, though the picture had its admirers, most critics shared the view of Herman G. Weinberg, who called it "a bad film with one or two good things"—notably José Ferrer's performance as the Dauphin; "for the rest it is childishly oversimplified, its battles papier-mâché, its heroine far too worldly, its spiritual content that of a chromo art calendar."

Fleming himself thought the film a failure. Adela Rogers St. Johns recalled meeting the director and telling him that she was going to see the picture; "he said 'Please don't. It's so bad. It's so dreadful.' And he was never the same again. It just killed him." In fact, Fleming made no more films and died the following year, after a heart attack at an Arizona dude ranch. He was survived by his wife, the former Lucille Rosson, and two daughters.

As Kevin Brownlow says, Fleming was a studio pro who in general accepted any assignment that was handed to him, for this reason "alternating from the sublime to the absolutely unspeakable." Enough of what he accomplished was sublime to insure him a place in the Hollywood pantheon. A formidable disciplinarian on set, he nevertheless inspired enormous devotion. Ingrid Bergman called him a "marvelous" director: "As soon as he came close to me I could tell by his eyes what he wanted me to do. . . . He got performances out of me which very often I didn't think I was capable of." His daughter Victoria described him as a loving father "but a cross between Patton and MacArthur."

FILMS: (with Ted Reed) When the Clouds Roll By, 1919; The Mollycoddle, 1920; Mamma's Affair, 1921; A Woman's Place, 1921; The Lane That Has No Turning, 1922; Red Hot Romance, 1922; Anna Ascends, 1922; Dark Secrets, 1923; The Law of the Lawless, 1923; To the Last Man, 1923; Call of the Canyon, 1923; Empty Hands, 1924; The Code of the Sea, 1924; The Devil's Cargo, 1925; Adventure, 1925; A Son of His Father, 1925; Lord Jim, 1925; The Blind Goddess, 1926; Mantrap, 1926; The Rough Riders (U.K., The Trumpet Call), 1927; The Way of All Flesh, 1927; Hula, 1927; Abie's Irish Rose, 1928; The Awakening, 1928; Wolf Song, 1929; The Virginian, 1929; Common Clay, 1930; Renegades, 1930; (with Douglas Fairbanks) Around the World in Eighty Minutes/Around the World With Douglas Fairbanks, 1931; The Wet Parade, 1932; Red Dust, 1932; The White Sister, 1933; Bombshell/Blonde Bombshell, 1933; Treasure Island, 1934; Reckless, 1935; The Farmer Takes a Wife, 1935; Captains Courageous, 1937; Test Pilot, 1938; The Wizard of Oz, 1939; Gone With the Wind, 1939; Dr. Jekyll and Mr. Hyde, 1941; Tortilla Flat, 1942; A Guy Named Joe, 1943; Adventure, 1945; Joan of Arc, 1948.

ABOUT: Hermetz, A. The Making of the Wizard of Oz, 1977; Lambert, G. Gone With the Wind, 1974; Parish, J. R. and Mank, G. The Best of MGM, 1981; Thomson, D. A Biographical Dictionary of the Cinema, 1980. Periodicals—Film Dope February 1979; Films and Filming December 1967, January 1968; Films in Review March 1983.

FORD, ALEKSANDER (November 24, 1908–April 29, 1980), Polish director and scenarist, was born at Lodz. He studied the history of art at Warsaw University and directed his first short films in 1928—Nad Ranem (Early Morning, 1929) and Tetno, Polskiego Manchesteru (Lodz, the Polish Manchester, 1929). A feature called The Mascot appeared in 1930 and Legion ulicy (Legion of the Streets) in 1932. The latter, a story about Warsaw newsboys, has been called the only Polish film "of any distinction" made in the 1930s.

About this time Ford joined START (Society of the Devotees of the Artistic Film), which had been founded in 1929 or 1930 by a group of students who included Wanda Jakubowska and Eugeniusz Cękalski. Jerzy Bossak and Jerzy Toeplitz also became members of this progressive organization, which encouraged the making of noncommercial films in Poland and sought to spread knowledge of foreign avant-garde cinema. The postwar development of the Polish film industry owed a great deal to START members, though the organization itself was dissolved in

ALEKSANDER FORD

1935. According to Philippe Haudiquet, Ford "systematically eluded" questions about his prewar films, which included Sabra (Chalutzim/Cactus, 1933), a pro-Jewish film made in Israel, and Przebudzenie (Awakening, 1934).

With the German invasion of Poland, Ford escaped to the Soviet Union and joined the first volunteer Polish division, the Kosciusko. He made several war documentaries and instructional films in Russian studios and then, with Jerzy Bossak and others, founded the Polish Army Film Unit, producing newsreels and compilation documentaries like Bitwa pod Lenino (Battle of Leningrad, 1944). When the provisional government of the Polish Republic was established in July 1944, Colonel Ford was named head of the government's film agency. Soon after, in collaboration with Jerzy Bossak, he made the harrowing documentary Majdanek (1944), about the Majdanek extermination camp.

Polish film production resumed in 1945 under the auspices of the government agency headed by Ford. Film Polski began production modestly enough in a Lodz gymnasium commandeered by Ford immediately after the Liberation. By 1946 it had three sound stages, and thereafter the rebuilding of the Polish cinema as a nationalized industry was rapid. As director general of Film Polski from 1945 to 1947, Ford played a central role in this process. Then, returning to active filmmaking, he quickly established himself as the leading Polish director of his generation.

Ford's first postwar feature was Ulica Graniczna (Border Street/That Others May Live, 1948). It is an attempt to give a picture of

Poland during the German occupation by following the fortunes of five young people and their families, concentrating in particular on the enclosure of the Warsaw ghetto, the uprising of 1943, and the bloody destruction of the ghetto and its inhabitants. The result seemed to Western critics rather oversimplified and schematic in its portrayal of human relationships, but with compensatory passages of visual brilliance. The regard and sympathy for young people that Ford had shown in *Legion of the Streets* is also evident in *Border Street,* as it is throughout his work, including his next film, *Mlodosc Chopina* (*The Youth of Chopin,* 1952).

The latter, written by Ford, is marred by the Stalinization of the Polish cinema that began to intensify in 1949. One reviewer wrote that the young musician is presented as if he had been born "with a Red flag clutched tightly in his infant fist," and the film conveniently overlooks the fact that Chopin was also an "indulged favorite of the ruling classes of Europe." Virginia Graham wrote that when Ford "cuts from one snippet of an episode to another, episodes as brief as animated snapshots in an album, his work takes on a curious, amateurish tinge"; however, when the director "allows his camera to rest for a few minutes on a broad canvas alive with movement, his brilliance . . . seems indubitable." There was praise for the performance in the lead of Czeslaw Wollejka—"a young man with a beautiful sensitive face and a genuine flair for pretending to play the piano"—and for the film's "real feeling and reverence for music."

Piatka z ulicy Barskiej (*Five Boys From Barska Street,* 1953) is one of the very few Polish films of any note produced during the period of maximum ideological control. It opens in Warsaw late in 1947. The authorities have launched a campaign to rehabilitate the young criminals, many of them orphaned by the war, who scrabble for a living amid the ruins of the city. The film concentrates on five youths, all found guilty of robbery, who under this scheme are put on probation and assigned to the care of a "guardian," a bricklayer named Wojciechowski (Ludwik Benoit).

This amateur probation officer throws himself wholeheartedly into his new task. He finds one of the boys a job in a newspaper office and another a place in a music school; the others he takes with him to work on the building of the city's new east-west thoroughfare. What Wojciechowski doesn't know is that the boys are still members of a gang devoted to sabotaging the reconstruction program. The gang leader Zenon uses violence, blackmail, and bribery to retain

the loyalty of the five and reclaims one of them, but a growing sense of achievement and self-respect enables the others to overcome Zenon's blandishments. Finally, in an exciting battle in the Warsaw sewers, they defeat his plan to blow up a section of the new highway on the eve of opening day.

Five Boys From Barska Street, adapted by Ford and Kazimierz Kozniewski from the latter's novel, is an excellent piece of propaganda. As Thomas Spencer wrote, it also "rattles along with the pace of a first-rate boy's yarn (which it very largely is). . . . In the process the boys and their associates . . . emerge as complete characters brought vividly to life as individuals." Not everyone agreed that the characters were much more than well-differentiated types, and there were complaints that the film was overlong and too overtly symbolic, but it was generally admired as an exciting and entertaining story, especially in the scene where the boys compete in a bricklaying contest, and in the climactic chase through the sewers. It brought Ford the award as best director at the 1954 Cannes festival.

Georges Sadoul called Ford "the most significant force in the artistic development of the Polish cinema"—partly, no doubt, on account of his achievements as first director of Film Polski, partly because of the quality and example of his own work, and partly because of his direct influence on the rising stars of the new Polish cinema. Andrzej Wajda was Ford's assistant on *Five Boys From Barska Street* and Ford supervised Wajda's *A Generation* (1955). Ford's influence widened after 1955, when he was named artistic director of Studio, one of the more or less autonomous film production units established in Poland that year.

The easing of ideological restrictions that followed the death of Stalin is reflected in Ford's next feature, *Osmy dzien tygodnia* (*The Eighth Day of the Week,* 1957), a Polish–West German coproduction. It is another study of young people in postwar Warsaw, but very different in tone from the patriotic optimism of *Five Boys From Barska Street.* Based on the novel by Marek Hlasko, it tells the story of a young man (Zbigniew Cybulski) and his girlfriend (Sonja Ziemann) who can find nowhere in the crowded and overworked city to go to bed together—the implication of the title is that unmarried lovers in modern Poland needed an extra day of the week. The frustrated couple have to make do with a fantasy "wedding" in a department store bedding display, and the girl is seduced by another man before they find their "eighth day."

This funny and touching film, with its picture of a dispirited nation and of young people more interested in sex than in the endless "challenges" of reconstruction, was too much for President Gomulka. The Polish version was withdrawn from the 1958 Cannes Festival, and when the German version was shown at Venice, the Polish delegation walked out. Hollis Alpert found the department store fantasy unconvincing and wrote that it was "the realism, and sharply human detail that save the film from the banality that a story of this kind would seem to indicate. Mr. Ford's direction of his own and Marek Hlasko's screenplay is clear and effective. . . . When an unpretentious, artfully made movie about a boy and girl in love can cause all this international fuss it probably says, more than anything else, something about the power of the medium."

By this time Polish filmmakers had largely worked through their preoccupation with the war and its aftermath, and had moreover built up production facilities capable of more ambitious projects than those previously attempted. Ford led the way with the historical epic *Kryzacy* (*The Knights of the Teutonic Order,* 1960), based on the novel by Henryk Sienkiewicz. It is set at the end of the fourteenth century and deals with the depredations of the Order of Teutonic Knights, whose rape and pillage raids were intended to convert the Poles to Christianity (a task that had inconveniently been accomplished some centuries earlier). In 1410, at the Battle of Grunwald (Tannenberg), the allied forces of Poland and Lithuania, with Russian, Tartar, and Czech support, defeated and destroyed the Order. Shooting began in July 1959 and the movie was completed a year later, in time to celebrate the millennium of the Polish state and the 550th anniversary of the Battle of Grunwald.

Kryzacy was the most expensive film ever made in Poland up to that time. Filmed in Eastmancolor and Dyaliscope, it involved about 1,800 actors, extras, and technicians and ran for 175 minutes. According to one British reviewer "the plot, which is thick, is sprung when the knights raid the home of a Polish border baron, Jurand, during his absence and kill his wife. . . . What with people being stuck with arrows during the subsequent feud, run through with pikes, having their limbs amputated by battle-axes, their eyes put out by red-hot daggers and their tongues pulled out with pincers—to mention but a few contemporary unpleasantnesses—life is shown to be brutish and short; but not, surprisingly, to be nasty in the sense one expects. For Mr. Ford is betrayed by his designer and color photography. So variegated and immaculate are the costumes that a great trade in dyes and stuffs is to be assumed, not to mention

dry cleaning." Most critics found the picture an impressive if sometimes confusing spectacle, and it had great popular success, both in Poland (where half of the entire population is said to have seen it within a year of its release) and abroad.

During the late 1950s and early 1960s, in spite of the box-office success of *Kryzacy,* Ford was somewhat eclipsed by Wajda, Munk, and the other idols of the "Polish School." He taught at the Lodz film school and continued to make films, if rather infrequently. In *Pierwszy dzien wolnosci* (*The First Day of Freedom,* 1964) he returned to a World War II theme with a story about a young Polish officer (Tadeusz Lomnicki) and the daughter of a "good" German doctor (Beta Tyszkiewicz) who love and lose each other in the last days of the war. Lomnicki also stars in *Der Arzt stellt fest* (1966), also known as *Angeklagt nach Paragraph 218* (*The Right to Be Born/The Doctor Speaks Out*), A Swiss–West German film, not widely released, about the need for a more thoughtful attitude to abortion.

During the political upheavals of 1968, Ford was dismissed from his teaching post at the Lodz film school. He emigrated to Israel and a few years later settled in Denmark. *Den Første Kreds* (*The First Circle,* 1972), filmed in Denmark, has been called a rather pale version of Solzhenitsyn's novel. It was followed three years later by an Israeli-German coproduction, *Der Martyrer* (*The Martyr*), also known as *Sie Sind Frei, Doktor Korczak,* which seems to have been his last film. Aleksander Ford was not a director of great originality but he was a man and an artist of integrity and a first-rate craftsman—the "doyen" of Polish cinema, who did more than any other single individual to make that cinema one to be reckoned with.

FILMS: Nad Ranem, 1929 (short); Tetno, Polskiego Manchesteru, 1929 (short); The Mascot, 1930; Legion ulicy (Legion of the Streets), 1932; Sabra (Chalutzim/Cactus), 1933; Przebudzenie (Awakening), 1934; Forward, Cooperation, 1935 (documentary); (with others) Ludzie Wisly (People of the Vistula), 1937 (documentary); Bitwa pod Lenino (Battle of Leningrad), 1944 (documentary); (with Jerzy Bossak) Majdanek (Majdanek, Extermination Camp), 1944 (documentary); (with Jerzy Bossak) Bitwa o Kolobrzeg (The Battle of Kolberg), 1945 (short); Ulica Graniczna (Border Street/That Others May Live), 1948; Mlodosc Chopina (The Youth of Chopin/Young Chopin), 1952; Piatka z ulicy Barskiej (Five Boys From Barska Street/Five From Barska Street), 1953; Osmy dzien tygodnia (The Eighth Day of the Week), 1957; Kryzacy (The Knights of the Teutonic Order/Knights of the Black Cross), 1960; Pierwszy dzien wolnosci (The First Day of Freedom), 1964; Der Arzt stellt fest, *also known as* Angeklagt nach Paragraph 218 (The Doctor Speaks Out/The Doctor Says/The Right to Be Born), 1966;

Good Morning, Poland, 1969 (documentary); Den Første Kreds (The First Circle), 1972; Der Martyrer (The Martyr), 1975 (*also known as* Sie Sind Frei, Doktor Korczak).

ABOUT: Haudiquet, P. Nouveaux cinéastes polonais, 1963; International Who's Who, 1980–81; Oxford Companion to Film, 1976. *Periodicals*—Avant-Scene December 1983; Cinéma (France) April 1974; Image et Son September 1980; Sight and Sound Winter 1957–1958.

FORD, JOHN (February 1, 1895–August 31, 1973), American director and producer, was born Sean Aloysius O'Fearna in Cape Elizabeth, Maine, thirteenth and youngest child of Irish immigrants who changed their name to O'Feeney. Shortly thereafter his family moved to Portland, Maine, where his father kept a saloon. In 1913, having graduated from Portland High School, he failed to gain entry to the Naval Academy at Annapolis, going to the University of Maine instead. After only a few weeks he moved on to Hollywood where an older brother, Francis, was already established at Universal as an actor, writer, and director. Francis had changed his name to Ford and Sean followed his example, signing himself Jack Ford in all his film credits until 1923, John Ford thereafter. He found a variety of employment in the booming industry, including stunt work and doubling for his brother, assistant cameraman, and riding with the Ku Klux Klan in *Birth of a Nation.* He became proficient as a cameraman and editor, and often functioned as such throughout his career. Although accounts disagree, he had definitely graduated to assistant directing by 1916.

The following year saw his debut as a Universal director. His first picture was *The Tornado* (1917), a bank robbery Western in which he himself played the stunt-riding hero. It was followed—more significantly for the future—by *The Soul Herder* (1917). This three-reeler was the first of twenty-six films that Ford was to make with Harry Carey, and the beginning of a burst of activity that produced at least thirty films by 1920. Few have survived, and it is possible that there were others of which records no longer exist. Ford himself described this series of Westerns as "character stories" built around Carey in the role of a saddle-tramp—a character of some integrity, but not a "hero" in the then conventional sense. Scripts were co-authored with Carey and shot on location within a week.

In those interviews in which Ford was forthcoming (rare events, in that he was famously uncooperative with most interviewers) he spoke fondly of this period and of his relationship with

JOHN FORD

Carey. A lifelong lover of location shooting, he evidently enjoyed the company of the (often real) cowboys used in the filming. There seems no doubt that these early films were cheerful pieces of storytelling through which Ford learned the essentials that were later to stand him in such good stead.

It is tempting to view a filmmaker's early work with the wisdom of hindsight, but, when a print of *Straight Shooting* (1917) was "discovered" in the late 1960s, only the most avid auteurist could claim to detect in it distinctively Fordian elements. Ford's longest film up to that point (five reels), *Straight Shooting* features the now familiar theme of powerful cattlemen persecuting small farmers; Carey is moved to come to the aid of the farmers. Carey himself cuts an impressive figure, and Lindsay Anderson rightly observes of him that "this combination of chivalry with strength is one which will characterise many a Ford hero to come." Indeed, it was to become one of the fundamental constituents of the whole Western genre. *Straight Shooting* is also distinguished by Ford's evident concern with photographic composition, by a tendency to sentimentality (hardly unique to Ford in this period, though a constant element in his later cinema), and by a pleasing sense of humor. If the other Carey-Ford ventures were like this one (and there is some reason to suppose that they were) then the three hectic years were well spent.

By the early 1920s Ford was firmly established in Hollywood. Westerns still dominated his output, but in 1920 he did take the opportunity to work in a different milieu with a comedy set among the New York Irish, *The Prince From Avenue A.* In 1921 Ford left Universal for Fox, where he worked for the next ten years.

In 1924, Fox employed Ford to direct his response to *The Covered Wagon,* Paramount's highly successful celebration of the pioneer spirit directed by James Cruze the year before. The result was *The Iron Horse* (1924), Ford's longest and most expensive film up to that point. Telling the story of the race to finish the transcontinental railroad, *The Iron Horse* was a considerable box-office success as well as bringing Ford widespread critical attention. Here Ford's romantic concern with American history emerges. Featuring a gallery of famous historical characters ranging from Lincoln to Wild Bill Hickock, *The Iron Horse* is an exciting epic which, in its warm celebration of "ordinary" people, gives early evidence of the populism that plays such a significant part in Ford's subsequent cinema.

For the rest of the 1920s Ford worked steadily in a variety of genres, completing a further sixteen films by the end of the decade. Westerns were now less prominent, as they would be until the late 1930s, and his last silent films concerned subjects as diverse as horse racing, boxing, and Irish history. The most notable movies of the period are *Three Bad Men* (1926) and *Four Sons* (1928). Set at the time of the Dakota land rush of 1876, *Three Bad Men* was notable for its striking location cinematography and for the evident affection with which Ford treated those caught up in these epic events. Commercially, however, it was less successful than *The Iron Horse,* and it was *Four Sons* that gave Ford his biggest commercial success of those years. His sentimentality, particularly where the family is concerned, is excessive in this story of a Bavarian woman, her four sons, and their experience of the First World War.

Ford visited Germany during the shooting of *Four Sons* and met F. W. Murnau and other German filmmakers. It is tempting to see their influence in his emerging visual style, doubly so in that he acknowledged no mentors other than his brother, Harry Carey, and D. W. Griffith. It is a difficult judgment to make. The clearest stylistic feature of Ford's early cinema is its inclination to pictorialism, to studied effects of composition and lighting, a tendency as much apparent before *Four Sons* as after it. Anderson argues that "at times in *Four Sons* the influence is strong, with movements that recall German camera handling and lighting effects that verge on the expressionistic." With so many films "lost," however, it is all but impossible to make the appropriate before-and-after comparisons, especially in a period when German influence

on American cinema was widespread. It may well be that Ford found in the German style new forms of expression for his already established pictorial concerns, and it is certainly an "influence" that marks his much admired work of the thirties.

By the coming of sound, then, Ford was established as an effective and efficient Hollywood director, who brought in his productions on time, and whose talent for location shooting gave a certain splendor to the look of his Westerns. It is generally conceded that no one viewing his silent output could possibly class him with the acknowledged masters of the period, and, at the time, no one did. Only *The Iron Horse* and *Four Sons* brought him serious critical attention—that was to come later, in the 1930s. It is possible, however, to see the beginnings of many Ford characteristics in the films of this period: in the character he and Harry Carey developed for their Westerns; in his concern for compositional effects; in his emphasis on family groups; and in his unselfconscious sentimentality. All these features were to be developed and extended in the years that followed.

Perhaps the most immediately significant factor in these developments was the emergence of his working relationship with the writer Dudley Nichols in *Men Without Women* (1930), about fourteen men trapped in a submarine. Ford found himself very sympathetic to Nichols' approach—"from then on, we worked together as much as possible, and I worked very closely with him. He had never written a script before, but he was very good, and he had the same idea I had about paucity of dialogue." The films they made together during the 1930s were to make Ford's reputation. While *Men Without Women* and *Judge Priest* (1934) are consistent with what we know of Ford's aesthetic and narrative preferences, *The Lost Patrol* (1934)—a World War I movie set in the Mesopotamian desert—and, even more strikingly, *The Informer* (1935), consciously set out to achieve specifically cinematic effects. The timing of this development gives some *prima facie* plausibility to the claim that Nichols had a crucially important influence upon Ford's work. New to the job in their earlier collaborations, by the time he came to adapt Liam O'Flaherty's novel *The Informer* Nichols had established his own artistic autonomy. This is not to suggest that *The Informer* is somehow Nichols' film. Rather, that Nichols provided the occasion, here and in a dozen other movies, for Ford to develop his own talents in specific—and not necessarily desirable—directions.

There is no question but that *The Informer* constitutes a sudden leap in the by then well established pattern of Ford's work. Ford in the 1930s (and, indeed, throughout his career) presented himself as a matter-of-fact craftsman. Although this was to some extent the public persona of an intensely private artist, much of his output testifies to Ford's willingness to function as a highly skilled artisan within the studio system. Against this background *The Informer* stands out as a remarkably self-conscious production. The elaborate care devoted to composition and photographic texture (the film was shot by Joseph August), the heavy symbolism found in many of its set-pieces, McLaglen's performance as the informer Gypo Nolan, and the almost expressionist settings, combine to create a film strikingly different from most other Hollywood products of the period. To the modern eye it has dated in ways almost unique in Ford, its techniques and experiments too weighty, too overt, to survive for fifty years.

The film brought Ford to a new level of critical respectability, but in so doing gave positive valuation to elements in his style that, in retrospect, are clearly not his most enduring contribution. It is easy enough to understand the adulatory response to *The Informer* at a time when the artistic credentials of the cinema remained to be established. The very self-consciousness of the movie's style delighted the film-as-art evangelists, and Ford's struggle to get the picture made could be (and was) construed as the battle of a serious artist against commercial philistinism. This view of Ford—as a director capable of greatness though generally constrained by commercial necessities—was to form the orthodox framework for critical discussion of his work for many years to come. It had the unfortunate consequence that many of his later films, particularly his Westerns, were systematically undervalued.

In the short run Ford, too, seems to have framed his aspirations in the terms formed by responses to *The Informer*. Inasmuch as Ford, Nichols, Victor McLaglen, and the composer Max Steiner earned Oscars, and Ford also received the New York film critics' Best Direction award, this is hardly surprising. That this should be achieved with a story of betrayal set in the Dublin of the Rebellion is all the more impressive, but there is a certain justice in Ford's own reply to Peter Bogdanovich when asked if *The Informer* was one of his favorite pictures: "I would say not. I think it lacks humor—which is my forte." (Elsewhere, however, he spoke enthusiastically of the film; he liked nothing better in an interview than to contradict what he had said in the last one.)

In that same year Ford's humor was much in evidence in the third of his films made with Will Rogers. *Steamboat Round the Bend* (1935) features Rogers as a quack who ends up running an ancient steamboat as a wax museum. Like the other films with Rogers—*Dr. Bull* (1933) and *Judge Priest* (1934)—*Steamboat Round the Bend* is shaped partly by Rogers' own quirky screen persona and partly by Ford's fascination with, and celebration of, small communities peopled by eccentrics and innocents. The two later films also include Stepin Fetchit playing the rolling-eyed black simpleton, a racial stereotype that is made no more acceptable by its period context than by the later claims made for its ironic effect. That aside, however, *Steamboat Round the Bend* survives remarkably well—better, some would argue, than the much more solemn *The Informer*. Ford was not to make as pleasurable a film until the end of the decade, when he embarked on the most strikingly creative years of his career. Although *The Prisoner of Shark Island* (1936) and *Wee Willie Winkie* (1937) are not without their (different) qualities, it is the series of films beginning with *Stagecoach* (1939) that best illustrate the flowering of John Ford's talent.

In many ways *Stagecoach* is the foundation stone of the modern Western, for, just as it was the occasion for Ford to find a mature outlook upon the landscape and characters of his early cinema, it also heralded a new seriousness and legitimacy for the Western genre. The French critic and theorist André Bazin saw it as the consummate classical Western, "the ideal balance between social myth, historical reconstruction, psychological truth, and the traditional theme of the Western *mise-en-scène.*" With its stagecoach laden with characters who were, or were to become, archetypes of the Western genre, it now looks far more clichéd than would have been the case in 1939. Modern audiences have long been familiar with Western gamblers, drunken doctors, and golden-hearted saloon girls, and, as with all classical genre pieces, it is impossible to see *Stagecoach* except through the perspective afforded by forty years of subsequent genre history.

Nevertheless, *Stagecoach* does mark Ford's triumphant return to a milieu in which he was completely at ease, thus opening up a new and vibrant phase in his work. It also brought John Wayne to stardom. A descendant of the Harry Carey figure in the early Ford Westerns, Wayne's Ringo Kid is in genesis the honest man of few words and profound actions who stands at the heart of Ford's Western vision. In genesis only, however, for *Stagecoach* viewed in the context of Ford's subsequent work seems a somewhat contrived sketch for what was to follow, not a fully realized achievement. It is a story very well told, and our pleasure in its magnificent Monument Valley setting, its compelling narrative, and its visual elegance, should not disguise the economy and skill with which its characters are presented to us and developed. In the end, though, it lacks the elegiac spirit of *My Darling Clementine* (1946), the irony of *The Searchers* (1956), and the richness of *The Man Who Shot Liberty Valance* (1962). Critically underrated on its first appearance (though it did gain Ford another New York critics' best direction award), it was later overvalued as *the* classic Western. Today critical opinion accepts neither proposition, preferring to see *Stagecoach* as Ford's first step toward his greatest achievements.

It also marked Ford's return to American history as a major source for his work, a concern found in the other two films he made in that productive year. *Young Mr. Lincoln* (1939) featured Henry Fonda (like Wayne, to become a Ford regular until they fell out during the filming of *Mister Roberts*) as the young Lincoln, both stiff and elegant in his stove-pipe hat. Ford (and his scenarist Lamar Trotti) gives us a Lincoln who is already the consummate peacemaker, the master bringer of order and justice, whether it be in judging a pie contest or successfully defending two brothers accused of murder. Sergei Eisenstein praised the film's "unity, its artistry, its genuine beauty," and named it as the American film he wished he had made.

Fonda also played in Ford's next film, his first in color ("a cinch to work in," according to Ford, "if you've any eye at all for color or composition"). *Drums Along the Mohawk* (1939) returned for the first time since *The Iron Horse* and *Three Bad Men* to a celebration of the pioneering spirit. Played out against a magnificent setting, the film follows the travails and joys of a young couple (Fonda and Claudette Colbert) settling in the Mohawk Valley at the time of the War of Independence. *Drums Along the Mohawk* is a particularly effective example of Ford's ability to combine the personal with the epic and historical. The Martins' battle for survival is also the battle for the founding of America, a conflation expressed in the stirring image of the new flag fluttering over the settlement. There is about *Drums Along the Mohawk* an affecting optimism, a joy in life and community that is central to Ford's cinema of the 1940s.

It is there powerfully in his next film, *The Grapes of Wrath* (1940). Adapted (by Nunnally Johnson) from John Steinbeck's novel about the Okies and the desolation of their circumstances, it won Ford both critical acclaim and his second

Oscar. Tom Joad, the elder son of the family, forced to wander the country in search of work, is played with startling beauty by Henry Fonda, his characteristic elegance of motion lending Tom a nobility around which the movie's ethical commitments revolve. Few could be unmoved by his final speech of affirmation, and few could miss the intensity of the film's commitment to these "simple people," as Ford described them.

Of course there is a certain romanticism about *The Grapes of Wrath*, not least in the portrait of Tom himself and in Ma Joad, here notably played by Jane Darwell (who collected the film's second Oscar). The movie is indubitably "on the side of" the people, but without going beyond that populism to find the anger and radicalism more apparent in Steinbeck's novel. Indeed, to some critics the movie robs the Joads' story of precisely that *social* awareness, especially at the end. It is hardly surprising that a Hollywood film of this period failed to use the novel's final scene in which Rose of Sharon, having lost her child, suckles a starving man, but Tom's departure and Ma's soliloquy give us the novel's humanity without its disturbing edge. Ford's film *is* a powerful experience, but apolitical and individualistic in its affirmation of human fortitude in the face of desperate adversity.

In visual style *The Grapes of Wrath* illustrates Ford's increasing confidence in his conception of how a film should look, here splendidly served by Gregg Toland's cinematography. Filled with striking compositions, the film only rarely seems studied in its photographic effects, something that could not be said of Ford's second film of that year. *The Long Voyage Home* (1940) proved his most stylized venture since *The Informer*, and was once more born of a collaboration with Dudley Nichols. Based on four of Eugene O'Neill's one-act plays, it centers on the adventures and travail of a group of seamen on a merchant ship. Again shot by Toland (but this time without the restraint of *The Grapes of Wrath*) it is a film of overwrought camerawork and almost expressionistic lighting. Much praised in some circles, it demonstrates the self-conscious artiness of which Ford was sometimes capable.

Ford was to make only two more films in Hollywood before war service took him away. Neither showed him at his best, although *How Green Was My Valley* (1941) proved the most honored of his films: Oscars for best picture, direction, supporting actor, photography, and art direction. A somewhat sentimental view of life in a disintegrating Welsh mining community, it was a "big production" that never approaches the power of *The Grapes of Wrath*, though it does serve to underline Ford's populist inclinations, and his unquestioning commitment to the family. That task completed, he was appointed chief of the Field Photographic Branch of the OSS with the naval rank of lieutenant commander (later rear admiral). There he made a series of war documentaries—most notably *The Battle of Midway* (1942), which he both shot and directed and which received an Academy Award. In 1944—and by all accounts reluctantly, in that the war continued—Ford returned to Hollywood to make a "propaganda film." In the event, *They Were Expendable* (1945) proved a more impressive effort than the "propaganda" label might suggest, though whether this story of the development and use of the PT Boat reaches the heights some have claimed remains a matter for debate.

No such reservations apply to Ford's first postwar film. *My Darling Clementine* (1946) is probably the most perfectly realized of his classic Westerns, holding in balance the thematic tensions that eventually overcame the apparently simple optimism of his Western vision. Wyatt Earp, played with a kind of elegant gaucheness by Henry Fonda, visits Tombstone as a relatively civilized resting place along the route of a cattle drive. The town is "wide open," and, in a splendidly skilled sequence, Earp deals with a drunken Indian who is terrorizing the town's ineffectual "respectable" population. Asked to stay on to bring law and order to the town, he refuses, only complying when the villainous Clantons murder his younger brother. On this situation Ford constructs a film of remarkable richness, exploring the tension between wilderness and civilization seen by so many critics as central to the Western and to Ford.

The difference between *My Darling Clementine* and later Ford Westerns (most notably *The Searchers* and *The Man Who Shot Liberty Valance*) is that in the earlier work the values deriving from both wilderness *and* civilization are sustained without apparent contradiction. To be sure, it is only the strengths brought from the wilderness that can defend the community from the threat of disorder and collapse—only Earp, unshaven and bedraggled from long weeks on the trail, can tame the "wild" Indian and clean up the town. But the community itself, in the person of Clementine the schoolteacher (Cathy Downs) and through its communal rituals, also "tames" Earp. Or nearly: as the thematic opposition requires, Earp rides on at the end of the film with the half-promise that someday he will return to Clementine.

Between this arrival and departure the film centers on two crucial relationships: one with the gunfighter Doc Holliday (Victor Mature), and the other with the community itself. Both are framed in terms of the central dichotomy, serving to give human substance to what might otherwise appear a didactic distinction. With Holliday, Earp's relationship is one of mixed respect and disapproval. Very much a product of Eastern values and institutions, the tubercular drunkard Holliday is seen as an attractively raffish figure who has betrayed Clementine's trust, who fails to defend his Mexican mistress Chihuahua, and who has not taken the town in hand in the way that Earp believes both responsible and necessary. Redeemed by his support of the Earps in the final showdown at the OK Corral, he nevertheless stands for the failure of Eastern "sophisticated" values, illustrating the necessity for a social order founded in the simple truths of Earp's Westerner. If that were all, of course, then it would be familiar enough: an expression of the conservative code of the strong man of integrity, the man who "must do what a man must do." What distinguishes Ford's version of this familiar Western theme is the emotional force with which the community itself takes on a positive role.

The heart of this aspect of the film is to be found in the justly famous Sunday morning sequence in which the town celebrates the founding of its new church. As the Stars and Stripes flutters above, Clementine and the shy and pomaded Earp join in a gloriously touching dance—both funny and exhilarating—on the unroofed new building's floor. It is one of Ford's most exquisite moments, and it nicely focuses the achievement of *My Darling Clementine* in holding a balance between a conservative commitment to order and a populist affirmation of community spirit. ("The dance," as Robin Wood writes in Richard Roud's *Cinema: A Critical Dictionary,* "is a central emblem in . . . [Ford's] work, the ritual expression of established community.")

This is not to say that the film is flawless. Clementine herself, like so many Ford heroines, is weakly drawn and individually uninteresting—a convenient aspiration for Earp, but little more than that. Victor Mature never seems entirely certain where to pitch his performance, Linda Darnell's Chihuahua leans more on racial stereotype than characterization, and Alan Mowbray's wandering Shakespearian actor is one of the broadest of many such caricatures to be found in Ford's cinema. Nevertheless, the film stands among Ford's most rewarding Westerns, and the world it so clearly defines is central to his later achievements. Critics of the time were inclined to dismiss such films as *My Darling Clementine* as "just another Western." As

Ford's own most famous comment might suggest—"my name's John Ford, I make Westerns"—it is the Westerns that are his most lasting achievement.

The film that followed *My Darling Clementine,* however, was not a Western, but a "serious" project that illustrated precisely where Ford's real talents did *not* lie. *The Fugitive* (1947), his last collaboration with Dudley Nichols, was adapted from Graham Greene's *The Power and the Glory,* and tended toward the studied pictorial splendor that also characterized *The Informer* and *The Long Voyage Home.* Ford told Bogdanovich that "it came out the way I wanted it to—that's why it's one of my favorite pictures," a judgment that seems to be based on "a lot of damn good photography—with those black and white shadows." The photographic and compositional effects are certainly striking, but serve no apparent purpose other than their own beauty or a heavily over-emphasized symbolism. In retrospect it seems extraordinary that Ford should feel that the Greene novel was a suitable subject for him (or, indeed, for Henry Fonda) and, in the event, the film loses most of what makes the novel so striking. It is perhaps Ford's most disappointing film, and there are those who have speculated that his new-found "freedom" as an independent producer (with Merian C. Cooper) momentarily cost him his customary sense of self-discipline.

Before the end of the decade, however, Ford was to make two more outstanding Westerns: *Fort Apache* (1948) and *She Wore a Yellow Ribbon* (1949), both scripted by Frank S. Nugent, who succeeded Nichols as Ford's most frequent collaborator, and made for his new production company Argosy Pictures. Together with *Rio Grande* (1950), they are sometimes thought of as Ford's cavalry trilogy; all are based on short stories by James Warner Bellah. John Wayne plays a very similar central character in all three, and in two (*Fort Apache* and *Rio Grande*) he appears first as Captain and then as Colonel Kirby York. Thematically, all three explore the obligations that a particular sort of community places on its members, and the responsibilities that such a community bears. Here, of course, the community in question is the isolated cavalry unit, and, precisely because it is so isolated, the structuring significance of the contrast between wilderness and civilization is particularly clear. The forts, and the homesteads the cavalry are called upon to protect, are bastions against the encroaching wilderness, outposts of civilized values in an antagonistic world.

As ever, Ford does not give his unqualified support to "civilization." Like Holliday in *My Darling Clementine,* Henry Fonda's martinet colonel in *Fort Apache* comes from the East. By conventional standards he is "civilized," yet he causes many unnecessary deaths because he is convinced of the superiority of his academic military knowledge over York's hard-won practical experience of fighting Indians. Ford's sympathies clearly lie with York and with the community, and finally with the greater good of the cavalry. At the end of the film we learn that Colonel Thursday has been enshrined as a hero, and York, now in command, promulgates the myth in order to sustain the public image of the military. Thus, although the film values York's individualism and his willingness to stand up to Thursday, it is an individualism that is tempered by sacrifice to the greater cause. As the troops ride out to battle, the women watch them go. "I can't see them any more," observes one, "all I can see is the flags." The whole is greater than the sum of the parts; the flags symbolically more potent than the men beneath them.

Unsurprisingly, then, most of the emotional weight of *Fort Apache* is carried in the cavalry rituals, expressed to perfection in the film's most famous sequence, the non-commissioned officers' ball. As the dancers form and reform in the repeated patterns of the Grand March, we are irresistibly drawn into the spirit of the military community. Although it is possible to see the end of the film as an ironic reflection on military values, such an interpretation runs so counter to the rest of the movie as to be virtually unsustainable. As more than one critic has observed, *Fort Apache* is an idealization of an organic community, a surrogate family within which individuals have their proper place. The significance of the movie's ending lies not in York's lie, but in the reason for that lie. The film closes with York's eulogy for the cavalry—the end that, for Ford at least, justifies the means.

This commitment to the ideal of the military community is also to be found in *She Wore a Yellow Ribbon* and *Rio Grande,* though more significantly in the former. While *Rio Grande* is acceptable enough, it has neither the polish nor the depth of *She Wore a Yellow Ribbon.* Shot in carefully stylized color designed to imitate the textures of Remington pictures, the latter is an often gentle story of an aging cavalry captain's last days before retirement, exciting, romantic, touching, and funny by turns. Distinguished by good performances from Wayne (as Captain Brittles) and McLaglen (as his broadly comic Irish sergeant), *She Wore a Yellow Ribbon* elaborates further upon the world of *Fort Apache.* Retirement for Brittles means the loss of what amounts to his family, and consistent with the film's sentiment (or, as some might have it, sentimentality) he is finally returned to it as chief of scouts.

The cavalry trilogy was not well received. Ford's persistence in making Westerns ran counter to the mandarin critical standards of the time, which systematically undervalued all popular genres. Recent criticism has proved less short-sighted, and *Fort Apache* and *She Wore a Yellow Ribbon* have been allowed their proper place in the Ford canon. Retrospect also allows us to see in *Fort Apache*, particularly, the developing tensions of Ford's Western vision—tensions that will come to the fore in *The Searchers*. In *Fort Apache* the actions of Wayne's individualist are unproblematic because they finally serve the cause of the military community. But what if they did not? The whole edifice of Ford's genre world is built upon a positive evaluation of both individual and community, wilderness and civilization, and their relation—in Ford's more optimistic period—is one of potential symbiosis. There are obvious difficulties inherent in such an ethical balancing act, and their first stirrings are apparent in the cavalry trilogy.

A number of films intervened before *The Searchers*, however, many of them much lighter in mood and weight. The most notable were *Wagonmaster* (1950), a gentle and humorous Western set in a Mormon wagon train; *The Sun Shines Bright* (1953), an affectionate portrait of a Kentucky town at the beginning of the century, partly based on Ford's earlier *Judge Priest* (1934); and *The Long Gray Line* (1955), a celebration of West Point that reaches (and barely survives) extraordinary heights of sentimentality. The virtues of these films—humor, affection, and a disarming willingness straightforwardly to express sentiment—were combined in the film that brought Ford yet another Oscar: *The Quiet Man* (1952). He had wanted to film Maurice Walsh's story for some time, and, unusually in Ford's cinema, the result was a touching and richly entertaining love story. Set in a green and magically pleasant Ireland—an Ireland as much of the imagination as Ford's West—*The Quiet Man* charts the tempestuous romance between John Wayne and Maureen O'Hara, the one an Irish-American boxer coming home, the other a splendidly fiery country girl.

For all its pleasures, however, *The Quiet Man* has not worn as well as some other of Ford's successes. Rightly much admired for the joy with which its central romance is developed, and for its careful color photography, it also serves to underline how few were the occasions on which Ford successfully focused upon a female character. His younger women, especially, are all too often like the insipid Clementine, or the stereotypical juvenile leads of *Fort Apache* and *She Wore a Yellow Ribbon*. In this gallery Maureen O'Hara's Mary Kate stands out, for, although she recognizably derives from the mythology of the "Irish colleen," she is at least allowed some autonomy and some development before she is "mastered" in a public spanking deeply offensive to modern sensibilities.

The Quiet Man was Ford's major success of the early 1950s. In 1956, however, he returned to the Western with *The Searchers*, a film now widely accepted as among his finest. It was not so recognized at the time, however, and even Lindsay Anderson (one of Ford's leading champions of the postwar years) saw in it a decline. It is instructive to see how *The Searchers* came to be reevaluated. For traditional criticism it presented no problem. As a Western it clearly could not involve the seriousness of purpose or stylistic sophistication of *The Informer* or *The Grapes of Wrath*, and could therefore be dismissed to the limbo of "mere entertainment." For those few, like Lindsay Anderson, who had appreciated Ford more generally, its failings seem to center on a loss of the "organic" quality that they considered typical of Ford, "the 'natural' which characterises Ford at his best." And for those critics who regard the film as Ford's masterpiece, the key is to be found in *The Searchers'* capacity to transcend the thematic limits of Ford's earlier work. How, then, are such divergent views to be reconciled?

It is first necessary to recognize that these views are *readings,* and, as such, they are highly dependent on the critic's perspective. For the traditionalist, committed to film-as-art in its most orthodox form, Ford hardly *ever* lived up to the appropriate criteria. For Anderson, however, Ford's work of the 1930s and 1940s marked one of the cinema's finest achievements, a commitment that perhaps leads him to interpret *change* as *decline*. To the later generation of critics Ford's work was available as a whole, and their perspective upon it was formed by a retrospective analysis. From that point of view *The Searchers* becomes a watershed movie, bringing to the fore tensions and themes apparent in the earlier work and preparing the way for change in the films that follow. To some degree, then, such views are irreconcilable; they are simply not looking at the same Ford. They can be compared, however, in terms of the empirical force and persuasiveness of their analysis, and on these grounds the more recent approach does seem more effective in expanding our understanding of a large and complex body of work.

The Searchers takes the thematic tensions of

My Darling Clementine and *Fort Apache* and welds them into a sad and beautiful film of some perception. Ethan Edwards, splendidly played by Wayne, is an embittered and isolated development of the familiar Wayne-Ford hero. At the beginning of the film he emerges from the wilderness, having been unseen by family and friends since the end of the Civil War. Our first view of him sets the mood. A door opens in blackness and sunshine floods in from the desert outside. A woman moves into shot and out through the door, taking us with her. She shades her eyes to look at a distant figure on horseback, the landscape behind him dominated by the great mesas of Monument Valley. It is Ethan, travel-worn, returning to his brother's house and family. Yet he is drawn only briefly into the calm and shelter of the family. For, as it emerges, there is Indian trouble, and while Ethan joins the Rangers in pursuit, the Indians attack the homestead. The Edwards adults and son are killed; the two daughters carried off.

This begins the search that occupies the rest of the film—a search for the surviving younger sister who grows up with the Comanches. Ethan, in company with the Edwards' adopted son (himself part Indian), pursues the hunt obsessively, determined to kill Debbie should she have become Indian. At the last minute he does not do so, and the film ends, as it began, with the wanderers' return. As Debbie's new family move toward us into the blackness, we are left looking through the sunlit door at Ethan. He turns and walks away, merging once more into the wilderness that is the only world open to him.

This bald description cannot begin to convey the riches and pleasures of *The Searchers*. It is visually magnificent, and not simply because of its pictorial splendor. The settings, the compositions, the color and the lighting constantly feed our sense of Ethan's state of mind. Characters emerge for us from the minutiae of their behaviour (though there are some caricatured exceptions), and, for an audience schooled in the Western, there is a constant awareness of depth and resonance. For *The Searchers* is more than simply a touching story. In its treatment of its central character it gives us *the* Western hero trapped forever in a world of his making, but a world to which he can no longer belong. It is this sustained reflection upon the major themes of the genre that finally raises *The Searchers* beyond Ford's other work, giving it the status of tragedy. When Ethan turns away at the end it is a profoundly moving moment. McBride and Wilmington, who believe this to be Ford's indubitable masterpiece, put it this way in their monograph on Ford: "[Ethan] . . . steps aside to

let the young couple pass him by and turns away to 'wander forever between the winds' like his Indian nemesis. Scar and Ethan, blood-brothers in their commitment to primitive justice, have sacrificed themselves to make civilisation possible. This is the meaning of the door opening and closing on the wilderness. It is the story of America."

If, on balance, critical opinion is inclining toward this positive evaluation of *The Searchers*, it must also be said that Ford did not follow it up with work of sustained quality. Of the twelve movies that he was to make over the next decade (including a brief episode for *How the West Was Won* [1962]), only one approaches the achievement of *The Searchers*. The rest are generally agreed to be of uneven quality as well as variable subject matter, ranging from Westerns (*The Horse Soldiers, Two Rode Together, Cheyenne Autumn*) through a biography of the pilot Spig Wead (*The Wings of Eagles*), a sentimental story of a Boston politician's last campaign (*The Last Hurrah*), and a historical drama about a black sergeant wrongly accused of rape (*Sergeant Rutledge*). It was only with *The Man Who Shot Liberty Valance* (1962) that Ford successfully returned to the ethically complex world of *The Searchers*.

That said, it must also be conceded that in some respects *Liberty Valance* is far from typical Ford. There are no grand landscapes (indeed, there are precious few exteriors) and the film's visual style makes it almost claustrophobic. It is frequently observed that Ford was ill at the time of shooting *Liberty Valance* and thus unable to work on location. While there is no doubt that he was ill, it is difficult to see how this particular story could have benefited from location work; as a narrative it is necessarily set in the town of Shinbone, and its thematic concerns are eminently suited to the "closed in" world suggested by Ford's careful framing and camerawork. Although lacking the tragic scale of *The Searchers*, it is a deeply sad movie, and there are critics who believe *Liberty Valance* to be at least the equal of Ford's finest.

As with *The Searchers*, the basis for this evaluation is to be found in Ford's apparently changing vision. *Liberty Valance* stands as his final word on the recurrent tensions between wilderness and civilization, individual and community. Not for the first time in Ford, but for the first time with such absolute consistency and clarity, these oppositions are captured in the casting of the movie's two central characters. Doniphon (John Wayne) and Stoddart (James Stewart) embody both the virtues and failings of, respectively, the individualist at home in the wilderness and the bringer of "civilized" legal order to the community. The fundamental narrative device has Stoddart, who is opposed to the rule of law by violence, forced into a situation in which he must face the notorious gunman Liberty Valance. He is victorious, and his success brings him fame and power as "the man who shot Liberty Valance." The truth, however, is otherwise. Doniphon, knowing Stoddart has no chance and impelled by his own standards of integrity, shoots Valance from the shadows, leaving Stoddart to take the credit and the girl whom Doniphon loves. Once more the traditional Man of the West has been sacrificed in the cause of civilization.

This story, already laden with saddening echoes of previous Westerns, is made all but unbearably poignant by its framing as a final revelation by the aging Senator Stoddart on the occasion of Doniphon's death. He tells the story to the editor of the Shinbone *Star* in explanation of his unannounced arrival at the funeral of an unknown pauper, fully recognizing the political price he might have to pay. But in one of the most famous lines in a Ford movie, the editor (Edmond O'Brien) declines to print: "This is the West, sir. When the legend conflicts with the facts, print the legend." The matter is not left there, however, which would have taken us no further than, say, the end of *Fort Apache*. Instead, in an exquisitely shot scene, we are returned to Doniphon's coffin where Hallie (one of Ford's stronger female characters, played by Vera Miles) is waiting, and, only as Stoddart turns for a last look, do we see that she has planted a cactus rose on the otherwise bare box. Both flower of the Garden and enduring survivor of the Wilderness, the cactus rose (which we have earlier seen as a gift from Doniphon to Hallie) becomes the perfect symbol for the film.

The train takes them away from Shinbone through lushly fruitful country. "Aren't you proud?" Hallie asks. "Once it was a desert and now it's a garden." Stoddart talks of retirement until, on the arrival of the train's conductor to attend his famous passenger, he reverts to the politician's front that has served him so well. The conductor's response to his thanks is sudden and sobering: "Don't you worry about that, Senator. Nothing's too good for the man who shot Liberty Valance." With that ironic line, and our final sight of Stoddart and Hallie lost in their regrets, we reach the last stop in Ford's journey through the West. The captivating optimism of *Drums Along the Mohawk* and *My Darling Clementine* has been replaced by the irony and sadness of *The Searchers* and *The Man Who Shot Liberty Valance*. Yet all is not regret, and Ford has shown us the benefits of civilization as well as its

price. He was never a filmmaker given to simple didacticism, and both these great achievements of his last years have a density of reference and a control of style that make them for many his richest reflections upon and within the Western genre.

Though he lived for a decade after *Liberty Valance*, illness effectively ended Ford's career in 1966. A strange end, too, in that *Seven Women* (1966) is hardly an obvious choice as a Ford subject. At root a melodramatic story of a group of mostly female missionaries in China in the 1930s, it is interesting in the context of Ford's *oeuvre* though hardly a memorable achievement. Recent reevaluators of Ford's work have seen in *Seven Women* qualities that have escaped earlier criticism, and Robin Wood suggests that the film represents "the disintegration of everything he [Ford] had believed in." While it is clear that *Seven Women* is consistent with the increasing disillusion found in Ford's late cinema, the fact of that consistency does not make it the summation that some have claimed. That honor surely falls to *Liberty Valance*.

Jack Ford died in 1973, his last years haunted by illness and by a series of projects that never got off the ground. He had made some one hundred and twenty films, not counting television work. He was survived by his wife, the former Mary Smith, whom he had married in 1920, and by their son and daughter. Ford disliked the Hollywood social scene, preferring the company of his family and a few old friends who were ordered to his house once a week to play cards.

According to one of his cronies, Ford was "a great shambles of a man" who on the set wore "mangy old khaki pants, tennis shoes with holes at the toes, a sloppy old campaign jacket, a beat-up fedora and a dirty scarf around the neck." His sight was always poor and he eventually became blind in one eye, appearing thereafter in a piratical black patch. He liked to work with a cup of brandy in his hand and a cigar in his mouth. The "Old Man" ran his set much as he did his home, surrounding himself with a "stock company" of favored technicians and actors whom he ruled with an imperious hand.

"Sheer longevity made Ford a major director," wrote David Thomson in his *Biographical Dictionary of the Cinema*; he was "bigoted, grandiloquent and maudlin," and "celebrated the tyrannical hero without any great qualification or demur." This view of Ford must be recorded, but is of course remote from the one commonly accepted. That is closer to the opinion expressed by Robin Wood—that Ford is "among the greatest artists the cinema has yet produced." Orson Welles, asked which American directors he most admired, replied "the old masters. . . . By which I mean John Ford, John Ford, and John Ford."

Ford himself resolutely avoided any such claim. "As a kid," he told Peter Bogdanovich, "I thought I was going to be an artist; I used to sketch and paint a great deal and I think, for a kid, I did pretty good work—at least I received a lot of compliments about it. But I have never thought about what I was doing in terms of art, or 'this is great,' or 'world-shaking,' or anything like that. To me, it was always a job of work—which I enjoyed immensely—and that's it."

—A.T.

FILMS: *as Jack Ford*—The Tornado, 1917; The Scrapper, 1917; The Soul Herder, 1917; Cheyenne's Pal, 1917; Straight Shooting, 1917; The Secret Man, 1917; A Marked Man, 1917; Bucking Broadway, 1917; The Phantom Riders, 1918; Wild Women, 1918; Thieves' Gold, 1918; The Scarlet Drop, 1918; Hell Bent, 1918; A Woman's Fool, 1918; Three Mounted Men, 1918; Roped, 1919; The Fighting Brothers, 1919; A Fight for Love, 1919; By Indian Post, 1919; The Rustlers, 1919; Bare Fists, 1919; Gun Law, 1919; The Gun Packer, 1919; Riders of Vengeance, 1919; The Last Outlaw, 1919; The Outcasts of Poker Flat, 1919; The Ace of the Saddle, 1919; The Rider of the Law, 1919; A Gun Fightin' Gentleman, 1919; Marked Men, 1919; The Prince of Avenue A, 1920; The Girl in No. 29, 1920; Hitchin' Posts, 1920; Just Pals, 1920; The Big Punch, 1921; The Freeze-Out, 1921; The Wallop, 1921; Desperate Trails, 1921; Action, 1921; Sure Fire, 1921; Jackie, 1921; Little Miss Smiles, 1922; (with Edwin Carewe) Silver Wings, 1922; The Village Blacksmith, 1922; The Face on the Barroom Floor, 1923; Three Jumps Ahead, 1923. *as John Ford*—Cameo Kirby, 1923; North of Hudson Bay, 1923; Hoodman Blind, 1923; The Iron Horse, 1924; Hearts of Oak, 1924; Lightnin', 1925; Kentucky Pride, 1925; The Fighting Heart, 1925; Thank You, 1925; The Shamrock Handicap, 1926; Three Bad Men, 1926; The Blue Eagle, 1926; Upstream, 1927; Mother Machree, 1928; Four Sons, 1928; Hangman's House, 1928; Napoleon's Barber, 1928; Riley the Cop, 1928; Strong Boy, 1929; (with Lumsden Hare) The Black Watch, 1929; Salute, 1929; (with Andrew Bennison) Men Without Women, 1930; (with Andrew Bennison) Born Reckless, 1930; (with William Collier) Up the River, 1930; Seas Beneath, 1931; The Brat, 1931; Arrowsmith, 1931; Air Mail, 1932; Flesh, 1932; (with William Collier) Pilgrimage, 1933; Dr. Bull, 1933; The Lost Patrol, 1934; The World Moves On, 1934; Judge Priest, 1934; The Whole Town's Talking (U.K., Passport to Fame), 1935; The Informer, 1935; Steamboat Round the Bend, 1935; The Prisoner of Shark Island, 1936; Mary of Scotland, 1936; The Plough and the Stars, 1936; Wee Willie Winkie, 1937; The Hurricane, 1937; Four Men and a Prayer, 1938; Submarine Patrol, 1938; Stagecoach, 1939; Young Mr. Lincoln, 1939; Drums Along the Mohawk, 1939; The Grapes of Wrath, 1940; The Long Voyage Home, 1940; Tobacco Road, 1941; Sex Hygiene, 1941 (documentary); How Green Was My Valley, 1941; The Battle of Midway, 1942 (documentary); Torpedo Squadron, 1942 (documentary); December 7th, 1943 (documentary); We Sail at Midnight, 1943 (documentary); They Were Expendable, 1945; My Darling Clementine, 1946; The Fugitive, 1947; Fort Apache, 1948; Three Godfathers, 1948; She Wore a Yellow Ribbon, 1949; When Willie Comes Marching Home, 1950; Wagonmaster, 1950; Rio Grande, 1950; This Is Korea, 1951 (documentary); What Price Glory, 1952; The Quiet Man, 1952; The Sun Shines Bright, 1953; Mogambo, 1953; The Long Gray Line, 1955; (with Mervyn Le Roy) Mister Roberts, 1955; The Searchers, 1956; The Wings of Eagles, 1957; The Rising of the Moon, 1957; The Last Hurrah, 1958; Gideon's Day (U.K., Gideon of Scotland Yard), 1959; Korea, 1959 (documentary); The Horse Soldiers, 1959; Sergeant Rutledge, 1960; Two Rode Together, 1961; The Man Who Shot Liberty Valance, 1962; How the West Was Won (Civil War episode), 1962; Donovan's Reef, 1963; Cheyenne Autumn, 1964; Seven Women, 1966. *Published scripts*—The Informer *in* Modern British Dramas, edited by Harlan Hatcher, New York, 1941 (*also in* Theatre Arts August 1951); The Grapes of Wrath, How Green Was My Valley, Stagecoach *in* Twenty Best Film Plays, edited by John Gassner and Dudley Nichols, Crown, 1943; Stagecoach, Lorrimer, 1971.

ABOUT: Anderson, L. About John Ford, 1981; Baxter, J. The Cinema of John Ford, 1971; Beylie, C. John Ford, 1975 (in French); Bogdanovich, P. John Ford, 1968, rev. ed. 1978; Gallagher, Tag John Ford, 1986; Haudiquet, P. John Ford, 1966 (in French); McBride, J. and Wilmington, M. John Ford, 1974; Mitry, J. John Ford, 1954 (in French); Place, J. A. The Western Films of John Ford, 1974; Roud, R. (ed.) The Cinema: A Critical Dictionary, 1980; Sarris, A. The John Ford Movie Mystery, 1976; Sinclair, A. John Ford, 1979; Thomson, D. A Biographical Dictionary of the Cinema, 1980; Wollen, P. Signs and Meanings in the Cinema, 1969. *Periodicals*—Cahiers du Cinéma July 1965, August–September 1970; Cinema (USA) Spring 1971; Film Comment Fall 1970, Spring 1971; Film Culture Summer 1962; Film Quarterly Winter 1963–1964; Films and Filming June 1962; Focus on Film Spring 1971; Image et Son February 1961; New Left Review January–February 1965; New York Times September 1, 1973; Positif 64–65 1964; Screen Autumn 1972; Sequence Winter 1947, Summer 1950, Autumn 1950, New Year 1951; Sight and Sound Summer 1956.

GALEEN, HENRYK or **HEINRICH** (1882–1949), director, scenarist, and actor, worked for most of his life in Germany but was probably born in Holland, though some sources give Denmark and others Czechoslovakia. Extraordinarily little precise information is available. According to Georges Sadoul, Galeen began as a journalist, then served as secretary to the novelist and scenarist Hanns Heinz Ewers. Another source places him in 1906 as an assistant to Max Reinhardt at the Deutsches Theater in Berlin

HENRYK GALEEN

and says that he later acted in Swiss, British, and French theatres.

By about 1910, Galeen was securing his first film roles, and in 1913 he served as assistant director of Stellan Rye's *Der Student von Prag* (*The Student of Prague*), written by Hanns Heinz Ewers and starring Paul Wegener. Two years later Galeen scripted *Der Golem* (*The Golem*), which he codirected with Wegener. In medieval Jewish legend, the Golem was a creature of superhuman strength—a great clay statue brought to life by Rabbi Loew, a cabalist, to defend the people of the Prague ghetto against persecution and eviction by the Emperor. Galeen's script extends the story into the present, imagining the Golem resurrected by an antique dealer. It falls in love with its new master's daughter and, rejected, becomes an all-destroying monster. Wegener himself played the Golem. The photography was by Guido Seeber, the best cameraman of his day, and the film was distinguished by its imaginative visual effects.

In 1915 Galeen scripted and acted in Stellan Rye's *Peter Schlemihl*, based on a *doppelgänger* story by Adalbert von Chamisso in which a young man sells his shadow. His first film as solo director was *Der verbotene Weg* (*The Forbidden Road*, 1920), subtitled "a drama with a happy ending," and another, *Judith Trachtenberg*, followed the same year. It was in 1920 also that Galeen scripted Wegener's second Golem movie, *Der Golem: Wie in der Welt kam*, which returns to the creation of the Golem and Rabbi Loew's victorious struggle against the Emperor's troops.

Many critics (but not some purists) describe this second Golem movie as Expressionist. This movement, which sought to depict not external reality but interior feelings and impulses, had been a factor in German art, literature, and theatre since before World War I. It gathered strength after 1918, partly on account of the traumatic effects of the war, partly as a reaction against naturalism, and partly because of Freud's discoveries. Some of its elements can be traced to the mysticism of the German Romantic tradition, and the pessimism and morbidity of that tradition, its preoccupation with the power of fate. Robert Wiene's *Caligari* (1920) was the first truly Expressionist film, and some maintain that it was also the last, but its concerns and some of the stylistic devices it borrowed from the Expressionist theatre are echoed in many movies of the period, including all of Galeen's best-known pictures.

There are certainly strongly Expressionist elements in the subject (as well as the visual style) of F. W. Murnau's *Nosferatu* (1922), written by Galeen—the first and arguably the greatest of all the many adaptations of Bram Stoker's novel *Dracula*—and in Paul Leni's masterpiece *Das Wachsfigurencabinett* (*Waxworks*, 1924), also scripted by Galeen. However, little seems to be known about the two films directed by Galeen himself at this time, *Stadt in Sicht* (*Town in Sight*, 1923) and *Die Liebesbriefe der Baronin von S . . .* (*The Loveletters of Baroness von S . . .*, 1924).

Galeen's own masterpiece was his 1926 version of *The Student of Prague,* a remake of the 1913 film on which he had served as Stellan Rye's assistant director. Galeen wrote his own script in collaboration with the author of the original version, Hanns Heinz Ewers, who had borrowed from Adalbert von Chamisso, E.T.A. Hoffmann, and the Faust legend in devising a story very much in the German Romantic tradition. In Galeen's remake, Conrad Veidt plays the poor student Baldwin who makes a deal with the devil—or rather with his representative Scapinelli (Werner Krauss). Baldwin exchanges his mirror-image (conjured into life by Scapinelli) for the promise of wealth. He marries a rich countess but is disgraced by his *doppelgänger*, masquerading as himself. When in the end, desperate, he maneuvers his double back into the mirror and shoots him, it is Baldwin himself who dies.

Siegfried Kracauer wrote that this story "introduced to the screen a theme that was to become an obsession of the German cinema: a deep and fearful concern with the foundations of the self." Galeen gave rather more weight than Stel-

Ian Rye had done to the psychological aspects of the story, clarifying the implication that Baldwin's *doppelgänger* represents the darker side of his own personality. Paul Rotha wrote that Galeen (who made the film entirely in the studio) had combined Expressionism and naturalism in a film that "had open spaciousness and dark psychology, wild poetic beauty and a deeply dramatic theme. Beyond this, it had Conrad Veidt at his best; a performance that he has never equaled before or since." Rotha went on: "The conflict of inner realities; the sadness and joy of changing atmosphere; the storm emphasizing the anguish of Baldwin; the rendering of the depths of human sorrow and weakness; the imagination and purity of treatment; the intensely dramatic unfolding of the theme: all these entitled the film to rank as great. The interior design was admirable, lit with some of the most beautiful lighting I have observed." C. A. Lejeune called it "one of the richest stories ever told in the film of any country. Galeen's sense of a narrative is violent and uncanny—he sees legend in every stick and stone, drawing from nature and the supernatural alike to strengthen his theme."

Galeen's next film was adapted from Ewers' novel *Alraune,* a fantasy about a scientist (Paul Wegener) who experiments with artificial insemination. From the test-tube union between a prostitute and an executed murderer he produces an elegant and mesmeric beauty (Brigitte Helm) who destroys those who love her, including her hubristic creator. The movie was beautifully shot by Franz Planer and drew a brilliant performance from Brigitte Helm. Lionel Collier, who saw a censored and partially reshot version in England in 1928 (with John Loder as one of Alraune's hapless lovers), wrote that even in its mutilated form it was "a great and extremely interesting picture," with "the same fine technical grasp" and distinctive style that had characterized *The Student of Prague*: "There is a wonderful power of dramatic picturisation and a complete understanding of the theme he is handling. There is symbolism and subtlety of a high order and a wonderful sense of character delineation."

After *Sein grösster Bluff,* made in 1927 in collaboration with Harry Piel, Galeen went to Britain and directed a thriller called *After the Verdict* (1929), about a young aristocrat charged with murdering a woman who is infatuated with him. It was not a success, and Paul Rotha said that Galeen's ideas were totally misunderstood and unappreciated in Britain. He made one more film in Germany, *Salon Dora Green,* released in 1933, the year Hitler came to power. Galeen emigrated to the United States, where he

disappeared into the same kind of obscurity from which he had come. As scriptwriter and director, he has nevertheless been described as possibly the most important single influence on the development of film Expressionism in Germany.

FILMS: (with Paul Wegener) Der Golem (The Golem), 1915; Der verbotene Weg: Ein Drama mit glücklichem Ausgang, 1920; Judith Trachtenberg, 1920; Stadt in Sicht, 1923; Die Liebesbriefe der Baronin von S . . . , 1924; Der Student von Prag (The Student of Prague/The Man Who Cheated Life), 1926; Alraune (Unholy Love/A Daughter of Destiny/Mandragora), 1927; (with Harry Piel) Sein grösster Bluff, 1927; After the Verdict, 1929; Salon Dora Green/Die Falle, 1933.

ABOUT: Kracauer, S. From Caligari to Hitler, 1947; Oxford Companion to Film, 1976. *Periodicals*—Film Dope 1979.

*GANCE, ABEL (EUGÈNE ALEXANDRE) (October 25, 1889–November 10, 1981), French director and screenwriter, was born in the eighteenth arrondissement of Paris, on the edge of Montmartre. He was the illegitimate son of a prosperous doctor, Abel Flamant, and Françoise Péréthon (or Perthon), a working-class woman from the Bourbonnais then living with a mechanic named Adolphe Gance. The child was baptized under the name of Péréthon and only given the surname Gance three years later. His early years were spent in the industrial town of Commentry, home of his mother's parents, where his grandfather worked as a coal-hauler; at six he was sent to the École Libre de la Mine, a charitable foundation set up by a local mining company. In 1897 Françoise Péréthon and Adolphe Gance were married, and the next year they returned with Abel to Paris and moved into the basement of an apartment house in the fashionable sixteenth arrondissement. Gance's mother worked as concierge, while Adolphe Gance acted as chauffeur for those residents progressive enough to own cars.

In later life, Gance suppressed this working-class background entirely, substituting a comfortable bourgeois upbringing as the son of a respectable doctor and his wife. This account was universally accepted, and only after his death did the facts emerge, as a result of research by Roger Icart.

Soon after the return to Paris, Gance's natural father provided funds to send him to the Collège de Chantilly, a privately run boarding school some miles north of the city. Gance was unhappy there and relieved when, at twelve, he was transferred to the Collège Chaptal in Paris,

°gäns

ABEL GANCE

which he could attend as a day pupil. In September 1904 he left school, apparently without graduating, and was articled to a solicitor specializing in divorce cases. (This apprenticeship too was probably paid for by Dr. Flamant.) Lacking all aptitude for the law, Gance was bored and miserable. Whenever possible he escaped to the Bibliothèque Nationale, where he lost himself in the works of Shakespeare, Hugo, Rostand, and other romantic playwrights for whom he had acquired a taste at school. Dreaming of a career in the theatre, he applied in October 1906 to enter the Conservatoire, but failed by a narrow margin to qualify. The next year he applied again—and failed by a wide margin. Disappointed but undiscouraged, he persisted, eventually making his stage debut in a tiny role at the Théâtre du Gymnase. In July 1908 he was engaged for a season at the Théâtre du Parc in Brussels, at a salary of 300 francs a month.

Gance spent a year acting with the Belgian company, with great enjoyment if no outstanding aptitude. He also wrote his first film scenario, *Mireille*, which he sold to the actor-director Léonce Perret. Back in Paris, he continued to take bit parts in various productions while writing plays of his own. As early as 1906 he had completed a one-act melodrama, *La Fugitive;* now he embarked on what was planned as a grand Arthurian trilogy, and for a time adopted the stage name of d'Arthus. To supplement his income he occasionally acted in films (making his screen debut in another Perret movie, *Molière*) and wrote more scenarios. Most went to Gaumont for 40 to 50 francs each, but for *Un Clair de lune sous Richelieu* the Film d'Art com-

pany paid all of 150 francs. Over fifty years later Gance reworked this scenario into his last film, *Cyrano et d'Artagnan.*

At this stage in his career his attitude to the cinema was dismissive: "All I saw in the moving image at that time was a meal ticket." His ambitions centered on the live theatre, where he was influenced by such orotund models as Rostand and d'Annunzio. But though his taste in theatre was traditional, he frequented avant-garde artistic circles, where his friends included Apollinaire, Léger, Chagall, Blaise Cendrars, and Honegger.

Gance's health had never been robust, and in 1910 tuberculosis was diagnosed. Luckily he secured an acting engagement at the Casino de Vittel, and after a few months at the spa he was pronounced cured. On his return to Paris he sold several more scripts (one of which, *Le Crime du Grand-Père*, was filmed by Feuillade). Deciding to take the cinema rather more seriously, he and some friends scraped together 1,000 francs to set up a production company, grandly named Le Film Français. It made four films, all directed and scripted by Gance; none of them has survived. *La Digue* (*The Dike*, 1912), a tale of seventeenth-century Dutch heroism, starred Pierre Renoir, elder brother of the future director. *Le Nègre blanc* (*The White Negro*, 1912) was an antiracist parable, and *Il y a des pieds au plafond* (*There are Feet on the Ceiling*, 1912), a spoof *policier* too badly mauled by the laboratory to be worth releasing. Only *Le Masque d'horreur* (*The Mask of Horror*, 1912) enjoyed any degree of public success. This Grand Guignol starred the great tragedian Edouard de Max as a sculptor struggling to create a truly horrific mask and eventually poisoning himself in order to use his own dying contortions as model.

The modest returns on *Le Masque d'horreur* were insufficient to offset the other losses, and the company collapsed in a morass of litigation. Gance abandoned the cinema in disgust and went back to writing plays, among them a "tragedy-comedy-ballet," *La Fin du monde*, and a grandiose classical verse-drama, *La Victoire de Samothrace.* In November 1912 he married Mathilde Thizeau, a journalist who shared many of his interests. In 1914 he completed *La Victoire* and sent it, with a recommendation from de Max, to Sarah Bernhardt. She liked it and promised to have it staged. Three weeks later war was declared, and theatrical activity was curtailed until further notice.

Gance was called up but then rejected on account of his poor health. Since there was little demand for plays, he wrote a scenario, *Les Morts reviennent-ils?*, and sent it to Louis Nalpas, the new head of Film d'Art. Nalpas expressed interest but requested something "more conventional." Gance supplied *L'Infirmière;* Nalpas paid him 350 francs and assigned the direction to Henri Pouctal. Watching Pouctal at work, Gance was unimpressed and told Nalpas as much, adding that he himself could do better. Nalpas took him at his word, offering him 5,000 francs and five days to film a script of his choice. Gance rewrote *Les Morts* as *Un Drame au Château d'Acre* (Drama at the Château d'Acre, 1915), a triangular melodrama, and brought it in within schedule and budget. Nalpas, pleased, gave him carte blanche on his next picture.

He soon regretted it. Instead of another routine melodrama, Gance came up with *La Folie du Docteur Tube* (*The Madness of Dr. Tube*, 1915), a surreal black comedy about a mad scientist (Albert Dieudonné) who discovers how to change the appearance of people and things— an excuse for Gance and his cameraman, Léonce-Henry Burel, to make resourceful use of distorting lenses. The earliest Gance film to survive, it provides a diverting and intriguing link between the theatrical effects of Méliès and the 1920s experimental avant-garde of Jean Epstein, Duchamp, and Man Ray. "For the first time," observed Roger Icart, "the cinema was aiming, not to reproduce an external reality (however much rearranged), but . . . to create an abstract universe of its own." Nalpas, however, was not impressed. He refused to release the film, and Gance received strict instructions to stay within acceptable limits.

Reluctantly, he complied, turning out a string of what he termed "movies for concierges" —standard thrillers and melodramas, of two or three reels each, all to his own scripts. None of these early films are known to survive, but it seems that Gance was taking every opportunity to experiment, though less obtrusively than in *Docteur Tube.* Nalpas was evidently happy enough; in 1916 he allowed Gance to graduate to feature-length films.

Gance's first two features were *Les Gaz mortels* (The Deadly Gas, 1916) and *Barberousse* (*Red Beard*, 1916), filmed simultaneously on location at Cassis—not as a technical experiment, but simply because of Film d'Art's usual parsimony over time and cash. Gance wrote both scenarios on the train. "I had to work it out so that the two films could be shot at the same time. Now let's see: did I have four or three actors? Was this one already dead in the film? Could he go on playing in the other? I had great fun. . . . The actors used to play their parts very seriously, but I knew the spirit in which the script had been written!"

Today, it seems hard to credit that anyone involved with these films took them seriously for an instant. Kevin Brownlow described *Les Gaz mortels*—in which the heirs of a scientist making poison gas plot to kill him by sabotaging his factory—as "extremely well photographed . . . and professionally edited, but the performances are ludicrous, even by the circus-tent standards of 1916. . . . Basically, *Les Gaz mortels* is a cheap little thriller which most directors of the time could have handled with ease." The plot of *Barberousse* was even sillier: a newspaper proprietor leads a double life as a ruthless bandit, complete with eye patch and pantomime beard, in order to create sensational items for his newspaper. Gance used this farrago to try out various experimental techniques—split screen, horizontal wipes, tracking from a motor-bike, and several extreme close-ups from dramatic angles which caused Nalpas some alarm. The public, though, seemed happy to take such audacities in its stride.

DeMille's *The Cheat*, recently shown in Paris, had caused a great stir, and Gance persuaded Nalpas to let him explore greater psychological depths, subtler lighting and editing effects. *Le Droit à la vie* (*The Right to Life*, 1916) turns on a standard melodramatic situation, frequent in Gance's films. A young woman (Andrée Brabant) is loved by two men, one poor and honorable (Léon Mathot), the other rich and corrupt (Paul Vermoyel); she loves the former but is obliged to marry the latter to pay her dying mother's debts. Wounded by an embezzling assistant, the jealous financier accuses Mathot but recants in a heated trial scene. It emerges that the older man is terminally ill. Ennobled by suffering, he dies blessing the young lovers.

The acting here still involved much grimacing and eye-rolling; but Gance and Burel (cinematographer on virtually all Gance's silent films) achieved striking results by shooting key scenes against black velvet, to concentrate audience attention on the action. There is considerable use of close-ups throughout and, as Richard Abel says, "the moral and psychological condition of the central characters (but only the men) is emphasized through several subjective images." The film was prefaced by a close-up of Gance himself, indicative of his growing status as a director.

Le Droit à la vie did well, and Gance received an even more generous budget for his next picture, *Mater Dolorosa* (1917). The story of a neglected wife (Emmy Lynn) who lapses into adultery and is punished by separation from her son, it surpassed its predecessor both in sententiousness and box-office success. *Mater Dolorosa,*

Jean Mitry wrote, "Surprises, astonishes, by means of lighting effects, the knowing use of light and shadow to intensify dramatic scenes, the intimate fidelity of the decors, singling out particular details, and a thousand unusual qualities for a French film." In fact it was the most successful French film of the year, and Nalpas offered Gance the artistic directorship of Film d'Art. He accepted, not without misgivings. "Am I not going to divert what remains of my energies," he mused in his journal, "in trying to teach everyone a language which I barely know how to stammer myself? . . . Cinema, this alphabet for the eyes of those too tired to think."

All prints of *La Zone de la mort* (*The Death Zone*, 1917) seem to have perished. According to Georges Charansol, it "introduced to the cinema that element of the fantastic later so effectively exploited in Germany." The plot echoes *Le Droit à la vie:* a rich perfume manufacturer, living in an old Breton château, plans to marry his young ward. She, however, is in love with his nephew, an astronomer, and the young couple are helped by a local sorcerer. By means of a drug, the plutocrat induces his ward to marry him; but a celebratory firework display turns into a holocaust, destroying the château and ravaging the surrounding countryside. (This vision of a blasted and fear-stricken landscape may have been Gance's metaphor for World War I, Death Zone par excellence.) Originally, *La Zone de la mort* ran to 3,000 meters, twice the length of *Mater Dolorosa*. Film d'Art cut it by half—the first, but far from the last, of Gance's works to suffer such a fate. In *Le Film*, Louis Delluc hailed the picture with enthusiasm: "Thank you, Gance. Never stop 'overreaching yourself.'"

Gance's view of cinema was changing rapidly. Initially he had seen himself as a playwright dabbling in this limited, and fairly ludicrous, medium until the live theatre should return to peacetime normality. But now he was coming to realize the vast undeveloped potential that cinema offered, and to consider that here, rather than on the stage, might lie his true metier. Contemporary Hollywood output, especially that of Ince, Griffith, and DeMille, had come as a revelation of what might be achieved, given sufficient imagination and resources.

La Dixième Symphonie (*The Tenth Symphony*, 1917), Kramer and Welsh wrote, "struggles even more valiantly than *Mater Dolorosa* against the constraints of the melodramatic structure." (It could be argued that neither here nor at any time did Gance "struggle against the constraints" of melodrama, within which he always seemed reasonably comfortable, but rather adapted them to his own idiosyncratic use.) A widowed composer, Enric Damor (played by Séverin-Mars in the first of his three major roles for Gance), remarries; his new wife, Eve (Emmy Lynn), is being blackmailed by an unscrupulous ex-lover who now proposes to Damor's daughter. Eve objects, arousing Damor's suspicions that she is herself infatuated with the suitor, and his emotional turmoil and anguish act as catalyst to his inspiration. He composes a symphony which, since he identifies strongly with Beethoven, he declares to be the Tenth Symphony that his idol never lived to complete.

Few critics would go quite so far as Kevin Brownlow in seeing *La Dixième Symphonie* as a "remarkably sophisticated marital drama" with which Gance proved himself "a sensitive, brilliantly imaginative director . . . the equal of any . . . in the world." Nonetheless, the picture demonstrates his growing mastery of visual and structural composition, of rhythmic editing, and of narrative technique. Roy Armes observed that "there is a constant interest to be found in Gance's use of masking and the play of silhouettes and shadows to create mood and his evident awareness of the ability of faces, movement and lighting to convey emotion."

For all the crudeness of its plot, *La Dixième Symphonie* can be seen as the first recognizably Gancian film, prefiguring certain recurrent elements in his later output. Damor stands as forerunner of a whole series of heroic figures—Jean Diaz, Napoleon, Jean Novalic, Beethoven, Columbus—"to whom," as Marcel Martin put it (*Revue du Cinéma*, May 1983), "Destiny has assigned an exceptional task because their visionary insight penetrates beyond that of ordinary mortals." The film also marks the first appearances of Gance's notorious literary intertitles: florid quotes from his favorite authors interrupting and clogging the action in a way that even his warmest admirers found hard to justify. In spite of them, the film was hugely successful; made at a cost of 63,000 francs, it grossed 343,000.

Before shooting *La Dixième Symphonie* Gance had finally been drafted and assigned to the Cinematographic Corps. He was soon discharged, thanks to an appeal from Film d'Art, but his few weeks in the army had given him the idea for a great cinematic statement about the war. By now he had come within the orbit of the art historian Elie Faure, the first major theoretician of French cinema and center of a group that included Louis Delluc, Jean Epstein, Germaine Dulac, and Marcel l'Herbier. Influenced by Faure's theories and those of Riciotto Canudo, Gance now aspired to create "cathedrals of light," "visible symphonies" that would "create for the whole of humanity a unique memory, a kind of music of faith, of hope, of recollections." The cinema, he believed, could become a great force for peace and understanding, playing a mystical, near-sacramental role: "People should go to the movies as they go to Mass."

The first step towards this ideal was to be *J'accuse* (*I Accuse*), Part One of a projected trilogy inspired by Woodrow Wilson's plan for a League of Nations, of which the other parts would be *Les Cicatrices* (*The Scars*) and *La Société des Nations*. Almost at once, though, this was set aside for a yet more ambitious plan: an apocalyptic trilogy centered around the figure of a Christ-like philosopher named Jean Novalic. Gance had gained the support and financial backing of the doyen of French producers, Charles Pathé, through whose company Film d'Art released, and in April 1918 began shooting *Ecce Homo*, first of the Novalic trilogy. Dissatisfied with the results, he abandoned filming after a few days, and with Pathé's agreement started work instead on *J'accuse*.

J'accuse (1919) is generally considered, in Kevin Brownlow's words, as "the first major pacifist picture in the cinema's history." This may not originally have been quite the case. Surviving prints (themselves incomplete) derive from the re-edited version released in 1922 when the patriotic fervor of war had cooled. The much longer version released in March 1919 was described by Gance in his spoken prologue as "an 'objective' and triumphant cry against German militarism and its slaughter of civilised Europe," and the script contained an episode (which may not have been filmed) in which a sneering, monocled Prussian is confronted at a World Tribunal by the crippled victims of his Hunnish bloodlust.

The bulk of the film, though, is concerned less with the war than with another love triangle. A poet, Jean Diaz (Romauld Joubé), and a violent but tender huntsman, François Laurin (Séverin-Mars), both love Edith (Maryse Dauvray)—who is married to François but loves Jean. The two men are both inducted into the French army and meet in the trenches, where mutual hatred gradually turns to friendship. Meanwhile Edith has been raped by a German soldier (a scene recalled with power and restraint as a series of threatening shadows), and returns home with a child; François, believing it to be Jean's, is once more roused to violent jealousy. When he learns the truth, he returns to the front and dies in Jean's arms. Jean, frantic with grief, goes home and recounts his vision of the dead rising from the battlefield to march through the countryside. The villagers flee in panic; Jean writes one last ode ("J'accuse") and dies.

On its release *J'accuse* had a staggering impact. It seemed to speak directly to the grief-stricken, war-weary population of Europe. Exhibitors reported whole audiences in floods of tears, women fainting and being carried from the auditorium. Whatever Gance's initial intentions, the film was hailed everywhere as a passionate outburst against the futility of war. "If this film," a Prague reviewer wrote, "had been shown in every country and every town in the world in 1913, then perhaps there would have been no war." Attention focused in particular on the Return of the Dead, a virtuoso sequence much argued over ever since. Where Brownlow saw "an allegorical scene of unique and bizarre power," Jacques Brunius referred to "an intolerably bombastic war film distinguished chiefly for the cliché of making dead soldiers rise in superimposition from the battlefield and pull tragic faces at the camera." David Thomson judged the sequence "an instance of emotional self-inducement on Gance's part, as moving but as contradictory as the shots of crowds in *Triumph of the Will*. . . . There is a naive passion in the conception that has more to do with melodramatic pageant than with true disenchantment."

J'accuse was astonishingly profitable, eventually grossing over 3.5 million francs. With Pathé's help, Gance now set up his own production company, Films Abel Gance. Recognized as the foremost French director, he was acknowledged (in Norman King's words) "not just as innovator but as filmmaker who blurred the distinction between the 'artistic' and the 'popular,' supplying films that were both prestigious and profitable," and thus a person ideally equipped to lead French cinema out of its financial and cultural depression. Conscious of these expectations, Gance spent some time searching for a suitable next subject. *Ecce Homo* was once again considered, and in November 1919 he travelled to Sussex to see Rudyard Kipling, to some of whose works Pathé held film rights. Finally he settled on a novel *Le Rail*, by the proletarian writer Pierre Hamp, which—with the help of Blaise Cendrars—he adopted as *La Roue* (*The Wheel.*)

During the war Gance had fallen in love with Ida Danis, a secretary at Film d'Art, and in June 1918 left Mathilde for her. The great flu epidemic of the winter after the war had left Ida with an infection which, just as work started on *La Roue*, was diagnosed as terminal tuberculosis. According to Gance's own romantic account, he tailored the scenario to Ida's medical requirements, setting the first half in Nice because she needed sunshine, then adding the second half on Mont Blanc when Alpine air was prescribed. On the other hand, the Pathé studios were at Nice; and in a diary entry predating the diagnosis of Ida's illness, Gance discussed his concept of a "symphony in black" (the railyard) followed by a "symphony in white" (the mountains).

The originality of Gance's ideas, impressive in matters of technique, rarely extended to the construction of plots. *La Roue* hinges, yet again, on male rivalry over a woman. Sisif (Séverin-Mars), an engine-driver, adopts a baby saved from a train wreck. When this girl, Norma (Ivy Close), grows up, both Sisif and his violin-maker son Elie fall in love with her. To protect her from both of them, Sisif marries her off to his boss, De Hersan. Sisif is partially blinded in an accident; faced with losing his job, he contrives a crash, wrecking his beloved engine, but fails to kill himself and is relegated to running the funicular on Mont Blanc. When Norma and her husband visit the area on holiday, Elie quarrels with De Hersan, and in the fight both are killed. Norma tends the now blind Sisif until he dies peacefully while she joins in the peasant's spring dance in the show.

La Roue took over a year to shoot, almost entirely on location. Sisif's house was constructed in the very middle of the railyards outside Nice, giant locomotives thundering past a few feet from the camera. The mountain scenes were shot on Mont Blanc itself. The budget, some two-and-half million francs, was the highest of any French film to date. In its original version the picture ran something over ten hours.

On the day that initial cutting was completed, Ida Danis died. Soon afterwards Gance made an extended visit to the United States. While there, he learned of the death of Séverin-Mars. Gance stayed five months in New York, where he presented *J'accuse* to an audience that included D.W. Griffith and the Gish sisters. (Griffith, deeply moved by the film, arranged to have it distributed by United Artists.) Watching the latest Hollywood films, Gance was greatly impressed by the fluency and precision of their editing. On his return to Paris he completely re-cut *La Roue*, which was premiered (in three parts) in December 1922. The previous month he had married Marguerite Danis, Ida's sister.

La Roue, Georges Sadoul wrote, "came over as something of tremendous verve, bubbling over, with much style but not a great deal of taste—a volcano emitting flame indeed, but also its quota of lava and slag." Many other critics, then and since, have concurred. Bardèche and Brasillach described it as "one of the monstrosi-

ties of the cinema, but an extraordinarily important monstrosity. . . . It would have been laughed off the screen had not everything else been effaced by its technical mastery, and by a very genuine, even nobly poetic, quality which this technique served to express." "As in romantic drama," René Clair commented, "you will find . . . a lack of verisimilitude, a superficial psychology, a relentless search for visual as well as verbal effects, and you will find passages of an extraordinary lyricism, . . . an inspired flow of the sublime and the grotesque. . . . If only he would renounce literature and have confidence in cinema!"

Not all critical reaction was qualified. Jean Cocteau roundly declared, "There is cinema before and after *La Roue* just as there is painting before and after Picasso," a verdict later echoed by Kevin Brownlow, who stated that with *La Roue* "Gance hurtled the cinema from timorous infancy into full-blooded maturity." Other reviewers, irritated by the heavy symbolism and the overblown pretensions of the characterization, found little or nothing to admire. "Everything in this film," growled the critic of the *Courrier Cinématographique*, "is abnormal, sickly, morbid and unwholesome. Nothing in it is true or human, neither in the plot nor in the feelings of the protagonists."

The most revolutionary aspect of *La Roue* lay in its unprecedented use of rapid, rhythmic cutting, which was to prove widely influential. Two sequences attracted particular notice: the death of Elie, and Sisif's first attempt to crash his train. Gance achieved a crescendo of narrative hysteria by steadily decreasing the length of his shots to near-subliminal level: close-ups of hands, faces, levers, wheels, hurtling railway tracks are intricately intercut; some shots are no more than a single frame in length. (Roger Icart has shown, through detailed comparison between the shooting script and the final movie, that none of this was planned in the shooting but stems from Gance's post-USA re-editing.) These sequences were internationally admired; Eisenstein, Pudovkin, and Dovzhenko all studied them in detail, and Kurosawa named *La Roue* as the film which first aroused his enthusiasm for the cinema.

By way of total contrast, Gance's next film was a comedy short with Max Linder. Early in his acting career he had appeared in one or two Linder films as Max's brother, and the two men had renewed their acquaintance in New York. Now back in Paris after the expiration of his American contract, the comedian half-jokingly suggested that a Linder short would be beyond Gance's capabilities. Never one to duck a challenge, Gance shot *Au secours!* (*Help!*, 1923) in twelve days. The plot also featured a challenge: Max is wagered by the owner of a haunted château that he will be unable to stay there until midnight without calling for help. Sadly, the results confirm Linder's original instinct; there are some enjoyable sight gags, but most of the humor seems protracted and heavy-handed. It was Linder's last French film; ill and tired, he made only one more movie (in Austria) before his death, in 1925, in a suicide pact with his wife.

Release of *Au secours!* was delayed by a dispute with Linder's American distributors, and the film only appeared a year later. By then, Gance was deep in the complex logistics of setting up his most famous film. Initially, it seems, he embarked on the idea of a biopic of Napoleon with some detachment, regarding it merely as "a commercial trampoline which will let me achieve the freedom to work as I want." But as so often happened, he got caught up as the project developed in a surge of self-generated enthusiasm, and was soon talking in terms of six, or even eight, vast films to cover Napoleon's life, "the greatest drama of all time." The problems of raising funds for such a project, daunting in any case, were often exacerbated by Gance himself. To Giuseppe Barattolo of Unione Cinematografica Italiana, who had financed *Au secours!*, he wrote: "My instinct is never wrong, my artistic conscience too great just for you to make money and expand your reputation." Backing from UCI for *Napoléon* was not forthcoming.

Pathé was prepared to put up some of the money, but most of the financial support for the project came from Germany—giving rise to much hostile sniping from the French press. Vladimir Wengeroff, a White Russian businessman based in Berlin, and Hugo Stinnes, one of the leading German industrialists, formed the Westi Consortium to provide the bulk of the budget, which was set at seven million francs. Gance retained absolute artistic control.

The first film was due for completion by the end of 1924, but shooting only began in January 1925. This initial episode covered Bonaparte's boyhood and experiences during the Revolution, ending as he led his army over the Alps to Italy, scene of his first great military triumph; originally it also included the Italian campaign itself, but Gance was obliged to cut this from his script, shortening it by almost a third. Even so, it would be the most expensive film that had ever been made in France, or anywhere outside America.

As the adult Bonaparte, Gance cast Albert Dieudonné, an old friend who had played the title role in *La Folie du Docteur Tube*. Antonin

Artaud was Marat, and Gance himself played Saint-Just, theoretician of the Revolution. The sixteen-year-old Annabella made her screen debut as Violine, a young woman of the people who adores Napoleon from afar. Bonaparte as a boy was played by Wladimir Roudenko, one of the singularly large number of Russians involved, both as actors and crew. This was mainly because the Billancourt studios, where Gance shot his interiors, was owned by Cinéfrance, whose head, the Russian Noë Bloch, had staffed his company largely with his fellow exiles. Two of Gance's assistants on *Napoléon* were established Russian directors—Viacheslav Tourjansky and Alexander Volkoff.

All accounts of Gance as director—especially on *Napoléon*—stress the exceptional personal magnetism he exercised over those who worked with him, persuading them to tireless, uncomplaining effort. Before shooting the battle scenes for the siege of Toulon, he made an impassioned appeal to his extras—most of them not professional actors, but strikers from the nearby Renault works: "Thanks to you, we are going to relive the Revolution and the Empire—an unheard-of task. You must find in yourselves the fire, the frenzy, the power, the mastery and the abnegation of those soldiers of the Year II. . . . My friends, all the screens of the universe await you!" Emile Vuillermoz, film critic of *Le Temps*, who watched much of the shooting, felt that Gance established such influence over his extras "he could have made them storm the Palais-Bourbon or the Elysée and had himself proclaimed dictator."

Five months into shooting, disaster struck. Hugo Stinnes died suddenly, and the Westi Consortium was dissolved. The budget now stood at nine million francs, of which five million had been spent. Gance had to halt the production for several months until fresh sources of finance could be found. At last, yet another Russian émigré—Jacques Grinieff, director of the newly formed Société Générale des Films—persuaded his board to back at least the first of the projected six movies.

Shooting was finally completed in August 1926, after which Gance spent seven months editing the film, restlessly recutting and rearranging, and driving his collaborators—especially Honegger, who was providing the score—to distraction. A shortened version (some four hours long) prepared especially for the premiere was finished with only hours to spare.

Napoléon vu par Abel Gance (*Napoleon as Seen by Abel Gance*) was premiered at the Opéra on April 7, 1927, before a glittering audience that included most of the senior dignitaries of the Republic. Despite the occasional hitch—a few frames, spliced in at the last minute, appeared upside-down—the response was intensely enthusiastic. Several sequences, such as Bonaparte's dashing horseback escape, in best Fairbanks style, from his Corsican enemies, were greeted with cheers and shouts of excitement, and when the film ended Gance received a fifteen-minute standing ovation.

If the startling originality of *La roue* had resided in its editing, imposed on the material almost as an afterthought, that of *Napoléon* lay, more intrinsically, in the shooting approach. Gance had aimed for an unheard-of degree of camera mobility. "I made [the camera] walk, run, turn its head, fall to its knees, raise its eyes to heaven; I made it into a living being with a brain and—even better—a heart." He also made it gallop on horseback, dive from a cliff, breast the waves, swing from a giant pendulum, and join in a snowball fight. (Despite persistent reports, though, he never hurled it through the air like a snowball.) His intention was not merely to astonish his viewers but to compel them to become totally involved as participants in the drama.

Throughout the film, Gance also experimented with the effects of blending and multiplying images. Sometimes by superimposition: "I had up to sixteen images on top of one another; I knew that, from the fifth image on, nothing more could be made out—but they were there, and therefore their *potential* was there too, just as in music when you have fifty instruments playing: you can't distinguish the sound of each instrument, but it's the orchestration which counts, as you're surrounded by it." Elsewhere he split his screen into multiple sections, as many as nine for the pillow fight at Brienne (reworked by Vigo for *Zéro de conduite*). And in the spectacular Double Tempest sequence, oscillating shots of Bonaparte's tiny boat, tossed by a raging storm, were intercut with, and overlaid on, the wild uproar in the Convention as Jacobins oust Girondists, Gance's camera swinging vertiginously above the brawling throng.

Most dramatic of all Gance's innovations were the triple-screen sequences, filmed in a process he named Polyvision. (He also, it seems, shot sequences in color and 3-D, but suppressed them as too distracting.) At two points in the narrative, curtains rolled back on each side of the main screen to produce huge triptychs: For the Bal des Victimes the screens showed three separate pictures, but for the grand finale of the Army of Italy the image extended into a full panorama; and in the closing shots the outer panels turned respectively blue and red, transforming the screen

into a giant Tricolor. "The audience," Emile Vuillermoz reported, "feels miraculously liberated. Reality and dreams no longer appear through a tiny casement; a whole wall grows transparent like crystal and opens up another universe. The spectators suddenly become a crowd watching a crowd. The onrush of this magical world cause an emotional shock of rare intensity."

Once the initial excitement had subsided, critical response was more mixed. Many reviewers, while hailing the triptychs with enthusiasm, found Gance's mobile camera an irritation. "The camera oscillates, shakes, slips," wrote Raymond Villette in *Mon Ciné*, "in short, bounces around, which has an unpleasant effect on the retina." Others objected, as always, to the all-too-frequent lapses of taste, the bombast, sentimentality, and crude attempts at humor that marred the grandeur of the overall conception.

Much of the controversy centered—as it still does—on the political implications of the film's romanticized view of its hero. In some quarters it was greeted with unabashed jingoism. "Glorification of France on the screen!" rhapsodized *La Semaine à Paris*. "Abel Gance's *Napoléon* is the most marvellous hymn to France—the Marseillaise of the image. . . . The whole world will say: 'It is true, the French are not as other men: if they were, they would not possess a living epic!'" On the left, if the verdict was similar, the tone was very different. In *L'Humanité* Léon Moussinac praised the film as "a major step forward for cinematography," but condemned its content as "not only false but dangerous. . . . A Bonaparte for apprentice fascists." More recent critics have reached similar verdicts. Peter Pappas, writing in *Cinéaste* (Spring 1981), called *Napoléon* "the greatest— and certainly the most profound—fascist film in the history of the cinema. . . . It strives to make the presentation and understanding of history an unintelligible act—or rather, an act intelligible only to a few seers privy to the mystery of an arcane universe. *Napoléon* is a testament to the capacity of fascism to function as the great equalizer, capable of reducing all humanity to one massive and common denominator of received intelligence. . . . We are compelled to confront an esthetic strategy whose singular intention is to superimpose the 'authentic' truth on what, according to Gance, is only the apparent, but quintessentially fallacious, fact of history. In *Napoléon*, all roads are paved with the same intention: the apotheosis of distortion."

Gance always maintained that his view of Napoleon was essentially democratic: that Bonaparte derived his power from the support of the people and stood as the embodiment of the popular will, "direct heir" of the Revolution. Even so, the standpoint is basically elitist: the people are never shown as taking charge of their own destiny, but always as needing to be inspired and directed by a strong leader, whose privileged vision marks him out from the crowd. Indeed, the leader is their destiny. Nor can Gance's description of Napoleon as a man who "does everything he can to avoid [war]" easily be reconciled with the film's final exultant vision of a conquering army on the march. "To adorn the figure of a despot with romantic traits, to decorate the statue of a tyrant with flowers, is heinous work both historically and philosophically," Émile Vuillermoz wrote in *Cinémagazine*. "To ennoble the technique of massacre through romanticism, to make killing respectable or simply enjoyable is to assume . . . a great responsibility towards mothers whose children will be gunned down tomorrow."

For all the éclat of its premiere, *Napoléon* received only a sparse and spasmodic release. Gaumont-Metro-Goldwyn, who had bought the distribution rights, preferred to concentrate their attention on the latest blockbuster from Culver City, *Ben-Hur*. The triptychs caused problems; with talkies imminent, and exhibitors nervously reckoning the cost of installing sound equipment, nobody wanted further complications in the shape of triple projectors and expandable screens. Shortened versions, minus the triptychs, were shown here and there, but the original (running some eight hours) was rarely to be seen. British and American showings were disastrous; the film was ruthlessly truncated (in New York, it ran about eighty minutes), with the triptychs projected across the middle of a single screen, leaving the audience peering at midget figures as if through a mail slot.

Further Napoleonic films were out of the question. Originally Gance had estimated twenty million francs for all six; *Napoléon* alone had cost around seventeen million. SGF was in deep financial trouble. (Its other major venture, Dreyer's *Passion de Jeanne d'Arc*, had also attracted much critical interest and very little revenue.) Gance sold the rights to the final episode to the German actor-director Lupu Pick, who made it as *Napoleon auf St. Helene* (1929), with Werner Krauss in the title role.

The future of the cinema, Gance believed, lay in his Polyvision process, in which he saw "the creation of visual harmonies, the transporting of the spectator's imagination into a new and sublime world." To help popularize it, he put together three "Polyvised" episodes from *Napoléon*: *Galops* (1928), Bonaparte's horseback escape across Corsica; *Marines* (1928), the storm at sea; and *Danses* (1928), the Bal des Victimes. To these he added *Cristaux*, a Polyvised version of a Dutch documentary (*Kristallen*, 1925, directed by J. C. Mol). They were shown at Studio 28, one of the few Paris cinemas fitted with triple screen, along with *Autour de Napoléon* (1927), a filmed record of the making of the epic.

Napoléon's financial failure did nothing to curb Gance's soaring imagination. In 1928 he sent a 57-page memorandum to the League of Nations, setting forth the means of harnessing "Universal Psychological Forces" in the cause of world peace. To this end, he would establish a World Cinema Corporation to make a series of films entitled *Les Grands Initiés*, planned to "bring to the screen the epic of human religion, to pour floods of light upon the summits of that immense mountain chain, on . . . the founding heroes of religions—Moses, Jesus, Mohammed, Buddha, Luther, etc.—who on each occasion have expanded the human heart and invented new forms of goodness. This vast symphony would embrace our modern world, extend into the beyond, and culminate in a personal revelation of which I hold the secret."

The League was polite but noncommittal, so instead Gance revived an earlier project: *La Fin du monde*, originally planned as the third of the Apocalyptic trilogy of which *Ecce Homo* was to be the first. Backing came from a recently formed company, L'Écran d'Art, run by yet another Russian, Vladimir Ivanoff.

A saintly visionary, Jean Novalic (played by Gance himself), preaches the message of universal love but is reviled and relegated to an asylum. Before disappearing, he entrusts his task to his brother Martial, an astronomer, who has just discovered a comet on collision course with Earth. News of the coming catastrophe causes panic; some throw themselves into a frenzy of pleasure-seeking, while others, inspired by Jean's message, come together in newfound solidarity. At the last moment the comet turns aside, and all the nations join in peace and brotherhood.

La Fin du monde (*The End of the World*, 1930) was announced as "The first great spectacle of the French talking cinema." Unlike many silent-era filmmakers, Gance welcomed the coming of sound, seeing its potential not only to echo the image, but to add further dimensions of meaning. To what extent he put these theories into practice in *La Fin du monde* is hard to tell, given the mutilation suffered by the film prior to release. Gance's 5,250-meter version was taken from him and cut by Ivanoff (with the help of his janitor, Gance alleged) to 2,800 meters of jerky, muddled, and often incomprehensible melodrama. Some reviewers, recognizing a travesty of Gance's intentions, reserved judgement; the majority were less sympathetic. "The film is painful to watch and to listen to," Philippe Soupault wrote in *L'Europe Nouvelle*. "It is a mixture of the pretentiously naive and the blatantly unrealistic, of the pompous and the trivial."

Ivanoff's butchery, Roger Icart suggested, "cannot alone explain the work's agonizing failure. The crucial reason—which *may* have motivated the mutilations—was a fundamental error less in the conception than in the execution of the dialogue scenes. . . . Faults such as lack of psychological depth, overblown sentiments, were amplified to a ludicrous degree by strained, exaggerated performances from actors—starting with Gance himself—unused to the requirements of the sound cinema. In his silent films, where these faults were already to some extent latent, they could be overlooked in the irresistibly lyrical surge of the images."

With this debacle, Gance's career collapsed with appalling suddenness. From being the standardbearer, the far-sighted pioneer boldly leading the French cinema over Alpine peaks towards its glorious future, he found himself dismissed, almost overnight, as an outdated relic, embarrassingly out of tune with the new age. A new generation of directors—Clair, Renoir, Feyder—were gaining recognition, and beside them Gance's style of cinema seemed irrelevant. Matters were hardly helped by an ill-advised remake of his first major success, *Mater Dolorosa* (1932). He hoped that this, filmed in eighteen days, would prove that he could stay within a modest budget and schedule; but the creaky old melodrama, fusty even on its first appearance, merely confirmed the general belief that he was hopelessly passé.

With one or two exceptions, Gance's films of the 1930's present a depressing picture of drastically diminished expectations. He told an interviewer in 1936; "I had to work, so I began to accept whatever was offered me—the most worn-out plots, the most undemanding projects. . . . I don't think my producers can complain: my films these days are commercial successes. I don't go to see them . . . that's a different matter." The veteran actor, Fernand Rivers, wanting to move into directing, approached him for help; Gance acted as "supervisor" on two adaptations of venerable theatrical hits, *Le Maître de forges* (1933) and *La Dame aux camélias* (1934), on which Rivers took directorial credit. In between these films Gance directed *Poliche* (1934), a melodrama so relentlessly lachrymose as to make *Mater Dolorosa* seem callous,

and married for the third time; his bride was Marie-Odette Vérité, who acted under the name Sylvie Grenade. They had one adopted daughter, Clarisse.

With the collapse of SGF in 1933, rights to the negative of *Napoléon* reverted to Gance. He took the opportunity to rework it as a sound film, recutting and shortening it, dubbing the voices, and shooting additional scenes, including a cumbersome prologue and epilogue; released as *Napoléon Bonaparte* (1935), it ran some two-and-a-quarter hours. Dialogue and sound effects were processed through "Perspective Sonore," a forerunner of multitrack stereo which Gance and André Debrie had invented for *La Fin du monde*. This sound system was found highly impressive, the film itself less so. The new footage, quickly and cheaply made, jarred with the original material; actors aged ten years from one shot to the next; and the explanatory dialogue was mostly clumsy and superfluous.

Frustrated in his bid for rehabilitation, Gance returned to making films "with my eyes closed"—trivial studio projects, adaptations of fashionable stage hits or popular novels, executed "not in order to live, but in order not to die." *Le Roman d'un jeune homme pauvre* (*The Story of a Poor Young Man*, 1935), *Jérôme Perreau, Héros des barricades* (*The Queen and the Cardinal*, 1935), and *Lucrèce Borgia* (1935) were all three filmed within five months, only the first to Gance's own script. If the first two were negligible, *Lucrèce Borgia* at least exhibited a crudely colorful energy, along with some profitably scandalous nude shots. It also boasted a pair of above-average performances, from Edwige Feuillère in the title role and Antonin Artaud as Savonarola.

In later years, Gance counted *Un Grand Amour de Beethoven* (*The Life and Loves of Beethoven*, 1937) the only one of his sound films worth preserving. A thoroughly fictionalized account of the composer's later life, focusing on his affair with Juliette Guicciardi, it was rated by Marcel Martin "without doubt Gances's most perfect film, the one which leaves itself least open to critics irritated by his usual excesses and bombast." Graham Greene, reviewing it in *The Spectator*, thought otherwise. "Terrific storms blow out his characters' cloaks, enormous chords bellow from the microphone: the actors gesture and moan and wring their hands in gargantuan griefs, and the banal symbols of blossom and thunder and dawn, all shot with a fine pictorial sense, magnify still further the human emotions. . . . This film never rises above the level of a cheap novelette." He was impressed, though, by Harry Baur in the title role: "That roughly carved monumental face never fails to convey a great reserve of power and when it drops into the hands it is as if a statue were to weep."

In the most famous sequence, the onset of Beethoven's deafness, Gance made striking use of expressionist sound technique: we first hear the various natural sounds that the composer can no longer detect, then see them being made (as he does) without hearing, and finally hear them once again as he recalls them, playing them over to himself in the tormented isolation of his brain. Elsewhere, though, what should be moving is trivialized by sentimentality and by inept attempts at humor. Not only is the aged Beethoven shown (wholly against the facts) as neglected and impoverished, he also helps himself to other people's beer behind their backs. Gance, Odile Cambier commented in *Cinémonde*, "has terrible faults laced with flashes of genius, and the same goes for this film. It remains nonetheless the richest, most personal, and most remarkable work currently to be seen."

One of the ironies of Gance's career was that, while films he threw off as commercial chores were released with scarcely a frame altered, those he cared about were invariably chopped and mangled. *Beethoven* was cut by its producers by nearly half to make it fit a double bill. A similar fate overtook his sound remake of *J'accuse* (*That They May Live*, 1938), cut by a third for release, and further shortened on rerelease in 1947.

The sound *J'accuse* is the more powerful of the two versions. Gance plays down the romantic triangle to concentrate on the effect of war on the sensitive nature of Jean Diaz, and his attempts to prevent its recurrence. Norman King found the sound version "much more strident in its indictment of war and of the capitalists who stood to gain from it. In contrast to Renoir's benign humanism [in *La Grande Illusion*], Gance's message was urgently and *aggressively* pacifist." Victor Francen played Diaz; if he was less convincing than Romauld Joubé (in the silent version) as the gentle poet, he carried far more weight as the deranged visionary summoning up the cadavers of Verdun. The film was weakened by over-wordy dialogue and by evidence of haste and corner-cutting in its making; sets are often visibly pasteboard, and footage of the final panic is blatantly lifted from *La Fin du monde*. Despite this, it was widely admired, except in the right-wing press where it was attacked for "defeatism."

Encouraged by the partial revival of his reputation, Gance began to plan various large-scale projects, in particular a color epic on the life of Christopher Columbus, to be shot in Spain. Meanwhile, he continued to turn out commercial assignments: *Le Voleur de femmes* (*The Robber of Women*, 1938), described by Louis Skorecki as "a bewildering mixture of Guitry and Mizoguchi"; a hilariously bad version of Charpentier's opera *Louise* (1938), with Grace Moore galumphing through the title role; and *Le Paradis perdu* (*Four Flights to Love*, 1940), the tale of a war widower who incestuously transfers his bereaved affection to his daughter, which Pierre Leprohon considered "a charming work, full of quiet emotion."

The outbreak of war disrupted all cinematic activity. Gance's planned Columbus epic, which had already run into difficulties, had to be shelved, and the authorities were unresponsive to ideas he suggested for patriotic propaganda movies. "I get the impression, when I mention cinema to them, that they see me rather like the fellow who, in the midst of a storm at sea, comes to the captain and proposes organizing a little party, or a round of deck-tennis." Instead, he made *La Vénus aveugle* (*Blind Venus*, 1941), a strange, overheated allegory about a woman who, learning she is going blind, drives her lover away by feigning infidelity; but she remains true to him, cares for his child, and is finally rewarded by his return and the restoration of her sight. Some critics have dismissed it as rubbish, but Roger Icart found it "a baroque, baffling and fascinating work . . . a passionate evocation, full of romantic fury and ingenuous touches." The heroine may be meant to stand for France, patient through adversity. *La Vénus aveugle* was premiered at Vichy, prefaced by a fulsome address to Pétain: "Since France is now personified in you, Marshal, allow me to dedicate [this film] in all humility to you."

Gance may have been playing it safe. His name apparently featured on a Nazi blacklist in Paris—partly for his membership in the early 1930s in the International Committee for the Defense of the Soviet Union, and partly because he was suspected of being Jewish. His next film (possibly also out of prudence) was a French-Italian coproduction: *Le Capitaine Fracasse* (1943), a swashbuckler based on a Théophile Gautier novel, with passages of rhymed dialogue à la Rostand. Soon after it was completed, Gance and his wife slipped across the border to Spain.

Gance's political attitudes have given rise to a good deal of debate. His consistently professed democratic, and on occasion socialist, beliefs hardly square with his boyish enthusiasm for autocrats: not only past figures like Napoleon, but Mussolini, De Gaulle, Mao Tse-tung—and Franco, whom in May 1938, with the Civil War still raging, he addressed as "the foremost paladin of our time." Sympathetic commentators have explained this as naive and often misguided idealism; other have seen it as blatant opportunism. At all events, once in Spain Gance made assiduous efforts to ingratiate himself with the authorities, whose cooperation he sought in making his long-planned *Christophe Colomb*. This was now to form part of a great Spanish nationalist trilogy, dealing with Columbus, El Cid, and Ignatius de Loyola. He also tried to promote his Pictographe invention—a form of deep-focus allowing for extensive use of artificial backgrounds. All these efforts proved abortive, as did a projected film about the celebrated bullfighter, *Manolete*, abandoned after Gance had shot some initial footage.

After the liberation, Gance returned to France to find himself virtually ostracized. For nearly ten years he directed nothing. He devised numerous projects and even traveled to London to try and interest J. Arthur Rank in a film to be called *Birth of an Empire*, a panegyric to the civilizing mission of British imperialism. The only one of his plans to come anywhere near fruition was *La Divine Tragédie*, a treatment of the life of Christ backed by the Office Familiale de Documentation Artistique, an anti-communist Catholic organization. Large sums of money, collected from pious believers all over the world, mysteriously trickled away before a frame had been shot, and the project collapsed in undignified legal squabbles.

In 1953 Gance was invited to give a tribute to his late friend Jean Epstein. "If my voice is broken, my thoughts wild, and my poor words unsure, it is because I too have earth in my mouth—I too have been killed by the French cinema. This is one dead man speaking to you of another."

He was rescued from this despair by Nelly Kaplan, newly arrived from Argentina. Kaplan, later to become a considerable director in her own right, constituted herself Gance's collaborator, muse, and cheering section. In particular, she urged the virtues of Polyvision, the subject of her *Manifeste d'un art nouveau: la Polyvision*, published in 1955. At her suggestion Gance, regaining his enthusiasm, made a ten-minute polyvised documentary on the July 14th festivities in Paris, *Quatorze juillet 1953* (1953), to demonstrate the system's potential. The next year he returned to feature films, thanks to Fernand Rivers (repaying the favor of twenty years earlier) who offered him an adaptation of a Dumas play, *La Tour de Nesle* (*The Tower of Lust*, 1954). This "cape and sword Western," as Gance described it, his first film in color, was a period adventure

generously laced with eroticism; it was shot in two versions, Italian (clothed) and French (rather less so). Gance shrugged off clerical complaints of indecency: "I simply evoked in images what is conveyed by the words, but I didn't tell anybody anything they didn't already know." François Truffaut reviewed it in *Cahiers du Cinéma*: "*La Tour de Nesle* is, if you like, the least good of Abel Gance's films. But, since Gance is a genius, it is also a film of genius. Gance does not *possess* genius, he *is possessed* by genius."

With *Cahiers* championing his cause and the sound version of *Napoléon*, with final triptych, revived for a run at Studio 28, Gance was re-emerging from limbo. To counter the invasion of Cinerama and show the superiority of his own system, he and Nelly Kaplan put together *Magirama* (1956), a compilation of short pieces: extracts from the 1927 *Napoléon* and the 1938 *J'accuse*, the July 14th film (renamed *Fête foraine*), two short films by Kaplan, and an extract from Norman McLaren's *Begone Dull Care*, reedited for triple screen. With interest stimulated by a television program on Gance's career, money was forthcoming for him to make the Napoleonic sequel he had planned thirty years before.

Austerlitz (1960) was filmed largely in Yugoslavia, amid a series of setbacks and disasters. The film covered events from the Peace of Amiens (1802) to the eponymous battle (1805), and was packed with international stars—Orson Welles, Martine Carol, Vittorio De Sica, Leslie Caron, Claudia Cardinale, Michel Simon, etc.— with Pierre Mondy as Napoleon. It was also static, wordy, and staggeringly dull, both verbally and visually, with (as Kevin Brownlow put it) "all the sweep and dash of moving day at Madame Tussaud's."

Gance, undeterred, continued tirelessly working on various elaborate projects: *Ecce Homo, Le Royaume de la terre* (Christ bringing peace to a post-atomic world), and the perennial *Christophe Colomb*. He visited China in 1964 to discuss with Chou En-lai plans for an epic treatment of the Long March, to be filmed in China simultaneously with a parallel revolutionary subject, *Les Soldats de l'an II*, in France. But he completed only one more film, *Cyrano et d'Artagnan* (1963)—less a swashbuckler than a romantic fantasy woven around the four-way love affair between the two swordsmen and the courtesans Marion Delorme and Ninon de l'Enclos, its eroticism spoken rather than shown. *The Times* described it as "an exquisite, eccentric entertainment, switching moods with a capricious sureness which recalls nothing more than a late Shakespearian romance."

For French television he directed an adaptation of Victor Hugo's play *Marie Tudor,* broadcast in April 1966, and a year later the first of three programs on the Napoleonic battle of Valmy. Despite his enthusiasm for the medium, no further commissions were forthcoming. "TV gives me tributes, but never commissions," he remarked sardonically. He was equally dismissive of the honors and restrospectives that came his way in his later years—the Légion d'Honneur, a César, an International Grand Prix du Cinéma: "So many baubles for an empty stomach!"

Even at this stage Gance was still obsessively tinkering with his silent masterpiece. In 1971, with financial support from Claude Lelouch, he released *Bonaparte et la révolution*—a ramshackle patchwork which included footage from the original silent *Napoléon,* some from the 1934 sound version, extracts from *Austerlitz* and the television program on Valmy, stills of documents and engravings, and some newly shot continuity. Voices were dubbed where necessary; Dieudonné, now eighty years old, dubbed himself, and Gance, at eighty-two, appeared on screen as Saint-Just. Press reaction was generally respectful, but for those familiar with the silent version it was a sad experience.

By now, an increasing number of people did know the silent *Napoléon* or at least a good deal of it. This was thanks largely to Kevin Brownlow, who put in years of work painstakingly reconstructing the film. Ancient prints were salvaged; footage long thought lost was recovered; conflicting versions were pieced together and reconciled. Brownlow also devoted to Gance the long final chapter of his book on the silent cinema, *The Parade's Gone By,* and a documentary film, *The Charm of Dynamite* (1968). In 1970 the reconstruction, still missing several key scenes and minus the triptychs, was shown at the National Film Theatre in London and hailed as a revelation. After a further nine years of reclamation Brownlow's version, now some five hours long, was shown at the Telluride Festival in Colorado, complete with final triptych sequence. (The earlier two triptychs seem to be lost for good; Gance claimed that he burnt them in 1940, in a fit of despair.)

The next year *Napoléon* was screened in London, accompanied by a full symphony orchestra playing a newly composed score by Carl Davis. It sold out, with tickets changing hands at blackmarket rates; the reviews were ecstatic and almost entirely uncritical. Showings in New York, presented by Francis Ford Coppola (with a score by his father Carmine Coppola), met with similar reactions. *Napoléon* was acclaimed, in terms far more glowing than any expressed on its first release, as a supreme masterpiece of the cinema, an unqualified triumph.

From now on, it seems likely that Gance's reputation will rest almost entirely on this one film, out of the fifty or so he directed. Perhaps rightly so—not only is *Napoléon,* as Bernard Eisenschitz noted, "technically . . . one of the richest films in the history of the cinema," it also represents, in its sprawling vitality and narrative bravura, the climax of Gance's greatest period, a summing-up of his silent cinema achievements before the decline of his sound films.

Evaluation of Abel Gance's work is to some extent hampered by the impossibility of seeing any of his major films in complete prints—or even, in most cases, of establishing just what would constitute "a complete print." *La Roue, J'accuse* (both versions), *Un grand amour de Beethoven, La Fin du monde* have survived only in truncated and mutilated form, and even *Napoléon,* despite Brownlow's devoted work, is still missing at least two hours of footage and two of the three triptych sequences. All the same, the character of what remains is consistent enough to suggest that, even were the gaps to be filled in, the final verdict on Gance might not be very different.

Almost everybody who has written about Gance's work, favorably or otherwise, has agreed on one salient point: its disconcerting unevenness. Not just from film to film, or even scene to scene, but within the same scene and almost the same shot the brilliant and the crass coexist, inextricably entwined—jolting us from admiration to derision in a split second. For some critics, especially those writing in the period of Gance's eclipse, the losses tended to outweigh the gains. In a famous phrase, Emile Vuillermoz summed him up as "a genius without talent."

Gance has often been compared to Victor Hugo, another artist whose towering aspirations could topple all too easily into bathos. Claude Mauriac observed that Gance's works, like Hugo's, "yoke together the best and the worst. We have to take them for what they are. . . . The unleashing of the elements, the storms of destiny, the furious tumult of crowds . . . these are the paroxysms of an inspiration in which the purest lyricism is so intimately mingled with grandiloquence and bad taste as almost to transform them."

Some recent critics have been readier to accept Gance at his own estimate—as a visionary genius whose innovations, deliberately suppressed by a timid and pusillanimous industry, could have led to a greater, more glorious future. Kevin Brownlow asserted that "the motion-picture industry . . . was alarmed by Gance's monumental talents, and frightened by his revolutionary ideas. They determined to control him, and to limit the length of his artistic leash. Unfortunately for all of us, they succeeded." Similarly, Brooks Riley wrote in *Film Comment* (Jan-Feb 1982): "The history of cinema since *Napoléon* could be described as a narrowing process, one which gave way to rules, definitions, and the congealing requisites of the market."

Roger Icart was less inclined to ascribe the collapse of Gance's career to envy and malignancy than to the same lack of judgement or proportion that mars his best films. "He seemed unable to impose on himself the discipline of following a thought through to its logical conclusion (there being so many others jostling for attention in his mind), which lent everything he undertook a muddle-headed quality which he never managed to shake off." In the same way, the deficiencies of his 1930s films can be attributed, Pierre Leprohon considered, "not to the obligations which were imposed on him, but often to his own naivety and astonishing lack of any critical sense."

It could also be argued that Gance's cinema, for all its emotional intensity, the ebullience and exhilaration of its headlong tumult, represented less a shining avenue to the future than a dead end. "Much silent cinema," David Thomson wrote, "now looks primitive, melodramatic, and naive—Gance's especially. To claim that it is superior, artistically, to the intelligence and emotional depths of, say, *La Règle du jeu*, *Citizen Kane*, *Ugetsu Monogatari* or *Viva l'Italia* is to prefer Dumas to Proust. . . . Gance tied himself to a stake—the triptych Polyvision—that was irrelevant to real cinema."

With the febrile enthusiasm that greeted the revived *Napoléon*—fueled partly, no doubt, by a feeling that amends were due to a venerable and neglected figure—Gance seems likely to find his place alongside Griffith as one of the great, flawed masters of silent cinema, unsurpassed in the zest and audacity of his visual imagination. As Georges Sadoul remarked: "Among compatriots whose first demand has always been for measure and proportion, he came as an untamed force of Nature—without logic or discipline, but of undeniable power."

Although only a few weeks short of ninety, Gance attended the Telluride screening of *Napoléon* and astonished his audience by addressing them on the subject of his "next film," *Christophe Colomb*. Nonetheless, in his final years he occasionally gave vent to a certain bitterness. "With the passing of time, I realize that I've made very few clever moves. . . . In all honesty, if I had my life over again, I wouldn't

make films." After the death of Sylvie Gance in 1978, he lived alone in his Paris apartment in the rue de l'Yvette, cared for by neighbors. He died of a pulmonary embolism two weeks after his ninety-second birthday.

—*P.K.*

FILMS: *Shorts*—La Digue, ou Pour sauver la Hollande (The Dike), 1912; Le Nègre blanc (The White Negro), 1912; Il y a des pieds au plafond (There Are Feet on the Ceiling), 1912; Le Masque d'horreur (The Mask of Horror), 1912; Un Drame au Château d'Acre (Drama at the Château d'Acre), 1915; La Folie du Docteur Tube (The Madness of Dr. Tube), 1915; L'Enigme de dix heures (The Ten o'Clock Mystery), 1915; La Fleur des ruines (The Flower of the Ruins), 1915; L'héroïsme de Paddy (Paddy the Hero), 1915; Strass et cie (Strass and Co.), 1915; Fioritures, ou La Source de beauté (Flourishes), 1915; Le Périscope (The Periscope), 1915; Ce que les flots racontent (What the Waves Tell), 1915; Au secours! (Help), 1923; Autour de Napoléon (About Napoleon), 1927; Marines, 1928; Danses, 1928; Galops, 1928; Quatorze Juillet 1953, 1953. *Features*—Le Fou de la falaise (The Madman on the Cliff), 1915; Les Gaz mortels (La Brouillard sur la ville/The Deadly Gas), 1916; Barberousse (Red Beard), 1916; Le Droit à la vie (The Right to Life), 1916; Mater dolorosa, 1917; La Zone de la mort (The Death Zone), 1917; La Dixième Symphonie (The Tenth Symphony), 1917; J'accuse (I Accuse), 1919; La Roue (The Wheel), 1922; Napoléon vu par Abel Gance (Napoleon as Seen by Abel Gance), 1927; La Fin du monde (The End of the World), 1931; Mater Dolorosa, 1932; Poliche, 1934; Napoléon Bonaparte, 1934; Le Roman d'un jeune homme pauvre (The Story of a Poor Young Man), 1935; Jérôme Perreau, héros des barricades (The Queen and the Cardinal), 1935; Lucrèce Borgia, 1935; Un grand amour de Beethoven (The Life and Loves of Beethoven), 1937; J'accuse (That They May Live), 1938; Le Voleur de femmes (The Robber of Women), 1938; Louise, 1938; Le Paradis perdu (Four Flights to Love), 1940; La Vénus aveugle (Blind Venus), 1941; Le Capitaine Fracasse, 1943; La Tour de Nesle (The Tower of Lust), 1954; (with Nelly Kaplan) Magirama, 1956; Austerlitz, 1960; Cyrano et d'Artagnan, 1963; Bonaparte et la révolution, 1971. *Published scripts*—La Digue *in* L'Écran 3 1958; La Fin du monde, ed. Renez, Tallandier 1931; Un Grand Amour de Beethoven *in* L'Avant-Scene du Cinema 213 1978; J'accuse (1919 version), ed. Moussinac, La Lampe merveilleuse, 1922; Lucrèce Borgia, Paris 1936; Mater dolorosa (1917 version),Villars 1927; Mater Dolorosa (1932 version), ed. Renez, Tallandier 1936; Napoléon vu par Abel Gance, Plon 1927; La Roue, ed. Arroy, Tallandier 1930.

ABOUT: Abel, R. French Cinema: The First Wave, 1984; Armes, R. French Cinema, 1985; Bardèche, M. and Brasillach, R. Histoire du Cinéma, 1935; Brownlow, K. The Parade's Gone By, 1968; Brownlow, K. Napoleon: Abel Gance's Classic Film, 1983; Brunius, J. En Marge du Cinéma Français, 1954; Daria, S. Abel Gance Hier et Demain, 1959; Icart, R. Abel Gance, 1960 (in French); Icart, R. Abel Gance ou Le Prométhée

Foudroyé, 1983; Jeanne, R. and Ford, C. Abel Gance, 1963 (in French); King, N. Abel Gance, 1984; Kramer, S.P. and Welsh, J.M. Abel Gance, 1978; Leprohon, P. Le Cinéma et la Montaigne, 1944; Leprohon, P. Présences Contemporaines Cinéma, 1957; Lopez, M.V. Cine Francés, 1947; Mauriac, C. Petite Littérature du Cinéma, 1957; Roud, R. (ed) Cinema: A Critical Dictionary, 1980; Sadoul, G. French Film, 1953; Thomson, D. A Biographical Dictionary of the Cinema, 1980. *Periodicals*—Bianco e Nero August–September 1953; Cahiers de la Cinémathèque 13–15 1974, Autumn 1981, Autumn 1982, Winter 1984; Cahiers du Cinéma October 1953, January 1955, August–September 1955, April–May 1968; Celulóide June 1982; Cineaste Spring 1981; Cinéma (France) February–March 1955, January 1971, December 1981; Cinema Journal Spring 1975; Cinématographe November 1982; Cinémonde January 1971; CTVD Winter 1984–85; L'Écran April–May 1958; Film (FFS) Spring 1969; Film (BFFS) August 1973; Film Collecting 1977; Film Comment March–April 1974; Film Dope September 1979; Film Faust December–January 1981–82; Films and Filming November–December 1969; Films in Review November 1952; Positif June 1982; Revue de Cinéma May 1983; Screen May–June 1984; Sight and Sound Spring 1976, Spring 1982; Take One July 1978; La Technique Cinématographique May 1953, October 1953.

GARNETT, TAY (June 13, 1894–October 4, 1977), American director, scenarist, and producer, was born in Santa Ana, near Los Angeles, the son of William Muldrough Garnett and the former Rachel Taylor. His father was a dentist and part-time inventor who had worked his way through college saddle-breaking horses. Garnett himself was educated at Los Angeles Polytechnic High School, Los Angeles High, and Sneed's Pool Room, whose other alumni included Frank Borzage and Leo McCarey. Besides pool, Garnett was interested in vaudeville, the nickelodeon, and girls. Too small to play football, he was a talented gymnast, once filling in (albeit briefly and disastrously) as "top-mount" with a visiting troupe of vaudeville acrobats.

When the United States entered World War I, Garnett volunteered for the Navy and trained as a flyer. He was serving as a flight instructor at San Diego when he was badly injured in a crash. It left him with a permanent limp and the walking stick that became his trademark. Garnett was not discharged from the Navy, however, but assigned by the San Diego commander to organize some morale-building entertainments. Drawing on his long and devoted study of vaudeville gags and routines, he devised a series of blackout sketches, recruited such amateur talent as the base could muster, and staged the first in a series of highly successful shows.

Some of these were seen and enjoyed by Alan

TAY GARNETT

Holubar, an independent movie producer and director who in 1922 shot a film called *Hurricane's Girl* at the San Diego base and hired Garnett to perform some flying stunts. Later the same year, when Garnett was discharged from the Navy, he was enlisted as a script doctor on two of Holubar's pictures, a Western called *Broken Chains* and *Slander the Woman,* a romantic adventure set in the north woods.

This experience was enough to hook Garnett on the movies and to land him a job with the Hal Roach studios, writing titles for such comics as Charley Chase and Will Rogers. John Gallagher, in his article about Garnett in *Films in Review* (December 1981), quotes him as saying that the average Hal Roach movie was "a slapdash affair in which the director came up with a story idea and the gag men went out [with the unit] and saw how many gags they could hang on it. When three or four days had passed, he brought it in and the cutter made a film out of it."

When this job came to an end, Garnett fell on extremely hard times. For some months he hustled occasional freelance assignments as a title writer, took appalling risks as an untrained stunt man, dug ditches, and when all else failed, starved. But by early 1924, thanks to a friend's intercession, Garnett was installed in Mack Sennett's famous "Tower"—the third-floor gag room of Sennett's frame office building, itself sometimes known as "the snake pit."

For the next two years Garnett wrote two-reelers for Sennett in collaboration with Hal Conklin, Vernon Smith, or Frank Capra, tailoring his scripts to the diverse comic talents of Harry Langdon, Ben Turpin, Slim Summerville, and Stan Laurel. He acknowledged the influence on him of Mack Sennett and his assistant Dick Jones, and said that at Sennett's studios, unlike Hal Roach's, "every film had to have a story line. Then it was Sennett's policy that the story line be pretty well buried in gags. Sennett used to say that when the audience goes to see it they'll have the satisfaction of feeling that the whole thing sticks together."

When Langdon and Capra left Sennett to make independent features under the auspices of First National, Garnett went with them to write gags and titles. He collaborated on the script of their very successful first film, *The Strong Man* (1926), and on others, and at about the same time signed a seven-year writing contract with Cecil B. De Mille's Pathé Studios in Culver City. The movies he wrote or coscripted for Pathé (and its subsidiary, Metropolitan Pictures) included among others *The Cruise of the Jasper B.* (1926), *White Gold* (1927), *Getting Gertie's Garter* (1927), *Power* (1928), *The Cop* (1928), and *Skyscraper* (1928).

By this time, Garnett was eager to direct. His chance came with a comedy-drama about a nearsighted fourth-rate boxer, Kid Reagan (Robert Armstrong). Garnett and George Dromgold had put together a script distantly derived from a Broadway show called *Celebrity*. One day Garnett was in the Pathé office when he learned that the assigned director, Howard Higgin, had quit after a studio row. De Mille arrived with his usual retinue, spotted Garnett, and "began to wave his riding quirt. 'Look. You want to direct. See what you can do with this one,' he ordered, then stalked out *en masse*."

Celebrity (1928) was successful enough to launch Garnett as a Pathé director. His second film was *The Spieler* (1928), scripted by himself with Hal Conklin and starring Alan Hale, Clyde Cook, and Renée Adorée. The studio converted to sound in the middle of filming, and Garnett was required to come up with spoken dialogue for the second half of this triangular love story. Like most of Garnett's films for Pathé, *The Spieler* was shot by Arthur Miller, whom the director regarded as one of the greatest cameramen he ever worked with.

Three more programmers followed, and then Garnett's first notable film, *Her Man* (1930). Based loosely on the song "Frankie and Johnnie," this was set in Havana, where backgrounds were shot by Garnett and his cameraman—in this case Edward Snyder. Helen Twelvetrees played the prostitute Frankie, Ricardo Cortez her pimp Johnnie, and Philip Holmes the romantic young sailor who tries to rescue Frankie from the dive where she works.

James Gleason provided hard-boiled comic relief as a sailor equally addicted to booze and one-armed bandits. This very successful picture was admired in particular for Garnett's command of the new sound medium—a modern critic, Andrew Sarris, speaks of the "extraordinarily fluid camera movements that dispel the myth of static [early] talkies."

Garnett made two more films for Pathé, then moved on to Universal. His first picture there, *Okay, America* (1932), was a hit. Lew Ayres starred as a wisecracking gossip writer, modeled on Walter Winchell, who foils a kidnapping attempt by a polished but ruthless gangster (Edward Arnold in a memorable movie debut). John Gallagher has commented on this film's "cracking tempo," quoting Garnett as saying of his work in general that "I have always very consciously striven for pace in every scene I ever shot. . . . Ninety per cent of the time, if a scene has a pace problem, it's . . . because it's too slow rather than too fast."

The same year, on loan to Warner Brothers, Garnett made what he considered his best film, *One Way Passage*. Scripted by Wilson Mizner and Joseph Jackson from a story by Robert Lord, it is set on a cruise ship where two doomed people enjoy a brief, bittersweet encounter. Kay Francis plays the gallant heroine, dying of heart disease, and William Powell a condemned murderer awaiting capture and execution. A skillful blend of comedy and tragedy, it achieves a supernatural "happy ending" through the famous running gag about the lovers' nightly tryst in the ship's bar over a Paradise champagne cocktail, and the ritual in which they break their glasses and leave the stems crossed on the bar. As the ship docks in San Francisco, they promise to meet again in Mexico on New Year's Eve, though both are aware that the parting is permanent. We nevertheless dissolve to a Tijuana nightclub and an orchestra playing "Auld Lang Syne." Two tired bartenders are cleaning up when there is an eerie tinkle of breaking glass. The men turn to stare at the bar, where lie the crossed stems of two champagne glasses.

One Way Passage won an Oscar for best original story and was a tremendous and much-emulated critical and financial success. Charles Higham describes it as "a quintessential Thirties film in its cruise ship setting and its languid playing" by the principals, whom another critic found "deliriously sophisticated." John Gillett had a special word of praise for Aline MacMahon's "beautifully judged performance" as a world-weary fake countess, but concluded that "the film's real distinction lies in Garnett's handling, helped by some superb lighting and Anton

Grot's realistically lived-in sets of ship's cabins and corridors. From the very beginning, with its long tracks along the Hong Kong bar, Garnett's camera is always revealing and pointing (if occasionally let down by some weak back projection). . . . Then in the epilogue, a final long track round a bar leads up to the last ghostly 'joke,' which Garnett makes seem absolutely right in the romantic convention created by what has gone before."

Back at Universal, Garnett made *Destination Unknown* (1933), with Pat O'Brien, Ralph Bellamy, and Alan Hale—a "strange, arty allegory about rumrunners adrift in the Pacific"—and then *S.O.S. Iceberg* (1933). This is something of a curiosity, an adventure story about a scientific expedition stranded on an iceberg, constructed around documentary footage shot by the German filmmaker Dr. Arnold Fanck and starring Fanck's protégée Leni Riefenstahl, later herself famous or infamous as the director of *Triumph of the Will* (1935) and other tributes to the Nazi movement.

Garnett's next major film, *China Seas* (1935), was made for MGM, where it was produced by Albert Lewin and supervised (too closely for Garnett's liking) by Irving Thalberg, whose infinitely detailed preparations delayed filming for over a year. For once, Thalberg wanted a money-maker and "to hell with art this time." The formula he arrived at featured the screen's favorite roughneck lovers, Clark Gable and Jean Harlow, and the equally popular roughneck villain, Wallace Beery, in a wisecracking adventure-romance adapted by Jules Furthman and James McGuinness from a novel by Crosbie Garstin. Gable plays the captain of the decrepit steamboat *Kin Lung,* carrying gold from Hong Kong to Singapore, and Beery is a trader in league with Malay pirates. Also on board are vulgar Harlow and aristocratic Rosalind Russell, both old flames of Gable's; lovable drunk Robert Benchley; and a cowardly third officer (Lewis Stone) who redeems himself by blowing up the pirates' junk at the cost of his own life.

Gable insisted on performing some of his own stunts in the action sequences and reportedly was almost killed in the terrifying scene in which a five-ton steamroller (packed with hidden gold) breaks loose during a typhoon and thunders back and forth among the wretched Chinese seamen on deck. The London *Times* complained that "there is too much torture and too many horrible accidents for any but perverted tastes," but the trade papers hailed the movie as "a showman's proposition" and "a cast-iron popular booking," and so it proved to be.

She Couldn't Take It (1935), a freelance as-

signment for Columbia, was a fast-moving comedy with Joan Bennett as a screwball heiress and George Raft as the ex-gangster who becomes her guardian. There followed three films for 20th Century–Fox, beginning with *Professional Soldier* (1935), starring Victor McLaglen and Freddie Bartholomew in a Graustarkian adventure story that received mixed reviews. Garnett's 1929 marriage to the silent star Patsy Ruth Miller had meanwhile failed, and in 1934 he had married another actress, Helga Moray. At the end of 1935 they took a delayed honeymoon in the form of a round-the-world cruise in Garnett's hundred-foot sailing yacht *Athene*. The cameraman James Shackleford went along, shooting 70,000 feet of travelog material, some of which Garnett later used in his films.

Back at work, the director made a trifling battle-of-the-sexes romp, *Love Is News* (1937), and then set to work on another big-budget adventure story, *Slave Ship* (1937). Highly successful in spite of its distasteful theme, the movie was adapted from George S. King's novel by an elite army of writers that included William Faulkner, Sam Hellman, Lamar Trotti, and Gladys Lehman. Beery is the villain again—a slave-runner whose young partner (Warner Baxter) tries to give up the trade when he marries Elizabeth Allan but has to contend with mutiny, fire at sea, and all kinds of skulduggery before he and his wife are free to start a new life.

The same year Garnett joined the independent producer Walter Wanger, working on a percentage basis and with full freedom to make his own films in his own way. Their first collaboration was *Stand-In* (1937), starring Leslie Howard as an efficiency expert sent to Hollywood by the New York office of a big production company to "rationalize" the chaotic West Coast operation. Guided by sardonic showgirl Joan Blondell, drunken producer Humphrey Bogart, and a Stroheimian director (Alan Mowbray) with a fanatical passion for authenticity, Howard learns that movie-making is a process not susceptible to logical analysis. *Time* called this "the most human as well as the most biting comedy yet written about Hollywood," adding that "the laughter is loud, warming, and contagious."

Stand-In was the first of three movies scripted for Garnett by Gene Towne and Graham Baker, the others being *Joy of Living* (1938), a musical screwball comedy with songs by Jerome Kern and Dorothy Fields, and *Eternally Yours* (1939), starring Loretta Young and David Niven—a light comedy about a professional magician and his neglected wife. In between came *Trade Winds* (1938), an international chase story that used (in back projection) some of the material shot by Garnett on his own round-the-world voyage. This comedy-drama, scripted by Dorothy Parker among others, had a formidable cast headed by Fredric March and Joan Bennett but seems not to have made much impact.

Slightly Honorable (1940), another comedy-drama featuring Garnett's friend Pat O'Brien, is said to have been drastically recut by Wanger's distributors, United Artists, and perhaps for that reason failed at the box office. Leaving Wanger, Garnett scored a major hit with *Seven Sinners* (Universal, 1940), teaming John Wayne and Marlene Dietrich in a boisterous adventure story, memorable for its marathon barroom brawl, set in the East Indies. Wayne plays a tough Navy lieutenant, Oscar Homolka is a charming villain and, as an itinerant *femme fatale* who causes riot and mayhem wherever she goes, Dietrich (according to William Whitebait) "sails back into her own. Not for years has she seemed so light, so alluring," photographed by Rudolph Maté "posing in black behind mosquito nets, set against sunlight lattices."

In 1941–1943 Garnett continued his collaboration with Wayne in the radio series *Three Sheets in the Wind*, about a boozy private eye. Wayne's costar was Garnett's wife Helga Moray, and Garnett, who directed and produced twenty-six episodes in the series, also wrote sixteen of them. Perhaps because of this involvement, his movie work during these years was uninspired—the grossly sentimental *Cheers for Miss Bishop* (1941), a tired comedy called *My Favorite Spy*, and two unusually realistic and very successful war movies, *Bataan* and *The Cross of Lorraine*, both made in 1943 for his new studio, MGM.

Mrs. Parkington (1944), from Louis Bromfield's novel, has Greer Garson as a rich and spunky old lady who saves her embezzling grandson from Sing Sing and lengthily remembers the days when she was a poor and spunky young lady and married Major Walter Pidgeon, identified by one reviewer as "a sort of knight of capitalism, staking his adventurous all on dangerous mines which blow up and kill everyone for miles." Old and young, Garson was prettily photographed, as always, by Joseph Ruttenberg, and her classy histrionics brought her her fourth consecutive Oscar nomination. But *Mrs. Parkington,* though it did well, was beaten hands-down in the box-office stakes by *Valley of Decision* (1945), Garnett's second family saga with the "Queen of Culver City."

Another adaptation (by John Meehan and Sonya Levien from Marcia Davenport), it opens in the 1870s in Pittsburgh, where an Irish servant girl (Garson) goes to work in the household of Donald Crisp, even though the latter is hated by her legless father (Lionel Barrymore), crippled in Crisp's steel mill. She falls in love with her employer's handsome son (Gregory Peck) and he with her, but, knowing her place, she declines marriage. Then things go from bad to worse, with Barrymore shooting Crisp and himself being killed by strikebreakers, and Peck marrying a nagging socialite. But Peck's mother (Gladys Cooper), who knows quality when she sees it, leaves her shares in the mill to the heroine, smoothing her path to marital bliss and higher social status. The film, wrote one reviewer, is the "Victorian servant's dream come true without a single cliché missing. . . . It's a pity that the one-dimensional quality of the acting should be corrupted by the intelligent performance of Gladys Cooper." Garson nevertheless copped yet another Oscar nomination, and the movie outgrossed even *Mrs. Miniver* ($5,560,000 on first release).

A very much better picture followed, *The Postman Always Rings Twice* (1946), preferred by many critics even to *One Way Passage* and widely regarded as Garnett's finest film. It was adapted by Harry Ruskin and Niven Busch from the novel by James M. Cain that had already inspired Visconti's *Ossessione* and Pierre Chenal's *Le Dernier Tournant,* and which has been filmed again since by Bob Rafelson. In Garnett's version, John Garfield plays Frank Chambers, the young drifter who takes a job at a roadside diner, falls in love with Cora Smith (Lana Turner), the owner's wife, and is seduced into murdering the boss for his insurance money. The lovers get away with the killing and collect the insurance, but then, in an ironic twist that combines the plots of *Thérèse Raquin* and *Payment Deferred,* Cora is accidentally killed and Frank is executed for her "murder."

Garfield was perfectly cast, and Lana Turner, dressed in white throughout the film until she changes to black at her moment of repentance, gave her best performance under Garnett's direction. Though this version of the story was considerably less erotic than Rafelson's remake, it was remarkably steamy by the standards of the day, and many contemporary reviewers condemned it as sordid, immoral, and brutal. Bosley Crowther, however, defended the film as "a sincere comprehension of an American tragedy. For the yearning of weak and clumsy people for something better than the stagnant lives they lead is revealed as the core of the dilemma, and sin is shown to be no way to happiness." A more recent critic, Charles Higham, praising the movie's "classic authority and concision," called it "the perfect *film noir,* harsh and heartless in its delineation of character, disclosing a rancid evil beyond the antiseptic atmosphere of the roadhouse diner."

Having completed his MGM contract, Garnett moved from one studio to another for the remainder of his career, producing no masterpieces but a number of excellent entertainments in various genres. The best of these was *Cause for Alarm* (1951), a low-budget suspense film tightly scripted by Mel Dinelli and Tom Lewis. Loretta Young stars as a woman whose husband (Barry Sullivan), a paranoid invalid, has sent a letter to the district attorney accusing her of planning to kill him. He boasts to her of what he has done, tries to kill her, and dies. The rest of the film deals with her increasingly frantic efforts to recover the letter before it reaches the DA—arguing with crass officials, heading off sympathetic neighbors and the dead man's suspicious aunt, and all the time enmeshing herself in a net of lies that seem to bear out the lie in the letter.

Time's reviewer wrote that the film "pulls off the old Hitchcock trick of giving commonplace people, events, and settings a sinister meaning. . . . Instead of the gloom-shrouded photography that has become standard in Hollywood melodrama, the movie wisely stresses the quiet, sunny atmosphere of a pleasant residential street." Loretta Young was reckoned to have succeeded in what one critic called "her bid to be considered as a high-powered dramatic actress," and there were excellent character sketches from Margalo Gillmore as a garrulous busybody and Irving Bacon as a footsore mailman.

Garnett went on making movies into the early 1970s (when he was nearly eighty), but none of his later films were of any great merit, and after the mid-1950s he became increasingly involved in television, directing shows for *Four Star Theatre,* the *Loretta Young Show, Gunsmoke, Death Valley Days,* and many other programs. In 1972 he directed a stage play, *84 Charing Cross Road,* derived from Helen Hanff's book, and in 1973 he published his autobiography, *Light Your Torches and Pull Up Your Tights.*

An extremely uneven director, Garnett was at his best a masterly storyteller, with a talent for the effective integration of background and plot. In his later years he was taken up by some French critics as an *auteur,* and Andrew Sarris, commenting on this, wrote that "Garnett's personality is that of a rowdy vaudevillian, an artist with the kind of rough edges that cause the over-civilized French sensibility to swoon in sheer physical frustration." The director, who had a daughter and a son by Hega Moray, made a third marriage in 1953 to Mari Aldon.

FILMS: Celebrity, 1928; The Spieler, 1928; The Flying Fool, 1928; Oh, Yeah!, 1929; Officer O'Brien, 1930; Her Man, 1930; Bad Company, 1931; Prestige, 1932;

Okay, America, 1932; One Way Passage, 1932; Destination Unknown, 1933; (with Arnold Fanck) S.O.S. Iceberg, 1933; China Seas, 1935; She Couldn't Take It, 1935; Professional Soldier, 1935; Love Is News, 1937; Slave Ship, 1937; Stand-In, 1937; Joy of Living, 1938; Trade Winds, 1938; Eternally Yours, 1939; Slightly Honorable, 1940; Seven Sinners, 1940; Cheers for Miss Bishop, 1941; My Favorite Spy, 1942; Bataan, 1943; The Cross of Lorraine, 1943; Mrs. Parkington, 1944; Valley of Decision, 1945; The Postman Always Rings Twice, 1946; Wild Harvest, 1947; A Connecticut Yankee in King Arthur's Court, 1949; The Fireball, 1950; Cause for Alarm, 1951; Soldiers Three, 1951; One Minute to Zero, 1952; Main Street to Broadway, 1953; The Black Knight, 1954; (with others) Seven Wonders of the World, 1956 (Cinerama); The Night Fighters (U.K., A Terrible Beauty), 1960; Guns of Wyoming (U.K., Cattle King), 1963; The Delta Factor, 1970; The Mad Trapper/Challenge to Be Free, 1975 (completed 1972); Timber Tramp, 1977 (completed 1972).

ABOUT: Gallagher, J. Tay Garnett, 1987; Garnett, T. and Balling, F. D. Light Your Torches and Pull Up Your Tights, 1973; Sarris, A. The American Cinema, 1968. *Periodicals*—Action September–October 1972; L'Avant-scène du Cinéma April 1, 1980; Écran April and May 1977; Films in Review December 1981; Velvet Light Trap Spring 1978.

*GERASIMOV, SERGEI APOLLINARI-EVICH (May 21, 1906–November 28, 1985), Soviet director, scenarist, actor, administrator, and teacher, contributed the following statement in English:

"Despite its pathetic brevity, life does not in the least resemble a questionnaire. I have tried here to measure it with films, although each of them was a result of much thought, of multiple encounters, arguments, collisions, evaluations, and reevaluations. But I will endeavor to give a compendious account of the main landmarks in my life.

"I was born on May 21st, 1906, into the family of a pre-Revolutionary political convict who lived in a village at Lake Chebarkul near the famous Miass factories in the beautiful Urals region. Times were hard; as a teenager I was for a while the only breadwinner in the family. And yet I dreamed of art, did some drawing; after the Revolution I made my way to Leningrad determined to become a painter.

"In the most unexpected way fate landed me at No. 2 Proletkult Street, where the FEKS Studio was housed—the Factory of the Eccentric Actor, headed by two young men, Grigory Kozintzev and Leonid Trauberg. Their cocky motto, borrowed from Mark Twain, was: Better be a young puppy than an old bird of paradise. ['Better a young June bug than an old bird of para-

SERGEI GERASIMOV

dise,' from *Puddenhead Wilson's Calendar.*
—Ed.] Thus I started on my way towards acting
and soon appeared in some of the talented films
produced at the Studio: *The Devil's Wheel, The
New Babylon, SVD,* and other others.

"In those days we openly rejected everything
that had been considered art, creating quite an
uproar. Still, after such a brawling start, FEKS
evolved into something most serious and fundamental. Out of the Studio emerged later on a
film that still holds a place of honor in the history
of the art—I mean the *Maxim* trilogy, which
tells the story of the Bolshevik party. That's the
way time molded people in those days.

"In the thirties, with the advent of sound in
films, I took my first steps as film director.

"I would like to mention here three films
which became milestones in my life; all of them
had a common theme—the development of vast
territories in our country, from the Kola Peninsula (*The Bold Seven,* 1936) to the Far East
(*Komsomolsk,* 1937), while *The Teacher* (1939)
depicted how new life came into being in the
Urals.

"Critics sensed in these films an original tone,
as well as a realistic style of direction. A gifted
young actor, Pyotr Alejnikov, made his film debut in these pictures and such performers as Boris Chirkov and Oleg Jakov demonstrated their
acting abilities in full measure. Tamara Makarova participated in all these films, a dedicated actress and my lifetime companion and
associate.

"War broke out, just as I completed
Masquerade, adapted from a drama of the same

title by M. Lermontov; I played the part of the
Stranger. The film was ready on a Saturday, and
on the next day at noon an official preview was
to take place in order to get the approval of a
committee appointed to prepare Lermontov's
anniversary celebration. Instead of the preview,
we heard an announcement of the war. We had
to face a crucial decision. For this purpose we
met, together with Tamara, with a close friend
of ours, Mikhail Kalatozov, who also worked at
the Lenfilm Studios. Tamara put it bluntly: 'I
shall not leave Leningrad. I was born here. I
have lived here all my life and will go nowhere
else.' And so it was.

"We went to Smolny and explained our intention to stay. After a brief discussion, it was decided that we would be attached to the Political
Department of the Leningrad front. Thus war
came into our lives.

"On August 13th, 1941, Tamara and I joined
the Party.

"These pages in my biography can hardly be
considered as purely cinematic as a reader of a
film director's life story might expect. But I
would not be giving an accurate account of my
life in art if I omitted this most important period
in my destiny.

"As the year 1942 came to its end, we were
summoned to go to Moscow. There, upon approval of the recently completed *The Invincible,*
we resumed our film work, this time at the Mosfilm Studios. There I directed *Mainland,* a film
about life at the famous Kirov works which had
been evacuated to the Urals. I still value some
episodes in this film for their truthfulness. To my
mind and taste, Tamara Makarova created the
character that remained her greatest artistic accomplishment.

"Soon after finishing work on *Mainland,* I got
an absolutely unexpected official appointment
as Vice-President of the Committee of cinematography responsible for the war-newsreel department. And at the same time I became the
Head of Central Documentary Film Studios.

"This period of my life was rich in various encounters, journeys, diversified and meaningful
discoveries about human existence. I had to supervise filming at the Yalta and later the Pots-
dam Conferences, I saw defeated Berlin,
liberated Budapest, Vienna, Prague. Ever since
those times, I have not been able to separate in
my mind fiction films from documentary cinema; more than once in following years, I felt
compelled to work in documentary films and
truly enjoyed it.

"My first important postwar production was
a fiction film based on Alexander Fadeyev's novel *The Young Guard.* The production was closely

linked with my activities at the All-Union State Film School (the VGIK). It was a difficult and yet a happy time. Never, since my work on the early film *The Bold Seven*, did I experience such unity and enthusiasm from a young actors' team. A phenomenon quite understandable, since everybody involved was indissolubly linked with the war that had just ended. Everyone had seen it face to face. Almost all the boys had fought at the fronts and come back with wounds and war decorations. In spite of their youth, war had been daily life to them. They did not have to imagine at all. They just had to remember. *The Young Guard* brought into our cinema a whole new group of young actors and directors.

"As years passed, the pace of my professional life changed: I measured time not so much with new film productions, but rather with new pupils' graduations. The workshop at the VGIK became a life priority.

"Way back in the thirties I had dreamed of making a screen adaptation of Mikhail Sholokhov's *And Quiet Flows the Don*. That dream did not come true in those years, but the idea, once conceived, remained alive.

"The project took in almost everything that I had lived, thought, and felt throughout those unforgettable years. The novel itself became closer, more lucid. As time went by, *And Quiet Flows the Don* came to be widely read throughout the world; it helped people not only to understand our history—the events of our revolution and civil war—but also to get the sense of our manifold age, of the social storms of the twentieth century that no one could escape or hide from, although quite a few would like to find their own personal hideouts.

"*And Quiet Flows the Don* attracted and fascinated me by the grandeur of its representation of class struggle and of the revolutionary reconstruction of the world. I saw it as a canvas on which social and psychological elements, ideology, and intimately personal, innermost feelings were fused with great mastery and were revealed with an unusual, I would even say, a piercing truthfulness. Being a genuine contemporary of the period described by Sholokhov, I perceived his novel not as an abstract, alien, purely literary system, but rather as my own true life.

"I suppose another circumstance should be taken into account: my conscious life began in the distinctive environment of the Orenburg Cossacks living around Chebarkul. I had the opportunity to observe their way of life, and I remember many details, such as their specific gait, their habits, sense of humor, their behavior in diverse situations—at table during meals, in the saddle on horseback, amid daily domestic chores. I felt quite familiar with this material—the life of Cossacks had attracted me since my early childhood—and thus I at once established a very special relation, I would even say a kind of kinship, with *And Quiet Flows the Don*. Having made the film I did not put aside Sholokhov's novel—it still is to me a kind of reference point.

"Meditating upon all that we have achieved within half a century of ordeals, havoc, starvaton, wars imposed on us, toil that was at times unbearable, I discover around me beautiful signs of moral conquest. They consist in the ability of plain people to live and act with deep concern for the destiny of humanity as a whole; this destiny concerns us all, and every single person among us is able and obliged to influence it in one way or another. This very idea prompted the making of such films as *Men and Beasts* and *The Journalist*.

"It might be interesting to note that all episodes in the *Journalist* that are set in the Soviet Union were filmed in Miass, the small Urals town of my childhood. Of course, everything that had changed throughout the country during the past decades had changed here too; only nature remained the same. Even the big stone on the shore of Lake Chebarkul, from which we kids used to jump into the cold water, even the hole in it where we left our rags. This amazing permanency of nature brought forth, perhaps, the first idea for a next film, later given the title *At the Lake*.

"Collision between the perpetuity, one might even say, the immobility of the lake and its quiet waters, on one hand, and all that had seethed on its shores in the past years, on the other, seemed to be a good start for a plot, for a main story in which I was personally involved. But soon this project somehow dissolved and transformed itself into a story of the prolonged and (as can be seen now) most effective polemic aroused by the construction of a pulp-and-paper mill at Lake Baikal.

"The problem is not only economic, but moral as well. This is why a very young seventeen-year-old girl became the main character of the film; daughter of a Siberian biologist, she is a pure, sympathetic creature, brought up by her father in the broad but strict spirit of the scientific concept of the world. The film encompasses four years of her life in which she will understand and reevaluate many things, experience the drama of her father's death and her own first love; in other words, she has to confront all her youthful criteria with the diversity of life, where everything moves through a continuous clash of contradictions.

"The title of my next film was not found immediately, although it supplied the essential key for understanding the whole idea. At first the script was called *The Town-Builders*. When the film was almost completed we thought of a new title— *For the Love of Man*, for it became obvious that we needed a straightforward way to express the thought underlying the architectural idea that engaged the film's protagonists. That idea determined the very substance of their lives: it evolved in the depth of the aesthetic and moral environment created by them. These people fulfilled an important duty by building a new world; their talent, their experience and hard work were called upon to mold individuals and society.

"The story was based on an actually-existing project elaborated by the architect Shipkov, who intended to fight the Far North climate by architectural means. His idea was to protect a whole town against the cruel northern cold by constructing an overall shelter.

"The success of the project depended on the main character Kalmykov. From the very beginning I knew that this role would be played by the actor Anatoly Solonitzyn. Why was I so certain that he was to play the part? Possibly because of his extraordinary likeness to my father, whose photograph—taken in the early days of his activity as member of the Social-Democratic Party— is always on my desk.

"According to the concept of the film, the protagonist was to be a very special person, obsessed by his idea, neglecting himself, a man of a unique passion that encompassed even his love for his wife-to-be; as people put it, 'a wholehearted man.'

"One is not supposed to meet such people at every crossroads. But their striving for truth and their craving for work seem to me noble and useful for our society, although these aspects are nowadays often totally disregarded in artistic explorations of every kind. Everybody claims to be on the search for truth, but for some reason it is expressed in threading one human flaw after another, and the more numerous they are and the viler they look, the closer the whole is supposed to be the real truth.

"Love for man . . . means being able to understand and forgive; to resist the temptation of getting angry; to control oneself for the sake of safeguarding the basic thing, human love—this main feeling in life—for love creates life itself. This has been set up by nature itself.

"Some time later a new script came into my life. It was *Mothers and Daughters* by Alexander Vilodin. . . . In my capacity as artistic head of a creative unit at the Gorky Film Studios (where I have worked for over thirty years) I have the regular task of reading scripts; thus I took *Mothers and Daughters* in order to help bring it into being by selecting a suitable director and also to get hold of a good author for the Studios. I read it in just an hour and a half with an ardor quite unusual to me nowadays. Thereupon I called the Studios and said: There is no need to look for a director. I'll make the film myself.

"While reading the script, I thought of one of our students, Liuba Poleknina, who was herself a kind of phenomenon. In one of our papers a reporter had published the story of her entering the Film School: she had come to Moscow from the provinces, had earned her living by being a street sweeper, and then became a film actress—a true film-fan's legend, although the story in itself was by no means unusual in our country. It seemed that Liuba had been born to play the leading part in *Mothers and Daughters*.

"By that time I had been elected to the Academy of Pedagogical Sciences; actually in my mature years I had never given up teaching. But from now on the profession seemed to me doubly important; it spread far beyond the limits of the workshop and faculty chair at the Film School. It extended, so to speak, to something on the scale of general education. What compelled me to decide to explicitly and so quickly to start working at *Mothers and Daughters*? I suppose it must have been the concept of Volodin's work that, in my view, completely conformed with the most important problems of modern educational and family life.

"After *Mothers and Daughters* I began to work on an adaptation of Stendhal's novel *Le Rouge et le noir*. As I remember, many people wondered why I had turned abruptly toward classic literature after two decades of work indissolubly linked to modern subjects. But there was actually no abrupt turn whatsoever. In all the previous years I never gave up the classics. Approaches and beginnings for the creation of a TV serial based on Stendhal's novel could be easily found in my teaching practice, the fact being that *Le Rouge et le noir* was constantly on our workshop's program at the VGIK during six generations of students. Among several other classics of world literature, such as *War and Peace, And Quiet Flows the Don, Père Goriot, Carmen,* and *Hamlet,* our workshop used *Le Rouge et le noir* as basic didactic material. Students were educated on it.

"My next work, not for TV but for cinema again, was *Peter the Great*. I was often asked, why did I decide to adapt the novel *Peter the Great* for the screen? There was already a good film, made by Vladimir Petrov with the personal participation of Alexei Tolstoy himself. The novelist's conception was so vast that the filmmakers were necessarily compelled to limit themselves. They chose the central part of Peter the Great's life, the story of his struggle against his son Alexei, leaving out the important period of the hero's coming of age, his fight for power, the gigantic creative activity at the beginning of his career. In Petrov's film Peter was shown as a strong man and a powerful statesman.

"Personally, I was more interested in the way A. Tolstoy's book showed the formation of Peter's character, the growth of his fierceness and impetuousness, of his angularities, his vices, but also of all the traits of his genius. Therefore our film is about Peter's youth. And Peter's youth means the first manifestations of cruelty, means the Russian Middle Ages magnified by his impetuous, frenzied character. It is also the riot against the Boyars' patriarchy. An indomitable diligence. Everything that laid down the foundations of the future great reformer's character.

"I happened to read a most interesting book: foreign guests, merchants, ambassadors, scholars who had had the opportunity to visit Peter the Great wrote about him and his times. It's unimaginable what fancies were included! Or let's take, for example, the Valishevsky book. In this bulky volume the author found nothing else to tell but dirty stories about a bloodthirsty, despotic emperor. He endeavored to render under this aspect the history of Peter the Great. Some foreigners might have, probably, seen it in this way, because Russian history was alien to them and the Czar Peter appeared to be an unknowable figure.

"Cinema is to me a book coming to life. While working at a screen adaptation I try to use as the main key in my artistic search the writer's perception of life. I want to see a literary work just as its authors visualized it. I want to to give the audience a precise impression of the environment in which the protagonists of the film are existing.

"They very fact that we were allowed to film inside the Kremlin itself tuned us up to the right register—we entered the sacrosanct center of Russian history. In my view, respect for the subject of one's creative work is the Alpha and Omega in everything. Of course, we learned this in the first place from Alexei Tolstoy himself: to respect Russian history, to be thrilled by its significant events, by its heroes.

"The idea of creating a film about Russia's great writer Leo Tolstoy came to my mind every now and again. By no means should it be a film of his works—his literary heritage, his fiction, especially, had been already widely used—it was to be a film about himself. I am deeply convinced that the most interesting object in any writing is the author himself. Which is particularly true when one has to do with such a personality as Leo Tolstoy—a man who had an amazing character, a phenomenal life-story, encompassing multitudes of diverse, sometimes contradictory gusts and essentials of his manifold existence.

"I thought the film should be focused on the authentic personality of Lev Nikolayevich Tolstoy, as he could be visualized through reading his many works, diaries, different documents, as well as through the evidence of his relatives and those who were close to him, including his biographers—Biryukov, Gussev, Bulgakov, Goldenweiser, Chertkov, Sergeyenko and many others—all of them having portrayed Leo Tolstoy during his lifetime, each according to his own understanding, his ability to observe, his appreciation of Tolstoy's place and importance in contemporary world.

"Of special importance, quite obviously, were the memoirs and diaries of Sofia Andreyevna, Tolstoy's spouse, as well as books by his sons and daughters, and also the extremely interesting and detailed day-by-day notes taken by his doctor Makovitzky.

"Along this path was molded and built up, step by step, the script of a film that was to be made in two parts. An idea came forth to focus the first part on Tolstoy's insomnia: during sleepless nights deeply intimate memories arise in his mind, resuscitating crucial moments and turning points in his astonishing life.

"Tolstoy's departure from Yasnaya Polyana and his ensuing death in the small, obscure railroad station Astapovo made up the film's second part; it comprised both the tragedy of this particular family and of the epoch, which was a turning point for Russia as a whole; it emphasized the heritage bequeathed to humanity by this death.

"Tolstoy believed that the world should and would, without fail, be full of harmony and happiness. But this would ensue only if man would eradicate from his soul egoism and indifference towards other people's destinies. This still remains a fundamental theme.

"At my mature (to put it mildly) age, the time has come to consider what I can leave to those who live after me. To leave a legacy means to create something that will, as much as possible, help people live and work. This very thought guided me towards Leo Tolstoy. Why do I, today, wish so eagerly to show Leo Tolstoy? Well, in the first place, because he is the receptacle of human conscience. And today, especially today, it would be most useful to 'buck up' our feeling of conscience. I would like to produce a story that would be congenial to all of us, a story about a man who is still close to us all, a story about a great human being whose problems became our own: problems of moral education and of shaping human individuals.

"Moral education—of our contemporaries and of the man of the future—is a theme and a task our society has to face today. History passed it on to us, and we are working at it, with the inevitable errands and searches. And with great victories that cannot be disregarded; and here again Tolstoy comes to our help by reinforcing our faith in ourselves, in our cause.

"The complexity of the leading role imposed on me the necessity of playing the part of Tolstoy myself and of suggesting to my constant companion and favorite actress Tamara Makarova that she perform the part of Tolstoy's wife.

"The film is preceded by an epigraph, in which one has the feeling of hearing the live voice of Lev Nikolayevich. It is as if he were to speak to us right now, almost eighty years after passing away. It is a note from his diary, dated October 26th, 1907: 'How strange it is that I have to be silent with the people living around me, and can talk only to those who are far away in time and space, but who will listen to me.'"

Gerasimov was excluded by illness from FEKS' first film, the fantastic comedy *Adventures of Oktyabrina* (1924), but participated wholeheartedly in most of the others, which in the course of a few years progressed from American-style slapstick comedies and thrillers to political engagement. He specialized in villainous roles and played them realistically, with a clear sense of psychological and societal motivation. The results, as Robert Dunbar says in *The International Dictionary of Films and Filmmakers,* were "very much more chilling than the antics of the usual silent film 'heavy.'" *Who's Who in the Soviet Cinema* gives this description of Gerasimov in the role of Medoks, the treacherous provocateur in *SVD* (1927), a drama about the Decembrist revolt in 1825: "Powerful, agile hands framed by lacy cuffs shuffle cards on a covered table in a murky room in a gambling house. Then the camera rises and we see a face with a large forehead and piercing eyes whose glance is as cold and hard as stone . . . and with a mouth drawn into a decisive and ominously thin line. . . . The role of Medoks shot Gerasimov into the front ranks of silent cinema actors."

Kozintsev greatly admired Gerasimov's talent for pantomime and wrote: "He could recreate a film in its entirety. He could act out a detective story all by himself: the murderer, the investigation, and the pursuit; or he would act out a slapstick scene: a brawl with the police, a farce with cream pies thrown in someone's face." In Kozintsev and Trauberg's *Alone* (1931), Gerasimov served as assistant director as well as playing the obtuse *kolkhov* chairman. Recalling his rural childhood, he "saw that the text for my role did not in any respect correspond to reality" and rebelled against the system under which an actor "blindly followed the will of the director. . . . I wanted to do something else, according to my own ideas. . . . From that moment, I think, dated my first real relationship with art. . . . Moreover, it is from this film that my path took a different turn from that of FEKS; this was our last work together" (though he took parts in several films directed by Kozintsev and Trauberg after the demise of FEKS).

By this time, as he tells above, Gerasimov had already become a director in his own right. From the outset, his work was fundamentally naturalistic, showing little of the FEKS "eccentricity." His first movie, directed in collaboration with another tyro, Sergei Bartenev, was *Twenty-Two Misfortunes* (1930), a satire on narrow-minded Philistinism. It was, according to Gerasimov, "a real disaster. . . . We were both of us spectacularly ignorant in the matter of *mise-en-scène.* . . . The film turned out as weak in sense as in talent and, thank heavens, no fragment of it survives today." Gerasimov's first solo effort, *The Forest* (1931), about the life of woodcutters, was somewhat more promising, and this film, he said, "marked my first steps on the thorny road of screenwriting. I must admit that I have always been very attracted to this literary exercise: I think I get most pleasure out of writing." After *The Heart of Solomon* (1932) came *Do I Love You?* (1934). Described by one critic as an "intelligent probing" into love, marriage, and family life in Soviet society, it showed a particular interest in the problems of young people (a perennial concern of Gerasimov's). Its message was that the time had come for an end to the freewheeling morals of the 1920s and a return to traditional values.

It was not until 1936 that Gerasimov was allowed to make a talkie. *Semero smelykh* (*The Bold Seven*), which he wrote in collaboration with the novelist Yuri Guerman, is a stirring tale about a group of young people battling against the rigors and perils of the Arctic to build a polar station. According to one account, "the film is full of the joy of discovery, when the young explorers find large tin deposits, and the sorrow of loss, when the meteorologist Osya dies in a fall from a cliff, and young love between the leader of the expedition, Ilya Letnikov, and the doctor, Zhenya Okhrimenko, and most important of all, it is filled with the sense of working together, the strength of each person in the working collective."

Gerasimov said this was "the first film I made in my own style. I had always been irritated by the intrusion of theatrical methods into the cinema. All those forced intonations, the fashion of playing to the public, facing the camera and the microphone, all the other borrowings from the theatre which marked the early sound period, seemed to me of heartbreaking naivety. . . . Guerman and I . . . wanted to try to give the impression of people spied on by the camera, something specifically cinematographic." The result was a great success with both the general public and the critics. Jay Leyda praised its "youthful originality," its selectivity and restraint, and its avoidance of "the temptations of melodrama," while Kozintsev wrote that Gerasimov's method was "the only manly and calm style in which to speak of heroes."

During his years with FEKS, Gerasimov had discovered a particular interest in and talent for the training of young actors, and *The Bold Seven* gave him an excellent opportunity to develop this skill—he said it marked "the debut of my pedagogic career: the unit was essentially my class, my pupils." The acting in the film was much admired, especially that of Nikolai Bogolyubov, who played the hero, and of Tamara Makarova (the doctor), the young actress whom Gerasimov had married in 1928 and who starred in the majority of his subsequent pictures.

Gerasimov was able to work with several of the same young actors (including Makarova) in his next film, *Komsomolsk* (*City of Youth,* 1938). This was a dramatized account (reportedly suggested by Stalin himself) of the building by Komsomol (Young Communist) workers of a new industrial community on the Amur River, in the Soviet Far East. Portraying the hardships faced by the young enthusiasts (and warning of the need for vigilance against class enemies), the movie was another great success, praised as a model of Socialist Realism. Unlike more propagandistic works in that style, Dunbar says, it depicted "ordinary young people as varied, breathing, living human beings rather than animated heroic sculptures."

In 1938, by now established as one of the leading filmmakers of his generation, Gerasimov became a teacher in the directors' seminar at the Lenfilm Studios. At the same time, he began work on a script for what became *Uchitel* (*The Teacher,* 1939), about a young graduate (Boris Chirkov) who, instead of pursuing a more ambi-

tious career, returns as a teacher to his native village. There he encounters considerable hostility but also a gifted young village girl (Makarova) who wants an education. Gerasimov's original scenario won first prize in a national competition and was published, setting off a nationwide debate. Some film critics objected to the "love interest" and touches of humor Gerasimov had introduced into his fundamentally serious examination of a critical problem in Soviet education, but hundreds of teachers and educators defended the script, providing a mass of facts, figures, and anecdotes in support of its thesis. Some of these suggestions were incorporated in a revised scenario, and the result was another financial and critical triumph.

The Soviet Union went to war against Germany in 1941 and the same year began the production of the monthly *Fighting Film Albums,* each made up of two or three short films—usually fictional—about some aspect of the war. "Meeting With Maxim," using the famous character (a young Bolshevik worker) created in Kozintsev and Trauberg's Maxim trilogy, was Gerasimov's contribution to the first of the *Albums.* The same year saw the release of *Maskarad* (*Masquerade*), an elaborate and gorgeously mounted adaptation of Lermontov's verse tragedy, starring Tamara Makarova. Gerasimov himself wrote the adaptation and played a secondary role. "I have always loved Lermontov, who comes next to Pushkin in my preferences," Gerasimov wrote, "perhaps because of certain romantic traditions which derive from Schiller. I adapted *Masquerade* with all the delight of a gourmet faced with his favorite dish" and "tried only to reproduce what Lermontov had created. There is a theatrical tradition of having Arbenin, the jealous husband and murderer, played by septuagenarians, although he is in fact at most twenty-six. And I made a youthful *Masquerade,* a story of young people, not something from a historical museum. The one question I never ceased to ask myself was 'How would Lermontov himself have wanted to see this?'"

Nepobedimye (*The Invincible,* 1943), directed in collaboration with Mikhail Kalatozov, was a mediocre but popular war drama about the defense of Leningrad. (The studios had been evacuated to Tashkent and the film was made by a cast sweltering in winter clothing amid imitation snowdrifts in the merciless heat of Central Asia). *Bolshaya zemlya* (*Mainland/The Great Earth,* 1944) was also a war film, this time dealing with a factory evacuated from Leningrad to the Urals, and the struggle to bring it back into full production. In 1944 Gerasimov was appointed vice-chairman of the Cinematographic Committee on War Reporting and head of the Central Newsreel and Documentary Studios in Moscow. There he was responsible for the production of some notable documentaries about the last stages of the war by such directors as Sergei Yutkevich, Josif Heifitz, Yuli Raizman, and others who (like himself) were otherwise best known for their feature films.

In 1945 Gerasimov joined the staff of the Moscow Film School (VGIK) as head of the Joint Acting and Directing Workshop. His first postwar film seriously dented his reputation. *Molodaya gvardiya* (*The Young Guard*) is a two-part adaptation of the Stalin Prize–winning novel by Gerasimov's friend Alexander Fadeyev about the heroic role of the Komsomol resistance organization in occupied Krasnodon in 1941. The cast and crew included many of Gerasimov's VGIK students, including such future notables as Sergei Bondarchuk and Samson Samsonov. The first part of the film was completed (and released, according to some accounts) in 1947 but was savagely criticized for including "negativistic" scenes of flight and panic in the withdrawal from Krasnodon and for giving too much credit to the Young Guard themselves (instead of their Communist Party seniors). Gerasimov rapidly revised the offending scenes, and when the complete film was released in 1948, it was warmly praised by the Party hacks and given a Stalin Prize.

Discussing this film, Jay Leyda refers to Gerasimov's prewar interest in making a film about Chekhov that would show "the meaning of modesty in combination with talent." Leyda writes that "this could have stood as Gerasimov's artistic credo up to that point—but something altered his direction during the war years; it may have been the handling of the beauties of *Masquerade,* it may have been his dissatisfaction with both his wartime films—*Invincible,* with Kalatozov, and *Mainland*—or some part of the reason may be sought in his decision to join the Communist Party in 1944, or in his work at the Documentary Film Studio. In any case the first film he made after the war is artistically one of the least modest films ever produced in the Soviet Union. In *Young Guard* the formerly acute observation of simple behavior is transformed into the grandiose, inflated mock heroics of popular nineteenth-century literature."

By 1949, at any rate, Gerasimov was back in official favor. He was part of the Soviet delegation to the Cultural and Scientific Conference for World Peace in New York. There he made his famous attack on Hollywood films for implicitly advocating the view that "to live better, to attain happiness, one must deceive, oppress and enslave, obtain profits by hook or by crook. . . . Irrespective of whether they deal with wages, honor, love or matrimony, the decisive argument in these films is violence, firearms, shooting, murder, and death." The same year Gerasimov went to China, where he stayed for almost a year and collaborated with a Chinese director on a film about the defeat of Chiang Kai-shek.

Gerasimov's next picture suggested that *The Young Guard* was a temporary aberration rather than a change of direction. *Selski vrach* (*The Country Doctor,* 1952) is an unexceptional but characteristically modest and observant story about the life and work of a woman doctor (Makarova) in a provincial town in Siberia, where her patients gradually come to accept her "advanced" ideas. It was followed by one of the most admired of all his films, *Tikhi Don* (*And Quiet Flows the Don,* 1957–1958), a loving and scrupulously faithful adaptation in three parts of the novels—until recently attributed to Dmitri Sholokhov—about the people of a Cossack village beside the River Don and the impact on them of the great events of the twentieth century. "Gerasimov's vast, tripartite screen fresco generally does not venture beyond illustrating the novel with dynamic images," Adam Garbicz and Jacek Klinowski write, but "the Russian spirit which pervades the whole is quite convincing; so is the sense of an individual being immersed in and determined by history, the attention to detail, and the expressively photographed scenery." *And Quiet Flows the Don* won prizes at Brussels, Karlovy Vary, and Moscow, and is regarded by some critics as one of the finest Soviet films of the 1950s. It is the last of the director's works to deal directly with the Russian revolution.

Gerasimov then embarked on a series of films, much discussed in the USSR, that take as their theme the moral development of the individual in a post-revolutionary society, often against a backdrop of contemporary social issues. *Lyudi i zveri* (*Men and Beasts,* 1962), a Soviet–East German coproduction, concerns a Russian veteran who has spent the years since World War II abroad, and the difficulties he encounters when he finally comes home. The London *Observer* compared it to "a Victorian sampler." Gerasimov made more effective use of similar material in *Zhurnalist* (*Journalist,* 1967), which follows a young newspaperman as he learns his trade (and discovers his true loyalties) on assignments that take him from a village in the Urals to the glittering and seductive capitals of the West. The film, wrote *Variety* "goes a long way to try to be objective . . . in its observations of the current Russian and European scene." Winner of the main prize at the Moscow Film Festival,

Zhurnalist was followed by *V ozera* (*At the Lake*, 1969), which received a state prize in the USSR and the jury prize at Karlovy Vary. The heroine of this two-part film is caught up in the controversy (an actual one) between engineers intent upon developing the resources of Siberia and biologists determined to protect the unique ecosystem of Lake Baikal. Considerable suspense is generated as she learns both the value and the limitations of scientific idealism.

Two of the most popular of all Gerasimov's films followed. *Lyubit cheloveka* (*For Love of Man*, 1972) centers on the love affair that flares up between two architects designing a complex of buildings in the far north. *Dochki-Materi* (*Mothers and Daughters*, 1974), based on a play by Alexander Volodin, tells the story of a young woman, abandoned as a child, who is caught up in a destructively obsessive search for her mother. She encounters a family of the same name, and though it emerges that they are not related, they take her in and provide her with a surrogate family that gives new meaning to her life. "I cannot divide social and political themes from personal themes arising from daily life," Gerasimov said. "I consider the cinema's purpose to be establishing tangible links between the universal and the specific."

In 1976 Gerasimov completed a much-praised five-part television adaptation of Stendhal's *Le Rouge et le noir*. He went on to direct three films that carefully recreate the Russian past. Characteristically, he centered his two-part biography of Peter the Great on the future czar's formative years. Dmitry Zolotukhin plays Peter, Natalia Bondarchuk the Princess Sofia, and Tamara Makarova the Czarina Natalia Kirilovna (Peter's mother). *Yunost Piotr* (*The Youth of Peter*) and *V natchale slavniykh del* (*At the Beginning of Glorious Deeds*), which continues the story, were both awarded a special prize at the Venice Film Festival but have not been widely seen in the West. Neither has Gerasimov's last film, *Lev Tolstoi* (*Leo Tolstoy*, 1984), in which he and Makarova play the leading roles.

In a statement in Luda and Jean Schnitzer's *Cinema in Revolution*, Gerasimov said: "I consider that the cinema . . . despite its reputation as a team activity, is absolutely and rigorously . . . an author's art. Who is the author? . . . It can be the writer, the director, the cameraman, the actor. It is always the one who is the real master of the original idea and of the *passions* of the work. . . . When I have adapted works of literature, I have never considered them as *my* films. *And Quiet Flows the Don* is Sholokhov's film."

In the same statement, made in 1964, Gerasimov commented on the "de-dramatization" movement sparked by the French New Wave: "De-dramatization, as I conceive it, is simply the rejection of the classical rules of dramaturgy in favor of the dramaturgy of real life. To depart from mechanical methods, tricks of the trade; to move towards the comprehension, the interpretation of real facts, things which actually exist in life, in all their complexity and all their contradictions—this is how I understand the new dramaturgy. . . . I am all for life, because life confounds art. It is so much more interesting." And on *mise-en-scène*, he said: "You must not limit yourself to depicting the elements of the action within a given frame. You must have a sense of the liberty which exists beyond the frame, 'out of shot.' You must have, and convey, the feeling of life effervescing on either side of the screen. You must give the impression that the screen is only a window open upon an immense life."

As head of the Acting and Directing Workshop of the VGIK for upwards of thirty years, Gerasimov had an incalculable influence on younger directors and on Soviet film in general. He was committed to a narrative, naturalistic cinema that would be, ideally, both true to human experience and faithful to the ideology of his party. If he saw any contradiction in this dual goal, he resolved it with an optimistic and assured professionalism. Throughout his teaching career, Gerasimov did much to maintain high professional standards at the Moscow Film School and to provide his students with a thorough grounding in the basics. Most Western critics believe that his own work suffered a decline in artistic quality during the Stalin years, and Robert Dunbar, for one, says that although "much of Gerasimov's post-Stalin output saw a return to his themes of the thirties . . . he never quite recaptured his freshness of approach and lightness of touch." His official duties were many. Besides holding a professorship at the VGIK, he served at various times as secretary of the Union of Cinematographers, on the editorial board of the journal *Iskusstvo Kino*, on the World Peace Council, in the Academy of Pedagogic Sciences, and as a deputy to the Supreme Soviets of the USSR and the RSFSR. In 1984 he was awarded his country's highest honor, the Lenin Prize. Previously he had been named a Hero of Socialist Labor (1974) and a People's Artist (1948). Gerasimov and his wife had one son.

FILMS: (with Sergei Bartenev) Twenty-Two Misfortunes, 1930; The Forest, 1931; (with M. Kressin) The Heart of Solomon, 1932; Do I Love You?, 1934; Semero smelykh (The Bold Seven/The Brave Seven), 1936; Komsomolsk (City of Youth/The Far North),

1938; Uchitel (The Teacher/The New Teacher), 1939; Maskarad (Masquerade), 1941; Meeting With Maxim *in* Fighting Film Album 1, 1941; The Old Guard, 1941 (medium length); (with Efim Dzigan and Mikhail Kalatozov) Film-Concert Dedicated to the 25th Anniversary of the Red Army, 1943; (with Mikhail Kalatozov) Nepobedimye (The Invincible/The Unconquerable), 1943; Bolshaya zemlya (Mainland/The Great Earth), 1944; Molodaya gvardiya (The Young Guard), 1948; (with Sui Sao-bin) Osvobozhdennyej Kitai (Liberated China), 1950; Selski vrach (The Country Doctor), 1952; Nadezhda, episode in Die Windrose (The Wind Rose), 1956; Tikhi Don (And Quiet Flows the Don), 1957–1958 (in three parts); (codirector) Sputnik Speaking, 1959; Lyudi i zveri (Men and Beasts/Menschen und Tiere), 1962; Zhurnalist (Journalist), 1967; V ozera (At the Lake), 1969; Lyubit cheloveka (For Love of Man), 1972; Dochki-Materi (Mothers and Daughters), 1974; Krasnoye i chyornoye (Le Rouge et le noir/The Red and the Black), 1976 (for television); Yunost Piotra (The Youth of Peter), 1981; V natchale skavnykh del (At the Beginning of Glorious Deeds), 1981; Lev Tolstoi (Leo Tolstoy), 1984. *Published scripts*—Uchitel, 1939; Bolshaya zemlya, 1943; Zhurnalist, 1968; V ozera *in* Isskustvo Kino 12 1968; Lyubit cheloveka, 1973.

ABOUT: Birkos, A. S. Soviet Cinema, 1976; Dolmatovskaya, G. and Shilova, I. Who's Who in the Soviet Cinema, 1979; Dunbar, R. *in* Lyon, C. (ed.) International Dictionary of Films and Filmakers, 1984; Garbicz, A. and Klinowski, J. Cinema: The Magic Vehicle, 1983; International Who's Who, 1980–81; Katz, E. The Film Encyclopedia, 1979; Leyda, J. Kino, 1960; Liehm, M. and A. The Most Important Art: Soviet and Eastern European Film After 1945, 1977; Schnitzer, L. and J. (eds.) Cinema in Revolution, 1973; Thomson, D. Biographical Dictionary of Film, 1976. *Periodicals*—Cinema Papers March–April 1976; Film (Britain) Spring 1969, Summer 1971; Film World October–December 1968; Films and Filming December 1958, March 1961; Iskusstvo Kino 8 1965, 5 1966, 12 1968, 5 1981, 3 1985, 7 1985; Soviet Film 3 1971, 6 1974, 6 1976, (261) 1979, 1 1981, 7 1981, 2 1982, 2 1985; Variety December 4, 1985.

GERMI, PIETRO (September 14, 1914–December 5, 1974), Italian director, scenarist, and actor, was born into a working-class family in Colombo, Liguria, and had to earn his own living from an early age. He worked as an errand boy, a bartender, and in various other casual jobs, and then entered the Genoa Instituto Nautice (naval college). Disliking the discipline, he left to study acting at the Italian film school, the Centro Sperimentale di Cinematografia. After completing the two-year acting course he stayed on at the CSC for another year to study directing, paying his way by working as an extra, a coscenarist, and a (reportedly cantankerous) assistant to Blasetti and others. At this time,

PIETRO GERMI

according to one account, Germi was a young man "who smoked strong Tuscan cigars, who was often unshaved, and argued hotly. . . . He was completely tactless, he didn't do anything to win approval, and his abrupt manners went well with his harsh little cigars."

Germi's first film, *Il testimone* (*The Witness*), was a thriller starring Marina Berti and Roldano Lupi, notable for its fresh and well-observed portrayal of suburban life. Released just after the war in the summer of 1946, it was shown in half-empty theaters to audiences more interested in the American movies that were then returning to their screens. All the same, a few critics noted that Germi's low-budget picture was of more than ordinary interest and gave it the Nastro d'Argento—the Italian Oscar—for its original screenplay, coauthored by the director.

This modest success was enough to bring Germi an assignment from Carlo Ponti. *Gioventù perduta* (*Lost Youth,* 1947), a story about teenage crime, has Jacques Sernas as a psychopathic student, Massimo Girotti as a detective, and Carla Del Poggio as the former's sister and the latter's girlfriend. The film upset the censors with its very detailed account of the planning and execution of various armed holdups, but was commercially successful and brought Germi another Nastro d'Argento, this time for the best Italian picture of 1948. The same year Germi gave a notable performance as a soldier in Mario Soldati's *Fuga in Francia*.

It was his own next film that established his international critical reputation, *In nome della legge* (*In the Name of the Law,* 1949), adapted by Germi and a whole team of writers (including

Federico Fellini) from Giuseppe Loschiavo's popular novel *Piccolo pretura*. It tells the story of Guido (Massimo Girotti), a young judge who comes to the Sicilian village of Capodarso and clashes with the local landowner and the Mafia. He forces the landowner to reopen a sulfur mine, providing work, but fails to win the trust of the people until, enraged by the murder of a youth he has befriended, he summons the whole village to an open trial, confronts Passalacqua (Charles Vanel), the Mafia chief, and wins his submission to the rule of law.

This upbeat conclusion is dramatically satisfying but obviously unrealistic. According to the Italian critic Ugo Casiraghi, Germi was obliged to submit his script to a Mafia leader and accept a compromise: "The film virtually idealizes the Mafia. The *mafiosi,* their leader in particular, are portrayed as knights of honor." There were also critical complaints about the love affair between Guido and the landowner's wife, obviously added by way of conventional romantic interest. But, as Roy Armes wrote, "the film also contains many incidental indications of the director's talent. The action scenes are well handled: the tense atmosphere surrounding Guido when he stands up to Passalacqua or the sudden void that opens up around a man known to be under sentence by the Mafia when he enters the bar. . . . Germi also contrives to touch briefly on a number of important social issues. . . . But the deepest impression left by *In nome della legge* is the quality of its visual style, its bold use of contrast, making full use of the possibilities offered by the arid Sicilian landscape, setting the black-garbed figures of the women against the dazzling whiteness of sun-drenched walls and focusing on the care-worn faces of authentic Sicilian workers."

Pierre Leprohon, in his account of the same movie, says that Germi "reveals considerable gifts for composition enhanced by austere, direct editing with no fading in or out, a sequence of shots captured by a fixed, objective camera. Like De Santis, Germi seems to have taken as his model the films of the Russian school—there is clear evidence of this in the sequence where the peasants, answering the summons of the alarm bell, gather on the village square, in the close-ups of tense faces, and in the social-documentary aspect" of the film.

Il cammino della speranza (*The Road To Hope*, 1950) was inspired by what Germi had seen in Sicily during the filming of *In nome della legge* and tackles another major social theme—that of emigration. It begins with a sit-in amid the fumes of a sulfur mine—an unsuccessful attempt to prevent its closure—and shows the dawning of hope when a stranger named Ciccio turns up, offering (for a price) to smuggle the villagers into France, where work is said to be plentiful. The body of the movie deals with the trek across Italy of a party of villagers led by the widower Saro (Raf Vallone) and guided by Ciccio. Along the way they are joined by Barbara (Elena Varza) and her gangster lover and at the Rome railroad station Ciccio provokes a gun battle between the gangster and police, absconding in the confusion. After this debacle, some of the peasants turn back, but the others press on in the face of every kind of adversity, and in the end a handful of them (including Saro and Barbara) reach their uncertain promised land.

Like its predecessor, *The Road to Hope* was photographed by Leonida Barboni, has a score by Carlo Rustichelli, and was coauthored by the director. But its treatment of its theme, most critics agreed, was considerably more honest, penetrating, and committed than in the earlier film. In spite of its melodramatic elements, it seemed to Roy Armes that "the social message of the film is not distorted. . . . There is no attempt to gloss over the bitterness produced by political unrest or to pretend that there are any easy solutions to the problems raised." It received the Selznick Golden Laurel at the Venice festival in 1951.

On account of their social concerns, their austerity of style, and even their weakness for melodrama, Germi's two Sicilian films are generally described as neorealist works and indeed are often listed among the more memorable products of the last years of that movement. Germi himself rejected the neorealist label, however, and Roy Armes makes the interesting suggestion that these pictures might owe more to the influence of John Ford, whom Germi greatly admired. *The Road to Hope* obviously has a good deal in common with *The Grapes of Wrath*—the journey across a whole country towards a "promised land," and even a scene in which honest workers are driven by events to become unwitting scabs. Beyond that, as Armes points out, both movies conform to the typical pattern of a Ford Western, being "built around the performance of an indestructible hero, played by an actor with star quality. The landscape plays an important part in expressing and visualising the essential conflicts."

After these two major efforts, Germi for a time seemed uncertain of his direction. *La città si difende* (*Four Ways Out*, 1951), a moderately interesting underworld story that picked up an award at Venice, was followed by a period piece, *Il brigante di Tacca del Lupo* (*The Brigand From Tacca del Lupo*, 1952), set in the period of confusion and warfare between soldiers and guerrillas that followed the collapse of the Kingdom of the Two Sicilys in the nineteenth century. Then came a successful social satire, *La presidentessa* (*Mademoiselle Gobette,* 1952), starring Silvana Pampanini as a cabaret star, investigated for appearing too scantily clad, who winds up as the influential mistress of the Minister of Justice; Pauline Kael called it a "neat little farce" combining "social ridicule and some light, deft horseplay." *Gelosia* (*Jealousy,* 1953) is a remake of a film made in 1942 by Ferdinando Poggioli.

When Germi returned to more serious concerns, he was seen to be addressing himself less to social questions than to the problems of the individual—though always the individual as a member of a carefully defined social group. *Il ferroviere* (*The Railroad Man,*/*Man of Iron,* 1956) centers on Andrea, a heavy-fisted, hard-drinking "man's man" and a crack railroad engineer. In his fiftieth year, the world suddenly begins to go wrong for Andrea—his son is a petty criminal, his daughter is bitterly unhappy in her shotgun marriage, and Andrea runs down a suicide in his locomotive. Demoted, he loses the last remnants of his pride when he scabs during a strike. He has a nearly fatal heart attack, but lives long enough for a happy, tearful family reunion at Christmas.

"Miraculously," wrote a reviewer in *Time,* "from this carload of sentimental clichés Germi weaves a compassionate, richly detailed reminiscence of the commonplace tragedies that every generation endures. . . . All of it seems familiar, all of it is quickened by a thorny sense of truth." *L'uomo di paglia* (*Man of Straw*/*The Seducer,* 1957) is a companion piece, dealing with a middle-aged factory engineer who has an affair with a young typist (sensitively played by Franca Bettoja) while his wife and child are away at the seashore. For the man the relationship is no more than a diversion, and it ends as soon as his wife returns; for the girl it is much more, and she kills herself.

Germi himself played the lead role in both of these films, earning a more consistently good press for his acting than for his directing. *Man of Straw* brought him an award as best director at Mar del Plata, but at Cannes, according to Pierre Leprohon, both films were "met mainly by sarcasm and indifference." This seemed to Leprohon unfair: "If his films are melodramatic it is because they are faithful reflections of reality, a reality closely defined in terms of race and class. . . . He is simple and direct, taking us straight to the heart of his milieu, those 'average' families continental critics and public detest,

though for different reasons. . . . The first part of *Man of Iron,* and even more that of *Man of Straw,* are quite remarkable in their way: the characters, the setting and the movement are absolutely authentic—an authenticity which is not confined, as in naturalism, to . . . outer appearances . . . but which delves to the very heart of the individual and gradually, through his eyes and his reactions, reveals to us the little universe in which he lives. . . . But [Germi's] plots drag on long after they have made their point; hence the forced endings, the calamities which suddenly rain down on his heroes and cause the human adventure to founder on the rocks of the romantic-jejune."

Germi again cast himself in an important role in the very different kind of film that followed, appearing as the police inspector in *Un maledetto imbroglio* (*A Sordid Affair,* 1959). Based on Carlo Gadda's extraordinary novel *Quer pasticciaccio brutto de via Merulana,* it takes off from a grotesque crime of violence in Rome. Germi could make little of the Joycean wordplay with which the novel abounds, but reveled in its baroque gallery of crooks, pimps, whores, and hypocritical *petits bourgeois,* and the film was both a critical and popular success.

Returning to Sicily to make his next movie, Germi reemerged not with an impassioned social document in the spirit of *The Road to Hope* but with a deeply cynical comedy of manners. *Divorzio all'Italiana* (*Divorce, Italian Style,* 1961) stars Marcello Mastroianni as a Sicilian aristocrat in love with his cousin Angela (Stefania Sandrelli). Forbidden by his country's antique laws to divorce his wife (Daniela Rocca), he maneuvers her into adultery and then "defends his honor" by killing her. After a brief jail sentence he returns home to a hero's welcome and Angela's eager arms; her gaze, however, is already wandering. This black comedy was the first resounding international hit of Germi's career—a huge critical and commercial success throughout Europe and in the United States, where it won an Oscar for best original screenplay.

Divorzio all'Italiana inspired a host of imitations, most of them inferior and several of them directed by Germi himself, like *Sedotta e abbandonata* (*Seduced and Abandoned,* 1963), an equally unsparing but relatively uninventive attack on Sicilian mores, about a family's frantic (and almost murderous) efforts to retrieve its honor after a daughter (Stefania Sandrelli) is deflowered. More a caricature than a satire, the movie was nevertheless another box-office hit, and in 1965 Germi, with L. Vincenzoni, launched his own production company, RPA. Its first film was another black comedy, set this time in a provincial town in northern Italy. *Signore e signori (The Birds, the Bees and the Italians,* 1965) shows us a bourgeois community of adulterers, voyeurs, and gossips, no whit better than their southern counterparts—except for one truly loving but unmarried couple who dare to live together openly, so affronting the local hypocrites that their destruction is inevitable. Admired by some critics for its "impeccable feeling for pace," this picture received the Palme d'or—the major prize—at Cannes.

Most of Germi's subsequent films were in a similar vein. *L'immorale (The Immoralist,* 1966) stars Sandrelli and Ugo Tognazzi in a story about a musician who works himself to death trying to support the three wives and families he has recklessly acquired. The hero of *Serafino* (1968) is a shepherd from the Abruzzi (played by Adriano Celentano)—a man who has grown up in such absolute freedom that the army is defeated in its attempt to discipline him and discharges him as "unadaptable to modern society." This comedy was followed by a romantic love story, *Le castagne sono buone (A Pocketful of Chestnuts,* 1970), and then by another satire on the Italian marriage trap, *Alfredo, Alfredo* (1972). Germi's last film, this stars Dustin Hoffman as a shy young bank clerk infatuated by the beautiful but mindless and sexually rapacious Mariarosa (Sandrelli). He is finally rescued by a coolly intelligent career woman (Carla Gravina).

Germi was an abrupt, silent man, said to "open his mouth every second day." An American critic has described him as "Italy's greatest film satirist of the postwar period." It seems a subject for satire that he achieved his greatest fame as the mordant observer of *Divorce, Italian Style;* his earlier films, which were more optimistic or more compassionate, were never so widely appreciated.

FILMS: Il testimone (The Witness), 1946; Gioventù perduta (Lost Youth), 1947; In nome della legge (In the Name of the Law), 1949; Il cammino della speranza (The Road to Hope), 1950; La città si difende (Four Ways Out/Passport to Hell), 1951; Il brigante di Tacca del Lupo, 1952; La presidentessa (Mademoiselle Gobette/The Lady President), 1952; Gelosia, 1953; *episode in* Amore di mezzo secolo, 1954; Il ferroviere (The Railroad Man/Man of Iron), 1956; L'uomo di paglia (The Seducer/Man of Straw), 1957; Un maledetto imbroglio (A Sordid Affair/An Ugly Mess/The Facts of Murder), 1959; Divorzio all'Italiana (Divorce, Italian Style), 1961; Sedotta e abbandonata (Seduced and Abandoned), 1963; Signore e signori (The Birds, the Bees and the Italians), 1965; La bomba, 1966; L'immorale (The Immoralist/Too Much for One Man/The Climax), 1966; Serafino, 1968; Le castagne son o buone (Pocketful of Chestnuts/Till Divorce Do You Part), 1970; Alfredo, Alfredo, 1972.

ABOUT: Armes, R. Patterns of Realism, 1971; Leprohon, P. The Italian Cinema, 1972; Schlappñer, M. Von Rosselini zu Fellini, 1958. *Periodicals*—Bianco e Nero June 1966; Cineforum August 1979; Cinéma (France) February 1975; Cinema Nuovo November–December 1974; Écran February 1975, September 1976; Film Dope December 1979; Films and Filming September 1966; New York Times December 6, 1974; Time December 16, 1974.

GILLIAT, SIDNEY. *See* **LAUNDER, FRANK**

GOSHO, HEINOSUKE (February 1, 1902–May 1, 1981), Japanese director, was born Heiuemon Gosho but later relinquished his "old-fashioned" given name. His father was a member of an old and rich family that derived its wealth from the tobacco industry, his mother a geisha famous for her beauty. Gosho was born and grew up in Tokyo, where his grandfather introduced him to the arts, his father to the geisha houses and the theatres in which he owned stock. It was in a geisha house that Gosho first saw the sketches of the artist Yumeiji Takehisa, whose delicate style is said to have influenced Gosho's film images.

With the early death of his father's only legitimate son, Gosho became his heir and was sent to Keio Commerce School in Tokyo to prepare himself for a career in the family tobacco business. By then, however, he was more interested in the theatre and, increasingly, in the cinema. He had his first taste of filmmaking when, as a student, he went before the cameras as an extra. By the time he graduated in 1923 his mind was made up, and in the face of family opposition, he joined the Shochiku company as an assistant director.

For the next two years, Gosho worked as an assistant to Yasujiro Shimazu, one of the pioneers of the *shomin-geki* genre—films of ordinary lower-middle-class life and its familiar economic and emotional problems. The realism, warmth, and humor of Shimazu's movies left their mark on the work of all his pupils, who included Kinoshita, Toyoda, and Yoshimura, as well as Gosho.

After a brief two-year apprenticeship, Gosho became a director in his own right, making five films in 1925 and no less than eight in 1926. None of these early movies was particularly successful, financially or artistically, though there was some interest in his second picture, *Sora wa haretari (The Sky Is Clear,* 1925). This quiet love story is said to show some of the hallmarks of his

HEINOSUKE GOSHO

mature style, including a predilection for close-ups and the use of an extraordinary number of very brief separate shots. Gosho, who came to be known as "the director who uses three shots where others use one," said that he developed this technique through a close study of Lubitsch's *The Marriage Circle* (1924), which he saw twenty times, and which he credited as the greatest foreign influence on his work, along with Chaplin's *A Woman of Paris* (1923). *The Sky Is Clear* also illustrated Gosho's penchant for *suikyo* settings—places located by rivers, lakes, or the sea.

The film that established Gosho as an important new talent was *Sabishiki ranbomono* (*Lonely Roughneck*, 1927), about the unlikely love affair between a rough but likable country boy and a middle-class girl from the city. A major critical and financial success, it was shot mostly on location—the method Gosho always preferred—and was admired as a "completely accurate reflection of Japanese village life." Gosho was married for the first time the same year, but his happiness was marred by the serious illness of a beloved younger brother, who contracted polio. Deeply distressed, Gosho said that he lost his way for several years—"my personal life began to fall apart." He even tried suicide, but in this "as in all my efforts during the period, I failed."

Gosho's depression is evident in the films he made during the late 1920s. *Karakuri musume* (*Tricky Girl*, 1927), which Gosho coscripted, was described by Sergei Eisenstein as "a melodramatic farce" that "begins in the manner of Monty Banks [and] ends in incredible gloom." In

Mura no hanayome (*The Village Bride*, 1928), a beautiful young woman, crippled in an accident, is replaced at the altar by her healthy sister (a not uncommon practice is rural communities), and *Kami eno michi* (*Road to God*, 1928) was said to be "little but a parade of cripples before the camera." Preoccupied as they are with poverty, suffering, and disease, some of these movies have been cited as examples of the "tendency" (left-wing) films of the period, but as Anderson and Richie point out in *The Japanese Film*, they have none of the socialist optimism of the "tendency" films and dwell on the prejudices and pettiness of peasant life.

Not surprisingly, these unhappy films failed at the box office, and it began to look as if Gosho's early promise would remain unfulfilled. Then in 1931 the Shochiku company, reluctantly embracing the new medium of sound, virtually forced Gosho to make their first talkie. All the other Shochiku directors had refused the chore, and Gosho was equally unenthusiastic, but his standing in the company was at that time too shaky to permit rebellious gestures. He agreed to make a two-reel trial talkie, liked the result, and expanded it to feature length as *Madamu to nyobo* (*The Neighbor's Wife and Mine*, 1931).

As far as the story is concerned, it is a fairly typical *shomin-geki* of suburban life. A young writer is distracted from his work by the noise of the jazz band practicing next door, and then distracted from his marriage by his thoroughly modern neighbor, but winds up safely back with his wife. Like many examples of the genre, it uses its slim plot as no more than a framework on which to hang observant little vignettes illustrating a way of life that would have been perfectly familiar to most of the members of its audience.

Many of these incidents are humorous, in a way that became increasingly characteristic of the *shomin-geki* after the coming of sound. We see the genteel young couple bullied into an unwanted purchase by a persistent door-to-door peddler; the husband putting aside his literary endeavours to take a child to the bathroom. At the end, on a family walk through the suburbs (conducted to the strains of "My Blue Heaven"), the reconciled couple recall in flashback the husband's adventure—he rather wistfully, his wife jealously—until they suddenly realize that they have left the baby parked far behind and hurry back for him, recalled to duty and responsibility.

There were no re-recording facilities in 1931, and dialogue, music, and natural sound all had to be recorded on the final track during shooting. The concealment of the large jazz band during exterior shooting caused problems worthy of a Marx Brothers movie, and massive soundproofing almost immobilized the camera. Like his contemporaries in the West, Gosho alleviated this handicap by shooting simultaneously with several cameras, thus achieving some variety in position and angle. And even in this first sound film, he resisted the temptation to use the new medium as a toy, keeping dialogue to a minimum and allowing the images to carry the story and reveal character.

The Neighbor's Wife and Mine was Japan's first successful talkie, winning first place in *Kinema Jumpo*'s poll of the year's best films. A Tokyo critic wrote that Gosho had "remained within cinematic traditions and borrowed none from the stage. . . . He knew from the start that film must remain film and must not attempt to be recorded theatre." More recently, Richard N. Tucker has referred to Gosho's inventive use of sound in this pioneer work, "employing telling silences and using sounds from off-screen actions to create a larger sense of reality." According to Anderson and Richie, the integration of sound and silent film techniques always remained for Gosho an absorbing problem, keeping him "from the extreme introspection which had caused his earlier depression."

Along with Ozu and Naruse, Gosho is a central figure in the development of the *shomin-geki,* to which he brought both richer humor and greater realism. "Goshoism" has passed into the Japanese critical vocabulary to mean "something that makes you laugh and cry at the same time." Anderson and Richie say that, like Ozu, Gosho "worked toward a simplicity in style," while his search for "a higher realism" tended towards "the elimination of plot for its own sake and . . . the development of the discursive, chronicle style, the simple recording of events" that became "a definite part of the Japanese film."

It was this "slice of life" quality that engaged Noël Burch in his discussion of *Jinsei no onimotsu* (*Burden of Life,* 1935). The film deals with the resentment felt by a father toward his small son when all the other children have grown up and left home; it ends with a promise of reconciliation. The story is filled out with portraits of members of the family, all equally "three-dimensional" in contrast to the "Western model of graded characterization," and with "irrelevant" events that are explored as thoroughly as those "articulated to the 'main theme.'" It seemed to Burch that at times the movie "anticipates and equals the most successful moments of Italian neorealism."

Gosho was also influential in the growth of the *junbungaku* movement that flourished during the 1930s—adaptations of works of "pure" (as distinct from commercial) literature. A notable example was *Izu no odoriko* (*Dancing Girls of Izu,* 1933), a late silent film based on the novel by Yasunari Kawabata. And for some critics, Gosho's best movie of this period was *Ikitoshi ikerumono* (*Everything That Lives,* 1934), adapted from a book by Yuzo Yamamoto and dealing with an embezzler and the girl who is blamed for his crime.

In 1938 Gosho contracted tuberculosis and was ill for three years, devoting the time to reflections on technique and on the relationship between literature and cinema that were eventually both fruitful and influential. He never resumed the vast output of his early years, and indeed made only six films during the entire decade of the 1940s. Poor health was only one of the reasons for this, however. Gosho was morally and temperamentally incapable of producing the nationalistic and militaristic works demanded by the authorities just before and during the war period.

In these years, most of his scripts were rejected, and those that were filmed were hardly to the liking of the Ministry of Information. *Mokuseki* (*Wooden Head,* 1940), intended as a "mother film" with "national policy" overtones, mysteriously turned into a complex psychological study of a woman doctor who adopts an illegitimate child to preserve its father's good name. And the propagandist elements built into *Shinsetsu* (*New Snow,* 1942) were almost entirely lost in the working out of the rather melodramatic plot. Only his continuing ill-health saved Gosho from official retribution.

Gosho left Shochiku in 1941 to work for the Daiei studio. He returned to make *Izu no musumetachi* (*The girls of Izu,* 1945), but then joined the Toho company. Soon, however, he found himself involved in the labor disputes that racked Toho for several years. Reports describe him marching with the workers, waving the red flag and singing the "Internationale." Gosho said, "I couldn't stand seeing people who had faithfully helped me to make films get fired. I was no communist, but I couldn't reject my friends' plight." When the union was eventually defeated, Gosho resigned from Toho, having made just two films for them. In 1948 he set up Studio 8 Productions (using the English name) in partnership with Shiro Toyoda and others; this new independent company was affiliated with Shin-Toho.

Studio 8 survived until 1954; there Gosho made *Entotsu no mieru basho* (*Where Chimneys Are Seen,* 1953), the best known of all his films. The setting is Tokyo's industrialized Kita-Senju district, dominated by a mysterious number of tall chimneys around a large factory. A couple, a *tabi* (Japanese footcovering) seller and his wife, whose first husband vanished in the war, live in a small, rickety house; they want a child but are prudently waiting for their financial condition to improve. They have rented their upstairs rooms to two lodgers. One, a kindly tax-office employee, has a crush on the other but is too shy to express his feelings in the face of her haughty indifference. Then a squalling baby is dumped on the doorstep, destroying the harmony of this sad quartet. At first resentful, the wife soon becomes attached to the child; so does her husband; so do the lodgers, who now have reason to speak. When the infant becomes seriously ill, all four devotedly nurse it, their moods changing with its condition. By the time the feckless parents have been identified and the baby returned, the married couple have decided to have a baby of their own and the two upstairs tenants are about to marry.

The multiple chimneys symbolize both the postwar industrialization of Japan and the film's philosophy. They are so placed that all are never visible at once—depending on the observer's point of view there seem to be four, three, two, or even only one. At the end of the movie, looking at the chimneys, the husband says, "Life is whatever you think it is. It can be sweet or it can be bitter . . . whichever you are." Based on a novel by Rinzo Shiina, the picture was a prizewinner at Berlin and a revelation to Western audiences whose knowledge of Japanese cinema had previously been limited to samurai films.

Anderson and Richie describe this as "one of the really important postwar Japanese films," and "*shomin-geki* at its purest. . . . Episodic in structure but with each event relating directly to the central philosophy of the film . . . Nothing is irrelevant, every detail adding to the effect of the whole world which is created." And William Whitebait thought its atmosphere "that of neorealism—with a difference. Here are the working-class lives, the rains . . . , the interminable radio. . . . In the end, six lives have been caught together dramatically, we have been taken into offices and bicycle stadiums, into the lowest depths of shack life. . . . Heinosuke Gosho has the kind of eye that has met us before in Japanese prints (witness not only his factory, but the reeds in the river, mist, rain, and bare flimsy interiors; he has compassion as well, which may surprise those who have known only the cruel austerities of history and legend)."

Gosho never abandoned the style he developed in his very first films, described by John Gillett as a form of "cut-up" montage—

"hundreds of short shots cut together to recreate a pattern of living revealing the characters' innermost feelings, using short, probing camera movements to fill in the perspective of a scene." There are over a thousand separate shots in *Osaka no yado* (*An Inn at Osaka*, 1954), a slice-of-life movie offering insights into the lives of guests and staff at an inn in Japan's commercial center. In the course of this powerful indictment of postwar materialism, we encounter a young man transferred from Tokyo, a geisha, an exploited hotel servant—and find that each is ruled, damaged, and diminished by the need for money.

Sentimentality is always a danger in the *shomin-geki* genre, and some Western critics found it in *An Inn at Osaka*—for example in the famous scene in which the hotel drudge studies the clumsy drawing of a cow sent to her by her little son in the country, and later, when the same woman is suspected of theft and forced to display her pathetic possessions, including a few shoddy toys cherished in the hope that she will one day be able to take them to the child. But these scenes are set off against others in a totally different mood—one showing the "ferocious cruelty" of the woman's employer and another very funny sequence in which the latter is overcome with remorse. It seemed to Donald Richie that "in the resulting conflict of emotion all idea of sentimentality is lost."

Gosho, who sometimes coscripted his films and always worked very closely with his art directors, is said to have been a perfectionist who showed an "almost fanatical concern over details." He personally visited fifty temples while designing the one used in *Takekurabe* (*Growing Up*, 1955) and for one scene is said to have polished the wooden floor himself to the requisite sheen. This film, based on a story by Ichiyo Higuchi and set in the Meiji period, tells the story of a carefree girl who, as she grows in maturity and beauty, comes gradually to realize that she is destined for the same fate as her prostitute sister.

Discussing Gosho's use of visual symbolism, Donald Richie cites an example at the end of this film when the heroine, crossing a bridge into the house of prostitution, drops the iris blossom given to her by a shy boy who loves her into the dirty canal. It is, as Richie says, "a hackneyed symbol which through careful usage manages to regain much of its original urgency." The same critic has described Gosho's brilliant use of his "cut-up" montage technique in this last section of the movie, which for ten minutes is entirely without dialogue: "The background score carries a full-scale passacaglia, a continuation of the opening-credit music. To this Gosho freely cuts a number of scenes, all short, all changing, all held together by the music and by a kind of cinematic logic which creates a great final coda, a kind of chaconne on film." Gosho's great skill as a director of actors is also evident in this film, not least in the extraordinary performance he drew from the young pop star Hibari Misora in her only serious role.

Kiiroi karasu (*Yellow Crow*, 1957) won a Golden Globe Award from the Hollywood Foreign Press Association. A boy's father is repatriated after ten years in China. The man attempts to make up for lost time in supporting his family but gives little thought to the son he barely knows. When a baby girl is born a year later, the boy feels altogether displaced. His uneasiness is manifested in his school drawings, in which he uses only blacks and yellows. When his teacher points this out to his parents, they resolve to pay more attention to him and promise to buy him a kite. However, they retract that promise when the baby is injured in an accident; they blame the boy and he runs away from home. Donald Richie cites *Yellow Crow* as an example of Gosho's "resolutely anti-traditional" subject manner: "The little boy . . . is shown as perfectly right in rebelling and running away. His parents learn a lesson and at the end of the film are about to reform."

Several of Gosho's later films focus on women and their traditonal social role. Although *Hotarubi* (*Firefly Light* 1958) depicts a well-known figure from Japanese history—Ryoma Sakamoto, a nobleman who sought to bring down the Tokugawa shogunate at the end of the Edo period—the film centers on Tose, the woman who runs the inn where he is a guest. To Joan Mellen, Tose's heroism "is revealed in her response to a momentous historical event . . . she is redeemed and fulfilled by her alliance with a person like Ryoma . . . Gosho sees Tose as no less heroic than Ryoma, notwithstanding her middle-class life, because her acts and her free spirit align her with a struggle for change."

Mark le Fanu compares Tose with the heroine from *Aru yo futatabi* (*Twice on a Certain Night*, 1956): "[Both women], elevated from the class into which they were born, repay their husbands, through the subsequent vicissitudes of the drama, with a loyalty that is not conceivably 'merited.' Wonderfully lively and intelligent in their interior selves, they yet measure their lives under the aegis of constancy. The intransigence of such faithfulness pushes these dramas toward genuine tragedy."

The melodramatic *Ryoji* (*Hunting Rifle*, 1961), based on Yasushi Inoue's acclaimed novel,

centers on a man who would appear to have everything except happiness. Mark le Fanu writes that Misugi, the protagonist, "is another of those doubles or shades of the director, brooding mature figures who seem to carry in their faces more than their mere role in the narrative. Misugi is a man who collects valuable vases, grimly unable to see his seduced mistress Saiko except in terms of a precious rare object."

Gosho continued making films until 1968, working with several different studios and often under considerable commercial pressure, damaging to his work. Donald Richie considers *Osorezan no onna* (*The Innocent Witch*, 1965) to be the director's last representative film, in which "a feudal society pushes the girl, played by Jitsuko Yoshimura, into a whorehouse, and a feudal religion kills her when a priest beats her to death trying to exorcise the evil spirits he believes live within her." John Gillett nonetheless enjoyed Gosho's final film *Meiji haru aki* (*Seasons of the Meiji Period*, 1968), "a feature-length marionette film with some pretty color and design and a splendidly animated ballroom scene (like all puppet films, it goes on rather too long)." After 1968, Gosho turned to television, primarily as a writer.

Gosho made nearly a hundred features, of which only a handful were seen in the West during his lifetime. The rediscovery of his work began in the mid 1980s, when the Japan Film Library Council sent a collection of his films on an international tour. During his lifetime, Gosho received several important honors: eleven of his films were among the top ten in the annual *Kinema Jumpo* poll, and one of those, *The Neighbor's Wife and Mine*, placed first; *Where Chimneys Are Seen* received the International Peace Award at the Berlin International Film Festival; *Ari no machi no Maria* (*Maria of the Ant Village*, 1958) won the Catholic (ICFC) Prize at the San Sebastian International Film Festival; the Hollywood Foreign Press Association honored *Yellow Crow* with a Golden Globe; and *Waga ai* (*When a Woman Loves*, 1960) won the Golden Harvest Awards for color photography and sound recording at the fourth Film Festival in Asia in 1960. Between 1964 and 1975 Gosho served as president of the Japanese Association of Film Directors and was also director of the Japanese Haiku Art Association. He was also awarded two special orders by the Japanese government, in 1941 and 1947.

Georges Sadoul called Gosho "one of the greatest Japanese directors, the peer of his better-known contemporary, Kenji Mizoguchi," and Donald Richie suggests that "if Mizoguchi had the eye of a painter, Gosho had the eye of a dramatist. The raw material of his pictures, people, what they are and what they do, creates the atmosphere of a Gosho film." In his films, unlike those of Ozu and Naruse, there is always "a sense of release. Something has happened: the circumstances remain the same but the outlook has changed and there is room for optimism." Gosho himself believed that "the purpose of a film director's life is to describe the real life around him and create works which express the true feelings of human beings . . . and only if we love our fellow human beings can we create."

FILMS: Nanto no haru (Spring in Southern Islands), 1925; Sora wa haretari (The Sky Is Clear/No Clouds in the Sky), 1925; Otoko gokoro (Man's Heart), 1925; Seishun (Youth), 1925; Tosei tamatebako (A Casket for Living), 1925; Machi no hitobito (Town People), 1926; Hatsukoi (First Love), 1926; Haha-yo koishi (Mothers' Love), 1926; Honryu (A Rapid Stream), 1926; Musume (Daughter), 1926; Kaeranu sasabue (No Return), 1926; Itoshino wagako (My Beloved Child), 1926; Kanojo (Girl Friend), 1926; Sabishiki ranbomono (Lonely Roughneck), 1927; Hazukashii yume (Intimate Dream), 1927; Karakuri musume (Tricky Girl), 1927; Shojo no shi (Death of a Maiden), 1927; Okame (Moonfaced), 1927; Suki nareba koso (If You Like It), 1928; Mura no hanayome (The Village Bride), 1928; Doraku goshinan (Debauchery Is Wrong), 1928; Kami eno michi (Road to God), 1928; Hito no yo sugata (Man's Worldly Appearance), 1928; Gaito no kishi (Knight of the Street), 1928; Yoru no meneko (Cat of the Night), 1929; Shin joseikan (A New Kind of Woman), 1929; Oyaji to sonoko (Father and His Son), 1929; Ukiyo buro (The Bath Harem), 1929; Jonetsu no ichiya (One Night of Passion), 1929; Dokushin-sha goyojin (Bachelors Beware), 1930; Dai-Tokyo no ikkaku (A Corner of Great Tokyo), 1930; Hohoemo jinsei (A Smiling Life), 1930; Onna-yo kimi no na o kegasu nakare (Woman, Don't Make Your Name Dirty), 1930; Shojo nyuyo (Virgin Wanted), 1930; Kinuyo monogatari (Story of Kinuyo), 1930; Aiyuko no yoru (Desire of Night), 1930; Jokyu aishi (Sad Story of a Barmaid), 1931; Yoru hiraku (Open at Night), 1931; Madamu to nyobo (The Neighbor's Wife and Mine/Madame and Wife), 1931; Shima no ratai jiken (Island of Naked Scandal), 1931; Gutei kenkei (Silly Younger Brother and Clever Elder Brother), 1931; Wakaki hi no kangeki (Memories of Young Days), 1931; Niisan no baka (My Stupid Brother), 1932; Ginza no yanagi (Willows of Ginza), 1932; Tengoku ni musube koi (Heaven Linked With Love), 1932; Satsueijo romansu, renai annai (A Studio Romance), 1932; Hototogisu (Cuckoo), 1932; Koi no Tokyo (Love in Tokyo), 1932; Hanayome no negoto (The Bride Talks in Her Sleep), 1933; Izu no odoriko (Dancing Girls of Izu), 1933; Juku no haru (The Nineteenth Spring), 1933; Shojo-yo sayonara (Goodbye My Girl), 1933; Aibu/Ramuura (Caress/L'Amour), 1933; Onna to umareta karanya (Now That I Was Born a Woman), 1934; Sakura ondo (Cherry Blossom Chorus), 1934; Ikitoshi ikerumono (Everything That Lives), 1934; Hanamuko no negoto (The Bridegroom Talks in His Sleep), 1935; Hidari uchiwa (Left-handed Fan/A Life of Luxury), 1935; Fukeyo koikaze (Breezes of Love), 1935;

Akogare (Yearning), 1935; Jinsei no onimotsu (Burden of Life), 1935; Okusama shakuyosho (A Married Lady Borrows Money), 1936; Oboroyo no onna (Woman of Pale Night/Woman of the Mist), 1936; Shindo (The New Road), 1936 (in two parts); Hanakago no uta (Song of the Flower Basket), 1937; Mokuseki (Wooden Head), 1940; Shinsetsu (New Snow), 1942; Goju no to (The Five-Storied Pagoda), 1944; Izu no musumetachi (The Girls of Izu), 1945; Ima hitotabi no (Once More), 1947; Omokage (Image), 1948; Wakare-gumo (Dispersing Clouds/Drifting Clouds), 1951; Asa no hamon (Morning Conflicts), 1952; Entotsu no mieru basho (Four Chimneys/Where Chimneys Are Seen), 1953; Osaka no yado (An Inn at Osaka/Hotel at Osaka), 1954; Ai to shi no tanima (The Valley Between Love and Death), 1954; Niwatori wa futatabi naku (The Cock Crows Twice/The Cock Crows Again), 1954; Takekurabe (Growing Up/Adolescence/Daughters of Yoshiwara/Skylark Growing Up), 1955; Aru yo futatabi (Twice on a Certain Night), 1956; Kiiroi karasu (Behold Thy Son/Yellow Crow), 1957; Banka (Elegy/Elegy of the North/Dirge), 1957; Hotarubi (The Fireflies/Firefly Light), 1958; Yoku (Avarice), 1958; Ari no machi no Maria (Maria of the Ant Village), 1958; Karatachi nikki (Journal of the Orange Flower), 1959; Waga ai (When a Woman Loves), 1959; Shiroi kiba (White Fangs), 1960; Ryoju (Hunting Rifle), 1961; Kumo ga chigieru toki (As the Clouds Scatter), 1961; Aijo no keifu (Love's Family Tree), 1961; Kaachan kekkon shiroyo (Get Married, Mother), 1962; Hyakuman-nin no musumetachi (A Million Girls), 1963; Osorezan no onna (The Innocent Witch), 1965; Kaachan to juichi-nin no kodomo (Our Wonderful Years), 1966; Utage (Rebellion in Japan), 1967; Onna to mishoshiru (Woman and Bean Soup), 1968; Meiji haru aki (A Girl of the Meiji Period/Seasons of the Meiji Period), 1968.

ABOUT: Anderson, J. L. and Richie, D. The Japanese Film, 1959; Burch, N. To the Distant Observer, 1979; Richie, D. Japanese Cinema, 1971. *Periodicals*—Cahiers du cinéma March 1984 (journal note 41); Cinéma (France) 83 1964; Film Dope April 1980; Revue du cinéma June 1986; Sight and Sound Autumn 1956, Summer 1970, Summer 1986.

GOULDING, EDMUND (March 20, 1891–December 24, 1959), American director, scenarist, songwriter, dramatist, and novelist, was born into a theatrical family in London, England, and reputedly began his working life as a butcher's boy in the Holborn district. Some sources claim that he made his stage debut at the age of twelve, but it seems more likely that his first appearance was in 1909, in a music-hall sketch called "Gentlemen, the King" at the Holborn Empire. Between then and 1914 Goulding had small roles in *Alice in Wonderland, Henry VIII, Macbeth, The Picture of Dorian Gray,* and other plays. His first screen appearance was in an adaptation of *Henry VIII*, directed by Louis N. Parker in

EDMUND GOULDING

1911, and he was also seen in Charles Raymond's *The Life of a London Shopgirl* (1914).

Richly and variously talented, Goulding was soon writing plays as well as acting in them. *Out of the Fog* was staged in 1912 and *God Save the King* in 1914. According to one gossip columnist, the latter was a one-acter written overnight when Britain declared war on Germany; Goulding "cast it the same day [war was declared—a Wednesday] and presented it in London at the Palladium Theatre the following Monday night with an all-star cast."

W. R. Meyer, in his *Warner Brothers Directors,* says that Goulding served with the British army in France in 1914–1915, received an honorable discharge after being wounded twice, and went to New York to study voice under Oscar Saenger. *Film Dope,* on the other hand, says that Goulding went to New York in 1915 to make his American stage debut; perhaps he did both. Back in Britain, Meyer says, Goulding "became an early favorite in English grand opera, with a repertoire of all the great baritone roles." Goulding was indeed a singer, good enough to perform during the 1930s on "international broadcasts," but Meyer is alone in claiming that he ever had a successful career in grand opera, and himself says that Goulding was appearing in London in *Kitty Darlin'*—as an actor rather than a singer—when in 1917 he broke his contract and re-enlisted in the army as a private, to drive trucks loaded with explosives.

In 1916, meanwhile, Goulding had written another play, *Ellen Young,* in collaboration with a Mrs. Enthoven. *Film Dope* notes that this was adapted for the screen the same year as *Quest of Life.* In 1917 Goulding provided the story for Marshall Neilan's *The Silent Partner* and in 1918 for Émile Chautard's *The Ordeal of Rosetta.*

The war ended in 1918 and the following year Goulding emigrated to the United States, soon finding work in Hollywood as a scenarist. In 1919–1920 he worked on scripts for Ralph Ince, George Irving, James Young, and Robert Ellis, among others. In 1921 he scripted Henry King's best silent film and first international success, *Tol'able David,* based on the novel by Joseph Hergesheimer, and subsequently wrote four of Robert Z. Leonard's Mae Murray vehicles—*Peacock Alley, Fascination, Broadway Rose,* and *Jazzmania.* Goulding published his only novel, the sea story *Fury,* in 1922; the same year he adapted it as a film, directed by Henry King. It was in 1922 also that he appeared in George Fitzmaurice's *Three Live Ghosts,* playing a Cockney revenant. More scripts followed for Victor Fleming, Sidney Franklin, and others, and in 1924 Goulding, in collaboration with Edgar Selwyn, wrote the play *Dancing Mothers,* a long-running hit on Broadway with Helen Hayes. It was filmed by Herbert Brenon in 1926.

Goulding directed his first film in 1925, when he joined MGM. He himself scripted many of his early pictures, including the first, *Sun-Up.* John Gillett, in his notes for the Goulding retrospective at Britain's National Film Theatre in 1984, describes *Sun-Up* as "a strong backwoods drama, atmospherically reminiscent of *Tol'able David,* about a feuding family and what happens when a son returns from World War I. A great performance by Lucille LaVerne as the crusty mother." The movie was based on a play by Lulu Vollmer, and a reviewer in the New York *Times* called it "a strong feature despite the amazing changes that have been wrought in transferring it to the screen."

Sally, Irene and Mary (1925), another play adaptation, stars Constance Bennett, Joan Crawford, and Sally O'Neil as Broadway chorus girls. Full of risqué sex and lively backstage detail, the film was a hit. It demonstrated Goulding's special talent as a director of actresses and set Joan Crawford on the path to stardom. *Paris* (1926) was a showcase for Crawford, here masquerading as a French café entertainer caught between a brutish hoodlum and a rich American. Goulding next drew a very sensitive performance from Pauline Starke in *Women Love Diamonds* (1927). Starke plays a woman of mysterious social origins torn—rather like Crawford in the preceding film—between a rich suitor and her chauffeur.

Goulding's first big chance came with his last silent picture, *Love* (1927). This was an updated version of *Anna Karenina* (its title in Britain), re-uniting Greta Garbo and John Gilbert immediately after their tremendous success in *Flesh and the Devil*—a success inspired partly by the real passion that so evidently underlay the filmic one: "Garbo and Gilbert in *Love*," brayed the posters. Adapted from Tolstoy's novel by Frances Marion (and, uncredited, Goulding), it was shot by Garbo's best photographer, William Daniels.

The received opinion has been that *Love* was inferior to Clarence Brown's later sound version of *Anna Karenina*, also with Garbo. However, John Gillett, seeing the earlier film again in the 1984 Goulding retrospective, called it "a major Garbo rediscovery: this . . . version of *Anna Karenina*, despite its simplifications, gets nearer to Tolstoy's moral analysis than the sound remake ('I shall leave you together and wait for you to destroy each other,' says Karenina to the lovers). A beautifully fluid production by Goulding, with outstanding settings and costumes and some of William Daniels' most breathtaking images." Douglas McVay thought that Garbo in *Love* "gives the most moving performance I've seen from any silent cinema star. Her two greatest scenes have an intensity beyond anything in her superb 1935 rendering of the part: Anna's tenderly joyous reunion with her young son is surpassed in power only by the poignant mock-nonchalance of her amorous adieu to Vronsky." The picture was made with two endings, one "happy," the other concluding with Anna's suicide.

Goulding left MGM after that, for the next few years dividing his time between Paramount and United Artists. Early in 1928 he was sent to New York by Adolph Zukor to study the Fox-Case Sound System. He was not impressed, writing in the *National Board of Review Magazine* (July 1928) that the first talkies were "but silent motion pictures accompanied by synchronized, but wholly mechanical and artificial sounding voices or instrumental music." If sound films were to succeed, he said, speech would have to be less stagey, proper attention would have to be given to camera movement, and "the new director will be more De Maupassant than Dickens—terse, tense, succinct." Goulding was still writing scripts at this stage of his career, though fewer and fewer of them, and dreamed up the plot of MGM's hugely successful first musical *The Broadway Melody* (1929).

Goulding's own first talkie was *The Trespasser* (United Artists, 1929), which he scripted and for which he wrote the hit theme song "Love, Your Magic Spell Is Everywhere." Despite the alleged operatic training, Goulding apparently could not write music but would hum or whistle his at-

tractive melodies to an arranger. *The Trespasser* was a melodrama about a gangster's widow (Gloria Swanson) trying to forget the past and was a flop, like most of Swanson's early sound films. Goulding next directed (and appeared in) the "Dream Girl" sequence in the portmanteau movie *Paramount on Parade* (1930), and then scripted, scored, and directed *The Devil's Holiday* (1930). *Reaching for the Moon* (United Artists, 1931), another Goulding script, starred Douglas Fairbanks as a millionaire playboy ruined by the Wall Street crash while on his honeymoon with Bebe Daniels. Bing Crosby has a small role in this movie, a mostly nonmusical version of an Irving Berlin show.

After *The Night Angel* (Paramount, 1931), for which Goulding's song melodies were arranged by Vernon Duke, he returned to MGM and directed the most famous of all his films, *Grand Hotel* (1932), adapted by William A. Drake from Vicki Baum's novel and play, produced by Irving Thalberg, and photographed by William Daniels. The movie, which won an Oscar as best picture of the year, is set in a cosmopolitan Berlin hotel where "nothing ever happens." Greta Garbo plays a great but fading ballerina who actually speaks the deathless line "I vant to be alone" before falling in love with an aristocratic jewel thief (John Barrymore). Lionel Barrymore is a dying clerk with his savings to spend, Wallace Beery a tycoon with a fortune at stake, and Joan Crawford makes the most of her small role as a poor but self-reliant stenographer.

Asked how he had handled this explosive mixture of talents and temperaments, Goulding said "I just worked secretly, and in the friendliest manner, behind the backs of my cast. . . . *Grand Hotel* was made at such a pace that nobody but myself knew how it was progressing. We made it in thirty-one days, with a fortnight for cutting. . . . The whole of the picture was worked out in secret, with instructions given in quiet corners, in the studio restaurant . . . or over a casual cigarette. . . . Greta Garbo was no trouble at all. She is what I would call director-proof. She is like a Strad violin. You play on her and produce a harmony. It is impossible to make an ugly sound on that instrument."

Garbo appears in only two long scenes in *Grand Hotel*, but she received top billing and widespread adulation. "She had about her," wrote Lincoln Kirstein, "that quality of gratuitous alchemy, of incandescent glamor which one hears associated with Réjane, Bernhardt, and Duse. . . . She wears nostalgia like a shawl, and when she dances around her suite . . . in an ecstasy of recaptured passion it is, simply, indescribable. *Grand Hotel* is the first picture in which Garbo has had a real chance to show what she could do free from the strictures of a close direction." Forty years later it seemed to Pauline Kael that "intellectually you have to reject *Grand Hotel* as an elaborate chunk of artifice and hocus-pocus. . . . But if you want to see what screen glamor used to be and what, originally, 'stars' were, this is perhaps the best example of all time."

Marion Davies, whose gifts as a comic actress are earning belated recognition, includes a marvelous imitation of Garbo in *Grand Hotel* in her "spirited but vulnerable" performance as *Blondie of the Follies* (1932), struggling out of the tenement and into the chorus. Reviewed in the NFT retrospective, the picture was warmly praised for its "potent theatrical atmosphere," the startling realism of its tenement scenes, and an excellent supporting cast that included Robert Montgomery, Jimmy Durante, and ZaSu Pitts. Anita Loos supplied the dialogue and Goulding himself makes a brief appearance as a Follies director.

Goulding directed another screen idol, Norma Shearer, in *Riptide* (1934), which has her married to faithful blueblood Herbert Marshall but passionately attached to rapacious Robert Montgomery. Pierre Sauvage, writing in Jean-Pierre Coursodon's *American Directors, Vol. 1,* notes that this was Irving Thalberg's first "personal" production at MGM (Shearer was his wife). According to Sauvage, the film "is remarkable now mainly for Adrian's costumes, which range from the outrageous (Herbert Marshall's insectile outfit for the costume ball) to the smashing (the willowy creations to which the soft-focus star does full justice). The upper-class plot line must have seemed outdated even then, although a seductive Miss Shearer and a rakish Robert Montgomery are suitably charming in their naughty scenes together."

The unfortunate Herbert Marshall had to stiffen his upper lip again in *The Flame Within* (1935), but collected the resigned heroine in the end. She was that other specialist in renunciation, Ann Harding, here a psychiatrist drawn to an alcoholic playboy, played with scene-stealing insouciance by newcomer Louis Hayward. She dries him out and then nobly surrenders him to her suicidally infatuated patient Maureen O'Sullivan. The latter also made a considerable impact in this melodrama, splendidly photographed and lit by James Wong Howe. A reviewer in the London *Times* found that "the eloquence of the camera is only too often paralysed by bathos" in Goulding's dialogue, "and sometimes a convincing phrase is pictorially distorted. On the whole the camera proves itself the better artist."

Moving on to Warner Brothers, Goulding directed Bette Davis for the first time in *That Certain Woman* (1937), a remake of his own *The Trespasser,* and another melodrama riddled with renunciations. Widowed in the Valentine Day massacre, and trying to forget the past, Davis marries rich young Henry Fonda. The marriage is annulled by his domineering father (Donald Crisp) and Fonda weds a suitable socialite. But then it emerges that the heroine has a child by the first marriage. . . . Bette Davis did her best with this wildly synthetic story but the result, as she acknowledged, "was not good" and this version of the picture, like the first, was a critical and commercial failure.

After *White Banners* (1938), a piece of nonsense based on a story by Lloyd C. Douglas, came another remake—of Howard Hawks' World War I flying classic *Dawn Patrol.* Errol Flynn gives an unusually restrained performance as the tormented British captain sending his half-trained young pilots out to certain death, and David Niven and Basil Rathbone provide excellent support as his brother officers. Goulding used some of the aerial footage from Hawks' original version but, as one reviewer remarked, "it is as a study of tension, heroism, and humor among a group of closely observed individuals that the film grips and impresses."

Goulding's second movie with Bette Davis, unlike the first, was hugely successful. *Dark Victory* (1939) was adapted from a Broadway play, with Davis in the role of Judith Traherne created on stage by Tallulah Bankhead. Davis pestered Jack Warner for six months to pay David Selznick $50,000 for the rights and he finally capitulated, groaning, "just get her off my back." Judith Traherne is a spoiled heiress who develops headaches and dizziness. She consults a physician (George Brent), who diagnoses brain tumor but conceals the fact that it is terminal. Doctor and patient fall in love and marry, setting up house in a pretty New England town where Judith begins to lose her sight. Disguising her condition from her dedicated husband, she sends away her agonized confidante (Geraldine Fitzgerald) and confronts death alone.

Although Casey Robinson received sole credit as scenarist, Goulding was responsible for the Geraldine Fitzgerald character, who did not exist in the original play. He explained that "no one will cry about anyone who cries about himself, so I wrote in a character who does all the crying for Miss Davis. . . . Miss Fitzgerald was in the position of the audience, weeping behind Miss Davis' back, and that gave Miss Davis a clear course for martyrdom."

Dark Victory is a film full of sharp alternations of mood. As Douglas McVay writes, Davis "progresses from youthfully aggressive brightness . . . to stunned anger and fake-casual, savagely black humour—until at last she achieves serenely reconciled courage." The actress and the picture were both nominated for Oscars, and Bette Davis always regarded this as her finest performance, describing Goulding in her memoirs as "one of the few all-time great directors of Hollywood." "Admittedly it is a great role," Frank Nugent wrote, "but that must not detract from the eloquence, the tenderness, the heartbreaking sincerity with which she has played it," while Goulding's direction had fused the film "into a deeply moving unity."

Davis starred again in *The Old Maid* (1939), a nineteenth-century drama based on a novel by Edith Wharton. She plays a woman whose lover is killed in the Civil War, leaving her pregnant. To preserve her daughter from the knowledge of her illegitimacy, she brings her up in the household of her scheming sister (Miriam Hopkins), herself masquerading as an unsympathetic "aunt." Graham Greene found "the whole picture . . . very lavish and competent," and Davis's performance "of extraordinary virtuosity— as the young girl, and the secret mother, and the harsh prim middle-aged woman with her tiny lines and her talcum. It is like a manual of acting for beginners in three lessons." George Brent costars again, and Jane Bryan plays the high-spirited daughter.

Another adaptation followed, *We Are Not Alone,* coscripted by Milton Krims and James Hilton from the latter's novel. Paul Muni plays a small-town doctor in 1914 England, wrongly accused of murdering his dreadful wife (Flora Robson) for love of a young Austrian dancer (Jane Bryan again). John Gillett thinks this "is probably Goulding's '30s masterpiece," touching "on many issues and emotions: marital incompatibility, war hysteria . . . , social bigotry and the perils of circumstantial evidence. Goulding moulds all these themes into an amazing tapestry of love, jealousy, and conscience, ending with one of his most disturbing climaxes."

After *'Til We Meet Again* (1940), an inferior remake of Tay Garnett's *One Way Passage* (1932), came *The Great Lie* (1941). George Brent stars woodenly yet again as the obscure object of desire of two women, scheming pianist Mary Astor and rich Bette Davis. The latter wins, in spite of Astor's unsporting attempt to wreck the marriage by revealing that she is the mother of Brent's child. As W. R. Meyer says, here as elsewhere Goulding "skillfully fuses melodramatic plots with a number of cynical supporting characters and comic players who add sparkle to humorous moments and thereby give the stories multi-level interest."

Mary Astor earned an Oscar nomination for her work in *The Great Lie,* and Joan Fontaine another for her poignant performance as the impetuous young charmer in Goulding's remake of *The Constant Nymph,* with Charles Boyer as the equally charming middle-aged composer who loves and loses her. The symphonic poem he provides for Fontaine to die by was actually written by Erich Korngold.

After that, Goulding joined 20th Century-Fox, where Dorothy McGuire rewarded him with another performance of enchanting eccentricity in *Claudia* (1943), her first movie. She plays (as she had on Broadway) a scattily childlike wife forced to come to terms with her mother's death and her own pregnancy. Robert Young is excellent as her husband. "I liked it, and was held by it," wrote C. A. Lejeune; "found myself interested, to my great surprise, in the affairs of a restless, chattering, sparrow-witted, subadolescent, expendable heroine of the type I normally detest."

In 1945 Goulding put $70,000 into a play, *That Ryan Girl,* written and directed by himself and starring Una O'Connor and Edmund Lowe. It flopped, and Goulding returned briefly to Warners for a remake of John Cromwell's *Of Human Bondage,* with Paul Henreid miscast as the clubfooted medical student and Eleanor Parker as the callous object of his obsessive passion. This also was a failure, and after it Goulding returned to Fox, where he spent the remainder of his career.

His next picture was another and better Somerset Maugham adaptation, *The Razor's Edge* (1946), notable for splendid performances from Gene Tierney and Anne Baxter, and a better than usual one from Tyrone Power as a troubled member of the Lost Generation who "finds himself" in India. Clifton Webb is also excellent as a malicious socialite, and the hedonistic 1920s are evoked in some memorable set pieces. Goulding wrote the moody background melody which became famous, with Mack David's lyrics, as "A Small Café, Mam'selle."

Tyrone Power excelled himself in his second film with Goulding, the extraordinary *Nightmare Alley* (1947). Power plays a ruthlessly ambitious young carnival barker who makes it big in cabaret by seducing soft-hearted Joan Blondell and stealing the intricate code that had once made her a star "mind-reader." He dumps her and moves on to a corrupt psychiatrist (Helen Walker) who guides him to power and wealth as a phony medium. Then he overplays his hand, his accomplice abandons him, and he winds up as what he has most feared, a carny geek who earns his hooch by biting the heads off live chickens. Along the way he has married young Coleen Gray, and a final reunion with her offers some hope of redemption but does little to relieve the impact of this dark film, based on a novel by William Lindsay Gresham and noirishly lit by Lee Garmes. Campbell Dixon called it "a dreadful little masterpiece."

A highly enjoyable farce followed in *Everybody Does It* (1949), a remake of Gregory Ratoff's *Wife, Husband and Friend,* from a story by James M. Cain. Celeste Holm is the tone-deaf socialite who believes she can sing, Paul Douglas the long-suffering husband who possesses a magnificent voice but doesn't know it, and Linda Darnell the ravishing prima donna who discovers him. There is a splendid climax at the opera when Douglas, stricken by stage fright and booze, makes his chaotic debut.

Mister 880 (1950), scripted by Robert Riskin, was based on the actual case of a small-time forger who, issuing only fifty deplorably bad one-dollar bills a month, eluded the authorities for a decade. Edmund Gwenn gives his familiar portrayal of anarchic innocence in the title role, and his criminal activities bring together Secret Service agent Burt Lancaster and Dorothy McGuire, his favorite suspect. There was general enthusiasm for this amiable piece of whimsy, which mildly parodies the quasi-documentary "from the files of the FBI" genre and features a brilliantly inventive scene played in dumb show through a shop window.

After *We're Not Married* (1952), an uneven comedy written by Nunnally Johnson and made up of six separate anecdotes, Goulding wound up his career with three movies of little or no interest, ending with the insipid Pat Boone vehicle *Mardi Gras* in 1958. The director died on Christmas Eve the following year at the age of sixty-eight.

In a characteristically frank and idiosyncratic note in *Film Culture* (67–69 1979), the actress Louise Brooks writes that in 1932, when Goulding learned that "his close friend, the English dancer Marjorie Moss had given up her fight with tuberculosis, he married her and filled the last three years of her life with beauty and the loving attendance of friends." According to Brooks, Goulding's name was "obliterated" because "his name evokes a vision of sex without sin which paralyzes the guilty mind of Hollywood. All for love he directed his sexual events with the same attention he gave the directing of films." For Brooks, Goulding was an "incomparable film director" and "the most joyful being I would ever meet." The screenwriter

Frances Marion said that his "spontaneous wit, Chesterfieldian manners, slightly manic behavior at times, and supreme self-confidence gave him an air of insouciant romanticism."

"Like Borzage, Stahl, Cukor, and Sirk," writes John Gillett, "Goulding was once classified simply as a purveyor of 'women's pictures'—but this was before melodrama ceased to be a dirty word and audiences and critics began to realise what certain writers and directors had achieved within this area. Goulding often concerned himself with what used to be called the battle of the sexes. . . . But Goulding invariably placed the emphasis on the women in the middle . . . and, working with most of Hollywood's 'strong' women, encouraged them to give their finest performances. . . . Like Mankiewicz, Goulding always believed in the value of a good script—he wrote many of them himself—taking in a fine flow of intelligent talk, designed, one suspects, with particular players in mind. Rhythm and pacing are his hallmarks, plus that facility for 'invisible' direction which so many Hollywood craftsmen possessed. . . . He could provide bravura displays when necessary. . . . , but his directorial style is concerned more with subtle camera placements (many two-shots and a curt, edgy way of moving characters in and out of frame as the drama intensifies)."

FILMS: Sun-Up, 1925; Sally, Irene and Mary, 1925; Paris (U.K., Shadows of Paris), 1926; Women Love Diamonds, 1927; Love (U.K., Anna Karenina), 1927; The Trespasser, 1929; (with others) Paramount on Parade, 1930; The Devil's Holiday, 1930; Reaching for the Moon, 1931; The Night Angel, 1931; Grand Hotel, 1932; Blondie of the Follies, 1932; Riptide, 1934; The Flame Within, 1935; That Certain Woman, 1937; White Banners, 1938; The Dawn Patrol, 1938; Dark Victory, 1939; The Old Maid, 1939; We Are Not Alone, 1939; 'Til We Meet Again, 1940; The Great Lie, 1941; (with others) Forever and a Day, 1943; The Constant Nymph, 1943; Claudia, 1943; Of Human Bondage, 1946; The Razor's Edge, 1946; Nightmare Alley, 1947; Everybody Does It, 1949; Mister 880, 1950; We're Not Married, 1952; Down Among the Sheltering Palms, 1953; Teenage Rebel, 1956; Mardi Gras, 1958.

ABOUT: Coursodon, J.-P. American Directors, Vol. 1, 1983; Meyer, W. R. Warner Brothers Directors, 1978. *Periodicals*—Film Culture 67–69 1979; Film Dope April 1980; Films and Filming July 1983; National Film Theatre (Britain) Booklet January 1984.

*GRÉMILLON, JEAN (October 3, 1901– November 25, 1959) was born in the cathedral city of Bayeux, in Normandy. His father was a railroad engineer of Breton origin and

°grä mē yoN´

JEAN GRÉMILLON

Grémillon spent part of his childhood in Brittany, attending the Brest *lycée* before going on to college at Dinan. Various careers were proposed for him—on the railroad, in medicine, in the merchant marine—but Grémillon's real vocation was music; indeed, Pierre Billard suggests that, in a sense, he was "more than anything else" a musician all his life. Since his father disapproved, the boy studied harmony secretly until he was able to go to Paris and enroll at the Schola Cantorum, studying violin and composition under Vincent d'Indy.

After that, in deference to his parents' wishes, Grémillon worked for a time as a clerk in a shipping firm at Le Havre. He found the work intolerably boring and frustrating and returned to Paris. There he earned his living by playing the violin in the small orchestras which at that time accompanied silent films in the great Paris movie theatres. A young cellist whom he met in this way introduced him to her husband, Georges Périnal, then a projectionist, later one of the greatest of French cinematographers. Grémillon and Périnal became friends and shared a growing interest in the cinema.

Grémillon entered the movie industry in the early 1920s, working as a title writer and then as an editor. Beginning in 1923 he directed a succession of short industrial documentaries with Périnal as his cameraman and assistant—films about road surfacing and the manufacture of cotton, cement, beer, ball bearings, and other products, in this way coming to know the trades, people, speech, and customs of many parts of France. In 1924 Grémillon edited shots from his first nine documentaries into a short experimental montage called *La Photogénie mécanique*, a sort of visual poem on the strangeness and beauty of machines and their products which was shown at Jean Tedesco's newly established avant-garde movie theatre, the Vieux Colombier.

More documentaries and training films were released in 1925, and the following year Grémillon went with the cameraman Lucien Lesaint to Brittany to make *Un Tour au large*, a full-length silent documentary about a Breton tuna fisherman. Grémillon himself wrote a musical accompaniment for the film, and this was recorded for performance on a player piano in careful synchronization with the images. Grémillon called *Un Tour au large* "a film of impressions, a marriage of music and imagery," and its first performance at the Vieux Colombier established him as a filmmaker to be reckoned with.

After this success Grémillon—still only twenty-five—was invited by a commercial producer to make his first feature, *Maldone* (1927). It stars Charles Dullin and Annabella in a story about a rich young man who abandons his inheritance to become a manual worker and vagabond and later, having settled down and married, sets off again in search of his lost freedom. Grémillon had Périnal and Christian Matras as his cameramen, and Périnal worked with him again on his second feature, *Gardiens de phare* (*Lighthouse Keepers*, 1928–1929). This had a script by Jacques Feyder based on a Grand Guignol play about two keepers, father and son, isolated in their lighthouse—and what happens after the son is bitten by a mad dog.

Grémillon's first sound film was *La Petite Lise* (*The Little Lise*, 1930), a melodrama about a man who is sent to prison for murdering his wife and emerges to find that his daughter has become a prostitute. Throught no fault of her own, Lise has killed a moneylender, and her father, making amends, for earlier failures, confesses to the killing and returns to jail. Jean Lenauer found the scenario clumsily constructed but had high praise for the director: "Grémillon's rhythm is slow—there is sometimes a danger that the spectator will find it too slow—but the rhythm is there and it is one peculiar to Grémillon himself. . . . Grémillon proves that he knows how to direct, that he knows how to create emotion by extremely simple means, and that he has already grasped a possible and intelligent alliance of sound and picture." A later critic found in this early sound film "a fusion of sound and image scarcely inferior to Renoir's in *La Nuit du Carrefour.*"

Unhappily the film lost money, and

Grémillon never recovered the full confidence of the financiers. After a brilliant and precocious beginning and a few years in the sun, his career became one of struggle and compromise, beginning with a long string of commercial films (1931–1937) in which he was able to show little of his style and originality. This bleak period included three years of work in Spain (where, however, one of his films had Luis Buñuel as producer) and three slightly more rewarding ones with the UFA studios in Germany. Grémillon's films for UFA included a remake in French of Hubert Marisch's *Königswaltz*; *Pattes de Mouches* (*A Scrap of Paper*), a Sardou comedy adapted by Grémillon and Roger Vitrac, and starring Pierre Brasseur and Renée Saint-Cyr; and *Gueule d'amour*, written by Charles Spaak, in which Jean Gabin plays a garrison-town Don Juan who gets his comeuppance from a cold-blooded Parisienne (Mireille Balin) and kills her. The most notable product of Grémillon's years with UFA *L'Étrange Monsieur Victor* (*The Strange Mr. Victor*, 1938); there is a wonderful performance from Raimu as a mild little criminal and excellent ones from Pierre Blanchar, Viviane Romance, and Madeleine Renaud, among others.

In the spring of 1939, back in France, Grémillon began work on *Remorques* (*Stormy Waters*). The war intervened a few months later, but work resumed in 1940 and the film was released the following year. It stars Gabin as a tugboat captain who falls in love with a girl (Michèle Morgan) he rescues from the sea, but leaves her for the sake of his dying wife (Madeleine Renaud). Written by Jacques Prévert, André Cayatte, and Charles Spaak, and with an exquisite performance from Michèle Morgan, it is very much in the fatalistic mode of "poetic realism" that dominated French cinema just before the war.

Remorques, one of the best known of Grémillon's films, was followed by what some regard as his masterpiece, *Lumière d'été* (*The Light of Summer*, 1943), also written by Prévert (in collaboration with Pierre Laroche) and brilliantly photographed by Louis Page. It centers on a Provençal hotel owned by Cri-Cri (Madeleine Renaud), an aging former dancer clinging desperately to her lover Patrice, a degenerate aristocrat (Paul Bernard). The innocent young Michèle (Madeleine Robinson) comes to the hotel to meet her fiancé Roland (Pierre Brasseur), an artist who is in fact a drunken failure. Michèle's youth and freshness attract the attention of Patrice and arouse Cri-Cri's bitter jealousy. Disillusioned by Roland and frightened by Patrice, Michèle is drawn to a straightforward young engineer (Georges Marchal) working

nearby on a hydroelectric dam. The contrast (and conflict) between the decadents at the hotel and the simple and positive values of the dam workers becomes increasingly overt. The tensions mount and reach a climax in a fancy-dress ball given by Patrice, where the characters appear in costumes reflecting their own natures—Patrice as the Marquis de Sade, Roland as Hamlet, and Cri-Cri as Manon Lescaut. The debauchery ends in a literal Dance of Death in the harsh morning light of summer—a horrible car crash in which Roland dies. Michèle and her engineer are united, leaving the aristocrats to their own futility.

Renoir's *La Règle du jeu*, on a similar theme, had been banned by the Vichy authorities, opposed to any suggestion of decadence in their "New France." Grémillon had to defend his film in long sessions before a censorship committee, and rather surprisingly secured its release. For many in occupied France, the triumph of working-class values in the film seemed to promise a return to sanity and freedom, and *Lumière d'été* was warmly welcomed. The British critic Hazel Hackett, who saw it just after the war, wrote that its "story of wasted and lost lives is set against a bare southern landscape, ravaged by the wind and burnt by the sun, whose desolation is broken only by . . . [the dam-building machinery] and by the slow flight of a massive eagle across the heavy air. There is something symbolical in the explosions which rip the earth asunder, and in the great bird of prey which hovers invulnerable and theatening . . . above the man-made confusion. . . . Grémillon throughout cunningly uses sound to heighten his cinematic effects. . . . *Lumière d'été* . . . is an unusual film that contains at the same time bitter satire, real human values, a sense of poetry and drama, and a wonderful feeling for landscape." The film's critical standing has if anything risen since then.

Another remarkable (and populist) film followed, *Le Ciel est à vous* (*The Woman Who Dared*, 1944), written by Charles Spaak and based on the true story of an ordinary woman in a French provincial town who became a record-setting pilot. The heroine, played by Madeleine Renaud, is married to a garage owner (Charles Vanel) who shares her passion for flying, and the couple are ready to sacrifice everything—from their piano and their business to their very lives—in order to reach their goal. Grémillon was a member of the underground Comité de Libération du Cinéma Français, and this film, even more than its predecessor, was welcomed in occupied France as a statement of faith in the national spirit, and a call to arms.

However, *Le Ciel est à vous* was an expensive film, and popular though it was, it failed to recover its costs, confirming Grémillon's reputation as a failure at the box office. The postwar years consequently brought him the same sort of frustrations and difficulties that had dogged him in the 1930s. Even his very personal documentary about the Allied landings in Normandy, *Le Six Juin à l'aube* (*The Sixth of June at Dawn,* 1945), was mutilated by the distributors. Grémillon had chosen to tell the story of the invasion mainly through maps, dwelling less on the landings themselves than their impact on the quiet countryside, the farmland at first devastated, then slowly coming back to life. With beautifully composed images (by four cameramen) enhanced by Grémillon's own expressive music, the film becomes a meditation on the persistence of fundamental human values, as the peasant farmers of Grémillon's native Normandy go about their immemorial tasks amid the debris and monuments of war. "Don't forget the materials I was working with," Grémillon said: "mines, stones, trees, fragments of statues. It was by arranging these images in time, according to a musical scheme, that I was able to give these inanimate and impassive objects a certain emotive quality."

Between 1945 and 1948 Grémillon worked on several ambitious projects, all of which failed for lack of backing. They included *Le Massacre des Innocents,* written with Charles Spaak, which was to have been a trilogy focusing on three critical events in contemporary history—the Spanish Civil War, the Munich Crisis of 1938, and the French Resistance in 1944. *Le Printemps de la Liberté,* on which Grémillon spent over a year, was intended as a celebration of the centenary of the revolution of 1848. Grémillon wrote the scenario, dialogue, and music himself and the work was broadcast in 1948, but was never filmed because the Ministry of Education withdrew its sponsorship.

Unable to proceed with any of his own projects, Grémillon accepted the job of directing *Pattes blanches* (*White Paws,* 1949), which the dramatist Jean Anouilh had written (in collaboration with Jean Bernard Luc) originally intending to direct it himself. Set in a Breton fishing village, which is brought to life with all Grémillon's sharp sense of reality, it is a powerful melodrama about the rivalry of the Comte de Keriadec's two sons (Paul Bernard and Michel Bouquet)for the innkeeper's beautiful but corrupt mistress (Suzy Delair). Grémillon's last two feature films were also made within the framework of the commercial cinema. *L'Étrange Madame X* (*The Strange Madame X,* 1951) has Henri Vidal as a young cabinetmaker who falls in love with a girl (Michèle Morgan) he imagines to be a chambermaid, though she is in fact a rich man's wife. *L'Amour d'une femme* (*A Woman's Love,* 1954), about a woman doctor torn between her work and love, is again set in Brittany, and was scripted by Grémillon himself. This tender and delicate story was an Italian-French coproduction, and some critics thought it somewhat marred by commercial considerations.

Grémillon turned once more to the documentary, now concerning himself mostly with the visual arts. With his former assistant Pierre Kast he codirected *Les Charmes de l'existence* (1950), a delightful seriocomic evocation of society in the half-century preceding the outbreak of the First World War, seen through the paintings of the period. He also wrote the commentary and music for Kast's *Les Désastres de la guerre* (1951), an account of the Napoleonic Wars as depicted by Goya. *Au coeur de l'Île-de-France* (1954) studies the art and architecture of central France from the Middle Ages to the Impressionist period.

Grémillon's last three documentaries, all filmed by Louis Page, use color to explore aspects of contemporary art. *La Maison aux images* (1955) shows the artists to Montmartre at work on etchings and engravings; *Haute Lisse* (1956) deals with the weaving of tapestries at the famous Gobelins works; while *André Masson et les quatre elements* (*André Masson and the Four Elements,* 1958), made in and around the painter's home and studio in Aix-en-Provence, relates his paintings to the Provençal landscape. This film (Grémillon's last) reflects on the process of artistic creation and itself becomes a work of art in which Masson's paintings and gestures are fused with Grémillon's words and music. Some critics consider this to be his finest documentary.

Grémillon is nowadays regarded by many critics as one of the half-dozen greatest of French directors—and one of the least fortunate, seldom permitted to give full expression to his exceptional abilities. Few of his contemporaries could equal his skill in the matching of sound and image, his subtle response to landscape, or his mastery of the technical resources of the medium. Grémillon was a populist and he wanted to create a popular cinema that would express his love and respect for the ordinary people of France; unhappily he seemed to lack the common touch that enabled directors like Renoir and Clair to make films in their own way and still succeed at the box office. He was a scholarly man, and one with a fatalistic sense of "the impossibility of harmony" that imbued many of his films with a disquieting melancholy.

Grémillon served from 1943 until shortly before his early death as president of the Cinémathèque Française, giving a great deal of time and effort to administrative work. He was married to Christiane Grémillon.

—K.B.

FILMS: *Early documentaries*—Chartres, 1923; La Revêtement des routes, 1923; La Fabrication du fil, 1924; Du Fil à l'aiguille, 1924; La Fabrication du ciment artificiel, 1924; La Bière, 1924; Le Roulement à Bille, 1924; Les Parfums, 1924; L'Étirage des ampoules électriques, 1924; La Photogénie mécanique, 1924; L'Éducation professionnelle des conducteurs de tramway (six brief training films), 1925; L'Électrification de la ligne Paris-Vierzon, 1925; L'Auvergne, 1925; La Naissance des cigognes, 1925; Les Aciéries de la Marine et d'Homecourt, 1925; La Vie des travailleurs italiens en France, 1926; La Croisière de l'Atalante, 1926; Un Tour au large, 1926; Gratuites, 1927; Bobs, 1928. *Features*—Maldone, 1927 (silent); Gardiens de phare (Lighthouse Keepers), 1929 (silent); La Petite Lise (The Little Lise), 1930; Daïnah la métisse, 1931; Pour un sou d'amour, 1932; Le Petit Babouin, 1932 (short feature); Gonzague/L'Accordeur, 1933; La Dolorosa, 1934 (Spain); Centinella Alerta!, 1935 (Spain); La Valse royale, 1935 (Germany); Pattes de mouches (A Scrap of Paper), 1936 (Germany); Gueule d'amour, 1937 (Germany); L'Étrange Monsieur Victor (The Strange Mr. Victor), 1938 (Germany); Remorques (Stormy Waters), 1941; Lumière d'été (The Light of Summer), 1943; Le Ciel est à vous (The Woman Who Dared), 1944; Pattes blanches, 1949; L'Étrange Madame X (The Strange Mrs. X), 1951; L'Amour d'une femme (A Woman's Love), 1954. *Later documentaries*—Le Six Juin à l'aube (The Sixth of June at Dawn), 1945; (with Pierre Kast) Les Charmes de l'existence, 1950; Alchimie, 1952; Astrologie, 1952; Au coeur de l'Île-de-France, 1954; La Maison aux images, 1955; Haute Lisse, 1956; André Masson et les quatre elements (André Masson and the Four Elements), 1958.

ABOUT: Abel, R. French Cinema: The First Wave, 1915–1929, 1984; Agel, H. Jean Grémillon, 1969 (France); Billard, P. Jean Grémillon, 1966; Armes, R. French Cinema Since 1946: 1, 1966; Kast, P. Jean Grémillon, 1960 (France); Leprohon, P. Présences contemporaines, cinéma, 1957; Roud, R. (ed.) Cinema: A Critical Dictionary, 1980; Sadoul, G. French Film, 1953. *Periodicals*—Bianco e Nero 1–2 1960; Ciné-Club January–February 1951; Cahiers du Cinéma September 1978; Cinéma (France) March 1960; Cinématographe October 1978; Image et Son January 1960, November 1970; Lettres Françaises December 3, 1959; November 24, 1960; Sight and Sound Summer 1947; Télérama July 5, 1978.

GRIFFITH, D(AVID) W(ARK) (January 22, 1875–July 23, 1948), the American director and producer who codified the cinematic means of storytelling, was born on a farm in Oldham

D. W. GRIFFITH

County, Kentucky, twenty miles from Louisville. He was one of the seven children of Jacob Wark Griffith and the former Mary Oglesby. His father was a half-trained physician, gold prospector, farmer, raconteur, orator, politician and soldier. He had fought with the United States Army in the 1846 Mexican War and against it as a lieutenant colonel in the Confederate cavalry.

Throughout his career D.W. Griffith revealed himself very much the product of his Southern childhood. His films always reflected a special fondness for rural life and rural people, a longing for an idyllic pastoral world, simpler, clearer, and sweeter than the urban present. He cherished the chivalric traditions of the antebellum South, just as his father Jacob cherished the sword that hung by his side as a soldier and over his mantel after the Civil War. Like his father, Griffith identified human feelings with concrete symbols. He also identified with Southern attitudes toward the proper places of whites and blacks. But if he was a racist—as we now define the term—he was also a populist, sharing the late-nineteenth-century agrarian suspicion of big business and meddlesome government. From childhood also came his initiation into the "finer things" of art. His father, the possessor of a famously powerful and resonant voice, introduced him as a small child to Shakespeare, Poe, Dickens, Longfellow, and the Bible, and also took him to his first magic-lantern show.

Griffith said that "the one person I really loved most in all my life was my father." But 'Roarin' Jake, who never entirely recovered from his Civil War wounds and was a heavy drinker, died in 1882, when his adoring son was only seven. In 1890 the Griffith family moved to Louisville. Griffith took what jobs he could find, working as an elevator operator in a dry goods store, clerk in a book store, reporter for the Louisville *Courier-Journal*—until he discovered his metier in the theatre. In 1896 Sarah Bernhardt's company came to Louisville. Griffith got a job as a super: "I deified myself by carrying a spear for the divine Sarah Bernhardt." Standing in the wings, Griffith was transfixed as "the golden voice of Bernhardt chanted . . . poetical lines." For the next dozen years Griffith's theatrical experiences would be less ethereal.

He became an itinerant actor in the American provinces, playing mostly minor roles with mostly undistinguished stock companies, for which he received little notice and little pay. Unlike his future colleague, Mack Sennett, who took to the stage at the same time, Griffith never played in New York, while Sennett worked both on Broadway and in the premier burlesque theatres of the Bowery. Griffith's theatrical apprenticeship was both more genteel and more shabby. What he was learning, without knowing it, were the techniques of theatrical melodrama—the sure-fire plot turns and emotional tugs that survived even mediocre playing and sloppy production. Both Griffith's strengths and his excesses could be traced to his clear understanding of what would play in Peoria at the turn of the century.

He met his first wife, Linda Arvidson, in 1904 in San Francisco, where both worked in the same theatrical company. They married in Boston in 1906 and moved to New York, where Griffith pursued a career as a writer. His first success was a free-verse poem published in *Leslie's Weekly*. According to Richard Schickel, Griffith's biographer, he "had a feeling he was destined to great things, but no specific idea of where or how he would realize the promise that was more apparent to him than to others." No less than his contemporary, Eugene O'Neill, Griffith's artistic career would be a battle between the poetic touch and the grandiose ambition. His play, *The Fool and the Girl*, had been optioned by the actor-manager James K. Hackett for production at the end of 1906. While he waited for rehearsals to begin, Griffith and his wife found work together on the stage—in a production of *The One Woman* by Thomas Dixon, author of *The Clansman*, on which Griffith was to base his most famous film.

The Fool and the Girl was the story of a poetic young man, a dreamer, a little like Griffith himself, whom everyone tries to swindle—including the girl of the title, with whom he falls blindly in love. After a disappointing week in Washing-

ton—some notices were kind, but most were devastating—and an even more dismal week in Baltimore, the production quietly folded on the road. Griffith immediately began work on his next play, *War,* an epic of the American Revolution in which an indentured servant becomes a heroic spy serving General George Washington and the American cause. As in so many later Griffith films, the historical epic served as background for a romantic drama of the common people. The patriot must choose between saving his country and saving his beloved from the barbarous Hessians. In *War* he makes the patriotic choice and abandons her to her fate, losing her forever. Later Griffith works would contrive ways for their heroes to take a political action that would also rescue the beloved. His most powerful films would take place at this same intersection of historical epic and romantic melodrama. Although *War* was never produced, some of its incidents found their way into Griffith's 1924 film *America*.

While he waited for the world to discover his poetic genius, Griffith struggled to keep the wolf from the door. His autobiographical manuscript "D.W. Griffith and the Wolf," edited by James Hart and published in 1972 as *The Man Who Invented Hollywood,* presented this "wolf" of poverty and hunger as his literal nemesis. One way for unemployed New York actors to keep the wolf at bay was to accept acting or extra work in the movies. Though it demeaned stage actors to perform in nonspeaking roles, a film job took only a day or two and no colleague was likely to witness their participation in such an ignominious enterprise; theatre people didn't go to movies. The rivalry between film and theatre had already begun by 1907, the year in which the movies first became a powerful force in American life.

After outgrowing the vaudeville houses, where films were merely one more item on the vaudeville bill, they began moving into their own theatres in 1902. By 1908 it was estimated that weekly attendance had reached one hundred million at American nickelodeons—little storefront theatres, seating about two hundred, where it cost a nickel or dime to see a sixty-minute program of short films. Those most possessed by "nickel madness" returned daily, if not twice a day, for different screenings. Stage actors, who grudgingly participated in what had seemed like a passing fad, found themselves involved in a vigorous young art form. It was no coincidence that D.W. Griffith and Mack Sennett both worked in films for the first time in 1907.

At the Edison studios in the Bronx, Griffith

applied for a job as a writer, his adaptation of *Tosca* under his arm. Griffith's bulky script was six years ahead of the infant industry's capabilities, defined by the ten-minute film, improvisational outdoor shooting, and cheap interior sets that only vaguely matched the exteriors which nature provided for nothing. Instead, Griffith accepted the Edison Company offer of an acting job at the standard rate of five dollars a day. In *Rescued From an Eagle's Nest* (1907), Griffith's first lead performance, he plays the lumberjack father of an infant stolen away by a huge bird. Griffith climbs into the eagle's nest (shot partially outdoors on the New Jersey Palisades, partially indoors on the ludicrous cardboard cliffs of the Edison studio) and slays the puppet eagle (dangling on clearly visible strings) to bring baby home.

Like Griffith's career as a whole, this little film stood poised between the conventions of film and theatre. Its director, Edwin S. Porter, America's most important filmmaker before Griffith, understood that narrative expectations provided the mental cement to join discontinuous pieces of space. That actual cliffs could be matched, however unconvincingly, with studio cliffs reveals that understanding. The attack on an innocent victim—child or defenseless woman—had also become a film staple by 1907, as it had been on the stage. The last-minute rescue from death (or worse) came directly from Victorian melodrama.

By 1908 Griffith was at Biograph—the American Mutoscope and Biograph Company, as it was formally known, at 11 East 14th Street. It was founded in 1896 by a syndicate of inventors and investors—William Kennedy Laurie Dickson, Elias Koopman, Herman Casler, and Henry Marvin. In 1908 it became an important member of the Motion Picture Patents Company, set up to block the encroachment of independent producers into the industry. Biograph films had not captured the audience imagination as fully as Porter's at Edison. Even with a superb cameraman, G.W. ("Billy") Bitzer, Biograph films, generally directed by Wallace C. ("Old Man") McCutcheon, were often plodding or incoherent.

After Griffith had been three months with the company as an actor and writer, Biograph asked him to direct films. The growing popularity of the nickelodeons generated an ever-increasing demand for films. Biograph needed more and better product. Griffith's thorough knowledge of theatrical conventions and techniques probably determined Biograph's decision. Uncertain about his new job and the movie business as a whole, Griffith accepted the assignment on the condition that he could return to acting at five dollars a day if he failed. He signed his contract and drew his salary as "Lawrence Griffith." Although later film scholars took the alias as a sign of Griffith's doubts about his new profession, he had in fact adopted the name a dozen years earlier as a stage actor.

Griffith directed his first film, *The Adventures of Dollie,* in July 1908, with his wife in the lead. Thus began four remarkable years, arguably the most remarkable in the history of the cinema. During this period Griffith personally directed some 420 films, most of them one-reelers (a 35-mm reel, with a maximum of 1000 feet of film, ran between ten and fifteen minutes). While the films could not grow in length—the one-reel restriction was imposed by the MPPC to fit the exhibition patterns of the nickelodeons—they grew steadily in narrative complexity, thematic subtlety, psychological integrity, and stylistic fluidity. In these four years, movies evolved from crude, clumsy skeletons of theatrical and novelistic fictions to evocative, autonomous, *cinematic* versions of the same kinds of narratives. The person most responsible for that evolution was Griffith. As Edward Wagenknecht noted, "Even we children sensed that Biograph pictures were different, although we could not tell wherein their difference might consist."

Although Griffith's accomplishment in this period is indisputable, critics and historians as well as children have had difficulty in describing it. The idea that recurs most often is that Griffith personally invented uniquely cinematic techniques. Robert M. Henderson summarized Griffith's accomplishment at Biograph by compiling a list of twenty-four techniques that Griffith was supposed to have contributed to the cinema. Lewis Jacobs wrote that "he repudiated theatrical conventions and evolved a method of expression peculiar to the screen." Underlying such assertions are two assumptions that dominated film history and theory for five decades.

Both Griffith and the movies were born in that era of American invention symbolized by Thomas Alva Edison and Alexander Graham Bell. The creation of a new and efficient machine or process seemed the highest human attainment. Invention and progress were synonymous; the patent and the copyright were instruments of destiny. To credit Griffith with the *invention* of devices first strikingly used in his Biograph films—close-ups, distant panoramas, cross-cuts—was to elevate his accomplishment into that American pantheon where art, science, and commerce met under the influence of historical inevitability. Griffith contributed to his own apotheosis when he laid claim to the invention of techniques and, late in life, regretted not having patented them. Later film historians, attacking this myth, actually succumbed to it when they demonstrated that Griffith only appropriated the techniques he claimed as his own. In proving that Griffith was no inventor, historians overlooked the problem of whether stylistic devices should properly be considered inventions at all.

The second assumption also arose from nineteenth-century certainties. Each art was supposed to have a unique mission, calling for unique tools: painting was pictorial, music melodic, the theatre verbal, and so forth. A tradition of film theory, stretching from Griffith to Eisenstein, determined that the unique tool of cinema was editing—the joining of disparate times and spaces into a single coherent artifact. It was editing or montage that distinguished cinema from theatre. While earlier films were "uncinematic" because they were "theatrical," composed of unedited shots spliced together in consecutive order, Griffith's films from 1908 to 1912 increasingly exploited the power of editing for both emotional and thematic impact. Kemp R. Niver's study of Griffith's years at Biograph was ruthlessly mathematical: the maturity of a film could be ascertained by counting the number of shots. Of course, the Biograph films reflect Griffith's growing mastery of many other elements no less essential to communicative cinema: effective composition, framing, and lighting; the telling use of both human personalities and inanimate objects; complex patterns of movement within the frame.

Intent on chronicling a unique cinematic art, historians took Griffith's editing as his "repudiation" of the theatre. Few early commentators realized, or remembered, that even Griffith's most famous editing device—the cross-cut during the last-minute rescue—came directly from the nineteenth-century stage. Increasingly complex theatrical machinery had made quick changes of location—from the victim on the railroad tracks to the hero rushing to her rescue—possible and popular. Griffith did not so much repudiate the stage as discover ways to translate its powerful effects into the terms of a new medium.

The real "discovery" of Griffith's 400-plus Biograph films is what we think of as "the movies" as a whole. From an inchoate collection of familiar plot motifs in 1908 we see the simultaneous emergence of genres, character types, expressive interior and exterior decor, a lexicon of shots, empathic film acting, and powerful rhythms and resources of movement within the frame

and between frames. When Griffith began making films in 1908 it was as if practitioners were barely able to construct the filmic equivalent of a coherent sentence; by the time he finished with the one-reeler in 1913 they were able to write "The Tell-Tale Heart."

Even his very first film, *The Adventures of Dollie*, reveals visual care, despite its hackneyed story of a child stolen by gypsies and saved from a plunge over the falls. The film's opening shots show the family, wearing their Sunday clothes on a bright summer day, walking in the woods beside a river. The outer harmony of nature and sunlight is echoed in the inner harmony of the family unit, about to be ruptured by a vengeful gypsy (a standard villain of early cinema, until replaced by a more American equivalent, the tramp). The river of Griffith's opening shot turns out to be the very river on which little Dollie will float toward her doom. As the family walks toward the camera, two boys carrying fishing poles walk in the opposite direction. Dollie will be rescued when one of the boys hears her cries and fishes her from the stream. However extraordinary the film's events, Griffith shapes them into a coherent pattern by preparing for the climax from the very beginning. Such narrative care was rare in 1908 cinema.

Other Griffith films of 1908 foreshadow his future predilections and preoccupations. His second film, *The Redman and the Child*, reverses the convention of *Dollie* by making the "foreigner," an American Indian, the heroic rescuer of a threatened child, assailed by mercenary white attackers. Griffith, whose racism did not usually extend to Indians, shared his generation's belief in the uncorrupted virtue of the Noble Savage. Griffith's taste for genteel literature also became evident in 1908 one-reel versions of *The Taming of the Shrew* and *After Many Years*, the latter the first of several versions of Tennyson's *Enoch Arden*. In shaping coherent film narratives, Griffith was also elevating popular taste, combining the books of the bourgeois parlor with motifs from the dime novel and penny dreadful. American films ever after would bounce between these two poles or, like Griffith, try to combine them. Already by 1908 Griffith had adopted abstract allegorizing to accompany Victorian moralizing. In *The Devil* the natural goodness of men and women is corrupted by the Evil One, who appears magically in the frame to whisper temptations into unsuspecting ears.

Of Griffith's sixty-nine 1908 films, *For Love of Gold* has received most critical attention—an adaptation of Jack London's "Just Meat," in which two thieves murder each other for money. To depict the climactic double killing, Griffith positions his camera closer to the two men than the standard far shot of 1908 films. The closer shot not only allows us to see crucial details—like the pouring of poison into a coffee cup—but enables us to observe the strategies and reactions of the two combatants. Although Griffith does not cut to a closer position *within* the scene, as many commentators claim, the setup he chose provides an early example of what Griffith called the photographing of thought.

Perhaps his most effective 1908 film is a family melodrama, so fluidly shot and edited that it hides its most powerful technical device. In *An Awful Moment* another vengeful gypsy invades a happy home, seeking revenge against the judge who sentenced her husband to prison. She trusses the judge's wife to a chair, aims a rifle at her breast, and ties a string from the trigger of the gun to the handle of the door. When the judge opens that door, he will unwittingly murder his own wife. The tragedy is prevented when their little child, sleeping in the mother's room, awakens to untie the string just before the husband opens the bedroom door.

To make this drama both comprehensible and suspenseful, it was necessary to define clearly the house's geography: three contiguous rooms—the judge's study, a sitting room, and the wife's bedroom. Only by showing the exact location of the fatal door in relation to the other rooms of the house could the awful moment make itself felt. By the husband's simple act of walking from right to left—leaving the frame at the far left and immediately entering the next frame, after a cut, at the far right—Griffith clearly defines the spatial connection of the rooms. It is so clear that there are three contiguous rooms that the viewer never doubts their existence. But the tiny Biograph studio, twenty-two feet wide, was too narrow to house more than one room at a time. Our belief in three contiguous rooms was a cinematic illusion produced by a combination of movement, editing, and framing.

Griffith's most productive Biograph year was 1909—both in quantity (138 films) and innovative quality. A frantic production schedule made it possible for Griffith to finish as many as three or four little films each week. The Biograph day often began as early as five a.m. with a ferry trip across the Hudson to Fort Lee, New Jersey. Outdoor location shooting would continue until about noon. Then the company would return to the Biograph studio, where an interior set had meanwhile been built and dressed. Interior shooting might continue until seven or eight at night. After dismissing the cast, Griffith would view the previous day's rushes until midnight, supervising the editing for his film cutter, Jimmie Smith. The whole process would begin again the next morning. The summer of 1909 brought a change of routine when Griffith took his entire company on location for a month to Cuddebackville, New Jersey, to take advantage of the brilliant weather, light, and scenery.

Griffith's 1909 films included further literary adaptations—of Poe (*Edgar Allen Poe* and *The Sealed Room*), Tolstoy (*The Resurrection*), Browning (*Pippa Passes*), Dickens (*The Cricket on the Hearth*), and Frank Norris (*A Corner in Wheat*). Griffith also paid his first film visits to distant historical periods that he would explore more fully in longer films: to Renaissance France (*The Golden Louis*), Revolutionary America (*1776*, or *The Hessian Renegades*), and the Civil War South (*In Old Kentucky*). This was the year in which Griffith's stock company of actors began to take shape. Mary Pickford, Mack Sennett, Henry B. Walthall, Robert Harron, Blanche Sweet, Miriam Cooper, and James Kirkwood all joined the Griffith company before the end of 1909.

This was also the year of Griffith's first use of cross-cutting to build the suspense of a last-minute rescue. In *At the Altar*, a young bride and her beloved move inexorably toward a fatal trap that has been prepared for them by a rejected suitor—another of those dastardly gun gadgets, rigged to go off just as the couple kneels at the church altar. Concerned friends and citizens, who have discovered the plot, race to warn the couple before they seal their doom. Griffith cuts back and forth between the happy wedding party inside the church and the grim race toward the church.

Similarly, at the climax of *The Lonely Villa*, a husband speeds home to save his wife and children from attack by the tramps who have invaded their home. Griffith cuts between the husband, racing furiously in a horse-drawn wagon, and his family under attack, withdrawing steadily into the inner rooms of the house (as in *An Awful Moment*, domestic geography is important to the film). Both the pace and the editing of this rescue are crisper than in *At the Altar*, as Griffith realized that a racing wagon demands faster editing rhythms than rushing people. Later Griffith rescues would take advantage of faster and faster vehicles—mounted riders, automobiles, trains.

Although these Griffith melodramas receive critical attention mostly on account of their editing, two Griffith mood pieces are among his most interesting films of 1909. In *The Drunkard's Reformation* Griffith depicts a husband whose heavy drinking brings grief to his wife and daughter. The lighting effect with which the film ends, the reunited family basking in the warm glow of a blazing fireplace, has attracted most of the critical approbation (although Edwin S. Porter had used the same lighting effect to a similar purpose in *The Seven Ages,* five years earlier). It was Griffith's first film to explore the curse of drink, which would become Griffith's own curse in his later years. The husband's reformation is inspired by a stage play that parallels his own life: a husband whose drinking destroys his family. That Griffith can tell the same story twice within the same film—one using deep film space and a relatively subtle style of film acting, the other using flatter stage space and broadly theatrical acting—reveals Griffith's awareness of the stylistic differences between the theatre he had left and the movies he had adopted.

The most remarkable single film of this remarkable year was *A Corner in Wheat.* This adaptation of Frank Norris' *The Pit* was not so much a story as a tapestry of American capitalism, invoking three different social groups, three sets of characters who never meet but whose lives affect one another profoundly. The film is distinguished not by the drive of its narrative but by its physical rhythms and visual texture. Griffith lyrically depicts the work of a farming family, tilling the fields in intimate contact with nature—fields, sky, tree, horses. Shot in the soft light of a November morning, these scenes have a visual texture that is luminous yet slightly barren and chilling. The farmer and his family move slowly and dreamily, almost in slow motion; their hand gestures are liquid and open, their clothing loose and soft, in the middle grays of the monochromatic scale. Griffith deliberately bases one composition on a painting, Jean-François Millet's "The Sowers"—not only the first shot in any film consciously derived from a painting, but also the first advertised as such.

At the opposite end of the social scale stands the Wheat King, the urban financier who manipulates the prices of the grain the farmer grows. Griffith emphasizes the distance of the Wheat King and his cronies from the natural processes of the farm with a consciously opposite principle of movement, acting, and decor. The Wheat King exists within crowded, confined interiors, movement is rapid, hand gestures grasping and pointed; clothing is tight, constricting, and formal, dominated by the extreme whites and blacks of the monochromatic scale.

Between the farmer and the Wheat King are the urban poor who suffer from his financial machinations. While for the farmer grain is a natural product and for the Wheat King merely a source of profit, for the urban poor it provides the bread which is their staff of life. In the film's most striking moment Griffith executes a kind of cross-cut which, unlike those in his last-minute rescues, has no narrative significance but simply makes a moral comment. Griffith cuts from a shot of the Wheat King and his friends, merrily celebrating at a festive banquet, to an absolutely still shot, a *tableau vivant,* of the poor standing in a breadline.

Nature, a powerful visual motif throughout the film, asserts its supremacy at the conclusion: the Wheat King falls into one of his own grain elevators to be "drowned in a torrent of golden grain." The film began with the hands of the farmer gently sifting grain and ends with the hand of the Wheat King, desperately grasping for air from beneath the pile of grain in which he is buried. Griffith had never before made a film so controlled in its structure, rhythms, decor, acting, composition, and editing—a film which made no conventional narrative sense but which was completely coherent as a result of its visual and metaphoric systems.

The next year brought fewer films (87), with fewer inventive leaps and fewer adaptations of literature. Griffith's most interesting films of 1910 followed the path of *A Corner in Wheat* and owed less to storytelling than to visual texture and poetic mood. Perhaps the most significant event of the year was Griffith's first winter trip to California. As he had done the previous summer in Cuddebackville, Griffith took his entire company for an extended shooting trip, where he and Bitzer could take full advantage of the California light and landscape. *The Way of the World,* a religious allegory of inevitable human failings, captured the silhouette of mission bells against the California sky and sunlight pouring through the windows of a California mission. *The Unchanging Sea* offered a poetic glimpse of suffering fisherfolk, especially the women who lose their men to the sea, shot beside the Pacific on the then unfamiliar beach at Santa Monica. *Ramona,* a film adaptation of Helen Hunt Jackson's novel (Griffith had earlier appeared in a stage version), used a striking mountain panorama, with simultaneous action in the distant rearground of the frame and in the foreground, at the very bottom of a canyon. This story of forbidden love between an aristocratic white woman and an American Indian predictably demonstrates the superior moral purity of the Noble Savage.

Among the films made elsewhere later in 1910 was *His Trust,* with its sequel, *His Trust Fulfilled.* This two-part film was Griffith's first move beyond the single-reel restriction. This story of a freed slave's fidelity to the master who died for the Confederacy reflects Griffith's usual fondness for the "Uncle Tom," the "simple soul" who knows his place. *The Two Paths* was, like *The Devil* and *The Way of the World*, a Griffith allegory of virtue and sin. The sister who takes the hard path is rewarded with familial contentment, but the sister who leaves the straight and narrow for the "House of Pleasure" finds that drinking cocktails and dancing the two-step is the road to a lonely death. Like his taste for melodrama and his sympathy for rural life, Griffith's tendency to allegorize began very early in his career.

Griffith's Biograph films of 1911 and 1912 continued the trend toward fewer films (70 and 67 respectively) invested with richer human and visual texture. Griffith cut his last-minute rescues more and more tightly as he moved from *The Lonedale Operator* of 1911 to *The Girl and Her Trust* and *A Beast at Bay* of 1912. In *An Unseen Enemy* two helpless girls—Lillian and Dorothy Gish in their first major roles for Griffith—are threatened from the next room by a hand holding a revolver, but eventually manage to telephone for help. Griffith roamed world history and world literature for backgrounds into which he could set his tales—from the Civil War (*Rose of Kentucky, The Battle*) to an allegorical struggle in the prehistoric past between Weakhands and Bruteforce (*Man's Genesis*). Many of Griffith's 1912 California films displayed not only the landscapes but the narrative conventions of a genre rapidly rising in public popularity, the Western (*Iola's Promise, The Goddess of Sagebrush Gulch*).

As in the preceding years, Griffith's most powerful films of 1912 were mood pieces rather than driving narratives, glimpses of either rural or urban life under moral and psychological duress. In *The Painted Lady* and *The New York Hat* Griffith attacks the severity of American puritanism, the destructiveness of mean-minded suspicion. In *The New York Hat*, the sharp tongues of small-town gossips, a favorite Griffith target, develop a salacious scandal out of the innocent friendship of Lionel Barrymore and Mary Pickford. *The Painted Lady* wilfully flouts the puritan ethic. Blanche Sweet, as the virtuous product of a repressive home, inadvertently kills the cad she loves and goes magnificently mad; her frivolous sister goes unpunished.

One Is Business, the Other Crime and *The Musketeers of Pig Alley* focus on the social problems of the modern city. While the poor man who robs the rich to feed his needy family is punished as a criminal in *One Is Business*, the rich man who steals far more by graft and bribery is applauded as a leading citizen. *The Musketeers of Pig Alley*, among the most remarkable of all Griffith's Biograph films, depicts a cross-section of American life on New York's teeming immigrant streets. Centering on the battle for mastery of those streets between two rival gangs, *Musketeers* is a forerunner of the gangster film, with a scrappy hood played by Elmer Booth in the jaunty manner of a James Cagney or Edward G. Robinson. The film also sketches the milieu for the modern story in Griffith's *Intolerance*. As opposed to the country films, in which innocence exists in a world of severely restricted opportunity, so that the principal menace is often a false accusation, Griffith's city films show innocence under perpetual attack by temptation and corruption. As in later American genre films, Griffith's Biograph split between rural and urban settings reflected not only a conflict of visual values but also of moral landscapes.

In 1913 Griffith made several key transitions: from short film to long, from staff director to auteur, from the MPPC studio Biograph to the independent company Mutual. The film business itself was in a similar state of change and growth. Spectacular feature films from Europe—*Queen Elizabeth, Quo Vadis?*—had become road-show attractions in legitimate theatres, while movie palaces were rising on Broadway. Like his coming to Biograph in 1908, Griffith's move in 1913 was both a cause and an effect of activity in the film business as a whole. In a full-page advertisement in the New York *Dramatic Mirror* of September 29, 1913, Griffith proclaimed himself the "producer of all great Biograph successes," listed 151 of them, and claimed the invention of the close-up, the long shot, cross-cutting, and "restraint of expression." Although his apparent purpose was to announce his availability, Griffith had already signed a contract with the Mutual Film Corporation for several program pictures as well as one personal production each year. The ad was mere trumpeting and puffery, the kind of flourish that not only became familiar in the film business as a whole but also accompanied the release of every future Griffith production.

Griffith films of 1913–14, whether for Biograph or Mutual, showed him groping toward longer narrative structures, grander moral themes, and more impressive visual settings. *The Battle of Elderbush Gulch*, Griffith's most spectacular Western, included a preliminary sketch for the climax of *The Birth of a Nation*: settlers trapped inside a cabin battle the encircling Indians, while the cavalry gallops to the eventual rescue. *Judith of Bethulia*, Griffith's first biblical epic and America's first four-reeler, similarly foreshadowed the battles around the besieged city of Babylon in *Intolerance*. Like so many Griffith projects, *Judith of Bethulia* combined cinematic spectacle and theatrical tradition, popular appeal and literary taste. It was based on Thomas Bailey Aldrich's famous play, in a production of which Griffith had appeared in 1905.

Home Sweet Home, another 1914 picture, also straddled film melodrama and genteel literature. Loosely based on Browning's *Pippa Passes*, which Griffith had filmed in 1909, *Home Sweet Home* replaces the wandering Pippa with various wandering musicians, all playing the strains of John Howard Payne's famous song. Like Pippa's melody, the song enters the lives of characters undergoing melodramatic struggles, converting strife and sorrow to peace and contentment. Linking four stories of temptation and redemption—each of them rather similar to a Biograph one-reeler—is the career of Payne himself, the Prodigal Son who left his small town and its wholesome values but could still summon the moral energy to write his nostalgic song. According to Richard Schickel, Griffith also saw himself as the artist who left a wholesome home to make his artistic mark on a sordid world. If *Home Sweet Home* looked back to *Pippa Passes,* it also looked forward to *Intolerance*—another quartet of stories bound together by visual and thematic motifs.

Griffith's final film of 1914, *The Avenging Conscience,* likewise mixed literature and film, past and future. Like several Griffith one-reelers, *The Avenging Conscience* drew on the fiction and imagery of Edgar Allan Poe. In this adaptation of "The Tell-Tale Heart," sprinkled with passages of "Annabel Lee," the guilt-stricken hero (Henry B. Walthall) kills only in his imagination. To increase our sympathetic identification, Griffith motivates the young man's homicide: his uncle is tightfisted and jealous, both unappreciative and unworthy of his nephew's care and attention. Though Griffith rationalizes Poe's inexplicable act of insanity, the young man's dream, which dominates the film, sustains the original mood of paranoia with haunting images, eerie light, and tortured visions. Griffith miraculously translates the aural torture of Poe's story—the remorseless thumping of the tell-tale heart—into visual correlatives, literal visions of demonic possession. For Gilbert Seldes, *The Avenging Conscience* remained Griffith's greatest film: "The picture was projected in a palpable atmosphere; it was *felt*. After ten years I recall dark masses and ghostly rays of light."

After six frantic years of production, averaging more than a film a week, Griffith invested three years in just two films. *The Birth of a Nation,* filmed over the final six months of 1914 and released in January 1915, was another blend of film technique and literary aspiration. Frank Woods' adaptation of Thomas Dixon's *The Clansman* (which Dixon himself had earlier adapted for the stage), incorporated passages from an even more luridly racist Dixon novel, *The Leopard's Spots.* The controversial result offered a romanticized view of the antebellum South, the devastating effects of the Civil War, and the struggle of white Southerners to survive the Reconstruction.

Two families, the Stonemans of the North and the Camerons of the South, are torn apart by the War Between the States but reunited at the conclusion in harmony and matrimony, aided by the heroic Ku Klux Klan. In a brilliantly edited last-minute rescue, the excitement of which is hard to resist, the Klan preserves Stonemans and Camerons alike from death and rapine by rampaging black hordes. Despite Griffith's softening of Dixon's most shocking passages, the film provoked the first massive American social protest against racist cinema propaganda. Both the infant NAACP and its white allies urged censorship of the most offensive scenes or sued to prohibit showings altogether. Although social activists learned much from this early campaign, civic agitation only helped publicize the film in 1915.

The Birth of a Nation cost more than any film ever had—over $100,000, which Griffith had to beg and borrow to complete the project. It also made more, in proportion to its cost, than any film ever would—almost twenty times its cost in its initial domestic run. It became the first blockbuster in film history—the first film that *had* to be seen, even at two-dollar ticket prices in special road-show presentations. The reason for its success was not its racist view of American history but its visual splendor, its care and detail with historical settings, and its tender depiction of human feelings.

Griffith's representation of Lincoln's assassination in Ford's theatre—step by step, moment by moment—was the first detailed reconstruction on film of a sensational historical incident, a resurrection of the dead past. The film's careful rendering of strategies on the battlefield (influenced by Mathew Brady's famous Civil War photographs), of injured soldiers in a Northern hospital, of Lee's surrender at Appomattox, were among the scenes that made audiences feel, as President Wilson did, that they were witnessing "history written in lightning." In addition to its mammoth spectacle, Griffith saturated his film with the emotions of his characters—the gallant Little Colonel (Henry B. Walthall), the demure Elsie Stoneman (Lillian Gish), the vivacious little sister (Mae Marsh): these were the same kinds of intimate human portraits that peopled his best Biograph films. Griffith brought to his epic the full arsenal of techniques he had mastered at Biograph—close-ups, cross-cuts, iris shots, tracking shots, distant panoramas, and the breathless climax of two interwoven last-minute rescues.

Although the film provoked the anger of antiracists—and still does—it remains an essential document in American cultural history. Most white Americans in 1915 shared Griffith's antipathy toward miscegenation and regarded social reformers who supported the black cause as meddlesome cranks. The "good" blacks in Griffith's film were "Uncle Toms," impersonated by white actors in blackface; however, at that time the blackface tradition dominated white America's depiction of black life—even on the Broadway stage. The enormous popular response to Griffith's film indicated that its depiction of blacks was neither offensive nor aberrational in the eyes of contemporary white audiences.

The film's enormous success converted an almost anonymous artisan into a famous public figure, speaking and writing widely and frequently about "the freedom of the screen" and the new art of the motion picture: "This is my art . . . whatever poetry is in me must be worked out in actual practice." Nowhere was Griffith's new role as visionary prophet more obvious than in his next film, *Intolerance*, perhaps the maddest, most idiosyncratic, most overwhelming and most overblown project in film history. While shooting *The Mother and the Law*, about gangs and crime in the city slums, Griffith got the notion that spectacular historical parallels could be found for its simple story. The most lavish was set in the ancient civilization of Babylon, which Griffith reconstructed on an enormous scale. The other historical settings were the Judea of Christ and the France of the St. Bartholomew's Day massacre. The theme of *Intolerance*—which Griffith subtitled "A Sun Play of the Ages"—was that social catastrophes always resulted from intolerant bigotry. The fall of Babylon, the death of Christ, the slaughter of the Huguenots, and the dissolution of the modern family could all be traced to the hypocrisy of "Uplifters." Although Griffith's war against intolerance may have been inspired by recent attempts to ban or censor *The Birth of a Nation*, the film's grandiose aspirations were also consistent with his new public persona. He was expected to top *The Birth of a Nation*. And he did.

Like its predecessor, *Intolerance* moved between gargantuan spectacle and human intimacy, from the topless towers of Babylon to the tender love between the Little Dear One (Mae Marsh) and her falsely accused husband (Robert Harron) in the modern city. Griffith's double last-minute rescue cross-cuts through the centuries—from chariots flogged by invading hordes toward Babylon to a speeding automobile and train, racing to save the boy from the gallows. Linking the four strands was the symbolic Mother (Lillian Gish) who "endlessly rocks the cradle, uniter of here and hereafter." *Intolerance*, like *The Birth of a Nation*, ends with a grandiose allegorical pageant—here one in which fields of flowers replace the walls of prisons.

Intolerance was released in 1916. Though for most critics and many viewers in the major cities it kept the artistic promise of *The Birth of a Nation*, it did not keep its commercial promise. With costs rumored at $2 million (but documented at about $400,000), *Intolerance* never repaid its original investment. Some historians have blamed the film's pacifist stance at a time when the nation was flexing its muscles for war; others its confusing metaphorical structure—the capricious leaps back and forth through history. Richard Schickel cites the lack of an intense dramatic focus: just as we are beginning to sympathize with one group of characters, we are transported elsewhere. A more probable reason for the film's disappointing performance is that it simply outstripped the capabilities of the 1916 film industry to return even a moderate profit on an immoderate investment. Though it did solid business, *Intolerance* was no cultural sensation. Griffith himself lost a lot of money on the project but was neither destitute nor desperate as a result. The lesson he had learned was not that it was a mistake to make grandiose films (he would make others) but that it was a mistake to put all his production eggs in a single basket.

After investing nearly two years of his creative life in *Intolerance*, Griffith returned to an earlier pattern: a diet of modest programmers, with one special project each year. His fame as a director of battle scenes brought an invitation from the British government to shoot propaganda footage on actual World War I battlefields. The documentary location footage he obtained in this way was woven into three fictional films of 1918—the major production, *Hearts of the World*, and two programmers, *The Great Love* and *The Greatest Thing in Life*. In each film, as in *The Birth of a Nation* and *Intolerance*, history intrudes into the lives and loves of simple families, here torn and tested by the Great War but with the courage, heart, and moral strength to endure all. In January 1919, Griffith joined Douglas Fairbanks, Mary Pickford, and Charles

Chaplin in forming the United Artists Corporation, the same year signing a three-picture contract with First National.

Griffith's program pictures of 1919 left war-torn Europe for the pastoral American idyll (*A Romance of Happy Valley, The Girl Who Stayed at Home,* and *True Heart Susie*), but his program pictures of 1920 took him to the exotic shores of the South Seas and West Indies (*The Idol Dancer* and *The Love Flower*). Griffith's major releases of those years—*Broken Blossoms* and *Way Down East*—were the last great commercial and artistic successes of his career. Both were adaptations of literary successes: *Broken Blossoms* was based on "The Chink and the Child" from Thomas Burke's collection of stories, *Limehouse Nights; Way Down East* on the old stage war-horse by Lottie Blair Parker, William A. Brady, and Joseph R. Grismer, which had been tugging hearts since 1897, one year after Griffith himself took to the stage.

In *Broken Blossoms,* a saintly Chinese (Richard Barthelmess) comes to offer his pacifistic Buddhism to the brawling, warring West. Instead, the Yellow Man, as he is called, falls victim to the opium-induced apathy of London's Chinese slum, Limehouse. Nearby lives the brutal prizefighter, Battling Burrows (Donald Crisp) and his delicate daughter Lucy (Lillian Gish), whom he mercilessly beats. Despite Lucy's sorrow and degradation, Burrows insists that she keep up a pretense of cheerfulness. Incapable of a spontaneous smile, she uses two fingers to poke one into her cheeks—one of the most memorable gestures in film history. When Lucy seeks the Yellow Man's protection from her father's beatings, her death, the Yellow Man's murder of Burrows in revenge, and his own *seppuku* suicide follow as inevitable consequences. There is very little action to this sustained mood piece, which is dominated by the rapt faces of Gish and Barthelmess; the delicate imagery of flowers; the tranced, hypnotic rhythms of the editing; and the moody lighting by Henrik Sartov, imported as Bitzer's photographic assistant for the Gish close-ups. Released in the same year as the German expressionist classic, *The Cabinet of Doctor Caligari, Broken Blossoms* is regarded by many as the first American art film.

Way Down East works in a very different key—with more violent action, moralistic commentary, and psychological detail. Seduced by a false marriage vow, Anna Moore (Lillian Gish) gives birth to an illegitimate child who dies in her arms. She recovers from her personal tragedy through hard work with a Maine farming family, which Griffith depicts with his familiar mixture of sympathy for their human warmth and criticism for their moral severity. When they discover Anna's "stain," she rushes out into a blinding snowstorm—which Griffith filmed during an actual New York blizzard. The literal and natural storm becomes an objective correlative of her emotional turmoil. The farmer's son David (Richard Barthelmess), who loves her, follows her into the storm and eventually rescues her from the ice floe on which she is drifting towards the falls. This was Griffith's final variation on the last-minute rescue—this time a race not between horses, automobiles, or trains but between tiny human protagonists and immense elemental forces. The tight cutting and powerful natural imagery of snow, wind, and ice create another of the most memorable sequences in the history of cinema.

In the final decade of his creative life Griffith fell steadily and drastically in public esteem. The three most impressive late Griffith productions—*Orphans of the Storm* (1922), *America* (1924), and *Isn't Life Wonderful?* (1925)—were commercial disappointments. Whatever their stylistic flourishes, all three reprised the theme of *The Birth of a Nation*—the family threatened by social tumult—simply redecorating the tumult as the French Revolution, the American Revolution, and contemporary Weimar inflation, respectively. Besides pictures like these, Griffith's output in the 1920s was characterized by an increasing proportion of programmers, and his customary fanfares of publicity upon the release of each new film seemed less and less appropriate to their object. For Lewis Jacobs, Griffith's sentimental Victorian moralism was inconsistent with the hedonism of the Jazz Age. For Richard Schickel, Griffith remained blind to the modernist literary currents around him, resolutely tied to the genteel literary fashions of his youth.

Various other factors contributed to Griffith's decline. Unlike his colleagues and contemporaries at United Artists, Griffith was a careless businessman who delegated the management of his financial affairs to apparently incompetent others. In 1920 he left Hollywood for a new studio in Mamaroneck, New York, the cost of which kept him severely in debt. If Griffith made a mess of his business affairs, he brought even less order to personal matters. The intensity of his films had always reflected emotional relationships with his women stars, especially Mae Marsh and Lillian Gish. In the 1920s Griffith transferred his emotional attention to a lesser actress, Carol Dempster. As Richard Schickel observes, "Whatever happiness we may imagine her bringing him in the years they were together, the cost of her presence at the center of his work for close on seven years was exorbitant." To accompany his disastrous relationship with an apparently inept Galatea, Griffith began drinking heavily.

While his personal life crumbled, his public drifted away. As ordinary program pictures, his films of the 1920s were not bad. But they bore the name of Griffith, from whom everyone—himself included—expected great things. In the context of the decade's cinematic explosion—the comedies of Chaplin, Keaton, Langdon, and Lloyd; the European challenges of Lubitsch, Lang, Murnau, Eisenstein, Gance, and Clair; the American genre epics of Ford, Vidor, Walsh, Cruze, and King—Griffith's films seemed frozen in the past. Although some critics, like Andrew Sarris, found Griffith's first sound film, *Abraham Lincoln* (1930), fluid beside its static contemporaries, Griffith's final film, *The Struggle* (1931), was a clumsy reprise of *The Drunkard's Reformation* of 1909.

Through the 1930s there was hope and talk of a Griffith comeback, and he even went to England to discuss a remake of *Broken Blossoms.* Griffith ruined most of those hopes with heavy drinking, irascible behavior, and incurable womanizing. His one Hollywood job in seventeen years was as advisor to producer Hal Roach in 1941 on *One Million B.C.*, a sound-film expansion of Griffith's 1912 Biograph fantasy of prehistoric life, *Man's Genesis*. Griffith retired to Kentucky, where he worked on plays, film scripts, and his memoirs: none was ever completed. Like Chaplin, Griffith settled late in life into a comfortable marriage with a younger woman, Evelyn Baldwin—but only for a while. They separated after a decade in 1947. He died in a Hollywood hotel room, not precisely broke but certainly alone. With his death Griffith became the hero of a sentimental melodrama that he himself might have filmed—the poetic genius crushed by crass commercial expediency.

Instead, one might see Griffith as a tragic rather than pathetic figure: the powerful embodiment of a particular place and time, with consummate skills suited exactly to that place and time, but to no others. James Agee said, "He lived too long, and that is one thing sadder than dying too soon. There is not a man working in movies or a man who cares for them who does not owe Griffith more than he owes anybody else." Griffith, who from 1908 to 1918 virtually *was* film history, was ultimately condemned by history to history.

—*G.M.*

FILMS: The Adventures of Dollie, The Redman and the Child, The Tavern Keeper's Daughter, The Bandit's Waterloo, A Calamitous Elopement, The Greaser's Gauntlet, The Man and the Woman, For Love of Gold, The Fatal Hour, For a Wife's Honor, Balked at the Altar, The Girl and the Outlaw, The Red Girl, Betrayed by a Hand Print, Monday Morning in a Coney Island Police Court, Behind the Scenes, The Heart of O'yama, Where the Breakers Roar, The Stolen Jewels, A Smoked Husband, The Zulu's Heart, The Vaquero's Vow, Father Gets in the Game, The Barbarian, Ingomar, The Planter's Wife, The Devil, The Romance of a Jewess, The Call of the Wild, After Many Years, Mr. Jones at the Ball, Concealing a Burglar, The Taming of the Shrew, The Ingrate, A Woman's Way, The Pirate's Gold, The Guerrilla, The Curtain Pole, The Song of the Shirt, The Clubman and the Tramp, Money Mad, Mrs. Jones Entertains, The Feud and the Turkey, The Test of Friendship, The Reckoning, One Touch of Nature, An Awful Moment, The Helping Hand, The Maniac Cook, The Christmas Burglars, A Wreath in Time, The Honor of Thieves, The Criminal Hypnotist, The Sacrifice, The Welcome Burglar, A Rural Elopement, Mr. Jones Has a Card Party, The Hindoo Dagger, The Salvation Army Lass, Love Finds a Way, Tragic Love, The Girls and a Daddy, 1908;

Those Boys, The Cord of Life, Trying to Get Arrested, The Fascinating Mrs. Frances, Those Awful Hats, Jones and the Lady Book Agent, The Drive for Life, The Brahma Diamond, The Politician's Love Story, The Joneses Have Amateur Theatricals, Edgar Allan Poe, The Roué's Heart, His Wife's Mother, The Golden Louis, His Ward's Love, At the Altar, The Prussian Spy, The Medicine Bottle, The Deception, The Lure of the Gown, Lady Helen's Escapade, A Fool's Revenge, The Wooden Leg, I Did It, Mama, A Burglar's Mistake, The Voice of the Violin, And a Little Child Shall Lead Them, The French Duel, Jones and His New Neighbors, The Drunkard's Reformation, The Winning Coat, A Rude Hostess, The Road to the Heart, The Eavesdropper, Schneider's Anti-Noise Crusade, Twin Brothers, Confidence, The Note in the Shoe, Lucky Jim, A Sound Sleeper, A Troublesome Satchel, 'Tis an Ill Wind That Blows No Good, The Suicide Club, Resurrection, One Busy Hour, A Baby's Shoe, Eloping With Auntie, The Cricket on the Hearth, The Jilt, Eradicating Auntie, What Drink Did, Her First Biscuits, The Violin Maker of Cremona, Two Memories, The Lonely Villa, The Peach Basket Hat, The Son's Return, His Duty, A New Trick, The Necklace, The Way of Man, The Faded Lilies, The Message, The Friend of the Family, Was Justice Served?, Mrs. Jones' Lover, or I Want My Hat!, The Mexican Sweethearts, The Country Doctor, Jealousy and the Man, The Renunciation, The Cardinal's Conspiracy, The Seventh Day, Tender Hearts, A Convict's Sacrifice, A Strange Meeting, Sweet and Twenty, The Slave, They Would Elope, Mr. Jones' Burglar, The Mended Lute, The Indian Runner's Romance, With Her Card, The Better Way, His Wife's Visitor, The Mills of the Gods, Pranks, Oh Uncle, The Sealed Room, 1776, or The Hessian Renegades, The Little Darling, In Old Kentucky, The Children's Friend, Comata, the Sioux, Getting Even, The Broken Locket, A Fair Exchange, The Awakening, Pippa Passes, Leather Stockings, Fools of Fate, Wanted, a Child, The Little Teacher, A Change of Heart, His Lost Love, Lines of

White on the Sullen Sea, The Gibson Goddess, In the Watches of the Night, The Expiation, What's Your Hurry, The Restoration, Nursing a Viper, Two Women and a Man, The Light That Came, A Midnight Adventure, The Open Gate, Sweet Revenge, The Mountaineer's Honor, In the Window Recess, The Trick That Failed, The Death Disc, Through the Breakers, In a Hempen Bag, A Corner in Wheat, The Redman's View, The Test, A Trap for Santa Claus, In Little Italy, To Save Her Soul, Choosing a Husband, The Rocky Road, The Dancing Girl of Butte, Her Terrible Ordeal, The Call, The Honor of His Family, On the Reef, The Last Deal, One Night and Then—, The Cloister's Touch, The Woman From Mellon's, The Duke's Plan, The Englishman and the Girl, 1909;

The Final Settlement, His Last Burglary, Taming a Husband, The Newlyweds, The Thread of Destiny, In Old California, The Man, The Converts, Faithful, The Twisted Trail, Gold Is Not All, As It Is in Life, A Rich Revenge, A Romance of the Western Hills, Thou Shalt Not, The Way of the World, The Unchanging Sea, The Gold Seekers, Love Among the Roses, The Two Brothers, Unexpected Help, An Affair of Hearts, Ramona, Over Silent Paths, The Implement, In the Season of Buds, A Child of the Ghetto, In the Border States, A Victim of Jealousy, The Face at the Window, The Marked Time-Table, A Child's Impulse, Muggsy's First Sweetheart, The Purgation, A Midnight Cupid, What the Daisy Said, A Child's Faith, The Call to Arms, Serious Sixteen, A Flash of Light, As the Bells Rang Out, An Arcadian Maid, The House with the Closed Shutters, Her Father's Pride, A Salutary Lesson, The Usurer, The Sorrows of the Unfaithful, In Life's Cycle, Wilful Peggy, A Summer Idyll, The Modern Prodigal, Rose o' Salem Town, Little Angels of Luck, A Mohawk's Way, The Oath and the Man, The Iconoclast, Examination Day at School, That Chink at Golden Gulch, The Broken Doll, The Banker's Daughters, The Message of the Violin, Two Little Waifs, Waiter No. 5, The Fugitive, Simply Charity, The Song of the Wildwood Flute, A Child's Stratagem, Sunshine Sue, A Plain Song, His Sister-in-Law, The Golden Supper, The Lesson, When a Man Loves, Winning Back His Love, His Trust, His Trust Fulfilled, A Wreath of Orange Blossoms, The Italian Barber, The Two Paths, Conscience, Three Sisters, A Decree of Destiny, Fate's Turning, What Shall We Do With Our Old?, The Diamond Star, The Lily of the Tenements, Heart Beats of Long Ago, 1910;

Fisher Folks, His Daughter, The Lonedale Operator, Was He a Coward?, Teaching Dad to Like Her, The Spanish Gypsy, The Broken Cross, The Chief's Daughter, A Knight of the Road, Madame Rex, His Mother's Scarf, How She Triumphed, In the Days of '49, The Two Sides, The New Dress, Enoch Arden, Part 1, Enoch Arden, Part 11, The White Rose of the Wilds, The Crooked Road, A Romany Tragedy, A Smile of a Child, The Primal Call, The Jealous Husband, The Indian Brothers, The Thief and the Girl, Her Sacrifice, The Blind Princess and the Poet, Fighting Blood, The Last Drop of Water, Robby the Coward, A Country Cupid, The Ruling Passion, The Rose of Kentucky, The Sorrowful Example, Swords and Hearts, The Stuff

Heroes Are Made Of, The Old Confectioner's Mistake, The Unveiling, The Eternal Mother, Dan the Dandy, The Revenue Man and the Girl, The Squaw's Love, Italian Blood, The Making of a Man, Her Awakening, The Adventures of Billy, The Long Road, The Battle, Love in the Hills, The Trail of the Books, Through Darkened Vales, Saved from Himself, A Woman Scorned, The Miser's Heart, The Failure, Sunshine Through the Dark, As in a Looking Glass, A Terrible Discovery, A Tale of the Wilderness, The Voice of the Child, The Baby and the Stork, The Old Bookkeeper, A Sister's Love, For His Son, The Transformation of Mike, A Blot on the 'Scutcheon, Billy's Stratagem, The Sunbeam, A String of Pearls, The Root of Evil, 1911;

The Mender of the Nets, Under Burning Skies, A Siren of Impulse, Iola's Promise, The Goddess of Sagebrush Gulch, The Girl and Her Trust, The Punishment, Fate's Interception, The Female of the Species, Just Like a Woman, One Is Business, the Other Crime, The Lesser Evil, The Old Actor, A Lodging for the Night, His Lesson, When Kings Were the Law, A Beast at Bay, An Outcast Among Outcasts, Home Folks, A Temporary Truce, The Spirit Awakened, Lena and the Geese, An Indian Summer, The Schoolteacher and the Waif, Man's Lust for Gold, Man's Genesis, Heaven Avenges, A Pueblo Legend, The Sands of Dee, Black Sheep, The Narrow Road, A Child's Remorse, The Inner Circle, A Change of Spirit, An Unseen Enemy, Two Daughters of Eve, Friends, So Near, Yet So Far, A Feud in the Kentucky Hills, In the Aisles of the Wild, The One She Loved, The Painted Lady, The Musketeers of Pig Alley, Heredity, Gold and Glitter, My Baby, The Informer, The Unwelcome Guest, Pirate Gold, Brutality, The New York Hat, The Massacre, My Hero, Oil and Water, The Burglar's Dilemma, A Cry for Help, The God Within, Three Friends, The Telephone Girl and the Lady, Fate, An Adventure in the Autumn Woods, A Chance Deception, The Tender-Hearted Boy, A Misappropriated Turkey, Brothers, Drink's Lure, Love in an Apartment Hotel, 1912;

Broken Ways, A Girl's Stratagem, Near to Earth, A Welcome Intruder, The Sheriff's Baby, The Hero of Little Italy, The Perfidy of Mary, A Misunderstood Boy, The Little Tease, The Lady and the Mouse, The Wanderer, The House of Darkness, Olaf—An Atom, Just Gold, His Mother's Son, The Yaqui Cur, The Ranchero's Revenge, A Timely Interception, Death's Marathon, The Sorrowful Shore, The Mistake, The Mothering Heart, Her Mother's Oath, During the Round-Up, The Coming of Angelo, The Indian's Loyalty, Two Men of the Desert, The Reformers, or the Lost Art of Minding One's Business, The Battle at Elderbush Gulch, In Prehistoric Days (*also known as* Wars of the Primal Tribes; *released as:* Brute Force), Judith of Bethulia, 1913;

The Battle of the Sexes, The Escape, Home, Sweet Home, The Avenging Conscience, 1914; The Birth of a Nation, 1915; Intolerance, 1916; Hearts of the World, The Great Love, The Greatest Thing in Life, 1918; A Romance of Happy Valley, The Girl Who Stayed at Home, Broken Blossoms, True Heart Susie, Scarlet Days, The Greatest Question, 1919; The Idol

Dancer, The Love Flower, Way Down East, 1920; Dream Street, Orphans of the Storm, 1921; One Exciting Night, 1922; The White Rose, 1923; America, Isn't Life Wonderful? 1924; Sally of the Sawdust, That Royle Girl, 1925; The Sorrows of Satan, 1926; Drums of Love, The Battle of the Sexes, 1928; Lady of the Pavements, 1929; Abraham Lincoln, 1930; The Struggle, 1931.

ABOUT: Aitken, R. (as told to Al P. Nelson) The Birth of a Nation Story, 1965; Balio, T. United Artists, 1976; Barry, I. and Bowser, E. D.W. Griffith, 1965; Bitzer, G.W. Billy Bitzer: His Story, 1973; Bowser, E. (ed.) Biograph Bulletins: 1908–1912, 1973; Brakhage, S. The Brakhage Lectures, 1972; Brown, K. Adventures With D.W. Griffith, 1973; Brownlow, K. The Parade's Gone By, 1968; Brownlow, K. Hollywood: The Pioneers, 1979; Brunetta, G. P. Nascita del racconto cinematografico Griffith: 1908–1912, 1974; Croy, H. Starmaker: The Story of D. W. Griffith, 1959; Eisenstein, S. M. Film Form, 1949; Everson, W. American Silent Film, 1978; Fulton, A. R. Motion Pictures, 1960; Geduld, H. (ed.) Focus on D. W. Griffith, 1971; Gish, L. with Pinchot, A. Lillian Gish: The Movies, Mr. Griffith, and Me, 1969; Goodman, E. The Fifty-Year Decline and Fall of Hollywood, 1961; Griffith D. W. The Man Who Invented Hollywood: The Autobiography of D. W. Griffith, ed. James Hart 1972; Griffith, L. A. When the Movies Were Young, 1922?; Hampton, B. B. History of the American Film Industry, 1931; Hastings, C. E. and Holland, H. A Biography of David Wark Griffith, 1920; Henderson, R. D. W. Griffith: The Years at Biograph, 1970; Henderson, R. D. W. Griffith: His Life and Work, 1972; Huff, T. Intolerance, The Film by David Wark Griffith: Shot-by-Shot Analysis, 1966; Huff, T. A Short Analysis of D. W. Griffith's Birth of a Nation, 1961; Humouda, A. and Cozzani, A. Ragioni di una proposta ovvera The Adventures of Dollie, 1975; Lewis, J. The Rise of the American Film, 1939; Koszarski, R. (ed.) The Rivals of D. W. Griffith: Alternate Auteurs, 1913–1918, 1976; Lahue, K. Dreams for Sale: The Rise and Fall of the Triangle Film Corporation, 1971; Lennig, A. The Silent Voice: A Text, 1969; Lindsay, V. The Art of the Moving Picture, 1915; Macgowan, K. Behind the Screen: The History and Technique of the Motion Picture, 1965; Marsh, M. Screen Acting, 1922; Mast, G. A Short History of the Movies, 4th ed., 1986; May, L. Screening Out the Past: The Birth of Mass Culture and the Motion Picture Industry, 1980; Mitry, J. Griffith, 1966 (in French); Münsterberg, H. The Photoplay: A Psychological Study, 1916; Niver, K. D. W. Griffith: His Biograph Films in Perspective, 1974; O'Dell, O. with Slide, A. Griffith and the Rise of Hollywood, 1971; Pickford, M. Sunshine and Shadow, 1955; Pratt, G. C. Spellbound in Darkness, 1966; Ramsaye, T. A Million and One Nights, 1926; Rotha, P. The Film Till Now, 1960; Sadoul, G. Le Cinéma devient un art, 1909–1920, 2 vols., 1952; Sarris, A. The American Cinema, 1968; Schickel, R. D. W. Griffith: An American Life, 1984; Silva, F. (ed.) Focus on The Birth of a Nation, 1971; Slide, A. The Griffith Actresses, 1973; Stern, S. An Index to the Creative Work of D. W. Griffith (BFI Index Series 2, 4, 7, 8, 10), 1944; Vardac, A. N. Stage to Screen: Theatrical Method From Garrick to Griffith, 1949; Wagenknecht, E. The Movies in the Age of Innocence, 1962; Wagenknecht, E. and Slide, A. The Films of D. W. Griffith, 1975; Williams, M. Griffith: First Artist of the Movies, 1980. *Periodicals*—AFI Report Winter 1973; Art Bulletin December 1972; Cinema Fall 1971; Cinema Journal Fall 1981; Critical Inquiry Fall 1984; Écran February 1973 (Griffith issue); Film Comment Fall–Winter 1967; Filmcritica August 1975 (Griffith issue); Film Culture Spring–Summer 1965 (Griffith issue); Film Heritage Fall 1965; Filmkritik April 1975 (Griffith issue); Film Quarterly Fall 1974; Films in Review July–August 1950, November 1951, February 1956, May, June, and July 1959, October 1975 (Griffith issue); Horizon Spring 1972; Image May 2, 1959; Journal of Popular Film Spring 1972; New York Times November 10, 1948; Quarterly Review of Film Studies Winter 1981; Salmagundi Winter 1965; Sewanee Review Fall 1948; Sight and Sound Autumn 1946, Spring 1947, Winter 1958–1959; Take One September–October 1971.

*GUITRY, SACHA (Alexandre-Pierre-Georges Guitry) (February 21, 1885–July 24, 1957), French film and theatre director, dramatist, scenarist, and actor, was born in Russia, where his father, the great French actor Lucien Guitry, was under contract to the Mikhailovsky Theatre in St. Petersburg. His mother was the beautiful Marie-Louise Renée Delmas. Lucien Guitry's contract committed him to a nine-season stay in St. Petersburg, but in 1889 his wife, unable to endure his philandering, returned to France with her two sons, Jean and Sacha. A few months after the separation, Lucien Guitry visited his family and literally kidnapped Sacha, taking him back with him to St. Petersburg.

Guitry made his debut at the age of five, in a pantomime performed before the Czar in the Imperial Palace. He and his father were very close, and he emulated the idolized actor in every way possible, trying on his costumes and memorizing his roles. Lucien Guitry took the boy regularly to the theatre and the circus, filling his head with stories of the great actors and clowns of the day.

In 1894 Sacha Guitry returned with his father to Paris, thereafter dividing his time between his mother's house and his father's, the latter crowded with famous performers, writers, characters, and wits. Sarah Bernhardt, Octave Mirbeau, Georges Feydeau, and Jules Renard were all regular visitors, and the most famous dramatists of the day brought their new plays to "the master." Guitry's parents were divorced in 1900, but he continued to see his mother, who herself enjoyed considerable success as an actress in Paris until her early death in 1902.

The same year Guitry's father abandoned his

°gē´ trē

SACHA GUITRY

struggle to keep the boy in school. Sacha Guitry had attended or boarded at a dozen different educational establishments between 1894 and 1902. He loathed his exile from the grandeur and glamor of life at home, refused to work or cooperate, and was invariably asked to leave. Guitry had already decided to follow his parents' profession, and thereafter studied acting under various masters, earning a little pocket money as a portraitist and caricaturist—arts in which he showed a precocious talent. Collaborating with his brother Jean, a year older than himself, he wrote his first theatrical piece at the age of sixteen, a one-act operetta in verse called *The Page*. It was staged the same year—1902—at the Théâtre des Mathurins, and enthusiastically received.

Seeking to explain Guitry's immense popularity in France, his obituarist in the London *Times* wrote: "The causes are many: his youth when he burst into immediate success in Paris at the age of sixteen; his impudence; his gaiety and easy wit; his frank hedonism; above all, his innate sense of the theatre and his constant association with it, which enabled him to use all its stalest tricks just twisted in a new way."

He gave proof of his hedonism and his impudence two years later, when he began a liaison with Charlotte Lysès, an actress eight years his senior. She was also his father's mistress. Lucien Guitry, intent on separating the two, took his son on a tour of the Dutch art galleries with his friend Eugène Demolder, an art critic who, Sacha Guitry later recalled, "infused excitement" into the great paintings they studied.

Back in Paris, Guitry made his professional debut in 1904 in a small role with his father's company at the Théâtre de la Renaissance. His relationship with Charlotte Lysès continued, however, and in 1905, after an argument about a fine imposed by Lucien Guitry for his son's late arrival for a performance, the two men were totally estranged for thirteen years.

It was through the influence of Charlotte Lysès that Guitry found work as an actor, and through her encouragement that he wrote his first full-length play, *Nono* (1905), a witty boulevard comedy about a young man tired of his older mistress. Two years later Guitry married his own older mistress. He continued to write plays, providing himself with starring roles in most of them, and had his first major success in 1911 with *Le Veilleur de nuit.* A string of stage hits followed, and growing fame, marred by the onset of the acute rheumatism that plagued him all his life.

In the course of his lifetime Guitry wrote about 150 plays, along with 900 newspaper articles, several volumes of memoirs and family biography, and two novels; hundreds of his caricatures were published from 1903 on, and he had two exhibitions of his paintings, in 1911 and 1921.

In 1915 Guitry visited the aged painter Auguste Renoir and conceived the idea of a film that would "eternalize" major French artists of the time and provide a response to the arrogant claims being made for German *kultur*. The result was *Ceux de chez nous (Those of Our Land,* 1915), a 22-minute documentary presenting portraits of Renoir, Degas, Rodin, Monet, Saint-Saëns, Sarah Bernhardt, André Antoine, Edmond Rostand, Lucien Guitry, Octave Mirbeau, Anatole France, and the lawyer Henri Robert. Each is shown in some characteristic attitude or activity, painting or writing, conducting or declaiming, in a lively mixture of closeups and long shots. Technically primitive in some respects, the film remains a valuable document.

Guitry's first involvement with the commercial cinema came in 1918, when he wrote the scenario of *Un Roman d'amour et d'aventures,* directed by René Hervil and Louis Mercanton, and starred in it. A couple of his plays were subsequently adapted by others for the silent screen. Otherwise Guitry, always wedded to the spoken word, had no more to do with the cinema until the advent of sound. Instead he consolidated his position as one of the most successful dramatists and most popular actors of the French boulevard theatre. At first he shared his triumph with his wife, who often starred opposite him in his plays.

In 1917, when he began a liaison with a much younger actress, Yvonne Printemps, Charlotte quietly packed her bags and left. They were divorced the following year.

Deburau (1918), Guitry's play about the great mime and his son, is full of apparently unconscious parallels with the relationship between the author and his father. Lucien Guitry went to see this play unannounced, and a reconciliation followed. Guitry's next play, *Pasteur* (1919), was written for his father. The same year, Guitry and Yvonne Printemps were married. He went from triumph to triumph with a succession of plays starring himself and his wife, or himself and his father, and sometimes all three together. In 1921 he leased a small Paris theatre of his own, where most of his plays were premiered over the next ten years (though sometimes he had as many as three plays running simultaneously in Paris). In 1923 Guitry was named a Chevalier of the Légion d'Honneur.

Guitry was a compulsive and immensely prolific worker, and the 1920s were richly productive and rewarding years for him, saddened only by the death of his brother Jean in 1920 and of Lucien Guitry in 1925. Sacha Guitry inherited his father's considerable debts but also his spectacular house near the Eiffel Tower. This mansion, with its soaring staircase and antique furniture, became the setting for Guitry's collections of first editions, of letters, of pottery and china and sculpture, and above all his legendary collection of paintings. Actor and dramatist, journalist and lecturer, wit and inimitable raconteur, Sacha Guitry was "the hero of *le tout Paris.*" In those days, as his *Times* obituarist wrote, a Guitry opening night "was the most typically Parisian thing in the world of the theatre—clear, lightly moving, brilliant, like the air of Paris itself, filled with the cynical but still happy tolerance of the author, and with the confident readiness of the audience to be amused and charmed."

In 1931 Guitry made another brief sortie into cinema, scripting a talking version of his play *Le Blanc et le noir* (*The White and the Black*), directed by Robert Florey and Marc Allégret and featuring, among others, Raimu and a young café entertainer whom Guitry had discovered, Fernandel. The script was marred by some pointless scene changes that slowed down the pace of the movie and reflected, it has been suggested, Guitry's uneasy suspicion that he was "betraying" the theatre by adapting his plays for the screen. In 1932 Yvonne Printemps left him for the actor Pierre Fresnay. Guitry soon found another mistress and leading lady in Jacqueline Delubac. They were married in 1934, when he was fifty and she was twenty-five, and remained together for four years.

Guitry adapted another of his plays for the cinema in 1935, *Les Deux Couverts* (*Two Place Settings*), directed by Léonce Perret, and the same year both scripted and directed an adaptation of his *Pasteur,* himself playing the great biologist—a role originally written for his father. The film was on the whole coolly received, most reviewers complaining that the action was constantly being halted by Pasteur's long monologues. Marguerite Tazelaar wrote that "for most of the time it appears to be simply an animated photograph of M. Guitry speaking French," and *Variety* concluded that "Guitry emerges as a good actor but a poor director."

For his part, Guitry made no secret of the fact that for him the text was central, the images in his films being selected mainly to reinforce and elucidate the dialogue. He never entirely overcame his sense of the film as something circumscribed and limited, stifled in a "metallic box," without the play's capacity to change and grow in response to a particular audience. "Theatre is the present," he wrote, "film is the past. Actors perform in the theatre. They have performed in the film. Audiences come to the theatre. Crowds go to motion pictures. . . . Theatre is the positive. Film is the negative." He recognized all the same that the movies could vastly increase his plays' audiences, and with characteristic professionalism set out to master the new medium.

He wrote his next film, *Bonne Chance* (*Good Luck,* 1935), as an original script—one of the few Guitry pictures not adapted from a Guitry play. It was the first of ten films starring himself and Jacqueline Delubac. This comedy is apparently a lost film, but Alain Resnais, an ardent champion of Guitry's work, remembers it fondly: "There was a tracking shot in it with Jacqueline Delubac, with the camera fixed on the hood of an automobile, in which Guitry explains to her that, 'You see, that's what cinema's like. . . . You put the camera on a car and'. . . . Suddenly I discovered the cinema within the cinema."

Le Nouveau Testament (*The New Testament,* 1936), codirected by Alexandre Ryder, was almost as static as *Pasteur* but considerably more entertaining, full of cynical wit in its story of a cuckolded husband and his cruel revenge: "Are there couples who have loved each other to the end?" "Yes, those who died at twenty." It was followed in 1936 by the film that is universally regarded as Guitry's masterpiece, *Le Roman d'un tricheur* (*The Story of a Cheat*), adapted by himself from his picaresque novel *Mémoires d'un tricheur* (1935).

Even the movie's credits are innovative—not printed, but read out by Guitry on the soundtrack while on the screen we see the studio and the crew members he names. The film proper then opens in a Paris sidewalk café. A middle-aged man (Guitry) sits down, orders a drink, and begins to compose a biography which (we eventually learn) is his own. The events he recalls are mimed by the cast to his voice-over narration. Even remembered dialogue is spoken by him rather than the actors on screen. Intermittently we return to the café, where the memoirist pauses in his labors to chat to the waiter or someone at a nearby table.

He traces his career as a *tricheur* back to an eventful day in his childhood. He had stolen eight sous from his peasant parents and by way of punishment had been excluded from the family meal of freshly picked mushrooms. The mushrooms had been poisonous toadstools, and that night all eleven members of his family had died in agony. This tragedy had forced him to the conclusion that dishonesty pays—a theory reinforced by the greed and hypocrisy he sees flourishing around him.

Basing his career on this perception, the *tricheur* had become successively a bellhop, an elevator boy, a croupier, a soldier, a jewel thief, and a card sharp. Women came and went: the amorous countess in a hotel at Monte Carlo; a beautiful thief; the adventuress who became his wife and gambling partner. Cheating had made him rich; his downfall had come when he had succumbed to the insidious temptations of honesty. An old lady who has entered the café turns out to be the Monte Carlo countess. When she invites him to join her in a modest safecracking project, he has to confess that he has become a private detective.

Basil Wright, reviewing this film in 1937, admitted that it was "done with a disarming wit and a discerning charm which successfully conceals the general immorality of the tale." However, he goes on to suggest that Guitry's work as a filmmaker was "chiefly distinguished by his total disregard for the real values of cinema. One almost feels that he perverts, rather than shapes it, to his own purposes." In *Le Roman d'un tricheur*, "Guitry takes the sound track and uses it merely as an accompaniment, in commentary form, to a film deliberately made in the style and atmosphere of pre-talkie days."

Forty years later, Richard Roud wrote: "I suspect it was because the film was so entertaining that its true originality was not highly regarded when it first appeared. Guitry uses many 'cinematic' devices—reverse motion, stop-motion, trick wipes—but they are so successfully integrated into the general flow of the film that their ingenuity was underrated. A *film d'auteur* if ever there was one." François Truffaut, who saw this film very many times, maintained that it originated the playback technique used by Orson Welles in *Citizen Kane,* and another critic has pointed out the specific advantage of this technique—"the introduction of a great deal of discursive and descriptive material which in the ordinary way simply could not be included in a film." For Bettina Knapp (in her monograph on Guitry), the narrator's repeated intrusion into the narrative functions like a Brechtian "alienation" device, imposing on the viewer not empathy but objective analysis.

Mon Père avait raison (My Father Knew Best), premiered only two months after *Le Roman,* was another hit—a relatively sentimental comedy-drama about the relations between a father and son before and after the mother's desertion. Sacha Guitry and Jacqueline Delubac played the roles created on stage by Lucien Guitry and Yvonne Printemps. Bettina Knapp suggested that this movie reflected Guitry's own loneliness as a child, as well as his "secret melancholy with respect to women. On the outside he was a great lover . . . [but] still living, unconsciously, in his father's shadow, he could not hope to compete with him where women were concerned. Lucien Guitry represented success in every domain."

A month later, in December 1936, Paris saw the premiere of an even greater success, *Faisons un rêve (Let Us Dream).* Another sour comedy about adultery, adapted from Guitry's 1916 play, it was remarkable on at least two counts. It mustered a dazzling cast: in the central story, Guitry, Delubac, and Raimu; in the party scene that served as prologue, among others, Arletty, Claude Dauphin, Yvette Guilbert, Michel Simon, and Jean Coquelin.

Even more admired and discussed than the cast was the long monologue in which Guitry, awaiting the arrival of his mistress, imagines her journey across Paris to join him. "The camera," writes Richard Roud, "is simply placed on Guitry for over three minutes. But the result, far from being stagey, is quite simply miraculous: 'Now she's getting into the taxi, now she's going up the Avenue George V; oh, the traffic light just turned red . . .' etc. And he shows us nothing but his own face, and yet we see the whole ride: extraordinary." Alain Resnais felt that this film "was an example of how real cinema could exist outside of any preoccupation with 'pure' cinema."

Le Mot de Cambronne (Cambronne's Word, 1937) was an oddity. A film in verse, it was dedicated to Guitry's friend, the dramatist Edmond

Rostand, who had suggested the idea to him years earlier. Guitry began the script one morning after breakfast, completed it by lunchtime, and filmed it in one day. He plays General Cambronne, Marguerite Moréno his formidable wife, and Jacqueline Delubac the compliant servant girl. The story turns wittily on Cambronne's famous response when, as commander of Napoleon's forces at Waterloo, he had been ordered to surrender. His wife has never been allowed to hear Cambronne's word, but the servant discloses it to her when she drops a tray: "*Merde!*"

An amateur historian, Guitry wrote and directed a number of historical and biographical plays and films that reflected his love of elegance and extravagance, his hero-worshipping patriotism, his distrust of revolution and love of monarchs, and his scant regard for facts. History, he maintained, was "a universal conspiracy made up of lies intended to fight truth." And in any case, court intrigue or the secrets of a royal bedchamber interested him far more than social injustice or reform politics.

The first of Guitry's historical extravaganzas, made in 1937 to commemorate the coronation of King George VI of England, was *Les Perles de la couronne* (*The Pearls of the Crown*), codirected by Christian-Jaque. Resnais and most other modern critics dismiss or dislike Guitry's grandiose historical confections, but Richard Roud makes an exception of *Les Perles:* "In many ways, this extraordinary mock-historical fresco is as inventive—or at least as ingenious—as . . . [*Le Roman d'un tricheur*]. For one thing, it is unique in being done in three languages—French, English, and Italian. French predominates, but the other languages contribute much—as in Godard's *Le Mépris,* which may well have been influenced by this film. The pretext is Guitry's explaining to his wife (Jacqueline Delubac) the amazing story of the seven pearls of the English crown, and how three of them were lost forever."

Roud goes on: "The story begins during the Renaissance, and everyone plays several roles. . . . Resnais is right to the degree that some of the historical episodes are dusty and laborious. But how can one resist the charm of Arletty as a snake-princess of Abyssinia? How can one forget the scene on the grand staircase of the S. S. *Normandie* when, by some preposterous conceit of Guitry's, Delubac is allowed to respond to the advances of a businessman from Marseilles (Raimu) using only adverbs—and succeeds in answering every question with a word ending in -*ment.*"

Désiré (1937), about a butler whose irresistible sexuality obliges him to move constantly from one infatuated employer to the next, produced a performance of rapt narcissism from Guitry. It was followed by *Quadrille* (1938), a witty boulevard comedy strongly reminiscent of Noel Coward's *Private Lives.* Guitry, who in general considered it naive and artificial to "open up" his plays for the screen, here very effectively introduced scenes in the street, in a taxi, and in a nightclub, making this one of the most satisfyingly "cinematic" of his movies.

Remontons les Champs-Elysées (*Champs-Elysées,* 1938), a historical extravaganza that failed to repeat the success of *Les Perles de la couronne,* was the last of Guitry's films to star Jacqueline Delubac. He had by then formed a new attachment, to Geneviève de Sereville, a beautiful and aristocratic aspiring actress thirty years his junior. She became his fourth wife in 1942 and, like her predecessors, appeared in several of his films.

There are some who hold that Guitry's next film was the last of any real merit. *Ils étaient neuf célibataires* (*Nine Bachelors,* 1939) was an original script about an amiable swindler (Guitry) who, when a new French law is passed requiring the repatriation of all foreigners, assembles a supply of decrepit bachelors prepared to bestow French citizenship on wealthy ladies. The movie has reportedly "lost none of its sparkle today." *Le Destin fabuleux de Desirée Clary* (*Mlle. Desirée,* 1942), about the woman (Gaby Morlay) who preceded Joséphine de Beauharnais in Napoleon's affections and later became queen of Sweden, was relatively well received. Guitry's other wartime films, *Donne-moi tes yeux* (*Give Me Your Eyes,* 1943) and *La Malibran* (1944), were both failures.

Throughout the German occupation of France, Guitry continued to lecture, to write and perform in his plays, and to make films. He took coffee with a German general and presented a volume of essays to Marshall Pétain. By 1942 his name had been placed on the blacklist of collaborators. His wife Geneviève left him in April 1944. In August, when the Allies liberated Paris, he was arrested and jailed for sixty days, then released for lack of evidence. He went home and devoted the next two years to accumulating evidence in his own defense. Among other things, he claimed that he had used his influence with German officials to save the lives or improve the lot of, among others, Henri Bergson, Tristan Bernard, André Antoine, and Colette's Jewish husband. In August 1947 he was cleared of all charges.

Guitry went back to work. His first postwar film was *Le Comédien* (*The Private Life of an Actor,* 1948), in which he portrayed both himself and his famous father but failed, it was agreed, to capture the depth and complexity of Lucien's character, let alone his range as an actor. Sacha Guitry always played himself—the quintessentially Parisian man of the world, speaking his cynically witty lines with grave relish. No one could surpass him in this role, but his father's was beyond him. As one critic wrote, "the dialogue is really a monologue." On the way to the opening of the film in Lyon, Guitry and his current companion, Lana Marconi, were "kidnapped" by a band of former Resistance fighters and taken to a monument commemorating one of their units in the city. There the couple was compelled to observe a moment of silence and then released.

In 1949 Guitry married Marconi, an indifferent actress who appeared in *Le Comédien* and many of her husband's subsequent movies. These included a number of "guitrizations" of history, most notably the lavish *Si Versailles m'était conté* (*Royal Affairs in Versailles*, 1954). It was immensely successful commercially, but Isabel Quigly expressed the modern view of it in a 1960 review: "It is a stupefying film: so stupefyingly wearisome that I could hardly believe, as I watched it, that it could go on and on and on much longer without breaking its tone of perfectly dropsical inflatedness."

The best of the films Guitry made in his prolific last decade—plagued as he was by illness and pain—were a series of amoral mysteries in which crime is generally shown to pay: *Le Poison* (*Poison*, 1951), *La Vie d'un honnête homme* (*The Virtuous Scoundrel*, 1953), *Assassins et voleurs* (*Lovers and Thieves*, 1956), and *Les Trois font la paire* (*Three Makes a Pair*, 1957). *Le Poison*, for example, is about a peasant (Michel Simon) who, intent on murdering his alcoholic wife, first seeks the advice of a lawyer as to the method most likely to secure acquittal in court, follows this advice to the letter, and goes home after the trial to a hero's welcome.

All of these mysteries except *Assassins et voleurs* starred Michel Simon, at whose request Guitry undertook to shoot each scene in them in a single take. The detailed planning it took to accomplish this extraordinary feat is said to have produced the sense of control and economy so admired by the *nouvelle vague* critics in these films. At the same time, Bettina Knapp suggests, they are "the works of a man who resents the suffering he has experienced, who never has really come to grips with his motivations or been able to face himself. Guitry's murder mysteries, although fascinating conceptually, are excuses—condemnations of a world which he felt had acted unjustly, unwisely, and cruelly toward him—a world he rejects."

In 1953, faced with a massive tax bill, Guitry was obliged to sell part of his art collection. The following year he made his last stage appearance in a revival of *Deburau*. He had undergone a serious stomach operation in 1951 and there was another in 1955. Suffering excruciating pain from polynephritis, he needed ever increasing injections of morphine but continued to work from a wheelchair. In 1957 there was a triumphant revival of *Faisons un rêve* at the Variétés. A few months later, Guitry died at the age of seventy-two. He was buried near his father at the Montmartre cemetery, where twelve thousand people attended the funeral.

As Richard Roud wrote in 1980, most of Guitry's films were popular successes, "though critics by and large maintained that they were only 'canned theatre.' But over the past two decades, the general view of his work has changed. In the late 1950s the *Cahiers du Cinéma* group acclaimed Guitry's last three works and reappraised the earlier films. But perhaps the decisive blow in Guitry's favour was struck by Alain Resnais, when he declared that he, Chris Marker, and Godard had all been influenced by Sacha Guitry. . . . Thanks to those masterpieces of wit and invention of the early 30s, Guitry's place in the history of the cinema is secure. And it is not fanciful to see in the work of Eric Rohmer a continuation of that *oeuvre*, though in a more serious vein."

FILMS: Ceux de chez nous, 1915 (documentary); Pasteur, 1935; Bonne chance, 1935; (with Alexandre Ryder) Le nouveau testament, 1936; Le Roman d'un tricheur (The Story of a Cheat/The Cheat), 1936; Mon Père avait raison, 1936; Faisons un rêve, 1936; Le Mot de Cambronne, 1937; (with Christian-Jaque) Les Perles de la couronne (The Pearls of the Crown), 1937; Désiré, 1937; Quadrille, 1938; Remontons les Champs-Elysées (Champs-Elysées), 1938; Ils étaient neuf célibataires (Nine Bachelors), 1939; Le Destin fabuleux de Désirée Clary (Mlle. Désirée), 1942; Donne-moi tes yeux, 1943; La malibran, 1944; Le Comédien (The Private Life of an Actor), 1948; Le Diable boiteux, 1949; Aux deux colombes, 1949; Toa, 1949; Le Trésor de Cantenac, 1950; Tu m'as sauvé la vie, 1950; Deburau, 1951; Le Poison, 1951; Je l'ai été trois fois, 1952; La Vie d'un honnête homme (The Virtuous Scoundrel), 1953; Si Versailles m'était conté (Royal Affairs in Versailles/Versailles), 1954; Napoléon, 1955; Si Paris nous était conté, 1956; Assassins et voleurs (Lovers and Thieves), 1956; (with Clément Duhour) Les Trois font la paire, 1957.

ABOUT: Bernard, A. and Floquet, C. Album Sacha Guitry, 1983; Delubac, Jacqueline Faut-il épouser Sacha Guitry? 1976; Guitry, S. If I Remember Right (translated by Lewis Galantiere), 1935; Guitry, S. Lucien Guitry raconté par son fils, 1930; Guitry, S. Quatre ans d'occupation, 1947; Guitry, S. Soixante jours de

prison, 1949; Et Versailles vos est conté, 1954; Harding, J. Sacha Guitry: The Last Boulevardier, 1968; Ja-
doux, H. Sacha Guitry, 1982 (in French); Knapp, B.
Sacha Guitry, 1981; Lorcey, J. Sacha, Guitry: Centans
de théatre et dèsprit, 1985; Lorcey, J. Sacha Guitry:
L'Homme et l'oeuvre, 1982; Lorcey, J. Sacha Guitry:
Raconté par les témoins de sa vie, 1976; Michalczyk,
J. J. The French Literary Filmmakers, 1980; Roud, R.
(ed.) Cinema: A Critical Dictionary, 1980; Séréville,
Geneviève de Sacha Guitry, Sacha Guitry, monmari,
1959; Siclier, J. Guitry, 1966 (in French).
Periodicals—Cahiers du Cinéma August–September
1957, October 1958, December 1965 (Guitry issue),
January 1984; Cinéma (France) May 1984;
Cinématographe February 1953 (Guitry issue); Cinemonde January 23, 1953; June 26, 1953; January 8,
1957; Image et Son March 1971; Lumière du Cinéma
October 1977 (Guitry issue); Positif January 1984; Revue du Cinéma 173 1971; Sight and Sound Autumn
1957, Winter 1980–1981; Times (London) July 25,
1957.

ALICE GUY-BLACHÉ

*GUY-BLACHÉ, ALICE (July 1, 1873–
March 24, 1968), French director, producer, and
scenarist, was born Alice Guy at Saint-Monde, on
the outskirts of Paris. She was the youngest of the
four daughters of a cultured businessman whose
enterprises apparently included publishing and/
or bookselling, and who was reportedly bankrupted on three separate occasions. One of his
projects took the family to Santiago, Chile, when
Alice Guy was four. They returned after two
years, and she was educated at convent schools
in Paris.

When her father died (as early as 1889, according to some accounts), Alice Guy decided to
acquire skills that would insure her independen-
dence. She learned stenography and typing, still
rare accomplishments in those days. Through
one of her mother's charity committees she met
members of the family of Léon Gaumont, who
in 1895 (?) hired her as his secretary. Hardworking and highly intelligent, she soon became his
"right arm."

Up to this time, Gaumont's company had
manufactured conventional photographic
equipment. According to Charles Ford's article
about Alice Guy in *Films in Review* (March
1964), Louis Lumière visited Gaumont in 1895
and demonstrated to him (and to his secretary)
the possibilities of the Cinématographe. By the
following year Gaumont was marketing a 60mm
camera of his own. In 1897 he launched a 35mm
combined camera-projector, and in 1898 an inexpensive mass-produced projector, the Gaumont Chrono-photographe.

In her *Memoirs* Guy recalls that "As the
daughter of an editor I'd read a lot and retained
a fair amount. I'd tried my hand at theater and

thought it could be done better. Summoning up
my courage, I timidly proposed to Gaumont to
write one or two short sketches and have friends
act them out. If the outcome of the affair had
been known in advance, I never would have
gotten the approval." Indeed, according to Guy,
Gaumont assented only on the condition that she
maintain her secretarial duties as well. Francis
Lacassin, in a thoroughly researched article in
Sight and Sound (Summer 1971), gives a somewhat different account, saying that, in order to
demonstrate his film cameras and projectors,
"Gaumont had . . . produced a few reels of factual or news footage" between 1896 and 1898.
The success of the Chrono-photographe "obliged
him to provide customers with fiction films
along the lines of those made by Pathé. He entrusted his active secretary with the organisation
of this new branch. With no resources and no
qualified staff, Mademoiselle Alice decided to
tackle the job herself."

Also in dispute is the date of Alice Guy's first
film, *La Fée aux choux* (*The Cabbage Fairy*, later retitled *Sage-femme de première classe*).
Charles Ford says it was made "early in 1896,"
shortly *before* Georges Méliès began his work as
the "father of the fiction film." Alice Guy herself
claimed that she preceded Méliès, but Francis
Lacassin thinks it unlikely "that Gaumont would
have envisaged producing fiction films before
they started mass-producing their projectors in
1898; or, at the very earliest, their combined
camera-projector in 1897." Whether or not Alice
Guy was "the mother of the fiction film," she
was certainly the first woman in the world to direct movies.

°gē blä shä´

La Fée aux choux was shot in the garden of Léon Gaumont's house, in the grounds of his factory at Buttes-Chaumont, Paris. There were a few painted backdrops and a cast comprised of the director and two amused friends. "In a picture postcard vein of humour," according to Lacassin, "it tells the story of a woman who grows children in a cabbage patch." Alice Guy enjoyed this experiment and Gaumont was obviously pleased with it. Up to 1901 she made dozens of very short films (about twenty meters), employing such professional entertainers as would work for Gaumont's fees—acrobats, singers, vaudeville performers. She is also credited with Gaumont's first narrative using sets, *Les Mésadventures dùn tête de veau* (1897).

By 1901, Gaumont was doing so well with these little films that he built a modest studio at Buttes-Chaumont and authorized Alice Guy to make longer movies. From *Les Apaches pas veinards* (twenty meters, 1903) she progressed to *La première cigarette* (sixty meters, 1904), showing in semi-closeup the reactions of a boy smoking a forbidden cigarette, observed by his frightened sister, and *L'Assassinat du courrier de Lyon* (122 meters, 1904). *Rélubilitation,* a "dramatic scene" also made in 1904, was 250 meters long. Lacassin says that "1904 was her year for children," who were the protagonists in many of that year's movies, including *Les Petits Coupeurs de bois vert.* In this "delightfully naive melodrama," two children whose mother is ill go into the forest to gather firewood for her. They are caught by a gamekeeper and brought before a magistrate. Instead of punishing them, he is so moved by their story that he gives them money.

Very little detailed information is available about Alice Guy's films, most of which are lost. Lacassin says that at Gaumont "she tackled every genre"—fairy tales and fantasies, religious subjects, "saucy" comedies, comedies that depended on cinematic tricks in the style of Méliès (including masking, double-exposure, and film run backwards), and films that simulated famous paintings and "came alive."

Guy said that virtually all the films produced by Gaumont up to the fall of 1905 were directed by her. The principal exceptions seem to have been the few pictures made by Ferdinand Zecca, formerly Charles Pathé's production chief, whom she happened upon in 1904 going door to door selling soap (and wetting it to make it weigh more). She immediately hired her fallen rival, who acted as her assistant and also directed several films himself before he made up his quarrel with Pathé and rejoined him.

By the fall of 1905, developing ever more ambitious projects, she found that she could no lon-

ger cope with Gaumont's production schedule singlehanded. She chose as her assistant Victorin Jasset, then producing historical spectaculars at the Paris Hippodrome. Jasset was for years erroneously credited as director of two of Alice Guy's most notable Gaumont productions, *Esmeralda* (290 meters, December 1905), an adaptation of Victor Hugo's *The Hunchback of Notre Dame,* and *La Vie de Christ* (*The Life of Christ,* 680 meters, January 1906). The latter was Gaumont's answer to Pathé's "super-production" on the same theme. It used three hundred extras and twenty-five wooden sets designed by Henri Ménessier, some of them mounted on mobile platforms and set up outdoors in the forest of Fontainebleau.

Victorin Jasset did direct several films at Gaumont, including the remarkable *Rêves d'un fumeur d'opium* (*Dreams of an Opium Smoker*), before Gaumont fired him for his amorous attentions to female extras. Meanwhile, Alice Guy had received a batch of scripts written by a journalist, Louis Feuillade. They impressed her so much that she invited Feuillade to direct them himself. He at first declined, suggesting that she might instead consider his friend Étienne Arnaud, a law graduate who was also a writer and a singer. Arnaud was duly hired and made his debut as a Gaumont director in January 1906 with Feuillade's first script, *Attrapez mon chapeau!* He remained with Gaumont until 1911.

Feuillade meanwhile became the company scenarist, turning in three scripts a week. Later in 1906 he gave up journalism to begin his career as a director, soon to emerge as the first major artist of the cinema. At about the same time, Feuillade and Arnaud were joined by two more directors, both former actors, Roméo Bosetti and J. Roullet-Plessis.

Alice Guy now turned her formidable energies to a new Gaumont enterprise, the Chronophone, which synchronized visual images with sounds recorded on a wax cylinder. In 1906–1907 she made about a hundred very short sound films, many of them musical pieces, including excerpts from operas featuring well-known singers. In 1906 she spent a month in Provence, filming the bullfights at Nîmes and shooting, on location, a number of pictures based on Provençal literature.

On the trip to Provence, she was accompanied by her scenarist, Louis Feuillade, who also directed portions of some of her films, and by a cameraman. Most accounts say that the cameraman was Herbert Blaché-Bolton, an Englishman of French descent who later dropped the second part of his surname. However, an unpublished memorandum by Anthony Slide, based on an interview with Alice Guy's daughter, maintains that Herbert Blaché was in Europe to study French production methods; when Gaumont sent Guy on some errand to Berlin, Blaché went along as her interpreter. It is quite conceivable that both stories are true. At any rate, Blaché and Alice Guy fell in love and were married in the spring of 1907.

Three days later they sailed for the United States, where Blaché had been made general manager of Gaumont's New York office. On Alice Guy-Blaché's recommendation, Louis Feuillade succeeded her as Gaumont's artistic director. The company's New York branch, like its other foreign offices, was intended to function only as an agency and print laboratory for the films made in Paris. While Herbert Blaché showed Gaumont productions to American exhibitors, ordered the required negatives, and made copies in his print laboratory at Flushing, New York, his wife kept house. In 1908 she gave birth to a daughter, Simone; a son followed some time later.

Three years of domesticity were enough for Alice Guy-Blaché. She pined for her lost career, and since Gaumont was not prepared to invest in foreign production and her husband was under exclusive contract, she launched her own production company, Solax, with a blazing sun as its logo. It was registered in September 1910, with herself as president. Although its office was in Manhattan, Solax actually operated from the Gaumont building in Flushing, on the outskirts of New York. Guy-Blaché used her husband's print laboratory, borrowed space for a studio, and shot most of her exteriors around Flushing, where there were still lakes and woods. She engaged a cameraman, John Haas, and brought Henri Ménessier over from Paris as her art director.

Between 1910 and 1914, according to Francis Lacassin, Solax turned out over three hundred films of various lengths and in every genre. Forty or fifty of them were directed by Guy-Blaché, the rest being assigned to the studio's two other directors, Edward Warren and Edgar Lewis.

Solax began production with Guy-Blaché's own one-reel *A Child's Sacrifice*, released in October 1910. Starring Magda Foy, the "Solax Kid," it tells the story of a little girl whose father is not earning because of a strike and whose undernourished mother is ill. Desperate to help, she sells her only doll to a junk-dealer. As kindly a man as the magistrate in *Les Petits Coupeurs*, he gives the doll back. Her faith in human goodness confirmed, the little girl steps in to prevent a fight provoked by the strike.

A Child's Sacrifice was a hit, beginning the Solax success story. From an initial production schedule of one one-reel movie a week, the company doubled its output beginning in March 1911, and in November of the same year, after enlarging its Flushing studio, announced that it would in future release a film every Monday, Wednesday, and Friday. A contemporary advertisement trumpeted: "Learn to swear three times a week: 'By the rising sun, I want Solax.'"

At first, Guy-Blaché seems to have thought it prudent not to draw attention to the fact that Solax was owned and run by a woman, but she grew more confident as the studio went from success to success. In November 1911 she granted an interview to a journalist from *Moving Picture World* who visited her enlarging studio. He reported that "all scenarios used by the Solax Company are edited by Madame Blaché and many of the pictures are personally directed by her. Those not made under her personal direction are viséd by her at some stage . . . so that she practically has a hand in the entire output of the company." The journalist also met Solax's leading players—Blanche Cornwall, Marion Swayne (or Sweyne), and Gladdon James.

Solax had always shown a particular interest in comedy, and in December 1911 Guy-Blaché announced "an emphatic effort to organize a perfect comedy stock company." Before the end of the year she held press conferences to boast of two notable additions to the Solax "stock company," Darwin Karr and Billy Quirk, both well-established comedians. Claire Whitney, who starred in a number of important productions, probably joined the company at about the same time. Another recruit was Guy-Blaché's small daughter Simone, who appeared in at least two Solax movies, in 1911 and 1913.

The company ended 1911 with *A Solax Celebration,* a curious movie in which most of the Solax luminaries (including Guy-Blaché) appear in allegorical roles celebrating their good fortune in working for Solax and its leader ("The Cause"). After this they all sit down to a banquet also attended by "A Relative"—Herbert Blaché. It is tempting to see Blaché as a specter at the Solax feast, as Gerald Peary does in his article in *Velvet Light Trap* (Fall 1972), but Lacassin maintains that "he was every bit as dynamic as his wife and was a great help in marketing her films," exploiting the contacts with exhibitors that came with his Gaumont job.

The Solax output was by no means confined to comedy. Gerald Peary says it was "generally half comedies and half dramas," and that "there was a period of several months in 1911 when all the dramas were of a military nature (filmed on location at a government post at Fort Myers, Virginia)." *In the Year 2000* (1912), probably but not certainly directed by Guy-Blaché herself, was a satire on the intriguing theme of a society ruled by women.

The same year, apparently continuing her work with Gaumont's Chronophone, Guy-Blaché filmed two operas, *Mignon* and *Fra Diavolo*, both three-reelers with orchestral accompaniment. A contemporary account by Louis Reeves Harrison describes the filming of the latter in June 1912, on location on Long Island: "I . . . came upon a fully equipped stage set up in the open, with Madame Blaché conducting rehearsals from an elevated camera platform. . . . Madame Blaché gives her signals with as much ease and composure as though there had been a month of dress rehearsals. She is never ruffled, never agitated. . . . With a few simple directions, uttered without apparent emotion, she handles the interweaving movements like a military leader might the maneuvers of an army."

In September 1912, two years after it was founded, Solax left Flushing and moved into new quarters in Fort Lee, New Jersey. Designed by Guy-Blaché herself and built at a cost of $100,000, the new studio could claim to be "the best-equipped moving picture plant in the world." Four stories of iron and glass, it provided five stages, projection rooms, prop rooms, carpenter shops, and laboratories capable of turning out 12,000 feet of positive film a day. The dressing rooms were elegantly furnished, and the men's recreation room was equipped with card tables and cuspidors.

Soon after, in November 1912, six Solax two-reelers were screened in a "Solax Night" at the town hall in Brewster, New York, as part of a campaign to demonstrate the growing respectability of the movies as a form of entertainment. The "best" people duly attended, including several who "came in automobiles," and "a millionaire and his family and other wealthy persons living in Brewster and its environs."

Solax had become one of the most successful and fast-growing of the East Coast independent production companies. To keep it in the vanguard, Guy-Blaché followed the trend to longer films, more carefully produced. Lacassin said that she "spared no effort or expense to achieve realism or sensational effect." In 1912 she had astounded the critics by setting fire to a real car ("a Darracq only three years old") for *Mickey's Pal*, a crime story. *The Sewer* (1913?), scripted by Henri Ménessier, featured an attack on the hero by sewer rats specially trained for the film.

The first three-reeler made by Solax was the spectacular *The Beasts of the Jungle* (1913), produced at enormous expense ($18,000) and directed by Edward Warren. Instead of the usual two days, Solax devoted an entire month to its production. The studio was converted into the "aromatic atmosphere of India and the treasure-laden hills of the Transvaal." An elephant, lions, monkeys, and parrots were assembled at Fort Lee, not to mention a tiger named Sarah who appeared in publicity pictures, submitting to a cuddle from the intrepid producer.

Beasts of the Jungle evidently justified the care and expense that had been lavished on it, initiating the jungle movie genre. Guy-Blaché herself directed Solax's next superproduction, *Dick Whittington and His Cat* (March 1913). Reconstructing Old England with twenty-six sets, the film had a cast of two hundred people, an army of rats, and a budget of $35,000. An anonymous reporter watched the filming of this epic and wrote: "Standing behind this gifted producer and listening to her quietly giving admonitions to her players, one gets a vivid impression of what her mind is drawing in her imagination. It seems magical, the closeness of the understanding between her and the player. . . . How sharp and clear-cut is her visualizing power and how thoroughly she knows just what she wants. . . . And yet, if anything humorous happens, Madame Blaché is the first to see its fun and the first to laugh . . . [even] when things happen that spoil the scene."

In the spring of 1913, when Guy-Blaché had brought her studio to a pinnacle of success, it was announced that Herbert Blaché had disassociated himself from his other commitments and "joined forces with his wife"; "together they will guide the destiny of the Solax Company." In August of the same year, a two-page advertisement proclaimed the birth of Blaché Features, which would produce feature films at the rate of one a month "under the personal direction of Herbert Blaché." Solax, Blaché explained, "will continue to produce its features under the direction and supervision of Madame Blaché with my advice."

However, in October 1913, Solax ceased production. As Gerald Peary puts it, "the coup was complete: Herbert Blaché was president of the new company, Alice Blaché was vice president and thus second in command. And although Alice Blaché returned to her first love of directing for most of the Blaché Features, she no longer owned a studio. Nor would any woman ever again in the film industry match Alice Blaché's control of Solax. . . . Alice Blaché's small step of handing away her power has proved historically a huge step backwards for women's rights in the cinema, perhaps irredeemable."

Lacassin reports that "unlike Solax, the new company made only dramas—especially adventure stories—and these were a minimum of four reels long. Alice Guy inaugurated the production side of the company on November 17 with *The Star of India*. Of the fourteen features made by Blaché Features Inc. from November 1913 until its disappearance in November 1914, nine were made by her; the others were directed by Harry Schenk or by Blaché himself."

In April 1914 Blaché set up another company, the United States Amusement Company, with himself as president and his wife as vice president. Its announced policy was to produce "masterpieces" by adapting literary classics and stage plays, in the latter case using actors who had successfully played in the stage versions. "This concern with quality and culture struck a new note in the materialist American cinema," wrote Francis Lacassin; "the scheme also offered all the disadvantages which Feuillade had denounced as early as 1911 . . . Namely, the death of the original script and the takeover of the cinema by the theatre."

Blaché directed most of the Amusement Corporation's films, his wife contributing only three, all released early in 1917—*The Adventurer* (from Upton Sinclair's novel), *The Empress,* and *A Man and a Woman* (based on Zola's *Nana*). Meanwhile, from October 1914 to August 1917, she directed about ten five-reelers (and supervised others) for another company with which Blaché was associated. This was Popular Players and Plays, which seemed to share the policies of the Amusement Corporation—all the films that Guy-Blaché directed for it were adaptations of stage plays or novels (except one, *My Madonna,* based on Robert Service's poem "The Call of the Yukon"). Most of them starred the Russian vamp Olga Petrova.

In January 1917, Blaché had rented the Solax studio to another company, and it was later sold and demolished. As Lacassin says, "the Blachés' departure from the Fort Lee studio signified the end of an era. By 1917 it was already impossible for independents to survive; the future belonged to the big companies." Guy-Blaché's last few films were released by Pathé-Exchange, including *The Great Adventure,* starring Bessie Love, and *Tarnished Reputation* (1920). Herbert Blaché went on working for another decade, serving for some time as production director at Universal.

Lacassin has it that, after Blaché's retirement, he and his wife opened "a small lampshade shop in downtown Los Angeles." Anthony Slide's 1973 memorandum, based on his interview with Simone Blaché-Bolton, offers a quite different account—that the Blachés separated in 1922, when Alice Guy-Blaché returned to France. She lectured, wrote children's books, and made several unsuccessful attempts to get back into the film industry. In 1927 she returned to the U.S. in hopes of retrieving her films, but was unable to locate them. In 1953, when she was seventy, her work was belatedly acknowledged by the French government with the award of the Légion d'Honneur. According to her daughter, "The only reason she is remembered at all now is that she made great efforts to stake her claim, to say 'I was the first person who ever did this. Now you've got to pay attention. You've got to take notice. I'm the one who did it.' Finally she was given the Legion of Honor for meritorious service. It was a great day in her life. . . . " Later, as a very old woman, she lived in Brussels, where Simone was working as secretary to the American ambassador. When Simone returned to the United States, her mother went with her. She died in Mahwah, New Jersey at the age of ninety-four.

Gerald Peary, discussing Guy-Blaché's work in sociopolitical terms, concludes sadly in his *Velvet Light Trap* article that the few Solax films dealing with labor-management relations "are stringently anti-strike, pro-management, and deal typically with a worker protagonist forced to strike against his will who discovers proof of the 'goodness' of the boss and leads the men back to work, and away from their 'unreasonable' demands."

Solax avoided the suffragist issue (unlike other studios in 1912–1913) and Guy-Blaché herself took a view of women close to that of a Victorian male. Peary refers to the director's essay on "Woman's Place in Photoplay Production," published in *Moving Picture World* (July 11, 1914) and reprinted with Peary's article in *Velvet Light Trap.* In it, she describes woman as "an authority on the emotions": "She has developed her finer feelings for generations, while being protected from the world by her male companions, and she is naturally religious. . . . A woman's magic touch is immediately recognized in a real home. Is it not just as recognizable in the home of the characters in a photoplay?" She concludes that "there is nothing connected with the staging of a motion picture that a woman cannot do as easily as a man, and there is no reason why she cannot completely master every technicality of the art."

So few of Guy-Blaché's films have been located and identified that Peary was unable to see a single one of them while researching his article. He suggests, however, that "although there are indications that Alice Blaché took more care than most producers in directing her films, it is romanticism to see Solax Studio as separate from the other companies in the choice of cinematic subject matter. The plots of most Solax movies were clichéd and melodramatic and familiar, typical of the hundreds of movies cranked out monthly at all the studios."

She remains a historical figure of the greatest interest and importance. As Peary says, she was "the most powerful woman executive ever to work in the film industry," running her very successful studio "with the kind of total authority that leads to theorizing about 'the studio head as *auteur.'*" Although she directed upwards of 270 films, and produced many more, she has until recently been totally ignored by most film historians, many of her pictures being attributed to other directors. A vast amount of research remains to be done.

FILMS (incomplete and probably inaccurate): La Fée aux choux, 1896? (in 1902 retitled Sage-femme de première classe); Les Mésadventures d'une tête de veau, 1898; Les Dangers de l'alcoolisme, 1899; La Danse des saisons, 1900; Au bal de flore, 1900; Hussards et grisettes, 1901; Le Pommier, 1902; Le Voleur sacrilège, 1903; Les Apaches pas veinards, 1903; Rapt d'enfants par les Romanichels, 1904; La Baptême de la poupée, 1904; La Première Cigarette, 1904; Les Petits Peintres, 1904; Les Petits Coupeurs de bois vert, 1904; Paris la nuit, 1904; L'Assassinat du courrier de Lyon, 1904; Le Crime de la rue du Temple, 1904; Un Noce au lac Saint-Fargeau, 1905; Esmeralda, 1905; Rélubilitation (Réhabilitation?), 1905; La Vie du Christ, 1906; Mireille, 1906; Le Fée printemps, 1906; Fanfan la tulipe, 1907; A Child's Sacrifice, 1910; Rose of the Circus, 1911; The Doll, 1911; The Violin Maker of Nuremberg, 1911; Sealed Lips, 1912; The Face at the Window, 1912; Mignon, 1912; Falling Leaves, 1912; In the Year 2000, 1912; Fra Diavolo, 1912; The Blood Stain, 1912; Playing Trumps, 1912; Phantom Paradise, 1912; Mickey's Pal, 1912; Flesh and Blood, 1912; At the Phone, 1912; The Paralytic, 1912; Dick Whittington and His Cat, 1913; Kelly of the Emerald Isle, 1913; The Pit and the Pendulum, 1913; A House Divided, 1913; A Terrible Night, 1913; The Little Hunchback, 1913; Western Love, 1913; Rogues of Paris, 1913; The Sewer, 1913(?); Ben Bolt, 1913; The Star of India, 1913; Blood and Water, 1913; Beneath the Czar, 1914; Shadows of the Moulin Rouge, 1914; The Monster and the Girl, 1914; The Dream Woman, 1914; The Woman of Mystery, 1914; The Lure, 1914; The Heart of a Painted Woman, 1915; My Madonna, 1915; What Will People Say?, 1916; The Girl With the Green Eyes, 1916; The Adventurer, 1917; The Empress, 1917; A Man and a Woman, 1917; Behind the Mask, 1917; The Great Adventure, 1918; A Soul Adrift, 1918; Tarnished Reputation, 1920; Vampire, 1920.

ABOUT: Beck, C. Scream Queens, 1978; Breton, É. Femmes d'images, 1984; Ford, C. Femmes cinéastes, 1972; Guy, A. Autobiographie d'une pionnière du cinéma, 1976; Martineau, M. Le Cinéma au feminisme (Cinémaction 9), 1979; Slide, A. Early Women Directors, 1977. *Periodicals*—Cinema (USA) 35 1976; Cinéma (France) January 1917; Écran August 1974, July 1976, September 1976, February 1977; Films in Review March 1964; Image et Son April 1974; Moving Picture World July 11, 1914; Sight and Sound Summer 1971; Velvet Light Trap Fall 1972.

HAMER, ROBERT (March 31, 1911– November 11, 1963), British director, scenarist, and editor, was born at Kidderminster in Worcestershire. He was educated at a public school, Rossall, and at Corpus Christi College, Cambridge University, where he read economics and showed some talent as a poet. Hamer entered the film industry in the time-honored fashion, joining the Gaumont-British studios as a number-boy in 1934—as he remarked, this was "before some genius thought of attaching the clapper to the number board." He moved on to Alexander Korda's London Film Productions as a tea boy and general dogsbody in the cutting rooms, in due course rising to assistant editor, editor, assistant director, and script collaborator.

At London Films he had "the inestimable good fortune to be put to work for Erich Pommer." He served as editor of Tim Whelan's *Saint Martin's Lane* (*Sidewalks of London*, 1938), Pommer's *Vessel of Wrath* (*The Beachcomber*, 1938), and Hitchcock's *Jamaica Inn* (1939), and then worked briefly with the General Post Office's famous Film Unit under John Grierson, editing among other things several of Cavalcanti's short films. In 1940 or 1941 he joined Michael Balcon's Ealing Studios, where he graduated from editor (of, for example, *The Foreman Went to France* and *Ships With Wings*) to coscenarist and associate producer of Charles Frend's *San Demetrio, London* (1943).

In his memoirs, Michael Balcon praises Hamer's "brilliant but mordant wit" and notes that he "engendered great affection in all who were allowed to know him well," but adds that "he was, alas, subject to great emotional stresses and strains in his private life. Despite his early brilliant success, he rarely came to terms with himself, and it almost seemed that he was engaged on a process of self-destruction"—a reference, presumably, to Hamer's drinking. These comments tend to bear out rumors of tension between Hamer and Balcon, who nevertheless recognized Hamer's talent. It was both a strength and a weakness of Balcon's administration that he tended to recruit his new directors from Ealing's own close-knit team of artists and technicians, and in 1945 he gave Hamer his chance as director of one of the episodes in that masterly anthology of supernatural stories, *Dead of Night*.

ROBERT HAMER

"The Haunted Mirror," the episode directed
by Hamer, stars Googie Withers and Ralph Michael in a story about an old mirror, given by a
woman to her fiancé, that reflects for him not his
orderly, superficial life but its own dark memories of murder and suicide. And these memories
connect with buried elements in his own psyche,
releasing a strain of obsessive sexual jealousy that
brings him close to madness. In the end, the
woman, recognizing what is happening, smashes
the mirror and saves them both from disaster.

In its clarity and dramatic unity, this piece
is—with Cavalcanti's "The Ventriloquist's
Dummy"—the most effective of the episodes in
Dead of Night. Charles Barr, in his thoughtful
study of the Ealing films, suggests that it is a key
work in the history of the studio, and an extremely ambivalent one. The confrontation with
the mirror had opened up "appalling conflicts
and inadequacies. But Ealing shuts the door on
them, smashes the mirror. It will not enter the
dark world, the Laurentian 'otherness' again; it
accepts instead, to use the terms articulated
within the film itself, *constraint* on *energy,*
meaning sexuality and violence. . . . Ealing became typed as the safe, responsible, U-certificate
British cinema *par excellence.*"

In fact, as Barr goes on to show, Hamer seems
to have been less willing to leave out the
"Laurentian 'otherness'" than most of Michael
Balcon's young men. His first feature, *Pink
String and Sealing Wax* (1945), scripted by Diana Morgan from the play by Roland Pertwee,
is a melodrama set in Victorian Brighton, where
the proper young hero (Gordon Jackson) is preparing to follow in his father's footsteps as a
pharmacist. One evening, driven to rebellion by
paternal repression, he visits a pub where he becomes infatuated by the libidinous Pearl (Googie
Withers), and before long he finds himself falsely implicated in the death by poisoning of her
husband.

In the end, her guilt apparent, Pearl drowns
herself, freeing the hero to make a suitable marriage. But, as Barr says, "the film has conjured
up a world of violence and sexuality with which
the respectable characters simply can't come to
terms." It seemed to John Russell Taylor that
"what was most distinctive about the film was
the intense and refined feeling for the period,
the extreme elegance of the visual style, and
Hamer's evident gift for producing a high level
of ensemble playing, all in accordance with the
slightly heightened artificial style he had set as
proper to the subject and ambience."

Googie Withers starred again in the very different movie that followed, *It Always Rains on
Sunday* (1947). Adapted (by Hamer among others) from a novel by Arthur La Bern, it introduces us to a poor, raffish, and rather
claustrophobically close-knit community in the
East End of London on a day when the ordinary
patterns of life are disrupted by the arrival of an
escaped criminal (John McCallum). He hides out
with Rose Sandigate (Withers), once his fiancée,
now married to a decent, boring, elderly man
(Edward Chapman). At first tempted to run off
with this revenant, she is soon forced to recognize his ruthless self-interest. He is recaptured,
and after a suicide attempt, she is reconciled to
her drab, ordinary life.

"In a manner reminiscent of Reed's thrillers
of the 1940s," wrote Roy Armes, "*It Always
Rains on Sunday* builds up a beautifully lit and
strikingly edited chase sequence, as Tommy
Swann is hunted down in a shunting yard. The
atmosphere of the East End is vividly captured
in its daily rhythms, its violence and sentimentality, but there is no social criticism, though the
characters' lives are bleak and stunted. Despite
a happy ending, there is only momentary escape
for them from a fatalism reminiscent of that pervading the 1930s work of Marcel Carné and
Jacques Prévert." John Russell Taylor, pointing
out that the movie was made almost entirely
without location work, apart from a few establishing shots, called it "a classic of studio
realism."

During the first half of 1949 Ealing released
three films that established the "Ealing comedy"
as a commodity recognized and welcomed all
over the world: Henry Cornelius' *Passport to
Pimlico,* Alexander Mackendrick's *Whisky
Galore* (*Tight Little Island*), and Hamer's *Kind*

Hearts and Coronets. Hamer's film, adapted by the director and John Dighton from a 1910 novel by Roy Horniman, is in fact a very atypical Ealing product—an extremely black comedy untouched by the "cosiness" associated with the studio. This had been attributed partly to the fact that much of it was shot at Pinewood (the Ealing stages being otherwise occupied), partly to Hamer's own temperament and intentions. He wanted, he said, to make "a film not noticeably similar to any previously made in the English language," and to use "this English language, which I love, in a more varied and, to me, more interesting way than I had previously had the chance of doing in a film."

This use of English is achieved in the coolly ironic and immensely witty diary read to us by the Tenth Duke of Chalfont (Dennis Price) as he awaits execution. It describes his humble beginnings as Louis Mazzini, son of a member of the Chalfont family who had been cruelly disowned after her elopement with an Italian singer; his suburban upbringing; his humiliations at the hands of his mother's family; and his elimination, in a series of ingenious murders, of the eight members of the hated family who stood between him and the dukedom. At the end of the film, in its original version, we are left unsure whether or not Louis will escape the gallows and, if he does, which of two eager and beautiful widows (Joan Greenwood and Valerie Hobson) he will choose as his duchess; the American censor insisted on a final shot establishing the certainty of his execution.

The film was universally admired for its wit and stylized elegance, for the excellence of the ensemble playing, and for the ingeniously differentiated grotesques created by Alec Guinness, who played all eight of Louis' victims. There were some objections to the movie's "uncinematic" reliance on a spoken commentary, but many praised the way this was used to complement and counterpoint the images. John Russell Taylor thought that it could "be compared more readily with the high comedy of Congreve and Wilde than with anything else in the cinema. And what gives it its special flavour is the distinctive tone of bitterness and strong feeling underlying the polished, formal surface." Charles Barr called it "the hardest of the Ealing comedies to write about . . . a particularly enigmatic and 'irreducible' work," but "quite possibly the most memorable of British films"—a large but not indefensible claim.

After this triumph, Hamer left Ealing, where Balcon had vetoed a project he had long been preparing, working thereafter for an assortment of production companies. His next film, scripted by Robert Westerby, was *The Spider and the Fly* (1949)—the only one of his pictures for which he did not receive a writing credit. It is set just before and during World War I in France, a country that Hamer loved and knew intimately. Guy Rolfe plays a gentlemanly criminal and Eric Portman the policeman who doggedly pursues him until the war converts them into a perfectly balanced team, assigned to steal vital documents from the German legation in Berne. The almost impossible task is brilliantly planned and achieved, but the documents reveal that the woman they both love (Nadia Gray) is an enemy spy. The thief goes off to die in the trenches; the policeman is left to live out his empty life alone.

Roy Armes wrote that *The Spider and the Fly* "shows Hamer's elegance and precision, as well as his taste for bitter irony, but it is a cold film which impresses with its intelligence while failing to involve us emotionally." This is the commonest criticism of Hamer's work—Lindsay Anderson had spoken of *Kind Hearts and Coronets* as "emotionally quite frozen"—but Charles Barr disputes such charges, calling *The Spider and the Fly* "on the contrary, one of the most moving of British films in its sympathetic analysis of emotionally crippled protagonists." It seems to Barr that Hamer was concerned in his movies to *diagnose* "emotional atrophy," and that to accuse him of this condition "is like ascribing to George Eliot herself, as the author of *Middlemarch,* the emotional atrophy of Mr. Casaubon."

Hamer returned briefly to Ealing to make *His Excellency* (1952), a rather "tame and stagebound" adaptation of a play by Dorothy and Campbell Christie about a plainspeaking trade union official (Eric Portman) sent by the postwar Labour Government to govern a small and rebellious colony. This was followed by *The Long Memory,* starring John Mills as a man who, after twelve years in prison for a murder he did not commit, comes out to hunt down the three people who framed him. Adapted from a novel by Howard Clewes, it is a rather slow-moving story, memorable mainly for the unfamiliarity of the setting—the wharves and mud-flats of the Thames Estuary. Though it was shot (by Harry Waxman) mainly on location, it was lit and framed in such a way as to give it a faint air of stylization and unreality, characteristic of Hamer. Like *It Always Rains on Sunday,* it evoked some comparisons with the melancholy work of Marcel Carné.

Some critics also detected "a bleak despair and a profound sense of the isolation of the individual" beneath the "surface humour and outward pieties" of *Father Brown* (*The*

Detective, 1954). Drawing on several of G. K. Chesterton's stories about a Catholic priest who is also a disarmingly eccentric amateur detective, it has Alec Guinness as Father Brown and Peter Finch as the well-bred thief he pursues through France, seeking to bring him not so much to justice as to redemption. This was the most successful of Hamer's later films, described by Gavin Lambert as "a little classic of its kind," though a few thought that Guinness was miscast and *Time*'s reviewer maintained that, with "the intellectual skeleton" of Chesterton's stories removed, "the film falls all of a sentimental heap."

Alec Guinness also stars in the two Hamer movies that followed, a puerile farce with slapstick elements called *To Paris With Love* (1955), and *The Scapegoat* (1959), adapted by Hamer and Gore Vidal from the novel by Daphne du Maurier. In the latter Guinness plays a lonely British teacher on vacation in France who meets his double, a raffish aristocrat, and is tricked into changing places. He thus suddenly acquires a glass factory on the verge of ruin and a family in much the same state—neglected wife (Irene Worth), formidable drug-addicted mother (Bette Davis), enigmatic sister (Pamela Browne), introverted daughter (Annabel Bartlett)—not to mention a mistress (Nicole Maurey). And soon there is a mysterious death to add to his problems.

The Scapegoat was produced by Michael Balcon, though it was not an Ealing film but an independent production financed and distributed by MGM. It is said that MGM was unhappy with Hamer's version of the picture and extensively re-edited the work, and this perhaps accounts for the gaps and inconsistencies that mar the film, described by Dilys Powell as "a bundle of first-rate loose ends." During the four years between *To Paris With Love* and *The Scapegoat* Hamer did some television work, notably a fine production of Turgenev's *A Month in the Country*.

His last film was *School for Scoundrels* (1960), a moderately entertaining comedy derived from Stephen Potter's books on the art of "one-upmanship." Ian Carmichael plays the born loser who learns at the feet of guru Alastair Sim "how to win without actually cheating," defeating his caddish rival (Terry-Thomas) and getting the girl (Janette Scott). By this time Hamer is said to have been drinking heavily and in poor health. He was coscenarist of Don Chaffey's *A Jolly Bad Fellow* (1963), a comedy faintly (and sadly) reminiscent of his own masterpiece, *Kind Hearts and Coronets*. He died later the same year, at the age of fifty-two.

Robert Hamer was one of the two directors—the other was Alexander Mackendrick—whose work transcended the self-imposed limitations of the Ealing style. Roy Armes wrote that his work "remains among the most deeply felt and personal in British postwar cinema." Gavin Lambert called his "the most civilised" talent in the British film industry.

FILMS: The Haunted Mirror *in* Dead of Night, 1945; Pink String and Sealing Wax, 1945; It Alway Rains on Sunday, 1947; Kind Hearts and Coronets, 1949; The Spider and the Fly, 1949; His Excellency, 1952; The Long Memory, 1952; Father Brown (The Detective), 1954; To Paris With Love, 1955; The Scapegoat, 1959; School for Scoundrels, 1960. *Published scripts*—Kind Hearts and Coronets *in* Taylor, J. R. (ed.) Masterworks of the British Cinema, 1974.

ABOUT: Barr, C. Ealing Studios, 1977; Belmans, R. Robert Hamer, 1976 (in French); Roud, R. (ed.) Cinema: A Critical Dictionary, 1980. *Periodicals*—Film Dope March 1981; Films and Filming July 1959; Screen Summer 1974; Sight and Sound October–December 1951, Spring 1959; Times (London) December 5, 1963.

HATHAWAY, HENRY (March 13, 1898–February 11, 1985), was born in Sacramento, California, where his mother was on tour. He was the only child of Rhoady de Fiennes, a theatrical manager, and Jean Hathaway, a stage actress. It is said that Hathaway could if he wished have styled himself the Marquis Henri Leopold de Fiennes, the title being inherited from his grandfather, who was commissioned by the King of Belgium to acquire the Sandwich Islands for his country. Ashamed to return home when his mission failed, he established himself as a lawyer in San Francisco in 1850. Rhoady, who was Henri's son, later adopted his wife's maiden name of Hathaway.

In 1908, thanks to these family contacts, Henry Hathaway joined the American Film Company as a child actor. He became a protegé of the prolific director Allan Dwan, whose output averaged a film a day, five days a week. Living and working on the Mexican border, Hathaway received little formal education but acquired an interest in Western lore, which he was to develop later as one of his prime professional assets. In 1912, he moved behind the cameras as a property boy at Universal, abandoning schooling altogether, but soon returned to acting.

America's entry into the First World War in 1917 ended Hathaway's acting career, and he spent the last part of the war as a gunnery instructor at Fort Wingfield School, San Francisco. Discharged in 1919, he worked briefly for the Morris Audit Company but was lured back to

HENRY HATHAWAY

Hollywood as property man for the producer-director Frank Lloyd, whose reputation rested on his consistently successful adaptation of literary classics. Lloyd inspired Hathaway to further his education, and this process continued when Hathaway became an assistant to the director Paul Bern. His passion for travel began when Bern encouraged him to visit India, where he spent nine months collecting material for a documentary on pilgrimages. Although the project fell through, the experience later led to his appointment as director of *The Lives of a Bengal Lancer.*

Hathaway also worked briefly for Sam Goldwyn before moving to Paramount, where he served during the 1920s as assistant director to Josef von Sternberg and Victor Fleming. He said of the latter, "Fleming never had a story conference without me, never went to the front office without me, never did any casting without me, not because he needed to do that but for me to learn. Fleming wasn't a joking man . . . he was a very serious, demanding man, and very positive in what he wanted to get, and most of his leading men were patterned after his own behavior; he was a real tough man. . . . With Fleming, I did *The Virginian.* I did all those early Westerns, all of the Zane Greys, the ones I did over again. I mostly learned from them how to handle people. I would take a script home and think: Now what would *I* tell these people to do to make the scene, how would *I* start it, where would be the climax, how would I get out of it, how do I get rid of the people, where would I do it? . . . And I'd make up my mind, and I'd make a lot of notes, and then I'd see what they did. Entirely different! But you learn."

Hathaway's debut as a director, *Heritage of the Desert* (1932), was the first in a series of eight low-budget Westerns—the Zane Grey stories he "did over again" between 1932 and 1934. Mostly starring Randolph Scott, and all running under sixty-five minutes, they were simple stories, packed with action, uncomplicated in characterization and narrative. Paramount seemed unsure where their novice director should go next. *Come On Marines!* (1934) was a comedy-drama in which the Marines rescue some shipwrecked "children" who turned out to be beautiful American girls (mostly fledgling contractees who were being tested for bigger roles—including Ida Lupino and Clara Lou [later Ann] Sheridan). Paramount then assigned Hathaway to *The Witching Hour* (1934), a love story involving thought transference and mysticism and featuring dependable but second-string players like Sir Guy Standing and John Halliday, before promoting him to direct Shirley Temple, Gary Cooper, and Carole Lombard in *Now and Forever* (1934), a mild romantic comedy about the reformation of a jewel thief. Hathaway had worked as an assistant on many of Gary Cooper's films before coming to direct him, and their mutual respect showed in the natural ease of Cooper's performances in his work for Hathaway.

Cooper also starred in *The Lives of a Bengal Lancer* (1935), along with Franchot Tone, Richard Cromwell, and other officers of the 41st Bengal Lancers serving on the North-West Frontier. They endure capture and torture in a spirit of wry banter before the enemies of the Raj are routed in a stirring cavalry charge. The film was made in California but incorporates some of the footage shot in India the year before by Ernest B. Schoedsack, who was originally assigned to direct. "It is superb cinema stuff," wrote C.A. Lejeune, "robust, eventful, and exciting, with good riding, good fighting, and, oddly enough, good talking, besides those sweeping cavalcades of extras that always do so much to brighten up the screen." It was deservedly an immense success, establishing Hathaway as an important action director (and boosting his salary from a few hundred to six thousand dollars a week).

He was teamed with Cooper yet again in *Peter Ibbetson* (1935), a romantic fantasy cleverly lit by cameraman Charles Lang, and imaginatively designed by Hans Dreier and Robert Usher. Based on George du Maurier's novel, it has elements in common with *The Witching Hour.* The shamelessly sentimental story concerns a young architect who is imprisoned for life for killing the husband of his childhood sweetheart (Ann Harding), but who nevertheless enjoys love and freedom in the dreams he mystically shares with her. The film has a mixed reception in 1935, when some critics though that the elaborate dream sequences failed completely, but a few years later it was discovered by the French surrealists and claimed by André Breton as "a triumph of surrealist thought," using the cinema to "turn our way of feeling upside down." As Garbicz and Klinowski note, "In *Peter Ibbetson* dreams are not treated as moody intrusions, but as independent antonomous entities—and this notion is dear to surrealist art."

The Trail of the Lonesome Pine (1936) was another prestigious project for Hathaway—the first three-color Technicolor film to be made on location. It stars Fred MacMurray and Sylvia Sidney in a story (already filmed twice before) about a young engineer who becomes involved in a long-standing "mountain family" feud. The distinguished cast also includes Henry Fonda, Nigel Bruce, and Beulah Bondi. The picture incorporates some material filmed purely for color effects, but it also gave Hathaway an opportunity to explore themes that have recurred in his later work—his interest in Americana and rural communities, revenge as motivation, and young men proving their manhood. The influence of Hathaway's mentor Victor Fleming has been seen in the consistency of the performances the young director drew from his cast and in his attention to visual detail, which is used both to further the narrative and in the revelation of character.

After *Go West, Young Man* (1936), a Mae West comedy vitiated by the stringent Hays Code regulations, came *Souls at Sea* (1937), co-starring Cooper and George Raft in a tale of skulduggery aboard a sailing ship. *Spawn of the North* (1938) continued this tradition of paired heroes, with Raft and Henry Fonda falling out as friends and partners when Russian pirates undermine the Alaskan fishing industry. Basil Wright praised the movie both for its "vivid and atmospheric" Alaskan location work and for Hathaway's "sensibility and sensitiveness on the set. Observe carefully his direction of the scenes between Raft and [Dorothy] Lamour. Note first the verisimilitude of the settings, second, the modest but unerring rightness of all his camera angles, and third, the sense of the ebb and flow of passion between two tough but inarticulate humans."

Again and again in these early films Hathaway demonstrated his ability to give fresh life to hackneyed material. None of these efforts did much to further his career, however, and after *Spawn of the North* he left Paramount and freelanced for a while. Goldwyn then hired him to direct *The Real Glory* (1939), in which Cooper, Broderick Crawford, and David Niven bat-tle heroically against Moro terrorists after the United States Army pulls out of the Philippines. The nature of the crisis is illustrated with powerful economy in the early scene where a priest is bidding farewell to the departing soldiery ("We who are about to die, salute you"); the camera moves to the end of the jetty, where a shaven-headed Moro swordsman climbs out of the water and charges through a hail of bullets to cut down the commanding officer. Authority figures in Hathaway's films are often dangerously flawed or vulnerable, and in *The Real Glory* the acting commanding officer (Reginald Owen) conceals the fact that he is going blind and makes a desperate situation worse by insisting on rigorous discipline instead of the commonsense initiatives favored by Dr. Canavan (Gary Cooper). Rudy Maté's photography skillfully conveys the isolation of the defenseless town, underlining the basis of the Filipinos' fear as well as setting the scene for the vividly staged action sequences.

Johnny Apollo (1940) was Hathaway's first film for 20th Century–Fox, where he remained for twenty years, making movies in virtually every genre except the musical. *Johnny Apollo* is a gangster yarn about a college graduate choosing crime as a career, and it teamed Hathaway with Tyrone Power, the studio's top star. It was not entirely successful, and interestingly Power is off-screen for long periods, as he was in other Hathaway films in which he starred. Returning briefly to Paramount, Hathaway filmed *The Shepherd of the Hills* (1941), another mountain feud film with John Wayne. It displays a more effective use of landscape than Hathaway's earlier films, and the presentation of violence in this film and in Fox's *Ten Gentlemen From West Point* (1942) demonstrated a new drive and a realistic brutality that derived from a keener visual awareness.

At this stage in his career Hathaway was well established as "a capable handler of big action thrillers and adventure." *The House on 92nd Street* (1945) earned him a new reputation as pioneer of the "semi-documentary" spy or crime thriller. It was Louis de Rochemont, former producer of the *March of Time,* who realized that the files of organizations like the police and the Federal Bureau of Investigation were full of filmable stories that were not only factual but highly dramatic. He sold the ideal of Darryl F. Zanuck of 20th Century–Fox, and Hathaway, with his wide experience of location shooting, was chosen to test the recipe in *The House on 92nd Street.* The FBI, always eager for uncritical publicity, supplied formerly secret information about their infiltration of a wartime ring of fifth columnists. The result, with its wealth of behind-the-scenes detail and authoritative-sounding commentary, captured the public's imagination and spawned many imitations.

Hathaway himself made a second "from the files of" thriller in *13 Rue Madeleine* (1946), a tribute to the work of the OSS in World War II. *Call Northside 777* (1948) is also a semi-documentary, this time about a cynical reporter (James Stewart) who goes from skepticism to a passionate belief in the innocence of a man convicted of murder, and vindicates him at the eleventh hour. The technical paraphernalia of telephoto cameras and lie detectors is used to great effect, and the film has fine performances from Stewart and from Lee J. Cobb as his crusading editor.

Fourteen Hours (1951), in which an intended suicide is poised on a ledge high above New York while a heartlessly fascinated crowd gathers (rather as in Wilder's *Ace in the Hole*), was also based on fact. All of Hathaway's semi-documentaries have certain elements in common, including outstanding second unit work (directed by Hathaway himself rather than by a specialist or assistant) and the characteristic use of a medium two-shot structure for dialogue sequences. By this time Hathaway's camera placement was reflecting an increasing concern with the aesthetic qualities of the image as well as with the information it conveyed.

During the same period Hathaway made some notable contributions to the related genre later dubbed *film noir*—thrillers characterized not only by their dark themes but by low-key location photography. In *The Dark Corner* (1946) Mark Stevens plays a tough private eye who turns to the bottle when he is framed for murder, but whose adoring secretary (Lucille Ball) pulls him together in the nick of time. The movie ends not in the traditional clinch between hero and heroine but in a burst of violent action.

The same is true of *Kiss of Death* (1947), in which Victor Mature stars as a small-time gangster left to defend himself against a killer he has unsuccessfully "fingered." The sentimentalization of such an unsavory "hero" disturbed some critics, but the film was a great commercial success, thanks in large measure to Richard Widmark's stunning debut as an even more unsavory villain, a gigling psychopath obsessed with revenge. Riveting tension is created from the outset, and the mood of quiet menace is sustained through Norbert Brodine's atmospheric camerawork on the streets and in the buildings of Manhattan (some of it shot with a 16mm hand-held camera). Hathaway said that when dialogue was being recorded, "if distant children were shouting or dogs were barking afar off, we went ahead, so that as in real street life noises and oth-er background sounds were recorded very naturally, with the close-to-camera conversation of the principals, with most realistic effect."

The Black Rose (1950), a costume adventure story in which a disinherited Saxon noble (Tyrone Power) becomes a soldier of fortune in Mongolia, has a cast that includes Orson Welles, Jack Hawkins, Cecile Aubry, Michael Rennie, Finlay Currie, Herbert Lom, James Robertson Justice, and Laurence Harvey. Shot largely in North Africa, it was one of the first American movies filmed on location abroad after World War II. For a picture of its sort it is unusual in that it contains no major battle scenes, the story's battles being represented by columns of soldiers marching away from the burning ruins of sacked cities. Tyrone Power plays another of Hathaway's flawed heroes, cynical and greedy, though ultimately triumphant. A technician who worked on the film confirmed the director's reputation as a hard taskmaster: "Hathaway seems to be everywhere at once, and does not recognize that the impossible exists, or that there are one hundred and twenty degrees of sunshine! He drives on, possessed with a fury of direction. Everyone curses, but everyone gets on with the job and the picture is made."

Tyrone Power also stars in *Diplomatic Courier* (1952), a neat thriller which is one of the director's own favorites. Quite untypically for Hathaway, its varied European settings were contrived almost entirely with transparencies in the studio. *Niagara* (1953) is of some interest for Marilyn Monroe's portrayal of a faithless wife, and *23 Paces to Baker Street* (1956) makes intelligent use of sound to underscore the predicament of its blind hero. *From Hell to Texas* (1958), a Western, has been greatly admired for its taut construction and convincing characterization, with excellent performances from Don Murray and Chill Wills (who plays the older mentor who so often appears in Hathaway's movies to guide the young hero in establishing moral priorities). *Legend of the Lost* (1957) stars John Wayne, Sophia Loren, and Rossano Brazzi in a story about a search in the Sahara Desert for a lost holy city. It was an independent production in which Hathaway had invested money of his own and it is visually one of the most interesting of his films, though it failed both critically and financially at the time of its release. Most of the movies Hathaway made for Fox during the 1950s were relatively pedestrian star vehicles, reflecting the general decline in the industry.

Hathaway's reputation began to recover during the 1960s. *Seven Thieves* (1960) is a highly effective "caper" movie about a casino robbery, and it was followed by a string of box-office hits starring John Wayne, among them *North to Alaska* (1960), *Circus World* (1964), and *The Sons of Katie Elder* (1965). In the latter, a Western, Wayne and his ne'er-do-well brothers team up to avenge their mother, whose funeral opens the movie. Andrew Sarris wrote that "the virtues of this kind of Western are largely negative; that is, anti-pop, anti-camp, and anti-pretentious. . . . Henry Hathaway has directed Wayne as he has directed him since *Shepherd of the Hills,* not with the classic force of John Ford and Howard Hawks, but with the serious craftsmanship one professional feels he owes another."

Nevada Smith (1966) is another revenge Western, a variation on the theme of *From Hell to Texas* starring Steve McQueen, and *Five Card Stud* (1968) is in effect a detective story, again set in the Old West, about the hunt for a homicidal religious maniac. Undoubtedly the most successful of Hathaway's late films was *True Grit* (1969), another Western, in which young Mattie Ross (Kim Darby) avenges her father's murder with the help of Rooster Cogburn, a cantankerous, hard-drinking, one-eyed old marshall (John Wayne). Marguerite Roberts' script, based very closely on the original novel by Charles Portis, is one of the most literate works Hathaway ever filmed, rich in humor and strikingly original turns of phrase. The photography, by the veteran cameraman Lucien Ballard, lovingly celebrates the traditional imagery of the Western, and the film is no less a tribute to John Wayne himself (who won a well-deserved Oscar for his performance). "Hathaway is seventy years old and has been making action films since 1933," wrote Richard Schickel, "so he knows instinctively, it seems, when he may invoke our laughter at the conventions of the Western, when he must retain his seriousness about them. His visual style is as simple as Mattie's moral style . . . and as direct as Portis' prose style."

Andrew Sarris has described Hathaway as a competent and unpretentious director, closer in style to William Wellman than John Ford or Howard Hawks, but neater. This has been very much the accepted view, but it is one that is challenged by Stuart M. Kaminsky in a reassessment of Hathaway in *Velvet Light Trap.* Kaminsky maintains that Hathaway "has worked steadily to fashion a remarkably unified and personal body of films as distinctive as any director in American popular film" and goes on to claim, in a surprisingly persuasive argument, that Hathaway's vision is fundamentally mythic and religious. According to Kaminsky, the "depiction of unreality, the conversion of supposedly 'real' settings into personal, unreal visions . . . [has been] a growing interest with Hathaway. Unreality frequently intrudes in

Hathaway's films, most strikingly as the painted backdrop and the optical effect. . . . This unreality is not arbitrary, but a central thematic concern for Hathaway." And Kaminsky cites among other examples the mirage city in *Legend of the Lost* (which he takes as his principal model) and, in the same film, the scene in which "the way to the treasure is pointed out by animated bats flying out of a well."

The heroes in Hathaway's films, Kaminsky maintains, are usually simple and humble men who drink too much or have other human weaknesses but who believe in God or at any rate in some superior force that is closely identified with nature: "They are, like John Wayne in *Legend of the Lost,* mystics in a strange landscape." Very often in Hathaway's mature work (which Kaminsky dates from 1952), his subject is a dangerous quest undertaken by a small group of people in a barren and hostile land. In the course of this quest, the hero shows his respect for the land, the villain exploits it. The villain, in fact, bases his life on illusion and is guilty of hubris (like Brazzi in *Legend of the Lost*). Nevertheless, the villain often seems *initially* a more admirable character than the earthy hero, and the woman on the quest (Sophia Loren in *Legend of the Lost*) prefers him until the true worth of the two men emerges under pressure.

Water in Hathaway's films is very often an agent of spiritual cleansing, according to Kaminsky, the hero in many cases being "immersed in a turbulent river, baptised under the watching eye of his paternal protector"—though the same element is dangerous for Hathaway's villains. Kaminsky also points out how often Hathaway's characters quote (for different purposes) from the Old and the New Testaments, and goes on to examine symbolism in *Legend of the Lost,* where the three skeletons discovered in the holy city unlock the past and seem to comment prophetically on the fate of the three living protagonists. Other such images are cited in support of Kaminsky's thesis that *Legend of the Lost* should be interpreted as a struggle between reality and illusion, body and (misguided) soul: "Hathaway's films are filled with striking mixtures of Christianity and paganism."

Henry Hathaway was married in 1933 to Blanca (Blanche) Estrella Gonzales. They had one son, John Henry. A tall, heavy-set man, Hathaway was a soft-spoken, widely informed conversationalist, his trademark a long cigar that never seemed to grow any shorter. Hathaway was a multimillionaire, the bulk of his fortune deriving from the formation, development, and sale of private corporations unconnected with the movie industry. He died in Los Angeles after a heart attack, at the age of eighty-six.

—*K.C.*

FILMS: Heritage of the Desert, 1932; Wild Horse Mesa, 1932; Under the Tonto Rim, 1933; Sunset Pass, 1933; Man of the Forest, 1933; To the Last Man, 1933; The Thundering Herd, 1933; The Last Round-Up, 1934; Come On Marines!, 1934; The Witching Hour, 1934; Now and Forever, 1934; The Lives of a Bengal Lancer, 1935; Peter Ibbetson, 1935; The Trail of the Lonesome Pine, 1936; Go West, Young Man, 1936; Souls at Sea, 1937; Lest We Forget, 1937 (short); Spawn of the North, 1938; The Real Glory, 1939; Johnny Apollo, 1940; Brigham Young—Frontiersman, 1940; The Shepherd of the Hills, 1941; Sundown, 1941; Ten Gentlemen from West Point, 1942; China Girl, 1942; Home in Indiana, 1944; Wing and a Prayer, 1944; Nob Hill, 1945; The House on 92nd Street, 1945; The Dark Corner, 1946; 13 Rue Madeleine, 1946; Kiss of Death, 1947; Call Northside 777 (also known as Calling Northside 777), 1948; Down to the Sea in Ships, 1949; The Black Rose, 1950; Rawhide (also known as Desperate Siege), 1950; U.S.S. Tea Kettle (retitled You're in the Navy Now), 1951; Fourteen Hours, 1951; The Desert Fox (U.K., Rommel—Desert Fox), 1951; Diplomatic Courier, 1952; The Clarion Call, *episode in* O'Henry's Full House (U.K., Full House), 1952; Niagara, 1953; White Witch Doctor, 1953; Prince Valiant, 1954; Garden of Evil, 1954; The Racers (U.K., Such Men Are Dangerous), 1954; The Bottom of the Bottle (U.K., Beyond the River), 1956; 23 Paces to Baker Street, 1956; Legend of the Lost, 1957; From Hell to Texas (U.K., Manhunt), 1958; Woman Obsessed, 1959; Seven Thieves, 1960; North to Alaska, 1960; The Rivers, The Plains, The Outlaws, *episodes in* How the West Was Won, 1962; Circus World (U.K., The Magnificent Showman), 1964; The Sons of Katie Elder, 1965; Nevada Smith, 1966; The Last Safari, 1967; Five Card Stud, 1968; True Grit, 1969; Raid on Rommel, 1971; Shootout, 1971; Hang-Up, 1973.

ABOUT: Canham, K. The Hollywood Professionals: 1, 1973; Garbicz, A. and Klinowski, J. Cinema: The Magic Vehicle, 1975; Sarris, A. The American Cinema: Directors and Directions 1929–1968, 1968. *Periodicals*—Action May–June 1970; Celuloide August, October, November, December 1970; Cinema (Italy) December 15, 1950; Film Daily April 11, 1952; Film Ideal March 15, 1964; March 1, 1965; Films and Filming November 1962; Focus on Film October 1971; Positif February–March 1972; Scen och Salanz N. 12 1962; Take One February 1976; Velvet Light Trap Winter 1975.

HAWKS, HOWARD (WINCHESTER) (May 30, 1896–December 26, 1977), American director, producer, and scenarist, was born in Goshen, Indiana. A child of the American midwest, like Thomas Edison, in the era of America's romance with inventors and inventions, Hawks would travel on his love of machines to

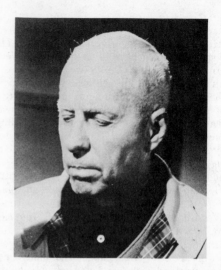

HOWARD HAWKS

the art of machines, the motion picture. The son of a wealthy paper manufacturer and grandson of a wealthy lumberman, Hawks moved west with his family in 1906. They settled in Pasadena, California, where the warmer and drier air was kinder to his mother's asthma. The movies themselves traveled west at about the same time. The young Hawks moved between east and west for his education—prep school at Phillips Exeter, graduation from Pasadena High School, and a degree in engineering from Cornell University. He began to spend his free time with the new movie companies that were turning Hollywood into a company town. In 1917 he worked as a prop boy for Famous Players–Lasky, assisting Marshall Neilan on Mary Pickford films. Later that year he joined the US Army Air Corps as a flying instructor. He would combine his two loves—for flying and filming—in years to come.

In the early 1920s, Hawks shared a Hollywood house with several young men on the threshold of movie distinction—Allan Dwan and Irving Thalberg among them. Thalberg recommended Hawks to Jesse Lasky, who in 1924 was looking for a bright young man to run the story department of Famous Players. For two years Hawks supervised the development and writing of every script for the company that was to become Paramount, the most powerful studio in 1920s Hollywood. William Fox invited Hawks to join his company in 1926, offering him a chance to direct the scripts he had developed. *The Road to Glory* was the first of eight films Hawks directed at Fox in the next three years, all of them silent except *The Air Circus* (1928) and *Trent's Last Case* (1929), part-talkies in the years of Hollywood's transition between silence and sound.

Of the Fox silents, only *Fig Leaves* (1926) and *A Girl in Every Port* (1928) survive. The former is a comedy of gender, tracing domestic warfare from Adam and Eve to their modern descendants. *A Girl in Every Port* is "a love story between two men," in Hawks' words—two brawling sailor buddies who fall for the same woman. The motif of two friends who share the same love would recur in many Hawks sound films, particularly in the 1930s (*Tiger Shark, Today We Live, Barbary Coast, The Road to Glory*). The motif of two wandering pals, enjoying the sexual benefits of travel, returns with a gender reversal in *Gentleman Prefer Blondes*, with Marilyn Monroe and Jane Russell playing the two traveling buddies. More than anything else, *A Girl in Every Port* declared male friendship one of Hawks' primary concerns. With the end of his Fox contract in 1929, Hawks would never again sign a long-term contract with a single studio.

It was the coming of synchronized sound that allowed Hawks to become so independent a film stylist. *The Dawn Patrol* (1930) was a remarkable early sound film in many respects. Its pacifism mirrored the reaction against the First World War in a period that produced such antiwar films as *What Price Glory?*, *The Big Parade*, and *All Quiet on the Western Front*. The flying sequences in *The Dawn Patrol* were as photographically brilliant as they were aeronautically accurate. Flying and filming had never before been so beautifully mated, and Hawks' flavorful dialogue sounded as if it were uttered by human beings, not orating actors. The affected, stilted diction that marred so many early talkies was entirely absent. Dialogue in Hawks' films would always suggest the feel and flavor of spontaneous conversation rather than scripted lines—he in fact not only permitted his players to improvise but deliberately hired players who would and could.

Scarface (1930–1932) brought this spontaneous quality down from the wartime skies to the urban streets. *Scarface* remains simultaneously one of the most brutal and most funny of gangster films—"as vehement, vitriolic, and passionate a work as has been made about Prohibition," in the opinion of Manny Farber. When Tony Camonte lets go with his new machine gun into a rack of pool cues, or the O'Hara gang shoots a restaurant to smithereens, they are murderous children having "fun," one of the most important words in Hawks' critical lexicon. Hawks' antihero Tony, a fanciful portrait of Al Capone sketched by Paul Muni, is not only a spiteful kid; he also nurses an unarticulated and repressed sexual attraction to his own sister and guns down the best friend (George Raft) who invades this

Freudian turf. Hawks' recurrent piece of physical business for Raft—the obsessive flipping of a coin—has survived ever after as the quintessential gangster's tic. It introduced the familiar Hawks method of deflecting psychological revelation from explicit dialogue to the subtle handling of physical objects. As John Belton notes, "Hawks's characterization is rooted in the physical."

Scarface also introduced Hawks to two important professional associates: Howard Hughes, who produced the film and would weave through Hawks' entire career as either ally or enemy; and Ben Hecht, the hard-drinking, wisecracking writer who, like Hawks, wanted to make films that were "fun." Hecht and Hawks were kindred cynics who would work together for twenty years. Hughes, however, had his own war to win. A lifetime foe of film industry censorship boards, Hughes resisted attempts to soften *Scarface*. He finally relented, not by toning down its brutal humor but by inserting a drab lecture on the social responsibility of voters. He also concluded the film with the fallen mobster's whining cowardice, to take the glamor out of his defiance. But Hughes was so enraged at being pressured into these emendations that he withdrew the film from circulation for four decades. Only his death returned it to American audiences.

Hawks traveled to other studios and genres in the 1930s. Columbia gave him a prison movie, *The Criminal Code* (1931). *The Crowd Roars* (1932) at Warner Brothers was his first picture about auto racing, another Hawks hobby; he designed the automobile that won the 1936 Indianapolis 500. *Tiger Shark* (1932), for Warners' subsidiary, First National, took Hawks to sea with Edward G. Robinson and the fishing fleet. Hawks depicted the professional business of tuna fishing in this film with the same documentary accuracy and regard for detail that he devoted to flying in *The Dawn Patrol* or driving in *The Crowd Roars*. His earliest talkies established a key pattern: in the words of Andrew Sarris, "the Hawksian hero is upheld by an instinctive professionalism."

Hawks returned to wartime professionals in *Today We Live* (1933) and *The Road to Glory* (1936). The former was adapted from "Turn About," a story by William Faulkner, and began Hawks' personal and professional association with the writer. Like Hawks, Faulkner loved flying and, like Hawks, had lost a brother in an air crash. Both men also liked drinking and storytelling. Hawks and Faulkner would drink, fly, and tell stories together over the next twenty years. *Today We Live*, made at MGM, began another Hawks pattern—walking off the set when studio bosses interfered with his filming. *Today We Live* was the only film Hawks completed under a three-picture agreement with MGM. After tolerating Louis B. Mayer's interference on this first film, mostly in the handling of star Joan Crawford, Hawks refused to finish two others (*The Prize Fighter and the Lady*, and *Viva Villa!*). He would never return to MGM.

Perhaps Hawks' most interesting genre films in the 1930s were screwball comedies. Hawks was a master of the genre that has come to represent one of the period's most revealing reflections of American aspirations. As the philosopher Stanley Cavell argued, the screwball comedy enacts the "myth of modern marriage," the basis of our culture's idea of happiness. While Hawks always added comic touches to serious stories—from *Scarface* in 1930 to *El Dorado* in 1967—the pure comedy provided much broader comic possibilities. Love and friendship had always been closely intertwined in his films, and since Hawks friends fight as much as they talk, fight because they are friends, each convinced of his own rightness, it was a very short step from male friends to male-female lovers. The Hawks screwball comedy is distinctive in that the hero and heroine are as much friends as lovers and as much fighting opponents as spiritual kin; it is a comedy of ego in which two strong personalities fight because they love.

Hawks' first work in this genre, *Twentieth Century* (1934), was adapted from a stage play by Ben Hecht and Charles MacArthur. Along with Frank Capra's *It Happened One Night*, made in the same year and at the same studio (Columbia), *Twentieth Century* was one of the films that defined the screwball genre. The two warring egos of *Twentieth Century* are the monomaniacal impresario Oscar Jaffe (played by the monomaniacal ham, John Barrymore) and his actress Galatea, Lily Garland (played by Hawks' own cousin, Carole Lombard, in her first major comic role). The film demonstrated several Hawks traits, including breakneck dialogue that refused to soften or sentimentalize the combat, and the revelation of internal psychological states through concrete external objects—the visible, photographic means of making clear inner feelings that his characters never verbally express. To free Lily from her inhibitions as an actress, Oscar jabs her in the buttocks with a pearl-headed pin; during their later separation, this becomes an ironic token of her hidden love for him, preserved in a little shrine of its own. The film also set the two essential Hawks patterns with movie stars: making a familiar star into a comic parody of his own persona (as Hawks would later do with Cary Grant, Hum-

phrey Bogart, John Wayne, and Marilyn Monroe); and inventing the persona of a total unknown (future Hawks Galateas included Frances Farmer, Rita Hayworth, Jane Russell, Lauren Bacall, Montgomery Clift, Joan Collins, and Angie Dickinson).

Bringing Up Baby (1938) at RKO, "the screwiest of the screwball comedies" for Andrew Sarris, was also the first of Hawks' four screwball comedies with Cary Grant. In these films, the smooth Grant not only becomes the alter ego of the icily smooth Howard Hawks behind the camera; he also becomes the butt of jokes that the world longs to inflict on the icily smooth. "Whereas the dramas show the mastery of man over nature . . . ," according to Peter Wollen, "the comedies show his humiliation, his regression." Hawks endlessly submits Grant to degrading attacks on his handsome masculinity, usually by removing his pants and putting him in a dress. In *Bringing Up Baby* Grant is a near-sighted zoologist who spends a midsummer night's eve with Katharine Hepburn, apparently chasing escaped leopards and lost dinosaur bones. What he finds instead is his love and his eyesight—indeed, his recognition that love is the secret of vision. In *His Girl Friday* (1940), adapted from *The Front Page*, another Hecht-MacArthur stage hit, Hawks changes the gender of the original newspaper reporter from male to female (Rosalind Russell), initiating a contest with her editor (Grant) that is both love and war. In the end, she too recovers her eyesight to discover love in their combative friendship.

I Was a Male War Bride (1949) took Grant and Hawks to postwar Germany for another love story that begins as a battle (with Ann Sheridan). But in *Monkey Business* (1952) Grant returns to domestic normalcy, discovering that placid married life (with Ginger Rogers) may be more appropriate to middle age than sexual adventure (with Marilyn Monroe). In this Darwinian comedy of youth and age, Hawks recognizes that both he and his colleagues (star Grant and writer Hecht) are a generation older than they were at the dawn of screwball comedy. Despite its careful symmetrical patterning—John Belton thought it Hawks' "most organic" comedy—the spirit of screwball comedy has itself grown old in *Monkey Business*. Hawks would make only one more comedy, *Man's Favorite Sport?* (1964), which seemed to prove how old both the genre and the director had become. Because Grant himself felt too old for the role, Hawks tried to disguise Rock Hudson as the young Cary Grant.

Grant made one film for Hawks that was not a comedy, *Only Angels Have Wings* (1939), a return to the professional world of flyers and the struggle between vocation, love, and friendship. Those involved in Grant's struggle were the close friend, Kid (Thomas Mitchell), and two women, Bonnie Lee (a homeless drifter played by Jean Arthur) and Judy (his former flame, played by Rita Hayworth in her first screen role). As usual, the Hawks hero finds both a testing ground and meeting place for his professional commitment, personal integrity, and human feeling.

Hawks spent the early 1940s with two personalities less slick, cool, and distant than Grant. Gary Cooper made two films for Hawks, both in 1941. *Sergeant York*, produced at Warners by Jesse Lasky, Hawks' first boss, features Cooper as the homespun pacifist who became a World War I hero. Hawks' most honored film in his lifetime, *Sergeant York* brought him his only Academy Award nomination for best director. *Ball of Fire* takes Cooper into a den of isolated academics, where seven emotional dwarfs are invaded by a Snow White stripper (Barbara Stanwyck). Produced by the ponderous Samuel Goldwyn and photographed by deep-focused Gregg Toland, *Ball of Fire*, was two beats slower but two heart-beats warmer than the products of Hawks' glidingly icy screwball style.

Another wartime alternative to Grant was Humphrey Bogart. The Bogart quality Hawks exploited—quite the opposite of Cooper's open warmth—was a tendency to hide the heart behind a tough mask of emotional indifference and vocal taciturnity. Hawks had always liked characters who did and felt more than they said and Bogart became an especially effective partner for Hawks' newest find, Lauren Bacall. Hawks chose Bacall's name, hair style and characteristic vocal register—much as Oscar Jaffe did Lily Garland's in *Twentieth Century*—and mated Bogart and Bacall in two films at Warners.

For *To Have and Have Not* (1944), Hawks bet his close friend Ernest Hemingway that he could make a good movie out of his "worst novel." Hawks, Faulkner, and frequent collaborator Jules Furthman set the adventures of a Hawks trio—Bogart, Bacall, and alcoholic old buddy Walter Brennan—against a background of wartime espionage in the Caribbean. Like *Casablanca*, Warners' wartime hit of 1942, *To Have and Have Not* brings the loner Bogart to a patriotic affirmation; unlike *Casablanca*, the affirmation comes not from a romantic renunciation but a reconciliation of love, friendship, and vocation—as is typical of Hawks. *The Big Sleep* (1946), a wittily sexual adaptation of the Raymond Chandler novel, plunged the combative lovers into a labyrinthine maze of plot points that Hawks deliberately refused to elucidate. In Bogart and Bacall, Hawks had found a matched

pair who contrasted warm interiors with cool exteriors, powerful feelings with protective reticence. They overcome their reticence in the usual Hawks way—by working together on a job and having fun together on a lark. His onscreen team generated even more interest with their offscreen romance and marriage.

If the decade and a half from 1938 to 1952 marked Hawks' Cary Grant period, split by the war years, the final two decades of Hawks' creative career marked his John Wayne period. *Red River* (1948) was both Hawks' first Wayne film and his first Western apart from *The Outlaw*, a Billy the Kid film that Hawks began in 1941 but quit on account of conflict with its producer, Howard Hughes. Hughes' resulting resentment had considerable impact on *Red River*, for he demanded that Hawks delete footage resembling scenes in *The Outlaw* or face a lawsuit. *Red River* was Hawks' most epic film, the story of a cattle drive from Texas to Kansas, in which the wanderers travel thousands of miles, facing both the external challenge of the physical universe and the internal struggle against their own psychological defects. Wayne plays the older rancher, Thomas Dunson, a man whose will, determination, and courage have built a cattle empire; Montgomery Clift, in his first film role, plays the young partner, Matthew Garth—Dunson's adopted son, friend, and "lover." When Dunson's unswerving commitment to his own values threatens the success of the drive, Matthew usurps Dunson's command in a Western *Mutiny on the Bounty*. Dunson swears to track Matthew down and kill him. He tracks him down, but as father faces son and friend faces friend, Dunson learns that a vow spoken in haste and anger is not worth defending. In *Red River* Hawks shaped the essential John Wayne persona—the inflexible man of honor, courage, and will whom no adversary can break but love can bend.

After *Red River*, Hawks and Wayne took three more trips to the Old West—in *Rio Bravo* (1959), *El Dorado* (1967), and *Rio Lobo* (1970). They also traveled to the wilds of Africa in *Hatari!* (1962), where Hawks' extended sequences of tracking wild animals provide another masterly film document of courageous and knowledgeable professionals performing an exotically difficult job. As both Wayne and Hawks grew older, their films together showed their age while defying it, settling into a comfortable social landscape with comfortable friends to perform tasks beyond the capacities of younger, less experienced men. If Robin Wood "were asked to choose a film that would justify the existence of Hollywood, . . . it would be *Rio Bravo*." This enclosed "chamber Western" returns to familiar moral and emotional terrain—the testing of friendship under duress (Wayne and the drunken Dean Martin); succeeding generations of competent professionals (Wayne, the cackling Walter Brennan in a final role for Hawks, and popular teen-star Ricky Nelson); and the comic clumsiness of professional men with provocative women (Wayne and Angie Dickinson). As the Hawks films move through the 1960s, they feel progressively less fast, frantic, and brilliant, more leisurely, relaxed, and warm, "with an overall serenity that grows steadily up to *Rio Bravo* and *Hatari!*" (Wood).

Those late Hawks films that do not saunter with Wayne explore other genre trails. *The Big Sky* (1952) and *Land of the Pharaohs* (1955) follow the historical path sketched by *Red River*—the former into the American past of Lewis and Clark, the latter into ancient Egypt for Hawks's last collaboration with William Faulkner before the novelist's death. *The Thing* (1950), produced by Hawks but directed by his editor, Christian Nyby, was Hawks' only expedition into the popular postwar genre of science fiction—confronting the cosmic unknown in a new era of nuclear bombs and space travel. *Red Line 7000* (1965) was Hawks' return to the race-car world of *The Crowd Roars*.

The final fifteen years of Hawks' life brought him wider public recognition than he had ever known in his busiest years of studio activity. Respected inside the industry as one of Hollywood's sturdiest directors of top stars in taut stories, Hawks acquired little fame outside it until the rise of the *auteur* theory in France, England, and America between 1953 and 1962. To some extent, it was the *auteur* theory that made Hawks a household name and Hawks that made the *auteur* theory a household idea. In their campaign against both European "art films" and solemn adaptations of literary classics, articulators of the *auteur* view—François Truffaut, Jacques Rivette, Peter Wollen, V. S. Perkins, Ian Cameron, Andrew Sarris, John Belton, William Paul—looked for studio directors of Hollywood genre films whose work displayed both a consistent cinematic style and consistent narrative motifs.

Hawks was the model of such a director. He spent fifteen years in interviews denying any serious artistic aspiration, claiming that all he wanted to do was tell a story. But a Hawks story had an unmistakable look, feel, and focus. His style, though never obtrusive, had always been built on certain basic elements: a careful attention to the sources and qualities of light (the lamps that always hang in a Hawks frame); the counterpoint of on-frame action and off-frame sound; the improvisationally casual sound of

Hawks' conversation; the reluctance of characters to articulate their inner feelings, and the transference of emotional material from dialogue to physical objects; symmetrically balanced frames that produce a dialectic between opposite halves of the frame. So too, Hawks' films, no matter what the genre, handled consistent plot motifs: a small band of professionals committed to doing their jobs as well as they could; pairs of friends who were also lovers and opponents; reversals of conventional gender expectations about manly men and womanly women. Dressed as routine Hollywood genre pictures, Hawks' films were psychological studies of people in action, simultaneously trying to be true to themselves and faithful to the group. In his classic conflict of love and honor, Hawks was the American movie descendant of Corneille.

He died at the age of eighty-one in Palm Springs, California, from complications arising from a broken hip when he tripped over one of his dogs. Even as he grew older he continued to ride his motorcycle and raise his martini. He was married three times and had four children, two of whom work in the film industry. His primary legacies are his films and his persona as the modest professional in a bombastic business, a man who could make the structures and strictures of that business work for him, so he could tell the stories he wanted to tell in the way he wanted to tell them.

—*G.M.*

FILMS: The Road to Glory, 1926; Fig Leaves, 1926; The Cradle Snatchers, 1927; Paid to Love, 1927; A Girl in Every Port, 1928; Fazil, 1928; (with Lewis B. Seiler) The Air Circus, 1928; Trent's Last Case, 1929; The Dawn Patrol, 1930; The Criminal Code, 1931; Scarface (Shame of a Nation), 1932; The Crowd Roars, 1932; Tiger Shark, 1932; Today We Live, 1933; (with Jack Conway; Hawks uncredited) Viva Villa!, 1934; Twentieth Century, 1934; Barbary Coast, 1935; Ceiling Zero, 1936; The Road to Glory, 1936; (with William Wyler) Come and Get It, 1936; Bringing Up Baby, 1938; Only Angels Have Wings, 1939; His Girl Friday, 1940; (with Howard Hughes; Hawks uncredited) The Outlaw, 1940, released 1943; Sergeant York, 1941; Ball of Fire, 1942; Air Force, 1943; To Have and Have Not, 1944; The Big Sleep, 1946; Red River, 1948; A Song Is Born, 1948; I Was a Male War Bride (You Can't Sleep Here), 1949; The Big Sky, 1952; "The Ransom of Red Chief" *episode in* O. Henry's Full House, 1952; Monkey Business, 1952; Gentlemen Prefer Blondes, 1953; Land of the Pharaohs, 1955; Rio Bravo, 1959; Hatari!, 1962; Man's Favorite Sport?, 1964; Red Line 7000, 1965; El Dorado, 1967; Rio Lobo, 1970. *Published scripts*—To Have and Have Not, edited by Bruce Kawin, University of Wisconsin, 1980; Bringing Up Baby, edited by Gerald Mast, Rutgers University Press (in preparation; 1988).

ABOUT: Belton, J. The Hollywood Professionals, Vol. 3 (Hawks, Borzage, Ulmer), 1974; Bogdanovich, P. The Cinema of Howard Hawks, 1962; Cavell, S. Pursuits of Happiness: The Hollywood Comedy of Remarriage, 1981; Giannetti, L. Masters of the American Cinema, 1981; Gili, J. A. Howard Hawks, 1971 (in French); McBride, J. (ed.) Focus on Howard Hawks, 1972; McBride, J. (ed.) Hawks on Hawks, 1982; Mast, G. The Comic Mind, 1979 (rev. ed.); Mast, G. Howard Hawks, Storyteller, 1982; Mast, G. and Cohen, M. (eds.) Film Theory and Criticism, 1979 (rev. ed.); Missiaen, J.-C. Howard Hawks, 1966 (in French); Peary, G. and Shatzkin, R. (eds.) The Modern American Novel and the Movies, 1978; Poague, L. Howard Hawks, 1982; Willis, D. C. The Films of Howard Hawks, 1975; Wood, R. Howard Hawks, 1982 (rev. ed.). *Periodicals*—Cahiers du Cinéma February 1956; Film Comment March–April 1974, July–August 1977, January–February 1978, March–April 1978; Films and Filming October 1968; Focus February and March 1967; Movie December 1962; New York Times December 28, 1977; Sight and Sound Spring 1971; Take One January–February 1971, July–August 1971; Wide Angle Summer 1976.

JOSIF HEIFITZ

HEIFITZ (or HEIFITS or HEIFETZ or KHEIFITZ, etc.), JOSIF (July 17, 1905–), Soviet director and scenarist, writes in Russian: "I was born on July 17, 1905, in a family of a provincial pharmacist and spent my childhood in a small White Russian town. When I was fifteen my parents moved to Kremenchug, a small industrial city on the banks of the Dnieper. There I finished school and left for Leningrad to continue my education. I think the story of my life will shed some light on my passions in art and the basis of my style, which consciously and subconsciously developed throughout my directing career. I tried to bring humor, which I believe accompanies men even in the most tragic and darkest moments, into my films as an integral reaction of the individual to reality. I learned this from Chekhov, whose work I have loved since childhood and from whom I learn even now. Chekhov is not only my teacher but also the author of three classic short stories, on which three of my films are based. I am referring to *Lady with a Lapdog, Ionych (In the Town C.)*, and the *Duel (The Bad Good Man)*.

"I do not believe those who claim to have loved their future professions since childhood. As a child I loved railway engines, and all the relatives said, 'He will be an engineer!' That was not to be; I hated math, and my achievements in physics were only mediocre. At fifteen, after losing my father, I started working to help my mother. A friend helped me find employment at a military tribunal. There my duties, like those of any other office boy, were not complicated.

However, twice a month I brought home bread, a jar of amber-colored butter, and a lump of sugar as hard as marble. I was given a uniform: combat boots with thick soles, and a large, shaggy sheepskin hat. So intimidating was my appearance in the sheepskin hat that ushers in local movie houses did not dare ask for my ticket. Taking advantage of this, I saw evey single movie, without straining my meager budget with the costs of admission. Thus began my fascination with cinematography. Regardless of whether or not all these dramas and Westerns appealed to me, they made me wonder about a mysterious and fascinating occupation, that allows its followers to imitate life and emotion with such perfection. I strove to comprehend how—the torrential rains, simooms and thunderstorms, fires, pursuits, and characters either swept by joy or crushed by fear, crying from hardship or surrendering to love—how all that was in control of a single person, whose name was prominent in the titles preceding the film. I ransacked the town's library for everything related to film, but there my endeavors stopped. To study? But where? Neither All-Union State Institute of Cinematography (VGIK), nor any other educational establishment where cinematography would be taught, existed at the time. Even if they had, they were so far away from our cosy town, and I had no money for a train ticket. Supporting myself and helping mother, I delivered official papers, swept the floor in the courtroom, and then remained there unnoticed, watching the trial proceedings. Before me passed a long line of types and personalities. Each one of the defendants had a past, rich with events and experiences. My eyes were fixed on their faces as I listened to the confused testimony of the witnesses and the quiet confessions of the guilty, sometimes contrived and delivered with theatrical pathos. That is how I, but a boy, became privy to the most intimate aspects of human nature and grew aware of its astonishing complexity. The defendants alternated between kulaks and officers of the White Army, anarchists and members of the (green) gangs, crooked supply sergeants and deserters. Many begged for mercy, but some met the condemning verdict with a smile. I saw crafty chicanery and compulsive greed, subhuman hatred and true remorse. In the evening, by the light of a dim lamp, I was dictated a list of items confiscated during searches. There were photographs of beautiful women, handsome men with neat haircuts, touching portraits of engaged couples, dried flowers in a book, bandits' knives fashioned from flat German bayonets, cards and cocaine, counterfeit money and a little cross in a candy box. How colorful and wondrous life is! As though in a film, (frames) of the civil war followed one another in quick succession before my boyish eyes, images of confused people who have lost forever their security and comfort in the crumbling of the old order. I never ceased wondering at how closely intertwined in a single character were valor and cowardice, good and evil. All these colorful experiences became useful much later, when I became a professional director.

"Once, after putting on my huge shaggy hat so terrifying to ushers, I saw myself in the mirror and realized that childhood was over. The time had come to venture into life, and a long forgotten dream of the cinema once again stirred in my soul. And at that moment I had a bit of luck. My uncle in Leningrad suddenly remembered his provincial nephew. Either from feelings of kinship or from fear of being forced out of his spacious apartment (at that time, due to a housing shortage, childless families were forced to move into smaller living quarters), he invited me to stay with him in Leningrad. And so I was in that beautiful city. In the first few months I was possessed by Leningrad. Hungry and wet, I splashed through the mess of March snow, regarded with great suspicion by doormen, along the banks of Neva, aimlessly walked the grim staircases of the Kolomna, imagining myself as Raskolnikov from *Crime and Punishment*. Imitating Gogol's Akak Akkyevich [from *The Overcoat*], I froze in the winds of Senate Square, and I read *Bronze Horseman* aloud before the statue of Pushkin on Marat street. There I understood and felt the tremendous influence of atmosphere and environment, which form what is generally referred to as background in the cine-

ma, on the mood, thoughts, and character of a human being.

"Time passed quickly, and it was necessary to look for work. Wandering throughout the city, living from earnings on occasional film reviews, I came upon a gorgeous town house, owned in the past by some great duke. Now the house was occupied by an institution known as a School of Screen Art, where I enrolled without hesitation. In the very recent past the school had housed such future stars of cinematography as the director Fredrick Ermler, and the brothers Vasiliev, the coauthors of an internationally acclaimed film *Chapaev*. However, we dreamed of creating a new and a revolutionary art, knowing that new words and forms would have to be found to express the new concepts. At this time the school was still dominated by the stale spirit of the prerevolutionary art, with its hackneyed views on acting, 'photogenety,' and other such concepts foreign to our perception. Sitting in lecture halls and watching rehearsals we laughed among ourselves, and openly challenged our instructors at oral examinations.

"Soon I ostentatiously left the school. It was a time of searching and experimentation in the arts, a time of gaudy and loud manifestos by various studios and groups, a time of artistic bankruptcy for many established and accepted movements. We realized then that no teachers were capable of teaching us anything, that we had to learn for ourselves and establish cinematography anew.

"The ambition of our dreams, however, was matched only by the modesty of our diets. When our wallets were depleted completely, we went off to the Labor Exchange. [The Labor Exchange was an institution in post-revolutionary Russia, similar in function to an unemployment office.] There people of various professions offered their services and there was a hall, where extras were engaged for mass scenes. My friends and I, without parting with the dreams of the new art, played 'the crowd' in the first historical films, falling into the snow 'cut down' by the rounds from cossack rifles. The romantic dreams of the great new art were far removed from the exhausting and prosaic filmings of the mass scenes, the jammed dressing rooms, the crude familiarity from assistants, the waiting in the cold, without food or drink, or with a hurriedly gulped-down sandwich, half stale bread, half hair from a badly glued-on beard. I calmed myself with the thoughts of the students to the great masters of Renaissance, who waited on their masters, lit fires in the studios and prepped canvases. As unpleasant as they were, my experiences from these days proved very useful in the future.

"On one summer day in 1928, I sacrificed dinner, bought the best paper I could find, hired a typist, and dictated my first script. With it I took my first steps through the front entrance of a famous film studio, later known as Lenfilm (as an extra I used the rear entrance). The halls were filled with the new generation of cinematographers. Future movie star Anna Sten, with large liquid eyes, stood in line for make up, Grigori Kozintzev and Leonid Trauberg hurried to the filming of the *New Babylon.*

"After lengthy deliberations my script was rejected, but my 'bookcase' knowledge and terminology from the famous book-manifesto by Bella Ballasha *Vidimyi Chelovek* (*Visible Man*) had an effect. I was given a job in the lowest possible capacity, that of an intern-assistant to the director. I led a dual existence. On one hand, I secretly nurtured ideas for future films, my head swelling with plots and visions. On the other hand, I was also a jack-of-all-trades, learning the skills of the profession as in the time of the Renaissance. I did more than anyone, both idlers and experienced administrators conspired to provide me with the benefits of all possible experiences. Everyone tried to shift all tasks onto my young shoulders. I had dozens of responsibilities. In the morning I made wake-up calls to actors, I was in charge of 'wind', 'blizzard', and 'snow', I laced up the tall boots of the heroine, and I waved flags and screamed the director's orders into a megaphone, to make them heard at the rear of the set. Learning the techniques of the profession the hard way was a great school and I am not sorry to have dedicated to it many of my best days. I moved up quickly, and once, at the initiative of the Young Communist League committee, my friend, Alexander Zarkhi, and I were given an opportunity to direct our own major film. The film was to deal with young people like us. The opening went off well, the film was written up and debated. The film had a symbolic title—*Into the Wind* (*Veter v Litso*). This was the beginning. Many, many years have passed since then. Thirty films are now behind me. Without false modesty I can say to have lived these years well, constantly working in the name of the ideal, for which we strive and in which we hold faith. In my best works I feel how vitally important was my experience of observations in the courtroom, how influential in the development of my sensitiveness and taste were the impressions of Leningrad, how useful was the store of practical knowledge acquired en route from a student to an apprentice and from an apprentice to master. Well then, when did I finally justify the exalted and proud title of a professional director? In any case much later than the completion of my first film. Maybe it was when, in spite of the scepticism of my peers, I tried to tell about the 'Deputy from the Baltics,' a great scientist, who plunges into the thick of the revolution. A child telling about an old man—it seemed ridiculous. Maybe I felt the power of the art, when I trembled while a fabulous actress Vera Maretskaya succeeded in portraying a spiritual awakening of a Russian peasant woman, who paid in suffering for her deliverance from slavery. And maybe it was later still, when I learned from Chekhov the humanity of art.

"Every new script in its very essence confronts me with that same dreaded question: are all your techniques, your technology, your system of norms and rules, are they still useful for the expression of your thoughts, your doubts, your pain and your convictions? And every time I pause before a new problem, choosing the most complex route, feeling my way in the dark, navigating by the stars, all past experience seems naive, all rules and laws outdated. And thus to the end!"

Heifitz was born in Minsk. In 1927 he left the Leningrad Technicum of Screen Arts along with his friend Alexander Zarkhi, who is a few years his junior. They began their careers together as scriptwriters at the Leningrad Sovkino studios and collaborated on several scenarios for silent films, including Alexander Ivanov's *Transport of Fire* (1929). According to some accounts, they had a hand in directing a movie called *A Song of Steel*, but the first film clearly attributed to them as codirectors was *Veter v litso* (*Against the Wind*, 1929), a story about Komsomols (Young Communists) struggling to eradicate vestiges of the bourgeois past. It encountered criticism for a scene in which the Komsomols, eager to stamp out alcoholism, make a violent raid on a tavern.

Thereafter, for the next twenty years, all of Heifitz's films were made in collaboration with Zarkhi. *Poldien* (*Noon,* 1931) was followed by *Moi rodina* (*My Country,* 1932), which looks at life on either side of the Sino-Soviet border, showing how similar the problems and aspirations of Vaska, a Red Army soldier, are to those of Vana, a Chinese worker. *Gorjace d eneki* (*Hectic Days,* 1935), set during the period of rearmament and military modernization of the Second Five-Year Plan, centers on a young tank officer and his girlfriend.

None of these movies attracted much attention, but Heifitz and Zarkhi's next film was a major success. The hero of *Deputat Baltiki* (*Baltic Deputy,* 1937) is Professor Polezhayev, a distinguished scientist well into his seventies who at first impatiently rejects the demands of the proletariat but is gradually won over to their cause. During the 1917 Revolution he risks everything to join the Bolsheviks and the sailors of the Baltic Fleet and is eventually elected to the Petrograd Soviet. The scenario, suggested by incidents in the life of the scientist K. A. Timiriazef, was written by the directors in collaboration with Leonid Rakhmanov and "D. Dell" (Leonid Lyubashevsky). Polezhayev is played with great subtlety by Nikolai Cherkasov, who at that time was best known for comedy roles (including one in *Hectic Days*). Cherkasov wrote later that "sooner or later every actor comes across a role that opens up new vistas before him, that perfectly suits his abilities." As soon as he read the script of *Baltic Deputy,* he was convinced that, although he was only thirty-two and Polezhayev was seventy-five, the role was "the chance I had been longing for. . . . I virtually forced myself on the directors."

According to Jay Leyda, *Baltic Deputy* became a model for films in the "historic realism" genre: "This youthful film about an old man derived its style from both *Chapaev* and *Maxim*—the full-bodied personal drama of the one, and the wise, selected reconstruction of the other. The style, so simple as to appear easily imitated, conceals itself behind the figure of Professor Polezhayev, acted by Nikolai Cherkasov, to whom this film brought world fame." It was, indeed, shown all over the world and warmly praised for its convincing revelation of how character develops and changes as a result of inner conflict.

Heifitz and Zarkhi repeated this triumph with another film about an individual transformed by the Revolution. *Chlen pravitelstva* (*Member of the Government/The Great Beginning,* 1940), from a script by Katerina Vinogradskaya, tells the story of Alexandra Sokolova, an exploited and almost illiterate peasant woman who, after the Revolution, fights her way up to become first the director of her collective farm and eventually a member of the Supreme Soviet. As in *Baltic Deputy,* the propaganda content is played down and the emphasis is on the careful and convincing exploration of character development. The result has been generally recognized as an interesting contribution to the theme of women's emancipation and one of the most accomplished Soviet films of the period. It made a star of Vera Maretskaya, an actress who (like Cherkasov) had previously specialized in comedy roles but who studied "a vast mass of materials" in her determination to play the part of Sokolova without "the slightest false note."

Yevo zovut Sukhe-Bator (*His Name Is Sukhe-Bator,* 1942), a war drama filmed in Mon-

golia, had Alexander Ginsburg as cinematographer and Cherkasov in the lead role, but was not much noticed. It was followed by *Malakhov Kurgan* (*The Last Hill,* 1944), a war film that was shelved, reportedly on aesthetic rather than ideological grounds. Heifitz and Zarkhi were then asigned to make a feature-length documentary, *The Defeat of Japan* (1946). This compilation film, assembled mostly from newsreels about the Soviet Far Eastern campaign against the Japanese in 1945, is one of the best of all Soviet war documentaries and received a Stalin Prize.

Heifitz and Zarkhi made three more movies together after the war. The most notable of these seems to have been *Vo imya zhizni* (*In the Name of Life,* 1947), about a doctor's fight against paralysis, but none of their postwar films attained the international success of their previous hits, and presumably for this reason, the partnership broke up. Zarkhi subsequently scored a great success with *The Heights* (1957), a love story with an industrial background, and made an interesting version of *Anna Karenina,* among other films; Heifitz went on to reveal talents not evident during his years of collaboration.

Apart from *Vesna v Moskve* (*Spring in Moscow,* 1953), a straightforward adaptation of a stage hit, Heifitz's first solo film was *Bolshaya semya* (*The Big Family,* 1954), based on the novel *Zhurbiny* by V. Kochetov. An absorbing and convincing study of a family involved in the shipbuilding industry, it combines low-key propaganda for Soviet industrial progress with Heifitz's characteristic concern for psychological exploration, and has a notable performance by Alexei Batalov as Matvei Zhurbin. It was well received on release but only later recognized as a forerunner—in its freedom from political sermonizing—of the brief renaissance in Soviet cinema that followed Stalin's death. *Delo Rumiantseva* (*The Rumiantsev Case,* 1955) was even more successful—an extremely enjoyable thriller about a truck driver wrongly accused of a crime and his workmates' efforts to prove his innocence.

Then, after *Dorogoi moi chelovek* (*My Dear Man,* 1958), based on the novel *Impudence* by U. Nazarov, came *Dama s sobachkoi* (*The Lady With the Little Dog,* 1959), a film in a very different vein from any of its predecessors and, in the opinion of many critics, a masterpiece. It was adapted (by the director himself) from Chekhov's story about the love affair that develops between two lonely people, both unhappily married, when they meet by chance on vacation in Yalta. For the man, the liaison at first seems almost boringly casual; it is only later, back in

Moscow and enduring his wife's trivial social round, that he realizes his life depends upon it. The relationship is resumed—snatched meetings in seedy hotel rooms—but the couple are caught "like two birds of passage locked in separate cages"; neither of them is quite brave enough to fly free: "It seemed that in a little while a solution would offer itself, a new, lovely life would begin."

There was universal praise for the sensitivity of Andrei Moskvin's black-and-white photography of Yalta in summer and Moscow in winter, and for the "exquisitely responsive" performances of Ya Savvina and Alexei Batalov. The film was called "effortlessly exact" in its period details—even in such things as the physiognomy and carriage of the actors—and in its period atmosphere: "the sense of that timeless world with its great stretches of yawning lethargy and its small gestures towards action." One critic complained of the "cumbersome and unrelenting rhythm" of the later sequences, but Isabel Quigly was one of several reviewers delighted by this quality of "reticence, stillness, the right degree of slowness; the marvellous atmospheric weight of moments in which nothing happens, or hardly, and the suggestiveness of very simple happenings, like someone leaning out of a window; the variety of light and weather and, even more, the variety of feeling that can be shown in two quite ordinary faces, conditioned . . . to control what they feel; a closeness to life that is the more striking because its conventions are those of another age."

Ingmar Bergman also praised the film for daring to be slow, and compared its scrupulous care with the looseness and "laxity" of the work of the *nouvelle vague*; he said it was "like having a glassful of healthy spring water after being forced to drink poor Pernod for a long time." There was general agreement that Heifitz had "never before achieved anything like this." *The Lady With the Little Dog* was called "the most satisfying translation of Chekhov the screen has ever given us" and "a rarely satisfying work of art in its own right." It received an award at Cannes.

After two other features came Heifitz's second Chekhov adaptation, *V gorodye "S"* (*In the Town of "S,"* 1966), based on a story called "Ionych." It traces the decline of Dr. Startsev (Anatoli Papanov) from an idealistic young physician to a fat, rich, and cynical exploiter of the poor. Richard Roud had written of *The Lady With the Little Dog* that it had "little to do with politics and yet its mood elegiac sadness helps one more fully to understand the world from which a Lenin came, and from which a Lenin

simply *had* to come." The same is true of *In the Town of "S,"* and more explicitly so—it is quite clearly the triviality, venality, and boredom of provincial society that destroys Dr. Startsev— that and his hopeless love for a product of that society, the spoiled and feckless Ekaterina (Nonna Terentieva). To point up (by contrast) the inertia of this doomed society, Heifitz introduced the figure of Chekhov himself into the film, showing him worn out by a lifetime of hard work in the service of humanity and art.

Some critics found this last device clumsy and unfortunate, and there were complaints also about the pace and structure of the film. It was greatly enjoyed, nevertheless, for its sidelong humor, warmth, and delicacy. One reviewer wrote that "the background is sketched in with deliciously leisurely wit: the cosy bourgeois home with its touchingly absurd literary salon where the mother reads her unpublished, leatherbound romances to an audience of dozing, politely applauding guests, and father livens things up with his banter and endless practical jokes; the orchard where the girl flirts with her ungainly suitor . . . the provincial ball with its wheezy orchestra and elderly gallants snoozing under the aspidistra, giving the girl a glimpse of the high life she yearns for. . . . Time passes, and time recurs. The doctor grows rich and fat, the girl comes back, weary and wiser. . . . And in one of the most touching scenes in the film, girl and doctor meet briefly . . . to stir a love that is dead and forgotten."

Saliut Marya! (*Salute Marya,* 1970) is a tribute to a Russian woman (played by Ada Rogovtseva) who married a Spaniard, lost husband and child in the Spanish Civil War, and returned to the Soviet Union to immerse herself in intelligence work. The most notable of Heifitz's subsequent films was *Asya* (*Love Should Be Guarded,* 1978), based on Turgenev's story about a love affair between a weak man and a strong woman; it brought Elena Korenova an award as best actress at Taormina. Heifitz's 1980 film *Vpervye Zamushem* (*First Marriage*) won first prize at Karlovy Vary.

Heifitz is not a stylistic innovator but an exceptionally gifted interpreter of good scripts (including his own), an acute observer, and a brilliant director of actors, many of whom have paid tribute to his patience, tact, and willingness to allow them their own interpretations of a role. In *The Lady With the Little Dog* he showed that "in the right hands conventional methods can achieve the most excitingly original and unconventional results."

FILMS: (*with Alexander Zarkhi*) Veter v litso (Against the Wind/Facing the Wind), 1929; Poldien (Noon),

1931; Moi rodina (My Country/My Motherland), 1932; Gorjace d eneki (Hectic Days/Red Army Days), 1935; Deputat Baltiki (Baltic Deputy), 1937; Chlen pravitelstva (Member of the Government/The Great Beginning), 1940; Yevo zovut Sukhe-Bator (His Name Is Sukhe-Bator), 1942; Malakhov Kurgan (Malakov Hill/The Last Hill), 1944; The Defeat of Japan, 1946 (documentary); Vo imya zhizni (In the Name of Life), 1947; Dragotsennye zerna (Precious Grain), 1948; Ogni Baku (Fires of Baku/Flames Over Baku), 1950. (*alone*)—Vesna v Moske (Spring in Moscow), 1953; Bolshaya semya (The Big Family/The Great Family), 1954; Delo Rumiantseva (The Rumiantsev Case), 1955; Dorogoi moi chelovek (My Dear Man/The Cause We Serve), 1958; Dama s sobachkoi (The Lady With the Little Dog), 1959; Gorizont (Horizon), 1961; Den schastya (A Day of Happiness), 1964; V gorodye "S" (In the Town of "S"), 1966; Saliut Marya! (Salute Marya), 1970; Plohoy Horoshii Chelovek (The Bad Good Man/The Bad Goody), 1973; Edinstvennaya (The One and Only/The Only One), 1976; Asya (Love Should Be Guarded), 1978; Vpervye Zamushem (First Marriage), 1980.

ABOUT: Birkos, A. S. Soviet Cinema, 1976; Leyda, J. Kino, 1960. *Perodicals*—Panoráma Autumn 1976; Soviet Film 2 1967, 12 1975, 9 1976, 10 1979; Variety December 29, 1982.

ALFRED HITCHCOCK

HITCHCOCK, Sir ALFRED (JOSEPH)

(August 13, 1899–April 28, 1980), Anglo-American director, producer and scenarist, was born in Leytonstone, at that time a village on the eastern outskirts of London. He was the third and youngest child of William Hitchcock, a greengrocer and poulterer, and his wife Emma (born Whalen). Hitchcock's father seems to have been a stern, rather distant figure; his mother he recalled as a placid woman, "shaped like a cottage loaf." Both his parents were Catholics, and he grew up in what he later depicted as a somewhat stifling atmosphere of working-class respectability and strict Catholic morality. "I was what is known as a well-behaved child. At family gatherings I would sit quietly in a corner, saying nothing. . . . I played by myself, inventing my own games." One such game was to travel over every route served by London Omnibus Company.

It was also to childhood experiences that Hitchcock attributed the insistent fear of punishment and the processes of law that pervades his films. A much-retailed anecdote relates how, when he was about five and had committed some childish misdemeanor, his father sent him to the local police station with a note. The sergeant read it, then locked the boy in a cell for five minutes or so, saying, "This is what we do to naughty boys." Hitchcock's preoccupation with guilt may have been further developed by

his education, from 1908 onwards, at St. Ignatius College, Stamford Hill, where the Jesuit fathers dispensed corporal punishment with pious rigor. "It wasn't done casually, you know. It was rather like the execution of a sentence. . . . You spent the whole day waiting for the sentence to be carried out." Not that he was often in trouble; he seems to have been a shy, quiet, slightly melancholy child, academically adequate but undistinguished, and with no aptitude for games.

When Hitchcock was fourteen his father died. A few months earlier he had left school, aware of no particular vocation, but with a talent for drawing and a vague interest in things mechanical. On the strength of this he was sent to the London School of Engineering and Navigation, where he studied mechanics, electricity, acoustics, and navigation. His training completed, he took a job with the W. T. Henley Telegraph Company as a technical clerk, and stayed there throughout the First World War. (He was turned down for active service on medical grounds, being then, as he would always remain, considerably overweight.) After some years of boredom checking estimates, his graphic skills got him transferred to the company's advertising department, where the work was a good deal more interesting. But by now his sights were set on a job in the movie industry.

As a child Hitchcock had been taken on numerous enjoyable visits to both the cinema and the theatre, but had always preferred the cinema. From the age of sixteen or so he began to study film journals—the trade and technical press, rather than the fan magazines—and realized that filmmaking was what he really wanted to do. His chance came in 1919, when he heard that Famous Players–Lasky (later to become Paramount) were opening a studio in Islington, North London. Hitchcock designed a number of drawings suitable for illustrating title-cards and took them around to the studio. The management were impressed enough to offer him some commissioned work and soon afterwards a full-time job.

Over the next two years Hitchcock designed title-cards for a dozen features produced at the Islington studios, while also serving the informal apprenticeship in every aspect of filmmaking that formed the basis of his formidable technique. Nearly all the other personnel, and the working arrangements, were American—giving him, he always said, a professional head start over most of his compatriots. "All my early training was American, which was far superior to the British." Being bright, industrious, and willing, Hitchcock soon found himself lending a hand with scriptwriting, set designing, editing, and even directing. "Sometimes when an extra scene was needed—but not an acting scene—they would let me shoot it."

Famous Players–Lasky soon discovered—as most other Hollywood companies would—that there was very little financial or artistic advantage in running a UK-based operation, and pulled out in 1922, renting out the Islington studios to various independent production companies. It was one of these that gave Hitchcock his first chance to direct, on a two-reel melodrama known either as *Number Thirteen* or *Mrs. Peabody*. Whatever its title, it was never completed and has since vanished—no great loss, according to Hitchcock. He also helped complete a one-reel comedy, *Always Tell Your Wife*; the star, Seymour Hicks, had parted company with the original director, and finished off the film with Hitchcock's assistance.

In 1923, a new company called Balcon-Saville-Freedman moved into the Islington studios. It was headed by Michael Balcon and Victor Saville, both at the start of their cinematic careers; with them they brought their star director, Graham Cutts. On the strength of his experience with Hicks, Hitchcock was hired as an assistant director and assigned to work with Cutts on the company's first picture, *Woman to Woman*. He also volunteered to write the script and serve as art director. The responsibilities of editing and script continuity (generally handled by one person in those days) were taken by a young woman named Alma Reville.

Little of Cutts' silent work has survived; by all accounts he was a competent if uninspired director. Hitchcock worked with him on three more films, one of which, *The Blackguard* (1925), was filmed in Germany as a coproduction with UFA. On a neighboring set at Neubabelsberg Murnau was shooting *Der letzte Mann*, and Hitchcock took every opportunity to watch him at work. "*The Last Laugh* was almost the perfect film. It told its story . . . entirely by the use of imagery, and that had a tremendous influence on me. . . . My models were forever after the German filmmakers of 1924 and 1925. They were trying very hard to express ideas in purely visual terms." Hitchcock was also impressed, in a rather different way, by the notoriously exotic nightlife of Berlin; he was at this time by his own description "an uncommonly unattractive young man," not just inexperienced but almost totally ignorant in sexual matters. On the boat returning to England he and Alma Reville became engaged.

Graham Cutts, whose chaotic sex life interfered considerably with his directorial duties, was by now becoming resentful of Hitchcock. The "wonder boy," he complained, was getting far too much credit on his (Cutts') films, and he refused to use him any more. Most studio bosses would have mollified their top director by firing the young man on the spot. Balcon instead offered Hitchcock a picture of his own to direct.

Not, admittedly, that it was much of a picture. *The Pleasure Garden* (1925) was to be another German coproduction, but not with the prestigious UFA; rather, with a shoestring Munich company called Emelka. The plot, a melodrama about the adventures of two chorus girls in London and the tropics, was thin in the extreme, and the budget even more so. More than once Hitchcock was reduced to borrowing money from his actors and crew in order to continue shooting. Nonetheless, with the help of Alma Reville as his assistant director, he managed to get the film completed. Balcon was pleased with the result, remarking that it looked less like a German picture than an American one, which Hitchcock took as high praise. He and Alma stayed in Germany to make another film, a melodrama set in the hills of Kentucky and called *The Mountain Eagle* (1926). This is the only Hitchcock feature of which no print seems to have survived; according to its director, it was "a very bad movie."

Hitchcock returned to London as a young director of promise. *The Pleasure Garden* had been cordially received by the critics, though not yet released; *The Mountain Eagle* was yet to be shown. Meanwhile he began work on what he always referred to as "the first true Hitchcock movie." *The Lodger* (1926) was based on a novel by Mrs. Belloc Lowndes inspired by the Jack the Ripper killings. A mysterious, taciturn young man takes rooms with a London family, who gradually come to suspect him of being the Ripper. And so he is—at least in the original novel. But Ivor Novello had been signed to play the lead in the film, and since it was unthinkable that the elegant young matinee idol should portray a deranged killer, the ending was changed. The Stranger, pursued through the streets by a baying, bloodthirsty crowd, proves to be not the Ripper but the brother of one of his victims, seeking to unmask his sister's killer. He thus became the first incarnation of that classic Hitchcockian figure, the wrongfully accused innocent, hounded and hunted by a self-righteous society.

The Lodger also contains much else that anticipates the later Hitchcock, including the first of his celebrated brief onscreen appearances. (In time, this would become a teasing personal trademark; but on this occasion it seems that another extra was needed to swell a scene or two and the director stood in for want of anyone else.) The technical ingenuity that distinguishes, and occasionally overpowers, his subsequent work is already on display: at one juncture, as the family gaze suspiciously upwards, the solid ceiling dissolves to one of glass, revealing their lodger's obsessive pacing across the floor above. Most characteristic of all is the film's moral ambiguity; ordinary decent people are shown relishing every detail of the sex-killings, yet eager to lynch any suspect on the flimsiest of pretexts.

Traces of Hitchcock's German mentors were much in evidence (far more so than in the German-made *Pleasure Garden*): heavy brooding shadows and oblique camera angles abounded, and several sequences recall the Lang of *Dr. Mabuse*. Alarmed by these stylistic excesses, Gainsborough (as Balcon's company was now named) hesitated to release the picture, particularly since the chairman and chief distributor, C. M. Woolf, found it incomprehensible. Ivor Montagu, the noted film theorist and co-founder of the London Film Society, was called in to advise; he was astonished to find such technical and artistic quality in a British film, but tactfully suggested a few small adjustments. Thus modified, *The Lodger* was released to ecstatic reviews and enormous box-office success. "It is possible that this film is the finest British production ever made," wrote the critic of *The Bioscope*. Overnight, Hitchcock found himself hailed as the foremost genius of British cinema.

If this seems excessive—*The Lodger*, though it stands up well today, hardly looks like a towering masterpiece—it has to be taken in the context of British films of the period. They were abysmal. Kevin Brownlow summed up British postwar silent movies as "with few exceptions,

crudely photographed; the direction and acting were on the level of cheap revue, they exploited so-called stars who generally had little more than a glimmer of histrionic talent, and they were exceedingly boring." Against this dismal background, Hitchcock's innately cinematic vision—American-trained, German-influenced—shone out with dazzling brilliance.

In December 1926, Hitchcock and Alma Reville (who had converted to Catholicism) were married. (Hitchcock, who loved to present himself as a straitlaced sexual innocent, always claimed that they had both preserved strict premarital chastity.) Alma continued to work closely with Hitchcock on his films, often collaborating on the scripts, and the marriage lasted, apparently without major strain, until his death fifty three years later. Their only child, Patricia, was born in 1928; she became an actress and appeared in small roles in several of her father's pictures.

With hindsight, and purely on the basis of *The Lodger*, Hitchcock's aptitude for thrillers seems obvious. At the time, though, it apparently didn't, since none of his remaining six silent films was a thriller. *Downhill* (1927), his next assignment, adapted from a mediocre stage play by Ivor Novello—who again took the film lead—concerned a public schoolboy who takes the blame for his chum and then goes spectacularly to the bad. It was fairly ludicrous stuff, though allowing Hitchcock the chance to explore new ideas in narrative technique. He could do less with *Easy Virtue* (1927), a static and verbose society drama also taken from a play, this time by Noel Coward.

Dissatisfaction with such uncongenial material, along with the promise of bigger budgets and greater freedom, lured Hitchcock to a newly formed company, British International Pictures, being set up by John Maxwell at Elstree. His starting salary was £13,000 a year, which by 1929 had risen to £17,000, making him the highest-paid director in Britain.

Hitchcock made a promising start at BIP with *The Ring* (1927), a boxing drama scripted by himself and Eliot Stannard, who had worked with him on *Easy Virtue*. The story was slight—fairground fighter taken up by reigning champ suspects that his wife and the champion are having an affair—but it was lifted out of the ordinary by Hitchcock's growing technical assurance and eye for significant detail. The opening fairground scenes in particular exude a rich and gamey atmosphere; later episodes, set in a milieu of moneyed decadence, carry rather less conviction. Hitchcock also inserted some virtuoso expressionist montage sequences, which were much admired at the time but now look uncomfortably self-conscious.

After this, *The Farmer's Wife* (1928), adapted from a ponderous rustic comedy by Eden Philpotts, represented something of a comedown. *Champagne* (1928), a comedy about an heiress forced to work for a living, was not much better—"the lowest ebb in my output," Hitchcock called it, though Donald Spoto discerned some "punctuations of inventive comedy" and Betty Balfour turned in a suitably bubbly performance as the heroine. His final silent movie, *The Manxman* (1929), was drawn from a then highly-regarded novel by Hall Caine, whose reputation obliged Hitchcock to stick closely to the book. The results, uncharacteristically stiff and humorless, were partly redeemed by some striking location photography (Cornwall standing in for the Isle of Man) from John Cox, cinematographer on all Hitchcock's BIP pictures.

Blackmail (1929) has become something of a historical landmark as the first British talkie. It started out, though, as a silent; despite Hitchcock's urgings, John Maxwell was reluctant to invest in this new and possibly ephemeral gimmick. Only when the silent *Blackmail* was nearly complete did he change his mind: the film would be "part talking" with sound added to the final reel. Hitchcock was already one jump ahead; anticipating Maxwell's decision, he had shot the whole film to allow for sound, making it relatively cheap and simple to produce two separate versions. The only serious problem was the star, Anny Ondra, whose strong Polish accent hardly fitted the ordinary London girl she was playing. Post-dubbing had yet to be devised, so an off-screen actress, Joan Barry, spoke the dialogue while Ondra mouthed silently to the camera.

With *Blackmail*, adapted from a play by Charles Bennett, Hitchcock returned with palpable relish to the thriller genre, further developing his perennial theme of the transference of guilt. After a row with her police detective boyfriend, a young woman lets herself be picked up by a raffish artist. His attempted seduction turns to rape; she stabs him in panic and is then blackmailed by a man who saw her leave the apartment. Her boyfriend, assigned to the case, begins to suspect the truth and contrives to focus attention on the blackmailer, who falls to his death during a chase. The girl, stricken by remorse, tries to confess but is forestalled by her boyfriend, who takes her home. Not such a happy ending as it might seem: the girl is still trapped, her crime still known—only the identity of her blackmailer has changed.

Far from letting the new medium inhibit him,

Hitchcock seized the opportunity to experiment with subjective sound techniques well ahead of their time. The most famous example occurs at the family breakfast table the morning after the killing: while a gossipy neighbor discusses the case with ghoulish pleasure, the heroine sits dazed, hearing the insistent monologue only as a drone punctuated by " . . . knife . . . knife . . . knife . . . " "Cut us a slice of bread," says her father; she reaches out reluctantly; "*Knife!*" shrieks the voice. Her hand jerks in horror, and the bread knife flies through the air.

Blackmail also introduced the favorite Hitchcock climax, a spectacular fall from a high place, a public monument for preference. In this case, it was the roof of the British Museum, through which the wretched blackmailer makes his fatal plunge. The film was hugely successful with both critics and public, and Hitchcock's status as the foremost British director seemed secure. Which was just as well, since his next few pictures might easily have demolished a lesser reputation for good.

Not that *Elstree Calling* (1930) was more than marginally a Hitchcock picture. A bid to rival the "showcase" revue movies put out by the Hollywood studios—Warner's *Show of Shows*, Metro's *Hollywood Revue of 1929*, and so on—it consisted of a dire series of feeble variety acts, roped together by the framing device of a frustrated family trying to tune in to the show on their newfangled TV. This framework was Hitchcock's contribution; responsibility for the rest of this "unmitigated footle" (James Agate's verdict) lay with Adrian Brunel.

Hitchcock's next assignment was another of the filmed stage plays which encumbered prewar British cinema. The play was at least a good one: Sean O'Casey's *Juno and the Paycock* (1930), well (if stagily) acted by an Abbey Theatre cast. "The film got very good notices, but I was actually ashamed, because it had nothing to do with cinema." Nor did *The Skin Game* (1931), adapted from an interminably talky Galsworthy play about social conflict.

In between these two came *Murder!* (1930), yet another adaptation from the stage. The subject at least was closer to Hitchcock's tastes, even though he always considered whodunits low in emotional involvement ("Murder mysteries are cerebral exercises, whereas suspense stories are emotional experiences."). In this case Sir John Menier, a prominent stage actor and a member of the jury at a murder trial, feels dissatisfied with the verdict and tracks down the real killer, who proves to be the accused woman's fiancé. A banal enough plot, which Hitchcock enlivened with some sophisticated decorations, including stylized choral dialogue, a stream-of-consciousness soliloquy—possibly the first on film—for Sir John (Herbert Marshall, excellent in his screen debut), and a covert homosexual subtext. This ironically detached treatment alienated both audiences and critics, and the film (made in English and German versions) did poorly on release. Its reputation in some quarters has since improved; Rohmer and Chabrol saw in it "a maturity, a seriousness, and a freedom of expression only rarely to be found in his films shot on British soil."

An even cooler reception greeted *Rich and Strange* (1932), a picture close to Hitchcock's heart and now generally considered his most interesting work of this patchy period. A dull, disenchanted suburban couple inherit money and set out on a world cruise, in the course of which they get cheated, bamboozled, shipwrecked, and nearly drowned. They finally return home as shallow and dreary as when they set out; no "sea-change" for them. At first sight, this might seem an unlikely subject for Hitchcock, but as Robin Wood noted, "the pattern established here is fundamental to Hitchcock's work: bourgeois normality is empty and unsatisfying, everything beyond it terrifying." Certain scenes—those on shipboard in particular—recall early Evelyn Waugh, as a facade of beady-eyed social satire parts to disclose the bleak spiritual abyss beneath. Several critics, among them Raymond Durgnat, have suggested that a better reception for *Rich and Strange* might have opened a more promising avenue of development for Hitchcock than the suspense thrillers to which he was to become restricted.

If so, Hitchcock's last film for BIP, *Number Seventeen* (1932), could almost be taken as a sardonic commentary on his future stock-in-trade. Landed with a rubbishy comedy-thriller by Jefferson Farjeon, Hitchcock and his scriptwriter Rodney Ackland retaliated by sending up the whole thing, packing the first half with every old-dark-house cliché in the book and devoting the rest to a demented chase involving a runaway train, a bus, and a cross-channel ferry, all blatantly staged with models. A spare 64 minutes long, the film retains an offhand, throwaway charm.

The relationship with John Maxwell had been deteriorating for some time, and after acting as producer on *Lord Camber's Ladies*, directed by his former scenario writer Benn Levy, Hitchcock quit BIP and signed a contract with Alexander Korda's London Pictures. After several months doing nothing on a large salary, he discovered that Korda, trapped in one of his recurrent financial crises, had no money to set up an

assignment for him. Hitchcock accordingly departed, and accepted a project from an independent producer, Tom Arnold, to make "a musical without music" about the elder and younger Strausses. Since Hitchcock felt nothing but loathing for this kind of confectionery, *Waltzes from Vienna* (1933) turned out to be the worst film he ever made.

From this low point in his career Hitchcock was rescued by Michael Balcon, now head of Gaumont-British at Shepherd's Bush. Here he was given a free hand (barring only the occasional tussle with his old enemy C. M. Woolf) to make subjects of his own choosing, and launched himself into his first great period: the unbroken run of six masterly thrillers that brought him international fame and mapped out the territory of which he was to become undisputed master.

As early as 1925, Hitchcock had told a meeting of the London Film Society that "actors come and go, but the name of the director should stay clearly in the mind of the audience." The name of Hitchcock, at any rate, was certainly intended to do so; he had always been assiduous in cultivating the press, and in 1930 set up a PR company, Hitchcock Baker Productions, whose sole function was to keep himself in the public eye. Interviews and articles on him appeared regularly in *Film Weekly*, *World Film News*, and so on, building up the carefully fostered image of Hitch, the plump, solemn joker with a taste for the macabre.

Many writers have suggested that a less amiable personality lurked behind the public facade (Donald Spoto, indeed, devoted a whole book to the thesis). Charles Bennett, Hitchcock's main scriptwriter during the 1930s, described him as a bully; and his predilection for putting his lead actresses though physical ordeals (both onscreen and sometimes, as with Tippi Hedren in *The Birds*, on set) has given rise to charges of misogyny. His weakness for practical jokes was famous; some, like serving his guests an all-blue meal, were pleasingly whimsical, but others—often involving subordinates—could be frankly sadistic. Hitchcock once bet a prop-man at Elstree £10 to spend a night in the studio handcuffed to a camera; before departing, he poured the man a brandy laced with a strong laxative.

The first of Hitchcock's Gaumont-British thrillers, *The Man Who Knew Too Much* (1934), derived from a script he had worked on at BIP with Charles Bennett. Maxwell had turned it down but Balcon liked it, and Hitchcock brought Bennett over from BIP to continue the collaboration. A young English couple, on vacation in Switzerland with their daughter, learn of a political assassination to be carried out in London. To keep them quiet, agents of the conspiracy kidnap their child. The parents return to London to track the plotters down, foil the assassination attempt during a concert at the Albert Hall, and finally manage to rescue the girl. The film, wrote John M. Smith in *Screen* (Autumn 1972), represents for Hitchcock "an amazing leap in technical accomplishment, part of a greater artistic discipline and precision, and of an increased ability to fully accommodate his characteristic themes within impersonal structures."

"Cinema," Hitchcock once remarked, "is the orchestration of shots." It was also, for him at least, the orchestration of the audience. Later films would refine and sharpen his technique, but *The Man Who Knew Too Much* displays Hitchcock's battery of audience-unsettling devices in full swing for the first time. Here can be found the tongue-in-cheek black humor; the disdain for mere surface plausibility; the evident delight in timing each buildup (or calculated letdown) to the second; the wry sense of incongruity, revealing the macabre or sinister lurking within the most drably mundane setting; and of course the sure, probing touch on our own fears and vulnerabilities, as in the scene in the dentist's office. "Throughout, terror and levity rub shoulders," Peter John Dyer noted in *Sight and Sound* (Spring 1961); "personal discomposure, never more than momentary, switches sides constantly."

The film reaches its climax in the famous Albert Hall sequence. Hitchcock's incisive editing builds up tension to the crucial moment of the gunshot, timed—as we know, but as the increasingly agitated mother, her eyes scanning the auditorium, does not—to coincide with a clash of cymbals in the orchestra. (The music, "Storm Cloud Cantata," was specially composed for the film by Arthur Benjamin.) As the parental couple, Leslie Banks and Edna Best effectively conveyed anguish dissembled by brittle banter, but the film's outstanding performance came from Peter Lorre (in his first English-language role), offering a subtly nuanced portrayal of the schizophrenic gang leader, soft-spoken and ruthless, the shy smile liable to twitch without warning into a convulsive spasm of fury.

The Man Who Knew Too Much was warmly acclaimed by the critics and would have been equally successful at the box office had not Woolf, still implacably hostile, released it as the lower half of a double bill. Still, Balcon was happy for Hitchcock to proceed with his next project, an adaptation of John Buchan's classic thriller *The 39 Steps* (1935). Working again with Reville and Bennett, and with a larger budget and bigger stars (Robert Donat and Madeleine Carroll), Hitchcock threw out large chunks of the novel and threw in a good deal more, but retained Buchan's essential framework of a man suspected of murder and hounded across country both by the police and by the spy ring responsible for the killing.

The most significant addition provided the fugitive with a female companion, to whom he spends much of the time handcuffed. Manacles, from *The Lodger* onwards, are something of a Hitchcock specialty, a vivid symbol of the humiliating processes of the law; but in *The 39 Steps* they serve mainly as a source of humor and teasing sexual innuendo, as when Carroll, the first of Hitchcock's long line of maltreated cool blondes, tries to remove her stockings while keeping Donat's hand off her thighs. The film also marks the first appearance of the McGuffin, Hitchcock's term (borrowed from Angus MacPhail) for a thriller's nominal motivating factor—secret plans, miracle ingredient, priceless jewelry; in short, something that matters vitally to the protagonists and not at all to the audience.

Drama, Hitchcock once suggested, is "life with the dull bits cut out," a definition that certainly holds good for *The 39 Steps*. The action buckets along from incident to incident with infectious gusto, maintaining a constant level of high-spirited excitement and never giving the viewer a second to reflect on the rampant non sequiturs. It was around this time, François Truffaut observed, that Hitchcock "began . . . to sacrifice plausibility in favour of pure emotion." Audiences evidently found the trade-off highly acceptable; the film scored a huge success not only in Britain, where it was voted best Film of the Year, but also in America. Hollywood, always on the alert for poachable European talent, started to put out feelers, most of which were quietly blocked by Balcon.

It was also Balcon who proposed Hitchcock's next subject, an adaptation of two of the Ashenden stories which Somerset Maugham based on his experiences as a British agent during World War I. In *Secret Agent* (1936) a novelist, Robert Ashenden (John Gielgud), recruited by British Intelligence, is sent to Switzerland to eliminate an enemy agent. Assigned to him to aid, or complicate, his task are a glamorous assistant (Madeleine Carroll) posing as his wife, and an eccentric double agent know as "the Hairless Mexican" (Peter Lorre in a frizzy wig). Through sheer incompetence the trio dispose of the wrong man; the real enemy agent, a charming American (Robert Young), is eventually killed in a train crash.

Unlike its two predecessors, *Secret Agent* carries a hint of a serious message, thanks perhaps to the left-wing sympathies of Ivor Montagu, Hitchcock's regular associate producer at this time. Raymond Durgnat detected a "quieter, internal movement, from espionage as patriotic fun to espionage as sickening duty," and John Russell Taylor considered it "the most substantial, though not therefore the best, of Hitchcock's films of the 1930s." As so often, the Hitchcockian hero (especially in Gielgud's chilly performance) comes across as far less attractive than the villain. All of which may have disconcerted audiences, since *Secret Agent* enjoyed only limited success—as did his next film, which shared its darker undertones.

Sabotage, uniquely among Hitchcock's films, draws on the work of a major writer—even if little of Conrad's original novel (entitled, confusingly, *The Secret Agent*) remains in the movie. An anarchist, Verloc (played with appealing melancholy by Oscar Homolka) runs a fleapit London cinema as a cover for his activities, which he conceals even from his wife (Sylvia Sidney). Suspecting that he may be watched, he entrusts the delivery of a lethal package to his young brother-in-law; the lad dawdles en route and is killed when the bomb explodes. Mrs. Verloc, dazed and grief-stricken, stabs her husband; her crime is concealed when an explosion caused by Verloc's associates wrecks the cinema, and she finds solace with the detective who had the gang under surveillance.

Several elements in *Sabotage* recall *Blackmail*—the semi-accidental murder (again with a bread knife), the unspoken complicity between the heroine and her policeman admirer, and the small drab details of domestic life. Writing in the *New Yorker* (September 11, 1971) about Hitchcock's English films, Penelope Gilliatt commended their "pungency and warm rapidity . . . a wonderful fighting humor and sense of social detail"—nowhere more vividly displayed than in *Sabotage*, with its shabby London street scenes which, for all the studio reconstructions, give off an authentic reek traceable back to Hitchcock's own childhood.

Raymond Durgnat considered *Sabotage*, with its "portrayal of moral tragedy," as "the profoundest film of Hitchcock's thriller period, and perhaps of his career." For Roy Armes, it was "an uneasy film—made with consummate professionalism but without the customary finesse in guiding audience reactions along predestined paths." Hitchcock felt likewise, finding it "a little messy. No clean lines about it." He also committed "a grave error" in allowing his time-bomb to kill a likable small boy, along with a cute puppy and a whole busload of Londoners;

the audience, he realized afterwards, having endured the remorseless buildup of tension, deserved a release and would resent being deprived of it.

Having learnt his lesson, Hitchcock reverted to a light, undemanding divertissement of the kind that had brought him success. *Young and Innocent* (1937) reworks *The 39 Steps*, with an innocent fugitive chased across country, hauling a reluctant female along with him—in this case, a young writer suspected of murder, and the daughter of the local police chief. Fast-paced, engaging, and adroit, the film contains one of Hitchcock's most dazzling technical coups. The girl (Nova Pilbeam) and an old tramp who witnessed the murder are scanning a busy hotel lobby for the killer, whose only identifying feature will be a convulsively twitching eyelid. While they gaze about them, the camera cranes back and up to the ceiling, through a wall to the next-door ballroom; then swoops down again, through the circling dancers, inexorably on past the conductor, through the blackfaced musicians to the drummer, and in to a massive close-up of his eye—which suddenly blinks, faced down by the camera's accusing gaze.

Meanwhile, Michael Balcon had been ousted from the Shepherd's Bush studios, as had Ivor Montagu, and Charles Bennett had taken up an offer from Hollywood. Hitchcock, increasingly tempted to follow his scriptwriter's example, was still contracted for one more picture—the best-remembered (and for many people, the best) of his English films.

For sheer entertainment, *The Lady Vanishes* (1938) is certainly Hitchcock's most accomplished film of the decade. Frank Launder and Sidney Gilliatt, then on the threshold of their own directorial careers, furnished a lithe, witty script that glanced tangentially off current political preoccupations (Munich, the Austrian *Anschluss*) without ever deviating into seriousness. Returning by train from a European holiday, a young Englishwoman (Margaret Lockwood) meets a nice old lady (May Whitty) who then vanishes without trace. All the other passengers deny that she ever existed. Aided by a young musician (Michael Redgrave), Lockwood ferrets out the truth: Miss Froy is a British spy, whom Teutonically sinister forces, headed by Paul Lukas, are about to abduct. With the reluctant help of some other passengers, the old lady is freed and makes her escape to London, where she delivers the vital message.

Much of the film's delight derives from its very absurdity, from the seeming effortlessness with which Hitchcock skims over the improbabilities of the plot, switching with insolent ease from tension to light comedy and back at a moment's notice. *The Lady Vanishes* boasts a rich gallery of incidental characters: the high-heeled nun, the traveling conjuror with his beret and deprecating grin, Cecil Parker's pompous adulterer—and of course Charters and Caldicott, the pair of silly-ass Englishmen obsessed with the Test Match, whom Basil Radford and Naunton Wayne were subsequently to develop into a much-loved double act.

Now free from contractual obligations, Hitchcock visited Hollywood and, from the numerous competing bids for his services, accepted a contract from David O. Selznick, at that time the most powerful of the independent producers. His first American project was to be a film about the sinking of the *Titanic*, but when Selznick ran into problems acquiring a suitable ship, Hitchcock found himself back in London with time on his hands. Fortuitously, he was offered a single-picture assignment by Charles Laughton, who together with the exiled German producer Erich Pommer had formed a company called Mayflower Productions.

Costume dramas were never Hitchcock's forte, and *Jamaica Inn* (1939) was as costumed as they come. Adapted from a creaky romantic novel by Daphne du Maurier, it concerned an innocent young orphan (Maureen O'Hara) arriving at her uncle's remote Cornish inn to find it a den of reprobates given to smuggling, wrecking, and gross overacting. She flees for help to the local magistrate, who of course turns out to be the leader of the gang. The latter role found Laughton at his most outrageously self-indulgent; since he was also the coproducer, there was little Hitchcock could do except grit his teeth and get it over with as best he could. This done, he departed for the States, along with his wife and daughter and his personal assistant, Joan Harrison.

Much critical dispute has centered around the respective merits of Hitchcock's British and American films. Robin Wood, firmly ensconced in the American camp, dismissed the British films as "little more than 'prentice work," and a preference for them as "analogous to preferring *A Comedy of Errors* to *Macbeth*." To Roy Armes, this constituted "a profoundly unhistorical judgement," Hitchcock's British work being comparable to that of Pabst and Clair, "constantly exciting in its exploration of the cinema's narrative potential and its expression of a consistent set of moral values." Armes conceded, though, that "by the end of the 1930s . . . Hitchcock gives the impression that he has worked through the possibilities of his chosen range of subject matter within the technical con-

fines of the British film industry, so that a move to Hollywood was both beneficial and inevitable."

Undoubtedly the American films benefit immeasurably from Hollywood's greater technical sophistication. They also, most writers would agree, frequently attain an emotional depth and resonance inconceivable in the earlier work. Against this, the British films have about them a vigor and spontaneity, an appealing freshness that the American films seldom recapture; nor can Hitchcock the Hollywood director often command his English predecessor's vivid sense of place.

For some critics, though (and not only British ones), the whole of Hitchcock's American output represents nothing but a lamentable decline. "It remains patently true," William S. Pechter asserted, "that the history of Hitchcock's American career must be told in terms of loss; for one, the loss of contact with a milieu he has known and depicted so well . . . ; instead of which, we are offered the pallid substitute of the drawing-room. . . . The world of these later films is without equilibrium, and, in this imbalance, even the most ingenious contrivances seem merely absurd." In William Rothman's opinion, on the other hand, "the Hollywood studio made it possible for Hitchcock to orchestrate the elements of cinematic expression to create incredibly rich and resonant emotional effects, although virtually every technique and formal device he comes to employ in his Hollywood films was already developed in his British films. . . . It is in America that Hitchcock solves the problem of exploiting the resources of the Hitchcock thriller while addressing the meaning of its conditions." His first American movie "clearly reveals Hitchcock's excitement at discovering the emotional weight, the sheer power, he can given to sounds and images by utilizing the sophisticated technology newly available to him."

By coincidence, this film was also based on a book by Daphne du Maurier and was equally untypical of Hitchcock's output, being more a novelettish romance than a thriller. It was, however, a much better film than *Jamaica Inn*. The plot of *Rebecca* (1940) rehashes *Jane Eyre*: a young woman (whose name we never learn) marries a handsome, distinguished older man and finds herself intimidated both by his exalted social status and by the spirit of his first wife. Unlike Mrs. Rochester, however, the first Mrs. de Winter is not lurking crazed in an attic; she is dead, but reincarnate in the malignant housekeeper, Mrs. Danvers, who tries to drive the new wife to suicide. When her scheme fails, Mrs.

Danvers burns down the great house and herself with it.

Hitchcock's description of *Rebecca* as "a completely British picture" holds true only in that the director, story, and nearly all the cast were British. In every other way *Rebecca* was very much a prestige Hollywood product—longer, glossier, more solemnly paced than anything he had made in Britain, bathed in the sheen of George Barnes' photography and Franz Waxman's opulent score. Apart from some early scenes featuring Florence Bates' richly fatuous American matron, the quirky Hitchcock humor was rarely in evidence. In the leading roles, Laurence Olivier was too stiff, and Joan Fontaine too submissive, to sustain sympathy; but as the reptilian Mrs. Danvers, Judith Anderson gave the performance of a lifetime.

Selznick, notorious for badgering his directors, for once interfered relatively little with the shooting. "It was my good fortune," Hitchcock later explained, "that he was extremely busy completing *Gone With the Wind.*" As it turned out, Selznick had no cause for concern. *Rebecca* was hugely successful, both with the critics and the public, and carried off the Academy Award for Best Picture—the only Hitchcock movie ever to win an Oscar (although, as Hitchcock pointed out with understandable pique, the award went not to him, but to Selznick as producer). His American career was off to an auspicious start.

In any case, Selznick had discovered, as had other producers before him, that thanks to Hitchcock's method of filming, his pictures were remarkably difficult to tamper with. Hitchcock was famous in the movie industry for the meticulous care with which he pre-planned his films, sketching out each shot and camera movement in detail, and editing in camera. As he once remarked, not without satisfaction: "I used to shoot . . . in such a way that no one else could put the pieces together properly; the only way they could be edited was to follow exactly what I had in mind." This "goddam jigsaw cutting" (as Selznick termed it) resulted in amazingly economic shooting ratios; *Rear Window* is said to have yielded a bare 100 feet of outtakes.

As a result of Hitchcock's systematic approach, the actual shooting and editing of a picture held (or so he claimed) little interest for him. "Creative work in the cutting is, for me, nonexistent, because it is designed ahead of time—pre-cut, which it should be. . . . I wish I didn't have to shoot the picture. When I've gone through the script and created the piece on paper, for me the creative work is done and the rest is just a bore." André Bazin, visiting the set of *To Catch a Thief,* was disconcerted to find the great director slumped comatose in his chair during a shot, inattentive or perhaps even asleep. (Asked once why he didn't simply delegate the shooting to someone else, Hitchcock responded, "They might screw it up.")

In the seven years during which Hitchcock was under contract to Selznick, he directed only three films for him. This was normal practice with Selznick, who liked to sign up sought-after artists and then loan them out, at a handsome profit, to other studios. Hitchcock's next assignment thus found him working for another of the independents, Walter Wanger, on a political thriller.

One of Hitchcock's virtually single-handed achievements was to raise the cinematic status of the thriller to parity with the other main movie genres. At the outset of his Hollywood career, thrillers, no matter how stylishly executed, were by definition B-Movie fodder, with players and budget ranked accordingly, and a major star like Gary Cooper could still turn down *Foreign Correspondent* (1940) as a "mere thriller," unworthy of his consideration. Hitchcock had to settle for Joel McCrea, whom he found "too easy-going," and Laraine Day as co-star.

Foreign Correspondent reunited Hitchcock with his old scriptwriter Charles Bennett and was the first of his films to include overt political propaganda, no doubt reflecting the apprehensions—and perhaps the guilt—of the two expatriate Englishmen. A brash, politically naive American reporter, sent to Europe on the eve of the war, meets a Dutch diplomat who is subsequently kidnapped by the Nazis. At the end of the film, having rescued the Dutchman and exposed the British head of a German spy ring, he broadcasts to America an impassioned plea against isolationism from a darkened London studio, as the bombs crash around him: "All that noise you hear isn't static, it's death coming to London. . . . Keep those lights burning, cover them with steel, ring them with guns . . . they're the only lights left in the world!"

"A dazzling directorial *tour de force,*" in the opinion of Charles Higham and Joel Greenberg, *Foreign Correspondent* "is still arguably the director's best American film. . . . Hitchcock has seldom equalled its parade of brilliantly inventive set-pieces." Few other critics have been enthusiastic to quite this degree. Raymond Durgnat commended the scene in which a double of the diplomat is assassinated amid a sea of rain-soaked Dutch umbrellas as "a superb textbook example of staging and cutting, developing a spatially complex action at breakneck speed with a force and clarity which . . . moves one by sheer aesthetic appeal," but found the film as a whole sluggish and stilted, "a superb exemplar of style without the spirit of poetry within it."

In the Hitchcock filmography, *Mr. and Mrs. Smith* (1941) stands out as a curious anomaly—a Hollywood screwball comedy in the classic mode, with not a single corpse in sight. Hitchcock took it on as a personal favor to its star, Carole Lombard; she and Robert Montgomery play a squabbling couple who discover that, through a legal technicality, they were never in fact married in the first place. "I really didn't understand the type of people who were portrayed in the film; all I did was photograph the scenes as written." His unease showed, and the film never sparkles as it should—and doubtless would have, in the hands of a Lubitsch or McCarey.

Suspicion (1941)—made, like *Mr. and Mrs. Smith*, for RKO—could almost be *Rebecca* rewritten along more Hitchcockian lines. Once more a shy, naive young woman (Joan Fontaine again) falls for a handsome, sophisticated man, and once more comes to fear that he may be a murderer. Only this time the possible victim is not the deceased first wife but the heroine herself. As the husband, Cary Grant (in the first of his four roles for Hitchcock) was impeccably cast—cheery, irresistibly dashing, just allowing the quietest possible hint of menace to slip into a passing gesture or half-glimpsed expression. "One of the main essentials in constructing a story," Hitchcock always insisted, "is to make sure that . . . your villain doesn't behave like one or even look like one. . . . He has to be charming, attractive. If he weren't, he'd never get near one of his victims."

As it finally turns out, Grant is not after all a villain—though not for want of trying by Hitchcock, who envisaged an ending in which Fontaine, before knowingly drinking poisoned milk, gives Grant a letter to mail in which she denounces him. This was more than the studio could take, and the star had to be cleared (although the final shot, with his arm falling protectively around her shoulders, can bear more than one reading). As so often, Hitchcock slyly banks on audience complicity; since we *want* to believe the worst, those scenes which confirm our darkest suspicions are the most effective, such as the famous glass-of-milk sequence, with Grant, features set in either solicitous concern or grim purpose, ascending shadowed stairs with the crucial drink (a light concealed inside it) glowing eerily on its tray, compelling our gaze.

Suspicion, like *Rebecca*, was set in England (or at least what passed for England in Hollywood). Only with his next film, *Saboteur* (1942), did Hitchcock venture an American-based thriller, and even then he played safe with a return to the picaresque format of *The 39 Steps* and *Young and Innocent*. The fugitive this time around is a young munitions worker arrested for industrial sabotage, who escapes (handcuffed, of course) in order to track down the true culprit. Hitchcock again failed to interest Gary Cooper and reluctantly made do with Robert Cummings; even less to his liking was the producer's choice for female lead, Priscilla Lane. The best things in this uneven and episodic film, "a potpourri of his English works" (Rohmer and Chabrol), were some witty dialogue contributed by Dorothy Parker, and Norman Lloyd's edgy, insidious performance as the real saboteur, who eventually slides slowly to his death off the Statue of Liberty in one of Hitchcock's best nail-biting climaxes.

If a certain uneasiness can be sensed in Hitchcock's output during the 1940s, it may be due, as John Russell Taylor suggested, to the problem of "coming to terms with the heavier, more fully worked-out style of the expensive Hollywood production . . . as compared to the slight, corner-cutting style he had perfected in his British films." The one virtually undisputed masterpiece of the decade—and one of his own favorite films—was *Shadow of a Doubt* (1943), the product of an harmonious working relationship with the playwright Thornton Wilder.

Hitchcock's view of the world, according to Thomas Hemmeter, is "a volatile duality of order and chaos, where the forces of order are but a frail hedge against arbitrary eruptions of disorder from nature, society, or from within the mind. The criminal, the psychotic and the demonic intrude with brutal violence into the lives of law-abiding, normal people; they are either destroyed or learn to see the world and themselves as Hitchcock does: as an anxious mixture of normal and abnormal, innocence and guilt, public and private, whose apparent duality is more a conventional illusion than a reality." This Manichean schema, adduced by some writers as evidence of Hitchcock the stern Catholic moralist, stands out clearly in *Shadow of a Doubt*, where heroine and villain are namesakes, two sides of a single nature.

To a small, sunlit California town comes Charlie Oakley, to stay for a while with his sister's family. They welcome him warmly—especially the teenage daughter, young Charlie, enchanted by this charming, sophisticated uncle for whom she was named. But Uncle Charlie is on the run, suspected of the murders of rich widows in cities all across the country. Alerted by a young detective, the incredulous girl gradually becomes aware of her uncle's psychotic nature. An alternative suspect is accidentally killed and the inquiry is closed. But by now young Charlie knows the truth and has divulged as much to her uncle. He tries to kill her, but dies himself in the attempt. At his funeral, Charlie Oakley is eulogized by the local citizens, while his niece and the detective stand apart, appalled by the knowledge they share.

If in general Hitchcock's American films lack the tangible sense of milieu of his English work, *Shadow of a Doubt* furnishes a notable exception. Much of the film—unusually for the Hollywood of the period—was shot on location, in the North California town of Santa Rosa, where Hitchcock and Wilder stayed for several weeks while working on the script. As Uncle Charlie, Joseph Cotten gave perhaps the finest performance of his career, skillfully disclosing the cold, crazed disgust beneath his engaging front, venting his spleen on the cozy Americana around him: "Do you know the world is a foul sty? Do you know if you ripped the fronts off houses you'd find swine?" His deranged vision of an impossible golden age when "everybody was sweet and pretty . . . not like today" is symbolized by a misty repeated shot of elegant couples circling to Strauss' *Merry Widow Waltz,* its title a reminder of his despised victims, "eating and drinking their money, stuffing themselves with their jewelry."

The excellence of Cotten's playing was matched by that of Teresa Wright as young Charlie, her frank, open gaze gradually shadowing as full realization of what the near-telepathic bond with her uncle implies creeps over her. She too, as she is forced to acknowledge, is capable of killing, and the world is indeed a darker place than she ever imagined. The heavy-handed reassurances of her detective boyfriend (Macdonald Carey, close kin to his equivocal colleagues in *The Lodger* and *Blackmail*) are scant consolation for the loss of her innocence.

After this, *Lifeboat* (1943), based on an idea by John Steinbeck, came as something of a disappointment. "A laboured allegory" (Higham and Greenberg) set in the eponymous vessel, it pitted a smiling, resourceful Nazi (Walter Slezak) against a stereotyped bunch of squabbling democrats, who finally unite to kill him in a scene of commendably unglorified brutality. The film's main interest, apart from an ingenious solution to the problem of featuring Hitchcock's habitual cameo (he turns up in a weight-loss ad on a scrap of salvaged newspaper), lay in the self-imposed technical challenge, the first of several which Hitchcock set himself around this period. In this case, every camera shot (barring one brief underwater angle) is taken from within the bounds of the lifeboat, the camera itself becoming one

of the passengers. Ingenious framing made this less visually oppressive than might have been feared, but the film still gave Hitchcock his first major American flop. Most reviewers objected either to the unflattering portrayal of the representatives of democracy or to the savagery of the Nazi's death. In the *New York Times,* Bosley Crowther accused the film of having "sold out democratic ideals and elevated the Nazi superman."

Though still a British national (not until 1955 would he take out US citizenship), Hitchcock had by now decided that his future, both personal and professional, lay in America. In 1942, after renting for a while, he and Alma had bought a house on Bellagio Road in the Bel-Air district of Hollywood. (A year later they also bought a vacation house in the hills north of Monterey near Santa Cruz.) The Bellagio Road house remained their home for the rest of their lives; among other refinements, Hitchcock added a huge kitchen, a walk-in freezer, and a capacious wine cellar. Not that he ever made any concessions in dress, speech, or personal habits to the California lifestyle. To the end of his days he retained his stage-Cockney accent, and whatever the temperature he invariably appeared in public wearing a soberly cut dark suit, a white shirt, and quiet tie—the costume of a respectable London clerk, often topped off with a bowler hat. He and Alma lived well (extremely well as far as food and wine were concerned) but they lived quietly, seeing only a small circle of friends, rarely going out, and avoiding all smart social gatherings.

Hitchcock's neatness and passion for order were legendary. "Evil," he once said, "is disorder," and his idea of happiness was "a clear horizon, no clouds, no shadows. Nothing." As far as he possibly could, he eliminated the unpredictable from his life, not only in his working methods but in everything he did. The family holidays were taken in the same places—New York, London, Paris, and St. Moritz—and even in the same suites of the same hotels, year after year. To some extent, this was part of the assiduously cultivated public persona; but many people, including Hitchcock himself, also ascribed it to genuine fear—of surprise, disorder, conflict, social disgrace, the police, the processes of law— of all the things, in fact, which he packed into his movies. "Under the invariably self-possessed and often cynical surface," observed Truffaut, "is a deeply vulnerable, sensitive and emotional person who feels with particular intensity the sensations he communicates to his audience."

In December 1943, Hitchcock paid a short visit to London, with the aim of making an overt contribution to the war effort; remarks made earlier in the war, by Michael Balcon among others, apparently still rankled. He stayed three months, during which he discussed the idea of forming a joint company with his old friend Sidney Bernstein, and made two short films in French for the Ministry of Information. *Bon Voyages* and *Aventure Malgache* (1944) were half-hour melodramas intended to support the cause of the French Resistance. The French, however, were not much interested, and the films never gained distribution.

Hitchcock returned to America in March 1944 and began work on the second of his films for Selznick. Freud, in suitably dilute form, was much in vogue in Hollywood, and in *Spellbound* (1945), Hitchcock, with Ben Hecht scripting, produced what might claim to be the first psychoanalytical thriller. Ingrid Bergman plays a doctor in a psychiatric clinic whose director (Leo G. Carroll) is about to retire in favor of a younger man. This Dr. Edwardes, when he arrives, proves to be Gregory Peck in a state of amnesia; concluding that he must somehow have disposed of the real Dr. Edwardes, he goes on the run. Bergman follows and enlists her old professor (Michael Chekhov) to unravel the mystery by analysing Peck's dreams. The culprit is revealed as Carroll, whose murder of Edwardes triggered off in Peck recall of a childhood trauma when he accidentally caused his brother's death.

Even the most fervent of Hitchcock's admirers have found little to like in *Spellbound*. Rohmer and Chabrol identified its "principal fault" as "aridity," and Robin Wood speculated that the director was "not much engaged with his material." Hitchcock himself described the film as "just another manhunt story wrapped up in pseudo-psychoanalysis," but even on this level it rarely generates much excitement. The dream sequence, for which Salvador Dali was called in amid great publicity, is sadly tame (though this may be due to drastic cutting by Selznick who reduced it from twenty minutes to a mere three or four). Nonetheless, *Spellbound* was hugely successful on release, despite James Agee's dismissal of it as "just so much of the Id as could be safely displayed in a Bergdorf Goodman window."

Notorious (1946) also started out as a Selznick project, but before shooting had commenced Selznick, deeply embroiled with the grandiose *Duel in the Sun*, sold the entire package to RKO, with Hitchcock taking over for the first time as his own producer. Relishing his increased independence and working with two of his favorite actors—Cary Grant and Ingrid Bergman—he produce a film which, in general estimation,

stands with *Shadow of a Doubt* as his finest work of the decade.

Ben Hecht's script traces patterns of emotional manipulation and betrayal. Devlin, a government agent (Grant), recruits Alicia Huberman (Bergman), daughter of a convicted Nazi spy, to help him infiltrate a circle of refugee Nazis in Rio de Janeiro. The two fall in love, but Devlin, despising Alicia for her family background and former fast life, pushes her into marriage with Sebastian (Claude Rains), a prominent member of the Nazi circle. With Alicia's help, Devlin penetrates the house and finds the McGuffin—uranium, in this case (a detail which apparently caused Hitchcock to be placed for a time under FBI surveillance). But Sebastian realizes that he has been betrayed; impelled by his formidable mother, he starts to poison Alicia. At the last moment Devlin breaks in and rescues her, leaving Sebastian compromised and at the mercy of his fellow Nazis.

For François Truffaut, *Notorious* "is the very quintessence of Hitchcock" having "at once a maximum of stylization and a maximum of simplicity." It was also, in William Rothman's view, "the first Hitchcock film in which every shot is not only meaningful but beautiful. . . . The camera's lush romanticism, for the first time, is equal and constant partner to its wit, elegance, and theatricality." Much of the film, including Ted Tetzlaff's soft lighting and sensuous camera movements, takes its tone from Bergman's warm, vulnerable performance. Claude Rains, another of Hitchcock's appealing villains, is cultured, charming, and far more sympathetic than the coldly censorious Devlin. As his mother, Leopoldine Konstantin inaugurates the gallery of monster mothers that culminated in *Psycho*—an element that enters Hitchcock's films (as Donald Spoto pointed out) only after the death of his own mother in 1942.

Notorious, Douglas McVay wrote in *Montage*, is "Hitchcock's most completely, rigorously stylized film . . . and perfect in its stylization." In one of the film's most famous moments, Hitchcock duplicates his virtuoso crane shot from *Young and Innocent*. During a lavish party at the Sebastian house, Alicia plans to steal down to the wine cellar, the key to which she has previously purloined. Starting high on a landing overlooking the thronged entrance-hall, the camera swoops smoothly down, past the elegant couples and the champagne-bearing servants, to where Alicia stands with Sebastian welcoming their guests, and into a close-up of her hand behind her back, which half-opens to reveal the one tiny, vital item in the whole bustling scene—the cellar key.

The Paradine Case (1947), third and last of Hitchcock's pictures for Selznick, was much the worst of them. A courtroom drama with a British setting, it concerns a barrister (played by Gregory Peck) falling in love with a client (Alida Valli) who has been charged with murdering her husband. Learning that she was in fact having an affair with her groom, the jealous lawyer badgers the man on the witness stand, driving him to suicide. Grief-stricken, the accused woman confesses her guilt and denounces her advocate in open court.

Either through luck or judgment, Selznick generally left Hitchcock alone—he once referred to him as "the only director I'd trust a picture with"—but on this occasion his interference proved disastrous. On his insistence, not only were Peck and Valli cast in the leads (both somewhat uncomfortably), but the role of the groom, supposedly a rough, earthy type, was assigned to the suave and cosmopolitan Louis Jourdan. Selznick also provided the script (adapted from a novel by Robert Hichens) and tinkered with it incessantly, sending down extensive rewrites just as scenes were about to be shot. Altogether the film suffered badly from "that distinctive Selznick atmosphere of soupy intensity and faint mustiness" (Penelope Houston); its only bright spot is a delectably malevolent performance from Charles Laughton as a lecherous old judge, crunching walnuts ("They resemble the human brain") while drooling over the prospect of hanging a beautiful woman.

Even while preparing *The Paradine Case*, Hitchcock was anticipating his imminent freedom, actively setting up his production company with Sidney Bernstein. Transatlantic Pictures would make films in both Britain and America and allow him virtually complete control over subject, casting, and budget. Their first project was one which Hitchcock had been toying with since the mid-30s, an adaptation of Patrick Hamilton's play *Rope's End*, loosely based on the notorious Leopold-Loeb case in which two rich young Chicagoans had murdered a third just for the hell of it.

Of all the abstruse technical challenges which Hitchcock set himself, *Rope* (1948) is the most elaborate. Not content with shooting in color for the first time, he decided to film the whole 81-minute picture in one continuous shot, without cuts. (At the end of each reel, the camera tracks in to a dark surface, and then out again as the new reel starts.) The famously meticulous pre-planning reached its apogee in this film: the intricate logistics of each 10-minute take were planned in minute detail and exhaustively rehearsed, with the camera roaming sinuously about the set on a mobile dolly while technicians, actors, and removable walls and furniture vanished silently out of its path.

For the technically minded, *Rope* is fascinating to watch; for the ordinary spectator, the lack of cutting and elision makes for visual tedium. But in either case, the story suffers; as he later acknowledged, Hitchcock had broken his own rule that technique should always serve the action. "I undertook *Rope* as a stunt. . . . I really don't know how I came to indulge in it." Even so, some critics have found the technique apt, in aiming "to create in the viewer," as Donald Spoto put it, "the most intense feelings of confinement and claustrophobia, the better to identify him with the main characters." Similarly, Higham and Greenberg observed that "the endlessly gliding takes . . . create an atmosphere as stifling as the interior of a coffin."

Farley Granger and John Dall effectively conveyed the sadomasochistic (and by implication homosexual) bond between the two young killers, though James Stewart, in the first of his four Hitchcock roles, seemed insecurely cast as the professor whose high-flown Nietzschean theories inspire their *acte gratuit*. Reviewers' reactions were mixed, ranging from *Newsweek*'s "unflagging suspense" to the "tedium" and "fizzle" endured by Bosley Crowther, but box-office response proved favorable enough for Transatlantic to embark on a second production, this time to be shot in Britain.

Since Hitchcock had never concealed his antipathy to costume drama—"One, I'm not good at it, and two, for me, nobody in a costumed picture ever goes to the toilet"—his choice of *Under Capricorn* (1949), a romance melodrama set in 1850s Australia, remains unaccountable. He subsequently insisted that he chose the subject to suit Ingrid Bergman, whose services he had secured against stiff competition: a strange assertion, given that the plot required her to play a high-born English lady. (Struggling valiantly with the accent, she finally compromised on a kind of Swedo-Irish.) Glum, dull, and ruinously expensive, the picture flopped calamitously, bringing Transatlantic down with it.

Cautious by nature, Hitchcock preferred in times of trouble to run for cover, and now, his bid for independence having misfired, he signed a multipicture deal with Warners, though one which allowed him a fair degree of creative freedom. Like *Under Capricorn*, his first film under the new contract was shot in England. *Stage Fright* (1950), a flaccid whodunut with a theatrical setting, nominally starring Marlene Dietrich and Jane Wyman, was largely hijacked by its supporting cast of British eccentrics, who included Alastair Sim, Sybil Thorndike, and Joyce Grenfell. "We are left," Raymond Durgnat wrote, "with . . . a classic, decorous, English story, located in some spiritual territory halfway between Ealing Studios and Agatha Christie-land, with the surface manners only too effectively setting the dramatic tone."

Hitchcock returned to the States with his career at its lowest ebb in two decades. Not since *Notorious* had he achieved a major hit, and he seemed to have lost his bearings. From this nadir he launched himself—as he had done in 1934—into the second of his great periods. Perhaps his greatest; among the eleven films he made between 1951 and 1960 are at least five which most critics would agree in rating among his finest work.

The work of this period also consolidated Hitchcock's public image as the Master of Suspense, the black humorist who transformed his own latent anxieties into practiced essays in applied terror, capturing his audiences through skillful appeal to the universal fear of finding ourselves helplessly entangled in events beyond our control or comprehension. In this he was in tune with the decade, insecure beneath its superficial complacency, ready to see nameless menace lurking behind bland quotidian appearance. As Andrew Sarris (*Film Culture,* Summer 1961) commented: "What has long been most disturbing in Hitchcock's films—the perverse ironies, the unresolved ambiguities, the switched protagonists—now marks him as a pioneer in the modern idiom in which nothing is what it seems on the surface."

Strangers on a Train (1951) found Hitchcock back in top form, with all the obsessional themes that fueled his art up and running. Adapted (with some ungracious help from Raymond Chandler) from Patricia Highsmith's first novel, the film tells of Guy Haines, an ambitious young tennis pro who is accosted on a train journey by an ostensible admirer, Bruno Anthony. Bruno proposes an exchange of murders: he will kill Guy's wife, who is refusing him the divorce he wants; in return, Guy will dispose of Bruno's obstructive father. Guy refuses to take the idea seriously, but Bruno goes ahead with his side of the bargain and pressures Guy to reciprocate by threatening to incriminate him. Increasingly agitated and under police surveillance, Guy finally catches up with Bruno just as he is about to plant evidence. In their struggle Bruno is killed, and Guy is cleared.

From its opening sequence—two pairs of feet, seen in alternate close-ups, arriving at a station and boarding a train, intercut with shots of merging and intercrossing rails—*Strangers on a Train* announces itself as an intricate pattern of doublings and parallels. Bruno (superlatively played by Robert Walker, in the finest role of his brief, troubled career) is the most unsettling of Hitchcock's charming psychopaths, whereas Guy, the supposed hero, comes across in Farley Granger's performance as self-serving and obnoxious. The two men, physically similar, are psychological mirror-images: Bruno would like to be Guy, with his fame and social success, while Guy yearns to do the things ("I'd like to break her foul, useless little neck!") that the less inhibited Bruno, embodiment of Guy's destructive urges, will readily perform.

Deftly photographed by Robert Burks—the beginning of a nearly unbroken thirteen-year association—*Strangers* includes several of Hitchcock's most accomplished set pieces: the fairground strangling reflected in the lens of the victim's glasses as in a distorted mind; the second strangling, at a vapid society party, that starts in fun and veers alarmingly into earnest; the gripping "double suspense" sequence, with Guy frantically striving to complete a tennis match while Bruno gropes to retrieve a lighter (the vital evidence against Guy) that has slipped down a grating. The virtuoso finale returns us to the fairground, with Guy and Bruno grappling aboard a carousel spinning wildly out of control, while children shriek, onlookers panic, and a little man crawls imperturbably beneath the hurtling boards towards the brake, pausing only (an ineffably Hitchcockian touch) to blow his nose.

The resounding success of *Strangers* restored Hitchcock's reputation. From now on, even during the period of critical and box-office disfavor in the 1960s, his status as one of the leading directors in the industry was never in serious doubt. His own producer, with his own choice of subject matter, he attained in the remaining twenty-five years of his career almost total autonomy over his projects, only limited on occasion by studio-imposed casting.

"There is not one of Hitchcock's films," Rohmer and Chabrol asserted, sparking off no end of critical argument, "that is not more or less marked by Christian ideas and symbols." Hitchcock himself always remained studiously noncommittal on the whole matter but his only film to deal explicitly with Christian, and indeed Catholic, matters turned out to be singularly cold and unengaging. *I Confess* (1952), adapted from a play by Paul Anthelme and relocated to a sombre, oppressive Montreal, presents the "transference of guilt" theme in its most literal form. A priest (Montgomery Clift) receives the confession of a murderer, whose victim (by useful coincidence) has been blackmailing this same priest for a past indiscretion. Bound by the sanctity of the confessional, he is then unable to clear himself when suspicion falls on him, and has to stand trial and public obloquy. Only when the killer's wife screams out the truth is he cleared, but his reputation has been ruined.

"Too serious" was Hitchcock's own verdict on *I Confess*. Most English-language critics, then and since, have agreed. Robin Wood found the film "earnest, distinguished, very interesting, and on the whole a failure," lacking the director's "characteristic complexity of tone," and "interplay of irony and humour." French critics, seizing on the religious theme, thought more highly of it, as for rather different reasons did William Rothman, who commended its "stark, tormented mood . . . accentuated by the poetic quality of its language," perceiving in it a covert allegory of McCarthyism.

Hitchcock, who always spoke of himself as "an exponent of pure cinema," often expressed dislike of films that he considered merely "photographs of people talking"—in which category he included his own *Dial M for Murder* (1954). Adapted from Frederic Knott's stage play, it was filmed in color and 3D but only released "flat," the short-lived craze having subsided. "A nine-day wonder," Hitchcock blandly observed, "and I came in on the ninth day." The plot might well be *Strangers on a Train* a dozen years later. An ex–tennis champion, tiring of his rich wife, plots her murder. When the scheme misfires, he adroitly switches tactics and succeeds in having her framed for murder instead, but is finally, thanks to the inevitable fatal flaw, trapped in his own machinations.

Avoiding any temptation to open up Knott's play, Hitchcock confined himself almost entirely to a single set (though with no attempt to repeat the continuous takes of *Rope*). The film's most effective sequence, however, was the wife's arrest, imprisonment, and trial, conveyed with brilliant economy by voices, sound effects, and changes in lighting, while the camera holds on a close-up of her anguished face. Grace Kelly, in the first of her three consecutive roles for Hitchcock, looked suitably lovely and appealing, while Ray Milland as her husband deployed just the right venal charm.

With *Dial M for Murder* Hitchcock had fulfilled the letter of his Warners contract (though feeling that he had given the studio poor value, he later volunteered to make one more film for them without fee). Meanwhile, through his agent Lew Wasserman at MCA, he signed an even more advantageous deal with Paramount, under which he would eventually gain one hundred–percent rights in the pictures that he made for them.

Of all those films where Hitchcock, as if with deliberate perversity, chose to set himself a technical challenge, only one can be accounted an unqualified success. In *Rear Window* (1954) he rooted his camera to the spot, observing all the action from the single viewpoint of a man immobilized in a chair with his leg in a plaster cast. The man is a top news photographer, L.B. Jeffries (James Stewart), whose leg was broken in a racetrack accident. Bored and frustrated, he takes to observing the neighbors visible from his Greenwich Village apartment, gradually focusing in one one of them who, he becomes convinced, has done away with a querulous and bed-ridden wife. At first sceptical, both his society fiancée (Grace Kelly) and his nurse (Thelma Ritter) are drawn into the investigation, accumulating evidence until the killer, alerted to the surveillance, turns on his helpless observer. The police arrive just too late to save Jeffries from defenestration; he falls, and breaks his other leg.

Hitchcock's subversive skill in implicating, even inculpating, his audience, forcing us to confront our own eager voyeurism and vicariously sadistic impulses, found its most overt statement in *Rear Window*. "Transference of guilt here," as Penelope Houston noted, "is really from the character to the audience." Stewart, pruriently swiveling his telephoto lens from one window to the next, stands as an obvious paradigm of the movie-going public, idly weighing up the rival attractions of a sex-comedy (the newlyweds, the nubile dancer), a weepie (the lonely spinster), or a bio-pic (the struggling young composer)—and finally settling, with the murder, for a Hitchcock movie. "Look at you and me," says Kelly when the evidence seems not to be holding up, "plunged into despair because we find out a man *didn't* kill his wife." Of course they are, and so are we—or would be, if we thought it were true. But our morbidity is punished, at least by way of our proxy; the monster that Jeffries has conjured up for his idle amusement breaks through the screen, invading the spectator's own sacrosanct territory.

In *Rear Window*, according to William Pechter, "the central invention is continually made ridiculous by the excrescence of easy clichés with which it is surrounded." His was a rare dissenting verdict: for most critics the film rates among Hitchcock's finest achievements. William Rothman called it "funny, touching, almost inhumanly brilliant, profound, completely worked out formally, dramatically and philosophically," and in Robin Wood's opinion, it was "perhaps the first of Hitchcock's films to which the term masterpiece can reasonably be applied." The script, resourcefully expanded from a Cornell Woolrich short story, was by John

Michael Hayes, who also scripted Hitchcock's next three films. In casting, Hitchcock no longer had to accept studio dictates, and it shows; there are no weak links, from Stewart's sweating, grumbling invalid to Raymond Burr's pitiable hulk of a killer. Kelly, in the best role of her career, was at her most coolly sensual. "Preview of coming attractions," she murmurs, displaying a flimsy negligee from her overnight bag.

Kelly likewise adorned *To Catch a Thief* (1955), her last performance for Hitchcock before moving on to a classier branch of show-business. The film was described by Hitchcock as "a lightweight story . . . not meant to be taken seriously," in which Cary Grant played a retired cat burglar living in ill-gotten comfort on the Riviera. When a spate of thefts brings him under suspicion, he has to identify the true criminal in order to clear himself. His task is complicated by a pair of American tourists—a nouveau-riche widow, played with ripe vulgarity by Jessie Royce Landis, and her seductive daughter (Kelly). The chance that Grant may really be a crook evidently increases his attraction in Kelly's eyes—a theme to be more thoroughly explored in *Marnie*.

By now, Hitchcock was probably the best-known film director in the world, rivaled only (barring actor-directors like Chaplin) by Cecil B. DeMille; one of the few whose name on a poster could attract an audience irrespective of the actors involved. But he was about to become even better known, as the first major Hollywood director to concern himself wholeheartedly with television. In October 1955, the first *Alfred Hitchcock Presents* was transmitted by CBS, produced by his old associate Joan Harrison. The series, and its successor *The Alfred Hitchcock Hour,* ran continuously until 1965; of the 350-odd episodes, Hitchcock himself directed twenty. Much of their huge success derived from the famous prologues and epilogues, scripted by James Allardice and invariably delivered by Hitchcock himself straight to camera in characteristic deadpan style. These lugubrious performances, preceded by his caricature self-portrait and bouncily sinister signature tune (Gounod's "Funeral March of a Marionette"), made him a national figure, better known than most movie stars. The Hitchcock publicity machine soon developed into a whole industry; spinoffs from the TV shows included short-story anthologies (*Stories They Wouldn't Let Me Do on TV,* and so forth), magazines, records, games, toys, and even an Alfred Hitchcock Fan club.

At the same time, Hitchcock's reputation was also receiving a boost on a more elevated intellectual plane. Serious critical opinion had largely tended to ignore him or dismiss him as a provider of skilled but trivial entertainments. In the 1950s, though, Hitchcock became, with Hawks, one of the chief beneficiaries of the *Cahiers* school of criticism. A mass of articles, culminating in Rohmer and Chabrol's controversial study and Truffaut's book-length interview, confirmed Hitchcock's status as one of the great cinematic *auteurs* and a fit subject for detailed critical exegesis. This evidently afforded him huge delight. To his numerous interviewers he was invariably polite and forthcoming, rarely venturing the discourtesy of straight disagreement; at most, he would evade the issue or deflect the question into one of his many well-polished anecdotes.

Critical opinion, always liable to diverge over this Hitchcock movie or that, split with a vengeance on *The Trouble With Harry* (1956). A "thumpingly bad film" (David Thomson), one which "showed Hitchcock's worst faults, archness, facetiousness, hollowness of content, at their most galling" (Charles Higham), "easily the nadir of Hitchcock's career, a leaden whimsy" (William Pechter), is also "that lightest of dark comedies" (Gordon Gow), "a sparkling *jeu d'esprit* . . . one of Hitchcock's most masterly works" (John Russell Taylor). Hitchcock himself ranked it among his favorites—"more than anything else it has the humor of the macabre." The film did poorly in America, only moderately well in Britain, but in Paris ran to packed houses for six months.

The trouble with Harry, of course, is that he is inconsiderately and obtrusively dead, a tastelessly clad corpse lying amid the autumnal glory of the Vermont hills. Various local people, including a retired sea captain (Edmund Gwenn), a respectable spinster (Mildred Natwick), and Harry's estranged wife (Shirley MacLaine, in her film debut), have reason to think they may have killed him, and Harry is buried, dug up, and reinterred several times before it comes out that he died of natural causes. The film's humor resides in its amorality; no one expresses the least shock or regret over Harry's death, and his remains are treated throughout as no more than a casual inconvenience. (Natwick, coming upon Gwenn lugging the body by the heels: "What seems to be the trouble, Captain?") Bernard Herrmann's score, the first of eight he wrote for Hitchcock, neatly captured the mood of cynical geniality.

As early as 1941, Hitchcock had contemplated remaking the first of his Gaumont-British hits, *The Man Who Knew Too Much.* Now he revived the project, working with Hayes to refashion the script but keeping the basic plot virtually intact. The venue of the initial killing was shifted from St. Moritz to Marrakesh, the parental couple (James Stewart and Doris Day) became Americans, and the skill whereby the mother rescues her child was no longer sharpshooting but, rather implausibly, singing. (This allowed for the inclusion of a syrupy theme-song, *Che Sera Sera*, which became a popular hit.) The most fundamental change, though—aside from color and VistaVision—lay in the pacing; where the 1934 film ran a lean 74 minutes, the new version lasted two hours.

The remade *Man Who Knew Too Much* (1956) has been elevated into something of a shibboleth in the battle over Hitchcock's British versus his American films. Truffaut had no doubt that "the remake is by far superior." (Hitchcock's response—"the first version is the work of a talented amateur and the second was made by a professional"—sounds, as so often, ostensibly like agreement while leaving the question wide open.) For Gordon Gow, the "overall crudity" of the British version "made the remake by comparison a paragon of balanced thrills and wit." Raymond Durgnat, on the other hand, considered the remake "painstakingly and boringly reworked for the family market," as did Penelope Houston, in whose view Hitchcock had traded in "the casual audacity of the 1934 version" for "an academic exercise in suspense-building that flatly misfires. . . . Where the earlier film went like a bullet, the remake weightily ambles." Audiences at the time, though, were happy enough—the picture was among the top box-office hits of the year.

Ironically, the film that Hitchcock now made to fulfill his sense of obligation to Warners turned out his biggest financial flop of the decade. Bleak, downbeat, almost Bressonian in its austerity, *The Wrong Man* (1957), for all its seemingly un-Hitchcockian visual style, constitutes the most direct expression of his central preoccupation from *The Lodger* onwards: the ordeal of the innocent individual trapped in the impersonal processes of the law. The story is based closely on a real-life case—that of a New York musician, Manny Balestrero, arrested for robbery in 1953 on the basis of an utterly fantastic string of coincidences. By the time he was cleared his wife, unhinged by the strain, had been committed to a sanitarium, and his family life was destroyed.

For Andrew Sarris, *The Wrong Man* ranked as "one of the great American films of the Fifties. . . . Not even Lang has presented such a scathing indictment of the police-dominated state." Shooting documentary-style, often in the actual locations concerned—shops, offices, prisons, the wife's sanitarium—Hitchcock concentrates his camera on all the petty indignities of arrest and incarceration. No one is brutal or even verbally abusive; indeed, the police officials are mostly friendly, in a dreadful, detached way: "Sure, Manny, of course, we understand." Much of the film's impact derives from the quiet, anguished intensity of Henry Fonda's performance as Balestrero, rare among Hitchcock protagonists in engaging our sympathy beyond a superficial level. It may well be, as Hollis Alpert suggested, that *The Wrong Man* failed because it had Hitchcock's name on it, arousing unsatisfied expectations; signed by Frankenheimer, say, or Lumet, it might have become a minor classic.

Vertigo (1958) *has* become a classic. At the time of its release, though, it was scarcely more warmly received than *The Wrong Man*, and Robin Wood, acclaiming it in 1966 as "Hitchcock's masterpiece to date, and one of the four or five most profound and beautiful films the cinema has yet given us," was consciously going out on a limb. (Today, most critics would go along with the first part of his assessment, if not altogether with the second.) "I deal in nightmares," Hitchcock often said; and the most effective moments in his work are those which partake most thoroughly of the dream-state, ruled by an emotional rather than an intellectual logic, where certainties dissolve, mundane appearances give way to terror and disarray, and nothing is what it seems to be. Such moments occur in all his best films; but *Vertigo*, with its mood of luminous, drifting obsession, its hallucinatory images which shift and disintegrate, enmeshes us in a dream-world of doomed romanticism.

During a rooftop chase a San Francisco police detective, Scottie Ferguson, contracts acrophobia and is obliged to resign from the force. An old school friend, Gavin Elster, offers him an assignment: to shadow Elster's wife Madeleine, who is deeply disturbed and potentially suicidal. Scottie falls in love with Madeleine, but because of his ailment fails to prevent her throwing herself from a high tower. Shattered, he suffers a breakdown. Subsequently he meets a woman, Judy, in whom he perceives a resemblance to Madeleine. (At this point Hitchcock reveals to us, though not to Scottie, that Judy *was* Madeleine, hired by Elster in a plot to dispose of his real wife.) Despite Judy's reluctance, Scottie begins to refashion her into the image of his dead love. When a chance discovery makes him suspicious, he drags her back to the fatal tower in an attempt to force the truth from her; she slips, and falls to her death.

Many reviewers at the time objected, not so much that the plot was riddled with improbabilities—which it certainly is—but that Hitchcock had "given away the surprise" halfway through. As always, though, Hitchcock wanted not surprise but suspense. (His favorite example was the bomb under a table where people are talking: unwarned, the audience has five minutes dull talk followed by a few seconds of surprise; warned, they get five minutes of nail-chewing suspense.) Vera Miles, who had been moving as Fonda's wife in *The Wrong Man*, was originally cast as Judy/Madeleine; when she became pregnant, Kim Novak took over. For some critics, and for Hitchcock himself, Novak's shallow performance weakened the film. It could be argued, though—and was, by Truffaut—that shallowness is apt for the role: "There was a passive, animal quality about her that was exactly right."

As Scottie, James Stewart deepened and darkened his *Rear Window* persona towards a lonely, agonized monomania. Where L. B. Jeffries stayed safely (or so he thought) detached from his puppet characters, manipulating them from a distance, Scottie takes the fatal step through the screen; trapped in his own fantasy, surrogate this time of the director rather than the viewer, he tries to reshape the object of his gaze according to an unattainable ideal. (The analogy with Hitchcock himself, avidly molding his ice-blonde heroines, has often been drawn.) No Hitchcock film has a bleaker ending: Judy/Madeleine is at last irrevocably dead, but Scottie is liberated, if at all, only into utter desolation. As Gabriel Miller (*Post Script*, Winter 1986) put it, "he is alone, helpless, and horrifyingly enlightened. . . . The tragedy of the dreamer's betrayal of reality is complete."

Vertigo was the last of the four films which Stewart made with Hitchcock. Comparing them with the four starring Cary Grant, Victor Perkins noted Hitchcock's habit of "casting Grant for films whose tones are predominantly light and in which Grant's presence acts as our guarantee that all will turn out well. At the same time, he centres his meaning on the moral weakness of the hero's disengaged attitude. In the Stewart films . . . the tone is much darker, reflecting the disturbing ambiguities of the central personality. Stewart's bemused detachment is seen as a mask which thinly disguises a deep and dangerous involvement." If *Vertigo* serves as a valedictory summation of Stewart's Hitchcockian persona, *North by Northwest* (1959) does the same for Grant. The most accomplished of Hitchcock's—or, probably, anybody else's—comedy-thrillers, it triumphantly concludes the series of cross-country chase movies begun by *The 39 Steps*.

"I plunder my films for ideas, but in my business self-plagiarism is hailed as style." *North by Northwest* (made, under a one-picture deal, for MGM) not only lifts ideas from its picaresque predecessors, it reworks *The Wrong Man* for laughs. Grant plays a smart Manhattan ad man, Roger O. Thornhill, who by a combination of absurd chances is mistaken for a CIA operative, George Kaplan. Thornhill ("the O stands for nothing") is a hollow man, superficial, self-satisfied, and emotionally undeveloped; but Kaplan is even more hollow: a tactical fiction created by the CIA, he never existed. From this point the wretched Thornhill, his smug world imploding about him, finds himself assaulted, framed for murder (in the lobby of the UN building), seduced and betrayed by a beautiful blonde agent, machine-gunned, and hounded across America to the inevitable dangling showdown on the vast stone presidential faces of Mount Rushmore. Ernest Lehman, Hitchcock's wittiest collaborator since John Michael Hayes, furnished a crisply sophisticated script whose ironies and thematic subtlety never for a moment impede our enjoyment.

The film features many of Hitchcock's most celebrated set-pieces: Grant, forcibly intoxicated and shoved behind the wheel of a car, cornering wildly on a precipitous road; the UN lobby sequence, with Grant gazing round in mounting desperation, a dagger in his hand and an expiring delegate at his feet; the auction, where he evades his pursuers by disrupting the proceedings with ludicrous bids; the Mount Rushmore cliffhanger; and of course the famous crop-spraying plane episode where Hitchcock, reversing all the *noir* conventions of the situation (dark, rainwashed street, sinister black limousine, etc.), sets up his victim in bright sunlight on a flat unpeopled plain, with not a tree, a house, or so much as a bush for miles. The casting, right down to the smallest role, is faultless: James Mason as the suavest of villains; Eva Marie Saint as the duplicitous blonde; Jesse Royce Landis, unshakeably complacent in another monster-mother role ("You men aren't *really* trying to kill my son, are you?" she inquires brightly of a pair of hit-men in an elevator); the ever-reliable Leo G. Carroll as a Dulles-like CIA boss. At two-and-a-quarter hours, *North by Northwest* is Hitchcock's longest film, but it never seems like it.

Faced with highbrow queries as to the prupose of his films, Hitchcock generally countered with the disingenuous assertion that his sole aim was "to put the audience through it." By this criterion, his supreme cinematic achievement must surely be *Psycho* (1960). For all that Hitchcock's films up to this time had dealt in thrills and suspense, there had been little in them that was actually terrifying; *Rear Window* or *Stranger on a Train* might keep audiences on the edge of their seats but can rarely have given rise to much out-and-out screaming. But with his first horror movie Hitchcock produced a classic of the genre; shot rapidly and cheaply in black and white, using a television-style team, *Psycho* still qualifies, even after three decades of successors, as one of the scariest films ever made.

In Phoenix, Arizona, Marion Crane (Janet Leigh) succumbs to the temptation of $40,000 entrusted to her boss by a client and lights out for California. Having driven as far as she can, she stops for the night at an isolated motel run by Norman Bates (Anthony Perkins), a sensitive young man dominated by his cranky, ailing mother. While Marion is showering, a grey-haired figure enters the bathroom and hacks her to death with a knife. Norman, horrified, cleans up the evidence and sinks Marion's car in a swamp, with her body and the money inside. Marion's fiancé Sam (John Gavin) and her sister Lila (Vera Miles) come looking for her, as does a detective, Arbogast (Martin Balsam), who visits the Bates house and is also stabbed to death. Sam and Lila, learning that Mrs. Bates has been dead for years, search the house, where Lila is saved by Sam from attack by a knife-wielding figure. This proves to be Norman, who having long ago killed his mother has assumed her identity along with his own.

Hitchcock described *Psycho* as "using pure cinema to cause the audience to emote," a view echoed both by Peter Bogdanovich ("Probably the most visual, most cinematic picture he has ever made") and by Donald Spoto ("Where Hitchcock succeeded . . . was in the manipulation of the audience's reaction at every moment. . . . It is *our* psyche that is being opened up, analyzed, searched"). Having led us to identify with Marion in her guilty flight, Hitchcock leaves us shattered and disoriented by her death (the more unexpected since, by all the rules, the star cannot be killed barely halfway through the movie). Deprived of any other viewpoint, we are forced to adopt Norman's—only to discover that from an embezzler we have switched allegiance to a psychotic killer. (As Norman tells Marion, "We all go a little mad sometimes.") *Psycho*, wrote Robin Wood, draws us "forward and downwards into the darkness of ourselves."

The shower killing, over 70 separate shots in 45 seconds, has become probably the most famous single sequence in all Hitchcock; and a prime example of his control over an audience's perception: we never see the knife contact the woman's flesh, but are led to think we do by sleight-of-editing, sound effects, Hermann's shrieking violins, and the assault on our emotions. The scene was storyboarded by Saul Bass, who also designed the titles (as he had for *Vertigo* and *North by Northwest*); to him, and to Hermann's masterly strings-only score, should go much of the credit for the film's lasting impact.

As a shrewd publicity move, *Psycho* was released with strict instructions that no one be allowed into the theater after the show had started. Most reviewers (possibly piqued by Hitchcock's insistence that the restriction applied to them too) panned the film with the same virulent hostility that had greeted Powell's *Peeping Tom* the previous year. "A reflection of a most unpleasant mind, a mean, sly, sadistic little mind," growled Dwight MacDonald in *Esquire*. The public, undeterred (or perhaps encouraged) by such outbursts, packed the moviehouses, giving Hitchcock the greatest hit of his career. Made for $800,000, *Psycho* grossed $15 million on initial release in the United States alone and inspired countless imitations; over twenty years later, two sequels could be made starring Perkins and relying confidently on audiences' recall of the original. Hitchcock, though provocatively referring to it as "a fun picture," was highly gratified by the public response. "It's tremendously satisfying . . . to be able to use the cinematic art to achieve something of a mass emotion," he told Truffaut. "It wasn't a message that stirred the audience, nor was it a great performance or their enjoyment of the novel. They were aroused by pure film."

Psycho was Hitchcock's last picture for Paramount. His agent Lew Wasserman had become head of MCA, which controlled Universal; and Hitchcock now moved to Universal Studios, where he was installed with his own autonomous unit, bolstered by a lucrative stock deal which made him one of MCA's largest shareholders. From 1925 to 1950 he had directed 47 features, well over one a year, but from now on his output slowed. In the last twenty years of his life he made only six more films, held by many critics to show something of a creative decline.

The Birds (1963), widely considered a disappointment when first released, has since been reassessed; by 1976 Donald Spoto could write of it as "an artistic culmination and a unique triumph." For the third time Hitchcock drew on Daphne du Maurier, adapting her short story in which birds suddenly launch inexplicable, lethal attacks on people—and, by implication, finally exterminate the whole human race. The first part of the film, though, focuses on the love-hate relationship of Melanie Daniels, a spoiled San Francisco socialite, and Mitch Brenner, a young lawyer whom she meets in town and follows to his family home up the coast. Thereafter, escalating feathered onslaughts take over, culminating in a concerted attack on the Brenner house in which Melanie is nearly killed. Next morning the survivors leave the house and drive away, watched by the massed, and temporarily quiescent, birds.

Reviewers indulged in endless speculation over why the birds attack, and what it means—an ecological parable, the wrath of God, a metaphor for the Bomb or for human destructiveness in general, and so on. Hitchcock himself would only vouchsafe that the film was "about complacency," a further example of his perennial delight in overturning his characters' (and his audiences') misplaced sense of security. A technical *tour de force*, the film deployed a barrage of trick photography and special effects masterminded by the veteran animator Ub Iwerks, all of which tended to upstage the rather dull leads, Rod Taylor and Tippi Hedren—the latter a discovery of Hitchcock's whom he hoped to groom into the new Grace Kelly.

For a while it seemed that the old Grace Kelly might return to play the title role of his next film, *Marnie* (1964). The Monegasques, though, objected to the idea of their princess portraying a frigid kleptomaniac, and Hedren was cast instead. She played a professional thief who robs successive firms where she works as a secretary, until recognized by Mark Ruthland (Sean Connery), who employs her, then after the expected theft tracks her down and blackmails her into marriage. Breaking his promise, he forces himself on her, after which she attempts suicide. Finally, Mark traces the origins of Marnie's problems to a childhood trauma, when she killed a sailor whom her prostitute mother had brought home.

On *Marnie*, again, critical opinion has divided sharply. At first it was largely dismissed as glib, novelettish, psychologically half-baked, and technically shoddy, with several reviewers singling out some glaringly obvious back-projections and crude painted backdrops. Since then, attempts at rehabilitation have been made. William Rothman coupled *Marnie* with *The Birds* as "great works, infused with a deep sense of loss, an urgency and an emotional directness that set them apart from other Hitchcock films;" and Donald Spoto defended the unrealistic settings as deliberate expressionism, "to suggest states of mind rather than representational realities." Robin Wood put forward similar views—although both Spoto and Wood subsequently retracted their earlier arguments, Spoto in his second book and Wood in a pseudonymous

Film Comment article (November 1972), whimsically signed "George Kaplan." Hitchcock himself repudiated the film's variable production values as "a technical mix-up, and something of which I did not approve."

Torn Curtain (1966) has found few advocates. Unwisely trumpeted as "Hitchcock's fiftieth film . . . a triumph of mystery," it emerged as slack and episodic, an uninvolving political thriller with Paul Newman and Julie Andrews (both miscast as, respectively, a brilliant physicist and his fiancée) racketing round East Germany in search of a secret formula. The best scene in it was a wrenchingly effective murder sequence devised "to show that it was very difficult, very painful, and it takes a very long time to kill a man." *Torn Curtain*, though, looked almost like a masterpiece beside *Topaz* (1969). This was an international spy intrigue loosely tied in to the Cuban missile crisis, and adapted from a sprawling novel by Leon Uris. The master of the meticulously planned movie found himself still hesitating, in final editing stage, between three different endings, all of them inadequate. *Topaz*, Hitchcock recalled, was "a most unhappy picture to make." Most people found it equally dispiriting to watch.

Hitchcock was now seventy, and there was speculation that his career might be over. His old team was beginning to break up; both his regualr cinematographer, Robert Burks, and his editor, George Tomasini, had died soon after *Marnie* was completed, and the irascible Bernard Herrmann had walked out following a quarrel over the score for *Torn Curtain*. There was scarcely much financial need for Hitchcock to work; he had become most likely the richest director in the history of the cinema. But he had no intention of retiring ("What on earth would I do?"), and his last two films, though neither could be counted among his finest, went some way toward restoring his reputation.

With *Frenzy* (1972) Hitchcock returned to Britain, and to the subject of his first British film, *The Lodger*. Once again London is thrilled and terrorized by a series of sex-murders, and once again an innocent man, snared by circumstances, is arrested as the killer. This time around, though, Hitchcock took advantage of relaxed censorship codes to be far more explicit—gratuitously so, some critics felt. Two scenes in particular—one in which a woman is raped and strangled, and another in which the killer struggles, amid a truckload of potatoes, to retrieve an incriminating tie-pin from the stiffened fingers of a nude victim—were criticized for dwelling gloatingly on lurid detail, as well as offering further evidence of Hitchcockian misogyny.

Though it was generally agreed that with *Frenzy* Hitchcock had regained his old command of narrative tension, some writers found the film overall a depressing experience. For Gabriel Miller it represented "a portrait of total decay. Civilization seems to have died and, with it, man's spirit." Joseph Sgammato (*Sight and Sound*, Summer 1973) thought it "Hitchcock's most exciting film since *Psycho*," but also "deliberately disappointing, sacrificing the richness which usually softens the edges of the Hitchcock cynicism in favour of shock appeal." In a notable food-obsessed movie, perhaps the most enjoyable scenes were those of the police inspector (Alec McCowen) discussing the case with his wife (Vivien Merchant) while dutifully consuming her unspeakable forays into gourmet cuisine.

After the overt ghoulishness of *Frenzy* Hitchcock's last film, *Family Plot* (1976), came as an unexpectedly light-hearted, even benign, diversion, weaving elegant patterns around a plot of playful intricacy. The convoluted story, scripted by Ernest Lehman from a novel by Victor Canning, followed two criminal couples (one pair likable, one less so) in their respective and intertwined quests—the twist being that the male of one couple, a kidnapper and jewel thief, is, unknowingly, the long-lost heir that the other couple are looking for. With particularly engaging performances from Bruce Dern and Barbara Harris as the less ruthless duo and some tongue-in-cheek set-pieces—a bishop in full regalia kidnapped in mid-service, a slow-motion geometric chase through a graveyard—*Family Plot* has the feel, in William Rothman's words, of "a curtain call: light, assured, intended for pleasure . . . an acknowledgment that the body of the concert is over." Appropriately enough, the final shot of Hitchcock's final film ends with a wink, delivered straight to camera.

Following the release of *Family Plot*, to generally favorable reviews, it was announced that Hitchcock's next film would be *The Short Night*, to be adapted from a novel by Ronald Kirkbride based on the exploits of the spy George Blake, who had escaped from Wormwood Scrubs to Russia. Ernest Lehman worked for a while with Hitchcock on a treatment, as did the playwright and screenwriter David Freeman. Hitchcock's health, however, was deteriorating rapidly—a pacemaker had been installed, and he was in constant pain from arthritis—and his drinking, which had never been stinted, was getting out of control. In May 1979 he admitted defeat, and his unit at Universal was closed down.

Although five times nominated for Best Director, Hitchcock never won an Oscar; in 1968 the Academy, perhaps slightly embarrassed by the omission, gave him a Thalberg Award "for production achievement." Numerous other awards and honors were bestowed on him, especially in his later years, including the Légion d'Honneur and, in 1979, a Life Achievement Award from the American Film Institute. In the New Year's Honours List of 1980, he made a knight—Sir Alfred Hitchcock, KBE. Four months later he died quietly at home, of kidney failure, at the age of seventy-nine.

If during the first half of his long cinematic career Alfred Hitchcock received less than his critical due, that situation has been amply remedied; he has now been more extensively written about, his work analyzed in greater detail, than any other film director. The flood of books and articles continues, and still the great Hitchcock debate shows no sign of subsiding. Joseph Sgammato neatly summarized the two main camps: "On the one hand are those who think that since Hitchcock's films have nothing to say, he is not a major artist, while on the other are those who think that since Hitchcock is a major artist, his films must be saying something." This may be oversimplifying matters a little. That Hitchcock is a great director is probably no longer in dispute; the point at issue is, just *how* great?

Hitchcock's status as an *auteur*—despite his having worked exclusively within the distorting pressures of the commercial Anglo-American cinema—is as secure as that of any director in the world; no one could deny his films a consistent stylistic and thematic vision. His technical expertise is immense. Yet when his admirers number him among "the world's greatest filmmakers" (Maurice Yacowar) or even among "the greatest living artists" (Jacques Leduc), doubts begin to surface. "The greatest" is playing for high stakes—line Hitchcock up alongside Renoir, Satyajit Ray, Ophuls, or Mizoguchi (to name only moviemakers), and at once a whole missing dimension becomes evident. (It must be admitted, though, that any one of those four would have made a fairly appalling hash of *North by Northwest*.) The famed control, the premeditated, pre-edited exactitude of his working method, preclude something to which the creative imperfection of less rigorous directors grants access—something which Robin Wood defined (apropos Renoir) as "the sense of superfluous life."

At its bluntest, the anti-Hitchcock position was stated by Lindsay Anderson in *Sequence* (Autumn 1949): "Hitchcock has never been a serious director. His films are interesting neither for their ideas nor for their characters." Similarly, if more sympathetically, Hollis Alpert wrote that "he is not more serious because it is impossible for him to be serious. He has tried to be, on occasion, but it hasn't really worked well. . . . Try to sum up his films in terms of their content, and you will discover at best an enigma, at worst a vacuum. . . . Throughout his long and successful career he has entertained and surprised, but he has said nothing."

Adverse criticism of Hitchcock has often focused on his characters, whom he regarded, according to one of his best screenwriters, John Michael Hayes, "not as people, but as means to an end." Small wonder, in that case, if the Hitchcockian universe appeared to Kirk Bond (*Film Culture*, Summer 1966) as "a drama of puppets, forever dancing to the tune of the puppet-master. The people have no life of their own, and the world is not a real world." The behavior of Hitchcock's protagonists can be read, as by Susan Jhirad (*Cineaste*, 1984), as a metaphor for the director's own detached, distanced attitude: "When James Stewart makes an unwilling Kim Novak into a character in his fantasy world in *Vertigo*, or views life through the end of a camera in *Rear Window*, he is creating the image of the director himself, shaping and observing reality, but never really participating."

Against this, Hitchcock's advocates would maintain that such critics confuse lucidity with superficiality. Truffaut observed that "the director who, through the simplicity and the clarity of his work, is the most accessible to a universal audience is also the director who excels at filming the most complex and subtle relationships between human beings. . . . Hitchcock belongs . . . among such artists of anxiety as Kafka, Dostoevsky, and Poe." From this angle, the mass appeal of Hitchcock's films derives not from cynical commercialism but from the universality of his concerns. "This guilt which he is so skillful in bringing to the surface," according to Rohmer and Chabrol, "is . . . part of our very nature, the heritage of original sin." Or, as Andrew Sarris put it, (*Village Voice*, May 12, 1980), in less theological terms: "Paradoxically, Hitchcock produced works of great and enduring artistry because he was fortunate enough to come upon the one medium for which his limited range of experience could be profoundly expressive of a universal malaise. . . . He imprisoned himself within certain genre conventions, and then liberated himself by an unusual mixture of formal premeditation and artful digression."

The perennial interest of Hitchcock's films to critics (as to audiences) is understandable enough. The dazzling surface—the visual and structural arabesques, the technical bravura, the sardonically sophisticated interplay posited between spectator and spectacle—offers a virtually inexhaustible field for critical analysis, material to dissect and refract from an infinity of angles. Some writers, though, have felt inclined to cite Peter Wollen's image of the Fabergé egg, beautifully constructed yet hollow at the center (and, it could be added, none too nourishing). "The bulk of his work," wrote David Thomson, "only illustrates the smallness of mastery." Charles Thomas Samuels put it less severely: "What Hitchcock supremely understood is that the line between perception and feeling can be manipulated by the director, can be sustained or broken, quickened or retarded so that the spectator feels only what the filmmaker intends. As a result, Hitchcock has produced a new experience, a new kind of art. It is low but powerful; it does not exploit the full range of his medium, but it takes to the limit one of the things that film can do more fully than any other art."

"Those who put him on a pedestal," Michael Wood commented in *New Society* (January 31, 1985), "ignore what is cheap or phony or shallow about him; those who knock him off ignore everything that brought him into the vicinity of the pedestal, and that keeps him there." At his finest, Hitchcock is the supreme cinematic exponent of control over his medium, over his material, and over his audience. Other directors plumb depths which his films rarely even approach and never equal; whole vast areas of human experience lie far outside the scope of his vision. Yet he defined and dominated his chosen genre as no other filmmaker in any other genre has ever done. Truffaut wrote in 1966 that when a director "sets out to make a thriller or a suspense picture, you may be certain that in his heart of hearts he is hoping to live up to one of Hitchcock's masterpieces." For the foreseeable future, at least, that seems likely to remain true.

—*P.K.*

FILMS: Number Thirteen (Mrs. Peabody), 1922 (short; unfinished); The Pleasure Garden (Irrgarten der Leidenschaft), 1925; The Mountain Eagle (Der Bergadler/Fear o' God), 1926; The Lodger (The Case of Jonathan Drew), 1926; Downhill (When Boys Leave Home), 1927; Easy Virtue, 1927; The Ring, 1927; The Farmer's Wife, 1928; Champagne, 1928; The Manxman, 1928; Blackmail, 1929; (with Adrian Brunel) Elstree Calling, 1930; Juno and the Paycock (The Shame of Mary Boyle), 1930; Murder! (Mary/Sir John greift ein!), 1930; The Skin Game, 1931; Rich and Strange (East of Shanghai), 1932; Number Seventeen, 1932; Waltzes From Vienna (Strauss's Great Waltz/The Great Waltz), 1933; The Man Who Knew Too Much, 1934; The 39 Steps, 1935; Secret Agent, 1936; Sabotage (The Woman Alone), 1936; Young and Innocent (The Girl Was Young), 1937; The Lady Vanishes, 1938; Jamaica Inn, 1939; Rebecca, 1940; Foreign Correspondent, 1940; Mr. and Mrs. Smith, 1941; Suspicion, 1941; Saboteur, 1942; Shadow of a Doubt, 1943; Lifeboat, 1943; Bon Voyage, 1944 (short); Aventure Malgache, 1944 (short); Spellbound, 1945; Notorious, 1946; The Paradine Case, 1947; Rope, 1948; Under Capricorn, 1949; Stage Fright, 1950; Strangers on a Train, 1951; I Confess, 1952; Dial M for Murder, 1954; Rear Window, 1954; To Catch a Thief, 1955; The Man Who Knew Too Much, 1955; The Trouble With Harry, 1956; The Wrong Man, 1957; Vertigo, 1958; North by Northwest, 1959; Psycho, 1960; The Birds, 1963; Marnie, 1964; Torn Curtain, 1966; Topaz, 1969; Frenzy, 1972; Family Plot, 1976. *Published scripts*—The Lady Vanishes, screenplay by Launder, F. and Gilliatt, S. (Lorrimer 1984); North By Northwest, screenplay by Lehman, E. (Viking 1972); Psycho, ed. Anobile, R.J. (Darien House 1974); Rebecca *in* Twenty Best Film Plays, ed. Gassner, J. and Nicholas, D. (Crown 1943); Spellbound *in* Best Film Plays 1945, ed. Gassner, J. and Nichols, D. (Crown 1946); Strangers on a Train *in* Avant-Scène du Cinéma 297–298, December 1982 (in French).

ABOUT Abruzzese, A. and others. Alfred Hitchcock: la critica, il pubblico, le fonte letterarie, 1981; Alpert, H. The Dreams and the Dreamers, 1962; Amengual, B. and Borde, R. Alfred Hitchcock, 1960 (in French); Armes, R. A Critical History of British Cinema, 1978; Barbier, P. and Moreau, J. Alfred Hitchcock, 1985 (in French); Bazin, A. Le Cinéma de la cruauté, 1975 (Eng. ed. 1982); Bellone, J. (ed.) Renaissance of the Film, 1970; Belton, J. Cinema Stylists, 1983; Bogdanovich, P. The Cinema of Alfred Hitchcock, 1963; Carlini, F. Hitchcock, 1974 (in Italian); Coursodon, J.-P. and Sauvage, P. American Directors, Vol I, 1983; Cowie, P. International Film Guide 1964, 1963; Derry, C. Dark Dreams: The Horror Film From Psycho to Jaws, 1977; Douchet, J. Alfred Hitchcock, 1967 (in French; rev. ed. 1985); Durgnat, R. The Strange Case of Alfred Hitchcock, 1974; Estève, M. (ed.) Alfred Hitchcock, 1971 (in French); Fernandez Cuenca, C. El cine britanico de Alfred Hitchcock, 1974; Fieschi, J.-A. and others. Hitchcock, 1981 (in French); Filmoteca Nacional de Espana. Alfred Hitchcock, 1978 (in Spanish); Freeman, D. The Last Days of Hitchcock, 1984; Geduld, H. M. (ed.) Film Makers on Film Making, 1967; Giannetti, L. Masters of the American Cinema, 1981; Gow, G. Hollywood in the Fifties, 1971; Haley, M. The Alfred Hitchcock Album, 1981; Harris, R. A. and Lasky, M. S. The Films of Alfred Hitchcock, 1976; Higham, C. and Greenberg, J. Hollywood in the Forties, 1968; Higham, C. and Greenberg, J. The Celluloid Muse: Hollywood Directors Speak, 1969; Hillier, J. (ed.) Cahiers du Cinéma: the 1950s, 1985; Lambert, G. The Dangerous Edge, 1975; LaValley, A. J. (ed.) Focus on Hitchcock, 1972; Low, R. The History of the British Film 1918–1929, 1971; Low, R. Film Making in 1930s Britain, 1985; Manz, H. P. (ed.) Alfred Hitchcock, 1982 (in French); Naremore, J. Filmguide to Psycho, 1973; Noble, P. Index to the Work of Alfred Hitchcock, 1949; Pechter, W. S. Twenty-Four Times a Second, 1971; Perkins, V. F. Film as Film 1972; Perry, G. The Films of Alfred Hitchcock, 1965; Perry, G. Hitchcock, 1975; Phillips, G.D. Alfred Hitchcock, 1984;

Robinson, W. R. (ed.) Man and the Movies, 1967; Rohmer, E. and Chabrol, C. Hitchcock, 1957 (in French; Eng. ed. 1979); Rothman, W. Hitchcock: The Murderous Gaze, 1982; Roud, R. (ed.) Cinema: a Critical Dictionary, 1980; Ryall, T. Alfred Hitchcock and the British Cinema, 1986; Samuels, C. T. Encountering Directors, 1972; Samuels, C. T. Mastering the Film and Other Essays, 1977; Sarris, A. Interview With Film Directors, 1967; Sarris, A. The American Cinema, 1968; Schickel, R. The Men Who Made the Movies, 1977; Simsolo, N. Alfred Hitchcock, 1969 (in French); Sinyard, N. The Films of Alfred Hitchcock, 1986; Spoto, D. The Art of Alfred Hitchcock, 1976; Spoto, D. The Dark Side of Genius: The Life of Alfred Hitchcock, 1982; Taylor, J. R. Cinema Eye, Cinema Ear, 1964; Taylor, J. R. Hitch, 1978 (rev. ed. 1981); Truffaut, F. and Scott, H. G. Le Cinéma selon Hitchcock, 1966 (Eng. ed. 1968; rev. eds. 1975, 1983; rev. Eng. ed. 1985); Tuska, J. (ed.) Close-up: The Hollywood Director, 1978; Villien, B. Hitchcock, 1982 (in French); Weis, E. The Silent Scream: Alfred Hitchcock's Sound Track, 1982; Whittemore, D. and Cecchettini, P. A. Passport to Hollywood, 1976; Wilson, G.M. Narration in Light, 1986; Wood, M. America in the Movies, 1975; Wood, R. Hitchcock's Films, 1965 (rev. ed. 1977); Wulff, H. J. and Heisterkamp, P. All About Alfred Hitchcock: Bibliographie, 1983 (in German); Yacowar, M. Hitchcock's British Films, 1977. *Periodicals*—Action, May–June 1968; American Cinematographer, May 1949, December 1952, February 1957, October 1966, May 1967; American Film January– February 1976, March 1976, October 1983, November 1983, November 1984; Avant-Scène du Cinéma 297–298 December 15, 1982; Cahiers du Cinéma April 1951, November 1952, August–September 1953, October 1954, February 1955, April 1956, August–September 1956, June 1957, February 1959, March 1959, September 1959, December 1959, November 1960, September 1963, October 1963, November 1963, July 1964, February 1965, January 1967, May 1967, October 1969, March– April 1971; Cahiers du Cinéma in English 2 1966, 10 1967; Camera Obscura Autumn 1977; Camera-Stylo November 1981; Chaplin November 1966; Cineaste 10/2 Spring 1980, 13/4 1984, 14/3 1986; Cineforum September 1980; Cinema (UK) 3 June 1969, 6/7 August 1970, 9, 1971; Cinema (USA) August–September 1963; Cinéma (France) December 1963, November 1971, May 1984; Cinema e Cinema October–December 1980; Cinema e Film Summer–Autumn 1970; Cinema Journal Spring 1976, Spring 1982, Winter 1986, Summer 1986; Cinema Rising August 1972; Cinemasessanta May–August 1980; Cinématographe July–August 1980, March 1984; Dialogue on Film 2/1, 1972; Dirigido Por . . . September 1974; Écran July–August 1972; Écran français April 6, 1948; February 8, 1949; January 23, 1950; Film (FFS) Summer 1966; Film (W. Ger) March 1967, August 1969; Film Comment November–December 1972, May–June 1973, March–April 1974, September–October 1978, March–April 1979, May–June 1979, June 1984; Film Criticism Spring 1986; Film Culture Summer 1961, Summer 1966; Film Heritage Spring 1969, Winter 1972–73, Winter 1973–74, Spring 1976; Film Ideal November 15–December 15, 1964; Film Quarterly Winter 1962–63 Summer 1968,

Spring 1985; Film Weekly May 2–May 30, 1936; Film-critica January 1981; Filmkritik August 1966, June 1977, June 1980; Filmmakers Newsletter December 1975; Films and Filming July 1959, November–December 1959, July 1963, February 1970, April–November 1970, February 1972; Films in Review December 1952, April 1966; Framework Autumn 1980, Spring 1981; Image et Son November 1960, December 1970, March 1978; Interview 4/8, 1974; L'Incroyable Cinéma Spring 1971; Literature/Film Quarterly 3/3 Summer 1975, 6/3 Summer 1978, 13/1 1985; Mise-en-Scène 1 1972, 2 Spring 1980; Monogram 5 1974; Montage 45 1980; Monthly Film Bulletin February 1984; Movie October 1962, January 1963, Spring 1965, Winter 1970/71; Moviegoer Summer–Autumn 1964; National Film Theatre Programme, August 1979, May 1983; New Left Review January–February 1966; New Society, January 31, 1985; New York Film Bulletin 33 May 1961; New Yorker, May 16, 1974; Nuevo Film Autumn 1969; Objectif April–May 1964; Positif November 1955, February–April 1960, April 1974, September 1980, July–August 1984, December 1984; Post Script Winter 1986; Revue Belge du Cinéma Autumn 1984, Winter 1984–85; Revue d'Esthétique April–September 1967; Revue du Cinéma July 1948, December 1982, January 1985; Rivista del Cinematografico July–September 1980; Rolling Stone 25 December 1980; Screen 11/4, 5 1970, 13/3 Autumn 1972, 28/1 Winter 1987; Sequence Autumn 1949; Sight and Sound Autumn 1963, Spring 1969, Summer 1973, Autumn 1975, Summer 1977, Summer 1980, Spring 1983, Spring 1985; Take One 1/1 September–October 1966, 2/2 November–December 1968, 5/2 1976; Thousand Eyes Magazine JulAugust 1976; Village Voice, June 22–29 1972; 12 May 1980; 24 Images 6, September/October 1980; Visions 19, June 1984; Wide Angle 1/3 1976, 4/1 1980.

HOWARD, WILLIAM K(ERRIGAN) (June 16, 1899–February 21, 1954), American director, was born in St. Mary's, Ohio, the son of Irish immigrants. He attended public schools in St. Mary's and then studied civil engineering at Ohio State University. Howard earned his degree but in the process lost interest in engineering. His first job was as a film salesman for Vitagraph in Cincinnati.

Not intending to remain in the movie industry, Howard next contemplated a legal career and began studying law at night school. Realizing that he would qualify faster if he studied days and worked nights, he got a job as manager of a movie theatre and entered the University of Cincinnati. After about a year of this he decided that the law interested him no more than engineering and returned to Vitagraph. Howard is said to have been an excellent if unorthodox salesman. William K. Everson, in his article about Howard in Films in Review (May 1954), says that "he used his instinct for drama by acting out his wares before reluctant theatre

WILLIAM K. HOWARD

managers." By the time America entered World War I, Howard was sales manager of Vitagraph's Minneapolis exchange.

Howard served as an artilleryman with the American Expeditionary Force until the end of the war. Back in the United States, he tried without success to find himself a place in the New York film industry and then decided to try his luck in Hollywood. There he persuaded Carl Laemmle that Universal needed a sales adviser who would develop sales pitches during the making of a film rather than after its completion. Installed in this position, Howard was able to observe every aspect of filmmaking, from script conference to post-production.

The experience confirmed his growing belief that his real metier was making films, not selling them. In 1920 he left Universal and joined Fox as an assistant director. The earliest Howard credit discovered by Film Dope's researchers was as assistant to James P. Hogan on The Skywayman (1920). In 1921 he was scenarist of Bernard J. Durning's The One-Man Trail and before that year was over he was a full-fledged director—one of the few ever to have made the switch from distribution to direction.

Three pictures are credited to Howard in 1921—Get Your Man, codirected by George W. Hill; his first solo film Play Square; and What Love Will Do. According to William K. Everson, the last was a vehicle for the athletic Johnnie Walker, who starred in several of Howard's early movies, most of which were "fast, virile action films that may have lacked the polish and subtlety of his later melodramas, but were notable for vitality and speed."

One of the few Howard pictures to survive from this period is *Let's Go* (1923), a routine stunt comedy in five reels produced by a small independent, the Carlos Film Corporation. The story was no more than a flimsy excuse for Richard Talmadge to demonstrate his prowess in a string of chases, fights, leaps, and tumbles. However, the film historian Kevin Brownlow, who has a copy of the original print in his private collection, writes in a program note that "the picture has a pleasant atmosphere about it" and "moves along briskly," when not overweighed by "some of . . . the lesser masterpieces" of the title writer, Ralph Spence. Keene Thompson was the scenarist, and the cast included Eileen Percy, George Nichols, and Tully Marshall.

In 1924 Howard made one film for Thomas Ince, *East of Broadway*, and later that year signed with Famous Players–Lasky, soon to become Paramount. Of the six pictures he made there, the most notable were four ambitious Westerns based on Zane Grey novels. The best of these, in Everson's opinion, was *The Thundering Herd* (1925), starring Jack Holt, Tim McCoy, and Noah Beery. It "featured a wonderfully staged stampede of massed covered wagons across a frozen lake. When it was remade as a talkie, most of Howard's original footage was retained, and as recently as 1940 his stampede scene was again used by Paramount." *Volcano* (1926) was another lavish production—a "disaster movie" set in Martinique and starring Bebe Daniels, Ricardo Cortez, and Wallace Beery. Containing elaborate carnival, earthquake, and volcano scenes, it suffered from a marked weakness in its special effects.

When Cecil B. DeMille quit Famous Players–Lasky and established the Producers Distributing Corporation, Howard joined him. He began with three Rod La Roque vehicles and then made a film that has come to be regarded as a high point of the American silent cinema, *White Gold* (1927). Adapted by Garrett Fort and Tay Garnett from the play by J. Palmer Parson, it was a story of sex and jealousy with a Western setting—the "white gold" of the title were sheep—but heavily influenced in mood and technique by Howard's idol, F. W. Murnau. The cast was headed by Jetta Goudal, Kenneth Thomson, and George Bancroft.

The cameraman Lucien Andriot recalled that when work began on *White Gold* virtually the whole studio was already taken up by DeMille's *King of Kings*. He and Howard were sent out to shoot their film on location, but found that the range sheep they saw were not white but almost black with dust. They returned to Culver City and begged for studio space. Finally the studio

manager found them a small stage. According to Andriot, "we got a scenic artist to build a panorama with the mountains and everything, and we imported about a dozen [clean] sheep. We did the whole picture on the stage, with double exposure—sometimes triple exposure as far as the sheep were concerned."

The strangely stylized film that resulted had an extremely mixed critical reception. Some, as Andriot said, "thought it was horrible," but many were profoundly impressed. One trade paper reviewer wrote: "From the standpoints of production, scenario construction, directing, and acting, *White Gold* compares most favorably with the best German films that have been brought to America. The production style is of the same order as *The Last Laugh*. Deeper psychology is revealed in this film than in any other ever produced in America." James Damico quotes another contemporary writer as saying that the film had made Howard "an idol, more discussed than Von Stroheim." Unfortunately, the paying public by and large took the negative view and this extraordinary picture was one of the few flops Howard ever made. He apparently took this disappointment philosophically—like many other Hollywood directors of that era, he insisted that he was simply a purveyor of entertainment and made no artistic claims.

With the collapse of DeMille's PDC, Howard returned with a lavish new contract to Fox, where over the next five years he directed a string of solid commercial successes featuring the studio's top stars and made with the collaboration of a hand-picked team of craftsmen. These included the art director Gordon Wiles and the editor Harold Schuster, both of whom has worked on Murnau's *Sunrise*, and the cinematographer James Wong Howe.

It was during this fruitful period at Fox that Howard made his first talkie, *The Valiant* (1929), teaming Johnny Mack Brown with two newcomers from the theatre, Paul Muni and Marguerite Churchill. He had a major success the following year with *Scotland Yard*, and in 1931 another with *Transatlantic*, a drama set aboard an ocean liner whose distinguished passenger list included Edmund Lowe and Myrna Loy. "Here was a picture that was hailed as technically the finest thing that had happened in Hollywood since talkies began," wrote the columnist John Carpenter. "Who will ever forget the first 400 feet of that picture, showing the departure of a liner? Howard drew marvelous cameo studies of the reactions of the parting: pathos, revelry, boredom and wonder: they were all there."

Surrender (1931), adapted from a novel of

World War I by Pierre Benoit, has Warner Baxter as a French POW saved from execution by the love of a German aristocrat (Leila Hyams). This was also generally well received, though *Bioscope*'s reviewer remarked that it was "couched in gloomy terms, with the slightest of comedy relief." Ralph Bellamy contributed a much-praised performance as the sinister camp commandant, maimed both physically and emotionally.

The Trial of Vivienne Ware (1932) brought Howard further plaudits for the mobile camerawork that enlivened the long courtroom scenes. After *The First Year*, a Janet Gaynor–Charles Farrell weepie, came *Sherlock Holmes* (1932), with Clive Brook polishing the authoritative reading he had first essayed in Basil Dean's *The Return of Sherlock Holmes* three years earlier. Reginald Owen played Dr. Watson; and Ernest Torrence, Moriarty. The New York *Times* reported that this "was a Holmes of 1932, who no longer stimulates himself with hypodermic injections, but who still clings to his pipe"; the movie offered "clever dialogue [by Bertram Milhauser], excitement, amusement and trickery" and "Mr. Brook is a well-nourished but otherwise quite engaging Holmes."

The most discussed of all Howard's films followed in 1933, *The Power and the Glory*. Produced by Jesse Lasky and photographed by James Wong Howe, this was Preston Sturges' first original script. Spencer Tracy plays Tom Garner, pursuer of the American Dream, the poor boy for whom success is all-important. He bullies his way to power and glory as a railroad magnate but loses the love of his wife (Colleen Moore) along the way. In the end, cuckolded and betrayed, he kills himself. His story is told by his secretary and life-long friend (Ralph Morgan) in flashbacks presented out of chronological order—a technique for which Jesse Lasky coined the term "narratage" (combining narrative and montage). The narrator's voice is synchronized with the lip movements of the characters Morgan is describing, so that he appears to be speaking their lines for them.

The Power and the Glory has been widely seen as a model for Orson Welles' *Citizen Kane*—in its subject and in its style, and also in its photography. As Robert Walker wrote in a CinemaTexas program note (September 19, 1974), "Richard Corliss describes *The Power and the Glory* as one of the earliest American *films noir* for its oppressive sense of predetermined pastness. . . . In this film the somber mood is emphasized by the lighting with its strong overtones of German expressionism. Areas of darkness dominate the frame even in the lighter

scenes such as at the swimming hole where Tom Garner . . . becomes friends with the boy who will later become his personal secretary, confidante, and powerless adorer."

The "narratage" technique, as Walker points out, provides opportunities for heavy irony: "For example, when Tom Garner goes in to see his newborn son and holds the infant aloft, vowing for him a fine and noble life, we already have been shown, through the use of flashback, that his son has turned out to be a wastrel." For Andrew Sarris, *The Power and the Glory* "remains one of the more impressive films of the thirties, and not at all an entirely unworthy precursor of *Citizen Kane* in the never very popular genre of grown-up pessimism about the American Dream. . . . Ultimately, *The Power and the Glory* depresses audiences not merely for its pessimism, which it shares with *Kane,* but for its sordidness, in which it is unique. What finally destroys the protagonist . . . is the moral corruption of the milieu into which his wealth has propelled him."

After that, Howard moved on to MGM, where his first film could scarcely have been more different from *The Power and the Glory*. Adapted from a Jerome Kern–Otto Harbach stage piece, *The Cat and the Fiddle* (1934) stars Jeanette MacDonald as a singer and songwriter, Ramon Novarro as a penniless operatic composer. Far from worshiping pelf, Novarro puts it to MacDonald that they should "love, laugh, eat, drink, starve together." A reviewer in the London *Times* enjoyed some Clair-like sequences at the beginning of the movie but thought that Howard's inspiration had then deserted him: "The film conveys the uncomfortable impression that it does not know what to do with its embarrassing 8,000 feet of length. The burst of Technicolor at the end comes as a distinct surprise, for, all through, regard for the conventions in the telling of a conventional story is positively subservient."

The picture nevertheless did well at the box office, and so did *Evelyn Prentice* (1934), which featured the stars of the "Thin Man" series, William Powell and Myrna Loy, in a relatively somber courtroom drama. Powell plays a brilliant lawyer obsessed with his work (and one of his female clients); Loy is his neglected wife, who drifts into an affair of her own with a despicable blackmailing poet whom she accidentally shoots dead. The plot thickens further when another woman (excellently played by Isabel Jewell) is accused of murdering the poet. C. A. Lejeune found it very efficiently made in a genteel and low-keyed way, and called for "a little less refinement and a few more bones and blood."

Vanessa, Her Love Story (1935) was an adaptation of the last part of Hugh Walpole's "Rogue Herries" cycle of novels, set in Victorian England and starring Helen Hayes in the title role and Robert Montgomery as Benjie, the black sheep of the Herries. The star-crossed lovers are separated by a tragic misunderstanding and marry others, but are reunited in the last reel. It was generally agreed that the amiable Bob Montgomery was miscast, entirely failing to convey Benjie's "fiery passion and recklessness," but there was a good deal of praise for May Robson's performance as Vanessa's centenarian grandmother, for Otto Kruger's as the heroine's insane husband, and for Hayes herself, as well as for the "attractively romantic setting among the Cumberland fells."

Rendezvous followed, a fast-moving and exciting World War I spy thriller, set in Washington, with William Powell as the dashing naval lieutenant who evolves a new code to confound a German spy ring, Rosalind Russell as his screwball girlfriend. "The unfolding is always interesting and often gripping," wrote *Motion Picture Daily*, "what with the matching of wits between American and German intelligence, laboratory experiments on invisible ink and the like." Another reviewer, however, warned that "some of the repartee is in questionable taste."

Moving back to Paramount, Howard made one of the best and most personal of his genre pictures, *Mary Burns, Fugitive* (1935). Mary Burns (Sylvia Sidney) is an innocent country girl who is swept off her feet by city slicker Babe Wilson (Alan Baxter). Wilson turns out to be a much-wanted gangster and Mary, falsely accused of complicity with him, is arrested and jailed. FBI agent Wallace Ford then engineers her escape, hoping that she will lead him to Wilson. Instead she goes to work in a hospital and falls in love with snow-blind explorer Melvyn Douglas. Babe Wilson shows up at the hospital, Mary shoots him, and everyone else lives happily ever after.

Acknowledging that the story was trite and the characterization less than convincing, some contemporary reviewers recognized the odd intensity of feeling in this thriller. One called it "high-voltage gangster melodrama, brilliantly approached from the woman's angle" and combining "comedy, stark melodrama, and genuine poignancy." Another wrote that "the plot moves to a strong climax and the acting is of high quality. Particularly noteworthy is the photography of the grim prison scenes with their symbolic lights and shadows." A later critic, James Damico, has described *Mary Burns* as expressionistic, and Richard Koszarski thinks it "one of the strangest American films of the period."

For David Thomson, at least, Howard's next picture was his best. *The Princess Comes Across* (1936) is set, like *Transatlantic*, on an ocean liner. King Mantell (Fred MacMurray), famous band leader, and "Princess Olga" (Carole Lombard) both have something to hide—Mantell a past jail sentence, Olga the fact that she is actually a Brooklyn chorus girl. These things (and much else) are known to the blackmailer Darcy, who winds up embarrassingly dead. The principals' difficulties are compounded by the presence aboard the S.S. *Mammoth* of no less than five detectives of assorted nationalities, en route to an international convention. The result is a perfectly balanced mixture of tension, romance, and comedy—a mix that few directors have ever handled with more frequent success than Howard.

Howard went to Britain to make his next film, the very successful and prestigious *Fire Over England* (1936). Produced by Erich Pommer (in association with Alexander Korda), it was adapted by Clemence Dane from the novel by A.E.W. Mason about the defeat of the Spanish Armada—a celebration of Britain's martial prowess at a time when the country was drifting towards another great war. Howard had the services of James Wong Howe as cinematographer, of Lazare Meerson as art director, and Richard Addinsell as composer. Flora Robson was the best Queen Elizabeth ever, Leslie Banks was the Earl of Leicester, and Morton Selten was memorable as the aged Lord Burleigh. The dashing young hero, sent as a spy into Spain, was played by Laurence Olivier, and Vivien Leigh was his beloved lady-in-waiting.

William K. Everson has described *Fire Over England* as "an excellent example of how to get the most out of a relatively limited budget. The fact that it was primarily designed, like *Alexander Nevsky*, for propaganda purposes, mattered not one iota. It was thrilling swashbuckling fare." It seemed to one contemporary writer that "the sea fights are less spectacular than they might have been, but less obviously faked than usual. The dialogue, usually so slow and so Wardour Street in costume pieces, is lively and even poetical, and the plot does not linger."

Howard stayed on in London, planning a lavish production of *Lawrence of Arabia* for Alexander Korda. It never materialized, and meanwhile Korda put the director to work on other projects. *Murder on Diamond Row* (1937) was based on Edgar Wallace's play *The Squeaker* (its title in Britain), and was a remake of a film directed by Wallace himself in 1930. Edmund Lowe, with whom Howard had made four pictures at Fox, starred as a tippling detective, Ann Todd was the heroine, and the supporting cast included Sebastian Shaw as the suave villain, and Alastair Sim. Moderately well received in England, the film was handled much more roughly by American reviewers, who found it badly written, badly lit and photographed, badly acted, and lacking in pace and excitement.

The same year Howard worked without credit on two other Korda films. *Over the Moon* (1937), begun by Thornton Freeland (to whom it was attributed), had Merle Oberon as the long-suffering niece of a miser who dies and leaves her millions; Rex Harrison was the village doctor whose pride stands in the way of their happiness. Based on an original story by Robert Sherwood and Lajos Biro, and filmed in Technicolor (partly in Monte Carlo, Venice, and other choice locations), it struck *Variety* as "conventional but exceptionally well worked out via witty dialog."

Altogether less distinguished was *The Green Cockatoo,* a thriller also known as *Four Dark Hours* and *Race Gang.* This was credited to William Cameron Menzies as director, and labeled "A William K. Howard production." According to Everson, Howard had been called in to reshoot this picture, "which had been so badly made as to be unplayable. Howard did what he could with the feeble plot and meager finances, but when the film was released it was universally graded C" (though it was subsequently much reissued in England, mostly on account of a good cast that included John Mills and Robert Newton).

When Howard had left the United States he had been at the top of his profession—the supremely "bankable" director of a long string of hits for major studios. After his return to Hollywood, he apparently could find no employment at all for a year or more, and even when he did get back to work it was on low-budget programmers. Referring to Howard's "mysteriously lost reputation," Everson implies that his mistake had been to let Korda involve him in B movies (an ironic switch, if that theory is correct, on the more familiar story of European directors destroyed by Hollywood extravagance). However, James Damico, in his brief note about Howard in Richard Roud's *Cinema,* offers an alternative explanation of the director's downfall, saying that his "big-studio career was abruptly ended in 1937, probably in retaliation for his having halted production on a Paramount film until the supervisor whom Howard had ordered off the set was withdrawn (in the first use of a newly won Screen Directors Guild right)."

"With typical gutsiness, " Damico goes on,

"the director responded by producing, directing, writing and acting in *Back Door to Heaven* (1939), remarkable for its demonstration of the intensely personal expression possible in the B-film form, and for its distillation of Howard's inseparably dark-and-light vision and style."

Back Door to Heaven was a very important film for Howard, and it was a failure. He made it for Astoria, a small New York company that gave him complete artistic control. Damico is wrong to say that Howard scripted the film, but he wrote the original story, based on the life and death of a boyhood friend in St. Mary's who became involved with the Dillinger gang and was shot down in an attempted escape from the condemned cell. From this Howard developed a narrative that set out to show how an "essentially good fellow" can be forced into a life of crime by "environment, heredity and adverse circumstances." Wallace Ford played the central character and the script was written by Howard's friends John Bright and Robert Tasker. Hal Mohr was the photographer and Gordon Wiles the art director.

William K. Everson, unlike Damico, found the movie's "pretentious approach . . . quite unsuitable to its content, and its market," maintaining that it "hastened Howard's decline." This is no doubt correct. One contemporary reviewer objected that the picture "lingers luxuriantly over its somber theory that once you have been sent to a reformatory for stealing a mouth organ you can't help being a criminal," and others complained of its excessive sentimentality.

Struggling on, Howard next made a couple of cheap programmers for Warner Brothers. *Money and the Woman* (1940) was a thriller based on a James M. Cain story about an embezzling bank official (Roger Pryor) and his apprehension by a colleague (Jeffrey Lynn) who loves his wife (Brenda Marshall). *Bullets for O'Hara* (1941) was a remake of a 1936 movie, *Public Enemy's Wife,* using some of the original footage. This time Roger Pryor is on the side of right, playing the police detective who persuades Joan Perry to divorce her criminal husband (Anthony Quinn) and marry himself, thus driving the wanted man into the arms of the law. "Action covers a multitude of weaknesses in the story," wrote *Variety*'s reviewer. "The acting is sufficiently virile to maintain its hold, and the direction moves briskly."

Klondike Fury (1942), made by King Brothers for Monogram release, tells the story of a brain surgeon who is disbarred after the failure of a difficult operation on his best friend. He becomes a ferry pilot, is shipwrecked in the Klondike, and there has to repeat the famous operation. Everson calls this "Howard's last really interesting film . . . a remake of *Klondike,* but a more elaborate, and psychologically a better developed film than its predecessor. . . . It was, for its type and budget classification, an ambitious film, and Howard was allowed a more or less free hand. He got Edmund Lowe to play the lead and used old friends from the silent era (Kenneth Harlan, Monte Blue) as extras. Some interesting editing effects—tense cross-cutting between clocks before a dangerous surgical operation—recalled some of the Howard glories of *White Gold* days, and one love scene, played in silhouette against a frost-encrusted cabin window, had much of the old Howard power."

The film was well received, and interest in Howard revived. As a result, William Cagney offered him *Johnny Come Lately,* an important project based on a novel by Louis Bromfield. With James Cagney miscast in the lead, and a poor script, this last chance failed. Howard made two more films: *When the Lights Go On Again* (1944), with Regis Toomey as a newspaperman trying to help Marine James Lydon find his lost memory, and a neat little thriller with strong romantic interest called *A Guy Could Change* (1945).

A Guy Could Change had been intended as the first in a series of B pictures that Howard was to direct for Republic. "What happened is uncertain," Everson says. "Howard's personal troubles may have prevented him concentrating. Intra-studio politics may have caused friction." At any rate, Howard made no more pictures for Republic or for anyone else, though he did try to find a producer for a remake of *White Gold.* Hailed in 1933 as "a director of genius," he died forgotten after a ten-year silence, aged only fifty-five. As he once remarked, "those who etch on celluloid live only for a day."

Interest in Howard has slowly revived. *White Gold* and *The Power and the Glory* already have a place in the history books, and it is surely time for a reappraisal of a director of such "puzzling versatility," who in the opinion of William K. Everson created "some of the best melodramas ever made." Andrew Sarris credited Howard with "a very personal touch" and "a deserved reputation for individual intransigence"; a contemporary described him as "highly sensitive, nervous . . . and curiously well read." He was active (and courageous) on behalf of the Directors' Guild and in one interview said: "This is a director's business. Directors have made it. At every critical stage in its growth the courageous decision, often of an individual director, has carried it forward."

FILMS: (with George W. Hill) Get Your Man, 1921; Play Square, 1921; What Love Will Do, 1921; Extra! Extra!, 1922; Lucky Dan, 1922; (with Al Kelley) Deserted at the Altar, 1922; Captain-Fly-by-Night, 1922; The Fourth Musketeer, 1923; Danger Ahead, 1923; Let's Go, 1923; The Border Legion, 1924; East of Broadway, 1924; The Thundering Herd, 1925; Code of the West, 1925; The Light of Western Stars, 1925; Red Dice, 1926; Bachelor Brides (U.K., Bachelor's Brides), 1926; Volcano, 1926; Gigolo, 1926; White Gold, 1927; The Main Event, 1927; A Ship Comes In (U.K., His Country), 1928; The River Pirate, 1928; Christina, 1929; The Valiant, 1929; Love, Live and Laugh, 1929; Good Intentions, 1930; Scotland Yard (U.K., Detective Clive, Bart), 1930; Don't Bet on Women (U.K., More Than a Kiss), 1931; Transatlantic, 1931; Surrender, 1931; The Trial of Vivienne Ware, 1932; The First Year, 1932; Sherlock Holmes, 1932; The Power and the Glory (U.K., Power and Glory), 1933; The Cat and the Fiddle, 1934; This Side of Heaven, 1934; Evelyn Prentice, 1934; Vanessa, Her Love Story, 1935; Rendezvous, 1935; Mary Burns, Fugitive, 1935; The Princess Comes Across, 1936; Fire Over England, 1936; Murder on Diamond Row (U.K., The Squeaker), 1937; (uncredited; with William Cameron Menzies) The Green Cockatoo (Four Dark Hours/Race Gang), 1937; Back Door to Heaven, 1939; Money and the Woman, 1940; Bullets for O'Hara, 1941; Klondike Fury, 1942; Johnny Come Lately (U.K., Johnny Vagabond), 1943; When the Lights Go On Again, 1944; A Guy Could Change, 1945.

ABOUT: Koszarski, R. Hollywood Directors, 1914–1940, 1976; Roud, R. (ed.) Cinema: A Critical Dictionary, 1980. *Periodicals*—Film Dope November 1982; Film Weekly August 3, 1934; Films in Review May 1954.

HUSTON, JOHN (MARCELLUS) (August 5, 1906–August 28, 1987), American director, scenarist, actor, and producer, was born in the town of Nevada, Missouri, where the Water and Power company—or, according to some accounts, the entire town—had been won by his maternal grandfather, John Gore, in a poker game. Huston's father, Walter, was at that time a small-time actor whose itinerant troupe had just gone bust in Arizona; John Gore therefore installed him as head of Nevada's public utilities. Totally without engineering training, he proved spectacularly unsuited for this post, and when a fire broke out he mishandled a valve, cutting off the water supply. Half of Nevada burned to the ground, and Walter, with his wife and infant son John, went back on the road.

Huston's parents' marriage—contracted at the St. Louis World's Fair—was never a great success, and in 1909 they separated, divorcing four years later. Huston spent his boyhood shuttling between them, spending most of the time with his mother, who became a journalist under

JOHN HUSTON

her own name of Rhea Gore. With her he traveled the midwest, picking up her taste for literature, horses, plush hotels, and gambling. He remained somewhat in awe of her, though, feeling that she despised him as a romantic fantasist. "Nothing I ever did pleased my mother," he later remarked.

He was far more at ease with his father, who when not acting in New York would take him on the vaudeville circuit, staying in hotels that were anything but plush. Huston thoroughly relished the contrast, and was enthralled by the theatrical low-life he encountered. But at twelve he was found to be suffering from Bright's disease and an "enlarged heart." The boy was placed in a sanatorium in Phoenix, Arizona, and told he must henceforth live as a cautious invalid. Rebelling, he took up secret midnight swimming in a nearby river. After some months, this pastime was discovered, and it was decided that he must have made a fortunate recovery.

His mother, who had remarried, moved to Los Angeles, where Huston attended Lincoln High School. As if making up for lost time, he plunged into a multitude of interests: abstract painting, ballet, English and French literature, opera, horseback riding, and boxing. At fifteen he dropped out of high school, becoming one of the state's top-ranking amateur lightweights (with a permanently flattened nose) while studying at the Art Students League in Los Angeles. He was also "infatuated" with the cinema, though as yet only as a spectator. "Charlie Chaplin was a god, and William S. Hart. I remember the enormous impact the UFA films had on me, those of Emil Jannings and *The Cabinet of Dr. Caligari*. I saw this many times."

Walter Huston had moved over from vaudeville to the legitimate theatre, and in 1924 achieved fame on Broadway with the lead in O'Neill's *Desire Under the Elms*. Watching his father's rehearsals, Huston was deeply impressed by O'Neill's work and fascinated by the mechanics of acting: "What I learned there, during those weeks of rehearsal, would serve me for the rest of my life." He himself acted briefly with the Provincetown Players in 1924. The following year, recovering from a mastoid operation, he took a long vacation in Mexico, where among other adventures he rode as an honorary member of the Mexican cavalry. On his return, Huston married a friend from high school, Dorothy Harvey. The marriage lasted barely a year.

He had begun to write short stories, one of which was published by H. L. Mencken in the *American Mercury*. Further pieces, clearly influenced by Hemingway, appeared in *Esquire*, the New York *Times*, and other journals. He also wrote *Frankie and Johnny*, "a puppet play with music" (the music being by Sam Jaffe). This was produced in Greenwich Village by Ruth Squires and published in book form. Through his mother, Huston was given a job on the New York *Graphic*. "I had no talent as a journalist whatever, and I was fired oftener than any reporter ever has been within such a limited time. There was a kind-hearted city editor who kept hiring me back." When even this man's patience ran out, Huston headed for Hollywood, where his father had moved with the coming of the talkies.

Huston was hired as a scenarist by Goldwyn Studios, spent six months there with no assignments, and then moved to his father's studio, Universal, where he collaborated on four scripts, two of them for films starring his father: *A House Divided* and *Law and Order*. His colleagues had no doubt of his talent, but one of them described him at this time as "just a drunken boy, helplessly immature." After a lethal automobile accident in which he was the driver, he "wanted nothing so much as to get away" and left Universal for a job with Gaumont-British in London. Unhappy there, he quit again and lived rough for a while, before bumming his way to Paris and eventually back to New York. After a brief stint as a journalist there and a few months with the WPA Theatre in Chicago, he returned to Hollywood in 1937 and went to work as a writer for Warner Brothers.

Newly married to Lesley Black, Huston now seemed ready to settle to a serious career as a screenwriter. His first credit was for William Wyler's *Jezebel* (1937); this was followed by *The Amazing Dr. Clitterhouse* (1938), and two of Warner's prestigious biopics, *Juarez* (1939) and *Dr. Ehrlich's Magic Bullet* (1940). *Dr. Ehrlich* won Huston an Academy Award nomination, as did his next script, for Howard Hawks' *Sergeant York* (1941). He was now successful enough to persuade the studio that, if his next script was a hit, he should be allowed a chance to direct. "They indulged me rather. They liked my work as a writer and they wanted to keep me on. If I wanted to direct, why, they'd give me a shot at it, and if it didn't come off all that well, they wouldn't be too disappointed as it was to be a very small picture."

Huston's next script was for *High Sierra* (1941). Directed by Raoul Walsh, it gave Humphrey Bogart, as a gunman on the run, his breakthrough to stardom, and provided Huston with the hit he wanted. Warners kept their word, and offered him his choice of subject. He chose Dashiell Hammett's thriller, *The Maltese Falcon,* which had already been adapted twice by Warners, both times badly. Wisely, Huston stuck closely to the original, taking over much of Hammett's dialogue unchanged, and filming with a clean, uncluttered style that provided a cinematic equivalent of the novel's fast, laconic narrative. He also benefited from a superb cast. George Raft was offered the role of the private eye Sam Spade but turned it down (as he had previously with the lead in *High Sierra*). Bogart, who liked Huston, was happy to take over, supported by Mary Astor, Peter Lorre, Sydney Greenstreet (in his first film role), Elisha Cook Jr., and—in a walk-on part "for luck"—Walter Huston.

The Maltese Falcon (1941) was made on a small, B-picture budget, and put out by Warners with minimal publicity. They were taken aback by the enthusiastic response of public and critics. The latter immediately hailed the film as a classic, and it has since been claimed as the best detective melodrama ever made. "It is hard to say," wrote Howard Barnes in the *Herald Tribune,* "whether Huston the adapter, or Huston the fledgling director, is more responsible for this triumph." Already, in his directorial debut, many of Huston's characteristic preoccupations appear. The plot is a web of deceptive appearances; characters and even objects (including the coveted falcon itself) are duplicitous and untrustworthy, and the hero himself is not what he seems. Spade, outwardly a cynical opportunist, proves to be driven by a scrupulous personal code. "When a man's partner is killed," he says, turning the woman he wants over to justice, "he's supposed to do something about it."

Huston's next two pictures were less impressive. *In This Our Life* (1942) was overheated melodrama, a routine Bette Davis vehicle. *Across the Pacific* (1942), though based on even poorer material, was vastly more enjoyable. A rickety tale of secret agents and Japanese spies, it reunited several of the *Maltese Falcon* cast (Bogart, Astor, and Greenstreet) and was treated by actors and director with cheerful insouciance. A few days before shooting was complete, Huston received his army induction papers. He promptly returned to the set, placed Bogart in the most inextricable predicament he could devise, and handed the unfinished picture over to his luckless replacement, Vincent Sherman. Lieutenant Huston then reported to Washington.

Appositely, his first assignment as a documentary filmmaker for the Signal Corps was across the Pacific—in the Aleutian Islands off Alaska. The resulting film, *Report From the Aleutians* (1943), was described in the New York *Times* as "one of the war's outstanding records of what our men are doing. It is furthermore an honest record." Promoted captain, Huston was sent to Italy to make *The Battle of San Pietro* (1944), regarded as one of the finest combat documentaries ever filmed. "No war film I have seen," wrote James Agee in *The Nation,* "has been quite so attentive to the heaviness of casualties, and to the number of yards gained or lost, in such an action; none has so levelly watched and implied what it meant, in such full and complex terms." Huston's ironic realism disconcerted the War Department. One general accused him of having made "a film against war," eliciting the response: "Well, sir, when I make a picture that's *for* war—why I hope you take me out and shoot me." Despite this, he was promoted to major and awarded the Legion of Merit.

His last film for the army was *Let There Be Light* (1945), on the rehabilitation of soldiers suffering from combat neuroses. The overtly optimistic message was constantly undercut by the compassionate objectivity of the filming, which for Huston was "practically a religious experience." The War Department shelved the picture, but it was finally given general release in December 1980. Noting "its voice-over narration [provided by Walter Huston], its use of wipes and dissolves, and its full-orchestra soundtrack music," Vincent Canby called it "an amazingly elegant movie."

Discharged from the Army in 1945, Huston returned to Hollywood, where he was divorced from his second wife. After a brief, spectacular affair with Olivia de Havilland, he married the actress Evelyn Keyes in 1946. About this time he coauthored the script for Robert Siodmak's *The Killers* (1946), taken from Hemingway's short story, but for contractual reasons took no screen credit on the film. He planned to film another of his scripts, *Three Strangers*, himself, but handed direction over to Jean Negulesco when the chance came to direct a play on Broadway. This was Jean-Paul Sartre's *Huis Clos* (*In Camera/No Exit*) which ran for thirty-one performances at the Biltmore. Reviews were excellent, and the New York critics chose it as best foreign play of the year; but the public was evidently not ready for existentialism, and Huston returned to the cinema.

At this period Huston had a reputation—which he did little to discourage—as one of the "wild men" of Hollywood. Along with such friends as Bogart and William Wyler, he indulged in frequent and well-publicized bouts of drinking, gambling, and general horseplay. "Huston has more color than ninety percent of the actors in Hollywood," Bogart asserted. Much of Huston's wayward humor was exercised at the expense of Jack Warner, whose frayed nerves were legendary. However, Warner, though autocratic, was ready to tolerate a lot in return for talent and box-office success. He even let himself be persuaded—though with considerable misgivings—to allow Huston to shoot his next film almost entirely on location, and in Mexico. At the time, this was a radical move.

The results justified it. *The Treasure of the Sierra Madre* (1948) is generally agreed to be one of Huston's finest films. Based on a novel by the enigmatic B. Traven, it tells of three drifters who band together to prospect for gold, find it—and eventually lose it again, destroyed by greed. Once more, Huston stuck closely to his source, preserving much of Traven's idiosyncratic dialogue and sardonic outlook. Bogart again starred, as the paranoid Fred C. Dobbs, and Walter Huston had the screen role of his career as Howard, the garrulous old prospector.

Treasure has often been cited as the archetypal Huston movie, though the director himself denies the presence of any authorial unity in his films. "I fail to see any continuity in my work from picture to picture—what's remarkable is how different the pictures are, one from another." In fact, though Huston's cinematic style varies according to the nature of his subject matter, clear thematic preoccupations can be seen to recur throughout his work. The classic "Huston movie" concerns a quest, often a parody of one of society's sanctioned forms of endeavor—the pursuit of wealth, power, religious knowledge, imperial sovereignty—which is destined, after initial success, to end in failure and futility. (This kind of denouement became known in the trade as "the Huston ending.") The protagonists will be a heterogeneous bunch, drawn into uneasy alliance by their common

goal; several, if not all, will be wearing masks, presenting themselves as other than they are. In the end, the survivors (if any) will be those who can detach themselves, accepting defeat with an ironic shrug. Those who perish are the obsessives, who let the quest take them over and eventually destroy them.

The studio was at first uncertain what to make of *Treasure*. Jack Warner personally detested it. However, the critical and public reception soon resolved their doubts. James Agee, always an admirer of Huston's work, called it "one of the most beautiful and visually alive movies I have ever seen," and *Time* thought it "one of the best things Hollywood has done since it learned to talk." The film triumphed at the 1948 Academy Awards. Huston won Oscars as best director and author of the best screenplay; his father was best supporting actor, and the film went on to gain several other awards in the USA and abroad. Huston was especially gratified since, despite their misgivings, the studio had demanded no changes. "The film is exactly as I wanted it," he declared.

The art, technique, and moral implications of *The Treasure of the Sierra Madre* (as of *The Maltese Falcon*) have since been discussed in great detail by many critics. Richard T. Jameson, who devotes four pages to it in his *Film Comment* article on Huston (May–June 1980), concludes: "There is not a department of the film's production, not a scene, not a performance, not even a 'flaw' that wouldn't merit lengthy commentary. Some of it—much of it—may finally be beyond criticism. . . . This film has impressed itself on the heart and mind and soul of anyone who has seen it, to the extent that filmmakers of great originality and distinctiveness like Robert Altman and Sam Peckinpah can be said to have remade it again and again . . . without compromising its uniqueness."

Warners were less circumspect over Huston's next film, his fourth with Bogart. *Key Largo* (1948) was adapted from a prewar play by Maxwell Anderson, originally written in blank verse. Huston and his co-scriptwriter, Richard Brooks, junked the verse and updated the plot, about a disillusioned returning veteran clashing with gangsters on a remote Florida key. Even rewritten, the action remained stage-bound and stilted, and the film was saved only by some outstanding performances, notably from Bogart, Lauren Bacall, Claire Trevor, and Edward G. Robinson. To Huston's annoyance, the studio cut several scenes from the final release. Not long before this, Huston had been refused permission, under the terms of his contract, to direct a play by his idol Eugene O'Neill for the Broadway stage. Angered by these incidents, Huston left Warners when his contract expired.

Together with Sam Spiegel and Jules Buck, Huston founded Horizon Films. The new company's first feature was a courageous failure. Huston had been among the strongest opponents of HUAC and the Hollywood blacklist, and when John Garfield came under pressure, Huston offered him the lead in *We Were Strangers* (1949) as a deliberate gesture of defiance—the more so since the prophetic plot concerned a revolution in Cuba against a corrupt dictatorship. It was attacked on release by both left and right. It was also a box-office disaster, and Huston admitted that "it didn't turn out to be a very good picture." Needing funds, he signed a short-term contract with MGM.

Having refused *Quo Vadis*—despite an amazing episode when Louis B. Mayer (according to Huston) "crawled across the floor and took my hands and kissed them" in order to persuade him to reconsider—Huston took on a far more congenial subject in *The Asphalt Jungle* (1950). Based on a novel by W. R. Burnett (author of *Little Caesar* and *High Sierra*), this was the progenitor of a long cycle of "caper movies," in which a crime (here a million-dollar jewel theft) is successfully carried out by sympathetically depicted criminals, only to fail through subsequent ill-chance or internal dissension. Huston was breaking new ground in presenting crime as an occupation like any other, "a left-handed form of human endeavor" carried out by ordinary people motivated not by the megalomanic will to power of 1930s movie gangsters, but simply by the desire to feed their families or realize some small private ambition. Once again, Huston focuses on a small group absorbed in an immensely difficult task and studies their reactions to success and to failure; the gritty atmosphere of the urban underworld is vividly evoked. Another HUAC victim, Sterling Hayden, took the lead, with Huston's old friend Sam Jaffe as the criminal mastermind and, in her first serious role, Marilyn Monroe. The film did well; Huston received Academy Award nominations for best director and best screenplay, and won the Screen Directors Guild Award.

That same year, 1950, Huston was amicably divorced from Evelyn Keyes; one day later he married Enrica Soma. In August, while *Asphalt Jungle* was still filming, his father died of a heart attack. Huston's second picture for MGM was only sixty-nine minutes long and is remembered, as he wryly acknowledges, more for the book it occasioned than for itself. *The Red Badge of Courage* (1951), taken from Stephen Crane's novel of the Civil War, fell victim to a power

struggle within MGM between Louis B. Mayer and Dore Schary. The wrangling, haggling, and compromising that ensued are charted in Lillian Ross' *Picture*, a classic piece of fly-on-the-wall reportage. As if this were not enough, Huston also had to contend with the studio's determination to boost the American fighting man (personified by war hero Audie Murphy); it is said that the director had originally planned to set this study of human bravery in a context of utter futility, a view of war (and of Crane) that alarmed his producers. The remnant of film that emerged from the MGM mangle garnered respectful critical notices and disastrous box-office returns—in the words of one studio executive, "a flop d'estime." By then Huston had left for Africa to make a film for Sam Spiegel, his partner in Horizon Films.

The script of *The African Queen* (1951) was taken from C. S. Forester's novel and written by Huston in collaboration with his greatest critical supporter, James Agee. The story of a spinster missionary and a drunken riverboat skipper who join forces to sink a World War I German warship held evident attractions for Huston. For once, though, he renounced the "Huston ending"; success is snatched from the jaws of defeat, and the protagonists survive. Filming, on location in the Congo and Uganda, took place under appalling conditions: not only extreme heat and humidity, but dysentery, malaria, mosquitoes, crocodiles, and safari ants beset actors and crew. Everybody became ill except Bogart, Lauren Bacall (who came to keep Bogart company), and Huston, who all ascribed their immunity to copious quantities of Scotch. Despite this, Bogart and Katharine Hepburn acted superbly together, playing off their contrasted acting styles to perfection, and Huston was in his Hemingwayesque element. The film was a huge popular and critical success, and won Bogart the only Oscar of his career.

Through some financial sleight-of-hand, little of the profits from *The African Queen* ever reached Huston, who consequently pulled out of Horizon Films. For his next three films, he acted as his own producer. *Moulin Rouge* (1952) was a heavily fictionalized life of the crippled and embittered painter Toulouse-Lautrec (played by José Ferrer wearing shoes on his knees). Visually, the film is impressive—Houston, working with cinematographer Oswald Morris, aimed at re-creating the palette of Lautrec's own paintings—and the long opening sequence is a dazzling explosion of music and dance. But the rest of the picture now seems trite and sentimentalized. *Beat the Devil* (1953), by contrast, was ahead of its time. Huston's sixth and last film with Bogart (who coproduced), it can now be seen as an early example of deliberately inconsequential black comedy, straightfacedly parodying Huston's favorite theme of the quest. At the time, it was greeted with incomprehension and dislike, flopped dismally at the box office, and only gradually built up a cult following.

Meanwhile, disgusted by the HUAC "witch-hunt" and the "moral rot" it had induced in the entertainment industry, Huston had moved to Ireland. He had bought a house in Galway, St. Clerans, and moved there in 1952 with his wife Enrica and their children Anthony and Anjelica. Twelve years later he took Irish citizenship. One of his neighbors was the writer Claud Cockburn, who had written the novel *Beat the Devil* under the pen name James Helvick.

For over ten years Huston had been planning to film Melville's *Moby Dick,* originally envisaging his father in the role of Captain Ahab, obsessed hunter of the Great White Whale. Instead, he cast Gregory Peck as "the man who shook his fist at God" (Huston's own reading of the character), and invited science-fiction writer Ray Bradbury to work on the script. Filming took nearly three years to complete, since Huston as usual shot largely on location. The fishing port of New Bedford was reconstructed on the waterfront of the Irish harbor of Youghal; Ahab's ship, the *Pequod,* was constructed to be fully seaworthy; and three hundred-foot whales were built of steel, wood, and latex to play the title role. Two of these were lost during filming on the open sea, several members of the crew and cast sustained injuries, and Peck, who gallantly refused doubles for some of the most hazardous scenes, more than once narrowly escaped drowning. Huston again worked with Oswald Morris to devise a distinctive visual texture. From the color film two negatives were taken, one in color and one in black and white, and these were superimposed in printing to produce the grainy, faded tonality of old whaling prints. Despite so much painstaking work, though, the film proved strangely lifeless and uninvolving. "Where Huston has failed," commented David Robinson, "is in suggesting the mysticism of the book. Without this, much of the story loses its significance."

After two financially unsuccessful pictures, with a large old house and a family to support, and paying multiple alimony, Huston was now deep in debt, and he accepted a lucrative three-picture contract with 20th Century–Fox. None of the three films gives the impression that Huston felt greatly involved with his material. *Heaven Knows, Mr. Allison* (1957), teaming Robert Mitchum and Deborah Kerr as a marine and a nun stranded on a Japanese-held island during World War II, struck many reviewers as an attempt to repeat *The African Queen.* Huston coscripted, and enjoyed working with Mitchum, whom he considers "one of the really fine actors of my time."

He felt less empathy with the star of his next picture, John Wayne. *The Barbarian and the Geisha* (1958) was based on the experiences of Townsend Harris, sent as the first United States Ambassabor to Japan in 1855. Huston had no hand in the script, disliked the title, and was appalled by the version that was released, heavily cut and partly reshot after his departure for Africa to make his third Fox assignment. Adapted from Romain Gary's novel about a crusade to save Africa's elephants from extinction by ivory hunters, *The Roots of Heaven* (1958) starred Errol Flynn in his penultimate role, with Trevor Howard as the eccentric idealist. As Huston readily admits, "*The Roots of Heaven* didn't come up to anything like what it might have been. I accept the blame fully. The depths of the novel were not touched."

During his stint at Fox, Huston had been offered by David Selznick the chance to direct a new version of *A Farewell to Arms.* He accepted enthusiastically, having long admired Hemingway, who for his part had described the Huston-scripted *The Killers* as "the only picture made out of my work that was any damn good." However, Huston soon realized that Selznick was intent on turning the film into a vehicle for his wife, Jennifer Jones, and after several disputes he quit the picture, which was eventually directed by Charles Vidor.

Despite his penchant for outdoor action movies, Huston had not so far made a Western. He was now offered one by Hecht-Hill-Lancaster, *The Unforgiven* (1960), taken from a novel by Alan LeMay. The film, which concerns a ranching family split apart by racial bigotry, has a brooding power and some strikingly surrealist images, but suffers from portentousness and a fragmented narrative. Huston felt at odds with the material and now dislikes the picture. "The overall tone is bombastic and overinflated. Everybody in it is larger than life."

A retrospective atmosphere of doom hangs over *The Misfits* (1961). Clark Gable died shortly after shooting was finished. Marilyn Monroe never completed another film. Montgomery Clift and Thelma Ritter were dead within a few years. While the film was being made, the marriage between Monroe and Arthur Miller (who had written the script) broke up, virtually on set. The story, about down-and-out modern cowboys who round up wild horses to be made into dog food, carries strong allegorical overtones as a metaphor for the trashing of the American dream of innocence and freedom, the closing of the frontier. Despite problems with Monroe, who by this stage in her career was in a desperate condition, Huston was pleased with the finished picture. "I had obtained the qualities I wanted." Critical and public reception was lukewarm, but the film's reputation has grown steadily ever since.

Huston had conceived the idea of making a film about Freud while working on *Let There Be Light*. He now invited Jean-Paul Sartre to prepare a script. Sartre did so—four hundred pages of it. Huston tactfully suggested that cuts might be necessary, and he and Sartre went over the script together. Sartre returned to Paris, and in due course submitted his revised script—of six hundred pages. With the help of Charles Kaufman, who had coscripted *Let There Be Light*, the scenario was pruned to a manageable hundred and fifty pages, although Sartre disowned it.

Freud: The Secret Passion (1962) is not a conventional biopic, but rather an intellectual detective story, in which Freud is shown tracking down, in himself as much as in others, the psychosexual source of the guilt which torments them. The film, like *The Misfits*, was shot in black and white, and includes an exceptionally high ratio of close-ups, and some startlingly unusual and disturbing dream sequences. Exceptionally for Huston, known as a courteous and considerate director who establishes good rapport with his actors, he had severe difficulties with his star. Montgomery Clift, who played Freud, was drinking heavily, taking drugs, and suffering from cataracts on both eyes. Huston described the making of the film as "hell for Monty and equally harrowing for me." There were critics who found *Freud* unintentionally funny, but Richard T. Jameson thought it "a brilliant picture, of a formal complexity all but unique in Huston's work. Its resonant script . . . and intricate *mise-en-scène* relate the substance of Freud's investigations and theories, the obsessiveness of the doctor's personal quest, and Huston's own art in rich and suggestive ways."

By way of relaxation, Huston turned to a spoof murder mystery, *The List of Adrian Messenger* (1963), in which the villain, played by Kirk Douglas, appears in numerous elaborate disguises. As an additional gimmick, the film featured various guest stars, also heavily disguised. Response was mainly puzzled. "This is a folly work in Huston's life," said Penelope Gilliat, guardedly, "but the casual authority of it is unmistakable and exciting." The film, like *Beat the Devil,* has since acquired a certain cult reputa-

tion and can be seen as a set of fantastic variations on Huston's running theme of disguise.

The "Huston ending," wherein all human activities culminate in ironic futility and disaster, was notably absent from *The Night of the Iguana* (1964). Huston and his co-scriptwriter, Anthony Veiller, took a characteristically overheated and doom-laden play by Tennessee Williams and transformed it into a melodramatic farce with a happy ending. Amazingly, Williams went along with their changes and even helped with the script. Shooting took place at Puerto Vallarta in Mexico, and the cast included Richard Burton, Ava Gardner, Deborah Kerr, and Sue Lyon, most of whom arrived with their various spouses and attachments, giving rise to some exceedingly well-publicized feuds and disputes on set. Huston rode the whole affair with cheerful insouciance, finishing five days ahead of schedule. "Everybody adored themselves and each other," he informed Hedda Hopper with a straight face. "A most serene experience."

While *Iguana* was doing well at the box office, Huston was visited in Ireland by Dino De Laurentiis, who planned to film *The Bible*. He envisaged a multiplicity of episodes, each with its own eminent director. Eventually, the producer modestly limited himself to half the Book of Genesis, with Huston as sole director. Huston also played Noah and the Voice of God—the former role allowing him to indulge his love of animals to the full. In the Ark sequence he established a most cordial relationship with his fellow actors, especially with the elephants, giraffes, and a hippopotamus "who broke into the damndest grin every time he saw me coming." The film finally cost eighteen million—by far the most expensive movie of Huston's career—and received atrocious notices. De Laurentiis, though, claimed to have recouped his costs several times over.

Huston directed, and acted in, an episode of *Casino Royale* (1967), a direly unfunny James Bond parody, while preparing his next film, *Reflections in a Golden Eye* (1967). Taken from Carson McCuller's novel of neurosis and sexual obsession at a peacetime army camp in the South, the picture could easily have toppled over into hothouse melodrama. Huston, however, handled his subject with faultless control, evoking the pervasive, drab claustrophobia of army life, and drawing from Marlon Brando a portrayal of emotional repression so intense as to be almost painful to watch. Again Huston worked with Oswald Morris to devise a creative use of color; taking his cue from the title, he filmed in a desaturated process that lent the whole film a cool, golden tone, aiming "to separate the audience somewhat from the characters, who were in various ways withdrawn from reality." The studio, Warners, regarded such sparing use of color as wasteful and reverted to full Technicolor for most of the release prints, to Huston's annoyance. This apart, he "found very little to fault in *Reflections.*" The paying public disagreed, however, and so did some of the critics. Andrew Sarris wrote that "Huston overdirects *Reflections* for the sake of a mass audience in which he has little confidence," and John Simon called it "a painfully artless film in a painfully arty shell."

There was an even harsher reception for *Sinful Davey* (1969), a picaresque adventure in the *Tom Jones* tradition set in early nineteenth-century Scotland (though filmed in Ireland). The film was a disaster, running for barely a week on release; Huston attributes its failure to insensitive recutting by the producer, Walter Mirisch, but in fact few of his films at this period were financially successful. This caused him to feel, he later wrote, "a certain responsibility and a deep disappointment, not only so far as I personally was concerned, but that others who wanted to do something original and new and away from the pattern would have my failure thrown up at them."

A Walk with Love and Death (1969), adapted by Hans Koningsberger from his own novel, concerns the brief, doomed love of two young people in fourteenth-century France, amid the wreckage of the Hundred Years War. For his leads, Huston chose two unknowns: his teenage daughter, Anjelica, and Assaf (son of Moshe) Dayan. He also cast himself in a key role as a sympathetic nobleman who joins the peasants' cause. The film was severely weakened by the evident inexperience of the two principals, but in the view of some critics conveyed a strikingly convincing, almost tangible, sense of the Middle Ages with something of the primary directness of an illuminated chronicle. Reviews in the USA were scathing, but the picture was enthusiastically praised in France, and ran in three movie theatres simultaneously in Paris for several months.

While *Walk* was being filmed, Huston's wife Enrica was killed in an automobile accident. This personal loss may partially account for the unremitting bleakness of his next film, *The Kremlin Letter* (1970). Based on a spy novel by Noel Behn, the film portrays a cold, amoral world, in which loyalty is no more than another commodity to be bought, sold, or bargained for as opportunity offers. The convoluted plot presents the most negative of all his variations on the quest theme; duplicity reigns supreme. "There are declines and declines," wrote William S.

Pechter in his review, "and Huston's is a prodigy: in the strict, classical purity of its prolonged downward movement, perhaps unrivaled even in the decline-crammed annals of the cinema." Pechter attributed Huston's deterioration to his "growing self-consciousness of his reputation as a serious artist, and his increasingly desperate efforts to satisfy the demands thought to attend Artistic Seriousness."

In 1971, Huston worked briefly as director on *The Last Run,* starring George C. Scott. He soon clashed with Scott and left the film, to be replaced by Richard Fleischer. In *Fat City* (1972) Huston drew on the boxing world of his youth. Unlike most fight movies, though, the film offered its characters no moment of glory in the big time; these were the small-time losers on the lower fringes of the sport, failures and derelicts never more than a step away from defeat. Filmed in muted, smoky tones in the bars, tenements, and pool-halls of dead-end Stockton, California, *Fat City* offers the clearest statement of Huston's fascination with defeat, and the small vestiges of dignity that can be salvaged from it. As a washed-up fighter, Stacy Keach gave the performance of a lifetime. Critics hailed the film as a return to form, and John Russell Taylor described it as "one of those late films by old masters that look effortless because they are effortless."

By way of total contrast, *The Life and Times of Judge Roy Bean* (1972) was a cheerfully inconsequential fantasy in the guise of a Western. Scripted by John Milius around the legend of a disreputable Texas hanging judge with a weakness for Lily Langtry, the film presented an episodic, freewheeling burlesque of Western conventions and occasionally lapsed into sentimentality. In the title role, Paul Newman gave a creditable impersonation of Huston and unconcernedly let a tame bear steal several of his scenes. While working on *Roy Bean,* Huston was married for the fifth time, to Celeste Shane. The marriage was to end in divorce after five years. During the course of it Huston sold his house in Galway and moved to Puerto Vallarta, where he had filmed *Night of the Iguana.*

Having established a good working relationship, Huston and Newman went on to make another picture together, *The Mackintosh Man* (1973). This was a spy film, but where *The Kremlin Letter* had been complex to the point of opacity, *Mackintosh* was straightforward, the motives of its characters rarely in question; they may aim to deceive each other, but not the audience. Despite some incidental felicities—such as a beautifully handled prison break—the overall effect was flat and somewhat impersonal.

Huston had long cherished an ambition to film Kipling's story *The Man Who Would Be King*. Originally, he had planned it with Gable and Bogart; then with Peter O'Toole and Richard Burton. It finally reached the screen with Sean Connery and Michael Caine in the leading roles, as the two British soldiers who set up a private kingdom in the wild mountains of Afghanistan. For once, delay proved beneficial. As Huston remarked, his modern actors brought "a reality to it that the old stars could not do. Today they would seem synthetic, so in a way I'm glad I didn't make the picture with them."

Certainly it would be hard to imagine the film done better. There is a sweep and grandeur, a legendary resonance to the narrative for which the misused term "epic" is for once wholly appropriate. Huston's screenplay, written with his long-time assistant Gladys Hill, used much of Kipling's dialogue, and expanded without distorting the original story, which once again furnished Huston with his perennial theme of the quest and the destruction of those who let it possess them. Afghanistan being inhospitable, the film was shot in Morocco, in the Atlas Mountains. For the first time in a decade, Huston achieved a success at the box office as well as with the critics, and he and Gladys Hill were nominated for an Academy Award for their screenplay.

After *The Man Who Would Be King,* Huston underwent heart surgery and as a result produced no feature films for four years. Any speculation, though, that his career as a director might be over was answered by *Wise Blood* (1979). Adapted from a characteristically gothic novel by Flannery O'Connor, this blackly comic parable about sin and salvation in the Bible Belt was handled with all Huston's cool irony and seemingly effortless control, observing its deranged and self-tormenting characters with wry compassion. "Its flair for narrative and atmosphere," said *Sight and Sound,* "unmistakably betrays the touch of a master."

The master's touch, however, was noticeably absent from his next two films. *Phobia* (1981) found Huston offhandedly dabbling in the horror genre, scarcely bothering to conceal the holes in a laughably improbable "mad-psychiatrist" plot. Even more ludicrous, though, were the schoolboy heroics of *Escape to Victory* (1981), a creaky World War II drama in which Allied prisoners, led by Michael Caine and Sylvester Stallone, take on their captors in a desperately hazardous game of soccer. After this debacle, the 75-year-old director ventured into his first musical and made a creditable job of it. *Annie* (1982) proved, despite some slightly cautious choreog-

raphy, to be consistently pleasurable to watch, and given its subject-matter—winsome orphan and lovable mongrel win over misanthropic billionaire—mercifully unmawkish for most of its duration. *Under the Volcano* (1984) was generally regarded as an honest but disappointingly matter-of-fact adaptation of an impossible novel—Malcolm Lowry's brilliant, densely symbolic account of a tormented alcoholic on a suicidal bender in Mexico. As the drunken British consul, Albert Finney gave an all-stops-out performance; his failure to win an award for the role provoked a flurry of protest at the 1984 Cannes Film Festival. Huston, on the other hand, received a special citation for "the entirety of his work and his extraordinary contributions to cinema," a salute he accepted with ironic grace.

An unmixed success was *Prizzi's Honor* (1985), based on the book by Richard Condon, starring Jack Nicholson, Katharine Turner, William Hickey, and Huston's daughter Anjelica (who won an Oscar for best supporting actress), and featuring a witty, opera-quoting score by Alex North. Huston's gift for eliciting definitive performances from his actors and his delight in labyrinthine plots were evident in this dark satire on the Mafia, American business, family honor, and romantic love. Nicholson, as Charley Partanna, a faithful enforcer for the Prizzi family, falls in love with a glamorous mystery woman (Turner), who turns out to be a professional killer as well. After a convoluted series of doublecrosses and unexpected revelations, Charley is forced to make the ultimate choice between personal happiness and family obligation. The film, wrote Vincent Canby, "does to *The Godfather* what Henry Fielding's *Joseph Andrews* did to Samuel Richardson's *Pamela*. It locates the deliriously comic center within all sentimentality." Many critics thought it a perfect Huston vehicle and the director's most fully realized film since *The Man Who Would Be King*. After this success, Huston set to work on an adaptation of James Joyce's story "The Dead," which he completed shortly before his death.

Robin Wood wrote of Huston in Richard Roud's *Cinema* that "the problem lies in tracing any significant unifying or developing pattern through his career as a whole. . . . This is but one of several signs—though a crucial one—that Huston is not a major artist, though he has at different stages of his career been mistaken for one." This is the view that has dominated serious discussion of Huston's work since the rise of auteurist criticism in the 1960s. But Andrew Sarris, once one of the director's most dismissive critics, wrote in 1980 that "what I have always tended to underestimate in Huston was how deep in his guts he could feel the universal experience of pointlessness and failure." And there are other signs that Huston's films are being reassessed—notably the thirty-page essay by Richard T. Jameson in *Film Comment* (May–June, 1980).

Although all of Huston's pictures are adaptations, in which he has sought "to find the particular style or look best suited to render a script into a persuasive and distinctive cinematic reality," Jameson maintains that "we do encounter a cohesive world-view, not only thematically but also stylistically; there *is* a Huston look," though one extremely difficult to define. Jameson might agree with James Agee that this "look" proceeds from Huston's "sense of what is natural to the eye and his delicate, simple feeling for space relationships." It is, moreover, Jameson's "considered opinion that with *The Misfits* Huston entered upon virtually a second career (after a few years of wandering in the contract wilderness) that includes some of the most mature, most personal, and most provocative films, not only of his *oeuvre* but also of the Sixties and Seventies at large."

In his last years, Huston pursued a parallel career as a film actor. In 1963 he was invited by Otto Preminger to portray a Boston prelate in *The Cardinal* and virtually stole the picture. Then, besides taking key roles in several of his own films, he appeared in a wide variety of works directed by others: most notably as the sinister patriarch Noah Cross in Polanski's *Chinatown* (1974), and as Teddy Roosevelt's advisor John Hay in Milius's *The Wind and the Lion* (1975). Huston evidently enjoyed acting and invariably denied that he took it at all seriously. "It's a cinch," he maintained, "and they pay you damn near as much as you make directing."

Suffering from emphysema, Huston spent some time in hospitals at the end of his life. When in Mexico, he lived at his home in Las Caletas, near Puerto Vallarta, in a clearing between the jungle and the Pacific Ocean accessible only by boat, together with various friends and a wide variety of animals. Living by the sea, he said, quoting an Irish saying, "lends tranquility to the soul. I'm content having arrived at this moment in eternity, but for the life of me I don't know how I got here."

—*P.K.*

FILMS: The Maltese Falcon, 1941; In This Our Life, 1942; Across the Pacific, 1942; Report From the Aleutians, 1943 (documentary); The Battle of San Pietro, 1944 (documentary); Let There Be Light, 1945 (documentary); The Treasure of the Sierra Madre, 1948; Key Largo, 1948; We Were Strangers, 1949; The Asphalt Jungle, 1950; The Red Badge of Courage, 1951;

The African Queen, 1951; Moulin Rouge, 1952; Beat the Devil, 1953; Moby Dick, 1956; Heaven Knows, Mr. Allison, 1957; The Barbarian and the Geisha, 1958; The Roots of Heaven, 1958; The Unforgiven, 1960; The Misfits, 1961; Freud, 1962; The List of Adrian Messenger, 1963; The Night of the Iguana, 1964; The Bible, 1966; (with others) Casino Royale, 1967; Reflections in a Golden Eye, 1967; Sinful Davey, 1969; A Walk With Love and Death, 1969; The Kremlin Letter, 1970; Fat City, 1972; The Life and Times of Judge Roy Bean, 1972; The Mackintosh Man, 1973; The Man Who Would Be King, 1975; Independence, 1976 (documentary); Wise Blood, 1979; Phobia, 1981; Escape to Victory, 1981; Annie, 1982; Under the Volcano, 1984; Prizzi's Honor, 1985. *Published scripts*—The Asphalt Jungle (Screenplay Library), 1980; High Sierra (University of Wisconsin), 1979; Jezebel (University of Wisconsin), 1982; Juarez (University of Wisconsin), 1982; Key Largo (University of Wisconsin), 1982; Let There Be Light *in* Film Book 2: Films of Peace and War (Grove Press), 1962; The Maltese Falcon (Flare Books), 1974 (with 1,400 frame blow-ups); Sergeant York (University of Wisconsin), 1982; Treasure of the Sierra Madre (University of Wisconsin), 1980.

ABOUT: Agee, J. Agee on Film, 1958; Benayoun, R. John Huston, 1966 (in French); Buache, F. John Huston, 1966 (in French); Current Biography, 1981; Gianetti, L. Masters of the American Cinema, 1981; Goode, J. The Story of *The Misfits*, 1963; Huston, J. An Open Book, 1980; International Film Guide, 1974; Kaminsky, S. John Huston: Maker of Magic, 1978; Leirens, J. Le cinéma et la crise de notre temps, 1960; McArthur, C. Underworld USA, 1973; Madsen, A. John Huston, 1978; Meyer, W. R. Warner Brothers Directors, 1978; Morandini, M. John Huston, 1980 (in Italian); Nolan, W. F. John Huston: King Rebel, 1965; Pratley, G. The Cinema of John Huston, 1977; Ross, L. Picture, 1952; Roud, R. (ed.) Cinema: A Critical Dictionary, 1980; Sarris, A. (ed.) Interviews With Film Directors, 1967; Silver, A. and Ward, E. Film Noir, 1980; Tozzi, R. John Huston: A Pictorial Treasury of His Films, 1971; Tuska, J. (ed.) Close-up: The Hollywood Director, 1978. *Periodicals*—Films and Filming September–October 1959; Film Comment May–June 1973, January–February 1976, March–April 1980, May–June 1980, January–February 1984; Film Culture 8 1956, 19 1959; Films in Review February 1950, October 1952; Film Quarterly Spring 1956, Fall 1965, Spring 1969; Newsweek January 9, 1956; New Yorker September 25, 1965; Positif 21 1957; Sight and Sound Spring 1952, Autumn 1958, Spring 1969, Summer 1975; Theatre Arts February 1952; Times Literary Supplement September 21, 1984; Transatlantic Review Autumn 1974.

"INGRAM, REX" (Reginald Ingram Montgomery Hitchcock) (January 15 or 18, 1893–July 22, 1950), American director and scenarist, was born in Dublin, Ireland. He was one of the two sons of Kathleen Ingram, daughter of Dublin's fire chief, and the Reverend Francis Ryan

REX INGRAM

Montgomery Hitchcock, a Church of England clergyman. His father, a talented amateur boxer in his youth, became a distinguished classical scholar and theologian, author of many books and Donnellan Lecturer at Trinity College, Dublin. During Ingram's childhood, however, Hitchcock was still a working clergyman, and the boy grew up in his father's various parishes in the beautiful countryside of rural Ireland.

In 1905 Ingram entered St. Columba's College at Rathfarnham in County Dublin. He was not academically gifted, but his father had instilled in him a love of literature and drama, and his mother of art and music. He won prizes for his essays, acted in school and other amateur productions, and was a talented graphic artist and caricaturist, selling his first drawings while he was still at school. Extremely handsome and possessed of great natural charm, he was also impulsive, quick-tempered, and something of a loner. His father had taught him to box, and he used this skill freely against school bullies, on several occasions challenging teachers as well as boys.

The death of his mother when he was fifteen affected Ingram deeply. He grew increasingly restless and intransigent at school and in 1909 was asked to leave. A year or so later he sailed for the United States, where a job had been arranged for him as a clerk in the New Haven freight yards. In his spare time he attended sculpture classes at the Yale School of Fine Arts given by Lee Oscar Laurie, who became a lifelong friend. Ingram's biographer, Liam O'Leary, suggests that his serious interest in the cinema was sparked at this time during a vacation spent with an old schoolfriend in New York,

where he met Thomas Edison's son Charles and also saw the first film that really impressed him, Vitagraph's three-reel A Tale of Two Cities (1911), starring the Irish actor Maurice Costello.

In 1913 Ingram went to New York and joined the Edison Company as a writer of subtitles, scene dresser, and bit-part actor. As Rex Hitchcock he had parts in many Edison two-reelers before moving on the following year to the Vitagraph Company in Brooklyn as scriptwriter and actor. In 1915 he joined the Fox Film Company. Ingram's talent as an actor was limited, and he was by then more interested in writing and, increasingly, in directing. He also continued to paint and sculpt, for a time sharing a studio with Thomas Hart Benton.

Ingram's chance came in 1916, when he joined Carl Laemmle's Universal-Bluebird Photoplays to direct his first film, The Great Problem, a five-reeler scripted by himself. It was a socially conscious drama about the rehabilitation of a criminal's daughter, with Lionel Adams as the girl's benefactor and Violet Mersereau playing both the heroine and her mother. Mersereau starred again in Broken Fetters (1916), a melodrama set partly in Hong Kong and partly in New York's Chinatown. This was followed the same year by Chalice of Sorrow, which placed the equally melodramatic plot of Tosca in a Mexican setting. Chalice of Sorrow, starring Cleo Madison and Wedgewood Nowell, was made not in New York but at Universal City, Laemmle's new Hollywood studios, formerly a 230-acre chicken farm.

None of the early Ingram films seems to have survived, but contemporary accounts suggest that these pictures—all scripted by Ingram himself—were lurid melodramas, generally set in exotic locales, and redeemed by excellent acting, careful evocation of mood and atmosphere, and a fine pictorial sense. Ingram had a sensational success with his next movie, Black Orchids (1916), in which Cleo Madison plays Zoraide, an evil temptress with occult powers who leads three men to their deaths. There was a strong element of Grand Guignol in this "high-class horror" movie, with its dungeons, duels, poisons, and bizarre passions. Some critics were troubled by hints of a "morbid" relationship between Zoraide and her familiar, the famous Hollywood chimpanzee Joe Martin.

The Reward of the Faithless (1917), adapted from a story by E. Magnus Ingleton, was a tale of intrigue and retribution in Russia, featuring Claire Du Brey and Nicholas Dunaew. There were brilliantly lit scenes in a tavern and in slum streets that have reminded some critics of Pabst in their low-life realism. These scenes were heavily populated by dwarfs, hunchbacks, and cripples, and indeed, as Liam O'Leary writes, "deformity amounted to an obsession in Ingram's work. Whether he used it as a superficial contrast to his handsome heroes and heroines, or whether it had a deeper motivation, it is hard to say."

Two more exotic tales in exotic settings followed, *The Pulse of Life* and *The Flower of Doom*, both made in 1917 and starring respectively Gypsy Harte and Yvette Mitchell, along with the Ingram regulars Wedgewood Nowell and Nicholas Dunaew. *The Flower of Doom*, a complex and deeply fatalistic tale of gang warfare in an American Chinatown, was again said to foreshadow Pabst in its murky recreation of sordid underworld settings.

The Little Terror (1917) was a considerable departure for Ingram—a romantic comedy with a circus setting. Violet Mersereau, who had played two roles in *The Great Problem*, did so again in *The Little Terror*, this time as rebellious "wildcat" and troubled mother. At that point, Ingram left Universal—or according to some accounts was fired—and joined a minor company, Paralta-Hodkinson. He made two films there, *His Robe of Honor* and *Humdrum Brown*, both starring Henry B. Walthall and neither, apparently, of much merit.

This was a dark time for Ingram. In March 1917 he had married a young actress named Doris Pawn. The marriage failed and the couple separated after a year, divorce following in 1920. In late 1918 Ingram joined the Royal Canadian Air Force as a flyer, but within months was invalided out after a bad crash. He returned to civilian life with his marriage in ruins, out of work, and penniless.

Universal took him back in 1919 and he directed two more pictures there. *The Day She Paid* (1919), the first of his films not scripted by himself, was adapted from a story by Fannie Hurst about the world of fashion models. Francelia Billington played a woman who sacrifices her own reputation to save her stepdaughter's. An action movie followed, *Under Crimson Skies* (1920), about gun-running in Latin America, with Elmo Lincoln as an adventurous sea captain. This was a success, but left Ingram frustrated and angry at the close supervision of the studio's managers. In 1920 he quit Universal and joined the Metro Picture Corporation.

Metro was at that time struggling for survival. It was in 1920 that Marcus Loew, Metro's principal backer, took control of the company, appointing Richard Rowland as studio head. Ingram's first film there was *Shore Acres* (1920), a "homespun" melodrama of the type then popular. It was adapted by Art Zellner from a hit play by James Herne about two brothers who tend a lighthouse and struggle to preserve their patch of land from a grasping speculator. It starred Edward Connelly, who was to appear in many of Ingram's later films, and Alice Lake.

A moderately successful beginning to Ingram's career at Metro, *Shore Acres* was momentous for him on other counts as well. It was shot by John F. Seitz, who became Ingram's regular photographer, soon to be recognized as the foremost "mood" cameraman in Hollywood (and the highest paid). The editor was Grant Whytock, another essential member of the team Ingram built up at Metro. And the film provided a small role for a young actress named Alice Terry, with whom Ingram had already worked in *The Day She Paid*. She and Ingram were married in 1921, and their professional and personal relationship lasted until Ingram's death.

Alice Terry played second lead in his next film, *Hearts Are Trumps* (1920), another melodrama derived from a stage play, this time with settings ranging from England to Switzerland, stately home to monastery garden. John Seitz and Grant Whytock were both involved, and the adaptation was by Metro's most influential scriptwriter, June Mathis. The same team worked on Ingram's next picture, *The Four Horsemen of the Apocalypse* (1921), which made them all famous.

According to some accounts (contradicted by others), it was June Mathis who persuaded Richard Rowland that Metro should film this popular war novel by Vicente Blasco Ibañez, and that Ingram was the man to direct it. It may also have been her inspiration to cast in the lead a little-known actor named Rudolph Valentino, previously typed as an oily "lounge lizard." At any rate, the package was accepted and generously backed to the tune of about a million dollars. Seizing his chance, Ingram strove for perfection in every aspect of the production, involving himself closely in the designing of sets, costumes, and props, and planning every camera setup with Seitz. He showed a concern for authenticity worthy of his friend Stroheim, for example insisting on correct 1914 clothing even for civilians (a rare consideration then in war films) and surrounding himself with technical advisors to insure the accuracy of the military scenes.

Valentino plays Julio Desnoyers, a wealthy young Argentinian of French extraction who goes to Paris during World War I. There he has a passionate affair with Marguerite Laurier (Alice Terry), a lonely married woman whose husband is in the trenches. When the latter returns blinded, Julio is racked by shame and guilt. He enlists in the French army and dies fighting his own German-born cousin. Marguerite atones for her sin by devoting herself to the care of her husband.

An elaborate premiere in February 1921 at the Ritz Carlton Hotel in New York launched *The Four Horsemen* as an immediate and almost unprecedented success, critical and financial. Valentino became a legend overnight, and the film's profits (estimated at $4 million) rescued Metro at a stroke from the financial doldrums. For years *The Four Horsemen* was the most talked-about movie in both America and Europe. As Liam O'Leary writes, "the streets of Paris, the war hysteria, the terrors of invasion, the horrors of the battlefield, the faithful depiction of social milieus, and the mystical tension binding the story together made for a film of overwhelming excitement. . . . Above all, the poignancy of the love scenes between Valentino and Alice Terry displayed a sensitivity rare to screen acting at that time." Another modern critic has praised in particular Ingram's "talent for precise recreation of another time and place, including some brilliantly photographed and realized war sequences, which have rarely been equalled."

The Four Horsemen established Rex Ingram for a time as the most adulated director in America, next to his idol D. W. Griffith. It also had some less happy effects. C. A. Lejeune saw it as "a production intelligent enough and emphatic enough to provide a deadly precedent," launching a flood of generally inferior war movies—"a whole new field of slaughter and sentiment." And, as Kevin Brownlow says, "while the mood of the film veered towards pacifism, with a mystical element which suited the nation's idealism, it opened all the old sores about German brutality. It also sparked off a new argument: who had won the war? The French were maddened by the emphasis on the Americans; the British by the fact that they were virtually left out; the Germans by the parody of their officers."

Given *carte blanche* at Metro after this triumph, Ingram chose to tackle Balzac's novel *Eugénie Grandet*, adapted by June Mathis as *The Conquering Power* (1921). Ralph Lewis played the miserly Pere Grandet, Alice Terry his ill-used daughter Eugénie, and Valentino the cousin from the city who falls in love with her and, in spite of Grandet's machinations, eventually wins her. An obvious act of homage to Griffith, admired for its "refinement of treatment," it had more success with the critics than with the paying public.

And Ingram's next picture had no success with anyone. He had quarreled with Valentino, who

had stormed off to Paramount; the infatuated June Mathis had followed him there. *Turn to the Right* (1922), based on a hit play by Winchell Smith, was adapted by Mary O'Hara and starred Jack Mulhall. It was a particularly fatuous "homespun" melodrama about a country boy who leaves his native village to seek his fortune, is wrongly imprisoned, but returns to find happiness in the arms of his village beloved (Alice Terry). Together they turn a run-down farm into a successful jam-making enterprise. A "cut-and-dried piece of hokum," it prompted speculation that the real credit for *The Four Horsemen* and *The Conquering Power* belonged to June Mathis—that without her Ingram was nothing.

Such rumors were promptly scotched by the success of *The Prisoner of Zenda* (1922), adapted from Anthony Hope's swashbuckling novel and again scripted by Mary O'Hara. Lewis Stone had the dual lead role as the threatened King Rudolf of Ruritania and Rudolf Rassendyll, the English soldier of fortune who takes his place. And Ingram demonstrated that he could live without Valentino as well, casting as the dashing villain, Rupert of Hentzau, an unknown young Mexican who had appeared as an extra in the *Four Horsemen*. This was Ramon Samaniegos who, as Ramon Novarro, leaped to fame as a "Latin lover" second only to Valentino himself.

A contemporary reviewer, Robert E. Sherwood, found in *The Prisoner of Zenda* "the same fertile imagination that had distinguished *The Four Horsemen of the Apocalypse*, the same sensitive feeling for form, in composition and in rhythm, and same intellectual alertness." Later critics, it must be said, have found it uneven, and marred by Ingram's rather crude sense of humor—altogether inferior to John Cromwell's 1937 version of the story.

After a series of films scripted by others, Ingram himself wrote (or rather rewrote) *Trifling Women* (1922), a remake of his 1916 movie *Black Orchids*, with Barbara La Marr as the evil enchantress previously played by Cleo Madison. This time around, her three victims were Ramon Novarro, Lewis Stone, and Edward Connelly. The result was described as a "feverish Gothic dream" in "a claustrophobic world of poisoned passions." This is another lost film, and one that would be well worth finding, if only for Leo Kutz's bizarre sets.

Ingram was again his own scriptwriter for *Where the Pavement Ends* (1923), adapted from a novel by John Russell. Set in the South Seas (and actually filmed in Florida and Cuba), it has Novarro as Motauri, a young islander who falls in love with Miss Matilda (Alice Terry), a lonely daughter of a lovable missionary (Edward Connelly). Threatened with marriage to the egregious trader Captain Gregson (played with gusto by Harry Morey), Matilda runs off with Motauri to a neighboring island where they are trapped by a great storm. Gregson pursues them and is killed in a fight with Motauri, who gives Matilda his horde of pearls before leaping to his death over the waterfall where they used to meet. Metro worried about this depressing conclusion and Ingram actually shot an alternative and happier ending in order to prove the superiority of his original conception. Robert E. Sherwood found it "gorgeously beautiful" but "too long for its substance—it exhausted several reels before it touched the surface of drama."

With his next film, Ingram added another important collaborator to his team, the scriptwriter Willis Goldbeck, who wrote the adaptation of Rafael Sabatini's novel *Scaramouche,* and stayed to script the best of Ingram's subsequent films. Scaramouche (Ramon Novarro) is a French nobleman during the Revolution who, to outwit his enemies, joins a troupe of strolling players. Alice Terry plays his beloved, and Lewis Stone contributed a fine performance as a cruel and cynical marquis.

Scaramouche (1923) was a major success, admired for its lavish sets (including an entire French village), authentic costumes, and convincing period detail. Lewis Jacobs found many similarities to Griffith's *Orphans of the Storm* "in its crowd scenes, tableaux, and the use of significant detail for atmosphere." Another critic, writing for the National Board of Review, praised some "fine sequences of action" but was most impressed by Ingram's ability to produce "motion in stillness," as when "Danton (most finely played by George Siegmann) turns upon the lords of the Assembly his pox-marked face and, motionless, regards them, and the power of the orator of liberty charges from the screen with a great dramatic force."

Ingram and his team went to Tunisia to film *The Arab* (1924), adapted by the director from a play by Edgar Selwyn—a conventional "sheikh story" about the romance between a missionary's daughter (Terry again) and the son of an Arab chieftain (Novarro). The film used authentic Arab dancers, costumes, and weapons, and was beautifully photographed by Seitz, but was otherwise undistinguished. However, Ingram fell in love with North Africa and the Arabs, who reciprocated his admiration. The Bey of Tunis presented him with the Order of Niftkan Itchkar and made him a gift of his own court jester, who stayed with Ingram for years and appeared in several of his films, as did Abd-el-Kader, an Arab boy whom the Ingrams adopted.

This happy interlude in Tunis only exacerbated Ingram's mounting detestation of Hollywood and the rigidities of the studio system. His disillusionment had begun in 1922, when he was assigned to direct the Goldwyn Company's lavish production of *Ben-Hur* and then replaced—accused of extravagance—first by Charles Brabin, then by Fred Niblo, who finally completed the film in 1925. Bitterly hurt, Ingram threatened to resign but was dissuaded by his close friend Erich von Stroheim. But in April 1924, when Metro became Metro-Goldwyn-Mayer, with the tyrannical Louis B. Mayer as studio head, Ingram decided that Hollywood had become unbearable.

And Ingram's standing at Metro was such that he was able to persuade the company to allow him to work in Nice, in the South of France. Seitz, Whytock, and Goldbeck went along, and Harry Lachman was appointed production manager. Ingram and Alice Terry installed themselves in the Villa Massena, once occupied by Napoleon's generals, and in this idyllic setting, far from Mayer's bullying interference, Ingram settled down to study Arabic, to work at his sculptures, and to hone a few films into idiosyncratic perfection.

Ingram became known as "the king of Nice," entertaining at the Villa Massena such luminaries as Bernard Shaw, the Scott Fitzgeralds, John Galsworthy, J. M. Barrie, Isadora Duncan, and Michael Arlen, as well as many friends from Hollywood, celebrated and otherwise. One of the latter was his young namesake Alfred Hitchcock; Ingram advised him to follow his own example and adopt a pseudonym, assuring him that he would never get anywhere under his own name.

The first and perhaps the best picture Ingram made at Nice was *Mare Nostrum* (*Our Sea,* 1925), an extraordinary espionage drama with mystical overtones adapted, like *The Four Horsemen,* from a novel by Blasco Ibañez. Antonio Moreno plays Ulysses Ferragut, Spanish captain of a sailing ship (the *Mare Nostrum*) who falls in love with Freya Talberg, a beautiful German spy played by Alice Terry in the performance of her life. She induces him to help in the refueling of a German submarine in the Mediterranean, but when his son dies in a torpedoed ship, Ulysses swears vengeance. He destroys the submarine, losing his life in the process. Freya is betrayed by her own organization to the French, and shot. The subsidiary mystical theme presents Freya as the sea goddess Amphitrite, who is reunited with Ulysses in death. There is an extremely perverse scene in the Naples Aquarium where Freya, erotically fascinated by death, bribes an attendant to stir up a fight between two octopuses and watches greedily to the end, when she turns to Ulysses and kisses him passionately.

Mare Nostrum was filmed in locations all over the Mediterranean, in France, Spain, and Italy. Ingram carried his perfectionism to almost insane lengths. One scene was shot 185 times before he was satisfied, and when Ulysses sinks the German submarine (actually a French one lent by the government), Ingram forced his wretched extras to plunge again and again into icy waters until some of them were half dead. Grant Whytock said "we must have thrown away ten or twelve cut reels and we still landed up with two-and-a-half hours of film." Herman Weinberg called *Mare Nostrum* "a love-poem to the Mediterranean," and Liam O'Leary described it as a "tragic story of an inflexible destiny told in images of great beauty," though another critic noted "some sluggish spots."

The Magician (1926) was, in the words of David Thomson, "an ornate fantasy with erotic undertones." Adapted from Somerset Maugham's novel based on the career of Aleister Crowley, it starred the German expressionist director and actor Paul Wegener as the necromancer, and was shot in an appropriately expressionist style. Alice Terry plays the magician's victim, and Ivan Petrovich the hero who struggles to rescue her from his evil domination. The future director Michael Powell had a small role in this film, and in Ingram's next, while learning the rudiments of filmmaking as a general factotum around the Nice studio.

Ingram's last film for MGM was a remake of *The Garden of Allah* (1927), scripted by Goldbeck from Robert Hichens' romantic novel about a Trappist monk (Ivan Petrovich) in North Africa who breaks his vows and flees to the desert. There he falls in love with a young Englishwoman (Alice Terry) and they marry. Caught in a sandstorm with his wife, he vows that if she is spared he will renounce her and return to the monastery. She is and he does.

The picture was shot on location in North Africa, in the region that had inspired Hichens' novel. Ingram had by then lost both Seitz and Whytock, but he had found an excellent substitute for the former in Lee Garmes. They filmed "only in the late afternoon, when the Mediterranean sun was subdued and the changing light and shadows lent a strange beauty to every scene"; the result was no doubt as pictorially beautiful as Ingram's other films of the period, though it was generally reckoned to be dramatically inferior to Richard Boleslavsky's 1936 talkie version in color, which starred Marlene Dietrich and Charles Boyer.

The filming of *The Garden of Allah* was by all accounts an unhappy experience, bedeviled by strife and bitterness. After it, Ingram bought the Nice studio from MGM, making his last two films as independent productions. The first of these was *The Three Passions* (1929), a sentimental drama about a wealthy shipowner (Shayle Gardner), his socialist son (Ivan Petrovich), and the woman (Alice Terry) who reconciles the two. Shot silent, it was issued with a post-synchronized soundtrack and musical score.

This was Alice Terry's last film before she chose to retire, and Ingram himself made only one more picture. This was *Baroud,* his only talkie—a story of French legionnaires and Berber tribesmen in the Atlas Mountains (actually shot mostly in Nice and the mountains behind it). Ingram cast himself in the lead, with Rosita Garcia as the heroine. Contemporary reviewers found the film a curious mixture of juvenile story development and "pleasantly" amateurish acting, but a charming evocation of Berber life. However, the wildly assorted accents of an international cast amused some reviewers, and this may have helped to convince Ingram that the sound medium was not for him.

At that point he retired from filmmaking, spending the next five years in North Africa with Alice Terry, living mostly in Cairo and Alexandria. He continued his researches into Arab life and the Muslim religion and some say that he became a convert to Islam, though his biographer denies this. In 1936 the Ingrams returned to Hollywood, where he devoted himself to sculpture and writing. He produced two novels, *The Legion Advances* and *Mars in the House of Death,* which are said to have been as luridly melodramatic as his filmscripts. During his last years, the Ingrams traveled around the Caribbean and Mexico. He died of heart disease in 1950.

At one time considered the equal of Griffith and Stroheim (who indeed thought him "the world's greatest director"), Ingram is, as Carlos Clarens says, now more often "linked with Maurice Tourneur as the other outstanding pictorial director in American silents"; both "sacrifice fluency, feeling, and characterization to the more physical aspects of *mise-en-scène*: sets, costumes, lighting, make-up," achieving a style of "isolated visual felicities rather than an organic filmic progression." Nevertheless, Kevin Brownlow maintains that Ingram "created some of the most beautiful films of the entire silent era," and Liam O'Leary calls him "the first great romantic of the screen," suggesting that "perhaps when we have passed through the current fashions of realism and neorealism his true achievements will appear more clearly."

It seemed to William K. Everson that "Ingram's art was essentially that of the painter"; perhaps it would be truer to say that of the sculptor. Ingram himself wrote that "without a knowledge of the construction and form of the human head, it is only by chance that a director can light it in such a way that the modeling is brought out. It is the modeling obtained by a judicious arrangement of lighting and shade that enables us to give something of a stereoscopic quality to the soft, mellow-tone closeups that take the place of the human voice on the [silent] screen and help to make audiences intimately acquainted with the characters."

FILMS: The Great Problem (U.K., Truth), 1916; Broken Fetters, 1916; Chalice of Sorrow (U.K., The Fatal Promise), 1916; Black Orchids (U.K., The Fatal Orchids), 1916; The Reward of the Faithless (U.K., The Ruling Passion), 1917; The Pulse of Life, 1917; The Flower of Doom, 1917; The Little Terror, 1917; His Robe of Honor, 1918; Humdrum Brown, 1918; The Day She Paid, 1919; Under Crimson Skies, 1920; Shore Acres, 1920; Hearts are Trumps, 1920; The Four Horsemen of the Apocalypse, 1921; The Conquering Power, 1921; Turn to the Right, 1922; The Prisoner of Zenda, 1922; Trifling Women, 1922; Where the Pavement Ends, 1923; Scaramouche, 1923; The Arab, 1924; Mare Nostrum (Our Sea), 1926; The Magician, 1926; The Garden of Allah, 1927; The Three Passions, 1929; Baroud/Love in Morocco/Passion in the Desert, 1931.

ABOUT: Brownlow, K. The War, the West, and the Wilderness, 1978; O'Leary, L. Rex Ingram: Master of the Silent Cinema, 1980; Prédal, R. Rex Ingram, 1970 (in French); Roud, R. (ed.) Cinema: A Critical Dictionary, 1980; Thomson, D. A Biographical Dictionary of the Cinema, 1980. Periodicals—Cinema Studies December 1961; Films in Review February and March 1975; Motion Picture Classic July 1921; The Word September 1973.

IVENS, "JORIS" (Georg Henri Anton Ivens)
(November 18, 1898–   ), Dutch documentarist, was born and grew up in Nijmegen, on the River Waal, one of the five children of Peter and Dorothea Ivens. The family had been involved with photography for two generations: his grandfather had introduced the daguerreotype into Holland, and his father was head of a family business, CAPI, that operated a chain of stores selling cameras and photographic supplies.

Bewitched by the traveling film shows that visited Nijmegen, Ivens made his own first movie in 1911, when he was thirteen. The script, he says, was inspired by the novels of Karl May: "There was a bad Indian who kidnapped a white boy, and a good Indian who rescued him. I was the good Indian. There were seven of us in the

JORIS IVENS

family . . . so that meant I had fourteen actors, seven white and seven redskins." Ivens shot the seven-minute film with a hand-cranked 35mm Pathé camera that his father had despaired of selling, and says that "the landscape exteriors turned out splendidly with sandhills and heather fields doing duty as the Mojave desert and the Rocky Mountains." Brandende Straal (Shining Ray, also called The Wigwam) is still preserved in the Royal Dutch Film Archive.

Intended for the family business, Ivens was sent in 1917 to the Rotterdam College of Economics. His education was interrupted by military service as an artillery lieutenant at the end of World War I, after which he returned to Rotterdam to complete his economics courses. It was at this time that he first became active in student politics and the trade union movement, and his political education continued when he was sent to study photochemistry at the University of Charlottenburg in Berlin. This postwar period was one of intense cultural as well as political ferment in Germany. Ivens had very little money, but the inflated mark made it possible for him to attend plays and concerts for practically nothing. In this way Ivens, in his early twenties, encountered the radical experiments of expressionism and Dada, the music of Schoenberg and Hanns Eisler, and the theatrical innovations of Erwin Piscator.

Still in Germany, Ivens went to Dresden to gain practical experience in the Ica and the Ernemann camera factories (where his participation in workers' committees and demonstrations strengthened his left-wing political commitment), and at the Zeiss plant in Jena, where he worked on optics and the mathematics of lens construction. In all, he spent four years in Germany, returning to Holland in 1926 to become head of CAPI's technical department and manager of the company's Amsterdam branch.

In Amsterdam Ivens made a close friend of the expressionist poet Hendrik Marsman and frequented the cafés favored by avant-garde and left-wing painters and sculptors. He and his friends shared a growing enthusiasm for the new cinema that was emerging from Germany and Russia. In 1927, when Pudovkin's *Mother* was banned in Holland, Ivens borrowed a projector from his shop and screened the film four times in a single evening at an Amsterdam artists' club; according to one account, it was "a tumultuous gathering which, owing to police action, threatened on more than one occasion to dissolve into chaos."

In September of the same year, Ivens and his associates founded the Dutch Film League (Filmliga), with Ivens as secretary. "Once in a hundred times we see film," they wrote in their manifesto, "the rest of the time we see movies. The herd, commercial clichés, America, *kitsch*. . . . We want to see the experimental work produced in the French, German and Russian avant-garde ateliers. We want to work toward film criticism that is in itself original, constructive and independent."

The Amsterdam Filmliga was immensely successful, and branches sprung up in cities and towns all over Holland. Major filmmakers came to Amsterdam to introduce their films, and in this way Ivens came to know directors of the caliber of René Clair, Jean Vigo, Luis Buñuel, and Vsevolod Pudovkin. The Dutch film industry scarcely existed at that time, the market being totally dominated by Hollywood products. Most of the young directors who now began to create the Dutch documentary tradition drew their first inspiration from Filmliga.

Ivens, who already had some experience making demonstration and publicity films for CAPI, began to use the company's resources—film stock, projection room, and personnel—for pictures of his own. A CAPI secretary, Helen van Dongen, became chief translator for Filmliga and before long was collaborating on Ivens' personal films as camera operator and editor. At that time and for years afterwards, his pictures were edited in an old loft building on Het Singel, one of Amsterdam's major canals. Ivens occupied the top two floors, the lower one housing his apartment and the beginnings of a film library, the upper containing a darkroom/laboratory and the crowded "montage room." According to Helen van Dongen, "the top floor of Het Sngel

was the real hub of the film-producing wheel where most of the original Filmliga members who eventually formed the nucleus of the avant-garde filmmakers in Holland could be found at one time or another."

Ivens was his own cameraman on his earliest films, using an Ica Kinamo—a very cheap 35mm camera that could shoot only about one hundred feet of film without reloading. His first adult film was *Zeedijk-Filmstudie* (1927), shot in an Amsterdam seamen's bar owned by the mother of a sculptor friend. Ivens wrote in *Theatre Arts* (March 1946) that "my camera moved a lot—too much—which is the usual fault of the beginner. But some of the movement does help me to catch the atmosphere and gestures of the men standing at the bar. . . . When I projected the printed footage I was surprised at how much of the quality of rough fun came across; and there was a certain pictorial accomplishment, giving some of the intensity of old Dutch paintings of dark interiors. I didn't edit the material because I realised that this was a purely amateur achievement; but I had tested my talent, and the test had been conducted in a real setting and not in the abstract angles and curves of [Walter] Ruttmann."

At this stage, Ivens wrote in his autobiography, *The Camera and I*, what he wanted "was to find some general rules, laws of continuity of movement. Music had its rules and its grammar on tones, melody, and counterpoint. . . . If anyone knew about the relation of motion on the screen he was keeping it to himself." In pursuit of these rules, he made shot-by-shot analyses of important sequences in films he particularly admired, including Eisenstein's *Battleship Potemkin* and Dovzhenko's *Arsenal*. At about the same time, on a visit to France, Ivens made *Études des mouvements* (*Studies in Movement*, 1928, 7 minutes), shot in the streets of Paris. But it was his next film that showed him the way forward, at the same time bringing him international attention in avant-garde circles.

De Brug (*The Bridge*, 11 minutes) is a study of the railroad bridge over the River Maas in Rotterdam, which could be raised to allow tall ships to pass beneath it. For Ivens, "the bridge was a laboratory of movements, tones, shapes, contrasts, rhythms, and the relations between all these. . . . I learnt from *The Bridge* that prolonged and careful observation is the only way to be sure of selecting, emphasizing, and squeezing everything possible out of the rich reality in front of you" (*The Camera and I*). In the influential avant-garde journal *Close-Up*, Jan Lenauer called *The Bridge* "a pure visual symphony, made with the highest technical understanding and an astonishing sureness of touch. . . . In its composition the film reveals a new talent, Joris Ivens' talent, which uses no tricks, no subterfuges, and from which we can undoubtedly look forward . . . to unsuspected levels of visual pleasure."

Received with enthusiasm at its Filmliga premiere in May 1928, *The Bridge* also achieved widespread and successful commercial release and was bought by UFA for distribution in Germany. More recently, Peter Cowie has described that short documentary as the film "that really inaugurated the Dutch cinema. . . . It is the smoothest of documentaries—a continuous flow of movement and a tribute to a feat of precision engineering. Ivens created a visual symphony of sliding wheels and swinging girders, ending with a train pouring through the bridge after it has been raised and lowered to allow a ship to pass beneath."

Ivens now turned his attention to the problem of working with actors and the human face in what was virtually his only fictional film, *Branding* (*Breakers*, 1929, 35 minutes). Based on a short story by Jef Last, this was scripted and codirected by Mannus Franken, a modest but influential figure in the development of the Dutch cinema, who at this time became Ivens' closest collaborator. Ivens was cameraman and editor, assisted in the former capacity by the fourteen-year-old John Fernhout (later known as Ferno), another recruit to Ivens' circle of disciples and later his principal cameraman. Acted by amateurs, the film was shot on location at the fishing village of Katwijk.

Breakers is a simple melodrama about an unemployed fisherman (played by the author, Jef Last) who loses his fiancée to a ruthless pawnbroker and in the end sails out alone to face an uncertain future. Flawed by bad acting and too many anguished close-ups, the film nevertheless featured some atmospheric shots of the little village and some extraordinarily dramatic ones of the sea and breakers. These were filmed by Ivens, wearing "a rubber sack with a glass front to contain my head and arms and camera"—a contraption that enabled him "to shoot while breakers rolled over my camera and myself."

Ivens' growing international reputation was confirmed by *Regen* (*Rain*, 1929, 12 minutes), for which Ivens spent four months filming every kind and degree of rain, editing the results in collaboration with Franken, who also worked on the script. One of the most admired of Ivens' films, *Rain* has been described by Peter Cowie as "a dazzling photographic exercise, starting with views of the sunny streets and then noticing the wind-troubled canopies above the shops, and

the first scattered drops of rain in the canals. As the shower intensifies, the streets themselves look like canals. Everywhere there are rivulets of water, drops that coalesce along the tumbled roofs. The pace of pedestrians caught in the rain increases—at first a mass of confused umbrellas crouching together, then a series of bustling figures hurrying home along the pavement."

Rosalind Delmar, in her introduction to Ivens' work, has drawn attention to the "strong narrative drive" that he builds into even his early experiments—in *Rain*, "the film is structured to give the impression of a single rain-shower, with a beginning—the warning signs; a middle—the shower and its effects; and a happy ending—the rain stops, the sun comes out." At the same time, *Rain* achieves effects that seemed to many critics close to the "pure cinema" of such experimentors as Henri Chomette, Richter, and Ruttmann. Although, even at this stage of his career, Ivens in theory rejected abstractionism, the Hungarian theorist Béla Balázs described both *The Bridge* and *Rain* as impressionist films in which "Ivens' moods and impressions dematerialize their theme. . . . Even when Ivens shows a bridge and tells us that it is the great railway bridge at Rotterdam, the huge iron structure dissolves into an immaterial picture of a hundred angles."

After two uncompleted experiments in the development of a "subjective" camera (one of them a study of the filmmaker's own feet as he skates over ice), Ivens set up a film production unit at CAPI and accepted his first commission. His sponsors were ANB, the Dutch building workers' union. Serving as producer, director, scriptwriter, cameraman, and editor, Ivens filmed examples of the many different kinds of work performed by the union's members, and assembled this footage into a recruiting film called *Wij Bouwen* (*We Are Building*, 1929, 110 minutes) composed of four parts: *Heien* (*Pile Driving*, 1929, 10 minutes); *Nieuwe Architectuur* (*New Architecture*, 1929, 5 minutes); *Caissonbouw Rotterdam* (1929, 6 minutes); and *Zuid Limburg* (*South Limburg*, 1929, 6 minutes).

C. Boost found *We Are Building* "satisfying, though not completely successful. The film was too long and not consistently interesting enough for exhibition to the general public . . . so that Ivens cut some passages from the whole and assembled these separately."

The same year Ivens worked as cameraman or editor on other short films for working-class organizations in Holland, also serving as film programmer for the leftist Association of Popular Culture. In December he spent three months in the Soviet Union at the invitation of Vsevolod Pudovkin, whom he had met when the Russian director had addressed the Filmliga earlier in the year. The young filmmaker stayed in Eisenstein's flat in Moscow, met Kozintsev and Trauberg in Leningrad, and Dovzhenko in Kiev.

Back in Holland, Ivens made four short films that have not survived, as well as *Zuiderzee* (1930, 45 minutes), the last of the documentaries that grew directly out of his ANB commission. Showing members of the union at work reclaiming land formerly covered by the Zuiderzee, it was hailed by Pudovkin as a "leap forward" from the "formalism" of Ivens' earlier work to the "cinematographic creation of 'living realities.'" This was the first of Ivens' films on which Helen van Dongen received credit, in this case as editor and as one of a team of five camera operators. Having studied sound recording and soundtrack editing in Paris and Berlin, she rejoined him for *Philips Radio* (1931, 36 minutes), his second commission and his first sound film.

Philips Radio was supposed to be a promotional documentary about the company's radio and lamp plant at Eindhoven. What Ivens delivered was something rather different. "In strong and striking images," wrote Leon Moussinac, "with a determined rhythm, it raises the spectre of the physical and moral ruin which threatens those workers who are the victims of capitalist rationalization. . . . Machines and muscles are held at work for shifts which use, ruin, and disorganize the poor human mechanism." Particularly disturbing was the evident physical damage done to the men who blew the giant neon lamps used in advertising. "To a certain extent," Moussinac concluded, "as well as being an accomplished piece of cinema . . . [*Philips Radio*] is an act of accusation against the present economic system." The same year, Ivens and his CAPI production team made another and less ambivalent promotional film, *Creosoot* (80 minutes), commissioned by the International Committee of Creosote Manufacturers.

Ivens made his next film in the Soviet Union—the first foreign director to do so. *Pesn o Gerojach* (*Komsomol/Song of Heroes,* 1932) deals with the building of a blast furnace by young workers in the Ural Mountains. This 35-minute sound documentary, directed and edited by Ivens, with music by Hanns Eisler, was one of ten films shown to celebrate the completion of Russia's first Five Year Plan. It is constructed around the experiences of a particular individual—a new recruit to the building project—and this means of developing narrative interest is used in a number of Ivens' subsequent documentaries.

Komsomol also introduced another Ivens technique, and one that has been much debated—the use of reenacted events alongside scenes that record unrehearsed events as they occur. Dziga Vertov was prominent among those who objected to this manipulation of "documentary truth," but Ivens maintained that "the distinction between letting the event dominate the filming and the attempt to film an event with maximum expressiveness is the difference between orthodox documentary (which today is represented by the newsreel) and the newer, broader form of documentary film."

Ivens was next invited by the Belgian director Henri Storck to make what became *Misère en Borinage* (*Borinage,* 1933, 34 minutes), about the atrocious conditions in Belgium's main coal-producing region in the aftermath of the strike of 1932. Making this film was a crucial turning-point for Ivens. He was "a suspect foreigner" in Belgium and to avoid the police and the danger of expulsion he often had to hide, taking refuge in the squalid homes of the miners. He wrote: "Faced with the terrible misery of these people I found I could not use the old techniques. So in *Borinage* you find that I am very modest in the use of the camera. After that I could not fall back into the old aesthetic style."

Finding that the oil lamps they had to use for lighting lent a certain charm even to filthy rags and dishes on a table, Ivens and Storck deliberately broke the edges of a pleasing shadow: they were determined that "every sequence should say I ACCUSE—accusing the social system which caused such misery and hardship." William Alexander in *Film on the Left* wrote that "Ivens was right to work out his anger and indignation in new cinematic terms, for a part of his indignation was directed at his own earlier cinematic practices. But the strength of his emotion may have caused an aesthetic overreaction, the result being that he neglected his greatest area of talent: his rare ability to feel and to work out . . . the physical force of an action, a stance, even a mood. . . . Had Ivens drawn more upon this talent . . . his film might . . . have been more unified, containing the continuous sense of involvement and conviction that sustain *New Earth* so well."

Nieuwe Gronden (*New Earth,* 1934) combines new material with footage originally shot for *Zuiderzee* and *We Are Building.* It shows a vast workforce reclaiming land from the sea and then closing the great barrier dyke across the north of the Zuiderzee to create an artificial inland sea or lake. "The sheer immensity of the landfill task creates a powerful dramatic tension," wrote William Alexander, "and that tension is reinforced by Hanns Eisler's score, which often works from a slow, measured, lyrical, workmanlike rhythm to another and much faster movement, a development that emphasizes both the enormous length of the undertaking and the quick energy it required. . . . A sustained dramatic tension also pervades sequence after sequence through the acute timing of man and machine and through the strain of men's bodies as they pit land against sea."

The film's climax comes in what Alexander calls "one of the most striking sequences in all of film: the final closing of the dyke. As we watch the gap narrow, the water moves more swiftly toward and through the diminishing opening, threatening to wash away every shovelful of clay as soon as it falls. Ivens' decision to have each of his three camera-people—John Fernhout, Helen van Dongen, and himself—*identify* with one of the contending forces, land, sea, and man, had brilliant results. The camera moves dramatically with the flying crane, it is held in close on the plunge of clay into the water, and it catches in close-up the power of the machinery. . . . The shots identified with the crane operator and his machinery increase towards the end until the title *Gesloten* (closed) appears on the screen, followed by a shot of water rushing to but halted by the land, and then a shot of a posed, fully opened shovel hanging triumphantly in the air, a visual and musical symphony that has seldom been surpassed."

But this "ecstatic burst of montage" is not the end of *New Earth*. If the first three-quarters of the film are a "hymn to humanity's commitment, energy, and effectiveness in pursuit of a great end," the rest is a savage indictment of the betrayal of that commitment—the overspeculation that threw the dike-builders out of work and led to the deliberate destruction of the first hard-won harvest from the new land. Ivens "edited stock-library footage, mostly newsreel, into an idea-montage of contrasting shots, accompanied by a biting narration and a final satirical ballad. With powerful effect, shots of wheat blown in the wind and shots of harvesters, stacks of wheat, and piles of grain are intercut with shots of grain pouring into the sea, milk dumped from trucks, coffee burnt, derricks inactive, children hungry, laborers homeless, and crowds marching in protest. The dearth of narration in the first three-fourths of the film renders doubly effective the constant, shouted narration here."

New Earth is widely regarded as one of the greatest of all documentaries, and for many is Ivens' masterpiece. However, Helen van Dongen, who collaborated on the editing, said in a 1976 interview that "there are several versions of *New Earth*. The one now ending with the economic crash . . . was not planned like that orig-

inally. . . . I think it could have been done better and with a more lasting effect by not using the sledge-hammer method. . . . It was in the beginning of using film as a political weapon, though, and as such it served probably a very good purpose."

After *New Earth,* Ivens made no more films in Holland for more than thirty years. He and Helen van Dongen worked in Moscow for a while and in 1936 went to the United States, where Ivens was the guest of the New York Film Alliance. Irving Lerner, Ben Maddow, and other independent filmmakers in America gave him a hero's welcome, afterwards recalling his visit as "a turning point . . . a shot in the arm." When the Spanish Civil War broke out in July 1936, a group of writers including Archibald MacLeish, Dorothy Parker, Lillian Hellman, and Clifford Odets set up a production company (Contemporary Historians Inc.) that sent Ivens to cover the fighting in Spain.

Ivens traveled to Madrid with his old cameraman John Ferno and the writer John Dos Passos, soon to be replaced by Ernest Hemingway. Their passage into Spain was arranged by Luis Buñuel, then cultural representative of the Spanish Republic in Paris. The film they made was shot in and around the town of Fuentidueña, on the key highway between Madrid and Valencia, and in Madrid itself. The action deals with the battles to defend Madrid and the highway, and with another battle—a Fuentidueña irrigation project that will enable the peasants to grow food for the Loyalist soldiers. "As *Spanish Earth* draws to a close," wrote William Alexander, "peasants hold high in the sunlight the last link of sluice that will insure the irrigation of the precious land, soldiers prevent Fascist rebels from taking the Arganda bridge, and, in a final montage, a single soldier pulls his rifle trigger as the water floods into the fields."

Spanish Earth (1937, 52 minutes) was directed and scripted by Ivens, and photographed by Ivens and Ferno, sometimes at the risk of their lives. Hemingway's spare, moving commentary, spoken by himself, has been called "a milestone in documentary form" and "a continuing influence," though its philosophical generalizations about war detract a little from the film's urgency. Ivens' new eschewal of visual poetry in favor of stark honesty was also regretted by some critics, and Archer Winston commented that "perhaps a theme so large and diffuse will not prove exciting to the general public." In fact, *Spanish Earth* achieved only limited commercial distribution. It remains what one reviewer called "a picture which, without sensationalism, gives a vivid and forceful idea of the horror and misery of the war in Spain." All of its profits went to buy ambulances for the Loyalist forces.

Ivens next set out for China, where an uneasy alliance of Kuomintang and Communist forces was falling back before the Japanese advance. Ivens and Ferno were attached to the Kuomintang forces, and *The Four Hundred Million* (1938, 53 minutes) was made in an atmosphere of defeat and intense political strain. As a result of censorship, too much of the film is limited to coverage of pious demonstrations in support of Chiang Kai-shek and boring meetings of the military council. Ivens did manage to contact the Communist forces before leaving China, however, donating to them a precious camera that now stands in the Museum of the Revolution in Peking.

From 1938 to 1945 Ivens worked in the United States. His first film there, commissioned by Pare Lorentz of the U.S. Film Service, was *Power and the Land* (1941, 33 minutes). Intended to demonstrate the benefits of rural electrification for the small farmer, it did so by showing how it affected the lives of one actual farming family, the Parkinsons of St. Clairsville, Ohio. After *Spanish Earth,* Ivens had relinquished the role of cameraman in his films, and *Power and the Land* was shot by Floyd Crosby and Arthur Ornitz, with a commentary by Stephen Vincent Benét. The film made very extensive use of reenactments to get its message across, turning the Parkinsons into a family of "flexible and adaptable" actors.

In making the film, Ivens learned that the power companies were in fact "not interested in sending their big lines to isolated farms or little villages where they don't get many customers," but Lorentz would not allow him to "include the drama of the conflict between farmers and the private utilities." Instead Ivens made a slow, dignified, undramatic film, much more carefully composed than most of his mature films, that succeeds in capturing a particular way of life lived by particular people. It was taken up for commercial distribution by RKO and very warmly received by the critics.

In 1941, Ivens joined the faculty of the University of Southern California, lecturing on the principles of documentary. The same year he made *Our Russian Front* (38 minutes), a plea for American intervention in World War II compiled by Ivens and Lewis Milestone from material shot in the embattled Soviet Union. *Oil for Aladdin's Lamp* (1943), made for Shell Oil, was a purely commercial venture undertaken to pay off debts Ivens had incurred by his habit of working without pay on projects close to his heart.

John Grierson's National Film Board of Canada sponsored his next project, *Action Stations* (1943, 50 minutes), an account of life aboard one of the small war ships that accompanied the Atlantic convoys. In 1943–1944 Ivens worked as scriptwriter on Frank Capra's compilation film *Know Your Enemy, Japan,* and (improbably) on *Woman of the Sea,* a proposed vehicle for Greta Garbo that was eventually abandoned. The following year he served as technical adviser on the documentary aspects of William Wellman's *The Story of G.I. Joe.*

Meanwhile, in October 1944, the Dutch government in exile had appointed Ivens Film Commissioner for the Dutch East Indies (then occupied by Japan), with Helen van Dongen as Deputy Commissioner. When Japan was defeated in 1945, Ivens went to Australia to visit members of the Indonesian government in exile. Discovering that the Dutch had no intention of granting independence to the colony, Ivens resigned his post in protest and offered his services to the Indonesians, who had proclaimed a republic.

Intent on reclaiming the colony, the Dutch tried to mobilize their colonial navy, stationed in Sydney. The mostly Indonesian crews of these ships went on strike, supported and financed by their Australian fellow trade unionists. Ivens' *Indonesia Calling* (1946, 22 minutes) is an account of this strike, with much reenactment filmed clandestinely in the Sydney docks. The film's photographer Marion Michelle, who had to work with Ivens' old Kinamo, recalled in an interview that the director "organised shooting like guerrilla warfare." Few of those involved received any payment (including the Australian-born actor Peter Finch, who read the commentary).

Michelle says that Ivens' editing of their sparse and rough material was "a real miracle. . . . Joris was a magician in the editing room. . . . I believe that the film was a passionate adventure for everyone—as much for those who saw it as for those who participated. . . . It has a spontaneity, an enthusiasm, a freshness which bursts on the screen, even now." A copy was smuggled into Indonesia through the Dutch blockade and did wonders for the morale of the new republic.

Indonesia Calling took a heavy toll on Ivens' health and cost him his Dutch citizenship, only restored in 1956. In the years between he worked in Eastern Europe, settling initially in Prague. *Pierwsze Lata* (*The First Years,* 1949, 99 minutes) illustrated the building of socialist societies in Czechoslovakia, Bulgaria, and Poland through a single incident filmed in each country.

In 1950 Ivens moved to Poland, where he taught at the Lodz film school and made *Pokoj Zwyciezy Swiat* (*Peace Will Win,* 1951, 90 minutes). The film, codirected with Jerzy Bossak, is a record of that year's World Peace Council, and two similar propaganda exercises followed.

The best of the films Ivens made in East Europe was *Das Lied der Ströme* (*Song of the Rivers,* 1954, 90 minutes), a celebration of the struggle of socialist trade unionists all over the world against oppression and exploitation. Sponsored by the communist World Federation of Trade Unionists, and produced by DEFA, the East German State production company, this compilation film applied classic montage techniques to material shot by photographers in thirty-two countries (including footage from *Borinage* and *New Earth*). A unifying motif is provided by the world's great rivers—and a human "river": the world-wide working-class movement.

The commentary was written by Vladimir Pozner and the score was provided by Dmitri Shostakovich, with song lyrics by Bertolt Brecht and Semyon Kirsanov, sung by Paul Robeson and Ernst Busch. Eighteen versions of the film were prepared, and though it was banned in many countries, it has been seen by an estimated two hundred and fifty million people. It won many prizes, including the International Peace Prize of the World Peace Council.

After that, Ivens worked as advisor or supervisor on several other DEFA films, including *Die Windrose* (1956), composed of episodes shot in five different countries. He also acted as adviser to Gérard Philipe on the French-German coproduction *Les aventures de Till L'Espiègle* (*The Adventures of Till Eulenspiegel,* 1956), and is sometimes credited as codirector of this fictional feature. The same year, when the Dutch government restored his passport, he returned to Western Europe. He settled in Paris, which has been his home ever since.

La Seine a rencontré Paris (*The Seine Meets Paris,* 1957, 32 minutes) has the lyricism of a homecoming. A record of the journey by barge up the Seine, it draws much of its strength from its commentary—a poem written by Marcel Carné's scenarist Jacques Prévert. The picture was produced by a new company, Garance-Film, set up by Betsy Blair, Roger Pigaut, and Serge Reggiani (who spoke the poem-commentary). As Rosalind Delmar says, "the commentaries in Ivens' films are never simply descriptive reinforcements of the image, and his use of montage usually operates according to a chain of associations. This is particularly open in his 'film-poem' *La Seine a rencontré Paris,*

where different aspects of the river from town to countryside are counterpointed by Prévert's poem. The poem is itself constructed as a chain of associations, through the different meanings the river can have for a child, a lover, a jaded tourist, and so on, as well as for the poet himself." The film was chosen as best documentary of the year at both the Cannes and the San Francisco festivals.

Ivens had been warmly remembered in China, and in 1958, at the invitation of Chou En-lai, he returned to teach a course at the Academy of Cinema in Peking. *Before Spring* (1958, 38 minutes), moving in three episodes from winter in Inner Mongolia to the coming of spring, was shot by Ivens' students and designed partly to test color film stock in various climatic conditions. Robert Grelier found it "an attractive and lively film," somewhat marred by a too didactic commentary. *Six Hundred Million With You* (1958, 12 minutes) is a short documentary showing the demonstrations in China against that year's British landings in Lebanon.

Back in Europe, Ivens was next commissioned by Enrico Mattei, head of ENI, the Italian State Natural Gas Monopoly. Mattei was supposed to be presiding over the demise of ENI; instead he expanded it, against opposition from the multinational oil companies and their political allies in Italy. *L'Italia non è un paese povero* (*Italy Is Not a Poor Country,* 1959) is in three parts, showing among other things how natural gas is produced, and the benefits it can bring to poor peasants. Made for television it cheerfully satirizes the methods of television documentary, especially the "on-the-spot" interview. Ivens had the young director Tinto Brass as his assistant and worked on the script with Valentino Orsini and the Taviani brothers, among others. In 1962 Enrico Mattei died in an air crash under mysterious circumstances that have been recorded in Francesco Rosi's film *The Mattei Affair* (1972).

Joris Ivens was already known as "The Flying Dutchman," and the pace of his peregrinations actually accelerated over the next few years. In 1960 he directed a film in the new Republic of Mali, and the following year he was in Cuba, where he taught at the Cuban Institute of Cinema Art and made two documentaries with his students. A stint followed at the Experimental Cinema Institute of the University of Santiago, Chile. Three films came out of this experience, including one of the finest of Ivens' later documentaries, *A Valparaiso* (1963, 37 minutes). An evocation of that sad city—a major port before the opening of the Panama Canal—it has a splendid commentary written by the French filmmaker Chris Marker. As Peter Cowie wrote,

"Marker's words, like Hemingway's in *Spanish Earth,* bring a dignity and a muted anguish to the picture of a city cramped almost to death against the hills." It won the Fipresci Prize at the Öberhausen Festival in 1964.

Ivens was sixty-five in 1963, and the occasion was marked by a major retrospective in Leipzig. There was another in Amsterdam in 1964, and the same year a jury of critics at the Mannheim Festival placed Ivens second only to Robert Flaherty among world documentarists—ahead of Vertov, Eisenstein, Ruttman, and Buñuel. Honored in this way, like a great filmmaker nearing the end of his career, Ivens soon showed that he was far from the end of anything.

In 1965 he made one of his rare nonpolitical films, *Pour le mistral,* which attempted to do for the winds of Provence what *Regen* had done for the rain, and the same year he paid his first visit to North Vietnam. The American bombing campaign had begun, and its effects (and the Vietnamese resistance to it) are shown in *Le ciel, la terre* (*The Threatening Sky,* 30 minutes). The profits from the film went to the struggling Vietnamese film industry, along with equipment begged on its behalf by Ivens from his friends around the world.

Ivens' first Dutch film in over thirty years followed, *Rotterdam-Europoort* (1966, 20 minutes), a somewhat fanciful film about the great modern port as it might strike the Flying Dutchman of legend. His assistant director on this film, Marceline Loridan, became Ivens' regular collaborator, and his wife. They returned to Vietnam in the spring of 1967 and filmed in and around Hanoi for four months. Some of this material was used in *Loin du Vietnam* (*Far From Vietnam,* 1967), a gesture of solidarity with the North Vietnamese initiated and edited by Chris Marker, with contributions from Alain Resnais, Jean-Luc Godard, William Klein, Claude Lelouch, and Agnès Varda, as well as Ivens.

Marceline Loridan was credited as codirector of all of Ivens' subsequent films, beginning with *Le dix-septième parallèle* (*The Seventeenth Parallel,* 1968, 113 minutes), dealing with life in a North Vietnamese village close to the border with the South. Ivens says that he and Loridan "lived completely with the population, the peasants and soldiers, day and night. For two months we had the same shelter, the same food, the same weapons, the same enemy, the same danger."

Loridan had previously worked with the *cinéma-vérité* directors Edgar Morin and Jean Rouch, and no doubt because of her collaboration *Seventeenth Parallel* was made, as Ivens says, "in a different style from the rest of my work, less lyrical, almost an anonymous form. I foreswore everything I found easy. In this film there are no fades, no dissolves, no dynamic montage—and I am known for active editing. . . . I also, consciously, expelled all exotic content, even so far as suppressing palm trees when cutting the image to the right or left! . . . In *Seventeenth Parallel* aesthetic problems, even of framing, have an ideological content." Rosalind Delmar has pointed out other changes in Ivens' style attributable to Loridan's influence, including the use of longer sequences and the employment of direct sound (here Vietnamese dialogue, used with subtitles).

Delmar regards *Seventeenth Parallel* as one of the best documentaries made about the Vietnam War, but Loridan was dissatisfied with it, saying that one could sit in front of it "and, to a certain extent, 'enjoy' one's emotions." She sought an even more rigorously political style, like that adopted by Godard in its eschewal of narrative devices and visual pleasures. For better or worse, this was achieved in *Le peuple et ses fusils* (*The People and Their Guns,* 1970, 97 minutes), shot during 1968 in Laos, in the cave barracks of the revolutionary Patriotic Front.

When Ivens and Loridan returned to Paris, shortly after the events of May 1968, they formed a film collective with other political militants to complete *The People and Their Guns.* The technique they adopted involved "a nondramatic, fragmentary construction" and "the use of many more and much longer explanatory captions," the latter intended to "allow the spectator at every moment to achieve a distance in relation to what is being seen." Much space is allotted to sequences showing political leaders and soldiers of the Patriotic Front seeking to arouse revolutionary fervor among the peasants. Regarded by the Film Control Commission as a propaganda document, hostile to the United States and the Laotian government, the film was refused a license for distribution outside France.

In 1971, Ivens and Loridan started work on what was intended as a four-hour film about life in China. After four years of planning, filming, and editing, they produced a monumental twelve-hour film in twelve parts, *Comment Yukong déplaça les montagnes* (*How Yukong Moved the Mountains,* 1976). The work was financed partly by the French Centre National du Cinéma, partly out of the fees that Ivens and Loridan earned by instructing Chinese cameramen and sound engineers.

The twelve episodes of *How Yukong Moved the Mountains* comprise seven shorts and five feature-length films varying in length from six minutes to two hours. Ivens and Loridan, permitted to film anywhere except at nuclear establishments, shot about half the episodes in and around Peking and also studied the effects of the Chinese Cultural Revolution at a generator factory and a huge pharmacy in Shanghai, at a barracks in Nanking, an oil well at Taking, and in the fishing village of Da Yu Dao. Abandoning the austerities of *The People and Their Guns,* they set out "to capture reality at its most intense, in daily life." They spent eight weeks at the Shanghai pharmacy alone, for example, showing how twenty-four workers, none of them doctors, diagnose ailments, prescribe and provide medicines, lecture on birth control in the surrounding villages, and apply acupuncture. We encounter characters like the irascible and rude young druggist whose self-criticism at group meetings is distinctly perfunctory, and the self-proclaimed "old capitalist" who avoids the enthusiastic group meetings altogether.

This "enormous fresco of contemporary China" was widely shown and admired, described by J. Hoberman as "the best first-hand glimpse we are likely to have of the late Cultural Revolution." But Nigel Andrews, while acknowledging that the film "has no precedent" as "a picture of the Chinese people at work and at play," suggested that it was also "the most insidiously Utopian portrait of China so far." He asks if the filmmakers visited China's prisons and labor camps and goes on: "If they did, none of their experience has survived on celluloid. Instead we have an endless gallery of indefatigably smiling peasant faces testifying to the improvement in their work conditions."

Reactions to Ivens' work as a whole tend to be colored by the political views of the commentator, and this is scarcely surprising since, as Rosalind Delmar points out, he is not an objective documentarist: "He does not set out to weigh all arguments in the balance and deliver judgment, but to act as a witness." For Peter Cowie, "the real tragedy of Ivens' career is that while his political commitment has intensified to a zealous degree, his talent as a filmmaker has dwindled, so that much of his recent work in Asia appears crude and naive." William Alexander, less sweepingly, points out that Ivens' films, in "their effort to feel out lives, rhythms, culture and country" have a looseness of structure that is "clear gain" where the attempt is successful, but otherwise leads to "a diffuseness that diminishes the film's intensity." Most critics would agree that Ivens is "the engaged reporter *par excellence,*" and "the most important documentarist of his period."

In 1976, according to David Robinson, Ivens was still "small, neat, fast-moving and strikingly handsome." His eightieth birthday in 1978 was celebrated with a complete retrospective of his work at the Amsterdam Filmmuseum, and there were further retrospectives during 1979 in the United States, Britain, France, and Italy.

FILMS: Brandende Straal (Shining Ray)/De Wigwam (The Wigwam), 1911 (amateur short); Zeedijk-Filmstudie (Filmstudy-Zeedijk), 1927; Études des mouvements (Studies in Movement), 1928; De Brug (The Bridge), 1928; (with Mannus Franken) Branding (Breakers), 1929; Regen (Rain), 1929; Schaatsenrijden (Skaters), 1929; 1K-Film (1-Film), 1929; Arm Drenthe (Poor Drenthe), 1929; NVV Congres, 1929–30; Jeudaag (Day of Youth), 1929–30; Wij Bouwen (We Are Building), 1929; Zuiderzee, 1930; Philips Radio (Symphonie Industrielle/Industrial Symphony), 1931; Creosoot (Creosote), 1931; Pesn o Gerojach (Komsomol/Song of Heroes), 1932; (with Henri Storck) Misère au Borinage (Borinage), 1934; Nieuwe Gronden (New Earth), 1934; Spanish Earth, 1937; The Four Hundred Million, 1939; Power and the Land, 1941; (with Lewis Milestone) Our Russian Front, 1941; Oil for Aladdin's Lamp, 1942; Action Stations, 1943; Indonesia Calling, 1946; Pierwsze Lata (The First Years), 1949; (with Jerzy Bossak) Pokoj Zwyciezy Swiat (Peace Will Win), 1951; (with Ivan Pyriev) Freundschaft Sieft (Friendship Triumphs), 1952; Naprozod Mlodziezy (Freundschaft Sieft/Friendship Triumphs), 1952; Wyscig Pokoju Warsawa-Berlin-Praga (Peace Tour), 1952; Das Lied der Ströme (Song of the Rivers, 1954); La Seine a rencontré Paris (The Seine Meets Paris), 1957; Before Spring, 1958; 600 Million With You, 1958; L'Italia non è un paese povero (Italy Is Not a Poor Country), 1959; Demain à Nanguila (Nanguila Tomorrow), 1960; Carnet de viaje (Travel Notebook), 1961; Pueblo armado (An Armed People), 1961; A Valparaiso, 1962; Le petit chapiteau (The Little Circus), 1963; Le train de la victoire (The Victory Train), 1964; Pour le mistral (Mistral), 1965; Le ciel, la terre (The Threatening Sky), 1965; Rotterdam-Europoort, 1966; (with others) Loin du Vietnam (Far From Vietnam), 1967; (with Marceline Loridan) Le dix-septième parallèle (The Seventeenth Parallel), 1968; (with Marceline Loridan and others) Le peuple et ses fusils (The People and Their Guns), 1970; (with Marceline Loridan) Rencontre avec le Président Ho Chi Minh (Meeting with President Ho Chi Minh), 1970; (with Marceline Loridan) Comment Yukong déplaça les montagnes (How Yukong Moved the Mountains), 1976 (in twelve parts); (with Marceline Loridan) Les Kazaks—minorité nationale—Sinkiang, 1977; (with Marceline Loridan) Les Ouigours—minorité nationale—Sinkiang, 1977. *Published scripts—In English:* A Valparaiso; La Seine a rencontré Paris (French and English); Song of the Rivers (edited version); Spanish Earth (excerpt) *all in* Delmar, R. Joris Ivens, 1979. *In other languages:* A Valparaiso *in* L'Avant-Scène du Cinéma December 1967 (in French); Le ciel, la terre *in* Positif June 1966 (in French); Le dix-septième parallèle, 1968 (Editeurs Français Réunis); Lied der Ströme *in* Tribune (Berlin) 1957 (in German); La Seine a rencontré Paris *in* Cinéma (France) May 1960 (in French).

ABOUT: Alexander, W. Film on the Left, 1981; Bellet, F. (and others) Muestra retrospectiva Joris Ivens, 1963 (in Spanish); Bellour, R. Le cinéma et la vérité, 1963; Brunel, C. Hommage à Joris Ivens, 1983; Cavatorta, S. and Maggione, D. Joris Ivens, 1979 (in Italian); Cinéma Politique. Joris Ivens, 1978 (in French); Cowie, P. Dutch Cinema, 1979; Dallet, S. (ed.) Guerres revolutionnaires: histoire et cinema, 1984; Delmar, R. Joris Ivens: Fifty Years of Film-making, 1979; Destanque, R. and Ivens, J. Joris Ivens ou la memoire d'un regard, 1982; Devarrieux, C. Joris Ivens: entretien, 1979; Gambetti, G. Joris Ivens, 1979 (in Italian); Grelier, R. Joris Ivens, 1965 (in English); International Film Guide, 1968; Ivens, J. The Camera and I, 1969; Ivens, J. and Destanque, R. Joris Ivens, ou le memoire d'un regard, 1982; Klaue, W. Joris Ivens, 1963 (in German); Kreimeier, K. Joris Ivens, 1976 (in German); Nederlands Filmmuseum. Joris Ivens, 1978 (in Dutch); Passek, J.-L. Joris Ivens, 1979 (in French); Wegner, H. Joris Ivens: Dokumentarist der Warheit, 1965; Zalzman, A. Joris Ivens, 1963 (in French). Periodicals—American Film June 1978; L'Avant-Scène du Cinéma January 1–15, 1981 (Ivens issue); Cahiers du Cinéma July, August–September, and November 1953, May 1976, January 1977; Cineaste 3 1980, 2 1982, 3 1983, 1 1984; Cineforum March 1979; Cinéma (France) February 1969, April 1976; Cinéma Politique November 1978 (Ivens issue); Cinema Sessanta May–June 1976; Cinematographe September 1982; Cinema Universatario 11 1960; Écran November 1978; Film (East Germany) 2 and 3 1963; Film Culture Spring 1972 (Ivens issue); Film Dope July 1983; Filmfaust December 1976, June–July 1977; Film Guide Summer 1955; FilmKritik November 1976 (Ivens issue); Positif 76 1966 (Ivens issue), February 1970; Sight and Sound Spring 1958; Theatre Arts March and April 1946; Times (London) November 25, 1976.

JENNINGS, HUMPHREY (1907– September 24, 1950), English documentarist, painter, poet, and sociologist, was the elder son of Frank Jennings, an architect. He was born in the seaside village of Walberswick, Suffolk, where his mother owned a pottery shop. Jennings' paternal great-grandfather had lost his fortune when the coming of the railroads ruined the coaching industry, but his grandfather, Tom Jennings, had become famous and wealthy as a trainer of racehorses at Newmarket. Horses and locomotives are potent and often related symbols in Jennings' iconography.

His parents were guild socialists and ardent admirers of peasant art, much influenced by A. R. Orage and his weekly magazine New Age. From early childhood Humphrey Jennings accompanied them on their long trips abroad— most often to Brittany—to buy pottery for his mother's shop. Largely on account of Orage's enthusiasm for the reforming educational theories of W.H.D. Rouse, Jennings was sent to study

under him at the Perse School in Cambridge. There he acquired a thorough grounding in the classical languages and literatures and came early under the influence of Milton, Shakespeare, Bunyan, and Blake. Thanks to his English teacher at the Perse, he also conceived an interest in the theatre, showing a precocious talent for scenic design.

In about 1925 Jennings entered Pembroke College, Cambridge University, where he was one of a brilliant generation that included Jacob Bronowski, William Empson, Kathleen Raine, and Charles Madge. What they had in common was an intense interest in the relationship between the material and the spiritual, technology and nature, science and art, prose and poetry. Left-wing politics were also very much a part of the Cambridge intellectual atmosphere, and though (unlike Madge) Jennings never joined the Communist Party, preferring Blake's vision of society to Marx's, he was attracted by the "imaginative materialism" of Marxism.

These assorted interests combined to produce his lifelong fascination with the Industrial Revolution and the way it transformed the world and our conception of the world—from the age of Reason and pure science (which for him was symbolized in Sir Christopher Wren's St. Paul's Cathedral) to the age of the machine and the factory. The latter excited him on account of its genius and daring, though at the same time he hated its greedy materialism and its exploitation of human beings, which he thought led to "the repression of the clear imaginative vision in ordinary folk."

Indeed, there seems never to have been any limit to the range of Jennings' interests. He wrote poetry, he painted, he involved himself in undergraduate theatre as an actor and designer, and, when he graduated in the English Tripos, did so with a starred first-class honors degree, an extremely rare distinction. Offered a chair in English literature at a Japanese university, he preferred to stay where he was and settled in a small flat in Cambridge with his wife Cicely, working on a definitive text of Shakespeare's Venus and Adonis and on a thesis about the poet Thomas Gray.

During these postgraduate years in Cambridge, he continued to design for the theatre, winning high praise even from the London critics for his sets for Denis Arundell's Cambridge productions of Stravinsky's The Soldier's Tale and Honegger's King David. When Arundell went to London, Jennings continued to work with him, designing his productions for the London Opera Festival in 1929 and The Bacchae in 1930. In 1931 he played Bottom in Arundell's version of Purcell's Fairy Queen.

But his real passion at this time was painting (and indeed, some of his friends maintain that Jennings always thought of himself as first of all a painter). The principal influence on his work was French Surrealism, for which he was a knowledgeable and effective advocate, though he disapproved of the Surrealists' use of purely private imagery. In his own paintings and collages he sought always to employ "public," familiar images, however incongruous their juxtapositions, just as he subsequently did in his films. His friend Julian Trevelyan maintained that Jennings was too much an intellectual to be a good painter, and most of his early work does seem to have been more interesting in conception than in execution. He himself was modest about his paintings, and seldom showed them in the small Experimental Gallery he opened in premises adjoining his Cambridge flat.

Gerald Noxon describes Jennings at this time as "rather tall, very angular and bony, with a wild crop of straggling fair hair" and "a large, sharp nose." He was "an acutely restless person" who "paced the floor as he talked . . . jerking and gesturing. . . . To say that Humphrey was a brilliant talker is a truth that does not in the least convey his impressive gifts in this area, which were beyond those of any person I have known. When Humphrey addressed himself to a subject he did so with a lucidity, a forcefulness, and a kind of internal illumination generated by his immense enthusiasm." If he "often spoke in outrageous hyperbole, made fantastically sweeping generalizations . . . it was all part of his technique of verbal exploration of the subject, of creating channels of communications with all those around him, even if he had to shock, outrage, and even seriously anger them in the process." And, "in spite of his brilliance and sophistication, Humphrey remained utterly nonsnob, utterly candid, utterly noninsular, essentially humble and completely and enthusiastically involved and in love with art and life everywhere."

It was thanks to Gerald Noxon that Jennings made his first film. In 1932–1933 a small legacy had made it possible for Jennings to devote himself full-time to painting, but by 1934 the money was all gone, the Jennings' first daughter had arrived, and they were in considerable financial difficulty. Noxon was by then working for an advertising agency, where he had a client who wanted a short film made to warn of the dangers of "Slum"—a mythical substance that was supposed to be deposited in automobile crankcases by rival motor oils. Noxon offered the chore to Jennings, fearing that he would be insulted: "I should not have hesitated. . . . He accepted the assignment instantly and in no time at all had made friends with the cameraman, written the script, charmed and amazed the oil company men . . . designed the set, and worked out the lighting." Finding that the actual contents of even the most ancient crankcases looked perfectly innocuous, Jennings then concocted a revolting and pernicious-looking substance that, for the purposes of the film, represented "Slum."

"The film turned out to be a minor triumph," Noxon says, "and Humphrey, it seemed, was from that moment destined to become involved in film work." The same year Jennings undertook his first freelance assignments for the General Post Office's Film Unit, though he had little in common with John Grierson, the Unit's famous chief. Grierson regarded documentary as "educative propaganda," whose purpose should be to foster "appreciation of public service and public purposes," and he at first considered Jennings something of an intellectual dilettante.

For his first GPO film, *Post Haste* (1934, 26 minutes), Jennings assembled a history of the post office through old prints and drawings, a technique that, according to some accounts, he originated. The same year he designed the sets for Cavalcanti's *Pett and Pott*, a whimsically surreal comedy remote from Grierson's conception of the Film Unit's function (Jennings also played a small role in this film). *The Story of the Wheel* (1934, 12 minutes), tracing the evolution of wheeled transport, was followed by *Locomotives* (1935, 21 minutes), a history of the steam engine and its uses: Both were photographed from models in museums and credit Jennings as editor, though this may mean (as some sources suggest) that he was in effect "director" as well.

In or about 1935 Jennings was briefly and improbably employed by J. Arthur Rank's Methodist film organization, for which he wrote a shooting script based on a novel by Leo Walmsley. At roughly the same time he served as color director on Len Lye's puppet film *The Birth of a Robot* (1936, 7 minutes), made in Gasparcolour for Shell Oil. But Jennings' main interests still seem to have been painting and the Surrealist movement, whose leader, André Breton, was by this time a close friend. Jennings was actively involved in preparations for the 1936 Surrealist Exhibition in London, in which he showed some paintings and collages. The same year he collaborated with David Gascoyne in translating twenty surrealist poems by Benjamin Peret for British publication.

Meanwhile, Jennings was also playing a leading role in what, on the face of it, seems a totally unrelated concern, the organization known as Mass Observation. This was a forerunner of contemporary opinion polls that sought "an anthropology of our own people" through the direct observation of their behavior and conversation—and in fact it showed a relish for the eccentricities of the British character that was at times positively surreal. Mass Observation's other prime movers were Jennings' Cambridge friend Charles Madge, who shared his interest in the impact of the Industrial Revolution, and the anthropologist Tom Harrison.

Jennings was responsible for coordinating and correlating the Mass Observation reports that were published in *May 12* (1937), a massive inquiry into the state of the nation at the time of George VI's coronation. Gerald Noxon believes that Jennings' involvement in Mass Observation "intensified his understanding and respect for people in all walks of life. It brought him into daily contact with men and women whose lives were utterly different from his own yet with whom he felt a bond of deep understanding and warm sympathy. It was this kind of experience that led Humphrey to make *Spare Time*, his first significant work as an artist in film."

Spare Time (1939, 18 minutes), written and directed by Jennings for the GPO Film Unit and produced by Cavalcanti, was an attempt to apply the methods of Mass Observation to the cinema. Jennings chose four communities shaped by the Industrial Revolution—the steel town of Sheffield, the cotton towns of Manchester and Bolton, and a Welsh mining community, Pontypridd—examining in each "the way people spend their spare time," and finding beauty and vigor as well as squalor in these industrial landscapes. *Spare Time* was attacked by more conventional documentarists for what seemed to them a satirical treatment of working people, especially in the sequence where a girl's kazoo band makes its almost surreal appearance on a bleak soccer field. It has since been recognized that, on the contrary, Jennings was trying to go beyond the accepted clichés about "the dignity of the working man" to the quirkish individual realities of working-class life.

With the outbreak of World War II in September 1939, the GPO Film Unit came under the control of the Ministry of Information and during the period of the "phoney war" (1939–1940), seems to have been seriously handicapped by bureaucratic interference. The first films Jennings made at this time were routine assignments of limited interest—*Speaking From America* (1939, 10 minutes), about the transatlantic telephone and radio link, and *SS Ionian* (1939, 20 minutes), about the wartime role of merchant ships in the Mediterranean. *The First Days* (1939, 23 minutes), made in collaboration with Harry Watt and Pat Jackson, was better—a

moody collage of impressions of the "strange new world" that the war had made of Britain—a world of barrage balloons, searchlights, partings, and denuded museums: a sense of a civilization endangered.

In April 1940 the GPO Film Unit became the Crown Film Unit. That year Jennings and Harry Watt made *London Can Take It* (10 minutes), intended primarily to win American support for the British war effort. The film, built around a *Collier's* article by Quentin Reynolds, is an evocation of London during a single evening, night, and morning in the early days of the blitz. It opens with leisurely views of the city as Londoners return from work, gathering momentum as people line up for air-raid shelters and searchlights and guns go on the alert. Then, as the skies darken, we hear the drone of approaching bombers and the first explosion, followed by a rapid montage of guns, men, and buildings. A bomb briefly lights up the dome of St. Paul's. We cut away to more peaceful scenes of people sleeping, men playing darts. And then, with dawn, comes the "All Clear" siren, and misty shots of the Thames and the Houses of Parliament. People survey the night's damage, and go off to work.

Jacob Bronowski said that he learned from Jennings that "a clown or a poet can impose his own macabre sense of fun on the imagination merely by treating extravagance as normal." There are several examples of what he means in *London Can Take It*, as when a woman casually enters a shop through its absent windows. Jim Hillier in *Studies in Documentary* calls the film Jennings' "first real evocation of the British people not so much at war as living with war. . . . Jennings' use of sound is already masterly. The commentary is used alongside images which complicate our response rather than illustrate the words. It is at the service of both the images and natural sounds. . . . On the whole, the images tend to make the general sentiments of the words more concrete and particular."

The day after the premiere of *London Can Take It*, Jennings and his colleagues are said to have scoured the papers in vain for reviews until someone thought to look at a front page, where they found the film treated as a news event. It was Jennings' first real success, and seems to have confirmed his commitment to film as a serious art form. At about this time Jennings, who had evacuated his wife and two children to the United States, called in at the London house of the Film Unit producer Ian Dalrymple, begged a bed for the night, and stayed for over two years. Free of domestic concerns, he worked during that period with intense concentration, though as always erratically, "in manic bursts."

Spring Offensive, also known as *An Unrecorded Victory* (1940, 20 minutes), deals very effectively with the wartime reclamation of farmland in Jennings' own part of Britain, East Anglia. Full of affection for the old ways, with its romantic images of men and horses toiling together in a misty landscape, it also shows his delight in the power and beauty of the new machines that the war brought into the immemorial scene. It was followed by *Welfare of the Workers* (1949, 10 minutes), an uninspired piece about wartime working conditions, codirected with Pat Jackson, and then by *Heart of Britain* (1941, 9 minutes), another meditation on the British way of life under the stresses of war.

In some of these early films, the power of the images had been diminished by the banality of their spoken commentaries. By now Jennings was learning to rely increasingly on music to supplement and at times to replace the commentary, as when the triumphant affirmation of the "Hallelujah Chorus" soars out over broken buildings in *Heart of Britain* with a power that derives as much from the homely faces of the Huddersfield Choral Society as from the music itself.

This liberation from the commentary is carried a step further in *Words for Britain* (1941, 8 minutes), in which images of ordinary British people at war are matched with Laurence Olivier's reading of stirring passages from Milton, Kipling, Churchill, Lincoln, and others and, for the last few minutes, are accompanied only by the music of Handel and the clatter of tanks driving into Parliament Square past Lincoln's statue: "and suddenly," wrote Lindsay Anderson, 'the camera is following a succession of men and women in uniform, striding along the pavement cheery and casual, endowed by the music, by the urgent rhythm of the cutting, and by the solemnity of what has gone before (to which we feel they are heirs) with an astonishing and breathtaking dignity, a mortal splendour."

In *Listen to Britain* (1942, 20 minutes), Jennings dispensed with verbal commentary altogether (apart from a superfluous introduction), relying entirely on natural sounds and music. Like some earlier Jennings films, but now with irresistible poetic force, *Listen to Britain* juxtaposes images reflecting the wartime menace to British culture with images that insist on the continuity of that culture. Fighter planes roar over fields rattling with the noise of harvesters; images of watchers on the coast, scanning the threatening horizon, frame scenes in a Blackpool dance hall; shots of the comedians Flanagan and Allen entertaining in a factory canteen merge into a lunchtime concert at the National Gallery, with Myra Hess playing Mozart—the transcen-

dent music carrying us over a montage of wartime scenes to a tank factory whose din leads us on to a street parade with a brass band, and then to the unabashed patriotism of "Rule Britannia," rising above juxtaposed shots of factories and cornfields.

"With the elimination of commentary," writes Jim Hillier, "the images or sequences often acquire a rich ambiguity which is a constant feature of Jennings' style (reminding us that Jennings was a product of the I. A. Richards school of criticism that produced Empson's concept of the ambiguity or multiplicity of the poetic statement). The meaning of an image, or more frequently the connections between images, are left to the audience's emotions for interpretation. . . . the Blackpool dancers, wedged between two shots of the watchers, on the dark shore, can be either gay or desperate. . . . *Listen to Britain* also expresses Jennings' sense of the indivisibility of Britain, not only of task but of landscape, especially the pastoral and the industrial. At one moment, as in the dissolve from birdsong and the wooded ridge at dawn to the sound of steps on cobbles and a grimy industrial landscape, the two are made to coalesce; at another, in the stunningly abrupt cut from hissing steam to shimmering, silent trees, they simply exist simultaneously."

Listen to Britain, Jennings' first masterpiece, was followed by the best-known of all his films and the only one of feature length, *Fires Were Started* (1943, 80 minutes). Conceived as a tribute to the part-time Auxiliary Fire Service and its work during the blitz, it was made when the bombing was over and the AFS had been disbanded, though all of the cast were members of the full-time National Fire Service that replaced it. One of these was the writer William Sansom, who plays the new recruit Barrett. His account of the making of the film suggests that Jennings worked from only the sketchiest outline, that dialogue was improvised on the spot, and that the simple but powerfully effective shape of the film was imposed largely in the cutting room.

Unlike most of Jennings' films, *Fires Were Started* has individualized characters and a straightforward linear plot. It begins in the early morning with the crew assembling at the fire station and follows them through the routine chores of the day, which, as Denis Forman says, "are shown as in a dream, the hideous work of the night ahead being the reality. This sense of living in a vacuum . . . is part of the experience of every solider who has had to wait for zero hour. In these periods the memory is acutely sensitive but strangely detached. An almond tree in blossom or a dog asleep in the sun [images from the film] will be remembered afterwards more vividly than the drastic events which follow."

As evening draws on there is an interval for relaxation, and then the night, sirens and swiveling guns, and the climactic struggle against the flames engulfing a dockside warehouse and threatening a munitions ship. A man dies, reinforcements arrive, and the editing rhythm grows less urgent as the fire is brought under control. In the gray, weary dawn, Barrett finds that he has taken the dead Jacko's place as an accepted member of the team. There is a brief funeral service for Jacko, images from which are juxtaposed with shots of the unharmed munitions ship setting off down the Thames.

Jim Hillier has drawn attention to the film's symbolic dimension—the treatment of the blitz less as enemy aggression than as a natural disaster in which Jacko's death takes on the character almost of a ritual sacrifice. Jennings was greatly interested in the symbolism of the Tarot pack and especially in the Maison-Dieu, the tower struck by fire from heaven. The Maison-Dieu is often associated with the alchemist's furnace and consequently with the search through the union of opposite elements (like fire and water) for the Philosopher's Stone. Denis Forman has called *Fires Were Started* "one of the most precious possessions of the cinema; alongside it most studio-made films look like pieces of confectionery. . . . It is without doubt the crowning achievement of the British documentary school." Some have gone further, calling it "the crowning achievement" of the British cinema as a whole.

The Silent Village (1943, 36 minutes) also blends documentary and narrative techniques to tell the story of Lidice, the Czech mining village wiped out by the Nazis as punishment for the miners' resistance. Jennings set the film in a similar mining village in Wales and the result, beautifully composed and often moving as it is, is unconvincing as a portrait of an occupied country, and further weakened by an almost immobile camera. Jennings himself was remembered with great warmth by the miners who worked on the film. According to one account, he would drop into their houses, "devour their books, teach their wives new cooking recipes and sometimes insist on cooking their dinners," afterwards keeping them awake for hours, reading to them: "He seems to have upset their households and lit up their lives."

The True Story of Lilli Marlene (1944, 30 minutes), Jennings' history of the song that caught the nostalgic imagination of two opposing armies, uneasily combines studio-staged scenes and newsreel sequences. It was followed

by *The Eighty Days* (1944, 14 minutes), about the renewed German attack on Southern England, this time using V-1 missiles—the "doodlebugs." Similar in technique to the early documentaries, it reflected a wearier but still determined Britain. A slightly shorter film on the same subject, *V1*, was made for overseas distribution.

The somber mood of *The Eighty Days* also dominates *A Diary for Timothy* (1945, 39 minutes), in which again, as in the early shorts, Jennings gives a central place to the spoken commentary. This commentary, written by E. M. Forster and spoken by Michael Redgrave, is addressed to the newborn Timothy. It takes the form of an introduction to his homeland as it passes from the dark days of autumn 1944 to the beginnings of hope with the build-up of the Soviet offensive at the turn of the year. We trace the changing fortunes during this period of various representative figures—a farmer, a wounded fighter pilot, a miner, an engineer, and Timothy himself—ending with victory assured but Britain's future (and therefore Timothy's) uncertain.

Many critics place *A Diary for Timothy* among Jennings' finest films. "With dazzling virtuosity," wrote Lindsay Anderson, "linking detail to detail by continuously striking associations of image, sound, music and comment, the film ranges freely over the life of the nation, connecting and connecting" full of "the intimate and loving observation of people, the devoted concentration on the gestures and expressions, the details of dress or behaviour that distinguished each unique human being from another." Others, however, agreeing that at its best the film deploys its images with an emotional effect beyond logical analysis, nevertheless found it marred sometimes by contrived or mechanical passages and not wholly free of sentimentality.

Jim Hillier, noting that *A Diary for Timothy* is "about a crisis of national morale," suggested that "for Jennings the filmmaker it also represents a crisis of style and subject matter. During the war he saw his ideas and feelings about British civilization and genius given an actuality from which he was able to create his best films. . . . Jennings' own attitudes survived into peacetime, but in peacetime how was he to find a context in which to express them?"

Jennings' first postwar film, *A Defeated People* (1946, 19 minutes), is about occupied Germany under the Allied Control Commission, dealing rather perfunctorily with the details of administration, more imaginatively and sympathetically with the German people themselves.

The Cumberland Story (1947, 39 minutes), promoting the postwar reorganization and development of the Cumberland coalfields, characteristically gives due weight both to the miners' resistance to change (and the historical reasons for it) and to the imaginative daring of the new plans. *Dim Little Island* (1949, 11 minutes) and *Family Portrait* (1950, 25 minutes) are both evocations of Britain and the British character, not very different from earlier variations on these themes. The latter was Jennings' contribution to the Festival of Britain, full of his sense of history but lacking the feeling of excitement and purpose of the war films.

More interesting were his detailed plans for a film about the London Symphony Orchestra, rich in invention and humor. It was put aside when Jennings began work on "The Good Life," a film about health intended as part of a series called "The Changing Face of Europe." In the autumn of 1950 he was scouting locations on the Greek island of Poros. He climbed a cliff to make a sketch for his cameraman and fell to his death. A copy of Trelawney's *The Last Days of Shelley and Byron* was found in his pocket.

During the last part of his life, Jennings was working hard on his long-projected book "Pandaemonium," a vast collage of annotated quotations and illustrations that was to have expressed his views on the Industrial Revolution. He also returned to painting, and with a new breadth and freedom of style. Some of his late work in this medium was included in the 1982 exhibition of his achievements in many fields at the Riverside Studios in London. John Russell Taylor found these paintings "astonishing . . . quite unlike anyone else painting, in Britain or anywhere at that time. Seldom can I remember receiving so forcefully, walking into a gallery, the impression of encountering a major new talent of complete originality. . . . By this time the Surrealist strain seems to have diminished in importance, and instead we have pure painting, of a discipline and seriousness which will come as a surprise even to those who know Jennings' films well."

Humphrey Jennings has been called "the British cinema's one undoubted *auteur*" and (by Lindsay Anderson, whom he so deeply influenced) "the only real poet the British cinema has yet produced." For his friend Gerald Noxon, it was above all his "power to see clearly yet love well that Humphrey Jennings brought to his films."

FILMS: Post Haste, 1934; The Story of the Wheel, 1934; Locomotives, 1935; Penny Journey, 1938; English Harvest, 1939; Spare Time, 1939; Speaking From America, 1939; SS Ionian/Her Last Trip, 1939 (shorter version released as Cargoes); (with Harry Watt and Pat Jackson) The First Days, 1939; (with Harry Watt) London Can Take it, 1940 (shorter version released as Britain Can Take It); Spring Offensive/An Unrecorded Victory, 1940; (with Pat Jackson) Welfare of the Workers, 1940; Heart of Britain/This Is England, 1941; Words for Battle, 1941; (with Stewart McAllister) Listen to Britain, 1942; Fires Were Started/I Was A Fireman, 1943; The Silent Village, 1943; The Eighty Days, 1944; The True Story of Lilli Marlene, 1944; VI, 1944; A Diary for Timothy, 1945; A Defeated People, 1946; The Cumberland Story, 1947; Dim Little Island, 1949; Family Portrait, 1950.

ABOUT: Belmans, J. Humphrey Jennings, 1970 (in French); Jennings, M.-L. (ed.) Humphrey Jennings: Film-Maker, Painter, Poet, 1982; Lovell, A. and Hillier, J. Studies in Documentary, 1972. *Periodicals*—Cinema Journal Spring 1972; Film Library Quarterly 3–4 1975 (Jennings issue); Film Quarterly Winter 1961–1962 (Jennings issue); Films and Filming May 1961; Films in Review February 1955; Literature-Film Quarterly 1 1979; Sight and Sound December 1950, May 1951, April–June 1954; Time Out January 8–14, 1982; Times (London) January 12, 1982; Twentieth Century January–February 1959.

*"KALATOZOV," MIKHAIL KONSTANTINOVICH (Mikhail Konstantinovich Kalatozishvili)

(December 28, 1903–March 27, 1973), Soviet director, cinematographer, and administrator, was born in Tiflis (now Tbilisi), Georgia. Leaving school at fourteen, he worked as a car mechanic and driver, meanwhile studying at home for his high school diploma. He graduated in or about 1920 and went on to a business school, studying economics until a job as a movie theatre projectionist convinced him that he wanted to become a filmmaker.

In 1925 Kalatozov entered the Tbilisi film studios, where he was soon taking small acting roles and learning both cinematography and editing. He worked as a cameraman on a number of documentaries and popular science films. At this early stage in his career, Kalatozov was particularly influenced by Dziga Vertov, master of the "camera eye" and prophet of *cinéma-vérité*, and Esther Shub, whom he met in 1927 and whose documentaries, compiled by the selection and brilliant editing of newsreel and other actuality material, he greatly admired.

18–28 (1928), Kalatozov's first attempt at directing, was made in collaboration with Nutsa Gogoberidze. They used Shub's compilation technique in a historical documentary about Georgia between 1918 and 1928, centering on the counter-revolutionary activities of the Mensheviks. Kalatozov's first important film was the documentary *Sol Svanetia* (*Salt for Svanetia*,

°kä′ lä tô′ zov

1930), shot on location in a beautiful, remote region of the Caucasus mountains, where some aspects of life had scarcely changed since the Middle Ages. According to a catalog description of the film, life in Svanetia was "patriarchal, primitive; the struggle for existence among the snow-capped mountains entails such constant want and hunger and, particularly, the tormenting hunger for salt, that each new birth is regarded as a terrible curse, while death becomes a solemn feast. Bloody offerings were made at the graves of the dead; horses . . . were slaughtered in honor of their pagan gods."

Kalatozov himself shot much of the film, which incorporates many on-the-spot departures from the scenario (by the notable dramatist and scriptwriter Sergei Tretyakov). The filming was observed by the American critic Harry Alan Potamkin, who wrote: "Kalatozov has established his point-of-view at once in the bold image and stern grand angles. . . . The funeral of the tuberculosis victim is excruciating in its dire grief. The widow, dripping her milk into the grave, condemns the collusion of paganism and Christianity conspiring against human happiness. 'We will not give our milk to the grave,' the women cry in revolt. The film calls and we respond: 'These people must be saved—roads and salt.'" Jay Leyda says that *Salt for Svanetia* will always be linked in his mind with Buñuel's *Land Without Bread*—"they are both sur-realist in the literal sense of the term, both with a harsh pity for the tragedies of their subjects that is far more moving than any appeal for sympathy."

However, some of Svanetia's leading citizens denied that the archaic customs shown in the film had ever existed and argued that, in any case, it was more important to show the modernization of the region. This early masterpiece was harshly criticized for "formalism" and "naturalism," and Kalatozov's next picture had an even more discouraging reception. *Gvozd v sapoge* (*A Nail in a Boot*, 1932) set out to illustrate the old adage: "For want of a nail the battle was lost," showing how the inferior quality of something so trivial as a nail in a soldier's boot leads inexorably to the capture of an armored train (albeit only on maneuvers). Kalatozov had intended to demonstrate the crucial and universal importance of efficiency in Soviet industry, but the generals decided that his fable gave a negative impression of the Red Army's capabilities and had it banned.

After this second misfortune, Kalatozov was obliged to shelve his career as a director. He studied for a time at the Leningrad Academy of Art (1933), then put his training as an economist and his talent for administration to work as head of the Tbilisi studios. Though he made one or two attempts to return to active filmmaking, it was not until 1939 that his next movie appeared. This was *Mut* (*Manhood*), a drama about Soviet aviation (and foreign espionage) that served as a preparation for the more considerable film that followed.

Valeri Chkalov (*Wings of Victory*, 1941) is a biography of the Russian aviator who was the first to fly from the USSR across the North Pole to the United States. An extremely popular and successful picture, it stars a young stage actor, Vladimir Belokurov, in the title role, and includes portraits of Stalin and Gorky, among other historical figures, as well as some unusually "credible and sympathetic" sketches of the Americans who greeted Chkalov on his arrival in the United States (one of them played by the director himself). Jay Leyda wrote, "The finished film conveys Kalatozov's excitement in the 'mere act of flying,' plus his sympathy with a hero whose temperament often got him into trouble. The photography by [Alexander] Ginsburg of *Valeri Chkalov* is extremely modest and direct, while Kalatozov encourages the performances to be passionately on the edge of exaggeration—and it may be in this stylistic reflection of the thematic conflict between discipline and passion that the film's power lies."

After this successful comeback, there was another hiatus in Kalatozov's career as a director. During the early years of World War II, he served in a consular post in Los Angeles, where he reportedly devoted his efforts to developing relations between Soviet and American filmmakers. In 1942 he returned to Russia to become chief administrator of feature film production and he retained that important post until 1946. The only movie he seems to have made during the war years was *Nepobedimye* (*The Invincible*, 1943), directed in collaboration with Sergei Gerasimov—an unexceptional if popular film about the defense of Stalingrad. From 1946 to 1949 Kalatozov was Deputy Minister of Cinematography and only after that returned to active filmmaking with *Zagavor obrechyonnykh* (*Conspiracy of the Doomed*, 1950), a Cold War exercise about a conspiracy between the Vatican and American intelligence to undermine communism in an East European country.

Verniye druzya (*True Friends*, 1954) is a work in an altogether different style and genre—a subtle and often very funny satire in which three friends band together in a struggle against the petty tyrannies and incompetence of the Soviet bureaucracy. The script (by Alexander Galich and Konstantin Isayev) had reportedly been "sat on" for two years before it was approved, and when the film finally appeared, only a year after Stalin's death, it was said to be the first genuine satire against any aspect of Soviet life to have been released in the USSR since the 1920s. It was warmly welcomed as a harbinger of a cultural thaw, and won the Grand Prix at Karlovy Vary.

After *Pervi eshelon* (*The First Echelon,* 1956), a patriotic drama about young settlers in the virgin lands, came Kalatozov's most famous film, *Letyat zhuravli* (*The Cranes Are Flying,* 1957), adapted by Victor Rosov from his own play and photographed by Sergei Urusevsky. It opens in Moscow with a marvelously lyrical sequence evoking the passionate, playful, tender love affair between Veronica (Tatiana Samoilova) and Boris (Alexei Batalov). The war begins and Boris goes off to fight. Left without news of him in a bombed and desolate city, Veronica in her confusion and despair marries a draft-dodger relative of Boris'. The marriage is a disaster and Veronica serves out the rest of the war as a nurse in Siberia, tormented by guilt and refusing to believe that Boris is dead (though he has long since been reported missing). Back in Moscow at the end of the war, she goes to the station to await his return, her arms full of flowers. She meets, not Boris, but a soldier who saw him die, and is at last able to begin to come to terms with reality, and herself.

It was extraordinary in 1957 to see a Soviet film that acknowledged the existence of draft-dodgers and black marketeers in wartime Russia, and that demanded sympathy instead of censure for a woman who has betrayed her soldier lover. And the picture was no less revolutionary in its style, reveling in elaborate crane shots, helicopter shots, hand-held camerawork, and all the devices forbidden in the "anti-formalist" Stalin years. "The beautiful opening passage with its variations of range and angle is quite unlike anything we have seen lately in a Russian film," wrote Dilys Powell. "There is a death-scene in which we look with the eyes of a dying man outward at whirling, blurring treetops, inward at his flickering vision of the past and the now unattainable future. Again and again the screen is filled with superimposed images, atmospheric effects."

Some of Kalatozov's effects in *The Cranes Are Flying* are intrusive, inappropriate, even preposterous, and most critics would agree with Penelope Houston that it is not a great film but "one of those rather special works which help unmistakably to fix a particular time and climate. It is as though a safety-valve has been unscrewed after all the years of pressure, and a film allowed to emerge like a violent jet of steam. It seems a long time since the cinema showed us anything

with just this air of urgent discovery about it— for all that some of the discoveries are by Western standards almost archaic." The irresistible virtuosity of Tatiana Samoilova's performance, as she progresses from frivolous girl to tragic heroine, established her as a major new star. The film received the Golden Palm at Cannes and took its place at once as a high point in the brief post-Stalin renaissance in the Soviet cinema.

None of Kalatozov's subsequent films equaled this triumph, though he obviously tried to do precisely that in *Neotpravlennoye pismo* (*The Letter That Was Not Sent,* 1960), using the same cameraman and again starring Samoilova. However, this drama about four young geologists searching for diamonds in Siberia had a mixed reception, and seemed to some reviewers as overwrought in its plot as in its self-indulgent technical bravura. The director's last two films were made abroad. *Ya-Kuba* (*I Am Cuba,* 1964), coscripted by Kalatozov and the poet Yevgeni Yevtushenko, is a tribute to Castro's Cuba in the form of four short stories about life there before the Revolution. *Krasnaya palatka* (*The Red Tent,* 1969), a Soviet-Italian coproduction, stars Peter Finch as the Italian aircraft designer and Polar explorer Umberto Nobile and Sean Connery as Raold Amundsen. Combining stolid and old-fashioned storytelling with Kalatozov's visual flamboyance, it was found an odd but interesting film.

FILMS: (with Nutsa Gogoberidze) 18–28, 1928; Blind, 1930; Sol Svanetia (Salt for Svanetia), 1930 (also known as Djim chuante); Gvozd v sapoge (A Nail in a Boot), 1932 (not released); Mut (Manhood/Courage), 1939; Valeri Chkalov (Wings of Victory/The Red Flyer), 1941; (with Sergei Gerasimov) Nepobedimye (The Invincible/The Unconquerable), 1943; Zagavor obrechyonnykh (Conspiracy of the Doomed), 1950; Verniye druzya (True Friends/Close Friends/Firm Friends), 1954; Pervi eshelon (The First Echelon), 1956; The Hostile Wind, 1956; Letyat zhuravli (The Cranes Are Flying), 1957; Neotpravlennoye pismo (The Letter That Was Not Sent/The Unsent Letter), 1960; Ya-Kuba (I Am Cuba/Here Is Cuba), 1964 (also known as Soy-Kuba); Krasnaya palatka (La Tènda Rossa/The Red Tent), 1969.

ABOUT: Birkos, A. S. Soviet Cinema, 1976; Kremlev, G. Mikhail Kalatozov, 1965 (in Russian); Leyda, J. Kino, 1960. *Periodicals*—Écran May 1973; Iskusstvo Kino August 1973; Kosmorama 54 1961; Soviet Film 8 1968; Times (London) March 3, 1973.

"KARLSON," PHIL (Philip N. Karlstein) (July 2, 1908–December 12, 1985), American director, was born in Chicago of Jewish-Irish parentage. His mother was Lillian O'Brien, who

PHIL KARLSON

began her stage career in Ireland, acted with the Abbey Players in Dublin, but wound up as a star of the Yiddish theatre in Chicago. Karlson, who became perhaps the most uncompromising enemy of organized crime the popular cinema has produced, grew up in Prohibition Chicago and remembered "getting 25¢ to stand on a corner, and if the cop was on this side of the street to whistle real loud, and if he was on that side of the street, just to whistle softly. I was keeping a brewery going by a little whistle."

Karlson attended Marshall High School and then studied painting at the Chicago Art Institute. Already attracted to show business, he worked up a song-and-dance act professional enough to take him on one occasion onto the stage of Chicago's Oriental Theatre, where he appeared with Paul Ashe and his orchestra. As a painter, Karlson was less successful. "I had a one-man show and never sold a painting," he said. "I realized then and there, in taking a critical look at my work, that I was no artist."

At his father's urging, Karlson settled on the law as a career. He enrolled as a scholarship student at Loyola University in Los Angeles and went on to the same university's law school, helping to pay his way with what he could earn as a gag writer for the old Buster Keaton studio. It became increasingly obvious to him that the movies excited him more than the law, and in 1927, a year away from graduation, he dropped out of school and joined Universal as a prop man.

A long, slow, and somewhat erratic climb followed. From the props department Karlson moved up to become a second, then a first assistant director; then second-unit director (and sometimes director) on *Leatherneck* and the Tom Mix series. He worked for a year (1932) in Universal's cutting rooms and the following year served as manager of the Bryan Foy Studios. In 1934–1936 he was assigned to the director Stuart Walker as technical and associate director, and between 1936 and 1940 he worked (as Phil Karstein) as assistant to an assortment of Universal directors, among them Stuart Walker, Karl Freund, Arthur Lubin, Tay Garnett, and Henry Koster.

In 1940 Karlson went to work for the USAAF as a civilian flight instructor. After three years, a bad crash in which he was seriously injured ended his flying career. He returned to Universal, but found that the studio was still not prepared to give him his chance as a director. It was not until 1944, when he moved to the cut-rate Monogram Picture Corporation, that he made his first movie, *A Wave, A Wac, and a Marine*. According to its director (at that time known as Philip P. Karlstein), "it was a nothing picture, but I was lucky because it was for Monogram and they didn't understand how bad it was because they had never made anything that was any good."

He stayed at Monogram, nevertheless, and scored something of a hit with *G.I. Honeymoon* (1945), an army farce of frustrated marital expectations starring Gale Storm and Peter Cookson. With his next picture, *The Shanghai Cobra* (1945), a Charlie Chan thriller about a poisoned juke box much relished by buffs, he adopted his last and best-known pseudonym, Phil Karlson. Sixteen more movies followed between 1946 and 1950, and none of them, it seems, has survived. Most were routine programmers made on minute budgets, often in as little as a week, but a few attracted more attention than Monogram products generally rated, like *Wife Wanted* (1946). Starring (and coproduced by) the aging Kay Francis (it was her last film), it was a lively and economical drama about an aging star who exposes a lonely-hearts racket.

Karlson himself spoke with some pride of a few of these early movies, like *Black Gold* (1947). This was the first film produced by the Monogram subsidiary Allied Artists, designed to disseminate more prestigious pictures than those associated with the parent company (which it subsequently devoured). Photographed by the excellent Harry Neumann, it starred Anthony Quinn as an Indian rancher in Oklahoma who adopts a Chinese boy (Ducky Louie) he finds orphaned in the desert, breeds a great race horse, but dies too soon to see it win the Kentucky Derby.

There are said to be some characteristic semi-documentary elements in *Black Gold* and also in *Louisiana* (1947), an indictment of political corruption in the South that looks forward both to *The Phenix City Story* and *Walking Tall*. Karlson also spoke enthusiastically of *The Big Cat* (1949), in which a city boy (Lon McCallister) transplanted to the mountains of southern Utah comes to manhood under the tutelage of his mother's former fiancé (Preston Foster), finally confronting the mountain lion that has killed his mentor. Others have drawn attention to *Adventures in Silverado* (1948), based on Robert Louis Stevenson's story and with Stevenson himself (William Bishop) as hero, mixing it up with a masked bandit: Brian Garfield called it a "strange little movie," and "better made than it ought to be." *Ladies of the Chorus* (1949), according to Andrew Sarris, "has acquired a retroactive cult composed of some of the admirers of the late Marilyn Monroe."

But it was not until the early 1950s, after Karlson had joined Columbia, that what Manny Farber called "chilly documentary exactness and . . . exciting shot-scattering belligerence" clearly emerged. These qualities were certainly evident in *99 River Street* (1953), an extremely black *film noir* in every sense—there are hardly any daylight scenes at all. Ernie Driscoll (John Payne) is a cab driver obsessed by his past glories as a boxer; his wife (Peggy Castle) fantasizes about the show business career she gave up to marry him. She is easily seduced by Victor (Brad Dexter), a flashy thief who involves her in a robbery, murders her when she loses her nerve, and frames Ernie for the killing. Helped by Linda (Evelyn Keyes), an ambitious actress who has previously duped him in furtherance of her career, Ernie goes out after Victor and his henchman and overcomes them in three battles of mounting savagery.

The purgative violence and seedy realism of this film were very much in the frustrated and disillusioned spirit of the times, as was the casual treachery of most of the characters, all of them in thrall to a corrupt notion of the American Dream. These elements remained central in Karlson's movies, the best of which, as Mark Bergman writes, "present a consistent theme of betrayal, violence, and revenge." After *They Rode West* (1954), a good Western scripted by Frank S. Nugent, Karlson returned to these *noir* themes in four notable films that were all released in 1955.

Tight Spot boasts a starrier cast than Karlson had handled before—Ginger Rogers as a convict persuaded to turn state's evidence against a powerful mobster, Edward G. Robinson as the government attorney, and Brian Keith giving a stylishly ironic performance as a crooked cop who falls in love with the woman he has been paid to kill. Even the humor in this dark drama is black, as it is also in *Hell's Island,* an extremely tough thriller that borrowed plot points from *The Maltese Falcon* and starred John Payne, an actor who in Karlson's opinion was much underrated.

But it was Karlson's next picture that confirmed his arrival as a director with a "distinctively personal" style. *Five Against the House,* adapted from a novel by Jack Finney, is set in Reno. Four vacationing college students, told that the casino they visit is thief-proof, decide to prove that it is no such thing. All agree to return the loot afterwards, but one of them, a disturbed Korean vet with homicidal tendencies (Brian Keith), privately makes other plans. The script (by Stirling Silliphant among others) is extremely witty and ingenious. There was high praise for Kim Novak's rendering of a sultry but wholesome nightclub singer who becomes involved in the plot, and even more for Brian Keith's "dazzling serio-comic performance" as the twisted vet. The result seemed to David Thomson "one of the most exciting planned-crime movies" the genre had produced.

Back at Allied Artists, on loan from Columbia, Karlson made what has remained the most widely admired of all his films, *The Phenix City Story.* As Geoff Brown says, it is "a powerful hybrid—a B-picture thriller with the tang of an investigative documentary." Scripted by Richard Mainwaring and closely based on fact, it was filmed on location in Phenix City, Alabama, where the events it recounts took place. Always a lawless town, Phenix City became notorious after World War II as the Deep South's "Sin City"—a haven for gambling, prostitution, and drugs, patronized mostly by soldiers from Fort Benning. In 1954 a local lawyer named Albert A. Patterson ran for nomination as state attorney general on a reform ticket. His campaign was met with increasing violence from the crime syndicate that ran the town, but Patterson persisted and in June 1954 won the Democratic nomination. The following day he was shot dead. The Governor was at last forced to take action. Martial law was declared and the National Guard was sent in. Patterson's son John was elected attorney general in his place, and some reforms followed.

The Phenix City Story begins and ends with footage of "real life" interviews with residents of the town, and this adds to the "raw documentary atmosphere" established by the sleazy natural locations and endlessly gray skies. The violence is horrific: a black child's corpse is thrown onto a lawn with a note threatening further killings; men and women are beaten at the polls and stagger away dripping blood; Patterson (John McIntire) is shot in the mouth. As J. Shadoian writes in *Dreams and Dead Ends*, the viewer is forced to share the film's paranoia—the sense that "we are in the grip of a dictatorship of evil"; "the movie makes you want to kill."

The film's authenticity of detail, accent, and atmosphere seemed to Jonathan Rosenbaum to be matched in the cinema only by Elia Kazan's Deep South movies. Mark Bergman drew attention to the vestigial *film noir* elements—"low angles, lights hanging low from ceilinged sets, sleek cars on wet streets, and the all-pervasive paranoia," which is exacerbated by the bleak implication that Tanner (Edward Andrews), the icily affable boss of the town's vice industry, is only a front for anonymous and far more powerful figures untouched by the investigations instituted by John Patterson (Richard Kiley). Shadoian wrote that "incidents are tied together like a closely-wound spring and dramatic pressure is gradually increased" in a film that is "a triumph of craftsmanship, of artistry, and economy of means."

Shadoian calls Karlson "the '50s' sternest moralist. . . . A plain, seemingly graceless stylist, his rather unpalatable movies, full of rabid, sloggingly orchestrated physical pain and psychic damage, picture crime as a monstrous, miasmal evil, divesting it of any glamour it ever had. He is the key figure of '50s violence, specializing in foreground placement of smashed, bloody faces. . . . His heroes stagger dully about as life's punching bags, until they can't take it anymore and go haywire. . . . For Karlson, criminals are the lowest scum on earth, and crime must be thoroughly destroyed. His hatred runs deep, and his cheap, sleazy, action movies are dead-serious assaults upon the audience's automatic receptivity to screen 'entertainment.'"

The criminals in *99 River Street* are a small band of corrupt individuals; in *The Phenix City Story* they have formed themselves into a syndicate powerful enough to control an entire town; and in *The Brothers Rico* (1957), as Shadoian points out, "all is lost. The hero acts, but clearly far too late. The infection has spread to national proportions." In this film, adapted from a story by Georges Simenon, Richard Conte plays Eddie Rico, a former Syndicate accountant who has gone straight and established a highly successful laundry business in Florida. When his two brothers tell him that their lives are in jeopardy from the gang run by their own uncle (Larry Gates), he dismisses their fears as groundless. It takes

their deaths to convince Eddie of the true monstrousness of the Syndicate and to turn him into an instrument of revenge. This is a cooler and more restrained film than Karlson's earlier crime movies, and there is, as Shadoian says, "very little violence because crime isn't like that anymore." Only moderately well received on release, it has come to be recognized as a model of the genre and is regarded by a few critics as superior even to *The Phenix City Story*.

Karlson's last film for Columbia was a Western, *Gunman's Walk* (1958). Like his earlier *They Rode West*, it was scripted by John Ford's scenarist, Frank S. Nugent, and photographed by Charles Lawton, who had worked with Ford, Budd Boetticher, and Delmer Daves. *Gunman's Walk* stars Van Heflin as Lee Hackett, a pioneer rancher who encourages his two sons to live as wildly as he had himself in his roisterous youth. One of them (James Darren), recognizing that times have changed, hangs up his guns and settles down with the part-Indian woman he loves; the other (Tab Hunter), seeking to outdo his father as a sharpshooting hell-raiser, winds up dead.

"It is the impact of some of the visuals with their graphic treatment of violence that lingers in the mind," wrote Allen Eyles: "the brutal murder of the unarmed deputy (Mickey Shaughnessy), the firm bracketing across the 'scope screen of the final confrontation between father and son, and the long shadows of the posse falling over Lee as he kneels by his son's body." Campbell Dixon wrote approvingly of the "maturity" of the film's handling of its Indian characters, who are presented more sympathetically than most of the whites.

Karlson had a major box-office hit (but a critical failure) with his next movie, *Hell to Eternity* (1960), based on the true story of Guy Gabaldon, an undersized Marine (played by six foot–two Jeffrey Hunter) who had been raised in Los Angeles by a Japanese-American family. During the bloody invasion of Saipan, Gabaldon went behind enemy lines and used his fluency in Japanese and his understanding of national mores to persuade one thousand men (or two thousand, according to the film) to surrender to him rather than fight to the death. Most reviewers found the film's heroics improbable and the obligatory sex scenes distasteful.

Having apparently peaked in the mid-1950s, Karlson's career declined during the 1960s, with relatively anonymous films like *Key Witness* (1960) and *The Young Doctors* (1961). His reputation picked up again with *The Scarface Mob* (1962), set in the Chicago of his youth. It is a taut, exciting, documentary-style account of the struggle between a dedicated Treasury Department agent, Elliot Ness (Robert Stack), and Al Capone (Neville Brand), ending with the destruction of Capone's booze empire and his jailing on tax evasion charges. The movie was assembled from two much-praised and honored programs Karlson had directed in 1959 for television (a medium that had little appeal for him), and became the pilot for the long-running television series *The Untouchables*.

After *Kid Galahad* (1962), a remake of the Michael Curtiz boxing drama that gave Elvis Presley one of his better roles, came the "anonymous" *Rampage* (1963), a jungle-jealousy concoction; then two contributions to the Matt Helm series, starring Dean Martin as the laid-back secret agent who outdoes James Bond both as a womanizer and a defender of the Free World against fiendish villains. Even critics who found the series disagreeable agreed that *The Silencers* (1966) and *The Wrecking Crew* (1968) were its most stylish and intelligent manifestations. There was also some critical interest in *A Time for Killing* (1967), a violent Civil War Western with Glenn Ford as a Union officer hunting down escaped Confederate prisoners, but none in either *Hornet's Nest* (1970) or *Ben* (1972).

Then came *Walking Tall* (1973), a film that has a good deal in common with *The Phenix City Story*. In Mort Briskin's script, based very loosely on the true story of Sheriff Buford Pusser, the hero (played by Joe Don Baker) is an itinerant wrestler who in 1957 returns with his wife and child to his home town in McNairy County, Tennessee. He finds that it has become a new "Sin City." When a friend is cheated in a dice game, Pusser complains and is beaten and slashed half to death.

Recovering, and finding the incumbent sheriff unwilling to take any action on his behalf, Pusser cuts himself a hickory club, returns to the casino, and breaks the arms of the crooked gamblers. He is charged wih armed robbery but is acquitted, acclaimed by the terrorized townpeople, and elected sheriff. With fists, club, and gun, Pusser proceeds to clean up the town, though at terrible cost to himself. His wife (Elizabeth Hartman) is murdered and he has his jaw shot away. But he rises, swathed in bandages, from his hospital bed, to lead the final assault on the forces of evil.

By and large, the establishment critics were appalled by this contribution to the vigilante genre that had begun with films like Don Siegel's *Dirty Harry* (1971)—movies in which the hero, despairing of legal process in a corrupt society, adopts the criminals' own methods in his fight against crime. Jay Cocks, for example, called *Walking Tall* "as smugly and viciously self-righteous as its hero. By the film's end, when Pusser and the aroused citizens storm the gangster stronghold, the film has ceased to apologize for lawless reprisals and turned to openly supporting them." Derek Malcolm, comparing it with *The Phenix City Story*, found it less sharply observed—"just more right-wing."

Pauline Kael's response was more ambivalent. Acknowledging the picture's "crummy cinematography," its "cheapie melodrama" and "tacky" script, its shameless whitewashing of Pusser and his methods, she nevertheless took this "shrewd, humble film" seriously as a return "to the moral landscape of the Western" and as "a volcano of a movie . . . in full eruption." And the general public adored the film. It grossed around $35 million before it even reached New York, and Kael said that "in parts of the South it is a ritual that at the end audiences stand in homage and cheer"; in New York, audiences shouted "their assent to each act of vengeance that the towering hero takes upon his enemies." There have been two sequels and a Buford Pusser television series. Joe Don Baker also starred in Karlson's last film, *Framed* (1974), again going outside the law to wreak terrible vengeance on his enemies—this time establishment figures who had framed him in a coverup of their own illegalities.

Karlson reportedly benefited from a healthy financial stake in *Walking Tall*, the greatest box-office success of his career. He is said to have had "a ferocious love and enthusiasm for his work and for the motion picture industry itself." Karlson was married to Dixie Pantages, a member of a well-known theatrical family, and had two daughters. A nine-handicap golfer, he lived in the Cheviot Hills section of Los Angeles.

FILMS: A Wave, a Wac, and a Marine, 1944; There Goes Kelly, 1945; G.I. Honeymoon, 1945; The Shanghai Cobra, 1945; Live Wires, 1946; Swing Parade of 1946, 1946; Dark Alibi, 1946; The Missing Lady, 1946; Behind the Mask, 1946; Bowery Bombshell, 1946; Wife Wanted (U.K., Shadow of Blackmail), 1946; Black Gold, 1947; Kilroy Was Here, 1947; Louisiana, 1947; Rocky, 1948; Adventures in Silverado (U.K., Above All Laws), 1948; Thunderhoof (U.K., Fury), 1948; Ladies of the Chorus, 1949; The Big Cat, 1949; Down Memory Lane, 1949; The Iroquois Trail (U.K., The Tomahawk Trail), 1950; Mask of the Avenger, 1951; The Texas Rangers, 1951; Lorna Doone, 1951; Scandal Sheet (U.K., the Dark Page), 1952; The Brigand, 1952; Kansas City Confidential, 1952; 99 River Street, 1953; They Rode West, 1954; Tight Spot, 1955; Hell's Island, 1955; Five Against the House, 1955; The Phenix City Story, 1955; The Brothers Rico, 1957; Gunman's Walk, 1958; Hell to Eternity, 1960; Key Witness, 1960; The

Secret Ways, 1961 (completed by Richard Widmark); The Young Doctors, 1961; The Scarface Mob, 1962; Kid Galahad, 1962; Rampage, 1963; The Silencers, 1966; A Time for Killing (U.K., The Long Ride Home), 1967; The Wrecking Crew, 1968; Hornet's Nest, 1970; Ben, 1972; Walking Tall, 1973; Framed, 1974.

ABOUT: Garfield, B. Western Films, 1982; McCarthy, T. and Flynn, C. (eds.) Kings of the Bs, 1975; Sarris, A. The American Cinema, 1968; Shadoian, J. Dreams and Dead Ends, 1977. *Periodicals*—Commentary November 1957; Film Ideal October 15, 1962; Monthly Film Bulletin (Britain) September 1973, January 1982.

HELMUT KÄUTNER

*KÄUTNER, HELMUT (March 25, 1908–April 20, 1980), German film and theatre director, actor, scenarist, and dramatist, was born in Düsseldorf. He studied philosophy, art history, and drama at the University of Munich; advertising, graphics, and interior decoration at the Cologne Academy of Arts. Käutner entered the theatre in 1931 as an actor and writer with the left-wing Munich student cabaret Die vier Nachrichter and secured his first small screen role a year later. He went on to work as an actor and director in theatres in Leipzig, Munich, and Berlin and, increasingly, as a film scenarist.

Käutner directed his first movie in 1939. *Kitty und die Weltkonferenz* (*Kitty and the World Conference*) is a sophisticated comedy of such wit and polish that it has earned comparisons with Lubitsch. However, its completion coincided with the outbreak of World War II, and its sympathetic and admiring portrait of a British diplomat angered Goebbels, who banned it. Käutner made nine films under the Nazis. They are uneven in quality, but share a scrupulous avoidance of the propaganda content that Goebbels sought to impose on directors. Although the German film industry was completely nationalized during the war and Goebbels controlled the department responsible for the licensing of films, it was possible to bypass the Minister's influence—for example by submitting to the licensing department a specially doctored version of each picture.

No one deviated more consistently and successfully from the official formula than Käutner, often by choosing non-contemporary subjects like that of *Kleider machen Leute* (*Clothes Make the Man,* 1940). Adapted from a novella by Gottfried Keller, and set in a small German town in the nineteenth century, it tells the story of a daydreaming tailor's apprentice who is transformed by a borrowed dress coat and the skills of an old con artist into a reasonable imitation of a visiting Russian aristocrat. As critics have pointed out,

the false Count is lionized and sought after with a veneration very much like that extended by twentieth-century Germans to petty officials transformed by their uniforms into Nazi supermen. There was much praise for the subtlety and sensitivity of Käutner's adaptation, for the performance in the lead of Heinz Rühmann, and for the music of Bernhard Eichhorn, a newcomer who went on to score many of Käutner's movies.

Romanze in Moll (*Romance in a Minor Key,* 1943) is also set in the nineteenth century, but even further away from contemporary German realities, in Paris. It is based on a Maupassant story about a bored wife who has an affair with a famous composer, is jilted, and kills herself. Käutner himself appears in the film as a resigned and cynical poet—a character, it has been suggested, not far from his own. This is one of Käutner's finest films, in which "composition, framing, camera movement, editing, [and] sound, remain, from start to finish, crystal clear," and in which "his direction of actors is magisterial."

Goebbels was not impressed, however, finding this escapist story, coming at a time when Germany was gathering itself for a great push to victory, nothing short of defeatist. The fact that it enjoyed far greater popular success than contemporary propagandist features incensed him even more. He summoned Käutner and told him that he was to direct a major epic about the German navy at war, but the director managed to convince him that his experience did not equip him for "this great task" and instead filmed a story of his own choice.

This was *Grosse Freiheit Nr 7* (*Port of Free-*

°kowt´ner

dom/La Paloma, 1944)—the title refers to a well-known street in Hamburg's red-light district. It is a tale about a seaman—very attractively played by Hans Albers—who falls in love, gets a nightclub job as a singer, but loses his girl, and goes sadder and wiser back to sea. A movie of considerable wit and great warmth, it was banned by Goebbels on moral and other grounds but was sold abroad very profitably and was a major hit in Germany after the war.

The last film Käutner made under the Nazis was Unter den Brücken (Under the Bridges, 1945), shot at great risk in the Berlin area in 1944, when the city was under heavy bombardment. It stars Hannelore Schroth, Carl Raddatz, and Gustav Knuth in a triangle story set among barge workers on the River Havel. A notable departure from its predecessors, it combines a harsh realism with a lyricism strongly reminiscent of the work of Marcel Carné and Jacques Prévert, rich in melancholy halftones and misty river scenes. The picture was thought to have been lost at the end of the war, but several prints were eventually discovered abroad and it was released to great acclaim. Some consider it Käutner's best film.

According to Erwin Leiser in Nazi Cinema, Käutner's wartime movies "upheld the individual's right to a life unfettered by the demands of discipline, emphasizing an independence in the private domain which invalidates the Führer's authoritarian claims on the individual." They were, Leiser writes, "celebrated examples of the kind of 'interior emigration' which even during the war could appear in German films." The only significant exception comes in Auf Wiedersehen, Franziska (1941), in which the heroine tries throughout the film to get her husband, a footloose journalist, to abandon his wanderings and settle down at home, only to send him off again in the last scene to fight for the Fatherland. Käutner explained after the war that this scene was added on the direct orders of the Ministry of Propaganda, and showed how he had attempted to signal this with an abrupt and otherwise inexplicable change of lenses.

After the war, the German cinema recovered more slowly in the west than in the eastern zone, where most of the production facilities were centered and where the occupying Russians established the state film company DEFA. The other occupying powers chose to issue licenses to individual commercial film units. One of the first companies to be licensed in the British zone was one established in Hamburg by Käutner, whose better work, according to Roger Manvell and Heinrich Fraenkel in The German Cinema, "stands out almost alone in the overwhelming tide of bad films made during this period."

Käutner's first postwar movie was In Jenen Tagen (In Former Days, 1947). Set during the Nazi era, it traces in seven episodes the fortunes of the various owners of an old automobile, seeking to show that even in those days there were always a few who tried to behave decently and humanely. Enno Patalas wrote that it "showed the same talent for psychological complexity as the decidedly unpolitical films he made during the Nazi period," and Roger Manvell called it "the first good film to be made under British sponsorship."

After collaborating on the script of Rudolph Jugert's Film ohne Titel (1947), Käutner directed Der Apfel ist ab (The Original Sin, 1948), based on one of the cabaret sketches he had written ten years earlier for Die vier Nachrichter. It is a modern version of Genesis, Expressionist in style, with Adam torn between profane love (Lilith) and the domestic kind (Eve)—a dilemma happily resolved when his two women are fused into one. The movie's sardonic humor, with its flashbacks to a hellishly boring vision of Paradise, caused it to be boycotted by some Catholics.

A string of unexceptional films followed, and then Die letzte Brücke (The Last Bridge, 1954). This war movie stars Maria Schell as a German woman doctor who falls into the hands of Yugoslav partisans, is gradually won over to their cause, and dies delivering medical supplies to them under fire. Manvell and Fraenkel commented that "Käutner directed the film with his usual technical efficiency, and Maria Schell managed to break through the comparative conventionalism of the script (on which Käutner had worked himself) and bring humanity to the part. The film, shot in Yugoslavia, was a very well-meant and, within its limitations, a genuine contribution to understanding of what the Nazi invasion of Yugoslavia signified to its people." Another critic called it "warm-hearted, high-minded and utterly convinced," and it won the main prize at Cannes, as well as the International Jury Prize at Berlin and the David O. Selznick prize.

No less than four Käutner films were released in 1955, the most notable of them being Der Teufels General (The Devil's General), based on a play by Carl Zuckmayer. Curt Jürgens gives a notable performance as General Harras, a German air ace (based on the famous aviator Ernst Udet) who, realizing that he has given his loyalty to an evil cause, tries to make amends and is hounded by the Gestapo to suicide. This attempt to remind postwar audiences that there had been "good" Germans even under Hitler was not welcomed by some critics, but the film was extremely successful. There was also a mixed reception for *Himmel ohne Sterne* (*Sky Without Stars,* 1955), in which a young East German worker (Eva Kotthaus) and a West German border guard (Horst Buchholz) make a brief "separate peace" before the Cold War claims their lives. Described by one reviewer as "a masterpiece of atmosphere and human characterisation," it was received with vociferous hostility in East Germany.

Ein Mädchen aus Flandern (1955), an adaptation of a Zuckmayer novella, was followed by an adaptation of a Zuckmayer play, *Der Hauptmann von Köpenick* (*The Captain From Köpenick,* 1956), previously filmed in 1932 by Richard Oswald. This famous satire on Prussian militarism, based on a true story, centers on an ex-convict who is desperate for papers that will give him the right to ply his newly acquired trade as a cobbler. When orthodox methods fail, he buys an officer's uniform from a pawnshop and proceeds to exploit the Prussian weakness for such symbols of authority, taking over the Köpenick town hall, arresting the mayor, and confiscating the treasury. Heinz Rühmann gives a marvelous performance in a role strangely similar to the one he had assumed sixteen years earlier in Käutner's *Clothes Make the Man.*

After two agreeable romantic comedies, *Die Zürcher Verlobung* (*Engagement in Zurich,* 1956) and *Monpti* (1956), came yet another Zuckmayer adaptation, *Der Schinderhannes* (1958), starring Curt Jürgens and Maria Schell. Käutner then went off to Hollywood, where he made two minor romances for Universal: *The Restless Years* (1958), a small-town drama starring Teresa Wright, and *Stranger in My Arms* (1959), with June Allyson and Jeff Chandler. "My work in Hollywood was not very successful but certainly interesting," Käutner said afterwards. "I have good friends in America and I like the country. . . . The two films I made in Hollywood, well, they were what I call unfortunate hybrids. They were too European for Americans and too American for Europeans."

Returning to Germany, Käutner made *Der Rest is Schweigen* (*The Rest Is Silence,* 1959), a modern version of the Hamlet story starring Hardy Kruger and transferred to the home of a rich industrialist. It was received with some critical interest but *Die Gans von Sedan* (1959), intended as a satire on the futility of war, was described as "disastrous," and there was an even more wounding reception for *Schwarzer Kies* (*Black Gravel,* 1960). A study of the effects on a West German town of the establishment of a NATO airbase, it was attacked by a Jewish organization as anti-Semitic. Deeply hurt, Käutner explained that the use of expressions like "filthy

Jew" did not represent his own feelings but rather was intended as a warning about the growth of neo-Nazism. However, this film and *Der Traum von Lieschen Müller* (1961) earned a special prize from young critics at Oberhausen in 1961 as "the worst achievement of a well-known director." Käutner announced that he would make no more political films: "an objective discussion on political things is no longer possible. . . . We have to skip political themes."

Käutner made a few more unremarkable pictures, and during the last part of his working life concentrated mainly on the theatre, opera, and television. He was also increasingly in demand as an actor and in 1974 received a West German award as best actor of the year for his performance in the title role of Hans Jürgen Syberberg's *Karl May.* Käutner was married in 1934 to the actress Erica Balqué, who often served as script-girl on his films. He died in Tuscany in 1980 after a long illness. Georges Sadoul thought him "the best West German director" of his generation, "sensitive, intelligent, and humanistic, despite the uneven quality of his work." And Louis Marcorelles wrote that his work is "a message of purity and elegance; he is the last German romantic."

FILMS: Kitty und die Weltkonferenz (Kitty and the World Conference), 1939; Kleider machen Leute (Clothes Make the Man), 1940; Frau nach Mass, 1940; Auf Wiedersehen, Franziska, 1941; Wir machen Musik, 1942; Anuschka, 1942; Romanze in Moll (Romance in a Minor Key), 1943; Grosse Freiheit Nr 7 (Port of Freedom/La Paloma), 1944; Unter den Brücken (Under the Bridges), 1945; In Jenen Tagen (In Former Days/Seven Journeys), 1947; Der Apfel ist ab (The Original Sin/The Fallen Apple/The Apple Is Picked), 1948; Königskinder, 1949; Epilog (Epilogue), 1950; Weisse Schatten, 1951; Käpt'n Bay-Bay, 1952; Die letzte Brücke (The Last Bridge), 1954; Bildnis einer Unbekannten, 1954; Ludwig II, 1955; Des Teufels General (The Devil's General), 1955; Himmel ohne Sterne (Sky Without Stars), 1955; Ein Mädchen aus Flandern, 1955; Der Hauptmann von Köpenick (The Captain From Köpenick/The Captain of Köpenick), 1956; Die Zürcher Verlobung (Engagement in Zurich), 1956; Monpti, 1956; Der Schinderhannes, 1958; The Restless Years/The Wonderful Years, 1958; Stranger in My Arms, 1959; Der Rest is Schweigen (The Rest is Silence), 1959; Die Gans von Sedan, 1959; Das Glas Wasser (A Glass of Water), 1960; Schwarzer Kies (Black Gravel), 1960; Der Traum von Lieschen Müller, 1961; Die Rote (The Redhead), 1962; Das Haus in Montevideo, 1963; Lausbubengeschichten, 1964; Die Feuerzangenbowle, 1970.

ABOUT: Goethe Institute Eighteen Films by Helmut Käutner, 1980; International Who's Who, 1980–1981; Leiser, E. Nazi Cinema, 1974; Manvell, R. and Fraenkel, H. The German Cinema, 1971.

KEATON, "BUSTER" (JOSEPH FRANK)

(October 4, 1895–February 1, 1966), American actor, director, and scenarist, was born in Piqua (pronounced, and sometimes spelled, Pickway), Kansas, the son of Joseph Hallie Keaton and Myra Edith Cutler. His parents had met in 1894 as members of the Cutler-Bryant Medicine Show, managed by Myra's father. They eloped together and joined the Mohawk Indian Medicine Company, which had reached Piqua when their eldest child was born.

Accounts of Keaton's eventful and accident-strewn childhood have become legendary. Keaton himself almost certainly believed them and later drew on them for the plots of his films, though it should be said that his father, Joe Keaton, had a ready imagination and an innate knack for effective publicity. The name "Buster" is said to have originated when the six-month-old child tumbled down a whole flight of stairs and was picked up, laughing delightedly, by another member of the company, the then unknown Harry Houdini. "That's some buster your baby took," remarked Houdini, and the name stuck. On other reported occasions the child nearly suffocated in a trunk, lost part of a finger in a mangle, and was sucked into the air and wafted four blocks by a cyclone. Keaton first appeared on stage at the age of nine months, when he crawled into the middle of his father's blackface routine, much to the audience's amusement. Over the next two years he continued to make unscheduled appearances until his parents gave in; Buster, not yet three, officially joined the act, and The Two Keatons became The Three Keatons.

Even in infancy, Keaton was beginning to develop the two most distinctive elements in his humor: phenomenal acrobatic agility and the famous deadpan face. Both were learned from working with his father: "I just watched what he did, then did the same thing. I could take crazy falls without hurting myself simply because I had learnt the trick so early in life that bodily control became pure instinct with me." And both father and son soon realized that audiences were convulsed by the child's immovably solemn reaction to all events. "If something tickled me and I started to grin the old man would hiss, 'Face, face!' That meant freeze the puss. The longer I held it, why, if we got a laugh the blank pan or the puzzled puss would double it."

Initially, Keaton's main role was to serve as butt for most of the violence in Joe's knockabout act: used to sweep the stage (as The Human Mop), picked up by a handle sewn to his clothes and slung bodily into the wings: "I'd just simply get in my father's way all the time and get kicked all over the stage." (Myra Keaton's part

BUSTER KEATON

was to take soubrette roles, play alto saxophone, and add a touch of class to the proceedings.) But as his own prodigious comic and athletic gifts developed, Keaton came to be seen as the main attraction: by the time he was six, the act was being billed as "BUSTER, assisted by Joe and Myra Keaton." In 1899 the family made the break from small-time provincial medicine shows to the glittering vaudeville circuit, and for the next eighteen years they played the halls in New York and all over the country, usually billed well up the program. In 1909 they made a trip to London, but it was a brief visit and not very successful.

The act broke up in early 1917. Joe Keaton was drinking ever more heavily and becoming dangerously violent towards Buster, both on and off the stage. By now a considerable stage star in his own right, Keaton had no difficulty landing a booking from the Shuberts for a show at the Winter Garden in New York, at $250 a week. Shortly before rehearsals were due to start, a chance meeting with an old friend led him to visit Joseph Schenck's film studios on 48th Street. Schenck, one of the leading independent producers, had just engaged Roscoe "Fatty" Arbuckle to make a series of comedy two-reelers, and when Keaton arrived the first of them, *The Butcher Boy* (1917), was in front of the camera. Arbuckle, who knew Keaton from vaudeville days, promptly invited him to take a role in the next scene. The following morning Keaton broke his Shubert contract and joined Arbuckle's team, without even asking what his salary woud be—as it turned out, it was $40 a week.

Throughout his life Keaton loved mechanical

devices and gadgets, and it was the technical no less than the creative aspects of filmmaking that had captivated him. "One of the first things I did was to tear a motion picture camera practically to pieces and . . . [find out about] the lenses and the splicing of films and how to get it on the projector. . . . This fascinated me." He seems to have grasped almost instantaneously what could, uniquely, be done with this enthralling new medium; he realized that, as Walter Kerr put it, "he had a mirror of the universe that altered the universe in certain subtle but important ways, which meant that between the record and the fact there was an exhilarating no-man's-land in which extraordinary but not necessarily untrue events could take place."

Keaton appears in *The Butcher Boy* in a long, intricate routine involving a canful of molasses; shot in a long single take, it was by all accounts perfect on the first run, with no retakes needed. Although he had never previously been before a film camera (Joe Keaton had despised the movies, and kept the act well away from them), Keaton's individual style of performance is evident from this very first moment of his cinematic career. "The scene is a village store," wrote Penelope Gilliatt. "Everyone else moves around a lot, to put it mildly. When Keaton enters, the unmistakable calm asserts itself." David Robinson made a similar comment: "He introduces a style in direct contrast to his fellow performers—the style which he was to develop and refine. While their movements are extravagant and overemphatic, excessive, he is quiet, controlled, unhurried, economical, accurate. His solitary calm already rivets attention."

Over the next three years Keaton made some fifteen two-reelers with Arbuckle's Comique Film Corporation, avidly exploring the possibilities of the new medium. The environment was ideal: everybody in the team was free to suggest gags, help with the editing, or do whatever was needed. Scripts were unknown. A rudimentary plot line was chosen and all the action was improvised around it, just as in the Keaton's vaudeville act. They had no outside interference to contend with, since Joe Schenck, wisely acknowledging that he knew nothing about comedy, left Arbuckle and his company to get on with the job as they thought best. He was justified by the results: their comedies were hugely popular, often more so than the feature films that nominally constituted the "main attraction."

In October 1917, having made six films, Arbuckle's company moved to California, where conditions were better for movie-making, and set up in new studios at Long Beach. Keaton made five more films there before being drafted

into the army in June 1918. He was sent to France but saw no combat: "By the time I hit the front, the Germans were in retreat. . . . I was tickled to death at that." Discharged in March 1919, he returned to California and made three or four final films with Comique. Arbuckle, as always, was listed as director with Keaton as uncredited assistant director, but in the later shorts a trend away from the earlier frenetic mugging towards a more controlled style of playing very probably derives from Keaton's influence. One of the last of the series, *Back Stage* (1919), looks very similar in style and execution to Keaton's earliest independent two-reelers.

All the Comique shorts had been released through Paramount, Adolph Zukor's studio. Schenck now arranged that Arbuckle should move to Paramount to make full-length features, while he set up for Keaton a new company to make shorts, releasing initially through Metro. The former Chaplin studios in Hollywood were bought and renamed the Keaton Studios, and Schenck also set up a separate deal with Metro for Keaton to star in a comedy feature. This was *The Saphead* (1920), directed by Herbert Blaché and adapted from a stage play that had starred Douglas Fairbanks. The film marks the first appearance of the rich, spoiled ninny character that Keaton was to refine in *The Navigator* and *Battling Butler,* but otherwise proved a pleasantly unremarkable light comedy, distinguished only by some spectacular acrobatics in the final Stock Exchange sequence. Before starting work on *The Saphead,* Keaton had already completed the first of his two-reelers, *The High Sign,* but, dissatisfied with it, withheld it from release.

As he had done with Arbuckle, Schenck took over all the business side of the operation and gave Keaton complete artistic freedom to make his comedies any way he wanted, paying him $1,000 a week plus twenty-five percent of the profits. Since Keaton had little interest in money and none whatsoever in business, this suited him perfectly. He apparently never even asked Schenck for a written contract.

In some of the early Arbuckle shorts, such as *Coney Island* (1917), Keaton had allowed himself to smile or even laugh; but from now on, in his own films, he never deviated from the grave deadpan that became his most famous attribute. However, to call Keaton's face (as James Agee did) "rigid" or "untroubled" is misleading: it was in fact far more expressive in its stoical restraint than the most frenzied grimaces of lesser comedians. As David Robinson noted, Keaton "is the only silent comedian with whom you are never for a moment in doubt as to what his thoughts are." "He could tell his story," his colleague

Clyde Bruckman recalled, "by lifting an eyebrow. He could tell it by *not* lifting an eyebrow." His face was also, as many writers have observed, exceptionally beautiful; Penelope Gilliatt referred to "the beautiful eyes, the nose running straight down from the forehead, the raised, speculative eyebrows, the profile that seems simplified into a line as classical as the line of a Picasso figure drawing."

From 1920 to 1923 Keaton directed and starred in nineteen comedy shorts, all of them—except the three-reel *Day Dreams* (1922)—two-reelers, perfecting and enriching his craft. The Keaton style, the recurrent Keatonian themes and situations, can all be seen developing in these films, later to be reformulated in the full-length features. Several of the shorts, indeed, can stand as fully achieved masterpieces in their own right. *One Week* (1920), the first of them to be released, "set the style for all the future Keatons," wrote Kevin Brownlow; "the opening gag sequence . . . the slow build-up . . . the frenetic climax . . . and then that climax outmatched by the final sequence." A build-it-yourself house, assembled according to maliciously altered instructions, slowly and inexorably disintegrates before Keaton's somber gaze. The house as intricate machine, either ingenious or infernal, frequently recurs in these shorts, turning up in *The Scarecrow* (1920), *The Haunted House* (1921), and *The Electric House* (1922). On one occasion the disaster was real: while filming the first version of *The Electric House* in 1921, Keaton caught his foot in an escalator and broke his ankle. The unsatisfactory *The High Sign* was released to fill the gap, and Keaton remade *The Electric House* a year later.

Seveal of Keaton's shorts, *One Week* among them, eschew the conventional happy ending, substituting instead the fatalism implicit in his stoical expression. *The Boat* (1921), a brilliantly structured chain of catastrophes, ends bleakly enough with an entire Keaton family shipwrecked and benighted. *Cops* (1922) finishes with an even blacker gag: Buster, with the whole city police force out for his blood, is spurned by his girl. Turning, he reenters the police station from which he has just escaped. We cut to a tombstone, topped by the unmistakable flattened porkpie hat. "There was in his comedy," James Agee remarked, "a freezing whisper not of pathos but of melancholia."

The near-surrealist quality of Keaton's visual imagination pervades *The Playhouse* (1921), made as a more "sedentary" subject while his ankle healed. In the opening sequence, by means of a multiple exposure technique that has rarely been equaled, let alone surpassed, Keaton plays every part in a theatre: the whole orchestra, the actors, all nine blackface minstrels, both halves of a dance act, and every single member of the audience, young and old, male and female. On principle, Keaton would never fake a stunt, but he was happy to exploit all the special effects that the movie camera could offer.

He was now building up the team of collaborators who would work with him (and play countless games of baseball, his second passion) on most of his silent features. Clyde Bruckman, Jean Havez, and Joe Mitchell were his main gag-writers, along with Eddie Cline, who received codirection credit on most of the shorts. The special effects technician was Fred Gabourie, and Elgin Lessley—described by Keaton as "a human metronome" in that age of hand-cranked, variable-speed cameras—the photographer. Among his regular actors were Joe Roberts, who played heavies, and Joe Keaton, grudgingly reconciled to being in movies so long as his son was directing.

In 1921 Keaton married Natalie Talmadge, whom he had met when they were both working for Arbuckle's company. Natalie was the second (and least famous) of the three Talmadge sisters, and sister-in-law to Joe Schenck, who had married Norma Talmadge in 1917. Keaton rapidly discovered that he had married the whole Talmadge clan: the grandiose mansion into which the couple moved was soon taken over by Norma, Constance, and their mother Peg, a formidable matriarch with great ambitions for her daughters. The Keatons had two sons: James, born 1922, and Robert, born 1924. Buster had planned, following long-established family tradition, to name his first-born Joseph but was overruled by unanimous Talmadge opinion.

In the summer of 1923, at Schenck's suggestion, Keaton moved into the production of full-length features. *The Three Ages* (1923) was clearly a hedged bet: three two-reelers skillfully intertwined, rather than an integrally constructed six-reeler. Parodying Griffith's *Intolerance,* it showed the vicissitudes of love through the ages—in the Stone Age, in Ancient Rome, and in modern times. In each age the Young Man, played by Keaton, attempts to win the Girl (Margaret Leahy) away from the Rival (Wallace Beery). There are some delightful gags, notably in the Roman episodes (Keaton, thrown to an affable lion, manicures its paws for it), but essentially the film marks no advance over the shorts.

Barely four months later, Keaton produced his first full-length masterpiece. *Our Hospitality* (1923) deploys impeccable dramatic logic, along with superb gags and some of Keaton's most breathtaking athletic feats. It is also beautiful to look at and filmed with a tangible sense of period and location. Keaton plays Willie McKay, orphaned survivor of a Southern blood feud. Returning to reclaim his ancestral estate (which turns out to be a derelict shack), he meets and falls in love with the daughter of his mortal enemies, the Canfields. Much of the humor stems from the rigid code of "Southern hospitality": the Canfields, itching to kill McKay, cannot lay a finger on him while he remains a guest in their house. At the film's climax Keaton performs one of his most spectacular geometric stunts (which regularly draws ecstatic applause from audiences), when he swings across the face of a waterfall to rescue his beloved as her canoe plunges into the depths.

Keaton's concern for historical detail is displayed in the delectable sequence of Willie's train journey to the South. Carefully setting the film in 1831, two years after trains were first introduced to the United States, he constructed a replica of Stevenson's Rocket, tagged on a string of stagecoaches with flanged wheels, and sent the whole endearingly ramshackle contraption chugging through the countryside to encounter derailments, collisions, and recalcitrant donkeys ("Onward sped the iron monster," comments a title). *Our Hospitality* was something of a Keaton family affair: Joe played the train driver, Natalie was the heroine, and the infant James Keaton represented Willie as a baby in the film's surprisingly serious, melodramatic prologue.

Our Hospitality clearly demonstrates, as much by its omissions as by its inclusions, how Keaton's style of comedy diverged from the conventions of the period. There is no speeded-up action, which he felt spoiled the timing of the gags, and none of the wild mugging and gesticulation that too often passed for comic acting at the time. Studio sets are avoided in favor of natural locations. Titles are kept to a minimum and close-ups are rare; Keaton preferred long shots whenever possible and insisted on them for stunts, to prove beyond doubt to the audience that nothing was being faked. Above all, the gags grow naturally and logically out of the action and are consistent with the characters that they involve, in accordance with Keaton's underlying principle that comedy, however hilarious, must be believable. "The thing is not to be ridiculous," he often remarked.

Daniel Moews has pointed out that almost all the Keaton features follow the same basic pattern, which could be summed up as adolescent wish-fulfillment. In the first half of the film the hero, who is presented as young, shy, and incapable, is confronted with some task or skill to be mastered, generally in order to gain the approval of the heroine. He attempts it, makes an utter fool of himself, and is ridiculed and despised for his incompetence. Disheartened, he sleeps—and wakes miraculously transformed. He is now bold, determined, and resourceful; with effortless proficiency he accomplishes all the feats that he previously bungled, gains universal admiration, and wins the heart of the girl. Furthermore, the skill to be mastered is usually one to which male adolescents traditionally aspire: to be a cowboy, detective, boxer, soldier, or champion athlete. This summary is schematic and of course takes no account of the infinite variety of gags with which Keaton adorned his bare storyline, but it does indicate a recurrent underlying pattern.

In *Sherlock Junior* (1924), the wish-fulfillment element is for once clearly presented as such, being shown as the hero's dream. A cinema projectionist and would-be detective, Keaton is framed for theft by his rival for the heroine's affections. Having failed dismally to solve the crime, he falls asleep and dreams of being the Great Detective, suave and infallible. When he wakes, he finds the crime has indeed been solved—by the heroine.

Of all Keaton's films, *Sherlock Junior* most richly displays his sheer delight in the endless possibilities of film for playing games with appearances. "Keaton's imaginative brain," wrote Gerald Mast, "has discovered both the ways that the cinematic universe defies nature and the way nature would try to copy cinema if it could." Taking advantage of the dream context, Keaton for once allows himself to stray into the fantastic—as in the famous montage sequence in which his dream self, having walked into a movie, is abruptly switched from a garden to a busy street, to a cliff-edge, to a jungle full of lions, and so on—all without any apparent cuts in his own movements. "Every cameraman in the business went to see that picture more than once," Keaton told Kevin Brownlow, "trying to figure out how the hell we did some of that."

The film also includes a virtuoso stunt sequence in which Keaton, riding on the handlebars of an otherwise riderless motorcycle, hurtles in a headlong trajectory through, over, and across numerous obstacles, before cannoning feet-first through the window of a cabin and into the stomach of the villain who is holding the heroine prisoner. The editing and framing of this sequence are no less masterly than the stunting; as ever, Keaton did all his own stunts in the film, and in one fall managed to break his neck. Ignoring intermittent headaches, he continued working and only discovered the fracture ten years later.

Much of Keaton's comedy derives from discrepancies of scale: the tiny, indomitable figure juxtaposed with some huge force or object. For *The Navigator* (1924), he provided himself with the biggest prop he could lay hands on—an entire ocean liner. The hero, one of Keaton's gallery of rich nitwits, finds himself alone on the ocean with a girl as rich and spoiled as himself. Used to having everything done for them, they must now do everything for themselves—two people, in a ship built for hundreds. Their incompetence in the vast galley is a delight to watch—as are the ingenious devices which, after a few weeks, they have rigged up to overcome their problems. Here, as so often in his films, Keaton draws on his lifelong joy in creating appealingly crazy mechanical gadgetry. Many critics have rated *The Navigator* Keaton's finest film, barring only *The General*.

His credited codirector on *The Navigator* was Donald Crisp, later well-known as an actor. Most of Keaton's films carry the name of someone else as codirector or even as sole director; Keaton himself was largely indifferent to credits. But by all accounts he was very much the dominant creative force in all his silent movies, thinking up most of the gags, choosing the camera set-ups, and editing the final cut. "I was often ashamed to take the money, let alone the credit," Clyde Bruckman later confessed. "Keaton could have graduated into a top director—of any kind of picture."

The relative weakness of his next film, *Seven Chances* (1925), can be ascribed mainly to the original material, a creaky old play that Joe Schenck had bought and now pressed on Keaton as a suitable property. The plot, which Keaton called "the type of unbelievable farce I don't like," concerned a young man who must marry by seven o'clock that evening in order to inherit a fortune. However, Keaton went ahead and made a passable job of it, thanks chiefly to an inspired new ending involving a frenzied chase, five hundred women, and a fifteen-hundred rock avalanche. The film also allowed ample opportunity to display the inimitable Keaton run, described by James Agee as progressing "from accelerating walk to easy jog trot to brisk canter to headlong gallop to flogged-piston sprint . . . as distinct and as soberly in order as an automatic gearshift."

In comparing, as they inevitably do, Keaton with Chaplin, critics have frequently noted that the often lachrymose sentimentality that plays so large a part in Chaplin's films scarcely figures in Keaton's. We side with the hero, of course, and sympathize with him, but are rarely invited to weep over his misfortunes. The sole exception, where Keaton seems to be edging a step or two in the direction of Chaplinesque pathos, is *Go West* (1925). The difference in tone is signaled from the start by the name of the hero, Friendless; a penniless orphan, he rides the freights to an Arizona ranch where he finally achieves both love and success. His beloved, though, is not the rancher's daughter but an appealing young Jersey cow.

Daniel Moews characterized the film as "an intelligent comic exercise in the sentimental. . . . We as audience are required both to feel the film's sentimental appeal and to laugh at its essentially nonsensical nature." There are few belly laughs in *Go West*; the humor throughout is quiet and pleasing rather than uproarious, and the final "chase," with a thousand head of cattle thronging the streets of Los Angeles, is slow and lacking in structure (mainly, as Keaton explained, because speeding things up could have set off a stampede for real). This sequence, however—during which Keaton dons a red devil costume to induce the cattle to follow him—does provide what David Robinson called "one of the cinema's great surrealist images: the line of policemen hanging on to one another's coattails, the first one hanging on to the devil's tail—the whole cortège pursued by bewildered bulls."

Another Broadway play, though a rather better one than *Seven Chances*, furnished the basis for *Battling Butler* (1926). The hero, Alfred Butler, is the most utterly helpless of all Keaton's rich milksops, unable even to flick the ash off his cigarette; required to take any action, he simply instructs his valet (the splendid, diminutive Snitz Edwards, who also appeared in *Seven Chances* and *College*): "Arrange it." But then, in order to impress his girl's family, Butler is trapped into pretending to be his namesake, a champion boxer. He is forced to fight and, spurred on by love, ends up thrashing the champ. As always, there are hilarious sequences—Alfred's disastrous attempt at duck-shooting from a canoe, filmed in one long unbroken take, is especially fine—but overall the film suffers from uncertainty of tone, veering between farce and realism, and the convincing brutality of the final fight seems particularly out of key. David Robinson found it "the least attractive of Keaton's features." Nonetheless, it did well at the box office, outgrossing even *The Navigator*, Keaton's biggest commercial success to date.

In 1926 Joe Schenck became chairman of United Artists, to whom he now switched the release of Keaton's pictures, away from his brother Nicholas at MGM. This made little difference to Keaton, who still had the freedom to make films in his own way, improvised around plots scribbled on the back of a postcard. (The story, Clyde Bruckman explained, was "as important as a tune to a jazz band, and no more.") Keaton reposed complete financial trust in Schenck, who was now paying him $1,000 per week, plus $27,000 for each film, and twenty-five per cent of the profits; Keaton owned no shares in Buster Keaton Productions, and apparently never asked for any. Both commercially and in critical esteem, he now ranked a respectable third to Chaplin and Harold Lloyd—both of whom, however, had shrewdly ensured that they kept full financial as well as artistic control over their pictures.

All Keaton's films, wrote Raymond Durgnat, "have an ascetic, yet dashing, beauty. . . . Perhaps The General is the most beautiful, with its spare, grey photography, its eye for the the racy, lungeing lines of the great locomotives, with their prow-like cowcatchers, and with its beautifully sustained movement." Most critics have agreed that The General (1926) is Keaton's finest film, and not for its visual beauty alone. Structured in a classically satisfying symmetrical pattern, its narrative line runs clean and uncluttered from start to finish. Little is superfluous or gratuitous; all the gags—and they include some of his finest—are designed to further the dramatic action. And in The General itself—a train, not a person—he found his ideal prop.

The action is set in Georgia, at the outset of the Civil War. Keaton plays Johnnie Gray, an engine-driver who suffers a double rejection—by the Confederate army, who tell him he is more useful driving an engine, and by his girl, who believes he has failed to enlist out of cowardice. His train, and fortuitously the girl, are kidnapped by Northern spies; he pursues them, manages to regain both, along with the enemy's secret plans, brings about a Southern victory, and is commissioned into the army, a hero.

Asked, years later, why his depiction of the Civil War era looked so much more authentic than that shown in Gone With the Wind, Keaton replied: "They went to a novel; I went to the history books." "Every shot," wrote David Robinson, "has the authenticity and the unassumingly correct composition of a Matthew Brady Civil War photograph." At the film's climax, the Union locomotive pursuing Johnnie Gray comes to a bridge that he has set on fire and begins to cross. The bridge collapses, hurling the train into the river beneath. Uncompromising as ever, Keaton refused to use a model; with full dramatic impact, a real train crashes through a real bridge—and, just to prove it, the frame includes some men on horseback moving on the river

bank. This single take—retakes were, obviously, hardly practicable—is said to have cost $42,000, an unprecedented sum.

Surprisingly, The General was received with indifference by most critics on its release. Motion Picture Classic considered it "a mild Civil War comedy, not up to Keaton's best standard," and the Herald-Tribune condemned it as "long and tedious—the least funny thing Buster Keaton has ever done." Box-office receipts were disappointing, the more so since the film had been so costly to make.

Perhaps feeling that he should play safe, Keaton modeled his next film on a proven success. If Go West saw Keaton straying into Chaplin's territory, College (1927) comes closest to the work of Harold Lloyd, virtually taking over the plot of The Freshman (1925), one of Lloyd's biggest hits. Keaton plays a bookish student who must succeed at college athletics in order to win the girl he loves. Pictorially flat and thinly plotted, College is perhaps the least interesting of Keaton's silent features, as well as the first on which he took no directorial credit. Not, apparently, that this was the cause of the film's weakness: Keaton described the nominal director, James Horne, as "absolutely useless to me. . . . I don't know why we had him, because I practically did College." (The film also contains the only instance when Keaton is known to have used a double, to pole-vault through a narrow second-floor window.)

With Steamboat Bill Jr. (1928), Keaton returned to form. Again, he was not credited as director, but all the evidence suggests that he was in charge as usual. The hero, Willie Canfield (the name signals another "feuding" plot), is the foppish, incompetent son of a Mississippi steamboat skipper whose livelihood is threatened by a flashy new craft. Willie, of course, is in love with the rival owner's daughter. When a cyclone flattens the town and wrecks the newer boat, Willie makes good, saving his father's boat and rescuing his sweetheart and both fathers from drowning, along with a convenient parson.

"Although . . . [Keaton's films] use standard cinema techniques unimpeachably," wrote André Martin in Cahiers du Cinéma (August 1958), "they avail themselves of a liberty of sequence much closer to that of animated films which, with their uniquely graphic technique, have no figurative difficulty." Nowhere is Martin's comment more apt than in the phantasmagoric cyclone sequence of Steamboat Bill, in which stunting is elevated into an elegant, dreamlike ballet. (Raymond Durgnat referred to Keaton as "the Fred Astaire of slapstick.") With all the forces of nature ranged against him, Keaton spins, slides, tumbles, and bounds through the deserted town, as apparently solid buildings collapse and vanish magically around him. At one point an entire house front falls on him, but (in a gag borrowed and refined from *One Week*) he remains miraculously untouched, framed by a tiny open window. He leans into the wind, at a sixty-degree angle; leaps into it, as though trying to take off; and does finally achieve flight, clinging to a tree that soars above the ruins of the town.

Aside from the sheer beauty of its hallucinatory images, this sequence illustrates Keaton's exceptional—and seemingly instinctive—sense of cinematic framing and composition. "The perfection and beauty of Keaton's form in space," wrote Jean-Patrick Lebel, "comes not merely from the serene equilibrium inherent in his body, but above all from its positioning in cinematic space, a perfect, harmonious positioning, marvelously suggesting his body's potential for power and balance." Louis Giannetti also commented on the unaffected rightness of Keaton's framing: "No one used the frame more organically. Almost any random shot demonstrates an acute sensitivity to how much—or how little—visual information is necessary to maximize the shot's impact."

In 1928, Keaton made what he called "the worst mistake of my life." *Steamboat Bill* had not done well at the box office, and with the coming of sound, times were growing hard for independent producers. Joe Schenck persuaded Keaton to sign a contract with MGM; since Schenck's brother Nick was president of the company, it was "all in the family." Despite the urgent warnings of Chaplin and Lloyd and his own misgivings, Keaton went along with the deal. MGM, and Irving Thalberg in particular, seem to have had all the best intentions. Keaton was, after all, a major star and, despite one or two financial disappointments, a considerable box-office attraction. The terms of his contract were generous—$3,000 a week, making him one of the studio's highest-paid actors. But his improvisatory working methods were utterly beyond the comprehension of the studio bosses, who thought strictly in terms of approved, closely-budgeted scripts, packed with carefully devised gags supplied by the MGM gagwriters' department.

Twenty-two writers were assigned to produce the initial script for *The Cameraman* (1928), which came complete with camera instructions for the director, Edward Sedgwick. Keaton, rebelling, persuaded a reluctant Thalberg to let him junk the script and shoot the film his way. The result is well up to the standard of Keaton's best independent features and (in the opinion of David Robinson) "betrays nothing of the struggle and strain that went into its preparation. It is a lucid, beautifully formed dramatic comedy." The hero is a street photographer with ambitions to become a newsreel cameraman. After numerous mishaps, and with the help of his girl (who works for a newsreel company) and a trained monkey, he finally comes up with some dramatic footage of a tong war and achieves his ambition.

The Cameraman includes some of Keaton's funniest improvised sequences, as when he and a short-tempered fat man (Edward Brophy, the unit manager, who had never acted before) find themselves sharing one tiny changing cubicle at a swimming pool and become hopelessly entangled in each other's clothes. Several of his old production crew were still with him on the film, including Clyde Bruckman, Elgin Lessley, and Fred Gabourie, but after *The Cameraman,* the team was split up. "I was again assured," Keaton sadly recalled, "that every effort would be made to let me continue working with my team whenever possible. It turned out to be possible very seldom."

Spite Marriage (1929), Keaton's second film for MGM, was his last silent feature, and—by general agreement—the last authentic Keaton film. (Sedgwick was again credited as director.) It was lost for many years, but John Gillett, writing in *Sight and Sound* (Winter 1970–1971) soon after it resurfaced, felt that "it lacks the character and density of the best Keaton." The hero is a humble admirer of a famous actress who, to spite her real lover, suddenly agrees to marry her devotee. On their wedding night she gets totally drunk. The couple become involved with a boatload of bootleggers; Keaton heroically routs them all and wins the actress's love. *Spite Marriage* is far from a total failure: the plot blatantly lacks narrative cohesion, and many of the gags are clearly rehashed from earlier Keaton movies, but much of it is extremely funny, notably the inspired sequence in which Keaton gallantly attempts to transport his hopelessly inebriated bride on to the bed. (Years later, Keaton revived this routine for stage performance with his third wife, Eleanor, as his partner.) Many of the gags, though, have the feel of the production-line about them, lacking Keaton's distinctively personal touch; the MGM machine, despite his efforts, was taking over.

Even had Keaton been temperamentally equipped to fight the studio, he had other battles on his hands. His marriage to Natalie, which had long been severely strained, was nearing breakdown, and he was drinking at a dangerous rate.

Matters were exacerbated by the coming of sound, which panicked the studios into ludicrous errors of judgment. "Talking pictures," it was held, must talk—or sing—virtually nonstop, whatever the innate talents of the actors. From 1929 to 1933 Keaton appeared in eight sound movies for MGM, ranging from the mediocre to the abysmal. Various directors were credited—mainly Sedgwick—but never Keaton, and indeed little trace of his talent can be detected in any of them.

Natalie Keaton was divorced from Buster in August 1932, taking custody of the children. Drunk and depressed, Keaton took to staying away from the studio. He was fired by MGM early in 1933. As far as Hollywood was concerned, he was a back number. The rest of the decade was a dismal story of drink, illness, and failure. A nurse who was helping him dry out after a binge joined him in a disastrous second marriage that lasted only a couple of years. He starred in a poor film in France and a terrible one in England, and appeared in a whole series of two-reelers for a Poverty Row company, Educational Films. His last directing assignment was for three undistinguished single-reelers in 1938—made, ironically, for MGM, for whom he also worked intermittently as a gag-writer.

In 1940, when he was forty-five, Keaton was married for the third time. His bride, Eleanor Norris, was a twenty-one-year-old dancer; it was a happy marriage, and lasted until his death. Gradually, as he gained some control over his drinking, he began to secure cameo roles in feature films—most famously, as one of Gloria Swanson's bridge four in *Sunset Boulevard* (1950). But his great silent films were largely forgotten, and Keaton himself believed that they had all been destroyed. He was remembered in France, though: the Cirque Médrano in Paris invited him over in 1947, and he was received with affectionate enthusiasm. He returned there several times and also played on variety bills in London.

An article by James Agee in *Life* (September 5, 1949), "Comedy's Greatest Era," did much to revive interest in Keaton. Prints of his films were tracked down and began to be shown. Briefly and unforgettably, he appeared with Chaplin in *Limelight* (1952)—their first and only film together. There was plentiful television work and in 1957 a film, *The Buster Keaton Story*, with Donald O'Connor in the title role. It was embarrassingly feeble, but Keaton's fee gave him financial security for the rest of his life, and enabled him and Eleanor to buy a house in Woodland Hills, San Fernando.

By 1960 the Keaton revival was in full swing.

Almost all his films had been rediscovered and restored, and were being shown in retrospectives and festivals around the world. Rather to his bewilderment, Keaton found himself elevated from near-oblivion to a position of equality with—or even superiority to—Chaplin in the pantheon of film comedians, a critical estimation that still holds good. "Keaton," stated Andrew Sarris, "is now generally acknowledged as the superior director and inventor of visual forms. There are those who would go further and claim Keaton as pure cinema as opposed to Chaplin's essentially theatrical cinema." Louis Giannetti felt that "even if Keaton never appeared before a camera, he would still be regarded as a great director," adding that "he was also a first-rate editor. . . . The shots are never merely decorative: each contributes its unique visual information." Keaton himself always disclaimed any theoretical basis to his filmmaking, insisting that he was simply "trying to make people laugh." The precision and lucidity of his directing style, the unfailingly satisfying compositions, were seemingly arrived at through an inherent instinct for narrating the story and setting up the gags by the most practical and effective method available.

Similarly, Keaton always deprecated attempts to trace any underlying philosophical attitude in his work. Several writers, following Agee's hint, have detected a melancholy fatalism and even an existential estrangement in the vision of a small, vulnerable human figure dwarfed by a vast universe of massive, impersonal forces and potentially hostile Things. André Martin referred to "Keaton's natural, contagious, and probably unconscious wisdom which reduces the representation of a hostile and sorrowful world . . . to a whole universe of fundamental adversity, of pure necessity." However, Keaton, as David Robinson pointed out, "can never remain pathetic for long, for he is also self-reliant, indomitable, endlessly resourceful." Even more categorically, Daniel Moews insisted that "the Keaton films do not belong among the works of art possessing significant social themes . . . and the attempt . . . to force a social or philosophical commentary out of them, is to do violence to their real nature."

The climax of Keaton's return to fame came at the 1965 Venice Film Festival, where *Film*, a 22-minute short written for him by Samuel Beckett, was premiered. Later that day, at the evening gala, Keaton was given a standing ovation of unparalleled fervor. He was touched and delighted, but told Lotte Eisner afterwards, "Sure it's great—but it's all thirty years too late." He continued working to within three months of his death, although there were now far more offers than he could fulfill. In October 1965, just after his seventieth birthday, lung cancer was diagnosed, and late the following January he suffered a terminal seizure. He no longer knew anybody but, active to the last, wandered all over the house, upstairs and downstairs, until he died in the early hours of the next morning.

—*P.K.*

FILMS: *Shorts*—(with Eddie Cline) One Week, 1920; (with Eddie Cline) Convict 13, 1920; (with Eddie Cline) The Scarecrow, 1920; (with Eddie Cline) Neighbors, 1920; (with Eddie Cline) The Haunted House, 1921; (with Eddie Cline) The High Sign, 1921, (completed 1920); (with Eddie Cline) Hard Luck, 1921; (with Mal St. Clair) The Goat, 1921; (with Eddie Cline) The Playhouse, 1921; (with Eddie Cline) The Boat, 1921; (with Eddie Cline) The Paleface, 1921; (with Eddie Cline) Cops, 1922; (with Eddie Cline) My Wife's Relations, 1922; (with Mal St. Clair) The Blacksmith, 1922; (with Eddie Cline) The Frozen North, 1922; (with Eddie Cline) Day Dreams, 1922; (with Eddie Cline) The Electric House, 1922; (with Eddie Cline) The Balloonatic, 1923; The Love Nest, 1923; Life in Sometown USA, 1938; Hollywood Handicap, 1938; Streamlined Swing, 1938. *Full-length*—(with Eddie Cline) Three Ages, 1923; (with Jack Blystone) Our Hospitality, 1923; Sherlock Junior, 1924; (with Donald Crisp) The Navigator, 1924; Seven Chances, 1925; Go West, 1925; Battling Butler, 1926; (with Clyde Bruckman) The General, 1926; (uncredited) College, 1927; (uncredited) Steamboat Bill Jr., 1928; (uncredited) The Cameraman, 1928; (uncredited) Spite Marriage, 1929. *Published scripts*—Buster Keaton's The General, edited by R. J. Anobile (with 2,100 frame enlargements), 1975.

ABOUT: Agee, J. Agee on Film, 1958; Arlorio, P. (ed.) Il cinema di Buster Keaton, 1972; Blesh, R. Keaton, 1966; Brownlow, K. The Parade's Gone By, 1968; Coursodon, J.-P. Keaton, 1973 (in French); Coursodon, J.-P. Keaton & Cie: les burlesques américains du 'muet,' 1964; Dardis, T. Keaton, 1979; Denis, M. Buster Keaton, 1971 (in French); Durgnat, R. The Crazy Mirror, 1969; Giannetti, L. Masters of the American Cinema, 1981; Gilliatt, P. Unholy Fools, 1973; Gunther, W. and Tichy, W. (eds.) Buster Keaton: eine Dokumentation, 1971; Keaton, B. and Samuels, C. My Wonderful World of Slapstick, 1960; Kerr, W. The Silent Clowns, 1975; Lebel, J.-P. Buster Keaton, 1964 (in French; English edition 1967); McCaffrey, D. W. Four Great Comedians, 1968; Manchel, F. Yesterday's Clowns, 1973; Mast, G. The Comic Mind, 1973; Moews, D. Keaton, 1977; Oms, M. Buster Keaton, 1964 (in French); Robinson, D. Buster Keaton, 1969; Rubinstein, E. Filmguide to The General, 1973; Turconi, D. and Savio, F. (eds.) Buster Keaton, 1963 (in Italian); Wead, G. Buster Keaton and the Dynamics of Visual Wit, 1976; Wead, G. and Lekkis, G. The Film Career of Buster Keaton, 1977. *Periodicals*—Bianco e Nero September–October 1963; Cahiers du Cinéma August 1958; September 1960, April 1962, February 1966, February 1969; Chaplin 63 1966; Cine Cubano 2–7 1962; Cineforum June 1964, January 1966; Cinéma (France) September–October 1958, August–September 1960, September–October 1962, March 1966, October 1981; Cinema Nuovo September–October 1963; March–April 1966; Encounter December 1967; Film November–December 1958, 42 1965; Filmcritica October 1963, February 1966, February 1967; Film Quarterly Fall 1958, Summer 1966; Films and Filming September 1961; Films in Review March 1975; Image et Son April 1964, November 1972; Positif Summer 1966; Roughcut Summer 1976; Sight and Sound April–June 1953, Winter 1959–1960, Winter 1965–1966, Spring 1968; Téléciné October– November 1962.

KEIGHLEY, WILLIAM (JACKSON)

(August 4, 1889–June 24, 1984), American director, was born in Philadelphia, Pennsylvania, the only child of William Jackson Keighley and the former Mary Hausel. His father, who was of British birth, died when the boy was very young and his mother made a second marriage to Christian Lauer, a kindly man who was a member of the Philadelphia Fire Department. Keighley's mother and grandmother were both ardent theatregoers and took him regularly to the Forepaugh Theatre, where Philadelphia's leading stock company presented "all the great romances, comedies, and melodramas of the day." He had his own first heady taste of amateur acting when his sandlot football team put on a play to raise funds.

Keighley was seventeen then, and a student at the Northeast Manual Training School where, in the course of the same year, he was publicly reprimanded for shuffling his feet when he walked. A teacher told him that this slovenly habit guaranteed that he "would never amount to anything" and Keighley, "a rather sensitive kid," felt himself "outraged and humiliated." He quit school without consulting his parents and got himself a job as a messenger boy, soon afterwards joining the Pennsylvania Railroad as a clerk. After two years of this, bored and looking for "new fields to conquer," he noticed a newspaper advertisement for the Ludlam School of Dramatic Art in Philadelphia, and signed up as a part-time student.

Ridiculed by his friends, he nevertheless "worked like a Trojan" and "received a wonderful training in Shakespeare and the drama generally," soon emerging as the school's star pupil. When a distinguished touring company, the Greet Players, visited Philadelphia in 1912, Keighley was recommended to Ben Greet and cast in a small role in each of the three Shakespeare plays Greet presented at the Academy of Music. When the season ended, Keighley was invited to join Greet's company. Quitting the Pennsylvania Railroad, he joined the tour as a professional actor.

WILLIAM KEIGHLEY

A major production of *A Midsummer Night's Dream* in Chicago was followed by four weeks of one-night stands in the sticks, with rehearsals whenever there was a layover between trains, and then a month at the Ben Greet Outdoor Theatre, improbably housed at the Cincinnati Zoo. During his first three-month season, Keighley had thirty-four parts in thirteen plays, most of them Shakespearean. A longer tour followed—forty weeks of one-night stands that took the company to forty-six of the forty-eight states. It was, Keighley says, "a great life."

Deciding that it was time to branch out professionally, Keighley went to New York. Working with Greet's largely English company had equipped him with a convincing British accent, and this helped land a part in the road company of *Officer 666*. Other such assignments followed, and then minor roles in various Broadway productions, including John Barrymore's *Richard III*. Beginning in 1918, Keighley promoted the idea of presenting contemporary plays on the Chautauqua circuit, which brought tent shows of classical works, lectures, and music to rural areas during the summer. The notion caught on, and for some years he staged Chautauqua productions with his own companies in Iowa, Missouri, and elsewhere, sometimes producing as many as sixteen plays in a single season and frequently appearing in them as well.

By 1924, Keighley had decided that he preferred directing to acting and, "feeling that one should be equipped with a knowledge of the continental theatre," spent two winters learning French and studying drama in Paris and London. In 1925 he joined Charles Hopkins' highly

successful Punch and Judy Theatre in New York and then, in association with William Tanner, independently produced *Penny Arcade,* a play that did well enough to launch the Hollywood careers of two newcomers, James Cagney and Joan Blondell. In 1930, on vacation with his mother in California, Keighley was invited to direct *Elizabeth the Queen* at the Belasco Theatre in Los Angeles. It was a major success, and a series of assignments followed for David Belasco over the next six years, including productions of *Cyrano de Bergerac* and *Camille* (both of which Keighley helped to translate).

It was during this period that he began to transfer his allegiance to the movie industry. In 1930 he served as dialogue director of Edwin Carewe's sound version of *Resurrection* for Universal, in which he also played the role of Schoenbock. He resumed his work at the Belasco Theatre, but in 1932 directed dialogue for William Dieterle's *The Jewel Robbery* for Warner Brothers–First National, the studio where Keighley was to spend almost his entire career as a filmmaker. His own first films, both directed in collaboration with Howard Bretherton, were *The Match King* (1932), a portrait of an industrialist modeled on the career of Ivar Kreuger, and *Ladies They Talk About* (1933), a shocker about woman criminals starring Barbara Stanwyck.

More dialogue work followed in 1933, and then Warners gave him his first solo assignment as director, *Easy to Love* (1934). A sophisticated marital comedy based on a popular play, it boasted a remarkable cast that included Mary Astor, Guy Kibbee, Edward Everett Horton, and Hugh Herbert, with Genevieve Tobin and Adolphe Menjou in the leads. Frank S. Nugent found it "bright, strenuous, and thinnish in equal proportions."

Five more Keighley movies followed during 1934, beginning with the much-praised *Journal of a Crime*. This starred Ruth Chatterton as a wife who murders her husband's mistress, goes into a guilt-induced decline, but recovers to live happily ever after with her chastened spouse (Menjou). It was said to have been directed with "great style and finish," and there was a generally warm welcome also for Keighley's version of Sinclair Lewis' novel *Babbitt,* with Guy Kibbee as the complacent and boastful Midwestern real estate agent who is unwittingly inveigled into a swindle and only rescued from ruin by the shrewdness of his long-suffering wife (Aileen MacMahon). If Keighley's *Babbitt* lost much of the satirical bite of the original, it succeeded very well in conveying the look and feel of small-town life.

Keighley was an urbane man who is said never to have raised his voice on set because "it would be embarrassing if anyone but the actors heard me." This being so, it is odd that his reputation should stand primarily on the group of taut and violent gangster movies that began in 1935 with *G-Men,* based on a story by Gregory Roberts. James Cagney plays a tough, wisecracking young lawyer who owes his education to a paternalistic mobster but who joins the FBI when his best friend is murdered. At first treated with suspicion by his boss (Robert Armstrong), he proves himself in a climactic and tightly edited gun battle that has not lost its excitement.

The choice of Cagney for this role was highly significant. His gleeful wickedness in William Wellman's *Public Enemy* (1931) had launched a genre in which gangsters were presented as fascinating outlaw-heroes, in a society pervaded with crime. The New Deal's optimistic respect for federal authority had no place for such antisocial attitudes, and contemporary critics thought it "a matter for general congratulation" that Warner Brothers had "found a way of getting a lot of gunplay back on the screen without falling foul of the Hays Office," in "a complete translation of the old gangster picture into terms of federal integrity." Will Hays himself commended the "healthy and helpful emphasis on law enforcement" in this picture, which is said to have been used by the FBI for inspirational and training purposes. Later commentators have nominated *G-Men* as a forerunner of the pseudo-documentary crime thrillers of the late 1940s, and William Everson maintains that it "was to the gangster film what *The Spoilers* is to the Western."

Special Agent (1935) was a variation on the same theme, starring George Brent and Bette Davis, and 1935 also saw the release of *Stars Over Broadway,* a likable musical scripted by Jerry Wald and Julius J. Epstein, with production numbers by Bobby Connolly and Busby Berkeley. Pat O'Brien plays a theatrical agent down on his luck, who discovers in hotel porter James Melton a crooner of cowboy songs with the makings of an opera star. The movie now seems more notable for a brief appearance by the blues singer Jane Froman than for Berkeley's staging of an aria from *Aida.* The following year Keighley made *The Singing Kid,* which provided Al Jolson with his last major role.

Another heavy came in from the cold in *Bullets or Ballots* (1936), with Edward G. Robinson following Cagney into the heroic ranks of the FBI, infiltrating Barton Maclane's gang and destroying it at the cost of his own life. Humphrey Bogart, still being cast on the wrong side of the

law, seemed to a contemporary reviewer "as sinister a racketeer as one could meet in a day's march," in what a later critic, David Thomson, has called a "racy piece of urban slaughter and conniving, without depth but sure of its pace."

After that, *The Green Pastures* (1936) was a considerable departure. The script was written by Marc Connelly—adapted from his own hit play based on the Southern sketches of Roark Bradford. An old black preacher (Rex Ingram) tells Old Testament stories to children in Sunday school who visualize the stories of Cain and Abel, Moses, Noah, and others in terms of their own experience, with heaven full of black angels fishing from puffy clouds and the preacher doubling as "de Lawd."

Connelly was to have directed the movie himself, but he was entirely without film experience and reportedly called for some thirty-six takes of his first scene. According to Keighley, "Jack Warner ordered me on the picture at once, and Connelly sat on the set while I directed the picture." *The Green Pastures* opened at Radio City Music Hall and was one of the most successful black movies of its era, praised for its skillful merging of painted backdrops and lush outdoor scenes, and for Ingram's dignified performance. Patronizing and even racist as it seems now, it was by the standards of its time a sympathetic and imaginative experiment.

A "big tree saga" called *God's Country and the Woman*—Keighley's first film in color—was followed by *The Prince and the Pauper* (1937), regarded by many as the best of the half-dozen versions of Mark Twain's novel. The atmosphere of sixteenth-century London was convincingly recreated and handsomely photographed by Sol Polito, and Laird Doyle's excellent script gave full weight to the novel's indictment of the social injustices of the period. Keighley drew remarkable performances from Billy and Bobby Mauch, the twelve-year-old twins who play the prince and the pauper that swap places, though Errol Flynn received star billing as Miles Hendon, the soldier who helps to restore the real prince to his throne.

Flynn also starred in Warners' splendid swashbuckler, *The Adventures of Robin Hood* (1938), most of it shot on location in the new three-color Technicolor process. The film was set up by Keighley but handed to Michael Curtiz eight weeks into shooting, apparently because Keighley had shown a "too lighthearted" approach to this, the studio's most expensive production up to that time. The film was commercially very successful and earned Oscars for music, art direction, and editing, though how much of the credit belongs to Keighley is a matter of speculation.

In spite of this rebuff, he stayed with Warners, the same year directing *Valley of the Giants,* a "rip-snorting sinewy flashback to the days of the strong and silent thrillers," a Kay Francis vehicle called *Secrets of an Actress,* and *Brother Rat.* The latter, adapted from a Broadway hit, starred Wayne Morris, Ronald Reagan, and Eddie Albert in a comedy about cadets at the Virginia Military Institute, with Priscilla Lane, Jane Wyman, and Jane Bryan as their girlfriends. Immensely popular, it inspired a sequel, *Brother Rat and the Baby,* and was remade in 1952 as *About Face.*

Another play adaptation, *Yes, My Darling Daughter* (1939), was followed by *Each Dawn I Die,* in which James Cagney is a reporter jailed on a frame-up who escapes with the help of a convict (George Raft) whom he helps to reform. The brutal large-scale shoot-out at the prison is constructed and cut rather like the climactic gun battle in *G-Men,* and here and elsewhere Cagney's performance contains hints of the insane rage he was to express so definitively in *White Heat* (1949). David Thomson wrote that the film "moves at great speed and even brings George Raft to life." Stalin reportedly told Roosevelt that this was his favorite film.

The Fighting 69th (1940), an all-male World War I saga about the famous New York regiment, stars Cagney as the hard-nosed kid who disgraces its traditions until chaplain Pat O'Brien talks him into line (and a hero's death). Jeffrey Lynn rhapsodizes as the poet Joyce Kilmer. It was, as one critic remarked, "pure hokum," but full of action and well-staged battles, and a major box-office hit. And *Torrid Zone* (1940) was another, with a "sparkling" script by Richard Macaulay and Jerry Wald, photography by James Wong Howe, and Mark Hellinger as producer. Pat O'Brien plays the manager of a struggling fruit company in Guatemala, using all his guile to keep his best man (James Cagney) on the job while coping with the depredations of bandit George Tobias. This was the eighth (and last) movie costarring Cagney and O'Brien, and it was stolen from them by Ann Sheridan's performance as a wisecracking nightclub singer.

Cagney was teamed with Bette Davis in *The Bride Came C.O.D.* (1941), a movie strongly reminiscent of Capra's *It Happened One Night,* with Cagney as a pilot who kidnaps a spoiled heiress at her father's request and falls in love with her. There followed two more comedies, both adapted from plays by George S. Kaufman and Moss Hart, *The Man Who Came to Dinner* and *George Washington Slept Here.* The best of the two was the first, in which Monty Woolley starred as Sheridan Whiteside, the role he had created on Broadway. He is an arrogant and vitriolically witty radio pundit (modeled on Alexander Woolcott) who is confined by an accident to a middle-class, Midwest home where he promptly creates bedlam. The splendid cast included Bette Davis, Ann Sheridan, Jimmy Durante, Billie Burke, and Reginald Gardiner. Most critics thought that Keighley had been wise not to "open up" a play whose point was the confinement of its venomous hero.

In 1938, meanwhile, the director had made a third and lasting marriage to the actress Genevieve Tobin, who had starred in his first solo film *Easy to Love.* Two years later, he was appointed as the first professor of cinema at the University of Southern California. Keighley had always felt close ties with Britain, his father's native country, and early in World War II he offered his services to England through the British Ambassador in Washington. The offer was not taken up, but in June 1942 he was asked to join the Motion Picture Division of the United States Army Air Forces to organize combat camera units in all operational theatres.

Keighley spent most of the next two years in the field in Europe, Asia, and Africa. In 1944 he went to England to make *Target for Today,* a feature-length documentary about the RAF's Bomber Command. Originally intended for RAF personnel only, it was subsequently released in the United States under the auspices of the *March of Time.* Keighley also made USAAF training films and, using miniature planes and models of the Japanese islands, filmed simulated bombing raids that enabled American pilots to recognize their targets on their first flights over Japan. He ended the war with the rank of colonel. Instead of returning to Warner Brothers, Keighley became host and producer of the *Lux Radio Theatre,* which featured well-known actors and actresses in radio adaptations of their film roles. *Newsweek* considered that Keighley "read lines with aplomb, in sharp contrast to the uninspired delivery of his predecessor"—Cecil B. DeMille.

It was not until 1947 that Keighley directed his first postwar film, an inconsequential romantic comedy called *Honeymoon,* made for RKO. *The Street With No Name* (Fox, 1948) was a very different matter—a return to the tough thriller genre at which Keighley excelled, and perhaps the best of all his films. The familiar story, drawn "from the files of the FBI," was scripted by Harry Kleiner. Richard Widmark, as the dangerously intelligent gang leader with a neurotic fear of drafts, delivers one of his most memorable studies in psychopathy, and Mark Stevens plays the young FBI agent who infiltrates his murderous mob.

The film is set in a fictitious Central City, but Joe MacDonald shot most of the footage on Los Angeles' skid row, a district of squalid streets, dark flophouses, and cheap bars and diners. *Variety* called the movie "a lean tough surface wrapped around a nucleus of explosive violence," and Robert Ottoson described it as "a combination of the fast-paced muscularity of the Warners' crime films of the 30s, and the postwar semidocumentary *film noir.*"

In 1950 Keighley returned to Warners, where he made three more films: *Rocky Mountain* (1950) and *The Master of Ballantrae* (1953), both with Errol Flynn, and *Close to My Heart* (1951), with Ray Milland and Gene Tierney. The most notable of these was *The Master of Ballantrae,* a lavish production filmed on location in Scotland, England, and Sicily, wih Jack Cardiff as photographer and a score by William Alwyn. It was well enough reviewed but only moderately successful at the box office.

Ballantrae was Keighley's last film. Tired of working with bad scripts, he turned to still photography, a field that had increasingly absorbed him. He and his wife settled in Paris, traveling all over Europe and the Near East to make systematic and detailed photographic studies of major architectural works. In 1958 Keighley was made an honorary citizen of Paris and a director of the Musée Carnavalet. The same year, still resident in Paris, he joined the staff of the New York Metropolitan Museum of Art, continuing his photographic work under its auspices. The Museum now houses (and makes frequent use of) Keighley's collection of 70,000 color slides. He and his wife returned to New York in 1972, settling into an apartment on Fifth Avenue. He died of a stroke twelve years later, at the age of ninety-four. Keighley was a Chevalier of the French Legion of Honor and of Arts and Letters, and had received awards for his photography also from Spain and Austria.

The director was a "chunky" man who has always dressed elegantly and conservatively. On set, he would isolate himself from everything but the camera and the actors, to whom he would whisper his instructions. He disliked conflict and was liable to defuse a potentially difficult situation by replying to a provocative remark in French. "I work with my eye on the cash register," Keighley said once. "It isn't gratifying to make an artistic triumph which only the chosen few appreciate. I'd rather serve the great masses who actually do know good entertainment when they get it." This attitude did not endear him to the more serious critics, but his films undoubtedly gave great pleasure to millions who wanted nothing more from the movies than entertainment. As William R. Mayer says, "his sense of humour and easy-going style camouflaged a consummate professional who knew how to motivate performers as well as the camera."

FILMS: (with Howard Bretherton) The Match King, 1932; (with Howard Bretherton) Ladies They Talk About, 1933; Easy to Love, 1934; Journal of a Crime, 1934; Dr. Monica, 1934; Kansas City Princess, 1934; Big-Hearted Herbert, 1934; Babbitt, 1934; The Right to Live (U.K., The Sacred Flame), 1935; Mary Jane's Pa (U.K., Wanderlust), 1935; G-Men, 1935; Special Agent, 1935; Stars Over Broadway, 1935; The Singing Kid, 1936; Bullets or Ballots, 1936; (with Marc Connelly) The Green Pastures, 1936; God's Country and the Woman, 1937; The Prince and the Pauper, 1937; Varsity Show, 1937; (with Michael Curtiz) The Adventures of Robin Hood, 1938; Valley of the Giants, 1938; Secrets of an Actress, 1938; Brother Rat, 1938; Yes, My Darling Daughter, 1939; Each Dawn I Die, 1939; The Fighting 69th, 1940; Torrid Zone, 1940; No Time for Comedy, 1940 (re-released in 1954 as Guy With a Grin); Four Mothers, 1941; The Bride Came C.O.D., 1941; The Man Who Came to Dinner, 1942; George Washington Slept Here, 1942; Target for Today, 1944 (documentary); Honeymoon (U.K., Two Men and a Girl), 1947; The Street With No Name, 1948; Rocky Mountain, 1950; Close to My Heart, 1951; The Master of Ballantrae, 1953.

ABOUT: Current Biography, 1948; Farber, M. *in* Talbot, D. (ed.) Film: An Anthology, 1966. Meyer, W. R. Warner Brothers Directors, 1978; Sennett, T. Warner Brothers Presents . . . , 1972. *Periodicals*—Cahiers de la Cinémathèque Summer 1978; Films in Review October 1974; Kino Lehti 2 1969.

KING, HENRY (January 24, 1888–June 29, 1982), American director and producer, was born in Christianburg, in western Virginia. His grandfather had fought under Lee in the Civil War and his father—in a family that produced many politicians—was a farmer and a railroad attorney. King attended public schools in Riverside and then Roanoke College, where a black-face routine he performed in a commencement program gave him his first taste of the pleasures of showmanship.

King quit school at fifteen to work in the machine shops of the Norfolk and Western Railroad. He was soon bored and, after a brief return to school, left home to tour the South as an apprentice actor with the Empire Stock Company. King entered the theatre against the wishes of most of his family, who had intended him for the Methodist ministry. Only his mother supported his choice. He said that "by this time my father was dead and my mother and aunt had become mortal enemies, because my aunt had said that

HENRY KING

she was glad to see my dad dead, so he wouldn't be able to see me in the theatre. . . . As long as she lived, my mother was my greatest booster."

Over the next few years, King toured all over the United States with a variety of repertory companies, appearing in everything from *The Jolly American Tramp* and *The Minister's Daughter* to Shakespeare with Anna Boyce, and gaining experience also as a set designer and almost certainly as a director as well. Nor was King limited to the legitimate stage—he is said to have tried his hand at virtually every kind of theatrical enterprise, including circus, vaudeville, and burlesque. Around 1912 he appeared (or even starred) in New York in a show called *Top o' the Morning*.

It was at about this time, almost by chance, that he entered the movie business. King accompanied his friend Pearl White—later famous as "the queen of the serials"—to an interview at the Lubin Company and was asked why he didn't go into movies himself: "I said, 'I have blue eyes and they don't photograph.' He said, 'Oh, that was in the old days. We photograph blue eyes now.' We got into a discussion and I got into motion pictures."

King was an exceptionally handsome man, but with rugged good looks of a sort that did not suit the vogue for pallid matinee idols. In his earliest pictures he was generally cast as the heavy. The first film in which King appeared, according to research done by James Card, was *A False Friend,* directed for Lubin by Bertram Bracken and released on April 3, 1913. Three more short features followed the same month, and another four were released in May 1913, an output that

continued at least into January 1914. Judging by their titles, most of these films were Westerns or romantic melodramas. The majority were directed by Bracken, though in those informal days King himself directed scenes occasionally.

In 1914 or 1915 he went west to join the Balboa Amusement Company, a subsidiary of Pathé in Long Beach, California. By then, film casting was less dominated by prevailing theatrical styles, and King had begun to acquire a following as a romantic lead in one-, two-, and three-reel comedies and dramas. At Balboa he also wrote some scripts and showed the first signs of exceptional directorial potential when he suggested an unorthodox way of filming a brawl scene. Drawing on recollections of a fight he had witnessed as a child, he tried to catch the violence and confusion of the scene in a montage of brief shots, each composed of only eight or ten frames. It was an unheard-of technique—so revolutionary that he had to show the editor how the shots should be spliced together.

Some sources say that King directed his first film in 1916, but there is evidence to support the claim that this stage of his career began in 1915—that he directed at least some of the twelve episodes of the Balboa serial *Who Pays?,* in which he also played the lead. He was certainly the director of *Little Mary Sunshine,* released by Pathé in March 1916. It starred the child actress Baby Marie Osborne and King himself. A reviewer in the New York *Dramatic Mirror* noted that his "handling of 'the little things,' the 'tremendous trifles' in the direction of this feature shows him to be an artist of depth and certainty." It was obviously a box-office success as well as a critical one, since King directed at least five more films for Balboa teaming Marie Osborne and himself—sagas of innocence and experience with titles like *Joy and the Dragon, Shadows and Sunshine,* and *Sunshine and Gold.*

In 1917 King joined the American Film Manufacturing Company at Niles, California, where he largely abandoned acting in favor of directing. He made a group of films starring Gail Kane, then several vehicles for Mary Miles Minter, a former child actress who by then was a childlike romantic lead. In 1918–1919 he directed William Russell in eleven five- or six-reel features, most of them Westerns. At American, King had the benefit of a brilliant cameraman in John F. Seitz, soon to become famous for his technical innovations and his moodily lit "art films" for Rex Ingram.

King moved on again in 1919 to the Thomas Ince Company, where he made his first major hit, an army comedy called *23¼ Hours Leave* (1919)—the title refers to the furlough granted to troops before they left the United States to fight in France. Adapted from a story by Mary Roberts Rinehart, it was called a fast-moving comedy "with the emphasis on small human touches." It made a star of Douglas MacLean but cost King his job. The studio manager fired him in Ince's absence for going over his budget; when Ince returned and saw the movie, he fired the studio manager. In 1919–1921, working for Robertson-Cole and other studios, King directed seven films starring H. B. Warner and three with Pauline Frederick. His own last screen role seems to have been in *Help Wanted—Male* (1920), in which he starred with Blanche Sweet.

In 1921 King established his own production company, Inspiration Pictures, distributing through First National. His partners in this enterprise were Charles H. Duell and D. W. Griffith's boyish star Richard Barthelmess. Their first project was a screen version of a book to which Griffith had originally owned the film rights, Joseph Hergesheimer's novel of Southern rural life, *Tol'able David*. Made at a cost of $86,000, it was shot by Henry Cronjager on location in the mountains of West Virginia, only a few miles from King's birthplace. Barthelmess gives a performance of "shining seriousness" as the young hero coming to manhood in the idyllic small town of Greenstream—his tender relationship with his mother (Marion Abbott), his first romance, the suspicion of cowardice that falls on him, and the climactic fight (to get the mail through) against a giant mountain man (played by Ernest Torrence as "a truly terrifying figure of moronic savagery").

As Richard Combs has said, "the static, almost stagey appearance of King's films is always contradicted . . . by the abundant flow of life within the frame. *Tol'able David* takes its time establishing the milieu and the inhabitants of tranquil Greenstream Valley, before the fateful and symbolic intrusion of the Hatfield family, leading to the textbook climax of David's protracted, punishing fight with the Goliath of the clan. But a wry lyricism generally excludes both nostalgia for a pastoral Eden and undiluted individual heroism; the film seems to lose its head in moments of melodramatic stress, and is at its sharpest in observing the small triumphs and disappointments, not just in David's sentimental education, but in the complete family experience. In fact, it stands at the head of a whole King cycle which pays tribute to the virtues of hard work, good will, and humour in the making of communities."

The quality of *Tol'able David* was recognized by no less a contemporary than Pudovkin, who praised it for the excellence of its construction and as an exemplary use of the plastic materials of the cinema. Paul Rotha maintained that it was "at its date the finest film America had produced," adding that "King robbed Griffith of all that was good, combining the spoil with his own filmic knowledge." A more recent program note by an anonymous critic also acknowledges Griffith's influence on the picture, in which however "there is much greater maturity of feeling than is found in Griffith. No egotism or self-consciousness stands between the creator of the film and the people he imbues with life." Griffith himself was impressed, and generous enough to say to King: "My boy, you're too good. . . . You're giving me a tough race." An immediate and widespread commercial success, *Tol'able David* received *Photoplay's* Gold Medal for 1921 and awards in France, Belgium, Austria, Italy, and Britain.

By these high standards, the four films that followed from Inspiration Pictures were not much more than melodramatic programmers. All four starred Richard Barthelmess, and in both *Sonny* (1922) and *The Bond Boy* (1922) he played dual roles. *Sonny*, adapted by Frances Marion and King himself from a contemporary play, is about two young men, one poor and the other aristocratic, who meet on the battlefields of France; the rich boy dies and the poor one goes home in his place. For Robert E. Sherwood, this film demonstrated that "a bad play may be made into a good movie," and the same critic also had a kind word for *Fury* (1923), a "two-fisted, red-blooded" sea adventure in which Barthelmess, Patrick Hartigan, and Dorothy Gish "give splendid performances as London waterfront types."

The White Sister (1923) was also a melodrama, but one that obviously fired King's imagination. Based on a popular novel by Francis Marion Crawford, it is set in Italy, where the aristocratic heroine (Lillian Gish) falls in love with a dashing officer (Ronald Colman), loses him in the war, and enters a convent. But her lover is after all not dead. He returns to her and begs her to renounce her vows. She is wavering when the decision is taken out of her hands by an act of God—an eruption of Vesuvius in which the hero dies.

King and his cameraman Roy Overbaugh shot *The White Sister* on location in Italy, penetrating for the volcano sequence into the actual crater of Vesuvius—the heat was so intense that Overbaugh's assistant fainted and King's eyebrows and hair were singed. Lillian Gish scored a personal triumph in the lead and Ronald Colman became a star overnight. This was Colman's Hollywood debut—he had previously appeared only in small roles in British movies, and had despaired of success as a screen actor until King recognized his potential and taught him how to realize it.

Clive Denton writes that King deepens the maudlin story of *The White Sister* by character exploration "and decorates his scenes with many details which reinforce conviction of the social time and place. The indolent pleasures of aristocratic Italian life before the 1914 war are captured with scenes of fox hunts . . . and trysts at the garden wall. The superbly framed and lit convent scenes suggest, through ritual and resignation, religion's dual face of serenity and fear. Most remarkably of all, King brings to his climactic scenes a sweep and fury which also gain from the leisurely tempo of all that has gone before."

King, who became a convert to Catholicism after making *The White Sister*, returned to Italy for his next film, *Romola* (1924), adapted from George Eliot's novel about a self-sacrificing heroine in the Florence of Savonarola. Finding Florence too full of traffic to pass as its fifteenth-century self, King and his art director Robert Haas recreated the Renaissance city on seventeen acres at the Vise studio. The tallest building on this gigantic set was nearly three hundred feet high, and in the interests of authenticity Haas used in the "stonework" plaster casts from the walls of the Davanzati Palace. With a cast headed by the two Gish sisters and Ronald Colman, this "lavish emotional film" seems to have been admired more for its visual magnificence than for its emotional impact.

Romola was the last film King made for Inspiration Pictures for some years, though the company continued to turn out movies by other directors. In 1925 he directed two mediocre films for Robert Kane, both starring Alice Terry, and then joined Samuel Goldwyn, for whom he worked on a profit-sharing basis until the end of the decade. King's first film for Goldwyn was one of his greatest, an adaptation (scripted by Frances Marion) of Olive Higgins Prouty's weepy novel of frustrated mother-love, *Stella Dallas*. Belle Bennett, who desperately wanted the part (and deliberately put on weight to get it) gave the performance of her life as Stella, a former mill worker and *petite bourgeoise* who slaves to educate her pretty daughter (Lois Moran), then walks out of her life when she comes to realize that her own vulgarity is all that might prevent the girl's marriage to rich young Ronald Colman.

Richard Roud found King's *Stella Dallas* "quite unforgettable, the only version of this (doubtless tawdry) novel that doesn't cheat. His

Stella, Belle Bennett, *is* vulgar, *is* an embarrassment, and thus the story becomes somewhat more believable than in the glamorous interpretation of the role by Barbara Stanwyck (1937). And the climaxes of the film—the birthday party to which no one comes and the wedding which Stella has to watch from outside in the pouring rain—have an effectiveness and a grandeur that are totally convincing."

Discussing King's comparatively rare but very telling use of close shots, Clive Denton refers to a moment in *Stella Dallas* that he finds "unique in the cinema." This comes when the daughter is enjoying the company of a group of "beautiful people" in an equally beautiful garden: "Suddenly her mother sails into view, lovingly but tactlessly seeking her out. The daughter, horrified, shrinks back and tries to hide. . . . The fat and aging Stella, dressed ridiculously in a hideous striped costume, advances over the grass towards the younger group. As she walks, the medium view is dissolved into a much closer one, with quite extraordinary impact. It is a bravura impact born of discretion beforehand. Henry King learned early the value of *relative* abandon within what might almost be called, in a modern phrase, 'minimal cinema.'"

After *Partners Again* (1926), one in a series of Goldwyn comedies starring Abe Potash and Mawruss Perlmutter, came another remarkable film, *The Winning of Barbara Worth* (1926), scripted by Frances Marion from a novel by Harold Bell Wright. According to Kevin Brownlow, "the picture was intended as a love story to exploit the appeal of Vilma Banky and Ronald Colman. But the romantic sequences pale into insignificance alongside the magnificent scenes of civil engineering and desert reclamation. Superbly photographed by George Barnes (assisted by Gregg Toland), the picture tells the story of Imperial Valley, California, an irrigation project long considered impossible."

The film was shot on location in the Black Rock Desert of Nevada, where three towns were constructed, a vast tent city erected to house the extras, and a new spur line built by the Western Pacific Railroad.

Brownlow claims that "the documentary reconstruction in *The Winning of Barbara Worth* is of such a high standard that it places the film on a level with the other Western epics, *The Covered Wagon* and *The Iron Horse*. . . . The picture is climaxed with a catastrophic flood—when the Colorado River burst its banks, flooded the valley, and created the Salton Sea. Ned Mann's special effects and miniatures are exceptional and the sequence has a terrifying reality." King has described how, when the actor cast as the engineer Abe Lee failed to show up, he took a chance with a young Montana cowboy who had been patiently waiting on the lot in hopes of a part. He tested him in a scene where he had to enter a room exhausted and collapse; Gary Cooper, who had been walked until he *was* exhausted, spoke his line and fell face downwards with such convincing disregard for his own profile that Goldwyn hired him on the spot.

The Magic Flame (1927), a circus melodrama with Vilma Banky and Ronald Colman, was King's last film for Goldwyn. In 1928, in collaboration with Sam Taylor, he made *The Woman Disputed,* a period drama borrowing somewhat from Maupassant's story "Boule de suif." Produced as well as directed by King for Joseph M. Schenck, it was released in two versions, one silent and the other with music and sound effects. There followed three films for Inspiration Pictures of which the second, *Hell Harbor* (1930), was King's first full talkie. A pirate story starring Lupe Velez and Jean Hersholt, it was shot on location in the Florida Keys and was one of the first sound films made outside the studio.

In July 1930 King joined Fox, which in 1935 became 20th Century–Fox. He worked for the studio for thirty-two years, becoming Fox's most popular and successful house director. "In the silent era," writes Clive Denton, "King was developing and perfecting a visual style that became marvellously direct, economical and free from clutter. It is not a style that lends itself readily to written analysis, if only because his cuts and set-ups draw so little attention to themselves. . . . He has always allowed a great deal to happen *within* the frame. His complete work must now include thousands of shots at middle distance from the lens, many of them without any camera movement at all. He will frequently open a scene on a person or object, shown very close, then pull into his full scene area and stay there. These simple, but eloquently judged, shots are the still centre of his pictorial world. . . . Many in themselves are of exquisite beauty, but this beauty can be as subtle and discreet as in some equally measured scenes of Jean Renoir." There are some who maintain that King's sound films, though the work of a "supreme craftsman," lack the personal signature he gave to the best of his silents.

Having earned his pilot's license in 1930, King adopted the practice of scouting locations from the air, becoming known as the "Flying Director." He did this first for his Fox debut film, a remake of John Ford's *Lightnin'.* King's version, scripted by S. N. Behrman and Sonya Levien, starred Will Rogers and Louise Dresser in this sentimental comedy-drama about a lov-

able drunk and his problems with his work and his wife. None of the three movies that followed were of much interest but *State Fair* (1933), a celebration of the rural American pursuits and the values that King so loved, showed that he had fully mastered the sound medium. An Iowa farmer and his wife (Will Rogers and Louise Dresser) drive to the state fair with their children (Janet Gaynor and Norman Foster). The farmer wins a prize for his Hampshire boar, the wife triumphs with her pickles (liberally spiced with apple brandy), and both of the young people have loving encounters—the boy's educational but fleeting, the girl's serious and perhaps lasting.

The story (from the novel by Phil Stong) could hardly be more slight, and the highly "typical" family is not strongly characterized. As Clive Denton writes, "King's great achievement here is to characterize the family as a unit. As with the Kinemons of *Tol'able David,* the Frakes in *State Fair* really do seem kith and kin—close and loving, picking up each other's ways, sometimes getting on each other's nerves but united by a warm, unspoken fellowship." Denton reserves some of his praise for the cameraman Hal Mohr and his "genius for lighting and angling," and concludes that King's *State Fair* (twice remade in musical versions) "has something of a musical's *joie de vivre,* without the need for music."

King worked with Hal Mohr again on *Carolina* (1934), another celebration of pastoral values about an old Southern family and its struggle to rehabilitate itself, and then resumed his collaboration with John F. Seitz for a series of four films. These were the spy drama *Marie Galante*; the wry Depression comedy *One More Spring* (from Robert Nathan's novel about an odd trio living in a tool shed in Central Park); a "surprisingly effective" remake of the old road-show melodrama *Way Down East,* previously filmed as a silent by Griffith; and *The Country Doctor,* a tribute to the devoted work of a physician (Jean Hersholt) in a small Canadian timber town. Based on the life of Dr. Allan Roy Dafoe, who brought the Dionne Quintuplets into the world, this last movie was an immense box-office success, and not only because it featured as its "guest-stars" the famous quints themselves: it was everywhere admired for its humor and "disarming simplicity, never losing touch with reality."

The Country Doctor (1936) was the first of King's movies edited by Barbara McLean, who worked on most of the films that followed, and the first of many produced by Darryl F. Zanuck, Fox's new head of production, whose taste for lavish entertainments emphasizing technical polish and visual gloss was soon evident. King used Technicolor for the first time in *Ramona* (1936), a hoary tale about an aristocratic white woman married to an Indian that had been screened three times before (once by Griffith), and over the next few years directed several contributions to a genre favored by Zanuck—the spectacular and more or less fictionalized biopic or historical reconstruction.

Zanuck had had his first major success in this mode with *The House of Rothschild* (1934), directed by Alfred Werker. King's *Lloyds of London* (1936) was an attempt to romanticize the famous insurance combine from its coffeehouse beginnings in 1770 to its dominant position at the time of the Battle of Trafalgar. T. J. Fitzmorris found the result "a fluffed-up spectacle with passages of stirring action and impressive dignity," though "very often the plot is unable to live up to the portentous atmosphere in which it is unfolded." It was, nevertheless, a huge success at the box office and launched a new star in Tyrone Power Jr.

After a feeble remake of *Seventh Heaven* (1937), with James Stewart badly miscast as a Parisian streetcleaner in love with a homeless waif (Simone Simon), Zanuck handed King two assignments that gave scope to his nostalgia for a bygone America. *In Old Chicago* (1938) traces the growth of that city from 1854 to 1871 through the history of a single family—the very O'Learys whose cow kicked over the lamp that started the great fire. This "early disaster movie" seemed to Roy Pickard to have an uncommon depth of feeling because "King placed as much emphasis on the human values of the story as he did on spectacle." *Alexander's Ragtime Band* (1938) follows the trials and triumphs of a mythical dance band of the 1920s, featuring more than thirty Irving Berlin songs and exhibiting, according to one critic, "a vitality that is not supplied in the sketchy plottings of the script."

Both films teamed Alice Faye and Tyrone Power, and the latter also starred in *Jesse James* (1939), with Henry Fonda as Jesse's brother Frank and John Carradine as Robert Ford, who earned an ignominious place in history by shooting the legendary outlaw in the back. Clive Denton places *Jesse James* very high among King's films. Although the Nunnally Johnson script whitewashes the James brothers, representing them as peaceful farm boys driven to crime by unscrupulous officials of the advancing railroad (Brian Donlevy and Donald Meek), the film, in Denton's opinion, "possesses a magnificent forward-pressing attack, a surge of images, not always present in his work, together with those moments of calm and reflection that are native to him."

A more ponderous semi-factual epic followed in *Stanley and Livingstone* (1939), with Spencer Tracy as the celebrated newspaperman who plunges into darkest Africa in search of Livingston (Cedric Harwicke) and a scoop. A string of generally agreeable but unmemorable movies followed in 1940–1941, and then a rousing pirate movie, *The Black Swan* (1942), which was one of fourteen pictures photographed for King between 1940 and 1961 by Leon Shamroy. At about this time King helped to form the Civil Air Patrol, a volunteer corps for which he flew during World War II with the Ferry Command, on submarine patrols, and on search and rescue missions.

The unassertive and generally unasserted religious faith that underlies all of King's mature work is for once overt in *The Song of Bernadette* (1943), adapted by George Seaton from Franz Werfel's novel about Bernadette Soubirous, the French peasant girl who in 1858 saw visions of the Virgin Mary and discovered the miraculous spring at Lourdes. James Agee, who loathed pseudo-religious movies, found this one almost inevitably limited by "middle-class twentieth-century genteelism" but went on: "Within those genteel limits I have seldom seen so tender and exact an attention to mood, to overall tone, to cutting, to the edging of an emotion, and to giving vitality, sometimes radiance, in terms of the image and the sound more than of the character, the story, the line, the music." *The Song of Bernadette* received four Oscars, including one for Jennifer Jones as best actress, and a Golden Globe award as the best production of the year.

Wilson (1944), an elaborate, expensive, and generally accurate biopic of President Woodrow Wilson (Alexander Knox), earned five Oscars, but is now regarded as one of the least exciting of King's historical reconstructions. The sets still command attention, nevertheless—especially the unprecedentedly massive ones built to house the 1912 Democratic National Convention. There were no Oscars but a warmer response to *A Bell for Adano* (1945), an often moving adaptation of John Hersey's novel, with John Hodiak as the American major trying to restore morale in a Sicilian village devastated by war. And *Margie* (1946), with Jeanne Crain reminiscing about her girlhood at a small American college, is one of King's best-loved pictures, "an exquisite slice of 1920s Americana"—though it seemed to Richard Combs that by now the director's "optimism and sentimentality" was complicated by a "regretful undertow"; that "the flood of nostalgia for shared experiences grows more melancholic as the focus becomes both more personalized and backward-looking."

King hit a bad patch after that, turning out

three tiresome films in as many years—the sentimental romance *Deep Waters* (1948) and two rambling costume epics, *Captain From Castile* (1947) and *Prince of Foxes* (1949), both adapted from novels by Samuel Shellabarger and both starring Tyrone Power. Just as inexplicably, he then produced two pictures that are regarded by some critics as the finest of all the films he directed in the sound era.

Twelve O'Clock High (1949), scripted by Sy Bartlett and Beirne Lay and photographed by Leon Shamroy, has Gregory Peck as a tough disciplinarian sent to take command of an American bomber base in Britain that has become demoralized by massive losses. He succeeds in restoring the unit's morale but cracks up himself under the strain. A flyer himself, King largely ignores the story's potential for exciting aerial sequences in order to concentrate on the psychology of his characters—only one raid is shown, though that is unusually lucid and convincing, intercutting reconstructed scenes with footage from official American and German records. Dean Jagger won an Oscar for his performance as Major Stovall, the humane, thoughtful officer who serves as the film's narrator.

The leisurely pace of King's films had grown more marked over the years, and there have been suggestions that the tautness and suspense achieved in *Twelve O'Clock High* should be attributed less to him than to Darryl F. Zanuck, the film's producer. This argument is vitiated by the fact that the same qualities are present in *The Gunfighter* (1950), produced by Nunnally Johnson. Perhaps in both cases King was stimulated by unusually intelligent scripts; *The Gunfighter* was written by William Bowers and André De Toth. Gregory Peck stars again as Jimmie Ringo, an aging gunfighter who wants to spend his last years in peace. He goes to the small Southwestern town where his wife lives, hoping for a reconciliation, but finds that he cannot shake the past. The picture was splendidly photographed by Arthur Miller in harsh black and white.

In this Western, wrote Robert Warshow, "the landscape has virtually disappeared. Most of the action takes place indoors, in a cheerless saloon where a tired 'bad man' contemplates the waste of his life, to be senselessly killed at the end by a vicious youngster setting out on the same futile path. The movie is done in cold, quiet tones of gray, and every object in it—faces, clothing, a table, the hero's heavy moustache—is given an air of uncompromising authenticity, suggesting those dim photographs of the nineteenth-century West." There was much praise for the sober restraint of Gregory Peck's performance in

this film, and Clive Denton has drawn attention to the extensive use, here and in *Twelve O'Clock High,* of deep-focus and wide-view photography "for dramatic isolation of a central character (Peck in each case). Did the two cinematographers have a chat in the studio restaurant—or is it possible that King knows something about visuals, after all?"

Two memorable exercises in nostalgia followed. *I'd Climb the Highest Mountain* (1951), shot by Edward Cronjager in the red hills of North Georgia, has William Lundigan as a circuit-riding Methodist minister (a vocation that might once have been the director's own) and Susan Hayward as his city-bred wife. They live through the ordinary sorrows and pleasures of such a life and end even more deeply in love than they began. If this film "shone with American sunlight and glowed with . . . nostalgic purity," a darker, more melancholic note underlies the humor and pathos of *Wait Till the Sun Shines Nellie* (1952). A small-town barber looks back over fifty years of his life and of the town's, and through what one critic called "the well-engineered contrivances of a professional script" there breaks an old man's slightly bitter conviction that the best days have gone.

And after that film, described by Clive Denton as a "virtually unknown minor masterpiece of nostalgia," King's best days as a director were gone too. He made nearly a dozen more movies before his retirement at the age of seventy-four, but none of them matched the achievements of his earlier days, though several had their admirers and champions—*Love Is a Many-Splendored Thing* (1955), with William Holden and Jennifer Jones; the Rodgers and Hammerstein musical *Carousel* (1956); a raw and uncharacteristically violent revenge Western, *The Bravados* (1958). There were also lavish, star-studded, but fundamentally misconceived adaptations of two works by Ernest Hemingway, *The Snows of Kilimanjaro* (1952) and *The Sun Also Rises* (1957), and King ended his career with equally stodgy versions of *Beloved Infidel* (1959), Sheilah Graham's memoir of her love affair with Scott Fitzgerald, and of Fitzgerald's autobiographical novel *Tender is the Night* (1962).

Six films by Henry King appear in a list of the hundred greatest movies compiled for the 1969 *International Motion Picture Almanac*—more than any other director. Commenting on this fact, Richard Combs wrote that "critical assessment has been less consistently kind, and at the moment King's reputation is probably at an all-time low. Part of the problem is the simple, unassertive craftsmanship with which he moved into territory—small-town and rural Americana—

which others more definitively made their own: his natural affinities with directors like Ford and Griffith have led to his subjects being merged with and swamped by theirs." Moreover, towards the end of his career "the uncomplicated strength and poetry of his treatment of simple emotions and rustic American subjects gave way to a certain literary heaviness" and evidence of a "pious and propagandizing spirit." Nevertheless, Combs maintains, "a number of lifelong characteristics in fact came intriguingly to fruition in King's generally maligned output of the 50s and early 60s," and all in all he "seems guaranteed a place as one of the genuine treasures of the art."

King was one of the founders of the Academy of Motion Picture Arts and Sciences, and served on the committee set up to organize its awards system—the Oscars. He was also a founder-member of the Director's Guild, and received its D. W. Griffith Award in 1956 for a lifetime's distinguished achievement. Up to 1978, Henry King was still logging around 12,000 miles a year in his own plane and was by then the oldest licensed pilot in the history of American aviation. His first wife, Gypsy, died in 1952 and he married again in 1959. When he died in his sleep at the age of ninety-four, he was survived by his second wife, Ida, and by a daughter and two sons. His brother Louis King was also an actor and film director.

FILMS: (Listing for early years uncertain; complete from 1919 onwards) Who Pays? (serial), 1915; The Brand of Man, 1915; Little Mary Sunshine, 1916; The Oath of Hate, 1916; The Sand Lark, 1916; Faith's Reward, 1916; Joy and the Dragon, 1916; Shadows and Sunshine, 1916; Twin Kiddies, 1917; The Climber, 1917; Told at Twilight, 1917; Sunshine and Gold, 1917; Souls in Pawn, 1917; The Bride's Silence, 1917; The Unafraid, 1917; The Upper Crust, 1917; Scepter of Suspicion, 1917; The Mainspring, 1917; Southern Pride, 1917; A Game of Wits, 1917; Mate of Sally Ann, 1917; Mlle. Tiptoes, 1918; King Social Briars, 1918; The Ghost of Rosy Taylor, 1918; Beauty and the Rogue, 1918; Powers That Prey, 1918; The Locked Heart, 1918; Hearts or Diamonds, 1918; Up Romance Road, 1918; All the World to Nothing, 1918; When a Man Rides Alone, 1918; Hobbs in a Hurry, 1919; Where the West Begins, 1919; Brass Buttons, 1919; Some Liar, 1919; A Sporting Chance, 1919; This Hero Stuff, 1919; Six Feet Four, 1919; 23½ Hours Leave, 1919; A Fugitive From Matrimony, 1919; Haunting Shadows, 1919; The White Dove, 1920; Uncharted Channels, 1920; One Hour Before Dawn, 1920; Dice of Destiny, 1920; Help Wanted—Male, 1920; When We Were Twenty-One, 1921; The Mistress of Shenstone, 1921; Salvage, 1921; The Sting of the Lash, 1921; Tol'able David, 1921; The Seventh Day, 1922; Sonny, 1922; The Bond Boy, 1922; Fury, 1923; The White Sister, 1923; Romola, 1924; Sackcloth and Scarlet, 1925; Any Woman, 1925; Stella Dallas, 1925; Partners Again, 1926; The Winning of Barbara Worth, 1926; The Magic Flame, 1927; (with Sam Taylor) The Woman Disputed, 1928; She Goes to War, 1929; Hell Harbor, 1930; The Eyes of the World, 1930; Lightnin', 1930; Merely Mary Ann, 1931; Over the Hill, 1931; The Woman in Room 13, 1932; State Fair, 1933; (with William Cameron Menzies) I Loved You Wednesday, 1933; Carolina, 1934; Marie Galante, 1934; One More Spring, 1935; Way Down East, 1935; The Country Doctor, 1936; Ramona, 1936; Lloyds of London, 1936; Seventh Heaven, 1937; In Old Chicago, 1938; Alexander's Ragtime Band, 1938; Jesse James, 1939; Stanley and Livingstone, 1939; Little Old New York, 1940; Maryland, 1940; Chad Hanna, 1940; A Yank in the R.A.F., 1941; Remember the Day, 1941; The Black Swan, 1942; The Song of Bernadette, 1943; Wilson, 1944; A Bell for Adano, 1945; Margie, 1946; Captain From Castile, 1947; Deep Waters, 1948; Prince of Foxes, 1949; Twelve O'Clock High, 1949; The Gunfighter, 1950; I'd Climb the Highest Mountain, 1951; David and Bathsheba, 1951; Wait Till the Sun Shines Nellie, 1952; The Snows of Kilimanjaro, 1952; The Gift of the Magi episode in O. Henry's Full House, 1952; King of the Khyber Rifles, 1953; Untamed, 1955; Love Is a Many-Splendored Thing, 1955; Carousel, 1956; The Sun Also Rises, 1957; The Bravados, 1958; This Earth Is Mine, 1959; Beloved Infidel, 1959; Tender Is the Night, 1962.

ABOUT: Brownlow, K. The Parade's Gone By, 1969; Brownlow, K. The War, the West and the Wilderness, 1979; Denton, C. (and others) Henry King, Lewis Milestone, Sam Wood (The Hollywood Professionals, Vol. 2), 1974; Roud, R. (ed.) Cinema: A Critical Dictionary, 1980; Tuska, J. (ed.) Close-Up: The Hollywood Director, 1978. Periodicals—Action November–December 1972; Écran June and July 1978; Films and Filming September 1971; Focus on Film Winter 1976; National Film Theatre (Britain) Booklet August 1977; Positif July–August 1982; Sight and Sound Winter 1977–1978; Variety July 7, 1982.

*KINOSHITA, KEISUKE (December 5, 1912–), Japanese director and scenarist, was born in Hamamatsu, Shizuoka Prefecture, where his parents ran a grocery store. He became addicted to the cinema when he was a small child, and by the time he was eight knew that he wanted to make movies—he says he is the only director he knows who "has always been this crazy about film."

However, Kinoshita's parents did not approve of his choice of career, and, after he graduated from technical high school in Hamamatsu, they insisted that he continue his formal education. He had resignedly begun to prepare himself for college entrance examinations when a film unit came to Hamamatsu. Some of the actors frequented the Kinoshita store, and the boy managed to persuade one of them, Junosuke Bando, to help him run away to the old Japanese capital of Kyoto, where many historical pictures were

°kē nō shē tä

KEISUKE KINOSHITA

made. His grandfather came after him and brought him back the next day, but this act of rebellion was enough to convince the family that Kinoshita was in earnest.

With his parents' help, Kinoshita managed to secure an interview at the Shochiku company's Kamata studios, where Ozu, Naruse, and Shimazu were at work on their films of lower-middle-class life, the *shomin-geki*. None of these heroes had been to a university, but Kinoshita was told that there would be no hope of directorial training without a degree, though there might be opportunities for a qualified photographer. His goal receded still further when, seeking to enroll at a Tokyo School of photography, he found that a prerequisite was six months' practical experience.

Still undaunted, Kinoshita found a job with a Tokyo photographer, acquired the necessary experience, and enrolled at the Oriental School of Photography. Armed with his diploma, he presented himself once more at Shochiku, where there was no longer any demand for camera assistants. There was a job in the film processing laboratory, however, and Kinoshita grabbed that, finally entering the film industry in 1933, when he was twenty-one. After a tedious stint in the laboratory, he was allowed to enter Shochiku's cinematography department as a camera assistant assigned to the director Yasujiro Shimazu. His original ambition undimmed, Kinoshita wrung everything he could out of this experience, studying composition and editing as he worked, and irritating his superiors by observing acting rehearsals instead of devoting himself solely to camerawork.

Shimazu took note of his young camera assistant's enthusiasm and skill and after three years had Kinoshita transferred to the directors' section as his assistant—a move that aroused the jealous wrath of all whom Kinoshita had bypassed in the rigid Shochiku hierarchy. Kinoshita worked for six years as assistant director to Shimazu and later to Kozaburo Yoshimura, learning most from the former. Shimazu was a tyrant, but he was also an extremely accomplished filmmaker with an intuitive approach greatly to Kinoshita's taste—he says it was from Shimazu that he learned to let his conception of a film grow "in fits and starts during the shooting process."

For Shochiku's assistant directors, the best hope of advancement was to write a script that would catch the attention of the company's president, Shiro Kido. Kinoshita churned out as many as two scripts a month with a feeling that he and Kido "were at war. As soon as one of my scripts was returned without comment I'd submit my next. I'd submit a tragedy, then a comedy, then a melodrama. It was to make the head of the studio remember the various talents I possessed." In spite of his energy and determination, a stint in the wartime Japanese army delayed Kinoshita's promotion, and it was not until 1943 that he directed his first film.

When at last he was given his chance, however, Shiro Kido was generous. Kinoshita was given a large budget, a starry cast, and sixty days' shooting time, including forty days on location at Amakusa. *Hana saku minato* (*The Blossoming Port*, 1943) is a comedy about two big-city crooks who embark on a large-scale confidence trick in a sleepy seaport town, planning to cheat the natives by pretending to revive the local shipyard. But one of them (Ken Uehara) falls in love with a local girl and in the end both are won over by the simple goodness of the people and by wartime patriotism, settling down in earnest to put the shipyard back into production.

Though Kinoshita had not been allowed to use one of his own scripts for his debut movie—his scenarist was Yoshiro Tsuji—*The Blossoming Port* has many of the characteristics that came to be associated with the director—a taste for beautiful locations, a faith in the basic goodness of ordinary human beings and in the redemptive power of love, and a talent for comedy. As Joseph L. Anderson and Donald Richie write in *The Japanese Film*, that nation's cinema has no lack of "slapstick, comedy of situation, comedy of manners," but "comedy of character is rare and satire is almost unheard of. And both would be even more rare were it not for the work of Keisuke Kinoshita," whom "the Japanese think of . . . in the same way that the French tend to think of René Clair."

The Blossoming Port came fourth in *Kinema Jumpo*'s annual poll of Japan's "Best Ten" films. It was followed by two wartime propaganda features—one promoting the need for increased food production and the other encouraging evacuation from the cities—and then by *Rikugun* (*Army*, 1944). The latter deals with three generations of a military family, and a father's fears that his son will fail to uphold family tradition and honor in the Pacific War. But the weakling child grows up strong and brave, and goes off to fight, a credit to his father and the Emperor.

Army has been attacked by Tadao Sato as a fascist and militaristic work—an accusation that could in fact be leveled at many of the movies made during the war under Ministry of Information regulations. But Audie Bock points out that the film's long last scene, graphically revealing the anguish of the young hero's mother as he marches away through a flag-waving mob, is hardly calculated to promote militarism. And indeed *Army* was condemned by the Ministry of Information on release as "antiwar," and on that account Kinoshita was considered unfit to direct a proposed propaganda movie about the Kamikaze suicide corps. Another script was rejected because it had nothing to do with the war effort, and after that Kinoshita settled back to await the coming of peace. "I can't lie to myself in my dramas," he said afterwards. "I couldn't direct anything that was like shaking hands and saying 'come die.'"

Kinoshita returned to the theme of *Army* with open bitterness in his first postwar film, which is also an invitation to female self-assertion in Japan's male-dominated society. *Osone-ke no asa* (*Morning for the Osone Family,* 1946), again set during the Pacific War, centers on a widow whose oldest son is jailed as a pacifist while his two younger brothers go off to die. By the time peace comes, the bereaved mother has come to understand the causes of Japan's tragedy and her own. She throws out her militaristic brother-in-law and welcomes home her pacifist son. Powerfully expressing a widespread feeling of disillusionment with the war, the picture came out at the top of *Kinema Jumpo*'s annual poll—the first of several Kinoshita movies so honored.

In spite of her enlightened and liberal sentiments, the mother in *Morning for the Osone Family* keeps her feelings to herself until it is too late and her sons are dead. Her progressive daughter is more outspoken, though her views are ignored by the villainous uncle. Audie Bock writes that "Kinoshita's women, the central figures in all of his tragedies, always know that war, political oppression, class distinctions and individual selfishness are evils. Their values always side with freedom of expression, love of family and, at the same time, romantic love, and overall honesty and straightforwardness. What they do in situations where their values are threatened is endure, sometimes in silence and suffering, sometimes protesting, but in extremity they choose death rather than forfeit the purity of their emotion and commitment."

After these polemics came a lyrical and haunting little love story, *Waga koi sashi otome* (*The Girl I Loved,* 1946), about a farm boy who adores but loses the orphan girl he grows up with. This movie, scripted by the director, was photographed like virtually all of his films by his brother-in-law Hiroshi Kusada. Kinoshita designs his own camera set-ups and says that he took Kusada on because he was willing to Do exactly as I wanted." *The Girl I Loved* is interwoven, in the Clair manner, with songs that comment on the action. These were the work of a new recruit to Kinoshita's team—his own brother Chuji, a music graduate who had found himself out of work at the war's end. Chuji Kinoshita has scored all of his brother's movies since then and has worked for other directors as well.

Under Shiro Kido, the Shochiku company at its Kamata studios had begun to specialize in the 1920s in *josei eiga* ("women's pictures"), inspired by a characteristic mixture of moral and commercial motives. "The old morality oppressed women," Kido said, "and in so doing gave rise to many dramatic situations. . . . Kamata movies try to cultivate obedience and gratitude on the part of the children toward mothers for their many sacrifices. We made women our allies and praised their virtues." After the war, when Shochiku moved to its new Ofuna studios, Kinoshita became the company's most prolific and accomplished purveyor of "women's pictures" with the warmly sentimental "Ofuna flavor." Early examples are *Kekkon* (*Marriage,* 1947), *Fushicho* (*Phoenix,* 1947), and *Onna* (*Woman,* 1948)—all minor pieces in praise of various womanly virtues. Kyoko Hirano writes that "*Marriage* and *Phoenix* surprised the audience with their bold and sophisticated expression of love, which pioneered the new social morality." *Shozo* (*The Portrait,* 1948), scripted by Kinoshita's friend Akira Kurosawa, has as its heroine a "kept woman" who is redeemed when a portrait is painted of her that brings out her natural goodness.

But Kinoshita is nothing if not versatile, and the other films he made during these early postwar years vary from *Hakai* (*Apostasy*, 1948), a somewhat sentimental adaptation of Toson's novel of social protest about the *eta*—a pariah caste resembling the Indian untouchables—to the delightful satirical comedy of *Ojosan kampai* (*A Toast to the Young Miss*, 1949), in which true love breaks down the barriers between *nouveaux riches* and impoverished aristocracy. *Yotsuya kaidan* (*The Yotsuya Ghost Story*, 1949) is rather stronger stuff—a two-part adaptation of a well-known Kabuki play about a scorned wife and the revenge taken by her ghost—while *Yabure-daiko* (*Broken Drum*, 1949) is a sharp and witty satirical attack on the rigidities of the Japanese family system, with a blustering authoritarian father finally defeated by his emancipated children. It was coscripted by Masaki Kobayashi, who was then Kinoshita's assistant and who even today, as a distinguished director in his own right, is an almost fanatical admirer of his mentor's art.

In 1951 Kinoshita scripted and directed one of his best-loved satirical comedies, *Karumen kokyo ni kaeru* (*Carmen Comes Home*), in which a good-hearted Tokyo stripper, Lily Carmen, and her friend Akemi visit the idyllic little country town where Carmen grew up. Innocently proud of her art, Carmen is bewildered to find herself scorned and shunned by all, until she and Akemi put on a benefit performance at the local school that winds up as a triumph of "art" over prejudice.

Shot mostly on location, *Carmen Comes Home* was Japan's first all-color feature, though the new Fuji color process was soon found to be unstable. (Fortunately, Kinoshita had with typical thoroughness shot the movie in black and white as well.) The dialogue is both funny and witty, and Hideko Takamine—usually cast in more serious roles—give extraordinary depth and charm to Carmen's character. She has starred in almost a dozen of Kinoshita's films and is one of the many artists and craftsmen who regard him with something close to reverence. Takamine speaks fondly of Kinoshita's "maternal" tenderness in dealing with actors, and has special reason to do so, since the director helped to arrange her marriage to his former assistant Zenzo Matsuyama.

Kinoshita spent part of 1951 in France, where he met his idol René Clair. He says that he went abroad because he "wanted to live for a while in a nice democratic country, a country where no matter how poor the people are they at least have heat in the winter; a country where no matter what kind of work a person does he at least gets a day off. . . . I really went to France so that I could see Japan better." Many believe that

he succeeded, producing in the years just after this sojourn abroad what Kobayashi calls his "most severe, most rigorous work."

There is some evidence of this new detachment even in *Karumen junjosu* (*Carmen's Pure Love*, 1952), in which we see the unshakeably romantic Tokyo stripper infatuated by a talentless playboy artist and drawn into his seedy circle. The movie is virtually a gallery of satirical portraits of postwar types, with tilted camera angles and eccentric camera movements expressing the moral and mental confusion of the era, when new ideas of social and sexual emancipation were in chaotic conflict with the old authoritarian and moralistic certainties.

This amiable satire was followed by what many regard as Kinoshita's masterpiece, *Nihon no higeki* (*A Japanese Tragedy*, 1953). When Kurosawa scripted *The Portrait* for Kinoshita, the latter promised to respond in kind and wrote *A Japanese Tragedy* for one of Kurosawa's former assistants at the Toho company. Kinoshita put a great deal of hard work and research into the script and was delighted when Toho rejected it as uncommercial. He promptly persuaded Shochiku to buy it back for his own use.

A Japanese Tragedy is a *haha-mono* ("mother film"), recognized as one of the finest examples of the genre. Yuko Mochizuki plays Haruko, an uneducated innocent whose husband had died in the war. To feed and educate her son and daughter, she had worked the black market and prostituted herself, as we learn through flashbacks. By now (1953) she is drudging as a maid at an Atami inn. Meanwhile her children, shaped by the hardships and lies of the war and the moral chaos of the American occupation, have grown up selfish, greedy, and obsessively materialistic. They no longer need Haruko and so they ruthlessly reject her. She throws herself under a train.

In content the film is an old-fashioned melodrama, but in form, as Audie Bock says, it "is one of the most modern of its time: a series of about twenty-one very fast-cut scenes showing the progress of the mood of the postwar reconstruction age precedes the title and credit sequences. These show montages of newspaper headlines on war crimes trials, the pardoned Emperor greeting the cameras, and jump through intertitles to the present-day political dissatisfaction and social unrest. . . . Before he focuses on his protagonists, Kinoshita uses an intertitle to warn—heavy kettle drums, bells, and cymbals on the soundtrack—that this story is an allegory about a problem that . . . could spread throughout Japanese soil. . . . Kinoshita's message explodes all over the screen through his montage and manipulation of time. He even worked out with Kusada how to get the contemporary dramatic footage to match the old newsreels. . . . The war was a case of insincerity [and] deceit, and the distortion of the meaning of democracy in the postwar era is just as impure, resulting in children who destroy their own parents."

Another work of unsparing social criticism followed in *Onna no sono* (*The Garden of Women*, 1954) about a private boarding school for girls ruled by a headmistress whose harshness is shown to be a product of tragedy in her own youth. She indulges her richer pupils but so persecutes a poor girl sent to the school to end an "undesirable" love affair that the girl commits suicide. A rebellion follows with which Kinoshita—almost always on the side of youth— is clearly in sympathy. But the director's reforming urge was fading—"the Japanese people did not take me seriously," he says, "and I decided it was useless to try to say anything meaningful to them."

And perhaps because of this, his next movie topped the *Kinema Jumpo* poll in 1954 (*Garden of Women* placed second) and became the most popular of all his films. This was *Nijushi no hitomi* (*Twenty-four Eyes*, 1954), which devotes nearly three hours to the career of a school teacher (Hideko Takamine) in a primitive Inland Sea village. During the years leading up to the war, we see the gradual erosion of freedom and individuality that turns the heroine's innocent first-graders into chauvinistic little robots until she resigns in impotent protest. All this is very perceptively and deftly handled, but Joan Mellen for one finds it hard to believe that the tough-minded and independent heroine would have managed no braver protest than resignation, and considers this a disservice to those who did have the courage to oppose the growth of Japanese militarism during the 1930s.

"As soon as . . . [she resigns]," Mellen writes, " . . . *Twenty-four Eyes* begins to degenerate into sentimentality. By the end, when the war is over and Miss Oishi attends a reunion with her seven surviving students (there were originally twelve, thus the 'twenty-four eyes' of the title), the director is wringing every last drop of feeling from his audience and the film becomes almost unwatchable. The characters cry, the audience cries, and the film finally loses all connection with the particularities of the thirties and forties in Japan to become a lamentation on all human suffering."

After this, Kinoshita seems increasingly to have embraced and defended the traditions and conventions he had once so sharply questioned, though his output continued as large and diverse as ever. "I loved Clair very much when I was young," the director says, "but Duvivier . . . I always wanted to be a director like Duvivier— he did everything." In fact, Kinoshita has also "done everything"—worked in every conceivable genre and in almost every cinematic style. He always tells his assistants that "after you've read the script, the biggest problem is not how you are going to direct individual scenes, but in what style are you going to make the entire film." That is the only kind of consistency that interests him, apart from that imposed by dedicated craftsmanship and his own personality and attitudes. Even within individual scenes, he likes to leave himself the maximum freedom for spontaneous invention. "In my direction," he says, "I'm always changing my ideas and set-ups at the last moment. I'm always getting sudden ideas on how to experiment with actors and action. I never rehearse in advance. . . . In every picture I try to do something that hasn't been done before."

One of Kinoshita's own favorites in *Nogiku no gotoki kimi nariki* (*You Were Like a Wild Chrysanthemum*, 1955), full of his "wonderful scenic long shots" of a beautiful mountain setting. An old man, revisiting his native town, remembers the cousin he loved as a youth but gave up at the insistence of his ambitious mother. He had achieved the material success demanded of him, but his cousin, submitting to an arranged marriage, had died in pregnancy without a word of protest. To convey the uncertainties of memory, the characters in the flashback sequences are masked—a characteristically daring device in what is otherwise "perhaps Kinoshita's most heartrendingly simple, sentimental film."

Yuyake-gumo (*Clouds at Twilight*, 1956) is a sensitive study of a dreamy boy forced to put his fantasies behind him and take over his father's shop when the family breaks up. It was scripted by Kinoshita's sister Yoshiko Kusada, wife of his cinematographer. With a score, as usual, by Chuji Kinoshita, this was even more a family affair than most of Kinoshita's movies. Since then, the director has written all his own scenarios except one. He maintains that all but the greatest scenarists are "very jealous of every word they've written. Trying to make corrections is too time-consuming and troublesome. My mind is always ahead of theirs by several steps anyway." Some critics believe that Kinoshita's sentimental later movies would have benefited from the stimulus of other creative minds.

There is nevertheless considerable wit and satirical bite in some of these films, even if true love does eventually conquer all with monotonous regularity. Notable among them are *Fuzen no tomoshibi* (*A Candle in the Wind*, 1957), about an avaricious suburban family whose beloved possessions prove equally attractive to a gang of semi-tough young thieves, and *Haru no yume* (*Spring Dreams*, 1960). The latter is a rather Capraesque comedy in which an upper-class family is thrown into disarray when an impoverished sweet-potato vendor has a stroke in their house and turns out to be the grandmother's first love.

There is grim tragedy as well as comedy in Kinoshita's later work. In *Narayamabushi-ko* (*The Ballad of Narayama*, 1958), set in the northern mountains during a time of famine, Orin (Kinuyo Tanaka), a spirited old woman, insists that her devoted son follow the savage local custom of leaving the old on the mountainside to die of exposure, so that more food can be given to the young. Bill Thompson points out that "although *The Ballad of Narayama* focuses on Orin's preparations and journey, Kinoshita clearly sympathizes with her simple son, whose heart disputes the deed," but whose respect for his mother and reverence for tradition force him to obey her, even in this.

The material is folkloric, and Kinoshita made innovative use of Kabuki stage techniques to frame the story. "A Kabuki narrator continually advances the film, which also incorporates spotlighting and curtains," Thompson writes. "All the shooting (except for the closing sequence) was done within the studio . . . the sets were a combination of Kabuki backdrops and natural elements. Kabuki is the most traditional of all Japanese theater forms, and at times *The Ballad of Narayama* takes on the veneer of filmed theater. Such techniques intentionally mute the harshness of the barbaric customs, occasionally inducing an atmosphere of fantasy. Shohei Imamura's 1983 remake of this film instead seeks to emphasize the cruelty of the customs, through a realistic atmosphere and a much stronger focus upon the frightful aspects of nature." Kinoshita wrote the words to the ballads that accompany the action, and had two authorities on Kabuki set them to appropriate music.

The Ballad of Narayama won virtually all of the 1958 film awards in Japan, including Kinoshita's third and final *Kinema Jumpo* "best one." In the West the response was mixed. Donald Richie has described *Narayama* as a "thoroughly conservative motion picture" that "failed to move audiences because the director was insisting upon naturalistic details in a theatrical and unnatural setting," but others have found the Kabuki framework both effective and resonant. Teiji Takahashi, who played Orin's son, received the best actor award at the Cork Film Festival.

Other distancing effects are used very successfully in *Fuefukigawa* (*The River Fuefuki*, 1960), Kinoshita's last important feature film. This is a stark antiwar chronicle of the sufferings over five generations of a poor farming family during the endless battles of the sixteenth century. It uses colors imitating those of early woodblock prints and other effects reminiscent of ancient picture-scrolls, and periodically freezes the action—for example of a battle scene—with an effect that reminded Donald Richie of the *kami-shibai*, "the old paper-slide theater which the boys and girls of Japan still love."

"The theme of the film would appear antitraditional," Richie writes. "The final scene, the true climax of this beautifully made and often compelling film, shows the last remaining member of the family picking up the banner of the ruling family, for which he and his ancestors have traditionally fought, as it floats by on the river, then, with a superb gesture of rejection, throwing it back into the river. What has also become apparent, however, is that Kinoshita is only rejecting the worst. The rest of traditional life he keeps and approves. . . . after all, the family is the most important thing."

The River Fuefuki finished fourth in the annual *Kinema Jumpo* poll. Two of Kinoshita's other works from the early 1960s were awarded "thirds." *Eien no hito* (*The Bitter Spirit*, 1961), which also received an Academy Award nomination, is set in rural Japan against the breathtaking scenery of Mount Aso. It is the story of a woman from a poor family forced to marry a man she hates. The action begins in the early 1930s, as Sadako (Hideko Takamine) awaits her lover Takashi's return from the Manchurian front. But Heibei (Tatsuya Nakadai), the son of a wealthy landowner, has decided he wants her for himself. When pressure against her family fails, he resorts to rape, and Sadako has no choice but to marry him. "Over the years," writes Audie Bock, "Sadako's hatred for Heibei never wanes, and when her daughter falls in love with Takashi's son, she helps them escape and marry without Heibei's knowledge. In their old age, Sadako and Heibei have spent their lives resenting each other, and it is Takashi, on his deathbed, who asks for Heibei's forgiveness."

Kobe (*The Scent of Incense*, 1964), the other third-place achiever, is a three-hour narrative of the geisha world. It relates the experiences of Tomoko (Mariko Okada) from age three, when her father dies, until her mother's death sixty years later. Sold into bondage as an apprentice geisha, Tomoko eventually becomes the toast of her district, then opens her own house to prepare for marriage. The great Kyoto earthquake and the war contribute to the ruin of her hopes, but more subtly devastating over the years is the conduct of her own mother, an exploitative and extravagant woman whom Tomoko deeply resents but always obeys.

Donald Richie uses *The Scent of Incense* to illustrate Kinoshita's fascination with time, drawing an analogy to Proust: "This chronicle film is—among other things—a detailed and deeply felt examination of the Japanese attitude toward the past. . . . It is assumed that any change is for the worse but, at the same time, there is the pleasure of understanding patterns and, hence, comprehending people. . . . Kinoshita's attitude quietly celebrates the changes which time makes because, after all, this is fit, and the reason for this is that the world is as it is. Thus, in Japan . . . time makes no monsters. Rather, it creates observers."

The Japanese film industry suffered a severe depression during the 1960s, and Kinoshita turned increasingly to television. Between 1964 and 1980 he produced (and often scripted and directed) three weekly series bearing his name. They were extremely popular, and he could "do whatever I want and a lot of it." Unfortunately, these programs have not been broadcast in the West.

During the decade following *The Scent of Incense*, Kinoshita made only one film, *Natsukashiki fue ya taiko* (*Eyes, the Sea, and a Ball*, 1967). This picture, Bill Thompson writes, "is set in Odeshima, a remote island in the Inland Sea. Because of its subject matter—teaching experiences with children in a far-away rural Inland Sea region—this film has been compared to Kinoshita's 1954 *24 Eyes*. But the focus differs in the protagonist's motivations for teaching there, as well as in the overall effect the instructor has on his pupils."

Since resuming his film career in 1976, Kinoshita has made five features. All have been extremely sentimental, four-hanky pictures, most containing social messages. *Sri Lanka no ai to wakare* (*Love and Separation in Sri Lanka*, 1976) is a cloyingly sweet love story whose plot is easily summarized by its title. *Shodo satsujin: Musukoyo* (*My Son*, 1979) centers on a factory owner whose son is killed by an underage *yakuza* who receives only a short prison sentence for his crime. The outraged father starts a campaign for tougher laws, tracking down and visiting families similarly victimized in the hope of uniting them to his cause. *Chichi yo haha yo* (*Parents, Awake!*, 1980) intertwines several stories about maladjusted teenagers and their families. For Audie Bock, "Kinoshita's message is clear: the selfishness of today's parents has brought about the unhappiness of today's children."

Konoko o nokoshite (*Children of Nagasaki*, 1983) recreates the life of Takashi Nagai, a young doctor who, thanks to an overdose of x-rays, was already ill with leukemia when the atom bomb was dropped. Nevertheless, he survived the blast (although his wife did not) and dedicated the remainder of his life to the treatment of other radiation victims. As his health deteriorated, he wrote several autobiographical novels to provide for his children after his death—works which became very popular, so that a generation of Japanese grew up reading Nagai's appeals for "absolutely no war." Like the novels, the film combines harrowing history with sentimentality and melodrama. It received special encomiums from Pope John Paul II and the official blessing of the Japanese Ministry of Education but did not greatly impress the critics: John Gillett, assessing Kinoshita's career, wrote that "in recent years, he has made a tentative return to the cinema, but it seems likely that his most memorable work will remain the sweetly scented romances and dramas of the '50s and '60s."

Earlier in his career Kinoshita had made the upbeat *Yorokobi mo kanashimi mo ikutoshitsuki* (*Times of Joy and Sorrow*, 1957), one of his personal favorites. Spanning a twenty-year period, it recounted the experiences of a couple and their family operating lighthouses in various parts of Japan. "The end assumption," Donald Richie wrote, "is that staying in relatively uncomfortable living quarters and doing their duty has paid off in all the joys and sorrows that they are, at the end of the film, able to remember." *Shin yorokobimo kanashimimo ikutoshitsuki* (*Big Joys, Small Sorrows*, 1986), Kinoshita's most recent film to date, is a very similar story about a lighthouse keeper, his family, and the grandfather who occasionally visits them as they move all over the country. According to Edna Fainaru, Kinoshita "considers this a sequel, rather than a remake, a further elaboration on the life of a lighthouse guardian first explored in the earlier picture, which is referred to lovingly in one of the early scenes. . . . This picture seems to sum up the director's world and his cinematic scope, insofar as it deals with subjects which have been close to his heart. . . . A feeling prevails that the film is the veteran director's tribute to his own country, and to an entire plethora of characters who have been parading through his films, in one disguise or another, for the last forty years."

Audie Bock places Kinoshita "among the postwar masters of the Japanese cinema," whose "devotion to a sentimental ideal of purity and beauty is precisely what lends his films their characteristic flavor. In his finest endeavors he succeeds in creating a nostalgia for these values that is next to excruciating. For the Japanese, who have revered simplicity, honesty, purity, devotion, and especially straightforwardness since the days of the samurai, the infallible attraction of the Kinoshita film has lain in seeing heroes who appear to be ordinary people like themselves, but are actually as pure, innocent and good as they would like to be." For Joseph L. Anderson and Donald Richie, his films are characterized "by a dedicated craftsmanship which is hard to find in any country and extremely rare in Japan. Whether satiric comedy or lyrical tragedy, the Kinoshita film is a unique experience, perhaps because it is so very personal, because it is so deeply felt."

The "small and gentlemanly" director, who is unmarried, is an odd mixture of arrogance and humility. The actress Hideko Takamine remembers him drawing attention to particularly skillful shots by saying, "See what a good director I am?"; but on another occasion he reflected sadly that "everything I've done has been somehow half-baked." Tenderly "maternal" as he was with his actors, he is said to have been demanding and possessive with his assistants and technical crew, though less of a martinet than his own mentor Shimazu. He was an excellent and careful teacher, whose unit at Shochiku was known as "Kinoshita's classroom."

FILMS: Hana saku minato (The Blossoming Port/Port of Flowers), 1943; Ikite iru magoroku (The Living Magoroku), 1943; Kanko no machi (Jubilation Street), 1944; Rikugun (Army), 1944; Osone-ke no asa (Morning for the Osone Family), 1946; Waga koi seshi otome (The Girl I Loved), 1946; Kekkon (Marriage), 1947; Fushicho (Phoenix), 1947; Onna (Woman), 1948; Shozo (The Portrait), 1948; Hakai (Apostasy), 1948; Ojo-san kampai (A Toast to the Young Miss/Here's to the Girls), 1949; Yotsuya kaidan, I–II (The Yotsuya Ghost Story, Parts I and II), 1949; Yabure-daiko (Broken Drum), 1949; Konyaku yubiwa (Engagement Ring), 1950; Zemma (The Good Fairy), 1951; Karumen kokyo ni kaeru (Carmen Comes Home), 1951; Shonenki (A Record of Youth), 1951; Umi no hanabi (Fireworks Over the Sea), 1951; Karumen junjosu (Carmen's Pure Love), 1952; Nihon no higeki (A Japanese Tragedy), 1953; Onna no sono (The Garden of Women), 1954; Nijushi no hitomi (Twenty-four Eyes), 1954; Toi kumo (Distant Clouds), 1955; Nogiku no gotoki kimi nariki (You Were Like a Wild Chrysanthemum/She Was Like a Wild Chrysanthemum), 1955; Yuyake-gumo (Clouds at Twilight), 1956; Taiyo to bara (The Rose on His Arm), 1956; Yorokobi mo kanashima mo ikutoshitsuki (Times of Joy and Sorrow/The Lighthouse), 1957; Fuzen no tomoshibi (A Candle in the Wind/Danger Stalks Near), 1957; Narayamabushi-ko (The Ballad of Narayama), 1958; Kono ten no niji (The Eternal Rainbow), 1958; Kazabana (Snow Flurry), 1959; Sekishuncho (The Bird of Springs Past), 1959; Kyo mo mata kakute ari nan (Thus Another Day), 1959; Haru no yume (Spring Dreams),

1960; Fuefukigawa (The River Fuefuki), 1960; Eien no hito (The Bitter Spirit/Immortal Love), 1961; Kotoshi no koi (This Year's Love), 1962; Futari de aruita iku shunju (The Seasons We Walked Together/Ballad of a Young Workman), 1962; Utae wakodo-tachi (Sing, Young People), 1963; Shito no densetsu (Legend of a Duel to the Death/A Legend, Or Was It?), 1963; Koge (The Scent of Incense), 1964; Natsukashiki fue ya taiko (Lovely Flute and Drum/Eyes, the Sea, and a Ball), 1967; Sri Lanka no ai to wakare (Love and Separation in Sri Lanka), 1976; Shodo satsujin: Musukoyo (My Son/The Impulse Murder of My Son), 1979; Chichi yo haha yo (Parents, Awake!), 1980; Konoko o nokoshite (Children of Nagasaki/Leaving These Children Behind), 1983; Shin yorokobi mo kanashimi mo ikutoshitsuki (Big Joys, Small Sorrows/The Lighthouse Keeper's Family), 1986.

ABOUT: Anderson, J. L. and Richie, D. The Japanese Film, 1959; Bock, A. Japanese Film Directors, 1978; Hirano, K. in Lyon, C. (ed.) International Dictionary of Films and Filmmakers, 1984; MacDonald, K. Cinema East, 1983; Mellen, J. The Waves at Genji's Door, 1976; Richie, D. Japanese Cinema, 1971; Sato, T. Currents in Japanese Cinema, 1982.

*KINUGASA, TEINOSUKE (January 1, 1896–February 26, 1982), Japanese director, scriptwriter, actor, and producer, was born Teinosuke Kogame in Mie Prefecture and attended the Sasayama Private School in Kyoto. As a child he worked in his father's rural tobacco business, "rolling cigars and assisting in the processing of *kizami* tobacco." It was his mother who introduced him to the theater, so that among his earliest memories were a *Yosei* comedy theater near their home and the touring Kabuki companies. At seventeen he ran away from home to begin his apprenticeship to a stage career in Nagoya, making his acting debut two years later. As was common for actors at that time, he performed both on stage and in films, joining the Nikkatsu Mukojima Studio in 1917 while still acting with the Kadoza theatre's *shimpa* company.

Kinugasa was an *oyama,* the male actor who in Japanese theatre and early films played the female role. His first screen part was in *Nanairo yubi wa (The Seven-Colored Ring)* directed by Chu Oguchi, and he played the heroine in Eizo Tanaka's *Ikeru shikabane (The Living Corpse)*, adapted from Tolstoy, which in 1917 began Nikkatsu's introduction of foreign techniques of expression into the Japanese film. Kinugasa's own early films were influenced by the Americans in their portrayal of emotion. In 1921 he wrote, under a pseudonym, and directed his first film, *Imoto no shi (The Death of My Sister)*, also playing the sister. This commercial success was a

°kē nōō gä sä

TEINOSUKE KINUGASA

melodrama about a girl who is raped by her brother's best friend and commits suicide by throwing herself under a train.

In 1922 he made *Niwa no kotori (Two Little Birds)* and *Hibana (Spark)*. According to Kinugasa's own cryptic account, the first had the same theme as *The Death of My Sister,* but with a change of characters from humans to birds. The second marks a step away from the theatre in his career. Before making this film he had been invited to take part in a show combining projected film with scenes played by actors. This was a popular kind of performance in which Kinugasa had often appeared as an *oyama*. He was dissuaded by Shozo Makino, a managing director at Nikkatsu, who thought a return to this old-fashioned form of entertainment by the already well-known Kinugasa would be bad for the studio's image. In working on *Hibana*, Kinugasa adapted the story from a famous serial novel, directed the filming, and played the juvenile lead—the daughter of a factory owner. Her worker lover was played by Tomu Uchida, who was himself later to become a director of *shomin geki*, realistic dramas, such as the semi-documentary *Tsuchi (Earth)*. In later years both men recalled with amusement this first encounter, when Kinugasa would issue his orders as director using his female acting voice.

In 1925 he made *Tsukigata Hanpeita (Hanpeita, Master Swordsman)*, an early example of *shomin geki*, and *Nichirin (The Sun)*, a mythological story about the origin of the Japanese imperial family that caused a stir at the time and was later suppressed for its right-wing sentiment. He made this and *Tenichibo to Iganosuke*

(Tenichibo and Iganosuke), another mythological subject, with Kabuki actors in the space of twenty-five days. He cut short the shooting of *Tenichibo* (without a scenario) to work on *Nichirin,* only returning to edit and devise titles for *Tenichibo* after the trouble with *Nichirin* had blown over. In an interview much later Kinugasa used these two films as examples of his working method—his belief in the desirability of improvisation and in the crucial importance of editing. "Creation only begins once the film is printed," he said, and he continued to hold that view, although he felt that improvisation as used in these films had ceased to be possible after the coming of sound.

Another practice that became a life-long habit was writing his own scripts, for which he gave three reasons. First, in the silent era it was usual to work that way, shooting the film from very summary notes. Second, he loved and was influenced by the films of Rupert Julian, who made the Lon Chaney *Phantom of the Opera* (1925), and who also combined directing and acting with writing scripts. A third reason was that he had already begun to write stage plays. The first of these, written when he was twenty-one, was based on a real-life incident involving a blind masseur who, after a fight with his wife, lay down on the railroad tracks to die, unaware that the train had already passed.

The 1920s were Kinugasa's most vigorously productive period. He worked mainly for the expanding Shochiku Company, achieving both critical acclaim and commercial success with romantic narratives based on popular historical fiction, and starring the current matinee idol, Kazuo Hasegawa. Robert Cohen, writing in *Sight and Sound* (Summer 1976), attributes to this association of actor and director the rise of Kinugasa to a reputation before World War II equal to those of Mizoguchi, Ozu, and Yamamoto, and to a position "as the preeminent creator of mood and romantic taste." Kinugasa was also politically active during this period, aligning himself with the new unions of actors and technicians and leading the famous strike at the Nikkatsu Studios in 1922 protesting the replacement of the traditional *oyama* in films by female players. (Paradoxically, he had always seen this change as inevitable and had himself used female players in some of his films.)

In the early 1920s, Kinugasa had become involved with Shinkankaku-Ha (the "neo-sensationalist" movement) led by Yasunari Kawabata and other contributors to the magazine *Bungei Jidai (The Age of Letters)*, who experimented with such western innovations as cubism, dadaism, futurism, surrealism, and the stream of consciousness. From his association with this group came his two most important films, *Kurutta ippeiji (A Page of Madness/A Crazy Page*, 1926), and *Jujiro* (1928). Hubert Niogret and others maintan that these films are a major landmark in the history not only of the Japanese cinema but of the medium as a whole.

Yasunari Kawabata is usually credited as scenarist or coscenarist of *A Page of Madness*, but there was apparently no script as such, and his initial idea was much modified in the filming, even the setting being changed from a circus to an insane asylum. The cinematographer was Kohei Sugiyama, thereafter Kinugasa's regular collaborator, and the film was made very cheaply over a period of a month—unheard of at a time when most movies were churned out in a week or less. The actors helped to paint sets and make props and slept in the studio—lent by Shochiku—the walls of which were painted silver to eke out the shortage of lighting. This was the source of the "unearthly luminosity" that suffuses some of the images.

The story concerns a retired seaman (played by the well-known actor Masao Inoue) working as an odd-job man in the asylum where his wife (Yoshie Nakagawa) is an inmate. Their daughter comes to visit them but is unable to communicate with either parent. The father recalls the family's happier early life together and the tragedy that led to his wife's commitment to the asylum. She had tried to drown herself and their infant son, and though she had been saved by their daughter, the baby had died. The old seaman steals a key and tries to free his wife, but she does not know him and refuses to leave the asylum, where a riot ensues. The old man settles back to his dreary duties, evidently intending to live out his life watching over the stranger who was once his wife.

It is Kinugasa's treatment of this material that makes the film remarkable, shifting in a dreamlike continuity between present and past, reality and hallucination. "Again and again," wrote Nora Sayre, "faces are seen through real or imaginary bars, while water—gushing through gutters or splashing in a sink—recalls the drowning of a baby. When a crazed young woman dances wildly alone in her cell, we see the drums that she thinks she hears." John Gillett was equally impressed by "the richness of Kinugasa's invention: a tracking camera moves down a corridor into a struggling melée of patients and doctors and then retreats back through the heaving bodies; the wife gazes moodily at a tree in the garden, which suddenly contracts as though in a fairground mirror; a girl dancing in her cell turns into an obscene blob as the crazy men ogle

her. . . . The film culminates in several hallucinatory sequences built up from layers of superimpositions in which we seem to be inside the minds of the patients . . . as the real world dissolves around them into anguish and unreason. . . . The whole *mise en scène*, as well as the mature acting style, suggests a phenomenal sophistication for the time."

This 60-minute film was designed to be presented without a *benshi* (a professional narrator) and without titles. Kinugasa wanted the audience to respond directly to his images, which he said were assembled in a way analogous to musical composition. Most critics have assumed that the film's rational sequences represented the husband's view of events, its irrationalities the distorted perceptions of inmates, as in Wiene's *Caligari* (1919). However, Anderson and Richie, in *The Japanese Movie*, contend that Kinugasa's method is not expressionist but impressionist—"concerned with the impression the creator himself felt when first confronted with his material. He picks and chooses scenes, the sum total of which is the impression of the emotion itself." This argument continues, but it is generally agreed that "on a psychological level the compassion and sympathy of Kinugasa's vision of the insane is very advanced," including "realistic portraits of catatonic schizophrenic withdrawal" (Toronto Film Society).

But the richness of the film's texture escapes purely psychological readings. The succession of images, as Noël Burch's detailed analysis has shown, subverts the understanding of montage then current in either Japan or the West, prefiguring the structures of "such advanced Soviet films as *The General Line, Earth,* or *The Man With a Movie Camera,*" all made three or four years later. A few avant-garde films from the West were shown in Japan in the 1920s, among them *Caligari* and Gance's *La Roue,* but, although many critics assume that Kinugasa must have learned from such films, he himself insisted that he had seen none of them before he made *A Page of Madness.*

The film was directed and produced by Kinugasa for the Shinkankaku-Ha Eiga Renmei (Neo-Sensationalist Film Federation), which subsequently developed into the Kinugasa Eiga Renmei (Kinugasa Film Federation). It was distributed by Shochiku through theaters that usually showed only imported films, but even so managed to make money, although it was received with hostility by most critics and seems to have had little or no influence on other Japanese filmmakers. It was later lost until, in 1971, Kinugasa accidentally discovered a copy in his garden storeroom. A sound track was added—

mostly music, with a few sound effects—and the film was received with acclaim in Europe and the United States. Tony Rayns wrote that it shows "a pioneering cinematic mind at work exploring and expanding the medium at high intensity." Charles Silver considered that "it ranks with the best of Murnau, Eisenstein, and Gance, and beyond its formal significance, it has an affecting quality which many of their films do not."

After *A Page of Madness,* Kinugasa went back to work for Shochiku, turning out nearly a score of conventional movies over the next two years before he could afford his second and last major independent experiment, *Jujiro (Crossways/Crossroads,* 1928). Produced for Kinugasa Eiga Renmei in association with Shochiku and scripted by the director, it was, as usual, shot by Kohei Sugiyama.

Jujiro is a *jidai-geki* (period drama) set in the Yoshiwara, the brothel quarter of eighteenth-century Tokyo. Rikiya, a young rake madly in love with the geisha O-ume, believes that he has killed his rival in an archery duel. Himself blinded, he takes refuge with his adoring sister Okiku, a virtuous dressmaker. Seeking help for him, Okiku is forced to submit to the advances of a bogus official, whom she eventually kills in self-defense, herself becoming a fugitive. Rikiya's sight returns and he in his turn now hides and protects his sister until, seeing his rival still alive and enjoying the favors of O-ume, he dies of shock.

As Anderson and Richie point out, Kinugasa's "basic unit for manipulation" in *Jujiro* "was the short, simple shot containing one small detail of motion. Just as he endeavoured in his story structure to anatomise pain, so too he tried to break down every action, however inherently complex, into each of its basic components. Instead of showing a full person, Kinugasa would often dissect him, using what the Soviets were calling 'analytical montage,' showing only such details as eyes, hands or bits of clothing." A memorable example is a huge close-up of the villain's gaping mouth and rotting teeth.

As in *A Page of Madness,* Kinugasa reportedly dispensed with intertitles, those in contemporary prints presumably having been added later. Again there are hallucinatory sequences, as when the wounded hero's room, in his pain and delirium, becomes a field full of jars containing boiling water that scalds him when he tries to quench his thirst. Disordered nonsequential flashbacks reveal the reasons for the duel and the myriad confused memories that flood his mind. But though *Jujiro* uses many of the same avant-garde devices as *A Page of Madness,* the experimentation is less radical and is presented as an expression of delirium: the film is altogether more accessible than its predecessor, if less startling and extreme.

Again critics suggested the influence of foreign film styles—of Soviet films in the editing, German expressionism in Bonji Taira's extraordinary decor. And again Kinugasa denied familiarity with such models, attributing his stark sets, painted dark gray, and low-key lighting partly to economic necessity, partly to his own state of depression at that time. He said *Jujiro* was "a film based on the *sumi-e"*—monochrome Japanese painting in ink. It has been described as "one of the masterpieces of Japanese cinema" and "one of the first major Japanese classics."

In the same year, 1928, Kinugasa set off for Russia and the West. Perhaps it is an indication of his limited knowledge of European cinema and genuine isolation from its influence that he chose to show only *Jujiro* on this tour, believing it would have more success than *A Page of Madness.* In fact he showed neither film in Russia, having despatched *Jujiro* to Hamburg before leaving Japan. As well as seeing films in the country that he believed held the future of cinema, Kinugasa met Eisenstein and had several conversations with him through interpreters. They discussed Eisenstein's manifesto on sound, and Kinugasa recalled their seeing together a visiting Kabuki production of *Chushingura (The Forty-Seven Ronin),* during which Eisenstein clapped him excitedly on the back and, pointing to the stage, exclaimed, "That is cinema!" Eisenstein gave him some stills from *October,* a film that had particularly impressed Kinugasa with what he described as the simultaneous simplicity and complexity of its shooting.

Kinugasa went on in 1929 to Germany and France, where *Jujiro,* under the title *Shadows of the Yoshiwara,* was a critical success but not a financial one. By the end of the year he had run out of money and returned to Japan to continue his work for Shochiku. Kinugasa Eiga Renmei produced no more films. For the rest of his career he was a successful director and writer of *jidai-geki,* earning a reputation, according to Douglas McVay, as "the pre-war founder of the spectacular period drama."

The leftist tendency implicit in his admiration for the Soviet cinema is evident in the first film made after his return. *Reimei izen (Before Dawn,* 1931) is a period story about a revolt among women sold into prostitution. There followed in 1932 the first period sound film, *Ikinokata Shinsengumi (The Surviving Shinsengumi),* and one of the most celebrated versions (now lost) of *Chushingura.* The great commercial success of *Koina no Gimpei* (*Gimpei From Koina*, 1933) enabled Kinugasa's star actor, Hasegawa, to begin a new career in talkies. The transition from silent stardom had been difficult at first owing to the actor's accent. The company now looked for a big film for him and chose *Yukinojo henge* (*The Revenge of Yukinojo*), based on a popular serial novel by Otokichi Mikami, and originally comprising three full-length features.

Yukinojo is a famous actor of female roles on the Kabuki stage who plots an intricate revenge on those responsible for the suffering and death of his parents. The action takes place both on and offstage, with Hasegawa's double role as man and female impersonator further complicated by his playing also a third character, a friendly thief. Kinugasa exploits these patterns wtih panache, creating an interplay between the artifice of the Kabuki stage and the psychological realism offstage, linked by Yukinojo's maintaining his female persona, as was the custom, in both worlds. The opening scene introduces us to the method and style. Yukinojo stands below the trapdoor awaiting his cue to appear on stage. The drum announcing his entrance calls up a vision of his mother superimposed on the backstage machinery, and further superimpositions and abstract visual patterns highlight the unfolding action. John Gillett thought that the film's best sections were "those concerned with the theatre and its physical atmosphere," praising Kinugasa's "very mobile camera and . . . exciting use of crowds."

Released in 1935–1936, the trilogy became one of the biggest box-office hits in Japanese cinema. It was reissued in 1952 as a single 100-minute feature, the resulting narrative incoherencies being reduced but not eradicated by the use of a narrator to bind together the "bleeding chunks." Interviewed in 1973, Kinugasa remarked pointedly that this was a film designed to please the public, unlike Ichikawa's brilliant version of the same story, made thirty years later in color and scope, with Hasegawa again in the lead and with a script again written in part by Kinugasa.

In 1939 Kinugasa moved from Shochiku to the Toho Company, accompanied by his leading man. In 1940 came *Hebi himesama* (*The Snake Princess*), another popular drama using a partly theatrical setting. Its merchant hero—an oriental Scaramouche—joins a troupe of traveling actors to conceal his identity in a struggle with corrupt enemies. *Kawanakajima kassen* (*The Battle of Kawanakajima*, 1941) exemplifies, according to Tadao Sato, a new current in the period drama, characterized by a strict adherence to historical accuracy, including details of medieval warfare. While not directly celebrating militarism, it is still an assertion of the principle of ideal chivalry and allegiance in the face of death, conveying a sense of the Japanese people as "a fated common body."

Aru yo no tonosama (*Lord for a Night*) in 1946 was a departure for the director, a high comedy romp mocking the feudal attitudes still rampant in contemporary Japanese society, but set in the Meiji period to avoid censorship. A musician is persuaded to impersonate a lord for the amusement of some businessmen on vacation. But he continues in the role so successfully as to win acceptance by a real aristocrat. The film, which also involves a melancholy romantic love story, has been seen as a contribution to the postwar "democratization" of Japan.

In 1947 Kinugasa made *Joyu* (*Actress*), which he described as a sort of moral essay on the profession. But his own beginnings in the theatre give a more personal interest to this biography of Sumako Matsui, the first great modern Japanese actress. Matsui and her director, Hogetsu Shimamura, were pioneers of realistic drama, introducing Ibsen and Tolstoy to Japanese audiences at a time when Kinugasa's own career was just beginning. Matsui was a controversial figure, on stage and off. Her love affair with the married Shimamura was an open secret, and her suicide following his death in 1918 has been interpreted as a public gesture of devotion. Kinugasa's theme therefore is the complex interplay between real life and theatrical art, and the conflict in both realms between tradition and the forces of change.

The first part of the film follows the creation of the revolutionary Art Theatre, and Matsui's pursuit of liberated personal fulfillment. The tragic conclusion is seen in relation to her last performance, in an avant-garde production in which her deathbed scene is intercut with her lover's actual death at home. Her own death is presented indirectly in a backstage scene—a friend discovers her body off-camera. A certain piquancy was contributed by Kinugasa's use of distinguished professionals from both film and theatre. His Shimamura was played by Yoshi Hijikata, a real and influential stage director, while the lead was taken by Isuzu Yamada, to whom Kinugasa himself was at one time married—one of her six husbands.

Robert Cohen praised the "remarkable Cocteauesque images" in the final play-within-the-film, and the "wonderful scene" in the dressing room, where the actors rehearse their lines as they apply their makeup, the camera cutting from one to another as they speak: "This visual badinage, one moment an actor as himself, the next another in character, reflected in the mirrors or shot directly, is a perfect metaphor not only for the central theme, but for Kinugasa's career itself: one moment a leader of the avant garde and the next master of the action epic."

In 1949 Kinugasa left Toho for the Daiei Company, where he spent the remainder of his career, though he also joined in 1950 the left-wing Shinsei Motion Picture Productions, a short-lived venture founded by the critic Akira Iwasaki. The films of this last period, despite beautiful and telling passages, are mainly undistinguished. *Daibutsu kaigen (The Dedication of the Great Buddha,* 1952) was a drama about the making of the gigantic copper Buddha at the Todaiji Temple in Nara, begun in 745 A.D. Though much less sophisticated, it has interesting resemblances to Andrei Tarkovsky's *Andrei Rublev* (1966). It was shown successfully in the Soviet Union and Europe but was a disappointment to its director, whose intentions for the film were frustrated by a shortage of money.

In 1953 he made *Jigokumon (Gate of Hell),* which reintroduced the director to western audiences at the start of a new era in the appreciation of Japanese cinema, launched in 1950 by Kurosawa's *Rashomon.* Although Japanese critics were unimpressed, *Gate of Hell* won the Grand Prix at the Seventh International Festival at Cannes in 1954 and the Oscar for Best Foreign Film in the same year. It was shot in Eastmancolor by Kohei Sugiyama, Kinugasa's constant collaborator since the days of *Page of Madness,* and was hailed by many critics as one of the most beautiful color films ever made.

The ancient story, well-known to Japanese audiences, tells of the samurai Moritoh (Kazuo Hasegawa), avid for the love of Kesa (Machiko Kyo), a woman whose life he has saved. He plots to murder her virtuous husband, but Kesa tricks him into killing her instead. Kinugasa contrasts images of vigorous action and ominous darkness with others of rich costume, moonlight, and diaphanous draperies to show a feudal aristocracy in a turbulent time. The layered compositions of color and moving figures deliberately copy Japanese paintings. Working without a true scenario, with the narrative in his head, Kinugasa used color to express the emotions of the three characters, especially in the final scenes, which take up a disproportionate amount of film time. This slowing of pace he himself attributed to the demands of the producers, who required a film of a certain length. Kinugasa found himself working to a deadline and having to extend the film by slowing the action. He confessed to unhappy memories of the production, even saying that the color composition was not as he had wished.

The Story of a River Downtown (1955), *Duel of a Snowy Night* (1954), and *Priest and Empress* (1963) have all been praised for their atmospheric images. *White Heron* (1958) makes interesting use of the split screen; Marcel Martin though it a banal story that nevertheless achieves real grandeur thanks to Kinugasa's mastery of color and composition. The director joined Daiei's board of directors in 1958 and the same year was awarded a Purple Ribbon Medal by the Japanese government for his services to the cinema and Japanese culture. His last film was *Chiisai tobosha (The Little Runaway,* 1967), a Soviet-Japanese coproduction codirected by Eduard Bocharov.

Kinugasa's career presents something of a paradox. It spans a large part of the history of the cinema in Japan, and for most of it he was creating commercial features exactly suited to the tastes of his public and backers. That prolific and successful career makes him a major figure in the Japanese industry. But on the other hand he was the first of the really independent creative artists to emerge in that industry, and his greatest film, *Page of Madness,* places him among the most original innovators of the cinema in any country. That film seems to be a largely intuitive response to "a cultural encounter, in a particularly sophisticated mind" between the cinematic codes of Japan and the West (Noël Burch).

After that all-too-brief achievement of a "purely cinematographic" expression, Kinugasa became in the main what has been described as "an academic master in a mildly traditional vein." It is noticeable that even the experimental *Page* and *Crossways* support traditional ideals of the family and personal happiness and justice, although Japanese audiences did not always understand these films in that way when they were first shown. Kinugasa's own view was of an inevitable conflict between his true cinema and the commercial one, in which (unhappily) the commercial dominated. In an interview in 1972 he wryly commented, "My work has consisted mainly in finding ways of making actresses laugh or cry, of finding artistic circumstances in which to have people die." He himself died ten years after that interview, at the age of eighty-six.

—D.W.

FILMS: Imoto no shi (The Death of My Sister), 1921; Niwa no kotori (Two Little Birds), 1922; Hibana (Spark), 1922; Hanasaka jijii (Happy Old Man), 1923; Jinsei o mitsumete (Ways of Life), 1923; Onna-yo aya-maru nakare (Lady, Be Not Wronged), 1923; Konjiki yasha (The Golden Demon), 1923; Ma no ike (The Spirit of the Pond), 1923; Choraku no kanata (Beyond Decay), 1923; Kanojo to unmei I-II (She Has Lived

Her Destiny), 1924; Tsuma no himitsu (Secret of a Wife), 1924; Koi (Love), 1924; Kiri no ame (Fog and Rain), 1924; Sabishiki mura (Lonely Village), 1924; Kishin Yuri Keiji (Detective Yuri), 1924; Kyoren no buto (Dance Training), 1924; Koi towa narinu (Thus It Turned Love), 1924; Shohin—Shuto (The Theft), 1924; Shohin—Shusoku (The Foot), 1924; Jasumon no onna (A Woman's Heresy), 1924; Koi to bushi (Love and a Warrior), 1925; Shinju yoimachigusa (Double Suicide), 1925; Tsukigata Hanpeita (Hanpeita, Master Swordsman), 1925; Wakaki hi no Chuji (Chuji's Early Days), 1925; Nichirin (The Sun), 1925; Tenichibo to Iganosuke (Tenichibo and Iganosuke), 1926; Kurutta ippeiji (A Page of Madness/A Crazy Page), 1926; Kirinji, 1926; Teru hi kumoru hi (Shining Sun Becomes Clouded), a trilogy, 1926; Hikuidori (Cassowary), 1927; Ojo Kichiza, 1927; Oni azami (The Horse Thistle), 1927; Kinno jidai (Epoch of Loyalty), 1927; Meoto boshi (A Star of Married Couples), 1927; Goyosen (The Government Vessel), 1927; Dochu sugoroku bune (The Ship), 1927; Dochu sugoroku kago (The Palanquin), 1927; Akatsuki no yushi (A Brave Soldier at Dawn), 1927; Gekka no kyojin (Moonlight Madness), 1927; Benten kozo (Gay Masquerade), 1928; Keiraku hicho (The Secret Documents), 1928; Kaikoku-ki (Tales From a Country by the Sea), 1928; Choken yasha (Female Demon), 1928; Jujiro (Crossways/Crossroads/Shadows of the Yoshiwara), 1928; Reimei izen (Before Dawn), 1931; Tojin Okichi (Okichi, the Mistress), 1931; Ikinokata Shinsengumi (The Surviving Shinsengumi), 1932; Chushingura (The Loyal Forty-Seven Ronin), 1932; Tenichibo to Iganosuke (Tenichibo and Iganosuke), 1933; Futatsu doro (Two Stone Lanterns), 1933; Koina no Gimpei (Gimpei From Koina), 1933; Kutsukate tokijiro, 1934; Fuyuki shinju (The Double Suicide in Winter), 1934; Ippon gatana dohyoiri (A Sword and the Sumo Ring), 1934; Nagurareta Kochiyama (The Beaten Kochiyama), 1934; Kurayami no Ushimatsu (Ushimatsu in the Darkness), 1935; Yukinojo henge I-II (The Revenge of Yukinojo/Yukinojo's Disguise), 1935; Yukinojo henge III, 1936; Osaka natsu no jiu (The Summer Battle at Osaka), 1937; Hito hada Kannon I-V (The Sacred Protector), 1937; Kuroda seichuroku (Loyalism at Kuroda), 1938; Hebi himesama I-II (The Snake Princess), 1940; Kawanakajima kassen (The Battle of Kawanakajima), 1941; Susume dokuritsuki (Forward, Flag of Independence!), 1943; Umi no bara (Rose of the Sea), 1945; Aru yo no tonosama (Lord for a Night), 1946; Koi no sakasu (The Love Circus/Circus of Love), episode in Yottsu no koi no monogatori (The Story of Four Loves/Four Love Stories), 1947; Joyu (Actress), 1947; Kobanzame I-II, 1949; Koga yashiki (Koga Mansion), 1949; Satsujinsha no kao (The Face of a Murderer), 1950; Beni komori (The Scarlet Bat), 1951; Tsuki no wataridori (Migratory Birds Under the Moon), 1951; Meigatsu somato (Lantern Under a Full Moon), 1951; Shurajo hibun I-II (The Castle of Carnage), 1952; Daibutsu kaigen (The Dedication of the Great Buddha/Saga of the Great Buddha), 1952; Jigokumon (Gate of Hell), 1953; Yuki no yo no ketto (Duel of a Snowy Night), 1954; Hana no nagadosu (End of a Prolonged Journey), 1954; Tekka bugyo (The Great Administrator), 1954; Kawa no aru shitamachi no hanashi (The Story of a River Downtown/It Happened in Tokyo), 1955; Bara ikuta-bi (A Girl Isn't Allowed to Love), 1955; Yushima no shiraume (The Romance of Yushima/White Sea of Yushima), 1955; Yoshinaka o meguru sannin no onna (Three Women Around Yoshinaka), 1956; Hibana (Spark), 1956; Tsukigata Hanpeita I-II, 1956; Ukifune (Floating Vessel), 1957; Naruto hicho (A Fantastic Tale of Naruto), 1957; Haru koro no hana no en (A Spring Banquet), 1958; Osaka no onna (A Woman of Osaka), 1958; Shirasagi (The White Heron/The Snowy Heron), 1958; The Red Cloak, 1958; Joen (Tormented Love), 1959; Kagero ezu (Stop the Old Fox), 1959; Uta andon (The Lantern), 1960; Midare-gami (Dissheveled Hair/Blind Devotion), 1961; Okoto to Sasuke (Okoto and Sasuke), 1961; San Jotai (Types of Women), episode in Uso (When Women Lie), 1963; Yoso (Priest and Empress/The Sorcerer), 1963; (with Eduard Bocharov) Chiisai tobosha (The Little Runaway), 1967.

ABOUT: Anderson, J. L. and Richie, D. The Japanese Film: Art and Industry, revised ed. 1982; Burch, N. To the Distant Observer: Form and Meaning in the Japanese Cinema, 1979; Richie, D. The Japanese Movie: An Illustrated History, revised ed. 1981; Sato, T. Currents in Japanese Cinema, 1982; Tucker, R. Japan: Film Image, 1973. *Periodicals*—Cinéma (France) 83 1964; Écran April 1975; Film Dope January 1985; Japan Film Yearbook various years; Les Lettres Françaises 1972; Monthly Film Bulletin April 1973, April 1974; Positif May 1973; Sight and Sound Winter 1972-3, Summer 1976.

"KORDA," Sir **ALEXANDER** (**Sándor László Kellner**) (September 16, 1893–January 13, 1956), British producer, director, and scenarist, was born in Puszta Turpásztó, a settlement on the outskirts of Túrkeve, on the Great Hungarian Plain. He was the oldest of the three sons of Henrik Kellner, a soldier who had become overseer of a bishop's estates, and the former Ernesztina Weiss. At his own insistence, he was enrolled when he was only five at the Jewish school in Túrkeve. Incorrect treatment of an eye condition damaged his sight in childhood and he always wore very thick glasses, but he was a voracious reader, mostly of popular fiction, and an eager student with an exceptional memory.

A scholarship took Sándor Kellner on to secondary school when he was nine. Four years later his father died of a ruptured appendix, leaving the family destitute. They moved in with Henrik Kellner's father, and soon afterwards Sándor left for the capital, Budapest, where he stayed with cousins and continued his education, earning a little by tutoring other students. Encouraged by a teacher named Oscar Faber, he developed a passion for Hungarian literature and history.

It was Faber who introduced him to left-wing politics and secured him—still in his early teens—his first assignments as a short story writ-

ALEXANDER KORDA

er and *feuilletonist* with a Budapest daily, *Független Magyarország* (Independent Hungary). On a visit to one of the city's music halls, Sándor noticed, inscribed in a wall, the injunction *sursum corda*—"lift up your hearts"—a phrase that he adopted as his pseudonym and later adapted as his name. He saw his first movie show—a program of shorts—in 1908 in a Budapest coffeehouse, and came away announcing to a friend: "This is the future! This is what I want to do!"

In 1908 Sándor's mother and brothers joined him in Budapest. They took in lodgers and his brother Zoltán found odd jobs, but their main source of income was what Sándor earned from tutoring and freelance journalism. It was not enough, and Sándor first took a night job with *Független Magyarország* and then, at sixteen, just before graduation, left school to join the paper as a full-time cub reporter. It was then that he began to sign himself Sándor Korda, under that pseudonym writing crime stories and reviews, and rising within eighteen months to become the paper's night editor.

It was poorly paid work, however, and Korda was in any case already determined on a dual career as a writer and a filmmaker. In 1911 he set off to seek his fortune in Paris. He spent most of his time there at the Pathé studios, observing, absorbing, and doing any odd jobs that came his way, living after a fashion on what he could earn by writing for Hungarian papers. In August 1912, when his money ran out, he returned to Budapest, where he soon afterwards joined the Projectograph company as secretary, publicist, and general factotum.

The Hungarian film industry was still in its infancy. A large proportion of all the films that could be seen in the country were produced or imported by Projectograph, which also dominated distribution and exhibition. The most instructive of Korda's jobs there was the translation of the titles and captions of the foreign films Projectograph imported, a task that involved close study of the movies themselves (and which incidentally introduced Korda to the half-dozen languages he eventually mastered). He also continued to work as a journalist, for a time writing the first regular film column to be published in Hungary. In October 1912, Korda and another newspaperman launched the country's first nontrade film magazine, *Pesti Mozi* (Budapest Cinema), a weekly sold in the movie theatres. It survived for eight months and was later twice revived under different titles.

At this time, Karol Kulik writes in an excellent biography, "Sándor Korda was a strikingly handsome young man. A portrait photograph of the time reveals a magnificent head, full lips, high cheekbones, straight nose, and hypnotic, slanting eyes. . . . This was the young man who lived at home but spent most of his days and nights in the Budapest cafés in heated debate with the rest of Budapest's young, idealistic community. . . . Korda thrived in this environment, and it was here that he met most of the men who would assist him in his filmmaking career."

None of Korda's Hungarian films has survived, but something is known of the circumstances of their creation. The first two were made in 1914 to be shown in schools and were codirected by Gyula Zilahy, an actor acquaintance of Korda's who also starred in them. Having talked himself into a directorial job at the educational film studio operated by the city of Budapest, he called in Korda to help him.

Lyon Lea (1915), adapted from a popular stage play, was codirected by a horticulturist named Miklós Pásztory, a movie enthusiast who had set up his own production company. He had met Korda through the latter's film magazine, by then called *Mozihet* and an extremely influential weekly journal that crusaded vigorously against the inertia and mediocrity of the Hungarian cinema. The direction of *A tiszti kardbojt* (The Officer's Swordknot, 1915), a wartime romance that Korda also scripted, was for complicated reasons credited to its producer, József Neumann, but this was in fact Korda's first picture as sole director. He borrowed soldiers and military installations from the army for this film, shot it in three days, and achieved a modest but encouraging success.

The following year Korda met Jenö Janovics,

director of the National Theatre of Kolozsvár, in Transylvania, where he had also established his own film studio, Corvin. The director Mihály Kertész (later better known as Michael Curtiz) had left Corvin, and Janovics needed a replacement. Korda moved to Kolozsvár in 1916, and before the year was out had directed (and in most cases scripted) at least seven films for Corvin, most of them adaptations of novels or plays, with casts drawn at least partly from Janovics' theatre company. The first of them, *Fehér éjszakák* (White Nights), based on Sardou's *Fedora*, was one of the first Hungarian films ever shown abroad, and all of the series seem to have been extremely well received, critically and commercially.

Soon, however, Korda began to chafe at the low budgets and tight schedules Janovics imposed on him. Early in 1917 he returned to Budapest and in April he and his friend Miklós Pásztory, the former horticulturist, established their own production company, financed by the wealthy Richard Strasser. They called it Corvin, buying rights to the name from Janovics, and built elegant and impressive studios at Zugló, the Budapest suburb where the vast Mafilm Studios now stand. From the outset, Korda, as head of production, established a policy stressing quality rather than quantity: "One good picture can make a company," he said, "a dozen good pictures can make an industry."

The new Corvin went into production in 1917. Because of Korda's insistence on care and quality, the studio made only seven films during its first year, four of them directed by Korda, including two literary adaptations and an atypical slapstick comedy, *Harrison és Barrison.* This was enough to establish the company's fortunes, however, and by the time the war ended in 1918, Korda was recognized to be Hungary's top producer. Since he was also the publisher of the country's most influential film magazine, he was undoubtedly the dominant figure in the Hungarian cinema, and he was still only twenty-five.

As he grew richer, Korda adopted an increasingly extravagant way of life, moving into a fashionable Budapest hotel and smoking ever larger cigars. His brother Zoltán [Korda] joined Corvin as a director in 1918, and another recruit was the beautiful dancer and actress Maria (then known as Antónia) Farkas, who starred in most of Korda's later Hungarian films and became his wife in 1919. Meanwhile, late in 1918, Korda had become Commissioner of Film Production in Károlyi's postwar coalition government, and early in 1919, when Károlyi relinquished power to the Hungarian Communist Party, he was appointed to the Communist Directory for the

Arts. Korda was not himself a Party member, but he saw a chance to weed out of the industry the distributors against whom he had inveighed as parasitic "middlemen" in *Mozihet.* At his urging, the Hungarian cinema became the world's first nationalized film industry in April 1919.

Two of the three pictures Korda directed during the next few months—*Ave Caesar!* and *Yamata*—were appropriately revolutionary in tone. Then the Communist government fell and was replaced by Horthy's right-wing regime and the White Terror—the persecution of Communists, liberals, Jews, and artists (especially filmmakers). Korda was obviously a prime target on most of these counts and he was arrested and briefly imprisoned. It is not clear how he gained his freedom, but he did so, completed the two movies he had been working on, and in November 1919 left Hungary forever, accompanied by his wife Maria.

Korda's brief reign as the "boy genius" leader of the Hungarian cinema was followed by eleven nomadic years during which he made films in four different countries. He went first to Vienna, where he had been invited to join Count Kolowrat's Sascha Film Company, and where he began to call himself Alexander rather than Sándor Korda. Here as elsewhere—partly to impress potential backers and partly from choice— the Kordas adopted a flamboyant lifestyle they could ill afford.

Korda's first picture for Sascha was an ambitious costume epic, *Seine Majestät das bettelkind* (1920), an adaptation of Mark Twain's *The Prince and the Pauper.* The scenarist was another Hungarian refugee, Lajos Biro, who thus began a long collaboration with Korda. Marred (like many of their collaborations) by a plodding narrative and an excess of pageantry and spectacle, it had a notable performance by Alfred Schreiber as Henry VIII and vigorously emphasized the contrasts between the wealth of the English court and the squalor outside. The picture was well received in Europe and was a hit in the United States. Korda directed two more films for Kolowrat and then went into partnership with another Hungarian to make *Samson und Delila* (1923). Combining a foolish contemporary story and the biblical one, and starring Korda's wife in both, it was a cut-rate imitation of Griffith's *Intolerance,* and a failure. By this time, Maria was much in demand, starring in films in several European countries. To emphasize her independence, she tried out several alternatives to her husband's name, winding up, confusingly, as Maria Corda.

With his credit and credibility exhausted in Vienna, Korda moved on to Berlin, where he conjured up backing for a new production company, Korda-Film. Its first product was *Das unbekannte morgen* (*The Unknown Tomorrow*, 1923), scripted by Korda and Ernest Vajda, a melodrama about a virtuous wife (Maria Corda) unjustly abandoned by her husband, who gets him back with the help of a Hindu mystic. The villain is played by Werner Krauss and the film is dramatically lit in the expressionist manner of *Das Cabinet des Dr. Caligari* (1919), in which Krauss had starred. It was a hit, and was followed by a string of less notable vehicles for Maria.

None of these films did much to advance Korda's career, and when First National invited him and his wife to Hollywood, he was happy to go (even though Maria's salary was to be higher than his). In fact, his Hollywood experience was extremely unrewarding. He disliked the rigid studio system and made only one film of any merit, *The Private Life of Helen of Troy* (1927), based on John Erskine's amusing novel demythologizing the ancient drama. The movie suffered from the lack of spoken dialogue but—thanks largely to the skill of its cameraman, Lee Garmes—was a polished production and a success, establishing Korda's reputation as an exponent of historical and sexual satire.

Korda made his first talkie in 1929, *The Squall*, "a ghastly picture" starring Myrna Loy. Two more insignificant films followed for First National and then two for Fox before Korda's unwillingness to grovel to the Fox studio head, Winfield Sheehan, ended his Hollywood career. And by this time his first marriage had also ended. With the coming of sound, Maria's strong accent disqualified her from English-language films, and her misery no doubt exacerbated the strains that already threatened the marriage; they were divorced in 1930.

Korda returned to Europe alone and virtually penniless, but determined to start again and to beat Hollywood at its own game. First he needed money. He went briefly to Berlin and then to Paris, where he found a job with Paramount's French subsidiary at Joinville. He made French and German versions of Harry D'Arrast's *Laughter*, and then *Marius* (1931), the screen adaptation of Marcel Pagnol's enormous stage hit about the *habitués* of a Marseilles waterfront café, the young man who yearns to go to sea, and the girl who loves him but lets him go.

The youngest Korda brother, Vincent, had until then been studying and working as an artist. Korda now brought him to Paris to design the sets for *Marius*, as he was to do for so many of Korda's later films. The splendid stage cast, headed by Raimu as Marius' father (and the café's cantankerous *patron*), was retained. Some contemporary critics found the movie stagebound, but Karol Kulik maintains that it makes skillful and sometimes imaginative use of lighting and camera point-of-view to support and clarify the play's psychological observations, and regards it as one of the most accomplished of Korda's films. It is certainly one of the most likable and—thanks largely to the marvelous dialogue and the richness of Raimu's performance—has become a classic of the period, still frequently revived.

In November 1931, Korda accepted a contract with Paramount British and moved on again to England. The native industry was then at a low ebb, almost totally dominated by Hollywood products. In an effort to control the situation, the government had introduced a quota system. It resulted in a spate of short and very cheap programmers, which were certainly made in England but did little credit to the British industry. Many, indeed, were actually made by the British subsidiaries of Hollywood companies, like Paramount British. Korda began his career in England as the director of what was intended as a "quota quickie," *Service for Ladies* (1932), but somehow managed to lay his hands on a rising young star, Leslie Howard. A trivial rags-to-riches comedy, the film nevertheless achieved in Korda's hands a polish that reminded one reviewer of Lubitsch, and it was financially extremely successful.

At that point, Korda launched another production company, London Film Productions, with a board of directors made up of its investors under the chairmanship of George Grossmith, offices in Mayfair, and Big Ben as its trademark. Vincent Korda was placed in charge of the art department, and Lajos Biro in charge of scripts. Finance for production was obtained through Paramount, which commissioned a series of quota films, and from Michael Balcon at Gaumont British. A stable of contract actors was recruited—mostly newcomers glad to accept a five-year contract at £20 a week. Among them were Merle Oberon, Wendy Barrie, Robert Donat, John Loder, and Maurice Evans. Better deals went to more established performers like Roland Young, Leslie Banks, and Edmund Gwenn.

London's first film, *Wedding Rehearsal* (1933), produced and directed by Korda, was a comedy about a bachelor marquis (Roland Young) who marries off to others the debutantes selected for him by his mother but finally falls in love with her secretary (Merle Oberon). Like many of Korda's films, it was more notable for its visual elegance than for its acting, which was highly uneven. Five routine quota films for Paramount followed in 1933, produced by Korda but directed by others, including Leontine Sagan, Zoltán Korda, and Allan Dwan. Meanwhile, Korda had returned to Paris to direct French and English versions of Georges Feydeau's play *The Girl From Maxim's,* to which he owned the rights. A lively musical comedy, it was the first film in which Korda had the services of the cinematographer Georges Périnal.

But Korda's ambitions far exceeded such modest entertainments, and before the end of 1933 he had completed London Films' most famous production, *The Private Life of Henry VIII.* Planned as a vehicle for Charles Laughton, it was written by Lajos Biro and Arthur Wimperis, seven complete scripts being dumped along the way. Money was scraped together from a variety of sources, costumes were kept to a minimum, and Vincent Korda designed the excellent sets so cheaply that the actors scarcely expected them to stand until the film was completed. Georges Périnal came over from Paris, and the shooting was completed in five weeks.

Virtually ignoring the religious and political implications of Henry's reign, the film offers an episodic "keyhole" history of most of the king's marriages, more titillating then lewd. Blustering and coarse on the surface, outrageous in his table manners, Henry is presented as vulnerable and affectionate underneath, and he ends as the helpless victim of manipulative women. There is a good deal of verbal wit, and a kind of chorus to the action is provided by Henry's subjects, who turn out to be very much like the thousands who attended the film's world premiere at Radio City Music Hall in October 1933. Laughton earned an Oscar for the "Shakespearian insolence" of his performance, and his wife Elsa Lanchester is splendid as the sexually ignorant Anne of Cleves.

Made at a cost of about £60,000, *Henry VIII* grossed £500,000 during its first world release, and was still taking in £10,000 a year twenty years later. It was the first British film to conquer the American market, and it was an enormous stimulus to the British industry as a whole. Even before its release, it so impressed United Artists that Korda was offered a contract to make a minimum of six films a year at an average cost of £100,000. Two years after his arrival in England, Korda was the most important single figure in the British cinema, touted as the industry's savior.

Capitalizing on this triumph, Korda pursued his rivalry of Hollywood with a series of films aimed at the international market—and particularly the American market. The deal with United Artists began with *The Rise of Catherine the Great* (1934), starring Elizabeth Bergner and Douglas Fairbanks Jr. It was directed by Bergner's husband, Paul Czinner, with much interference from Korda, and was admired by the critics, though the public seemed to prefer Marlene Dietrich's version of Catherine in von Sternberg's *The Scarlet Empress,* released simultaneously. This was followed by the solitary product of Korda's dalliance with documentary, Julian Huxley's Oscar-winning *The Private Life of the Gannets* (1934).

Korda himself directed *The Private Life of Don Juan* (1934), with the middle-aged Douglas Fairbanks as a middle-aged Don, running out of swash and buckling down to respectability. The ironic script was by Biro, Wimperis, and Frederick Lonsdale, with uncredited contributions from Korda, who in fact always participated vigorously in story conferences. The weakness of this, as of so many of Korda's scripts, was that it hammered home its plot points so remorselessly that the life was crushed out of the story. After this flop, however, came the enormous success of *The Scarlet Pimpernel* (1934), starring Leslie Howard and Merle Oberon and made mostly by imported Hollywood talent.

A 1935 poll showed that Korda was Britain's favorite filmmaker. That year he returned to Hollywood in triumph—to "genuflections by the greatest and hosannas from the highest"—to accept a full partnership in United Artists, along with Fairbanks, Chaplin, Sam Goldwyn, and Mary Pickford. In June 1935, with the death of George Grossmith, he became chairman of the London Films board, and the same year work began on the construction of the company's new studios on a 165-acre estate at Denham, on the outskirts of London.

Rejecting plans for sterile offices, Korda retained the estate's mansion as his administration building, adapting stables as editing rooms and a cottage as the music department. With its splendidly equipped workshops, projection theatres, infirmary, restaurant (with French chef), and seven sound stages, Denham was the biggest and most up-to-date film studio in Europe. Nearby, at Denham Laboratories, Korda had the first Technicolor laboratories in England. And to Denham he brought some of the finest technicians in the film world—so many of them foreign that it was claimed that the five British flags which flew at Denham represented the number of British employees there.

As he became increasingly involved in administration, Korda spent less and less time on the studio floor. In a 1935 article, Freda Bruce Lockhart suggested that this was all to the good—that

Korda's work as a director was polished and pictorially beautiful but lacked vitality, and that his real genius was as a producer and impresario. A courageously unorthodox opinion when it appeared, at the height of Korda's fame, it is the view that has persisted.

In fact *Rembrandt* (1936), the first film to be shot in its entirety at the new Denham studios, was the only picture Korda was to direct there. He was an art lover and collector, and the film was conceived as a deeply sincere tribute to an uncompromising genius and to art in general. Scripted by the German dramatist Carl Zuckmayer in collaboration with Biro, Wimperis, and June Head, it begins at the turning point in Rembrandt's career in 1642, when his beloved wife died and his technical experiments began to lose him the patronage of the Dutch bourgeoisie. It goes on to trace his decline into poverty, his love affair with a servant girl, and his solitary last years.

For the starring role, Charles Laughton immersed himself in research and achieved a portrayal of real insight. Vincent Korda's sets and Périnal's photography created scenes that might almost have been painted by Rembrandt. Karol Kulik called the result "a series of *tableaux* often without dramatic links between them. On the other hand, there is scarcely a superfluous scene in the whole film; each one is thematically linked to the overall portrait of the artist which Korda is trying to express." *Rembrandt* did not succeed financially, but it is widely regarded as Korda's finest achievement as a director.

Meanwhile, other London Films productions were taking the company from success to success. *Sanders of the River* (*Bosambo*, 1935), directed by Zoltán Korda, was a hugely popular tribute to the British Empire, with Paul Robeson as the childlike tribal chief learning wisdom at the feet of the white administrator Sanders (Leslie Banks). Robeson was embarrassed by the role but achieved a great personal success (and a worldwide hit with the recording of his "Canoe Song"). Equally profitable was *The Ghost Goes West* (1935), with Robert Donat as both the Glourie Ghost (exported to philistine America along with his castle) and the Ghost's living descendant. In spite of much interference from Korda, the film retains something of the lightness of touch associated with René Clair, its director.

The most ambitious of all London Films products, *Things to Come* (1936), cost some $1.5 million. It was based on an essay by H. G. Wells, prophesying a world redeemed by science (whose advance is opposed by demagogic artists). In spite of Vincent Korda's brilliantly conceived models for a science-fiction world of the future and Arthur Bliss's memorable score, the film was more prestigious than profitable, stodgily directed by William Cameron Menzies.

The patriotic *Fire Over England* (1937), with Flora Robson as Elizabeth I, was a hit, but Korda's next major project became the most discussed nonevent in British film history. Josef von Sternberg was recruited to direct *I, Claudius*, and the script was adapted from Robert Graves' novel by Graves himself, together with von Sternberg, Carl Zuckmayer, Biro, Wimperis, and Lester Cohen. Georges Périnal had Robert Krasker as his camera operator, the designer was Vincent Korda, and the choreographer was Agnes De Mille. The clips from the film shown in a BBC documentary about it suggest that it might have been a masterpiece, but Laughton had great difficulty in "finding" the role of Claudius, and when Merle Oberon (Messalina) was injured in a car accident, the film was abandoned.

Other notable London movies of the period include *Elephant Boy* (1937), directed by Robert Flaherty (who discovered Sabu and shot fifty-five hours of background footage) and Zoltán Korda (who added the story line at Denham); Jacques Feyder's excellent *Knight Without Armour* (1937), starring Marlene Dietrich and Robert Donat in a James Hilton story about the Russian Revolution; and another action-packed epic of empire, *The Drum* (1938), directed by Zoltán Korda.

By this time, the boom in British filmmaking stimulated by *The Private Life of Henry VIII* had run out of steam. The hope that British movies could conquer world markets had on the whole not been realized, and the financiers were calling in their loans. Korda himself lasted longer than many of his rivals, using his extraordinary powers of persuasion to raise more and more money in what was becoming a financial desert. He was finally undone by the sheer size of the Denham Studios, which were only viable if the seven stages could be kept occupied. He rented them to independent producers and himself promoted more films than he wanted to, but it was not enough. By 1938, London Films' liabilities exceeded a million pounds, and its principal backers, the Prudential Assurance Company, took Denham out of Korda's hands. It was his greatest defeat, and the end of what to many of his employees had been something like "a modern-day Camelot."

Korda was still chairman of London Films and still had his partnership in United Artists. He continued at Denham as a tenant producer and in March 1939 started work on *The Thief of*

Bagdad. A few months later he married Merle Oberon, took off on a honeymoon, and returned to scrap much of the work on *The Thief* that had been done in his absence. Examining one of the sets, he shouted at his brother: "Vincent, you are crazy! Go away, get a lot of men, build it four times as big and paint it all crimson." Work on the movie was interrupted again soon afterwards by the outbreak of World War II, when Korda threw all his resources into the making of *The Lion Has Wings,* a propaganda movie about the Royal Air Force for which he pawned his last life insurance policy in a gesture of passionate British patriotism. Made with immense speed and efficiency, this uneven but not uninteresting film was released two months after its inception. *The Thief of Bagdad* finally had its premiere in October 1940, by which time half-a-dozen directors had had a hand in it. A rather wooden and humorless version of the story, it is nevertheless magnificently spectacular "family entertainment" and made a respectable profit.

By this time Korda was in the United States, where he spent most of the war years until the spring of 1943. He directed one film in Hollywood, *That Hamilton Woman (Lady Hamilton,* 1941), starring Laurence Olivier as Nelson and Vivien Leigh as his inamorata. Korda's intention in making the film was to arouse pro-British sentiment, and he succeeded so well that a Senate investigating committee was appointed to look into the work of British propagandists in the still neutral United States—an investigation ended by the Japanese bombing of Pearl Harbor. There were also objections from the American censor that Nelson's adultery with Lady Hamilton was not sufficiently condemned (even though the story is told in flashback by a heroine reduced by her sinful love to a drunken waterfront whore).

Such criticisms apart, the film is sometimes moving and often amusing, with a too-solemn performance by Olivier but a fine one from Vivien Leigh. It was one of the favorite films of Korda's friend Winston Churchill, and helped to bring Korda a knighthood in June 1942. (There are rumors that this knighthood also reflected the government's gratitude to Korda for his work as a courier for the OSS and a similar British organization, and for certain intelligence-gathering services before and during the war.) Korda produced two other movies during his war years in America, *Lydia* (1941), a remake by Julien Duvivier of his own *Carnet de bal,* and Zoltán Korda's spectacular and successful *Jungle Book.*

In March 1943 a merger was announced between London Film Productions and MGM-British, and Korda returned to England to take charge. An ambitious program was promised, but the only film actually completed by the new company was *Perfect Strangers (Vacation From Marriage,* 1945), directed as well as produced by Korda himself. It starred Robert Donat and Deborah Kerr as a drab married couple who are both called up for wartime service and transformed by danger and responsibility into quite different people. A modest but absorbing and assured film, with excellent dialogue, it brought Clemence Dane an Oscar for best original story and was a commercial and critical success.

Korda's marriage to Merle Oberon ended in 1945. He was deeply hurt, and the same year had his first heart attack. In September of that year he resigned from MGM, but in 1946 he set about reviving London Film Productions as a private company. His wartime films had been profitable and he had sold his shares in United Artists for $900,000, so for once he had adequate capital. He bought controling interests in Shepperton Studios and in the distributing company British Lion, and for offices secured a mansion in Piccadilly where "you walk on Aubusson and sit upon Gobelins."

In 1947 Korda directed his own last film, an adaptation of Oscar Wilde's *An Ideal Husband* starring Paulette Goddard, Michael Wilding, and Diana Wynyard. It was gorgeously designed by Vincent Korda and Cecil Beaton but was otherwise of very little interest. Other superproductions like *Anna Karenina* and *Bonnie Prince Charlie* also failed, but a £3 million government loan kept British Lion in operation until June 1954, when it was put into the hands of a receiver.

Korda was by then sixty years old and in poor health. For a time he considered retirement. Instead he persuaded an American property investor, Robert Dowling, to put up $15 million and announced that London Films was back in business. Returning to his original policy, he now concentrated on ambitious color films, some of them in Cinemascope, and scored a series of hits with movies like David Lean's *Summer Madness,* Zoltán Korda's *Storm Over the Nile,* and Olivier's *Richard III.* London Films, a profitable business when he died in January 1956, died with him.

Korda, who had become a British citizen in 1936, had soon abandoned the left-wing idealism of his youth. He was a romantic Anglophile and a snob, and his own films reflect this, centering uncritically on the antics of the British monarchy and upper classes. He was at his best in *Rembrandt,* a deeply felt tribute to an uncompromising artist, but most of his films were diminished by his own passion for international market success on the Hollywood model. The fact remains that he created a handful of excellent entertainments and allowed others to create very many more, singlehandedly revitalizing the moribund British film industry in the process.

In 1953 Korda had made a third marriage to a young Canadian named Alexandra Boycun. He had a son, Peter, by his first marriage. Immensely intelligent and cultured, he was a splendid conversationalist in several languages and the possessor of a "hypnotic" charm that was equally successful with temperamental artists and suspicious financiers. He was unique.

FILMS: (The source of this filmography is K. Kulik's *Alexander Korda*, 1975.) *Hungary*—(with Gyula Zilahy) A becsapott újságíró, 1914; (with Gyula Zilahy) Tutyu és Totyo, 1914; (with Miklós Pásztory) Lea Lyon, 1915; (uncredited) A tiszti kardbojt, 1915; Fehér éjszakák (Fedora), 1916; A nagymama, 1916; Mesék az írógépről, 1916; A kétszívű férfi, 1916; Az egymillió fontos bankó, 1916; Ciklámen, 1916; Vergödö szívek, 1916; A nevető Szaszkia, 1916 (attribution to Korda uncertain); Mágnás Miska, 1916 (attribution uncertain); Szent Péter esernyöje, 1917; A gólyakalifa, 1917; Mágia, 1917; Harrison és Barrison, 1917; Faun, 1918; Az aranyember, 1918; Mary Ann, 1918; Ave Caesar!, 1919; Fehér rózsa, 1919; Yamata, 1919; Se ki, se be, 1919; A 111-es, 1919. *Austria*—Seine Majestät das bettelkind (Prinz und bettelknabe/The Prince and the Pauper), 1920; Herren der meere, 1922; Eine Versunkene Welt, 1922; Samson und Delila (Samson and Delilah), 1922. *Germany*—Das unbekannte morgen (The Unknown Tomorrow), 1923; Jedermanns Frau (Jedermanns Weib), 1924; Tragödie im Hause Habsburg (Das Drama von Mayerling/Der Prinz der legende), 1924; Der Tänzer meiner frau (Dancing Mad), 1925; Madame wünscht keine kinder (Madame Wants No Children), 1926; Eine Dubarry von heute (A Modern Dubarry), 1927. *Hollywood*—The Stolen Bride, 1927; The Private Life of Helen of Troy, 1927; Yellow Lily, 1928; Night Watch, 1928; Love of the Devil, 1929; The Squall, 1929; Her Private Life, 1929; Lilies of the Field, 1930; Women Everywhere, 1930; The Princess and the Plumber, 1930; That Hamilton Woman (Lady Hamilton), 1941. *France*—Rive Gauche and Die Manner um Lucie, 1931 (French and German versions of Harry D'Arrast's Laughter); Marius, 1931; Zum Goldener Anker, 1931 (German version of Marius); The Girl From Maxim's, 1933; La Dame de Chez Maxim, 1934 (French version of The Girl From Maxim's). *Britain*—Service for Ladies (Reserved for Ladies), 1932; Wedding Rehearsal, 1933; The Private Life of Henry VIII, 1933; The Private Life of Don Juan, 1934; Rembrandt, 1936; Perfect Strangers (Vacation From Marriage), 1945; An Ideal Husband, 1947. *Published scripts*—The Private Life of Henry VIII, ed. by E. Betts, 1934.

ABOUT: Armes, R. A Critical History of the British Cinema, 1978; Cowie, P. Korda, 1965 (in French); Current Biography, 1946; Korda, M. Charmed Lives: A Family Romance, 1979; Kulik, K. Alexander Korda: The Man Who Could Work Miracles, 1975; Nemeskürty, I. Word and Image—History of the Hungarian Cinema, 1974; Read, A. and Fisher, D. Colonel Z—The Secret Life of a Master of Spies, 1985; Tabori, G. Alexander Korda, 1966. *Periodicals*—British Film Academy Journal Spring 1956; Cinema Quarterly Autumn 1933; Collier's February 15, 1936; Film Weekly June 20, 1936; Films and Filming March 1963, March 1968; Image et Son July 1961; Life June 30, 1967; New York Times Magazine March 14, 1962; Quarterly of Film, Radio and Television Spring 1957; Saturday Review December 2, 1961; Sight and Sound Spring 1956; Time September 9, 1935; April 6, 1936; Time Out February 13–19, 1976.

"KORDA," ZOLTÁN (Zoltán Kellner) (May 3, 1895–October 13, 1961), British director, editor, and scenarist, was born near Túrkeve, Hungary, the second of the three lavishly talented sons of assimilated Jews, Henrik and Ernesztina (Weiss) Kellner. His father was estate manager for the Salgo family in Puszta Turpásztó, on the edge of the Hungarian plain. Like his elder brother Sándor [Alexander Korda], Zoltán was enthralled as a boy by the writings of Jules Verne and other tales of adventure in exotic locales, a predilection reflected in all of his most successful films.

Like his father, formerly a noncommissioned officer in the Hussars, Zoltán Kellner had in his youth a fiery temperament that often got him into fights. Sándor frequently had to intercede or join the fray, and the two brothers became very close. Their father's early death from a misdiagnosed case of appendicitis increased the family's cohesion, especially when the widow and her three sons were forced to move in with unsympathetic in-laws. Sándor soon moved to Budapest, where he began to earn a little money as a journalist and tutor while continuing his education. It was at this time that he adopted the name Korda, originally using it as his byline.

In 1908 the rest of the family joined Sándor in Budapest. Despite Zoltán's desire to become a writer, practical considerations obliged him to enroll in a commercial high school. Upon graduation he worked as a clerk for a coal merchant until the summer of 1914, when he was drafted into the Austro-Hungarian army. Commissioned as a lieutenant, he fought on the Galician front, where his lungs were seriously damaged in a gas attack. He never fully recovered, for the rest of his life suffering periodic bouts of disabling illness.

Meanwhile, in 1912, Sándor Korda had entered the developing Hungarian film industry, where he moved rapidly from success to success.

ZOLTÁN KORDA

By the time the war ended in 1918 he had built his own film studio on the outskirts of Budapest and was established as Hungary's top producer, as well as an important director and editor of the country's most influential film magazine. Zoltán joined his brother's Corvin studio in 1918, adopting the new family name of Korda. Beginning as an editor, he made his first film, *Karoly-Bakak,* later the same year, codirecting with Sándor's partner Miklós Pásztory.

Though not himself a communist, Sándor played an important part in the nationalization of the Hungarian film industry under a communist government early in 1919. A few months later the communists were replaced by Horthy's vengeful right-wing regime, and the "White Terror" followed—the murderous persecution of communists, Jews, and liberal artists. Obviously a prime target, Sándor was arrested but gained his freedom thanks to the efforts and influence of his wife and of Zoltán, a wounded veteran and former officer.

Like many other Hungarian filmmakers, Sándor went to Vienna, where he anglicized his first name to Alexander and joined the Sascha film company. The rest of the family followed—Zoltán, the younger brother Vincent, then an art student, and their mother. Zoltán became a cameraman and editor for Sascha, and probably also edited *Samson und Delila,* a sub-Griffith epic made by Alexander as an independent production. This was the Kordas' last film in Austria. They moved on again to Berlin, where Alexander launched a new production company and made half a dozen movies. Zoltán worked once more as his editor and in 1927 di-rected his own first solo feature, *Die Elf Teufel* (*The Eleven Devils*).

The same year, Alexander Korda and his first wife Maria went to Hollywood, where neither had much success and where their marriage ended. Alexander returned to Europe and made one notable film in Paris, *Marius* (1931). The excellent sets were the work of Vincent Korda, who thus began his distinguished career as an art director. In November 1931, Alexander went to England. Zoltán had belatedly followed Alexander to Hollywood, where he worked as an editor and coscripted his brother's movie *Women Everywhere* (1930). Again delayed by ill-health, he rejoined Alexander in 1933 in England.

By this time Alexander had established yet another new production company, London Film Production, with Vincent in charge of the art department and Lajos Biro—another of "Korda's magyars"—heading the script department. London Films began as a manufacturer of "quota quickies"—low-budget programmers designed to meet the quota of British-made films demanded by the 1927 Cinematograph Act to combat Hollywood's domination of the British market. As Karol Kulik says, the results were often "an affront to both British filmmakers and the British public, and gave British films a bad reputation." On the other hand, these programmers did provide opportunities for young directors, writers, and performers to practice their crafts with a minimum of financial risk. In 1933 Zoltán Korda directed one such item, *Men of Tomorrow,* in collaboration with Leontine Sagan. Later the same year came his first British solo feature, a "quota quickie" called *Cash* (*For Love and Money* in the United States).

Alexander Korda was not content to churn out such modest entertainments. Still smarting at his failure in Hollywood, he was determined to beat the dream factory at its own game. Before the end of 1933 he scored his first great success with *The Private Life of Henry VIII.* It was the first British film for many years to capture an international market, and it established Korda as the "savior" of the British film industry (as he had been fifteen years earlier of the Hungarian industry). Another enormous success for London Films followed with *The Scarlet Pimpernel* (1934), directed like *Henry VIII* by Alexander himself.

In 1935 Zoltán matched his brother's triumphs with his second feature, *Sanders of the River* (U.S., *Bosambo*). Based on Edgar Wallace's stories about a British district commissioner in darkest Africa, the film was scripted by Lajos Biro and Jeffrey Dell and photographed by Georges Périnal, Osmond Borrodaile, and Louis

Page. Zoltán Korda and a crew of twelve spent four months in West Africa filming the dances of half-a-dozen different tribes and recording their songs. Many of the songs are used in the film, either as they were recorded or—like the hit "Canoe Song"—in arrangements by the composer Mischa Spoliansky and the picture's musical director Muir Matheson. According to Zoltán Korda, the movie used 3,000 feet of film shot on location. London's publicity department reported that "the 20,000 African Negroes who take part in this picture received most of their wages in the form of cartons of cigarettes." Produced by Alexander Korda, with Vincent as art director, this was the first film on which all three Korda brothers worked together.

Leslie Banks plays the wise administrator who maintains the king's peace more by his moral strength than by force of arms. Paul Robeson was recruited to play the chieftain Bosambo, who learns the truth of Sanders' dictum "the job of a ruler is not to be feared, but to be loved." However, as Raymond Durgnat remarked, the movie "wobbles deliciously" between this thesis "and a plot which proves the exact opposite. Indeed the natives, with childlike wisdom, observe 'We realise that we must live in peace and love one another for if we do not O white master you will punish us most cruelly.'"

Sanders of the River was an international hit. *Kinematograph Weekly* called it "spectacular adventure drama, a fine tribute to British rule in Africa. Although spectacle predominates, it is not allowed to impose upon the author's narrative skill, for the story comes first all the time, and it carries with it an immense amount of general entertainment. The locale is new to screen drama and the virgin territory has been explored with real showmanship. . . . The casting of Paul Robeson as Bosambo is a clever move. He not only acts well, but has a commanding screen presence and a fine voice which is shrewdly utilized."

In fact, Robeson disowned the picture for its condescending racism, and in 1957, when *Sanders* was revived on British television, it drew a protest from the Nigerian Commissioner, who said it brought Disgrace and disrepute to Nigerians." There have been suggestions that the film's Anglophilia was imposed by Alexander Korda, Zoltán being responsible for the more or less respectful (and often valuable) ethnographic content of this and other Korda epics of empire. On the other hand, in his accounts of the filming, Zoltán reported almost reverently on the British administrators he met in Africa, while describing tribal ways with something closer to amiable contempt. In any case, David Thomson, discuss-

ing *Sanders* in his *Biographical Dictionary of the Cinema* (1980), wrote that "in retrospect . . . the imperial offensiveness seems peripheral to an engaging taste for adventurous nonsense. It was the feeling for romance that inspired the Korda empire."

Whether or not Zoltán and Alexander clashed over this aspect of *Sanders of the River,* there was certainly no shortage of fraternal conflict between them. Zoltán, who was inclined to feel that the poor were morally superior to the rich, criticized his big brother for his legendary extravagance and called his lavish dinner parties a "waste of bloody time." Their disputes frequently spilled over onto the set, where they would quarrel violently, to the bewilderment of their British employees, in a mixture of Hungarian, German, and heavily accented English. In times of trouble, however, the brothers' loyalty to each other was absolute. Zoltán played an important role in foiling a bid by disgruntled stockholders to wrest London Films from Alexander's control, and he cared for his brother devotedly when his health began to fail.

In the mid-1930s, Zoltán was one of several Korda directors involved (uncredited) in the piecemeal creation of *Conquest of the Air,* a feature-length semi-documentary about the history of aviation finally completed by Charles Frend in 1940. After *Forget Me Not* (1936; U.S., *Forever Yours*), an inconsequential romance, came *Elephant Boy* (1937). The film was originally assigned to Robert Flaherty, who disappeared with his crew into the Indian jungles and spent a year shooting fifty-five hours of "background." Zoltán Korda was given the unenviable task of adding studio material that would turn this mass of mostly documentary footage into an economically viable feature.

Korda had a considerable asset in Sabu, a twelve-year-old charmer who had been working as a stable boy at the court of an Indian maharajah when Flaherty discovered him and cast him in the film's lead role. Based loosely on Kipling's story "Toomai of the Elephants," the film is about a boy with a hereditary genius for handling elephants, his friendship with the great bull elephant Kala Nag, and his involvement with Peterson (Walter Hudd), a white hunter who uses Kala Nag and Toomai in an expedition to capture wild elephants.

Elephant Boy was attacked both by lovers of Kipling and admirers of Flaherty. Graham Greene, for example, complained of "the bad cutting, the dreadful studio work, the pedestrian adaptation so unfair to Kipling's story" and especially to its climax, the secret dance of the elephants witnessed—alone among humans—by

Toomai. Greene wrote that "to use the gathering of the wild elephants at their jungle dance-floor merely to resolve the problem of Petersen Sahib who has got to trap a certain number of elephants for labour if he is to retain his job—that it to throw away the whole poetic value of the original."

Sabu starred again in *Drum* (1938; U.S., *Drums*), adapted by Lajos Biro and others from the novel by A.E.W. Mason. This time he plays the young heir to a mountain kingdom on the Northwest Frontier of India. He is threatened by the evil machinations of his anti-imperialist uncle but ultimately triumphs, thanks to his own resourcefulness and the heroism of the British troops who befriend him. The film was much admired for its splendid location photography in Technicolor and for Korda's characteristic use of authentic Indian music and dances. However, even in 1938 some critics resented its jingoism: Otis Ferguson called it "a bang-up adventure job though particularly anachronistic for this time and pregnant with Raymond Massey and other bad jokes in black face."

Another A.E.W. Mason novel of imperialist adventure, *The Four Feathers,* had already been filmed two or three times before Korda made what is generally regarded as the definitive version of the story, and his masterpiece. John Clements plays Harry Faversham, sensitive son of an army family who as a boy had listened terrified to the bloodthirsty dinner-table recollections of his father, the general (C. Aubrey Smith). Being a Faversham, Harry takes a commission, but he loses his nerve and resigns when his regiment sails for the Sudan to put down the Khalifa's uprising. He receives white feathers—the symbol of cowardice—from three of his brother officers and from his beloved Ethna (June Duprez).

Ostracized by family, friends, and fiancée, Faversham goes alone to Egypt, disguises himself as a mute tribesman, and joins the Khalifa's army as a spy. After a desert engagement, he finds his former friend John Durrance alone and blinded by the sun. Without revealing his identity, he leads him back to the British lines. As he hands him over, he slips Durrance's white feather into his pocket and returns to the Khalifa's camp. Here he joins his other two friends in prison and, during the Battle of Omdurman, frees them and helps win victory for the British. Back in England, he is reinstated and marries Ethna.

"What is new is the drive—and in the Sudanese sequences the conviction—of this new version," wrote Graham Greene. "Even the thickest of the ham—the old veterans discussing the Crimea in the Faversham home, among the portraits of military ancestors—goes smoothly down, savoured with humour and satire. . . . So in *The Four Feathers* the plot hardly matters: what is important is the colour, which is almost invariably pleasant and sometimes gives a shock of pleasure. . . . What is important is nocturnal London smoking up through Faversham's grey windows; the close-up of mulberry bodies straining at the ropes along the Nile; the cracked umber waste round the dried-up wells; the vultures . . . dropping like weighted parachutes. It is impossible to divide the credit between Mr. Zoltán Korda, the director, who has wiped out the disgrace of *Sanders of the River,* and Mr. R. C. Sherriff, author of the film play."

There was universal praise also for the scope and excitement of the battle scenes, some of which have been re-used in at least four other films, and for the quality of the acting. Ralph Richardson, who played the blinded Durrance, growing from panic to serene acceptance, created in about fifteen minutes of screen time a performance that, as C. A. Lejeune wrote, "is deliberately scaled to heroic size. . . . This is real acting, in an industry that barely knows the meaning of the word."

London Films' *The Thief of Bagdad* (1940), like *Conquest of the Air,* was a much-delayed project in which a number of Korda directors had a hand, Zoltán Korda among them. By the time it appeared, the Kordas were in Hollywood, where Zoltán directed the last of his films with Alexander as his producer, *Jungle Book* (1942), a commercial if not a critical success. Sabu was cast as Mowgli, the boy raised by wolves, and the scenarist Laurence Stallings tacked a plodding story about wicked treasure-hunters onto Kipling's original fable. Dilys Powell wrote that the movie had "a great deal of jungle and very little Book," and Bosley Crowther found in it "a semblance of a super–Tarzan film in Technicolor."

When Alexander Korda returned to Britain in 1943, Zoltán remained in Hollywood, where he next made *Sahara* (Columbia, 1943). The picture was suggested by a notable Soviet film, *The Thirteen,* and scripted by John Howard Lawson and the director. Humphrey Bogart starred as Sergeant Joe Gunn, commanding an American tank in the Libyan desert. He picks up an assortment of stranded Allied soldiers after the fall of Tobruk, as well as a repentant Italian and an arrogant German pilot. In the end, the goodies decide to make a stand at a desert waterhole against five hundred thirsty German troops. Filmed with army cooperation in the American southwest, the movie was praised for its originality and realism and described by Alton Cook as "the most exciting movie of desert warfare we have had from this war."

Counter-Attack (Columbia, 1945) was also scripted by John Howard Lawson from a Soviet original, in this case a stage play that had already been seen on Broadway. A Russian commando (Paul Muni) is trapped in a cellar with a group of German prisoners and one Soviet partisan (Marguerite Chapman). For three days and nights, while the Germans maneuver to turn the tables on their exhausted captors, Muni uses an assortment of psychological tricks and tactics to wring vital military information from them. His performance as the ill-educated but shrewd interrogator was generally admired, but most reviewers found the picture wordy and static.

Korda returned to Africa for *The Macomber Affair* (1947), from Hemingway's story "The Short Happy Life of Francis Macomber." Robert Preston plays the rich, blustering, but fundamentally likable Macomber who, on safari in Kenya, is shot dead by his destructive wife (Joan Bennett). Gregory Peck is the professional hunter attracted to this dangerous lady. Beginning with the husband dead, the film tells its story in flashback. It was on the whole respectfully received, though critics objected more or less vehemently to its modifying of Hemingway's harsh story—its suggestion that Macomber's murder might after all have been an accident.

Another literary adaptation followed, *A Woman's Vengeance* (1948), adapted by Aldous Huxley and others from his own short story and play *The Giaconda Smile*. Wearer of the mysterious smile is Jessica Tandy—a jealous woman who, spurned by philandering Charles Boyer, poisons his wife and lets him face the gallows for the murder. Cedric Hardwicke gave one of his best performances as the doctor who worms out the truth in the nick of time. A reviewer in the London *Times* wrote that "much of the astringency and intellectual satire of the story had been lost" in the adaptation, but found it "a relief to hear in the cinema conversation with an interest in ideas."

It was, wrote David Thomson, "as if to make amends for *Sanders of the River*" that Korda next filmed Alan Paton's novel about the racial tragedy in South Africa, *Cry the Beloved Country*. Its hero is a black clergyman (Canada Lee), a simple, inarticulate man who leaves the back country around Natal and sets out for Johannesburg in search of his sister and his son. His sister has become a shanty-town prostitute; the son has murdered in a hold-up a man who turns out to have been a white liberal activist for racial equality. The Job-like sufferings of the hero are alleviated when the murdered man's father (Charles Carson) is won over to the side of racial justice. "Although its contents are explosively melodramatic," wrote John McCarten, "it is nev-

er shrill, and when it points up man's inhumanity to man, it does so with a compassionate rather than a fanatical air." The film won the David Selznick award for its contribution to world brotherhood.

Korda's failing health limited his output thereafter, but in 1955 he codirected with Terence Young a Cinemascope remake of *The Four Feathers* called *Storm Over the Nile*. It was enjoyed for its visual splendors, though most reviewers found Anthony Steel and Laurence Harvey poor substitutes for Clements and Ralph Richardson.

A quiet and self-effacing man, always overshadowed by his larger-than-life brother Alexander, Zoltán Korda survived that titan by five years, dying of a heart attack in Los Angeles in 1961. He was himself survived by his English wife, the former actress Joan Gardner, and two sons.

—*L.R.*

FILMS: (with Miklós Pásztory) Karoly-Bakak, 1918; Die Elf Teufel, 1927; (with Leontine Sagan) Men of Tomorrow, 1933; Cash (U.S., For Love and Money), 1933; Sanders of the River (U.S., Bosambo), 1935; Forget Me Not (U.S., Forever Yours), 1936; (with Robert J. Flaherty) Elephant Boy, 1937; The Drum (U.S., Drums), 1938; The Four Feathers, 1939; Jungle Book, 1942; Sahara, 1943; Counter-Attack, 1945; The Macomber Affair, 1947; A Woman's Vengeance, 1948; Cry, the Beloved Country, 1952; (with Terence Young) Storm Over the Nile, 1955.

ABOUT: Armes, R. A Critical History of the British Cinema, 1978; Cripps, T. Slow Fade to Black, 1977; Durgnat, R. A Mirror for England, 1970; Korda, M. Charmed Lives: A Family Romance, 1979; Kulik, K. Alexander Korda, 1975; Richards, J. Visions of Yesterday, 1973; Tabori, P. Alexander Korda, 1959; Thomson, D. A Biographical Dictionary of the Cinema, 1980. *Periodicals*—Australian Journal of Screen Theory 5–6 1980.

"KOSTER, HENRY" (Hermann Kosterlitz) (May 1, 1905–), American director and producer, was born in Berlin to Albert and Emma Kosterlitz. His father was a lingerie wholesaler, and his mother a frustrated musician. With her encouragement and tutelage, the boy drew and painted and briefly studied the piano. At fifteen, he won a minor scholarship to the Academy of Fine Arts in Berlin, afterwards taking an assortment of jobs in which he made use of his artistic training. The advertising signs he painted for a department store brought him an offer from a "trick film" company, where he made animated commercials to be shown between features in local movie theatres. Noticing that audiences chat-

HENRY KOSTER

ted through his offerings, he "added some gags and they started laughing at my commercials." This burgeoning talent for comedy took him into the film industry proper when a director hired him to "punch up" a weak script with gags.

Kosterlitz was soon devoting much of his time to screenwriting. His first script reached the screen in 1924, aptly titled *Die grosse gelegenheit* (*The Big Opportunity*). The Hungarian director, Lorand von Kapdebo, was if anything less experienced than Kosterlitz. Before shooting was completed, the latter had some directorial experience under his belt, albeit uncredited. *Die grosse gelegenheit* "wasn't great," he says, "but at least it reached the screen." Until he was able to support himself completely by screenwriting, Kosterlitz also wrote film criticism and fiction, worked for a time as a newspaper reporter, operated a newsreel camera, and (briefly) acted.

In 1925 he wrote the screenplay for a version of *Jane Eyre* called *Die waise von Lowood* (*The Orphan From Lowood*), directed by Kurt Bernhardt. This was the beginning of a four-year partnership between the two men, who concentrated on dark melodramas and social tracts like the antiabortion *Kinderseelen klagen an* (1927). Kosterlitz's true gifts lay in comedy, however, and eventually he drifted away from Bernhardt and teamed with another screenwriter, Hans Wilhelm. Their first collaboration was a risqué comedy called *Suendig und suess* (*Sweet and Sinful*). It was a turning point in Kosterlitz's career; his gift for humor, kept under wraps for so long, was soon much in demand. By 1929, in addition to his regular writing chores, he was sup-

plementing his income by working for Paramount's Berlin office. There, with the help of an English translator, he "Germanized" (and sometimes added gags to) the intertitles of imported American movies.

His first sound script teamed him again with the director Kurt Bernhardt for *Die letzte kompanie* (*The Last Company,* 1930), starring Emil Jannings and Conrad Veidt. One of Germany's first talkies, it was, according to Henri Langlois, "celebrated for the sound montage that serves as a curtain-raiser but also distinguished by the sobriety of its acting and direction." Soon after he was hired by Joe Pasternak, head of Universal's Berlin studio, to script *Fünf von der Jazzband* (*Five in a Jazzband,* 1932), directed by Erich Engel. According to Koster, Engel "had never been in a studio. . . . I had to help him with the camera angles and the cuts and the technique of making motion pictures. I did the technical part of directing and . . . [Engel] did the acting directing. He was one of the great stage directors, but he had never tackled a motion picture."

Joe Pasternak was impressed by Kosterlitz's ability and took him onto Universal's payroll as a full-fledged director. His first two projects were *Das Abenteuer der Thea Roland* (*The Adventure of Thea Roland,* 1932) and *Das hässliche mädchen* (*The Ugly Girl,* 1933). Both were well received, but at that point Kosterlitz's career in the German film industry was cut short by Hitler's accession to power. Kosterlitz was Jewish, and seeing what lay ahead for his people in Germany, he fled to Paris on April 5, 1933. Once there, he found that foreigners were prohibited from joining the screen directors' guild and was obliged to resume his career as a scenarist. His *Le Sexe faible* (*The Weaker Sex,* 1933), directed by Robert Siodmak, was so successful that he soon had to hire ghostwriters to help him deal with a flood of commissions.

In 1934, his mentor Joe Pasternak invited Kosterlitz to join him in Budapest. His first picture in Hungary was *Peter* (1934), an enormously successful comedy. Shown in 1935 at the International Exposition of Motion Picture Arts in Moscow, it received a gold medal as best comedy of the year. *Kleine mutti* (*Little Mother,* 1934), his next picture, was similarly well received and was later remade in Hollywood as *Bachelor Mother*. According to some accounts, Kosterlitz next made a film in Holland (*Kribbe bejter,* 1935), and then moved on to Vienna, where he directed two pictures, *Katherina die letzte* (*Katherina the Last,* 1935) and *Maria Baschkirtzeff* (1936), about the tragic love affair between Guy de Maupassant and the painter

Maria Baschkirtzeff (Lili Darvas). This film was later released in the United States as *Affairs of Maupassant*.

When Carl Laemmle decided to close down Universal's European operations, he ordered Joe Pasternak back to Hollywood. Pasternak insisted that Kosterlitz be allowed to return with him, though the young director could not speak a word of English. Laemmle was not enthusiastic, remarking that he was "up to his ass in German directors," but eventually capitulated. Hermann Kosterlitz, translated into Henry Koster, landed alone in New York, where he spent three weeks watching American movies by way of a crash course in the English language. He particularly favored the Astaire-Rogers musical *Follow the Fleet*, which he saw countless times. These studies bore fruit on at least one occasion shortly after Koster's arrival in Hollywood. Negotiating with Universal (Pasternak translating), Koster suddenly pronounced, "Ziss guy's not all he's crecked op to be," flummoxing the opposition, who had assumed they were dealing with a greenhorn.

Koster's initial negotiations with Universal were difficult in the extreme. The studio was in deep financial trouble, and by the time Koster arrived, Carl Laemmle had been forced to sell out. "Uncle Carl" had not much wanted Koster's services, and his hard-headed successors wanted them not at all. Koster threatened a lawsuit, and it was finally agreed that he and Pasternak could make one film, on condition that they used only standing sets, contract players, and a miniscule budget. Koster suggested a story he had written in Germany about three teenage girls who mend their parents' broken marriage. He wanted Edith Fellows to star in *Three Smart Girls*. Informed that her fee was too high for such a low-budget production, he turned to his second choice, a fourteen-year-old singer named Deanna Durbin.

Universal expected the movie to fail, providing them with an excuse to fire Koster. Ironically enough, it was hugely successful, setting the studio on the road back to financial health. The Hollywood *Reporter* said that "Universal has taken a story of little consequence and, through fine writing, acting, direction, and production, has made one of the best pieces of entertainment this reviewer has seen in many months. . . . The three smart girls of the picture are Deanna Durbin, Nan Grey, and Barbara Reed, all newcomers, all from the Universal stock company and all certain to go far, particularly Miss Durbin, who is assuredly the greatest find of the year. . . . [She] is one of the most astonishing personalities to come to the screen in a long time.

She can act, sings gloriously and is most pleasant to look at."

Koster's contract was renegotiated. "They paid me more," he says, "and everybody was a little friendlier to me." He directed Durbin again in *100 Men and a Girl* (1937), costarring Adolphe Menjou, Eugene Pallette, and the popular conductor Leopold Stokowski. The hundred men in this Depression movie are unemployed musicians who make a desperate bid for success by trying to persuade the great Stokowski to conduct their orchestra. This is accomplished, of course, through the determined but charming machinations of the film's young star.

Most critics reviewed the picture almost entirely in terms of Durbin. "Histrionically," said *Variety*, "she does everything like a veteran, scores with comedy, charms with her naivete and registers at the tear-ducts with her persuasive emotional passages." The same writer went on to point out that "much of the distinctive nature of the film . . . lies in the vastly improved mechanical skill of tone reproduction. This has been so adroitly and expertly contrived, in combination with camera shots of various instrumental sections, that the effect is startling."

After another bright and well received comedy, *The Rage of Paris* (1938), with Danielle Darrieux and Douglas Fairbanks, Jr., Universal put the Koster-Pasternak-Durbin team back to work on their increasingly popular series. *Three Smart Girls Grow Up* (1939), a sequel to their first hit, even melted the stony heart of Graham Greene. Noting sternly that "the awkward age has never been so laundered and lavendered and laid away," he went on to confess that "it is all charming, very charming. There is no longer any doubt of Miss Durbin's immense talents as an actress; any undertones that there are in this amusing, astute and sentimental tale are supplied by her. Singing 'The Last Rose of Summer' to her preoccupied Wall Street father, blundering into her sisters' love affairs and rearranging them with crude, unscrupulous success, she swings the picture along in her gauche and graceful stride. The competence of the director, Mr. Henry Koster, matches hers: a kind of national value emerges from the *schwärmerei*—it is all Fifth Avenue and girlish freedom—tea at the Waldorf and cold, clear New York spring."

Durbin received a highly publicized first screen kiss from Robert Stack in *First Love* (1939). Graham Greene, by now hopelessly besotted, called it "an honest fairy tale, based even to the slipper and the midnight sanction on *Cinderella* . . . , adroitly directed, amusingly written, and acted with immense virtuosity by a fine cast. It isn't true . . . but that doesn't matter, because there is nothing shabby or hypocritical in the dream which Miss Durbin expresses with the drive of irresistible conviction."

Basil Wright wrote no less warmly of *Spring Parade* (1940), set in the "escapist paradise" of a mythical Old Vienna, where peasant-girl Durbin falls in love with a handsome corporal who turns out to be a brilliant composer as well, and sings for him and the Emperor Franz Josef at the court ball. "Shot after shot swings along to the rhythm of the music," Wright reported, "the camera splendidly gyrates, and the Joe Pasternak repertory company puts up a row of good performances again" (including Mischa Auer's memorable impersonation of a wild and moustachioed *czardas* dancer). Durbin made one more film with Koster and Pasternak before they left Universal, *It Started With Eve* (1941). Her career declined after that, until she retired in 1948, and it might be said that Koster himself never fully recaptured the freshness and authenticity of feeling he achieved in his films with her.

He made one more picture at Universal. *Between Us Girls* (1942) starred Kay Francis as a woman intent on remarriage and on that account pretending to be younger than she is. Diana Barrymore plays her daughter—a twenty-year-old actress who, to further the illusion, passes herself off to her mother's suitor (John Boles) as a child of twelve, in the process almost wrecking her own incipient romance with Robert Cummings. Joe Pasternak had moved over to MGM earlier in the year and the film was produced by Koster himself—he says it was "not so much that they trusted me but that they could save money." Koster believes that in this, the second film of her tragically brief career, Diana Barrymore was not "fully equipped to play so difficult a part. She has to play an actress on the stage, a lover in her private life, and a child with her mother." Most of the critics emphatically disagreed, praising her "brilliantly versatile performance" and announcing that "a new star has quite definitely risen" in this "irresistible" comedy.

That year, 1942, was a momentous one for Koster. He wrapped up his Universal contract, following Pasternak to MGM, received United States citizenship, and in November married Peggy Moran, a twenty-one-year-old actress who had played a small role in *First Love*. It was Koster's second marriage—he had been married briefly in 1935 to Katherine Kiraly—and proved to be both happy and permanent.

Koster's first film at MGM, *Music for Millions* (1944), featured the talented child star Margaret O'Brien as a waif who is adopted by a symphony orchestra conducted by José Iturbi. An obvious

attempt to emulate the successful formula of *100 Men and a Girl,* it was considerably less popular, partly because Koster felt stifled by the "overprogrammed" MGM production style. "They had a coach for this, an aide for that, a department for this," he complains, "more than at any other studio. In most cases it was right, but sometimes it was not so good for the picture, I think. A whole high command was there. Not that it was unpleasant, and you felt very safe there, but it interfered."

Nevertheless, his second MGM assignment, *Two Sisters From Boston* (1946), is one of his favorite pictures: "I had no children in that. I could get a little deeper into the lives of human beings." Another contribution to the contemporary vogue for films featuring pop classics, it has Kathryn Grayson as a proper Bostonian girl ambitious for an operatic career and June Allyson as her even more proper sister. The road to the Metropolitan takes a detour via the Golden Rooster beerhall on the Bowery, presided over by Jimmy Durante. The result pleased almost everyone except serious opera lovers.

Koster felt very differently about his last film for MGM, *The Unfinished Dance* (1947). Another venture into pop culture—this time the ballet—it was a watered-down version of *La Mort du Cygne* (*Ballerina*), made in 1937 by Jean Benoit-Lévy and Marc Epstein. Koster's advice to a recent interviewer was "Don't look at it." Despite the best efforts of Cyd Charisse, Margaret O'Brien, and Danny Thomas (in his movie debut), it was a critical and commercial failure. One reviewer said that it "glitters and crackles in Technicolor. It is spectacular, sentimental, superficial."

Koster's fortunes revived with his next project, made for Sam Goldwyn. The producer, dissatisfied with the original director (and third script) of *The Bishop's Wife,* handed the picture to Koster five weeks into production. The film was based on a novel by Robert Nathan and tells the whimsical story of a young Protestant bishop whose obsession with his new cathedral estranges him from his beautiful wife (Loretta Young). Help arrives in the shape of a debonair and alarmingly attractive angel named Dudley. With the scenarist Robert E. Sherwood, Koster revised the script yet again and switched the two male leads in their roles, handing the miter to David Niven and the supernatural powers to Cary Grant.

The result, released in 1947, was one of Koster's most popular films, a likable Christmas fantasy with strong supporting performances from Monty Woolley as an irascible historian, James Gleason as a philosophical taxi driver, Elsa

Lanchester as an eccentric maid, and Gladys Cooper as a headstrong matron. Cecilia Ager found it "a handsomely accoutered, shrewdly manipulated batch of movie entertainment," including "some first-class comedy and effective sentimentality," while Archer Winsten thought that "never before has one of Robert Nathan's imaginative fantasies been translated so successfully to the screen." It received an Oscar for its sound recording and was nominated for best film and best direction. In Britain it was chosen for the annual Royal Command Performance.

After that, Koster signed a contract with 20th Century–Fox, the studio with which he spent the remainder of his career. His first film there was *The Luck of the Irish* (1948), with Tyrone Power as an American newspaperman who on a visit to Ireland does a kindness to a leprechaun (Cecil Kellaway). The latter follows his benefactor back to New York, sets up as his butler, and rescues him from the boss's daughter so that he may pursue true love and Responsible Journalism with colleen Anne Baxter. Koster says that he likes "stories that are a little pixie-ish, a little fairytale-like, and telling a truth in them"; most reviewers saw his point. Philip Dunne's script (based on a novel) was found "amiably witty," and Kellaway's performance "ravishing."

The majority of the critics seemed happy to swallow a further dose of whimsy in *Come to the Stable* (1949), starring Loretta Young and Celeste Holm as a dashing pair of French nuns trying to build a children's hospital in New England. There was a somewhat more mixed reaction to Koster's version of Gogol's *The Inspector General* (1949), made on loan to Warner Brothers. The "watered-down and gagged-up" adaptation by Philip Rapp and Harry Kurnitz turned the satire into what one reviewer called "a circus with Mr. Danny Kaye as the chief clown."

Koster next delivered two bright Betty Grable vehicles, *Wabash Avenue* (1950), a remake of Walter Lang's *Coney Island* (which had also starred Grable), and *My Blue Heaven* (1950), a comedy-drama costarring Dan Dailey about a show-biz couple's efforts to adopt a child. Koster followed these with one of the most enduring favorites among his films, *Harvey* (1950), made on loan to his old studio, Universal. Based on the hit play by Mary Chase, *Harvey* is about the friendship of gentle boozer Elwood P. Dowd (James Stewart) with a six-foot, three-inch white rabbit visible (for the most part) only to him. Koster recalls it as "a complete, one-hundred-percent pleasure, the whole picture, and I still think it's one of my best."

The public and most of the critics agreed. "If you're for warm and gentle whimsy, for a charmingly fanciful farce and for a little touch of pathos anent the fateful evanescence of man's dreams," gurgled Bosley Crowther, "then the movie version of *Harvey* is definitely for you." Dilys Powell wasn't so sure. It seemed to her that the play had been "farce with a touch of sentiment," whereas Koster had given it "the tone of comedy with a touch of farce. I won't say the result isn't pleasant now and then. Dowd's account of his first meeting with Harvey and his talk with the young lovers become touching; but in contrast the rougher scenes in the mental home seem odious as they weren't odious in the theatre."

James Stewart also starred in Koster's next picture, another success, made in England at Fox's studio there. *No Highway in the Sky* (1951) was adapted by R. C. Sherriff and others from Nevil Shute's novel *No Highway* (the film's British title). Stewart plays Mr. Honey, a vague, eccentric, but brilliant mathematician in an airplane factory whose research has convinced him that the company's newest passenger model has a lethal design flaw. Marlene Dietrich plays a sympathetic movie star who flies with Honey in one of the threatened planes, and Glynis Johns is the stewardess who decides to take him and his much put-upon daughter under her wing. Otis L. Guernsey called the movie "a quietly amusing and occasionally suspenseful comedy-drama . . . that is at least unusual and at best wryly funny."

There followed three films starring Clifton Webb. In *Mr. Belvedere Rings the Bell* (1951) he plays the omniscient snob Lynn Belvedere, first seen in *Sitting Pretty* (1947). Here he applies his theories on rejuvenation to the inmates of an old people's home, with results that few found even remotely funny. *Elopement* (1951) was better liked—a domestic comedy with Webb as an irascible father in pursuit of his errant daughter (Anne Francis). Webb then played John Philip Sousa in *Stars and Stripes Forever* (1952), a highly fictionalized but entertaining biography of the March King. This movie was scripted by Lamar Trotti, who also wrote "The Cop and the Anthem," Koster's episode in the omnibus film *O. Henry's Full House* (1952).

My Cousin Rachel was adapted from Daphne du Maurier's novel by its producer, Nunnally Johnson. Richard Burton made his very successful Hollywood debut in this film as Philip Ashley, a rich young Cornishman who falls in love with his guardian's mysterious widow, Rachel (Olivia de Havilland), even though he suspects her of killing her husband. Fearing that she is trying to poison him also, Philip engineers her death, only to find that she was blameless (perhaps). The picture was generally well received, though some critics, like Otis Guernsey, found it in the end "more puzzling than mysterious . . . a minor thriller all dressed up in a big production."

After that, Koster went to work on *The Robe,* based on Lloyd C. Douglas's novel about Christ's robe (gambled away at the Crucifixion) and its effect on several lives. Fox had owned the rights for about ten years when Koster was assigned to make the picture. Having considered the new three-projector Cinerama process, the studio settled on CinemaScope as the most suitable medium for their Biblical epic, but took no chances. The cinematographer Leon Shamroy shot every scene twice, once in CinemaScope and once in the standard 1:33 × 1 ratio for theatres not yet equipped for wide screen.

Most critics gave more attention to the film's process than to its content. Bosley Crowther, indeed, called it "a historical drama less compelling than the process by which it is shown," and went on: "The shape of the screen—wide and narrow—makes for an occasional oppressiveness. A sense of the image being pressed down and drawn out inevitably occurs"; nevertheless, "the expanse of the screen across the theatre gives opportunity for panoramic scenes of overwhelming beauty." *The Robe* turned out to be the top grosser of 1953 and one of the most profitable films ever. It also garnered Academy Award nominations for best picture, best actor (Richard Burton), cinematography, and costume design. All of Koster's films after that were made in CinemaScope or, later, Panavision.

Marlon Brando contributed a stiff, tense, powerful study of Napoleon to *Desirée* (1954), an epic more of the bedchamber than the battlefield, and a flop. Koster found a more sympathetic subject in *A Man Called Peter* (1955), a respectful adaptation of Catherine Marshall's adulatory biography of her husband (Richard Todd), the Scottish minister who became chaplain to the U.S. Senate. There was an even warmer reception for *Good Morning, Miss Dove* (1955), from the novel by Frances Gray Patton, with Jennifer Jones as the redoubtable and much-loved New England schoolmarm.

Although it is clear that Koster was at his best with warm human dramas like *Miss Dove,* Fox persisted in handing him wide-screen epics, costume and otherwise. *The Virgin Queen* (1955), with Bette Davis raising tight-lipped hell as the eponymous Elizabeth, was followed by *D-Day: The Sixth of June* (1956), which in fact deals less with the Normandy invasion than with the romantic problem (Dana Wynter) shared by two of the invaders, Robert Taylor and Richard Todd. Taylor also starred, with Elisabeth Mueller, in the big-business saga *The Power and the Prize,* made on loan to MGM and including "some unintentionally hilarious scenes from English life."

After an ill-advised remake of Gregory La Cava's *My Man Godfrey,* best forgotten, Koster returned to his native Berlin in 1958 to film *Fraulein,* set just after World War II. An American officer (Mel Ferrer) finds a girl (Dana Wynter) who had helped him when he was an escaping prisoner and rescues her from the chorus line to which she has been reduced. "It was to me a sentimental journey," Koster says, "because the picture was shot in Berlin, in the ruins, and on the Rhine River, which I had fond memories of [from] when I was a young student." The movie was praised for its "convincing atmosphere of bombed buildings and moral decay," but found less persuasive as an account of human relationships.

From Germany, Koster moved to Italy for *The Naked Maja* (1959), about the artist Goya (Anthony Franciosa) and his turbulent relationship with his model and mistress the Duchess of Alba (Ava Gardner). These stars had an equally turbulent relationship with the director. "Really, out of such friction and mutual irritation there can't come out a good picture," Koster mused, and he was right.

Back in Hollywood, Koster directed an uninspired but successful adaptation of the Rodgers and Hammerstein musical *Flower Drum Song,* made for Ross Hunter at Universal, returning to Fox for *The Story of Ruth.* Another Biblical drama, though not an epic, the latter had a mixed but generally favorable reception, one reviewer calling it "a warm and moving film, several cuts above the religious films that cinema viewers have been used to."

The Story of Ruth—Koster's last film set in the past—was followed by three comedies starring James Stewart. *Mr. Hobbs Takes a Vacation* (1963), about the tribulations of a family man on his annual seaside vacation, seemed to *Variety* a movie "peppered with refreshingly sharp, sophisticated references and quips," though Nunnally Johnson's screenplay "falls down in development of its timely premise, leaving the cast and . . . Koster heavily dependent on their own comedy resources in generating fun. Koster manages, more often than not, to keep the bubble bubbling."

Mr. Hobbs made a respectable showing at the box office, as did its successor. *Take Her, She's Mine* (1963) was adapted by Johnson from the play by Phoebe and Henry Ephron about an all-

American father's assorted anxieties over his politically liberated and all too nubile daughter (Sandra Dee). Most reviewers enjoyed the movie, praising especially the endeavors in well-written supporting roles of Robert Morley as a complaisant British parent and John McGiver as a fatuous school-board chairman. Stewart was a harassed father again in *Dear Brigitte* (1965), this time of an eight-year-old mathematical prodigy. The latter makes a pen-pal of Brigitte Bardot, who insists on meeting him. "Nothing in my memory is so embarrassing as this scene," wrote Patrick Gibbs, "and I might almost say the same for the film as a whole."

The failure of finesse and conviction in this picture was even more evident in *The Singing Nun* (1966), made on loan to MGM and starring Debbie Reynolds. It was inspired by the career of a Belgian nun who sang pop religious songs and made the charts with one of them. Pauline Kael, kinder than some, wrote that the film's characters "behave like animals in a Disney movie; they are so cute and full of tricks." Years later, Koster remembered life on that set as a nightmare of clashing wills (his and Debbie Reynolds') and backstabbing. "So that makes it tough," he says, "I'm a nervous man and I went home and I was really tired. I was finished. I didn't want it anymore."

He halfheartedly considered a few more projects but in practice sat out the remainder of his Fox contract. He did direct a Pat Boone television pilot, *My Island Family,* but the series was not picked up. In 1967 Koster retired with his wife Peggy to a comfortable home in Pacific Palisades, California. They have two grown sons, Nicholas and Peter. A son from Koster's first marriage, Robert, is a television producer. In retirement, Koster's childhood interest in art has revived. Interviewed by Irene Atkins in 1982 for the Directors Guild of America *Oral History,* he said "I have a studio. I do portraits of people and I've had several shows."

Koster's Hollywood films, up to and including *The Robe* in 1953, were for the most part admired by critics and extremely popular with audiences. Like his contemporary Jean Negulesco, Koster was not at home with the wide screen or the expansive epics it demanded. After *The Robe,* there were few really good films, and the endearing touches of whimsy with which Koster "signed" his work became crassly sentimental viewed through the giant eye of the Cinema-Scope lens.

Nor did Koster benefit from the rise of *auteurist* criticism, perhaps because his movies were so unfashionably "decent." He said: "I don't believe in making pictures about dope fiends, lesbianism, cannibalism, deviations, etc. I know such people exist but it is not for me and I do not believe their problems have anything to do with entertainment." His regard for family relationships—often more important in his films than sexual relationships—and his fondness for religious themes are equally alien to the contemporary climate.

Perhaps Koster's time will nevertheless come round again. The Deanna Durbin films and some of the later comedies were works of undeniable charm and invention. If he lacked Lubitsch's interest in the salacious, Koster shared his flair for the offhand but revealing remark, the subtly suggestive gesture. And he was the most humane of filmmakers; there are virtually no villains in his pictures.

—F. T.

FILMS: Das Abenteuer der Thea Roland, 1932; Das hässliche mädchen, 1933; Peter, 1934; Kleine mutti, 1934; Kribbe bejter, 1935; Katherina die letzte, 1935; Maria Baschkirtzeff (also made in German, Italian, and French versions; released in the United States in 1938 as Affairs of Maupassant), 1936; Three Smart Girls, 1936; 100 Men and a Girl, 1937; The Rage of Paris, 1938; Three Smart Girls Grow Up, 1939; First Love, 1939; Spring Parade, 1940; It Started With Eve, 1941; Between Us Girls, 1942; Music for Millions, 1944; Two Sisters From Boston, 1946; The Unfinished Dance, 1947; The Bishop's Wife, 1947; The Luck of the Irish, 1948; Come to the Stable, 1949; The Inspector General, 1949; Wabash Avenue, 1950; My Blue Heaven, 1950; Harvey, 1950; No Highway in the Sky (U.K., No Highway), 1951; Mr. Belvedere Rings the Bell, 1951; Elopement, 1951; (with others) O. Henry's Full House, 1952; Stars and Stripes Forever, 1952; My Cousin Rachel, 1953; The Robe, 1953; Desirée, 1954; A Man Called Peter, 1955; The Virgin Queen, 1955; Good Morning, Miss Dove, 1955; D-Day: The Sixth of June, 1956; The Power and the Prize, 1956; My Man Godfrey, 1957; Fraulein, 1958; La Maja Desnuda/The Naked Maja, 1959; The Story of Ruth, 1960; Flower Drum Song, 1961; Mr. Hobbs Takes a Vacation, 1963; Take Her, She's Mine, 1963; Dear Brigitte, 1965; The Singing Nun, 1966.

ABOUT: Atkins, I. K. A Directors Guild of America Oral History, 1982 (unpublished?); Cook, D. A History of Narrative Film, 1981; Dooley, R. From Scarface to Scarlet, 1981; Eames, J. D. The MGM Story, 1975; Hirschhorn, C. The Warner Bros. Story, 1979; Hirschhorn, C. The Hollywood Musical, 1981; Hirschhorn, C. The Universal Story, 1983; Jewell, R. B. and Harbin, V. The RKO Story, 1982; Johnson, D. and Levanthal, E. The Letters of Nunnally Johnson, 1981; Koszarski, R. Hollywood Directors 1941–1976, 1977; Stack, R. and Evans, M. Straight Shooting, 1980; Thomson, D. A Biographical Dictionary of the Cinema, 1980. *Periodicals*—Citizen News November 13, 1961; September 9, 1964; Film Weekly January 28, 1939; Friday September 20, 1940; Los Angeles Herald Examiner April 21, 1962; Los Angeles Times June 30, 1950; February 9, 1965; New York Times July 2, 1950; New York Times Magazine October 26, 1952; Universal News Flashes June 9, 1941.

*KOZINTSEV, GRIGORI MIKHAILO-VICH (March 22, 1905–May 11, 1973), Soviet film and theatre director, scenarist, and theoretician, was born in Kiev, the capital city of the Ukraine, and attended the gymnasium there. In his autobiographical statement in Luda and Jean Schnitzer's *Cinema in Revolution,* he wrote: "It was a queer kind of education we had in the first years of the Revolution. Classes were frequently interrupted by artillery fire, and when I left school in the evening, with my satchel stuffed with books, you could never be sure who was currently occupying the town. . . . At Petchursk, not far from the gymnasium, the twisted corpses of shot men lay in the ditch. . . . People spoke of death with no respect. . . . I saw with my own eyes Shchors' troops enter the town, and the detachment of the First Cavalry Army. This was in 1919. . . . And immediately, in the revolutionary town, every kind of art began to flourish. . . . Everyone took to art with passion, and with passion people taught it."

While still attending the gymnasium, Kozintsev went in the evenings to painting classes given by Alexandra Exter. "In fact," he said, "I did not do at all well with still-lifes; but I invented parodies, I drew caricatures, I designed décors for imaginary plays." When some of the class's older students were entrusted with the task of decorating a propaganda train, they took Kozintsev along to help and he used a freight wagon as a stage for a short agit-sketch or propaganda play—his first work as a director, staged at the age of fourteen! Soon afterwards, Kozintsev got a job as a stage designer's assistant at the Solvtzovsky Theatre. One day he showed his sketches to the director, Konstantin Mardjanov, and—still in his mid-teens—was assigned to design the décor for the operetta *La Mascotte* in collaboration with an equally youthful painter named Sergei Yutkevich.

Yutkevich and Kozintsev shared their generation's passion for the poems and plays of the Futurist Vladimir Mayakovsky and, even before they had completed their designs for *La Mascotte,* had gathered a group of young actors around them who "all worshipped the same god." With Mardjanov's help, they launched a little theatre of their own in a Kiev cellar formerly occupied by a cabaret. They opened with a clown show written by Kozintsev and followed this with a Petrushka play, a puppet version of a Pushkin story, and popular melodramas, per-

GRIGORI KOZINTSEV

forming in clubs and on the street as well as in their own theatre.

Kozintsev was still only fifteen or sixteen when the Kiev Union of Art Workers sent him to continue his studies in Petrograd (formerly St. Petersburg, later Leningrad). He set off with a pillowcase containing a spare shirt, a volume of Mayakovsky's poems, and a set of Picasso reproductions, traveling by cattle train and freight car. The country was in the throes of the Civil War and the great city was half empty. Kozintsev found Mardjanov at the Palace Theatre (and was immediately signed on as a director) and then enrolled at the Academy of Fine Arts; it was desperately short of teachers, students, equipment, and heating, but rich in "the same kind of joyful brotherhood" Kozintsev had known in Kiev. "No one bothered about cold or hunger. Life seemed marvelously interesting, and there was no doubt at all that this moment marked the coming of a new era, the era of art. This art had to be as bold as the workers' power itself, as pitiless towards the past as the Revolution. Everyone argued fiercely about 'contemporary rhythms' and 'industrial poetry' whilst chopping wood and lighting the stove."

In Petrograd Kozintsev observed the great poet Alexander Blok observing a circus show, saw the "one-man *avant-garde*" Vsevolod Meyerhold, heard Mayakovsky himself thundering out his verses. "The life of art simmered around us," he wrote. "The extent to which we were crazed about art in those difficult years now seems quite astonishing." And the art had to be new, raw, proletarian, iconoclastic, and as noisy as possible—"creativity," "sensibility," and "feeling" were dirty words. The slogan was Mayakovsky's: "Prance if you like or kick if you like,/ But I want the racket of tempests!"

Kozintsev struck up a friendship with a young dramatist named Leonid Trauberg and soon they were joined by two old friends from Kiev—Sergei Yutkevich and the actor and writer Alexei Kapler. A new group was born, captivated by the circus, by Chaplin, by fairs, posters, advertisements, and all the "street arts," and by what little vaudeville they had seen. They called themselves FEKS—Fabrika eksentricheskovo aktyora (Factory of the Eccentric Actor). It was December 1921 and Kozintsev was sixteen.

The following year FEKS issued its *Eccentric Manifesto*. For Kozintsev and his friends, "it was a case of trying to demolish all the usual theatrical forms and to find others, which could convey the intense sentiment of the new life. Unless this last point is recognized, our creations of that period would become incomprehensible. All these experiments, all these quests for new forms came because we had an intense feeling of an extraordinary renewal of life. . . . What we were doing then we were doing in the cold and famine of a devastated country. . . . The State, occupied with a full-scale Civil War, was undergoing enormous difficulties. Yet the dominant sentiment was the affirmation of life. . . . In the midst of every kind of privation a sort of fair was going on."

FEKS' first production in 1922 was a joyously unorthodox version of Gogol's *Marriage*, which ended with the "author" dying in despair on the stage. The play was presented as a spectacle combining elements of circus, cabaret, and cinema—passages from a Chaplin comedy were projected at the back of the stage while the actors cavorted in front. The Petrograd theatres were so much in demand that the cast had to rehearse elsewhere, stepping onto their stage for the first time two hours before the curtain was due to rise on the first show. This dress rehearsal took place while the audience clamored in the foyer and a young visitor "with a huge forehead and a lot of hair" assured them that their production was much too slow—Sergei Eisenstein. The same year Kozintsev and Yutkevich exhibited their posters and collages at the famous "Left Stream" Exhibition, placarding them with slogans in support of the "street arts"; the important "Leftist" art critic Nikolai Punin, reading these, remarked scornfully: "If you carry on like this, you will end up by saying that the cinema is an art as well."

Other "eccentric" productions followed, and FEKS established a studio where young actors were trained in circus and pantomime techniques. The future film director Sergei Gerasimov went to his first FEKS workshop in 1923 (by which time Yutkevich and Kapler had left Petrograd) and found himself in a huge room where "a score of youngsters of my own age were performing somersaults under the direction of two masters, the older of whom, Leonid Trauberg, was twenty-one. Grigori Kozintsev was scarcely eighteen, but his authority over this rowdy crew was already absolute and without appeal. . . . FEKS rejected, overthrew and negated in every possible way pre-existing forms of theatrical art. To this effect, its members possessed a whole arsenal of whistles and rattles which allowed them to organize demonstrations in the 'academic' theatres. . . . I joined them with joy. In this workshop they were doing absolutely unimaginable things! The avowed end of our activity was the overthrow of all the old values. . . . We had contacts with Mayakovsky and his 'LEF' group. Meyerhold also played a role in our group. We made a lot of racket, but we were so young that people accepted us cheerfully. . . . Then the cinema came and swept us off our feet. We were all of us precipitated into this path which, it (rightly) seemed to us, offered a much vaster field and richer means to express ourselves."

Having decided that "all our tendencies and our instincts drew us" to the cinema, Kozintsev and Trauberg wrote a scenario and took it to the offices of Sevzapkino (North-Western Cinema), where they made friends with the young secretary of the studio—another future director, Friedrich Ermler. To everyone's surprise, Sevzapkino accepted the scenario, and with one of the studio's directors (B. V. Tchaikowski) as guide and mentor, Kozintsev and Trauberg made their first movie, *Pokhozhdeniya Octyabrini* (*The Adventures of Octyabrina*, 1924).

This short fantastic comedy centered upon an American attempt to screw tsarist debts out of Soviet workers—a capitalist scheme which is foiled by the daring young komsomol Octyabrina (played by the dancer Z. Tarakhovskaya). The picture made no great impact—a few years later the critic Yuri Tinyanov wrote that "this small film, which was made under heaven knows what conditions, does not belong among the important films of any genre. *The Adventures* made liberal use of all the tricks that the FEKS people had been panting to utilize once they had entered that paradise—the cinema. The least pretentious episode I can remember from it is a crowd bicycling across roofs! Nevertheless, the FEKS are right to love their *Octyabrina*. It taught them not about 'monumental epics' or 'fundamental comics,' where there were already footprints to guide them, but it helped them to discover, even to invent, elements of cinema."

Making this first film, Kozintsev wrote, "we tamed the old wild beast with three legs and a great glass eye: an ancient Pathé camera, practically worn out. The handle turned with an asthmatic panting noise. All at once the panting turned to a rattle. . . . The side was opened and out fell the film, concertina'd. But this prehistoric beast seemed to us a miracle. We could hoist its three feet to the highest point in the town and bend its glass eye downward. We could bury it or stride over it. The handle could turn faster or slower; we could wind back the film and superimpose one, two (five, ten) other images. The discomfort of the places in which we chose to shoot was to play an important part in our destiny. The director assigned to the film, Tchaikowski, listened sympathetically to our ideas but when he discovered that the first shot was to be made on the sloping roof of a very tall building, he declined to be present at the start of the shooting. As our next viewpoint was the spire of the Admiralty Building . . . , we found ourselves working alone, without supervision."

In spite of the knockabout anti-American propaganda in these early films, Gerasimov recalls that the FEKS group (like most of their contemporaries) were "infatuated with the American cinema. Detective film, burlesques, melodramas and of course all the films of Griffith were for us revelations and models." They moved into a commandeered mansion in Leningrad (as the city became in 1924), where the Gobelins tapestries competed for wall space with the brashest kind of American movie posters. Gerasimov and the other young actors practiced gymnastics, acrobatics, horseback-riding, boxing—"vital disciplines of the actor's profession"; they studied theory with Trauberg and, at the feet of their "undisputed master" Kozintsev learned the art of "cinegesture," which was "based on the mathematical precision of American comic and detective films. The actor was required not to 'feel.' The very word 'feeling' was . . . pronounced with derisive grimaces accompanied by scornful laughter from the whole troupe."

FEKS' second movie was *Mishki protiv Yudenica* (*Mishka Against Yudenich,* 1925), a comedy-thriller for children about treachery and espionage during the Civil War. Gerasimov (who appeared in it) says that "the whole scenario was written on a little scrap of paper; everything had to be improvised in the course of shooting, and we might—had to—do anything that came into our heads. This adventure passed all imagining, and when I think back to it, I tell myself that only our robust good health saved us from certain death. . . . We leapt from signals onto moving trains; we galloped along railroad tracks, breaking the legs of our horses—and our own. It was an accumulation of the most audacious tricks, dizzy falls, the maddest inventions."

"Eccentricity" ceased to be enough for Kozintsev after he saw Eisenstein's *Strike* (1925). According to Gerasimov, he came back to the studio and announced: "All that we've been doing up to now is baby stuff. We have to review our whole way of thinking, everything. We have to look for serious links with real life." The effects of this decision can already be seen in Kozintsev and Trauberg's next film (and first full-length feature) *Chyortovo koleso* (*The Devil's Wheel,* 1926), about a sailor who misses his ship because he spends too long at a fair with a pretty girl, but who vindicates himself by destroying one of the gangs who preyed on the citizens of Petrograd during the Civil War.

The Devil's Wheel is still experimental and even bizarre in style, but according to Jay Leyda "the clash between the realistic material and the eccentric treatment by the FEKS seems to have increased the force of the film. All disparate elements were pulled together by the dramatic, expressive, Germanic photography of their new cameraman, Andrei Moskvin, who was to identify himself with the whole film career of Kozintsev and Trauberg." David Robinson found "odd anticipations of Hitchcock in the scenes set in the fairground, and in the memory man who turns out to be associated with the gang."

Expressionist tendencies were even more overt in *Shinel* (*The Overcoat/The Cloak,* 1926), adapted by Yuri Tinyanov from Gogol's famous story. The picture brilliantly unifies FEKS' stylized, acrobatic, and deliberately melodramatic acting techniques, Moskvin's camerawork—veering between the romantic and the grotesque—and the richly atmospheric interiors and street scenes of the designer Yevgeni Enei, who had also become a permanent member of Kozintsev and Trauberg's team. After *Bratishka* (*Little Brother,* 1927), a lyrical little comedy about the love affair between a truckdriver and a streetcar conductor, came *S.V.D.* (*Soyuz Velikogo Dela—The Club of the Great Deed,* 1927), dealing with an episode in the Decembrist Revolt of 1825. This was noticeably more naturalistic in its style than its predecessors, and considerably more ambitious in scale. Gerasimov, who scored a great personal success as the *provocateur* Medoks, called it the first FEKS film "in which human and social elements and historic problems at last appeared"—even if these elements were somewhat overshadowed by Enei's spectacular sets and costumes and Moskvin's dramatically-lit photography.

S.V.D. established Kozintsev and Trauberg's

reputation, and their next picture was their first truly mature work. Another and even more lavish historical drama, *Novyi Vavilon* (*The New Babylon*, 1929), presents a succession of incidents during the Paris Commune of 1871 to reflect the conflict between the Paris workers and the bourgeoisie. The heroine is Louise (Elena Kuzmina), a clerk in a luxury store—the New Babylon—who provides a link between the two classes; recognizing the selfish materialism of the people she serves, she joins the Communards and dies for her principles. When the Germans attack, the heroism of the workers is contrasted with the cowardice of the rich. Scripted by the directors, photographed by Moskvin, and designed by Enei, the film took a year and a half to complete.

Jay Leyda wrote that *The New Babylon* forms "a consistently magnificent climax to the silent films of Kozintsev and Trauberg. The performances have just the right mixture of warmth and caricature, and the chiefly studio photography . . . is irreproachable. . . . It is a glittering film in which the glitter plays a calculated dramatic role. It is one of the most sardonic of Soviet films, and succeeds where most Soviet films about the past or the capitalist world do not; the trip to Paris made by Kozintsev and Trauberg just before filming their scenario must have been an extremely rewarding excursion." According to Alexander Birkos, however, the film appeared "at a time when the whole atmosphere in the Soviet film industry was changing. Critics were not too happy with the film's expressionistic style which they saw as similar to Eisenstein's *October,* which had been criticized for being too intellectual. Only today is *New Babylon* considered by the Soviets to be the climax of Soviet silent film art." It did not help that the score written by Dmitri Shostakovich to accompany this silent movie was so advanced in its orchestral combinations that it defeated the première orchestra, convincing contemporary observers that the conductor was drunk.

The New Babylon was Kozintsev and Trauberg's last wholly silent film. *Odna* (*Alone*), which followed in 1931, was also shot silent, but had music (again by Shostakovich) and fragments of dialogue added afterwards by Lev Arnshtam. Kuzmina plays a young teacher assigned to a post in the remote and freezing wilderness of the Altai, whose bleakness is vividly captured in the location photography (and underlined by the fine score). At first she yearns desperately for the civilization of Leningrad (as Kozintsev and Trauberg themselves reportedly did during the filming), but gradually comes to terms with the wilderness and its people. A tense, subtle, and psychologically convincing film, it was consider-

ably more popular with contemporary audiences and critics than its predecessor, but is said to have dissatisfied its directors.

For their next project, Kozintsev and Trauberg set out to trace the whole history of the Bolshevik Revolution, recording these enormous events through the political education and development of a typical young party worker. The resulting trilogy was the product of prolonged and careful study of contemporary memoirs and of all that the directors had learned together about filmmaking. The first part of the trilogy, *Yunost Maksima* (*The Youth of Maxim,* 1935) is set in St. Petersburg in the period of tsarist repression that followed the abortive revolution of 1905. It shows how young Maxim (Boris Chirkov) becomes involved in clandestine political work through his love for the wise and beautiful Natasha (Valentina Kibardina), an activist schoolteacher, and through the influence of an old militant whom he meets in prison.

The "synthetic Bolshevik" Maxim miraculously emerges as a wholly believable and likeable human being—tough, stubborn, funny, and optimistic. The film's narrative is made up of a rigorously selected series of episodes from Maxim's life—many completed sections were reportedly sacrificed in the editing. Shostakovich provided music for the prologue, but elsewhere the score relied on songs and accordion music that might actually have been heard in the St. Petersburg slums—including one tune that after much research and debate was chosen as Maxim's theme. Moskvin's photography also eschews self-conscious virtuosity, showing us the buildings and streets of the city as if through Maxim's eyes. This fresh, cheerful, and witty film refuses easy heroics, retaining something of the old FEKS ability to see the humorously incongruous even in potentially ugly scenes. It was received with pride and delight by both critics and public, winning first prize at the Moscow Film Festival in 1935 and bringing Kozintsev and Trauberg the state's highest cultural award, the Order of Lenin.

Vozvrashcheniye Maksima (*The Return of Maxim,* 1937) is set in the months before World War I. The hero is now a fully committed Bolshevik revolutionary, and there are fewer touches of FEKS grotesquerie. Here, as in the first film in the trilogy, the directors used with excellent effect a technique recommended by Stanislavsky, rehearsing members of the cast in improvised scenes that were never intended to be filmed, so as to help each actor "to a more explicit comprehension of his whole image." (Chirkov even worked for a time in a Vyborg factory in order to master his role.) Vyborg is the industrial suburb of Leningrad, and provides the title of the third film in the series, *Vyborgskaya storona* (*The Vyborg Side*, 1939). This deals with the events of 1918, from the capture of the Winter Palace to the dispersal of the Constituent Assembly. Maxim becomes a political commissar in charge of the State Bank, and Natasha is made a judge. In this movie the actor Maxim Strauch appears as Lenin, Mikhail Gelovani as Stalin—roles they were both to repeat many times.

The Vyborg Side is inevitably a duller and more earnest film than its predecessors, but the trilogy as a whole remains, as Georges Sadoul concluded, the finest of the works created in the collaboration between Kozintsev and Trauberg, "a perfect example of socialist realism at its best." "At a time when American films were concentrating on compressed and swift narrative," Sadoul wrote, "Kozintsev and Trauberg luxuriated in lengthy and detailed exposition. They managed, in spite of this, to avoid heaviness, overcrowding, vulgarity, and the serious nature of the subject was tempered with a robust humor." Maxim was adopted a national hero, and he and his theme song passed into modern Soviet folklore.

Indeed, Maxim became so much a symbol of the revolutionary spirit that he was subsequently resuscitated in films by other directors, including Sergei Gerasimov's "Meeting With Maxim" in *Fighting Film Album No. 1* (1941), which launched a monthly series of excellent wartime anthologies of short films by distinguished directors. Kozintsev himself contributed to *Album No. 2* (1941)—a brief gag called "Incident at the Telegraph Office" in which Napoleon sends a warning to Hitler. He did not resume his collaboration with Trauberg until late in the war, when they made *Prostiye lyudi* (*Plain People*, 1945). This film was intended as a tribute to the workers on the home front and dealt with the difficulties caused by poor leadership in evacuating a Leningrad factory to Uzbekistan. It was released and then banned, presumably on account of its criticisms of the Party leadership. Kozintsev and Trauberg, together with Pudovkin and Eisenstein, were all condemned in the infamous Central Committee resolution of September 4, 1946 for their "erroneous" interpretations of Russian history.

Plain People was quietly re-released ten years later, in a version that was probably much cut and revised, but Kozintsev and Trauberg never worked together again. The latter seems to have born the brunt of the criticism in 1946, being barred from filmmaking until after Stalin's death. The nature of their long collaboration was never made explicit, but Sadoul wrote that Trauberg "appears to have been mainly the scriptwriter on the remarkable series of films the two made together. Perhaps less artistic and refined than Kozintsev, he would seem to have contributed to their films a particular emotional tone and his sense of observation of everyday life." At any rate, when Trauberg returned to direction in the late 1950s, his few films were of no great merit.

Meanwhile, Kozintsev tried to regain official approval with *Pirogov* (1947), a biography of the nineteenth-century surgeon which seems to have been of no more interest than its successor, *Belinsky* (1953), another orthodox biography. After that, Kozintsev concentrated for a time on the theatre, which attracted less official attention, directing *Hamlet* and other Shakespeare plays in Leningrad. He returned to international attention four years after Stalin's death with *Don Kikhot* (*Don Quixote*, 1957), adapted by Yevgeni Shvartz from Cervantes' masterpiece. The film stars the veteran actor Nikolai Cherkasov, who had played the old knight in a number of stage productions, while Yuri Tolubeyev is a "vulnerably human" Sancho Panza.

The film was warmly received all over the world. "Visually," wrote Isabel Quigly, it is "one of the most magnificent spectacles you could hope to see, particularly the outdoor scenes that have caught the empty brown landscapes of central Spain to perfection; and the two main figures are almost uncannily what one had hoped for. . . . No one, luckily, has tried to look Spanish, and somehow the film, without appearing specifically Spanish, has caught instead what applies beyond Spain, the spirit that has made what on the face of it is a literary satire of a limited and quite local appeal . . . into a profound and powerful allegory whose central character is one of the recognisable figures . . . of the world's metaphorical imagination." David Robinson found the movie's use of color "exceptional in the period for its sophistication and restraint" and called it "arguably the best of all the many screen adaptations of Cervantes."

There were similar comments about Kozintsev's screen version of *Hamlet* (1964), the preparation and making of which occupied him for the intervening eight years. (Indeed, Kozintsev had been fascinated by the play since the earliest days of FEKS.) In one of the several essays he published while he was actively planning the film, he describes how he had inspected various medieval castles as possible locations and rejected them all: "Historical and geographical authenticity are not the authenticity of poetry. . . . What one sees in the mind cannot easily be translated into visual terms." However, "the cinema is first and foremost a visual art. A screen version entails a decisive alteration of the play's structure. . . . The poetic texture has itself to be transformed into a visual poetry, into the dynamic organisation of film imagery. What I have in mind is the possibility of conveying both a sense of human fate and the atmosphere of a political poem—of finding the inner connections between People, Nature, and History itself."

For example, working from this thesis, it seemed to Kozintsev significant that Ophelia's mad scene takes place during Laertes' revolt: "In our film Ophelia walks about a palace that is paralyzed by alarm. . . . The sounds of battle, fear, hatred, reign everywhere. And in the general confusion there is only one happy person—Ophelia. To be out of one's mind here is to be happy." Similarly, Hamlet's loneliness is emphasized when his first soliloquy is spoken in the midst of a bustling, jostling crowd excited at the start of a new reign. "The process tracing the spiritual life of Shakespeare's plays," Kozintsev wrote, "cannot be separated from tracing the historical process. The essence of the art of filmmaking, it seems to me, consists in the linking of these two viewpoints. The close shot catches the barely perceptible spiritual movement, while the general view shows the movement of historical time. This isn't just a question of the technical possibilities of montage, but is a means of depicting the fate of human beings which differs from the means employed in the theatre." Of the available Russian translations of *Hamlet*, Kozintsev chose to use the free version of Boris Pasternak, which seeks to capture "the living relevance of Shakespeare" rather than to ape the verse patterns of the original. The score was assigned to Shostakovich and the 150-minute film was shot in black and white and scope by Jonas Gricius and designed by Enei.

An anonymous Canadian critic has explained how the whole line of the film is laid down in the opening sequence: "Shots of a restless, frothing sea are succeeded by the sight of one black flag after another being thrust from the castle's windows to mark the King's death. Hamlet gallops full pelt across the sands towards Elsinore, and into the great sombre castle. Claudius's rule is proclaimed in the crowded courtyard; the drawbridge is pulled up, shutting the castle in on itself. . . . The castle and the court . . . are used to create a feeling of encirclement by iron, stone and the watchful eyes of the courtiers. 'Denmark's a prison'—shots of a massive portcullis, the vast drawbridge, guards with muskets and a harsh iron corset into which Ophelia is strapped as she dresses in black to mourn Polonius. . . . Shostakovich's score lifts the film onto an epic plane" and Innokenti Smoktunovsky's Prince is

"strong, volatile, and direct; neither poet nor intellectual, this Hamlet brushes aside those enigmatic hesitations on which Olivier based his screen reading of the part." (Kozintsev maintains that Hamlet lived and died fighting for man's conscience—"into this State, where everyone swims with the stream, there comes a person who is against all this.")

Most critics had reservations about one aspect of Kozintsev's *Hamlet* or another, but almost without exception they agreed that it was magnificent. Kenneth Tynan called it "the most striking evocation of Hamlet's Elsinore that we are ever likely to see." It received a Lenin Prize, shared between the director and Smoktunovsky. There is a detailed account of the making of the film, together with essays on the problems of staging Shakespeare, in Kozintsev's *Nash sovremennik Viliam Shekspir* (1962; translated by Joyce Vining as *Shakespeare: Time and Consciousness*, 1966).

In *Korol Lir* (*King Lear*, 1971), Kozintsev again sought "the inner connections between People, Nature, and History." Here the setting seemed to him of critical importance. The play suggested to him images of a country stripped bare: "There is nothing to eat and no shelter. Here, in the specific concreteness of life, lies the source of tragedy. The spatial world which is *King Lear* is not just the location for the action but the root and cause of the action itself. . . . In attempting to embody the poetry in the figurativeness of film imagery, I looked for it in the fluidity, the changeability, the conflicts of a landscape—the way out of enclosed places into the wide spaces of Nature. Man is surrounded by a crowd and alone in a limitless void." Indeed, Kozintsev suggests, the crowds around his Lear are there to emphasize his desolation when it comes, "so that a sense is obtained of just how much one person is . . . and then two persons, father and daughter. . . . These situations weren't just abstract ones as far as I was concerned. They determined the composition of a shot—the relation between people and the surrounding space." And beneath all the movement and hubbub and flames of war and destruction can be heard in Shostakovich's score "the still voice of suffering"—the almost human voice of a Fool's wooden pipe, and later a requiem that drowns the noise of battle: "the eternal, inconsolable lament of human kind."

The Fool in Kozintsev's *King Lear* (Oleg Dal) is a shaven-headed starveling—this figure was suggested to the director by an account he had read of prisoners in Auschwitz forced to form an orchestra to entertain their murderers—and Lear himself is played by the frail and diminutive Estonian actor Yuri Jarvet—a stroke which troubled some critics used to seeing the King as a towering, bear-like figure. For David Robinson, this casting seemed wholly in keeping with Kozintsev's notion of the play as "a tragedy of reclamation rather than retribution. Humiliated, cast out, tormented into madness and death, Kozintsev's Lear nevertheless grows larger in human stature. The tyrant becomes a philosopher."

Lear and Edgar, as Robinson points out, are never solitary in this film: "they are part of a Breughel-like caravan of vagabonds and idiots and victims of a merciless feudal world. . . . From the opening, with a vast multitude of ragged, sad, and silent people waiting on a hillside to hear the King's decree, to the end, where these same people are seen as the victims of the holocaust that the King's caprices have wrought, the screen seems always full of people. The main point, then, of Kozintsev's interpretation is that the King shares the very sufferings he has bequeathed to his subjects, and in sharing their sufferings becomes one with them, a man and a human being." Though this film was rather less warmly received in the West than its predecessor, in retrospect, as Robinson says, "his last film may well seem the culmination of Kozintsev's creative career."

Kozintsev taught in the directors' workshop at the Leningrad film studios and lectured all over the world. *Prostranstvo Tragedii: Dnevnik Regissera* (1973; translated by Mary Mackintosh as *King Lear: The Space of Tragedy*, 1977) is more than an account of the filming of *Korol Lir.* J.I.M. Stewart called it "a wonderful book, full of technical chat, green-room gossip, apparently irrelevant reminiscence of one Russian theatrical movement or another—yet we are never many pages removed from some deep aesthetic revelation." *Glubokil ekran* (1971), which also combines theorizing (about the importance of depth of image) and personal reminiscence, has not yet been translated. A "gentle, slightly diffident person," Kozintsev is said to have been an extremely stimulating and entertaining speaker, fluent in several languages (including English). He always looked many years younger than he was, and his sudden death at the age of sixty-eight was a shock to his many friends. David Robinson wrote that "despite the events of the intervening years you still sensed in his presence a little of the wonder and elation of those heroic days of Soviet art . . . when no extravagance was too great; when the whole future seemed to belong to the very young."

FILMS: *With Leonid Trauberg*—Pokhozhdeniya Octyabrini (The Adventures of Octyabrina), 1924; Mishki protiv Yudenica (Mishka Against Yudenich), 1925;

Chyortovo koleso/Moyak s Aurora (The Devil's Wheel/The Sailor From the Aurora), 1926; Shinel (The Overcoat/The Cloak), 1926; Bratishka (Little Brother), 1927; S.V.D. (Soyuz Velikogo Dela; The Club of the Big Deed/The Club of the Great Deed/Bleeding Snows), 1927; Novyi Vavilon (The New Babylon), 1929; Odna (Alone), 1931; Yunost Maksima (The Youth of Maxim), 1935; Vozvrashcheniye Maksima (The Return of Maxim), 1937; Vyborgskaya storona (The Vyborg Side/Maxim at Vyborg/New Horizons), 1939; Prostiye lyudi (Plain People/Ordinary People/Simple People), 1945 (re-released 1956). *As sole director*—Slutshai na telegrafe (Incident at the Telegraph Office) *in* Fighting Film Album No. 1, 1941; Pirogov, 1947; Belinsky, 1953; Don Kikhot (Don Quixote), 1957; Gamlet (Hamlet), 1964; Korol Lir (King Lear), 1971. *Published scripts*—The Trilogy of Maxim (in Russian), 1939.

ABOUT: Birkos, A. S. Soviet Cinema, 1976; Dobin, E. Kozintsev i Trauberg, 1963 (in Russian); Gregor, U. Wie sie filmen, 1960; International Film Guide, 1972; Kozintsev, G. King Lear: The Space of Tragedy, 1977; Kozintsev, G. Shakespeare: Time and Conscience, 1966; Leyda, J. Kino, 1960; Oms, M. Grigori Kozintsev, 1976 (in French); Roud, R. (ed.) Cinema: A Critical Dictionary, 1980; Schnitzer, L. and J. (eds.) Cinema in Revolution, 1973; Verdone, M. and Amengual, B. La Feks, 1970 (in French); Vesnin, M. (eds.) Grigori* Kozintsev, 1967 (in Russian). *Periodicals*—Avant-Scène du Cinéma December 1978, July–September 1976 (Kozintsev supplement); Bianco e Nero July–August 1965; Films and Filming March 1961, September 1962; Iskusstvo Kino 11 1966, 7 1971, 11 1974; New Yorker August 28, 1965; Panoráma Winter 1976; Positif June 1977; Sight and Sound Summer 1959, Winter 1962–1963, Summer 1973; Times (London) May 14, 1973; May 19, 1973.

*KULESHOV, LEV (January 13, 1899–March 29, 1970), Soviet director, was born in Tambov, a provincial market town southeast of Moscow. He was the son of Vladimir Sergeyevich Kuleshov and the former Pelegeya Aleksandrovna Shubina, a country school teacher. Kuleshov's father was in a peculiar way a victim of technology. Trained as an artist, he could find no better use for his skill than to draw enlargements of photographs, while his dexterity at the piano equipped him to work not as a musician but as a typist. (It might be said that Lev Kuleshov followed a similar path when he went from "pure" art to the movies, except that he turned the tables by showing how art could be created out of the technological gimmickry of the cinema.)

After his father's death in 1910, Kuleshov was taken to Moscow by his mother. At the age of fifteen he enrolled in the School of Art to study painting, but became more and more interested in stage design. It was as a designer that Kuleshov entered the cinema, recommended to

*koo´ li shôf

LEV KULESHOV

the Khanzhonkov Studios by the film director Andrew Gromov, father of a fellow-student at the School of Art. The year was 1916, and Kuleshov was seventeen years old.

As he later recalled, Kuleshov "was to do the décors for a film by a very celebrated director of those times, Evgeny Bauer. Already in tsarist Russia there were two progressive directors: Bauer and Protazanov. I made several films with Bauer, became friendly with him and learnt a great deal from him; but unhappily he died very soon afterwards, in 1917. Then I began to design for other directors, always dreaming of directing myself. But of course, people were hesitant about entrusting me with a first film! This lack of confidence was understandable: I wanted to direct in a way which at that time was not allowed and seemed unallowable. I was the first in Russia to speak the word 'montage,' to speak of the action, of the dynamic of the cinema, of realism in the art of the film. At that time all this seemed very strange indeed. They regarded me as a Futurist—the name under which they lumped together all artists with leftist tendencies."

In fact, Kuleshov's ideas developed initially out of what he had seen of the American silent cinema, which "enormously influenced" him, and especially the work of D. W. Griffith. By 1917, Kuleshov's first published articles were expounding his belief in the key role of design in the expressive means of the cinema. The same year (at the age of eighteen) Kuleshov was given the chance to apply his theories as director of a short film called *Proyekt inzhenera Praita* (*Engineer Prite's Project*), a sort of detective sto-

ry with an industrial theme. It was, Kuleshov believed, one of the first Russian films consciously to explore the possibilities of editing—to be constructed "dynamically and editorially, with the use of close-ups."

In 1918 Kuleshov worked for the Central Administration of Cinema Affairs, first as head of the re-editing section, then as director of the newsreel section. The following year he participated in the founding of the First State Film School in Moscow. He then left the city to play his part in the Civil War of 1919–1920, working on Eastern Front agit-trains with a team of newsreel cameramen. Returning early in 1920 to the State Film School, he found that it was being run on lines that seemed to him more theatrical than cinematic. In March 1920 Kuleshov began to work with a group of student actors who had failed their examinations, developing a teaching system so effective that on reexamination all of his students passed with distinction. At about this time two of the students presented an extremely funny parody of Kuleshov's step-by-step teaching method; one of them was Alexandra Khokhlova, later described as Russia's "first genuine cinema actress." She was then married to the actor Konstantin Khokhlov, whom she left in 1920 to live with Kuleshov. They were eventually able to marry in 1956. According to some accounts Kuleshov, in order to support Khokhlova and her son, was obliged in 1921 to direct a purely commercial film, a vehicle for the star Vitold Polonsky called *The Unfinished Love Story*.

From Kuleshov's first class of "bad" students developed his famous workshop. The group moved into its first quarters, in a Moscow mansion, in May 1920. Almost at once it was sent off to the western front, ordered to make a short film celebrating the deeds of the Red Army in its latest struggle (against the Poles, who had attacked in April 1920). The result was *Na krasnom fronte* (*On the Red Front,* 1920), directed by Kuleshov, with Pyotr Yermolov as cameraman, and a cast of three (including Khokhlova). Combining documentary and fictional sequences, and emulating the technique of American chase films, it involves a horse, a train, and an automobile in an exciting race between a Red soldier and a Polish spy for possession of an important dispatch. The film, made on washed, recoated (and positive) stock, has not survived, but Lenin is said to have praised it, and Kuleshov and his students learned a great deal from the exercise.

Back in Moscow, Kuleshov's group threw themselves into their studies and their experiments. "Our first task," Kuleshov said, was to develop "a firm theoretic basis for the training of film actors. . . . As part of this training we prepared several instructional *études* in the form of complete little plays, arranged with 'montage' changes and without pauses. . . . Why didn't we make films? There was no raw film." The training Kuleshov offered was not only in the principles of film and film acting. His students were expected to perform all of their own stunts, and as one of them later recalled, "we ran, jumped, boxed, rode horses, climbed from cars into streetcars, and so on." Boris Barnet and Pudovkin were only the most famous of the many Soviet filmmakers whose work grew out of the principles they learned from Kuleshov; Eisenstein himself was a member of the workshop during 1923.

In his "films without film" and in experiments with existing footage and with the scraps of raw stock he was able to obtain, Kuleshov worked out the first principles of editing and montage. A number of the devices he developed in those heady early days have become part of the grammar of film editing, like his "creative geography"—assembling shots taken at different times in different places into a single sequence so as to suggest (for example) that the American White House faces Gogol's monument on Prechistensky Boulevard, Moscow. Perhaps the most significant of these techniques—the so-called "Kuleshov effect"—is described by Pudovkin in *Film Direction*. It involved a long close-up of the perfectly expressionless face of an actor, undercut with shots of (for example) a bowl of steaming soup, a woman in a coffin, and a child playing with a toy bear. Pudovkin says: "The public raved about the acting of the artist. They pointed out the heavy pensiveness of his mood over the forgotten soup, were touched and moved by the deep sorrow with which he looked at the dead woman, and admired the light, happy smile with which he surveyed the girl at play. But we knew that in all three cases the face was exactly the same."

At last, in 1923, the opportunity came for the Kuleshov collective to make their first feature film. They needed a story that would give them the widest possible scope to test the theories they had developed—in particular their belief in the superiority of actors trained specifically for film work. They decided on a fast-moving satirical comedy, and a script was prepared by Pudovkin and the Futurist poet Nikolai Aseyev for what became *Neobychainiye priklucheniya Mistera Vesta v stranya bolshevikov* (*The Extraordinary Adventures of Mr. West in the Land of the Bolsheviks*). A U.S. Senator goes to Russia, expecting to encounter there all the suffering and horror he has read about in the American press. He falls into the hands of a gang who play up to his fantasies and hold him to ransom, but in the end he is rescued by the G.P.U. and shown the real Russia. The film is as full of chases and visual trickery as a Mack Sennett comedy, and stars the actor Porfiry Podobed, who greatly resembles Harold Lloyd. *Mr. West* was a huge success in Russia in 1924, and was warmly praised by Eisenstein for its "refined" and "Western" craftsmanship. Many years later, when it was finally seen in the West, a British critic found it "still a marvellously funny film" which had "lost none of its edge as an object lesson in the idiocy of all Cold Wars."

Hoping to cap this success, the Kuleshov workshop made their second film in emulation of the popular adventure and science fiction serials of the time. Written by Pudovkin from an idea by Kuleshov, *Luch smerti* (*The Death Ray,* 1925) has to do with the theft of a laserlike secret ray, stolen from its Soviet inventor by a group of fascists. Kuleshov admitted later that the film "was too conscious an imitation of the American cinema. There were too many tricks in it: I wanted to demonstrate all the resources of my students, all that they could do; and in consequence it is a catalogue of devices." The Soviet critics agreed, and although *Luch smerti* did well commercially, it was bitterly criticized for its extravagance and its lack of social relevance. All the same, as Kuleshov pointed out, in its use of mobile cameras and fast cutting, in its handling of crowd scenes, and in other ways, the film had a great deal of influence on the young Soviet cinema (though not an altogether healthy influence, encouraging as it did an excessive concern with technique at the expense of feeling).

The Kuleshov collective was in disgrace for a year and a half after the release of *The Death Ray,* and when they were given another chance it was on the understanding that the new film must be made very quickly and cheaply. Kuleshov and his cowriter Viktor Shklovsky settled on Jack London's story "The Unexpected," set in a log cabin in the Yukon during the Gold Rush. It examines the impact of murder on the minds and values of three people who are cut off by the Arctic winter from civilization and its laws. *Po zakonu* (*By the Law/Dura Lex,* 1926), using a single interior set and only three salaried actors, and with each day's shooting carefully rehearsed the evening before, remains the cheapest feature film ever produced in Russia. Coolly received at home, it was greeted with excitement by foreign critics who were intrigued by its eschewal of many standard cinematic elements—the film has no real villain, no hero, and no changes of locale. It was the great psychological tension Kuleshov achieved with such limited means that so impressed the foreign reviewers—

the American poet H. D., who saw it in Lausanne, confessed that it induced in her sensations of catalepsy and hysteria. It is now generally recognized to be the finest of Kuleshov's films.

Thereafter, Kuleshov's reputation went into a decline from which it did not recover for thirty years. *Vasha znakomaya (The Girl Journalist/ Your Acquaintance,* 1927), *Veselaia kanareika (The Gay Canary,* 1929), and *Dva, Bouldej, dva (The Great Buldis,* 1930), all silent feature films, were all unsuccessful, critically and commercially. Kuleshov's first sound film, *Gorizont (Horizon,* 1932), is (as David Thomson points out) rather like a *Mr. West* in reverse—a story about a Jew who emigrates from tsarist Russia to an unconvincingly nightmarish America. Melodramatic as it is, the film is not without interest. Kuleshov tried to bring to his sound track the kind of rigorous realism he had sought in visual terms in his silent films. There is no background music—only music called for in the course of the narrative—and scrupulous attention is paid to sound perspective: to the quality as well as the volume of sound as it is heard from a specified distance.

These techniques were used to better advantage in *Veliky uteshitel (The Great Consoler,* 1933), the most notable of Kuleshov's later films. The "consoler" of the title is the American writer O. Henry, who is depicted as sentimentalizing in his stories the wretched lives of his fellow inmates in a federal penitentiary. The question of the responsibility of the artist was a very relevant one in the Soviet Union at that time, when artists were being required by the doctrine of Socialist Realism to portray society in misleadingly optimistic terms. In spite of the American setting, it seemed to Ronald Levaco a film "in which a weary and assailed Kuleshov attempted to pose his own dilemma as a Soviet artist."

The Great Consoler has been much discussed for its technical innovations. It was made very cheaply and filmed in only forty days, thanks to careful rehearsals on a miniature studio floor. "In fact," according to Pudovkin, "prior to the shooting of the film, Kuleshov staged a performance consisting of very short scenes each in length identical with the piece later to be edited. As far as possible, Kuleshov played each scene through on the studio floor in such a way that subsequently, after most careful rehearsal, it could be transferred back to and shot without alteration on the actual floor used in shooting." As Pudovkin points out, this method gives the director the closest possible control over his actors and allows him and others to "see" and in effect to edit the film before it is shot; on the other hand the technique imposed its own limitations on the

film, which has few characters, no crowd scenes, and "sparse and limited exteriors." Pudovkin considered it a most interesting experiment, but not one to be generally adopted, and the result struck a western critic, Catherine de la Roche, as "tense, disciplined, logical"—a film with "intellectual power but little emotional appeal."

At any rate, Kuleshov was one of those denounced for "formalism" at the infamous First Congress of Film Workers in 1935, and he directed nothing more after *The Great Consoler* until 1940. During the war years he was allowed to make several films for children and young people, the last of them being *My c Urala (We Are From the Urals,* 1944). The same year, thanks to Eisenstein's intervention, he was appointed director of the State Film School in Moscow (the VGIK) which he had helped to establish in 1919. He became a doctor of arts in 1947. "I love the job of professor," he said in 1965. "At present it is not easy to recruit teachers to VGIK, because people do not want to teach, to instruct others. Directors prefer to make their own films. I on the contrary have always thought that it was more important to create men of the cinema than to make films myself. . . . Just think: eighty percent of Soviet filmmakers are old VGIK students. And fifty percent are my students."

Kuleshov's first important book was published in 1929 as *Iskusstvo kino (The Art of the Cinema);* half a dozen more appeared in the 1930s and 1940s, including the massive manual *Osnovy kinorezhissury (The Fundamentals of Film Direction,* 1941). None of these works has appeared in English, but a selection from Kuleshov's writings has been translated and edited by Ronald Levaco as *Kuleshov on Film* (1974). In the post-Stalinist years, Kuleshov's work as a writer and teacher, and the respect in which he was held by his former students, brought a slow recovery in his reputation. There was a retrospective showing of his films in Moscow in 1966, and the same year *The Extraordinary Adventures of Mr. West* was shown abroad for the first time. In 1967 Kuleshov was awarded the Order of Lenin. The director was a small man, addicted to travel, hunting, and cigarettes, which he chain-smoked all his adult life. He was also an automobile enthusiast, the proud owner at various times of a Model-A Ford and a Mercedes.

Kuleshov is generally recognized to be the founder of montage theory and a great codifier and coordinator of previously undefined techniques. Jay Leyda wrote that "the basic technical contribution of Kuleshov, the artistic legacy that he handed over to Pudovkin and Eisenstein for further investment, was the discovery that there were, inherent in a single piece of unedited film, two strengths; its own, and the strength of its relation to other pieces of film." And David Robinson suggests that "Griffith's discovery had been to use editing to assemble individual elements into a continuous story. Kuleshov had gone further, to show how the juxtaposition of shots can alter the intrinsic meaning of each shot." Most critics would agree that Kuleshov, having shown the way, was outshone as a filmmaker by the greatest of his students, but Pudovkin disputed this, writing in *Art of the Cinema*: "The rise of the cinema began with Kuleshov. Formal problems were inevitable, and Kuleshov undertook to solve them. He was hounded because he was a pioneer. . . . Kuleshov is the first filmmaker who began to talk about an alphabet, organizing unsegmented material, and he worked with syllables, not words. This is his guilt before the court of vague thinkers. Some of us who worked in Kuleshov's stock company are defined as having 'outshot' our teacher. Such a statement is extremely superficial. We crossed through the sargasso into the open sea on his shoulders. We make pictures—Kuleshov made the cinema."

—K.B.

FILMS: Za schastem (After Happiness), 1917; (begun by Evgeny Bauer, completed by Kuleshov): Proyekt inzhenera Praita (Engineer Prite's Project), 1918 (short); Na krasnom fronte (On the Red Front), 1920 (short); Neobychainiye priklucheniya Mistera Vesta v stranye bolshevikov (The Extraordinary Adventures of Mr. West in the Land of the Bolsheviks), 1924; Luch smerti (The Death Ray), 1925; Po zakonu (By the Law/Dura Lex), 1926; Locomotive No. 10006, 1926 (experimental short); Vasha znakomaya (The Girl Journalist/Your Acquaintance), 1927; Veselaia kanareika (The Gay Canary), 1929; Dva, Bouldej, dva (The Great Buldis), 1930; Gorizont (Horizon), 1932; Veliky uteshitel (The Great Consoler), 1933; Sibiriki (The Siberians), 1940; Sluchai v vulkane (Incident on a Volcano), 1941; (with Alexandra Khokhlova) Klyatva Timura (The Oath of Timur), 1942; Yunye Partizany (The Young Partisans), 1942; My c Urala (We Are From the Urals), 1944.

ABOUT: Levaco, R. *introduction to* Kuleshov on Film, 1974; Leyda, J. Kino, 1960; Pudovkin, V. Film Technique, 1929 (and other works by Pudovkin); Schnitzer, L. and D. (eds.) Cinema in Revolution, translated by David Robinson, 1973; Thomson, D. A Biographical Dictionary of the Cinema, 1975; World Encyclopedia of Film, 1972. *Periodicals*—Afterimage April 1970; Bianco e Negro October 1947; Cahiers du Cinéma May–June 1970; Film Culture Spring 1967; Film Journal Fall–Winter 1972; Film Quarterly Spring 1976; Sight and Sound Spring 1971; Silent Picture Autumn 1970.

*KUROSAWA, AKIRA (March 23, 1910–   ), Japanese director and scriptwriter, was born in the Omori district of Tokyo. His father, Yutaka Kurosawa, a native of Akita Prefecture and of samurai descent, was an army officer who became a teacher and administrator of physical education. A graduate of the Toyama Imperial Military Academy, he earned a moderate income at the Ebara Middle School, famous for its spartan program. The director's mother, whom he has described as a self-sacrificing realist—'a typical woman of the Meiji era'—came from an Osaka merchant family. Akira was the last of the couple's children, following four sisters and three brothers. The oldest sister had already left home and married by the time Kurosawa was born, and the oldest brother left while he was still a child. The second brother had died before Kurosawa was born, so that Akira grew up with three sisters and the one elder brother who was later to be a great influence in his life. The youngest of the sisters, to whom Kurosawa was closest, died at the age of sixteen while he was in the fourth grade.

Kurosawa characterizes himself in childhood as at first backward at school and physically weak, to the disappointment of his father. In spite of that weakness, he soon came to share his father's enthusiasm for physical challenge, developing a lifelong interest in sports, especially baseball, and an attitude of "single-minded devotion to a discipline." As a child of ten he practiced *kendo*, traditional Japanese swordsmanship, and "assumed all the affectations of a boy fencer." His father's influence extended in another significant direction. In a time when films were considered frivolous entertainment, Yutaka Kurosawa insisted on their educational value, and took his whole family regularly to the movies as well as to the traditional storytellers in the music-halls around Kagurazaka. Kurosawa's first two years at school (at Morimura Gakuen) were years of misery which he was later to compare to the experiences of the retarded children in Inagaki Hiroshi's film *Wasurareta kora* (*Forgotten Children*, 1949). But in his second year his family moved to the Koishikawa district, and he was transferred to the Kuroda Primary School. Here the young Kurosawa's intelligence was awakened and a rapid development began, encouraged by the protective presence of his elder brother Heigo and by the unusually progressive teaching of Seiji Tachikawa, the school principal, who introduced Kurosawa to the fine arts. No longer teased as a crybaby, the boy became class president and a popular figure in the school. At this time too began his close friendship with Keinosuke Uekusa, who was to become a scriptwriter, working on several of Kurosawa's own films.

°koo rŏ sä wä

James Wentzy

AKIRA KUROSAWA

The great Kanto earthquake of 1923 occurred during Kurosawa's second year at the Keika Middle School. His brother took him on "an expedition to conquer fear," forcing him to look at scenes of horrifying destruction. At this time Kurosawa was reading everything he could. While walking between home and school he read the novels of Ichiyo Higuchi, Doppo Kunikida, Soseki Natsume, and Ivan Turgenev. He had good teachers, but in his third year compulsory military training began. Kurosawa resented the imposition, was in continual conflict with his army instructor, and failed the course on graduation. By that time he had expressed a wish to become a painter. Despite the family's declining fortunes, his father did not object, but insisted that he go to art school. In 1927, his year of graduation from Middle School, he is said to have enrolled at the Doshusha School of Western painting, but he himself recalls failing the entrance examination and pursuing his studies, as a lover of Van Gogh and Cézanne, free from academic constraints. At any rate, in the following year he had the first of two paintings accepted for the prestigious Nitten exhibition, a show of modern works established in opposition to traditional government-supported art.

Kurosawa found it hard to give his mind to his artistic career during the Depression. His family could not afford to buy the materials he needed, and the distractions of those disturbed times were many. He explored literature, especially the works of Dostoevsky and Gorki; he went to the theatre; he listened to classical music; he became fascinated by movies. In this last he was guided by his brother, who wrote program notes for movie theatres and took part in shows himself as a *benshi*, a professional commentator, specializing in foreign films. Kurosawa was later to list nearly a hundred films that particularly impressed him in the years up to 1929. The list is mainly composed of films from Russia and the West, and includes most of the great names from *Caligari* to Chaplin. In 1929 Kurosawa joined the Proletarian Artists' League, not so much from a commitment to Marxism as out of a fashionable interest in all new movements. He became involved in illegal direct political action, dodging the police because of his role "in the lower reaches" of an organization that produced underground proletarian newspapers. He left home at this time, ostensibly to live with his brother, but actually moving between various rented rooms and the homes of Communist friends.

Increasingly disillusioned both with the political movement and with his painting, Kurosawa left the League in the spring of 1932 and went to share the bohemian life of his brother, who lived, to the disapproval of the family, with a woman in the tenement district of Kagurazaka. The movie-going continued, of course, but now came the first of the foreign talkies that would mean the end of Heigo's career. The *benshi* was no longer required for sound films, and the strike organized to persuade the studios to resist the change was doomed to fail. Heigo found himself a leader of the strike, and it was this painful role above all that led, in Kurosawa's view, to his brother's suicide attempt. Kurosawa tried to reconcile Heigo to the family by arranging his marriage to the woman he lived with, but in 1933, at the age of twenty-seven, Heigo's second suicide attempt succeeded. The effect on Kurosawa was profound, and he came to describe the brother, whom he saw as a more pessimistic version of himself, "as a negative strip of film that led to my own development as a positive image."

Kurosawa had by this time lost faith in his talent as a painter. He felt himself too easily influenced by the vision of whatever artist he was studying. "In other words, I did not—and still don't—have a completely personal, distinctive way of looking at things." It was in any case impossible to make a living as an artist. He had to undertake hack work producing cartoons and illustrations for magazines, and visual aids for cookery instruction. He began to cast about for another profession and in 1935 (although until that moment he had never thought of entering the film industry) he answered a newspaper advertisement put out by the newly established PCL (Photo Chemical Laboratory, later to become Toho Motion Picture Company). Applicants for jobs as assistant directors were required first to submit an essay on the fundamental deficiencies of Japanese films and how to correct them. The subject appealed to Kurosawa's sense of mischief, and he wrote the essay "in a half-mocking spirit," but with all his accumulated knowledge of foreign films and his simmering dissatisfaction with the Japanese product. Out of more than five hundred applicants, over one hundred and thirty were selected on the basis of the essay, but only seven passed the next test, which involved writing a scenario from a newspaper story. Kurosawa was one of the five who came through the final interview, having already established a rapport with Kajiro Yamamoto, whom he impressed with his knowledge of the visual arts.

Kurosawa joined PCL in 1936, when the company was only two years old, a vigorous, open-minded organization that encouraged experiment and trained its assistant directors by giving them every job in the production process. After an uneasy start, Kurosawa joined the group led by director Yamamoto, in whom he discovered "the best teacher of my entire life." Yamamoto encouraged confidence in his young assistants by allowing them great freedom and independence, even to the detriment of his own films. Kurosawa learned in this school of hard work the importance especially of scriptwriting, editing, and dubbing. From the first, Yamamoto said, he saw Kurosawa as the inspired type, rather than a determined plodder. Between 1937 and 1941 Kurosawa moved from third to chief assistant, occasionally working for other directors; Takizawa, Fushimizu, Naruse. On location for Takizawa on *Sengoku guntoden* (*Saga of the Vagabonds*, 1937), Kurosawa developed a feeling for Gotemba and the plains at the foot of Mount Fuji, and for the people and horses of the area. Yamamoto was to recall in particular Kurosawa's work on the film *Uma* (*Horses*, 1941), where the young man, officially second-unit director, acted rather as the director's "other self," spending a whole year on location in the Tohoku district, allowing Yamamoto to return to Tokyo to work on another film.

Kurosawa now began to win prizes from the Ministry of Education for his filmscripts—a second prize for *Shizuku nari* (*All is Quiet*) and a first for *Yuki* (*Snow*). He sold scripts to Daiei (although Toho took a percentage), and his first published screenplay, *A German at the Daruma Temple*, appeared in 1941. It was the the story of Bruno Taut, the Bauhaus architect "who discovered the plain and simple beauty of the Japanese sense of form to which the Japanese themselves, over-familiar, had become apathetic, and brought it once more into Japanese consciousness." Kurosawa was interested in Taut as one who pointed the way to an understanding of what was characteristically Japanese—in Akira Iwasaki's opinion, a constant concern of Kurosawa's. A chance to direct this story came to nothing because of wartime restrictions. Another of Kurosawa's scripts, *Tekichu odan sanbyakuri* (*Three Hundred Miles Through Enemy Lines*), although exactly the sort of patriotic action story the censors might approve, was shelved as being too big to give to a novice. (It was eventually directed by Kazuo Mori, in 1957.)

Kurosawa resigned himself for a time to turning out formulaic scripts and drinking up the proceeds, usually in the company of his old friend Uekusa, who had come to Toho as an extra and stayed on to write scripts himself. The drinking led to a preulcerative stomach condition, which Kurosawa attempted to treat by making strenuous expeditions into the mountains. Then one day he saw an advertisement for a new novel, *Sugata Sanshiro*, by Tsuneo Tomita. Reading through the summary of the story, he knew instinctively that here was the subject for a film that would not only be acceptable to the censors but ideal for himself to direct. Toho's head of planning, Nobuyoshi Morita, was astonished when Kurosawa asked him to buy the rights to a book that was not yet even available. He insisted on waiting till Kurosawa had at least read the novel, but then found Toho in competition with other studios for the rights. Luckily, the novelist's wife had heard of the promise of young Kurosawa and influenced her husband to accept the Toho offer. Kurosawa was duly given the job of directing, and shooting began in Yokohama in 1942.

Sanshiro Sugata (the Western order for the name) is a Meiji period story about the origins of judo, tracing the rise of one of its first practitioners. The film was made in accordance with national policy dictated by the Information Bureau. Since the film's content was thus restricted, Kurosawa took the opportunity to concern himself with its form. At a time when the received idea was that a Japanese film should be as simple as possible, "I disagreed and got away with disagreeing—that much I could say," and he said it by making "a really movie-like movie." Several critics remark how many of the characteristic features of Kurosawa's style are already apparent here. Richie points to the kind of story (a young man's education), to the tendency to "cyclic form," to the interest in how things are done (in this case the method of judo itself), and to "the extraordinary economy of the way in which he shows his story." Already Kurosawa is making use of his favorite punctuation device, the wipe, between scenes. Noël Burch singles out the scene of the final combat as "a *tour de force* that already hints at the mastery to come." The scene takes place at night amid the tall grasses of the windswept Sengokuhara plain, with the antagonists poised in complete stillness before the swift action. The combat is practically invisible, being suggested rather by the movement of the grasses, an elliptical effect which Max Tessier sees as foreshadowing Kurosawa's treatment of the final battle in *Kagemusha*, forty years later. The decision to shoot the scene on location was taken at the last minute, and the director recalls the anxious waiting before the arrival of the ferocious wind for which the location was famous.

Sanshiro Sugata brought Kurosawa immediate recognition, Tadashi Iijima seeing him as injecting new life into Japanese cinema. The same critic, writing of the film many years later, gave his view of the contention (familiar both in Japan and in the West) that Kurosawa is too "Western." Iijima believes that despite the deliberately Western appearance of many of his films, Kurosawa retains a typically Japanese spirit, evident from the outset of his career. It is a spirit not to be confused with simple patriotic fervor. Many films produced in wartime are hard for a later audience to watch, but Audie Bock considers that "compared to almost any American film of similar vintage and subject matter, the tone of Kurosawa's national policy films hardly qualifies as propaganda," and finds it surprising that a novice director could get approval from the authorities to make films "so scant in fanaticism."

Some critics of *Sanshiro Sugata* felt that Ryunosuke Tsunagata, playing the villain Higaki, overacted and was too dominant. But Kurosawa claims that Higaki's prominence was deliberate and says he found this character strangely attractive, an example of the "proud and uncompromising" who are destroyed by circumstances; the victorious Sugata (played by Susumu Fujita in his first major role) he describes as "straightforward and flexible"—a temperament Kurosawa sees as close to his own. In 1965 Kurosawa would edit Toho's remake, directed by Seiichiro Uchikawa.

Kurosawa's next film, *Ichiban utsukushiku* (*The Most Beautiful*, 1943), belongs to a cycle of "national policy" projects designed to encourage increased industrial production. Unusually for him its subject is women. They are workers in a factory making optical instruments in wartime conditions. The story is a series of episodes concerning each of the girls as they continue their work through various personal crises. Although

the cast were professionals, Kurosawa wanted to create the effect of a documentary, portraying the women as a group. He went to great lengths to make the actresses lose their professional polish and play themselves. They had to sleep in the dormitory of the real factory where the filming took place, go on runs together, and even march in the streets as a fife-and-drum corps—a regimen that caused considerable conflict between the women and their director.

The style of *The Most Beautiful*, according to Richie, was influenced by German and Russian documentary. but he notes also the beginnings of a number of techniques, not especially associated with documentary, that Kurosawa was to develop later as his own, such as the "short-cut" for narrative transitions, and a "peculiarly personal use of the flashback." Richie finds manipulative and sentimental a climactic scene in which Yoko Yaguchi, as the group leader, searches all night for a lost lens. But Audie Bock believes "the heroine emerges as a real person despite the propaganda." Max Tessier considers this film, and most of those made between *Sanshiro Sugata* and *Rashomon* in 1950, as uneven works with good sequences, but marred by Kurosawa's "bad tendencies," especially "his inclination towards a pathos pushed to the limits of what a rationalist Western viewer can endure," and a yielding to sentimentality "to the extent sometimes of forgetting to direct." Noël Burch, on the other hand, justifies the protracted scenes of pathos in the early films not only on the grounds that a Japanese audience might find them appealing, but precisely because of the "mastery of editing and of the direction of actors" which makes them convincing.

Kurosawa was now asked by the studio to make a sequel to the very successful *Sanshiro Sugata*, and the result was equally popular, except with the critics. Kurosawa did not enjoy what he called "refrying" old material, although he confessed to an interest in the fact that Part II enabled him to show Higaki the villain observing himself in earlier days through the impetuous actions of his younger brother Tesshin as he seeks revenge on Sugata. On February 15, 1945, the month *Sanshiro Sugata Part II* was released, Kurosawa married the star of *The Most Beautiful*, Yoko Yaguchi (whose real name was Kato Kiyo), at the Meiji shrine in Tokyo, with Yamamoto and his wife as matchmakers. They were at first very poor, his salary being less than a third of what his wife's had been as an actress. Their son Hisao was born in December of the same year; a daughter, Kuzuko, was born in 1954. As Japan's defeat in the war approached, Kurosawa wrote a script for a film called *Dokkoi kono yari* (*The Lifted Spear*), but it was abandoned in the pre-production stage because of a shortage of horses. This led to the hastily assembled production of *Tora no o o fumu otokotachi* (*They Who Step on the Tiger's Tail*), during which Japan surrendered. Kurosawa clashed angrily over this film with the Japanese censors, who had remained at their post even after the government collapsed. They pronounced it an insult to Japanese traditions. The American censors who succeeded them also banned the film, some say for its feudalism, but according to Kurosawa because the Japanese had failed to submit it for approval. His first encounter with an American censor, with whom he discussed a one-act play he had written, Kurosawa found "a strange kind of pleasure," after "having lived through an age that had no respect for creation." *Toro no o* was not released until 1952. Kurosawa wrote the scenario in one night, and the shooting was carried out on only one modest set, with some location shots in the imperial forest, conveniently close to the studio. American soldiers were in the habit of visiting the set during production, among them on one occassion John Ford, who left a message which Kurosawa never received. He only learned of the visit when the two met at last in London years later.

The story of *They Who Step on the Tiger's Tail* is taken from the Kabuki play *Kanjincho* and concerns the young general Yoshitsune (1159–1189), fleeing from his brother Yoritomo. He and his retainers, led by Benkei, arrive at one of Yoritomo's check-points disguised as priests. To convince the commander Togashi, Benkei reads from an empty scroll, pretending that it is a list of subscribers to their temple. When Yoshitsune is recognized, Benkei averts complete discovery by beating his master, who is acting the part of a porter. Togashi sees through the deception but is so moved by this action, unthinkable in the world of traditional feudal allegiance, that he lets the party pass. Kurosawa's version follows the original play closely, except for the addition to the cast of the comedian Kenichi Enomoto (known as Enoken) as another porter, in a role that broadens the meaning of the whole story. Kurosawa had worked with Enoken when acting as assistant to Yamamoto. Now he wanted him to provide a thread unifying the whole film, to "make the picture come alive" in the straitened circumstances of production. Enoken was to appear in his usual popular role—"a parody of the ordinary man," overreacting to everything—and as a baffled outsider in the feudal world of noblemen, draw the audience into the story. Richie notes Kurosawa's careful use of music to define different levels of the plot. Kurosawa later discussed the possibility of a more elaborate remake with his great friend the composer Fumio Hayasaka, but this project was prevented by Hayasaka's death.

Asu o tsukuru hitobito (*Those Who Make Tomorrow*, 1946) was codirected by Kurosawa with Kajiro Yamamoto and Hideo Sekigawa, but Kurosawa denies his own and his colleagues' responsibility for it. The film was designed as propaganda for the Toho union campaign; "it was really made by the labor union and is an excellent example of why a committee-made film is no good." It was a critical and commercial disaster. Kurosawa's next film, *Waga seishun ni kuinashi* (*No Regrets for Our Youth*), made in the same year, was intended as a personal statement, but it too suffered because of union activity. It was produced in the seven months between the two great strikes at Toho, during which time communist membership increased, and a union committee insisted that Kurosawa rewrite the original script because another director, Kiyoshi Kusuda, was working on a similar subject. The story is based on the Takikawa Incident in 1933, when a professor was forced to resign from Tokyo University because of his Communist sympathies. The film concentrates on the subsequent fate of his daughter Yukie (Setsuko Hara) in love with Noge (Susumu Fujita), one of her father's pupils, with whom she lives until he is arrested and executed as a spy. She makes the extraordinary decision to take her lover's ashes to the home of his poor parents in the country, and to remain there, working as a peasant in the fields, enduring hardship and the enmity of the neighbors. A brief return home at the end of the war shows her she has no place in the city, and she goes back to the harsh life of the peasants. The heroine, as Audie Bock says, "remains an uncompromising idealist despite social and political opposition as well as physical exhaustion." She also embodies Kurosawa's belief that in Japan after the war there could be no freedom and democracy "without the establishment of the self as a positive value." About this time Kurosawa had resumed his study of traditional Japanese culture, especially of pottery and the Noh theatre. He felt that his better understanding of and pride in Japanese aesthetics gave him greater self-confidence. In postwar Japan he looked for a respect for the individual self unusual (so far) in Japanese society, and presented it in his portrait of Yukie. The character proved unpopular with some Japanese critics who, it seemed to Kurosawa, would have had no objections had she been a man. Some critics regretted the contemporary subject-matter, urging a return to the style of *Sanshiro Sugata*. But others saw the film as among the best of the director's postwar works, and its second place in the 1946 *Kinema Jumpo* list of best films marked the first major recognition of his career. Even now *No Regrets for Our Youth* is considered (by Tessier, for example) one of the most interesting of the pre-*Rashomon* films, while the testimony of Tadao Sato, writing in 1969, to the fascinating power of the portrayal of Yukie and its effect on his own youth, suggests that something of Kurosawa's intention survived the alterations to the script.

During the second union dispute in October 1946, the stars of *No Regrets for Our Youth*, in opposition to the strike, formed, with other leading actors, the Flag Group of Ten, starting a Second Toho Production Branch which eventually broke away as Shin Toho. The new company, according to Kurosawa, was to be based on stars, whereas the original Toho, where he continued to work, now became more emphatically "director-based." It began by publishing a schedule of new releases, including *Four Love Stories*, one of which was scripted by Kurosawa; *Ginrei no hate* (*To the End of the Silver Mountains*), which he coscripted with Yamamoto; and *Subarashiki nichiyobi* (*One Wonderful Sunday*), his next film as director. The idea for the latter came from an old D. W. Griffith picture about a couple, after the First World War, planting potatoes and persisting in the face of misfortune. Kurosawa's film follows a young factory worker and his fiancée (played by Isao Numasaki and Chieko Nakakita) through their one weekly day off on thirty-five yen, a sum that gradually diminishes as the episodic story proceeds: a baseball game with some boys means they must pay for some damaged cookies; the young man is beaten up when trying to buy some cheap tickets for a concert; finally the couple stage their own fantasy concert. Donald Richie invokes Capra as well as Griffith, and calls the film "a kind of musical" because of the constant presence in it of music, popular tunes as well as the melodies of Schubert, who is the couple's favorite composer. Kurosawa had Uekusa working with him on the script for the first time. The friends had some disagreement over the climactic scene in the empty amphitheatre, where the young man pretends to conduct an imaginary orchestra. He falters, and the girl turns to the camera, asking the cinema audience to encourage him with applause. Uekusa wanted to put the requested applause on the soundtrack and provide a source for it in the film, but Kurosawa wanted to rely entirely on the reaction of the live audience. Kurosawa's version of the scene was shot, but Japanese audiences did not respond, although a later audience in Paris played their part as the director wished. Richie sides with the Japanese audiences, disliking not only this scene "straight from Henry Koster's

One Hundred Men and a Girl but also the extreme length and slowness of the scenes in the young man's room. But *One Wonderful Sunday* was generally well received. It was placed sixth in the *Kinema Jumpo* list for 1947, and together with *No Regrets for Our Youth* earned for Kurosawa the Mainichi best director award. But for Kurosawa himself, "It is certainly by no means my favorite picture. I had a lot of things to say and I got them all mixed up. I remembered this in *Drunken Angel* and kept my eyes open."

Yoidori tenshi (*Drunken Angel*, 1948) is set in a city slum surrounding a polluted, refuse-filled pond, beside which Sanada, an alcoholic doctor, runs a clinic. Matsunaga, one of the young gangsters who control the neighborhood, comes to the clinic to have a bullet removed from his hand. The doctor finds that Matsunaga also has tuberculosis, and tries to treat him. Just as Matsunaga is at last willing to be saved, his former boss returns from prison, displacing him in the neighborhood and reclaiming his girl, who is also Sanada's nurse. Matsunaga tries to kill the boss but is himself killed in a final struggle where the two slip and slide clumsily among ladders and buckets of white paint. The style of this sequence Noël Burch calls "sinister slapstick. It is not a parody, but the symbolic defilement of a *lumpen* underworld, dismissed as pathetically irretrievable." He compares it with the final chase of *Stray Dog* (1949) for its sudden break with the pathos of the body of the film. The real theme of *Drunken Angel* is the fate of postwar Japanese society. The festering pond outside Sanada's office, and Matsunaga's illness, Joan Mellen suggests, symbolize the corruption of that society. "Matsunaga represents Japanese youth emerging from the war, wounded yet full of energy and courage." The alcoholic doctor offers only "a very limited alternative" because "the problem is bigger than the individual."

"In this picture," said Kurosawa, "I finally discovered myself. It was *my* picture: *I* was doing it and no one else." The film came to life out of a number of contradictions. First came the script problem. As the story developed, Kurosawa and Uekusa found the doctor, originally conceived as a young idealist, becoming more and more lifeless beside the dynamic gangster. So they made the doctor a "drunken angel" along the lines of a real character they had met in a Yokohama bar. But the balance between the two main characters continued to be a difficulty, above all because of the remarkable performance of Toshiro Mifune as Matsunaga. Realizing that in Mifune he had come across "a kind of talent I had never encountered before in the Japanese film world," Kurosawa wanted to allow scope for the actor's extraordinary vitality. At the same time he worried that the young gangster's attractiveness would disturb the balance of the film and defeat his own purposes (he had begun, after all, from his impatient disgust with the world of the *yakuza*). The dilemma "did indeed warp the structure of the drama," but Kurosawa acknowledged that part of the liberation from outside influences he felt in making this film came from the experience of directing Mifune. "It was, above all, the speed with which he expressed himself that was astounding. The ordinary Japanese actor might need ten feet of film to get across an impression; Mifune needed only three feet. . . . He put forth everything directly and boldly, and his sense of timing was the keenest I had ever seen in a Japanese actor. And yet with all his quickness he also had surprisingly fine sensibilities." The overshadowed doctor was played by Takashi Shimura, who had been in almost all of Kurosawa's films starting with the first, and was to appear in almost all of those made in the next twenty years, as was Mifune himself until *Red Beard*. Kurosawa says that his practice of using the same actors again and again, forming what has been called a "repertory company" or "family," was not the result of design; but that he selects actors with whom he is likely to become friends. He *is* deliberate in choosing two or three new faces for each film, and in giving the familiar players new roles to challenge them and prevent their becoming typed. *Drunken Angel* was the first picture on which the composer Fumio Hayasaka worked with Kurosawa. They became close friends as well as collaborators and worked together until the composer's death, making nine pictures and developing from the first what Kurosawa characterizes as a "counterpoint [rather than a union] of sound and image."

Drunken Angel was both a popular and a critical success. It was placed first in the *Kinema Jumpo* list, gained a Ministry of Education prize, and the Mainichi award for best picture. Tsuneo Hazumi recognized that "out of an atmosphere of self-destruction and deterioration, a most important new Japanese film style is created." Max Tessier considers *Drunken Angel*, with *No Regrets for Our Youth* and *Stray Dog*, the best of the earlier films, which deal with "the acquisition of self-consciousness, the acceptance of responsibilities, a certain painful moral apprenticeship," themes that will reappear in many of Kurosawa's works up to and including *Kagemusha*.

While *Drunken Angel* was still in production, Kurosawa's father died. In April 1948, just as the film was released, the third union dispute broke out at Toho, and Kurosawa, who was attending Buddhist memorial ceremonies for his father,

was called back to the studio. It was a bitter and disillusioning experience, with Kurosawa caught between the two groups of employees of Toho and Shin Toho. The strike ended on October 19, leaving the studio in the hands of a management apparently willing to countenance the destruction of a cooperating work force. Kurosawa dates the decline of the Japanese film industry from the sacking of assistant directors during this strike. He transferred his allegiance to the Film Art Association (Eiga Geijutsu Kyokai) which he and three other directors—Yamamoto, Naruse, and Taniguchi—had established before the strike began. His first job outside Toho was to direct *Shizukanaru ketto* (*The Quiet Duel*) for Daiei, for whom he had written scripts in the early days. It was based on a popular stage play which starred Minoru Chiaki in a part Kurosawa saw as right for Mifune to give him a change from gangster roles. Kurosawa also chose the subject as being suitable for the inexperienced talents of his new young crew.

During the war a young doctor (Mifune) accidentally cuts his finger during an operation and contracts syphilis from the patient through the wound. On his return to a peacetime practice with his father, played by Takashi Shimura, he does not reveal to his fiancée of six years the reason for his refusal now to marry her, although one of their nurses learns the truth. Encountering again the man who infected him, the hero tries to help him and his wife, whose baby is born dead and deformed. The film ends with the fiancée arranging to marry someone else, and the doctor dedicating himself anew to his work. Donald Richie finds the film meticulous, slow, and lifeless, while Kurosawa himself felt that "only the early scenes in the field hospital have any validity." There were script problems as a result of alterations demanded by the Civil Information and Education Section of the American Occupation force: they removed the depiction of the more alarming stages of the disease in case it should discourage people from seeking treatment, and objected to the original ending in which the hero became insane. The result was a modest success and placed seventh in the 1949 *Kinema Jumpo* list.

In the same year Kurosawa made *Nora inu* (*Stray Dog*), because, he said, he felt he had not been fully understood in *The Quiet Duel* and wished to make his point more clearly. The story was based on a real incident in which a policeman lost his pistol. In the film, it is stolen from the young detective Murakami on a crowded bus. Afraid of losing his job, he sets about the seemingly impossible task of recovering it. While the search proceeds, Murakami (played by Mifune) begins to identify with his quarry, especially when the gun is used in a murder. But finally, helped by his chief (played by Shimura), Murakami tracks down the murderer and recovers the pistol. Kurosawa saw the original anecdote as a chance to do something in the manner of Georges Simenon, which was why he took the unusual step of first writing the story as a novel and only then adapting it for the screen with the collaboration of Ryuzo Kikushima. The film is another comment on postwar Japanese society, with the hero's search, in oppressive summer heat, taking us through all levels of Tokyo's social life, but especially the lowest. Seeing in its style similarities to American crime pictures, Richie and Anderson regard *Stray Dog* as probably the best Japanese detective film, with its depiction of the social milieu "an active part of the film rather than just exotic background." Burch points to American postwar realism and compares Dassin's *The Naked City*. Kurosawa himself felt he had failed to do justice to the Simenon inspiration, that the film was too technical and lacked depth of character, except perhaps in the case of the criminal, played by Ko Kimura in his first film part. But the production was a happy experience. Shin Toho's involvement meant that Kurosawa was reunited with technicians who were old friends from the days of PCL, including second-unit director Inoshiro Honda and cameraman Asakazu Nakai. *Stray Dog* placed third in the *Kinema Jumpo* list for 1949, but first in the Motion Picture Art Magazine (*Eiga Geijutsu*), and received a Ministry of Education award.

Shubun (*Scandal*, 1950) was Kurosawa's first film for Shochiku. A protest about the power of the exploitative press in Japan, what Kurosawa called its "habitual confusion of freedom with license," *Scandal* tells of the accidental and innocent meeting between a successful young artist, played by Mifune, and a well-known singer, played by Yoshiko Yamaguchi. This chance encounter is discovered by an unscrupulous gossip magazine and publicized as a great affair. The painter sues, but his lawyer, played by Takashi Shimura, is bribed by the magazine to lose the case. In the end the lawyer confesses and the magazine is restrained by the court. The lawyer's bedridden daughter, for whose sake he accepted the bribe, dies.

Throughout his career Kurosawa has been famous for his reserve towards the press. Protecting his private life with secrecy, he has been reluctant to give interviews until very recently, when it seems to have become necessary to encourage financial backing for his films. Donald Richie notes that Kurosawa was himself the subject of gossip after the war, concerning a supposed romance with Hideko Takamine, the star

of *Uma*. Whether or not the "outrage" Kurosawa felt at the scandal sheets had a personal motive, one critic, Noël Burch, nevertheless describes *Shubun* as "the one wholly *anonymous* film that bears Kurosawa's signature." Tadao Sato feels that it "lacks both the thematic strength and the formal beauty of Kurosawa's best work." But the film does have a certain interest because of the part it gave to Takashi Shimura as the lawyer, stronger than his role in *Drunken Angel* to the extent that it is he, not Mifune, who dominates the second half of the film. Kurosawa believes that the "characters in a film have their own existence," so that, for instance, once he had hit upon the corrupt Hiruta as a solution to his problems with the script of *Scandal*, the character "quite naturally took over the film and nudged the hero aside." Although Kurosawa has traced the origin in Hiruta to another real-life encounter, the character is also one of those in whom some critics, such as Audie Bock, have seen Russian literary prototypes, along with the doctor in *Drunken Angel*, the heroes of *Ikiru*, *Record of a Living Being*, and *The Bad Sleep Well*, and the criminals of *Stray Dog* and *High and Low*.

Kurosawa's next film, *Rashomon*, also made in 1950, was a landmark, not only in his own career but also in the history of Japanese cinema and its relation to the cinema of the West. Critics see continuity and gradual change rather than marked turns in the course of Kurosawa's career. Max Tessier notes a displacement of the early interest in humble, suffering humanity towards a hero of stronger personality. Audie Bock sees the topicality of *Drunken Angel* and *Stray Dog* giving way to something more universal. Noël Burch compares the films between 1946 and 1950 to the neorealism of Rosselini and De Sica, but finds in their style the "disjunctiveness, pathos, and excess" which will also be "constants in the mature work of the 1950s," together with the "characteristic *stubbornness* of Kurosawa's protagonists" which affects the structure as well as the theme of many of his films. Even so, *Rashomon* still marks a change, not only because of its unexpected success at the 1951 Venice Festival, but because of the unusual nature of the project itself. *Rashomon* came together in Kurosawa's mind from a number of stimuli. He felt that films had lost something of "peculiar beauty" from the days of silent film. In particular he felt "there was something to be learned from the spirit of the French avant-garde films of the 1920s." *Rashomon* would be a "testing ground" where he could apply his ideas on the aesthetics of those silent films, using "an elaborately fashioned play of light and shadow" to express the "strange impulses of the human heart" explored by the original short story, "In a Grove," by Ryunosuke Akutagawa.

The story had been made into a script by Shinobu Hashimoto, but it was too short for a feature film until Kurosawa added material from a second Akutagawa story called "Rashomon" as a frame to the first, the whole being set in the Heian period (794–1184). In a dense forest, a triangular encounter takes place between a samurai and his bride and a bandit. The bride is raped, the samurai killed, and the scene is witnessed by a woodcutter. The narrative of the film presents four main versions of this story, each told from the point of view of one of the participants. The captured bandit tells of tying up the husband, raping his bride, then, at her entreaty, dueling with the husband and killing him. The woman's version is that after the rape her husband rejected her, and she killed him in her angry grief. The third account is spoken through the lips of a medium by the spirit of the dead samurai. He says that after the rape the woman agreed to follow the bandit, but that the bandit rejected her when she insisted that he kill her husband; then the samurai found the woman's dagger and killed himself. The fourth version is the woodcutter's, altered by himself as he tells it. He says that he found the bandit, after the rape, pleading with the woman to run away with him. She insisted that the two men fight for her. The bandit killed the samurai, then he and the woman left separately. We see these versions as told partly before the police, but also retold and discussed by three men sheltering from torrential rain in the ruins of the great Rashomon gate of the medieval city of Kyoto. One of these men is the woodcutter himself, another a priest who was also present at the police interrogation, and the third a common man who questions and comments. Finally, as these three consider the baffling tale, they hear a baby cry. The commoner, finding an abandoned child, steals its clothes, but the woodcutter, who has earlier been suspected of stealing the woman's dagger, picks up the baby to take it home, while the priest comments that his faith in humanity has been restored.

The apparent relativism of this intriguingly complex structure, which may have had much to do with its popularity in the West, created some problems in Japan. Daiei were reluctant to approve production because they did not understand the story. The studio head, Masaichi Nagata, was particularly scornful, until the film's success abroad. Although *Rashomon* did well at the box office in Japan, audiences were inclined to miss the point, searching for the one "true" version of events. Some theatres appointed a sort of *benshi* to help. Kurosawa explained the script to three baffled assistants, one of whom refused to cooperate and was sacked, by comparing its

difficulty to the difficulty of understanding the psychology of human beings who "are unable to be honest with themselves about themselves." Donald Richie confirms such a reading, distinguishing the rich suggestiveness of Kurosawa's film from the simpler questioning of all truth in Akutagawa's original. Turning attention away from any supposed message Tadao Sato says, "*Rashomon* is a masterpiece because of the way it is made," citing in particular the editing of the scene in which the woman yields to the bandit. Noël Burch notes Kurosawa's revival of the device of the 180-degree reverse-angle cut as "a basic element of his rough-hewn, jagged editing," and his use of "frequent and sharply contrasting juxtapositions of close-up and long shot, of moving and fixed shots, or shots of contrary movement." Richie on the other hand emphasizes the unobtrusive connecting of the mostly very brief but unusually numerous shots (420 in all). Kurosawa has acquired the reputation among his collaborators of being, as his production chief Hiroshi Nezu said, "the best editor in the world." He sees editing as the most important phase of production, giving life to the film, while pointing out that nothing can rescue a bad script. His method is unusual. Instead of shooting scenes in a random order of convenience, he prefers to shoot chronologically, following the script, as far as possible, scene by scene. He then edits the rushes when each day's shooting is over, so that he can maintain the involvement of his crew in the film's progress, and so that "I have only the fine cut to complete when the shooting is finished." Although his selection of shots, including the split-second shots of action, excludes those that draw attention to the camera, with *Rashomon* he begins to use more frequently that obtrusive punctuation mark, the hard-edged wipe. Kurosawa himself acknowledges that the powerful visual impression of this film is largely due to the work of cameraman Kazuo Miyagawa, with whom he worked here for the first time, and praises in particular the introductory section "which leads the viewer through the light and shadow of the forest into a world where the human heart loses its way." Miyagawa says that till then he had been shooting for Daiei "in a rather soft key," but that Kurosawa required many "special effects." He instances the forest love-scene of Machiko Kyo as the bride and Toshiro Mifune as the bandit: "He wanted Mifune to be like a big sun, like the Hinomaru [the red sun of the Japanese flag] in high contrast with the softness of Machiko Kyo. . . . [As that required] contrast between black and white, not the usual grey tone, I even used mirrors against the sun to get that effect, which was something I had never done before." In the same interview

Miyagawa recalled a plan Kurosawa had had, which remained only a plan, for combining tracking shots by four different cameras. Despite Daiei's doubts, *Rashomon* was released with a certain flourish and, although accounts differ about its success, it was reasonably well received. Patricia Erens says that it "managed only to earn back its production costs" on first release, but it was placed fifth in the Kinema Jumpo list for 1950, and, according to Richie and Anderson it was Daiei's fourth best money earner out of fifty-two films distributed that year. The Tokyo Motion Picture Reviewers' Club awarded their Blue Ribbon for the screenplay. But wider recognition was yet to come.

Meanwhile Kurosawa was at work on *Hakuchi*, his version of Dostoevsky's *The Idiot*. It was his opportunity to make a film from his favorite author but, perhaps because it was so close to his heart, it proved one of the great disappointments of his career. Kurosawa felt that, precisely because Dostoevsky was not a visual novelist but a psychological one of great objectivity, his novels could be recreated in images; but he confessed that the effort of recreation almost destroyed him. In interpreting Dostoevsky's novel, he thought he had "said simply a very simple truth," although some said he had made a film too heavy and difficult. His film follows the original story very closely, but transfers it to Japan, in particular to snow-covered Hokkaido. Akama, the Rogozhin of the original, played by Toshiro Mifune, loves Taeko Nasu (Nastasya Filippovna, played by Setsuko Hara). Kameda (Prince Myshkin, Masayuki Mori) loves both Taeko and Ayaka (Aglaya, Yoshiko Kuga) the daughter of his kinsman Ono (Takashi Shimura). The conflict between Kameda and Akama over Taeko, and between the two women over Kameda, ends when Akama stabs Taeko and, in a change from the novel, joins Kameda in madness, the two men huddling together in the icy room. Japanese critics condemned the adaptation; Tadashi Iijima is typical in seeing Kurosawa defeated by the realistic tendency inherent in the very nature of his medium. Donald Richie amd Audie Bock agree that the problem may well have been his very "refusal to tamper with Dostoevsky." Kurosawa himself refused to believe he had failed and was gratified by interested letters from members of his audience, more than for any other film. When the picture was released in America in 1963, the reviews were still bad. Recently in Europe, however, critics have taken a different view. Noël Burch sees *Hakuchi* as "probably the only adaptation of Dostoevsky to the screen which carries something of the complexity and dramatic intensity of the original." Aldo Tassone describes it as a point of departure, where *Rashomon* was an arrival: "This rich, limitless work points the way to the masterpiece of *Ikiru*." Claude Beylie's approval (comparing Murnau's *Faust* and Dreyer's *Gertrud*) is echoed by Tom Milne, who admires the "central metaphor of snow" which "instantly captures the essence of Dostoevsky's novel"; the stylization of movement and gesture; the simple stylistic device of triangular groupings that conveys "the interlocking despair of human relationships" and leads "almost mathematically to the extraordinary climax of the ice carnival . . . where all the characters, as though summoned by demonic invocation, converge tangentially, at different moments, upon the fixed point of the Idiot." Milne judges this "strange, poetic" film among Kurosawa's best. But in 1951 it was a critical and commercial failure, and a setback for Kurosawa, who angrily objected when Shochiku, whom he had chosen as the best studio to produce this kind of film, insisted on cutting its original length of 265 minutes to 166. The film's reception caused the Daiei Company to withdraw its offer to make another picture with Kurosawa. Arriving home from an abortive attempt to console himself with a fishing trip, Kurosawa was met by his wife with the news that *Rashomon* had won the Grand Prize at the Venice Film Festival.

Kurosawa had no idea that the film had been entered. Daiei themselves were reluctant, but the recommendation of Giuliana Stramigioli, head of Unitalia Film in Japan, had prevailed. *Rashomon* went on to win the American Academy Award for best foreign film and awards from the New York film critics and the National Board of Review. It was the first Japanese film for fourteen years to play commercially in the United States. Its worldwide success created some cross-cultural confusion. Western critics, ignorant of the output of the Japanese industry, heralded the "birth of a great national cinema." The film's visual style and the artifice of its complex narrative—as unusual in Japan as anywhere else at that time—were seen as typically Japanese. The vigorously expressive acting, especially of Mifune and Machiko Kyo, was compared to Kabuki theatre (in fact, Kurosawa dislikes Kabuki, considering it a worn-out form). Only later did the story become famous of his encouraging Mifune to act like the lion the crew had seen in a jungle film, and Donald Richie further undermine the Kabuki theory by explaining that the acting in *Rashomon* was rather a "grand" version of Japanese naturalistic. Arguments went on over whether the film was humanist or expressed despair about humanity; in particular, whether or not the "sentimental" conclusion was forced. Once Mizoguchi's new films began to appear,

from 1952 on, he and Kurosawa became the opposite poles in critical debates among French
New Wave critics, generally to the detriment of
Kurosawa. But *Rashomon*'s influence was wide:
Robbe-Grillet declared it had inspired *L'Année
dernière à Marienbad* (1961) and Bergman
called his own *Virgin Spring* (1959) "a pale
imitation." The Japanese were equally confused
by *Rashomon*'s foreign success, suspecting uneasily that the film appealed in the West because
it was "exotic," or alternatively because it was
"Western." At any rate, according to Kurosawa,
Toho were still reluctant to send his next film,
Ikiru, abroad, for fear of its not being understood; this although it was an immediate popular
and critical success at home, was placed first on
the *Kinema Jumpo* list for 1952, given the
Mainichi Film Concours award for best picture
and best screenplay, and awarded a Ministry of
Education prize. When the film was finally
shown abroad, it was very well received, and at
a 1961 Kurosawa retrospective in Berlin, it was
awarded the David O. Selznick Golden Laurel.

Ikiru (*Living*) tells the story of Watanabe, a
minor official in the city administration, widowed, and alienated from his married son. He
learns that he is suffering from cancer and has
only six months to live. He tries to lose himself
in pleasure, visiting bars and night spots accompanied by a writer who acts as a sort of Mephistopheles. He forms a friendship with a young
girl from his office. Finally he resolves to spend
his time creating a children's playground on
some waste land, against the resistance and delays of the local bureaucracy. But what distinguishes the film is the way it is told. *Ikiru* breaks
into two parts: after about two-thirds of its 143
minutes, when Watanabe has decided on the
playground project, a narrating voice informs us
of our hero's death five months later; the remainder of the film is devoted to his funeral ceremony, at which he is eulogised by his fellow
officials, whose hypocritical and increasingly
drunken discourse produces brief flashbacks,
filling in the five-month gap, and telling how
Watanabe's project succeeded. The first part of
the film also contains flashbacks, equally brief,
depicting Watanabe's recollections of his relations with his son: the mother's funeral, a baseball game, an appendix operation, the son's
leaving for the war. The flashbacks in the second
part show, as Burch points out, not the decisive
moments in the progress of Watanabe's project,
but rather glimpses of Watanabe himself engaged in various typical activities, concluding
with the famous shot of him sitting on a swing
in his completed playground (where he dies) as
the snow falls, singing softly the song "Life is so
short" that he had sung in the bar in part one.

"At no time do we see decisive papers being
signed, an official throwing up his hands in surrender, or any other definitive stage of the
struggle." This off-centered use of flashbacks, in
Burch's view, results in the "sense of distancing
which the spectator experiences in passing from
the first to the second part." Richie interprets the
division into two as a division between the
"reality" of Watanabe's life in part one and the
"illusion" of various views of it in part two. The
film is full of changes of tone and mood, as well
as of narrative and visual method. It begins with
an x-ray picture of Watanabe's stomach, and the
narrating voice telling us about his cancer. We
next see Watanabe in his office surrounded by
piles of papers. The narrating voice dismisses
him as uninteresting, scarcely alive. What follows is a satirical presentation of the way the bureaucracy frustrates the needs of citizens: a series
of the briefest scenes, divided by wipes, shows a
group of women complaining about the unsanitary waste ground. They visit each of the city's
offices until they return to where they started.
Then we join Watanabe in the hospital, absent
from his desk for the first time anyone can remember.

Richie calls the theme existentialist, comparing Dostoevsky and quoting with approval Richard Brown: "It consists of a restrained
affirmation within the context of a giant
negation." It is clearly possible in interpretation
to emphasize one strand more than another in
the structure of this very various film. Burch, in
considering it "Kurosawa's first full-blown masterwork and the most perfect statement of his
dramatic geometry," also finds it "somewhat
marred by its complicity with the reformist ideology dominant in that period." Tadao Sato too
feels that Kurosawa, in expressing a principle of
"work for work's sake," was presenting an idealized view of the world. The central performance
by Takashi Shimura did not entirely satisfy the
director, who "would have preferred something
a bit more relaxed." Peter John Dyer also found
the effect "a shade calculated," complaining too
that the pathos is "at times played upon rather
than suggested." This is a not uncommon criticism of Kurosawa's work in general. John Gillett,
for instance, attacks "his fondness for making his
actors give out *fortissimo* for much of the time,
and his tendency to stress obvious things in an
equally obvious way," and includes among his
examples the birthday party scene at the end of
the first part of *Ikiru*. Kurosawa saw himself
reaching "a certain maturity" in this film, which
he felt was the culmination of the "researches"
he had carried out since the war; nevertheless
the film left him dissatisfied, and it contains
blunders that still embarrassed him when inter-

viewed in 1966 by *Cahiers du Cinéma*. Asked if he considered himself a realist or a romantic, he replied, "I am a sentimentalist."

Kurosawa collaborated on the script for *Ikiru* with two other writers, Shinobu Hashimoto and Hideo Oguni. Since the earliest films he had preferred not to write alone, because of the danger of one-sidedness in interpreting a character, for a character is usually the starting point. The process of writing Kurosawa describes as "a real competition." The team retires to a hotel or a house isolated from distractions. Then, sitting around one table, each one writes, then takes and rewrites the others' work. "Then we talk about it and decide what to use." Although he finds scriptwriting the hardest part of his work, he always lays great emphasis on its importance. It is the first stage in an essentially collaborative process, of which the next is the careful rehearsals with the cast before any filming takes place. The scripts are often written with particular actors in mind. "We don't just rehearse the actors, but every part of every scene—the camera movements, the lighting, everything."

For his next film, *Shichinin no samurai (Seven Samurai*, 1954), that process with Kurosawa's "family" of collaborators took more than a year, by which time it had become not only Toho's most expensive undertaking but the most expensive film ever made in Japan. Much of the shooting was done on location a long way from the studio. Toho, fearful of their investment, tried to recall the director but relented when he threatened to abandon the production. His intention, long planned, was to make something outstanding in the genre of *jidai-geki,* the period film. Kurosawa dislikes in Japanese film the tendency towards the simple and wholesome. "I think we ought to have richer foods, richer films. And so I thought I would make this kind of film, entertaining enough to eat, as it were." The achievement of this aim cost "intense labour," because Kurosawa was seeking authenticity, to present seriously the issues of a sixteenth-century world, and to convey a sense of that world with convincing realism. Kurosawa's admiration for that very different director, Mizoguchi, is significant here: "His greatness was that he never gave up trying to heighten the reality of each scene." Kurosawa is equally renowned for his exacting concern for sets and properties, sensitive to the effect they have not only on the audience but also on the actor's performances.

After an explanatory caption locating the action in the Sengoku period of civil wars in Japan, *Seven Samurai* opens explosively with rapid shots of a band of brigands on swiftly galloping horses silhouetted against a dawn sky. Their chief decides to put off an attack on the village huddled below until its barley has been harvested. News of the threat is conveyed to the villagers, who decide that to defend themselves they must hire samurai. Ordinarily an outrageous notion—that such aristocratic warriors should associate with these peasants, let alone be employed by them—now in troubled times there are many *ronin* (masterless samurai) who may be hungry enough to be persuaded. The film tells the story, first of the search for a band of seven such men, then of the epic defense of the village against the brigands, in which four of the seven die, leaving their leader to reflect that the peasants, now happily planting their rice crop, are the real winners of the battle, not the warriors who led them. "What makes the film remarkable," in Audie Bock's view, "is the portrayal of the characters and the development of socio-philosophical themes." For example, the characterization of Kanbei, the leading samurai, played by Takashi Shimura, "suggests a theme of the breakdown of class distinctions," also a favorite concern of Jean Renoir, a director much admired by Kurosawa. Kanbei is discovered by the incredulous peasants when having his head shaved (thus removing the top-knot that denotes his privileged rank) to disguise himself as a priest in order to rescue a child held hostage by a thief. He of course agrees to help the villagers and assembles a band of five of his kind. They are introduced to us in a long sequence of interwoven scenes, variations on a repeated pattern of encounters, characterizing each samurai economically and memorably. Striking among these is Kyuzo (Seiji Miyaguchi), discovered fighting a duel with unostentatious skill, who at first refuses Kanbei's overtures because his only concern is to perfect his own art. Most significant of the remainder are the youthful Katsushiro (Ko Kimura), who embarrasses Kanbei by insisting on becoming his disciple, and Kikuchiyo (Toshiro Mifune in a *tour de force* of idiosyncratic characterization), who adds himself to the band as a seventh "unofficial" samurai. In his relationship to Kyuzo as well as to Kanbei, the young Katsushiro embodies a variation on a repeated theme in Kurosawa's work, that of the influence of an older, experienced mentor on a pupil. The Mifune character, Kikuchiyo, turns out to be a peasant himself, orphaned by the destruction of his home by bandits. He complicates and illuminates the story by his alarmingly unpredictable behavior, and in an important scene reverses the view of the relationship between the peasants and the samurai which the film has encouraged till that point. Speaking passionately to camera in close-up, as Joan Mellen says, "he defends the peasants as a class and as historical victims of the entire feudal order. . . . If they are foxy beasts—mean, stingy, and murderous—it is samurai who have made them so." The admiration Kurosawa makes us feel for his chosen samurai can only be for them as individuals, and for a noble tradition of behavior that no longer survives in the social system. "All seven regain their heroic role only in relation to what they can teach the villagers about a collective unity now gone forever from their own lives." The elegiac conclusion is enriched by a contrast, as the exhaustion and grief that end the battle are suddenly relieved, as Donald Richie describes: "We sit in darkness and then we hear music. It is the music of the farmers, and the screen lightens to reveal one of the most heartbreaking of sequences: the rice planting." This change of pace and mood is typical of the film's rhythm, what Audie Bock calls the "push-and-release" rhythm of Kurosawa's best films. Kurosawa himself explains: "The spectator's receptiveness has limits. It cannot endure a number of undisguised truths brought to a culmination at the same time. They have to be pondered. So there have to be scenes that are amusing although appearing to serve no purpose." Such scenes might include the lyrical treatment of the adolescent love between Katsushiro and a village girl, but also the haunting shot within the bandits' fortress as it catches fire and the captive wife of one of the villagers wakes dreamily in her stolen finery.

With *Seven Samurai* Kurosawa had emerged as a "notorious technical revolutionary" (Bock). Here he began in the battle scene to shoot using several moving cameras running simultaneously (because of the danger of repeating a take). It became his regular practice in conjunction with ruthlessly selective editing. His answer to the objection that this wastes film is that, on the other hand, it saves time. In addition he uses frequently, but again with particular force in the great battle of *Seven Samurai*, extreme telephoto lenses "to bring the action directly into the laps of the audience" (Richie), but also, as he himself explained, to ensure that the actors would not be distracted by the presence of the camera, and would therefore behave more naturally.

Seven Samurai is considered by many to be the best of all Kurosawa's films, and some would go further, as Anderson and Richie suggest, putting it "among the best films ever made not only in Japan but anywhere in the world." It was a popular success on first release, although some Japanese critics had reservations. Tadao Sato, for example, while acknowledging "an incomparable masterpiece" as a film of action, complained at the unfair treatment of the peasants in comparison to the samurai. There were some complaints about the film's length. Originally it was

three hours and twenty minutes long, but is more usually seen in a version cut to two hours and forty minutes. A cut version shown at the Venice Festival made the first part especially difficult to follow, but was nevertheless awarded a Silver Lion. *Kinema Jumpo* gave *Seven Samurai* third place in its 1954 list. Speaking of the film's affirmation of the grace and dignity represented by Kurosawa's seven heroes, Joan Mellen comments, "Kurosawa's films will never again be as lyrical as *Seven Samurai*. Nor does he ever again allow himself to feel so much for anything. The satiric works that follow seem, by comparison, like those of a person who had been hurt too deeply to allow himself to love again. Kurosawa's remaining *jidai-geki*, *Throne of Blood*, *The Hidden Fortress*, *Yojimbo*, and *Sanjuro*, portray landscapes without faith."

During the filming of *Seven Samurai*, Fumio Hayasaka, who composed its music, lay dying in the hospital. When Kurosawa went to see his great friend, Hayasaka spoke of how hard it would be to work well if a person knew that he was dying. He was not referring to himself, as Kurosawa at first thought, but to "everyone: all of us." The experiments at Bikini had just become news. The two men began to work on a film dealing with this subject. The original plan, on the advice of others, was to make it a satire, but as Kurosawa worked on the script with Oguni and Hashimoto, it turned into something else, which Richie describes as a tragedy, and which, Kurosawa acknowledged, might seem chaotic and incoherent as a result. During the filming Hayasaka died, so that Kurosawa had difficulty finishing the work. The score was completed by Masaru Sato.

The thirty-five-year-old Toshiro Mifune plays Nakajima, a seventy-year-old industrialist who, terrified by the threat of the atom bomb, attempts to persuade his large family, including his mistresses and their children, to move to a farm in Brazil to escape destruction. When he fails, and the family have him declared incompetent, he burns down his own factory. Confined in a mental hospital, he is visited by Harada (Takashi Shimura), a member of the court that tried his case. The film ends as Nakajima, seeing the setting sun from the window, cries, "It's burning. The earth is burning. Burning. At last finally it's burning!" *Ikimono no kiroku* (*Record of a Living Being*, 1955) was one of Kurosawa's biggest commercial failures, perhaps because, as he himself thought, it was made too soon. It placed fourth in the *Kinema Jumpo* list and eighth in the Tokyo Movie Reviewers' list. It was well received in 1961 at the Berlin Festival Kurosawa Retrospective. Anderson and Richie complain of "a wandering story that lacks direction. Kurosawa fails to make the fear of the atom bomb a universal phenomenon by showing it only through the distorted imagination of his crazy old man." Joan Mellen agrees in finding the film inconclusive, but still considers it "the finest Japanese film on atomic war." Noël Burch, noting the "class content" in attacks on the film, sees it as "one of Kurosawa's finest dramaturgical achievements" and considers that, "in contrast with the reformist idealism of *Living*," it "objectively offers a compassionate and yet critical image of the lucid social rebel, conscious of hidden historical reality and unable to act because of his isolation." Chris Auty finds that, "for all its symmetry and logic, the film remains relatively unmoving"; that the pathos "works at the level of spectacle rather than feeling, despite Mifune's consistently fine performance." But he also sees it as "less concerned with the objective memory of Nagasaki and Hiroshima than with the course of an obsession, and with the problems of traditional Japanese family structures in the nuclear age." He finds its themes "constantly, almost overwhelmingly, Shakespearian," calling to mind especially *King Lear* and *Hamlet*.

Kurosawa now wrote the screenplay of a long projected version of *Macbeth*, *Kumonosu-jo* (*The Throne of Blood*, 1957), intending it for a younger director. But Toho saw the finished script, as usual richer in visual material than scripts for his own direction, saw how expensive it would be, and asked Kurosawa to direct it himself. As in *Seven Samurai*, his intention was to improve on the "historically uninformed" *jidai-geki*, especially by introducing modern film techniques. With his designer Yoshio Muraki, he studied the plans of real Japanese castles, deciding on black, armored walls, to go with an ink-painting effect to be created with much mist and fog. The main location was on the black volcanic soil of Mount Fuji, where an elaborate castle was built for exteriors. Interiors were shot in the studios, to which soil had to be brought from Fuji and where even the lacquerware had to be specially copied from museum specimens. Another location, miles away in the Izu peninsula, was chosen for the mansion of Washizu (the Macbeth of the film, played by Mifune). The art consultant was Kohei Esaki, an inheritor of the Japanese tradition of scroll-painting. But Kurosawa was to reject his ideas for a towering castle, wanting instead to create an oppressive atmosphere with a low, squat one, and to carry this atmosphere through in low-ceilinged interiors.

The story follows Shakespeare's quite closely, with some minor differences, but Washizu is a less complex figure than Macbeth, more simply obsessive and ambitious from the start. The narrative is framed by images of the ruins of the castle to which Washizu's ambition brings him. The moving camera shows the foundations of posts, drifting fog, as a chorus chants the whole story of ambition and its end. The formality of this frame matches the style of the whole film which, of all Kurosawa's works, is the one most deliberately derived from the Japanese Noh theatre. David Desser sees this as a problem, because the method of Noh runs counter to the concrete nature of the film medium. "The Noh theatre presents the relation of events not their reproduction." Action takes place offscreen. He cites the neighing of the horse that signifies the murder of Washizu's friend Miki. Kurosawa himself felt that the Noh had affinities with Shakespearian theatre, and recommends Noh as a structural principle suitable for a screenplay: "*jo* (introduction), *ha* (destruction), and *kyu* (haste)." He also points out that "in the Noh, style and story are one." The dialogue in *The Throne of Blood* is spare, the actors' movements economical and formalized, as in the famous scene where the Lady Asaji (Washizu's wife, played by the great Isuzu Yamada) waits for the first murder to be accomplished, and there is a predominance of full-shots instead of close-ups. This last feature Kurosawa acknowledged as experimental, recalling the way it disturbed his crew, who were accustomed to moving in close for moments of emotion. Noël Burch sees the structure of *Throne of Blood* as founded on "an opposition between extreme violence or pathos and moments of static, restrained tension." He cites, among other sequences, "the headlong ride through the storm-swept forest, which signifies the gathering of occult forces" and precedes the tension of the first meeting with the witch. The opposition between these two types of scene is resolved, Burch argues, in the famous final scene, a "bravura passage . . . usually recognized by Western critics as such but nothing more." This is the scene in which Washizu is suddenly made the desperate target of the deadly arrows of his own troops, who stand silent in the courtyard below him. The film is full of similarly memorable inventions, such as the ominous invasion of the castle by a flock of birds, panicked by the cutting of the forest to disguise the advancing enemy, and the relentlessly formalized confusion when Washizu and Miki are lost in the fog, riding towards and away from the static camera a full twelve times. For exemplifying at its extreme what he calls Kurosawa's "geometry," Burch considers *The Throne of Blood* its director's "finest achievement." Richie searches rather for his preferred humanist message, a warning against rigidity and formalism itself. Desser argues more generally of Kurosawa's work, that "Kurosawa's primary interest in the cinema, despite his humanism and all that implies, is a formal one." The film placed fourth in the 1957 *Kinema Jumpo* list and was well received at the Venice Film Festival. As a version of Shakespeare, it has had both severely adverse criticism and praise as among the finest of screen adaptations.

Later the same year, Kurosawa realised another long-cherished ambition, bringing Gorky's *The Lower Depths* to the screen in *Donzoko*. The scenario follows the play very closely, but moves its interpretation in the direction of comedy and transfers the scene to Japan in the Edo period. Audie Bock considers that here Kurosawa is looking again at "the *Rashomon* problem of people's images of themselves," and to do so "adapted the setting and costumes to a kind of timeless poverty." But it is clear that Kurosawa was more interested than that suggests in the particular milieu he chose: "In Edo during this period the Shogunate was falling to pieces and thousands were living almost unendurable lives. Their resentment can still be felt in *senryu* and *rakushu* [satires] of the period. I wanted to show this atmosphere." Nevertheless he also wanted to make "a really easy and entertaining movie" and reported how easy and enjoyable an experience the production proved. Shooting time was brief but was preceded by a forty-day rehearsal period on the single set, with all the actors in full costume, with cameras empty but running. During this time all movements of actors and cameras were worked out and, above all, the performers were enabled to play as an ensemble. This was important in a film without starring roles (although the cast is full of stars: Toshiro Mifune, Isuzu Yamada, Kyoko Kagawa, Ganjiro Nakamura), and one in which the effect, as Richie suggests, is that of a performance rather than an interpretation. Deliberately theatrical too is the shock ending, in which the comic *bakabayashi* music, performed by the cast, is interrupted by the news that the actor (played by Kamatari Fujiwara) has killed himself, to which the gambler (Koji Mitsui) says, in close-up directly to camera, "The idiot—just as the fun was beginning." Donald Richie reports that Japanese audiences were disturbed by this, and that most disliked the film as a whole. Patricia Erens describes it as a qualified success. It was tenth on *Kinema Jumpo*'s list for 1957. In October of that year Kurosawa traveled abroad for the first time, visiting London for the opening of the new National Film Theatre, where *Throne of Blood* was shown. There he was honoured along with other great directors, including René Clair, Vittorio de Sica, and John Ford. In an interview at that time Kurosawa spoke of an ambition to make a film of the life of Van Gogh.

Kurosawa's next production, *Kakushi toride no san-akunin* (*The Hidden Fortress*, 1958), was filmed partly around Gotemba, at the foot of Mount Fuji, and beset by difficulties of location shooting. The rapid weather changes slowed up the shooting even before a typhoon destroyed the scenery. Wind has so often been an accompaniment to Kurosawa's filming, since *Sanshiro Sugata*, that he has acquired among his crew the nickname *kaze-otoko* (wind-man)—his own staff do not use the name *tenno* (emperor) devised for him by the press. However difficult and delayed the production, *Hidden Fortress* became Kurosawa's biggest box-office success before *Yojimbo*. The story is set in his favorite samurai period of the sixteenth-century civil wars. Referring to that time, before the lives of samurai were subject to social restriction in the Tokugawa era, Kurosawa has said, "It's the strong, colorful personalities of the earlier period that fascinate me." A princess (Misa Uehara), disguised, and protected by one of her generals (Toshiro Mifune), is trying to reach the safety of a friendly province, pursued by the enemy forces. She and the general are captured at the barrier station, along with the gold they are carrying, and two peasants the general has pressed into service. Their captor turns out to have personal reasons for befriending them, and joins in their escape to safety, where the peasants are rewarded. Most critics see the film as a light entertainment, a more than usually well-made *chambara*, with its spectacular scenes of the fire festival and the rebellion of the slaves. But it is also important as the first film in which Kurosawa used the wide screen, and he exploits it strikingly throughout, in compositions that emphasize the shape and boundaries of the frame in a way that Burch believes to be distinctively Japanese. The influence of the Noh is again apparent, as Kurosawa explains, not only in the music but in the very style and rhythm, for example, of the scene of the duel with lances. The *Hidden Fortress* placed second on the 1958 *Kinema Jumpo* list and received the NHK Network award, a Blue Ribbon prize, and the Golden Bear at the 1959 Berlin Festival. It was the last film Kurosawa was to make directly for Toho.

On January 29, 1959, Kurosawa gave his first press interview and announced the formation of his own company, Kurosawa Productions. Toho was to put up one million yen in an agreement requiring three films over two years, with profits and losses to be shared equally with Kurosawa. It was the first independent company headed by a working director in the history of the Japanese cinema. Three days later, production began on *Warui yatsu hodo yoku nemuru* (*The Bad Sleep Well*).

"Making a film just to make money did not appeal to me—one should not take advantage of an audience." Kurosawa wanted his first independent production to have "some social significance" and chose the subject of corruption. The story opens at a wedding reception, the formal ritual disturbed by accusations of murder, suspicion of the bridegroom's opportunism, and a police arrest. It is a sequence of economical, ironic storytelling, described by Richie as "twenty minutes of a brilliancy unparalleled even in Kurosawa." Nishi (Toshiro Mifune), private secretary to Iwabuchi (Masayuki Mori), president of a government housing corporation, is marrying his boss's daughter. It turns out to be his first step in a revenge against the firm that forced his father to jump from a window five years before. The police try to expose a case of bribery, but one of the men they arrest commits suicide, while the other, Wada, is saved by Nishi. They kidnap Moriyama, vice-president of the corporation (Takashi Shimura), starving their captive in an air-raid shelter and forcing him to confess. Matters are complicated by the love that has grown up between Nishi and his crippled wife (Kyoko Kagawa). Mistakenly trusting her father, she reveals to him Nishi's hideout. Nishi is murdered by *yakuza*, who inject alcohol into his veins. Iwabuchi makes a phone call, not for the first time, to an unknown government official. The plot seeks not only to expose corruption but to show how it taints even those who look for justice. Although Burch suggests that *The Bad Sleep Well* is underrated, most critics agree that the film does not live up to its brilliant opening, where a macabre cake, decorated with the single rose, is wheeled into the wedding reception. *Kinema Jumpo* gave the picture third place. Kurosawa told Paul Schrader that this was the most difficult of all his scripts to write, because of its topicality and because of the impossibility of speaking directly and explicitly. Joan Mellen believes that the concentration on the psychology of Nishi obscures the political point, and she attributes the shift of emphasis to a "sense of futility before the crucial question at the heart of his own subject." But Richie considers the film's failure "much more interesting than many successes."

Defending Kurosawa against Tado Sato's opinion that the director's work shows a decline after *Record of a Living Being* (1955), Joan Mellen points to "three masterpieces, *Yojimbo* (1961), *Sanjuro* (1962), and *High and Low* (1963)." In the first two, she says, "Kurosawa discovers Japan through critical moments of transition in Japanese history when decaying values have lost their universal acceptance and new modes have neither clearly emerged nor fully displaced the old." "The samurai in *Yojimbo*," Kurosawa explains, "is not the same as the samurai in *Seven Samurai*. During the peaceful era of Tokugawa those who had secured their jobs long ago had ceased to be warriors. . . . Those who were out of jobs were to remain permanently unemployed . . . so they had to take a job, any job available, and some became the bodyguards of gamblers." Mellen considers *Yojimbo* "one of Kurosawa's darkest films," expressing "the hopelessness of all the intellectuals of Japan who have watched their country pass into its modern technological stage guided by nothing but the pursuit of profit." Richie, however, insists that Kurosawa's concerns are more moral than political. The plot of *Yojimbo* turns on the rivalry between Tazaemon, a silk merchant, and Tokuemon, a saké brewer, each with his gang of henchmen. Into this town split by the conflict between two evils (Kurosawa says he was expressing his anger at the *yakuza* again), comes Sanjuro Kuwabatake, an independent "samurai of the imagination," as Kurosawa describes him, who plays one side off against the other until both are destroyed. It is a film of macabre humor and elaborately choreographed combat, presided over by Toshiro Mifune's off-hand, world-weary, tooth-picking, chin-stroking Sanjuro. For the second time, Kazuo Miyagawa was Kurosawa's photographer, and Audie Bock believes him responsible for the successful pans and for avoiding the static, staged look of Kurosawa's other widescreen pictures.

This film, like many of Kurosawa's *jidai-geki*, has been compared to American westerns, and the director has acknowledged that he has learned from "the grammar" of the genre. But he in turn has made his own contribution. *Yojimbo* appeared again in 1964 as Sergio Leoni's "spaghetti western" *For a Fistful of Dollars* just as *Rashomon* and *Seven Samurai* had earlier spawned Martin Ritt's *The Outrage* and John Sturges' *The Magnificent Seven*. *Yojimbo* was Kurosawa's biggest commercial success and placed second on the Kinema Jumpo list.

Kurosawa had already written a script for his next picture based on a story by Shugoro Yamamoto, about a *ronin* who makes up in brains for what he lacks in strength and skill. The success of *Yojimbo* led to rewriting and therefore to the more athletic hero, better with the sword, who appears in *Tsubaki Sanjuro* (*Sanjuro*, 1962), played again, of course, by Toshiro Mifune. It was another big success with audiences and placed fifth on the *Kinema Jumpo* list. Kurosawa feels the film to be very different from *Yojimbo* and detected a different response from audiences. "The youngsters loved *Yojimbo,* but it was the adults who liked *Sanjuro.* I think they liked it because it was the funnier and really the more attractive of the two films."

In this story, Sanjuro helps Iito Izaka and a group of fledgling samurai in support of Izaka's uncle, clan leader Mutsuta, in a struggle with his political enemy Kikui. They rescue first Mutsuta's kidnapped wife and daughter and then the lord himself, using a trick of floating camellias down a stream to signal an attack. Skipping the celebratory banquet in his honor, Sanjuro, in a final duel with Kikui's henchman Muroto (Tatsuya Nakadai), kills him with one swift stroke that produces a sudden spurt of blood from the villain's heart. Sanjuro sternly reprimands the eager young samurai who applaud this feat, quoting a remark made earlier by Lady Mutsuta, when she compared him to an unsheathed sword: "Really good swords are kept in their scabbards. Yours had better stay in yours. And don't try to follow me or I'll kill you." Nigel Andrews calls this "the most autumnal of Kurosawa's Japanese Westerns" and suggests some affinities with *True Grit,* comparing Mifune's "shaggy, truculent samurai" with John Wayne's Rooster Cogburn as "reluctant exiles" both. He appreciates too "the choreographic formalism of Kurosawa's style, making an entertainingly quaint chorus of Sanjuro's hangdog disciples, and giving a hilarious unity to the demure utterances of the kidnapped official's wife and daughter." Akira Iwasaki, however, finds in *Sanjuro* neither the extravagance, irony, or force of *Yojimbo.*

The Story of *Tengoku to jigoku* (*High and Low,* 1963) is based on an Ed McBain detective story called *King's Ransom.* The son of Gondo, production head of a shoe company (Toshiro Mifune), has apparently been kidnapped and a ransom is demanded. When it turns out that the son of Gondo's chauffeur has been taken by mistake, Gondo must decide whether he will still pay the ransom—to do so will would ruin him and allow his rivals to take over the company. Agreeing to pay, he is instructed to throw a briefcase containing the money from a high-speed train. We then learn the identity of the kidnapper: Takeuchi, a poor medical student, provoked by the sight of Gondo's ostentatious house on a hill overlooking the Yokohama slums where he himself struggles to live. As the police close in, Takeuchi (also a pusher of heroin) kills his accomplices. He is finally captured, and Gondo visits him in prison. The first part of the film (65 minutes of 143) takes place entirely in Gondo's hilltop house, the action restricted to phone calls and conversations, filmed in long takes shot with

several cameras. Three identical sets were built to represent the scene at different times of day, according to Richie; cameras followed the actors' movements closely but were positioned outside the set itself. "The effect is one of complete freedom within a very constricted area," and the camerawork makes the hour-long sequence seem much shorter. It also provides a context for the explosive action that follows, the four-minute sequence on the speeding train. The rest of the narrative is full of incidents, sights and sounds, punctuated by the famous moment when red smoke, in color on the black-and-white screen, appears from a chimney to reveal the location of the discarded briefcase, after which the action accelerates for the final chase. This bold two-part structure is seen by Burch as another outstanding example of Kurosawa's distinctive "dramatic geometry." Richie sees it as marking two areas of thematic interest, the first emotionally involving, the second intellectual. Joan Mellen considers it fortunate that the "rather obvious moral dilemma" of the first part is replaced by the "much more interesting treatment of the personality of the kidnapper." The second part, after the train sequence, begins by deliberately destroying the pattern of suspense, revealing the kidnapper in his miserable daily existence. For Mellen, this part, with its descent into the slums and its satirical presentation of police and press, "comes close to developing into one of the finest critiques of the inequitable class structure of Japan ever offered in a Japanese film." She answers Tadao Sato's objection that a man destined to become a doctor would never have risked his future as Takeuchi does, by reading it as a deliberate irony confirming "the depth of Kurosawa's social vision." In the final confrontation, which Richie reads as Dostoevskian, the faces of Gondo and the kidnapper begin to merge with each other's reflections in the glass screen dividing them, indicating their underlying identity. *High and Low* placed second on the *Kinema Jumpo* list and received the Mainichi Concours award for best picture and screenplay. Some French critics, however, saw it as Kurosawa's worst picture. Informed of this, Kurosawa wondered if they had not liked it because of the Americanness of Gondo's style of life—something he had to show, since it is a part of real Japanese society.

Kurosawa began work on his next film, *Akahige* (*Red Beard*) with "something special in mind," saying that he wanted to make "something so magnificent that people would just have to see it." The hard work and attention to detail this necessitated meant that the film took almost two years to shoot, longer than any previous Japanese film. The main set was in effect an entire small town, authentic in every detail. Kurosawa fell ill twice during the production, and his two leading men, Mifune and Kayama, once each. The script, on which Kurosawa worked with Ryuzo Kikushima, Hideo Oguni, and Masato Ide, was based on a novel by Shugoro Yamamoto, but Kurosawa also had Dostoevsky in mind, in particular *The Insulted and Injured* for the character of Otoyo. The story, set in the late Tokugawa period, concerns Yasumoto, a young medical student (Yuzo Kayama) recovering from a failed love affair, who unwillingly joins a public clinic run by Dr. Niide, nicknamed Red Beard (Toshiro Mifune). The ambitious young man is at first repelled by the place, which is understaffed and overcrowded with poverty-stricken patients. But Red Beard, despite his rough arrogance, impresses him, so that he learns and matures under his influence until at the end of the film he himself is insisting, against Niide's gruff discouragement, that he remain at the clinic. The numerous complicatons of the plot include an attempt on Yasumoto's life by an insane woman patient, and the rescue from a brothel and gradual rehabilitation of twelve-year-old Otoyo, Yasumoto's first patient. The resemblance, especially in Mifune's role, to the earlier samurai films is underlined by such scenes as Red Beard's fight with the bouncers at the brothel. The narrative is in two parts with a break, the second part beginning with the story of Otoyo's slow recovery. Both Burch and Richie remark on the absence of a clear formal structure, Richie comparing Dickens, and believing that "the film discloses through characterization and parallels of action."

Akahige was an immediate success with Japanese audiences, and critics saw it as a masterpiece. It was number one on the *Kinema Jumpo* list for 1965, received a Blue Ribbon award, and the award for best picture in the Mainichi Concours. In the same year Kurosawa received the Ramon Magsaysay Memorial Award in Manila. The reputation of *Akahige* has varied since that time. It was inevitable that it should be compared to televison hospital series. The justice of the comparison is vigorously denied by David Wilson and Donald Richie. Akira Iwasaki notes a political dimension: "Kurosawa makes it clear that the enemy confronting both Red Beard himself and Noboru (Yasumoto) is not simply disease but a political set-up which creates poverty and ignorance without the means to remedy them." Richard N. Tucker describes it as "probably Kurosawa's greatest film" and its director's "most perfect statement" of his favorite theme of an education in humanist values "absorbed by the pupil through the observation of the master." But Tucker also believes that "it

is almost as though we were watching his final statement." Audie Bock agrees, finding a "didactic remoteness" in it and in Kurosawa's next film, a distance between Kurosawa and his audience explained by "the alienation of contemporary society from humanist values." She also finds the technical virtuosity of *Red Beard* unconvincing: "Filmed in 'scope, it is a very frontal film, and as expertly as the visuals are handled, they lack the depth and movement of a film like *Seven Samurai*." Kurosawa himself described the picture as a dream; if a man like Red Beard existed and could gain a following, the world would change. Although it is a black story, he wanted the audience to leave with light hearts full of hope. He felt that the look of the film (using extreme long-distance lenses and a new, highly sensitive film stock) created a sense of freshness and vitality, where critics, as Richie suggests, have rather seen *sabi*—an appearance of aging or patina. *Akahige* marks the end of an era if for no other reason that that it is the last of Kurosawa's films in which Toshiro Mifune appears. The actor whose face and physique had been so closely identified with the expression of Kurosawa's vision quarreled with the director, partly because *Akahige's* two-year production period (during which he had to maintain his beard) interfered with other work.

In the five years before his next production, Kurosawa was involved in a number of unhappy projects. Japanese companies refused him support, so he sought financing in the United States. When bad weather postponed shooting in Rochester, New York, of a script called *The Runaway Train,* Fox invited Kurosawa to direct the Japanese sequences of *Tora! Tora! Tora!* After a few weeks' shooting, bitter disagreements with the studio ended with Fox claiming that Kurosawa had resigned because of bad health (meaning mental health), and with Kurosawa insisting that he had been misled (for instance, about the other director supposed to work with him—he had been promised David Lean) and then dismissed against his will.

Disillusioned, Kurosawa returned to Japan, where an independent company was formed, called Yonki no Kai (The Four Musketeers), consisting of Kurosawa, Keisuke Kinoshita, Kon Ichikawa, and Masaki Kobayashi. It was an attempt to reassert the power and independence of the director in what Kurosawa has referred to as the Dark Ages of Japanese cinema. Kurosawa's first venture for the company was *Dodes'kaden* (1970), his first picture in color. He has said, "I made this film partly to prove I wasn't insane; I further tested myself with a budget of less than one million dollars and a schedule of only twenty-eight days." Based on *The*

Town Without Seasons, a collection of stories by Shugoro Yamamoto, it consists of loosely interwoven episodes in the lives and fantasies of the inhabitants of a garbage-dump shantytown, but its "dialectic of suffering and reverie" (Joan Mellen) is treated by Kurosawa in a manner consciously designed, as he said, to be "bright, light, endearing." The title is an onomatopoeic rendering of the sound of a tram on its rails. It is the sound uttered by Rokkuchan, a boy who makes the rounds of the dump driving an imaginary streetcar. His delusion is only an extreme version of the self-deceptions of the other characters, a group presided over by Tamba, "an old craftsman and beneficent spirit," as Joan Mellen describes him, who seems to act as Kurosawa's mouthpiece in the structure. There is also a chorus in the form of the chattering women who gather at the pump.

Dodes'kaden is shot in standard format, and the use of color combines the naturalistic with what Philip Strick calls a "departure into surrealistic shades for points of crisis." When it rained on the painted shacks built in the real Tokyo dump where the shooting took place, the ground turned a variety of colors, to Kurosawa's delight, as a result of a reaction with chemicals in the soil. Without his customary long rehearsal, Kurosawa asked his actors to behave spontaneously and improvise, while he filmed, unusually for him, in long takes. The picture was a financial failure, and the new company foundered. But it was liked by Japanese critics, and came third in the Kinema Jumpo list. Many believed, with Joan Mellen, that with this picture "Kurosawa abandoned the glorification of supreme individuals and focussed on the courage and endurance of the weak and the forgotten." The change moved Kurosawa closer to his younger contemporaries. Noël Burch suggests a similar affinity in the style: "Its theatricality of acting, sets and lighting is an interesting response to the experiments of the younger generation." The same influence appears in "the extravagant accumulation of symbolic parable. The shantytown is clearly Japan." But Richard Tucker is not alone in feeling that this relaxed film "lacked the power and cohesive force that the world had come to expect from such a great artist." It was awarded a Special Prize at the Seventh Moscow International Film Festival.

Kurosawa next made a television documentary, *Uma no uta* (*The Song of the Horse*). Then, on December 22, 1971, a housemaid found him lying in his half-filled bath, wounded with twenty-two slashes on his neck, arms, and hands. He had attempted suicide. Joan Mellen has discussed this attempt in the context of Japanese attitudes toward death and suicide; Kurosawa

himself spoke of neurosis, low spirits, and the realization (after an operation for a severe case of gallstones) that he had been in pain for years. His eyesight too had begun to fail. "Letters and telegrams came from all over the world; there were offers from children to help finance my films. I realized I had committed a terrible error." His spirits were fully restored by an offer in 1972 from the Soviet Union to direct a subject of his choice. Kurosawa chose to write a script based on the writing of Vladimir Arseniev, which he had read in the 1940s. Arseniev was a Russian soldier who, while mapping the Russian-Manchurian border in the early 1900s, formed a friendship with Dersu Uzala, an old hunter who acted as guide for him and his party. In the film the story of the relationship between the two men, and the portrayal of Dersu's life of pantheistic unity with the great Ussuri forest and its creatures, are given in flashbacks. The opening scene takes place in 1910, when new settlements have changed the area, and Arseniev (Yuri Salomin) cannot even find Dersu's grave. The first flashback tells of his introduction to Dersu (Maxim Munzuk, in an engaging performance), culminating in the scene of the great blizzard in which the old man saves both their lives, as the two men urgently cut reeds to form a shelter on a frozen lake, and ending as Arseniev returns home. Five years later, a title informs us, the soldiers return to the region, enabling the two men to meet again. Dersu is now going blind, and when he fears that he has offended the forest spirit by killing a tiger, he is persuaded to accompany Arseniev to his home in Khabarovsk to live with him and his family. But the old man is unable to settle down. At last he returns to the forest with a modern rifle given him by his host. When he is murdered for the rifle, Arseniev is called to identify the body and buries Dersu in a final scene in the snow-filled forest.

Dersu Uzala took almost four years to complete, two of which were spent filming in the Siberian winter. It was shot in 70-mm with six-track stereophonic sound. Kurosawa was not entirely happy with the color, or with his limited success under these arduous conditions in depicting the natural world. Mellen finds *Dersu Uzala* "a rather lifeless film" showing a "decline in Kurosawa's powers." But John Gillett, with reservations about the "touch of early Kipling" in a "hymn to nature and friendship," nevertheless appreciates the "strictly classical style" of this "intimate epic." Tom Milne sees its theme saved from sentimentality "by direction as calm and matter-of-fact in its elegiacs as the best of John Ford." Yikichi Shinada also noticed here a new objectivity in Kurosawa's work. The film was popular in Japan, and played widely in Russia. When Sovexport cut twenty minutes from its length for its distribution in Italy, Kurosawa made them restore it, threatening never to work again with the Russians. *Dersu Uzala* ranked fifth on *Kinema Jumpo*'s list for 1975. It was given the American Academy Award for best foreign picture, a Federation of International Film Critics Award, a Gold Medal at the Ninth Moscow Festival, and in Italy in 1977 the Donatello Prize. In 1976 Kurosawa was given by the Japanese government the high-ranking cultural award of Order of the Sacred Treasure, designating him a Person of Cultural Merits, the first such in his profession; and in 1978 he received an award for "Humanistic Contribution to Society in Film Production" from the European Film Academy.

Another five years went by before Kurosawa made his next film. He worked on the script for *Ran*, his Japanese *King Lear*, and on a project based on Edgar Allen Poe's "Masque of the Red Death." With Masato Ide he wrote the script that was to become *Kagemusha*. But although this was a film that had to be shot in Japan, no Japanese company was willing to risk money unless it was assured of large returns. Meanwhile Kurosawa produced hundreds of colored drawings, planning every detail of a film that might never be seen. To supplement his own finances he even appeared in whiskey commercials. Since his recovery in 1972, he had become a much more public person, more open to television and the press. He traveled in 1978 to Europe (visiting his daughter and grandchild in Italy) and to the United States. There he met Francis Ford Coppola and George Lucas, two of his admirers, who consider themselves his students. Realizing Kurosawa's difficulties, the two American directors approached Alan Ladd Jr. of 20th Century–Fox, who in turn made a deal for *Kagemusha* with Toho, to whom Fox was to give one-and-a-half million dollars for all the foreign rights. The total cost of six million dollars made it the most expensive film made in Japan, but with gross earnings of ten million on its first run, it was one of the most successful Japanese films of 1980. That year it shared the Grand Prize at Cannes.

The plot of *Kagemusha* returns to sixteenth-century Japan. During the clan wars, a thief is spared from execution because of his resemblance to Shingen, lord of the Takeda clan, for whom he will act as a *kagemusha* (shadow warrior), a double to deceive his enemies in battle. When Shingen is mortally wounded by a sniper, he gives instructions to keep his death secret for three years. Reluctant at first, the *kagemusha*, coached by Shingen's brother Nobukado, grows into his role, deceiving Shingen's little grandson

and heir, Takemaru, and his concubines. The *kagemusha* does well, despite the resentment of Shingen's illegitimate son Katsuyori, and rallies the clan forces by imitating Shingen's legendary fortitude during a confusing night battle, so that the Takeda clan triumphs. His downfall comes when Takemaru persuades him to attempt Shingen's unrideable horse, and he is thrown. He is ignominiously expelled, and Katsuyori succeeds his father. Then, in 1575, the Takeda clan launches its army against the combined forces of its three rivals, Nobunaga Oda, Ieyasu Tokugawa, and Kenshin Uesugi, and is destroyed at Nagashino by the use of guns. The banished thief, wandering on the battlefield, also dies, carried away in a stream with the banner of Shingen. In this final sequence, Kurosawa rejects as unsatisfactory the film convention of cavalry battles, where riders are shot and seen to fall, in favor of "something different, more effective for the sophisticated film audiences of today—to show the final effect of the battle rather than those shootings themselves." Having seen nothing of the murderous battle directly, we now contemplate, in detail and slow motion, the stricken soldiers and wounded horses trying to rise from a field of dead. Kurosawa says that the script grew from that fateful battle—a turning point in Japanese history because Nobunaga Oda and Ieyasu Tokugawa represent the beginning of a new kind of Japan. He sees the defeat of the Takeda clan as the paradoxical result of the powerful love that Shingen inspired in his followers, so that in effect they were willing to commit suicide to join him in death. Shingen "is really the hero of the film. Everyone else is moving under his shadow." He haunts the picture in various forms from first to last. The film begins with a static six-minute shot in which Shingen, played by Tatsuya Nakadai, sits facing us in the middle. His brother Nobukado sits on the left, dressed identically because till now it has often been his task to impersonate Shingen. On the right sits the prospective *kagemusha*, also played by Nakadai, and dressed identically by Nobukado, who is demonstrating to his brother how convincing the thief will be in the role. This shot, "teasing the audience to spot the process work" (Richard Combs), is a calculated opening to what David Desser calls "a tragedy of signification, for Kurosawa has detailed the manner in which signs come together to shape events." He calls *Kagemusha* "as stylized and formalized a film as Kurosawa has ever produced (excepting *Throne of Blood* perhaps)," but still one concerned with the human condition. John Pym calls it a "deliberately populist movie," citing the "deft, small-scale, comic moments" of the story of the sniper, and the gentle play with

"Shingen's decidedly Western grandson," but considers these to be self-indulgent interludes "incidental to the rather plodding business of the development of the *kagemusha*'s character." Richard Combs acknowledges the film's "grandiloquence, the Shakespearian design in which the story of the *kagemusha* becomes an interrogation of the very notions of power and kingship," but misses "any feel for the crunch of history on ordinary lives." For Max Tessier it is a "triumph of 'pure mise-en-scène'" and "a political fable about the appearance of power." David Robinson thought that *Kagemusha* marked "perhaps the first time the cinema has produced a tragedy of truly Shakespearian resonance." Donald Richie enumerates the disasters that befell the film during its nine months of production. The eyesight of the great cameraman Kazuo Miyagawa began to fail, so that Takao Saito and Masaharu Ueda had to replace him, supervised by a familiar member of Kurosawa's team, Asakazu Nakai. Kurosawa fell out with composer Masaru Sato, who was replaced by Shinichiro Ikebe. Then the star who was to play the double lead, Shinaro Katsu, a popular comic actor, turned up on the set with his own camera and cameraman to record his performance. Kurosawa's response was, "we don't need two directors on this movie," and Katsu was replaced by Nakadai. Whether or not any of this materially affected what Kurosawa had already planned so meticulously, Richie reads in the finished film "an unsparingly bleak statement, a profoundly pessimistic view."

If some critics were tempted to see *Kagemusha* as an old man's culminating statement, his latest picture, *Ran* (1985), has proved even more tempting. The story resembles that of Shakespeare's *King Lear*, but concerns the sixteenth-century Japanese lord Hidetora, who retires from active leadership of his clan while retaining an over-all title, and transfers power to the eldest of his three sons, Taro Takatora, and in lesser degree to the other two, Jiro Masatora and Saburo Naotara. Saburo scorns Hidetora's sentimental belief that family ties will prevent conflict and is consequently banished, along with a retainer, Tango, who supports him. Saburo takes sanctuary with a neighboring lord, while Tango, like Kent, tries to serve Hidetora unrecognized. Goaded by his wife, Kaede, Taro siezes full power from his father, and Jiro backs him. Only Saburo's castle is prepared to shelter Hidetora, but when Taro and Jiro attack (and Taro is killed by one of Jiro's snipers), the old man wanders crazily, accompanied by his fool, Kyoami, and Tango. In the same wilderness are other wanderers: Sué, wife of Jiro who now seeks to kill her, having been seduced by his brother's widow Lady Kaede; and Sué's brother Tsurumaru, blinded in childhood by Hidetora. The conflict among the forces of Jiro, Saburo, and their opportunist neighbors leaves Kaede dead, Sué beheaded, Saburo shot, and Hidetora dead of grief. In the final scene, the blind Tsurumaru stands on the edge of a precipice and releases a scroll-painting of the Buddha into the void. Critics were quick to notice similarities between Hidetora and Kurosawa himself, both the same age. It is said that the relationship between Hidetora and the fool is paralleled by Kurosawa's relationship with Peter, the transvestite actor who plays Kyoami. The twelve-million-dollar budget for *Ran* was put together by French producer Serge Silberman in negotiation with Japanese companies, Nippon Herald, Toho, and Fuji TV; and once the film was completed Kurosawa set off around the world on a promotional tour. A tall, amiable figure, wearing dark glasses to shield his sensitive eyes and surrounded by a busy, protective retinue, he was described by one of his interviewers as "the quiet eye of the storm that blows all around him." Four months of rehearsal were followed by nine months shooting, extended because of mourning for the death of Kurosawa's wife early in 1985. The spectacular production took Kurosawa's unit once again to the black volcanic slopes of Mount Fuji, where a castle had to be built and then burned down for the scene of Hidetora's descent into madness.

The Japanese word *ran* means "war," "riot," or "conflict," but has too an older, broader significance—"chaos." Tony Rayns describes the vision of the film as "one step further down the road to hell from the ending of *Kagemusha*." After a startling opening scene depicting a boar hunt, the narrative begins with Hidetora handing over power and giving a little lesson in the value of family unity, declaring that while one arrow alone can be broken, three together cannot. Saburo breaks all three arrows across his knee, saying, "This is a world where men's cruel and evil instincts are only too evident, where one can survive only by suppressing one's humanity and all one's higher feelings." Rayns sees the film as "essentially an extended dramatisation" of this scene, "a tautologous gloss on Saburo's pragmatic pessimism." He finds the parallel of Shakespeare's original a problem. Hidetora is denied tragic stature because Kurosawa is more concerned with his hero's past than with his moral regeneration. To Rayns, Hidetora is credible neither as a "brilliant military leader on the verge of senility nor as a madman in second childhood stricken with remorse." Tom Milne takes a more positive view, describing a film in which "a certain classicism seems to replace the ferment of invention as virtuosity no longer feels the need to be *seen* to exist. One is moved, as often as not, less by what is expressed than by what is implied." Reviewers were impressed by the spectacle of the battle, with its forces sharply differentiated by their colors in the blackness of their world, and by some performances, notably that by Mieko Harada as the startling Lady Kaede. Vincent Canby, reviewing *Ran* in the twenty-fifth week of its New York run, felt that the audience which applauded "had been swept up in the kind of all-embracing movie experience that's rare in any era." In March 1986, Kurosawa visited London to be made a Fellow of the British Film Institute.

Throughout his career, from his earliest encounters with the Japanese censors, it has been suggested that Kurosawa is too "Western" to be a good Japanese director. In the West a kind of purism began to prefer Ozu and Mizoguchi. But Kurosawa has always insisted on his Japanese outlook. "I am a man who likes Sotatsu, Gyokudo, and Tessai in the same way as Van Gogh, Lautrec and Rouault. . . . I collect old Japanese lacquerware as well as antique French and Dutch glassware. In short, the Western and the Japanese live side by side in my mind naturally, without the least sense of conflict." Akira Iwasaki agrees, pointing out that, unlike Ozu and Naruse, "Kurosawa belongs to a more recent generation which must look to the West for help in defining Japan, which verifies and analyses the one by constant reference to the other." Audie Bock insists that he "has never catered to a foreign audience and has condemned those that do." But from his Japanese center, Kurosawa from the first was in touch with international film culture, as the lists in his autobiography, of films he admired, show. Interviews from the 1960s onwards show his interest also in the latest films. He has always believed cinema should take advantage of technical developments. Among his Japanese "teachers," either literally or as models, Kurosawa names first "Yama-san" (Kajiro Yamamoto), along with his great friend Sadao Yamanaka then Mizoguchi, Ozu, and Naruse. Of Western directors he speaks with most reverence perhaps of John Ford and Jean Renoir. Kurosawa is himself a teacher in his turn. Among more recent examples in the West alone, Altman, Penn, Coppola, and Lucas have all testified to his influence. The younger Japanese directors, on the other hand, have felt the need to react against the world that Kurosawa represents.

Interpreters of Kurosawa, especially the influential Richie, have always been concerned with his "humanism," although Richard N. Tucker takes issue with Richie and finds in other direc-

tors a less feudal version of that humanism. David Desser suggests that it is Kurosawa's very "humanist" reputation that has excluded him from the pantheon of the "neo-formalist" critics. An exception among those critics is Noël Burch, who admires Kurosawa above all for his construction of "a formal system whose rigor and originality are comparable, on their own grounds, to those of certain Western masters," and here he names Lang, Von Sternberg, Dreyer, and Eisenstein, while insisting on Kurosawa's "specifically Japanese dimension." Like many artists, Kurosawa himself complains of critical over-determination. "I have felt that my works are more nuanced and complex, and they have analyzed them too simplistically." In 1961, he said his aim as a filmmaker was "to give people strength to live and face life; to help them live more powerfully and happily." At the time of *Kagemusha* he said, "I think it's impossible in this day and age to be optimistic," but that, seeing the possibilities still in the medium of film, "I would like to be able to create hope somewhere." He believes that to treat contemporary questions directly is impossible in Japan today. A film like *Ikiru* would be suppressed as too critical. But with a head full of projects still, he does not think of retirement. "When I die I prefer to just drop dead on the set."

—D.W.

FILMS: Sugata Sanshiro (Sanshiro Sugata), 1943; Ichiban utsukushiku (The Most Beautiful/Most Beautifully), 1944; Zoku Sugata Sanshiro (Sanshiro Sugata Part Two), 1945; Tora no o o fuma otokotachi (They Who Step on the Tiger's Tail/Walkers on the Tiger's Tail), 1945; Asu o tsukuru hitobito (Those Who Make Tomorrow), 1946; Waga seishun ni kuinashi (No Regrets for Our Youth/No Regrets for My Youth), 1946; Subarashiki nichiyobi (One Wonderful Sunday), 1947; Yoidori tenshi (Drunken Angel), 1948; Shizukanaru ketto (The Quiet Duel/A Silent Duel), 1949; Nora inu (Stray Dog), 1949; Shubun (Scandal), 1950; Rashomon, 1950; Hakuchi (The Idiot), 1951; Ikiru (Living/To Live/Doomed), 1952; Shichinin no samurai (Seven Samurai/The Magnificent Seven), 1954; Ikimono no kiroku (Record of a Living Being/I Live in Fear/What the Birds Knew), 1955; Kumonosu-jo (The Throne of Blood, The Castle of the Spider's Web/Cobweb Castle), 1957; Donzoko (The Lower Depths), 1957; Kakushi toride no san-akunin (The Hidden Fortress/Three Bad Men in a Hidden Fortress), 1958; Warui yatsu hodo yoku nemuru (The Bad Sleep Well/The Worse You Are the Better You Sleep/The Rose in the Mud), 1960; Yojimbo, 1961; Tsubaki Sanjuro (Sanjuro), 1962; Tengoku to jigoku (High and Low/Heaven and Hell/The Ransom), 1963; Akahige (Red Beard), 1965; Dodesukaden (Dodes'kaden), 1970; Derusu Usara (Dersu Uzala), 1975; Kagemusha, 1980; Ran, 1985. *Published scripts*—Dodesukaden, Sugata Sanshiro, No Regrets for Our Youth, One Wonderful Sunday, Drunken Angel, Quiet Duel, Stray Dog, The Idiot,

Ikiru, The Hidden Fortress, The Bad Sleep Well *in* The Complete Works of Akira Kurosawa (Kurosawa Eiga Taiken), Tokyo: Kinema Jumpo-Sha, 1970–71; Ikiru, translated by Donald Richie, London and New York: Lorrimer/Simon and Schuster, 1969; Rashomon, translated by Donald Richie, New York: Grove Press, 1969; Seven Samurai, translated by Donald Richie, London and New York: Lorrimer/Simon and Schuster, 1970–1971; Kagemusha, Tokyo: Kodansha International, 1980.

ABOUT: Anderson, J. L. and Richie, D. The Japanese Film: Art and Industry, rev. ed. 1982; Bock, A. Japanese Film Directors, 1978; Bock, A. *in* Lyon, C. (ed.) International Dictionary of Films and Filmmakers, 1984; Burch, N. To the Distant Observer: Form and Meaning in the Japanese Cinema, 1979; Desser, D. The Samurai Films of Akira Kurosawa, 1983; Erens, P. Akira Kurosawa: A Guide to References and Resources, 1979; Ezratti, S. Kurosawa, 1964; Kott, J. The Bottom Translation, 1987; Kurosawa, A. Something Like an Autobiography, 1983; Mellen, J. Voices from the Japanese Cinema, 1975; Mellen, J. The Waves at Genji's Door: Japan through its Cinema, 1976; Mesnil, M. Kurosawa, 1973; Richie, D. The Films of Akira Kurosawa, rev. ed. 1984; Richie, D. (ed.) Focus on Rashomon, 1972; Roud, R. (ed.) Cinema: A Critical Dictionary, 1980; Tassone, A. Akira Kurosawa, 1983; Tessier, M. Images du Cinéma Japonais, 1981; Tucker, R. N. Japan: Film Image, 1973. *Periodicals*—American Film September 1985; Cahiers du Cinéma 69 1957, 182 1966; City Limits 14–20 March 1986; Écran April 1973; Études Cinématographiques Spring 1964; Film Comment November 1980; Film Quarterly 34 1980–81; Films and Filming August 1959, May 1986; Image et Son November 1970; Monthly Film Bulletin January 1969 July 1970, January 1971, March 1974, May 1975, January 1978, December 1980, May 1982, April 1986; New York Times April 27, 1980, October 4, 1981, December 15, 1985; Sight and Sound Spring 1955, Summer 1964, Autumn 1970, Summer 1970, Winter 1970–1971, Autumn 1975, Summer 1979, Spring 1980, Winter 1980–1981, Summer 1981, Autumn 1985, Spring 1986; Stills Spring 1981; Take One March 1971, March 1979. *Films about*—Akira Kurosawa: Film Director (by Donald Richie), 1975; AK (by Chris Marker), 1985.

LA CAVA, GREGORY (March 10, 1892–February 3, 1952), American director, scenarist, producer, and animator, was born in Towanda, Pennsylvania. His father Pascal was a musician of Calabrian origin. La Cava's first ambition was to be a painter, and he studied at the Chicago Institute of Art and the New York Art Students League until financial necessity forced him to look for a job. After a stint as a cub reporter in Rochester, New York, he became a newspaper cartoonist, working for the New York *Globe* and the *Evening World* among other journals. Around 1913 he began to work occasionally as an animator for the Barré studio, showing exceptional ability in this medium.

GREGORY LA CAVA

In December 1915, when the newspaper publisher William Randolph Hearst established his own animation studio, the twenty-four-year-old La Cava was appointed editor-in-chief. He set up eight units, each producing an animated cartoon featuring characters from the Hearst comic strips. La Cava reportedly drew storyboards for all of these units and supervised all productions, himself working with Walter Lantz and others on such famous series as *The Katzenjammer Kids* and *Silk Hat Harry*. When the Bray studio took over the Hearst products in 1918, La Cava followed them there, remaining until these cartoons were discontinued in 1921.

He had become increasingly interested in live-action cinema, and at that point he went off to Hollywood to try his luck. He began as a gagwriter, working on one- and two-reel comedies featuring Lloyd Hamilton and on Johnny Hines' "Torchy" series. La Cava's first feature—and possibly the first film he directed—was *His Nibs,* a rural comedy starring Charles Sale and Colleen Moore, released in January 1922 by Exceptional Pictures. From 1922 to 1924 he directed a series of All Star Comedy two-reelers featuring Charlie Murray. He returned to feature direction in 1924, when he made two films for C. C. Burr Pictures, both starring Doris Kenyon. The first was a melodrama called *Restless Wives,* the second a comedy-drama, *The New School Teacher,* scripted by the director.

The following year, La Cava joined the Famous Players–Lasky Corporation, where he worked for four years—his longest stint with any one studio. He directed ten silent features there, five of them vehicles for Richard Dix. One of these, included in the British National Film Theatre retrospective in December 1976, was *Let's Get Married* (1926), a mildly satirical comedy in which Dix plays a disaster-prone young man who escapes from jail and tries to marry his girl (Lois Wilson) before the cops catch up with him. Edna May Oliver is featured as a perennially inebriated peddler of hymnals.

La Cava also made two comedies starring W. C. Fields. *So's Your Old Man* (1926) casts Fields as a small-town would-be inventor, scorned by all for his vulgarity, who confounds his wife and snobbish neighbors when he is selected as the official escort of visiting princess Alice Joyce. Roger McNiven, in his article about La Cava in *Bright Lights* (8 1979), points out that Fields' apotheosis follows a three-day binge (on his own potent roach-killer) and suggests that "La Cava, an alcoholic, presented an absurdist view of the world, delightfully distorted through a whiskey bottle. . . . Drunkenness plays a large role in the lives of most of his protagonists. It goes hand in hand with their fantastic shifts from one economic stratum to another."

La Cava's other Fields movie was *Running Wild* (1927), in which the comedian plays the unlikely victim of a massive inferiority complex. Eventually cured under hypnosis by a stage magician, he sets out to reverse twenty years of disparagement by his family, his boss, and dogs. W. C. Fields credited La Cava with the best comedy mind in Hollywood (next, of course, to Fields' own). John Gillett maintains that "La Cava did for W. C. Fields what Capra did for Langdon," and attributes to the director's training as a cartoonist "the prevalence of sight gags and beautifully timed visual 'business'" in these and later comedies.

According to the same critic, "running gags are built up to hysterical climaxes" in *Feel My Pulse* (1928), perhaps the best of La Cava's silent comedies. Bebe Daniels plays a sheltered and hypochondriac heiress who inherits an island sanatorium and discovers that it is doubling as the hideaway of a bootlegger (William Powell). After exchanging "medicines" with one of the rumrunners, the heroine is transformed into an athletic extrovert who sorts out both patients and crooks in a series of ingenious gags. Scripted by Keene Thompson and Nick Barrows, with titles by George Marion Jr., the movie features a splendid performance by Bebe Daniels and touches of real originality in the visuals, like the sequence in which ether is released and the action shifts to slow motion, with (as *Bioscope* put it), "the bootleggers floating and curvetting among their barrels in graceful aerial evolutions."

La Cava's other films for Famous Players–Lasky were *Tell It to Sweeney* (1927), a farce centering on an old railroad engineer who refuses to retire, and *Half a Bride* (1928). The latter—rather similar in situation to *Feel My Pulse*—stars Esther Ralston as a spoiled heiress who embarks on a trial marriage when she is shipwrecked on a desert island with the handsome skipper of her yacht (Gary Cooper).

Saturday's Children, made for Walter Morosco, was a screen version of Maxwell Anderson's romantic comedy starring Corinne Griffiths and Grant Withers. Released in March 1929 as a silent, it was reissued a month later with some hastily added talking sequences. *Big News* and *His First Command,* neither of which made much impact, were released in 1929 by Pathé Exchange in both silent and sound versions. La Cava seems to have been unemployed in 1930, but the following year he joined RKO, for whom he directed five pictures in 1931–1932.

His first film there, *Laugh and Get Rich,* was scripted by himself and explored one of La Cava's favorite subjects—a well-assorted collection of eccentric characters gathered together in one building: family home, hospital, or—as here—a run-down boardinghouse. Hugh Herbert and Edna May Oliver lead as indolent husband and waspish wife, and the movie examines the unforeseen consequences for them of sudden wealth (another La Cava preoccupation).

Smart Woman (1931) is a sly marital comedy with Mary Astor as a society woman who discovers her husband's infidelity and gives him a taste of his own medicine. This was followed in 1932 by two melodramas, *Symphony of Six Million* and *The Age of Consent,* the latter a collegiate shocker dealing with co-education and the "permissive society." *Symphony of Six Million* is more interesting, a tearjerker based on a Fannie Hurst novel about a slum doctor (Ricardo Cortez) who is seduced away to Park Avenue. Irene Dunne plays the poor crippled girl who reawakens his idealism. The contrasts between life in the ghetto and uptown are sharply drawn, and the film features a Max Steiner score—one of his first to attract attention—that embodies melodies from popular songs of the period.

The Half-Naked Truth (1932) is notable in different ways. It is a comedy about a circus barker (Lee Tracy) who boosts his protégée, fairground dancer Lupe Velez, to Broadway stardom. Roger McNiven has described Velez' performance as "one of the lewdest on film." He suggests that this movie, in its "outlandish publicity stunts and in the freakish sexuality and pathos-tinged stupidity" of the heroine, "is the direct antecedent of the Jayne Mansfield films,

Will Success Spoil Rock Hunter? (1957) and *The Girl Can't Help It* (1956)" directed by another former cartoonist, Frank Tashlin.

This picture completed La Cava's relatively prolonged stint with RKO. Thereafter, the director—whose drinking habits and independent spirit led him into constant battles with his employers—never made more than three movies in succession for any one studio. It was at MGM, with Walter Wanger as his producer, that La Cava made his first major hit, *Gabriel Over the White House* (1933). Walter Huston plays Judson Hammond, a newly elected President of the United States who comes to office as a party puppet, amiable, weak, and more interested in his mistress than in unemployment, crime, or the mounting threat of war.

Then Hammond is concussed in a car accident—engineered, it is hinted, by the Archangel Gabriel for the good of America and the world. As a result, he is transformed into an inspired and decisive leader. He disposes of Congress, shoots all the gangsters, blows up the Navy, and makes peace with all the nations of the world. This accomplished, he passes out again and comes to horrified by what he has done. Gabriel intervenes again before it can be undone.

This piece of propaganda for a "benevolent" American dictatorship has been condemned in some quarters for its "vigilante spirit," but is apparently far less fascistic than the peculiar novel on which it was based, the work of a British brigadier named Thomas Tweed. It seems, in fact, an odd assignment to have been handed to La Cava—remote from the amiable satires on the follies of the rich in which he was most at home. Nevertheless, the picture was praised by many contemporary reviewers for the excellence of its acting and the economy and lucidity of its direction and was immensely successful with Depression audiences hungry for magical solutions to their problems.

La Cava had a more congenial subject in *Bed of Roses* (1933), starring Constance Bennett as an ex-convict who forsakes hard-up barge captain Joel McCrea in favor of millionaire John Halliday, whom she blackmails by claiming that he has raped her while drunk. She eventually learns that true love is worth more than money, but on the way to this conventional conclusion is invested with a ruthlessness remarkable even in the "gold-digger" genre, though this is balanced by an impulsive streak of nobility in her character.

Roger McNiven has explained that La Cava's scripts, like Leo McCarey's, "were subjected to considerable manipulation during shooting. Situations, lines of dialogue and gestures were freely invented with a view to creating very idiosyncratic characters. Consequently, the narrative structures are often episodic and unpredictable in tone. Sequences which begin farcically suddenly turn darkly melodramatic, and vice versa. These shifts are manifested in the performances, which are given maximum expressive weight by long takes and fluid camerawork which intimately observes the characters." In *Bed of Roses,* McNiven writes, "what could have been a trite tale of a bad girl's reputation became a scathing comedy of manners mocking every level of society. This is where La Cava's greatness lies: in balancing the absurdities of social extremes in comic and dramatic contexts, with unexpected nuances of feeling."

There is little of this kind of complexity in *Gallant Lady,* released by United Artists in 1934 and starring that paragon of patient suffering, Ann Harding, in a melodrama about unmarried motherhood. *The Affairs of Cellini* (United Artists, 1934) is both more cynical and more entertaining, with Fredric March swashbuckling fetchingly around Renaissance Florence as the amorous goldsmith of the title, Frank Morgan and Constance Bennett equally libidinous as the Duke and Duchess, and a lovely portrayal by Fay Wray of Cellini's model Angela, a beauty of impenetrable stupidity.

After a remake of J. M. Barrie's *What Every Woman Knows* (1934), produced by Irving Thalberg at MGM and starring Helen Hayes, came *Private Worlds* (1935), made at Paramount. Adapted by Lynn Starling and (uncredited) La Cava from a novel by Phyllis Bottome, this drama about the staff and inmates of a mental hospital mustered a distinguished cast, including Claudette Colbert, Charles Boyer, Joel McCrea, and Constance Bennett. Otis Ferguson thought it an improvement on the book, and called it a film of "dignity and honest intelligence."

The first of La Cava's classic comedies followed from Columbia the same year, with a notably witty and civilized script by Sidney Buchman. *She Married Her Boss* has Claudette Colbert in one of her most beguiling performances as the romantic (and ambitious) secretary who marries her rich employer (Melvyn Douglas). She finds that she has to cope not only with his pomposity and sulkiness (he misses her help at the office) but with his dreadful family, including his snobbish sister (Katharine Alexander), constantly adjusting the curtains to keep sunlight from touching the carpet, and one of the most awful children in the whole history of the cinema, played with gusto by Edith Fellows.

"Once again," wrote John Gillett, "La Cava

shows his great skills in linking and sustaining long dialogue scenes with the direction of the players, always moving scenes along with astutely judged camera movements and close-ups and never for one moment allowing it to fall back on static, stagy techniques. . . . La Cava weaves his favourite theme of how a stuffy society of wealth, privilege and allegiance to the familiar American ideals of success . . . can be punctured and liberated by a freer spirit who comes in and starts to blow the cobwebs away."

A basically similar situation is explored in the most famous of La Cava's comedies, *My Man Godfrey* (Universal, 1936), produced as well as directed by La Cava, who also collaborated on the script with Morrie Ryskind and the author of the original story, Eric Hatch. The movie opens with a "scavenging party" at the Waldorf-Ritz. The drunken, shrieking competitors are handed a list of objects to be scavenged—including a "forgotten man"—and sent out to get them. Debutante Irene Bullock (Carole Lombard) locates *her* derelict on a garbage dump under the Brooklyn Bridge and impulsively hires him as butler to her family of rich nincompoops (Eugene Pallette, Alice Brady, Gail Patrick). Godfrey Parke (William Powell) turns out to be no ordinary servant. He is a universal fixer with a Harvard degree who straightens out everyone's personal problems, saves the Bullocks from bankruptcy through his knowledge of the stock market, and winds up marrying his beautiful employer.

Graham Greene found this "adventure of a sane man among the witless wealthy" acutely funny for most of its length, but regretted that the film's social conscience becomes in the end overt: "Mr. Powell is made to preach a sermon to the assembled family on social reform . . . and—curious moral—a huge luxury club rises on the site of the rubbish-dump in which his old down-and-out friends are given employment in elegant uniforms."

A more recent critic, Richard Corliss, finds an element of cruelty in the film's humor: "*My Man Godfrey* is one screwball comedy in which almost everyone seems . . . really insane. And La Cava's matter-of-fact *mise-en-scène* imparts a kind of documentary detachment to the film. You get the feeling psychosis is being rouged up as humor." Corliss calls the picture "a manic Messiah story," in which "Godfrey is God come to free the people from selfishness and pretense." Another critic, Lauren Rabinowitz, has scrutinized the movie in terms of Vladimir Propp's structuralist study *The Morphology of the Folktale,* identifying Godfrey as "the fairy tale prince who disguises himself as a peasant."

Another enormously successful film followed, *Stage Door* (RKO, 1937), adapted by Morrie Ryskind and Anthony Veiller from the hit play by Edna Ferber and George S. Kaufman. The setting is a New York boardinghouse inhabited by aspiring young actresses. Many of the wittiest exchanges come in the running battle between highbrow socialite Katharine Hepburn and her working-class roommate Ginger Rogers. Andrea Leeds plays the sad girl who kills herself when Hepburn gets the part she covets, and Adolphe Menjou excels as a theatrical impresario "with one eye on the stage and another on the bedroom."

John Grierson noted in his review that *Stage Door* was "booked by half a dozen critics as a masterpiece." He questioned this assessment, finding "something theatrical and lightweight about the whole business," but conceded that "it is certainly a remarkably directed description of a theatrical boarding house. Keeping a dozen young women flowing in a single stream for the best part of a film, and maintaining the while their separate little characters and stories is a difficult feat in cinema. It means a huge ingenuity in the shaping of exits and entrances and the still more considerable business of holding the central necessarily fast narrative through the detail." Richard Roud wrote in 1980 that the film had "gained rather than lost with the passage of time," and drew attention to dialogue "almost as overlapping as in the films of Robert Altman."

Another of La Cava's discontented rich families is disrupted and redeemed by a liberated outsider in *Fifth Avenue Girl* (RKO, 1939), with Ginger Rogers as a poor girl bribed by millionaire Walter Connolly to pose as a gold digger in order to scare his spoiled family into line. This film, wrote John Gillett, was scripted by Allan Scott "with a splendid flow and bite of both dialogue and situations. . . . Apart from being a superb director of actors (everyone in the cast plays with a most precise nuance and timing), La Cava is primarily a director of social attitudes—there is only the thinnest of 'plots' but an abundance of character interaction, with each adding his own little surprise to the overall scheme. . . . Utilising a variety of mid-long shots and reserving close-ups for precise moments of punctuation, La Cava's camera stealthily picks out and follows the characters as they move around Walter Connolly's vast mansion (Van Nest Polglase's design, possibly utilising a standing set, is a masterpiece in itself)."

La Cava was his own scenarist (with Allan Scott) on *The Primrose Path* (RKO, 1940), one of the gentlest of his films. Under his direction,

Ginger Rogers gives another performance of unusual restraint and control as a girl from the wrong side of the tracks tempted by prostitution (a subject seldom ventured upon at that time). Miles Mander, playing the heroine's father, also contributes a notable study of a disappointed intellectual who has settled down to drink himself to death. Set in the shantytown district of a California coastal city and filmed on location, it seemed to Richard Roud to look "almost like an Italian neorealist film."

Unfinished Business (Universal, 1941) has Irene Dunne as an Ohio music teacher who comes to New York in pursuit of fame as an opera singer, marries rich Robert Montgomery instead, and then goes off with his charming brother (Preston Foster). There are passages of sharp social observation, and a charming performance from Irene Dunne, but the film is marred by Eugene Thackrey's wordy and poorly structured script.

Irene Dunne also stars in *Lady in a Jam* (Universal, 1942), playing a screwball heiress who cracks up when her fortune disappears and decides that the only way her psychiatrist (Patric Knowles) can cure her is to marry her. By this time, La Cava's intransigence and the "recurrent illnesses" caused by his drinking were seriously affecting his career. Five years passed before he made his next—and last—film, a musical called *Living in a Big Way* (MGM, 1947) that showed nothing of his old brilliance.

Frank Capra wrote that "the meteor Gregory La Cava . . . was an extreme proponent of inventing scenes on the set. Blessed with a brilliant, fertile mind and a flashing wit, he claimed he could make pictures without scripts. But without scripts the studio heads could make no accurate budgets, schedules, or time allowances. . . . He stuck to his off-the-cuff guns. Result: fewer and fewer film assignments for him—then none. . . . So he mixed his exotic fuels with more mundane spirits, and brooded himself into oblivion. . . . La Cava was a man out of his time—a precursor of the New Wave directors of Europe."

Roger McNiven also maintains that La Cava's fondness for improvisation, his impressionistic *mise-en-scène,* and his constant and disturbing shifting of "the spectator's involvement with characters" distinguished him among directors of the 1930s and looked forward to later trends. For John Gillett, La Cava "imposed his own view on a variety of subjects and combined a surface brilliance with a subversively bitter view of American society which makes him, in his best work, at least the equal of his better-known contemporaries."

La Cava was married twice—to Beryle Morse, by whom he had a son, and in 1940 to Grace Garland. Both marriages ended in divorce. He was living alone when he died of a heart attack at the age of fifty-nine.

FILMS: His Nibs, 1922; Restless Wives, 1924; The New School Teacher, 1924; Womanhandled, 1925; Let's Get Married, 1926; So's Your Old Man, 1926; Say It Again, 1926; Paradise for Two, 1927; Running Wild, 1927; Tell It to Sweeney, 1927; The Gay Defender, 1927; Feel My Pulse, 1928; Half a Bride, 1928; Saturday's Children, 1929; Big News, 1929; His First Command, 1929; Laugh and Get Rich, 1931; Smart Woman, 1931; Symphony of Six Million (U.K., Melody of Life), 1932; The Age of Consent (U.K., Are These Our Children?), 1932; The Half-Naked Truth, 1932; Gabriel Over the White House, 1933; Bed of Roses, 1933; Gallant Lady, 1934; The Affairs of Cellini, 1934; What Every Woman Knows, 1934; Private Worlds, 1935; She Married Her Boss, 1935; My Man Godfrey, 1936; Stage Door, 1937; Fifth Avenue Girl, 1939; Primrose Path, 1940; Unfinished Business, 1941; Lady in a Jam, 1942; Living in a Big Way, 1947.

ABOUT: Canham, K. Gregory La Cava (annotated filmography), 1975; Roud, R. (ed.) Cinema: A Critical Dictionary, 1980. *Periodicals*—Bright Lights 8 1979; Écran May 1974; National Film Theatre Booklet (Britain) December 1976–February 1977.

*LANG, "FRITZ" (FRIEDRICH CHRISTIAN ANTON)

(December 5, 1890–August 2, 1976), Austrian-American director and screenwriter, was born in Vienna, the only child of middle-class parents. His father, Anton Lang, was a municipal architect. His mother, Paula Schlesinger Lang, had been born Jewish but had converted to Catholicism early in life. Lang was educated at the local *Volksschule* (primary school), and moved on to the *Realschule* (secondary school) in 1901, where he specialized in architecture, since Anton Lang intended his son to follow the paternal calling. "Yet I had heard too many of his complaints about the disadvantages of his profession to feel much enthusiasm at the prospect," Lang said. His own ambition at the time was to become a painter. He was also, like his parents, a regular and enthusiastic theatregoer.

Early in adolescence Lang suffered a serious illness, during which he had a vision of Death. As he later described it: "I saw myself face to face, not terrifying, but unmistakable, with Death. Made of black and white, light and shade, the rib cage, the naked bones. . . . I don't know whether I should call the feeling I experienced at that moment one of fear. It was horror, but without panic. . . . I recovered

°läng

FRITZ LANG

quickly. But the love of death, compounded of horror and affection . . . stayed with me and became a part of my films."

Still following his father's wishes, Lang enrolled in 1908 at the *Technische Hochschule* to study architecture. He was very soon bored and instead began studying art at the Vienna Academy of Graphic Arts, where he was strongly influenced by Klimt and Egon Schiele. He also made the most of other opportunities that Vienna offered: "I was precocious and started having affairs very early. Viennese women were the most beautiful and the most generous women in the world." To help pay for his studies, Lang occasionally worked as master of ceremonies at two of the city's cabarets, *Femina* and *Hölle* (Hell). This activity finally exhausted his father's patience, so around 1909 Lang ran away from home—"something every decent young man should do"—and made his way to Brussels, where he lived by selling sketches in the cafés.

After unwittingly getting himself involved in an art-faking racket, Lang headed for Munich, where he studied art at the School of Arts and Crafts under Julius Dietz. In 1910 he embarked on a long sea journey, which took him to North Africa, Asia Minor, China, Japan, and Bali. On his return to Europe he settled in Paris, renting a studio in Montmartre and studying at the Académie Julien. He made a living by designing clothes and selling postcards, watercolors, and cartoons, and also began to take a serious interest in the cinema: "I already subconsciously felt that a new art . . . was about to be born." Painting, though, was still his main interest, and he was preparing his first exhibition when war was de-

clared. Lang just managed to get himself on the last train across the French border and safely back to Vienna, where, despite defective eyesight, he was called up for active service in the army.

Promoted to lieutenant, Lang served on the Russian, Balkan, and Italian fronts, received several wounds (one of which cost him the sight of his right eye), and various decorations. "For four years I saw life stripped to its rawest, hunger and desperation and death—scenes that neither fiction nor the screen can ever picture." While in military hospital he began writing filmscripts and sold two of them to Joe May, at that time one of Germany's leading producer-directors. Both *Die Hochzeit im Exzentrikklub* (*The Wedding in the Eccentric Club*, 1917) and *Hilde Warren und der Tod* (*Hilde Warren and Death*, 1917)— in which Lang played Death, plus three other roles—seem to have had reasonable success, though Lang was irritated to find, when he took a party of friends to see *Die Hochzeit*, that Joe May had credited himself as scenarist.

Early in 1918 Lang was declared unfit for further service. Whiling away his time in Vienna, he was offered a part in a Red Cross play, and after driving the fee up to 1,000 kronen he accepted. Among the audience was Erich Pommer, head of the Decla film company in Berlin. Pommer was unimpressed with Lang's acting ability but struck during a subsequent meeting by his ideas on the cinema, and offered him a contract with Decla as a scriptwriter.

Lang arrived in Berlin in September 1918, shortly before the end of the war. His first scripts for Decla, *Pest in Florenz* (*Plague in Florence*, 1919), *Totentanz* (*Dance of Death*, 1919) and *Die Frau mit dem Orchideen* (*The Lady With the Orchids*, 1919), were all three directed by Otto Rippert, and received good reviews. By the time they were released, Lang had already persuaded Pommer to let him direct a film. *Halbblut* (*The Half-Caste*, 1919), filmed in five days to Lang's own script, was a triangular melodrama with as its apex the half-caste of the title, first of the many *femmes fatales* in Lang's films. No prints of *Halbblut* are extant, nor of his next picture, *Der Herr der Liebe* (*The Master of Love*, 1919), of which little is known; but both were successful enough for Pommer to let Lang embark on a major production, the first episode of an adventure serial, *Die Spinnen* (*The Spiders*).

The influence of Feuillade (whose *Fantômas* series Lang would have seen in pre-war Paris) and of Hollywood's Pearl White–style cliffhangers can be detected in the episodic, comic-book construction of *Die Spinnen*. The first part,

Der Goldene See (*The Golden Lake*, 1919), contained all the standard ingredients: a sinister, all-powerful secret society, with masked minions to execute its nefarious designs; a (supposedly) irresistibly beautiful and demonic temptress; an intrepid and resourceful hero; hidden Inca treasures, exotic locations, last-minute rescues, human sacrifices, snakes; all thrown together with a blithe disregard for verisimilitude or narrative structure. The acting was none too subtle, either. But Lang and Pommer evidently knew their public; the film was hugely successful on release, establishing Decla as one of the major German companies.

Before continuing *Die Spinnen*, Lang was assigned to direct *Harakiri* (1919), a version of David Belasco's oriental weepie, *Madame Butterfly*, on which Puccini had based his opera. The film survives only in one fragile, rarely-shown print, but was praised at the time for its "vivid realistic picture of life as it is." Lang's next film was to have been *Das Kabinett des Dr. Caligari* (1919), on the scenario of which he collaborated; but distributors were clamoring for the next part of *Die Spinnen*, and *Caligari*, much to Lang's disappointment, went instead to Robert Wiene. *Das Brillantenschiff* (*The Diamond Ship*, 1920), episode two of *Die Spinnen*, provided the mixture as before, with an even more convoluted plot.

By this stage in his career Lang had already evolved his working method, which entailed meticulous preparation of every aspect of filmmaking. Carl de Vogt, who played the hero of *Die Spinnen*, noted that Lang "was dominated by a fanatical love for the cinema and the demands he made on his actors were enormous. . . . In contrast to other directors he always knew exactly what he wanted. He was indefatigable in his work and never self-indulgent." Theo Lingen, another of Lang's actors, recalled that "one did what one was told to do to the letter of the timetable, by which I mean that no improvisation was tolerated. Everything . . . was fixed and calculated in advance. This might suggest . . . pedantry, but that is the exact opposite of the truth: the mastering of all aspects, the intelligent use of this method, and the conviction that technology can only be mastered by technology—these were probably Lang's main strengths as a film director."

To supplement his income, Lang had continued to take on occasional assignments for Joe May while working at Decla, and had been assistant director on May's *Die Herrin der Welt* (*The Mistress of the World*, 1919). Now, annoyed over the loss of *Caligari* and the rejection of his *Spinnen* scripts, Lang signed a contract with May to direct *Das Wandernde Bild* (*The Wandering Image*, 1920). No prints are known to exist of this film, a triangular melodrama set in a remote mountain village, but surviving stills suggest that Lang made impressive use of exterior locations. It was also his first collaboration with Thea von Harbou, the popular novelist who was to coscript all his films until his departure from Germany in 1933.

Lang and von Harbou next wrote a two-part exotic adventure, *Das Indische Grabmal* (*The Indian Tomb*), which Lang expected to direct but which May arrogated to himself. Since he had never much liked May but had a high personal regard for Pommer, Lang returned to Decla (or Decla-Bioscop, as it had become through a merger), taking von Harbou with him, and directed the last of his "lost" films, *Kämpfende Herzen* (*Struggling Hearts*, 1920). The film's alternative title was *Die Vier um die Frau* (*Four Around a Woman*), apparently a fair summary of the plot.

In Germany Lang was by now recognized as one of the foremost directors, though he was as yet little known abroad. His status, and the consistent box-office success of his pictures, enabled him to insist on his own choice of subject for his next film, *Der Müde Tod* (*Destiny*, 1921). Initially, Pommer may have regretted his concession. The film was poorly received in Germany—one critic referring to it as *Der Mühsame Tod* (*The Tiresome Death*)—and ran only two weeks in Berlin. In France, though, the response was immediate and enthusiastic; Dürer and Grünewald were invoked, and the film was rated with *Caligari* and Wegener's *Golem* as a supreme masterpiece of German cinema. Encouraged, Pommer re-released it in Germany, where the critics hastily reversed their previous judgements.

"In Europe," Lang later wrote about the postwar period, "an entire generation of intellectuals embraced despair. . . . Young people engaged in the cultural fields, myself among them, made a fetish of tragedy." *Der Müde Tod* clearly expresses that "love of death, compounded of horror and affection," that Lang had experienced in his boyhood vision. Two lovers arrive at a tiny, timeless German town, near which a mysterious stranger has built a huge walled estate. The stranger (Death, of course) takes the young man away with him. The young woman comes to plead for her lover, and Death shows her, in three tales (set in Caliphate Baghdad, Renaissance Venice, and a mythical China), the impossibility of saving a doomed life. Finally the woman also resigns herself to death, and the lovers are reunited in the afterworld.

Lang always deprecated references to his films as "expressionist," maintaining that he never restricted himself by conforming to a single artistic fashion. Nonetheless, expressionism—the visual distortion and stylization of reality to express psychological states and heighten emotional response—undeniably influences many aspects of Lang's films, if never to the extremes of Wiene's *Caligari*, with its contorted, aggressively two-dimensional sets. In *Der Müde Tod*, the vast wall, extending beyond the confines of the screen, that surrounds Death's realm, the misty vastness of the cathedral in which burn countless candle-souls of humankind, and the storybook German toy-town, all draw on expressionist elements in their design. Lotte Eisner even regarded much of the film as deliberate parody of expressionism, especially the Chinese episode: "The overturned baroque roofs built higgledy-piggledy together, the little bridges, the warped trees with their tortured curves and bends, are a good rendering of the bizarre contortions of expressionism. . . . The magician, turned into a cactus by his daughter, is stretched into a grotesque expressionist diagonal."

This episode also featured the film's most impressive special effects, including a miniaturized army and a journey by flying carpet. These were much admired and emulated. In the United States, Douglas Fairbanks bought the distribution rights but delayed the release until after the premiere of his own *Thief of Bagdad*, which copied several of Lang's best tricks. Meanwhile Lang, now internationally famous, began work with von Harbou on a two-part crime thriller, *Dr. Mabuse der Spieler* (*Dr. Mabuse the Gambler*, 1922).

In some ways *Dr. Mabuse* returns to the world of *Die Spinnen*. Mabuse is a fiendish mastermind, a man of a thousand disguises, gifted with sinister hypnotic powers, leader of a gang of criminals and cutthroats. During the course of the complicated plot, he manipulates the Stock Exchange, steals treaties, murders, runs crooked gambling dens, abducts women; finally, brought to bay by a determined public prosecutor, he goes mad, and is taken away babbling incoherently.

Von Harbou and Lang took pains to stress the contemporary relevance of the *Mabuse* films. The two parts, *Der Grosse Spieler* (*The Great Gambler*) and *Inferno*, were respectively subtitled *Ein Bild der Zeit* (*A Portrait of the Age*) and *Ein Spiel von Menschen unseren Zeit* (*A Play About People of Our Time*). Today, to claim any kind of documentary realism for such overblown melodramatics may seem ludicrous, but at the time the suggestion was evidently found credible. "The film is a document of our time," wrote a reviewer in *Die Welt am Montag*, "an excellent portrait of high society with its gambling passion and dancing madness, its hysteria and decadence, its expressionism and occultisms." An article in *BZ am Mittag* described the films as "a condensation of the spirit of the age, a playful re-enactment. . . . Not one important symptom of the postwar years is missing." Writing with hindsight, Siegfried Kracauer detected the shadow of coming events: *Dr. Mabuse*, in his view, "is revealed to be not so much a document as one of those deep-rooted premonitions which spread over the German postwar screen."

Despite some narrative longueurs—far too much time is taken up with static conversation pieces, interspersed with intolerably wordy intertitles—the *Mabuse* films mark a considerable advance in dramatic structure over the amorphous one-damn-thing-after-another of *Die Spinnen*. The protean personality of Mabuse—resourcefully played by von Harbou's first husband, Rudolf Klein-Rogge—dominates the action, manipulating all the other characters and events. Even the police seem reduced to a mere rival gang—as so often in Lang's films, villains and heroes, crime and justice tend to become interchangeable. *Mabuse* remains memorable not for its limping and flawed plot but for the darkly brooding atmosphere that Lang creates, a disturbing compound of hysteria and fatalistic passivity.

In August 1922, a few months after the release of *Dr. Mabuse*, Fritz Lang and Thea von Harbou were married. It was a second marriage for both of them. Von Harbou had separated quite amicably from Klein-Rogge, who readily continued to appear in Lang's films. Lang's first wife, about whom little is known, had been a Russian Jew from Vilna. She had died in 1920—according to some accounts, she killed herself on learning of the passionate affair between her husband and von Harbou.

Dr. Mabuse was enormously successful, both in Germany and abroad, and on the strength of it Pommer announced an even more ambitious project: a two-part epic superproduction, *Die Nibelungen* (1924). The basis for Lang and von Harbou's script was not Wagner's operatic tetralogy but the original medieval epic, *Das Nibelungenlied*, on which Wagner had also drawn. Preparations for the massive production took nearly two years, and shooting lasted nine months. During filming, Decla-Bioscop merged with UFA; Lang was now the star director of the world's largest studio outside Hollywood.

Siegfried, the first part of *Die Nibelungen*, tells how the hero slays a dragon, meets and marries the Burgundian princess Kriemhild, and is killed through the treachery of Hagen and the jealousy of Brunhild, an Icelandic princess whom he has wooed on behalf of Kriemhild's brother, Gunther. "For sheer pictorial beauty of structural architecture, *Siegfried* has never been equalled," wrote Paul Rotha. Most critics have agreed, adding that the monumentally symmetric architecture leaves little room for the human element. "[Lang's] decorative compositions," observed Georges Sadoul, "seem often like frozen bits of life, as if any movement would disturb the geometry." The actors, perhaps trying to live up to their surroundings, tended to lapse into slow-motion heroic gestures, often to ludicrous effect.

The two parts of *Die Nibelungen* were intended by Lang to contrast with each other. After the monolithic stasis of *Siegfried, Kriemhilds Rache* (*Kriemhild's Revenge*)—in which Kriemhild marries Etzel, King of the Huns, and brings about the massacre of the Burgundians—is dynamic, though no less stylized. In Luc Moullet's description, "the climax is a long battle lasting three-quarters of an hour, with encirclements and identical attacks, defences against the encirclements, and renewed attacks; the movements of the assailants are similar, but Lang . . . builds a rhythm of variations." Kriemhild, like many of Lang's protagonists, is reduced by her obsession with vengeance to the level of those who wronged her, dragging herself and all around her down to destruction. "Nemesis drives the action onwards," wrote Lotte Eisner, "as the introduction of the Asian elements destroys the monumental stillness of the heroic epic, and as Kriemhild's revenge acts upon all the other characters like a violent maelstrom."

Arguments over whether Lang, however unwittingly, was creating fascist cinema have inevitably clustered around *Die Nibelungen.* Hitler and other leading Nazis certainly admired *Siegfried* greatly (*Kriemhilds Rache* less so), and after Lang's departure from Germany it was revived in a sound version, complete with chunks of Wagner. The film's grandiose architecture evidently influenced Speer in his staging of the Nuremberg rallies, as well as Leni Riefenstahl's notorious propaganda film, *Triumph des Willens.* Siegfried Kracauer was in no doubt that Lang had anticipated Nazi attitudes: "It is the complete triumph of the ornamental over the human. Absolute authority asserts itself by arranging people under its domination in pleasing designs." Lang's own stated intention, in recreating heroic myth, was "to show that Germany was searching for an ideal in her past . . . could draw inspiration from her past" to restore self-confidence after the debacle and chaotic aftermath of the Great War—an aim with which Hitler would hardly have quarreled.

Die Nibelungen, and especially *Siegfried,* was enthusiastically received and even recouped its huge cost. In October 1924, partly to help publicize the film and partly to study the latest Hollywood methods, Lang and Pommer sailed for the United States. Disembarkation at New York was delayed by quarantine restrictions, and Lang had time to study the city's skyline, which greatly impressed him. He was also struck by New York itself, "the crossroads of multiple and confused human forces," driven "to exploit each other and thus living in perpetual anxiety." Back in Germany, he set to work with von Harbou to distil his experience into a towering vision of the future.

Metropolis (1926), "an exaggerated dream of the New York skyline, multiplied a thousandfold and divested of all reality" (Lotte Eisner), was by far the most ambitious film ever produced in Germany. Originally budgeted at 1.9 million marks, it eventually cost over 5 million, took nearly a year to shoot, and ruined UFA. The company was refused a state subsidy and passed into the control of Alfred Hugenberg, a millionaire industrialist and press baron with Nazi sympathies.

Lang envisioned a repressive technological future (set in the year 2000), in which the gulf between the classes has become brutally absolute. The ruling aristocracy lead lives of idle luxury in sunlit gardens, while the workers, housed in subterranean caverns, have been reduced to a soulless army of slaves. Fredersen, the Master of Metropolis, commissions a sinister inventor, Rotwang, to construct a robot provocateur to stir up the workers to revolt. (Quite why he should want to is never made clear). Through the efforts of Frederson's son and a saintly woman, Maria, both sides are finally reconciled.

Luis Buñuel, reviewing *Metropolis* in 1927, described it as "two films glued together by their bellies." Most critics, then and since, have agreed with him. The plot of the film is puerile, incoherent, and feebly motivated, culminating in an embarrassingly trite and sentimental ending. Lang himself claimed that he "detested [the film] after it was finished," and admitted that "you cannot make a social-conscious picture in which you say that the intermediary between the hand and the brain is the heart—I mean that's a fairytale—definitely."

Visually, though, *Metropolis* is superb, and remains so even in the face of modern megaproductions. The great city itself, luminous and immense, with its soaring geometric buildings, art deco towers, and overhead freeways (around which hover charmingly dated biplanes), pays tribute to Lang's architectural training; but perhaps the most memorable sequence is our first vision of the workers, shuffling mindlessly, heads bowed, in close-packed phalanxes, human slabs that might have been manufactured by the very machines they slave for. "In this silent film," Lotte Eisner observed, "sound has been *visualized* with such intensity that we seem to hear the pistons' throb and the shrill sound of the factory siren." Much of the film's graphic impact can be credited to the cinematographer, Eugen Schüfftan, who invented for it the mirror process that bears his name.

Although a commercial disaster, *Metropolis* was widely shown and hugely influential. Countless science-fiction films owe a debt to it; and the sequence in Rotwang's gothically cluttered laboratory where, amid spouting vapors and electrical arcs, the evil robot-Maria is brought to life, was reworked five years later for Whale's *Frankenstein* and passed thence into the standard iconography of the horror movie. Brigitte Helm played both Marias, the good and the evil, embodying Lang's recurrent theme of the morally schizoid personality.

Disappointed by the financial failure of *Metropolis*, Lang now formed his own production company, Fritz-Lang-Films, to release through UFA. For its first project, Lang and von Harbou cautiously reverted to the proven box-office values of *Dr. Mabuse,* applying them with minor modifications to the world of international espionage. *Spione* (*The Spy,* 1928) centers around the machinations of Haghi (or Haighi, in some versions), the master-spy, who operates through a network of ruthless agents and skilled seductresses. He also doubles as an eminent banker and—like Mabuse—performs a vaudeville act under yet another disguise. (As before, Rudolf Klein-Rogge—who had also played Rotwang in *Metropolis*—took the role of the arch-villain.) A dauntless government agent finally corners him, and he shoots himself.

Despite all the parallels, *Spione* improves greatly on *Dr. Mabuse* in both pacing and atmosphere. Paul Jensen found it "far better made; aside from a superb sense of composition, an element missing from the earlier work, this imitation is technically more creative and fluid, with a faster pace and admirably controlled acting." In a retrospective review in *Monthly Film Bulletin* (May 1976), Jonathan Rosenbaum commented that "*Spione* strips the spy-thriller form down to basics and reveals . . . its underlying mechanism. . . . The remarkable elliptical editing . . . contrives to organise the extraordinary density of the overlapping intrigues into a lucid pattern." Once again, Lang conceded scant moral superiority to the forces of law; espionage

and counterespionage operate in the same ethical jungle.

Lang had originally planned to include a space-ship sequence in *Metropolis* but was forced to abandon it by the film's spiraling costs. He now returned to the idea for his last silent picture, *Die Frau im Mond* (*The Woman in the Moon,* 1929), in which an ill-assorted band of scientists, capitalists, and stowaways travel to the moon in search of gold. Lang took great trouble over the technical details of the rocketship and its launching, calling in Hermann Oberth and Willy Ley as scientific advisors. The plot, though, was confused and perfunctory, lacking in interest or tension. For one large-scale scene at the launching, Lang simulated a distant crowd by means of "pins with large glass heads." The film's main characters, unfortunately, seemed to have been devised along similar lines.

Some of the disjointed plotting of *Die Frau im Mond,* to be fair, may be due to clumsy recutting, which seems to have affected most surviving prints. Many of Lang's silent films—especially *Metropolis* and *Dr. Mabuse*—suffered extensive mutilation at the hands of foreign distributors. Lang was much angered by this, though he could do nothing about it; but he could and did object when UFA proposed that *Die Frau,* along with their other current films, should be converted to sound. Since the film had been planned silent, that—he insisted—was how it should be shown, without even added music or sound effects. As a result of this quarrel, Lang broke completely with UFA and even contemplated giving up filmmaking to become a scientist. Luckily, he reconsidered, and went on to make what is generally recognized as his finest film.

When Lang announced his new project, his first sound film, under the working title of *Mörder unter uns* (*Murderers Among Us*), he encountered unexpected hostility. Anonymous threatening letters arrived, and he was refused use of the studios he wanted. Not until he explained that the film was to be about a sex murderer did opposition cease. The Nazis, apparently, had assumed that the title referred to them.

Based on the real-life case of Peter Kürten, who had terrorized Düsseldorf in the 1920s, *M* (1931) shows a city shaken by mounting hysteria as children are murdered and the police flail ineffectually, arresting suspects at random. Finally the underworld organize themselves to trap the killer, since the increased police vigilance is disrupting their activities; child-murderers, Lang suggests with Brechtian irony, must be discouraged, since they are bad for business.

In *M,* for the first time in Lang's work, style and content fuse into a taut, effective whole. The brooding urban menace that he had brought to *Dr. Mabuse* and *Spione,* the dark fatalism of *Der Müde Tod,* the acute spatial instinct of *Siegfried* and *Metropolis,* are at last placed at the service of a plot that needs no apology. Sound is used creatively and dramatically, with no hint of inexperience, to counterpoint and enrich the images, often overlapping across scenes to achieve fast narrative ellipses. Violence, as Lang always preferred, is suggested rather than shown: a child's killing is conveyed by a ball rolling out of a bush, a stray balloon caught in overhead wires—thus (as Lang wrote) "forcing each individual member of the audience to create the gruesome details of the murder according to his personal imagination."

As Franz Becker, the murderer, Peter Lorre's performance made him deservedly world-famous. Squat, chubby, and vulnerable, obsessively whistling his snatch of Grieg (performed by Lang, since Lorre couldn't whistle), smiling with shy kindness as he buys his victim a balloon, grimacing before a mirror in an attempt to grasp his own monstrosity, he presented a chillingly plausible incarnation of helpless schizophrenia. Cornered at last by a grim-faced jury of sanctimonious thugs, cringing, eyes bulging in terror, Lorre could still lend pathetic dignity to his agonized plea: "But can I . . . can I help it? Haven't I got this curse inside me? The fire? The voice? The pain? . . . Who knows what it feels like to be me?" (Worth noting, since von Harbou is often blamed for the worst inanities of Lang's German movies, that Lang always credited her with sole authorship of this searingly despairing speech.)

Although it encountered censorship problems in a few countries, *M* enjoyed widespread success. Some critics found the subject-matter "disgusting," but most were enthusiastic. Graham Greene vividly likened the film to "looking through the eye-piece of a microscope, through which the tangled mind is exposed, laid flat on the slide: love and lust; nobility and perversity, hatred of itself and despair jumping at you from the jelly." *M* rapidly achieved classic status, confirmed by Joseph Losey's ill-advised remake of 1951, in which the action was transferred to Los Angeles. Lang drily commented that, when Losey's film was released, "I had the best reviews of my life."

Seymour Nebenzal, for whose Nero Films Lang had made *M,* urged him to make a new Dr. Mabuse film. Initially reluctant, Lang gradually began to see possibilities in the idea of his master-criminal directing operations from within

the lunatic asylum in which, at the end of the earlier film, he had been incarcerated. In later years Lang consistently maintained that *Das Testament des Dr. Mabuse* (*The Last Will of Dr. Mabuse,* 1933) was intended as "a veiled comment on Nazism," and that he put Nazi slogans into the mouth of the deranged criminal. This seems slightly improbable, since von Harbou, who coscripted as usual, was by this time a keen member of the Nazi party. On the other hand, the film was certainly found subversive enough to be banned by Goebbels.

Mabuse himself dies midway through *Das Testament*; but by then he has gained control over the mind of the director of the asylum, Dr. Baum, through whom his orders are transmitted to his gang. After Mabuse's death his spirit continues to possess Baum, who goes steadily out of his mind and by the end of the film has been completely taken over, like Norman Bates in *Psycho,* by his alter ego. As Mabuse/Baum's chief opponent, Lang reintroduced the stolidly humorous Inspector Lohmann (played by Otto Wernicke), who had headed the police investigation in *M.*

As with *Spione* and the earlier *Mabuse* films, the plot of *Das Testament* is less interesting than the atmosphere of intangible menace that Lang creates. The opening sequence is especially effective: a huge factory, filled with an ominous pounding roar, in which a terrified man is watching some mysterious activity. He is discovered, and flees. In the street, a huge lump of masonry crashes down just behind him. A group of men appear, waiting quietly on the corner; as he turns back, a barrel rolls off a cart, just missing him, and explodes into fragments. Menace is inexplicable, impersonal, and ubiquitous.

Soon after *Das Testament* had been banned by the newly elected Nazi government, Lang was summoned to an interview with Goebbels. Apprehensively, he presented himself in the customary formal dress. Goebbels—"he was a charming man when he wanted to be" —explained that both he and Hitler had much admired *Metropolis* and *Die Nibelungen,* and invited Lang to head the Third Reich's film industry. Lang expressed his gratitude and delight. "I could only think 'How do you get out of here?' I wanted to get some money out of the bank. Outside the window, there was a big clock, and the hands went slowly round." Goebbels talked on. At last Lang could make a polite departure, but the banks had closed. He rushed home, grabbed all his loose cash and portable valuables, and caught a train that evening for Paris, leaving behind his wife, his money, his extensive art collection, and his position as Germany's foremost director. "I must begin over again. It is not easy. But, yes, it was good. I was *arrivé*—fat in my soul, fat around the heart. Darling, too much success . . . oh, it is not good for the man." Thea von Harbou remained behind in Germany, where she continued to make films for the Nazis. She and Lang were divorced about a year later.

Erich Pommer, who had also left Germany and was working in Paris as head of Fox's European operations, offered Lang a project: a version of Molnár's play *Liliom* (1934), on which the musical *Carousel* was later based. It is the tragicomedy of a selfish fairground barker (played by Charles Boyer) who is allowed a posthumous chance to redeem himself for the sake of his wife and daughter—an uncomfortable mix of sentiment and satirical fantasy that might have been better suited to René Clair. Harry Wilson, though, writing in *Film Quarterly* (Summer 1947) found it "lighthearted, gay, inconsequential, with a fine satiric flavour," and Don Willis, generally dismissive of Lang's work, rated it "perhaps his finest film."

Like most prominent European filmmakers, Lang had received frequent offers from Hollywood, but he had always turned them down. Now, however, when David O. Selznick arrived in Paris on a talent hunt, Lang accepted a contract with MGM, and sailed for America in June 1934. Not for the first time, Hollywood, having acquired its "trophy" (Lang's own term), had trouble deciding how to display it. For eighteen months he stayed on MGM's payroll without directing a single foot of film. Part of the reason was that the studio heads had grown wary of "Prussian autocrats" like Stroheim and Sternberg and suspected that Lang, with his monocle, formal manner, and exacting reputation, might prove another of the breed. Various projects were mooted but came to nothing.

Though frustrated at not working, Lang had no intention of wasting his time and set out to learn the language and customs of his adopted country, becoming an American citizen in 1935. "I read a lot of newspapers, and I read comic strips—from which I learned a lot. . . . I drove around the country and tried to speak with everybody. I spoke with every cab driver, every gas station attendant—and I looked at films. Naturally, I was also very interested in the Indians, and I went to Arizona and lived there with the Navajos for eight weeks." Eventually MGM decided to drop him. Lang protested to Eddie Mannix, Louis B. Mayer's chief hatchet man, and was finally allowed to make his first Hollywood movie.

If a single consistent theme can be isolated from Lang's oeuvre, it would be the struggle of the individual against fate. But fate, for Lang, is not a metaphysical concept or a supernatural power. Even when—as in *Der Müde Tod* or *Die Nibelungen*—supernatural elements are introduced, they never decide the outcome; Siegfried's Tarnhelm is merely an enabling device, an instrument, like a gun or a fast car. Lang's fate is always some human force or factor—a criminal organization, social pressure, a psychological impulse within the individual. The socially critical aspect of this theme, implicit in his German films, became increasingly overt in his Hollywood output.

Fury (1936), as Gavin Lambert has pointed out, "is not . . . *about* a lynching, but an almost abstract study of mob hysteria; this hysteria has a number of results, of which the attempted lynching is one and the ferocious destructive bitterness it arouses in the victim . . . is another." A man is arrested on suspicion of kidnapping, and held in a small town's jail. The townsfolk, worked up to frenzy, burn down the jail; but the man escapes, unseen, and lets his supposed murderers be brought to trial. Joe Wilson's lust for vengeance, like Kriemhild's, degrades and dehumanizes him; his fury, no less than the mob's, gives the film its title. Once again, Lang shows the divisions between guilt and innocence, respectability and crime, to be hopelessly blurred, and the law all too readily manipulated and duped.

"Every serious picture that depicts people today," Lang once remarked, "should be a kind of documentary of its time." The vivid portrayal of small-town life (especially remarkable in a foreigner's first American film) lends frightening credibility to the superbly paced sequence in which idle, almost good-humored gossip builds into uncontrollable mob violence. Lang drew fine performances from Spencer Tracy and Sylvia Sidney, and the film was marred only by some nudging symbolism (scandalmongering women intercut with cackling geese), and a crassly happy ending that Lang detested. *Fury*, much to the studio's surprise, scored a commercial and critical success; Alistair Cooke, in a typical review of the time, called it "the best film of this and maybe of any other coming year."

Nonetheless, MGM failed to renew Lang's contract. His next film was an independent production for Walter Wanger, released through United Artists. *You Only Live Once* (1937), with its pair of ill-fated young fugitives, is the direct ancestor of Nicholas Ray's *They Live by Night* and Penn's *Bonnie and Clyde*. It can also, set as it is in a "doomed imaginary country of night, rain, penumbral mist and darkness" (Gavin Lambert), be counted one of the earliest authentic examples of the *film noir*, of which Lang has as good a claim as anyone to be the originator.

Though he apparently detested working with Lang, Henry Fonda gave one of his best early performances as Eddie, the three-time loser who tries to go straight in the teeth of society's indifference and hostility. "Light is never in Lang used merely decoratively, atmospherically," observed John Russell Taylor (*Sight and Sound*, Winter 1961–1962), "but always psychologically, to convey emotional states." This applies well to *You Only Live Once*, whose dense visual texture thickens ever more claustrophobically around its protagonists as the traps close upon them. The bank robbery sequence—later lifted wholesale for use in *Dillinger* (1945)—takes place in driving rain, drenched figures floundering in mud and tear-gas. Fog envelops Eddie's nocturnal jailbreak, in which (Alain Silver wrote) "searchlight beams reach out for him like white, spectral fingers; and the whole nightmarish array of mists, massive walls, blurred lights, hazy figures, and loudspeaker voices becomes an extension of Eddie's frightened and disoriented state of mind."

Lang's "social trilogy," as his first three Hollywood films are sometimes called, ended with a flop. *You and Me* (1938) was intended as a comedy—never Lang's forte—with a moral; a satirical, socially conscious *Lehrstück* in the Brechtian tradition. Kurt Weill, indeed, provided some of the songs which, unintegrated into the narrative fabric, stuck out embarrassingly. Further encumbered with George Raft at his most wooden, the mixture utterly failed to jell, as Lang readily conceded: "It was the only really lousy picture I ever made precisely because I wasn't being myself." Brought into the project well after its inception, Lang hardly deserved to be held solely responsible, but the film's failure seriously damaged his career, and for some time he had trouble getting work.

His reputation as a cinematic perfectionist probably contributed to his difficulties. Though not reckoned a tyrant like Sternberg or a slavedriver like Michael Curtiz, Lang had become known for his tireless (and, some thought, wearisome) insistence on detail. Drinking endless cups of black coffee, rarely eating, wearing a different sweater for each day of the week, he prowled the set, checking on everything. Lewis Jacobs described him at work: "From the moment he arrived in the morning until he dismissed the company at night, he never let up on his drive. The man was all energy, roaming the set with a viewfinder; climbing chairs or lying on the floor in search of a camera angle; conferring with his cameraman time and again about the tempo of a dolly shot; dashing to a corner to rehearse the players; rearranging lights and props so they would function organically in the composition; suggesting business to an actor; studying every set-up through the camera lens."

Not all actors resented Lang's methods. Joan Bennett, who made four films with him, found the effort well worth while: "Fritz was terribly exacting and demanding and working with him was sometimes abrasive, but he commanded great respect, and I performed better under his direction than at any other time in my career." But Henry Fonda, not generally known as a temperamental actor, said, "I couldn't get along with him at all. He is an artist certainly. A creative artist. But he has no regard for his actors. . . . It just doesn't occur to him that actors are human beings with hearts and instincts and other things." Fonda summed Lang up as "a master puppeteer."

After two years of idleness, Lang was finally offered an assignment by Darryl F. Zanuck at Fox—his first color film, and his first Western. *The Return of Frank James* (1940), a sequel to Henry King's *Jesse James* of the previous year, dealt with Frank's quest for vengeance on the Fords, who shot his brother. For once, revenge is gained without loss of integrity, and at the end Frank (Henry Fonda, in his second and last Lang film) returns to his peaceful farm. Charles Higham and Joel Greenberg thought it "a fairly routine sequel," but commended "its beautiful feeling for the outdoors, established in a lovely opening sequence showing Henry Fonda ploughing."

The Return did well enough for Zanuck to offer Lang another Western to direct. *Western Union* (1941) recounted, in highly fictionalized form, the saga of the first telegraph line being laid across the West. Once again Lang's direction was thoroughly competent, but detached; his Westerns, as Luc Moullet wrote, "make for very austere works, even down to the choice of landscapes, which are a little too bleak . . . This lyrical rigor reminds one of Hawks, minus the humor."

The outbreak of war allowed Lang to return to a far more congenial genre. The sinister, pervasive criminal organizations of his German movies, dedicated to terror, destruction, and world domination, had become awful reality and taken over most of Europe; who better than Fritz Lang to depict the struggle against them? Lang's anti-Nazi films, wrote Peter Bogdanovich, are "characterized by an intense personal involvement, a vivid awareness of the fascist mind, missing from other similar movies of the period."

Fox had originally assigned John Ford to direct *Man Hunt* (1941); when he turned it down the studio, pleased with the success of the two Westerns, gave Lang the project instead. The film was based on Geoffrey Household's novel *Rogue Male*, about an English sportsman (Walter Pidgeon) who stalks Hitler, not quite certain in his own mind if he means to shoot the Führer or not. Captured and tortured, he escapes and is pursued by the Nazis back to England; the hunter becomes the hunted. Much of *Man Hunt* takes place in an improbable, chiaroscuro London redolent of Pabst's *Dreigroschenoper*, where shadows lurk down cobbled alleys, and the most stolidly British face may suddenly twitch with Nazi fanaticism. Lang builds the tension slowly and inexorably, tightening the trap of the hero's isolation—his sole ally a Cockney prostitute, touchingly played by Joan Bennett.

Lang next began work on *Confirm or Deny,* a romantic melodrama set in wartime London, but fell ill and—rather to his relief—was replaced by Archie Mayo. His next assignment was *Moontide,* the studio's inept attempt to provide a suitable vehicle for the exiled Jean Gabin. Lang, who was "very unhappy about the whole thing," clashed with Gabin after four days' shooting and was once again replaced by Mayo. The final result amply justified Lang's misgivings; meanwhile he had quit Fox.

Among the European refugees recently arrived in California were Arnold Pressburger, a producer Lang had known in Berlin, and Bertolt Brecht. When in May 1942 news came of the assassination in Prague of Heydrich, the *Reichsprotektor* of Czechoslovakia, Lang decided to coscript a film with Brecht for Pressburger to produce. Since Brecht spoke little English, a left-wing American playwright, John Wexley, was called in to help. By the time *Hangmen Also Die* (1943) was released, Wexley had secured sole screenplay credit, and Brecht and Lang were no longer on speaking terms.

Whatever its true authorship, the film abounds in Brechtian touches, such as the theme song, "No Surrender" (music by Hanns Eisler), or the climactic scene in which the Czech people unite in solidarity of deception to throw the blame for Heydrich's death on a pro-Nazi traitor. Like most Hollywood propaganda pieces of the period, *Hangmen* suffers from an excess of sententious speeches and a conspicuous lack of local atmosphere—studio-bound sets, and the miscasting as central Europeans of such Hollywood regulars as Brian Donlevy and Walter Brennan. One performance, though, stands out from the prevailing blandness—Alexander Granach's Nazi detective, sordid, bowler-hatted,

and thoroughly *unherrenvolk*—a debased version of *M*'s Inspector Lohmann. In an article in *Cahiers du Cinéma* (March 1978), Jean-Louis Comolli and François Géré pointed out how Lang frequently traps his audience into "forced identification" with the detective's viewpoint, to disquieting effect.

François Truffaut identified Lang's "favorite theme" as "moral solitude, a man alone, conducting a struggle against a semi-hostile, semi-indifferent universe"—an apt summary of *Ministry of Fear* (1944). Lang much admired the Graham Greene novel, though not the script that had been drawn from it; his agent had neglected to include in the contract Lang's regular clause allowing him to modify the script if he wanted. Nonetheless, in texture and atmosphere this is one of his most characteristic films, plunging the hero (Ray Milland) into a *noir* nightmare world in which the most innocuous people and things suddenly turn inexplicably hostile. Since the film begins with his release from an asylum, he—and we—can never be sure that what seems to happen is not (shades of *Caligari*) simply a madman's paranoid vision. The rational denouement—that an undercover Nazi organization is behind all the bizarre events—comes as something of an anti-climax.

Lang's film—or Seton Miller's script—loses the emotional bleakness, the subtle inward despair of Greene's novel, but replaces them, as David Thomson put it, with "a narrow but intense visualisation of action conveying fear, claustrophia and malign fate." No ground is solid; anything and anybody can prove deceptive. A blind man's blankly pious stare flicks into sighted malice; a box of books lethally explodes; an urbane and courteous tailor (Dan Duryea, always well used in Lang's films) flourishes murderous shears, then turns them against himself. Even the inane happy ending can do little to dispel the chilling darkness of Lang's conception.

His next film (made after, though released a few days before, *Ministry*) also partakes, and more explicitly, of the quality of nightmare. *The Woman in the Window* (1944) enmeshes a respectable, middle-aged psychology professor (Edward G. Robinson) in an implacable pattern of fatality and guilt. Succumbing to a momentary impulse of repressed desire, he finds himself, helpless and horrified, caught in a downward spiral of homicide, blackmail, and premeditated murder. As he sinks lower in culpability, so his unconscious urge to self-incrimination grows, facilitated—through an overly deterministic twist of the plot—by his friendship with the local district attorney. Finally, as the trap closes, suicide offers the only escape. At which point, he wakes up—the nightmare was indeed just a dream.

For once, the happy ending was no studio imposition, but Lang's own express intention, which he later defended. "I rejected this logical ending [in which the Professor dies] because it seemed to me a defeatist ending, a tragedy for nothing brought about by an implacable Fate." Few critics have found this convincing; Paul Jensen called the dream ending "a cheat used to rescue the director, who had painted himself into a corner." Once again, though, Lang made up for a flawed plot with evocatively detailed visual textures, suggesting with encroaching shadows and expressive lighting the moral nightworld into which his complacent bourgeois has been hurled. He also drew fine performances from his principals: Robinson, Joan Bennett as the object of his fantasy, and Duryea as the vicious blackmailer.

Woman in the Window was independently produced by Nunnally Johnson, who also scripted. Lang enjoyed the freedom from studio constraints, working with the kind of overall control he had been used to in Germany, and now set up an independent production company, Diana Productions, together with Joan Bennett and her then husband, the producer Walter Wanger. Diana's first film, *Scarlet Street* (1945), was in many ways a companion piece to *Woman,* starring the same three principals. Once again Robinson played a hitherto respectable bourgeois obsessed with Bennett, with Duryea as the low-life who came between them. But the tone of *Scarlet Street* takes an altogether bleaker and sleazier turn, with no hope of a happy ending. Robinson's downtrodden and henpecked clerk becomes infatuated with a mercenary streetwalker who despises and uses him, caring only for her brutal pimp. Eventually the clerk murders her, and the pimp, snagged by circumstantial evidence, goes to the chair. When Robinson tries to confess to the murder, the police laugh at him; tortured by guilt and hearing the lovers' voices echoing in his ears, he sinks into derangement and destitution.

The plot was taken from *La Chienne,* a novel already filmed by Renoir in 1931. But where Renoir sets his sordid story against the richly detailed background of Montmartre, Lang places it in clinical isolation. In the opinion of Louis Giannetti, Lang generally "remains aloof from his characters and their feelings. Emotions are presented objectively, as scientific variables." This is certainly true of *Scarlet Street,* most dispassionate of all his films. Even the protagonist's name, Chris Cross, is schematic; not a person, but a psychological diagram. Only in the final

shot, as Chris shuffles listlessly down a bustling Christmas street and the crowds fade from around him, leaving him utterly alone with his unceasing voices, does a hint of pity color Lang's contempt. *Scarlet Street* is a brilliantly sustained *tour de force* of *noir* filmmaking, but ice-cold. Unprecedentedly, since an innocent man is executed while the murderer goes (at least by human justice) unpunished, *Scarlet Street* was passed by the Hays Office. The New York State board was less permissive, and banned the film; the resultant notoriety did its box-office returns no harm at all.

As a postscript to his wartime anti-Nazi films, Lang directed *Cloak and Dagger* (1946) for a Warners offshoot, United States Pictures. Burdened with a talky script, an episodic plot, and the miscasting of Gary Cooper as a top physicist turned undercover agent in occupied Europe, the film was further weakened by the removal of its concluding scenes. Lang had intended to end with a warning against the horrors of nuclear power: "God have mercy on us if we think we can wage other wars without destroying ourselves"; but Warners suppressed the entire final reel, and no complete copy of the film seems to have survived.

Lang's second and last film for Diana, *Secret Beyond the Door* (1948), was, according to its director, "jinxed from the beginning—trouble with cameraman, trouble with script." (Trouble, also, between Bennett and Wanger, whose marriage was breaking up.) A ludicrously unconvincing reworking of the Bluebeard legend, laced with dime-store Freudianism, the film at least offered Lang a showcase for some of his most impressive visual compositions. Henri Chapier, writing in *Combat* (February 20, 1968), noted "a baroque profusion which reminds us of . . . Sternberg, but Fritz Lang imbues it with that Germanic coldness of delirium which has the purity of a diamond." Less indulgently, James Agee commented that "Lang gets a few wood-silky highlights out of this sow's ear, but it is a hopeless job and a worthless movie."

Beset by financial and personal problems, Diana Productions folded, and Lang, having had two flops in succession, found himself little in demand. It was two years before his next picture, made for Herbert Yates' cut-rate B-factory, Republic Pictures. *House by the River* (1950) suffered, like its predecessor, from a shaky script and implausible plotting; but Lang endowed the flimsy story of a third-rate writer turned sex murderer with a pervasive dream-like atmosphere and (in Bertrand Tavernier's phrase) "a harrowing romanticism" that at least partly redeemed the banalities.

Few of Lang's films are totally without interest, but *An American Guerilla in the Philippines* (1950) comes close. Adequately summarized by its title, it was made (for Fox) because "even a director has to eat," as Lang laconically remarked. He moved on to RKO to direct the last, and most individual, of his three Westerns, *Rancho Notorious* (1952).

Don Willis, in an article in *Film Quarterly* (Winter 1979–80), described *Rancho Notorious* as "striking, garish, fast-moving, always faintly ridiculous, sometimes . . . wholly ridiculous." The plot recalls *Fury* and *Kriemhilds Rache*: a quest for vengeance that leaves the revenger cauterized, devoid of human feelings, his triumph bitter and futile. A rancher (Arthur Kennedy) sets out to track down the gunmen who raped and murdered his fiancée; the trail leads him to an outlaws' hideout run by an ex–saloon dancer (Marlene Dietrich). Lang had problems both with Dietrich—"by the end of the picture, we didn't speak to each other any more"—and with the studio, then undergoing the trauma of being taken over by Howard Hughes. For economy, most of the exteriors were shot in the studio, against gaudily blatant backdrops, their hothouse effect enhanced by a lurid Technicolor process.

Some critics have commended the film's lack of realism as dramatically effective. Lotte Eisner suggested that "*Rancho Notorious* would not have worked half as well had it been shot on locations. The world of the film is a closed one, in which moral alternatives are limited, in which literally there is nowhere to go." Lang further stylized the narrative through the use of a linking ballad, whose refrain ("Hate, murder and revenge") he often liked to quote; the first time, if regrettably not the last, that this technique was used in a Western. Little noticed at the time, the film has since acquired something of a cult reputation; Peter Bogdanovich praised it as "uniquely Langian—visually, temperamentally, thematically. . . . Despite budgetary limitations . . . it is among Lang's finest pictures."

By way of contrast, Lang's next film opened with five minutes of pure documentary, lyrically shot, on the sardine fishing and canning industry of Monterey. *Clash by Night* (1952), from a play by Clifford Odets, had originally been set on Staten Island; the action was shifted to the West Coast at the suggestion of the producer, Jerry Wald. Odets's play, a triangle drama full of gritty metaphor and elaborate set speeches, plus a wealth of secondary characters, provided untypical material for Lang. He made an effective, if slightly impersonal, job of it, helped by strong central performances from Barbara Stanwyck

and Robert Ryan. Lang particularly enjoyed working with Stanwyck, whose patience and professionalism he appreciated.

Lang's career was now at a low ebb. None of his recent films had done well, either commercially or critically, and producers were increasingly reluctant to employ him. One reason for this, he discovered, was that he was considered politically suspect, having associated with such "premature anti-fascists" as Brecht, Eisler, and Ring Lardner Jr.; he had therefore, as a "potential Communist," been blacklisted. He was only rescued from limbo after eighteen months, by Harry Cohn, with whom Lang, unlike most people, got on well. Cohn arranged for him to direct a small-budget crime movie at Warners and also offered him a two-picture contract at Columbia.

Lang never developed Curtiz's trick of creating lavish results on shoestring budgets, and *The Blue Gardenia* (1953) looks like what it was—a cheap programmer, shot in twenty days. Both plot and characterization are perfunctory, but Lang and his cinematographer, Nicholas Musuraca (who also worked on *Clash by Night*), exploited the film's limited resources to create a convincingly stifling sense of shallow, paltry lives.

Lang's Hollywood career has sometimes been seen as a steady, disheartening decline from the glories of his German years. Even from this viewpoint, though, *The Big Heat* (1953) has to be acknowledged as a decisive break in the pattern, and many critics rate it the finest of all his American movies. Colin McArthur considered it "his most formally restrained and beautifully constructed film . . . in which the narrative proceeds apace but each scene is resonant with subtle, characteristically Langian meanings." Within its compact narrative (tightly scripted by Sidney Boehm), *The Big Heat* unites all Lang's primary themes: the dehumanizing quest for vengeance; the remote master-criminal, whose power reaches into every corner of society; the lone individual struggling against seemingly hopeless odds; and (both in the hero and, more graphically, in Gloria Grahame's lopsidedly disfigured face) the morally split personality, good and evil in one.

The plot is classic genre material. A conscientious police detective, Bannion (Glenn Ford), investigating the suicide of a colleague, finds himself being quietly, then heavily, warned off. When he persists, his car is booby-trapped, killing his wife. Bannion resigns from the force but continues his crusade, and finally, with the help of a gangster's moll scarred by her sadistic lover, brings down "the big heat" on the whole corrupt syndicate. "The basic material of *The Big Heat* resembles that of a score of American thrillers," wrote Gavin Lambert, "but a personal imagination transforms it and relates to the artist's own created world."

The film's rich, dark texture is shot through with violence, often directed against women. Of five killings, women are victims of four. In the picture's most horrific scene a mobster, Vince Stone (Lee Marvin at his heaviest), throws boiling coffee in the face of his girlfriend Debby (Grahame); elsewhere he burns another woman with a cigarette. In contrast—disproving allegations that "Lang was incapable of depicting happiness convincingly" (Giannetti)—stand the warmth and affection of the domestic scenes between Bannion and his wife Katie (a likeable, humorous performance from Jocelyn Brando). The authenticity of their relationship increases our shock at Katie's abrupt death, and renders Bannion's bitter fury and determination wholly credible.

Lighting and decor further point up the contrasted worlds, and mark Bannion's descent into hell. His home is clean, simply furnished, brightly lit; the police precinct is functional, slightly shabby. Elsewhere lies the shadowed, *noir* world of crime: stifling, softly-lit luxury surrounding Lagana, the affluent racketeer; the same ambience tawdrily imitated in Vince Stone's apartment; cheap hotel rooms, used-car lots, nocturnal streets and bars. This, after his wife's death, becomes Bannion's world, just as his methods come to emulate the ruthlessness of his enemies. For once, Lang's ending seems wholly appropriate—neither inanely happy, nor melodramatically wretched. Justice is done, the criminal network is destroyed, and Bannion rejoins the force, respected by his colleagues, but no less embittered by his loss. A call comes through; wearily, Bannion goes out on the case. Life goes on.

The Big Heat was Lang's first box-office hit for several years. To complete his Columbia contract, he directed *Human Desire* (1954), an adaptation of Zola's novel *La Bête Humaine*, which Renoir had filmed in 1938. Andrew Sarris, comparing the two, observed: "Where Renoir's [film] is the tragedy of a doomed man caught up in the flow of life, Lang's remake . . . is the nightmare of an innocent man enmeshed in the tangled strands of fate. What we remember in Renoir are the faces of Gabin, Simon, and Ledoux. What we remember in Lang are the geometrical patterns of trains, tracks, and fateful camera angles. If Renoir is humanism, Lang is determinism. If Renoir is concerned with the plight of his characters,

Lang is obsessed with the structure of the trap." Lang himself had a low opinion of the film, disliking the script modifications that had been forced on him; whereas Renoir's hero (played by Jean Gabin) had been a sexual psychopath, "in an American movie you cannot make the hero a sex killer. . . . So Glenn Ford has to play it, you know, like Li'l Abner coming back from Korea. . . . It was a great success in France, I don't know why. It certainly doesn't deserve it."

Lang's main reason for accepting *Moonfleet* (1955), he maintained, was that it was an MGM assignment. "After *Fury* I was banned from MGM for twenty years, and it was a kind of satisfaction to come back." A period swashbuckler, complete with smugglers, buried treasure, and all the rest of the stock romantic apparatus, *Moonfleet* was scarcely Lang's usual material; but he succeeded in creating from it a mood of encroaching gothic menace, especially in the graveyard sequence, all spooky camera angles and teetering headstones. This was Lang's only film in Cinemascope, a ratio that he later dismissed (in an often-quoted line from Godard's *Le Mépris*) as "for snakes and funerals."

The last films that Lang made in America, Richard Roud wrote, "are stripped down to their bare functional essentials, and their beauty is in their structure." Opinions have differed widely about these two films. Paul Jensen thought *While the City Sleeps* (1956) "routine . . . so profoundly ordinary as to be worth even less notice than a disaster." Against this, Jean Domarchi (*Cahiers du Cinéma*, October 1956) described the film (one of Lang's own favorites) as "a contribution of the first order to the aesthetics of the abject. . . . It's not a question of documentary realism . . . [but] of an analysis which only retains certain determining details. . . ." Like *M*, the film deals with a series of sex killings, but the narrative focuses less on the murderer than on a group of journalists who try to catch him, egged on to compete with each other by their manipulative employer. Mercenary and unscrupulous, the newsmen are revealed as little better than the criminal they pursue, without even his excuse of mental instability. The "hero," played by Dana Andrews, callously sets up his own fiancée as bait for the killer, and Lang frequently suggests, through parallel framing and action, that the two men may not be very different from each other.

Moral ambiguity, the disputed borderland between guilt and innocence, is again the territory for *Beyond a Reasonable Doubt* (1956). Appearances in Lang's films are generally deceptive, and here more so than ever: the whole plot functions as a trap, both for the hero (Dana Andrews again, ideal casting with his shifty good looks) and for the audience. To build a case against capital punishment, two men plan an elaborate hoax, constructing a net of circumstantial evidence that appears to implicate one of them, Tom Garrett, in a recent killing. He is duly arrested and tried; his partner, bringing the further evidence to clear him, dies in a road accident. Garrett's fiancée fights to prove his innocence, and succeeds; a pardon is about to be granted. At the last moment Garrett betrays himself—he is, after all, the murderer. His fiancée decides to tell the authorities, and Garrett must die.

As in *While the City Sleeps,* nobody comes out well. Garrett himself, premeditated killer scheming to trick the law; the murdered woman, who had been blackmailing him; his fiancée, coldly sending him to his death; the reporter who wants her, and therefore encourages her to "do the right thing"—"who then," as Lang asked, "is the worse human being?" Lang's last American films present us with a corrupt world, bleak and comfortless.

During the making of these films (both for RKO) Lang clashed repeatedly with his producer, Bert Friedlob. It was the last of a long series of battles. After twenty years, he decided, he had had enough of Hollywood. "I looked back over the past—how many pictures had been mutilated—and since I had no intention of dying of a heart attack, I said, 'I think I'll step out of this rat race.' And I decided not to make pictures here anymore." Instead, he went to India at the invitation of the government, to research a project for a period love story to be called *Taj Mahal.* Though the proposal came to nothing, it may well have made Lang more receptive to the next offer that came his way.

Artur Brauner, head of CCC Films in Germany, had acquired the rights to the script of *Das Indische Grabmal,* which Lang and von Harbou had written together in 1920, but which Joe May had not let Lang direct. Perhaps the old slight still rankled; perhaps the promise of working in Germany once more with a completely free hand—just like the old days—was too tempting to resist. When Brauner invited him to direct a two-part remake, with a lavish budget, Lang willingly accepted.

Some critics have found a lot to admire in *Der Tiger von Eschnapur* (1959) and *Das Indische Grabmal* (*The Indian Tomb,* 1959). Lotte Eisner noted "the balancing of colours and structures . . . the formal perfection, the masterly use of decor and spatial structures," and Robin Wood saw in them "the thematic patterns of Lang's German period . . . executed with the purity of line and economy of means learned in Hollywood." For many of Lang's admirers, though, these films came as an embarrassment, a ludicrous throwback to the melodramatic conventions and pasteboard exoticism of *Die Spinnen.* Though almost all the exteriors were shot on location in India, the interiors were patently studio sets, and browned-up European actors impersonated Indians. Four years after *Pather Panchali,* such artifice was no longer acceptable.

The *Eschnapur* films attracted little attention in Britain or the United States, where they were mostly shown combined into a single, mutilated film; but they did well enough in Europe for Brauner to offer Lang another project. Lang firmly rejected the first suggestion, a remake of *Die Nibelungen,* and was no keener on remaking *Das Testament des Dr. Mabuse.* However, he agreed to try updating the Mabuse theme in a new film: *Die Tausend Augen des Dr. Mabuse* (*The Thousand Eyes of Dr. Mabuse,* 1960). He later admitted that he "would rather not have made it," and his lack of enthusiasm showed. Although technically superior to the *Eschnapur* films, *Die Tausend Augen* proved an equally doomed attempt to resuscitate long-dead conventions: slow, short on excitement and—despite references to atomic weapons—irredeemably dated.

Referring to all three of his last German films, Lang subsequently, and rather sadly, confessed: "I didn't make these pictures because they were important, but because I was hoping that if I made somebody a great financial success I would again have the chance—as I had with *M*—to work without any restrictions. It was my mistake." Lang was now seventy, and the sight in his remaining eye was beginning to fail. Over the next few years he worked on various projects—including a promising idea for Jeanne Moreau, *Death of a Career Girl*—but none of them was realized.

The former critical consensus, that Lang was once a great "classic" director whose unique creative abilities were mangled by the insensitive Hollywood machine, no longer commands much acceptance. With the rise of auteurist criticism in the fifties, and the resultant elevation of Hollywood movies to intellectual respectability, Lang's American films began to be considered on a par with those of his earlier German period. No one would now be likely to assert that, say, *Die Frau im Mond* should automatically be seen as superior to *Ministry of Fear* simply because Lang enjoyed near-total control over making the former, while the latter was a mere studio assignment.

On the other hand, Lang's stature within the industry—and to a lesser degree among critics—*was* diminished during his years in Hollywood. From the mid-1920s until 1933, Lang was recognized as the greatest director in Germany, and perhaps in Europe. By the time he arrived in the States, he was no more than one of many distinguished European refugees; by 1950, he had become just another directorial hack, and politically dubious at that. (Lang's own independent temperament, and refusal to stay tied to any one studio, most likely contributed to Hollywood's dismissive stance towards him.) The hope that he might repeat earlier glories by returning to Germany was disappointed. It was mainly during his retirement, when the overall shape of his career could be assessed, that Lang regained his status as one of the cinema's greatest artists. Pauline Kael rated him with Eisenstein, Gance, Griffith, and Welles as one "whose prodigious failures make other people's successes look puny."

Lang's films, by general agreement, are distinguished above all by the visual potency of his images, which carry an emotional charge far beyond their ostensible content. Hence, perhaps, his preeminence in *film noir,* where (as Michael Wood put it) "nothing that happens *in* the films quite lives up to the eerie menace contained in the looks of these movies." Claude Chabrol observed (*Cahiers du Cinéma,* December 1955) that "his thematic, the fatality of the fall, vengeance, the occult power of secret societies and the networks of espionage, has no more importance in his eyes than his aesthetic, which illustrates and produces it, surrounding the characters with a frame of which they are the slaves. . . . The decor, even the edges of the screen, have in their design as much importance as the actors. . . . The work of Fritz Lang is based on a metaphysic of architecture." Or in John Russell Taylor's words: "He makes films with ideas rather than films of ideas . . . in the end it is his power to embody his ideas visually which accounts for the lasting effect of his films. The main conflict in them is not primarily on the intellectual level, between good and bad, order the disorder, but on the intuitive, between darkness and light."

Throughout his films, both American and European, Lang created a distinct world, consistent and unmistakable, marked by the intensity of his vision. "Fritz Lang's America is not essentially different from Fritz Lang's Germany," maintained Gavin Lambert; "it is less openly macabre, its crime and terror exist on a comparatively realistic level, but both countries are really another country, a haunted place in which the same dramas constantly occur. The shadow of outrage lies across *Fury, You Only Live Once, Scarlet Street, The Big Heat,* as it does across *Dr. Mabuse* and *M,* and the obsessed little New York cashier is trying, like the child-murderer of Düsseldorf, to escape 'the man behind you'."

At his best, Lang is the greatest exponent of the Cinema of Paranoia. His films feed upon, and nourish, the irrational fear that nothing is as it seems, that a hidden menace lurks behind all bland appearances, and that even the most amiable of individuals—*especially* the most amiable—is a member of some vast malign conspiracy, from which we alone are excluded. "No other director," wrote David Thomson, "convinces us that the melodramatic threat of extinction in the crime movie is the metaphor of a much greater danger. . . . Lang's films begin in top gear and then advance into higher ratios unknown to other directors."

In 1963, Lang was invited by Jean-Luc Godard to appear in his film *Le Mépris (Contempt)* in the role of a film director. Since he took a close interest in the work of the *nouvelle vague,* Lang was happy to accept, and greatly enjoyed himself. "There are two monsters in this picture," he explained later. " . . . Jack Palance, who plays a producer, and myself. I play Fritz Lang." He also developed a great liking and admiration for Godard, despite the considerable differences in their approach to filmmaking, Godard's improvisatory methods running counter to all Lang's beliefs in meticulous preparation. Within the film, Lang was shown directing a few scenes of a rather bizarre version of *The Odyssey*; he performed with imperturbable dignity, no doubt bringing personal experience to his scenes with Palance's crassly overbearing producer.

After *Le Mépris* Lang returned to the United States, and settled down for the rest of his life in the house in Beverly Hills that he had bought in 1945. After his divorce from Thea von Harbou, he never remarried; his friend and companion throughout most of his years in America was Lily Latté, whom he had known when she was a writer in Berlin in the early thirties. Lang's on-set image as a dour and doom-obsessed perfectionist did not carry over into his private life, where he was known as charming and hospitable; David Overbey, who knew him well, remembered him as "a generous friend, an immensely intelligent companion with a highly developed sense of ironic humour not only about life in general but, above all, about himself and his work." Until old age and illness slowed him down, Lang was always physically active; he rode, swam, boxed, and played a formidable game of tennis. At home, he surrounded himself with books, primitive art, and cats.

Hollywood never gave Lang an Academy Award or even nominated him for one, though in his later years he received honors and awards from various governments and cinematic bodies, and his films were shown at countless festivals and retrospectives. Lang received these tributes politely, with a certain detached irony ("I am the last of the dinosaurs"). Towards the end of his life he became almost completely blind. He died at the age of eighty-five, after a long illness, at his home in Beverly Hills.

—P.K.

FILMS: Halbblut (The Half-Caste), 1919; Der Herr der Liebe (Master of Love), 1919; Die Spinnen (The Spiders), Part 1: Der Goldene See (The Golden Lake), 1919; Harakiri (Madame Butterfly), 1919; Die Spinnen, Part 2: Das Brillantenschiff (The Diamond Ship), 1920; Das Wandernde Bild (The Wandering Image), 1920; Kämpfende Herzen (Die Vier um die Frau/Struggling Hearts/Four Around a Woman), 1921; Der Müde Tod (Destiny/The Weary Death/Beyond the Wall/Between Two Worlds/The Three Lights), 1921; Dr. Mabuse der Spieler (Dr. Mabuse the Gambler), Part 1: Der Grosse Spieler (The Great Gambler), Part 2: Inferno, 1922; Die Nibelungen, Part 1: Siegfried, Part 2: Kriemhilds Rache (Kriemhild's Revenge), 1924; Metropolis, 1926; Spione (Spies/The Spy), 1928; Die Frau im Mond (Woman in the Moon/By Rocket to the Moon), 1929; M, 1931; Das Testament des Dr. Mabuse (The Last Will of Dr. Mabuse), 1933; Liliom, 1934; Fury, 1936; You Only Live Once, 1937; You and Me, 1938; The Return of Frank James, 1940; Western Union, 1941; Man Hunt, 1941; Hangmen Also Die, 1943; Ministry of Fear, 1944; The Woman in the Window, 1944; Scarlet Street, 1945; Cloak and Dagger, 1946; Secret Beyond the Door, 1948; House by the River; 1950; An American Guerilla in the Philippines (U.K., I Shall Return), 1950; Rancho Notorious, 1952; Clash by Night, 1952; The Blue Gardenia, 1953; The Big Heat, 1953; Human Desire, 1954; Moonfleet, 1955; While the City Sleeps, 1956; Beyond a Reasonable Doubt, 1956; Der Tiger von Eschnapur, 1959; Das Indische Grabmal (The Indian Tomb), 1959; Die Tausend Augen des Dr. Mabuse (The Thousand Eyes of Dr. Mabuse), 1960. *Published scripts—*Fury *in* Twenty Best Film Plays, 1953; Hangmen Also Die (French trans.) *in* Présence du Cinéma 10 1962; M, Marion von Schröder Verlag, 1963 (also published in English translation by Lorrimer, 1968, and in Masterworks of the German Cinema, Lorrimer, 1973); Metropolis (in English translation), Lorrimer, 1973; Die Nibelungen (novelization with 24 stills) *in* Das Nibelungenbuch by Thea von Harbou, 1923; Spione *in* Filmregie und Filmmanuskript, edited by W. Pudowkin, 1928.

ABOUT: Albrecht, G. (ed.) Retrospective Fritz Lang: Dokumentation, 1964; Armour, R. A. Fritz Lang: 1978; Barlow, J. German Expressionist Film, 1982; Bazin, A. *et al.* La Politique des Auteurs, 1972; Bogdanovich, P. Fritz Lang in America, 1967; Courtade, F. Fritz Lang (in French), 1963; Dürrenmatt, D. Fritz Lang: Leben und Werk, 1982; Eibel, A. (ed.) Fritz Lang, 1964 (in French); Eisner, L. The Haunted House, 1973; Eisner, L. Fritz Lang, 1976; Gesek, L. Gestalter der Filmkunst von Asta Nielsen bis Walt Disney, 1948; Giannetti, L. Masters of the American Cinema, 1981; Grafe, F. *et al.* Fritz Lang, 1976 (in German); Higham, C. and Greenberg, J. Hollywood in the Forties, 1968; Higham, C. and Greenberg, J. The Celluloid Muse, 1969; Humphries, R. Fritz Lang: Cinéaste Américain, 1982; Jacob, G. Le Cinéma Moderne, 1964; Jenkins, S. (ed.) Fritz Lang: The Image and the Look, 1981; Jensen, P. M. The Cinema of Fritz Lang, 1969; Kaplan, E. A. Fritz Lang: A Guide to References and Resources, 1981; McArthur, C. Underworld USA, 1972; Maibohm, L. Fritz Lang: seine Filme, sein Leben, 1981; Manvell, R. and Fraenkel, H. The German Cinema, 1971; Moullet, L. Fritz Lang, 1963 (in French); Ott, F. W. The Films of Fritz Lang, 1979; Petley, J. The Films of Fritz Lang: the Cinema of Destiny, 1973; Rhode, E. Tower of Babel, 1966; Rosenberg, B. and Silverstein, H. The Real Tinsel, 1970; Rotha, P. Celluloid: The Film Today, 1931; Roud, R. (ed.) Cinema: A Critical Dictionary, 1980; Sarris, A. The American Cinema, 1968; Silver, A. and Ward, E. Film Noir, 1980; Simsolo, N. Fritz Lang (in French); Truffaut, F. The Films in my Life, 1978; Weinberg, H. G. Index to the Creative Work of Fritz Lang, 1946; Whittemore, D. and Cecchettini, P. A. Passport to Hollywood, 1976; Wollenberg, H. H. Fifty Years of German Film, 1972. *Periodicals*—Avant-Scène du Cinéma January 1981; Bianco e Nero March–April 1978; Cahiers du Cinéma September 1959, November 1959, June 1964, August 1965, June 1966, March 1978; Chaplin December 1960; Cinéaste November 1953; Cinema (UK) August 1970; Cinéma (France) November 1962, December 1979, June 1982; Cinématographe February 1981; Critique March 1966; Dialogue on Film April 1974; Écran October 1976; Film (UK) Summer 1962; Film (W. Ger.) 12 1965; Film Comment November–December 1974; Film Quarterly (UK) Summer 1947; Film Quarterly (US) Winter 1979–1980; Film und Fernsehen 8 1983; Filmcritica March 1962, September 1964, September 1967; Filmkritik 12 1965; Filmograph Summer 1970; Films and Filming June 1962; Films in Review June–July 1956; Filmstudio September 1964, November 1964; First Cut 11 1981; Focus on Film Spring 1975; Image et Son January 1964, February 1968, April 1968, November 1982; Kosmorama December 1965; Mise-en-Scène 1 1972; Monthly Film Bulletin June 1976; Movie November 1962; National Film Theatre Booklet January 1978, February 1978, May 1981; New Republic June 23, 1941; June 30, 1941; July 7, 1941; Penguin Film Review 5 and 6 1948; Positif March 1963, April 1968, December 1976, March 1980; Revue du Cinéma February 1947; Séquences October 1976, January 1977; Sight and Sound Summer 1955, Autumn 1955, Winter 1961–1962, Summer 1967, Autumn 1975, Spring 1977, Autumn 1977; Sub-Stance 9 1974; Take One November–December 1968, March 1977; Theatre Arts December 1947; Vampir 22 1981; Wide Angle 3 1979.

*LATTUADA, ALBERTO (November 13, 1914–), Italian director and scenarist, was born in Milan, the son of the composer Felice Lattuada, and grew up in the "magical atmosphere" of the opera, receiving his vocation at the age of eight: "It was in the wings of La Scala in Milan, alongside my father . . . that I discovered the art of directing and the power of the artifices of spectacle." At home he constructed a miniature theatre and made sets for it, becoming fascinated by "the phenomenon of lighting." Roy Armes believes that "the sense of affinity with opera and melodrama" lies "at the root of Lattuada's conception of the cinema."

During his teens, Lattuada's interests extended to embrace all the visual arts and literature as well. Though he does not share the Marxist commitment of many of his friends in the Italian cinema, he was opposed to the fascist regime and at university and after he wrote critical articles, poems, and short stories for such anti-conformist magazines as *Corrente* (which he helped to found) and *Domus*. By the time he qualified as an architect at the age of twenty-three, Lattuada had decided that his real métier was the cinema. He had had his first taste of filmmaking while still a student, working as a designer on one movie—Mondadori's *Cuore rivelatore* (1933)—and as color consultant on the first Italian color film, Mario Baffico's *Il museo dell'amore* (1935). Soon after, with Luigi Comencini and Mario Ferreri, he established Italy's first film archive in Milan, laying the foundations of the Cineteca Italiana.

For the seventh Milan Triennale in May 1940, just before the invasion of France, Lattuada and his friends organized an international retrospective film festival in which, disregarding official warnings, they insisted on screening Renoir's *La Marseillaise*. "Its showing was a memorable event," according to Pierre Leprohon. "At the point where the characters sing the Marseillaise, the audience applauded and joined in the singing; fighting broke out, the police intervened, and Lattuada avoided arrest by escaping through a skylight in the projection room. . . . the affair was finally swept under the carpet to avoid compromising more important personages [and] Lattuada settled in Rome." In 1941 he published a volume of photographs, *Occhio quadrato,* which caused him to be "summoned by the police and accused of showing only the imperfections of the regime and not its grandeurs."

Lattuada served as coscenarist of Mario Soldati's *Piccolo mondo antico* (1940) and Ferdinando Poggioli's *Sissignora* (1942), both works in the mode described pejoratively by Giuseppe De Santis as "calligraphist." Prevented by the fascist

ALBERTO LATTUADA

censorship from making films that would reflect the realities of life in wartime Italy, the calligraphists turned to literary adaptations, to the past, to the pursuit of pure style—a style that was often emptily decorative and melodramatic.

These terms have been applied to Lattuada's own first film, *Giacomo l'idealista* (*Giacomo the Idealist,* 1942), adapted by Emilio Cecchi and Aldo Buzzi from a nineteenth-century novel by Emilio De Marchi, and with a score by Felice Lattuada—the first of many he wrote for his son's films. Alberto Lattuada has described the movie as being "the story of a dreamer who lives outside reality and gets out of his depth when faced with the mysteries of life." It introduces the theme of solitude, a central preoccupation in Lattuada's work, but deals with it melodramatically and romantically, dwelling on shots of misty lakes and leafless trees. De Santis found it "a deplorable regression," denouncing this "marriage between cinema and literature as totally arid and sterile, frigid and uninteresting." Nino Frank agreed that it was a cold film but thought it was also compelling, and many shared this view.

The release of *Giacomo* apparently reminded the authorities of Lattuada's involvement in the incidents at the Milan Triennale, and for a time he was obliged to lie low in Rome. When he did try to resume work, the authorities turned down scripts based on works by Moravia, Robert Louis Stevenson, Dostoyevsky, and Matilde Serao, and it was not until 1944 that Lattuada's second film appeared. This was *La freccia nel fianco,* another calligraphist literary adaptation, derived by a team of writers (including Ennio Flaiano, Alberto Moravia, and Lattuada himself) from a novel by Luciano Zuccoli.

But, as Lattuada has said, the cinema "reflects moments of crisis, that is to say, of social metamorphosis. As soon as there are reactions with regard to reality, artists react more or less. They translate these upheavals." And with the fall of fascism, the German occupation, and the liberation, Lattuada lost interest in calligraphic cinema: "My friends Vittorini, the painter Gottuso, Pavese, Cassola and I . . . felt the necessity of living outside these romantic complacencies. Our preoccupations were political and realistic." The first evidence of this was *La nostra guerra* (*Our War,* 1944), a documentary about the partisan contribution to the liberation. And in 1945 Lattuada published an article in *Film d'oggi* that stands as one of the first manifestos of neorealism: "We are in rags? Then let us show everybody our rags. We are defeated? Let us look at our disasters. . . . Let us pay all our debts with a fierce love of honesty and the world will participate with emotion in this great game with truth. This confession will illuminate our crazy secret virtue, our belief in life, our superior Christian brotherhood."

And Lattuada's next feature was a work in the neorealist mainstream which had surfaced a year earlier in Rossellini's *Open City. Il bandito* (*The Bandit,* 1946), from an original screenplay of which the director was one of the authors, was shot silent by Aldo Tonti with a 120 camera and post-synchronized. This was a common enough procedure at the time, but no doubt contributed to a quality of "strangeness" that reminded Paul Eluard of the silent cinema. It opens with Ernesto (Amedeo Nazzari) returning to Turin from a prisoner-of-war camp. These scenes, wrote Carlo Lizzani, are "breathless and anguished, with crowded railroad stations, packed trains, people seeking an aim in life, views of Turin by night with its ruined houses, its deserted poverty-stricken streets, where the only sign of life is a jazz tune or an open-air gambling hell for down-and-outs in search of easy money."

Ernesto finds his own house destroyed, his family dead or scattered. Following a girl to a brothel, he discovers that it is his own sister (played by Lattuada's wife, Carla Del Poggio). She dies in a brawl and Ernesto kills her pimp. A fugitive, he is drawn inevitably into crime, joining a gang led by the seductive Lydia (Anna Magnani). Even then he tries to abide by a certain code of decency, and he eventually dies saving the life of a child who has come to symbolize for him his lost innocence and goodness.

After the harsh realism of its opening scenes, the film deteriorates into a more or less routine crime melodrama, though with touches (like Ernesto's death in the snow) that reminded critics of the "poetic realism" of Marcel Carné and other masters of the prewar French cinema. Roy Armes found in this movie evidence of "Lattuada's basic approach, which is to create drama and significance out of material extracted from life rather than to seek an authentic and direct documentary-style transcription of reality. . . . Lattuada has always worked strictly within the commercial structure of the film industry and the original and penetrating insights of *Il bandito* are set firmly in the context of a conventional gangster plot." This film was rather surprisingly followed by a regression to the calligraphist mode—an adaptation of D'Annunzio's novel *Il delitto di Giovanni Episcopo.* Set in Rome at the turn of the century, it was written by Lattuada in collaboration with Suso Cecchi d'Amico, Federico Fellini, Piero Tellini, and Aldo Fabrizzi, who also stars as the shy middle-aged clerk led astray by a wicked woman (Yvonne Sanson).

Senza pietà (*Without Pity,* 1947) returns to the social chaos of the immediate postwar period in an original screenplay set in liberated Leghorn, a center for black marketeering and every kind of corruption. It was filmed on location in the bars, streets, and docks of the city, using extras recruited on the spot. Commenting on this aspect of neorealism, Lattuada has said that "the experience of the war was a determining one for all of us. Everyone felt a mad desire to throw into the air all the old stories of the Italian cinema, to plant the camera in the middle of real life, in the middle of everything which struck our astonished gaze. We sought to liberate ourselves from the weight of our faults, we wanted to look each other in the eyes and tell the truth, discover what we really were, and seek salvation."

The movie tells the tragic love story of Jerry (John Kitzmiller), a black American GI, and Angela (Carla Del Poggio), an Italian girl who has been driven into prostitution. Desperate to rescue her from this situation, Jerry becomes involved in the black market, and the result is death for them both. Some critics have seen an implication of Christian redemption in the fact that Angela is shot soon after she and Jerry have visited a church and prayed together. This element in the film—if indeed it was intended at all—has been credited to Lattuada's coscenarist Fellini rather than to the director himself: Lattuada has often expressed his disapproval of films too firmly anchored to any one ideological preoccupation, Catholic or socialist.

Senza pietà was acclaimed for its humanity,

its pace and vigor, and its raw authenticity. Again, there were critical references to the "poetic realism" (and the defeatism) of pre-war French cinema, which was so often drawn to similar stories of hopeless love affairs between doomed social outcasts. There is a good deal of violence in the film and Lattuada considers that this was justified, explaining that violence always ensues when "the lack of balance at the heart of society pushes man into unaccustomed paths and compels him to confront conflicts which upset and break his life." In another interview, Lattuada said in 1963: "If I think back to *Il bandito* and *Senza pietà*, I'd say that the most valuable parts of these films are also those most detached from events and from actuality. They are the most symbolic, with a significance intended to be universal." This is not the common view, most critics valuing the two films, as Armes says, primarily for their "precise and forceful capturing of the realities of the postwar situation."

The most admired of all Lattuada's contributions to neorealism is in fact set in the past. *Il mulino del Po* (*The Mill on the Po*, 1949) was adapted by Riccardo Bacchelli, Lattuada, Fellini, Pinelli, and others from Bacchelli's famous novel about the nineteenth-century agrarian struggles in northern Italy and the birth of socialism there. The clash of interests comes to a head in an agricultural strike during which both the local landowner and the socialist organizer show themselves more concerned with ideology than with human beings, and in the end neither side is wholly victorious. In spite of its historical setting, the film was highly relevant to contemporary developments in Italy, its release in 1949 coinciding with a national strike of agricultural workers.

In the foreground of these events is the Romeo and Juliet love story of Berta (Carla Del Poggio), a member of a semi-bourgeois family of millers, and the socialist tenant farmer Orbino (Jacques Sernas). The great river itself plays an important role in the story—a source of fear for Orbino and of solace for Berta. The deep and violent passions of the film are conveyed through the river's moods and in a series of powerfully managed crowd scenes that reminded critics of such masters of the Soviet silent cinema as Eisenstein and Dovzhenko, like the chaotic montage when the mill is burned down, and the scene in which a ragged cluster of peasant women outface a long menacing black line of soldiers.

Roy Armes has described *The Mill on the Po* as "a crucial film in the development of neorealism, a most striking and successful attempt to unite formalism and the study of the poor, contemporaneity and an awareness of the historical process. . . . Despite his concern with social issues and with the political attitude of his characters, Lattuada's prime interest remains not commitment but solitude. He has defined his approach on numerous occasions, claiming that the one constant in his work is 'the state of solitude of the individual faced with society, a solitude inseparable from the individual's aspiration to rejoin in the heart of society all those who hope and struggle with him. An attitude of rebellion, engendered by solitude and directed against it but resulting, in most cases, only in the confirmation of this solitude.'" Lattuada has recalled with satisfaction that *The Mill on the Po* was attacked both by the communists and the right, and Armes finds in this fact evidence that "Lattuada is an authentic neorealist in that he sees problems in terms which do not allow neat formulas or glib assertions of right and wrong."

After this epic film came *Luci del varietà* (*Variety Lights*, 1950), which Lattuada co-authored, co-produced, and co-directed with his friend Fellini, whose first picture it was. A series of anecdotes about a touring vaudeville company, it has a cast that includes Peppino De Filippo, Carla Del Poggio, Giulietta Masina, John Kitzmiller, and Folco Lulli. The theme of human solitude is central in this picture, but Pierre Leprohon attributes this element to Fellini rather than Lattuada, maintaining that the characters "were undoubtedly chosen to meet the wishes of Fellini. These touring music-hall artists, with their gilded poverty, their delusions of grandeur, and their nostalgia for the open road, are typically Fellinian characters—a blend of the chimerical and the real, always ready to exchange the disappointments of actual life for the consolations of a mirage. The irony here is biting and sometimes cruel."

The artist, Lattuada says, "must work towards authenticity and the clarification of ideas, must contribute to progress, struggle against conformity, seek modestly and humbly—that goes without saying—to say the things he feels capable of contributing to the redressing of errors, must be a guide, a 'detector' for society, but must in no case be transformed into a mere instrument of political propaganda." At the same time, Lattuada believes it wrong to "cut yourself off from the mass audience, for if you make a film to be shown only to a few friends, it would be better to write a pamphlet." For this reason, even his most passionately felt films contain compromises and "concessions coldly agreed to," and he has made a good many movies that seem to aim at nothing more than popular success. There are times, indeed, when the urge to success seems for long periods to have supplanted his ambition to "contribute to progress" and "struggle against conformity."

Lattuada's first strictly commercial venture was *Anna* (1951), a polished entertainment starring Silvana Mangano and Raf Vallone which did indeed achieve great success at the box office, but which disappointed the critics. They were much happier with *Il cappotto* (*The Overcoat*, 1952), an adaptation of the Gogol story written by Lattuada with Cesare Zavattini, Leonardo Sinisgalli, and others. In this rather Kafkaesque version of the famous story, the central figure (played by the comic actor Renato Rascel) is a petty official haunted by great aspirations (as well as his yearning for a warm overcoat). Leprohon suggests that "he is cold because he is alone, rejected, even more than because the wind is cutting through his rags." When he gets his overcoat, he becomes ridiculous in his delusions of grandeur, but is rescued from these by a thief, and soon by death. Leprohon went so far as to call this "a great film, complex, moving, satiric . . . a homage to humility and a criticism of all material success, even among the poor."

La lupa (*The She-Wolf*, 1953), a very bad adaptation of a story by Verga, was followed by an episode in the omnibus film *Amore in città*, and then by *La spiaggia* (*The Beach*, 1954). This was Lattuada's first color film, an interesting and ironic piece in which Martine Carole plays a prostitute who finds romance with Raf Vallone while taking a seaside vacation with her child. *Scuolo elementaire* (*Elementary School*, 1954) is a touching drama, filmed in black and white, about the experiences of a young teacher from the south who gets a job in a northern city. Lattuada has an avowed fondness for juvenile heroines and their problems, and in *Guendalina* (1957) gives a sensitive portrait of the spoiled daughter of rich parents whose flirtation with a working boy turns into something more serious. He returned to the subject in *I dolci inganni* (1960), about the sexual awakening and subsequent disillusionment of a young student.

In between came the elaborate and ambitious *La tempesta* (*The Tempest*, 1958), adapted from two stories by Pushkin—an international coproduction with a cast that includes Silvana Mangano, Van Heflin, Viveca Lindfors, Vittorio Gassman, Oscar Homolka, Agnes Moorehead, Finlay Currie, and Robert Keith. Set in Russia at the time of Catherine the Great, it tells the story of a young officer cadet who becomes involved with Emil Pugachev, the rebel leader who called himself Czar Peter III. *Lettere di una novizia* (*Letter From a Novice*, 1960), another literary adaptation, was written by Roger Vailland among others and based on Guido Piovene's novel about a girl (Pascale Petit) forced against her will into a convent from which she eventually escapes.

After *L'Imprevisto* (*The Unexpected*, 1961), in which Anouk Aimée plays a woman who becomes involved with her schoolmaster husband in a kidnapping, came a Chekhov adaptation, *La steppa* (*The Steppe*, 1962), and then *Mafioso* (*The Mafia*, 1962). The latter has Alberto Sordi as a Sicilian who, having made good in Milan, comes home with his young wife and two daughters and suddenly finds himself abducted by the Mafia, taken to the United States, and forced to commit murder. Perhaps because Marco Ferreri and Rafael Azcona were among its scenarists, this film has an edge of ferocious satire that sharply differentiates it from its immediate predecessors. It received the Grand Prix at San Sebastian in 1963.

Lattuada's next film also attracted a good deal of attention. This was *La mandragola* (*The Mandrake*, 1965), adapted from Machiavelli's libertine comedy about a young man's bold and ingenious campaign to win a night with a beautiful woman who is inconveniently married to a possessive old fool. Hollis Alpert called it "a fully satisfying film, played with exactly the properly cynical, irreverent spirit by Philippe Leroy, Jean-Claude Brialy, Rosanna Schiaffino, and Romolo Valli. Alberto Lattuada . . . has gone in for richness and opulence in re-creating the atmosphere of Renaissance Florence." In the United States, the film was condemned by the National Catholic Office for Motion Pictures (but not banned, as the story had been four hundred years earlier).

Of Lattuada's later movies, the more notable include *Fraülein Doktor* (1969), an entertaining piece of nonsense about a female spy (Suzy Kendall) in World War I, and *Venga a prendere il caffè da noi* (*Come Have Coffee With Us*, 1970), in which Ugo Tognazzi plays a middle-aged bachelor who decides that he needs a woman to take care of him. *Cuore di cane* (*Heart of a Dog*, 1975), based on Bulgakov's novel about an eminent scientist who turns his dog into a human being with disastrous results, was more ambitious than successful.

Lattuada has never ceased to be fascinated by the opera, in which he "steeps" himself in the intervals between films. He has published a volume of poems and one of short stories. Edgardo Cozarinsky writes that Lattuada's "eclecticism has obstructed an evaluation of his unusual achievement. . . . For over thirty years he has turned out films of considerable interest . . . without surrendering to opportunism. . . . Most of Lattuada's minor films look considerably better years after they were made. . . . The capacity to work with given materials and achieve something else, in quality and tone, has been one of Lattuada's elusive talents: very much isolated in the Italian cinema of the 1970s, his solid, unadventurous films often prove more biting, more complex even than the flashy concoctions of most 'new' Italian directors."

In an interview in 1961, Lattuada said "the protagonists of my films are, for the most part, I won't say anarchists, but rebels who find themselves in a situation of revolt and polemic, and it would be equally fair to say that in the heart of this struggle they find themselves somewhat isolated." And in 1966 he made this statement of faith: "A free, isolated, independent man, recognizing neither parties nor dictatorships, neither fanaticisms nor religions, an individual man struggles, and the army of free men becomes more and more numerous."

FILMS: Giacomo l'idealista, 1942; La freccia nel fianco, 1944; La nostra guerra (Our War), 1944 (documentary); Il bandito (The Bandit), 1946; Il delitto di Giovanni Episcopo (Flesh Will Surrender/Giovanni Episcopo), 1947; Senza pietà (Without Pity), 1947; Il mulino del Po (The Mill on the Po/The Mill on the River), 1949; (with Federico Fellini) Luci del varietà (Variety Lights), 1950; Anna, 1951; Il cappotto (The Overcoat), 1952; La lupe (The She-Wolf/The Vixen), 1953; Gli Italiani si voltano in Amore in Città (Love in the City), 1953; La spiaggia (The Beach), 1954; Scuolo elementare (Elementary School), 1954; Guendalina, 1957; La tempesta (The Tempest), 1958; I dolci inganni, 1960; Lettere di una novizia (Letters From a Novice/Rita), 1960; L'imprevisto (The Unexpected), 1961; La steppa (The Steppe), 1962; Mafioso (The Mafia), 1962; La mandragola (The Mandrake/The Love Root), 1965; Matchless, 1966; Don Giovanni in Sicilia, 1967; L'amica, 1969; Fraülein Doktor, 1969; Venga a prendere il caffè da noi (Come Have Coffee With Us), 1970; Bianco Rosso e . . . (White Sister), 1973; Sono stato io (I Did It), 1973; Le faro da padre, 1974; Cuore di cane (Heart of a Dog), 1975; Cosi come sei (Stay As You Are/The Daughter), 1978; Cristofero Columbus, 1983.

ABOUT: Armes, R. Patterns of Realism, 1971; Bondanella, P. Italian Cinema, 1983; Bruno, E. Lattuada o la proposta ambigua, 1968 (in Italian); Camerini, C. Alberto Lattuada, 1981; De Sanctis, F. M. Alberto Lattuada, 1965 (in Italian); Jarratt, V. The Italian Cinema, 1951; Leprohon, P. The Italian Cinema, 1972; Liehm, M. Passion and Defiance—Film in Italy from 1942 to the Present, 1984; Roud, R. (ed.) Cinema: A Critical Dictionary, 1980; Schlappner, M. Von Rossellini zu Fellini, 1958; Who's Who in Italy, 1980; Zanellato, A. L'uomo (cattivo sorte), 1973 (in Italian). Periodicals—Bianco e Nero June 1961; Cinéma (France) May 1960, April 1981; Cinestudio November 1963; Écran June 1972; Image et Son February 1962, June 1966, December 1974, July 1979; Jeune Cinéma December 1974—January 1975; Positif June, September, October 1978.

LAUNDER, FRANK (1907–) and **GILLIAT, SIDNEY** (February 15, 1908–), British directors, scenarists, and producers. Launder was born in Hitchin, Hertfordshire, the son of a builder, and educated in Brighton, where he also began his career in the office of the Official Receiver in Bankruptcy—an excellent preparation, as he says, for the movie business. He spent his evenings acting with the semiprofessional Brighton Repertory Company, which in 1928 produced his first play, *There Was No Signpost.*

Gilliat was born in Edgeley, Cheshire, but grew up in London, where his father worked as a journalist and eventually became the editor of a national daily, *The Evening Standard.* Sidney Gilliat studied English and history at London University and was expected to follow his father's career. However, in 1928 the *Standard's* film critic, Walter C. Mycroft, became scenario chief with British International Pictures at Elstree studios, and Gilliat joined him as his assistant. He began by writing titles for silent movies, among them Arthur Maude's *Toni* (1928), Alfred Hitchcock's *Champagne* (1928), and Harry Lachman's *Week-End Wives* (1928)—the latter from a script by Victor Kendall that Gilliat had rescued from the "tripe heap."

The same year, Frank Launder also arrived in Mycroft's office, having been hired on the strength of a good review of his Brighton play. The studio had agreed to match his civil service salary of four pounds, ten shillings a week—a sum so munificent that it was generally assumed that he must be the bastard son of the managing director. After a brief stint as a title-writer, Launder was assigned to script a "piffling" adaptation of Thomas Hardy's *Under the Greenwood Tree* (1928). This was very nearly the first full-length British talkie, but its director, Harry Lachman, worked so slowly that Hitchcock got there first with *Blackmail.*

As it happened, Gilliat had also been involved with this film at an earlier stage, making a synopsis of the plot and researching the costumes, before leaving Elstree to join Nettlefold Films in December 1928. There he worked at an assortment of jobs—gag-writer, bit-part actor, assistant director—mostly on films directed by Walter Forde. When Forde moved on to other studios, Gilliat continued to help him with his scripts, but unofficially. It was not until 1932 that he received his first screenplay credit, as coscenarist of Sinclair Hall's *A Gentleman of Paris.* His first important assignment was as scenarist of Forde's *Rome Express* (1932), starring Conrad Veidt. There followed several years of less prestigious work, mostly as coscenarist of comedies and musicals starring Jack Hulbert and

SIDNEY GILLIAT

others, until in 1936 he became an associate producer at Gainsborough Pictures, working with Edward Black on Robert Stevenson's *Tudor Rose* (*Nine Days a Queen*) among other movies.

Launder's career was meanwhile proceeding rather more smoothly at Elstree, where he had remained. After stints as writer of additional dialogue and coscenarist he wrote—alone, but under the watchful eye of the dramatist himself—the first screen version of a play by George Bernard Shaw, *How He Lied to Her Husband* (1931), directed by Cecil Lewis. Launder subsequently adapted Arnold Ridley's *Keepers of Youth* (1931), Harold Brighouse's *Hobson's Choice* (1931), John van Druten's *London Wall* (filmed as *After Office Hours*, 1932), Shaw's *Arms and the Man* (1932), and a number of other plays (including *The Taming of the Shrew*, in a modernized musical version written with and starring Stanley Lupino).

In 1934 Launder left British International Pictures and went freelance, working over the next two years on a string of indifferent movies. During this period he wrote several scripts in collaboration with Gilliat, none of them produced until, in 1936, Gaumont-British hired them to adapt a very bad stage thriller. The result was Albert de Courville's *Seven Sinners*, very well recieved for its "ideas and wit" and its ingenious plot twists.

Twelve Good Men (1936), their second collaboration (though released first), was another thriller. After that Gilliat and Launder worked separately for a while. Gilliat wound up his contract as an associate producer at Gainsborough and returned to scriptwriting, while Launder

(recommended by Gilliat) joined Gainsborough as script editor, working mostly on Will Hay and Crazy Gang comedies. Gilliat was prominent among the thirty or so writers involved in the first MGM British production, Jack Conway's *A Yank at Oxford* (1938)—a painful experience but a major hit.

The collaboration was revived with immense success when Launder and Gilliat adapted a novel called *The Wheel Spins* into a film called *The Lady Vanishes* (1938), directed by Alfred Hitchcock for Gainsborough. This witty and ingenious thriller, set mostly on a transcontinental express, has Dame May Whitty as the dotty old lady who disappears, Margaret Lockwood as the girl who wonders why, and Michael Redgrave as the young folklorist who gets drawn with her into the thick of a spy intrigue. The picture is stolen by two minor characters—imperturbable upper-class Englishmen named Charters (Basil Radford) and Caldicott (Naunton Wayne), who are moved by nothing on earth except the test match cricket scores. Launder and Gilliat were shrewd enough to copyright these surreal characters, who appeared in two subsequent films and in two radio serials (which themselves gave birth to a further film called *Crooks' Tour*, made without the direct participation of Gilliat and Launder).

The two scenarists then worked separately on a number of movies, each being involved in films directed by Carol Reed, and came together again to write Reed's *Night Train to Munich* (1940), a picture very much in the tradition of *The Lady Vanishes* and featuring Charters and Caldicott. In 1940 the Launder-Gilliat play *The Body Was Well Nourished* was staged with great success. It has been frequently revived, much translated, and filmed (as *The Green Man*).

By this time World War II had begun. Gilliat worked on several propaganda pictures and collaborated with Launder in writing Reed's *The Young Mr. Pitt* (1942), a historical film centering on the struggle against Napoleon that itself carried a propaganda message for a newly embattled Britain. They subsequently coscripted *Partners in Crime* (1942), a propaganda short chiefly of interest because it was also the first movie they codirected. *Millions Like Us*, their first feature as codirectors, followed in 1943.

Millions Like Us was originally conceived as a propaganda film for the Ministry of Information, which wanted a tribute to the war effort on the "home front," but finally produced by Gainsborough Pictures. The product of much research, it shows how women from all levels of British society are directed into factory work, and their gradual adjustment to their new life.

It incorporates contemporary documentary material and some filming with models, but was otherwise shot mostly on location in actual factories and hostels. The story centers on an upper-class girl (Anne Crawford) who comes to terms with her new environment when she falls in love with the blunt North Country foreman (Eric Portman); a working-class country girl (Megs Jenkins); and the lower-middle-class Celia (Patricia Roc), who meets, marries, and loses a young flyer (Gordon Jackson) who is killed in action.

In his excellent study of Launder and Gilliat, Geoff Brown notes that they had been in the forefront of the attempt to make British films more British—to replace the "wisecracking puppets" modeled on Hollywood movies with what Launder called "real people—people we know—people that live next door to us—that travel with us in the bus—that we meet in the shops and street." By 1943, such people had begun to appear in British documentaries and— much more rarely—in feature films but, as Roy Armes says, *Millions Like Us* is nevertheless "a key document of the period, posing questions about class and the durability of national unity which are smoothed over in the work of Humphrey Jennings [and other documentarists]." Gilliat himself says of this moving, funny film that "I still think it gives you, at times at any rate, the feeling of what it was like to be in a town in Britain around 1943"; most people would agree.

Millions Like Us was the only film that Launder and Gilliat codirected side by side. It was followed by Launder's first movie as sole director, *Two Thousand Women* (1944), which he also scripted. The setting is a camp where the Germans interned two thousand women after the fall of France, and the cast includes Phyllis Calvert, Pat Roc, Renée Houston, Flora Robson, and Jean Kent. Believing that his war-stricken audience needed light relief, Launder elected to play his potentially grim theme for laughs, but came to agree with critics who thought this an unfortunate decision.

There were more of the "real people" that Launder had called for in Gilliat's first solo film, *Waterloo Road* (1945), set in the working-class area around Waterloo Station in London. John Mills plays a young soldier who, hearing that a local punk (Stewart Granger) is pursuing his wife (Joy Shelton), goes absent without leave to put the matter right in a brilliantly shot and edited fight that introduced a new level of violence in British cinema. Alastair Sim gives a characteristically whimsical performance as a philosophical local doctor (and chorus). Scripted by Gilliat with Val Valentine, the film seemed to Geoff

Brown aesthetically less satisfying than *Millions Like Us*, though it digs deeper "into the fabric of working-class wartime life."

The same year, Launder and Gilliat launched their own production company, Individual Pictures, under the financial umbrella of J. Arthur Rank's Independent Producers. Its first picture was *The Rake's Progress* (*The Notorious Gentleman*, 1945), coproduced and scripted by Launder and Gilliat from a story by Val Valentine and directed by Gilliat. It finds a contemporary parallel for Hogarth's famous series of etchings in the story of Vivian Kenway (Rex Harrison), a rich young wastrel whose anarchic and destructive pursuit of excitement throughout the 1930s finds an arguably acceptable outlet in World War II. Sharply observed, caustic, and tough-minded, this uneven movie remains, of all Gilliat's films, the one closest to his heart.

Individual Pictures' next film was again scripted by its two producers but directed, this time, by Frank Launder. *I See a Dark Stranger* (1946), called *The Adventuress* in the United States, was mostly shot on location in Ireland. Deborah Kerr gives an award-winning performance as a naive Irish girl talked into spying for the Nazis, Raymond Huntley is superb as the disenchanted German agent, and Trevor Howard is there to save the day. This "delectable comedy-thriller" enjoyed great commercial success, as did Gilliat's *Green for Danger* (1946), in which Inspector Cockrill (Alastair Sim) investigates a murder in a hospital rent with suspicion and intrigue.

Green for Danger, based on a novel by Christianne Brand, was scripted by the director in collaboration with another writer (in this case Claud Gurney) but coproduced with Frank Launder—a pattern in many of the Launder-Gilliat films that followed. The picture was shot by Wilkie Cooper almost entirely in the studio, exteriors and all—the operating theatre set was built twice over, "so that to reverse shots one simply moved a couple of yards to the 'spare' theatre." A particular pleasure in this film was that, without surrendering tension, it made "capital of the very clichés of the detective novel," turning the omniscient Inspector Cockrill (as Gilliat put it) into a "spritely conceived extrovert . . . with a dash of mild sadism and a decided tendency to jump to the wrong conclusion."

A more serious and ambitious film followed from Launder, *Captain Boycott* (1947), about the plight of the Irish peasantry in the days of absentee landlords. Raymond Durgnat found it "refreshingly on the side of the rabble. It returns us to Ireland, with Cecil Parker as the English landlord, the English army playing a fascist role, and Stewart Granger saving the peasantry from a doomed uprising by inventing the boycott," though "the end result is a decidedly rosy view of Anglo-Irish history."

It was Gilliat's turn next, and he chose to adapt Norman Collins' bestseller *London Belongs to Me,* about the assorted inhabitants of a London boardinghouse in 1939, one of them (Richard Attenborough) accused of murder. As Launder said, it had "too many characters going their diverse ways in different stories." Launder's own next picture had, for most of its length, only two characters—the boy and girl who grow to maturity on a desert island in *The Blue Lagoon,* based on the novel by H. de Vere Stacpoole. Starring Jean Simmons and Donald Houston, it was Launder and Gilliat's first color film, shot by Geoffrey Unsworth partly in the studio, partly on what were then uncharted islands in the Fijis. Regarded by most critics as a cloying piece of dated romanticism, it was Launder and Gilliat's greatest box-office success.

By this time, however, Rank's Independent Producers was disintegrating and Launder and Gilliat left that organization, moving on to Alexander Korda's London Films, which offered similar facilities but more freedom. *State Secret* (*The Great Manhunt,* 1950), their first film for Korda, was directed and scripted by Gilliat, with Douglas Fairbanks Jr. as a surgeon who is abducted and taken to a mythical totalitarian country called Vosnia to operate on its dying dictator. The tyrant dies and the hero is on the run, with no one to help him but a young cabaret performer (Glynis Johns). The plot of this film is remarkably similar to that of Richard Brooks' *Crisis,* released the same year, but the setting is quite different and so is Gilliat's approach to the subject. He is said to be "a fanatic for the precise detail," and he went so far in *State Secret* as to employ a linguist to invent a fully fledged language for his Vosnians, creating in this and other ways "one of the few believable nonexistent countries in cinema."

The last movie made under the banner of Individual Pictures was also one of the most successful of them, *The Happiest Days of Your Life* (1950), directed by Launder and scripted by him and John Dighton from the latter's play. It examines what happens when a boys' school is, through bureaucratic error, sent to occupy premises already occupied by a girls' school. Margaret Rutherford plays the formidable headmistress, Alastair Sim the pained headmaster, and the result seemed to Raymond Durgnat "one of the brightest postwar comedies." Indeed, Geoff Brown called it "a well-nigh perfect example of farce balanced by sprightly dialogue" and went on: "The film has not only survived the years with its comic mechanisms still in splendid working order, it has also picked up considerable period interest" as a "picture of Britain in the years of postwar reconstruction."

Individual Pictures was replaced in 1950 by Launder-Gilliat Productions Ltd., whose first two films for Korda were both directed by Frank Launder. *Lady Godiva Rides Again* (1951), about a provincial girl (Pauline Stroud) who achieves fame and disillusionment as a beauty queen, was a rather weak farce, making little of the theme's potential for satire, but *Folly to Be Wise* (1952) was modestly successful. Adapted from James Bridie's play *It Depends What You Mean,* it has Alastair Sim as an army chaplain who organizes a quiz show that lurches into disaster when a question about marriage is put to a team that comprises husband, wife, and lover.

Gilliat's *The Story of Gilbert and Sullivan,* a much more ambitious movie, provided potted biographies of W. S. Gilbert (Robert Morley) and Arthur Sullivan (Maurice Evans), together with extracts from the famous operettas, but was disappointingly dull. Not so Launder's *The Belles of St. Trinian's* (1954), inspired by Ronald Searle's drawings of monstrous schoolgirls and starring Joyce Grenfell and Alastair Sim (the latter playing both the headmistress, Miss Fritton, and her wastrel brother Clarence). A comedy in the tradition of *The Happiest Days of Your Life,* though broader and rougher in its humor, it was hugely successful and has been followed by a string of popular sequels. Launder had another hit in *Geordie* (1955), about a Scottish weakling (Bill Travers) who takes a muscle-building correspondence course and winds up throwing the hammer for Scotland in the 1956 Olympics.

But by this time Launder and Gilliat's output was diminishing, and it slowed still further after February 1958, when they joined the board of British Lion and became increasingly involved in its vicissitudes (Gilliat as chairman of Shepperton Studios). Their most notable movie of the next few years was *Only Two Can Play* (1962), directed by Gilliat and scripted by Bryan Forbes from Kingsley Amis' novel *That Uncertain Feeling.* Peter Sellers plays John Lewis, a randy, underpaid Welsh librarian whose career potential burgeons when he catches the eye of the mayor's promiscuous wife (Mai Zetterling)—but only until his gloomy reluctant honesty reasserts itself.

Full of "relish for the endless little miseries, cruelties and vulgarities of ordinary life," this seemed to Pauline Kael "the funniest script since the heyday of Ealing." She sees John Lewis as a timid man whose "spurts of impossible behavior come out of a deep and often self-sacrificial resolve to earn the scorn of people he knows to be phony" (including Richard Attenborough's Gareth Probert, local bard and prophet of self-conscious Welshness). Gilliat apparently did a good deal of uncredited work on the script, especially the splendidly authentic scenes between Lewis and his nagging, unglamorous, but real and likable wife (Virginia Maskell).

Only Two Can Play resurrected in more sophisticated terms the concern with "real people" that distinguished the early work of Gilliat and Launder, but was the last of their films to do so. Launder's *Joey Boy* (1965), an embarrassingly old-fashioned war comedy, was followed by the most profitable of all the St. Trinian's movies, *The Great St. Trinian's Train Robbery* (1966). This was the first film since *Millions Like Us* codirected by Launder and Gilliat, though here they worked with two separate units. Neither made any more pictures until 1972, when Gilliat directed *Endless Night,* an Agatha Christie adaptation starring Hayley Mills and Hywel Bennett that earned him "the worst reviews I've ever had."

No one would claim that either Launder or Gilliat is a major artist, but as scenarists, directors, and producers they have been responsible for an extraordinary number of good films, some of them key works in the partial demolition of the class barriers that so limited and diminished the prewar British cinema. Raymond Durgnat praises in particular their "wily irreverence . . . their consistent freshness and mischief, their cheerful lightly-and-slightly anarchism, their relaxed romping in and out of the system's little loopholes and bye-ways."

Frank Launder is said to be an easy-going, optimistic, absentminded man, fond of the races. Sidney Gilliat is more intellectual in his interests and has written libretti for two operas—Malcolm Arnold's *The Open Window* (1956), based on a story by Saki, and Malcolm Williamson's *Our Man in Havana* (1963), from Graham Greene's novel. He is also less predictable in temperament than Launder, more caustic in his wit. Both men are married, with children, and both have become rich. But neither, according to Theo Richmond, has ever "been known to indulge in double-dealing, credit-stealing, backstabbing or financial thuggery. In the movie business this alone entitles them to some kind of immortality."

FILMS: *Codirected by Launder and Gilliat*—Partners in Crime, 1942 (short); Millions Like Us, 1943; The Great St. Trinian's Train Robbery, 1966. *Directed by Frank Launder*—Two Thousand Women, 1944; I See a Dark Stranger (The Adventuress), 1946; Captain Boycott, 1947; The Blue Lagoon, 1949; The Happiest Days of Your Life, 1950; Lady Godiva Rides Again, 1951; Folly to Be Wise, 1952; The Belles of St. Trinian's, 1954; Geordie (Wee Geordie), 1955; Blue Murder at St. Trinian's, 1957; The Bridal Path, 1959; The Pure Hell of St. Trinian's, 1960; Joey Boy, 1965; The Wildcats of St. Trinians, 1980. *Directed by Sidney Gilliat*—The Tryst, 1929 (amateur short); Waterloo Road, 1945; The Rake's Progress (The Notorious Gentleman), 1945; Green for Danger, 1946; London Belongs to Me (Dulcimer Street), 1948; State Secret (The Great Manhunt), 1950; The Story of Gilbert and Sullivan (Gilbert and Sullivan), 1953; The Constant Husband, 1955; Fortune Is a Woman (She Played With Fire), 1957; Left, Right and Centre, 1959; Only Two Can Play, 1962; Endless Night, 1972.

ABOUT: Armes, R. A Critical History of the British Cinema, 1978; Brown, G. Launder and Gilliat, 1977; Durgnat, R. A Mirror for England, 1970; Rubenstein, L. The Great Spy Films, 1979. *Periodicals*—Film Dope December 1979, November 1985; Films Illustrated November 1979; Monthly Film Bulletin June 17, 1982; Sight and Sound Autumn 1956, Autumn 1958.

LEAN, Sir DAVID (March 25, 1908–), British director and editor, was born in Croydon, London, the son of Francis William le Blount Lean and the former Helena Tangye. Lean was very strictly raised by his Quaker parents and forbidden the cinema, but in his early teens became a secret addict. "It had an immediate magic for me," he says, "that beam of light travelling through the smoke. I used to go regularly to the films at the Philharmonic Hall, Croydon, and travelled all the world in the cinema. I remember . . . movies like Griffith's *Way Down East* with the camera floating downriver on an ice floe: I think this early passion for outdoor films explains why I've been drawn to exterior pictures all over the world. But the man who really got me going was Rex Ingram . . . in everything he did the camerawork was impeccable."

Lean's academic record at Leighton Park School, a Quaker institution near Reading, was not particularly distinguished. On leaving he went straight to work as a trainee in the office of his father, a chartered accountant. He had no liking or aptitude for the work and in 1928, in spite of his parents' disapproval, he got himself a job as tea boy at the Gaumont British studios in London. Over the next few years Lean worked his way up through the studio hierarchy to become an editor.

It was upon this aspect of film production that Lean built his reputation, and he says that he has remained an editor at heart: "I can't keep my

DAVID LEAN

hands off the scissors." By 1930 he was chief editor at Gaumont British News, often writing and speaking the commentary as well as editing the newsreels that were then an integral part of most movie programs. In the mid-1930s he began working on feature films, and his editing credits include Gabriel Pascal's *Pygmalion* and *Major Barbara* and Michael Powell's war films *49th Parallel* (*The Invaders*) and *One of Our Aircraft Is Missing*. It was an early indication of David Lean's fastidiousness that during this period he turned down chances to direct shoddy "quota quickies," content to work as "the highest paid cutter in Britain" until in 1942 he was invited by Noel Coward to codirect a screenplay Coward had written and intended to star in.

This was *In Which We Serve* (1942), a wartime drama that follows the career of a British destroyer from its launching to its sinking in combat. The narrative focuses on three members of the crew: the captain (Coward), chief petty officer (Bernard Miles), and an ordinary seaman (John Mills). After the sinking, as they cling to a tiny life raft in the sea, their stories and the story of the ship are recalled by these three in overlapping flashbacks. In spite of some clumsy contrivances in these sequences and a good deal of class stereotyping in the characterizations, the film has a tension and realism that were warmly received by the critics and the public, though Coward inevitably received more acclaim than the unknown Lean. (In fact, much of the hard work of direction seems to have been left to Lean, who nevertheless says that Coward "taught me more about directing actors than anyone else.")

Out of *In Which We Serve* emerged the partnership of Lean, Coward, the producer Anthony Havelock-Allan, and the cameraman (later director) Ronald Neame to form Cineguild, a production company that was to be responsible for David Lean's next seven films. This development was part of a pattern that helped to establish and sustain a thriving British film industry during the 1940s, with small companies like Cineguild, The Archers, Individual Pictures, and Ealing Studios retaining their own creative freedom while benefiting from the financial backing of such larger organizations as Two Cities and the Rank Organization.

Lean's first three films as solo director were all derived from Coward plays, beginning a career that has involved him almost exclusively in literary adaptations or collaborations with distinguished writers. *This Happy Breed* (1944) follows the fortunes of a lower-middle-class family living in a small suburban house in Clapham, London, between the wars. It begins with a long shot of the rooftops of London, closing in on one particular window. The camera advances through this window just as the Gibbons family moves in, and twenty years later withdraws from the same window as they move out. Celia Johnson and Robert Newton play Ethel and Frank Gibbons, Kay Walsh (Lean's first wife) their waspish daughter, and John Mills her sailor boyfriend.

The picture was shot in color, using one of only four Technicolor cameras then in England. This was employed (by Ronald Neame) with a realism and delicacy well in advance of most contemporary color work in the United States. The problem of transposing an episodic play to the screen was not entirely overcome, but most reviewers greatly enjoyed what one in *Time* called "the many plotless little human studies which Coward wrote with such relish—Frank's advice to his bridegroom son . . . ; snappish, jagged family quarrels; a touching drunk scene between two aging ex-soldiers; Ethel's silent, terrible way of absorbing bitter news. The real hero of the film is time." It might be added that the real enemy of the film is time, also, since it has not worn well. Coward's depiction of the family, with their stoical humor and homespun philosophizing, nowadays seems irritatingly patronizing, a defect that Lean's direction fails to overcome, in spite of the formal excellence of his use of cinematic time and space.

No such problem was involved in filming the stage farce *Blithe Spirit*, since in this case Coward was writing about his own milieu. A successful novelist (Rex Harrison), researching a book about spiritualism, invites an eccentric medium to his house. As an unfortunate by-product of her activities, the spirit of his first wife (Kay Hammond) is materialized, much to the dismay of her successor (Constance Cummings). Lean's version is very much a filmed play, only very discreetly modified to take advantage of the cinema's capacity for optical illusion, but this, together with Coward's witty and irreverent dialogue, an accomplished cast, and above all Margaret Rutherford's unforgettable performance as the medium, Madame Arcati, made the movie a hit with the war-worn British public.

Brief Encounter (1945), Lean's last collaboration with Coward, was adapted from a playlet called *Still Life*. Laura (Celia Johnson) is a middle-class woman in early middle-age, contentedly married. She goes on a shopping trip to the neighboring town and at the railroad station, by chance, meets Alec (Trevor Howard), an equally conventional doctor. Without warning, they find themselves passionately in love. After a few chaste but furtive meetings, they decide to go to bed together, but their plans go awry and, shocked out of their dreams, they realize that they must part. Laura, from whose viewpoint the story is told, relives her brief encounter in her own living room with her own patient husband, listening to the poignant melodies of Rachmaninoff's Second Piano Concerto on the radio.

Lean believes that "sex is the trigger of the emotions" but also that "to reveal the animal beneath the skin of us all" can be very dangerous—that libidinal urges are "the more precious for being kept bottled up." This puritanical and peculiarly British spirit of self-sacrifice and renunciation—a recurring theme in his work—is nowadays likely to be scorned as the product of socially-induced guilt feelings and repression. Nevertheless, *Brief Encounter,* not particularly successful on release, has come to be recognized as a minor classic of the cinema—even as "the first British screen masterpiece."

From such mundane settings as the railroad station, a movie theatre, and a city park Lean draws powerfully romantic images, and he makes subtle but telling use of symbolism, like the chain that halts the couple's rented rowboat, foreshadowing the end of their affair. It was in this film also that Lean first demonstrated his mastery of subjectification, revealing Laura's state of mind through her changing reactions to the same scene, as when a lady cellist first seen as eccentrically humorous is later recalled as a figure of pathos. As John Russell Taylor says, the visual tension created by these charged images, together with the film's economy of expression and the delicacy of the acting, "fuse perfectly to capture with extraordinary vividness the tone of the time: a sort of bittersweet romanticism."

Great Expectations (1946), adapted by Lean and Ronald Neame from Dickens' novel, was a project on a much bigger scale. In spite of his devotion to literature Lean says "I'm not a word man. I'm a picture man." The truth of this is evident from the moment at the beginning of the film when the boy Pip, kneeling alone by his father's grave, rises and turns straight into the arms of the terrifying escaped convict Magwitch. Lean took full advantage of a magnificently visual story, an accomplished crew, and a cast that included John Mills (Pip), Valerie Hobson (Estella), Bernard Miles (Joe Gargery), Finlay Currie (Magwitch), Martita Hunt (magnificent as the tragically perverse Miss Havisham), Francis L. Sullivan (Jaggers), and Alec Guinness (in his first film) as Herbert Pocket.

The novel's criticism of the British class system and the spiritually crippling effects of the industrial revolution are implicit in the film also, and Lean imbues his black-and-white exteriors (shot by Guy Green on the Kent marshes) with his own kind of pantheism. Alain Silver and James Ursini in their monograph on the director describe how "Lean rapidly establishes the figurative tug of natural versus artificial impulses in Pip," and show how faithfully and skillfully he "adapts Dickens's literary tropes" into visual terms. The film enjoyed great critical and popular success, earning Oscars for best black-and-white photography, art direction, and set decoration.

Lean used much the same crew in his adaptation of *Oliver Twist,* which is more stylized than its predecessor, with a greater use of sets and interiors (meticulously recreated from the novel by John Bryan), low-key expressionistic camerawork, and deliberately melodramatic characterization. Ron Pickard has given this account of the famous opening scene (which does not exist in the novel): "It begins with a long shot of a moorland hill. A rough cart track runs down from the top of the hill towards the camera. As the camera remains motionless the faint figure of a woman, silhouetted in extreme long shot, can be seen topping the brow of the hill. Lightning flashes suddenly and Lean cuts to a close-up of the woman's agonized face. As the rain begins to fall, the woman sees the lights of a building in the distance. There is a medium shot of the woman emphasizing, as she bends under extreme pain, the advanced state of her pregnancy. Intercut is a shot of briar bending in the sudden wind, its thorns harsh and sharp against the sky, symbolizing the woman's suffering. As she staggers towards the light in the distance the camera follows from behind. She reaches the building and a man with a lantern opens the huge iron gates and helps her through. There is another flash of lightning and the words 'Parish Workhouse' above the gates are lit up. The picture fades and opens again on a tranquil night sky. On the left of the frame is the towering silhouette of the workhouse. The silence is broken suddenly by a baby's cries. The first human sounds in the entire film are those uttered by Oliver Twist as he is born. The whole scene takes six minutes. It is pure cinema."

There are other scenes almost as effective in *Oliver Twist,* including those in the workhouse, establishing with brilliant economy the drudgery, starvation, and regimentation of that institution; the scene in which Fagin instructs Oliver in the art of picking pockets; and the accelerating chase by an ever-growing crowd after Bill Sykes' dog. Alec Guinness's make-up and his highly mannered performance as Fagin provoked accusations of anti-Semitism; in fact the make-up was modeled on the original engravings by Cruikshank, but the film caused riots in Germany, and in the United States was banned for three years until cuts were made. Some critics maintain that *Oliver Twist* lacks the fine edge of observation of *Great Expectations* and is a little more romanticized, but as Ron Pickard says, it "stands as a masterly work of great visual excitement."

After these two triumphs came Lean's first failure. *The Passionate Friends (One Woman's Story* in the United States), adapted by Eric Ambler from a novel by H. G. Wells, is an "eternal triangle" story involving a millionaire banker (Claude Rains), his wife (Ann Todd), and a young scientist (Trevor Howard). In effect, it is a more glamorous version of *Brief Encounter,* transposed from the London suburbs to the Swiss Alps and marred by confusing flashbacks-within-flashbacks. Ann Todd, who was Lean's second wife, starred again in *Madeleine* (1950), another investigation of sexual transgression in a repressive age, based on a famous nineteenth-century murder trial.

Madeleine Hamilton Smith, born into the Scottish gentry, came home to Glasgow from a London finishing school and, the prosecution asserted, began a love affair with a social inferior whom she poisoned when he became an inconvenience. The charge was "not proven" and Madeleine Smith went free. Contemporary reviewers found the film stylish but excessively slow and somber, clogged with "little vignettes of persons and places." To Silver and Ursini it seems "Lean's most serious examination of nineteenth-century Great Britain. . . . Unlike most

of Lean's dreamers and visionaries, who are either destroyed by their dream or compelled to abandon it, Madeleine [at the end] has retained her integrity and isolation. . . . the enigma is all that remains."

Lean spent the next twelve months working on a screenplay that was never used. The influx of American capital at this time was sapping the strength of the British film industry, leading to a crisis that only the most resilient of the small production companies survived. For this and other reasons the Cineguild partners—Lean, Neame, and Havelock-Allan—decided to go their separate ways, and Lean joined Alexander Korda's London Films. According to Richard Griffith, he had by then established himself as "a brilliant technician, sensitive and serious about the cinema, probably the most skillful of all the young British directors, obviously waiting for real material of contemporary importance to come into his hands." What did come into his hands was a newspaper story about a jet plane that had disintegrated in flight for no known reason, though it was speculated that the cause might have been an invisible entity called the sound barrier. Lean was fascinated and spent three months visiting aircraft factories and talking to test pilots, designers, and scientists. He made a twenty-thousand-word summary of what he learned and passed it to the playwright Terence Rattigan to be fashioned into a screenplay.

Rattigan came up with a story about a tyrannical aircraft manufacturer, John Ridgefield (Ralph Richardson), who sacrifices both his son (Denholm Elliott) and his son-in-law (Nigel Patrick) in his singleminded passion to create a supersonic plane, and whose ruthlessness alienates his bereaved daughter (Ann Todd). Most reviewers found the domestic confrontations no more than conventional but thought that in the flying scenes Lean had "expressed with unequalled brilliance the conflicts between the beauty of flying and its perils, between pride of exploration and its terror." The film seemed to some a return to the documentary style of *In Which We Serve,* but others have recognized in Ridgefield one of Lean's "dreamers and visionaries," a "modern Prometheus" snatching powers from the gods on behalf of humanity, regardless of the risks. *The Sound Barrier* was selected by the British Film Academy as the best picture of 1952.

Lean took his last look at Victorian England in *Hobson's Choice* (1954), which was also his last film in black and white. Based on Harold Brighouse's play, it tells the story of Henry Hobson, a boozy petty tyrant, owner of a boot shop in Salford, Lancashire, who gets his comeuppance from his strongwilled daughter (Brenda de Banzie) and her despised beloved (John Mills). The film is an observant comedy of manners, never descending to caricature, with a tremendous larger-than-life performance by Charles Laughton as the Lancashire King Lear and some notable scenes (including an almost surreal one when the drunken shopkeeper attempts to capture the moon, chasing its reflection from puddle to puddle across the wet street, the images supplemented by Malcolm Arnold's "rumbustious, brilliantly orchestrated" music).

The second stage in Lean's career, when he ceased to be a purely British director and became an international one, began modestly but successfully with *Summertime* (1955), adapted from Arthur Laurents' play *Time of the Cuckoo*. Shot by Jack Hildyard on location in Venice, it stars Katharine Hepburn as an American spinster on vacation and Rossano Brazzi as the Venetian antique dealer she learns to love and decides to leave when he confesses that he is already married. It is another variation on the theme of *Brief Encounter*—bittersweet, frequently funny, and rescued from sentimentality by the richness of Hepburn's performance as the vulnerable, clumsy, but tough-spirited heroine and by the subtlety and intelligence of Lean's direction. Lean had already demonstrated exceptional skill in framing and angling shots so as to express the psychological states and status of his characters; here he adds color to his resources, using it to reflect the progress of the love affair, from the prosaic browns of the opening scenes, through the multi-colored skyrockets of the couple's grand passion, to the dying fires of the setting sun at the end. He had filmed in color before, but never so tellingly.

Summertime was released by Lopert Films and United Artists, and *The Bridge on the River Kwai*, which followed in 1957, was produced by Sam Spiegel for Horizon Pictures–Columbia. It was the first of the mammoth international productions for which Lean is most widely known. With American financing allowing for extended production time, starry casts, huge crews, and the most sophisticated technical resources, his films have become increasingly spectacular and increasingly perfectionist.

The Bridge on the River Kwai was made on location in Ceylon, under extremely difficult conditions, and took sixteen months to prepare and film. It was adapted from the novel by Pierre Boulle, itself based on an actual incident in World War II. The setting is Southeast Asia, where British prisoners of war are being forced by the Japanese to construct a railroad from Bangkok to Rangoon. The British commanding officer, Colonel Nicholson, agrees to help the Japanese to build a bridge across the Kwai. He sees the project first as a morale booster for his men, then as a personal memorial to which he is prepared to sacrifice anything (rather like John Ridgefield in *The Sound Barrier*). As the work nears completion, a team of Allied commandos are parachuted into the jungle to destroy the bridge before the Japanese can move vital supplies across it.

Alec Guinness plays the obsessive Colonel Nicholson and Sessue Hayakawa his Japanese opposite number, a man of a very similar type. The commandos are led by an Englishman (Jack Hawkins) and a cynical American (William Holden). The film cuts back and forth between the sufferings and psychological dramas of the prisoners and the adventures of the advancing commandos, while the conflicts of character, motive, and nationality, and the mounting suspense over the fate of the bridge, cohere to make a classically structured adventure film. It was showered with awards, bringing Lean himself an Oscar, and has enjoyed great financial success. Lean intended the film as "a painfully eloquent statement of the general folly and waste of war" but Ron Pickard calls it a picture "that does not bear too close a re-examination. Most of it today seems hollow and its antiwar attitudes are often lost in the more routine aspects of the story."

Lean worked with Sam Spiegel again on *Lawrence of Arabia* (1962). Based on T. E. Lawrence's autobiographical *Seven Pillars of Wisdom*, it was the first of Lean's films to be written by Robert Bolt, who became an indispensable collaborator. Peter O'Toole plays Lawrence, the young British officer who united the desert tribes against the Turks in World War I, and the cast also includes Omar Sharif, Alec Guinness, Anthony Quinn, Jack Hawkins, Claude Rains, and Arthur Kennedy. Starting from Lawrence's memorial service in London, the film chronicles his achievements in a sustained flashback. There are as many different interpretions of what Lawrence did as there are interpreters. Lean's Lawrence is another of the director's obsessive dreamer-heroes, a visionary in the desert, struggling in the teeth of a rigidly limiting social structure (the army) and his own human weakness to become a god and ending as something like a demon.

Lawrence of Arabia was filmed on location in Super Panavision 70mm in Jordan, Spain, Morocco, and England. It employed thousands of extras, involved the partial reconstruction of several cities, and cost fifteen million dollars. It took three years to prepare and make, and in its original form ran for almost four hours. Nevertheless, according to Silver and Ursini, "the end result can objectively be viewed as a textbook example of economic and direct filmmaking." Every scene serves a purpose in furthering the narrative or revealing character, and not even the most beautiful sunset or stirring battle scene is extended for its own sake. In fact, as Steven Ross points out, the desert landscape becomes "a presence with as much dramatic and thematic force as any character in the film"—it is "necessarily alien, inhospitable and challenging, offering a source of escape and self-discovery." One critic called this "the first truly satisfying film epic" and it received seven Oscars—for best picture, best director, best color photography, color art direction, editing, music, and sound. It remains Lean's most impressive formal achievement.

There was a more equivocal critical reception for his next picture, *Doctor Zhivago* (1965), which was nevertheless even more successful financially. Bolt's adaptation of Pasternak's immense novel arrived at what Steven Ross calls a "modified epic structure" in which the earth-shaking events of the Russian Revolution are reflected primarily in their effects on the destinies of a few individuals—the doctor-poet Yuri Zhivago (Omar Sharif), his mistress Lara (Julie Christie), and their friends and families. Unfortunately the subsidiary characters are reduced largely to stereotypes (arrogant Czarists, ruthless Bolsheviks). Ross found the film notable for "a startling, highly stylized narration flashback device that freely intermingles narration from the present with dialogue and visuals from the past," but there is no doubt that the movie owed its great popular success mostly to its poignant love story and spectacular production values. It was filmed on location in Spain, where a huge mock-up of Moscow was built on a ten-acre site outside Madrid. *Doctor Zhivago* carried off Oscars for best screenplay, color art direction, color photography, color costume design, and for Maurice Jarre's music (including the haunting "Lara's Theme"), another important factor in its success. One critic called it *"Gone with the Wind* with snow."

Lean worked with Robert Bolt for ten months on the script of *Ryan's Daughter* (1970), an original screenplay. "I spend so much time on a film's script not because I consider myself a writer, but because I consider it my homework for directing the film," Lean says, and his fidelity to the completed scenario is well known. *Ryan's Daughter* is another exploration of sexual transgression, set this time in a remote Irish village during World War I. The heroine is Rosy Ryan (Sarah Miles), a young woman whose marriage to the worthy but dull village schoolteacher (Robert Mitchum interestingly cast against type) leaves her romantic aspirations unfulfilled; she enters into a passionate affair with a shell-shocked English officer (Christopher Jones) and tragedy follows. As in *Brief Encounter,* the love story, as Lean said, is portrayed "in a purposely over-romantic way, almost like an erotic dream" so as to make all the more dramatic Rosy's "fall back to earth" and her discovery that "something has to be paid for everything."

This small-scale story is set in the spectacular landscape and seascape of the west of Ireland and against the backdrop of the Troubles. Jean Paul Torok wrote that "to insert in this monumental panorama an intimate little love story, give it a luxurious surface like the flamboyant facade on some piece of romantic architecture, elevate hidden passions to cataclysmic and tempestuous proportions, in short, to use millions of dollars to transform a banal story of adultery into a turbulent super-spectacular was a gamble which compels respect if only for being so disarmingly naive in its intentions and unique in its formula." Torok concludes that the result "could either be sublime or ridiculous and it succeeds in being both."

After *Ryan's Daughter,* there was a long hiatus in Lean's career. For a time he hoped to bring to fruition a long-cherished project, a film biography of Gandhi, but the movie was never made. Lean spent the 1970s traveling, researching, or living quietly in his villa just outside Rome. In 1978 he began work with Robert Bolt on a new version of *Mutiny on the Bounty,* but after problems over financing and Bolt's heart attack, he left the project. (The film was eventually produced as *The Bounty* [1984], directed by Roger Donaldson.) In 1984, in his mid-seventies, Lean came out of a fourteen-year retirement to direct *A Passage to India,* his own adaptation of the E. M. Forster novel and one of the finest movies of his career. Both the New York Film Critics' Circle and the National Board of Review chose Lean as the best director of the year, and one of the film's principals, Peggy Ashcroft, received an Academy Award as Best Supporting Actress. In October 1984, Lean (who had previously received a CBE in 1953) was knighted by Queen Elizabeth.

Reviews of *A Passage to India* were highly favorable, although Lean was criticized for being less than faithful to the novel. As Michael Seitz pointed out, the cast of Indian characters in the book was effectively reduced in the film to two, Dr. Aziz and Professor Godbole, with other Indians appearing as undifferentiated supernumeraries. In the role of Professor Godbole, Alec Guinness was widely regarded as an embarrassment. "Though not quite a Peter Sellers pastiche Indian," John Simon observed acidulously, "the performance seems to come not from life but from a theatrical warehouse." The fault, however, was not entirely Guinness', since he had little to work with in the way of dialogue. In the film, Godbole merely dispenses banalities, whereas in the Forster novel he is, as one critic expressed it, "a key-brahmin, emblematic of the muddle-mystery of India." Perhaps the chief flaw of the screen adaptation was the happy ending imposed by Lean on Forster's resonantly unresolved and more troubling one. Yet despite reservations expressed, critics were impressed by Lean's direction of the nearly three-hour film. John Coleman spoke of it as an "intelligent and sympathetic" work that was not only good but even marvelous; and Stanley Kauffmann found it a perfect choice for Lean's most striking talent, "his ability to deal beautifully with the large scale and the intricate, his insistence on juxtaposing them." Certain scenes particularly—the nocturnal encounter of Mrs. Moore and Dr. Aziz in a deserted mosque, the scenic train trips to Chandrapore and Marabar, and the colorful, elephant-led procession to the caves—have a haunting visual opulence. Two performances were especially praised—those of Victor Banerjee as the ingratiating and put-upon Aziz, and Dame Peggy Ashcroft as the aging Mrs. Moore.

Lean's 1960 marriage to Lelia Devi, whom he met during the filming of *The Bridge on the River Kwai*, was dissolved in 1978. At seventy-eight, the director is a handsome man, austerely elegant, reticent about his private life. He admits that "making a film does get to be a drug for me and once started, it's hard for me to stop." Lean's films have won over twenty-five Oscars and earned huge profits. He has remained highly selective about the projects he is prepared to undertake, and is one of the few directors in the world able to command almost unlimited financial backing. His kind of compulsive perfectionism is unfashionable, however, as are his commitment to stories with "a beginning, a middle and an end" and his liking for mammoth international productions. Young *cinéastes* and critics tend to dismiss him as "a masterly technician without any very marked personal approach." His admirers, on the other hand, contend that even his late films "are supremely personal works, made within the unfashionable conventions of the international 'blockbuster.'" Those who seek to identify his approach place him in the English romantic tradition, citing his admiration for individualistic visionaries, his pantheism, his poignant sense of what "might have been."

—*T.G.*

FILMS: (with Noel Coward) In Which We Serve, 1942; This Happy Breed, 1944; Blithe Spirit, 1945; Brief Encounter, 1945; Great Expectations, 1946; Oliver Twist, 1948; The Passionate Friends (U.S., One Woman's Story), 1949; Madeleine, 1950; The Sound Barrier/Breaking Through the Sound Barrier (U.S., Breaking the Sound Barrier), 1952; Hobson's Choice, 1954; Summertime (U.K., Summer Madness), 1955; The Bridge on the River Kwai, 1957; Lawrence of Arabia, 1962; Doctor Zhivago, 1965; Ryan's Daughter, 1970; A Passage to India, 1984. *Published scripts*—Doctor Zhivago, 1965.

ABOUT: Current Biography, 1953; Durgnat, R. A Mirror for England, 1970; Forman, D. Films 1945–1950, 1952; International Who's Who, 1979–80; Manvell, R. New Cinema in Britain, 1969; Pratley, G. The Cinema of David Lean, 1974; Sarris, A. (ed.) Interviews with Film Directors, 1967; Silver, A. and Ursini, J. David Lean and His Films, 1974; Who's Who, 1980. *Periodicals*—Action November–December 1973; Filmmaker's Newsletter 12 1973; Films and Filming August 1959, January 1963; Films in Review May 1974, 5 1975; London Magazine January 1965; Monogram 3 1972; New Republic January 21, 1985; New York Times Magazine May 23, 1965; Picture Post August 2, 1952; Saturday Review November 14, 1970; Take One November 1973; Time December 24, 1965; Times (London) December 5, 1970.

LEENHARDT, ROGER (July 23, 1903–December 4, 1985), French director, producer, and critic, was born into a wealthy Protestant family in Montpellier in southern France. The son of a university professor, he was sent to Paris at the age of eighteen to pursue his studies and completed a higher degree in philosophy at the Sorbonne. In 1927, however, the combination of a "romantic setback" (the object of his affections married someone else) and "a taste for adventure" impelled him to drop his studies and set out for Corsica to launch a citrus plantation. Two years later, having spent almost all of his inheritance, he made his way back to Paris and passed a foreign-service exam that got him an administrative post in French colonial Africa. When he returned to France in 1932, it was to marry "the woman of my life," Yvonne Gerber, the same woman whose first marriage had precipitated his flight to Corsica and with whom he remained for the rest of his life. They had one son, Blaise.

By the time Leenhardt had resettled himself in Paris, he had become quite interested in the cinema, as he had never been (he readily admitted) during his childhood and student years, when intellectuals still largely ignored the new medium. But even though he went several times a week to the specialized cinémathèques that were opening up all over the city, he did not at

ROGER LEENHARDT

first think of a film career; instead, he saw himself as an aspiring man of letters, practicing journalism, literary criticism, and fiction. Following the example of many French writers, he sought to enter the civil service as a way of gaining a steady income. By his own account, it was because of a hiring freeze that he wound up in the film industry instead: his cousin, a sound engineer at the Éclair Studios outside Paris, got him a trainee post as a newsreel editor, and within a short time, Leenhardt became the assistant editor of the *Éclair-Journal.* He made his first short film, *Lettre de Paris,* in 1933 and the following year set up his own production company, Les Films du Compas.

Leenhardt began to write film criticism in 1933 and in 1936–1939 contributed an extremely influential column on the cinema to the review *Esprit.* The most eminent of his disciples was André Bazin, prophet of the *nouvelle vague.* Bazin regarded Leenhardt as the first serious film critic (a view that some would dispute) and as the subtlest of them all. He has been described in Bazin's magazine *Les Cahiers du Cinéma* as "the spiritual father of the New Wave" and the formulator of its principles.

"I tried to base my criticism," Leenhardt said, "on an overall moral and intellectual view of life at the time, in line with *Esprit*'s philosophy." *Esprit* had been founded in 1932 by Emmanuel Mounier, an adherent of Personalism. This is a philosophy which in some respects resembles existentialism, and which pins its hopes for a better world on the existence of free and creative individuals. Leenhardt was the first serious European critic to champion the American cinema

which, with "that famous Anglo-Saxon pragmatism," had "showed us how to overcome the apparent incompatability between sound and image and so started us on the road towards the modern cinema." Bazin shared Leenhardt's admiration for some Hollywood directors and joined him in his advocacy of deep-focus cinematography and the moving camera. After the war, when Bazin succeeded his master as *Esprit*'s regular film columnist, Leenhardt said that Bazin's work "was a continuation of what I was doing and he took it beyond what I was trying to do." Leenhardt wrote regularly on film for *Lettres françaises* in 1944–1946 and just after the Second World War directed a program on the cinema for French radio. He also contributed to *Fontaine, Cahiers du cinéma,* and *L'Écran français,* where he made his mark with the famous declaration: "Down with Ford! Long live Wyler!" In line with his commitment to *auteur* cinema, he also helped to found several filmmakers' associations and the film festivals at Tours and Annecy.

The strength of Leenhardt's criticism derived partly from the fact that he knows the problems and possibilities of filmmaking at first hand. He made his first short, *Lettre de Paris,* in 1933—the same year that he began his critical career—and by the beginning of World War II was established as an intelligent and skillful documentarist. However, it was not until 1946 that he made a film that attracted widespread attention. This was *Naissance du cinéma,* a study of the history of the cinema that won the Grand Prix at Brussels. "Here," wrote Lo Duca, "his direction, his scrupulous accuracy, his efficient cutting, his patient reconstructions—even his voice as commentator, full of feeling and almost hierarchical, make him stand out in the inner circle of the great." At about the same time Leenhardt wrote two scripts for other directors: Pierre de Hérain's *L'Amour autour de la maison* (1946) and Jean Lods' *Aubusson* (1946).

The most famous of Leenhardt's films, and his first feature, followed in 1947—*Les Dernières Vacances (The Last Holidays).* Written by the director with Roger Breuil, it is set in 1932 in the Cévennes, in a country house whose owners have gathered to decide whether or not they must sell the property and to pursue their amorous intrigues. Against this background is set a beautifully delicate study of the first awakenings of adult feeling in two adolescents (played by Odile Versois and Michel François) who have spent all their vacations together in that house.

As Lo Duca wrote, the two themes—the end of childhood and the end of a family heritage—"complement each other, and sometimes merge into each other. . . . The decline of the bourgeoisie and of their particular virtues can have a tragic aspect . . . and one of the virtues of the scenario lies in the fact that it never allows mere mockery . . . to touch a theme which is concerned deeply with a whole civilization. . . . The scenario takes its inspiration directly from its author—his Protestant turn of mind and the influence of the Cévennes, where he was born. . . . Leenhardt has brought all his subtlety, his discretion and wisdom to the direction of the film . . . [which] attains greatness through its style, and its unity of imagination and expression." Roy Armes finds in the film "all the personal style and scope of an autobiographical novel," and other critics have warmly praised the work of the cameraman Philippe Agostini and the designer Léon Barsacq, as well as the conviction and sensitivity of Odile Versois's performance.

Les Dernières Vacances has achieved the status of a minor classic but it was not a financial success, and after several feature projects fell through, Leenhardt returned to the documentary field. Not until 1961 was he again able to make a feature film on his own terms. This was *Le Rendez-vous de minuit* (*Rendezvous at Midnight*, 1962), described by Leenhardt as a "dramatic entertainment." It concerns a woman, Eva, who becomes obsessed by a film she sees and identifies herself so completely with its heroine that she is drawn helplessly to emulate her suicide. Lili Palmer plays both Eva and the woman in the film, differentiating the two roles with great subtlety and skill, and Michel Auclair is the journalist who tries to save her. The picture, written by the director with Jean-Pierre Vivet, represents the working out of an idea that had interested him for years—that of the film within a film. David Thomson called the result "a poetic rhapsody on the beguiling nature of filmmaking," but to most critics it seemed a rather impersonal movie, though a very competent and interesting one. Leenhardt also made a feature film for television, *Une Fille dans la montagne* (1964), based on a novel written by his brother-in-law Roger Breuil, and adapted by the director and his nephew Sidney Jézéquel. Dealing with the struggle of a young woman from the Pyrennees to save her native forests, it was, in Claude Beylie's words, "an 'ecology' film before its time."

Reflecting on the fact that he made so few features, Leenhardt told Patrick Laroche in 1983 that "If I didn't make more, it's because I don't have this terrifying will that a big film demands. It takes money, and while the people who succeed with the 'big film' certainly have talent, they're also the determined types who say

'I have to have backing.' . . . Myself, maybe because the businessman's legacy is still there, I've never wanted to, and I've always been afraid of ruining a producer. . . . I'm satisfied with modest little films."

Apart from *Les Dernières Vacances*, Leenhardt's reputation as a filmmaker rests on his documentaries, most of which were made either for Les Films du Compas or its successor, Les Films Roger Leenhardt. He directed over fifty short films, many of which he had written himself; some were commercial projects undertaken for clients but others were his own productions. His regular collaborators included the cameramen Pierre Levent and Daniel Sarrade, the composer Guy Bernard, and the editor Suzanne Gaveau. Leenhardt made travelogues, documentaries on such assorted topics as charcoal, noise, and the automatic transmission, and in 1950 a notable film called *La Fugue de Mahmoud* about the modernization of agriculture in Morocco as it seems to a young Arab and to the French teacher who has become his friend. However, as a documentarist he is best known for perceptive biographies of writers and artists, including *Victor Hugo* (1951), made in collaboration with Yvonne Gerber; *François Mauriac* (1954); *Jean-Jacques* (1957), about Rousseau, made with Jean-Pierre Vivet; *Daumier* (1958); *Paul Valéry* (1959); *L'Homme à la pipe* (1962), about Gustave Courbet; and *Corot* (1965). Throughout the 1970s he continued to collaborate with Sidney Jézéquel on films for television, including a series on the history of French printmaking, *La Vie des estampes* (*The Life of Prints*, 1976). In 1979 he retired to Calvisson, in the south of France; in the remaining years of his life, he was honored with retrospectives at Bordeaux, Montpellier, Nîmes, Munich, and Padua.

Lo Duca suggests that "there are many affinities between Leenhardt and the cinema. Both of them have often lost their way, though they have always gained by the experience; both of them have searched in documentary truth for the proof of their greatness and for the strict rules which govern both mathematics and poetry." Leenhardt calls himself "an ardent admirer of a scriptwriter's cinema"—he believes that, unlike the theatre, the cinema is fundamentally "not a spectacle . . . not a public phenomenon, but a personal form of expression rather similar to novel-writing." The director appears in Jean-Luc Godard's *Une Femme mariée* (1964), addressing the camera, as David Thomson says, as the very "voice of intelligence."

FILMS: *Shorts*—Lettre de Paris, 1933 (remade in 1945); (with René Zuber) L'Orient qui vient, 1934; (with

René Zuber) Le Rezzou, 1934; Le Vrai jeu, 1934; Métro, 1934 (remade in 1950); Le Pain de Barbarie, 1934 (remade in 1949); Le Père Hugo, 1934; R.N. 37, 1937; Revêtements routiers, 1938; La Course au petrole, 1938; Fêtes de France, 1940; À la poursuite du vent, 1943 (remade for television in 1973); Le Chant des ondes, 1943; Le Chantier en ruines, 1945; Departs pour L'Allemagne, 1946; Naissance du cinéma (in English as two films: Animated Cartoons and Biography of the Motion Picture Camera), 1946; Le Barrage de l'aigle, 1946; La Côte d'Azur, 1948; Entrez dans la danse, 1948; L'Heritage du Croissant, 1950; Les Hommes du champagne, 1950; La Fugue de Mahmoud, 1950; (with Yvonne Gerber) Victor Hugo, 1951; Du Charbon et des hommes, 1952; La France est un jardin, 1953; François Mauriac, 1954; (with Jean-Pierre Vivet) Louis Capet, 1954; Ordinations, 1955; La Conquête de l'Angleterre, 1955; Notre sang, 1955; Les Transmissions hydrauliques, 1955; Le Bruit, 1955; (with Sidney Jézéquel) Bâtir à notre âge, 1956; (with Jean-Pierre Vivet) Jean-Jacques, 1957; Paris et le desert français, 1957; (with Sidney Jézéquel) En plein midi, 1957; Daumier, 1958; Paul Valéry, 1959; Le Maître de Montpellier, 1960; Entre Seine et mer, 1960; (with Sidney Jézéquel) La Traversée de la France, 1961; L'Homme à la pipe, 1962; Le Coeur de la France, 1962; Des femmes et des fleurs, 1963; 1989 [title], 1963; Monsieur de Voltaire, 1963; George, 1963; Demain Paris, 1964; Europe, 1964; Daguerre, or ou la naissance de la photographie, 1964; Corot, 1965; Monsieur Ingres, 1967; Le Beatnik et le minet, 1967; (with Sidney Jézéquel) Douze Mois en France, 1970; Abraham Bosse, 1972; Otto Dix ou la nouvelle objectivite allemande, 1973 (for television); Il y a cent ans: 1875, 1975 (for television); Pissarro, 1975; La Languedocienne, 1976; Var-matin, 1976; La Vie des estampes, 1976 (series for television); Cent Mille Images, 1977 (for television); Anjou, 1977; Du plaisir à la joie, 1978; Manet ou le novateur malgré lui, 1980 (unreleased). *Features*—Les Dernières Vacances (The Last Holidays), 1947; Le Rendez-vous de minuit (Rendezvous at Midnight), 1962; Une Fille dans la montagne (A Girl in the Mountains), 1964 (for television).

ABOUT: Armes, R. French Cinema Since 1946: 1, 1970; Bazin, A. What Is Cinema?, volume 2, 1971; Chirat, R. Le IVe République et ses films, 1985; Leenhardt, R. Chroniques du cinéma, 1986; Leenhardt, R. Les Yeux ouverts; The Oxford Companion to Film, 1976; Sadoul, G. Dictionary of Film Makers, edited and translated by Peter Morris, 1972; Thomson, D. A Biographical Dictionary of the Cinema, 1975. *Periodicals*—Avant-scène du cinéma November 1, 1980; Cahiers du cinéma January 1986; Calades (Nîmes) December 1983; Cinéma (France) January 1962; Revue du cinéma February 1986; Sight and Sound Autumn 1963.

LEISEN, MITCHELL (October 6, 1898–October 28, 1972), American director, designer, and producer, was born in Menominee, Michigan, where his father was a partner in the Leisen and Hennes Brewing Company. His parents

MITCHELL LEISEN

were divorced soon after he was born and he grew up in St. Louis with his mother and her second husband. At the age of five he was operated on to cure a club foot, and for many years after was slightly lame. This handicap made him a lonely and introspective child who spent his time designing model theatres and devising elaborate flower arrangements. In order to counteract these "unmanly" tendencies, his parents sent him to a military school. His limp kept him out of World War I, though the army hired him to drill recruits.

Leisen trained as an architect at Washington University in St. Louis, and then moved to Chicago. He worked there in the advertising department of the Chicago *Tribune* and for the architectural firm of Marshall and Fox, in his spare time acting with a little theatre company. In 1919, hearing that the war had let to a shortage of leading men in Hollywood, Leisen took some time off from Marshall and Fox and went west to reconnoitre the situation. Staying in Hollywood with Ruth St. Denis and Ted Shawn, who were family friends, he secured one small screen role but "didn't get anywhere as an actor." However, the stage sets he designed for the Hollywood Community Theatre were much admired and discussed, and brought him an introduction to Cecil B. DeMille, by then the main creative force in Famous Players–Lasky.

"DeMille was doing *Male and Female,* and he wanted some costumes designed," Leisen recalled many years later. "I had never designed any clothes in my life, but I thought, 'What the hell.'" DeMille liked his trial sketches and offered him a contract, and that was the end of

Leisen's career as an architect. After *Male and Female*, Leisen said, "I did clothes for some other pictures, but I forget what they were." Growing bored, he asked for a more challenging job and for a time worked with Cecil B. DeMille's brother William as a set dresser, then in the same capacity for Cecil himself.

Leisen was constantly at odds with DeMille's art director, Paul Iribe, and in 1922, hearing that Douglas Fairbanks needed someone to design costumes, quit to join United Artists. At about this time he met Marguerite DeLaMotte, heroine of Fairbanks' *Three Musketeers*, beginning a relationship that lasted several years. After it broke up, Leisen married Sondra Gahle, a would-be opera singer whose real name was Stella Yeager. They were married for twenty years though they seldom lived together, and Leisen, who was bisexual, continued to have other liaisons with both men and women.

He did costumes for four United Artists films—the Douglas Fairbanks *Robin Hood* (1922), *Rosita* (1923), *The Thief of Bagdad* (1924), and *Dorothy Vernon of Haddon Hall* (1924). While working on *Robin Hood*, Leisen lived for weeks on end at Pickfair, the Fairbanks-Pickford mansion, sharing the hectic work-and-play schedule of that legendary couple with Chaplin and other members of the Pickfair "court." For *The Thief of Bagdad*, he said, "we had 3,000 extras a day . . . and I had to design different costumes for all of them." Leisen was "a fiend for authenticity," and for *Dorothy Vernon* made Elizabethan costumes that were completely authentic, "even the underwear."

In 1925, when Cecil B. DeMille launched his own production company, Leisen rejoined him as set dresser on *The Road to Yesterday*. He was promoted to co–art director on *The Volga Boatman* (1926) and subsequently worked as art director, alone or with others, on nearly a score of DeMille pictures between 1927 and 1932. Leisen always took on many duties not normally assigned to the art director, and was credited also as assistant director of his last four films with DeMille: *Dynamite* (1929), *Madam Satan* (1930), *The Squaw Man* remake (1931), and *The Sign of the Cross*. After Leisen left DeMille, according to the costume designer Natalie Visart, the latter "had to hire about ten people to cover all the things Mitchell did by himself, and he was never satisfied." Leisen himself said that he owed DeMille "everything I ever learned about making pictures. The most important thing of all is the power of concentration, never deviating from your objective."

Leisen's first studio, Famous Players–Lasky, had been restructured in 1927 as the Paramount Pictures Corporation. He joined Paramount in 1933 and worked there for twenty years. His first assignment was as "associate director" of *Tonight Is Ours*, though it seems to be generally accepted that Leisen directed the movie more or less singlehanded, while the credited director, Stuart Walker, "sat alone on the set offering occasional suggestions." Adapted from Noel Coward's play *The Queen Was in the Parlor*, the picture was shot in eighteen days for $86,000 but achieves an impression of lavish elegance, thanks to Theodore Sparkuhl's heavily diffused photography and Leisen's inventive lighting and rearrangement of sets left over from *The Smiling Lieutenant* and other Lubitsch films.

Claudette Colbert stars as a Ruritanian aristocrat who meets a charming American (Fredric March) in Paris. They are about to marry when she is summoned home to assume the duties of queen. She is glumly preparing for a marriage of political convenience when she is rescued by a revolution whose leaders demand her marriage to a commoner—like the March character, who at that point conveniently appears. In spite of the clumsiness of the adaptation, this "dreamily romantic" movie impressed reviewers with its "wonderful quality of sensuousness."

Leisen was again credited only as associate director of *The Eagle and the Hawk* (1933), though Stuart Walker reportedly had even less to do with this film than with its predecessor. It tells the story of a World War I air ace, Jeremiah Young (Fredric March), idolized as a hero but anguished by the deaths on his conscience. After a brief encounter on leave with "the Beautiful Lady" (Carole Lombard), he returns to the front. Unable to bear the slaughter any longer, he kills himself.

As John Baxter says, "his suicide is shot from below the bare springs of a stripped bed—that of . . . [a colleague], killed that morning—and his dead face stares down at us while, in the background, his friend (Cary Grant) walks in to discover the body." In a misguided attempt to protect Jeremiah's reputation, his buddy takes his body on a last flight and riddles it with machine-gun bullets, so that it will seem that Jeremiah died in action. This powerful and sometimes brilliant film was reissued in 1939 with Leisen now credited as codirector, but with its pacifist message diluted. Among the scenes cut was the final one showing Cary Grant as a drunk haunted by the mockery he had made of his friend's death.

The first picture credited to Mitchell Leisen alone was *Cradle Song* (1933), a sentimental and unsuccessful vehicle for the German actress

Dorothea Wieck. It was followed by *Death Takes a Holiday* (1934), Leisen's first big commercial success. Adapted by Maxwell Anderson and others from Anderson's play, it tells how Death comes to earth in the shape of the recently deceased Prince Sirki (Fredric March). For three days, nothing and nobody dies, while Death tastes all the earthly pleasures, seeking to understand why human beings fear him and cling so desperately to life. In the end, through Grazia (Evelyn Venable), he discovers the beauty and the power of love, and she returns with him to his own country.

Leisen had Ernst Fegté as his art director on this film, set in a Florentine *palazzo* whose great rooms and "drooping Italianate gardens" are of critical importance in establishing the mood. Leisen regarded Fegté as one of the greatest of art directors, and would "move heaven and earth" to secure his services. Fegté was equally complimentary about Leisen—"just about the only director I've ever known who could read blueprints . . . and visualized the whole thing." The film's photographer, Charles Lang, spoke no less admiringly of Leisen's abilities: "Mitch had a tremendous feel for the cameras; I guess it was because of his experience as an art director. He always placed the cameras himself. I'd give him the finder and he'd tell me what angles he wanted."

These quotations are from David Chierichetti's book about Leisen, *Hollywood Director* (1973), a Louis B. Mayer American Oral History Project based on prolonged interviews with the director just before his death, and with many of his associates. In the same work, Leisen describes how he achieved two of the movie's most remarkable effects—that of Death's apparent transparency in a scene where another actor appears "solid," and the sequence in which March's face changes gradually into a skull.

For the first effect, Leisen said, "we duplicated certain parts of the set in black velvet. Then we put a mirror in front of Freddy that was only thirty percent silvered so that you could shoot through it. In order to make him transparent, we simply lit up portions of the black set which reflected in the mirror superimposed over Freddy, giving the appearance that he was transparent." For the skull effect, March's face was made up in red like a skull: "Under red light, the make-up didn't show and he looked normal. Then by dissolving the red light out and bringing the green light in, the make-up slowly began to show until his face became a skull."

John Baxter found the result of all this ingenuity and talent "a strange film . . . skating the delicate line between poetry and comedy"; other modern opinions of the picture suggest that it may have worn less well than Leisen's comedies, but in 1934 it secured the director's position at Paramount. It was followed by a work of a startlingly different nature, *Murder at the Vanities* (1934). A combination of backstage musical and murder mystery, it featured Jack Oakie as the hard-pressed stage manager of Earl Carroll's Vanities and Victor McLaglen as the police sergeant investigating the two killings that disrupt the opening night.

Leisen insisted on staging the musical numbers within the bounds of a life-sized proscenium, refusing on principle to "do a Buzz Berkeley routine with a stage that's acres big." Within these spatial confines, writes David Chierichetti, he "pushed the limits of bawdiness and nudity further than they would go in any American film until the 1960s." The film's most notorious number is "Sweet Marijuana," in which Gertrude Michael sings of being reunited with her lost lover in drug-induced dreams before being shot dead on stage.

After the melodramatic *Behold My Wife* came another thriller with a musical revue setting, *Four Hours to Kill*, and then an excellent "screwball" comedy, *Hands Across the Table* (1935). Carole Lombard stars as a manicurist in search of a rich husband and Fred MacMurray (then little known) as an impoverished playboy in search of an heiress. Critics found a new complexity in Leisen's style—tender or introspective moments that deepen the characterization. It was the first of Leisen's many "role-reversal" movies in which, as Chierichetti says, the woman is presented as "self-sufficient, successful and aggressive, man as a sexual object valued more for his looks and charm than intellect or ability."

Thirteen Hours by Air, an early example of the disaster movie genre, was followed by *The Big Broadcast of 1937*, with Jack Benny as manager of a radio station, Burns and Allen as his sponsors, and a gallery of guest artists that included Leopold Stokowski, Benny Goodman, and Martha Raye. Entertaining as it was, the film offered little scope for Leisen's talents, but ushered in the period of his greatest triumphs, beginning with *Swing High, Swing Low* (1937).

This comedy-drama was adapted by Virginia Van Upp and Oscar Hammerstein II from a stage play, *Burlesque*, already filmed as *The Dance of Life*. Maggie King (Carole Lombard), an incompetent hairdresser on a cruise liner, falls in love in Panama with Skid Johnson (Fred MacMurray), a talented, witty, self-destructive trumpet player. She jumps ship and gets herself a job as a singer in a nightclub, where Skid joins her. They are married, but Skid is seduced away to New York by Anita (Dorothy Lamour) and divorce follows. Skid declines into alcoholism, drinking himself almost to death. His last chance is a radio audition for which he can hardly stand, but Maggie reappears and, with her physically supporting him, he somehow gets through an irresistibly moving performance of their old song, "A Call to Arms."

Until recently a "lost" film, *Swing High, Swing Low* enshrines what some regard as Carole Lombard's greatest performance. In it, wrote *Photoplay's* reviewer, "by turns beautiful, comic, drab, heart-stirring," she "reaches glory." Leisen spoke of his extraordinary rapport with the "profane angel" Lombard, attributing it to the fact that they were both Librans, born on October 6th. He discusses her in less superstitious terms in his illuminating account of the difference between stage and screen acting, quoted by Chierichetti: "In a play, you're working out of a cone to a proscenium arch that's at least thirty feet across. On the screen, it's just the reverse. You're working down to the point of the cone, to a proscenium arch the size of your lens, approximately two inches. As you get closer to your camera, the action becomes more mental and less physical. With a close-up, the actor only thinks. Subtle changes take place in the musculature of the face from the thoughts. If an actor has an expressive face, as Garbo did, it was quite wonderful. . . . Carole Lombard had the same quality. . . . The principal problem then is to get them to think what their character would be thinking."

Much better known today is *Easy Living* (1937), wittily scripted by Preston Sturges from a story by Vera Caspary. During an argument, millionaire Edward Arnold throws his wife's fur coat out of the window. It lands on the back of poor working girl Jean Arthur, who on this account is promptly identified as Arnold's mistress. Far from making her a social outcast, this misunderstanding elevates her to a position of great prestige and power, so that a casual remark from her is enough to precipitate a stock market crash. All ends happily, with Jean Arthur in the arms of the millionaire's son (Ray Milland).

Only moderately successful on release, *Easy Living* is nowadays regarded as one of the classic social comedies of the 1930s, though in some ways it is atypical of Leisen's best work—a comedy of situation rather than of character. More successful in its day was *The Big Broadcast of 1938,* set on an ocean liner but more or less following the formula of its predecessor of 1937. It was in this movie that Bob Hope first sang (with Shirley Ross) what became his theme song, "Thanks for the Memory." Making this picture

was an ordeal for Leisen, who was in constant conflict with its arrogant star, W. C. Fields. When shooting finished in November 1937, he went home and had his first heart attack. After six weeks in bed he returned to work on another successful if unexceptional musical, *Artists and Models Abroad* (1938).

Leisen's next film was of a very different caliber, and indeed is regarded by many critics as his masterpiece although (like *Easy Living*) it was underrated in its day. *Midnight* (1939) was produced by Arthur Hornblow Jr., with whom Leisen always worked well, photographed by Charles Lang, and provided by Charles Brackett and Billy Wilder with an excellent script. Stranded in Paris, feather-brained "gold digger" Eve Peabody (Claudette Colbert) is ardently pursued by Tibor Czerny (Don Ameche), a wisecracking taxi-driver. A rich man (John Barrymore) sets her up in society, where she is to lure the handsome Francis Lederer away from Barrymore's wife (Mary Astor). Eve is posing as a countess when Czerny intrudes, posing as the count her husband. This ploy enforces a fake divorce, which is followed by Eve's realization that she actually loves Czerny—and this in turn by the revelation that the latter drives a cab only by vocation, and really is a count.

John Baxter writes of *Midnight,* "one of the best comedies of the Thirties," that "there is a happy ending, but no plot twist can dispel the film's essential bitterness. Like all Leisen films, it is callous and cynical, its style faultless, its design superb." David Chierichetti agrees that the picture conveys "a vague feeling of cruelty and deceit sugar-coated by wit and the conventions of a genteel society," but attributes these qualities to the script rather than to the "optimistic" Leisen who, in Chierichetti's opinion, makes even the avaricious heroine "human and sympathetic." And David Stewart Hull has described this as "a genuinely great film . . . in many ways the swansong of Thirties comedy, a last great gasp before the advent of Preston Sturges as a director of a new kind of comedy."

Leisen (serving for the first time as his own producer) had Sturges as his scenarist on *Remember the Night* (1940), called "a warmly sentimental comedy-drama." Fred MacMurray plays a decent district attorney who takes jewel thief Barbara Stanwyck home for Christmas when her trial is adjourned. The warmth and affection she finds in the bosom of his family (headed by Beulah Bondi) cracks her tough shell, in one of several Leisen films contrasting big-city values with those of Middle America.

After a year of unrealized projects came Leisen's first war movie since *The Eagle and the*

Hawk. Arise My Love (1940) was produced by Hornblow, photographed by Lang, and scripted by Charles Brackett. It begins in Spain just after the civil war, when reporter Claudette Colbert rescues American flyer Ray Milland from a firing squad by pretending to be his wife. Moving on to Paris and elsewhere, they fall in love in the deepening shadow of World War II, sail for America, are torpedoed, and decide to stay in Europe to fight Nazi tyranny. William Whitebait called it "a love story in the Hemingway tradition. . . . Realism, relish of the picaresque and a certain playfulness about human relations in an erupting world give this film its touch of authenticity."

Leisen made two more movies with Hornblow as his producer. *I Wanted Wings* (1941) follows the fortunes of three young trainee pilots (Ray Milland, William Holden, Wayne Morris). A great box-office success, it has a scene-stealing performance by Veronica Lake in her movie debut. *Hold Back the Dawn* (1941), written by Brackett and Wilder from a story by Ketti Frings, was considerably more original. The setting is a Mexican border town, where assorted refugees from war-torn Europe cluster in the hope of gaining entry to the United States.

One of the few Leisen films with any serious social content, the picture makes a strong case against the inhumanity of the quota laws in a series of vignettes illustrating the pathetic plight of the immigrants. The central character, however, is the least deserving of the refugees—a shady Romanian (Charles Boyer) who charms and marries a naive schoolteacher (Olivia de Havilland) in order to acquire American citizenship, but in the end falls genuinely in love. Paulette Goddard plays his former accomplice and mistress.

The story is told in flashback by Boyer to a film director (played by Leisen himself) after most of it has happened. William Whitebait wrote that Leisen uses flashback to brilliant effect, so that "we get the benefit of all those inflexions of irony and later knowledge belonging to personal narrative. . . . And the background of the little Mexican town—with its fiestas and bullfights; its gates opening to let tourists pop in and closed against refugees who want to slip out; its immigrant officer [sympathetically played by Walter Abel], cafés, colonnades and main square in the sun—is splendidly realized. There is one hotel, ironically named the Esperanza, which we get to know in every cranny of its shabby and queerly derelict living; and the view widens to an empty coastline and to a nearby village where there is a marriage festival in progress." Revived in 1982, it seemed to Howard Thompson a "luminous romantic drama."

Leisen was loaned to Columbia for *The Lady Is Willing* (1942), a "witless" comedy-drama with Marlene Dietrich as a Broadway star intent on a marriage of convenience so that she can adopt an abandoned baby. Back at Paramount he made two middling comedies scripted by Claude Binyon, both dealing with a "career woman" who meets an *homme fatal*. In *Take a Letter, Darling,* Rosalind Russell is an advertising executive who hires Fred MacMurray as her personal secretary; in *No Time for Love,* photographer Claudette Colbert falls for a rugged sandhog (also played by MacMurray) after dreaming about him in the role of Superman.

Dreams play a critical role in the much more ambitious film that followed in 1944, *Lady in the Dark,* adapted from the Moss Hart play inspired by the dramatist's experience of analysis. Leisen had also spent many years in analysis, and completely revised the script credited to Frances Goodrich and Albert Hackett. As he did for many of his pictures, Leisen designed some of the costumes for the movie's very large cast (including the fabulous mink dress worn by Ginger Rogers).

Rogers is the "lady in the dark," a dynamic fashion magazine editor who suddenly finds herself unable to make decisions. She consults an analyst (Barry Sullivan) and, after experiencing three colorful dreams (complete with songs by Kurt Weill and Ira Gershwin), comes to understand that she loves the man she had thought of as her *bête noire,* the magazine's insolent advertising manager (Ray Milland).

Using the three-strip Technicolor process for the first time, mostly in a remarkably restrained fashion, Leisen allowed full saturation only for the dream sequences: the "blue dream" in which Rogers sees herself posing for a portrait that will adorn the new two-cent stamp; the "gold dream" in which she envisages her marriage to her fatherly suitor and realizes that she dislikes the idea; and the surrealistic "circus dream" in which she is brought to trial for refusing to make up her mind.

C. A. Lejeune prophesied that "this combination of elementary Freud and advanced flummery" would be an immense success, and so it was. But, as David Chierichetti says, it also "contains the first signs of . . . Leisen's decline as an artist" in that, for the first time in his career, "he let the form . . . overpower the content." Gilbert Adair similarly saw it as the movie in which "the Paramount style curdled into . . . rampant window-dressing."

Numerous explanations have been offered for the inadequacies of *Lady in the Dark.* The size and complexity of the project necessitated the use of technicians who were not members of Leisen's devoted team, and this led to long-lasting resentments. The director found Ginger Rogers very difficult to work with, and said afterwards that the production had aged him ten years. Some of the film's best moments were reportedly mangled by the studio.

According to David Chierichetti, there was another and more personal reason for Leisen's loss of control. Around 1938 he had become infatuated with Billy Daniels, a dancer in the revues that Leisen regularly staged at the Coconut Grove, and a bit-player in *Lady in the Dark* and other Leisen movies. Chierichetti writes that "although homosexuality *per se* was hardly uncommon in Hollywood, most of Leisen's friends found Daniels vulgar and distasteful, and while they continued to work with Leisen at the studio, they stopped seeing him socially. . . . By the mid–1940s, Daniels was having a clearly deleterious effect on Leisen's career. The trouble Daniels caused on the set of *Lady in the Dark, Dream Girl* and *Bride of Vengeance* was particularly evident, as was a profound loss of self-confidence in everything Leisen did. By the time of his final break with Daniels, Leisen was in his early fifties and his era as one of Hollywood's top directors was over."

In 1944, however, this eventuality was still years away and, if Leisen never equaled his triumphs of the 1930s, he made a number of notable films after *Lady in the Dark,* beginning with his adaptation of Daphne Du Maurier's *Frenchman's Creek* (1944). Gilbert Adair said that it was "claptrap from start to finish," but enjoyed it nevertheless as "a sumptuous costume melodrama . . . ravishingly designed [by Leisen and Ernst Fegté, who earned an Oscar], exquisitely photographed, [and] amusingly played by Joan Fontaine."

Kitty (1945) starred Paulette Goddard as a Cockney street girl in Restoration London, painted by Gainsborough and transmuted into a marriageable lady of fashion by a penniless Pygmalion on the make (Ray Milland). It won citations for its historical accuracy and was a major box-office hit. One British critic wrote that the "shoddy story" was "enshrined in the most beautiful and meticulously faithful English period settings ever filmed in Britain or anywhere," and added: "There are, in the unfolding of this story, sequences which have an insight and poetry rarely encountered outside the French cinema."

There was no less praise for *To Each His Own* (1946), produced by Charles Brackett (who also scripted with Jacques Thery). Olivia de Havilland won an Oscar for her performance as a middle-aged businesswoman, long separated from her illegitimate son, who reencounters him as a young American flyer in World War II London. John Lund plays both the heroine's lover, killed in the first World War, and his son—a casting, Molly Haskell suggested, that "revealingly suggests the extent to which an American woman's feelings for son and lover are identical." In spite of the banality of the story, David Thomson called this "the most serene and moving of women's pictures. . . . The plastic harmony of the film is more than Lubitsch ever achieved, and more tranquil than Sirk has ever managed."

The hit comedy *Suddenly It's Spring* (1947), with Paulette Goddard as an army marriage counselor and Fred MacMurray as her restive husband, was followed by an equally successful farrago of nonsense called *Golden Earrings.* These adornments are worn by Marlene Dietrich in her role as an earthy, sensual gypsy woman in World War II Germany who rescues stuffy Ray Milland simultaneously from the Nazis and his own inhibitions. Ian Christie thought it "an archaic mixture of fairytale and melodrama, yet surprisingly effective in Leisen's sympathetic hands."

It was after this exotic entertainment that Leisen's decline became obvious, exacerbated by his personal unhappiness, his difficult relationship with the producer Richard Maibaum, and the fact that many of his key collaborators had by then left Paramount. Losing his best writers, Andrew Sarris wrote, Leisen found himself in "the unenviable position of an expert diamond cutter working with lumpy coal."

Dream Girl (1948), starring the egregious Betty Hutton in an adaptation of Elmer Rice's play, was a flop. *Song of Surrender* (1949) was scarcely more successful, though some consider that this off-beat period piece set in rural New England deserves reconsideration. *Bride of Vengeance* (1949), with Paulette Goddard miscast as Lucretia Borgia, was excoriated by the critics, and *Captain Carey, USA* (1950), an art-and-espionage thriller, seemed to David Chierichetti "the worst film of . . . [Leisen's] entire career." It is remembered, if at all, for its Oscar-winning theme song "Mona Lisa," not for its "hopeless script."

No Man of Her Own (1950), a bleak, despairing *film noir,* showed something of Leisen's old quality. He had liked *I Married a Dead Man,* the novel by "William Irish" (Cornell Woolrich), and (uncredited) virtually wrote the adaptation himself. Barbara Stanwyck is the heroine, pregnant and unmarried, who impersonates a more fortunate woman killed in a train accident and then is blackmailed by her unfaithful lover.

Leisen's Indian summer continued with *The Mating Season* (1951), produced and coscripted by Charles Brackett, and shot by Charles Lang. Thelma Ritter gives a characteristically bravura performance as a wisecracking New Jersey hash-slinger who visits her ambitious son (John Lund) and his rich wife (Gene Tierney) and is taken for the new cook. She more or less graciously accepts this role—until Tierney's autocratic mother (Miriam Hopkins) moves in. Ian Christie found this "a sharp and sensitive social comedy."

After *Darling, How Could You!* (1951), a comedy of less interest, Leisen went freelance. He believed that Paramount had been feeding him weak scripts quite deliberately to make him relinquish his lavish contract, and in the end he did so. His first non-Paramount picture, made for MGM in 1952, was *Young Man With Ideas,* starring Glenn Ford as a young lawyer who goes west to seek his fortune; it was the first Leisen movie to be released as a second feature.

Tonight We Sing (Fox, 1953), ostensibly a biopic of the impresario Sol Hurok (David Wayne), was primarily a showcase for popular operatic, ballet, and concert artists (and a bid to repeat the success of *The Great Caruso*). Seeking to counter his damaging reputation as a spend-thrift director, Leisen used great ingenuity to achieve expensive effects very cheaply. It seemed to Ian Christie "interesting for Leisen's fastidious . . . *mise-en-scène* in the musical se-quences and as one of the relatively few exam-ples of his impressive use of colour . . . an inventory of stylistic segments, a repertoire of problems elegantly 'solved.'"

Nevertheless, Leisen remained unemployed for a year after this film. In 1953 he began work on *Red Garters* back at Paramount, but a few days into shooting was taken off the picture without explanation. Another period of unem-ployment ended in 1954, when he directed a plodding thriller, *Bedevilled,* for MGM. His last feature, *The Girl Most Likely* (1957), was also the last picture made at RKO. A return to the theme of *Lady in the Dark* and *Dream Girl,* this not uninteresting film starred Jane Powell as a girl who finds herself engaged simultaneously to three men and dreamily imagines what mar-riage to each would be like.

Beginning in 1955, Leisen turned to televi-sion, directing episodes in *GE Theatre, Shirley Temple's Storybook, Twilight Zone, Wagon Train,* and worse. His health deteriorated rapid-ly after 1960. Afflicted with ulcers, emphysema, and impaired vision, he nevertheless went on working until 1966. In 1967 he was credited as codirector of *Spree,* a documentary that used footage Leisen had shot a few years earlier in Las Vegas. In 1970 he was hospitalized and his left leg was amputated. Two years later he died.

In his heyday, Mitch Leisen had been at the very center of Hollywood society. According to Chierichetti, "the whole town turned out twice a year for the openings of his lavish revues at the Coconut Grove," and people begged and lied for invitations to his parties. The hangers-on disap-peared when Leisen's reputation began to slip, and his old age was lonely as well as painful. "To me," said Ernst Fegté, "Mitch's career was like a star that got brighter and brighter until it ex-ploded and the remnants fell to earth."

Robin Wood has said that he has "difficulty in understanding, or feeling any sympathy with, the intermittent attempts to elevate . . . Leisen to *auteur* status," though "one can credit Leisen with being an effective and decently reticent coordinator." Gilbert Adair called him "a minor, derivative filmmaker" who was, "unlike Wilder or Sturges, incapable of forging a personal vision out of the Paramount 'look.'"

More generous critics, like David Thomson, maintain that in fact Leisen was "the man most responsible for the lustrous look of Paramount films." Thomson goes on: "There is a dreaming lightness and grace in the way Leisen's stories move, a wealth of meaning in the decor and a gallery of enchanting performances from his actresses." His decline "should not conceal Leisen's proper position as a leading American director." For John Gillett, the "very precision and economy" of Leisen's best films "testify to the effectiveness of this 'invisible' director." John Baxter agrees that Leisen was "a major di-rectorial talent."

FILMS: (as associate director) Tonight Is Ours, 1933; (as associate director) The Eagle and the Hawk, 1933; Cradle Song, 1933; Death Takes a Holiday, 1934; Mur-der at the Vanities, 1934; Behold My Wife, 1935; Four Hours to Kill, 1935; Hands Across the Table, 1935; Thirteen Hours by Air, 1936; The Big Broadcast of 1937, 1936; Swing High, Swing Low, 1937; Easy Liv-ing, 1937; The Big Broadcast of 1938, 1938; Artists and Models Abroad, 1938; Midnight, 1939; Remember the Night, 1940; Arise My Love, 1940; I Wanted Wings, 1941; Hold Back the Dawn, 1941; The Lady Is Will-ing, 1942; Take a Letter, Darling, 1942; No Time for Love, 1943; Lady in the Dark, 1944; Frenchman's Creek, 1944; Practically Yours, 1944; Kitty, 1945; Mas-querade in Mexico, 1945; To Each His Own, 1946; Suddenly It's Spring, 1947; Golden Earrings, 1947; Dream Girl, 1948; Song of Surrender, 1949; Bride of Vengeance, 1949; Captain Carey, USA, 1950; No Man of Her Own, 1950; The Mating Season, 1951; Darling, How Could You!, 1951; Young Man With Ideas, 1952; Tonight We Sing, 1953; Bedevilled, 1955; The Girl Most Likely, 1957; (with Walon Green) Spree, 1967 (documentary).

ABOUT: Baxter, J. Hollywood in the Thirties, 1968; Chierichetti, D. Hollywood Director: The Career of Mitchell Leisen, 1973; Roud, R. (ed.) Cinema: A Critical Dictionary, 1980; Sarris, A. The American Cinema, 1968; Thomson, D. A Biographical Dictionary of the Cinema, 1980. *Periodicals*—Action November–December 1969; Cinema (USA) Spring 1973; Film Digest (Australia) February 1966; Journal of Popular Film and Television Fall 1980; National Film Theatre Booklet (Britain) September 1979; Sight and Sound Summer 1980.

*LENI, PAUL (July 8, 1885–1929), German director, art director, and scenarist, was born in Stuttgart. He went to Berlin when he was fifteen and studied painting there at the Academy of Creative Arts. According to some accounts he was a member of the Berlin *Sturm* group, which advocated expressionism in all the arts, and beginning in 1903 he worked as a set designer in various theatres in Berlin and elsewhere—notably for Max Reinhardt, the prophet of expressionism in the theatre, and for Reinhardt's disciple Leopold Jessner. He also designed posters for both plays and films before entering the cinema as an art director.

The first movie Leni designed seems to have been Joe May's *Das Panzergewölbe* (1914) and his debut as a director came two years later with *Das Tagebuch des Dr. Hart* (*Dr. Hart's Diary*). In 1917 he was assistant or associate director of Alexander von Antalffy's *Das Rätsel von Bangalor* (*The Riddle of Bangalor*), which he also scripted in collaboration with Rudolf Kurtz, later the author of *Expressionismus und Film*. During the next four years Leni designed films by E. A. Dupont, Joe May, and others while directing six movies of his own. These were *Dornröschen* (*Sleeping Beauty,* 1917); *Die Platonische Ehe* (*The Platonic Marriage,* 1919); *Prinz Kuckuck* (*Prince Cuckoo,* 1919), based on a novel by Otto Julius Bierbaur, and starring Conrad Veidt; *Patience* (1920), also with Veidt; *Fiesco* (1921); and *Das Gespensterschiff* (*The Ghost Ship,* 1921).

The same year, working in collaboration with his former employer Leopold Jessner, Leni made *Die Hintertreppe* (*Backstairs,* 1921), the first of his films to attract serious critical attention. Written by Carl Mayer, it was a pioneer example of the so-called *Kammerspielfilm,* a form devised by Mayer in imitation of Max Reinhardt's *Kammerspiele* (chamber plays). Mayer went on to write better examples of the genre, including Murnau's *Der Letzte Mann,* but the intention remained the same—intimate psychological dramas devoted to the analysis of a demoralized lower middle class, and distinguished

PAUL LENI

by the eschewal of narrative titles in favor of a total reliance on cinematic means.

Die Hintertreppe is about a servant girl (played by an overweight and badly miscast Henny Porten) whose letters from her absent lover are intercepted by a jealous and somewhat deranged postman (Fritz Kortner). Thinking herself abandoned, the girl in her misery visits the postman in his squalid basement, where she is discovered by her returning lover (Wilhelm Dieterle, later better known as the director William Dieterle). The maddened postman murders the lover with an ax and the girl, equally distracted, throws herself off the roof. Jessner seems to have been responsible for directing the actors, Leni for the photography and the design. There are some telling images and some memorable sets, but neither director seems to have resolved the conflict between the naturalism of the *Kammerspielfilm* and their shared proclivity for expressionism.

Expressionism, which achieved great influence in all the arts in Germany after World War I, rejects surface naturalism, seeking through various kinds of distortion to represent symbolically the deepest emotions and instincts of the artist or his characters. It was when Leni was able wholeheartedly to explore the cinematic possibilities of expressionism that he had his first major success. This was in *Das Wachsfigurenkabinett* (*Waxworks,* 1924), which he modeled on the prototypical expressionist movie, *The Cabinet of Dr. Caligari,* and which was scripted for him by the expressionist scenarist and director Henryk Galeen.

As in *Caligari,* the story opens at a fairground,

where a showman employs a hungry young poet (Wilhelm Dieterle) to write stories about three of the wax figures he is exhibiting in his chamber of horrors. The stories are enacted as he writes them. The first deals with Haroun-al-Rashid (Emil Jannings) and takes the form of a fairly lighthearted burlesque on the foibles of Oriental despots. Ivan the Terrible (Conrad Veidt), by contrast, is a monstrous tyrant who uses his power to indulge his passion for torture (and who goes mad when one of his own ingenious torments is turned against himself). The exhausted poet falls asleep and in his nightmare he and the showman's pretty daughter are pursued through the deserted fairground by the third wax figure, Jack the Ripper (Werner Krauss). A fourth episode was planned but abandoned for lack of funds.

Leni designed *Waxworks* himself in collaboration with Ernst Stern. Lotte Eisner pointed out the contrast between the "puffy, dough-like settings" used in the encounter between Haroun-al-Rashid and the baker's wife and the "misty chiaroscuro" of the Ivan episode, in which "the low ceilings and vaults oblige the characters to stoop, and force them into those jerky movements and broken gestures which produce the extravagant curves and diagonals required by Expressionist precept."

The openly artificial painted sets of *Caligari* are most closely imitated in the third episode, described by Siegfried Kracauer as "a very short sequence which must be counted among the greatest achievements of film art. It evolves outside the waxworks, in the fair with which the audience has already been familiarized by the framing story. But what in the framing story was no more than a crowded pleasure spot is now a deserted hunting ground for specters. Expressionist canvases, ingenious lighting effects and many other devices at hand in 1924 have been used to create this eerie phantasmagoria, which substantiates more forcibly than the analogous decor in *Caligari* the notion of chaos. Disparate architectural fragments form pell-mell complexes, doors open of their own accord and all proportions and relations deport from the normal."

Leni himself explained that in *Waxworks* he had "tried to create sets so stylized that they evince no idea of reality. My fairground is sketched in with an utter renunciation of detail. All it seeks to engender is an indescribable fluidity of light, moving shapes, shadows, lines, and curves. It is not extreme reality that the camera perceives, but the reality of the inner event, which is more profound, effective and moving than what we see through everyday eyes. . . . It will be seen that a designer must not construct 'fine' sets. He must penetrate the surface of things and reach their heart. . . . It is this which makes him an artist. Otherwise I can see no reason why he should not be replaced by an adroit apprentice carpenter."

Waxworks was a great success, critically and commercially. According to Lotte Eisner, Eisenstein himself used it as a model in the filming of *Ivan the Terrible*, "particularly in the disposition of the figures on the screen, and the way in which they are reduced to ornaments, their gestures frozen to the point of a carefully elaborate abstraction." Eisner was one of the very few critics to have serious reservations about *Waxworks*; she thought it a regression to the decorative expressionism of *Caligari* and wrote that, for all the film's manifest virtuosity, "a sort of resolute perfectionism, an over-refined composition, an excessive mannerism, can make the spectator feel uncomfortable."

Throughout the early 1920s, in spite of his burgeoning reputation as a director, Leni continued to design movies for such other filmmakers as Dupont, Joe May, Richard Oswald, and Alexander Korda, and also did occasional stints as scenarist and even as an actor. He was also something of a cinema theorist, as the quotation above shows. Henri Langlois asserts—on what evidence he does not say—that "in all the films on which Leni worked as a designer . . . the dominant personality is Leni's, all the more so in that . . . he was more than a designer." According to Langlois, "From 1919 to 1924 . . . Paul Leni had been—along with the script-writer Carl Mayer—a veritable *éminence grise* to the German cinema."

In 1927, however, Leni joined the German invasion of Hollywood, invited by Carl Laemmle to become a Universal director. The first and best of the films he made there was *The Cat and the Canary* (1927), based on the Broadway hit by John Willard. The setting is the mansion of an eccentric millionaire and the movie opens with a famous shot of the old man on his deathbed, "dwarfed by gigantic bottles and snarling cats," which dissolves into our first view of his "spiky old castle." It emerges that his entire fortune is to go to the young and beautiful Annabelle West (Laura La Plante)—so long as she is certified sane by the old man's doctor (who eventually arrives in a costume modeled on that worn by Werner Krauss as Dr. Caligari). Needless to say, things promptly begin to happen that are horrifying enough to threaten Annabelle's reason.

A Museum of Modern Art program note points out that Leni did not design his own sets for his Hollywood films: "The touch of Leni is evident rather in the dramatic lighting of the interiors and particularly in the gothic effect obtained in the long entrance hall. The oblique camera angles, the scene looking downward on the assembled characters, the shot through the high back of a chair were expected not only of any German director at the time but of directors in Hollywood generally." Nevertheless, the film was recognized as outstanding in its use of these so-called German angles—some critics indeed thought them rather gimmicky in their ingenuity. There were also complaints about the weakness of the film's comic touches and suggestions that a director of Leni's stature should have been found an assignment "more appropriate to his peculiar talent for evoking spiritual rather than physical terror."

Most reviewers, however, shared the view of one in the New York *Times* who wrote that it was "the first time that a mystery melodrama has been lifted into the realms of art." And Lotte Eisner considered that Leni only really mastered his craft in Hollywood: "In the United States Paul Leni was to realize the necessity of intensifying the 'mood' and of going beyond mere enjoyment in the baroque and in the use of a superabundance of forms. The set stops being a game or a subterfuge and becomes part of the action. In *The Cat and the Canary* a long dark corridor, light-colored richly draped curtains falling over the numerous windows, the enigmatic housekeeper holding an oil-lamp in the foreground while her black form throws a heavy shadow—all these details provoke an inexpressible feeling of horror. Having learnt how to master his settings, Leni made films which have close links with the universe of Hoffmann. He no longer needed facile accessories."

The Cat and the Canary launched a whole cycle of Universal horror movies and was itself remade in sound in 1930 as *The Cat Creeps* and again in 1939 as a comedy vehicle for Bob Hope and Paulette Goddard. Hitchcock was influenced by it, and indeed it introduced so many now familiar devices—clutching hands, sliding panels, bodies falling out of cupboards into the camera—that it has suffered from its own inventiveness. Joe Franklin listed it in his *Classics of the Silent Cinema* as one of the "Fifty Great Films," noting that it "doesn't survive the years without creaking a little, but this is not so much due to defects in the film itself as to the fact that it was really a blueprint of its own species."

After this triumphant debut, Leni's second Hollywood film, *The Chinese Parrot* (1927), seems to have made little impact, but *The Man Who Laughs* (1928) is a gothic extravagance of some interest, based on a novel by Victor Hugo. Conrad Veidt plays Gwynplaine, heir to a rebel peer tortured to death by James II. As a small child his own face had been mutilated into a permanent hideous grin, and he had been raised by a traveling showman along with Dea, a blind waif who loves him but et cetera. Working for the first time with a large budget, Leni seemed to Paul Rotha to have become slack and slovenly, his film "a travesty of cinematic methods"; Carlos Clarens called it "the most relentlessly Germanic film to have come out of Hollywood." All the same, it has its admirers, who commend its "architectural style" and strong sense of mood.

The Last Warning (1929), set in a theatre beset by mysterious "accidents," is closer to the style of *The Cat and the Canary*, mixing "pleasant comic episodes" with macabre effects achieved by the use of ultra-mobile cameras and elaborate lighting and design, and again starring Laura La Plante. It was the first—and, as it turned out, the only one—of Leni's films to include some sound sequences. He died suddenly soon after it was completed, apparently of blood poisoning.

FILMS: Das Tagebuch des Dr. Hart, 1916; Dornröschen (Sleeping Beauty), 1917; Die Platonische Ehe, 1919; Prinz Kuckuck (Prince Cuckoo), 1919; Patience, 1920; Fiesco/Die Verschwörung zu Genua, 1921; Das Gespensterschiff, 1921; (with Leopold Jessner) Die Hintertreppe (Backstairs), 1921; Komödie der Leidenschaften, 1921; Das Wachsfigurenkabinett (Waxworks), 1924; The Cat and the Canary, 1927; The Chinese Parrot, 1927; The Man Who Laughs, 1928; The Last Warning, 1929.

ABOUT: Buache, F. Paul Leni, 1968 (in French); Eisner, L. The Haunted Screen, 1969; Kracauer, S. From Caligari to Hitler, 1947; Kurtz, R. Expressionismus und Film, 1926; Oxford Companion to Film, 1976; Petrie, G. Hollywood Destinies: European Directors in America, 1922–1931, 1986; Rotha, P. The Film Till Now, 1930; Roud, R. (ed.) Cinema: A Critical Dictionary, 1980. *Periodicals*—Films in Review November 1969.

LEROY, MERVYN (October 15, 1900–September 13, 1987), American director and producer, was born in San Francisco, the only child of Harry LeRoy and the former Edna Armer. His father owned the Fair, a small department store in the city. Both parents came from Jewish families that, LeRoy says in his autobiography, "had been in San Francisco for a couple of generations" and had become "assimilated to the point of complete absorption."

LeRoy had two older cousins, Jesse and Blanche Lasky, who were vaudevillians, a circumstance that "helped kindle my interest in show business." His mother was also devoted to

MERVYN LEROY

vaudeville and the theatre, though only as a spectator. Thanks to her contacts, LeRoy made his stage debut at six months, carried on at the Alcazar Theatre as the papoose in *The Squaw Man*. (A few years later the infant George Stevens appeared on the same famous stage in *Sappho*.)

When LeRoy was five, his mother went off with the man who subsequently became her second husband, Percy Teeple. They moved no further than Oakland, where LeRoy and his father frequently visited them, but the event was the first trauma of the boy's childhood. The second followed within a year—the San Francisco earthquake of 1906. It ruined LeRoy's father, destroying both the family home and Harry LeRoy's beloved store. He subsequently found work as a salesman, but "he was a beaten man."

LeRoy never went hungry, but he wanted more than bare subsistence and, at the age of twelve or thirteen, quit school to become a newsboy. "I saw life in the raw on the streets of San Francisco," he says. "I met the cops and the whores and the reporters and the bartenders and the Chinese and the fishermen and the shopkeepers. . . . When it came time for me to make motion pictures, I made movies that were real, because I knew at first hand how real people behaved." Newsboys "had to battle it out for choice corners" and LeRoy, who was small but wiry, fought his way from a corner in Oakland to the two pitches he most desired, "the lucrative corner at the Saint Francis Hotel in the morning, and the exciting corner in front of the Alcazar Theatre in the evening."

When he was fourteen, hawking his papers outside the Alcazar, the actor Theodore Roberts noticed him and gave him a one-line role in a play called *Barbarie Frietchie*. After that, he says, "the stage bug had bitten, and the itch would never leave me." He began to compete in amateur talent contests as "The Singing Newsboy," before long promoting himself to "Mervyn LeRoy, the Boy Tenor of the Generation." According to some accounts, he appeared around this time as a child actor in one or more of Bronco Billy Anderson's films.

In 1916, LeRoy met another would-be vaudevillian, Clyde Cooper, and teamed up with him as "LeRoy and Cooper, Two Kids and a Piano." After a while they were signed by one of the vaudeville circuits and toured all over the country with growing success. LeRoy says: "I learned show business from the bottom up. I learned the value of dialogue, the value of music, the value of timing." After three years, the act broke up. Stranded in New York and penniless, LeRoy swallowed his pride and went to see his cousin Jesse Lasky, who had quit vaudeville and risen to power and wealth as one of the first movie moguls, chief of Famous Players–Lasky. Jesse gave him his train fare to Los Angeles and a note to the studio.

LeRoy arrived in Hollywood in 1919 (not in 1923, as for some reason he states in his autobiography). He found that he had a menial job in the wardrobe department at $12.50 a week. Whenever he could, he would "visit the stages and watch them make movies," soon deciding that "the director seemed to be at the center of the artistic universe" there.

Tiring of the smell of mothballs, LeRoy talked himself into a job in the lab as a film tinter, at the same time trading on his extraordinarily youthful appearance to secure juvenile roles in two or three forgotten movies. One day, William DeMille was directing a movie that called for the effect of moonlight shining on water. No one knew how to achieve this, but that night LeRoy stayed late at the lab and rigged the shot with a black box full of distilled water and a spotlight. This coup brought LeRoy a back-breaking job as assistant cameraman, and after about six months as an undersized beast of burden, he was promoted to second cameraman, responsible for loading the camera and pulling focus. That advance was short-lived, ending when LeRoy ruined the first footage he handled.

Deciding that his movie career was finished, he returned to vaudeville. Within a year he was back in Hollywood, intent on a new career as an actor. LeRoy played a ghost in Alfred E. Green's *The Ghost Breaker* (1922), a crooked jockey in Arthur Rosson and Johnny Hines' *Little Johnny*

Jones (1923), a bellboy in Lloyd Ingraham's *Going Up* (1923), and three or four other small roles in 1923–1924. He was evidently only moderately talented as an actor, but had impressed Alfred E. Green with his gifts as a gagman during the filming of *The Ghost Breaker*. In 1924, when Green offered him a job as gagwriter, he moved behind the camera "with no regrets."

LeRoy worked with Green and others as a "comedy constructor" on a series of films that included *In Hollywood With Potash and Perlmutter* (1924), *Sally* (1925), *The Desert Flower* (1925), *The Pace That Thrills* (1925), *Ella Cinders* (1926), *Irene* (1926), and *Orchids and Ermine* (1927). The majority of these pictures starred Colleen Moore, who became a close friend. It was through her influence at First National that LeRoy secured his first directorial assignment, *No Place To Go* (1928), starring Mary Astor as a banker's daughter who sails to the South Seas in search of romance and finds more than she bargained for.

No Place To Go was adapted from a *Saturday Evening Post* story that LeRoy had found himself. In his first film he initiated a number of policies that he was to follow throughout his career—wide and constant reading in search of stories with "heart"; insistence that the script be complete before shooting began (by no means as general a policy as might be supposed); and the equally thorough advance working-out of camera angles. Shot in five weeks at a cost of about $70,000, *No Place To Go* made a modest profit—another useful precedent. LeRoy claimed that "all my pictures—and I made seventy-five of them—have been money-makers."

His second film, *Harold Teen* (1928), certainly was. Based on Carl Ed's popular comic strip, and starring Arthur Lake and Alice White, it apparently grossed a million dollars. By the end of 1928, LeRoy was making a thousand dollars a week. A string of comedies and romances followed in 1928–1930 from First National and its successor, Warner Brothers. LeRoy's first sound film was the backstage romance *Broadway Babies* (1929), in which the heroine (Alice White) is briefly infatuated with a gangster. A similar situation is central in *Playing Around*, made in 1930 and also starring Alice White, while in *Numbered Men* (1930), the hero (Raymond Hackett) is a convict, jailed for counterfeiting.

But LeRoy's most important contribution to the burgeoning gangster genre was *Little Caesar* (1930), scripted by Francis Faragoh from the novel by W. R. Burnett. It traces the rise and fall of Rico Bandelli, a Chicago mobster modeled on Al Capone, ending with his death in a back alley

and the famous last words: "Mother of Mercy, is this the end of Rico?" LeRoy had to fight for permission to film Burnett's rawly realistic novel, the Warners' front office then being of the opinion that Depression audiences wanted only light relief. The director lost a lesser battle with his employers—to cast as Rico's crony Joe Masara an unknown young actor he had discovered in a play called *The Last Mile*. He was told that he had wasted a screen test on a man whose ears were too big for a screen career, so the part went to Douglas Fairbanks Jr. and Clark Gable joined MGM.

Rico Bandelli is a primitive in pursuit of the American Dream, self-righteously convinced that hard work, clean living, and murder are the poor man's way to the top. The psychological complexity and brutal vitality of Edward G. Robinson's performance made him a star overnight. Equally admired was the almost documentary realism with which the film portrays the criminal milieu and, as Kingsley Canham writes, "the ethnic and family-orientated customs and loyalties that it openly portrayed became iconographical features of the genre." William Wolf suggests that it was also the "landmark film" in its use of the new sound medium: "The incessant noise of the machine guns, the chilling scream of brakes . . . dramatically impressed upon the public the blessings of sound."

Richard Watts Jr. called *Little Caesar* "the truest, most ambitious and most distinguished" of the contemporary rash of gangster movies, "pushing into the background the usual romantic conventions of the theme and concentrating on characterization rather than on plot." Dwight Macdonald went so far as to call it "the most successful talkie that has yet been made in this country," with "a dynamic driving pace which carried through to the very end"; LeRoy had "adroitly modulated the tone from tense drama (as in the gangsters' inner sanctum scenes) to satire (as in the superb banquet episode) to the bleakest realism (as in the last reel)." Forty years later Peter Waymark found it "still as fast and abrasive as when it was made." Though there was a good deal of criticism of the film's callousness and violence, it was an overwhelming box-office success.

LeRoy made six films in 1931, two of them vehicles for the rubber-mouthed comedian Joe E. Brown. The most notable of the year's output was *Five Star Final*, a tough newspaper story in the tradition of *Front Page*, scripted by Robert Lord from a play by Louis Weitzenkorn. Edward G. Robinson stars again as Randall, a cynical city editor who, stuck for a story, dredges up a twenty-year-old one involving a woman who had killed her lover. One of Randall's reporters impersonates a priest (Boris Karloff played this part with relish) to secure a photograph of the wretched woman's daughter, and Randall publishes it, causing so much anguish that the woman kills herself. Seeing what he has done, Randall reforms and delivers a great diatribe against yellow journalism.

Five Star Final was chosen as one of the year's ten best movies by *Film Daily,* and nominated for an Oscar. William K. Everson, discussing a recent revival of the film, wrote that "of all the gangster, newspaper and 'social' melodramas of the early 1930s that together form a kind of loose genre all their own, *Five Star Final* is far and away still one of the best—and least dated. . . . Despite a preponderance of dialogue, one hardly ever thinks of . . . [it] as having come from the stage. . . . What must have been a difficult and possibly tedious scene on stage (the mother trying desperately to get the managing editor on the phone) becomes simultaneously poignant and exciting thanks to some of the best utilisation of a split screen ever seen."

Two Seconds (1932), one of the most original of the Warners low-life dramas, was scripted by Harvey Thew from a story by Lester Elliott and this time casts Robinson as a convicted killer. Reporters gather to watch his execution. The condemned is led in, contemptuously studies his audience, and is strapped into the chair. The switch is thrown and, in the two seconds before his heart stops, he relives the events that had brought him to this end. It had been a life of almost unrelieved bleakness. He had worked as a scaffolder, sharing a squalid room with his best friend (Preston Foster) until the day when, drunk on speakeasy gin, a teacup grotesquely still stuck on his finger, he had married a dancehall "hostess" (Vivienne Foster).

The death of his friend in a shocking fall from a high scaffold begins his mental collapse, and his wife's open scorn for him and his poverty completes the process. From the top of his scaffolding, people begin to look "like flies" to him, and one day he kills the fly who happens to be his wife. The trial, according to Kingsley Canham, is a brilliantly conceived affair of "abstract low-key lighting with a single spot illuminating Robinson's face, leaving the judge and jury barely discernible in the gloom."

This Zolaesque drama was followed by *Big City Blues* (1932), a relatively lightweight but highly efficient entertainment. It has Eric Linden as a hick in New York. He is conned by his city slicker cousin, falls in love with a chorus girl (Joan Blondell), and is wrongly accused of mur-

der before he retires to the safety of Indiana. Guy Kibbee contributes a notable supporting performance as a dimwitted hotel detective who prowls the corridors, intermittently fortifying himself with shots of illicit booze in the laundry room.

Lucien Hubbard wrote *Three on a Match* (1932), a fast-paced melodrama following the fortunes of three old school friends after a reunion. Joan Blondell has become a showgirl, Bette Davis a hard-working stenographer, and Ann Dvorak a wealthy but dissatisfied socialite. After the fateful reunion, Dvorak falls for a hustler and leaves her rich husband. The latter marries Blondell, who engages Davis as a nanny. The climax comes when Dvorak's lover kidnaps her child. The mother, by now a drink-sodden wreck, spectacularly commits suicide, defenestrating herself with the kidnapper's whereabouts lipsticked on her nightdress.

John Baxter thinks this "an unconventional film for LeRoy. The social message is there, but he betrays also a Curtiz-like concern with pace not especially typical of him. There are some neat transitions. Dvorak's quick slide to the gutter is summed up in a brief scene, with two chauffeurs chatting while they wait for their employers. . . . One points out a ragged figure standing on the other side of the street, and confides that she is the woman who used to employ him, his present boss being a girl who, until a year ago, had been a friend of hers. The camera moves in to Dvorak, ashamed and down at heel, then to Blondell leaving the beauty shop. The point is made quickly, and with intelligence."

The picture that followed remains the most admired of all LeRoy's films, *I Am a Fugitive From a Chain Gang* (1932). An escaped convict named Robert Elliott Burns sold Warners a fictionalized account of his own experiences and worked with the dramatist Sheridan Gibney on the screenplay. In the film, Burns is called Jim Allen and played by Paul Muni. A veteran of World War I, he is wrongly convicted of theft and condemned to the inhuman cruelties of a Georgia chain gang, eventually escaping to live as a fugitive in Los Angeles.

As William R. Meyer says, LeRoy largely avoids the graphic depiction of brutality, relying on the power of suggestion—when Muni is flogged, "the main sound heard is that of screaming, while the images portrayed are the shadow of a whip thrashing a back and the men's horrified faces." In the famous final scene, Jim Allen's girl asks him how he manages to stay alive in Los Angeles without a job, and he hisses: "I steal," before vanishing into a pool of darkness. This brilliant effect was achieved accidentally, when a klieg light blew a fuse. Recognizing its power, LeRoy retained it, only substituting a more gradual dimming to darkness.

I Am a Fugitive broke box-office records and shared an Oscar as best picture with *Forty Second Street*. It was received with adulatory reviews everywhere except in Georgia, whose state government brought a libel suit against Warner Brothers. LeRoy was warned never to set foot in the state. Nevertheless, as a direct result of the film and the public outrage it caused, various reforms were instituted in the state's penal system including (eventually) the abolition of shackles and leg irons.

LeRoy had yet another hit with his next movie, *Hard to Handle* (1933), starring James Cagney as a heartless con man who believes that "the public's like a cow bellowing to be milked," but who meets his match in Ruth Donnelly, the social-climbing money-grubbing mother of his beloved (Mary Brian). Dwight Macdonald wrote that it was "a commonplace affair as to plot and dialogue . . . but LeRoy keeps the mechanism purring along at such a smooth, swift pace that one is not bored. . . . He gets impetus every now and then by a quick succession of short shots dissolving into each other every five seconds or so. Above all, he doesn't dot his i's. Once his point is made, he moves on at once. Essentially, it is the vaudeville black-out technique." There are some who believe that this little-known film is one of the best of LeRoy's "golden age."

After a couple of minor pieces came the "ebullient and witty" *Gold Diggers of 1933*, generally regarded as one of the classic film musicals of the 1930s. The "gold diggers" are Ruby Keeler, Ginger Rogers, Joan Blondell, and Aline MacMahon—showgirls looking for work. Ned Sparks plays a producer looking for an "angel," and Dick Powell is the playboy songsmith who writes, subsidizes, and stars in the show that makes all their dreams come true. The movie features some of Busby Berkeley's most spectacular production numbers, including the stunning opening with Ginger Rogers garbed in gold dollars and the Depression-conscious finale, "My Forgotten Man."

The World Changes (1933) stars Paul Muni as an industrialist of immigrant stock who cuts himself off from his family roots as he climbs to wealth and power. This somewhat tedious film has a memorable performance by Aline MacMahon as the hero's embittered mother. The same underrated actress starred in *Heat Lightning* (1934), a powerful melodrama set in an Arizona small town. She plays a middle-aged woman with a past whose attempts to save her younger sister (Ann Dvorak) from involvement

with a petty crook (Preston Foster) lead her to murder. MacMahon did her best work under LeRoy's direction; after he left Warners, she drifted back into supporting roles.

A musical comedy, *Happiness Ahead* (1934), was followed by *Oil for the Lamps of China* (1935), from the novel by Alice Tisdale Hobart. The book deals with the activities of a ruthless American oil company in China, centering on an executive (Pat O'Brien) whose devotion to the company costs him the love of his wife and the life of his child. The novel's indictment of the methods and morals of big business is considerably softened in Laird Doyle's screenplay, but the picture has nevertheless been much admired for the quality of its direction and acting and for Tony Gaudio's photography. John Baxter calls it "one of the few films of the Thirties to deal exclusively with the problems of work," and "a brave attempt to generalise about the conflict between individuality and social allegiance."

After three routine movies came the most ambitious of LeRoy's Warner Brothers pictures, the $2 million adaptation of Hervey Allen's sprawling historical novel *Anthony Adverse*. It had Fredric March in the title role, Olivia de Havilland as the heroine, Claude Rains and Gale Sondergaard as the villains. The film had a mixed reception, some critics finding it too long and too slow, but it collected four Oscars—for best supporting actress (Sondergaard), best photography (Tony Gaudio), best musical score (Leo Forbstein), and best editing (Ralph Dawson).

One of the finest movies of LeRoy's career followed in 1937, *They Won't Forget*, adapted by Robert Rossen and Aben Kandel from a novel by Ward Greene. Claude Rains plays an unscrupulous Southern district attorney ambitious for the governorship who sees his chance when a coed is found murdered. (The coed, in a tight sweater, is Lana Turner, one of LeRoy's discoveries.) Aided by the gutter press, the DA builds up a sensational case on circumstantial evidence against the dead girl's teacher Robert Hale (Edward Norris), a Northerner. Mob fury mounts when the verdict of "guilty" is set aside by the governor, and Hale is hanged by a lynch mob. "I wonder if he really did it," a journalist says to the DA at the end; "I wonder," echoes the DA.

The poisonous claustrophobia and demoralizing heat of small-town Southern life are powerfully conveyed in a film that Frank S. Nugent called "a brilliant sociological drama and a trenchant film editorial against intolerance and hatred." It contains some of LeRoy's most telling and memorable images—the corpse crumpled at the bottom of an elevator shaft, lit fitfully by the beams of torches; a high angle shot of a terrified black janitor lying on a cell cot surrounded by sweating cops intent on a confession; above all the images accompanying the lynching, which occurs off screen, after the mob has snatched Hale from the train carrying him to safety. As Lewis Jacobs describes it, we cut from the mob scene to "a mailbag suspended from a crosstree beside the railroad tracks. At the moment of the lynching . . . , a train roars by, emitting an unearthly shriek as a steel hook extended from the mail car catches the sack and whirls it away."

LeRoy also acted as producer of James Whale's *The Great Garrick* in 1937, and the following year he directed his last film for Warners, a comedy called *Fools for Scandal.* After that he moved to MGM, succeeding Irving Thalberg as supervisor of production at the phenomenal salary of $6,000 a week. He produced four films, including the hugely successful *The Wizard of Oz* (1939), but found himself increasingly frustrated in the role of executive. In the end, MGM gave way and let him return to directing. At the MGM "glamor factory," LeRoy became a very different kind of filmmaker from the socially conscious realist he had been at Warners, as was evident from his first film there.

This was *Waterloo Bridge* (1940), one of three screen versions of Robert E. Sherwood's melodrama about the doomed love affair in World War I between a beautiful young ballet dancer (Vivien Leigh) and an aristocratic Scottish officer (Robert Taylor). The film, in Bosley Crowther's words, "spins a dream-world of sentiment," but spins it very skillfully. Basil Wright noted that "the sequence where the heroine, standing solitary and despairing on Waterloo Bridge, is fascinated by the wheels of a passing convoy of ambulances and eventually flings herself under one of them, is very well constructed, its mounting rhythm recalling some of the thrills of the early Russian films. The scenes dealing with prostitution are also handled with a tact which depends on a subtle, almost casual, registration of minor details."

LeRoy directed Greer Garson and Walter Pidgeon in *Blossoms in the Dust* (1941), a highly romanticized biography of Edna Gladney, the campaigner for the rights of illegitimate children; and Garson again in *Random Harvest* (1942), James Hilton's tearjerker about the love affair between an impulsive Scottish lass and an amnesiac officer (Ronald Colman). James Agee recommended the latter to those "who could with pleasure eat a bowl of Yardley's shaving soap for breakfast" and it was, of course, immensely successful. "The sheer lavishness of the décor and design," wrote Kingsley Canham, "the loud romantic score, and the measured pace of

the acting, camerawork, and narrative development, illustrate the difference between Warner and MGM product." Garson and Pidgeon discover radium in *Madame Curie* (1943), described by Agee as "safe, smooth, respectable, an epitome of all that the bourgeois likes what he calls his art to be."

Thirty Seconds Over Tokyo (1944) was one of the better American films of World War II. Scripted by Dalton Trumbo, it stars Van Johnson as Lieutenant Ted Lawson, who led the first bombing raid on Tokyo and lost a leg in the process. Spencer Tracy plays General Jimmy Doolittle. LeRoy's remake of *Little Women* (1949), with June Allyson, was a work of "picture-postcard prettiness," much inferior to George Cukor's 1933 version starring Katharine Hepburn. LeRoy's decline into mere glossiness continued with his $12 million remake of *Quo Vadis?* (1951), a critical flop. More entertaining was *Million Dollar Mermaid* (1952), a romantic biopic of the swimming star of the silents, Annette Kellerman, starring her modern counterpart Esther Williams, and with lavish aquatic numbers staged by Busby Berkeley.

LeRoy had been finding life at MGM increasingly difficult after the enthronement of Dore Schary, and in 1955 he returned to Warners. Some critics see evidence of a renewal in the movies LeRoy made at his old studio, but it is a claim that is hard to substantiate. Perhaps the best of his late films were the naval comedy-drama *Mister Roberts* (1955), completed by LeRoy when John Ford became ill, and *Home Before Dark* (1958). The latter stars Jean Simmons as a woman obsessively in love with her cold-hearted college professor husband (Dan O'Herlihy). Her only hope of sanity is to overcome her jealous dependency. For Arthur Knight, the picture was raised "far above the level of tract or treatise" by "the performances that Mervyn LeRoy has drawn from his entire cast, but particularly from Jean Simmons as the insecure, uncertain, and frightened girl determined to keep her precarious hold on sanity."

Raymond Rohauer suggests that LeRoy's "range and diversity have seldom been equaled by any other producer-director," but the same could be said for the unevenness of his work. His worst films, as John Baxter remarks, are "impossible to watch." But, working for Warners in the 1930s, he made eight or nine movies that fully justify Peter Waymark's description of him as "one of the great Hollywood craftsmen," and John Baxter's claim that he was, at his best, "an artist of ideas." LeRoy was first married to Harry Warner's daughter Doris, by whom he had a son and a daughter. After their divorce in 1943, LeRoy made a second marriage to Kitty Spiegel.

FILMS: No Place To Go/Her Primitive Mate, 1927; Harold Teen, 1928; Flying Romeos, 1928; Oh, Kay!, 1928; Naughty Baby (U.K., Reckless Rosie), 1929; Hot Stuff, 1929; Broadway Babies/Broadway Daddies, 1929; Little Johnny Jones, 1929; Playing Around, 1930; Showgirl in Hollywood, 1930; Numbered Men, 1930; Top Speed, 1930; Little Caesar, 1930; A Gentleman's Fate, 1931; Too Young To Marry/Broken Dishes, 1931; Broad-Minded, 1931; Five Star Final (on TV called One Fatal Hour), 1931; Local Boy Makes Good, 1931; Tonight or Never, 1931; High Pressure, 1932; Heart of New York, 1932; Two Seconds, 1932; Big City Blues, 1932; Three on a Match, 1932; I Am a Fugitive From a Chain Gang, 1932; Hard to Handle, 1933; Tugboat Annie, 1933; Elmer the Great, 1933; Gold Diggers of 1933, 1933; The World Changes, 1933; Heat Lightning, 1934; Hi, Nellie!, 1934; Happiness Ahead, 1934; Oil for the Lamps of China, 1935; Page Miss Glory, 1935; I Found Stella Parish, 1935; Sweet Adeline, 1935; Anthony Adverse, 1936; Three Men on a Horse, 1936; The King and the Chorus Girl, 1937; They Won't Forget, 1937; Fools for Scandal, 1938; Waterloo Bridge, 1940; Escape, 1940 (reissued as When the Door Opened); Blossoms in the Dust, 1941; Unholy Partners, 1941; Johnny Eager, 1941; Random Harvest, 1942; Madame Curie, 1943; Thirty Seconds Over Tokyo, 1944; Without Reservations, 1946; Homecoming, 1948; Little Women, 1949; Any Number Can Play, 1949; East Side, West Side, 1950; Quo Vadis?, 1951; Lovely to Look At, 1952; Million Dollar Mermaid (U.K., The One Piece Bathing Suit), 1952; Latin Lovers, 1953; Rose Marie, 1954; Strange Lady in Town, 1955; (with John Ford) Mister Roberts, 1955; The Bad Seed, 1956; Toward the Unknown (U.K., Brink of Hell), 1956; No Time for Sergeants, 1958; Home Before Dark, 1958; The FBI Story, 1959; Wake Me When It's Over, 1960; The Devil at 4 O'Clock, 1961; A Majority of One, 1961; Gypsy, 1962; Mary, Mary, 1963; Moment to Moment, 1965.

ABOUT: Baxter, J. Hollywood in the Thirties, 1968; Canham, K. Mervyn LeRoy in The Hollywood Professionals, Vol. 5, 1976; LeRoy, M. (as told to Dick Kleiner) Mervyn LeRoy: Take One, 1974; Meyer, W. R. Warner Brothers Directors, 1978; Roud, R. (ed.) Cinema: A Critical Dictionary, 1980. Periodicals—Action November–December 1974; Cinematographe October 1982; Cine Revue September 2, 1982; Film Ideal 220–221 1970; Photoplay December 1974.

LEWIN, ALBERT (September 23, 1894–May 9, 1968), American director, scenarist, and producer, was born into an immigrant family in Brooklyn, the youngest of the three children of Marcus and Yetta Lewin, and grew up in Newark, New Jersey. According to Lewin's autobiographical note in The Real Tinsel, his father had held a variety of jobs: waterboy on a railroad construction gang, machine-operator in a shirt factory, and at one time "the only newsdealer in Flatbush." He was a bookish man who read

ALBERT LEWIN

Shakespeare (in German) as well as Lessing and Schiller. But the dominant figure in Lewin's childhood was his mother. "She was illiterate, but an extraordinary, intelligent and quite marvelous person; very, very capable. The Jews didn't educate their daughters. Her brothers were schooled, but she wasn't. My mother was passionately determined that her children would have the education she didn't have. Out of a little neighborhood ice-cream store in Newark, she sent three children through college."

Despite his family's relative poverty, therefore, Lewin had a highly cultured upbringing, "uncorrupted by any religious training whatever." Both his parents loved music, and took him regularly to opera at the Met. Lewin took to all this with enthusiasm, studied assiduously, and won several scholarships to help himself through school. At New York University he majored in literature, played mandolin in the Glee Club, and "thought I was Keats and Shelley and Coleridge all wrapped into one." After graduating from NYU in 1915—head of his class and Phi Beta Kappa—he spent a year reading for his English MA at Harvard, where he was a charter member of the Poetry Society. ("We wrote bad verses and read them at each other.") He then taught briefly at the University of Missouri, before joining the American Jewish Relief Committee, of which he became Assistant National Director. In 1918 he was married to Mildred Mindlin.

At NYU, Lewin had helped pay his way through college by writing occasional pieces for the Newark Evening News. Now his friend Bernard Bergman, who was editing the Jewish

Tribune, offered him the post of drama critic—unpaid, apart from the free theatre tickets. Since both Lewin and his wife loved the theatre, he readily accepted, the more so since Bergman gave him a free hand to review whatever he liked. This soon came to include cinema. Lewin was particularly impressed by the films coming out of Italy and Germany: "What really got me going was *The Cabinet of Dr. Caligari,* which I still think was the finest film ever made. I decided I didn't want to be a mediocre poet. . . . I wanted to do something in films."

Through a friend of Bergman's, a major exhibitor in Philadelphia, Lewin contacted Sam Goldwyn, who gave him a $50-a-week job as a reader—reading novels with an eye to their screen potential and writing synopses of them. Lewin found the work like being "a squirrel in a cage," but stuck it out in New York for nearly a year, before heading in 1923 for Goldwyn's Culver City studios and demanding something nearer the action. After some persistence, since he was reckoned to be "overeducated," he landed a job as a script clerk (responsible for continuity), in which capacity he worked with King Vidor and Victor Sjöström. "It was a tremendous education—how they directed and how they worked, how they handled the actors, how they staged the scenes." He also worked, unofficially, in the cutting room, picking up further useful skills.

In 1924 Lewin moved to Metro as a screenwriter. His first assignment was to produce a script from a novel by Charles Norris, unpromisingly entitled *Bread.* Several other writers, he later discovered, had failed to make anything of this stodgy material, but Lewin succeeded in turning out a usable script, which was filmed (1924) with Victor Schertzinger directing. While the film was in production, Metro was merged into the new MGM, with Louis B. Mayer as head of studio. In charge of production was the twenty-five-year-old prodigy, Irving Thalberg.

Thalberg was impressed with Lewin's work on *Bread* and steadily promoted him. Initially, though, Lewin had to serve his time scripting "quickies which I agreed to write on one condition—that I got no screen credit. They put my name on one of those stinkers, and I made them remake the main title." But gradually the quality of his assignments improved, together with his status at the studio. Two of his most successful scripts at this period were adaptations of English stage hits, both directed on screen by Sidney Franklin: *Quality Street* (1926), from J. M. Barrie's play, starring Hearst's protegée Marion Davies; and *The Actress* (1928), based on Pinero's *Trelawney of the Wells,* with Norma Shearer as Rose Trelawney. By now, Lewin had been made head of the studio's script department, and in 1928 he also became Thalberg's personal assistant, working closely with him "twenty-eight hours a day. It was terrible. I never had time for myself."

In 1929 Lewin became a producer, entrusted with those projects in which Thalberg took the closest interest. His first production was Garbo's last silent movie, *The Kiss* (1929), directed by Jacques Feyder; he also assisted Thalberg in making MGM's belated but triumphant entry into sound, *Broadway Melody* (1929). Over the next few years, Lewin produced some of the studio's glossiest and most prestigious pictures: *The Guardsman* (1931), with Alfred Lunt and Lynn Fontanne; *Red-Headed Woman* (1934), with Jean Harlow; *Mutiny on the Bounty* (1935), with Gable and Laughton; *The Good Earth* (1937), with Muni and Luise Rainer. Occasionally he suggested that he might try directing, but always allowed Thalberg to dissuade him.

When Thalberg died in 1936, Lewin promptly quit MGM, thus greatly offending Louis B. Mayer, and joined Paramount, where he produced three films. Two of them did well: a screwball comedy with Carole Lombard called *True Confessions* (1937), and *Spawn of the North* (1938), an Alaskan melodrama. The third, *Zaza* (1939), a comedy with Cukor directing, flopped disastrously. Lewin, finding that his ideas were now being blocked, left Paramount and formed an independent company in partnership with David L. Loew to produce films for release through United Artists.

Their first film was *So Ends Our Night* (1941), an anti-Nazi drama based on a novel by Erich Maria Remarque, directed by John Cromwell. Despite a strong cast, the film had little success in the United States (thanks possibly to isolationist sentiment), though it was well received in Britain. The company's next production, it was evident, had to be made cheaply. Loew was keen to make a film of Somerset Maugham's novel *The Moon and Sixpence* and had bought the rights from MGM. "I hadn't written a script in fifteen years," Lewin said. "David wanted to save the price of a writer, so he turned to me, 'You're a writer. For God's sake, write.'"

Lewin's screenplay earned Maugham's enthusiastic praise, and Loew, still looking to cut costs, now suggested that Lewin should direct the film as well. After some token resistance he agreed, bringing the picture in well within schedule and budget. "I found directing a big challenge," Lewin wrote in *The Real Tinsel,* "I didn't have a great deal of facility, but I loved doing it. Everybody felt we'd make, at most, an artistic flop.

They said, the story of a disagreeable character, a painter whose paintings are burned and who dies of leprosy—this is entertainment?"

Apparently, it was. *The Moon and Sixpence* (1942) was a commercial and critical success, and gave George Sanders the first worthwhile part of his career as Charles Strickland, a dull stockbroker who deserts his family to become a Gauguinesque painter, finding his soul as he dies of leprosy in Tahiti. The film introduced a new technique to American cinema. The main obstacle that had prevented Maugham's novel being filmed by MGM—or by Warners, who had previously owned the rights—was its narrative structure: the story is recounted by an author-figure who also, from time to time, participates in the action. No scriptwriter had been able to translate this into cinematic form. Lewin, however, had seen a film by Sacha Guitry, *The Story of a Cheat* (1936), that featured voice-over narration by a character who also appeared on screen, and realized that the device was ideal for *The Moon and Sixpence*. "After that, everybody used narrative technique like mad, even when it wasn't necessary."

In Charles Strickland, Lewin presented the first of his gallery of obsessive and generally self-destructive protagonists. As always with Lewin, the script was literate to a fault, retaining much of Maugham's original dialogue as well as the novel's assured narrative pacing. The film was in black and white, apart from a final color sequence to show Strickland's paintings—a combination Lewin used again, to even better effect, in his next movie. "An admirable film until the end," James Agate commented, "when it lapses into Technicolour and techni-pathos." This was a minority view, however, and most reviewers agreed with C. A. Lejeune, who was moved by "that sudden flowering into Technicolour in the painter's hut in Tahiti," and called this "a real translation" from literature to cinema. Higham and Greenberg, in their survey of '40s Hollywood, found it "an unorthodox and often beautiful film, finely acted."

At this point Loew, in spite of the partnership's sudden success, decided to do war work, and Lewin was out of a job. Somewhat unexpectedly, he found himself back at MGM, after his old friend Sidney Franklin had arranged for Louis B. Mayer to see *The Moon and Sixpence*. "A fine movie," Mayer conceded. "A pity it wasn't made by a nice guy instead of that son-of-a-bitch." Nonetheless, he re-employed Lewin, and assigned him to direct *Madame Curie* (1943), a prestige production with Greer Garson and Walter Pidgeon.

After ten days, Lewin was taken off the pic-ture. "I thought I was going mad. I just couldn't make these people come to life. Perhaps I couldn't direct at all. Mervyn LeRoy took over, and I used to sneak on to the set, to see if I could divine the great mystery to which he must have the key. I never managed to find out!" Fortunately, the studio retained enough faith in Lewin's abilities to invite him to choose a project of his own. Lewin settled on Oscar Wilde's Faustian fable, *The Picture of Dorian Gray*, the story of a rich young man about town in *fin-de-siècle* London whose ever-deepening moral corruption is reflected not in his own beautiful face but in the portrait he hides in his attic.

One intriguing casting possibility came to nothing. Greta Garbo, it seemed, wanted to play Dorian Gray. Lewin "moved heaven and earth to set it up. But everyone had a fit: the censorship problem, formidable anyway, would become insurmountable with a woman *en travesti* playing the role. I had to give up, but I've always regarded that as one of the screen's great lost opportunities." Instead, the title role went to Hurd Hatfield, with George Sanders stealing the film as his bad angel, Lord Henry Wotton, and Angela Lansbury as the ill-fated Sybil Vane, who kills herself when Dorian rejects her.

Visually, *The Picture of Dorian Gray* (1945) is consistently superb. Lewin's complex, slightly mannered style provided an excellent cinematic equivalent for Wilde's studied prose; and his intention of making each scene exquisite down to the last detail was well served by Hans Peter's baroque sets, and Harry Stradling's elegant cinematography. As before, Lewin mixed monochrome and color, reserving the latter for periodic glimpses of the eponymous portrait (painted for the film by Ivan Albright) deliquescing into vividly lush decay. As always, Lewin wrote his own script (working in frequent references to his favorite poem, *The Rubáiyát of Omar Khayyám*). Opinions varied as to its quality, but the general feeling was that Lewin had improved on the original by "rooting out all the preciousness which gets in the way of the melodrama." James Agee dismissed the whole affair as "respectful, earnest and, I'm afraid, dead," but another critic, objecting to "the spoken narrative which interrupts the visual flow of the story," went on: "But then Mr. Lewin is a literary director . . . and it is, probably, his literary sensibility which has enabled him to translate into such elaborate and beautiful pictorial terms the elaborate artificialities of Wilde's writing."

Dorian Gray earned Harry Stradling an Oscar, plus a nomination for Angela Lansbury, and more than recouped its costs; but Lewin had run over schedule and budget, and it was felt at MGM that he had been unnecessarily extravagant. He therefore quit the studio once again, and reformed his partnership with David Loew, for whom he directed his third film, *The Private Affairs of Bel Ami* (1947). Based on Maupassant's novel *Bel Ami,* it starred Lewin's perennial favorite George Sanders as the charming, unscrupulous journalist who achieves success at the expense of the women who love him.

Once again the film was a constant pleasure to the eye, with lavish sets recreating the opulent, artificial world of Paris in the Belle Époque. It features a commissioned painting by Max Ernst ("The Temptation of St. Anthony"), and Darius Milhaud contributed a fine score. But Lewin's script, witty and literate as ever, tended at times to slow down the action, and the film was marred by a moralistic ending, imposed by the censors, in which Bel Ami meets his deserts in a fatal duel. (Lewin did, however, take the opportunity to stage this scene superbly, in a torrential downpour with lights gleaming off dark wet umbrellas.) *Bel Ami* failed at the box office, and Lewin—now on excellent terms with the unpredictable Louis B. Mayer—returned to MGM as an executive.

After doing "a hell of a lot of anonymous doctoring" on other people's films, Lewin took a year's leave of absence to make *Pandora and the Flying Dutchman* (1951) as an independent production. This was the first film in which Lewin set out from an original idea of his own, rather than adapting someone else's novel. The story transposed the legend of the Flying Dutchman to modern Spain, where the hero, condemned to sail the Seven Seas forever, meets the reincarnation of his dead love in a small Costa Brava fishing port. Ava Gardner and James Mason took the title roles, and Lewin shared production costs with a British company, Romulus Films. Once again, there are references to *The Rubáiyát* and a significant painting but, unusually for Lewin, most of the movie was shot (by Jack Cardiff) on location, and for the first time he filmed entirely in color.

In *Pandora,* Lewin's taste for the bizarre, the operatic, and the romantic reaches its apotheosis. Reflecting the influence of such surrealists as Delvaux and de Chirico, the film unrolls in a dream-like, unreal atmosphere where past and present exist in startling juxtaposition. On any literal level, the plot is clearly ludicrous, and at the time most critics reacted in contemptuously literal terms. Dilys Powell found in it "film compositions of a romantic delicacy which you do not easily forget," but C. A. Lejeune called it "conspicuous in its confident assumption of

scholarship and its utter poverty of imagination and taste," and Richard Winnington was only marginally more indulgent: "It might have been enjoyably silly but for Lewin's striving to be classy and an air of third-rate decadence that hangs about it." More recently, though, there have been signs that the film is being revalued, and may even be acquiring cult status. Georges Sadoul saw it as a "symbolic paean to feminine beauty," and David Thomson found it "impressive in a romantic, thundery way." In an article in *Cinématographe* (January 1982), Claude Arnaud commended Lewin's attempt to "create cinema which, for all its weaknesses, gathers together the fragments of the great legends, from Faust to Eve, from Tristan to the Ghost Ship, and tries to express the unutterable."

After *Pandora,* Lewin returned to MGM, for whom he made his two last films: *Saadia* (1954), based on a novel by Francis d'Autheville, in which a young French doctor (Mel Ferrer) rescues a Berber girl (Rita Gam) from local superstition; and *The Living Idol* (1957), a drama of reincarnation set in Mexico. Both films were disappointing, marred by weak casting, and overwhelmed by the preciousness which had always threatened Lewin's work.

Claude Arnaud has suggested that Albert Lewin was always likely to fall between two stools: "Europeans sneered at the 'Yankee's' intellectual pretensions; his designs mixed spots with stripes, like ties worn by a *nouveau riche.* And Americans had little relish for the acid which he splashed on their healthy morality." Artiness, pretension, and vulgarity have been the criticisms most frequently levelled at Lewin's films, as in David Thomson's verdict that his "arty aspirations showed like a teenage slip. He cultivated a garish sophistication—in subject, setting, style and actors—and sometimes achieved real vulgarity." Ephraim Katz, more sympathetically, summed up Lewin's output as "a curious but interesting mixture of the naive and the sophisticated, the dilettantish and the fascinating, the vulgar and the refined." As yet, his films have attracted little serious critical attention, even though so eminent a figure as Jean Renoir rated him as a conscious artist, "indispensable to the health of our times." It may be, as Claude Arnaud suggests, that Lewin's highly individual romanticism, with its protagonists "tormented by a need for excess, by a blind longing for which they can find no satisfaction," is due for a return to fashion.

After completing *The Living Idol,* Lewin suffered a heart attack, and retired from filmmaking. Soon afterwards, he and his wife Mildred left California and moved to New York, where they lived in an apartment overlooking Central Park, the rooms crowded with books, musical scores, ancient Minoan fragments, modern paintings, and numerous other *objets d'art*. In 1966 Lewin published a novel of the supernatural, *The Unaltered Cat*. He died of heart failure at the age of seventy-three.

—*P.K.*

FILMS: The Moon and Sixpence, 1942; The Picture of Dorian Gray, 1945; The Private Affairs of Bel Ami, 1947; Pandora and the Flying Dutchman, 1951; Saadia, 1954; The Living Idol, 1957.

ABOUT: Rosenberg, B. and Silverstein, H. The Real Tinsel, 1970. *Periodicals*—Cinématographe January 1982; Sight and Sound Winter 1967–1968.

JOSEPH H. LEWIS

LEWIS, JOSEPH H. (April 6, 1900–), American director, was born in New York City and educated at De Witt Clinton High School. Nothing else has been published about his early life until he joined MGM as a camera boy at the age of seventeen. His brother Ben was already an MGM editor, and Joseph Lewis followed his example. He worked as an assistant editor and editor for nineteen years, first at MGM, then at Mascot, and in 1935–1936 at Republic Pictures.

At Republic, Lewis designed elaborate main titles for more than a dozen forgotten movies, in this way gaining experience in directing actors and devising lighting and editing effects. He apparently also worked as a second-unit director, though none of the published filmographies lists his credits in this role. In 1937 Lewis joined Grand National and codirected with Crane Wilbur a thriller called *Navy Spy*, scripted by Wilbur and featuring Conrad Nagel. After that he moved on to Universal, where in 1937–1938 he directed five low-budget B pictures, all produced by Trem Carr. Four of these were "singing cowboy" Westerns, featuring Bob Baker and Fuzzy Knight. Reviewing the first of them, *Courage of the West* (1937), *Variety* said it was "marked by smarter scripting and directing" than most such programmers, and many years later, at a Berkeley retrospective, it was found "notable for extremely enterprising camera movements, framings, and editing devices."

The Spy Ring (1938), the only non-Western Lewis made for Universal, was even more inventive. Filming a polo game, the director decided that he "wanted to have the movement of the horses [and] the men." He strapped a portable camera to his protesting photographer and sent him into the thick of the game. Interviewed by

Peter Bogdanovich in *Cinema* (Fall 1971), Lewis said that at this stage of his career "it hadn't occurred to me that performance was the most important thing. I learned that later. . . . What interested me most was telling the story . . . through the eye of the camera. And I didn't like words. Whenever I could, I cut words out, and told it silently through the camera. I still do that."

In 1939 Lewis went to Columbia and made five more cut-rate Westerns, all starring Iris Meredith and either Charles Starrett or Bill Elliott. A stint with Monogram followed in 1940–1941—three contributions to the "East Side Kids" series, with Leo Gorcey and Bobby Jordan, and a Bela Lugosi horror film called *The Invisible Ghost*.

Lewis's whole career was a demonstration that (as one critic put it) "even on miniscule budgets and virtually nonexistent sets, style was still possible." There is strong evidence of this in at least one of the three pictures he made for the Producers Releasing Corporation in 1941–1942. *Secrets of a Co-Ed* contains a courtroom scene shot in a single ten-minute take that predated Hitchcock's experiments with the long take by almost a decade. Lewis shot the sequence at the end of a day of rehearsal and in those ten minutes, as he says, "you saw close-ups, long shots, medium shots, over-the-shoulder shots, you name it." Myron Meisel, in his essay on Lewis in *Kings of the B's,* called this "a bit of brilliance without purpose that cannot redeem a worthless film," but which suggests "a developing talent hungry for meaningful assignment." Lewis told Bogdanovich that "in those days when it took a week to shoot a film, it would be nothing for me to come on [the job] ten weeks before. Because I enjoyed it, you know. This was my hobby."

In 1942, nevertheless, Lewis found himself back at Universal, churning out more Fuzzy Knight Westerns (and one horror movie, *The Mad Doctor of Market Street*). His army service followed, then a return to PRC for a sentimental musical, *The Minstrel Man* (1944), then an "undemandingly watchable" contribution to the Falcon series, made for RKO in 1945, and starring Tom Conway as Michael Arlen's debonair private eye.

The impression that Lewis was trudging a hopeless circle seemed to be confirmed later the same year when he rejoined Columbia. However, the studio had just embarked upon a "fewer and better" B-film policy, and Lewis seized the opportunity this offered with his first picture there, *My Name Is Julia Ross* (1945). It was adapted from Anthony Gilbert's novel *The Woman in Red,* a modern Gothic in the *Rebecca* mold. The heroine (Nina Foch) is hired as secretary by a charming old lady (Dame May Whitty) who lives in a lonely clifftop house and who, it becomes increasingly clear, is prepared to go to any lengths whatever to save her psychopath son (George Macready) from a murder rap.

The English setting was achieved by a tirelessly imaginative use of studio sets, stock footage, back projection, fog, and low-key lighting. The result was Lewis's first recognizable contribution to the *film noir* genre in which, as Richard Thompson says, he "found his metier, if not his personal vision. From *Julia Ross* on, all his successful films were either outright *films noirs* . . . or contained *maudit* elements. . . . Though it seems difficult to claim for Lewis a consistently black vision, his visual style contained several elements conducive to the genre: a taste for Bazinian depth of focus; and for its temporal twin, the long take; for camera movement (relativity) rather than alternating static cuts (isolated specificity); for cinematographers with dramatic, concrete styles, often harshly black and white; for naturalistic location shooting, or, failing that, for modestly scaled back-lot work stressing character/environment interfaces rather than explicit spectacle."

James Agee in his reviews said of *Julia Ross,* "the film is well planned, mostly well played, well directed and, in a somewhat boom-happy way, well photographed—all around, a likable, unpretentious, generally successful attempt to turn good trash into decently artful entertainment." Few modern critics would quarrel with this account. Louis Black wrote that "most of the film is beautiful to look at, the atmosphere

of paranoia and confusion created as much by camera movement and lighting as by the story." But Black thought that Lewis, mining the same vein as Hitchcock, "gets nowhere near the mileage out of his material"; David Thomson, making the same comparison, maintained that "Dame May Whitty blithely tolerating her maniac son . . . is not much less disturbing than *Strangers on a Train.* "

Although it was gnerally agreed that this was the first of Lewis's movies in which a sense of personal relationships comes through, the director still seemed to most critics more successful at creating atmosphere than in handling his actors and the sometimes weak dialogue. Nevertheless, *Julia Ross* was Lewis's first hit, attracting much admiring critical attention and grossing somewhere between $4 and $5 million. Allocated a twelve-day shooting schedule and a budget of $125,000, Lewis had exceeded the first by five days and the second by $50,000, but was vindicated by the film's success. This secured his position at Columbia as a director who could make gold bricks with very little straw, and he remained at the studio for four years—his longest stay with any one company.

He directed the musical numbers in Alfred E. Green's *The Jolson Story* (1946) and then made *So Dark the Night* (1946), which Myron Meisel thinks superior to *Julia Ross.* Based on a *Readers' Digest* story set in France, it was, like its predecessor, photographed by Burnett Guffey. Stephen Geray is cast as what Meisel calls "the first distinctive Lewis hero, a man precariously balanced on the edge of control." He plays Cassin, a brilliant and dedicated Parisian police detective who, overworked and close to a breakdown, is sent to recover his equilibrium in a small provincial town. There he falls in love with a much younger woman (Micheline Cheirel) and they become engaged. At a celebratory party, the girl and her former fiancé disappear. Both are later found murdered. Cassin undertakes the investigation, but more murders follow before and after the detective recognizes the truth—that he himself is the schizoid killer.

Lewis found his French village on the Columbia back lot—a bombed-out set of which little remained but a half-demolished steeple in a field. Lewis added a winding dirt road, a thatched roof, and a couple of flats, and that was his village. We observe Geray's arrival from the viewpoint of one of the villagers. Lewis said: "when the peasant is looking out of the window, we had nothing to shoot as . . . [Geray's] car drove by. We took a black velvet drop because we had no set . . . And we put this woman in front of the black velvet looking out the window and shot into the window, reflecting the dirt road, and showed the car come winding all the way down through the eyes of the woman as reflected in the pane of glass."

Meisel discusses *So Dark the Night* at some length to illustrate Lewis's "complete visual control" in this "absurd low-budget project." For example, "when the subject of marriage is seriously broached, Lewis pans up from an idyllic contemplation of Geray's image in the murky pond to Geray himself, the first of many such images emphasizing the separation within Geray between a submerged murderous identity and a gentle, sympathetic character. It is only the challenge of marriage to a much younger woman that forces the hidden identity out into the open. Lewis also perceptively uses point-of-view shots from interiors looking outward to designate separations between characters. On several stunning occasions, from an outside position looking at a group of people, he dollies back through a window to reveal others observing them from the inside, thus interposing the physical separation of the set's walls rather than using the less obtrusive temporal device of cutting. . . . In this manner, whoever is being observed . . . is directly related to the view others are taking of them."

It seemed to Paul Schrader that the film has "very intriguing, baroque qualities, but you have to overlook a great deal to notice them." But for Meisel, *So Dark the Night* reveals Lewis "as a filmmaker of astonishing complexity," presenting "in the most direct fashion the preoccupations of this deviously effacing artist." It introduces "two essential Lewis motifs: the plot structure of hunter and hunted; and the progressive discovery of the inseparability of individual identity from social action." The picture, Meisel concludes, "succeeds as a matchless stylistic exercise, marking it as the first major film in the Lewis canon."

No great claims have been made for Lewis's next two Columbia assignments, *The Swordsman* (1947), a "Scottish clan costumer" starring Larry Parks, and *The Return of October* (1948). The latter was an unsalvageable comedy starring Glenn Ford as a psychology professor intrigued by a girl (Terry Moore) convinced that her dear dead uncle has been resurrected as a race horse. However, Lewis's next picture, *Undercover Man* (1949), produced by Robert Rossen and photographed by Guffey, was the first of the three movies on which the director's cult reputation rests.

The Sydney Boehm script (adapted by Jack Rubin), based on the fall of Al Capone, relates in the quasi-documentary style of the period the efforts of three agents of the US Treasury Department to nail a big-city racketeer on a tax-evasion charge. At the heart of the film, however, is the relationship between one of the agents, Frank Warren (Glenn Ford), and his wife Judith (Nina Foch)—his struggle to reconcile his duty to society with his responsibility to his family—always a profoundly important concern with Lewis.

Richard Combs praised, among other elements in the film, a police line-up that "features threatening low angles and intimidated witnesses and a brilliant chiaroscuro division of space" and a climax that "lucidly lays out the action and throws in one unbeatable shot of a major villain's death." Richard Thompson noted that Lewis's "unfailing response to *noir* genre films has been to play down generic concerns and play up relationships and the role of women." Lewis himself said the movie "was about Capone and gangsters and what not, yet . . . truly they all have to have the same thing, and that's love."

At that point, Lewis left Columbia and made *Gun Crazy* (1949) for the comparatively unknown King Brothers (distributing through United Artists). The film was scripted by "Millard Kaufman" (the blacklisted Dalton Trumbo) and Mackinlay Kantor from the latter's story. It was shot by Russell Harlan, partly on location in the California town of Montrose. Lewis has nothing but praise for Frank and Maurice King, who gave him a free hand and a relatively generous budget (about $450,000) and shooting schedule (thirty days). The result is generally regarded as Lewis's masterpiece and is one of the most lengthily and lovingly analyzed B pictures ever made.

Bart Tare (John Dall) is a gentle marksman obsessed by guns but incapable of killing. After a period in a reform school for robbing a gunsmith, and service in World War II, he comes home. Visiting a carnival, he accepts a barker's challenge and outshoots Annie Laurie Starr (Peggy Cummins). They fall passionately in love and begin a penniless marriage. Hungry for money and kicks, Laurie has none of Bart's scruples and seduces him into a life of crime. In spite of his efforts to avoid killings, she shoots down two people in a raid on an Armour plant (festooned with animal carcasses silently commenting on socially approved butchery). They prudently agree to separate for a time, but neither can bear the parting. In the end they are cornered in a fog-bound swamp by a posse led by two of Bart's boyhood friends. There Bart kills for the first and only time in his life; he shoots Laurie to prevent her from firing on his friends, and dies himself in the posse's fire.

Ed Lowry, in a Cinema Texas program note, writes that the film's "conflicts, the emotions and attitudes of the characters, and the plot itself are conveyed not through the scripted dialogue, but through visual and aural imagery. . . . The characters are viewed from the outside and we are never presented with their motivations. We sympathize with them, but never really understand them. . . . The film's style embodies its content, conveying a world of feelings, emotions, and physical action through the most visual-visceral methods available."

Describing the opening scene (shown under the credits) when we see the young Bart robbing the gunsmith's shop, Lowry points out that when he stumbles in his panic and drops the stolen gun, which slides to the feet of a towering cop, "the resemblance to the adolescent's initiation to sexuality is painfully evident, and the boy is left on the ground defeated beneath the ominous gaze of a father figure." The Freudian implications in this marvelously economical sequence, conscious or not, run "throughout the film: guns are clearly related to sex, both are repressed by a benevolent castrating authority, and the individual's exercise of the power they represent takes the form of clearly antisocial acts."

Lowry goes on to discuss the film's use of mirrors and glass: "Breaking glass becomes a physical expression of violent self-assertion." For example, when Bart comes to take Laurie away from Packett, the carnival owner she is living with, "the spurned lover grabs a mirror from the wall to throw it at Bart; but before he is able to take it in his hands, Bart shoots it to pieces and Packett is left staring at his own image in the shattered mirror, reflecting his shattered self-image springing from his inability to prove 'man enough' for Laurie." The role of costume is also explored in the film, especially the cowboy clothes that Bart and Laurie both wear at times—an expression of "both Laurie's glamorized conception of outlawry and Bart's attitude about the noble use of guns, concepts which are undercut by the action of the film."

Gun Crazy's most famous sequence is a bank robbery, occupying three and a half minutes of screen time, that was filmed in a single shot. Lewis rigged his camera in the back seat of the couple's car, with sound equipment inside and out. We see only the backs of their heads as they drive towards the bank, chattering nervously, watching for a parking space. One offers itself, they pull in, and Bart enters the bank, leaving Laurie at the wheel. When a cop appears, Laurie gets out and distracts his attention until Bart hurries out of the bank. Laurie clubs the cop, they both jump into the car, and we ride with them out of town.

By refusing to cut to another angle, Lewis makes the spectator an accomplice to the robbery, forced to play out the whole scene in real time and from the viewpoint of the protagonists, sharing with Laurie an acute awareness of Bart's absence within the bank stretching into an eternity. Lewis filmed the sequence in "about three hours in the morning rather than four days of shooting," and obviated the need for sets. It was generally assumed within the industry that he must have used back projection, and "every studio in the country . . . wanted to know how we used four or five projection machines at the same time." Fourteen years later, as Lowry says, reviewers of Bande à part hailed Godard's "innovatory" placing of his camera in the back seat of a moving car.

Howard Thompson in the New York Times called Gun Crazy "pretty cheap stuff," though he allowed that Lewis "has kept the whole thing zipping along at a colorful tempo." However, a year later the French surrealist critic Gerard Legrand called the film "a rigorous love poem," directed by Lewis "with a technical brio equaled only by his openly subversive intentions." Ado Kyrou, in Le Surréalisme au cinéma (1953), worte that it was "an admirable film, which alone of all cinema marks the road which leads from l'amour fou to la revolt folle."

American and British critics came more slowly to recognize the film's merits. In 1971, the American magazine Cinema, then edited by Paul Schrader, published three articles about Lewis (by Schrader, Richard Thompson, and Robert Mundy), a filmography, and the Bogdanovich interview. Schrader's essay called Gun Crazy "one of the best American films ever made." He rejected psychological interpretations, calling the picture "an exhilarating tribute to reckless love and non-stop action. . . . In no film has the American mania for youth, action, sex and crime been so immediately portrayed." For the British critic Chris Auty it is "a B-picture classic. . . . Compulsive genre cinema, wearing its low budget and its Freudian motifs with almost equal disdain, it simply knocks spots off senile imitations like Bonnie and Clyde."

Lewis went to MGM for A Lady Without Passport (1950). Like Undercover Man, it belongs to the quasi-documentary cycle of crime films of the post-war years. John Hodiak plays an officer of the Miami Border Patrol who goes to Cuba posing as a would-be illegal immigrant. In Havana he falls in love with concentration camp survivor Hedy Lamarr, and begins to sympathize with the plight of the refugees. This is one of the several Lewis films that reaches its climax in a misty swamp, with Hodiak trying to rescue Lamarr from the clutches of Palinov

(George Macready), cynical mastermind of the organization that smuggles refugees into Florida.

Tim Pulleine admired Paul Vogel's elegant camerawork and Lewis's capacity for "animating routine story-telling with unexpected invention," but thought the "perfunctory plotting wins out over any stylistic intensity." Myron Meisel disagreed, rhapsodizing about the effortless virtuosity of the director's *mise-en-scène* and the excellence of the performances he extracted from his "indifferent" players in what was, he thought, "perhaps the loveliest of Lewis's neglected works." *Retreat, Hell!* (Warner Brothers, 1952), a conventionally propagandist Korean War movie, was rather coolly received, but there has been a good deal of interest in Lewis's next two films, both made for MGM.

Desperate Search has flyer Howard Keel combing the Canadian wilderness for the lost children of his first marriage, accompanied by their mother (Patricia Medina) and his second wife (Jane Greer). Richard Thompson wrote that "the sexual problems of the grown-ups are almost mirrored in the problems of the lost boy and girl—a fascinating 'almost,' but Lewis doesn't break loose for it." In *Cry of the Hunted* (1953), prison officer Barry Sullivan pursues fugitive Vittorio Gassman into the Louisiana swamps. Meisel called this "a very personal work. . . . Both men are odd, sympathetic characters, drawn to each other by a personal bond so obscure in its detailed moral accounting as to be nearly incomprehensible."

The Big Combo (Allied Artists, 1955) was the last of the three remarkable B films on which Lewis's reputation rests (the others being *Gun Crazy* and *Undercover Man*). Cornel Wilde stars as Diamond, a police lieutenant searching for evidence to pin on racketeer Brown (Richard Conte). What drives him past the bounds of duty and reason is his sick devotion to Brown's classy mistress Susan (Jean Wallace), herself torn between hatred of Brown and helpless lust for him. Susan, questioned after a suicide attempt, hands Diamond the clue that eventually cracks the case. Along the way, Diamond is tortured and his stripper girlfriend murdered, while Brown's own empire is threatened by his lieutenant McClure (Brian Donlevy), eventually eliminated by Brown's hit men, Fante (Lee Van Cleef) and Mingo (Earl Holliman).

"The contributions of writer Philip Yordan and cameraman John Alton," wrote Myron Meisel, "inescapably stamp this as Lewis's most classical exploit in the [*noir*] genre. . . . What gives *The Big Combo* distinction beyond an original,

superbly realized genre piece is Lewis's revulsion at much of the behavior in the film, a distaste not conveyed by a criticism of the form . . . but instead by establishing his values through finely attuned visual symbols. . . . The key is his treatment of Wallace. . . . Lewis continually enshrouds her in light, setting her eerily aglow amid the blackness and the concentrated *maudit* style. . . . Her iconic significance is made most explicit when Conte makes love to her, kissing her ears and neck and dropping down out of the shot as we stare intently at the impassive absorption on her inscrutable face, bathed in quivering light. This beacon of light transmutes itself from a passive quality into an assertive gesture when Wallace punctuates the climactic shoot-out by turning the sharp beam of a spotlight on Conte, preventing his getaway."

Meisel goes on: "The value Lewis places on emotional sensitivity figures in the film's famous set pieces, the two scenes where Brian Donlevy's hearing aid figures in the action. Robert Mundy has noted how Lewis effectively manages to underplay the violence both times by objectively shooting a torture scene in which the hearing aid is placed in Wilde's ear with the volume screaming into his brain (i.e., we see Wilde writhing in agony but hear the dialogue normally), and then by subjectively shooting Donlevy's death scene without the aid (we see the bursts of machine-gun fire without hearing anything). . . . Lewis further gives highly sympathetic shticks to the many minor characters who are exposed to danger through Wilde's insensitivity to their fates, which ensures that our sympathy remains withheld from Wilde. . . . The most impressive contrast to the ruthless solipsism of Wilde and Conte is the deep mutual affection displayed by a pair of hired killers, a devotion of which the protagonists are sadly incapable."

Tom Milne maintains that *The Big Combo*, "often held to be inferior to *Gun Crazy* . . . , is probably at least its equal, and certainly more consistent within itself. . . . Rarely since the Expressionist Twenties in Germany, in fact, has torment so invaded the screen, with virtually every character either in mortal terror . . . or nursing an aspiration of love, however tainted, that is crushed beneath the burden of corruption. . . . At the very end . . . , Susan offers a symbolic ray of light; but as she and Diamond walk away together, into an enveloping fog, the happy ending looms more like merciful oblivion." Richard Thompson similarly regards this as "the most completely, evenly, successfully realized of all Lewis's films. If it does not reach the archetypical peaks of *Gun Crazy,* it also does not break down in the memory into sequences and transitions." Louis Black, on the other hand, called *The Big Combo* "an undeniably interesting film, full of fascinating scenes . . . [that] still only hints at the brilliance of *Gun Crazy*."

A common criticism of *The Big Combo* is that it plagiarizes Fritz Lang's *The Big Heat*. Paul Kerr, in his article about Lewis in *Screen* (July–October 1983), acknowledges the similarities but points out that *film noir* depended on "repetitions, conventions and familiar formulas," and goes on to show that *The Big Heat* itself has a good deal in common with an earlier Columbia film, also scripted by Sydney Boehm and starring Glenn Ford: "The film was called *Undercover Man* and it was directed by Joseph H. Lewis." Meisel sees *The Big Combo* (Lewis's last film in black and white) as a transitional work between "Lewis, the man of tactful compassion, and the Lewis of the last four Westerns," which are "more resolutely male-oriented" and "grow more eccentric in substance and quirky in method."

The first of these, *A Lawless Street* (1955), stars Randolph Scott as a town marshall eager to quit, but forced to stay in office when a vengeful gunman rides in. Apparently killed in a gun fight, Scott is resurrected to destroy the outlaws, hang up his guns, and reclaim his estranged wife (Angela Lansbury). Richard Thompson wrote of the film: "It grows in the memory; I can't wait to see it again. The script, with its terrible dialogue, was written by people not heard from before or since; but somewhere within it there hatched a background vision of civil order and disruption more commonly found in Ford."

The Seventh Cavalry (1956), a more routine Randolph Scott Western, was followed by *The Halliday Brand* (1957), with Ward Bond as a tyrannical and racist landowner-sheriff and Joseph Cotten as his intransigent son. The interesting script (by George W. George and George S. Slavin) and the film's "visual intelligence and compositional sense" have been analyzed in almost as much depth and detail as *The Big Combo*.

Lewis' last feature film was *Terror in a Texas Town* (1958)—characteristically shot in ten days on a laughable budget of $80,000. It was scripted by Ben L. Perry and (uncredited) the blacklisted Nedrick Young, who also appears in the movie as a gunman hired by landowner Sebastian Cabot to drive off the small ranchers around Prairie City, where oil has been discovered. Sterling Hayden plays the Swedish-American seaman who comes home to find his father murdered and who eventually confronts Cabot, harpoon against six-gun.

Richard Combs found Lewis in his swansong "stylistically at full stretch with almost nonexistent content—or at least material so banal that it is distended beyond meaningful interpretation by the director's mannerisms. . . . If ever Lewis made an 'art' film, this is arguably it." Meisel agreed that "the film isn't exactly good, yet it is marvelous; involving and colorful, personal and awful." Lewis subsequently did some work for television, directing episodes of *The Rifleman*, *Gunsmoke*, and other series until his retirement in the early 1960s.

Various attempts have been made to discern an *auteurist* consistency of theme in Lewis' work—a "hunter-hunted motif," "a thematic concern for memory and its loss," "an obsession with neurotic sexuality." The commonest feeling is that stated by Richard Combs: "It is quite easy to find evidence of a director with a strong personality—and just as much evidence of one who never really found a subject. Lewis might almost embody the kind of caricature figure that an *auteurist* critic would hold up as the epitome of the cult of the director: stylistic authority operating in a vacuum." However, Paul Kerr maintains that Lewis' "stylistic signature"—however difficult to identify—"did preempt some of the attributed innovations of the *nouvelle vague* and yet at the same time functioned as a symptom of and a valediction for a certain sort of American cinema."

FILMS: (with Crane Wilbur) Navy Spy, 1937; Courage of the West, 1937; Singing Outlaw, 1937; The Spy Ring/International Spy, 1938; Border Wolves, 1938; The Last Stand, 1938; Two-Fisted Rangers (U.K., Forestalled), 1939; Blazing Six Shooters (U.K., Stolen Wealth), 1940; Texas Stagecoach (U.K., Two Roads), 1940; The Man From Tumbleweeds, 1940; Boys of the City, 1940; The Return of Wild Bill (U.K., False Evidence), 1940; That Gang of Mine, 1940; The Invisible Ghost, 1941; Pride of the Bowery (U.K., Here We Go Again), 1941; Criminals Within, 1941; Arizona Cyclone, 1942; Bombs Over Burma, 1942; The Silver Bullet, 1942; Secrets of a Co-Ed/Secret Witness, 1942; The Boss of Hangtown Mesa, 1942; The Mad Doctor of Market Street, 1942; The Minstrel Man, 1944; The Falcon in San Francisco, 1945; My Name Is Julia Ross, 1945; (with Alfred E. Green) The Jolson Story, 1946; So Dark the Night, 1946; The Swordsman, 1947; The Return of October/Date With Destiny, 1948; Undercover Man, 1949; Gun Crazy/Deadly Is the Female, 1949; A Lady Without Passport, 1950; Retreat, Hell!, 1952; Desperate Search, 1952; Cry of the Hunted, 1953; The Big Combo, 1955; A Lawless Street, 1955; The Seventh Cavalry, 1956; The Halliday Brand, 1957; Terror in a Texas Town, 1958.

ABOUT: Belton, J. Cinema Stylists, 1983; McCarthy, T. and Flynn, C. Kings of the Bs, 1975. *Periodicals*—Cinema (USA) Fall 1971; Films and Filming October 1983; Monthly Film Bulletin March, April, and October 1980; Positif July–August 1975; Screen July–October 1983; Time Out May 2–8, 1980; Velvet Light Trap Summer 1983.

*L'HERBIER, MARCEL (April 23, 1888–
November 26, 1979), French director and scenarist, was born in Paris, the son of Hector
L'Herbier, a consular magistrate, and the former
Marie L'Homme de Braux. He was educated at
the Institution Sainte-Marie at Monceau, the
Lycée Voltaire in Paris, and in the faculties of
law and literature at the Sorbonne, becoming a
licentiate in law. He subsequently entered the
École des Hautes Études Sociales and studied
musical composition.

An admirer of Debussy and, in literature, of
Proust, Paul Claudel, Oscar Wilde, and Villiers
de l'Isle-Adam, L'Herbier was the complete
young Parisian aesthete. His ballet and theatre
reviews began to appear in 1913, and a volume
of verse, *Au jardin des jeux secrets* (*In the Garden of Secret Games*), was published in 1914. His
first play, a reflection on war written while he
was serving with the artillery in World War I,
was produced two years later at the theatre
workshop run by Madame Lara, mother of the
film director Claude Autant-Lara.

L'Herbier is said to have had little regard for
the cinema until 1917, when he saw Cecil B. De-
Mille's *The Cheat,* a film whose technical
sophistication was a revelation to the Paris intelligentsia. The same year L'Herbier wrote two
scripts for the directorial team of Mercanton and
Hervil, *Le Torrent* and *Bouclette,* and played a
small role in the latter, and late in 1917 he transferred from the artillery to the army's film unit.
His articles in defense of the cinema as an art
form started to appear in 1918, when he also
made his first films. L'Herbier soon emerged
with Abel Gance and Jean Epstein as a leader of
the so-called impressionist school, also known as
the "first avant-garde."

At that time, the French cinema desperately
needed some kind of renewal, having declined
into what Jacques Brunius called "a second-rate
poor man's theatre, photographed and bereft of
speech." Serious film criticism first began to
make an impact towards the end of World War
I, combining with the excitement that gripped
all the arts at that time, producing dada, surrealism, and cubism. The new critics, led by Louis
Delluc, called for a rediscovery and refining of
the technical inventiveness of such pioneers as
Méliès, and pointed to the example of the best
American directors—Ince, Griffith, Mack Sennett, Chaplin.

Before long, as Brunius says, "there came to
light another discovery that was to lead to the
notion of a cinema entirely sufficient to itself,
free of all anecdote, and from there to 'pure' and
then to 'abstract' cinema. Certain newcomers
laid emphasis on the extreme potence of cine-

MARCEL L'HERBIER

matic images considered as *poetic material,* a
quality doubtless inherent in the atmosphere of
a film's projection in a dark theatre filled with
men and women strangers to one another. However that may be, a quite new and unsuspected
force came into being, owing even less to the poetry of words and images than a film drama
owes to a stage play. A new claim was advanced
now for the right of a film, as of poetry or painting, to break away from both realism and didacticism, from documentary and fiction, in order
to refuse to tell a story, if and when it pleases,
and even to create forms and movements instead
of copying them from nature."

Between 1918 and 1922 L'Herbier was, in his
own words, "attached to the giant Gaumont
company," and he made eight films for them.
The first, *Phantasmes* (1918), was never finished, though fragments of it survive. It was followed by *Rose-France* (1918), commissioned by
the propaganda ministry, and already showing
L'Herbier's "impressionist" predilection for
maskings, superimposition, and experimental
lighting effects. Its subtitle describes it as "a song
composed and visualized by Marcel L'Herbier."
Noël Burch, writing in Richard Roud's *Cinema:
A Critical Dictionary,* said that "this genuinely
experimental film . . . embodies an idea which
casts even further than the major works to come:
the idea of narrative as plastic by vocation. Here
there is no dramaturgy, virtually no story, only
a succession of symbolic actions articulating an
'impressionist' evocation through the indetermi-
nately placed titles and inserts. Bu although this
technique derives from *fin de siècle* conventions,
it looks forward to our own times, to our concern

°ler bē ā´

with discontinuity, heterogenous materials, irrational narratives. And beyond the frenzied patriotism it expounds so faithfully, *Rose-France* emerges today as the 'visual music' dreamed of by L'Herbier, Gance and Dulac."

At the time, however, *Rose-France* was coolly received by the critics, and L'Herbier's next two films were conventional works in which he had obviously settled down to complete his apprenticeship. *L'Homme du large* (*Man of the Open Seas*, 1920) was more personal and much more notable. It was adapted from a Balzac story about a Breton fisherman "who loves only the seaman's life and the son who is attracted to the troubled life of the big towns." Described as "a pantheistic poem of man and nature," it shows a characteristic concern with the dual claims of documentary and stylization, experimenting with the dramatic uses of rhythmic cutting in a way that at times approaches abstraction (and makes it difficult to understand why contemporary critics admired it as a powerful piece of naturalism).

After the Oscar Wilde pastiche *Villa Destin* (1920) came the immensely innovative *El Dorado* (1921). It was written (like most of L'Herbier's pictures) by the director, filmed on location in Spain, and runs 141 minutes. Louis Delluc's wife Eve Francis, one of the finest of the early screen actresses, plays the tragic cabaret dancer Sybilla. The movie, utilizing a visual style influenced by Spanish painting, is full of brilliantly original effects: a scene in which Sybilla, lost in reverie, is seen as a blur while those around her remain in focus; an almost surrealist use of distorting mirrors; some masterly and ingenious examples of cross-cutting and split-screen; and the famous sequence of Sybilla's death, played against a gauze backcloth on which move the shadows of dancers. *El Dorado* was also the first film made in France (and probably in the world) to have a score composed especially for it (by Marius-François Gaillard) and intended to be played in synchronization with the images.

Problems with Gaumont over his next film, *Don Juan et Faust* (1922), prompted L'Herbier to set up his own company, Cinégraphic, which later fostered the film debuts of Jacques Catelain and Claude Autant-Lara, among others, and also produced Louis Delluc's last film. L'Herbier's own films were mostly coproductions that varied greatly in style and subject, beginning with several literary or theatrical adaptations. *L'Inhumaine* (*The New Enchantment*, 1924) was an extraordinary experiment financed in part by its star, the singer Georgette Leblanc, and intended to exhibit for the American market

the best that French art had to offer in the fields of painting, music, dance, architecture, design, and fashion. The plot, conceived by L'Herbier in collaboration with Pierre Mac Orlan, centers on a famous singer, talented but heartless, with an army of admirers. The young scientist who truly loves her awakens her dormant emotions by pretending suicide, but the heroine is then bitten by a poisonous snake sent by a jealous maharajah: can her scientist lover and the marvelous machine he has invented save her life? This absurd story, strongly reminiscent of a Feuillade serial, provides a framework for a series of bravura sequences, each in a different location (the Théâtre des Champs-Élysées, the Ballets Suédois), or on a set created by a different artist (Cavalcanti, Autant-Lara, Léger, Mallet-Stevens). A score was specially composed by Darius Milhaud.

The film was a disastrous failure, earning L'Herbier a reputation for aesthetic dilletantism that he was never quite able to shake off. Georgette Leblanc was an extremely bad actress, and much too old for her role. Jacques Brunius wrote unkindly that "the incredible and prodigiously boring adventures of this Baucis and Adonis were enacted against sets . . . , modern to be sure, but already tottering more unsteadily than any ruin. In the midst of all this a laboratory scene suddenly bursts into view. . . . It was a would-be cubist set by Fernand Léger, though why it tried to be cubist is impossible to say, and it merely succeeded in looking incongruous."

Later critics have been less harsh, praising the skill with which L'Herbier established a different mood and rhythm for each set or location. The fabulous sets have also found admirers, though largely among devotees of camp. The scene in which a riot breaks out at the heroine's concert has more than one claim to attention. With little time to prepare this sequence, L'Herbier simply arranged a concert at the Théâtre des Champs-Élysées by the immensely controversial composer George Antheil, and installed hidden cameras. The audience reacted with outrage or enthusiasm according to their lights, fights broke out, seats were thrown into the orchestra, and L'Herbier had his riot. According to Antheil, distinguished rioters who can be seen in the film include Erik Satie, Milhaud, James Joyce, Picasso, Man Ray, and Ezra Pound, among others.

Feu Mathias Pascal (*The Living Dead Man*), which followed in 1925, was adapted by L'Herbier from Pirandello's novel about a man who, when he is falsely reported dead, seizes the opportunity to begin a new life in fresh surroundings. The Russian *émigré* actor Ivan

Mozhukhin (or Mosjoukine) gives a brilliantly sustained performance as the detached and cynical Pascal, and a very funny character sketch is contributed by Michel Simon in one of his first screen roles. Ranging easily from fantasy to comedy of manners, and with a strong story line (altered by L'Herbier to provide a romantic happy ending), this is the least coldly intellectual of the director's early films, and has been regarded by many critics as his masterpiece.

Noël Burch, however, describes *Feu Mathias Pascal* as "a retrograde step both in the history of the cinema and in L'Herbier's work." He credits L'Herbier with the discovery that "through the mediation of the *découpage,* the shot structure, dramaturgical methods can *also* be structure." In *L'Homme du large,* for example, "a confrontation scene starting with comparatively brief shots and ending with a slow dissolve between the last shot and reverse angle, followed by an iris out, will inevitably bestow a double function on the *découpage,* appealing to the spectator in double guise: as narrative medium and as pure structure (rhythm), because this doubly 'cushioned' fall, in opposition to the previous progression along a series of peaks, carries the narrative but at the same time asserts its abstraction." In *Feu Mathias Pascal,* however, "the double function of the *découpage* which L'Herbier had already outlined in three of his films" seems to Burch to be entirely missing: "each shot simply invents a new trick designed to display the Mathias-Mozhukhin character, and each sequence a new style which will 're-flect' the next stage in the story," taking us back "to the notion of *mise en scène* as being solely *at the service of a story.*"

For Burch and for many other recent critics, L'Herbier's real masterpiece is *L'Argent* (*Money*), a Franco-German coproduction made with a very large budget in 1928. Based on Zola's novel about greed, love, and corruption in the world of international finance, and with some sequences shot on location in the Paris stock exchange, it has a running time of three hours. *L'Argent* was first screened in December 1928 with some sound effects (airplane engines and crowd noises) recorded on phonograph records and played in synchronization. The splendid cast includes Brigitte Helm, Alcover, Alfred Abel, Jules Berry, and Antonin Artaud.

Tom Milne writes that "the film has a subtle and intricate narrative fluidity that never for a moment betrays its origin in a densely plotted novel," and is "full of delicate metaphorical touches—the fretwork of a radio receiver, for instance, ominously suggests a stilled propellor as a wife fearfully awaits news of her aviator husband on his dangerous long-distance flight. . . . What chiefly amazes, though, is the extreme sophistication of L'Herbier's visual approach. Vast architectural sets, stark and grey, impassively dwarfing the human beings scurrying in frenzied quest of fame and fortune. . . . Strange, gliding movements of the camera, constantly zeroing in to isolate the private motivations of a character, or withdrawing to reorientate the context, to make new connections, to suggest wider implications."

Noël Burch goes further, maintaining that *L'Argent* was the culmination of the experiments of the French avant-garde "and even, to a certain extent, of the entire Western cinema." Burch believes that the film "gave birth to modern *découpage"* because "here, for the first time, the *style* (framing, camera placement and movement, positioning of actors, entries or exits from the frame, shot changes) systematically assumes a double role, dramaturgic and plastic, and . . . the interpenetration of these two functions creates an authentic cinematic dialectic. . . . For over forty years established film historians, parroting the contemporary view, have described *L'Argent* as a ponderously boring white elephant. It is only recently that the evolution of cinematographic language has enabled us to *see* a film which must have remained totally *invisible* at the time."

Nuits de prince (1928) was chiefly remarkable for its introduction of music, songs, and sound effects, and L'Herbier's next film, *L'Enfant de l'amour* (1929), based on a play by Henry Bataille, was the first French talkie, made in French and English versions (and also in a German version with some speech). Sound is used more creatively in *Le Mystère de la chambre jaune* (*The Mystery of the Yellow Room,* 1930), a mock-serious adaptation of a famous thriller by Gaston Leroux, full of ominous chiaroscuro and with an astonishingly sophisticated use of overlapping dialogue. The journalist-detective in this movie (Roland Toutain) reappears in its even more remarkable sequel, *La Parfum de la dame en noir* (*The Perfume of the Lady in Black,* 1931), about a woman haunted by the presence of her supposedly dead husband. This "deliriously sinister" film, with brilliant sets by Jacques Manuel, is distinguished according to Noël Burch "by its disorienting effects (mirror images, spatially elusive sets, fragmented *découpage*) and by some wonderfully inventive sound (the mysterious noises which silence the hallucinatory hubbub at the sinister dinner)."

After that, L'Herbier made no more films for two years, and when he did go back to work it was to direct a conventional adaptation of a successful boulevard play, *L'Épervier* (*Bird of Prey,* 1933), starring Charles Boyer. Similar chores followed, and although L'Herbier made some thirty films during the sound era, few of them show any of the capacity for formal invention that characterized his silent movies. Asked to explain this, L'Herbier said, "it is sometimes hard to know yourself what you did or what you didn't do. What is certain, however, is that when sound came, conditions of work became very difficult for a filmmaker like me. For economic reasons, you couldn't consider making sound films like the ones we had done in the silent days, sometimes even at our own expense. You had to exercise a good deal of auto-censorship, and, as far as I was concerned, even accept forms of cinema which were the very ones I had always avoided. Because of the dialogue, we were suddenly obliged simply to can plays."

As critics have pointed out, however, this does not take account of the fact that, in his Gaston Leroux adaptations, L'Herbier had showed as much inventiveness in his use of sound as he had with the images in his silent movies. It seems more likely that the director's own attitude to his work had changed. Even before he made *L'Argent,* he had told Jean Dréville that perhaps the period of experimentation was over—that in his opinion the "first avant-garde" was played out, and it was time to pass on to more serious matters.

L'Herbier's later films are not all negligible, however, as was demonstrated when the National Film Theatre in London mounted a major retrospective of his work in 1979. *Nuits de feu* (*The Living Corpse,* 1936), adapted from Tolstoy, deals with a public prosecutor who has to revise his view on marital fidelity when his own wife takes a lover. It was found fascinating for its careful recreation of the character's social background, and draws excellent performances from a cast that includes Gaby Morlay, Madeleine Robinson, and Victor Francen (who stars in many of L'Herbier's later films). *La Citadelle du silence* (*The Citadel of Silence,* 1937), a brooding study of life and death in a vast czarist prison, has dialogue by Jean Anouilh, lavish sets designed by Andreyev, and music by Honegger and Milhaud. It was followed by *Forfaiture* (*The Cheat,* 1937), an *hommage* to Cecil B. DeMille in the shape of a remake of the movie that had so stirred the young L'Herbier twenty years earlier.

L'Herbier himself recalled that "after two years of unemployment and hesitation" in the mid-1930s, he "again tried to retrieve, through various filmic routes," his own film form with adaptations such as *Nuits de feu* and *Les Hommes nouveaux* (also 1936), but he felt that this route had become almost impracticable and so turned toward a new genre, "exorcised of the theater," which he called the *chronique filmée,* or "filmed chronicle." Beginning in 1938 with *La Tragédie impériale* (about Rasputin), L'Herbier made a series of such films— grandiose costume movies more remarkable for their elaborate sets and starry casts than for their historical or psychological authenticity. A more personal film was the "supple and brilliant" *La Comédie du bonheur* (*The Comedy of Happiness,* 1940), in which Michel Simon plays a banker who escapes from the clutches of the psychiatrists, moves into a boardinghouse, and engages a group of carnival entertainers to brighten the lives of his gloomy fellow residents. Benefiting from a cast that includes Ramon Novarro, Louis Jourdan, and Micheline Presle, the movie has additional dialogue by Jean Cocteau and music by Ibert.

The most admired of L'Herbier's later films was *La Nuit fantastique* (*The Fantastic Night,* 1942), with Fernand Gravey as a young student who meets the mysterious woman in white (Micheline Presle) who has been haunting his dreams. The dream sequences include several references to L'Herbier's early preoccupations, including a temple of false magic and a parade of conjurors, mountebanks, and lunatics. Subsequent works included versions of *La Vie de bohème* (1943), and *The Last Days of Pompei* (1945), an *Hommage à Debussy* (1963), and two anthology movies providing a history of the fantastic film "from Lumière and Méliès to Jean-Luc Godard."

In fact, L'Herbier virtually abandoned the cinema at the end of the 1940s, turning instead to television, for which he made numerous documentary series on the arts—especially the cinema—as well as adaptations of various literary works. In 1944, during the German occupation, and with the deliberate aim of proving that there was a future for the French cinema, L'Herbier founded IDHEC (L'Institut des Hautes Études Cinématographiques), the French film school, serving as its president until 1969. He was also the first president of the Cinemathèque Française, founded in 1936. A volume of L'Herbier's essays, *Intelligence du cinématographe,* appeared in 1946, and his memoirs, *La Tête qui tourne,* in 1979. The director was married in 1923 to Marcelle Pénicaud, and had a daughter.

When he died in 1979 at the age of ninety-one, L'Herbier was described as the doyen of French film directors. Paul Rotha once called him "the supreme technician of the French cinema," and John Gillett said he was its "great imagist." Gillett suggests that, if L'Herbier has remained insufficiently appreciated in Anglo-American film circles, it is perhaps because his best films were extremely long and stylistically complex—"perhaps too complex for British and American distributors to handle. Also, given the pronounced literary bent of many critics in the 1930s and 1940s, the strong visual content of his work, the often extremely fanciful subject matter and a decorative stylisation utilising some of the most important artists and designers of the times, suggested a rarified form of aestheticism which contradicted the then much favoured notion of 'realism.'" Alain Resnais has acknowledged L'Herbier's influence on his work, and Tom Milne, discussing *L'Argent,* found in it "an unmistakable premonition . . . of the quintessence of Resnais's style."

FILMS: *Silent films*—Phantasmes, 1918 (incomplete); Rose-France, 1918; Le Bercail, 1919; Le Carnaval des vérités, 1919; L'Homme du large (Man of the Open Seas), 1920; Villa Destin, 1920; El Dorado, 1921; Prométhée . . . banquier, 1921; Don Juan et Faust, 1922; L'Inhumaine (The New Enchantment), 1924; Feu Mathias Pascal (The Living Dead Man), 1925; Le Vertige, 1926; Le Diable au coeur, 1927; L'Argent/ Geld, geld, geld (Money), 1928; Nuits de prince, 1928. *Sound films*—L'Enfant de l'amour, 1929; La Femme d'une nuit, 1930; Le Mystère de la chambre jaune (The Mystery of the Yellow Room), 1930; Le Parfum de la dame en noir (The Perfume of the Lady in Black), 1931; L'Épervier (Bird of Prey), 1933; Le Scandale, 1934; L'Aventurier, 1934; Le Bonheur, 1934; La Route impériale, 1935; Veille d'armes (The Vigil), 1935; Les Hommes nouveaux, 1936; La Porte du large (The Great Temptation), 1936; Nuits de feu (The Living Corpse), 1936; La Citadelle du silence (The Citadel of Silence), 1937; Forfaiture (The Cheat), 1937; La Tragédie impériale, 1938; Adrienne Lecouvreur, 1938; Terre de feu, 1938; La Brigade sauvage (The Savage Brigade), 1938; Children's Corner, 1938 (short); Entente cordiale, 1939; La Mode révée, 1939 (short); La Comédie du bonheur (The Comedy of Happiness), 1940; Histoire de rire (Foolish Husbands/Just for Fun), 1941; La Nuit fantastique (The Fantastic Night), 1942; L'Honorable Catherine, 1942; La Vie de bohème, 1943; Au petit bonheur, 1945; L'Affaire du collier de la reine (The Queen's Necklace), 1946; La Révoltée (Stolen Affections), 1947; Les Derniers jours de Pompei (The Last Days of Pompei), 1948; (with Robert Paul Dugan) Le Père de mademoiselle, 1953; Hommage à Debussy, 1963; Le Cinéma du diable, 1967; La Féerie des fantasmes (unfinished), 1978.

ABOUT: Abel, R. French Cinema, The First Wave: 1915-1929, 1984; Brossard, J.-P. Marcel L'Herbier et son temps, 1980; Brunius, J. B. En marge du cinéma français, 1954; Burch, N. Marcel L'Herbier, 1973 (in French); Catelain, J. Marcel L'Herbier, 1950 (in French); Filmoteca Nacional de España Marcel L'Herbier, 1980 (in Spanish); Lawder, S. D. The Cub-

ist Cinema, 1975; Leprohon, P. Présences contemporaines, 1957; L'Herbier, M. La Tête qui tourne, 1979; Manvell, R. (ed.) Experiment in the Film, 1949; Roud, R. (ed.) Cinema: A Critical Dictionary, 1980; Who's Who in France, 1979–1980. *Periodicals*—L'Avant-Scène du Cinéma June 1978, January 1980, October 1981; Cinéma (France) December 1954; Écran January 1976; Image et Son January 1980.

"LINDER, MAX" (Gabriel-Maximilien Leuvielle) (December 16, 1883–October 31, 1925), French comedian, director, and scenarist, was born in the village of Caverne, near Saint-Loubès in the Bordeaux region of France. His wealthy parents owned vineyards which they hoped Linder would take over, but he had other ideas: "Nothing was more distasteful to me than the thought of a life among the grapes," he later wrote. He was stagestruck from an early age, fascinated by the touring shows and circuses that occasionally visited the area.

In 1899 he was admitted to the Bordeaux Conservatoire, a prestigious academy of acting where he won first prize for comedy and second prize for tragedy. He was offered a contract at the Bordeaux Théâtre des Arts, and for the next three years he played in the French classics: Molière, Corneille, and Musset. At this time he met and struck up a friendship with M. le Bargy of the Comédie Française. In 1904, encouraged by le Bargy, he applied to the Paris Conservatoire. He was rejected—perhaps fortunately for the future of film comedy, because he was forced to play instead in the more popular comic theatres, such as the Olympia and the Théâtre de l'Ambigu.

It was at this time that he started calling himself Max Linder. There is some controversy about the origins of this name: some say that it was derived from the names of two fellow performers, Max Dearly and Marcelle Lender, but Jean Mitry thinks this unlikely and cites instead Linder's middle name: Maximilien. One thing is certain—it was not adopted because of the ignominy of appearing in films, as some claim—Linder used it for some of his theatre work too.

His debut in the cinema is shrouded in myth: it is said that Charles Pathé saw him at the Ambigu theatre and sent an admiring note: "In your eyes lies a fortune. Come and act in front of my cameras, and I will help to make it." The truth is somewhat less dramatic: he applied for work at the Pathé studios in the Paris suburb of Vincennes, probably at the suggestion of Louis Gasnier, formerly the "chef de claque" at the Ambigu (and future director of *The Perils of Pauline*); from July 1905 he started appearing in bit parts there. He was paid at the rate of twenty

MAX LINDER

francs per day, plus an extra fifteen if his clothing was damaged in the (often slapstick) films. Linder was by no means committed to the cinema at this point, and for another two years continued to appear in the evenings at the Paris music halls.

Linder's first important film role was in *The Young Man's First Outing* (*La première sortie d'un collégien*, 1905), playing a high-spirited student. Like many early films it was shot in a matter of hours. Linder appeared in dozens of other Pathé shorts at this time, often as a supporting player. By no means all of these were comedies: *Serpentine Dances* (1906), for example, was a Méliès-like fantasy, as was *La légende de Polichinelle* (1907), in which Linder played the lead.

The French film industry was then the biggest in the world, and was to remain so almost until World War I, when it was overtaken by the American. The two largest production companies were Pathé and Gaumont, each of which released hundreds of short films a week for screening in France and export around the world. The most popular genre from the beginning was comedy: a recent study has shown that, in the early years of the century, around forty percent of Pathé films were comedies. The style was usually slapstick, with very broad acting, exaggerated costumes and makeup, and many frenetic chases. *The Aeronaut's First Appearance* (1907) shows Linder piloting a balloon and causing havoc with a dangling anchor: a woman is lifted into the air, then a pram with a baby inside, and finally the entire roof is taken off a house. An angry crowd finally catches the balloon, and Linder and his copilot are severely chastised.

Linder's hammy performance in this film is indistinguishable from that of the dozens of other slapstick comedians of the period. But a change in his style was imminent and, like Chaplin (and Harold Lloyd) in later years, he may have been inspired by a new costume. For some time the actor René Gréhan had been playing a dandyish character called Gontran. In late 1907 Gréhan left to join the Éclair company and Linder promptly took over his high-class style of dress. It was to be his trademark for the rest of his career. As David Robinson says, Linder "was no grotesque: he was young, handsome, debonair, immaculate . . . in silk hat, jock coat, cravat, spats, patent shoes, and swagger cane."

His first film in the new garb was shot in the winter of 1907. Lake Daumesnil was frozen over and Louis Gasnier took him there to make *The Skater's Debut* (*Les débuts d'un patineur*). Linder, dressed immaculately, makes his way onto the ice. Unable to skate, he does the "windmilling" routine that Chaplin was to make famous in *The Rink*, his hat drops off, and he promptly falls onto it (Linder later recalled that he ruined his new clothes and lost a pair of cufflinks during the shooting). Slapstick elements are still present in *The Skater's Debut*, but Linder has abandoned the exaggerated mugging of earlier films; he is a foppish but believable human being—the character that was soon to make him the most popular comedian in the world. It is surprising then that the film was considered uninspired both by the studio—which reshot parts of it—and by the public. To make matters worse, at this point the director Gasnier left for Italy, and Linder was virtually put on the shelf by Pathé for the rest of 1908.

Meanwhile, however, an Italian film company, Itala, was looking for a new star comedian and chose André Deed, Pathé's leading knockabout comic. His departure gave Linder a chance to prove himself, and he received another fillip from Italy when Gasnier returned from his sojourn there with plans for him to star in a whole series. The films Gasnier started to make in 1909 had Linder playing various roles—a short-sighted old man (in *Le duel d'un Monsieur Myope*); a young woman in *Une jeune fille romanesque*—but soon it became obvious that it was the character of the dandy that the public really liked.

A Young Lady Killer (*Le petit jeune homme*, 1909) shows Linder's style, even at this early stage, fully developed. The dapper Max is following two pretty young women; they lead him into a dentist's where, before he can stop it, he has a tooth pulled. Undeterred, he follows the girls to their house, lights a cigar they have given him, and is promptly sick out of the window onto a passing gentleman. It is important to note that the cruder elements of comedy were not excluded by Linder, although they were relegated to a subsidiary role in his films. "I prefer the subtle comedy," he later said, "but it is a mistake to say that I do not use slapstick. I do not make it the object, I do not force it, but I use it when it comes naturally."

It is instructive to compare a film made by Linder in 1909 with another using the same plot and made the same year by someone else. Linder's *The Cure for Cowardice* (*La timidité vaincue*) features Linder as a man bullied by his wife, his mother-in-law, and his servants. He reads in a newspaper of a medical cure for cowardice; the treatment works, and he goes home and slaps his family around without mercy. *Elixir of Strength* (*Elixir d'énergie*) was also produced by Pathé and follows Linder's plot closely, but rather than using his naturalistic playing, makeup, and costume, it employs the broad, slapstick, acrobatic acting typical of this era; the "hero" even wears an obviously fake theatrical wig. Nothing could better illustrate the change in film comedy style that Linder was helping to bring about: his film still seems funny, the other is a bore.

Pathé could see that they had a success on their hands. In early 1910, when Gasnier had gone to oversee Pathé's production in America, Linder was placed under the direction of Lucien Nonguet, and his character was formally given the name "Max." Titles like *Max fait de la photo*, *Max fait du ski* and *Max et le téléphone* started to flow onto the world's screens. It is difficult to establish how many films Linder made in his career; generally it has been thought to be over 350, but Jean Mitry has checked the available catalogues, and believes the true figure is nearer half that. What is clear is that once Linder had found "Max," he stayed with him. Max was the archetypal boulevardier or man about town. He lived in a fashionable residence tended by servants and, of course, never did a stroke of work—Georges Sadoul notes that Max's character was at least partially based on fact: in France at this time there were at least one million "*gens de maison*" who lived off their investments. Max often drank too much and usually got into scrapes either through this, or through the pastime he adored above all else, the pursuit of women.

Through 1910, Linder's films show an increasing confidence. Typically he takes a simple situation and allows events to develop without being forced. In *Max Takes a Bath* (*Max prend un bain*) he tries to fill his bath with teacups of water, but, finding this process slow he decides he must move the bath into the hall where the faucet is. His neighbors, however, object to his bathing naked there, and Max, protesting, is carried off to the police station, still in the tub. *Max Linder's Film Debut* (*Les debuts de Max au cinéma*) is one of his most interesting films of the year—a recreation of his own beginnings in the movies. An interview with Charles Pathé (playing himself) is followed by Linder's parody of the knockabout films he first made—he is schooled in being thrown out of windows, having furniture hurled on top of him and water sprayed in his face, winding up bedraggled and thoroughly annoyed.

This first series of "Max" films immediately achieved enormous popularity all over the world, and he became, as Sadoul says, "the first major international star." In Russia he was voted the most popular film actor, ahead of Asta Nielsen; the Czar himself was a loyal fan, and Linder was paid the ultimate compliment of having a well-known imitator there, Zozlov. In Bulgaria the first feature film ever made was a version of a Linder comedy. And at home in Paris, a Max Linder movie theatre opened in 1910. Even among the intelligentsia he had a large following: Bernard Shaw wrote approvingly of the comic Frenchman in one of his letters to Mrs. Patrick Campbell.

Linder's career was brought to an abrupt halt at the end of 1910 by appendicitis—only one of the succession of illnesses that dogged him. The Paris newspapers published daily bulletins on his condition, and Pathé released recut versions of some of his earlier films to keep the public satisfied. Eventually rumors started circulating that Max had died, and to counter this two documentaries were made showing Linder returning to his family in Saint-Loubès and being nursed back to health.

By May 1911 he was back at work, and with increased control over his films. He had been coscenarist for the first "Max" series, but now he took sole script credit and also codirected, with René LePrince, who would act as a kind of producer for Linder right up to the World War. This increase in authority brought excellent results; one of the best films of the period—"his masterpiece," according to Sadoul—was *Max, Victim of Quinine* (*Max victime du quinquina*, 1911; apparently reedited and rereleased in 1914 as *Max et le quinquina*). Max, prescribed quinine as a tonic, takes far too much and becomes intoxicated. He quarrels with a man over a taxi—it turns out to be the minister of war, who presents his card and challenges Max to a duel. Then Max gets into arguments with an ambassador and with the police commissioner, collecting more challenges and more cards. A succession of police escort this drunken troublemaker "home" to the various addresses, but each time he is thrown out again. Finally he is discovered in bed with the minister's wife and is hurled out the window onto a trio of policemen, who belabor him unmercifully. Deceptively simple in technique, this film is one of the most accomplished comedies before the era of Chaplin and Keaton.

Though he was achieving enormous success in the cinema, Linder did not lose his passion for live performance, and periodically undertook tours. In 1910 he was offered $12,000 for a month of personal appearances with his films in Berlin; in 1911–1912 he traveled in Spain and was met by thousands of fans at the Barcelona station; the following year he toured Austria, Poland, and Russia (where he was accompanied on the piano by a young Dimitri Tiomkin, later famous as a Hollywood composer). Linder liked to film on location and made full use of the attractive and exotic settings discovered on his tours and vacations.

It was partly these tours that opened Linder's eyes to the true extent of his international popularity. He demanded (and got) an increase in salary to 150,000 francs, and then in 1912 to the unprecedented figure of one million. This, at a time when the average French salary was 100 francs per month, made him the best-paid actor in the world. Charles Pathé took what advantage he could from paying these huge amounts, quoting them in his publicity: "We understand that the gilded shackles which bind Max Linder have attained the value of a million francs a year. . . . The imagination boggles at such a figure!" Before Linder, film actors had generally taken what they were given. But he set his own conditions of employment, and in so doing heralded what was to become the Hollywood star system. It must have been with mixed feelings that the Pathé publicity machine dubbed Linder "The Napoleon of the Cinema."

The two years before World War I were Linder's heyday. His films, now directed by him alone, were made with increasing skill. In *Max Virtuoso* (*Max virtuose*, 1913) he pretends to be a skilled pianist to impress his upper-class girlfriend's family. But in fact the piano he plays is a mechanical one, and he is exposed when he tries to demonstrate his abilities at a party and the piano goes wrong. Linder's humor continued to be based upon these kinds of romantic complications—there is a delightful scene in *Max Does*

Not Speak English (*L'Anglais tel que Max le parle*, 1914) when he finds himself alone in a railway coach with a pretty English girl and can only communicate with her by exchanging drawings. Linder's films benefited from the services of some talented costars: Stacia de Napierkowska, Jane Renouardt, and Gaby Morlay often played the all-important female leads. Other occasional performers included a very young Maurice Chevalier and Abel Gance.

When war was declared in 1914, Linder was eager to help the Allied cause. He made a short film, *The Second of August* (*Le 2 Août 1914*), but his attempt to join the army met with a refusal on grounds of unfitness. Instead he was given a job delivering dispatches between Paris and the front in his large limousine. There are many stories of the wounds he sustained, but according to Jack Spears the truth is rather unromantic: he developed pneumonia from standing in icy water under a bridge to avoid a German patrol. Denied further military service after his recovery, Linder spent the rest of the war performing for the troops and making one or two films, including the superb spoof of the Pearl White serials, *Max and the Clutching Hand* (*Max et la main qui étreint*, 1916). During the war he also suffered the first in a series of depressions that were to plague him for the rest of his life.

During this low point, in the summer of 1916, he was visited by George K. Spoor, president of the Essanay company. Spoor offered Linder $5,000 a week to make twelve 3-reelers, and despite a counter-offer from Pathé (to costar in a serial with Pearl White), Linder accepted and headed for Chicago. Spoor needed a new comic star because Charlie Chaplin had just left him for more lucrative work at the Mutual company. And Essanay's advertising campaign for Linder gave off more than a whiff of sour grapes. In the words of Terry Ramsaye, "it was laden with innuendo. It [implied] that Chaplin was sloppy, unclean and sordid on the screen, whereas M. Linder in his new Essanay comedies was to be revealed a Beau Brummel, a Chesterfield— and very funny."

This was a large billing to live up to, especially since (as Chaplin had found) the Essanay Chicago studios were poorly equipped and difficult to work in. Linder's first film, *Max Comes Across* (1917), was not a success—as Ramsaye put it, "Max came across, but he did not go over." His next film, *Max Wants a Divorce*, was more in his old romantic style, but it too did badly. His third attempt, *Max and His Taxi*, shot in California, was fairly successful but Spoor was not impressed and arranged with a dispirited Linder to cancel the contract. (Unfortunately, none of the three films from this period have survived).

Back in Paris, Linder opened a movie theatre, the Ciné Max Linder, but could not settle back down to work. The war was depressing him deeply, and he often referred to its horrors in press interviews. But with the Armistice, Linder's spirits revived. He agreed to star in a feature-length comedy, *The Little Café* (*Le petit café*, 1919), directed by Raymond Bernard and based on a popular play by the director's father. Linder played a waiter who inherits a fortune but who has been tricked into a twenty-year contract by the café owner. Max becomes a gay man-about-town in the evenings and a very disgruntled waiter during the day. From the fragments available, Linder appears as sharp and witty as ever, and the film, after initial problems in finding a distributor, did very well in Europe, being one of the most popular films of the year in France. According to Richard Abel, it cost 160,000 francs and grossed over a million. In America it made no impression; nevertheless, Linder decided to try his luck in that country once more and, using his own money, launched an independent production company in Hollywood.

His first feature there, *Seven Years Bad Luck* (1921), is perhaps the best film he ever made. The first sequence has become a classic: Max's butler breaks a mirror and the cook, who resembles Linder, is persuaded to stand in the frame and pretend to be Max's reflection, copying every move he makes. This was not the first or the last time this gag was used, but no one has improved on Linder's style and timing. However, neither this film nor *Be My Wife*, which followed, was a success with the American public.

Linder decided on a total change of image. His *The Three Must-Get-Theres* (1922) was a parody of Dumas (and Douglas Fairbanks), relying largely on gags of anachronism: the Musketeers slide down fire-poles onto their horses; Cardinal Richelieu (played bizarrely by Bull Montana) uses a telephone concealed in a tree. There is a wonderful gag when "Dart-in-Again" (Linder) is surrounded by a circle of swordsmen: as they lunge toward him for the kill, he simply ducks and they all skewer each other! But generally, the film is ineffective and lacks the charm of Linder in his "Max" incarnation, and again it did poorly at the box office. Nevertheless it delighted both Douglas Fairbanks and a man who was very important to Linder at this time: Charlie Chaplin.

On his previous trip to Hollywood, Linder had met and formed a friendship with Chaplin. Now the two became frequent companions at boxing matches or car races, and at Linder's parties. Jack Spears writes: "While working on a picture Linder would go next door to Chaplin's home and discuss the day's shooting. The two often sat up until dawn, developing and refining the gags. Chaplin's suggestions were invaluable, Linder said." But it was a friendship of unequals, and Linder was becoming increasingly depressed by his lack of success compared to Chaplin.

Director Robert Florey, who accompanied the dispirited Linder to a preview of *The Three Must-Get-Theres*, quotes him as saying: "You see, Bob, I sense that I'm no longer funny; I have so many preoccupations that I can no longer concentrate on my film character. . . . The public is mildly amused by my situations, but this evening where were the explosions of laughter that we hear when Charlie's on the screen?. . . . 'Make people laugh,' it's easy to say, 'make people laugh,' but I don't feel funny any more."

Sick at heart, Linder returned once more to Europe and a short time later did indeed make a serious (or semi-serious) film. *The Haunted House* (*Au secours/Help!* 1923), directed by Abel Gance, is a rather uneven exercise in *grand guignol*; the best moments are when Linder undercuts the horror with touches of comedy: Max tries to hold a door shut against some horrifying power on the other side; eventually it is forced open and a tiny duckling waddles over to him. The film was well received when released in Britain in 1924, but due to rights litigation it remained unscreened in the USA or France.

Linder's last film, *The King of the Circus* (*Der Zirkuskönig*, 1924), was initiated by Jacques Feyder, with whom Linder had formed a short-lived film company. Made in Vienna in 1925, the plot had Max joining a circus to be near his sweetheart; one scene showed him waking up in a department store after a night on the town, a scene that was to be used by many other comedians later. Chaplin himself may have been influenced by the Linder film in his *The Circus*, released three years later.

In 1923 Linder had eloped with Helène Peters, an eighteen-year-old from a wealthy background. But despite this match, and despite starting work on a new film (*Barkas le fol*), Linder's depressions continued. There were rumors of drug addiction and of suicide attempts. After attending a performance of *Quo Vadis*, in which the principals bleed themselves to death, Linder seemed to be in despair and told friends he had nothing to live for. On October 31, 1925, Linder and his young wife were found in a hotel room, their wrists slashed. Their baby daughter Maud was in the room with them, and there were suicide notes. Later that day both died.

Linder's films were quickly forgotten after his death. It was not until the 1960s that, due to the efforts of Maud Linder, his rediscovery began.

His last three American comedies formed the basis of her film *En compagnie de Max Linder* (*Laugh With Max Linder*, 1963) and another compilation film followed, *L'Homme au chapeau de soie* (*The Man in the Silk Hat*). Some eighty of his films are wholly or partly preserved. What do these tell us about Linder the comic? It is often said that Linder's comic style was totally different from the slapstick of other early film comedians. In fact this is something of an exaggeration: others in this era did employ a "comedy of character"—Léonce Perret, for example, in the "Léonce" series, and Max's greatest rival, Charles Prince, who is today virtually forgotten. Prince, known in France as "Rigadin," also worked at Pathé and was as popular as Linder in the period before World War I: if Max was "the King of laughter," Prince was "the Emperor of the smile."

The similarity between the two comics is worth pursuing. The Rigadin character, like Max, was a bourgeois who never worked and was perpetually falling in love. The two comedians worked with similar plots and sometimes even used the same sets, such as the lovers' balcony in Max's *Voisin, voisine* and in *Le nez de Rigadin*. Seen today, the best of Rigadin's films, like *Rigadin, Winetaster* (*Rigadin, degustateur en vins*, 1913), are better than many of Linder's, which occasionally lack pace and gags. However, while Linder steadily improved over the years, his rival continued in the same, somewhat predictable vein. This must be partly the fault of Prince's director, Georges Monca (who in fact had also directed Linder in some uninspired films in late 1909); Linder for much of his career had one of the best comic directors in the business: himself.

The two comedians also shared a training in the legitimate theatre, though the effect of this on their work has never been critically examined. The influence of the bourgeois theatre on French cinema had really begun in 1908 with the Films d'Art, which aimed to bring classical French authors and actors into the lowbrow cinema. Until recently this movement has been thought a retrograde influence, a taming of the youthful exuberance of the cinema, but recently historians have claimed some positive results. Linder himself was very impressed by the Films d'Art and, according to Henri Fescourt, consciously decided to make his comedies in the same restrained style: "He said to me that he dreamed of making a series of playlets, each ten to fifteen minutes long, based on a situation that was comic yet possible in everyday life, needing the skill of an actor and not just hamming." This admiration for "class" stayed with Linder all his life; he always hated purely slapstick films—

Florey says that when Linder went to the movies he would always be very careful to find the exact time a feature film started, so that he would be sure to miss the slapstick short that preceded it.

It is in his contribution toward the changing of comic styles that Linder was most appreciated by later comedians. It is partly due to him that the knockabout school of comedy—dominated by people like André Deed and Mack Sennett— was slowly overtaken in public affection by the Chaplins of the comic world. (The claim by Mack Sennett that Linder influenced his comedy is largely spurious—their styles are virtual opposites, and in any case the first film in which Sennett appeared as a Frenchman—*Father Gets in the Game*—was made in 1908 before Linder was widely known).

On the other hand, Charlie Chaplin's debt to Linder was considerable, as has often been said. Both played a dapper, quick-witted rogue, though Chaplin added the ingredient of pathos to Linder's carefree clowning. Both supplemented the actor's art with that of the director, Chaplin being far more of a perfectionist in this area—Linder would usually be satisfied with one take on a scene and this is sometimes apparent in his weaker films. Chaplin often borrowed Linder's comic business and even his plots, and himself acknowledged the debt in a famous photograph which he inscribed: "To Max, the Professor, from his disciple, Charlie Chaplin."

With other comedians the influence has been less direct, but the whole tone of comedy that Linder helped create was certainly absorbed by Keaton and to some degree by Lloyd. And Max's persona finds a clear echo in the comic elegance of Raymond Griffith, of Adolphe Menjou, and more recently of Pierre Étaix.

Outside the immediate realm of comedy Linder had a more general impact: even King Vidor acknowledged in his autiobiography that he "learned much from Max." If one were to summarize Linder's contribution to the cinema, it would surely be that he popularized subtlety over crudity; he showed, as Charles Ford has written, that "to suggest is more effective than to underline."

—*S.B.*

FILMS: As actor and director (codirector at first) and usually scriptwriter.
Max dans sa famille, Max en convalescence, Max est charitable, Max est distrait, Max et son âne, Voisin voisine, Max a un duel, Max victime du quinquina, Max veut faire du théâtre, Max et Jane font des crêpes, Max et Jane en voyage de noces, Max lance la mode, Max reprend sa liberté, Max et son chien Dick, Max amoreux de la teinturière, 1911;
Max Linder contre Nick Winter, Max bandit par

amour, Que peut il avoir?, Max escamoteur, Une nuit
agitée, La malle au mariage, Max cocher de fiacre,
Match de boxe entre patineurs à roulettes, Max professeur de tango, Max et les femmes, Une idyll à la ferme, Un pari original, Max peintre par amour, La fuite
de gaz, Max boxeur par amour, Le mal de mer, La vengeance du domestique, Max collectioneur de chaus-
sures, Max jockey par amour, Voyage de noces en
Espagne, Max toréador, Max emule de tartarin, Amour
tenace, Max et l'Entente Cordiale, Max veut grandir,
Un mariage au téléphone, Le roman de Max, Max pratique tour les sports, 1912;
Comment Max fait le tour du monde, Max fait des
conquêtes, Max n'aime pas les chats, Max et le billet
doux, Max part en vacances, Max à Monaco, Max a
peur de l'eau, Un enlèvement en hydroplane, Max as-
thmatique, Le rendezvous de Max, La rivalité de Max,
Le duel de Max, Un mariage imprévu, Le hasard et
l'amour, Qui a túe Max?, Max au couvent, Les escar-
pins de Max, La ruse de Max, Le chapeau de Max, Max
virtuose, 1913;
Max sauveteur, Max décoré, Max et le comissaire, Max
pédicure, Max illusioniste, N'embrassez pas votre
bonne, Max et le bâton de rouge, L'anglais tel que Max
le parle, Max et le mari jaloux, Max et la doctoresse,
Max maître d'hôtel, Max médecin malgré lui, Max
dans les airs, Le 2 août 1914, 1914;
Max devrait porter des bretelles, Max et le sac, Max et
l'espion, 1915;
Max et la main-qui-étreint, Max entre deux feux, 1916;
Max Comes Across, Max Wants a Divorce, Max and
His Taxi, 1917;
Seven Years Bad Luck, Be My Wife, 1921;
The Three Must-Get-Theres, 1922.

ABOUT: Abel, R. French Cinema: The First Wave,
1915–1929, 1984; Fescourt, H. La foi et les montagnes,
1959; Florey, R. La lanterne magique, 1966; Ford, C.
Max Linder, 1966 (in French); Institut Jean Vigo. Les
premiers ans du cinéma français, 1985; Kerr, W. The
Silent Clowns, 1975; Mitry, J. Filmographie Universelle, 1964 to date; Mitry, J. Max Linder, 1966 (in
French); Sadoul, G. Histoire générale du cinéma, vols.
2–6, 1949–1980. *Periodicals*—Bioscope 1908–1914;
Film Comment September–October 1984; Films in
Review May 1965; Moving Picture World 1907--1914.

LITVAK, ANATOLE (Mikhail Anatol
Litvak or Litwak) (May 10, 1902–December
15, 1974), American director, scenarist, and producer, was born into a Jewish family in Kiev,
Russia. His father, a bank manager, moved the
family to St. Petersburg when Litvak was still a
child. He reportedly entered the University of
St. Petersburg as a student of philosophy at the
age of fourteen, continued his studies through all
the upheavals and chaos of the revolution and
the civil war, and emerged in 1921 with a doctorate.

Meanwhile, Litvak had become involved as a
stagehand and actor in the burgeoning

ANATOLE LITVAK

avant-garde theatre of the immediate post-
revolutionary years. He even visited Moscow
while still in his teens, meeting and working in-
formally with such innovators as Meyerhold and
Vagtangov. In 1922, after his graduation, he
joined an avant-garde theatre company in Leningrad (as St. Petersburg had become) and soon
afterwards gained entry to the State School of
Theatre. He continued to work for his fringe
theatre, and by 1923 was directing as well as acting there. "I would have stayed at the little
theatre," he said later, "had it not been transformed into an immense place absolutely unsuited for being an experimental theatre. It was at
that time that I chose cinema."

In 1923, Litvak joined the Nordkino studios in
Leningrad as an assistant director and set decorator. The following year he directed two short
films, *Tatiana,* "a film about kids," and *Hearts
and Dollars,* an anti-American piece that was released in France as *Le Coeur.* Litvak worked on
other Soviet films as assistant director or coscenarist, but no details are available—partly because of his own reticence about his early career,
partly because Soviet filmographies omitted all
references to Litvak's work until the "thaw." After that, he was credited in some sources as
coscenarist with K. Derszhavin of the latter's
Samii Yunii Pioner (*A Very Young Pioneer,*
1925), a comedy about a teenaged activist.

It has never been explained how Litvak was
able to leave the Soviet Union, as he did in 1925.
His stated destination was Paris, but the same
year he turned up at the UFA studios in Berlin,
where he was known as Anatol Lutwak. At UFA
he had a hand in the editing of Pabst's *Die*

freudlose Gasse (*The Joyless Street*, 1925), and afterwards worked as assistant and general factotum to the flamboyant expatriate director Nikolai Alexander Volkoff, who had escaped from Russia with a large fortune just after the Bolshevik revolution.

Volkoff and his retinue lived lavishly in Paris, commuting to Berlin to work on his UFA films. Litvak was involved in various capacities in a number of Volkoff's pictures and was actually credited as assistant director of three of them: the Ivan Moszhukin vehicles *Casanova* (1927; released in the United States in 1929 as *The Loves of Casanova*) and *Der weisse Teufel* (*The White Devil*, 1930), and *Scheherazade* (1929; released in the United States in 1932 as *Secrets of the Orient*). Litvak was entrusted with the direction of the talking and musical sequences that were added to *The White Devil* when it was converted to sound, and it has been said that it was his facility with languages—at a time when some early European talkies were being made in as many as eight languages—that earned Litvak his chance as a director.

His first film at UFA was *Dolly macht Karriere* (*Dolly's Way to Stardom/Dolly Gets Ahead*, 1929), a backstage musical starring Dolly Haas that was highly successful at the box office. The following year Litvak directed his first multiple-language picture, a shipboard musical comedy, in the German version called *Nie wieder Liebe*. Litvak, who collaborated with Irma von Cube on the script, had the young Max Ophuls as his assistant and a cast headed by Harry Liedke, Lilian Harvey, and Felix Bressart. The French version, *Calais-Douvres*, also directed by Litvak, was shot simultaneously in Berlin, with virtually the same bilingual cast.

A much more personal film followed, *Coeur de Lilas* (1932), made not in Germany but for Artistes Associés in France. Litvak scripted the movie himself, from the play by Tristan Bernard. It is a raw and remarkably authentic account of low life in the bars and streets of the Porte de Lilas district of Paris, with Jean Gabin—then little known—as a gangster, and Fernandel in a bit part.

A publicity handout of the time quotes Litvak as saying: "It may seem reckless of me to try to direct grim and cruel subjects which unfold at the lower depths of life when such subjects have been treated with great technique by directors of great talents. My cast speaks only when it's necessary for the drama, and words are not the only sound effects. We use street noises and the sounds of motor cars. . . . It is necessary nowadays to remember that sounds are another support for a film's images, heightening their pictorial values, underscoring their visual beauty."

Coeur de Lilas was a success, financial and critical, and Litvak returned to Berlin with his reputation enhanced. He had another hit with *Das Lied einer Nacht* (1932), made for Cine-Allianz Tonfilm (successor to Volkoff's old company). Scripted by Irma von Cube, this was a musical about a famous Italian singer traveling incognito but unable to conceal his "sex appeal." It starred Jan Kiepura and Magda Schneider (mother of Romy), and the same pair appeared in the English version, directed by Litvak as *Be Mine Tonight*, and the French, called *La Chanson d'une nuit*. (The latter was directed by Henri-Georges Clouzot and Pierre Colombier "under the artistic supervision" of Litvak.)

In 1933, when Hitler came to power in Germany, Litvak went to Paris. His first picture there was the comedy-drama *Cette vieille canaille* (Pathé, 1937), coscripted by Litvak and Serge Veber from Fernand Nozier's play. Harry Bauer plays a doctor who nobly saves the life of the man (Pierre Blanchar) who had stolen his mistress. The same year Litvak accepted a one-picture deal with Gaumont British to make *Sleeping Car*, which miscast Ivor Novello as an amorous sleeping-car attendant on a transcontinental train carrying, among others, Madeleine Carroll. The movie seems to have vanished without trace—fortunately so, by all accounts.

Back at Pathé, Litvak directed a remake of Maurice Tourneur's silent *L'Équipage* (*Flight Into Darkness*, 1935), with a script by Joseph Kessel and the director. Charles Vanel was cast as the middle-aged air ace Maury, Annabella as his wife Denise, and Jean-Pierre Aumont as Herbillon, the young flyer who falls in love with the faithless Denise. The film features a twenty-minute aerial battle cut to Arthur Honegger's score.

Basil Wright called this "an undistinguished film, redeemed only by a few moments of sincerity," and "humdrum" in its direction. This was a minority view, however, and *Variety*'s reviewer found "camera work and direction . . . outstanding" in this "gripping, human story." *Boxoffice* likewise praised it as "absorbing, although somewhat grim entertainment."

It was Litvak's next picture that established his international reputation. *Mayerling* (1936), based on Claude Anet's novel and adapted by Irma von Cube and Joseph Kessel, stars Charles Boyer and Danielle Darrieux in an intensely romantic version of a much-filmed story—the forbidden love affair between the dissolute Archduke Rudolph, heir to the Hapsburg empire, and the beautiful Maria Vetsera. The couple's mysterious death in 1890 in the hunting lodge at Mayerling, which has so exercised the imaginations of writers and historians, is here presented unequivocally as the product of a suicide pact.

Litvak made the film in five weeks, apparently because Boyer had commitments elsewhere. It was greeted with an international chorus of praise as "one of the most compelling love stories the cinema has produced" and "a romantic tragedy of the highest order." Lincoln Kirstein, commending Litvak's "comprehension of psychological nuance, his tactful and judicious recreation of the strict Hapsburg etiquette," said the film had become "a kind of standard for the romantic film in an historical setting." A more recent writer, Jack Edmund Nolan, in his article about Litvak in *Films in Review* (November 1967), wrote that his direction "was replete with the camera trackings, pans and swoops which later became the trademark of Max Ophuls. *Mayerling* well illustrates Litvak's extreme ambivalence toward royalty and the Europe that existed before World War I. And, typically, his visualizations in *Mayerling* of the glories of the Austro-Hungarian empire are more memorable than his depiction of its corruption."

The immense worldwide success of *Mayerling* brought Litvak to Hollywood (along with both Boyer and Darrieux). Various projects were mooted for various studios, including a version of *Joan of Arc* that was to have starred Claudette Colbert. As it turned out, Litvak made his first American film at RKO—a remake of *L'Équipage* called *The Woman I Love* (1937). Ethel Borden wrote the script, altered to center on the Lafayette Escadrille. Paul Muni, Miriam Hopkins, and Louis Hayward replaced the original stars, and Henry Rust re-edited the *L'Équipage* dogfight scenes with some new footage. Admired as it was by some, it was said not to "hang together" as successfully as the French film.

The same year, Litvak and Miriam Hopkins began a marriage that lasted for only two years. Meanwhile, he joined Warner Brothers, where he worked as a contract director until the end of 1941, directing nine films, many of them in the socially conscious mode the studio had by then embraced.

Tovarich (1937), based on Robert F. Sherwood's adaptation of Jacques Deval's popular play, has White Russian nobles Claudette Colbert and Charles Boyer, ruined and exiled by the revolution, working incognito as servants for a fatuous Parisian banker (Melville Cooper). Penniless as they are, they will not touch the fortune entrusted to them by the czar to help finance a counterrevolution. Commissar Basil Rathbone shows up and eventually convinces them that it is their duty to hand over the hoard for the benefit of the new Russia.

The movie was well enough received by contemporary critics, though several complained that Litvak's direction sometimes "sacrifices the subtle humor of the original for broader comedy effects." It seemed to Jack Edmund Nolan that "Litvak's exceptional ability to carry political water on both shoulders has never been better exemplified than here. The banker for whom the noble couple work . . . is broadly caricatured; the commissar . . . can be taken any way your political predilection prefers."

Litvak produced as well as directed his next film, as he did frequently thereafter. *The Amazing Dr. Clitterhouse* (1938) was adapted by John Wexley and John Huston from the successful stage play by Barre Lyndon. Edward G. Robinson stars as a distinguished psychologist who, to further his investigation of the roots of crime, joins a gang of jewel thieves, showing such talent and panache that he becomes the gang's leader. Blackmailed by "public enemy" Humphrey Bogart, he next tries his hand at murder and, in an extremely funny trial sequence, escapes retribution by pleading insanity.

In a role previously played on the stage by Ralph Richardson and Cedric Hardwicke, Robinson gives a performance of polished and sardonic assurance, and there is excellent support from Bogart, Claire Trevor, and (as a bemused jury foreman) Irving Bacon. The picture was enjoyed equally for its suspense and for its black humor, and Otis Ferguson was reminded of Hitchcock by the film's "dramatic irony."

The Sisters (1938) follows the marital fortunes of three Montana girls at the turn of the century. It concentrates on Bette Davis' sufferings as the wife of a hard-drinking newspaperman (Errol Flynn), culminating in her miscarriage after much travail in the San Francisco earthquake. In spite of the lachrymose story, Graham Greene thought it "worth seeing for the sake of the adroit period direction and the fragile, popeyed acting" of the star. The historical background, including the elections of Theodore Roosevelt and Taft, is carefully sketched in—early evidence of Litvak's fondness for stiffening his fictions with facts.

This tendency comes to the fore in *Confessions of a Nazi Spy* (1939), which pits FBI agent Edward G. Robinson against a Nazi spy ring that includes Paul Lukas and Francis Lederer—the latter giving the performance of his life as the egocentric failure whose vanity destroys the spy network. No masterpiece, this well-constructed drama is of exceptional interest on two counts. Based on fact, it mixes convincing reconstructions of Gestapo activities in America and elsewhere with actual newsreel footage of Nazi Bund rallies in New York and New Jersey. The dramatized incidents, as David Wolff wrote, are "connected and explained by a commentator" as though the film were a full-length version of MGM's "Crime Does Not Pay" series: "It has the same general method, the same plain people and utilitarian dialogue, the same emphasis on clarity of situation."

In fact, the movie can be seen as a prototype of the quasi-documentary thrillers of the postwar years. It is historically no less interesting as one of Hollywood's first contributions to World War II propaganda. Wolff said it was "a crusading picture, and an immensely successful one, for the audience invariably comes out of the the-atre discussing not the film as such, but its content." Another reviewer suggested that "its public exhibition may prove a milestone in the history of the cinema as a political force."

Graham Greene, in a moving review in the London *Spectator* (June 23, 1939), wrote: "Well, the war of nerves is on, and the Censor who refused last autumn to pass a *March of Time* issue criticising the Munich settlement now allows an actor made up as Dr. Goebbels to refer to 'our glorious victory at Munich': he even gives the U. certificate, which he refuses most Westerns, to this picture of methodical violence and treachery. Our children must be allowed to hate, and we can really feel, when the Board of British Film Censors abandons the policy of appeasement, that it is really dead at last. So—repressing a slight shudder—let us give as whole-hearted a welcome as we can to this magnificently constructed engine-of-war."

Litvak next prepared and began shooting the gangster movie *The Roaring Twenties*. He was replaced by Raoul Walsh, for reasons that have never been entirely clear, and turned his attention to *Castle on the Hudson* (1940), loosely based on the memoirs of Sing Sing warden Lewis E. Lawes. John Garfield starred as an arrogant racketeer with his own code of morality who keeps his word to the warden, even though he goes to the chair for it. It was generally well received as an effective drama with good performances by Garfield, Ann Sheridan, Pat O'Brien, and Burgess Meredith.

All This and Heaven Too (1940) was considerably more ambitious. Set in Paris in 1847, it is (like *Mayerling*) a recreation of a famous historical scandal—the love affair between the Duc de Praslin (Charles Boyer) and his children's governess (Bette Davis) which ended with the mur-der of the neurotic duchess and the suicide of the duke. Casey Robinson's script draws as much on historical accounts of the affair as on Rachel Field's novel about it, and there is again a documentary element in the film's style. Contemporary reviewers baulked at the movie's "enormous length" (two and a quarter hours), but most admired its "delicate" direction, and the relatively subdued performance Litvak had extracted from Bette Davis.

Jack Edmund Nolan nominates as Litvak's worst film *City for Conquest* (1940), a "mish-mash of infantile leftisms" about a boxer (James Cagney), blinded by a crooked opponent, who draws comfort from his brother's success as a composer. Ann Sheridan is the wisecracking heroine, Arthur Kennedy the sensitive brother, and the film also provides roles for Anthony Quinn and Elia Kazan. It was followed by *Out of the Fog* (1941), from Irwin Shaw's play *The Gentle People,* set in the Sheepshead Bay district of Brooklyn. Local girl Ida Lupino, seduced by protection racketeer John Garfield, learns the hard way to appreciate the sterling qualities of the boring boy next door (Eddie Albert).

Robert Rossen, who had collaborated on the script of *Out of the Fog,* also wrote *Blues in the Night* (1941), about an itinerant jazz band, led by Richard Whorf, that finds success and happiness in a nightclub run by friendly gangster Lloyd Nolan. The agreeable songs were by Johnny Mercer and Harold Arlen. *Blues in the Night* was rather coolly received on first release, but Richard Winnington, after seeing a reissue in 1946, concluded that it had been underrated. He found it "a film of sincerity and character, an odd and successful fusion of Musical and Gangster [genres] developed with a minimum of explanation and acted to the bone by Richard Whorf, Priscilla Lane, Betty Field, Lloyd Nolan, Jack Carson, and Howard da Silva. . . . *Blues in the Night* under the direction of Anatole Litvak moves swiftly and exists in its own right as a tough, rasping melodrama."

It was Litvak's last film for Warner Brothers, where he was apparently a casualty of Jack Warner's chronic itch to dispose of expensive talent. His next film, *This Above All,* was made in 1942 for 20th Century–Fox. Scripted by R. C. Sherriff from the novel by Eric Knight, it stars Tyrone Power as the disillusioned British soldier who deserts near the beginning of World War II but rediscovers his duty in the arms of aristocratic WAAF Joan Fontaine. Power was badly miscast, but the movie was nevertheless effective as a touching love story and in its portrayal of the London blitz, contrived through a skillful combination of newsreel footage and model work.

Litvak was by this time an American citizen, and in 1942 he joined the Special Services Film Unit of the United States Army. After helping to film the North African landings, he worked with Frank Capra on the "Why We Fight" series, co-producing and co-directing four of them, and directing *War Comes to America* solo. These two-reelers combined actuality and fictional footage in a way that Litvak had long since mastered, and the films were edited by Willis Hornbeck with such skill that the "joins" seldom showed. All of the "Why We Fight" films directed by Litvak were scripted by Anthony Veiller and narrated by Walter Huston, with music by Dmitri Tiomkin. Litvak subsequently supervised the filming of the Normandy landings and recorded aerial warfare with the Eighth Air Force. He ended the war a full colonel, with awards from the governments of Britain, the United States, and France (including the Légion d'Honneur and the Croix de Guerre).

He returned to Hollywood as a freelance, attached to no one studio. In fact, his first postwar project was not a film at all but a stage play, *Meet Me at Dawn*, which he wrote in collaboration with Marcel Achard. Set in *fin de siècle* Paris, it concerns a plot to dispose of a politician by forcing him into conflict with a deadly duellist—a storyline more familiar in the context of the Western. The play was filmed in 1947 from a script written not by Anatole Litvak but by Lesley Storm and James Seymour, directed by Thornton Freeland.

Litvak's own first postwar picture was *The Long Night* (RKO, 1947), a remake of Marcel Carné's *Le Jour se lève*, with Henry Fonda in the Gabin role, Vincent Price doubling for Jules Berry as the obscene showman who steals Fonda's girl, and Ann Dvorak attempting the part of the enigmatic prostitute so magnificently portrayed by Arletty in the original. As Roger Manvell wrote, "the shell of the place and the story is there" but "the richer feeling for human life and instinct and love always present in the French film is gone." RKO's attempts to buy and destroy all prints of Carné's great film in the interests of their own version were bitterly attacked and, in the end, fortunately unsuccessful.

A screen version of Lucille Fletcher's radio shocker *Sorry, Wrong Number* followed from Paramount in 1948, with Barbara Stanwyck as the rich bedridden neurotic who, thanks to a crossed line, learns that two professional hit men plan to kill a woman at 11:15 that night. Subsequent phone calls establish that the killer's client is her own husband (Burt Lancaster) and that the proposed victim is herself. The rest of the film deals with her increasingly frantic attempts to invoke help before the all too literal deadline arrives. The picture was a box-office hit and earned Stanwyck an Oscar, though most critics thought it altogether less intense, credible, and coherent than the original radio play.

Litvak had himself bought the film rights to *Sorry, Wrong Number,* which he coproduced with Hal B. Wallis. He did the same with Mary Jane Ward's novel *The Snake Pit,* snapping it up while it was still in galleys and eventually persuading Fox to back it. Olivia de Havilland stars as the tormented heroine whose sufferings in a barbarous mental hospital were so harrowingly portrayed as to provoke immense controversy, a good deal of censorship and, according to some accounts, reforms in the relevant legislation.

There was universal admiration for Olivia de Havilland's performance, and she was nominated for an Oscar (as was the film itself). Otherwise, critical opinions varied widely between those who thought the film "compassionate, understanding, and informed with truth" (Fred Majdalany), and those who, like Herman G. Weinberg, considered that "everything has been put in to shock or move or entertain an audience" in "a film of superficial veracity . . . of a subject that requires a bigger man than Litvak."

Twenty years later, Eileen Bowser in *Film Notes* called the picture dated but "still convincing and deeply moving, thanks to an expert manipulation of film techniques . . . the terrible isolation of the mentally ill is made felt by the camera placements and movements and the use of the nonsynchronous sound track. . . . Sometimes the sound track contrasts with the objectivity of the camera, and we hear the patient narrating her thoughts or hear loud, discordant music at her greatest moments of panic. Objective and subjective angles alternate. The camera dwells on the patient's face, but when we cut away, as often as not we are seeing from her viewpoint. . . . The various points of view are woven together very skillfully, without apparent discrepancies, comparable to the combined use of first and third person in a novel."

Another notable picture followed, *Decision Before Dawn* (1951), scripted by Peter Viertel from George Howe's novel *Call It Treason,* itself based on fact. Oskar Werner plays "Happy," an anti-Nazi German medic captured by the Americans in early 1945. Hoping to hasten the end of the war, he agrees to spy against his own country. Richard Basehart and Gary Merrill are American intelligence officers, and Hildegard Knef a German girl demoralized by the war.

Decision Before Dawn was shot by Franz Planer on location in various devastated cities.

Arthur Knight wrote that "Anatole Litvak has planned his shooting to involve his audiences at all points. His long, sweeping pan shots across the chaos of a newly bombed city, ground troops fleeing a raid by P-47s, the sudden choke of traffic at a Nazi checkpoint—all these mass scenes are handled so that we can pick out from the crowd, the figure of Happy. . . . For us the camera builds the German scene with such detail, such depth, and such dimension that it becomes impossible to accept it all as merely a recreation. This is Germany 1945 just as long as it remains on the screen." Another critic said that "the raw emotions, prejudices, and loyalties arising out of the theme are treated with real understanding," and for Jack Edmund Nolan this was Litvak's "masterpiece, and, in my opinion, the best film about Nazism made anywhere."

Decision Before Dawn was Litvak's second film in succession to be nominated for an Oscar. By this time, however, he had left Hollywood and settled in Paris, where he married a former fashion model named Sophie Bourdeen. Most of his subsequent films were made in Europe and reflected his desire to secure maximum control over his work—a policy that was not always beneficial to it.

His next picture, for example, *Act of Love* (1953), was financed and produced by the director, who also coscripted it (with Irwin Shaw) from Alfred Hayes' novel *The Girl on the Via Flamina*. The adaptation shifted the story from Italy to liberated Paris, where GI Kirk Douglas takes in a homeless French girl (Dany Robin) and begins a doomed love affair. The film struck most critics as too long and sadly lacking in the poignant lyricism Litvak had achieved in *Mayerling* and elsewhere. And reviewers found virtually nothing to commend in his screen version of Terrence Rattigan's play *The Deep Blue Sea*, made in Britain.

Litvak's fading reputation was rescued by *Anastasia* (1956), scripted by Arthur Laurents from a play by Marcelle Maureth. Yul Brynner plays a former White Russian general on the make who attempts to pass off an amnesiac French waif (Ingrid Bergman) as the youngest daughter of Czar Nicolas, miraculously saved from the slaughter at Ekaterinburg. Coached and groomed by her bald Pygmalion, the girl grows ever more convincingly regal, seeming oddly to remember more than she has been taught of her fabricated past.

"And still the best is to come," wrote the critic of the London *Times*, "the scene between the girl and the Empress in Copenhagen, the girl longing for the love and sense of security that only knowledge of her own identity can give, the old woman steeling herself to resist a too easy surrender to the desire to be deceived. Miss Helen Hayes and Miss Bergman make this scene one of the most moving and memorable in the history of the cinema." Ingrid Bergman earned an Oscar for her performance in this, her Hollywood comeback.

Litvak's only television film followed, an expensive but sadly static remake of *Mayerling*, starring Mel Ferrer and Audrey Hepburn. *The Journey* (1959) was written by George Tabori around a situation suggested by Litvak (who also produced). A well-assorted busload of Western neutrals trying to leave Hungary after the uprising of 1956 are stopped at the border by a Soviet officer (Yul Brynner) uncertain of the political allegiance of a wounded Hungarian. Various stories are played out in this dangerous limbo, including a near romance between an English passenger (Deborah Kerr) and the decent Russian officer. Then the latter sends the bus on its way in a quixotic gesture that for him proves fatal.

Shot on location in and around Vienna, not far from the Hungarian border, it seemed to Jack Edmund Nolan another opportunity "to watch Litvak carrying political water on both shoulders." The director himself proudly defended the film's "fair play" in presenting a Soviet officer who was not "all black"—its eschewal of Cold War stereotypes. Steven Marcus thought that in this movie "we are back in the . . . 1930s with Alfred Hitchcock and that glamorous band of international characters trapped in Mitteleuropa"— a band that includes Jason Robards Jr., Robert Morley, Anouk Aimée, E. G. Marshall, and Anne Jackson.

After two fatuous films, *Goodbye Again* (1961) and *Five Miles to Midnight* (1962), Litvak made no more for five years. *The Night of the Generals* was a distinct improvement over its predecessors. Adapted from a novel by Hans Helmut Kirst, it casts Peter O'Toole as a psychopathic German general who, having murdered and mutilated girls in Warsaw and Paris during World War II, continues this practice afterwards until he is unmasked by a dedicated German intelligence officer (Omar Sharif). Marred as it was by O'Toole's mannered performance, the movie was generally admired as "a good old-fashioned psychological thriller . . . elegantly decked out in the trappings of Hitler's New Europe." David Robinson wrote that "in recent years Anatole Litvak has become very much a *realisateur* in the literal sense of directly, cleanly, faithfully, elegantly (not to say glossily) realising, rather than interpreting scripts. His films therefore tend to be as good as their screenplays, and this is a good one."

The same could not be said for Litvak's next movie, which turned out to be his last, *La Dame dans l'auto avec des lunettes et un fusie (The Lady in the Car With Glasses and a Gun,* 1969). Samantha Eggar plays the hapless heroine, an English secretary in France who finds herself framed for a murder she is not quite certain she did not commit. In spite of photography by Claude Renoir and a cast that includes Oliver Reed and Stéphane Audran, it seemed to Jan Dawson that the film "failed to establish either credible situations or humanly recognisable characters."

Jack Edmund Nolan, noting that Litvak had been called "a politically conscious Ernst Lubitsch," wrote: "Politically conscious Litvak certainly is, but politically 'committed' I doubt. I infer, from his pictures, that he is merely anti whatever establishment happens to be established." But *Decision Before Dawn,* Nolan concluded, "makes one wonder what Litvak might not have accomplished in the way of illuminating the human destiny, had the turmoil of our times not swamped his spirit and corroded his mind." As it is, the critical enthusiasm that has tended to greet revivals of his best films suggests that, like so many other half-forgotten Hollywood craftsmen, Litvak and his work are due for reassessment.

FILMS: Tatiana, 1924 (short); Hearts and Dollars, 1924 (short); Dolly macht Karriere (Dolly's Way to Stardom), 1929; Nie wieder Liebe, 1931; Calais-Douvres, 1931 (French version of Nie wieder Liebe); Coeur de Lilas, 1932; Das Lied einer Nacht, 1932; Be Mine Tonight, 1932 (English version of Das Lied einer Nacht); Sleeping Car, 1933; Cette vieille canaille, 1933; L'Équipage (Flight Into Darkness), 1935; Mayerling, 1936; The Woman I Love (U.K., The Woman Between), 1937; Tovarich, 1937; The Amazing Dr. Clitterhouse, 1938; The Sisters, 1938; Confessions of a Nazi Spy, 1939; Castle on the Hudson, 1940; City for Conquest, 1940; All This and Heaven Too, 1940; Out of the Fog, 1941; Blues in the Night, 1941; This Above All, 1942; (with Frank Capra) The Nazis Strike, 1942 ("Why We Fight"); (with Frank Capra) Divide and Conquer, 1942 ("Why We Fight"); (with Frank Capra) The Battle of Russia, 1943 ("Why We Fight"); (with Frank Capra) The Battle of China, 1944 ("Why We Fight"); War Comes to America, 1945 ("Why We Fight"); The Long Night, 1947; Sorry, Wrong Number, 1948; The Snake Pit, 1948; Decision Before Dawn, 1951; Act of Love, 1953; The Deep Blue Sea, 1955; Anastasia, 1956; Mayerling, 1957 (for television); The Journey, 1959 (retitled Some of Us May Die); Goodbye Again (U.K., Aimez-vous Brahms?), 1961; Five Miles to Midnight, 1962; The Night of the Generals, 1967; La Dame dans l'auto avec des lunettes et un fusil (The Lady in the Car With Glasses and a Gun), 1969.

ABOUT: Meyer, W. R. Warner Brothers Directors, 1978; Thomson, D. A Biographical Dictionary of the Cinema, 1980. *Periodicals*—Films in Review November 1967.

LLOYD, FRANK (February 2, 1886–August 10, 1960), American director, scenarist, and producer, was born in Glasgow, Scotland, and grew up in the Shepherds Bush district of London. According to George Geltzer's article about Lloyd in *Films in Review* (May 1981), his father Edmund "traveled all over the British Isles, from port to port, he being one of the first engineers to instal turbine engines in ships." This is puzzling, since most other sources maintain that Edmund Lloyd was a musical comedy actor.

As it happens, Frank Lloyd showed a taste for both of his father's putative professions. A love of the sea—evident in some of his best films—inspired an early ambition to become a sailor, but at fifteen, when he ended his education in London state schools, Lloyd embarked on a show-business career. As a singer specializing in imitations of Albert Chevalier and Harry Lauder, he performed in concert parties in West London, in time graduating to musical comedy and operetta, and to straight acting with repertory companies in various parts of Britain.

In 1909 or 1910 Lloyd emigrated to Canada, armed with a letter of introduction to a London member of Parliament to the Winnipeg entrepreneur C. P. Walker. His stint with Walker Theatrical Enterprises seems to have been brief, and a period of hardship followed during which Lloyd worked at an assortment of jobs, including one as a telegraph lineman. He eventually resumed his acting career with the resident stock company in Edmonton, Alberta, where he met and married Alma Heller, the troupe's German-American soubrette. The couple moved to the United States, where Lloyd turned to vaudeville, touring up and down the West Coast on the Pantages circuit. In 1913 he was playing in burlesque at the Century Theatre in Los Angeles when an actor acquaintance arranged for him to meet Carl Laemmle of Universal, who hired him.

Lloyd's first film credit was a small role in *Shadows of Life* (1913), a two-reeler coscripted and codirected by Lois Weber. In 1913–1915 Lloyd appeared in more than fifty Universal movies, most of them one- or two-reelers. Many of his early pictures were directed by Otis Turner, a competent professional from whom Lloyd learned much. He directed his own first two-reeler, *A Prince of Bavaria,* in 1914. Later the same year he tried his hand as a scenarist,

FRANK LLOYD

coscripting with Philip Walsh *The Link That Binds*, which he also played in and directed. During 1915 Lloyd directed no less than thirty-three short features, acting in eighteen of them and scripting or coscripting fifteen.

According to George Geltzer, Lloyd "was an efficient writer, but as an actor . . . it was a toss-up as to whether he or W. S. Van Dyke was the poorer." Lloyd "shed no tears" when he moved to Pallas-Morosco in 1915, abandoning his acting career almost completely. At Pallas-Morosco he was for the first time directing five-reel (full-length) features. He began there with *The Gentleman From Indiana* (1915), adapted by Julia Crawford Ivers from the novel by Booth Tarkington, and starring Dustin Farnum and Winifred Kingston. The same pair were featured in *David Garrick* (1916), another Ivers script. Lloyd's other stars during his year with Pallas-Morosco included Charlotte Greenwood, Constance Collier, Forrest Stanley, and Vivian Martin. Florence and King Vidor both appeared in *The Intrigue* (1916).

Lloyd broke into the big time the same year, when he joined the Fox Film Corporation. He made fifteen pictures there between 1916 and 1919, most of them scripted or coscripted by himself. After the melodrama *Sin of the Parent* (1916) he made *The Price of Silence* (1917), working for the first time with Dustin Farnum's brother William. The latter also starred in Lloyd's first major success, his seven-reel version of Dickens' novel of the French Revolution, *A Tale of Two Cities* (1917).

Faced with the first real challenge of his career, Lloyd had decided it would be "more dis-creet to bring the work of Charles Dickens before (possibly) many million people, than the work of Lloyd. For that reason I followed as closely as possible the story of the book. Every historical detail was absolutely correct; all the settings were the result of careful, patient research; and the characterizations and theme of the story were transferred to the screen in such a manner as to accurately follow the author's ideas."

Peter Milne, in his review, wrote that in *A Tale of Two Cities* Lloyd had "earned himself a place in the hall of fame of directors. Better than his masterly handling of the mob scenes, his delightful reproduction of the atmosphere of the period; better than his remarkable double-exposure scenes and the selection of proper types, is the manner in which he has handled the plot itself," wringing from the story "every possible atom of suspense."

Lloyd worked exceptionally well with William Farnum, who starred in most of the pictures he directed for Fox, including a ten-reel *Les Misérables* and two Zane Grey Westerns, *Riders of the Purple Sage* and *The Rainbow Trail*, both made in 1918.

After World War I, Lloyd moved on again to the Goldwyn company, where his first assignment was *The World and Its Women* (1919), an elaborate drama of the Russian Revolution starring Geraldine Farrar. Lloyd directed thirteen films for Goldwyn, the most notable of them being *Madame X* (1920) and *The Sin Flood* (1921). The first, based on a play by Alexandre Bisson, was a tearjerker set in France about a woman (Pauline Frederick) who sinks into alcoholic degradation after she is spurned by her husband, but nevertheless commits murder to save him from blackmail. In the famous trial scene, the woman is defended by a tyro lawyer who never learns that he is fighting for the life of his own mother. This outrageous piece of flummery was subsequently remade twice.

The Sin Flood, based on an American adaptation of Henning Berger's play *Syndafloden*, sounds considerably more original. According to George Geltzer, it was "a drama of regeneration when the great vault-like doors of a cellar bar are closed and locked, shutting out the waters . . . [that have overflowed] the New Orleans levee, locking in the human dregs that have sought refuge there. Starring Richard Dix, with Helene Chadwick and James Kirkwood, it was an unusual and gripping drama."

Lloyd made some of his best silents after his move to First National in 1922, including several vehicles for the reigning queen of Hollywood, Norma Talmadge. She starred in his first film for the studio, *The Eternal Flame* (1922), adapted by Frances Marion from a Balzac novel, *La Duchesse de Langeais.* The cast of this unusually erotic Napoleonic drama also included Conway Tearle and Adolphe Menjou. Next came a version of *Oliver Twist,* with Jackie Coogan as Oliver and Lon Chaney as Fagin. Robert E. Sherwood wrote that "*Oliver Twist* was a coherent story on the screen, and this was entirely due to Frank Lloyd's deft weaving of the various strands of plot."

By 1923, Lloyd was so well established at First National that he was given his own production unit there. Its first project was *Black Oxen,* from the novel by Gertrude Atherton—"a strong drama of rejuvenation" starring Corinne Griffith and newcomer Clara Bow. *Photoplay* concluded that Lloyd's next picture was his best since *A Tale of Two Cities.* It was a lavish version of Rafael Sabatini's novel *The Sea Hawk* (1924), with Milton Sills as the swashbuckling hero. The adaptation was the work of J. G. Hawks, who had scripted *The Sin Flood* and who wrote a number of Lloyd's First National films as well. *Photoplay* found the movie overlong at twelve reels, but said that the battle scenes were done "with spirit and skill," while those dealing with the hero's stint as a galley slave were powerfully graphic.

Lloyd directed his last movie with his First National unit in 1926, did a two-picture stint with Paramount, and then returned to First National as an ordinary (but highly successful) contract director. He earned his first Oscar as director—the second ever awarded—for *The Divine Lady* (1929), a sumptuous historical drama about Nelson (Victor Varconi) and Lady Hamilton (Corinne Griffith).

The two Richard Barthelmess vehicles that followed also earned Oscar nominations —*Weary River* (1929), Lloyd's first "all-talking" film, and *Drag* (1929), costarring Lila Lee as a virtuous nagger who drives her husband to drink. These two were the first in a series of eight movies scripted for Lloyd by Bradley King. They included *The Way of All Men,* a remake with sound of *The Sin Flood,* and a very popular version of *East Lynne* (1931), starring Ann Harding and Clive Brook. One contemporary reviewer called Lloyd "a sentimentalist with a Scottish reserve, which took him at a bound across the gulfs of bathos" that yawn throughout Mrs. Henry Wood's melodrama.

Lloyd had made *East Lynne* on loan to Fox, and its success brought him a contract with that studio, for which he made five pictures, including the one that elevated him into the front rank of American directors, *Cavalcade* (1933), faithfully adapted from Noel Coward's play by Regi-nald Berkeley. It is a panorama of thirty years of Victorian and Edwardian English life, including the Boer War and World War I, unfolding through the experiences—tragic and joyful—of Jane Marryot (Diana Wynyard), her husband Robert (Clive Brook), their children, friends, and servants.

The Observer's reviewer wrote that *Cavalcade* was "perhaps the greatest reproach that has ever been levelled at the British film industry. . . . There was no reason in the world, except lack of vision, why the film rights of Noel Coward's play should not have been snapped up by a British production company as soon as its success became apparent at Drury Lane. They were not. They were snapped up by the Fox Film Company of America. The entire stage performance of *Cavalcade* was shot one afternoon by Movietone News, and shipped to Hollywood for reference. . . . The cast was handpicked from British players already in America and others recruited from the London stage . . . [and] a large proportion of the technical staff was British."

The same anonymous critic goes on: "The film is Noel Coward's *Cavalcade,* patriotic, sentimental, swaggering, moving, packed with hysteria, and dodging any real constructive issue, but so close to the emotional memories of every British man and woman that it must sweep British audiences off their feet wherever it is shown. . . . I cannot think of any way in which the stage spectacle could have been better transferred to the screen. You miss colour, perhaps, and the screen seems at moments too small to hold the thrusting crowd of images. But on the whole, the sense of space and movement is wonderfully contrived. Close-ups are used not to interrupt, but to correlate the action. Crowd scenes, where a single American voice might break the illusion, are played silent against a fanfare of music. Diana Wynyard's lovely playing of Jane Marryot gives the scattered episodes a central meaning. . . . *Cavalcade* is the best British film that has ever been made, and it was made in America."

Another reviewer wrote that "no other film, as far as I know, has received a critical tribute so nearly unanimous on both sides of the Atlantic." *Cavalcade* won Oscars as best film of 1932–1933, for best direction, and for best art direction (William S. Darling). Made on a lavish budget of about $1.25 million, it grossed over $5 million.

Another hit followed for Lloyd the same year with *Berkeley Square,* scripted by Sonia Levien and John L. Balderston from the latter's play, itself based on Henry James' story "The Sense of the Past." Leslie Howard plays Peter Standish, a young American who inherits an old house in London and finds himself translated back into the eighteenth century, in love with a woman (Heather Angel) of that time, and still aware—with an effect that is sometimes comic and sometimes tragic—of the shape of things to come. "The thought is fragile and evasive," wrote one reviewer, "presented through quiet acting and imaginative dialogue; the hero can go back into the past, the heroine can see ahead into the future, and they meet in an odd world of ephemeral and shifting time." Howard was nominated for an Oscar.

Lloyd turned out two less remarkable movies for Fox, *Hoopla* (1933), and *Servants' Entrance* (1934), and then made the most famous of all his films, *Mutiny on the Bounty,* produced for MGM by Irving Thalberg. Lloyd himself had bought (for $12,500) the rights to Nordhoff and Hall's fictional account of the famous mutiny. He sold the rights to MGM on condition that he should direct the picture, and Fox obligingly released him for the two years he devoted to it. Some background material was shot in Tahiti, but most of the two-and-a-quarter hour film was, as one writer said, "Hollywood studio craftsmanship at its most accomplished."

The mutiny took place in 1879, when HMS *Bounty* was sailing from Tahiti to the West Indies with a cargo of breadfruit plants. It is not clear whether it was inspired by the captain's tyranny, as in the novel, or by the crew's reluctance to leave the women they had found in Tahiti. At any rate, the mutineers sailed back to Tahiti and some of them subsequently colonized the Pitcairn Islands. Captain Bligh and eighteen loyal crew members sailed an open boat four thousand miles to Timor in the East Indies—an astonishing feat of seamanship.

The film follows the novel in presenting Captain Bligh (Charles Laughton) as a tyrant of monstrous inhumanity. Even before the *Bounty* sails a seaman, as Otis Ferguson wrote, "is flogged through the fleet" at Bligh's command, "the flesh stripped from his bones in accordance with the printed word of Article XXI. . . . when they do leave, there is a certain coordination of cameras, sound recordings, and cutting that makes something strange and beautiful out of old hulk the movies bought up and glued their properties to. The whole tone of the picture, in fact, is set by this beauty they have found in ships and described with the true care and knowledge of craftsmen."

For Ferguson, *Mutiny on the Bounty* was "one of the best pictures that have ever been made," primarily because of Lloyd's success in "the putting together of static fragments into a live sto-

ry. . . . And the incidents leading up to the violent overthrow are made vivid in terms of the medium—the swish and pistol crack of the lash, the sweating, lean bodies, the terrible labor, and the ominous judgment from the quarterdeck. The ship and the ship's life open out here, but the film becomes grand by virtue of something more than quarterdecks and hurlyburly. It is the reworking of a large tragedy—men not only against the sea but against their own forces, both universal and particular." Clark Gable played master's mate Fletcher Christian, reluctant leader of the mutineers, and Laughton "gave a savage and overbearing performance as Captain Bligh which provided music-hall impersonators with material for years."

Mutiny on the Bounty (1935) brought Lloyd another Oscar (for best picture). Back at Fox, he next directed a remake of *Under Two Flags* (1936) from the melodramatic Foreign Legion novel by Ouida. Claudette Colbert was rather uncomfortably cast as Cigarette, the tough Legion groupie who falls in love with an aristocratic British legionnaire (Ronald Colman) and has the privilege of dying in his arms at the end. Mixing such scenes with some exciting battle footage, Lloyd scored another box-office success.

After that, the director joined Paramount, where he once more established his own production unit. His first film there, *Maid of Salem* (1937), again starred Claudette Colbert, this time protected by Virginian Fred MacMurray from an epidemic of witch-burning in Colonial Massachusetts. *Stage*'s reviewer thought the movie had been "glamorized to the extent of dwelling for some luscious moments on the romance. . . . Once the panic of witchcraft starts (and you know what director Frank Lloyd did with panic in *Cavalcade* and *Mutiny*) you are carried along on a vicious crescendo of madness and terror."

Wells Fargo (1937), with Joel McCrea and Frances Dee, was a history of the formation of the Wells Fargo Express Company and the development of its coast-to-coast delivery service. It was admired as an "epic Western" of "panoramic scope," and it was yet another money-maker. So was *If I Were King* (1938), scripted by Preston Sturges from the play by J. H. McCarthy (and the operetta *The Vagabond King*). Ronald Colman stars as François Villon, the rabble-rousing poet-thief of fifteenth-century Paris. We see this colorful scoundrel save France from the invading Burgundian army, thus earning the jealous gratitude of Louis XI (splendidly played by Basil Rathbone) and the rather chilly hand of Frances Dee. Colman was a somewhat genteel Villon, but the movie was enjoyed for its "acres of Gothic sets" and for Lloyd's "transparent delight in the picturesque."

There was also a generally favorable reception for *Rulers of the Sea* (1939), Lloyd's last film for Paramount. Will Fyffe plays a Scottish machine-shop worker who, abetted by Douglas Fairbanks Jr., fulfills his dream of sending a paddle wheeler across the Atlantic. Some critics have detected a certain ambivalence in Lloyd's attitude towards this victory of steam over sail.

After that, the director freelanced for most of what remained of his career, which was relatively undistinguished. The best of his late films was *Blood on the Sun* (1945), independently produced by William Cagney, and starring his brother James as an American journalist in Tokyo, trying to smuggle out evidence of a Japanese warlord's plans for world domination. C. A. Lejeune, praising the "brilliantly imaginative" *film noir* photography, Cagney's masterly performance, and the adroitly built tension of the climactic manhunt, called this a "top flight" melodrama. Reviewers also found much to admire in Lloyd's last picture—one of two he made for Republic—*The Last Command* (1955). An account of the Battle of the Alamo, with Sterling Hayden as Jim Bowie, it seemed to one British reviewer "a smashing piece of cinematic carnage."

Ephraim Katz described Lloyd as "a highly skilled craftsman . . . [with] few pretensions about the significance of film other than as a means of entertainment, or about his own role as a director. . . . Accordingly, he is shortshrifted by most film historians. But films like *Cavalcade, Mutiny on the Bounty,* and *Wells Fargo* reveal not only technical mastery but also a cohesive style and a keen visual sense." And it seemed to Henri Agel that "for the period 1930–1940 Frank Lloyd remains one of the masters of adventure, one of those who introduced into the epic, the story of time past, the exoticism, that undefinable soft and trembling feeling that is the attribute of American cinema."

According to Hedda Hopper, Lloyd was an extremely economical director, who rehearsed his actors every evening and the next day knew exactly what he was going to shoot and how. "When the picture is three-quarters finished," Hopper reported, "the entire company gets a look at it, and if any actor is unhappy about his scene, he talks it over with Frank and it is retaken." He himself maintained that "what a film director mainly requires is common sense, good taste along with plenty of hard work and not even a dab of genius. Likewise, he must realize that every six months the whole movie business rolls over and is no longer what it used to be."

Lloyd's first wife Alma died in 1952. A few years later he married the scenarist Virginia Kellogg. He had a daughter by his first marriage. Lloyd has been described as a calm, slow-spoken man, generous with his time and money, modest, and well-liked by almost everyone he worked with. He owned a small ranch near Whittier, California, as well as a house in Beverly Hills.

FILMS: *Short features*—A Prince of Bavaria, 1914; As the Wind Blows, 1914; The Vagabond, 1914; The Link That Binds, 1914; The Chorus Girl's Thanksgiving, 1914; Traffic in Babes, 1914; A Page From Life, 1914; Pawns of Fate, 1915; The Temptation of Edwin Swayne, 1915; Wolves of Society, 1915; His Last Serenade, 1915; Martin Lowe, Financier, 1915; An Arrangement With Fate, 1915; To Redeem an Oath, 1915; The Bay of Seven Isles, 1915; His Last Trick, 1915; The Pinch, 1915; His Captive, 1915; Life's Furrow, 1915; When the Spider Tore Loose, 1915; Nature's Triumph, 1915; A Prophet of the Hills, 1915; $100,000, 1915; The Little Girl of the Attic, 1915; The Toll of the Youth, 1915; Fate's Alibi, 1915; Trickery, 1915; Their Golden Wedding, 1915; From the Shadows, 1915; Little Mr. Fixer, 1915; Eleven to One, 1915; Billie's Baby, 1915; Martin Lowe, Fixer, 1915; His Superior's Honor, 1915; According to Value, 1915; Paternal Love, 1915; The Source of Happiness, 1915; In the Grip of the Law, 1915; A Double Deal in Pork, 1915; Dr. Mason's Temptation, 1915. *Features*—The Gentleman From Indiana, 1915; Jane, 1915; The Reform Candidate, 1916; The Tongues of Men, 1916; The Call of the Cumberlands, 1916; Madame la Presidente, 1916; The Code of Marcia Gray, 1916; David Garrick, 1916; The Making of Maddalena, 1916; An International Marriage, 1916; The Stronger Love, 1916; The Intrigue, 1916; Sin of the Parent, 1916; The Price of Silence, 1917; A Tale of Two Cities, 1917; American Methods, 1917; When a Man Sees Red, 1917; The Heart of a Lion, 1917; The Kingdom of Love, 1917; Les Misèrables, 1918; The Blindness of Divorce, 1918; True Blue, 1918; Riders of the Purple Sage, 1918; The Rainbow Trail, 1918; For Freedom, 1918; The Man Hunter, 1919; Pitfalls of a Big City, 1919; The World and Its Women, 1919; The Loves of Letty, 1920; The Women in Room 13, 1920; The Silver Horde, 1920; Madame X, 1920; The Great Lover, 1920; A Tale of Two Worlds, 1921; Roads of Destiny, 1921; A Voice in the Dark, 1921; The Invisible Power, 1921; The Man From Lost River, 1921; The Grim Comedian, 1921; The Sin Flood, 1921; The Eternal Flame, 1922; Oliver Twist, 1922; The Voice From the Minaret, 1923; Within the Law, 1923; Ashes of Vengeance, 1923; Black Oxen, 1923; The Sea Hawk, 1924; The Silent Watcher, 1924; Her Husband's Secret, 1925; Winds of Chance, 1925; The Splendid Road, 1926; The Wise Guy, 1926; The Eagle of the Sea, 1926; Children of Divorce, 1927; Adoration, 1928; The Divine Lady, 1929; Weary River, 1929; Drag, 1929; Dark Streets, 1929; Young Nowheres, 1929; Sons of the Gods, 1930; The Way of All Men, 1930; The Lash, 1930; East Lynne, 1931; The Right of Way, 1931; The Age for Love, 1931; A Passport to Hell, 1932; Cavalcade, 1933; Berkeley Square,

1933; Hoopla, 1933; Servants' Entrance, 1934; Mutiny on the Bounty, 1935; Under Two Flags, 1936; Maid of Salem, 1937; Wells Fargo, 1937; If I Were King, 1938; Rulers of the Sea, 1939; The Howards of Virginia, 1940; The Lady From Cheyenne, 1941; This Woman Is Mine, 1941; (with others) Forever and a Day, 1943; Air-Pattern Pacific, 1944 (documentary); Blood on the Sun, 1945; The Last Bomb, 1946 (documentary); The Shanghai Story, 1954; The Last Command, 1955.

ABOUT: Katz, E. The International Film Encyclopedia, 1980. Periodicals—Écran May 1975; Films in Review May 1981.

LORENTZ, PARE (December 11, 1905–), American documentarist, film critic, journalist, and author, was born in Clarksburg, West Virginia, and grew up in Buckhannon, a small town in the same state. His father, Pare Hanson Lorentz, was a printer whose German Pietist ancestors had come to America in the eighteenth century to escape religious persecution. Buckhannon had been founded by Pare Lorentz's great grandfather Jacob who, upon receiving land grants from the Governor of Virginia, had cut a road and made his way, with a hundred-mule train, from Pennsylvania over the Allegheny Mountains, into the wilderness of northern West Virginia. Lorentz's mother, the former Alma Ruttencutter, was a professional singer. The house was always full of music and musicians, and Pare Lorentz himself studied music for ten years.

Graduating from Buckhannon High School in 1921, Lorentz spent a year at West Virginia Wesleyan College, then transferred to the University of West Virginia. He edited the university's humor magazine and became president of the Southern Association of College Editors. Shortage of funds forced him to leave the university before graduation, and at nineteen he went off to New York with some idea of becoming a music critic. Instead he became the editor of the Edison Mazda Lamp Company's house organ, in his spare time writing humorous articles for a new magazine called the New Yorker. In 1926 he joined the staff of the weekly magazine Judge as its film reviewer (and was then the youngest critic of any kind writing regularly for a national magazine).

Lorentz retained his Judge column for eight years and during this period also reviewed films for the New York Evening Journal, Vanity Fair, and Town and Country. In 1935 he became film critic of McCall's. "No other reviewer for this magazine has ever evoked such a violent reaction among readers," wrote the editor of McCall's in 1938, "yet you will find that, month

PARE LORENTZ

in and month out, his reviews are never deliberately belligerent. Rather, they reflect Lorentz's profound conviction that motion pictures represent an important means of expression. When he pierces the fog of feverish movie ballyhoo he does so with a surgeon's eye and a surgeon's intent." In 1934–1936 Lorentz also wrote a syndicated movie column for Hearst's King Features. However, the political column he began under the auspices of the same organization ended abruptly when he sent in a piece praising the New Deal's farm program.

Meanwhile Lorentz had published his first books, beginning with one about film censorship written in collaboration with Morris Ernst. Censored: The Private Life of the Movies (1930) was an attack, with examples, on "the unlearned and stupid heckling of the censor" and on Will Hays in particular; this outspoken book may account for some of the obstructionism Lorentz later encountered in Hollywood. The Roosevelt Year: 1933 (1934) was a largely photographic account of the achievements of the president's first year in office. It had been planned as a documentary film, to be assembled mostly from newsreel footage, but the project found no backers.

During the 1930s the New Deal's Resettlement Administration sent its photographers all over the United States in a program designed to "educate the city dweller to the needs of the rural population"—Walker Evans' Let Us Now Praise Famous Men is one of the products of this program. In 1935 the RA decided that motion pictures were needed—specifically to convey the extent of the Dust Bowl, which by then stretched from Texas to North Dakota, and the violence of the dust storms that were rapidly enlarging it. Pare Lorentz was called to Washington as a consultant. It was an odd choice, in that Lorentz had no direct experience whatever of filmmaking. But he was well known as a serious movie critic; he had toured the Dust Bowl researching an article for *Newsweek* and had subsequently tried to raise funds for a film on the subject; and *The Roosevelt Year* had demonstrated his loyalty to the New Deal.

In Washington, Lorentz began by screening some of the informational, educational, and public relations films that had already been produced by various government agencies, and studied distribution and production systems. He came to the conclusion that very few of these early attempts at government filmmaking were suitable for release in ordinary commercial movie theatres and that they were therefore doomed to achieve only limited distribution, mostly to the converted. Instead of the series of pictures envisaged by the director of the Resettlement Administration, Rexford G. Tugwell, Lorentz proposed that the RA concentrate its resources on one "film of merit" that would be technically accomplished and entertaining enough to compete successfully with Hollywood feature films.

Tugwell agreed, and Lorentz embarked on his pioneering project with a budget of six thousand dollars. He accepted from the outset that he would have to work without professional actors or studio sets, shooting on location and without direct sound. Lorentz proposed to write the film himself and, failing to find suitably talented people prepared to work within his tiny budget, soon realized that he would have to serve as producer and director as well.

He signed up a crew of three experienced cameramen—Ralph Steiner, Paul Strand, and Leo Hurwitz—all of them strongly influenced by the great Russian documentarists, and in September 1935 began shooting. The team worked its way from Montana through Wyoming, Colorado, western Kansas, and the Texas Panhandle, encountering blizzards and dust storms. Relations became strained between the cameramen and Lorentz, who knew what he wanted but could not express himself in the jargon of his new profession. As soon as location shooting was completed, he fired his crew and went to Hollywood in search of stock shots of the Great Plains in their former glory. The studios were not interested in succoring a New Deal project, however, and Lorentz got his stock shots only with the help of King Vidor and other sympathetic directors. While in California he also shot some footage of migrants arriving there from the Dust Bowl, using Paul Ivano as his cameraman.

The budget was almost spent and Lorentz still had no editor and no score. Deciding that he would have to be his own editor as well, he went to New York, where he rented laboratory space and hired a technician to teach him the rudiments of the craft. Music was a bigger problem, since Lorentz attached great importance to this element. After interviewing twelve composers he picked Virgil Thomson, whose work he already knew and who was able to draw on an exceptionally wide knowledge of American music. Thomson had no experience of film work, but he was interested, prepared to accept a small fee, and to work closely with his equally inexperienced director. He was also able to persuade Alexander Smallens to conduct the score with a small orchestra drawn from the New York Philharmonic.

Lorentz had already put his film roughly into shape, but he now recut it to fit the recorded score. It is an unusual approach to editing but, as Robert Snyder says, the music gave Lorentz a form: "He could tighten the visual sequences to match the emotional content of Thomson's score, letting the latter serve as counterpoint at times, a technique Lorentz had learned from René Clair."

The Plow That Broke the Plains was completed early in 1936. Its story is extremely simple, beginning with "lush, billowy grass," then showing how ranching and homesteading were followed by the railroads, then by the massive overplowing of the economic boom and the Great War, with drought and terrible winds completing the destruction of the plains. In the end, there is only "a dead tree surrounded by sun-baked desert." An epilogue shows the RA relocating Dust Bowl refugees on small farms elsewhere. In the end, Lorentz had considerably exceeded his minute budget, and the film's final cost was $19,260. Inexperienced in the handling of vouchers and receipts, the director never recovered some of the money he had paid out of his own pocket.

Lorentz's next challenge was to obtain commercial distribution for his film. He managed to arrange a screening at the White House in March 1936; President Roosevelt was impressed, as were the Hollywood directors who saw it soon after (among them King Vidor, Rouben Mamoulian, and Lewis Milestone). A triumphant full-dress premiere followed in Washington in May. But because of the opposition of Will Hays, or a more general Hollywood dislike of the New Deal, or resentment of government-sponsored competition, no commercial distribution company would touch it. Lorentz therefore set out with a team of government press agents, taking the film to press previews in town after town and urging the critics to ask for the film to be shown in local theatres. A breakthrough came when Arthur Mayer put it on at his Rialto Theatre in Times Square, billing it as "the picture they dared us to show." Other bookings followed in first-run houses from coast to coast. Some reviewers found it a little slow in tempo and erratic in structure, but there was more or less universal praise for its photographic technique, its score, and its commentary, and it was called "an immensely emotional, powerful, and important human document."

The Plow That Broke the Plains made no money because it was distributed free, but it was unmistakably a success (in spite of complaints from politicians that it libeled "the greatest section of the United States"). However, there was still a good deal of jealous, self-centered, or merely ignorant opposition to Lorentz's film program within the government. He himself was earning less than his cameramen and had virtually no office staff or backing for what he wanted to do. In June 1936, frustrated and disillusioned, he walked into Tugwell's office and resigned. Turning to leave, he noticed a profile map of the Mississippi on the wall: "There," he said, "you people are missing the biggest story in the world—the Mississippi River." On July 4, at home at Sneeden's Landing, New York, Lorentz received a call from the RA offering him a salary of $30 a day and a budget of $50,000 to make his film about the Mississippi.

Lorentz began work on *The River* in the summer of 1936. Virgil Thomson was immediately engaged to write the score and Lorentz selected a new team of cameramen: Floyd Crosby, Willard Van Dyke, and Stacy Woodard. (Crosby subsequently worked with Lorentz on several other projects and all three had distinguished later careers.) Bad weather held up filming but brought a bonus in the form of a major flood on the Ohio River—a disaster that provided "some of the most thrilling unstaged photography ever included in a motion picture." Filming the flood and the suffering it caused, Lorentz and his cameramen sometimes worked for thirty-six hours at a stretch, and in the end they had traveled twenty-six thousand miles up and down the Mississippi and its tributaries. When shooting was finished in March 1937, they had eighty thousand feet of film, which had to be reduced to three thousand. Over the next six months Lloyd Nosler and Lorentz edited the film in close collaboration with Virgil Thomson, whose score grew step by step as the movie was cut into shape. "For the human episodes," wrote Kathleen Hoover, Thomson "drew on folk tunes, but his idiom was modern and individual. For the landscape sequences he invented material that captures the Mississippi's changing moods with electric immediacy." The score was to have been accompanied by a purely functional narration, but a highly lyrical report on the flood that Lorentz published in *McCall's* was received with such tremendous public enthusiasm that he used this piece, scarcely changed, as his narration.

Robert Snyder wrote that the picture's opening sequence, "which traces the course of the river from its minute beginnings in an upland forest to the Gulf of Mexico, accompanied by the roll call of rivers and Thomson's music, is one of the unforgettable moments in films. The sequence begins with the musical river motif, a simple trumpet call, and shots of clouds. Mists break, first to reveal the Rockies and then the Appalachians, with appropriate descriptive words by the narrator. The river is built from close-ups of its dripping beginnings on the side of a hill through ever-expanding shots of larger and larger streams of water. The movement of water is from top to bottom and usually from left to right. When the river itself is reached, the left-to-right flow of water is continued as the boat on which the camera is mounted moves to the left against the flow. Throughout the sequence, Thomson's music builds on the river motif and takes on a hymnlike quality."

Although *The River* had cost $50,000, government grumbles were stifled after the film had had its premiere at the White House in September 1937; the President pronounced it "a grand movie" and asked what he could do to help. Lorentz told him and an informal discussion followed on the role of film in government—a discussion that led directly to the formation of the United States Film Service. *The River* was just as obviously a work of propaganda for the New Deal as its predecessor, but this time there were no distribution problems: Paramount agreed to distribute the film, which was shown in more than five thousand movie theatres in the United States and televised in Britain. Excluded from consideration for an Oscar (ostensibly because it didn't fit any of the existing categories), it took first prize at the 1938 International Cinematographic Exposition in Venice, winning over Leni Riefenstahl's *Olympiad*.

V. F. Calverton called *The River* "a masterpiece of social documentation and cinematic dramatization" and A. R. Fulton said it was "a great documentary, if not the greatest that the art of the motion picture has produced." In 1971 Andrew Bergman found it, in spite of its brilliant photography, "somehow cold and self-serving, too concerned with becoming instant myth, too wrapped up with its role in an historical saga of the thirties." But meanwhile *The River* had become "the most quoted, the most exhibited and the most taught short motion picture ever produced in America."

President Roosevelt established the U.S. Film Service in August 1938, with Lorentz as director. The great success of *The River* was a major factor in this decision; others were the popularity of the "March of Time" film magazines, the achievements of John Grierson's Post Office Film Unit in Britain, and a growing recognition that documentaries were powerful instruments of education and propaganda. The Film Service was to make pictures for the education of government employees and to inform the public about contemporary problems. It was also to coordinate filming by other government agencies, to develop standards of quality for government films, to control their distribution, and to provide a film library and information service. Funds were supposed to come from the WPA and PWA, and the Farm Security Administration. In fact, however, it proved to be extremely difficult for the new service to obtain any funds at all. In July 1939 the President transferred the service to the Federal Security Agency as part of the Office of Education, but its financial situation remained extremely precarious.

Meanwhile, Lorentz went on with his work as best he could. In 1938 CBS radio had broadcast his play about unemployment, *Ecce Homo!*. It had been voted the best dramatic presentation of the year and Lorentz decided to adapt it as a film. A great deal of background footage was shot in factories and on construction sites, but there were administrative and financial problems and delays, and *Ecce Homo!* was never completed. Instead, in the spring of 1939, Lorentz was recalled to Washington by President Roosevelt, who wanted a film that would promote the major health program he intended to put before Congress. It was decided that Lorentz should make a film based on the first part of Paul de Kruif's book *The Fight for Life*; it was to give "a picture of human erosion" and to dramatize "the efforts which are being made in a certain area by modern science in reducing the infant and maternal mortality rate."

This semi-documentary was to have a fictional "story," and for the first time Lorentz worked with professional actors, including Myron McCormick, Storrs Haynes, Will Geer, and Dorothy Adams, who all agreed to work for twenty-five dollars a day (like Lorentz himself). McCormick, Haynes, and Geer were given elementary medical training in the interests of authenticity, and a research worker prepared an exhaustive report on the workings of the Chicago Maternity Center, founded in 1932 by the pioneering obstetri-

cian Joseph B. De Lee in the city's slums. (The research worker was Elizabeth Meyer, who became Lorentz's second wife in 1943.) On the basis of this report, Lorentz prepared his first detailed shooting script. The rest of the acting parts were taken by "mothers in the waiting rooms of the Maternity Center, undernourished children playing dangerously in the streets—the people of the tenements themselves."

Lacking a score, Lorentz directed many of the hospital scenes to the beat of a metronome, in this way sustaining the rhythm he knew he wanted. Most of the film was shot on location in the Maternity Center (where all equipment had to be sterilized) or in the streets and tenements of the surrounding slums. Floyd Crosby and his camera crew often worked with a hidden camera, capturing "some of the most candid footage of human life ever caught by the camera," improvising their way around the lighting and other problems this technique involved.

The film's music was crucial in Lorentz's plan and he finally commissioned Louis Gruenberg, who worked with the director for twenty-two weeks, producing a brilliant fifty-five minute score. A jazz sequence that Gruenberg could not provide was improvised by pianist Joe Sullivan and his band to the beat set by Lorentz's metronome. The director's detailed instructions to Gruenberg have survived and are of the greatest interest. For example, in the famous early scene in which a mother dies in childbirth, the situation is expressed on the soundtrack by a double heart beat—the mother's and the child's, which is one-and-a-half times faster. "For 360 feet we had a time dominated by the mother's heart," Lorentz wrote; "the tympani concentrates on this beat. The minute the child is born, the baby's fluttering heart dominates the beat, so for this transition . . . a trumpet cry, a crescendo— any device you may wish to use for the birth pain—is merely a cue for a different beat." Then the mother begins to fail and her heart—the bass drum—builds in volume "like a heavy truck struggling under a load to climb a hill until it suddenly cuts out completely, and the faint tenor drum beat carries on."

After the woman dies, the young intern who had been attending her (McCormick) walks out into the jazzy, squalid streets beset by doubts about himself, his profession, and the economic system that had contributed to the death. He leaves the hospital where he has been working and takes a job at the Chicago Maternity Center, where he learns the exacting routine of the Center's prenatal examinations and its fanatical concern for hygiene and sanitation, and finally saves the life of a hemorrhaging mother.

The Fight for Life (1940) was Lorentz's first feature-length film (sixty-eight minutes). It was distributed by Columbia and on the whole warmly received. Howard Barnes called it "a stirring and eloquent drama, as well as a document of profound significance. . . . Here is a memorable tribute to the medical profession, accented by challenging social overtones." Paul Rotha considered that in it Lorentz had "attacked and solved a problem which documentary makers had been evading for a decade: how to make dramatic and emotional use of real people in their everyday surroundings." The film was selected by the National Board of Review as the best documentary of the year. It was also received with enthusiasm by many doctors and obstetricians, but others questioned Lorentz's statistics on childhood mortality rates and accused him of scaremongering. However, the resultant controversy only increased public interest in the film, which enjoyed great popular success.

The Fight for Life, the first production of the US Film Service, was followed the same year by *Power and the Land*, directed by Joris Ivens for the Rural Electrification Administration. Lorentz was too involved in *The Fight for Life* to contribute much to the film, and some conflict developed between Ivens and Lorentz, who had to bear the responsibility when the picture fell behind schedule. There were similar problems with the Film Service's other major project, *The Land*, written and directed by Robert Flaherty to dramatize the agricultural conservation program. Meanwhile, the Film Service was struggling to perform its other functions, clearing films made by other government agencies for distribution, and cataloguing and promoting them.

However, personality conflicts were developing between Lorentz and the Commissioner of Education, and there was growing resistance from Hollywood to "Uncle Sam's invasion of the motion picture field." In March 1940 the House Appropriations Subcommittee decided that there was "no existing law that would authorize the carrying on" of the Film Service, and refused an appropriation. The Senate failed to restore the appropriation, and the US Film Service came to an end in June 1940.

In 1940–1941 Lorentz served as National Defense Editor of *McCall's*. The following year he joined Air Transport Command to form the Overseas Technical Unit, taking Floyd Crosby and Lloyd Nosler with him. The unit's function was to fly the airways of the world, filming the scenes and checkpoints on the ground below and assembling briefing films that gave pilots a visu-

al preview of their routes. The filmed material was augmented by maps and charts, and by a narration giving advice about weather, recommended altitudes, and radio ranges. Lorentz ended the war with the rank of lieutenant colonel, and received the Air Medal and the Legion of Merit. In March 1946 he was appointed Chief of Motion Pictures, Theatre and Music in the Civil Affairs Division of the War Department in occupied Germany. Among other things he produced the official war department film on the Nuremberg trials (mysteriously never released in the United States).

After the war Lorentz went into business as a consultant on public interest films and television, serving as president and treasurer of Pare Lorentz Associates until his retirement in 1978. He has continued to interest himself in conservation and land use and served as a member of the Democratic Advisory Council on Natural Resources. A collection of Lorentz's early reviews were published in 1975 as *Lorentz on Film: Movies 1927 to 1941*. He frequently lectures on film, and has honorary degrees from the University of Wisconsin–Oshkosh, West Virginia Wesleyan, and the University of West Virginia. There have been many retrospectives and festivals of his three films. In 1961 Station WGBH Boston produced a series of four ninety-minute television shows called *Lorentz on Film* for National Educational Television, and these were widely shown around the country. Lorentz has two children by his first wife, the actress Sally Bates.

FILMS: The Plow That Broke the Plains, 1936; The River, 1937; The Fight for Life, 1940. *Published scripts*—The River, 1938; The Fight for Life *in* Gassner, J. and Nichols, D. (eds.) Twenty Best Film Plays, 1943.

ABOUT: Barnouw, E. Documentary History of the Nonfiction Film, 1974; Current Biography, 1940; Kauffmann, S. (ed.) American Film Critics, 1972; Jacobs, L. The Documentary Tradition, 1979; Snyder, R. L. Pare Lorentz and the Documentary Film, 1968; Thomson, V. Virgil Thomson, 1966. *Periodicals*—Film Comment Spring 1965; Focus Autumn 1972.

*LUBITSCH, ERNST (January 29, 1892–November 30, 1947), German and American director, scenarist, producer, and actor, was born in Berlin. He was the son of Simon Lubitsch, a Jewish tailor who owned a profitable men's clothing store in the city. Ernst Libitsch was educated at the Berlin Sophien-Gymnasium. He acted in school plays and at sixteen announced that he wanted a career in the theatre. He was a

°lōo´ bich

ERNST LUBITSCH

small, clumsy, and homely boy and his father assured him that he would be better off working in the family business. For a time Lubitsch had to accept this judgment, though he was so inept in the store that his father relegated him to the back office as a bookkeeper. Then he met and became the friend of the comic actor Victor Arnold, who tutored him and helped him to find evening work as an actor and low comedian in Berlin music-halls and cabarets. In 1911, after a year of this hard training, Arnold introduced him to Max Reinhardt, who hired him as a member of his famous company at the Deutsches Theater—a company that included Emil Jannings, Paul Wegener, Rudolph Schildkraut, Albert Basserman, and Conrad Veidt, among other great names.

Lubitsch was nineteen when he abandoned bookkeeping and became a full-time actor. During the next year or so he appeared in a variety of minor classical and other roles, and in one major one, as the hunchback clown in the pantomime Sumurun, and he traveled with the Deutsches Theater to Vienna, Paris, and London. Beginning in 1912, he began to eke out his small salary as a property man and general dogsbody at the Bioscope film studios in Berlin. The following year he went to work as a comic actor for Paul Davidson, one of Germany's first cinema entrepreneurs. Having built over fifty movie theatres, Davidson decided that it would be more profitable to make his own films than to rent those of others, and established the Union-Film production company. Lubitsch's first screen appearance was in the title role in Meyer auf der Alm (Meyer in the Alps, 1913). Thereaf-

ter he appeared in a succession of short Union-Film comedies, often as the archetypal Jewish dummkopf who makes good in the end, thanks to his indestructible optimism, good luck, and a winning way with the ladies.

These comedies were very popular and successful, and when the studio ran out of ideas, Lubitsch came up with some of his own, offering his services as director into the bargain. According to Herman G. Weinberg, author of the wonderfully detailed biography The Lubitsch Touch, Lubitsch's first film as director-author-star was Fräulein Seifenschaum (Miss Soapsuds, 1914), a slapstick one-reeler about a lady barber. Others maintain that his directorial debut was Blinde Kuh (Blindman's Buff), made the following year. By 1915, at any rate, Lubitsch was directing most of the comedies in which he starred, and sometimes writing them as well. In the evenings, nevertheless, he would appear in some topical sketch at the Apollo Theater and then go on to eat at a show-business cafe called Mutter Maentz's. There he would often stay till dawn, swapping anecdotes and wisecracks with his circle of Berlin wits, and puffing on his endless cigars.

Lubitsch's first big success as a director was Schuhpalast Pinkus (Shoe Salon Pinkus, 1916). It was written partly by Hans Kräly, soon to become the director's regular scenarist, and starred Lubitsch not as a clownish Meyer or Moritz but as Solomon Pinkus, a bumptious young man-about-town. The following year Paul Davidson and his temperamental new star Pola Negri persuaded a reluctant Lubitsch to direct his first serious drama (and first feature) Die Augen der Mumie Ma (The Eyes of the Mummy Ma, 1918), starring Negri as a temple dancer in ancient Egypt and Emil Jannings as her fanatical pursuer. World War I ended soon after its release and Berlin became a madhouse of inflation, black-marketeering, hunger riots, drug peddling, and every kind of prostitution and pornography. But the arts flourished and so did the escapist cinema, greatly aided by the devaluation of the Reichsmark (which meant that production costs could quickly be recovered if a film was sold abroad).

In this atmosphere Lubitsch made his second film with "that temperamental Polish witch" Pola Negri. This was Carmen, adapted by Kräly and another writer and told in flashback, with some hand-tinted scenes. Released at the end of 1918, it was voted the best German picture of the year and some years later was a success also in the United States (as Gypsy Blood). However, Jay Leyda, who saw it in 1967, found it devoid of Lubitsch's characteristic wit and "film logic."

After directing two or three comedy shorts (and starring in one of them, *Meyer aus Berlin*), Lubitsch then embarked on another feature, *Die Austernprinzessin* (*The Oyster Princess,* 1919). It has Ossi Oswalda as the spoiled daughter of an American "oyster king" who sets out to buy a Prussian aristocrat for a husband, and satirizes with equal good humor Prussian snobbery and American materialism. Lubitsch thought it his "first comedy that showed something of a definite style." Another hit, it was followed by a drama called *Rausch* (*Intoxication*), based on Strindberg's *There Are Crimes and Crimes.*

Paul Davidson, the entrepreneur behind all this, then decided that he should make "the greatest film of all time." He raised funds from UFA, the government-sponsored production company in which his Union-Film was already an important element, and put Lubitsch and Negri to work on *Madame Dubarry*. Emil Jannings begged for and got the role of Louis XV, and Lubitsch engaged over two thousand extras to fill his carefully researched costumes and his studio-built Paris. The film shows what he had learned from Reinhardt about the direction of crowd scenes and also his own unique talent as a "humanizer" of history. Running over two hours, it was supplied with a specially written score, played at the Berlin premiere by a full orchestra. It was a huge success in Germany, then all over Europe, and finally in the United States. Some critics, it is true, objected to the presentation of the French Revolution as the outcome of an affair between a king and his *midinette* mistress. There was also some resistance to the picture in the United States, even though its distributor there, aware of the virulent anti-German feelings of the time, had retitled it *Passion* and removed all traces of its German origin from the credits (including Lubitsch's name). Nevertheless, with this film, as Andrew Sarris says, "Lubitsch almost singlehandedly lifted Germany into the forefront of film-producing nations."

After this triumph, Lubitsch demonstrated his versatility in a string of successes for Union-UFA. *Die Puppe* (*The Doll,* 1919) is an E.T.A. Hoffmann fantasy that makes audacious use of all the movie camera's capacity for visual trickery (and opens with an extraordinary shot of puppet-master Lubitsch himself assembling a miniature set). Another hit (in spite of charges that it was anti-clerical), it was followed by *Kölhiesels Töchter* (*Kölhiesel's Daughters,* 1920), a peasant *Taming of the Shrew* shot on location in Bavaria, then by a screen version of the ballet-pantomime *Sumurun* (*One Arabian Night,* 1920), with Lubitsch repeating his stage performance (and vigorously overacting) as the hunchback clown in love with a beautiful dancer (Negri).

Anna Boleyn (*Deception,* 1920), starring Jannings as Henry VIII, was another spectacular essay on the influence of lust on history. Gerald Mast writes that if *Dubarry* "is convincingly eighteenth-century France, *Anna Boleyn* is even more magnificently convincing as Renaissance England. Lubitsch's control of lighting gives the wood of sets and the faces of people the glow of Renaissance painting." At the same time, in this as in all his historical epics, Lubitsch sought to "de-operatize" and to "humanize" his characters: "I treated the intimate nuances just as importantly as the mass movements and tried to blend them both together." *Die Bergkatze* (*The Wildcat,* 1921) is by contrast an anti-militaristic satire, unique among his films in that its bizarre sets and stylized acting were evidently influenced by expressionism (and, in its day, a complete failure).

The last and most elaborate of the historical spectacles Lubitsch made in Germany was *Das Weib des Pharao* (*The Loves of Pharaoh,* 1922), which crowded the UFA lot with palaces and pyramids and many thousands of extras (at a total cost, according to one account, of only $75,000). It is a movie on the scale of *Intolerance* or *Ben Hur* and took almost a year to make. There are notable performances from Jannings as the Pharaoh Amenes and Paul Wegener as the King of Ethiopia, who go to war for the love of the beautiful slave girl Theonis (Dagny Servaes). In December 1921 Lubitsch paid his first visit to the United States, taking *The Loves of Pharaoh* with him. It opened in New York a few months later and was hailed as "a magnificent production and stirring testimony to the genius of Ernst Lubitsch."

Much interviewed in the United States, Lubitsch expressed his admiration for Chaplin, Griffith, De Mille, Stroheim, and the American cinema in general, but with one reservation: "The American moviegoing public has the mind of a twelve-year-old child: it must have life as it isn't." Back in Berlin, Lubitsch made one last film there, *Die Flamme* (1923), a relatively small-scale story set in *fin-de-siècle* Paris about a *cocotte* (Negri) who falls in love with a composer (Hermann Thimig), loses him, and kills herself. It was released in the United States as *Montmartre* (1924), with an unsatisfactory happy ending tacked on for the public that "must have life as it isn't."

In December 1922, meanwhile, Lubitsch had committed himself to that public. The "greatest director in Europe," the "European Griffith," had been invited to Hollywood by "America's sweetheart," Mary Pickford, who starred opposite Douglas Fairbanks in Lubitsch's first American movie, *Rosita* (1923). It is an agreeable fantasy about a street singer in nineteenth-century Spain who attracts the attention of the libidinous king with a satirical song about him. Lubitsch and Pickford clashed incessantly, personally and professionally, throughout the three months of filming, and the picture, perhaps because it gave Pickford her first grown-up role, was not a financial success. However, the critics, then and since, have praised it warmly as a "distinguished and lovely film," and Lotte Eisner was put in mind both of Goya and of Sternberg's later *The Devil Is a Woman.*

As Gerald Mast says, *Rosita* "closed Lubitsch's first period"; after it, romanticism gave way to irony, the crowded canvas was exchanged for the telling detail. The move to Hollywood must have had something to do with this dramatic change of style; marital comedies were then in vogue, and Lubitsch no doubt learned from the achievements of Stroheim and De Mille in this genre. But by far the greatest influence on Lubitsch at this time was Chaplin's *A Woman of Paris* (1923), which tells its story about a provincial girl who becomes a "kept woman" with absolute moral detachment, great economy of means, and brilliantly suggestive imagery.

Much of what Lubitsch learned from Chaplin is already evident in *The Marriage Circle* (1924), the first of the five movies he made for a relatively new and still minor studio called Warner Brothers. It is a sophisticated comedy studying the collision between a hopeful new marriage (Florence Vidor and Monte Blue) and one that is failing (Marie Prevost and Adolphe Menjou). It impressed Iris Barry that Lubitsch "has shown, not told, the story. Everything is visualized, all the comedy is in what the characters are seen or imagined to be thinking or feeling, in the interplay, never expressed in . . . [subtitles], of wills and personalities. . . . Gestures and situations, so lucidly presented that one is perfectly aware from the 'pictures' alone of what is happening, give rise to other gestures and other situations which—because of the permanence of visual memory—one recognizes as the logical outcome of what has occurred before." The *New Yorker* called it "a champagne picture in a beery movie world."

In a moment of exasperation Mary Pickford had referred to Lubitsch as a "director of doors," and there is justice in the charge. As Arthur Knight has pointed out, "prior to *The Marriage Circle,* almost any decoration would do—either wholly nondescript for a routine film or, for a more elaborate production, rooms choked with bric-a-brac and overstuffed chairs set off by loudly ornamental drapes and busy wallpaper. Lubitsch cleared away the clutter, providing clean playing areas for his action. The advantages were so immediately apparent that they were incorporated into the majority of pictures from that moment on. Few directors, however, have quite his ability to use settings to their fullest advantage. To Lubitsch, a door was always more than simply a way to get into or out of a room; it was a way to end an argument, to suggest pique or coquetry or even the sexual act itself. Corridors, stairways, windows—all had a dramatic function in the Lubitsch films."

Three Women (1924) is a harsher picture about a "lady-killer" (Lew Cody) who plays mother (Pauline Frederick) against daughter (May McAvoy)—the first for her money, the latter as a recruit to his "harem." It was the first of Lubitsch's American films to be written by Hans Kräly, who had followed him to Hollywood and who was thereafter his principal scenarist until 1928. Pola Negri had also arrived in Hollywood, and she starred in *Forbidden Paradise* (1924) as Catherine the Great of Russia, equally interested in power and virile young officers. The visual economy of this satire has been much discussed—for example the officers' revolt which is put down in three shots: the general's hand moving to his sword; the chamberlain's hand pulling out a checkbook; the general's hand releasing his sword. The movie's general air of mockery extends to the totally unrealistic sets and the deliberate anachronisms, which endow eighteenth-century Russia with automobiles and flashlights to underline the universality of human frailty.

Lubitsch's sexual comedies always preserve this mood of sardonic but affectionate amusement at the dismal antics of his characters, and it was this, as much as the obliqueness of his innuendos, that earned him his apparent immunity from censorship in both Germany and America. He demonstrates both qualities again and again in *Kiss Me Again* (1925), adapted from a Sardou farce and starring Marie Prevost as a wife who wants to divorce Monte Blue in favor of a long-fingered pianist (John Roche). Much loved scenes include one in which Blue, to facilitate the divorce, is urged by all concerned to strike his wife but cannot bring himself to do so; and the final scene in which Roche, awaiting his beloved (and unaware that she and her husband are reconciled), serenades her on the piano. Blue enters in pajamas and urges him to play more softly before hurrying back to the marital bedroom. It was strokes like this, crystallizing in a single shot the whole essence of a (generally outrageous) situation, that became known as "the Lubitsch touch." Robert Flaherty, asked to name his favorite film, usually said it was Dovzhenko's *Earth* because "that's what they expect me to say." But, he told Weinberg, "between you and me, my favorite film is Lubitsch's *Kiss Me Again*."

That movie was chosen as one of the ten best of 1925; so was *Forbidden Paradise* and so was Lubitsch's adaptation of *Lady Windermere's Fan:* an unparalleled achievement. *Lady Windermere*, as Ted Shane wrote, substituted Lubitsch's "own great sense of cinematic wit and the dramatic" for Wilde's "perfumed sayings." A notable example is the famous sequence at Royal Ascot, where the disgraced Mrs. Erlynne is scrutinized through binoculars by the British establishment as if she were herself a dark horse in the next race. Irene Rich gave the performance of her life as Mrs. Erlynne and the cast also included May McEvoy (Lady Windermere) and Ronald Colman (Lord Darlington). Georges Sadoul considered this Lubitsch's best silent film, full of "incisive details, discreet touches, nuances of gestures, where behavior betrays the character and discloses the sentiments of the personages. With Lubitsch a new art carried on the subtleties of Marivaux, and the comedy of manners made its debut on the screen."

So This Is Paris (1926) was another "sophisticated comedy, full of marital complications, petty jealousies, and humors of the married but otherwise unemployed," and another huge success for Warner Brothers. It captures the frenetic spirit of the twenties in the sequence which shows us "a host of dance-crazed revelers performing the Charleston. Like an animated cubist painting, . . . [Lubitsch's] camera has caught the pulsing pandemonium of the scene, and the tempo of his dissolving scenes has the swing of a futuristic rhapsody. The kaleidoscopic sequence discloses a blazingly illuminated ballroom where hundreds are hitting the highspots with the Charleston. It glows, it fades. . . . Now are seen misty, tipsily lifted glasses, faint swift-swept fiddle bows, laughing or leering faces, twinkling toes, rattling drums—all intermingling, tantalizing, exhilarating, a chaos of impressions." No less telling than this spectacular scene was Lubitsch's brilliant use throughout the film of a man's cane, which doubles as plot device and sexual symbol.

Lubitsch was then thirty-four and one of the most admired and successful film directors in the world—some placed him second only to Griffith among Hollywood directors. According to Weinberg, his directorial technique was "simple, direct, patient. He didn't believe in many rehearsals, feeling they tired the actor and robbed him of his spontaneity. If a scene *had* to be done over several times, he never lost his patience or courtesy. . . . Sitting on a small camp chair, he would lean forward in his intensity. . . . And his face would mirror all the emotions of the player, male or female. Sometimes he would jump up and show an actor how to do a scene. . . . Some directors liked to improvise—not he. It must all be down in the scenario, everything thought and worked out. . . . Each scene has to 'grow' out of the preceding one; a film was a series of propulsions or combustions, like an engine which keeps a vehicle going." Because his scripts were "complete blueprints," very little footage was wasted; in effect, his pictures were edited before they were shot.

By this time all the major studios were putting their directors to work on Lubitschean comedies, the master's many imitators including Richard Rosson, Lewis Milestone, and Malcolm St. Clair. Lubitsch himself was naturally much in demand, and in 1926 he left Warner Brothers and, under the auspices of MGM, returned to Germany to shoot exteriors for *The Student Prince*. Based on the operetta *Old Heidelberg*, this was a shrewd "fusing of sentiment and highbred comedy," charmingly played by Norma Shearer and Ramon Navarro (though according to Weinberg it was considerably "doctored" by the studio).

Lubitsch's next picture began his ten-year tenure at Paramount. The "German invasion" of Hollywood had continued and Emil Jannings was now on the scene. Lubitsch starred him in *The Patriot* (1928) as the mad Czar Paul I, who is eventually assassinated by his best friend Count Pahlen (Lewis Stone) for the good of Russia. "Though the picture is essentially a tragedy," wrote Richard Watts, "Ernst Lubitsch has made at least half of it that sort of sly, brilliant sex comedy that mocks the czar's amorousness without ever obtruding on the tragic mood of the drama." Jannings' performance was acclaimed and at least one reviewer called this "the greatest motion picture ever made." However, Dwight Macdonald was not alone among later critics when he found "something static, cumbersome and dead" about the film, and financially it was a failure.

The Patriot, made on the eve of the advent of sound, was given a synchronized musical score, together with some sound effects and occasional voices (like the czar's pathetic cries for his friend Pahlen when he realizes that death is near). *Eternal Love* (1929) was Lubitsch's last silent film and the last written for him by his old friend Hans Kräly (whose "intrusion" into his marriage he never forgave). Not much seems to be known about this movie, which was drowned in a tidal wave of talkies. Lubitsch's own first talkie was *The Love Parade* (1929), adapted by

Ernest Vajda and Guy Bolton from a successful play, with songs by Victor Schertzinger and Clifford Grey. The cameraman was Victor Milner, the art director Hans Dreier, and the cast included Jeanette MacDonald in her first screen role as the Queen of Sylvania, Maurice Chevalier as her bored and erring consort, Lupino Lane as his valet, and Lillian Roth as the Queen's maid (with Jean Harlow as an extra).

Lubitsch had had his doubts about sound, but when it came he took to it with the greatest ease and panache. *The Love Parade* is witty in its dialogue, lavish in its settings, startling in its sexual innuendos, and adroit in its introduction of songs. As Kenneth White wrote, "Lupino Lane's opening song snapped the picture off as if it had been flung out by a rubber band. Chevalier's singing of 'Nobody's Using It Now' seemed only the end to a series of exasperations. And when a song . . . came in the middle of an episode, Lubitsch did not let it die out but multiplied its effects in a comic mood to carry the farce that much farther." Theodore Huff called this "the first truly cinematic screen musical in America."

Its success was so great that Lubitsch had to follow it with another, similar musical, *Monte Carlo* (1930), famous for the exhilarating sequence in which Jeanette MacDonald sings "Beyond the Blue Horizon" as a speeding train carries her to her happy ending. C. A. Lejeune pointed out that "faced with the facts of sound, and more, of quite incidental and irrelevant musical sound, Lubitsch has invented for himself a curious hand-over-hand method of treating his visual and sound images: climbing, as it were, towards his conclusion with alternate grips of sight and voice, the two held firmly together, but one always a handhold ahead. . . . He sets the 'Blue Horizon' song to the rushing images of the Riviera express, a chorus of peasants waving from the fields below, Jeanette MacDonald's edged voice matching the whistle and the wind and the speed of the steely rails. Our intellects may tell us that material like this is emotional claptrap, but our senses will take it like an electric contact, sudden and sure. It is a bit of pure ciné-opera, in which every line advances the action, every chorus comments on the individual, every situation develops through song. The man who can create it . . . is a master of his craft." There was no less enthusiasm for *The Smiling Lieutenant* (1931), based on Oscar Straus's operetta *A Waltz Dream*. Matching Chevalier with Claudette Colbert and Miriam Hopkins, Lubitsch here used dialogue almost as sparingly as René Clair had in *Le Million,* relying on music and the camera to tell his story.

From time to time throughout his career, Lu-bitsch seems to have become dissatisfied with his court jester role and to have set out to demonstrate a capacity for something more serious than sexual comedies. He did so in *Rausch, The Patriot,* and *Eternal Love,* and he tried again with *The Man I Killed* (1932), adapted from a Maurice Rostand play by Samson Raphaelson and Ernest Vajda. It is a somber pacifist tract about a young Frenchman who kills an enemy soldier in World War I and later goes to Germany to beg the forgiveness of the dead youth's parents. Adulated by the critics, it failed at the box-office. More recently, Andrew Sarris has suggested that the public knew better than the critics—that the film is "Lubitsch's least inspired and most calculated effort, all surface effect, all ritualistic piety towards a 'noble' subject."

At any rate, Lubitsch returned to his métier with *One Hour With You* (1932), a remake with music of *The Marriage Circle* that apparently was directed mainly by George Cukor (credited only as dialogue director), and followed it with *Trouble in Paradise* (1932). This masterpiece stars Miriam Hopkins and Herbert Marshall in a totally amoral comedy about a couple of high-class thieves in Venice. The tone is set in the opening sequence, when a gondola gliding through the moonlit canals is seen to be collecting garbage; the gondolier throws a pail of slops aboard and launches into a heartfelt rendition of "O Sole Mio." There is never the slightest hint that the protagonists might be redeemed by love or anything else: they are thieves; never mind, they only steal from the rich, and the rich are thieves too. Gerald Mast writes that "the delights, the gags, the comic business, the brilliant dialogue, the technical grace and ingenuity of camera, cutting, and sound have never been surpassed by any Lubitsch film"; many would agree. It was the director's own favorite among his pictures and marked the high point in his career.

For his screen version of Noel Coward's *Design for Living* (1933), Lubitsch set Ben Hecht to work rewriting Coward's dialogue, explaining that the play was too static for the cinema and that "things on the screen should happen in the present," not be recalled in conversation. This effrontery worried contemporary critics, who also found Lubitsch's cast (Fredric March, Miriam Hopkins, Gary Cooper) inferior to the soigné trio of the stage original (the Lunts and Coward himself). There was a mixed reception also for *The Merry Widow* (MGM, 1934), a sumptuous Chevalier-MacDonald adaptation of the Lehar operetta that failed to recover its costs.

In November 1934, tired and a little shaken, Lubitsch acquired a new job as production chief at Paramount. He supervised Sternberg's *The Devil Is A Woman* and Borzage's *Desire*, but in 1936 was abruptly replaced by William Le Baron. Lubitsch's own next film, *Angel* (1937), was his greatest failure. Set in London and Paris in the mid-1930s, and with a cast headed by Marlene Dietrich as a neglected wife, Herbert Marshall as her oblivious husband, and Melvyn Douglas as an amorous bachelor, it builds its plot around the fact that the "salon" where Dietrich and Douglas meet is in fact an elegant brothel. Given the ever-increasing puritanism of the period, this was a very nearly impossible theme, but Lubitsch found ways of telling his story without ever mentioning its real content.

Discussing *Angel*, Gerald Mast found in Herbert Marshall's acceptance of "his wife's present sexuality and past profession" evidence that Lubitsch was mellowing—allowing that human beings are capable of growth and change. Andrew Sarris maintains that the film was "simply misunderstood as a failed bedroom farce . . . rather than as a rhyming exercise in Pirandellian role-playing." Indeed, Sarris suggests, this film and its two predecessors, "far from being failures . . . mark an evolution in Lubitsch's style away from the sparkling balancing acts" of the earlier boudoir comedies to "the somewhat heavier, but richer, concoctions of the 1940s."

The decline in Lubitsch's reputation was halted by the enormous popularity of *Bluebeard's Eighth Wife* (1938), his last film for Paramount. It has Gary Cooper as a much-married American millionaire who finally succumbs to the daughter (Claudette Colbert) of an impoverished French marquis, and the brilliant dialogue was supplied by Charles Brackett and Billy Wilder. The same team, supplemented by Walter Reisch, wrote *Ninotchka* (MGM, 1939), Lubitsch's only film with Greta Garbo. She plays a dour and dedicated Soviet commissar sent to Paris to straighten out three comrades who have been seduced from the path of duty by capitalist self-indulgence. She meets an aristocratic French playboy (Melvyn Douglas) and herself succumbs to Paris, glamour, and romance. Cheerfully satirizing both communism and capitalism (and thus antagonizing some Marxist critics), it is one of the wittiest and also one of the warmest of Lubitsch comedies. It is not particularly well endowed with "Lubitsch touches" but remains perhaps the best loved of all his works, largely because of Garbo's ineffable impersonation of a beautiful iceberg slowly lighting up from within and melting into imperfect but irresistible humanity. Garbo herself once said that "*Ninotchka* was the only time I had a great director in Hollywood."

A leather goods and novelty shop in Budapest is the setting of *The Shop Around the Corner* (MGM, 1940). James Stewart is the head clerk, Margaret Sullavan a salesgirl, and they quarrel so much that they eventually realize that they must be in love. It is one of the few Lubitsch films not concerned with the antics of the rich and idle, and it is difficult to understand why it did not fare better at the box office. James Shelley Hamilton wrote "it has those warm qualities that Lubitsch seems to have discovered within himself of late, not over-sentimentalized and presented with a humorous kindness." *That Uncertain Feeling* (United Artists, 1941) was a disappointing and much altered remake of *Kiss Me Again,* translated from Paris to New York.

It was followed by the controversial comedy *To Be or Not To Be* (United Artists, 1942), in which a Warsaw theatre company during the Nazi occupation combines its work with a little sabotage against the invaders. According to Theodore Huff, the piece was called "callous, a picture of confusing moods, lacking in taste, its subject not suitable for fun-making." It didn't help that it was released shortly after the death in a plane crash of its star, Carole Lombard. In fact, the film is rich in the kind of "black humor" that only became acceptable years later. Peter Bogdanovich wrote in 1972 that it "survives not only as satire but as a glorification of man's indomitable good spirits in the face of disaster— survives in a way that many more serious and high-toned works about the war do not."

In 1943 Lubitsch joined 20th Century–Fox as a producer-director, performing both functions for his first movie there, *Heaven Can Wait* (1943). Set in the 1890s in New York and Kansas (and in hell), it is a pleasant fantasy described by Huff as "a series of animated tintypes, poking sly fun at the manners, decorations and naughtiness of the gay nineties." It was Lubitsch's first film in color, which he used well enough to earn an admiring comment from D. W. Griffith. In 1945 the director had his first heart attack while working on a remake of *Forbidden Paradise* called *A Royal Scandal.* Otto Preminger took over and Lubitsch was credited as producer, though the film has nothing of his style. The same is true of *Dragonwyck* (1946), of which he was also the nominal producer.

Lubitsch went back to work in the spring of 1946. He produced and directed *Cluny Brown,* an excellent satire on English society with a fine cast headed by Charles Boyer and Jennifer Jones and including Reginald Gardiner, C. Aubrey Smith, Peter Lawford, and other pillars of Hollywood's "British colony." In 1947 Lubitsch began work on *That Lady in Ermine,* a screen version of an operetta starring Betty Grable. After a week's shooting he became ill and Preminger again took over. Lubitsch died later the same year at the age of fifty-five.

Theodore Huff defined the "Lubitsch touch" as a "swift innuendo or rapier-like 'comment' accomplished pictorially by a brief camera shot or telling action, to convey an idea or suggestion in a manner impossible in words." Lubitsch himself thought that "one shouldn't single out 'touches.' They're part of a whole. The camera *should* comment, insinuate, make an epigram or a bon mot, as well as tell a story. We're telling stories with pictures so we must try to make the pictures as expressive as we can." Gerald Mast thought Lubitsch the American cinema's greatest technician after Griffith and wrote: his "art is one of omission. . . . he consistently shows less than he might, implies more than he shows." In this way Lubitsch "transformed melodramatic and sentimental tripe into credible human stuff and forged deeper into sexual desires, needs, frustrations, and fears than most of his contemporaries (and descendants) dared to go." Jean Renoir thought that Lubitsch "invented the modern Hollywood."

Robert E. Sherwood described the director as "an extremely short, dark, thickset man, with ponderous shoulders and huge, twinkling eyes. In appearance he resembled a combination of Napoleon and Punchinello; in character he combines the best features of each." Lubitsch's 1922 marriage to Irma Kraus ended in divorce in the early 1930s. Some years later he married an Englishwoman, Sania (whom he called Vivian); they were divorced towards the end of World War II. Lubitsch had a daughter, Nicola, by this second marriage. He was a hyperactive man who drove himself relentlessly, a gourmet, a wit, and a practical joker; he never lost his music-hall German accent nor relinquished the big black cigars that became his trademark. He loved to dance, and he played the piano and the cello badly but with enthusiasm.

For Lubitsch, the crucial stage in making a film was the preparation of the script, and he worked so closely with his writers that they could seldom remember afterwards who contributed what to the finished product. Many of his writers became close friends. Samson Raphaelson, his favorite scenarist of the post-Kräly period, remembered him like this: "Lubitsch loved ideas more than anything in the world, except his daughter Nicola. It didn't matter what kind of ideas. He could become equally impassioned over an exit speech for a character in the current script, the relative merits of Horowitz and Heifetz, the aesthetics of modern painting,

or whether now is the time to buy real estate. And his passion was usually much stronger than that of anyone else around him, so he was likely to dominate in a group. Yet I never saw, even in this territory of egotists, anyone who didn't light up with pleasure in Lubitsch's company. We got that pleasure . . . from the purity and childlike delight of his lifelong love affair with ideas. . . . As an artist he was sophisticated, as a man almost naive. As an artist shrewd, as a man simple."

FILMS: (Films not certainly directed by Lubitsch are preceded by a question mark.) *Germany*—? Fräulein Seifenschaum, 1914; Blinde Kuh, 1915; Auf Eis geführt, 1915; ?(with F. Matray) Zucker und Zimt, 1915; ?Leutnant auf Befehl, 1915; Wo ist mein Schatz?, 1916; ?Als ich tot war, 1916; Der Schwarze Mortiz, 1916; Schuhpalast Pinkus/Schuhsalon Pinkus, 1916; Der gemischte Frauenchor, 1916; Der GMBH Tenor, 1916; ?Seine neue Nase, 1917; Ossis Tagebuch, 1917; Der Blusenkönig, 1917; Wenn Vier Dasselbe Tun, 1917; Das Fideles Gefängnis, 1917; Prinz Sami, 1918; Der Rodelkavalier, 1918; Ich Möchte Kein Mann Sein, 1918; Der Fall Rosentopf, 1918; Die Augen der Mumie Ma (The Eyes of the Mummy Ma), 1918; Das Mädel vom Ballett, 1918; Carmen (Gypsy Blood), 1918; ?Fuhrmann Henschel, 1918; ?Marionetten, 1918; Meyer aus Berlin, 1919; Meine Frau, Die Filmschauspielerin, 1919; Schwabenmädle, 1919; Die Austernprinzessin, 1919; Rausch, 1919; Madame Dubarry (Passion), 1919; Die Puppe, 1919; Kölhiesels Töchter, 1920; Romeo und Juliet im Schnee, 1920; Sumurun (One Arabian Night), 1920; Anna Boleyn (Deception), 1920; Die Bergkatze (The Wildcat), 1921; ?Vendetta, 1921 (or 1918); Das Weib des Pharao (The Loves of Pharaoh), 1921; Die Flamme (Montmartre), 1923. *United States*—Rosita, 1923; The Marriage Circle, 1924; Three Women, 1924; Forbidden Paradise, 1924; Kiss Me Again, 1925; Lady Windermere's Fan, 1925; So This Is Paris, 1926; The Student Prince, 1927; The Patriot, 1928; Eternal Love, 1929; The Love Parade, 1929; (with others) Paramount on Parade, 1930; Monte Carlo, 1930; The Smiling Lieutenant, 1931; The Man I Killed/Broken Lullaby, 1932; One Hour With You, 1932; Trouble in Paradise, 1932; (with others) If I Had a Million, 1932; Design for Living, 1933; The Merry Widow, 1934; Angel, 1937; Bluebeard's Eighth Wife, 1938; Ninotchka, 1939; The Shop Around the Corner, 1940; That Uncertain Feeling, 1941; To Be or Not To Be, 1942; Heaven Can Wait, 1943; Cluny Brown, 1946; (completed by Otto Preminger) That Lady in Ermine, 1948. *Published scripts*—Ninotchka (excerpts) *in* Wald, J. and Macaulay, R. (eds.) The Best Pictures, 1939–1940, 1940 *and in* Weinberg, H. G. The Lubitsch Touch, 1977.

ABOUT: Bergman, A. We're in the Money, 1971; Bogdanovich, P. Pieces of Time, 1973; Carringer, R. and Sabath, B. Ernst Lubitsch: A Guide to References and Resources, 1978; Corliss, R. Talking Pictures, 1974; Durgnat, R. The Crazy Mirror, 1969; Eisner, L. The Haunted Screen, 1967; Eisenschitz, B. Lubitsch, 1967 (in French); Fink, G. Lubitsch, 1977 (in Italian); Haskell, M. From Reverence to Rape, 1974; Huff, T. An

Index to the Films of Ernst Lubitsch, 1947; Mast, G. The Comic Mind, 1973; Poague, L. The Cinema of Ernst Lubitsch, 1978; Roud, R. (ed.) Cinema: A Critical Dictionary, 1980; Sarris, A. (ed.) Interviews with Film Directors, 1967; Verdone, M. Ernst Lubitsch, 1964 (in French); Weinberg, H. G. The Lubitsch Touch, 1977. *Periodicals*—American Cinematographer July 1947; American Film May 1978; Cahiers de la cinémathèque Summer 1976; Cahiers du Cinéma February 1968 (Lubitsch issue); Cinéma (France) June 1973; Cinestudio July, August–September 1971; Film Comment Winter 1971–1972; Film Culture 63–67 1977; Focus on Film April 1979; Image 4 1975; Kosmorama Spring 1976 (Lubitsch issue); Literature/Film Quarterly Fall 1975; Positif April 1972; Revue du Cinéma September 1948; The Silent Picture 11–12, 1971.

LOUIS LUMIÈRE

*LUMIÈRE, LOUIS (October 5, 1864–June 6, 1968), inventor, pioneer filmmaker, and entrepreneur recognized as the father of the French cinema, was born in Besançon in northeastern France; his surname, appropriately, means "light." He was the third of six children in a family that came to enjoy increasingly good circumstances over the years. When his parents, Jeanne Josephine Castille and Antoine Lumière, moved to Besançon from Paris as newlyweds, his father was working as a sign painter and decorator. Around the time of Louis' birth, Antoine Lumière became interested in photography, and after the Paris Commune of 1870 he moved the family to Lyons to set up a portrait studio with another photographer. Within four years he was able to expand his one-room shop into a two-story building and later to send Louis and his elder brother, Auguste, to the highly respected professional and industrial school of La Martinière.

Nonetheless, Antoine Lumière never became a conventional businessman; rather, as Louis described him, he remained a "poet," someone who spent his money as fast as he earned it, who had no respect for science or its practitioners, and who preferred to spend his free time among the magicians and other entertainers in the local café-concert. According to Louis, Antoine was also authoritarian and given to violent behavior, in reaction to which, it seems, the son became a quiet, introverted child who suffered from chronic headaches. He and Auguste were both outstanding students at La Martinière, distinguishing themselves in physics and chemistry respectively, and Louis was graduated in 1880 at the head of his class. But while Auguste continued his studies (and went on to become a distinguished physician), Louis was unable to go on to the Polytechnic because of the headaches. As a distraction from the pain, he took up the study

of Greek with a family friend and also attended classes in drawing, sculpture, and piano at the Lyons Conservatory, but his primary involvement became his father's photography business.

Since the introduction of van Monckhoven's improved dryplate technique in 1878, Antoine Lumière had been trying to perfect the emulsion used to coat the plate; after a few months' experimentation in his father's lab, Louis developed a formula that not only produced a finer image but streamlined the entire developing process. When clients began to request the new plates, Antoine decided to move into the manufacture of photographic supplies, and the seventeen-year-old Louis was soon supervising ten workers in a converted warehouse. Initially the business did not do well: by the time Auguste returned from military service in 1882, there was a debt of 275,000 francs. At this point, it was decided that the two brothers should take over the financial operation of the company, which became Lumière and Sons. In this way, Auguste and Louis entered a thirty-five-year partnership that encompassed both scientific research and commercial enterprise in still photography and motion pictures. From 1882 on, as Auguste later wrote, "It was formally acknowledged that we should collaborate in the most complete and most absolute fashion, not only on the task of recovery and creation that was incumbent upon us, but also on all the projects that we might later undertake and that would invariably be published in common."

When Louis was able to perfect the secret-formula emulsion that came to be known as "Etiquette bleue," the family business took a

°lŭ myâr´

dramatic turn for the better, earning some 500,000 francs the first year. By the middle of the 1890s, Lumière and Sons had three hundred employees and was producing about fifteen million plates a year, second only to Kodak in Rochester, New York. As Louis later described the experience: "Asleep to the world, so to speak, as adolescents, we woke up grown men when success came."

In 1893, he married Rose Winkler, the daughter of a Lyons brewer and sister of Auguste's wife; the two families lived in facing apartments in the same villa while the two brothers worked side by side in the same laboratory. During this period they were investigating color photography based on the Lippmann interference color process. Late in the summer of 1894, Antoine Lumière, now retired to La Ciotat, on the Mediterranean, told his sons about a new invention he had seen in Paris—the Edison Kinetoscope, a coin-operated machine that displayed through a peephole a brief sequence of human figures moving against a black background. Years later the conversation was described by Charles Moisson, the head mechanic of the Lumière factory, who was with Louis Lumière when Antoine came with the news. According to Moisson, Antoine showed them a strip of film that the Kinetoscope promoters had given him and told his son, "This is what you should be making, because Edison is selling it for crazy prices, and those agents are trying to manufacture the strips here in France to get them at a better price." The strip of film, Moisson recalled, was "exactly like film today: four perforations per frame, same width and same pitch. It showed a scene at a hairdresser's." Antoine Lumière was so taken with the device that he bought one for 6000 francs (then about $1225).

In fact, Edison was only one of a number of inventors who by then were working on moving pictures of one kind or another. In October 1894, Georges Demeny, the former assistant of Jules Marey, invited the Lumière brothers to join him in his effort to commercialize two "inseparable" devices: a camera that he called the Chronophotograph (the name of the photographic "gain" that Marey had patented in 1889) and a projector, the Phonoscope. Demeny and Louis Lumière met in Paris around the end of 1894, but as Lumière wrote to Demeny in March 1895, describing the Cinématographe he and his brother had just patented, "This device was already under consideration when we had the pleasure of meeting."

According to Auguste Lumière, "We had observed, my brother and I, how interesting it would be if we could project on a screen and show before a whole gathering animated scenes faithfully reproducing objects and people in movement." It was Auguste who first began working on the project, during the summer of 1894; his device, based on Edison's Kinetoscope, introduced a notched cylinder and unperforated film, which did not produce the desired results. Louis then steeped in. On the occasion of the fortieth-anniversary celebrations for the Cinématographe, Auguste recounted the now famous story of how his brother had come up with the key innovation during a sleepless night: "One morning, toward the end of 1894, I went to the bedroom of my brother, who was not feeling well and was confined to bed. He told me that, unable to sleep, he had, in the calm of the night, pinned down the conditions necessary to reach the desired result and envisioned a mechanism. It consisted, he told me, of transmitting to a claw device a movement produced by a mechanism analogous to that of a sewing machine presser foot . . . That was a revelation, and I quickly understood that I could only abandon the precarious solution I had imagined . . . In one night, my brother had just invented the Cinématographe."

The first patent, issued on February 13, 1895, described a still-nameless "device for obtaining and viewing chronophotographic prints." As usual, the original patent and later additions to it were claimed jointly by Auguste and Louis. Consequently, the invention was for some time attributed to both. After Louis was nominated to the French Academy of Sciences in 1919, the two brothers were obliged to distinguish their respective contributions, and Auguste clearly renounced any claim to the discovery.

Five weeks after the patent was obtained, on March 22, 1895, thirty-one-year-old Louis Lumière gave the first demonstration of his invention to the Society for the Encouragement of National Industry, which was meeting in Paris. In fact, Lumière devoted most of the session to a talk on the photography industry and projections of the work he and Auguste had been doing with the Lippmann color process. It was only at the end of this presentation that he showed the audience of some two hundred people, including his father and brother, a fifty-second moving picture called La Sortie des usines (Workers Leaving the Factory).

The factory in question was that of Lumière and Sons, which Louis had filmed head-on from across the street. The resulting footage shows a crowd of men and women streaming out of the factory door for their lunch break; the Lumières' own carriage makes a brief appearance at the end. Although limited to less than a minute's time because of the capacity of the camera-projector, the "story" is nonetheless complete: the factory door swings open; the workers pour out; the door is closed. Equally well defined is the visual structure: the doorway frames the view horizontally and vertically, while the diagonal push of the workers to the two bottom corners of the frame emphasizes the very essence of the feast: movement.

As the event was reported in the Society's 1895 *Bulletin*, "The exhibition of a *kinetoscope for projections*, as yet unpublicized, excited the keenest interest and was often interrupted by applause from the audience." The demonstration was repeated on April 17, 1895, this time by Auguste, before the Congress of Learned Societies in Paris. In the interim, on March 30, they had filled an addition to their patent to modify the crucial claw mechanism by replacing the round cam of the original design with a triangular one. This addition also introduced the name Cinématographe, which was derived from the Greek *kinema* or *kinematos* (movement) and *graphein* (to write), probably via the name of Edison's camera, the Kinetograph. In fact, even the name Cinématographe was not new: Léon Bouly, whose earlier work had influenced Auguste's experiments, had already used it on patents for both a camera (February 12, 1892) and a projector (December 27, 1893). Warning his sons of the danger of copyright infringement, Antoine Lumière tried to get them to use a name of very different inspiration—Domitor (apparently from *dominer*, to dominate). But his sons held to their choice; Bouly's designs were never realized, and, as Georges Sadoul has pointed out, the name Cinématographe generated what became the universal word for motion pictures: cinema.

The next demonstration of the Cinématographe was held on June 10, 1895, at the Congress of French Photography Societies in Lyons. With this program, Lumière introduced seven new "views" in addition to *Workers Leaving the Factory*. These were *Lyon, Place de la Bourse* (*Lyons Stock Exchange*), *La Voltige* (*Mounted Gymnastics*), *Forgerons* (*Blacksmiths Hammering Iron*), *Pêche aux poissons rouges* (*Fishing for Goldfish*), *Pompiers: Attaque de feu* (*The Fire*), *Le Jardinier* (*The Gardener*, later known as *L'Arroseur arrosé*, literally *The Sprinkler Sprinkled*), and *Le repas de bébé* (*Feeding the Baby*). Once again, as reported in *Le Moniteur de la photographie*, "the large audience that filled the hall of the Stock Exchange, where the projections took place, applauded and stamped their feet after each exhibition of a new series [of moving pictures]." Two days later Lumière further delighted Congress members

when he was able to show them two views of their own activities recorded the day before: the landing of the delegates after an excursion on the Saône Riber (*Débarquement des Congressistes à Neuville-sur-Saône*) and a conversation between the distinguished astronomer-inventor Jules Janssen and M. Lagrange, president of the Lyons photo-club (*Discussion de M. Janssen et de M. Lagrange*).

Like *Workers Leaving the Factory*, the new subjects presented to the Congress were basically glimpses of Lumière's own world, both public and private—a street scene in his home town, a military exercise, artisans from his own factory, local firefighters, the Congress "newsreels," and perhaps most telling, vignettes of family life featuring his brother's year-old daughter playing with a goldfish bowl under the eyes of her doting parents at a well-laden breakfast table.

Even with his filmed comedy, *The Gardener*, the story was acted out by the Lumière family gardener, François Clerc. This landmark venture into fiction was a staged sight-gag where the gardener's assistant steps on the hose to keep the water from flowing and then removes his foot as the gardener peers into the nozzle, so that the water gushes into his face. According to Clerc, the youngest Lumière brother, Edouard, had actually played this trick on him, although it was also popular in children's books and magic-lantern shows.

At the end of his life, Lumière was quite adamant about his intentions with these early films: "When I used the expression 'staging' (*mise-en-scène*) in front of him," Georges Sadoul recalled, "Mr. Louis Lumière . . . wrinkled his shaggy black brows. Then he told me that his films of 1895 were intended above all to 'reproduce life.'" Indeed, when the Janssen-Lagrange conversation was projected at the closing session of the Photography Congress, Lagrange sat behind the screen and read his words aloud. Some historians have perceived in these flickering images the beginnings of all the various movements and genres of modern cinema; others claim the Lumières as the source of a distinct realist or documentary tradition, attributing the tradition of fantasy and fiction to Georges Méliès. Lumière himself later described Lagrange's dubbing as "the first projection of talking cinema, but in a crude form." Nevertheless, these early films have roots in preexisting forms of popular culture, including journalism, photography, and theatrical entertainments.

Lumière associated his visual style with his study of drawing and painting. "My master," he told Georges Sadoul, "was a certain Borel who worked in my father's photography shop. What always preoccupied me in my views was the framing (*mise-en-page*) of my subjects." But he had also been an active outdoor photographer since his youth, and for him, as well as for his audiences, fifty years of still photography undoubtedly exerted a powerful influence on the way the new medium was perceived. In a letter to Demeny after the first public demonstration of the Cinématographe, for example, Lumière described what he had shown as "a chronophotographic series of eight hundred prints." Similarly, at the closing banquet of the Lyons Congress, Janssen (himself the inventor of a photographic "revolver") told the gathering that "thanks to the Lumières, photography, which I propose to name *animated photography* in order to distinguish it from the analytic photography of movements, has taken a great step forward."

By this time, articles about the Cinématographe were appearing in professional publications, but the device was far from perfected. Film stock presented a particular problem: celluloid film was not available in the necessary fifty-foot strips because Edison had a monopoly on the output of the sole manufacturer, Eastman. Raw celluloid was no longer made in France, and the photographic film that Lumière's own company produced was a gelatin stock. As the original patent indicates, Louis Lumière had began his own experiments with emulsioned paper strips, using very strong arc lamps for projection. After an unsuccessful attempt to make his own film strips from sheets of celluloid imported from London, he began buying raw stock from the New York Celluloid Company and managed to produce a usable film (which, Vincent Pinel suggests, may have differed from that of Edison and Dickson just enough to avoid a copyright suit). The problem was finally resolved when he located a Paris film manufacturer, Planchon, who was able to duplicate the American product and subsequently agreed to transfer his factory to Lyons.

The Cinématographe itself posed no fewer problems. The original model, based on Louis Lumière's sketches, had been built by Charles Moisson early in 1895. After the first demonstration that March, Jules Carpentier, a Paris engineer who had already constructed his own portable camera and was soon to patent a projector, approached the Lumières about manufacturing the Cinématographe for them, and after the prototype was completed in mid-October, twenty-five more were ordered. Even then, as can be seen from the correspondence between Louis Lumière and Carpentier over the next four months, the perfection of the machine remained a laborious process of trial and error.

"One always thinks 'that's it,' but utilization shows you that there's still something else," Lumière wrote to Carpentier on December 10, adding, "However, I firmly believe that we're 'coming into the port of call.'" In that letter he indicated that there was a problem with the feeding mechanism and sought to reduce the length of the claws; four days later he wrote to say that the new claws were fine, but the heat from the projection lamp was bending the ebony discs in the mechanism and these would have to be changed. The next day he announced that "We are running up against a new difficulty"—the perforations in the film no longer matched the new claws. Throughout this period Lumière had only two machines to work with, the original Cinématographe and Carpentier's prototype, which was sent back and forth between Paris and Lyons for adjustments.

This inconvenience was not the only reason the Lumières were anxious to perfect the prototype and begin large-scale production: they were fully aware of the commercial possibilities of the invention and did not want to lose out to competitors. In the same November 2 letter, Lumière told Carpentier, "They're breathing down our necks from all sides, and my father in particular wishes [the first batch] were already available because he wants to deal with this matter. On the other hand, de Bedts (American Import Office) is still making the loudest possible noise with his chronos [i.e., chronophotographs], and it would really be quite regrettable if he were to show something before us."

The particular "matter" that Antoine Lumière wanted to get underway was the commercial exhibition of the Cinématographe in Paris to promote the eventual sale of equipment, raw film, and recorded views. Working with his former partner Clément Maurice (the person who had originally taken him to see Edison's Kinetoscope the summer before), he arranged to rent the elegant but unpatronized Salon Indien in the basement of the Grand Café, located on the fashionable Boulevard des Capucines in Paris. When the owner refused to gamble on a percentage of the receipts, they signed a one-year lease at a fixed rental of 30 francs a day (then less than $7) and set the opening date for Thursday, December 28—the holiday weekend between Christmas and New Year's.

Ten films were included in the opening program: six that had been demonstrated during the summer (*Working Leaving the Factory, Mounted Gymnastics, Fishing for Goldfish, Blacksmiths, The Gardener, Feeding the Baby*); one newsreel from the photographers' congress (*The Landing at Neuville-sur-Saône*); another street scene in Lyons (*Place des Cordeliers*), a military game (*La Brimade—The Hazing*), and a view of the sea (*La Mer*). Journalists and various theatre and music-hall directors, including Georges Méliès from the Théâtre Robert-Houdin, Gabriel Thomas of the Grévin wax museum, and M. Lallemand of the Folies-Bergère, were invited to a preview that afternoon.

Among those not invited was Jules Carpentier, who had delivered the first twenty-five Cinématographes on December 25; writing to apologize for this embarrassing oversight, Louis Lumière explained that "My father tortured us to let him organize these presentations in Paris, and we were intent on not getting mixed up in it at all." In fact, neither brother was present on the opening day. Charles Moisson came from Lyons to operate the Cinématographe, and Clément Maurice stood by the door to collect the price of admission.

The first day's revenues, at one franc a head, amounted to only thirty-five francs, barely enough to cover the rent, but after these modest beginnings, word spread. Although the program was not mentioned in the major newspapers, two smaller dailies published glowing accounts on December 30. Calling the Cinématographe a "photographic marvel," *Le Radical* reported that "a new invention, which is certainly one of the most curious things of our era, . . . was produced last evening. . . . Whatever the scene shot in that way, and however many people thus caught unaware in the doings of their life, you see them again, in natural size, with the colors, the perspectives, the distant skies, the houses, the streets, with every illusion of real life."

Similarly, *La Poste* told its readers to "Picture a screen placed at the end of a hall as large as one can imagine [in fact, the Salon Indien accommodated only about 120 people]. This screen is visible to a crowd. On the screen appears a photographic projection. So far, nothing new. But suddenly, the image of natural size or smaller, according to the size of the scene, starts to move and comes alive." Describing *Workers Leaving the Factory*, the article continues, "It's the door of a factory opening to let out a flood of men and women workers, with bicycles, dogs running, carriages; all that is moving, swarming. It's life itself, it's movement taken from life."

By January, some 2000 to 2500 people a day were flocking to the Grand Café. There were twenty half-hour screenings daily, from ten in the morning to one-thirty the next morning, with breaks for lunch and dinner. Clément Maurice, the ticket-taker, later described how passersby who saw the Lumière poster on the street above would peer in to find out what a Cinématographe could be. "Those who decided to enter soon left in a state of bewilderment. Then you'd see them return quickly, bringing with them people they knew whom they'd been able to find on the boulevard. In the afternoon there was a line stretching all the way to rue Caumartin [three to four hundred meters away]."

The repertoire of views seems to have included at least thirty-five films made by Louis Lumière the previous year. With the exception of one effort by Auguste, *Mauvaises herbes (Bad Plants)*, which showed women burning weeds in a field, Louis was the only person to use the Cinématographe while it was still in the experimental stage, but Auguste and other family members and Lumière employees regularly appear as amateur actors. *Démolition d'un mur (Demolition of A Wall)*, for example, shows Auguste directing workers as they knock down a wall inside the Lumière factory; this film became a favorite at the Grand Café when the projection was followed by one in reverse, an early example of cinematic trickery that allowed the wall to resurrect itself with the same compelling realism of detail that had accompanied its demolition. A varied group of views were shot at Antoine Lumière's property at la Ciotat, where the brothers and their families spent summer vacation in 1895. Of particular interest was *Arrivée d'un train à La Ciotat (Arrival of a Train at La Ciotat)*, which apparently had audiences at the Grand Café jumping back from the screen as the train moved forward. Positioning the Cinématographe at eye level, Lumière was able to track the train from its inconspicuous appearance on the horizon to its lumbering entry into the station (where his mother and his older daughter were standing on the platform). Owing to the precision of the lens, the image retains its clarity at every distance, as the heaving, smoking engine looms closer and closer until it fills the screen.

Another impressive view from La Ciotat is *Barque sortant du port (Boat Leaving the Harbor)*, a majestic seascape that shows three men in a rowboat making their way from a jetty, with Lumère's wife and two daughters watching from the side. Louis and Auguste together staged a comedy during the summer, a satire on the Chicago meatpacking industry called *Charcuterie mécanique (Mechanical Butcher Shop*, originally *Charcuterie américaine)*; it first showed a live pig coming out of a box as a string of sausages, then the string of sausages going into the box and emerging as a live pig. *Partie d'écarté (The Card Party)* probably comes from the La Ciotat vacation as well. A classic genre subject contemporary with the famous *Card*

Players of Cézanne (and soon taken up by Georges Méliès in his first film), it features Antoine Lumière, the illusionist Félicien Trewey, and the Lumières' father-in-law, Winkler the brewer, around the card table; at the end of the game, Louis Lumière's valet comes in with a round of beers and an impromptu vaudeville routine.

Public response to these and other films shown at the Grand Café focused on the same element singled out in the earliest newspaper accounts—what was most often referred to as "nature in the raw." If the approaching train somehow threatened to jump out of the screen, the movement of the waves in *Boat Leaving the Harbor*, the smoke from the blacksmiths' forge, or the cloud of dust that rose from *Demolition of a Wall* similarly captivated viewers; in his recollection of the very first screening at the Grand Café, Georges Méliès made special mention of the leaves that fluttered far in the background of *Feeding the Baby*. As Georges Sadoul pointed out, such details would hardly be noticed today, but they seem to have conveyed then a special power—to represent not only what was tangible, predictable, manageable, but also what was ephemeral, unexpected, and uncontrollable. David Thomson suggests other effects: "Used to the frozen mirror of stills, people began to see for the first time how they walked, smiled and gestured, how they looked from the back, and how other people watched them. Introspection and exhibitionism were thus simultaneously stimulated."

At the end of March 1896, the Cinématographe was added to the evening program at the Eldorado café-concert; by mid-April, in response to requests from the residents of the tenth arondissement, the Eldorado was converted to a theatre for afternoon screenings. Around the same time, the Lumières opened another theatre down the street from the Grand Café at the Musée Oller, and by the end of the month, a fourth Lumière theatre was operating in a meeting hall of the Dufayel department store. A fifth was soon opened by photographer Eugène Pirou at the Café de la Paix, also on the Boulevard des Capucines, and yet another was set up in St.-Denis in March of the following year.

But even these mushrooming theatres in Paris did not represent the main thrust of the Lumière operation. On November 25, 1895, Louis Lumière had written to Jules Carpentier, "When we launch this business commercially, we want to be ready for the largest possible expansion." Three days after the Paris premiere, satisfied that Carpentier's prototype was "definitive," he told the engineer to go ahead with the construction of two hundred more machines. Requests

for purchase had been received well before the public screenings; between the end of October 1895 and mid-February 1896, some one hundred inquiries had arrived, not only from France, but from the rest of Europe, England, and Russia, as well as Egypt, Turkey, and Mexico. Louis Lumière's standard response was that no date had yet been set for the sale of the new device. On the very afternoon of the preview at the Grand Café, at least three of the entrepreneurs in the audience—Méliès, Thomas, and Lallemand—tried to buy the Cinématographe for prices ranging from 10,000 to 50,000 francs (at that time $2000 to $10,000). According to the classic account presented by Méliès in his memoirs, Antoine Lumière refused their offers and told them, "It's a big secret, this device, and I don't want to sell it. I want to develop it myself, exclusively."

Within little more than a week, that development was underway. As a prelude to selling the Cinétographe itself, the Lumières began to hire traveling operators to set up exhibitions quite literally all over the world. The first and most prominent of these was Alexandre Promio, who had seen the demonstration at the Lyons photography congress. Appraching the Lumières through a mutual friend, he entered their employ at the beginning of January 1896. Another early operator was Félix Mesguich, a young Algerian who presented himself at the Lumière factory only a few days after his discharge from the Zouaves, a crack French infantry unit recruited in Algeria. Although he had no technical experience, Louis Lumière was impressed with his manner and passed him along to Promio for training. First assigned to the Lumière theater in Lyons, which was opened on January 25, Mesguich was next sent into the provinces. In his autobiography, he recalls that Louis Lumière hired him with the warning that "this is not a position with a future that we're offering you; rather, it's an itinerant trade—it could last six months, a year, maybe more, maybe less." It turned out to last some eighteen months, by the end of which Mesguich was in Russia, and about one hundred other Lumière operators had reached every continent but Antarctica.

The first commercial presentation in a foreign capital took place in London, where Antoine Lumière's friend Félicien Trewey (from *The Card Party*) organized a show at the Empire theatre on March 9, two weeks after he had given a demonstration at the Polytechnic Association. In May, Promio was sent to Madrid (he introduced the Cinématographe two days after the presentation of Edison's Cinetoscopio). Early in June, Mesguich set sail for New York, where he organized a public screening at the Keith Music

Hall on June 28 and was carried to the stage amid ovations at the end. In a few days, he later wrote, the fame of the Lumière Cinématographe had swept the entire country. "My refuge on Twenty-third Street, Beef à la Mode, was invaded at all hours by reporters, whose articles helped to publicize the enterprise still further." In response to this overwhelming demand, Mesguich himself traveled to Washington, DC, Philadelphia, Baltimore, Chicago, and St. Louis, and, he recalled, "Every week for almost six months, a transatlantic steamer brought a new operator from France."

The Cinématographe reached Berlin on April 30 (four days after the Isola brothers' Isolatographe was introduced there), St. Petersburg on May 4, Moscow on May 5 (with the mechanic Charles Moisson and Francis Doublier), Helsinki and Malmo on June 28, Bombay on July 7. Promio eventually made his way to Italy, Switzerland, England, Ireland, Turkey, and Palestine; Doublier, to Asia; Maurius Sestier, who had organized the Bombay screening, continued on to Australia; others went to Mexico and Latin America. The usual procedure was to begin with a modest showing in a small theatre or hotel, and if that proved successful, to move to a larger hall with additional screenings. The operators were paid a weekly salary (Mesguich indicates that he received seventy francs) plus one percent of the box-office receipts. They were instructed that no one else was to handle the Cinématographe, that its operation was to remain a secret, and that they were to keep it with them at all times.

Like the Cinématographe itself, this commercial enterprise was "self-complementary"; wherever the operators went, they were able to produce new footage because their projector also functioned as a camera and a printer. In his travel notes, Alexandre Promio indicates that he, at least, was sent abroad primarily to obtain new material: "At that time, there were only a very small number of films recorded by M. Lumière, but this quite modest stock quickly became inadequate, and after he had me try my hand at shooting, M. Louis Lumière asked me to set out on a journey in order to collect as quickly as possible some new views to meet the demand."

Filming in well-frequented public places provided valuable publicity for the screenings, and spectators were often drawn to attend in hopes of catching a glimpse of themselves on the screen. But if the lightweight (5 kilo), hand-cranked Cinématographe was well suited to such a venture, there were other complications—harsh climates, difficult travel, unfamiliar terrain, and the inevitable encounters with foreign bureaucracies. Promio, for example, recalled his difficulties in Ottoman Turkey, where "any instrument equipped with a crank was suspect," and he was forced to rely on the assistance of the French ambassador as well as "some pieces of money handily forgotten in the palm of some functionary" in order to gain entry. Moisson and Doublier were even less fortunate in Russia: after they filmed an otherwise unreported accident that killed some five thousand people at Czar Nicholas II's first public audience, they were arrested and their equipment was confiscated.

Despite these difficulties, a great amount of material was sent back to Lyons for redistribution. Mesguich's programs in New York, for example, included views from London, Venice, Milan, Germany, and Austria; by 1897, as Eric Barnouw observes, "the Cinématographe was already giving its audiences an unprecedented sense of seeing the world."

In spite of the number of operators involved, the geographical spread, and the potential range of themes, these foreign views display a uniformity of style and subject that eventually became repetitious. The nature of the equipment itself (especially the lack of a viewer and the limited film capacity), and the close involvement of Louis Lumière in the training and supervision of the operators, as well as the absence of alternative models, all contributed to a consistent visual approach. Like Louis Lumière's own views, those of the operators tended to combine a basic two-dimensional orientation to fixed horizontals and verticals for framing (buildings, trees, roads) with strong diagonal movements in depth (trains, processions, military exercises).

Similarly, what was available to be filmed, coupled with what audiences at home wanted to see, encouraged a fairly fixed repertoire of themes: city subjects, first of all, because they were more accessible by major routes of travel; tourist sights, emphasizing the modern in European centers and the traditional or "exotic" elsewhere; and increasingly, as the newsreel aspect of motion pictures came to the fore, topical events and ceremonies. As many film historians have observed, heads of state were able to memorialize themselves worldwide, not only because their activities were popular with the audiences, but also because of the power and patronage they wielded: among the sponsors of Cinématographe exhibitions abroad were the czarina Alexandra in St. Petersburg, King Oscar in Stockholm, the queen mother in Madrid, Emperor Franz-Joseph in Vienna, King Karel I in Bucharest, and King Milan of Serbia in Belgrade.

Louis Lumière, who was clearly a skilled camera operator to begin with, improved the quality of his own work by shooting multiple versions and selecting the best for public display. (Thousands of unprinted negatives are still preserved at the Musée du Cinéma in Lyons.) He also exercised control over the material sent back by his operators; Marius Sestier, for example, was berated for his views of Bombay, which were deemed unusable. Other operators were encouraged for their innovations, most notably the traveling shot or panorama introduced by Promio in Venice. "Going from the station to my hotel in a boat," he later recalled, "I watched the banks recede in front of the gondola, and then I thought that if the immobile cinema could reproduce mobile objects, perhaps one could reverse the proposition and try to reproduce immobile objects with the help of the mobile cinema." While the Cinématographe itself had to remain fixed, the gondola, and later the steamboat or train, provided the necessary movement for the shot.

In the Lumière catalogues issued in 1897, well over 400 of the 691 titles are views from other countries—the rest of Europe, England, the eastern Mediterranean and North Africa, the U.S. and Mexico; the 1898 catalogue includes views from Japan, the Indies, and Australia as well. But already the novelty was wearing off. Not only had audiences begun to lose interest in travelogues, but the Lumières' competitors—among them Edison in the U.S., Birt Acres and William Paul in England, the Skladanowskys in Germany, not to mention Charles Pathé, Georges Méliès, and Léon Gaumont in France—had quickly absorbed the technological breakthroughs of the Cinématographe and set up their own tours and sales operations. In Paris, fliers for the Grand Café now carried the warning "Not to be confused with the crude imitations of the Lumière Cinématographe." The morning programs there were ended, then the number of films in each screening was doubled and the price of admission cut to 50 centimes, but even so the house was not always full. In July 1897, the Lumière office in New York was abruptly closed when its director, Francais Lafont, increasingly beset by US customs officials and fearful of a patent war with Edison, sneaked onto a steamer and returned to France. At the end of the year, the Lumière company ended the rest of its direct operations outside of Paris and made the Cinématographe available for purchase along with raw film and printed views.

Seeking to expand the sale of their own films the Lumières turned to various forms of staged productions in response to the popular new themes introduced by their competitors. At the urging of Antoine Lumière and Clément Mau-

rice, Georges Hatot was brought in to supervise comedies. A number of stag films were made, including at least one by Promio. Another vogue that peaked in 1897 and 1898 was the historical reconstruction, which drew heavily on the theatre; Lumière productions ranged from ancient Rome (*Néron essayant des poisons sur des esclaves—Nero Testing Poisons on Slaves*) to the French Revolution (*Mort de Robespierre —Death of Robespierre*). Late in 1897 Hatot produced a 250-meter version of *La Vie et la passion de Jésus-Christ* (*The Life and Passion of Jesus Christ*) in thirty tableaux, notable for its length if not its content.

Catalogues for the next few years continued to offer, on a greatly reduced scale, genre subjects and scenic views from France and abroad, military scenes, and newsreels featuring heads of state, along with Hatot's comedies and a few of the trick-photography transformations that Georges Méliès had pioneered. Lumière film production ended altogether in 1905 with a group of twenty-three "vues fantasmagoriques" in the manner of Méliès, including titles such as *La Maison hantée* (*The Haunted House*), *Le Marmite diabolique* (*The Diabolical Kettle*), and *L'Illusioniste au café* (*The Illusionist at the Café*). Within a few years, all sales rights were ceded to Pathé.

After 1896, Louis Lumière had little if anything to do with actual film production, not simply for lack of interest in the new directions the medium was taking, but because he seems to have considered himself primarily an inventor, a man of science. "My works," he told Georges Sadoul in his last interview, "are works of technical research. I have never done what is called '*mise-en-scène.*' And I can't see myself very well in a modern studio." Indeed, he remained a researcher and inventor to the end of his working life and, in particular, continued experimenting with the Cinématographe to modify it and develop new applications for it.

On August 20, 1896 he patented a combined Cinématographe-phonograph for the simultaneous recording of movement and sound. In 1897, after a disastrous fire caused by an ether-fueled projector killed one hundred people at the Bazar de la Charité in Paris, he developed a safety condenser for the Cinématographe, and in 1898 he patented a threading device to correct film displacement with prisms. The same year, he approached officials of the impending Universal Exposition of 1900 with a plan for giant outdoor Cinématographe projections under the Eiffel Tower. Wind problems (the danger of capsizing the screen) greatly reduced the scale of the project from the beginning, and the program ultimately took place indoors on a screen measuring 16 by 21 meters. Still hoping for an outdoor demonstration, Lumière's twenty-five-minute program of moving-picture projections and color photographs attracted some five thousand people a day for almost six months.

Over the next few years Lumière was engaged in several projects with still photography. On December 29, 1900, he patented the Photorama, a device to project still panoramas on a circular screen by means of twelve lenses; in 1901 he set up a projection hall in Paris, where daily shows were presented for the next two years. At that point, he and Auguste made a major break-through with what he later called "the largest preoccupation of my existence": color photography. On October 17, 1903 they patented the panchromatic emulsion process that substituted a single photographic plate, known as the Auto-chrome, for the separate plates of the three-color process. As was the case with the Ciné-matographer, the invention was not limited to a single device, but required the creation of all the supporting equipment as well—special vats, canvas rollers, dying materials, laminators. Within a decade, the Lumière factory was man-ufacturing some six thousand Autochrome plates a day, and they continued to be used until the commercialization of color film in the 1940s. Lumière himself later tried to adapt the auto-chrome process for Cinématographer film with finer, more sensitive emulsions, but his research was interrupted by the onset of the Second World War.

In 1907, meanwhile, Lumière and Jules Car-pentier perfected the Défileur Carpentier-Lumière, a threading device that accommodat-ed long reels of film up to 400 meters. The fol-lowing year Lumière took out a patent for a loudspeaker with a folded-paper diaphragm, which was used first in phonographs and later in radios. In 1909 he developed a nonflammable film on an acetate base to replace nitrate stock, and he and Carpentier patented the Cinématobale, a rather cumbersome camera with a 120-meter film magazine. During World War I, the Lumière factory was converted to a hospital, and Louis Lumière put his skills at the service of the military, inventing among other things a sound detector, a combustion device to prevent the thickening of airplane motor oil, protective glasses for welders, and an artificial hand for amputees.

After 1920, Louis Lumière withdrew from the management of the family factory to pursue his own research interests. In a note to the French Academy of Sciences that year, he described a project he was working on with "stereo-

synthesis" or "relief" images in still photography; by the middle of the next decade, he had made significant advances with an analogous "cinema in relief," known today as 3-D. As early as 1900 he and Auguste had taken out a patent for "a de-vice intended to record and show stereoscopic images of moving objects," but it was not until 1934 that he began shooting his first 3-D films. By early 1935 he was able to present his discov-ery (a collaboration with Pierre Cuvier) before the Academy of Sciences, and the "cinema in relief" premiered in Paris on May 1, 1936.

As he finally developed the relief process, the films were viewed through special yellow-and-blue glasses which, like the stereoscope (and un-like the nineteenth-century anaglyph system based on the subtraction of images), functioned additively, with two separate projections on the screen. Significantly, Lumière included among his new films a "remake" of the *Arrival of a Train at La Ciotat*, which had already anticipat-ed somewhat the effects of 3-D movies in 1895. By the 1937 Paris Exposition he had made fur-ther refinements of his technique, although a *Variety* reviewer found that the blue-and-yellow viewing glasses still tired the eyes. But once the novelty wore off, and color films caught on, the "cinema in relief" lapsed into the domain of sci-ence until the 1950s.

It was rather the fortieth anniversary of the invention of the Cinématographe that brought Lumière back into the public view, with jubilee celebrations throughout the world. He was feted at the Sorbonne in November 1935, and a "Louis Lumière Week" was declared at the end of the year. Similar commemorations were held in London the following February, and in the USSR a special biography was published to show "that the Soviet Union knows and values him as nowhere else in the world." In the United States, as Sadoul points out, the jubilee was recognized as the "fortieth anniversary in France," politely retaining for Edison the founder's role in world cinema.

After the death of his wife in 1925, Lumière had settled in Neuilly, on the outsdkirts of Paris; in 1938 he moved to Bandol, in the south of France, to continue his scientific work. The fol-lowing year he was awarded the French Legion of Honor. When the Cannes Film Festival was established in June 1939, he was asked to serve as honorary president, and the highest award was to be named after him, but plans for the fes-tival were interrupted by the outbreak of the war and the German occupation. Remaining in Bandol under the government of Marshall Pétain, Lumière was appointed as a science rep-resentative on the advisory council that was to frame the Vichy constitution in 1941, but he soon withdrew. His health failed after the war—when he wrote to Georges Sadoul to confirm what was to be his last interview in January 1948, Lumière urged him to move quickly "because my health is not improving, quite the contrary . . . in my case, the human machine doesn't have a backup." He died exactly five months later in Bandol at the age of eighty-four.

At the end of his long and productive life, and in spite of the string of honors he had accumulated, Louis Lumière seemed to feel that the world of cinema had passed him by. The fact that he was not invited to the Cannes Film Festival when it finally took place in 1946 was, according to Sadoul, a particular source of bitterness. "Now they've put me aside, now they've put me on the shelf," Lumière told him and then added his familiar refrain: "Besides, in the cinema the time of the technicians is past; it's the age of theatre." In fact, his preeminent role in the history of French cinema was and is unchallenged; as Vincent Pinel has aptly put it, Louis Lumière received his "canonization" with the Jubilee of 1935. If he is most often enshrined in the trinity of French film founders as Lumière the inventor (alongside Méliès the director and Pathé the promoter), for Georges Sadoul he was also the pioneer director who first captured "nature in the raw"; for Jacques Deslandes, his "invention" was not simply the Cinématographe but the cinema, insofar as he also developed the means of utilizing the new technology.

Lumière himself freely acknowledged his debt to others in the field. "What have I done? It was in the air," he told those gathered to honor him at the Sorbonne in 1935. "Sooner or later the works of Janssen, of Edison, and especially of Marey and his students would have led to the result." Yet, as Maurice Bessy and Jean-Louis Chardans have pointed out, echoing Lumière's own words, "All the ideas that led to the Cinématographe of Louis Lumière were in the air for fifty years, but it was he who made it all seem clear, who developed the invention decisively and with absolute perfection."

The same might be said for the rest of the operation as well. There are ample precedents for every aspect of Louis Lumière's involvement with what is, thanks to him, know as cinema—his "views" drew heavily on photography, painting, and popular entertainments; the operators continued the tradition of any number of traveling merchants; the much-heralded program at the Grand Café was not even the first of its kind for moving pictures, since Max Skladanowsky had begun projecting his Bioskope at the Winter Garden in Berlin nearly two months earlier. But it was Lumière who brought the disparate currents together, as inventor, manufacturer, operator, director, producer, and promoter. This is not to say that he originated, anticipated, or even prefigured subsequent developments (as the teleological reading of film history would have it), but rather, that he realized the possibilities of his own time, with the science, the art, and the industry of the Cinématographe, and in so doing, he enabled others to recognize and develop the possibilities of the future.

—*M.R.*

FILMS: Of the fourteen hundred views listed in the final Lumière catalogue of 1907, no more than fifty or sixty were made by Louis Lumière, and these in the first years of the operation. Lumière's own recollections to Maurice Bessy and Georges Sadoul were neither precise nor consistent, and in the absence of written records, it is impossible to establish a definitive filmography for him. At best, thirty-eight views known to have been made in 1895 can be attributed to him on the basis of the fact that he was the only person using the Cinématographe at that time. According to Sadoul these include the following (those identified for Sadoul by Lumière himself are marked with an asterisk).

1895: La Sortie des usines (Workers Leaving the Factory, first version, around mid-March); La Sortie des usines (second version, prior to Lyons congress of 10 June); Le Jardinier/L'Arroseur arrosé (The Gardener/ The Sprinkled, before 10 June); Forgerons (Blacksmiths, before 10 June); Pompiers: Sortie de la pompe, Mise en batterie, Attaque du feu, Sauvetage (Firefighters: Bringing Out the Pump, Getting Ready, Attacking the Fire, The Rescue, before 10 June); Le Repas de bébé (Feeding the Baby, before 10 June); Pêche aux poissons rouges (Fishing for Goldfish, before 10 June); La Voltige (Mounted Gymnastics, before 10 June); Débarquement des congressistes à Neuville-sur-Saône (Landing of the Congress Participants at Neuville-sur-Saône, 11 June); Discussion de M. Janssen et de M. Lagrange (Conversation between M. Janssen and M. Lagrange, 11 June); Saut à la couverture/Brimade dans une caserne (The Blanket Game/ Hazing in the Barracks, before 11 July); Lyon, place des Cordeliers (before 11 July); °Lyon, place Bellecour (before 11 July); Recreation à la Martinière (Student Games at La Martinière, July); °Charcuterie mécanique (Mechanical Butcher Shop, summer); °Le Maréchal-ferrant (The Farrier summer); Lancement d'un navire à La Ciotat (Launching of a Ship at La Ciotat, summer); °Baignade en mer (Bathing in the Sea, summer); Ateliers de La Ciotat (Workshops at La Ciotat, summer): °Barque sortant du port (Boat Leaving the Harbor, summer): Arrivée d'un train à La Ciotat (Arrival of a Train at La Ciotat, summer—Lumière identified a similar view, Arrival of a Train in the Station, as his own, but this was apparently a mistake on his part); °Partie d'écarté (The Card Party, probably summer, La Ciotat); °Assiettes tournantes (Spinning Plates, possibly summer, La Ciotat): Chapeaux à transformations (Transformations With

Hats, possibly summer, La Ciotat); °Photographe (Photographer, possibly early 1896); °Démolition d'un mur (Demolition of a Wall, possibly spring 1896); °Querelle enfantine (Children's Quarrel); °Aquarium; Bocal aux poissons rouges (Goldfish Bowl); °Partie de tric-trac (Backgammon Game); Le déjeuner du chat (The Cat's Lunch); Départ en voiture (Setting Out in a Carriage); °Enfants aux jouets (Children's Games); °Course en sac (Sack Race); Discussion ([comedy in a garden]).

1900: Lumière's 73mm films shot for the Universal Exposition in April 1900 include: Inauguration de l'Exposition universelle (Opening of the Universal Exposition), La tour Eiffel (The Eiffel Tower), Le Pont d'Iéna (Iéna Bridge), Danses espagnoles (Spanish Dances).

1930s: Lumière also made several "films in relief" in the mid-thirties, including Arrivée d'un train en gare de La Ciotat (Arrival of a train in La Ciotat Station), 1934.

ABOUT: Armes, R. Film and Reality, 1974; Barnouw, E. Documentary, 1974, reprinted 1981; Bazin, A. Qu'est-ce que le cinéma? Vol. 1, 1958; Bessy, M. and Duca, L. Louis Lumière, inventeur, 1948; Coissac, G.-M. Histoire du cinématographe, 1925; Deslandes, J. Histoire comparée du cinéma, Vol. 1, 1966; Deslandes, J. and Richard, J. Histoire comparée du cinéma, Vol. 2, 1968; Fell, J. Film Before Griffith, 1983; Godard, J.-L. Jean-Luc Godard par Jean-Luc Godard, 1968; Kubnick, H. Les Frères Lumière, 1938; Leroy, P. Au seuil du paradis des images avec Louis Lumière, 1939, reprinted 1948; Mesguich, F. Tours de manivelle, 1933; Pinel, v. Louis Lumière, 1974 (in French); Sadoul, G. Louis Lumière, 1964 (in French); Rittaud-Hutinet, J. Le Cinéma des origines, 1985; Sauvage, L. L'Affaire Lumière: du mythe à l'histoire, 1985; Thomson, D. A Biographical Dictionary of the Cinema, 1980. Periodicals—L'Avant-Scène du Cinéma November 1984; Cinéma (France) 2 1955, January 1955, January 1971; La Cinématographe française March 1935, November 1935; Cinetrack Summer and Fall 1981; Dossiers du Cinéma 2 1971; L'Exportateur films français November 7, 1935; Filmkritic August 1978, November 1981; Iris 2/1 1984; Journal of Aesthetics Summer 1978; Quarterly of the Library of Congress Winter 1981; Revue Belge du Cinéma Winter 1984–1985; Singt and Sound Spring 1981; Wide Angle 3 1 1979. Films about Lumière—Duvivier, J. and Lepage, H. La machine à refaire la vie, 1924 (sound version, 1933); Licot, L. Quarante ans de cinéma, 1935; Dècharme, P.-E. Cinématographe Lumière, 1946; Duca, J.-M. Le cinématographe en 1895, 1949; Paviot, P. Lumière, 1953; Allegret, M. Lumière, 1966; Rohmer, E. Louis Lumière, 1968; Chapot, J. Les Années Lumière, 1970; La Voie Lumière, 1983 (compilation film).

*MAMOULIAN, ROUBEN (October 8, 1897–), American film and theatre director, was born in Tiflis, in the Caucasus Mountains of

°mä moo˙ lē an

ROUBEN MAMOULIAN

Georgia, then a Russian province, now a Soviet Socialist Republic. He is the son of Armenian parents, Zachary Mamoulian and the former Virginia Kalantarian. His father was a bank president in Tiflis (now Tbilisi) who served with distinction in the Russian army in World War I. Both parents were cultivated people, interested in the arts and devoted to the theatre. Virginia Mamoulian was for many years president of the Armenian Theatre in Tiflis.

When Mamoulian was seven the family moved to Paris, where they lived for nearly six years. The boy attended the Lycée Montaigne and was an exceptional student. After their return to Georgia he continued his education at a private school in Tiflis and then at the local gymnasium. There followed two years at Moscow University, where he graduated in criminal law. His evenings were spent at the Moscow Art Theatre, studying acting, writing, and directing under Eugene Vakhtangov, a distinguished disciple of Stanislavsky. After the 1917 Revolution Mamoulian went home to Tiflis. He was an actor and director in local theatres and wrote drama criticism for a Tiflis newspaper.

Mamoulian has said that his passion for the theatre began with Shakespeare, whose plays he saw as a child in Tiflis. Eager to learn Shakespeare's own language, he went in 1920 to stay with his married sister in London. There he secured his first important assignment as a director, a production of Austin Page's The Beating on the Door at the St. James's Theatre in November 1922. Mamoulian directed the play with a relentless naturalism worthy of Stanislavsky himself. He later said that this "was the first and last production that I directed in this manner. . . . In my subsequent work, my aim always was rhythm and poetic stylization." Nevertheless, the production was a success, and brought Mamoulian a long telegram from George Eastman, inviting him to help organize and direct the new American Opera Company at Eastman's equally new theatre in Rochester, New York.

During the two and a half years he spent in Rochester, Mamoulian directed the American Opera Company in about a dozen major productions. It was then that he began to work towards "a truly dramatic theatre, a theatre that would combine all the elements of movement, dancing, acting, music, singing, decor, lighting, color, and so on." During 1926 Mamoulian directed several plays at the Theatre Guild's School of Acting in Scarborough, New York, and in October 1927 he staged his first play in New York City, DuBose and Dorothy Heyward's Porgy, which ran for three hundred and sixty-seven performances at the Guild Theatre. This famous production began with a brilliantly orchestrated "symphony" of street noises, which Mamoulian later reproduced in the movie Love Me Tonight. It is a triumphant early example of what Tom Milne sees as the "real distinguishing mark" of Mamoulian's films, "their unerring sense of rhythm in exploring the sensuous pleasures of movement."

Several notable stage productions followed, and then in 1929 Mamoulian joined Paramount to make his first film. He spent five weeks at the Astoria Studios in New York, studying the techniques in use there, and soon decided he could do better. Mamoulian found a novel by Beth Brown about a fading burlesque queen who sacrifices herself for her daughter, wrote an adaptation in collaboration with Garrett Ford, and in October 1929 set to work with a cast of actors all of whom were as new to the cinema as he was.

Mamoulian says that in Applause, as in the films that followed, he set out to combine poetry and psychological truth. However, between his conception and its realization there stood massive technical barriers. In those first days of sound, movie cameras were enclosed in soundproof booths that were almost immovable. Mamoulian wanted his cameras to recover the mobility of silent days—"the movement of the camera along with the delight of movement which constitutes the attraction of the screen." His cameraman George Folsey said it couldn't be done. Sound was another problem, especially in a scene where his star Helen Morgan sings a burlesque song to her daughter by way of a lullaby, and the child simultaneously whispers her prayers. The single microphone picked up the

song but not the prayer, so Mamoulian suggested using two microphones, recording sound on two channels, and mixing it later. He was told this was impossible.

At that point Mamoulian threw down his megaphone and stormed upstairs into a meeting of Paramount moguls that included Adolph Zukor and Jesse L. Lasky. Zukor called the technicians in and told them, with no great enthusiasm, that the young director must be given his head. Mamoulian filmed one scene and went home convinced that his movie career was finished. When he arrived at the studio next morning the resplendent Irish doorman, who in the past had ignored him, greeted him with elaborate courtesy. The studio chiefs had had the laboratory working all night, had seen rushes of Mamoulian's first scene, and were converted. The word had gone out that he was to get everything he wanted. Applause, according to one critic, was "edged from melodrama into tragedy by Helen Morgan's superb performance and by Mamoulian's cunning juggling of naturalism and expressionism into a stylized reality." After this film, a major critical success, Mamoulian returned to Broadway, where he directed five plays (including his own adaptation of Turgenev's A Month in the Country) and an opera, Schönberg's The Hand of Fate.

In City Streets (Paramount, 1931), based on a Dashiel Hammett story, a gangster's daughter and the young man she recruits into the mob finally escape to make a new life together. Though by contemporary standards the plot is banal, the film is anything but. Its most famous innovation comes in the scene where Nan (Sylvia Sidney in her first starring role) is in jail. While the camera moves into a long close-up of her face, we hear not her own voice but what she is remembering—the voice of her lover, The Kid (Gary Cooper). Mamoulian was assured that audiences would not understand this device but in fact, as he says, it was immediately accepted, becoming a standard part of movie technique. Tom Milne, in his study of Mamoulian, has drawn attention to other remarkable aspects of this film, like the brilliant (and characteristic) economy with which the young lovers are introduced and the plot established, the "sensuous grace of the camera movement," and the telling use of symbolism. As Milne says, City Streets shows again and again that "Mamoulian knew and had thoroughly absorbed the techniques of the silent film. As always in his work at its best, dialogue is strictly an adjunct" to the visual images.

There followed one of the most admired of Mamoulian's films, Dr. Jekyll and Mr. Hyde

(Paramount, 1931), on which for the first time he served as producer as well as director. The screenplay, by Samuel Hoffenstein and Percy Heath, is remarkably frank in attributing Hyde's monstrous lusts to the frustration by a prudish society of Jekyll's perfectly natural desires. The film contains several of the innovations which audiences had begun to expect of a Mamoulian movie: the celebrated opening sequence in which the audience is shown only what Jekyll sees—his own hands playing the organ, the butler coming in to remind him of his lecture, his own reflection in the mirror as he puts on his cloak, and so on; the dramatic use of a device Mamoulian had introduced in *Applause*, with two scenes playing simultaneously on a diagonally divided screen; and the scene in which the handsome Jekyll is transformed (by the use of color filters) into the devilish Hyde in one continuous shot. The scene was given an extra dimension of strangeness by what was probably the first cinematic use of synthetic sound. Mamoulian's *Jekyll and Hyde* surpasses its numerous rivals not only in its technical mastery but in its psychological coherence and in its powerfully atmospheric incarnation of Stevenson's gaslit, fogbound London, brilliantly photographed by Karl Struss. The film won first prize at the 1931 Venice International Film Festival and collected Academy Awards for best actor (Fredric March) and best photography.

"If you were to see *Love Me Tonight*," Mamoulian said in an interview in 1970, "although it is a very light, gay musical, you'd see in it most clearly what motivates me, what I like. The whole of *Love Me Tonight* is a poem, from beginning to end. Everything is rhythm, counterpoint, stylization. . . . " This film, made for Paramount in 1932, had a cast that included Maurice Chevalier, Jeanette MacDonald, Charlie Ruggles, and Myrna Loy, and music by an almost unknown team of songwriters, Richard Rodgers and Lorenz Hart. The witty script was by Samuel Hoffenstein, Waldemar Young, and George Marion Jr., but the style of the movie, its subtlety and inventiveness, its gentle parody of other films in the genre, its "ineffable mixture of absurdity and enchantment," are Mamoulian's own. David Robinson wrote that in this film, "which is for me still the most enchanting of all musical films, . . . [Mamoulian] used sound *metaphorically*. For instance, when a trio of awful old ladies are gossiping excitedly, the noise that comes from their mouths is the yapping of little dogs. And when Jeanette MacDonald, in a moment of extreme embarrassment, drops a vase, the impact with the floor is a dynamite explosion."

In *Song of Songs* (Paramount, 1933), Ma-

moulian borrowed Marlene Dietrich from her mentor Josef von Sternberg to decorate a sometimes rather melodramatic account of innocence destroyed. This flawed attempt to build a film around one of Hollywood's great love goddesses was followed by a minor masterpiece starring the cinema's principal female deity, Greta Garbo. *Queen Christina* (1933), for which Mamoulian was signed by MGM at Garbo's personal request, tells the tragic story of the young queen of seventeenth-century Sweden. Two sequences in particular have a permanent place in film history. One is the beautifully lyrical scene in which Christina moves around the room in which she has found love, gently touching its clumsy furniture, committing it all to memory. The rhythm of the scene was actually set by a metronome, Mamoulian has explained. He told Garbo: "The movement must be like a dance. Treat it the way you would do it to music." At the end of the film, her country lost to her, her lover dead, Christina sails for Spain. She moves serenely into the bows of the ship and looks out to sea as the camera advances steadily from long shot into a close-up that holds for ninety feet of film. Mamoulian's instruction to Garbo was that throughout this long close-up, her face was to be a *tabula rasa*, a blank sheet of paper. "So in fact there is *nothing* on her face: but everyone who has seen the film will tell you what she is thinking and feeling. And always it's something different."

Anna Sten starred with Fredric March in Mamoulian's next film, *We Live Again* (Samuel Goldwyn, 1934). Adapted from Tolstoy's *Resurrection,* and with magnificent camerawork by Gregg Toland, the film was marred by some embarrassingly ill-conceived scenes. By this time, nevertheless, Mamoulian had become "one of the most discussed men in Hollywood." According to *Film Weekly* (March 16, 1934), he was threatening Lubitsch's position as Hollywood's most popular director, and there were rumors of a possible marriage to Garbo. In January 1935 he took over from Lowell Sherman (who died shortly after shooting began) the direction of Pioneer Pictures' *Becky Sharp*, based on Langdon Mitchell's stage version of Thackeray's novel *Vanity Fair*. It was the first feature film to use the new three-color Technicolor process and arguably the first film to employ color to specific dramatic ends.

The most famous example of Mamoulian's approach comes in the Duchess of Richmond's great ball, which is interrupted by the first rumble of cannons from the Battle of Waterloo. In this sequence it would have been logical for the many uniformed officers at the ball to hurry out as soon as the gunfire began, but Mamoulian made them leave last. His reason for this was simply that British officers of the period wore scarlet, and he wanted this powerful and dangerous color to dominate the *end* of the sequence. Mamoulian believes that "colors on the screen should be used as emotions. If you use them for their emotional and dramatic values, the aesthetics of colors take care of themselves." This principle is applied throughout *Becky Sharp.* The unfaltering pace and stunning theatricality of Mamoulian's direction were matched by shrewd casting, Miriam Hopkins as Becky being vigorously supported by Alan Mowbray, Cedric Hardwicke, Nigel Bruce, Frances Dee, and Billie Burke.

After *Becky Sharp,* Mamoulian returned to Broadway to direct *Porgy and Bess,* Gershwin's operatic version of *Porgy.* It is the usual critical view that Mamoulian's work in the cinema after 1935 showed a marked decline—that his later films are for the most part trivial entertainments, expert but uninspired. "Mamoulian's tragedy," says Andrew Sarris, "is that of the innovator who runs out of innovations." This view is strongly disputed by a growing number of critics who maintain that Mamoulian has always been more than an innovator, and assert that his later films contain some of his best work.

The Gay Desperado (Pickford-Lasky, 1936) is a musical comedy about a Mexican bandit who tries to modernize his techniques after seeing an American gangster movie. This engaging film, which has a splendidly eccentric characterization of the bandit chief by Leo Carrillo, brought Mamoulian both the New York Critics' Award and the Foreign Press Society's Award as the best director of the year. It was followed by *High, Wide and Handsome* (Paramount, 1937), starring Irene Dunne and Randolph Scott. This "musical Western," which has been shamefully underrated, impressed Richard Roud as "an extraordinary fusion of Brecht and Broadway." It has some memorable songs by Oscar Hammerstein and Jerome Kern.

Mamoulian's screen version of Clifford Odets' sentimental play *Golden Boy* (Columbia, 1939) was not a success, in spite of a cast that included Barbara Stanwyck, Adolph Menjou, and Sam Levene, and a fine performance in the lead by the totally unknown William Holden. Mamoulian kept his tongue firmly in his cheek in his next film, *The Mark of Zorro* (20th Century–Fox, 1940). A number of reviewers found Tyrone Power a poor substitute for Douglas Fairbanks, star of a famous silent version, but the film is increasingly admired as a masterpiece of the swashbuckling genre, a work of the greatest visual wit and elegance. Of Mamoulian's later films, the one that has been most seriously discussed is *Blood and Sand* (20th Century–Fox, 1941), which again starred Tyrone Power, and again faced comparison with a notable silent version. It is based on the novel by Vicente Blasco Ibáñez about a young matador's progress from rags to riches, his courting of the pure and beautiful Carmen (Linda Darnell), his seduction by the faithless society woman Doña Sol (Rita Hayworth), and his death in the ring. Mamoulian conceived the film as a series of "moving paintings," basing his use of color on the work of Murillo, Goya, El Greco, and other painters. *Blood and Sand* received an Academy Award for the best color photography of the year, and Mamoulian says that in it "colors come closer to achieving their aesthetic and dramatic potential than in any other film I have done."

In 1942 Mamoulian made *Rings on Her Fingers* (20th Century–Fox), a comedy starring Gene Tierney and Henry Fonda. For five years after that he devoted himself to the musical theatre. He directed two Rodgers and Hammerstein blockbusters—*Oklahoma!* (which opened in 1943 and closed in 1948 as the longest running musical in history) and *Carousel* (which brought him the Donaldson Award as the best director of 1945)—as well as *Sadie Thompson* (1944) and *St. Louis Woman* (1946). Mamoulian returned to Hollywood to make *Summer Holiday* (MGM, 1948). It is a musical based on Eugene O'Neill's *Ah, Wilderness!,* a nostalgic (and partly autobiographical) celebration of American small-town life at the turn of the century. The film had a mixed reception, and many critics balked at Mickey Rooney's broad playing of Richard, the rebellious young aesthete whom O'Neill had modeled partly on himself.

It was not until 1957, after another ten years in the musical theatre, that Mamoulian went back to Hollywood to make his controversial last film, *Silk Stockings,* for MGM. Starring Cyd Charisse and Fred Astaire, it is a screen adaptation of a Cole Porter musical based on one of the most famous of Lubitsch's films, *Ninotchka* (1939). It tells the story of a dourly dedicated Russian official who, in the course of her duty, is exposed to the delights of Paris and, to her shame, falls in love with a capitalist.

Ninotchka had drawn a miraculous performance from Greta Garbo, and for most critics Cyd Charisse was an unacceptable substitute. It seems to Tom Milne that such critics missed the point—"the equivalent of Garbo-Ninotchka's face in close-up is not Charisse-Ninotchka's expression but her movement." Milne goes on: "Quite apart from its use of dance to narrate the progress of the love story, *Silk Stockings* is so rich in invention that it gives the lie even more forcefully than *The Mark of Zorro, Blood and Sand,* or *Summer Holiday* to the myth of Mamoulian's decline. . . . Perhaps, one day, critics, historians, and those who write about the cinema will at last realise that it is one of the great musicals."

In 1959 Mamoulian prepared a shooting script for the Goldwyn movie version of *Porgy and Bess,* but the sets were destroyed by fire, disagreements arose between Mamoulian and Goldwyn, and for the second time a film begun by Mamoulian was completed by Otto Preminger. (The same thing had happened with *Laura* in 1944.) Later the same year Mamoulian was signed as director of *Cleopatra,* starring Elizabeth Taylor. He worked on the project for more than a year but in the end resigned because of the studio's insistence that the film should be shot in England rather than in Egypt. Thereafter Mamoulian made no more films, and for years his contribution to the cinema seemed almost forgotten. He occupied himself with various literary projects. *The Devil's Hornpipe,* a play written in collaboration with Maxwell Anderson, was filmed in 1958 as *Never Steal Anything Small,* directed by Charles Lederer. *Abigayil, Story of the Cat at the Manger* (1964) is a story for children. Mamoulian's *Hamlet: A New Version* was published in 1965 and staged the following year at the University of Kentucky.

The rediscovery of Rouben Mamoulian began in the early 1960s, and in 1967 there was a retrospective showing of all his films at the Gallery of Modern Art in New York. The National Film Theatre in London arranged a similar tribute the following year, and since then there have been Mamoulian festivals and retrospectives in many American cities, in Canada, Russia, Armenia, Soviet Georgia, Spain, France, Italy, Lebanon, Egypt, Australia, and Iran. A newly restored print of *Becky Sharp* was a highlight of the 1984 New York Film Festival. Mamoulian's place in the history of the cinema now seems secure, as a supreme stylist and "great inventor of the cinema's forms."

Mamoulian has been described as a person of "civilized ease and grace"—"a tall, slender, scholarly figure . . . with round black-rimmed spectacles over mysterious stone-grey eyes." He was married in 1945 to Azadia Newman, who is a portrait painter. They live in a sprawling neoclassical house in Beverly Hills. Mamoulian speaks Armenian, Georgian, Russian, French, German, and, as he misleadingly says, "a smattering of English." He is a collector of books, of paintings, of rocks, and of cats. A student of philosophy and literature (especially the literature of the American frontier), he writes poetry, makes pressed flower portraits, plays the violin, and enjoys swimming and riding. He belongs to the Armenian Apostolic Church.

FILMS: Applause, 1929; City Streets, 1931; Dr. Jekyll and Mr. Hyde, 1931; Love Me Tonight, 1932; Song of Songs, 1933; Queen Christina, 1933; We Live Again, 1934; Becky Sharp, 1935; The Gay Desperado, 1936; High, Wide and Handsome, 1937; Golden Boy, 1939; The Mark of Zorro, 1940; Blood and Sand, 1941; Rings on Her Fingers, 1942; Summer Holiday, 1948; Silk Stockings, 1957.

ABOUT: American Film Institute Rouben Mamoulian: Style Is the Man, 1971; Anobile, R. J. (editor) Rouben Mamoulian's Dr. Jekyll and Mr. Hyde, 1975; Baxter, J. Hollywood in the Thirties, 1968; Castello, G. C. Rouben Mamoulian, 1964 (Italy); Contemporary Authors 25–28 1st revision, 1977; Current Biography, 1949; Higham, C. and Greenberg, J. The Celluloid Muse, 1969; International Motion Picture Almanac, 1979; International Who's Who, 1978–79; Jacobs, L. Rouben Mamoulian, 1973; Knight, A. The Liveliest Art, 1957; Milne, T. Rouben Mamoulian, 1969; Oxford Companion to Film, 1976; Rohauer, R. A Fortieth Anniversary Tribute to Rouben Mamoulian, 1967; Sarris, A. (editor) Interviews with Film Directors, 1967; Thomson, D. A Biographical Dictionary of the Cinema, 1975; Who's Who, 1979; Who's Who in America, 1978–1979. *Periodicals*—Action September–October, 1974; American Cinematographer June 1941; American Classic Screen September–October, November–December 1976, January–February 1977; Cahiers du Cinéma February 1965; Film Journal January–March 1973; Films in Review August–September 1973; Financial Times April 18, 1968; International Photographer July 1935; New Statesman and Nation November 26, 1932; Picturegoer July 13, 1935; Positif Autumn 1964; Saturday Evening Post December 13, 1947; Sight and Sound Summer 1961.

MANKIEWICZ, JOSEPH L(EO) (February 11, 1909–), American director, scenarist, and producer, was born in Wilkes-Barre, Pennsylvania, third and youngest child of Frank (or Franz) and Johanna (Blumenau) Mankiewicz. Both parents were German-Jewish immigrants who met and married in New York. Frank Mankiewicz, a "rip-snorting atheist" with a fervent belief in education, had moved to Wilkes-Barre to take a job as editor of a German-language newspaper, later becoming a language instructor at the local Hillman Academy. In 1913 the family returned to New York, where Frank Mankiewicz took up a post at Stuyvesant High School.

Since his father, as well as teaching high school and tutoring privately, was also studying nights for his master's degree, the young Joseph Mankiewicz was raised mostly by his mother, "a round little woman who was uneducated in four

JOSEPH L. MANKIEWICZ

languages." He grew up "an only child in the sense that my brother and sister were a generation older than I was, and I was a very tiny little fellow among screaming, articulate giants. . . . We moved as many as six times a year, and I found new friends every three months. . . . There were always new neighborhoods, new gangs of kids, new adjustments. I became skillful at taking the color of my environment without absorbing it." Meanwhile Frank Mankiewicz completed a doctorate and went on to become a professor at City College and editor of the prestigious *Modern Language Quarterly.* A brilliant man but a demanding and authoritarian parent, he expected his children to distinguish themselves, preferably along the path he had broken.

After graduating from Stuyvesant at the age of fifteen, Joseph Mankiewicz enrolled at Columbia to study psychiatry. He got no further than the pre-med course. Repelled at the prospect of dissecting worms and frogs, he flunked with the nethermost grade and switched to liberal arts. When he graduated in 1928, having majored in English, his father rewarded him with further study in Europe. The plan was for Joseph to enroll at the University of Berlin, proceed from there to the Sorbonne and Oxford, and then return to America to teach. "That was my father's idea, but not mine," Mankiewicz has recalled. "When I hit Berlin in 1928, I was dazzled by the theatre." Using contacts established by his brother Herman, he quit the academic life in favor of more exciting employment. Three employments, in fact: as a junior reporter in the Berlin office of the Chicago *Tribune,* as the Ber-

lin stringer for *Variety,* and—his first contact with the film world—translating intertitles from German to English for UFA silents. "I was earning about $100 a week and living like a king. I learned more about everything in those four months in Berlin than I think I've learned in the rest of my life." Living in an "absolute intoxication of theater, excitement, glamor and sex," Mankiewicz rapidly overspent his triple income, and had to leave town when the checks started bouncing. After three miserably penurious months in Paris he was rescued by Herman, by now well established as a writer at Paramount. Since part of Herman's job was to lure talented writers to the studio, and nepotism was a Hollywood tradition, he saw no reason to ignore his younger brother. (A year later he also fixed his sister Erna up with a job, but she never took to screenwriting and soon resumed her teaching career.)

Mankiewicz started at Paramount on $60 a week, writing titles for sound movies that in some venues still had to be shown silent. His first assignment was *The Dummy* (1929), which Herman had scripted; other early movies included Sternberg's *Thunderbolt* and Victor Fleming's *The Virginian.* In his first eight weeks at the studio, he titled a record six movies; his fluency attracted the attention of David Selznick, who had him upgraded to dialogue writer for a Jack Oakie vehicle, *Fast Company* (1929). The film did well, and Mankiewicz went on to script another half-dozen pictures for the comedian. Best-remembered of them today are two that also featured W. C. Fields: *Million Dollar Legs* (1932), an anarchic comedy, and *If I Had a Million* (1932), an eight-episode movie that employed seven directors, eighteen writers, and most of the studio's acting roster. The previous year Mankiewicz had gained his first Oscar nomination as screenwriter on *Skippy* (1931), a sentimental juvenile comedy based on a popular comic strip.

Mankiewicz's last film for Paramount was a prestige production of *Alice in Wonderland* (1933), stuffed with stars and stupefyingly dull. David Selznick, who had returned to MGM, now offered him a contract, and assigned him to coscript *Manhattan Melodrama* (1934). A routinely competent crime movie, it achieved fortuitous fame as the movie Dillinger had been watching just before he was gunned down, and earned Mankiewicz his second Academy Award nomination. In May of that year, he married Elizabeth Young, an actress, having overcome the opposition of her patrician New York family. Their son Eric was born in 1936.

For a nominal fee, Mankiewicz provided dialogue for King Vidor's independently produced, naive agrarian parable, *Our Daily Bread* (1934), before turning out two frothy studio comedies for Joan Crawford. "It was at this time that dysentery was very prevalent . . . and whimsy spread through Hollywood in even greater proportions. I was badly taken with it." Whimsy or not, this was evidently what the public wanted. Mankiewicz, having scripted three hits in a row and now earning $1,250 a week, approached Louis B. Mayer and asked to direct his own material.

Mayer turned him down; first, he must become a producer. "You have to learn to crawl before you can walk," he told Mankiewicz, who considered this "about as good a definition of a producer as any." So began his "black years" at MGM, during which "I produced a great many films which I am embarrassed to have associated with my name." He had no cause, though, to feel ashamed of *Fury* (1936), Fritz Lang's first American film, a harsh, dispassionate account of lynch-mob violence. He then marked time with a series of vehicles for Joan Crawford, with whom he was currently involved. His marriage to Elizabeth Young ended in divorce in 1937.

"If I go down at all in literary history, in a footnote, it will be as the swine who rewrote F. Scott Fitzgerald." *Three Comrades* (1938), taken from a novel by Remarque, carried Fitzgerald's only screenwriter credit, though his dialogue was extensively revised by Mankiewicz. The changes prompted Fitzgerald's famous, pathetic plea: "Oh, Joe, can't a producer ever be wrong? I'm a good writer—honest." "You should have seen . . . [Fitzgerald's] screenplay," Mankiewicz later observed in his own defense. "Some novelists cannot write dialogue and Scott Fitzgerald was one of them."

In July 1939 Mankiewicz married for the second time. His new wife was Rosa Stradner, a prominent Austrian actress under contract to MGM. The couple had two sons, Christopher (born 1940) and Thomas (born 1942), both now working in Hollywood. The year after his marriage, Mankiewicz produced the comic masterpiece of his decade at MGM. ("I'm going to be fired," he remarked in the studio refectory. "I've made a good picture.") *The Philadelphia Story* (1940), impeccably cast, written, and performed, was rapturously received, and still ranks as a classic of elegant, sophisticated comedy.

In 1941, soon after Herman Mankiewicz's Academy Award for his *Citizen Kane* screenplay, Frank Mankiewicz died of a cerebral hemorrhage. The fact that their father had lived to see Herman's triumph, while he himself was still stuck in the inglorious role of a Metro producer, intensified Mankiewicz's dissatisfaction. His re-

maining films at MGM were unremarkable, apart from *Woman of the Year* (1942), the witty and stylish comedy in which Katharine Hepburn and Spencer Tracy were first teamed.

Mankiewicz finally quit MGM in 1943, after a furious row with Louis B. Mayer. (The immediate cause was Mankiewicz's affair with Judy Garland, in whom Mayer alleged a paternal interest.) He moved to 20th Century–Fox, where after a final job as producer—*Keys of the Kingdom* (1944), a stolidly worthy religious piece—he was at long last permitted to direct.

Despite his fifteen-year apprenticeship, there was little that was distinctively personal—or particularly distinguished—about Mankiewicz's first five films as director. *Dragonwyck* (1946) offered sub-Brontean Gothickry, with Vincent Price waving his eyebrows as a despotic landowner planning to bump off his beautiful wife (Gene Tierney). The producer was Ernst Lubitsch, whom Mankiewicz revered, but the two men quarreled disastrously, and Lubitsch took his name off the film.

Though negligible in itself, *Dragonwyck* does mark an early appearance of a theme that recurs in many Mankiewicz films, through *All About Eve* and *Five Fingers* right up to *The Honey Pot* and *Sleuth*. Steve Fagin, writing in *Film Reader* (1975), defined it as "the clash between patricians and parvenus"—the challenge to a socially or culturally well established figure by a younger, brasher outsider, who often succeeds in supplanting the other by sheer force of ambition.

Mankiewicz wrote his own script for *Dragonwyck* (from a novel by Anya Seton), and coscripted his second film, *Somewhere in the Night* (1946), a *noir*-ish thriller with a tortuous plot and an amnesiac hero. For his next three pictures, he elected to leave the scripting to someone else while he "concentrated upon learning the technique and craft of directing—indeed, upon disassociating myself as far as possible from the writer's approach."

His choice as screenwriter was Philip Dunne, whose urbane, literate style meshed perfectly with Mankiewicz's. *The Late George Apley* (1947), from a novel by John P. Marquand, was described by a *Time* critic as "a friendly, quietly amusing, rather slow picture." Most of the novel's social satire was lost in Dunne's adaptation, which substituted a conventional happy ending for the ironic posthumous epilogue (thus making nonsense of the title), and allowed Ronald Colman to deploy his habitual gentlemanly charm as the eponymous Boston patriarch.

If *The Ghost and Mrs. Muir* (1947) was livelier, it was thanks largely to Rex Harrison, in the first of his four Mankiewicz films. As the ghost of a raffish sea captain, complete with nautical beard and vocabulary (skillfully bowdlerized by Dunne to suit the prevailing censorship), his stylish brio prevented the fantasy from sliding into whimsy—at least while he was on screen. "A thing of lightness and grey charm," thought Gordon Gow, "[characterized by] an astringent romanticism." The movie later served as the basis for a successful television series.

Though none of Mankiewicz's films had so far been an outstanding hit, all had shown respectable box-office returns. *Escape* (1948) was his first flop. Filmed in Britain under a tax-settlement agreement, it was adapted by Dunne from a 1926 Galsworthy play, and again starred Rex Harrison (who had suggested the subject to Zanuck) as a convict escaped from Dartmoor. Much of the filming was done on location, but the picture bogged down less in the terrain than in Galsworthy's trite moralizing. Some critics, though, among them Pauline Kael, have considered the film unfairly neglected.

Back in Hollywood, Mankiewicz set about making a film that at last bore his own personal stamp. "Sol Siegel showed me an adaptation . . . of a novel called *A Letter to Five Wives* by John Klempner. I read it and knew I had looked upon the Promised Land." *A Letter to Three Wives* (1949)—Mankiewicz dropped one wife and Zanuck, "in an almost bloodless operation," persuaded him to excise another—scored a hit with both public and critics, and won Mankiewicz two Oscars, for writing and for directing. The film displays all his characteristic virtues (or virtuosities): an intricate plot-line, woven around deftly handled multiple flash- backs; crisp, intelligent dialogue; mordant social satire; incisively depicted characters, deployed in taut, dramatic situations. All the qualities, in short—as Mankiewicz himself would readily concede—of the best stage comedy. David Thomson noted that Mankiewicz "creates the atmosphere of a proscenium arch, a little Shavian in the way he arranges action for an audience."

Letter also marks the first appearance of another Mankiewicz feature, the ironic, omniscient commentator—although in this case, "appear" is just what she never does. Addie Ross, local siren and writer of The Letter, remains a silky off-screen voice (that of Celeste Holm), felinely taunting the three friends whose lives she has disrupted. She has, she informs them, made off with the husband of one of them. Cut off from their homes on a May Day picnic, they must agonize until evening over which man she has taken. Since all three marriages are, in different ways, under strain, each wife can indulge in a long, anguished flashback before the final reve-

lation. This denouement, in fact, falls rather flat, but what precedes it more than compensates—especially Thelma Ritter, delectably caustic in her first major screen role, and Paul Douglas as a rich businessman inflamed into matrimony by the cannily withheld allurements of Linda Darnell.

Mankiewicz also scripted most of *House of Strangers* (1949), though a dispute with his co-writer, Philip Yordan, let to Yordan taking sole writer credit. The picture did poorly in America, "because it was a bad film," Mankiewicz remarked sourly, though he later revised his opinion. It was much better received in Europe, where Edward G. Robinson won Best Actor award at Cannes for his portrayal of the immigrant Italian barber-turned-banker who dominates his family and the film. *House of Strangers* also attracted the attention of the young French critics, and founded Mankiewicz's high reputation among the *nouvelle vague*. Jean-Luc Godard, writing in the *Gazette du Cinéma*, hailed him as "one of the most brilliant of American directors," and added that *House* incorporated "one of the finest flashbacks in the history of the cinema." More recently, Andrew Sarris has called it "a movie that becomes more memorable with each passing year."

Zanuck, whose carefully packaged dramas of racial prejudice such as *Gentleman's Agreement* (1947) and *Pinky* (1949) had proved good box-office, now offered Mankiewicz another in the same tradition. *No Way Out* (1950) pitted a young black intern (Sidney Poitier in his screen debut) against a psychotic racist (Richard Widmark) whose brother's death the intern was unable to prevent. Though often vivid and dramatic, the film stacked its cards too blatantly for conviction: deploring the persecution of saintly black medics by white psychopaths scarcely constituted a bold attack on racism.

It is often asserted that Mankiewicz's films are essentially theatrical—François Truffaut, with no implication of disparagement, has classified him as a master of *théâtre filmé*. One reason for this is surely his lifelong fascination with the theatre's "creative commune . . . the quirks and frailties, the needs and talents of the performing personality." This fascination, deeply sentimental behind a cynical facade, informs the quintessential Mankiewicz movie, *All About Eve* (1950). Widely regarded as his masterpiece, it traces the irresistible rise to stardom of a sweet-faced young predator, Eve Harrington (Anne Baxter), who attaches herself to a great lady of the theatre, Margo Channing (Bette Davis, magisterial). The film is structured around Mankiewicz's favorite format, the extended multiple flashback: from the ceremony at which Eve is to receive the coveted Sarah Siddons Award, we backtrack through the voice-over memories of three characters scarred in her climb, finally returning full circle to the presentation.

"I don't think," Mankiewicz had often responded to charges of excessive verbiage, "that there can ever be an excess of good talk." Not all the talk in his films, unfortunately, *is* good; but in *Eve*, it rarely fails to be less than brilliant. His script, as Neil Sinyard has commented, "seems not so much written as detonated," sparkling with epigrams, wisecracks, and five-star bitchery. (Celeste Holm, one of the film's leads, felt that "Joe was in love with the concept of the theatre as a wolverine's lair of skulduggery and bitchcraft.") Many of the best lines go, as usual, to the resident Mankiewicz-surrogate, in this case the coolly venomous dramatic critic, Addison DeWitt—George Sanders, delicately placing the witticisms like poisoned banderillas, gave the performance of his life and reaped a well-deserved Best Supporting Oscar. Nevertheless, wrote Jacques Doniol-Valcroze, "what really interests Mankiewicz in *All About Eve* as well as in most of his other films are the women, and through them the permanence of a certain femininity, the archetype of a certain way of being female."

Two more Oscars went to Mankiewicz, again for scripting and directing, making him the only person so far to win two Academy Awards two years running. *Eve* was also chosen as Best Picture and gained a record number of nominations (fourteen), plus awards in New York, Cannes, London, and elsewhere. Reviewers, with a few exceptions, frothed with enthusiasm. Those who complained of a lack of realism, Hollis Alpert pointed out in the *Saturday Review*, were rather missing the point: "[Mankiewicz] obviously knows how to get the most out of his players, but more important than this is his ability to *stylize* a picture. The documentary approach is not for him; rather he likes to get as *fictional* a quality as possible, so that . . . the audience remains entirely in the realm of illusion." Over the years, *Eve* has sustained its reputation as a highpoint of sophisticated comedy with "the highest quotient of (verbal) wit of any film made before or since" (David Shipman).

In 1950, soon after winning his first pair of Oscars, Mankiewicz had been elected president of the Screen Directors Guild. He was nominated for the post by Cecil B. DeMille, who at that time had the Guild in his pocket. However, the virulently right-wing DeMille, perhaps having overheard Mankiewicz's opinion of his films ("DeMille has his finger up the pulse of America"), decided that his erstwhile protégé was a dangerous lefty and initiated maneuvers to have Mankiewicz ousted from the presidency. There followed several weeks of conspiratorial shenanigans, loyalty oaths, ballots, and petitions, culminating in what Mankiewicz termed "the most dramatic evening in my life"—a seven-hour emergency meeting of the Guild, at which he and his supporters, who included John Huston, William Wyler, and George Stevens, decisively defeated DeMille and forced his resignation from the committee. Nonetheless Mankiewicz, a middle-of-the-road liberal and "the least politically minded person in the world," felt revolted by the whole affair. Shortly afterwards he announced his intention of "getting the hell out of Hollywood" and moving east.

Something of his Guild experience was reflected in *People Will Talk* (1951), adapted from Curt Goetz's 1933 German film *Dr. Praetorius*, in which an unconventional medical professor (played by Cary Grant) suffers an assault on his professional and private life by malicious colleagues. Both plot and hero were frankly implausible; Mankiewicz, wrote the *Time* critics, "tests Bernard Shaw's theory that people will listen to anything so long as it is amusingly said." Either the theory was wrong or the talk was insufficiently amusing, for the film did poorly at the box office, though it remains one of its director's personal favorites.

For his last film at Fox, Mankiewicz turned for the only time in his career to factual material—albeit substantially transformed. *Five Fingers* (1952) was adapted from L. C. Moyzisch's book *Operation Cicero*, which told how the British Ambassador's valet in Ankara sold military secrets to the Germans during World War II. "If Hitchcock had ever collaborated with Lubitsch," Neil Sinyard wrote, "the result might have resembled *Five Fingers*." As Diello, valet turned master-spy, James Mason gave one of his finest performances, subtly conveying the cold ambition beneath a surface of urbane deference. He was well matched by Danielle Darrieux, as an exiled Polish countess short of money and scruples. For contractual reasons Michael Wilson, author of the original adaptation, took sole screenwriting credit, but the dialogue, and the sardonic slant on patriotism and loyalty, betray Mankiewicz's touch. Gordon Gow observed that "the oblique comment upon the absurdities which are promoted by conflicting nations braced the romanticism with a cynical wit," and Richard Corliss praised the film as "a graceful blending of political intrigue and sexual politics, with as mordant a tone as any of the black comedies it prefigured."

Quitting Fox on reasonably amicable terms, Mankiewicz and his family exchanged the "intellectual fog belt" of Los Angeles for midtown Manhattan. His plan was "to make my pitch for the theatre"; but an offer from MGM, whence he had departed under a cloud ten years earlier, proved too much to resist. The project was in any case calculated to appeal to him: a film version of Shakespeare's *Julius Caesar* (1953), to be produced by John Houseman, who had staged the famous Mercury Theatre version with Orson Welles in 1937.

Critical opinion, then and since, has divided over the Mankiewicz-Houseman *Caesar*. Lindsay Anderson approvingly quoted Houseman's description of the play as "a political thriller," adding: "[Mankiewicz] has appreciated the sensational excellence of the writing, and has filmed it directly, powerfully and dramatically. There are no visual tricks to distract one from the marvellous words. . . . If the later scenes in the film lack the brilliance and tension of the first half, the fault is largely Shakespeare's." Bernard Dick, though, found the film "only occasionally cinematic. . . . Everything seemed cabined and confined; except for the assassination and the funeral oration, there were few surprises. . . . Much of *Julius Caesar* looks like the aftermath of a budget cut." Dick singled out, as have other critics, the glaringly artificial mound on which Cassius kills himself, and the bizarre decision to stage the battle of Philippi in a canyon "like an ambush in a B Western."

The lead performances, too, have been widely debated (with the exception of Louis Calhern's Caesar, generally agreed to be inadequate). James Mason's thoughtful, sensitive Brutus was found colorless by some, while Gielgud's vibrant portrait of embittered malice as Cassius struck others as over-theatrical. Most controversial was the casting of Marlon Brando as a "thrillingly histrionic Antony, contemptuously inspecting his hand after having it shaken in friendship by the murderers, and displaying Caesar's body to the crowd as a bloodcurdlingly effective prop" (Neil Sinyard). Jack L. Jorgens, commending Mankiewicz and Houseman's "refusal to sentimentalize, popularize, or oversimplify," regretted that the film contained "memorable dramatic moments, but no memorable images. In seeking restraint and a distancing effect, Mankiewicz often succeeded only in making scenes bland and visually dull." He concluded, though, that "few Shakespeare films can match it for its integrity in dealing with the original, its narrative drive, and its fine characterizations."

MGM announced a further Shakespeare project for Mankiewicz: a version of *Twelfth Night*, with Audrey Hepburn playing both Viola and Sebastian. The idea fell through, and he returned to New York to direct a new production of *La Bohème* at the Met, in which he tried to rid the opera of some of the sentimental detritus that had accrued to it over the years. Reviews were lukewarm, and Mankiewicz, disappointed, reverted to movie-making, setting up a deal between United Artists and his own newly-formed independent company, Figaro Inc.

Shortly before the premiere of *Julius Caesar,* Herman Mankiewicz had died at the age of fifty-five. The mingled admiration and envy that Joe had felt towards his brother, and the guilty triumph at seeing his own fortunes prosper while Herman's faded, perhaps contributed to the "slough of ill-humor" in which he made his next movie. Mankiewicz's first film in color—and the first that he wrote, directed, and produced—*The Barefoot Contessa* (1954) was summed up by Pauline Kael as "a trash masterpiece." Like a soured, overripe counterpart to *All About Eve,* the film traces in flashback a woman's rise to fame. Maria Vargas (Ava Gardner) is discovered in a Madrid nightclub by a Hughes-ish movie tycoon, shoots to stardom, joins the international set, and is eventually murdered by the jealous Italian count she has married. Her story is narrated by three mourners at her funeral: the Count (Rossano Brazzi); a publicist, Oscar Muldoon (a sweating, sycophantic *tour de force* that won Edmond O'Brien an Academy Award); and the inevitable Mankiewicz-figure, writer-director Harry Dawes (Humphrey Bogart).

"Joseph Mankiewicz, one begins to think," observed Penelope Houston, "looks on a film as a sort of expanding suitcase . . . and in *The Barefoot Contessa* the suitcase has split wide open under the strain. . . . He has buried this fundamentally novelettish story in an immense cocoon of verbiage." Most English-language reviewers concurred, and Henry Hart accused Mankiewicz of "an ambivalent hatred and envy for the aristocracy; an ambivalent distaste for and truckling to the proletariat." In France, though, *Contessa* was hailed as its director's masterpiece. "This is not a film to be picked apart," wrote François Truffaut; "either one rejects it or accepts it whole. I myself accept and value it for its freshness, intelligence and beauty." Similar laudatory comments were made by Godard (who called Mankiewicz "the most intelligent man in all contemporary cinema") and other French critics. Fellini later claimed *Contessa* as his direct inspiration for *La Dolce Vita.*

Sam Goldwyn, who had acquired the rights to Frank Loesser's smash-hit musical *Guys and*

Dolls against fierce competition, offered Mankiewicz the chance of directing and scripting the movie version. Mankiewicz jumped at the idea and made a very respectable job of it: if not one of the great screen musicals, *Guys and Dolls* (1955) is consistently lively, likeable, and passably Runyonesque. Surprisingly, the pair of "non-singers," Marlon Brando and Jean Simmons, came off better than Frank Sinatra and Vivian Blaine, the professional vocalists. Michael Kidd choreographed exhilaratingly, most notably in the fight sequence when a drunken Jean Simmons takes on all comers in a Cuban bar. Brando and Sinatra, by all accounts, detested each other, but none of their hostility comes across in the picture which, as Goldwyn aptly put it, "has warmth and charmth."

Figaro Inc.—intended by Mankiewicz "to do a little bit of everything"—now embarked on its sole theatrical venture. It was a resounding flop: Carson McCullers' *The Square Root of Wonderful*, which opened on Broadway in October 1957, received appalling notices and closed after eight weeks. This was altogether a bad period for Mankiewicz, professionally and privately; his wife Rosa was becoming mentally unstable. His next picture was as ill-starred as the McCullers play; he later described it as "the very bad film I made during a very unhappy time of my life."

Even Mankiewicz's warmest admirers have reservations about *The Quiet American* (1958). "Such delicacy in the scenario, so many gems in the dialogue, are staggering," Jean-Luc Godard wrote. "But is this not a reproach rather than praise? It all looks, in fact, as though everything had been planned on paper, the actual shooting adding very little. . . . He is too perfect a writer to be a director as well." Graham Greene's novel, on which Mankiewicz based his script, warned with remarkable prescience of the perils of American moral naivety in what was then French Indochina. Mankiewicz, however, jettisoned Greene's subtle ambiguities in favor of a crassly pro-American ending. The American turns out to have been not just naive but innocent of any harm; Fowler, the English journalist who brings about his death, was duped by the devious Communists. The resultant fable, far too black-and-white to be Greene, found little favor with critics or audiences, though Michael Redgrave's "acidly intelligent playing" (Penelope Houston) as Fowler was widely praised, as was Robert Krasker's atmospheric cinematography.

In September 1958, Rosa Mankiewicz committed suicide in a summer home the family had rented in upstate New York. She had often threatened, and attempted, suicide; this time she had carried through.

Suddenly, Last Summer (1959) had made up half of a Tennessee Williams double bill off-Broadway. Sam Spiegel bought the movie rights and invited Mankiewicz to direct. Williams, together with Gore Vidal, took screenplay credit but later repudiated the film, complaining that "a short morality play, in a lyrical style, was turned into a sensationally successful film that the public thinks was a literal study of such things as cannibalism, madness, and sexual deviation." It seems highly improbable that the public thought anything of the sort; the film is evidently and unashamedly a roaring Grand Guignol melodrama, played several inches past the hilt. A rich recluse (Katharine Hepburn in her nuttiest *grande dame* vein) tries to pressure a young psychosurgeon (Montgomery Clift) into lobotomizing her niece (Elizabeth Taylor) into permanent amnesia. The doctor finds out what is supposed to be forgotten: the niece was being used by her cousin, a pederastic poet, to entice young Spanish urchins, some of whom had eventually torn him apart and eaten him. "The violent poetry of the writing is given eloquent expression in every aspect of the film's visual design," wrote Neil Sinyard, "and the performances are extraordinary." Both Hepburn and Taylor were nominated for Oscars, and *Suddenly* gave Mankiewicz his biggest box-office hit since *All About Eve*.

His reputation restored, Mankiewicz signed a contract to write and direct for his old studio, Fox. A planned adaptation of Stephen Vincent Benét's epic Civil War poem, *John Brown's Body*, came to nothing, but Fox then offered him a project greatly to his taste: Lawrence Durrell's kaleidoscopic series of novels, The Alexandria Quartet. Durrell's multiple-viewpoint structure and highly-colored prose offered Mankiewicz scope for just the kind of filmmaking he liked, full of witty prolixity and complex patterns of flashbacks.

Mankiewicz later described his failure to direct this film as "the greatest disappointment of my career. . . . If ever I were to summon up enough talent to make a definitive film about anything, this would have been it." He had completed around half of his first draft of *Justine* (some 674 pages) to Durrell's whole-hearted approval when he received an emergency call from Spyros Skouras, head of Fox. The studio was in deep trouble with its ambitious epic production, *Cleopatra*. Would Mankiewicz take over and rescue them? Despite severe misgivings, he let himself be persuaded. "It was, on my part, knowingly an act of whoredom—I was handsomely paid. And, in the end, in turn, I paid. Most unhandsomely indeed." (*Justine* eventually reached the screen in 1969, in a dismally inadequate version. Durrell, who had always dreaded "a sort of *Peyton Place* with camels," saw his worst fears realized.)

The Fox executives had reason to be desperate about *Cleopatra*. It had now been two years in the making. The $6 million budget had already been overspent by $1 million, and Rouben Mamoulian, the director, had just ten and a half minutes of film in the can. Elizabeth Taylor, playing the title role for a record $1 million fee, was thoroughly unhappy with Mamoulian and asked for Mankiewicz. Skouras, a nervously impulsive man given to panicky snap decisions, readily agreed to Mankiewicz's exorbitant terms: one and a half million dollars to buy the director's half interest in Figaro; the same again to buy out NBC, who owned the other fifty percent; plus, of course, a generous salary and expenses.

Mankiewicz hoped to finish *Cleopatra* in fifteen weeks. In fact it took him eighteen months. "The toughest three pictures I ever made," he ruefully remarked. "*Cleopatra* was first conceived in emergency, shot in hysteria, and wound up in blind panic." As error piled on disaster, costs spiraled to $35 million (still, allowing for inflation, the most expensive film ever made), and the production became a public joke, compounded by press obsession with the increasingly overt affair between Taylor and Richard Burton (playing Antony). Walter Wanger, the original producer, was sacked. Three weeks later Skouras was ousted from the presidency of Fox, and Darryl F. Zanuck took over. One of his first acts was to fire Mankiewicz from the picture. Though later rehired, Mankiewicz had no hand in the final cut.

Predictably, *Cleopatra* (1963) was slammed on release. No one but Andy Warhol seemed to like it, and he liked it because it was "long and boring." Of the principal actors, only Rex Harrison as Caesar came off with honor (and an Oscar nomination). Burton was found dull, and Taylor hopelessly underequipped for her role, utterly lacking in "infinite variety." Dilys Powell was more restrained than most in her judgment: "Mr. Mankiewicz has made a film about the barge she sat in. The trouble is that there is nobody, or next to nobody, sitting in it. The barge itself, I admit, really is something. . . . There is a kind of vulgarity which by its own boldness becomes beautiful, and this is it." But most critics treated the picture as the definitive Hollywood Edsel. Although commentary has become more temperate in recent years, the verdict on *Cleopatra* has not been reversed.

This debacle permanently damaged Mankiewicz's reputation but clinched his third marriage. Rosemary Matthews, an Englishwoman, had met Mankiewicz in Rome during the filming of *The Barefoot Contessa*, and acted as his personal assistant on *Cleopatra*. They were married in December 1962, and their daughter Alexandra Kate was born in 1966.

In 1964 Mankiewicz directed a film for ABC-TV, *A Carol for Another Christmas*. An update of Dickens in the form of a political satire, it amply confirmed Mankiewicz's claim that he was not "politically minded." His next feature film also modernized a literary classic, Ben Jonson's *Volpone*, throwing in a murder mystery for good measure. *The Honey Pot* (1967) is set in contemporary Venice where Cecil Fox (Rex Harrison), a man of reputedly immense wealth, summons three women from his past to what they believe to be his deathbed. Even for Mankiewicz, this was an exceptionally verbose film, further marred by a general uncertainty of tone. It had its admirers, nevertheless, and Stephen Farber wrote that the two scenes between Harrison and Maggie Smith "are as masterful examples of high comic writing as we can hope to see in movies."

Will, a Shakespeare biopic to be scripted by Anthony Burgess, proved abortive, as did a proposed version of John Updike's *Couples.* Instead, Mankiewicz rather unexpectedly directed his first Western. *There Was a Crooked Man* (1970), written by Robert Benton and David Newman (Oscar-winners for their script of *Bonnie and Clyde*), combined two genres in one: Western and prison movie. A richly cynical comedy, it was structured around the dealings between a charmingly ruthless convict (Kirk Douglas with granny glasses and unfazable grin) and the conscientious prison warden (Henry Fonda, in a parody of his own solemnly liberal image) who tries to reform him. In support the film assembled a "parade of beautifully defined, rounded characterisations of amiable rogues," as Tom Milne put it, adding that *Crooked Man* "comes closer to the true spirit of Ben Jonson than *The Honey Pot. . . .* One shouldn't be too hard on a film which revels so persistently in dry, civilised ironies." Many critics, though, found the moral ambiguity self-defeating: Paul Zimmermann called it "a piecework movie in which individual sequences work well but contradict each other until total moral confusion reigns."

Mankiewicz's last film to date was *Sleuth* (1972), scripted by Anthony Shaffer from his own stage hit. The convoluted plot entailed an elaborate and ultimately murderous passage of game-playing between two men, an elderly thriller-writer and the successful hairdresser who has seduced the writer's wife. The cast of two, Laurence Olivier and Michael Caine, provided virtuoso playing, but the blatant artificiality that had seemed audacious on stage looked merely hollow on screen. David Thomson described the film as "a grotesque throwback to theatricality, indicative of Mankiewicz's readiness to be fooled by cleverness and of his lack of creative personality." *Sleuth*, nonetheless, proved his first box-office success for over a decade, and earned him an Oscar nomination for Best Director.

Criticisms of Joseph Mankiewicz have centered, inevitably, on the allegedly uncinematic priority of words over images in his work. Comparing *The Barefoot Contessa* to *Pandora and the Flying Dutchman*, Andrew Sarris commented, "Mankiewicz's sensibility is decidedly more refined than Lewin's, but his technique is almost as pedestrian." "Pungent situations, witty dialogue and smart playing," wrote David Thomson, "conceal his indifference to what a film looks like or his inability to reveal the emotional depths beneath dialogue." For himself, Mankiewicz has always maintained that "I don't believe the word is of prime importance. I believe that the word is worthy of equal respect," and that film is "a medium for the exchange of ideas and exchange of comment as well as purely visual effects."

It seems unlikely that Mankiewicz will ever regain the status he achieved at the zenith of his fame in the early 1950s. His stock remains high in France, though, where he has often been honored by festivals and retrospectives; in 1983, he was the subject of a full-length film, *All About Mankiewicz*, made by Luc Béraud and Michel Ciment. At his finest, he was an acknowledged master of "quintessential Hollywood movies, with all the glamour and brittle sophistication of the best American high comedy" (Richard Corliss), and some of his detractors have subsequently had second thoughts. Andrew Sarris, who had dismissed Mankiewicz's work as "a cinema of intelligence without inspiration," later detected "a pattern of intelligence, charm and subtlety that I had tended to take too much for granted. . . . What makes him truly admirable . . . is his defiance of a historical process that in its viciously simple-minded way is striving to make intelligent liberalism obsolete in a world sinking into the chaos of aimless absurdism." (*Show*, March 1970.)

Mankiewicz's own view of current cinematic trends is similarly damning. Modern Hollywood films he describes as "cartoons, with balloon dialogue, for fourteen-year-old minds." As for the industry itself: "The Mayers, the Thalbergs, the Schencks, the Goldwyns, the Cohns . . . they were the Medici compared to the money-grabbers we have today. They were picture-makers, not deal-makers. The flesh-peddlers, the agents, are now in charge, and never before has the industry been such a con-game. The pimps have taken over the whorehouse." Formerly known for his gregariousness, Mankiewicz is said to have become increasingly embittered and reclusive in recent years. He lives mainly on his estate at Bedford, New York, with his wife and daughter. Ostensibly, he remains willing to direct more films; but "the oldest whore on the beat," as he likes to call himself, has for the last ten years fastidiously turned down all propositions.

—*P.K.*

FILMS: Dragonwyck, 1946; Somewhere in the Night, 1946; The Late George Apley, 1947; The Ghost and Mrs. Muir, 1947; Escape, 1948; A Letter to Three Wives, 1949; House of Strangers, 1949; No Way Out, 1950; All About Eve, 1950; People Will Talk, 1951; Five Fingers, 1952; Julius Caesar, 1953; The Barefoot Contessa, 1954; Guys and Dolls, 1955; The Quiet American, 1958; Suddenly, Last Summer, 1959; Cleopatra, 1963; The Honey Pot/It Comes Up Murder, 1967; (with Sidney Lumet) King: A Filmed Record, 1969; There Was a Crooked Man, 1970; Sleuth, 1972. *Published scripts*—All About Eve *in* More About All About Eve (Random House, 1972); The Barefoot Contessa (French translation) *in* L'Avant-Scène du Cinéma 68 (1967); The Ghost and Mrs. Muir (French translation) *in* L'Avant-Scène du Cinéma 237 (1979).

ABOUT: Alpert, H. The Dream and the Dreamers, 1962; Dick, B. F. Joseph L. Mankiewicz, 1983; Farber, S. and Green, M. Hollywood Dynasties, 1984; Geist, K. L. Pictures Will Talk: The Life and Films of Joseph L. Mankiewicz, 1978; Gow, G. Hollywood in the Fifties, 1971; Jorgens, J. L. Shakespeare on Film, 1977; Mankiewicz, J. L. More About All About Eve (with Gary Carey), 1972; Mauriac, C. Petite Littérature du Cinéma, 1957; Roud, R. (ed.) Cinema: A Critical Dictionary, 1980; Sarris, A. The American Cinema, 1968; Taylor, J. R. Joseph L. Mankiewicz: An Index to his Work, 1960; Thomson, D. A Biographical Dictionary of the Cinema, 1980. *Periodicals*—American Film April 1978; Cahiers du Cinéma May 1951, March 1964, May 1966, October 1980; Cahiers du Cinéma in English February 1967; Cinéma January 1960, June 1981, July–August 1981; Dirigido January 1974; Film Ideal January 1, 1964; Film Reader 1 1975; Films and Filming January 1960, August 1963, September 1963, November 1970, November 1982; Focus Spring–Summer 1973; National Film Theatre Booklet (Britain) August 1982; Positif September 1973, February 1984; Présence du Cinéma 18 1963; Sight and Sound Autumn 1970; Show March 1970; Skoop December 1968.

"MANN, ANTHONY" (Emil Anton Bundsmann) (June 30, 1906–April 29, 1967), American director and producer, was born in Point Loma, near San Diego, California. Much about his early life is obscure: some sources give his birth date as 1907, and his given name is variously quoted as Emil, or Anton, or both. His parents, Emil T. Bundsmann and Bertha (Waxelbaum) Bundsmann, were both philosophy teachers. Mann's taste for theatre showed up early: he was a child actor in San Diego, before the family moved to the New York City area around 1917. He continued to act in school theatricals at East Orange Grammar and Central High, New York, playing the title role in a Central High production of *Alcestis*. (A fellow cast member was Dore Schary.)

Mann left school in 1923, after the death of his father, and took a night job with Westinghouse at $35 a week, looking for theatre work during the daytime. He was eventually taken on by the Stagers company as general handyman and bit player at $10 a week. For that he quit Westinghouse, and from there transferred to the Triangle Theater in Greenwich Village. The name Anton Mann turns up in small roles in the programs of such Broadway productions as *The Dybbuk* (1925) and *The Little Clay Cart* (1926). Around 1930, after working with various theatre groups and stock companies, Mann joined the prestigious Theater Guild as their production manager, and began directing for the stage. The following year he married Mildred Kenyon, an executive at Macy's. The couple had two children: Anthony (born 1938) and Nina (born 1944).

In 1933 Mann directed his first Broadway production, *The Squall*. He formed his own summer stock company in 1934, playing on Long Island and around New England; one member of the cast was the young James Stewart. Altogether Mann directed eight Broadway productions, several for the Federal Theater, including *Cherokee Night* (1936), *So Proudly We Hail* (1936), and *The Big Blow* (1938). None of them was more than moderately successful, but Mann had established enough of a reputation to attract the attention of Hollywood. Towards the end of 1938 he was hired by David O. Selznick to work as a talent scout and casting director for the Selznick company. In this capacity Mann shot screen tests for *Gone with the Wind*, *Rebecca*, and *Intermezzo*. One of the unknown newcomers he tested was Jennifer Jones.

After a few months with Selznick, Mann moved to Paramount as an assistant director, working with Preston Sturges among others. "He let me go through the entire production, watching him direct—and I directed a little. I'd stage

ANTHONY MANN

a scene and he'd tell me how lousy it was." After three years, Mann got the chance to direct a film of his own. MacDonald Carey, a former member of his stock company, had been imported from Broadway by Sol Siegel to star in a comedy-thriller, *Dr. Broadway* (1942), and asked to have Mann direct it. Since the picture was a low-budget programmer, Paramount agreed.

None of the ten B films that Mann directed from 1942 to 1946 are of much interest, except as they prefigure themes and stylistic traits in his later, more accomplished work. Cheaply made, clumsily scripted, and for the most part indifferently acted, they would probably have sunk without trace long ago but for Mann's name on the credits. He himself recalled most of them with scant affection, understandably in view of the conditions under which he usually had to work. On *Dr. Broadway*: "They promised me three whole days for the street scenes, so I made my shooting plans accordingly, and marked off some interesting angles. At the end of the first day they ordered me literally to get off the stage, C. B. DeMille having decided to set up his cameras there."

John Howard Reid (*Films and Filming*, January 1962) characterized *Dr. Broadway* as "a series of phoney events that portray Broadway not as it ever was, but as the picture-people like to think the hicks think it was." (The story was by Borden Chase, later to script several of Mann's finest Westerns.) Mann did his best to play down the sub-Runyonesque hokum and lend the more menacing aspects as much atmospheric interest as possible. There was little he could do, though, with his next assignment, *Moonlight in Havana* (1942), a threadbare musical for Universal.

Not surprisingly, neither of these two caused any great stir, and Mann had trouble finding further employment. After nine months without work he fetched up at Republic, home of B-minus movies, and directed *Nobody's Darling* (1943). This ugly-duckling-makes-good story, according to Jeanine Basinger, "might have killed a lesser talent. Fortunately, nobody remembers it." Nor would many recall *My Best Gal* (1944), a musical following the well-worn "Hey gang, let's put on a show!" formula. Mann's next two for Republic, though, showed something of an improvement. *Strangers in the Night* (1944), about a crazed old lady obsessed with a fictitious beautiful daughter, was breathlessly over-plotted, but featured expressively textured photography by Reggie Lanning. In the eponymous hero of *The Great Flamarion* (1945), a *Blue Angel*-style melodrama, Phil Hardy noted "the prototype of the Mannian hero, a man wounded in the past who carries the scar with him into the present." The role was played by Erich von Stroheim, with whom Mann had his problems: "He was a personality, not really an actor. . . . He drove me mad. He was a genius. I'm not a genius: I'm a worker."

Moving to the B-unit at RKO, Mann made a lumbering comedy-thriller, *Two O'Clock Courage* (1945), and another inane musical, *Sing Your Way Home* (1945), before returning to Republic for his last film with the studio, *Strange Impersonation* (1946). Writing in *Bright Lights*, Robert E. Smith described this surrealist melodrama, about a woman scientist who samples her own experimental anaesthetic, as "the most impoverished film of Mann's career," but added that it "points the way to what would be Mann's forte during this period: a nightmare landscape of pain, trapped characters and vicious, unscrupulous villains."

Mann left Republic without regrets ("Grim, grim days") and rejoined RKO to direct two more films. One was a negligible romantic comedy, *The Bamboo Blonde* (1946); but the other, *Desperate* (1947), marked a major step forward. For the first time, Mann had some control over his script (even sharing credit for the story), and he created with George Diskant's moody cinematography a tannibly menacing urban underworld, into which a young couple find themselves inexorably drawn—chief focus of evil being Raymond Burr's bloated gang boss. *Desperate* is generally held to have initiated the seven-picture *film noir* cycle directed by Mann between 1947 and 1949. In Silver and Ward's *Film Noir*, Carl Macek praised the film for its "raw impact unmatched in most *noir* films of the period. Even in an early Mann film . . . the visual quality of the violence is well defined."

Railroaded (1947), Jeanine Basinger considered, "is perhaps his first really unified film," pointing towards "the coherence of Mann's later works." The first of four Mann films scripted by John C. Higgins, it was made for PRC, the poverty row studio for whom Edgar Ulmer directed his shoestring masterpieces. It might have been an even better film if its story, about a woman's fight to clear her unjustly jailed brother, had not derived from the same real-life case that inspired 20th Century–Fox's *Call Northside 777*. To Mann's annoyance, Fox persuaded PRC to make plot changes.

Around this time PRC's precarious finances were revived by a merger with the Rank Organisation, transforming the company into Eagle-Lion International, and allowing for slightly more lavish production values on Mann's next film, *T-Men* (1948). "This is what I call my first film," Mann later commented. "I was responsible for its story, for its structure, its characters, and for actually making it. This was my first real break towards being able to make films the way I wanted." It was also his first teaming with the brilliant cinematographer John Alton, whose "intense downbeat virtuosity," wrote Stephen Handzo (*Bright Lights*, Summer 1976), lent their five films together "an unmistakable style: deep perspective compositions with half-illuminated faces in the foreground . . . distant backgrounds, ceilinged sets, pervasive darkness and gloom created through high-contrast lighting and filters, angular composition, all creating a screen space at once expansive yet oppressively fatalistic."

T-Men, which purported to relate an actual investigation by US Treasury agents, provided Mann with his first box-office success and helped to spark off a whole series of pseudo-documentary thrillers in the late 1940s. But despite the flagwaving confidence of its narration, most of the film is set deep in the alienated shadowland of *film noir*, where nothing and nobody can be relied on. In one memorable sequence, an undercover agent must stand by helplessly and watch his colleague gunned down; in another, a suspected informer is locked inside a steam bath and scalded to death.

An even darker vision informed *Raw Deal* (1948), which Robert Smith found "one of the most visually stylish and striking of Mann's early films . . . also one of the most fatalistic." In its story of a convict who escapes to take revenge on a treacherous associate, it marks an early appearance of one of Mann's favorite themes, that of former comradeship betrayed, as well as a prototype of the flawed Mann hero. Another criminal anti-hero (played by Richard Basehart) featured in *He Walked by Night* (1948), a film scripted by Higgins, photographed by Alton, and mainly directed by Mann, although Alfred Werker (who took over the project) received sole director credit.

Reign of Terror (1949), set in the French Revolution, falls into that fairly rare category, the *noir* costume drama. Most critics have found it disappointing, bogged down by a feeble love interest and the risible dialogue of Philip Yordan's script. ("Don't call me Max!" snarls Basehart as a tetchy Robespierre.) Mann himself, though, was "very fond" of the film, and Higham and Greenberg commended it as a "somber, broodingly handsome . . . melodrama made pictorially compelling by William Cameron Menzies' designs and John Alton's Germanic low-key black-and-white camerawork."

On the strength of his work for Eagle-Lion, and *T-Men* in particular, Mann was now invited by Dore Schary to work for MGM. Playing safe, he took Alton and Higgins over with him, and with *Border Incident* (1949) produced a close reworking of his earlier success. The undercover agents this time come from the Immigration Office, and once again one of them is forced to watch impotently as his colleague dies (in a vividly horrible manner, beneath the blades of a cultivator). There were two crucial differences from *T-Men*, though: the evidently far plusher budget that even a B-unit could command at Metro, and the fact that almost all of *Border Incident* was shot on location, in the San Joaquin Valley where the story took place. For the first time, Mann was let loose on exterior landscapes; the result, as Stephen Handzo observed, came as "a major revelation. . . . A director of gritty, urban crime films emerged as a rival to John Ford in the mythic use of locale."

Side Street (1950), the last of Mann's *noir* thrillers, was weakened by overly sentimental treatment of its trapped young couple—played by Farley Granger and Cathy O'Donnell, reteamed from Nicholas Ray's *They Live by Night*. Nonetheless, Mann made telling use of the urban landscape, especially in the final car-chase sequence.

"If it can be argued that the fifties were as brilliant a decade as any other in Hollywood history," wrote Jean-Pierre Coursodon, "it is to a large extent thanks to the superior quality of the Westerns, and to the artistry of the foremost specialist of the genre, Anthony Mann." From 1950 to 1958 Mann directed seventeen films, of which ten were Westerns—six of them now widely reckoned to rank among the finest ever made.

Mann himself seems to have felt an immedi-ate affinity with the genre, recognizing it as the perfect vehicle for the kind of filmmaking he aspired to. The Western, he explained, "has the essential pictorial qualities, . . . the sweep of anything you feel, the joy of sheer exercise, of outdoorness. It is legend—and legend makes the very best cinema. . . . Legend is a concept of characters greater than life." Or, as Jim Kitses put it, "Mann's response to the Western was not a response to history, as with Ford or Peckinpah, but to its most archetypal form, the mythic patterns deeply embedded in the plots and characters of the genre." Mann also relished the ample scope furnished by Westerns for location shooting, which he vastly preferred to studio work, maintaining that it resulted in far better performances. "Actors achieve far more truth on location. In a studio everything's quiet, everything's set up for the scene, the lights are lit. But when an actor has to play it on top of a mountain, by a river or in a forest, you've got the wind, the dust, the snow, the creaking of branches interrupting him, forcing him to give more; he becomes that much more alive."

Even so, Mann apparently had no prior intention of making Westerns. "I was under contract to MGM. . . . Nick [Nayfack, producer of *Border Incident*] called me and said: 'How would you like to make a Western? I've got a script here that looks interesting.' In fact it was more than interesting, it was the best script I had ever read." The script, by Guy Trosper, was for *Devil's Doorway* (1950). Robert Taylor played the hero, a Shoshone who returns home from the Civil War with a Congressional Medal of Honor to find that an Indian, war hero or no, has no legal rights. Ahead of its time both racially and politically, the film demonstrated "with merciless logic," as Paul Willemen noted (*Framework*, Summer 1981), "that the law is there to oppress people and that political power grows out of the barrel of a gun."

Neatly transitional, *Devil's Doorway* carries much of the *noir* style over into its Western setting, with frequent use of interiors and nocturnal sequences. Mann's next film, though, clearly launches the great series of classic Westerns on which his reputation rests. *Winchester '73* (1950) was originally slated by Universal for Fritz Lang, with James Stewart in the lead. When Lang withdrew, Stewart, who had been impressed by *Devil's Doorway*, suggested Mann as replacement. Mann readily accepted, but threw out the script, calling in Borden Chase to work on a complete rewrite. "This film," stated Jeanine Basinger, "is Mann's first real Western. . . . Beginning with *Winchester '73*, a new simplicity and clarity entered his work, bringing with it the psychological intensity of the *noir* period, but realized in a more direct visual manner."

The film also marks the emergence of the ambivalent, morally flawed Mann hero, whom the director once defined as "a man who could kill his own brother." In Mann's Westerns, the protagonist is shown as an hysterical psychopath, driven by unexalted motives of gain or revenge to destroy a villain who mirrors all his own worst impulses—who is spiritually, and sometimes physically as well, his own brother. "The greatest danger for the Mann protagonist," Robert Smith suggested, "is the possibility of becoming completely what he so closely resembles, the Mann villain." Jim Kitses similarly commented that "the revenge taken by the character is taken upon *himself.*"

Kitses also noted, as have many writers, the distinctively psychological use of landscape in Mann's Westerns, where he took "an unparalleled opportunity to explore through the dialectic of landscape and hero the interior and finally *metaphysical* conflict of his characters. . . . The terrain is so colored by the action that it finally seems an inner landscape, the unnatural world of a disturbed mind." Thus in *Winchester '73,* as Stephen Handzo wrote, "we regress through the verdant landscapes of Colorado to the parched New Mexico desert studded with grotesque cacti and finally to the climactic fratricide on a desolate craggy rockpile."

The plot of the film centers around the eponymous and much-prized rifle. Won by Stewart in a Dodge City shooting contest, stolen from him by the villain, the gun passes from hand to hand (often bringing death upon its temporary possessor) and is finally regained by Stewart after a fatal battle with the man who first stole it—now revealed as Stewart's brother, killer of their father. The image of the enclosed, self-lacerating family unit, with its mythic overtones, would constantly recur in Mann's Westerns, a deliberate transferal of the dimensions of Greek tragedy to the equally legendary setting of the Old West.

Winchester '73, released before *Devil's Doorway* though made later, gave Mann his first major box-office hit, and Universal their most successful film of the year. At the invitation of Hal Wallis, Mann directed his third Western of 1950 for Paramount. *The Furies* (1950), as the title suggests, proved "a further variation on The House of Atreus Goes West" (Handzo), with Barbara Stanwyck as the Electra-like daughter clashing with her rancher father, played by Walter Huston in his final role. (The Niven Busch novel from which the film was adapted, though, was apparently inspired by Dostoyevsky's *The Idiot.*) Filmed in a reversion to Mann's *noir* style and weighted down by its heavy load of cultural allusions, *The Furies* sank into melodrama. Mann was in any case never at his best handling strong female characters. However, he paid warm tribute to Huston: "He was everything that one hopes an actor will be."

Back at MGM, Mann spent some weeks working as assistant director on *Quo Vadis* (1951), one of the earliest of the post-war blockbuster epics. Apart from Peter Ustinov's ripely histrionic Nero, Mann's virtuoso handling of the burning of Rome provided the sole relief in an otherwise painfully dull movie. His only film as director that year was *The Tall Target* (1951), an impressively controlled period thriller in which a police agent foils an attempted assassination of Lincoln just prior to his inauguration. Tim Pulleine (*Monthly Film Bulletin,* March 1982) praised the "seductive accomplishment in the way Mann—proceeding from an elegantly constructed screenplay—modulates the movie's rhythms, admitting periodic bravura touches without ever overplaying his hand."

All of Mann's next seven films starred James Stewart, an unbroken partnership with few precedents in movie history. (Later in the decade, Budd Boetticher would equal it with a run of seven Westerns with Randolph Scott.) The Mann films marked a decisive change of direction in Stewart's career, which had been faltering, trapped in a prolonged adolescence. But beneath the endearingly shambling hick of Stewart's comic persona Mann detected a colder, edgier individual: a neurotic, selfish to the point of obsession, harboring a deep mistrust of society. (Hitchcock later pounced on this new side to the actor, exposing further aspects in *Rear Window* and *Vertigo.*) For two of Mann's non-Westerns, though, *Strategic Air Command* and *The Glenn Miller Story,* Stewart was allowed to revert to lovable diffidence.

The theme of a journey, or quest, provides the framework for all Mann's major Westerns. In *Winchester '73* it was Stewart's pursuit of the rifle and his murderous brother; in *Bend of the River* (1952) he plays the leader of a wagon train, guiding a band of settlers over the mountains to the Oregon Territory. Behind him lies his guilty past as a Missouri border raider, which is resurrected when he encounters a former comrade (Arthur Kennedy at his most engagingly duplicitous). Eventually, of course, Kennedy double-crosses him, making off with the settlers' supplies, and Stewart must track down and kill him—and, with him, a part of his own nature.

Once again scripted by Borden Chase, *Bend of the River* was Mann's first color film, making still more effective use of landscape as a correlative to the psychology of his characters. When Stewart is ambushed and beaten, high on the mountainside, and the stores stolen from him, the coldly beautiful scenery emphasizes first his isolation and seeming impotence and then, as he sets off doggedly in pursuit, the chill determination of his vengeance, a solitary inexorable figure against the immensity of the snowfield. "The great value of using locations," Mann believed, "is that it enhances everything: it enhances the story; it enhances the very action and the acting. I'll never show a piece of scenery . . . without an actor in it."

The cinematic style of Mann's Westerns is generally unobtrusive: he creates classically satisfying compositions within the frame without drawing attention to the means by which they were achieved. Jim Kitses identified "the hallmark of Mann's style" as "a mobile camera, moving fluidly with the action, its pace and direction dictated by the drive of the character." For Mann the story was always primary, determining his approach; he liked to quote Lubitsch's dictum that "there are a thousand ways to point a camera, but really only one." David Thomson found "a mathematical element in his lateral camera movements and infinite perspectives, but this clarity and balance are indications of the elemental newness of the frontier situation."

In *The Naked Spur* (1953) Mann stripped his narrative archetype down to the bare minimum, almost to the linear simplicity of a geometrical diagram. With only five characters (barring some briefly-glimpsed Indians), and not a single interior sequence, it constitutes, in Jean-Pierre Coursodon's view, "a perfect masterpiece," as well as offering the clearest portrait in all Mann's films of the hero as neurotic obsessive. Stewart plays a bounty hunter who has at some point been cheated out of his ranch, apparently by a woman he loved. To recoup his loss, he stubbornly hunts down outlaw Robert Ryan (another of Mann's charming, humorous villains) for the $5,000 on his head. Reluctantly, he finds himself obliged to take on partners. "The almost unholy force" of the film, Kitses suggested, "stems in part from the resemblance of the five characters to a malignant family bent on murdering each other at the first opportunity."

Donald Phelps singled out two sequences in *The Naked Spur* to illustrate how Mann's "octopus-armed sense of form" can subvert "the conventional and frequently boring values" of the Western genre: "An Indian attack . . . is delivered as a pile-driver of half-naked bodies, ramming down a rocky slope again and again,

the camera sidling to and fro at its usual discreet distance. . . . A shooting-match is presented with the same deceptive bluntness; none of the usual suspense-begging variations, big close-ups of reactions, etc.; but an intercutting of distant figures, rock shelf, and pistol-volleys as elegantly co-ordinated as piano arpeggios; until, eventually, one realizes that orthodox suspense, and its gratifications, have been deposed by beautifully oblique narrative rhythm."

With *The Naked Spur* Mann completed his contractual obligations to MGM—much to his relief, since he always disliked being under contract. His next three films were made for Universal. *Thunder Bay* (1953), about a clash between fishermen and oilmen off the Louisiana coast, badly lacked the dramatic tension of the Westerns. Mann admitted that "its story was weak and we never were really able to lick it." *The Glenn Miller Story* (1954) was scarcely more exciting ("The story of the mediocre jazz trombonist, Glenn Miller, whose personality was of no great interest," summed up Jean Wagner laconically), but Stewart, back in his nice-guy persona, exuded relaxed charm in the title role, and the film was hugely successful.

Mann's last collaboration with Borden Chase, *The Far Country* (1955), is in some ways the most light-hearted of his Westerns—though as Jeanine Basinger pointed out, the humor is cool and ironic, pointing up the violence rather than lessening its impact. Stewart's character this time is not so much scarred as deliberately withdrawn, an emotionally frigid outsider who rejects social involvement. His sole close relationship is with his old partner, played by Walter Brennan, and its takes Brennan's murder to force him into action. Once again Mann provided an affably unprincipled villain to set against Stewart's dourness, and used landscape to counterpoint action and character. In a key scene, Stewart leads his section of a wagon train on a detour around a treacherous mountain pass. The rest of the train enter the pass, where they will be hit by an avalanche. Stewart merely watches them go, with no attempt to warn them—as coldly indifferent as the mountain snows themselves.

Strategic Air Command (1955) reunited Stewart (who had had a distinguished flying record in the war) with June Allyson from *The Glenn Miller Story*, though as Mann readily conceded, the real stars were the planes. "I went into it purely as a service to the Air Force . . . the characters were papier-mâché."

Last of the Mann-Stewart Westerns, and their final film together, was *The Man From Laramie* (1955). It was also the most successful financially, thanks partly to an astutely plugged theme song. Mann saw the film as a summary of their collaboration: "That work distilled our relationship. I reprised themes and situations by pushing them to their paroxysm." Most violent of all the series (Stewart is pinioned, dragged through salt flats, shot in the hand at point-blank range), *Man From Laramie* returns to the guilt-torn family of *Winchester '73* and *The Furies*. Its focus is a stubborn, near-blind old patriarch (Donald Crisp) with two sons: a real one who despises him and an adoptive one who craves his love; also a niece who hates him for having cheated her father, his brother. Into this Freudian tangle rides Stewart, seeking the gun-runners who caused the death of *his* brother. (Mann intended to make Stewart yet another son to the old man, but was vetoed by the producer.)

The apparently motiveless attack on Stewart in *Man From Laramie* was cited by Alain Silver and Elizabeth Ward in support of their thesis that all Mann's Westerns (not merely the dark-toned *Devil's Doorway* and *The Furies*) can be seen to carry over elements of the *noir* vision into his later films: "The entire sequence has an almost surreal quality—remote, highly emotional, and yet ultimately lifeless—more typical of *film noir* than of the Western." As in his thrillers, "Mann would often manipulate the environment to permit the fatalistic nature of his narrative to be echoed in the landscape." Noting a similar continuity of vision, Stephen Handzo observed that Mann portrayed "the dark side of the heroic and majestic West hymned by Ford. Mann's West is lonely, tragic, timeless and primal—a brutal setting for brutal men."

Following the success of *Man From Laramie*, Mann was invited to direct another film with Stewart—*Night Passage*, a thriller-Western scripted by Borden Chase—but found the script weak and confusing, and withdrew from the project. "Jimmy was dead set on the film. He had to play the accordion and do a bunch of stunts that actors adore. . . . The film was a near total failure, and Jimmy always held it against me."

Laramie's scriptwriter was Philip Yordan, who also scripted Mann's fourth film of that year, *The Last Frontier* (1955). One of the dullest of Mann's Westerns, it starred Victor Mature as a noble savage whose untamed wilderness is invaded by the army. Mann disliked the film, regarding it as a "damp squib" ruined by studio interference. His next, though, was even worse: *Serenade* (1956), a windily melodramatic adaptation of a James M. Cain novel, with Mario Lanza inadequate in the lead role. "One tries in vain to see what could have attracted Mann to this,"

wrote a bemused Jean Wagner; the answer, apparently, was sympathy for Lanza, whose career was in a bad way. "It was one of those things . . I should never have approached, but I'm glad I did it," Mann remarked later. "At least it got him a couple more pictures before he died."

In 1956, after twenty-five years, Mann's marriage to Mildred Kenyon ended in divorce. The next year he married the Mexican actress, Sarita Montiel, who had played Lanza's wife in *Serenade*.

Tired of battling with studios, Mann now formed his own production company, Security Pictures, with Philip Yordan, releasing through United Artists. Security produced only two films, both of them interestingly atypical of Mann's output. *Men in War* (1957), his only true war movie (*Heroes of Telemark* is adventure with a wartime setting), frankly presents itself as an archetype. "Tell me the story of the foot soldier, and I will tell you the story of all wars," states the opening title, neatly undercutting the exactitude of what follows: "Korea, September 6, 1950." As in his Westerns, Mann aimed for the universality of legend, war stripped down to the grim basics of survival or death in a hostile terrain.

"With the possible exception of Sam Fuller," wrote Phil Hardy, "no other American director has so vividly caught the atmosphere of battle." An infantry patrol, cut off from their battalion, struggle across open country to a meaningless objective, dying one by one. Mann discards all the clichés of war films of the period. There are no heroics, no stock characters, no speeches extolling freedom or democracy; instead, a fatalistic nihilism. "Regiment doesn't exist. Battalion doesn't exist. The USA doesn't exist. . . . We're the only ones left to fight this war," says Robert Ryan, the lieutenant, whose sole purpose is to keep his patrol alive. Even in that, he fails. By the end, all his men have succumbed to the enemy—or to the landscape, since Mann presents them as virtually identical. "All I can get out of the air is Korean," complains the radio operator—the very atmosphere is enemy territory.

Men in War was shot in black and white, as were Mann's subsequent two films. *The Tin Star* (1957) is his most static Western, and the most didactic—"a lesson in apprenticeship," as Mann described it. Henry Fonda plays an ex-sheriff turned bounty hunter, who passes on his expertise to an insecure young sheriff (Anthony Perkins) before moving on. Both situation and characters lack credibility, and the script (by Dudley Nichols, Ford's regular scriptwriter) is over-explicit, lacking the understated resonance of Mann's finest Westerns.

Security Pictures' second and last production was an adaptation of Erskine Caldwell's notorious Deep South novel, *God's Little Acre* (1958). Critical opinion, then and since, differed widely. The French, usually champions of Mann's work, loathed it: "as depressing as it was catastrophic" was Godard's verdict. David Thomson dismissed it as "a restrained attempt at the cheerful bawdiness of Erskine Caldwell." Mann himself, though, always thought it one of his best films, and Donald Phelps found it "remarkable for the dance-like movement which Mann and Yordan and their company set going behind every sequence, quite fluently and appositely." Robert Ryan, always good in Mann's films, turned in a beautifully judged performance as Ty-Ty Walden, the disreputable patriarch obsessively excavating his land for buried treasure.

Mann reverted to color, and widescreen, for his last major Western, *Man of the West* (1958). Gary Cooper, aging and visibly ill, played the most haunted of all Mann's heroes. "In attempting to destroy the past that holds him to ransom," Jim Kitses wrote, "the hero is driven inescapably to relive it, the violence and evil that he has tried to bury forced to surface by the situation he is in." An ostensibly respectable citizen, stranded when his train is attacked, Cooper tracks the robbers across country—only to be revealed, when he finds them, as a former member of the gang, nephew of their leader, the deranged and malevolent Dock Tobin (Lee J. Cobb). For his own safety and that of his two fellow-travelers, a saloon singer and an elderly con man, he must pretend to rejoin the gang in order to destroy it—and his past.

For Robin Wood, *Man of the West* is "Mann's greatest film and one of the half dozen or so 'essential' Westerns," in which "all his major preoccupations are bound together in a satisfying unity." "Each shot," Jean-Luc Godard maintained, "gives the impression that Anthony Mann is reinventing the Western. . . . *Man of the West* is the most intelligent of films, and at the same time the most simple." More cautiously, Philip French called it "perhaps his finest, and certainly his most pessimistic, movie. . . . Few Westerns can match its integration of setting, dramatic development and moral progress." The film's main weakness lies in Reginald Rose's heavily schematic screenplay, which often over-points the allegory: the Cooper character is nudgingly named Link (between old West and new, savagery and civilization), and the ghost town where the gang are trapped in a final shoot-out is called Lasso. Despite her interestingly off-beat reading of the role, Julie London's saloon girl seems an egregious figure, the statutory female-in-jeopardy to motivate and hamper the hero. (Mann wanted her to be Cooper's wife, but was overruled.) Nonetheless, the somber power of Mann's direction, and Cooper's agonized performance, easily outweigh such flaws.

Man of the West is starker in its cruelty than any of the Stewart Westerns. Both Cooper and his alter ego—his cousin, played by John Dehner—are shown as capable of extreme brutality, and Dehner shares little of the deceptive charm of Ryan or Kennedy in the earlier films. As ever, the landscape mirrors the hero's journey: from the bustling town amid green rolling hills where he catches the train, to the outlaws' squalid shack, and finally to the barren rocks around the ghost town, Cooper, stripped of his civilized veneer, must travel into the hell of his former self. This bleakness, Jean-Pierre Coursodon felt, "strikes a disquietingly decadent note"; the film "appears as the twilight effort of a classicist reluctantly surrendering to 'modern' trends; it points to the downbeat Western of the sixties, with its embittered losers and phased-out old-timers."

The 1950s, by general agreement, was Mann's finest decade; of his five remaining films, none—except at rare moments—attains the same level of achievement. It may well be, as Jeanine Basinger suggests, that after *Man of the West* "there was no point in his making another Western," that he had said all he could in the genre, and needed to make a break as radical as that of ten years earlier, when he had switched from thrillers to Westerns. This time, his move was into that most problematic of all cinematic genres, the costume epic.

It was a logical enough development. Epics were currently booming, seen by a demoralized movie industry as a means of beating off the encroaching threat of television. And Mann, though still largely ignored by "serious" critics (except in France), was acknowledged an exceptionally skilled director of outdoor action films, with an innate feel for locale and a taste for larger-than-life narrative. As a director of epics, he was clearly a natural.

His first two assignments, though, were hardly propitious. After a few weeks shooting on *Spartacus* (1960) Mann clashed with the film's producer and star, Kirk Douglas ("He wanted to insist on the message. . . . A film has to be visual") and left, being replaced by Stanley Kubrick. Instead, he went to MGM to direct *Cimarron* (1961). Another conveniently transitional film in Mann's career, this was an epic Western, based on a typically sprawling novel by Edna Ferber (previously filmed by Wesley Ruggles in 1931) about the Oklahoma land rush and the settling of the West. Already burdened with a simpering Maria Schell as the heroine, *Cimarron* was irretrievably sunk when Metro decided, in mid-production, to reshoot most of the exteriors on studio sets. Mann quit in disgust, disowning the final release: "I don't consider it a film. I just consider it a disaster."

Mann's next two films were made for Samuel Bronston's grand and short-lived production empire in Spain. *El Cid* (1961), which relates the legend of Spain's great medieval champion against the Moors, is generally regarded, along with Schaffner's *The War Lord*, as the most intelligent and satisfying of the epics produced during this period. Certainly much of the film is visually superb, especially the great final battle for Valencia when, in perhaps the supreme moment in all epic cinema, the dead Cid, strapped to his horse, is borne out along the seashore at the head of the Spanish charge, even his corpse enough to strike terror in the enemy. Throughout, Mann makes evocative use of seascapes, the interpenetration of land and sea suggesting the clash of Moorish and Christian cultures within the embattled realm. David Thomson considered *El Cid* "an astonishing departure and a total success. . . . The simplicity of the conception . . . relates to the cinema's earliest portraits of the virtuous hero and to the medium's power to combine physical and moral tension." Moral tension, though, was just what others found missing, since the film—as Robin Wood remarked—"lacks the fallible, divided protagonist to whom . . . [Mann] naturally gravitated": the Cid (played, inevitably, by Charlton Heston) starts off noble and gets steadily nobler for the next three hours. Any brief moments of human hesitation are promptly overcome, never seriously impeding the mythic progress. For all its austere grandeur, and the clarity of Yordan's script (which avoids most of the direst pitfalls of epic-speak), much of *El Cid* is dull.

In 1963 Mann was divorced from Sarita Montiel. The same year he settled in London, and married Anna Kutzho, a Russian-born ex-ballerina. Their son Nicholas was born in 1965.

El Cid was well received critically and commercially. Mann's second epic for Bronston, *The Fall of the Roman Empire* (1964), was a lot less successful on both counts. Starting from the premise (which furnished an epilogue to the film) that "no civilization can be destroyed from without, but it destroys itself from within," Mann pinpoints the beginning of Rome's decline as the moment when the Stoic philosopher Marcus Aurelius is succeeded as emperor by his corrupt and licentious son Commodus. By the end of the film Commodus is dead, the barbarians are crossing the frontiers, and the imperial throne is up for auction to the highest bidder. The theme, of Mann's own devising, is massive—so much so, that the human actors are dwarfed by the vast sweep of history. Individual sequences, though, work well: most notably the opening, played strikingly against the conventional image of bare-kneed legions marching over torrid hills. Instead Mann presents the chill northern frontier of empire, torches flaming in the frosty night air and sentries gazing out across the impenetrable German forests. Against this setting Alec Guinness as Aurelius, graciously receiving tributary kings in snowbound pomp, convincingly embodies calm majesty; but after his death the film flounders, losing impetus in episodic plotting.

Fall never recouped its huge production costs, bringing down the Bronston empire in its wake. In Britain, Mann directed *Heroes of Telemark* (1965), a sadly undramatic account of a wartime Resistance raid on a German heavy-water plant in occupied Norway, redeemed only by Mann's feeling for mountainous snowscapes, superbly photographed by Robert Krasker.

The morally cleft Mann hero, shadowed by his evil counterpart, reached a logical culmination in his final movie, *A Dandy in Aspic* (1968), where hero and villain are one and the same. A weary double agent, Eberlin, is assigned the task of killing his opposite number—who is of course himself. "The powerful simplicity of Mann's conception," Phil Hardy commented, "is clouded in the film itself, as one by one the conventions of the spy film crumble under the weight of despair Mann invests them with." While on location in Berlin, Mann suffered a heart attack, and died in his hotel room. The film's concluding scenes were directed by its star, Laurence Harvey.

At the time of his sudden death, Mann was working on a number of possible projects. One of them would have been a return to the Western: *The King*, a version of *King Lear*, to star John Wayne as ruler of a vast cattle empire, who loses it through misjudgement of his sons. (As Robin Wood points out, the theme had been foreshadowed in *The Man From Laramie*.)

During Anthony Mann's lifetime and for some years after his death, critical opinion on his work was broadly unanimous: his films were either ignored or dismissed as negligible. Gordon Gow, in *Hollywood in the Fifties*, was not untypical: having briefly noticed *God's Little Acre* and *The Glenn Miller Story*, he summarized the remaining films of Mann's outstanding decade as "otherwise concerned with the war and the old West." And when, in 1970, *Action* magazine polled 250 newspaper and magazine critics for their choice of the best dozen Westerns ever made, not only did no Mann film make it to the top twelve, but not one was mentioned among the runners-up.

One possible explanation for this neglect may be that almost all Mann's work falls into three genres—thriller, Western, epic—which at that time lacked critical respectability. (Epic, indeed, still does.) Westerns made by directors who specialized in the genre tended to be taken less seriously than those by prestige directors venturing into the field to make "significant" statements—such as Wellman's *Ox-Bow Incident*, Zinnemann's *High Noon*, and Stevens' *Shane*, all of which qualified for *Action*'s greatest dozen. (The obvious exception, of course, was Ford—but even he was perhaps more highly regarded at the time for having made *The Informer* and *The Grapes of Wrath*.)

If without honor in his own country, Mann was amply appreciated in France from the mid-1950s onwards. His films were enthusiastically received in the pages of *Cahiers du Cinéma* by Truffaut and Godard; in 1955 Rivette listed him, along with Nicholas Ray, Richard Brooks, and Robert Aldrich, as "one of the four great directors of postwar Hollywood." In Henri Agel's *Le Western* (published 1961), Claude-Jean Philippe compared Mann's work to that of Hawks, with no disparagement of either: "The beauty of Anthony Mann's Westerns is not that of a fluid classicism, but of a romanticism shot through with lightning-flashes."

In recent years English-language criticism has moved closer to the French view, though Coursodon asserted in 1983 that Mann's achievements "continue to be underrated to this day." His finest work, by near-unanimous agreement, lies in the six key Westerns—the five with Stewart, plus *Man of the West*—to which some would add *Men in War* and *El Cid*. "The work of Anthony Mann," David Thomson wrote, "is unrivalled for its development of the themes in the Western form, combining the visual sensitivity to terrain of a frontier scout with a deliberate but uncontrived sense of morality worked out through spatial authenticity," in short the "ability to place every action in perfect physical and moral context at the same time." Mann's influence on the Western is seen as radical and lasting, no less significant (in Jim Kitses' view) than that of Ford: " [Mann's] contribution was in its way equally unique, the incarnation of his tragic world darkening the genre as no one else has." Stephen Handzo categorically described Mann as "the key figure in the post-war

Western." Ten years ago such evaluations might have seemed bizarre—today they would probably command widespread, if not universal, assent.

—*P.K.*

FILMS: Dr. Broadway, 1942; Moonlight in Havana, 1942; Nobody's Darling, 1943; My Best Gal, 1944; Strangers in the Night, 1944; The Great Flamarion, 1945; Two O'Clock Courage, 1945; Sing Your Way Home, 1945; Strange Impersonation, 1946; The Bamboo Blonde, 1946; Desperate, 1947; Railroaded, 1947; T-Men, 1948; Raw Deal, 1948; (uncredited; with Alfred Werker) He Walked by Night, 1948; Reign of Terror (The Black Book), 1949; Border Incident, 1949; Side Street, 1950; Devil's Doorway, 1950; Winchester '73, 1950; The Furies, 1950; The Tall Target, 1951; Bend of the River (U.K., Where the River Bends), 1952; The Naked Spur, 1953; Thunder Bay, 1953; The Glenn Miller Story, 1954; The Far Country, 1955; Strategic Air Command, 1955; The Man From Laramie, 1955; The Last Frontier, 1955; Serenade, 1956; Men in War, 1957; The Tin Star, 1957; God's Little Acre, 1958; Man of the West, 1958; Cimarron, 1961; El Cid, 1961; The Fall of the Roman Empire, 1964; The Heroes of Telemark, 1965; (with Laurence Harvey) A Dandy in Aspic, 1968.

ABOUT: Agel, H. (ed.) Le Western, 1961; Basinger, J. Anthony Mann, 1979; Coursodon, J. P. and Sauvage, P. American Directors, vol. 1, 1983; French, P. Westerns: Aspects of a Movie Genre, 1973; Hardy, P. Aspects of the Western, 1969; Higham, C. and Greenberg, J. Hollywood in the Forties, 1968; Kitses, J. Horizons West, 1969; Missaien, J. C. Anthony Mann, 1964 (in French); Phelps, D. Covering Ground: Essays for Now, 1969; Roud, R. (ed.) Cinema: A Critical Dictionary, 1980; Silver, A. and Ward, E. Film Noir, 1980; Thomson, D. Movie Man, 1967; Thomson, D. A Biographical Dictionary of the Cinema, 1980; Wagner, J. Anthony Mann, 1968 (in French); Wright, W. Sixguns and Society: A Structural Study of the Western, 1975. *Periodicals*—Bright Lights Summer 1976, Fall 1976, 2/1 1977; Cahiers du Cinéma March 1957, August 1965, May 1967; Cahiers du Cinéma in English December 1967; Celulóide September 1968; Films and Filming January–February 1962, March 1964; Film Ideal May 15, 1964; September 1, 1964; Focus on Film November 1978; Framework Summer 1981; Monthly Film Bulletin January 1982, March–April 1982; Movietone News Fall 1978; National Film Theatre (Britain) Booklet August 1978; Oltro Cine September–October 1962; Positif April 1968; Screen July–October 1969; Sight and Sound Autumn 1965.

MARSHALL, GEORGE (December 29, 1891–February 17, 1975), American director, was born in Chicago, the son of a jeweler. He was educated at St. John's Military Academy and expelled from the University of Chicago. Marshall began his career as a portrait salesman, cycling from one Illinois farm to another. Ac-

GEORGE MARSHALL

cording to a studio press handout, he subsequently played professional baseball and worked on the Chicago, Milwaukee, St. Paul and Pacific Railroad, as well as in his father's jewelry shop. He also tried journalism for a while, as a cub reporter for the Seattle *Post-Intelligencer* and as west coast representative of *Collier's* magazine.

Marshall arrived in Hollywood in 1912 on a visit to his mother. The burgeoning movie industry caught his interest, and he went to work as an extra at Universal. During his six months as an actor, he appeared as an extra or bit player in Wallace Reid productions, in serials directed by Francis Ford, and in Al Christie comedies. Over the next few years he gradually broadened his experience, working as a prop man, make-up man, scenarist, editor, cameraman, and assistant director.

He directed his first films in 1915 or 1916—mostly short Westerns, with an occasional feature like *Love's Lariat* (1916) and *The Man From Montana* (1917). Marshall was a first lieutenant in the Coast Artillery of the National Guard, and in 1917, when the United States entered World War I, he volunteered for the army. By the afternoon of the same day, he was in uniform as a sergeant, in command of 191 men. Mustered into the Signal Corps, he was first sent to lay cables in France, then transferred to the Corps' Photographic Section.

This move "sounded good after the mud and slop we were bathing [in]," Marshall told Kevin Brownlow. "But the Photographic Section! It was the most slipshod outfit you could possibly imagine. . . . I was still a first sergeant, and I was so annoyed when I walked in there, to see

the barracks and to see the way they were living. I raised hell for about two weeks. . . . It was useless. You couldn't beat them down. I had all these characters, like those fabulous New York cameramen from Hearst News; they'd never taken orders in their life. . . . We made up newsreels to send back home. We'd take a piece of film from here and a piece from there—they had no connection with each other whatsoever. We'd make up a big bombing episode, showing people carrying bodies which had been photographed fifty miles away. . . . They were screaming for film, but there was nobody to make decisions as to what sort of film they wanted."

Marshall ended the war as a lieutenant and returned to Hollywood with the girl he had met and married in France, Germaine Minet. His first assignment was to direct two Pathé serials starring Ruth Roland, Pearl White's principal rival as "Queen of the Serials." After a stint with Fox, where among other things he scripted and directed the Tom Mix Western *A Ridin' Romeo* (1921), he joined Educational Pictures, directing a series of two-reel comedies featuring Lloyd Hamilton.

Returning to Fox, Marshall worked on the Richard Harding Davis "Van Bibber" series, among other shorts, as well as directing occasional features, some of which he scripted. In 1925 he was appointed supervisor of all Fox short films, responsible for eight different series. In that capacity at Fox (and in 1928–1929 at Pathé), Marshall gave initial breaks to a number of directors later well known, among them Lloyd Bacon, Sidney Lanfield, David Butler, and Lewis Seiler. He himself directed scores of shorts in the series he supervised, including some W. C. Fields vehicles and the Bobby Jones golfing comedies (which Marshall devised). Marshall's short films are not listed in the filmography below; he made over three hundred of them.

He returned to features in 1932 with the full-length Laurel and Hardy comedy *Pack Up Your Troubles,* codirected with Raymond McCarey. Two Laurel and Hardy shorts followed and then, between 1934 and 1969, some seventy features in almost every genre. David Thomson maintains that Marshall "disliked real violence" and avoided crime, horror, and the "serious" war picture: "His happiest forte was mild, satirical comedy."

An early example was *In Old Kentucky* (1935). It stars Will Rogers (in his last role) as a racehorse trainer who calls on the services of a professional rainmaker to improve the chances of his star pupil, a horse that goes best on a wet track. The film was enjoyed as "a warm, human, and jolly comedy." However—David Thomson's claims to the contrary notwithstanding—Marshall showed the same year that he could indeed handle violence, in a movie inspired by the Weyerhaeuser kidnapping.

Show Them No Mercy, featuring Rochelle Hudson, Bruce Cabot, and Cesar Romero, begins with a young couple, their baby, and a lovable terrier *en route* to California. When their car mires down in a storm, they take shelter in a lonely house that turns out to be the refuge also of a quartet of kidnappers. Tracked down by dedicated G-men, the gang finally comes to grief through internal dissension and jealousy. Even this violent and exciting film, however, was marked by "cleverly interspersed comedy touches" that "somewhat relieve the emotional tension." André Sennwald wrote that, "as a modern morality tale, made out of cold brutality and macabre humor, it presents the screen in its raciest journalistic vein."

There was also a great deal of brutality—including scenes of torture—in *Message to Garcia* (1936), based on the true story of the hazardous delivery by Lieutenant Andrew S. Rowan of President McKinley's famous message to General Garcia in Cuba before the Spanish-American War. Wallace Beery, Barbara Stanwyck, and John Boles star in a "thin story" that emerged as "mediocre melodrama." The satirical musical *Can This Be Dixie?* (1936) was even more coolly received as an "unfunny" hodgepodge of synthetic caricatures, silly gags, and tasteless production numbers."

Marshall made most of his early features for Fox. An exception was *The Goldwyn Follies* (1938), a musical comedy with a Hollywood setting. It was mainly a showcase for the variegated talents of Edgar Bergen and Charlie McCarthy, Helen Jepson, the Ritz Brothers, and Kenny Baker, with Adolphe Menjou as the ruthless producer with a heart of gold, and Andrea Leeds as the country girl he hires to inject "a sense of humanity" into his latest movie.

After this excursion, Marshall returned to Fox in 1938 to make *Battle of Broadway* and *Hold That Co-ed,* the latter an extremely successful musical comedy scripted by Karl Tunberg, Don Ettlinger, and Jack Yellen. It satirized both college football and politics in its portrait of a state governor modeled on Huey Long (whose influence over the Louisiana State University's team was well known). John Barrymore plays this "bibulous, back-slapping, vote-getting genius" with great gusto, and romantic interest is supplied by George Murphy (as a homespun football coach) and Marjorie Weaver (as the

Governor's amiable secretary). Howard Barnes wrote that the movie "combines huddles, end runs, satirical reflections on the current scene, romance and hotcha collegiate doings in a vastly entertaining show."

Moving over to Universal, Marshall made *You Can't Cheat an Honest Man* (1939), with W. C. Fields in fine fettle as Larson E. Whipsnade, a shoestring circus owner whose unfortunate daughter (Constance Moore) has to introduce this outrageous huckster to her fiancé's snobbish family. Marshall's best-known film, *Destry Rides Again,* followed the same year from the same studio. Adapted by Felix Jackson, Henry Myers, and Gertrude Purcell from the novel by Max Brand, and photographed by Hal Mohr, this was a remake of Ben Stoloff's Tom Mix movie of 1932. In Marshall's version, James Stewart stars as Tom Destry, diffident but ultimately formidable son of a famous fighting sheriff, sent to tame the wild western town of Bottleneck. There he meets his future bride (Irene Hervey) and is also loved by the quixotic harlot Frenchy (Marlene Dietrich), who stops a bullet meant for him and dies in his arms.

The previous year, Dietrich had been among those listed in a public advertisement by the Independent Theatre Owners Association of New York as "box-office poison." It seemed that her career was finished until the producer Joe Pasternak cast the exquisite sex icon of the 1930s as a frontier *chanteuse,* belting out "See What the Boys in the Back Room Will Have," and brawling in the mud with Una Merkel. The film resuscitated her career. Cecil Wilson, seeing a revival in 1977, wrote that "what gives the film the gloss of greatness and assures it an honored place among the classics is Marlene Dietrich's showstopping performance as Frenchy." Another critic suggested that, "while sacrificing none of the drama and action traditional in the Western, *Destry Rides Again* introduced a new style with its debunking of the genre."

And in his next movie, *The Ghost Breakers* (1940), Marshall did the same for the horror film. In this, the third sceen version of a popular stage thriller, Bob Hope stars, with Paulette Goddard as the inheritor of a Cuban castle infested by zombies (Hope assumes that they must be Democrats). Willie Best rolls his eyes in one of his numerous impersonations of a permanently terrified black servant. According to Basil Wright, the film's "thrills, set in a frame of jocosity, are none the less valid—the chest full of dusty and cobwebbed clothes, the shapeless figure under the fourposter's counterpane, the organ's ghostly music, and the shadowy hand across the unwitting mouth." Leslie Halliwell, thirty years later, found it "an oddly successful combination of laughs and horror."

There is a good deal of humor also in the Randolph Scott–Kay Francis Western *When the Daltons Rode* (1940), treasured by genre buffs for the famous Yakima Canutt stunt, never repeated without faking, in which the Dalton brothers jump on horseback from a fast-moving train. *Texas* (1941), with William Holden, Glenn Ford, and Claire Trevor (and Edgar Buchanan as a villainous dentist), was another "light and likable" Western.

Perhaps the most admired of Marshall's films of this period was *Murder He Says* (1945), an original Lou Breslow script satirizing both the horror genre and such Deep South melodramas of the 1940s as Ford's *Tobacco Road*. Fred MacMurray plays a likable nincompoop hunting for a gangster's missing moll (Helen Walker). He winds up in Marjorie Main's hillbilly menage, where murder is everyone's hobby and corpses glow fitfully in the dark from radium poisoning. Hughes and Greenberg, in *Hollywood in the Forties*, called this "a neglected masterpiece and perhaps the forties' funniest farce."

A year later, however, Marshall demonstrated once more that he was as capable of directing straightforward genre violence as anyone in Hollywood. *The Blue Dahlia*, an excellent original script by Raymond Chandler, stars Alan Ladd as a navy flier home from the war whose unfaithful wife is murdered. The rest of the picture, as C. A. Lejeune wrote, "is a manhunt, with the police after the husband and the husband after the killer." Veronica Lake is there to bind Ladd's physical and emotional wounds, Howard da Silva is a convincingly shady nightclub owner, and William Bendix is both frightening and touching as Ladd's buddy, whose wartime head wound has left him liable to outbursts of uncontrollable violence.

Simon Harcourt-Smith found the movie "austerely free of artistic aspirations" but, in "its speed and its wit . . . a model of adroit filmmaking." Campbell Dixon called it "a thriller with characters sharply etched, an ingenious plot, exciting incident and laconic wit. . . . The action moves fast without creaking. The detail is brilliant in its significance and economy."

The Blue Dahlia was financially as well as critically successful, and so was *Monsieur Beaucaire*, the totally different kind of entertainment that followed from Paramount the same year. A remake of the 1924 silent based on Booth Tarkington's story, it burlesqued the swashbuckling original in a way that Marshall had made peculiarly his own. In the Rudolph Valentino version, the hero was an aristocratic swordsman posing as a barber; in the Marshall version, Bob Hope is a craven barber posing as a dueling duke.

Marshall produced nothing of much interest after that until *My Friend Irma* (1949), in itself a tedious radio-derived comedy about a dumb blonde (Marie Wilson), but arguably significant as the first film in which Dean Martin and Jerry Lewis worked together. *Fancy Pants* (1950) is a feeble variation on the theme of *Ruggles of Red Gap* that also has unacknowledged debts to *Monsieur Beaucaire*, with Hope as a ham actor masquerading as a butler masquerading as an English earl in the Wild West.

Marshall's run of poor scripts continued into the early 1950s and included *Scared Stiff* (1953), a Martin and Lewis remake of *The Ghost Breakers*. Things picked up a little with *Houdini* (1953), an "enjoyable piece of hokum" with Tony Curtis as Houdini and Janet Leigh as his assistant and wife, and *Red Garters* (1954). This musical spoof Western, starring Rosemary Clooney and Jack Carson, made little impact on release but has since been described (by David Thomson) as a stylized musical "years ahead of its time."

After that, mediocrity settled in again until, in the midst of what seemed like an irreversible decline, came a "droll Western" called *The Sheepman* (1958), an engaging and characteristic Marshall movie much closer in spirit to *Destry Rides Again* than *Destry* (1955), his middling remake of his masterpiece, with the egregious Audie Murphy in the James Stewart role.

The Sheepman stars Glenn Ford as the newcomer who insists on raising sheep in cattle country. "In the early scenes," wrote *Time*'s reviewer, "the script sets up all the principal cowtown clichés, and one by one the hero neatly knocks them over. As he saunters down Main Street, he outtalks the Town Character, outsmarts the Local Merchant, outtrades the Horse Dealer, outfigures the Marshal (Slim Pickens), outfights the Big Bully (Mickey Shaughnessy), outshoots the Dirty Villain (Leslie Nielsen), outflirts the Prettiest Girl in Town (Shirley MacLaine)." Ford also starred (somewhat miscast) in the interesting black comedy *The Gazebo* (1960), playing a television thriller writer who applies his skills to disposing of a blackmailer.

The best of Marshall's remaining films was *Advance to the Rear* (1964), again starring Glenn Ford, with Stella Stevens, Melvyn Douglas, and Joan Blondell. Based on William Chamberlain's novel *The Company of Cowards*, it is another spoof Western, set just after the Civil War. It centers on an incompetent cavalry troop of misfits and near-criminals that is sent west by river boat to battle Indians and outlaws. They win the climactic battle only by making use of their talents for thieving and arson (and of such unorthodox weapons as ballistas improvised from brassieres). The movie was generally enjoyed as a "slapdash, non-wounding joke at the expense of cavalry epics and traditions," showing that George Marshall had not lost his "flair for this kind of casual, balloon-pricking parody."

Marshall made his last movie, a disappointing Jerry Lewis comedy called *Hook, Line, and Sinker,* in 1968, when he was seventy-seven, but even then did not retire, turning his attention to television. He appeared as an actor in the *Police Woman* series, directed several Lucille Ball shows, and ended his career with an episode of the Richard Boone *Hec Ramsey* series, made when he was eighty-one years old.

No one would claim that George Marshall was a major artist of the cinema—least of all Marshall himself. But his craftsmanship and gentle humor gave much pleasure to millions in the course of a career that, as David Thomson says, had "few equals for labour and survival." Called a "wiry-framed fountain of incredible energy," he once expressed some impatience with the Method actors who came his way, complaining that "by the time they get into the part and know what the character is all about, I've already finished the picture." He was inducted into the Hall of Fame of the Academy of Motion Picture Arts and Sciences in 1975, three days before his death. He and his wife Germaine had a son and a daughter, and four grandchildren.

FILMS (features only): Love's Lariat, 1916; The Man From Montana, 1917; The Embarrassment of Riches, 1918; The Adventures of Ruth (serial), 1919; Ruth of the Rockies (serial), 1920; Prairie Trails, 1920; Why Trust Your Husband?, 1921; Hands Off, 1921; A Ridin' Romeo, 1921; After Your Own Heart, 1921; The Lady From Longacre, 1921; The Jolt, 1921; Smiles Are Trumps, 1922; Haunted Valley (serial), 1923; Don Quickshot of the Rio Grande, 1923; Where Is This West?, 1923; Men in the Raw, 1923; (with Raymond McCarey) Pack Up Your Troubles, 1932; Ever Since Eve, 1934; Wild Gold, 1934; She Learned About Sailors, 1934; He Learned About Women, 1934; 365 Nights in Hollywood, 1934; Life Begins at Forty, 1935; Ten Dollar Raise, 1935; In Old Kentucky, 1935; Music Is Magic, 1935; Show Them No Mercy, 1935; A Message to Garcia, 1936; The Crime of Dr. Forbes, 1936; Can This Be Dixie?, 1936; Nancy Steele Is Missing, 1937; Love Under Fire, 1937; The Goldwyn Follies, 1938; Battle of Broadway, 1938; Hold That Co-ed, 1938; You Can't Cheat an Honest Man, 1938; Destry Rides Again, 1939; The Ghost Breakers, 1940; When the Daltons Rode, 1940; Pot o' Gold, 1941; Texas, 1941; Valley of the Sun, 1942; The Forest Rangers, 1942; Star Spangled Rhythm, 1942; True to Life, 1943; Riding High, 1943; As the Angels Sing, 1944; Murder He Says, 1945; Incendiary Blonde, 1945; Hold That Blonde, 1945; The Blue Dahlia, 1946; Monsieur Beaucaire, 1946; The Perils of Pauline, 1947; Variety Girl, 1947; Hazard, 1948; Tap Roots, 1948; My Friend Irma, 1949; Fancy Pants, 1950; Never a Dull Moment, 1950; A Millionaire for Christy, 1951; The Savage, 1952; Off Limits/Military Policeman, 1953; Scared Stiff, 1953; Houdini, 1953; Money From Home, 1954; Red Garters, 1954; Duel in the Jungle, 1954; Destry, 1955; The Second Greatest Sex, 1955; Pillars of the Sky, 1956; The Guns of Fort Petticoat, 1957; Beyond Mombasa, 1957; The Sad Sack, 1957; The Sheepman, 1958; Imitation General, 1958; The Mating Game, 1959; It Started With a Kiss, 1959; The Gazebo, 1960; Cry for Happy, 1961; The Happy Thieves, 1962; The Railroad *episode* in How the West Was Won, 1962; Papa's Delicate Condition, 1963; L'Intrigo/Dark Purpose, 1964; Advance to the Rear/Company of Cowards, 1964; Boy, Did I Get a Wrong Number, 1966; Eight on the Lam, 1967; The Wicked Dreams of Paula Schultz, 1968; Hook, Line, and Sinker, 1968.

ABOUT: Brownlow, K. The War, the West, and the Wilderness, 1979; Garfield, B. Western Films, 1982.

*MAURO, HUMBERTO (April 30, 1897– November 6, 1983), Brazilian director, producer, scenarist, cinematographer, editor, etc., was born in Volta Grande, a small town in the state of Minas Gerais. His father, Caetano Mauro, was of Italian extraction; his mother, Tereza Duarte Mauro, a native of Minas. Humberto Mauro was the oldest of six children. Before he was two years old the family moved to Saõ José d'Alem Paraíba, also in Minas, and the *mineiro* landscape and people remained important to him and to his work.

Graduating from high school in the nearby town of Leopoldina, Mauro enrolled at the School of Engineering, then dropped out to follow a correspondence course in electricity and electric trams. Thus equipped, he moved to Rio de Janeiro, where he worked for various manufacturers of electrical apparatus. Returning to Minas Gerais, he settled in the small town of Cataguases, 120 miles north of Rio, where he opened his own electromechanical workshop. Among other things, he made telephone receivers which he sold to local farmers and businessmen. He meanwhile explored a succession of other passions—as a radio amateur, stamp collector, photographer, and local chess champion. When he was twenty-three he married Maria Villela de Almeida and was soon struggling to support a growing family.

These new responsibilities did not deter his forays into the arts and sciences. With characteristic ardor, Mauro next threw himself into acting with the amateur theatre in Cataguases. He also

HUMBERTO MAURO

tried his hand as a dramatist before deciding
that it might be more exciting to involve himself
in the manufacture of gliders. This dream evaporated in its turn when Mauro discovered his final, lasting passion, the cinema.

There had been sporadic attempts at filmmaking in Brazil from 1908 onwards, but the
pictures that fired Mauro's imagination when he
saw them in the mid-1920s at the Recreio movie
theatre in Cataguases were all Hollywood products. He immediately recognized in this marriage of art and technology his true vocation,
and in 1925, with a Baby Pathé 9.5mm movie
camera, he made *Valadião, o Cratera (Valadião,
the Disaster)*. Inspired by the serials of Pearl
White and the Westerns of Thomas Ince, this
short amateur feature follows a band of desperadoes out of the mountains of Minas Gerais and
into the town, where they kidnap a young girl.
In the end, the girl is safe and the baddies behind
bars. No masterpiece, the movie served "to
frighten the children" and to whet Mauro's appetite for more.

This exercise also helped him to win the support of his friends Homero Côrtes and Agenor
Côrtes de Barros, two Cataguases businessmen.
In 1927, ignoring all those who openly questioned their sanity, they founded Sul América
Filme (South America Films). On the face of it,
it was indeed a lunatic enterprise: these provincial idealists were proposing to make pictures
without a studio or equipment, without professional actors or technicians, without access to a
distributor, and with no knowledge of the market. In a climate of ridicule, Sul América Filme
began work on a full-length feature, *Os Dios
Irmãos (The Two Brothers)*, directed by another
recruit, Pedro Comello, and starring Mauro.

This project proved abortive, and the first feature actually completed by Sul América was *Na
Primavera da Vida (In the Springtime of Life,
1926)*. Scripted and directed by Mauro, this was
produced by Homero Côrtes and photographed
by Comello, with two local actors in the lead
roles: Eva Nil and Mauro's brother Bruno. Its
melodramatic plot centered on the social problems connected with bootleg rum. Made at the
trifling cost of 12,000 cruzeiros, it achieved a
showing at a movie theatre in Rio de Janeiro.
There it was seen by another Brazilian film pioneer, Ademar or Adhemar Gonzaga, who
praised this provincial phenomenon in the
"National Cinema" column he wrote in the magazine *Para Todos*. This led to a meeting in Rio
between Mauro and Gonzaga that began a long
friendship and collaboration.

Gonzaga introduced his new friend to Griffith's *Broken Blossoms* and Henry King's
Tol'able David, both of which impressed Mauro
profoundly and had an acknowledged influence
on his second feature, *Tesouro Perdido (Lost
Treasure, 1927)*. This society melodrama,
scripted as usual by Mauro, starred his wife, Maria de Almeida Mauro, under the exotic pseudonym "Lola Lys," and, again, Bruno Mauro.
Both brothers took a hand, with Pedro Comello,
at the camera, and Humberto also acted in the
film, which was backed to the tune of 20,000
cruzeiros by his new company, Phebo Brasil
Filme.

Indeed, as Mauro said, "all the family acted,
and we filmed the typical townsman and coun-
tryman in their everyday occupations." He had
come a long way since *In the Springtime of Life*,
in both technical skill and style, and *Tesouro
Perdido* is said to show not only the influence of
Griffith and Henry King, but of German expressionism and the French "first avant-garde."
Landscape played an important part in this, as
in all the films in the so-called Cataguases cycle,
and Mauro declared that his formula was "the
bush, the waterfall, the women." The influential
Rio magazine *Cinearte*, another of Gonzaga's
contributions to the development of the Brazilian cinema, awarded the movie its prize as best
film of the year.

Brasa Dormida (Dead Embers, 1928) continued the cycle with a story about a poor young
man, working in a sugar refinery, who uncovers
a sabotage plot and gets to marry the boss's
daughter. This time Mauro had the services of
a first-class cinematographer, Edgar Brasil, and
the result, though coolly received by the commercial press, was eulogized by more serious

critics like Octávio Gabus Mendes, who called it (in *Cinearte*) "the best Brazilian film yet." More recently, Georges Sadoul wrote that "the plot is ordinary and dull but the direction is often superb," showing "a remarkable ability to use details in close-up and create a sense of 'filmic space.' There is also a lyrical use of the drama of natural sets, such as the love scene in a large tropical forest involving a snake." The film actually achieved distribution by Universal, which, however, handled it so half-heartedly that this relatively expensive production (36,000 cruzeiros) was a financial failure.

Impressed by Walter Ruttmann's poetic documentary *Berlin,* Mauro emulated it in *Cataguases* (1929), a twelve-minute study of his hometown, photographed and edited by himself and financed by local businessmen. Mauro went on to make the last film in his Cataguases cycle, *Sangue Mineiro (Blood of Minas,* 1930), again photographed by Edgar Brasil, and made by Phebo at a cost of 48,000 cruzeiros. In fact, only part of the film was shot in Cataguases, some sequences being made in Belo Horizonte and others in Rio. For the first time, Mauro was working with a real star, Carmen Santos, whom he had met through Ademar Gonzaga (who himself took a small part in the picture). However, once again a Mauro film suffered at the hands of its distributor (Urânia), and Phebo Brasil Filme went out of business.

With the advent of sound, a wave of optimism swept the Brazilian film industry. It was supposed that Hollywood movies, incomprehensible to native audiences on account of the language barrier, would be purged from Brazilian screens. In the grip of this plausible fantasy, Ademar Gonzaga established his Cinédia Studios in Rio and invited Mauro to direct his silent first production, *Lábios sem Beijos (Lips Without Kisses,* 1930). Some critics regard this as a sterile imitation of Hollywood comedy—a decline from the integrity and spontaneity of the Cataguases cycle. Others maintain that Mauro benefited from his access to professional technicians and actors, and praise the film for a bittersweet subtlety and intelligence reminiscent of René Clair. Carlos Ortiz calls it "a milestone in Brazilian cinema in the field of comedy."

Mauro's second film for Cinédia is generally regarded as his masterpiece. This was *Ganga Bruta* (1933), sometimes translated as *Rough Diamond,* though *Brutal Caress* would seem more literal. Produced by Gonzaga, it was directed by Mauro from a script by Octávio Gabus Mendes and photographed by Afrodísio de Castro and Mauro. The score by Radamés Gnatelli, sound effects, and a word or two of dialogue were synchronized and recorded on discs by the Vitaphone method.

Discovering on his wedding night that his wife is not a virgin, Marcos kills her. He is absolved by an understanding judiciary and goes off to Guarahiba to build a factory while rebuilding his life. There he inspires the devotion of Sonia, adoptive sister of his assistant Decio, and gradually, in spite of his obsessive immersion in work, he comes to return her love. Mad with jealousy, Decio rapes Sonia and attacks Marcos, but Marcos wins the fight, Decio dies, and Marcos and Sonia live happily ever after.

"Despite its silly and conventional plot," wrote Georges Sadoul, "this is Humberto Mauro's best film and a landmark in the history of Brazilian cinema. . . . Excellent sequences: the wedding in a luxurious villa like El's in Buñuel's film; the depiction of a large factory under construction; the lovemaking in a park; the final battle. The editing is very forceful, using industrial elements as erotic symbols—a penchant that earned Mauro the name of 'The Freud of Cascadura' (a suburb of Rio)." Glauber Rocha, the prophet of Brazilian Cinema Novo in the 1960s, wrote that "the riches of *Ganga Bruta* are unlimited," its editing "suggesting today a relationship with the syncopated rhythms of a Godard or the speculative rhythm of a Resnais."

Mauro's first full talkie, *A Voz do Carnaval (The Voice of Carnival,* 1933), was also his last film for Cinédia. This was a much slighter picture than *Ganga Bruta,* an early *chanchada* (musical) featuring the "Brazilian Bombshell," Carmen Miranda. Meanwhile, the actress and producer Carmen Santos, who had starred in *Sangue Mineiro,* had left Gonzaga to establish her own production company, Brasil Vita Filme. In 1934 Mauro joined her as technical director, beginning with three short documentaries photographed and edited by him and produced by Santos, all now unfortunately lost.

An even greater loss was *Favela dos Meus Amores (Favela of My Loves,* 1934), all prints of which are believed to have been destroyed by fire. Carmen Santos produced and starred, and Mauro was director, cameraman, editor, and even sound engineer and electrician on this film, evidently a labor of love. His earlier pictures had dealt mostly with the middle and upper classes, but for this he went into the *favelas*—shanty towns—on the hills around Rio to record the life and the songs of the poor: "I simply grabbed life in the *favelas* as it was. I documented it."

According to Paulo Perdigão in his article about Mauro in *Filme Cultura* (January–February 1967), the script by Henrique Pongetti "represented the style of popular narrative in terms of the dramatic fable." The cast included the ordinary people of the favelas as well as professional actors, and for the first time here Mauro achieved a creative integration of music and images. The result is regarded by Perdigão both as an important step towards the development of a truly Brazilian cinema and as a precursor of neorealism. Others have found it particularly reminiscent of early De Sica (though Mauro commented: "What is neorealism? Isn't it simply realism?"). *Cidade Mulher (City Woman,* 1934), also combining the talents of Santos, Mauro, and Pongetti, has been seen as a pale imitation of *Favela dos Meus Amores.* It marked the end of the most fruitful phase of Mauro's career as a director of features.

In 1936 the director became resident filmmaker at the Instituto Nacional de Cinema Educativo (National Institute of Educational Cinema), a newly formed branch of Brazil's Department of Education. There he spent the remainder of his career, over a period of thirty years turning out more than two hundred and thirty documentaries. At first he was his own cinematographer and editor, but increasingly often he surrendered these roles, first to Manoel P. Ribeiro, then to his own sons, José Almeida and Luis.

Perdigão's article in *Filme Cultura* includes a complete and detailed filmography of Mauro's work up to 1967, showing the immense range of subjects tackled in his INCE documentaries, which vary in length from two to forty-two minutes. There are instructional films on the use of tools and machines, on the preparation of vaccines, on surgical technique; there are substantial documentaries about historical and literary figures, about astronomy and geography, botany and zoology, about Brazilian industries and institutions. National events and celebrations are covered as well, including ballets, folk dances, and concerts of classical and of folk music (as in the notable series called *Brasilianas,* begun in 1945).

In spite of this immense output of documentaries, providing a great panorama of thirty years of Brazilian life, Mauro did not entirely abandon the feature film. Somewhere between feature and historical reconstruction was the full-length *Descobrimento do Brasil (The Discovery of Brazil,* 1937), about the voyage of Pedro Álvares Cabral to claim Brazil for Portugal in 1500. The score by Heitor Villa-Lobos was probably the most notable element in this film, commissioned by the Instituto do Cacau of Bahia.

In 1940 came *Argila (Clay),* a Brasil Vita film scripted and directed by Mauro, who also collaborated with Manoel P. Ribeiro on the photography. This was another of the several Mauro films scored by Villa-Lobos. Carmen Santos produced and starred as a sophisticated city woman who falls in love with a potter in the interior and "renews" the ceramic arts of the Indians. This film was praised by Georges Sadoul for "a refined visual sense of atmosphere and the countryside."

O Segrêdo das Asas (The Secret of Wings, 1944) was a medium-length (45 minutes) feature based on a story by Maria Eugênia Celso. And Mauro made his last feature in 1952, *O Canto da Saudade (The Song of Yearning).* The director had bought an estate, Rancho Alegre, in his birthplace, Volta Grande, and the film was shot there by his son, José Almeida Mauro. It was scripted and produced by Mauro, who also provided his own score and acted in the picture. A thoroughly authentic portrait of life in the Brazilian interior, it combined comedy and sadness in a characteristically Brazilian way that nevertheless reminded critics of both René Clair and Vittorio De Sica.

And indeed, as Richard Peña has pointed out, it was "by concentrating on mostly regional ways of life and themes" that Mauro "created the single body of film work [in Brazil] of any universal significance before the explosion of Cinema Novo in the early 1960s." His importance was fully recognized by the creators of Cinema Novo, Glauber Rocha describing him as Brazil's first auteur and "a forefather in the search for Brazil's particular language."

For Richard Peña, Mauro was "one of the greatest of all Latin American filmmakers—a fascinating, deeply original talent whose best work exhibits a lyrical integration of characters and environment reminiscent of Dovzhenko." Georges Sadoul agreed, referring to Mauro's "profoundly cinematic vision, ingenuous but not naive," and describing him as "a great filmmaker who will inevitably one day receive the international reputation he deserves."

Humberto Mauro died at home in Volta Grande at the age of eighty-six. He was survived by his wife, six sons and daughters, seventeen grandsons, and nine great-grandsons. "Cinema here in Brazil will have to emerge from our Brazilian milieu," he wrote in 1977. "If American cinema already accustomed us to the luxuriousness and the variety of its productions, it has not yet robbed us of our natural enthusiasm for the faithful representation of everything we are or that we wish to be."

FILMS: Valadião, o Cratera (Valadião, the Disaster), 1925 (amateur short feature); Na Primavera da Vida (In the Springtime of Life), 1926; Tesouro Perdido (Lost Treasure), 1927; Brasa Dormida (Dead Embers),

1928; Cataguases, 1929 (documentary), 1929; Sangue Mineiro (Blood of Minas), 1930; Lábios sem Beijos (Lips Without Kisses, 1930); Ganga Bruta (Rough Diamond), 1933; A Voz do Carnaval (The Voice of Carnival), 1933; Favela dos Meus Amores (Favela of My Loves), 1934; Cidade Mulher (City Woman), 1934; Descobrimento do Brasil (The Discovery of Brazil), 1937; Argila (Clay), 1940; O Segrêdo das Asas (The Secret of Wings), 1944; O Canto da Saudade (The Song of Yearning), 1952; *and* approximately 230 documentaries for the Instituto Nacional de Cinema Educativo.

ABOUT: Andrade, R. and others Il cinema Brasiliano, 1961; Gomes, P. E. S. Humberto Mauro: Cataguases, Cinearte, 1974 (in Portuguese); Hennebelle, G. and Gumúcio Dagron, A. Les Cinémas de l'Amérique Latine, 1981; Johnson, R. and Stam, R. Brazilian Cinema, 1982; Viany, A. Humberto Mauro: sua vida, sua arte, sua trajetoria no cinema, 1978 (in Portuguese). *Periodicals*—Celuloide June 1966, January 1984; Contracampo August–September 1982; Filme Cultura January–February 1967.

LEO McCAREY

McCAREY, (THOMAS) LEO (October 3, 1898–July 5, 1969), American director, scenarist, and producer, was born in Los Angeles, California, the son of Thomas J. McCarey and the former Leona Mistrot, who was of Pyrenean-French descent. His Irish father, "Uncle Tom" McCarey, was the leading boxing and sports promoter on the Pacific coast, staging bouts for such heroes as Jim Jeffries, Jess Willard, and Jack Johnson; he was also an immensely popular man of huge personality and charm. Thomas Leo McCarey relinquished his first name to avoid confusion with his father. His younger brother Ray (1904–1948) followed him into the film industry, among other things directing comedy shorts with Laurel and Hardy, Our Gang, and The Three Stooges in the early 1930s.

"I was a problem child," Leo McCarey told an interviewer, "and problem children do the seemingly insane because they are trying to find out how to fit into the scheme of things." He attended Los Angeles High School, where his friends included the future directors Tay Garnett and David Butler, and where he began a brief career as an amateur middleweight boxer. This distressed his parents, who had no wish to see their firstborn caught up in a trade they knew only too well, and at their urging McCarey enrolled at the University of Southern California's law school.

McCarey was riding in a USC elevator one day when the cable snapped and the car fell four floors down the shaft. He escaped with a broken leg and then collected $5,000 in damages, which he invested in a copper mine. It failed, and McCarey, graduating, had no choice but to go to work, first with Rufus Thayer's law firm in San Francisco, then in his own practice in Los Angeles.

"I was a very poor lawyer," McCarey told Peter Bogdanovich (*Esquire* February 1972). "In the first place, I started out very young, so they mistook me for the office boy." Things soon "got so bad that I used to beat the office boy in the morning to get some papers to serve. You got ten cents a mile for serving papers. And I made more money that way than I did trying to practice law. Another discouraging factor in my legal career is that I lost every case. One time an irate client literally chased me out of the courtroom, and as I was running down the street, a friend of mine saw me and yelled, 'What are you doing, Leo? And I yelled back, 'Practicing law!' After about three blocks, I lost the client, but I kept running out to Hollywood."

In fact, McCarey tried vaudeville before he tried Hollywood, writing sketches and songs with his friend Chuck Reisner (e.g., "When the Eagle Flaps His Wings and Calls Upon the Kaiser"). He turned to the movies when these efforts went unrewarded, but failed in his attempts to find film work either as an actor or as a gag writer.

McCarey's first break came when his schoolfriend David Butler introduced him to the director Tod Browning at Universal. He was taken on (or so he claimed) as a "script girl," working his way up to assistant director on Browning's *Bonnie, Bonnie Lassie* (1919), with David Butler and Mary MacLaren, and *The Virgin of Stamboul* (1920), with Priscilla Dean and Wallace Beery. In July 1920 MaCarey married his high school sweetheart Stella Martin.

Tod Browning let McCarey direct Lon Chaney in one sequence in *Outside the Law* (1921) and then helped him to land his first directorial assignment on a Universal five-reeler called *Society Secrets* (1921), a satire about a finishing school starring Eva Novak and George Verrell, photographed by Browning's regular cameraman William Fildew. This appears to be a lost film, which may be just as well—Universal, at any rate, were sufficiently dissatisfied with it to fire McCarey altogether.

McCarey joined the Hal Roach Studios in 1923 as a gag writer and director. He wrote for the Our Gang series and was teamed as a writer-director with the comedian Charley Chase on dozens of two-reel comedies, such as *Publicity Pays* (1924), *Why Husbands Go Mad* (1924), *Bungalow Boobs* (1924), *All Wet* (1924), *What Price Goofy?* (1925), and *Mighty Like a Moose* (1926). Leonard Maltin called *Mighty Like a Moose* "a superb comedy, which deftly blends sophistication and sight gags and depends as much on *acting* and *personality* to bring it off as any other element. This is where Chase stood out from the crowd of second-echelon comics." When Chase died in 1940, McCarey said: "He was a great man, had a keen sense of comedy values and we were together in fifty pictures at Hal Roach Studios. I received credit as director, but it was really Charley Chase who did most of the directing. Whatever success I have had or may have I owe to his help because he taught me all I know."

In 1926, Roach promoted McCarey to vice-president and supervisor of all the studio's two-reel comedies. McCarey supervised three hundred shorts, including the Charley Chase series, a short-lived series starring Mabel Normand, and the Hal Roach Comedy All Stars. In a *Cahiers du Cinéma in English* interview (January 1967), McCarey said that as supervisor he had "the function of being responsible for practically everything in the film: writing the story, cutting it, stringing the gags together, coordinating everything, screening the rushes, working on the editing, sending out the prints, working on the second editing when the preview reactions weren't good enough and even, from time to time, shooting sequences over again."

McCarey is said to have been responsible, during his reign as Roach's supervisor, for assembling one of the greatest of all comedy teams, Laurel and Hardy. They had coincidentally appeared together in a film called *Lucky Dog* (1917), but it was apparently McCarey who saw the possibilities of this juxtaposition of opposites. He provided the stories, selected the directors, and supervised over thirty Laurel and Hardy shorts, which were produced at a rate of one ev-

ery three weeks and usually photographed by the future director George Stevens.

Three of Laurel and Hardy's best two-reelers were directed by McCarey himself: *We Faw Down* (1928); *Liberty* (1929), featuring the young Jean Harlow; and *Wrong Again* (1929). Discussing *Wrong Again* in Richard Roud's *Cinema*, Robin Wood writes that "the action reaches the point where Laurel and Hardy, delivering a racehorse called Blue Boy to the owner of a missing painting called Blue Boy, are told by the (off-screen) owner to 'put it on the piano.' Most directors would have been content to stop there. Not McCarey: the profoundly satisfying effect of the short depends on the visible evidence of a real racehorse on a real (and collapsing) grand piano." In his *Cahiers* interview, McCarey said of this collaboration: "This work represented a great deal to me; nothing could have replaced such an experience. . . . it caused me a lot of pain to leave Laurel and Hardy."

He did so because he knew that he was ready to direct features, resigning from the Roach Studios in 1929 to free-lance. For Pathé, he directed and co-wrote a collegiate comedy, *The Sophomore* (1929), with Eddie Quillan, derided by the New York *Times* for its "low order of humor" and "feeble production," and the musical comedy *Red Hot Rhythm* (1929), with Alan Hale, dismissed by McCarey himself as "one of the worst films I ever made."

Moving on to Paramount, he produced and directed *Let's Go Native* (1930), another musical comedy, reminiscent of J. M. Barrie's *The Admirable Crichton*, which has Jeanette MacDonald stranded on a tropical island where Jack Oakie, a sailor from Brooklyn, has established himself as ruler. George Marion Jr. and Percy Heath scripted, and there were some pleasant songs by Marion and Richard Whiting in this "fast-moving, wisecracking comedy." It was McCarey's first successful feature but after it, having clashed with Paramount executive B. P. Schulberg, he left that studio and moved on to Fox, where he directed two pictures.

Wild Company (1930) was McCarey's first attempt at drama—a story of conflict between father (H. B. Warner) and son (Frank Albertson). It was not successful, and Jean-Pierre Coursodon, in his *American Film Directors, Volume I*, called it "a dreary indictment of parental permissiveness filmed in static long takes and clumsily edited"; McCarey himself thought it "mediocre."

Part-Time Wife (1930) was more to his liking—a domestic comedy in which a wife (Leila Hyams) is so addicted to golf that the husband

(Edmund Lowe) has to take it up in order to save the marriage. The movie was adapted from a *Saturday Evening Post* story called "The Shepper-Newfounder." When S. L. Rothafel screened it at his famous Roxy Theatre in New York, he restored the original title and took out ads proclaiming it "one of the greatest films ever shown at my theatre." The campaign generated strong business, and Fox circulated subsequent prints of the picture as *The Shepper-Newfounder.*

This success brought McCarey the prestigious job of directing Gloria Swanson in *Indiscreet* (1931), produced by Joseph Schenck for United Artists. Originally intended as a full-scale musical, the film was shorn of all but two of its songs at the last moment, and McCarey was reportedly forced to rewrite the script only ten days before production began. The result was an uneven comedy-drama, redeemed if at all only by the Ray June–Gregg Toland camerawork, though the New York *Times* allowed that McCarey "reveals a certain aptitude for handling farcical incident."

He had better luck with his next assignment, *The Kid From Spain* (1932), a Sam Goldwyn production also released by United Artists. Goldwyn provided McCarey with a characteristically well-mounted production and his popular comedy star Eddie Cantor, playing an American on the run in Mexico, masquerading as a famous bullfighter. It was scripted by the Marx Brothers' scenarists Bert Kalmar and Harry Ruby, who also collaborated with Harry Akst on the songs. Busby Berkeley staged the dance sequences featuring the Goldwyn Girls (Betty Grable and Paulette Goddard among them). The result, hailed as "an uproarious farce," was highly successful at the box office and is often claimed as Eddie Cantor's best picture, though some modern critics find both Cantor and the script dismally unfunny.

Courted by several studios, McCarey decided on a return to Paramount, where Emanuel Cohen had replaced B. P. Schulberg as production chief and had offered him a lucrative contract. McCarey was anxious to avoid being typed as a comedy director, but ironically his first assignment at Paramount was the Marx Brothers' *Duck Soup* (1933), originally called *Cracked Ice.* According to McCarey, he initially refused this assignment, even though the Marx Brothers demanded him as their director. They then broke their own contract in protest, and McCarey signed with Paramount, "believing myself secure. . . . Soon, the Marx Brothers were reconciled with the company . . . and I found myself in the process of directing the Marx Brothers.

The most surprising thing about this film was that I succeeded in not going crazy, for I really did not want to work with them: they were completely mad. It was nearly impossible to get all four of them together at the same time."

Kalmar and Ruby's screenplay, with additional dialogue by Arthur Sheekman and Nat Perrin, was set in the mythical land of Freedonia (or America), where the infinitely wealthy Mrs. Teasdale (Margaret Dumont, who never learned) hires Rufus T. Firefly (Groucho) as president, hoping that he will save her country, which is threatened by the neighboring state of Sylvania. Firefly wreaks havoc at cabinet meetings, appoints an enemy agent (Chico) as Secretary of War, and leads Freedonia into war over a teaparty tiff with the Sylvanian envoy (Louis Calhern).

There has to be a war, anyway, because Firefly has paid a month's rent on the battlefield. Assuming a variety of picturesque military costumes from assorted historical periods, he shoots at his own men, sends generals out to buy trenches, and recommends bicarbonate of soda for a gas attack. When Harpo is dispatched for reinforcements, Groucho boosts his morale by telling him that "while you're out there risking life and limb through shot and shell, we'll be in here thinking what a sap you are." In *Duck Soup,* as Allan Eyles wrote, "war has become an absurd farce: without meaning, without logic." So have politics, diplomacy, espionage, and patriotism. When Mrs. Teasdale rises to sing a victory anthem at the end, the Brothers pelt her with fruit.

Many critics regard *Duck Soup* as the best of the Marx Brothers' films, "the most inventive and the most disciplined." It is hard to judge how much of the credit is due to McCarey, but he is said to have eliminated two of the elements that weaken most of the Brothers' movies—musical interludes with Harpo on the harp and Chico on the piano, and a romantic subplot (here to have involved Zeppo and Raquel Torres). He is also credited with developing the marvelously funny and prolonged scene in which Harpo and Chico break into Mrs. Teasdale's house at night, the battle between peanut vendor Harpo and lemonade vendor Edgar Kennedy, and the extended variation on the old mirror routine. If all these claims are correct, his contribution to the film's success was definitive. And despite his disdain for the project, it remains his most frequently revived picture.

Six of a Kind (1934), originally called "Republicans and Sinners," was a showcase for Paramount's comedy stars. George Burns and Gracie Allen, Charlie Ruggles and Mary Boland, are two married couples on a cross-country auto tour with an enormous Great Dane. In Nuggetville, Nevada, as if they did not have problems enough, they encounter W. C. Fields as a crooked and drunken sheriff, and his indomitable foil Alison Skipworth. "With no less than three comic couples vying for the spotlight," wrote Jean-Pierre Coursodon, "McCarey was confronted with an embarrassment of riches, but . . . managed to bring some degree of unity to the proceedings" in this "minor, uneven" but "likable" comedy.

After W. C. Fields, Mae West. In *Belle of the Nineties* (1934), her own script, she plays a music hall diva in love with a boxer (Roger Pryor) but separated from him by the machinations of his manager. Thanks to the newly established Production Code, West was denied her usual level of creative lewdness, and McCarey apparently enjoyed very little about the film apart from the chance to work with Duke Ellington and his orchestra.

Much more to his taste was *Ruggles of Red Gap* (1935), Paramount's sound remake of a story previously filmed in 1918 and again (by James Cruze) in 1923, and drawn from a novel and play by Harry Leon Wilson. Marmaduke Ruggles (Charles Laughton) is an English gentleman's gentleman of ineffable snobbery, dedicated to servitude. His fatuous employer Lord Burnstead (Roland Young) loses him in a poker game to Egbert Floud (Charlie Ruggles), a rowdy though good-hearted Western millionaire, and his social-climbing wife Effie (Mary Boland).

Translated to Red Gap, Washington, Ruggles is at first appalled to find himself in the service of barbarians, but comes to learn the meaning of equality and freedom; he goes into business as a restaurateur, with ZaSu Pitts as his prospective partner. McCarey is said to have improvised the marvelous scene in which the saloon owner Nell Kenna (Leila Hyams) teaches Lord Burnstead to play "Pretty Baby" on the drums, outraging the snobbish elite of Red Gap. He was also responsible for the even better scene where Laughton, with quiet but irresistibly moving eloquence, recites from memory Lincoln's Gettysburg Address to an audience of barflies ignorant of their own heritage.

Thoroughly at home with this mixture of good-humored clowning and unstrident patriotism, McCarey made what is arguably his best comedy and "a classic populist fairy tale" (Jeffrey Richards). The often acerbic British reviewer C. A. Lejeune had "no hesitation in saying that *Ruggles of Red Gap* is one of the most moving pictures—honestly, simply moving, without

a trace of catchpenny sentiment—that I have ever seen on a screen." More recently, Jean-Pierre Coursodon wrote that "the film is typical of McCarey in its bringing together of thoroughly heterogeneous types, yet it is predicated upon a firm belief in a utopian melting pot within which the ideological and psychological worlds of such alien and potentially antagonistic characters can be reconciled. Everybody in the story eventually learns something, becomes more tolerant and more enlightened."

McCarey, by now something of a specialist in directing vehicles for famous comics, next tackled Harold Lloyd in *The Milky Way* (1936), based on the play by Lynn Root and Harry Cork. Lloyd plays a timid Brooklyn milkman, adept at ducking, who in this way acquires an undeserved reputation as a fighter and ends up competing for the middleweight championship of the world against William Gargan. Adolphe Menjou plays a gum-chewing and vociferous fight promoter—a breed McCarey knew well—and Verree Teasdale is a wisecracking blonde in the Jean Harlow mold.

"Harold Lloyd may be the 'starred' attraction in *The Milky Way*," wrote a reviewer in the Boston *Transcript*, "but he should be prepared to share the glory of its inevitable popularity with every principal member of his supporting cast and with the scenarists and director who helped so substantially in its creation. For this picture is a gilt-edged cinematic bond with a guaranteed income." *Variety* went so far as to call it "one of the funniest comedies since the advent of the talkies," and later critics have pointed out that the comedy starts slowly and accelerates to a final burst of sustained insanity—a technique traced back to McCarey's training on two-reel comedies at the Roach Studios. The film was remade by Norman Z. McLeod in 1946 as *The Kid From Brooklyn*, with Danny Kaye.

Promoting *The Milky Way*, McCarey drank some contaminated milk and was hospitalized for months with Malta fever. Returning to Paramount in March 1936, he dismayed the front office by his insistence on filming Josephine Lawrence's novel *The Years Are So Long*. A harrowing story about a family in which the five grown children neglect and humiliate their aging parents, it was rightly considered a poor box-office project. McCarey was adamant, however, offering to go off salary and take a flat rate for his services as both director and producer. Paramount reluctantly gave in and let him make the picture, adapted by Viña Delmar as *Make Way for Tomorrow* (1937).

Victor Moore and Beulah Bondi gave the performances of a lifetime as the old retired couple who lose their home to a bank. None of their children can (or will) take them both in, and soon Lucy is placed in an old people's home, while Bark is sent off to California for his health. Briefly reunited, they spend their last afternoon together in the hotel where they had honeymooned fifty years earlier—"a perfect, magical moment during which time is suspended, the past recaptured, the present sorrow annihilated . . . a privileged cinematic experience" (Jean-Pierre Coursodon). Then they separate, talking of a possible future in California, but knowing that they will most probably never meet again.

What could have been the grossest sentimentality is constantly undercut by saving humor, as when Bark, in bed with a bad cold, refuses to say "ninety-nine" for the young doctor and eventually bites him. Such *Lear*-like touches, showing the old couple to be ignobly human, make the tragedy seem unbearably real, forcing the viewer to consider how well he or she might behave in the same circumstances as the children.

Make Way for Tomorrow is McCarey's most personal picture. He appears in it in three bit parts, and often spoke of it as his favorite among his films. "If I really have talent," he said in his *Cahiers* interview, "this is where it appears." Jeffrey Richards, in *Visions of Yesterday,* called it an "unsung masterpiece, one of the enduring classics of personal filmmaking to come out of Hollywood." And for Charles Silver it is "a film of so devastating an emotional impact, of such indescribable inner beauty, as to make a critic throw his typewriter out of the window in frustration over his inability to capture in mere words the feelings McCarey's sensibility evokes. Only the director's sometimes awkward visual style prevents it from ranking among the cinema's greatest masterpieces." Although contemporary critics also praised the film, it flopped at the box office, whereupon Paramount fired its director.

Frank Capra had just left Columbia, and Harry Cohn was intent on proving that he could get along without him. He hired McCarey to direct and produce the third screen version of Arthur Richman's 1922 stage comedy *The Awful Truth,* to star Cary Grant, Irene Dunne, and Ralph Bellamy. McCarey was not impressed by the material, but, needing the money, he set to work and, with Viña Delmar as his scenarist, transformed it into one of the best screwball comedies. In an interview with Frank Nugent, he said "it wasn't until we got on the set that the story began to show itself. One character took over. After ten days we had to suspend production and begin rewriting. We still didn't have a script when we re-

sumed. We worked nights on scenes to be shot the next day. You can't tell about a story until you begin shooting, and even then you get surprises."

In fact, it seems that a good deal of the picture (which in the end bore little resemblance to Richman's play) was actually improvised on the set, including the excellent scene in which Dunne and Bellamy perform "Home on the Range." This was reportedly a response to McCarey's discovery that Bellamy could not sing, and Dunne was an indifferent pianist. Robin Wood places McCarey with Renoir and Howard Hawks as an "actor-centered director"—one for whom actors are not puppets but "responsive human beings, with particular gifts, particular limitations, particular reactions, out of which the film develops: that is the foundation of their 'humanism.'"

As the film opens, Jerry Warriner (Grant) is just returning from "a trip to Florida" (though he tells a friend that he had actually stayed in New York and played poker). His wife Lucy (Dunne) gets home even later, accompanied by her handsome French singing teacher, and attributes her all-night absence to a car breakdown. Mutually mistrustful, they begin divorce proceedings. Lucy takes up with a wonderfully boring Oklahoma millionaire (Bellamy), Jerry with a dumb Southern belle, but gradually both come to recognize how much they value the marriage they have so nearly scuttled.

Favorably compared by contemporary reviewers with Capra's *It Happened One Night,* the picture also reminded critics of W. S. Van Dyke's *The Thin Man* in its treatment of "the *idea* of marriage as the subject of an affectionate comedy." Otis Ferguson called it "a true director's triumph" and "thorough comedy, a whole pattern that is neither actor's vehicle nor technician's holiday. . . . The dialogue is good, clever, or uproarious, but dialogue fades so quickly in the air, and here there is the necessary visual play to complement it." And Basil Wright said that "McCarey deals with his actors with more than skill, he gets inside them as persons, as well as the parts they have to play. . . . The people move and speak, not according to the rules of acting or even of directing, but because there is, out of all the hundreds of possible courses of speech or action, not any other which these particular people could *in nature* follow."

The Awful Truth (1937) was one of the year's top grossers and brought McCarey his first Oscar for direction, along with nominations in five other categories (including best picture). After that, he was able to name his price and project. Cohn tried to lure him to Columbia with *You Can't*

Take It With You, and all of the major studios bid for his services, including an embarrassed Paramount. McCarey chose a lucrative contract with RKO Radio that included profit participation and, riding on a wave of success, was even able to sell an ad-libbed storyline to Sam Goldwyn for $50,000: *The Cowboy and the Lady* (1938), with Gary Cooper and Merle Oberon, directed by H. C. Potter.

His first RKO production was *Love Affair* (1939), which had a curious history. Irene Dunne and Charles Boyer were to star under McCarey's direction in a film called *Love Match,* about an illicit (albeit tragic) love affair between a married woman and a French diplomat in the 1850s. The French Embassy, facing a war, refused to allow this to be made, for fear it might damage relations with the United States. McCarey dragged his friend Delmer Daves out of bed at 6 a.m. and demanded a new story for his two stars. Since the script was nowhere near complete when the film went into production, it was shot in continuity and involved at least as much overnight writing and on-set improvisation as *The Awful Truth.*

What emerged was *Love Affair,* a bittersweet story about an irresponsible playboy (Boyer) and a nightclub singer (Dunne) who fall in love on an ocean liner. Beginning as something close to screwball comedy, the picture modulates into a wistful interlude in the South of France, then plunges into melodrama when Dunne, hurrying to a reunion with Boyer at the top of the Empire State Building, is hit by a car and paralyzed from the waist down. Boyer finally tracks her down and in a long, beautifully managed scene, with him pacing bewildered around her chaise longue, she conceals her condition, spurning him bravely until he discovers the truth and convinces her that happiness can be theirs nevertheless.

Frank Nugent wrote that McCarey "has taken a story which might have been an airy comedy or a sentimental romance and has blended its components so skillfully that it has become both and neither—a film as unclassifiable as life itself and best described perhaps as leaving a delightful afterglow." It won a sheaf of Oscar nominations, and brought RKO a much-needed box-office success.

McCarey next started work, with Sam and Bella Spewack, on "Woman Overboard," a script originally intended for Helen Hayes and Leslie Howard. This was in pre-production when, in late 1939, on their way home from McCarey's vacation retreat at Lake Arrowhead, he and Gene Fowler were seriously injured in an automobile accident. "Woman Overboard" became

My Favorite Wife (1940), starring Irene Dunne, Cary Grant, and Randolph Scott; it was directed by Garson Kanin, with McCarey producing from a wheelchair. Called "one of the last and best screwball comedies," it collected three Academy Award nominations.

In July 1940, McCarey signed a contract with Howard Hughes to direct an Adela Rogers St. John story called *Hollywood Legend.* He went to work on the script with Morrie Ryskind but found that Hughes was absolutely impossible to contact. It was not until March 1942 that the California courts freed McCarey from this abortive contract. He returned to RKO with two new projects, a medical comedy called "The Bedside Manner," which went unproduced, and a Sheridan Gibney script, "International Honeymoon," eventually filmed as *Once Upon a Honeymoon* (1942).

Opening in the late 1930s, it has Cary Grant as an American newspaperman pursuing former showgirl Ginger Rogers around Europe (in spite of her marriage to a German aristocrat). This comedy then turns into an anti-Fascist tract. The fun-loving Rogers is gradually brought to recognize the evil of Nazism, until in the end she pushes her fifth-columnist husband overboard on their way to America. One of the strangest of McCarey's hybrids, the film had an uneasy reception. Philip Hartung wrote that "the underlying note of tragedy . . . makes the lighthearted humor seem too irresponsible."

The greatest box-office success of McCarey's career followed in *Going My Way* (1944), made for Paramount and scripted by Frank Butler and Frank Cavett from the director's original story. It centers on the conflict between an old-fashioned and lovably cantankerous parish priest, Father Fitzgibbon (Barry Fitzgerald), and his progressive young curate, Father O'Malley (Bing Crosby), who smokes a pipe, plays baseball, and writes songs.

This villified newcomer turns a street gang into a boys' choir, redeems a runaway girl by crooning "The Day After Forever" at her, and pays off the church's mortgage by selling his songs. There is a setback when the church burns down, but this also turns out to be a blessing in disguise. The grasping landlord (Gene Lockhart), who has always wanted the site for a parking lot, sees the light and agrees to a new mortgage, everyone rallies round to raise funds, and, after a happy Christmas Eve finale wherein old Fitzgibbon is reunited with his ancient Irish mother, Father O'Malley goes his way through the softly falling snow.

Jean-Pierre Coursodon maintains that most of McCarey's plots "revolve around a denial—

either voluntary or imposed by circumstances—
of . . . sexual and/or emotional fulfillment."
He thinks "it was almost inevitable . . . that
McCarey should some day hit upon the ideal
variation upon this favorite theme by using as a
hero a man pledged to celibacy." Jeffrey Richards, writing in *Visions of Yesterday*, sees the
film as marking McCarey's relinquishment of
the populism of such pictures as *Ruggles of Red
Gap* and *Make Way for Tomorrow*, "and a turning towards the older teachings of the Catholic
Church."

Though some reviewers gagged on the sentimentality of *Going My Way*, and the "almost
nauseating" celebration of motherhood in the finale, the public loved it. A huge financial success, it also swept the board of Academy Awards,
receiving Oscars for best picture, best actor
(Crosby), best supporting actor (Fitzgerald), best
screenplay, and best song (Johnny Burke and
James Van Heusen's "Swinging on a Star").
McCarey himself won two Oscars, for his direction and his original story.

A sequel to this blockbuster was promptly
cobbled together, *The Bells of St. Mary's* (1945),
produced and directed by McCarey for his own
newly formed Rainbow Productions, releasing
through RKO. The original story was his once
more, and virtually identical to that of *Going My
Way*. Dudley Nichols wrote the screenplay, with
uncredited contributions from McCarey's
friends Tay Garnett and James Kevin McGuinness. This time, Bing Crosby's Father O'Malley
is assigned to solve the financial problems of a
parochial school run on old-fashioned lines by a
baseball-playing nun, Sister Benedict (Ingrid
Bergman). Again there is conflict between the
two protagonists, but here there is the additional
frisson of a potential sexual attraction between
the charming priest and the beautiful nun.

David Selznick was opposed to releasing Bergman for the role, but she wanted to work with
McCarey and insisted. James Agee took exception to the star's "sex appeal" in this role, asserting that "she has and uses a lot too much to play
a Mother Superior" and comes "painfully close
to twittering her eyes in scenes with Crosby."
Richard Corliss added that the picture "chokes
on its own calculated treacle," and most found
it inferior to its predecessor, apart from a genuinely moving Nativity play performed (and
scripted) by kindergartners. This did not prevent
it from garnering Oscar nominations in most
major categories, though it actually received
only one Academy Award, for Stephen Dunn's
sound. An American cardinal disloyally declared
that *Going My Way* and *The Bells of St. Mary's*
did more for Catholicism than a dozen bishops

could have done in a year. They did a lot for
McCarey, too; he had profit participation in
both films and in 1945 was listed as the highest
paid employee in the United States, with an income in 1944 of over $1 million.

After that, he presumably need never have
worked again, but, according to Peter Bogdanovich, the decline in McCarey's output after
1939 was primarily due to an increasing addiction to drink and drugs, aggravated perhaps by
the effects of his almost fatal auto accident. At
any rate, his next picture did not appear until
1948. This was *Good Sam*, a Rainbow-RKO release from a story by McCarey and James
Klorer, scripted by Ken Englund.

Gary Cooper starred in this domestic comedy
about a man whose obsessive benevolence almost
destroys his marriage (to Ann Sheridan). His tendency to lend their car to people who smash it
up and their money to people who never return
it, while filling their house with assorted spong-
ers who won't leave, seems to her the behavior
of "a double-crossing, two-faced, sneaking
Samaritan." In the end, Sam comes to see that
charity must begin at home.

There were the usual complaints about
McCarey's sentimentality, and doubts about his
moral values, but the movie was otherwise generally well received by reviewers, who enjoyed
its genial wit and polished performances. Audiences were for some reason less responsive.
McCarey told his *Cahiers* interviewers that "the
film had a certain success but when, after two
immense successes, you have a small one, it is
considered a failure."

By this time, McCarey had become obsessed
with the menace of Communism. He testified on
Communism in the film industry before the
House Un-American Activities Committee and
was very active in the Society for the Preservation of American Ideals. He sold Rainbow Productions to Paramount, where in 1951 he made
a picture embodying his preoccupations, *My Son
John*. McCarey produced and directed, devised
the story, and wrote the script in collaboration
with Myles Connolly and John Lee Mahin.

Helen Hayes, in her first major screen role for
many years, was teamed in *My Son John* with
Dean Jagger as the small-town parents of three
sons. Two of the boys go off to fight in Korea;
the third (Robert Walker) is a government employee in Washington. On a visit home, he confronts his parents in a series of ideological
clashes, railing against their all-American bigotry and anti-intellectualism and in favor of democratic tolerance. This persuasive and clever
young man, having won the audience to his side,
is then revealed as a Communist agent. The

film's apparent message is reversed: "plain folks" know best after all, and liberal intellectuals are Communists and traitors *manqués*. Threatening to turn him in, John's Mom persuades him to give himself up instead, but he is gunned down in the street by a carload of Commies.

The making of *My Son John* was almost halted by the death during filming of its star, Robert Walker. McCarey solved the problem with great ingenuity by shifting the emphasis in the second half of the film to the character of the FBI agent investigating John (Van Heflin), by using doubles, and (in a gruesome borrowing) by inserting a close-up of a dying Robert Walker from Hitchcock's *Strangers on a Train*. Walker had already recorded the long speech, played to his old university on graduation day, in which he confesses to the sin of intellectualism.

Most critics were enraged by this McCarthyist film, described by Robert Warshow as "an attack on Communism and an affirmation of Americanism that might legitimately alarm any thoughtful American whether liberal or conservative." Later critics have been kinder, and Coursodon believes that the movie's first half "comes close to being McCarey's best work of writing and direction." And George Morris suggests that "perhaps no other film in the history of the American cinema has been so unjustly maligned. . . . *My Son John* is not really *about* Communism at all. . . . Neither is it the simplistic, jingoistic call-to-arms for Mom, America, and apple pie that its detractors claim. On its most immediate level, it is a rousing melodrama about the deceptions parents and children practice on one another."

McCarey dissolved Rainbow Productions after *My Son John*. He directed a twenty-minute short for a Catholic organization, The Christophers, called *You Can Change the World* (1951), whose dazzling cast included Bing Crosby, Bob Hope, Loretta Young, Irene Dunne, William Holden, Ann Blyth, and Jack Benny, among others. He then invested a good deal of money in a pet project—a musical adventure about Marco Polo that was to star Mario Lanza. He bought the rights to Donn Byrne's *Messr. Marco Polo* and commissioned a score by Harold Adamson and Harry Warren, but Lanza's recurring weight problem and studio apathy quashed the project. Turning briefly to another medium, McCarey directed the debut episode of Screen Directors' Playhouse, a TV anthology series, in 1955.

An Affair to Remember (1957), made at the request of Cary Grant for 20th Century–Fox, is a remake in color and 'Scope of McCarey's own *Love Affair*, with Grant and Deborah Kerr in the Boyer-Dunne roles and Jerry Wald as producer. At Grant's insistence, the original script was followed very closely, but in the hands of Grant and Kerr a very different film emerged—lighter, funnier, and less poignant—but not less successful with critics and audience.

McCarey's last two pictures were disappointing. *Rally 'Round the Flag, Boys* (1958), adapted from the Max Schulman novel, starred Paul Newman, Joanne Woodward, and Joan Collins in a very uneven comedy about life and lust in suburbia. *Satan Never Sleeps* (1962), based on a Pearl Buck story, is a crassly anti-Communist drama set in China in 1949. William Holden uneasily plays a young priest whose initial conflict with his waspish superior (Clifton Webb) echoes the Crosby-Fitzgerald strife in *Going My Way*.

McCarey left *Satan Never Sleeps* complaining of constant interference from the Fox front office, and the last five days of shooting were completed by an assistant. He remained in retirement throughout the 1960s, and was interviewed at length by Peter Bogdanovich for the American Film Institute's Oral History Project. He was already very ill with emphysema but, Bogdanovich says, still smoking cigarillos—"a gesture of folly and defiance that seemed to me to epitomize the most enduring elements in his work."

"I like my characters to walk in clouds," McCarey once said. "I like a little bit of the fairy tale. As long as I'm there behind the camera lens, I'll let someone else photograph the ugliness of the world." On another occasion he asserted that "it's larceny to remind people how lousy things are and call it entertainment. A lot can be done using wit to get a point over without giving offense." As Jeffrey Richards pointed out in *Visions of Yesterday*, when McCarey "broke his own rule about not photographing the ugliness of the world and lectured us on the evils of Communism, the films failed to convince."

There was a striking similarity between the careers of McCarey and Frank Capra, and the two directors are often compared, usually to McCarey's disadvantage. "He had none of the narrative drive or epic sweep of Capra," wrote Jeffrey Richards. "His films were often amusing, sometimes moving, but rarely inspiring in the way that Capra's were. . . . McCarey will probably be remembered as a director of great moments rather than great movies."

It was characteristic of McCarey's approach to filmmaking that he would keep a piano on set and play it between takes while thinking up new bits and ideas. As Andrew Sarris says, "Leo McCarey represents a principle of improvisation in the history of the American film. Noted less for his rigorous direction than for his relaxed digressions, McCarey has distilled a unique blend of farce and sentimentality in his best efforts." However, George Morris considers that McCarey's work "is more misunderstood than that of any other director comparable in stature. . . . Like Renoir and Hawks, his art lies in his artlessness." And Renoir himself said that "McCarey understands people better perhaps than anyone else in Hollywood."

—J.A.G.

FILMS (Features Only): Society Secrets, 1921 (silent); The Sophomore, 1929; Red Hot Rhythm, 1929; Let's Go Native, 1930; Wild Company, 1930; Part-Time Wife (The Shepper-Newfounder), 1930; Indiscreet, 1931; The Kid from Spain, 1932; Duck Soup, 1933; Six of a Kind, 1934; Belle of the Nineties, 1934; Ruggles of Red Gap, 1935; The Milky Way, 1936; Make Way for Tomorrow, 1937; The Awful Truth, 1937; Love Affair, 1939; Once Upon a Honeymoon, 1942; Going My Way, 1944; The Bells of St. Mary's, 1945; Good Sam, 1948; My Son John, 1951; You Can Change the World, 1951 (short); An Affair to Remember, 1957; Rally 'Round the Flag, Boys, 1958; Satan Never Sleeps, 1962. *Published scripts*—Duck Soup, Simon and Schuster, 1972; Going My Way *in* Best Film Plays of 1943–44, Crown, 1945.

ABOUT: Coursodon, J.-P. American Film Directors, Volume 1, 1983; Eyles, A. The Marx Brothers, 1966; Gehring, W. Leo McCarey and the Comic Anti-Hero in American Film, 1980; Kanin, G. Hollywood, 1974; Lourcelles, J. Leo McCarey, 1972 (in French); Maltin, L. The Great Movie Comedians, 1982; Mast, G. The Comic Mind, 1979; Poague, L. Wilder and McCarey (The Hollywood Professionals,Volume 7); Richards, J. Visions of Yesterday, 1973; Roud, R. (ed.) Cinema: A Critical Dictionary, 1980; Thomson, D. A Biographical Dictionary of the Cinema, 1980. *Periodicals*—Action September–October 1969; Cahiers du Cinéma February 1965; Cahiers du Cinéma in English January 1967; Esquire May 1943, February 1972; Film Comment September–October 1973, January–February 1976; Films and Filming April 1983; Films in Review November 1979, February 1980; Focus on Film Spring 1973; Journal of Popular Film 1 1978; Liberty May 26, 1946; Variety January 1970.

*MÉLIÈS, GEORGES (Marie-Georges-Jean Méliès) (December 8, 1861–January 21, 1938), French director, producer, designer, and performer of the earliest cinema spectacles, was the third son of a successful Paris shoe manufacturer, Jean-Louis-Stanislas Méliès, and his Dutch wife, Johannah-Catherine Schuering. The family's wealth was newly acquired. Louis Méliès had come to Paris in 1843 as a journeyman shoemaker and met his future wife in the boot factory where they both worked. She was the daughter of the former bootmaker to the Dutch

GEORGES MÉLIÈS

court, who had been ruined by a fire. She helped Louis to educate himself, and before long he set up a mechanized workshop for high-quality boots on the boulevard Saint-Martin. By the time his youngest son was born, Louis had become a prosperous and propertied factory owner.

Georges Méliès grew up in the tumultuous period of the Paris Commune and the Franco-Prussian War. At the age of seven he was sent to the Lycée Michelet outside Paris for a classical education, but two years later, when the school was bombed during the war, the students were evacuated to the prestigious Lycée Louis-le-Grand in the city's Latin Quarter. In the memoirs that he composed near the end of his life, Méliès stresses the formal, literary training he received in school, in order to counter the accusation that the pioneers of the cinema were "illiterates incapable of producing anything artistic." But already his "innate tastes" favored the visual arts and the theatre. Writing about himself in the third person, he explains that "the artistic passion was too strong for him, and while he would ponder a French composition or Latin verses, his pen mechanically sketched portraits or caricatures of his professors and classmates, if not some fantasy palace or an original landscape that already had the look of a theatre set." Notebooks and textbooks covered with drawings, he recalls, brought countless punishments from teachers, but he remained undeterred. At the age of ten, he was building puppet shows and cardboard stage sets and, as a teenager, created marionettes for his nieces.

In spite of these pronounced artistic inclinations, Méliès was expected to enter the family

°mā lē āz

business like his older brothers, Henri and Gaston. After completing his *baccalauréat* in 1880, he spent a short time in the shoe factory supervising accounts, taking the opportunity to familiarize himself with the workings of the stitching machines. Three years of military service followed, and then his father sent him to London for a year to improve his English and his business skills. Installed as a clerk in the department store of a family friend, he quickly involved himself in another art form. "It was during the year in London," he writes, "that, still not understanding English well enough to follow plays, he began to frequent the Egyptian Hall directed by Maskeline, the famous English illusionist, a theatre that featured conjuring, fantasies, and great scenic illusions," with the result that he soon became a "great enthusiast for magic."

When he returned to Paris, he sought to study painting at the École des Beaux-Arts, but his father objected, declaring "that with such a profession one could die of hunger." Consigned again to the family factory, he took over supervision of the machinery while continuing to pursue his interest in magic. He attended performances at the Théâtre Robert-Houdin (founded by the renowned conjurer Jena-Eugène Robert-Houdin) and took lessons from Émile Voisin, the proprietor of a magic supply store. He soon began giving private shows to family friends and then, with Voisin's help, moved on to public performances at the Cabinet Fantastique of the Grévin Wax Museum and later the Galérie Vivienne. By this time Méliès had evaded another family plan for his future as well: marriage to the younger sister of his brothers' wives. In 1885, soon after his return from London, he married Eugénie Génin. She was Dutch, like his mother—a timid convent student who was the natural daughter of a family friend and who brought Méliès a sizeable dowry from her guardians.

When Louis Méliès retired in 1888, Georges sold his share in the family business to his two brothers and bought the Théâtre Robert-Houdin. It had been equipped by its founder with the requisite machines, lights, levers, pulleys, and trap doors for all sorts of conjuring and "marvels," including several robotic mechanical figures or "automata." The facilities were, as Méliès said, "superb," but the repertoire of illusions sadly out of date. Even after Méliès made renovations, attendance was minimal. Determined to turn the situation around, Méliès set out to create his own illusions and over the next nine years introduced some thirty new "theatrical compositions."

What set these productions apart from the streamlined illusions of Robert-Houdin was not only the infusion of drama and pageantry, clearly inspired by the Egyptian Hall tradition of John Nevil Maskelyne, but also Méliès' own penchant for comedy. In *American Spiritualistic Mediums ou Le Décapité récalcitrant* (*The Recalcitrant Decapitated Man*, 1891), for example, a loquacious Professor Barbenfouillies (literally "Tangled-Beard") babbles on about spiritualism until a conjurer lops off his head with a scimitar. After various antics involving the conjurer and his two-part victim, the professor recovers his head and instantly resumes his monologue. At about the same time (1889–1890) Méliès enjoyed a brief subsidiary career as a political cartoonist in *La Griffe* (*The Talon*), edited by his cousin Adolphe Méliès. Anagrammatically signing himself "Geo. Smile," he demonstrated his liberal republicanism in savage caricatures of the Royalist reactionary General Boulanger.

With a thought to the spectacles mounted at larger theatres like the Châtelet and the Folies Bergère, Méliès put together ambitious programs for the Robert-Houdin that included various feats of conjuring, a fairy pantomime with illusions, a display of Robert-Houdin automata during the intermission, and a magic lantern show at the end. He had inherited his chief mechanic, Eugène Calmels, when he took over the theatre; among the performers who stayed on was Jehanne D'Alcy (born Charlotte-Stéphanie Faes), the actress who became Méliès' mistress and later his second wife. With the improving fortunes of the theatre, famous conjurers were brought in, including the top-ranking Joseph Baultier de Kolta, Raynaly, and others.

Méliès' own stage appearances remained infrequent, but his involvement behind the scenes was all-encompassing: he was producer, director, author, and set and costume designer for the stage pieces; with Calmels' help he reconstructed the Robert-Houdin automata (in a workshop he set up in the Méliès shoe factory), and he put together the magic-lantern shows using his own caricatures as well as special effects for snowfalls, lightning, and the like. Above all, he brought out the best in his performers. "M. Méliès is absent," Duperrey the conjurer noted in his journal. "Every time he's absent, my tricks flop." By 1895, his prestige was such that he was elected president of the Chambre Syndicale des Artistes Illusionistes, an office he retained for forty years.

As a theatre entrepreneur, Méliès was among those attending the first public showing of the Lumière Cinématographe held on December 28, 1895 at the Grand Café. As he reports in his memoirs, he and the other guests "were left gaping, struck with amazement, surprised beyond all expression" by the series of fifty-second moving pictures that were projected onto a small screen at the front of the room. Immediately after the program Méliès offered what he considered the "enormous sum" of 10,000 francs (then about $2000) for one of the machines, but Lumière refused him, as well as M. Thomas of the Grévin Wax Museum (who tried 20,000 francs) and Lallemand of the Folies-Bergère (who was willing to pay 50,000).

In fact, the Lumière Cinématographe was one of many moving-picture devices—albeit the most technically developed—that were being introduced throughout Europe, England, and the United States. Jehanne d' Alcy apparently saw Robert W. Paul's experiments with the Animatograph while she was on tour in England, and in February 1896 Méliès traveled to London and bought an Animatograph (which was basically a pirated version of Edison's Kinetoscope) and a limited number of films that were available from Paul and the Edison Company. By the first week in April, "Kinétographe moving photographs" were advertised among the entertainments at the Théâtre Robert-Houdin.

Using Paul's projector as a model, Méliès also began working on a camera of his own, which he put together, with the help of the mechanic Lucien Korsten, from machine parts used for the automata and special effects at the theatre. Describing the "Road to Calvary" that ensued, Méliès notes in his memoirs that even though he was able to construct a camera, there was no raw film stock available in Paris. He returned to London in March hoping to buy some trial spools from Paul, but the Englishman refused, and he was forced to take an entire case of Eastman stock at a cost of 45,000 francs. Once he got back to Paris, he found that the film was unperforated and had to commission a special perforating device.

Developing and printing evolved by trial and error as well. The earliest spools of film were cut into sections, developed like still photographs, and then spliced back together. In order to avoid this tedious process, which often resulted in streaked, finger-printed negatives, Méliès began wrapping the entire spool of film around a glass bottle, which he then dipped in pails of chemicals. This process was later refined by replacing the bottles with wooden drums that could be rotated inside semicircular tanks, first by cranking and then by electricity. Printing, which was done by running the negative through the camera mechanism with a strip of raw positive film, still posed problems because the natural light fluctuated in the course of a day's shooting. In order to compensate for the irregularities of the negative, Méliès devised a system to vary the speed of the hand-cranked printer frame by frame: instructions were posted on a large placard, and the operator counted aloud as he turned the crank to the beat of a metronome.

Méliès began shooting his first films in May 1896, and by the beginning of August he was screening—and selling—"personal views" at the Théâtre Robert-Houdin. On September 2, he filed a joint patent with Korsten and his promoter Lucien Reulos for the Kinétographe Robert-Houdin, a cumbersome cast-iron camera-projector that Méliès called his "coffee grinder" or "machine gun" because of the racket that it made. As other cameras came on the market, he quickly abandoned his own version, opting first for Demeny's Chronophotographe, manufactured by Gaumount, then for the Lumière Cinématographe, which went on sale at the end of 1897, and years later, for Pathé's Kinetographe.

By the end of 1896, Méliès and Reulos were operating as the Star Film Company. Their motto, reflecting the larger spirit of the age as much as the ambitions of a budding industry, was "The World Within Reach of the Hand." In fact, the promise of such a motto was being fulfilled in its literal sense by the Lumière Company, whose operators had already been dispatched all over the world to promote the Cinématographe, and in the process, to provide home audiences with thousands of foreign views. Star Films was a different kind of operation altogether: it was aimed largely at the fairground clientele who had already been buying Méliès' theatrical illusions through Émile Voisin, the magic supply dealer. Moreover Méliès' own overriding interest was not the industry but the art of film.

In his first film ventures (known only from their catalogue descriptions), Méliès closely emulated the original Lumière models with cityscapes, scenic views, and domestic vignettes —Arrivée d'un train, Gare de Vincennes (Arrival of a Train at Vincennes Station; Lumière's famous train arrived at La Ciotat); Barque sortant du port de Trouville (Boat Leaving the Harbor of Trouville; Lumière's boat was filmed in La Ciotat, where he vacationed in 1895, while Méliès' 1896 vacation was spent at Trouville); Les Forgerons (Blacksmith in His Workshop, same as Lumière). Even Louis Lumière's pioneering Sortie des usines (Workers Leaving the Factory) has its parallel in Méliès' Sortie des Ateliers Vibert (Closing Hours at Vibert's Perfume Factory). Méliès' L'Arroseur (Watering the Flowers) was simply a remake of Louis Lumière's earliest venture into comedy, L'Arroseur arrosé (The Sprinkler Sprinkled), just as the very first item in the Star Film catalogue, *Une Partie de cartes* (*A Game of Cards/Playing Cards*) reconstitutes a similar occasion filmed by Lumière during the summer of 1895.

While such films were shameless imitations of a popular craze (by January 1896, more than two thousand people a day were flocking to the Grand Café to see the Lumière programs), they were not the totality of Méliès' initial output. Even among the seventy-eight Star Films produced in 1896, there is ample evidence of the innovative subjects and techniques that were to establish Méliès (in the words of Louis Lumière himself) as the "creator of the cinematic spectacle."

The earliest surviving film, *Une Nuit terrible* (*A Terrible Night*), for example, is an abbreviated (fifty-second) comedy showing a hotel guest attacked by giant bedbugs. Like Lumière's *l'Arroseur arrosé*, it is a cross between popular entertainment and home movies—a variety-show joke reenacted in Méliès' garden at Montreuil outside of Paris. But Méliès' theatrical vision and ambition are already displayed: the garden, a natural setting for Lumière's horticultural joke, is here transformed into a rudimentary stage set, with hanging curtains for a backdrop, bedroom furniture, and a rug on the "floor" next to the bed. The guest, costumed in nightshirt and cap, has just demonstrated his preparedness for sleep by blowing out a candle (although the outdoor light obviously remains undimmed), when the cardboard bedbugs, manipulated by stage wires, begin their advance and a broom-and-shoe battle ensues.

Not surprisingly, magic acts provided Méliès with another early subject, beginning with *Séance de prestidigitation* (*Conjuring*), the second item in the Star Film catalogue. As with the staged comedies, these works were initially no more than filmed records of a theatrical performance, but by the late summer of 1896, Méliès began experimenting with techniques that allowed him to create illusions not on the stage but in the camera itself.

According to Méliès' own account, the original discovery was a matter of chance—he was shooting at the Palace de l'Opéra when the camera jammed, forcing him to stop for a minute or so to fix the film. "During this minute," he explained, "the passersby, buses, carriages had moved of course. When I projected the film, joined at the place where the break had occurred, I suddenly saw a Madeleine-Bastille bus changed into a hearse, and men changed into women. The substitution trick, called stop-motion, had been discovered." In fact, the stop-motion effect had been used for the execution

scene of Edison's *Mary Queen of Scots*, filmed on August 28, 1895, and most likely shown by Méliès at the Théâtre Robert-Houdin. But whatever the source of his inspiration, Méliès' use of the camera magic was unique.

The stop-motion effect first turns up in *Escamotage d'une dame chez Robert-Houdin* (*The Vanishing Lady*), the one other film that survives from 1896. The well-known theatrical illusion of the same name, invented by Bualtier de Kolta, accomplished its stated aim through the use of a camouflaged trap door and a chair with a collapsible seat. In the filmed version, featuring Méliès and Jehanne d'Alcy, the setting and props recreate the theatrical model (down to the newspaper used to hide the trap door), just as the stop-motion effect simulates the on-stage illusion. But Méliès adds a final twist—a second camera stop produces a skeleton in place of the vanished lady, while a third allows her to reappear in the chair. In a final assertion of their theatrical identity (itself of course an illusion), the two actors bow to the audience.

In September 1896, recognizing the limitations of outdoor shooting, Méliès began to build a film studio on his property at Montreuil, outside Paris. The glass-enclosed structure was, in his words, "the union of the photography workshop (in its gigantic proportions) and the theatre stage." Its dimensions were identical to those of Théâtre Robert-Houdin, and, as in the theatre, a three-meter pit in the stage area was equipped with various ramps, traps, set banks, and winches for mechanical effects. A two-story shed behind the studio contained dressing rooms, while a separate hangar came to be used for set construction.

For the next sixteen years, Méliès divided his time between Montreuil and Paris. Although he ceased to create stage illusions between 1897 and 1904, he remained in charge of Théâtre Robert-Houdin: "My theatrical career and my cinematographic career," he emphasized, "took place simultaneously." According to his memoirs, he arrived at the studio at seven a.m. to put in a ten-hour day building sets and props. At five he would change his clothes and set out for Paris in order to be in the theatre office by six to receive callers. After a quick dinner he was back to the theatre for the eight o'clock show, during which he sketched his set designs, and then returned to Montreuil to sleep. On Fridays and Saturdays he shot scenes prepared during the week, while Sundays and holidays were taken up with a theatre matinee, three film screenings, and an evening presentation that lasted until eleven-thirty. The result of these gigantic efforts amounted in the end to some five hundred films, ranging from the earliest fifty-second reels of 1896 to the elaborate production of later years that ran as long as twenty-six minutes.

By the end of 1897, Méliès had already introduced just about all of the genres that he was to develop for the remainder of his filmmaking years. As Georges Brunel wrote that year, in a publicity brochure for the Robert-Houdin Cinématographe. "MM. Méliès and Reulos have above all made a specialty of fantastic or artistic scenes, reproductions of theatre scenes, etc., so as to create a special genre, entirely distinct from the ordinary cinematographic views consisting of street scenes or genre subjects." In fact, of the fifty-three films he made in 1897, about a dozen were outdoor views in the familiar Lumière manner, but others included comedies, historical reconstructions, dramatic adaptations, magical transformations, and the *féeries*, or fairy stories, that were to become his most important idiom of expression.

One pioneering venture was stimulated early in the year when the popular singer Paulus requested films of some of his performances, apparently to be screened along with sound recordings in the dance halls. In order to show the singer on the stage of Théâtre Robert-Houdin, Méliès set up a battery of arc lamps and mercury lights, thus introducing the use of artificial lighting to the cinema. After the Montreuil studio was completed in March 1897, he made several more of his fifty-second comedies, including *Le Malade imaginaire (An Imaginary Patient)* and *Le Musulman rigolo (A Funny Mahometan)*, as well as *Le Château hanté (The Haunted Castle)*, which was based on one of his stage illusions. Like his competitors Lumière and Pathé, Méliès also began to stage what were referred to in the Star Film catalogue as "mature subjects"—stag films—with titles like *L'Indiscret aux Bains de mer (Peeping Tom at the Seaside)*, *En cabinet particulier (A Private Dinner)*, or *Le Magnétiseur (A Hypnotist at Work)*. The one surviving film from this group, *Après le bal (After the Ball)*, shows Jehanne d'Alcy stripping down to a flesh-colored leotard and receiving a bath from her maid (Jeanne Brady); for the sake of the camera the "water" consisted of charcoal or sand.

In June Méliès embarked on a different sort of reenactment, the reconstructed newsreel (*Actualité reconstituée*). This was used to portray current events from the Greco-Turkish War of 1897 (*Épisodes de guerre/War Episodes*; *La Prise de Tournavos/The Surrender of Tournavos*; *Exécution d'un espion/Execution of a Spy*; *Massacres en Crête/Massacre in Crete*; *Combat naval en Grèce/Sea Fighting in Greece*)

and later that year, anti-British riots in India (*Combat dans une rue aux Indes/Fighting in the Streets in India*; *Attaque d'une poste anglais/Attack on an English Blockhouse*). An incident from the Franco-Prussian War of 1870 likewise provided him with material for *Les Dernières Cartouches (The Last Cartridges)*, which was based on a painting by Alfred de Neuville. These proto-docudramas were basically studio alternatives to the very popular travelogues and newsreels that the Lumière operators were able to provide. They were made with small-scale models and theatrical enhancements that were not intended to simulate events but, like the drawings and engravings used to illustrate the newspapers and magazines of the day, to evoke them. The focus for Méliès, as the titles suggest, was clearly the spectacle. Along with these dramatic moments in contemporary history, he was also pursuing the drama of the imagination with fantasies like the three-reel *Le Cabinet de Mephistophélès (The Laboratory of Mephistopheles)*, where he made the first of his many appearances as the devil; *L'Auberge ensorcelée (The Bewitched Inn)*, based on a well-known Châtelet *féerie*; and the last film of the year, *Faust et Marguerite*, which was his first adaptation of a literary theme.

One other form that Méliès' flair for spectacle took on during this period was the advertisement—between 1896 and 1900 he made about ten of these films. As Méliès described these efforts for products ranging from whiskey, chocolates, and baby cereal to corsets, combs, and hair restorers, they were "very amusing, even exaggeratedly burlesqued, mixing in some tricks that would intrigue the public, short views, briskly executed but very substantial nonetheless, and ended naturally with slogans promoting the product in question." The Bornibus mustard commercial, for example, showed diners in a restaurant hurling mustard at each other in the course of a violent argument, but because the mustard was so good, a dog promptly licked it from the floor. "There was a little trick," Méliès later admitted: "the famous mustard in the pots was really chocolate cream." But the best part of the commercial, he explained, was the ending: a pile of white letters suddenly appeared on a black table filling the entire screen and quickly assembled themselves into the familiar slogan for the mustard, with the exception of the final "s" in Bornibus, which was unable to find its place and bumped its way around the table until it finally settled into the end of the manufacturer's name. "The effect was tremendous," he recalled. "People doubled over with laughter."

Making the most of their entertainment value, Méliès used such commercials to advertise himself as well: his daughter Georgette was posted outside Théâtre Robert-Houdin with a projector to screen them for the passersby. In September 1897 he attempted to turn the theatre into a cinema by cutting back on the magic shows and instituting nightly film screenings with piano music, sound effects, and narration, but after the Christmas break that year separate screenings were resumed only on Sunday evenings.

By this time the Montreuil studio was in full operation, and although Méliès made only thirty films in 1898, all but three were studio productions, with more elaborate casting, sets, and camera tricks than he had attempted before. During the spring and summer he turned out five ambitious reconstructed newsreels on the sinking of the battleship *Maine* in Havana harbor and the subsequent US confrontation with Spain in the Philippines. In the one film that survives, *Visite sous-marine du "Maine" (Divers at Work on the Wreck of the "Maine")*, the action takes place behind a strip of gauze painted with images of seaweed to simulate an underwater setting—a common theatrical device—while a large fish tank set up in front of the camera makes it appear that fish are swimming around the divers.

Méliès then seems to have turned his attention back to in-camera manipulations with a series of short magic demonstrations based on the stop-motion effect. The most sophisticated of these is *Illusions fantasmagoriques (The Famous Box Trick)*, which features ten stop-substitutions in the course of a one-minute performance. With *La Lune à un mètre (The Astronomer's Dream)*, Méliès' distinctive blend of camera magic and stage magic reached maturity. In this three-minute film, adapted from his own 1891 theatre piece, an astronomer (Méliès) finds himself in the company of demons and goddesses as the moon (with the help of the camera-stop) works a series of magical transformations on his laboratory. Similarly, in the phantasmagoric *Tentation de Saint Antoine (Temptation of Saint Anthony)*, a subject that was brought to the Paris stage by the late eighteenth-century illusionist Robertson, the camera-stop is used to transform a statue of Christ on the cross into a seductive woman. The Méliès touch is apparent in the blatant parody of religious morality; with himself in the title role and Jehanne d'Alcy as one of the temptresses, the film may have had autobiographical associations as well.

Three new camera tricks introduced during this period further enhanced Méliès' ability to create fantasies on film. The simplest of these illusions was the reversed action, which appears for the first time in the thirty-second *Salle à manger fantastique (A Dinner Under Difficulties)*. Here a diner's table accidentally knocked to the floor magically restores itself and the food it carries, apparently by the simple device of cranking the camera backwards after the film had been run through with the lens covered.

Méliès' other experiments were considerably more complicated, involving carefully staged actions as well as camera manipulations. According to Georges Sadoul, the 1897 publication of Albert Allis Hopkins' compendium on *Magic, Stage Illusions, and Scientific Diversions, Including Trick Photography* was directly for Méliès' adaptation of superimpositions and multiple images on a black ground; others maintain that such devices were common knowledge, and superimpositions, at least, had already been used by W. K. L. Dickson and possibly by George Albert Smith. In any case, a repertoire of transparent ghosts (so-called spirit photography) and composite images (from multiple exposures) soon made its way into Méliès films. *La Caverne maudite (The Cave of the Demons)*, for example, is populated with ghosts photographed on a black ground before the setting itself was recorded. In *Un Homme de tête (Four Troublesome Heads)*, Méliès the magician removes his head three times over, strikes up a song with the resulting chorus, and then causes the extra heads to disappear by smashing them with a banjo. Here the individual heads are removed (and later made to disappear) with a basic camera-stop: when Méliès reached up, the camera stops, his head is covered with a black bag (virtually invisible against the black ground), and a papier-mâché head is placed in his hands to be set on the table. The camera is stopped again, the bag is taken off, and the head is removed from the table. After the last head is removed, the film is wound back to the end of the first removal, and Méliès' singing head is then photographed three times, up to the point where it disappears.

Méliès himself managed to avoid any detailed explanation of the techniques he used, but in an article on cinematographic views ("Les vues cinématographiques," published in 1907), he stressed the precision that was required in filming such transformations: "Every second the actor playing different scenes ten times [a slight exaggeration—the maximum appears to be seven] has to remember, while the film is rolling, exactly what he did at the same point in the preceding scenes and the exact place where he was on the stage." Because of these difficulties, camera stops and superimpositions were never used as strictly in-camera devices, but rather were combined with darkroom editing of the negatives to ensure smooth transitions from one image to another. Unlike the less sophisticated edits of Edison and Zecca, which are noticeable in the lower part of the frame, Méliès carefully made his splices in the upper quarter or fifth, where they get lost in the backdrop.

Méliès continued to perfect his camera tricks during 1899; in *Le Portrait mystérieux* (*A Mysterious Portrait*), for example, he used a matte shot with double exposure to strike up a dialogue with a lifesize portrait of himself, while in *L'Homme protée* (*The Lightning-Change Artist*), a succession of camera-stops allowed him to put the conjurer and quick-change artist Leopoldo Fregoli through twenty character changes in two minutes. But in fact, with the invention of the dissolve for scene transitions in *Le Diable au Couvent* (*The Devil in a Convent*, another jibe at the Church), he basically completed the repertoire of camera devices he was to draw on for the remainder of his career. At this point he seems to have turned his attention from individual problems of technique to the possibilities of large-scale film productions.

In late summer 1899, Méliès began his longest film to date, a reconstructed newsreel based on the notorious Dreyfus Affair, which had divided all France into two camps. The scandal had just entered a second round with the retrial of Captain Alfred Dreyfus, the French Jew sentenced to life imprisonment on false charges of selling military secrets to the Germans. Méliès himself took a pro-Dreyfus stand, which is clearly reflected in the episodes he chose to dramatize— Dreyfus' arrest and sentencing, his incarceration on Devils Island, a meeting with his wife, and so forth. Public response was so heated, Méliès recalls in his memoirs, that the so-called Dreyfusards and anti-Dreyfusards got into fights with each other in the theatres; as a result, police halted screenings after the eleventh segment, which depicted Dreyfus' return to prison after the retrial failed to acquit him. Despite the possibilities for spectacle inherent in the subject itself (to say nothing of Méliès' own inclinations), the approach is generally straightforward and heavily reliant on newspaper illustrations of the day. As John Frazer suggests, "his willingness to undertake a genre basically alien to his own sense of what he did best is a testament to his own feelings about the case."

After this film, Méliès did in fact return to "what he did best" with *Cendrillon* (*Cinderella*), a seven-minute spectacle divided (for the first time) into twenty scenes. As the Star Film catalogue noted, there were "over thirty-five people" in the cast, which represented no small acting enterprise. In the beginning, he recalls with some amusement in his memoirs, professional actors were not interested in the new and untried medium, so he had to look elsewhere:

"All the employees of his Théâtre Robert-Houdin, neighbors, family, even his servants, right up to the gardener, were promoted to the rank of actors and didn't do such a bad job. As for the extras, they were supplied, men and women, by the workers employed in Montreuil itself, in the nearby factories or mills." "But alas!" he continues, "In spite of their good will, period costumes cut a poor figure on people who weren't used to wearing them, and the bearing of the gentlemen or grand ladies perhaps left something to be desired." As a result, he turned to Châtelet dancers, and as word spread about the chance to earn extra money (he paid them one gold louis a day plus the midday meal), they were joined by the dancers from the opera, café-concert singers, and eventually, the actors. Even then, he points out, "great talents of the Comédie Française were not necessarily well equipped for the demands of silent film. Deprived of the word, their very soul, and being used to gestures on the stage that were very restrained and not expressive without the speech that accompaned them, most of their acting was lost on the audiences." But when Méliès finally learned to match up the talents of various artists with the appropriate roles, "he wound up with a troupe that was quite complete and well trained."

Cinderella was very successful in music halls and fairgrounds, not only in France but elsewhere in Europe and in the United States. The competition for markets was a bitter one from the very beginning, with Edison and other American companies waging an aggressive campaign to keep out foreign productions. In 1900, French film producers formed the Chambre Syndicale des Éditeurs Cinématographiques, a trade union aimed at warding off the American companies. Méliès was chosen to be the first president, a position he held until 1912, and Théâtre Robert-Houdin served as the group's headquarters.

The success that he was enjoying with his "artificially arranged scenes," as they were called in the Star Film catalogue, encouraged him to pursue his distinctive form of filmmaking. The Montreuil studio was enlarged in 1899 and again in 1900 to allow for more elaborate stage manipulations as well as set and costume production and storage. After his first films, which had been shot by himself or Reulos, he trained Leclerc, the piano player at Théâtre Robert-Houdin, for the job; when Leclerc was arrested in 1910 for selling obscene photographs, the role of cameraman passed on to Michaut, who had been in charge of the printing operation at the laboratories in the Passage de l'Opéra.

Méliès' set designs were carried out by a team of artists, including Claudel, Parvillier, and Lecuit-Monroy. In order to avoid the false values registered on the black-and-white film of the day, all the sets and props were executed in grisaille (tones of gray), as were the costumes and even the actors' makeup. "Sets in colors come out horribly bad," Méliès wrote in 1906: "The blue becomes white, the red, the greens, and the yellows become black. It's necessary therefore that the sets are painted like the backgrounds of photographs. Unlike theatre sets, the painting is extremely careful. The finish, the exactitude of the perspective, the *trompe-l'oeil* skillfully executed and linking painting to real objects as in a panorama, it's all necessary to give the appearance of reality to things that are entirely artificial and that the camera will photograph with an absolute precision. Anything badly done will be faithfully reproduced in the camera."

As Méliès described the actual filming process, rehearsals would begin with a general explanation of a given tableau, followed by a run-through of the main action and then the lesser episodes. "All of that," he wrote in the 1907 article, "calls for great practice, a concise and absolute precision in explanations, and requires the cooperation of intelligent actors and extras who understand what is asked of them from the first word." In his view, "it cannot be forgotten that the sun turns relentlessly, and that if everything isn't known, planned, and ready to photograph on time, the favorable hour when the day presents itself head on will pass, and it will be necessary to postpone until the next day; the result: double expense." In the eyes of his cast and crew, Méliès was an autocratic father figure, demanding, impatient, and difficult to follow. According to Astaix, another worker in the film laboratories, actors who did not catch on quickly were summarily fired.

The inseparability of the virtuoso and autocrat is uncannily reflected in *L'Homme Orchestre* (*The One-Man Band*), a 1900 film where Méliès multiplies himself into a seven-strong musical ensemble. Also among the thirty-three films he made that year was *Jeanne d'Arc* (*Joan of Arc*), a thirteen-minute historical epic in twelve tableaux (now lost), and *Les Sept Péchés capitaux* (*The Seven Deadly Sins*), a short extravaganza full of dancing girls in exotic settings. The other major effort was *Le Rêve de Noël* (*The Christmas Dream*), a fairy story combining the pageantry of traditional Christmas pantomimes with the special effects of the movie camera.

By 1901 Méliès was reaching the peak of his fame as a master of filmed comedy, magic, and fantasy. The interweaving of all three trends can be seen in *le Brahmane et le papillon* (*The Brahmin and the Butterfly*), a two-minute exotic fairy tale in which Méliès the brahmin turns a caterpillar into a flying butterfly woman, only to be turned into a caterpillar himself. The two major productions of the year were also fairy tales: *Le Petit Chaperon Rouge* (*Little Red Riding Hood*) and *Barbe Bleue* (*Bluebeard*). The ten-minute Bluebeard (with Méliès in the title role) transforms the Charles Perault story into a melodramatic pantomime with a music-hall apotheosis at the end; it is, in John Frazer's words, "not the most enjoyable Méliès film," but it is nonetheless significant for two pronounced departures from the fixed viewpoint: an early use of parallel cross-cutting and successive shots of a character moving from one room to another. One distinctly vulgar venture from this period is *L'Omnibus des toqués*, also called *Échappés de Charenton* (*Off to Bloomingdale Asylum*), a crude burlesque in blackface that ends with four bus passengers turning into one large black who gets blown up by the conductor for refusing to pay the fare.

In several films made early the following year, Méliès experimented with actual camera movement to create illusions of changing size. In *Le Diable géant, ou le miracle de la Madonne* (*The Devil and the Statue*), for example, a Méliès-Satan reaches giant proportions before a terrified Shakespearean Juliet and then, through the intercession of the Virgin Mary, shrinks to the size of a dwarf and dissappears. A much more elaborate device (and an inverse traveling shot superimposed on a black ground) is used to create a similar illusion in the well-known *L'Homme à tête de caoutchouc* (*Man with the Rubber Head*), which shows Méliès, now a chemist, inflating his head with an air pump until it explodes. As Méliès noted with no small satisfaction in his 1907 article on "Les vues cinématographiques," his competitor Ferdinand Zecca tried to imitate the illusion by bringing the camera forward, but Zecca was unable to keep the head from expanding over the plane of the table it was sitting on. "I did it otherwise," Méliès explains, "advancing toward the camera." The device he used was a chair drawn by pulley along a ramp; the ramp itself was precisely marked to allow the cameraman to readjust the focus of the lens continuously; at the same time, Méliès rose as he approached the camera so that his head would remain aligned with the table on which it was later superimposed.

All the while that these experiments were underway, Méliès was also engaged in his longest and most eleaborate film project to date, *Voyage dans la lune* (*A Trip to the Moon*), completed in

May 1902. Picking up the basic theme of *The Astronomer's Dream* from 1898, this science-fiction fantasy in thirty tableaux draws on the plots of Jules Verne's *From the Earth to the Moon* (1865) and H. G. Wells' *The First Men on the Moon* (1901), but injects the basic lunar adventure story with a combination of pageantry and parody that speaks to the mixed response to modern science itself among popular audiences. Professor Barbenfouillis (Méliès), now president of the Astronomers' Club, proposes a rocket journey to the moon to his colleagues and is selected to head a six-man mission. The rocket is built in a factory modeled on Méliès' own studio at Montreuil, and the launch is assisted by a chorus line of sailor girls from the Châtelet who load the space vehicle into a cannon and wave to the audience. The journey through the heavens is marked by an ever-approaching image of the moon (which repeats the illusion in *The Man with a Rubber Head*); after a double landing—once in closeup and once in a distance shot that reveals the lunar surface—the explorers disembark and to go sleep. As they dream, the planets and constellations dancy by; the moon causes a snowstorm, and an army of Sélénites—moon men, played by acrobats from the Folies-Bergère—attacks them. The mission retreats to the spaceship and returns to earth; a sea landing superimposed on a real image of the sea is followed by a second version in a fish tank. In the final tableau, the adventurers receive a public celebration of their feat.

As Jean Mitry has suggested, *A Trip to the Moon* evokes something of the painter Henri Rousseau's childlike dream world, especially in the pictorial naïveté of the sets, but at the same time the chorus lines exploit a knowing adult sexuality. The extravagant production, which cost about 10,000 francs, was sold in black and white for 1.5 francs per meter (420 francs), with hand-tinted versions available for double that amount. Méliès later described how his fairground clients reacted to the steep price with such amazement and disapproval that he finally offered to loan one of them a copy for free screenings, just to see how the public would react. The applause from the first show, he recalled, was enough to pack the theatre until midnight. The showman, as Méliès told the story, was frantic to buy the film and, when reminded of his earlier lack of interest, offered to pay an extra 200 francs "for his inconvenience."

About the time he was completing *A Trip to the Moon,* Méliès made his last three reconstructed newsreels. Two of these were brief encapsulations of recent disasters—*Éruption volcanique à la Martinique* (*The Terrible Eruption of Mt. Pelée and Destruction of St. Pierre,*

Martinique) and *Catastrophe du ballon "Le Pax"* (*The Catastrophe of the Balloon "Pax"*), but the third, *Le Sacre d'Edouard VII* (*The Coronation of Edward VII*), was a major production, completed in advance of the event it supposedly "reconstructed." The project was initiated by Charles Urban, head of Warwick Trading Company, who had been denied permission to film the actual ceremony inside Westminster Abbey (where the light would have been inadequate anyway). Urban, the Star Film representative in London, supplied Méliès with pictures of the site, costumes and props, and a detailed description of the impending ceremony from the royal protocol officer. With Urban's advance of 80,000 francs, Méliès built a miniaturized version of the abbey's north transept and assembled a forty-member cast, featuring a bathhouse attendant with a fortuitous resemblance to Edward VII. The five-minute film was ready for the June 26th ceremony, but when the coronation itself was postponed six weeks because of the king's ill health, the "reconstruction" was released after the event with actual footage of the carriage procession tacked on to the beginning and the end.

Edward VII was supposedly quite pleased, as was the public, nothwithstanding one Parisian critic in *Le Petit Bleu* who lambasted what he called "Edward VII at Montreuil" as "a put-on, a bluff, amateur theatrics." With the money that the film brought in, Méliès was able to undertake two more ambitious projects before the end of the year: a four-minute *Voyage de Gulliver* (*Gulliver's Travels*) that brought both Lilliputians and giants to the screen by means of superimpositions, and a fifteen-minute *Robinson Crusoe*—the longest film to date—inspired by an 1899 Châtelet pantomime.

The Méliès himself later noted, success brought mixed results—the renown went to him, but the profits went increasingly to foreign distributors who pirated his films. *A Trip to the Moon,* in particular, established Méliès' name in the United States, but it made the rounds of American music halls through the illegal copies by Edison, Siegmund Lubin, and Carl Laemmle. In order to gain direct access to the United States market (and US copyright protection), Méliès' brother Gaston, who had not fared well in the shoe business after all, went to New York in November 1902 to establish a branch office of Star Films. As the introduction to the English-language Star Films catalogue declared: "In opening a factory and office in New York we are prepared and determined energetically to pursue all counterfeiters and pirates. We will not speak twice, we will act!"

Because of the high import duties on film

prints, Méliès had begun to shoot all his productions with two cameras (the second was operated by his daughter), so that the extra negative could be shipped to New York for printing and distribution. Between June 1903 and May 1904, paper prints of all new films were deposited in the Library of Congress for copyright purposes, and as a result, this is the best-documented period of Méliès' career; all but one of the twenty-nine films in 1903 have survived through the paper prints, along with eighteen of the thirty-five made in 1904. Among the works of these peak years were a number of short films abounding in devils, dreams, and magical transformations, but apart from the use of dissolves against a white ground, introduced with *La Guirlande merveilleuse* (*The Marvellous Wreath*, 1903), these pieces offered no particular innovations. Rather, they brought to perfection Méliès repertoire of camera tricks, as in *La Parapluie fantastique* (*Ten Ladies in One Umbrella*, 1903), with its witty and fast-paced transformations, or *Le Mélomane* (*The Melomaniac*, 1903), where an unprecedented seven multiple exposures allow Méliès the singing teacher to create a musical score with notes fashioned from multiples of his own head.

The major production of 1903 was *La Royaume des Fées* (*The Kingdom of the Fairies*), the twenty-minute fairy-tale extravaganza that Jean Mitry regards as "undoubtedly Méliès' best film, and in any case the most intensely poetic." Based on a well-known nineteenth-century pantomime, the thirty tableaux chronicling the adventures of Prince Belazor and his beloved Princess Azurine feature some eighteen different sets that range from a medieval castle to an underwater grotto, with the latter once again shot through a fish tank. *The Kingdom of the Fairies* is Méliès' most theatrical film in its staging, but at the same time it introduces several structuring devices that can be seen, in John Frazer's words, as "protoeditorial": cross-cutting and parallel construction to present simultaneous actions, as well as cutaway shots for multiple views of the same action.

At the end of 1903 Méliès returned to a favorite theme with his eight-minute *Faust aux enfers* (*The Damnation of Faust*). Inspired by Berlioz' opera, Méliès' sixteen-scene journey through hell is less a narrative than a sequence of visual effects, with subterranean grottos, walls of water and fire, and the like. A few months later Méliès made *La Damnation du docteur Faust* (*Faust and Marguerite*), yet a fourth version of the Faust legend, this time based on Gounod's opera; a music sheet with a special arrangement of the main arias, intended to accompany both *Faust and Marguerite* and its "natural sequel," *The*

Damnation of Faust, was sold to theatre owners for an additional $2.50. A twenty-two minute *Barbier de Seville* (*The Barber of Sevilla* [sic]), made soon afterwards, was faithfully drawn from the Beaumarchais play and likewise provided with a musical score based on Rossini's opera. Despite the uneasy mix of high art and popular culture that such opera films entailed— modern critics have found them stilted—they were well received by contemporary audiences.

Another major production from 1904 is the twenty-four minute *Voyage à travers l'impossible* (*Impossible Voyage*, 1904), which, like the Faust operas, was also based on a successful formula, here the fantastic journey first presented in *Trip to the Moon*. In the new version, the target is the sun; Professor Barbenfouillis and the Astronomers' Club are replaced by Engineer Mabouloff and the Institute of Incoherent Geography, and their spaceship has become a land-air-sea vehicle called the Automobouloff; again, despite the lack of innovation, the polish of the performance is unrivaled. For Lewis Jacobs, "this film expressed all of Méliès' talents. . . . The complexity of his tricks, his resourcefulness with mechanical contrivances, the imaginativeness of the settings and the sumptuous tableaux made the film a masterpiece for its day."

By this time the cinema was well entrenched in popular entertainment, and for the 1904 Folies Bergère revue, director Victor de Cottens invited Méliès to create a special film sequence. The result was *Le Raid Paris-Monte Carlo* (*The Adventurous Automobile Trip*), a topical spoof on Belgium's playboy king Leopold, which enjoyed three hundred screenings in the revue before Méliès offered it for sale as a Star Film. In 1905 de Cottens asked him to collaborate on another revue for the Châtelet, *Les Quatre Cent Coups du diable* (*The Merry Deeds of Satan*), a reworking of a nineteenth-century theatre spectacle. Méliès, clearly in his element with the Faustian theme, not only provided two short film segments, *Le Voyage dans l'éspace* (*The Space Trip*) and *Le Cyclone* (*The Cyclone*) but worked with de Cottens on the script of the highly successful revue, which ran for five hundred performances.

It was also at this point, on the occasion of the centennial celebration for Robert-Houdin, that Méliès went back to creating stage illusions at his own theatre with *Les Phénomènes du spiritisme* (*Spiritualist Phenomena*). But this activity hardly signaled a retreat from filmmaking, for he was simultaneously making major improvements in his Montreuil production facilities, installing electric lights, building a second studio, and buying out a vast costume collection.

Among the twenty-two films issued in 1905 were several very proficient magical transformations, including *Les Cartes vivantes* (*The Living Playing Cards*), a stage illusion brought to the screen through white-ground dissolves. A nineteen-minute *Palais des Mille et Une Nuits* (*Palace of the Arabian Nights*) serves up an exotic romance in elaborate settings that are, notwithstanding the film's title, identifiably Indian, while an eighteen-minute *Légende de Rip van Winkle* (*Rip's Dream*), with Méliès in the title role, brings Robert Planquette's opera *Rip* almost directly to the screen. Similar fare appears among the eighteen films produced in 1906, including an ambitious remake of his 1905 Chatêlet revue, now retitled *Les 400 Farces du diable* (*The Merry Frolics of Satan*) and embellished with twenty-three new scenes. *La Fée Carabosse ou le poignard fatal* (*The Witch*), another extravaganza about fifteen minutes long, recasts *The Kingdom of the Fairies* in the form of a Breton legend, which, according to Georges Sadoul, may have been aimed at Méliès' English audiences.

In his 1933 memoirs, Félix Mesguich, one of the original Lumière camaramen, expresses his exasperation with the cinema fantasies that had overshadowed his own documentary mode in the first years of the twentieth century: "If the public applauds them," he writes, "I suppose that they appreciate above all the surprise effects that amuse them with their extravagance." But in his view, "It's no longer acrobatics. It's trickery." Within a few years, popular taste followed suit: three of Méliès' fairy tales—*Cinderella, Bluebeard,* and *Robinson Crusoe*—put up for resale by an exhibitor at drastically reduced prices in August 1905, remained unsold four months later, and at the end of the year, his brother Gaston cut back the rental price of Star Films in New York by 20 percent, a move that greatly increased revenues.

Méliès himself was already beginning to move into the melodramas, comedies, and literary adaptations that were bringing success to his competitors. An eight-minute film, *Détresse et Charité* (*The Christmas Angel*, 1905), for example, is described in the Star Film Catalogue as "a grand picture of Pathos and Humor with a Moral." Similarly *Les Incendiaires* (*A Desperate Crime*, 1906) was based on the story of a real murderer and included outdoor scenes interpolated at the insistence of Lallemand and Michaut, Méliès' former assistants who were now distributing his films. Advertised as a "great realist drama," the twenty-minute film also owed a considerable debt to his rival Ferdinand Zecca's popular *Histoire d'un Crime* (*Story of a Crime*, 1901). Another 1906 production, *Robert*

Macaire et Bertrand, which includes the second portion of Méliès' Chatelet film of the year before, is built around the cops-and-robbers chase popularized by English filmmakers.

Rather than abandoning the world of magic and fantasy, Méliès again pursued it through the theatre, creating three new illusions for the Théatre Robert-Houdin during 1907. The nineteen films he produced that year include various fantasies and farces, a parody of Jules Verne's *2000 Leagues Under the Sea*, a political satire on Anglo-French relations, and a nine-and-a-half-minute *Hamlet*, but no single work seems to stand out. In fact, it is with the films of 1907 that critics such as Georges Sadoul and Jean Mitry begin to speak of a decline in Méliès' work, a lapse into the repetition of old formulas on the one hand and an uneasy imitation of new trends on the other.

By this time, the industrialization of filmmaking was well under way. The Nickelodeon, invented in 1905, had greatly increased the demand for films in the US, but at the same time, the major producers, notably Edison and Pathé, were moving to take over the markets there and in Europe. Early in 1908 Edison formed the Motion Picture Patents Company to control American film production and distribution. Méliès, with his Star Film office in New York, joined the venture and as a result was committed to supplying 1000 feet of film a week for American distribution. In order to fulfill this obligation, Gaston Méliès set up a second production unit in Chicago, the Méliès Manufacturing Company, but during the first year, the quota was met from Montreuil, where Georges Méliès produced sixty-eight films, the equivalent of his entire output from 1898 to 1903. Many of these were short fairy stories, although, as John Frazer has noted, in a film like *Le Rêve d'un fumeur d'opium* (*The Dream of an Opium Fiend*, practically the same title as Victorin Jasset's 1905 film for Gaumont), the tendency toward direct, naturalistic acting is noticeably in conflict with the fantastic decor.

The vogue for slapstick is reflected in a number of comedies, including one clever science-fiction farce, *La Photographie électrique à distance* (*Long-Distance Wireless Photography*) with Méliès in the role of Louis Marconi. In February Méliès came out with a major work, *Le Civilisation à travers les âges* (*Humanity Through the Ages*), which is notable for its ambition on the one hand and its dire pessimism on the other. Most likely inspired by the success of historical spectacles coming from Pathé, Gaumont, and the Italian film studios, this reconstruction in eleven tableaux traces the seemingly eternal path of human transgression from the story of Cain and Abel to a final apotheosis of death and destruction following the Hague Peace Conference that had been held the year before. It was, according to the Star Film catalogue, "one of the most artistic films ever made," and Méliès remained quite proud of it throughout his life, but the public was not equally responsive to this effort, as Jean Mitry put it, to "sift through all of human history in less than fifteen minutes."

Early in 1909, faced with the general upheaval of the film industry and the falling demand for his own films, Méliès suspended production altogether. In February, he presided over the first meeting of an international filmmakers congress convened in Paris to counter Edison's monopolistic tactics in the United States. Méliès' own preoccupation seems to have been the adoption of a uniform standard for film perforation, a measure that the congress finally agreed to, but the really significant result of the conference was the decision to follow a growing trend and replace outright film sales with four-month rentals restricted to members of their association. Méliès, along with the fairground exhibitors who had been his main clients over the years, opposed this move toward increasing commercialization: "I am not a corporation," he wrote in a fairground trade journal," I am an independent producer."

Resuming production that autumn, he made nine films, none of which has survived. During the same period, Gaston Méliès completed the first three films of the Méliès Manufacturing Company, which he had now relocated to Fort Lee, New Jersey, the site of Pathé and Éclair's American studios. Early in 1910 he set up a Star Film Ranch in San Antonio, Texas, where he began to turn out large numbers of successful Westerns; by the spring of 1911, the company, now called American Wildwest, was in southern California, and his films were meeting the entire Star Film quota for Edison's Motion Picture Patent Company.

Between 1910 and 1912, Gaston produced some 130 films; during the same period, which was to be the last phase of his filmmaking career, Georges Méliès produced 20. In 1910 he went back to active theatre involvement with a revue adapted from his last stage illusion, *Spiritualist Phenomena*; the fourteen films he made during this year similarly recapitulate his vintage magic and fantasy, and in one of them, *Les Illusions Fantaistes* (*Whimsical Illusions*) he performs once again as a stage magician.

Around this time the Gaumont Company apparently took over distribution of Star Films; the following autumn Méliès signed a contract with Charles Pathé, now the largest producer in the world. Under their agreement, Méliès put up his home and studios at Montreuil as security against a personal advance from Pathé, who was to have the right not only to distribute subsequent films, but also to edit them if necessary. Méliès resumed work in grand style, but the first two films produced in 1911 under the new agreement, *Les Hallucinations du Baron de Münchausen* (*The hallucinations of Baron de Münchausen*) and *Le Vitrail diabolique* (*The Haunted Window*), were failures.

For Georges Sadoul, *Münchausen*, the one of the pair that has survived, provides "rather distressing proof of Méliès' decline," but the filmmaker himself was apparently undaunted and began 1912 with a twenty-minute science fiction story, *A la conquête du Pôle* (*Conquest of the Pole*). While it drew on earlier works of literature (Verne) and film (Lumière and Robert W. Paul), Méliès' ambitous adventure had topical associations as well—Peary's visit to the North Pole in 1909 and Amundsen's to the South Pole in 1911. In spite of a celestial voyage, a griffin-headed aerobus, and a giant Monster of the Pole (operated by twelve stagehands), this third variation on the fantastic journey theme failed to capture popular attention as the earlier *Trip to the Moon* and *Impossible Voyage* had done.

Pathé then began to exercise his right to edit. Another revived subject, *Cendrillon ou la pantoufle mystérieuse* (*Cinderella or the Glass Slipper*), now filmed out of doors with deep-focus photography, was ineptly cut down from fifty-four to thirty-three minutes by an apparently jealous Ferdinand Zecca. Late in 1912 Méliès made two more films, *Le Chevalier des neiges* (*The Snow Knight*), which was a fairy story, and *Le Voyage de la famille Bourrichon*, a music-hall adaptation. When they suffered a similar editing fate, Méliès broke with Pathé but was unable to repay his debts to the giant film entrepreneur. Only a moratorium declared during the First World War prevented Pathé from repossessing the Montreuil properties. By this time Gaston Méliès, whose Westerns had kept Star Films solvent for several years, was also out of business. In July of 1912 he had left for Tahiti with family and film crew numbering twenty-two and over the next year filmed his way through the South Seas to Cambodia and Japan. When it turned out that much of the documentary footage he shipped back to his son in New York was damaged and the rest evoked little interest, he decided to give up his company. After losing some $50,000 on the Asian adventure, Gaston sold out to Vitagraph and returned to Europe. The two brothers remained estranged until his death in 1915.

By Méliès' own account, it was "a whole series of unlucky circumstances" that led him to abandon filmmaking in 1913. His own dire financial straits (which he attributes to his inability to adapt to the rental system) and Gaston's "unfortunate idea" coincided with the death of his wife, which apparently dealt him a serious emotional blow and also left him with two children to raise alone. The "final catastrophe," he writes in his memoirs, was the outbreak of war in 1914: the Théâtre Robert-Houdin was shut down for a year, and Méliès, fearing a German invasion, left Paris with his children during that time. In 1917 the main studio at Montreuil was converted into a hospital for the war wounded, and Méliès and his children began to use the second studio as a variety theatre where they staged some twenty-four productions over the next seven years. Pathé was finally able to take over the Montreuil holdings in 1923, the same year that the Théâtre Robert-Houdin was razed for the construction of Boulevard Haussmann.

During the war, some four hundred of Star Films films stored in the Paris offices were melted down by the army in order to retrieve their silver and celluloid content. In rage and despair, Méliès himself destroyed the negatives kept at Montreuil when he lost the property, and for a time it seemed that he as well had disappeared from the French film world. By the mid-1920s he was in fact eking out a miserable livelihood in a small candy and toy stand at the Montparnasse train station with Jehanne d'Alcy, his former star and mistress, whom he married in 1925. But through the efforts of several journalists and critics, articles by and about him began to appear in the film press, and in December 1929, a gala retrospective was held at the Salle Pleyel, where, Méliès wrote in his memoirs, "he experienced one of the most brilliant moments of his life."

Nonetheless, public acclaim did not alleviate his day-to-day situation. "Luckily enough, I am strong and in good health," he wrote to another forgotten filmmaker, Eugène Lauste, early in 1931, "but it is hard to work fourteen hours a day without getting my Sundays or holidays, in an ice-box in winter and a furnace in summer." Later that year he was awarded the Cross of the Legion of Honor, but it was only in 1932 that a more practical form of recognition was forthcoming: the Mutuelle du Cinéma, a mutual assistance organization, installed Méliès, his wife, and the granddaughter who lived with them, in the retirement home recently acquired at the Château d'Orly. "My best satisfaction in all," he wrote to the American journalist Merritt Crawford, "is to be sure not to be one day *without bread and home!*"

While at Orly he began working with Hans Richter on a scenario for another *Baron Münchausen* and with Marcel Carné and Jacques Prévert on a projected *Fantôme du métro (Phantom of the Metro).* and he acted in several commercials with Prévert. To the end of his life, he continued to draw, write, and receive admirers from the younger generation of theatre and film artists. He died of cancer at the age of seventy-seven and was buried in the Père Lachaise cemetery, where, according to Maurice Bessy and G. M. Lo Duca, "deep inside, each [of the mourners] was hoping . . . to witness a resurrection performed, or at least believed that Méliès would conjure himself up one last time."

It is perhaps only fitting—and as Méliès himself might have wished—that the master of illusion and transformation has remained a contradictory and ultimately elusive figure in the history of Western cinema. For René Clair (echoing Louis Lumière), he was the "inventor of the cinematic *spectacle*"; for Henri Langlois, the first "auteur"; for Georges Sadoul, the father of the art film; for Bessy and Lo Duca, the "magus" of the cinema. David Thomson, on the other hand, insists that Méliès remained a conjuror—an ingenious inventor who "failed to see that audiences might be more interested in people than in magic."

It is, in any case, the fanciful, visionary aspect of his work that has most influenced later filmmakers, from Clair and Jean Cocteau to Walt Disney. But Sadoul could also see in Méliès' films the beginnings of engaged cinema (notably with *The Dreyfus Affair*), while Gerald Mast has recognized him as "the first filmmaker who deliberately pushed himself into the illusion of the film. He was conscious of making films and informing his audience that it was watching film." Likewise John Frazer, invoking a comparison with early cubism, suggests that "Méliès' films can certainly be considered the first sources worthy of study as forerunners of modernism," and while the cubist connection seems tenuous, at least one avant-garde filmmaker, Stan Brakhage, recalls that "I took my first sense of the individual frame life of a film from Méliès."

Bessy writes that between 1896 and 1914 Méliès "invented everything: technique, commercial exploitation, direction, corporate organization, sets, shooting, tricks, scenario, editing, studio management, advertising, acting, extras." But, for all his innovations, as John Frazer acknowledges, "Georges Méliès was finally a man of the nineteenth, not the twentieth century. . . . both a pioneer of the cinema and the last man of the theatrical fairy pantomime spectacles." Even more forcefully, Jacques Deslandes, recalling that "the birth of the cinema was not the doing of a few but of a multitude," concludes: "For me, Méliès . . . is not a pioneer, in the sense of someone who has made the cinema advance, but above all a man of his own epoch." And finally, Alain Masson contends that "the historians don't like Méliès: they feel sorry for him."

The protean quality of Georges Méliès—the diversity, complexity, and sheer quantity of his work—partly accounts for the array of critical responses his films have evoked over the years. But the situation is compounded by the fact that less than one third of the 500 or so films now attributed to him (145 at latest count) have been preserved. Two years before his death, Méliès himself lamented what he saw as the necessarily incomplete appreciation of his work: "Young people," he told Bessy and Lo Duca, "don't know anything of my productions except a few fairy stories from the Dufayel collection. . . . And that's why, while they bury me with praise, they often accuse me of naiveté, clearly unaware that I touched all the genres." He might have added that he touched all the emotions as well, for even his humor was often laced with violence; his futuristic voyages in fact ridiculed current events; and his devilish romps universal questions of human morality.

As Méliès was doubtless aware, the intent of the filmmaker and the impact of his films were not necessarily the same, and the afterlife of the films has clearly colored the perception of their maker. In the balance, it seems equally unlikely that Méliès would have chosen to describe himself, once and for all, as either a magician or a modernist. Rather, as André R. Maugé wrote in 1931, in a judgment the old man chose to quote at the end of his memoirs, "Méliès did what he wanted to do; it's for that reason that his oeuvre preserves, in spite of the years, such a marvelous innocence, a purity that has been lost and won't be recovered, He expressed simply, with the means at his disposal, what his genius dictated to him."

—M.R.

FILMS: The following list is based on *Marvelous Méliès* by P. Hammond (1975) and *Essai de reconstitution du Catalogue Français de la Star Film, suivi d'une analyse catalographique des films de Georges Méliès recensés en France*, published by the Centre National de la Cinématographie (1981). Asterisks indicate extant films. Titles given in English were used in the United States or in Britain: a few films, however, were shown abroad under their French titles.

1896: Une Partie de cartes (Playing Cards); Séance de prestidigitation (Conjuring); Plus fort que le maitre (Smarter Than the Teacher); Jardinier brulant des her-

bes (Gardener Burning Weeds); Les Chevaux de bois (A Merry-Go-Round); L'Arroseur (Watering the Flowers); Les Blanchisseuses (The Washerwomen); Arrivée d'un train Gare de Vincennes (Arrival of a Train at Vincennes Station); Le Chiffonier/Une bonne farce (The Rag-Picker/A Good Joke); Place de l'Opéra, 1er aspect (Place de l'Opera, 1st View); Place du Théâtre Français; Un Petit Diable (A Little Devil); Couronnement de la rosière (Coronation of a Village Maiden); Bébé et fillettes (Baby and Young Girls); Défense d'afficher (Post No Bills); Bateau-Mouche sur la Seine (Steamboats on River Seine); Place de l'Opéra. 2e aspect (Place de l'Opéra, 2nd View); Boulevard des Italiens; Un Lycée de jeunes filles (Academy for Young Ladies); Bois de Boulogne (Touring Club); Bois de Boulogne—Porte de Madrid; Sauvetage en rivière (Rescue on the River, 1st part); Sauvetage en rivière (Rescue on the River, 2nd part); Le Régiment (French Regiment Going to the Parade); Campement de bohémiens (Gipsies at Home); °Une Nuit terrible (A Terrible Night); Déchargement de bateaux—Le Havre (Unloading the Boat—Havre); Plage de Villiers par gros temps (The Beach at Villiers in a Gale); Les Quais à Marseilles (The Docks at Marseilles); Jetée et plage de Trouville—1er partie (Beach and Pier at Trouville—Part One); Barque sortant du port de Trouville (Boat Leaving the Harbor of Trouville); Jetée et plage de Trouville—2e partie (Beach and Pier at Trouville—Part Two); Jour de marché à Trouville (Market Day—Trouville); Panorama du Havre pris d'un bateau (Panorama of Havre Taken From a Boat); Arrivée d'un Train—Gare de Joinville (Arrival of a Train—Joinville Station); Salut malencontreux d'un déserteur (A Soldier's Unlucky Salutation); Dessinateur express: M. Thiers (A Lightning Sketch: Mr Thiers); Les Forgerons (Blacksmith in His Workshop); Tribulations d'un concierge (A Janitor in Trouble); Baignade en mer (Sea Bathing); Enfants jouant sur la plage (Children Playing on the Beach); Dix chapeaux en 60 seconds (Conjuror Making Ten Hats in Sixty Seconds); Effects de mer sur les rochers (Sea Breaking on the Rocks); Danse Serpentine (A Serpentine Dance); Miss de Vère (Miss de Vère/English Jig); Départ des automobiles (Automobiles Starting on a Race); Revue navale à Cherbourg (A Naval Review at Cherbourg); Cortège de Tzar allant à Versailles (The Czar and His Cortège Going to Versailles); Les Haleurs de Bateaux (Towing a Boat on the River); Cortège de Tzar au Bois de Boulogne (The Czar's Cortège in the Bois de Boulogne); Sortie des Ateliers Vibert (Closing Hours at Vibert's Perfume Factory); La Voiture du potier (The Potter's Cart); Le Papier protée (The Mysterious Paper); Place de la Concorde; La Gare Saint-Lazare (St Lazare Railroad Station); Grandes Maneuvres (Maneuvres of the French Army); Dessinateur: Chamberlain (A Lightning Sketch: Chamberlain); Place de la Bastille; Marée montante sur brise-larmes (Tide Rising Over the Breakwater); Retour au cantonnement (Return to the Barracks); Dessinateur; Reine Victoria (A Lightning Sketch: H.M. Queen Victoria); Réunion d'officiers (French Officers' Meeting); Tempête sur la jetée du Tréport (The Pier at Tréport During a Storm); Le Bivouac (The Bivouac); Batteuse à vapeur (Steam Threshing-Machines); Sac au dos (Sacks Up!); Libération des territoriaux (Breaking up of the Territorial Army—France); Départ des officiers (Officers of French Army Leaving Service); Place Saint-Augustin; °Escamotage d'une dame chez Robert-Houdin (The Vanishing Lady); Le Fakir, mystère Indien (The Fakir, a Hindoo Mystery);

Winter 1896–1897: L'Hôtel empoisonné (A Badly Managed Hotel); Dessinateur: Von Bismark (A Lightning Sketch: Von Bismark); Les Indiscrets (The Peeping Toms); Tom Old Boot (Tom Old Boot, a Grotesque Dwarf); Les Ivrognes (The Drunkards); Le Manoir du diable (The Devil's Castle/The Haunted Castle); Chicot, Dentiste américain (An Up-to-Date Dentist); Le Cauchemar (A Nightmare); Le Cortège du Boeuf Gras passant Place de la Concorde (The Mardi Gras Procession); Cortège du Boeuf Gras boulevard des Italiens (The Mardi Gras Procession); Une Cour de ferme (A Farm Yard); Les Apprentis militaires (Military Apprentices); Paulus chantant: Derrière l'Omnibus (Comedian Paulus Singing "Derrière l'Omnibus"); Paulus Chantant: Coquin de Printemps (Comedian Paulus Singing "Coquin de Printemps"); Paulus chantant: Duelliste marseillais (Comedian Paulus Singing "Duelliste Marseillais"); Paulus chantant: Père la Victoire; Paulus chantant: En revenant d'la revue; Défilé des pompiers (Firemen on Parade); Danseuses au Jardin de Paris (Dancing Girls, Jardin de Paris); Le Malade imaginiare (An Imaginary Patient); Le Musulman rigolo (A Funny Mahometan); L'Hallucination de l'alchimiste (An Hallucinated Alchemist); Le Château hanté (The Haunted Castle/The Devil's Castle);

1897: Cortége de la Mi-Carême (Mid-Lent Procession in Paris); Bataille de confettis (Battle with Confetti); Sur les toits (On the Roofs); D. Devant, Prestidigitateur (D. Devant, Conjuror); L'École des gendres (The School for Sons-in-law); Épisodes de Guerre (War Episodes); Les Dernières Cartouches (The Last Cartridges); La Prise de Tournavos (The Surrender of Tournavos (The Surrender of Tournavos); Exécution d'un espion (Execution of a Spy); Massacres en Crète (Massacre in Crete); Passage dangereux, Mont Blanc (A Dangerous Pass, Mont Blanc); Combat navel en Grèce (Sea Fighting in Greece); Gugusse et l'automate (Gugusse and the Automaton); °Entre Calais et Douvres (Between Calais and Dover); L'Indiscret aux bains de mer (Peeping Tom at the Seaside); Dans les coulisses (Behind the Scenes); Tourneur en poterie (A Potterymaker); La Cigale et la fourmi (The Grasshopper and the Ant); Ascension d'un ballon (A Balloon Ascension); Le Cabinet de Mephistophélès (Laboratory of Mephistopheles); Figaro et l'auvergnat (The Barber and the Farmer); °l'Auberge ensorcelée (The Bewitched Inn); Auguste et Bibb (Auguste and Bibb); Chirurgien américain (A Twentieth-Century Surgeon); Arlequin et charbonnier (The Charcoal Man's Reception); En Cabinet particulier (A Private Dinner); °Après le bal: le tub (After the Ball); Le Magnétiseur (A Hypnotist at Work/While Under a Hypnotist's Influence); Le Modéle irascible (An Irritable Model); °Danse au sérail (Dancing in a Harem); °Vente d'esclaves au harem (Slave Trading in a Harem); Combat dans une rue aux Indes (Fighting in the Streets in India); Attaque d'une poste anglais (Attack on an English Blockhouse); Match de Boxe—Ecole de Joinville

(Boxing Match); Vision d'ivrogne (A Drunkard's Dream);

Winter 1897–1898: °Faust et Marguérite (Faust and Marguerite); Carrefour de l'Opéra (Place de l'Opéra, 3rd View); Magie Diabolique (Black Art/Devilish Magic); Les Rayons X (A Novice at X-Rays); Collision et naufrage en mer (Collision and Shipwreck at Sea);

1898: Quais de la Havane (The Blowing up of the Maine in Havana Harbour); Visite de l'épave du Maine (A View of the Wreck of the Maine); °Visite sous-marin du Maine (Divers at Work on the Wreck of the Maine/Divers at Work on a Wreck Under Sea); Assaut d'escrime—Ecole de Joinville (Fencing at the Joinville School); Le Maçon maladroit (A Clumsy Mason); Combat naval devant Manille (Defending the Fort at Manila); °Panorama pris d'un train en marche (Panorama from Top of Moving Train); Corvée de quartier accidentée (A Soldier's Tedious Duty); °Le Magicien (The Magician/Black Magic); Sorti sans permission (A Soldier's French Leave); °Illusions fantasmagoriques (The Famous Box Trick); Pygmalion et Galathée (Pygmalion and Galatea); Montagnes Russes nautiques (Shooting the Chutes); Damnation de Faust (Damnation of Faust); Guillaume Tell et le Clown (Adventures of William Tell); °La Lune à un mètre/L'Homme dans la Lune (The Astronomer's Dream, or the Man in the Moon); Prenez garde à la peinture (Fresh Paint); La Caverne maudite (The Cave of the Demons); Rêve d'artiste (The Artist's Dream); Atelier d'artiste, farce de Modèles (The Painter's Studio); °Un Homme de téte (The Four Troublesome Heads); Dédoublement cabalistique (The Triple Lady);

Winter 1898–1899: °Tentation de saint Antoine (Temptation of Saint Anthony); Reve du Pauvre (The Beggar's Dream); °Salle à manger fantastique (A Dinner Under Difficulties); Creations spontanées/Illusions fantastiques (Fantastical Illusions); Funérailles de Félix Faure (Funeral of Felix Faure);

1899: Cléopâtre (Robbing Cleopatra's Tomb); Le Coucher de la mariée ou Triste Nuit de Noce (The Bridegroom's Dilemma); Duel politique (A Political Duel); Luttes extravagantes (An Extraordinary Wrestling Match); Richesse et misère ou La Cigale et la fourmi (The Wandering Minstrel); L'Ours et la sentinelle (The Sentry's Stratagem); °L'Impressioniste fin de siècle/Illusioniste fin de siècle (An Up-to-Date Conjuror); Le Spectre (Murder Will Out); Le Diàble au Couvent (The Devil in a Convent/The Sign of the Cross); La Danse du Feu (Haggard's "She"—The Pillar of Fire); La Crémation (The Spanish Inquisition); °Un bon lit (A Midnight Episode); Force doit rester à la Loi (The Slippery Burglar); Pick-pocket et Policeman (A Drop Too Much); Combat de Coqs (Lively Cock-Fight); Automaboulisme et Autorité (The Clown and Automobilé/The Clown and Motor Car); °Le Portrait mysterieux (A Mysterious Portrait); Le Conférencier distrait (Absent-minded Lecturer); La Pierre philosophale (The Philosopher's Stone); Le Miroir de Cagliostro (Cagliostro's Mirror); Neptune et Amphitrite

(Neptune and Amphitrite); Panorama du Port de St-Hélier (Bird's-Eye View of St Helier, Jersey); Entrée d'un Paquebot, Port de Jersey (Steamer Entering the Harbour of Jersey); Débarquement de Voyageurs, Port de Granville (Passengers Landing at Harbour of Granville); Le Christ marchant sur les flots (Christ Walking on the Water); Evocation spirite (Summoning the Spirits); °L'Affaire Dreyfus (The Dreyfus Affair/Dreyfus Court Martial); La Pyramide de Triboulet (The Human Pyramid); °Cendrillon (Cinderella); La Statue de neige (The Snow Man); Le Chevalier Mystère (The Mysterious Knight); L'Homme protée (The Lightning Change Artist/The Chameleon Man); Charmant voyages de noces (The Interrupted Honeymoon);

Winter 1899–1900: Panorama de la Seine (Panorama of River Seine); Tom Whisky ou l'Illusioniste toqué (Addition and Subtraction); Fatale méprise (The Railroad Pickpocket/The Railway Pickpocket); Un Intrus dans une loge de Figurantes (An Intruder Behind the Scenes); Les Miracles du Brahmane (The Miracles of Brahmin); Farce de marmitons (Schullion's Joke on the Chef); Les Trois Bacchantes (The Three Bacchants); La Vengeance du Gâte-Sauce (The Cook's Revenge); Les Infortunes d'un Explorateur (The Misfortunes of an Explorer);

1900: °Exposition de 1900 (Paris Exposition, 1900); °L'Homme Orchestre (The One-Man Band); °Jeanne d'Arc (Joan of Arc); Les Sept Péchés capitaux (The Seven Capital Sins); Le Prisonnier récalcitrant (The Tricky Prisoner); La Réve du Rajah ou la Forêt enchantée (The Rajah's Dream or the Bewitched Wood); Les Deux Aveugles (The Two Blind Men); L'Artiste et le Mannequin (The Artist and the Manikin); Le Sorcier, le Prince et le bon Génie (The Wizard, the Prince, and the Good Fairy/The Sorcerer, the Prince, and the Good Fairy); Ne Bougeons plus! (Don't Move); Le Fou assassin (The Dangerous Lunatic); °Le Livre magique (The Magic Book); Vue de Remerciements au public (Thanking the Audience); Spiritisme abracadabrant (Up-to-Date Spiritualism); L'Illusioniste double et la tête vivante (The Triple Conjuror and the Living Head); Le Songe d'or de l'Avare (The Miser's Dream of Gold/The Miser or the Gold Country); °Le Rêve de Noël (The Christmas Dream); Gens qui pleurent et Gens qui rient (Crying and Laughing); Coppelia ou la Poupée animée (Coppelia, the Animated Doll); °Nouvelles Luttes extravagantes (Fat and Lean Wrestling Match/The Wrestling Sextette); Le Repas fantastique (A Fantastical Meal); Le Déshabillage impossible (Going to Bed Under Difficulties/An Increasing Wardrobe); Le Tonneau des Danaides (The Danaids' Barrel/Eight Girls in a Barrel); Le Malade hydrophobe (The Man With Wheels in His Head/The Gouty Patient);

Winter 1900–1901: Une Mauvaise Plaisanterie (Practical Joke in a Bar Room); Le Savant et le Chimpanzé (The Doctor and the Monkey); L'Homme aux cent trucs (The Conjuror With A Hundred Tricks); Guguste et Belzebuth (The Clown Versus Satan); Le Reveil d'un Monsieur pressé (How He Missed His Train); La Chirurgie de l'Avenir (Twentieth Century Surgery);

La Maison tranquille (What is Home Without the Boarder?); La Congres des nations en Chine (China Versus Allied Powers); Mésaventures d'un Aéronaute (The Balloonist's Mishap); La Tour maudite (The Bewitched Dungeon); °La Chrysalide et le Papillon d'or/Le Brahmane et le Papillon (The Brahmin and the Butterfly); Bouquet d'illusions (The Triple-Headed Lady);

1901: °Dislocation mystérieuse (Dislocation Extraordinary); Le Petit Chaperon rouge (Little Red Riding Hood); L'Antre des esprits (The Magician's Cavern/The House of Mystery); Le Chimiste repopulateur (A Maiden's Paradise); Chez la sorcière (The Bachelor's Paradise); Le Temple de la magie (The Temple of the Sun); °Le Charlatan (Painless Dentistry); Une Noce au village (Fun in Court/Contempt of Court); Le Chevalier demontable et le Géneral Boum (A Good Trick/The Fierce Charger and the Knight); Excelsior! (Excelsior!/The Prince of Magicians); L'Omnibus des toqueés/Échappés de Charenton/Off to Bloomingdale Asylum/Off to Bedlam; La Fontaine sacrée ou la Vengeance de Boudha (The Sacred Fountain); °Barbe-Bleue (Blue Beard); Le Chapeau à surprises (The Hat With Many Surprises); La Phrénologic burlesque (A Phrenological Burlesque/The Phrenologist and the Lively Skull); La Libellule (The Dragon-Fly); L'École infernale (The Trials of a Schoolmaster);

Winter 1901–1902: Le Réve du pariah (The Dream of a Hindu Beggar); Le Bataillon élastique (The Elastic Batallion); °L'Homme à la tête de Caoutchouc (The Man With the Rubber Head/A Swelled Head); Le Diable géant ou le miracle de la Madonne (The Devil and the Statue/The Gigantic Devil); Nain et géant (The Dwarf and the Giant/The Long and Short of It); Spring 1902: L'Armoire des Frères Davenport (The Cabinet Trick of the Davenport Brothers/The Mysterious Cabinet); Les Piqueurs de fûts (Wine Cellar Burglars/The Burglars in the Wine Cellar); Douche du Colonel (The Colonel's Shower Bath/The Painter's Mishap in the Barracks); L'Oeuf du Sorcier/L'Oeuf Magique Prolifique (Prolific Magical Egg/The Egg in Black Art); La Danseuse microscopique (The Dancing Midget/Marvellous Egg Producing With Surprising Developments);

1902: °Eruption volcanique à la Martinique (The Eruption of Mount Pelee/The Terrible Eruption of Mount Pelee and Destruction of St Pierre, Martinique); Catastrophe du Ballon "Le Pax" (The Catastrophe of the Balloon "Le Pax"); °Le Voyage dans la Lune (A Trip to the Moon); La Clownesse fantôme (The Shadow-girl/Twentieth Century Conjuring); °Le Sacré d'Édouard VII (The Coronation of Edward VII); °Les Trésors de Satan (The Treasures of Satan/The Devil's Money Bags); °L'Homme-Mouche (The Human Fly); °La Femme volante (Marvellous Suspension and Evolution); L'Equilibre impossible (An Impossible Balancing Feat); Le Pochard et l'inventeur (Drunkard and Inventor/What Befell the Inventor's Visitor); Une Indigestion/Chirurgie fin de siècle (Up-to-Date Surgery/Sure Cure for Indigestion); Le Voyage de Gulliver à Lilliput et chez les Géants/Voyages de Gulliver (Gulliver's Travels Among the Lilliputians and the Giants);

Winter 1902–1903: Les Aventures de Robinson Crusoe (Robinson Crusoe); La Corbeille enchantée (The Enchanted Basket); °La Guirlande merveilleuse (The Marvellous Wreath/The Marvellous Hoop); Les Filles du Diable (Beelzebub's Daughters/The Women of Fire); °Un Malheur n'arrive jamais seul (Misfortune Never Comes Alone/Accidents Never Happen Singly); °Le Cake-walk infernal (The Cake Walk Infernal/The Infernal Cake Walk); °La Boite à malice (The Mysterious Box/The Shallow Box Trick); Les Mousquetaires de la Reine (The Queen's Musketeers/The Musketeers of the Queen);

1903: °Le Puits fantastique (The Enchanted Well); °L'Auberge du Bon Repos (The Inn Where No Man Rests/The Inn of "Good Rest"); °La Statue animée (The Drawing Lesson, or the Living Statue); °La Flamme merveilleuse (The Mystical Flame); °Le Sorcier (The Witch's Revenge/The Sorcerer's Revenge); °L'Oracle de Delphes (The Oracle of Delphi); °Le Portrait spirite (A Spiritualistic Photographer); °Le Mélomane (The Melomaniac); °Le Monstre (The Monster); °Le Royaume des Fées (Fairyland, or The Kingdom of the Fairies/Wonders of the Deep); °Le Chaudron infernal (The Infernal Cauldron and the Phantasmal Vapours); °Le Revenant (The Apparition, or Mr. Jones' Comical Experience With a Ghost/The Ghost and the Candle); °Le Tonnerre de Jupiter (Jupiter's Thunderbolts, or the Home of the Muses); °La Parapluie fantastique (Ten Ladies in One Umbrella/The Girls in One Umbrella); °Tom Tight et Dum Dum (Jack Jaggs and Dum Dum/The Rival Music Hall Artistes); °Bob Kick, l'Enfant terrible (Bob Kick the Mischievous Kid); °Illusions funambulesques (Extraordinary Illusions/The 20th Century Illustrationist); °L'Enchanteur Alcofrisbas (Alcofrisbas, the Master Magician/The Enchanter); °Jack et Jim (Jack and Jim/Comical Conjuring); °La Lanterne magique (The Magic Lantern); °Le Rêve du Maître de Ballet (The Ballet-Master's Dream/The Dream of the Ballet Master); °Faust aux Enfers/La Damnation de Faust (The Damnation of Faust/The Condemnation of Faust);

Winter 1903–1904: °Le Bourreau turc (The Terrible Turkish Executioner, or It Served Him Right); Les Apaches (A Burlesque Highway Robbery in "Gay Paree"); °Au Clair de la Lune ou Pierrot malheureux (A Moonlight Serenade, or the Miser Punisher); °Un Prêté pour un rendu/Une bonne Farce avec ma tête (Tit for Tat, or a Good Joke With My Head); Match de Prestidigitation (A Wager Between Two Magicians, or "Jealous of Myself"); Un Peu de feu, S. V. P. (Every Man His Own Cigar Lighter); Siva l'Invisible (The Invisible Silvia); °Le Coffre enchanté (The Bewitched Trunk); °Les Apparitions fugitives (The Fugitive Apparitions); °Le Roi du Maquillage (The Untamable Whiskers); °Le Rêve de l'Horloger (The Clockmaker's Dream); °Les Transmutations imperceptibles (The Imperceptible Transmutations);

1904: °Un Miracle sous L' Inquisition (A Miracle Under the Inquisition); °Benvenuto Cellini ou une curieuse évasion (Benvenuto Cellini, or A Curious Evasion); °Damnation du Doctor Faust (Faust and Marguerite/Faust); Le Joyeux Prophète russe (The Fake Russian Prophet); °Le Thaumaturge chinois (Tchin-Chao, the Chinese Conjuror); °Le Merveilleux Éventail vivant (The Wonderful Living Fan); °Sorcellerie culinaire (The Cook in Trouble); La Planche du Diable (The Devilish Plank); Le Dîner impossible (The Impossible Dinner); °La Sirène (The Mermaid); Les Mésaventures de M. Boit-sans-Soif (The Mischances of a Drunkard); La Providence de Notre-Dame des Flots (The Providence of the Waves, or the Dream of a Poor Fisherman); La Fête au père Mathieu (Uncle Rube's Birthday); Le Barbier de Seville (The Barber of Sevilla, or the Useless Precaution) two versions; Les Costumes animés (The Animated Costumes); Les Invités de M. Latourte/Une Bonne Surprise (Simple Simon's Surprise Party); Le Cadre aux surprises (The Astonishing Frame); Le Rosier miraculeux (The Wonderful Rose-Tree); La Dame fantôme (The Shadow Lady); Mariage par correspondence (A Wedding by Correspondence); °Le Voyage à travers l'Impossible/Voyage (An Impossible Voyage/Whirling the Worlds) two versions;

Winter 1904–1905: °Le Juif Errant (The Wandering Jew); °Le Cascade de feu (The Firefall); La Grotte aux surprises (The Grotto of Surprises); °Détresse et charité (The Christmas Angel/The Beggar Maiden); °Les Cartes vivantes (The Living Playing Cards); Le Roi des Tireurs (The King of Sharpshooters); °Le Diable noir (The Black Imp); °Le Phenix ou le Coffret de cristal (The Crystal Casket); °Le Menuet lilliputien (The Lilliputian Minuet); °Le Baquet de Mesmer (A Mesmerian Experiment);

1905: Le Peintre Barbouillard et le Tableau diabolique (Mr. Dauber and the Whimsical Picture); Le Miroir de Venise. Une Mésaventure de Shylock (The Venetian Looking-glass); Les Chevaliers du chloroforme (The Chloroform Fiends); °Le Palais des Mille et Une Nuits (The Place of the Arabian Nights) two versions; °Le Compositeur toqué (A Crazy Composer); La Tour de Londres et les Dernières Moments d'Anne Boleyn (The Tower of London); °La Chaise à porteurs enchantée (The Enchanted Sedan Chair); °Le Raid Paris–Monte Carlo en 2 heures (An Adventurous Automobile Trip); °L'Ile de Calypso. Ulysse et le géant Polypheme (The Mysterious Island); °Un Feu d'artifice improvisé (Unexpected Fireworks); °La Légende de Rip van Winkle (Rip's Dream); Le Cauchemar du pêcheur ou l'Escarpolette fantastique (The Angler's Nightmare, or a Policeman's Troubles); Le Système du Docteur Sonflamort (Life-Saving Up-to-Date); °Le Tripot clandestin (The Scheming Gamblers' Paradise);

Winter 1905–1906: Le Dirigeable fantastique ou le Cauchemar d'un Inventeur (The Inventor Crazybrains and his Wonderful Airship); °Une Chute de cinq étages (A Mix-up in the Gallery); °Jack le Ramoneur (The Chimney Sweep); Le Maestro Do-mi-sol-do (Professor Do-mi-sol-do); La Magie à travers les âges (Old and New Style Conjurors); L'Honneur est satisfait (Who Looks, Pays!); °La Cardeuse de matelas (The Tramp and the Mattress Makers); °Les Affiches en goguette (The Hilarious Posters); °Les Incendiaires/Histoire d'un crime (A Desperate Crime); L'Anarchie chez Guignol (Punch and Judy); Le Fantôme d'Alger (A Spiritualistic Meeting); °L'Hotel des voyageurs de commerce (A Roadside Inn); °Les Bulles de savon animées (Soap Bubbles); °Les 400 Farces du Diable (The Merry Frolics of Satan); Le Rastaquouère Rodriguez y Papanaguaz (A Seaside Flirtation); L'Alchimste Parafaragamus ou la Cornue infernale (The Mysterious Retort); °La Fée Carabosse ou le Poignard fatal (The Witch);

Winter 1906–1907: Robert Macaire et Berrand (Robert Macaire and Bertrand); Le Carton fantastique (A Mischievous Sketch); °La Douche d'eau bouillante (Rogues' Tricks); 1907: Deux cent mille lieues sous les mers ou le cauchemar d'un pecheur (Under the Seas); Les Fromages automobiles (The Skipping Cheeses); °Le Mariage de Victorine/Le Mariage de Victoire (How Bridget's Lover Escaped); °Le tunnel sous la Manche ou le Cauchemar franco-anglais (Tunnelling the English Channel); La nouvelle peine de mort (A New Death Penalty); Le Delirium Tremens ou la fin d'un alcoolique (Drink! A Great Temperance Story); °L'Éclipse du soleil en pleine lune (The Eclipse); Le Placard infernal (The Bewildering Cabinet); La Marche funebre de Chopin (Chopin's Funeral March Burlesqued); Hamlet (Hamlet, Prince of Denmark); Bernard le Bucheron ou le Miracle de saint Hubert (A Forester Made King); Shakespeare. La Mort de Jules César (Shakespeare Writing "Julius Caesar"); °Pauvre John ou les Aventures d'un buveur de whiskey (Sightseeing Through Whisky); °La Colle universelle (Good Glue Sticks); °Satan en prison (Satan in Prison); °Ali Barbouyou et Ali Bouf à l'huile (Delirium in a Studio); La Boulangerie modèle (Bakers in Trouble); La Perle des savants (An Angelic Servant); °Le Tambourin fantastique (The Knight of Black Art); La Cuisine de l'ogre (In the Bogie Man's Cave); François 1er et Triboulet (The King and the Jester); °Il y a un dieu pour les ivrognes (The Good Luck of a "Souse"); Seek and Thou Shalt Find; Le Civilisation à travers les âges (Humanity Through the Ages); Les Torches humaines (Justinian's Human Torches); °La Génie du Feu (The Genii of Fire); °Why That Actor Was Late; °Le Rêve d'un fumeur d'opium (The Dream of an Opium Fiend); Nuit de Carnaval (A Night With Masqueraders in Paris); °La Photographie électrique à distance (Long Distance Wireless Photography); La Prophétesse de Thèbes (The Prophetess of Thebes); °Salon de coiffure (In the Barber Shop); 1908: Quiproquo (A Mistaken Identity); Mariage de raison et mariage d'amour (A Lover's Hazing); L'Habit ne fait pas le moine/Le Fabricant de Diamants (A Fake-Diamond Swindler); La Curiosité puniée/Le Crime de la rue de Cherche-Midi à quatorze heures (Curiosity Punished); °Le Nouveau Seigneur du Village; °L'Avare (The Miser); °Le Conseil de pipelet (Up-to-Date Clothes Cleaning [?]); Le Serpent de la rue de la Lune (Pranks With a Fake Python); High Life Taylor/Sideshow Wrestlers [?]; °Lulli ou le Violon brisé (The Broken Violin); Tartarin de Tarascon ou une chasse à l'ours (Hunting the Teddy Bear); Le Trait d'Union (The Little Peacemaker); Rivalité d'amour (A Tragedy in Spain); Le Raid Paris–New York en automobile (Mishaps of the N.Y.–Paris Race); On ne badine pas avec l'amour (No Trifling With Love [?]; Love and

Molasses; Mystery of the Garrison; Magic of Catchy Songs; °Woes of Roller Skates; Le Fakir de Singapoure (Indian Sorcerer); Le Jugement du Garde-Champêtre (The Forester's Remedy) [?]; °Mischances of a Photographer; Two Crazy Bugs; °His First Job; °French Interpreter Policeman (French Cops Learning English); At the Hotel Mix-Up; Oriental Black Art; °Tricky Painter's Fate; Two Talented Vagabonds; Conte de la Grand'mere et Rêve de l'Enfant/Au pays des Jouets (Grandmother's Story); Le Main secourable (Helping Hand); °Buncoed Stage Johnnie; °Not Guilty; Le Mariage de Thomas Poirot (Fun With the Bridal Party); Trop Vieux! (Old Footlight Favourite) [?]; Anaie ou le Balafré; Pour l'étoile S.V.P.; Pour les p'tiots; La Fontaine merveilleuse; L'Ascension de la rosière; Voyage de noces en ballon (Honeymoon in a Balloon); Aventures de Don Quichotte (Incident From Don Quixote); Rude Awakening; Wonderful Charm; The Duke's Good Joke; Pochardiana ou le rêveur éveillé; La Tiole d'araignée merveilleuse; La Fée libellule/Le Lac enchanté; La Génie des cloches/La Fête du sonneur; Moitié de polka; °Hallucinations pharmaceutiques/La Truc du potard; °La bonne bergère et la méchante princesse; La Poupée vivante;

1909: Cinderella Up-to-Date; For the Cause of Suffrage; Hypnotist's Revenge; For Sale: a Baby; A Tumultuous Elopement; Count's Wooing; Mrs. and Mr. Duff; Fortune Favours the Brave; Seein' Things;

1910: °Hydrothérapie fantastique; Le Traitment 706/Guérison de l'obésité en 5 minutes [?]; °Le Locataire diabolique; Un Homme comme il faut; °Les Illusions fantaisistes; Si j'étais le roi!!!; Le Roi des Médiums/Apparitions fantômatiques; Le Papillon fantastique; La Gigue merveilleuse; Le Mousquetaire de la Reine; Le Conte du vieux Talute; Les sept barres d'or; Galatée; L'Homme aux mille inventions; Le Secret du Médécin (The Doctor's Secret); Fin de réveillon; °Les Hallucinations du Baron de Münchausen; Le Vitrail diabolique; °À la Conquête du Pole (Conquest of the Pole); °Cendrillon ou la pantoufle mystérieuse (Cinderella, or the Glass Slipper); °Le Chevalier des neiges; Le Voyage de la famille Bourrichon.

PRINCIPAL WRITINGS: Star Film Catalogue, 1905; "Les vues cinématographiques" in Annuaire général et international de la photographie, 1907, reprinted in La revue du cinéma October 1929, Anthologie du cinéma 1946, and Sadoul, G. Georges Méliès, 1961; "Le merveilleux" in L'echo du cinéma May 1912; "L'invention des trucs" in Coissac, G. M. Histoire du cinématographe, 1925; "En marge de l'histoire du cinema" in Ciné-Journal August 1926; "Le Théâtre Robert-Houdin" in Passez muscade 41–44, 1928; "Allocution" (speech at the Méliès gala) in Le nouvel art cinématographique January 1930; "Importance du scénario" in Cinéma-Ciné pour tous April 1932; "Les phénomènes du spiritisme" in Journal de l'association française des artistes prestidigitateurs 90–91, 1936; "Mes memoires" in Bessy, M. and Lo Duca, G. M. Georges Méliès, mage, 1945 (reprinted 1961); "Histoire d'un film: Le voyage dans la lune" in Ce soir, December 1937; "J'ai construit le premier studio du monde il y a quarante ans" *in* Pour vous December 1937; "The Silver Lining," *in* Sight and Sound Spring 1938.

ABOUT: Barnouw, E. The Magician and the Cinema, 1981; Bessy, M. and Lo Duca, G. M. Georges Méliès mage, 1961; Bessy, M. Méliès, 1967; Brakhage, S. Film Biographies, 1977; Cherchi Usai, P. Georges Méliès, 1983; Costa, A. La morale del giocattolo, 1980; Cuenca, C. F. El mundo de Georges Méliès, 1961 (in Spanish); Deslandes, J. Le Boulevard du cinéma à l'époque de Georges Méliès, 1963; Deslandes, J. and Richard, J. Histoire comparée du cinéma, 1968; Exposition commemorative du centénaire de Georges Méliès (catalogue), 1961; Fell, J. Film Before Griffith, 1983; Ford, C. Georges Méliès, 1959; Frazer, J. Artificially Arranged Scenes, 1979; Fulton, A. R. Motion Pictures, 1980; Hammond, P. Marvellous Méliès, 1975; Jenn, P. Georges Méliès cinéaste, 1984; Kyrou, A. De Méliès à l'expressionisme, le surréalisme au cinéma, 1963; Malthête-Méliès, M. Méliès, l'enchanteur, 1973; Malthête-Méliès, M. (ed.) Méliès et la naissance du spectacle cinématographique, 1984; Mitry, J. Histoire du cinéma, vol. 1, 1967; Roud, R. (ed.) Cinema: A Critical Dictionary, 1980; Sadoul, G. Georges Méliès, 1961 (in French); Thomson, D. A Biographical Dictionary of the Cinema, 1980. *Periodicals*—Afterimage Spring 1981; Cahiers du cinéma March 1952, April 1979; Cahiers de la Cinémathèque Autumn 1982, Winter 1984; Ciné Journal March 1930; Cine-Tracts Winter 1981; Cinéma (France) January 1971, May 1977, May 1979, September 1979; Cinema Journal Fall 1976; Cinématographe April 1977, April 1979, January 1981; Écran April 1979; Film (London) January–February 1957; Films and Filming December 1961; Filmcritica January 1977; Film Culture 48–49 1970, 67–69 1979; Film Quarterly Fall 1979; Iris 2/1 1984; The Listener June 2, 1938; Nouvel art cinématographique (Brest) 3–5 1929–1930; Positif June 1977, December–January 1977–1978, June 1979, April 1985; Revue belge Winter 1984–1985; Revue du cinéma October 15, 1929; October 1, 1946; March 11, 1948; Sight and Sound 11 1947, Autumn 1961, Autumn 1979; Village Voice December 25, 1978. *Films about Méliès*—Bianchi, G. Méliès, [n.d.]; Cavalcanti, A. Film and Reality, 1943; Franju, G. Le grand Méliès, 1952; Franju, G. Méliès père et fils, 1976; Malthête-Méliès, M. Georges Méliès, 1969; Montgomery P. Georges Méliès: Cinema Magician, 1977; Schmitt, F. (comp.) Méliès et ses contemporains, 1981.

---

*MICHEAUX, OSCAR (1884–April 1, 1951), black American director, scenarist, and producer, was born on a small farm near the Ohio River, about forty miles above Cairo, Illinois. He was the fifth child in a family of thirteen. Both of his parents had been slaves. Micheaux is said to have enjoyed what little schooling he had, and evidently decided early on that he would not be content with a life of drudgery on the family farm.

He left home at seventeen and, after working

The Bowser Black Film Collection

OSCAR MICHEAUX

as a shoeshine boy and as a laborer, became a Pullman porter on the Chicago-Portland run. He liked the West and in 1904 left the railroad and bought a "relinquishment on a homestead" in Gregory County, South Dakota—a state which, according to a contemporary census, had at that time fewer than two hundred black inhabitants.

Micheaux's entry in the *Dictionary of American Negro Biography* says that he was at this time "a hardworking, bookish, somewhat priggish young man, a great admirer of Booker T. Washington." He was "successful as a farmer, got along well with his exclusively white neighbors, and was scornful of Negroes unwilling to leave the bright lights of the cities for the agricultural opportunities of the West." There is reason to believe that, during this period of his life, he had a frustrated romance with a white woman and subsequently married the daughter of a black minister—a man whose financial chicanery may have caused Micheaux to lose his land.

At any rate, this is the story he told in his first novel, *The Conquest: The Story of a Negro Pioneer* (1913), and retold, with variations, again and again in his books and films. The hero of *The Conquest* is "Oscar Devereaux," a young black man who achieves success as a farmer and falls in love with a girl of Scottish descent. Since he is opposed on principle to interracial marriage (which in any case was illegal at that time in South Dakota), he decides that he must forget his true love. He marries a black woman, the daughter of a lecherous, dishonest, and hypocritical Methodist minister who eventually breaks up the marriage.

Micheaux published the novel anonymously

and at his own expense. He had apparently had it polished by a professional or semi-professional writer who was responsible for its style—more or less literate, but dull and pedestrian. The book would probably have sunk without trace if Micheaux had not possessed a positive genius for salesmanship. He embarked on aggressive promotional tours all over the west and south, calling meetings in churches and schools and selling the book—and later shares in his Western Book Supply Company—to both black and white audiences. Even at this stage of his career, it was said, Micheaux stepped into a meeting hall as if "he were God about to deliver a sermon." His experiences on tour provided the plot of a second novel, *The Forged Note: A Romance of the Darker Races* (1915), which he promoted and sold in the same way.

Robert Bone, in *The Negro Novelist in America*, places Micheaux with those assimilationist writers who "stoutly maintain that there is no barrier to success which diligence and perseverance cannot hurdle. Rather than face the harsh realities of caste, these novelists prefer to indulge in crude success fantasies. . . . The Negro protagonists are invariably modeled after white culture-heroes. . . . Their antagonists are not prejudiced whites but rather those 'lazy' and 'indifferent' members of the [black] race who, in their view, willfully refuse to succeed." Micheaux himself was determined to succeed, and to do so precisely in the terms of white American capitalism—he was, he wrote, "stimulated to effort by the example of my white friends and neighbors who were doing what I admired, building an empire."

Micheaux's third novel, *The Homesteader,* appeared in 1917. It is a reworking of the later chapters of *The Conquest,* but far more melodramatic. The hero, now named Jean Baptiste, again falls in love with a Scottish girl but marries the daughter of a villainous minister; however, in this version of the story the wife goes mad, killing her father and herself. One obstacle to a "happy" ending is thus removed, and the remaining hurdle falls when it emerges that the white heroine is actually "of Ethiopian extraction."

Written by Micheaux without professional assistance, *The Homesteader,* according to the *Dictionary of American Negro Biography,* was "a literary disaster, with an unbelievably complicated plot, long-winded, pretentiously awkward writing, stilted conversations, and the grotesque misuse of words. Nevertheless, the author's promotional methods won for it considerable circulation." More than that, in 1918 Micheaux was approached by the Lincoln Mo-

tion Picture Company for the film rights to the novel.

Lincoln was the most respected of the black independent production companies that were then emerging. Micheaux, recognizing in this exciting new industry fresh possibilities for empire building, said that Lincoln could have the movie rights only if *The Homesteader* was filmed as a major eight-reel production. According to Thomas Cripps, in his *Slow Fade to Black,* the "prim men of Lincoln" disapproved of Micheaux, whom they regarded as a "rough Negro who had got his hands on some cash," and in the end the negotiations collapsed. With characteristic *chutzpah,* Micheaux decided to film the novel himself.

The black American cinema began as a direct response to the racist bigotry of D. W. Griffith's *The Birth of a Nation* (1915)—the first black film was *The Birth of a Race,* made by Booker T. Washington's secretary E. J. Scott. The picture was a failure, but other black producers entered the arena with more success, showing their products in ghetto movie theatres and in schools and churches, as well as at segregated matinees or midnight showings in white theatres. As Thomas Cripps says, there was never more than "a thin stream of movies created by blacks for black audiences. Stifled by short capital, muddled by the tangle between cultural nationalism and NAACP assimilationism, stunted by lack of outlets, rendered comic by inexperience and artlessness . . . the all-black cinema failed miserably." Nevertheless, throughout the 1920s, Micheaux was the major figure in "an underground cinema that attempted a black aesthetic to fill the vacuum left by Hollywood."

In 1918 Micheaux established the Micheaux Book and Film Company, which in subsequent manifestations became the Micheaux Pictures Corporation and the Micheaux Film Corporation. The enterprise seems actually to have begun in Sioux City, Iowa, but soon moved to Chicago and then to Harlem. Sending his wife home to her family, Micheaux set out to sell stock in the new company to the same white farmers who had backed his books. In between he wrote a script of 600 shots and 400 titles, hustled bookings, and recruited actors—mostly amateurs chosen for their physical suitability. The only "name" in the cast was Evelyn Preer, a veteran of the black stage company The Lafayette Players.

The Homesteader was filmed in eight reels under Micheaux's direction at the old Selig studio in Chicago, and cost about $15,000. It opened in Chicago early in 1919, supported by a brassy publicity campaign, and reportedly grossed around $5,600—only a third of its cost, but still more than most black movies earned. Reviews are hard to come by, and *The Homesteader,* like most of Micheaux's films, is lost; Pearl Bowser wrote that its depiction of the hero's father-in-law—a minister who is "the embodiment of vanity, deceit, and hypocrisy" —caused a certain amount of controversy, always welcomed by Micheaux as an aid to sales.

Micheaux tackled the crucial problem of distribution much as he had that of selling his books. Twice a year he would take to the road, touring ghetto movie theatres and white theatres that might be persuaded to show black films (especially films like his, many of which contained raunchy cabaret scenes that earned them midnight showings for white audiences). Micheaux would take stills from his latest movie (and sometimes his star performers themselves) and show them off to theatre managers as an inducement to bookings. At the same time he would tout the script of his next picture, asking for an advance against *its* bookings. "A hefty six-footer, given to wearing long Russian coats and extravagant wide-brimmed hats," Micheaux, according to one of his principal leading men, Lorenzo Tucker, was "so impressive and charming that he could talk the shirt off your back."

When he had raised the production money, Micheaux would settle down and shoot his next film, usually in about six weeks. All of his pictures, but especially the early ones, suffered from the shortage of funds (and Micheaux's own reluctance to part with his hard-won cash). There were no black technicians, and the white journeymen prepared to work for blacks were seldom the best. In any case, Micheaux used the cheapest available equipment and a minimal crew, usually hiring his cameraman by the day. Most of his scenes, however complicated, were shot in a single take and he discarded almost nothing. As one of his actors said, "if you made a mistake or missed a line, he'd leave it in . . . , saying maybe the audience would get a laugh."

For economic rather than aesthetic reasons, Micheaux shot on location whenever he could, interiors as well as exteriors, often using homes or offices belonging to friends and acquaintances who could be flattered into providing the director with free sets. He was particularly fond of Harlem nightclub scenes featuring half-naked chorus girls—locations like these sold movies, and they came cheap or free when he explained to the club owners what excellent publicity he was giving them.

Micheaux freely mixed amateur and professional actors, often to ludicrous effect. The professionals he recruited mostly from black theatre companies; the beginners he discovered much as he did his locations. He met Shingzie Howard, for example, while selling books to her father in Stelton, Pennsylvania. She played bit parts in several films and doubled as Micheaux's secretary before finally achieving a starring role in *The House Behind the Cedars* (1923). Race-conscious critics were continually incensed by the director's preference for light-skinned performers, who would be billed as the "black Valentino," the "sepia Mae West," or the "colored Cagney." Many of his players were so pale-skinned that they could be cast without difficulty in white roles.

This failing, however, was not unusual in "race" cinema of the time. And Micheaux did address himself to subjects that no other black filmmaker of his day dared touch. In the storm of publicity surrounding the arrest and lynching of Leo Frank, a Jewish grocer, in Atlanta, Micheaux saw an opportunity to draw attention to the plight of his own people. *Within Our Gates* (1920) starred Evelyn Preer, Lawrence Chenault, and Charles Lucas, and dealt with the lynching of a black. Billed as a "spectacular screen version of the most sensational story on the race question since *Uncle Tom's Cabin,*" the film included scenes so horrific that, when it opened in Chicago and Denver, both blacks and whites opposed its release as conducive to race riots. Micheaux responded angrily that "our people do not care—nor the other race for that matter—for propaganda."

Perhaps because of its dangerous theme, *Within Our Gates* did badly, but was soon followed by *The Brute* (1921), a commercial if not a critical success. Teaming Evelyn Preer and the black boxer Sam Langford, it included many scenes of black low-life as well as fight sequences, and touched on the mistreatment of black women by black men. Southern police shut it down as "a very dangerous picture," and there was trouble with the Chicago censors, understandably nervous about racial violence so soon after the riots. Black critics objected to scenes showing wife-beating and crap games in black dives, complaining that the story "was not elevating."

The Brute, according to Cripps, "opened in New York in the late summer [of 1921] supported by nine prints, every one 'in action' in both North and South; by a strong package of lobby cards and stills; and by the teamwork of Micheaux and his brother, who in concert were able to promote the New York opening while cutting and polishing their next film. The prerelease campaign drew enthusiastic audiences who cheered the boxing sequences of Langford." As Cripps says, "Micheaux had arrived," but knew very well that there was "something missing"—"the bad lighting concealed action, the unmatched textures marred shots made under varied conditions, the jerky rhythms worked to false climaxes. . . . None of the black filmmakers could afford the luxury of a cutter who could edit a bad shot and control pacing and texture merely by good selection, but at least the Micheaux group knew the problem and gave their attention to it."

By the fall of 1921, Micheaux was already clearly established as the leading black producer. Cripps says that "he could get $500 per engagement in the urban houses . . . and in New York's Lafayette he once cleared $2,000 on a gross of $10,000. . . . Still, though he earned $40,000 in 1920 and hoped for $100,000 in 1921, he was not above taking $25 for a one-nighter in Mound Bayou or Arkadelphia. Indeed, his 'bread and butter' was down home in the South, where he had more dates than in the North."

Symbol of the Unconquered (1921), in which a black girl goes west to take possession of a mine inherited from her grandfather, attacked both the Ku Klux Klan and the folly of blacks trying to pass as white, and threw in a love story. Its reception showed that Micheaux had at least some supporters among black critics, including Kennard Williams of the Baltimore *Afro-American,* who asked for "sensible support of Negro producers like Micheaux" with "organized protest" against Hollywood movies and their caricatured blacks. One of the reasons why so little support was forthcoming was illustrated in Micheaux's *The Gunsaulus Mystery,* a whodunnit, now lost, that judging from contemporary accounts was blatantly cobbled together from outtakes from *Within Our Gates.*

But Micheaux turned more seriously to the problems of urban life in *The Wages of Sin* (1921), while *The Dungeon* (1922) dealt in part with residential segregation and a campaign for a black seat in Congress. However, the latter irritated a columnist in the Chicago *Defender* because it had "nothing to indicate that the feature is colored, as the . . . [actors are] almost white." Subsequent pictures attracted less and less attention from press and public, and *The House Behind the Cedars* (1923), one of two Micheaux films adapted from novels by Charles Waddell Chesnutt, was almost ignored, in spite of a vigorous promotional campaign.

So was *Birthright* (1924), said to have been one of Micheaux' better films. Based on a novel by T. B. Stribling, and starring Evelyn Preer and J. Homer Tutt, it tells the story of an idealistic black Harvard graduate who returns to his Tennessee home town determined to found a college and "uplift the race." He encounters bigotry and brutality not only from whites but from blacks who agree that education "ruins a Negro." As Donald Bogle writes, "in its own silly and sly way, *Birthright* made a definite plea for black unity while seriously satirizing the old-style toms."

The best of Micheaux's silent pictures followed the same year, *Body and Soul.* One of the few Micheaux films to have survived, it starred Paul Robeson in his first movie as a young jackleg preacher in Georgia. The New York censor objected to the portrayal of the preacher as a man of unrelieved venality, and so Micheaux added a confusing sequence in which it emerges that he is actually an agent assigned to break up a bootlegging ring. James Hoberman saw an even more complicated version of the story during the Micheaux centennial in 1984, reporting that "Robeson's role has been split in two—the bogus preacher (here an ex-con) and a timid inventor named Sylvester. The presence of these identical twins is never explained, but most of the film turns out to be a hallucination anyway ("only a nightmare—the dream of a tortured soul").

But, Hoberman wrote, "however bizarre this seems at the narrative level, Robeson's schizoid figure makes perfect allegorical sense: he represents what Micheaux saw as the two alternatives open to the black man, namely the hustler-trickster . . . or the bourgeois disciple of Booker T. Washington. (By all accounts, the director was a bit of both.)"

For Thomas Cripps, the film "represented the highest level of achievement for Micheaux. For the first time he wrestled with the nature of the black community, without recourse to shoddy devices . . . or interracial sensationalism. . . . In a dual role . . . [Robeson] brought power to the gambler's cynical smile and to the preacher's practical piety. Micheaux gave him tight closeups that tilted up to capture a virility long missing from black figures. . . . Micheaux too reached high. In spite of the stagey, unmatched cutaway shots inherent in low-budget shooting, the garbled plot, and the broad comedy relief, he pulled off a modestly successful black movie. The exteriors had the rough and unpainted texture of Auburn Avenue, Beale Street, or some other black Southern promenade. . . . The dense life of the ghetto with its many alternative life-models, close-packed upon each other and in competition, had never appeared before on film."

It has been suggested that the success of *Body*

and Soul may have been one factor in the brief revival in black cinema during the mid-1920s. For a while, Micheaux himself increased the social thrust of his pictures. *The Devil's Disciple* (1926) touched on prostitution in New York and *The Spider's Web* (1927) centered on the numbers game. But black filmmakers were losing the fight with Hollywood, and by the end of the decade were turning increasingly to cheap melodramas like Micheaux's *The Millionaire* (1927), about a black pioneer in Argentina. Grace Smith starred as the vamp who tries to trap the self-made millionaire into marriage on behalf of her criminal master, but winds up redeemed by true love. This movie, incidentally, was advertised as the screen version of the director's own novel—one of several pieces of evidence that Micheaux did not abandon literature when he invaded the film industry.

The end of an era came in 1928, when Micheaux went into voluntary bankruptcy, unable any longer to survive Hollywood's penetration of the black market, the tight credit presaging the crash of 1929, and the irresistible but hopelessly expensive novelty of sound. Alone among black independents, he went on making movies, but financial control in his company had passed into white hands.

Micheaux' first sound film was *The Exile* (1931), a reworking of the theme of his first silent, *The Homesteader*. Jean Baptiste leaves corrupt Chicago, where his fiancée Edith has become a brothel madam, and becomes a successful pioneer in South Dakota. He falls in love with Agnes, a white girl, but cannot face the burden of miscegeny and returns to Chicago. Edith conveniently dies in a sex-murder, and Agnes turns out to possess enough "black blood" to license their union. *The Exile* had some dialogue and synchronized music, and was padded out with cabaret routines. It was found generally crude and old-fashioned.

Ten Minutes to Live (1932) was even worse. Recording voice and image together was an expensive operation and, as James Hoberman wrote, "Micheaux makes elaborate use of deaf-mute characters, letters and telegrams, flashbacks, long lyrical interludes to narrate the two separate murder stories that punctuate the dizzying stream of entertainment that flows from the single set that is called 'Club Libya.'" When all else failed, Micheaux broke the talkies' ultimate taboo and used an intertitle.

He made no movies for three years after that, but in 1935 he was back again with *Harlem After Midnight*, presumably black exploitation. *Swing: The Story of Mandy* (1936) follows its heroine from drudgery in support of a faithless husband in Birmingham to fame as a singer in Harlem and was said to be "relatively slick and straightforward for a Micheaux film." *Temptation* and *Underworld,* both released in 1936, each imitated a Hollywood genre. The first, with Ethel Moses in the title role, attempted the sophisticated sex drama; *Underworld* the gangster movie. But, here as elsewhere, Micheaux could not match Hollywood's technical skills, making do perforce with semi-amateur casts, tacky backdrops, and a padding of vaudeville acts.

All of Micheaux's racial confusion and disillusionment broke loose in *God's Step Children* (1938), again starring Ethel Moses. She plays Naomi, a light-skinned mulatto foundling adopted by a kindly widow and raised in "Coloredtown." Naomi is pale and presumptuous enough to try to "pass" and, in the film's most intensely lyrical sequence, she runs away to enroll in a white school. Unmasked, she returns to Coloredtown, where she breaks another taboo by showing sexual interest in her foster brother. Her punishment is marriage to the blackest black in town, a rich farmer who is portrayed as a cackling coon. She bears his child and then jumps off a bridge, under a caption reading "As ye sow, so shall ye reap."

When *God's Step Children* opened at an RKO theatre in Harlem, there was a storm of protest from liberal, political, civic, labor, and youth groups. A spokesman for the Young Communist League said that the film "slandered Negroes, holding them up to ridicule, playing light-skinned Negroes against their darker brothers"; it also implied that "Negroes fall for any kind of gambling game" and that only "one Negro in a million tries to think." The theatre was picketed until the movie was withdrawn from circulation at all RKO theatres and Micheaux promised to mend his ways. James Hoberman called this "horrific" film "Micheaux's inside-out imitation of *Imitation of Life*"—a "nightmarish account of self-directed racism and misplaced mother love," but also "the director's antimasterpiece, as profound and powerful an embodiment of American racial pathology as D. W. Griffith's *The Birth of a Nation* or John Ford's *The Searchers*, and as amazing a movie as either of them."

In his final years as a filmmaker, Micheaux concentrated on genre movies, continuing his unsuccessful attempt to compete with the Hollywood models. He made a talking version of *Birthright* in 1939 and then *The Notorious Elinor Lee* (1940), a boxing story strongly reminiscent of *Golden Boy* and starring two of the best black actors of the era, Edna Mae Harris and

Robert Earl Jones. By this time Micheaux had gone into partnership with Colonel Hubert Julian, the "Black Eagle" of the Ethiopian Air Force—a man whose flair for publicity at least equaled Micheaux's. *Elinor Lee* had a splendiferous premiere at the RKO Regent, but the producers' fanfaronade could not conceal the slowness and improbability of the story (in which the *deus ex machina* is a parrot). *Lying Lips* (1940), in which the heroine is framed for murder when she refuses to prostitute herself, had the same cast as *Elinor Lee* and was probably patched together from its outtakes.

After that, Micheaux made no more films for eight years, returning to his career as a writer and book drummer. In 1948 he attempted a come-back with *The Betrayal*, yet another reworking of the story of *The Homesteader*. It achieved a Broadway opening, at which it was excoriated. A characteristic review (from the New York *Herald-Tribune*) called it "a preposterous, inept bore. . . . Acting that is worse than amateurish . . . [and] dialogue even worse, with senseless and unmouthable lines. . . . [Micheaux's] concept of human beings is absurd and his direction somewhat less artful than one would expect of home movies. The fact that Micheaux expects one to watch this trashy *The Betrayal* for more than three hours is a monstrous piece of miscalculation."

Oscar Micheaux died three years later, on April 1, 1951, while on a promotional tour in North Carolina. He was survived by his (second?) wife, the former Alice B. Russell. After his death she retired into seclusion, refusing to comment in any way on her husband's life and career.

It seemed to Donald Bogle that "Oscar Micheaux's greatest contribution . . . is often viewed by contemporary black audiences as his severest shortcoming. That his films reflect the interests and outlooks of the black bourgeoisie will no doubt always be held against him. His films never centered on the ghetto; they seldom deal with racial misery and decay. Instead they concentrate on the problems of 'passing' or the difficulties facing 'professional people.' But to appreciate Micheaux's films one must understand that he was moving as far as possible away from Hollywood's [black] jesters and servants. He wanted to give his audience something 'to further the race, not hinder it.' Often he sacrificed plausibility to do so. He created a fantasy world where blacks were just as affluent, just as educated, just as 'cultured,' just as well-mannered—in short, just as white—as white America."

James Hoberman, who calls Micheaux "the unknown titan and Black Pioneer of American cinema," maintains that "Micheaux's films 'fail' with a resonance that far surpasses Hollywood's or Europe's greatest successes. In their capacity to inspire consciousness of both the process and plastic possibilities of cinema they are all but unequalled. In their utter nuttiness, their moment-to-moment unpredictability, their blunt ingenuity, they are unique. Micheaux's films re-invent the language of cinema and their value cannot be overestimated."

FILMS: (All of the films listed were made by Micheaux's company, but it is possible that a handful of them were directed not by Micheaux but by his brother or another colleague): The Homesteader, 1919; Within Our Gates, 1920; The Brute, 1921; Symbol of the Unconquered, 1921; The Shadow, 1921; The Gunsaulus Mystery, 1921; The Hypocrite, 1921; The Wages of Sin, 1921; Uncle Jasper's Will, 1922; The Dungeon, 1922; The Ghost of Tolston's Manor, 1922; The House Behind the Cedars, 1923; Deceit, 1923; A Son of Satan, 1924; Birthright, 1924; Body and Soul, 1924; Marcus Garland, 1925; The Conjure Woman, 1926; The Devil's Disciple, 1926; The Spider's Web, 1927; The Millionaire, 1927; The Girl From Chicago, 1927; The Broken Violin, 1927; Thirty Years Later, 1928; When Men Betray, 1928; A Daughter of the Congo, 1930; Easy Street, 1930; The Exile, 1931; The Veiled Aristocrats, 1932; Ten Minutes to Live, 1932; Harlem After Midnight, 1935; Lem Hawkins' Confession/The Brand of Cain, 1935; Swing: The Story of Mandy, 1936; Temptation, 1936; Underworld, 1936; God's Step Children, 1938; Birthright (remake), 1939; The Notorious Elinor Lee, 1940; Lying Lips, 1940; The Betrayal, 1948.

ABOUT: Bogle, D. Toms, Coons, Mulattoes, Mammies, and Bucks, 1973; Cripps, T. Slow Fade to Black, 1977; Cripps, T. Black Film as Genre, 1978; Dictionary of American Negro Biography, 1982; Encyclopedia of Black Americans, 1981; Leab, D. J. From Sambo to Superspade, 1975; Powers, A. Blacks in America Movies: A Selective Bibliography, 1974; Sampson, H. T. Blacks in Black and White: A Source Book on Black Films, 1977. *Periodicals*—Cinema (USA) Fall 1970; Negro Digest December 1969; No Rose Fall 1976; Village Voice May 29, 1984; Whitney Museum Program Note 17, May 22–June 10, 1984.

"MILESTONE," LEWIS (Lewis or Lev Milstein) (September 30, 1895–September 25, 1980), American director, screenwriter, editor, and producer, was born in Chisnau, near Odessa, Russia, into a prosperous Jewish family. (A younger cousin was the violinist, Nathan Milstein.) His father, Emanuel Milstein, was a successful clothing manufacturer. In 1900 the family moved to Kishinev, capital of what was then Russian Bessarabia (now the Moldavian SSR), where Milestone attended local Jewish schools.

LEWIS MILESTONE

His family, though liberal and cultured in their outlook, were not pleased to find that their adolescent son was developing a taste for acting. In 1912, after he finished high school, he was sent off to a college at Mitweide, in Saxony, to study engineering.

At Christmas 1913 his father sent him money for a trip home; Milestone used it instead for a passage to the United States, along with two equally adventurous (or equally bored) classmates. They arrived in Hoboken, New Jersey, with six dollars between them. At first an aunt who lived in New York provided Milestone with money; when that ran out, he optimistically cabled his father for more funds. The reply came: "You are in the land of opportunity—use your own judgment."

Having little choice, Milestone followed the parental advice, and found work sweeping floors for a raincoat manufacturer. He subsequently worked as a janitor, door-to-door salesman, and machine operator in a lace factory, before landing a job as a photographer's assistant in 1915. Finding himself, for the first time, in a congenial profession, he eagerly sought experience of both the technical and aesthetic aspects of photography, and then moved closer to his hopes of a stage career by becoming assistant to a theatrical photographer, at seven dollars a week. In 1917, when the United States entered the war, Milestone enlisted, and after basic training was assigned to the photographic division of the Army Signal Corps. Posted to Washington, he helped to make training films, edited combat footage, and took an occasional acting role. Among his colleagues were Victor Fleming, Wesley Ruggles, and (as he then was) Jo Sternberg.

Discharged in February 1919, Milestone took American citizenship, acclimatizing his name to mark the occasion. After the excitement of making movies, portrait photography seemed tame, and at the first opportunity he headed for Hollywood, arriving there flat broke. A friend from the Signal Corps, Jesse D. Hampton, now an independent producer, gave him a job as cutting room assistant at twenty dollars a week. In between sweeping floors and running errands, Milestone acquired further filmmaking skills, and in 1920 became general assistant to Henry King, working with him on *Dice of Destiny* (1920) and *When We Were Twenty-One* (1921). Later in 1921 he moved to the Ince Studios, where he perfected his editing technique, and began a four-year association with one of Ince's directors, William A. Seiter. Seiter, a fluent director of unremarkable light comedies, employed Milestone as general assistant on *The Foolish Age* (1921), soon promoting him to screenwriter and assistant director.

According to Milestone, Seiter was more interested in golf than in filmmaking, and was happy to let his assistant take over much of the directing. This suited Milestone perfectly, and he stayed with Seiter when the latter moved from Ince to Warners in 1923, and then to Universal in 1925. Besides gaining experience as an uncredited director, Milestone worked nights and weekends as an editor, establishing a reputation as an accomplished "film doctor" for his rescue work on the first Rin Tin Tin feature, *Where the North Begins* (1923). He also coscripted many of Seiter's films, and worked with Raymond Griffith on the scenario of *The Yankee Consul* (1924), directed by James W. Horne. His first solo writing credit came on *Bobbed Hair* (1925), an adaptation of a satirical farce originally written by twenty different writers.

After five years' apprenticeship, Milestone decided that it was time to show what he had learned; he offered an original story idea to Jack Warner on condition that he be allowed to direct. His co-writer on *Seven Sinners* (1925), a crime comedy in which seven crooks independently try to burgle the same Long Island mansion, was another keen young beginner, Darryl F. Zanuck. The film, which starred Marie Prevost, was reasonably well received, and Milestone and Zanuck followed it up with *The Cave Man* (1926), a mildly satirical social comedy in which a coalman is passed off as an eccentric professor in smart society. Marie Prevost again starred, with Myrna Loy making her screen debut in a bit part.

Warners were now paying Milestone $400 a week, a substantial salary. He discovered, though, that they were loaning him out at $1,000 a week as a film doctor, and demanded to be paid the difference. When they refused, he quit; the studio sued him for breach of contract and won. To avoid payment, Milestone had himself declared bankrupt, and moved into a two-room apartment with his friends David and Myron Selznick. Despite an attempt by Warners to have him blacklisted, he soon found work at Paramount, where he made a film with the silent star Thomas Meighan, *The New Klondike* (1926). Loosely based on a story by Ring Lardner, the plot centered around the Florida real estate boom then at its height; with considerable audacity, Milestone hauled his actors and a forty-man crew off to Miami to shoot on location, picking up local color and writing the script as they went along.

Reviews were mixed, but Paramount thought well enough of Milestone to feature him as himself in a showcase film for the studio's up-and-coming talent, *Fascinating Youth* (1926), and to assign him to a comedy with their top star, Gloria Swanson. Star and director clashed during the shooting of *Fine Manners* (1926), and Milestone left the film, which was completed by Richard Rosson. By now he had gained the reputation of being talented but awkward, which could be one reason that he signed a four-year contract with another notorious maverick, Howard Hughes, then just starting out in movies as an independent producer.

Milestone's first film for Hughes, *Two Arabian Knights* (1927), was also his first excursion into war films. Not that the war featured much beyond the opening scenes, in which two feuding American doughboys (Louis Wolheim and William Boyd) are taken prisoner by the Germans; the rest of the action concerns their escape from a POW camp and some highly improbable adventures in Palestine. The film's cheerfully coarse tone and bickering buddies were clearly inspired by *What Price Glory?*, Raoul Walsh's recent smash hit. But despite these derivative elements, the film was received with enthusiasm by public and critics alike, and Milestone was awarded an Oscar for best comedy direction in that year's first-ever Academy Award ceremony.

By way of contrast, *The Garden of Eden* (1928) was a sophisticated comedy in the Lubitsch vein, scripted by Hans Kraly, who often wrote for Lubitsch. The plot was routine Cinderella stuff, redeemed by the humor of Corinne Griffith's performance as the heroine, and some impressive sets by William Cameron Menzies. Further extending his range, Milestone now turned to the hard-bitten gangland genre initiated by Sternberg's *Underworld* (1927). *The*

Racket (1928)—"one of the best silent gangster films" in Derek Malcolm's opinion—united three of Milestone's previous stars: Louis Wolheim as a Chicago bootlegger, Thomas Meighan as the honest police captain, and Marie Prevost as a chorus girl. Notably realistic for its period—it was based on a successful Broadway play by Bartlett Cormack, a Chicago news reporter—the film was nominated for an Oscar as best picture of the year.

Milestone was loaned out to Paramount for his last silent film, *Betrayal* (1929)—a creaky, studio-bound melodrama, supposedly set in the Swiss Alps, and burdened with Emil Jannings at his most ponderously hammy. Milestone's first sound movie, *New York Nights* (1929), was if anything even worse: an overwrought backstage gangster story, shot with an immobile camera and a cast elocuting painfully into ill-concealed microphones. After seeing the producer's cut, Milestone demanded (without success) to have his name taken off the picture.

Erich Maria Remarque's first novel, *Im Westen nichts Neues (All Quiet on the Western Front)*, had been published in 1929 and achieved immediate international success. The screen rights were acquired by Universal, whose ambitious young head of production, Carl Laemmle Jr., began looking for a suitable but inexpensive director. On the strength of *Two Arabian Knights*, and thanks to some astute dealing by his agent, Myron Selznick, Milestone was chosen, and given relative freedom from studio interference.

All Quiet on the Western Front (1930), wrote Clyde Jeavons, "has become, if not the most praised, then certainly the most reappraised of all war films." At the time of its release, the film was instantly hailed as a classic, a profoundly moving humanist and pacifist statement . Closely following Remarque's novel, the plot traces the progress of a group of young German recruits on the Western Front, from initial recruitment, through increasing disillusionment, to their gradual extermination, one by one. In the film's final moments the last of them, Paul Baumer (Lew Ayres), is shot dead by a French sniper only days before the Armistice.

One reason for the film's signal success, undoubtedly, was its timing. Midway between the wars, before the rise of Hitler, was the ideal moment for an eloquent antiwar statement, seen sympathetically from a German viewpoint. "But above all, " maintained Kingsley Canham, "it was the technique of Milestone's film that rightly led to its fame." Abandoning all the stilted immobility of early sound-movie convention, Milestone restored to the camera much of the freedom of the silent era, shooting and cutting with a fluid, rhythmic style and great pictorial elegance. Most effective of all were the battle sequences: filmed with the fast lateral tracking shots that were to become Milestone's stock-in-trade, they still communicate with fierce immediacy. "Milestone's eloquent silent editing style and his camerawork," wrote Karel Reisz in *Sequence* 14 (1952), "generate an overwhelming sense of impersonal horror."

"I shot very little footage on the battles because the film was all figured out," Milestone told Kevin Brownlow. "Being an editor myself, I pre-edited the thing. . . . The front office was always sitting there waiting for me to say, 'Tomorrow I want 10,000 men.' I made the whole battle scene with 150 fellows, 75 Frenchmen and 75 Germans." He also created, in those sequences, some memorably lasting images: Ayres trapped in a shellhole with a dying French soldier (the silent comedian Raymond Griffith, in his last film role); the coveted soft-leather boots, passed from soldier to soldier as each successive occupant is killed; Ayres carrying the wounded Katczinsky (Louis Wolheim) on his back and chatting cheerfully to him, not realizing that he is already dead; and of course the final, famous shot of the hand reaching out for a butterfly as a sniper takes aim. "The scenes at the front," Clyde Jeavons observed, "have an authentic feeling of waste, desolation and menace, and the relentlessly grey, chaotic, drawn-out panoramas of trench warfare are justly celebrated."

Yet much of the film now seems distinctly uneven, lapsing into sentimentality or didacticism —Eisenstein is said to have called it "a good PhD thesis." The scenes at home with Paul's mother and sister equal the worst emotional excesses of D. W. Griffith, and equally embarrassing is Paul's habit of praying out loud (internalized dialogue in the novel) at moments of stress. Despite its weaknesses, though, *All Quiet's* technical brilliance and compassionate intensity justify its status as what Richard Cutts called "the most powerful indictment of war's stupidity, waste, carnage, agony and confusion yet captured on film."

All Quiet was awarded an Oscar as best film of the year, with another going to Milestone as best director. His reputation was further enhanced by his next picture, which was also his last for Howard Hughes: *The Front Page* (1931), an adaptation of Hecht and MacArthur's 1928 Broadway hit. The archetypal tough, cynical newsroom drama, it offered a wealth of wise-cracking dialogue strung around a two-pronged plot—the shameless exploitation of a newsworthy hanging, and the efforts of an unscrupulous Chicago editor, Walter Burns, to prevent Hildy Johnson, his crack reporter, from getting married and leaving for New York.

Milestone filmed the piece at a cracking pace, with a restlessly mobile camera that made not the least concession to sound-recording restrictions. Most of the action is confined to the court newsroom, but Milestone moves outside (as James Shelley Hamilton wrote) "often enough to create a sense of the life of a city." Lewis Jacobs considered it (with *All Quiet*) "one of the first talkies to recapture the spirit and movement of the silent film." Adolphe Menjou, cast against previous lounge-lizard type as Walter Burns, turned in a superbly judged performance, though Pat O'Brien's Hildy was no more than adequate (Milestone had wanted Cagney or Gable for the role, but Hughes vetoed them both). The film still works well, though later versions by Howard Hawks (1940) and Billy Wilder (1974) are generally reckoned even better.

Milestone's reputation was now at its height. *The Front Page* was nominated for an Oscar as best picture, though it lost out to Wesley Ruggles's sprawling *Cimmaron*. In a poll of three hundred movie critics organized by *Film Daily*, Milestone topped a list of "Ten Best Directors." Now that his contract with Hughes had expired, he hoped to achieve greater independence. However, an attempt by David Selznick to set up an independent production unit with Milestone, Lubitsch, and King Vidor came to nothing. Instead, Milestone accepted the job of production head for United Artists.

From this point, it seems, dates the beginning of Milestone's long decline as a director. Certainly his next five films fell far short of his previous standards. *Rain* (1932) was a stagey remake of the much-adapted Somerset Maugham short story, with Joan Crawford uncomfortably cast (against Milestone's wish) as Sadie Thompson. It did poorly, but *Hallelujah, I'm a Bum* (1933) fared even worse. An uneasy mish-mash of fantasy, musical, and inept social satire, it features "rhythmic dialogue" by Lorenz Hart, an unsympathetic lead performance from Al Jolson, and an embarrassing one from Harry Langdon as a half-baked left-wing theorist. Not all critics agree in writing it off, though; Charles Shibuk, comparing it to Pabst's *Dreigroschenoper* and the work of René Clair, called it "one of the most underrated films ever made, and one of Milestone's best."

After a series of aborted projects, Milestone accepted a contract from Harry Cohn at Columbia, where he made *The Captain Hates the Sea* (1934), a starry *Grand Hotel*–style showcase that included the sad spectacle of the alcoholic and ulcer-ridden John Gilbert in his final film role. The picture was shot aboard a rented steamer off the California coast, in reportedly chaotic conditions that showed up all too clearly in the finished product. In spite of these moments of "queer confusion," however, Otis Ferguson recalled it in 1936 as "the absolutely best neglected picture of two years . . . carried out with an ease of direction that is as simple and right as the principle of cantilever." However, the movie was half-heartedly promoted, and flopped. Milestone departed from Columbia without much regret on either side, and moved to Paramount.

While shooting *Rain*, Milestone had met Kendall Lee Glaezner, who was acting the supporting role of Mrs. McPhail. They were married in July 1935. It was a childless marriage, and by all accounts a very happy one, lasting until Mrs. Milestone's death in 1978.

Milestone began at Paramount with (in his own words) "two insignificant musicals," *Paris in Spring* (1935) and *Anything Goes* (1936). His third film for the studio, though, marked a distinct return to form. John Baxter described *The General Died at Dawn* (1936) as "a film which, for style and content, is one of the thirties' undoubted masterpieces," and other writers, though not quite so laudatory, have agreed that it "holds up very well both as entertainment and art." Here, as in most of Milestone's more personal films, the theme is of individuals caught up in the turmoil of social movements beyond their control. The plot, taken from an unpublished pulp novel, is set in contemporary, war-torn China: an American adventurer, played by Gary Cooper, tries to aid the peasants against a brutal warlord (Akim Tamiroff), and is first betrayed, then helped, by a girl (Madeleine Carroll) whose father is in the warlord's pay. "A melodrama of more than usual skill," wrote Graham Greene in *The Spectator*. "If it were not for a rather ludicrous ending, this would be one of the best thrillers for some years."

Clifford Odets, then just achieving fame as a left-wing playwright, wrote the script, mixing political cynicism with lyrical effusions. ("We could have made beautiful music together," Cooper tells Carroll, possibly providing the line's first public outing.) Visually, the film is often superb, not least in the opening sequence, as the warlord's forces move with chillingly impersonal menace across the ravaged landscape. In a generally excellent cast, Madeleine Carroll gave the performance of her career, lost and world-weary beneath a facade of cynical toughness.

It was three years before Milestone completed another film. Several projects fell through, or were handed over to other directors. Working again with Odets, Milestone prepared a script for Sam Goldwyn, based on Sidney Kingsley's Broadway hit, *Dead End*; Goldwyn, however, assigned the job (with a different script) to William Wyler. Hal Roach then invited Milestone to direct *Road Show*, taken from a novel by Eric Hatch about a traveling carnival, but fired him after ten weeks' shooting on the grounds that the director was making a serious drama out of a comedy. Milestone sued Roach for damages and arrears; Roach countersued; and the dispute was finally settled out of court, with Roach agreeing to finance Milestone's projected version of Steinbeck's *Of Mice and Men*. While the production was in preparation, Milestone turned out a routine programmer for Paramount, *Night of Nights* (1939).

In the opinion of many critics, *Of Mice and Men* (1940)—on which Milestone acted as his own producer—ranks with *All Quiet* as the finest of his films. Based closely on the play that Steinbeck drew from his own short novel, it offers, wrote William K. Everson in *The Modern American Novel and the Movies*, "a good case for suggesting that occasionally a movie *can* improve on and enhance the values of the original fiction." The film opens with what may well be the first use of a precredit sequence, as George (Burgess Meredith) and his friend, the half-witted giant Lennie (Lon Chaney Jr.), flee from a posse, thus setting the mood and theme of the rest of the action. In the final scene, after Lennie has inadvertently killed a woman and the two men's fragile plans for happiness are in ruins, the posse catches up with them—a different posse, except that all posses are the same.

Milestone's direction faithfully served the wider social implications of Steinbeck's melancholy fable. "Under the surface of a western wheat ranch," observed Richard Griffith, "his camera discovered the menace and insecurity of industrialised existence, and the loneliness of men forced to adapt to it." Milestone, like Steinbeck, was evidently responding to the social and political climate of the period; Joseph Millichap suggested that "the visual ambience of Milestone's film, like John Ford's adaptation of *The Grapes of Wrath*, seems strongly influenced by the documentary film and photography of the 1930s." Eschewing his usual ultramobile camera, Milestone kept the shooting style cool and unobtrusive, making effective use of deep-focus composition and carefully detailed *mise-en-scène*. The film also boasted an evocative score from Aaron Copland and uniformly excellent acting, especially from Meredith and

Chaney—the latter making the most of the only worthwhile role in his whole career.

Critical response to *Of Mice and Men* was unanimously enthusiastic, but the picture flopped at the box office. However, Milestone's reputation was enhanced, and he signed a contract with RKO, who gave him his own production team. All he did with it was produce two feeble comedies starring Ronald Colman, *Lucky Partners* (1940) and *My Life with Caroline* (1941). These assignments, he later remarked, "were of the kind you did if you hoped to stay in motion pictures, in the expectation that the next film might give you a chance to redeem yourself."

America's entry into the war allowed Milestone to return to the genre in which he had made his name. None of his later war films, though, maintained the unequivocal pacifist stance of *All Quiet*; as a left liberal with a Russian Jewish background, Milestone may well have felt that pacifism was no longer appropriate. But for the most part (*Halls of Montezuma* being the glaring exception) he managed to avoid the cruder excesses of gung-ho patriotism, continuing to depict war as a chaotic, tragic (if sometimes unavoidable) waste, in which ordinary individuals find themselves uncomprehendingly caught up.

The great Dutch documentary maker, Joris Ivens, then working with Pare Lorentz of the United States Government Film Service, had acquired 15,000 feet of film from the Eastern Front, shot by Soviet news photographers. He invited Milestone to work with him as editor and coproducer, and together they fashioned a somber, strikingly dramatic 45-minute documentary, *Our Russian Front* (1942), with music by Dmitri Tiomkin and a commentary spoken by Walter Huston. Milestone's next two films also aimed at celebrating the valor of America's allies, but at several removes further from actuality.

Warners offered him a one-picture contract, and Milestone started work on a version of *Moby Dick,* to star Errol Flynn. Perhaps fortunately, the project was scrapped, and instead Milestone directed Flynn in *Edge of Darkness* (1943), a melodrama of Norwegian resistance to the Nazis. Despite an intelligent script by Robert Rossen, the film is now impossible to take seriously, given Flynn and Ann Sheridan (not to mention Ruth Gordon) passing themselves off as Norwegians, and the Monterey waterfront doing duty for a Nordic fjord. Nevertheless, as Richard T. Jameson says, "the swooping, rushing, craning, even (this was 1943) *zooming* coverage of action sequences in *Edge of Darkness* generated

some of the most thrilling Second World War footage ever shot."

The North Star (1943) displayed highly impressive production credits: script by Lillian Hellman, music by Aaron Copland, sets by William Cameron Menzies, photography by James Wong Howe. Milestone directed it for Sam Goldwyn, who interfered constantly, much to the director's irritation. Depicting the impact of the German invasion on one small Russian village, the film succeeded in being occasionally moving, frequently pretentious, and now and again downright ridiculous—notably in an early scene of simple peasant festivities, in which the entire Bolshoi Ballet appear to have dropped by for an impromptu workout. However, the invasion sequence, with German tanks thundering through the smoke of the burning village, comes over powerfully, with much effective use of Milestone's characteristic lateral tracking shots. The film, which later became something of a political embarrassment to all concerned, was subsequently reissued in a heavily cut version as *Armored Attack,* overlaid with an anticommunist commentary.

Moving from a fake Russia to an even more synthetic Japan, Milestone made *The Purple Heart* (1944) for Darryl F. Zanuck (who also scripted under a pseudonym) at Fox. A conjectural account of the trial of eight American airmen captured—and allegedly tortured—by the Japanese, the film built up a tellingly claustrophobic atmosphere, but today seems badly flawed by the emotional overkill that made it, at the time, such effective propaganda.

After another aborted project, Milestone began work on the best of his World War II films, *A Walk in the Sun* (1945). Scripted by Robert Rossen, it follows the progress of an infantry platoon landing at Salerno, and sent to capture a German-held farmhouse six miles inland. "Here is war not as excitement and ultimate triumph," commented David Parker and Burton Shapiro in *The Contract Director,* "but war as infinitely boring and unrelated to a larger view." Kingsley Canham concurred: "A sense of purposelessness pervades the film; a blind serving of a plan whose shape and final outcome means nothing to the men who are fighting the war." Even in the climactic assault, Milestone avoids glamor or heroics, and most of the action has a downbeat, near-documentary flavor.

"*A Walk in the Sun* is not pacifist in the sense that Milestone's *All Quiet on the Western Front* is pacifist," wrote Clyde Jeavons, "but it is distinguished by an intense compassion and humanity which, in the context of a war which had to be fought, comprise an equally strong statement about the futility and tragedy of war." The main false note—apart from some occasionally self-conscious dialogue—is sounded by an archly romantic ballad, sung over the credits and reprised at later points in the film. (Milestone seems to have pioneered this dubious practice, which was to be imitated in countless war movies and Westerns over the next twenty years.) The film was started for United Artists, who pulled out during production, claiming the property lacked commercial potential. Milestone continued shooting, using his own funds, and sold the completed film to Zanuck, who had no cause to complain of his bargain. On release, it was received with general enthusiasm as a sensitive, honest war movie, although James Agee, writing in *Nation,* voiced a dissenting opinion: "an embarrassing movie . . . more related to ballet than to war."

Milestone's third and last film scripted by Rossen, whose own directing career was about to take off, was *The Strange Love of Martha Ivers* (1946), the director's sole, and remarkably accomplished, excursion into *film noir.* Many of the classic *noir* elements are present: ancient, buried guilt resurfacing; a ruthlessly ambitious *femme fatale* (Barbara Stanwyck, cast exactly to type); self-destructive obsessions; an all-pervasive atmosphere of hopelessness, corruption, and greed. In conformity with the conventions of the genre, much of the action takes place at night; Milestone skillfully deploys high-contrast lighting and disconcerting camera angles to enhance the already emotionally charged situations.

One Hollywood expression of the restless, dissatisfied mood of the postwar years was Enterprise Studios, set up by a group of producers, directors, and actors to operate in freer, more cooperative conditions, away from the dictatorial grasp of the big studios. Enterprise planned a broad spread of quality films, but its ace project was *Arch of Triumph* (1948), a guaranteed, cast-iron box-office smash, starring Ingrid Bergman and Charles Boyer in an adaptation of Remarque's bestselling novel, set in the soon-to-vanish world of pre-war Paris. Milestone was the natural choice to direct, having never fitted comfortably into the studio system, and also having achieved his greatest success with an earlier Remarque novel. But the cast-iron smash proved to be a lead balloon: *Arch of Triumph* turned out long, lifeless, and inert, and failed dismally at the box office, bringing Enterprise down in ruins.

Before the studio finally collapsed, Milestone threw off a quick comedy "to keep the gates open." By the time *No Minor Vices* (1948) appeared, though, Enterprise had already folded, and the film was in any case poorly received. A triangle comedy with psychoanalytic trimmings, it may have been before its time; William K. Everson found it "a most welcome oasis of sophistication in the rather barren comedy field of the mid-forties."

Ever since making *Of Mice and Men,* Milestone had planned to adapt another of Steinbeck's shorter fictions, *The Red Pony.* He now made it as his first color film, both producing and directing. Despite a script by Steinbeck, one of Copland's finest scores, and an effortlessly assured performance from Robert Mitchum, the result was trite and lacking in excitement; some ill-advised animated fantasy sequences apparently stemmed from a desire by the studio, Republic, to turn the film into a "children's Western."

In 1946, Milestone had been one of the first to be subpoenaed by the House Un-American Activities Committee: of Russian origins, and a lifelong leftist, he was an obvious target for the witch-hunters. Citing the Fifth Amendment, he refused to testify, and was not called before the Committee; but over the next few years he suffered sporadic attacks from such strident anti-Communists as Hedda Hopper. Since he continued to work, it seems that he escaped the worst effects of the Hollywood blacklist; but the pressures and tensions of the period may partly explain the depressing mediocrity of most of his later films. "A fear psychosis pervades [Hollywood]," he wrote in *New Republic* in January 1949, "engendered by witch hunts on the national, state, and community level. Producers are asking for and getting pictures without ideas. . . . We ought to . . . get back to making films with content, substance and meaning." In his own case, such aspirations were to remain largely unrealized.

Milestone began the 1950s with three films for Fox. *Halls of Montezuma* (1951), an account of a Marine attack on Okinawa during the Pacific War, is probably the worst of Milestone's war movies; moments of realism and sensitivity are eventually swamped by a blare of patriotic clichés. Fox, which had funds frozen in Australia, now sent Milestone there to make *Kangaroo* (1952)—a period drama set in the Outback, and his worst film of all, according to Charles Shibuk. The third Fox assignment was a dispirited version of Hugo's much filmed *Les Miserables* (1952). "It had been done before," commented Milestone drily; "I hope it will never be done again." He then made two pictures in Britain. *Melba* (1953) purported, without much justification, to be a biopic of the famous soprano; Milestone observed that it "should have been called

Melba like I should have been christened Napoleon." *They Who Dare* (1953), a dull war film starring a miscast Dirk Bogarde, was set (and partly shot) on Rhodes. Moving on to Italy, Milestone directed an Anglo-Italian romantic weepie, *La Vedova X* (*The Widow,* 1955), before returning to the United States.

For the next four years Milestone directed no more films; instead he took on some television work "in order to find out what it was all about." What it was about, he concluded, was mostly "slavery," and he returned to filmmaking with his last war movie, *Pork Chop Hill* (1959). Set during the final days of the Korean War, it was Milestone's first interesting film in ten years, and might even, had it not suffered subsequent distortion, have qualified as one of his best. Like *A Walk in the Sun,* it follows the action of a single infantry platoon, ordered to take a hill of minimal strategic value simply to strengthen America's hand at the Panmunjon peace negotiations. Parker and Shapiro reckoned it "one of his most courageous, most thoughtful films . . . arguably a new kind of war film." Several scenes, in particular a night attack disrupted by an accidentally lit "friendly" searchlight, are visually and dramatically outstanding, and the ironic futility of the men's sacrifice is well conveyed. However, the picture was clumsily recut against Milestone's wishes by its star, Gregory Peck. It ends with a voice-over statement totally at variance with Milestone's intentions, claiming that the costly victory at Pork Chop Hill secured the freedom of "millions."

Ocean's Eleven (1960) furnished an undemanding vehicle for the self-indulgent antics of Frank Sinatra's clan. The last film to carry Milestone's name was the remake of *Mutiny on the Bounty* (1962), with Marlon Brando as Fletcher Christian. It was an unhappy assignment: the original director had been Carol Reed, who pulled out after clashing with the temperamental Brando. Milestone took over in February 1961 and soon ran into the same problem. "I wasn't directing Brando, just the rest of the cast. He was directing himself and ignoring everyone else." Eventually Brando took charge of both script and direction, while Milestone "went off to sit down somewhere and read the paper." The film ran heavily over schedule and budget; when it was finally released, critical response was mixed, but commercially it was a disaster. Milestone received sole directorial credit.

In 1963 he began shooting *PT 109,* based on John F. Kennedy's wartime experiences, but left the film after a dispute with Jack Warner, Milestone claiming that the script was inadequate. The eventual film, which was completed by Leslie Martinson, largely confirmed his allegations. Two years later he was contracted to direct an episode of an international coproduction, *The Dirty Game,* but was replaced on account of illness before shooting had started.

With equal justification, Lewis Milestone could be considered unusually fortunate, or unusually unlucky. Early in his career, he directed a film that was instantly hailed as a classic of the cinema—and which, despite its unevenness, still retains that status. On the strength of that film, some writers have suggested, he rarely thereafter lacked work throughout a not especially distinguished directorial career. A more sympathetic view might be that, through a fortuitous combination of circumstances, he peaked too soon, and spent the rest of his life shadowed by unfulfilled expectations that he would repeat his early triumph.

Writing in Richard Roud's *Cinema,* Richard T. Jameson suggested that it "is biographically irrelevant but mythically appropriate that a [Russian-born] director . . . should have cleaved obsessively to an insistently montage-oriented style. . . . But, though Milestone entered movies as a cutter, his first pictorial experience came as a photographer's assistant, and from his earliest films he manifested a commendable concern for integral composition as well as shot juxtaposition. Foregrounds and backgrounds rarely go unfilled, and his frequently moving camera recedes or penetrates almost as often as it drifts laterally." All the same, as Richard Griffith says, though Milestone at his best had a style of his own, "it would be difficult, even for a connoisseur, to tell who directed the majority of his films."

Like most American directors of his generation, Milestone had to contend with the restrictions of the studio system. But as Joseph Millichap points out, artists like Capra, Ford, or Huston "could take an unpromising genre idea and turn it into something truly artistic and uniquely [their] own, . . . Milestone never quite managed to transform his material, trash or classic, in this manner. . . . More than most directors of talent, Milestone was the prisoner of his literary property; if it was great he could soar with it, but if . . . mediocre he could only rarely rise above it." Although he earned a reputation for stubborn independence, Milestone often chose to walk away from problems rather than confront them, as with *Pork Chop Hill*: "I didn't agree with the way Mr. Gregory Peck wanted to edit it, so I simply walked out and he edited it the way he saw fit."

Milestone's skill and flamboyant technical brilliance are widely acknowledged; his pioneering work in freeing the movie camera from the tyrannical confines of static sound equipment achieved lasting and valuable effects. But all too often his work is undermined by an ultimate disengagement that, at its worst, amounts to indifference: in his own words (about *Les Miserables*), "Oh, for Chrissake, it's just a job—I'll do it and get it over with." Expounding his view of the director's role, he once said: "My approach, my style is governed by the story, not the story by my style. The story is the important thing and the director has no business intruding."

During the latter part of his life, Milestone's declining health prevented him from working, and in his last years a serious stroke confined him to a wheelchair. In July 1979 the Directors Guild, of which he had been one of the original founder members, awarded him a Pioneer Tribute. He died the following year, a few days short of his eighty-fifth birthday.

—*P.K.*

FILMS: Seven Sinners, 1925; The Cave Man, 1926; The New Klondike, 1926; Two Arabian Knights, 1927; The Garden of Eden, 1928; The Racket, 1928; Betrayal, 1929; New York Nights, 1929; All Quiet on the Western Front, 1930; The Front Page, 1931; Rain, 1932; Hallelujah, I'm a Bum (U.K., Hallelujah, I'm a Tramp), 1933; The Captain Hates the Sea, 1934; Paris in Spring, 1935; Anything Goes, 1936; The General Died at Dawn, 1936; The Night of Nights, 1939; Of Mice and Men, 1940; Lucky Partners, 1940; My Life with Caroline, 1941; (with Joris Ivens) Our Russian Front, 1942 (documentary); Edge of Darkness, 1943; The North Star, 1943; The Purple Heart, 1944; A Walk in the Sun, 1945; The Strange Love of Martha Ivers, 1946; Arch of Triumph, 1948; No Minor Vices, 1948; The Red Pony, 1949; Halls of Montezuma, 1951; Kangaroo, 1952; Les Miserables, 1952; Melba, 1953; They Who Dare, 1953; La Vedova X (The Widow), 1955; Pork Chop Hill, 1959; Ocean's Eleven, 1960; Mutiny on the Bounty, 1962. *Published script*—The North Star: A motion picture about some Russian people, by Lillian Hellman (Viking Press, 1943).

ABOUT: Basinger, J. The World War II Combat Film, 1986; Baxter, J. Hollywood in the Thirties, 1968; Brownlow, K. The War, the West, and the Wilderness, 1979; Canham, K. Lewis Milestone *in* The Hollywood Professionals vol. 2, 1974; Higham, C. and Greenberg, J. The Celluloid Muse: Hollywood Directors Speak, 1969; Jeavons, C. A Pictorial History of War Films, 1974; Millichap, J. R. Lewis Milestone, 1981; Peary, G. and Shatzkin, R. (eds.) The Modern American Novel and the Movies, 1978; Rotha, P. and Griffith, R. The Film Till Now, 1960; Roud, R. (ed.) Cinema: A Critical Dictionary, 1980; Sarris, A. The American Cinema, 1968; Shibuk, C. An Index to the Films of Lewis Milestone, 1958; Shindler, C. Hollywood Goes To War, 1979; Suid, L. Guts and Glory, 1978; Tuska, J. (ed.) Close Up: The Contract Director, 1976.

Periodicals—Action July–August 1972; Classic Film Collector Fall 1975; Film Comment March–April 1974, March–April 1980; Film Culture September 1964; Film Ideal November 1, 1962; Film Quarterly Fall 1959; Films and Filming April 1963; Sequence 14 1952; Theater Arts February 1943; Views and Reviews Spring 1972.

MINNELLI, VINCENTE (February 28, 1903–July 25, 1986), American director, was born in Chicago. His Italian-born father and uncle ran the Minnelli Brothers' Dramatic Tent Show, which toured the Midwest presenting plays and concerts. His father served as orchestrator and pianist, his mother as director and leading lady. Minnelli himself made his debut with the troupe in *East Lynne* at the age of three, but "retired" five years later when the show folded.

While still in high school Minnelli worked for a sign painter and designed the drop curtain for the local movie theatre. Graduating at sixteen, he was briefly apprenticed to a photographer, then went to the Marshall Field department store as a trainee window-dresser, studying for a time at the Chicago Art Institute. In 1929 he was hired by the Balaban and Katz chain of movie theatres in Chicago, working as assistant stage manager and designing sets and costumes for the live shows that preceded screenings.

In 1931 Minnelli went to New York as set and costume designer at the Paramount Theatre. He designed the sets for Earl Carroll's *Vanities* that year and sets and costumes for the *Vanities* of 1932, as well Grace Moore's costumes for *Du Barry*. In 1933 Minnelli moved on to Radio City Music Hall. Initially a costume designer there, he was soon art director and producer, turning out a new show every month, including the ballet "El Amor Brujo" and the song-and-dance spectacle "Scheherazade." His debut as a Broadway director came in 1935 with the revue *At Home Abroad*, for which he also designed sets and costumes: his flair for staging dance was demonstrated in a much-praised bullfight number. Minnelli supplied sets and costumes for the *Ziegfeld Follies* of 1936 and was director and set designer for the 1936 revue *The Show Is On*, which featured two balletic sequences. Even at this stage, Minnelli's work reflected his interest in modern art and especially surrealism.

Established as one of Broadway's most promising young directors and designers, Minnelli began to receive offers from Hollywood. He went there first in 1937, engaged by Paramount not as a director but as a producer. In fact, apart from devising the "Public Melody Number One"

VINCENTE MINNELLI

sequence in Raoul Walsh's *Artists and Models*, Minnelli's time at Paramount was unproductive and frustrating. He said, "I prepared several projects, one for Marlene Dietrich, but they weren't willing to support the kind of musicals I wanted to do, only bad ideas, like the *Big Broadcast* pictures."

After six months Minnelli bought himself out of his Paramount contract and returned to Broadway. He directed and designed the sets for the popular musical *Hooray for What!* (1937), then for Jerome Kern's less successful *Very Warm for May* (1939). The following year he was invited to MGM by the innovative producer Arthur Freed, with whom he made his greatest screen musicals.

Recalling his attitudes at that time, Minnelli wrote that "though I liked the idea of musical films, I wasn't impressed by the quality of the early ones." An exception was Rouben Mamoulian's *Love Me Tonight*, "a marvel of sophistication"; and "if there was one picture that embodied my fascination in art and my attitude toward style it was Jacques Feyder's *Carnival in Flanders*. He'd taken the story of a Spanish general bringing his troops north and told it with the artful detail and luminosity of the Flemish masters. . . . Perhaps I could bring a similar perspective to American films."

Freed had offered him a no-strings, no-contract arrangement: MGM would pay his living expenses, and he would be free to return to New York whenever he wished. He spent his first months at MGM studying all aspects of filmmaking there while advising on scripts and musical numbers, and providing ideas like the

use of fruit as "musicians" in Busby Berkeley's *Strike Up the Band* (1940). Minnelli confessed that Berkeley's "large-scale numbers never moved me," and he showed his own capacity for visual elegance in his handling of Judy Garland's numbers in the "Ghost Theatre" section of Berkeley's *Babes on Broadway* (1941). Minnelli also directed four numbers in Norman Z. McLeod's *Panama Hattie* (1942), including Lena Horne's "Just One of Those Things."

His appetite whetted, Minnelli then embarked on his first film as director, *Cabin in the Sky*, released in 1943. Adapted from the all-black Broadway musical, this centered on an injured gambler (Eddie "Rochester" Anderson), hovering between life and death. In an extended dream sequence (the first of many in Minnelli's films), God's General (Kenneth Spencer) and Lucifer Jr. (Rex Ingram) battle for the gambler's soul, a contest echoed in the struggle for his body between his virtuous wife (Ethel Waters) and a vampish Lena Horne.

It was a difficult production on account of real-life conflict between the two actresses, and Minnelli's decorative talents were constricted by the fact that the film was shot in sepia. His pictorial sense is nevertheless evident in several passages. The nightclub episode in which "Bubbles" (John W. Sublett) renders "Shine" is a vivid example of stylized action, the performer's shadow and those of his audience thrown on a white background as he struts up the stairs. The church service in the first reel was much admired at the time, as was Anderson's duet with Lena Horne, "Consequences."

Although some writers criticized the film for perpetuating black stereotypes, this was scarcely unusual at the time, and *Cabin in the Sky* had a generally enthusiastic reception. Minnelli himself was proudest of touches that "involved an inquisitive, restless camera"; Max Ophuls, whose films "swirled with movement," had become his "spiritual leader." Minnelli next took over the direction of *I Dood It* (1943), a farce about a pantspresser (Red Skelton) infatuated with a stage star (Eleanor Powell)—in fact a scrappy remake of Buster Keaton's silent *Spite Marriage*.

Then, with *Meet Me in St. Louis* (1944), Minnelli achieved one of his most enduringly popular musicals. Adapted by Irving Brecher and Fred Finklehoffe from the *New Yorker* stories of Sally Benson, and with songs by Hugh Martin and Ralph Blane, it was set in St. Louis in 1903–1904. Minnelli obtained flawless service from the cinematographer George Folsey and dance director Charles Walters, as well as from designers Lemuel Ayers and Jack Martin Smith and costumer Irene Sharaff.

The forthcoming World's Fair is the sole topic of conversation in the summer of 1903, when the film opens in St. Louis. It is also the theme of the title song, which is picked up by various members of the Smith family in their plushly furnished bourgeois home. But this mood of family harmony is soon marred by a visit from handsome neighbor John Truett (Tom Drake), who is blithely unaware that Esther Smith (Judy Garland) has a crush on him. (This inspires her plaintive song "The Boy Next Door.") Disaster threatens when Esther's authoritarian father (Leon Ames) announces the family's imminent removal to New York, where he has been offered an important new post.

Out of this family crisis, Minnelli and his collaborators fabricated an almost unbroken series of delights, beginning with the framed lithographs that announce each of the film's four seasons, from summer to spring; then slowly acquire color, begin to move, and come completely to life. Garland, on a visit to the fairground, belts out "The Trolley Song" amid a colorfully costumed chorus of straphangers. The party sequence and the Christmas ball are remarkable for their groupings (guests repeatedly glimpsed in recessive compositions), their movement within the frame, and their cutting (particularly in the dance "Skip to My Lou"). The party is followed by a sequence in which Esther and John Truett linger to turn down the lights, and Minnelli here achieves a marvelous intimacy, craning gently down past a gleaming chandelier to the loving couple, and ending with Garland's bewitching delivery on the staircase of "Over the Banisters."

The threat of exile from St. Louis, love, and the Fair is modified and finally dispelled in a succession of memorable passages: Father and Mother (Mary Astor) sing "You and I" at the piano and the rest of the household congregate to listen in an image of family harmony at least temporarily restored; after the ball, in a superbly framed sequence, Esther sings the poignant "Have Yourself a Merry Little Christmas" to her little sister Tootie (Margaret O'Brien)—and Father, overhearing Tootie's heartbroken sobs, decides not to uproot his family.

One other highlight was evoked by James Agee when, eulogizing the remarkable child actress Margaret O'Brien, he wrote: "Her walk on Halloween, away from the bonfire into the deepening dark of the street, her fear and excitement intensifying as she approaches her destination (the insulting of the most frightening man in the neighborhood) and follows the camera (which withdraws a few feet ahead of her in a long soft curve) are a piece of acting, of lovely, simple camera movement, and of color control which combined, while they lasted, to make my hair stand on end."

John Russell Taylor and Arthur Jackson in *The Hollywood Musical* wrote that in *Meet Me in St. Louis* "we can for the first time see Minnelli's talents whole, or nearly whole (there is still almost no real dance for him to cope with). And it is here that we begin to appreciate the secret of his special way with musicals. It is that while phenomenally sensitive to music (he is a pianist himself) and to the subtlest variations of pacing and rhythm within a scene, a movement, and possessed of great visual flair . . . , he is fundamentally a *dramatic* director. *Meet Me in St. Louis* is conceived and directed as a coherent drama, a story about believable people in a believable situation. The musical episodes are all judged from the outset according to their power to advance the story, epitomize a situation, intensify a mood; they all have their dramatic raison d'être."

Simon Harcourt-Smith took a somewhat different tack, calling this "a real work of imagination," blending "fantasy and operetta with such airy skill as almost to provide a new pattern for the musical of the future." And Joel E. Siegel, in Penny Yates' *The Films of Vincente Minnelli*, wrote that Garland, under Minnelli's direction, gave "one of her sweetest, least neurotic performances," while her "severity, her emotional intensity," released "a depth of feeling never before evident in Minnelli's work." Garland and Minnelli were married in 1945, and Liza Minnelli was born the following year.

To the revue-film *Ziegfeld Follies* (shot in 1944–1945, released in 1946), Minnelli contributed six items, including a stylish staging of "Libiamo" from *La Traviata*, Garland's satirical "Madame Crematon," and the buoyant song-and-dance by Fred Astaire and Gene Kelly, "The Babbit and the Bromide." The film's summits, though, were furnished by two ballets—"This Heart of Mine" and "Limehouse Blues"—in which the director matched and sometimes surpassed the virtuosity in color, design, and dance production that he had displayed in *Meet Me in St. Louis*. Both numbers star Astaire and Lucille Bremer, and both owe much to the choreography of Robert Alton and Jack Martin Smith's designs.

"This Heart of Mine" is danced on an immense surreal set in white, blue, and scarlet. Joel E. Siegel wrote that this "Raffles-like dance of thievery and passion is the last word in outrageous stylization with its treadmills, turntables and rhinestone-studded, antler-shaped trees . . . , the perfection of the icily sophisticated sets, color schemes and costuming that Minnelli developed at the Music Hall and on Broadway." "Limehouse Blues," telling in dance and pantomime the story of a tragic love affair between two denizens of London's old Chinatown, draws on a tradition that includes Thomas Burke's Limehouse stories and D. W. Griffith's *Broken Blossoms*. Among its special glories is the passage in which the scarlet-clad Bremer and Astaire execute an intricate, ravishing series of movements with four Oriental fans.

Minnelli's first nonmusical film followed, a World War II romance called *The Clock* (1945), adapted by Robert Nathan and Joseph Schrank form a story by Paul and Pauline Gallico. It is set in New York City, with Robert Walker as a confused, ingenuous GI, Judy Garland as his working-class angel. Though not a musical, the movie has frequent musical overtones, like the sequence where the couple listen to the sounds of the city, move raptly towards each other, embrace, and raptly depart. There are surreal elements in the recurring coincidences that unite or separate the lovers, and a hint of Kafka in their struggle to obtain a marriage license. After the wedding, for their first breakfast together, Minnelli cut four pages of "noble" dialogue from the script, leaving the characters to express their happiness entirely through glances and gestures, in a way that René Clair would have approved. James Agee, in one of many favorable reviews, wrote that Minnelli's "extras and their gaits and groupings and clothes, and their stammering collisions and multiplicities of purpose and aimlessness, beat anything I can remember out of Hollywood."

In the 1945 *Yolanda and the Thief*, Minnelli reverted to song and dance with a vengeance. The script, based by Irving Brecher on a story by Jacques Thery and Ludwig Bemelmans, is a trifle about a gambler (Fred Astaire) who sets out to swindle an heiress (Lucille Bremer) by masquerading as her guardian angel, only to fall in love with her. The film was coolly received at the time, though the *Tribune*'s reviewer noted the influence of the French surrealist painters on its use of color.

Since then, however, the reputation of *Yolanda and the Thief* has risen steadily. Joel E. Siegel wrote that the film was "an important step, perhaps the critical step, in the evolution of the modern MGM musical style. Jack Martin Smith's imaginative sets are the height of baroque eccentricity, and Charles Rosher's camerawork is filled with vibrant hues and bold tonal contrasts. The film's surrealistic ballet surpasses the more acclaimed ballets in *The Red Shoes* and Minnelli's own *An American in Paris*.

And "Coffee Time," with its subtle 5/4 rhythms, superb Eugene Loring choreography, and sweeping camera movements around and over a pulsating Copacabana floor, is one of the milestones of screen dance."

Jean-Pierre Coursodon, in *American Directors, Volume II*, makes even larger claims for the film, which he regards as "Minnelli's musical masterpiece" and "one of Minnelli's most personal films. For the first time the dominant themes of his work—the ordeal of coming of age, the lure of the dream world, the tension between fantasy and reality and the effort to reconcile them—took shape and coalesced into a coherent whole. Yolanda . . . is the first of several Minnelli heroines . . . who are deceived, ostensibly by men, but actually by their own romantic imaginations. . . . Chronologically, *Yolanda and the Thief* can be considered the first of the modern film musicals."

Minnelli's next enterprise was the direction of Judy Garland's scenes (as Marilyn Miller) in Richard Whorf's *Till the Clouds Roll By*, a biopic of Jerome Kern filmed in 1945–1946 but not released until 1947. The Minnellian stamp is evident in sequences like the opening tracking shot into Marilyn Miller's crowded dressing room (excited conversations overlapping on the soundtrack), and in the way this contrasts with her lonely walk out to the empty, shadowed stage.

Undercurrent (1946), which followed, was Minnelli's first melodrama, a "wife-in-distress" thriller about an intellectual (Katharine Hepburn) who marries a millionaire (Robert Taylor) and then falls for his brother (Robert Mitchum), in this way discovering her husband's psychopathic tendencies. The failure of both husband and wife to live up to each other's "dream" is a Minnellian theme, but there are few traces of the director's style in this movie, and the performances are mediocre or worse.

Minnelli returned spectacularly to form with his next musical, *The Pirate* (1948), scripted by Albert Hackett and Frances Goodrich from S. N. Behrman's Broadway comedy, and with songs by Cole Porter. Judy Garland stars as Manuela, a well-bred young woman growing up on a Caribbean island in the nineteenth century. She is reluctantly betrothed to the plump bourgeois Don Pedro (Walter Slezak) but dreams of being carried off by the notorious buccaneer Macoco. Serafin (Gene Kelly), leader of a troupe of actors, masquerades as Macoco in order to woo Manuela. It emerges, ironically, that the real Macoco is Don Pedro. Manuela joins Serafin's troupe, and the film ends with the salute to show-biz escapism, "Be a Clown."

Where *St. Louis* radiates nostalgic warmth, *The Pirate* offers ceaseless pace and panache. Gene Kelly's "Niña," danced with a brightly-clad female *corps de ballet*, is one of the most inventively shot and choreographed numbers in the genre; there is an intoxicatingly exciting bolero performed by Kelly and three women in a scarlet and white pavilion. In "Mack the Black," Manuela is under mesmeric influence, and this is powerfully conveyed in her convulsive movements and the accelerating hand-clapping of the supporting dancers. The "Pirate Ballet Fantasy" that Manuela envisions and Kelly dominates is a flamboyant Fairbanks pastiche.

Lindsay Anderson, in a contemporary review, called the "Pirate Ballet" "a dream-fantasy in color and movement (scarlet and black and great sweeping crane shots, all to a bold and brassy orchestration) which demonstrates with what excitement dance and cinema can be mated by a director, a dancer and a designer sensitive to the resources of both mediums." David Vaughan praised "the dazzling virtuosity of the big dance sequences, the complete assurance with which Minnelli handles large crowds . . . and above all the use of color and lighting."

These encomiums expressed a minority view at the time of the film's release and box-office failure, but *The Pirate*, like *Yolanda and the Thief*, has grown in critical esteem, bearing out Arthur Freed's contention that it was twenty years ahead of its time. J. P. Telotte, writing in the *Journal of Popular Film and Television* (Winter 1982), called it "the premier example of Minnelli's fantasy musicals," whose characters "participate in a carefully choreographed interaction with the culture depicted," illustrating "man's capacity not only to sing the self, but to find a place in society, and paradoxically, not despite but by means of that very effort of individuality . . . In setting himself apart and playing a role, the performer comes to recognize his part in . . . [the] social context, at least his own need for an audience. Far from being antithetical to society, then, the assertion of individuality in Minnelli's films serves to demonstrate man's capacity to find an attunement with his world." Leo Braudy has made a similar point, suggesting that *The Pirate* shows how "the perfect couple" can become "the center of an ideal community."

Madame Bovary (1949), adapted by Robert Ardrey from Flaubert's novel, appealed to Minnelli because Emma Bovary is a dreamer who refuses to accept the harsh realities of life, like Yolanda and Manuela; the film has been seen as a vindication of the romanticism that Flaubert condemns. Extravagant chatter and careful groupings at Emma's disastrous party are recognizably in Minnelli's mocking vein, as is the set-piece waltz, with frenzied subjective traveling shots cut to the "neurotic" music, and windows smashed to relieve Emma's claustrophobia. But for most critics, the film was not a satisfactory cinematic equivalent of the novel, in spite of a cast that included Jennifer Jones, James Mason, Van Heflin, and Louis Jourdan.

Minnelli was on altogether surer ground with *Father of the Bride* (1950), scripted by Hackett and Goodrich from Edward Streeter's novel about the tribulations of a Midwestern banker (endearingly played by Spencer Tracy) during the ruinously expensive preparations for the wedding of his daughter (Elizabeth Taylor). George Morris called this "a gentle but profound examination of the absurdities and human foibles which surface" around this social ritual, ultimately endorsing "those traditional values it lightly satirizes." Coursodon disagreed, maintaining that this "melancholy" film takes "a bitter look at middle-class mores," and includes a dream sequence which is "an actual nightmare that spells out the real fear underlying the jocularity." The picture was, in any case, immensely successful, and was followed a year later by a sequel, *Father's Little Dividend*.

In between came another major musical, *An American in Paris* (1951). This won five Academy Awards, including Best Picture, and remains one of Minnelli's best-known films, though the Oscar-winning script by Alan Jay Lerner has not worn well. It centers on the relationship between Jerry, an aspiring expatriate painter (Gene Kelly), and the *gamine* Lise (Leslie Caron). Complications are provided by a voracious socialite (Nina Foch) and a charming singer (Georges Guetary), and Oscar Levant plays Jerry's wise-cracking buddy Adam, a concert pianist whose only performance is in a dream sequence in which he plays all of the instruments of the orchestra and makes up the audience as well. The songs are by George and Ira Gershwin, the choreography by Gene Kelly, and the art direction by Preston Ames.

The number most generally admired today is the Kelly-Caron "Love Is Here to Stay." The couple stroll through a crowd at dusk, the hubbub fading as they reach a deserted spot beside the Seine, all muted blue except for the dim glow of the bronze streetlights. Kelly's delivery of the ballad has a tenderness which is echoed in the grave beauty of the intimate, sauntering *pas-de-deux*.

Critical opinion is nowadays less unanimous as to the merits of the climactic "American in Paris" ballet, danced to Gershwin's tone poem. Evoking Gerry's loss of Lise and her return to him, this seventeen-minute tour de force is one of the most famous dance sequences in the history of the cinema. It employs all the resources of the dance, from ballet to tap, and draws on the styles of impressionist and postimpressionist French painters to depict various parts of Paris and various moods. For Coursodon this remains "the greatest set-piece not only in Minnelli's career but in the entire history of the film musical"; other modern critics find it undistinguished in its choreography and dancing, and tedious in its cultural pretensions.

Minnelli and Judy Garland were divorced in 1951. Minnelli went on to direct the fashion show sequence in Mervyn LeRoy's *Lovely to Look At* (1952); it bears his signature in its fast tracking shots, dramatic shifts of color and light, bizarre costumes, and formalized groupings. His trademarks were less apparent in "Mademoiselle," the episode he contributed to the omnibus film *The Story of Three Loves* (1953).

One of the most admired of Minnelli's nonmusical films followed, *The Bad and the Beautiful* (1953), produced by John Houseman and scripted by Charles Schnee. It centers on a demonic Hollywood producer, Jonathan Shields (Kirk Douglas), who will sacrifice anything and anyone (including himself) to the cause of art. We see Shields from the points of view of three of his victims: a director (Barry Sullivan), an actress (Lana Turner, in what was perhaps her best performance), and a writer (Dick Powell). Each of these people is manipulated by Shields in his quest for artistic greatness; each is damaged emotionally but enlarged creatively.

Shot in black and white by Robert Surtees, the film is full of memorable moments, like the Beverly Hills party in which an impression of rampant egotism is underlined by the cacophony of overlapping conversations (a device often attributed to Robert Altman who used it in *M°A°S°H* seventeen years later). There is a brilliantly visualized scene in which Shields explains that horror is most effectively achieved in film by suggestion, illustrating the point with a hand sinisterly outlined in light (the reference is to *Cat People*, produced by Val Lewton, on whom Shields is partly modeled). Another justly famous sequence is the frenzied one in which Lana Turner, arriving to celebrate her new film's premiere, finds Shields with another woman; watched by an immobile camera, she hurls herself into her car and hurtles out into the night and the pelting rain, her suicidal acceleration keeping pace with her mounting hysteria until the car skids to a halt and she collapses weeping over the wheel.

Thomas Elsaesser, in Rich Altman's *Genre: The Musical*, writes that Minnelli habitually presents psychological conflict "as a clash of settings, an imbalance of stylistic elements, such as a contrast of movements or a disharmony of colours or objects. . . . when Barry Sullivan in one of the opening scenes of *The Bad and the Beautiful* slams down the telephone, an incongruous but highly dramatic contrast is created in opposition to the dream-like setting in which Lana Turner is being filmed by the camera-crew. Minnelli constantly reduces his stories to their moments of visual intensity, where he can project the dramatic conflicts into the decor." Coursodon sees the film as the clearest exposition of one of Minnelli's central themes, the choice that must be made between "art" and "love." It is widely regarded as one of the best of all Hollywood self-examinations.

The Band Wagon, appearing the same year, is yet another candidate for the title of Minnelli's best musical. Wittily scripted by Betty Comden and Adolph Green and with attractive songs by Arthur Schwartz and Howard Dietz, it features another Faustian producer, Jeffrey Cordova (Jack Buchanan), who is in fact embarked on a grandiose plan to make a musical out of the Faust legend. Some critics believe that both this character and Jonathan Shields are wry parodies of Minnelli himself, as an artist who famously strove for a fusion of show business and high culture.

The film's protagonist, however, is not Cordova but Tony Hunter (Fred Astaire), a washed-up dancer making his comeback in Cordova's musical, opposite ballerina Gaby (Cyd Charisse). When Tony arrives in New York, the reporters at the station turn out to be waiting not for him but for a new star (Ava Gardner). His sense of rejection inspires the film's melancholy and introspective first number, "By Myself." But Cordova's high-toned musical soon collapses of its own weightiness, and Tony finances a more traditional entertainment. This is a hit, of course, leading to Tony's rehabilitation as a member of the show-biz community and a happy resolution of his troubled affair with Gaby. The film ends with a reprise of the central number, "That's Entertainment," echoing the escapist sentiments of "Be a Clown" in *The Pirate*.

The Band Wagon is Minnelli's only backstage musical, but it is a remarkably downbeat and ambiguous variation on the time-honored theme, mixing exuberance and self-questioning. High spots in Michael Kidd's memorable choreography include the "Girl Hunt Ballet," a parody of Mickey Spillane, and the rapt and lyrical *pas de deux* in which Charisse and Astaire, after an accident-prone beginning, discover their artistic and emotional rapport while "Dancing in the Dark" in Central Park.

Opinions differ about *The Long, Long Trailer* (1954), a nonmusical comedy adapted by Hackett and Goodrich from Clinton Twiss' novel. Lucille Ball and Desi Arnaz star as newlyweds uncomfortably honeymooning in the gigantic yellow trailer of the title. The film received some good reviews on release and was a box-office success, but has not been very successful with later critics.

There have also been mixed responses to Minnelli's screen version of the stage musical *Brigadoon* (1954). This Alan Jay Lerner story is a fantasy about an American tourist (Gene Kelly) who renounces all to live with the woman he loves (Cyd Charisse) in a village of another century, magically preserved amid the Scottish mists. Like all of Minnelli's musicals, this one has its devotees, but most thought it marred by stagey sets, drab AnscoColor photography, and Minnelli's uncertain handling of CinemaScope. Compensations include Kelly's solo, "Almost Like Being in Love," and the Charisse-Kelly duet "The Heather on the Hill," in which the effect of several graceful lifts is intensified by Minnelli's use of tracking and crane shots.

All in all, most critics preferred *Brigadoon* to *Kismet* (1955), another CinemaScope adaptation of a Broadway musical—one that used musical themes from Borodin in an Arabian Nights fantasy about a wily Bagdad beggar-poet (Howard Keel), with Dolores Gray as the object of his affections. Coursodon found it "lavish and stupefyingly lifeless," pointing out that "Minnelli's instinctive ploy when faced with weak material . . . was to overload the screen with production values, feeling that, at least, the audience would have something to look at."

The same year, reverting to the melodrama, Minnelli made *The Cobweb*, derived from William Gibson's novel about the seething tensions in an expensive psychiatric clinic. Richard Widmark and Lauren Bacall starred, and Gavin Lambert wrote that Minnelli handles their relationship "in his best, intimate, deftly observant style." There was also praise for the appropriately disorienting camera movements, but once again some critics demurred, suggesting that Dr. Widmark and his staff sometimes seemed madder than their patients.

Even more feverish was *Lust for Life* (1956), based on Irving Stone's novelized biography of Vincent Van Gogh, with Kirk Douglas as the tormented hero. This was Minnelli's favorite among his films, "the only time I ever asked a studio to make a picture." The Minnellian choice

between art and love is central here; Van Gogh is denied the latter by the very intensity of his artistic sensibility. One of Hollywood's more serious attempts to treat the life of an artist, *Lust for Life* earned an Oscar for Anthony Quinn in the supporting role of Paul Gauguin, and an Oscar nomination for Douglas.

Thomas Elsaesser wrote that Minnelli, paying homage to a greater artist, "sharpens his own theme to paroxysm. The Nietzschean intensity of Van Gogh's vision produces paintings of life as no human eye has ever seen it, but it is also a demonic urge that dissolves and severs all human bonds and finally destroys Van Gogh himself. In the film, the two sides are linked symbolically. As his isolation grows, the yellow colours of a superhuman light invade the canvas."

After a forgettable adaptation of Robert Anderson's play *Tea and Sympathy* (1956) came *Designing Woman* (1957), one of the most successful of Minnelli's later films. Scripted by George Wells, this marital comedy has Gregory Peck as a sports reporter, Lauren Becall as a fashion designer, their marriage on the rocks because of the gulf between their milieux. The movie has several musical touches—Dolores Gray belting out "There'll Be Some Changes Made" on television, the choreographer Jack Cole (playing a choreographer) adding an element of frenetic dance, and the culminating brawl combining ballet with the martial arts.

The French critic-director Eric Rohmer wrote that "after *Designing Woman*, there is no further possibility of doubt. The *auteur* of *An American in Paris* is not only an excellent director of musical comedies, but an excellent director of comedies, period." This review was moderate indeed compared to the huge claims that were by then being made for Minnelli by some of Rohmer's colleagues. As Minnelli's star fell in his native country, it rose ever higher in France, where the New Wave critics had identified him as one of the greatest of *auteurist* directors.

But even in America there was a generally favorable response to Minnelli's next comedy, *The Reluctant Debutante* (1958), from the stage piece by William Douglas Home. Rex Harrison and Kay Kendall starred as the elegant parents striving—through what one critic called "a Roman orgy of dinner parties and debutante balls"—to marry off their reluctant Jane (Sandra Dee). There were costumes by Balmain, sets by Jean d'Eaubonne.

By this time the French critics were in full auteurist cry. Jean Wagner in *Cahiers du Cinéma* thought *The Reluctant Debutante* a minor work in the Minnelli canon but interesting as "a latent ballet" in which "the characters glide and soar, talk too much or not at all, separate, come together and bustle about in activities as vain as they are futile." Another *Cahiers* critic, Luc Moullet, praised the "admirably inhuman mechanized playing" of the principal and concluded that, in spite of the "remarkable imbecility" of the plot, this was in fact "Minnelli's masterpiece"!

The theme of *The Reluctant Debutante*—a young woman being groomed and maneuvered by her family into a role that repels her—is also the theme of *Gigi* (1958), the best of Minnelli's late musicals. Adapted from a novel by Colette, it has Leslie Caron as a girl who is being educated for a career as a courtesan in *fin de siècle* Paris. There is a lilting and jaunty Lerner-Loewe score, excellent performances from Maurice Chevalier and Hermione Gingold as elderly hedonists and, above all, superb Paris settings (Preston Ames) and costumes (Cecil Beaton).

"Whatever else it may or may not be," wrote Joel E. Siegel, "*Gigi* is a superlative visual accomplishment, one of the most beautiful movies ever made. . . . But the director appears to have been more concerned with the surface of the film than with its essence. Because we are never allowed to feel much of the anguish of Colette's coltish child as she is forced against her will to become part of an artificial, hypocritical society, the film remains remote from us, a perfectly preserved musical in amber." *Gigi* nevertheless carried off nine Oscars, including Best Picture and Minnelli's sole Oscar as Best Director. It was also highly successful at the box office, returning the director, for the moment, to the top of the tree.

Minnelli followed this triumph with two less successful melodramas. *Some Came Running* (1959), adapted from the partly autobiographical novel by James Jones, stars Frank Sinatra as a war vet and blocked novelist who returns to the small Indiana town where he was born and is at once thrust into a hotbed of hypocrisy and bigotry. He is resented by his brother (Arthur Kennedy), now married into a rich family, encouraged in his writing by the beautiful but repressed schoolteacher (Martha Hyer), and uncritically adored by the golden-hearted prostitute he has picked up along the way (Shirley MacLaine).

"Sinatra's blocked writer contains the Minnellian conflict in one of its purest forms," wrote George Morris. "He is divided between Martha Hyer and everything she represents . . . and Shirley MacLaine, who appeals to his baser instincts, and that world of gambling dives and one-night stands to which he is inexorably

drawn. . . . [But] the moral issues are not clear-cut at all, and the film's tragic ending leaves them disturbingly unresolved. . . . Minnelli's *mise-en-scène* in this film is extraordinary. . . . The neon that flashes from the signs over Kenney's jewelry store, various motels, liquor stores, and the jukeboxes and pinball machines in Smitty's Bar, literally explodes in the carnival at the film's climax. Signaled by a drunken shadow silhouetted against an inferno-red blaze of neon, this set-piece is one of the most superbly realized sequences in Minnelli."

Discussing this film with Jean Domarchi and Jean Douchet for *Cahiers*, Minnelli explained that he had tried to make the low-life characters look as if they were living "inside a jukebox. . . . You can't separate the character from his milieu, isolate him arbitrarily by close-ups. His milieu, his way of life, the chairs where he sits, the room he lives in, all that is part of his personality. It's this man's history."

Home From the Hill (1960), based on the novel by William Humphrey, is another of the numerous Minnelli movies claimed as his best by at least some of his admirers. It tells the story of a Texas dynasty torn by Freudian guilts. Robert Mitchum plays Wade Hunnicutt, the patriarch, with Eleanor Parker as his wife Hannah, George Hamilton as his son Theron, and George Peppard as Theron's illegitimate brother Rafe. The film was shot in CinemaScope and Metrocolor by Milton Krasner, who at this time became Minnelli's regular cinematographer.

George Morris pointed out that the film "has a quasi-symphonic structure of three movements, the climax of each movement marked by George Hamilton's increasingly violent thrusts toward personal freedom. The first movement reaches its climax in the boar hunt, during which Hamilton proves himself in that world his father inhabits with natural ease. This boar hunt with its breathtaking parallel tracking movements attests to Minnelli's skill in creating movement within the frame." The second movement takes place in the kitchen, "that bastion of harmony in the American home," where Theron learns that Rafe is his brother. The third returns us to the forest, where Theron kills his father's murderer (Everett Sloane) and in this way frees himself to invent his own life. Morris found in this film "a perfect fusion of performance, narrative and *mise-en-scène*," and drew attention to Minnelli's use of decor to convey information about its inhabitants, most notably in Hunnicutt's "den," with its guns, dogs, beer cooler, and red leather chair.

Bells Are Ringing (1960), with Judy Holliday as a lovelorn telephone operator, was a rather lackluster Comden-Green musical. This was followed in 1962 by a remake of *The Four Horsemen of the Apocalypse*, updated to World War II, with Glenn Ford in the Valentino role. Minnelli was not happy with the casting (he had wanted the then-unknown Alain Delon) or the script (Robert Ardrey and John Gay). As usual under such circumstances, he "decided it should be as stunning visually as I could make it. The flaws in the story might be overlooked."

Jean Douchet described Minnelli's pre-war Paris in this film as a set invaded by another set, with "the Nazi dream, a collective and uniform dream, unfurling over France, destroying town after town, set after set." There was praise for Milton Krasner's rich, Ophulsian camerawork, but the film's reception was generally cool.

The same was true of *Two Weeks in Another Town* (1962), from Irwin Shaw's novel about the Italian film world. Kirk Douglas, once again Minnelli's anguished artist-protagonist, plays Jack Andrus, a star recovering from a breakdown. He flies to Rome to resume his career and finds himself drawn back into the old world of lies and illusion. Thomas Elsaesser identifies this as one of the Minnelli films in which "tragedy is present as a particular kind of unfreedom, as the constraint of an emotional or artistic temperament in a world that becomes claustrophobic, where reality suddenly reveals itself as mere decor, unbearably false and oppressive. That is when the dream changes into nightmare, when desire becomes obsession, and the creative will turns into mad frenzy."

The Courtship of Eddie's Father (1963), from a novel by Mark Toby, starred Glenn Ford as a personable widower pursued by three women (each with her own distinctive style and decor). Ron Howard plays his precocious small son Eddie, who helps him make up his mind and even teaches him how to mourn his dead wife. T. L. French, describing Howard as "America's answer to Jean-Pierre Leaud," credited this "brash, tiny and *weird*" child with communicating such energy to the other players that Minnelli could "exact from Glenn Ford and Shirley Jones the performances of their lives. The result was one of his loveliest and most personal films."

But, as Coursodon says, "there is as much pathos as laughter" in this film, "where cracks keep appearing in the surface cuteness to reveal depths of anguish. This is a world in which the death of a goldfish can take on traumatic proportions. Minnelli is too fascinated with the workings of the human psyche to play the [dehumanizing] rules of comedy straight." Once again the American reviewers were dismissive or hostile, and now even Minnelli's French admirers

were deserting him. The *Cahiers* critic Michel Mardore wrote that "the aesthetic concepts exposed in *The Courtship of Eddie's Father* justify our former infatuation and our violent disavowal of the recent productions. Today we see the worm and the apple inseparably."

Things picked up a little with *Goodbye Charlie* (1964), made not for MGM but for 20th Century–Fox. This adaptation of George Axelrod's comedy about a macho male who undergoes an involuntary sex-change starred Debbie Reynolds as the hero/heroine, Tony Curtis as his/her embarrassed buddy. This movie had a moderately encouraging reception, but was followed by what is arguably Minnelli's worst film, *The Sandpiper* (1965), a farrago about the tormented liaison between a priest (Richard Burton) and a painter (Elizabeth Taylor). With an abysmal script by Dalton Trumbo and self-parodic hamming from the stars, Minnelli's "all-powerful" decor, as one *Cahiers* critic wrote, becomes pointless: "Everything crumbles, and the set becomes just painted paper again." In 1966, having failed to set up a screen musical using Irving Berlin songs, Minnelli ended his MGM contract. In 1967 he directed the stage musical *Mata Hari*, another flop.

Minnelli made his last musical, *On a Clear Day You Can See Forever* (1970), at Paramount. Adapted by Alan Jay Lerner from his Broadway show, it has Barbra Streisand as Daisy Gamble, a university student who, under hypnosis, regresses to a previous incarnation as Melinda, a seductive charmer in Regency England. Yves Montand was miscast as the psychologist who falls in love with the girl from long ago. No one has claimed this as a masterpiece, but the Regency scenes, shot in Technicolor and Panavision and costumed by Cecil Beaton, have a sophisticated opulence. And Minnelli worked well with Streisand, notably in Melinda's ballad "Love With All the Trimmings," filmed in enticing close-shots, and Daisy's probing of her identity crisis in "What Did I Have That I Don't Have?," with the camera tracking her restless wanderings.

Six years passed before Minnelli completed his next picture, *A Matter of Time*, adapted by John Gay from a novel by Maurice Druon and made at American-International. It was Minnelli's last film, and the only one on which he worked with his daughter Liza. She plays a rising young musical-comedy star, and the film centers on her relationship with an aging, impoverished, and mentally unstable aristocrat (Ingrid Bergman). The piece suffered from front-office alterations and Minnelli disowned it, but it has its riches, providing an autumnal summation of the director's themes in its portraits of a young artist and an old dreamer, and an anthology of his stylistic traits—the crane and tracking shots, the telling decors and figure groupings. Bergman, in a magnificent summatory performance of her own, outshines Liza Minnelli, but the latter is often spirited and touching. During her solo "Do It Again," her father and the cinematographer Geoffrey Unsworth send the camera questing forward over a gondola-strewn lagoon, among glimmering torches, carnival streamers, and fantastically garbed revellers: a final moment of Minnelli magic. George Morris, not unjustly, hailed the film as "a glorious tone poem composed by the American cinema's greatest aesthete."

Minnelli died ten years later in Beverly Hills, having spent the last day of his life with his daughter Liza. He had another daughter, Christina, by his second wife, Georgette Magnani, and subsequently was married twice more, to Denise Gigante and Lee Anderson.

Thomas Elsaesser called Minnelli "the virtual father of the modern musical," and not many would disagree with that. The same critic goes on to suggest that "the Minnelli musical celebrates the fulfillment of desire and identity, whose tragic absence so many of his dramatic films portray. Looked at like this, the dramas and dramatic comedies are *musicals turned inside out,* for the latter affirm all those values and urges which the former visualize as being in conflict with a radically different order of reality." Even before Minnelli sank under a deluge of bad scripts during the 1960s, his "exaltation of artifice" had put him out of favor with the "realist" critics: Andrew Sarris accused him of believing "more in beauty than in art." However, as Jean-Pierre Coursodon points out, "'realism' being a highly relative and constantly redefined concept, artificiality . . . stands a better chance of convincing, and aging well."
　　　　　　　　　　　　　　　　　　—D.McV.

FILMS: Cabin in the Sky, 1943; I Dood It (By Hook or by Crook), 1943; Meet Me in St. Louis, 1944; The Clock (Under the Clock), 1945; Yolanda and the Thief, 1945; Ziegfeld Follies, 1946; Undercurrent, 1946; The Pirate, 1948; Madame Bovary, 1949; Father of the Bride, 1950; An American in Paris, 1951; Father's Little Dividend, 1951; The Bad and the Beautiful, 1953; Mademoiselle *episode in* The Story of Three Loves, 1953; The Band Wagon, 1953; The Long, Long Trailer, 1954; Brigadoon, 1954; The Cobweb, 1955; Kismet, 1955; Lust for Life, 1956; Tea and Sympathy, 1956; Designing Woman, 1957; Gigi, 1958; The Reluctant Debutante, 1958; Some Came Running, 1959; Home from the Hill, 1960; Bells Are Ringing, 1960; The Four Horsemen of the Apocalypse, 1962; Two Weeks in Another Town, 1962; The Courtship of Eddie's Father,

1963; Goodbye Charlie, 1964; The Sandpiper, 1965; On a Clear Day You Can See Forever, 1970; A Matter of Time, 1976.

ABOUT: Altman, R. (ed.) Genre: The Musical, 1982; Brion, P. (and others) Vincente Minnelli, 1985 (in French); Casper, J.A. Vincente Minnelli and the Film Musical, 1977; Coursodon, J–P. American Directors, Vol. II, 1983; De La Roche, C. Vincente Minnelli, 1959; Guérif, F. Vincente Minnelli, 1984 (in French); Higham, C. and Greenberg, J. (eds.) The Celluloid Muse: Hollywood Directors Speak, 1969; International Film Guide, 1978; Knox, D. The Magic Factory: How MGM made An American In Paris, 1973; Marchelli, M. Vincente Minnelli, 1979 (in Italian); Minnelli, V. (with Arce, H.) I Remember It Well, 1974; Roud, R. (ed.) Cinema: A Critical Dictionary, 1980; Taylor, J. R. and Jackson, A. The Hollywood Musical, 1971; Truchaud, F. Vincente Minnelli, 1966 (in French); Vidal, M. Vincente Minnelli, 1973 (in French); Yates, P. (ed.) The Films of Vincente Minnelli, 1978. *Periodicals*: Cahiers du Cinéma August–September 1957, February 1962; Cinema Nuovo January–February 1975; Cinématographe January 1978; Dirigido Janaury–February 1973; Film Notebooks Winter 1978; Film Quarterly Winter 1958 and Spring 1959; Films and Filming June 1959; Films in Review March 1964; Image et Son October 1981; Journal of Popular Film Winter 1982; Movie June 1962, October 1963; Objectif February–March 1964; Positif November–December 1954, March 1963; Sight and Sound January–March 1952.

*MIZOGUCHI, KENJI (May 16, 1898– August 24, 1956), Japanese director, was born in the middle-class district of Hongo, in Toyko, near the Yushima shrine. His father, Zentaro, was a roofing carpenter, and his mother, Masa, the daughter of an unsuccessful trader in Chinese herbal remedies. When Mizoguchi was seven, they had to move to the poorer downtown district of Asakusa because of the failure of a business venture in which his father tried to sell raincoats to the army during the war with Russia. In that same year his younger brother, Yoshio, was born, while his sister, Suzu, then fourteen, was given up for adoption to help the family finances, and soon afterwards sold by her foster parents to a geisha house. She was eventually to find a wealthy patron who married her in 1925.

These early experiences were to have a powerful influence on Mizoguchi's films, like much else in his turbulent personal life. At the time of the move to Asakusa he suffered his first attack of the rheumatoid arthritis that was to recur throughout his life, and which left him with an odd gait and a tendency to raise his right shoulder when angry. In June 1907 he entered Isihama elementary school and there met Matsutaro

°mē zō gōō chē

KENJI MIZOGUCHI

Kawaguchi, who became a successful novelist and Mizoguchi's collaborator on many of his best-known films.

When Mizoguchi was eleven, after a total of six years schooling, his father was forced by lack of money to send him to live with relatives in the northern city of Morioka, where he was apprenticed to an uncle who worked as a hospital pharmacist. He returned home in 1912, but his father, whom he hated, refused to send him to school again. The resulting sense of inferiority about his lack of formal education stayed with him all his life.

In 1913 Mizoguchi's sister found him a job with a designer of patterns for kimonos. Two years later, when their mother died, Suzu installed their father in an old people's home, and took her two brothers to live with her. Watching an artist who lived across the street, Mizoguchi began to be interested in painting, and studied Western-style oil and watercolor painting at the Aiobashi Institute. At the same time he was absorbing the city life of Tokyo and going to the Japanese variety theatre and Western-style shows in Asakusa. He read Zola, Maupassant, and Tolstoy, but preferred Japanese novelists: Kafu Nagai for his naturalism, Soseki Natsume for a philosophical view, Koyo Ozaki, for his panoramic and allegorical narratives, and Kyoka Izumi for the aestheticism of his sentimental Meiji melodramas.

Mizoguchi went to Kobe in 1918 to take up a job as a designer of advertisements for a newspaper there. He enjoyed the city's progressive atmosphere and the company of new drinking companions, dabbled in theatrical ventures, and wrote poems which the newspaper printed; but homesickness soon drove him back to Toyko. He moved in with a friend who worked at Nikkatsu's Mukojima film studios and through him came to know Osamu Wakayama, one of the progressive directors. At this time Nikkatsu was modernizing its methods of production in response to competition from other studios. Mizoguchi was fascinated. He offered himself in 1922 as an actor, but found himself doing various jobs such as transcribing scripts. "I remember my first day in the studio perfectly," he said years later, "I was a flunky, that's all, but at the end of that day, I thought—this is good work for me."

Mizoguchi worked for Eizo Tanaka, organizing sets for his *Kyoya Collar Shop* (1922) so effectively that Tanaka recommended him as a director. This was the year of the famous walkout of directors and actors protesting at the studio's new policy of casting actresses in women's roles instead of female impersonators—the traditional *oyama*. Because of the strike, a directorial vacancy appeared almost at once. Mizoguchi's first film, *Ai ni yomigaeru hi* (*The Resurrection of Love*) was released on February 3, 1923, heavily cut by the censors because of its resolutely naturalistic treatment of a "proletarian ideology." Its realistic style was influenced by the innovative critic and director Norimasa Kaeriyama. Mizoguchi used a great many intertitles—his first attempt to dispense with the traditional *benshi*, the narrator who sat on a special platform and explained what was happening on the silent screen behind him.

Ten more films followed in the same year, the average shooting time being about a week for each. *Foggy Harbor*, based on O'Neill's *Anna Christie*, had a formally framed story beginning one evening and ending the following dawn, and was as richly melancholy in atmosphere as the title suggests. It continued the innovative tendency toward making the *benshi* redundant, but this time by using the camera to tell the story so clearly that few titles were required. *Blood and Soul* showed the expressionist influence of *Caligari*, which had appeared in Japan in 1921. The variety of Mizoguchi's early output is further demonstrated on the one hand by *813*, based on an Arsène Lupin detective story by Maurice Leblanc, and on the other by *The Song of the Mountain Pass*, which derives from a play by Lady Gregory, a founder of the Irish Literary Theatre. The great Tokyo earthquake on September 1, 1923 caused the evacuation of Suzu and their father to the studios for safety; Mizoguchi himself was filming the disaster for American newsreels and for use in the feature film *In the Ruins*, which opened to great success the following month.

Mizoguchi was now moved to Nikkatsu's Kyoto studios, where he continued to make many films according to front office requirements. He found the atmosphere of the ancient city, with its traditions and its distinctive Kansai dialect, so much to his taste that he made it his permanent home. Beginning with *Turkeys in a Row* in 1924, most of Mizoguchi's films until the advent of sound were scripted by Shuichi Hatamoto, over whom he exercised a domineering control of the kind his more famous collaborator Yoshikata Yoda suffered in later years. Hatamoto was not even allowed to return home after work, but was enlisted as Mizoguchi's unwilling drinking partner. Mizoguchi was living with Yuriko Ichijo, a call girl who moved into the flat he shared with his assistant director Koji Asaka. In the summer of 1925, she attacked Mizoguchi in a jealous rage, wounding him in the back with a razor. The scandal that followed led to Mizoguchi's suspension from the studio, interrupting the shooting of *Shining in the Red Sunset*; it was completed by his friend Saegusa.

J. D. Andrew has suggested that the films Mizoguchi made after his return to the studio in October 1925 begin to take on a different character, but that from this time began both his obsessive perfectionism and his preoccupation with the suffering and hostility of women; it is difficult to judge since almost none of these early films survive. The first of his pictures still extant, *Furusato no uta* (*The Song of Home*), is a studio assignment remote from Mizoguchi's personal concerns, lauding traditional rural values over those of the wicked city, although it contains some montage experiments in the manner of Minoru Murata. The script by Ryunosuke Shimizu won a Ministry of Education award.

Then came the success of *A Paper Doll's Whisper of Spring* (1926), praised for its sensitive portrayal of an emotional conflict created by male egotism. The film was ranked seventh in the first *Kinema Jumpo* list of the ten best movies of the year. After that Mizoguchi was able to persuade his old school friend Matsutaro Kawaguchi for the first time to write him a script. The result was *The Passion of a Woman Teacher,* and pleased both Nikkatsu and the public so well that it became the first of Mizoguchi's films to be exported to Europe, where it had some success. French interest in that film led him to make one with foreign audiences specifically in mind—a portrait of the traditional Japan based on Kyoka Izumi's novel *Nihonbashi.*

This was the era of the "tendency film" (*keiko eiga*), a manifestation of the new socialist consciousness. The extent of Mizoguchi's own commitment to this movement is much discussed. Kawaguchi saw his friend as an opportunist

merely following the Marxist fashion of the time, but Richie and Anderson may be right in regarding the ambiguity of Mizoguchi's position as a characteristic shared by many Japanese. At any rate the leftist tendency led Mizoguchi into a clash with Minoru Murata, a right-winger who was not only Mizoguchi's chief rival as a director but had become Nikkatsu's secretary in charge of production. Nevertheless Mizoguchi's own position as head of the script department enabled him to make *Tokyo March* (1929), of which a fragment survives showing a use of newsreel techniques. It had success enough for the company to sanction *Metropolitan Symphony* (1929), coscripted by the Marxist Fusao Hayashi who had a great influence on Mizoguchi at this time. The film ran into trouble with the censors and brought a police reprimand for the director and jail for Hayashi, but it still placed tenth in the *Kinema Jumpo* list.

No less influential than politics in Mizoguchi's life and perhaps his work in this period was his impulsive marriage to Chieko Saga, an Osaka dance-hall girl whom he met in 1926. Chieko's attempts to regulate her husband's life led to violent fights and brief separations, repeatedly resolved with his promises of reform.

Mizoguchi's first sound film, *Furusato* (*Home Town*), made in 1930, was also one of the first in Japan, and like other pioneer talkies was marked by primitive recording techniques. The silent film that followed, *Mistress of a Foreigner,* is regarded as the first in which the director systematically employed the long take or "one scene—one shot" method that became so essential a part of his mature style. He found justification for the technique in the psychological experiments of his friend Dr. Konan Naito. As the director himself explained, "During the course of filming a scene, if I feel that a kind of psychological sympathy has begun to develop, then I cannot without regret cut into this. Rather, I then try to intensify, to prolong the scene as long as possible." Around this time Mizoguchi began to interest himself in the study of music, starting with Beethoven. He was also a member of a folk art group including the philosopher Kitaro Nishida, and wore clothes of a material woven and dyed by himself.

And Yet They Go (1931), a late "tendency" film, was followed in 1932 by *The Man of the Moment,* which was Nikkatsu's first success in sound despite production difficulties as a result of a strike of *benshi* that year. It also marks the end of an uninterrupted series of films for the studio. For some time he had been discontented with his salary and the company's policies, especially since a new management had instituted an even more dictatorial regime. Mizoguchi signed a contract with Shinko Studios, and began work for them by spending two months on location in China shooting *The Dawn of Manchuria and Mongolia* (1932), a propaganda piece that failed embarrassingly and led to Mizoguchi's refusal to undertake another project for six months.

Having been shown a version of Kyoka Izumi's novel *Giketsu, Kyoketsu*, Mizoguchi set out in 1933 to adapt it for the screen. But the novelist, who had greatly disliked the director's earlier adaptation of *Nihonbashi*, would not cooperate. The studio arranged a meeting at last, and the silent film *Taki no Shiraito* was made in the face of continuing disagreement. Izumi had objections to the cast Mizoguchi wanted, but the director got his way, while demanding freedom to shoot at his own pace. Beginning without a completed script, so that changes had to be made from day to day, Mizoguchi spent forty days shooting. The result of his obsessive care was a success with both critics and public, ranking second in the *Kinema Jumpo* list for 1933.

The film tells the story of the tragic love of the heroine Taki no Shiraito for a weak and passive young student, Kinya. Taki, a stage performer specializing in a kind of juggling display with water jets, is a prototype of the rebellious women who appear in many of Mizoguchi's films, working for her financial independence, taking the initiative in the love affair. In the face of terrible difficulties, Taki contrives to support Kinya through his studies to become a lawyer, only to have him as her prosecutor when she is accused of murder. The story ends with the suicide of both lovers. Close-ups and the normal procedures of narrative editing are freely used, but the film shows Mizoguchi's increasing tendency to favor the long shot and the long take. It is remarkable also for its subtle but intense eroticism.

Gion Festival, made in the same year, had to be shot in haste to be in time for the festival of its title, a great annual celebration in Kyoto. An unexceptional studio assignment, it marked the beginning of Mizoguchi's association with art director Hiroshi Mizutani, who had been impressed with *Taki no Shiraito* and was to remain with the director for the rest of his career. As obsessed as Mizoguchi himself with detailed research in the interests of authenticity and historical accuracy, Mizutani's sets became an essential part of the one scene–one shot method, leading at least one Japanese critic to suggest that the setting is the central factor, even the "hero," in Mizoguchi's films, though others have found the scrupulously detailed settings too museum-like. Mizoguchi himself, speaking to film students, stressed the importance of atmosphere,

saying that atmosphere to a film is like light to painting. According to the critic Yasuzo Masumura, it determines the very nature of Mizoguchi's realism, since his motive in devoting such attention to set detail was to provide an atmosphere that would draw the most authentic performances from his actors.

Up to *Jinpuren* (1934), Mizoguchi's films for Shinko had been subcontracted to a production company headed by the actress Takako Irie. The director resented this arrangement, and left Shinko as soon as his contract expired in March 1934. He returned to Nikkatsu for long enough to make *Aizo toge* (*The Mountain Pass of Love and Hate*), about the love between a Liberal Party activist and a blind actress, but was negotiating at the same time with Shochiku in an attempt to overcome his financial difficulties. In 1933 Shochiku had founded a new subsidiary, Daiichi Eiga, which was to be headed by Masaichi Nagata (formerly of Nikkatsu). This was the company that Mizoguchi joined. Nagata, whose collaboration and support were to be important throughout Mizoguchi's career, now gave the director freedom to work in his own way he made a number of films between 1934 and 1936 of the greatest importance in his development as an artist, and perhaps for the Japanese cinema itself.

Orizuru Osen (*The Downfall of Osen*), another Kyoka adaptation, tells the story of Sokichi, a young man who wants to be a doctor, and Osen, a beautiful prostitute who rescues him from suicide. She works for a gangster who puts Sokichi to work too, treating him brutally until the pair contrive to escape, betraying the gang to the police. To send her lover to medical school Osen, unknown to him, returns to prostitution, is unjustly imprisoned for theft, and disappears from Sokichi's life. Years later, having become a doctor, Sokichi re-encounters Osen when she faints in a crowded railroad station. He finds she is both incurably ill and insane, quite unaware of her former lover. The complicated story, of which this is the barest summary, is told in a boldly complex manner, starting with the scene at the station and using a double set of flashbacks representing the past as remembered by each of the main characters. The opening sequence mingles present and past in a masterfully edited series of images, using close-ups and the moving camera with panache. *The Downfall of Osen*, with its emphatically dramatic treatment of emotional conflict, is called, by Burch "a splendidly baroque poem"—a judgment that might be illustrated by the terrifying final scene in hospital where Osen, now living entirely in her fantasies, attacks her lover's enemies with a razor and then returns in pathetic contentment to her bed.

Two more films followed in 1935: *Maria no Oyuki,* a transposition of Maupassant's "Boule de Suif" to the Japan of 1878, for which Mizoguchi showed little enthusiam, disliking Kawaguchi's script; and *Gubijinso (Poppy),* adapted from a novel by Soseki Natsume. Both films show Mizoguchi continuing to experiment with method. *Gubijinso,* for instance, almost completely abandons the moving camera and the long take, which had already begun to represent the main trend in his work, in favor of Western-style editing using close-ups and reverse-field to intensify dramatic tension. The story, as in *Maria no Oyuki,* concerns a contrasted pair of women, in this case the dutiful innocent betrothed to the ambitious hero Ono by her father, and the sophisticated older woman to whom Ono teaches English. Neither film had much critical or popular success at the time or since, but Mizoguchi's next, *Osaka Elegy* (1936), ranked third in the *Kinema Jumpo* list and is often considered by Japanese critics to be his first masterpiece.

Isuzu Yamada, a favorite actress of the director's ever since she worked for him on *Aizo toge,* plays Ayako, a characteristic Mizoguchi heroine. She is a young telephone operator, working in a pharmaceutical company. When she needs money to keep her embezzling father out of jail, Asai, the owner of the company, offers help in return for sexual favors. She is shocked, but her fiancé Nishimura will not help, and further difficulties at home persuade her to become Asai's mistress, until his wife discovers them in bed. Nishimura fails her, and Ayako resorts to prostitution for the sake of her family. They spurn her while accepting her money, and finally she is arrested and tried for defrauding her boss, Fujino, of money paid for her favors. To this and all her other humiliations, Ayako responds with ironic defiance, demanding to know what cure there is for the "disease" of delinquency for which family and society condemn her, and staring challengingly into the camera in the final close-up shot.

The setting is modern Osaka, and Mizoguchi went to great trouble to give it substance in the film, especially through the careful use of the authentic Kansai dialect. Keiko McDonald describes Osaka as a city associated by the Japanese with cunning merchants intent on profit and pleasure. Mizoguchi conveys the city's atmosphere and significance typically in nocturnal scenes, such as that on the bridge at the end, and shows Ayako's predicament by images of confinement and by close-framing, although with a sparing use of close-ups, so that the audience is simultaneously drawn in and held at arm's length. Often considered "the forerunner of realism in the Japanese cinema," *Osaka Elegy* also shows a concern for the formal beauty of its images that is equally characteristic of its director.

An immediate critical success, this was Mizoguchi's first association with the long-suffering scriptwriter Yoshikata Yoda, which lasted until the director's death. He was the ideal collaborator for so demanding a master, submissively revising the script, in this case more than ten times, before it was grudgingly accepted. Yoda was never told precisely what was wrong (Mizoguchi habitually placed all his associates in the same state of uncertainty), but was repeatedly instructed to create characters so real that the audience would smell their human odor. "Describe for me the implacable, the egoistic, the sensual, the cruel . . . there are none but disgusting people in this world." Yoda himself described the pent-up emotion that charged Mizoguchi's formally meticulous films: "He does not have the courage to face persons, things, and ideas that assail him. The anger and resentment which he cannot deal with makes him cry hysterically. This is the source of that intensity revealed in *Osaka Elegy* and *Sisters of the Gion.*" Admired as it was by the critics, *Osaka Elegy* was a financial failure. The director was summoned before the Ministry of Internal Affairs, and the film was only just passed by the censors, so that its distributors, Shochiku and Nikkatsu, were nervous of publicizing it.

After Osaka, Mizoguchi turned his attention to another district of the Kansai region, the Gion or pleasure quarter of Kyoto, in *Sisters of the Gion.* Despite some censorship problems, this was placed above its predecessor by *Kinema Jumpo* as best picture of 1936. Determined to convey the reality—the "earthiness"—of Kyoto, where Yoda was raised and Mizoguchi lived, they again made significant use of the local dialect. The director wanted his film to contain the rich complexity of the ancient city, its deceptive subtleties as well as the "uncouthness" of its citizens, and disregarded the financial restrictions placed on him, bankrupting the Daiichi Company in the process. Yoda claimed that the idea for the story was his, while admitting the inspiration of Kuprin's novel *The Pit,* which Mizoguchi had made him read. The two sisters of the title are geisha. The elder, Umekichi, is conscientious and submissive in her role of pleasing men; while Omocha, the younger, is a modern, despising the traditions of her profession and intent on exploiting it for her own advancement. Umekichi owes allegiance to a merchant, now bankrupt, and invites him to live in their house in the Gion, but Omocha has other plans and gets him to leave. Omocha obtains expensive kimono cloth by flirting with a shop clerk. When his boss fires him and takes up with Omocha himself, the young man kidnaps and abuses her, and she is seriously injured in a fall from a speeding taxi. In her hospital bed, with her sister, also abandoned finally by her merchant, sitting beside her, she curses men and the life of the geisha.

The most familiar features of Mizoguchi's style are here fully developed. The long take, with the camera distanced from its object, is exemplified in the scene where Omocha gently hustles her sister's patron from their house. During most of this scene, the characters occupy only the lower left quarter of the screen, seated at a table, so that while responding to the characters and their drama we must also be continuously aware of the details of the world in which it takes place. The effect of this "disengaging distance" (Donald Richie) is often remarked, combining as it does a "steady gaze" (Motohiko Fujita) with a detachment that leads Noël Burch to speak of the "ultimately non-anthropocentric quality of Mizoguchi's mature style."

The film opens with a striking use of the moving camera in a "scroll-shot," so-called from a resemblance to the traditional Japanese art of painting on a long paper roll. A lateral track through the merchant's house reveals in succession evidence of his former wealth and of his present bankruptcy: first the auction itself, then a room full of creditors, then another where objects are being sorted for sale, then a dissolve to a shot revealing the merchant himself, still linked with the rest by the sounds of the auction. The conflict of values between old and new represented by the sisters extends its implications beyond the particular case partly as a result of Mizoguchi's distancing method. The audience's sympathies may be moved either way, and the choice is still open in the problematic ending. In a discussion with critics at the time, the director apologised for what they regarded as the unsatisfactory nature of this open conclusion.

Mizoguchi intended to follow this with a third picture, set in Kobe, to complete a Kansai trilogy, but the company's financial difficulties and his doubts about the Tanizaki novel he hoped to adapt caused the project to be dropped. In 1937 the Daiichi Eiga Company went out of business, and Mizoguchi returned to Shinko Kinema in Tokyo, where he first made *Aien kyo* (*The Straits of Love and Hate*), adapted from Tolstoy's *Resurrection* in collaboration with Yoda and Kawaguchi. Ofumi, played by Fumiko Yamaji, has been described by Audie Bock as Mizoguchi's "one heroine who retains both love and moral courage" as she struggles against her fate to achieve a kind of resigned happiness. Made pregnant by the son of her innkeeper employer, she runs away to Tokyo where, abandoned by her lover, she eventually joins a band of traveling players. Returning to her home town, and reject-

ed by her lover's parents, she marries the actor who partners her in comic sketches, and returns to the road. In the final scene the camera tracks away, so that we are among the audience in the theatre watching a farce performed by the couple.

Mizoguchi said that he was influenced by Von Sternberg in this film, especially in the use of sound, and critics have noticed in particular his debt to *The Docks of New York* (1928). In 1936 Mizoguchi had spent an afternoon with Von Sternberg in Kyoto, insisting that the protesting visitor watch a bad print of one of Von Sternberg's own movies. It was during the making of this film that his associates begin to talk about Mizoguchi's obsessive concern to perfect his actors' performances. It is said that over three days he rehearsed one scene with Fumiko Yamaji almost seven hundred times. Yoda records that with actors, as with the writer himself, the director gave only a general idea of what was required, leaving the performers "to live and create themselves." Designer Mizutani recalled that if a long scene was failing to work, Mizoguchi would have the actors rehearse it on their own and tell him when they felt ready.

In 1938, much against his will, Mizoguchi made *The Song of the Camp*, a "patriotic potboiler" (McDonald) and, apparently also with little enthusiasm, *Ah, My Home Town*, his last for Shinko. His younger brother Yoshio, under political pressure for participation in a Western idealistic philosophical movement led by Kiyoshi Miki, died suddenly in the same year. Mizoguchi was appointed a national film consultant and sent in 1939 with five other directors on a visit to Manchuria. Despite overtures from Toho, Mizoguchi now went to Shochiku and began work on what was to be a trilogy of films about the theatre in the Meiji period. This return to a historical setting and the *shinpa* mode of his earliest successes was a response to the censorship problems provoked by the social criticism in the Kansai movies, and to the increasingly repressive atmosphere of militarism at the time of the war in China. But although *Zangiku monogatari* (*The Story of the Late Chrysanthemums*, 1939) has been seen as escapist, Noël Burch describes it as "one of his most deeply 'feminist' films."

It is ostensibly the story of Kabuki actor Kikunosuke (Shotaro Hanayagi), adopted son of an illustrious acting family. He falls in love with the servant Otoku (Kakuko Mori), the real subject of the film, who has dared to tell him just how bad an actor he is. When the family forces Otoku to leave, Kikunosuke goes too and, with Otoku's support and love, works to perfect his acting in the hard school of provincial tours. When he is reunited with his family five years later, Otoku withdraws from his life, seeing that she would be an obstacle to the career of the now great actor. During the river procession with which the public honors its Kabuki stars, Kikunosuke is told that Otoku is seriously ill and goes to her. But she sends him back to his triumph, and dies while the actor is acknowledging the admiration of the crowd from his barge.

The self-sacrifice of this typical Mizoguchi heroine, stronger and more intelligent than the men around her, is counterpointed by ironic ambiguity, for example in the fact that Kikunosuke's specialty is playing women's roles, and in the challenge of the final shot of the great artist bowing to the camera. The theme is further enriched by the extraordinary power of the film's style. As John Pym writes, the sets are "crammed with human detail," and one effect of this, "sometimes offset by shots of notably uncluttered spaces, is to highlight the isolation of the two principals in a teeming world dominated by class prejudice, harsh economics, and sheer blank human indifference." The "sequence-shot," the long mobile take, is developed to a new and pure extreme governing the whole film apart from the Kabuki scenes, set off by their sharp editing. Richard Tucker says that the opening scenes, introducing us to the backstage world, work "in a way which makes even the weavings of the camera and the sound control in Altman's *M°A°S°H* look heavy-handed." Burch analyzes in detail the scene following Otoku's dismissal, describing how the camera, itself continuously moving, discovers fixed "tableaux" illustrating the progress of the drama. The film was an immediate success, coming second in the *Kinema Jumpo* list and winning Mizoguchi an Education Ministry Award and a place on the National Film Committee. Tony Rayns regards it as "the peak of Mizoguchi's art," and many agree.

In July 1940 Mizoguchi began again on an earlier idea, a film on the puppet master Danpei Toyozawa. As the heroine he had the actress he had wanted all along, Kinuyo Tanaka, who became a close friend as well as his favorite female lead in his remaining films. When she arrived for her first day's work, Mizoguchi gave her a set of volumes on the Bunraku theatre and told her to immerse herself in its world. She was to find this typical of Mizoguchi's thoroughgoing approach, as she explained in interviews later. The original idea and first preparations for a film might come two years ahead of shooting; then came reading, planning, getting the right cast. Actors had to study the background of their roles, but their lines had to be learned fast. Mi-

zoguchi used a blackboard on which was written the dialogue for each day's shooting, to be learned that day. The long takes made this particularly difficult, and Hisakazu Tsuji, planner and assistant director on Mizoguchi's last films, confirms that the blackboard in effect represented the only definitive text since, of the numerous revisions of the script demanded by the director, none was ever final. He also reported that Mizoguchi rarely improvised on the set itself, simply writing last-minute revisions on the blackboard.

Despite the exhausting nature of Mizoguchi's method, Kinuyo Tanaka found it justified by its effect. It worked because of the tension it created in everyone. In spite of what many thought, she believed he had a great respect for actors and what they could do in the space he gave them. His instructions were few and general. She heard him say a hundred times: "Be a mirror to the character, reflect it, be natural"; never much else. Tanaka's role in *Woman of Osaka* (1940) was modeled on Mizoguchi's own wife Chieko. The film, of which the print is lost, had some success, as did the third of the trilogy, *The Life of an Actor* (1941), also lost. But by now Shochiku was less supportive to Mizoguchi about films so apparently out of tune with the times. Mizoguchi himself seems to have been affected by the contemporary jingoistic fervor, but Dudley Andrew questions the seriousness of patriotic public statements made by him at this period.

Mizoguchi's next film, *Genroku Chushingura* (*The Loyal Forty-Seven Ronin of the Genroku Era*), seemed to give him the opportunity for a major film on a subject exactly fitted to the government's current requirements. The story, based on events that occurred in the early eighteenth century, is one of the great heroic legends of Japan. It had already appeared often in films, including the celebrated Kinugasa version, as well as in the theatre. The script by Yoda and Kenichiro Hara was based on a current stage hit.

Asano, one of two *daimyo* (provincial lords) appointed to arrange festivities for an imperial visit to the Shogun in Edo, is provoked by the deceit and insults of his more experienced fellow, Kira, and assaults him with his sword. Serious injury is avoided, but Asano has to commit *seppuku*, ritual suicide, for the crime of drawing a weapon in the Shogun's palace. Asano's property is forfeit, and his retainers become *ronin*, masterless samurai. But a group of these, led by Oishi, swear vengeance, delaying for months with extravagant deceptions to still Kira's fear of reprisal. After a year, the loyal band storms Kira's house and kills him, retiring to a nearby temple. When their courage and loyalty become known, they are allowed the honorable course of committing *seppuku.*

The government was eager to have the film made as a tribute to the heroic *bushido* spirit, and allowed Mizoguchi a huge budget and an extended shooting schedule. The film was made and released in two parts between June 1941 and February 1942, with the director overspending to the extent of ruining the newly founded Koa Eiga Company that produced it. The first part alone cost five hundred and thirty thousand yen (when a major film rarely cost more than a hundred thousand), and part two almost as much. Although the film was a financial disaster, it apparently pleased the government. All Mizoguchi's lavish attention to detail produces a narrative of powerful austerity which disdains any kind of spectacular action (for example, the attack on Kira's mansion and the final suicides are not shown), concentrating instead on ritual and the discussion of issues, and generating a sternly elegiac mood, searching and ambiguous. Noël Burch was moved to call this film "the most important work of art drawn from the famous episode."

Chushingura is an extraordinary stylistic achievement, with camera movements displaying at times a new extravagance, while following what Burch calls an "inner logic." Mizoguchi had a crane at his disposal for the first time, and in the scene where Asano is questioned after his crime, and again at his suicide, the craned camera seems to be trying to gain access to ritually restricted spaces—partly in sympathy with the anguish of the loyal Oishi, but perhaps also with a more impersonal exploratory purpose. The extent to which the film affirms or questions traditional codes in this and other ways has been much discussed. Some Japanese critics, including Keiko McDonald, have suggested that the director simply did not understand the samurai ethos; others, like Leach, see a more complex vision, avoiding simple propaganda. For example, we learn of the climactic attack on Kira's mansion through a message read by Lady Asano: "Her excitement reveals her identification with the samurai code, but the substitution of her personal response for the expected scene of heroic action distances the film from that code, which supposedly supports the genre to which it belongs."

During the filming of the second part of *Chushingura*—but without interrupting it, as McDonald notes, for even a day—Mizoguchi's wife Chieko went finally insane and was committed to an institution for the rest of her life. Mizoguchi went to live with her war-widowed sister Fuji and her two children. He was made

president of the Directors' Society, and engaged in researching projects for state policy films. His other accommodations to wartime requirements included two more ventures into the unfamiliar and uncongenial territory of the samurai film, *Miyamoto Musashi* (1944) and *Meito Bijomaru* (1945), undistinguished work done without enthusiasm. *Danjuro sandai* (1944), a theatrical subject, he himself later dismissed: "A very bad historical film—let's not talk about it." *Hisshoka* (*Victory Song*) was another patriotic piece made in 1945 at the instigation of the Information Bureau.

After the Japanese surrender, Mizoguchi found himself elected president of the labor union organized at Shochiku in response to the policy of the occupation forces. After three months, unwilling even to consider the notion of halting film production by strikes, he resigned. His first hesitant attempt at conformity with the American forces' demand for "democratic" subjects was *The Victory of Women* (1946), described by Keiko McDonald as "an outspoken celebration of women's rights." Scripted by Kogo Noda and Kaneto Shindo, it tells the story of a woman lawyer, Hiroko, played by Kinuyu Tanaka. Her lover, Yamaoka, lies in hospital mentally and physically broken after imprisonment as a dangerous liberal during the war. Hiroko is called on to defend an old school friend, desperately poor, who, on the death of her husband, has smothered her child. The prosecutor is the conservative husband of Hiroko's conventional sister, and the man responsible for Yamaoka's imprisonment. The verdict is not announced in the film, but in the course of the trial Yamaoka dies, leaving Hiroko more than ever determined to fight for social justice, while her sister decides to leave her husband and seek her independence. Keiko McDonald's view is representative of critical response: "one of the greatest flaws in the film is that Hiroko and the two male characters are rigidly stereotyped. From the outset they become, as it were, mere mouthpieces for political maxims and textbook illustrations."

At this time, despite shortages and inflation, the film industry was able to expand thanks to a demand for escapist entertainment. Mizoguchi's next film is partly a response to this climate, but *Five Women Around Utamaro*, called by Tony Rayns "a fascinatingly labyrinthine exploration" of the life and loves of the famous color print artist, is also more complex and personal. Yoda confessed that, when writing the script, he created in Utamaro, "almost unconsciously," a portrait of the director himself, explaining too "the confusion and dispersion of the film's theme" as a consequence of his own complicated and "muddled" view of its hero.

The eighteenth-century setting made it difficult to get the project accepted by the Occupation Forces, who rejected period pieces as "feudal." Mizoguchi argued that the subject was no samurai but an artist of liberal views and a "man of the people," and promised that the film would look in a modern way at women's rights, and this convinced the authorities, although they demanded frequent consultations with Mizoguchi during production. He complained about this some years later, saying it left him without enough time to work.

Five Women Around Utamaro (1946) tells the interconnected and highly dramatic stories of various of the artist's models, lovers, and friends. Utamaro's work offends the authorities, and he is sentenced to fifty days in handcuffs to prevent him from working. Utamaro is released and eagerly returns to his drawing, taking as his themes the stories in the film. A succession of prints is cast in profusion before the camera over the closing credits.

Usually considered a minor work, *Utamaro* nevertheless refuses to be dismissed. Jonathan Rosenbaum sees it as a "highly complex reflection on the director's art," comparing its expressive intensity with *Montparnasse 19* or *A King in New York*. The difficulties it gives the viewer are related to its achievements. The distanced camera resists easy identification with the numerous strands of the plot, with its many characters and "a periodic displacement of narrative centers." Utamaro's work has only an abstract status in the film whose real theme has "less to do with art itself than with the conditions and consequences of its place within society . . . Utamaro is an elusive character whose significance principally rests upon the identity and importance he confers upon others."

In 1947 Shochiku had Mizoguchi make *Joyu Sumako no koi*, about the life of Sumako Matsui, the pioneer actress of modern drama in the Japanese theatre; the film was designed to rival the Toho Company's version of the same subject, *Actress*, directed by Kinugasa. It opens at a lecture by the scholar and director Hogetsu Shimamura, where a discussion follows on his proposal to produce Ibsen's *A Doll's House* in a country with no tradition of women playing on the stage. His problem is solved by the appearance of the headstrong Sumako Matsui at his acting school. The film goes on to relate the rise of modern Western drama in Japan through the story of the stormy career and relationship of actress and director, which ended with Shimamura's death and Matsui's suicide.

The themes of the new theatre and of a woman's liberation are gradually submerged in the melodrama of the love affair. Yoda felt that his script was at fault for the absence of any searching exploration of the personalities of the two principals, although it seems also that Mizoguchi was forced to give Matsui more audience appeal than he might have intended. At the time, although generally considered artistically less satisfactory than Kinugasa's version, Mizoguchi's film was the greater financial success. Kinuyo Tanaka, who played Matsui, received the 1947 Mainichi Film Concours award for best actress.

Mizoguchi was in a creative and emotional depression in these postwar years, shocked and confused by the Japanese surrender. Critics were inclined to regard him as a "grand old man" clinging to outdated styles. His politics were as confused as ever: again heading a left-wing union in 1948, in 1949 he was made president of the right-wing Directors' Association, a post he held for the rest of his life. Audie Bock believes that "the accusation that he did not really grasp the new postwar humanism proves itself in the similarity of the prostitutes' dismal fate in the 1948 *Women of the Night* and the 1931 *And Yet They Go*." During the filming of *Women of the Night* Mizoguchi broke down in front of prostitutes in a Yoshiwara hospital, cursing the villainy of all men, including himself. Scandal linked him in an affair with his favorite actress Kinuyo Tanaka, although their close friendship probably remained platonic to the end. Meanwhile he had to make money, the more so because his sister Suzu now needed his financial support.

Women of the Night was a commercial success and ranked third in the *Kinema Jumpo* list, while Tanaka's performance as Fusako again contributed to a Mainichi Concours award. It is a stark and pessimistic "view of prostitution seen as the epitome of the social and economic evils suffered by postwar Japan" (Keiko McDonald). Fusako, widowed by the war, feeds herself and her tubercular son by pawning her possessions, until the child dies. After working for Kuriyama, a black marketeer, and becoming his mistress, she ends the relationship when she discovers her younger sister's involvement with him, and turns to prostitution as her only means of survival. Natsuko, the sister, more easily accepts a life as Kuriyama's mistress and a cabaret dancer, but she contracts venereal disease, and her child by Kuriyama is stillborn. The third main strand in the narrative concerns Fusako's sister-in-law Kumiko, who joins the prostitutes after being raped. The three characters have considerable strength and try to rise above their circumstances. Fusako in particular takes the lead in understanding and even lecturing the other prostitutes on the reasons for their predicament. But there is no sense that any real change will come.

Waga koi wa moenu (*My Love Has Been Burning*), made cheaply and hurriedly in 1949, was a commercial failure and was attacked by Japanese critics as the work of "a wild animal." In an interview with Tsuneo Hazumi, Mizoguchi allowed that it was a "barbaric" film, arising from the frustrations of wartime and inspired by Picasso's work immediately after the war, and said that he had wanted "to grapple with themes hand-to-hand." Tom Milne detects this feeling, combining rage and pity, in "the factory sequence, where a kaleidoscope of contrasting moods and tempi—police dispersing rioters in the streets, a meeting in a tranquilly moonlit forest, Eiko's stealthy infiltration of the factory, the lurid brutalities inside, the cleansing flames as it burns—are fused into a genuine fury of protest."

The story of Eiko Hirayama is based on the autobiography of Hideko Kageyama, who in the 1880s was one of the first feminist political activists in Japan. Despite the strength of its overt polemic and the brilliance of its more abstract moments, Tom Milne sees the main weakness of the film in its melodrama and "its formulary characters." But James Leach believes it to be "less concerned with propagating liberal values than with examining the tensions and contradictions of a period of transition," and suggests that "the fusion of detachment and engagement that Eiko achieves can also be seen as the goal of Mizoguchi's style."

After a fruitless battle with Shochiku to get the company to finance his proposed film of *Saikaku ichidai onna* (*The Life of Oharu*), based on a popular seventeenth-century classic, Mizoguchi left in 1950 and joined the rival Shin Toho Studios. During that year and the next he made a trio of films about women, two of them challenging social and sexual taboos. The first, *A Picture of Madame Yuki*, was adapted from a magazine serial, and tells the story of Yuki, a beautiful heiress. Married and sexually devoted to the dissolute Naoyuki, she longs to escape with the more sympathetic *koto* teacher Masaya, but he proves weak and unresponsive. When Naoyuki has squandered most of her fortune, Madame Yuki is forced to convert her family home into an inn. The inn is taken over by Ayako, her husband's unscrupulous mistress, and Yuki, estranged from both her husband and Masaya, drowns herself.

Some critics have complained of weaknesses in characterization, particularly in Yuki herself. Sato and McDonald agree that Michiyo Kogure is too robust a type to represent "the remote, troubled beauty" required by the role, but Anderson and Richie, among others, have admired her sensitive playing of this woman "in love with the sex act itself." The same critics describe *A Picture of Madame Yuki*, "with more bed scenes than were ever shown before on the Japanese screen," as the most advanced of the films about sex that were testing the new postwar freedom of cinematic expression. Among many atmospherically beautiful scenes, those taking the viewpoint of Hamako, Yuki's innocent maid, are striking. The strength of Yuki's sexual passion is conveyed through her response and through expressively indirect images using flowing curtains, discarded clothing, a fluttering butterfly. In the final scene, the moving camera looks down "on a landscape strewn with empty chairs" (John Gillett), as it follows Yuki in the early morning mist to the lake. The last shot descends with Hamako to the water where she screams after her dead mistress.

Miss Oyu (1951), adapted from Junichiro Tanizaki's novel *Ashikari*, had neither critical nor commercial success, but its sensitive mobile camerawork marks Mizoguchi's first collaboration with Kazuo Miyagawa, who was to contribute so much to the virtuoso style of his later films. Hisakazu Tsuji noticed that the director always took Miyagawa's advice and the cinematographer himself, interviewed in 1979, said that he "never found Mizoguchi particularly difficult to work with, though that is part of the legend, often built up by people who didn't really know him . . . though he was indeed short of compliments." Mizoguchi always began by creating a mood or atmosphere "and then placed his actors and scenes inside that mood." Most scenes were shot in deep focus because Mizoguchi wanted nothing out of focus "even very slightly, even in the background—he wanted everything as neat as possible. That is why he had the characters in the background either very clearly shown or completely dark, almost invisible, since he hated those intermediate 'out-of-focus' effects."

In Stephen H. Barr's view, the "themes of passion, sacrifice, and transcendence" in *Miss Oyu* point away from issues of social justice towards the later works. The story challenged taboos because it tells of Shinnosuke who, contracted to marry Oshizu, falls in love with her elder sister, the widow Oyu, and goes ahead with the marriage in order to be near his love. The understanding Oshizu offers to let the marriage remain one in name only, but the relatively happy triangular relationship breaks down; Oyu marries a rich merchant and Oshizu dies bearing Shinnosuke's child, which he leaves for Oyu to raise. In a final scene of pathos and transcendence dispassionately observed, Shinnosuke disappears among tall reeds bordering a river, singing a song from a Noh play recalling an earlier happier moment with Oyu.

Mizoguchi dispensed with the elaborate layers of narration in the original novel, but used camera movement to shift narrative perspective among the three main characters. For example, in the sequence where Oyu collapses from sunstroke and is watched as she sleeps by Shinnosuke, the camera is at first occupied with the hero and his nearly uncontrollable feelings, then picks up Oyu at the moment her eyes open. A contemporary critic, Futaba, admired the long takes and the sets they explore, but regretted what he saw as the resulting slow tempo and oppressive atmosphere. Mizoguchi himself was dissatisfied, although much involved with Tanizaki's novel.

The Lady From Musashino, made in the same year, was no more successful. Like *Miss Oyu*, it was compared unfavorably with the original novel, this time by Shohei Ooka. More recent critics have been able to admire qualities in it familiar from superior works. Richard Tucker compares the camera movement in the opening scene with *The Story of the Late Chrysanthemums*: "A single, long, looping crane shot introduces the characters and the neighbouring houses that are the conflicting elements of the story." The heroine is Michiko, a sensitive woman of traditional views, incapable of adapting to the postwar world, and trying to protect herself and her inheritance from exploitation in a commercially minded society. That world is represented by her cousin Eiji and his wife Tomiko, willingly seduced by Michiko's husband. Tsutomu, her platonic lover, appears to be different, attached to the old world as well as the new. But he too betrays Michiko, joining in the mutual recriminations of the rest of the family when she commits an honorable suicide and relinquishing the inheritance left to him in her will. The film uses the setting of the beautiful Musashino Plain, with the contrasting ugliness of downtown Tokyo encroaching upon it, to underscore its theme.

According to Yoda, Mizoguchi was provoked into making his next film, *The Life of Oharu* (1952), by the irritation he felt at the success of Kurosawa's *Rashomon* at Venice the previous year. Whatever the truth of this, it was a consciously ambitious film, a high point in the director's career, initiating a new phase. Collaborating from the start with Kinuyo Tanaka, recently returned from America, Mizoguchi began without normal studio finance, subcontracting the production through Shin Toho. Shooting was done in a "bombed-out park" near Kyoto where the noise of trains passing every fifteen minutes determined the schedule, but nothing could disturb the director's legendary concentration. Since *Miss Oyu* he had

taken to using a portable urinal to avoid having to leave the set. Nothing could begin till the crane arrived from Kyoto, and authentic props had been collected from museums. As usual, scenes were shot and reshot again and again. Strict controls on the budget were ignored, and production cost forty-six million yen. The obsessive perfectionism paid off. Although in Japan it was a commercial failure and only a modest critical success, *The Life of Oharu* was chosen for the 1952 Venice Film Festival and shared a Silver Lion for best direction with John Ford's *The Quiet Man*. It was the beginning of Mizoguchi's belated international recognition, only four years before his death.

Most of the story, set in the seventeenth century, is told in flashback as Oharu, now fifty, contemplates a statue in a Buddhist temple and recalls her past. In her beautiful youth, daughter of a samurai at the Imperial Palace in Kyoto, she had fallen in love with Katsunosuke (Toshiro Mifune) a man of low class. He was punished on discovery by beheading, while she and her parents were exiled. After attempting suicide, Oharu was taken as a mistress by Lord Matsudaira in Edo, bearing him a son. Dismissal forced her to work as a courtesan, then a maid, before marriage brought her an interlude of happiness, cut short when her husband was murdered. She took refuge in a convent but because men forced sexual attentions on her was expelled, and sank to begging and prostitution. The flashback ends as she collapses from illness. Informed by her mother that her son has succeeded Lord Matsudaira, Oharu returns to Edo, only to be humiliated by her past. She resumes her vagrant life.

The Life of Oharu was adapted by Yoda from a famous picaresque novel by the seventeenth-century writer Saikaku Iharu. Jonathan Rosenbaum finds in this film a combination of the detailed historical realism of Saikaku's original novel and something of the social criticism of Mizoguchi's films about modern geishas. However, the persistence of Oharu's spirit in the face of her endless misfortunes seemed to Jun Izawa to make the film more romantic than realistic. The new philosophical breadth often remarked in Mizoguchi's later works is strong here. "For Mizoguchi the rights of women are merely a logical extension of the rights of man," wrote Andrew Sarris and, of the ending, "Just one misfortune after another. Yet Oharu endures. She sees her son one last time, and then wanders into eternity as a street singer, a pagoda-shaped hat forming her last silhouette. In the last frames of the film Oharu pauses, turns to look at a distant pagoda, her spatial and spiritual correlative, and passes off the screen while the pagoda remains." Rosenbaum calls it "a coda that tells us nothing and, by doing so expresses everything." But where he finds a "relentless polemical thrust," Sarris sees Mizoguchi's "sublime directional purpose" as "a manner of looking at the world rather than as a means of changing it."

The rigorously controlled style is both a vehicle for the theme and a means of eliciting such varied responses. Tadao Sato considers Mizoguchi's style, which had been used for "outward picturesque beauty" in the films of the previous two years, to have here a more expressive purpose. He refers, as do many critics, to the early scene of the banishment of Oharu and her parents. The camera at first remains static, seeming to watch the family crossing the bridge in "cold abandonment," but when they have reached the far side, the camera advances to glimpse them from beneath the girders of the bridge, the movement expressing solicitude for the victims. The power of the scene's final image, according to Richard Tucker, "comes from the parallel between the crushing of the three people by social regulations and the visual crushing of the small figures by the enormous black masses on the screen." Sato connects such effects, and in particular the constant shifting of the camera between points of momentary fixity, with the methods of traditional Japanese arts and theatre, and with Buddhist thought itself, which "apprehends society and man in their ever-changing aspects." Burch suggests that the spectacular use of the long take in *The Life of Oharu* may also have been stimulated by Mizoguchi's desire to outdo the William Wyler of such films as *The Little Foxes* or *Best Years of Our Lives*.

The moving camera is naturally much occupied with Oharu herself—Kinuyo Tanaka in one of her most poignant roles. Typically the reserved distance of the shot (and the frequent choice of a back view) throws emphasis on the posture of her whole body to express her condition and relation to the world. It is an example of Mizoguchi's obsession, noted by Dudley Andrew, "with the gait of women, with their swoons, with their averted or penetrating gaze." Ichiro Saito's "prodigious musical score" also contributes powerfully to the film's effect and helped gain the composer a Mainichi Concours award.

Beginning with the success of *The Life of Oharu* in Venice, Mizoguchi began to be adopted as a hero by the critics and young filmmakers of the French New Wave. Jacques Rivette, writing in *Cahiers du Cinéma* in 1958, pointed out how Mizoguchi's films communicated across barriers of culture in a familiar tongue, "the only language to which a filmmaker should lay claim: the language of *mise-en-scène*." In particular the young French enthusiasts admired Mizoguchi's long take and what Audie Bock calls the "centrifugal force applied to the edges of the frame." In their critical polemics Kurosawa and Mizoguchi (then the two best-known Japanese directors) were seen as opposites, with the latter much preferred.

Following the foreign success of *Oharu*, Masiachi Nagata of Daiei Studios, an old friend, offered the director a rare carte-blanche contract for *Ugetsu monogatari* (1953)—and even so Mizoguchi found himself influenced by the company to provide *Ugetsu* with a less bitter conclusion than he had wanted. The script was adapted by Yoda and Kawaguchi from two stories in an eighteenth-century collection of the same title by Akinari Ueda, with borrowings also from Maupassant's short story "Décoré!" During the civil wars of the sixteenth century the potter Genjuro leaves home eager to sell his wares and becomes lost in a dream world of dangerous beauty, seduced by the ghost of a long-dead princess. When the dream breaks he returns to his village, to a vision of his wife whom we have seen murdered by starving soldiers, and to humble toil to raise their young son. In a parallel narrative, Genjuro's brother Tobei, eager to be a great soldier, cheats his way to brief eminence as a general. When he is confronted by his wife in a brothel, where she works after being raped by soldiers, he returns contritely with her to the village to join his brother.

In one of many letters to Yoda, Mizoguchi explained what he wanted to emphasize as the main theme of the film: "Whether war originates in the ruler's personal motives or in some public concern, how violence, disguised as war, oppresses and torments the populace, both physically and spiritually!" And this theme is expressed not through documentary realism, but through a grippingly realized vision of the past in which natural and supernatural, grim reality and distracting dream, deceptively coexist. Such critics as Dudley Andrew and Max Tessier have noted the relevance of the subject, and in particular of Genjuro's story, to the director's own case as creator of artistic illusions in a violent world.

Mizoguchi told his cameraman Miyagawa that he wanted the film "to unroll seamlessly like a scroll-painting," and the transitions of mood and atmosphere, for example from the bustling market to the mansion of the ghost princess, are achieved largely by rhythmically fluid camera movement. In one of the most famous scenes, at the climax of the haunted love affair, Genjuro and the ghost Wakasa make love by a spring while the camera shifts uneasily away, following the stream, until a swift dissolve brings us smoothly to a long shot of the lovers in fluttering kimonos, playing on the shore of Lake Biwa in the glittering sunshine. Miyagawa remembered the creation of these shots as the only occasion Mizoguchi ever praised him for his work. Lake Biwa is also the setting for another celebrated scene when, in the enveloping mist, the boat carrying the two families encounters another containing not a ghost but a boatman dying of wounds. Donald Richie draws attention to the formal beauty and conservative moral message of *Ugetsu* as exemplified and framed by the opening and closing shots. "*Ugetsu* opens with a long panorama around a lake, a shot which begins on the far shore and then tilts down to reveal the village at the conclusion. It closes with the child and the father offering a bowl of rice at the mother's grave . . . with the camera moving off into an upward tilting panorama which describes the movement of the opening." These "separate but similar" shots are "like brackets to the film" suggesting "a sameness, a spiral-like quality of experience," echoing "the stories of the two women, separate yet inverted: the wife moves from life to death, the ghost from death to life."

Some Western critics, such as Max Tessier, are suspicious of the seductive appeal of *Ugetsu,* designed perhaps too pointedly for foreign audiences, and look elsewhere for Mizoguchi's highest achievement, but others, like Anderson and Richie, still incline to see it as "one of the most perfect movies in the history of Japanese cinema." It was well enough received in Japan, coming third in the *Kinema Jumpo* list. The Mainichi Concours gave awards to Kisaku Ito for art direction and to Iwao Otano for sound, and the Ministry of Education one to Miyagawa. But the immediate reception of the film in the West was more significant. Mizoguchi made his first trip abroad, accompanying the film to the Venice Festival, along with Yoda and Tanaka. Tanaka found him keeping to his hotel room praying before an image of the Buddhist saint Nichiren, whose sect he had joined under the influence of Nagata. Mizoguchi had an uncommunicative meeting with the once-admired Wyler, whose *Roman Holiday* was a rival to *Ugetsu* for the Silver Lion. Mizoguchi's prayers were answered, and his film also won the Italian Critics' Award.

His next film, *Gion bayashi* (*Gion Festival Music*) was a virtual remake in 1953 of the 1936 *Sisters of the Gion*. Sugiyama Heiichi, reviewing it at the time, found it a more relaxed, confident, and mature film, displaying a colder, more objective attitude. The views and lives of the two geisha are less polarized than in the earlier film.

The younger woman, played by Ayako Wakao, is now the daughter of the ex-patron of the elder (Michiyo Kogure), who trains her, reluctantly, in the traditions of her profession. According to McDonald, "the first half of the film develops contrasts between the two types of women adapting to their surroundings" but the second half unites them "in a determined resistance to exploitation." Finally the two are resigned, in mutual support, to the sacrifices imposed on them. Critics remark on the sensitive playing in even the minor roles, but the film was coolly received in Japan and was not shown abroad till after Mizoguchi's death.

In 1954 Mizoguchi and Kinuyo Tanaka quarreled over Tanaka's project to direct a film with the support of Ozu and Naruse. But it was still a prolific year for Mizoguchi, with three films, two of them considered among his finest. *Sansho dayu* (*Sansho the Bailiff*) is described by John Gillett as "not only a great classic of world cinema, but one of Mizoguchi's most probing and rigorously worked period pieces." Tessier calls it one of the director's most moving works, "fully meriting the adjective 'sublime' often abused in reference to Mizoguchi."

In eleventh-century Japan, a provincial governor teaches his children that "a man without pity is no longer human," but his concern for human rights causes him to be exiled. Traveling to join him, his wife Tamaki (Kinuyo Tanaka) is sold into prostitution on Sado Island, while his son Zushio and daugher Anju are enslaved on an estate under the brutal bailiff Sansho. After ten years, Zushio has compromised his humane principles to the extent of becoming an overseer, shocking his sister by branding an aged runaway. When they hear news that their mother is still alive, Anju persuades Zushio to escape, giving her own life to cover his tracks. Seeking justice from the prime minister, Zushio is appointed governor of the province, the post once held by his now dead father. He frees all the slaves and banishes Sansho, then goes in search of his mother, whom he finds living blind and maimed on the shore of Sado Island. He convinces her of his identity and they embrace.

Although the script is based on a version by the novelist Ogai Mori, the story is a very well known legend in Japan. By presenting this familiar tale "in an unfamiliar, challenging framework," explains Tony Rayns, Mizoguchi produces "an almost visionary account of the wheels of history turning." Images of ancient stone relics, which open the film and recur to mark each ten-year interval, are used to "evoke the period in which the story is set from a present-day perspective," both "actualising" the narrative and asserting "the film's meditative stance," inviting the audience's reflection. On the other hand, the political and moral choices facing all the characters, by being centered on the inner conflict of Zushio himself, "become highly engaging issues cutting across the schematization of the melodrama." This "coexistence of direct engagement and reflective distance" means that the images are used both literally and figuratively. Rayns cites for instance the opening scenes of the journeying family, "developed through chiaroscuro images whose fragility intimates the precariousness of the family unit." The mode of narration is calculatedly equivocal, with flashbacks and "languorous dissolves" to express shifts of time and the divisions between individual members of the family. Mizoguchi refuses to make of all this one single statement; "his subject is as much the lines of male/female force within a family as it is the historical struggle between totalitarianism and liberal humanism." The various themes and images are united in a final shot where the camera cranes up from the pitiful reunion of mother and son, panning away to a seaweed gatherer at work on the wave-washed beach, taking the film out of the world of the individual and historical into the contemplative detachment of Mizoguchi's Buddhism.

Like its immediate predecessor, *Sansho the Bailiff* had a better reception abroad than in Japan, in 1954 sharing the Silver Lion at Venice with Kurosawa's *Seven Samurai*. Mizoguchi now made *Uwasa no onna* (*A Woman of Rumor*), a modern subject set in a high-class brothel run by a mother who herself loves the young doctor her daughter hopes to marry. The two women are finally reconciled in rejecting the young man. Mizoguchi's approach is cool and detached in a style colored, according to McDonald, by "Western cinematic devices: close-ups, intercutting, and many reverse-field shots." *Chikamatsu monogatari* (*A Story by Chikamatsu*), Mizoguchi's third film of the year, became perhaps the best-loved of all his works among his colleagues and the Japanese critics, possibly because of its close adherence to its source, a seventeenth-century Bunraku (puppet-theatre) play by the popular master Chikamatsu Monzaemon. It received a number of awards, and Mizoguchi himself was honored by the Ministry of Education for achievements in this film and in the past. Daiei gave him a seat on its board of directors.

Chikamatsu (also known as *The Crucified Lovers*) is set in seventeenth-century Kyoto, where crucifixion is the punishment for adultery. Mohei, played by the popular star Kazuo Hasegawa, is a designer and foreman in the workshop of wealthy scroll-maker Ishun. When Ishun refuses to help his beautiful wife Osan pay her brother's debts, Mohei comes to her aid, but is arrested for forgery. A servant girl tells Osan how Ishun tried to seduce her, and they exchange beds in an attempt to trap the husband. The plan miscarries and Mohei is found with Osan, innocent but compromised. Refusing Ishun's demand that she commit suicide, Osan joins the fleeing Mohei. They confess their love but, after a single night together, are captured. Ishun is banished for trying to conceal his wife's crime, and the lovers are "united" again, bound together on their way to their crucifixion. One of Osan's maids, looking on, remarks that she has never seen her mistress so happy.

The theme is one more example of the "pessimistic individualism" Noël Burch sees in Mizoguchi's postwar films. Belton defines it as an escape from social confinement and oppressive isolation through love, and sees this also as a metaphor for the director's own role as an artist. The style is a particularly striking instance of Mizoguchi's apparent attempt in these later films to integrate the "one shot–one cut" method into what Ian Christie calls "a more complex and varied visual syntax," though Christie also regrets "the more prosaic passages with their standardized angles of vision and conventional cutting." The opening of *Chikamatsu*, unlike the long introductory takes of *Sisters of the Gion* or *Ugetsu*, consists of a staccato series of shots that McDonald interprets as "an almost impatient assembling of the forces which bring the socially incompatible hero and heroine together only to destroy them." The few examples that remain of the long take with deep focus are reserved, as Christie points out, for the "crucial moments of emotional rapport" between the lovers, notably in the pivotal four-minute take in the boat on Lake Biwa when Mohei and Osan declare their mutual passion. The boat, surrounded by fog, lies sideways to the camera, making a two-dimensional image until, stirred by the lovers' clumsy movements, it "turns in a complicitous arc and disappears into the darkness of the lake." Noël Burch has written of Mizoguchi's collaboration in this film with composer Fumio Hayasaka to explore "in remarkable fashion the 'sound-track continuum,' establishing frequent relays between music, sound effects (noise), and the spoken word."

Mizoguchi's next two films were his only ones in color, and neither was a happy experience for the director, in spite of his interest in this expansion of the medium's possibilities. He was also interested at this time in wide-screen processes, eagerly discussing the Vistavision camera and CinemaScope with Miyagawa, who had returned from studying them in Hollywood. But *Yokihi* (*The Empress Yang Kwei Fei*), which went into production in 1955, was made against the director's will. It was a very commercial venture involving Daiei with the Shaw Brothers of Hong Kong and designed with an eye on Western markets. The director was ill, irritably wearing a plaster cast for a back injury, and already feeling the effects of leukemia (as yet undiagnosed). There were many changes of script and scriptwriters, and the actress Takako Irie was sacked by Mizoguchi, perhaps still nursing a grudge from the time he worked for her company. Eventually he got Machiko Kyo for the lead, with Masayuki Mori playing opposite her as in *Ugetsu*.

Based on a Chinese lyric poem by Po Chü-i, *Yokihi* is the story of an emperor of China who falls in love with Yang Yu-huan, a kitchen maid brought to him by an ambitious courtier. In a brief interlude of happiness, the kitchen maid teaches the emperor the joy of life and then, when court intrigue demands her execution, the sterner virtues of self-sacrifice. The narrative is a long flashback framed by the old retired emperor remembering the affair and finally looking to a reunion with his beloved in death. Few critics have been happy with the work, dismissing it as "tasteless and empty" (Toyoshi Okuro) or "rather dull if pictorially beautiful" (Anderson and Richie). The film was taken to Venice where it gained no prize but was praised for its color photography.

The color consultant on *Shin heike monogatari* (*New Tales of the Taira Clan*) also released in 1955, was Mitsuzo Wada, Mizoguchi's old art teacher, who also painted the background for the film's credits. Yoda felt that the director showed little interest in the film. Set in the twelfth century, the story is certainly an unusual one for Mizoguchi, chronicling the rise to power of the successful rebel Kiyomori against the background of a conflict between soldier monks supported by the old nobility, and the new samurai class. Critical reception was (and is) mixed. While admitting the interestingly restrained use of color in Miyagawa's photography and the success of Raizo Ichikawa in the central role, some critics have seen the film as a rather conventional exercise in the genre of historical spectacular. But John Gillett found it "a gripping narrative of political intrigue," while Richard Tucker saw it as unjustly neglected evidence that Mizoguchi should be considered "Japan's finest director of the period film." Tsuji detected in it the influence of John Ford's *She Wore a Yellow Ribbon*.

Mizoguchi's last film was a return to a contemporary subject, to black and white, and to a familiar theme. *Akasen chitai* (*Street of Shame*, 1956) depicts the red-light district of modern Tokyo through the stories of five prostitutes of various backgrounds and character who work at the "Dreamland" brothel. The director's original plan was for a semidocumentary shot on location, but the brothel owners refused to cooperate. The action takes place, as Anderson and Richie explain, against the background of one of the "heated and widely publicized" debates on prostitution in the Diet, and was released while the actual debates were continuing.

The film proved to be one of Mizoguchi's biggest successes at the box office; despite the cool objectivity of its approach, condemned at the time by some Japanese critics, it may have helped to bring about the reforms of 1957. It was also "the very first outstanding film on Japanese contemporary life to command a large American audience." Philippe Demonsablon compared Mizoguchi to a composer working with rhythm and tonality, and wrote that "like Ophuls and Preminger, Mizoguchi's entire art, with all its artifice, is aimed at allowing actors to reveal the fugitive truths of their being." Osamu Takizawa complained of an overly theatrical display of talents by the five principal actresses, but John Gillett found the performances, "led by Machiko Kyo's ebullient Mickey," full of insight.

Mizoguchi began a new project in May 1956. *Osaka monogatari* (*Osaka Story*) was to depict the rise of the merchant class in the Genroku era through a story of a miser's tyranny over his own family. Yoshimura completed it the following year. Mizoguchi was still working on the script in his hospital bed when he died, aged fifty-eight.

Mizoguchi was a perfectionist, as Keiko McDonald says, "in all things and sometimes calamitously." His working method tested the endurance of his collaborators, who nevertheless testify to its success, as well as the affection he inspired. Yoshikata Yoda recalled the demanding nature of their collaboration and something of Mizoguchi's purpose: "To finish my scenarios I would help my weak body by thinking, almost desperately, of all the obstacles I had to overcome, and which were set in front of me by Mizo-san. 'Be stronger, dig more deeply. You have to seize man, not in some of his superficial aspects, but in his totality. We have to know that we lack, we Japanese, all ideological visions: the vision of life, the vision of the universe . . .' Completely discouraged by these words from Mizo-san, and making myself sorrier by thinking of the weakness of my brain, I tried to write, without ever being sure of myself." Mizoguchi's old friend and rival Kawaguchi worked gladly on his scripts although he felt "devoured" by the director in the process. He saw Mizoguchi as an opportunist, but nevertheless found in his work a persistent personal quality—"a certain 'Mizoguchism'"—which he defined as a search for the beauty of the everyday, and for which he loved him, saying "Mizoguchi and I, we are men without ideas."

Mizoguchi's eclecticism—what Burch calls "ideological plasticity"—has concerned many critics, especially in the West and on the left. But to Japanese eyes Mizoguchi did not conform quite so readily to fashionable trends as his detractors suggest. *Chushingura* was hardly conventional propaganda, while *The Life of Oharu* was too far outside tradition to gain studio support. Tadao Sato, considering the extent to which the recognition of Mizoguchi's genius had been left to Western (and in the first instance to French) critics, wrote that in Japan, "while Mizoguchi was greatly applauded as a realist, as an inquirer into human nature, and as an aesthetic artist, a great deal of criticism asserted that his strong attachment to old manners was a form of escape, and that the length of his shots and the slackness of his tempo reflected conservatism in cinematic methodology." However, Sato pointed out, Japanese critics could no longer call Mizoguchi old-fashioned when the French *nouvelle vague* took him as a model.

The treatment of women, Mizoguchi's favorite theme, is a key to his work. Dudley Andrew believes he saw women as "representative of culture, of the artistic impulse, of the downtrodden, of history, and of revolt," and that increasingly for him social problems were seen "as emanations of a cosmic fiction" to which the only possible response was a stoic awareness. Women critics have been sharper in their comments, Amy Taubin for instance noting an element of sadism. Audie Bock finds "an ambivalent attitude towards women" connected with Mizoguchi's "enigmatic political stance toward oppression, poverty, and even the Japanese family." She stresses the extent to which this ambivalence derives from his turbulent personal life, quoting Matsuo Kishi's view that the director was "unusual in the extent to which he suffered at the hands of women. He hated women; he was contemptuous of women. On the other hand, when he fell in love, it was with the sincerity of a little boy." Sato considered Mizoguchi's work "the purification of a national resentment" about the tragic role of women, while Anderson and Richie identify a recurrent motif in the films as Mizoguchi's favorite myth: "A man's soul is saved by a woman's love."

Western responses to Mizoguchi's work, as Stephen Barr points out, "were based initially on the films from the end of Mizoguchi's career." More recent criticism tends to concentrate on the earlier work, Burch in particular even rejecting the films after 1947 as showing a decline resulting from opportunistic adoption of Western techniques. His view has not found general support. As influences, Mizoguchi himself acknowledged L'Herbier, Von Sternberg, Wyler, and Ford, while others have proposed Murnau, Ophuls, and Cukor. When Mizoguchi died, Kurosawa, a director often seen as his exact opposite, said, "Now that Mizoguchi has gone, there are very few directors left who can see the past clearly and realistically." Acknowledged as one of the greatest of all movie directors, Mizoguchi himself said, at the height of his international success, "Today and as always I am interested in showing how a particular people live. Since I do not want my spectator to be driven to despair by the spectacle, however, I also want to make a sense of the new for him, so that he will not despair. And yet I cannot altogether disregard the old. I love the past and I have but little hope for the future."

—D.W.

FILMS: Ai ni yomigaeru hi (The Resurrection of Love/ The Day When Love Returns), 1923; Kokyo (Hometown/Native Country), 1923; Seishun no yumeji (The Dream Path of Youth/Dreams of Youth), 1923; Joen no chimata (City of Desire), 1923; Haizan no uta wa kanashi (Failure's Song is Sad), 1923; 813 (813: The Adventures of Arsène Lupin), 1923; Kiri no minato (Foggy Harbor), 1923; Haikyo no naka (In the Ruins), 1923; Yoru (The Night), 1923; Chi to rei (Blood and Soul), 1923; Toge no uta (The Song of the Mountain Pass), 1923; Kanashiki hakuchi (The Sad Idiot), 1924; Akatsuki no shi (Death at Dawn), 1924; Gendai no jo-o (The Queen of Modern Times), 1924; Josei wa tsuyoshi (Women Are Strong), 1924; Jin kyo (This Dusty World), 1924; Shichimencho no yukue (Turkeys in a Row), 1924; Samidare zoshi (A Chronicle of May Rain), 1924; Kanraku no onna (A Woman of Pleasure), 1924; Kyokubadan no jo-o (Queen of the Circus), 1924; Musen fusen (No Money, No Fight), 1925; Gakuso o idete (Out of College), 1925; *episode in* Daichi wa hohoemu (The Earth Smiles; a three-part film), 1925; Shirayuri wa nageku (The White Lily Laments), 1925; Akai yuhi ni terasarete (Shining in the Red Sunset), 1925; Gaijo no suketchi (Street Sketches), 1925; Ningen (The Human Being/Humanity), 1925; Furusato no uta (The Song of Home/The Song of the Native Country), 1925; Nogi taisho to Kumasan (General Nogi and Kumasan), 1925; Doka o (The Copper Coin King), 1926; Kaminingyo haru no sasayaki (A Paper Doll's Whisper of Spring), 1926; Shin ono ga tsumi (My Fault, New Version/My Fault Continued), 1926; Kyoren no onna shisho (The Passion of a Woman Teacher), 1926; Kaikoku danji (The Boy of the Sea), 1926; Kane (Money), 1926; Ko-on (The Imperial Grace/Gratitude to the

Emperor), 1927; Jihi shincho (The Cuckoo/Like the Changing Heart of a Bird/The Bird of Mercy), 1927; Hito no issho (A Man's Life; in three parts), 1928; Musume kawaiya (My Lovely Daughter), 1928; Nihonbashi (Nihon Bridge), 1929; (with Seiichi Ina) Asahi wa kagayaku (The Morning Sun Shines/The Rising Sun Shines), 1929; Tokyo koshinkyoku (Tokyo March), 1929; Tokai kokyogaku (Metropolitan Symphony), 1929; Furusato (Home Town), 1930; Tojin okichi (Mistress of a Foreigner), 1930; Shikamo karera wa yuku (And Yet They Go), 1931; Toki no ujigami (The Man of the Moment/Timely Mediator), 1932; Manmo Kenkoku no Reimei (The Dawn of Manchuria and Mongolia), 1932; Taki no Shiraito (White Threads of the Waterfall/The Water Magician), 1933; Gion matsuri (Gion Festival), 1933; Jinpuren (The Jinpu Group), 1934; Aizo toge (The Mountain Pass of Love and Hate), 1934; Orizuru Osen (The Downfall of Osen/Osen of the Paper Cranes), 1935; Maria no Oyuki (Oyuki the Virgin/Oyuki the Madonna), 1935; Gubijinso (The Field Poppy/Poppy), 1935; Naniwa hika/Naniwa ereji (Osaka Elegy), 1936; Gion no shimai (Sisters of the Gion), 1936; Aien kyo (The Straits of Love and Hate), 1937; Roei no uta (The Song of the Camp), 1938; Aa Kokyo/Aa furusato (Ah, My Home Town), 1938; Zangiku monogatari (The Story of the Late Chrysanthemums/The Story of the Last Chrysanthemums), 1939; Naniwa onna (The Woman of Osaka), 1940; Geido ichidai otoko (The Life of an Actor), 1941; Genroku Chushingura (The Loyal Forty-Seven Ronin/The Loyal Forty-Seven Ronin of the Genroku Era), 1941–1942; Danjuro sandai (Three Generations of Danjuro), 1944; Miyamoto Musashi (The Swordsman/Musashi Miyamoto), 1944; Meito Bijomaru (The Noted Sword/The Famous Sword Bijomaru), 1945; Hisshoka (Victory Song), 1945; Josei no shori (The Victory of Women), 1946; Utamaro o meguru gonin no onna (Five Women Around Utamaro/Utamaro and his Five Women), 1946; Joyu Sumako no koi (The Love of Sumako the Actress), 1947; Yoru no onnatachi (Women of the Night), 1948; Waga koi wa moenu (My Love Has Been Burning/My Love Burns), 1949; Yuki fujin ezu (A Portrait of Madame Yuki/A Picture of Madame Yuki), 1950; Oyusama (Miss Oyu), 1951; Musashino fujin (The Lady From Musashino/Lady Musashino), 1951; Saikaku ichidai Onna (The Life of Oharu), 1952; Ugetsu monogatari (Ugetsu/Tales of the Pale and Silvery Moon After the Rain), 1953; Gion bayashi (Gion Festival Music), 1953; Sansho dayu (Sansho the Bailiff), 1954; Uwasa no onna (A Woman of Rumour/The Woman of the Rumor/The Crucified Woman), 1954; Chikamatsu monogatari (The Crucified Lovers/A Story From Chikamatsu), 1954; Yokihi (The Empress Yang Kwei-Fei/The Princess Yang Kwei-Fei), 1955; Shin Heike monogatari (New Tales of the Taira Clan), 1955; Akasen chitai (Street of Shame/Red Light District), 1956. *Published scripts*: Osaka Elegy, Sisters of the Gion, and Straits of Love and Hate *in* Mizoguchi Kenji Sakuhin Kyakuhon Shu, Tokyo: Bunka Shobo, 1937; The Loyal Forty-Seven Ronin (Part I) *in* Jidai Eiga September 1941; Lady Musashino *in* Kinema Jumpo August 1, 1951; A Story from Chikamatsu *in* Kinema Jumpo November 25, 1954, *reprinted in* Sato, T. (ed.) Kyakuhon: Nihon Eiga no Meisaku, vol. 2, Tokyo: Futosha, 1975; Ugetsu

Monogatari (an extract in French) *in* Mesnil, M. Mizoguchi Kenji, Paris: Éditions Seghers, 1965 (also in Japanese translation, Tokyo: Sainichi Shobo, 1970); Ugetsu Monogatari (in French) *in* L'Avant-Scène du Cinéma January 1977; Sansho the Bailiff (in French) *in* L'Avant-Scène du Cinéma May 1979.

ABOUT: Anderson, J. L. and Richie, D. The Japanese Film: Art and Industry, revised edn. 1982; Andrew, J. D. and P. Kenji Mizoguchi: A Guide to References and Resources, 1981; Andrew, J. D. Film in the Aura of Art, 1984; Apra, A. (ed.) Il Cinema di Kenji Mizoguchi: La Biennale, Mostra Internazionale del Cinema, 1980; Belton, J. Cinema Stylists, 1983; Bock, A. Japanese Film Directors, 1978; Burch, N. Theory of Film Practice, 1973; Burch, N. To the Distant Observer: Form and Meaning in the Japanese Cinema, 1979; Freiberg, F. Women in Mizoguchi Films, 1981; Gillett, J. and Rayns, T. Kenji Mizoguchi: London, National Film Theatre Programme, 1978; McDonald, K. Kenji Mizoguchi, 1984; Mellen, J. The Waves at Genji's Door: Japan Through its Cinema, 1976; Mesnil, M. Mizoguchi Kenji, 1965; Richie, D. The Japanese Movie: An Illustrated History, rev. ed. 1981; Roud, R. (ed.) Cinema: A Critical Dictionary, 1980; Sato, T. Currents in Japanese Cinema, 1982; Serceau, D. Mizoguchi: De la Révolte aux Songes, 1983; Tessier, M. Images du Cinéma Japonais, 1981; Tucker, R. N. Japan: Film Image, 1973; Vê Hô Kenji Mizoguchi, 1963; Wood, R. Personal Views, 1976. *Periodicals*—Anthologie du Cinéma November 29, 1967; Cahiers du Cinéma 81 1958, 95 1959, 116 1961, 158 1964, 166 1965, 169 1965, 172 1965, 174 1966, 181 1966, 186 1966, 192 1966, 206 1966; Cinema (USA) Spring 1971; Écran August 1974; Études Cinématographiques Summer 1960; Film Comment March 1973; Film Criticism Spring 1980, Fall 1983; Film Quarterly Fall 1971; Monthly Film Bulletin August 1973, March 1975, March 1976, December 1976, May 1977, September 1979, April 1981; Positif November 1978, December 1980, January 1981; Sight and Sound Autumn 1955, Spring 1958, Winter 1972–1973, Spring 1978, Summer 1979; Village Voice May 28, 1964; June 24, 1971.

MOLANDER, GUSTAF (November 18, 1888–June 21, 1973), Swedish director and scenarist, was born in Helsinki, Finland, the son of the director of the Swedish National Theatre there. He joined his father's company as an actor in 1909 and two or three years later went to Sweden as a member of the Royal Dramatic Theatre in Stockholm. Molander's qualities as an actor and his exceptionally melodious voice took him to the top of his profession—he is said to have been a notable Hamlet. He also taught for two years at the Royal Theatre's drama school, where Greta Garbo was among his students.

The Swedish cinema flourished during World War I, and while continuing his stage career Molander began to write scenarios for the Svenska Bio company, which in 1919 was incorporated

GUSTAF MOLANDER

into Svensk Filmindustri—still Sweden's principal production company. Molander scripted or coscripted Konrad Tallroth's *Millers dokument* (1916), Victor Sjöström's seminal *Terje Vigen* (1917), based on Ibsen's poem, and then a series of films for Mauritz Stiller, like himself a native of Helsinki. His scenarios for Stiller included *Thomas Graal's Best Film* (1917), *Thomas Graal's First Child* (1918), *Song of the Scarlet Flower* (1919), the epic masterpiece *Sir Arne's Treasure* (1919), and *Gunnar Hede's Saga* (1923). The two sparkling romantic comedies about the scriptwriter Thomas Graal, full of sharp satire on the artificialities of the movie world, starred Victor Sjöström and Karin Molander, who was Gustaf Molander's wife from 1910 to 1918.

Meanwhile, Molander had directed (and scripted) his own first film, *Bodakungen* (*King of Boda*, 1920), with Victor Sjöström in the lead. This was followed two years later by an addition to the Thomas Graal series, *Thomas Graal's Ward*, again starring Sjöström and also featuring Molander's younger brother Olof, later himself distinguished as a film and theatre director. After that, Gustaf Molander began to sever his connections with the theatre to concentrate on his new career as a filmmaker, directing more than a dozen pictures between 1922 and 1930. Sadly little is known about these early movies, but they are said to have shown an unusual sympathy with the problems of adolescence, and to have tended towards expressionism in style.

The radical shortage of information about Molander's work is all the more frustrating in view of what he achieved in the film that must—

on the available evidence—be regarded as his masterpiece, the early talkie *En natt* (*One Night*, 1931). Scripted by R. Hylten-Cavallius, and set during the Finnish civil war, it tells the story of a young soldier (Björn Berglund) who falls in love with a Russian mill girl (Ingert Bjuggren) and fights for her class against his own. Captured and sentenced to death, he is granted a night's freedom to be with her. At dawn, in spite of her pathetic efforts to detain him, he rides back to face the firing squad.

In Molander's hands, it was said, this melodramatic theme acquired "something of the quality of a noble legend." The acting was called "beautifully grave" and Åke Dahlquist's photography "luminous and serene." A reviewer in the London *Observer* wrote that "there is a sense of *texture* about the interiors that we have not known since Sjöström left Sweden ten years ago." Other contemporary critics also recognized the film's affinities with the golden age of the Swedish silent cinema, while noting that Molander had "been learning a great deal from Soviet models."

Vernon Young, writing forty years later, suggested that Molander had been influenced by his young production adviser, Gösta Hellstrom, who had studied Soviet film at close range. Young is no admirer of Molander's work as a whole, but he acknowledged that this "was a phenomenal case of filmmaking in the context of the early sound movie. No film made in Sweden at that period . . . had anything like its pace, its adroit metaphors, or its handsomely graded light effects. . . . The montage organisation, the cutting-for-contrast, the witness points of the camera, the arbitrary selection of closeup details, all are reminiscent of Eisenstein or Pudovkin."

Learning, perhaps, from Fritz Lang or Hitchcock, Molander showed equal sophistication in his handling of that unfamiliar element the soundtrack. Vernon Young's notes on the film include references to a "tickertape machine announcing War [that] becomes the sound of a train" and a "cut from scream of train whistle to overhead shot of couple embracing." Young concludes that *En natt*'s "style of antithetical cutting . . . might have served as an object lesson, if nothing else, in the making of a movie." In fact, the Swedish cinema had already sunk into a decline from which it did not emerge for fifteen years. Most of its major talents had been seduced away across the Atlantic, and the native industry, abandoning any hope of an international market, contented itself with churning out operettas and trivial comedies.

During the next ten years, as Rune Waldekranz has said, Molander, "the dominant director of the decade, still managed to preserve a semblance of quality in a series of popular comedies," keeping alive something of the great tradition of the silent era. In this "artificial atmosphere of stylish production," Molander also "discovered" and "groomed for stardom" a number of notable young players of whom the most famous was Ingrid Bergman. She appeared under his direction in *Swedenhielms* (1935) and *Pa solsidan* (*On the Sunny Side*, 1936), and became an international figure with her performance in Molander's *Intermezzo* (1936).

In *Intermezzo*, Bergman plays Anita Hoffman, a shy young Stockholm piano teacher. She falls deeply and passionately in love with Holger Brandt (Gösta Ekman), a world-famous violinist whose daughter is one of her pupils. He returns her love and they enjoy a glorious interlude of happiness when they make a European concert tour. But illicit love is not for the likes of Anita, and her agonized conscience forces her to end the affair. Holger eventually returns to his family responsibilities and she devotes herself to her own musical career—a choice of which the bitter outcome, it might fancifully be supposed, can be observed in the actress's last film: Ingmar Bergman's *Autumn Sonata*. Scripted by Molander with Gösta Stevens, it was photographed by Åke Dahlquist.

Intermezzo is cloying by today's cynical standards, but in its time it was wept and raved over as profusely as *Casablanca* was seven years later by critics and audiences excited by the intensity of its forbidden passions and enraptured by the dignified vulnerability of its young star. Indeed, it still has its champions, like Peter Cowie, who writes that "the music provides a dramatic link between sequences; and Holger's soul seems to flow through his violin, so concentrated is his feeling for the instrument. . . . The familiar scene on the bridge in Stockholm, when everyone else has gone home and Holger and Anita talk together, is charged with an intoxication completely foreign to later Swedish films." It was the first Swedish movie for many years to achieve an international success, and brought both star and director invitations to Hollywood.

Ingrid Bergman joined Selznick, for whom her first assignment was a remake of *Intermezzo* (1939, called *Escape to Happiness* in Britain) opposite Leslie Howard. Molander chose to stay home, perhaps remembering what happened to his friend Mauritz Stiller when he followed *his* star—Greta Garbo—to Hollywood. In Sweden, his standing as the country's leading director had been confirmed by the success of *Intermezzo*, which for many represented the "first stirrings

of new life" in a moribund industry. Its release coincided with a protest meeting by Swedish film workers against the abysmal artistic standards that prevailed. For the next few years Molander, like everyone else, continued to churn out trivial entertainments. But the seeds had been sown, and in the early 1940s Molander laid the groundwork for the renaissance that began with the innovations of Alf Sjöberg and culminated in the work of Ingmar Bergman.

The first of the three notable films that Molander made then was *Rid i natt!* (*Ride Tonight*, 1942). It was adapted from a novel by Vilhelm Moberg that lightly veiled a denunciation of the Nazi occupation in an account of a historical situation—the seizure of feudal power by foreign vassals of Queen Christina after the Thirty Years' War. The story centers on an obdurate peasant (Oscar Ljung) who refuses to pay excessive taxes to the German squire. Branded as an outlaw, he escapes into the woods but is hunted down by his own neighbors and killed by the professional hangman (Erik Hell), with whom he had once refused to drink. This injustice inspires the community to belated rebellion, with riders carrying the burning cross from village to village.

Vernon Young found the picture marred by a poor score and an irrelevant love story, but thought these weaknesses "more than redressed . . . by the generally firm handling of place and people, by the unsparing evaluation of Svedje's fellowmen as boneheaded superstitious traitors. Many visual touches in this film, such as strained sunlight on a clearing in the woods, shots of a log-house interior framed by a low, heavy-lintel doorway . . . suggest a provenance for similar effects and closeups in Bergman's *The Seventh Seal*. . . . *Ride Tonight* can be seen as a forceful precedent of the woodland mode to which . . . both *The Seventh Seal* and *The Virgin Spring* belong." It was "a poem of northern darkness, shot through with pastoral touches which yet remained subordinate to the stern drift of the narrative. It was Sjöström and Stiller, preserved in Molander's memory . . . and the atmosphere was in no small measure the contribution of the cinematographer, Åke Dahlquist."

The German occupation of Scandinavia in World War II was quite openly the theme of *Det brinner en eld* (*There Burned a Flame*, 1943), which studies the psychological effects of the occupation on a number of people in Oslo—particularly a woman who falls in love with a German officer. The film was attacked in some quarters for showing the invaders in too favorable a light, but Rune Waldekranz suggests that "its sympathies were exactly as clear-cut as the censor would permit them to be," and points out that "the heroine's emotional conflict proved strong and moving mainly because the German officer (Lars Hansen) was presented as an ordinarily complex human being." Waldekranz thought the result superior to the contemporary American movies on this theme, "with their cliché-ridden, black-and-white characterizations."

The Molander film that "galvanized" the Swedish film industry, and did most to precipitate its often-heralded renaissance was *Ordet* (*The Word,* 1943), adapted from Kaj Munk's play by Rune Lindström. The latter also plays the young pastor Johannes who, in the midst of his first sermon, realizes that his faith is not strong enough for the work he has chosen. He leaves his west coast village and, racked by a sense of worthlessness, breaks off his engagement. This indirectly causes the death of his fiancée in a car accident, and Johannes, unhinged by so much guilt and grief, loses his sanity. These are not the only sorrows that his Job-like father Knut has to endure—there is another tragedy when his daughter-in-law Inger dies in childbirth. But then Johannes recovers his sanity and his faith and, returning for the funeral, prays for Inger with such passionate intensity that she is recalled to life.

This "strange and disturbing climax" is handled with great tact and restraint, and with what Peter Cowie called "a naturalism that transforms [the apparent miracle] into something a good deal more disturbing and less mystical than it is in Carl Dreyer's later (1954) version" of *Ordet*. Vernon Young also preferred Molander's "spacious, open-air treatment" to Dreyer's. The film gave Victor Sjöström one of the finest roles of his later years as the patriarch Knut Borg, and there was much praise also for Lindström's "impressive, idiosyncratic" performance as Johannes.

Molander's star fell after that as Sjöberg's and then Bergman's rose. It was Bergman who scripted his only other major success, *Kvinna utan ansikte* (*Woman Without a Face,* 1947). Alf Kjellin plays the young man who leaves his wife (Anita Björk) and deserts from military service in the throes of an insanely destructive passion for a heartless "nymphomaniac" (Gunn Wallgren). The critics were not kind to the picture, attributing its success less to Molander's direction than to Åke Dahlquist's photography, Wallgren's "ambiguous performance," and the film's general air of steamy eroticism. But Bergman, admitting that the script was based on a youthful experience of his own, said that Molander had

"tidied it up very cleverly, to make it acceptable to the audiences of those days."

Two more of Molander's late films were scripted by Bergman. *Eva* (1948), based on the latter's unstaged play *The Station,* deals with a young man afraid to commit himself to marriage on account of a childhood trauma—an escapade that had cost the life of another child. An unrelievedly pessimistic film with a totally unconvincing happy ending, it seemed to Vernon Young "happily refreshed for the eye by the numerous social anecdotes that introduce a variety of characters and places," though "rarely has the invention of scissors been so ungratefully ignored."

Critics found even less to admire in Molander's third collaboration with Bergman, *Frånskild* (*Divorced,* 1951), in which a widow who seems to have every reason to commit suicide fails to do so and finds happiness instead in the arms of a young neighbor. The most interesting of Molander's later films were remakes, in color, of two that he had scripted as silent movies for Mauritz Stiller, *Sir Arne's Treasure* and *The Song of the Scarlet Flower*. His last work was an episode in the Scandinavian portmanteau film *Stimulantia* (1967)—an adaptation of Maupassant's story "The Necklace" starring his great "discovery" of the 1930s, Ingrid Bergman.

Gustaf Molander is generally placed with Stiller and Sjöström as one of the triumverate that created the golden age of the Swedish silent film. Though his was the least of the three talents, he was the only one of them to survive the lean years of the 1930s in the Swedish cinema, preserving virtually alone something of the old spirit, and leading the way towards the rebirth of the 1940s. "I've tremendous respect for Gustaf Molander," Ingmar Bergman told an interviewer. "I've learned a lot from him, and he was always generous and friendly and helpful."

FILMS: Bodakungen (King of Boda), 1920; Thomas Graals myndling (Thomas Graal's Ward), 1922; Amatör filmen (The Amateur Film), 1922; 33.333, 1924; Polis Paulus paskamäll (Constable Paulus's Easter Bomb), 1925; Ingmarsarvet (The Ingmar Inheritance), 1925; Till Österland (To the Orient), 1926; Hon, den enda (She the Only One), 1926; Hans engelska fru (His English Wife/Discord), 1927; Förseglade läppar (Sealed Lips), 1927; Parisskor (Women of Paris), 1928; Synd (Sin), 1928; Hjärtats triumf (Triumph of the Heart), 1929; Fridas visor (Frida's Song), 1930; Charlotte Löwensköld, 1930; En natt (One Night), 1931; Svarta rasor (Black Roses), 1932; Kärlek och kassbrist (Love and Deficit), 1932; Vi som gar köksvägen (We Go Through the Kitchen), 1932; Kära Släkten (Dear Relatives), 1933; En stille flirt (A Quiet Affair), 1933; Fasters Millioner (My Aunt's Millions), 1934; Ungkarlspappan (Bachelor Father), 1934; Swedenhiel-

ms, 1935; Under flask flagg (Under False Colors),
1935; Bröllopsresan (The Honeymoon Trip), 1936; Pa
solsidan (On the Sunny Side), 1936; Intermezzo, 1936;
Familjens hemlighet (The Family Secret, 1936; Sara
lär sig folkvett (Sara Learns Manners), 1937; Dollar,
1938; En Kvinnas ansikte (A Woman's Face), 1938; En
enda natt (One Single Night), 1938; Ombyte förnöjer
(Variety Is the Spice of Life), 1939; Emilie Högquist,
1939; En, men ett lejon (One, But a Lion), 1940; Den
Ljusande framtid (Bright Prospects), 1941; I natt ellet
aldrig (Tonight or Never), 1941; Striden gar vidare
(The Fight Goes On), 1941; Jacobs stege (Jacob's Ladder), 1942; Rid i natt (Ride Tonight), 1942; Det Brinner en eld (There Burned a Flame), 1943; Älskling, jag
ger mig (Darling, I Surrender), 1943; Ordet (The
Word), 1943; Den Osynliga muren (The Invisible
Wall), 1944; Kejsarn av Portugallien (The Emperor of
Portugal), 1944; Galgamannen (Mandragora), 1945;
Det Är min modell (It's My Model/Affairs of a Model),
1946; Kvinna utan ansikte (Woman Without a Face),
1947; Nu börjar livet (Live Begins Now), 1948; Eva,
1948; Kärleken segrar (Love Will Conquer), 1949;
Kvartetten som Sprängdes (The Quartet That Split
Up), 1950; Fästmö Uthyres (Fiancée for Hire), 1951;
Frånskild (Divorced), 1951; Trots (Defiance), 1952;
Kärlek (Love), 1952; Glasberget (Unmarried), 1953;
Herr Arnes penningar (Sir Arne's Treasure), 1954; En-
horningen (The Unicorn), 1955; Sangen om den
eldröda blomman (The Song of the Scarlet Flower),
1956; Smycket (The Necklace), *episode in* Stimulantia,
1967.

ABOUT: Cowie, P. Sweden (Screen Series), vols. 1 and 2,
1970; Waldekranz, R. Swedish Cinema, 1959; Young,
V. Cinema Borealis, 1971. *Periodicals*—Chaplin (Sweden) 5 1970; Times (London) June 22, 1973.

*"MURNAU," F. W. (Friedrich Wilhelm
Plumpe)** (December 28, 1888–March 11, 1931),
German director, was born in Bielefeld, West-
phalia, into a prosperous middle-class family of
Swedish origin. His father, who had inherited a
thriving textile business, bought a large country
estate near Kassel, to which the family moved
when Murnau was seven. "We children were
delighted," his brother Robert recalled. "There
was everything we could wish for in that garden. . . . It was a miniature paradise." Their elder half-sister set up a theatre in the attic, which
captivated Murnau; when she left for boarding
school he took over as director.

An ill-fated business speculation put an end to
this idyll. The estate was sold and the family
moved to a rented apartment in Kassel. For a
while Murnau made do with a puppet show, but
before long with the help of his brothers he had
designed and constructed a chamber theatre
with a full-scale stage. Performances were
mounted every Sunday, to paying audiences.
Murnau's father was less than appreciative of

F. W. MURNAU

these activities, or of his son's passion for literature, but Murnau was encouraged by his mother
Ottilie and by his father's sister Anna. After
graduating from high school, where according to
Robert he had been an outstanding pupil,
Murnau enrolled at Heidelberg, where he studied literature and art history. He also acted in local amateur productions, and was noticed in one
of them by Max Reinhardt, who invited him to
join his Deutsches Theater company.

For a stage-struck young man, an offer from
the famous Reinhardt was too good an opportunity to miss. Somehow contriving simultaneously
to continue his studies, he embarked on an acting career. It was then that he adopted the stage
name of Murnau (a small town in Bavaria)—
apparently less for euphony than to prevent his
father finding out what was happening. The
ploy failed dismally; easily recognizable by his
exceptional height, he was soon spotted by a
family friend, and his irate father cut off all
funding. Luckily his maternal grandfather came
to the rescue, and Murnau was able to complete
his studies. Having graduated he joined Reinhardt on a full-time basis as an actor and assistant director, touring with the company in
Germany and Austria-Hungary.

While still a student, Murnau had formed a
close and lasting attachment to a young poet,
Hans Ehrenbaum Degele, whose parents, a Jewish banker and a noted opera singer, treated
Murnau with great kindness and became a second family to him. Degele's death early in the
First World War deeply affected Murnau, further darkening his already melancholic temperament.

°mo͞or´nou

On the outbreak of war, Murnau was drafted into the infantry and saw service on the Russian front before being commissioned and transferring to the air force as a pilot. He survived seven crashes without serious injury, but in 1917, while on a combat mission, got lost in fog and landed in Switzerland, where he was interned for the duration. Conditions were by no means onerous; the Swiss authorities allowed him to direct theatrical productions and even to help compile propaganda films for the German Embassy in Bern.

This first contact with the cinema evidently fired Murnau's imagination. Released at the Armistice, he returned to Berlin determined to dedicate himself exclusively to filmmaking. In 1919, along with the actor Conrad Veidt and other colleagues from his Reinhardt days, he formed the Murnau Veidt Filmgesellschaft. The company's first production was *Der Knabe in Blau* (*The Blue Boy*, 1919), of which—as of most of Murnau's early work—no prints are known to survive. A Gothic melodrama inspired by Gainsborough's famous painting, it involved an impoverished young aristocrat (Ernst Hofman) haunted by an ancestral portrait, a missing emerald bearing a family curse, and a troupe of traveling players of whom one, a beautiful gypsy, ensnares the hero to his ruin.

No reviews of *Der Knabe in Blau*, good or bad, have been traced. Murnau and his associates proceeded to a more ambitious project: *Satanas* (1919), a three-episode film modeled after the then influential pattern of Griffith's *Intolerance*. In various guises, Lucifer (played by Conrad Veidt) contemptuously manipulates human affairs in Egypt, Renaissance Italy, and revolutionary Russia. (Carl Dreyer followed a very similar scheme in *Blade af Satans Bog*, made around the same time.) The script was by Robert Wiene, director of *Das Cabinett des Dr. Caligari*, and the cinematographer was Karl Freund, making the first of his nine films with Murnau. Again, no prints are extant, but contemporary reviews suggest that Murnau's gift for creating visual beauty was already evident.

Even less is known about *Sehnsucht* (*Longing*, 1920), which may also have been called *Bajazzo*, and seems to have concerned a Russian dancer (Conrad Veidt) who falls in love with a Grand Duchess. *Der Bucklige und die Tänzerin* (*The Hunchback and the Dancer*, 1920) marked Murnau's first collaboration with the scriptwriter Carl Mayer. Mayer, who had coscripted *Caligari*, was one of the key figures of German silent cinema, perhaps the first writer to think wholly in cinematic terms. "A script by Carl Mayer," wrote Karl Freund, "was already a film. The appearance of a Meyer script was that of a dramatic poem—a detailed recording of every shot and rhythm that he had formed in his imagination. . . . If one man should ever be given credit for the best film-work to come from Germany, it would have to be Carl Mayer."

Mayer is also generally credited with initiating the *kammerspiel* genre—pictures dealing with intimate, human situations, handled realistically and often set in relatively humble surroundings, like Murnau's *Der Letzte Mann* (1924). *Der Bucklige und die Tänzerin*, though, hardly sounds like *kammerspiel*. A rich hunchback (John Gottowt) tries to buy the love of a dancer (Sacha Gury); when she rejects him, he gives her poisoned cosmetics (having secretly fed her the antidote), thus rendering her kisses fatal to her other lovers. The critic of *Film Kurier* (February 3, 1920) found the action less than plausible but commended Murnau's fine images, adding: "I have never seen a production in which the characters are bathed in such atmosphere; it has a kind of psychic perfume."

Of Murnau's total output of twenty-one films, nine are currently thought to be lost; of these, *Der Januskopf* (*The Janus Head*, 1920) sounds the most intriguing. Based without acknowledgement on Stevenson's *Dr. Jekyll and Mr. Hyde*, it was scripted by Hans Janowitz, Mayer's co-writer on *Caligari*, and starred Conrad Veidt as Dr. Warren, a respectable London physician who, under the influence of a double-faced antique bust, becomes the bestial Mr. O'Connor. Reviewers singled out Veidt's dual performance for praise, but Murnau's direction attracted little attention. He gained still less notice—and may well have been glad of it—on his next film, *Abend . . . Nacht . . . Morgen* (*Evening . . . Night . . . Morning*, 1920). This was a detective story with, according to Lotte Eisner, a "horribly banal" plot. The reviewer of *Film und Presse* even suggested, tactfully, that it might be better not to mention the director's name.

The earliest of Murnau's films known to survive is *Der Gang in die Nacht* (*Journey into the Night*, 1920), rediscovered by Henri Langlois in the vaults of an East Berlin film archive. Carl Mayer's script was based on a play by Harriet Bloch, who often wrote for the Danish cinema, and the film shows the influence of contemporary Scandinavian models: the lead role is taken by Olaf Fønss, a prominent Danish actor of the period, and Murnau's lighting and composition frequently recall Stiller or Sjöström. The plot concerns a doctor who loses his wife to a young painter whom he cured of blindness. Years later, she returns to beg his help: the blindness has recurred. Bitterly he rejects her, declaring that he would only cure the artist if she did not exist. She kills herself. The painter rejects the offered cure, choosing, now his love is gone, to remain in darkness. Next day the doctor is found dead in his study.

In *Film Kurier* of December 14, 1920, Willy Haas, later to work with Murnau as a writer on *Der Brennende Acker,* warmly commended *Der Gang in der Nacht.* Everything about it, he wrote, was perfect—script, acting, and direction; he spoke of eloquent facial expressions, almost imperceptible gestures. Modern viewers are more likely to be struck by the resounding clash of acting styles, Fønss's old-fashioned staginess colliding with the expressionistic angularity of Conrad Veidt as the artist. Much of the action now seems ponderous or embarrassingly melodramatic, redeemed only by Murnau's subtle lighting and atmospheric use of natural landscape. Already, Eric Rhode observed, Murnau "had discovered the means by which he could use location shooting to present unusual states of mind in an unforced manner." Lotte Eisner singled out two sequences of a boat sailing through the dusk: "the surface of the water and the shore combine to form in each case a perfect image, full of rhythm and movement, and vibrant with atmosphere."

Murnau's cycle of peasant films, which reached its apotheosis in *Sunrise,* opened with the crisply titled *Marizza, genannt die Schmuglermadonna (Marizza, the Smugglers' Madonna,* 1921), another of the "lost" movies. Scripted by Hans Janowitz and set somewhere in southern Europe, it involved a complicated story—suggesting a cross between *Carmen* and *Tess of the D'Urbervilles*—about a beautiful peasant girl, forced to act as decoy for smugglers, who is made pregnant by the son of a local landowner and runs away with his bookish brother. Karl Freund's photography attracted much praise.

The "perfect form" of the silent movie, Murnau once stated, would be one without a single intertitle—an ideal famously realized in *Der Letzte Mann.* By this criterion, *Schloss Vogelöd* (1921) is very far from perfection; a surfeit of title-cards clogs its action, most of them superfluous. Despite the English-language title, *The Haunted Castle,* this is no ghost story but a psychological drama drawing on Gothic imagery to enhance its suspense. The members of a hunting party of a remote castle become obsessed with the mystery surrounding two of the guests: a beautiful baroness, whose husband died in ambiguous circumstances, and her saturnine brother-in-law, suspected of being implicated in the death. Finally the mystery is cleared up; guilt is assigned and expiated. The plot, though, scarcely matters. Atmosphere, as Whittemore and Cecchettini noted, is the all-important factor: "Murnau works in basic patterns of light just as he works in basic character traits. This story of criminal guilt is practically reduced to a series of visual abstractions in which the moral significance of each act is conveyed by the spatial configuration."

"Perhaps no other filmmaker has used space more rigorously or inventively than Murnau," Eric Rohmer commented. Already, in *Schloss Vogelöd,* that spatial skill is clearly in evidence. In one scene a man confronts the woman whose husband he has just killed, an act which she has half-consciously desired, in a narrow, high-ceilinged room whose gloom is pierced only by two tall windows like accusing eyes. The couple stand as far as possible from each other, leaning backwards against opposite walls, the expanse of the desolate room between them—each isolated, yet trapped in the aridity of their mutual guilt.

Midway through the film, perhaps feeling that its bleak austerity needed some leavening, Murnau and Mayer (who scripted) introduce a nightmare by way of light relief. This is dreamt by a nervous guest, unsettled by the strange happenings around him: as he sits up in bed, peering apprehensively into the darkness, a claw-like hand emerges from behind the curtains and takes him by the throat. Though played for comedy, even perhaps parody, this sequence hints at the film Murnau was about to make—his first masterpiece, and one of the greatest of all horror films.

"A chilling draught from the world beyond," in Béla Bálazs's phrase, blows through *Nosferatu* (1922), far colder than anything in the many subsequent versions of the Dracula story, for all their greater technical sophistication. In the whole span of horror movies, perhaps only Dreyer's *Vampyr* matches it for sheer unearthliness. Henrik Galeen, who scripted—and who later directed another gothic masterpiece of the era, *Der Student von Prag*—adheres broadly to the plot of Bram Stoker's novel *Dracula* (used without acknowledgement. Both Galeen and Murnau were sued for infringement of copyright.)

Hutter, a real-estate broker's clerk, travels to the remote castle of Count Orlok, who plans to buy property in the old Hanseatic city of Bremen, where Hutter lives. Orlok, of course, is Nosferatu, the undying vampire who feeds on human blood, and Hutter narrowly escapes becoming his prey. Hutter returns home, but Nosferatu is also en route, traveling by ship in an earth-filled coffin. His arrival spreads plague and death in the old city, and the curse is lifted only by the self-sacrifice of Hutter's wife Nina (or Ellen—names vary from print to print), who entices the vampire to her bedroom and detains him there, sucking her blood, until dawn. In the rays of the rising sun Nosferatu is destroyed, and Nina dies in her husband's arms.

Most German horror films of the period, following *Caligari,* were claustrophobic, studio-bound, filled with heavy shadows and distorted expressionist sets. Murnau rejected this convention; much of *Nosferatu* was filmed on location, in rugged mountain landscapes and on quiet northern streets. And these authentic surroundings, far from rendering the horror prosaic, seem themselves to be infected by Nosferatu's monstrous presence. "For all the increased directness, all the unyielding photographic naturalism of these scenes," Gilberto Perez Guillermo wrote in *Sight and Sound* (Summer 1967), "something, one senses, remains beyond what the camera can capture. The physical world, placed almost tangibly before our eyes, is somehow still distant, inscrutable, ghostly. . . . Appearances are not deceptive, they are simply opaque, inherently incomplete." And David Thomson, in his *Biographical Dictionary of the Cinema,* suggests that "Murnau's greatness lies in this realisation—that it is possible to photograph the real world and yet invest it with a variety of poetic, imaginative and subjective qualities."

The Nosferatu of Max Schreck is unforgettably grotesque from his first manifestation—no hint of the superficial urbanity of Lugosi or Christopher Lee. Tall, cadaverously thin, bald, bat-eared, rabbit-toothed, he moves with short jerky steps, taloned hands close to his sides, as though permanently confined by the shape of his diurnal coffin. The effect is near-ludicrous, chilling, and ultimately even pitiful—the creature's need for blood, for living warmth, is palpably urgent to the point of agony. Beside him, the other characters fade to insignificance. Hutter and Nina, through whose mutual devotion Nosferatu is finally overcome, remain conventional figures, never approaching the dramatic stature of the similarly threatened couple in *Sunrise* (except perhaps in the hints that Nina is secretly not immune to the attractions of Thanatos-Nosferatu).

Nosferatu was made on a modest budget for the small Prana company, one reason perhaps for the sparing use of trick effects. At one point, as Hutter approaches the sinister castle, the film slips into negative, with ghastly white trees waving stricken limbs as though even Nature had been sucked dry. Two brief episodes of stop-action cause figures to move with a deranged clockwork rapidity. But generally Murnau relies on subtly off-center framings and disorienting camera angles to convey the insidious menace of his vision, often focusing on some small, allusive detail—like the sailor's hammock, still gently swinging after its occupant, along with all his fellow crew-members, has succumbed to Nosferatu and to death. Most telling of all is the scene in which Nosferatu, approaching Nina's bedroom, is seen only as a huge, tormented, spiderlike shadow.

Within Germany, *Nosferatu* established Murnau's reputation as a major director, and remained famous enough to be reissued eight years later with the coming of sound, in a botched-up version with additional sequences and a dubbed soundtrack. (This version, entitled *Die Zwölfte Stunde* [*The Twelfth Hour,* 1930], was not authorized by Murnau, who probably never even saw it.) For a time the film's critical standing slumped; writing in 1948, Theodore Huff could dismiss it as "a rather crude picture . . . no more 'profound' than the American *Dracula* or *Frankenstein,*" though conceding that it "did show Murnau's flair for pictorial effect."

More recently the film has been reestablished among Murnau's finest works. For Robin Wood (*Film Comment,* May–June 1976) it constituted "one of the cinema's finest and most powerfully suggestive embodiments of . . . one of those universal myths that seem fundamental to human experience." Jean-André Fieschi, in Richard Roud's *Cinema,* writes that "Murnau was one of the first systematically to consider the shot . . . as a space negotiable in every way . . . inviting the most unpredictable courses. Like a stage whose specific (variable) scale induces the precedence of gesture, movement, attitude over plot or decor. Murnau's discoveries on that score in *Nosferatu* were of great importance; here, liberation from the theatre was finally and decisively achieved." And Fieschi concludes with this large claim: "The genius of Murnau: *Nosferatu* marks the advent of a total cinema in which the plastic, rythmic and narrative elements are no longer graduated in importance, but in strict interdependence upon each other. With this film the modern cinema was born." In 1979 Werner Herzog paid Murnau characteristically obsessive tribute with a remake (*Nosferatu: Phantom der Nacht*) that reproduced much of the original almost shot for shot.

A recurrent theme in Murnau's work is of individuals who cut themselves off from some form of primal innocence (often represented by a simple country life) in order to plumb forbidden depths, physical or emotional. By doing so, they release dark, chthonic forces that threaten to destroy them. Variations on this theme underlie *Faust, Sunrise* and *Tabu*; a relatively crude version provides the plot of *Der Brennende Acker (The Burning Earth,* 1922), the most recently rediscovered of the supposedly lost films. Another peasant drama, this involves the two sons of an old farmer (Werner Krauss), one of whom inherits the land and farms it contentedly. His ambitious brother marries a widowed countess, not for love but for a tract of oil-bearing land that she owns. Oil is struck, but the well is sabotaged by the countess's jealous daughter, and the chastened young man returns to his village and the simple peasant girl who loves him.

The ponderousness of the plot is matched by the acting, which entails a good deal of sustained glowering, but once again the film's visual qualities partly compensate for its dramatic shortcomings. With the aid of Karl Freund's photography and Rochus Gliese's atmospheric sets, Murnau creates—in John Gillett's description—"a darkly claustrophobic mood with much concentration on faces and objects and exquisite interiors." Reviewers at the time were greatly impressed by the audacious lighting effects, especially in the climactic scene of the oil-well burning furiously amid nocturnal, snow-covered fields.

Phantom (1922), made for Erich Pommer at Decla-Bioscop, was adapted from a novel by Gerhart Hauptmann, at that time considered Germany's foremost living dramatist. Hence, perhaps, the virulent attacks launched on the film—most of them directed not at Murnau but at Thea von Harbou, whose script was found "pretentious," "superficial," and "picture-postcard stuff." The plot, recounted in a long flashback, traces the downfall of an indigent clerk (played with quivering furtiveness by Alfred Abel) who is struck—literally—by fate in the form of a carriage bearing a beautiful young woman. Disgusted by the contrasting shabbiness of his own existence, he embarks on an increasingly demented campaign to win her love, culminating in fraud, robbery, and murder.

Due possibly to the influence of von Harbou, Fritz Lang's wife and regular scriptwriter, *Phantom* conforms more closely to the Expressionist conventions of the period than any other surviving Murnau film. Most of the action is filtered through the distorting glass of the protagonist's crazed perception. Two virtuoso sequences in particular aroused much comment. In one, as the guilt-ridden clerk scurries along a street, all the tall, gabled houses lean over as if to crush him, their pointed black shadows stabbing ferociously at his fleeing figure. Later, as he sits in

a bar, the whole room, with its chairs, tables and customers, begins to spin round him, and he himself, trapped at the center of the whirlpool, finds himself drawn down helplessly into a dark, whirling tunnel. Striking though these effects are, they seem to belong—as indeed does the whole film—to a style of brash melodrama alien to the cool fantasy of Murnau's vision.

The last of Murnau's lost German films, *Die Austreibung (The Expulsion,* 1923), was based on a play by Karl Hauptmann, Gerhart's brother. A peasant drama, again scripted by von Harbou, it told of the son of an old Silesian couple who sells the family farm in order to please his unfaithful wife. *Film Kurier* commended it as "the first peasant film dealing with nuances rather than with broad effects"; other reviewers thought it overburdened with titles, but again praised Murnau's visual sense and feeling for landscape.

Most critics would accept Jean Domarchi's assertion that Murnau's is essentially "a tragic universe, characterized by an ever deepening obsession with death." His sole attempt at a comedy, *Die Finanzen des Grossherzogs (The Finances of the Grand Duke,* 1923), bears out this judgment. A lumbering farce revolving around an attempted coup in a comic-opera Grand Duchy, it was filmed on the Dalmatian coast and performed by most of the cast at a high level of misplaced energy. The script, her last for Murnau, was once more by von Harbou; she too evidently had little knack for comedy.

"All our efforts must be directed towards abstracting everything that isn't the true domain of the cinema," Murnau said, "everything that is trivial and acquired from other sources—all the tricks, devices and clichés inherited from the stage and from books." With his next film, Murnau came close to realizing his ideal. The effort reunited him with Carl Mayer, a writer who also worked in "the true domain of the cinema," and together they produced a work generally recognized as a highpoint of German cinema, and one of the most influential movies ever made.

Der Letzte Mann (The Last Laugh, 1924), according to Lotte Eisner, "is preeminently a German tragedy, and can only be understood in a country where uniform is King, not to say God. A non-German mind will have difficulty in comprehending all its tragic implications." There may be some truth in this, but the film nevertheless quickly achieved worldwide success, established Murnau's international reputation, and led in due course to his departure for Hollywood.

The theme—universal enough, beneath its

surface detail—is that of dignity dethroned, pomposity brought humiliatingly low. A hotel doorman (Emil Jannings), magnificent in his braided greatcoat and flowing whiskers, lords it not only over the hotel foyer but also over the humble tenement where he lives and where his return each evening resembles a royal progress. As Siegfried Kracauer wrote, "all the tenants, in particular the female ones . . . [revere the uniform] as a symbol of supreme authority and are happy to be allowed to revere it."

But age is catching up with the doorman; one day the manager notices him stagger beneath a heavy trunk. A younger man gets his job, and the old fellow, stripped of his majestic livery, is given a white jacket and put in charge of the men's lavatory. Crushed, broken, mocked by his neighbors, evicted from his apartment, he sinks into terminal decline—at which point a title announces ironically that, out of pity for the old man, a happy ending has been provided. The ex-doorman inherits all the wealth of an eccentric millionaire who dies in his lavatory, and departs the hotel in triumphant luxury.

For Paul Rotha, writing in 1929, *Der Letzte Mann* "definitely established the film as an independent medium of expression. . . . Everything that had to be said . . . was said entirely through the camera. . . . *The Last Laugh* was cine-fiction in its purest form; exemplary of the rhythmic composition proper to the film." C. A. Lejeune, who considered it "probably the least sensational and certainly the most important" of Murnau's films, observed that "it gave the camera a new dominion, a new freedom. . . . It influenced the future of motion picture photography . . . all over the world, and without suggesting any revolution in method, without storming critical opinion as *Caligari* had done, it turned technical attention towards experiment, and stimulated . . . a new kind of camera-thinking with a definite narrative end."

If *Der Letzte Mann* no longer stands quite so high in critical estimation, it remains impressive in its technical ingenuity and seamless narrative fluency. The ironic "happy ending" apart, intertitles are completely dispensed with; the story is told purely in visual terms, with perfect lucidity. (This was not quite such an innovation as is sometimes claimed: Arthur Robison's *Schatten* (1923) had also managed without titles, as had *Scherben* (1921) and *Sylvester* (1923), both scripted by Mayer and directed by Lupu Pick. Pick had been scheduled to direct *Der Letzte Mann* until he and Mayer quarreled.)

The film attained an unprecedented degree of camera mobility and camera subjectivity. Working closely with Karl Freund, Murnau and Mayer devised means of liberating the apparatus from its tripod, letting it wheel and soar around and within the action. For the opening shot in the hotel, Freund, the camera strapped to his chest, descended in the hotel elevator mounted on a bicycle. As the doors opened he rode out across the foyer, through the huge revolving doors, and into the street. Elsewhere, the camera seemed to fly up to a high tenement window, an effect achieved by letting it slide down a wire, then reversing the film. The visual fluidity gained by this *entfesselte Kamera* ("unchained camera") was hailed as a great liberation by such young filmmakers as Marcel Carné, who wrote: "The camera . . . glides, rises, zooms or weaves where the story takes it. It is no longer fixed, but takes part in the action and becomes a *character* in the drama."

Der Letzte Mann was filmed entirely in the studio, where Robert Herlth and Walter Röhrig created a glittering, impressionistic cityscape of dark, angled buildings and flashing neon. Lotte Eisner noted Murnau's delight in "opalescent surfaces streaming with reflections, rain, or light: car windows, the glazed leaves of the revolving door reflecting the silhouette of the doorman dressed in a gleaming black waterproof, the dark mass of houses with lighted windows, wet pavements and shimmering puddles. . . . His camera captures the filtered half-light falling from the street lamps . . . it seizes the reflections of toilet articles seen in the lavatory mirrors, and the slanting shadow of street railings through the basement window." Murnau himself said that "on account of the way . . . [objects] were placed or photographed, their image is a visual drama. In their relationship with other objects or with the characters, they are units in the symphony of the film." As the doorman, Emil Jannings gave the performance of his career, his orotund acting style for once perfectly in tune with the role.

Some critics have speculated whether the prime creative impulse behind *Der Letzte Mann,* as behind *Sunrise,* should not be credited to Carl Mayer, who scripted both films. Karl Freund lent credence to this view, recalling that Murnau never looked through the viewfinder, had nothing to do with the lighting, and that "Carl Mayer used to take much more interest than he did in the framing." Other former colleagues, such as Robert Herlth and Charles Rosher, have strongly disagreed however, insisting that Murnau, though always receptive to other people's ideas, knew exactly what he wanted and would take infinite pains to achieve it.

It may well be that Murnau's habitually diffident and courteous manner was taken for a lack of creative drive—especially by anyone used to the peremptory ways of Lang, with whom Freund also worked. Herlth first encountered Murnau as "a tall slim gentleman in his white work-coat, issuing directions in a very low voice," and described him as "always good-humored. . . . Our team was extremely happy, always ready for jokes and teasing one another. . . . But this is not to say that Murnau did not work like a demon. He worked fast, but he was so interested in every detail that he did not bother about questions of time. . . . He wanted to know about everything, to try everything from every possible angle." Other collaborators have mentioned the long, meticulous preparation prior to shooting, and the unifying and seemingly instinctive visual grasp that Murnau brought to bear on each picture. Edgar G. Ulmer, his assistant on several films (including *Sunrise*), recalled him as "a man who had the camera up there, a man who saw pictures and built pictures in his head. . . . He always saw a film as a whole."

Der Letzte Mann was Murnau's first film for UFA, now headed by Erich Pommer. Its success encouraged Pommer to assign him two big-budget, prestige projects, based on major literary classics, beginning with *Tartüff (Tartuffe*, 1926). Adapted from Molière's satire on religious hypocrisy, this had Jannings in the title role of the greedy lecher battening on a credulous bourgeois (Werner Krauss) under a cloak of pious austerity.

In no other Murnau film is his training as an art historian more in evidence. The elegant, stylized compositions and formal sets constantly recall the work of Watteau, Boucher, or Chardin. The action, too, is stylized, the carefully patterned movements of actors and camera suggesting a musical structure, the groupings of individuals and ensembles reminiscent of Mozartian opera. Doors open and close, figures ascend and descend curving, ornamental staircases, the camera dwells on rich, delicate textures: silks and velvets, lace and brocade, soft skin in shadowed lamplight. The effect is visually sumptuous but tends to reduce Molière's characters to lay figures, patterns of light and shade.

This impression is strengthened by the framing of the play within a modern-day prologue and epilogue. In a misguided attempt to lend Molière contemporary relevance, the story of Tartuffe becomes a film within the film, shown by a young man to alert his gullible uncle to the designs of a mercenary housekeeper. In Gilberto Perez Guillermo's view, "the performance is not of the Molière play but of a coarsening and reduction of it. Yet . . . somehow this version of

Molière turns out as a faintly comic variation of *Dracula,* with Jannings as Tartuffe suggesting a fat Nosferatu . . . and a sense of unexpressed horror pervading the soft lighting and the graceful architecture of the sets."

Murnau's final film for UFA (and his last film in Germany) tackled one of the commanding heights of German literature—Goethe's *Faust.* Of all Murnau's pictures, *Faust* (1926) has aroused the most violently divergent critical opinions. Many writers, then and since, have seen it as a grandiose and vapid display of theatrical artifice. C. A. Lejeune found in it "all the tinsel and bombast of a world-circus," and Siegfried Kracauer thought that not even its technical ingenuity and its Gerhart Hauptmann titles "could compensate for the futility of a film which misrepresented, if not ignored, all significant motives inherent in its subject-matter. The metaphysical conflict between good and evil was thoroughly vulgarized."

On the other hand, Herman G. Weinberg, writing in *cinemages* (1/1, 1955), hailed it as "a great fresco painted with lights and shadows. . . . Never before or since was there . . . such an exultant flight of the cinema spirit." Theodore Huff considered it "one of the most pictorially beautiful films ever made, a supreme example of German studio craftsmanship, at times seeming like a Dürer or a Breughel come to life." And, in a book devoted entirely to a detailed study of this film, Eric Rohmer observed that here "Murnau put into effect his total mastery of cinematic space. . . . No other cinematic work has left so little to chance."

These categorically opposed views suggest that it all depends which bit of *Faust* is being considered. At times the film superbly measures up to the metaphysical stature of its theme—never more so perhaps than in the prologue in heaven, which Lotte Eisner described as "the most remarkable and poignant images the German chiaroscuro ever created. The chaotic density of the opening shots, the light dawning in the mists, the rays beaming through the opaque air, and the visual fugue which diapasons round the heavens, are breathtaking." Elsewhere, Murnau's pictorial genius creates masterly effects: the misty, Rembrandtesque scenes in Faust's study, darkness swirling ominously at the imminence of the fatal pact; the spreading out of Mephisto's cloak into a monstrous black cloud hovering above the little town, pestilence and death lurking in its folds; Faust's aerial journey, borne up on that same cloak, over brilliantly modeled rooftops, plains, rivers, and mountains to the sea; the nocturnal duel between Faust and Valentin, shadows weaving and lunging across a little square beneath lowering gables.

At other times, though, the film veers disastrously into inflated kitsch, as in the embarrassingly sentimental love scenes between Faust and Marguerite, the lumbering comic flirtation between Mephisto and Marthe, Marguerite's complaisant aunt, or the Duchess of Parma's ball, likened by Georges Sadoul to a 1920s German music hall. Some of these lapses can be traced to Hans Kyser's script, which drew not only on Goethe but also on Marlowe and (rather unwisely) on Gounod. *Faust's* main weakness, however, lies in its uniformly deplorable casting. The feeble Faust of the Swedish actor, Gösta Ekman, is matched by the insipidity of Camilla Horn's Marguerite (a role originally offered to Lillian Gish, who regrettably turned it down). The future director Wilhelm Dieterle, hamming valiantly as Valentin, fades beside the "amateur-night-at-the-opera performance" (Robin Wood) of Emil Jannings's Mephistopheles, grinning and grimacing at his most corpulently histrionic.

Faust failed to achieve the success Pommer had hoped for. By the time of its release, though, Murnau was already in Hollywood, preparing his first American film. The studio heads, always on the lookout for prestigious European talent, had registered the worldwide acclaim for *Der Letzte Mann,* and enticing offers rolled in. Murnau needed little persuading and soon signed a four-picture contract with William Fox. In America, he hoped, he would find "new opportunities to develop my artistic aims." He may also have hoped to find greater personal freedom; as a homosexual, he had always felt oppressed by the threat of Germany's savage penal code. He arrived in Hollywood in July 1926. Under the terms of his contract, Fox's "German genius" had complete freedom to choose his own subject, could spend as he liked, and would be wholly free from studio interference—at least, on his first film.

Sunrise (1927) may well be the most German film ever made in Hollywood. Watching it, one can easily forget that it is, in fact, an American movie, made with American actors and a largely American crew; the look and feel are so entirely consistent with Murnau's previous work. The script, taken from a story by Hermann Sudermann, *Die Reise nach Tilsit* (A Trip to Tilsit), was again by Carl Mayer, who had been invited to accompany Murnau to America. (He refused, preferring to stay in Germany and deal with Hollywood at a safe distance.) The happiness of a young rural couple is threatened by a seductive city woman, who captivates and obsesses the husband; at her urging, he evolves a plan to drown his wife on a supposed pleasure outing to the nearby city. At the last moment he shrinks

from the deed, but the wife, guessing his intention, flees in terror. He catches up with her, filled with remorse, and during their day in the city manages to regain her confidence. Their mutual love is reborn. But on the way home across the lake a storm overturns the boat, and the wife is apparently drowned. The husband, wild with grief, violently attacks the city woman when she comes to him. Then the wife is found, alive. As day breaks the couple embrace ecstatically, while the temptress returns defeated to the city.

Many critics have seen *Sunrise* as structured—over-simplistically, some have maintained—around a pattern of paired opposites, "between sunrise and sunset, the country and the city, good and evil, divine grace and black magic, natural and unnatural acts, and finally the blonde, beatific wife . . . and the dark, sultry city woman . . . in their struggle for The Man's soul," as Molly Haskell summarized it (*Film Comment,* Summer 1971). The dichotomies are not quite so clear-cut; it is after all through the glittering excitements of the city that the couple are reunited. As if to emphasize their archetypal, mythic nature, the three characters—there are only three that matter—have no names, being referred to simply as The Man (played by George O'Brien), The Wife (Janet Gaynor), and The Woman from the City (Margaret Livingstone). Many expressionist plays use the same device, and *Sunrise,* for all its Hollywood provenance, has often been regarded as (in David Robinson's words) "the apogee of the German expressionist cinema."

"Real art," Murnau once observed, "is simple, but simplicity requires the greatest art." *Sunrise* was shot almost entirely under studio conditions, but achieves—especially in the first half of the film—a cool, unforced atmosphere in which naturalism and expressionism seem to merge in a dream landscape, real and unreal at once. Murnau and his designer, Rochus Gliese, took full advantage of their carte blanche to construct hugely elaborate sets: wild, desolate marshes, a lakeside village, a refulgent amusement park and, for the young couple's first awed view of the city, a vast urban square—complete with traffic, streetcars, subway entrances, neon signs, and towering buildings—which covered some twenty acres of studio lot. Around these expanses the camera prowled and glided, outdoing even *Der Letzte Mann* in its tireless motion. "The premise of the film," Rodney Farnsworth wrote, " is that the camera will move; and that it will have any excuse to move. Plot and characters seem pretexts for movement and light."

Sunrise, in Jean Domarchi's opinion, is unquestionably "the most beautiful film there is" and was voted to be so in a 1958 *Cahiers* poll. If not all critics would go quite that far, most have agreed that it is a pictorial feast, full of hauntingly beautiful scenes—the brooding marshland, lit by a mist-swathed moon, through which the Man treads somberly, as though under a malign compulsion, to meet the City Woman; the dazzling restaurant-cum-dance-hall, enchanting and bewildering the eye with shimmering lights reflected in multiple vistas of glass, all brilliance and ceaseless movement; the peaceful journey home across the wind-rippled lake, before the storm strikes, with a vision of distant festivities, dark Goyaesque figures around a flickering bonfire. Probably the most famous sequence is the long trolley-ride bearing the agonized, estranged couple, just after the abortive murder attempt, from the countryside into the city. This sequence, for which two miles of trolley-track were laid, extending from real forest into the constructed cityscape, was described by Molly Haskell as "one of the most ecstatic movements in all cinema. The psychological suspension between anguish and relief is exquisitely, and physically, sustained by the breathtakingly lyrical, delirious motion of the trolley through real space."

Sunrise received three Academy Awards—best actress, best cinematography (Charles Rosher, Karl Struss), and "artistic quality of production"—and was hailed by American critics as a masterpiece. Robert Sherwood, reviewing it in *Life,* called it "the most important picture in the history of the movies." In *New Republic* Louise Bogan wrote: "Here is camera technique pushed to its limits, freed from pantomime and parade. . . . Not since the earliest, simplest moving pictures . . . has there been such joy in motion as under Murnau's direction." Some—wrongly, in fact—deduced studio interference in the happy ending and in episodes of clumsy comedy in the city scenes. In the second half of the film, Lewis Jacobs considered, "the lyricism was dissipated by comic relief; the universality was destroyed by melodrama," but overall "this synthesis of all factors to create a particular mood for a scene or a sequence imbued *Sunrise* with a psychological intensity and a rare style."

In Europe, not all critics were so enthusiastic. "Faces and bodies are to . . . [Murnau] simply vehicles for light or masses of shadow," Harry Kahn noted in *Die Weltbühne,* and Paul Rotha scornfully dismissed the film as the work of a major European talent hopelessly vulgarized by Hollywood, "a masterpiece of bluff, insincerity, unsubstantial nonsense." The critical consensus inclined towards Rotha's view during the years

when it was supposed that little good could come out of Hollywood, but the film's reputation began to revive in the 1960s, and most writers would now rate it Murnau's finest work.

On release, the critical success of *Sunrise* was far from matched by its box-office takings, and the film failed to recoup its formidable costs. Fox, no doubt feeling that genius could be purchased at too high a price, tightened his grip; the remaining two films that Murnau made for the studio were subjected to close control and released in forms very different from his original intentions.

It is not clear whether or not *Four Devils* (1928) should be numbered among Murnau's lost films. According to Lotte Eisner, a negative is preserved in the Fox archive, and in recent years there have been recurrent, though unfulfilled, rumors that a print was about to surface. At all events, nobody appears to have seen the film since well before World War II, although Mayer's original script still exists. The Devils of the title are a circus act—four young acrobats, two male and two female, who have grown up together in the care of an old clown. One of the men falls into the toils of a seductive vamp, to the despair of his female partner. His work deteriorates dangerously. Finally he makes a fatal error; his partner saves him, but then lets go, and they both fall to their deaths.

This was Mayer's original conception, as adapted from a novel by Hermann Bang. The studio, though, imposed a happy ending: the female acrobat alone falls, sustaining minor injuries, and her partner remorsefully begs her forgiveness. Sound was also added to the final two reels. Contemporary reviewers praised the film's pictorial brilliance, especially in the intricately lit trapeze routines, but found the plot trite and sentimental—Dupont's *Variété,* "swiped, denatured and lollypopped" (*New Masses*).

Murnau's last film for Fox ran into even more problems. It was to be called *Our Daily Bread,* and he had envisaged a series of rhapsodic documentary sequences punctuating the action, a "symphony of wheat" tracing the progress from field to finished loaf, "a tale . . . about the sacredness of bread, about the estrangement of the modern city dwellers and their ignorance about Nature's sources of sustenance." This was to be grafted on to an adaptation of a play called *The Mud Turtle,* by Elliot Lester, about a country lad who brings home a bride from the city, arousing his father's hostility.

Delighted to be working in the open again after the studio-bound *Four Devils,* Murnau had bought a farm in Oregon (using studio money) and was planning endless tracking shots through the ripe wheat. William Fox, alarmed at what seemed to be incipient Teutonic megalomania (the dread name of von Stroheim was being whispered), viewed a rough cut and called a halt. The film, he told Murnau, was too long and the peasants were "not at all American." All the documentary sections were jettisoned, and the Fox gag-writers were wheeled in to "give it some fun."

Eventually, the film, now renamed *City Girl* (1930), was made in two versions. One, with post-synchronized sound, ran slightly over an hour, was given a half-hearted release, and taken off after doing poor business. Much of it is said to have been shot by someone other than Murnau—by William K. Howard, according to Edgar Ulmer, though others credit Murnau's assistant director, "Buddy" Erickson. The other was a silent version, some 88 minutes long, which was apparently never released. Long believed lost, it was rediscovered in 1970 and premiered in a Murnau retrospective at the Museum of Modern Art.

Judging by appearances, the silent *City Girl* is pure Murnau—entirely his work, albeit probably truncated—and though it limps in places, and the editing is often abrupt, it includes scenes as fine as anything he ever shot. Richard Koszarski (*Film Comment*, Summer 1971) singled out a sequence when the newly married couple arrive in the country for the first time—"The sense of space comes as an explosion after the claustrophobic city sequences"—and run joyfully through sunlit fields of wheat, the camera following in "one of the screen's most breathtakingly romantic tracking shots." The plot, as several critics have pointed out, can be read as a reversal of *Sunrise*, with the disenchanted city girl coming to realize that the country is no idyllic refuge, but harbors no less cruelty and greed than the city from which she has escaped.

In February 1929, disgusted and disillusioned with Hollywood, Murnau broke his contract with Fox. While shooting *City Girl* he had met David Flaherty, brother of Robert Flaherty, director of *Nanook of the North* and *Moana*, and the idea of a joint venture arose. Flaherty, after the failure of his attempted collaboration with Woody Van Dyke on *White Shadows of the South Seas*, was equally jaded with the Hollywood system. This, and their shared idealism, may have prevented the two men from realizing that their respective approaches to filmmaking had in fact very little in common.

Murnau had bought a luxurious yacht, which he named the *Bali*, and planned to sail it to the South Seas, in his eyes an unspoilt paradise.

Flaherty, keen to revisit the islands where he had made *Moana*—and perhaps to exorcise memories of the *White Shadows* debacle—readily agreed to accompany him and offered as the first of a planned series of joint projects a story about pearl fishers exploited by local Chinese merchants. The film was budgeted at some $150,000, and a contract was signed with a newly established company, Colorart. At the end of April 1929 Murnau sailed for Tahiti, where Flaherty met him with the news that Colorart was bankrupt. Murnau, who had been well paid at Fox, decided to finance the film out of his own savings—thus giving himself the final say over what kind of film should be made.

Though far from an anthropological purist, Flaherty found himself increasingly unhappy over what he saw as Murnau's desire to impose a fictional plot and European cultural values on the Polynesian material. After some months he resigned from the project, leaving Murnau to complete the picture by himself. The disagreement, though profound, seems to have been without rancor; Flaherty always afterwards spoke of Murnau and his work with respect.

Just how much of *Tabu* (1931) should be attributed to Flaherty, credited as co-writer and co-director, is unclear. Most writers have agreed with Richard Griffith's assessment of the film as "a Murnau treasure, not a Flaherty one. . . . It is a beauty filtered and refracted through the imagination of a European of the twenties, who saw what he had come to see and had eyes for nothing else." Two young islanders, Matahi and Reri, fall in love. But Reri is a sacred virgin, consecrated to the gods, and when the lovers run away together they violate a powerful taboo. Hitu, the old priest-chief, pursues them and takes Reri back. Matahi, swimming desperately after their boat, is drowned.

As Gary Lewis noted (*Film Heritage*, Spring 1966), *Tabu*, like so many of Murnau's pictures, is "a film about Fate and Death . . . the ultimately metaphysical and tragic themes which always interested him." Robin Wood, considering *Nosferatu*, *Sunrise*, and *Tabu* as a trilogy, pointed out that each involves "three central figures: a couple, and a force that threatens to destroy them. In all three films the couple present no interpretative problems, but the 'force' remains to some extent mysterious . . . shadowy or equivocal in meaning." Jacques Fieschi (*Cinématographe*, February 1981) even saw the film as a Polynesian idyll recast in expressionist terms: "The face of the old priest is carved into an Expressionist Destiny. . . . From the joys and nightmares of Matahi, Murnau still extracts the ontological drama of his German protagonists."

For all its thematic consistency with the rest of Murnau's oeuvre, *Tabu* transports us into a new, idyllic world, a vision of the South Seas perhaps not as they were but as Murnau wanted to believe them to be, where lithe brown male bodies dive and disport through sun-dappled water, erotic in their prelapsarian innocence. The camera, intoxicated with light and movement, seems for long stretches to forget the slight, simple story around which it weaves its fascinated arabesques. As Lotte Eisner wrote: "The plot becomes a faint melody caught from time to time; finding its place like distant figures appearing in a landscape, like some desirable ornament."

Alexandre Astruc identified "the key to all of Murnau's work" as "this fatality hidden behind the most harmless elements in the frame." Even in this remote, sunlit paradise, Fate is omnipresent and inescapable. The shadow of old Hitu, falling across Reri's sleeping body, recalls that of Nosferatu cast on the wall outside Nina's room.

Most of *Tabu* was filmed with a nonprofessional cast on Tahiti, where Murnau had built a bungalow. He wrote to his mother: "When I think I shall have to leave all this I already suffer all the agony of going. I am bewitched by this place. . . . Sometimes I wish I were at home. But I am never 'at home' anywhere—I feel this more and more the older I get—not in any country nor in any house with anybody."

Before shooting was complete, money had run out. Flaherty came to the rescue, persuading Paramount to take the film on a fifty-fifty distribution deal. *Tabu* had been filmed silent; sound effects and a banal music track were added, to Murnau's annoyance, and the film opened to great critical acclaim. "Not a shot is displayed which does not concern and accentuate the story and the mood. . . . The landscape folds into the mood of the picture," Kenneth White wrote in *Hound and Horn*. Other reviewers were equally appreciative, and for once public and critical response were at one. *Tabu*, made in staunch independence, far from the crass commercial concerns of Hollywood, proved the sole boxoffice hit of Murnau's American career. But by the time it opened, on March 18, 1931, Murnau was no longer alive to savor the irony.

A week earlier, he had driven with friends up the coast from Los Angeles in a hired Rolls-Royce. A chauffeur came with the Rolls, but Murnau objected to him as "too ugly." One of his companions was Garcia Stevenson, a young Filipino whom Murnau had engaged as chauffeur on a forthcoming trip to Germany—more for his looks, apparently, than for his driving ability. Near Santa Barbara, Stevenson persuaded Murnau to let him take the wheel. The car went off the road and overturned, but all the passengers escaped unhurt—except Murnau. His head hit a post, and he died a few hours later.

According to Kenneth Anger, in *Hollywood Babylon*, rumors circulated round the movie colony that Murnau had been fellating the young Filipino at the time of the accident. Hollywood, scandal-conscious as ever, played safe; only eleven people attended the funeral. Among them were George O'Brien, Edgar Ulmer, and Greta Garbo, who for many years afterwards kept Murnau's death mask above her desk.

By general consent, Murnau ranks as one of the great film directors. Jean Domarchi, never one to balk at unqualified superlatives, called him "the most important filmmaker of the twentieth century . . . the greatest director of all time." Alexandre Astruc, with slightly more restraint, described him as "the greatest poet the screen has ever known . . . the most *magic* director in the history of the cinema." Fluid terms such as "magic," "poetic," "lyrical" constantly recur in critical comment on Murnau, suggesting perhaps that while almost everybody agrees that Murnau's work is masterly and highly influential, defining just what makes it so is rather less easy. Lotte Eisner, who considered him "the greatest film-director the Germans have ever known," linked his achievement to his melancholic, sexually tormented temperament: "He created the most overwhelming and poignant images in the whole German cinema. . . . All his films bear the impress of his own inner complexity, of the struggle he waged within himself against a world in which he remained despairingly alien."

The chief weakness of Murnau's films—apart from his inept handling of comedy—lies in his delineation of character. Set beside, say, *Greed, The Wind,* or *Die Büchse der Pandora*—to look no further than the work of his nearcontemporaries—no Murnau film can offer a single rounded, convincing character. Instead we are given simplified, universal figures; as Andrew Sarris put it: "His Everyman in *Faust, The Last Laugh, Sunrise,* and *Tabu* is no man in particular, and paradoxically, no man in general." It could be objected, though, that this is simply to say that Murnau's art, dealing as it does in mood, rhythm, and visual imagery, comes far closer to that of the painter, or even the composer, than to that of the novelist. (No one, after all, reproaches Monet or Chopin for failing to create rounded characters.) Robin Wood, arguing along these lines, observed that Murnau "shows remarkably little of the novelist's interest in the development and interaction of individualized characters. His characters are certainly not shallow—they are capable of the most intense and ultimate emotional commitments—but their depth is that of universal archetypes rather than of detailed individual studies."

The essentially nonverbal nature of Murnau's films may be partly what makes his achievement so difficult to define in words. His art at its finest is deliquescent—shifting, constantly in flux, evading the grasp. Attempts to fit him into neat pigeonholes—expressionist, *kammerspiel*—have had little success. The tendency, once common, to see him as a wholly formalist, artificial director—"a studio product, a manipulator of artificial effects, a manager of exaggeration, introspective, perverse: an artist who never smelt an honest wind in his life," in John Grierson's truculent judgement—now seems even more misguided than André Bazin's attempt to recruit him as a "realist."

Vague and unsatisfactory though the term is, "poetry" may perhaps sum up Murnau's work— if by poetry we understand the attempt to endow words, or in this case images, with the greatest possible resonance, to deepen and extend meaning beyond the readily expressible. Murnau, as many writers have noted, seems in his best work to be trying to show us more than we can see, to be about to seize the intangible. Even a relatively unsympathetic critic like Siegfried Kracauer recognized Murnau's "unique faculty of obliterating the boundaries between the real and the unreal. Reality in his films was surrounded by a halo of dreams and presentiments, and a tangible person might suddenly impress the audience as a mere apparition." Or, as Gilberto Perez Guillermo expressed it, "Nothing in his images quite accounts for their disturbing intensity, nothing in the physical world they display and no emotion that the characters feel. . . . We seem . . . to be inside the director's head; the gaze we turn towards things, charging them with an emotional significance which they don't possess in themselves, we sense as the gaze of the director himself."

Murnau would not have disowned such implications of subjectivity. In a phrase which anticipates Astruc's "caméra-stylo" and the theorists of auteurism, he once wrote: "The camera is the director's pencil. It should have the greatest possible mobility in order to record the most fleeting harmony of atmosphere." In this statement, perhaps, lies the key to Murnau's lasting cinematic influence, his twofold legacy to subsequent filmmakers. By "unchaining" the camera, he freed it to play a fluid, intimate role in a dynamically versatile narrative structure; and through his haunted, visionary, romantic temperament, he extended the scope of the cinema into a whole new territory of subtle, emotionally charged imagery, elusive and disconcertingly potent.

—*P.K.*

FILMS: Der Knabe in Blau (Der Todessmaragd/The Blue Boy), 1919; Satanas, 1919; Sehnsucht (Bajazzo/ Longing), 1920; Der Bucklige und die Tänzerin (The Hunchback and the Dancer), 1920; Der Januskopf (Schrecken/The Janus Head), 1920; Abend . . . Nacht . . . Morgen (Evening . . . Night . . . Morning), 1920; Der Gang in die Nacht (Journey into the Night), 1920; Marizza, genannt die Schmugglermadonna (Marizza, Called the Smugglers' Madonna), 1921; Schloss Vogelöd (The Haunted Castle), 1921; Nosferatu—Eine Symphonie des Gravens/Nosferatu the Vampire, 1922 (revised version, with sound, released as Die Zwölfte Stunde, 1930); Der Brennende Acker (The Burning Earth), 1922; Phantom, 1922; Die Austreibung (The Expulsion), 1923; Die Finanzen des Grossherzogs (The Finances of the Grand Duke), 1923; Der Letzte Mann (The Last Laugh), 1924; Tartüff (Tartuffe), 1926; Faust, 1926; Sunrise/A Song of Two Humans, 1927; Four Devils, 1928; City Girl (Our Daily Bread), 1930; with Robert Flaherty) Tabu, 1931. *Published scripts*—Faust in L'Avant-Scène du Cinéma, July–September 1977; *Der Letzte Mann* in Filmregie und Filmmanuskript by V. Pudovkin, 1928, *also* in L'Avant-Scène du Cinéma, July–September 1977; *Nosferatu* in Films of Tyranny edited by R. Byrne, 1966, *also* in Murnau by L. Eisner, Secker & Warburg 1973, *also* in Masterworks of the German Cinema, Lorrimer 1973, *also* in L'Avant-Scène du Cinéma, May 1979; *Sunrise* edited by H. Graap, Wiesbaden 1971, *also* in L'Avant-Scène du Cinéma, June 1974; *Tabu* in Film Culture 20, 1959; *Tartüff* in L'Avant-Scène du Cinéma, July–September 1977.

ABOUT: Barlow, J. D. German Expressionist Film, 1982; Desilets, E. M. F. W. Murnau's *Sunrise*: A Critical Study, 1979; Dittmar, P. F. W. Murnau: Eine Darstellung seiner Regie und seiner Stilmerkmale, 1962; Domarchi, J. Murnau, 1965 (in French); Eisner, L. The Haunted Screen, 1969; Eisner, L. Murnau, 1973; Huff, T. An Index to the Films of F. W. Murnau, 1948; Jacobs, L. The Rise of the American Film, 1939; Jameux, C. F. W. Murnau, 1965 (in French); Kracauer, S. From Caligari to Hitler, 1947; Lejeune, C. A. Cinema, 1931; Manvell, R. and Fraenkel, H. The German Cinema, 1971; Prawer, S. S. Caligari's Children: The Film as Tale of Terror, 1980; Robinson, D. Hollywood in the Twenties, 1968; Rohmer, E. L'Organisation de l'espace dans le Faust de Murnau, 1977; Rotha, P. The Film Till Now, 1930; Roud, R. (ed.) Cinema: a Critical Dictionary, 1980; Sarris, A. The American Cinema, 1968; Thomson, D. A Biographical Dictionary of the Cinema, 1980; Tone, P. G. F. W. Murnau, 1976 (in Italian); Whittemore, D. and Cecchettini, P. A. Passport to Hollywood, 1976. *Periodicals*—Avant-Scène du Cinéma June 1974, July–September 1977; Backtrack May–June 1968; Bianco e Nero April 1951, June 1953; Cahiers du Cinéma December 1952, March 1953, January 1958; Cahiers du Cinéma in English January 1966; Cinéma (France) May 1963, Cinema Journal

Spring 1985; March 1964; Cinemages 1/1 1955; Cinemasessanta March–April 1979; Cinématographe January 1977, February 1981; DIF March 1971; Film
(West Germany) June 1965; Film Comment Summer
1971, May–June 1976; Film Culture 20 1959; Film Da-
nas April–June 1959; Film Heritage Spring 1966; Film
und Fernsehen May 1981; Filmcritica July 1974; Filmfaust February 1979; Filmkritik September 1967; Image et Son 214 1968; Kosmorama April 1965; National
Film Theatre Booklet March 1981; Positif December
1966, February 1972; Quarterly of Film, Radio and
TV Spring 1955; Retro October 1983–February 1984;
Sight and Sound Summer 1967; Take One January–
February 1970.

MIKIO NARUSE

*NARUSE, MIKIO (August 20, 1905–July 2,
1969), Japanese director and scenarist, was born
in central Tokyo in the district now called
Wakabacho. He grew up there, in a family that
was never far from destitution, the third and
youngest child of an embroiderer and his wife.
Naruse was a bookish boy and an excellent student at his Wakabacho elementary school. He
would have liked an academic education at middle school, but this was financially out of the
question and instead he attended a two-year
technical school. His studies there bored him and
he sought solace in literature, developing a precocious enthusiasm for the works of Shusei
Tokuda and Toson Shimazaki, among others.

Naruse graduated from technical school in
1920, when he was fifteen. The death of his father ended any hope of a university education
and he had to find work. With a friend's introduction, Naruse got a job as a prop man at the
Kamata studios of the newly formed Shochiku
film company. Leaving home to live in rented
rooms near the studio, he was intensely lonely
and unhappy: "I had immediately to become an
adult," he said. "It was the darkest period of my
life." The pessimism of Naruse's films can readily be traced to the poverty and insecurity of his
childhood and the bleakness of his adolescence.
He acknowledged that "from the earliest age, I
have thought that the world we live in betrays
us; this thought still remains with me. . . .
Among the people in my films, there is definitely something of [this]. . . . If they move even a
little they quickly hit the wall."

But others have scrabbled their way free of
equally grim beginnings, and Naruse's nihilism
must be attributed in some measure to his own
temperament. He entered the film industry in
1920, when it was in a state of youthful ferment
and more forceful recruits climbed quickly to
directorial status at Shochiku. Naruse was handicapped in the intensely competitive world he
had entered by his obstinate humility and a

sulky reluctance to push himself forward—he
would always rather suffer in silence than demand his rights.

Naruse never made many friends, but those
he had, he kept, and it was their efforts rather
than his own that secured his painfully slow advancement. While he was still drudging in the
props department at Shochiku he struck up a
friendship with Yoshinobu Ikeda, who had
joined the company as an assistant director.
Naruse helped Ikeda to write his first script, and
in 1921, when the latter became a director (after
only a year at Shochiku), he took Naruse onto his
staff—at first as a general factotum and in 1922
as an assistant director.

Six years later Naruse was still Ikeda's assistant, while Ozu, Gosho, and others who had
joined the company after him were already
making their names. It has been suggested that
Shiro Kido, Shochiku's ebullient president, personally detested the morose Naruse, and ignored
the determinedly comic scripts he regularly submitted. Naruse was close to resigning when, in
1929, he made a fresh start by joining the staff
of his friend Heinosuke Gosho. The following
year he was given his first directorial assignment—a slapstick comedy short scripted by
Shiro Kido himself and called *Chambara fufu*
(*Mr. and Mrs. Swordplay*).

Kido denied the rumor that he disliked
Naruse, but the almost impossible shooting
schedule he gave him for his first movie throws
doubt on this. Characteristically, Naruse accepted Kido's intolerable conditions without complaint, cast the film the day he received the
script, chose locations the day after, and filmed

°nä rōō sä

for thirty-six hours without a break. At that point he collapsed, but the film (of which no trace survives), was edited for him by Gosho and was fairly successful, leaving Kido no choice but to give Naruse further assignments.

Junjo (Pure Love, 1930) was a medium-length movie aimed at the teenage market. It impressed Yasujiro Ozu, who said: "Someone who can do that well on only his second film has real directorial strength." The four pictures that followed during the next year were all made more or less to the Kido formula—an uneasy blend of slapstick and melodrama. But *Oshikiri shinkonki (A Record of Shameless Newlyweds,* 1930) brought Naruse further evidence of Kido's disapproval. He was accused of copying Ozu's style and the film was shelved for some months, leaving Naruse to search for a new kind of subject matter. He eventually found it in his own experience of life.

Throughout his years as a Shochiku director, Naruse received an insultingly low salary. His mother had died, his relations with his brother and sister were cool, and he had neither the money nor the inclination for a conventional middle-class social life. He rented a second-floor room from a family with a failing *sushi* business, moving with them to progressively poorer quarters in the new suburbs. Most of his spare cash went on lonely drinking sessions at a cheap restaurant, where he would spend hours watching the small dramas unfolding around him, and chatting with the waitresses. One of these fell in love with him and, when he ignored her letters, committed suicide. The tragedy was the subject of eager gossip in the film world, earning Naruse great hostility and increasing his sense of failure and isolation.

At this time, he was writing or originating most of his own scripts. Gradually he learned that, so long as he injected a ration of gags into each scenario, he could interest Kido in stories about the seedy world he knew best—life in the new Tokyo housing developments or in the old *shitamachi* ("lower city") of dark, back-to-back wooden houses, cheap bars, restaurants, and open-fronted stores unknown to tourists, where financial failure is never very far away. There are already signs that he had learned this lesson in *Nikai no himei (Screams From the Second Floor,* 1931), dealing with white-collar workers in one of the new suburbs.

Naruse took firm hold on this theme in his next picture, *Koshiben gambare (Flunky, Work Hard!,* 1931). It is a dark comedy about a desperately poor insurance salesman who plots and grovels frantically to sell accident coverage to a rich woman, but reassesses his priorities when his own uninsured child is injured by a train. During the next three years Naruse directed fourteen silent movies. Most of them are now lost, but they all seem to have blended in varying proportions the Shochiku mixture of comedy and melodrama, often with a touch of Naruse's own sad lyricism. And all were *shomin-geki*—stories of everyday life—dealing often with such *shitamachi* types as geishas and street musicians as well as the ill-paid "salarymen" and store clerks who were crowding into the new suburbs.

Of the few surviving examples of Naruse's Shochiku films, the most admired is *Kimi to wakarete (Apart From You,* 1933). It was made from his own script, though he had little faith in his abilities as a scenarist and by this time was writing very few of his own films. A youth, ashamed because his mother Kikue is a geisha, drifts into delinquency but is redeemed by the love of Teru, a young apprentice geisha. She takes him to visit her family on the coast and makes him understand the financial imperatives that have driven his mother (and herself) into the profession. Then, trapped by the family responsibilities that cripple so many of Naruse's characters, she has to leave him for more lucrative work elsewhere.

The aging geisha Kikue is observed with great sympathy, as in her dawning panic when, searching the mirror for gray hairs, she finds there are simply too many to pluck out; and later when, slighted by her patron in favor of a younger woman, she gets pathetically drunk: there are many characters like Kikue in Naruse's mature films. And Teru is an early sketch for the typical Naruse heroine. There is still something in her of the woman-as-martyr that Shiro Kido favored, but there is also a kind of irrational courage that refuses to accept the hopelessness of her situation, and is pure Naruse.

Apart From You is significant in form as well as content. Naruse's earlier films, following the fashion of the time, had been full of the acrobatic camera movements, trick transitions, and rapid montage sequences copied from Russian and European models. *Apart From You* shows him (like Ozu at the same period) beginning to pare down his effects in pursuit of a chastely unassertive style that would not distract the spectator from his close scrutiny of his characters' slightest movements and changes of expression.

In 1934 Naruse finally gave up on Shochiku and joined PCL, which three years later merged with another company to form Toho. He made his first talkie in 1935, and had his first major success the same year with *Tsuma yo bara no yo ni (Wife! Be Like a Rose!),* scripted by himself. The heroine is a "modern" girl (Sachiko Chiba) who works in an office and lives with her mother, a poet. Her runaway father has set up house with a former geisha in the country, but the heroine, about to marry, is determined that he should come home and face up to his responsibilities. She is less certain when she visits him and finds him living in happy rural poverty with two children and a devoted mistress. He comes to the city for her wedding, but it is clear that his heart is elsewhere, and equally clear that her mother is better at writing odes to an idealized notion of her spouse than living with him in the imperfect flesh. In the end, the father returns to his other family with his daughter's blessing.

The year's winner in *Kinema Jumpo*'s annual poll and a box-office success as well, the movie was the first Japanese film to be shown in the United States. It introduced, in the heroine's poet mother, what one critic called "the comic prototype for the more fully developed, exacting, perfection-seeking women" of Naruse's major films. This "lightest" and "most urbane" of the director's works has been criticized by Joan Mellen for its scornful caricature of a woman who puts her emotions into her art instead of her marriage, and its evident approval of the self-sacrificing *hausfrau* mistress—a "reactionary" view that would be reversed in Naruse's later work.

Meanwhile, in 1937, the melancholy loner Naruse astonished his colleagues by marrying the vivacious star of *Wife! Be Like a Rose!*, Sachiko Chiba. The marriage lasted seven years and produced a child, after which Naruse returned to the life of rented rooms and bars until, many years later, he quietly remarried. Throughout the period of his troubled marriage and indeed for a long time after it, Naruse produced very little of any real merit—Anderson and Richie in *The Japanese Film* called this "the most serious . . . [slump] any major director has ever experienced."

One bright spot, however, in this period is *Tsuruhachi Tsurujiro* (*Tsuruhachi and Tsurujiro*, 1938), a film only recently discovered in the West. A young ballad singer (matinee idol Kazuo Hasegawa) and a female samisen player (Isuzu Yamada), students with the same instructor, form a popular duo near the turn of the century. Despite their harmony in performance, they bicker constantly backstage. Believing that the singer dislikes her, Tsuruhachi marries a favorite patron, thus breaking up the act. Tsurujiro's career quickly declines, and finally their old instructor asks the samisen player to help save her former partner. After their reunion, she realizes the true nature of their feelings for one another; sensing danger in this, Tsurujiro picks

a quarrel with her and makes her return to her husband. Audie Bock writes that "as the militaristic spirit that would culminate in the Pacific War intensified, the 'performing artists piece' became more and more common as a means of avoiding censorship, but Naruse manages in this film to give the genre remarkable freshness with his own script and the unusually fine acting he elicits from Hasagawa."

Naruse succeeded better than most of his colleagues in avoiding the propaganda features of the period. *Hataraku ikka* (*The Whole Family Works*, 1939), a "national policy" film depicting a family's struggle to survive during the Depression, makes almost ironic use of contemporary patriotic posters. Among the characters is a boy who dreams of becoming a soldier simply because soldiers are well fed. Audie Bock regards this film as "one of the best from Japan in this era." Naruse directed only one straightforward propaganda piece, shown to the troops abroad, and one historical film, *Sanjusangendo toshiya monogatari* (*A Tale of Archery at the Sanjusangendo*), made in Kyoto at the very end of the war and probably never released.

After the war, Japanese filmmakers found themselves under new pressures, ordered by the American occupation authorities to make movies celebrating the virtues of democracy. Naruse directed two such pictures during this "noisy age" (as he called it), neither of much interest. He left Toho in the midst of the company's labor troubles of the late 1940s and became a freelance, making for various companies a further series of indifferent movies. The first of his postwar films to give him any pleasure was the regional comedy *Ishinaka sensei gyojoki* (*Conduct Report on Professor Ishinaka*, 1950). In 1950 he joined the short-lived Motion Picture Art Association, an independent company formed by Akira Kurosawa, Kajiro Yamamoto, and others.

Naruse finally emerged from his fifteen-year slump with *Ginza gesho* (*Ginza Cosmetics*, 1951), about a bar hostess approaching middle age, her struggles to support herself and her daughter, and the brief flowering of hope when she meets a rich and poetic young man from the country. Then he falls in love with a younger woman, and harsh reality reasserts itself. Naruse and his scenarist Matsuo Kishi both knew the Ginza bars well and this movie, sentimental as it often is, has the feel of truth. It was at this point, Naruse said later, that things began to improve for him—"It seemed to suit my temperament. I seemed to have relaxed."

In fact, *Ginza Cosmetics* had taken Naruse back to the world he knew best and to his favorite theme: "women on their own," usually enmeshed in family responsibilities that force them into occupations frowned on by society—virtually the only ones available to unmarried or widowed women in Japan. There is no way out of this trap for Naruse's heroines: "If they move even a little they quickly hit the wall." They may succumb to fleeting illusions of love and security, but they can never close their eyes for long to the hopelessness of their situations, the inadequacy of their lovers. But these women never give up. As Audie Bock says, "it is always their own limitations they are pushing, their own ideals they are testing." They are not pathetic like Mizoguchi's self-sacrificing heroines, but tough, willful, and demanding.

The married women in Naruse's films are no better off than their single sisters: they may have more security, but they have even less freedom. The first of his mature *shomin-geki* about "the petrification of a marriage" was *Meshi (Repast,* 1951), adapted from a novel left unfinished at her death by Fumiko Hayashi (1904–1951). Made under the editorial supervision of the novelist Yasunari Kawabata, later a Nobel prizewinner, it is a subtle study of a childless couple living in the Osaka suburbs. The husband (Ken Uehara) is a "salaryman"—a low-paid white-collar worker, dull and apparently unfeeling, bored after five years of marriage. Poor as they are, he treats himself to expensive new shoes and, when his pretty niece comes to visit, begins an affair with her.

The wife (Setsuko Hara), equally disappointed by the marriage, has no money for treats and is too virtuous for extramarital romance. She drudges self-righteously at her housework until she discovers her husband and his niece in a compromising situation. Freed by this treachery, she runs off to her parents' house in Tokyo, dreaming of a new life. But there are no jobs to be had in Tokyo, she denies herself a possible love affair, and her mother nags her to rejoin her husband. When the latter, recognizing his dependence on her, comes after her, she realizes that his life is as unrewarding as her own and that they at least have habit in common. She decides that "my happiness is seeking happiness with him."

Repast came second in the *Kinema Jumpo* poll and is regarded by many as one of Naruse's finest films. It seemed to John Gillett marred by "a typically '50s music score" and a banal final scene, but he thought it nevertheless showed Naruse's "mastery in composition and cutting—the movement around the little living room and kitchen area, the selective use of close-ups, and the feeling for an atmospheric sequence (like the coming of the storm) which also tells a good deal about the characters' emotional and psychological states." Joan Mellen disliked the resignation of the conclusion but, comparing it favorably to a similar work by Ozu (*Ochazuke*), described Naruse as "a man of more ambiguous and complex sensibility" than his more famous contemporary, with " a sympathy with the trials of the Japanese woman of which Ozu was incapable."

Mellen was less kind to *Okasan (Mother,* 1952), which in her view "almost obscenely" idealizes the Japanese woman in her domestic role. Scripted by Yoko Mizuki and based on the winning story in a competition for children, it is nevertheless one of the sunniest and most popular of Naruse's films, and has been widely seen abroad. Kinuyo Tanaka, Mizoguchi's favorite actress, plays the madonna-like mother, forced to send her youngest daughter away to live with childless relatives as she struggles to run her late husband's dry-cleaning business.

Naruse warmed to this simple and shamelessly sentimental theme, for once allowing his characters a happy ending. The picture is further brightened by *jeux d'esprit* of a sort rare in his work. At one point the bewildered audience is suddenly confronted with scenes that have apparently been shot upside down, and then discovers that it is seeing the world as it appears to a little boy standing on his head. Later, just as the film's various themes are reaching a climax, "The End" flashes on the screen. Again the audience is aghast—until it realizes that it has joined the characters in a movie theatre, from which they emerge to work the story out to its end.

Another *Kinema Jumpo* "Number Two" followed the same year in *Inazuma (Lightning)*. This was Naruse's second adaptation of a work by Fumiko Hayashi, whose childhood had been as impoverished as his own and who shared his compassion for what she called "the pitiful assiduousness of human beings" in a hostile universe, as well as his particular interest in the stubborn courage of downtrodden women. Though he never met her, Naruse seems to have regarded Hayashi as a kind of soul-mate, and is said to have behaved like a man bereaved when, having based six films on her novels and stories, he had to face the fact that "there's nothing left of Hayashi's any more."

In *Lightning* we encounter a whole gallery of Naruse women. Osei, a weak-willed natural victim, has four children by as many fathers. There are two married daughters—one as helpless as her mother, the other more predatory—and a spoiled and lazy son. The fourth child is Kiyoko, played by Naruse's favorite actress Hideko Takamine, with whom he made seventeen films in twenty-five years. Attractive, but still unmarried in her early twenties, Kiyoko lives with her mother and half-brother, and works as a bus conductor. Pressed to accept the marriage proposal of a lewd but wealthy middle-aged baker, and realizing that she is being used as sexual bait by her own family, Kiyoko finally moves away to lodgings in the suburbs, where her escape from the *shitamachi* world to one more cultured and genteel is symbolized for her by the Western piano music she hears coming from the house next door. Greedy and manipulative as they are, Kiyoko's relatives are portrayed without contempt and indeed with some humor and affection, as in the final reconciliation (not in the original novel) between Kiyoko and her mother.

Lightning is a sprawling film, with little in the way of a conventional dramatic structure. What is has instead, according to Audie Bock, is Naruse's "finely woven continuity and Sumie Tanaka's eloquently understated dialogue. . . . As inconclusive as Naruse's marriage cycle films, it deals with the same narrow, virtually static world of the home and family that Ozu portrayed, but in a very different and disapproving way. . . . Much of the atmosphere . . . resides in nonverbal effects. . . . The lonely sounding *chindonya* (parading costumed musicians who publicize the opening of a new small business establishment), children playing in alleyways, and sounds of street vendors' calls create the world and the mood of the Naruse film. It is the . . . [*shitamachi*] atmosphere—poor, crowded, traditional . . . that comforts at the same time it imprisons the poor."

The marriage cycle to which Bock refers continued with *Fufu (Husband and Wife,* 1953), planned as a sequel to *Repast* and starring Ken Uehara and Yoko Sugi as a married couple living in a rented room and slowly drifting apart. The trilogy ended with Naruse's next Hayashi adaptation, *Tsuma (Wife,* 1953), with Uehara again playing the "salaryman" husband and Mieko Takamine as the wife who battles desperately to save their dying marriage. "One knows the house in *Wife* architecturally," wrote Donald Richie, "for emotionally we have spent an hour and a half in it. The atmosphere becomes palpable; the same kind of shot, from the same general angle, appears again and again. Monotony is successfully suggested, but one is kept from monotony through the interest one feels in character and story and, perhaps most important, in structure."

Richie goes on to discuss the way Naruse's single theme—"the petrification of a marriage"—is enriched by using it as a minor as well as a major theme: "Thus early in the film the troubles of the couple upstairs are a presage of what eventually occurs downstairs. . . . This canon-like structure—all themes being segments of the same theme—creates a number of parallels which both continue and intensify our interest. At the same time it adds an ironic flavour to the film. Naruse forces us that step backwards towards objectivity which ensures interest yet thwarts our native sentimentality." Speaking no doubt out of his own bitter experience, Naruse himself said of these three "marriage cycle" films that they "have little that happens in them and end without a conclusion—just like life."

By this time, Naruse had not only found his *metier* and his strength but, having returned to Toho, had assembled there a team of collaborators accustomed to his peculiar working methods. Most of his scripts at this time were written by either Sumie Tanaka (who found him extremely strict, unhelpful and ungracious, but says she nevertheless learned from him everything she knew about scriptwriting) or Yoko Mizuki (who thought him the easiest person in the world to work with). From 1952 to 1964 almost all of the music he used so unobtrusively in his films was composed by Ichiro Saito, and his favorite cameraman at this time was Masao Tamai, who plain style was perfectly in accord with Naruse's insistence that nothing should distract the audience from total concentration on the actors.

According to a note prepared at the Tokyo Film Center, Naruse in his postwar films had purged his style of camera movements (except for tracking shots of two people conversing as they walk) and of variety for its own sake in his choice of camera angles, limiting himself to 90° and 45° level shots. This required him (like Ozu) to use a large number of shots—about 570 in the 85 minutes of *Lightning,* for example. These many transitions are unobtrusive "because of the restricted angles and locations. Both Ozu and Naruse follow traditional methods of changing time and place—with fadeouts, music or sound over, and a sequence of establishing shots with a gradual progression from long shot to medium closeup for dialogue. Like Ozu, Naruse prefers a restricted setting"—he was always happiest filming in the interior of a small Japanese house, where his "relentless" camera could observe every nuance of his characters' behavior.

All this placed great responsibility on his actors, who nevertheless received no guidance from Naruse, being expected to develop their own interpretations. If Naruse was dissatisfied, they would be asked to try again and again until the director decided that nothing better was going to emerge. Tatsuya Nakadai called him "the most difficult director I ever worked for. He never said a word. A real nihilist." But Hideko Takamine, who seemed to know intuitively what Naruse wanted, did some of her finest work for him. He was equally uncommunicative with his other collaborators, never giving praise or blame, and often accepting inferior or unsuitable work rather than make a fuss. Kurosawa, Naruse's assistant on the 1937 *Avalanche,* also thought him "the hardest director of all to work under," though he admires his films.

Naruse had two more successes in 1954, both of them among *Kinema Jumpo's* "Best Ten." *Yama no oto (Sound of the Mountain),* adapted from the Kawabata novel by Yoko Mizuki, was shot partly in the studio, with sets modeled on Kawabata's own house, and partly on location near the house itself. Setsuko Hara plays a married woman whose bored husband has a child by another woman while she herself has an abortion. Only her odd, tender relationship with her father-in-law gives her the courage to survive. Anderson and Richie found it outstanding in the way that Naruse's "microscopic" use of the camera reveals emotions the characters themselves are trying to hide. There was similar praise for *Bangiku (Late Chrysanthemums),* which draws on three short stories by Fumiko Hayashi and returns to a subject Naruse had first explored twenty years earlier in *Apart From You*—the loneliness and emotional insolvency that awaits the geisha once her youth has passed.

The most popular and successful of all Naruse's films followed in *Ukigumo (Floating Clouds),* which topped the *Kinema Jumpo* poll in 1955. Another Hayashi adaptation, it is a study of *amour fou.* Hideko Takamine plays Yukiko, a young nurse who falls in love with a sardonic forestry expert (Masayuki Mori) while they are both stationed in Indonesia during the Pacific War. In Tokyo after the war they meet again and Yukiko discovers that her lover is married. Jobless and penniless, she offers herself to him nevertheless, and is rejected as an embarrassment. She turns to prostitution, grows bitter, but cannot forget him. Later, when she is desperately ill with tuberculosis and he is financially ruined, she steals money for him and joins him on the remote island where he has taken a job, knowing that the climate will kill her. She dies there in his arms.

What lifts the story above melodrama is Yukiko's clear-sighted realism. She knows perfectly well that her lover is selfish, weak, and insensitive—that she has little chance of happiness with him—but she accepts the risks and makes her existential commitment with her eyes open. As Audie Bock says, the movie reflects Naruse's "admiration for human obstinacy and irrational-ity as a kind of courage in the face of meaninglessness." It is said to have been a very important film to Nagisa Oshima, who paid his own homage to *amour fou* in *Empire of Passion.*

With his next assignment, an episode in a Toho portmanteau film called *Kuchizuke (The Kiss,* 1955), Naruse recognized that he was on the verge of another slump. Two relatively weak films followed, and then Naruse recovered his self-confidence with *Nagareru (Flowing,* 1956), about the postwar decline of the geisha tradition into simple prostitution. The hopeless struggle against this decline by a proud but aging geisha is observed by her humble maid (Kinuyo Tanaka), though as one critic said "the observing eyes" are really Naruse's own, "clear and cold," while the geisha's "determined and critical daughter speaks for him."

At the end of *Flowing,* the maid (and the audience) knows that the geisha house is sold, that there is only a little time left, though her employer is still full of hope for the future. Donald Richie sees "a kind of beauty, a kind of strength" in this "fortunate innocence," doomed as it is, and elsewhere describes the film's conclusion, which is entirely without dialogue: "We leave the geisha house and move backwards, as it were, along the river, down to the sea—by showing us more Naruse has suddenly begun to show us less as the camera leaves behind those we know and care about. At the same time the tempo slows and finally stops. The film unravels as though its very restrictions can no longer hold it together—both spatially and temporally the picture dissolves into that great, final and only true restriction: nothingness."

For this film Naruse had the services of all his favorite collaborators, and virtually the same team worked with him on *Arakure (Untamed,* 1957), adapted by Yoko Mizuki from a novel by Shusei Tokuda. It opens in the 1920s when Oshima (Hideko Takamine), having walked out on her first husband on their wedding night, makes a second marriage to a lazy, nagging, and unfaithful grocer. Rejected by him when she has a miscarriage, Oshima eventually takes the startling step (for a Japanese woman) of launching her own tailoring business. Tireless (and tyrannical) though she is, the shop fails but Oshima starts again with a rented sewing machine and makes enough money to revive her business on more successful lines. She begins a love affair with an enterprising and talented young employee, and the film ends with her full of hope, striding through the rain under a new umbrella.

"Naruse's style is that of the chronicler," wrote Joan Mellen, "his editing workmanlike but undramatic, his shot compositions adequate but nowhere approaching the visualization of woman's servitude we find in Mizoguchi. Instead, Naruse relies on full, close shots of Takamine as she is struck by each new blow of her husband's arrogance. Each episode of her oppression is punctuated by the unambiguous determinism of the fade." At the end, "in long shot we finally lose sight of her, if not of her spirit. She is all that the Japanese woman—and all women—can be. She has never flinched from paying the price of her freedom, including facing the indignation of women less courageous than she."

It must be said that other critics found Oshima unattractive in her ruthless "egoism" and (in Takamine's performance) not without "a quality of neuroticism." Naruse himself remarked in a 1960 interview that "the people won't turn out for stories about a strong, independent woman. The audience prefers and is pleased only with stories about a weak woman's torment and abuse. But I shared none of their feelings that untraditional women are unattractive, that strong-hearted women are despicable and disgusting."

There is another "strong-hearted" woman in *Onna ga Kaidan o Agaru Toki (When a Woman Ascends the Stairs, 1960)*, though in this case her strength is insufficient to overcome the obstacles placed in her way by society. Takamine here plays the proprietess of a bar in the Ginza, beset by creditors and intense competition, and handicapped by her loyalty to her dead husband. Worn down by the struggle, she allows herself to fall in love with an affluent executive (Masayuki Mori) who seems to offer an escape. He gives her money but won't in the end leave his wife. When he is posted to Osaka, she returns his gifts and, once more, wearily climbs the stairs to her bar— an ascent that is really a descent.

Naruse's subsequent output was uneven in quality but includes several interesting works. *Horoki (Lonely Lane, 1962)* is an adaptation of Fumiko Hayashi's autobiography and a clear labor of love for the director. In this sixth and final adaptation of Hayashi's writings, he traces his favorite author's life from her menial jobs and first encounters with leftist writers through her failed loves and marriages, impoverished solitude, and eventual success as a writer, to her death from overwork while writing *Repast*. Her most outstanding quality throughout is her single-mindedness. Naruse's affinity for this woman who felt compelled to go it alone after many difficult relationships becomes clear in the course of the film: Philip Lopate calls *Lonely Lane* the director's "final, beautiful tribute to her." About Hideko Takamine, who played the lead and considered it her favorite Naruse role,

Lopate writes, "The quintessential Naruse actress was Hideko Takamine . . . who was certainly as important to Naruse's realization of his vision as was Fūmiko Hayashi. This beautiful star has large, vulnerable, somewhat prideful eyes given to flashes of obstinacy and annoyance. . . . In what is probably her greatest performance, the autobiographical film about Fumiko Hayashi, . . . Takamine even succeeds in making herself look homely, curling her mouth into a sarcastic grimace as she threads her way through Tokyo's literary bohemia, sloughing off insults and condescension or retaliating when it suits her, contrarily falling in love with the wrong men. In all of Takamine's roles, her face shows so abjectly when she is fond of a man that the object of her desires starts taking her for granted right away. He would be wrong to think her easily gotten rid of, however, because a Takamine character in love can be quite a nuisance."

Two years and one more failure later, Naruse made the melodramatic *Midareru (Yearning, 1964)*, a very believable depiction of a war widow who has continued living with her in-laws for the eighteen years following her husband's death, and her relationship with her late husband's wild younger brother. Audie Bock writes, "This film because of its theme becomes one of the best for studying Naruse's techniques of directing nonverbal communication, through glances and body-language revealing the thoughts of the would-be lovers and the hypocrisy of the family. It is also a contemporary problem film, as are many of Naruse's late works, in that it shows the changes taking place in provincial life with the advent of such modern conveniences as the supermarket, and the failure of the traditional values held by the heroine to help her cope with new emotions in this setting."

Midaregumo (Scattered Clouds, 1967), Naruse's final film, placed fourth on the *Kinema Jumpo* annual poll. It concerns a pregnant woman whose husband is killed by a car. Her financial woes, abortion, and chance meetings with the car's driver permit Naruse to develop a keen analysis of her character. Audie Bock rates *Scattered Clouds* "among . . . [Naruse's] finest. . . . Yumiko represents the final transition of the Naruse heroine from the proud, self-sufficient woman whose men aren't good enough for her, to the woman whose experience of life is so painful that she chooses to remain alone. . . . The bleakness of this tale, so delicately and beautifully told, must reflect something of Naruse's own feelings when he was facing the end of his life."

Naruse's works after 1960 never equaled the

products of his great creative burst of the 1950s, showing less control and more sentimentality, though most had moments of clearsighted psychological perception. Shortly before his death in 1969 he told Hideko Takamine that his conception of the ideal film would be one with no exteriors and no sets—only actors working in front of white backdrops.

Naruse's pessimism alienated some critics, and his feminism others. Having produced no major works in his last years, he was already half-forgotten by the time of his death. It is only recently that his work has been rediscovered and reassessed. Many consider him the equal—or even the superior—of his contemporaries Ozu and Mizoguchi. Unlike them, "he never lets go of the human," and his films have reminded critics of the work of Satyajit Ray and the Italian neorealists. "It is the honesty with which Naruse treats his theme that commands our respect," wrote Anderson and Richie; "it is his faithfulness to this theme which creates his style; and it is our suspicion that, painful though it be, he is telling the truth, that creates his greatness."

FILMS: (The source of this filmography is Audie Bock's *Japanese Film Directors,* 1978.) Chambara fufu (Mr. and Mrs. Swordplay), 1930 (short); Junjo (Pure Love), 1930; Fukeiki jidai (Hard Times), 1930; Ai wa chikara da (Love Is Strength), 1930; Oshikiri shinkonki (A Record of Shameless Newlyweds), 1930; Nee kofun shicha iya yo (Now Don't Get Excited), 1931; Nikai no himei (Screams From the Second Floor), 1931; Koshiben gambare (Flunky, Work Hard), 1931; Uwaki wa kisha ni notte (Fickleness Gets on the Train), 1931; Hige no chikara (The Strength of a Moustache), 1931; Tonari no yane no shita (Under the Neighbors' Roof), 1931; Onna wa tamoto o goyojin (Ladies, Be Careful of Your Sleeves), 1932; Aozora ni naku (Crying to the Blue Sky), 1932; Eraku nare (Be Great!), 1932; Mushibameru haru (Motheaten Spring), 1932; Chokoreito garu (Chocolate Girl), 1932; Nasanu naka (Not Blood Relations), 1932; Kimi to wakarete (Apart From You), 1933; Yogoto no yume (Every Night Dreams), 1933; Boku no marumage (A Man With a Married Woman's Hairdo), 1933; Sobo (Two Eyes), 1933; Kagirinaki hodo (Street Without End), 1934; Otome-gokoro sannin shimai (Three Sisters With Maiden Hearts), 1935; Joyu to shijin (The Actress and the Poet), 1935; Tsuma yo bara no yo ni (Wife! Be Like a Rose!/Kimiko), 1935; Sakasu gonin-gumi (Five Men in the Circus), 1935; Uwasa no musume (The Girl in the Rumor), 1935; Tochuken kumoemon (Kumoemon Tochuken), 1936; Kimi to iku michi (The Road I Travel With You), 1936; Asa no namikimichi (Morning's Tree-Lined Street), 1936; Nyonin aishu (A Woman's Sorrows), 1937; Nadare (Avalanche), 1937; Kafuku (Learn From Experience), 1937 (in two parts); Tsuruhachi Tsurujiro (Tsuruhachi and Tsurujiro), 1938; Hataraku ikka (The Whole Family Works), 1939; Magokoro (Sincerity), 1939; Tabi yakusha (Traveling Actors), 1940; Natsukashi no kao (A Face From the Past), 1941; Shanhai

no tsuki (Shanghai Moon), 1941; Hideko no shasho-san (Hideko the Bus Conductor), 1941; Haha wa shinazu (Mother Never Dies), 1942; Uta andon (The Song Lantern), 1943; Tanoshiki kana jinsei (This Happy Life), 1944; Shibaido (The Way of Drama), 1944; Shori no hi made (Until Victory Day), 1945; Sanjusangendo toshiya monogatari (A Tale of Archery at the Sanjusangendo), 1945; Urashima Taro no koei (The Descendants of Taro Urashima), 1946; Ore mo omae mo (Both You and I), 1946; Wakare mo tanoshi (Even Parting Is Enjoyable) *episode in* yottsu no koi no monogatari (Four Love Stories), 1947; Haru no mezame (Spring Awakens), 1947; Furyo shojo (Delinquent Girl), 1949; Ishinaka sensei gyojoki (Conduct Report on Professor Ishinaka), 1950; Ikari no machi (The Angry Street), 1950; Shiroi yaju (White Beast), 1950; Bara gassen (The Battle of Roses), 1950; Ginza gesho (Ginza Cosmetics), 1951; Maihime (Dancing Girl), 1951; Meshi (Repast), 1951; Okuni to Gohei (Okuni and Gohei), 1952; Okasan (Mother), 1952; Inazuma (Lightning), 1952; Fufu (Husband and Wife), 1953; Tsuma (Wife), 1953; Ani imoto (Older Brother, Younger Sister), 1953; Yama no oto (Sound of the Mountain), 1954; Bangiku (Late Chrysanthemums), 1954; Ukigumo (Floating Clouds), 1955; Onna doshi (Women's Ways) *episode in* Kuchizuke (The Kiss), 1955; Shu-u (Sudden Rain), 1956; Tsuma no kokoro (A Wife's Heart), 1956; Nagareru (Flowing), 1956; Arakure (Untamed Woman/Untamed), 1957; Anzukko, 1958; Iwashigumo (Herringbone Clouds), 1958; Kotan no kuchibue (Whistling in Kotan/A Whistle in My Heart), 1959; Onna ga kaidan o agaru toki (When a Woman Ascends the Stairs), 1960; Musume tsuma haha (Daughters, Wives and a Mother), 1960; (with Yuzo Kawashima) Yoru no nagare (Evening Stream), 1960; Aki tachinu (The Approach of Autumn), 1960; Tsuma toshite onna toshite (As a Wife, As a Woman/ The Other Woman), 1961; Onna no za (Woman's Status), 1962; Horoki (Lonely Lane/Her Lonely Lane/A Wanderer's Notebook), 1962; Onna no rekishi (A Woman's Story), 1963; Midareru (Yearning), 1964; Onna no naka ni iru tanin (The Stranger Within a Woman/The Thin Line), 1966; Hikinige (Hit and Run/Moment of Terror), 1966; Midaregumo (Scattered Clouds/Two in the Shadow), 1967.

ABOUT: Anderson, J. L. and Richie, D. The Japanese Film, 1959; Bock, A. Japanese Film Directors, 1978; Bock, A. Mikio Naruse: A Master of the Japanese Cinema (booklet published by the Film Center of the Chicago Art Institute), 1984; Burch, N. To the Distant Observer, 1979; Mellen, J. The Waves at Genji's Door, 1976; Richie, D. Japanese Cinema, 1971; Roud, R. (ed.) Cinema: A Critical Dictionary, 1980; Sato, T. Currents in Japanese Cinema, 1982; Tessier, M. Images du Cinema Japonais, 1981. *Periodicals*—Cahiers du Cinéma February 1983; Film Quarterly Summer 1986; Positif January 1984; Revue du Cinéma February 1984.

NEGULESCO, JEAN (February 29, 1900–), American director and producer, was born at Craiova, Romania, where at the age of twelve (according to his publicists) he won a prize as the nation's most brilliant primary school pupil. Two years later he ran away from home and, on the advice of an old sculptor who befriended him, made his way to Paris. There he washed dishes, scrubbed floors, and eavesdropped eagerly on the conversations of the artists and bohemians who patronized the cafés where he worked.

With the outbreak of World War I in 1914, Negulesco went home. After service as a front-line hospital orderly, he began his first career as a self-taught and apparently highly successful painter—it is claimed that all one hundred and fifty pictures in his first exhibition sold within three days. Thus financed, Negulesco resumed his travels, visiting Constantinople, Greece, and Italy before making his way back to France. In Paris he found unorthodox employment with an art school, touring the cafés to bad-mouth all the other academies. He quit when he won an income of fifty francs a month in a drawing contest, and for a time worked for little or no pay designing sets for the avant-garde theatres that flourished in postwar Paris.

Returning once more to Romania, Negulesco held a second exhibition of his work, which was now decidedly modernist. Romania was not ready for the new Negulesco. The exhibition not only failed but created a scandal. His father barred him from the house, there was no work to be found, and Negulesco returned to Paris.

All this information is drawn from studio press releases. However, in his interview in Higham and Greenberg's *The Celluloid Muse*, Negulesco omits most of the details summarized above, saying merely that he "lived and worked as an artist for fifteen years in Paris" prior to 1929; "Brancusi [also a Romanian expatriate] was my teacher, and about 1918 I got to know Modigliani, spending a lot of time in his studio."

In 1929, at any rate (or in 1927 according to some accounts), Negulesco went to the United States, where he had arranged exhibitions in New York and elsewhere. He was already intensely interested in the cinema, and made his first Hollywood contacts when he visited California and painted portraits of Dolores del Rio and other stars. An exhibition in Seattle earned Negulesco $19,000, which he invested in his first film, *Three and a Day*, written and directed by himself. His technical ignorance was such that none of the sequences matched, but twenty-one cans of film reportedly still repose in the vault of a Hollywood storage company.

JEAN NEGULESCO

Negulesco's expensive gamble was not entirely wasted. His friend Mischa Auer, who had appeared in *Three and a Day*, introduced him to the Paramount director Frank Tuttle. Negulesco began his professional film career as technical director on Tuttle's *This Is the Night* (1932), starring Lily Damita _(and introducing Cary Grant). Thereafter he worked in various capacities till the end of the 1930s for Paramount and Universal, "doing second-unit things, working mainly on camera angles because of my painter's pictorial sense." Negulesco was credited as second-unit director on Frank Borzage's *A Farewell to Arms* (1933), assistant director of Harlan Thompson's *Kiss and Make Up* (1934), second-unit director of Michael Curtiz's *Captain Blood* (1935), and director of the action sequences in William Nigh's *Crash Donovan* (1936).

From 1933 to 1935 Negulesco also served as assistant to the Paramount producer Benjamin Glazer. He says that "being an assistant producer was a little more complicated than being an assistant director. I acted as a sort of a go-between between the producer and the director because they were usually feuding. However, I gained an extraordinary amount of experience through that, because I sat in on every story conference, fought over the cutting of pictures with the editor in the cutting-room, and examined all the rushes in detail." In the late 1930s, Negulesco turned to scriptwriting, collaborating on the scenarios of *Expensive Husbands* (1937), *Fight for Your Lady* (1937), *The Beloved Brat* (1938), *Swiss Miss* (1938), and *Rio* (1939).

In 1940 Negulesco was hired by Warner Brothers as a director of short subjects, beginning with *Flag of Humanity,* a "Technicolor Special" about Clara Barton and the Red Cross. Between then and 1944, Negulesco directed fifty short films in various Warner Brothers series: "Melody Masters" (showcasing the talents of such as the Carioca Serenaders, the Don Cossack Chorus, and Borrah Minnevitch and His Harmonica School); "Featurettes" (like *Alice in Movieland,* with Joan Leslie); and "Brevities" (*The Spirit of Annapolis, The Spirit of West Point*). It was two shorts made in 1942 in the "Technicolor Special" series that attracted most attention—*Gaieté Parisienne* (*The Gay Parisian*) and *Capriccio Espagnol* (*Spanish Fiesta*), both featuring Léonide Massine's Ballet Russe de Monte Carlo. Though the dance critic Arlene Croce has complained that "Negulesco competes with Massine in bravura and cancels every choreographic effect," these two movies were almost the first ever devoted to ballet performances specially staged for the camera; in 1942 they were received with great enthusiasm, and then and for years afterwards were very widely shown.

Negulesco was of course avid to direct full-length features. He says in *The Celluloid Muse* that Warners originally assigned him to direct *The Maltese Falcon,* but replaced him after two months' work when John Huston asserted a prior claim. The same year, 1941, he directed part of *Singapore Woman,* a B-movie about the romance between a rubber planter and a café singer starring Brenda Marshall, David Bruce, and Virginia Field. Though Negulesco was credited as the film's director, he was in fact fired in midproduction and returned to the salt mines of "Technicolor Specials" and "Melody Masters."

His moment finally came in 1944, when Warners put him to work on *The Mask of Dimitrios,* an excellent script by Frank Gruber, based on Eric Ambler's novel *A Coffin for Dimitrios.* Peter Lorre plays Cornelius Leyden, a Dutch thriller writer who first sees Dimitrios Makropoulos (Zachary Scott in his debut film) when the latter is lying on a slab in the Istanbul morgue. Scenting a story, the nervous but determined Leyden begins to unravel the tangled history that took Dimitrios from the Levant to Geneva and Paris, and from a modest first murder, through every kind of treachery and double-dealing, to a dangerous pinnacle of success as an international criminal. Along the way, Leyden meets Grodek (Victor Francen), "an employer of spy labor" who is writing a biography of St. Francis, and the unctuous and ubiquitous Mr. Peters (Sydney Greenstreet).

There was much praise for the script and for Arthur Edeson's photography. Edgar Anstey commended "the extremely competent direction of Mr. Jean Negulesco, who comes fully grown to his trade from the making of many excellent short films. His shots are always well composed and adapted to the sudden visual surprise, the alarming revelation. The complexities of the film's crimes are made credible by uniformly good acting (Mr. Greenstreet has never been better), but it is the performance of Mr. Lorre which comes back into your mind after the film is over. In spite of the fact that he is handicapped by the sinister associations of his usual roles, he has given a moving portrait of a frightened yet obstinate little man, not gallant, dashing nor heroic, but a citizen fallen among thieves."

Negulesco himself, in *The Celluloid Muse,* said that "Lorre was the most talented man I have ever seen in my life. If you watch *The Mask of Dimitrios,* you'll find that the whole picture, its entire mood, is held together by him. Without him, you're a little bored by it. . . . I allowed Lorre complete freedom to improvise." In the same interview, the director remarked that he had "established a sombre, low-key mood" in this movie "that I followed in a number of subsequent films. I learned that the public loves to share the actor's situation, to be a vicarious part of the action. It's curious that when you see actors moving and talking in semi-darkness it's always more exciting than seeing them plainly, because you identify with them more."

This technique worked less successfully in *The Conspirators* (1944), an attempt to combine winning ingredients from *The Mask of Dimitrios* and *Casablanca.* Adapted from the novel by Frederic Prokosch, and set in World War II Lisbon, it has Lorre, Greenstreet, and Francen in supporting roles, Paul Henreid as a Dutch underground leader, and Hedy Lamarr as a woman of mystery. All this shrewd packaging produced a "slow, mediocre spy story."

Three Strangers (1946), from a script by John Huston and Howard Koch, was also disappointing in box-office terms, but enjoyed a much warmer critical reception. To Jack Warner's astonishment, Negulesco insisted on casting Peter Lorre in a role for which David Niven, Leslie Howard, and Errol Flynn had all been considered—an alcoholic small-time hoodlum finally redeemed by the love of a good woman. He is one of three strangers who meet in London and split the price of a sweepstakes ticket. They rashly invoke the aid of Kwan-Yin, a Chinese goddess of "fortune and destiny, life and death," agreeing to share their winnings. Before the film is over, they also share an involvement in murder. Lorre's partners are Geraldine Fitzgerald, neurotically intent on ruining her husband's career, and a crooked lawyer (Sydney Greenstreet again).

Todd McCarthy, who was strongly reminded of Huston's *The Maltese Falcon,* wrote that "the story of three dubious types bound together in a common questionable enterprise also bears other favorite Huston motifs, such as gambling, horses, the bluff, drinking, somewhat specious Freudian character motivations and even a bit of sadism with a cigarette which anticipates *The Kremlin Letter* by over forty years. Characters instinctively blame everyone but themselves for the failings of the tenuous group, and the script is without question more absurdist and existentialist than any of Huston's other early writing jobs. Given Jean Negulesco's efficient, moody direction, it really doesn't matter that Huston didn't actually direct himself, and the intentions of the script come across as fully as could be desired."

Geraldine Fitzgerald also appears in *Nobody Lives Forever* (1946), this time opposite John Garfield, a soft-centered con man who falls in love with his intended victim. Adapted by W. R. Burnett from his own novel, this was generally dismissed as no more than a "formula melodrama."

Not so *Humoresque* (1946), probably Negulesco's best-known film, distantly derived by Clifford Odets and Zachary Gold from a short story by Fannie Hurst. It is, Geoff Brown suggests, virtually a variation on Odets' *Golden Boy,* with John Garfield as Paul Boray, a tough, talented, and ambitious violinist fiddling his way out of the ghetto. Oscar Levant (who is said to have written much of his own dialogue) provides the light relief as Boray's wisecracking friend, and Joan Crawford the tragedy. She plays Helen Wright, a bored and boozy socialite in a loveless marriage who almost smothers Boray's talent with her obsessive passion for him ("I need a hot towel or a cold shower, either or both, or vice versa"). In the end, after an ironic toast to love, she walks into the moonlit Pacific in a black sequined dress, the sobbing melodies of the *Liebestod* crashing around her.

Humoresque seemed to Geoff Brown "the perfect delirious fusion" of Odets and Hollywood; "in many ways Garfield makes an odd violinist, and the director had a big task making him wield his instrument sensibly. The arms doing the fingering and bowing in close-ups really belong to two violinists standing on either side. . . . But the character of Paul Boray needs the violence of the embattled proletariat to make dramatic sense, and this Garfield abundantly provides. . . . The participation of Oscar Le-

vant and Isaac Stern (the soundtrack's violinist) helped ensure that the portrayal of concert life kept touch with reality. . . . For once there is a consistent visual panache to match the exuberance of Odets' dialogue. This is the dream factory working overtime: luscious black-and-white photography from Ernest Haller; flashy dissolves from a rolled-up window blind to a piano keyboard, from a china statuette to the Atlas figure at Rockefeller Centre; Joan Crawford, bitching, fretting and going quietly mad in dresses by Adrian. *Humoresque* is the Forties' apotheosis of Hollywood madness."

Thanks to a Hollywood strike, Negulesco made his next film on location at Big Sur. *Deep Valley* (1947) has Ida Lupino as a stammering backwoods drudge who leaves her miserable parents and squalid shack and runs off with chain gang escapee Dane Clark for a brief, doomed, but glorious idyll in the forest. Coolly received on release as "a gloomy little study in degeneracy," it has been admired by later critics for its originality and for Ida Lupino's touching performance.

A somewhat similar but far more successful film followed, *Johnny Belinda* (1948), adapted by Irmgard von Cube and Allen Vincent from Elmer Harris's play. Like *Deep Valley,* it was shot on location. Fort Bragg, California, stood in for Cape Breton Island, Novia Scotia, the primitive and puritanical fishing community where bewildered deaf-mute Jane Wyman, raped by drunken Stephen McNally, gives birth to a child. Abominated for this by the villagers, she is befriended and taught sign language by Dr. Lew Ayres. Her delight and pride in this achievement and in her son are short-lived. She has to shoot McNally in defense of the baby and stand trial for murder before her happy ending finally arrives.

Johnny Belinda was Negulesco's favorite among his films, partly because he had an entirely free hand in directing it, partly because it was "the only time in my career when everybody connected with the film—including actors, cameramen, still-photographers, etc.—felt themselves an integral part of the project. . . . We stayed back at night, met every evening to discuss it. . . . That was the first time I'd seen actors altruistically trying to improve a picture at the expense of their own parts."

This time, the contemporary reviewers were ecstatic, especially about Jane Wyman. "With only her eyes and gestures to speak the lines," wrote one, "she maintains a dramatic grip on the film and the audience that is overwhelming. One will not easily forget her trembling, animal eagerness when, with the doctor's help, she is first struggling to burst out of the loneliness, aching and total, which has previously imprisoned her; or the silent screams in the seduction sequence; or the mute bliss of the young nursing mother. This is the outstanding acting performance of the year." Later critics have tended to be less enthusiastic, David Thomson finding the characters "one-dimensional and blatant."

This was Negulesco's last film for Warners—he said, rather surprisingly, that "Jack Warner was opposed to offbeat pictures at this time" and therefore "he fired me." If this is the whole story, Warner may have regretted his decision when *Johnny Belinda* was nominated for eight Oscars (receiving only one, for Jane Wyman as best actress). "Feeling very low," Negulesco went off for a trip to India. He was recalled by his agent Charlie Feldman to join Twentieth Century-Fox, where Darryl F. Zanuck, greatly impressed by Negulesco's location work on *Deep Valley,* had a film for him using the same star, Ida Lupino.

In his *Celluloid Muse* interview, Negulesco said that "working at Warners had been wonderful because it was a very tough training-ground. They had strict schedules which you couldn't exceed by so much as a day. I had to make shorts there at the rate of one reel daily; often I had to make do with existing sets and invent stories of my own. Budgets were very tight. . . . Fox was very different to work for from Warners. It was not as tight or as strict; it was much more liberal. If they liked what you were doing, there was no limit to your budget, no restriction on your way of shooting, or your casting or anything."

Idyllic as this sounds, Negulesco made few films of any real merit at Twentieth Century–Fox, where he spent most of the rest of his career; he was by no means the only director who did his best work for the parsimonious but socially conscious Warners. One of his most notable Fox pictures was his first, *Road House* (1948), which in fact has some of the toughness and sophistication associated with Negulesco's old studio. Scripted by Edward Chodorov, it was described by William R. Meyer as "a *film noir* transplanted from the city." Cornel Wilde is the hero, persecuted by roadhouse owner Richard Widmark, here giving one of his celebrated impersonations of a psychotic killer. But the movie belongs to Ida Lupino, as a sultry chanteuse whose husky songs and sardonic wisecracks set the film's mood.

Two negligible movies followed, *The Forbidden Street* (1949) and *Under My Skin* (1950), and then a set of more considerable films scripted and produced by Nunnally Johnson. The most admired of these was *Three Came*

Home (1950), based on Agnes Newton Keith's autobiographical account of the sufferings endured by the inmates—European women and children—of a Japanese prison camp in Borneo during World War II. Claudette Colbert gives a moving performance, especially in her scenes with the sympathetic Japanese commander (Sessue Hayakawa), though the film was somewhat marred by "easy sentimentalities and meretricious dramatic effects."

The Mudlark (1950), with Andrew Ray as a Cockney urchin who breaks into Windsor Castle to meet Queen Victoria (Irene Dunne), was found charming, innocuous, and rather dull (as befits a Royal Command Performance picture), but ameliorated by Alec Guinness's magisterial performance as Disraeli. Negulesco's third film with Nunnally Johnson (after a feeble attack on college sorority snobberies called *Take Care of My Little Girl*) was *Phone Call From a Stranger* (1952). This was an effective multi-plot drama in which lawyer Gary Merrill, surviving a plane crash, seeks out the families of those who died—an alcoholic doctor (Michael Rennie), a stripper (Shelley Winters), and a loudmouthed salesman (Keenan Wynn) with a heart of gold and an invalid wife (Bette Davis). Johnson's neat screenplay was chosen as the year's best at Venice.

Lydia Bailey, Lure of the Wilderness, and *Scandal at Scourie* were all potboilers, mediocre or worse, but "The Last Leaf," Negulesco's contribution to *O. Henry's Full House* (1952), was much enjoyed as a "touching, ironic vignette" about a young woman (Jean Peters) who enlists the aid of an artist (Gregory Ratoff) to trick her ailing sister (Anne Baxter) back to health. Most critics preferred it to any of the other episodes, directed by Howard Hawks, Henry King, and Henry Koster. Negulesco's next film, *Titanic* (1953), earned an Oscar for its script (by Charles Brackett, Walter Reisch, and Richard Breen). However, most reviewers seemed more impressed by the visual reconstruction of the great sea disaster than by the "novelettish" problems of the passengers, prominent among whom were Clifton Webb and his absconding wife (Barbara Stanwyck).

Working again with Nunnally Johnson as his producer and scriptwriter, Negulesco next directed *How to Marry a Millionaire* (1953), only the second Cinemascope movie to be made. Marilyn Monroe, Betty Grable, and Lauren Bacall are more or less good-hearted "gold diggers" pursuing rich husbands in locations (New York City and Maine) that make attractive use of the wide screen. Nina Nichols suggested that the spendthrift deployment of three female stars was partly inspired by the same "problem of filling the vast lateral space of the wide screen." For many, Monroe stole the picture from her more experienced sisters, portraying a desperately shortsighted beauty denied spectacles by Dorothy Parker's adage about girls who wear glasses.

The great success of How to Marry a Millionaire reinforced Fox's commitment to Cinemascope. Most of Negulesco's subsequent films used the wide screen, and tended to emphasize glamorous locations at the expense of character and plot. Andrew Sarris, indeed, wrote that "Jean Negulesco's career can be divided into two periods labeled B.C. and A.C., or Before Cinemascope and After Cinemascope. . . . Everything After Cinemascope is completely worthless. Negulesco's is the most dramatic case of directorial maladjustment in the fifties."

Typical of his work A.C. is Three Coins in the Fountain (1954). It interweaves the romantic adventures in the more photogenic bits of Rome of three American women (Dorothy McGuire, Jean Peters, Maggie McNamara), with Clifton Webb, Louis Jourdan, and Rossano Brazzi as the men they appear to want in their lives. Handsomely photographed by Milton Krasner, and with the added attraction of a hit title song by Victor Young, it was another huge success at the box-office.

Negulesco was condemned to repeat the package in a long succession of scenic "women's pictures"—A Woman's World (1954); the musical Daddy Long Legs, with Fred Astaire and Leslie Caron; The Rains of Ranchipur (1955), a fatuous remake of Clarence Brown's The Rains Came; The Gift of Love (1958), a "slick sudser" based on the same novel that had inspired Walter Lang's Sentimental Journey; A Certain Smile (1958), from Françoise Sagan; Count Your Blessings (1959), from Nancy Mitford; The Best of Everything (1959), from Rona Jaffe's novel about sex in the glamorous world of paperback publishing; The Pleasure Seekers (1964), a translation to Madrid of Three Coins in the Fountain; and Hello-Goodbye (1970), another wide-screen peek at swinging Europe.

There were occasional departures from this formula, but even these only confirmed that Negulesco's spirit, too long stretched on the Cinemascope rack, was broken. Boy on a Dolphin (1957), which introduced Sophia Loren to English-speaking films, was called a "dull adventure film." Jessica (1962), produced as well as directed by Negulesco, was slightly better—a mildly amusing romp in which Angie Dickinson plays an American nurse pitching in as midwife in an Italian village.

The best of Negulesco's late films was, significantly, not made for Fox but produced independently in Iran by Mostafa and Morteza Akavan. The Heroes (1969), given limited release in the United States as The Invincible Six, was based on a novel by Michael Barrett, but closely resembled an innumerate version of The Magnificent Seven, with six criminal fugitives committing themselves to the defense against bandits of a helpless village, and regenerating themselves in the process. With music by Manos Hadjidakis, and a cast that includes Stuart Whitman, Curt Jurgens, and Elke Sommer, this "tough little B film" shows more than a glimmer of Negulesco's old style. "For the most part," wrote William R. Meyer, "the actors are properly cynical, the parched Iranian locations are chokingly arid yet picturesque, and well-cut violence is plentiful."

In Negulesco's best films, wrote David Thomson, "there is an entrancing, velvety quality of dream world brought to life. The timing, mood and nuance are as precise as in Casablanca, and Negulesco seems as assured a director as Michael Curtiz." After he left Warners, he "lost the chance to continue the romantic treatment of 'hard' people, and gave himself up to the sentimental view of cosiness."

Negulesco was married in 1946 to the model and actress Dusty Anderson, who is said to make a hobby of dealing in real estate. That may explain why the Negulescos own or owned three houses in the best residential district of Los Angeles, as well as property in sundry world capitals. During the 1970s, after making The Heroes, the director made frequent visits to Tehran, advising on the development of the Iranian film industry. Negulesco is said to be "a generous, intelligent, highly cultured man, who is justly proud of his excellent art collection" (including "his own elegant line drawings and oil paintings").

FILMS: Shorts—The Flag of Humanity, 1940; Joe Reichmann and His Orchestra, 1940; Alice in Movieland, 1940; Henry Busse and His Orchestra, 1940; The U.S.C. Band and Glee Club, 1941; Carioca Serenaders, 1941; Jan Garber and His Orchestra, 1941; Skinny Ennis and His Orchestra, 1941; Cliff Edwards and His Buckaroos, 1941; Freddy Martin and His Orchestra, 1941; Marie Green and Her Merrie Men, 1941; Hal Kemp and His Orchestra, 1941; Those Good Old Days, 1941; At the Stroke of Twelve, 1941; Dog in the Orchard, 1941; Gaieté Parisienne (The Gay Parisian), 1942; Capriccio Espagnol (Spanish Fiesta), 1942; Californian Junior Symphony, 1942; A Ship Is Born, 1942; The Daughter of Rosie O'Grady, 1942; The Spirit of Annapolis, 1942; The Spirit of West Point, 1942; Carl Hoff and His Band, 1942; Playgirls, 1942; Leo Reishmann and His Orchestra, 1942; Richard Himber and His Orchestra, 1942; The Don Cossack Chorus, 1942; Emil Coleman and His Orchestra, 1942; Glen Gray and His Casa Loma Band, 1942; The Army Air Force Band, 1942; Six Hits and a Miss, 1942; The U.S. Marine Band, 1942; Borrah Minnevitch and His Harmonica School, 1942; Women at War, 1943; Army Show, 1943; The Voice That Thrilled the World, 1943; Over the Wall, 1943; The U.S. Navy Band, 1943; Ozzie Nelson and His Orchestra, 1943; The U.S. Army Band, 1943; The All-American Band, 1943; Childhood Days, 1943; U.S. Service Bands, 1943; The Hit Parade of the Gay Nineties, 1943; Sweetheart Serenade, 1943; Cavalcade of the Dance, 1943; Grandfather's Follies, 1944; Roaring Guns, 1944; South American Swing, 1944; All Star Melody Masters, 1944; Listen to the Bands, 1944. *Features*—Singapore Woman, 1941; The Mask of Dimitrios, 1944; The Conspirators, 1944; Three Strangers, 1946; Nobody Lives Forever, 1946; Humoresque, 1947; Deep Valley, 1947; Johnny Belinda, 1948; Road House, 1948; The Forbidden Street (U.K., Britannia Mews), 1949; Under My Skin, 1950; Three Came Home, 1950; The Mudlark, 1950; Take Care of My Little Girl, 1951; Phone Call From a Stranger, 1952; Lydia Bailey, 1952; Lure of the Wilderness, 1952; The Last Leaf *episode in* O. Henry's Full House, 1952; Scandal at Scourie, 1953; Titanic, 1953; How to Marry a Millionaire, 1953; Three Coins in the Fountain, 1954; A Woman's World, 1954; Daddy Long Legs, 1955; The Rains of Ranchipur, 1955; Boy on a Dolphin, 1957; The Gift of Love, 1958; A Certain Smile, 1958; Count Your Blessings, 1959; The Best of Everything, 1959; Jessica, 1962; The Pleasure Seekers, 1964; The Heroes/The Invincible Six, 1969; Hello-Goodbye, 1970.

ABOUT: Higham, C. and Greenberg, J. The Celluloid Muse, 1969; Meyer, W. R. Warner Brothers Directors, 1978; Negulesco, J. Things I Did . . . and Things I Think I Did, 1984; Thomson, D. A Biographical Dictionary of the Cinema, 1980. *Periodicals*—Films in Review April 1973, August–September 1973, January 1974.

*OLIVEIRA, MANOEL (CÂNDIDO PINTO) DE (December 12, 1908–), Portuguese director, scenarist, and producer, was born in Oporto, the son of Francisco José de Oliveira, a prominent and innovative industrialist who was the first Portuguese manufacturer of electric lamps, also involved in the manufacture of machinery and knitwear and in the hydroelectrification of the River Ave.

Manoel de Oliveira enrolled for a time in the Colégio Universal in Oporto and the Colégio de La Guardia, Galiza, but left before completing his studies. An imaginative and creative youth, he was nevertheless expected to join his brothers in the administration of his father's factories, and did so when he was seventeen. As a young man, Oliveira was an athlete, a gymnast, and a racing driver, in the latter sport winning prizes in Portugal, Spain, and Brazil. But this handsome young executive had less conventional in-

MANOEL DE OLIVEIRA

terests as well—in the condition of the poor, in the arts, and especially in the cinema.

Oliveira's first notions of montage and cinematic rhythm came from his devoted scrutiny of the films of griffith, of the French impressionists and the German expressionists, of Stroheim and Sternberg and Chaplin. He has recalled the special impact on him of Dreyer's *The Passion of Joan of Arc,* Eisenstein's *The General Line,* and Pudovkin's *Mother.* Oliveira had virtually no Portuguese models to draw upon, the meager film industry there being restricted to naive comedies, literary adaptations, and historical romances made for local audiences and innocent of artistic ambitions.

According to John Gillett, in his article in *Sight and Sound* (Summer 1981), Oliveira "seems to have spent most of his life in business," making films when circumstances allowed. "Oliveira's actual output over the years is sparse: less than a dozen shorts and documentaries and only six features [now eight]. Fastidiousness and a reluctance to compromise place him alongside other solitary filmmakers, from Dreyer to Dovzhenko. But other factors, including [the rigorous censorship imposed by] the Salazar regime during the major part of his career, and the baffled response of the Portuguese industry, hardly encouraged productivity in an artist concerned to probe his own society. Furthermore, the extreme variations in tone, style, and method from film to film mean that his work can't be pigeonholed and contained in the manner beloved of bureaucrats and critics."

In 1927, when he was nineteen, Oliveira was involved with others in an unrealized project to

°ō lē vād´ ä

make a film about Portugal's participation in World War I. The following year he appeared in *Fátima Milagrosa*, a picture made in Oporto by Rino Lupo, and in 1929 he worked with the painter Ventura Porfírio on an animated film—another project that had to be abandoned. By then, Oliveira had already embarked on what became his first completed film, *Douro, faina fluvial (Hard Labor on the River Douro*, 510 meters), a documentary portrait of his native Oporto. He borrowed the money to buy a 35mm camera and filmstock, and himself served as producer, scenarist, and editor. The cameraman on this and most of Oliveira's other early films was his friend António Mendes, a bookkeeper and amateur photographer who shared his passion for the cinema.

John Gillett, discussing the film in 1981, fifty years after its first screening, wrote that "seen again today, it has all the vigour and self-awareness of a first film, nicely shot but somewhat overcut in an attempt to sustain a flow of meaningful, 'symphonic' images. It is also defiantly unromantic in its portrayal of poverty and deprivation, a fact which caused a rumpus at an international congress in the early 30s when Portuguese officials protested at a spectacle which showed such severe working conditions." Francisco Aranda agreed that the picture emulated the rhythmic "symphonic" treatment of Walter Ruttmann's *Berlin* while avoiding the cold abstract formalism of that film; here "the workers are victims and heroes in the middle of the steel masses and mechanical movements."

After that, more than ten years passed before Oliveira was able to complete another film of comparable importance. There were a number of ambitious projects during the 1930s—an abstract film, another that Oliveira describes as "surrealistic," two studies of workers—but all of these proved abortive; he actually produced only a few relatively insignificant documentaries. *Estátuas de Lisboa (Statues of Lisbon,* 1932), only one hundred meters long, was apparently released against Oliveira's wishes, before he was satisfied with it. In 1933 he had a substantial role in Cotinelli Telmo's *A canção de Lisboa (Song of Lisbon)*, Portugal's first all-sound film, and in 1934 *Douro, faina fluvial* was re-released with a score by Luís de Freitas Branco. According to Raphaël Bassan, the three documentaries Oliveira made at the end of the decade—*Já se fabricam automóveis em Portugal (Now They Make Automobiles in Portugal,* 1938); *Miramar, praia de rosas (Miramar, Beach of Roses,* 1939); and *Famalicão* (1940)—"offer no great artistic interest." The director was married in 1940 to Dona Maria Isabel Brandão Carvalhais Oliveira.

Oliveira's first feature was *Aniki-Bóbó* (1942), a children's film produced by António Lopes Ribeiro and adapted by the director from a story by Rodrigues de Freitas. The cast was headed by two professional actors, Nascimento Fernandes and Vital dos Santos, but was otherwise composed mostly of children recruited from the streets of Oporto, where the film was shot in black and white by António Mendes. According to one critic, it "tells a story of children in whose games . . . [Oliveira] mirrors the ethical conceptions of adults." Many critics have seen in Oliveira's naturalistic use of location shooting a kind of neorealism "before the letter," although, as J. Hoberman points out, the film's "overscored alfresco lyricism" is perhaps closer to Jean Vigo's poetic realism. At the time, critics called the film immoral and it was rejected by the public, but forty years later, according to Oliveira, it was one of the most popular films in Portugal, showing on television three or four times a year.

Following *Aniki-Bóbó* there was an even longer silence—fourteen years—during which Oliveira involved himself in farming and, as before, wrote scripts and pursued financing for projects that never came to fruition. A less committed filmmaker would have given up, but in 1955 he traveled to Germany to study new color techniques, and the following year he completed his own color film, *O pintor e a cidade (The Painter and the City)*. Like his very first movie, it was a documentary about Oporto—this time setting photographic images of the city against those created on canvas by the Oporto painter António Cruz. Francisco Aranda called the result a "philosophical essay in film language about the behavior of the human being in a town." It was shown at a number of film festivals and very well received. For this 45-minute color film, Oliveira was not only director, scenarist, and editor, but producer and cameraman as well. The same was true of *O pão (Bread)*, which followed in 1959.

O pão, originally 1,620 meters long (75 minutes) but later cut to 660 meters, was a documentary commissioned by Portugal's National Federation of Industrial Millers. John Gillett writes that it "opens with a shot of wheatfields in brilliant colour and then proceeds, without commentary, to enact a little parable on bread production. Small individual country bakeries merge into vistas of the big city, with factories at work (taking in witty shots of machines puffing and blowing out their sacks of flour), international corporations doing deals, people actually buying and eating the product. Finally, there is a slow regression back to the gleaming wheatfield. Throughout, Oliveira's associative editing is masterly, yet there is no forced didacticism. The film works most effectively as a kind of polemical poem, without words."

Poetry and documentary are combined with even more powerful effect in *Acto da primavera (The Passion of Jesus,* 1963), a two-hour record of the Passion Play performed every year during Holy Week by the peasants of Curalha, Trás-os-Montes, in the northeast of Portugal. A British National Film Theatre program note says that the work "is transformed by Oliveira from a mummers' play by willing amateurs into a strange, hieratic rite (both religious and erotic), far removed from the commercial representations of other cinemas." According to Oliveira, *The Passion of Jesus* profoundly altered his conception of cinema: "I realized that I was working with a sixteenth-century text and depicting an event about two thousand years old, to be shown today. This stressed the idea of not simulating reality but merely representing it." To this end, Oliveira incorporated footage of himself filming the event alongside the event itself, and to signal its contemporary import, ended with images of the atomic bomb. The Portuguese critic Henrique Costa wrote that "what Oliveira portrays here openly, no one among us has ever dared to say. And I will go one step further. *The Passion of Jesus* is the first political film from Portugal—because what was done to Jesus was a political act."

It was at this time that the world began to take note of Oliveira's long and solitary struggle. There were various tributes to him in Portugal in 1963, including a special issue of *Filme.* In 1964 *Acto da primavera* received the *grand prix* at the Siena film festival and there was an Oliveira retrospective at Locarno—the first of many.

Continuing as a one-man production team and again working with amateur actors, Oliveira next made a short (twenty minutes) fictional film, *A Caça (The Hunt,* 1964). Two boys encounter a bizarre hunting party in marshy country near their village, have an argument about the morality of hunting, and separate. The younger falls into a bog. His friend musters a rescue party of hunters and villagers (including a cobbler whom the boys had earlier angered). A human chain is formed to pull the boy out, but snaps. Arguments begin but, at the urging of the cobbler, everyone joins hands again for another rescue attempt. Praising the film's "disturbing, hypnotic images and Buñuelian undertones," John Gillett asks: "A parable about solidarity or an ironic attack on violence, as some Portuguese critics have suggested? Oliveira never quite tells us. His formidable camera eye, however, is used to sustain a mood of palpable disquiet." In fact,

Oliveira himself intended another ending—one that would have stopped with the failed rescue attempt in order to stress the difficulty of understanding among people—but the censors imposed the more optimistic version.

As pinturas do meu irmão Júlio (My Brother Julio's Paintings, 15 minutes, 1965) was the last of Oliveira's films photographed by himself. The film had in fact been made in 1959 as part of a projected documentary on Portugal as seen by its artists, abandoned for lack of funds. The artist whose works are the subject of this piece was Júlio Régio, brother of Oliveira's friend the writer José Régio, who provided the picture's poems and commentary. The paintings, many of which portray scenes from the brothers' lives, were photographed at the family home, the Vila do Conde, and Carlos Paredes contributed a guitar score improvised as "he watched the pictures passing before his eyes."

Another long silence followed, not broken until the release in 1972 of *O passado e o presente (Past and Present),* Oliveira's first full-length fictional feature for adults, made when he was already sixty-three. Financed by the Gulbenkian Foundation, it was adapted by the director and Vicente Sanchez from the latter's play, a satirical comedy on marriage and the upper classes. Oliveira describes his filmmaking career up to this point as "the stage of the people," characterized by the constant interplay of documentary and fiction; with *Past and Present,* he says, he embarked on "the stage of the bourgeoisie," with its markedly romantic and literary sensibility. The first in a cycle of films about "frustrated loves," *O passado e o presente* is, according to Alan Brien, "a boulevard farce, set in a luxurious city mansion, frequented by a gang of spoilt, self-absorbed, upper-crust figures who tolerate each other's foibles and quirks, however weird, buoyed up by a hierarchy of servants who bustle around dealing with suicide attempts, deliveries of coffins and memorial paintings, endless arrivals and departures of funeral and wedding guests, the alternating humiliation of living spouses and sanctification of expired ones. . . . The waspish queen of this disturbed hive . . . is Vanda—a sour, pettish performance by the poisonously attractive Maria de Saisset—who has decided the only good husband is a buried one. Oliveira plays off the stage conventions against themselves with his winged camera . . . , hovering just around the corner until our expectations almost burst. . . . I cannot help registering the indelible impression of an obliquely subversive parody of high life under a conservative, respectable dictatorship, deliberately paced to spark a rejection of its callously trivial values."

John Gillett was even more enthusiastic, praising Oliveira's "wonderful use" of Mendelssohn's *Midsummer Night's Dream* music, "alternating with passages of silence," and calling this "Oliveira's most accessible film"—"a rich and heady feast" which "could have become a world success" if properly distributed. Others, it must be said, were less impressed. John Coleman thought it "an undernourished oddity," full of "visual ado about nothing," over which "the ghost of Buñuel . . . hovers uneasily."

Oliveira's cycle of frustrated loves continued with *Benilde ou a Virgem Maê (Benilde: Virgin and Mother,* 1975), his first film after the fall of the Salazar dictatorship. Subsidized by the Portuguese Cinema Fund and the Gulbenkian Foundation , it was based on a play by Oliveira's friend José Régio. It is a fable set in the 1930s about an overprotected girl (Maria Amélia Aranda), raised in a deeply religious household in the Alentejo, who becomes mysteriously pregnant. "When I made *Benilde,*" Oliveira recalls, "I tortured myself figuring out how to do cinema without falling into theatre, because this film started out as a three-act play, which I wanted to respect in preserving the whole text." But as he worked on the filmscript, Oliveira realized that he was destroying the play, and that in fact, since the cinema is a process of "fixing" audiovisually, "it was just as legitimate to fix a word or a speech as an image. . . . That's why I chose to make *Benilde* as a kind of ironic reaction . . . marking 'first act,' 'end of first act,' et cetera, all the while insisting that it wasn't theatre."

Amor de Perdição (Ill-Fated Love, 1978) was financed by an assortment of institutions and organizations, including Radiotelevisão Portuguese, and was first screened on television in six episodes. Released to movie theatres in 1979, it still ran for four hours and twenty minutes. For financial reasons, the movie was shot (by Manuel Costa e Silva) in 16mm, and suffers somewhat from this. It was scripted by Oliveira from the famous 1861 novel by Camilo Castelo Branco, who based it on an actual incident from the history of his own family. With a characteristic disregard for the box office, Oliveira cast amateurs in the principal roles, theatre actors in the others.

The story concerns the Romeo and Juliet tragedy of two young lovers, Simão (António Sequeira Lopes) and Teresa (Cristina Hauser), who live in Viseu, Brazil, and whose aristocratic families are implacably hostile to each other. When Teresa refuses an arranged marriage, she is consigned to a convent. Simão kills his rival and is jailed. The lovers exchange anguished letters—Simão with the help of Mariana (Elsa Wallenkamp), a servant who selflessly adores

him. Simão is exiled to India, both he and Teresa die of broken hearts, and Mariana drowns herself.

Amor de Perdição was widely shown at festivals in Europe (and in the United States at Los Angeles). Admired for the beauty of its images, it seemed to many critics too long, too slow, and too subdued in tone—even "matter of fact"—for the passionate story it unfolds. Oliveira explained in an interview that he had found himself "making a film from a romantic work—but this work operates at two distinct levels. One is superficial, anecdotal, sentimental and very explicit; the other is much more profound. I didn't wish to remain with the first level. . . . Since I was adapting a work of literature to an audiovisual medium—a work of great beauty, moreover—I thought it would be legitimate to concentrate on the text, the words, and to let the images have a more serene form."

Serge Daney suggested in *Cahiers du Cinéma* that the coolness of the Portuguese critics could be attributed to their resentment of Oliveira's "tampering" with the most widely read of all Portuguese novels (which had been more conventionally filmed twice before). Daney himself considers this a great film, dealing with Oliveira's "favorite theme . . . this suspension of social rules and norms and exchanging them for those his heroes create and which they obey until death or madness." Louis Marcorelles wrote that the director had "created the most astonishing and impressive approximation one could possibly conceive of a period and of a sensibility." Several critics were reminded of Mizoguchi, and John Gillett also found resemblances to Dreyer.

With *Amor de perdição,* Oliveira had concluded what he originally conceived as a trilogy of "frustrated loves." He then turned to the preparation of a comedy, but a dispute with the author forced him to abandon that project. At this point, he was offered the opportunity to adapt a novel by Agustina Bessa Luís, a distinguished contemporary Portuguese writer. *Fanny Owen,* which became Oliveira's *Francisca* (1981), is the story of an English girl loved, to no avail, by Castelo Branco, the author of *Amor de perdição.* She is passionately in love with the writer's friend, José Augusto, but once they marry, he inexplicably rejects her and she dies a heartbroken virgin.

Agustina Bessa Luís based her book on the letters of Castelo Branco and Augusto, which "constitute a reflection on life, women, love, fatalism, unhappiness." Oliveira, whose wife's family was related to Fanny Owen, had access to additional documents, which he worked into the film. But while underscoring the primacy of such texts—presented in dialogue, voice-overs, intertitles—his adaptation creates striking visual counterparts (rather than illustrations) in the form of carefully stylized tableaus. According to one critic, "many observers believe Manoel de Oliveira sharpened his directorial style on this film. He reduced the story to a conceptual game without retreating from the literary quality of the dialogue," deliberately rejecting naturalism in the language of the film while faithfully reconstructing nineteenth-century literary society.

Francisca was "the event" of the Directors' Fortnight at Cannes in 1981, according to Emmanuel Decaux, who considered it "a masterpiece that can't even be compared with the films in the official competition." With this conclusion to the cycle of "frustrated loves," Oliveira turned to nonfiction projects. In 1982, he made the autobiographical *Memórias e confissões* (*Memories and Confessions*), recounting his own family history "as a pretext for saying something that must be said," but decided that the film should not be released until after his death. Two documentaries followed, *Lisboa cultural* (*Cultural Lisbon*, 1983), an Italian production, and *Nice à propos de Jean Vigo* (1984), made for French television as part of a series on French cities a seen by foreign directors. As his title indicates, Oliveira first saw Nice in Vigo's classic documentary, *À propos de Nice*, and this 1930 film becomes a point of reference for an idiosyncratic exploration of the present-day city (with its Portuguese community) and of the cinema itself.

After this initial venture into France (generally thought to have suffered by comparison with the Vigo original), Oliveira embarked on a much more ambitious project. *Sapato de cetim* (*The Satin Slipper*, 1985) is a six-hour and fifty-minute version of Paul Claudel's 1929 verse drama, *Le Soulier de satin*, which presents in four monumental sections a mystical romance of the sixteenth-century Spanish empire. The slipper of the title is pledged to the Virgin by the devout Dona Prouhèze (Patricia Barzyk) in anticipation of a meeting with the man she loves, Don Rodrigue (Luis Miguel Cintra), so that she, a married woman, will be unable to hurry along the path toward sin. Her vow is dreadfully effective, for the meeting never takes place and the lovers endure a lifetime of separation. But their undying passion is sublimated to the benefit of the imperial Catholic cause, helping to fuel the conquest of the New World and the defeat of the Moors, as well as producing a spiritual child, Marie des Sept-Épées (Ann Cosigny), the symbol of purified love. At the end of the story, as the aged and disgraced Don Rodrigue is led away to the galleys, he hears the cannon heralding the marriage of Marie to Don John of Austria, the great champion who won the victory at Lepanto.

Oliveira began working on *The Satin Slipper* early in 1983, after the Portuguese Ministry of Culture let it be known that money was available for coproductions with France. In August 1984 he began seven months of shooting with a ninety-six member cast, seventy-five technicians, and a twelve-million-dollar budget. With the conclusion of "frustrated loves," Oliveira had begun to consider a new theme, "lost wars." The Claudel play, with its evocation of a vanished empire, provided "a means of moving from one theme to another, while still maintaining a continuation." The historical setting had a special significance in that Spanish ambitions of the period entailed the subjugation of Portugal (accomplished, in part, by John of Austria). In addition, Oliveira sensed in Claudel's drama a "certain cinematographic vision, a preview of the cinema." The fact that the play is rarely performed in its entirety and has never been popular did not deter him: "It's necessary to shape the public's taste. It's difficult, but you have to do it."

In this instance, Oliveira quite literally leads the public to the stage, opening the film at the entrance to the theatre and moving the camera forward until it comes to rest . . . on a movie screen. The creative tension between cinema and theatre is maintained throughout the film by the inclusion of the stage set itself, the insistence on a frontal camera (with no reaction shots until the end of the film), and the delineation of episodes with long sequence-shots. Cinema, Oliveira maintains, "should not represent theatre, it should do it. Theatre is the representation of life; cinema is the representation of life, not of theatre. Theatre and cinema are the same thing with different possibilities." And as Marcel Martin, among others, pointed out, it was precisely in this context that *The Satin Slipper*, "far from being filmed theatre, exploits all the stylistic resources of stage expression while imposing a plastic vision and fascination with image and sound that only the cinema can provide, beyond the figurative realism and imitation most often found on the screen."

Critics got a glimpse of "Fourth Day"—the last section of Claudel's play, which both the playwright and the filmmaker completed first—at Cannes in the spring of 1985. When the entire film was screened at Venice that fall, the seventy-seven-year-old director received a special Golden Lion for his achievement. Serge Toubiana noted that Oliveira had won his "bet" in taking on the whole of the text, "for the argument about the length doesn't hold up very long in the face of the film's beauty, which often attains a veritable splendor. Or in the face of the humor, the fantasies, and the intelligence of the direction."

A year later, the director was back at Venice to open the festival with *Mon cas* (*My Case*, 1986). This film was not another venture into the "lost wars" but a somewhat lighter variation on the theme of film and theatre, a kind of "cinema of the absurd." *My Case* begins with a one-act play by José Régio, in which a 1920s boulevard actress (Bulle Ogier) has her performance interrupted by the Unknown One (Luis Miguel Cintra), who is trying to present "his case." A second version of the same play is performed silently, accompanied by a voice-over of Samuel Beckett's text on The Other, while a third runthrough is accompanied by a reversed sound track. For the finale, Ogier and Cintra act out the biblical story of Job and his wife.

John Gillett wrote of Oliveira in 1981 that "on meeting this tall, alert figure, who looks twenty years younger than his official age, one feels that his tense, rather reserved manner may disguise a Hawksian man of action. His words have the force and conviction of someone who has had to fight every foot of the way." Indeed, while his filmmaking career goes back to 1929, it was only in the 1960s that he began to attract even limited attention; and then, as J. Hoberman writes, "at an age when many men think of retirement, Oliveira emerged from obscurity as one of the '70s' leading modernists, a peer of Straub, Syberberg, and Duras."

FILMS: *Documentaries*—Douro, Faina Fluvial (Hard Labor on the River Douro), 1931; Estatuas de Lisboa, 1932; Já se fabricam automóveis em Portugal/Em Portugal já se fazem automóveis, 1938; Miramar, Praia de Rosas (Miramar, Beach of Roses), 1939; Famalicão, 1940; O Pintor e a Cidade (The Painter and the City), 1956; O Pão (Bread), 1959; Coração (The Heart), 1960; Acto da Primavera (The Passion of Jesus), 1963 (full-length); As Pinturas do Meu Irmão Júlio (My Brother Julio's Paintings), 1965; Memórias e confissões (Memories and Confessions), 1982 (unreleased); Lisboa cultural, 1983 (for television); Nice à propos de Jean Vigo, 1984 (for television). *Features*—Aniki-Bóbó, 1942; A Caça (The Hunt), 1964 (short); O Passado e o Presente (Past and Present), 1972; Benilde ou a Virgem Maẽ (Benilde: Virgin and Mother), 1975; Amor de Perdição (Ill-Fated Love), 1978; Francisca, 1981; Sapato de cetim (The Satin Slipper), 1985; Mon cas (My Case), 1986. *Published scripts*—Aniki-Bóbó, 1963.

ABOUT: Cinemateca Portuguesa. Manoel de Oliveira, 1981; Costa, A. Breve Historía do Cinema Portugues, 1978 (in Portuguese); Dos Santos Fonseca, M. *in* Lyon, C. (ed.) International Dictionary of Films and Filmmakers, 1984; Passek, J.-L. Le cinéma portugais, 1982 (in French); Passek, J-L. (ed.) Dictionnaire du cinéma, 1986. *Periodicals*—Bianco e Nero July–August 1976; Cahiers du Cinéma February 1966, May 1977, October 1981, August 1983, May 1985, October 1985, January 1986; Celuloide March 1972, January 1976, January 1981, September 1981, July 1983; Cineforum November 1976; Cinéma (France) March 1980 (Oliveira issue), June 8, 1986; Cinématographe June 1981, November 1981, July–August 1983, May 1985; Contracampo January 1981; Film Comment May–June 1981; Filmkritik January 1982; Films and Filming June 1960; Frauen & Film February 1982; Image et Son February 1977, February 1980; Jeune Cinéma April–May 1980; National Film Theatre (Britain) Booklet July 1981; Positif March 1980; Revue du cinéma hors série 33 (1986); Sight and Sound Summer 1981; Village Voice November 13, 1984; November 20, 1984.

OLIVIER, LAURENCE (KERR) (Baron Olivier of Brighton) (May 22, 1907–   ), British film and theatre actor and director, was born in Dorking, Surrey, the youngest of the three children of an Anglican clergyman, Gerard Olivier, and the former Agnes Crookenden. His father was a stern and rather remote man, though he is said to have conducted his services with a distinctly theatrical flair. Olivier was closer to his mother, who died when he was thirteen—he said once that he had been looking for her ever since.

Olivier seems always to have wanted to act, and had his first success at the age of ten, playing Brutus in a production of *Julius Caesar* at All Saints Choir School in London. He went on to St. Edward's School, Oxford, and at thirteen played Katharina in a special boys' production of *The Taming of the Shrew* at the Stratford Shakespeare Festival. In 1924, when he was seventeen, he entered Elsie Fogarty's Central School of Speech and Drama in London. His professional career began the same year (presumably during vacations), when he toured with Ruby Miller in a sketch called *Unfailing Instinct* and appeared in Lena Ashwell's production of *Henry VIII*.

This mixture of classical and commercial roles characterized Olivier's early career. In 1927–1928 he appeared with the excellent Birmingham Repertory Company in important or lead roles in *She Stoops to Conquer*, *Uncle Vanya*, and Elmer Rice's expressionist drama *The Adding Machine*, but strove no less eagerly for "matinée idol" success in popular entertainments like John Drinkwater's *Bird in Hand* (1928) and a 1929 stage version of *Beau Geste* (for which he grew a "Ronald Colman" mustache).

At this stage in his career, Olivier was a flamboyant, athletic actor who capitalized shamelessly on his dark good looks and great physical presence. Cedric Hardwicke found him "noisy and lacking in subtlety" (but "knew instinctively that he'd be a great actor"). Playing second lead to Noël Coward in *Private Lives* is said to have

LAURENCE OLIVIER

taught him something about comedy timing and the advantages of underplaying. The same year, 1930, he made his movie debut in George King's thriller *Too Many Crooks,* and married his first wife, the actress Jill Esmond.

Olivier had first appeared on Broadway, unnoticed, in 1929. He returned in 1931 with *Private Lives* and again in 1934 (*The Green Bay Tree*). His first important Shakespearian role came in 1935 in John Gielgud's production of *Romeo and Juliet,* when he and Gielgud alternated as Romeo and Mercutio. Olivier's sexy and hot-blooded Romeo, and his insistence on speaking the poetry as if it were contemporary prose, appalled some critics but delighted audiences: "I had the voice," Gielgud said ruefully; "Larry had the legs."

Meanwhile, Olivier pursued his movie career, appearing—usually as romantic lead—in films like *Murder for Sale* (made in Germany), Maurice Elvey's *Her Strange Desire (Potiphar's Wife,* 1931), Raoul Walsh's *The Yellow Ticket* (1931), Jim Stafford's *No Funny Business* (1933), and Anthony Asquith's *I Stand Condemned* (1935), among others. In 1937 he was Orlando to Elisabeth Bergner's Rosalind in Paul Czinner's poor screen version of *As You Like It.* A boyishly handsome hero, Olivier was not yet at home in front of the cameras, moving stiffly and speaking beautifully but inexpressively. He believed at the time that an actor "has no creative part, whatever, in pictures. . . . he has no opportunity to build up and explore a character."

One of those who had admired Olivier's Romeo was Tyrone Guthrie, who in 1937 invited him to join the famous Old Vic theatre compa-

ny. That year Olivier played Hamlet, Sir Toby Belch, and Henry V, and in 1938 he was Macbeth, Iago, and Coriolanus. He was then thirty years old, and Guthrie later wrote that "the voice already had a marvellous ringing baritone brilliance at the top; he spoke with a beautiful and aristocratic accent, with keen intelligence and a strong sense of rhythm. He moved with catlike agility. He had, if anything, too strong an instinct for the sort of theatrical effect which is striking and memorable. . . . it was evident that here was no ordinary actor, not everyone's cup of tea . . . but inevitably destined for the very top of the tree."

Olivier finally came into his own as a screen actor with his darkly romantic performance as Heathcliff in William Wyler's *Wuthering Heights* (1939), a passionate young savage who becomes a tortured instrument of revenge. Although the film softened and sentimentalized Emily Brontë's anarchic novel, it brought Olivier his first great popular screen success, and he has always credited Wyler with teaching him the rudiments of movie acting. He learned more from another master, Alfred Hitchcock, when he played the enigmatic Maxim de Winter in *Rebecca* (1940), and his star status was confirmed by his noble performance as Mr. Darcy in Robert Z. Leonard's *Pride and Prejudice* (1940).

Instead of capitalizing on these screen successes, however, the erstwhile matinée idol had by then set his sights on fame as a classical actor in the theatre. In 1940 he presented his own production of *Romeo and Juliet* in New York, with Vivien Leigh as his Juliet. It was a disastrous failure, condemned for the fussy realism of the sets and his own violent and unpoetic performance as Romeo. The same year, still in the United States, he and Vivien Leigh were married. Throughout the 1940s and most of the 1950s, they were the most celebrated theatrical couple in the world, courted by the powerful and the famous, the darling of the gossip columnists. Before they returned to England, Olivier and Leigh were persuaded to star as Nelson and Emma Hamilton in Alexander Korda's intensely patriotic *That Hamilton Woman* (1941; called *Lady Hamilton* in Britain).

Olivier had been rejected by the Royal Air Force at the beginning of the war, but had taken flying lessons and accumulated two hundred flying hours. Back in Britain, he was commissioned in the Fleet Air Arm, though restricted mostly to administrative duties. His reading of patriotic speeches from Shakespeare's *Henry V* on a radio program inspired the producer Filippo del Guidice with the idea of filming the play—at least partly for its propaganda value at a time when Britain was poised for the invasion of France. Olivier was not enthusiastic about the project—Shakespeare had never been satisfactorily filmed, largely because the literalness of the medium jarred against the fantasy and soaring language of the plays. However, he finally agreed to produce and direct the film, and to star as Henry, and was temporarily released from military service to do so.

His central inspiration was a brilliantly direct way of leading the cinema audience into the conventions and language of the play. A contemporary playbill for a seventeenth-century production of *Henry V* at Shakespeare's Globe Theatre flutters into close-up and then, from a panoramic aerial view of Elizabethan London (a meticulously detailed model) we enter the reconstructed Globe itself. We watch its actors prepare, its boisterous audience settle down for the play's Prologue—which is in fact Shakespeare's apology for attempting so vast a theme within the confines of a small theatre! Expository scenes set out the grounds—morally extremely dubious—for Henry's decision to invade France.

Once Henry sets out for France and conquest, we leave the "wooden O" of the Globe Theatre behind, but the great world beyond is still not the real one. Instead, Olivier and his designers (Paul Sheriff and Carmen Dillon) lead us out onto a vast stage, where the landscapes end in painted backdrops, and the effete French court minces through gorgeous sets with the naive perspectives and rich unnatural colors of a medieval Book of Hours. It is not until the night before Agincourt, when Henry moves anonymously among his sleepless soldiers, that the film finally arrives at a chiaroscuro naturalism.

There follows the magnificent ten-minute battle scene, shot by Robert Krasker in completely realistic style on the lush green fields of Ireland. Olivier had studied Uccello's painting *The Rout of San Romano* and the famous battle scene in Eisenstein's *Alexander Nevsky*. As Foster Hirsch writes in his useful monograph on Olivier, "his symmetrical arrangement of archers, his long shots of soldiers silhouetted against the horizon, and his dynamic cutting, acknowledge his debt to Eisenstein's epic. He creates tension by editing on conflicting directions of movement . . . [and] cuts are matched to the swelling cadences of William Walton's pageant-like score, which parallels Prokofiev's for *Alexander Nevsky* in its enhancement of the images." We return to the Book of Hours set for the last scenes (including Henry's courtship of the French princess, played by Renee Asherson), and end as we began in the Globe Theatre.

David Thomson wrote that *Henry V* "is filled with the stage artist's delight in so many new tricks and machines," and indeed Olivier shows extraordinary confidence in his exuberantly inventive use of dissolves, pans, and tracking shots (the latter brilliantly exploited as the camera follows the accelerating charge of the French knights). The performances, as another critic noted, are "solidly within the conventions of the classical theatre"—and permissibly so, since the movie keeps one foot on the stage. Olivier was co-author with Alan Dent and Reginald Beck of the adaptation, which—in this "patriotic" reading of the play—eliminates scenes that detract from Henry's image as a figure of absolute nobility. Pistol (Robert Newton) and his low comic friends remain to undercut the heroics a little, and the dying Falstaff is movingly played by the comedian George Robey.

As Foster Hirsch says, "no film had ever looked quite like this before; no film, especially for general audiences, had risked such glaring departures from the tradition of cinematic realism." There were objections to its mixture of visual styles and to its jingoistic Elizabethan militarism, but most critics recognized it as the first successful screen version of a Shakespeare play. James Agee, in a two-part review in the *Nation,* said that its "branching, nervous interpretive intelligence, so contemporary in quality, except that it always keeps the main lines of its drive and meaning clear . . . is vivid in every way during all parts of the film. . . . I am not a Tory, a monarchist, a Catholic, a medievalist, an Englishman, or . . . a lover of war: but the beauty and power of this traditional exercise was such that, watching it, I wished I was, thought I was, and was proud of it." Made at a cost of £500,000, it was a major financial as well as critical success, and did much to stimulate the postwar British film industry.

Henry V established Olivier as a major figure in the cinema, both as a director and as an actor. By the time it appeared, he had achieved equal distinction on the stage. In 1944 he was invited to assume the management of the Old Vic, together with Ralph Richardson and John Burrell. There followed the legendary seasons of 1944–1946, when Olivier gave a string of astonishingly varied performances that established him beyond question as the greatest living actor—dimwittedly gallant as Sergius in *Arms and the Man,* mordant as Richard III, wanly charming as Astrov in *Uncle Vanya,* a tempestuous, stammering Hotspur in *Henry IV, Part I* and a wizened Justice Shallow in *Part II.* In a double bill of arrogant virtuosity, he gave what was arguably the greatest performance of the decade as Sophocles' Oedipus, returning after a brief interval as the foppish Mr. Puff in Sheridan's *The Critic.* In 1946 the Old Vic went in triumph to New York, and the following year Olivier was knighted.

At the urging of del Guidice, he then undertook the production and direction of a screen version of *Hamlet.* Unlike *Henry V,* sprawling across "the vasty fields of France," *Hamlet* is confined to the castle at Elsinore, and Olivier decided that he should accept and exploit these spatial limitations. Though Roger Furse's castle is realistic enough, it has an almost Expressionist function—it deliberately suggests no "particular point in time or space," and its bare, cavernous chambers, broken up by pillars, arches, and staircases, fitfully lit, reflect the tortuous, deeply shadowed labyrinths of the Prince's mind.

Henry V was all color, pageantry, and extrovert action; *Hamlet* could scarcely be more different in conception. Shot by Desmond Dickenson in starkly contrasting black and white, it combines long takes with a restlessly mobile camera in a way more reminiscent of Orson Welles than Eisenstein. In place of the magic lantern cuts of *Henry V,* there is a dreamlike fluency of movement as we track from one chamber to another along corridors and up and down stairways. Wellesian deep focus is much used in scenes where the emotional separation of the characters is expressed in their physical remoteness from one another.

Here and there, the claustrophobic world of Elsinore is exchanged for a glimpse of other worlds outside—the Gravedigger (Stanley Holloway) digs real earth, the drowned Ophelia drifts in Millaisian beauty, and the pirate attack on Hamlet's ship is enacted with what are all too obviously model boats. These half-hearted attempts to "open up" the drama are on the whole clumsily handled. There is a more telling use of sound: the noise of waves that punctuates dialogue spoken on the ramparts; the ominous heartbeat heard whenever the Ghost appears.

When Hamlet himself first confronts his father's Ghost, the image zooms in and out of focus in time with the heartbeats, and there are other virtuoso visual effects, like the extreme high-angle shot of the night watch, isolated in swirling fog on the high ramparts. ("You feel dizzy when you look down from a great height," said Jean Renoir. "So what? What has that to do with Shakespeare?") Some scenes only described in the play are acted out on screen; on the other hand, most of the "To be or not to be" soliloquy is carried on the soundtrack while Hamlet muses unspeaking on the battlements. The duel scene is marvelously composed and edited, culminating in Olivier's tigerish leap upon Claudius (Basil

Sydney) from a high balcony. There follows the extraordinary conclusion, when Hamlet's body is carried up and up towards the topmost tower like a dead god, while lightning picks out the rooms in which his drama has been enacted.

Wanting an accessible *Hamlet* of acceptable feature-film length, Olivier and Alan Dent removed Fortinbras, Rosencrantz, and Guildenstern, and excised much else, including several of the soliloquies. Olivier was drawn to Freudian interpretations of the play and provided himself with a Gertrude (Eileen Herlie) young and attractive enough to justify the Oedipal fixation which accounts for Hamlet's misuse of Ophelia (touchingly played by Jean Simmons). This Oedipal reading, overt in the passionate intensity of the closet scene, is elsewhere played down, and a spoken prologue defines the Prince simply as "a man who could not make up his mind."

Few critics regard Olivier as one of the great Hamlets—he is magnificent in action and comedy, in evil and madness, but he has always had to push himself to the very limits of his range to convey self-doubt and the victories and tragedies of introspection. But if his Hamlet falls short of greatness it is still an intelligent, absorbing, and noble reading, and there were Oscars for Olivier as best actor and for *Hamlet* as best film of the year. There were critics who found its cinematic virtuosity self-conscious and others who complained, on the other hand, that it was no more than "canned theatre"; for David Thomson, it was the only one of Olivier's Shakespeare adaptations that was a true film, "rooted in the actual quality of the image."

During 1948 Olivier toured Australia with the Old Vic company, directing himself and Vivien Leigh in *The School for Scandal* and *The Skin of Our Teeth,* and playing Richard III under the direction of John Burrell. He and the other members of the famous triumvirate were then removed from the management of the Old Vic—he and Ralph Richardson, it was thought, were by then too much in demand as actors to be able to give their full attention to the company. Olivier nevertheless appeared with the Old Vic in 1949, and the following year took over the management of the St. James Theatre. His intention was to produce the best of contemporary drama there, but his choices were unfortunate and his intermittent tenancy of the St. James was not among his successes.

William Wyler brought Olivier back to the cinema in 1951 for *Carrie,* based on Dreiser's novel and co-starring Jennifer Jones. In 1953 he played MacHeath in Peter Brook's *The Beggar's Opera.* A rather unrewarding period in Olivier's career ended in 1955 when, at the Shakespeare

Memorial Theatre in Stratford-on-Avon, he burst back into the public eye with a splendid triptych of performances as Malvolio, Macbeth, and Titus Andronicus, the latter in Peter Brook's Grand Guignol production. The same year—in seventeen weeks—Olivier produced and directed his screen version of *Richard III* for Alexander Korda's London Films.

Olivier's Richard III, unlike his Hamlet, is one of his great roles. He plays this upstart who murdered his way to the throne as a capering hunchback of Machiavellian cunning and absolute evil—and then takes the audience into his confidence, makes it a party to his crimes, forces it —almost—to love him. In the film, Olivier cast Ralph Richardson as the Duke of Buckingham, John Gielgud as the Duke of Clarence, and Claire Bloom as Lady Anne—formidable competition. Nevertheless, in a way that he had scrupulously avoided in the two earlier Shakespeare films, Olivier built this one around his own "incomparably witty, incisive, vaudevillian performance" as a demonic "master of the revels."

Roger Furse's sets for *Richard III* are stylized rather like those for *Henry V*, suggesting illuminated manuscripts, though the climactic battle scene is again shot realistically on location (bare Spanish earth standing in for Bosworth Field). On the other hand, the movie is full of the long takes and careful compositions in deep focus that characterized *Hamlet*. As Foster Hirsch says, "Richard and his victims are often in the same frame, separated by arches or platforms or by the vast space of the throne room. Richard often spies on his intended victims from windows or raised galleries; he is dominant in the foreground, hatching his Machiavellian schemes, while his unsuspecting victims are confined to the depth of the frame. . . . The sense of flow and movement made possible by the long takes is suggested, with spectacular results, by Olivier's opening soliloquy, which is filmed in a single nine-minute take as the actor beckons the camera to follow him around the vast throne room that he plans to claim for himself."

Each of Olivier's Shakespeare adaptations has been claimed as the finest by a coterie of fans, of which *Richard III* has as many as any, though the play itself is scarcely a masterpiece. Discussing the three films in 1970, fifteen years after the last was released, Raymond Durgnat wrote of them in oddly ambivalent terms: "Their lack of conviction," he said (making a charge that many would reject), "results, not only from Olivier's acquiescence in the spirit of their age, but from a scepticism which is not quite aware of itself. For what Olivier treats with unconscious criticism is not the film medium, but the plays. The shifting stylizations of *Henry V* oddly prefigure Godard's use of the non-realistic, the non-conviction of life seen through the filter of an art which distorts."

Durgnat goes on: "The theme Olivier saw in *Hamlet* is a Godardian one—'Hamlet is the story of a man who cannot make up his mind'—and its surface conventionality is belied by something in Olivier's screen personality, something hard, stony, resentful, something that rebels, from within, against Hamlet's sensitivity, because it sees through it, as a Commissar or a Castro might have seen through it. If Richard III confides to the audience, it is because Olivier has gone more than half way to converting him from villain to hero; only a little more cynicism would have been needed for Machiavellian realpolitik to have cut through the whole iridescent spiderweb of Tudor propaganda. Beyond all these plays looms the shadowy figure of—The Entertainer. Which helps to explain why these strange films, with their interpenetration of energies and hollows, make so much more impact than the far more correct Castellani version of *Romeo and Juliet* (1954) . . . or the stylistic puffs and curls of Shakespeare à la Zeffirelli." *Richard III* won three British Film Academy awards and the Silver Bear at Berlin.

The death of Alexander Korda ended Olivier's plans for a screen version of *Macbeth,* but he remained eager to try his hand at directing a contemporary subject, and in 1957 he made, for Warner Brothers, *The Prince and the Showgirl.* This was an adaptation by Terence Rattigan of his own play *The Sleeping Prince*, in which Olivier had appeared on stage with Vivien Leigh. It is set in 1911 in London, where the crowned heads of Europe have gathered for the coronation of King George V. Among those present is Grand Duke Charles (Olivier), an ambitious foreign princeling who, requiring relaxation, seduces a chorus girl and then finds to his horror that she has taken his amorous protestations seriously. Olivier enjoyed himself as the imperious, disagreeable Grand Duke, but Marilyn Monroe was sadly miscast as the wistful heroine, and this stagey, trivial piece was not a success.

The same year Olivier scored a triumph with his stage performance as the seedy comedian Archie Rice in John Osborne's play *The Entertainer* (hence Durgnat's reference above). In 1959 he was Coriolanus at Stratford and in 1960 starred in Ionesco's *Rhinoceros.* Olivier's marriage to Vivien Leigh had been under increasing strain. A manic-depressive, she was desperately unsure of her own talent, and her condition was exacerbated by suggestions that

Olivier gallantly "acted down" to her when they appeared together, so as to conceal her inadequacies. She became increasingly unbalanced and abusive and, after a period of estrangement, they were divorced in 1961, when Olivier married Joan Plowright.

It was in 1961 also that Olivier accepted the directorship of the Chichester Festival Theatre, where he was a splendid Astrov in his immensely successful production of *Uncle Vanya*. Two years later he was named as the first director of Britain's new National Theatre. He retained the post for a decade, earning a predictable mixture of praise and brickbats, and appearing himself in *Uncle Vanya, The Recruiting Officer, Othello, Love for Love, The Dance of Death, The Merchant of Venice*, and *Long Day's Journey Into Night*. In 1970 he was created Baron Olivier of Brighton—the first British actor ever to receive a life peerage.

Olivier has directed only one other film, a screen version of Chekhov's *Three Sisters* (1970), with himself as Dr. Chebutykin and Joan Plowright as Masha. Made for the American Film Theatre, it was photographed by Geoffrey Unsworth, with music by William Walton. Although it uses a semi-naturalistic set, it is basically a record of a rather uninspired theatrical performance.

A number of Olivier's major stage performances have also been preserved (though generally diminished) in movies or television films directed by others—his Archie Rice in *The Entertainer* (Tony Richardson, 1960); his extraordinary macho black Othello (Stuart Burge, 1966); his Astrov in *Uncle Vanya* (Burge, 1964); the captain in Strindberg's *Dance of Death* (David Giles, 1969); James Tyrone in O'Neill's *Long Day's Journey Into Night* (1973); his controversial (because arguably racist) Shylock in *The Merchant of Venice* (1973). In 1977 Olivier undertook to produce and star in a series of American plays for British television, but got no further than relatively unsuccessful productions of Tennessee Williams' *Cat on a Hot Tin Roof* and William Inge's *Come Back, Little Sheba*.

Olivier has continued to accept roles in movies unconnected with his stage career, among them *The Devil's Disciple* (1959), *Spartacus* (1960), *Term of Trial* (1962), *Bunny Lake Is Missing* (1965), *Khartoum* (1966), *The Battle of Britain* (1969), *Sleuth* (1972), and *Love Among the Ruins* (1975). By 1976 he had survived three extremely serious illnesses, including cancer and thrombosis, but he has gone on working in films, generally in "cameo" roles. In 1982 he took the lead role in John Mortimer's *A Voyage Round My Father*, produced for British television and generally admired, and in 1983 gave one of his greatest Shakespearean performances in the Granada Television production of *King Lear*.

Almost beyond question the finest stage actor of his generation, Olivier has only intermittently achieved equal success on the screen—one critic suggests that "he is too big for the screen. He gives off so many volts that he upsets the camera." As a film director, his status has slumped in recent years, when many critics have tended to dismiss adaptations from other forms as irrelevant to the real business of the cinema, and to remain unmoved by claims that Olivier brought Shakespeare to millions all over the world. The fact remains that, as Foster Hirsch writes, this interloper from the theatre showed "extraordinary sensitivity to the texture and rhythm of films. In addition to his skillful handling of actors, he proved highly sophisticated in his composition of images, his use of camera movement and camera placement, his transitions in time and place, his pacing, and his creation of mood and atmosphere." His three Shakespeare films may outlast his doctrinaire critics.

Olivier has a son by Jill Esmond and three children by Joan Plowright. A domineering man, but with "a marvelous gift for intimacy," he had a reputation for volcanic rages and rough language, but is said to have mellowed in his old age (though not to have lost his ability to drink anybody else under the table without damage to his capacity for work). He is loaded with honorary degrees and assorted honors from all over the world; in 1979 he was awarded a special Oscar for "the full body of his work, the unique achievement of his entire career, and his lifetime of contribution to the art of film."

FILMS: Henry V, 1944; Hamlet, 1948; Richard III, 1955; The Prince and the Showgirl, 1957: Three Sisters, 1970.

ABOUT: Barker, F. The Oliviers, 1953; Cottrell, J. Laurence Olivier, 1975; Cross, B. (ed.) The Film Hamlet, 1948; Daniels, R. L. Laurence Olivier: Theatre and Cinema, 1980; Dent, A. (ed.) Hamlet: The Film and the Play, 1948; Durgnat, R. A Mirror for England, 1970; Eckert, C. W. Focus on Shakespearian Films, 1972; Geduld, H. M. Filmguide to Henry V, 1973; Gourlay, L. (ed.) Olivier, 1974; Hirsch, F. Laurence Olivier, 1979; Jorgens, J. Shakespeare on Film, 1977; Kiernan, T. Olivier, 1981; Lefevre, R. Sir Laurence Olivier, 1980 (in French); Morlay, M. (ed.) Olivier, 1978; Silviria, D. Laurence Olivier and the Art of Film Making, 1985; Spiel, H. Sir Laurence Olivier, 1958; Who's Who, 1982. *Periodicals*—American Film July–August 1977; Australian Journal of Screen Theory 7 1980; Film Quarterly Summer 1967; Films and Filming April 1955; Films in Review December 1979;

Focus on Film Spring 1973; Hollywood Quarterly Spring 1948; Kenyon Review Summer 1949; Times (London) May 17, 1982.

*"OPHULS," MAX (Max Oppenheimer; also signed himself **"Ophüls"** and **"Opuls")** (May 6, 1902—March 26, 1957), film and theatre director and scenarist, was born in Saarbrücken, Germany, an industrial town in the Rhine valley, not far from the French border. Jewish, rich, and well established, the Oppenheimer family owned an important Saarbrücken department store. The Saar was occupied by France from 1919 to 1935. Ophuls grew up speaking French fluently and chose to become a French citizen in 1938, but he usually wrote in German and always retained a German accent.

Passionately devoted to the theatre and without the slightest desire to enter the family business, Ophuls published his first theatre reviews in about 1920 and toyed with the idea of becoming a performer in the circus or music hall, entertainments that he loved all his life. Instead he became an actor—attracted, so he said, by the notion of having beautiful girls waiting for him at the stage door. Entering this [disreputable] profession at the age of eighteen, he adopted a pseudonym out of consideration for his bourgeois family. (Ophuls later insisted on the removal of the umlaut from his name, finding it disagreeably German; the American version, Opuls, never really caught on.)

Between 1920 and 1923 Ophuls appeared with repertory companies in Stuttgart, Aachen, and Dortmund, playing small parts in a great variety of plays and operas. Evidently he was notably untalented as an actor, as he was the first to admit. According to his own account, he was so bad in a comedy role at a Dortmund theatre that the manager threatened to cut his salary unless he doubled as a director. That was in 1923, and Ophuls found direction so much to his taste that he abandoned his acting career forthwith.

Ophuls is said to have staged some two hundred plays in Dortmund before moving on to Elberfeld-Barmen, where he directed operettas. He always lived beyond his means, and supplemented his income by working for radio, first as a literary critic, then as a poetry reader, adaptor, director, and writer of stories and plays. According to Paul Willemen, "he was to continue this radio work throughout his life, developing a format that could be described as a 'literary show': a mixture of extracts from novels, poetry, etc. ranging across a wide variety of styles, combined with improvisational pieces, reflections and comments, parodies and so on, the whole interwoven with sound and music effects."

MAX OPHULS

In 1926, when he was twenty-three, Ophuls became one of the youngest directors ever hired by the Burgtheater in Vienna, where he met and married the actress Hilde Wall. After a stint at the New Theatre in Frankfurt (1927), Ophuls joined the municipal theatre in Breslau, where between 1928 and 1929 he staged plays by Shakespeare, Molière, Kleist, Shaw, Pagnol, and Ben Hecht, among others. During this period he wrote the popular marching song "Murmeln," and he continued to write songs and revue material in Berlin, where he was invited in 1930 to direct a left-wing political play at the Lessing Theatre and remained to stage others at the Barnowski Theatre.

In those days Ophuls was an occasional moviegoer, an admirer of Chaplin, Fritz Lang, and Murnau. He was particularly "drawn to films which were absolutely non-naturalistic." After he had seen his first talkie he began to think that there might be a place for him in the cinema as a director accustomed to dealing with dialogue, though he still had reservations about the medium. He had his own first taste of filmmaking in 1930, when UFA hired him as a dialogue director on Anatole Litvak's *Nie Wieder Liebe*, which was made simultaneously in French and German.

The producers were impressed by Ophuls' work, and his own first film followed the same year. It was a forty-minute fantasy called *Dann schon lieber Lebertran* (*Rather Cod Liver Oil*), adapted by Ophuls and Emeric Pressburger from a story by Erich Kästner. (Ophuls said that he took the book from the shelf of the studio library just ahead of another young director with

°ō füls´

the same idea, Billy Wilder.) His second film, *Der Verliebte Firma* (*The Company in Love*, 1932), was a longer comedy in which a group of movie people become collectively infatuated with a beautiful young telegraph operator. They give her a lead role in the movie they are making but find that she is completely without talent. The girl winds up happily married instead.

Then came Ophuls' extraordinary screen version of Smetana's comic opera *The Bartered Bride* (1932). An entire Czech village was constructed in the hills near Munich, and Ophuls hired local inhabitants and professional circus entertainers as well as actors for the film. The great clown Karl Valentin gives a marvelous performance as the circus director—a man (according to Frieda Grafe) "who is always tripping up, lousing up the most apparently straightforward procedure or simplest statement," an elemental anarchic force. Bertolt Brecht is known to have learned much about the nature of spectacle from Valentin and Masao Yamaguchi has suggested that the techniques Ophuls shared with Brecht—especially his repeated use of a narrator or ringmaster to distance the audience from the action—may have been inspired in the same way.

In Ophuls' version of *The Bartered Bride* the songs are recited to music rather than sung, and he was equally unorthodox in his interpretation of the plot, turning it from a bourgeois comedy into an anarchic celebration of love and sex, fairs and circuses, full of puns and cheerful vulgarity. Trude Weiss, who disapproved of Ophuls's handling of the songs, nevertheless praised the skill with which he fitted visual rhythms to the music, and concluded that "the aim of the film seems to be to drag the lavish rhythms from their frame and dissolve the opera into a whirl of rapture and movement."

Frieda Grafe, discussing the same movie, wrote that "for Ophuls realism is a literary process, not a recipe for depicting reality. That is why for him there is no such thing as a model with a claim to priority, but simply images of images. . . . The things he introduces into his films take on multiple values, polyvalences, which dissolve the boundaries between high and low art. . . . The sense of freedom that you feel when you see *The Bartered Bride* (how funny it will be when everything falls apart) comes from Ophuls' lack of respect towards his source material."

Not much is known about *Die Lachende Erben* (*The Happy Heirs*), which followed in 1933; it is said to have been a musical based on the Romeo and Juliet story. It was *Liebelei* (1933) that brought Ophuls his first major suc-

cess. Freely adapted from Arthur Schnitzler's play and shot in four weeks, it was for Ophuls the most "simple, calm, tranquil" of all his films. *Liebelei* is set in Hapsburg Vienna, where a shy girl, Christine (Magda Schneider), falls in love with Fritz, a philandering young officer (Wolfgang Liebeneiner). In the film (though not in the play) he fully reciprocates her love, expressed in an unforgettable scene when the couple ride together in a sleigh through snow-covered woods. They have a brief interlude of happiness, and then Fritz, as a result of an earlier and more trivial affair, is forced to fight a duel. He is killed and Christine jumps to her death from the window of their flat.

With its virtuoso camerawork, its inspired use of music and sound, and its sparse dialogue, *Liebelei* has been much discussed as early evidence of Ophuls' view of the cinema as an essentially non-verbal art. ("The highest reaches of the actor's art," he wrote, "begin, I believe, at the point where words cease to play a part.") Many of Ophuls' films contain excerpts from operatic productions, and *Liebelei* begins at a performance of *The Abduction from the Seraglio*. Frieda Grafe has shown how Ophuls uses this scene "to create complicity between actor and audience": "The first act is over. The stage manager is looking out through the gap in the curtains into the auditorium. Perspectives are reversed." It is made known that the Emperor is arriving and "the audience rises, turns its back on the stage and looks up at the Emperor's box, which is now the stage, while the stalls have changed their function for a second time. The visual attention of the audience in the cinema is activated by seeing the people in the stalls first as subject, then as object, then as subject again. . . . The interchange between stage and auditorium becomes increasingly a stylistic device and a theme in Ophuls' films."

Other critics have drawn attention to other scenes in *Liebelei*, like the waltz in the café where the dancers swing around clockwise while the camera revolves in the opposite direction. The duel scene takes place off-screen and is brilliantly orchestrated with a section of Beethoven's Fifth Symphony which we then see is being played in rehearsal by Christine's father. At the end of the film, the camera looks down at Christine's body and the crowd around it in the snowy street, and then wanders around the empty apartment where she and Fritz had been happy, finally tracking through the snow-clad woods of the sleigh ride. Many of Ophuls' films are about love in the elegant, febrile society of Hapsburg Vienna or in other societies like it, but usually, as Jon Halliday points out, it is unrequited love or loveless desire: "Where true love does occur, as in *Liebelei*, it is blocked by social circumstances. . . . . All his characters are prisoners of social circumstances and of class."

When Hitler came to power in 1933, Ophuls and his family left Germany for Paris. There he quickly made *Une histoire d'amour*, a French version of *Liebelei* with different actors in the main parts: "All we redid was the close-ups," he said. "The rest was the German version, dubbed into French." After completing *On a volé un homme* (*A Man Has Been Stolen*, 1934), an unexceptional mystery story and an acknowledged pot-boiler, Ophuls moved on to Italy where he had been invited by Angelo Rizzoli, an newspaper publisher then beginning a new career as a film producer. For Rizzoli Ophuls made *La Signora di tutti* (*Everybody's Lady*, 1934), about the life and death of a famous movie star, Gaby Doriot (Isa Miranda).

The story is told in flashback as Gaby, anesthetized in an operating theatre after a suicide attempt, relives her life. Blessed and cursed with beauty, she has brought misery or death to almost everyone who has loved her. The operation fails and Gaby dies. The printing press we see at the beginning of the film churning out posters for her latest movie grinds to a stop. Claude Beylie called this melodramatic picture "the most musical of Ophuls' films" and Richard Roud thought it interesting in that "for the first time we see Ophuls' technique of telling a story in fragments. For there is not only long flashback (Gaby under ether), but this is broken up into many smaller flashbacks, thus announcing the technique of *La tendre ennemie* and *Lola Montès*."

Divine (1935), made in France from a scenario by Colette, is about a pretty country girl who goes to Paris to work as a dancer, becomes involved with a satanic music-hall snake charmer, and returns with relief to simple domesticity in the country. The music-hall background is brilliantly captured, and François Truffaut found this film "a little masterpiece of verve, health and life, a real little Renoir, with naturally that Ophulsian fury that drives the camera up staircases, into the flies, in and out of the wings." Other critics have been less impressed and Ophuls himself called the movie "my biggest flop." *Komedie om geld* (*The Trouble with Money*, 1936), which Ophuls made in Holland, is a complicated ironic comedy about the misfortunes of a bank clerk, with a shamelessly improbable happy ending (announced by a street singer, just as in Brecht's *Threepenny Opera*). Few copies survive but critics who have seen the film found it heavy going, in spite of some notable camerawork by Eugène Schufftan.

Back in France, Ophuls contributed two shorts, *Ave Maria of Schubert* and *La valse brillante*, to *Music and Cinema*, an anthology film compiled by Émile Vuillermoz. The five pictures that followed were also made in France. *La tendre ennemie* (*The Tender Enemy*, 1936), adapted from a play by André-Paul Antoine, is a study of a woman (Simone Berriau), prevented from marrying the man she loves, who drives both her husband and her lover to their deaths. Their ghosts turn up to prevent her from committing her own daughter to a similar marriage of convenience. The film is said to be one of considerable charm. Arthur Vesselo called it "a high achievement"—"the ingenuity of the original idea is equalled only by the subtle facility with which it is carried out."

Late in 1936 Ophuls visited the Soviet Union, where he had been offered a two-year contract. He was apparently not greatly impressed by what he saw there, and returned two months later to France. His next movie, *Yoshiwara* (1937), a triangular love story set in Tokyo and involving a Russian naval officer, a high-born *geisha*, and a young rickshaw coolie (Sessue Hayakawa), was a fiasco. *Werther* (1938), an adaptation of Goethe's novel, was, as Ophuls sadly recognized, not much better. On the other hand *Sans lendemain* (1940), starring Edwige Feuillère in a melodrama about a nightclub stripper who sacrifices herself for love, was found surprisingly delicate and effective—a better film than its foolish story line would suggest.

The last film Ophuls made before leaving France in 1940 was *De Mayerling à Sarajevo*, in which Feuillère plays the Czech Countess Sophie Chotek and John Lodge her royal lover, the Archduke Franz-Ferdinand. Once the couple are safely married, not a great deal happens in the film until the assassination at Sarajevo, and William Whitebait concluded that the movie's principal appeal lies in its portrait of court life, "seen with an eye that delights equally in elegance and absurdity."

Inducted into the French army in 1939, Ophuls had served briefly with an Algerian regiment before being granted leave to complete the Mayerling film. He next began work on a propaganda movie about the Foreign Legion. This project had to be abandoned because so many potential extras were being mobilized, and Ophuls then worked for a time on anti-Nazi radio propaganda. In 1940 he and his family joined the exodus from Paris, fleeing first to Aix-en-Provence and then to Marseilles and narrowly escaping arrest by the Vichy police. Finally they were permitted to leave for Switzerland, traveling with Louis Jouvet and his theatre company.

In Geneva Ophuls planned a film version of Jouvet's production of Molière's *L'École des femmes*. This scheme collapsed when their backer withdrew. Ophuls had more success in the Swiss theatre, directing two plays in Zurich. He needed a work permit to remain in Switzerland, however, and found that he could obtain one only by declaring himself a deserter from the French army. Ophuls refused to do this and instead set off for the United States. He finally arrived in Hollywood with his wife and child late in 1941. For four years he could find no work and was forced to accept financial help from European colleagues already established in Hollywood. At last, after many disappointments and some hardship, Preston Sturges (who had seen and admired *Liebelei*) invited Ophuls to work on a movie called *Vendetta*. His troubles were not over, however; disagreements soon developed between Ophuls and the producer, Howard Hughes, and Ophuls was fired, the film being completed by others.

After that, things began to improve. On the recommendation of his friend Robert Siodmak, Ophuls was hired by Douglas Fairbanks, Jr. to direct *The Exile* (1947), a costume drama about Charles II and his fleeting romance with a Dutch girl during his exile in Holland. Ophuls enjoyed making the movie and began to feel at home in Hollywood. The finest of his American films followed, *Letter from an Unknown Woman* (1948). Produced for Universal-International by John Houseman, and adapted by Howard Koch from Stefan Zweig's novella, it was photographed (like *Liebelei*) by Franz Planer in black and white. Zweig's story is in the form of a letter from Lisa Berndle to Stefan Brand, recalling the bleak history of their relationship. Loved and then abandoned by Brand, Lisa had been forced into prostitution to support herself and their son. She had become a successful courtesan until, meeting Stefan by chance, she had slept with him once more, finding that he had no idea who she was. Soon after this their son had died of typhus and Lisa herself was now fatally ill. Stefan, reading this letter from a woman now dead, is saddened to find that he still cannot remember her.

Ophuls (who worked on the script with Koch) considerably softened this grim story, as he almost invariably did in his adaptations of literary works. Lisa (movingly played by Joan Fontaine) does not become a courtesan but instead marries an older man who is kind to her. Nor does she go to bed with Stefan (Louis Jourdan) when they meet again. Her husband nevertheless challenges Stefan to a duel and, after reading the letter, Stefan accepts the challenge, knowing it means death. This adaptation is no doubt an example of "the sense of purity" that critics have discerned in Ophuls' work. He himself said that "the theme of purity may not be immediately apparent in a subject, but the story can develop towards that conclusion. A conclusion that has no explanation, that certainly doesn't find its explanation in real life. . . . Maybe I'm always looking for that beautiful purity without knowing it. It's the most wonderful thing when you find it."

The film had no great success in the United States at the time of its release there but admiration for it has grown. Karel Reisz, one of a group of critics who were responsible for its belated release in Britain, wrote in *Sequence* in 1952 that "It is typical of Ophuls' approach that while he has softened the ending he has also expanded and intensified the bitterness of Lisa's last encounter with her lover. . . . It is perhaps because of these inconsistencies that the film leaves one, in retrospect, with a slight sense of dissatisfaction. . . . But when this has been said, there remains a richness of observation and a feeling for the small situation that is deeply rewarding." Nicholas Wapshott, reviewing a revival twenty-seven years later, made the [interesting] point that, throughout the story, it is Lisa who takes the lead, both as "predator and victim." Wapshott goes on to praise Ophuls' evocation of old Vienna, its opera house, fairground, fashionable restaurants, and "cluttered drawing rooms." He writes: "Whether it is rug-beating day at a tenement, the courtyard filled with servants, dust and scampering children, or the bourgeoisie out for their Sunday strut, the camera weaves in and among them, illuminating the spectacle of the whole while eavesdropping on a more intimate scene to hear a snatch of conversation."

In *Caught* (1949), an ambitious young girl marries a monster of a millionaire (Robert Ryan) but eventually, after much suffering, finds happiness with a young doctor. There was much praise for the performances of Barbara Bel Geddes and James Mason, for Arthur Laurents' dialogue, and for the "elegantly low-keyed camerawork." Paul Dehn wrote that the film had been made in an idiom that he associated with Orson Welles—"overlapping conversation, dramatic lighting, a sultry sense of claustrophobia; but it is an idiom on which the director, Max Ophuls, has magnificently improved."

James Mason also starred in *The Reckless Moment* (1949), produced by Walter Wanger for Columbia and shot largely on location. Joan Bennett plays Lucia Harper, innocently involved in murder and threatened by blackmail, and Geraldine Brooks is her mother, who averts disaster by winning over the blackmailer (Mason). Gavin Lambert found the story unconvincing but wrote that "Ophuls' handling of it and a well-constructed script with some excellent dialogue . . . make it unexpectedly absorbing. Where the film excels is in its incidental observation of family life, in making the mother's predicament real and immediate."

Wanger then conceived the idea of tempting Greta Garbo back to the screen to star opposite James Mason in a film version of a Balzac story (*La Duchesse de Langeais*), to be filmed in France with Ophuls as director. The latter was sent to Paris in 1949 but nothing came of Wanger's scheme and in 1950 Ophuls started work for Sacha Gordine on *La Ronde,* a screen adaptation of Arthur Schnitzler's play *Reigen,* which he much admired. (Ophuls once said of Schnitzler that, reading him, "I *see* each thing. . . . I see it at once, and not in two different ways. I see how it has to be.")

Ophuls' script (written with Jacques Natanson) deals with ten characters from various walks of life, all living in an idealized Vienna in 1900. A prostitute picks up a soldier, who leaves her for a chambermaid, who leaves him for another man, who leaves her for a married woman, and so on in an endless round-dance of love. Ophuls had the benefit of a marvelous cast that included Anton Walbrook, Simone Signoret, Serge Reggiani, Simone Simon, Daniel Gélin, Danielle Darrieux, Fernand Gravey, Odette Joyeux, Jean-Louis Barrault, Isa Miranda, and Gérard Philipe. His crew (basically the same that worked on all his subsequent films) was equally distinguished—Christian Matras as director of photography, sets by Jean d'Eaubonne, costumes by Georges Annenkov. The result had an international box-office success that few European films have ever equalled.

The critical response was more ambivalent. Some saw the film as no more than a "bitter-sweet sexual comedy" of great technical virtuosity. Roy Armes wrote that "the film is full of cynicism and worldly wit and Ophuls takes an apparent delight in the manipulation of his characters, exploiting to the full the irony of their situation: the fact that their partners change but their gestures remain the same, that they are in turn deceivers and deceived, involuntarily echoing each other's words and sentiments. The film is episodic . . . and great ingenuity is shown by the authors in varying the routine of encounter, seduction and desertion. To link the episodes Ophuls used the famous waltz written for the film by Oscar Straus, the recurring image of the roundabout [carousel], and the very important character played by Anton Walbrook, that of master of ceremonies or *meneur de jeu* [a character who does not exist in the original play]. He

is a sort of personification of the director himself, manipulating the characters and making them dance to the tune of the waltz. . . . The fact that the circle is never broken gives a sense of fatality to the coupling of the characters and the dialogue is littered with epigrams about the impossibility of love and happiness." Henri Agel wondered whether the film's "bitter, angry libertinage . . . is not an inverse form of the nostalgia for purity," and Claude Beylie said that he did not know "of any more despairing work, crueller under a frivolous surface, of a more immaculate quality, and, beyond its swirling frenzy, more bare and stark."

Ophuls followed that triumph with *Le Plaisir,* based on three stories by Guy de Maupassant: "Le Masque" is about an old man who goes dancing every night in a youthful mask; "La Maison Tellier" discloses what happens when Madame Tellier shuts down her brothel for the day so that she and her employees can attend her niece's first communion (at which all the prostitutes weep for their lost innocence). In "Le Modèle" an artist drives his mistress to attempt suicide. The attempt fails but she is crippled and, in remorse, he marries her and devotes his life to caring for her. Ophuls assembled another brilliant company of actors, among them Madeleine Renaud, Danielle Darrieux, Jean Gabin, Pierre Brasseur, Daniel Gélin, and Simone Simon. Once again he used a narrator to connect the episodes as so many illustrations of the misery we endure in the pursuit of pleasure; he is played by Jean Servais in the French version of the film, by Peter Ustinov in the British version.

Unusually for Ophuls, parts of *Le Plaisir* were shot on location. However, the interior of the brothel in "La Maison Tellier," the longest of the three stories, was constructed in great detail in the studio—and then not used. Instead, the camera contents itself with scrutinizing the façade, climbing the walls, peering in at the windows. Ophuls jokingly (but perhaps significantly) explained that this was because the Maison Tellier was, after all, a *maison close*—a closed house. "Behind its doors and windows," as Paul Willemen puts it, "is locked away what a rigorous social morality excludes from its legal order."

Indeed, *Le Plaisir* is full of the tracking and crane shots that characterize Ophuls' work. Richard Roud has praised in particular the church sequence in "La Maison Tellier," "when the camera moves up a diagonal line of sculptured angels, following a shaft of light, cuts outside to the steeple, then back to the topmost angel, and then slowly descends the beam of light back to the congregation." Jon Halliday, discussing a literally indescribable quality in

Ophuls' cinema, mentions the inexplicable emotion "which Ophuls can conjure up as we follow the masked dancer, circling till he falls," in "Le Masque."

Madame de . . . was adapted by Ophuls, Marcel Achard, and Annette Wadement from a novella by Louise de Vilmorin. Ophuls said it was the story's construction that attracted him: "there is always the same axis around which the action continually turns, like a carousel. A tiny, scarcely visible axis: a pair of earrings." The earrings had been given to Madame de . . . (Danielle Darrieux) by her husband (Charles Boyer). The hopelessly extravagant heroine sells them to pay off her debts and tells her husband they were lost. But the jeweler sells them back to her husband, who gives them to his mistress as a farewell gift. She is returning to her own native country in Latin America, where the earrings are again sold. This time they are bought by a diplomat (Vittorio de Sica) who is then posted to Paris. He falls in love with Madame de . . . and gives her the earrings. Her husband sees them, discovers her infidelity, and tells the whole story to the diplomat. Shocked, he discards the adoring Madame de . . . , but she cannot forget him. Her husband, now furious, challenges the diplomat to a duel, and Madame D . . . dies of shock as the fatal shot is fired. (The duel was a dramatic inspiration of Ophuls'; in the book, the heroine simply expires of heartbreak, giving one earring to her husband, the other to her lover.)

Lindsay Anderson wrote that in *Madame de . . .* "the camera is never still; every shot has the tension of a conjuring trick. The sleight of hand is dazzling, but fatally distracting. . . . With a supple, ingenious, glittering flow of images that is aesthetically the diametric opposite of Mme de Vilmorin's chaste prose, he has made the film an excuse for a succession of rich decorative displays. . . . In all this visual frou-frou it is not surprising that the characters become lost, and the interior development of their drama is almost completely unobserved." This was a widely held view when the film was first released but, like many of Ophuls' late films, its stock has risen high since then. When it was revived in England in 1979, Derek Malcolm called it "a supreme piece of film-making which hardly puts a foot wrong for two hours . . . a magnificent and utterly timeless dissection of passion and affection, the game of life and love itself."

Lola Montès, Ophuls' last and greatest film, followed in 1956. It was an ambitious international coproduction, the most lavish of his movies, shot partly on location in Bavaria, on the Côte d'Azur, and in Paris. It is his only film in color. The script was adapted by Ophuls and others from a [trashy] popular novel by Cécil Saint-Laurent. There are echoes in the adaptation of the harsh fate of great stars like Judy Garland, but Lola Montès herself was not really the center of Ophuls' interest—her role, he said, "is roughly the same as that of our pair of earrings in *Madame de . . . ."*

The film opens in a circus in New Orleans in the late nineteenth century. The ringmaster (Peter Ustinov) introduces Lola (Martine Carol) and tells the audience that they are to hear her life story. The camera moves from a line of chorus girls to make a 360 degree revolution around Lola, chandeliers begin to rise and fall, the screen turns red, and we cut to the first flashback, recalling the end of Lola's affair with Franz Lizst. After a brief return to the circus there follows an astonishing sequence of crane shots of people at various levels of a staircase, which Lola ascends to meet the man her mother had once arranged for her to marry. In fact she had left home with someone quite different— her mother's lover.

We return to the circus, where Lola and her husband revolve clock-wise on a carousel while the camera revolves in the opposite direction. Further flashbacks deal with Lola's brief marriage, her first stage appearances, an affair with a married musician. Back in the circus, Lola is hauled up on the platform from which she is to make a death-defying jump. We then cut to a long flashback about Lola's period of happiness as mistress of the King of Bavaria (Anton Walbrook). In the circus again, Lola makes her jump. She is then placed in a cage, and men queue to kiss her hand at a dollar a time. In a very long crane shot, we move back along the line of men until the cage is only a shape in the distance. Curtains fall and the film ends.

Color is used in *Lola Montès* both for dramatic and psychological effect. Ophuls fills the circus scenes with colored light and dazzling costumes, and keys each of the principal flashbacks to a dominant color scheme corresponding to one of the seasons of the year (and of Lola's life). He is equally inventive in his handling of cinemascope, using the wide screen to excellent effect but also securing the advantages of close-ups by masking the unwanted parts of the screen with veils or panels. The camerawork throughout is incomparably brilliant. However, the film was not the simpleminded sexual romp the public had been led to expect but an unorthodox and disturbing masterpiece, and it failed at the box office. The producers cut the 140-minute original by thirty minutes, and cut again (to ninety minutes) for the British version. This cutting did no good; the film (which had cost over 650 million francs) was a commercial disaster and the producers were bankrupted.

The critics were more appreciative, warmly praising d'Eaubonne's sets, Annenkov's costumes, Matras' photography, Auric's musical score, and above all Ophuls' direction. Roy Armes called the film "awe-inspiring" technically, and went on: "All the features of Ophuls's style, all his favourite situations and love of opulence and intricacy are here. *Lola Montès* seems at times a synthesis of his life's work of twenty-one films. But what is lacking is depth: the whole tour de force is dazzling but ultimately quite remarkably hollow." Armes goes on to say that Ophuls "is virtually a test case of one's approach to the cinema. For those whose concern is purely visual and whose ideal is an abstract symphony of images, Ophuls has the status of one of the very great directors. For spectators and critics who demand in addition to the images the sort of human insight and moral depth that a play or a novel can give, he is merely a minor master."

Subsequent criticism has tended to confirm Ophuls' status as "one of the very great directors," and to deny that he is a mere formalist. Armes himself allowed that "it is possible to see Ophuls' films as a critique of elegant society"—one that points out for us the void that yawns "beneath those who base their lives on the search for pleasure." This view of Ophuls as a moralist *manqué* is strongly held by some French Catholic critics, especially in relation to *Lola Montès*. For Dominique Delouche, Lola is "a daughter of Eve, inheritor of Original Sin, still dizzy from the Fall" in a film that "brings us to the very foot of the Cross." Others, like Karel Reisz, see Ophuls as a social critic—although he "is clearly fascinated by the world he depicts," he "never allows his surface charm to obscure the price that has to be paid for its preservation." Jon Halliday concurs in this opinion, calling Ophuls a filmmaker "well aware of the structure of exploitation" and especially the exploitation of women by men.

The *nouvelle vague* critics in France have praised Ophuls as an *auteur* who, in the face of financial pressures and conflicts with producers, managed to impose an astonishingly consistent style and view of life on more than twenty films made in five different countries over a period of twenty-five years. André Bazin and others (including Henri Agel and Alexandre Astruc) particularly admired him for his relative lack of interest in montage (the juxtaposition of individual shots during editing) and his preference for extremely fluid camera movements within the sequence during shooting. Ophuls never totally rejected montage, however, and Andrew Sarris

and others have studied the combination in his work of the two methods.

Music is used to great effect in Ophuls' films and, as Richard Roud says, he "also used words, phrases, images musically—the recurring leitmotif of 'Vergogna' in *Signora di Tutti*; 'Ça va aller' in *Lola Montès*; 'quarante francs par jour' in *Divine*. These phrases are used almost operatically: they identify characters, they denote themes, they mark transitions." Roud also draws attention to Ophuls' "passion for decor: cages, mirrors, staircases (there are sixty shots of staircases in *Madame de . . .*), laces, gauzes, hangings, chandeliers. This heavily-charged decorative style is not to everyone's taste. . . . But it *is* a style, and a style in most cases in keeping with his subject."

In *Ophuls* (1978), Paul Willemen has offered another reading of the director's work as "a machine for the entrapment of the look" —particularly the scrutiny of the body of a woman, forbidden by social conventions but desired by the repressed victims of those conventions. Hence the obsessive circling of the *maison close* in "La Maison Tellier," and the entire structure of *Lola Montès*, "where the woman is explicitly and directly put on show, offered to the fixed and fixing gaze of viewer (in the film and of the film) and camera. But what the look finds is a mask, the woman as masquerade, as screen. . . . the look is offered (moves to) scene after scene, each constituting a trap for it, something in which it can lose itself . . . but nevertheless always lacking what it is looking for, and thus forever launching the wish to look again or to look elsewhere." Willemen goes on to show how this approach can be used to explain the fragmentation of narrative in Ophuls' work, the restlessness of his camera, the proliferation of detail in his sets: "Ophuls' cinema can be seen as the dramatisation of repression."

In 1957 Ophuls went to Hamburg to direct a production of Beaumarchais' *Mariage de Figaro*. He had been suffering for years from heart disease and in February 1957 he became ill and was admitted to a Hamburg clinic. He died there the following month at the age of fifty-four and his ashes were buried in a Paris cemetery. His son Marcel is also a filmmaker, a documentarist of distinction. François Truffaut and Jacques Rivette have said of Max Ophuls that "He was as subtle as he was thought ponderous, as profound as he was thought superficial, as pure as he was thought vulgar. . . . Luxury and insouciance only provided a favorable framework for this savage painter."

Late in his life, in an essay translated in *Ophuls* (1978), the director wrote: "Just one thing seems certain to me—that one ought not to be completely certain that one has found the story for a film until one feels that this vision is unalterably fixed in a succession of images or before one feels in oneself the almost physical desire to bring this sequence of images onto the screen. . . . The masters of our profession, René Clair or Jean Renoir, for example, Jacques Becker in his late work, or John Ford in many of his early films, in their best moments of 'in-sight' transcend both dramatic structure and dialogue, and create a new kind of tension which, I believe, has never existed before in any of the other forms of dramatic expression: the tension of pictorial atmosphere and of shifting images."

FILMS: Dann schon lieber Lebertran, 1930 (Germany); Die Verliebte Firma, 1932 (Germany); Die Verkaufte Braut (The Bartered Bride), 1932 (Germany); Die Lachende Erben, 1933 (Germany); Liebelei, 1933 (Germany); Une histoire d'amour, 1933 (French version of Liebelei); On a volé un homme, 1934 (France); La Signora di Tutti, 1934 (Italy); Divine, 1935 (France); Komedie om Geld (The Trouble with Money), 1936 (Netherlands); Ave Maria de Schubert, 1936 (France; short); La Valse Brillante, 1936 (France; short); La tendre ennemie, 1936 (France); Yoshiwara, 1937 (France); Werther, 1938 (France); Sans lendemain, 1940 (France); De Mayerling à Sarajevo (Mayerling to Sarajevo/Sarajevo), 1940 (France); Vendetta, 1946 (USA; completed by Preston Sturges, Stuart Heisler, Howard Hughes, Mel Ferrer); The Exile, 1947 (USA); Letter from an Unknown Woman, 1948 (USA); Caught, 1949 (USA); The Reckless Moment, 1949 (USA); La Ronde, 1950 (France); Le Plaisir, 1952 (France); Madame de . . . (The Earrings of Madame de . . .), 1953 (France); Lola Montès (The Fall of Lola Montès), 1955 (France/Germany). Published scripts—La Ronde in L'Avant-Scène du Cinéma April 1963; Lola Montès in L'Avant-Scène du Cinéma January 1969.

ABOUT: Annenkov, G. Max Ophuls, 1962 (in French); Armes, R. French Cinema Since 1946: 1, 1970; Astre, G. G. (ed.) Cinéma et roman, 1958 (in French); Beylie, C. Max Ophuls, 1963 (in French); Leprohon, P. Présences Contemporaines, Cinéma, 1957 (in French); Mancini, M. Max Ophuls, 1978 (in Italian); Ophuls, M. Spiel im Dasein, 1959 (in German; translated into French as Max Ophuls, 1963); Rhode, E. Tower of Babel, 1966; Roud, R. (ed.) Cinema: A Critical Dictionary, 1980; Roud, R. Max Ophuls: An Index, 1958; Sarris, A. (ed.) Interviews with Film Directors, 1967; Willemen, P. (ed.) Ophuls, 1978. Periodicals —Cahiers du Cinéma June 1957, March 1958; Cinéma (France) May 1957; Cinema (Switzerland) 29–30 1962; Cinématographe December 1977; Film Comment Winter 1969, Winter 1970–1971, Summer 1971; Filmkritik December 1977; New York Times March 27, 1957; Seventh Art Summer 1964; Sight and Sound Summer 1957; Time Out August 18–24, 1978; Yale French Studies Summer 1956.

OZU, YASUJIRO (December 12, 1903–December 11, 1963), Japanese director and scenarist, was born in the old Fukagawa district of Tokyo, one of the five children of a fertilizer merchant. When he was ten his father ordained that the children should be educated at Matsuzaka, in Mie Prefecture, the family's ancestral home. Ozu grew up there, separated from his father and indulged by his mother. This imbalance in his own family life presumably accounts for the obsessive analysis in his films of the Japanese family as an institution—especially the role of the father—as well as his preoccupation with themes of separation and loneliness.

By the time he entered Uji-Yamada Middle School at the age of sixteen, Ozu was an intransigent and hard-drinking youth, intellectual in his interests but without academic ambitions. When he was seventeen, an indiscreet letter to a younger boy got him expelled from the school dormitory (though such billets-doux were common enough in single-sex schools like his). Thereafter he had to commute daily from home. Ozu adroitly exploited this punishment to gain greater freedom than ever, and this was typical of his contempt for restrictions of any kind, and his skill in bypassing them.

If his studies did not interest Ozu, literature did, and in middle school he developed a precocious taste for the work of such contemporary writers as Junichiro Tanizaki, Ryunosuke Akutagawa, and Naoya Shiga. And he had an even greater passion for Hollywood movies, playing truant in Tsu and Nagoya to follow the latest exploits of Pearl White and William S. Hart, and writing fan letters to *benshi* (film narrators) in Kobe. He boasted that, when he should have been sitting the entrance examination to Kobe Higher Commercial School, he was actually in a movie theatre watching Rex Ingram's *Prisoner of Zenda*.

Having failed such examinations as he did take, Ozu was unemployed for a time after leaving middle school, then worked for a year as an assistant teacher in a village school near Matsuzaka. By the time the family was reunited in Tokyo in 1924, his heart was set on a film career. His bourgeois father naturally opposed this choice but Ozu, who became famous for his stubbornness, went ahead anyway and, through a family friend, secured an introduction to the Shochiku company, formed a few years earlier. The executives at Shochiku's Kamata studios were astonished to learn that, in all his youthful years of dedicated moviegoing, he had seen only three Japanese films, but they hired him nevertheless as an assistant cameraman—in those days a menial who served as the cameraman's caddie.

YASUJIRO OZU

Ozu spent most of 1925 in the army reserve, feigning tuberculosis by "dipping the thermometer in warm water and coughing," and thus contriving to pass the time restfully in hospital. A year after his return to Shochiku he talked his way into a job as assistant director to Tadamoto Okubo, who specialized in risqué "nonsense" comedies. Apart from his fondness for bathroom humor, there is no evidence in Ozu's own films that Okubo had the slightest influence on him. Though he eventually made up for his ignorance of Japanese cinema by studying the work of his seniors at Shochiku, Ozu maintained that he then "formulated my own directing style in my own head, proceeding without any unnecessary imitation of others. . . . For me there was no such thing as a teacher. I have relied entirely on my own strength."

Notoriously hard-working in later years, Ozu enjoyed his stint as an assistant director primarily because he "could drink all I wanted and spend my time talking." He was nevertheless promoted before the end of 1927, joining the Shochiku division devoted to churning out period films. He made his debut as a director with *Zange no yaiba* (*The Sword of Penitence*, 1927), based on a Hollywood movie called *Kick-In* by the French-born director George Fitzmaurice. The script was by Kogo Noda, who was to write all of Ozu's major films of the 1950s and 1960s. The young director was called up for another session in the reserve before shooting was complete, and when he finally saw the movie he disowned it.

This was Ozu's only period picture. He switched once and for all to contemporary themes with his second film, *Wakodo no yume* (*The Dreams of Youth,* 1928), a comedy of college life made in imitation of American movies on the same popular subject. Between the beginning of 1928 and the end of 1930, Ozu made eighteen films on an assortment of topics— student life, the problems of young married couples, and the lighter side of life in the Depression. All of them were comedies, and some were made in as little as five days.

It was a hectic apprenticeship. Ozu said it was not until he had made four or five movies that he really knew what he was doing and "began to like being a director." Even then, however, he was building up a team of regular collaborators, some of whom worked with him for the rest of his life. These early pictures were generally scripted by Ozu in collaboration with Kogo Noda, Akira Fushimi, or Tadao Ikeda, and photographed by Hideo Shigehara. Early recruits to the director's stable of actors included Takeshi Sakamoto, Choka Iida, and Chishu Ryu (who appeared in all but two of Ozu's fifty-three films).

At this stage, Ozu's work still showed the influence of the Hollywood movies he had so loved during his adolescence. But increasingly he was finding his own way and moving in the direction of the *shomin-geki*—the "home drama" of everyday life among the lower middle-classes, in a Japan that was evolving at bewildering speed from feudalism to Western-style capitalism.

The first of his films to bear the hall-marks of the genre was *Kaishain Seikatsu* (*The Life of an Office Worker,* 1929), scripted by Noda. It is a wry comedy about a hard-up married couple who dream all year about the husband's expected annual bonus, then have to come to terms with the fact that, because of the Depression, he loses not only his bonus but his job as well. Here, for the first time in Ozu's work, "nonsense" comedy gags took second place to the demands of social and psychological realism. There was a further advance in *Tokyo no gassho* (*Tokyo Chorus,* 1931), a much darker comedy with a very similar plot about a "salaryman" who bravely defends an unjustly dismissed colleague, is fired himself, and endures many "painfully comic" misadventures before he is rescued by old friends.

Tokyo Chorus finished third in *Kinema Jumpo's* annual poll of the year's ten best films, the second consecutive year his work received this honor (in 1930 the now-lost *Ojosan* (*Young Miss*), a comedy centering on a woman journalist, had also been awarded third place). The following year Ozu topped the poll for the first time with *Umarete wa mita keredo* (*I Was Born, But . . .*). In the course of his career, Ozu would receive six *Kinema Jumpo* "best ones," more than any other director in the history of Japanese cinema.

An original script from an idea of Ozu's own, *I Was Born, But . . .* centers on two small boys whose admiration for their father leads them into a battle with his boss's son. They are shocked when they see their "great man" toadying to his employer and, when he explains that he needs his job in order to feed them, they resolve to eat no more. But their hunger is stronger than their idealism. They abandon martyrdom and, their bellies filled, cheerfully accept the status quo.

This moving comedy was a great success, critically and financially, and is generally recognized to be Ozu's first major film. The father is shown to be weak, foolish, and inconsistent—for example smoking a cigarette while exercising—but his lazy and pompous boss is an equally ridiculous figure, and there is obviously no moral justification for the difference in status between the two men. When the boys learn to accept this injustice they consign themselves, as their parents realize, to "the same kind of sorry lives that we have." However amusingly presented, it is a bleak perception of the sort that has antagonized activist critics of Ozu's work, while establishing him in other eyes as "the artist of life as it is."

The conformity and regimentation of Japanese society is wittily pointed up when a tracking shot of children drilling at school is echoed, "in a marvelous use of matched cutting," by one of yawning office workers at their ranked desks. However, as Audie Bock says, "Ozu would later dispense with such associative editing, camera movement and cutting on action." He was already deeply immersed in the exploration of cinematic theory and technique, and working his way steadily towards the chaste simplicity of his mature style. He only used dissolves once in his entire career (in *Life of an Office Worker*), promptly rejecting the device as "uninteresting," and by 1932 he was finding the fade equally pointless. "Generally dissolves and fades are not a part of cinematic grammar," he remarked. "They are only attributes of the camera."

Another *Kinema Jumpo* "best one" followed in 1933, the "subtle, beautiful" *Dekigokoro* (*Passing Fancy*), also scripted from an original idea of Ozu's. It deals, not with the "people like you and me" of the conventional *shomin-geki,* but with the relationship between an illiterate brewery worker and his better educated son. The father, long since abandoned by his wife, becomes infatuated with a much younger woman who has no interest in him. The son's recognition of his father's foolishness leads to a fight that brings the latter to his senses. The boy

becomes seriously ill and afterwards, to pay for his medical expenses, his father sets off for Hokkaido as a hired laborer. As the boat leaves Tokyo harbor he recognizes a more important responsibility, jumps overboard and swims ashore to rejoin his son, happily repeating a silly joke the boy had told him. "This is a sequence rare in Ozu," wrote Joan Mellen, "involving a human being immersed in the elements and there achieving peace with himself. Kihachi's swimming is filmed as a natural and beautiful act, expressive of an emotional resonance Ozu attaches to the return to his son."

Ozu's own father had become reconciled to his choice of career, and by then he was living in the parental home in Tokyo, as he did for the rest of his life. He was terrified of women and, though he frequently fell in love with his actresses, and sometimes went so far as to arrange meetings, nothing ever came of these assignations and he remained unmarried. His father died in 1934, choosing him as head of the family "though he knew that I was the last person to be relied upon." Much moved, Ozu seems to have taken his responsibilities very seriously and to have matured considerably, though he always remained a heavy drinker.

The director's first picture had been based on one by George Fitzmaurice, and another Fitzmaurice movie, *The Barker* (1928), inspired *Ukigusa monogatari* (*A Story of Floating Weeds,* 1934), which was infinitely superior to its model. Ozu won his third consecutive *Kinema Jumpo* "best one" for his rendering of a traveling theatre troupe's visit to a mountain village where the group's leader, now married to a jealous actress, encounters a former mistress and the son he had casually fathered. Donald Richie called this "a picture of great atmosphere and intensity of character, one in which story, actors, and setting all combined to create a whole world, the first of those eight-reel universes in which everything takes on a consistency somewhat greater than life: in short, a work of art."

Ozu held out against sound long after all the other Shochiku directors had adopted it—he was intent on reducing his means rather than extending them and he had, besides, promised his photographer Hideo Shigehara to wait until the latter had perfected a sound system of his own. "If I can't keep promises like this," Ozu wrote in his diary in June 1935, "then the best thing would be to give up being a director—which would be all right, too." He finally succumbed the following year, afraid that he was being "left behind by the other directors." The new medium affected his working methods less than he had expected: indeed, the stationary microphone gave him even greater control over his actors than before, forcing them to rely on the small stylized movements and changes of expression that for him spoke more clearly and precisely than more expansive actions.

His first talkie was *Hitori musuko* (*The Only Son,* 1936), adapted from an old script by "James Maki" (Ozu). The heroine is an elderly woman worn out by her struggle to put her son through college. After a long separation, she uses up her meager savings to visit him in Tokyo and finds that her grand hopes for him have come to nothing—he is an ill-paid schoolteacher, scarcely able to support his wife and child. Nevertheless, he borrows enough to entertain her, and promises to resume his studies; she goes home ready to "die in peace." In fact, the son seems already quite defeated by life and this is one of the darkest and most poignant of Ozu's films.

He made one more picture before the outbreak of the Sino-Japanese War, a gently ironic study of a marital crisis called *Shukujo wa nani o wasuretaka* (*What Did the Lady Forget?,* 1937). The first film Ozu made at Shochiku's new sound studios at Ofuna, it was also the first in which he addressed himself to the problems of upper middle-class professional people, the subjects of many of his later movies. The same year he was drafted and sent to China as an infantry corporal—an experience he could scarcely bring himself to speak of either in his diaries or in subsequent conversation.

When Ozu returned to Shochiku in 1939, his cameraman Hideo Shigehara had moved on to another company. The two films he made during the war were shot by Shigehara's former assistant, Yuharu Atsuta, who became his regular cameraman. The first was *Toda-ke no kyodai* (*The Brothers and Sisters of the Toda Family,* 1941), an account of the tensions that arise when a widow and her daughter move in with a married son. Like several of Ozu's prewar pictures, it topped the *Kinema Jumpo* poll and was a great critical success; much more unusually, it was also a box-office hit—perhaps because the Japanese public, educated by the suffering, separations, and losses of war, was by then better able to understand Ozu's point of view.

His new-found popularity was confirmed by *Chichi ariki* (*There Was a Father,* 1942), with Chishu Ryu in one of his finest performances as a schoolteacher who gently guides his son through the vicissitudes of childhood and adolescence, conscription and marriage.

Ozu's admirers claim that, in his two wartime films, he refused to exploit his subjects for propaganda purposes. Joan Mellen agrees that he was neither a propagandist nor an imperialist, calling him in fact "the least overtly didactic of any Japanese director," but argues that the movies he made during and after the war nevertheless endorse a reactionary Japanese spirit: "Ozu evoked traditional ideas not because the militarists forced him to, but because he believed in them," and he "accomplishes his propaganda for the war [which is scarcely mentioned] through appeals to a traditional style of obedience, which is, however, only a brief step away from enlisting that obedience in the service of the State."

The facts remain that at least one of Ozu's wartime scripts was rejected by the censors as "unserious," that he somehow avoided making a single militaristic or imperialist film, and that he took serious risks in defending against the censors the work of fellow-directors like Akira Kurosawa. According to Masahiro Shinoda, "he always made such funny jokes, always got everyone in such a good mood, and was so expert in saying a serious thing in a light way, that nothing ever happened to him." In 1943 Ozu was sent to Singapore to make propaganda films and even then managed to do no such thing. He passed the time viewing confiscated American movies and was impressed above all by one absolutely remote from his own style, Orson Welles' *Citizen Kane.* After six months as a prisoner of war, Ozu was repatriated in February 1946.

By this time, he was very clear about what he wanted to do and how he wanted to do it. Like many Japanese, he had begun by exploring Western styles and attitudes, but as he grew older turned more and more to the traditional Japanese ideals, defined by Donald Richie as "restraint, simplicity, and near-Buddhist serenity." The conflict between the radical individualism of the young and the older generation's nostalgic devotion to these qualities is often a source of tension in his films, whose theme is almost invariably the Japanese family—most often the relations between parents and children.

"Pictures with obvious plots bore me now," Ozu said after the war. He thought that conventional drama made it easy for a director to arouse emotions in his audience, but was only an "explanation" of human motivations that concealed the real truth. His endless variations on a few simple and archetypal themes gave him all the scope he ever needed for his purpose, which was the rigorous exploration of character as a revelation of what was fundamental in the human condition. It was an approach that had much in common with the work of one of Ozu's favorite writers, Naoya Shiga, who in his novels also eschewed plot and dramatic effect to study in minute detail the often irrational interactions that take place within the microcosm of the family.

Donald Richie writes that "Ozu's later films are probably the most restrained ever made, the most limited, controlled, and restricted." They are typically built up as a mosaic of brief shots—often one for each line of dialogue—taken from directly in front of the actor who is speaking, and from a very low angle. The "Ozu shot," Richie says, is "taken from the level of a person seated in traditional fashion on *tatami* [matting]. Whether indoors or out, the Ozu camera is always about three feet from floor level, and the camera never moves. There are no pan shots and, except in the rarest of instances, no dolly shots. This traditional view is the view in repose, commanding a very limited field of vision but commanding it entirely. . . . It is the aesthetic passive attitude of the haiku master who sits in silence and with painful accuracy observes cause and effect, reaching essence through an extreme simplification." Audie Bock maintains that Ozu consistently shot from a height of even less than three feet, however, and suggests that the effect of this on the audience "is to force [it] to assume a viewpoint of reverence . . . toward ordinary people. Its power is not one of contemplation but of involuntary veneration."

As Bock says, Ozu placed his characters in film after film in similar settings—"the home, the office, the tea salon, the restaurant or bar are the places in which the plain but deeply illuminating conversations occur." And the director was notoriously perfectionist about the positioning of objects within these sets, often "demanding that furniture, teapots, cups, vases be moved one or two centimeters this way or that until he got exactly the composition he wanted, whether it maintained continuity from shot to shot and satisfied logic or not."

Ozu was no less demanding in his direction of actors, Bock says. He "would allow no one to dominate a scene. . . . Like the stories, the settings, and the events, if the acting became individualized and special, Ozu's balance would be upset." Chishu Ryu, who gave his finest performances under Ozu's direction and in the later films became in effect the director's spokesman, said he felt he "was only the colors with which Ozu painted his pictures. . . . I once heard Ozu say, 'Ryu is not a skillful actor—that is why I use him.'" Less modest performers naturally resented Ozu's habit of making them rehearse some minute gesture twenty or thirty times in pursuit of an effect that he would not bother to explain, even though his purpose would become clear when the film was finally edited.

The first film Ozu made after the war was *Nagaya no shinshi roku* (*The Record of a Tenement Gentleman,* 1947), a rather uncharacteristic piece drawing on one of his old scripts. *Kaze no naka no mendori* (*A Hen in the Wind,* 1948) was also somewhat atypical, with its relatively melodramatic story about a woman forced into a single night of prostitution during the war, when her husband is away and their child needs medical treatment she cannot otherwise afford. When her husband is finally repatriated and she confesses her fall from grace, he knocks her down the stairs, but gradually comes to understand and accept that she had had no choice. It seemed to Joan Mellen that Ozu had "brilliantly and honestly confronted the postwar moment," showing how Japan—like the heroine—had become prostituted to the sleazy values of the Occupation. Ozu himself thought the movie "a bad failure."

For his next picture, *Banshun* (*Late Spring,* 1949), Ozu was reunited with his favorite scenarist Kogo Noda, with whom he wrote all of his subsequent scripts. They would begin with the dialogue, always written with particular actors in mind, and let character and setting emerge from that. Both men worked best late at night while consuming large quantities of sake or whiskey at some inn, and they hardly ever disagreed. Ozu maintained that the quality of a film was directly proportionate to the number of bottles he and Noda emptied.

Late Spring launched the series of almost plotless masterpieces that crowned Ozu's career. A young woman (Setsuko Hara) lives with her widowed father (Chishu Ryu) and will not consider marriage, preferring her state of cosy dependence to the responsibilities of childbearing and household management. The father, afraid that she faces a lonely and barren future after his death, lets it be known that he himself intends to remarry, and she then sadly and reluctantly takes a husband. The father remains alone, as he had always intended, condemned by his sense of duty to a solitary and empty old age.

Ozu's late films typically open with a sequence establishing a mood of quiet, dispassionate observation. *Late Spring* starts with one in a temple in Kamakura, the old Japanese capital. "Nothing happens," wrote Donald Richie. "No one is visible. The shadows of the bamboos move against the *shoji*; the tea kettle is boiling, the steam escaping. It is a scene of utter calm. There is no subject, no theme, unless it is the gratefulness of silence and repose. This quality having been established, one of the characters enters and the story begins. Empty rooms, uninhabited landscapes, objects (rocks, trees, tea kettles), textures (shadows on *shoji*, the grain of *tatami*, rain dripping) play a large part in Ozu's world."

The most discussed scene in *Late Spring* comes at the very end, after the daughter has left. The father sits alone, methodically peeling a pear. He lets the peel drop and his head falls slightly. "Is it too much to suggest that Ozu . . . designed the film to set off this one shot?" asked Don Willis. "The slight falling movement of Ryu's head is the suggestive emotional centre of *Late Spring*, as Setsuko Hara's great performance is the expressive centre." And Richie wrote that "the end effect of an Ozu film . . . is a kind of resigned sadness. . . . The Japanese call this quality (an essential manifestation of the Japanese aesthetic spirit) *mono no aware*, for which the nearest translation might be *lachrimae rerum*, Lucretius' reference to those tears caused by things as they are."

From the lonely figure of the father, Ozu cuts away to a deserted shore, and the film ends with an image of gentle waves. Audie Bock believes that the director uses images of this sort not as "symbols in the western sense, but [as] vehicles for the transcendent, ineffable quality of life that takes us outside of mere human emotion."

This aspect of Ozu's work is discussed at considerable length by Paul Schrader in *Transcendental Style in Film: Ozu, Bresson, Dreyer*, in which he defines transcendental style as "a form which expresses something deeper than itself, the inner unity of all things." Schrader continues, "In Ozu's films, as in all Oriental art, the form itself is the ritual which creates the eternal present (*ekaksana*), gives weight to the emptiness (*mu*), and makes it possible to evoke the *furyu*, the four basic untranslatable moods of Zen. . . . The greatest conflict (and the greatest resulting disillusionment) in Ozu's films is not political, psychological, or domestic, but is, for want of a better term, 'environmental.' . . . Ozu responds to the disunity in Japanese life by evoking the traditional verities of Zen art in a contemporary, cinematic context."

Late Spring, called "one of the most perfect, most complete, and most successful studies of character ever achieved in Japanese cinema," was a *Kinema Jumpo* "best one," and so was *Bakushu* (*Early Summer*), which followed in 1951, after the comparatively minor *Munekata Shimai* (*The Munekata Sisters*). It has been pointed out that Ozu's theme is not so much the Japanese family as its dissolution, and this is very much the case in *Early Summer*, in which Setsuko Hara again plays the woman whose late, reluctant marriage unravels a close-knit family— in this case one of three generations.

Ochazuke no Aji (*The Flavor of Green Tea Over Rice*, 1952), dealing with a middle-aged childless couple, builds to a somewhat more conventionally dramatic crisis than usual. The refined and arrogant wife, scornful of her unsophisticated husband, realizes how much he means to her when it seems that he is to be sent away on business. At the end they share a quintessentially Japanese meal of rice soaked in green tea, which is "simple and unpretentious. It's how a married life should be." Their "modern" niece, whose story provides a subplot, comes to recognize over the same period that "feudal" arranged marriages can sometimes make sense.

Joan Mellen compared this film, to its disadvantage, with Mikio Naruse's similar *Repast* (1951), saying that in Ozu's movie "the wife's side is finally given very little credibility. . . . Where Naruse blames the wife's unhappiness in part on social conditions . . . , Ozu, more conservative, suggests that it is in the nature of things for . . . people sometimes to be thwarted in their desires. . . . In his insight into the silent, forced submission to circumstance of the Japanese wife, Naruse shows a sympathy with the trials of the Japanese woman of which Ozu was incapable." In fact, Ozu said that he had "wanted to show something about a man from the viewpoint of a woman," but acknowledged that this film, adapted from an old script, "wasn't very well made."

For many critics, the simplicity and purity of Ozu's mature style reached its apotheosis in *Tokyo monogatari* (*Tokyo Story*, 1953), described by Robert Boyers as "a work that fairly epitomizes transcendental style." An elderly couple (Chishu Ryu and Chieko Higashiyami), living by the sea at Onomichi in the south of Japan, visit their married children in Tokyo. They find that their son and daughter have become mean and selfish, dehumanized by life in modern Tokyo, and they are kindly treated only by Noriko (Setsuko Hara), their widowed daughter-in-law, who in spite of her poverty has retained the traditional Japanese virtues.

The old people are bundled off to the hot spring resort at Atami, which they hate. They return to Tokyo, where the wife spends a happy night in Noriko's small apartment while the husband is out drinking with old cronies. On the way home, the wife becomes ill and the family, concerned at last, assembles briefly at her deathbed. When the others leave to pursue their own affairs, Noriko stays behind to console the old man and it is he who urges her to forget her duty to his dead son and marry again. In the end he is alone but outside, in Onomichi harbor, life goes on.

Richie points out that Ozu could have provided some consolation by ending the film "with a final shot of the daughter-in-law going off into a happier future." He does not do so partly because he does not believe in such consolations, partly because he "refuses to compromise his theme. . . . By ending the drama (the daughter-in-law) before he ends the film, by returning to the father, by showing us the by-now familiar port shots, which reoccur like closing chords in this final coda, by referring, finally, to the larger context of city, sea, mountains, he also suggests that what we are seeing occurs every day, that it is common, that it has happened before and will happen many times over, that it is the way of the world." Stanley Kauffmann, rating this film as one of his ten personal favorites of all time, writes, "By holding to truth, much more than to naturalism, he [Ozu] gives us a process of mutual discovery, the characters' and ours."

In *Soshun* (*Early Spring*, 1956), a white-collar worker in Tokyo, bored with his job and his marriage, has an affair with a girl at work. He and his wife separate but, when he is transferred to the provinces, she accompanies him and they make a fresh start. As Joan Mellen writes, "the husband's transfer allows them the opportunity to renew feelings weakened by the environment of sleazy bars, gigantic glass office buildings compartmentalizing men into robots, packed trains, and streets filled with black smoke spewed out as factory waste. Ozu associates, quite brilliantly, the man's abuse of his wife, such as his mindless anger at dinner's not being ready and his infidelity, with alienation at the workplace."

The same critic described *Tokyo boshoku* (*Tokyo Twilight*, 1957) as "the darkest and strongest of Ozu's films about the disintegration of the family." Chishu Ryu plays a father living alone with his two daughters. The elder (Setsuko Hara) has left her husband and the younger (Ineko Arima) is having an affair that results in an abortion. When they discover that their mother, whom they presumed dead, is actually living with another man, the younger daughter commits suicide and the elder returns to her husband, leaving the father alone. The extreme and unrelieved pessimism of this film, which displeased some critics, is, as Don Willis says, "understated, distilled in sounds and silences. . . . The meaning of the film rests in the pointed silences of the characters. Those silences are like psychic dead ends, intimations of defeat."

After the "harsh" and "cheerless" black and white of *Tokyo Twilight* came Ozu's first film in color, *Higanbana* (*Equinox Flower*, 1958), "a warm comedy of reconciliation which brings its characters together as convincingly and movingly as *Tokyo Twilight* leaves them scattered and alone." An old-fashioned father (Shin Saburi) is hurt when his daughter (Ineko Arima) becomes engaged without his consent, and the film turns on the efforts of the mother and a friend from Kyoto to win him over. There is a characteristically broad running gag concerning the Kyoto woman, who rushes to the lavatory whenever she becomes excited. However, as Audie Bock remarked, "even the jokes and gags in late Ozu have a sharply ironic edge to them, often centering on aging. Ozu never, to the very end, condescended to offer palliatives for the pain of living."

Ozu's next three pictures were all variations on themes he had used in successful earlier films, beginning with *Ohayo* (*Good Morning*, 1959), a less sharply ironic version of *I Was Born, But . . .* Another silent film, *A Story of Floating Weeds*, was remade in 1959 as *Ukigusa* (*Floating Weeds*), with the action shifted from the mountainous north of Japan to the island of Shijima in Wakayama. One of the handful of pictures Ozu made for a company other than Shochiku, this was magnificently photographed in color by the great Daiei cinematographer Kazuo Miyagawa. Donald Richie found "an autumnal sadness" in the new film, but less bitterness in the portrayal of the misery of the twice-abandoned mistress. Don Willis thought the remake "a much greater film" than the original because of "the way Ozu and Noda tighten, loosen, distill and in general deploy the narrative elements—comic, dramatic, atmospheric—so that one intersects, punctuates, extends and qualifies another."

In *Akibiyori* (*Late Autumn*, 1960), as in *Late Spring* (1949), a woman marries in the belief that her only surviving parent is about to do the same, though in the 1960 film it is not a father who is left alone at the end but a widowed mother. She is played by Setsuko Hara—the daughter in *Late Spring*. Ozu said of this picture that "life, which seems complex, suddenly reveals itself as very simple—and I wanted to show that in this film." He may have succeeded in his own terms, but for some critics the result was considerably more opaque than *Late Spring*.

Kohayagawa-ke no aki (*The End of Summer*, 1961) begins as a rich and earthy comedy, full of amusing character vignettes, about an Osaka merchant whose three grown daughters are appalled when he takes up again with a discarded mistress (the mother of a fourth girl). In the midst of their attempts to reform him, the old reprobate dies of a heart attack. As Richie says, "the surface is mundane, marvelously so, but with no hint of the depths we are later to view.

With humor, with affection, we are willingly led deeper and deeper until we are faced with death. And death triumphs. . . . It is perhaps the only Ozu picture in which there is no spiritual survivor. One of Ozu's most beautiful films, it is one of his most disturbing."

Ozu's last film, *Samma no aji (An Autumn Afternoon,* 1962), was yet another variation on his favorite theme, with yet another widower marrying off his daughter and then facing his own loneliness. Tom Milne wrote that this film (like its predecessor) is mainly light and even ribald in tone, but "closes on a strangely moving, almost cathartic note of mingled grief, resignation and tranquillity when Harayama, alone at home after his self-sufficient son had gone to bed, breaks down and weeps quietly. . . . Nothing, apparently, has prepared for the emotional depth of the last scene, yet it is a perfectly natural climax towards which the whole film has been imperceptibly moving through a mosaic of characters and incidents which interlock, sometimes obviously and sometimes obliquely, to illuminate the underlying theme of loneliness." Ozu's mother died while he was working on this film, and the following year he himself became ill with the cancer that killed him on the eve of his sixtieth birthday.

Younger and more militant filmmakers in Japan, believing that the world can and should be changed, have in recent years tended to reject and scorn Ozu's theme of acceptance and resignation, the "uncinematic" stasis of his late films, and his fondness for the arts and conventions of the feudal past, in particular condemning his nostalgia for the traditional Japanese family structure, which they regard as perniciously conformist and authoritarian. At the same time, this "most Japanese" of directors has acquired a devoted following abroad, where the purity of his "transcendental" style and the universality of his insights into the "ordinary sorrows" of life established him during the 1970s as one of the masters of world cinema.

FILMS: Zange no Yaiba (The Sword of Penitence), 1927; Wakodo no Yume (The Dreams of Youth), 1928; Nyobo Funshitsu (Wife Lost), 1928; Kabocha (Pumpkin), 1928; Hikkoshi Fufu (A Couple on the Move), 1928; Nikutaibi (Body Beautiful), 1928; Takara no Yama (Treasure Mountain), 1929; Wakaki Hi (Days of Youth), 1929; Wasei Kenka Tomodachi (Fighting Friends—Japanese Style), 1929; Daigaku wa Deta Keredo (I Graduated, But . . .), 1929; Kaishain Seikatsu (The Life of an Office Worker), 1929; Tokkan Kozo (A Straightforward Boy), 1929; Kekkon Gaku Nyumon (An Introduction to Marriage), 1930; Hogaraka ni Ayume (Walk Cheerfully), 1930; Rakudai wa Shita Keredo (I Flunked, But . . .), 1930; Sono Yo no Tsuma (That Night's Wife), 1930; Erogami no On-

ryo (The Revengeful Spirit of Eros), 1930; Ashi ni Sawatta Koun (Lost Luck/Luck Touched My Legs), 1930; Ojosan (Young Miss), 1931; Shukujo to Hige (The Lady and the Beard/The Lady and Her Favorite), 1931; Bijin Aishu (Beauty's Sorrows), 1931; Tokyo no Gassho (Tokyo Chorus), 1931; Haru wa Gofujin Kara (Spring Comes From the Ladies), 1932; Umarete wa Mita Keredo (I Was Born, But . . .), 1932; Seishun no Yume Ima Izuko (Where Now Are the Dreams of Youth?), 1932; Mata Au Hi Made (Until the Day We Meet Again), 1932; Tokyo no Onna (Woman of Tokyo), 1933; Hijosen no Onna (Dragnet Girl/Women on the Firing Line), 1933; Dekigokoro (Passing Fancy), 1933; Haha o Kawazuya (A Mother Should Be Loved), 1934; Ukigusa Monogatari (A Story of Floating Weeds), 1934; Hakoiri Musume (An Innocent Maid/The Young Virgin), 1935; Tokyo no Yado (An Inn in Tokyo), 1935; Daigaku Yoi Toko (College Is a Nice Place), 1936; Hitori Musuko (The Only Son), 1936; Shukujo wa Nani o Wasuretaka (What Did the Lady Forget?), 1937; Toda-ke no Kyodai (The Brothers and Sisters of the Toda Family), 1941; Chichi Ariki (There Was a Father), 1942; Nagaya no Shinshi Roku (The Record of a Tenement Gentleman), 1947; Kaze no Naka no Mendori (A Hen in the Wind), 1948; Banshun (Late Spring), 1949; Munekata Shimai (The Munekata Sisters), 1950; Bakushu (Early Summer), 1951; Ochazuke no Aji (The Flavor of Green Tea Over Rice/Tea and Rice), 1952; Tokyo Monogatari (Tokyo Story), 1953; Soshun (Early Spring), 1956; Tokyo Boshoku (Tokyo Twilight/Twilight in Tokyo), 1957; Higanbana (Equinox Flower), 1958; Ohayo (Good Morning!), 1959; Ukigusa (Floating Weeds), 1959; Akibiyori (Late Autumn), 1960; Kohayagawa-ke no Aki (The End of Summer/Early Autumn/The Last of Summer), 1961; Samma no Aji (An Autumn Afternoon), 1962. *Published screenplays*—Tokyo Story in Hibbett, H. S. (ed.) Contemporary Japanese Literature, 1977; New Yorker Films (ed.) The Major Works of Yasujiro Ozu, 1976.

ABOUT: Anderson, J. L. and Richie, D. The Japanese Film, 1960; Bock, A. Japanese Film Directors, 1978; Bordwell, D. *in* Lyon, C. (ed.) The International Dictionary of Films and Filmmakers, 1984; Burch, N. Theory of Film Practice, 1973; Burch, N. To the Distant Observer, 1979; Gillett, J. and Wilson, D. (eds.) Yasujiro Ozu: A Critical Anthology, 1976; MacDonald, K. Cinema East, 1982; Mellen, J. The Waves at Genji's Door, 1976; Richie, D. Japanese Cinema, 1971; Richie, D. Ozu: His Life and Films, 1974; Roud, R. (ed.) Cinema: A Critical Dictionary, 1980; Sato, T. Currents in Japanese Cinema, 1982; Schrader, P. Transcendental Style in Film: Ozu, Bresson, Dreyer, 1972; Tessier, M. Yasujiro Ozu, 1971 (in French). *Periodicals*—Art and Cinema Fall 1986; Art Forum June 1970, October 1985; Australian Journal of Screen Theory 7 1980; Avant-Scène du Cinéma March 15, 1978 (Ozu issue); Cahiers du Cinéma March 1978, April 1980, May 1980, December 1985; Cineforum July–August 1982; Cinéma (France) January and February 1981; Cinema (US) Summer 1970, Winter 1972–1973; Dossiers du Cinéma: Cinéastes 1 1971; Écran December 15, 1979; Filament 4 1984; Film (UK) Summer 1965; Film Comment Spring 1971, Summer 1972; Film Criticism 3

1980, 1 1983; Film Journal Fall–Winter 1972; Film
Reader 4 1980; Film Quarterly Fall 1959, Winter
1963–1964, Fall 1983; Georgia Review Spring 1978;
Jeune Cinéma December–January 1979–1980; Jump
Cut August 1978; Les Lettres Françaises December 19,
1963; National Film Theatre Booklets December
1975–January 1976, June–August 1976; Positif February
1978 (Ozu issue), January 1979, December 1980,
February 1981; Rolling Stone April 13, 1972; Screen
Summer 1976; Sight and Sound Autumn 1963, Spring
1964, Summer 1975, Winter 1978–1979; Take One
January–February 1974, May 1975; Wide Angle 4
1977, 2 1979. *Films about*—Inoue, K. (dir.) Ikitewa
mitakeredo (I Lived, But . . .), 1985; Wenders, W.
(dir.) Tokyo-ga, 1985.

PABST, G(EORG) W(ILHELM) (August 27,
1885–May 29, 1967), Austrian director and scenarist,
was born in Raudnitz, Bohemia, then part
of the Austro-Hungarian empire, now in
Czechoslovakia. His father, August, was a railroad
official whose career took the family to Vienna
when Pabst was still a child. At his father's
urging he at first studied engineering. He soon
abandoned this, toyed for a time with the idea
of a military career, and finally—to his parents'
distress—opted for the stage. In 1904 he entered
the Vienna Academy of Decorative Arts, where
he studied acting for two years.

In 1910, after varied experience at theatres in
Switzerland and Germany, Pabst went to the
United States to join the Deutsche Volkstheater
in New York, appearing in plays by Hauptmann,
Schnitzler, and others. The theatre was controlled
by labor unions and he met a number of
prominent American socialists, including Upton
Sinclair. It was at the Volkstheater that Pabst
first tried his hand as a director, soon realizing
that he had a much greater talent for this than
as an actor. In 1914 he returned to Europe to recruit
new performers but, with the outbreak of
war, was detained in France as an enemy alien.
Pabst spent nearly five years in a prison camp
near Brest, where he organized a theatre company
and presented French plays for the entertainment
of prisoners and guards alike. In this way
he acquired his lifelong admiration for French
culture, but his imprisonment was nevertheless
a painful experience which marked him deeply.

Released at the end of the war, Pabst directed
a season of plays in Prague, including two controversial
works by Frank Wedekind. His stage
productions at this time are said to have been in
the Expressionist style then dominant in Germany.
In 1920 he became artistic director of a Vienna
theatre, the Neuen Wiener Bühne, where he
staged avant-garde plays by Sternheim and
Georg Kaiser among others. It was the German

G. W. PABST

cinematographer and film pioneer Carl Froelich
who brought Pabst into the cinema. When
Froelich formed his own production company,
he gave Pabst an acting role in his first movie,
Im Banne der Kralle (1921), then took him on
as assistant director and scenarist of *Der
Taugenichts* (1922) and *Luise Millerin* (1922).

Pabst's first film as a director followed in
1923, *Der Schatz* (*The Treasure*). Financed
mainly by Froelich, it was adapted by the director
and Willy Hennings from a story by Rudolph
Hans Bartsch. The setting is an imaginary medieval
locale "on the shadowy edge of an Austrian
forest" where a murky fable about love and
greed unfolds at the house of the bell-founder
Balthasar. His villainous assistant is played by
Werner Krauss, who was to appear in many of
Pabst's films, and the Expressionistic sets were
the work of Walter Röhrig (who had worked on
Caligari) and Robert Herlth.

It seemed to Lotte Eisner that "the main influence
felt is that of *The Golem*: those thick, rough
dilapidated walls, familiar to us already from
many a German film, lurk like carnivorous
plants ready to devour any mortal who comes
close. There are staircases everywhere, and on
all sides dark sunken corridors lead off with sudden
steps and sharp curves." Freddy Buache noted
that Pabst's use of *chiaroscuro* "allows him to
put into relief the presence of objects, the weight
of things, the material of a table or piece of
clothing. These qualities return in several sequences
. . . in counterpoint with the fantastic
pictorial effects that justify the intrigue." Interesting
as it is, the film has seemed to many critics
a clumsy and heavy-handed melodrama, remote

from Pabst's real concerns in both style and content.

Der Schatz did poorly at the box office and Pabst's next assignment, secured for him by Froelich, was a routine commercial vehicle for the popular actress Henny Porten, *Gräfin Donelli* (*Countess Donelli,* 1924). It was made very quickly and cheaply, but enjoyed great popularity and commercial success. Its producers, Maxim Films, urged Pabst to make other similar entertainments, but he had no wish to settle into a rut as a commercial director, and was looking for a story that would allow him to express his developing social consciousness. He found it in *Die freudlose Gasse* (*The Joyless Street*), a controversial novel by the Viennese journalist Hugo Bettauer, and in due course also found backers for what developed into an extremely ambitious project.

Bettauer's novel, originally a serial, is a portrait of Viennese society in the postwar period of inflation, which brought an accelerating breakdown in economic, social, and moral values. Pabst engaged Willi Haas to write the script and Guido Seeber as his photographer, signing Werner Krauss and Asta Nielsen as his stars. He also selected Valeska Gert, a popular cabaret entertainer, to play the madam of a brothel, and agreed to pay the then outrageous sum of $4,000 for the services of an almost unknown young actress named Greta Garbo, whose promise he had recognized in Mauritz Stiller's *The Saga of Gösta Berling.*

"Abandon hope all ye who enter here," says the opening title. Set in the winter of 1923, the film begins with a long line of desperate people waiting outside a butcher's shop. They include Maria Lechner (Nielsen), daughter of an impoverished cripple, and Greta Rumfort (Garbo), daughter of a respectable city councillor. Both are turned away by the brutal and libidinous butcher (Krauss), while the brothel keeper is welcomed obsequiously into the shop. Through these characters we examine the effects of the economic breakdown on various levels of society—the misery of the working class and the pauperized middle-class, the expensive pleasures of the speculators and blackmarketeers who batten on them.

For the most part, *The Joyless Street* eschews Expressionist symbolism and indeed it has been recognized as an important contribution to a very different movement—the so-called "Neue Sachlichkeit" (New Objectivity). The term had been coined in 1924 to define the glum realism that had emerged in painting as a reflection of a national mood of disillusionment. Reacting against the Expressionists' romantic probing into the depths of the human psyche, the artists of the Neue Sachlichkeit limited themselves to a resigned scrutiny of what people did to each other in visible and material terms, refusing speculations about why. "What need is there for romantic treatment?" Pabst asked once. "Real life is already far too romantic, too disturbing."

All the same, there are Expressionist touches in the film, like the scene in which Garbo, dressed by the procuress in a revealing gown, is reflected in a three-fold mirror and joined there by the triple silhouette of a drunken lecher—his real presence shown only by a shot of his clutching hand at the edge of the screen. And there is a famous shot of Garbo's threadbare coat hanging beside the opulent gray fur that she is supposed to earn. Objectivity is moreover constantly diluted by Pabst's taste for melodrama, especially in the improbable character of the "kept woman" driven to murder (Asta Nielsen) and the happy ending contrived for Garbo and her father.

But in 1925 the film's unblinking portrayal of squalor and depravity was startling. In spite of the wholesale mutilations imposed by the censors of various countries, it was a major international success, establishing Pabst as a significant figure in world cinema, and in particular as a brilliant director of women. Edgardo Cozarinsky wrote of this movie in the 1970s that "Pabst used hard facts as a painted backdrop for melodrama, for starkly defined types and immediately recognizable situations, thus setting a pattern which would be that of his best films."

In the course of his career Pabst became involved in an assortment of political and cultural movements, but his deepest concern as a filmmaker was always the revelation through visual images of human character. He was greatly interested in psychology and psychoanalysis, as his next picture showed. This was *Geheimnisse einer Seele* (*Secrets of a Soul,* 1926), a dramatization in Freudian terms of the case history of a chemistry professor (Werner Krauss) troubled by dreams in which he murders his wife (just like the hero of the film Ingmar Bergman made in Germany in 1980, *From the Life of the Marionettes*). He consults an analyst who unravels his problems and cures his impotence.

The script was prepared with the help of two of Freud's associates, Hanns Sachs and Karl Abraham, and the film is presented in a coolly documentary manner except for the astonishing dream sequences. These use superimposition, miniaturization, split screen, and every kind of visual and optical distortion in a burst of Expressionistic virtuosity, packed with sexual symbolism. It is almost impossible to believe that these effects were achieved—as they necessarily were—in the *camera*, through endless rewinding and multiple exposures. A great deal of credit for the movie's prestigious success belongs to Pabst's photographers, Seeber and Curt Oertel, and his designer, Ernö Metzner. Standish D. Lawder regards it as "an important but little-known prototype of the Surrealist film." The same year—perhaps as a vacation from this marathon of concentration—Pabst knocked out a foolish little historical romance called *Man spielt nicht mit der Liebe* (*Don't Play With Love,* 1926).

In 1927 Pabst's political commitment was intensified by his involvement with Dacho, a German film workers' syndicate. The following year he joined with Heinrich Mann, Erwin Piscator, and Karl Freund in the Volksverband für Filmkunst (Popular Association for Film Art). The Volksverband was dedicated to the overthrow of bourgeois reactionary cinema, but Pabst was not prepared to relinquish the established industry entirely; he believed that he could subvert it from within, as he sought to do when he somehow persuaded UFA to back his adaptation of Ilya Ehrenberg's pro-Bolshevik novel *Die Liebe der Jeanne Ney* (*The Love of Jeanne Ney,* 1927).

Jeanne Ney (Edith Jehanne) is the daughter of a French diplomat. Her father is assassinated by Bolsheviks, but she nevertheless falls in love with another dedicated young Communist, Andreas (Uno Henning). They have a brief interlude of happiness in Paris but are haunted by the sadistic adventurer Khabiliev (Fritz Rasp), who eventually murders Jeanne's uncle and pins the crime on Andreas. The study of German decadence in *The Joyless Street* is here extended into a general indictment of the European bourgeoisie. "The reality is postwar Europe in full disintegration," wrote Siegfried Kracauer. "Its ghastliness unfolds in scenes which are unique not so much for their unhesitating frankness as for their insight into the symptoms of social morbidity. . . . Surveying various strata of the population, the film sometimes assumes the character of a report on the diseases of European society" (though one that is weakened—in spite of Pabst's revolutionary intentions—by bowdlerization and sentimentality).

Technically, the film marked an important advance in Pabst's work. His cameraman, Fritz Arno Wagner, was instructed to avoid artificiality in lighting and effects, and some scenes were shot not in the studio but on location in Paris. "At Pabst's will," wrote Paul Rotha, "Wagner's camera nosed into the corners and ran with the players. . . . Every curve, every angle, every approach of the lens was controlled by the mate-

rial that it photographed for the expression of mood." Titles were used as little as possible, settings and objects being put to work to illuminate character and atmosphere, as in the opening sequence in whch the camera pans from Khabiliev's shabby boots, insolently propped on a café table, to the ashtray full of cigarette butts, to the newspaper covering his face. We see his arrogant treatment of a waiter, explore the smoky café, and encounter Andreas through his reflection in a mirror. Khabiliev begins to paw through a telephone directory, and the story is underway.

Pabst had been learning from Eisenstein, and the editing is equally sophisticated. "Every cut," he said, "is made on some movement. At the end of one cut somebody is moving, at the beginning of the adjoining one the movement is continued. The eye is thus so occupied in following these movements that it misses the cuts." Kracauer wrote that Pabst "utilizes tiny pictorial particles to capture the slightest impressions, and he fuses these particulars into a finespun texture to mirror reality as a continuity"; to *mirror* reality: in fact most critics agree that even in this film Pabst is not truly a realist. Iris Barry wrote that he organized his shots so as to reinforce "the illusion of reality" and Lotte Eisner that "for Pabst, reality was simply another convention. . . . Even if Pabst wanted us to say 'how true' rather than 'how beautiful,' he never managed to reject a shot which was both forceful and picturesque."

No doubt partly for this reason, *Jeanne Ney* was another triumph, critical and financial. A slighter work followed: *Abwege* (*Crisis,* 1928), starring Brigitte Helm, who had given a touching performance as a blind girl in *Jeanne Ney.* In *Abwege* she plays a middle-class woman, neglected by her ambitious husband, who joins a set of what would nowadays be called "swingers," but in the end rediscovers her husband's love. Paul Rotha remarked that Helm's "curious, fascinating power had never been exploited with such skill," and Pabst's ability to recognize and develop the unique, individual talent (and erotic style) of his actresses was to make a masterpiece of his next picture.

Ever since he had staged Wedekind's play *Erdgeist* in Prague just after the war, he had wanted to film it and its companion piece, *Die Büchse der Pandora.* In 1928 he saw a couple of Paramount movies featuring a young starlet named Louise Brooks and recognized in her the combination of intelligence and intuition, innocence and eroticism, that he saw in Wedekind's Lulu. As it happened, she had just been refused a salary increase by Paramount and at once accepted Pabst's offer. "In Berlin," she later recalled, "I stepped to the station platform to meet Mr. Pabst and became an actress. . . . It was just as if Mr. Pabst had sat in on my whole life and career and knew exactly where I needed assurance and protection." Discussing Pabst's directorial technique, she said "it was the stimulus that concerned him. If he got that right, the actor's emotional reaction would be like life itself. . . . by some magic he would saturate me with one clear emotion and turn me loose."

Die Büchse der Pandora (*Pandora's Box,* 1928) was drawn by Ladislaus Vajda from Wedekind's two Lulu plays (which also inspired Alban Berg's great opera *Lulu*). In his *demimondaine* Lulu, Wedekind created a "personification of primitive sexuality" who uses up and destroys the men that love her until she meets an even more destructive sexual monster than herself, Jack the Ripper. Where Berg in his opera heightened the theatricality of the plays, Pabst and his scenarist subdued them to a more subtle and cinematic naturalism. However, Pabst does not hesitate to use Expressionist devices when they suit his purpose—especially towards the end of the film, as in the extreme *chiaroscuro* of the floating casino, or the disturbing psychological details picked out by the camera as Jack is briefly distracted from his need to kill by Lulu's irresistible sexuality.

Other scenes seem closer to Impressionism, like the sequence in which Lulu takes part in a cabaret. Lotte Eisner wrote of this that "nobody has ever equalled Pabst's portrayal of the backstage fever on the opening night of a big show, the hurrying and scurrying between scene changes . . . the rivalry, complacency, and humour, the bewildering bustle of stage-hands and electricians—a stupendous whirl of artistic aspirations, colourful detail, and a facile eroticism. . . . Lulu appears like some pagan idol, tempting, glittering with spangles, feathers, and frills, against a wavering, out-of-focus background."

Pandora was cruelly mutilated by the censors, but it was only partly for this reason that contemporary reviewers greeted it so coolly. Some were shocked; others regretted Pabst's apparent retreat from political engagement; many concluded that "Lulu is inconceivable without the words that Wedekind made her speak." More recently—with different preconceptions and with something like a complete print to study—critics have recognized "the miracle of Louise Brooks" and the dimensions of Pabst's achievement, marred though it is by a lack of stylistic unity. Lee Atwell wrote that "Pabst's film reincarnates Lulu as a modern myth. Pabst sees her as a dangerously free and alluring innocent, without any

notion of sin in the Christian sense . . . a liberated figure of pure untrammelled feminine desire." The movie has been compared with Carl Dreyer's *Passion of Joan of Arc* "for the intense, intimate way it uses the camera to watch the processes of thought and feeling through close shots of the face."

In 1929 Pabst co-directed with Arnold Fanck *Die Weisse Hölle vom Piz Palü* (*The White Hell of Piz Palü*). Starring the young Leni Riefenstahl, it proved one of the most successful of Fanck's exciting "mountain films." The same year, Pabst returned to his own concerns in *Das Tagebuch einer Verlorenen* (*Diary of a Lost Girl*), based on a best seller by Margarethe Böhme. Undeterred by the reception given to *Pandora,* he starred Louise Brooks in another study of a sexually generous girl. She plays Thymiane, a pharmacist's daughter made pregnant by his wicked assistant (Fritz Rasp) and incarcerated for this sin in a reform school run by a voyeur and a sadist (Valeska Gert). Escaping in the midst of a rebellion, Thymiane winds up in a brothel. There are two conclusions to the story: one in which Thymiane, rejecting spurious respectability, herself becomes the madam of a brothel, and another, substituted by Pabst to secure the film's release in Germany, in which she marries the old Count Osdorff but retains her courage and honesty.

Freddy Buache has described Thymiane's initial seduction in the brothel as "one of the purest, most iridescent, and the most ineffably magnificent in the cinema's collection of erotica." Even more directly than in *Pandora,* Pabst contrasts the basic innocence and honesty of his "lost girl" with the hypocrisy and decadence of bourgeois society, though Kracauer and others complained that he does not take his social criticism far enough and instead "elaborates upon the decadence itself." There is little of the Expressionistic virtuosity or atmospheric richness of *Pandora* in this film, which is characterized by an almost documentary restraint and a new concern for stylistic unity.

By this time, the movies were becoming talkies. Pabst said some years later that he remained "convinced that in the cinema, the text counts for little. What counts is the image." He nevertheless recognized that sound could not be ignored and in 1929 went to London to study the new production methods. He reached the conclusion that the early talkies he saw there merely exploited sound as a novelty instead of recognizing it as an addition to the filmmaker's vocabulary.

Returning to Germany early in 1930, he began work on his own first sound film, *Westfront*

1918, adapted by Ladislaus Vajda and P. M. Lampel from Ernst Johannsen's anti-war novel *Vier von der Infantrie.* He engaged his well-tried designer Ernö Metzner and used Fritz Arno Wagner as his cameraman on this and on his next three films. *Westfront* traces the fortunes in the Great War of four German infantrymen from various social backgrounds. It shows that almost surreal horrors of battle and also the emotional wounds inflicted by the war, the long periods of boredom, the camaraderie. It ends with a wounded French soldier clutching the hand of a dead German one and telling him that he is not his enemy but his comrade.

The film, made almost entirely in the studio, eschews the close-ups and montage effects of Pabst's previous movies (which indeed would have been impossible with early sound equipment). Pabst relies instead on fluid, mobile camerawork and inventive composition within the frame to make his points and retain the attention of the spectator. At that time most filming was done with a static camera in a soundproof booth but Wagner, to give Pabst what he needed, "blimped" his cameras and made them almost as maneuverable as in the silent days. Lee Atwell wrote of one sequence that "the approach to the front at dawn is treated like a large newsreel tableau. The camera tracks relentlessly along the desolate lunar landscape, encompassing a succession of seemingly trivial details, part of an aesthetically designed, yet realistic appearing pattern: piles of corpses, mazes of barbed wire, ruined buildings jutting out of the smoldering atmosphere."

Pabst provides the musical episodes that were *de rigueur* in early talkies—a military band, a nostalgic song, a vaudeville show—but these are firmly integrated into the narrative. The dialogue is often banal, but otherwise sound is used with great ingenuity to amplify rather than to duplicate the messages of the visual images. Given the crudeness of the contemporary technology, Atwell considers that "the complexity of overlapping sound in the final hospital scene is still astonishing enough to be placed in an anthology of early aural accomplishments."

Though he had long been regarded as a realist director, it was in this grim and powerful film that Pabst achieved for the first time the goals of the "New Objectivity," with none or few of the concessions to picturesqueness and sentimentality that marred other war films of the period (as well as many of his own earlier pictures). It was released in May 1930 at a time when Germany was already gearing itself for another great war, and Pabst's insistence on the futility and dreary monotony of militarism was not wel-

comed by most German critics, though the movie was greatly admired in Britain and France.

Westfront was made for Seymour Nebenzahl's Nero Films, where Pabst was given more freedom than most contemporary directors ever dreamed of. As a favor to Nebenzahl, Pabst next made a lightweight comedy called *Skandal um Eva* (1930), Henny Porten's first talkie. It grieved Pabst's more serious admirers, but was a great popular success. This was followed by a much more considerable work, but one that was almost equally unexpected, in that it led Pabst back to the Expressionist style—a screen version of Bertold Brecht and Kurt Weill's famous *Die Dreigroschenoper* (*The Threepenny Opera,* 1931). The adaptation was written by Vajda, Leo Lania, and Bela Belàsz in a way that outraged Brecht with its disregard for his political and stylistic intentions. He and Weill sued Nero Films, seeking to abort the production, but without success.

Set in Victorian London, Pabst's version centers on the love between the gangster Mack and Polly Peachum, daughter of the King of the Beggars. Peachum opposes their marriage and plots against it with Tiger Brown, the corrupt police commissioner. Lotte Eisner, who sympathized with Brecht, nevertheless conceded that "the vigorous starkness of the original was not entirely lost. . . . The dialogues and the poignant rhythm of the songs created under Brecht's instructions are counterpointed by a visual theme which is not unworthy of it. . . . [Andrei] Andreiev's misty London for *Pandora* was a first version of his sets for *Die Dreigroschenoper.* Pabst and Andreiev contrived to clothe everything in *chiaroscuro* and mist, making the brick walls of the Thames-side docks and Soho slums both real and fantastic at the same time. Swirls of dust and smoke wreath the dwellings of the beggar king and cling to the bare walls, where the wretches' rags are like ornamental blobs of paint, and hover in the nuptial shed on the docks, softening the splendour of the tables brimming with fruit and silverware amid the reflections of the gentle candlelight. . . . The encounter of the renaissance of 'Impressionism' and the waning of Expressionism is a happy one."

Like René Clair in his first sound films, Pabst reduces dialogue to a minimum, concentrating instead on gesture and image. Mack's marriage proposal to Polly is filmed through a window, so that it emerges as pantomime, and when Mack's gang plunder London stores to furnish the wedding, the whole sequence is a sort of ballet, set to music but wordless. Released in Germany in 1931, *The Threepenny Opera* was a critical and popular success, but it was soon recognized as a veiled criticism of contemporary Germany and it was banned by the Nazis in 1933, together with *Westfront*. The French version was acclaimed as a masterpiece, and a shortened version was successful in London and New York.

Returning to the style of *Westfront*, Pabst made one of his finest films in *Kameradschaft* (*Comradeship*, 1931). Set in the immediate postwar period, it is based on an incident that actually occurred in 1906, when German miners crossed the border to help rescue French miners trapped underground in a disaster at Courrières. The theme lent itself admirably to an expression of Pabst's humanistic distaste for the growing nationalism of the 1930s, and the film was organized as a Franco-German coproduction, with French and German actors speaking their own languages throughout. The mine interiors were constructed at vast expense on the Staaken sound stages near Berlin, the remainder of the film being shot on location in France and Germany.

After opening scenes establishing the film's terms of reference, the explosion in the French mine draws anxious crowds; thereafter Pabst cuts regularly from the drama underground to the anguish and turmoil on the surface. Roger Manvell wrote that "with a cunning montage of shots involving static cameras gathering telling details and travelling cameras identified with the running crowd, while the sound track represents the ebb and flow of human cries and the clatter of running feet, Pabst builds up a sympathetic identification between the mining community and the audience which is to watch their suffering. Working in the early, exciting days of sound, Pabst often had the imagination to impose complete silence on a scene. Often, too, he makes prolonged use of the simplest kind of natural sound, like the moaning roar which comes up from the mine-shaft when the old man climbs down to find Georges, his grandson, or the intense pulsation of an artificial respirator."

We cut to the German mine, where miners ending the night shift gather in a vast shower room where long ropes carry their filthy clothes up into the rafters and light reflects off the naked bodies of the men in the showers. The Germans decide that they must go to help their comrades (even though the French "are richer than we"). They arrive at the French mine, demolish the underground iron trellis marking the 1919 frontier, and join the search. There is a memorable, almost surreal scene in which a French miner is found by a German wearing a gas mask. Groggy with fumes, the Frenchman imagines himself back in the war and attacks his rescuer. The film ends with a rather unnecessary

assertion of working class solidarity, followed by an ironic postscript (missing from the German version) in which the trellis forming the underground frontier is reinstated by officials.

Kameradschaft has been recognized as a masterpiece of the fictional documentary and was an important influence on such British directors as Basil Wright and Humphrey Jennings. In France, it brought Pabst the Legion of Honor. In Germany, however, the film was condemned by the reactionary press as unpatriotic and it failed at the box office. Finally disillusioned, Pabst went to France.

None of Pabst's later films equaled the major achievements of his first German period, but some are of considerable merit. The first movie he made in France was *L'Atlantide* (1932), a remake of Feyder's 1921 silent picture. A colorful piece of exotica starring Brigitte Helm as a destructive love goddess, it was a great success and in Germany actually enhanced Pabst's reputation. Pabst's *Don Quixote* (1933), the first sound version of the story, stars Chaliapin as the old knight, has an animated prologue by Lotte Reiniger, and a score by Ibert. At the end, when Quixote is dying, his books are consigned to a bonfire like those lit by the Nazis in Germany. But mindless evil is denied its victory; the flames themselves are consumed and from them emerges a title page reading "Don Quixote de la Mancha by Miguel de Cervantes." There are a number of such fine moments but the film was spoiled by the fact that Pabst, for financial reasons, was unable to complete it as he had planned, and had to pad it out with songs. *De haut en bas* (1933), a "slice of life" movie set in a Vienna boarding house, was found generally unconvincing and unsatisfactory.

Short of funds, Pabst then accepted an invitation to make a film for Warner Brothers in Hollywood. He settled on Louis Bromfield's novel *A Modern Hero*, about an ambitious young circus performer who grows rich and unhappy as an automobile manufacturer. This also was a flop and Pabst returned to France, bitterly disillusioned with Hollywood's assembly-line methods. Lee Atwell suggests that he simply lacked the ruthlessness and arrogance it took to survive there. He made three more films in France, two of them intermittently distinguished by the splendid camerawork of Eugen Schüfftan, and in April 1939 returned to his family home near Vienna.

Pabst's reputation has never recovered from the fact that he elected to spend the war years in Austria and Germany. According to his wife, he had in fact intended to emigrate to the United States, but at the last moment was trapped in

Europe by a traveling accident. There is evidence to support this claim, but he was also the only great German *cinéaste* of the prewar period to make films under the Nazis, and this has been found harder to justify. *Komödianten* (*Comedians*, 1941), a big-budget production about the eighteenth-century actress and producer Karoline Neuber, marred by poor dialogue, was followed by a highly fictionalized biography of the mystical physician Paracelsus. There are touches of Pabst's old brilliance in this film, which some rate highly among his works, but many critics find its adulatory treatment of Paracelsus as a visionary leader ahead of his time uncomfortably close to Nazi tributes to Hitler. *Der Fall Molander,* shot in 1943 at the Barrandov Studios in Prague, was destroyed unedited during the Russian attack on the city.

After the war, Pabst remained for a time in Austria. *Der Prozess* (*The Trial,* 1947) is set in nineteenth-century Hungary and centers on a lawyer famous for his defense of Jews persecuted during a wave of anti-Semitic hysteria. Like *Paracelsus,* it has been much praised for its cinematic qualities (which brought Pabst the award as best director at Venice in 1948), but rancorously attacked on ideological grounds. One French reviewer remarked that Pabst "defends the Jews . . . but ten years too late." It should be said that he had been anxious to make a movie on this theme as early as 1933, but had then been unable to obtain French backing for the project.

In 1949, Pabst founded his own production company in Vienna, supervising three films by other directors and making one himself, *Geheimnisvolle Tiefen* (*Mysterious Shadows,* 1949), written by his wife with Walter Hollander. An insignificant piece, it was followed by three equally uninspired movies, two of them made in Italy (where Pabst had gone to try his hand as an opera director). The best of his late films was *Der letzte Akt* (*The Last Ten Days,* 1955), a recreation of the insane dance of death that preceded Hitler's suicide in his Berlin bunker. There are powerful performances from Albin Skoda as the dictator and from Oskar Werner as a humanistic young officer, and Pabst's old mastery of lighting and framing gives the film great psychological intensity.

Es Geschah am 20 Juli (*The Jackboot Mutiny,* 1955), a companion picture about the 1944 plot by German officers to assassinate Hitler, was by comparison a failure. Two strictly commercial romances followed in 1956, but none of Pabst's subsequent projects came to anything. In 1957 he developed Parkinson's Disease, and complications made him an invalid until his death ten years later.

Jean Mitry found in Pabst's work "an incomparable mastery in the art of creating atmosphere and a social climate; a flagrant incapacity to deal with political and social problems other than through the individual or the couple; an anarchistic ethic and a bourgeois humanism nearer that of Proudhon or Gustav Landauer than that of Karl Marx." Jean Renoir said in 1963 that Pabst "knows how to create a strange world, whose elements are borrowed from daily life. Beyond this precious gift, he knows, better than anyone else, how to direct actors. His characters emerge like his own children, created from fragments of his own heart and mind."

Lee Atwell is no doubt correct to say that "Pabst's strength as a director was not ideological and, second, that while pursuing a new vein of realism, he remained temperamentally still profoundly romantic." Atwell suggests that Pabst was not strictly speaking an *auteur,* imposing a consistent vision on all his work: "With each new film . . . his restless sensibility sought a fresh approach; thus each work must be judged according to its merits." Perhaps for this reason—because he cannot be neatly categorized—Pabst has received less attention than most other directors of his caliber, though few would deny his greatness. Henri Agel called him "the most indefinable of German directors: to the ambiguous and fugitive character of his German temperament is added a strange duality always oscillating from non-realism to objectivity."

Pabst was married in 1924 to Gertrude Henning, by whom he had two children. Louise Brooks described her mentor as "a short man, broad-shouldered and thick chested, looking heavy and wilful in repose. But in action his legs carried him on wings which matched the swiftness of his mind." Alexandre Arnoux said that he possessed "a Viennese charm that nobody I know can resist, an extraordinary power of seduction; the demon of intelligence in his look and a certain fullness and direct humanity that pierces the soul."

FILMS: Der Schatz (The Treasure), 1923; Gräfin Donelli, 1924; Die freudlose Gasse (The Joyless Street), 1925 (post-synchronized version released as The Street of Sorrow, 1937); Geheimnisse einer Seele (Secrets of a Soul), 1926; Man spielt nicht mit der Liebe (Don't Play With Love), 1926; Die Liebe der Jeanne Ney (The Love of Jeanne Ney), 1927; Abwege/Begierde (Crisis/Desire), 1928; Die Büchse der Pandora (Pandora's Box), 1929; Das Tagebuch einer Verlorenen (Diary of a Lost Girl), 1929; (with Arnold Fanck) Die Weisse Hölle vom Piz Palü (The White Hell of Piz Palü), 1929 (reissued with synchronized music score, 1935); Westfront 1918 (Comrades of 1918), 1930; Skandal um Eva, 1930; Die Dreigroschenoper (The Threepenny Opera), 1931; Kameradschaft (Comradeship), 1931;

L'Atlantide/Die Herrin von Atlantis, 1932; Don Quichotte (Don Quixote), 1933; De haut en bas, 1933; A Modern Hero, 1934; Mademoiselle Docteur (Street of Shadows/Spies from Salonika), 1936; Le Drame de Shanghai, 1938; Jeunes filles en détresse, 1939; Komödianten (Comedians), 1941; Paracelsus, 1943; Der Prozess (The Trial), 1947; Geheimnisvolle Tiefen (Mysterious Shadows), 1949; La Voce del Silenzio (The Voice of Silence), 1952; Cose da Pazzi (Droll Stories), 1953; Das Bekenntnis der Ina Kahr (Afraid to Love), 1954; Der letzte Akt (The Last Ten Days/Ten Days to Die), 1955; Es Geschah am 20 Juli (The Jackboot Mutiny), 1955; Rosen für Bettina (Ballerina), 1956; Durch die Wälder, durch di Auen, 1956. *Published scripts*—Pandora's Box, translated by Christopher Holme, 1971; The Threepenny Opera *in* Manvell, R. (ed.) Masterpieces of the German Cinema, 1973.

ABOUT: Amengual, B. Georg Wilhelm Pabst, 1966 (in French); Atwell, L. Georg Wilhelm Pabst, 1977 (in English); Aubry, Y. and Petat, J. Georg Wilhelm Pabst, 1968 (in French); Buache, F. Georg Wilhelm Pabst, 1965 (in French); Eisner, L. The Haunted Screen, 1969; Hull, D. S. Film in the Third Reich, 1969; Hunter, W. Scrutiny of Cinema, 1932; Joseph, R. S. (ed.) Der Regisseur; G. W. Pabst, 1963; Kracauer, S. From Caligari to Hitler, 1947; Manvell, R. Film, 1946; Rotha, P. The Film Till Now, 1967; Roud, R. (ed.) Cinema: A Critical Dictionary, 1980; Tyler, P. Classics of the Foreign Film, 1962. *Periodicals*—Avant-Scène du Cinéma December 1, 1976; Bianco e Nero April 1949; Cahiers du Cinéma September 1967; Cinema (USA) Winter 1967; Cinéma (France) April 1981; Cinemages 3 1955 (Pabst issue); Close Up December 1927; Film Kunst 18 1955 (Pabst issue); Film Quarterly Fall 1960; Films and Filming April 1961, April 1967; Films in Review February 1964; Hound and Horn January–March 1933; Image September 1956; Sight and Sound Summer 1965, Autumn 1967.

MARCEL PAGNOL

*PAGNOL, MARCEL (February 25, 1895– April 18, 1974), French director, scenarist, producer, and dramatist, was born at Aubagne, near Marseilles, in Provence, the eldest of the four children of Joseph Pagnol and the former Augustine Lansot. His father, son of a stonemason, fought his way into teachers' training college and became a school principal—a gentle humanist who was also passionately devoted to hunting and fiercely anticlerical. His mother's health was delicate and, beginning in the summer of 1903, his father regularly rented a villa in the hills outside Marseilles. The summers Marcel Pagnol spent there, wandering alone or hunting with his father, are lovingly recalled in his memoirs.

In 1905 Pagnol entered the Lycée Thiers in Marseilles, where he was an exceptionally able student. By 1909 he was publishing Virgilian pastoral verse in a Marseilles magazine. His mother died in 1910, when he was fifteen—a savage blow to the close and happy family. Pagnol wrote his first play when he was seventeen—a verse drama called *Lesbie*—and in 1913 was co-founder of *Fortunio,* the literary journal which subsequently established itself as *Cahiers du Sud.*

Leaving the Lycée Thiers in 1914, Pagnol became a teaching assistant at *lycées* in Digne and Tarascon while studying English at Montpellier University. He received his degree in 1916 and the same year married Simonne Colin. Pagnol was expected to follow in his father's footsteps, but he neglected his pedagogic studies in favor of his literary activities, and it was increasingly obvious that a writing career was his real aim. Meanwhile, he continued to teach at various schools in and around Marseilles, including his *alma mater* the Lycée Thiers (1920–1922). By this time he was publishing fiction as well as verse in *Fortunio.*

In October 1922 Pagnol left Provence and went to Paris to take up a post as auxiliary teacher at the famous Lycée Condorcet, and to seek his fortune as a writer. Through an acquaintance named Paul Nivoix he met the editor of *Comoedia,* an influential literary and theatrical review. He became a contributor, in this way gaining access to the whole Parisian theatre world. Pagnol was soon at work on a play of his own, *Tonton,* written in collaboration with Nivoix. It had a brief run at a theatre in Marseilles, launching his career as a professional dramatist. Pagnol wrote two more plays with Nivoix: *Les Marchands de gloire,* a sharp social satire about a war hero who unexpectedly returns from the dead to the embarrassment of all, was performed in Paris in 1926, while *Un Direct au coeur,* dealing with corruption in professional boxing, had a short run in Lille.

Pagnol's first success was *Jazz,* which he wrote alone. It centers on a university professor who ruins his life by pursuing academic distinction at the cost of love and friendship. The play was staged in Monte Carlo and in Paris in 1926–1927, and generally well received. This was all the encouragement Pagnol needed to resign from the Condorcet and take his chances as a full-time writer. At that time Pagnol seems to have been an idealistic and ambitious young man, exceptionally hard-working but highly sociable. According to his best friend, Marcel Achard, his Paris apartment was dominated by piles of unwashed clothing and a bizarre machine with which Pagnol hoped to solve the problem of perpetual motion.

Achard went on to become famous as a dramatist, and the same is true of several other members of Pagnol's circle, including Henri Jeanson, Paul Vialar, and Armand Salacroux. These and others formed themselves into a group called Les moins de trente ans ("The Under-Thirties"), which met regularly to read each other's plays and to criticize the lamentable state of the Paris theatre. Their own plays were slow to gain acceptance, tending to be too savage in their social satire for the boulevard theatres, too "well-made" to interest the avant-garde directors.

For Pagnol himself, success came swiftly with a play called *Topaze,* first performed in Paris in 1928. Topaze is a humble and dedicated teacher in a scruffy private school. Dismissed for speaking too frankly to an aristocratic parent, Topaze is taken up by a crooked politician who needs a gullible front-man to head one of his phoney companies. Then Topaze discovers that he has been conned and is transformed. He takes on the authority that is legally his, ousts his crooked boss, and acquires his mistress. A pungent indictment of political corruption, it became one of the most successful plays of its era and was repeatedly revived. Achard wrote that Pagnol, "who lived an impoverished existence before the play, suddenly found fame—fame of a kind that is just impossible to convey to people nowadays."

Topaze was the last of Pagnol's satirical thesis plays. While he was writing it, he had turned for a change of pace to a very different kind of play—an affectionate, free-wheeling portrait of life in the old port of Marseilles called *Marius* (1929). Set in a waterfront bar presided over by the cantankerous César, it tells the story of César's son Marius, torn between the call of the sea and his love for Fanny, who runs the fish stall outside. In the end, the self-sacrificing Fanny feigns indifference so that Marius can sail away from her. Full of Marseilles jokes and *patois,* interspersed with some memorable card games, rich in colorful characters, solidly based on the traditional virtues, this zestful and ebullient work ran for over a thousand performances at the Théâtre de Paris, breaking all contemporary box-office records.

A large factor in the play's phenomenal success (and in Pagnol's subsequent career) was Raimu, a bear-like actor and music hall entertainer from Marseilles. He was a dogmatic, irascible, intuitive genius of the theatre, a character several times larger than life. Pagnol offered him the part of Panisse, but Raimu declined this, announcing that he would instead play César, provided that Pagnol revised and expanded the part to fit his own temperament. Raimu then demanded parts for former associates from the Marseilles music hall and to a large extent took charge of preparations for the production. With Raimu's grudging permission, Pierre Fresnay (a northerner and a Protestant to boot) was allowed to play the part of Marius, and the role of Fanny went to Orane Demazis, a young actress who was Pagnol's companion and leading lady for almost ten years.

As C.E.J. Caldicott wrote, *Marius* developed as "the result of a corporate effort. This first experience of work with a team . . . made a profound impression upon Pagnol and his work. . . . Not only was the experience extremely enjoyable to all concerned but the work, written by a Marseillais, set in Marseilles, developed and modified by a team of experienced southerners . . . was able to catch and hold the elusive note of genuine authenticity. It is to Pagnol's eternal credit that he recognized the value of a corporate contribution and admitted it; it was to become his particular style and the team of *Marius* would be the nucleus for most future enterprises."

Marius established Pagnol as the most successful and famous French dramatist of the day, but he was already looking for new fields to conquer. In 1930 he went to London expressly to see one of the first talkies, *Broadway Melody.* Returning, he wrote an immensely controversial article in *Le Journal* claiming that talking pictures were the ultimate form of dramatic art. Attacked on all sides, Pagnol proceeded to write the screen adaptation of *Marius,* filmed by Alexander Korda for Paramount with the original cast. At Korda's insistence, the production was closely supervised by Pagnol, who took advantage of his position to learn everything he could about all the crafts and skills involved in making and marketing a film. *Marius* emerged as virtually a screen record of the original play. It was one of the most successful Franco-American productions ever made, though hostile critics condemned it as "théâtre en conserve" (canned theatre).

The same year, 1931, saw the opening of *Fanny*, a stage sequel to *Marius* and another great success, though neither Raimu nor Fresnay were available to appear in it. Marius is still at sea when Fanny discovers that she is pregnant by him—one of the many husbandless mothers in Pagnol's work. With no word of Marius, she marries the sailmaker Panisse, who loves her and will provide for her child. She finds herself contented with this good and devoted man and, though she still loves Marius, sends him away when he eventually returns.

The screen version of *Topaze* was completed in 1932, with Louis Jouvet in the lead. Paramount assigned Louis Gasnier to direct it and infuriated Pagnol by employing Léopold Marchand (rather than Pagnol himself) to write the dialogue. Already eager to produce his own films, he was now determined to do so. He went into partnership with a French distribution company, Braunberger-Richebé, and reassembled the cast of *Marius* for a movie version of *Fanny* (1932), with Marc Allégret as director. He similarly wrote and co-produced two lesser movies, *Un Direct au coeur* (1932), adapted from his own play and directed by Roger Lion, and *L'Agonie des aigles*, directed by Roger Richebé. In December 1933 Pagnol launched a new journal called *Les Cahiers du Film*. In the first issue he announced that "Le muet est mort, le théâtre est à l'agonie" (The silent cinema is dead, the theatre is dying). This headlong assault on the already anxious artists and technicians of two industries resurrected and heightened the nationwide controversy that had greeted Pagnol's *Le Journal* article three years earlier, earning him a host of enemies.

His successes had made him rich. In 1933, turning his back on the theatre, and on Paris, Pagnol formed his own production company, Les Auteurs Associés, staffing it with relatives and old friends. He equipped his own studios in Marseilles, where he also bought several movie theatres. The new company went into production with a film called *Léopold le bien aimé* (1933), and this was followed by Pagnol's first film as a director, *Le Gendre de Monsieur Poirier* (1934), adapted from a play by Émile Augier and Jules Sandeau, and entirely unmemorable.

Les Auteurs Associés (soon renamed La Société des Films Marcel Pagnol) was intended from the outset to concentrate on adaptations of works by novelists and dramatists. All of Pagnol's finest films were based on novels or stories by Jean Giono—a Provençal writer like Pagnol himself, but one whose passionate and lyrical pantheism was far removed from the director's earthy humanism. Their first collaboration was *Jofroi* (1934), an hour-long movie based on a Giono short story, adapted and directed by Pagnol. Jofroi is an old peasant who grows too old to work his land and sells it to a neighbor—sells it on paper but not in his heart. When the new owner proposes to uproot the worn-out fruit trees that Jofroi had planted as a young man, he threatens suicide.

Pagnol moved the story from Giono's upper Provence to his own birthplace of Aubagne, but otherwise stayed close to the original, which is warmer and more humorous than most of Giono's work. C. E. J. Caldicott wrote that "the reticent humor and humanity of the peasants, interpreted by Vincent Scotto, Poupon, and Blavette, blend naturally with the beauty of the landscape in the hills behind Marseilles. . . . The team for *Jofroi* . . . was to change little in subsequent productions. The cameraman, Willy Faktorovitch, was rarely absent from Pagnol's future movie sets; his apparently relaxed style was a direct consequence of the emphasis placed by Pagnol on the reproduction of the actors' performance. Aiming the camera in the general direction of the actors, Willy alternated between the close-up (which Pagnol treasured as a dramatic ploy) and longer shots which allowed the audience to register a change in scenery." *Jofroi* was received with general enthusiasm and in 1950, when it was first seen in America, Vincent Scotto (better known as a Marseilles songwriter) won an Oscar for his performance as Jofroi.

During the same busy year of 1934, Pagnol wrote and directed an adaptation of Courteline's play *L'Article 330,* produced a documentary about Marseilles, adapted Daudet's novel *Tartarin de Tarascon* for filming by Raymond Bernard, and produced Jean Renoir's *Toni*. Renoir wrote later: "I lived as best I could, making poor films from time to time until Marcel Pagnol gave me the opportunity to make *Toni*. With *Toni* I learned much: it was a film that gave me the courage which was necessary to try something new in different directions." And Caldicott points out that "in Renoir's films, the long shot is hailed as a technical innovation; it is baptized 'depth of field' and acclaimed as the first introduction of outdoor realism into sound movies in France. It should be recalled that these techniques were only developed after Renoir made *Toni* in Pagnol's studios with Pagnol's troupe of actors and with Pagnol's technical team."

All of the next eight pictures produced by Films Marcel Pagnol were directed by Pagnol himself, beginning with *Angèle*, also made in 1934, and based on a Giono novel called *Un de Baumugnes*. The book is in Giono's most high-flown and mystical manner, and Pagnol took considerable liberties to bring it closer to his own more earthy style. As filmed, it tells (at a length of two and a half hours) the story of a country girl (Orane Demazis) left pregnant by a villain from Marseilles but redeemed by a pure young man from the mountains (Jean Servais) and the equally devoted but comic farmhand Saturnin. The latter part was taken by an actor named Fernand Contandin, later better known as Fernandel. Filmed on location in a derelict farm-house rebuilt by Pagnol's construction team (and with access roads blasted out with dynamite), it was even more successful than *Jofroi*.

Ever since the bitter controversies of 1930–1933, Pagnol's detractors have accused him of making movies that, though they were immensely popular, were simply "canned theatre." The calumny persisted until the 1950s, when André Bazin and others began a reassessment of Pagnol's work. In fact, from the very beginning, films like *Jofroi* and *Angèle* showed how far the accusation was from the truth. Richard Roud suggests that Pagnol, "all unknowing, had discovered intuitively what Bazin and the Nouvelle Vague were later to work out theoretically; i.e. that sacrosanct 'montage' was not necessarily the essence of the cinema. That what happened during a shot was just as important as the relationship between the shots. . . . In 1934 he made *Angèle*, his most important achievement in historical terms. . . . Pagnol left the studios, went into the hill towns of Provence and made what we can consider the first neo-realist film, and with direct sound as well: the creaking of the windmills and the chirping of the crickets providing a continual background accompaniment to the dialogue"—in fact, precisely the same is true of the earlier *Jofroi*.

Merlusse (1935), based on one of Pagnol's early short stories, is about an ogrish schoolmaster (Henri Poupon) who turns out to be better than he seems. This was followed by *Cigalon* (1935), a romance involving two rival restauranteurs, and then by a remake of *Topaze* (1936), starring the character actor Arnaudy. For *César* (1936), the last film in the Marseilles trilogy, written expressly for the cinema and only subsequently staged, Pagnol re-assembled the splendid cast of the first two movies. Recording the death of Panisse and the reconciliation of Marius and Fanny, it is a highly enjoyable film, if a little less vigorous than its predecessors.

Pagnol's next Giono adaptation was *Regain* (*Harvest*, 1937), set in a dying Provençal village with only one remaining able-bodied inhabitant, the poacher Panturle (Gabriel Gabrio). Inspired by the witchlike old seer La Mamèche, Panturle sets out to save the village, taking as his helpmate Arsule (Orane Demazis), whom he rescues from bondage to an itinerant tinker (Fernandel). Arsule's pregnancy by Panturle coincides with their first phenomenal harvest; people and life begin to return to the village. Again, Pagnol filmed on location, building a complete replica of the deserted village that had inspired Giono's story. He retained Arthur Honegger to write and direct the score, bringing Honegger and his orchestra to live for months on location, recording as the movie progressed. The huge crew of technicians, actors, musicians, stonemasons, builders, and catering staff became a kind of ongoing party, and every participant, however humble, was listed in the credits.

Regain, like *Angèle*, runs for 150 minutes. Derek Prouse, seeing a 1956 revival, found it not a great film but one with "some great moments. The vivid Midi peasants do not always suit a narrative which shows its literary bones too clearly. With the comic or ironic scenes (the film is almost a series of *vignettes*) Pagnol captures the essence of his people; but in the more romantic dealings he is apt to fall into sentimental tedium. . . . Technically, the film is crude, even for its time; the camera often takes up its position like a spectator at a football match and solidly entrenches itself. In some scenes this makes for *longueurs;* in others the sturdy authenticity of the characters grips one in warm and instant sympathy. . . . And, as in the old trilogy, the spirit of Provence breathes through this strange film, imposing dignity on its untidy narrative and ensuring its charm."

Le Schpountz (*Heartbeat*, 1938), from an original Pagnol script, is an uneven comedy about a moviestruck grocery store clerk (Fernandel) who thinks he has the making of a great tragic actor but finds fame instead as a brilliant comedian. The last movie Pagnol made with Orane Demazis, it was followed by the best known of all his pictures, *La Femme du boulanger* (*The Baker's Wife*, 1938). It was adapted from Giono's *Jean le Bleu*, but so loosely that, after a bitter court case, Giono finally broke with Pagnol.

In *La Femme du boulanger*, the baker's pretty wife Aurélie (Ginette Leclerc) is seduced by a handsome shepherd and runs off with him. The baker (Raimu) collapses into despair. He takes to drink, tries to hang himself, and—worst of all—loses interest in supplying the village with his superlative bread. The whole village conspires to find her and bring her back, whereupon the baker and everyone else tactfully welcome her home as if nothing had happened. The comic drinking scenes and the attempted suicide were among Pagnol's additions to the story, as was the rivalry (reminiscent of the Don Camillo stories) between the *curé* (Robert Vattier) and the anticlerical schoolteacher (Robert Bassac). As usual, Raimu played a more than actorly part in the production, altering the baker's character to fit his own, and developing many of his own gags.

Basil Wright found the movie "enchanting," but complained that "the poor film critic is once again baffled by the phenomenon of a film that eschews much of the technique and polish of cinema and yet achieves an undeniable greatness. One might, indeed, almost accuse it of being shoddily made. The photography is certainly no more than competent, and most of the film is shot in mid-shots or long-shots notable for their extreme length and unoriginality of angle or lighting. . . . It must be conceded that much of the film depends on the dialogue, which it would be impossible to overpraise, and on the quality of the acting. . . . [Raimu] makes of his conjugal love, of his overpowering grief at his wife's absence, and of his resulting lapse into outrageous drunkenness, an epic portrait of man, simple and human, and he gives to Giono's dialogue that poetic translucence which is its just due. . . . It is probable that no review can give a satisfactory explanation of the film's beauty. Of all films since Vigo's *Atalante*, it remains most gratefully in the memory."

La Fille du puisatier (*The Welldigger's Daughter,* 1940) stars Josette Day (who had replaced Orane Demazis in Pagnol's household) as Patricia, daughter of a widowed welldigger (Raimu). The year is 1939 and the young poacher who seduces her turns out to be a rich young officer in the French air force. By the time Patricia discovers that she is pregnant, her lover has been posted overseas, where he is reported killed. Discovering that they have a grandchild, the flyer's rich and snobbish parents visit the welldigger and his family but are rebuffed. Then it emerges that the boy is not dead after all, but has been a prisoner of war. He returns, and the happy ending follows.

The welldigger's assistant, devoted to Patricia, is played by Fernandel in a role very similar to that of Saturnin in *Angèle,* and the movie can be regarded as a revamped version of that work, though a somewhat inferior one. *La Fille du puisatier* includes a scene in which the charac-

ters listen to a radio broadcast by Marshall Pétain announcing France's armistice with Germany in 1940; mainly for this reason, the film was attacked by Gaullists as "political propaganda for Pétain and the Vichy regime." Others maintain that these charges are unjustified and unjust, pointing out that Pagnol resigned in 1941 from the Comité d'Organisation de l'Industrie Cinématographique, a Vichy institution, and that he made no films during the German occupation. In a post-Liberation revision of *La Fille du puisatier,* a speech by de Gaulle was substituted for Pétain's.

In 1945 Pagnol wrote *Naïs,* adapted from a short story by Zola, and gave it to Raymond Leboursier to direct. Its heroine, Jacqueline Bouvier, became Pagnol's second wife the same year. By 1946 the political attacks on Pagnol had subsided sufficiently to permit his election to the Académie Française—an immense honor never before accorded to a filmmaker. The following year Pagnol published his translation of *Hamlet* and his *Notes sur le rire* ("Notes on Laughter"), and in 1948 he made *La Belle meunière,* a disastrously bad film biography of Franz Schubert which he codirected with Max de Rieux. The picture was savaged by the critics, and Pagnol characteristically struck back at them in *Critique des critiques* (1949).

After yet another remake of *Topaze,* this time starring Fernandel, came the best of Pagnol's late films, *Manon des sources* (*Manon of the Springs,* 1952), a three-hour work written and directed by him as a kind of homage to his wife, who was its star. Manon is the daughter of a hunchback who inherits a farm in a Provençal village. Covetous neighbors seal off the spring that waters his land and he dies, worn out by the labor of carrying water. Manon goes to live alone in the hills, feared as a witch and pursued for her beauty. She revenges her father by blocking the spring that brings water to the village. Her principal enemy, regarding this as divine retribution for his crime, confesses all and commits suicide. Manon marries the village schoolteacher (Raymond Pellegrin).

Jacqueline Pagnol perfectly embodies the combination of sensuality and sensitivity in the character of Manon, who has something of the animal wildness of her namesake in Prévost's novel. Pagnol's scenario also shows obvious debts to Giono and to Zola and the *Naïs* script. The film is too long and prolix, but is nevertheless a work of great richness and some grandeur, and a moving expression of the director's love and admiration for his young wife. Pierre Leprohon said of Pagnol that "his mistakes, his foibles and his naiveté are more endearing than faultless techniques," and André Bazin thought that the film came close to being the finest of all French screen epics.

Pagnol's last movie followed in 1954, adapting three of the stories in Alphonse Daudet's *Lettres de mon moulin*. It was well enough received at the time, but has seemed to later critics a minor and rather lackluster parade of familiar Provençal characters and clichés. Thereafter Pagnol devoted himself largely to literary activities, including three greatly admired volumes of autobiography, translations of Virgil's *Bucolics* and Shakespeare's *A Midsummer Night's Dream,* and a two-volume novel, *L'Eau des collines* (1963), based on *Manon des sources.* There were two more plays, *Judas* (1955) and *Fabien* (1956), and Pagnol also tried his hand at the new medium of television, writing an adaptation of Dumas' *La Dame aux camélias* (1962) and directing a television film called *Le Curé de Cucugnan* (1967).

In 1959 Pagnol welcomed his old friend Marcel Achard into the Académie Française with a famously witty speech, and in 1971 he himself was named a Grand-officier of the Légion d'Honneur. He died three years later at the age of seventy-nine and was survived by his wife and his son Frédéric, a daughter having died in infancy. His epitaph, written by himself, was *"Fontes, amicos, uxorem dilexit"* (He loved the fresh-water springs, his friends, and his wife).

André Bazin wrote of him that, "in his best films at least, Pagnol demolished the formalist myth of Cinematographic Art. A heritage of silent cinema, this was the feeling that cinema should be pure, specific and unable to be reduced to its content; the cinema was to be an art of moving images and depended totally on the rhythm of its montage. Quietly but irrefutably, *Angèle* and *The Baker's Wife* disproved this idea. Not because, as Pagnol believed, his successes contradicted the existence of the cinema as a specific means of expression, but because his ignorance of those technical habits and customs current in professional circles led him unconsciously to the discovery of other, no less cinematographic values which only his turning to realism could reveal. Pagnol's *oeuvre* is there to negate not only those who believe that the cinema has only to do with framing, lighting or *découpage*; it also demonstrates the foolishness of Pagnol's own belief in the future of 'filmed theatre.' Alas, his failures, more numerous than his successes, are sufficient proof that a contempt for technique is an even more dangerous recipe than formalism." Pagnol has increasingly been seen as a forerunner of neorealism, and both Vittorio De Sica and Roberto Rossellini acknowledged a debt to him.

Pagnol's reputation languished somewhat after his death, but in 1986 Claude Berri based two very successful films, *Jean de Florette* and *Manon des sources*, on Pagnol's novel, *L'Eau des collines*, rekindling interest in the earlier director's work. "His characters come across as mythic representatives of the tics and foibles that belong to . . . village France and to no other place in the world," Richard Bernstein wrote. "At a time when most serious French film consists of modern urban drama involving glossy, chic, world-weary characters, Pagnol returns to the scene with a kind of primitive, archaic force, telling . . . rough-edged stories of a world that has disappeared."

FILMS: Le Gendre de Monsieur Poirier, 1934; Jofroi (Ways of Love), 1934; L'Article 330, 1934 (medium-length); Angèle, 1934; Merlusse, 1935; Cigalon, 1935; Topaze, 1936; César, 1936; Regain (Harvest), 1937; Le Schpountz (Heartbeat), 1938; La Femme du boulanger (The Baker's Wife), 1938; La Fille du puisatier (The Welldigger's Daughter), 1940; La Belle meunière, 1948; Topaze, 1951 (remake); Manon des sources (Manon of the Springs), 1952; Les Lettres de mon moulin (Letters From My Windmill), 1954. *Published scripts*—All of Pagnol's scripts are included (in play form) in his Oeuvres dramatiques, 1954 and most have also been published in French as individual works.

ABOUT: Bazin, A. Qu'est-ce que le cinéma? 2, 1959; Beylie, C. Marcel Pagnol, 1974 (in French); Blavette, C. Ma Provence en cuisine, 1961; Caldicott, C.E.J. Marcel Pagnol (in English), 1977; Castans, R. Il était une fois . . . Marcel Pagnol, 1978; Clair, R. Réflexion faite, 1951; Leprohon, P. Marcel Pagnol, 1976 (in French); Pagnol, M. The Days Were Too Short, 1960; Pagnol, M. The Time of Secrets, 1962; Roud, R. (ed.) Cinema: A Critical Dictionary, 1980; World Authors: 1950–1970, 1975. *Periodicals*—L'Avant-Scène du Cinéma July–September 1970; Cahiers du Cinéma December 1965, June 1969; Cinéma (France) March 1969, June 1974; Écran June 1974; Films in Review April 1970; Image et Son May 1969, September 1973; New York Times December 7, 1986; June 21, 1987.

PORTER, EDWIN S(TANTON) (April 21, 1870–April 30, 1941), American director, producer, cameraman, scenarist, exhibitor, and equipment designer and manufacturer, was born and spent the first twenty-three years of his life in Connellsville, Pennsylvania, fifty miles southeast of Pittsburgh. He was the fourth of seven children. His father, Thomas Richard Porter, was an undertaker and furniture salesman who worked for his more successful brothers. His mother, Mary Clark Porter, was descended from a signer of the Declaration of Independence. Porter's family were small businessmen in a

EDWIN S. PORTER

town dominated by conflict between absentee owners of large coke works and coal miners and coke workers. The class antagonism and violent strikes that Porter witnessed as a youth helped to shape the ideological values he subsequently expressed in his work. Porter's films generally reveal a distrust for a society based on the conflict between labor and capital and for its social counterpart, the impersonal city. Correspondingly, Porter refused to adopt the large scale, systematized production methods that came to dominate the American film industry by the 1910s.

As he grew up, Porter participated in many aspects of Connellsville's cultural life. He worked at the local theatre as an usher and ticket-taker, a job that allowed him to see a range of theatrical entertainment. He was also an exhibition skater at the local roller-skating rink in the mid-1880s. A poor student, Ed Porter became a telegraph operator at fifteen and co-invented an electrical regulating device at the age of twenty. He worked as a tailor in the early 1890s and opened his own tailoring establishment in Connellsville early in 1893. That year of severe economic depression ruined him financially. On June 5th, 1893, he married Caroline Ridinger of Somerset, Pennsylvania; on the 15th he declared bankruptcy; and on the 19th he enlisted in the navy as a telegraph operator.

Porter's enlistment record reported his height as 5´4 and 3/4´´, his weight as 150 pounds. He had brown hair and eyes and a sunburned complexion. In later years he retained a weakness for "eats" and big cigars, and became "heavy-set" with a "full round face." Porter never had chil-

dren, his greatest personal tragedy. His wife had many miscarriages, and the recurring loss became an obsession that worked its way into his films. Although the threatened loss of a child was a common theme in American popular culture, Porter returned to it with unusual frequency in films such as *Life Of an American Fireman* (1903), *Lost in the Alps* (1907) and *Rescued From an Eagle's Nest* (1908).

Porter spent his three years' enlistment first in Philadelphia and then at the Brooklyn Navy Yard, where he helped develop the Fiske electric rangefinder and invented and improved electrical devices for the navy's communication service. Porter eagerly followed developments in the electrical field, particularly the activities of Thomas Edison, whom he admired and emulated. In the winter of 1895–1896, as his enlistment approached its end, Porter learned of plans to introduce projected moving pictures as a public amusement. He persuaded a group of Connellsville friends to purchase the exhibition rights to Edison's Vitascope for California and Indiana. He learned as much as he could about the new projecting machine and helped exhibit the Vitascope in Koster and Bial's Music Hall in New York. Leaving the navy in June 1896, Porter joined his friends who were showing films in San Francisco and Los Angeles. Although their enterprise soon folded, Porter remained in the motion-picture field, showing films in New York City and also in the Caribbean and Central America, where he presented himself as Thomas Edison, Jr.

By 1898, Porter had returned to New York, where he began to work for the Eden Musee on West 23rd Street near Madison Square. The Musee, which presented waxworks and musical entertainments to middle-class audiences, had added motion pictures to its repertoire in December 1896. Among the works that Porter screened as a motion-picture operator were *Passion Play*, produced by Musee president Richard Hollaman, and films of the Spanish-American War. Porter was one of several Musee employees responsible for combining short films into more complex programs often based on a single subject. Programs constantly changed, allowing Porter to experiment with a range of editorial possibilities. Many tasks generally now performed in the post-production phase of filmmaking were then executed during the exhibition stage, including editing. The exhibitor often provided a spoken narrative or lecture to clarify the images, elaborate characterization, or insert local references.

Porter also used his mechanical and electrical ingenuity to produce motion-picture equipment. During the 1890s, he and Frank Cannock built and then frequently improved the Eden Musee's projector. In 1899 Porter also built the cameras, printing machines, and projectors for the American Sportagraph Company. These used a special-sized film and were to be employed to photograph and exhibit films of the Palmer-McGovern fight. The fight was filmed but lasted less than one round, and the company failed. After a brief stint as a traveling exhibitor, Porter was hired in November 1900 by the Edison Manufacturing Company to improve and redesign its cameras, projecting machines, and perforators.

In the fall of 1900, the Edison Company had contracted to build an indoor film studio at 41 East 21st Street in New York City. By February 1901 Porter was placed in charge of the newly completed studio, where he served as producer, cameraman, and director. At the turn of the century, the cinema was conceived largely as a "visual newspaper." The Edison Company's motion picture department, headed by James White, gave primary emphasis to the filming of local news events. Porter provided the cinematic equivalents of comic strips and political cartoons as well as reenactments of important news events that had not been or could not be filmed. Porter's *The Kansas Saloon Smashers*, perhaps the first film made in the new studio, was a one-shot reenactment of Carrie Nation wrecking a Wichita saloon. The set was based on a photograph that appeared in a New York newspaper. Porter, however, burlesqued the scene in the style of a political cartoon.

Porter's sense of popular taste was noted by his employers and this solidified his appointment as studio chief. *Pie, Tramp and the Bulldog*, one of the many one-shot comedies Porter made in early 1901, ran for five weeks in several New York vaudeville theaters. Many spectators must have seen the film several times, but this simple story about a tramp who uses stilts to steal a pie from a windowsill—in an unsuccessful effort to elude the guard dog—kept audiences amused. *Terrible Teddy, the Grizzly King* was a two-shot comedy based on two panels of a political cartoon series in the *Journal*. It burlesqued the much-publicized hunting expeditions of Vice President–elect Theodore Roosevelt. For this latter production, Porter took studio resources (camera, actors, props, etc.) to exterior locations.

Several of Porter's first comedies were multi-shot films. In *Another Job for the Undertaker*, for instance, a country rube stays in a city hotel room. Since he cannot read, he ignores the warning "Don't Blow Out the Gas." The brief second shot shows a hearse on its way to the cemetery,

providing a punchline to the main scene. *The Tramp's Dream* used a three-shot dream structure already explored by Porter's contemporaries. In the first shot, the tramp goes to sleep on a park bench. Porter then dissolves to the central shot of the tramp's dream—the familiar confrontation between tramp and bulldog. In the final shot, Porter dissolves back to the tramp as he is rudely awakened by a policeman. In all these films, additional shots are dependent on the main scene for their meaning.

Although a newcomer to films, Porter's position in the American industry proved unique. His employer, Thomas Edison, was suing rival producers for infringement of his motion-picture patents and in July 1901 won a victory in the lower courts. For the next eight months, Porter may have been the only person making fictional films in the United States. Assured of its supremacy, however, the Edison Company pursued a conservative business policy and took no risks on expensive productions. The studio was often idle when Porter was away shooting travel and news films for his employers.

In September 1901, after President McKinley's assassination by the anarchist Leon Czolgosz, Porter and other Edison cameramen filmed the funeral ceremonies in Buffalo, Washington, and Canton (Ohio). These short films could be bought separately, but the Edison Company also marketed them as a set in a prearranged sequence with dissolves between each film. Editorial control was beginning to shift from the exhibitor to the production company, and the process continued with Porter's *The Execution of Czolgosz*, a four-shot film. The first two shots were exterior views of Auburn State Prison where Czolgosz was executed. The last two scenes reenacted the execution in accordance with newspaper reports. Again, the exhibitor was given a choice and could buy the film with or without the opening panoramas. In this well-made and relatively elaborate picture, Porter established exterior-interior relations between the shots and spatial contiguity. The film also implied a temporal simultaneity of scenes, since actions in the third and fourth shots occurred at the same time, a narrative construction equivalent to the term *meanwhile*.

When Edison's court victory was reversed on appeal in March 1902, the threat of competition drove the Edison Company to make story films. The first, Porter's *Appointment by Telephone* (May 1902), was a three-shot comedy about a man who makes an assignation with an attractive woman at a restaurant, only to be discovered there by his wife. The story unfolds smoothly from scene to scene. The exterior of a restaurant, shot on a city street, is followed by a reverse-angle interior filmed in the studio. Porter used similar storytelling methods in *Jack and the Beanstalk* (May–June 1902), which told a version of the fairy tale in ten scenes. Photographed entirely within the studio, it was indebted to European fairy tale films, particularly Georges Méliès' *Bluebeard.*

Porter studied Méliès' productions carefully, particularly *A Trip to the Moon*, which reached the United States by October. The rocket landing, shown twice from different points of view, was particularly seminal. A shot of the rocket hitting the Man in the Moon in the eye is followed by a view of the rocket landing on the moon and its passengers disembarking. The overlapping action made the temporal relation between the two shots explicit. Porter experimented with this form of continuity and pushed it to new extremes. In the three-shot film *How They Do Things on the Bowery* (October 1902), a country rube comes to New York City and is picked up by a prostitute. Scene 1: The prostitute lures him into a bar. Scene 2: She administers a Mickey Finn, steals his money, and leaves. The bartender then throws him and his suitcase out onto the street. Scene 3: A police patrol wagon comes down the street and waits outside the bar—for the rube. The ejection of the rube and his suitcase is shown at the end of both the second and third scenes, establishing the temporal relations between the shots. The continuity comically suggests that the rube is the victim of a coordinated urban conspiracy between prostitute, bartender, and police—an unholy triumverate.

Porter explored these methods of continuity still further in *Life of an American Fireman* (November 1902–January 1903). James White, head of Edison's Kinetograph Department, was a lieutenant in the Orange, New Jersey, Volunteer Fire Department. He produced the film and played the heroic fireman. One of the most elaborate and advanced examples of the pre-Griffith mode of representation, *Fireman* has been a key and controversial film in American film historiography. Unfortunately, the film could not be seen for many years. The historian Terry Ramsaye adopted a fanciful description of the picture provided by Porter: it suggested the use of parallel editing, interpolated close-ups, and other modern storytelling techniques. The notion that the grammar of the new medium was established from the start—that *Life of an American Fireman* in particular and early cinema in general displayed in primitive form the Hollywood conventions of later years—seemed to be confirmed when a print of *Fireman* finally came to light in the early 1940s. In fact, this print had been doctored: the last two scenes were

intercut, creating a rudimentary form of cross-cutting. Much film history was written based on this modernized version. By the late 1970s, it became apparent that another copy of *Fireman*, restored by the Library of Congress in the 1960s, was the correct version. This forced a major reevaluation of early cinema in general and Porter's career in particular.

As Noel Burch has pointed out, Porter's method of storytelling differed in many of its most basic assumptions from the method of filmmakers who worked less than ten years later. Porter's narrative did not move forward in a direct linear sequence but allowed for digressions and recapitulations. Action at the end of one scene might be repeated at the beginning of the next. In the film's third shot, firemen are awakened, get into their clothes, and slide down the brass pole. In the following scene, also inside the firehouse but now on the ground floor, the firemen come down the pole again, hitch their horses to the fire engines, and dash off. In the fifth scene, the exterior of the firehouse is shown, the doors open, and from this new vantage point we again see the engines dash out and off to the fire. The recognizable repetition of actions identifies the relations between adjacent scenes.

The temporal construction of the final two shots is the most remarkable. In the eighth shot, a complete rescue is shown from the inside of the burning house: a fireman enters the bedroom by the door, breaks out the window, takes the unconscious woman out the window, and then returns to rescue the child. In the next and final scene, the same events are shown from the exterior of the house. From this second perspective, Porter records new elements of the action: the fireman carrying the woman down the ladder, the revived woman pleading "Save my child!", the fireman going back up the ladder, etc. The repetition is thus complementary, rather than redundant. The two scenes are also complementary in their use of "real time." In the interior view, everything that happens inside the house takes place in real time, while whatever may be assumed to be happening outside the building seems to occur in the twinkling of an eye—the fireman carries the woman out the window and almost instantly reappears to rescue the child. In the exterior perspective, the reverse is true: now the business with the ladder and the pleading mother occupies real time, and the business inside the house is radically foreshortened. (This treatment has been seen as an adaptation of the theatrical convention by which time is compressed or speeded up for off-stage activity.) In watching the film, the spectator must fit these two scenes together, dovetailing the complementary time-frames in order to "see" the complete action. *Fireman* (and most other Porter-Edison films) seems today more like a related series of self-contained scenes than a single seamless narrative. Although editorial responsibility had been centralized in the production company, individual scenes are similar in many respects to the single-shot films of an earlier era.

The Edison Company's ownership rights to both *Jack and the Beanstalk* and *Life of an American Fireman* were called into question in January 1903 when a lower court refused to recognize Thomas Edison's method of copyrighting films. As its films were duplicated and sold by a rival firm, the Edison Company abandoned production until the issue was resolved in its favor—a period of several months. Porter did not actually resume large-scale studio production until that summer, when he made *Uncle Tom's Cabin* (July 1903). Although Edison's salesmen called this the most elaborate story film ever attempted, the 18-minute picture was really canned theatre. Porter hired an *Uncle Tom's Cabin* troupe and photographed a condensed version of their play, a type of cinema that Porter found increasingly interesting in later years.

The Edison Company expected Porter to produce many different kinds of subjects—news and travel films, dramatic spectacles, and comedies. Among the latter was *The Gay Shoe Clerk*. In this three-shot comedy, a salesman helps a young woman try on a shoe. Porter cuts to a close view of her ankle as the clerk's hand travels up her calf; then returns to the establishing shot as the woman's chaperon thumps the forward saleman on the head with her umbrella. An early example of an interpolated close-up, the match in action between shots is excellent, except that the petticoats are black in the establishing shot, white in the close-up. The leg in close-up belonged to someone else, possibly even one of Porter's male employees.

Porter's films at this time were often part fiction, part actuality. In showing *Life of an American Fireman*, an exhibitor could emphasize either its fictional elements (by focusing on the story), or its documentary aspects by specifying, for instance, the various fire departments participating in the production). *Rube and Mandy at Coney Island* (August 1903) was part comedy, part travelogue. In some shots, Porter focused on the antics of two stage comedians, Coney Island merely providing the background. In others the actors were made subservient to the setting as Porter featured America's foremost amusement park. A short comedy, *Romance of the Rail* (October 1903), also exemplifies the railroad subgenre of the travelogue, an exhibition format that culminated in Hale's Tours. In this genre, the spectator sat in a mock Pullman car and assumed the role of passenger observing the passing scenery, which had been photographed from the front of a train. To heighten the illusion, its car would sway and bang, and to prevent audiences from becoming bored, exhibitors inserted comic vignettes of train travel into these views. *Romance of the Rail* was one such vignette, a lighthearted burlesque of the Lackawanna Railroad's advertising campaign in which Phoebe Snow rode the coal carrier to the slogan "My gown stays white/From morn to night/Upon the Road of Anthracite." In the course of Porter's four-minute film, Phoebe Snow meets her male equivalent, falls in love, and is married. Although only one scene of this film features the scenery as much as the story, exhibitors used their editorial prerogative to find their own balance between the scenic and fictional elements.

Porter's best known film, *The Great Train Robbery* (November 1903), was an unprecedented commercial success that remained immensely popular for many years after its first release. One reason for its popularity was that Porter contrived to incorporate so many different trends, genres, and strategies into this single film. Twelve minutes long, it pushed the railway subgenre to new heights and was often shown in Hale's Tours. In such a format, the film was usually preceded by the customary travel views. Spectators, having started out as railway passengers, were suddenly assaulted by a close-up of the outlaw Barnes firing his six-shooter directly into their midst. (This shot could be shown either at the beginning or the end of the film—in a Hale's Tour's situation it would seem more effective at the beginning.) The viewers, having assumed the roles of passengers, were held up. The close-up of Barnes reaffirmed the spectators' assumed role, bringing them into the narrative that followed and intensifying their identification with the bandits' victims. As the robbery unfolds during the next eight scenes the train is kept in almost constant view: through the station window as the telegraph operator is knocked unconscious, as a fight unfolds on the tender, from the inside of the mail car, or along the tracks as the locomotive is disconnected from the cars and the passengers are relieved of their money. The Hale's Tours conventions are abandoned in the later scenes as the bandits flee, the posse gives pursuit, and the final shootout occurs. For these end scenes, the exhibitor usually stopped the simulated swaying and sounds of a moving train and let the viewers assume a more familiar spectatorial position.

Another popular cinematic genre utilized in *The Great Train Robbery* was the reenacted contemporary news events (sections were modeled after recently reported crimes). The film's title referred to a well-known stage melodrama by the same name. Porter was moreover consciously working within the violent crime genre begun in England by Sheffield Photo's *Daring Daylight Robbery* and Walter Haggar's *Desperate Poaching Affair* earlier that year. Porter's success, in turn, encouraged other films in this genre—William Paley's *Burned at the Stake* and Sigmund Lubin's *The Bold Bank Robbery* (August 1904). *The Great Train Robbery* was also Porter's first chase film, another genre that was just beginning to establish its popularity. However, the picture was not originally seen as a Western, as some historians have assumed. It was interpreted from this perspective only much later, after the Western emerged as an important genre in the nickelodeon era.

The Great Train Robbery, like many earlier films, utilizes temporal repetition within an overall narrative progression. The robbery of the mail car (scene 3) and the fight on the tender (scene 4) occur simultaneously according to the catalog description, even though they are shown successively without intercutting. As André Gaudreault has pointed out, this return to an earlier moment in time recurs in more extreme form later. After the bandits make their getaway in scene 9, the film goes back to pick up another line of action: the telegraph operator regaining consciousness and raising the posse. Although these two scenes (10 and 11) are supposed to take place at the same time as the actions in scenes 2–9, Porter's narrative construction here lacks the continuity cues of *Life of an American Fireman*. The two lines of action are only united, and the relationship between them clarified, in scene 12, a chase between the posse and the bandits.

Porter had developed a repertoire of storytelling methods that he utilized throughout his remaining years at Edison. Yet the production of original story films did not immediately assume a central role in the Edison production schedule. For the following two months, Porter concentrated on the production of short comedies and actualities. In making the *Buster Brown* series (February 1904), Porter presented not a unified narrative but a group of one-shot comedies that shared a common character, the hero of R. F. Outcault's comic strip. *How a French Nobleman Got a Wife Through the New York "Herald" Personal Columns* (August 1904) and *Maniac Chase* (October 1904) imitated comedies produced by the rival Biograph company and were made strictly for commercial purposes. *Capture of the Yegg Bank Burglars* (September 1904) shows remarkable similarities to Lubin's earlier *The Bold Bank Robbery*. For *Parsifal* (October

1904), Porter merely photographed selections from a dramatic version of Wagner's opera.

Only late in 1904 did Porter begin to produce a steady flow of fictional narratives. *The Ex-Convict* (November 1904) and *The Kleptomaniac* (February 1905) were two of Porter's most explicitly political films. In the first, the hero loses his job when his employer learns that he is an ex-convict. A good family man, he is driven to steal to save his sick child. He enters a wealthy man's house but is caught. However, the daughter of the house recognizes him as the man who had earlier risked his life to save hers from an onrushing automobile. The ex-convict is forgiven and a shared recognition of paternal responsibility allows the two men to transcend their class differences and become friends. Family and societal responsibilities again come into conflict in *The Kleptomaniac*. To feed her child, a desperate woman steals bread from an unattended basket of groceries. She is caught and taken to the police station. "Mrs. Banker" visits Macy's where she steals some merchandise. Both women are tried by the same court. Mrs. Banker is let go because she is excused as a "kleptomaniac" while the poor woman is sent to prison: justice is shown blinded by money.

Porter alternated between serious subjects and comedies during 1904–1905. *The Strenuous Life or Anti–Race Suicide* (December 1904) satirized two of President Roosevelt's more famous slogans. *How Jones Lost His Roll* (March 1905), *The Whole Dam Family and the Dam Dog* (May 1905) and *Everybody Works But Father* (November 1905) amused audiences with "jumble titles," an early form of object animation in which the letters of intertitles moved around the background. *On a Good Old Five Cent Trolley Ride* (May 1904) and *Everybody Works But Father* were based on popular songs and designed for possible accompaniment by a singer. *The Little Train Robbery* (August 1905) had children imitate the action of Porter's most famous film. They rob a miniature train and relieve their young victims of popcorn and candy. Meant in good fun, Porter's film illustrated the very issue that was beginning to worry social reformers: crime films like *The Great Train Robbery* inspired young viewers to emulation.

By July 1905, Porter was collaborating with Wallace McCutcheon, who had worked for many years at Biograph as a director and cameraman. McCutcheon directed the actors and assumed other responsibilities. Porter did the camerawork and editing. While Porter maintained ultimate control as head of production, he preferred this method of working and sought similar collaborations throughout his career.

In *The Miller's Daughter* (October 1905), Porter reveals a nostalgia for the innocent life of rural America. The miller's daughter, rather than marry a local farmer as her father desires, elopes with an artist. He proves to be already married and the heroine, banished from her rural Garden of Eden, lives in urban misery as a garment worker. She returns home desperate and ill, but her wrathful father does not forgive her. She is saved from suicide by her faithful suitor, the local farmer, and they start life afresh together.

In Porter's work, the large city is often a place of anonymous misery, where class distinctions are not softened by personal contact and where people do not feel responsible for their neighbors' welfare. In *Life of an American Policeman* (December 1905), the policeman is identified with the familial values that the city apparently needs. The policeman's family breakfast is shown before he leaves for work. On his rounds he befriends a hungry, lost child. Other cops save a woman attempting suicide and capture a burglar—this latter scene was based on an actual incident, with many police officers reenacting their original roles. The professionalized nature of urban law enforcement is in marked contrast to the intimacy of rural vigilante justice depicted in *The White Caps* (October 1905). After a brutish man ignores the White Caps' warning and beats his wife, her family and neighbors—anonymous in white hoods—tar and feather this wayward member, riding him out of town on a rail. Porter presents the vigilantes as members of an organic, self-policing community.

In Porter's fictional worlds—as in others at that time—many groups outside "proper" society were excluded from serious consideration. In *Watermelon Patch* (October 1905), a "comedy" with many similarities to McCutcheon's earlier Biograph film, *The Chicken Thief*, blacks are depicted as lazy petty thieves. Tramps, as in *Burglar's Slide for Life* (April 1905), and Jews, in *Cohen's Fire Sale* (May 1907), were frequent objects of comic ridicule or condemnation. *Stolen by Gypsies* (July 1905) was part of a popular genre that labeled gypsies as child-stealers. Women were usually marginal to his films' concerns as well.

Porter was an employee who operated within constraints established by Edison Company executives. By the end of 1905, with his comedies consistently outselling the social-problem films, Porter generally avoided controversial subjects. *The Train Wreckers* (November 1905) pitted all social classes against malevolent outlaws attempting to derail passenger trains. *Dreams of a Rarebit Fiend* (February 1906), a remake of Pathé's *Rêve a la Lune* (1905), appropriated the title of Winsor McCay's popular comic strip and sold 182 copies during the following year. *The Terrible Kids* (April 1906) and *How the Office Boy Saw the Game* (June 1906) were in the popular "bad boy" genre. They shared a nostalgic memory of a lost male childhood before social rules and responsibilities were inculcated. In both films, the boys escape punishment for their misdeeds.

Porter frequently relied on his viewers' knowledge of popular culture for an understanding and appreciation of his films. *Waiting at the Church* (July 1906) is a nonsensical chase film unless the spectator knows the hit song of the same name. Then the film becomes comprehensible and clever. *Kathleen Mavourneen* (May 1906) and *Daniel Boone* (December 1906) were both adaptations of plays commonly found in the repertoire of traveling theatrical stock companies. *The "Teddy" Bears* (February 1907) evoked the craze for the stuffed toy bears. It begins by telling the children's story of "Goldilocks and the Three Bears." When the bears (costumed actors) discover Goldilocks in their bed, they chase her through the snowy countryside. She is rescued by Teddy Roosevelt who shoots the adult bears but spares the cub, reenacting the circumstances that were at the origins of the craze (the stuffed toy was named after a bear cub Roosevelt captured on a hunting expedition in 1902). Porter listed *The "Teddy" Bears* among his favorite films, although he remembered it chiefly for an animated scene in which toy bears perform acrobatic feats: the short scene took the director a week to film.

The number of storefront theatres mushroomed in 1906, but Porter did not increase his production rate to meet the tremendous demand for new films. If anything, he took more time over each subject because the increased number of print sales could justify higher production costs. Moreover, he had multiple responsibilities. He continued to improve the projecting kinetoscope, Edison's motion picture projector. Kinetoscope sales yielded larger profits than film sales during the early nickelodeon era, when the demand for projectors was at its peak. Porter also spent much time supervising the building and outfitting of Edison's new film studio in the Bronx. This opened in July 1907.

A few months before the new studio opened, McCutcheon left the Edison Company, ending his collaboration with Porter. Porter found a new collaborator in J. Searle Dawley, a young playwright and stage manager: *The Nine Lives of a Cat* (July 1907) was their first film together. With the new studio completed, Edison executives considered increased production to be of paramount importance. The Edison studio staff grew, and the pace of work quickened. By January 1908, when he made *Rescued From an Eagle's Nest*, which starred D. W. Griffith in his first leading film role, Porter was making four one-reel films a month.

Most of Porter's films made prior to February 1908 survive. After this date, only a handful can be found. Contemporary reviews and other paper documentation become central to understanding the changes affecting Porter's career. Porter's films from the first months of 1908 indicate that his storytelling methods had not changed. He continued to rely on nonlinear narrative structures. The overlapping action found in the early scenes of *Life of an American Fireman* is still present. By mid-1908, this approach to cinema was becoming antiquated. Linear narrative, parallel editing, and other modern techniques were being employed at Vitagraph, Pathé, and Biograph with increasing authority. Porter resisted these changes. More than any of his contemporaries, he had elaborated a pre-nickelodeon representational system. Now in the nickelodeon era, his once-popular films came under increasingly severe criticism. His rapid production schedule made it difficult to spend time on the small details that had given his earlier films a distinctive quality.

In June 1908, the Edison Company expanded its production capabilities by forming a second unit. Dawley was placed in charge of this second unit. Porter acted as both studio head, overseeing the new unit, and as producer-cameraman for the first unit. He was not comfortable with the hierarchical structure of this emerging studio system. Porter often called Dawley away from the second unit to advise on his current production, disrupting the studio's organizational structures and creating inefficiencies. Nor did multiple responsibilities improve his films. In a caustic but typical review, the New York *Dramatic Mirror* called Porter's *The Tale the Ticker Told* (December 1908) "a confused unintelligible series of scenes" presented in "an unknown picture-language." In January, Frank Dyer, general manager of the Edison Manufacturing Company, reorganized the studio. Porter was no longer in charge of the first unit. He remained as studio head, supervising the two units and making only an occasional film himself. He had little talent for administration, and Edison productions continued to be condemned by the trade press and by exhibitors.

At the end of February 1909, as the Motion Picture Patents Company began its operations, Porter was deposed as studio head. He remained with the Edison Company, testing film stocks and acting as a technical advisor. Porter made a few more films for Edison but outside its studio system. In August 1909 he went to Colorado, where he filmed *Bear Hunt in the Rockies* and an industrial short. Shortly after his return, on November 1909, he was fired.

Porter maintained his interest in motion picture technology, developing the Simplex projector with Frank Cannock. This machine, promoted by Richard Hollaman of the Eden Musee, was first used commercially in 1911. Porter also worked briefly with Will Rising for the Actophone company. In 1910, Porter formed the Defender film company with Joseph Engel, a theatre owner, and William Swanson, a Chicago distributor and exhibitor. The New York–based company released its first films on June 10, 1910. Little is known about Defender and much of that is contradictory. Trade journals paid it surprisingly little attention. However, a report in *Moving Picture World* (July 30, 1910) mentioned that Defender releases were originally made by the World Film Company of Portland, Oregon—a company earlier put out of business by a studio fire. These releases were expected to continue until the new Defender studio was completed. On the other hand, Arthur Miller, who worked with Porter, claims that Porter was responsible for all the company's productions. Porter might simply have added a few exterior shots to these films, such as a view of Ellis Island for *Russia, the Land of Oppression*, the company's first release. Was *The Cattle Thief's Revenge* shot in Oregon or on Staten Island, where Porter did most of his location work? Not one Defender film is available to answer these questions.

Defender films received generally adverse criticism in trade publications, and the company stopped releasing in November 1910. Was it considered best to disassociate Porter's own productions from those made by a defunct firm? Or did Porter continue to encounter the same problems he faced at Edison, finally forcing the partners to reorganize their company? In either case, the same trio—Porter, Engel, and Swanson—formed Rex which began to release films in February 1911. By then Porter had already completed more than twenty productions at the Rex studio at 573 Eleventh Avenue in New York City. The first production, *Heroine of '76*, starred Gordon Sackville, who had acted for Porter as far back as 1904, and the future director Lois Weber. Porter soon developed a Rex stock company which featured Weber, her husband Phillips Smalley, and Cleo Ridgely. Smalley worked closely with Porter, assuming the position held earlier by Dawley and McCutcheon. Weber wrote many of the scenarios.

Only one film we can definitely attribute to Porter survives from this period: *Fate*, released on July 16, 1911. By this time Porter had simplified his storytelling methods, eliminating the deviant, antiquated elements that had been so harshly criticized in his Edison films. But the veteran director did not enrich his representational repertoire with the methods being developed by Griffith and others, and the result was a kind of filmed theatre. It nevertheless found favor in some circles, one critic praising Rex productions for photographing actors in full shot, keeping distance enough that the camera did not cut off the actors' feet. Readers were urged to "study their work for consistent and praiseworthy effort to keep the full figure on the screen." This critic's view was a minority one.

In January 1912, Rex began to release a second subject each week. Porter's films with Weber and Smalley were released on Thursdays, subjects starring Marion Leonard and produced by her husband Stanner E. V. Taylor on Sunday. In May, Porter and Rex were instrumental in the formation of the Universal Film Manufacturing Company, ultimately controlled by Carl Laemmle. Porter was also pursuing other plans. In July he, Daniel Frohman, and Adolph Zukor acquired the American rights to *Queen Elizabeth*, a three-reel French-made feature directed by Louis Mercanton and starring Sarah Bernhardt. They launched their Famous Players Film Company to market it. At a point when the American industry was looking for respectability, Bernhardt's "immortal" name and art generated coverage in reputable newspapers that customarily ignored moving pictures unless to condemn them. *Queen Elizabeth* played to standing room only on the Loew circuit and in other theatres. As Porter became increasingly involved in Famous Players, he spent less time at Rex. Smalley and Weber assumed more and more responsibility, including the direction of many Rex films. They left in September and Porter sold his shares in Universal in October.

By the fall of 1912, Famous Players had decided to film American plays with famous American theatrical stars. Bernhardt set the example, Daniel Frohman provided ties to the theatrical world, Porter the expertise in film production, and Zukor the business acumen and much of the financing. Porter directed James O'Neill (father of Eugene) in *The Count of Monte Cristo* late in 1912. When the Selig company quickly released their own version of the story, Famous Players shelved its version for almost a year before releasing it. In any case, this remarkable record of nineteenth-century theatrical technique may not have been an appropriate way to launch the company. The next Famous Players production, *The Prisoner of Zenda* with James Hackett, proved to be more successful, particularly after Hackett recognized the need to adapt his style to the moving picture medium. According to the New York *World*, *The Prisoner of Zenda*, released in February 1913, "proved to be more the visualization of the novel on which the play was based than a reproduction in moving pictures of the play itself." Four acts were transformed into over a hundred scenes. Although Porter's camera was considered too far from the actors by some critics, the film was "unexpectedly successful." A viewing of the film shows Porter in full control of his mise-en-scène.

Zukor acquired the services of many of America's leading actors including Lillie Langtry, Maclyn Arbuckle, and William Farnum. Porter was given the responsibility of making a filmed version of Belasco's *A Good Little Devil* with Mary Pickford. Another disappointing effort, its release was postponed for many months. His filmed version of the play *A Bishop's Carriage* proved to be a more successful vehicle for Pickford and was released next. Although Famous Players hired J. Searle Dawley to work with Porter, the protégé soon headed his own production unit.

Porter took Pickford out to California for several months of filming in late 1913 and early 1914. There they made *Tess of the Storm Country* (1914), one of Pickford's most popular films. Despite its success, *Tess* shows a director who had not adopted modern techniques of storytelling. Other people directed Pickford's films in the future as Porter began to work with his last collaborator, Hugh Ford. They traveled to Europe where Famous Players planned to make a series of dramas. These plans were curtailed by World War I before *The Eternal City* (1915) was completed. The two collaborators finished it in New York City.

Shortly before his directing career ended, Porter reminisced: "Looking back upon the past eighteen years in motion pictures—back to the day when no one knew what a motion picture was—and realizing the wonderful strides the industry had taken since then, I am more than impressed. I am thrilled. Artistically and mechanically the motion picture has forged its way forward until today it is recognized as the greatest amusement factor in the world and the greatest educational force in the history of civilization."

One wonders if Porter believed what he wrote. By 1915 feature productions were becoming the dominant product of the industry: production was even more standardized and large staffs even more stratified than they had been at the Edison Company. At Famous Players, Porter was considered something of an oddity. He refused to change his working methods which, though collaborative, simultaneously involved him in all aspects of filmmaking. He insisted on photographing his own productions. His predicament replayed, in many respects, his experience at the Edison Company, but now more was at stake than the production of one-reelers. Feature production was too elaborate and expensive for an individual like Porter to start his own company. With no place else to go, Porter was forced to retire from film production. His final break with Zukor came after the burning of the Famous Players studio at 213 West 26th Street on September 11, 1915. Porter remained to supervise the hastened completion of a new studio in northern Manhattan and then sold his share in Famous Players for $800,000.

Porter used some of his proceeds to buy shares in the Precision Machine Company and became its president. At least he no longer had to work for someone else. Under his supervision, the company's Simplex projector became the industry standard. Porter returned to his passion for mechanical invention and developed several pieces of new equipment—for example, an inexpensive camera that exhibitors could use to take local pictures. These new devices were not notably successful. When the Precision Machine Company merged with the International Projecting Company in 1925, Porter did not become an officer of the new corporation, sliding quietly into retirement. Although he lost much of his money in the stock market crash of 1929, the retired filmmaker continued to tinker, becoming ever more a recluse. He and his wife lived in the Taft Hotel off Times Square until he died at the age of seventy-one.

Kevin Brownlow quotes the cinematographer Arthur Miller as saying that "Porter was a director by necessity. He never had the ego to make a *great* director, or to be an actor. He was softspoken, kindly, completely unselfish, and always answered a question as briefly as possible, in order to make the other person think for himself. He never thought of himself as just a director. He thought of himself as a manufacturer of motion pictures, capable of handling personally every phase of filmmaking, from turning the crank of the camera to printing and toning the final positives. His life was devoted to movies, and he did more to create the motion picture business than those who invented the camera."

—C.M.

FILMS: *Edwin Porter produced, directed, and photographed the following films unless noted in parentheses. Titles for many early films varied: the following*

filmography of Porter/Edison films uses the copyright title when available. An alternate, catalog title is sometimes supplied in parentheses when commonly used.

1901: Follow the Leader; Joke on Grandma; Kansas Saloon Smashers (Carrie Nation and Her Hatchet Brigade); Terrible Teddy, the Grizzly King; The Finish of Brigit McKeen; The Old Maid Having Her Picture Taken; The Old Maid in the Drawing Room; The Old Maid in the Horse Carriage; Why Mrs. Nation Wants a Divorce; Why Brigit Stopped Drinking; Love by the Light of the Moon; The Donkey Party; The Automatic Weather Prophet; Happy Hooligan April-Fooled; Happy Hooligan Surprised; Stage Coach Hold-up in the Days of '49; The Tramp's Dream; Pie, Tramp and the Bulldog; Laura Comstock's Bag Punching Dog; Fun in a Butcher Shop; Gordon Sisters Boxing; How the Dutch Beat the Irish; Tramp's Strategy That Failed; Another Job for the Undertaker; The Tramp's Unexpected Skate; The Finish of Michael Casey or Blasting Rocks in Harlem; Building Made Easy, or How Mechanics Work in the Twentieth Century; Little Willie's Last Celebration; The Tramp's Miraculous Escape; The Photographer's Mishap; Photographing a Country Couple; Aunt Sallie's Wonderful Bustle; Sampson-Schley Controversy; Weary Willie and the Gardener; The Tramp and the Nursing Bottle; What Happened on Twenty-Third Street, New York City; The Reversible Divers; Soubrette's Troubles on a Fifth Avenue Stage; The Farmer and the Bad Boys; Rubes in the Theatre; Life Rescue at Long Branch (Life Rescue at Atlantic City); Lukens, Novel Gymnast; The Musical Ride; Faust Family of Acrobats; The Lovers, Coal Box, and Fireplace; The Martyred Presidents; Pan-American Exposition By Night; Catching an Early Train (Trying to Catch an Early Train); Execution of Czolgosz with Panorama of Auburn State Prison; Panorama of Esplanade by Night; A Phenomenal Contortionist; Trapeze Disrobing Act.

Porter served as cameraman on a number of actualities produced by James White during 1901, including films of the Pan-American Exposition taken in the Spring and Summer, of President McKinley's funeral in September, the America's Cup Races in September–October, and films taken in the Far West in November. Since other cameramen, including White, were available for these assignments it is usually impossible to pinpoint Porter's contributions in the absence of detailed records. The same limitations hold for detailing Porter's contributions as cameraman in 1902. For instance, Porter took films of Prince Henry's visit to the United States, but so did Jacob (James) B. Smith.

1902: Happy Hooligan Turns Burglar; Facial Expression (Female Facial Expressions); The Twentieth Century Tramp, or Happy Hooligan and His Airship; Uncle Josh at the Motion Picture Show; The Capture of the Biddle Brothers; The Burning of Durland's Riding Academy; New York City in a Blizzard; Kaiser Wilhelm's Yacht "Meteor" Entering the Water (cameraman); Prince Henry [of Prussia] at Lincoln Monument, Chicago, Ill. German and American Tableau; Fun in a Bakery Shop; Burlesque Suicide; Appointment by Telephone; Mt. Pelee Smoking Before Eruption (studio re-enactment); Mt. Pelee in Eruption and Destruction of St. Pierre (studio re-enactment); Burning of St. Pierre (studio re-enactment); Jack and the Beanstalk; The Interrupted Bathers; The Interrupted Picnic; The Bull and the Picnickers; How They Do Things on the Bowery; Rock of Ages.

After 1902, detailed production information exists for the Edison Company, linking Porter's name to the following titles:

1903: Electrocuting an Elephant; Goo Goo Eyes; Life of an American Fireman; Panorama of Blackwell Island; Panorama of Riker's Island, New York; Steam Scow "Cinderella" and Ferryboat "Cincinnati"; New York Harbor Police Boat Patrol Capturing Pirates (with cameraman Jacob Smith); New York City Police Parade (with Smith); The Still Alarm (with Smith); Panorama Water Front and Brooklyn Bridge from the East River; Sorting Refuse at Incinerating Plant, New York City; Lehigh Valley Black Diamond Express; 69th Regiment N.G.N.Y.; Africander Winning the Suburban Handicap; Uncle Tom's Cabin; The Unappreciated Joke; Street Car Chivalry; Little Lillian, Toe Danseuse; Subub Surprises the Burglar; The Gay Shoe Clerk; Rube and Mandy at Coney Island; Down Where the Wurzburger Flows; Seashore Frolics; Old Fashioned Scottish Reel; New York Caledonian Club's Parade; Throwing the Sixteen Pound Hammer; Miss Jessie Dogherty, Champion Female Highland Fling Dancer; Miss Jessie Cameron, Champion Child Sword Dancer; East Side Urchins Bathing in a Fountain; New York City Public Bath; A Romance of the Rail; Casey and His Neighbor's Goat; The Extra Turn; The Animated Poster; Two Chappies in a Box; Heavenly Twins at Lunch; Heavenly Twins at Odds; The Messenger Boy's Mistake; East River Novelty; The Animated Poster; Buster's Joke on Papa (later part of the Buster Brown Series); What Happened in the Tunnel; The Great Train Robbery; The Office Boy's Revenge; How Old is Ann?; Under the Mistletoe.

1904: Circular Panorama of the Horse Shoe Falls in Winter; Crossing Ice Bridge at Niagara Falls; Sliding Down Ice Mound at Niagara Falls; Ice Skating in Central Park, N.Y.; Treloar and Miss Marshall, Prize Winners at the Physical Culture Show in Madison Square Garden; Casey's Frightful Dream; Cohen's Advertising Scheme; Midnight Intruder; Wifey's Mistake; Old Maid and Fortune Teller; Little German Band; Animated Painting; Halloween Night at the Seminary; Ice Boating on the North Shrewsbury, Red Bank, N.J.; Sleighing in Central Park, New York; The Buster Brown Series (Buster Brown and His Dog Tige); Skirmish Between Russian and Japanese Advance Guards; Battle of Chemulpo Bay; Babe and Puppies; Dog Factory; The Cop Fools the Sergeant; Japanese Acrobats; Hold-up in a Country Store; Annual Parade, New York Fire Department; Elephants Shooting the Chutes at Luna Park; Inter-Collegiate Athletic Association Championships, 1904 (with Alfred C. Abadie); Weary Willie Kidnaps the Child; Inter-Collegiate Regatta, Poughkeepsie, N.Y.; White Star S.S. "Baltic" Leaving Pier on First Eastern Voyage; Canoeing on the Charles River, Boston, Mass.; Scenes in an Infant Orphan Asylum; Fire and Flames at Luna Park; How a French Nobleman Got a Wife Through the New York "Herald" Personal Columns; From Rector's Bank to Claremont; European Rest Cure; Railway Smash-up;

Capture of the Yegg Bank Burglars; Nervy Nat Kisses the Bride; Maniac Chase; Parsifal; City Hall to Harlem in 15 Seconds Via the Subway Route; A Rube Couple at the Country Fair; Miss Lillian Shaffer and Her Dancing Horse; Opening Ceremonies, New York Subway, Oct. 27, 1904; The Ex-Convict; Scarecrow Pump; Bad Boys' Joke on the Nurse; The Strenuous Life or Anti-race Suicide.

1905: The Kleptomaniac; The Seven Ages; President Roosevelt's Inauguration (with Robert K. Bonine); How Jones Lost His Roll; The Burglar's Slide for Life; Opening of Belmont Park Race Course; A Five Cent Trolley Ride; Start of Ocean Race for Kaiser's Cup; The Whole Dam Family and the Dam Dog; Empire State Express, the Second, Taking Water on the Fly; Hippodrome Races, Dreamland, Coney Island; Coney Island at Night. *In mid-1905 Porter began collaborating with Wallace McCutcheon, a partnership that continued until McCutcheon left in early 1907. They worked on many of the following films together:* Raffles, the Dog; June's Birthday Party; Stolen by Gypsies; Mystic Shriner's Day; [Industrial for George Keyes of Portsmouth, New Hampshire]; Scenes and Incidents, Russo-Japanese Peace Conference, Portsmouth, New Hampshire; The Electric Mule; The Little Train Robbery; Boarding School Girls; The White Caps; Poor Algy; The Watermelon Patch; The Miller's Daughter; Down on the Farm; Everybody Works But Father; Phoebe Snow; The Train Wreckers; Life of an American Policeman; The Night Before Christmas.

1906: Dream of a Rarebit Fiend; A Winter Straw Ride; Three American Beauties; The Terrible Kids; Life of a Cowboy; How the Office Boy Saw the Ball Game; Waiting at the Church; Kathleen Mavourneen; Getting Evidence; The Honeymoon at Niagara Falls; Minstrel Mishaps (with and for Lew Dockstader).

1907: Daniel Boone; Vesta Victoria Singing "Poor John"; Vesta Victoria Singing "Waiting at the Church"; The "Teddy" Bears; Colonial Virginia—Historical Scenes and Incidents Connected with the Founding of Jamestown, Va.; Lost in the Alps; Cohen's Fire Sale. *Porter made the following 1907 films with J. Searle Dawley:* The Nine Lives of a Cat; Stage Struck; The Rivals; A Race for Millions; Jack the Kisser; Three American Beauties No. 2; Midnight Ride of Paul Revere; The Trainer's Daughter; College Chums; Laughing Gas; A Little Girl Who Did Not Believe in Santa Claus.

1908: A Suburbanite's Ingenious Alarm; Rescued From an Eagle's Nest; Fireside Reminiscences; A Yankee Man-o-Warman's Fight for Love, an Incident during the Pacific Cruise of the American Fleet; A Sculptor's Welsh Rabbit Dream; Nellie, the Pretty Typewriter, A Romance Among the Skyscrapers; Animated Snowballs; Stage Memories of an Old Theatrical Trunk; A Country Girl's Seminary Life and Experiences; The Cowboy and the Schoolmarm; Tale the Autumn Leaves Told; Nero and the Burning of Rome; The Merry Widow Craze; Bridal Couple Dodging Cameras; The Gentleman Burglar; Curious Mr. Curio; The Painter's Revenge; Skinny's Finish; The Blue and the Gray or The Days of '61; Honesty is the Best Policy; Love Will Find a Way; Pioneers Crossing the Plains in '49; The Little Coxswain of the Varsity Eight. *In early July the Edison Company formed a second production unit. Porter supervised the second unit run by Dawley and headed the first unit for which he continued to act as cameraman. The following films were made by Porter's unit:* Fly Paper; The Face on the Barroom Floor; When Ruben Comes to Town; Tales the Searchlight Told; A Comedy in Black and White; Heard Over the Phone; The Devil; Wife's Strategy; Buying a Title; Pocahontas—A Child of the Forest (with Will Rising); Sandy McPherson's Quiet Fishing Trip; Ten Pickaninnies; A Voice From the Dead; Ex-Convict #900; The Army of Two—An Incident During the American Revolution; Saved by Love; The New Stenographer; The King's Pardon; Old Maid's Temperance Club; Miss Sherlock Holmes; The Angel Child; Cocoa Industry, Trinidad, British West Indies (studio work, with James White); An Unexpected Santa Claus.

1909: A Persistent Suitor; A Burglar Cupid; A Modest Young Man. *After being removed as studio head, Porter made the following films outside the studio system:* A Road to Love or Romance of a Yankee Engineer in Central America; The Doctored Dinner Pail; Bear Hunt in Rockies.

Porter may have produced and directed some of the following Defender films:

1910: Russia, the Land of Oppression; Married in Haste; Too Many Girls; Saved from Himself; The Girl Who Dared (The Girl Strike Leader); A Bridegroom's Mishaps; Retribution; Repaid with Interest; Indian Squaw's Sacrifice; Shanghaied; Hazing a New Scholar; Great Marshall Jewel Case; That Letter From Teddy; Wanted: an Athletic Instructor; Cowboy's Courtships; A Game for Life; An Attempted Elopement; The Cattle Thief's Revenge; A Schoolmarm's Ride for Life; Wild Bill's Defeat; The Tale the Camera Told; The Heart of a Cowboy; A Clause in the Will; Cohen's Generosity; The Last Straw; The Education of Mary Jane; Forgiven.

Porter produced and usually directed and photographed the following films at the Rex Motion Picture Manufacturing Company:
1911: A Heroine of '76; The Story of a Prayer Rug; By the Light of the Moon; The Fall of a Knight; Where the Shamrock Grows; Five Hours; As Ye Sow; The Heiress; The Little Major; A Daughter of the Revolution; The Realization; The Ultimate Sacrifice; The Guardsman; An Exception to the Rule; Called Back; The Monogram "J.O."; From Death to Life; The Twins; On the Brink; Securing Evidence; Fate; The Vagabond; Sherlock Holmes, Jr.; Her Way; The Artist Financier; The White Red Man; The Colonel's Daughter; Castles in the Air; The Torn Scarf; Faith; The Rose and the Dagger; The Derelict; Lost Illusions; Chasing a Rainbow; Her Sister; A Breech of Faith; The Tale of a Cat; Saints and Sinners; The Return; The Price; The Strangers; The Measure of a Man; The Martyr; An Unwelcome Saint.

1912: The Parting of the Ways; A Boarding House Mystery; Angels Unawares; A Sane Asylum; Fine Feathers; The Bargain; Taming Mrs. Shrew; Under Her Wing; The Final Pardon; Eyes That See Not; The Price of Money; Love's Four Stone Walls; Modern Slaves; A Tangled Web; Beauty and the Beast; State's Warning; Drawing the Line; The Eternal Conflict; Grandfather's Clock; The Price of Peace; The Flirt; The Power of Thought; The Weight of a Feather; A Prophet Without Honor; The Greater Love; The Hidden Light; The Hand of Mystery; The Lash of Fate; The Troubadour's Triumph (dir: Louis Weber); The Greater Christian; An Old Fashioned Girl; A Japanese Idyll; From the Wild; The Squatter's Rights; Faraway Fields; The Old Organist; Bob's Deception; If Dreams Come True; The Wedding March; Leaves in a Storm; A Kentucky Feud; Through a Higher Power.

With the Famous Players Co. Porter produced, directed and photographed the following films:

1912: The Count of Monte Christo (but released in 1913 after In the Bishop's Carriage).

1913: The Prisoner of Zenda; A Good Little Devil (but released in 1914 after Hearts Adrift); In the Bishop's Carriage (directed with J. Searle Dawley); Tess of the D'Urbervilles (with Dawley?).

1914: Hearts Adrift; Tess of the Storm Country. *Porter shared directing with Hugh Ford on the following films:* Such a Little Queen; Monsieur Beaucaire.

1915: The Eternal City; The Prince and the Pauper; Sold; Zaza; Bella Donna; Lydia Gilmore (released in 1916).

ABOUT: Brownlow, K. Hollywood; The Pioneers, 1979; Cook, D. A History of Narrative Film, 1982; Deslandes, J. and Richard, J. Histoire Comparée du Cinéma, Vol. II, 1968; Fulton, A. R. Motion Pictures: The Development of an Art, 1980; Jacobs, L. The Rise of the American Film, 1939; Leyda, J. Voice of Film Experience, 1977; Mast, G. A Short History of the Movies, 1976; Miller, A. and Balshofer, F. J. One Reel a Week, 1967; National Cyclopedia of American Biography, Vol. XXX; National Film Archive and International Federation of Film Archives (eds.) Cinema 1900–1906: An Analytic Study, 1982; Pratt, G. Spellbound in Darkness, 1973; Ramsaye, T. A Million and One Nights, 1926; Sadoul, G. Histoire Générale du Cinéma, Vol. II, 1948; Sklar, R. Movie-Made America, 1975; Vardac, A. Stage to Screen, 1949. *Periodicals*—Afterimage Spring 1981; Cinema Journal Fall 1979; Film and History December 1981; Films in Review June–July 1970; Framework August 1983; Iris ler semestre 1984; Moving Picture World July 30, 1910; February 24, 1912; July 11, 1914; New York Dramatic Mirror March 15, 1911; Screen Winter 1978–1979. *Films about*—Musser, C. Before the Nickelodeon: The Early Cinema of Edwin S. Porter, 1982.

POWELL, MICHAEL (September 30, 1905–   ), British director, producer, and scenarist, was born in Bekesbourne, near Canterbury, Kent, the younger son of Thomas Powell, a hop grower, and the former Mabel Corbett. He grew up on the family farm and was educated at King's School, Canterbury, until 1918, when he took his brother's place at Dulwich College, the older boy having died. Meanwhile, Powell's father, who had been posted to France at the beginning of World War I, had decided to stay there and buy a hotel, a decision that effectively ended his marriage. Michael Powell remained with his mother in England. Reading the first issue of *Picturegoer* in 1921, when he was sixteen, he decided that he wanted to make films, but the following year began his career in a branch of the National Provincial Bank.

He immersed himself in films, nevertheless. In 1925, on his way to visit his father, who had acquired a hotel on the Riviera, he stopped off in Paris to catch up with the work of Buñuel and Dali and "that lot, involved in surrealism," as he put it to an interviewer, adding that "of course, all films are surrealist . . . because they are making something that looks like a real world but isn't." He entered the film industry the same year when his father introduced him at a party to Harry Lachman, an artist and filmmaker then working with Rex Ingram on *Mare Nostrum* at the Nice studios.

Powell joined the unit and "worked all through" *Mare Nostrum*, an extravagant spy story. He says "it was a great film to come in on because, being a spectacular film, full of enormous tricks with a great theme and an international cast, it gave you ideas which stayed with you all through your life. . . . My first job was really to stick around—that was how Harry Lachman put it. Then I was a grip, but I was unofficially attached to Lachman as the strange, cultured young Englishman who had a remarkable gift for falling over things."

Some of these qualities were put to work in Ingram's next two films, *The Magician* (1926) and *The Garden of Allah* (1927), in both of which Powell had small roles providing "comic relief." These were great days in the film industry in France: "everyone was mad about the cinema," and in Nice Powell met celebrated painters, sculptors, and writers all eager to contribute to the medium. Then Ingram decided to take a break from films. Lachman launched a series of comedy travelogues featuring Powell, but this project was ended after a few months by the arrival of the talkies and, Powell says, "we closed up the studio, said goodbye to the sun and headed for the fogbelt." Lachman joined British International at the Elstree studios, where he

MICHAEL POWELL

found work for Powell also, first as stills photographer on Hitchcock's *Champagne* and then as a cutter on Lupu Pick's *A Knight in London*. Powell's last assignment at Elstree was as an uncredited contributor to the script of Hitchcock's *Blackmail*—he says it was he that suggested the final chase over the roof of the British Museum: "Being an East End boy, Hitch had never been there."

In 1930 Powell joined a young American producer named Jerome Jackson, then entering the British "quota quickie" market. Alarmed by the fact that only about five per cent of movies shown in Britain were made there, the government had instituted a quota system that was supposed to improve the situation. The result was a flood of generally rubbishy cut-rate pictures, most of them less than an hour in length, that were shown as second features with Hollywood movies. Some were churned out by small independent producers like Jerome Jackson and many, in fact, were made by Hollywood companies through British subsidiaries.

Powell's first assignment for Jackson was as scenarist of *Caste* (1930), a comedy adapted from the play by T. W. Robertson and directed by Campbell Gullan. He was co-scenarist of Albert de Courville's *77 Park Lane* (1931), and then directed his own first film, *Two Crowded Hours* (1931), a comedy-thriller scripted by J. Jefferson Farjeon and running forty-three minutes. It was distributed by Fox, who paid £1 per foot, and was unexpectedly well received by the critics and the paying public.

The same formula was repeated in Powell's second four-reeler, *My Friend the King* (1931) which, like its predecessor, starred Jerry Verno as a comic cab driver but which flopped. However, *Rynox* (1931), adapted from a Philip MacDonald thriller, confirmed Powell's promise. Over the next five years he turned out twenty more quota films for Jerome Jackson and others, developing an exceptional talent for unfolding a story in strikingly visual terms, and an equally valuable capacity for working within his tiny budgets.

Something of Powell's individual creative personality began to impose itself on the films he made towards the end of this apprenticeship. The otherwise conventional *Red Ensign* (1934), about a Clydeside shipyard, includes a burst of Eisensteinian montage—"rolling trucks, frantic pistons, a burning fiery furnace"—and Powell's predilection for fantasy emerges strongly in *The Phantom Light* (1935). This deals with an insurance investigator (Ian Hunter) who is sent to a Welsh village to find out why so many ships are going aground there. "The plot, contrived and trivial as with most quota films, is redeemed by Roy Kellino's photography, the quality of the sound with the cawing of the gulls and the roll of the sea, and the strength of Powell's images," wrote Kevin Gough-Yates. "The train emerges from a tunnel and the steam, which is hanging like mist, gradually gives way to a dream-like Wonderland in which Ian Hunter looks lost and suspicious."

One of the last of Powell's "quickies" was *The Man Behind the Mask* (1936), made for an American producer named Joe Rock. Powell says that the script was very poor but "I did my best to make it into a rather German type expressionistic thriller. . . . The only good that came out of it was that I met Joe Rock." For five years—ever since he had read a newspaper report on the depopulation of the Scottish islands—Powell had been trying to find backing for a film on that subject. Joe Rock encouraged him to write a script, and then sent him off to the remote Shetland island of Foula to make what became *The Edge of the World*, his first personal film.

Powell worked on Foula from June to October of 1936, with three cameramen and a cast composed partly of professionals like John Laurie, Belle Chrystall, and Finlay Currie, partly of Foula islanders. He himself appears in a prologue as a visitor to whom the story is told. The filming was fraught with problems—abrupt changes in the weather, local prejudice, technical and transport difficulties, personality clashes, and the strain that all these anxieties placed on Powell's relationship with his future wife, Frances Reidy, who had accompanied him. He

wound up with 200,000 feet of exposed film and no idea how to cut it into the shape he wanted. Powell begged Joe Rock for the services of a talented young editor named Derek Twist, and says the picture "was entirely saved for me by the editor."

The Edge of the World tells the story of two men whose friendly rivalry ends in the death of one and the frustration of the other's love for the dead man's sister. This is set against a broader conflict, the crofters as a community being torn between their traditional relationship to the laird and the new attractions of the mainland and the trawler fleet, in a way that has reminded some critics of Visconti's *La terra trema*. As John Russell Taylor says, the film "was accepted at the time as a semi-documentary on the Flaherty model, but in retrospect the mystical aspects of the story, with its visions and premonitions, the romantic advocacy of traditional ways of life over material progress . . . , mark it as a recognizable Powell film." Marred as it is for today's audiences by stagey performances and an unconvincing happy ending, it remains impressive in its use of wild scenery and authentic island faces, and in its bold use of visual symbolism. In 1937 it was chosen by the New York Film Critics as the best foreign movie of the year, and in 1938 Powell published an account of the making of the picture, *200,000 Feet on Foula*.

At that point Powell was considering going to Hollywood, but Alexander Korda, impressed by *The Edge of the World*, offered him a contract. His first film for Korda was *The Spy in Black* (1939), a fast-moving and often amusing spy thriller set during World War I. Conrad Veidt plays the heroic German agent, assigned to introduce a U-Boat into the British naval base at Scapa Flow, and Valerie Hobson is his beautiful adversary. It opened just before the beginning of World War II and, Powell says, "during the run of the picture a submarine did get into Scapa Flow and torpedoed one of our best battle ships. It just made people go more, because at least it was about what was happening. It was such a success that it was immediately retitled *U-Boat 29* and sent to America, where it cleaned up."

More important, *The Spy in Black* began Powell's collaboration with the Hungarian-born scenarist, Emeric Pressburger. After *The Lion Has Wings* (1939), a propaganda film that Powell co-directed with Brian Desmond Hurst and Adrian Brunel, he worked with Pressburger again on *Contraband* (called *Blackout* in America). Designed to capitalize on the success of their first picture, it is another Hitchcockian comedy-thriller starring Veidt and Valerie Hobson, and set in a blacked-out wartime London rich in atmosphere. This was the first of Powell's films in which he had Alfred Junge as his art director. The same year saw the release of Korda's splendid version of *The Thief of Bagdad,* which had engaged the talents of half-a-dozen different directors, and for which Powell had shot some of the most spectacular sequences.

Powell himself produced *49th Parallel* (1941), financed by the Ministry of Information. A story about the crew of a wrecked German submarine on the run in Canada, it was intended to counter isolationism in North America. The film was shot mostly on location in Canada with a starry cast that included Laurence Olivier, Leslie Howard, Anton Walbrook, and Glynis Johns as representatives of various aspects of Canadian life, and Eric Portman as the ruthless Nazi commander. Vaughan Williams provided the score, Pressburger's script won him an Oscar, and the movie was a great financial success (though it nowadays seems rather embarrassingly crude at times in its defense of the Western cultural heritage against the Nazi threat—"That's for Thomas Mann, and that's for me," cries Leslie Howard, as he pummels one of the Germans who have destroyed his paintings and books).

The plot of *49th Parallel* is virtually reversed in *One of Our Aircraft Is Missing* (1942), co-scripted and co-produced by Powell and Pressburger, in which the crew of a British bomber are forced to bail out over Holland and are smuggled to safety under the noses of the Germans by the Dutch Resistance. Made in the documentary style typical of the period, it opens with an extraordinary shot of an empty bomber sailing eerily across the Channel.

The same year, 1942, Powell and Pressburger established their own production company, The Archers, under the financial umbrella provided by J. Arthur Rank's Independent Producers. Most of the films they made for The Archers credited Powell and Pressburger as joint directors, producers, and scenarists, though it seems fairly clear that Pressburger dominated the writing, Powell the directing. The latter told an interviewer that "what we always did was that he would write the script and then I would rewrite it completely in *my* version, sometimes with very little change and sometimes with a very great deal of change. The changes would be because I was naturally interested in how to present it, how to create the actual atmosphere of the place, and how to get over Emeric's story line in the most effective way."

After *The Silver Fleet* (1943), a story of the Dutch Resistance that they produced but neither wrote nor directed, came their first collaboration, *The Life and Death of Colonel Blimp*

(1943). The hero's real name is Clive Candy (Roger Livesey)—the title refers to a character, created by the cartoonist David Low, depicted as an ultra-conservative old officer senior enough to impose his antiquated ideas on the modern army. When we first encounter Clive Candy, early in World War II, he is indeed a Blimp, outraged by the ungentlemanly ruthlessness of a younger officer. But this, as the film proceeds to demonstrate, is in the nature of institutions like the British army—forty years earlier Candy had himself been a reckless young officer, frustrated by the monolithic inertia of his superiors.

Deborah Kerr plays Candy's "ideal woman" (three red-headed generations of her) and Anton Walbrook is a "good German"—the enemy who becomes Candy's lifelong friend. Apart from *The Thief of Bagdad,* this was Powell's first film in color. It was gorgeously designed by Alfred Junge and beautifully filmed by an illustrious team of photographers—Jack Cardiff and Geoffrey Unsworth, under the direction of Georges Périnal.

Colonel Blimp is an ambivalent film—apparently intended as a warning against the dangers of leaving too much power in the hands of bumbling old diehards like Clive Candy, it is in fact full of nostalgia for a more heroic and gallant notion of warfare than seemed viable in 1943. The Ministry of Information thought it defeatist, and encouraged by Winston Churchill himself, did everything it could to prevent its production. Army help was denied and Laurence Olivier, who was to have played the lead, was refused release from military service. In fact Roger Livesey gave the performance of his life, making Candy an irresistibly likable old warhorse, while the government's attempts to suppress the movie only increased its immense box-office appeal.

The Volunteer (1943), a medium-length recruiting film in which Ralph Richardson plays himself (and Othello), was followed by *A Canterbury Tale* (1944). This cuts from Chaucerian pilgrims on their way to Powell's birthplace to three modern pilgrims and their intertwined destinies in World War II, showing again and again the more or less mystic connections between past and present. This complex structure is woven around a plot about the hunt for a mystery man with a penchant for pouring glue on girls' heads, and Powell acknowledges that the film was overly complicated.

The Archers had more success with *I Know Where I'm Going* (1945), in which Wendy Hiller goes to the Western Isles of Scotland to marry a millionaire but falls under the spell of Celtic mysticism and winds up in the arms of the haunted young laird (Roger Livesey). Pamela Brown gives an extraordinary performance as an aristocratic sorceress. It was clear to Raymond Durgnat that "Powell's film reveals a serious belief in the wayward natural forces. Their fierce power is asserted in constant hints and jabs (a close-up of the eagle's beak ripping off a rabbit's ear) which sees nature as a Nietzschean whirl of blood and death. . . . But the hero, sailing . . . [the heroine's] boat through the treacherous whirlpool, overcomes these forces with that protective manliness which . . . is itself a force of nature" This is one of the most personal and original of Powell's films, and one of the best loved—Nora Sayre has recalled that she was almost deprived of her allowance when she was twelve because she went to see it week after week.

Asked by the Ministry of Information for a film that might help to reverse the postwar decline in Anglo-American relations, Powell and Pressburger came up with *A Matter of Life and Death* (*Stairway to Heaven* in the United States). David Niven plays a British pilot (and poet) who jumps from his blazing plane without a parachute and apparently survives to fall in love with June, an American airforce radio operator (Kim Hunter). But his survival has been a cosmic oversight, and an official is sent from a monochrome heaven to claim him for death. The rest of the film deals with the struggle to save him—both on earth, where surgeons fight for his life, and in heaven, where an all-American jury is selected from the illustrious armies of the dead to insure a fair trial. In a reversal of the Orpheus myth, it is June who saves him, proving that nothing in the universe is stronger than love.

The script is full of the kind of erudite and witty paradoxes that Powell regards as characteristic of the Hungarian Pressburger—"They always see the world inside out. All their jokes are reverse jokes." For the director, this was "the most perfect film . . . a wonderful conjuring trick to get handed. It is all the more fascinating to me because all this fantasy actually takes place . . . inside somebody's damaged head, so there was a good sound medical reason for every image that appears on the screen."

Roy Armes writes that "with its huge escalator to heaven and its skilful use of model shots," this is "very much a studio movie"—"an amazing amalgam of colour and black and white images, audacity and conventionality. . . . Powell is never afraid of mixing fact and fantasy and handles the spectacle and rhetoric with equal assurance, dwelling on such moments as the huge pink eyelid closing over the camera lens or the catching of a woman's tear in a red rose."

Some reviewers, it must be said, found the characters unconvincing and the story therefore emotionally uninvolving, and others responded uneasily to the film's departures from the tradition of realism in British cinema. There was also a strange outburst from E. W. and M. M. Robson in their *The World Is My Cinema* (1947). They called the picture decadent, sadistic, and fascist, equating its distinctly unattractive heaven with the Nazi state. Later critics tend to see it rather as a caricature of a bureaucratic socialist utopia—evidence of what Durgnat calls the director's "High Tory" morality.

Black Narcissus (1947), in which Anglican nuns set up a new mission in the Himalayas, was also shot in the studio, Powell having decided that pictures made partly on location "are nearly always pastiche or hotch-potch." Like *I Know Where I'm Going,* the film centers on the conflict between a "civilized" (here specifically Christian) notion of order and pagan nature, personified in the flailing Himalayan winds, local superstition, and a naked holy man. Nature wins when one of the nuns (Kathleen Byron) is driven to homicidal madness by her repressed lust for the hairy knees of David Farrar.

Powell worked out the climactic final scene with his composer, Brian Easdale (who was also in charge of the film's sound effects), and prerecorded the scene's soundtrack before filming the images. He took this decisive step towards the development of a musical structure for his movies because he believes that "composers and film makers think very much alike. Their tempos are very closely related to our cutting tempos, their longueurs and their statements are very similar to ours. Whereas, even with a writer as clever and subtle as Emeric, I always had this continual battle with words." Jack Cardiff's color photography for the film won him an Oscar.

Moira Shearer, one of the most striking of Powell's red-haired heroines, is a ballet dancer fatally torn between love and art in *The Red Shoes* (1948), originally written by Pressburger for Alexander Korda but bought back by The Archers. Anton Walbrook is magnificent as the diabolical impresario Lermontov, the choreographer is played by Leonid Massine, and the heroine's co-dancers are Ludmilla Tcherina and Robert Helpmann (the film's actual choreographer). Music was again in the hands of Brian Easdale, and Hein Heckroth's spectacular sets were lyrically photographed in Technicolor by Jack Cardiff. The film went nearly £200,000 over budget and Powell says that "when the Rank Organisation saw it they thought they were sunk. . . . It's probably grossed $20 to $30 million."

The Red Shoes seems to Roy Armes "Powell and Pressburger's most explicit statement of the relationship of art and life," and "the high point of their career in both commercial and artistic terms. . . . All [their] central themes and stylistic concerns find expression in *The Red Shoes:* the Romantic opposition of art and life, the concern with a choreography of film whereby overwhelming passions are acted out rather than expressed through words, and the creation of a dynamic inter-relationship of vivid visual imagery and an immensely rhythmic soundtrack. In a memorable climax the ballerina dies but the ballet goes ahead without her, the audience being made to imagine her presence by the conviction of music and production."

A much more modest but no less accomplished film followed, the first of four made by The Archers for Korda's London Film Productions. Filmed in black and white from a taut novel by Nigel Balchin, *The Small Back Room* (*Hour of Glory,* 1949) has David Farrar as an embittered bomb disposal expert in World War II, handicapped by bad conscience, alcoholism, and a tin leg, while struggling with an appallingly complex booby-trap bomb. Raymond Durgnat called it an expressionist film, and wrote: "Faces moving through alternately opposite spotlights in dark rooms; shadow webs from camouflage netting, window stickytape or elevator grilles . . . uneasy depths half-obscured by darkness; the then all-but-unique absence of background music . . . achieves an oppressiveness as massive as Lang's."

A critical success, *The Small Back Room* inexplicably failed financially. And Powell's next two films for Korda flopped more comprehensibly and comprehensively. Korda had set up a deal with David Selznick to make *Gone to Earth* (1950), adapted by Powell and Pressburger from Mary Webb's novel of passion in Shropshire, and starring Selznick's wife Jennifer Jones. Powell thought that "we never licked the script—it's doubtful if Mary Webb can be licked," and Selznick (who produced) hired Rouben Mamoulian for extensive re-shooting for the shorter American version, called *The Wild Heart.* And the Korda-Archers version of the Scarlet Pimpernel story, *The Elusive Pimpernel,* was "another disaster" for Powell, though some sequences have been extravagantly admired by recent critics.

The Tales of Hoffmann (1951), from Denis Arundell's adaptation of Offenbach's operetta, was The Archers' last film for Korda and a much happier production, using much the same team as *The Red Shoes.* Its romantic excesses embarrassed some reviewers but it took the Special

Jury Prize at Cannes and delighted Raymond Durgnat, who wrote: "this gallimaufry of Gothicisms, this pantechnicon of palettical paroxysms . . . this massive accumulation of immemorial Mighty Wurlitzerisms, follows Offenbach's operetta relatively faithfully and fills in filmically by ballet, decor and by-play, seeking, moreover, an operatic visual style with a splendid disdain of plausibility. . . . If often overblown, the film is intermittently breathtaking, an effect which survives repeated viewings."

In 1944 Powell had directed a stage production of Hemingway's *The Fifth Column,* and in 1951 he returned to the theatre with Raymond Massey's play *Hanging Judge.* At about the same time he also tried without success to set up two ambitious screen projects—a short film of a scene from *The Odyssey* that was to have had words by Dylan Thomas and music by Stravinsky, and a version of Shakespeare's *The Tempest,* with Moira Shearer and John Gielgud. In fact his next picture was a short ballet film, *The Sorcerer's Apprentice* (1955), distributed by Twentieth Century–Fox. The Archers went back into production with *Oh Rosalinda!!* (1955), based on Strauss's opera *Die Fledermaus.* This "had some lovely things in it," Powell thought, but "is one of our failures."

The Archers' last two productions, both unexceptional war films, were *The Battle of the River Plate* (*Pursuit of the Graf Spee,* 1956) and *Ill Met by Moonlight* (*Night Ambush,* 1957). Working separately, neither Powell nor Pressburger ever really established a consistent pattern of production again. Powell's next picture, another ballet film called *Luna de Miel* (*Honeymoon*), was made in 1961 in Spain. Then he met a writer and former cypher expert named Leo Marks, who proposed a picture in the sadistic horror-movie genre then being exploited by Anglo-Amalgamated. The result was *Peeping Tom* (1960).

The film centers on Mark Lewis (Carl Boehm), who works in a film studio by day as a focus-puller, and in the evening sometimes makes pornographic films of an appallingly specialized nature. It is his pleasure to stab beautiful girls through the throat with a blade concealed in his tripod and to film their dying agonies in close-up, a mirror on the tripod allowing them to share this experience. This voyeur psychosis is traced back to Mark's childhood, during which his father, an authority on the psychology of fear, had used him as a guinea pig, filming his reactions to terrifying situations, natural or contrived.

And all these horrors were, of course, set up

and filmed by Michael Powell and *his* camera-man (Otto Heller), so that the movie becomes an extremely complex essay on the voyeurism involved in making and watching films, as Powell clearly recognized. He himself plays Mark's father in *Peeping Tom,* and he has said that he "felt very close to the hero, who is an 'absolute' director, someone who approaches life like a director, who is conscious of and suffers from it. He is a technician of emotion. And I am someone who is thrilled by technique, always mentally editing the scene in front of me in the street, so I was able to share his anguish."

Except in the trade press, where the film was praised for its commercial potential, the critical response was almost totally negative—a passionate chorus of disgust and loathing that is examined at some length in Ian Christie's *Powell, Pressburger and Others.* The first dissenting voice of any weight was that of a French critic, Jean-Paul Török, writing in *Positif* (36 1960). Pointing out that the real "Peeping Tom" is the audience, who watches the voyeur watch, Török said that the film was "beautifully done. The fragments of 16mm footage shot by Mark Lewis are edited and inserted into the action with great skill, so that the same sequence can be seen simultaneously from the point of view of the character observing it through his camera, and from the point of view of the director making the film. Certain moments achieve a quite extraordinary sort of black poetry. . . . And of course the only person to see clearly through this whole voyeur business is a blind woman."

As Török put it, Mark completes his "documentary" by turning his blade and his camera on himself. In a final hallucination, he is reconciled with his dead father (who says: "Don't be a silly boy. There's nothing to be afraid of"). A later critic, Raymond Durgnat, has pointed out that "here art reveals, again, its diabolic root, and reconciliation with the diabolic is an underlying *leitmotif* in Powell." Durgnat and others have explored at length the multiple levels of perception in this Chinese box of a film, its endless jokes and puns, verbal and visual. Roy Armes is reminded of Resnais and for many *Peeping Tom* is Powell's masterpiece, though in Britain in 1960 it virtually ended his career, while the shortened version seen in the United States was largely ignored.

Its immediate successor was *The Queen's Guards* (1961), a "High Tory" tribute to the Brigade of Guards starring both Raymond and Daniel Massey, of no special interest. After that, shunned by backers and distributors, Powell was reduced to directing episodes of *Espionage, The Defenders,* and other television series, or to filming abroad. *Bluebeard's Castle* (1964) is a straightforward record of a Zagreb production of Bartók's opera, and this was followed by two "romps" made in Australia, *They're a Weird Mob* (1966) and *Age of Consent* (1969), co-produced with James Mason, who also stars as a painter entangled with a youthful Helen Mirren. Back in Britain, and re-united with Pressburger, Powell made a prizewinning children's film, *The Boy Who Turned Yellow* (1972).

But meanwhile, a reassessment of Powell's work had begun in such British journals as *Motion* and *Movie,* and in such foreign ones as *Image et Son* and *Midi-Minuit Fantastique.* Since 1970, there has been an apparently endless series of Powell retrospectives all over the world. He has been increasingly in demand as a lecturer and teacher, and in 1981 he was "senior director in residence" at Francis Coppola's Zoetrope Studios in Los Angeles, working on a long-planned film about the Russian dancer Anna Pavlova. The same year, Gilbert Adair said that he was "fast turning into one of the most widely discussed of all filmmakers."

Raymond Durgnat has compared Powell to Abel Gance in his "weakness for patriotic sentiment" and for "optical shocks," but rejects the once fashionable view of him as a mere stylist, "camouflaging an absence of ideas by a weakness for the grandiose, out-of-context effect." Durgnat suggests that Powell "remains an upholder, through its lean years, of the Méliès tradition . . . a school of 'Cinema' which is always exquisitely conscious of not only its cinematic effects but its cinematic *nature.*"

Powell regards not Gance but Walt Disney as "the greatest genius of us all," but probably accepts Durgnat's assessment of his own work. He said once that "the majority of film makers of my generation have a style very much their own. . . . Not me, *I live cinema.* I chose the cinema when I was very young, sixteen years old, and from then on my memories virtually coincide with the history of the cinema. . . . I'm not a director with a personal style, *I am simply cinema.*"

In 1981, when he was seventy-six, Michael Powell was described as "a rubicund, avuncular figure," full of energy and enthusiasm, and distinctly Blimpish in appearance, with a trimmed moustache, tweed suit, and brown bowler hat. He has two grown sons, Kevin and Columba, from his marriage to Frankie Reidy; after her death he married the film editor Thelma Schoonmaker, in 1984. *A Life in the Movies,* the first volume of his autobiography, appeared in 1986.

FILMS: Two Crowded Hours, 1931; My Friend the King, 1931; Rynox, 1931; The Rasp, 1931; The Star Reporter, 1932; Hotel Splendide, 1932; C.O.D., 1932; His Lordship, 1932; Born Lucky, 1932; The Fire Raisers, 1933; Red Ensign (Strike!), 1934; The Night of the Party (The Murder Party), 1934; Something Always Happens, 1934; The Girl in the Crowd, 1934; Lazybones, 1935; The Love Test, 1935; The Phantom Light, 1935; The Price of a Song, 1935; Someday, 1935; Crown vs. Stevens, 1936; Her Last Affaire, 1936; The Brown Wallet, 1936; The Man Behind the Mask, 1936; The Edge of the World, 1937; The Spy in Black (U-Boat 29), 1939; (with Brian Desmond-Hurst and Adrian Brunel) The Lion Has Wings, 1939; Contraband (Blackout), 1940; (with others) The Thief of Bagdad, 1940; An Airman's Letter to His Mother, 1941 (short); 49th Parallel (The Invaders), 1941; One of Our Aircraft Is Missing, 1942. *With Emeric Pressburger*— The Life and Death of Colonel Blimp (Colonel Blimp), 1943; The Volunteer, 1943; A Canterbury Tale, 1944; I Know Where I'm Going, 1945; A Matter of Life and Death (Stairway to Heaven), 1946; Black Narcissus, 1947; The Red Shoes, 1948; The Small Back Room (Hour of Glory), 1949; Gone to Earth (The Wild Heart), 1950; The Elusive Pimpernel, 1950; The Tales of Hoffmann, 1951; Oh Rosalinda!!, 1955; The Battle of the River Plate (Pursuit of the Graf Spee), 1956; Ill Met by Moonlight (Night Ambush), 1957. *As sole director*—The Sorcerer's Apprentice, 1955 (short); Peeping Tom, 1960; Luna de miel (Honeymoon), 1961; The Queen's Guards, 1961; Bluebeard's Castle, 1964; They're a Weird Mob, 1966; Age of Consent, 1969; The Boy Who Turned Yellow, 1972.

ABOUT: Armes, R. A Critical History of British Cinema, 1978; Cameron, I. Movie Reader, 1972; Christie, I. (ed.) Powell, Pressburger and Others, 1978; Current Biography, 1987; Durgnat, R. A Mirror for England, 1970; Gibbon, M. The Red Shoes Ballet: A Critical Study, 1948; Gibbon, M. The Tales of Hoffmann, 1951; Gough-Yates, K. Michael Powell, 1973; Powell, M. The Battle of the River Plate: Graf Spee, 1957; Powell, M. A Life in the Movies, 1986; Warman, E. (ed.) A Matter of Life and Death, 1946. *Periodicals*—American Film November 1980; Cahiers du Cinéma March 1981; Écran January and February 1979; Film Comment May–June 1979; Films and Filming November 1955, November and December 1981; Films in Review August–September 1980; Image et Son June–July 1971, May 1981; Midi-Minuit Fantastique October 1968; Monthly Film Bulletin August 1981, September 1981, November 1982, October 1984; Movie Autumn 1965; New York Times November 30, 1980; Positif February, March, April 1981; Sight and Sound Autumn 1978, Winter 1978–1979; Time Out May 19–25, 1978; November 3–9, 1978; World Review April 1947.

PREMINGER, OTTO (LUDWIG) (December 5, 1905 or 1906—April 23, 1986), American director, producer, and actor, said in his autobiography that "one set of documents lists Vienna as my birthplace but another set . . . places my

OTTO PREMINGER

birth at my great-grandfather's farm some distance away. One records that I was born on the fifth of December, 1906, the other exactly one year earlier." It was an appropriate beginning for a man so fond of ambiguity.

His father, Markus Preminger, was a well-known lawyer, chief prosecutor for the Austro-Hungarian Empire and then for the imperial army, unusually high positions for a Jew in that anti-Semitic society. Josepha Fraenkel, Preminger's mother, described by him as "sweet, warm hearted, and easily worried," was the daughter of a lumberyard owner. Otto was her first child, followed by another son, Ingo, five years later. Preminger's childhood was a privileged and happy one. He said that he "had a wonderful relationship" with his father: "We were like two brothers." A loyal monarchist, Markus Preminger left public office with the consolidation of the Austrian republic after World War I, beginning a lucrative private practice in Vienna.

The city's rich cultural life in the 1920s was far more attractive to Preminger than the study of law, to which his family urged him. He dreamed of acting from the age of nine, and made his stage debut at twelve, the only child among adults at a poetry reading. Preminger spent his time writing and learning poetry, memorizing dramatic speeches, and angling for stage parts. His father, though he was dismayed by the boy's outlandish ambitions, simply asked him to get his law degree first.

Preminger did no such thing. While he was still at school he auditioned for the great Max Reinhardt and was taken on as an apprentice at the Josefstadt, the beautiful old theatre Reinhardt bought and lavishly refurbished in Vienna. As Preminger told Gerald Pratley (*The Cinema of Otto Preminger,* 1971), Reinhardt opened the Josefstadt in 1924 with Goldoni's *Servant of Two Masters.* There was no curtain "and the scene changes were effected by . . . young actors who carried out furniture. . . . I was one of . . . [them]. That was my first acting job. I also played in the park the part of Lysander in *A Midsummer Night's Dream.* . . . That was not Reinhardt—it was done by somebody else. . . . I stayed in the theatre, playing a few more small parts, and then became bored and took on a job to go to Prague where there was a German theatre."

After Prague, Preminger moved on to Zurich, but his career as a juvenile lead was increasingly handicapped by premature baldness, a condition he eventually adopted as his trademark. In 1925 he joined the German theatre in Aussig (now in Czechoslovakia) and asked to be allowed to direct. To his surprise, he was making his directorial debut with a production of Klabund's *Kreiderkreis* (*The Chalk Circle*).

Finding that he preferred directing to acting, Preminger returned to Vienna where he launched a theatre of his own, the Kömedia, and then, after two years, another—the Schauspielhaus—"in a huge building, a popular theatre, with very low prices." Simultaneously he pursued his legal studies at the University of Vienna and, after flunking once, earned his law degree.

Having made something of a reputation, Preminger was invited back as an assistant director to the theatre where he had begun his acting career, Max Reinhardt's Josefstadt. He had his first great success in 1931 as director of a play called *Voruntersuchung* (*Preliminary Inquiry*), following this the same year with an adaptation of Hecht and McArthur's *The Front Page*. It featured a young actress called Marion Mill who had come to Preminger in great distress, seeking his legal advice in a breach-of-contract suit brought against her by a nightclub owner. In his only recorded action as a lawyer, Preminger helped her to settle the case. He also gave Marion Mill a part in *The Front Page* and, the following year, married her.

Preminger had meanwhile directed his first film, *Die Grosse Liebe* (*The Great Love,* 1931), based on a true story about a returning veteran of World War I and a woman who believes him to be her son. Preminger told an interviewer that this tragicomedy was "a film I would rather forget," but a print apparently survived at least into the 1970s, when the Cinémathèque

Française revived it in their Preminger retrospective. *Die Grosse Liebe* was released in Austria in December 1931 and "was quite successful."

For all its great prestige, the Josefstadt at this point was losing money. Reinhardt went into semi-retirement after the 1932–1933 season, and Preminger, still in his mid-twenties, took over as director, making the theatre once more a paying proposition with a series of mostly contemporary plays and musical comedies. Preminger told Gerald Pratley that during this period he was invited to become head of the State Theatre in Vienna, "a tremendous honor for a young man." The only condition was that he would have to convert to Catholicism—"just a formality." Although Preminger "never went to any [Jewish] religious prayers or services," he refused, and his contract was torn up.

Then "one day a man from America came to Vienna called Joseph M. Schenck. . . . He had just merged a small company—20th Century—with Fox, and he needed young people." Schenck knew of Preminger's reputation and invited him to Hollywood. "It was a very old dream of mine," Preminger said, "and nothing to do with Hitler, to go to America." He started learning English at once, and sailed for New York on October 16, 1936.

On the *Normandie* he met the American producer Gilbert Miller, an old friend, and arranged to stay in New York long enough to direct *Libel,* an English play he had staged at the Josefstadt. Preminger was "absolutely overwhelmed" by New York and always loved it "more than any city in the world." With his unerring instinct for the better things in life, he went straight from the boat to 21, the fashionable midtown restaurant that was to be his East Coast headquarters for half a century. *Libel* opened in December 1935 at the Henry Miller Theatre and ran for 159 performances.

Preminger arrived in Hollywood in January 1936 and was joined there by his wife, who became a well-known hostess in New York and Hollywood. For eight months Preminger studied the process of making films on the sound stages at 20th Century–Fox, then was assigned *Under Your Spell* (1936), a routine musical comedy starring the opera singer Lawrence Tibbett, whose first film had bombed but who refused to be parted from his contract.

Danger, Love at Work (1937) brought Preminger's first clash with the autocratic Darryl F. Zanuck, who wanted his young protégée Simone Simon to star in this screwball comedy about an eccentric family. Preminger insisted that the French actress would not be able to handle the script's rapid-fire wisecracks and won, winding up with Ann Sothern and a success. Preminger's next falling-out with Zanuck cost him his job and almost his career. He was assigned an expensive production of Robert Louis Stevenson's *Kidnapped.* Knowing nothing about Stevenson or Scotland, where the film was set, Preminger wanted to turn the assignment down but was warned not to. Within a week he had had a shouting match with Zanuck over the script and had been replaced by Alfred Werker.

Preminger was still under contract, but Zanuck gave him no work. Schenck would not see him, and no other studio would hire him. Preminger returned to his beloved New York, worked on his English, and resumed his career as a stage director. At about this time his parents joined him in the United States, having escaped from Vienna by the skin of their teeth as Hitler arrived there. Between 1938 and 1941 Preminger directed seven plays, including Laurette Taylor's triumphant comeback in Sutton Vane's *Outward Bound.*

One of the most successful of these stage productions was Clare Boothe Luce's play *Margin for Error.* Because of the defection of another actor, Preminger himself was obliged at the last moment to take the role of a bullying Nazi consul. He received excellent reviews, and was then invited by the writer-producer Nunnally Johnson to return to 20th Century–Fox as an actor, playing a Nazi officer in *The Pied Piper.* Zanuck was overseas with the army, the coast was clear, and Preminger agreed. Fox also wanted him to repeat his role in their film version of *Margin for Error.* Preminger saw his chance to direct again and carved out a deal with William Goetz, who was heading the studio in Zanuck's absence. He offered to act in *and* direct the film for his actor's fee alone, undertaking to step down as director if Goetz was not pleased with his first week's work; Goetz could hardly refuse.

When Preminger read the screenplay, however, he found it was "awful." At his own expense, he hired a young novelist on leave from the army to help him revise the script—the future director Samuel Fuller. The film is a comedy-thriller in which a Jewish policeman (Milton Berle) in an American city is given the distasteful job of protecting a tyrannical German consul (Preminger) who is eventually murdered. Goetz was delighted with the first rushes, and Preminger wound up with a contract as actor, director, *and* producer. The film was generally well received, described by G. E. Blackford as "a good movie—entertaining, amusing and sufficiently melodramatic in its melodramatic moments."

At this point Zanuck returned from the army, picking up his fight with Preminger where it had left off seven years before and assuring him that he would "never direct again." Assigned as a producer to B movies, Preminger found a story he liked called *Laura,* based on a mystery novel by Vera Caspary. In Gerald Pratley's book, Preminger gives a detailed account of his long struggle to overcome the studio's dislike of the script and opposition to his casting in it of Clifton Webb. By the risky process of appealing directly to Zanuck, whose professionalism overcame his pique, he won both battles. After further conflict between Preminger as producer and Rouben Mamoulian, the assigned director, Zanuck took the latter off the picture and gave it to Preminger to direct. *Laura's* troubles were still not over. Zanuck was unhappy with the rough cut and demanded a new ending; the situation was only saved by the columnist Walter Winchell, who sat in on a screening and pronounced the movie "big-time."

Laura (1944) begins with a dark screen and the voice of the effete, acidly witty columnist Waldo Lydecker (Clifton Webb): "I shall never forget the weekend Laura died." The beautiful socialite Laura Hunt (Gene Tierney) has been murdered, disfigured beyond recognition by a shotgun blast. Mark McPherson (Dana Andrews), the glum detective investigating the case, is entranced by her portrait, her favorite record, her perfume. As he uncovers ever more decadence and corruption in her glittering world, he becomes obsessed with this dead woman who can never be his—until one day she walks in on him as he gazes at her image. It emerges that another woman has been killed in Laura's place while she was away. Blundering into her own murder investigation, she becomes a suspect. As in many a *film noir,* the detective must discover the true nature of the beauty that fascinates him, and which has also enticed a killer—Waldo Lydecker, Laura's Pygmalion, whose unrequited love for his "creation" has finally claimed his sanity.

Laura is no doubt Preminger's best-remembered film. Andrew Sarris, his principal American champion, called it "Preminger's *Citizen Kane,* at least in the sense that Otto's detractors, like Orson's, have never let him live it down." Though uncredited, the director claimed that he had rewritten the script into a tighter and more suspenseful shape. He convincingly evoked a social milieu he himself knew well. Under his direction, such unresponsive players as Tierney and Andrews gave of their best, while Vincent Price (as Laura's fiancé) and Judith Anderson (as her aunt) were restrained from chewing the scenery. The vein of dark sardonic humor that Preminger had discerned in Clifton Webb carried that aging musical comedy performer to an Oscar nomination as best supporting actor and launched him on a new career. Added to all this was the haunting title ballad by David Raksin, who worked on many of Preminger's subsequent films at Fox.

The film was a major financial success, garnering an Oscar for Joseph La Shelle's dreamlike cinematography and a nomination for Preminger's direction. *Laura* introduced many of the themes and motifs that characterized Preminger's work. Waldo Lydecker remained the most memorable of his "grotesques," as Molly Haskell called them—characters who might be alter egos of the director himself "with their droll, shaggy-dog impertinence that is never quite domesticated by the main plot." And Gene Tierney's Laura is the first of Preminger's enigmatic women, "never more mysterious," in Haskell's words, "than when they meet, in the mirror, their own impassive gaze, revealing all and nothing." Above all, there was a certain moral objectivity or neutrality in Preminger's direction—a quality that increasingly exercised the critics, disliked by some, admired by others as the source of what Haskell called "a disconcertingly autonomous reality."

Laura established Preminger's international reputation also. In Britain, Campbell Dixon said it was "one of the best thrillers ever made" and called Preminger's direction "superb in its timing and understatement." A French critic in *Revue du Cinéma* wrote: "The characters in *Laura*—the situation is rare—have a real existence. . . . In the final analysis it matters little that the story is a detective story. Laura could also be put in a family or love story without in any way altering her destiny as an attractive and troubling girl who does nothing either to provoke or retain men and who only very soberly profits from her gifts in order to protect herself. . . . The miracle is to have brought her to life."

Preminger next made *In the Meantime Darling* (actually released a month before *Laura*, in September 1944). This was a forgettable wartime romance with Jeanne Crain as an heiress who learns the common touch when she marries a soldier and goes to live on an army base. Preminger's growing reputation as a tyrant on the set was confirmed by a story about an unfortunate bit player in this film who froze under his direction and could not speak his lines. When haranguing him had no effect, Preminger reportedly grabbed the man by the shoulders and shook him like a doll, shouting into his face: "Relax! Relax! Relax!"

Not everyone thought Preminger a backstage bully—Gene Tierney said "he could charm you and intimidate you at the same time"—but accounts of his infamous temper followed him throughout his career. His admirers tended to regard his temper as the mark of a perfectionist, which he indeed was. Tierney recounts how he rejected a full-length portrait of her commissioned for *Laura* and instead sent her to be photographed by a studio glamour specialist. The photo was then brushed with paint to make it look like a portrait in oils.

Royal Scandal (1945, called *Czarina* in Britain), was adapted from an old Lajos Biro play, already filmed at least twice, about an amorous interlude between Catherine the Great of Russia and a handsome young Guards captain. Catherine was played by Preminger's friend Talullah Bankhead, who had used her influence to obtain immigrant status for his parents when they came to the United States. The film had originally been assigned to Ernst Lubitsch but was passed to Preminger, with Lubitsch as producer, on account of the latter's poor health. The "Lubitsch touch" was notably absent, and the film was both a financial and a critical failure.

Preminger was more at home with his next picture, *Fallen Angel* (1945), the second film in what has been called his "Fox quintet" of notable melodramas. Like the first, *Laura*, it starred Dana Andrews, "the ideal Preminger hero, whose presence encourages moral uncertainty." Jonathan Rosenbaum, writing in Richard Roud's *Cinema: A Critical Dictionary,* points out that Preminger's "narrative lines are strewn with deceptive counterpaths, shifting viewpoints, and ambiguous characters who perpetually slip out of static categories and moral definitions. . . . Preminger frequently mystifies the spectator who is looking for a fixed moral reference."

This is certainly true of *Fallen Angel,* in which Andrews plays Eric Stanton, down on his luck, who drifts into a small town where he falls for a cafe waitress, the provocatively attractive Stella (Linda Darnell). Needing money to impress her, Stanton seduces the wealthy June Mills (Alice Faye), planning to marry her for her money and then divorce her in favor of Stella. June marries him secretly, but then Stella is murdered. Stanton is suspected and flees with June, whom he discovers he loves. With her support he returns to clear his name, proving that the mysterious detective Judd (Charles Bickford), another of Stella's admirers, is the real killer.

Fallen Angel has elicited considerable affection in some quarters. Jean-Luc Godard wrote that he loved "that moment in *Fallen Angel* when the camera, in order not to lose sight of

Linda Darnell as she walks across a restaurant, rushes so fast through the customers that one sees the assistants' hands seizing two or three of them by the scruff of the neck and pulling them aside to make way for it." The film rings interesting changes on the themes of *Laura*—obsession, guilt, and perverted sexuality, in an ever-shifting perspective on the central characters, whose significance and moral tone change as the action progresses. Even Pauline Kael, Preminger's most influential detractor, found the film "tolerable, in a tawdry sort of way."

After this Preminger found it a "welcome change" to do a musical, *Centennial Summer* (1946). A period piece about an American family's adventures in Philadelphia during the centenary exhibition of 1876, this had songs by Jerome Kern and Oscar Hammerstein II and a cast headed by Linda Darnell, Jeanne Crain, Cornell Wilde, and Walter Brennan. Most thought it an inferior but generally agreeable attempt to emulate the phenomenal success of Minnelli's *Meet Me in St. Louis* (1944).

An adaptation followed of Kathleen Winsor's steamy "historical" novel *Forever Amber*. Preminger took over the picture from John M. Stahl at Zanuck's behest and "was unhappy with it." So were the critics, but the public flocked to see it, even though the studio had mollified the Catholic Legion of Decency by cleaning up the more sensational scenes in this story of a farmer's daughter (Linda Darnell) who sleeps her way into the bed of Charles II (George Sanders), all the while pining for the gallant Lord Carlton (Cornell Wilde). Illegitimacy, prostitution, and other vices were all suitably punished, and a crawl after the credits cautioned the ambitious against following Amber's example. With a plush David Raksin score and Leon Shamroy's luxurious color photography, *Forever Amber* has worn well as a typically florid forties extravaganza.

Daisy Kenyon (1947) is one of the surprising number of Preminger films that the director claims not to remember "at all." He explained to Gerald Pratley that "part of my makeup or character, perhaps part of my self-education, is that I don't collect any old reviews, scrapbooks, anything. I always try to finish whatever I have to do and go on to something new. This is perhaps an almost neurotic fear of being caught up in the past. I feel that in order to be able to work I need to forget what I have done." ·

Daisy Kenyon (Joan Crawford) is torn between an ambitious (and married) lawyer (Dana Andrews) and a sensitive, shell-shocked yacht designer (Henry Fonda). Here again are the themes of *Laura* and *Fallen Angel*—sexual ob-

session, redemptive love, the forces of light and darkness embodied in competing lovers. Dismissed at the time, this movie has acquired something of a cult reputation; Jonathan Rosenbaum described it as "a stately soap opera with some of the ambience of a *film noir*." Another writer has gone so far as to call it "arguably the masterpiece of this period," and Godard inserted a characteristic *hommage* in his *Made in USA*, where a loudspeaker can be heard paging Daisy Kenyon. No great claims have been made for *That Lady in Ermine* (1948), a farrago of costumed nonsense begun by Lubitsch just before his death, or *The Fan* (1949), a clumsy remake of Lubitsch's screen version of *Lady Windermere's Fan*.

Things picked up when Preminger returned to the *film noir* and the psychology of obsession in *Whirlpool* (1949), based on a novel by Guy Endore and scripted by Ben Hecht under the pseudonym Lester Barlow. Gene Tierney plays Ann Sutton, the kleptomaniac wife of a psychiatrist (Richard Conte). She comes under the influence of Dr. Korvo (Jose Ferrer), a sinister hypnotist who dispatches a troublesome lover and frames Ann for the killing. Korvo has an apparently perfect alibi: at the time of the murder, he was in the hospital recovering from surgery, too weak to move, (in fact, self-hypnosis has enabled him to leave his bed and kill). The dogged detective Colton (Charles Bickford) remains skeptical, however. He takes Ann back to the scene of the crime, where they find Korvo trying to recover incriminating evidence. The victim of his own delusions of supernatural powers, Korvo bleeds to death and Ann is exonerated.

Fifteen years after their first appearance, Preminger's "Fox quintet" were the subject of much critical controversy. Andrew Sarris posited them as evidence of the director's right to *auteur* status, a claim hotly contested by Pauline Kael. She particularly disliked *Whirlpool*, which she called an "atrocity," while Sarris placed it among Preminger's best films—"all moodily fluid studies in perverse psychology." Godard's *Made in USA* has a reference to this picture also—a character named Dr. Korvo—as well as one to the hero of the next film in the cycle.

This was *Where the Sidewalk Ends* (1950), another pseudonymous Ben Hecht script, attributed to "Rex Conner." Mark Dixon (Dana Andrews) is a tough cop with a reputation for beating confessions out of criminals. When he accidentally kills a murder suspect, he tries to cover it up as a gangland slaying perpetrated by the mobster Scalise (Gary Merrill). But a complication arises: the dead man had been involved with the beautiful Morgan Taylor (Gene Tierney), and her father is accused of the murder. Dixon falls in love with Morgan and decides to make amends by deliberately provoking his own death at the hands of Scalise's mob, confident that they will be convicted. Instead, he captures the gang singlehanded. Acclaimed for his heroism but purified by love, Dixon confesses all and prepares for judgment as the film ends, Morgan at his side.

Treasured though it is by Preminger's admirers, the director himself could "remember nothing about" this film or the one that followed, *The Thirteenth Letter* (1950), a remake of H. G. Clouzot's *Le Corbeau* (1943). This story of a small French town paralyzed by a flurry of poison-pen letters was translated to Canada in Preminger's version, and shot by Joseph La Shelle partly on location. Critics have found it a "somewhat marginal" rendering of Preminger's typical concerns of the period, with an obsessive doctor (Charles Boyer) bending his young wife (Linda Darnell) to his deranged will. After that Preminger returned for a while to the New York theatre, in early 1951 directing two comedies: Joseph Kesselring's *Four Twelves Are Forty-Eight* and F. Hugh Herbert's *The Moon Is Blue*. Preminger had been divorced from Marion Mill in the late 1940s, and in 1951 he made a second marriage to "a pretty New York model," Mary Gardner.

The last of his "Fox quintet" was in fact made on loan to RKO. In *Angel Face* (1952), Robert Mitchum replaced Dana Andrews as the ambiguous Preminger hero. He plays Frank Jessup, an ambulance driver who arrives at the Tremayne mansion just in time to save the life of Mrs. Tremayne, who has been gassed in what she claims was a murder attempt.

Jessup becomes involved with the aloof daughter of the house, Diane (Jean Simmons), who adores her millionaire father (Herbert Marshall) but hates her stepmother. Signing on as the family chauffeur, Jessup witnesses Diane's second attempt to kill Mrs. Tremayne. It is successful, but accidentally claims her father's life as well, and Diane and Frank are charged with both murders. On the advice of a smart lawyer, they play for sympathy by marrying in jail, and they are acquitted. Frank has had enough, but when he tries to leave Diane, she drives their car backwards off a cliff, killing them both in one of the cinema's most startling conclusions. Paul Mayersberg called this film "the only lyrical nightmare in cinema," and Jacques Rivette described Preminger's *mise en scène* as "the creation of a complex summary of characters and sets, a web of connections, an architecture of relations."

Many would agree with Jonathan Rosenbaum that the melodramas Preminger directed while under contract to 20th Century–Fox "comprise the bulk of his durable work." Discussing this "unique collection of haunting masterpieces" in *American Directors*, Jean-Pierre Coursodon wrote that these films are "not only thematically similar, they *look* alike, and generate the same kind of atmosphere. . . . The fluidity of the camerawork is the concrete expression of his attitude to his material. The camera unobtrusively but relentlessly follows the characters around in medium shots and long boom or dolly shots, so as to integrate them to the surroundings. Preminger's vision is a global one, he strives to capture the whole, not details—hence the paucity of close-up and reaction shots in his films. . . . This stylistic option is consistent with Preminger's unfailingly objective attitude toward characters and situations. . . . If the harmony of form and content, expression and intention, is the mark of 'classic' art, Preminger is one of the great classics of the American film."

The last film Preminger made on his Fox contract was *River of No Return* (1954), a Western and so an unusual choice for this intensely urban and theatrical sensibility. Marilyn Monroe and Robert Mitchum star as a saloon singer and a widowed farmer thrown together in the wilderness, where they try to make their way down a raging river (with Mitchum's son in tow) so that Mitchum can settle accounts with Monroe's nogood husband, who bushwhacked him and left him for dead. It was Preminger's first exercise in widescreen aesthetics, indeed the first CinemaScope Western, and André Bazin, for one, said that it was the "one film in CinemaScope that added anything of importance to the *mise-en-scène*." V. F. Perkins noted its carefully articulated plot and symbolic decor, the opposing "moral extremes" of Mitchum ("static and unbending") and Monroe ("lacking purpose and definition") carefully modulated by the child Tommy Rettig, "whose equal affection for both" is the locus of the spectator's desire for compromise. "The symbolism is so completely absorbed into the action that it may pass unnoticed."

By the time Preminger made this Western, he was already an independent producer. His first project was a film remembered largely for its historical significance—*The Moon Is Blue* (1953), the innocuous comedy of misunderstandings that Preminger had successfully directed on the stage. Adapted and coproduced by the play's author, F. Hugh Herbert, the movie starred William Holden, David Niven, and Maggie McNamara, and was set mostly in the Holden character's New York bachelor apartment. The Breen Office of the Motion Picture Association of America insisted that six lines of the finished film be changed to qualify for the Production Seal (without which, it was assumed, no movie theatre would book the film). The forbidden words were "virgin," "pregnant," and "seduce," and the Breen Office objected also to the line: "You are shallow, cynical, selfish, and immoral, and I like you!" It was for just such a confrontation that Preminger had gone independent, and his contract with his distributor, United Artists, gave him final cut. He refused to make the changes, saying afterwards, "I am not a crusader or anything like that, but it gives me great pleasure to fight for my rights."

Without a Production Seal or much of a recommendation from the reviewers, *The Moon Is Blue* played, according to Preminger, "in something like eight or nine thousand theatres in the US" and grossed over $6 million. This coup left the industry's antiquated self-censorship apparatus in disarray, contributing to the sweeping revision of the Code in 1966. Otto Preminger became a household name, a development he relished and shrewdly used to promote his films.

During the 1950s, Preminger gravitated towards productions on a much grander scale than the films he had made at Fox. *Carmen Jones* (1954) was an updating to World War II of Bizet's opera *Carmen*. The all-black cast was headed by Dorothy Dandridge as the beautiful factory worker, Harry Belafonte as the soldier destroyed by his love for her. The film has elicited ambiguous praise from Preminger's admirers. Sarris wrote that it "succeeds on its own questionable terms as the Preminger musical par excellence—drab, austere, and completely depoeticized."

Preminger bolstered his reputation as an uncompromising purveyor of controversial subjects with *The Man with the Golden Arm* (1955), in which drug addiction, a strictly taboo subject, was treated frankly on the screen for the first time. Frank Sinatra played the hero of Nelson Algren's novel, a musician fighting the ravages of heroin. Frankie Machine is saddled with a neurotic wife (Eleanor Parker) but buoyed by a faithful girlfriend (Kim Novak), who ultimately helps him kick the habit. But not before he's suspected of murdering a sadistic drug dealer, the victim in fact of Frankie's crazed wife, who kills herself when her crime is discovered.

Like *The Moon is Blue*, this film is more interesting historically than aesthetically, although it should be noted that Preminger films have unusually volatile critical careers, and sooner or later may all be "recuperated" into the auteurist canon. Again the MPAA Seal was withheld from the film, which Preminger refused to change, although he did cut one 30-second scene of Frankie preparing heroin for injection in order to avoid condemnation by the Legion of Decency. It was the first time the Legion did not condemn a film that had been refused the MPAA Seal.

At this point Preminger turned his attention to various social institutions, in a cycle of films that occupied him for over a decade. He began with the army, in *The Court Martial of Billy Mitchell* (1955), which starred Gary Cooper as the maverick World War I general who sacrificed his own career in an attempt to persuade the army that air power was the only hope for military supremacy in the future. The static courtroom drama, which exposed the inflexibility of the military, gave Preminger an opportunity to indulge his legal training and his penchant for relying on *mise-en-scène* rather than montage. "This is another of my independent films when I was not entirely independent and had a producer [Milton Sperling]. I was asked to do it."

In 1956, having acquired the rights to George Bernard Shaw's play *Saint Joan*, Preminger launched a well-publicized search for a talented unknown to play the Maid, settling finally on impressionable Iowa teenager Jean Seberg, who embarked on a sometimes brilliant but ultimately destructive acting career by starting at the top. Graham Greene wrote the screenplay, and Saul Bass designed the first of his distinctive title logos, henceforth a Preminger trademark. The trial scene was singled out for praise, but for all its pageantry and publicity, *Saint Joan* was a flop.

Seberg appeared again in *Bonjour Tristesse* (1957), as Cécile, the spoiled daughter of Raymond, a wealthy widower (David Niven) pursuing his pleasures on the Riviera. When Raymond is attracted to Anne (Deborah Kerr), who criticizes Cécile's abominable behavior, the girl casually plots to thwart their romance, and succeeds. Tragedy follows when Anne, distraught, is killed in an auto accident. Raymond and Cécile resume the round of cocktail parties and nightclubs, but the old pleasures seem empty now, soured by unspoken quiet. The story is told in flashback by Cécile during the winter after the events; Preminger filmed the past—Cécile's memories—in color, and the present in black and white. "I'm not particularly fond of flashbacks. I probably tried to make it more agreeable or interesting by doing that," he explained to Peter Bogdanovich.

What Preminger did remember of it, he remembered fondly, and he thought the American critics treated it unfairly ("They said it wasn't French enough"). But *Bonjour Tristesse*, based on Françoise Sagan's precocious novel, was very popular in France and had an incalculable influence on the critics who were about to embark as directors of France's New Wave. Godard, making *À bout de souffle* (*Breathless*), which also starred Jean Seberg, two years later, used some scenes from Preminger's film in composing his own shots. Seberg's role, he wrote, was "a continuation" of her role in *Bonjour Tristesse*. "I could have taken the last shot of Preminger's film and started after dissolving to a title, 'Three years later.'" François Truffaut saw in its plot a "remake" of *Angel Face*, "a pretext to embroider his [Preminger's] favorite theme: the child-woman and her sadness at approaching age."

In 1958 Preminger ended his "forgettable marriage" (as he called it) to Mary Gardner and married Patricia Hope Bryce, the fashion coordinator on *Bonjour Tristesse*. They had twin sons in 1960. It was to be Preminger's last and happiest marriage, though he did add another son to his family. In 1971, after the death of Gypsy Rose Lee, he revealed that he was the father of her twenty-six-year-old son, Erik Kirkland, and adopted him. Kirkland changed his name to Eric Lee Preminger and worked for his father as a writer and associate producer.

Porgy and Bess (1959), like *Carmen Jones*, was a musical with an all-black cast. Based on Gershwin's "folk opera," it had Sidney Poitier as Porgy, Dorothy Dandridge as Bess, and Sammy Davis Jr. as the corrupt and corrupting Sportin' Life. This was not a Preminger production but an assignment for Sam Goldwyn; for the second time in his career Preminger replaced Rouben Mamoulian, director of the original stage production, who had had a fight with Goldwyn. In spite of the excellent cast (which also included Pearl Bailey, Brock Peters, and Diahann Carroll), the film was a flop.

Preminger's legal training and family background have often been suggested as the source of his fondness for courtroom dramas and perhaps also of his relativistic view of life. Both elements were prominent in *Anatomy of a Murder* (1959), adapted by Wendell Mayes from the novel by Robert Traver, and with a jazz score commissioned from Duke Ellington. James Stewart stars as a canny country lawyer who takes on the city slickers in a sensational murder trial. His client is an army lieutenant (Ben Gazzara) who has killed a bartender, claiming that he did so because the man had raped and beaten his wife (Lee Remick). This defense looks more and more shaky as it emerges that the lieutenant has a history of violence, his wife of promiscuity, but in the end the lawyer wins the case with a plea of "irresistible impulse." When he calls for his fee, he finds a note explaining that his client had succumbed to an irresistible impulse to get out of town.

The utterly frank discussion of rape in *Anatomy of a Murder* again made history, making the Production Code even more of an anachronism. Preminger also successfully challenged the prevailing notion that the proper length for a non-epic was ninety minutes, sustaining the film's tension for nearly three hours. Moreover, by raising doubts about the innocence of the defendant, Preminger put the audience—as David Thomson pointed out—"in the position of the jury: the workings of the film became the due process of law." *Anatomy of a Murder* received six Oscar nominations (including best picture) and is ranked by some critics even above *Laura*. When *Anatomy* was sold for television, the director himself lost a landmark lawsuit to prevent the network from editing his film, arguing that his contract assured him of final cut. However, in a later battle, Preminger did win some concessions from CBS over the editing.

Jean-Pierre Coursodon has written persuasively about the stylistic transition Preminger made from his Fox period to his independent work, and how *Anatomy of a Murder* typifies the concerns of the latter period while keeping faith with the former. The later films "may seem to be the exact opposite of his earlier works, as they represent efforts—often doomed, albeit stunning—to piece together multitudes of fragments, whereas the Fox films had been prime examples of self-contained tightness. Still, there is logic in what could be called Preminger's evolution from a microcosmic to a macrocosmic vision. His commitment to an impartial, detached outlook was bound to lead him to projects of increasingly broader scope, encompassing as many characters, episodes, and points of view as possible, so that the issues involved . . . might be dealt with as fairly as possible."

Macrocosmic indeed were his next four films. *Exodus* (1960) followed the travails of Jews fighting for a homeland in Palestine. Paul Newman played the rugged hero who attracts a Gentile widow (Eva Marie Saint) to his cause. Preminger made headlines again when he ignored the industry's fading McCarthyite blacklist and credited Dalton Trumbo for the screenplay, adapted from the novel by Leon Uris. *Exodus* was long, popular, and received by most critics with skepticism or rage. "Preminger's matzoh opera" was one comment, and Gideon Bachmann wrote that "for one who has lived through that period and that time in that place, *Exodus* is sacrilege." It has not weathered the passage of time with as much grace as Preminger's next film.

"One of Preminger's great underrated virtues in *Advise and Consent* is clarity—the pristine sharpness and intelligibility with which he handles complex materials," Molly Haskell wrote of this 1962 film, based on a novel by Allen Drury. It is the story of the machinations behind a presidential appointee's interrogation by the Senate. Suicide, homosexuality, demagoguery, unbridled ambition, and the closing of the ranks of the old guard all figure in the plot. Once again Preminger shifts between several points of view in following Robert Leffingwell (Henry Fonda) as he fights such formidable opponents as the seasoned politician Seabright Cooley (Charles Laughton) and the idealistic young Brigham Anderson (Don Murray), who each oppose his nomination as Secretary of State for far different reasons. Leffingwell has an unsavory backer in the unscrupulous and ambitious Van Ackerman (George Grizzard), who threatens Anderson over a youthful homosexual indiscretion and causes his suicide. The Senate is shocked and deadlocks on Leffingwell's nomination, only to have the ailing President die as the Vice President prepares to break the tie vote. The new President reserves judgment—and the right to name his own Secretary.

Coursodon feels "it was in *Advise and Consent* that Preminger's objectivity began to show its limitations, and to lapse into occasional blandness and complacency," its plot beset by contrivances. Sarris, on the other hand, termed it one of Preminger's four "masterpieces of ambiguity and objectivity," along with *Laura, Bonjour Tristesse,* and the 1965 psychological mystery, *Bunny Lake Is Missing.* Rosenbaum has made the provocative suggestion that these late, issue-oriented films, vaunted for their objectivity, only give the appearance of it. "He will welcome antagonistic points of view within a single shot so that he can watch them co-exist, mingle, synthesize, or compete for supremacy, but he always makes sure that the overall composition of these elements conveys a given slant, and the ostensible appeal to the spectator to 'use his own intelligence' is often a very clever means of directing and programming that intelligence. . . . The journey taken is implacably one from A to B, but we are given a choice of diverse routes by which we may traverse the distance."

Coursodon felt considerable reservation too about the subsequent blockbusters of this Preminger period, *The Cardinal, In Harm's Way,* and *Hurry Sundown:* "each is great in parts, and a failure as a whole." Each was also sensationally publicized, as Preminger maintained his high public profile. *The Cardinal* (1963) was a controversial portrait of a fictional young priest from his seminary days to his annointing as a prince of the Church, with episodes on abortion, the rigors of celibacy, and prejudice and rivalry within the priesthood. Tom Tryon played the central character, Stephen Fermoyle. John Huston's performance as a wily old cleric was nominated for a supporting actor Oscar, but reviews for the film as a whole were decidedly cool. Stanley Kauffmann called it "a polychrome heartstring-tugger, nothing more."

In Harm's Way (1965), which followed the difficulties of the peacetime navy in gearing up for World War II, featured an opening sequence that struck one admirer as "one of the most impressively directed sequences in Preminger's career." It followed a couple from a party to a remote beach, where their lovemaking is interrupted by the attack on Pearl Harbor. John Wayne plays an aggressive officer who leads a gallant but disastrous pursuit of the enemy after Pearl Harbor and is disgraced. His private life is complicated by a botched reunion with his estranged son, now in the service, his new romance with a wordly nurse (Patricia Neal), and the downward spiral of his old friend (Kirk Douglas), who is embittered by the death of his faithless wife (the party-goer in the film's opening). A climactic battle ties up all the loose ends neatly—perhaps too neatly, according to some critics.

Only one of the director's late films has captured the imagination of his critics, and that primarily in retrospect, as is so often the case with Preminger. In *Bunny Lake Is Missing* (1965), Ann Lake (Carol Lynley) is terrified when her small daughter Bunny, just arrived in London with her, disappears. But the policeman assigned to the case (Laurence Olivier) begins to doubt the child exists, when he can find no trace of her at all, and Ann's brother Stephen (Keir Dullea) subtly contributes to this view. Ann discovers that Stephen, obsessed with jealousy, has abducted the child and plans to kill her. Ann holds him off with a desperate series of childhood games until the detective arrives to save her. While this exercise in obsession was another commercial failure for Preminger, critics have noted in its mobile camera, it claustrophobic relationships, and its night scenes an echo of Preminger's Fox melodramas, even an extension of them. It is the last film his admirers agree on. Sarris notes that "Preminger's wondrous control of CinemaScope enables him to establish a multiplicity of viewpoints in this crisis-induced rediscovery of childhood by bemused adults." Coursodon, pointing out its many similarities to *Laura* in particular, calls it a technical tour de force; "Preminger's last great film, and it is somehow fitting that it should evoke the memory of what, for many, will remain his best period—a period of intimist explorations, before inflated ambitions took over."

Racism was the theme of Preminger's last "big" film, *Hurry Sundown* (1967), generally reckoned the weakest of the cycle. At the end of World War II, two poor Southern farmers, one black and one white, form an unprecedented partnership to resist a ruthless land-grabber (Michael Caine), who ultimately tries to run them out with violence. Jane Fonda co-starred as Caine's sexually dependent wife, who eventually frees herself from him and his schemes. Neither the critics nor the public warmed to the film, described by Bosley Crowther as "Otto Preminger's awful glop of neo–Uncle Tomism."

There followed the disaster of *Skidoo* (1968), a strong candidate for Preminger's worst picture, with its frantic slapstick farce of gangsters and hippies; *Tell Me That You Love Me, Junie Moon* (1970), a tragicomedy about three variously disabled friends striving for readjustment, strong on lugubrious pathos; and a bitter comedy about a woman who discovers her dying husband's infidelity, *Such Good Friends* (1971). None of them fared well, being variously described as obnoxious, aimless, and heavy-handed even by Preminger's admirers. Preminger did not make another film until *Rosebud* (1975). It was another disaster—the story of a terrorist kidnapping, conceived on the same huge scale as *Exodus*. According to Coursodon, "people are not just dwarfed by the physical scope of the narrative, they are given up as individuals from the moment they first appear."

Preminger managed to surprise all those who had written him off with his last film, *The Human Factor* (1979), an intimate political drama adapted by Tom Stoppard from Graham Greene's novel about a minor Secret Service functionary, Castle, who long ago became a double agent out of gratitude for the rescue of his black African wife by a communist friend. Inevitably, though, the coldly efficient department catches up to him, and life falls apart suddenly and shockingly, forcing his departure, sans all he "turned" for, to Moscow. Nicol Williamson's performance as Castle was praised for its subdued irony, as was Preminger's integration of camera movement and characters. However far from truly great Preminger work, Coursodon concluded, *The Human Factor* "would not be an unworthy conclusion to an exceptionally diversified, if uneven, career."

One of the most visible of Hollywood directors, Preminger became well-known to the public as an independent producer-director in the 1950s, and was also known for his occasional appearances as an actor, most famously as the con-

centration camp commandant in Billy Wilder's *Stalag 17*. Preminger was noted not only for his distinctive personal style and marketing genius, but for his choice of controversial subject matter and his stubborn challenges to political and censorship taboos. His high profile in the film industry made him a controversial figure to critics as well. "His enemies have never forgiven him for being a director with the personality of a producer," Sarris writes. He enjoyed high esteem among proponents of the *auteur* theory, was a favorite in France of the New Wave critic-directors and in England of the academics clustered around the influential magazine *Movie*.

In the United States his work served as a bone of contention between Andrew Sarris, chief American champion of the *auteur* theory, and Pauline Kael, its prime challenger. Sarris admired Preminger's "impassive gaze—accepting the good with the bad, the beautiful with the ugly, the sublime with the mediocre." William Pechter bestowed on Preminger the ambivalent but evocative epithet, "renaissance hack." V.F. Perkins saw in him "the enemy of preconceptions, snap judgments, closed minds." Pauline Kael, on the other hand, wrote that "his films are consistently superficial and facile."

Few directors so divide critics into fanatics and foes, although even Preminger's most ardent defenders concede that his later films display regrettable excesses and failures of imagination. Nevertheless, Sarris wrote upon the director's death that he thought he had underestimated his career, that only *Rosebud* "seems utterly beyond revisionism" and suggested that "a massive re-evaluation seems in order on both the thematic and stylistic fronts."

—P.D.

FILMS: Die Grosse Liebe (The Great Love), 1931; Under Your Spell, 1936; Danger Love at Work, 1937; Margin for Error, 1943; In the Meantime Darling, 1944; Laura, 1944; Royal Scandal (U.K., Czarina), 1945; Fallen Angel, 1945; Centennial Summer, 1946; Forever Amber, 1947; Daisy Kenyon, 1947; That Lady in Ermine, 1948; The Fan, 1949 (U.K., Lady Windermere's Fan), 1949; Whirlpool, 1949; Where the Sidewalk Ends, 1950; The Thirteenth Letter, 1951; Angel Face, 1952; The Moon Is Blue, 1953 (filmed simultaneously in German as Die Jungfrau auf dem Dach); River of No Return, 1954; Carmen Jones, 1954; The Man With the Golden Arm, 1955; The Court Martial of Billy Mitchell (U.K., One Man Mutiny), 1955; Saint Joan, 1957; Bonjour Tristesse, 1958; Porgy and Bess, 1959; Anatomy of a Murder, 1959; Exodus, 1960; Advise and Consent, 1962; The Cardinal, 1963; In Harm's Way, 1965; Bunny Lake Is Missing, 1965; Hurry Sundown, 1967; Skidoo, 1968; Tell Me That You Love Me, Junie Moon, 1970; Such Good Friends, 1971; Rosebud, 1975; The Human Factor, 1979.

ABOUT: Cameron, I. (ed.) Movie Reader, 1972; Coursodon, J.-P. American Directors, Volume 1, 1983; Frisch-
auer, W. Behind the Scenes of Otto Preminger, 1974;
Lourcelles, J. Otto Preminger, 1965 (in French); Mour-
let, M. Sur un Art Ignoré, 1965; Perkins, V. F. Film as
Film, 1972; Pratley, G. The Cinema of Otto Preminger, 1971; Preminger, M. M. All I Want Is Everything, 1957; Preminger, O. Preminger: An
Autobiography, 1977; Roud, R. (ed.) Cinema: A Critical Dictionary, 1980; Sarris, A. The American Cinema,
1985; Sarris, A. Interviews With Film Directors, 1967.
Periodicals—Avant-Scène du Cinéma July–September
1978; Cahiers du Cinéma December 1953, July 1961,
July 1962; Cinéma (France) April, May and June 1971,
May 1975; Cinemonde May 30, 1961; Current Biography June 1986; Dirigido January 1977; Esquire October 1958, March 1961; Film Comment Summer 1965;
Film Ideal November 15, 1963; Films and Filming
November 1959, February 1961, March 1961, May
1962, November 1963, June 1965, November 1979;
Films Illustrated January 1980; Focus on Film August
1979; Image et Son November 1962; Intercine 1 and
2 1963; Interview July 1972; Journal of Popular Film
and TV Summer 1983; King July 1965; Lumière
March 1974; Movie September 1962 (Preminger issue), Summer 1965; New Yorker February 19, 1966;
Playboy July 1961; Positif June 1971; Présence du
Cinéma February 1962; Saturday Evening Post April
8, 1967; Theatre Arts January 1961; Village Voice May
27, 1986; Visage du Cinéma March 1963.

YAKOV PROTAZANOV

PROTAZANOV, YAKOV (1881–August 8,
1945), Russian director and scenarist, was born
in Moscow. Dependable information about his
early life is scarce, but he seems to have begun
as a stage actor in 1905 and to have been involved in the cinema as early as 1907, presumably as an actor. The first film credited to him
as a director was called *The Fountains of
Bakhisarai* (1909), which he also scripted, but
the first of his movies noted by the historian Jay
Leyda in *Kino* was *Pesnya katorzhanina* (*The
Prisoner's Song*), made for the Thiemann and
Reinhardt company in 1911. Inspired by a popular song of the period and scripted by the director, its cast included N. Saltikov, Vladimir
Shaternikov, and M. Koroleva.

The Prisoner's Song was photographed by
Giovanni Vitrotti, who was also Protazanov's
cameraman on *Anfisa* (1912), adapted by Leonid Andreyev from his own play. *Ukhod
velikovo startza* (*Departure of a Grand Old Man*,
1912), a tribute to Tolstoy with Shaternikov in
the lead role, was condemned as a caricature by
Tolstoy's widow at a special premiere and never
publicly shown in Russia, though Leyda describes it as both "innocent" and "daring."

Beginning in 1913 Thiemann and Reinhardt
launched their "Golden Series" of movies—most
of them sentimental "psychological" dramas

about elegantly dressed men and women living
in luxurious houses: an art director's cinema.
Many of the most successful films in the series
were directed by Protazanov—tear-jerkers like
Razbitaya vaza (*The Shattered Vase*, 1913) and
the hugely profitable *Klyuchi shchastya* (*Keys to
Happiness*, 1913). The latter, the greatest box-
office success of pre-Revolutionary Russia, was
based on a popular novel and co-directed by
Protazanov and Vladimir Gardin, with Vladimir
Maximov and Olga Preobrazhenskaya in the
lead roles. Thiemann and Reinhardt were able
to re-equip their studios on the profits of this
film.

By 1915 the demand was for another kind of
escapism—the murder mystery or serial, modeled on *Fantômas* or *The Perils of Pauline*. Joining the flamboyant new producer Josef
Yermoliev, Protazanov and Gardin co-directed
an imitation of the latter, the four-episode
Peterburgskiye trushchobi (*Petersburg Slums*,
1915), with Olga Preobrazhenskaya as the intrepid heroine. She also starred as Natasha in
Protazanov and Gardin's much-admired two-
and-a-half-hour version of *Voina i mir* (*War and
Peace*, 1915), with Gardin as Napoleon. Protazanov's other literary adaptations of this period
included *Plebei* (*Plebeian*, 1915), a version of
Strindberg's *Miss Julie*, with Preobrazhenskaya
and Nikolai Radin; *Nikolai Stavrogin* (1915),
based on Dostoevsky's *Devils* and starring Ivan
Mozhukhin; and a faithful and handsomely
dressed adaptation of Pushkin's *Pikovaya dama*
(*The Queen of Spades*, 1916), scripted by the
youthful Fyodor Otsep. The latter also starred
Mozhukhin, with whom Protazanov made twenty-six films between 1915 and 1919.

The public demand for sensational escapist entertainment continued in the years leading up to the 1917 revolutions, and Protazanov made some notable contributions—*Zhenshchina s kinzhalom* (*Woman With a Dagger*, 1916); the three-part *Grekh* (*Sin*, 1916–1917); and *Satana likuyushchii* (*Satan Triumphant*, 1917). The latter, perfectly reflecting the contemporary interest in sin, demonology, and the occult, starred Mozhukin and Natalia Lissenko in a fantasy about a clergyman tempted by a mysterious Stranger and eventually committing adultery in his own church, which is promptly struck by lightning.

A new genre emerged after the February Revolution of 1917—the anti-czarist film. Protazanov's *Andrei Kozhukov* (1917), based on an autobiographical novel by the terrorist Stepniak, is an example of this short-lived vogue, and so is *Otets Sergii* (*Father Sergius*), a much more considerable film. It is based on Tolstoy's story about a dashing young officer at the court of Nikolai I who, discovering that his *fiancée* had been the czar's mistress, breaks off his engagement and enters a monastery. He becomes famous as a hermit and a healer, but cannot entirely obliterate his sexual appetites (though he goes to brutal lengths to subdue them, at one testing moment lacerating his finger tips with a chopper). Finally he does succumb to temptation and in bitter remorse leaves his monastery to become a wandering beggar.

With its revelations of corruption and weakness both at court and in the priesthood, the original story had caused a great scandal, but in the permissive and anti-czarist mood that followed the February Revolution it seemed to Protazanov possible to film it—it was indeed the last Russian film completed before the October Revolution, though it was not shown until the following year. (Protazanov's *Taina korolevy* [*The Queen's Secret*], based on Elinor Glyn's *Three Weeks*, was begun in Moscow but completed in Yalta in 1919.) According to Jay Leyda, the anti-czarist film served one useful purpose—the need to lend conviction to revelations of Romanov wickedness demanded more realism and more historical accuracy or verisimilitude than had previously been considered necessary in historical films, and Protazanov in particular "immediately profited from these lessons in naturalism to give his films . . . more atmosphere and more life."

Writing in 1960, Leyda said that *Father Sergius* "is still dramatic and compels . . . attention. . . . Only the actors' make-up obtrudes. Its episodic story is told and the stages in the life of Father Sergius are shown with a skill exceptional anywhere in 1917. . . . Mozhukin

never excelled this performance in its convincing complex ageing of a man eternally pursued by the desires of the flesh, and Lissenko portrays an astonishingly sensual creature." Another critic wrote that "the opulence of the palace scenes with their careful grouping of players and tastefully coordinated movement, the authentic feeling of the monastery scenes with their attention to detail and the realistic exteriors at the end of the film give a sense of variety and liveliness to a story which is primarily static and psychological."

Many filmmakers, faced with an uncertain future, left Russia after the October Revolution. Josef Yermoliev persuaded virtually his entire staff to leave with him, Protazanov and Mozhukin among them. For two years they and other refugees settled at Yalta in the Crimea, a seaside resort where there were some studios, and filming continued rather half-heartedly there and in Odessa as the latter changed hands with ever-increasing frequency. When the Allies abandoned Odessa, Yermoliev and his entourage moved themselves and their equipment on to Constantinople for a while and then, in August 1920, made their way to France. In Paris Yermoliev promptly showed some of his Russian-made films, including *The Queen of Spades,* and soon established a new French company, Ermolieff-Films, at Méliès' old studios.

Protazanov made a number of films in France, including *L'Angoissante aventure,* which had evolved gradually during Yermoliev's wanderings and which established Mozhukin (now known as Ivan Mosjoukine) as an idol of French movie-goers. Details of Protazanov's European films are hard to come by—there is some evidence that he was filming in France before Yermoliev arrived there, and it is certain that he worked for several producers apart from Yermoliev and made among other films a French version of *Prokuror* called *Justice d'abord* and adaptations of Zola's *Pour une nuit d'amour* and Paul Bourget's *Le Sens de la mort* (which provided a minor acting role for the young René Clair); he also made several movies for UFA in Berlin.

In 1924 Protazanov was invited back to the Soviet Union to direct one of the first productions of the new Mezhrabpom-Russ company, *Aelita,* adapted by Fyodor Otsep and Alexei Faiko from a novel by Alexei Tolstoy. It tells the story of an engineer named Los who, tired of earthly miseries, and pursued for the murder of his wife, escapes to Mars on a flying machine of his own invention, accompanied by the detective investigating the murder and a good-hearted Red Army soldier. On Mars Los falls in love with the planet's ruler Aelita but is also imprisoned, enslaved, and involved in a revolution. In the end he is relieved to find that it has all been a dream—that he is safely back on his own formerly despised planet.

The Martian sets and costumes designed in the constructivist manner by Alexandra Exter and Isaac Rabinovich were extravagantly admired at the time, though later critics have found them overly theatrical, and have reserved their praise for the broad comedy acting of Igor Ilinsky (as the detective) and Nikolai Batalov (as the soldier). Nevertheless, *Aelita* was the most widely publicized Soviet film of the era and is still one of the best known.

Yevo prizyv (*His Call,* 1925) was Protazanov's first work of Communist propaganda and is an unusually civilized example of the form, with convincing characterization even of the villains. It was followed by *The Tailor From Torzhok* (1925), commissioned to publicize a state lottery. This turned out to be a satirical comedy of considerable charm, with notable performances from Igor Ilynsky, Anatoli Ktorov, and Olga Zhizneva. It was so successful that Protazanov used the same team again in a similar satire, *Protsess o tryokh millyonakh* (*The Three Million Case,* or *Three Thieves,* 1926), adapted by Protazanov and Oleg Leonidov from a novel by Umberto Notari.

The Three Million Case turns on a love affair between a banker's wife (Zhizneva) and a thief named Cascarilia (Ktorov), and its point is that the banker (Mikhail Klimov) is a bigger and better crook than the thief. It was another box-office hit, but a contemporary Soviet reviewer complained that Protazanov had done nothing to sharpen or deepen the "rosewater" satire of the original. A Western critic, commenting years later on this review, maintained that on the contrary Protazanov's "sly and gentle" humor retained "a genuinely satirical punch. The comings and goings in the big house, although nicely orchestrated, certainly have something of the boulevard farce flavour, yet Protazanov often appears to be sending up the convention, as in the very funny, constantly interrupted love scenes between Cascarilia and the wife. . . . Similarly, there is a good deal of edge and virtuosity in the staging of the final, mad trial scene set in [Isaac] Rabinovich's wonderful decor."

A very different film followed, *Sorok pervyi* (*The Forty-First,* 1927), based on a story by Boris Lavrenov and set in Tashkent during the civil war. This strange and intensely romantic movie deals with the forbidden love affair that develops between Maryutka, a Red Army marksman, and a captured White Guard officer when they are marooned together alone on an island. When rescue arrives for the guardsman, Maryutka recovers her sense of duty and her lover becomes the forty-first victim of her unerring aim.

Maryutka was to have been played by Vera Maretskaya, but when she fell ill Protazanov's assistant Yuli Raizman hastily recruited as her replacement an unknown young actress named Ada Voitsik, just graduated from the film school in Moscow. The film's great international success owed much to her intense, half-savage performance. She herself gave the credit to Protazanov, who "would always explain everything to us in advance, and in the fullest detail: not only what shot was to be filmed and how many metres it was to be, but also what in the final film would precede and follow it . . . [and even] why we were waiting for this shadow, or why [Pyotr] Yermolov was using that lens." In spite of its financial success, the film was much criticized for its sympathetic portrayal of the White officer, though it is now regarded as a Civil War classic. It was remade thirty years later by Grigori Chukrai, but most critics prefer Protazanov's version.

There was also a good deal of official hostility to *The Man From the Restaurant* (1927), with Mikhail Chekhov as a waiter in pre-Revolutionary Russia humiliated by the restaurant's wealthy customers but achieving through his suffering an inner strength. The Mezhrabpom-Russ studios having been almost totally destroyed by fire, Protazanov made the film on location in the once-famous Yar Restaurant in Moscow, lighting some scenes with the restaurant's own chandeliers. It was presumably the opulence of the setting that caused Party critics to condemn the film for "appeals to bourgeois taste," though the wretched waiter obviously symbolized the indomitable spirit of the Russian masses and the movie has since gained official approval—it always had that of the general public. *Don Diego and Pelageya,* made the same year, is an agreeable satirical comedy about a provincial bureaucrat so carried away by his own sense of power that he imprisons an old woman for a minute breach of the law, but gets his comeuppance from the Young Komsomols.

Protazanov's last three silent films were all written by the director in collaboration with Oleg Leonidov and, as Jay Leyda says, each of them was "in its quiet, solid way, an experiment." *Byeli orel* (*The White Eagle,* 1928), based on a story by Leonid Andreyev, was the first Soviet film to show a czarist official as a human being with a conscience and was predictably condemned for "misplaced sympathies." It is nowadays chiefly remarkable for preserving the only surviving film performances of the great theatre director Vsevolod Meyerhold and the Moscow Arts Theatre actor Vasili Kachalov, as well as the last performance in a Russian film of Anna Sten, later touted by Sam Goldwyn as a rival to Garbo.

Two more luminaries of the Moscow Arts Theatre, Ivan Moskvin and Mikhail Tarkhanov, appeared in *Chiny i liudi* (*Ranks and People,* 1929). Stringing together three short stories by Chekhov, it was the first ever such anthology of miniatures, according to Leyda, and the first Soviet film to draw on Chekhov. *Prazdnik svyatovo Iorgene* (*The Feast of St. Jorgen,* 1930), featuring Protazanov's favorite comedy team of Ktorov, Ilinsky, and Klimov, is set in a small town on its annual saint's day, and points up with great relish the resemblances between the activities of two visiting thieves and the equally corrupt exploitation of the occasion by the church. It remains one of the most enjoyable and admired of Protazanov's later films.

Protazanov's first talkie was *Tommy* (1931), based on Ivanov's play *Armored Train 14-69* about foreign intervention during the Civil War as it strikes an ordinary British soldier. A work of no great interest, it was followed by one of the weakest of Protazanov's films, *Marionettes* (1934), a satire on political intrigue set in an imaginary European country. It was not until he made *Bespridannitsa* (*Without Dowry*) in 1936 that Protazanov seemed fully to have mastered the use of sound; this adaptation of N. A. Ostrovsky's satirical play about the status of women was one of the first Soviet talkies to escape theatricality and take on a cinematic life of its own.

Protazanov's health was failing, and his next film was not made until 1941. This was *Salavat Yulayev,* dealing with the revolutionary struggles of the Bakshir people of Central Asia, whose landscapes and colors Protazanov discovered with delight. He returned there to make his last film at the Tashkent Studio. *Nasreddin v Bukhare* (*Adventures in Bokhara,* 1943) draws on the large body of stories about the eighteenth-century folk hero Nasreddin, the ever-resourceful and witty enemy of Ottoman tyranny and defender of the poor.

Nasreddin is played with great *élan* by Lev Sverdlin, and the film was splendidly shot on location in Uzbekistan by Dovzhenko's cameraman Danylo Demutsky. The result was an excellent swashbuckling comedy, described by William Whitebait as "buoyant, racy and both fanciful and down to earth"—"the first real whiff of Asia we have known in the cinema for many months." Protazanov suffered a serious

heart attack during the filming of *Nasreddin* but continued to work after it. When he died in August 1945 he was collaborating with Boris Barnet on a proposed adaptation of Ostrovsky's play *Wolves and Sheep.*

Protazanov has until recently been given short shrift by Soviet critics because of his breaches of Party dogma, and by Western critics suspicious of his popular success. He was indeed not an innovator of the caliber of Eisenstein or Vertov, but he was the best of the Russian pioneer filmmakers, an eclectic master of all the resources of the silent cinema, a fine (if sometimes overindulgent) director of actors, and the creator of a large body of work that enriched the Russian cinema almost from its beginning—civilized, intelligent, and courageous in its quiet assertion of human rather than commercial or doctrinaire values. A great deal of work remains to be done on Protazanov's early and European movies, but his reputation is rising both in the USSR and abroad as his films begin to be assessed on their merits.

FILMS: *Partial list only*—The Fountains of Bakhisarai, 1909; Pesnya katorzhanina (The Prisoner's Song), 1911; Anfisa, 1912; Ukhod velikovo startza (The Departure of a Grand Old Man/The Life of Tolstoy), 1912; Kak khoroshi, kak svezhi byli rozi (How Fine, How Fresh the Roses Were), 1913; Razbitaya vaza (The Shattered Vase), 1913; (with Vladimir Gardin) Klyuchi shchastya (Keys to Happiness), 1913; Drama by Telephone, 1914; (with Vladimir Gardin) Voina i mir (War and Peace), 1915; (with Vladimir Gardin) Peterburgskiye trushchobi (Petersburg Slums), 1915; Plebei (Plebian), 1915; Nikolai Stavrogin, 1915; Pikovaya dama (The Queen of Spades), 1916; (with Georgi Azagarov) Grekh (Sin), 1916–1917; Zhenshchina s kinzhalom (Woman With a Dagger), 1916; Prokuror (Public Prosecutor), 1917; Andrei Kozhukhov, 1917; Ne nado krovi (Blood Need Not Be Spilled), 1917; Prokliatiye millioni (Cursed Millions), 1917; Satana likuyushchii (Satan Triumphant), 1917; Otets Sergii (Father Sergius), 1918; Taina korolevy (The Queen's Secret), 1919; Aelita, 1924; Yevo prizyv (His Call/Broken Chains), 1925; The Tailor From Torzhok, 1925; Protsess o troyokh millyonakh (The Three Million Case/Three Thieves), 1926; Sorok pervyi (The Forty-First), 1927; The Man From the Restaurant, 1927; Don Diego and Pelageya, 1927; Byeli orel (The White Eagle), 1928; Chiny i liudi (Ranks and People/An Hour With Chekhov), 1929; Prazdnik svyatovo Iorgena (The Holiday of St. Jorgen/The Feast of St. Jorgen), 1930; Tommy (Siberian Patrol), 1931; Marionettes, 1934; Bespridannitsa (Without Dowry), 1936; Seventh Grade, 1938 (for children); Salavat Yulayev, 1941; Nasreddin v Bukhare (Nasreddin in Bukhara/Adventures in Bokhara), 1943. *Films made in France and Germany (1919–1923) include*: L'Angoissante aventure; L'Amour et la loi; Pour une nuit d'amour; Justice d'abord (remake of Prokuror); Le Sens de la mort; L'Ombre du péché (or Les Ombres qui passent?); Der Liebe Pielgerfahrt; etc.

ABOUT: Birkos, A. S. Soviet Cinema, 1976; Leyda, J. Kino, 1960. *Periodicals*—Soviet Film 6 1981.

*PUDOVKIN, VSEVOLOD ILLARIANO-VICH (February 16, 1893—June 20, 1953), Soviet film director, scenarist, actor, and theorist, was born in Penza, a small town in the Volga region, where his father, of peasant origins, was a traveling salesman. Pudovkin was not involved in acting or filmmaking until relatively late in his life. He spent his formative years in Moscow, where his family moved after young Pudovkin turned four, and was about to complete his chemistry degree at Moscow University when World War I broke out and interrupted his studies.

During the war Pudovkin served at the front, was seriously wounded and captured by the Germans. He spent three years in a Pomeranian prisoner-of-war camp, where he undoubtedly heard about the revolutionary turmoil back home, the fall of the czar in February of 1917 and the fall of the provisional government in October. On his second try, Pudovkin escaped, and, eight months later, in December 1918, he was back in Moscow. After the war, Pudovkin completed his degree and worked as a chemist in a factory laboratory until Lenin's historic decree of August 27, 1919 nationalized the Russian film industry and mobilized the studios to serve the Red Army cause during the Russian Civil War. In 1920, at the age of twenty-seven, presumably after viewing D. W. Griffith's *Intolerance*, Pudovkin changed his whole life by enrolling in the newly formed State Film School (VGIK), the first institution of its kind in the world.

Soviet cinema was born during a turbulent era under the very difficult conditions of civil war and foreign intervention. It had to discover its social purpose and ideological identity quickly and with little past experience to fall back upon. Private filmmaking of the period, largely characterized by melodramatic despair and pessimism, had largely been done by emigrés who fled the revolution. During the summer of 1919, the Russian film industry was virtually nonexistent; only one theatre operated in Moscow and the St. Petersburg theatres had no films. The development of a Soviet cinema, adjusted to new socialist realities, was left, for the most part, to young filmmakers who were struggling for the independence of the new "toiler's republic" and who learned their trade by propagandizing the revolution and its promise of a better future for the working masses. Lenin proclaimed film "the most important art" and the revolutionary poet Vladimir Mayakovsky, leader of the avant-garde

VSEVOLOD PUDOVKIN

LEF group, called it "the director of progress." It was the visionary spirit of this volatile period, demanding social and political commitment, more than any artistic influence, that made Pudovkin realize the great potential of film to form and express the will of the masses.

Like most Soviet filmmakers, Pudovkin made his debut in agit-prop shorts that tried to explain what the Red Army was fighting for and why its popular cause had to be supported. His first acting role was as the Red Army commander in Ivan Perestiani's 1920, 600-meter-long *agitka* (agitational propaganda film), *V dni borbi* (*In Days of Struggle*), about the fighting on the Polish front. In the same year, along with the Latvian cameraman Edward Tisse (soon to be famous for his collaboration with Sergei Eisenstein), Pudovkin worked on the first Soviet full-length feature film, essentially an extended *agitka* entitled *Serp i molot* (*Hammer and Sickle*) and directed by Vladimir Gardin, head of the State Film School. Not only did Pudovkin serve as Gardin's assistant director, he also starred in the leading role as Andrei Krasov, the peasant proletarian turned Red Army soldier who, wounded, returns home from the front and exposes greedy kulaks hoarding grain while others starve. In 1921 Pudovkin again assisted Gardin on the theatrical dramatization of Jack London's novel *The Iron Heel*, which involved some filming, as well as on *Golod, golod, golod* (*Hunger, Hunger, Hunger*), an *agitka* about the famine in the Volga region also filmed by Tisse. While assisting Gardin on the script of the film adaptation of Anatoli Luncharsky's play *Sluzar i kanzler* (*Locksmith and Chancellor*), Pudovkin took a step toward inde-

°pə dŏf´ kĕn

pendence by joining Lev Kuleshov's pioneering workshop that laid the groundwork for constructivist Soviet filmmaking.

Under the influence of the much younger Kuleshov, Pudovkin admits in his autobiography, he became for the first time an impassioned adherent of film art, realizing its enormous possibilities. What Kuleshov taught his students (among them some of the greatest Soviet directors, from Eisenstein to Sergei Paradjanov) was the creation of "artificial landscape" through montage. By examining the narrative devices of Leo Tolstoy and those of American filmmakers, especially D. W. Griffith, Kuleshov came to regard montage as the basic means of filmmaking. He insisted that the ordering of film shots was far more important than their subject matter; the meaning and emotional valence of an image would be determined by its context, by the shots juxtaposed to it in the editing process.

Pudovkin remained with the struggling workshop for more than two years, learning the new techniques of editing, *mise-en-scène*, and film acting. The Kuleshov workshop often practiced making "films without film," the international blockade having created a drastic shortage of film stock in the Soviet Union. When the blockade ended, Kuleshov was permitted to make *Neobychaine prikluchania Mistera Vesta v stranie bolshevikov (The Extraordinary Adventures of Mister West in the Land of the Bolsheviks)* which came out in 1924, followed by *Luch smerti (The Death Ray)* in 1925. Pudovkin assisted him in a general capacity as scenarist, designer, and actor, playing the villain in both films (and nearly killing himself in a fall from a three-story building). The first film, a political satire mimicking American detective thrillers, was very successful. The film's protagonist Mr. West, an American senator and YMCA official, is purged of his ideological preconceptions about the Soviet Union after he is liberated by the Soviet police from a band of extortionists who pander to his wild illusions. But the film *The Death Ray*, in which Pudovkin was even more directly involved, was largely a flop, criticized for its lack of political perspective and excessive formalism. It both contributed to Kuleshov's personal difficulties, nearly causing his dismissal from the studio, and caused the breakup of the workshop. Kuleshov later called this prophetic science-fiction allegory, about a fascist-religious plot to steal a laser-like ray from the Soviets, a primer in the grammar of film.

Owing perhaps to the failure of *The Death Ray*, Pudovkin's own films developed subjectively, underscoring the importance of pathos. The spectator has to identify with the humanity and the realistic detail engendered and intensified by the film narrative. For Pudovkin, reality always outpaces its intellectualization. The objective of acting and filmmaking, he says in *Film Technique and Film Acting*, is the creation of "the whole life-image" that will encompass the living complexity of being in the world, which is beyond purely conceptual understanding: "The eager desire to discover, beyond each generalization, the living complexity of life, ever new-faceted, inevitably gives rise to a desire to embrace a maximum number of events in the work of art and consequently expand it over a maximum embrace of time and space." The problem of *The Death Ray* was not so much its "formalism," its semiological orientation, as the film's ideological critics have contended, as its entangled plot, for which Pudovkin was largely responsible. However, it is worth noting that this idealistic, pure pursuit of technical virtuosity led to an inward, psychological turn, not only in Pudovkin's own filmmaking, where it found its most profound expression, but in Soviet constructivist cinema as a whole, including Kuleshov's subsequent work.

Pudovkin's first two films—*Mekanika golovnovo mozga (Mechanics of the Brain)*, a documentary about Pavlov's famous experiments in conditioning animal behavior, which were begun in 1925, and a quickly shot, comic short *Shakmatnaya goriachka (Chess Fever)*, about a chess craze during the International Chess Tournament held in Moscow in November 1925—are Kuleshov-inspired. *Mechanics of the Brain* is widely acclaimed as the best scientific educational film of the silent era. It marked the beginning of Pudovkin's enduring partnership with cameraman Anatoly Golovnia, similar to that of Eisenstein and Tisse, Dovzhenko and Demitzky, and the Vertov brothers. A montage spectacle and a tribute to Kuleshov, *Chess Fever* relies on newsreel footage to tell the tale of a chess fanatic who abandons his fiancée (played by Pudovkin's wife, Anna Zentsova) for the love of the game. On the brink of committing suicide, the lovers are saved by the chess fever, which appears to be catching, and they are reunited by the international chess champion José Capablanca, who is made to "star" in the film by means of editing. What followed was Pudovkin's film triumph *Mother*, which, like Eisenstein's *Potemkin*, was made to commemorate the twentieth anniversary of the 1905 Revolution.

Eisenstein's *Potemkin* shocked the world in 1925; Pudovkin's *Mother*, a year later, demonstrated to the world the remarkable achievement and power of young Soviet cinema. "If Eisenstein's film is a pathetic shout," observed Leon Moussinac, "Pudovkin's is a lyrical song." Owing to the success of his earlier films, Pudovkin was asked by Mezrabpom-Rus (International Worker's Aid—Russian Art Collective) to take over from Yuri Zheliabutsky the adaptation of Gorki's novel *Mother*. The problem apparently was finding a suitable actress to play the title role and preserving Gorki's ideological texture without entirely rewriting the novel. Persuaded by his assistant director, Mihail Doller, for whom he had worked a year earlier as an actor in *Kripichki* (*Little Bricks*), Pudovkin used two accomplished actors from the Moscow Arts Theatre—Vera Baranvskaya as the mother and Nicolai Batalov as her Bolshevik son Pavel—both of whom were trained by Constantin Stanislavsky. A Kuleshov student, A. P. Christiakov, played the father, while Pudovkin himself, in one of his most memorable roles, played the police officer who interrogates the mother about her son's subversive activities after the strike.

This choice of character-actors represented a significant departure from Kuleshov's teaching in the direction of exploration of psychological motivations. For Kuleshov, the actor in film should be naturalized and reduced to signifying functions, existing only as an externalized iconographic complex, a "super-marionette." The choice of actors enhanced Pudovkin's intent to use montage as a commentary on the action, exposing its motives and psychological depth. In the film, the narrative exists for the purpose of clarifying what is hidden beneath it—the deeply integrated network of relations that constitutes human reality. It is the objective of montage to lay it bare and make it comprehensible. For, like Dziga Vertov, Pudovkin wanted to affect and profoundly alter the spectator's perception of space and time by means of the camera.

Gorki's *Mother*, written in exile in the United States, is based on events that occurred in the writer's hometown, Nizny Novogrod (now Gorki), in Krasnoye Sormovo, which, at the time of the failed insurrection of 1905, was one of the largest factories in Russia. The novel is widely recognized as a classic of revolutionary literature and is the prototype for Socialist Realism, the style that dominated the Russian cultural milieu during the Stalin era. It has been translated into more than twenty-eight different languages and has been adapted several times for the screen— never as successfully as by Pudovkin—as well as for the stage, notably by the German playwright Bertolt Brecht. Pudovkin's *Mother* refines Gorki's novel ideologically along the lines of post-revolutionary Bolshevik thinking. The substantial changes, however, are generally in the spirit of the work, even though Gorki himself was not wholly satisfied with the adaptation.

The differences between the film and the novel are significant. The novel is essentially pacifist with religious overtones. For the mother, the socialist struggle is the realization of Christian aspirations; even though not everyone agrees with her, the "world work" of her comrades is more important than what they call it. Gorki's novel is a plea for a better, more humanitarian, socialist future. It is meant to appeal to all who value the principles of social justice to join this international cause, whose triumph is inevitable. More specifically, it is a story of Pelegaya Vlasova, an aging, illiterate, working class woman, who is brutalized by her husband, and who (after his death in the first chapter) becomes involved in the subversive political work of her son Pavel and his young comrades. By the end, she is more than just a mother who cares about her children. She is also an agitator spreading the word, the socialist new world gospel. In effect, she becomes the revolutionary pieta, the maternal ideal representing the emerging political consciousness of Russia.

Pudovkin's *Mother*, relying on the script by Nathan Zarkhi, enlarges the role of the father to underscore the depth of social oppression, which is felt most critically when it is personally experienced. Significantly, Pudovkin does not stereotype the older Vlasov, in contrast to some of the blackguards who are used to break the strike. Vlasov is a misguided worker, a victim of social corruption, who joins the strikebreakers to support his drinking habit and is killed accidentally in self-defense by one of his son's friends. Pudovkin's young revolutionaries harbor guns, not just political literature. They are the self-sacrificing revolutionary vanguard leading the workers on. The worker's cause is just: from a trickle to a swelling river (Gorki's metaphors foreshadow Pudovkin's famous montage sequence), the film culminates in the May Day demonstration to free the imprisoned strike leaders, which is like the ice breaking on the river in springtime.

Pudovkin's *Mother* ends lyrically: Pelegava eases to the ground her dead son, shot down by the soldiers, and lifts the red banner to lead the proletarians aganst the cossack cavalry. The detailed close-ups of these final shots provide a startling stylistic contrast to a similar, more schematized montage sequence in Eisenstein's *Potemkin*; during the Odessa Steps episode, a mother carries her dead son up the stairs against the descending line of czarist soldiers who mechanically shoot down the fleeing crowd of demonstrators. Eisenstein admired the powerful, seemingly spontaneous intimacy of Pudovkin's shots, which overwhelmed the spectator with their lyrical pathos. *Mother* is heroic realism, perhaps a centaur—as the LEFist formalist critic, Victor Shklovsky, described it—half-prose and half-poetry, but one that was to dominate the Soviet screen with its passionate close-ups for some time to come.

Revolutionary spring, the awakening of consciousness into revolutionary insight, is the central motif of Pudovkin's *Mother*. It reappears again and again in the director's most captivating and successful films: *Konets Sankt Pyotersburga* (*The End of St. Petersburg*), and *Potomok Chingis-Khan* (*The Heir of Genghis Khan* or *Storm Over Asia*). In *The End of St. Petersburg*, which like Eisenstein's *October* was commissioned for the tenth anniversary of the Bolshevik Revolution, a young peasant from Penza (played by Ivan Chuvelov) becomes the vehicle for revolutionary enlightenment. Pudovkin's film personalizes the revolutionary struggle by a kind of a *bildungsroman* approach that traces the making of a Bolshevik, out of dim and humble peasant-working class origins to social illumination and revolutionary sacrifice. *The End of St. Petersburg*, initially entitled *Petersburg-Petrograd-Leningrad*, is also a story of the transformation of a city and the emergence of political consciousness in Russia, ending in rebirth in a new city, in a new socialist world. While Eisenstein's *October* is an anti-narrative epical history, a sociopolitical discussion of monumental proportions that would lead the director to dream of filming Marx's *Capital*, Pudovkin's film demonstrates how politically overwhelming "literary" persuasion can be. *The End of St. Petersburg* de-intellectualizes complex ideas and values by making them comprehensible to all.

Forced to migrate to the big city to find work after his wife dies in childbirth, the young peasant joins his kinsman (Christiakov), a communist steel worker in St. Petersburg who is organizing a strike against extending the work day. Unwelcome to the worker's wife (Baranovskaya), who sees him as one more mouth to feed with only a few potatoes left for her hungry daughter, the young man goes out looking for work; inadvertently, he joins the strike breakers and betrays a comrade to the factory managers. After the worker is arrested, the young man pleads for his release with the owner, only to end up in jail himself, charged with assault. When World War I breaks out, he is "volunteered" by the police to fight for the motherland and the czar and sent off to the front. The czar falls, but nothing changes. The provisional government continues the war. The young man helps his kinsman to persuade his fellow soldiers to go over to the Bolsheviks, then is wounded while storming the Winter Palace. The morning after, no longer in St. Petersburg but in "the city of Lenin," he is reconciled with the working-class mother, who dresses his wounds and offers him her potatoes. *The End of St. Petersburg* ends lyrically, with the humble-looking mother, with her potato can, walking through the empty ornate corridors of the Winter Palace and up the grand staircase to greet her Bolshevik husband.

The End of St. Petersburg, as Jay Leyda observed in *Kino: A History of the Russian and Soviet Film*, is really an indictment of war even more than it is a revolutionary film commemorating the Bolshevik triumph. Nationalistic bombast and chauvinism are exposed as cruel and cold-hearted sentiments, as a false ideological charade for which a bourgeois gentleman sacrifices little more than his foreign-made hat and cane, while a proletarian or a peasant is asked to give up his life. War is fought for profit, and for the frivolities of the decadent bourgeois class. Pudovkin's film treats the Bolshevik coup almost anticlimactically. It fades when it is contrasted with the powerful montage sequences at the front (the rain-drenched battle scenes, the muddy trenches flooded knee-deep, the frightened, huddling soldiers simply trying to survive) juxtaposed to the stock market fever, to the scenes of bourgeois gentlemen in bowler hats in ecstasies over stock prices hitting the roof.

In *The End of St. Petersburg* and *Storm Over Asia*, just as he did in *Mother*, Pudovkin tried to make his audience come to grips with the new socialist realities, to form the political consciousness of the post-revolutionary society. As portrayals of self-deception, sociopolitical naïveté and ideological abuse, all three films were meant to foster reconciliation in a deeply divided country that had been shaken by several revolutions, a civil war, and a famine in which more than five million people had died. But the technical and narrative means by which Pudovkin tried to dispel social illusions are far more mature in *The End of St. Petersburg* and *Storm Over Asia*, which have been overshadowed by the success of *Mother*. What is most appealing about Pudovkin's films is his ability to disclose the human character of ideological struggles.

Storm Over Asia, made without Zarkhi or Doller, and based on a brief scenario of fifteen typewritten pages (as opposed to sixty-two for *Mother*) by the poet and LEFist formalist critic Osip Brik, owes its title to its German editors, who tried to depoliticize the film by cutting the British Occupation Forces out of the picture. Originally titled *The Heir of Genghis Khan*, this anecdote about imperialism is deepened by its human interest. It is a story of a simple Mongolian hunter, Bair, whose revolutionary consciousness is raised after he had been conned out of a rare fox skin by a British fur trader, nearly executed by British Occupation Forces, and then duped into becoming a puppet ruler because of an amulet traced to Genghis Khan that never really belonged to him. Bair, marvelously interpreted by a Kuleshov-trained Mongolian actor, Valeri Inkizhinov, finally turns on his enemies. In the end, riding at the head of the Mongol horde, he unleashes a mighty storm that sweeps across Asia. What makes the film remarkable are not only its complex ironies about history but also its authentic portrayal of oriental life and traditions, never before presented in such realistic detail on the screen.

Soviet historians Yuri Vorontsov and Igor Rachuk in *The Phenomenon of the Soviet Cinema* blame the failure of Pudovkin's next three films, *Prostoi sluchai (A Simple Case)*, *Dezertir (Deserter)*, and *Pobeda (Victory)*, on LEFist aestheticism "borrowed from prerevolutionary decadent art." Just how decadent or unrealistic the LEFists actually were is open to question. The fact that the avant-garde represented the dominant tendency after the Revolution and produced works of enduring appeal becomes difficult to erase. Independent creative groups, such as the experimental Mayakovsky-led LEF or the Proletcult organizations, were disbanded by the Communist Party resolution of April 23, 1932. With the consolidation of political power under Joseph Stalin at the beginning of the era of five-year plans emphasizing the development of heavy industry, the cultural climate in the Soviet Union changed dramatically. Art had to toe the party line.

The Leninist call for partisan culture was reformulated into the party-sanctioned stylized canon of Socialist Realism, which became the yardstick for cultural production during the Stalin period. Formal experimentation became the equivalent of cultural decadence and Westernizing bourgeois sentiments. Many progressive Soviet artists were repressed, became creatively disillusioned, or were forced into exile; Pudovkin's actors, Vera Baranovskaya and Valeri Inkizhinov, eventually emigrated. Not only Pudovkin, but just about every major Soviet filmmaker (Kuleshov, Eisenstein, Vertov, Dovzhenko, not to mention other cultural workers), was accused of formalism and excessive LEFism. This is particularly ironic since the futurist LEFists were among the first and generally the most ardent supporters of Bolshevism throughout the twenties.

What may have contributed to some of the failures were not only the political changes but also the coming of sound. *A Simple Case*, shot without Golovnia (who did not like Alexander Rzheshevsky's impressionistic scenario) and begun in 1929 after Pudovkin's lecture tour to England and Holland, was to be a sound film entitled *Life's Very Good*. But technical difficulties made sound impossible. The film had to be reworked several times to make it more acceptable ideologically before it finally came out in 1932, four years after *Storm Over Asia*. In the end, Pudovkin settled on a story with which he was not entirely satisfied, about personal choices coming into conflict with social obligations. A Red Army commander, Pavel Langvoi, gives up his wife, Mashenka, to whom he owes his life, for another woman; in the end, he returns to her because of his comrades.

The *Deserter*, inspired by Pudovkin's visit to Hamburg in 1931, was affected by Hitler's putsch in January 1933. It was the director's first sound feature and was made four years after the manifesto calling for asynchronous use of sound, which he co-signed with Sergei Eisenstein and Grigori Alexandrov. It is a story of a Hamburg dock worker, Karl Renn, who, after "deserting" to the Soviet Union, has the choice of working freely in a Soviet factory or returning home to struggle agains the reactionaries. *Victory*, initially *The Happiest One*, is an account of a heroic Soviet mother who, after one of her sons dies in an attempt to circle the globe, sends another on his "Victory" flight. The film had to be completed by Doller, after an automobile accident that seriously injured Pudovkin and killed his passenger, the scenarist Natan Zarkhi.

Minin and Pozharsky and *Suvorov* were Pudovkin's contributions to the patriotic historical genre that dominated Soviet cinematography during the late thirties and forties. These years saw Eisenstein's *Alexander Nevksy*, Dovzhenko's *Shchors*, Petrov's *Peter the First*, Shevchenko's *Bogdan Khmelnitsky*. In contrast to the films of the twenties, which immersed themselves in contemporary history by celebrating the triumph of the Revolution and its accomplishments, the historical sagas valorized the past. History was displaced into edifying memories intended to arouse patriotism. "He who attacks Russia," warns Pudovkin's Suvorov, "will find his tomb!" The threat of Nazi invasion was imminent. History was mustered as an emotional moral commentary that assured Soviet audiences of the inevitable triumph over the enemy.

In contrast to Eisenstein's *Alexander Nevsky*, which allegorically expresses its anti-fascist sympathies, Pudovkin's historical films are intensely felt period pieces. *Minin and Pozharsky*, based on a scenario by Victor Shklovsky, is a historically matter-of-fact portrayal of Moscovite life at the beginning of the seventeenth century during the "Time of Troubles" after the death of Ivan the Terrible. Prince Pozharsky and Kuzma Minin gather resistance forces to defend Russia against the invading Poles who take Moscow, and the Swedes who threaten the Baltic coast. After the initial loss during the week before Easter 1611 and the burning of Moscow by the Poles, Minin and Pozharsky regroup to defeat the Poles near Moscow, on August 24–25, 1612. Minin, a Novogrod butcher, becomes the real popular hero, commanding all to vanquish the invaders and not, as Pozharsky wishes, to die honorably for the country. For all its historical accuracy, the film is excessively didactic and "monumental."

Pudovkin's very successful *Suvorov*, which won the Stalin Prize in 1941, is a more human portrayal of history than either *Alexander Nevsky* or *Minin and Pozharsky*. It shows the legendary Russian military hero as an ordinary person. The simple-mannered, somewhat eccentric general—interpreted by Nikolai Konstantinovich Cherkasov, who was over sixty at the time—has no use for superficial aristocratic formalities, hates Prussian military discipline, and perfers to live like a common soldier. The film encompasses Suvorov's later years, after the death of Catherine the Great, beginning after his triumph in Warsaw and for the most part concentrating on his Italian and Swiss campaigns against the French revolutionary armies. With the exception of Suvorov's crossing of the Alps and final victory, Pudovkin eliminates spectacular battle scenes and develops the emotional make-up of the general's character, which was said to resemble the director's own. After *Suvorov*, Pudovkin began working on another film about a heroic figure, *Admiral Nakhimov*, about the brilliant tactician who, during the Crimean War, defended Sevastopol to the death. But the film was put aside because of the war.

On June 22, 1941, Hitler's army invaded Soviet territory, and the Soviet film industry once again was mobilized for the purposes of war reportage and propaganda. According to Soviet film historian Sergei Drobashenko, within three weeks after the German attack, sixteen film crews with eighty-nine filmmakers were operating at the front. Pudovkin worked on war cinejournals which were modeled on post-revolutionary *agitkas*; seven were made between September 2 and December 5, 1941 under the general title, *The Victory Is Ours*. The sixth, and one of the most effective, was Pudovkin's contribution, *Pir v Jermunkie* (*The Feast at Jirmunka*) about a peasant woman, Prascovia, who sacrifices herself to poison German soldiers. According to his biographer A. Mariamov, after the evacuation of the Moscow and Leningrad film studios to Alma Ata, Pudovkin made another cine-journal, *Ubitsy vykhodiat na dorogu* (*The Murderers are on the Way*), subtitled "The Face of Fascism," based on a dramatic sketch by Bertolt Brecht. However, the film was never publicly released because it was deemed inadequate as war propaganda. It empathized with the victims of the Nazi terror without really explaining the roots of fascism. *V imia rodiny* (*In the Name of the Fatherland*), about a woman who is rescued by Soviet soldiers led by her fiancé after she has fallen into the hands of the SS, was hastily made and is regarded as Pudovkin's least memorable film, in spite of its immediate popularity when it opened July 20, 1943. What attracted Pudovkin to the source, Konstantin Simonov's play *The Russian People*, was its portrayal of the struggle and the personal sacrifices of ordinary men and women.

After the war, Pudovkin returned to *Admiral Nakhimov*. The task of the Soviet film industry at the time was defined by Stalin: quality not quantity, fewer films but all masterpieces. This in practice meant that the filmmaker had to adhere to the principles of Socialist Realism to win the Stalin prize and thereby legitimate his film's ideological and cultural worth. When Pudovkin's film about the legendary military hero who opposed the French, British and Turkish forces at Sevastopol first came out, it was severely criticized by the Communist Party resolution of September 4, 1946, for historical inaccuracies. The initial version of the film apparently had too many balls and dances and not enough battle scenes. The substantial revision met with unanimous critical success and won the Stalin prize. *The Return of Vasily Bortnikov*, based on Galina Nikolaievna's popular novel *The Harvest*, is, on the one hand, about a soldier who returns from the front after being taken for dead to find his wife remarried to another man; and, on the other, a propaganda piece for the mechanization of the countryside. Three months after the film's release, on June 20, 1953, Pudovkin died of a heart attack while vacationing on the Baltic coast near Riga.

Mother, The End of St. Petersburg, and *Storm Over Asia* remain Pudovkin's most widely acknowledged classics, but his entire film career is an enduring monument to realism in cinema. His theoretical essays, collected in *Film Technique and Film Acting*, are notable for their clarity and infectious enthusiasm. He was awarded the Order of Lenin, his country's highest honor, in 1935 and in 1953.

—M.S.

FILMS: Shakmatnaya goriachka (Chess Fever), 1925; Mekhanika golovnovo mozga (Mechanics of the

Brain), 1926; Mat (Mother), 1926; Konyets Sankt
Pyoterburga (The End of St. Petersburg), 1927; Potomok Chingis-Khan (Storm Over Asia or The Heir of
Genghis Khan), 1928; Prostoi sluchai (A Simple Case)
or Ochen khorosho zhevyotsa (Life Is Very Good),
1932; Dezertir (Deserter), 1933; (with Mikhail Doller)
Pobedal (Victory), 1938; (with Mikhail Doller) Minin
and Pozharsky, 1939; (with Esther Shub) Kino sa XX
let (Twenty Years of Film), 1940; (with Mikhail Doller) Suvorov, 1940; Pir v Jirmukie (The Feast at Jirmunka) *episode in* The Victory Is Ours, 1941; (codirector) Ubitsy vykhodiat na dorogu (The Murderers
Are on the Way), subtitled "Litso Fashizma" ("The
Face of Fascism"), 1942; (with Dimitri Vasiliev) Vo
imya rodiny (In the Name of the Fatherland), 1943;
Admiral Nakhimov, 1946; (with Sergei Yutkevich and
Alexander Ptushko) Tri Vstrechi (Three Encounters),
1948; (with Dmitri Vasiliev) Zhukovsky, 1950; Voz-
vrashchenie Vasilia Bortnikova (The Return of Vasily
Bortnikov), 1953.

ABOUT: Dart, P. Pudovkin's Films and Film Theory,
1974; Dobrashenko, S.V. Dokumientalnaya Kinemato-
gafia. Ocherki Istori Sovietskovo Kino. Vol. 2, 1959;
Leyda, J. Kino: A History of the Russian and Soviet
Film, 1983; Mariamov, A. Narodnyi Artist SSSR:
Vsevolod Pudovkin, 1952; Pudovkin, V. I. Film Tech-
nique and Film Acting, 1960; Schnitzer, L. and J. Pou-
dovkine, 1966; Schnitzer, L. and J. Cinema in
Revolution, 1973; Schnitzer, L. and J. Histoire du
Cinéma Sovietique, 1979; Vorontsov, Y. and Rachuk,
I. The Phenomenon of the Soviet Cinema, 1980.
Periodicals—Cahiers du Cinéma (special issue) Au-
gust–September 1953; Cinéma (France) June 1972; Le
Cinéma Pratique September–October 1966, November–December 1966, March 1967; Cinemage May
1955; L'Écran Français September 11, 1950;
Esthétique July–August 1963; Film und Fernsehen
May 1974, June 1974, April 1977; Films in Review August–September 1953; Hound and Horn April–June
1933; Image et son October 1953; Iskusstvo Kino (special issue) February 1973; Journal of Aesthetic Education No. 2, 1979; Journal of Popular Film and
Television Summer 1981; Les Lettres Françaises July
9, 1953; Revue du Cinéma December 1, 1931; Sight
and Sound Summer 1933, November 1948, October–
December 1953.

*RAIZMAN, YULI (YAKOVLEVICH) (December 2, 1903–   ), Soviet director, producer,
and scenarist, was born in Moscow and studied
literature at Moscow University. Graduating in
1924, he began his career as a literary consultant
at the Mezhrabpom studios. He spent nearly a
year in this capacity, mostly reading scripts—a
useful beginning for a director who would later
be known for the quality of his scenarios.

In 1925 Mezhrabpom assigned Raizman as assistant to Konstantin Eggert on *Medvezhya
svadba* (*The Bear's Wedding*). The same year
Raizman played a small role (as the assistant

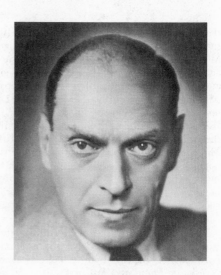

YULI RAIZMAN

pharmacist) in Pudovkin's witty two-reeler
Shakhmatnaya goryachka (*Chess Fever*).

Raizman's mentor was not Eggert, with whom
his relations were difficult, but the veteran
Yakov Protazanov. He assisted Protazanov on
Protsess o tryokh millyonakh (*The Three Million
Case*, 1926), a popular comedy, and on *Sorok
pervyi* (*The Forty-First*, 1926), shot partly on location in Turkestan. The heroine is a soldier of
the Red Army—a sharpshooter who falls in love
with an enemy officer before she dutifully
makes him the forty-first victim of her marks-
manship. When Vera Maretskaya fell ill, Raizman had to find an immediate replacement. He
discovered Ada Voitsik in a student film, and under Protazanov's direction this unknown actress
gave a performance of disturbing intensity that
helped to make the picture an international success.

Raizman admired Protazanov as "a complete
professional"—a term that has since been applied to Raizman himself. He says of Protazanov
that "the actors were always the most important
element for him. He advised me to expect to
have to compromise on many things in filmmaking, but never to begin shooting until I was satisfied that the actors understood their roles."

It was Protazanov who gave Raizman his
chance as a director. When the young assistant
became dissatisfied with his situation at
Mezhrabpom, Protazanov handed him a project
that he himself had agreed to direct for Gosvoyenkino (State Army Films), a studio which
up to that time had produced nothing of distinction. Raizman's debut film was no exception. A
modest comedy revolving around a trial, *Kpyr*

(*The Circle/The Ring,* 1927), codirected by A. Gavronsky, did however serve as Raizman's introduction to Sergei Yermolinsky, his scenarist on this and the three films that followed.

Kpyr went almost unnoticed by the critics; not so Raizman's second film for Gosvoyenkino, *Katorga* (*Penal Servitude,* 1928). Scripted by Yermolinsky and photographed by Leonid Kosmatov, it is a grim study of a brutal czarist prison camp for political offenders in Siberia, climaxing in an unsuccessful revolt against the sadistic warden. This film, as Galina Dolmatovskaya writes in *Who's Who in Soviet Cinema,* "showed that Raizman was capable of using grotesque perspective, sharp transitions in editing, and shot compositions similar to paintings—all the refinements of montage cinema. Nevertheless Raizman, above all a portrait artist, did not lose his bearings in this metaphorically intense work. He closely examined the figure of the prison warden . . . , seeking to show social evil through his physical deformity and his malicious, boarish eyes." Contemporary party hacks attacked the film for its "pessimism" and "expressionism," but it was championed by the Moscow branch of the Society of Political Exiles as a highly realistic portrayal of conditions in the czarist camps.

A later critic, John Gillett, allowed that "the 'expressionism' and 'pessimism' are certainly there in parts (the first manifested in the strongly German-influenced lighting of the prison, the latter in the miserable, tormented lot of the political prisoners) but nowadays one also sees influences from the Eccentric movement of the time . . . which gives the film a strangely ambiguous colouring. . . . Raizman, in fact, adopts an extremely stylised method to contrast the scenes with the prisoners (notably the scary off-screen riot) and those concerning the warden and his [dandified] entourage. . . . He uses a mixture of satire and caricature which is both venomous and non-naturalistic, requiring his actors to preen and gesticulate in a broad parody of old vaudeville styles. But such is the strength of the film's concept that it accommodates all these disparate elements, rising to truly surreal flights of fancy in the concluding passages, with the advancing revolutionary army (seen only as a whirl of horses, harness, and wheels) intercut with the last drunken contortions of the dinner party and ending with slowed-down motion and freeze frames—a gesture which suddenly advances the film across fifty years to the present age."

Raizman moved on to the Vostok-kino studios for his next picture, *Zemlya zhazhdyot* (*The Earth Thirsts,* 1930), shot by Kosmatov in the Kara Kum desert of the Turkmen Republic in Central Asia. By this time the doctrine of Socialist Realism had gained its stranglehold on the Soviet cinema—formal experiment was banned and plots had to conform rigidly to the formula demanding "optimistic" stories about the class struggle. Thus, *Zemlya zhazhdyot* depicts the efforts of a team of Komsomols (members of a Communist youth organization) to bring the benefits of irrigation to a remote village, despite the passivity of the peasants, the opposition of a feudal landlord, and the malevolence of nature. This early "docudrama" had the distinction of being the first Soviet sound film. Released silent in 1930, it was reissued in 1931 with a synchronized soundtrack of music and background noises.

Expressing a suitably romantic view of Soviet technology and progress and eschewing the frowned-upon montage experiments of *Katorga,* this film firmly established Raizman's reputation with the Party critics. Like all his films since, however, it showed that he would surrender no more to expediency than he must. Its visual compensations include bravura set pieces of railroads and a sandstorm, and as Dolmatovskaya writes, "the scenes where water flows onto parched earth have become models of their type." The picture also demonstrates Raizman's growing narrative fluency and his gift for characterization. According to N. Zorkaya, "the human image always retains its undisputed primacy for Raizman. . . . Human character is the point of departure into life and into time."

Raizman's last collaboration with Yermolinsky, a short feature called *Rasskaz oh Umare Hapsoko* (*The Story of Omar Hapsoko*), was released in 1932 but had perhaps been made earlier, since this village anecdote showed some of the visual stylization of *Katorga.* At any rate, it did not prevent Raizman's move to the major studio, Mosfilm, where he has made most of his subsequent films.

His first assignment at Mosfilm—and his first talkie—was *Lyotchiki* (*Flyers/The Aviators,* 1935). Intended as propaganda for the government's plans to expand and modernize the Soviet air force, it is set in a pilot training school. It follows the fortunes of a group of trainees—women as well as men—and is thus able to incorporate a triangular romance involving two young would-be flyers and an older instructor. The unit's commander is played by Boris Shchukin in his first screen role.

Lyotchiki was the first in a whole string of Soviet aviation dramas, most of them inferior imitations showing little of Raizman's grasp of characterization and narrative tension. John Gillett wrote that he "virtually transforms a routine moralistic tract . . . into a lyrical celebration of flying. Amazing, too, how he employs a Hawks-like camera style to equate movement with character; thus, the stern but kindly commander is accompanied by slow, deliberate tracking shots across the tarmac, while the headstrong young pilot is characterised by faster movements in the opposite direction, culminating in a wild, virtuoso run across the entire length of the airport." Gillett attributes the movie's excellence partly to the laconic script by Alexander Macheret and Yuri Olesha. According to Jay Leyda an even more eminent writer, Isaac Babel, had a hand in the final draft, taking his salary but no credit—a choice he had cause to regret when the film became a success.

A central concern in Raizman's work has been the conflict between love and duty, and this theme emerged powerfully in *Poslednaya noch* (*The Last Night,* 1937), based on Yevgeney Gabrilovich's story "Quiet Brovkin." Gabrilovich, an old schoolfriend of Raizman's, gave up his job as a journalist to collaborate with the director on the script, beginning a long if intermittent partnership that was very fruitful for them both. Dmitri Vasiliev has been credited variously as associate director and as codirector of the film, though it is obviously Raizman's picture.

The Last Night is a broad and teeming canvas of life in Bryansk on the eve of the 1917 Revolution, with the trivial concerns and elegant parties of the rich set off against bitter poverty and injustice, ominous rumors, and mounting insurrection. These contrasts are summed up in a moving *Romeo and Juliet* affair between an industrialist's daughter and the son of a worker. The film ends with a famous sequence in a dark railroad station. A train packed with soldiers steams in, and no one knows whether they have joined the Revolution or come to crush it until, in a "ludicrous yet sublime tailpiece," an old woman totters forward to ask.

John Gillett praised the movie for its "flow of small character sketches" and "the onward drive of the narrative," sustained by a camera style of "almost Ophuls-like mobility, tracking briskly through battle-torn streets and round corners and alleys. Also embedded in the almost continuous flow of movement is a faintly satirical tone centering on the exploits of the bombastic young Bolshevik who always seems to be doing the 'right' things at the wrong time. . . . It is Raizman's willingness to combine elements of a political adventure story and a family chronicle with the flights of fancy of the conclusion which gives the film its undeniable appeal." Some critics have gone further, claiming this as Raizman's masterpiece.

Podnyataya tzelina (*Virgin Soil Upturned,* 1940) was based on the first part of Sholokov's massive novel about the struggle (against the ruthless opposition of evil *kulaks*) to turn a Cossack village into an agricultural collective. Adapted by Sholokov and Raizman's old collaborator Sergei Yermolinsky, this sprawling film was excellently photographed by Leonid Kosmatov.

It was followed by one of the most popular of Raizman's films, *Mashenka* (1942), another collaboration with Gabrilovich and another study of the conflict between love and duty. As the unassuming telegraph operator Mashenka, Valentina Karavayeva scored an international success. Her portrayal "of a girl at the height of an early and happy love" seemed to a reviewer in the London *Times* "delightfully fresh in line and colour."

Mashenka has to contend with the temporary disaffection of the handsome mechanic Alyosha (Mikhail Kuznetsov), and then both face the greater threat of the war with Finland, which turns Masha into a front-line nurse and Alyosha into a soldier. They part and meet again on the snowy battlefields of Finland, and the film ends with another farewell that reminded one critic of Borzage in its poignancy. The Russian audience took *Mashenka* to its bosom, and foreign critics praised its "terrifying battle scenes" and relative freedom from sloganizing. *Mashenka* was first released on March 31, 1942, nine months after Hitler invaded the USSR; it seems that in some versions of the picture, the battles are presented as being in defense of the homeland against the Germans, rather than against the Finns.

By this time the Soviet film industry, dispersed and undermanned as a result of the invasion, was mobilizing its resources to fight the propaganda war. Sergei Gerasimov, now in charge of the Central Documentary Filmstudios in Moscow, recruited prominent feature directors to make documentaries like Raizman's *Za pneremirie c Finlandia* (*Towards an Armistice With Finland,* 1944).

In 1945 Raizman was put in command of the more than forty cameramen (including Roman Karmen) who covered the battle for Berlin. He set out to edit the enormous footage that resulted "so that spectators would sense what we had seen, thought, and understood out there at the front," also making ironic use of captured footage showing the city in its Nazi heyday. Assisted by Yelizaveta Svilova and Nikolai Shpikovsky, Raizman cut the film into shape in sixteen days. The result was *Berlin* (1945, 69 minutes), somewhat marred by an inflated commentary but otherwise universally admired as one of the most impressive of the Russian war documentaries. In between these two documentaries, Raizman made a feature film, *Nebo Moskvy (Moscow Sky,* 1944), a fulsome tribute to the Soviet fighter pilots who defended Moscow against the Luftwaffe.

Raizman's first postwar film was *Poezd idet na Vostok (The Train Goes East,* 1947). A sort of travelogue of the Soviet Union from Vladivostok to Moscow, it was built around a story reminiscent of American screwball comedies of the 1930s. Soviet critics who caught the allusion frowned on this aping of Western film models; the others were simply nonplussed. As a result, the movie received only limited distribution, while there is no clear evidence that *Rainis,* made in 1949 at the Riga studios, was ever released at all.

Between the end of the war and Stalin's death in 1953, political control of the cinema tightened convulsively as the dictator sank deeper into paranoia. One film after another was eviscerated or banned, and production declined until in 1950 only six features were completed. Raizman had survived thus far by toeing the party line in terms of plot and style, while ameliorating his Socialist Realism with romance, humor, and a generous humanism. In the dark days of the early 1950s, even these "cosmopolitan" elements had to go.

Back at Mosfilm by 1951, Raizman directed the Soviet "super-production" *Kavaler Zolotoi Zvezdy (Cavalier of the Golden Star,* 1951), an almost unrelieved act of homage to the Stalinist "cult of personality." Sergei Bondarchuk, in his first major screen role, stars as a war hero who returns to his native village as head of the local *kolkhoz,* unites all the other agricultural collectives in the region, and builds an electrical power plant in the bargain. *Kavaler* was marred by such technological uncertainties as tractors apparently plugged into the new power plant by long cables. All the same, Georges Sadoul considered that Raizman's "very beautiful imagery" gave the movie "a certain sensitivity." It was the director's first color film.

The gradual loosening of controls that followed Stalin's death is already evident in *Vrok zhizni (A Lesson in Life/Conflict,* 1955). Dealing with a group of young people working on a new construction project, it views them less as propaganda fodder than as idealistic but fallible human beings. The story centers on an impetuous and arrogant engineer who alienates his colleagues and his dreamy young wife until he learns a lesson in humility and social responsibility. Reuniting Raizman with his friend and fa-

vorite scriptwriter Yevgeny Gabrilovich after a separation of thirteen years, the film shows much of the romanticism tempered by shrewd observation that had distinguished their earlier collaborations.

Gabrilovich scripted most of Raizman's subsequent films up to 1977, beginning with *Kommunist (The Communist,* 1957). This is a tribute to a humble Party member, Vassili Gubanov (Yevgeny Urbansky), who joins in the construction of a power plant just after the revolution and eventually sacrifices his life to the task. Raizman and Gabrilovich characteristically humanize their hero by allowing him a passionate, lyrical, but after all illicit relationship with the wife of a saboteur.

Intense controversy greeted their next film, *A esli eto lyubov (Can This Be Love?,* 1961), which shows how bigotry and self-righteousness destroy the love between two teenagers, driving the girl to attempt suicide. A program note for the British National Film Theatre describes this as Raizman's best black-and-white 'scope film, saying that he "skilfully uses the wide expanses of the tenement courtyard as a stage for the conflict between the lovers and their prying neighbours. Sharply acted and edited . . . [the film] moves inexorably towards its disturbing climax."

Though the movie was hotly debated and construed in some quarters as an attack on established moral values, Raizman seems to have survived unscathed. In fact, here as elsewhere, he takes care to offer his social criticisms within an acceptable context, attacking individual or group failings on the grounds that they might impede the progress or well-being of Soviet society in general.

In this way he was able to criticize the Soviet bureaucracy in *Tvoy sovremennik (Your Contemporary,* 1967), a two-part, 140-minute sequel to *Kommunist* centering on Vassili Gubanov's son. As an elderly and distinguished engineer, he goes to Moscow to champion a new liquid fuel but runs up against an arrogant and reactionary bureaucracy. A secondary theme concerns the protagonist's anxieties over his own son, who is in love with an unmarried mother. The film conveys a strong sense of everyday life in Moscow and contrasts the robust optimism of one generation with the complex social and political dilemmas of the next. Nikolai Plotnikov, who plays Gubanov, was chosen as best actor of the year at Karlovy Vary in 1968.

From *The Last Night* onwards, Raizman has shown a sympathy with the aspirations of women that is rare in the Soviet cinema. In *Strannaya zhenshchina (A Strange Woman,* 1977), the heroine Zhenya is a law consultant married to a diplomat. She suddenly abandons the comforts and rewards of her affluent life—including her children—to pursue a romantic love affair. When this sours she takes a job in a small town, continuing her quest for self-realization.

Another two-part film, running 150 minutes, this was the last of Raizman's fruitful collaborations with Yevgeny Gabrilovich. There was much praise for Irina Kupchenko's performance in the lead, which movingly conveyed both the determination and the uncertainties of this "strange" woman. A writer in the *Economist* (October 13, 1984) found the movie "full of sharp character vignettes. It covers a wide range of sexual politics, played against detailed backgrounds of life in city offices and quiet country backwaters."

This was followed by one of the most widely distributed and discussed of all Raizman's films, *Chastnaya zhizn* (*Private Life,* 1982). Coscripted by the director and "Anatole Grebnev" (Mikhail Ulyanov), it concerns a powerful factory executive who is suddenly forced into early retirement and faced with the task of rebuilding his relationships with family and friends whom, he discovers, he scarcely knows. Janet Maslin wrote that Raizman "presents these events with a gentle knowingness, and directs them in a plain and forthright style. . . . Structurally, the film is a series of encounters that are individually compelling, perhaps more so than the conclusion towards which they build. . . . In appearance, the film seems almost like a documentary, with street and indoor settings . . . that reveal much about how life must be conducted in these places." *Chastnaya zhizn* was nominated for an Oscar as best foreign film, the first such honor for Raizman in almost sixty years of filmmaking.

The director was eighty-one years old by the time he completed his next picture, *Vremya zhelanii* (*A Tale of Wishes,* 1984). It is another portrait of a woman—a member of the "special generation" that grew up in a society deeply scarred by the excesses of Stalinism and the losses of war. We first meet Svetlana (Vera Alentova) at a summer resort where she is scouting for a suitable husband. Finding nothing more exciting than a minor civil servant, she applies her skill and determination to molding his career in the way she wants it to go. "Although full of humour," wrote the *Economist*'s critic, "it is not a pretty picture. It is a portrait of a person who has seen it all and survived. So, in a different way, has Raizman."

The oldest working director in the Soviet Union, Raizman is indeed a survivor, having weathered all the aesthetic and political changes and reversals inflicted on the Soviet film indus-

try over seven decades. He has retrenched when he had to, moved forward when he could, and never lost his candor, courage, and humanism. If he has escaped the martyrdom that befell some of his great contemporaries, he has also failed to equal their fame, but is now the subject of an increasingly respectful reappraisal.

In their introduction to the major Raizman retrospective at the British National Film Theatre in 1984, John Gillett and Ian Christie wrote that, in collaboration with Gabrilovich, Raizman "developed a synthetic 'realism' that admits both humour *and* heroism. Viewing the films for this season, we have been struck by the consistency of Raizman's concerns throughout his long career. . . . The tension between private needs and public duties is ever-present for his characters. . . . Raizman remains committed to posing questions about Soviet society, the quality of life it makes possible and the extent to which the ideals of October [1917] are still at work in it." Georges Sadoul considered that Raizman is, "with Frank Borzage, one of those rare filmmakers who have been able to communicate effectively and movingly the warmth and empathy of human love. . . . Since he avoided fashionable effects it is perhaps his restrained, economical style that led to his being underestimated."

Raizman supervises the Third Production Group at Mosfilm. The Group produces seven or eight films a year, and includes such rising young directors as Vadim Abdrashitov, for whom Raizman nurses high hopes. Raizman himself is said to be a perfectionist on set; Yevgeny Gabrilovich said that he was "difficult" but always rewarding to work with. The director lives in a Moscow apartment and, according to Galina Dolmatovskaya, "barely changes with the years: he is thin and always elegant, with a spritely gait, a firm gaze, and eyes that have not lost their color with time."

FILMS: (with A. Gavronsky) Kpyr (The Circle/The Ring), 1927; Katorga (Penal Servitude/Forced Labor), 1928; Zemlya zhazhdyot (The Earth Thirsts), 1930 (sound version, 1931); Rasskaz ob Umare Hapsoko (The Story of Omar Hapsoko), 1932 (short); Lyotchiki (Flyers/The Aviators), 1935; Poslednaya noch (The Last Night), 1937; Podnyataya tzelina (Virgin Soil Upturned), 1940; Mashenka, 1942; Za pneremirie c Finlandia (Towards an Armistice With Finland), 1944 (documentary); Nebo Moskvy (Moscow Sky/Moscow Nights), 1944; Berlin/The Fall of Berlin, 1945 (documentary); Poezd idet na Vostok (The Train Goes East), 1947; Rainis, 1949; Kavaler Zolotoi Zvezdy (Cavalier of the Golden Star/Dream of a Cossack), 1951; Vrok zhizni (A Lesson in Life/Conflict), 1955; Kommunist (The Communist), 1957; A esli eto lyubov? (Can This Be Love?), 1961; Tvoy sovremennik (Your Contemporary), 1967; Visit vezhlivosti (A Courtesy Call), 1973;

Strannaya zhenshchina (A Strange Woman), 1977; Chastnaya zhizn (Private Life), 1982; Vremya zhelanii (A Tale of Wishes), 1984.

ABOUT: Birkos, A. Soviet Cinema, 1976; Gerasimov, S. and others. Il mestiere di regista, 1954 (Italian); Leyda, J. Kino, 1960; Leyda, J. Voices of Film Experience, 1977; Liehm, M. and A. J. The Most Important Art, 1977; Raizman, Y. Vchera i segodna rasskaz o tvorcheskom puti narodnogo artista, 1949 (autobiography); Who's Who in Soviet Cinema, 1978. *Periodicals*—Cinéma (France) May 1983; Economist October 13, 1984; Film World April–June 1969; Iskusstvo Kino 1 and 2 1967, December 1973, February 1979; National Film Theatre (Britain) Booklet October–November 1984; Soviet Film 1 1974.

RAPPER, IRVING (1898–), American director, was born in London, England. According to William R. Meyer in *Warner Brothers Directors*, he went to the United States after World War I to study law at New York University, though other sources claim that he was in America from the age of eight. At any rate, it seems clear that he joined the Washington Square Players as a stage director while still a student at NYU, and then "got caught up in the flourish of theatrical activity in the Manhattan of the 1920s." Interviewed by James Bawden in *Classic Images* (June 1982), he said he was "a struggling actor and not a very good one at that" before becoming "Gilbert Miller's protegé" and a Broadway director.

Meyer says that Rapper first went to Hollywood in 1929, assisting Robert Florey on *Hole in the Wall* for Paramount. He returned in 1933 "during a lull on Broadway called the Depression," when MGM hired him as dialogue director on Robert Leonard's *Dancing Lady*, with Joan Crawford. After that Rapper returned to Broadway for a few more years, until the success of a stage thriller called *Crime* secured him a contract with Warner Brothers. Beginning in 1936, Rapper was a dialogue director there for five years, coaching actors in the delivery of their lines and often the execution of movement during both rehearsals and filming. Dialogue directors were much in demand during the early years of sound, when filmmakers trained in the silents lacked experience of the spoken word.

As he told James Bawden, Rapper's "guide and mentor" during those early years at Warners was Michael Curtiz: "By working so closely with him I received a crash course in film directing." Rapper served Curtiz as dialogue director on *The Walking Dead* (1936), *Kid Galahad* (1937), and *The Private Lives of Elizabeth and Essex* (1939), among other films. He also worked with

IRVING RAPPER

William Dieterle on *The Story of Louis Pasteur* (1936) and several other Warner biopics, with Anatole Litvak (*All This and Heaven Too*, 1940), and Curtis Bernhardt. "Many of these pictures," he says, "were made for the producer Henry Blanke, the most sympathetic, versatile and intelligent producer at Warners." And these films "were made with such care that a dialogue director really was a necessity so the actors could come on the floor thoroughly prepared. They really need dialogue directors today—it's a poor economy not to have them."

By 1938 Warners had decided that Rapper was ready to direct films of his own. However, he was at first offered nothing but "really bad 'B' pictures," and astonished his colleagues by turning them down. "I just kept doing dialogue and waiting my turn." He saw his opportunity with *Shining Victory* (1941), a modest melodrama adapted from a play by A. J. Cronin. James Stephenson plays an ambitious and sexist psychobiologist pursuing his researches in a Scottish sanatorium. Geraldine Fitzgerald, as his unwelcome assistant, wins his reluctant admiration and his heart before sacrificing her life to save his research notes from a fire set by a jealous rival (Barbara O'Neil). The solid cast also included Donald Crisp and Sig Ruman, and Bette Davis, a friend of Rapper's since *Kid Galahad,* made an uncredited walk-on appearance as a nurse.

Though he seems to have relinquished the practice later, Rapper says in *The Celluloid Muse* that he preplanned *Shining Victory* and other early pictures: "I'd plot out the opening and closing of a sequence, and its highest dramatic point. . . . I'd sometimes begin with fully detailed plans and sketches, but then Bette or someone would yell out, 'Why did you do that?' and I'd throw them all away. I would improvise a good deal, but I always followed the scripts I was given to the letter. At Warners they would give you a finished script, and if you refused to do it, you were out on suspension." Rapper reportedly collected ten suspensions in that way at Warners: "I would refuse, say, a crime picture I wouldn't even know how to begin, or some Nazi picture when I thought people were tired of them, or nonliterate scripts."

Shining Victory was moderately well received, though some found it pedestrian, and Rapper had a critical and commercial success with his second feature, a nostalgic piece of Americana called *One Foot in Heaven* (1941), assigned to him when Anatole Litvak was taken off the film. Scripted by Casey Robinson, it deals with the vicissitudes of thirty years in the life of a hard-up Methodist minister (Fredric March) and his wife (Martha Scott). Bosley Crowther found it "cheerful and warmly compassionate . . . one of the finest pictures of the year," and Howard Barnes thought that the "challenging subject matter has been handled with great skill and authority." The British critic C. A. Lejeune liked its "human and salty" humor and put it "very high up" on her list of favorite movies—"special films, not necessarily great or celebrated, which . . . are remembered with a glow when better films have been forgotten." It was nominated for an Oscar as best picture.

Barbara Stanwyck starred in Rapper's next film, *The Gay Sisters* (1942). She plays one of three impoverished heiresses struggling through years of litigation in an attempt to gain control of their father's estate. George Brent plays her opponent (and the father of her child) and the movie gave a young actor named Byron Elsworth Barr his first featured role as second leading man Gig Young—the name that thereafter appeared on his credits. Rapper says that he had "tried to use Chekhov's *Three Sisters* in a modern Manhattan location" but "it didn't jell." Some reviewers liked the film nevertheless for its "good narrative sense" and acting.

The film that followed, *Now, Voyager* (1942), is generally regarded as Rapper's masterpiece. Adapted by Casey Robinson from a novel by Olive Higgins Prouty, it was originally assigned to Michael Curtiz, who promptly fell ill (or pretended to; he reportedly loathed its star, Bette Davis). Rapper, who had just completed *The Gay Sisters*, was in great distress over the death of his mother and desperately needed a break, but was ordered to take over with only two weeks' preparation time. "I think I ploughed my

own emotions right into it," he says. The picture was already partly cast, but the director was able to hire Gladys Cooper as the heroine's autocratic mother, and Ilka Chase and Bonita Granville as a couple of spiteful socialites. For the romantic lead he wanted Charles Boyer but had to "make do" with Paul Henreid.

Davis plays Charlotte Vale, plump, plain, and repressed in thick-lensed glasses, slumping into middle-age in a Boston Back Bay mansion. Fleeing from despair into a nervous breakdown, she finds a friend and confidant in Dr. Jacquith (Claude Rains), America's greatest psychiatrist. After repairing her battered psyche, he packs her off on a luxury cruise that introduces her to Jerry (Henreid), an unhappily married architect. They fall in love in Rio, and Charlotte is transformed into a passionate and beautiful woman with 20/20 vision. Contentedly assuming the role of Other Woman in Jerry's life, she also becomes surrogate mother to his teenaged daughter, rescuing her from the kind of repression she herself had escaped. "Don't let's ask for the moon," Charlotte admonishes herself at the end. "We have the stars."

"This very clever wish-fulfillment fantasy . . . ," wrote Higham and Greenberg in *Hollywood in the Forties*, "is directed by Rapper with mesmerising skill. Max Steiner's hypnotic variations on a series of cellophane love-themes ('Wrong, could it be wrong to kiss?' is the most famous of these) underline every scene and give the film a strong romantic coherence. Sol Polito's glamorous photography evokes the shimmering paradise of the Bahamas, the Boston mansion, the soft moonlight of the African coast." David Thomson called it "a gorgeous, wallowing film," and "rather better Litvak than Anatole could have managed."

Rapper was already establishing his reputation as a director of actors, and he elicited from Bette Davis a "precision and control" that delighted her admirers. Paul Henreid, in his first Hollywood film, distinguished himself chiefly by lighting two cigarettes at once and handing one to his lover. He was hailed as the "creator for all time of the two cigarette routine," but Rapper says he stole the gimmick from Alan Dwan, "so you can see nothing is new." Some reviewers found the picture weakly structured—"diffuse and overlong"—but the public didn't care, making it one of the top moneymakers of the year. And there were Oscar nominations for best actress, best supporting actress (Gladys Cooper), and Steiner's score.

Having cut his teeth as a dialogue director on Warner biopics, Rapper was finally assigned one of his own, *The Adventures of Mark Twain*

(1944). He was not happy with Alan Le May's screenplay, which lacked "the close feeling of progressive excitement that a script should have," but once again had Sol Polito as cinematographer and Max Steiner as his composer, as well as a fine cast headed by Fredric March. Centering on Mark Twain's career as a steamboat pilot on the Mississippi (splendidly evoked in Steiner's score), this rambling film (130 minutes) is another amiable exercise in Americana—Higham and Greenberg called it "a *tour de force* of historical reconstruction." It ends with a scene in which the dying author is led over the brow of a hill into the sunrise of immortality by the children of his imagination in miniature—Huckleberry Finn, Tom Sawyer, and their friends. Found sentimental by some, this remains one of Rapper's favorite sequences.

The director again had the services of some of his most congenial collaborators in *The Corn Is Green* (1945), from the play by Emlyn Williams about a surly young Welsh miner with great academic gifts (John Dall) who is cajoled and bullied into an Oxford scholarship by a dedicated village schoolteacher. Bette Davis played this tough-minded idealist, and the film was scripted by Casey Robinson and Frank Cavett, photographed by Polito, and scored by Steiner.

"The sets in *The Corn Is Green* are appalling," wrote a critic in the London *Times*, "the singing is overdone, and an occasional false note is struck, but it is . . . a most courageous, exciting film." Most reviewers, whatever their reservations, shared this last conclusion, praising in particular the "sharp vitality" and "unique sincerity" of Davis' performance and the fidelity with which the scriptwriters had preserved "the witty, human, nervous dialogue" of the play. Rapper has agreed that the Carl Weyl sets were poor: "If you strain you can see the painted backdrops, which distressed me a bit." But "shooting in Wales was impossible with the war on."

Rapper's second screen biography was *Rhapsody in Blue* (1945), about George Gershwin's progress from a penny arcade pianola on the Lower East Side to fabulous success and tragic death. The script was credited to Howard Koch and Elliot Paul, from an original story by Sonya Levien, but it is rumored that the film also draws on an earlier script by Clifford Odets, written with Odets' friend John Garfield in mind as the composer. The front office apparently concluded that Garfield "wouldn't look right in a full dress suit," and Odets eventually recycled his Gershwin script as *Humoresque* (1946).

Rhapsody in Blue had a mixed reception. The unknown Robert Alda, cast in the lead, resem-

bled the composer more than Garfield did, but made a colorless Gershwin (though his faked piano playing was found reasonably convincing). Some reviewers were perfectly happy to sit through two hours of Gershwin music performed by the likes of Anne Brown, Hazel Scott, and Gershwin's old colleagues Paul Whiteman and Oscar Levant (who has a sizable role as himself). But many complained that the story was heavily stereotyped and fictionalized (and Levant himself called it "preposterous").

There is also a good deal of music (by Beethoven) in *Deception* (1946), not to mention the three stars of *Now, Voyager*. This time, Paul Henreid is an Austrian cellist who comes to America from war-torn Vienna in search of his lost beloved (Bette Davis), slowly arriving at the distressing discovery that she has kept herself in Bechsteins by accepting the post of mistress to an egocentric composer (Claude Rains). The movie seemed to Virginia Graham "intelligently written, produced and acted," while Leonard Mosley thought that Hollywood had "at long last made a genuine and successful film about music and musicians."

Deception ends with Davis shooting Rains and going off to the clink. According to Rapper, this outcome was imposed by the all-powerful star herself, who demanded a conclusion that she could get her histrionic teeth into, in place of the "gay, light, natural, 'so what' ending" of John Collier's original script. It was also at Davis' insistence that Rapper's usual cameraman Sol Polito was replaced by Ernest Haller, who specialized in "making the stars look beautiful," and who "used those wonderful deep-focus shots that gave the story so much weight." Rapper maintains that this collaboration gave rise to a well-known Haller anecdote usually supposed to have involved either Garbo or Dietrich. Davis apparently reproached Haller for failing to make her look as good in *Deception* as he had in *Jezebel*, to which he tactfully replied, "But Bette, I was eight years younger then."

A series of play adaptations followed. *The Voice of the Turtle* (1947) derived from John van Druten's comedy about a naively romantic actress (Eleanor Parker) in New York who gives a bed in her apartment to a young army sergeant on leave (Ronald Reagan). The film was found "coyly prurient where the play was most pleasantly candid," and Rapper thought that Reagan "really didn't have a light touch for comedy."

Most critics agree that Rapper directed his best films during his years with Warner Brothers. He left the studio in 1947, and has since explained that he was angry about the casting of Robert Alda in *Rhapsody in Blue*. His first movie as a freelance was *Anna Lucasta* (1949), produced by Philip Yordan from his own play about incestuous yearnings in a Pennsylvania mill town. No one was much impressed, and Paulette Goddard was thought hopelessly miscast in the title role, where she "distinguished herself chiefly for her decor."

Rapper returned to Warners to direct his adaptation of Tennessee Williams' *The Glass Menagerie* (1950) because he "couldn't resist that one." Gertrude Lawrence was inexplicably cast as the one-time Southern belle reduced to a shabby St. Louis apartment and obsessively intent on finding a husband for her desperately shy and crippled daughter (Jane Wyman). She bullies her son (Arthur Kennedy) until he brings home a glib "gentleman caller" (Kirk Douglas), with results desolating in the play, less so in the movie. *Time*'s reviewer concluded that the picture "tries conscientiously to rework the frail story in movie terms. But the charm, the magic, and the vague sadness of the play are lost."

Bette Davis took Rapper to his native England for their last collaboration, *Another Man's Poison* (1952), based on a play by Leslie Sands. Davis plays a murderous thriller writer who lives in a lonely house on the Yorkshire moors and poisons almost everyone except her horse. Frank Hauser recommended the movie to "the audience which specialises in bad films . . . slap-up, expensive, pretentious stinkers. . . . No one has ever accused Bette Davis of failing to rise to a good script; what this film shows is how far she can go to meet a bad one. . . . *Another Man's Poison* is not to be missed; it is safe to say there are few things in the cinema like it."

Rapper went to Columbia for the insignificant *Bad for Each Other* (1953) and to Paramount for the slightly better *Forever Female* (1953), which stars Ginger Rogers as a middle-aged actress who wants to play ingenues. *Strange Intruder* (1956), for Allied Artists, is a turgid melodrama about a temporarily deranged vet wrestling with his promise to murder his dead buddy's children.

The best of Rapper's post-Warner films, *The Brave One* (1956), was made for the King Brothers. It is a variation on the Androcles story. Leonardo (Michel Ray), a Mexican peasant boy, raises a bull calf, Gitano, on the ranch where his father works. He gains and loses ownership of the animal and in the end follows it to the bullring in Mexico City, expecting to see it die there. But Gitano shows such courage the crowd demands the *indulto*—the rare sparing of a fighting bull's life. Leonardo runs into the arena, calms the still frenzied animal, and leads it away to freedom.

The Brave One was shot in CinemaScope and Technicolor by Jack Cardiff on location in Mexico, apart from a few sequences filmed in the Churubusco Studios. The script, written under a pseudonym by the blacklisted writer Dalton Trumbo, won an Oscar. The film was warmly received by the critics, and Rapper says in *The Celluloid Muse* that this was "one picture of mine in recent years [that] wasn't compromised. . . . My friends and my agent even advised me against making it. . . . They all said, 'What do you see in it?' And I said, 'It's so simple, it reads like a fairy tale.' And it cost $430,000 to make, and grossed eight and a half million. After that, I'll follow my own judgment, all the time."

If he did so, his judgment let him down. His next assignment took him back to Warners for an adaptation of Herman Wouk's bestseller *Marjorie Morningstar,* about growing up Jewish and middle-class in New York City in the 1950s. Natalie Wood played the virginal Marjorie and Gene Kelly the second-rate hoofer she falls in love with while working one summer as a drama counselor on the borscht circuit. Two more non-Jews, Claire Trevor and Everett Sloane, played her loving but overprotective parents. Reviewers found the film competent but unexciting.

The Miracle (1959) was based on Max Reinhardt's famous stage piece about a medieval nun who falls in love with a knight, forsakes her vows, and after many colorful adventures returns contrite, to find that a statue of the Madonna had left its pedestal to cover for her during her absence. Frank Butler's script transposes the story to Spain in the early nineteenth century. The nun is now only a postulant (Carroll Baker) and her lover a dashing English officer (Roger Moore). Hollis Alpert suggested that this was "the kind of movie they don't make any more—but they did, unfortunately."

Now typed as a "religious director," Rapper next found himself involved in two spaghetti biblical epics, neither of any merit: *Joseph and His Brethren* (1960), the English-language version of a film by Luciano Ricci, and *Ponzio Pilato* (*Pontius Pilate,* 1962). Eight years passed after that before Rapper went back to work on *The Christine Jorgensen Story,* about the first American male to undergo a sex-change operation. David Watts wrote that Rapper had "sealed it with the depressing glaze of old Hollywood" but "does give the pulpy script certain disturbingly sinister accents by means of cheesy old-style lighting and a pseudo-Tchaikovsky score." For David Thomson, however, this was "possibly the most bizarre departure by any director once in steady work."

Rapper reached the dismal end of his career

in 1978 with another religious assignment, *Born Again*, based on the experiences of Charles W. Colson, Nixon's former special counsel, who had undergone a religious conversion while serving time for obstruction of justice in the Pentagon Papers case. Warmly received by evangelical Christians, the film was largely ignored by the godless critics.

According to *The Celluloid Muse*, Rapper lives in a luxurious apartment crowded with fine paintings and "set high in a glistening white building in the very heart of Hollywood. . . . Comfortably plump and relaxed, with an elegant and cultivated personality, he is utterly unlike the brisk new generation of grey-suited, fiercely efficient Hollywood men. His best known films were made with Bette Davis . . . but his unacknowledged technical skill, his tremendous flair for the cinema, were perhaps more formidably displayed in his biographies." David Thomson says that "the mark of Curtiz, Dieterle, and Litvak shows in his . . . films—if nothing else, Rapper learned a gilded craft."

FILMS: Shining Victory, 1941; One Foot in Heaven, 1941; The Gay Sisters, 1942; Now, Voyager, 1942; The Adventures of Mark Twain, 1944; The Corn Is Green, 1945; Rhapsody in Blue, 1945; Deception, 1946; The Voice of the Turtle, 1947; Anna Lucasta, 1949; The Glass Menagerie, 1950; Another Man's Poison, 1952; Bad for Each Other, 1953; Forever Female, 1953; Strange Intruder, 1956; The Brave One, 1956; Marjorie Morningstar, 1958; The Miracle, 1959; Joseph and His Brethren/Sold Into Egypt, 1960; Ponzio Pilato (Pontius Pilate), 1962; The Christine Jorgensen Story, 1970; Born Again, 1978.

ABOUT: Higham, C. and Greenberg, J.The Celluloid Muse, 1969; Meyer, W. R. Warner Brothers Directors, 1978; Thomson, D. A Biographical Dictionary of the Cinema, 1980. *Periodicals*—Classic Images June 1982.

REED, Sir CAROL (December 30, 1906–April 25, 1976), British director and producer, was born into a large and moderately affluent family in Putney, London, and educated at King's School, Canterbury. He spent much of his leisure time in the London theatres, and by the time he left school was stagestruck. His middle-class parents did not regard acting as a desirable career and insisted that he try something else first, but after six miserable months on a brother's chicken farm in Maine he came home determined to act.

Reed made his first stage appearance in 1924, when he was eighteen, and the same year had a small part in a famous production of *Saint Joan*, helping Laurence Olivier drag Sybil Thorndike to her trial. Reed was not a particularly good ac-

CAROL REED

tor, and four years later was still touring in relatively minor roles. Then he had a small success as Oberon in a production of *A Midsummer Night's Dream*, and this earned him a part in Edgar Wallace's *The Terror* at the Lyceum Theatre, where he also became an assistant stage manager.

Edgar Wallace, who in those days sometimes had two or three plays running simultaneously in London, was as stagestruck as Reed had been. He used to beg to be allowed to operate the trapdoor that figured crucially in the plot, paying for the privilege by taking Reed out to dinner at Ciro's. They became friends, and in 1927, when Wallace accepted the chairmanship of the new British Lion Film Corporation, Reed joined him as his personal assistant, keeping an eye on British Lion's adaptations of Wallace's thrillers (and learning in the process a great deal about filmmaking, as well as about Wallace's techniques for building atmosphere and suspense). "We had our studios at Beaconsfield," Reed recalled, "and we made *Valley of Ghosts*, *Alias*, and *Chick*. I would keep him informed about how things were going, and in the evening I would rush back to London to act in his plays and be assistant stage manager. We never minded how long we worked in those days. Everything was such tremendous fun."

Later Reed also produced some of Wallace's plays on tour, and their hectic partnership continued until 1932, when Wallace died. That was the end of Reed's theatrical career. The talkies had arrived, and he joined the exodus of theatre people to the cinema, becoming a dialogue director with Basil Dean's Associated Talking Pictures at their studios at Ealing, in the London suburbs. He is credited as dialogue director of Basil Dean's *Nine Till Six* (1932), as assistant director of Dean's *Autumn Crocus* and *Sing As We Go* (both 1934), and second unit director of J. Walter Ruben's *Java Head* (1934). Some sources list him as codirector with Robert Wyler of *It Happened in Paris* (1935), but Reed himself maintains that he only shot retakes for this movie.

His first picture as sole director was *Midshipman Easy* (US, *Men of the Sea*, 1936), based on Captain Maryat's adventure story. It starred Hughie Green as the gallant young officer with an argumentative passion for egalitarianism, and Margaret Lockwood as the lady he rescues from assorted dastardly foreigners. Like Reed's next three films, it was scripted by Anthony Kimmins. This debut was well received, and followed by an adaptation of *Laburnum Grove*, J. B. Priestley's play about a suburban father who rids himself of a sponging brother-in-law by revealing his own past as a forger. It was this extremely successful film that first drew Hollywood's attention to Cedric Hardwicke and Edmund Gwenn.

Graham Greene, who had warmly praised the "sense of cinema" shown in *Midshipman Easy*, found this promise confirmed in *Laburnum Grove*: "Both films are thoroughly workmanlike and unpretentious," he wrote, "with just a hint of a personal manner. . . . One remembers the opening sequence of *Midshipman Easy*; the camera sailing with the motion of a frigate before the wind down the hedge and the country lane to Easy's home, when the camera in Mr. Reed's new film leads us remorselessly down Laburnum Grove up to the threshold of the tall grim granite church at the bottom. . . . Mr. Reed's camera has gone beyond the dialogue, has picked out far more of the suburban background . . . and presents its own equally dramatic commentary."

Carol Reed was an excellent mimic, and in his early days at Ealing discovered that he got better service from the property room if he imitated Basil Dean's voice on the telephone. It was this experience that suggested the plot of his next film, *Talk of the Devil* (1937), in which the villain uses his talent for mimicry to secure information vital to the future of a Tyneside shipyard. However, there was more to this now vanished movie than that. According to Basil Wright, its motivation "arises from a real situation—unemployment. It arises too from the single-mindedness of Findlay [Randle Ayrton], who is represented as a man who has risen from the ranks of the workers and never forgotten

them. . . . Particularly notable are the two scenes in the Boardroom in which Reeds' assurance in direction and in the pacing and movement of his camera will stand up to comparison with his later work. The film is also remarkable in that it has no . . . [background] music. Instead, we hear only the roar of the riveters as the shipyard swings back to life."

Who's Your Ladyfriend? (1937), based on a German stage comedy about plastic surgery, has also disappeared, but Reed's next film was his first real hit. *Bank Holiday* (1938), called *Three on a Weekend* in the United States, is an episodic piece on the model of *Grand Hotel*. It records the experiences of a group of Londoners spending an August weekend at the seaside, centering on a young nurse (Margaret Lockwood), her boyfriend, and a man whose wife has died in childbirth. It shows Reed's exceptional talent for drawing the best from his actors (most memorably in a tour de force cameo performance by Wilfred Lawson), and includes some location work at Waterloo Station and at a coastal resort—a rare phenomenon in British movies at that time. In spite of this, the film seemed to a recent critic, John Russell Taylor, "very studiobound, its treatment of its working-class characters rather stiff and literary—but its vividness remains as a picture of England at a particualr time, an evocation of a particular atmosphere. It has become a documentary almost in spite of itself."

After *Penny Paradise* (1938), a comedy with Edmund Gwenn as a tugboat captain who thinks he has won a fortune, came the Jessie Matthews farce *Climbing High*, in which wealthy Michael Redgrave is reduced to impersonating a male model to win the girl. There is more role-playing in *A Girl Must Live* (1939), with a schoolgirl posing as an actress's daughter to foil a blackmail plot against the Earl of Pangborough. This robust comedy, with its provincial theatre setting, was scripted by Frank Launder. It shocked some contemporary reviewers but delighted others with its vigor and cheerful vulgarity, and has been described as "one of the best British comedies to be made before the Second World War." The excellent cast includes Margaret Lockwood, Renee Houston, Lilli Palmer, George Robey, and Hugh Sinclair.

The film that finally established Reed's reputation as a major British director was *The Stars Look Down* (1940), from A. J. Cronin's novel about a Welsh coalminer's son (Michael Redgrave), his struggle to become a member of Parliament, and his battle for responsible public ownership of the mines. The mine disaster scene evoked comparisons with Pabst's

Kameradschaft, but some critics have complained that Reed gave too little attention to the social and political issues, too much to the romantic subplot involving the hero and Margaret Lockwood. (And in fact Reed later acknowledged that he had no strong feeling about nationalization—"one could just as easily make a picture on the opposite side.")

Reed's first war film, *Night Train to Munich* (1940), was in a much lighter vein, a comedy-thriller about a British agent (Rex Harrison) posing as a Nazi officer to rescue a Czech inventor and his daughter (the ubiquitous Margaret Lockwood). With a witty script by Frank Launder and Sidney Gilliat, who also wrote Hitchcock's *The Lady Vanishes,* it borrows shamelessly from that small masterpiece—to the extent of resurrecting its brace of cricket-obsessed, ultra-British muttonheads Charters and Caldicott (played again by Basil Radford and Naunton Wayne).

Most critics agree that, having challenged Hitchcock on his own ground, Reed survived the inevitable comparisons very well, and the movie was extremely successful. The director himself characteristically gave most of the credit to his scriptwriters, who "were so brilliant at this kind of story," and made light of his temerity in assuming Hitchcock's mantle: "in those days, one made four pictures a year, each shot in five weeks"; he was by that time under contract to Gainsborough "and was handed scripts, with whose authors I was given opportunity to work for perhaps two weeks. There wasn't the importance put on films that there is now. You never even knew when the picture was finished—another department took care of that. . . . You have a job and you do the best you can."

Another thriller followed, *The Girl in the News* (1941), also scripted by Gilliat, and with Margaret Lockwood this time playing a nurse framed for murder, and then an adaptation of H. G. Wells's novel *Kipps.* Michael Redgrave was miscast as a provincial shop assistant in Edwardian England trying to counterjump his way into high society, but Cecil Beaton's elegant settings earned the film considerable success. *A Letter From Home,* a propaganda short about British evacuees in the United States, was also a hit in America.

Viscount Castlerosse, an authority on William Pitt the Younger, had pointed out to Reed the parallels between Britain's situation in 1941, under threat of German invasion, and the Napoleonic menace of Pitt's day. At Reed's invitation, Castlerosse wrote a plot outline bringing out these ultimately encouraging parallels, and Launder and Gilliat drew from it their script for

The Young Mr. Pitt (1942), a handsomely mounted panorama of Georgian England (again designed by Cecil Beaton) that was also an effective work of propaganda. There is a fine performance by Robert Donat in the lead, and vigorous historical cameos by Robert Morley, John Mills, Raymond Lovell, Phyllis Calvert, and half the character actors in England.

At that point Reed joined the Army Kinematograph Service, where Eric Ambler and Peter Ustinov scripted for him a training film called *The New Lot* (1942). It impressed the authorities, who saw in this short the basis of a film that might be the army's answer to Noël Coward's *In Which We Serve,* which had done so much for the navy's public image. The Ministry of Information eventually parted with the necessary funds, and *The New Lot* was extended by the same scenarists into a memorable feature film, *The Way Ahead* (1944).

The plot is simple enough—a motley group of civilians, inducted into the army from their offices and shops and factories, and gradually transformed from a reluctant rabble into a disciplined platoon that we last see advancing steadily into the smoke and carnage of battle in the African desert. The fine cast was headed by David Niven, Stanley Holloway, William Hartnell, Raymond Huntley, and Jimmy Hanley. The movie's low-key heroics have dated, but even recent critics have found it hard to resist "the wit and accuracy of the writing" and Reed's "talent for speed, for split-second timing and the creation of emotional suspense."

The True Glory (1945), an Anglo-American coproduction directed by Reed in collaboration with Garson Kanin, is a compilation documentary using combat footage shot by the many cameramen who followed the Allied landings in Europe and the advance into the heart of Germany. The soundtrack, similarly, interweaves with moving effect the voices and varied accents of dozens of British and American servicemen and women. It received an Oscar as best documentary of the year. By the time the war ended, Carol Reed was among the best known and most admired of all British directors. He chose as his first postwar subject *Odd Man Out,* adapted by R. C. Sherriff and F. L. Green from the latter's novel, rights to which Reed had acquired as soon as he read it. The picture was produced by Reed for Filippo Del Giudice's Two Cities.

Odd Man Out (1947) begins with a raid on a Belfast linen mill by terrorists seeking funds for their (unspecified) party. Their troubled, idealistic leader Johnny (James Mason) has recently escaped from jail and is not fit enough for such a project. Things go wrong, the cashier is shot dead, and Johnny is badly wounded. In the gateway, he falls from the speeding car and staggers away to hide in an old air-raid shelter. It is 4 p.m. For the next eight hours, as the afternoon drags on toward night and rain turns to snow, the whole city focuses its attention on the wounded fugitive. Children act out his escape, the police hunt him like a dangerous animal, his girl and his comrades search for him in the hope of saving him.

And meanwhile Johnny moves on, in pain and weakening, evolving slowly from a hurt individual into a symbol of all human suffering in his encounters with a garish assortment of friends and enemies. Some wish him well but want him gone. An old priest (W. G. Fay) is only interested in his soul. The pathetic little jackal Shell (superbly played by F. J. McCormick) will sell him to the highest bidder as soon as he is sure who that is. The mad artist Lukey (Robert Newton) is frantic to paint the death he sees in his eyes. Only his girl Kathleen (Kathleen Ryan) shows him true compassion when, at the end, she provokes police gunfire to put him out of his misery, and dies with him in the snow.

Odd Man Out was the first of three succeeding films that constitute Reed's principal claim to an important place in cinema history, and it had one of the best presses ever accorded to a British picture. It was Reeds's first personal film and his first open attempt to create a work of art—one American critic called it "a reckless, head-on attempt at greatness" that "frequently succeeds." Moodily lit by Robert Krasker, it evoked in its "humane pessimism" many comparisons with the films of Carné and Prévert, but seemed to some reviewers flawed by ambitious stylistic effects not entirely under control, and by Newton's overly theatrical performance as Lukey. Nevertheless, Basil Wright found in it "that symmetry, that tautness of construction, that wholeness, which one associates with poetic drama." Many called it a masterpiece and some thought it simply the best film ever made. For Richard Winnington it was "a work that announces once and for all the maturity of the British cinema," and it brought Reed the award as best director at Brussels.

Dilys Powell called *Odd Man Out* "a superb canvas of figures and movement" and said that its mastery was most clearly seen in its evocation of the life of the Belfast streets. Roger Manvell was one of a number of critics who drew attention to the brilliance of the soundtrack and of William Alwyn's score, which "becomes itself part of the dramatic action." Manvell goes on: "In the closing moments when death is very near, Johnny's girl . . . finds him at last near

the docks through which she had hoped to arrange for his escape at midnight. But it is evident that he is dying, and the police are closing in on them. Alwyn's deeply emotional music for these last minutes combines with both speech and natural sounds—the ship's siren, the gunshots, the chiming of the clock which counts the lonely hours of Johnny's pain and wandering."

Reed made his next five films for Alexander Korda's London Films, where his first project was *The Fallen Idol* (1948), scripted by his old admirer Graham Greene from Greene's own short story "The Basement Room." As adapted, it tells the story of an eight-year-old boy, Felipe (Bobby Henrey), lonely son of a foreign ambassador in London, who develops a regard on the order of hero worship for the embassy's butler, Baines (Ralph Richardson). When Baines' hated wife dies in an accident, Felipe believes that Baines, who is in love with another woman (Michèle Morgan), has murdered his wife. Lying to protect his hero, he almost incriminates him, in the process discovering the man's mediocrity.

The Fallen Idol won a Danish Oscar and brought Reed the New York Film Critics' Award as best director. Roy Armes wrote that "Reed captures beautifully the child's misunderstanding of adult emotional entanglements and, like David Lean, he is excellent at conveying the frustrations of romances conducted in English tearooms. The tone remains light and humorous, despite two bravura passages—a game of hide-and-seek played in the darkened embassy and Felipe's terror-stricken run through the night after witnessing Mrs. Baines' death." Not everyone would place this among Reed's major films, however—Raymond Durgnat wrote that "its plush visuals offer neither a common denominator nor a bridge between the mind of the hero-worshipping child . . . and the adult realm."

What was universally acknowledged was the brilliance of Reed's direction of his untrained child actor, and he once offered some tips on directing children and amateurs: "You must always shoot very far or very close. When shooting close, you repeat everything, keeping only the few bits you want. I never let a child speak in a scene with professionals because . . . [the professionals] keep worrying that he'll forget his cue. What I do is shoot the scene until the child's line is due. Then I cut, do a separate take of the line reading, and then start again. This relaxes the professionals. And I never use a number board with a child because it breaks his thoughts: when he hears it, he looks at the clapper boy and wishes they could change places. . . . Amateurs and children always remember their dialogue, but they always forget their cues."

Odd Man Out and *The Fallen Idol* were both major box-office hits as well as critical successes, and the same was true of Reed's next film, *The Third Man* (1949), another collaboration with Graham Greene and this time an original scenario. Over the studio's opposition, the picture was shot on location in Vienna, albeit with an almost impossibly tight schedule. As Reed described the filming, "we had a day and a night unit. The actors we used at night didn't work in the day and vice versa. We worked from 8 p.m. to 5 a.m., then went to bed, got up at 10 a.m., worked with the day unit until 4, and then went back to bed until 8. That way we got double the work done in the same time. It's a bit of a rush, but it's better to rush than not to get it all and have to match things in the studio."

Like *The Fallen Idol,* the film is among other things an exploration of the contradictions of innocence and experience. Innocence is represented by Holly Martins (Joseph Cotten), a writer of Westerns and a man of boyish simplicity who arrives in postwar Vienna and is from the beginning at a loss to comprehend this bizarre, corrupt, and raddled relic of an older civilization. Holly has come to Vienna at the request of his old friend Harry Lime (Orson Welles), but arrives in time to attend Harry's funeral. He makes tentative overtures toward Anna, Harry's beautiful refugee mistress (Alida Valli), but she is still obsessed by memories of her dead lover.

Then it begins to appear that Harry may not be dead after all. He is in fact in hiding from the military police, led by the sardonic Major Calloway (Trevor Howard). Holly's brilliant old friend has become a monster of absolute cynicism, who traffics in penicillin intended for dying children and who, when he and Holly finally meet, attempts a casuistic defense of his corruption. In the end, it is Holly himself who shoots Lime down in the Vienna sewers. The way is now clear for a rapprochement between Holly and Anna, but Reed rejected this simplistic happy ending (which Greene advocated), substituting the famous long last shot in which, after Lime's burial, Holly waits for Anna beside his car and she simply walks on past him down the cemetery road with its litter of fallen leaves and out of the picture.

Reed was never averse to improvisation, and in an interview with C. T. Samuels he explained how he cobbled together the much-discussed sequence in which Holly tries to play with a cat on Anna's bed and is told that the animal "only liked Harry." The cat runs away from Holly and goes down into the street, where it approaches the shoes of someone waiting in the shadows. "So far as we know, it might be anyone. But by going

over to him and playing with his lace, the cat establishes that it's Harry." Another important element in the film's success was its exclusive reliance for musical accompaniment on the haunting zither music of Anton Karas, whose "Harry Lime Theme" became a worldwide hit. Reed himself had discovered Karas, playing for coins in a tiny beer-and-sausage restaurant.

The Third Man took the Grand Prix at Cannes in 1949. It was universally praised for Greene's "beautifully ambiguous" dialogue, for Welles' disturbingly brilliant performance as Harry Lime, and for Reed's "ability to make every aspect of a production serve the final dramatic effect." Roger Manvell called it "the most richly atmospheric of all Carol Reed's films," creating "a certain kind of dramatic poetry" out of its world of "shadows and the half-light." (Vincent Korda was the art director.) There were some reservations about Reed's too frequent use of off-angle shots, intended to reflect the moral distortions of the city, and Manvell thought that the chase through the sewers was too crudely violent, destroying the film's atmosphere. But most agreed with Derek Malcolm that Reed's "sharp, nervous style, which piled detail upon detail without ever seeming to obtrude on the main business of storytelling, was never put to better effect."

At this stage in his career, Carol Reed was regarded, if briefly, as one of the greatest of living film directors. For many critics (but not all), his decline began with his next film, *Outcast of the Islands,* which appeared after a three-year silence in 1952. Much of the delay is accounted for by the fact that, having spent some time scouting locations in Borneo, Reed was forced by the outbreak of the Korean War (and the consequent nervousness of insurance companies) to start all over again in Ceylon, though some background footage was shot in Borneo by army cameramen.

Conrad's novel, adapted by William Fairchild, is a study of the destructive force of passion. The vain and unscrupulous Peter Willens (Trevor Howard) falls insanely in love with Aissa (Kerima), a half-Arab girl of sullen beauty. Possessed by this passion, he lurches from degradation to degradation, finally betraying his benefactor Captain Lingard (Ralph Richardson) and destroying the trading post Lingard had built on his "secret river" in Borneo. Contemporary critics were entranced by Kerima (who speaks not a word throughout), but many were embarassed or puzzled by the use of Conrad's own grave and sonorous dialogue and the rather theatrical acting style which that called for. Richard Winnington thought *Outcast* Reed's "first serious failure," and it was no more successful with the public than with the reviewers.

Since then, however, the critical standing of *Outcast of the Islands* had steadily improved. Raymond Durgnat calls it "Reed's stylistic tour de force," and finds in it "visual continuities whose deft intricacy rivals Pabst's." C. T. Samuels described it as the director's best and most passionate film, and Derek Malcolm writes that "more than any of his films [it] betrayed his true aesthetic concerns. Perhaps because those concerns went deeper than the public was at that time prepared to explore, the film was not a commercial success and he never made another in which he so exposed the basis of his art. This lay, above all, in an innate pessimism about the world and an instinct about its cruelty that would have been much more fashionable today than it was in a world struggling to forget the Second World War." In that determinedly optimistic world, Reed found himself with nothing personal to say. He continued to make films of immaculate craftsmanship, but most of his later work, as Roy Armes says, demonstrated "the separation of technique from meaning, so that the director's role becomes merely the highly professional presentation of trivia."

The Man Between (1953), a thriller set in postwar Berlin and starring James Mason, has seemd to most critics an inferior pastiche of *The Third Man,* though it has its admirers. *A Kid for Two Farthings* (1955), Reed's first film in color, is a screen version of Wolf Mankowitz's "soft-centre fairy-tale" about life in the East End of London, where a boy buys a unicorn that is really only a baby goat. A financial success, it was Reed's last movie for British Lion. Its successors were mostly big-budget projects made in a "mid-Atlantic" style with American financing.

The first of these, *Trapeze* (1956), with Burt Lancaster, Tony Curtis, and Gina Lollobrigida, offered "superb aerial thrills to make up for a rather conventional circus story." According to Reed himself, it was the most profitable of all his pictures. The romantic drama *The Key* (1958), despite a cast headed by Sophia Loren, William Holden, and Trevor Howard, fared less well, mostly on account of a portentous script by Carl Foreman (who also produced). Another collaboration with Graham Greene followed, *Our Man in Havana* (1960). Alex Guinness stars as an English vacuum-cleaner salesman in Cuba who is recruited by British Intelligence (in the person of Noël Coward) and finds that it is easier to invent secrets than to discover them. An entertaining satire, it is also a prime example of the expenditure of great talent and skill on a trivial subject.

Reed then began work on the remake of *Mutiny on the Bounty,* eventually resigning in favor of Lewis Milestone over difficulties with the script and the star, Marlon Brando. *The Running Man* (1963), scripted by John Mortimer, had dogged insurance investigator Alan Bates pursuing Laurence Harvey and Lee Remick across Spain—a promising formula that somehow "turned out flat." And *The Agony and the Ecstasy* (1965), from Irving Stone's foolish novel about the conflicts between Michelangelo (Charlton Heston) and Pope Julius II (Rex Harrison), never really had a chance.

The only major success of Reed's last years was his screen version of Lionel Bart's musical *Oliver!* (1968), filmed in 70mm Panavision. With a excellent cast headed by Oliver Reed (Bill Sykes), Ron Moody (Fagin), and Mark Lester (Oliver Twist), Reed captured at times a real Dickensian gusto, and was rewarded with a clutch of Oscars (best film, best director, best art direction, best sound, best musical score adaptation).

Reed made only two more movies after that, both of them disasters. In *The Last Warrior* (US, *Flap,* 1970), Anthony Quinn impersonates a troublemaking Indian in a farcical comedy with serious overtones about the miseries of reservation life. *Follow Me* (US, *The Public Eye,* 1972) is an insipid adaptation by Peter Shaffer of his play about a private eye (Topol) who falls in love with the young wife (Mia Farrow) he is supposed to be investigating. Reed later explained that he had accepted this assignment because he had "nothing on my plate" when it was offered to him: "If you like making pictures, you've got to go from one to the other—within reason. It's like being a boxer—there's no good just sitting there."

Carol Reed was known as an easygoing, self-deprecating man with an excellent sense of humor. He was married twice, on both occasions to actresses—to Diana Wynyard in 1943 and to Penelope Dudley Ward in 1948. He had a son by his second marriage. He was knighted in 1952 for his services to the British cinema. Reviewing *The Third Man,* Richard Winnington wrote that Reed was "probably the most brilliant craftsman of the modern cinema, yet one who is devoid of the urges that make a really great director. Sensitive and humane and dedicated, he would seem to be enclosed from life, with no specially strong feelings about the stories that come his way to film other than that they should be something he can perfect and polish with a craftsman's love."

This is very much the impression that Reed himself promulgated. Asked in 1971 for his opinion of the *auteur* theory, he replied, "This is something I am not familiar with." Reed went on to say that "the audience should be unconscious that the damned thing has been directed at all. . . . I know there are great directors, like Visconti and Bergman, who have a certain view of life, but I don't think that a director who knows how to put a film together need impose his ideas on the world." The director he himself held in the highest regard was William Wyler. And yet there seems to be growing dissatisfaction with this view of Reed as being above all a "technician's director," an interpreter rather than a creator. Derek Malcolm wrote that "there was more than this in his best work, which could well be revalued upwards in the future." And *Time* magazine called him "a director of loneliness and betrayal, an artist fascinated by the somber contemplation of the outcast from society."

FILMS: Midshipman Easy (Men of the Sea), 1936; Laburnum Grove, 1936; Talk of the Devil, 1937; Who's Your Lady Friend?, 1937; Bank Holiday (Three on a Weekend), 1938; Penny Paradise, 1938; Climbing High, 1939; A Girl Must Live, 1939; The Stars Look Down, 1940; Night Train to Munich (Night Train), 1940; The Girl in the News, 1941; Kipps (The Remarkable Mr. Kipps), 1941; A Letter From Home, 1941 (short); The New Lot, 1942 (short; not released?); The Young Mr. Pitt, 1942; The Way Ahead, 1944; (with Garson Kanin) The True Glory, 1945; Odd Man Out, 1947; The Fallen Idol, 1948; The Third Man, 1949; Outcast of the Islands, 1952; The Man Between, 1953; A Kid for Two Farthings, 1955; Trapeze, 1956; The Key, 1958; Our Man in Havana, 1960; The Running Man, 1963; The Agony and the Ecstasy, 1965; Oliver!, 1968; The Last Warrior (Flap), 1970; Follow Me (The Public Eye), 1972. *Published scripts*—The Third Man, *in* Masterworks of the British Cinema, 1974.

ABOUT: Armes, R. A Critical History of the British Cinema, 1978; Current Biography, 1950; Davies, B. (Ed.) Carol Reed, 1978; Hadsell, J. Classics of the Film, 1965; Moss, R. The Films of Carol Reed, 1987; Roud, R. (ed.) Cinema: A Critical Dictionary, 1980; Samuels, C. T. Encountering Directors, 1972; Samuels, C. T. (ed.) Mastering Film, 1977; Screen Education Yearbook, 1969; Who's Who, 1976; Year's Work in the Film 1949, 1950. *Periodicals*—Film Culture Spring 1963; Film Heritage Summer 1971; Films and Filming December 1954, September and October 1957, January 1962; Films in Review March 1959, August–September 1982; Focus on Films Spring 1974; Guardian April 27, 1976; Hollywood Quarterly July 1947; New York Times Magazine January 15, 1960; Theatre Arts May 1947; Times (London) April 27, 1976; Washington Post April 27, 1976.

*RENOIR, JEAN (September 15, 1894–February 12, 1979), French director and scenarist, was born in Montmartre, second of the three sons of Pierre-Auguste Renoir, the impressionist painter, and his wife Aline, née Charigot.

°ren wär´

JEAN RENOIR

"When the midwife held me up, my mother exclaimed: 'Heavens, how ugly! Take it away!' My father said: 'What a mouth; it's a regular oven! He'll be a glutton.' Alas, his prediction was to come true." Renoir grew up in three environments: in Paris, in his mother's Burgundian village of Essoyes, and in Provence, where the family often spent winters. Much of his upbringing was entrusted to his adored Gabrielle, Aline Renoir's young cousin, who lived with the family. "I was a spoiled child. Family life surrounded me with a protective wall, softly padded on the inside. Outside, impressive personages bustled about. I would have liked to join them and be impressive myself. Unfortunately nature had made me a coward. As soon as I detected a crack in the protective wall, I yelled with terror."

By the time his second son was born, Auguste Renoir was fifty-three, and his paintings, scornfully rejected twenty years earlier, were becoming accepted and salable. Jean Renoir (who often served as his father's model) was brought up in comfortable, though never luxurious, surroundings, which he recalled as full of laughter, light, friendship and vivid physical sensation, "a simple environment in which nothing trashy was tolerated." His first experience of the cinema, which took place in 1897, was inauspicious ("I howled as usual and had to be taken out"), but his introduction to the Guignol theatre at the Tuileries, two years later, sparked off a lifelong enthusiasm for the stage, as well as "a taste for naive stories and a deep mistrust of what is generally called psychology." Since his father considered all attempts to train children a waste of time, it was not until Renoir was seven that he was sent to school—to the Collège Saint-Croix at Neuilly, where he had been preceded by his elder brother Pierre.

Unlike his brother, Renoir was unhappy at Saint-Croix. He ran away several times before his parents moved him to the less strict École Sainte-Marie de Monceau, where he greatly enjoyed the weekly movie show featuring a carmad comedian named Automaboul. From there he moved to the École Masséna in Nice, and in 1913 earned his Baccalauréat in mathematics and philosophy from the University of Aix-en-Provence. He had taken to writing poetry, and there was talk of his becoming a writer. However, "I began to realize that my father was an important artist, and it rather frightened me, and I tried to set my mind to everything that was contrary to art. . . . I was very fond of horses, and so I wanted to be a cavalry officer." He therefore enlisted as a sergeant in the Chasseurs Alpins. At the outbreak of World War I he was commissioned second lieutenant and sent to the Vosges front, where "a Bavarian sniper did me the service of putting a bullet in my thigh." Hospitalized with a fractured femur, he was only saved from having his leg amputated by the intervention of his mother, by then gravely ill with diabetes. She died two months later.

Renoir's wound healed, but he was left with a permanent limp. While convalescing, he developed a passion for the cinema, often seeing twenty or more pictures a week, almost always American pictures. On a friend's recommendation, he sought out Chaplin's films. "To say that I was enthusiastic would be inadequate. I was carried away. The genius of Charlot had been revealed to me." He even persuaded his father, now confined to a wheelchair, to buy a projector so that they could watch Chaplin movies together in the studio.

In 1916, returning to active duty, Renoir transferred to the Flying Corps and became a pilot. After several successful missions, he crashed, thereby aggravating his leg injury, and decided that he had seen enough combat. "French aviation lost little by this. I was not a very good pilot." Securing the undemanding post of chief military censor at Nice ("There was never anything to censor"), he spent most of his time at his father's studio, a few miles away in Cagnes. Though immobilized, Auguste Renoir was still actively painting; his most frequent model was a young Alsatian woman, Andrée Heuschling, with whom Jean fell in love. They were married in January 1920, a few weeks after Auguste Renoir's death. Their son Alain, Renoir's only child, was born in 1921.

For four years Renoir worked at pottery and ceramics, in company with his wife, his younger brother Claude, and various friends, but his interests were turning towards filmmaking. Two pictures in particular decided him: Volkov's *Le Brasier ardent* with Mosjoukine; and Stroheim's *Foolish Wives*, which he saw ten times, stirred by the cinematic possibilities it revealed. "I started out in the cinema because I was interested in trick shots . . . purely in technique and trick shots," he later recalled, although elsewhere he stated that "I only ventured into cinema in the hope of making my wife a star. . . . I did not foresee that, once caught up in the machinery, I would never be able to escape." Whatever the reason, in March 1924 he began work on *Catherine*, otherwise known as *Une Vie sans joie*, with Andrée starring under the name of Catherine Hessling. The director was the actor Albert Dieudonné (who played Napoleon in Gance's grandiose epic), though some surviving prints credit Renoir with codirection. He certainly produced and scripted, besides taking a small role as a lecherous *sous-préfet*.

The plot of *Catherine* revolved around a pure young heroine, wickedly exploited and persecuted by everybody in sight. Apart from Dieudonné, few of the participants had much professional experience, and it showed. In his autobiography Renoir expressed the hope "that no trace exists of this little masterpiece of banality." After its brief release in 1924, Dieudonné withdrew the film for re-editing, and re-released it three years later; in neither version did it achieve much success. But Renoir, eager to direct on his own account, proceeded with most of the same team to make *La Fille de l'eau* (1924).

Once again Hessling played a victimized heroine, daughter of a canal boatman who drowns, leaving her at the mercy of her brutal and lecherous uncle—a villain sneeringly portrayed by Renoir's friend Pierre Lestringuez, who also provided the scenario. Pierre Renoir, by now a leading stage actor, made a brief appearance as a pitchfork-wielding peasant. Most of the film was shot on location in the forest of Fontainebleau and on the banks of the Loing, showing Renoir, in Richard Roud's view, "already capable of capturing on the screen the atmosphere and beauty of landscape, and of suggesting that almost pagan reverence for nature which was to run through much of his work." Together with this pictorial realism came a strong element of fantasy, in particular some hallucinatory dream-sequences ("reminiscent of *Alice in Wonderland*," thought Leo Braudy) which attracted the interest of the avant-garde. Jacques Brunius, who later often worked with Renoir, wrote that *La Fille de l'eau* was the first film to show "a really dream-like dream."

The general public, though, was not much taken with the picture, and Renoir, temporarily despairing of the cinema, opened an art gallery in Paris. Since he never had much head for business, this foundered after a few months. In any case, the pull of movie-making proved too strong, and towards the end of 1925 he began work on an ambitious new project: an adaptation of Zola's novel *Nana*, planned as the first Franco-German coproduction and lavishly budgeted at over a million francs. The script was again by Lestringuez, in collaboration with Renoir himself and Zola's daughter, Denise Leblond-Zola, and the sets and costumes were designed by Claude Autant-Lara, the first of several future directors whose careers Renoir helped to launch.

Renoir's first two films introduce two of the primary themes of his work: nature and the theatre. Generally reckoned the best of his silent movies and visibly influenced by Stroheim, *Nana* (1926) traces the rise to fame, via the stage and the bedroom, of a slum-born girl in Second Empire Paris. Hessling again took the lead, with Werner Krauss as the most infatuated of her lovers. In Noël Burch's view, *Nana* can be regarded as "a key film in the development of a cinematic language" for its structural use of off-screen space: "More than half the shots . . . begin with someone entering the frame or end with someone exiting from it . . . leaving several empty frames before and after each shot. . . . Sometimes . . . the character off screen . . . becomes as important as, if not more important than, the person who is visible in frame and the actual screen-space." Already, it seems, Renoir is developing that distinctive quality of his films which Robin Wood referred to as "the sense of superfluous life"—the impression that any amount of things are going on all around the point on which the camera has happened to focus, that his characters and locations have retained their own autonomous existence.

Critical verdicts on *Nana*, as on several of Renoir's silent films, tend to be colored by individual reactions to Catherine Hessling's highly idiosyncratic style of acting. Quite deliberately, Renoir had decided to turn her into "a kind of puppet, though a puppet of genius," plastering her face with heavy makeup for a doll-like parody of Mae Murray, and limiting her movements to a weirdly convulsive pantomime. "I had got it into my head, and into hers, that since filming depended on the jerks of a Maltese cross, acting should also be jerky." The results, for some critics effectively expressionistic or even "zany, spontaneous and amusing" (Truffaut), seemed to others wooden and intolerably mannered. Richard Roud described her performances as "both touching and abominable."

Nana was premiered in Paris to a very mixed reception. In some quarters the film was attacked for being part-German, and Renoir himself encountered a good deal of professional hostility, being seen as a rich amateur trying to buy his way into the industry. He had, it was true, invested a million francs of his own money, raised by selling pictures left him by his father; and when *Nana*, despite some very favorable reviews, proved a financial disaster, he had to sell a lot more to meet the bills. Realizing that, for a while at least, he would have to make commercial potboilers if he wanted to work in cinema at all, Renoir "deserted the ranks of the avant-garde for those of the industry."

Before doing so, though, he used up the short ends of film left over from *Nana* on a twenty-minute *jeu d'esprit*, shot in three days on a single, elaborate (and uncredited) set representing a ruined, post-cataclysm Paris. Inspired by Renoir's recent discovery of jazz, to which Jacques Becker had introduced him, *Sur un air de Charleston* (1927) featured Hessling performing a highly erotic dance for the benefit of a visiting black aeronaut (played by the tap dancer Johnny Higgins). The only other characters were a pair of angels, played by Pierre Lestringuez and another of Renoir's friends, Pierre Braunberger, who had helped set up the coproduction deal on *Nana*.

Renoir's first venture into crass commercialism was *Marquitta* (1927), the story of a Russian prince who takes a street singer as his mistress. It was scripted by Lestringuez, "who had sardonically loaded it with every conceivable cliché and banality." Made as a vehicle for Pierre Renoir's wife, Marie-Louise Iribe, it seems to be the only Renoir film of which no print has survived; by all accounts no great loss. Having completed it, Renoir indulged himself (and Hessling) in another short fantasy piece, *La Petite Marchande d'allumettes* (1928), a half-hour adaptation of Andersen's sentimental fable, *The Little Match Girl*. With the aid of his cinematographer, Jean Bachelet, he devised lighting that would let him shoot interiors on panchromatic stock, allowing far more subtle gradations of tone; previously, studio work had been limited to orthochromatic film, with its harsh tonal contrasts. Delayed by a lawsuit brought by Edmond Rostand for alleged plagiarism, the film was finally released in 1930, with an added soundtrack.

The best of Renoir's commercial chores of the period was his contribution to the popular genre of *comique troupier* (military farce), *Tire au flanc* (1928). A boisterously episodic account of a young man's induction into the army, "it does for barracks life," wrote Bernard Mylonas, "what Vigo's *Zéro de Conduite* was to do for life in a boarding school," and it gave Michel Simon, playing the recruit's valet, his first substantial screen role. Richard Abel considered it "Renoir's most underrated silent film" and "a first-rate social satire."

Renoir's last two silent features were large-scale period pieces made on ample budgets for the Société des Films Historiques. *Le Tournoi dans la cité* (1928), shot in the walled city of Carcassonne, was set amid the religious turmoil of sixteenth-century France, and *Le Bled* (1929) marked the centenary of the French colonization of Algeria. Neither project was much to Renoir's liking. "I bitterly regret," he told an interviewer at the time, "that I have been obliged to make films of a type so alien to my taste and to my way of thinking." Some ten years later he added the hope that "all trace of those celluloid masquerades has disappeared, and that no knight in armor from my early days will play me a dirty trick by charging suddenly on to some screen and covering me with embarrassment."

Nonetheless, Renoir took advantage of these "anodyne films" to explore areas of technique and creative expression, building up experience against the day when he would once again be able to make the films he wanted. He was also taking occasional acting roles in other people's movies, partly to understand filmmaking from the actor's viewpoint, and partly for sheer enjoyment. With Hessling he appeared in two short films directed by his friend Alberto Cavalcanti: *La P'tite Lili* (1927) where he played a pimp; and *Le Petit Chaperon Rouge* (1929) where, strikingly attired in bowler hat, dungarees and tartan bedroom slippers, he played the Wolf to Hessling's Little Red Riding-Hood. (He may also have lent a hand with the direction.) Around this time, according to his own recollection, he took a small role in a Pabst film, possibly *Skandal um Eva* (1930), and appeared with Hessling in Rochus Gliese's *Die Jagd nach dem Glück* (1930). It was their last film together; they separated later that year.

Renoir welcomed the coming of sound with delight, hailing it as "a magical transformation, as if someone had opened a secret door of communication between the filmmaker and his audience." For a time, though, it seriously hampered his career; in the wake of *Nana*, *Le Tournoi* and *Le Bled*, he was seen as a director of cumbersome and costly period pieces, incapable of working with the speed and efficiency demanded by the new technology. For two years he was unable to find backing, until in 1931 his friend Pierre Braunberger set up a production company with Roger Richebé and took over the old Billancourt studios. Even then Renoir had to prove himself, and to do so shot his first sound film in six days for 200,000 francs. This was a scatological Feydeau farce, *On purge Bébé* (1931), concerning the constipated son of a manufacturer of unbreakable chamber pots, with a cast that included Michel Simon and (in his screen debut) Fernandel. It found instant success, recouping its cost within a week of opening; the fidelity with which the soundtrack captured the flush of a lavatory was widely appreciated.

Looking back on his earliest films, Renoir reflected that he had been over-influenced by his American models. "I had not yet understood that the individual . . . is derived from the soil that nourishes him, from the conditions of life which fashion his body and mind, and from the landscape which . . . passes before his eyes. I hadn't yet realized that a Frenchman living in France, drinking red wine and eating Brie, before the grey vistas of Paris, can produce work of real quality only by drawing on the traditions of those who have shared his way of life." No such reproach could be leveled at the films he directed during the 1930s; a more quintessentially French body of work would be hard to imagine. Despite this—or perhaps because of it—they include, by general consensus, some of the supreme masterpieces of world cinema.

Having passed his test, Renoir was allowed to start work on the first of his major films, *La Chienne* (1931), adapted from a novel by Georges de la Fouchardière. A middle-aged bank clerk and amateur painter, Maurice Legrand, oppressed by a nagging wife, falls in love with a young prostitute, Lulu. At the urging of her pimp Dédé, she leads him on, and passes off his paintings as her own, with some success. But Legrand, catching her with Dédé, becomes furiously jealous and kills her; Dédé is executed for the crime. Legrand becomes a tramp, while his misattributed paintings sell for large sums.

Michel Simon, playing Legrand with doggy resignation, at once ludicrous and moving, nonetheless brought to his scenes with Janie Marèze's Lulu the animal urgency of a man grasping a late, unlooked-for chance of sexual abandon. (Marèze, an actress of evident potential, died in a car crash two weeks after the film was completed.) Exteriors for *La Chienne* were shot—and recorded—on location in Montmartre; the colorful streetlife—petty crooks rubbing shoulders with respectable citizens—lent a rich visual and aural texture to an otherwise predictable anecdote. The same intimation of complex and abundant life extended to the interiors; David Thomson singled out a scene in which "Michel Simon, while shaving, hears and sees a woman singing at a window across the yard. The pull of the focus as it moves to sharpen on the woman, and then back to Simon, is a presentiment of the depth Renoir was soon to obtain. For Renoir this technical integration was the necessary expression of his social awareness . . . in the conception of life as a pattern of personalities and principles, all equally justifiable, and all fascinating." When Lang, fourteen years later, remade the story as *Scarlet Street*, this social dimension was largely excised; his film, though effective in its cold detachment, rarely rises above its material.

"During the making of *La Chienne*, I was ruthless and, I must admit, intolerable. I made the film the way I wanted it, with no reference to the producer's wishes. I never showed an inch of film or a scrap of dialogue, and I arranged for the rushes to remain invisible until the film was complete." The producer, Roger Richebé, who had expected a farce, "found himself watching a sombre, hopeless drama with a murder for light relief" and banished Renoir from the studio, calling in Paul Fejös to re-edit the material. When Fejös refused, Renoir was allowed back, and the film opened to a mixed but lively reception. The dispute with Richebé, though, earned Renoir a reputation for being difficult, and various projects—including a filmed *Hamlet* with Michel Simon in the title role—fell through for want of backing. Instead, he acquired the rights to a Simenon novel, *La Nuit du carrefour*, casting his brother Pierre as Inspector Maigret.

Renoir later recalled *La Nuit du carrefour* (*Night at the Crossroads*, 1932) as "a completely absurd experiment that I cannot think of without nostalgia." The film is a mystery in more ways than one. The soundtrack is so indistinct, and existing prints so murky, as to make it hard to tell not only what is being said, but sometimes even who is saying it. The confusion was compounded by the future film historian Jean Mitry, acting as assistant editor, who apparently lost three reels of film (or, according to Mitry himself, allowed them to be accidentally double-exposed), leaving the picture to be assembled from what was left. "Even at the time, you know," Renoir admitted, "it wasn't very clear. I don't think anyone of us understood anything. Least of all me."

The story, insofar as it can be deciphered, concerns the killing of a diamond-merchant at a dismal crossroads some way outside Paris. But if the plot is tenuous, the atmosphere is thick enough to slice; eerie and haunted, its poetic gloom prefigures the Carné-Prévert collaborations of a few years later. Most of the action takes place in darkness or in a greyish half-light filtered through fog and drizzle; even scenes in Maigret's Paris office are obscured by swirling clouds of tobacco smoke. As the Inspector, Pierre Renoir contributed a dourly incisive presence and a drooping, disenchanted eye: the first and in Simenon's view the best of the many screen Maigrets. Few people, perhaps, would go so far as Jean-Luc Godard in hailing *La Nuit du carrefour* as "the only great French thriller," but it could well claim to be the only one of its kind.

"My work as a director," Renoir once observed, "starts with the actor. . . . I don't want the movements of the actors to be determined by the camera, but the movements of the camera to be determined by the actors." Rather than mold his players into a predetermined scheme, he would readily modify scenes, dialogue, even the whole drift of a film in the light of insights that emerged from a developing performance. One inspired result of such creative collaboration was *Boudu sauvé des eaux* (*Boudu Saved From Drowning*, 1932), a long-neglected film now widely considered the first of Renoir's masterpieces; in *Sight and Sound* (Summer 1960) Peter John Dyer described it as "a film of such fresh, simple joy and total harmony between actor, director and setting that one can only regard it as a perfect example of collective evolution."

Taken from a popular boulevard farce by René Fauchois (who was outraged at what he considered a distortion of his work), *Boudu* is built around Michel Simon's colossal performance in the title role. Boudu is a shaggy and disreputable vagabond who, having lost his beloved dog, decides to throw himself into the Seine. He is observed by Lestingois, a bookseller living on the *quai*, who leaps in to rescue him. Fancying himself as a philanthropist, Lestingois decides to take Boudu into his household, there to be fed, clothed, and rehabilitated. The tramp, however, proves ungratefully resistant to the bourgeois virtues; he spits in first editions, cleans his shoes on the bedspread, seduces Lestingois' wife, and makes a pass at his mistress, the housemaid. To regularize the situation, Boudu is married off to the maid. As the wedding party floats merrily along the river, Boudu topples overboard; while the rest mourn his death, he surfaces downstream, wades ashore, swaps clothes with a scarecrow and strolls off across the summer meadows.

Boudu has sometimes been represented as a pointed and virulent attack on the bourgeoisie (Gerald Mast referred to "the venomous energy of Renoir's spitting . . . on the whole history of Western civilization"), but such a reading seems difficult to sustain in the face of the film's genial exuberance—even if no opportunity is missed of satirizing the pretensions of the Lestingois household. (Asked why she has a piano when no one can play it, Mme. Lestingois responds: "Because we're respectable people"; and, on discovering the devastation wreaked by Boudu's shoe-cleaning activities: "This has gone too far! One should only rescue people of one's own class.") But the satire remains essentially good-natured; as Raymond Durgnat suggested, "If Lestingois had gone to the cinema to see *Boudu* . . . he would undoubtedly have taken Boudu's side and laughed heartily at the 'other' Lestingois."

Not that *Boudu* is devoid of any political dimension. Christopher Faulkner noted the film's "social concentration upon settings in which character and environment are a function of one another," indicating "Renoir's awareness that social reality and character are historically produced" and prefiguring his commitment to the socialist ideals of the Popular Front. Much of the richness of *Boudu* derives from this intensely immediate sense of milieu: the sunlit parks and bridges of Paris, the deep-focus geography of the Lestingois apartment (activity in one room glimpsed from another through two windows and across an airshaft), and the final exhilarating grassy warmth of the August riverbank, where the camera celebrates Boudu's regained freedom with a joyful 360-degree pan.

The anarchistic irreverence of *Boudu* owes a good deal to the political climate of the time; a similar spirit suffuses the Prévert brothers' *L'Affaire est dans le sac* and (in a cooler mode) Clair's *À nous la liberté*. Renoir, though never formally a member, had close contacts with several people in the left-wing agit-prop Groupe Octobre, including the Préverts (Pierre Prévert had lent a hand with *On purge Bébé* and *La Chienne*) and Jacques Brunius. Brunius, in turn, was among those who during the thirties formed part of Renoir's informal stock company, acting or otherwise assisting as occasion demanded. Other frequent collaborators (or "accomplices" as Renoir preferred to call them) included Jacques Becker as assistant director, Claude Renoir (Pierre Renoir's son) on camera, the composer Joseph Kosma, and the editor Marguerite Houllé. The latter, also sometimes called Marguerite Mathieu, was Renoir's regular companion for most of the decade; though they were never married, she took the name Marguerite Renoir, which she used for the rest of her professional life.

Renoir followed *Boudu* with another adapted stage comedy, *Chotard et Cie* (1933), about a greengrocer's assistant who achieves fame as a poet. This time, though, a routine farce on stage

remained a routine farce on the screen; in Daniel Serceau's opinion, *Chotard* is "Renoir's only negligible film." (The director evidently agreed. Asked about the picture in 1959, he responded, "I don't remember it.") After an ill-timed trip to Berlin with Pierre Braunberger in search of financing (their arrival coincided with Hitler's accession to power), Renoir accepted a commission from the publisher Gallimard to direct a version of Flaubert's *Madame Bovary*.

Madame Bovary (1934), the tragedy of a romantically discontented woman in a nineteenth-century provincial backwater, is a difficult film to assess, since no prints of Renoir's original version seem to have survived. Exteriors were shot on location in Normandy, as far as possible in the settings that Flaubert had in mind. Renoir's aim was realism rather than costume drama: "No big scenes, just daily life. No characters in costume, but people living in the clothes that they're used to wearing. A straightforward picture, without exaggeration, a bit grey and monotonous—like life, in fact!"

When completed, *Madame Bovary* ran well over three hours. Cut down to two hours at the insistence of the distributors—and to Renoir's annoyance—it was poorly received, reviewers finding it dull and lacking dramatic impact. Most later critics have agreed. "The whole film," Roy Armes wrote, "has the slightly embalmed air of a too solemn and faithful adaptation"—a view recalling Renoir's own remark that "the participants in that adventure were all petrified when faced by Flaubert." André Bazin, though, appreciated the film's "fidelity . . . compatible with complete independence from the original," and Richard Roud commended Valentine Tessier's performance in the title role, as well as "the use of the Normandy landscape, and the contrast between that beauty and Emma's despair."

The failure of *Bovary*, following three films which had enjoyed only modest box-office success, left Renoir's career at its lowest ebb. He was rescued by Marcel Pagnol, whose filmed productions of his own plays *Marius* and *Fanny* had proved hugely popular, and who now offered Renoir financial backing and the use of his Marseille studios. Following Pagnol's own example with *Angèle*, Renoir decided to film exclusively on location, using direct sound and largely nonprofessional actors, the intention being "to give the impression that I was carrying a camera and microphone in my pocket and recording whatever came my way, regardless of its comparative importance." The plot of *Toni* (1935) was taken from a dossier in the files of the local police. Toni, an Italian immigrant laborer, falls in love with Josefa but loses her to the brutal Belgian foreman Albert, and instead marries Marie, his landlady. Josefa, driven to desperation, kills her husband; Toni tries to cover up for her but is caught in the act. He flees in panic, and is shot down beside the tracks, as a train brings in a new consignment of immigrants.

With *Toni*, Renoir anticipated the Italian neo-realists—and may even have directly influenced them through Luchino Visconti, who worked as his assistant on this and several other pictures. It was also a key film in his own development, and one from which, as he later remarked, he "learned a lot." If the plot, with its looming fatal-ism and deterministic structure (the arriving trainload of immigrants as framing device) re-calls elements of Renoir's early Zolaesque melo-dramas, his later style is heralded by the relaxed, improvisatory working out of the story, "often permitting the accidental and random to take precedence over the deliberate, the individual detail over the general design," as Jonathan Rosenbaum put it (*Monthly Film Bulletin*, Octo-ber 1974). Rosenbaum also noted the intense physicality of the film, the actors' sometimes stilted performances subsumed in the immedia-cy of their presence in the parched Provencal landscape: "One remembers heat and light—the warmth of the sun as well as that of the charac-ters . . . denoting generosity and luminosity in a bleak and difficult environment."

On his return to Paris, Renoir found himself caught up in the surging exhilaration of the Pop-ular Front, in which many of his closest friends were involved, and whose aims and aspirations were to color all his remaining films of the de-cade. In later years, particularly after taking up residence in America, Renoir tended to play down his political commitment at this period—as have several of his critics, such as Truffaut—in favor of the serenely detached humanism of his postwar films. Indeed, Pierre Leprohon went so far as to state that "any 'commitment' is an abandonment of freedom, of that freedom with-out which there can be no art." By this logic, ei-ther Renoir was not, at this time, a politically committed filmmaker, or the films that he made from *Le Crime de Monsieur Lange* to *La Règle du jeu*—on most counts, the finest work of his ca-reer—are not art. Either position seems hard to sustain.

Though nearly all films are works of collabo-ration, and Renoir's more than most ("When I make a film, I am asking others to influence me"), *Le Crime de Monsieur Lange* (1936) is es-pecially so; it bears Renoir's signature as director but should perhaps be credited to the Groupe Octobre, whose first film it was. Aptly enough, the plot celebrates collectivity. Amédée Lange

(René Lefevre, hero of Clair's *Le Million*) works in a publishing house run by the unscrupulous Batala (Jules Berry, charmingly despicable), and writes pulp Westerns in his spare time. Batala, discovering this, offers to publish them for a pit-tance; the stories make a hit with the public, and a fat profit for Batala. But creditors are closing in; he absconds and is reported dead. His em-ployees band together and run the company as a cooperative with great success, and Lange de-clares his love to Valentine (Florelle), Batala's former mistress. But Batala returns, delighted to find everything flourishing, and prepares to re-sume control. Lange shoots him dead and flees with Valentine. In the final scene, the clientele of a cafe on the Belgian border, to whom Valen-tine has told the story in flashback, agree unani-mously to let the lovers escape.

Most of the action of *Lange* revolves around the courtyard of the building which houses both the printing press and many of the characters; the original title of Jacques Prévert's script, based on an idea by Renoir and Jean Castanier, was *Sur la cour*. Around this informal amphi-theatre lives a gregarious and verbose communi-ty, tirelessly discussing everything that occurs and constituting a world (in Penelope Gilliatt's words) "suffused with light and the possibility of happiness and a sense that life is simultaneously serious, absurd, impossible and inescapably interesting." Reviewing the film in *Esprit*, Roger Leenhardt found it "all the more remarkable in that the work owes its witty style to the harmony of . . . two unshakably original tempera-ments. . . . Prévert contributed his vivacity and mordant humour, and Renoir the resonance of his true romanticism."

Christopher Faulkner called *Lange* "a film thoroughly conscious of its politicisation." The benefits of communal action are made abun-dantly clear. "Who paid when Estelle had her baby?" demands one character. "The Co-op! Who paid for Charles' doctor's fees? The Co-op!" Similarly, we are left in no doubt that Jules Berry's Batala ("one of the truly great per-formances in French cinema," in Alexander Se-sonske's opinion) stands for all the innate arrogance of the boss class. "A cooperative?" he scoffs, on his return from the dead. "It's ridicu-lous, old man, it's . . . chaos! What's necessary is authority, someone who gives orders, a man! Me!" In this, the famous confrontation between Lange and Batala, the camera sweeps (left-wards) round the courtyard in a 360-degree pan before Lange fires, reminding us of everything that has happened there, and indicating that he kills not just for himself but for the good of the whole community.

The film's message is optimistic, less socialist than anarchist: left to themselves, freed from hierarchical structures, people can order their own lives to far better effect—just as, in the framing scenes, the people's court of the bistro can reach a truer verdict than any law court. All the same, Peter Harcourt, who called *Lange* "in a sense the most *intelligent* film . . . [Renoir] ever made," found a desolate sadness in the final image of Lange and Valentine "crossing the border into some unspecified country, walking away from the scenes of happiness. . . . It is as if to act is to alienate yourself."

Predictably enough, *Lange* was vituperated by the right-wing press, but otherwise warmly received. Renoir, now considered the leading cinematic spokesman for the Left, was invited by the Communist Party to make a propaganda film in preparation for the forthcoming national elections. His exact role in the making of *La Vie est à nous* (*People of France*, 1936) has been variously defined: "supervising director" probably comes closest. Even more than *Lange*, *La Vie* was a collaborative project, made (according to the credit titles) "by a team of technicians, artists, and workers." Scenes were shot by half-a-dozen other directors besides Renoir, including Jacques Becker, Jacques Brunius and Henri Cartier-Bresson. The script, though sometimes credited solely to André Zwobada, seems also to have been a joint effort.

All prints of *La Vie est à nous* were long believed lost. Writing in *Le Nouvel Observateur* (September 9, 1969) soon after its reappearance, Jean-Louis Bory described it as "an election speech in the form of a long dramatic tract" proclaiming "that happiness . . . has never been anything but an idea for most people, and that it is time it became a reality—a *political* reality." A mixture of newsreels, dramatized sequences, and addresses direct to camera, the film presents a France whose beauty and abundance, ample for all its people, are appropriated by a small greedy minority, the "200 families," supported by the forces of right-wing repression. In three vignettes, presented in the guise of letters to the editor of *L'Humanité*, the Party is shown providing solidarity and support to three beleaguered individuals—a factory worker, a peasant, and a student. Many critics have found the film something of an embarrassment; André Bazin spoke of "tremendous didactic naivety." Georges Sadoul, however, roundly declared it "unarguably a brilliant work of art, stylistically characteristic of Renoir during his best period."

Denied a certificate by the French censor, *La Vie est à nous* could only be shown at party meetings, cultural centers, and film societies.

Even so, it may well have contributed to the sweeping victory of the Left in April 1936. Shortly before this, the CP set up a film cooperative called Ciné-Liberté to make and distribute left-wing movies, with Renoir as its guiding spirit. At this period, he later recalled, "I breathed the exalted air of the Popular Front. For a short time the French really believed they could love one another. One felt oneself borne on a wave of warm-heartedness." (The phrase recalls a dictum of his father's which he liked to quote: "You must let yourself go along in life like a cork in the current of the stream.") He was also contributing regularly to the CP journal *Ce Soir* and the antifascist *Commune*, and acting as artistic advisor to the left-wing theatre organization, Théâtre de la Liberté.

Accounts of Renoir's working methods at this period often present him as a caring, earth-father figure, bathing his extended family of collaborators in the inspirational warmth of his benevolence. Though he certainly believed in filmmaking as a communal and informal activity, hints of a tougher, more ambivalent individual occasionally filter through. Sylvia Bataille considered his behavior over *Partie de campagne* "unforgivable" and never acted for him again; Leopold Scholsberg, who worked on several Renoir pictures as a production assistant, recalled him as "a brawler . . . sociable, but not kind. . . . Jean was slovenly, truculent, he worked with his guts and heart. . . . He was scoffing all the time."

Those who were used to more disciplined directors often found Renoir's open, collaborative approach disconcerting. Scholsberg again: "If you look at Renoir's films, you'll see that there is a unity at the level of the characters, but there's no camera style of Renoir's own. . . . He took everybody's good ideas, even the technicians. . . . He only understood the job when his friends were around him; he never chose the camera angles." That Renoir relied on others for ideas he never denied—"I'm a sort of opportunist. I ask others to give me all the ingredients. For my part I contribute nothing"—but that his films lack a distinctive camera style is disputable; André Bazin certainly thought otherwise. "He forced himself to look back beyond the resources provided by montage, and so uncovered the secret of a film form that would permit everything to be said without chopping the world up into little fragments, that would reveal the hidden meanings in people and things without disturbing the unity natural to them."

Similarly, Elizabeth Strebel pointed out how Renoir's style contrasted with the *découpage classique*, the alternating angle/reverse-angle close-ups favored by most French (and American) directors of the time: "He put less emphasis on montage and exhibited instead a marked preference for long takes, in-depth shooting with foreground and background equally clear, panning, tracking, movement within a fixed frame, all indicative of that respect for the continuity of dramatic space and time which gives his films a unique sense of organic wholeness." This style, Strebel suggested, can be linked to the ideological and political stance of the films themselves: "In opposition to arbitrarily assigned technical teams and hierarchically determined decisions, he offered his own conception of cooperative filmmaking. In opposition to a cinematography of classical *mise en scène* and montage, he offered his own freewheeling camerawork."

Renoir's own rationale for his camera style was his belief in the primacy of the actor as focus of cinematic interest and source of inspiration. "My work as a director starts with the actor," he always maintained. "The reason for my camerawork was to have the camera hanging on the actor, following the actor, the camera being just a recording instrument, not a god." His technique of coaxing performers, persuading through praise, was summed up by Gaston Modot as *dressage à douceur*, gentle breaking-in: "Gently, without seeming to, he dismantles everything and begins all over again. Seduced, the actors purr, stretch, arch their backs under the velvet glove. They recommence the scene, quite confident, docile, attentive. The smiling trainer flatters them, leads them on his invisible leash."

After *La Vie est à nous*, Renoir began work on what was envisaged as the first of two medium-length Maupassant adaptations, to be released together as a single feature. As it turned out, only one—*Partie de campagne* (*A Day in the Country*, 1936)—was made, and even that was probably never finished. In a 1961 interview, Renoir maintained that, at 37 minutes, the film is complete as it stands and that he never intended anything longer, although "a producer subsequently asked me to make it into a 90-minute film. I tried to write some more material, but couldn't manage it." However, *Partie* was not released for a decade; when it finally appeared in 1946, recut by Pierre Braunberger and Marguerite Renoir from the original negative, it bore a title explaining that "for reasons of *force majeure*" it had never been finished, and that two brief intertitles had been added to explain missing sequences. Other members of the team, such as Sylvia Bataille, certainly believed it to be incomplete. Despite Renoir's statement, it seems that the film should have run some 50 minutes, but that bad weather and his commitment to *Les Bas-Fonds* prevented its completion.

In any case, it hardly matters. In its brief, seemingly artless simplicity, *Partie de campagne* must be the most perfect unfinished film ever made. The action, based on Maupassant's short story, takes place in the 1860s. A Parisian ironmonger, M. Dufour, takes his family out for the day: his wife, daughter, and aged mother, and his assistant and prospective son-in-law, the doltish Anatole. Two young men, staying at the riverside inn where the family stop for lunch, decide to make a play for mother and daughter. Mme. Dufour readily accedes to the lecherous Rodolphe; the daughter, Henriette, succumbs to the more soulful passion of Henri. A rainstorm ends the idyll. Years later Henriette, with her husband, returns to the same spot and meets Henri. They exchange a few melancholy words before Anatole awakes, braying for his wife.

One of Renoir's most personal works, filmed at Marlotte on the Loing where Auguste Renoir used to paint, *Partie de campagne* was shot almost *en famille*. Alain, Renoir's son, took a small role, as did Marguerite Renoir and the director himself, hamming throatily as the *patron* of the inn. Claude Renoir was cinematographer, and most of the stock company lent a hand with the filming. For all this, the atmosphere on the shoot seems to have been poisonous. Sylvia Bataille, whose hauntingly vulnerable performance as Henriette holds the film's emotional center, recalled days of miserable waiting, bitter quarrels, drunkenness, and recrimination—none of which shows in the film's mood of elegiac nostalgia and bittersweet regret. "This," wrote Richard Winnington, "is everybody's lost love." As an example of the visual intensity which Renoir so often brought to deep-focus shots through windows and doors, Alexander Sesonske cited "that almost enchanted instant . . . when Rodolphe rises from the table and pushes open the shutters: the world floods through the window. The shallow space bursts open as the compositional center of the shot leaps to the deep exterior, with the interior becoming a mere frame."

"I can't imagine cinema without water. The movement of cinema has something ineluctable about it like the current of a stream." From *La Fille de l'eau* onwards, the ripple of light on water forms an essential element in Renoir's films. In *Partie* the river itself becomes a character: not just a metaphor (brief, evanescent joys carried away on the flux of life), but a very tangible presence, its changing moods mirroring those of the protagonists. From the broad satire of the opening scenes—the two Parisian males are caricatured, in both costume and gesture, into something very close to Laurel and Hardy—the tone shifts through pastoral lyricism into the aching poignancy of the close, intensified by Joseph Kosma's yearning score.

Renoir's fourth film of the year, *Les Bas-Fonds* (1936) was an adaptation—coscripted with Charles Spaak—of Maxim Gorky's most famous play, *The Lower Depths*. Not enough of an adaptation, perhaps. Though the script kept relatively close to the original (and received Gorky's approval), Renoir explicitly stipulated that he should not be expected to create an authentically Russian atmosphere. Yet neither characters nor setting ever become wholly French, leaving the film hovering somewhere in limbo, in a half-world whose unreality blunts the edge of any intended social comment. Kurosawa's 1957 version, though more faithful to Gorky, works far better—as Renoir himself acknowledged—for being transposed to a richly-detailed nineteenth-century Japan.

Renoir intended *Les Bas-Fonds* as "a realistic poem on the loss of human dignity." The bulk of the action takes place in a riverside flophouse owned by Kostilyev, an elderly miser, and inhabited by a vivid assortment of social outcasts, including Pepel, a professional thief (Jean Gabin), and a ruined baron (Louis Jouvet). This was the only film that Gabin and Jouvet made together, and it remains memorable chiefly for their performances, and that of Jany Holt as a prostitute. Renoir tended to play down the despairing squalor of the original in favor of comedy and added an up-beat, almost Chaplinesque coda, in which Pepel, having killed the repellent Kostilyev, wanders off down the open road with the girl he loves. "I admit," François Poulle wrote, "that the film is well acted, well edited, well designed, well lit—but it still bores me."

At the time, though, Russian subjects were much in vogue in French cinema, and *Les Bas-Fonds* became one of Renoir's biggest box-office successes. It also earned him the Prix Louis Delluc, and he was made a Chevalier of the Légion d'Honneur by the socialist government of Leon Blum. With this prestige, and the support of Jean Gabin, Renoir finally managed to secure backing for a project he had been working on for three years. *La Grande Illusion* (1937) was based on the experiences of a wartime fellow pilot, Adjutant Pinsard, who had made seven escapes from enemy prison camp; but what started out as a rousing adventure film was gradually deepened in its conception—and in this, the enforced delay may have proven beneficial—into one of the great cinematic statements on class and war and the roots of human conflict. "If the film celebrates the possibility of demolishing boundaries," Robin Wood observed, "it also acknowledges, within the existing social system, their inevitability."

As Renoir and Spaak (again coscripting) had first planned it, the film was to center on three socially diverse French officers thrown together in captivity. But while things were being set up, the producers secured Erich von Stroheim for the relatively small part of the camp commandant. Overwhelmed by the idea of working with the man whose films had inspired his own career, Renoir set about reshaping the script; together with Stroheim and Spaak he expanded the commandant's role, adding a whole further dimension: the power of class affinities to cut across national allegiances. The casting of the Jewish actor Marcel Dalio introduced yet another theme, that of racial prejudice.

Two French fliers, the aristocratic Captain de Boeldieu (Pierre Fresnay) and the working-class Lieutenant Maréchal (Gabin), are shot down behind enemy lines and taken prisoner. After several attempted escapes they are transferred to a high-security camp whose commandant, von Rauffenstein (Stroheim), is an ex-pilot, now crippled; he and Boeldieu, both upper-class professional soldiers, establish a friendship. After several attempts, Maréchal succeeds in escaping, along with another prisoner, Rosenthal (Dalio), while Boeldieu, helping to cover them, is shot dead by Rauffenstein. The fugitives take refuge on a German farm, and Maréchal enjoys a brief idyll with the widowed owner Elsa (Dita Parlo) before the two Frenchmen struggle on to reach the Swiss border.

La Grande Illusion, Renoir explained, is a war film without heroes or villains, in which "the villain is the war." But not simply the war as such; all the divisive barriers—of nation, class, race, or religion—which preclude fraternity, and which lead to wars, are equally indicted. In the self-contained microcosm of the prison camp, the conflicts engendered by social and political rifts stand out with ironic clarity, as do the friendships that, despite everything, transcend such divisions. The Germans are no less prisoners than the men they guard, and Rauffenstein, with the corset and neck-brace imposed by his injuries, especially so—a man visibly locked into a rigid code whose logic constrains him to kill his only friend. The realistic use of language (contrary to cinematic custom of the period, all the characters speak in their own tongues) provides another factor in the mix, serving as connection or barrier according to circumstance. Maréchal and Elsa, unable to communicate verbally, evolve their own warm nonverbal language; while Boeldieu and Rauffenstein talk together in English, the international upper-class tongue, effectively excluding their own compatriots.

"I made *La Grande Illusion* because I am a pacifist," Renoir affirmed, although he also suggested that the film owed its initial success to being a prison-break movie. "The escape story has nothing to do with my film. But it's a mask, a disguise, and this disguise made *La Grande Illusion* a big money-maker." Whether or not this was so, the pacifist message seems to have come across clearly from the first. The film was widely acclaimed, both in France and abroad, as a masterpiece. In New York it ran for twenty-six weeks; it was nominated for an Oscar, and President Roosevelt declared that "all the democracies of the world should see this film." Other countries paid it more back-handed tributes. At the Venice Biennale, pressure was put on the jury not to award it the top honor, the Mussolini Cup; a special award, the International Jury Cup, had to be created instead, after which the film was banned in Italy. It was also banned in Germany, and in Belgium (by order of the Foreign Minister, Henri Spaak, who was Charles Spaak's brother). During and immediately after the war the film suffered various cuts (although it had been suppressed by the Nazis, it was attacked after the liberation for being pro-German), but the complete version was restored in 1958, in time to be voted fifth greatest film of all time at the Brussels World Fair.

In recent years the reputation of *La Grande Illusion* has slipped a little, supplanted as Renoir's supreme achievement—at least in most critics' estimation—by *La Règle du jeu*, and criticized, by Bernard Chardère among others, for showing "war in lace ruffles. . . . The ocean of mud, tedium, sweat and death of the years 1914–18 has become some kind of chivalry." Similarly, with historical hindsight, Roy Armes suggested that the film "presents almost too benign a view of war in view of the holocaust which was about to engulf Europe." It could be argued, though, that evoking the horrors of the trenches (or indeed of the death-camps) to demonstrate the hell of war is to state the obvious; Renoir is concerned to show that, even under relatively civilized circumstances, war is still utterly unjustifiable.

Jacques Brunius recalled that, though the dramatic focus of *La Grande Illusion* was intended to concentrate on Maréchal and Rosenthal, the men of the new order, during the course of filming "the characters of Fresnay and Stroheim interested . . . [Renoir] so much more than those of the proletarians that the two aristocrats became the true heroes of the film." A similar shift of sympathy seems to have affected the balance of *La Marseillaise* (1938), a historical pageant supposedly celebrating the triumph of the populace in the French Revolution, but whose most engaging and moving scenes are those involving Louis XVI (partly thanks to Pierre Renoir, giving one of the finest screen performances of his career as the luckless monarch).

La Marseillaise was planned as a great popular commemorative production, "a film for the People and by the People," to be made by Ciné-Liberté and financed by two-franc subscriptions from the members of the CGT, the leading left-wing trade union. The initial scenario, covering the events of 1787 to 1792, was soon judged impracticable, and Renoir decided to concentrate on a few crucial weeks during the summer of 1792, leading up to the taking of the Tuileries palace and the fall of the monarchy. Linked to these events was the march to Paris of the Marseilles battalion—five hundred volunteers who came to offer their services against counterrevolutionary foreign aggression. Renoir aimed to demystify history, to scrape away the accretions of grandeur and heroic posturing to reveal everyday people, as preoccupied with their own basic needs as with the great events in which they were taking part. Thus the marchers en route from Marseilles discuss, not high-flown revolutionary abstractions, but how best to stop their feet hurting; Louis, reviewing his remaining loyal troops, is bothered about his wig, which keeps slipping. "I tried to make the film as if the camera had existed two hundred years ago and I had shot a documentary."

Renoir always referred to *La Marseillaise* as one of his favorite films. Few critics of any persuasion have felt able to agree with him. For Pierre Leprohon, the picture revealed the director at well below his best: "Trying, in this committed film, to prove something, to serve a cause, he was unable to allow free rein to his faults, which are also his virtues: his freedom, his untidiness, his improvisation." Truffaut thought more highly of the film, but at the cost of depoliticizing it: "Renoir serves up an entire world, where all causes are presented with the objectivity, generosity and intelligence that mark all of his work. Renoir is above the struggle." Coming from a very different angle, François Poulle arrived at a similar verdict, seeing the film as "a kind of anti-*Potemkin* . . . all we witness is a clash between individuals, revolutionary characters against monarchist characters. Adherence to the Revolution becomes a question of temperament rather than of social position." An evasion, suggested Bernard Chardère, "glorifying the Great Revolution of '89 to avoid staging that of '37."

"Insofar as the film identifies the interest of the nation with that of its lower-class majorities," Raymond Durgnat remarked, "it is more Marxist than it seems. Insofar as it sees some hope of class reconciliation, Marxists must consider Renoir a bourgeois liberal. . . . The film is permeated by its play of contradictions." Hence, perhaps, the tendency of *La Marseillaise* to resolve itself, not into the narrative tapestry that Renoir seems to have intended, but into a series of memorable episodes: the scenes with Louis, the shadow-play (designed by Lotte Reiniger) of King and Nation, the assault on the Tuileries, the death of Bomier (one of the Marseillais) while, framed in a gateway, the victorious forces of the Revolution march joyfully by. Such sequences, fine though they are, never quite sustain a two-and-a-quarter-hour length, and *La Marseillaise* failed to achieve its hoped-for popular success (except in Russia, where it broke box-office records).

Renoir was now generally recognized, even by those who disliked his political stance, as one of the foremost directors in France. Despite this, he could rarely find anyone willing to back the films he wanted to make. "Even after *La Grande Illusion* had made a fortune for its producer I had difficulty in raising money for my own projects. I was not, and still am not, 'commercial.'" The failure of *La Marseillaise* having done little to further his box-office standing, he accepted an assignment from the Hakim brothers' company, Paris Film, to direct Jean Gabin in a 1938 version of Zola's *La Bête humaine* (*The Human Beast*)—mainly, he later insisted, "because Gabin and I wanted to play with trains."

"Of all Renoir's works of this period," Alexander Sesonske wrote, "only *La Bête humaine* fits snugly into the mold of the most popular French films of the day," sharing with the Carné-Prévert cycle "a dark atmosphere, an air of hopelessness, and the presence of Gabin in his classic role of doomed tragic hero." Renoir's script, written like *Nana* with the help of Denise Leblond-Zola, follows Zola's novel in its broad essentials. Gabin plays Jacques Lantier, a train driver with a family history of mental illness. On his way back to Le Havre from a Paris run, he witnesses a murder: the jealous stationmaster Roubaud, learning that his wife Séverine had an affair with her guardian, kills him with her unwilling help. To keep Lantier quiet, Séverine seduces him, and also urges him to kill her husband. Lantier agrees, but at the last moment lacks the will to do it; instead, he kills Séverine in a fit of madness, and throws himself from his speeding train.

Graham Greene, reviewing the film in *The Spectator,* commended Renoir's ability "to get the most out of the everyday life of his characters, the routine of their work," noting how he "works the depot and a man's job into every scene—conversations on platforms, in washrooms and canteens, views from the stationmaster's window over the steaming metal waste: the short, sharp lust worked out in a wooden platelayer's shed among shunted trucks under the steaming rain." The opening, near-documentary sequence, filmed without studio trickery from the footplate of a speeding locomotive (with Gabin actually driving the train) and trenchantly edited, has been widely praised. Gabin's subtle performance is finely matched by the feline sensuality of Simone Simon as Séverine, and by Fernand Ledoux's sullen, menacing Roubaud. (Renoir himself took a small role, as a poacher.) Where *La Bête humaine* lacks conviction is in the mechanics of the plot; Renoir, least deterministic of directors, can have felt little sympathy with Zola's rigid genetic determinism.

For some time Renoir had been contemplating a modern adaptation of Musset's tragicomedy of amorous intrigue, *Les Caprices de Marianne,* and in November 1938, together with his brother Claude and three friends, he set up his own production company in order to film it. La Nouvelle Edition Française was envisaged as a French equivalent of United Artists, which would allow Renoir and other directors of independent temperament to make the pictures they wanted, under their own control. As it turned out, the fledgling company made only a single film before collapsing in financial ruin. That one film, however, was Renoir's masterpiece, though not for twenty years would it be generally recognized as such.

Of all Renoir's films, *La Règle du jeu* (*The Rules of the Game,* 1939) is the richest and most complex, the most subtly composed both in the interweavings of its narrative intrigue and in its wider implications. Inspired not only by Musset but by the eighteenth-century tradition of Beaumarchais and Marivaux (whose best-known play, *Le Jeu de l'Amour et du Hasard,* could have furnished an alternative title), and by the composers of the French baroque, it exploits—as did *La Grande Illusion*—the convention of the microcosm: here using the events of a house-party at a country chateau to comment, with irony and despair, on the state of France on the eve of disaster. It is, Penelope Gilliatt wrote, "not only a masterpiece of filmmaking, not only a great work of humanism in a perfect rococo frame, but also an act of historical testimony." Renoir himself, describing the film as "a sort of reconstructed documentary . . . on the condition of society at a given moment," added: "It is a war film, and yet there is no reference to the war. Beneath its seemingly innocuous appearance the story attacks the very structure of our society."

Very broadly, the plot of *La Règle du jeu* centers round three emotional triangles. André Jurieu, an aviator, loves Christine, wife of the Marquis de la Chesnaye. La Chesnaye, for his part, is tiring of his affair with Geneviève, which he has contrived to conceal from his wife. And la Chesnaye's gamekeeper, Schumacher, is violently jealous of his wife Lisette (who is Christine's maid), suspecting her of an affair with the poacher-turned-valet Marceau. Around all these hovers the figure of Octave, mediator, confidant, and go-between, welcome everywhere and at home nowhere. During a weekend at la Chesnaye's chateau, Christine, discovering her husband's infidelity, resolves to go away with Jurieu, but when he expresses scruples drops him for Octave. Meanwhile the enraged Schumacher, who has been pursuing Marceau with a revolver, is led to believe that Octave has designs on Lisette; mistaking Jurieu for Octave, he shoots him dead. There has been, la Chesnaye tells his assembled guests and servants, a deplorable accident; no one is to blame.

Renoir once described his preferred style of filmmaking as "improvisation . . . built on a firm basis." Believing that "one discovers the content of a film only in the process of making it," he rejected total, unfettered improvisation as unsuited to his purpose, since "I have to know in advance what I'm going to film; but even though I know what I'm going to do, what I finally film turns out to be something quite different." A film's ostensible subject-matter was no more than the starting-point, like a theme for a jazz musician, or (as he himself put it) "a landscape for a painter." His own role in this process he liked to term not "director," with its connotations of rigid control, but rather "le meneur du jeu" (which might be translated "master of the revels"). Nowhere is that role more manifest than in *La Règle du jeu*, with his casting of himself as the pivotal figure of Octave—seen by David Thomson as "Renoir's admission that the director, supposedly the authoritative and manipulating figure, is as much victim as originator of circumstances."

La Règle, Joel Finler remarked, "truly *evolved* during its making, as Renoir worked on writing and rewriting the script, balancing and rebalancing the characters and relationships, plots and subplots." On one level, the film can be taken as the tragicomedy of those who find themselves unable to fit the neat, predetermined boxes society, or conventional wisdom, has constructed for them. The aviator, stepping down from his record-breaking flight as the flashbulbs pop, is no modest and laconic hero but a tearful, petulant creature, complaining that the woman he loves is not there to welcome him. The poacher, Nature's free spirit, wants only to don the livery of a flunky; the gracious aristocrat is sneered

at in the servant's hall for being a Jew; while Octave, shambling miserably between the strata of society, reviles himself as a failure and a parasite. The rules of the game are designed to exclude those who fail to grasp the unspoken assumptions behind them.

"Everyone has his reasons"—Octave's remark has become the most famous line in all Renoir's films. In context, though, it ceases to be the comfortably tolerant dictum it might seem. Given its full form—"You know, in this world there's one thing that is terrible: that everyone has his reasons"—it stands revealed as an insight into the awful incompatibility of human desires. Drawing on the classic conventions of French theatre—Molière's comedy of obsession, Marivaux's master-servant entanglements, Feydeau's bedroom fugues—the film swerves unpredictably between farce and tragedy, climaxing in the after-dinner sequence, a sustained tour de force of orchestrated chaos. Through the tattered remnants of amateur theatricals, with some guests clad as skeletons, others as Bavarian peasants, and Octave lumbering round seeking help in shedding his bear costume, erupts the gun-wielding Schumacher, blasting in all directions while Lisette tries to restrain him and Marceau dodges behind furniture and people. Jurieu meantime is begging Christine to run off with him and offering to fight all and sundry. La Chesnaye, proudly displaying his prized collection of mechanical toys, registers that some sort of disruption is in progress. "Stop this farce!" he orders Corneille, his major-domo. "Which one, sir?" the servant inquires.

Renoir films this sequence as though the camera were itself one of the guests—wandering, bemused and mildly intoxicated, from room to room, catching glimpses of events through a doorway or over someone's shoulder, uncertain whether to laugh, or take cover, or intervene. His experiments with deep-focus, multilevel composition—as revolutionary, in their less flamboyant way, as those of Welles—here reach their apogee: the roaming, inquisitive viewpoint constantly reframes, without seeking to contain, the intricate flux of movements and events. "The spatial relationships are so engrossing," David Thomson wrote, "that . . . one has the impression of a camera that is always moving to cover as much as possible. One does not notice cuts, one delights in a continuity which is often on the verge of chaos and finally leads to tragedy in the intrusion of subplot into plot, of the theatrical into the real, and of disaster into balance."

Perfection was never Renoir's aim, and *La Règle*, though a great film, is by no means a perfect one. The acting in particular is highly uneven; if Marcel Dalio (la Chesnaye), Julien Carette (Marceau), Pauline Dubost (Lisette), and Gaston Modot (Schumacher) are rarely less than superb, and if Renoir himself turns his limitations as an actor to advantage, Nora Gregor's Christine creates a void at the center. The supposed object of every man's passionate adoration, she seems stiff and insipid, "as haunting and bewitching" (in Gerald Mast's brutal phrase) "as a plaster giraffe." (Renoir, apparently temporarily infatuated, insisted against all advice on casting her when Simone Simon proved too pricey, but became increasingly disillusioned as shooting progressed.) For many critics, though, Renoir's imperfections are a strength; Truffaut wrote that his work "unfolds as if he had devoted his most brilliant moments to fleeing from the masterpiece, to escape any notion of the definite and the fixed, so as to create a semi-improvisation, a deliberately unfinished 'open' work that each viewer can complete for himself."

This quality of openness, by which a range of possible attitudes seem to be offered for our consideration rather than dropped ready-packaged in our laps, is what lends many of Renoir's films, but La Règle du jeu in particular, their singularly modern feel. Where Le Jour se lève, for example, for all Carné and Prévert's skill, seems frozen in its period, a prime specimen preserved in the aspic of poetic realism, La Règle contrives to be both of its time and of now, offering no "definitive statement," but fresh readings on each repeated viewing. The looseness and fluidity of texture stemming from Renoir's informal approach to filmmaking creates in the viewer an impression of freedom, of the rich untidy ambiguity of "real life." In William Pechter's words, "the sense of liberation with which Renoir's films leave us is not only our own but that of . . . [the] characters themselves."

During the course of filming, La Règle ran seriously over budget; estimated at 2.5 million francs, it ended up costing 5 million, and the company was obliged to turn to Gaumont for extra funds, thus sacrificing their independence. As cut together by Marguerite Renoir, the picture ran 113 minutes, which Gaumont insisted was too long. Renoir reluctantly agreed, and 13 minutes were taken out before the premiere.

The opening of La Règle du jeu was calamitous. Audiences howled, whistled, ripped up seats and set newspapers afire in protest. The film was attacked as frivolous, unpatriotic, clumsy, and downright incomprehensible. Devastated, Renoir agreed to further cuts in the hope of salvaging both the film and his company. Two amputated versions were prepared, one of 85 and one of 90 minutes, both of them lacking several crucial plot points; baffled audiences proved even less receptive. In October 1939 the picture was banned as "demoralizing" by the authorities, a ban reimposed when the Germans reached Paris the following June. After the war La Règle received occasional showings in versions ranging from 80 to 90 minutes, and was generally written off as "one for the buzzards" (as the New York Times put it in 1950).

The film's rehabilitation began with the providential discovery, in 1956, of 200 cans of outtakes. With Renoir's help, all but one minute of the original, 113-minute version was restored, and the resurrected film was premiered at Venice in 1959, where it was hailed as a lost masterpiece. Since then its reputation has steadily grown, among audiences and critics alike, as Renoir's supreme achievement and one of the greatest pictures ever made. Robin Wood described it as "one of the cinema's few truly inexhaustible films"; for Alain Resnais it provided "the single most overwhelming experience I have ever had in the cinema."

"The failure of La Règle du jeu so depressed me that I resolved either to give up the cinema or to leave France." As things worked out, Renoir chose the latter option. It would be fifteen years before he made another film in France. In July 1939, shortly after the disastrous premiere of La Règle, he left for Rome, where he had been invited by the Scalera company to direct a film of Puccini's Tosca. His relationship with Marguerite Renoir having ended, his companion on the Italian trip (and henceforward) was Dido Freire, Cavalcanti's niece, who had worked with him as his secretary and continuity assistant.

When war broke out in September 1939 Renoir returned home. For the time being, though, Mussolini remained neutral, and a few months later Renoir was persuaded by the French Ministry of Information, anxious to preserve good relations with Italy, to go back and resume filming in Rome. He did so, but had directed only a few shots when in June 1940 Italy declared war on France and Renoir departed hastily, leaving the film to his assistants Carl Koch and Luchino Visconti. La Tosca (1941) finally appeared with Koch credited as sole director.

As the Germans advanced on Paris, Renoir and Dido Freire joined the trek southward, finally reaching Auguste Renoir's old house at Cagnes, where Renoir's brother Claude now lived. While there, he received an invitation, couched in seductive terms, to make films for the German government. "So attractive and dazzling did their offers become . . . that I felt it might be better for me to leave." Through the influence of Robert Flaherty and Albert Lewin, who had met him in Paris before the war, Renoir was granted an entry visa to the United States. In December 1940, having travelled via Algiers, Casablanca, and Lisbon, he and Dido took ship for New York; Renoir found himself sharing a cabin with Antoine de Saint-Exupéry.

Renoir arrived in Hollywood in January 1941 and signed a one-year contract with Darryl F. Zanuck at Fox—a relationship characterized, on both sides, by well-meaning incomprehension. Renoir suggested various subjects, including Saint-Exupéry's *Terre des hommes*, which the studio turned down as "too European." Fox, for their part, came up with a range of action-packed melodramas which Renoir politely declined. Eventually agreement was reached on *Swamp Water*, a script by Dudley Nichols based on a recent novel by Vereen Bell, set in the Okefenokee Swamp in Georgia. In its subject—a man falsely accused of murder and driven to take refuge in the swamp—Renoir may have seen the opportunity for an exploration of the relations between man, society, and nature. As things turned out, he felt that he had "passed by a great subject without penetrating it . . . but it is still something to be able to direct a film with a story that is not completely idiotic."

"What bothered me in Hollywood wasn't interference," Renoir later explained. "I love interference; it produces discussion, and discussion frequently helps you improve your work. . . . People believe that Hollywood producers are very greedy and think only of earning lots of money, but that's not true. The defect is much more dangerous: they want their films to be technically perfect." The shooting of *Swamp Water* (1941), he had assumed, would allow him to escape from the studio and film on location in the Okefenokee itself. Zanuck maintained that Fox could build a swamp as good as or even better than Nature's in the controllable environment of the studio. In the end, Renoir was allowed to film a few exteriors in Georgia with his lead actor, Dana Andrews, but with none of the other players, nor any sound equipment. Swamp sound effects would be created back in the studio, along with the rest of the film.

Renoir completed *Swamp Water* in a state of misery. Though he got on well with his cast and crew, the Fox approach to filmmaking baffled and depressed him. "I ask you not to judge my work in America by this film, which will be Mr. Zanuck's and not mine," he told Dudley Nichols. "I would rather sell peanuts in Mexico than make films at Fox." He was further hampered by his limited English, and by worries about his son Alain, who was still in Vichy territory. The

end result, according to Higham and Greenberg, was "an indifferently-made rustic tale," although Tom Milne detected, both here and in *The Southerner,* "a good deal of the old Renoir bite in the rough, warm humanity of their themes." Despite Renoir's unhappiness, *Swamp Water* got good notices and received the New York Critics Award.

Having severed his Fox contract, to the relief of both parties, Renoir found himself out of work but under no urgent financial pressure. Towards the end of the year he managed to secure his son's passage to America; Alain Renoir arrived in December and soon afterwards enlisted in the US Army. In February 1942 Renoir signed a long-term deal with Universal, but after a few days' work on a Deanna Durbin vehicle, *Forever Yours,* he asked to be released from his contract. (The film eventually appeared as *The Amazing Mrs. Holliday,* credited to Bruce Manning; an article in the August 1986 *Films in Review* suggests that Renoir may in fact have shot most of it.) While making *Swamp Water,* he had formed a close friendship with Dudley Nichols, and they now began to collaborate on a script to be filmed as an independent production for RKO, with Renoir and Nichols as joint producers.

When, after the war, Renoir's American films were eventually released in France, none of them aroused much enthusiasm. The most hostile reception of all greeted *This Land Is Mine* (1943). Set in a Nazi-occupied country which, although unidentified, is clearly France, it tells of a timid schoolteacher, Albert Lory (Charles Laughton), who meekly obeys orders and shuns any contact with the Resistance. But events conspire to prick his conscience; he publicly denounces the Nazis and is arrested while reading his pupils the Declaration of the Rights of Man. This simplified, sterilized version of the Occupation was contemptuously rejected by the French, who had so recently experienced the real thing. Renoir pointed out, however, that the film was never intended for their consumption; it was aimed at those Americans who despised all the occupied peoples as cowards and collaborators, to show that "when one was under the boot of the occupying power, it wasn't perhaps quite so easy to play the hero."

With its pasteboard studio sets, well-nourished Hollywood faces (Maureen O'Hara, Kent Smith), and ringingly sententious dialogue, *This Land Is Mine* seems now absurdly remote from any kind of reality. All that saves it from inanity is the passionate sincerity of Renoir's intentions, detectable even through Laughton's barnstorming peroration. The same emotional commitment can be felt in *Salute to France* (1944), a

half-hour propaganda film codirected by Renoir
and Garson Kanin for the Office of War Information. Alternating staged sequences with documentary footage, it was intended to offer GIs
some understanding of the country they were
about to liberate. (Renoir also recalled having
worked, uncredited, on other propaganda films
around this time, but never identified them.) In
February 1944, while *Salute to France* was in
preparation, Renoir and Dido Freire were married.

Looking back on his Hollywood films, Renoir
reflected that "while not regretting them, I'm all
too well aware that they come nowhere near my
ideal." The least unsatisfactory, he felt, was *The
Southerner* (1945); many critics have agreed.
Made for Producing Artists, an independent
company set up by Robert Hakim and David
Loew, the film was based on a novel by George
Sessions Perry, *Hold Autumn in Your Hand,*
about the struggles of a poor farming family in
Texas. Renoir wrote his own script (with some
uncredited help from William Faulkner), and
was given complete freedom to film as he wanted, largely on location with a small crew and rel-
atively unknown actors. His set designer was
Eugène Lourié, who had worked on *La Grande
Illusion* and *La Règle du jeu.*

The Southerner has little plot as such. It
chronicles a year in the life of the Tucker family
as they try to set up their own farm, battling disease, the elements, hostile neighbors, and the
stubborn intractability of the soil. Eric Rohmer,
reassessing the American films in *Cahiers du
Cinéma* (January 1952), observed that "Renoir
presents these cotton-farmers . . . with entirely
appropriate austerity. . . . There is something
noble in their meager lives, something dramatic,
to which Renoir gives an added dimension, as he
has always enriched the characters he is given to
work with." The harsh poetry of survival in a
desolate landscape at times recalls *Toni,* as does
the vividly realized sense of place. "Physically,"
James Agee wrote in *The Nation,* "it is one of the
most sensitive and beautiful American-made
pictures I have seen. . . . It gets perfectly the
mournful, hungry mysteriousness of a Southern
country winter." He was less happy with the actors, most of whom he found "screechingly, unbearably wrong. They didn't walk right, stand
right, eat right, sound right or look right,
and . . . it was clear that the basic understanding and the basic emotional and mental . . . attitudes were wrong, to the point of unintentional
insult."

Surface verisimilitude, as Raymond Durgnat
remarked, was not necessarily Renoir's aim.
Many of Agee's fellow-southerners, though,

thought that it was, and considered the film,
with its seemingly definitive title, a deliberately
derogatory image of them and their region. *The
Southerner* was picketed and boycotted throughout the South and banned in Agee's native Tennessee. Elsewhere, though, it was warmly
received, winning an Oscar nomination (for best
director) and several other awards, and becoming the only commercial hit of Renoir's American period.

Since the silent era Renoir had cherished the
idea of making a film of Octave Mirbeau's scathing social satire, *Le Journal d'une femme de
chambre.* His motives in choosing to film such
an innately French work in a Hollywood studio
have never been quite clear; he explained, rather
oddly, that "I very much wanted to make a film
with Paulette Goddard," but regretted his failure to "draw from this goldmine of a subject all
that I should have done. . . . I hoped to bring
out the baroque, odious, chillingly cruel side of
the work; starting out with the best intentions,
I let myself be over-influenced by public
opinion." Like *The Southerner, The Diary of a
Chambermaid* (1946) was made for an independent company—in this case Camden Productions, set up by Goddard's husband, Burgess
Meredith, who also coscripted, coproduced, and
took a major role in the film.

Mirbeau's novel paints a scurrilous picture of
the turn-of-the-century *haute bourgeoisie*
through the pitiless eyes of Célestine, the mercenary chambermaid who observes (and avidly exploits) the meanness, snobbery and sexual foibles
of her employers. Renoir, no doubt constrained
by the Hays Code, omitted much of Mirbeau's
seamier detail (unlike Bunuel in his 1964 version, who dwelt on it with relish). For some critics, these omissions, and the Hollywood casting,
constituted major weaknesses. "The film turns
on the spunky, wholesome frolics of Paulette
Goddard," Christopher Faulkner wrote, "whose
Celestine displays none of the vulgarity and sexuality of the Mirbeau original." The film
flopped badly when released in France, where
the studio sets and artificial lighting, the alien
cast and language appeared a betrayal, not just
of Renoir's material, but of the principles on
which he had based his own earlier work.
François Poulle saw it as "an exile's film, full of
abortive intentions."

More recently, though, the film has come in
for reappraisal, and some critics would now
agree with Higham and Greenberg in rating it
"unquestionably Renoir's best American film."
André Bazin, at first outspoken in his disappointment, later reconsidered: "The meticulously exact reconstruction, rather than having the effect

of creating an impossible, synthetic France, on the contrary gave the images the clarity of a nightmare. . . . There is no film in all Renoir's output which shows greater freedom of style." In its overt theatricality, it can be seen to foreshadow the mood of his postwar French films, with their implied (or sometimes explicit) proscenium-arch framing. In *Sight and Sound* (Autumn 1964) Tom Milne described it as *"La Règle du jeu* on a wider register. Everything is carried to greater extremes: on the one hand, the fantasy and artificial comedy, on the other, the paroxysmal cry of anger. . . . He constantly undercuts the charade element by twisting his puppets to reveal flesh and blood." *Diary of a Chambermaid,* Milne added, is "one of the normally gentle Renoir's most violent films"; and as Joseph, the saturnine and brutal valet, Francis Lederer created one of Renoir's few wholly despicable characters.

For the last film of his American period, Renoir returned to RKO, for whom he had made *This Land Is Mine.* As with *Madame Bovary,* it is difficult to assess *The Woman on the Beach* (1947), since the original (which no longer survives) was heavily cut and reshot. This time, though, no heavy-handed executive can be blamed; the butcher was Renoir himself.

A brooding, atmospheric affair that might have suited Fritz Lang, the film brings together on a wreck-strewn shore a trio of social misfits: a blind ex-artist, his sensual and unhappy wife, and a war-shocked veteran haunted by nightmares of drowning. The first third or so of the picture—which runs only 71 minutes—builds up a bleak, sexual intensity as the wife and the veteran (well played by Joan Bennett and Robert Ryan) meet and are attracted: more through shared despair, it seems, than through any hope of lasting happiness. But thereafter the action starts to meander, losing direction and dissipating the initial tension—weaknesses resulting, by all accounts, from Renoir's revisions. Previewed in Santa Barbara in its initial version, the film was greeted with giggles and jibes. "I was suddenly scared of losing contact with the public, and I lost my nerve." About a third of the footage was reshot and a lot more scrapped before the picture was eventually released—only to flop disastrously.

By mutual consent, Renoir's contract with RKO was terminated. Together with Burgess Meredith, he set up an independent company, the Film Group, planning to shoot low-budget versions of stage classics. Their first project was to be an adaptation of Clifford Odets' *Night Music,* starring Dana Andrews and Joan Bennett, but they were unable to find funding, and the company folded without making a single picture.

For Renoir, as for other European exiles with a history of prewar leftist sympathies, the political climate in the USA was starting to turn cold; for this and other reasons, he was coming to feel himself alienated from Hollywood. "Since the death of Lubitsch," he observed sadly, "the idea of the filmmaker, as such, has vanished from Hollywood. It happens all too often that the post of director consists of little more than a folding chair with his name on it." California remained his second home; his son Alain was studying at Santa Barbara, with a view to an academic career, and just after the war Renoir had become a naturalized American, retaining dual French-US citizenship. But America no longer seemed a good place to make films in, although some unspecified reluctance prevented Renoir returning directly to France. Instead, he embarked on a long detour, by way of India and Italy.

While still struggling to salvage *Woman on the Beach* Renoir had come across Rumer Godden's *The River,* a semi-autobiographical novel based on her own Anglo-Indian childhood, and had secured an option on it. Backing proved hard to come by; India, as far as Hollywood was concerned, meant elephants, maharajahs and tiger hunts, none of which featured in Godden's story. Eventually Kenneth McEldowney, a prosperous florist who wanted to be a film producer, helped raise the necessary funds partly in the US and partly in India. Working closely together, Renoir and Godden devised a script which, with each successive draft, diverged further from conventional narrative structure to incorporate documentary and lyrical episodes, ending up as (in Renoir's words) "an Occidental meditation on the Orient. . . . I wanted to bear witness to a civilization which wasn't based on profit." The picture was to be shot entirely on location in India, and in color—the first color film that either Renoir or his nephew Claude, the cinematographer, had ever worked on.

The narrative element of *The River* (1951), such as it is, centers on the relationship between a young war-wounded American, Captain John, and three teenage girls: the impetuously self-assured Valerie; the Indo-European Melanie; and Harriet, awkward and shy, who aspires to be a writer. Through and around this tenuous plot flows the timeless, gaudy, self-renewing life of India, endlessly changing and endlessly the same, like the great river itself. Renoir, Gerald Mast noted, "used color 'musically' as he had previously used music for tonal colouring. . . . *The River* comes alive with its shots of the blue-gray-green Ganges, the red dust of the soil, the sharp greens, whites, yellows and reds of the Indian villages, houses, and foliage." India, in its overwhelming presence, dominates the film—the more so since the stilted performances of Renoir's largely amateur cast scarcely compete with it for our attention.

Renoir's experience of India made a deep impression on him, consolidating a change in his philosophical outlook that had begun with his departure from Europe in 1940. Henceforth his films are suffused with a spirit of benign, universal acceptance (or, some would say, complacency). "Before the war, my way of contributing to the universal concert was by trying to add a voice of protest. . . . Today, the new being that I've become realizes that sarcasm is no longer timely, and that the only thing I can bring to this illogical, irresponsible and cruel world is my 'love.'" In *The River*, the death by snakebite of Harriet's young brother is merely a darker note in the eternal harmony, a loss to be mourned but no cause for lasting despair—and implicitly, in the birth to the family of a new child, part of the cycle of constant renewal. "How can you carry on as if nothing had happened?" Harriet screams at her parents. "We don't," her mother replies. "We just carry on."

The River, in Pierre Leprohon's view, "is one of Renoir's greatest films. . . . Its apparent disorder corresponds to the reality of life and of dreams, whose complexity and richness it expresses like a poem." Most critics have agreed on the film's lyrical and plastic beauty; but some objected to what they regarded as its fatalistic, depoliticized stance. Marcel Oms described it as "a long, slow hymn to the glory of the Eternal. The misery and overpopulation of India are not seen. . . . Renoir has preferred the fruitbasket of Rabindranath Tagore to the anticolonial protests of Gandhi." Even so sympathetic a writer as Satyajit Ray (who had met Renoir in Calcutta, and been greatly encouraged in his ambition to direct) expressed dissapointment that Indians figured so little, and Europeans so much. "After the nightmarish versions and perversions of India perpetrated by Hollywood," he wrote in *Sequence*, "I was looking forward with real eagerness to the prospect of a great director tackling the Indian scene. . . . I could not help feeling that it was overdoing it a bit, coming all the way from California merely to get the topography right."

In July 1951 Renoir arrived in Italy, a few days before *The River* won the International Critics Prize at the Venice Biennale. This was fortuitous; he had come to direct an Italian-French-British coproduction, *The Golden Coach* (1953), originally planned for Visconti. (It was released in three languages, but Renoir always considered the English version to be the original, since the other two were post-synched.) A particular attraction for him was the chance to work with Anna Magnani, who had already been cast in the leading role. The plot was derived, at some distance, from a play by Prosper Merimée, *Le Carrosse du Saint-Sacrament* (which also provided the libretto of Offenbach's operetta *La Périchole*). A troupe of *commedia dell'arte* actors arrive in eighteenth-century Peru, led by the fiery Camilla (Magnani), who attracts the attention of three suitors: Felipe, a young soldier; Ramon, a bullfighter; and the Viceroy, who gives her the eponymous coach. The gift arouses the fury of the court. To save the Viceroy from public humiliation, Camilla donates the coach to the church, and rejects all three suitors in favor of her only true love, the theatre.

The Golden Coach is the first of what has sometimes been termed Renoir's "theatre trilogy"—the other two components being *French Cancan* and *Elena et les hommes*. In these films play-acting—the literal or metaphorical adoption of public roles—is presented as a means of reconciling art and life, reality and aspiration; as an alternative, in other words, to the political idealism of Renoir's prewar movies. In *The Golden Coach*, Merimée's anticolonial and anticlerical satire has been transmuted into what Leo Braudy called "a world of ormolu fantasy, happily protected from the rhythms of a world outside art"; all conflict is illusory, since "the world is a stage, the state is stuffed with comic fools, and the theatrical can absorb the rest of the world into itself." All scenes, whether nominally onstage or not, are framed and composed as through a proscenium arch, and characters fall instinctively into hieratic postures, or move to the stately rhythms of Vivaldi's music. Renoir, Tom Milne commented, "is not creating art out of life, but life out of art."

With *French Cancan* (1955), Renoir made his long-awaited return to the French film industry, and also to the Montmartre of his boyhood. Conceived as a riposte to the Hollywood view of the Bel Époque shown in Huston's *Moulin Rouge*, the film offers a romanticized account of the founding of the Moulin by Ziegler (called Danglard in the film, and played, in his fourth and last role for Renoir, by Jean Gabin). The plot is standard backstage-musical stuff: Danglard discovers a young laundress, Nini (Françoise Arnoul), takes her as his mistress and trains her as his star dancer. This incurs the animosity of his previous mistress, who persuades her rich protector to withdraw his backing from Danglard's projected night-spot. But Danglard finds alternative funding and the Moulin is built. On the opening night

Nini, learning that Danglard has transferred his affections to another potential star, refuses to appear; he tells her that he belongs not to her nor to any woman, but to the audience—and so must she. Nini goes on and joins in the final tempestuous cancan.

Bernard Chardère, for whom *French Cancan* marked "the beginning of . . . [Renoir's] downfall," detected "a tangible sign of lassitude and declining powers. . . . Objects lose their dramatic role. The rhythm is slack. . . . This kind of cinema is regressive and boring." By contrast, Gerald Mast saw the film as a "magnificent jewel of color, music, movement, structure and human performance," in which Danglard stands as "a surrogate for Renoir himself . . . a man who produces whole universes of art." John Belton, writing in *Movie* (Spring 1977), also drew parallels between the director and his protagonist: "Renoir sees his passionate interest in life as the sign of a true artist and uses Danglard's role as director to express his own notion of art as the recognition of the beauty that exists in the life around the artist. . . . Art, for Danglard (and Renoir), is everywhere—in the cafes, in the streets, in neighbouring apartments, in unconscious gesture and song. The ability to recognise, develop and encourage other artists makes Danglard himself an artist, and Renoir acknowledges, through Danglard, the importance of his own role as director."

Like *The Golden Coach, French Cancan* is frankly and unashamedly theatrical, its Montmartre an idealized studio construction complete with crescent moon. "The film's images," Raymond Durgnat wrote, "are those of a past reality, selective and heightened, as subjectively real, that is, as superreal, as moments polished by memory." Renoir himself referred to it as "a piece of tapestry, a composition in colors." For all Chardère's strictures, the climactic twenty-minute cancan sequence, a dazzling explosion of choreographed exuberance, must be one of the most exhilarating scenes ever filmed. John Belton noted how "the spirit of the event overrides everything. . . . Renoir's cutting and the cancan itself even lure the film's audience, as it does the Moulin Rouge audience, into this swirl of movement. . . . As few other musicals do, *French Cancan* erases the distinction between audience and performers."

French Cancan was an elaborate and expensive production, and Renoir was unable to retain final control. Several scenes seem to have been shortened or excised, and in places the editing is jarringly uneven. The film enjoyed a decidedly mixed critical response, but audiences liked it, making it Renoir's only postwar commercial success.

Renoir's preoccupation with theatre at this period was not limited to the subjects of his films; he was also branching out as a playwright and stage director. On 10th July 1954 he directed a single open-air production of Shakespeare's *Julius Caesar* in the Roman arena at Arles to commemorate the 2,000th anniversary of Caesar's founding of the city. A year later, in Paris, he directed his own first play, *Orvet*, with Leslie Caron—for whom it was written—in the title role of a young forest girl who becomes involved with the inhabitants of the local chateau. Reviewers were largely unimpressed, but the play ran a respectable sixty performances.

Perhaps no other film has divided Renoir's critics more radically than *Elena et les hommes* (1956). Tom Milne rated it "Renoir's most brilliant if not most perfect film . . . a joyous operetta of love's surprises," and Jean-Luc Godard enthused over "the most intelligent of films . . . a spectacle of profoundly moving comedy." Marcel Martin (*Cinéma 58*) thought otherwise: "How could Renoir have reached such a level of insignificance and vacuity? . . . Renoir has caricatured himself. Here is nothing but platitude and mediocrity." Georges Sadoul was less broadly dismissive, finding some merit, and even the occasional "brief, too brief, flash of genius" in the earlier sequences; but "the action doesn't so much resolve itself as unravel. The final 'triumph of love' . . . rings abominably false," leaving the audience "bored and depressed by the feeble farce that it has been put through."

As originally conceived, the film was to deal with General Boulanger, the war minister who nearly seized power by coup d'état in 1889; it seems, as Christopher Faulkner suggested, that Renoir had in mind something in the spirit of *La Règle du jeu*, "part farce, part tragedy, a bitter satire of our own age seen through the follies of another." If this was the idea, it turned out rather differently. The producers, fearing legal action, obliged Renoir to drop all mention of Boulanger. The decision to film a simultaneous English-language version caused the plot to be simplified and lightened, to suit American audiences. And the casting of Ingrid Bergman in the title part shifted the dramatic center of interest, pushing General Rollan (as the Boulanger-figure was now called) into a peripheral role. In the form in which it finally emerged, *Elena et les hommes* (like *French Cancan* and *The Golden Coach*) concerns a woman faced with a choice between three men. The Polish princess Elena (Bergman), exiled and impoverished in Paris, meets elegant *flâneur* Henri de Chevincourt (Mel Ferrer), who introduces her to Rollan (Jean Marais), the Minister of War. Elena is also being courted by a rich, elderly boot manufacturer,

Michaud, whose money is backing Rollan's bid for power. At first excited by the idea of becoming a dictator's consort, Elena comes to realize that she really loves Henri, while Rollan, compromised in some way that never becomes wholly clear, vanishes alone into the night. In any case, he could never have succeeded, since—as Henri explains—"dictatorship has no chance in a country where affairs of the heart are so important."

In making *Elena*, Renoir was fulfilling a long-standing ambition to shoot a film with Ingrid Bergman, and especially one in which she could be seen "laughing and smiling." Filming, as it turned out, was a less than happy experience, owing to linguistic problems; neither Bergman nor Ferrer spoke French, and the rest of the cast knew little English. Despite this, the warmth and gaiety of Bergman's performance glow from the screen, and almost contrive—with the help of Claude Renoir's vibrant color photography—to carry the film over its dramatic and political inadequacies. At least, they do so in the French version; the American version, which Warners truncated, partially reshot, and released under the title *Paris Does Strange Things*, is probably beyond redemption. Renoir, furious, disowned it.

"I've spent my life trying to raise money for my productions," Renoir once ruefully remarked. "With a few exceptions, I've never succeeded—and then only thanks to the intervention of Providence." The commercial and critical failure of *Elena*, which had been far from cheap to make, exacerbated his difficulties; during the remaining twenty-three years of his life, he was able to direct only four more films. Not from lack of subjects; all through his career, and especially in the latter years, he was working on scripts and outlines for films which were never made. (Most of them were assembled by Claude Gauteur, after Renoir's death, into a sizable volume.) But with backing increasingly hard to come by, he turned to other modes of expression—books and stage works. Soon after completing *Elena* he started work on a biography of his father, and in 1957 his translation of Clifford Odets' play *The Big Knife* was staged in Paris. About this time he also finished his own second play, *Carola* (though it was not produced until three years later, in California) and wrote the scenario for a ballet, *Le Feu aux Poudres*.

Disliking what he saw as a pursuit of bland technical perfection in the contemporary cinema (something which the Nouvelle Vague, with their rough-edged vigor learned from Renoir himself, were about to change), Renoir began to investigate the potential of a younger medium.

Television, he believed, was "in a technically primitive state which may restore to artists that fighting spirit of the early cinema, when everything that was made was good." In the hope of revitalizing the cinema through the introduction of fast, cheap TV techniques, he planned a film to be shot live for television, which would then receive immediate cinematic release.

Le Testament du Docteur Cordelier (*Experiment in Evil*, 1959) relocated Stevenson's much-filmed *Dr. Jekyll and Mr. Hyde* to modern-day Paris, with Jean-Louis Barrault in the double role of the ascetic scientist Cordelier and his brutal alter ego Opale. Live shooting proved impracticable, but Renoir adopted an approach aimed at capturing the greatest possible spontaneity, shooting—generally in a single take—with multiple concealed cameras and microphones to avoid cutting within scenes; he thus allowed his actors great freedom of movement, while relying on the creative response of his technicians. "My work consists solely in placing several forces in relation, as a watchmaker would assemble the various wheels of his mechanism. Then everything is set going, and each wheel plays its personal note in the final concert." Exteriors were filmed *cinéma-vérité* style on the streets of Paris, where unsuspecting citizens politely disregarded Opale's eccentric behavior. The whole production was completed within a month—two weeks for rehearsals and two more for the actual filming.

The widely-held view of late Renoir as mellowing into a warm haze of honeyed benignity is undercut by the somber tone of *Cordelier* (and by that of *Le Caporal épinglé*, also filmed in monochrome). The theme which runs through so much of Renoir's work, of the dichotomy between nature and intellect and of the dangers that result when one is sundered from the other, here receives its most overt statement—perhaps too overt, given the heavily moralizing voice-over commentary, spoken by Renoir himself. The film stands or falls, though, by Barrault's performance, a tour de force of expressive mime. Tom Milne described him "prancing, twitching, moving with the animal grace of a dancer . . . creating an extraordinary, chimerical figure whose intrusion into real Paris streets lends them a bizarre, unsettling air of menace," but felt that Renoir had often overindulged his star, causing "a curious lack of balance . . . one begins ultimately to feel Barrault's performance as an exercise in technique rather than as a characterisation."

The idea that *Cordelier* might inaugurate an era of fruitful cooperation between cinema and television backfired badly. The movie industry, regarding the film as "unfair competition," organized a boycott, and apart from a premiere at the 1959 Venice Biennale the picture was not shown, either on TV or in the cinema, for over two years. When it did finally appear, reviewers generally dismissed it as visually and thematically uninteresting. Even before *Cordelier's* Venice premiere, though, Renoir had completed another film using many of the same rapid, multi-camera techniques, but destined this time solely for cinematic release.

In *Le Déjeuner sur l'herbe* (*Picnic on the Grass*, 1959), as its title suggests, Renoir paid his most direct homage to the world of the impressionist painters in which he grew up. Filmed in and around the Provencal estate of Les Collettes, where Auguste Renoir spent the last years of his life, it offers a long lyrical hymn to nature, luxuriating in the warm southern summer landscape. *Déjeuner* can be seen as *Cordelier's* counterpart, the second half of a diptych: color rather than monochrome, rural instead of urban, playful where the other was somber. Both are concerned with scientists who attempt the Cartesian division of mind from nature; but while Cordelier splits himself in two and perishes, Etienne Alexis reintegrates himself and learns to live.

The action of *Déjeuner* takes place in a vaguely-defined future. Alexis, specialist in artificial insemination and president-elect of Europe, and his German fiancée Marie-Charlotte, leader of a girl-scout movement, celebrate their engagement by inviting their colleagues on a picnic. As unwary of the powers of nature as were M. Dufour and family in *Partie de campagne*, they find their lunch disrupted by a windstorm summoned up by the flute-playing goatherd Gaspard. Alexis, separated from the others, comes upon a beautiful peasant girl, Nénette, bathing naked in a pool and makes love with her. Afterwards, back in the world of science and seriousness, he resumes his responsibilities, preparing for his wedding and for high office. But at the last minute he meets Nénette again, pregnant with his child, and marries her instead of Marie-Charlotte. Nature and intellect, united, will lead Europe.

"Every creative genius has a message to give the world," Renoir commented apropos of his father. "Yet the moment he is aware that he is uttering it, by a strange contradiction the message sounds hollow and loses its value." The dictum might well be applied to *Déjeuner*, whose message is altogether too conscious, too brashly simplistic, to convince. On the one hand, the representatives of intellectual progress, inhibited and sterile; on the other, the repositories of rough peasant wisdom, of unjaded appetite and sunlit sensuality. The figures are cardboard, and the contest is rigged from the start. And by treating what he acknowledged to be an "extremely serious" subject as "a kind of farce," Renoir defuses his own message; were the forces of technological oppression to be deflected from their course by a quick roll in the hay, they would scarcely be worth worrying about. The film, Charles Samuels commented, "reduces its thesis to an incompatibility of styles."

Most critics have appreciated the ripe visual beauty of *Déjeuner*, Renoir's most "painterly" picture, even if few have found it satisfying on a conceptual or dramatic level. Opinion has diverged more sharply over *Le Caporal épinglé* (*The Elusive Corporal*, 1962). Generally dismissed on initial release as a lightweight remake of *La Grande Illusion*, "perilously close to standard army farce" (Roy Armes), it has since been reassessed, in some quarters at least, as the most complex and subtle of Renoir's postwar films.

The parallels with *Illusion* are evident enough: both films deal with French soldiers held in German prison camps and bent on escape. But *Le Caporal* is set in the Second World War, not the First; the soldiers are not officers; and France is no longer facing the enemy, but has ignominiously capitulated. Codes of chivalry and gentlemanly conduct have no place here, where the highest good is personal survival on the best available terms. "The characters in *La Grande Illusion*," Renoir pointed out, "acted according to solid and unshakeable values, but here they are people who are walking on shifting sands: the world around them is collapsing." The hero of the film, the Corporal (we never learn his name), is possessed by a determination to escape, but not for any patriotic or ideological reason. He acts purely on instinct—the instinct for freedom.

Patriotism, the film makes clear, is a mug's game. Renoir punctuates the action with assorted newsreels of the period—all of them, French and British no less than German, stuffed with bluster and bombast. The French officers in the camps readily cooperate with their German counterparts to enforce discipline and *Ordnung* on their compatriots. On the run, the Corporal and his friend Pater encounter a Frenchman who (like Maréchal in *Illusion*) is helping a German war-widow with her farm; but unlike Maréchal, the man plans to stay and marry the woman. "You never made a dash for it, to the land of your ancestors?" asks the Corporal. The man shrugs: "My ancestors never had any land."

For all its humor—and much of the drab routine of prison-camp life is played for laughs—and despite Jean-Pierre Cassel's resilient performance in the title role, *Le Caporal épinglé* leaves an oddly desolate impression. Renoir called it "my saddest film," and Don Willis (*Sight and Sound*, Autumn 1977) saw it as "Renoir's most pessimistic deliberation on the subject of detachment," the comedy "growing out of or into something unsettling and unstated, just intimated by the images." The overall mood is grey; even the final successful escape brings little sense of release, let alone exhilaration. In the bleak coda, set on a bridge over the Seine, Pater and the Corporal exchange a few uneasy words before walking away, each alone, into a Paris seemingly drained of life and light.

It was eight years before Renoir was able to make another film—eight years during which the man generally acknowledged as France's most distinguished filmmaker could find no one to back his projects. It was, Penelope Gilliatt remarked, rather as though Mozart had been denied music paper. *La Clocharde*, a film about a female tramp planned for Jeanne Moreau, came to nothing, as did *Julienne et son amour*, an erotic comedy about a man who can only get a good night's sleep in the arms of a prostitute. A scenario for a multi-episode film, entitled *C'est la révolution!*, was submitted to the officially-funded Centre Nationale du Cinéma and rejected as being "idiotic and obscene."

Meanwhile Renoir busied himself with writing. The biography of his father, entitled simply *Renoir* (*Renoir, My Father* in the English translation), appeared in 1962, followed in 1966 by his first novel, *Les Cahiers du Capitaine Georges*. He also taught various courses at the University of California at Berkeley, where his son Alain had become a professor of English literature.

C'est la révolution, renamed *Le Petit Théâtre de Jean Renoir* (1970), was eventually realized with the help of funding from Italian and French television. As finally filmed, it consisted of four episodes, each introduced by Renoir himself as master of ceremonies. In "Le Dernier Réveillon," a sentimental fable recalling, in both style and subject matter, *La Petite Marchande d'allumettes*, two old tramps enjoy a final meal before dying together in the snow. "La Cireuse électrique" is social satire, with a sung commentary à la Jacques Demy, about a woman whose obsession with her floor-polisher proves fatal. Jeanne Moreau then sings, rather uncomfortably, an old song entitled "Quand l'amour se meurt." The fourth episode, "Le Roi d'Yvetot," is the most substantial. An elderly husband, blissfully happy with his young wife, is shaken to find her in bed with their friend, the local doctor. But on reflection, he realizes that they all

three enjoy a friendship too valuable to sacrifice for mere convention, and they cheerfully defy the mocking gossip of the village.

Le Petit Théâtre was premiered on Italian television early in 1970 and on French TV a few months later. It was subsequently given theatrical release in other countries, but not in France in Renoir's lifetime. Most critics found the first two episodes excessively whimsical (and were puzzled by the third), but succumbed to the relaxed charm of "Le Roi d'Yvetot," "a little comedy of manners which—brief, lighthearted and limpid as it is—can take its place beside *Partie de campagne*, *La Règle du jeu* and *Déjeuner sur l'herbe*," wrote David Robinson. Tom Milne pointed out, though, that the film should be taken as a whole and that the fourth episode, though the only one shot in a real setting, "is also the most artificial," its resolution being "pure theatrical contrivance, with no truth, psychological or otherwise, except in the never-never land of the imagination."

At the end of "Le Roi d'Yvetot" the whole cast, laughing merrily, line up and bow to the camera, which pulls back to show them framed in the proscenium arch of a toy theatre. It looks like a valedictory gesture, and so it proved; *Le Petit Théâtre* was Renoir's last film. He offered as excuse his old war wound: "I directed films as much with my legs as with my head, and the result of that wound, which never healed, was that . . . at the age of seventy-five, I had to abandon a career which, to my mind, was only just beginning." It seems likely, though, that he was also weary of the dispiriting struggle to find backing.

Renoir's last years were spent mainly in California. He was paid all the expected honors and tributes; in April 1975 he received a special Academy Award for his "grace, responsibility, and enviable competence" as a filmmaker. An autobiography of sorts, *Ma vie et mes films*, appeared in 1974, and he wrote three more novels: *Le Coeur à l'aise* (1978), *Le Crime de l'anglais* (1979) and *Geneviève* (1979). He died at his home in Beverly Hills, at the age of eighty-four.

Before the war, and even for some time after it, Jean Renoir was ranked as one of the leading French directors, but by no means supreme. Carné, Clair, Feyder, and Duvivier were all considered at least his equals, or even his superiors. His work, by comparison with theirs, was felt to lack polish and dramatic shape; both technically and morally it seemed rough, often tentative. Around the early 1950s, with the advent of the *Cahiers* school of *auteurist* criticism, his stock began to rise, as that of the other '30s directors (with the sole exception of Jean Vigo) fell. Truffaut, speaking for his fellow critics and New Wave directors, hailed Renoir as "the father of us all." His prewar films were received, on re-release, with an enthusiasm they had rarely aroused the first time round; they had become (as Peter Harcourt commented) "more contemporary as the world itself has changed. Their uncertainty of moral position . . . is the very quality that today makes them seem so modern. . . . We no longer expect art to be rigorously shaped to create a grand emotion. We have come to value works that are more tentative and self-questioning, that seem more personal in their apparent casualness of technique."

Today few would dispute Renoir's status as one of the greatest of all filmmakers, and most would accept that the films he made between 1932 and 1939 (from *Boudu*, that is, to *La Règle du jeu*) include half-a-dozen of the supreme masterpieces of the cinema. Where disagreement sets in is with the subsequent films, from 1940 onwards. There are those who feel that with his departure for America Renoir's career went into a decline from which, despite some fine moments, it never really recovered. Susan Bennett found in the late movies "an impression—of great beauty, yet with a dimension missing—that is often gathered from an Auguste Renoir painting," and Roy Armes, while appreciating their "affectionate humour, zest for life and warm humanity," also noted the overall "schematisation of character and the paucity and superficiality of ideas." Ado Kyrou went further, rejecting the later work *in toto*: "The Renoir whom I loved has become a sickeningly indulgent old man, a boy scout of the camera, an advocate of bungled work, and what's worse, he has repudiated some of his best films. But I shall remember only the pre-war Renoir."

For many critics, on the other hand, the late films are no less great than the earlier ones, merely different: masterworks of pantheistic humanism, produced by a supreme filmmaker mellowing into a tranquil, autumnal richness. The love of life, the sense of nature, the texture and density of the earlier films remain, but the concern with transient social objectives is transmuted into an all-embracing affirmation, a belief in art as expression of the ultimate harmony of existence. "The impatient, crusading young filmmaker," as Tom Milne put it, "became the serene and watchful artist of maturity, with some loss of attack perhaps, but an immense gain in wisdom." Gary Carey (*The Seventh Art*, Summer 1963) likewise concluded that "his films in recent years have become more alive, more invigorating than ever before, but the zest is tempered by the wisdom and the mellowness that come with age well lived." The argument often

takes on a political dimension. Many of those disappointed by the later films ascribe Renoir's decline (as they see it) to his abdication from political commitment; conversely, their opponents have tried to play down or explain away the polemical content of the prewar pictures, suggesting that *Le Crime de M. Lange* "smells altogether too strongly of Prévert" (Eric Rohmer), or that Renoir, tolerant and obliging as ever, made *La Vie est à nous* mainly to gratify his friends. The tendency, Christopher Faulkner commented, "has been to read Renoir backwards. Drawing upon the films, interviews and writings produced after 1950, critics have applied what these sources can yield to an analysis of Renoir's work in the thirties. . . . By ignoring important forces of production and social relations in favour of a confidence in the authority of the single, presiding imaginative intelligence of the artist, Renoir and his films have been systematically de-historicized." Ironically, Marcel Oms, by no means an admirer of the later work, adopted a similar procedure: reacting violently against the "ultra-fascistic affirmations" of *Le Déjeuner sur l'herbe*, he detected beneath the left-wing gestures of the '30s films a Renoir who had always been, at heart, a reactionary and a nationalist. While not going quite so far, François Poulle concluded that Renoir was never a true leftist, merely a parlor radical dabbling in the Marxist chic of the era.

Ultimately, though, debate over Renoir's "true" political views may be beside the point. If the aspirations of the Popular Front lend an added bite and immediacy to Renoir's films of the period, they hardly account for the consistent richness and vitality of his output, and even less for its curiously pervasive melancholy. "Why is it," William Pechter asked, "that in a world so free of malevolence as is that of Renoir's films, things seem always to end so sadly?" Even overtly optimistic pictures such as *Lange* and *French Cancan* are tinged with poignancy, and sadness suffuses the comedy in *Règle du jeu* and *Le Caporal épinglé*. It is this complex of co-existing emotions, the ambiguities, tensions, and uncertainties underlying all his work, that make the earlier pictures so rewarding on each reviewing, and redeem the later ones from triteness. Renoir's films, Leo Braudy wrote, "are not categorical and theoretical, but capacious and ironic. . . . Nothing is ever single-valued . . . no set of ideas has automatic consent." It may be that, had Renoir felt more secure in his political beliefs, his films would have been the worse for it.

Gerald Mast called Renoir "one of those artists who can assert a position passionately and then add his own 'Yes, but. . . .'" From these innate contradictions he created films which, despite (or even because of) their weaknesses, seem to breathe life. Not that Renoir himself made any such claim. "It is pretentious to appear to be presenting real life on screen. Real life is too big," he wrote, and again: "Reality is always more amusing and audacious than our inventions." Nonetheless, few other directors have succeeded in conveying so intensely the sense of messy, turbulent, unstructured reality. His influence has been immense but diffuse—and almost wholly for the good, affecting directors as diverse as Truffaut and Visconti, Becker, Altman, and Satyajit Ray. Since Renoir's death his reputation has shown no sign of diminishing, and it seems unlikely that it will.

—*P.K.*

FILMS: (with Albert Dieudonné) Catherine (Une Vie sans joie), 1924–27; La Fille de l'eau (The Water Girl/The Whirlpool of Fate), 1924; Nana, 1926; Sur un air de Charleston (Charleston/Charleston-Parade), 1927 (short); Marquitta, 1927; (with Jean Tedesco) La Petite Marchande d'allumettes (The Little Match Girl), 1928 (short); Tire-au-flanc, 1928; Le Tournoi (Le Tournoi dans la Cité), 1928; Le Bled, 1929; (with Alberto Cavalcanti) Le Petit Chaperon Rouge (Little Red Riding-Hood), 1929 (short); On purge Bébé, 1931; La Chienne, 1931; La Nuit du carrefour (Night at the Crossroads), 1932; Boudu sauvé des eaux (Boudu Saved From Drowning), 1932; Chotard & Cie, 1933; Madame Bovary, 1934; Toni (Les Amours de Toni), 1935; Le Crime de Monsieur Lange (The Crime of Monsieur Lange), 1936; (with others) La Vie est à nous (People of France . . .), 1936; Partie de campagne (A Day in the Country/Country Excursion), 1936 (short); Les Bas-Fonds (Underworld/The Lower Depths), 1936; La Grande Illusion (Grand Illusion), 1937; La Marseillaise, 1938; La Bête humaine (The Human Beast/Judas Was a Woman), 1938; La Règle du jeu (The Rules of the Game), 1939; (with Carl Koch) La Tosca (The Story of Tosca), 1940; Swamp Water (The Man Who Came Back), 1941; This Land Is Mine, 1943; (with Garson Kanin) Salute to France, 1944 (short); The Southerner (Hold Autumn in Your Hand), 1945; The Diary of a Chambermaid, 1946; The Woman on the Beach, 1946; The River, 1950; La Carrozza d'oro (Le Carrosse d'or/The Golden Coach), 1953; French Cancan (Only the French Can), 1955; Elena et les hommes (Paris Does Strange Things), 1956; Le Testament du Docteur Cordelier (Experiment in Evil), 1959; Le Déjeuner sur l'herbe (Picnic on the Grass/Lunch on the Grass), 1959; Le Caporal épinglé (The Elusive Corporal/The Vanishing Corporal), 1962; Le Petit Théâtre de Jean Renoir, 1969. *Published scripts*—La Chienne *in* L'Avant-Scène du Cinéma October 1975; La Direction d'Acteurs par Jean Renoir *in* L'Avant-Scène du Cinéma July 1980; La Grande Illusion (by C. Spaak and J. Renoir) La Nouvelle Edition 1949; *also in* L'Avant-Scène du Cinéma January 1965, *also in* Lorrimer 1968 rev. ed. 1974 (English translation by M. Alexandre and A. Sinclair), *also in* Balland 1974 (edited by G. Vaugeois); Partie de campagne *in*

Image et Son April–May 1962, *also in* L'Avant-Scène du Cinéma December 1962; La Petite Marchande d'allumettes *in* L'Avant-Scène du Cinéma July 1980; La Règle du jeu *in* L'Avant-Scène du Cinéma October 1965, *also in* Lorrimer 1970 (English translation by J. McGrath and M. Teitelbaum); The Southerner (by Butler, H.) *in* Best Film Plays of 1945 (edited by J. Gassner and D. Nichols, Crown 1946; Le Testament du Docteur Cordelier *in* L'Avant-Scène du Cinéma July 1961; This Land Is Mine (by D. Nichols) *in* Twenty Best Film Plays (edited by J. Gassner and D. Nichols, Crown 1943; Toni *in* L'Avant-Scène du Cinéma July 1980; La Vie est à nous (excerpts) *in* Premier Plan May 1962.

ABOUT: Abel, R. French Cinema: The First Wave, 1915–1929, 1984; Agel, H. Les Grands Cinéastes, 1959 (rev. ed. 1967); Armes, R. French Cinema Since 1946, Vol I, 1966 (rev. ed. 1970); Armes, R. French Cinema, 1985; Bandy, M. L. (ed.) Rediscovering French Film, 1983; Bazin, A. (edited by F. Truffaut) Jean Renoir, 1971 (Eng. ed. 1973); Bazin, A. et al. La Politique des auteurs, 1972; Bennett, S. Jean Renoir, 1967; Beylie, C. Jean Renoir: le spectacle, la vie, 1975; Braudy, L. Jean Renoir: The World of His Films, 1972; Brunius, J. En marge du cinéma français, 1954; Burch, N. Praxis du cinéma, 1969 (Eng. ed. 1973); Campassi, O. 10 anni di cinema francese, Vol. 1, 1948; Canziani, A. Cinema francese 1945–1967, Vol. 1, 1968; Cauliez, A-J. Jean Renoir, 1962; Chardère, B. (ed.) Jean Renoir, 1962; Durgnat, R. Jean Renoir, 1975; Faulkner, C. Jean Renoir: A Guide to References and Resources, 1979; Fernandez Cuenca, C. Jean Renoir, 1966 (in Spanish); Gauteur, C. Jean Renoir: La Double Méprise (1925–1939), 1980; Gilliatt, P. Jean Renoir: Essays, Conversations, Reviews, 1975; Gregor, U. (ed.) Jean Renoir und seine Filme: eine Dokumentation, 1970; Harcourt, P. Six European Directors, 1974; Henderson, R. (ed.) The Image Maker, 1971; Higham, C. and Greenberg, J. Hollywood in the Forties, 1968; IDHEC. Analyse des films de Jean Renoir, 1966; Leprohon, P. Présences contemporaines: Cinema, 1957; Leprohon, P. Jean Renoir, 1967 (Eng. ed. 1971); McBride, J. (ed.) Filmmakers on Filmmaking, Vol. 2, 1983; Martin, J. W. The Golden Age of the French Cinema, 1929–1939, 1983; Mast, G. The Comic Mind: Comedy and the Movies, 1973 (rev. ed. 1979); Mast, G. Filmguide to The Rules of the Game, 1973; Mauriac, C. L'Amour du cinéma, 1954; Pechter, W. S. Twenty-four Frames a Second, 1971; Poulle, F. Renoir 1938, ou, Jean Renoir pour rien?, 1969; Reader, K. Cultures on Celluloid, 1981; Renoir, J. Ma vie et mes films, 1974 (Eng. ed. 1974); Renoir, J. Écrits 1926–1971, 1974; Renoir, J. Entretiens et propos, 1979; Renoir, J. (edited by C. Gauteur) Oeuvres de cinéma inédites, 1981; Renoir, J. Lettres d'Amerique, 1984; Roud, R. (ed.) Cinema: A Critical Dictionary, 1980; Sarris, A. (ed.) Interviews With Film Directors, 1967; Sadoul, G. French Film, 1953; Samuels, C. T. Encountering Directors, 1972; Samuels, C. T. Mastering the Film, 1977; Serceau, D. Jean Renoir, l'insurgé, 1981; Serceau, D. Jean Renoir, 1985; Sesonske, A. Jean Renoir: The French Films, 1924–1939, 1980; Siclier, J. La Femme dans le cinéma français, 1957; Strebel, E. G. French Social Cinema of the Nineteen-Thirties, 1980; Thiher, A. The Cinematic Muse:

Critical Studies in the History of French Cinema, 1979; Thomson, D. Movie Man, 1967; Thomson, D. A Biographical Dictionary of the Cinema, 1976 (rev. ed. 1980); Venegoni, C. F. Jean Renoir, 1975 (in Italian); Vincendeau, G. and Reader, K. (eds.) La Vie est à nous!: French Cinema of the Popular Front 1935–1938, 1986. *Periodicals*—Action May–June 1972; American Film January–February 1985; American Cinematographer March 1960; Avant-Scène du Cinéma July 1980; Bianco e Nero August–September 1953, November–December 1968; Bright Lights 2–3, 1978; Cahiers de l'Écran 1, 1947; Cahiers du Cinéma January 1952, April–May 1954, August–September 1954, June 1956, Christmas 1957, February 1958, May 1959, October 1959, December 1959, September 1961, May 1964, July 1966, January 1967, December 1967, April–May 1968, March 1970, July 1977; Cahiers du Cinéma in English 9, 1967; Chaplin Summer 1965; Cineaste Fall 1979, Summer 1980; Ciné-Club April 1948; Cinéma (Switzerland) 4, 1975; Cinema (USA) February 1964, Spring 1968, Spring 1970; Cinéma (France) December 1954, October–November 1956, May 1958, September–October 1958, February 1959, July 1959, February 1960, November–December 1960, May–June 1967, January 1968, November 1969, June 1978, January 1979, March 1979, April 1979, July–August 1984; Cinema Journal Fall 1972, Fall 1973; Cinema Nuovo May–June 1963; Cinématographe April 1984; Cine-Technician March–April 1939; Dirigido Por . . . September 1979, October 1979; Eco del Cinema January 15, 1953; Écran December 1974, November 1978, April 1979; Film October 10, 1974; Film (FFS) September–October 1956, November–December 1960; Film (West Germany) November 1966, July 1969; Film Comment July–August 1974; Film Journal July 1964; Film Quarterly Winter 1960, Winter 1967–68, Winter 1970–71, Spring 1971; Film World February 1970; Filmcritica July–August 1969; Filmkritik January 1965, November 1975, October 1980; Films and Filming June–July 1960, November 1962; Films in Review March 1952, August–September 1986; Focus on Film Autumn 1975; Griffith 6 1966; Image et Son April–May 1962, Summer 1962, May 1965, December 1968, 233 1969, December 1972, February 1973, August 1973, March 1977; Intermede 1 1946; Journal of the Producers Guild of America March 1969; Kinema Autumn 1971; Kosmorama July 1967, December 1967; The Listener June 12, 1986; Montage 31, 1975; Movie 4 1962, Summer 1965, Spring 1977; Moviegoer 2 1964; National Film Theatre Programme, February–March 1975, July 1979; New Left Review May–June 1964; New Yorker August 23, 1969; November 2, 1974; Il Nuovo Spettatore Cinematografico November 1961–February 1962; Positif March 1968, February 1970, July–August 1973, September 1975, July–August 1982; Quarterly of Film, Radio and Television Fall 1954; Rivista del Cinematografo December 1970; Screen January–February 1970, Winter 1972–73, Summer 1978; The Seventh Art Summer 1963; Sight and Sound July–September 1954, Winter 1958–59, Summer 1960, Spring 1962, Autumn 1964, Spring 1965, Spring 1968, Summer 1968, Winter 1974–75, Autumn 1977, Winter 1979–80, Autumn 1981; Substance 9, 1974; Take One 1/7 1967, July–August 1968; Télé-Ciné July–August 1955; Theatre Arts August 1951; Velvet Light Trap Summer 1973, Spring 1974; Yale French Studies Summer 1956.

RICHTER, HANS (1888–February 1, 1976), German filmmaker, painter, sculptor, and writer, was born into a wealthy and cultured if conservative bourgeois family. His father was a diplomat and his mother a talented amateur pianist—Richter said that "music really was my first experience with art, with the spiritual, with something above our daily, banal experiences." At the age of fourteen he discovered a talent for portraiture, and the "freedom and self-assurance" this success gave him drew him on. In 1908 he joined Gari Melchers' art class in Weimar; he also learned a great deal from copying the masters—especially Velasquez—in the Berlin museums.

Richter had his first real experience of "the gods of modern art" in 1913, at Herwarth Walden's Herbstsalon in Berlin. He was an immediate convert to cubism, and this contact with "the problems of contemporary art" led to "contact with contemporary artists, with individuals and groups as well as with magazines." He was soon contributing drawings, linocuts, and portraits to Franz Pfemfert's magazine Die Aktion, the literary center of the avant-garde in Germany before and during the First World War.

In 1914 Richter was living in Berlin with a Javanese dancer named Taka-Taka. He came home one day and found her in tears: a letter had arrived, inducting him into the German army. Richter served with a reconnaisance unit in Russia, where he was often "frozen into the ground." After a year or so of this he was lucky enough to be wounded and repatriated to a Berlin hospital. He fell in love with his nurse, Elisabeth Steinert, who turned out to be the daughter of a very rich Berlin businessman. They were married, but not for very long: "In spite of our great love, it was a tragic thing," Richter said.

By 1916, meanwhile, he was painting again. His work was honored in a special issue of Die Aktion, and the same year he shared a two-man show in Munich with Erich Heckel, exhibiting work that reflected the cubist influence. In 1917 Richter went to Zurich, Switzerland, ostensibly to consult a specialist about the lingering effects of his war wound, which had slightly damaged his spine. His real interest was the dada movement, newly established in Zurich by Tristan Tzara and others. Already dissatisfied with cubism, Richter joined the dadaists, excited by the movement's spontaneity, its celebration of meaninglessness and chance, its contempt for

HANS RICHTER

bourgeois values. At the same time he became an anarchist—euphoric, after his experience of war and the army, with this "new ticket" to life and freedom, "the fight against everything that limited our energies."

The first important products of Richter's dada period were his "visionary portraits," executed in fluid shapes and explosive colors. He soon returned to more rigorous forms—abstract portraits in black ink exploring not the psychology of his sitters but the balance between figure and background, black and white. In these drawings he was seeking "a positive principle, a method, an order" for his own life, as well as for his art. The Italian composer Ferruccio Busoni, then living in Zurich, suggested that his problem was related to the problem of counterpoint in music, and urged him to study the preludes and fugues of Bach. Richter said that exploring "the up and down, the movements and countermovements all leading to a definite unity . . . helped me enormously and gave me the idea that it could be done on a piece of paper"—that the paper could be "used like a musical instrument."

In 1918 Tzara introduced Richter to the Swedish artist Viking Eggeling. It turned out that Eggeling was conducting related experiments, seeking a "vocabulary" of basic pictorial forms which he then organized according to a kind of contrapuntual grammar, a compositional scheme of contrasting opposites. Richter recalled of their first meeting that "our complete agreement on aesthetic as well as on philosophical matters, a kind of 'enthusiastic identity' between us, led spontaneously to an intense collaboration, and a friendship which lasted until his death in 1925."

In 1919 Richter, Eggeling, and Eggeling's wife retired to Klein-Kölzig, the Richter family estate near Berlin. For three years—until inflation ruined Richter's parents and they had to sell the estate—the two men battled together with their separate problems. Eggeling was preoccupied with line, Richter with surfaces, but both were concerned less with their individual elements than with the interplay and interaction between them. "For both of us," Richter said, "music became the model. In musical counterpoint, we found a principle that fitted our philosophy: every action produces a corresponding reaction . . . and in this model we saw an image of life itself: one thing growing, another declining, in a creative marriage of contrast and analogy."

"Month after month," Richter went on, "we studied and compared our analytical drawings made on hundreds of little sheets of paper. . . . It was unavoidable that, sooner or later in these experiments, these drawings, which were spread about on the floor of our studio, would begin to relate systematically to each other. We seemed to have a new problem on our hands, that of continuity, and the more we looked, the more we realized that this new problem had to be dealt with . . . until, by the end of 1919, we decided to do something about it. On long scrolls of paper Eggeling developed a theme of elements into [a compostion called] 'Horizontal-Vertical Man,' and I developed another into 'Preludium.'"

In these scrolls, as Standish Lawder writes, Richter and Eggeling "had formed a new artistic syntax in which the eye traveled a prescribed route from beginning to end, and in which sequential images created an art of becoming, of unfolding, of constant reference forward and backward in space and time." According to Richter, they had also "arrived at a crossroad: the scroll looked at us and seemed to ask for real motion. That was just as much of a shock to us as it was a sensation. Because in order to realize movement, we needed film."

Neither Richter nor Eggeling knew anything whatever about film, and by this time they had no money. With a donation from a banker interested in their work, they produced a pamphlet describing their intentions amd sent it to a long list of influential people. The testimonials garnered in this way (including one from Einstein) were enough to persuade the giant production company UFA to provide them in 1920 with an animation studio and a technician. The technician turned out to be unsympathetic and the problem of turning the scrolls into films enormous. The results were totally unsatisfactory but instructive, and Richter and Eggeling perservered.

Rhythmus 21 (*Rhythm 21*), 250 feet long, and designed and photographed by Richter himself in 1921, is almost certainly the first abstract film. Lawder calls it "a kinetic composition of rectangular forms of black, grey, and white. Perhaps more than in any other avant-garde film, it uses the movie screen as a direct substitute for the painter's canvas, as a framed rectangular surface on which a kinetic organization of purely plastic forms was composed. . . . In the opening passages, the screen is divided into large dynamically interacting areas of black and white. Thus, a black screen is closed over by two white rectangles sliding in from either side, a white screen splits in the middle to reveal a black background, a white square in the center of a black void advances and recedes, expanding and diminishing in size. By eliminating image content and greatly simplifying pictorial composition, Richter created a world of pure visual rhythm in which these large areas of light and dark fill the screen with movements."

Richter worked with cutouts in *Rhythmus 21* but for his next film, *Rhythmus 23*, he designed a system of shutters on strings and movable slides that enabled him to film light reflected on a screen. Photographed by Charles Métain, and studying the interplay of lines as well as squares, *Rhythmus 23* caused a furor when it was screened in Berlin, delighting some critics and infuriating the philistines. *Rhythmus 25*, now lost, followed two years later and added a new element: color, applied to the film by hand. A further development was the introduction of photographed images as well as geometrical shapes, first seen in *Filmstudie* (1926), a dreamy and more or less surrealist sequence whose images are connected by free association and analogy. By this time the influence of Richter's pioneering experiments (and those of Eggeling and Walter Ruttmann) had spread to France, where the devotees of the abstract film (or *cinéma-pur*) included Henri Chomette, Jean Gremillon, Marcel Duchamp, and Fernand Léger.

Richter subsidized his experiments by accepting a variety of commercial assignments. He designed catalogs, made illustrations for various film companies, and even served for a time as head of a fashion magazine's drawing office. The interest aroused by his experimental films brought him an assortment of filmmaking jobs as well (including a short advertising the prowess of an escape artist named Albertini). In 1927 he went to work for Epoche, a company turning out screen commercials for showing in the UFA theatres. He remained there for a year and half, making a ten-minute publicity film every week, and incidentally learning all he could about the uses of the camera. Richter had made a second marriage—even briefer than the first—in the early 1920s. In 1927 he married Erna Niemeyer, a girlfriend of five years standing, but the relationship did not long survive its formalization.

About this time, Richter made *Inflation,* a kind of preface to the UFA feature film *The Lady With the Mask,* directed by Wilhelm Thiele. UFA had asked for a documentary but Richter, applying the principles of contrast and analogy, created a montage described by one critic as a chain of associations in which "thirst for pleasure and desire for living were contrasted with need and suicide, stock exchange booms with empty warehouses" to illustrate "the dreadful contrasts" of the inflation years in postwar Germany. Herman G. Weinberg said that in its use of "facts, abstract forms, symbols, comic effects, etc." it "set the pattern for Richter's later essay-films."

One of Richter's best-known movies followed, *Vormittagspuk* (*Ghosts Before Breakfast,* 1928). It was made at the invitation of Paul Hindemith for the 1928 International Music Festival at Baden-Baden, where Hindemith's score was performed live and the film was screened synchronously. Richter shot it in his Berlin studio with the Hindemiths and the Darius Milhauds as his actors. He described it as "the very rhythmical story of the rebellion of some objects (hats, neckties, coffee cups, etc.) against their daily routine. . . . The style of the film shows, in my opinion, more of my dadaistic past than other films I have made."

Ed Lowry notes that *Ghosts Before Breakfast* was subsequently suppressed by the Nazis as "degenerate art," and goes on: "The liberation of hats, teacups, and firehorses from their functional roles, in a total rebellion against their owners, against logic, against the laws of time and space, becomes a joke on the narrowly defined, stuffy lives of the bourgeoisie, the society which defines itself by the clock. . . . Richter explores the uniquely cinematic qualities of film—its ability to manipulate the illusions of time and, space. Utilizing time-lapse photography, pixillation, split screen, the reversal of the image both in time (running the film backwards) and in negative, and the juxtaposition of shots through editing, Richter creates . . . a delightful bit of film trickery that challenges our perceptions of the cinema while exploiting its possibilities to the fullest."

"Before I began to understand film, in making my first *Rhythms,*" Richter said years later, "I saw it only as a medium of occasional *experiments,* extending my paintings, not as a new form of plastic expression. But slowly the beauty of this new muse uncovered itself. I saw, suddenly, to which freedom, to which liberties the film invited us. I succumbed to this temptation to such a degree that I neglected, over a period of twelve years, my work as a painter." His delight in the new medium's possibilities is evident even in commercial films like *Zweigroschenzauber* (*Twopence Magic*, 1929), advertising an illustrated magazine, and "composed exclusively of related movements of diverse objects, one movement going over the other, telling the 'story' of the contents of . . . [the magazine]. It translated the poetry of *Filmstudie* into the commercial film."

Richter's first sound film was the three-reel *Alles dreht sich, alles bewegt sich* (*Everything Revolves, Everything Moves*, 1929). The director described it as "a fantastic documentary of a fair after a script by Werner Graeff, who also played the leading role. . . . Walter Gronostay, nineteen years old when I met him at Baden-Baden the year before, was the most understanding film composer, or should I say 'sound dramatist,' I ever met. He cooperated with me intensely to give the film the tumbling rhythm of the merry-go-round. The boy-meets-girl . . . story in the film was not very strong and was not very seriously followed through. What mattered more to us was to translate the uninhibited fun-making of the fair into real fantasy." Words as well as music and sound were used rhythmically rather than naturalistically, and this apparently offended the sensibilities of two Nazi S.S. men who attended the premiere in Baden-Baden. They accosted Richter after the show, called him a "Kultur Bolshevik," and beat him up.

The same year Richter was invited to join an avant-garde film workshop in London, and there made a movie called *Everyday* (in which Eisenstein, also visiting Britain, appears as a London policeman). Overwhelmed at the time by *Potemkin, Earth,* and the other Soviet films he had recently seen, Richter set out to make a film with social content. *Everyday* is about a city clerk who wakes up, goes to work tired, is yelled at by his boss, goes to the movies exhausted, goes to bed and dreams frustrated dreams, wakes up, goes to work, and so on, over and over again, in an accelerating tempo, until he falls down dead. Richter lost confidence in the picture when it was finished and didn't edit it until 1966, when he discovered the rushes at a laboratory in Basle.

Neus Leben (*New Living*, 1930), made in Switzerland, is a documentary about architecture, and especially the new architecture of Switzerland. It was the first of a number of "essay-films" made by Richter in the course of his career, using paintings, prints, engravings, and other static pictures as well as cinematography in support of some thesis. *Europa Radio* (1931), also made in Switzerland, was commissioned by the international radio company Philips, soon to come to Richter's rescue at a difficult moment in his life.

The Nazi attack on Richter as "Kultur Bolshevik" had been widely reported, and in 1931 this incident brought him an invitation to make an anti-Nazi film to be produced by the left-wing Prometheus Film company of Germany in cooperation with a Soviet company. Work began that year and continued intermittently into 1933, the movie meanwhile developing from a documentary into a full-scale fictional feature. Centering on a strike at an iron foundry in Hennigsdorf near Berlin, *Metall* was filmed partly there and partly in Russia, with Richter "commuting" between the two and growing increasingly disillusioned by the need to adjust the film to follow changing political lines in both Germany and Russia.

Richter was actually in Russia when Hitler came to power in Germany. *Metall* was scrapped and Richter found himself unattracted by the alternative projects suggested by his hosts and by the Soviet system. He left without saying goodbye, arriving in Prague with only the clothes he stood in. Meanwhile, in Berlin, the Nazis stripped his apartment and destroyed virtually all of his paintings, drawings, and manuscripts. It was at that point that an offer came from the Philips Company in Holland. Richter made his way there and directed a documentary called *Hallo, Everybody* (1933), with music by his friend Milhaud. Other commissions followed, and Philips advanced Richter enough money, as he put it, "to rent an apartment in Paris, to buy a car and a suit."

Between 1933 and 1940 Richter produced mostly documentaries, "essay-films," and commercials, filming in Holland and in Switzerland, where he went to live. As the German army overran Europe, he became increasingly desperate to leave, and in 1941, with many misgivings, he accepted an invitation from the Guggenheim Foundation to lecture in New York on his work with Eggeling. At first Richter was terrified by "the incredible and audacious arrogance of the buildings" and worried about the inadequacy of his English. He improved the latter by reading Raymond Chandler and Dashiel Hammett and began to feel more at home when he encountered old friends in New York, among them Fernand Léger, Max Ernst, Man Ray, and Marcel Duchamp, as well as a former student, the film scholar Jay Leyda. Thanks to Leyda, Richter was invited to lecture to a group of documentarists and there met Irving Jacobi, who offered him a teaching post at his newly founded City College Film Institute. The same year Richter married his fourth wife, Frieda, his companion for the rest of his life.

Richter taught at the Film Institute for fourteen years, at first as a substitute supervisor and then as director. During that period the Institute grew until it had twenty-three classes and fourteen instructors, and "there was not a single film or television studio in New York in which at least one of my students didn't work." In 1943, with Fernand Léger, Richter began work on what developed into his most famous film, *Dreams That Money Can Buy*. In a borrowed loft on 21st Street, with borrowed cameras, Richter worked nights and weekends for four years to make the movie, drawing his old friends into the project, squandering his salary on it, and surmounting horrendous problems and accidents.

The film opens with a framing story about a young man named Joe (Jack Bittner), down on his luck, who discovers that he has the power to create dreams and goes into business to sell these commodities. The first dream he sells, based on stream of consciousness monologues by Max Ernst, centers on a young man eavesdropping on the dream talk of his sleeping beloved. The second dream, suggested by Léger, is the love story of two shopwindow dummies, and the third, from a story by Man Ray, satirizes the impressionability of a movie theatre audience. After an animated collage by Marcel Duchamp, "Discs and Nudes Descending a Staircase," come two episodes using mobiles by Alexander Calder, a kind of cosmic ballet and a circus of wire figures. The final episode, Richter's own, is called "Narcissus," and shows the dream salesman Joe, previously filmed in black and white, happily turning blue as he discovers his true self.

Not surprisingly, given the circumstances of its creation, *Dreams That Money Can Buy* is lacking in continuity. It is also, at times, painfully slow. Nevertheless, it is recognized to be one of the most important and influential of American avant-garde films and is of great musical interest as well, including contributions by Milhaud, Paul Bowles, Edgard Varèse, and John Cage, lyrics by John Latouche, and songs by Libby Holman and Josh White. At the 1947 Venice Film Festival, it was honored as the "best original contribution to the progress of cinematography." Many of the artists involved in *Dreams* are also represented in an anthology of experimental films compiled by Richter in 1944, *The Movies Take a Holiday*, while the early explorations of Eggeling, Richter, and Ruttmann are surveyed in *Thirty Years of Experiments* (1951).

Richter retired from his City College post in 1956. He thereafter divided his time between studios in Connecticut and in Locarno, Switzerland, where a number of his friends had settled. *Dadascope I* (1956) and *Dadascope II* (1957) were made there and consist of images set by Richter to poems composed and read by such former dadaists as Man Ray, Duchamp, Tzara, Arp, Raoul Hausmann, Kurt Schwitters, and Richard Hülsenbeck. Speaking of *Dadascope I,* Richter said that the film itself has been "conceived as freewheeling poetry; and, as such, it is in my opinion the best filmmaking I have done. But the poetry is so free that in several instances the sensations or analogies cannot be established at all. It is just as much chance which directs the flow of images as I do. But the fact remains that it is *my* chance."

Richter's last major film was *Acht mal acht* (*Eight by Eight,* 1957), which extends his experiments into the realm of sound. He explained that "the film begins with two chess figures in a tree, the Queen and the old White King (Marcel Duchamp) who is sleeping. Julian Levi as a Knight, Yves Tanguy as a Bishop and Hülsenbeck as a Castle are all trying to seduce the White Queen. I shot this scene and nothing else. I put it in my pocket and went to Europe. And in Europe my friends Arp, Cocteau, Peggy Guggenheim, Sandberg, etc. offered their cooperation for further individual episodes." Thus, in the third episode, Alexander Calder blows his breath into a whole forest of tiny mobiles to bring them to life. In the seventh, Jean Cocteau plays a pawn which, by reaching the eighth square, is transformed into a Queen.

Each of the film's eight episodes depicts a common human situation in chess terms, and each involves a different approach to the use of sound. This is Richter's account of the fifth episode, dealing with the problem of frustration: "A man is playing chess with himself. He seems to be nervous and disturbed by the problems on the board. And rightly so, because there is a wrong figure on the chess board, a kind of miniature clothes hanger which handicaps and frustrates his game and inhibits him. To solve the problem of sound for this episode, I decided to use *stuttering* as a theme—the desire to express something, to go ahead, but to be unable to do so: a stuttering trumpet with a melody that never comes through, people speaking stutteringly, machine sounds accelerated and retarded, voices counting from one to ten but never getting there, etc. But finally the player overcomes his emotional block, eliminates the disturbing element. At this moment, the Muse, as a nude, appears as the logical and biological opposite of the male. He is freed from his frustration. Everything falls into place and the trumpet finally blows its melodious theme to the end."

Though he found it difficult to make progress with his painting in the years of upheaval between 1930 and 1950, Richter never abandoned it. There was an exhibition of his drawings, paintings, and collages in New York in the late 1960s. He also published a number of books on cinema and a variety of other subjects, the best known of these being his history of dada, published in English in 1965 as *Dada: Art and Anti-Art.*

Cleve Gray, editor of *Hans Richter by Hans Richter,* describes him at the age of eighty-three "still tall, straight and alert," with an extraordinary recall of the people and events of his long life. Gray calls him "a Classicist with a keen appreciation of Romanticism" and "a profound understanding of the importance of liberty. . . . The world of Chance is for Richter the world of Chaos and Death. It is man, and only man, who has the ability to conquer this world. Death and Chaos are to be challenged everyday anew in every form, for out of them comes life." He has been described as "the high priest of the experimental film"—a pioneer whose work was a crucial influence on the development of abstract film in both Europe and the United States.

Richter himself always recognized that "the combination of spontaneity and the desire for order . . . these two things have always popped up in my life." He maintained that he was not really a *cinéaste* but "a painter who makes films," but nevertheless spoke of film as "the most powerful art medium of our time"—"the art of the twentieth century."

FILMS: Rhythmus 21 (Rhythm 21), 1921; Rhythmus 23, 1923; Rhythmus 25, 1925; Filmstudie (Film Study), 1926; Inflation, 1928; Vormittagspuk (Ghosts Before Noon/Ghosts Before Breakfast), 1928; Rennsymphonie (Race Symphony; prelude to Robert Dinesen's Ariadne in Hoppegarten, 1929; Zweigroschenzauber (Twopence Magic), 1929; Alles dreht sich, alles bewegt sich, 1929; Everyday, 1929 (completed 1966); Neus Leben, 1930; Europa Radio, 1931; Hallo, Everybody, 1933; Metall, 1931–1933 (unfinished); Vom Blitz zum Fernsehbild, 1936; Eine kleine Welt im Dunkelen (A Small World in the Dark), 1938; Die Enstehung der Farbe, 1938; Die Eroberung des Himmels (Conquest of the Skies), 1938; Hans im Glück, 1938; Die Börse (The Stock Exchange), 1939; (as compiler) The Movies Take a Holiday, 1944; (with others) Dreams That Money Can Buy, 1946; (with others) Thirty Years of Experiments, 1951; Dadascope I, 1956; Dadascope II, 1957; Acht mal acht (Eight by Eight), 1957; Chessce-tera (Passionate Pastime), 1957; (with others) From Dada to Surrealism: Forty Years of Experiment, 1961 (in two parts); (as compiler) Alexander Calder: From the Circus to the Moon (episodes from Dreams That Money Can Buy and Eight by Eight), 1963.

ABOUT: Lawder, S. D. The Cubist Cinema, 1975; Richter, H. Hans Richter, 1971; Weinberg, H. G. An Index to the Creative Work of Two Pioneers, 1957. *Periodicals*—Art in America January 1968; Bianco e Nero February 1939, September–October 1968, January–February 1978; Écran May 1977; Film Culture Winter 1955, Winter 1963–1964; Film Forum July 1952, April 1959; Film Library Quarterly 1 1974; Films in Review December 1951; New York Times February 3, 1976; Sight and Sound Winter 1962.

*RIEFENSTAHL, "LENI" (Berta Helene Amalia Riefenstahl) (August 22, 1902–), German director, scenarist, producer, actress, and photographer, was born in Berlin, the oldest daughter of Alfred Riefenstahl, owner of a plumbing engineering firm, and the former Berta Scherlach. She was a romantic and artistic child, drawn to painting and dancing and entranced by nature. She told an interviewer that she had read nothing but fairy tales until she was in her late teens: "I didn't want to have anything to do with reality. We had a weekend house by a lake near Berlin, and I spent hours in the woods, watching trees, bushes, animals, beetles, and butterflies. I turned them into human figures, like Walt Disney. I always looked for a fantasy image in nature."

Leni Riefenstahl attended *gymnasium* in Berlin and went on to art school at the urging of her father, who envisaged a career for her as a commercial artist. She herself wanted passionately to become a dancer, and took lessons in both classical ballet and modern dance. In the end, when she was twenty-one, she persuaded her father to finance a solo dance recital on the understanding that she would relinquish her ambitions if the performance was a flop. It was, on the contrary, successful enough to attract the attention of the great director and impresario Max Reinhardt, who sent her on a tour of Europe in a program of modern dances of her own creation.

Her brief career as a dancer was ended by a knee injury in 1924. It was during her convalescence that she happened to see a movie by Arnold Fanck, a geologist and climber who became famous for his "mountain films." At a time when most German movies were shot entirely in the studio, Fanck trained a team of technicians who were also expert climbers and skiers, and made on location a series of documentaries, travelogues, and fiction films. Magnificently photographed and celebrating the most dramatic and grandiose kinds of natural beauty, these films also embodied an inflated spirit of heroic idealism that Siegfried Kracauer believed "was rooted in a mentality kindred to [the] Nazi spirit," a point of view echoed by Susan Sontag in her

°rē´ fen stäl

LENI RIEFENSTAHL

study of Riefenstahl, the essay "Fascinating Fascism," reprinted in *Under the Sign of Saturn*.

Excited by Fanck's film, Leni Riefenstahl went to see him. She was promptly taken on as the only female member of his team, and taught to ski and to climb. It was from the same "professor," she says, that she learned the fundamentals of *mise-en-scène*: "I also found myself somewhat involved in the camera work and at times collaborated with the directorial crew." She made her screen debut as the star of a movie that Fanck had written especially for her, *Der Heilige Berg* (*The Holy Mountain*, 1926), in which she plays a dancer turned climber who inspires a dangerous rivalry between two young mountaineers. The film was extremely successful and so was its star: "After all the sensuous vamps and hothouse beauties who for so long had reigned in the German cinema," wrote one contemporary critic, "she was a breath of fresh air; the new Germany of athletes and freedom saw in her a symbol."

Leni Riefenstahl starred again in Fanck's routine comedy *Der grosse Sprung* (*The Big Leap* 1927) and then as Marie Vetsera in *Das Schicksalderer von Habsburg* (*The Fate of the Habsburgs*, 1929), an Austrian film by a different director. Another spectacular and immensely successful mountain drama followed: *Die Weisse Hölle von Piz Palü* (*The White Hell of Piz Palü*, 1929). Directed by Fanck in collaboration with G. W. Pabst, it combined daring mountain ascents and the equally hair-raising aerial stunts of the aviator Ernst Udet. In her first talkie, Fanck's *Stürme über dem Montblanc* (*Avalanche*, 1930), Riefenstahl successfully survived both the transition to sound and the elemental furies of Mont Blanc to rescue the man she loved.

An agreeable skiing comedy, *Der Weisse Rausch* (*White Frenzy*, 1931), also for Fanck, confirmed Riefenstahl's status as one of Germany's most popular movie stars, and the same year she established her own production company, Leni Riefenstahl Studio Films. At that point she was recalled to make one more picture with Fanck, who could find no other actress with the necessary stamina and skills. This was *SOS Eisberg* (*SOS Iceberg*), a German-American coproduction shot on location in Iceland under the supervision of the explorer Knud Rasmussen (who, according to the ballyhoo, housed his cast in Eskimo huts and fed them on seal meat).

The first production of Leni Riefenstahl Studio Films was *Das blaue Licht* (*The Blue Light*, 1932), starring Riefenstahl, directed by her, and written by her with Béla Balázs, the Hungarian film theorist. Balázs also shared the role of producer with Riefenstahl and the movie's cinematographer Hans Schneeberger, formerly a member of Fanck's team. Set in the Italian Dolomites, it was based on a folk tale about the mysterious blue light that suffuses the peak of Mount Cristallo at full moon, luring young climbers to their death. Only Junta (Riefenstahl), an innocent child of nature who lives alone in the high mountains, can reach the light and survive; the local villagers are certain that she is a witch. A young Viennese painter (Mathias Wieman) visiting the mountains is enthralled by Junta and follows her up Mount Cristallo, discovering that the source of the light is a grotto of precious crystals. He reveals the secret to the villagers, who greedily remove this treasure. Climbing again at the next full moon, but without the crystals to guide her, Junta falls to her death.

Riefenstahl would have preferred to make the movie in the studio but, short of funds, was obliged to shoot it on location and to persuade the Dolomite peasants to appear as themselves (thus anticipating the methods of neo-realism by twenty years). The harshness of the mountain landscapes, and the almost equally strong and weather-worn faces of the peasants, provide a powerful contrast to the romanticism of this fairy story, with its lament for a world that prefers hard cash to the pure and mysterious light of crystals.

Jonathan Rosenbaum found a strong parallel between Leni Riefenstahl's vision in this film (and others) and Walt Disney's, citing "the intense pantheism and towering vistas of the film's landscape shots, the poetic innocence and purity of the heroine, the telepathy and empathy shown by animals . . . towards her moods," as well as a general "predilection for primal myths of unity and perfection." Moderateley successful in Germany, the film received a silver medal at Vienna in 1932 and was a hit in Paris and London. Leni Riefenstahl said farewell to the "mountain film" in an illustrated autobiography called *Kampf in Schnee und Eis (Struggle in Snow and Ice,* 1933).

Adolf Hitler himself greatly admired *Das blaue Licht,* and in 1933, at his direct invitation, Leni Riefenstahl shot a documentary about the Nazi party's annual rally at Nuremberg. *Sieg des Glaubens (Victory of Faith),* as it was called, was withdrawn after Hitler's purge of the party leadership in 1934.

An enormous edifice of statements and counterstatements, charges and denials, now obscures the facts about Riefenstahl's relationship with Hitler and the Nazis. She is said to have thought Hitler "faultless" and "the greatest man who ever lived"; he reportedly described her as "a perfect example of German womanhood" and an artistic genius. Many photographs exist of them together, and her enemies maintain that she was the dictator's mistress, a charge that she emphatically denies. "In the early days," she says, "like many millions of people, I believed in Hitler and had been impressed by him. But it is absolutely false to say that we were intimate friends." Goebbels was bitterly jealous of her success and influence with Hitler, and he and his propaganda ministry did all they dared to disparage and obstruct her—among other things spreading the rumor that she was half-Jewish (a claim she also denied).

There is no doubt, at any rate, that Hitler assigned Riefenstahl to film the Nazi rallies in Nuremberg in 1934, and that she performed this task with disturbing brilliance in a film released in 1935 as *Triumph des Willens (Triumph of the Will).* Speaking of this work, she told a *Guardian* reporter in 1976 that "It is always said that I worked for the Nazis, that the Nazis helped me. But I was not in the Party and they made only difficulties for me. . . . The Party did not pay for the film. I hired my own cameras. I had my own contract, my own company and I arranged the distribution. It was hard work; it was horrible. For six days I just filmed everything that happened. But it did not seem a sinister event to me. Remember this was long before the war; all the diplomats were coming to Nuremberg. Many were saying that it was a good thing that Germany had such a leader. All the horror came later." (Riefenstahl's account is described as self-serving in Sontag's essay.)

It is true that *Triumph of the Will* was re-leased by Riefenstahl's own Studio Film company and financed by UFA, but it is also clear that it was made with the full support of Hitler, if not of all of his colleagues. In her book *Hinter den Kulissen des Reichsparteitag-Films (Behind the Scenes of the National Party Congress Films,* 1935) Riefenstahl herself asserts that the ecstatic parades, involving hundreds of thousands of carefully drilled participants, were stage-managed for the benefit of her cameras—that "the preparations for the Party Convention were made in concert with the preparations for the camerawork." She and her director of photography (Sepp Allgeier) had thirty cameras with the latest wide-angle and telescopic lenses, and a total staff of a hundred and twenty. Special camera lifts were built for her in Nuremberg.

John Russell Taylor suggests that *Trimph of the Will* can be seen "both as a documentary and as a mythic fantasy. Documentary it certainly is . . . [but] everything is selected and manipulated to a larger, more mystical end. The very opening of the film . . . a factual account of Hitler's arrival in Nuremberg by air, becomes also an evocation of a god's descent to earth—from the endless vistas of clouds, seen from the god's-eye viewpoint of the plane, we pass to the plane's shadow moving majestically, inexorably over the summer city as those in the streets gaze up in rapturous expectation. . . . The rest of the film adopts the same approach. Constantly we lose all sense of perspective, are cut off from the basic realities by alternations of extreme long-shot and gigantic close-up. . . . The torchlit celebrations are turned into abstract patterns of sight and sound."

The film shows a mastery of editing, Taylor thought, that is comparable to Eisenstein's, transcending its political context and compelling "one to judge it absolutely as a film." Many have disagreed, including Siegfried Kracauer, who attributed his "deep feeling of uneasiness" to the fact "that before our eyes palpable life becomes an apparition. . . . The film represents an inextricable mixture of a show simulating German reality and of German reality maneuvered into a show." Paul Rotha wrote that this powerful film "reeked" of National Socialism and "unqualified idolatry for Hitler and all Nazism stood for." In *Sight and Sound* Brian Winston argued against the idea that the visual power of *Triumph of the Will* derives primarily from Riefenstahl's aesthetic vision. He wrote: "Given our taste for the spectacle of dehumanized mass (that part of fascist aesthetics which we all share), shots of 200,000 men in close formation become impressive not through the fact of filming, but because of the formation itself. Riefenstahl is as impressive as the next film-maker when she has that sort of spectacle to work with. . . . " It is now universally regarded as a propaganda masterpiece, however distasteful. It received the German state prize in 1935 and the gold medal at Venice in 1936, among other awards. Albert Speer, principal architect of the 1934 rally, wrote of Leni Riefenstahl: "The Nazis were by tradition anti-feminist and could hardly brook this self-assured woman, the more so since she knew how to bend this men's world to her purposes. . . . But the . . . partly rally film . . . convinced even the doubters of her skill."

Triumph of the Will had celebrated the Nazi party but not the German army and, to mollify the high command, Leni Riefenstahl next made a short documentary about the Wehrmacht called *Tag der Freiheit* (*Day of Freedom*, 1935). This was followed by the most ambitious of her films, *Olympische Spiele* (*Olympia/Olympiad*), a two-part record of the 1936 Olympic Games in Berlin, shot by a team of forty-five cameramen. Part I, *Fest der Völker* (*Festival of the Nations*), begins with a lyrical evocation of classical Greece and a reconstruction of the ancient beginnings of the Games. It follows the Olympic flame to Berlin for the opening parade, presided over by Hitler, before covering some of the contests themselves. The rest of the events are recorded in Part II, *Fest der Schönheit* (*Festival of Beauty*), which begins with sequences in the Olympic village—loving studies of muscular bodies in the steam of Turkish baths, or plunging at dawn into misty woodland pools. Later there is a long montage of midair shots of high divers "falling out of the sun" that comes close to total abstraction.

For the filming of *Olympia,* Riefenstahl mounted cameras on steel towers, lifted them on ballons, sunk them in trenches, floated them on rafts. The famous diving sequence includes shots taken underwater by a cameraman specially trained as a diver, and the director also makes brilliant use of slow-motion photography, a technique she learned from Fanck. By the time the Games were over, Leni Riefenstahl had some two hundred hours of film in the can and faced the monumental task of reducing this to four hours, with variant versions in several different languages. The editing occupied her for nearly two years and was, if anything, an even greater achievement than the filming itself. (Riefenstahl's enemies have suggested that it was not she but the master editor Walter Ruttmann who was mainly responsible for this, but there seems to be no evidence that he was more than her assistant and adviser.)

Olympia was released in April 1938, in time for the festivities in honor of Hitler's forty-ninth birthday, and was accepted by the Olympic Committee as the official film of the 1936 Games. As a paean of praise to physical strength and beauty (and to Hitler and his entourage), it has seemed to some critics tainted by the same anti-intellectual and pagan spirit that disfigured *Triumph of the Will*—just as "outspokenly fascistic in spirit." On the other hand, though Goebbels had reportedly ordered Riefenstahl to play down the embarrassing successes of "non-Aryan" athletes, she completely ignored him, giving special prominence to the achievements of the black American track star Jesse Owens.

"The individual spectator must make up his own mind on the political implications of the film," wrote David Stewart Hull, "but it is hard to deny that *Olympia*, examined purely as *film,* is one of the most beautiful and exciting works the medium has produced." For John Russell Taylor, it remains "a masterpiece undimmed by time, one of the cinema's supreme celebrations of the mystery, beauty and grandeur of the human body." And Arlene Croce, in an essay on dance in film in Richard Roud's *Cinema*, wrote that "although it is not a dance film, it is unsurpassed as a study of physical motion. . . . Accompanied by a fine musical score composed by Herbert Windt, *Olympia* transcends its obligations as a documentary. . . . The editing is so lyrical and so exactly timed to the differently charged proportions of regular or slowed motion that we are often displaced before we know it from one plane to the other, from stadium to 'theatre.'" Mussolini's Italy gave the movie the gold medal at Venice in 1938. Ten years later the International Olympic Committee awarded Leni Riefenstahl a gold medal and a diploma, and in 1955 a Hollywood jury voted *Olympia* one of the ten finest motion pictures of all time.

In the winter of 1938, Riefenstahl went to the United States to promote *Olympia* but was cold-shouldered by Hollywood (except by Walt Disney, who invited her to his studios). Returning to Germany, she resumed work on an earlier project—an adaptation of Kleist's drama *Penthesilea*—but had to abandon this when World War II began. To her subsequent regret, she served briefly as a war correspondent, following the advancing German army into Poland with a camera team. In 1940, refusing Goebbels' invitation to make propaganda films, she went back to work on another long-planned movie of her own, a non-musical version of Eugen d'Albert's opera *Tiefland*. Starring the director herself as a poor girl ensnared by a powerful lowlander but rescued by a highland shepherd, *Tiefland* (*Lowlands*) is a characteristic affirmation of faith in "simple people living close to nature." The opening scenes show the heroine dancing with a troupe of gypsies—real gypsies, whom Riefenstahl recruited from a concentration camp. By her account, neither she nor they realized that these extras were destined for Auschwitz. There were constant interruptions during the filming, but the movie was apparently completed in 1944 at the Barrandov Studios in Prague, though it was not released until ten years later. Riefenstahl's 1944 marriage to Peter Jacob, an army major, ended in divorce two years later.

At the end of the war she was imprisoned for a total of more than three years, first by the American army and then by the French authorities. The latter confiscated her films and equipment, and she also lost her houses in Kitzbühel (Austria), Berlin, and Munich. Released, she continued her battle to clear herself of her reputation as a devoted supporter of the Nazis. The most damning piece of evidence against her was a photograph, published in 1951 or 1952 in a German illustrated weekly. It showed her watching the massacre of civilians by German troops in the Polish village of Konsky in September 1939. In 1952, at her own request, an inquiry was held in a West Berlin denazification court. According to her own account, she had followed the German army into Konsky on her first day as a war correspondent. She had chanced upon the massacre and had tried to end it at some risk to herself, subsequently protesting to the German commander and withdrawing from all war-oriented filmmaking. Witnesses supported what she said, and the court decided that she had engaged in "no political action in support of the Nazi regime which would warrent punishment."

In 1953 Leni Riefenstahl's equipment and films were returned to her, and the following year Tiefland was released with some success in Germany and Austria. Various other projects (including a collaboration with Jean Cocteau) came to nothing, and in 1956 Riefenstahl went to Africa to make Schwarze Fracht (Black Cargo), a semi-documentary about the modern slave trade. Various complications (includng a serious car accident) aborted this film also.

However, she had fallen in love with Africa and with "native people as yet untouched by the destructive hand of civilization." In 1962 she went to the southern Sudan to film and photograph the Nuba, a group of mountain tribes whose people are of great physical beauty. She learned their language, lived among them, and returned repeatedly to record their daily lives, their ceremonies, and their athletic contests. A volume of her magnificent photographs was

published in 1973 (English version in 1974), but her long-promised film about the Nuba has still not appeared. She has also undertaken photographic commissions for various newspapers and magazines (including coverage of the 1972 Olympics in Munich) and at seventy-one lied about her age and took a diving course, mastering underwater photography to produce, among other things, the pictures collected in Coral Gardens (1980).

Formally cleared by the denazification courts, Leni Riefenstahl has continued to encounter controversy and hostility and is said to have fought over fifty court cases since World War II. In 1960, an invitation to lecture at the National Film Theatre in London was cancelled after protests. In 1974 she was honored at the Telluride film festival in Colorado, but the event was marked by protests and demonstrations by Jewish organizations. John Russell Taylor has suggested that anti-female prejudice may have contributed to all this, since "the directors of far more politically objectionable Nazi films, like Veit Harlan, maker of the notorious Jew Süss, were happily reinstated and went back to work" while "she suffered continuing boycotts and protests, as a sort of solitary scapegoat for the cinematic sins of Nazi Germany."

Suzanna Lowry, who interviewed Leni Riefenstahl in 1976 for the Guardian, wrote that, at seventy-four, she was still "sportlich, freckled and even a little sinewy from her ceaseless photographic adventures—ranging the world and returning to labour away in her own cutting room in Schwabing, Munich's trendy-elegant quarter." In the same interview, speaking of The Blue Light, Riefenstahl said that, for her, the film symbolized her life: "Junta, the heroine, is a girl with a very wild nature; she is very poor but very happy. The people of the valley where she lives hate her and think she is a witch."

FILMS: Das blaue Licht (The Blue Light), 1932; Sieg des Glaubens (Victory of Faith), 1933 (short); Triumph des Willens (Triumph of the Will), 1935; Tag der Freiheit—Unsere Wehrmacht (Day of Freedom), 1935 (short); Olympische Spiele (Olympia/Olympiad): Part I, Fest der Völker (Festival of the Nations); Part II, Fest der Schönheit (Festival of Beauty), 1936–1938; Tiefland, 1954.

ABOUT: Barnouw, E. Documentary, 1974; Barsam, R. M. Filmguide to Triumph of the Will, 1975; Berg-Pan, R. Leni Riefenstahl, 1980; Burden, H. T. The Nuremberg Party Rallies, 1967; Current Biography, 1975; Ford, C. Femmes cinéastes, 1972; Ford, C. Leni Riefenstahl, 1978 (in French); Hinton, D. B. The Films of Leni Riefenstahl, 1978; Hull, D. S. Film in the Third Reich, 1969; Infield, G. B. Leni Riefenstahl, 1976 (in English); Kracauer, S. From Caligari to Hitler, 1947;

Leiser, E. Nazi Cinema, 1975; Mandell, R. The Nazi Olympics, 1971; Petley, J. Capital and Culture: German Cinema 1933–1945, 1979; Richards, J. Visions of Yesterday, 1973; Riefenstahl, L. Kampf in Schnee und Eis, 1933; Riefenstahl, L. Schönheit im Olympischen Kampf, 1937; Roud, R. (ed.) Cinema: A Critical Dictionary, 1980; Sarris, A. Interviews With Film Directors, 1967; Sontag, S. Under the Sign of Saturn, 1984; Who's Who in Germany, 1980. *Periodicals*—American Film March 1984; Cahiers in English 5 1966; Film Comment Winter 1965, November–December 1973; Film Culture Spring 1973 (Riefenstahl issue); Film Heritage Fall 1969; Filmkritik August 1972 (Riefenstahl issue); Film Quarterly Fall 1960; Films and Filming April 1965; Guardian October 15, 1976; Interview January 1975; London Times August 21, 1982; Modern Photography February 1974; New York Review of Books February 6, 1975; March 3, 1975; Quarterly Review of Film Studies November 1977; Sight and Sound Spring 1981; Take One October 1976.

MIKHAIL ROMM

ROMM, MIKHAIL ILYICH (January 24, 1901–November 1, 1971), Russian director, was born in the little town of Zaigraievo, on the River Selenga, in the Buryat Republic. He was the son of a doctor. The facts concerning his early life are somewhat complicated, as he explained: "My father had been deported and my family lived in Siberia, beyond Lake Baikal. I was a Jew, and the nearest rabbi was a Irkutsk, very far from our village. To register my birth entailed a very long journey and my father put it off from one day to the next. Eventually he did get round to it, but six months had gone by, and he had quite forgotten the date of my birth—he was a very absentminded man. He entered the date as being February 8, 1901, when in reality I was born earlier, in January—24 January to be exact. He had made the trip to Irkutsk in company with a friend, an old Social Democrat who had also just had a son. On the way my father asked him, 'What are you going to call yours?' 'Ilya, of course, in honor of you. What are you calling yours?' My father blushed, embarrassed and, out of simple delicacy, replied, 'Mikhail of course—in your honor!' Now the point was that for six months they had been calling me Yura, the name which my mother had chosen. My father registered me as Mikhail, but he didn't tell my mother. Two years later we were moved to another place of deportation. Only then, seeing our identity papers, did my mother perceive with horror that her son was called Mikhail. She flatly refused to call me Misha—Misha, she said, was not her little boy, he was a stranger. Finally, after a family council, they invented the name Moura for me. But Moura is a girl's name. Still people got used to it and it stuck to me right up

to school. Then, when my school chums discovered that I was called Moura, like a girl, and surnamed Romm [meaning 'rum'] into the bargain, they started to bully me. This was a very formative experience, and after the third year nobody beat me any more—I had learned to defend myself."

In his late teens Romm went to Moscow to study sculpture at the Academy of Fine Arts. He fought in the Red Army during the civil war of 1918–1921, and then returned to Moscow to complete his studies as a sculptor, graduating in 1925, and subsequently turning his attention to literature and the theatre. These immediate post-revolutionary years were a time of great creative ferment, when the different arts were cross-fertilizing each other and artists themselves often moved from one medium to another. Romm wrote: "The idea of going into the cinema came to me rather late. I was twenty-eight when I earned my first payment for a scenario for a children's short which I had written in collaboration with three other people. Until then I had practiced all the arts except for ballet and the trombone. . . . Frustrated, eager and full of joy, I tirelessly sought a real vocation. My different artistic activities did not feed me."

From scriptwriting Romm moved on to become Alexander Macheret's assistant on *Dela y lyudi* (*Men and Jobs*, 1932). This was an early sound film, and Romm's own first feature as a director turned out to be the last Russian film of the silent era. According to him, "it was extremely easy for a young man with even a little energy to get a film to direct. . . . To be able to write a scenario for one's film—that was really the most important thing. Everyone who could write a scenario was launched into direction at that time. . . . I was the last to win my promotion. After me the doors were closed. A new era had just begun—the era of sound cinema."

Romm made his debut with *Pyshka* (1934), an adaptation of Maupassant's story *Boule de suif*, about a prostitute who saves a coach party fleeing from Rouen during the Franco-Prussian war and then finds herself despised by them. Romm told many stories about the making and reception of the film, including one about a discussion with Eisenstein concerning to correct way to handle the story. Eisenstein's attention centered on Maupassant's description of Rouen and the entry of the German troops, while Romm was more interested in the travelers. As he said, "When Eisenstein was starting, the essential thing was monumental spectacle built around mass scenes. The rest—the coach and its occupants—was only an optional and incidental detail. Now for me this detail was precisely the central thing, and I rejected all the rest. . . . There then are two different methods of work and two different generations, however amiably linked we were."

Gorky liked the film, and took Stalin to see it, but then kept explaining to the dictator exactly how it differed from the original story. (Among other things Romm had added a love story between a servant and a Prussian soldier.) In the end "Stalin told him: 'But look, the film is a completely different art!' That was enough to make me a great director on the spot." Jay Leyda thought the film "little more than an acceptable, stiff student adaptation," but later criticism has been much more respectful, and Georges Sadoul called it "the best film adaptation ever made of a Maupassant story."

Romm's second film, *Trinadtsat* (*The Thirteen*, 1937) was inspired by John Ford's *The Lost Patrol*, and Romm left a characteristically wry account of how this came about. Boris Shumyatsky, head of the Soviet film industry, called in the director and his scriptwriter and described Ford's film (which they hadn't seen): "'The action takes place in a desert: an American patrol is wiped out in a battle with the natives, but succeeds in doing its duty . . . ' 'Can we see the film?'—'No, it's already been sent back. But that is of no account. What is important is that you need a desert (we have some very good ones), frontier guards, counterrevolutionary pillagers and that almost all of the men are wiped out. Almost all, but not quite.' So they called the film *The Thirteen* because it sounded like a nice title, hoping that no one would count the characters, since there were actually only twelve. And they

shot everything realistically, enduring the heat and thirst of the Central Asian desert, only to find everything looked delightfully cool on the screen, so that they had to bring a truckload of sand to the studio and *act* the heat and thirst of all the close-ups."

In August 1927 the twentieth anniversary of the October Revolution was at hand. Alexei Kapler's script for a picture about the revolution had already been approved, and Romm was ordered to film it in time for the celebration. The film went into production on August 10 and was ready for release on November 7 as *Lenin v Octyabre* (*Lenin in October*). This lively piece enjoyed great success, and was held up as an example of economical and efficient production in the shakeup of the Soviet film industry that took place in 1938. Lenin was played in the movie by the distinguished stage actor Boris Shchukin, who also appeared in Romm's sequel *Lenin v 1918 godu* (*Lenin in 1918*, 1939), centering on the attempted assassination of Lenin in August 1918. According to Nina Hibbin, Shchukin "put so much nervous energy into practising mannerisms and gait that his health weakened and he died not long after the second film was completed."

At the time of the Nazi invasion in June 1941 Romm was making a film called *Mechta* (*The Dream*) in the western Ukraine. The film unit had to be hastily evacuated to Central Asia, and *Mechta* was only finally completed in Tashkent in 1943. *Chelovek 217* (*Girl No. 217*, 1944) tells the story of one of the many Russian girls deported during World War II to Nazi Germany. Acquired as slave labor by a German family, she is later driven to kill a member of the SS. Jay Leyda wrote that "no dramatic or cinematic device for underlining villainy" was overlooked by the director, by his camera team (Volchok and Savelyova), by the scriptwriter (Yevgeni Gabrilovich), or by Yelena Kuzmina, who played the lead. All the same, it seemed to Catherine de la Roche that "all the characters, even the Germans, were convincing, and the terrible drama had a measure of restraint which made it all the more moving."

Not much can be said in favor of Romm's cold war movie *Russky vopros* (*The Russian Question,* 1948), an uneasy screen version of Konstantin Simonov's anti-American play of the same name. And Romm himself condemned *Admiral Ushakov* (1953) and its sequel *Korabli shturmuyut bastiony* (*The Ships Attack the Fortifications,* 1953). They were made in the paranoid atmosphere of Stalin's last days, and practically every line of dialogue had to be scrutinized by a committee before filming. The result, Romm said later, was that "the people were depicted as a faceless mass—clay in the omnipotent hands of the flawless hero." In 1954 Romm became artistic director of the Cinema Actors' Theatre Studio, later serving in the same capacity at Mosfilm Studios. In 1957 he became a professor at VGIK, the state film school in Moscow, and he is said to have been a "splendid teacher."

The most notable of Romm's later films is *Devyat dnei odnogo goda* (*Nine Days of One Year,* 1961), in which Alexei Batalov plays a young nuclear physicist so obsessed by his work that he neglects his wife (Tatiana Lavrova) and his own health, exposing himself to an excessive amount of radiation. The film ends with his life in the balance. Peter Cowie thought it "a remarkably taut, gripping film about problems of science and private life in the Soviet Union, and it is Romm's triumph that it assumes a universality that is rare in contemporary Soviet films. . . . The camerawork is immaculate and the background of the Research Institute is brilliantly used; the gigantic machines and reactors seem to dominate their operators. . . . Alexei Batalov, with his abstracted face, and controlled—almost mocking—performance . . . gives the film the spirit of untiring ambition that makes it so memorable." Some critics regard this as Romm's finest work, and one of the best Soviet films of the early 1960s. *Obyknovennyi fazhism* (*Ordinary Fascism,* 1963) is a highly intelligent compilation of documentary material, with a commentary delivered by Romm himself, showing how the rise of Nazism was abetted by the complacency of ordinary men and women.

A "lean, ascetic, poker-faced figure," Romm was "a man of great culture, wit and intelligence." In the 1960s he emerged as an increasingly outspoken opponent of political interference in the arts and of anti-Semitism in Russian life. He was one of the sixty-four signatories of a famous letter to the Central Committee of the CPSU protesting against re-Stalinization in the late 1960s. Romm served as a member of the presidium of the Union of Cinematography Workers, and chairman of the Union's film drama section. He held the Order of Lenin and five Stalin Prizes, among other distinctions.

FILMS: Pyshka (Boule de suif), 1934; Trinadtsat (The Thirteen), 1937; Lenin v Octyabre (Lenin in October), 1937; Lenin v 1918 godu (Lenin in 1918), 1939; Mechta (The Dream), 1943; Chelovek No. 217 (Girl No. 217), 1944; Russky vopros (The Russian Question), 1948; (with Vasily Belyaev) Vladimir Ilyich Lenin, 1948 (compilation); Sekretnaia missia (Secret Mission), 1950; Admiral Ushakov, 1953; Korabli shturmuyut bastiony (The Ships Attack the Fortifications), 1953; Ubiystvo na ulitse dante (Murder on Dante Street), 1956; Devyat dnei odnogo goda (Nine Days of One Year), 1961; Obyknovennyi fazhism (ordinary Fascism), 1965 (compilation).

ABOUT: Biographical Directory of the USSR, 1958; International Film Guide, 1965; Leyda, J. Kino, 1960; Logoyheva, L. Mikhail Romm, 1967 (Russia); Oxford Companion to Film, 1976; Prédal, R. Mikhail Romm, 1974 (France); Schnitzer, L. and J. (eds) Cinema in Revolution, translated by David Robinson, 1976. *Periodicals*—Cahiers du Cinéma April 1970; Classic Film Collector Spring 1972; Commentary December 1963; Film Comment Fall 1968; Films and Filming September 1961, August 1966, July 1970; Iskusstvo Kino February 1972; Movieland October 8, 1965; Observer (London) November 17, 1963; Positif March 1972.

ROSSELLINI, ROBERTO (May 8, 1906–June 3, 1977), Italian director, scenarist, and producer, was born in Rome into a family claiming ancient origins; the Renaissance sculptor Rossellino was probably an early ancestor. Rossellini was the eldest of the four sons of an architect who contributed to the plans for the development of modern Rome. He was, according to his son, "quite an exceptional man"; he enjoyed all sorts of intellectual interests and entertained some of the best-known artists and writers living in Rome, among them many film people. As a result, his son met "only intellectual, never business people." Roberto, as he said in a short autobiography, pursued "literary, philosophical and artistic studies" at school but developed an early passion for things mechanical, setting up a home workshop in which he produced a number of ingenious optical and other devices.

Rossellini's father built the Corso movie theatre in 1918 and later a second theatre, the Barberini, both in downtown Rome. Roberto Rossellini had free entrance to both and visited them frequently. Of all the films he saw, he was most impressed by King Vidor's *The Crowd* (1928) and *Hallelujah* (1929); he said later that these were "perhaps the only 'classical' films I had the opportunity of seeing at the time."

With the death of his father, the family's income diminished and Rossellini took a more practical interest in cinema. Beginning around 1934, thanks to his father's contacts in the industry, he worked for a time editing, dubbing, and even writing screenplays, albeit anonymously. At about the same time he built a small studio in the family villa in Ladispoli, a small resort town north of Rome.

Rossellini's first amateur experiments, which he conducted with the help of his brother, were

ROBERTO ROSSELLINI

documentaries of sorts. *Prélude à l'aprés midi d'un faune* (1937–1938) was not, he said, "a visual ballet, but a documentary on nature," containing "an autobiographical element. . . . In fact, one can find in it my childhood fantasies about the discovery of life." The Italian public never saw the film; the government censor judged some of the scenes indecent and prevented its commercial distribution.

For his next project, Rossellini built a small aquarium in the family villa, filled it with several varieties of fish, and then proceeded to shoot *Fantasia soHomarina* (*Underwater Fantasia*, 1939). He wanted to tell the story of two fish, the vicissitudes of their lives, and the dangers they daily incurred. After carefully studying his subjects, he set to work. To move these nonprofessional actors in accordance with his script, he tied and controlled them with long human hairs, at times procured over the protests of their owners. It took a few months of hard work and various tribulations to complete this ten-minute filming but a national distributor bought the result and it was shown widely. Heartened by this success, Rossellini made three more amateur shorts in 1939–1941.

During this period the Fascist government, recognizing that the cinema was both a profitable business and powerful propaganda tool, took over the industry as a state monopoly, developing in the suburbs of Rome the largest complex of sound studios in Europe, Cinecittà, and establishing a school of cinema, the Centro Sperimentale di Cinematografia. These policies attracted many young bourgeois intellectuals— by no means all of them supporters of the Fascist

regime. Rossellini gained his first screen credit as writer of *Luciano Serra, Pilota* (1938), which eulogizes an Italian pilot fighting in the war against Ethiopia. The film was directed by Goffredo Alessandrini, and Rossellini contributed more than the script; indeed he apparently shot most of the scenes set in Africa. The son of the Duce, Vittorio Mussolini (his name rearranged as Tito Silvio Mursino), wrote the original story and supervised the production, which shared the Mussolini Prize at Venice with Leni Riefenstahl's *Olympiad.*

Rossellini's involvement in this project raises the question of his political allegiance. He himself said: "I have never been a member of the Fascist Party or any of its organizations. I was very anxious to work and found a job with a film company. At a certain moment, Vittorio Mussolini—whom I met and found to be a pleasant lad—joined the company and brought with him the entire *Cinema* group. I was not well acquainted with them, but later on, as was unavoidable, I met all the people gathered around the magazine *Cinema.*"

During this time, the late 1930s, Francesco De Robertis, at that time a naval officer, caused a great sensation in Roman film circles, particularly among the young directors, with his new style of shooting film. De Robertis produced some short documentaries and later a full-length, fictional feature, *Uomini sul fondo* (*Men of the Deep,* 1940). In the film, shot entirely aboard a submarine, he utilized some of the techniques of documentaries, including the use of nonprofessional actors, and for this reason he is considered a forerunner of Italian neorealism.

Appointed to direct the navy's film production unit, De Robertis commissioned Rossellini to make a documentary about a hospital ship. The director had already shot some fifteen thousand meters of film when the decision was made to insert into the script a love story that transformed the documentary into a morale-boosting feature for general release on the home front. *La nave bianca* (*The White Ship,* 1941) was thus Rossellini's first feature film as a director. Robin Wood, writing in Richard Roud's *Cinema* (1980), called this "a war movie made from the Italian viewpoint, it suggests that Italian sailors were largely likeable, Italian nurses humane and dedicated, and Italian hospital ships efficiently run. It is, in other words, no more (though no less) a 'Fascist' movie than most of its British and American counterparts of that period."

The two films that followed, *Un pilota ritorna* (*A Pilot Returns,* 1942) and *L'uomo della croce* (*The Man of the Cross,* 1943) share a strong propagandist tone, much more explicit than in the generically humanitarian *La nave bianca*. Rossellini's collaborators in the production of these films included Michelangelo Antonioni, Massimo Mida, and Alberto Consiglio; the latter two continued to work with Rossellini in several films after the war, as did the director's brother Renzo Rossellini, who wrote the scores for both pictures and became Rossellini's regular composer (for better or worse—many have found Renzo's music sentimental and manipulative).

L'uomo della croce differs substantially from Rossellini's earlier efforts: bound to a martial treatment of the suffering and heroism of simple men, it tells the story of a chaplain on the Russian front killed while carrying out his mission. That movie finished, in the summer of 1943 Rossellini began shooting a film called *Rinuncia* (*Renunciation*). Meanwhile, political events were coming to a head. As Fascism brought Italy closer to catastrophe, the film was left unfinished. It was eventually completed in 1946 by Rossellini's friend Marcello Pagliero, who played Manfredi, the protagonist in *Roma, città aperta*. Not without interest, it was disowned by Rossellini.

In 1944 meanwhile, even before the Germans left Rome, Rossellini began preparing a new film. War had nearly destroyed the movie industry in Italy, and there were very few producers and very little money available to revive it, though sporadic efforts were made by a few directors. Rossellini found an elderly Roman lady willing and able to finance a documentary on Don Pietro Morosini, a priest who was shot by the Germans for having helped the partisan movement. Rossellini wanted Aldo Fabrizi to play the priest, and in order to persuade him to accept the role, he contacted Federico Fellini, a close friend of the Roman actor and music-hall comedian. When his patron offered to finance a second documentary on the actions of Roman children against the Germans, Fellini and Sergio Amidei, who had joined the group as scriptwriters, suggested making one full-length feature film instead of two documentaries. Rossellini welcomed the proposal, and the new film, *Roma, città aperta* (*Rome, Open City*), set out to evoke the history of the Roman people under the German occupation.

In spite of the generosity of the sponsor, the money was never sufficient, and the film had to be shot under primitive conditions. The studios at Cinecittà were unusable, electric power was uncertain, and the film stock was of substandard quality. However, the desperate postwar conditions resulted in certain advantages. The hardship and devastation the filmmakers wanted to portray didn't have to be artificially produced—

they existed right there in the city. The mostly nonprofessional cast, "taken from the street," had themselves lived through the privations and horrors of the occupation. Rossellini called this "a film about fear, the fear felt by all of us but by me in particular. I too had to go into hiding, I too was on the run, I had friends who were captured and killed."

Open City begins with a German patrol searching for the resistance leader Manfredi (Marcello Paglieri). Manfredi escapes and goes to the home of Francesco and his fiancée Pina (Anna Magnani), already pregnant by him. With their help, Manfredi enlists the aid of the priest Don Pietro (Aldo Fabrizi) to smuggle funds to the resistance. The growing militancy of the Roman people as a whole is shown in a riot over bread shortages and an act of sabotage performed by children, among them Pina's son by her first marriage.

The next day Francesco is arrested by the Nazis. Running frantically after the truckload of prisoners, Pina is shot dead—"few scenes in cinema," wrote William Wolf, "have the force of that in which Magnani, arms outstretched, races toward the camera and her death." Manfredi and Don Pietro are soon also arrested. Manfredi is horribly tortured but will not speak. Before Manfredi dies, the Nazi officer tries to win over Don Pietro by pointing out that Manfredi is a subversive opposed to religion, but the priest replies that the resistance leader, by fighting for liberty and justice, "walks in the pathways of the Lord." Manfredi dies, and Don Pietro is taken out to be shot on a hill above Rome, to the accompaniment of rebellious whistling by Pina's son and his friends. The Italian firing squad deliberately misses, but the priest is executed by one of the Germans. Heads bowed, the children trudge off down the hill towards the city.

Open City (1945) had a mixed reception when it was first shown in Italy, where audiences wanted to forget the miseries and divisions of the recent past. Acceptance there grew after the film was acclaimed abroad, including in the United States, where the New York Film Critics chose it as the best foreign picture of 1946. It was praised for the powerful performances of Fabrizi and Magnani, and the use of nonprofessional actors, chosen for their physical appearance, was triumphantly vindicated. The employment of real locations and even the roughness of the filmstock contributed to the film's raw immediacy, its appearance of newsreel authenticity. Rossellini's direction was guided, he said, by the "situation of the moment" and reflected his own changing perceptions and an actor's mood during shooting rather than strict adherence to the script.

It was the great success of *Open City* that first drew international attention to Italian neorealism, and it has been claimed by some as the first full-fledged example of that style. However, Rossellini himself traced the movement back at least as far as *La nave bianca* (1941), and some critics maintain that neorealism was simply a continuation of tendencies already evident in the 1930s, especially in the work of De Robertis and Alessandro Blasetti. There have been objections from left-wing writers that the film ultimately celebrates the spiritual strength of the martyred priest (and therefore of the Catholic church) over the physical courage of the Communist resistance leader.

The criticisms came later, however, and meanwhile Rossellini continued his exploration of the recent past in *Paisà (Paisan,* 1946), produced by the director with funds from a variety of sources, including American ones. The film consists of six short stories about the liberation of Italy, suggested by six different writers: Victor Haines, Marcello Pagliero, Sergio Amidei, Fellini, Rossellini, and Vasco Pratolini. These anecdotes evoke the period from the Allied invasion in 1943 to the liberation in 1945, and each was filmed in a different location, moving north from Sicily to the Po Valley.

Improvisation was carried further than in *Open City,* the script being thrown together almost from day to day. The first episode reportedly acquired its final shape only when the two protagonists were on the set. In this story about a brief and ultimately tragic encounter between an American GI and a Sicilian village girl, the heroine was played by Carmela Sazio, an almost illiterate peasant who, with Rossellini's coaching, contributed a performance of touching freshness.

As José Luis Guarner writes in his book about Rossellini, the camera in this episode "keeps still throughout the long conversation, content to look and record, like a film by Louis Lumière. A lot more is suggested than can actually be seen: the soldier's loneliness, his need to talk to someone, his longing for home and family, the girl's growing confidence. . . . To show all this with such economy of means is one of the great secrets of the cinema. The whole of *Paisà* witnesses the same pressing need to portray a complex reality directly, at one go."

In Naples, a street urchin befriends a black GI and, in a sudden access of goodwill, begs him not to fall asleep because he will then inevitably steal the soldier's boots; in Rome a drunken American spends a night with a prostitute, never recogniz-

ing her as the girl he had fallen in love with earlier; in Florence an English nurse searches for her fiancé, eventually learning by chance that he died in the resistance. Three American chaplains in the Romagna find refuge in a monastery, where the brothers fast for the conversion of the two who are not Catholic. In the Po Valley an American soldier dies alongside the partisans when they are captured by the Germans.

"The episodes set in Florence and the Po Valley move in a series of leaps," wrote Guarner, "leaving enormous gaps. . . . Participation by the audience is greatly increased in this way, since we have to fill in the gaps and understand that other things exist beyond what we can see. By this expedient, sentimentality is ruled out. *Paisà* is presented above all as simple reporting, but it can easily be seen now to express as personal a viewpoint as a film by Hitchcock. . . . Throughout *Paisà* there is . . . [the] will to show individual conflicts in the midst of collective ones, never to separate characters from their environment, and at all times to respect the immediate reality of events, giving them their full duration. The search by Rossellini to find an ideal continuity to form a medium for synthesis finds its logical outcome in the single-shot *plan-séquence.*" Guarner concludes that *Paisà* was Rossellini's "first masterpiece, a masterpiece of neorealism as well as one of the peaks of film history."

Andŕe Bazin, in *What Is Cinema?* (Volume 2, 1971), also drew attention to the "enormous ellipses" in Rossellini's narrative technique: "The mind has to leap from one event to the other as one leaps from stone to stone in crossing a river. It may happen that one's foot hesitates between two rocks, or that one misses one's footing and slips. The mind does likewise. Actually it is not of the essence of a stone to allow people to cross rivers without wetting their feet. . . . Facts are facts, our imagination makes use of them, but they do not exist inherently for this purpose. . . . The unit of cinematic narrative in *Paisà* is not the 'shot,' an abstract view of a reality which is being analyzed, but the 'fact.' A fragment of concrete reality in itself multiple and full of ambiguity, whose meaning emerges only [afterwards] . . . thanks to other imposed facts between which the mind establishes certain relationships."

Another aspect of *Paisà*—its supposed and acclaimed realism—is discussed by Robin Wood: "That we are conditioned to accept . . . something approximating the look of newsreel as 'realistic' accounts partly for the immediate impact *Rome, Open City* and *Paisà* had when they first appeared, but it is also responsible for false assumptions and false expectations (Rossellini's reputation has never recovered from this initial international acclaim)." Wood goes on to compare the Po Valley sequence—the rounding up and execution of partisans and American soldiers—with the Odessa Steps sequence in Eisenstein's *Battleship Potemkin*, with its poetic montage of fragmented close-ups: "Rossellini, on the contrary, works in fairly long takes, almost entirely in long-shot, the camera in almost constant movement. . . . Yet it is arguable that the emotional effect of the Po valley episode is at least as immediate and overwhelming . . . , and the spectator, supposedly left 'detached' by the 'objective' style, can scarcely be in doubt as to which side Rossellini is on, what his position is with regard to the action, and how he means us to react."

Rossellini's war trilogy was completed by *Germania, anno zero* (*Germany, Year Zero*, 1947). An exploratory trip to postwar Germany had proved to him that its people were, after all, as human as anyone else: What had brought them to the nightmare of Nazism? He decided to "tell the story of a child, of an innocent creature which a distorted 'utopian' education induced to commit murder in the belief that he was performing a heroic gesture. But a feeble light of morality is not yet extinguished in him; driven by these small gleams of conscience, confused, he commits suicide." The child is thirteen-year-old Edmund (Edmund Moeschke) and the man he kills is his own sickly father, whom he poisons in accordance with the Nazi doctrine of the survival of the fittest preached by his old teacher Henning (Erich Gühne), now a homosexual pimp.

The film was condemned as biased, melodramatic, and "hysterical," and also disappointed neorealist critics because it was shot mostly in the studio, with the Berlin landscape in back projection. There are some brilliant moments, nevertheless, like the one in which Hitler's voice, played over a portable phonograph, rings out in the city his doctrines have reduced to rubble and chaos. Above all there is the final sequence, ending with shocking suddenness in Edmund's suicide. After the murder, cast off in horror even by the abominable Henning, the child wanders alone through the ruined city, pausing sometimes to play desultory little games until, climbing aimlessly about a half-finished building, he covers his face with his hands as if he has suddenly seen something too awful to bear, and throws himself into space. Tom Milne wrote: "It is this detachment of Rossellini's, in creating characters who are as much to be condemned as pitied (or vice versa), which saves the film from the neorealist disease of miserabilism and turns it into a devastating analysis of human folly. That, and the extraordinary skill with which Rossellini paces an essentially contemplative film almost as an action thriller."

In 1947 Rossellini made *Una voce umana* (*The Human Voice*), a vehicle for Anna Magnani adapted by himself from a one-act play by Jean Cocteau. Recognizing that this 45-minute piece was unmarketable, Rossellini added to it another medium-length film, *Il miracolo* (*The Miracle*), scripted by himself and Fellini. This has Magnani as a deranged peasant seduced by a vagabond (played by Fellini) whom she believes to be St. Joseph. Pregnant, she announces that she is going to give birth to the Son of God and, when the other villagers ridicule her, drags herself off to have her baby alone in an abandoned sanctuary. The two films were released together in 1948 as *L'amore* (*Love*) and presented as "a homage to the art of Anna Magnani."

The Human Voice is a monologue in which Magnani, alone in her apartment, pleads feverishly on the telephone with her bored lover, who is deserting her in favor of a "good" marriage. Rossellini explained his intentions thus: "This new art can take us by the hand and lead us to discover things that the eye cannot perceive. Better than any other subject, *Una voce umana* offered me the opportunity to use the camera as a microscope, all the more so in that the phenomenon to be scrutinized was called Anna Magnani. Only the novel, poetry, and cinema allow us to look into a character and to discover his or her reactions and the causes of those reactions." In spite of the enormous bravura of Magnani's performance, the more serious critics were unimpressed, asserting that this enclosed and static film was not cinema.

Il miracolo is very similar in its theme to *Adega*, a novella by the Spanish writer Valle-Inclán that had caused a sensation in 1901. Rossellini's film provoked even stronger reactions, in Italy and abroad. Some American Catholics accused the director of making money "by using blasphemy" and proscribed not only this film but practically every picture he had made. The intense sensuality of Magnani's performance no doubt added to the sense of outrage, as did images that relate her sufferings to Christ's Passion.

Rossellini allowed that what the peasant woman believes "may be blasphemous . . . but her faith is so strong that her faith redeems it. The last thing she does is completely human and normal: she gives her breast to the child. Some Catholics praised it." Eric Rohmer in *Cahiers du Cinéma* praised the film warmly for its depiction of the loneliness of the human condition and especially the female condition, but Louis Leguin, writing some years later in *Cahiers'* more political rival *Positif*, found in it only "contempt for women and for 'desire.'"

What followed was a comedy of sorts, a considerable departure for Rossellini. The fatal gadget in *La macchina ammazzacattivi* (*The Machine That Kills Bad People*, 1948) is the camera possessed by Celestino Esposito (Gennaro Pisano), a photographer in a small town in southern Italy. This magical machine petrifies everyone it photographs, and Celestino sets out to rid the town of its corrupt authorities and other evildoers.

Peter Bondanella, discussing the picture in *Film Criticism* (3 2 1979), wrote that "Rossellini is chiefly concerned with the symbolic importance of the camera and, by extension, the nature of photography itself. In good neorealist fashion . . . Celestino views the camera as a means of separating reality from illusion, good from evil. . . . It enables him, so he believes, to penetrate the surface of events . . . and to fulfill a God-like role in his small village (not unlike that of a film director on the set). Interestingly enough, Celestino does not perform this miraculous photographic feat with a direct duplication on film of objects in the 'real' world. Instead, he must first take a photograph of another photograph. . . . As any good Platonist knows, he is two steps removed from the world of tangible objects . . . and is engaged in the essentially self-reflexive act of producing a work of art from another work of art. . . . In a comic manner . . . [Rossellini] tells us emphatically that photography (and by extension the cinema . . .) is incapable of separating good from evil or of readily distinguishing reality from appearance" and is "a fallible instrument which reflects not reality but human subjectivity and error."

On May 8, 1948 (his birthday), Rossellini received a letter from Ingrid Bergman, then at the height of her success as a Hollywood star. She had seen *Open City* and said that she would like to work with its director "for the sheer pleasure of the experience." Rossellini was already working with Sergio Amidei on the script of *Stromboli* and offered her the lead role. In January 1949, after much correspondence, he arrived in Hollywood to conclude the contract. Sam Goldwyn was interested in the project but stipulated that Rossellini would have to abandon his improvisational method and adhere to a detailed shooting script. The director declined, but one evening was summoned with Bergman to a Goldwyn press conference and was astonished to hear the mogul announce *Stromboli* as a Gold-

wyn production. Pictures were taken of the director and his star signing a fake contract. When Rossellini read the real document he found that it would deprive him of any artistic freedom, and broke off his dealings with Goldwyn.

Soon afterwards Rossellini signed a more acceptable contract with RKO and returned to Italy, where Bergman joined him. Shooting began in April 1949 on the island of Stromboli, off the Sicilian coast. Then came the international scandal of a liaison between Rossellini and Bergman, the Catholic director and the Protestant actress, both of them already married. They themselves were married in 1950, but the furor continued—orchestrated, in Rossellini's opinion, by Hollywood. The marriage produced a son and two daughters but had a nearly disastrous effect on both careers. Their films were unofficially boycotted in America and elsewhere.

Stromboli, terra di Dio (*Stromboli, Land of God/Stromboli*, 1949) casts Bergman as Karin, a Lithuanian refugee in an internment camp after the war. To get out, she marries Antonio (Mario Vitale), an Italian fisherman and ex-POW, and goes home with him to Stromboli. Her husband beats her as a matter of course, and the barrenness of the island and the harshness of life there are exacerbated for her by the hostility of the other women, jealous and suspicious of her beauty. She is even more a prisoner than in the camp, and more hopelessly one when she becomes pregnant. After an eruption of the volcano she tries to escape, making her way towards the harbor on the far side of the island.

Lost on the mountain, blinded by volcanic gases, exhausted and in despair, Karin cries herself to sleep. As José Luis Guarner writes, "this is the turning point in the film's strange dialogue between a woman and an island, and is expressed with outstanding sensuality." Waking up next morning, oddly serene, Karin looks back at the village and bursts into tears, calling on God to help her. It seemed to Guarner that, "although the narrative framework of *Stromboli, terra di Dio* is disconcertingly simple, the film itself is fairly obscure and difficult to interpret. The theological conclusion is only relative, and the structure of the film itself makes it more pantheistic than Catholic. . . . We are not allowed to draw any conclusions as to whether the woman will come back in submission to the village, escape from the island, or finish up dying lost on the mountain. We only know that from the moment she recognises that she is enslaved by her environment, she becomes in some way free."

In fact, in the version shown in Britain and the United States, RKO cut nearly half an hour of the 107-minute film and edited the ending to suggest that Karin will return to her husband. The picture was in any case a critical and commercial disaster, excoriated by neorealist critics for its unsympathetic portrayal of the Stromboli peasants, by communists for its Catholicism, and by Catholics as the work of adulterers. Thus began and continued the second phase of Rossellini's career, the years with Bergman. Things have changed, however, and the ridicule and outrage that originally greeted these films has been drowned out by a growing chorus of adulation.

At about this time, Rossellini made a statement that amounted to a manifesto: "I need a depth which perhaps only the cinema can provide, both the ability to see characters and objects from any angle and the opportunity to adapt and omit, to make use of dissolves and internal monologue (not, I might add, Joyce's stream of consciousness, but rather that of Dos Passos), to take or leave, putting in what is inherent in the action and what is perhaps its distant origin. I will combine my talent with the camera to haunt and pursue the character: the pain of our times will emerge just through the inability to escape the unblinking eye of the camera."

If the elements are at first the heroine's enemies in *Stromboli*, they are the dear friends of the childlike holy men in *Francesco giullare di Dio* (*Francis, Jester of God*, 1950). In this tribute to Francis of Assisi, the saint even remonstrates mildly when one of his followers beats out the fire which is about to consume his robe: "Why do you want to do it harm?" One brother turns up naked, having given his habit to the poor; Francis kisses the leper; Brother Ginepro overcomes a dreaded tyrant by his terrifying humility.

The film was improvised from a screenplay of twenty-eight pages and about seventy lines of dialogue, with Aldo Fabrizi as the tyrant and the friars recruited from a Franciscan monastery. Delighting some and repelling others, this exuberantly devout movie seemed to Marcel Oms "a monument to stupidity" but to Geoffrey Nowell-Smith "crude, simple and wonderful," and "the (infinitely superior) prototype of Pasolini's medieval films. Rossellini's may be a fairy-tale Middle Ages, but the fairy-tale has the feel of truth as well as charm." For François Truffaut, it was simply the most beautiful film in the world.

The perfect charity of the Franciscans is seen again in *Europa '51* (*The Greatest Love*, 1952), but this time in a modern context where saintliness is interpreted as madness. Irene (Ingrid Bergman), a frivolous bourgeois, is transformed by the suicide of her neglected young son. Advised by a communist cousin, she goes into the slums

and even does a day's factory work on behalf of a woman in need. Unsatisfied by these efforts, she cares devotedly for a dying prostitute and then helps a young delinquent to escape from the police. Her husband (Alexander Knox) sends her to a psychiatrist, and because she insists that she is in the grip of absolute moral imperatives—not simply a temporary breakdown—she is consigned to an asylum. It is a strange film, passionate and at times almost incoherent in its intensity, and was another failure, though Bergman received several prizes for her performance.

Dov'è la libertà? was made mostly in 1952, but not completed and released until 1953. It tells the story of a barber (played by the comic actor Totò) who, as the result of a crime of passion, spends most of the Fascist years in prison. Released into postwar Italy, he finds the outside world so disagreeable that he hastens back to jail. His experiences are recounted in flashback in the course of a trial scene shot (not by Rossellini) after the rest of the film was complete—hence the somewhat disjointed quality of this fable. At this time Rossellini contributed episodes to several of the portmanteau movies then in vogue in Italy, and also directed a number of stage works, including productions of Verdi's opera *Otello* and of Honegger's oratorio *Jeanne au bûcher* (*Joan at the Stake*), from Paul Claudel's play.

While Rossellini's reputation as a filmmaker declined in Italy and elsewhere, it was soaring in France among the contributors to *Cahiers du Cinéma*, the young cinephiles soon to become the epoch-making *cinéastes* of the French New Wave. The definitive split between Rossellini's French admirers and the left-wing Italian critics, disenchanted with their former hero, came with *Viaggio in Italia* (*Journey to Italy/ Strangers/The Lonely Woman*, 1953).

In this script by Rossellini and Vitaliano Brancati, Ingrid Bergman and George Sanders play Katherine and Alexander Joyce, an English couple who have inherited a property in Naples and go there to dispose of it. Separated from their familiar social and professional routines, and under the passionate influence of Italian life and scenery, the Joyces—and especially the prudish Katherine—begin to reassess themselves and their relationship. They see how little binds them together, and after a foolish quarrel they decide on a divorce. But at a religious procession, swept along and separated by the crowd in the excitement occasioned by a miraculous healing, they discover their need for one another.

The making of this film was reportedly an extremely unhappy experience for all concerned. George Sanders in particular objected to receiving his lines the evening before shooting and complained about Rossellini's unprofessionalism. When the film was released, the Italian critics denounced the actors' flat delivery of their lines, the deliberately unbalanced compositions, and the weakness of the film's construction. They pointed out that there were long periods when "nothing happened" except that the characters visit museums or the ruins of Pompeii, gaze at the sea, and attend social functions, these longueurs alternating with abrupt and unprepared-for developments like the divorce decision and the equally unexpected and "miraculous" resolution of the conflict. The left wing lamented Rossellini's abandonment of social realism in favor of an increasingly overt religious message. Audiences stayed away.

But in France, André Bazin, editor of *Cahiers du Cinéma*, wrote a long letter—"In Defense of Rossellini"—to Guido Aristarco, editor of *Cinema Nuovo*. He suggested that Naples in *Viaggio* is "Naples filtered through the consciousness of the heroine . . . a mental landscape at once as objective as a straight photograph and as subjective as pure personal consciousness." He praised Rossellini's "integrity of style and a moral unity only too rare in cinema," saying that "there is no Italian director in whose work aims and form are more closely linked." Bazin goes on: "Neorealism is a description of reality conceived as a whole by a consciousness disposed to see things as a whole. Neorealism contrasts with the realist aesthetics that preceded it . . . in that its realism is not so much concerned with the choice of subjects as with a particular way of regarding things"—in Rossellini's case "a presentation which is at once elliptic and synthetic." Bazin claims that "of all Italian directors Rossellini has done the most to extend the frontiers of the neorealist aesthetic. . . . The art of Rossellini consists in knowing what has to be done to confer on the facts what is at once their most substantial and their most elegant shape—not the most graceful, but the sharpest in outline, the most direct, or the most trenchant."

Another *Cahiers* critic, Jacques Rivette, went so far as to compare Rossellini with Matisse, Goethe, and Mozart on various counts; he said that, on the appearance of *Viaggio*, "all other films suddenly aged ten years"—that it opened "a gap through which the whole cinema must pass or die." Jean-Luc Godard, the New Wave director most directly influenced by Rossellini's improvisational and documentary tendencies, later made *Le Mépris* (1963) as a reflection on some of the themes of *Viaggio*. And Bertolucci, an Italian influenced both by Godard and Rossellini, has the cinephile in *Before the Revolution*

(1964) say: "I saw *Journey to Italy* fifteen times. . . . Remember, you cannot *live* without Rossellini."

More recently, Robin Wood has placed *Viaggio* with *Stromboli* and *Europa '51* as "the three greatest Rossellini movies I have seen. . . . If his art is faithful to certain neorealist principles, it also transcends them. One can state the relationship thus: all art is poised somewhere between exploration and statement. . . . It is a question of which is the dominant impulse; and one can see that Rossellini's art, though it certainly makes statements, is primarily motivated by the drive to understand. This implies that Rossellini's camera is used primarily to record what is before it, without tricks and fakery, and with a minimum (though not an absence) of rhetoric; and that his work with actors, decor, landscape is a process of investigation rather than an expression of foregone conclusions. The central paradox of Rossellini's cinema is that, while he sees the function of the camera as necessarily restricted to photographing the actual, material world, he is of all filmmakers the most rigorously and single-mindedly preoccupied with the spiritual and invisible. Nowhere is this paradox more vividly exemplified, nowhere are its seeming contradictions more successfully resolved, than in the Bergman films."

Rossellini's 1953 stage production of Claudel and Honegger's oratorio *Jeanne au bûcher*, with Bergman as Joan of Arc, had been a great success. A screen version followed in 1954, *Giovanna d'Arco al rogo*, again starring Bergman and with dubbed singing voices. Rossellini remarked that this "very strange film" was "not in any way filmed theatre but cinema, I would even say neorealist cinema in the sense that I have always understood it." Most critics vehemently disagreed, but Guarner, describing the film's cyclical structure and circular camera movements, saw it as "a meditation on space, movement and time, a meditation on the cinema."

La paura (*Fear*, 1954), was an Italian-German coproduction, adapted by Sergio Amidei and Franz Graf Treuberg from a story by Stefan Zweig, "Angst" (the film's German title). Bergman this time plays Irena, the wife of Albert Wagner, an important German scientist (Mathias Wiemann). Irena is remorsefully pursuing an affair with a young composer. She is blackmailed, but eventually learns that the blackmailer is a tool of her husband, who is trying to make her confess her infidelity. When she discovers this, Irena comes close to suicide, but decides that she must live for the sake of her children.

This deeply shadowed film reminded one critic of *film noir*, both in its lighting and in its psychological suspense. It ends with Irena returning to her children in the country—a long tracking shot from darkness into the clear light of moral sanity. When *La paura* failed at the box office, the distributors issued a new version, *Non credo più all'amore* (1955), ending in a reconciliation between husband and wife; this was no more successful.

Nevertheless, like other products of Rossellini's so-called "dark period," *La paura* has grown in critical stature. Jill Forbes wrote in 1981 that Rossellini had transformed the original story "into a film which discusses the value of moral beliefs, the aims of science and the proper role of women. Vivisection is a subtext in this story, and Irena is the possible victim of a kind of moral surgery, performed by her husband who treats her like the [laboratory] guinea pigs. . . . Irena's increasingly frenetic movements, as the cage Alberto has constructed closes around her, mirror those of the animals. . . . *La paura* addresses the issues of domestic politics with a fundamentally liberal understanding of the female condition which makes it extraordinary in its time—and indeed in ours."

La paura was Rossellini's last film with Ingrid Bergman, and marked also the end of their marriage, as well as of an entire phase in the director's work. He made no more films for three years, devoting himself to reading and reflection and spending long periods in Paris as adviser and mentor to the New Wave critics and filmmakers. In 1957–1958, originally with the blessing and backing of Nehru's government, Rossellini worked in India on what was planned as a massive documentary evocation of the subcontinent. When it emerged that he was having an affair with his collaborator and intermediary Sonali Das Gupta, a married woman, a new scandal erupted. Rossellini was denounced by Nehru, and government support was withdrawn.

Nevertheless, from the mass of material that had been shot Rossellini derived a full-length documentary, *India* (1959), and a highly successful ten-part television series, shown in Italy in 1959 as *L'India vista da Rossellini* and in France as *J'ai fait un beau voyage*. The documentary feature *India* comprises four episodes: the marriage in Kalepur of a peasant and a peddler's daughter; a laborer's farewell to the great dam at Hirakud, on which he has worked for five years; the story of an old man who tries to save a man-eating tiger from hunters; the bewilderment of a trained monkey when its master dies, leaving it lost between the human and the animal worlds.

According to Guarner, "the whole method of the film [is] based on resonances between shots and on abridgements in the narrative, which form a climax to the experiments in *Paisà* and *Viaggio in Italia*. Each shot in *India* gives rise to innumerable reverberations, which in turn inspire other shots, without ever moving from the original theme of the integration of Man and Nature." And Jean-Luc Godard wrote that "*India* runs counter to all normal cinema: the image merely complements the idea which provokes it. *India* is a film of absolute logic, more Socratic than Socrates. Each image is beautiful, not because it is beautiful in itself, like a shot from *Que Viva Mexico!*, but because it has the splendor of the true, and Rossellini starts from truth. He has already gone on from the point which others may perhaps reach in twenty years' time."

India was also well received at Cannes, even by the Italian critics, who welcomed it as a return to neorealist principles. Thus "rehabilitated," Rossellini was able to return to the feature film with an Italian-French coproduction, *Il generale Della Rovere* (*General Della Rovere*, 1959), from a novel by Indro Montanelli. Set during the German occupation, and based on a true story, it stars Vittorio De Sica as Bardone, a seedy swindler who is forced by the Nazis to impersonate a dead Italian general. His assignment is to discover the identity of the Italian resistance leader Fabrizio but, disgusted by the brutality of his masters and at the same time caught up in the operatic heroism of his role, he chooses to die with other patriots rather than betray Fabrizio.

General Della Rovere represented a painful compromise for Rossellini; he said that it, with *Anima nera*, were the only movies he ever made for money—"purely alimentary films"—and he bitterly regretted both of them. This melodramatic entertainment, played with relish by De Sica, was nevertheless a huge financial success and shared the Golden Lion at Venice.

Another story of the resistance followed in *Era notte a Roma* (*It Was Night in Rome*, 1960). An English officer (Leo Genn), an American pilot (Peter Baldwin), and a Russian sergeant (Sergei Bondarchuk) escape from a German camp and are hidden in a loft by Esperia (Giovanna Ralli), a young black marketeer. They are tracked down by Tarcisio (George Petrarca), an unfrocked priest working for the Germans, who is eventually strangled by the British officer.

Rossellini believed that "neorealism consists of following someone with love and watching all his discoveries and impressions. . . . The camera does not leave the actor, and in this way the camera effects the most complex journeys." Given these views, it is not surprising that he had always favored the long take. In *Era notte*, however, this preference is carried to quite extraordinary lengths, with whole sequences of often violent action being shot from a single set-up by a camera that is nevertheless capable of following the characters closely as they move, gesture, and react.

This was achieved with the use of a zoom camera adapted by Rossellini himself, who had never abandoned his youthful experiments with optical devices. His Pancinor Zoom, as he explained, "has two interlocking motors, and one of them acts as a counterweight to stop the lens oscillating as it moves, so that you don't get the zoom effect. . . . The camera works more like an eye." With the Pancinor, "the director can put the accents where he wishes, during the shooting of the scene. Moreover, this device removes any of the rigidity attached to cutting and speeds up the rhythm because changes in angle also bring their own tempo. The dolly is used specifically for changes of angle, while moving in and out is done with the Pancinor. . . . The director can thus steal the expressions of his actors without them noticing him, while their performance goes on." This statement, wrote Guarner, "implies a whole new idea of *mise-en-scène* and space in the cinema."

Rossellini's next two films were commissioned projects, produced as part of the celebrations for the 1961 centennial celebrations of the unification of Italy. *Viva L'Italia* (1960) commemorates the conquest of southern Italy by Garibaldi and his thousand Redcoats in 1860, the campaign that virtually completed the unification. Unlike romantic earlier accounts, Rossellini's is detached, clear, and almost documentary in its exposition, making effective use of the Pancinor Zoom to show troop movements over vast stretches of landscape. Garibaldi (Renzo Ricci) is not a dashing young hero but a middle-aged man with gout and a cough, calmly determined and profoundly human.

Andrew Sarris, discussing this film four years later, said that "the zoom not only supplements the devices by which Rossellini expresses a unified and circular vision of the world; it enables him to endow his later . . . work with a double vision of history as a remote and immediate experience. It is as if a painter could establish a dynamic relationship between his painting and one of its internal details. Garibaldi's men fight on a hill. Long shot equals *then*. Zoom shot equals *now*. The two shots in tandem are no longer limited to an imitation of an event. What we are watching is our own aesthetic and ideological

distance from the event. We are also watching the capacity of man to act as if he were watching his acts from a great distance away in time (history's) through space (cinema's)."

The other commissioned film, *Vanina Vanini* (*The Betrayer*, 1961), is set thirty years earlier and tells in similar style the story of the tragic love affair between the young princess of the title (Sandra Milo) and Pietro Missirilli (Laurent Terzieff), a leader of the *Carbonari*, a secret society fighting for Italian unity. Drawn from *Chroniques italiennes* and other works by Stendhal, it was mutilated by its producer and dismissed by most critics. However, Paul Mayersberg, writing in *Movie* (6 1963), wrote that "*Vanina* is shot almost entirely with a zoom. Quite apart from the fact that this technique is admirably suited to the presentation of a historical subject, as its flattening of perspective gives the impression of a moving fresco, it has at last liberated the zoom from its status as a mere device in the filmmaker's vocabulary. In *Vanina* the zoom is not used in the accepted way for 'effect,' to make isolated dramatic points, but is as much a part of Rossellini's style as the tracking shot is a part of Preminger's. The zoom serves two distinct but related functions: to incorporate surprise within a single fluid movement . . . and to follow the characters without the artifice of contrived camera set-ups, allowing them great freedom in their actions."

Rossellini also contributed a documentary to the unification celebrations, the 45-minute *Torino nei Centi ' anni* (1961), a montage of stills, documents, newsreels, clips, etc., covering the history of Turin from 1860 to 1960. The potboiling feature *Anima nera* followed in 1962, a superficial melodrama with a few good scenes. Rossellini was a contributor—along with Godard, Pasolini, and Ugo Gregoretti—to the 1962 portmanteau film *RoGoPaG*. After that he turned to television, beginning with a five-episode historical documentary called *L'Età del Ferro* (*The Age of Iron*, 1965). It is a history of the world seen in relation to the development of the iron and steel industry, from the Etruscan origins of smelting to the present. Written and supervised by Rossellini but directed by his son Renzo, it can be seen as a rather fumbling first step towards the series of didactic historical films that Rossellini subsequently made for television.

The failure of his later films, and above all the fact that they were not understood by the masses (whose opinion he valued above that of critics), led Rossellini in 1965 to conclude that he was "useless." As early as 1957, in an interview with André Bazin, he had spoken enthusiastically about television: "In modern society, men have an enormous need to know each other. Modern society and modern art have been destructive of man; but television is an aid to his rediscovery. Television, an art without traditions, dares to go out to look for man. . . . The television audience is quite different from that of the cinema. In television you're talking not to the mass public but to ten million individuals; and the discussion becomes much more intimate, more persuasive." And a few years later, in 1963, he said that "history, through teaching visually, can evolve on its own ground rather than evaporate into dates and names. Abandoning the usual litany of battles, it can surrender to its social, economic and political determinants. It can build, not on fantasy, but on historical knowledge, situations, costumes, atmospheres, and men who had historical significance and helped the social developments by which we live today."

Rossellini inaugurated the program implied by these statements with *La Prise de pouvoir par Louis XIV* (*The Rise to Power of Louis XIV*, 1966), made for French television with a cast of little-known actors and nonprofessionals. Beginning in 1661 with the death of France's First Minister Cardinal Mazarin, it shows how the young king (Jean-Marie Patte) tightens his grip, step by step, on the court, the government, and the nation until, in 1682, he shuts himself away in Versailles as the Sun King, the very embodiment of lonely power.

From the outset, the film rejects all the conventions of the historical movie. The characters, from Louis down, speak in the flat tones of ordinary conversation (or of the television interview). The elaborate settings and costumes are there not for their own picturesque sake but as evidence and instruments of the king's power—he imprisons his rebellious nobles in complicated structures of dress and convention. And though there is spectacle in plenty, scenes are included only when they add to our understanding of Louis' power games—never *because* they are spectacular (or amusing or exciting or romantic).

The distinguished historian Philippe Erlanger collaborated on the script, which is full of details of fascinating strangeness, like the doctors' dependency upon their sense of smell in diagnosis, and the queen clapping to announce to the court that the king has performed his husbandly duty. As Martin Walsh wrote in *Jump Cut* (15 1977), the audience at the beginning of the film "are taken . . . into the court world of intrigue and power-struggle in a manner which suggests the voyeurist presentation of another time—we are literally transported into an alien world as observers." All this seems to bear out Rossellini's claim that "I don't interpret. I don't transmit any message. I avoid expressing theories and forcing meanings. I reconstruct documents, I offer information which leaves to the spectator the entire responsibility for his own judgments." To the extent that this is true, it makes all the more remarkable and admirable the immense success of this and his other historical films for television.

However, Walsh goes on, "it gradually becomes apparent that there is a decisive 'constructivist principle' in operation, and it is one that establishes a central link between Louis' grasping of power and the primary techniques of bourgeois cinema: this principle is that of spectacle as a means to power. Indeed it is probably not too much to say that *Louis XIV* is one of the most extraordinary meditations on the nature and power of spectacle that the cinema has yet produced. . . . Rossellini makes clear that Louis' accession to domination is the result of Louis' contrivance, the result of his successful imposition of a fiction upon his people. And that fiction is presented in various ways: Louis is not seen in the opening minutes of the film; by the end we have no other visual reality. . . . The opening scenes have a confused, if not quite chaotic, aura as everyone jockeys for position while Mazarin's death is awaited; by the end formality rules, everything is neatly ordered hierarchically. The opening scenes are sombre with deep reds, black, and the paleness of death, while by the end gaudy colours vibrate from every corner of the frame. . . . And Rossellini crystallizes Louis' centrality by putting the audience in the position of the courtiers who watch Louis as he wakes, dresses, hunts and eats. . . . the further the film progresses, the more inexorably Rossellini moves us toward an understanding of both Louis' power over his world and the film's power over us."

After *Idea di un'isola* (*The Idea of an Island*, 1967), a documentary about Sicily made for American television, came *La lotta dell ' uomo per la sua sopravvivenza* (*Man's Struggle for Survival*, 1967), another vast television feature in twelve one-hour episodes. Written and supervised by Rossellini, and like *L'Età del Ferro* directed by his son Renzo, it traces humanity's long battle for mastery over nature from Neolithic times to the present day.

The careful research and documentary techniques used in *Louis XIV* are seen again in *Atti degli Apostoli* (*Acts of the Apostles*, 1968), a five-part television series directed by Rossellini in collaboration with Renzo. There is a characteristic stress on the simple humanity of the Apostles, their occasional weaknesses and confusions, and also their revolutionary commitment to political and religious equality and freedom. There is a marked element of demythologization in the presentation of their visions and miraculous visitations, which are recounted as dreams. The series was very warmly received and very successful.

The renewal of Rossellini's reputation was confirmed in 1969 by his election as president of the Centro Sperimentale di Cinematografia, which incorporates the national film archive and the national film school. He resigned a year later, saying that the Centro's financial structure made it impossible for him to run the school as he had wished, as a place where students could "find their own way" by making their own movies.

The series of historical features for television continued with *Socrate* (*Socrates*, 1970). As Guarner said, "the continual shifting between the general and the particular" in this film—greatly facilitated by the Pancinor—"is intended to make *Socrate* the chronicle of a civilization, as well as of a particular personal experience. . . . This approach seems typical of Rossellini and has emerged as a deliberate method of exposition"—a method that goes some ways towards answering the criticism that Rossellini subscribed to the "great man" theory of history. He himself said that his historical films "show the customs, prejudices, fears, aspirations, ideas and agonies of an epoch and a place. I show a man—an inventor—confront these." On the other hand, speaking specifically of *Socrate*, he said that "history was . . . written to glorify power. But the real history is to discover man, the simple man whose life was never written."

Blaise Pascal (1972), an account of the life and times of the French philosopher and mathematician (1623–1662), was shot mostly in Italy. Pascal was played by Pierre Arditi, a Parisian baker chosen simply on account of his facial resemblance to the great man. Rossellini set out to show "the drama of a man who develops scientific thought which is in conflict with the dogmatism of his deep religious faith." The result seemed to Geoffrey Nowell-Smith "a triumph of lucid exposition and storytelling, rich in historical detail and compelling in its presentation of both intellectual issues and of personal suffering." Though the subject hardly seems one of mass appeal, this television film was seen by sixteen million people in a single broadcast. Considerably less successful was *Agostino d'Ippona* (*Augustine of Hippo*, 1972), a biography of St. Augustine set against the fall of the Roman Empire. Rossellini pointed out that "now we live in a destructive historical era, similar to the one that preceded the fall of the Roman Empire; and it is obvious that our civilization is [also] braced on the brink of an abyss."

The series continued with *L'Età di Cosimo de'Medici* (*The Age of Cosimo de'Medici*, 1972). This four-hour film, televised in three parts, combined what had been two separate scripts, one on the artist Leone Battista Alberti and the other on his patron, Cosimo de'Medici. Jill Forbes wrote that "in the absence of real financial resources, Rossellini proceeds more by emblems than reconstructions. . . . But though it cites all the great events mentioned in the manuals, *Cosimo* is much more than a school textbook. It is not difficult to see why the early Florentine Renaissance should interest Rossellini. Not simply because Cosimo is a figure comparable in many respects to Louis XIV . . . but also because the Florentine Renaissance was the moment when art and (primitive) capitalism achieved a perfect equilibrium. . . . On the other hand, Rossellini's approach is explanatory rather than nostalgic, a history rather than a celebration, expository rather than moralistic, and completely open-ended."

Cartesius (*Descartes*) followed in 1973, representing (according to the director) "among other things, the advent of a method in which human thought becomes more rational and definitively moves toward the age of technical and scientific development." After that, Rossellini returned to the cinema with *Anno uno* (*Italy, Year One*, 1974), a theatre film made in the same "didactic" style as the television series. It is an account of Italian history from World War II to the mid-1950s, centered upon the career of the Christian Democrat leader Alcide De Gasperi. This centrist view was received by the Christian Democrats with disdain and by the left with outraged hostility. Financially it flopped.

Unable to find a backer or distributor for his next film, *Il Messia* (*The Messiah*), Rossellini nevertheless went to Tunisia in the summer of 1975—the location he had used for *The Acts of the Apostles*. He recruited nonprofessional actors and in six weeks, in spite of the unbearable heat, completed the film. His choice of such a subject for what turned out to be his last film inevitably raises the question of Rossellini's religious beliefs. Don Ranvaud, editor of the British Film Institute's *Dossier* on Rossellini (1981), speaks of his "unfathomable mysticism, generated by a profound Catholicism." Adriano Aprá, however, in an essay in the same publication, suggests that "all those films which were considered to be 'spiritualistic' or 'mystical' and which had attracted the scorn and irony of Italian critics for that very reason, had been made in order to be able to diagnose and fight against precisely such residues." Rossellini's own statements tend to bear out the latter view: "I'm not religious at all. I'm the product of a society that is religious among other things, and I deal with religion as a reality. We are capable of thinking in metaphysical terms—that's a reality and it has to be dealt with."

Rossellini said that he had "tried to make *The Messiah* acceptable to everybody, with the intention of putting people together, not dividing them. People find belief in the fact that Jesus performed miracles. I find tremendous importance, rather, in what he said. 'The Sabbath was made for Man, not Man for the Sabbath' is, I think, one of the most revolutionary sentences ever spoken." The picture was not well received, however, critics complaining that it "retails information but makes no attempt to reveal its meaning"; that it was "all talk and no action."

Rossellini had completed a script on Karl Marx and was also planning a film on the history of Islam when he died suddenly of a heart attack at his home in a Rome suburb. As Sam Rohdie said, he had "been at the center of three important events in the history of the cinema . . . : he was one of the filmmakers most responsible for the creation of neorealism in Italy in the 1940s; both through his films and by direct personal encouragement he helped make the New Wave in France in the late 1950s a possibility; and his engagement with television in the 1960s . . . [was] more serious than that of any other established filmmaker." For many, he was the greatest postwar Italian director.

—P.R.

FILMS: *Shorts and documentaries*—Daphne, 1936; Prelude à l'après midi d 'un faune, 1938; Fantasia sottomarina, 1939; Il tacchino prepotente, 1939; La vispa Teresa, 1939; Il ruscello di Ripasottile, 1941; L'India vista da Rossellini, 1959; India, 1959; Torino nei cent'anni, 1961; Idea di un'isola: La Sicilia, 1967; Intervista con Salvador Allende, 1973; Concerto per Michelangelo, 1977; Le Centre Georges Pompidou, 1977. *Features*—La nave bianca (The White Ship), 1941; Un pilota ritorna (A Pilot Returns), 1942; L'uomo della croce (The Man of the Cross, 1943; Roma, città aperta (Rome, Open City/Open City), 1945; Paisà (Paisan/ Ordinary People), 1946; Germania, anno zero (Germany, Year Zero/Evil Street), 1947; L'amore (Love): in two parts, Una voce umana (The Human Voice) and Il miracolo (The Miracle), 1948; La macchina ammazzacattivi (The Machine that Kills Bad People), 1948; Stromboli, terra di Dio (Stromboli), 1949; Francesco, giullare di Dio (Francis, God's Jester/The Flowers of St. Francis), 1950; L'Invidia (Envy) *episode in* Les Septs Péchés capitaux (The Seven Deadly Sins), 1952; Europa '51 (The Greatest Love), 1952; Ingrid Bergman *episode in* Siamo donne (We Are the Women), 1953; Dov'è la libertà?, 1953; Viaggio in Italia (Journey to Italy/Strangers/The Lonely Woman), 1953; Napoli '43 *episode in* Amori di mezzo secolo, 1954; Giovanna d'Arco al rogo (Joan at the Stake), 1954; La paura/Angst (Fear), 1954 (re-released in 1955 as Non

credo più all 'amore); Il generale Della Rovere (General Della Rovera), 1959; Era notte a Roma (It Was Night in Rome/Once Upon a Night in Rome), 1960; Viva L'Italia (Garibaldi), 1960; Vanina Vanini (The Betrayer), 1961; Anima nera, 1962; Illibatezza (Chastity) *episode in* RoGoPaG, 1962; La Prise de pouvoir par Louis XIV, (The Rise to Power of Louis XIV), 1966; Atti degli Apostoli (Acts of the Apostles), 1968; Socrate (Socrates), 1970; Blaise Pascal, 1972; Agostino d 'Ippona (Augustine of Hippo), 1972; L'Età di Cosimo de'Medici (The Age of Cosimo de'Medici/The Age of the Medici), 1972; Cartesius (Descartes), 1973; Anno uno (Italy: Year One), 1974; Il Messia (The Messiah), 1975.

ABOUT: Baldelli, P. Roberto Rossellini, 1972 (in Italian); Bazin, A. What Is Cinema? (Volume 2), 1971; Bergman, I. and Burgess, A. Ingrid Bergman: My Story, 1980; Boucard, M. Roberto Rossellini, 1972 (in German); Brunette, P. Roberto Rossellini, 1987; Bruno, E. Roberto Rossellini, 1979 (in Italian); Ferrara, G. L'Opera di Roberto Rossellini 1973; Guarner, J. L. Roberto Rossellini, translated by Elisabeth Cameron, 1970; Godard, J. -L.Godard on Godard, edited by Tom Milne, 1972; Hovald, P. Roberto Rossellini, 1958 (in French); Menon, G. (ed.) Dibattito su Rossellini, 1972; Mida, M. Roberto Rossellini, 1961 (in Italian); Ranvaud, D. (ed.) Roberto Rossellini (BFI Dossier 8), 1981; Rondolino, G. Rossellini, 1974 (in Italian); Roud R. (ed.) Cinema: A Critical Dictionary, 1980; Trasatti, S. Rossellini e la Televisione, 1978; Verdone, M. Roberto Rossellini, 1963 (in French). *Periodicals*—L'Avant-Scène du Cinéma February 15, 1979; Bianco e Nero February 1952 (Rossellini issue); Cahiers du Cinéma July 1953, July 1954, May 1955, May 1956, May 1962, July 1962, July 1963, August 1965, October 1966; Cinema (Italy) October 1948; Cinéma (France) February 1976, March 1978; Cinema e Film Spring 1967; Cinema Journal Fall 1985; Cinema Nuovo November, December 1955, February 1956; Cinema Sessanta January–February 1974; Écran July 1977; Film Comment Fall 1964, July–August 1974; Filmcritica April–May 1965, May–June 1966, August 1968, April–May 1977; Film Culture Spring 1964, Spring 1971; Filmkritik October 1978, March 1982; Image et Son/Écran April 1982; Monogram Summer 1971; National Film Theatre (London) Booklet May 1974, April 1981; Positif April 1958; Rivista del Cinematografo July–August 1977 (Rossellini issue); Screen Winter 1973–1974 (Rossellini issue); Sight and Sound April 1950; Take One January–February 1974; Times (London) June 4, 1977.

"ROSSEN," ROBERT (Robert Rosen) (March 16, 1908–February 18, 1966), American director, scenarist, and producer, was born in New York City. The son of Russian-Jewish immigrants, he grew up on Rivington Street on the Lower East Side—not in an exclusively Jewish neighborhood but in a racially mixed one that gave him early lessons in "the impact of environment on character and vice versa." It was a

ROBERT ROSSEN

tough world and Rossen learned to defend himself, for a while boxing—sometimes professionally—as a welterweight.

Perhaps because he was the grandson of a rabbi and the nephew of a Hebrew poet, Rossen was also and increasingly drawn to the intellectual life, especially to literature and the study of history. He attended various courses at New York University and in his early twenties turned to the stage, involving himself as an actor, writer, and director in several of the radical and/or avant-garde little theatres that flourished in those years, most notably the Washington Square Players and the Maverick-Woodstock Players.

The first play Rossen directed was *The Tree,* an anti-lynching drama by Richard Maibaum produced in either 1931 or 1932. In 1932 Rossen directed John Wexley's *Steel* under the auspices of the *Daily Worker,* and the following year Maibum's *Birthright,* one of several anti-Nazi dramas staged in the year of Hitler's accession to power. At about the same time Rossen wrote a play of his own set in a poolroom, *Corner Pocket.* This forerunner of *The Hustler* was never produced, but Rossen's play *The Body Beautiful* made it to Broadway in November 1935. Though it survived only four performances, it impressed the Warner Brothers director Mervyn LeRoy, who brought the twenty-eight-year-old Rossen to Hollywood in 1936.

Rossen earned ten writing credits at Warners between 1937 and 1943, also working on eight uncompleted projects. The poverty and injustice he had seen as a boy had led him into the radical theatre, and in 1937, like many other idealistic young filmmakers, he joined the Hollywood branch of the Communist Party. Rossen explained later that he had been looking for "new horizons, a new kind of society"; the Party at that time seemed to offer "every possible kind of thing . . . which could fulfil your sense of idealism."

Rossen could not have found a studio more sympathetic to his concerns than Warner Brothers. The most socially-conscious of the majors, taking many of its subjects from contemporary headlines, it actively supported Roosevelt's New Deal. Jack Warner was indeed a personal friend of the president. And, though Warner was notoriously parsimonious, the studio was popular with writers. Rossen said that "subjects were not just shoved under your nose. Within reasonable limits you were able to choose from what went through the story department. Hal Wallis, the production chief, respected the writers and did not force them to accept assignments they didn't agree with. Within the necessary limits of a certain discipline, I was remarkably free."

His first script, written in collaboration with Abem Finkel, was *Marked Woman* (1937), directed by Lloyd Bacon and inspired by Thomas E. Dewey's successful battle against Lucky Luciano's prostitution empire. Humphrey Bogart played the tough young prosecutor, with Bette Davis as his star witness. Frank Nugent praised the "dramatically concise script," which eschewed a conventionally happy ending; it showed that the trial, which launched the prosecutor's political career, did little to improve the circumstances of the "hostesses" whose testimony had won the case for him.

Mervyn LeRoy directed *They Won't Forget* (1937), adapted by Rossen and Aben Kandel from a novel by Ward Greene. The film features Claude Rains as a cynical Southern DA and introduced Lana Turner as the "sweater girl" whose murder leads to the indictment and eventual lynching of a man who may well be innocent. Praised as "a brilliant sociological drama and a trenchant film editorial against intolerance," it showed that Rossen had indeed learned something about "the impact of environment on character and vice versa."

Teamed with Leonardo Bercovici, Rossen returned to the transcripts of Thomas Dewey's New York racket trials and produced a well-researched original script, *Racket Busters* (1938). Dealing with extortion and murder in the trucking industry, it (like *Marked Woman*) was directed by Lloyd Bacon, with Bogart this time on the wrong side of the law. Brian Neve, in his article about Rossen as a scriptwriter in *Film and History* (February 1984), finds the movie political in its insistence on worker solidarity as the answer to intimidation, but adds that it suffers from "some unlikely plotting and characterization," as well as poor production values and casting.

Rossen's first solo writing credit was on *Dust Be My Destiny* (1939), another "problem" picture centering on the struggles of a young man (John Garfield) during the Depression. This was followed by an exiting Warners gangster melodrama, *The Roaring Twenties* (1939), then by two less interesting films, *A Child Is Born* (1940), set in a maternity ward, and the disappointing jazz movie *Blues in the Night*. Rossen's 1941 version of Jack London's *The Sea Wolf*, directed by Michael Curtiz, and with Edward G. Robinson as the Nietzschean sea captain Wolf Larsen, is regarded as the best of the novel's numerous adaptations. After another exposé of economic corruption and intimidation, this time on the docks, in *Out of the Fog* (1941), came Rossen's last Warners assignment, *Edge of Darkness* (1943), a wartime drama about Norwegian resistance to the Nazis.

A Walk in the Sun, Harry Brown's notable short novel about an American infantry platoon in Italy in World War II, was scripted by Rossen and directed for 20th Century–Fox by Lewis Milestone. This moving and humane picture is regarded by some as one of the best films to have come out of the war. Rossen then followed Milestone to Paramount for *The Strange Love of Martha Ivers* (1946), a remarkable *film noir* set in a small town. Barbara Stanwyck stars as a rich woman twisted by greed and guilt, with Van Heflin as the returned wanderer who may know her secret. Milestone, wrote one reviewer, had been "greatly helped by his script writer, Robert Rossen, who had decorated an exiting and never quite predictable script with much American wit."

Rossen began his directorial career the following year at Columbia. Having scripted *Johnny O'Clock*, a tough underworld thriller of no particular social significance, he was allowed to direct it at the insistence of its star, Dick Powell, who plays a gambler wrongly suspected of having murdered a crooked cop. Contemporary reviewers found the movie sordid, if occasionally suspenseful, reserving their praise for Lee J. Cobb's performance as a lumbering, implacable detective.

After scripting *Desert Fury* (1947), directed by Lewis Allen, Rossen made his own second feature—one much closer to his real concerns than *Johnny O'Clock. Body and Soul* (1947), made for the independent Enterprise Productions, was written not by Rossen but by Abraham Polonsky, who shared the same political convic-

tions. John Garfield plays Charley Davis, a boxer who has fought his way out of the ghetto slums of the Lower East Side. Hungry for success, he signs up with a crooked promoter and becomes a "money machine," alienating his mother (Anne Revere) and his artist girlfriend Peg (Lilli Palmer). As world champion, he agrees to take a dive in a big-money fight but recovers his integrity in the last round, winning the fight, his self-respect, and Peg.

A critic for the National Board of Review found in this picture "the gin and tinsel, squalor and sables of the Depression era, less daring than when first revealed in *Dead End* or *Golden Boy* but more valid and mature because shown without sentiment or blur. The old tenement films with 'social significance' had general reform in mind. . . . But *Body and Soul* gets deeper into its milieu, makes specific the blame, and tightens up the conflicts of its cast with logic." There was universal praise for the direction of the fight scenes, especially the climactic bout, whose "tour-de-force photography," as Alan Casty writes, "combines an immediacy and fluidity of camera work (James Wong Howe reputedly shot the scenes while on roller skates) with decisive, exclamatory editing (especially in the use of close-ups) and a steady rhythmic progression towards the crescendo of the final knockout."

In 1949, under contract to Columbia, Rossen produced Joseph H. Lewis' interesting *film noir Undercover Man*, now a cult movie; then scripted, directed, and produced one of the most admired of his own pictures, *All the King's Men* (1949). This was adapted from the Pulitzer Prize–winning novel by Robert Penn Warren, a fictionalized account of the career of Huey Long, demagogic governor of Louisiana. Long appears as Willie Stark (Broderick Crawford), a redneck idealist corrupted by power. His story is told by the journalist Jack Burden (John Ireland), who is seduced by Stark's rhetoric and charisma and becomes his stooge, flacking for the governor and condoning his corruption on the grounds that he gets things done. It is only after Stark has stolen his girlfriend and driven his best friend to suicide that Burden stops blurring the issues with a whiskey bottle and sets out to destroy the would-be dictator.

Alan Casty, writing in *Film Quarterly* (Winter 1966–1967), says that in *All the King's Men* Rossen's "techniques are similar to and probably influenced by those of the Italian neorealists, and especially Roberto Rossellini; Rossen [and his photographer Burnett Guffey] shoots the film entirely on location with the available light in all kinds of weather conditions, uses many non-actors, catches his performers unawares and spontaneous, and generally employs documentary camera and cutting methods."

For Casty, "it is the social side of the film that is most effective; the intricate set of personal relationships that are to parallel the political corruption are left shadowy and fragmented, never fully integrated into the social context." Bosley Crowther expressed similar reservations about the film's characterization and consistency of structure, but praised its "superb pictorialism which perpetually crackles and explodes. . . . From ugly illustrations of back-room spittoon politics to wild illuminations of howling political mobs, it catches the dim but dreadful aspect of ignorance and greed when played upon by theatrics, eloquence, and bluff." *All the King's Men* received more acclaim from contemporary critics than any of Rossen's other films and garnered some thirty awards, including Oscars for best picture, best actor, and best supporting actress (Mercedes McCambridge, as Stark's hard-boiled assistant and mistress); Rossen was nominated for both best direction and best screenplay.

Alan Casty maintains that "in all his major works, Rossen was concerned with the search of a young man for something which he does not recognize as himself, his identity. He is a character of a certain natural inner force . . . , but he cannot fully identify or control this energy, skill, or potential, this source of grace and power." Misguided by a corrupt society, his natural *élan* "turns aggressive, perverse, destructive," and he pursues such "illusory symbols of the self" as "power, status, wealth, violence, domination, love turned inside out into violation."

Charley Davis in *Body and Soul* obviously fits this account of Rossen's films, and in *All the King's Men,* Casty suggests, "the Rossen hero is split into two—the rootless intellectual Jack Burden and the dynamic activist Willie Stark." In *The Brave Bulls* (1951), adapted from Tom Lea's novel, the hero is Luis Bello (Mel Ferrer), a poor Mexican peasant who achieves fame and wealth through his skill and courage as a matador. Asked why he fights bulls he says: "It's what I do. Without it, I am nothing." Spoiled by parasitic crowds and corrupt promoters, he loses his nerve but, like Charley Davis, recovers himself during a climactic fight. This takes place at a village fiesta before an audience of country people; their simplicity returns Bello to his roots and the real source of his spirit.

Produced and directed for Columbia by Rossen but scripted by John Bright, the film had a mixed reception. It was generally admired for the excitement and technical accuracy of the bullfight scenes, shot in black and white on location by James Wong Howe. However, it seemed to most reviewers diffuse and clumsily structured, while Bello's apotheosis struck many as an arbitrary and unconvincing reversal of the movie's predominant mood of defeated bitterness.

Soon after the release of *The Brave Bulls,* Rossen fell foul of the House Un-American Activities Committee. He had already been named as a Communist in 1947 but had denied the accusation. At new HUAC hearings early in 1951, he was again named by several witnesses, and Columbia took steps to break his contract. To avoid a subpoena Rossen returned for a time to Mexico, but in June he went home to testify, repeating that he was not at that time a member of the Communist Party but refusing to discuss his past activities or to name others as Communists.

Rossen was blacklisted for two years. In May 1953 he testified again, now admitting his previous membership in the Party and describing his disillusionment and final break with it in 1947. He also supplied the names of nearly sixty other members of the Party. He explained that he had initially refused to testify because he "didn't want to give any names," but that after two years of reflection he no longer believed that "any one individual can indulge himself in the luxury of individual morality or put it against what I feel very strongly is the security and safety of this nation."

Even after this purgation, Rossen could not at first find employment in the United States, and indeed he never made another picture in a Hollywood studio. His next film, *Mambo,* was made in 1954 in Italy for Carlo Ponti–Dino de Laurentiis. Atrociously dubbed, it might almost be a parody of Rossen's earlier films, telling the inspiring story of a girl from the Venetian slums who rises to giddy heights as a mambo dancer, is temporarily corrupted, but decides in the end to dedicate herself to her art. Obviously aimed at the American market, it stars not only Silvana Mangano and Vittorio Gassman but Shelley Winters and Michael Rennie. Duly released in 1955 by Columbia, it was met with general derision.

Alexander the Great (1956) was written and directed by Rossen and produced by his own Rossen Enterprises, which distributed through United Artists. This three-hour historical epic in Technicolor proved to be a surprisingly serious treatment of a characteristic theme. Rossen discovers in the Macedonian conqueror qualities similar to those of Charley Davis, Willie Stark, and Luis Bello. Driven by a lust for personal glory (and an obsessive rivalry with his father), Alexander seeks to create a world order by force of arms. His armies spread destruction and suffering everywhere, while his victories turn to ashes in his mouth. He conquers the world but dies praying for peace and brotherhood.

A reviewer in *Saturday Review* expressed the general reaction when he praised the film for its avoidance of the usual clichés of historical spectacle and for "sticking reasonably close to such facts as have come down to us," but damned it for its lack of "a coherent storyline," finding the result neither good drama nor good cinema. Isabel Quigly, sharing most of these reservations, found the picture so full of memorable incidents and illuminations that it nevertheless seemed to her "an achievement of outstanding intelligence and power." There was widespread admiration for Fredric March's performance as Alexander's father, Philip of Macedon. Richard Burton, in the lead, was thought to have done the best he could with an almost impossibly complex role. Burton, incidentally, thought Rossen's script for this film the best he had ever read, and hinted that pressures from the distributors imposed changes that weakened it.

Rossen's next project was a potboiler, produced by Darryl Zanuck and scripted by Alfred Hayes from Alec Waugh's novel *Island in the Sun*. The setting, lushly photographed in CinemaScope by Fred Young, is a Caribbean island on the verge of independence, and the plot gingerly considers how racial prejudice affects the romantic attachments and political plans of various residents and visitors, among them Joan Fontaine and Harry Belafonte, John Justin and Dorothy Dandridge, Joan Collins and James Mason. "So far as exploring any of these issues with sensitivity goes," wrote Hollis Alpert, "the movie is a total loss."

Back with Columbia, Rossen directed *They Came to Cordura* (1959), a 148-minute, four-million-dollar epic Western in Eastmancolor and CinemaScope, coscripted by the director and Ivan Moffat from Glendon Swarthout's novel. The movie is set in Mexico in 1916, when the American cavalry was skirmishing wih Pancho Villa. Gary Cooper plays Major Thorn, an officer who has demonstrated his cowardice to the world and to himself. Ironically, he is assigned to choose candidates for the Medal of Honor, and to lead his band of heroes across a waterless waste to receive their decorations. Rita Hayworth, a prisoner charged with giving aid and comfort to the enemy, completes the explosive package. In the course of the journey, Thorn discovers that the heroism of his charges was in most cases based on the ugliest of motives and finds a truer courage in himself.

Time's reviewer wrote that Rossen examines "the nature and conduct of a hero at considerable depth, and he finds in his moral conflicts a stronger motive for the usual violent action, which in this film is intensified and refined into a genuine parable of the journey of the soul, a sort of *Pilgrim's Progress* through the Mexican badlands." Another critic, in *Saturday Review*, noted that most of the action occurs early in the picture and that, "just when you would expect the tensions to be mounting to a climax, the characters sit down and start analyzing each other. It makes a long film seem longer—particularly since the dialogue, which up to this point has been laconic and pointed, suddenly becomes literary and stilted. But the cast, most of them playing notably offbeat roles, provide an intensity that carries off all but the most unlikely scenes."

The Hustler (1961) was the first film since *Alexander the Great* over which Rossen had full artistic control as director, producer, and coscenarist (with Sidney Carroll). He returned in it to his favorite theme of a young man in search of himself, but now with a richer apprehension of the kind of realism he wanted to achieve—"not a matter of a servile reproduction of reality; rather, it will be necessary to capture things as they are and modify them so as to give them a poetic significance" and to get at "this whole question of the inner life."

Eddie Felson (Paul Newman) in *The Hustler* is an itinerant young pool shark, who lures amateurs into games by pretending incompetence, then takes them for the money they greedily bet against him. Fast Eddie has real talent and, as the film begins, takes on the champion, the immaculate Minnesota Fats (Jackie Gleason), in a thirty-six-hour game. Fats wins, not because he is a better player but because he has a stronger will. The brash and overconfident Eddie is a loser—the quintessential Rossen hero with great ability but no self-knowledge.

Eddie meets a girl (Piper Laurie), a crippled alcoholic drifter who nevertheless offers the possibility of mutual salvation through love. But Eddie, still hungry for success, throws in his lot with a sinister professional gambler, Bert Gordon (George C. Scott), a demoniacal figure in love with power. Gordon introduces him to big-time hustling in Louisville during Derby Week. Eddie wins money but loses his girl, whom Gordon deliberately drives to despair and suicide. At last realizing what he has lost, and coming to understand his own nature, Eddie is able to take on Minnesota Fats and beat him, at the same time freeing himself from Gordon.

Not for the first time in a Rossen film, the conclusion seemed to many critics unconvincing and/or inappropriate, but there was universal praise for the intense excitement generated by the pool games, the almost documentary realism of the film's various milieus, and for the performances Rossen had elicited from his principals and above all from George C. Scott, established here as an actor of the first rank. *The Hustler* was nominated for Academy Awards in every major category but received only one, for Eugen Shuftan's moody black-and-white photography. André Fieschi has suggested that the film's "ultraclassical" skill in the ordering of spectacle and suspense "often masked the real originality of the thesis that . . . [it] supported, that developed as if underground a fragile network of hauntings and obsessions."

Rossen was already ill when he produced and directed his last film, *Lilith* (1964), adapted by himself and Robert Alan Arthur from J. R. Salamanca's novel, and magnificently photographed by Shuftan, again in black and white. Warren Beatty plays Vincent Bruce, a young vet who goes to work in a plush mental hospital. One of the inmates is Lilith (Jean Seberg), a beautiful schizophrenic who seems to offer him perfect love. Slowly it emerges that, as she says of herself, Lilith "wants to leave the mark of her desire on every living creature in the world"—that there is something in her of the ancient Lilith of Jewish folklore, demon and child corrupter. Vincent's helpless jealousy grows into madness and ends fatally.

Lilith was entered by Columia for the 1964 Venice film festival, then withdrawn in the face of harsh comments from the chairman of the festival's organizing committee. In America the picture was a critical and commercial failure, but it was profoundly admired in France and its international reputation has continued to grow; some now regard it, rather than *The Hustler,* as Rossen's best film.

It seemed to Tom Milne that "the only puzzle about *Lilith* is why so many people should have reacted so violently against this extraordinarily beautiful, intelligent film. Perhaps—who knows?—because Rossen and Shuftan between them have created a siren song so insidiously persuasive about the strange, tranquil attraction of madness that we, like Vincent Bruce, are almost caught by it. . . . The question the film asks and leaves unanswered—and unanswerable—is who is the victim, who the villain between Lilith and Vincent. . . . *Lilith* is a remarkable attempt to dig a little deeper in an almost untilled field, and to throw some light on that mystery of mysteries—the relationship between madness and the creative imagination."

Part of the reason for *Lilith*'s initial harsh reception was its apparent remoteness from Rossen's usual realistic concerns. In fact, Alan Casty suggests, it is not a complete departure from Rossen's earlier work, nor a fashionable imitation of French models (as some critics suggested), "but an extension of his own developing concern for film realism" in which he achieves "a more complex and ambiguous sense of motive, character, and existence. . . . Why we do what we do as we seek to define ourselves is left an awful mystery."

For André Fieschi, *Lilith* was Rossen's "incontestable masterpiece—which serves as well to wipe out past errors (*An Island in the Sun, Mambo*) as to relegate successes (*All the King's Men, The Hustler*) to the second rank. This man, said to be rough, grumpy, gauche, and preoccupied with pounding first truths without much nuance, came, against all expectation and thanks to a single film, to confuse the more or less vague ideas that critics maintained about him. . . . Nothing could let us suppose that Rossen carried in him a diamond as brilliant and as cutting as *Lilith.* Yet one masterpiece is enough to change the face of a man."

Rossen died in 1966 at the age of fifty-seven. He was survived by his wife Sue, whom he had married in 1934, and by a son and two daughters.

FILMS: Johnny O'Clock, 1947; Body and Soul, 1947; All the King's Men, 1949; The Brave Bulls, 1951; Mambo, 1955; Alexander the Great, 1956; Island in the Sun, 1957; They Came to Cordura, 1959; The Hustler, 1961; Lilith, 1964.

ABOUT: Casty, A. The Films of Robert Rossen, 1969; Coursodon, J. P. American Directors, Vol. II, 1983; McBride, J. (ed.) Persistence of Vision, 1968; Roud, R. (ed.) Cinema: A Critical Dictionary, 1980. *Periodicals*—L'Avant-Scène du Cinéma October 1967; Cahiers du Cinéma April 1966; Cahiers in English January 1967; Cinema (UK) August 1970; Cinema (USA) Fall 1968; Film and History February 1984; Film Ideal 213 and 217–219 1969; Film Index 11 and 12–13 1971; Film Quarterly Winter 1966–1967; Films and Filming August 1962, February 1972; Films in Review June–July 1962; Monthly Film Bulletin (Britain) 416 1968.

"ROTHA," PAUL (Paul Thompson) (June 3, 1907–   ), British director, producer, scenarist, film critic, and historian, was born in London, the youngest of the four children of Dr. C.J.S. Thompson and the former Ethel Tindall. His father was curator of the Welcome Historical Medical Museum in London and conservator at the Royal College of Surgeons, as well as the author of many medical books. Paul Thompson (who later changed his name to Paul Rotha) in-

PAUL ROTHA

herited his father's conservatorial mind and applied it to his childhood passion, the cinema. Even in his schooldays, he scrupulously recorded his impressions of the movies he saw and collected and clipped fan magazines, laying the foundations of what became a huge and unique archive.

Rotha's brother became a journalist and his sisters both entered the book trade, but he himself was from the beginning drawn to the visual arts, showing early promise in drawing and painting. He was educated at Highgate School in London, and from 1923 to 1925 studied at the Slade School of Fine Arts. Rotha began his career while still a student as a painter, book illustrator, and theatre designer. He won an international award for theatre design at the Paris Exhibition in 1925, and in 1927 became art critic of *The Connoisseur.*

These successes did nothing to deflect Rotha from his first love, the cinema. In 1928, he cycled one day to Elstree studios on the outskirts of London, and talked himself into a job with British International Pictures. Beginning as an "outside man"—hiring furniture and props—he was soon promoted to assistant designer. He was just as swiftly fired when *Film Weekly* (November 12, 1928) published an article by him containing harsh satricial comments on the British movie industry.

"Virtually the whole film industry on the production side was then out of work," Rotha says. "So I did what I have always done since then; if I couldn't make films, the next best thing was to write about them." The suggestion that Rotha should write came from Norah C. James of Jona-

than Cape, and the writings became *The Film Till Now.* With the contract came a £50 advance that Rotha invested in a study trip to Paris (where he met René Clair, Alberto Cavalcanti, and others) and Berlin. Written during 1929, the book was published in 1930, when Rotha was twenty-three.

The Film Till Now was the first comprehensive survey of the scientific, commercial, and aesthetic development of the silent film from its beginnings in the 1880s, and it immediately established itself as the standard history. Rotha "seemed to have seen every film, whatever its nationality and however old," wrote Richard Griffith. "He spoke with authority, imagination, assurance." Beyond its "superb command of fact," however, it was "a young man's book," passionate in its enthusiasm for Russian and European cinema, equally passionate in its contempt for the "glittering, metallic" products of Hollywood. In 1930, it "reached people all over the world with the excited realization that there *was* an art of the film."

Richard Griffith collaborated with Rotha on a revision of *The Film Till Now* in 1949, and it remained a standard work until changing critical standards in the 1960s made some of its judgments seem dated. Hugely successful as it was, it seems to Rotha that the book "probably did me more harm in the film industry than any other of the rash acts I have committed. To write a serious book about films and then expect to be employed by the industry is too much to expect." In fact, in 1931, the year he published a sequel to *The Film Till Now* called *Celluloid,* Rotha was invited by John Grierson to join the film unit of the Empire Marketing Board, where Grierson and his disciples were hammering out the socially idealistic policies that characterized the developing British documentary movement.

Rotha shared Grierson's social consciousness but stayed with him for only six month before leaving the EMB to work on scripts for the actor and director Miles Mander. He made his own first film in 1932 on commission from Shell-Mex and Imperial Airways, the four-reel documentary *Contact,* which he wrote and produced as well as directed. It is a romantic account of the airline's operations, from the building of a plane to Imperial's routes across Africa and India. It pleased Grierson, who called it "the most ambitious documentary film since Elton's *Voice of the World*"—"the first work of a very able critic who knows all the rules and all the theories. . . . Its impressionistic method is vivid, its photography beautiful, the sense of great distance wonderfully captured."

There followed three documentaries made for

various sponsors with the facilities of Gaumont-British Instructional, all of them scripted and edited by the director. *The Rising Tide* (25 minutes, 1933) about the construction of a dock at Southampton, attracted very little attention, but showed a concern with the social effects of such a development that became central in *Shipyard* (24 minutes, 1935). Sponsored by the Orient Shipping Line and Vickers-Armstrong, it follows the building of a new liner, the SS *Orient*, at Barrow-in-Furness in Lancashire, at the same time tracing the social and economic effects of the project on an industrial area so impoverished and depressed that Rotha was moved to give away £45 of his minute budget in hand outs to the needy.

Rotha believes that *Shipyard* was "the first British documentary film to express a social purpose," and it is the only one of his early pictures that he remembers with affection. Critics were reminded of Eisenstein by Rotha's use of cross-cutting, superimposition, and rigorously selective editing to build up an impressionistic portrait of life in Barrow during the Depression. There was also much praise for Rotha's use of natural sound—though apparently there was in fact no money for location sound and the soundtrack was entirely fabricated in the laboratory.

For a year, Rotha and his team traveled regularly from London to Barrow to follow the progress of the *Orient*. On these journeys they shot the material that was eventually assembled as *The Face of Britain* (19 minutes, 1935). Rotha says its "theme embraces the confusion brought about by the Industrial Revolution with its canopies of smoke and steam and the coming of a New Power in the Second Industrial Revolution— Electricity." According to Roger Manvell, the photography of all these early Rotha films was outstandingly beautiful, and they "were carefully cut (sometimes to excess) in order to achieve the maximum possible effects in mobile composition."

Rotha published another extremely important book in 1935, *Documentary Film*, still a standard work, and followed this in 1936 with *Movie Parade*, done in collaboration with Roger Manvell. Alistair Cooke called the latter "the first, and already indispensable, photographic history of the movies," and said that Rotha was "rapidly qualifying as the Grove of the cinema." At about this time he became a member of the British Labour Party's film advisory committee, and also found time to make two relatively conventional documentaries, *Steel* (10 minutes, 1935) and *Death on the Road* (17 minutes, 1936).

In *Documentary Film*, Rotha writes: "Real and creative thought must be about real things. Let cinema explore beyond the limits of what we are told constitutes entertainment. Let cinema attempt the dramatization of the living scene and the living theme, springing from the living present instead of from the synthetic fabrication of the studio. Let cinema attempt film interpretations of modern problems and events, of things as they really are today. . . . Let cinema recognize the existence of real men and women, real things and real issues."

Rotha showed what he meant in *Peace Film* (1936), made in collaboration with Ruby Grierson and others. A response to news that Britain was rearming against Hitler's Germany, this very short, rhythmically cut film used slogans to urge people to write to their political representatives demanding "peace by discussion." The Labour statesman Sir Stafford Cripps was among those who contributed to its costs, and Benjamin Brittten donated its musical score. *Peace Film* was at first denied a certificate by the British Board of Film Censors but was eventually widely distributed. In the *Morning Post,* Rotha was called "a Pacifist infecting the public mind with mischievous . . . propaganda," though many were just as ardent in his defense. *Peace of Britain* (17 minutes, 1936) appears to be a longer version of the same film.

In 1936, with Ralph Keene and Donald Taylor, Rotha founded Strand Films. For the next years he worked mainly as a producer, though one who often played a considerable creative role. For example, he both coordinated and edited *The Way We Live* (1937), directed by Ralph Bond and Ruby Grierson and examining the economic and social effects of the Depression in two contrasting areas of Britain—the Rhondda Valley coalmining region in Wales and the agricultural Cotswolds.

It was during this period, in the winter of 1937–1938, that Rotha visited the United States as an advisor on documentary film to the Rockefeller Foundation and the Museum of Modern Art's film library. In New York he saw some of the Federal Theatre's *Living Newspaper* productions, and was very greatly impressed by their techniques—the way they addressed themselves to a current social issues in an assortment of theatrical modes and from a variety of viewpoints. He began to consider ways of applying this dialectical method of documentary film, though it was to be some years before he could put his ideas into practice.

Meanwhile, back in Britain, Rotha was cofounder in 1939 of *Documentary News Letter* and the same year began work on a major documentary commissioned by the London

Times—a picture of Britain as seen through the pages of that newspaper. Scripted, directed, and edited by Rotha, *The Fourth Estate* was completed in 1940 after a year and a half of work, and promptly buried in the *Times*' vaults—the war had begun, and the film's images of peacetime Britain, beautiful as they were, seemed quite irrelevant. It was finally shown in 1964, cut from sixty to forty-five minutes, and was said to convey perfectly the *Times*' "characteristic blend of starchy dignity, and rather self-conscious loyalty to an historic tradition."

When the London blitz began, Rotha went off to the slums of the East End and supervised a mobile canteen for bombed-out workers. In 1941 he established his own documentary production company, Paul Rotha Productions Ltd., which during World War II made about 150 instructional and propaganda films for the Ministry of Information. They included some notable investigations of social problems that looked beyond the present crisis—documentaries like Donald Alexander's *Five and Under* (1941), Budge Cooper's *Children of the City* (1944), and Rotha's own memorable and innovatory *World of Plenty* (46 minutes, 1943).

Scripted by Rotha with Eric Knight and photographed by Wolfgang Suschitzky and Peter Hennessy, *World of Plenty* was a plea for solutions to the problems of global food distribution that would have to be faced after the war. It was in this film that Rotha first made full use of the techniques he had learned from the *Living Newspaper*, using an assortment of materials—newsreel footage, interviews with experts, diagrams by the Isotype Institute—and also a variety of narrators expressing conflicting views. As Richard Griffith wrote, "previous documentaries had been narrated by a 'voice of God' commentator who . . . explained the visuals with an authority that brooked no back-talk"; *World of Plenty* "provided several commentators, each with a mind of his own, who argued the issues of the film from varying points of view—and in doing so, for the first time let the audiences into the argument too."

The pioneer documentarist Edgar Anstey called *World of Plenty* "one of the very few completely individual contributions to the art of the cinema." He praised Rotha's "virtuosity as one of the screen's great editors" and called the film a "carefully composed piece of nonfictional drama which is as mindful of its emotional climaxes as is the most popular piece of escapist melodrama." A critic in the London *Times* said it was "much more than a first-class documentary. It is a political event. It is the first satisfactory use of modern technique to explain to the public

one of the great world problems. . . . *World of Plenty* is a front-page story and a leading article thrown at the heads of filmgoers." A "book of the film" was published in 1945.

In 1944 Rotha set up Films of Fact Ltd. as a subsidiary of Paul Rotha Productions, and over the next three or four years made some fifty documentaries for the Ministry of Information and its successor, the Central Office of Information. In 1945 Rotha produced a long and detailed memorandum at the request of Sir Stafford Cripps, suggesting a postwar program for relations between the government and the film industry (a program that was never instituted). He was also a member of the committee that wrote the Arts Enquiry report *The Factual Film* (1946) and around the same time became a founding member and the first chairman of the Federation of Documentary Film Units.

Land of Promise (64 minutes, 1945), made by Films of Fact for the British Gas Council and directed and coscripted by Rotha, used the techniques developed in *World of Plenty* in "an argument about homes and houses." In this film, indeed, the dialectical method is carried further, with professional actors portraying representative types—an "enemy of progress" (Miles Malleson), and a young soldier (John Mills) speaking for those who would need decent housing in the postwar years—as well as argumentative "voices from the audience." William Alwyn provided the score, as he had for *World of Plenty*.

"Rotha has out-plentied *World of Plenty*," wrote a reviewer in *Documentary News Letter*. "From the experience gained in the earlier film, he has achieved a greater concentration of fact and emotion, and has at the same time sought, not unsuccessfully, to simplify his argument by personalising it. . . . As a result, *Land of Promise* grips you. What is more important, the film has passion . . . passion in the sense that the wickedness of the slums . . . is pushed home to you. . . . Vivid images, brilliant editing, dramatic and frightening in some of the sequences, ingenious soundtrack." It seemed to Roger Manvell that, "in spite of an overloading of statistics, this film remains one of the most courageous documentaries yet made in Britain." Thirty years later, large sections of the film were used in Christopher Booker's *Where We Live Now*, a television indictment of postwar architecture and planning.

A City Speaks (65 minutes, 1947) is a city planning film made for and about the city of Manchester, notable for a final fifteen-minute sequence showing the city's amusements and leisure activities, reminiscent of Walter Ruttmann's *Berlin* and cut to the music of "The Ride of the Valkyries." Rotha returned to the subject of world food problems in *The World Is Rich* (36 minutes, 1947), centering on the work of the Food and Agriculture Organization of the United Nations. A compilation film, it was assembled from some 800,000 feet of stock footage collected from innumerable sources, with a script by Arthur Calder-Marshall and music by Clifton Parker. A less didactic, more lyrical film than *World of Plenty,* it received a special award from the British Film Academy.

When, after a four-year silence, Rotha returned to directing, it was with his first fictional feature, *No Resting Place* (1951). The film was produced by Colin Lesslie, who scraped together the budget of £60,000 and also collaborated with Rotha and Michael Orrom on the script, based on Ian Niall's novel. Orrom was the editor, William Alwyn wrote the score, and Walter Suschitzky shot the film in black and white (and under dreadful weather conditions) entirely on location in the Wicklow Mountains of Ireland. The cast was drawn mostly from the Irish theatre.

As adapted, *No Resting Place* deals with a family of wandering Irish tinkers—rough and illiterate people, unwanted in any respectable community, and hostile to everyone except their own kind. One of them (Michael Gough) accidentally kills a gamekeeper who has wounded his small son and, though his guilt is unproven, he is remorselessly hounded by a Civil Guard (Noel Purcell) that he has bested in a brawl. The film was shown at the Venice and Edinburgh festivals, but failed to achieve general distribution.

No Resting Place is said to be Rotha's own favorite among his films. It was universally praised for the beauty of its photography, but the critical response was otherwise extremely mixed. One reviewer found the acting "consistently ghastly, in keeping with the script," and others complained of its slow pace, its lack of variation in pitch and tempo, and a certain remoteness in its approach to the emotions of its characters. Its champions liked its semi-documentary style, its compassion for "the illiterate, underprivileged and dispossessed," and were reminded of the work of the Italian neorealists. For Eric Shorter, it "survives with a strange and endearing compulsion as a severely amoral fable of oppression, opportunity, and Irish independence."

In 1952 Rotha went to Mexico to shoot his portion of *World Without End* (60 minutes, 1953), a documentary about the work of UNESCO in that country and in Thailand (covered by Basil Wright). Cutting back and forth between the two countries, it effectively illustrates the basic similarities between people everywhere. The film was acclaimed at the Edinburgh film festival and won an award from the British Film Academy. The same year, 1953, Rotha was elected chairman of the BFA, and began a two-year stint as head of documentaries at BBC-TV, where he produced nearly eighty films.

Another feature film appeared in 1958—a modestly budgeted suspense thriller written, directed, and produced by Rotha, and called *Cat and Mouse.* Lee Patterson plays a deserter from the American army, Ann Sears the English girl he makes a prisoner in her own house. After this film, which seems to have sunk without a trace, came *Cradle of Genius* (1959), a documentary about the Abbey Theatre in Dublin, and then *Das Leben von Adolf Hitler* (*The Life of Adolf Hitler,* 1961). The latter is an excellent compilation film made at the invitation of the producer Walter Koppel, who had suffered in a concentration camp and wanted a film "to show the German people what Hitler had been about." Rotha spent two years gathering archive material from all over Europe and checking its authenticity.

Rotha's next film was also made abroad, produced by Rudolph Meyer for Sapphire Film Productions of Amsterdam. *De Overval* (*The Silent Raid,* 1962) is a fictional film, scripted by Rotha with Dr. L. De Jong, but based with scrupulous accuracy on an actual incident that took place towards the end of World War II in Holland, when resistance fighters raided the Nazi prison at Leeuwarden and liberated important political prisoners. Made with a Dutch crew and cast and shot on the actual locations, the result is said to have been an exciting action picture that conveys an impression of documentary authenticity.

Though *De Overval* enjoyed considerable financial success, Rotha has made no more films because, he says, "no one has asked me to." He has continued to write about the cinema in British and foreign journals and has published several more books, including *Television in the Making* (1956), which he edited; *Rotha on the Film* (1958); and *Documentary Diary* (1973). *The Innocent Eye* (1963), Arthur Calder-Marshall's biography of Robert Flaherty, was based on research by Rotha and Basil Wright. Derek Hill said of *Rotha on the Film,* a collection of seventy essays and articles, that it "remainds one just how determined and vigorous he has always been on the cinema's behalf," in the forefront of campaigns for film societies, a film archive, and a national film institute, and "a keen, knowledgeable observer of the tortuous affairs of the whole British film industry."

Michael Orrom, who worked with Rotha on a number of pictures, says that he was "regarded by many as *l'enfant terrible* of British documentary, the teller of unpalatable truths. Hence he has been rather the odd man out—of the main stream, yet outside it. His purpose has always been clear and political, his commitment complete. . . . Rotha's standards were exacting: nothing slipshod, nothing glossed over. Every shot had to have a meaning, and be fitted together with craftsmanship." And Richard Griffith says that in his best documentaries Rotha "tries to speak for modern man, lost in the chaos of the machine civilization he has created, and now seeking to create a new life on a more human scale. For these films of complex social and economic argument touch at every turn the humblest levels of living—birth and death, feast and famine, beauty and ugliness, the elements of experience common to all."

Rotha is married to the Irish actress Constance Smith, his third wife. They have been in considerable financial difficulty in recent years, and Rotha has been obliged to sell parts of his unique collection of books, scripts, photographs, letters, and press clippings.

FILMS: *Documentaries*—Contact, 1933; The Rising Tide, 1933 (reissued as Great Cargoes, 1935); Shipyard, 1935; The Face of Britain, 1935; Steel, 1935; Death on the Road, 1936; Peace Film, 1936; Peace of Britain, 1936; (with Sidney Cole) Roads Across Britain, 1939; The Fourth Estate, 1940 (not shown until 1964); Mr. Borland Thinks Again, 1940; World of Plenty, 1943; Soviet Village, 1944; Land of Promise, 1945; Total War in Britain, 1945; A City Speaks, 1947; The World Is Rich, 1947; (with Basil Wright) World Without End, 1953; Cradle of Genius, 1959; Das Leben von Adolf Hitler (The Life of Adolf Hitler), 1961. *Features*—No Resting Place, 1951; Cat and Mouse, 1958; De Overval (The Silent Raid), 1962.

ABOUT: Current Biography, 1957; International Who's Who, 1981–82; Rotha, P. Documentary Diary, 1973; Rotha, P. Rotha on the Film, 1958. *Periodicals*—Film Forum January 1963; Quarterly of Film, Radio and Television Fall 1955; Screen Summer 1972.

*ROUQUIER, GEORGES (June 23, 1909–) was born at Lunel-Viel, Hérault, in the French Massif Central. He began as a typographer and linotype operator but he was passionately interested in the cinema, inspired particularly by the films of Robert J. Flaherty. At the age of twenty he made an amateur documentary in the Flaherty spirit—an impressionistic study of the grape harvest in the south of France called *Vendanges* (*Vintage*, 1929). Rouquier wrote, photographed, and directed the film single-handed, and on the

GEORGES ROUQUIER

strength of it secured himself a post as artistic director of the shorts section of International Films, where he worked from 1929 to 1942.

In 1942, during the German occupation, Rouquier returned to directing with a short documentary, *Le Tonnelier* (*The Cooper*, 1942). The work and traditions of the barrel maker are described with great understanding and respect, and Rouquier followed this study with one of the equally ancient craft of the wheelwright, *Le Charron* (1943). He made two more shorts before embarking on the full-length documentary *Farrebique*, which was not released until after the liberation in 1946.

Farrebique, depicting the life of a peasant family on a farm in the Massif Central, is Rouquier's masterpiece. The farm was one in the district where he was born and the family was well known to him; in that sense, as he says, the film is "a diary of childhood memories." Rouquier and his cameramen (André Dantan and Daniel Sarrade) spent an entire year on the farm, from December 1944 to November 1945, and Rouquier wrote the scenario himself, as he did for virtually all his documentaries. As Basil Wright says, Rouquier records the everyday life of the family—ploughing and harvesting, cooking, evening prayers and trips to church and bistro—with "an intensity of observation which is rare in cinema," and which can turn a routine task like the making and baking of bread into "a ritual, a symbolic act." In the course of the year the family realize their long-standing ambition to install electricity at the farm; otherwise they pursue a way of life that has changed very little for more than a century. The old grandfather, aware that his life is coming to an end, talks to his sons about the family's history; before the year is over he is dead. But the film ends not with this sadness but with a reassertion of continuity and rebirth—the engagement of the younger son and the promise of spring, lyrically evoked in stop-motion shots of flowers opening and microphotographs of rising sap.

Rouquier was clearly influenced in *Farrebique* by the Russian masters of the 1920 and 1930s, especially Alexander Dovzhenko, but unlike them (and Visconti in *La terra trema*, made two years after *Farrebique*), Rouquier was not concerned to make political points. There are no capitalist or kulak villains in *Farrebique*, and the hard life of the French peasants is seen as natural and satisfying. André Bazin, discussing the differences between that film and *La terra trema*, pointed out that "half the dialogue in *Farrebique* is spoken offstage because Rouquier could not get the peasants not to laugh during a speech of any length." For this reason, Bazin suggested, Rouquier had to rely on montage to infuse his film with its poetry and symbolism. There is no doubt that he succeeded, however, and Roger Manvell called *Farrebique* "the finest, closest observation of French rural life which has been made."

Admired as it was and is by critics and filmmakers, the picture had no great commercial success—Georges Sadoul described it as "an excellent *cinéma-vérité* film in advance of its time." Rouquier, ambitious to try his hand at fictional features, could for some years find no backers. He resumed his career as the director of short and medium-length documentaries with films about the achievements of Louis Pasteur (made in collaboration with Jean Painlevé) and about the craft of the coppersmith (*Le Chaudronnier*, 1949).

Le Sel de la terre (The Salt of the Earth, 1950) is a more personal film, closer in feeling to *Farrebique*. It is a portrait of the Camargue, an area of salty marshland in southern France, the haunt of flamingos and fighting bulls, then in process of partial reclamation for rice growing. Beautifully photographed by Marcel Fradetal and with a fine score by Guy Bernard, the film is a poetic celebration both of the natural world and of man's capacity to meet the challenges nature sets him. Here again there are echoes of Dovzhenko and Eisenstein, as there are in *Malgovert* (1952), a documentary about the building of a hydroelectric station in the Savoie mountains. The cost of the project (in terms of the loss of lives and homes) is movingly recorded, but as in *Le Sel de la terre* the final effect is one of exultation in human courage and

achievement, splendidly captured in the meeting of two parties of miners who have been tunneling towards each other through a mountain.

Rouquier's first fictional film followed in 1953, *Sang et lumière (Blood and Light)*. Adapted by Maurice Berry and Michel Audiard from a novel by Joseph Peyre, it stars Daniel Gélin and Zsa Zsa Gabor in a rigmarole about a bullfighter and a *femme fatale*. An international coproduction, it was made in two versions—in French by Rouquier and in Spanish by Ricardo Munoz-Suay. Neither version has much to recommend it. Rouquier's only other feature, *SOS Noronha* (1957), is set in a Latin American country torn by revolution, where Jean Marais struggles to keep a beleaguered radio station on the air. In spite of a script by Pierre Boileau, Thomas Narcejac, and Rouquier himself, this film also sank without a trace.

The director's later work includes a perceptive study of the composer Arthur Honegger and *Lourdes et ses miracles* (1954), a full-length documentary about the Lourdes phenomenon in three parts. The theme is handled with great objectivity—we see those who have been cured at Lourdes and those who have been disappointed, and we are left to form our own conclusions. "My taste has always been towards authenticity," Rouquier said of it, "more so with regard to this film than to any other."

Claude Goretta has compared Rouquier with his close friend Georges Franju and says that, unlike that other great documentarist, Rouquier "creates his rhythms by quick cutting," infusing his films with a "rough, serene, optimistic poetry." Goretta praises "the talent and conviction which Rouquier can bring to bear on simple things and people," and writes: "The emotional suspense with which Rouquier is able to invest the construction of a dam or the boring of a tunnel has only found its equal in the Russian cinema."

FILMS: *Documentaries*—Vendanges, 1929; Le Tonnelier, 1942; Le Charron, 1943; L'Économie des métaux, 1943; Le Part de l'enfant, 1943; Farrebique/Les Quatre Saisons (The Four Seasons), 1946 (full-length); (with Jean Painlevé) L'Oeuvre scientifique de Pasteur, 1947; Le Chaudronnier, 1949; Le Sel de la terre, 1950; Malgovert, 1952; Le Lycée sur la colline, 1953; Un Jour comme les autres, 1953; Lourdes et ses miracles, 1954 (feature-length film in three parts); Arthur Honegger, 1955; La Bête noire, 1956; Une Belle Peur, 1958; Le Bouclier, 1960; Sire le Roy n'a plus rien dit, 1964 (France/Canada). *Fiction films*—Sang et lumière, 1953; SOS Noronha, 1957.

ABOUT: Armes, R. French Cinema Since 1946: 1, 1970; Issari, M. A. and Paul, D. A. What Is Cinéma Vérité?, 1979; Rouquier, G. Album de Farrebique, 1947

(France); Sadoul, G. Dictionary of Film Makers, edited and translated by Peter Morris, 1972; Wright, B. The Long View, 1974. *Periodicals*—Ciné-Club December 1947; Sight and Sound Winter 1956–1957.

*RUTTMANN, WALTHER (December 28, 1887–July 15, 1941), German director and editor, was born in Frankfurt. He studied architecture in Zürich and Munich, then painting with Angelo Jank and Übelohde, and was an accomplished violinist. During World War I, according to his friend Albrecht Hasselbach, he painted many small watercolors at the front, both representational and abstract, but by 1918 was no longer satisfied with this medium. He is reported to have said: "It makes no sense to paint anymore. This painting must be set in motion."

After the war, Ruttmann worked in Munich as a poster designer. It had been supposed that his interest in the cinema grew out of the abstract animation experiments of Viking Eggeling and Hans Richter, but Standish Lawder in *The Cubist Cinema* maintains that Ruttmann began his own experiments in animated art quite independently. His *Opus I* had its premiere in 1921 and, according to Lawder, had apparently been made on "some sort of animation table in which designs were painted on sheets of glass, then distorted and made to move by mirrors. Color, probably applied by stencil, was an important expressive ingredient of the film. A musical accompaniment was composed for the film by Max Butting."

Herman G. Scheffauer, who attended the Berlin premiere, described *Opus I* as a "visible symphony" whose "opening notes" were "iridescent atmospheres surcharged with an intense and vibrant light" that "served as backgrounds, melting and flowing into one another—dawnlight and sunburst and twilight, infinite reaches of space. . . . The separate notes and cadences of the symphony darted and floated into these luminous fields" like "a river of flamboyant color. . . . Some of the forms these colors assumed were already familiar to us in the restless paintings of the cubists and expressionists . . . all the usual fragmentary and activist geometry. But here the writing, shifting, interlacing, interlocking, intersecting elements were fluent and alive, moving to the laws of a definite rhythm and harmony, obedient to an inherent will and impulse. . . . Globes and discs of harmonious colors came rolling into the field, some cannoning furiously against others, some buoyant as toy balloons, some kissing or repulsing or merging with one another like white or red blood corpuscles. Triangles sharp as splinters

WALTHER RUTTMANN

darted across the rushing torrent of forms. Clouds rolled up, spread, vanished. Serpents of flame blazed through this pictured music, a colored echo, no doubt, of some dominating note. . . . Then the color equivalents of the strong, clear finale poured themselves like a cataract upon the scene—masses of oblongs and squares fell crashingly, shower upon shower. The silent symphony was over."

Ruttmann's rivals, Richter and Eggeling, were considerably less ecstatic about the film. They saw *Opus I* and *Opus II* early in 1922 and Richter wrote that they felt "deeply depressed. Our forms and rhythms had 'meaning,' Ruttmann's had none. What we saw were improvisations with forms united by an accidental rhythm. There was nothing of an articulate language (which was for us . . . the one and only reason to use this suspicious medium, film). . . . But on the other hand, we had to admit that Ruttmann's films were technically better than ours, that he understood more of the camera and used it."

According to Lawder, "Richter and Eggeling used music as a structural model to analyze the movement through time and space," but Ruttmann "was more interested in translating the emotional overtones of music into moving colored images. . . . Ruttmann produced three more abstract shorts which he christened *Opus II, III,* and *IV* . . . and these, too, were apparently colored in their original form. Only black-and-white prints seem to have survived, yet, even so, his sense of rhythm is clearly evident in the organic flow of forms across the screen." Victor Schamoni has said that these later films were more precisely structured than *Opus I,* perhaps

°rŏŏt´ măn

because of the influence of Richter and Eggeling.

Ruttmann made several more short films in the early 1920s, at least one of them being an advertising film combining abstract forms with slogans. *Romanze in der Nacht* (1924) set landscape and scenic motifs to Schumann's piano music, and the same year Ruttmann created "Der Falkentraum" ("Dream of the Hawks"), an animated sequence in Fritz Lang's *Die Nibelungen* in which two semiabstract black hawks and a white dove form a pattern of rhythmic movements. At about the same time he painted the backgrounds for Lotte Reiniger's animated silhouette film *Die Abenteuer der Prinzen Achmed* (1923–1926). By this time the abstract or "absolute" cinema of Ruttmann, Eggeling, and Richter—cinema conceived as a plastic art form like painting rather than as a narrative medium—was having a good deal of influence, especially in France, where it partly inspired the *cinéma-pur* of Henri Chomette, Jean Grémillon, Marcel Duchamp, Fernand Léger, and others. Meanwhile, Ruttmann himself was moving forward into experiments of a different nature.

In 1925 the scriptwriter Carl Mayer had conceived the idea of a "city symphony" which would evoke the spirit of Berlin in "a melody of pictures." The cinematographer Karl Freund shared Mayer's disenchantment with studiomade films; he seized eagerly on the idea and sold it to Julius Aussenberg, European managing director of 20th Century–Fox. The following year, equipped with hypersensitive stock that enabled him to shoot without artificial light, and with cameras concealed in trucks and in suitcases, Freund set out with three other cameramen to film Berlin.

At what point Ruttmann became involved is disputed. Siegfried Kracauer implies that the film was shot by Freund and his colleagues and handed to Ruttmann for editing. Ruttmann himself said that he was involved from the outset and "knew straight away that the sole responsibility for each picture, for the lighting, tempo, background atmosphere, in short every foot of film, rested on me." He referred to Heimar Kuntze rather than Freund as his principal cameraman, and described how "for weeks we met at 4 a.m. in the morning in order to photograph 'the dead city' (before sunrise)." He said that the film was processed daily and edited as it came to hand: "After every cutting session I discovered what was still missing, here a shot for a tender crescendo, there an andante, and yet another brass sound or another flute sequence. I was continuously flexible about what to absorb and what to create afresh—I constantly reformed my script while shooting."

As this statement suggests, the film's symphonic form was very much in Ruttmann's mind as he edited the vast amount of "candid camera" material assembled by the photographers. What resulted was an account of a single spring day in Berlin. It begins *allegro moderato* at dawn, as the night express pulls into the sleeping city. Berlin wakes up, and the tempo changes to *allegro vivace* as people set off to work and the machines of business and industry begin to turn. Lunchtime, and the poor, the rich, and the animals in the zoo all pause to refresh themselves before the city goes back to business (and one woman jumps to her death from a bridge). The evening sequence is a *presto finale*—a frenzied montage of neon lights, dancing, concerts, movies, young lovers—the pursuit of every kind of pleasure.

Carl Mayer, who had devised the film and written the first treatment, had envisaged a movie that would celebrate the beauty of Berlin but would also indict its social injustices. Ruttmann had seemed the ideal director for a picture conceived as a symphony, but his approach to the material led to Mayer's early withdrawal from the production. Ruttmann's overwhelming concern was with form. The movie is full of social contrasts—hungry children in the streets and lavish meals in restaurants—but they are used to provide visual counterpoint, not social criticism. Released in 1927 as *Berlin, die Sinfonie der Grosstadt* (*Berlin, Symphony of a Great City*), it is indeed a silent symphony composed in patterns of movement—an "absolute" film more than a documentary, imposing its own rhythms on people, animals, buildings, and pounding machines, and using the city's scurrying crowds much as Ruttmann had used the abstract shapes in his early experimental films.

The use of *cinéma-vérité* material and montage in *Berlin* prompted comparisons with Dziga Vertov and Eisenstein, but socially committed critics were quick to assert that Ruttmann had none of those masters' social idealism. Hans Richter called the film a work of impressionistic art, "revolting to people who had grown up to understand more about the soul and problems of the big city than Ruttmann showed. The splendid musical rhythm of the pictures seemed abused and ran suddenly empty in a vacuum." John Grierson wrote of *Berlin* and other symphonic films that they used tempo and rhythm to "capture the eye and impress the mind in the same way as . . . a military parade might do. . . . For this reason I hold the symphony tradition of cinema for a danger and *Berlin* for the most dangerous of all film models to follow." Nevertheless, for those who were prepared to accept the film on its own terms, *Berlin* was a cinematic landmark, establishing Ruttmann among Germany's major directors and inspiring many imitations in that country and abroad. Years later, it still seemed to C. A. Lejeune "the best example of the topographical film, the best illustration . . . of the gigantic effects to be created from the commonplace details of daily life."

In 1927 Ruttmann collaborated with Erwin Piscator on two filmed sequences used by Piscator in his production of Ernst Toller's play *Hoppla! Wir leben,* and the following year made *Deutscher Rundfunk,* celebrating the new world of sound offered by the invention of radio. *Die tönende Welle (The Sounding Wave),* described by Richter as a short feature on the same theme as *Deutscher Rundfunk,* appeared the same year (and may even be the same film under a different title—there is still a good deal of uncertainty about Ruttmann's filmography).

It must also have been in 1928 that Ruttmann was commissioned by the Hamburg-Amerika Line to make a promotional movie that would encourage sea travel; he turned this commercial assignment into the "cosmic hymn" *Die Melodie der Welt (World Melody,* 1929). A fictional story about a seaman leaving his girl in Hamburg and setting out on a voyage leads into footage shot all over the world, organized around a variety of themes such as architecture, love, transportation, religious faiths, military forces and militarism, sports, and entertainments. The material is edited according to the rhythmic principles Ruttmann had pioneered in *Berlin,* but this time his montage includes music (by Wolfgang Zeller) and natural sounds as well as images.

Die Melodie der Welt was Germany's first full-length sound film. Hans Richter reported that it was a box-office hit and went on: "Besides being a success it had some unforgettable scenes. The nearly abstract symphony of ship sirens at the beginning of the film: deep and high, long and short in different rhythms in the harbor of Hamburg, became soon a standard device for any film which could manage somehow to get into the neighborhood of a port. Pudovkin raved about this scene, and declared it the true way of handling sound problems. The great variety of musical themes (all over the world) with the changing scenery (all over the world) gave Ruttmann an ideal playground to connect musical and pictorial movements. His good eye for the plastic value of the frame and for movement made for good editing, and such a 'sea voyage' certainly was an editor's job if it was anything."

All the same, for Richter the film had the same faults as *Berlin* and "got lost in a meaningless kind of picture-postcard montage . . . fascinating but empty." Kracauer condemned its undiscriminating "neutrality" and "wholesale acceptance of the universe," but Georges Sadoul welcomed the implication that "everyone in the world, whatever their color, shares the same feelings and participates in the same basic daily routines." And Henri Langlois, a more recent critic, found the movie "infinitely richer" than *Berlin,* "thanks to its experimentation with sound, to the scope of its subject (the globe), and to the vividness of the newsreel material which Ruttmann was obliged to resort to, since he could not film everything himself, and which brings a breath of air to it; but also because the simplicity of the unifying idea that governs it— the desire to show everything common to mankind—corresponds to the montage method."

Ruttmann's most extreme experiment with sound was the so-called "imageless film" *Wochenende* (Weekend, 1930). In fact it is not a film at all, but a soundtrack—a short (three hundred feet) montage of sounds telling the story of two young lovers from the moment the train leaves the city for their weekend in the country until they are separated by the homegoing crowd. For once, Richter was unequivocally impressed, calling *Wochenende* "among the outstanding experiments in sound ever made," showing Ruttmann "as a true lyrical poet with untiring inventiveness. . . . It was a symphony of sound, speech fragments and silence woven into a poem. It made a perfect story in all its primitiveness and simplicity. If I had to choose between all of Ruttmann's works I would give this one the prize as the most inspired." It was followed by something entirely different, *Feind im Blut* (Enemy in the Blood, 1931), an educational film about venereal disease. According to Ernst Iros, it was "made with artistry, yet never concealing its true purpose." The same year Ruttmann collaborated with Abel Gance on the editing of *La Fin du monde.*

Ruttmann was almost the only major German filmmaker to stay in his country after Hitler came to power; he explained in a letter to Richter that he refused to leave his fatherland "at such a time." In fact he did leave it in 1933, but only to make a movie in Mussolini's Italy. This was *Acciaio (Steel),* an unsuccessful attempt at a feature film freely adapted from a Pirandello theme. Thereafter he collaborated with the Third Reich. He acted as adviser and assistant to the youthful Leni Riefenstahl on *Olympiad* (1936–1938) and made films celebrating several German cities, on the model of *Berlin.* He also directed a number of propaganda documentaries for Goebbels, among them the powerful *Deutsche Panzer (German Tanks,* 1940), glorifying the German conquest of France. He was working on a similar film on the Russian front when he was fatally wounded.

Henri Langlois wrote that, at the time of *Melodie der Welt,* Ruttmann "was held to be one of the cinema's geniuses, but one need only glance at his subsequent films to realize the extent to which he was incapable of incorporating life into his art as a source of inspiration and richness. Whether making a film about the ravages of syphilis or on some proletarian theme, he reduced everything to abstraction and schematism, forgetting man to see only a pattern of lines, constantly mistaking the mechanics of the metronome for the art of the fugue." Nevertheless, Ruttmann's early experiments had great influence on avant-garde filmmakers in Germany and abroad, and *Berlin* and *Melodie der Welt,* as Georges Sadoul wrote, "played a determinant role in the development of the documentary."

FILMS: Opus I and Opus II, 1921 (shorts); Der Sieger, 1923 (short); Das verlorene Paradies, 1923 (short); Kantorowitz, 1923 (short); Gesolei, 1923 (short); Romanze in der Nacht, 1924 (short); Der Falkentraum *in* Fritz Lang's Die Nibelungen, 1924; Opus III and Opus IV, 1924 (shorts); Berlin, die Sinfonie der Grosstadt (Berlin, Symphony of a Great City), 1927; Deutscher Rundfunk, 1928 (short); Die tönende Welle, 1928 (short); Melodie der Welt (World Melody), 1929; Wochenende (Weekend), 1930 (short soundtrack); Feind im Blut (Enemy in the Blood), 1931; Acciaio (Steel/Arbeit macht Frei), 1933; Altgermanische Bauernkultur, 1934; Metall des Himmels, 1934; Stadt der Verheissung, 1935; Kleiner Film einer grossen Stadt: Düsseldorf, 1935; Stuttgart, Grosstadt zwischen Wald und Reben, 1935; Schiff in Not, 1936; Mannesmann, 1937; Hamburg—Weltstrasse See, 1938; Im Zeichen des Vertrauens, 1938; Im Dienste der Menschlichkeit, 1938; Heinkel—ein deutsches Werk in seiner Arbeit, 1938; Die deutsche Waffenschmiede, 1940; Aberglaube, 1940; Deutsche Panzer (German Tanks) 1940; Volkskrankheit Krebs/Jeder Achte, 1941.

ABOUT: Domburg, A. van Walter Ruttman en het Beginsel, 1956; Eisner, L. The Haunted Screen, 1969; Gebauer, D. and Wolf, S. (eds.) Bilddokumente zur Geschichte des Films, 1968; Kurz, R. Expressionismus und Film, 1926; Lawder, S. D. The Cubist Cinema, 1975; Kracuer, S. From Caligari to Hitler, 1947; Manvell, R. (ed.) Experiment in the Film, 1949; Roud, R. (ed.) Cinema: A Critical Dictionary, 1980. *Periodicals*—Celluloide 43 1961; Film Culture Summer 1961; Film Forum April 1959; Films and Filming August 1961.

"SENNETT, MACK" (Mikall or Michael Sinnott) (January 17, 1880–November 5, 1960), American director, producer, and scenarist, was born in Danville, near Richmond, Quebec, into a family of Irish Catholic farmers who later op-

MACK SENNETT

erated small hotels and boardinghouses. The Sinnott clan had emigrated to Canada early in the eighteenth century, well before both the French and Indian War and the American Revolution. Michael Sinnott was one of the four children of John Francis Sinnott and the former Catherine Foy. A strapping youth, he was remarkable for his size, his strength, and his booming bass voice. The family moved in 1897 from Canada to East Berlin, Connecticut, where Michael Sinnott took a job in an iron foundry. His dream at that time was to sing bass at the Metropolitan Opera.

In 1900 a twenty-year-old Sennett made his way to New York City, encouraged by the vaudeville star Marie Dressler. She had been introduced to him by the Sinnott family lawyer, one Calvin Coolidge, and she in turn gave him a letter of introduction to the impresario David Belasco. Years later Sennett would repay the favor by bringing Dressler to Hollywood for her first film role—*Tillie's Punctured Romance.* In their initial interview, Belasco convinced the naive young iron puddler that his clownish bulk and deafening voice did not equip him for the Met. Although he performed in the chorus of several uptown musical shows (including the 1902 hit *Wang,* starring DeWolf Hopper, and the 1905 Victor Herbert operetta, *Mlle. Modiste*), Sennett found his real home on the burlesque stages of New York's Lower East Side. His first New York stage appearance was, literally, as a horse's ass—the rear (and funny) part in the traditional burlesque sketch in which two men impersonate one horse. Featured on the same burlesque bill in 1900 was Little Egypt, the most famous belly dancer of her age, who brought the bump and grind to Chicago's Columbian Exposition of 1893.

If D. W. Griffith became known as "the Belasco of the Screen," the director who translated Belasco's genteel literary tastes, heart-stopping melodrama, and dazzling scenic effects into film terms, then Mack Sennett could be called the Minsky of the screen. To understand Sennett's impact on the early silent cinema is to understand the cultural and artistic role of the turn-of-the-century American burlesque theater: predominantly male, predominantly working-class, predominantly immigrant, and decidedly vulgar. For its exclusively male audience, the burlesque hall provided loud, bawdy fun—a welcome escape from the loneliness of boarding-house life, the demands and obligations of job and family, or the stifling proprieties of more genteel recreation. A product of the same double standard that allowed American males such outlets as the saloon and the sporting house, the burlesque show eventually climbed out of the rowdy, male, working-class milieu and into the proper middle-class environments of Broadway (Florenz Ziegfeld's annual *Follies*) and Hollywood. The movies themselves made the same journey in the same period—from cheap nickelodeons to grandiose Picture Palaces.

Many motifs of American burlesque moved directly into Sennett films. All respectable members of the middle and moneyed classes were treated with comic disdain as stiff snobs or stuffed shirts. Representatives of the legitimate social institutions were particular targets: doctors, lawyers, professors, judges, financiers, inventors, politicians, and, especially, cops. Sennett said of his first experience at a burlesque show: "They whaled the daylights out of pretension. They made fun of themselves and the human race. They reduced convention, dogma, stuffed shirts, and Authority to nonsense." One way to make fun of themselves and the human race was to reduce the proper bourgeois home and the sexual relationships on which it depended to vulgar, venal nonsense: wives were always domineering battle-axes; chambermaids were always pretty and always for the pinching. Women came in three sizes with temperaments to match: shapely and alluring; bean pole-thin and grim; roundly fat and, after a few drinks, bouncy. Another way to ridicule the human race was to put down its high art—for example, by parodying the legitimate theatre hits uptown, making nonsense of their posturings and pretensions.

The traditional ethnic traits of America's urban and immigrant population provided another rich source of material. The American burlesque theatre was both a mirror and a product of immigration patterns, dominated by the stage Irishman (in the same era as the shows of Harrigan and Hart and George M. Cohan), the "Dutch" dialect comedians ("Dutch," slang for *deutsch,* usually meant Yiddish), and the "coon" shows (which grew out of earlier minstrel shows to become the performance rage early in the century). The dominant producers and performers of burlesque were generally Jewish—Joe Weber and Lew Fields, the Minsky brothers, the Howard brothers—and many would move from the cheap novelty shows into the infant movie business. By the more enlightened standards of today, the explicit jokes based on racial and sexual stereotypes would seem unkind at the least and often grossly racist or sexist. Many Sennett films are so offensive in later American terms that they have not been shown for sixty years.

In March 1908 Sennett moved from the Bowery to Fourteenth Street, where he took a job with the American Mutoscope and Biograph Company—"Biograph," as it was called—just three months before D. W. Griffith began to direct Biograph films. Griffith and Sennett acted together in a Biograph comedy, *After the Ball,* in May 1908, a month before Griffith directed his first film, *The Adventures of Dollie.* That the former legitimate actor Griffith and the former burlesque clown Sennett should come by different roads to the same place indicates both the growing commercial power of the movies and their progress toward achieving a balance between the high and low forms of American theatrical entertainment.

For three years Sennett worked both with and under Griffith. He wrote some of Griffith's scripts and acted in many of Griffith's films as well, usually in small comic roles. Sennett wrote *The Lonely Villa,* Griffith's powerful 1909 melodrama in which a husband races home to save his wife and children from tramps, and also played a clownish servant in the early scenes of the film. In *The Curtain Pole,* a slapstick Griffith comedy of 1908, Sennett appears as a clumsy Frenchman who wreaks chaos all over town in his drunken search to replace a broken curtain rod. Sennett's clownish Frenchman was an acknowledgment of the reigning style of comedy coming from France in 1908. As Sennett noted, "It was those Frenchmen who invented slapstick and I imitated them," though "I never went as far as they did." *The Curtain Pole* went as far as it could. Though Griffith directed the film, it already contains the seeds of the Sennett style: broad slapstick clowning, clear but simple motivation, rapid physical movement, the reduction of rational human beings to irrational venality, and the ceaseless rhythm of the chase.

Sennett became an important assistant to Griffith in 1910, accompanying him on his winter trips to California in 1910 and 1911, taking over direction of the Biograph films that Griffith himself could not manage. The growing commercial success of the Biograph product, as well as the increasing devotion to film style that slowed Griffith's pace of production, gave Sennett more and more to do at Biograph. By 1911 Sennett had assumed responsibility for all of Biograph's comic films and, like Griffith, had built his own stock company of actors—including Fred Mace, Ford Sterling, and the gifted comedienne Mable Normand, Sennett's companion for several years.

In 1912, Sennett left Biograph for the independent company Keystone. As with his move from stage to films, this step mirrored a movement in show business as a whole. The American film industry, dominated and shackled since 1908 by the ten powerful Eastern film companies, banded together as the Motion Picture Patents Company, or "Edison Trust," was growing into its Golden Age, which would be dominated by the film studios, distribution offices, and theatre chains called "independents" in 1912 but known colloquially as "Hollywood" by 1920. A year after Sennett's departure, Griffith would also leave Biograph, one of the Patent companies, for the independent Mutual company.

In his autobiography, Sennett claims that he founded Keystone by convincing his bookies, Charles Bauman and Adam Kessel, to forget his $100 pony tab and invest $2500 in a new production company. Like many of Sennett's stories, it was more colorful than true. Kessel and Bauman had been out of the bookie business and in the movie business for four years, like Sennett and Griffith, producing very successful Westerns directed by Thomas Ince and starring William S. Hart. Sennett, with a proven track record at Biograph, was a sensible choice to direct a series of physical comedies to accompany the Hart Westerns. Sennett went to work at his Keystone studio in Edendale, California, just north of Hollywood in the San Fernando Valley, in January 1912.

Throughout the next twenty-three years—the remainder of his career in silent and sound comedies—Sennett was more significant as a producer and a presence than as a director of a coherent body of work. Keystone produced over 150 short films in 1913 alone. More than anything else, Sennett provided the bridge that brought burlesque from the Bowery to Hollywood. For his characters, Sennett borrowed the usual burlesque assortment of ethnic stereotypes: Jews named Cohen, blacks named Rastus, Irish

named Riley, Germans named Meyer, Schultz, and Heinie, and country bumpkins, usually played by Sennett himself. Women were bathing beauties or battle-axes. Motivation was simple and clear: lechery, liquor, theft, and revenge. The traditional "slapstick" of burlesque evolved into a variety of comic objects to bash the head or bat the butt: the brick, the nightstick, the broom, and the one comic object which Sennett claimed to have discovered, the custard pie.

To these burlesque conventions, Sennett added the uniquely cinematic possibilities that he had learned in his years at Biograph. Sennett's best Keystones were outdoor films, their action rarely confined to domestic interiors. The outdoors meant space to move, a freedom denied even the most violent chases on the burlesque stage. By slightly undercranking the camera, Sennett could magnify the power and delight of outdoor movement by accelerating it—"just a shade faster and fizzier than life," according to James Agee. And Raymond Durgnat wrote that "much of Sennett's comedy is about the shock of speed, the . . . concept of man as an impersonal object existing only to work rapidly, rhythmically, repetitively." The outdoors also gave Sennett the opportunity to display other speeding objects that could never appear on a burlesque stage. "A chase . . . built up such a majestic trajectory of pure anarchic motion," observes Agee, "that bathing girls, cops, comics, dogs, cats, babies, automobiles, locomotives, innocent bystanders, sometimes what seemed like a whole city, an entire civilization, were hauled along head over heels in the wake of that energy like dry leaves following an express train."

If the outdoors gave Sennett both space to move in and time to play with, it became more than merely a backdrop for frantic activity. Setting became a major character in Sennett films. Many Keystones were improvisational sketches built around the setting: a stretch of railroad track (*Barney Oldfield's Race for a Life*, 1913), a reservoir (*A Muddy Romance*, 1913), a dance contest (*Tango Tangles*, 1914), an afternoon of automobile races (*Kid Auto Races at Venice* and *A Busy Day*, both 1914); and innumerable films on the beaches and piers of the Pacific waterfront, or on the benches and in the bushes of any city park. Setting rather than story determined the action of a Sennett film. Once the Keystone crew knew where a film would be shot and what went on in such a place, the gags, stuck together with the thinnest pretense of narrative paste, inevitably followed.

A final Sennett trait combined a lesson from the Bowery and Biograph: comic timing depended on an attuned ensemble of comic players. Sennett assembled the most dextrous band of physical comedians ever to share a frame, a stage, or a studio. It took an extraordinary physical instrument to compete successfully with the antics of an automobile, a train, or a pack of lions. Sennett performers were not simply comic goons with silly facial expressions; they had to be able to run, leap, fall, jump, twirl, and tumble fast enough and well enough to outmaneuver the cars, boats, bricks, trains, horses, wells, and walls that perpetually attacked them in the Keystone world. "Words can scarcely suggest," suggests James Agee, "how energetically they collided and bounced apart . . . how hard and how often they fell on their backsides; or with what fantastically adroit clumsiness they got themselves fouled up in folding ladders, garden hoses, tethered animals, and each other's headlong cross-purposes." Virtually every major performer of silent film comedy began with Sennett: the cross-eyed Ben Turpin, the beady-eyed Chester Conklin, the walrus-moustached Mack Swain, the cherubic Fatty Arbuckle, the lithe Mabel Normand, the huffing Ford Sterling, the skinny Slim Summerville, the brash Billy Bevan, the child-man Harry Langdon, and the most enduring and accomplished of all silent clowns, Charles Chaplin. Gloria Swanson, Carole Lombard, Harold Lloyd, Charley Chase, Leo McCarey, and Frank Capra also learned their trade with Sennett. The only major figures of American silent comedy never to work for Sennett were Buster Keaton, Stan Laurel, and Oliver Hardy—and they began in films with Sennett disciples. Whatever his personal artistic accomplishment, Sennett's influence on the entire tradition of American film comedy is immeasurable.

In his film technique, Sennett shared Griffith's commitment to editing as the quickest and liveliest way to construct a film. Sennett's Keystones dart about in space, cutting between locations, from racing car to speeding train to pursuing cops, as freely as any Griffith melodrama. Since many Sennett films are deliberate burlesques of that kind of melodrama, their editing both parodies the style of the original and captures its energy. Sennett also cut avidly within scenes, breaking groupings of characters into separate frames. Many Keystones seem overly dependent on this kind of editing—an economical shortcut that fails to convince the viewer that two persons actually inhabit the same space. This principle of cutting led to a Sennett battle with Chaplin. While Sennett liked to keep space jumping, Chaplin liked to settle into a clearly defined space to observe the counterpoint of mental action and physical movement within it. Future comic film technique would support

Chaplin, not only in his own films but in the films of Lloyd, Langdon, Keaton, and Laurel and Hardy as well, which depend on human action within contiguous space and continuous time.

James Agee divides Sennett films into two types: "parody laced with slapstick, and plain slapstick." Almost all of them were short—one- and two- reel films of ten to twenty frantic minutes. Like Griffith and Chaplin, Sennett began making films in the nickelodeon era when the one-reeler dominated the American market. Unlike Griffith and Chaplin, Sennett never outgrew the short film, even when film distribution consigned the comedy short to a supporting role, merely the appetizer on a bill constructed around the full-length feature. As a result, Sennett's complete filmography rolls on for several thousand titles of which he personally directed about two hundred. His active directorial career falls into three distinct phases: 1911–1914, from his final year at Biograph through the years of establishing the Keystone Company; 1929–1931, the difficult transitional period between silent and sound filming; and 1935, his final year as a filmmaker. In his peak periods of power and success, 1915–1927 and 1932–1933, Sennett did not soil his hands with day-to-day shooting on the set.

The films that Agee identified as "parodies laced with slapstick" revealed Sennett's burlesque training. *Barney Oldfield's Race for a Life* was a classic parody of the life-or-death race between automobile and locomotive featured in several D.W. Griffith melodramas—the damsel (Mabel Normand) tied to the railroad tracks, the villain (Ford Sterling) speeding toward her body on a train, the hero (Mack Sennett) racing alongside the train in a car driven by a famous driver of the day, Barney Oldfield. Sennett would make a fancier version of the same film in 1916, *Teddy at the Throttle* with Gloria Swanson as the damsel, Wallace Beery as the villain, and tiny Bobby Vernon as her hero. Another parody used the motif of Griffith's *The Ingrate* (1908) and *Love in the Hills* (1911), in both of which a man rescued from death in the forest steals the wife of his rescuer. Sennett reduced this drama to farce in *Love, Speed, and Thrills* (1915), in which Mack Swain plays the dogged husband and Chester Conklin the ungrateful lecher. Like burlesque on the Bowery, Sennett's parodies reveal the ludicrous underside of melodrama by assigning the passions to clowns and playing them at impossible speeds.

Other Sennett films parodied ordinary domestic relations rather than specific film plots. Mabel Normand found herself in a series of films with two intolerable husbands—the perpetually drunk and cowardly Charlie Chaplin in 1914 (*Mabel's Married Life; His Trysting Places*) and the perpetually round and rowdy Fatty Arbuckle in 1915 (*Mabel and Fatty's Wash Day; Mabel and Fatty's Simple Life; Mabel, Fatty, and the Law*). Another favorite target was the film business itself, and many Sennett comedies invade a studio or movie theatre to burlesque the activities of players and audiences (*Mabel's Dramatic Career*, 1913; *The Masquerader*, 1914). After Ben Turpin joined the Sennett ensemble in 1917, he made a specialty of mimicking Hollywood's reigning romantic idols as cross-eyed clowns: Douglas Fairbanks in *A Small Town Idol* (1921), Rudolph Valentino in *The Shriek of Araby* (1923), and Erich von Stroheim in *Three Foolish Wives* (1924).

The "plain slapstick" films were perpetual-motion machines, a breathless succession of running, racing, jumping, hitting, dodging, and crashing, anchored (loosely) by the physical setting: a muddy lake (*A Muddy Romance*), a race-car track (*The Speed Kings*, 1913), a boxing ring (*The Knockout*, 1914), a beach (*The Sea Nymph*, 1912; *The Surf Girl*, 1916), a highway (*Mabel at the Wheel*, 1914; *Love, Loot, and Crash*, 1915; *Lizzies of the Field*, 1924; *Super-Hooper-Dyne Lizzies*, 1925). "The essence of these Keystones was movement," Gerald Mast writes in *The Comic Mind*, "dash, crash, smash, and splash. Figures ran after things they wanted, ran away from things they wanted to avoid, ran over mountains, over dangerous ledges, fields, beaches. . . . And they kept running from the start of the film until they smashed into something that stopped them."

Given the length of Sennett's filmography, the rapidity of his production, and the scale of his films, it is difficult to single out any particular work as either typical or extraordinary. Perhaps *Tillie's Punctured Romance* of 1914 is both. At six reels (approximately 90 minutes at silent projection speed), *Tillie's Punctured Romance* was the first feature-length comedy produced in America, mirroring the general movement of the American film industry from the short to the feature. It was also the only feature film Sennett ever directed, and one of only three he ever produced (*Mickey* 1918, and *Molly O*, 1921, two Mabel Normand vehicles, were the others). In recognition of its specialness, Sennett combined his usual ensemble of Keystone players— Chaplin, Normand, Conklin, Swain, and the Keystone Kops—with a famous star imported from the stage, Marie Dressler.

Like Sennett's career itself, *Tillie's Punctured Romance* combined film and theatre traditions.

The film was loosely based on Dressler's most famous stage vehicle, *Tillie's Nightmare*, in which the comic star endures numerous sufferings, including being jilted by a faithless lover. In *Tillie's Nightmare* Dressler sang her famous trademark song, "Heaven Will Protect the Working Girl." A stage star for over two decades, Dressler had evolved into something resembling the comic Fat Lady of burlesque—too brash and bulky to be mistaken for a delicate damsel in distress. This was the parodic premise of the play and quite consistent with the burlesque flavor of the Keystones. Sennett decorated the Dressler vehicle with both Keystone patterns: parody and slapstick. In the first reel of the film, Tillie is an innocent farm girl wooed by a city slicker—Charlie Chaplin, in a jaunty straw hat rather than his tramp's bowler. The disproportion in their sizes—huge Tillie and little Charlie—fit both Sennett's parody and burlesque's reduction of sexuality to the absurd. Many Sennett one-reel films were based on comic contrasts between country hick and city slicker.

When Tillie inherits a pile of money from an uncle presumed dead, Charlie lures her to the Big City, where he and his pretty accomplice, Mabel Normand, try to swindle her of her cash. "Charlie and Tillie move into a posh house," writes Mast, "pretend to be swells, dance the tango, and do all the other naughty things that rich city folks were wont to do" in both early movies and on the burlesque stage. The masquerade ends when Charlie's treachery is exposed. Tillie summons the Keystone Kops, who race speedily if incompetently to the rescue. The chase ends on the Santa Monica pier, a favored setting for Keystone fun, where almost everyone rides, leaps, or slips into the surf. Like most Keystones, the film simply stops when everyone is too wet, exhausted, or dazed to continue. As an ordinary Keystone comedy stuffed, padded, and decorated beyond its means, *Tillie's Punctured Romance* reveals all that Sennett could and could not accomplish.

In 1915, Keystone became part of the newly formed Triangle Film Corporation, functioning there as an autonomous unit. As Ephraim Katz has noted, this put "under one roof the creative talents of the three biggest names in the American silent cinema—D.W. Griffith, Thomas H. Ince, and Mack Sennett."

With bigger budgets, Sennett's films became less primitive and more diversified. He had already introduced cheesecake (or a parody of it) with the famous Bathing Beauties, as well as the "Kid Komedies," a prototype for Hal Roach's "Our Gang" series. Now he instituted a series of romantic comedy shorts featuring Gloria Swanson and Bobby Vernon, and a variety of comedies relying more on situation than on slapstick.

Griffith left Triangle early in 1917, after the financial disaster of *Intolerance* ; Ince and Sennett soon followed. The Keystone trademark disappeared with Triangle, but in June 1917 Sennett launched a new company which released comedies initially through Paramount, then in the early 1920s through Associated Producers and First National. From 1923 to the end of the silent era in 1928, Sennett was associated with Pathé, where he launched three new series—"Handy Andy," "Taxicab," and "The Smith Family"—and three big stars: Harry Langdon, Ben Turpin, and Billy Bevan.

In 1929–1932 Sennett worked with Educational films, a small company producing only shorts, where he directed his first sound films. In 1932 he renewed his association with Paramount, producing a number of shorts with W. C. Fields (*The Dentist, The Fatal Glass of Beer, The Barber Shop, The Pharmacist*) and Bing Crosby (*The Singing Plumber, Blue of the Night, Sing Bing Sing*). Not only did these films introduce two major stars to film audiences, they also played a major role in shaping the stars' screen personalities, presenting Fields as the incompetent professional and malevolent commentator on American life, Crosby as the imperturbable crooner. But Sennett was no longer the "king of comedy," and in 1933, thanks partly to the financial crisis at Paramount, his own company went bankrupt. He retired altogether from filmmaking in 1935 and went home to Canada, virtually penniless. Sennett returned to Hollywood in 1937 to receive a special Academy Award for "his lasting contribution to the comedy technique of the screen," and in 1939 accepted a nominal post as an associate producer at 20th Century–Fox. The same year he served as technical adviser on *Hollywood Cavalcade*, in which he also appeared as himself. He spent the last part of his life in a show business retirement home, surviving on social security payments. Sennett began his film career with Griffith and ended up the same way, broke and alone.

Georges Sadoul placed Sennett with Ince and Griffith as "one of the three great pioneers who fashioned the art of the American cinema." It would be difficult to overestimate his influence on film comedy, both through his own anarchic work as a producer and director, and that of the clowns, stars, and filmmakers he trained at Keystone. One of his earliest serious admirers was the novelist Theodore Dreiser, who interviewed him for *Photoplay* (August 1928) and wrote that "to me his is a real creative force in the cinema world—a master at interpreting the crude primary impulses of the dub, the numbskull, the weakling, failure, clown, boor, coward, bully. The interpretive burlesque he achieves is no different from that of Shakespeare, Voltaire, Shaw or Dickens, when they are out to achieve humorous effects by burlesquing humanity. To be sure, these others move away from burlesque to greater ends. It is merely an incident on a great canvas. With Sennett it is quite the whole canvas. But within his range, what a master!"

—*G.M.*

FILMS (*directed personally by Sennett*):
1910: The Lucky Toothache, The Masher;
1911: Comrades, Priscilla's April Fool Joke, Cured, Priscilla and the Umbrella, Cupid's Joke, Misplaced Jealousy, The Country Lovers, The Manicure Lady, Curiosity, A Dutch Gold Mine, Dave's Love Affair, Their Fates Sealed, Bearded Youth, The Delayed Proposal, Stubbs' New Servants, The Wonderful Eye, The Jealous Husband, The Ghost, Jinks Joins the Temperance Club, Mr. Peck Goes Calling, The Beautiful Voice, That Dare Devil, An Interrupted Game, The Diving Girl, $500,000 Reward, The Baron, The Villain Foiled, The Village Hero, The Lucky Horseshoe, A Convenient Burglar, When Wifey Holds the Purse Strings, Too Many Burglars, Mr. Bragg—a Fugitive, Trailing the Counterfeit, Josh's Suicide, Through His Wife's Picture, The Inventor's Secret, A Victim of Circumstances, Their First Divorce Case, Dooley's Scheme, Won Through a Medium, Resourceful Lovers, Her Mother Interferes, Why He Gave Up, Abe Gets Even with Father, Taking His Medicine, Her Pet, Caught with the Goods, A Mix-up in Raincoats;
1912: The Joke on the Joker, Who Got the Reward?, Brave and Bold, Did Mother Get Her Wish?, With a Kodak, Pants and Pansies, A Near Tragedy, Lily's Lovers, The Fatal Chocolate, Got a Match?, A Message from the Moon, Priscilla's Capture, A Spanish Dilemma, The Engagement Ring, A Voice from the Deep, Hot Stuff, Oh those Eyes, Those Hicksville Boys, Their First Kidnapping Case, Help Help, The Brave Hunter, Won by a Fish, The Leading Man, The Fickle Spaniard, When the Fire Bells Rang, The Furs, A Close Call, Helen's Marriage, Tomboy Bessie, Algy the Watchman, Katchem Kate, Neighbors, A Dash Through the Clouds, The New Baby, Trying to Fool Uncle, One-Round O'Brien, The Speed Demon, His Own Fault, The Would-Be Shriner, Willie Becomes an Artist, The Tourists, What the Doctor Ordered, An Interrupted Elopement, The Tragedy of a Dress Suit, Mr. Grouch at the Seashore, Through Dumb Luck, Cohen Collects a Debt, The Water Nymph, Riley and Schultz, The New Neighbor, The Beating He Needed, Pedro's Dilemma, Stolen Glory, The Ambitious Butler, The Flirting Husband, The Grocery Clerk's Romance, At Coney Island, Mabel's Lovers, At It Again, The Deacon's Troubles, A Temperamental Husband, The Rivals, Mr. Fix It, A Desperate Lover, A Bear Escape, Pat's Day Off, Brown's Seance, A Family Mixup, A Midnight Elopement, Mabel's Adventures, Useful Sheep, Hoffmeyer's Legacy, The Drummer's Vacation, The Duel, Mabel's Strategem;

1913: Saving Mabel's Dad, A Double Wedding, The Cure that Failed, How Hiram Won Out, For Lizzie's Sake, Sir Thomas Lipton Out West, The Mistaken Masher, The Deacon Outwitted, The Elite Ball, Just Brown's Luck, The Battle of Who Run, The Jealous Waiter, The Stolen Purse, Mabel's Heroes, Her Birthday Present, Heinze's Resurrection, A Landlord's Troubles, Forced Bravery, The Professor's Daughter, A Tangled Affair, A Red Hot Romance, A Doctored Affair, The Sleuth's Last Stand, A Deaf Burglar, The Sleuths at the Floral Parade, A Rural Third Degree, A Strong Revenge, The Two Widows, Love and Pain, The Man Next Door, A Wife Wanted, The Rube and the Baron, Jenny's Pearls, The Chief's Predicament, At 12 O'Clock, Her New Beau, On His Wedding Day, The Land Salesman, Hide and Seek, Those Good Old Days, A Game of Poker, Father's Choice, A Life in the Balance, Murphy's IOU, A Dollar Did It, Cupid in the Dental Parlor, A Fishy Affair, The Bangville Police, The New Conductor, His Chum the Baron, That Ragtime Band, Algie on the Force, His Ups and Downs, The Darktown Belle, A Little Hero, Mabel's Awful Mistake, The Foreman of the Jury, The Gangster, Barney Oldfield's Race for a Life, Passions—He Had Three, Help! Help! Hydrophobia!, The Hansom Driver, The Speed Queen, The Waiter's Picnic, The Tale of a Black Eye, Out and In, A Bandit, Peeping Pete, His Crooked Career, For Love of Mabel, Safe in Jail, The Telltale Light, Love and Rubbish, A Noise from the Deep, The Peddler, Love and Courage, Professor Bean's Removal, Cohen's Outing, The Firebugs, Baby Day, Mabel's New Hero, Mabel's Dramatic Career, The Gypsy Queen, When Dreams Come True, Mother's Boy, The Bowling Match, The Speed Kings, Love Sickness at Sea, A Muddy Romance, Cohen Saves the Flag, Zuzu the Band Leader;
1914: In the Clutches of the Gang, Mabel's Strange Predicament, Love and Gasoline, Mack At It Again, Mabel at the Wheel, A New York Girl, His Talented Wife, Tillie's Punctured Romance (feature);
1915: Hearts and Planets, The Little Teacher, My Valet, A Favorite Fool, Stolen Magic;
1916: The Surf Girl;
1921: Oh, Mabel Behave;
1927: A Finished Actor;
1928: The Lion's Roar;
1929: The Bride's Relations, The Old Barn, Whirls and Girls, Broadway Blues, The Bee's Buzz, The Big Palooka, Girl Crazy, The Barber's Daughter, Jazz Mamas, The New Bankroll, The Constable, Midnight Daddies, The Lunkhead, The Golfers, A Hollywood Star, The New Half-Back;
1930: Scotch, Sugar Plum Papa, Bulls and Bears, Match Play, Honeymoon Zeppellin, Fat Wives for Thin, Campus Crushes, The Chumps, Goodbye Legs, Average Husband, Vacation Loves, The Bluffer, Grandma's Girl, Divorced Sweethearts, Racket Cheers, Rough Idea of Love;
1931: A Poor Fish, Dance Hall Marge, The Chiseler, Ghost Parade, Hollywood Happenings, Hold'er Sheriff, Monkey Business in Africa, Movie-Town, The Albany Branch, Fainting Lover, I Surrender Dear, Speed, One More Chance;
1932: Hypnotized;
1935: Ye Olde Saw Mill, Flicker Fever, Just Another Murder, The Timid Young Man, Way Up Thar.

ABOUT: Durgnat, R. The Crazy Mirror, 1970; Fowler, G. Father Goose: The Story of Mack Sennett, 1934; Katz, E. The International Film Encyclopedia, 1979; Kerr, W. The Silent Clowns, 1975; Lahue, K. C. Dreams for Sale: The Rise and Fall of the Triangle Film Corporation, 1971; Lahue, K. C. Mack Sennett's Keystone, 1971; Lahue, K. C and Brewer, T. Kops and Kustard: The Legend of Keystone Films, 1968; Lejeune, C. A. Mack Sennett, 1931; Mast, G. The Comic Mind: Comedy and the Movies, 1979; Mast, G. and Cohen, M. (eds.) Film Theory and Criticism: Introductory Readings, 3rd ed., 1986; Roud, R. (ed.) Cinema: A Critical Dictionary, 1980; Sennett, M. (as told to Cameron Shipp) King of Comedy, 1954; Turconi, D. Mack Sennett, 1966 (in French). *Periodicals*—Cinéma (France) August–September 1960 (Sennett issue); Classic Film Collector Summer 1971; Colliers November 5, 1927; Films and Filming August 1958, October 1965; Films in Review December 1968; Focus on Film Autumn 1974; Image et Son April 1964 (Sennett issue); Photoplay May 1915, August 1928; Saturday Review December 18, 1954; Vanity Fair May 1926.

SIDNEY, GEORGE (October 4, 1916–), American director and producer, was born in Long Island City, New York, the son of Louis K. Sidney and the former Hazel Mooney. It was a show-business family on both sides. Sidney's father was a pioneer film exhibitor, a producer of radio and stage shows, and (eventually) a vice-president of MGM. His mother was one of the famous Mooney Sisters, stars of the Winter Garden, and the granddaughter of Henry Mooney, a producer of tent shows.

Having made his theatrical debut at ten months, when he was carried onstage as somebody's baby, Sidney received his movie education "sitting in the balcony of my dad's Denver theatre and watching Tom Mix Westerns and later getting to play a small part in a film Mix made near Denver." His other great love was music, and at some point in his itinerant youth he attended the Pittsburgh Musical Institute, studying composition and conducting. He eventually mastered piano, clarinet, violin, and saxaphone, and in his teens played with bands and worked in vaudeville.

The family moved to Hollywood around 1930, and in 1933, when he was seventeen, Sidney joined MGM as a messenger boy. He soon found his way into the studio's sound department as a boom operator, subsequently trying his hand at orchestration, choreography, and music editing. By 1935 he was an assistant director and second unit director, sometimes doubling as composer and conductor. "I always seemed to gravitate to musicals," Sidney told James Bawden (*Films in Review*, June–July 1983). "I was always working on some facet of a Jeanette MacDonald, Nelson Eddy musical."

GEORGE SIDNEY

In 1936, aged twenty, Sidney began directing MGM screen tests, including those of future stars like Judy Garland, Rosalind Russell, Robert Taylor, and Lana Turner. The same year he submitted a script to Pete Smith, producer of the "Pete Smith Specialties" series of comedy shorts. He was assigned to direct it and subsequently made over eighty one- and two-reelers in this and other MGM series, including "Crime Does Not Pay" and "Our Gang." One of his Pete Smith comedies, *Quicker'n a Wink*, using ultraslow motion, won an Oscar as best one-reeler of 1940, and there was another Oscar the following year for *Of Pups and Puzzles*, a contribution to the "Passing Parade" series.

After these successes, MGM handed Sidney a medium-length feature, *Free and Easy* (1941, 56 minutes), based on a play by Ivor Novello and starring Robert Cummings and Ruth Hussey. The full-length feature *Pacific Rendezvous* followed in 1942 and *Pilot No. 5* in 1943. The last had Franchot Tone as a crusading antifascist lawyer who becomes a heroic flyer against the Japanese in Java, and costarred newcomer Gene Kelly as his best friend and rival for the hand of Marsha Hunt.

None of these low-budget programmers made much impact. Sidney then started work on another B-movie—a musical originally called *Private Miss Jones*, with Kathryn Grayson as a colonel's daughter who falls in love with a disaffected GI (Gene Kelly). With the help of Kelly's family, who happen to be circus acrobats, the colonel teaches his future son-in-law something about *esprit de corps* and the team spirit.

"When I got into it," Sidney says, "I kept get-

ting more ideas to expand it and expand it." Louis B. Mayer and the film's producer Joe Pasternak were impressed, and decided to swing the whole resources of the studio behind the project. They approved a switch from black and white to Technicolor, and the ridiculous story line was used as an excuse for a series of musical and/or comedy routines featuring many of MGM's top stars, among them Judy Garland, the conductor José Iturbi, Ann Sothern, Lucille Ball, Eleanor Powell, Lena Horne, Mickey Rooney, Red Skelton, and June Allyson.

"I worked in free form—that was possible then," Sidney recalled in an *Action* interview (May–June 1974). "I improvised scenes, dialogue, whole musical numbers. It was creatively exciting; everything was spontaneous, exhilarating. Some scenes were shot before they were written. Stanley Donen was my dance assistant. Gene Kelly was just beginning his gigantic screen career. We had a hundred players in the orchestra under contract, and they were the best available. If you needed more, you sent for more." Retitled *Thousands Cheer* (1943), this MGM showcase ran to 126 minutes. For all its absurdities, it was enjoyed for its "slick glitter and glamour" and was a financial hit, establishing Gene Kelly as a star and Sidney as a director of lavish musicals characterized by stylistic bravura and a special fondness for exhilarating crane shots.

Sidney had another success with *Bathing Beauty* (1944), a frothy (and often bubbly) musical that introduced another new star, the former swimming champion Esther Williams. The first in a long series of opulent aquatic vehicles for Williams, *Bathing Beauty* presented Sidney with a variety of technical problems: "We had to have cameras with mobility under water, and the lighting had to be adjusted for the refraction in the pool. Water acts as a conductor, so the girls' ear-drums were almost shattered until we could adjust the volume. . . . Still, the new equipment we had devised was a great help when I made *Jupiter's Darling* ten years later."

Anchors Aweigh, which followed in 1945, was even more successful and earned an Oscar nomination as bst picture of the year. Sidney had a penchant (or weakness) for long movies, and this one ran a full 140 minutes. Another morale-boosting wartime musical, it stars Gene Kelly and Frank Sinatra as two bemedaled sailors on shore leave, and Kathryn Grayson as a singer craving an audition with José Iturbi. The movie was praised for its energy and high spirits, condemned as "sprawling and undisciplined." George Morris, writing in *Film Comment* (November–December 1977), described it as "a hybrid, combining the worst excesses of the wartime Pasternak product with intimations of the revolutionary developments the genre would shortly undergo. . . . Although William Hanna and Joseph Barbera designed, and Fred Quimby directed, the famous cartoon sequence in which Kelly dances with Jerry the Mouse, the dancer's three other big numbers in *Anchors Aweigh* . . . are distinguished by the sweeping cranes and tracking shots characteristic of Sidney."

The director's next MGM assignment was produced not by Pasternak but by Arthur Freed, and is arguably his best musical. *The Harvey Girls* (1946), based on the novel by Samuel Hopkins Adams and full of memorable songs by Johnny Mercer and Harry Warren, is set in pioneer days in New Mexico. Judy Garland plays a spirited but virtuous Easterner who crosses the continent to work as a waitress in one of the chain of depot lunchrooms established by a precursor of Howard Johnson named Fred Harvey. She falls for a dour but sensitive gambler (John Hodiak) and makes her own contribution to the taming of the Wild West.

For George Morris, *The Harvey Girls* is the only one of Sidney's musicals "that can bear comparison with the masterpieces of Minnelli and Donen. . . . [It] has a rhythmic lilt and flow that seems to elude Sidney in his other musicals. The structure of the film is seamless—song, dance, and story effortlessly integrated into a cohesive whole. The musical numbers are especially felicitous, not only as entities within themselves but also in the manner in which they reinforce and complement character and narrative. . . . The justly famous 'On the Atchison, Topeka and the Santa Fe' number that accompanies the train's arrival in Sandrock, New Mexico, is not only one of the most superbly realized sequences in film musicals, it is also a particular type of number at which Sidney excels. Sidney has a unique way with large-scale ensembles, using his camera to choreograph the most spectacular effects around his star (or stars). The result is a fascinating mosaic of color, decor, and performance. In this number, for instance, he uses elaborate pans, cranes, and tracking movements to involve the entire populace with Judy Garland's arrival in Sandrock."

Back with Joe Pasternak, Sidney made a relatively trivial musical, *Holiday in Mexico* (1946), and then asked for a break from the genre. MGM gave him *Cass Timberlane* (1947), adapted by Donald Ogden Stewart from Sinclair Lewis' novel about a small-town judge (Spencer Tracy) who marries a girl from the wrong side of the tracks (Lana Turner). it was coolly re-

ceived, one reviewer writing that, "stripped bare of all Lewis' acute social observation, a story remains which is embarrassing, banal and very, very long"(119 minutes).

There had already been at least eight versions of Dumas' *The Three Musketeers* when Sidney made his in 1948. It had Lana Turner interestingly cast as a villainous Milady plotting with Vincent Price to dethrone Louis XIII, and Gene Kelly as an acrobatic D'Artagnan on the Douglas Fairbanks model. This energetic romp has worn remarkably well, in spite of the rather slighting reviews that greeted its first appearance. Not so the Cold War thriller *The Red Danube* (1949) or *Key to the City* (1950), in which Clark Gable plays the two-fisted mayor of a California city who meets his match in an ostensibly genteel colleague from Maine (Loretta Young). *Time* concluded that the picture "tries anything for a laugh, and sometimes succeeds. But the effort is more conspicuous than the fun."

Sidney returned to the musical with *Annie Get Your Gun* (1950). Its exuberance was perhaps a measure of his relief at finding himself once more on familiar territory and with Arthur Freed as his producer. This Sidney Sheldon adaptation of the Berlin-Fields stage musical features the raucous Betty Hutton as Annie Oakley, the hillbilly sharpshooter who rose to international fame with Buffalo Bill's Wild West show. Howard Keel plays her beloved rival Frank Butler. The movie was received with unanimous enthusiasm, grossing over $8 million on first release.

Freed also produced Sidney's next picture, a second remake of the Jerome Kern musical *Show Boat* (1951). Handicapped by Kathryn Grayson's wooden performance in the lead, the film nevertheless achieves some passages of genuine poetry—notably the beautifully built excitement of the opening, as the entire population spills out of shanties and mansions to greet the approaching showboat, and the pathos of the moment when the showboat's star (Ava Gardner), forced out of the company by the discovery that she has mixed blood, bids farewell to the fog-enshrouded steamer as William Warfield sings "Ol' Man River."

Rafael Sabatini's novel *Scaramouche*, set in prerevolutionary France, tells the story of a young aristocrat of populist sympathies who sets out to avenge the murder of his friend by a malevolent monarchist. Pursued by the authorities, he joins a troupe of traveling players. Sidney's remake of the 1923 silent version casts Stewart Granger as a dashing Scaramouche and Eleanor Parker as the fiery Pierrette with whom he squabbles and makes love until he wins the wan and virtuous hand of Janet Leigh.

Received without too much enthusiasm on release, *Scaramouche* is another Sidney movie whose reputation has grown over the years. George Morris, who regards it as one of the director's three best pictures, concentrates in his discussion on the relationship between Granger and Eleanor Parker, here playing a character that recurs in Sidney's films from *The Harvey Girls* on—the "sacrificial whore, at once vulnerable and resilient." When Granger rejects the theatre and Parker in favor of his fellow aristocrat Janet Leigh, his choice ironically "reinforces the class distinctions he has been fighting to obliterate throughout the film, irrevocably isolating Eleanor Parker in the lower-class world of the theatre. Her final moments in the film have a depth of feeling rare in Sidney. . . . The film's ending is both melancholy and euphoric, however, for Sidney dissolves to a closeup of the exploding bouquet Parker will toss to Granger and Leigh as their wedding carriage passes beneath her balcony where she is entertaining her next conquest—Napoleon."

For Morris, *Scaramouche* is "Sidney's most meticulously structured work. The diverse elements and themes of the film are woven into an elaborate fabric, heightened at every point by a precise coordination of color, psychological detail, and camera placement. Its formal richness amplifies its narrative and thematic resonance, for Sidney has never before (or since) exercised such control over his more flamboyant tendencies. . . . First and foremost though, *Scaramouche* is superb fun. The duels alone place it squarely among the finest adventure films ever made."

Kiss Me Kate (1953) reunited Kathryn Grayson and Howard Keel in an adequate adaptation of the Cole Porter musical. There was a revival of interest in 3-D movies at this time, and *Kiss Me Kate* was made in both two- and three-dimensional versions. It was a large nail in the coffin of 3-D when Radio City Music Hall chose to premiere the "flat" print.

An agreeable historical romance followed, an adaptation of Margaret Irwin's novel *Young Bess*, which finds an explanation for Queen Elizabeth's famous celibacy in her doomed love for Admiral Thomas Seymour, done to death by his powerful brother Ned. Jean Simmons and Stewart Granger have the leads, and Charles Laughton hams and belches outrageously as Henry VIII. *Jupiter's Darling* (1954) was a less persuasive costumer, though it has its champions. It showed how Esther Williams saved Ancient Rome by seducing Hannibal (Howard Keel), to music and sometimes underwater. After this, both Esther Williams and George Sidney parted company with MGM, the former to attempt a straight dramatic career on dry land. Sidney himself says, "I didn't really leave the studio. They left me with the new emphasis on Method pictures."

At that point Sidney established his own production company, releasing through Columbia. His first independent picture was *The Eddie Duchin Story* (1956), a biopic of the pianist and bandleader of the 1930s and 1940s. Tyrone Power plays Duchin, and the film records his marriage to a socialite beauty (Kim Novak), her early death, Duchin's struggle for fame, and his second marriage to his son's governess before leukemia ended his career. As a boy, Sidney had taken piano lessons from Duchin, and his admiration for the musician emerges emerges in the movie as sentimental hero worship. There has been a good deal of praise for the first half of the film, lyrically evoking young love in a romanticized New York, but it seemed to Hollis Alpert that "for a movie based upon known facts it has an unaccountable air of unreality, a lugubriousness, a prettying-up that eventually becomes morbid and offensive."

Kim Novak also starred in *Jeanne Eagels* (1957), another show-business biopic and the first of a number of films that Sidney produced as well as directed. Jeanne Eagels was a fairground dancer who, thanks to a combination of talent and ruthless determination, fulfilled her ambition to become a star of the legitimate theatre, only to return via drink and drugs to the ignominy of Coney Island vaudeville. Novak was found acceptable and even touching in her portrayal of ambition and decline, but quite inadequate in her attempt to match Jeanne Eagels' tour de force performance in Somerset Maugham's *Rain*. At that point, wrote one reviewer, "this film cracks and comes to pieces."

Since then the movie has acquired a certain notoriety as a camp classic, a judgment that George Morris emphatically rejects: "Here the thread separating illusion and reality has become so thin that the film assumes the dimensions of a hallucination, paralleling the trancelike visage of its heroine. Its fevered rhythms accommodate the familiar contradictions in Sidney's work: intuition and control, trash and art, and theatre and reality are balanced more delicately than in any of his other movies. And yet the balance is perfect, embracing as it does Sidney's fusion of good and evil into his penultimate fallen woman. . . . *Jeanne Eagels* is a profound examination of the American Dream and its concomitant equation of stardom and success with personal happiness. . . . It is certainly Sidney's most surreal film, capturing the phantasmic nature of stardom in a series of striking, disturbing images."

After *Pal Joey* (1957), a reasonably tough-minded screen version of the stage musical about a reprobate nightclub singer (Frank Sinatra), came *Who Was That Lady?* (1960), adapted by Norman Krasna from his own play. Tony Curtis plays a chemistry teacher who, caught kissing a student, persuades his wife (Janet Leigh) that his delinquency stems from his secret work for the FBI. Her loyal enthusiasm for this heroic role involves him and his friend (Dean Martin) with the real FBI and with a murderous spy ring. Well played and often funny, the movie suffers from one of Sidney's prevailing weaknesses, running 115 minutes on material adequate for 90.

Pepe (1960), a tedious vehicle for the Mexican comic Cantinflas, was even more grossly inflated at 195 minutes. Bolstered though it was by guest appearances by a whole galaxy of stars, it flopped. Nor was there much enthusiasm for Sidney's screen version of the stage musical *Bye Bye Birdie* (1963). A critic in *Saturday Review* complained about its "blatant, eye-damaging color," adding that "the cheerful satire of the original has given way to some bloated production numbers and long stretches of cornball dialogue."

After that, Sidney returned to MGM for two more movies—the unfunny comedy *A Ticklish Affair* (1963) and an Elvis Presley musical, *Viva Las Vegas!* (1964). The latter costarred Ann-Margret, whose "startling mixture of brazen sexuality and kittenish naivete," George Morris maintains, "was formed by Sidney in such barometers of sixties mass taste as *Bye Bye Birdie, Viva Las Vegas!* and *The Swinger.* For Morris, *Viva Las Vegas!* "is a combustible fusion of Sidney's kinetic style and the non-stop gyrations of its two stars. . . . This is not only Sidney's best Sixties movie; it is also *the* Presley movie and *the* Ann-Margret movie. Audaciously directed and outrageously performed, *Viva Las Vegas* gets its juices from the perpetual movement before—and behind—the camera."

Sidney next produced and directed *Who Has Seen the Wind?* (1965), one of a series of television films sponsored by the United Nations. Scripted by Don Mankiewicz from a story by Tad Mosel, this one was meant to draw attention to the work of the UN's Commission for Refugees, and did so with a melodramatic story of steamy passions on a decrepit freighter whose stateless crew are condemned to roam the seas like so many Flying Dutchmen, never able to go ashore. In spite of an impressive cast headed by Edward G. Robinson, Maria Schell, and Stanley Baker, the film failed to overcome the limitations of its script.

Sidney's directorial career ended at Paramount with one bad film, the prurient comedy *The Swinger* (1966), and one moderately good one, *Half a Sixpence* (1967). The latter, adapted from H. G. Wells's novel *Kipps* and the stage musical based upon it, was filmed in England by Geoffrey Unsworth, with the young British entertainer Tommy Steele as Kipps, a humble draper's assistant in Edwardian England who briefly acquires a fortune, hobnobs in high society, but returns gratefully to his own kind in the end. Coolly received in the United States, where it was found excessively opulent and stagey, *Half a Sixpence* was a hit in Britain. John Russell Taylor found it "a bit too long" (at 148 minutes) but otherwise "an almost continuous delight" in which "George Sidney's fluently mobile camera creates a real screen-musical elation."

Since then, Sidney has occupied himself with the financial aspects of the industry—interim financing, completion bonding, postproduction, and distribution. He served for some years as president of Hanna-Barbera Productions, the animation company. From time to time he has spoken of returning to directing with a new musical, but in 1983 he told James Bawden that "musicals are as dead as the studio system, destroyed by incompetents who don't understand how to make them. . . . The studio system furnished us with choreographers, set designers, orchestras, everyone who learned from past mistakes and went from one musical to another. The tradition is gone and cannot be revived."

After thirty years of filmmaking, Sidney has resumed his formal education, studying law and traveling to East Africa on archaeological digs. He has retained his interest in music, both classical and popular, and has also made a considerable reputation as a photographer, with credits in such publications as *Life, Look,* and the New York *Times.* An amateur painter himself, he owns a notable collection of French Impressionists. He is a car buff and a crack rifle shot who reportedly did some of the trick shooting in *Annie Get Your Gun.* Seldom seen without a pipe in his mouth, Sidney is an amiable man whose unprecedently long tenure as president of the Directors Guild is an indication of his popularity in the industry. He has been married twice, in 1941 to Lillian Burns, former MGM dramatic coach, and in 1978 to Jane Robinson, widow of Edward G. Robinson.

"Sidney is a genuine curiosity," writes George Morris, "a man whose career simultaneously reflects the central paradox of the American cinema (the uneasy alliance between commerce and art), and one of its most familiar characteristics: that tension between primal energy and aesthetic discipline. Sidney maintains a delicate balance between instinct and control in his movies, and more often than not, his impulsive energy will tip the scales, lending his film an anarchic style bordering on surrealism. A close look at George Sidney's oeuvre is exasperating. The good and the bad blithely coexist in his filmography, sometimes within the very same film, and there are no easy divisions into periods or trends. . . . Indeed, Sidney's work indicates a man with neither good taste nor bad taste, but, quite simply, no taste at all. In this respect George Sidney may be the most supremely intuitive director of all. When his movies work, they work beautifully. When they don't they can be excruciating." Alain Masson likewise maintains that "no absurdity was too much" for Sidney, but that his best work showed a "boisterous virtuosity" in his "intuitive conception of space."

FILMS: (Features only)—Free and Easy, 1941; Pacific Rendezvous, 1942; Pilot No. 5, 1943; Thousands Cheer, 1943; Bathing Beauty, 1944; Anchors Aweigh, 1945; The Harvey Girls, 1946; Holiday in Mexico, 1946; Cass Timberlane, 1947; The Three Musketeers, 1948; The Red Danube, 1949; Key to the City. 1950; Annie Get Your Gun, 1950; Show Boat, 1951; Scaramouche, 1952; Kiss Me Kate, 1953; Young Bess, 1953; Jupiter's Darling, 1954; The Eddie Duchin Story, 1956; Jeanne Eagels, 1957; Pal Joey, 1957; Who Was That Lady?, 1960; Pepe, 1960; Bye Bye Birdie, 1963; A Ticklish Affair, 1963; Viva Las Vegas! (U.K., Love in Las Vegas), 1964; Who Has Seen the Wind?, 1965 (for television); The Swinger, 1966; Half a Sixpence, 1967.

ABOUT: Coursodon, J.-P. American Directors Vol. II, 1983. Periodicals—Action (U.S.) May–June 1974; Bright Lights Vol. 3 No. 1 1980; Film Comment November–December 1977; Films in Review June–July 1983; New York Times October 28, 1945; Positif April 1976.

SIEGEL, DONALD (October 26, 1912–) was born in Chicago, Illinois. His parents, Sam and Anne Siegel, were vaudeville artists before settling in Chicago and establishing a school that taught music by correspondence. Siegel's childhood years were spent in Chicago and New York. Although his parents were Jews with strong family religious connections, Siegel had a secular upbringing and is an atheist who denies that his Jewish background has affected him. In the late 1920s the family moved to London where Sam Siegel managed an American business. Don Siegel continued his education in Britain, studying at Jesus College, Cambridge University. His father had encouraged him to become a musician, but Siegel became more interested in the theatre and while in Britain he

DONALD SIEGEL

studied for a time at the Royal Academy of Dramatic Art. Siegel moved with his parents to Paris before returning to the United States in 1932, when he was twenty. His early ambition to be an actor had waned and, casting around for a job, he wrote to an uncle who was a film editor in Hollywood. In 1934 Siegel went to work as an assistant librarian in the stock-shot library at Warner Brothers.

His first real experience of the craft of filmmaking was as an assistant editor, but he found the work dull and moved with relief to the inserts department. "We shot newspapers, closeups of guns or railroad signs, anything the director wanted," Siegel says. "It was extraordinary. There I was in my mid-twenties with a whole camera crew at my disposal. . . . I became eager to shoot film. Rapidly I convinced directors that inserts were anything they were too lazy to shoot. . . . I was soon shooting a tremendous amount of film."

This basic education in filmmaking continued when Siegel took charge of montage work at Warners. Montage sequences were widely used at that time—for example to indicate the passage of time (calendar pages falling like leaves) or to summarize the rise or fall of a character's career. Siegel virtually created the montage department, greatly expanding the scope of the work, experimenting with "revolutionary things like having dialogue in montages." Siegel's years as head of montage at Warner's were "the most exciting part of my film career." It was, as he says, "a most marvelous way to learn about films, because I made endless, endless mistakes just experimenting with no supervision. And the result was that a great many of the montages were enormously effective." Before long, he was shooting more film than anybody else working at Warners at that time, and directing stars like James Cagney, Humphrey Bogart, Walter Huston, and Fredric March. Examples of his work are to be found in many Warner films of the late 1930s and early 1940s, including *The Roaring Twenties, Casablanca, They Drive by Night,* and *Across the Pacific.* In 1940 Siegel began to receive assignments as a second unit director—work which often involved action scenes. He believes it was this that turned him from a director with "no gift for violence" into a "a specialist in brawls and fights . . . filed among the action directors."

In fact, however, Siegel's first film as director was a sentimental account of the nativity of Christ, updated to the American West, and called *Star in the Night* (1945). This short film won an Oscar, as did *Hitler Lives,* a propaganda short assembled mostly from newsreel footage. Siegel's first feature followed in 1946: *The Verdict,* a mystery story set in Victorian London and starring Sydney Greenstreet and Peter Lorre. It was moderately successful, but of no particular interest. Over the next seven years Siegel directed a miscellaneous bunch of films for Warners, RKO, Universal, and Columbia. They included a chase film with Robert Mitchum (*The Big Steal*), a Western with Audie Murphy (*Duel at Silver Creek*), and an anti-communist comedy with Viveca Lindfors (*No Time for Flowers*). All of them were very modestly budgeted and frequently made in difficult production circumstances—for example, Siegel started shooting *Duel at Silver Creek* before the writer had decided who was going to get the girl; when he had finished, the picture ran fifty-four minutes, and a prologue had to be quickly thought up and shot to expand it to seventy-seven.

By the mid-1950s, the films Siegel had directed seemed to identify him as a run-of-the-mill Hollywood director of no obvious distinction. He began to establish a critical reputation when he directed *Riot in Cell Block 11* for Allied Artists in 1954. The story of a prison riot, the film was praised for its realistic and uncompromising handling of the subject and its avoidance of the clichés of the prison movie genre. There are no stars, no women, no easy liberalism. Like many Siegel heroes, the convicts' leader Dunn (Neville Brand) is a violent and passionate man, though intelligent enough to control his instinctive responses. Thanks to him, the rioters win their demands, though Dunn himself pays a high price for his leadership. The picture also demonstrates very simply and directly another Siegel characteristic—the division of society into the conflict-

ing forces of law and crime (with no very clear indication of which side Siegel favors). *Karel Reisz* wrote in *Sight and Sound*: "*Riot in Cell Block 11* is said to have been made on a B-picture budget but is technically in complete control of its material: it proceeds in so craftsmanlike a manner that one is not tempted to analyse the contributions of producer (Walter Wanger), director (Don Siegel) and writer (Richard Collins). . . . The narrative as a whole has a crisp, purposeful tempo about it. *Riot in Cell Block 11* is, in fact, one of the most effective pieces of film journalism to have come our way for a long time."

The importance of Walter Wanger's contribution has been acknowledged by Siegel. Wanger had himself served a jail sentence and was an important inspiration in the making of the picture. He also produced the film that confirmed Siegel's reputation, *Invasion of the Body Snatchers* (1956). Adapted from a science-fiction novel by Jack Finney, it is set in a well-observed midwestern small town, orderly and parochial, whose inhabitants are taken over by aliens from space. The people commandeered in this way become "pods"—physically unchanged but without minds or feelings of their own. (Siegel makes no secret of the fact that he thinks most people *are* "pods," without any interference from outer space.) The story centers on a doctor, a man of independence and honest emotion who resists the takeover, becoming ever more isolated in a community populated by blank and ultimately murderous vegetables. This bleak parable (the reassuring ending was added at the insistence of the studio, Allied Artists) was widely interpreted as an attack on McCarthyism, but the film has outlasted the senator and may, as Susan Sontag suggests, reflect popular fears of the depersonalizing aspects of modern life. Siegel made a brief courtesy appearance as a taxi driver in Philip Kaufman's 1978 remake of the picture.

Baby-Face Nelson (1957), a gangster film with Mickey Rooney playing the title role, was very cheaply and rapidly made. When first shown, it was much criticized for its extreme violence. More recently it has been studied respectfully as an "exemplary action film" and as a prime example of Siegel's interest in reckless heroes who struggle to control their violent impulses. The same characteristics are divided between the two drug smugglers in *The Line Up* (1958), Julian (Robert Keith) providing the intellectual control, Dancer (Eli Wallach) the violence. The film, a spinoff from a television series, was praised for the vivid and detailed picture it gives of a criminal organization and the community (San Francisco) in which it operates.

Although the films Siegel directed during the middle and late 1950s achieved some critical and commercial success, his position in the film industry was not a secure one. The decline in the number of films made in Hollywood had a disproportionate effect on directors who worked on low budget films, and Siegel turned to television. In that medium, he says, "You have less time to work, less time to prepare and absolutely no post production time. . . . Most of the work done on television is poor, as far as directing is concerned." However, Siegel is a pragmatist. He started to work in television in 1953 and his involvement with the medium reached a peak in the 1960s, when he directed the pilot for *The Legend of Jesse James* and produced all thirty-four episodes of the series. In the mid-1960s Siegel also made three feature films intended for television presentation: *The Killers, The Hanged Man,* and *Stranger on the Run.* The first, based on the Hemingway short story, was described by its director as a "brutal and sensual film"; it had a distinguished cast (including Lee Marvin, John Cassavetes, and Angie Dickinson), but not everyone thought it an improvement on Robert Siodmak's 1946 version of the story. *The Hanged Man* was also a remake (of Robert Montgomery's *Ride a Pink Horse,* 1947).

Of the cinema feature films Siegel directed during the same period the best received were *Hell Is for Heroes* and *Flaming Star.* Both have similar qualities to *Riot in Cell Block 11.* They deal with large social issues—war in *Hell Is for Heroes,* race prejudice in *Flaming Star*—come to no easy conclusions, and are bleakly violent in tone. *Flaming Star* is also notable for the excellent performance Siegel drew from Elvis Presley in what is basically a straight dramatic role.

Siegel's position and reputation were greatly strengthened in the late 1960s when he began to work with Clint Eastwood. Their relationship began almost accidentally when the first director of *Coogan's Bluff* quit the film while it was being scripted. Since then Siegel has directed Eastwood in *Two Mules for Sister Sara, The Beguiled, Dirty Harry,* and *Escape From Alcatraz.* Their working relationship was reversed when Siegel played a small part in the first film Eastwood directed, *Play Misty for Me.* As the most popular Hollywood star of the late 1960s and 1970s, Eastwood made it possible for Siegel to work on more ambitious and expensive projects. This new situation was highlighted by *Dirty Harry* (1971). The film was very successful at the box office, and its central character, the heroic renegade cop Harry Callahan, became a cinematic legend whose exploits were the subject of two subsequent films. *Dirty Harry* was highly controversial because of its apparent advocacy of hard-nosed attitudes to law enforcement. (It features a psychopathic killer who taunts the police from behind constitutional safeguards; only Dirty Harry, who fights fire with fire and torture with torture, can bring him to savage justice.) The criticism was all the harsher because Siegel had previously been identified as a liberal. He has denied that *Dirty Harry* represented a change of attitude, pointing out that his direction of the film did not necessarily identify him with its protagonist.

Siegel's arrival as a director of major commercial importance coincided with the development of the *auteur* theory promulgated by André Bazin and the *Cahiers du Cinéma* writers. Siegel's films, like those of Samuel Fuller, Bud Boetticher, Nicholas Ray, and other Hollywood stalwarts, were now scrutinized by serious critics as the work of an artist *manqué.* Seasons of his films were organized in London, Paris, and Vienna, and books and articles were written about his work. So much heady praise had its effect on at least one Siegel-Eastwood movie, a "bizarre and haunting" piece called *The Beguiled* (1970). The film, which tells a misogynistic story about an army fugitive seeking refuge in a girls' school during the American Civil War, has a self-conscious "art film" quality, and Siegel's awareness of his new critical status is indicated by the hand-written credit "a Siegel film." *The Beguiled,* though it gained some critical support and still seems to Siegel "the best film I have done," was not a commercial success. The best of his subsequent films, *Charley Varrick* (1973) and *Escape From Alcatraz,* were closer to Siegel's usual style, though there is an interesting and well-controlled use of symbolism in *Escape From Alcatraz* (1979).

Charley Varrick stars Walter Matthau as a crop-duster who sidelines as a small-time bank robber, and gets into trouble when he accidentally makes off with Mafia money on one of his heists. Steven H. Scheur praised the film as a "very slick, entertaining crime yarn." *Escape From Alcatraz* is a prison film based on the true story of Frank Norris, an inmate who tried to break out of Alcatraz in 1962 and was never heard from again. With Eastwood playing Norris and Patrick McGoohan cast as the warden, the film was generally well received by critics.

The off-beat comedy *Jinxed!* (1982) was an atypical film for Siegel. It deals with a young blackjack dealer (Ken Wahl) who, after having been consistently and maddeningly bested by a loutish gambler (Rip Torn), attempts to break the jinx by taking something from his nemesis. What he takes, in this case, is the gambler's wife (Bette Midler), a small-time casino singer. Together, in fact, they plan to do away with the Wahl character for the insurance money they hope to collect. Reviews were generally regative. Vincent Canby remarked that *Jinxed!* is occasionally "good fun . . . but otherwise it's desperate," veering from comic melodrama to romantic comedy to an out-and-out vehicle for Midler. "One can understand why Mr. Siegel might have been originally drawn to the idea of the film," Richard Schickel noted, "but the material remains undeveloped." Schickel was also unhappy with the movie's script, which "keeps waffling off into farce, romance and just plain improbability. The often estimable Don Siegel brings little conviction, comic or otherwise, to the picture."

"Ninety-five percent of my time on . . . most pictures which I don't produce myself is spent outwitting, outfoxing, and putting on an act for the producer," Siegel said once (he nowadays produces most of his own films). He has been equally outspoken about other aspects of the studio system, but he has accepted these constraints and worked within them. A typical Siegel film opens with an irresistibly gripping and often violent episode—"the hook"—and is developed very rapidly and economically, without subplots or much detail, and generally through action rather than dialogue. This unfaltering pace is achieved partly by careful initial planning, but to an unusual extent in the editing. "After shooting a picture I stay away from it for a while," Siegel says. "Then when I look at the first assembled picture, I don't want anyone to talk to me. I just look at it as a whole. . . . The result is almost always the same. I'm livid with myself for some of the terrible things I okayed. I go home thoroughly depressed. But an anger is building up and I come back the next day and I just can't wait to get at the goddam film and rip it to shreds. For, at that point, nothing in the film is sacred. . . . If I don't think it works it goes."

The central dramatic situation in a Siegel movie is almost always organized around a male character torn between violence and self-control, and the drama is emphasized by the naturalistic use of mundane settings. The reckless hero is often pitted against an unfeeling, coldly efficient organization, and often he is destroyed by it. The most satisfactory outcome is when the hero manages to bring the two aspects of his nature—instinct and calculation—into balance. The films express an almost Hobbesian view, of a world dominated by greed, revenge, suspicion, and betrayal. Brutality and savagery are shown as facts of life, and little attempt is made to excuse or explain them in psychological terms. The forces of law and the forces of crime are presented as if there were little or no moral difference between them.

In some of Siegel's later films (since about 1962) there is some modification and "fleshing-out" of these elements—a greater use of irony and comedy, a willingness to allow slightly more importance to female characters, a degree of moral indignation (directed especially against eroticism). His basically straightforward shooting style remains, but he has occasionally allowed himself rhetorical flourishes. With the relaxation of censorship, violence in his films has become, if anything, more extreme.

Siegel, a "very trim and handsome" man, lives near Los Angeles. He has a son by his first marriage to the actress Viveca Lindfors and four adopted children from his marriage to Doe Avedon, also an actress. Siegel is said to be easy to work with but possessed of a hard-won "assurance and decision that awes crew and actors." Peter Bogdanovich has written that Siegel "has managed, often against stifling odds, to bring a disquieting ambiguity as well as a unified viewpoint to assignments which, in other hands, could easily have been routine. . . . his films are unpretentious and as precisely executed as they are unconventional in their implications."

—An.L.

FILMS: Star in the Night, 1945 (short); Hitler Lives, 1945 (short); The Verdict, 1946; Night unto Night, 1948; The Big Steal, 1949; No Time for Flowers, 1952; Duel at Silver Creek, 1952; Count the Hours (In Britain, Every Minute Counts), 1953; China Venture, 1954; Riot in Cell Block 11, 1954; Private Hell 36, 1954: An Annapolis Story (In Britain, The Blue and the Gold), 1955; Invasion of the Body Snatchers, 1956; Crime in the Streets, 1956; A Spanish Affair, 1957; Baby-Face Nelson, 1957; The Gun Runners, 1958; The Line Up, 1958; Edge of Eternity, 1959; Hound Dog Man, 1959; Flaming Star, 1960; Hell Is for Heroes, 1962; The Killers, 1964; The Hanged Man, 1964; Stranger on the Run, 1967; Madigan, 1967; Coogan's Bluff, 1968; Two Mules for Sister Sara, 1969; The Beguiled, 1970; Dirty Harry, 1971; Charley Varrick, 1973; The Black Windmill, 1974; The Shootist, 1976; Telefon, 1977; Escape From Alcatraz, 1979; Jinxed!, 1982.

ABOUT: Farber, M. Negative Space, 1971; Kaminsky, S. M. Don Siegel: Director, 1974; Kaminsky, S. M. American Film Genres, 1974; Lovell, A. Don Siegel: American Cinema, 1975; McArthur, C. Underworld USA, 1972; Rosenthal, S. and Kass. J. M. The Hollywood Professionals, 1975; Who's Who in America, 1978–1979. *Periodicals*—American Film December–January 1978–1979; L'Avant Scène du Cinema July 1979; Cahiers du Cinéma December–January 1964; Cinema (Britain) February 1970; Cinema (USA) Spring 1968; Films and Filming May and June 1968, January 1969, November 1973; Image et Son May 1976; Journal of Popular Film Winter 1972; Kinema June 1969; Millimeter July–August 1976; Monthly Film Bulletin October 1980, February 1984, March

1984, July 1985; Movie Spring 1968; New York Times October 22, 1982; Positif September 1965; Sight and Sound Autumn 1973; Take One March–April 1971; Velvet Light Trap Spring 1972.

*SIODMAK, ROBERT (August 8, 1900– March 10, 1973) was born in Memphis, Tennessee, but always considered Germany to be his homeland. He was the son of a Jewish banker who took the family back to Germany when Robert Siodmak was a year old. Schooled in Berlin and then at Marburg University (1917–1920), Siodmak's first ambition was to become an actor. He studied with the innovative theatrical director Erich Ponto and subsequently joined a touring repertory company. However, because a fight with another pupil in kindergarten had resulted in permanent damage to his eyes, Siodmak did not achieve much success as an actor; looking prematurely aged, he was always cast in the part of an old man. Dissatisfied, and yielding to his father's pressure, Siodmak gave up the stage and joined the family banking business. By the time the rising inflation of the interwar years ruined banking and investment prospects in Germany, Siodmak had already left the bank, trying his hand at magazine editing and wholesaling, "anything I could turn into profit." It is important not to minimize the effect this period of desolation that followed World War I in Germany was to have on the kind of subject matter and concerns depicted in Siodmak's mature films.

In 1925 the ambitious Siodmak landed a job writing subtitles for American films imported into Germany. Exploiting this foothold in the German film industry, Siodmak joined UFA Studios in Berlin in 1927. Under Erich Pommer, he worked as a cutter, script assistant, writing scout (he "discovered" Emeric Pressburger), and assistant director. Convinced of his own abilities he battled for some time to secure financing for a project of his own. The resultant film, *Menshen am Sonntag* (*People on Sunday, 1929*), launched at least six careers: Siodmak and Edgar G. Ulmer directed; Curt Siodmak (Robert's brother, himself to become a successful Hollywood scriptwriter) and Billy Wilder (Siodmak's roommate) assisted on the script; and Eugen Schüfftan was cameraman, with Fred Zinnemann as his assistant. Regarded by many critics as a classic of German silent cinema, the film depicts a Sunday outing by a varied cross section of Berliners to the outskirts of the city. Lighthearted and neo-realist in tone, the film is distinguished by its refusal to politically categorize its characters (the bane of so much of the German film industry at

ROBERT SIODMAK

the time) and by its technical competence, especially the showy, freewheeling, hand-held camera work, and its use of flashback and stop motion. Siodmak recalls that it was "amazing how simply you could film then. . . . We just thought of a scene and filmed it right away." John Gillett says "it is impossible to know how many [other filmmakers] were influenced by it."

Certainly its promise was clear to Erich Pommer, who offered Siodmak the chance to direct a series of films for UFA Studios. He made six films for Erich Pommer in the next five years. The first, *Abschied* (*Farewell*), made in 1930, had a script written by Emeric Pressburger. A drama set within the enclosed world of a small boardinghouse and tracing its various tensions and levels of conflict, the film was not a critical or popular success, though Siodmak was praised for the "inventiveness of his direction." His next four films—*Der Mann, der seinen Mörder sucht* (*The Man Who Seeks His Own Murderer*), *Voruntersuchung* (*Preliminary Investigation*), *Stürme der Leidenschaft* (*Storm of Passion/ Tempest*), and *Quick*—were all commercial successes, and they helped to confirm Siodmak's growing reputation. But more important, they introduced techniques and themes that were to distinguish Siodmak's mature work—his expressionistic use of claustrophobic interiors, his neat, precise camera movement, the atmospheric interplay of light and shadow, and his flair for psychological suspense.

A number of these concerns are evident in Siodmak's best but last film for UFA, *Brennendes Geheimis* (*The Burning Secret,* 1933). A psychological drama based upon a Ste-

°sē´ od mäk

phan Zweig story about the effect on a son of his mother's affair with a racing driver, the film delicately uses its setting, an off-season hotel, to underline the disintegration of the relationships. The film was attacked by Goebbels, who alleged that Siodmak's preoccupation with extramarital relationships and dubious morality made him a "corrupter of the German family." Alarmed by the political situation in Germany and by the growing anti-Semitism, Siodmak took the first available train to Paris.

Joining an already well-established German exile community that included Fritz Lang and Wilder, Siodmak found work quite easily. Over the next six years he directed most of the major French stars of the period, among them Danielle Darrieux, Louis Jouvet, Charles Boyer, and Maurice Chevalier. Siodmak's films of this French period have been characterized as slight and often uneven, primarily because economic pressures forced him to make specifically entertainment-oriented pictures. Working on unsympathetic themes and struggling to satisfy public expectations, Siodmak cannot be said noticeably to have increased his reputation over this period.

However, three of his French films do stand out (along with the salty seaport locations of *Mollenard,* 1937). These are *Mister Flow* (1936), a slick, American-style comedy for which Siodmak was accused of too closely imitating Lubitsch; *Cargaison blanche* (*French White Cargo/Traffic in Souls,* 1937), a thriller about the white slave trade to Rio, memorable for its acute characterizations (especially that of Jules Berry as a pimp) and its steamy atmosphere of exotic sexuality; and the most powerful of them all, *Pièges* (*Snares,* 1939), a crime melodrama starring Pierre Renoir, Erich von Stroheim, and Maurice Chevalier. Creating a world that looks forward to the *films noirs* of his American period, *Snares* stylishly evokes the eddying cross-currents of murder, deception, and sexuality within the loosely constructed story of an amateur detective's attempts to discover the murderer of a dancer. As an indication of the direction that Siodmak was to follow the film is indispensable, and in its own right it is an effective and moody crime drama (barring an unfortunate burst of song by Chevalier).

Siodmak left for America in 1940, the day before Hitler's army marched into Paris. With the help of his brother Curt (who had gone to Hollywood some years earlier), he landed a two-year contract with Paramount. For the first six months of this contract he did nothing but collect his paycheck and invest in the stock market, and when he was put to work he was at first given only B pictures to direct. Indeed, he dismissed

his first seven Hollywood films as "hack work," saying that the only good thing about them was that their "villains were either Japs, Germans, or Italians so I could make them as wicked as I wanted." Among these the only notable films are *Son of Dracula* (1943), interesting for its complex use of Christian symbols and its fusing of European and American movie traditions, and *Cobra Woman* (1943), his first color film. The success of the former drew him to the attention of Universal, who signed him to a seven-year contract in 1944. It was only then that Siodmak began to receive scripts worthy of his talent.

A chance meeting in 1944 with Joan Harrison, Hitchcock's producer, led to one of Siodmak's best films, *Phantom Lady.* It is his first *film noir*—a name given to some American films of the mid-1940s and 1950s by French critics who noted in them a darkening, paranoiac tone, a preoccupation with the psychology of the criminal and social outcast, and an implicit critique of American society in the aftermath of World War II. *Phantom Lady* offers an excellent recreation of New York City, sweltering in summer heat, steaming with tension. It traces the efforts of Kansas Richman (Ella Raines) to locate an elusive woman her boss (Alan Curtis) claims he met in a bar—the only person who can prove that he didn't murder his wife. When a deranged little drummer named Cliff March (Elisha Cook Jr.) admits that he had been bribed to forget the "phantom lady," Kansas intensifies her efforts, discovering in the end that the murderer was in fact her boss's best friend. Franchot Tone's playing of the murderer and Cook's performance as the drummer are of a piece with the world of dimly lit bars and glistening, shadowy streets which skillfully evoke the latent violence and paranoia at the film's center. As Robert Porfirio comments, "Siodmak and his brilliant cinematographer, Woody Bredell, have provided *Phantom Lady* with the essential ingredients . . . from the desperate innocent at loose in New York City . . . to the details of threatening shadows, jazz emanating from low-class bars, and the click of high heels on the pavement. The whole *noir* world is developed here."

Two other atmospheric dramas followed: *Christmas Holiday* (1944) and *The Suspect* (1944), a Victorian period piece starring Charles Laughton. Siodmak's next film, *The Spiral Staircase* (1945), is a unique mixture of the thriller and the horror film. Described by one critic as "quintessential Siodmak," the movie is almost an anthology of *film noir* ingredients—corridors, pools of shadow, stairways striped in light and dark, and the isolation and ultimate entrapment of the heroine within a claustrophobic interior. The plot is thin—a young servant girl

(Dorothy McGuire) and a crippled old woman (Ethel Barrymore) are terrorized by an insane killer in a crumbling mansion—but the film is unforgettable for its creation of an atmosphere of horror. The theme—of "helpless victims . . . being enveloped by shadows"—is one that Siodmak handles with precision and subtlety. The effectiveness of this picture owes much to the editing, which Siodmak was for once able to handle himself because of a strike at the studio. It was his own favorite among his films.

In 1945 Siodmak coscripted *Conflict*, another *film noir*, for his old friend Curtis Bernhardt, and himself directed one of his richest psychological studies, *The Strange Affair of Uncle Harry*. A complex story of suppressed (and incestuous) passion, confused loyalties, and domestic conflict, it explores the frustrations—eventually leading to murder—of a man and his two sisters who share a gloomy house in a small town in New Hampshire. The jealousy that ensues when the man (George Sanders) takes a lover (Ella Raines) precipitates the final tragedy: Sanders tries to poison his meddling sister, Lettie (Geraldine Fitzgerald), who had attempted to ruin his romance, but actually kills the other sister (Moyna MacGill), a crime for which Lettie is convicted. Such twists are characteristic of Siodmak. Nevertheless, the Hays Office code, still strong in 1945, demanded that the killer pay for the crime. To Siodmak's disgust, Universal tacked on a postscript showing that the whole story had been a dream, a conclusion that completely invalidates the psychological drive of the narrative. Siodmak thought the film no longer credible, but many critics, like Alain Silver, regard its anatomy of repression as one "that ranks with the most severe in *film noir.*"

Siodmak's next film, *The Killers* (1946), was the first of three exceptional forays into the gangster genre and has the status of a minor classic. Based loosely upon the Hemingway story of the same name, the picture (written by but not credited to John Huston) is a series of flashbacks. Slowly the puzzle of the murder of the Swede (Burt Lancaster) is pieced together by an obsessive insurance investigator (Edmond O'Brien). Step by step he uncovers the Swede's connection with a gang led by Colfax (Albert Dekker) whom, it turns out, the Swede had doublecrossed, and with Kitty Collins (Ava Gardner), who had seduced him and then betrayed him to the gang. The use of time, nonlinear and overlapping, is substantially responsible for the unique texture and atmosphere of the film; as Colin McArthur wrote, "yet again, the flashback structure, the raking over of time and memory to reveal obsession and betrayal, seems characteristic of Siodmak." The movie also includes

one of the most memorable set pieces in forties cinema: the robbery sequence is filmed in one long swooping crane take, the camera diving and panning like a demented bird. But it is the creation of the violent, alienated, amoral world into which the Swede is plunged that is the film's most important achievement. As Carl Macek commented, "the overwhelmingly corrupt universe in which the young boxer-turned-criminal involves himself is simply the *noir* world . . . in Siodmak's vision, the *noir* universe endures."

The Dark Mirror (1946) is the last of Siodmak's movies for which he accepts credit, dismissing the rest as "nothing more than potboilers." Written by Nunnally Johnson, it is an extended psychological study of two identical twins (played by Olivia De Havilland), one kind and gentle, the other a ruthless murderer, who confuse and confound both a police inspector (Thomas Mitchell) and a psychologist (Lew Ayres). Aided by trick photography and a sharp and precise *mise-en-scène*, the film again demonstrates Siodmak's mastery of psychological conundrums, its characters once more "lost and confused in a world that seems to reward alienation and depression."

Some of Siodmak's later Hollywood movies *were* potboilers but two at least were not, and it is difficult to understand why he chose to repudiate them. Indeed, with the quasi-documentary approach and brilliant location shooting of *Cry of the City* (1948) he achieved a realism and authenticity that represents one of the high points of *film noir*. It was followed by *Criss Cross,* about an armored truck guard (Burt Lancaster) who is drawn into a conspiracy (with Dan Duryea and Yvonne De Carlo) to rob his employers, and the complex network of doublecrosses and sexual convolutions that results. These two films best represent the section of Siodmak's work that Howard Mandelbaum calls "urban nightmares." The gritty location shooting, the restless, doom-laden atmosphere, the almost pathological reaction to the city (described by McArthur as "a Dali-like landscape") all combine to represent a world that is imploding with its own greed and lust.

Siodmak's view of society is shared by other directors of the period, including Fritz Lang, Otto Preminger, and Jules Dassin. Rejecting Hollywood and its values, these directors sought to infuse American films with a kind of expressionistic extension of the violence, persecution, and repressed sexuality that they found in the world around them—a world of insecurity, fear, and failure, in which the gangster was the last of the rugged individualists and people were "constantly trapped by their own greed and obsessions." The foreign filmmakers, especially, brought to their American material some of the desperate anxieties of pre-war Europe; Andrew Sarris has gone so far as to say that Siodmak's Universal pictures "are more Germanic than his German ones."

The plot of *Cry of the City* represents the confluence of a number of Siodmak's thematic obsessions. In it, an escaped criminal, Martin Rome (Richard Conte), is pursued by Lieutenant Candella (Victor Mature) with a zeal that borders on madness. Candella's "Dostoyevskian pursuit of Rome," who uses friends and family to shelter him, becomes an elaborate cat-and-mouse game of deception and investigation. That they grew up in the same neighborhood becomes the central point of narrative: "It is clear that Candella sees in Rome what he himself might have, perhaps wants to, become." This desperate pursuit tramples everything in its path, Candella abusing the law, Rome leaving only pain and betrayal in his wake, until their final confrontation in an empty church and the death of the gangster on a dimly lit, rain-soaked street. This combination of psychological probing with explicit social criticism gives it "as much of an oppressive atmosphere as Siodmak's earlier studio films," even though he himself was dissatisfied with the lack of control location shooting entailed. *Cry of the City* and *Criss Cross* set a standard against which other *noir* films of the fifties can be assessed.

After *Thelma Jordan* (1950), a dark melodrama that starred Barbara Stanwyck and Wendell Corey, playing the "*noir* hero unwittingly pulled into a nightmare," came Siodmak's last two American films, *Deported* (1950) and *The Whistle at Eaton Falls* (1951), neither of any particular interest. He returned to Germany in 1952, depressed because in Hollywood "the studio always wanted to change my psychological endings into physical ones," and bitter about the creative limitations placed on a filmmaker in America, where "the director is nothing much more than a glorified cameraman." Siodmak looked forward to the more relaxed structure of the European film industry: "In Europe I'm much freer to do what I want and make films as I like."

Sadly, of the films of his second European period, few are outstanding, too many thoroughly inconsequential. Most of the films Siodmak made between 1952 and his final project in 1968 could be summed up in the comment he himself made on *The Rough and the Smooth*, an adaptation of a Somerset Maugham story he made in 1958: "I've seen worse, but not much." Carlos Clarens declares that these years "were spent lifelessly churning out whatever producers asked for. He lost interest in moviemaking. He just worked for the money."

At least three films must be excepted from this sweeping condemnation: *The Crimson Pirate* (1952), *Die Ratten* (*The Rats,* 1955), and *Nachts, wenn der Teufel kam* (*The Devil Strikes at Night,* 1957). The first of these, an adventure yarn starring Burt Lancaster as an eighteenth-century Caribbean pirate, harkens back to the light comedy "entertainments" he directed in France in the mid-1930s. Both a tribute to and a gentle parody of the swashbuckling films of Douglas Fairbanks, the film demonstrates Siodmak's ability to work in a different genre and has an ease and verve conspicuously absent from his American films. *The Rats,* on the other hand, is a gloomy and pessimistic portrayal of the shattered Germany to which Siodmak had returned. A loose adaptation of Hauptmann's play, the film conveys his utter despair at the war's destruction of a generation (Maria Schell sells her child to finance her escape to West Berlin, only to be deserted by her lover upon her arrival), and the ruin of his homeland (signified by the rats of the title, gnawing on furniture and scurrying into corners). If the desperation of the interwar years was significantly responsible for the world-view reflected in his best American films, the desolation of the Europe to which he returned in the 1950s had as appreciable an effect on his films of that period.

Perhaps the best film Siodmak directed on his return to Europe was *The Devil Strikes at Night*. Like *The Rats,* it was made for the West German producer Arthur Brauner. A thinly disguised attack on Nazism, the film chronicles the story of Bruno Ludke, a real-life psychopath of the early 1940s, who strangled more than seventy women in Nazi Germany. Siodmak uses his story to draw a subtle parallel between the career of Ludke (Mario Adorf) and the mass genocide practiced by the Nazis (who in fact found it politically expedient to engage in an elaborate cover-up of Ludke's reign of terror). Precise and direct in its narrative, the film seemed to John Gillett to belong "to the great German thriller tradition, and Mario Adorf's disturbing portrait of the killer pulls the story full circle back to Lang's *M*."

Such late films as *Custer of the West* (1966), a project both Kurosawa and Zinnemann rejected, or the two Lex Barker adventures, *Der Schatz der Azteken* and *Die Pyramide des Sonnengottes,* along with earlier American features like *Fly by Night* (1942) and *The Whistle at Eaton Falls* (1951), tend to support Kenneth Tynan's assertion that Siodmak wasted a genuine talent on bad films; Siodmak himself said that he was obliged to accept such assignments "so that I could get my own way from time to time." A more useful assessment might be the *Times* obituary writer's: "Robert Siodmak tended to be underestimated among serious film students because his best work was done in the despised genres of the psychological thriller and the horror film, but within [these] limits . . . his mastery was complete."

Siodmak's films of the 1940s remain important contributions to the cinema, distinguished by the virtuosity of their dramatic lighting and camera placement, acute characterization, and a powerful blend of psychological analysis with suspenseful narrative. Unlike the characters of Fritz Lang and Jules Dassin (to whose films Siodmak's are perhaps closest), who are manipulated by a ruthless fate, Siodmak's characters "are driven from within by intense loves or hatreds," and it is this characteristic that gives his films their emotive center. Colin McArthur writes that "darkness, cruelty, obsession, betrayal and death are the hallmarks of Siodmak's work," and this is true; but it is also true that, as Howard Mandelbaum says, his "constancy of tone and artful lighting transform reality into poetry." The director himself, sadly, said: "I have done little that has pleased me. Perhaps one scene, five minutes, no more in each picture."

Robert Siodmak died in Locarno, Switzerland, not far from his home in Ascona. His wife, the former Bertha Odenheimer, had died only seven weeks before. At the time of his death, he was planning a film version of Thomas Mann's *The Magic Mountain.*

—*C.L.*

FILMS: Menschen am Sonntag (People on Sunday), 1929; Abschied (Farewell), 1930; Der Mann, der seinen Mörder sucht (The Man Who Seeks His Own Murderer), 1930; Voruntersuchung (Preliminary Investigation), 1931; Stürme der Leidenschaft (Storm of Passion/Tempest), 1931; Brennendes Geheimnis (The Burning Secret), 1933; Le Sexe faible, 1933; La Crise est finie (The Slump Is Over), 1934; La Vie Parisienne, 1935; Mister Flow, 1936; Cargaison blanche/Le Chemin de Rio (French White Cargo/Traffic in Souls), 1937; Mollenard, 1937; Pièges (Snares), 1939; West Point Widow, 1941; Fly by Night (UK, Secret of G.32), 1942; The Night Before the Divorce, 1942; My Heart Belongs to Daddy, 1942; Someone to Remember, 1943; Son of Dracula, 1943; Cobra Woman, 1943; Phantom Lady, 1944; Christmas Holiday, 1944; The Suspect, 1944; The Spiral Staircase, 1945; The Strange Affair of Uncle Harry, 1945; The Killers, 1946; The Dark Mirror, 1946; Time Out of Mind, 1947; Cry of the City, 1948; Criss Cross, 1949; Thelma Jordan (UK, The File on Thelma Jordan), 1949; Deported, 1950; The Whistle at Eaton Falls (UK, Richer Than the Earth), 1951; The Crimson Pirate, 1952; Le Grand Jeu (Card of Fate), 1953; Die Ratten (The Rats), 1955;

Mein Vater, Der Schauspieler, 1956; Nachts, wenn der Teufel kam (The Devil Strikes at Night), 1957; Dorothea Angermann, 1958; The Rough and the Smooth, 1959; Katia, 1959; Mein Schulfreund/Der Schulfreund, 1960; L'Affaire Nina B., 1961; Tunnel 28 (Escape from East Berlin), 1962; Der Schut, 1964; Der Schatz der Azteken, 1965; Die Pyramide des Sonnengottes, 1963; Custer of the West, 1966; Der Kampf um Rom 1. Teil, 1968; Der Kampf um Rom 11. Tiel, 1969. *Published scripts*—Custer of the West, 1966.

ABOUT: Borde, R. and Chaumeton, E. Panorama due Film Noir American, 1955; Higham, C. and Greenberg, J. Hollywood in the Forties, 1968; Koszarski, R. Hollywood Directors 1941–1976, 1977; McArthur, C. Underworld USA, 1972; Silver, A. and Ward, E. Film Noir, 1979. *Periodicals*—Bright Lights 8 1979; Film Journal February 1958; Films and Filming June 1959; Films in Review April 1969; Life August 25, 1947; Monthly Film Bulletin June 1978; New York Times March 12, 1973; Sight and Sound Summer-Autumn 1959; Time Out August 15–21, 1980; Velvet Light Trap 5 1972.

"SIRK, DOUGLAS" (Claus Detlev Sierk or Sierck) (April 26, 1900–January 16, 1987), American director, was born in Hamburg, Germany of Danish parents. A good deal of contradictory information has been published about his early life, but it seems that he grew up mostly in Skagen, Denmark, receiving a good classical education, and that he may have attended the University of Copenhagen for a time before returning to Germany soon after World War I. At first a law student at Munich University, he apparently found that not to his taste, subsequently studying philosophy at Jena and the history of art under Erwin Panofsky at Hamburg. In 1921 he also attended Einstein's lectures on relativity.

In 1920, while still a student, he began writing for the *Neue Hamburger Zeitung* and entered the theatre as assistant *Dramaturg* at the Deutsches Schauspielhaus, germanizing his name to Hans Detlef Sierck. He was promoted to *Dramaturg* the following year and became director of the Kleines Theatre in Chemnitz in 1922, when he also published his translations of Shakespeare's sonnets. Sierck was only twenty-three when he was appointed artistic director of the Bremen Schauspielhaus. Over the next six years he directed often audacious productions of plays by Hofmannsthal, Grillparzer, Werfel, and Brecht, as well as Shakespeare (in his own translations), Sophocles, Calderón, Strindberg, Ibsen, Shaw, and many others, establishing himself as one of the most inventive young directors in Germany, avant-garde in his techniques and left-wing in his political orientation.

In 1929 Sierck became director of the Altes

DOUGLAS SIRK

Theatre in Leipzig. The following year his production of Bernhard Blume's sympathetic play about Sacco and Vanzetti, *Im Namen des Volkes,* scandalized Nazi critics. Sierck was undeterred, but things came to a head three years later, when (in the year the Nazis came to power) he staged Georg Kaiser and Kurt Weill's *The Silver Lake.* The official Nazi newspaper *Volkischer Beobachter* called the authors "salon bolshevists" and said that Sierck "has rendered a service to the Berlin literary intelligentsia and its outdated intellectual satellites which stands to cost him very dear indeed."

Thus threatened, Sierck turned to the cinema which, because of its international markets, was at first less rigidly controlled by the new regime than the theatre. In 1934 he joined UFA, beginning his film career by directing three shorts of about thirty minutes each: *Der Eingebildete Kranke* (*The Imaginary Invalid*), *Dreimal Liebe* (*Three Times Love*), and another whose title is unknown.

UFA assigned Sierck his first feature in early 1935—a semi-musical which he made both in German (*April April*) and in a Dutch version ('*T was éen April,* codirected by Jacques van Pol). The German version starred Albrecht Schoenhals, a well-known actor of the time. According to Jon Halliday, in his article about Sierck's German films in *Screen* (Summer 1971), both versions are now lost but the trade reviews "indicate the director managed to do a surprising amount of transformation on basically recalcitrant material."

Das Mädchen vom Moorhof (*The Girl From the Marshcroft,* 1935), another studio assign-

ment, was a remake of Sjöström's successful silent adaptation of the novel by Selma Lagerlöf. It tells the story of a poor girl, scorned as the mother of an illegitimate child, who is taken in by the compassionate son of a landowner. When, after a tavern brawl, her benefactor faces a murder charge, the heroine works devotedly to prove his innocence, winning his love and the respect of the community.

Jon Halliday says that this film, "while showing some uncertainties, also reveals several of . . . [Sierck's] predilections: many mirror shots and reflections in water; the deliberate dismantling of 'suspense' . . . ; considerable use of the local church, and the relationship to it of the local burghers; the exposure of pretense and hypocrisy. Sirk here, too, for the first time makes a major excursus into what seems to have been favorite terrain: the waterfront, fishing nets, mist and fog, sleazy bars, and lighting reminiscent of Sternberg."

Already established at UFA as a successful director, Sierck was next given Heinrich George, then Germany's leading stage actor, for *Stützen der Gesellschaft* (*Pillars of Society,* 1935), an adaptation of Ibsen's play, which Sierck had directed on the stage in 1923. George plays Consul Bernick, a shipowner with a shameful but well-concealed past. His small-town life of spurious respectability is shattered by the return from America of his victim Tönnessen (Albrecht Schoenhals). Sierck eliminated several of Isben's characters and pared the story to the bone, reducing suspense by placing Bernick's exposure very early in the film, but strengthening Ibsen's social criticism and adding a long sequence set in the American West, where Tönnessen is seen preparing for his return.

David Stewart Hull says that *Stützen der Gesellschaft* "ranks among the best literary adaptations of the period [in Germany]. Halliday draws attention to Sierck's evident delight in his "Wild West" sequence, and goes on: "The return from the American West to Europe (Norway) allows for a stunning demonstration of Sirk's gift of transition: as Tönnessen raises his glass to the Norwegian flag in his hut in the West, it falls away to reveal a statue of Bernick which is being unveiled under the hostile stares of the local proletariat back in Norway. . . . In fact, it would be possible to see the whole film as a cultural parable: the influx of energy and honesty from the West into a stultified, dishonest small town in Europe. Schoenhals charges through at the head of his circus, detonating paroxysms of pretense, terror, and deceit."

Sierck then turned to the genre with which he is primarily associated, the melodramatic "woman's picture." *Schlussakkord* (*Final Accord/Ninth Symphony*, 1936) starred Willy Birgel as a successful conductor married to neurotic Lil Dagover. They have adopted a little boy (Peter Bosse) whose real mother (Maria von Tasnady) they employ as his nanny. The unhappy Dagover falls into the clutches of a clairvoyant and dies under suspicious circumstances, but a verdict of suicide frees Birgel and his beautiful employee to live happily ever after. Sierck said that when he read this script he "got the smell of a tremendous success." He decided to accept this mawkish tale and turn it into something new—not by subduing the melodramatic elements but by intensifying them. This he did so thoroughly that the scenarist removed his name from the credits—and so effectively that the movie became a huge success all over the world. It was followed by *Das Hofkonzert* (1936), also made in a French version as *La Chanson du souvenir*. This lost film was a period musical with a score by Edmund Nick and photography by Franz Weihmayr, who was Sierck's cameraman also on his two subsequent German films.

Late in 1936, UFA made Sirk responsible for building its new discovery, Zarah Leander, into a star. Sierck first cast the talented and very beautiful Swedish singer in *Zu Neuen Ufern* (*To New Shores*, 1937). The film opens in nineteenth-century England, where Gloria Vane (Leander) takes the blame for offenses committed by her lover Sir Albert Finsbury (Willy Birgel), a weak and decadent army officer. Condemned by a class-conscious court, she is transported to Paramatta, the women's prison in Australia. To escape his gambling debts, Sir Albert also goes to Australia, but by the time Gloria is released he is engaged to another woman. Broken-hearted, she takes a job singing in a sleazy casino, but in the end finds happiness as the (purchased) bride of an honest farmer.

"Stylistically, *Ufern* is one of the most extraordinary films ever made," Halliday writes; "the main tradition to which it belongs is clearly that of Brecht and Weill—not just in the combination of music, songs, and dialogue, but in the assemblage of contrasts, of light, of class, of geography. One scene in particular, the trial of Gloria Vane, represents a highly successful attempt to put the Weill-Brecht advances on the screen. The scene is introduced with an old woman singing a song about Paramatta . . . ; she has a large placard with a number of pictures of Paramatta on it: the camera passes from her into the courtroom, where Leander is sentenced, back out to the woman in the street and then *through* a picture of Paramatta to Paramatta itself, baking in the bright Australian sun, as the camera moves straight to the prison church, whence issue the voices of the prisoners singing hymns. Cut to the governor's mansion where Birgel is languidly pursuing the governor's daughter."

At *Ufern*'s Berlin premiere there were an unprecedented seventy-eight curtain calls. The film established Sierck as UFA's most successful director and Zarah Leander as its biggest star. Sierck was immediately put to work on another vehicle for Leander, *La Habañera* (1937). This time she plays a Swedish woman who jumps ship in Puerto Rico (actually Tenerife) and marries a local plantation owner (Ferdinand Marian). Ten years later she is desperate to escape from her husband, the heat, and her life of idle affluence. A plague strikes the island and her husband tries to suppress news of it to protect his fruit exports. The plague kills him and the heroine is rescued by a young Swedish doctor (Karl Martell).

Sierck himself wrote the lyrics of Leander's songs, which are integral to the structure of the film. *La Habañera* and *Ufern*, Halliday says, are both "quite uncompromisingly tough critical films—the one directed against the British ruling class and colonialism . . . , the other against big business in the colonies. . . . At the same time, both films are shot in a style which is usually associated with the 'exotic': the nearest comparison being Sternberg, although several sequences, particularly a long cab ride in the fog in *Ufern*, unequivocally recall Ophüls. . . . The surprise of the films (quite apart from their excellence) is both political—to see what could still be made in Germany in 1937—and 'stylistic.'"

Other projects that Sierck worked on in Germany but was not allowed to realize included screen versions of Chekhov's *The Shooting Party* and William Faulkner's *Pylon*, both filmed later in Hollywood. Sierck also wanted to make a film about the Children's Crusade, a project he never did find backing for. In 1937 he coscripted Han Hinrich's *Liebling der Matrosen* and also collaborated on a script that he intended to direct himself, *Dreiklang*, which drew both on Turgenev's *First Love* and Pushkin's *The Shot*. Sierck actually completed the preparation of the latter but left Germany before shooting began; in the end, that script also was filmed by Hinrich.

It was in 1937 that UFA fell under direct state ownership. The already repressive and philistine atmosphere at the studio intensified. Sierck was also worried about his wife, the actress Hildegard Jary, who was Jewish. In December 1937 the Siercks left Germany, ostensibly to scout locations for a film called *Wilton's Zoo*. Actually they went via Zurich to Paris, where Sierck began what became a long search for work. In 1938 he spent two months on an abortive plan to turn

Renoir's *Une Partie de campagne* into a full-length feature. No other assignments came his way until the following year, when he supervised for France Suisse Film a picture called *Accord Final* (perhaps a remake of *Schlussakkord*?). The same year, 1939, he went to Holland to direct another obscure movie called *Boefje* and then received an invitation from Warner Brothers to come to the United States for a remake of *Zu Neuen Ufern*. He arrived in Hollywood before the end of 1939.

Nothing came of the *Ufern* project, and in 1940 Warner Brothers terminated Sierck's contract. He and his wife—mostly his wife—made an improbable stab at running a chicken farm in Southern California and, when that failed, grew alfalfa for a time. They had no close friends in the film industry apart from the actor George Sanders, who moved in with them for a year, but were acquainted with the Hollywood colony of German exiles that included Mann, Werfel, Reinhardt, Lubitsch, and Lang. Sierck disliked their almost obsessive contempt for everything American, preferring the company and friendship of the "ordinary Americans" they lived among, who treated them with a "simple creative generosity" that he and his wife remembered with gratitude and affection.

In 1941 Sierck made a short documentary about a wine-producing California monastery, and the same year he was invited to direct a light opera company in San Francisco. This project collapsed with Pearl Harbor and America's entry into World War II. Sierck's situation began to improve in 1942, when Columbia signed him as a writer. Though the studio at first kept him in demoralizing idleness, they did allow him to work as a director on loan to other producers. His first American feature—and the first credited to "Douglas Sirk"—was *Hitler's Madman* (1943). It was made for Angelus Pictures, a group set up by German emigrés and subsequently purchased by MGM.

Hitler's Madman was one of several contemporary films (including Lang's *Hangmen Also Die*) dealing with the Nazi massacre in 1942 of the people of Lidice, a small Czech village. The slaughter was ordered as a reprisal for the assassination by Czech resistance fighters of Reinhard Heydrich, the murderous Reichsprotektor of Bohemia and Moravia. Heydrich is played with satanic gusto by John Carradine and the film was shot by Eugene Shuftan (credited only as "technical consultant" because he was not then a member of the cinematographer's union). Reportedly much mauled by MGM, it was dismissed as "another occupied country picture."

Sirk's second Hollywood film was *Summer Storm* (1944), a far more personal and ambitious project. Columbia had still found nothing for him to do apart from one writing assignment, *Malta*, well received by the studio but then shelved. Nevertheless, when Sirk worked at MGM on some additional scenes for *Hitler's Madman* and was offered a directorial job there, Columbia refused to release him from his contract. *Summer Storm* was again made on loan to Angelus (for release by United Artists) and like its predecessor was shot (uncredited) by Shuftan.

Summer Storm is an adaptation of the script Sirk had written in Germany from *The Shooting Party,* Chekhov's only novel. The film (unlike the book) begins after the Russian Revolution, then goes into flashback to examine—through one man's confessional memoirs—the decadence of the aristocracy that made the Revolution inevitable. The man in question is Fedor Petrov (George Sanders), a provincial magistrate in the summer resort of Tenovo. Cynical, world-weary, and weak, Petrov is well aware that he and his class are doomed, but still capable of yearning for a past in which hope was still possible—and still capable of falling destructively in love with the avaricious *femme fatale* Olga (Linda Darnell). When he learns that she intends to take up with Count Volsky (Edward Everett Horton), he murders her, allowing her peasant husband to pay for the crime. Consumed by guilt and self-disgust, Petrov decides to confess, then loses his nerve. Ironically, he is killed while attempting to retrieve his confession.

Contemporary reviewers, anticipating nothing but embarrassment from a Hollywood version of Chekhov, reacted with pleased surprise. Some complained about Sirk's tampering with the original's narrative structure, but there was much praise for the excellence and appropriateness of the casting and the sets and for a "most delicate accuracy of atmosphere." Michael Stern, in his monograph on Sirk, analyzes "his first major American film" at considerable length. He points out that "the first shot following the titles is a close-up of a pair of feet walking hesitantly along a cobblestone street. Many of Douglas Sirk's films begin with similar shots, showing first the feet and then pulling back to reveal the context and the character. . . . This figure of style that characterizes Sirk's *mise-en-scène* immediately establishes the primacy of the camera's point of view. We are viewing a drama created in the camera's eye."

And this opening image tells us something else about Sirk's vision. Stern writes: "so much of Sirkian cinema works to express the impotence of human will . . . in the face of fate, accident, and . . . time. The tension between the charac-

ters' needs and desires to break free and the irre-
vocability of the human condition is what
energizes Sirkian melodrama. . . . We know
from this first shot that *Summer Storm* will be
a film about uncertainty, doubt, and choice."
The use of flashback and voice-over narration,
emphasizing that the events described are already past, the characters' hopes forever unfulfilled, is a "characteristically fatalistic dramatic
device" expressing Sirk's "European" pessimism.

Stern goes on to discuss Sirk's "ironically detached point of view toward his characters' folly. . . . Object-symbols like the rainbow, the
cupid, and the dance card that says 'I love you'
represent not what the director sees as signs of
true romance, but rather what the characters
see. . . . The dance card, which represents
Petrov's hope of what he might have been, is important not because it is Sirk's image of True
Love, but because it has become Petrov's."
Moreover, the dance card also plays a part in
Sirk's underlying political allegory: "The final
image of the film, showing . . . [it] among the
trash, is an almost literal rendering of Trotsky's
prophecy about the aristocracy winding up in
the dustbin of history."

A Scandal in Paris (1946), made for Arnold
Pressburger, recounts the rise of Eugène
François Vidocq from a life of crime in nineteenth-century Paris to become the first director
of the French Sûreté. The screenplay, based very
loosely on Vidocq's memoirs, was by Ellis St. Joseph and (uncredited) Sirk himself, who generally had a hand in his scripts. Shuftan (also and
again uncredited) worked on the photography
and another famous exile, the composer Hanns
Eisler, contributed to the score. George Sanders
starred as Vidocq—witty, cynical, but deeply
unsure of himself and his goals—with Akim
Tamiroff as his scoundrelly sidekick and straight
man.

This picaresque and deeply ironic film, again
using voice-over narration, had a mixed critical
reception and, according to Sirk, was "not very
successful. This was presumably because I
adopted a position which brought out the irony,
and that doesn't go down well at all with an
American audience." All the same, Sirk says that
St. Joseph's script contained "the most brilliant
dialogue" he ever worked with and "in fact if
you talk of art, I consider *A Scandal in Paris* my
best picture. . . . But it's a European film really—in a totally European style."

Two entertaining but more routine assignments followed. *Lured* (also known as *Personal
Column*, 1947) was the better of the two, a remake for Oakmont Pictures of a film made in
France by Robert Siodmak. It has Lucille Ball

working for the London vice squad early in this
century to trap a murderous white slaver with a
taste for Baudelaire. The excellent sets are by
Nicolai Remisoff, photography by William Daniels, and the notable cast includes George Sanders, Charles Coburn, Boris Karloff, Sir Cedric
Hardwicke, and Alan Mowbray. Leo Rosten's
script is bizarrely ironical, full of false leads and
quirky characters, but Howard Mandelbaum
complained that the latter "have eccentricities
rather than depth."

The same is true of *Sleep, My Love* (1948), another Rosten script. It is a thriller in the *Gaslight*
tradition, though with touches of comedy. Claudette Colbert stars as a rich woman whose husband (Don Ameche) is trying to drive her mad
for the benefit of his mistress (Hazel Brooks).
The reviewers were lukewarm, finding the movie "above the average in its own particular class"
but weakened by its threadbare plot and "many
laggard passages."

After *Sleep, My Love,* made for Triangle, Sirk
finally directed a film for his own studio, Columbia. It was a minor musical called *Slightly
French* (1949), with Dorothy Lamour as a Coney Island dancer passing herself off as a French
starlet. A much more interesting picture followed, *Shockproof* (1949), also for Columbia.
Patricia Knight plays a woman who (like Zarah
Leander in *Ufern*) takes the rap for the heel she
loves (John Baragrey). After five years she is pa-
roled to Cornel Wilde, who falls for her. Against
parole regulations they are married and, when
Baragrey threatens to wreck Wilde's political career by exposing them, she shoots him. A tense
flight from the police follows, and an improbable happy ending.

Shockproof was written as an original script
by Samuel Fuller. Sirk liked it because it contained "situations of love. Love that cannot be
fulfilled. Love in extreme circumstances." In
spite of major script changes (by Helen
Deutsch), studio reediting, and the imposed happy ending, it seemed to Michael Stern that "the
film nevertheless prefigures attitudes that were
to prevail in Sirk's work during the 1950s, and
it is the film's posture as a *folktale* . . . that
marks it as a precursor of Sirk's major forays into
'the folklore of American melodrama.'" Contemporary reviews were generally favorable,
praising the movie as "tense and hard-hitting,"
with "torrid romantic sequences" and some good
acting both by the principals and the supporting
players, especially Esther Minciotti as Wilde's
blind mother and Ann Shoemaker as a prison
psychiatrist.

However, Sirk had resented Columbia's tinkering with his film, and after it he left the stu-

dio, "completely fed up with Harry Cohn and really sick of the whole business." Washing his hands of Hollywood, he went back to Germany. He found the film industry there in a "catastrophic" state and after about a year returned to the United States "feeling very demoralized." Back in Hollywood he made one independent film, *The First Legion* (Sedif Pictures/United Artists, 1951). Scripted by Emmet Lavery from his own play, it was coproduced by Rudolph Joseph and Sirk himself.

The First Legion is set in a troubled Jesuit seminary in California. The imminent resignation of a disillusioned young priest is averted by an apparent miracle—the paralyzed Father Sierra (H. B. Warner) rises from his deathbed and walks. The seminary quickly becomes a minor Lourdes, where the halt and the sick flock in hope of healing. Father Charles Boyer, formerly a criminal lawyer, remains skeptical, however, and seems to be justified when an agnostic doctor confesses that he had engineered the famous miracle by medical means. But Terry Gilmartin (Barbara Rush), the doctor's crippled girlfriend, refuses to accept this reductionist account. She prays in the chapel—and is cured.

Sirk, who had set out "to merge melodrama with the religious film," says that he "wanted the picture to be very ironical." There is no doubt that he succeeded, manipulating the audience's responses by switching from the piety of the first miracle to a cynical exposure of it, and ending with an apparent reaffirmation of faith—the healing of Terry Gilmartin. However, this climactic scene is filmed with no attempt at conviction, as some contemporary reviewers remarked; it is indeed more ominous than uplifting, and modern critics agree that the effect was deliberate. The casting as Jesuit priests of actors better known as heavies, like Leo G. Carroll and George Zucco, was no doubt another covert example of Sirk's irony.

In 1950 Sirk joined Universal-International, where he spent the remainder of his career. His first picture there, a routine war movie called *Mystery Submarine* (1951), was actually released before *The First Legion*. More interesting was *Thunder on the Hill* (1951), an adaptation of Charlotte Hastings' play *Bonaventure* (the film's British title). The story is set in nineteenth-century England. Ann Blyth plays Valerie Carns, a woman condemned to hang for murder. En route to her execution, she and her guards are forced by floods to take refuge in a Norfolk convent. One of the nuns (Claudette Colbert) detects Valerie's innocence. Investigating in the face of growing repression from her superiors, she forces the real murderer—the convent's doc-

tor—into the open. Here, in the words of a National Film Theatre program, is "one of Sirk's recurrent themes: the discovery of 'reality' and the uncovering of pretense and deceit."

After that, Sirk embarked on a series of comedies for Universal. He says that his "idea at this time was to create a *comédie humaine* with little people, average people—samples from every period of American life. Now I had something in mind, a definite design; but of course I had to grab the opportunities as they came." He has described his early Universal comedies as *contes moraux*—"not so much moral tales, as tales about people's morality."

The series began with *The Lady Pays Off* (1951). Linda Darnell stars as America's "Teacher of the Year," a paragon in the classroom but an uptight failure in romance. On vacation in Reno, she gambles herself tipsily into debt to a tough casino owner (Stephen McNally), who happens to have a troublesome pre-teen daughter (Gigi Perreau) in need of a governess and/or stepmother. Thanks to the latter's precocious machinations, the unlikely couple are finally brought to the altar (in spite of the irruption of Virginia Field as "an old flame down to burn over the weekend"). Reviewers, it must be said, failed to recognize that they were in the presence of a new *comédie humaine*, finding the picture at best "far-fetched but funny," at worst "silly, sloppy, and vulgar."

There was even less enthusiasm for *Weekend With Father* (1951), in which Gigi Perreau plays a similarly manipulative role. To break the news of their impending marriage, widowed Patricia Neal and widower Van Heflin visit the summer camp in Maine where they have consigned their respective children. The news is not well received, and Heflin's daughter (Perreau) leads the other in maneuvers to wreck the romance. She succeeds but then, recognizing that the wretched couple do actually love one another, sets out to undo her work of destruction.

Most reviewers disliked the film, finding the comedy cruel and painfully broad, far beneath the talents of Heflin and Neal, and the children entirely loathsome. Sirk has explained that for him, "children are not . . . symbols of purity, far from it. Children are usually used at the ends of films to show that a new generation is beginning. In my films, I want to suggest exactly the opposite: I think it is the tragedies that begin again, always."

More easily identifiable as a *conte moral* was *Has Anybody Seen My Gal?* (1952), set in the 1920s. Aging multimillionaire Charles Coburn poses as a feckless artist and takes a room in the small-town home of Mrs. Blaisdell (Lynn Bari).

He had once loved the lady's mother and is looking for suitable heirs. When he tests them with an anonymous gift of $100,000, the results are disastrous. Mrs. Blaisdell and her husband—decent "ordinary Americans"—immediately put on grotesque airs. They move into a chilly mansion, trade their friendly mongrel for a poodle, and demand that their daughter (Piper Laurie) replace her soda-jerk boyfriend (Rock Hudson) with a spoiled playboy in a raccoon coat. In the end the Blaisdells go broke and drop their pretensions.

Sirk's first color film, and his first with Rock Hudson, it was generally well received and praised for its humor and period atmosphere. Fred Camper, in his article about Sirk in *Screen* (Summer 1971), writes that "Sirk makes systematic use of narrative situations which place an individual outside of an action which he would like to be a part of. Sirk is then able to explore the relationship between, really the distance between, the character and the action." The Coburn character in this film who can only relate to the Blaisdells "through the mask of the identity he has assumed," seems to Camper a particularly clear example of this.

This amusing fable was followed by a much more savage satire, *No Room for the Groom,* adapted by Joseph Hoffman from a novel by Darwin Teilhet. Small-town boy Alvah Morell (Tony Curtis) marries his girlfriend Lee (Piper Laurie) and spends the rest of the movie trying to consummate the union. First he is stricken with measles, then the army claims him. When he returns, he finds his house packed with a proliferating plague of freakish and greedy in-laws, all working at the local cement plant, a profitable industry because of the Korean War. The cement boom has turned the whole town into a ghastly industrial park. When Morell protests, he is called un-American and finally declared insane, so that his vineyards can be appropriated for a spur line to the cement plant. There is no happy ending to this "excruciating comedy," but total victory for the forces of greed and hypocrisy.

Another piece of small-town Americana followed in *Meet Me at the Fair* (1953), a musical comedy set at the turn of the century. Dan Dailey plays Doc Tilbee, an itinerant salesman of patent medicines and teller of tall tales—a good-hearted rogue who is not nearly as crooked as the "respectable" local politicians who are milking funds from the town's orphanage, and whose machinations he uncovers. There is a notable scene in which Tilbee introduces "the newest thing in the entertainment field"—a motion picture—and then slips in the revelatory pictures of conditions at the orphanage that awake the town's conscience. However, as Howard Mandelbaum wrote, Sirk on this occasion "neither deepens nor counteracts the heavy sentiment of the script," and the film suffers accordingly.

Take Me to Town (1953) is also set at the turn of the century, but this time amid the forests of Oregon. Ann Sheridan stars as Vermillion O'Toole, a woman with a past as colorful as her name. Sterling Hayden is a widowed lumberman and part-time preacher whose three young sons yearn for a mother. They sensibly choose Sheridan but, like Gigi Perreau in *The Lady Pays Off,* are then faced with the problem of imposing their wishes on their ostensibly ill-assorted elders. Sheridan quickly falls in with their plans when the sheriff comes looking for her, but has to cope single-handedly with an angry bear and a chorus of prim gossips before Hayden sees the light. The memorable ending has melodrama on stage and "real life" drama off it.

Michael Stern called this "one of Sirk's most likable forays into nostalgic Americana. . . . There is an 'openness' that characterizes the world of *Take Me to Town* which is atypical of Sirk's work. Characters are free to recreate their lives." It is "a picture of Eden before the fall . . . Sirk's own nostalgic looking backwards to an America he at one time imagined, an innocence that had vanished from the contemporary landscape. . . . Much of it is shot outdoors . . . freed of the visual oppression of staircases, furniture, and all of the things that represent social pressure in Sirk's other films." This was the first of his pictures to be produced by Ross Hunter, and the first photographed by Russell Metty, both to become frequent collaborators.

The "visual oppression" Stern mentions is very much in evidence in *All I Desire* (1953), another study of small-town life but this time a melodrama, set in Wisconsin early in the present century. Naomi Murdoch (Barbara Stanwyck) goes home to the husband and children she had deserted years earlier after a scandalous affair. At the end of her tether, she dreams of forgiveness and welcome, meeting instead hostility and vicious gossip in a house that is a claustrophobic maze of staircases and corridors. (The film's set designer, Russell A. Gausman, made important contributions to all of Sirk's Universal pictures; Bernard Herzbrun was his art director until Alexander Golitzen took his place on Sirk's team with *Sign of the Pagan.*) *All I Desire* was based on Carol Brink's novel *Stopover,* which ends with Naomi leaving home again, preferring the seedy life of a second-rate entertainer to what Jeanine Basinger called "the fishbowl existence of an American small town." The film's "happy" ending, with Naomi settling down and cheerfully accepting her responsibilities, was apparently imposed by Ross Hunter.

After this, the last of Sirk's *contes moraux*, came his only Western, *Taza, Son of Cochise*. Taza (Rock Hudson) becomes chief of his Apache tribe upon the death of his father, at a time when the American government is shamelessly trampling on his people's few remaining rights. Unlike his militant brother, who joins the rebel Geronimo, Taza argues for peaceful coexistence and then, when Washington steps up the pressure, for surrender as the only alternative to genocide. Written by Sirk's favorite scriptwriter, George Zuckerman, and shot by Metty in Technicolor and 3-D, the movie was a flop, its vacillating hero seeming more like a product of Old World moral exhaustion than of the primitive American West.

In the five years between 1954 and 1959, Sirk made, among other films, a series of tear-jerking melodramas that were commercially immensely successful. Originally scorned by the reviewers, they were rediscovered by *auteurist* critics and eventually identified as works that in their thematic and stylistic excesses ritualized the clichés of the "woman's picture" and deliberately subverted its inanely optimistic materialism, sexism, and sentimentality.

If this reading is correct, Michael Stern suggests, its rationale can be traced back through Sirk's career as far as the 1920s when, the director told Stern, he and his colleagues in the disillusioned European theatre "were looking for something completely different" from the available postwar modes and "there arose a belief in style—and in banality."

Stern says that "like e. e. cummings, Marcel Duchamp, and Bertolt Brecht, Sirk sought in popular culture a source from which high art could draw the energy it needed to escape the burden of a dead or dying culture. . . . The full-blown melodramas for which he is best known today are in this sense the fulfillment of the general search during the 1920s for an art that would defy the tradition-bound and rational strictures by which society allows art to exist. His definitive melodramas—charged as they are with coincidence, artifice, and magic—are, along with Dada and Pop art, a major rebellion against the repressive qualities of acceptable culture and good taste." Most of these "definitive melodramas" were produced by Ross Hunter and photographed by Russell Metty, and four of them starred Rock Hudson.

The series began with *Magnificent Obsession* (1954), a remake of John M. Stahl's 1935 adapta-

tion of the novel by Lloyd C. Douglas. In Sirk's version, scripted by Robert Blees, Hudson plays Bob Merrick who, after the death of his rich and dynamic father, abandons his medical studies and becomes a recklessly self-destructive playboy. At the beginning of the film, Merrick has an almost fatal accident in his speedboat. The respirator used to resuscitate him is also needed by Dr. Wayne Phillips, saintly leader of an underground religious organization devoted to doing good by stealth. Deprived of the respirator, the good doctor dies. Merrick falls in love with his widow Helen (Jane Wyman) but precipitates another accident in which Helen is blinded.

Instructed by Dr. Phillips' disciple Edward Randolph (Otto Kruger), Merrick becomes a devotee of Phillips' "magnificent obsession" —and a great eye surgeon. He seeks Helen out in Switzerland and cares for her under an assumed name (unaware that she "sees" through his masquerade). Finally, when Helen is ill and dying, Merrick draws on the "infinite power" his new faith has given him and performs a miraculous operation, not only saving the life of his beloved but restoring her sight.

Sirk says that he was "attracted by something irrational" in the script of *Magnificent Obsession*. "Something mad, in a way—well, obsessed." As he had with *Schlussakkord*, Sirk made no attempt to subdue the "craziness" of the script but instead embraced it, dressing it, as Michael Stern says, in "a system of signs with meaning that stand for an absurdist vision." The nonnaturalistic lighting, the violent colors, the restless camerawork, and the unconvincing back projection, Stern maintains, "are an assertion of directorial power. . . . the director/artist is a god who denies his characters clear perception, free will, or effective movement. . . . The absolute inability of his main characters to act in a positive, potent manner to alter their own lives is an expression of Sirk's own sense that 'drama is impossible today. Drama used to be the belief in guilt, and in a higher order. This absolutely cruel didactic is . . . unacceptable for us moderns. But melodrama has kept it. You are caged. In melodrama you have earthly prisons rather than godly creations.'"

Elsewhere Sirk says that his use of "almost surrealistic" lighting operates as a Brechtian device: "You must never forget that this is not reality. This is a motion picture. It is a tale you are telling." The absurd and tragic gap between appearance and reality is indeed a central theme in Sirk's work, evinced in his fondness for mirrors, for scenes shot through windows—"through a glass darkly"—and by his preoccupation with characters who are blind. In a much-quoted in-

terview in *Cahiers du Cinéma* (April 1967), he
said that "everything, even life, is eventually
taken away from you. You cannot feel, cannot
touch the expression, you can only reach its reflections. If you try to grasp happiness itself,
your fingers only meet a surface of glass, because
happiness has no existence of its own, and probably exists, if only by the simple fact that it can
be destroyed." And Martin Rubin has said that
"Sirk depicts metaphorically blind characters
stumbling about a mirror-world of deceptive appearances, a modern equivalent of Plato's
cave. . . . Sirk is admired by *cinéastes* today
for . . . his profound comprehension of the per-
ceptual causes of twentieth-century anxiety."

If *Magnificent Obsession* is the "craziest" of
Sirk's films, it is also, according to Stern, "the
Sirk film laced most richly with classic motifs
and patterns—and for that reason, one of the
most difficult to penetrate." This is borne out by
Sirk's account of the film in *Sirk on Sirk,* his
book-length interview with Jon Halliday. "This
saintly woman's husband, Dr. Phillips, dies so
another can live. It is Euripidean irony—the
theme of *Alcestis.*" It is also possible to read the
film in classical and Freudian terms as a version
of the Oedipus myth, with Merrick killing his
godlike "father" (Dr. Phillips) and thereby gaining sufficient potency to marry the "father's"
wife. Or again, as Stern says, it can be seen as "a
commentary on the role of the artist in a world
where God has died."

After this, it would have been interesting to
see what Sirk would have made of his proposal
to film Marlowe's *Tamburlaine*. However, that
project was diluted by Universal into *Sign of the
Pagan* (1955), a CinemaScope historical epic
about Attila the Hun. The result was generally
enjoyed as "a first-class example of good
hokum," benefiting greatly from Jack Palance's
striking performance as Attila.

Another costume picture followed, *Captain
Lightfoot* (1955), with Rock Hudson as a dashing
Irish outlaw who winds up as a revolutionary
leader. Shot on location in Ireland by Irving
Glassberg, the movie has a good script by W. R.
Burnett and Oscar Brodney. According to a National Film Theatre program note, "the revolution is seen as a merry, almost lighthearted
affair, even though terrible things happen. . . .
Sirk plays the film mainly for comedy, but also
for true love, a sure sign he is far away from contemporary America."

There Sirk returned for the second of his major melodramas, *All That Heaven Allows* (1956),
a studio-inspired follow-up to *Magnificent
Obsession,* with the same stars. Set in suburban
Connecticut, it casts Jane Wyman as Carey

Scott, a widow who falls in love with Ron Kirby
(Rock Hudson), a young gardener on her estate.
Unlike her politely oppressive, spiritually empty
social equals, Ron is a free man, in touch with
nature—as someone says, he has never read
Walden, "he just lives it." Carey's age, her snobbish friends, her dead husband, and her rigidly
conventional children are all marshaled against
this unorthodox love, and she gives it up. Only
then does she understand that love is more important than convention; fortunately for the box
office, this revelation does not come too late.

Less "crazy" in its subject matter than
Magnificent Obsession, the film is sharper in its
social observation and more naturalistic and accessible in its style. It contains one of Sirk's most
admired sequences—the scene in which Carey,
having resigned herself to loveless solitude, is rewarded by her ghastly children with the gift of
a television set. The TV is wheeled in and the
camera dollies up to its screen, where we see
Carey's reflection, trapped, ghostlike, alone—
and the salesman assures her that in this box she
will find "drama . . . comedy . . . life's parade at your fingertips." Fred Camper called
this "one of the most chilling moments in any
film."

Jon Halliday wrote that "on the surface,
Heaven is a standard women's magazine weepie—mawkish, mindless, and reactionary. Yet
just beneath the surface it is a tough attack on
the moralism of petit bourgeois America." Jean-
Pierre Coursodon, in *American Directors* (Volume 1, 1983), takes issue with Halliday, arguing
that on the contrary the film's social criticism is
"quite overtly made its central theme. . . . [It]
is a wonderfully naive and earnest picture.
There is nothing ambiguous about its message,
and one does it a disservice by pretending otherwise. While watching the film, one feels no condescension toward the genre, which is perhaps
the greatest praise it could receive."

The director Rainer Werner Fassbinder, who
greatly admired Sirk, discussed this, among
other films, in an article first published in German in *Film und Fernsehen* (February 1971)
and translated by Halliday and Laura Mulvey:
"Women *think* in Sirk's films. . . . Usually
women are [shown] always reacting, doing what
women are supposed to do, but in Sirk they
think. . . . Then, in Sirk, people are always
placed in rooms already heavily marked by their
social situation. The rooms are incredibly exact.
In Jane's house there is only one way in which
one could possible move. Only certain kinds of
sentences could come to mind when wanting to
say something. . . . When Jane goes to another
house, to Rock's, for instance, would she be able

to change? . . . That's why the happy ending is not one. Jane fits into her own home better than she fits into Rock's."

Sirk worked with Ross Hunter and Metty but not Rock Hudson on his next picture, *There's Always Tomorrow* (1956), scripted by Bernard C. Schoenfeld from a story by Ursula Parrott. Fred MacMurray plays Clifford Groves, owner of a California toy factory, affluent, married, and the father of three children. On the face of it he has realized the American Dream, and yet he is not happy. A man of some sensibility, his creativity has been channeled into business administration; he cannot communicate with his mindless wife (Joan Bennett); his children are prying Sirkian monsters. He lives in an expensive house so cluttered and claustrophobic that banisters and furniture are forever cutting across the lines of communication. When he reencounters a former girlfriend, Norma Vail (Barbara Stanwyck) and realizes that she still loves him, a new and richer life seems possible. They have a brief interlude of happiness, but then Norma, failing to perceive the emptiness of his life, decides that his family is more important than her love and flies back to New York.

Groves' wife has never suspected his romantic yearnings and, with Norma gone, the household returns to "normal." All that has changed is that Groves now fully recognizes the bleak meaninglessness of his life. As Jeanine Basinger wrote (*Bright Lights* Winter 1977–1978), this dark fairy tale "ends with the Sleeping Beauty having kissed the prince awake into his own fantasy world. Her kiss is a romantic curse. He remains behind, himself forever trapped in the gilded cage of American middle-class life."

His situation at the end of the film is expressed in a famous image. Norma has gone and Groves is alone in his office except for the company's newest product, "Rex, the walkie-talkie robot man." Rex is shown in huge close-up, marching towards the camera, with Groves staring hopelessly out through the bars of the window frame at rain falling on the gray industrial landscape: like Rex, he will go on marching mechanically along a set path until his springs give out. "In tragedy," Sirk says, "the life always ends. By being dead, the hero is at the same time rescued from life's troubles. In melodrama he lives on— in an unhappy happy end."

The most widely admired of Sirk's melodramas followed, *Written on the Wind* (1957). It was produced by Albert Zugsmith, photographed by Metty, and scripted—from a novel by Robert Wilder—by George Zuckerman. In the flamboyantly brilliant scene that opens the film, a car screeches up the drive of a Colonial-style mansion in Texas. A drunken man staggers out and enters the house in a flurry of dead leaves, observed by a woman in an upstairs window. The camera pans on a desk calendar and, as the leaves swirl in the great entrance hall, the leaves of the calendar blow back to the beginning of the story.

The man is Kyle Hadley (Robert Stack), another of Sirk's self-destructive, speed-hungry playboys. Heir to the millions pumped up by the oil derricks that march across the barren landscape, he is rootless, violent, and desperately insecure. His sister Marylee is as tormented as himself, expressing her self-contempt in casual sexual liaisons. Kyle finds a measure of peace and self-esteem when he marries Lucy Moore (Lauren Bacall), an elegant New Yorker, and brings her home.

Marylee loves Kyle's best friend Mitch Wayne (Rock Hudson), who is everything the Hadleys are not—poor, decent, and serene. When she can't get Mitch, Marylee takes her revenge by hinting falsely that he has cuckolded Kyle—that he is the real father of the child that Lucy is pregnant with. This confirms Kyle's fear that he is impotent, and in his agony he beats up Lucy, destroying their child. Mitch throws him out of the house and, after more drinking, Kyle returns, as we saw at the beginning of the movie. Seeking to murder Mitch, Kyle is accidentally killed himself. Mitch is charged with murder but is exonerated by a reformed Marylee. In the end Mitch and Lucy drive away together, leaving Marylee to rule the Hadley empire.

Written on the Wind, as Michael Stern writes, "is a wildly mannered film, characterized by formal extravagance in almost every respect. The excessive look of the film functions as in a dream—or as in surrealist art—to conjure states of being below the level of consciousness." Sirk himself says that "almost throughout the film I used deep-focus lenses whch have the effect of giving a harshness to the objects and a kind of enamelled, hard surface to the colors. I wanted this to bring out the inner violence, the energy of the characters which is all inside them and can't break through."

"In no film is the circularity of Sirk's dramatic vision more clear," Stern writes. "The end is revealed at the beginning . . . and the plot is therefore a circle . . . telling us that for Kyle Hadley there is no way out." Stern goes on to quote many examples of the way in which "the circular motif runs throughout the film"—for instance in the juke joint scene just before Kyle's fateful return to the house, when we watch the balls in a pinball machine ricochet around their obstacle course with meaningless noise and violence (like Kyle himself), then come to rest where they began.

Sirk says that "it has been proven medically that if you think too much of the sex act, you lose your sexual powers." For Michael Stern, "the direct relationship Sirk creates between obsession with sex and impotence is the dialectic of the film," and "the sexual nature of the plot and characters is woven into a metonymic pattern of signs, gestures, and kinetic rhythms all of which function as a sexual language." Thus, "the first images of the film show a darkened landscape and phallic oil wells . . . that seem to haunt the film." At the end, Marylee is sitting at her father's desk, dressed in a blue-gray business suit like her father's, clutching a small model of an oil derrick: "it represents the unlimited energy of the Hadley dynasty. But we realize that for Marylee the oil well is a mockingly inadequate phallus. The Hadley dynasty has come to an end."

R. W. Fassbinder was one of a number of critics who recognized that "in *Written on the Wind* the good, the 'normal,' the 'beautiful' are always utterly revolting; the evil, the weak, the dissolute arouse one's compassion." Fassbinder goes on to discuss the Hadley mansion, "governed, so to speak, by one huge staircase. And mirrors. And endless flowers. And gold. And coldness. . . . Human emotions have to blossom in the strangest ways in the house Douglas Sirk has built for the Hadleys. Sirk's lighting is always as unnatural as possible. Shadows where there shouldn't be any make feelings plausible which one would rather have left unacknowledged. In the same way, the camera angles in *Written on the Wind* are almost always tilted, mostly from below, so that strange things happen on screen, not just in the spectator's head. Douglas Sirk's films liberate your head."

Battle Hymn (1957) tells the true story of Colonel Dean Hess (Rock Hudson). As a pilot in World War II, Hess accidentally bombed a German orphanage. During the Korean War, he expiated his guilt by airlifting hundreds of children to safety and establishing an orphanage for them. Hollis Alpert, who pointed out that the film "could easily have been called *Magnificent Obsession at War*," praised "some good flying scenes, and some taut moments," but complained (like most reviewers) about the movie's excessive sentimentality.

Sirk's second remake of a John Stahl melodrama followed. *Interlude* (1957) was based on Stahl's *When Tomorrow Comes* (1939), but transported the story from New York to Munich, where American cultural officer June Allyson falls in love with an Italian conductor (Rossano Brazzi) whose wife is insane. Tim Pulleine wrote that the remake lacked "the mutedly screwball comedy" of Stahl's version, while "the original's precise formal structure, with the action concentrated within a single weekend, is dissipated by a scenario that confusedly incorporates not only a swath of local colour but also an indeterminate period of time." Others found Allyson and Brazzi poor substitutes for Stahl's stars, Irene Dunne and Charles Boyer.

Sirk had first read William Faulkner's novel *Pylon* in 1936 and wanted to film it while he was still working in Germany. UFA turned it down, worried by its black pessimism at a time when the Nazi regime was demanding positive thinking. Sirk had better luck with Universal and made his film there in 1958 as *The Tarnished Angels*, with Albert Zugsmith as his producer and a script by George Zukerman that gave Faulkner's elusive novel—a stylistic experiment seeking to capture "a folklore of speed"—a more solid dramatic (or melodramatic) structure.

The film, shot by Irving Glassberg in black and white, is set in New Orleans during the Depression. The story is told in flashback by newspaper reporter Burke Devlin (Rock Hudson). He had set out to write a story about a team of stunt flyers: World War I ace Roger Shumann (Robert Stack), his parachutist wife Laverne (Dorothy Malone), and their mechanic-sidekick (Jack Carson). Devlin had fallen in love with these "crazy gypsies of the air," seeing them as a new breed of people with "crankcase oil in their veins." He had tried to gain acceptance in their world but failed, lacking the necessary madness. Laverne is virtually prostituted to an airplane dealer to further her husband's obsession with flying, and in the end Shumann goes up in a dangerously damaged plane and is killed. As James McCourt wrote in *Film Comment* (November–December 1975), "the flyers . . . cannot live on the ground. . . . When they betray themselves as human beings, they vanish."

McCourt goes on: "Working in black-and-white, shooting planes against worried skies, planes zooming around pylons in lunatic aeriel carousel, shooting Malone, blown into the wind and hurtling toward earth until the parachute opens, Sirk is right in the realm of sudden and violent movement he favors. The scenes on the ground, crowded, crammed rooms eerily lit and as indebted to the grotesque in German cinema as anything he has done, point up the ironic treatment of the desperate, not-truly-heroic fliers—the Sirkian alternative response to, say, Hawks' *Dawn Patrol* or Walsh's *Fighter Squadron,* where the men prove themselves heroically. The tarnished angels don't prove a thing."

Michael Stern describes *The Tarnished Angels* as "a *danse macabre,* a vision of hell populated with animated corpses." He points out that "the race around the pylons which thrills the audience and forms the centerpiece of their festivity is also a ritualized invocation of death. The Mardi Gras itself, a time for merrymaking, is visualized as a hellish inversion of happiness peopled with death's heads and leering clowns. . . . The most tender moment of the film—a scene in which it appears that Laverne and Burke Devlin are really making contact . . . is violently interrupted by a death's head bursting in their door. . . . It is a devastating moment, signifying death's ascendance and life's impotence in its face." Jon Halliday called this "outstandingly the best adaptation to the screen of any Faulkner, acknowledged as such by Faulkner himself."

Another adaptation followed, *A Time to Love and a Time to Die* (1958), scripted by Orin Jannings from the World War II novel by Erich Maria Remarque and shot by Metty on location in Germany. It opens on Germany's Russian front, where infantryman Ernst Graeber (John Gavin) is sickened by the cold-blooded shooting of Russian prisoners. Returning on leave to Berlin, he meets and falls in love with Elizabeth (Lilo Pulver). They marry and have an interlude of great happiness amid the ruins and madness of the dying city. Returning to the front, he receives a letter from his wife telling him that she is expecting a baby. He is ordered by an SS officer to shoot four captured guerrillas but instead, liberated by love, he kills the officer and releases the prisoners, throwing away his rifle. One of the Russians retrieves the gun and kills him.

Although this was not quite Sirk's last film, it seemed to Jean-Pierre Coursodon that it "deserves to be remembered as his fitting farewell to the cinema. One of his most balanced and controlled, yet most moving films, it brings together the diverging threads of his work, reconciles the restraint and the madness. . . . Sirk's visual style here is bare and sober, far removed from the baroque flamboyance of *Written on the Wind.* . . . With muted compassion and immense tenderness, Sirk simply records a few brief moments of happiness snatched from the engulfing darkness by two young people. . . . Fate always pulls the strings in Sirk's cinema. In *A Time,* individual fate is played against the background of history, of an entire country's fate. . . . The poetry of Sirk's cinema is indeed a poetry of happiness threatened, crumbling, or destroyed, and each of his films . . . is his *Love Among the Ruins.*"

Sirk ended his Hollywood career with *Imitation of Life* (1959), his third remake of a John Stahl melodrama, based on the novel by Fannie Hurst but considerably modified. Whereas Hurst's heroine made a fortune by marketing pancakes from her black friend's secret recipe, Lora Meredith (Lana Turner) fights her way to success in the fantasy world of the theatre, neglecting her daughter (Sandra Dee) and her faithful admirer Steve Archer (John Gavin).

Lora's black friend Annie Johnson (Juanita Moore) is no longer her business partner but her servant. Susan Kohner very nearly stole the picture as Annie's rebellious daughter Sara Jane, who disowns her mother and tries to pass as white—also in show business, but in its lowest and most demeaning reaches. Heartbroken, Annie dies, and her funeral brings Sara Jane to repentance, Lora and Steve to reconciliation. (But, Sirk said, "you don't believe in the happy ending, and you're not really supposed to.")

Villified by contemporary reviewers as "about the wettest wallow in cheap sentiment that Hollywood has sent us for years" and an "almost unbelievably ridiculous film," it has since been hailed by Sirk's admirers as "a great crazy movie about life and death" (Fassbinder); "an astonishing demonstration of lighting, camera movement and angles" (National Film Theatre); and "a grand, diffuse, and elaborate receptacle for everything that composed the body of his previous work in America" (Michael Stern). Many have recognized that the film's true subject is not Lora Meredith but Annie and her daughter, and Sirk has been praised for covert hints that Sara Jane was justified in repudiating her mother's servile devotion to her white employer.

Not everyone shares this enthusiasm for Sirk's *Imitation of Life.* Jean-Pierre Coursodon, for one, preferred Stahl's "quiet, almost unprepossessing" version to "Sirk's slick, deliberate hysteria." Coursodon also puts in a heretical word in favor of some of Sirk's early work, suggesting that "the taste and restraint he brought to so many modest projects is as effective as, and in some ways more appealing than, the hysterical quality critics admire in his most famous pictures. It *is* possible to prefer *All That Heaven Allows* to *Imitation of Life.*"

Made for around $1.5 million, *Imitation of Life* grossed a reported $15 million, making it the most successful movie in Universal's history. And at that point, perhaps because he could afford to, Sirk terminated his contract with the studio. He turned his attention to an independent production, a biographical film about the painter Utrillo. This project was abandoned when Sirk fell ill, and he and his wife then moved to Lugano, Switzerland, where they settled.

Sirk's rediscovery began in the early 1960s,

when the *auteurist* critic Andrew Sarris wrote that "time, if nothing else, will vindicate Douglas Sirk as it has already vindicated Josef von Sternberg. Formal excellence and visual wit are seldom as appreciated at first glance as are the topical sensations of the hour." In 1972 came Jon Halliday's book-length interview, *Sirk on Sirk,* which first revealed the sophistication of the director's vision. The same year Halliday and Laura Mulvey published an anthology of critical approaches to Sirk's work for a major retrospective at the Edinburgh Film Festival that was repeated at the National Film Theatre. Once dismissed as a vulgar purveyor of the cinema's most despised genre, Sirk is now as Michael Stern says, generally recognized as "a major, unique figure among the last classical directors in the swan song decade of Hollywood."

In 1960–1969, resuming the name Detlef Sierck, the director staged plays in Munich and Hamburg. In the late 1970s (of the century and of his own life) he supervised students at the Munich Academy of Film and Television in the making of three short films based on one-act plays. These were *Sprich zu mir wie die regen* (1975, 14 minutes), based on Tennessee Williams' *Talk to Me Like the Rain; Sylvestersnacht* (*New Year's Eve,* 1977; 18 minutes), from a play by Arthur Schnitzler, with Hanna Schygulla and Christian Berkel; and *Bourbon Street Blues* (1978, 24 minutes), from Tennessee Williams' *The Lady of Larkspur Street.*

The last is actually credited to Sirk as director. It features Annemarie Düringer as a woman rather like Blanche DuBois in *A Streetcar Named Desire.* Tom Allen wrote that "Düringer's revelatory confrontations with a dressing mirror, a mercenary landlady (Doris Schade), and a compassionately mocking tenant (Fassbinder) begin under sunlight pouring through French shutters and end in a dusk lit by Tiffany lamps and garish neon signs. The Sirkian magic of characters transfigured by exquisitely stylistic artifice is once again resurrected."

FILMS (features only): April April (Dutch version, 'T was éen April, with Jacques van Pol), 1935; Das Mädchen vom Moorhof (The Girl From the Marshcroft), 1935; Stützen der Gesellschaft (Pillars of Society), 1935; Schlussakkord (Final Accord/Ninth Symphony), 1936; Das Hofkonzert (French version, La Chanson du souvenir) 1936; Zu Neuen Ufern (To New Shores/Life Begins Anew), 1937; La Habañera, 1937; Boefje, 1939; Hitler's Madman, 1943; Summer Storm, 1944; A Scandal in Paris, 1946; Lured/Personal Column, 1947; Sleep, My Love, 1948; Slightly French, 1949; Shockproof, 1949; Mystery Submarine, 1951; The First Legion, 1951; Thunder on the Hill (U.K., Bonaventure), 1951; The Lady Pays Off, 1951; Weekend With Father, 1951; Has Anybody Seen My Gal?,

1952; No Room for the Groom, 1952; Meet Me at the Fair, 1953; Take Me to Town, 1953; All I Desire, 1953; Taza, Son of Cochise, 1954; Magnificent Obsession, 1954; Sign of the Pagan, 1955; Captain Lightfoot, 1955; All That Heaven Allows, 1956; There's Always Tomorrow, 1956; Written on the Wind, 1957; Battle Hymn, 1957; Interlude, 1957; The Tarnished Angels, 1958; A Time to Love and a Time to Die, 1958; Imitation of Life, 1959.

ABOUT: Belton, J. Cinema Stylists, 1983; Coursodon, J.-P. American Directors, volume 1, 1983; Halliday, J. Sirk on Sirk, 1972; Hernandez, M. Douglas Sirk, 1979 (in Spanish); Mulvey, L. and Halliday, J. (eds.) Douglas Sirk, 1972; Stern, M. Douglas Sirk, 1979. *Periodicals*—Australian Journal of Screen Theory 3 1977; Bright Lights Winter 1977–1978 (Sirk issue); Cahiers de la Cinémathèque Spring 1981; Cahiers du Cinéma April 1967, October 1978; Cinema (Switzerland) August 1978 (Sirk issue); Cinéma (France) October 1978; Cinema Journal Summer 1983; Cinématographe July–August 1982; Film Comment Summer 1972, November–December 1975, July–August 1978, March–April 1980; Filmkritik November 1973; Film Notebooks Winter 1977; Literature-Film Quarterly Summer 1977; Monthly Film Bulletin November 1981; Monogram 4 1972; Movie Winter 1977–1978; National Film Theatre Booklet August–September 1972; Positif April 1972, September 1972, July–August 1976, September 1982 (Sirk issue); Screen Summer 1971 (Sirk issue), Winter 1972–1973; Velvet Light Trap Fall 1976; Wide Angle 4 1980.

*SJÖBERG, ALF (June 21, 1903–April 17, 1980), Swedish film and theatre director and scenarist, was born in Stockholm a few years after the birth of the Swedish film industry. As a schoolboy Sjöberg's loyalties were divided between the cinema and the theatre—he acted in and even directed high school plays, at the same time filling hundreds of notebooks with "treatments" for imaginary movies.

From 1923 to 1925, Sjöberg studied at the famous drama school of the Royal Dramatic Theatre in Stockholm (where he was a contemporary of Greta Gustafsson, later better known as Greta Garbo). He was a stage actor until 1929, but retained his interest in the film and was powerfully impressed and influenced by the early works of Eisenstein, which he saw in 1928.

In 1929, after working for a time as a radio producer, Sjöberg wrote and directed his own first film, *Den starkaste (The Strongest),* which he made in collaboration with Axel Lindholm. It is a dramatic tale with a strong flavor of documentary about the Greenland farmers who every winter left their lands to hunt seal and bear. The story centers on one of these seasonal hunters, Ole (Anders Henrikson), and his rivalry with the stranger Gustaf (Bengt Djurberg) for the

ALF SJÖBERG

hand of Ingeborg (Gunn Holmquist) and for supremacy on the hunting grounds, where "right
belongs to the strongest." The location work was
directed by Lindholm, the studio scenes by
Sjöberg, with Lindholm and Åke Dahlquist sharing the photography.

The Strongest was widely acclaimed for the
excellence of its characterization, the beauty of
its images, and the "mesmeric" rhythms of its
editing, which in the climactic bear hunt was
said to show a "grace and fluidity" worthy of
Eisenstein. The film seemed to presage "a new
realism, a vigorously matter-of-fact and laconic
film style," and it established Sjöberg at once as
a director of great promise. But *The Strongest*
was one of the last silent films made in Sweden,
and with the coming of sound the native cinema
sank into mediocrity. Sjöberg could not or would
not lend his talents to the kitsch that filled the
Swedish studios throughout the 1930s, and made
no more movies for ten years.

Instead he pursued his career in the theatre,
where he became the most respected director of
his generation. His work in that field was enriched by his interest in social and political
developments, as well as in avant-garde movements in all the arts, and not only in Scandinavia.
He traveled widely, visiting England, Germany,
France, Russia, and Hungary. In Paris he was
fascinated by the theatre of Russian emigrés, especially the Jewish Habima theatre, and in Russia itself he saw and admired Meyerhold's work.
Beginning in 1931, he was the principal director
at the Royal Dramatic Theatre and taught in its
drama school.

By the mid-1930s there were intermittent

signs of a revival in the Swedish cinema, but
most historians date the real beginning of the renaissance from Sjöberg's return to filmmaking in
1940. The picture he made then was *Med livet
som insats (They Staked Their Lives)*, a remake
of a Finnish film which, under the guise of an
adventure story, dealt with tyranny and resistance in an unspecified Baltic country. Completed just after the outbreak of World War II, it was
premiered in January 1940. It is an intensely fatalistic film, with the resistance workers too busy
quarreling among themselves in gloomy rooms
to offer much hope of liberation. Edgardo Cozarinsky suggests that it struck its first Swedish
audiences "as almost a foreign film. Not only because of the enduring Swedish tradition that
equates political subject matter with foreign settings . . . but also because its visual elaboration,
eclectic and brilliant, looked unlike any Swedish
film of the period."

If Sjöberg's first picture had shown the influence of Eisenstein, *They Staked Their Lives*
seemed more in the mood of French "poetic
realism," reminding some critics of the
Carné-Prévert films of the 1930s. Many were
disappointed, finding the movie altogether less
cinematic and more theatrical than *The
Strongest*, but Rune Waldekranz regards it as "a
challenging and provocative experiment. A film
of ideas, the first one for decades. . . . With its
curious blend of overemphasized camera-
consciousness and stagey dramatic sequences,
They Staked Their Lives today may appear in
retrospect as an attempt to revive the film expressionism of the twenties. But in January 1940,
Sjöberg's appearance as a film director was a signal of rebellion against the flat conventionalism
of Swedish film production."

Den blomstertid (Blossom Time, 1940) tells a
story about a teacher on one of Sweden's western
islands, her obsession with her dead lover, and
her eventual realization that life and love go on.
The content is novelettish, but there was praise
for Sjöberg's effective use of his island setting
and of light and shade. A later critic, Edgardo
Cozarinsky, detects irony in the director's handling of his material both in this film and in
Hem från Babylon (Home From Babylon, 1941),
whose hero, having had his fill of adventure in
foreign lands, finds when he at last gets home
that his patient fiancée is now eager to embrace
the wandering life. "Both films deal with Bo-
vary-like cases of self-delusion," Cozarinsky
says; "both are ironical in espousing conventions
of cheap fiction only to expose them, as it were,
between quotation marks; both present Sweden
as an island, diseased with the very neutrality
that protects it."

A much more considerable work followed in 1942. *Himlaspelet (The Road to Heaven)* was adapted by Sjöberg and Rune Lindström from the latter's verse drama—a modern morality play that is or was performed annually at Leksand in the province of Dalarna, where it is set. Lindström himself appears in the film as the naive but determined young peasant Mats Ersson, whose innocent fiancée is killed as a witch. Inspired by the primitive religious paintings in the local church, Mats sets off on the "road to Heaven" to get this injustice righted by God himself, but is waylaid by the Devil and lured into the City of Desire. He wastes his life in the pursuit of pleasure and power, grows rich and heartless, but is saved on his deathbed by the Good Father (Anders Henrikson) who has always watched over him. He dies repentant and is gathered up into a flowery paradise where his lost beloved awaits him.

The play had achieved the simple piety of a piece of folk art and it seemed to most critics that this quality had been captured in the screen version, thanks partly to Lindström's extraordinary performance, partly to Sjöberg's visual borrowings from the peasant art of Dalarna (also used by Bergman, but to very different effect, in *The Seventh Seal*). In this film, wrote Rune Waldekranz, "the folklore and the poetic atmosphere of the old Sjöström pictures arose anew, but in a modern and dynamic form"—Sjöberg has united "the realistic and allegorically stylised elements of his film language into a clear and expressive form."

Many Swedish critics regard *The Road to Heaven* as "one of the finest products of the Scandinavian cinema between 1920 and 1950," and as an assertion (in the face of the Nazi occupation) of traditional Swedish values. Forsyth Hardy said that it "helped to give spiritual status to the revival of the Swedish cinema." But in this film, as in the two that preceded it, Edgardo Cozarinsky found ironies that eluded other critics, insisting that it was in fact "utterly sceptical, its underlying world image . . . an absurd and existentialist one."

Kungajakt (The Royal Hunt, 1943) is another veiled attack on totalitarianism—an exciting and often funny swashbuckler set in the latter part of the eighteenth century, when Russia was seeking to overthrow the Swedish king Gustav III. "No other Swedish director," wrote Peter Cowie, "could evoke the extremes of eighteenth-century life so well as Sjöberg does in the opening sequences, with, at first, a duel being fought under a bright afternoon sun and the patronising eyes of the courtiers, and then a tavern brawl set in motion by night, with gnarled faces looming out

of the smoke and the shadows. The hunt itself is a regal centre-piece, a Watteau canvas come to life as the white horses spread over the fields to the accompaniment of Lars-Erik Larsson's martial music."

It was Sjöberg's next film that established him as an international figure, at the same time directing world attention to the revival in the Swedish cinema. Significantly enough, it was the first picture scripted by its assistant director, Ingmar Bergman. *Hets (Torment/Frenzy*, 1944) is set in contemporary Stockholm, where Jan-Erik (Alf Kjellin) is studying for his matriculation examinations in a school that has a good deal in common with a concentration camp. There he is harassed and humiliated by his sadistic Latin teacher, known as Caligula (Stig Järrel in his finest performance), who wears a Himmler-like mustache and reads the Nazi newspaper *Dagsposten*. Denied the sympathy of his aloof bourgeois parents, Jan-Erik shares his troubles with Bertha (Mai Zetterling), who works in a tobacconist's kiosk.

Bertha has troubles of her own—a mysterious stranger who follows her at night like a ghost. She becomes too frightened to go home, and Jan-Erik finds her wandering in a state of drunken despair. He spends the night with her and falls deeply in love. One evening he calls her flat and finds her dead, with a trembling Caligula hiding behind some coats. The authorities attribute the death to heart failure, and when Jan-Erik attempts to indict Caligula he is simply disqualified from taking his examinations. At the end of the film, lonely but free, Jan-Erik is beginning to pick up the pieces of his shattered life.

There are those who attribute the film's power to Bergman's script—"the first Swedish script reflecting the melancholy and rebellion of the new generation"—but it is said to have been Sjöberg who added the touches that turned a psychological study into an indictment of the totalitarian mentality, and it was certainly he who was responsible for the film's "powerfully expressionistic visual style"—"the brooding shadows of Bertha's room . . . and the silhouette of Caligula's hand stretching out across the hall"—in a way that reminded Peter Cowie of a famous image in Murnau's *Nosferatu*.

Similar stylistic devices are rather self-consciously employed in *Resan bort (Journey Out*, 1945), and few found much to admire in this complicated wartime story. It was followed by three of Sjöberg's most notable films, the first and slightest of which was *Iris och löjtnantshjärta (Iris and the Lieutenant*, 1946). This reunited the young stars of *Torment* in a contemporary story about the love affair between a parlormaid and her employers' son, an aristocratic young Guards officer who is killed on maneuvers, leaving her pregnant. Offered the disinterested help of her lover's elder brother, Iris decides to raise her child alone and unaided.

Though the plot could scarcely be more trite, it supports what was generally recognized to be "an exceedingly subtle and moving film." The love affair was called "heartrending in its sharp intensity," filmed with "a warmth and intimate poetry that is rare with Sjöberg." The tenderness and gaiety of this relationship is effectively contrasted with the behavior of the lieutenant's high bourgeois family—"icy, unloving people, devouring one another with polite hatred," and struggling to preserve the status quo in the face of postwar disillusionment with the old order. Peter Cowie calls this "a film that has dated with the utmost charm."

Bara en mor (Only a Mother, 1949) was adapted by Sjöberg and Ivar-Lo Johansson from the latter's Zolaesque novel about the *statarna* —grossly exploited itinerant field workers whose condition was abolished in the 1930s. Eva Dahlbeck plays Rya-Rya, a high-spirited girl who scandalizes the community by bathing naked. Spurned by her fiancé, she is made pregnant by and married to a boorish peasant, beginning an endless cycle of childbearing that only ends when she is worked literally to death on the local estate. In the process she grows into an archetypal figure of suffering and enduring motherhood. Dahlbeck's account of this transition has been described by responsible critics as "one of the greatest performances in the history of the cinema" in its "strength and transparent beauty."

Rich in character and incident, the film echoes in its rhythms the transition that takes place in Rya-Rya, from the excitement of the country dance where she is seduced to the dragging, exhausted movements at the end. Disparate scenes along the way are linked by huge close-ups of Rya-Rya, and in one early and much-discussed sequence Sjöberg explores a more original means of indicating the passage of time and the heroine's changing apprehensions. "In the early part of the film," he said, "the leading actress is kept in the center of the picture and her surroundings are changed. She moves as in a dream. She has no contact with reality, until her character is changed later by another disappointment. At this point the picture technique changes and becomes naked, hard and real."

Similar experiments in his next film are developed into what Peter Cowie has called a "new cinematic language." Sjöberg himself adapted Strindberg's one-act play *Fröken Julie (Miss Julie)*, moving the action out of Strindberg's single claustrophobic chamber and into the rooms and gardens of the Count's country estate, photographed "with a brilliant clarity" by Göran Strindberg, the playwright's grandson. Anita Björk plays the Count's daughter, Miss Julie, an arrogant, passionate, wretched girl whose mother has shaped her as an instrument of revenge against the whole male sex.

On a bored impulse, she attends the Brueghelesque Midsummer Eve dance of her father's employees, where she dances with his groom Jean (Ulf Palme). They become lovers and the vulgar opportunist Jean, initially servile and adoring, soon turns the tables, teaching his mistress the pleasures of self-abasement. Jean relents and the lovers plan to elope, but the entwined class and sexual hatreds that propel them flare up again, and when the Count returns to reestablish the old order, Miss Julie cuts her throat.

Some critics felt that, by "opening up" the play, Sjöberg had vitiated its intensity, but Richard Roud thought that "what it lost in intensity it gained in breadth," and Richard Winnington called the film "a fresh work that uses Strindberg as raw material for its own design and purpose." At times, when Julie is recalling her childhood schooling in emotional warfare, Sjöberg relinquishes naturalism and brings figures from the past into the same room as her adult self. "Strindberg's single act explodes in all directions," wrote Edgardo Cozarinsky— "memories of the characters' past, as well as their dreams, and even intimations of the future, are worked into an exciting structure of flashbacks . . . , where the past is always pressing upon the present." After the acclaim that greeted Eva Dahlbeck's performance in the previous film, Sjöberg's skill as a director of actresses must be given some of the credit for the extraordinary tributes earned by Anita Björk's Julie—Richard Roud said it was "perhaps the most absolutely compelling study of controlled passion in the history of the cinema."

Miss Julie shared the Palme d'Or at Cannes with De Sica's *Miracle in Milan*. Rune Waldekranz has described it as "a national masterpiece and among the unique achievements of the cinema medium," and in 1964 the Swedish critics voted it the finest product of the nation's cinema. To a modern eye, some of its *trouvailles* seem more theatrical than cinematic, and its reputation has slumped a little, along with Sjöberg's own, but it is still regarded by most critics as the director's masterpiece.

Sjöberg's next film was planned as a prestige venture by Sandrews, its producers—an ambitious and expensive adaptation of *Barabbas*, Pär

Lagerkvist's novel about the imagined fate of the thief whose life was spared in exchange for that of Jesus Christ. Working in the Cyprus copper mines as a Roman slave, Barabbas (Ulf Palme) is converted to Christianity and is crucified along with hundreds of other martyrs. But he dies perplexed, unable to reconcile the loving gentleness of the new faith with the violence that his motherless childhood has made instinctive in him.

It seemed to Peter Cowie that Barabbas's crisis is "to a certain extent that of modern man, torn between doubt and belief, between darkness and light," and that "Sjöberg is at his best when suggesting this conflict in visual terms. . . . the exteriors, shot in Israel and Rome, afford him plenty of scope for pictorial comment." For most critics, the novel "never acquired enough flesh on the screen to dress its allegorical bones," and the movie was found ponderous, slow, and often boring. It failed at the box office and so did Sjöberg's next picture, *Karin Månsdotter* (1954), about the peasant girl who became the mistress of Erik XIV, the mad king of sixteenth-century Sweden.

Karin Månsdotter opens with an extraordinary prologue—a "broadside ballad" in color that uses titles and painted backdrops and speeded-up action to tell the fairy-tale story of the farm girl and the prince, reminding critics of both puppet shows and silent film comedies. The comedy ends when Karin realizes that she is to go to bed with the king but not to become queen, and color gives way to plain black and white for the main body of the film, drawn from Strindberg's *Erik XIV*, and shot by Sven Nykvist in various Swedish castles.

Erik (Jarl Kulle) is already petulant and unpredictable to the point of madness. Though Karin (Ulla Jacobsson) bears him two children, he has no intention of marrying her, being intent on marriage to Elizabeth I of England. He has nevertheless been seen as a kind of proto-radical in that he chose both his mistress and his chief counselor Göran Persson (Ulf Palme) from the common people. And when Elizabeth rejects his suit, he does in fact make Karin his queen. This is too much for the entrenched Swedish nobles. Persson is executed, Erik is overthrown and imprisoned, and Karin and her children sent into exile. This section of the film has been described by Cozarinsky as "an exercise in larger-than-life theatricality, a play of solitary figures which cast enormous shadows on imposing decors," evoking many comparisons with Eisenstein's *Ivan the Terrible*. There follows an epilogue, scripted by Sjöberg from the sad and scattered diaries of Karin's exile and final reconciliation with the

dying Erik, in which it emerges that the bewildered peasant girl has become truly a queen.

The film's fairy-tale prologue seemed to Peter Cowie "a foolish preparation for the lengthy and deeply serious recreation of history that Sjöberg is about to present," and audiences were also bewildered and offended by the film's harsh treatment of a pretty rags-to-riches story and of the whole notion of royalty. *Karin Månsdotter* failed in Sweden and has been very little seen abroad. But Edgardo Cozarinsky has described the film's critical reception as "obtuse," and praised the boldness of its structure, pointing out that the three sections are *meant* to clash dialectically in a work that he considers the finest of Sjöberg's films.

Torment had installed Sjöberg as the leading figure in the renovation of the Swedish cinema, and *Miss Julie* had confirmed his right to that position, but his reputation began to decline after that as Ingmar Bergman asserted his supremacy, and *Vildfågler* (*Wild Birds*, 1955) only accelerated the process. Based on a novel by Bengt Anderberg, it tells a tragic love story faintly reminiscent of *Miss Julie* and includes some brilliant scenes and set pieces, but is finally unconvincing and sometimes ludicrous in its characterization, while its naturalistic Göteborg locations clash awkwardly with its intimations of metaphysical evil.

Sista paret ut (*Last Pair Out*, 1956), scripted by Bergman and sharing some of the preoccupations of *Torment*, had none of the latter's success and was said to wear "a weary, old-fashioned look." Sjöberg made only two films over the next ten years: *Domaren* (*The Judge*, 1960), adapted from a play by Vilhelm Moberg about a young poet ruined by his former guardian, a judge, and committed to a mental institution, but saved by the efforts of a young lawyer; and *Ön* (*The Island*, 1966), a fable about a Hamlet-like aristocrat striving to organize the inhabitants of an island in the Stockholm archipelago against government plans to turn it into a military training area. Both films were said to be smothered by "a high-flung allegorical treatment." Sjöberg made only one more picture, a record of his production at the Royal Dramatic Theatre of Strindberg's *Fadern* (*The Father*, 1969).

Michael Meyer described Sjöberg as a man "seemingly without envy." Ousted from his position as the foremost Swedish film director, he re-adopted the theatre as his principal medium of expression, staging superb productions of Shakespeare, Lorca, and Pär Lagerkvist, of Ibsen and Strindberg, of Eugene O'Neill and Arthur Miller. He scored "brilliant late successes" with plays by Witold Gombrowicz, and at the age of

seventy-five—a year before his death as the result of a road accident—directed a new Swedish
play about a Russian revolutionary "with undi-
minished authority and panache."

Lasse Bergström has pointed out that all of
Sjöberg's late films center on a single character
who is in conflict with society, and Rune
Walderkranz agrees that "philosophically, the
common denominator in Sjöberg's work is his vision of the individual's helplessness in an alien,
and almost always menacing, enviroment." Peter Cowie, on the other hand, can distinguish no
"personal vision" in Sjöberg's work and maintains that, for that reason, he failed to create "a
world to which one returns with an immediate
feeling of recognition and empathy. Each of his
films is a solitary achievement."

But Edgardo Cozarinsky, writing ten years
later in Richard Roud's *Cinema* (1980), suggests
that "critics irritated by . . . [Sjöberg's] over-
elaborate compositions, his intricate patterns of
lighting, his too brilliant editing . . . should see
again so-called minor films (*Resan bort*, even
Hem från Babylon) in the light of such an acclaimed modern film as the *The Conformist*
(1970). Bertolucci's ironical reworking of '30s
rhetoric coincides almost constantly with
Sjöberg's own treatment, even to the point of
achieving an almost dreamlike continuity of
brief sequences. It would not be too surprising
if Sjöberg's *oeuvre*, confined for today's taste to
outmoded keys of sensibility and intellectual
commitment, turns out to be ripe for reappraisal."

FILMS: (with Axel Lindholm) Den starkaste (The
Strongest/The Strongest One), 1929; Med livet som in-
sats (They Staked Their Lives), 1940; Den blomstertid
(Blossom Time/Flowering Time), 1940; Hem från
Babylon (Home From Babylon), 1941; Himlaspelet
(The Road to Heaven), 1942; Kungajakt (The Royal
Hunt), 1943; Hets (Torment/Frenzy), 1944; Resan
bort (Journey Out), 1945; Iris och löjtnantshjärta (Iris
and the Lieutenant/Iris), 1946; Bara en mor (Only a
Mother), 1949; Fröken Julie (Miss Julie), 1951; Barab-
ba (Barabbas), 1953; Karin Månsdotter, 1954;
Vildfågler (Wild Birds), 1955; Sista paret ut (Last Pair
Out/The Last Couple Out), 1956; Domaren (The
Judge), 1960; Ön (The Island), 1964, released 1966;
Fadern (The Father), 1969.

ABOUT: Béranger, J. La Grande Aventure du Cinéma
Suédois, 1960; Cowie, P. Sweden (Screen Series), vols.
1 and 2, 1970; Lundin, G. Filmregi Alf Sjöberg, 1979;
Waldekranz, R. Swedish Cinema, 1959; Widerberg, B.
Visionen i svensk film, 1962; Young, V. Cinema Borealis, 1971. *Periodicals*—Film Forum November
1959; Film Ideal 216 1969; Kosmorama 49 1960.

***SJÖSTRÖM,   VICTOR   ("Victor
Seastrom")** (September 20, 1879–January 3,
1960), Swedish director, scenarist, and actor, was
born in Silbodal, a small rural community in the
central Swedish province of Värmland. He was
the son of Olof Sjöström, a farmer, and the former Elisabeth Hartman, who had been an actress.

The conditions into which Sjöström was born
were markedly similar to those evoked in Jan
Troell's film *Utvandrarna* (*The Emigrants*,
1970), about the homesteaders and tenant farmers of Småland, a heavily forested region much
like Värmland. The desperate hardships involved in wresting a livelihood from a small
farm on poor soil led in the mid–nineteenth century to a great exodus in which thousands of
homesteaders emigrated to the United States.
Sjöström's family joined this exodus in 1880, arriving in New York when he was seven months
old.

Most of the emigrants went on to farm in Minnesota, but the Sjöströms remained in Brooklyn,
where they ran a small boardinghouse. Elisabeth
Sjöström died a few years later and her husband
soon remarried. He was a religious bigot and a
domestic tyrant who had made his son's early
childhood wretchedly unhappy; now there was
conflict with the new stepmother as well. At the
age of seven, Victor Sjöström was shipped back
to live with an aunt and uncle at Uppsala, the
university town north of Stockholm. He was educated there, but not at the university. Like his
mother, his uncle Victor was an actor, then employed at the Royal Dramatic Theatre in Stockholm. Entranced by an exciting new world
remote from the dour puritanism of his early
years, Sjöström plunged into amateur theatricals
at the age of fourteen and three years later, in
1896, joined a theatre company touring Finland.

Sjöström was married for the first time around
1900 to Sascha Stjagoff, an actress of Russian descent who died a few years later. Between 1900
and 1911 he became well known in both Sweden
and Finland as an actor of exceptional power
and intensity and—with his long, sensitive face
and sad eyes—something of a matinée idol. He
also traveled abroad, visiting theatres in Paris,
London, and Berlin. For a time he was a director
at the Royal Theatre, Copenhagen, and it was
there that he met his second wife, Lili Bech.
Sjöström's interests turned increasingly to production, and in 1911, with Einar Fröberg, he established his own theatre company in Malmö, in
southern Sweden.

By this time, the Swedish film industry was
gaining strength, led by the Svenska Bio company under its able production manager Charles

VICTOR SJÖSTRÖM

Magnusson. He had joined the company in 1909, initiating a policy of filming adaptations of popular classics using actors and directors already established in the theatre. The movies were still regarded as a vulgar and probably pernicious form of entertainment, but a few films of real quality were beginning to appear in Sweden, especially after Svenska Bio added the brilliant cameraman Julius Jaenzon to its staff in 1911.

Sjöström joined Svenska Bio in June 1912, when he was thirty-two—a few months after another Magnusson discovery, Mauritz Stiller, soon to become a close friend. "The thing that brought me to filmmaking," Sjöström said, "was a youthful desire for adventure and a curiosity to try this new medium of which I then did not have the slightest knowledge." Looking back long after at his beginnings in the cinema, he said, "I am sure that it did not for a moment occur either to Stiller or to me that in those days we were doing something that would be remembered or talked about many years later. We happened to enter the job at a lucky time."

It was as an actor that Sjöström made his film debut, appearing in Paul Garbagny's *I livets vår* in 1912. The same year he had the lead roles in two movies directed by Stiller, *De svarta maskerna* (*The Black Masks*) and *Vampyren* (*The Vampire*), as well as in the first film he himself directed, *Trädgårdsmästaren* (*The Gardener*), scripted by Stiller. Nothing seems to be known about this picture except that it also featured Sjöström's wife, Lili Bech, and "Sweden's John Barrymore," Gösta Ekman, and that (according to the director himself) it was banned by the Swedish censors and never released.

Peter Cowie says that as an actor Sjöström "was as intrepid as Fairbanks or Flynn, with the [same] capacity for suggesting nobility, dignity, and emotional stress." He continued to work as an actor for Svenska Bio, usually in his own films or Stiller's, but devoted himself increasingly to direction, turning out an average of eight films a year between 1912 and 1916. Most of them were three-reelers—the commonest length for features at that time—but some were as long as modern features, like Sjöström's first notable work, *Ingeborg Holm* (1913).

Adapted by the director from a play by Nils Krook (itself based on an actual case), this was a tense social drama about a woman (Hilda Borgström) who, after her husband dies, is confined to a poorhouse while her children are auctioned off to speculators in forced labor. Hearing that her daughter is ill, she escapes from the poorhouse to help her but is caught by the police and returned, white-haired and insane with grief, cradling a piece of wood as if it were her baby. There is an unconvincing happy ending—a bow to the conventions of the time—but otherwise this early movie shows a scrupulous concern for detailed authenticity, including some scenes shot on location. The stark photography (by Julius Jaenzon's brother Henrik) intensifies the force of this savage indictment of the barbaric poor laws of the time.

A critical and financial success, *Ingeborg Holm* was greeted as the first Swedish film with any real claim to artistic merit. It is also the only one of Sjöström's early movies to have survived. The rest—like other Swedish films of the period—were mostly trite melodramas or thrillers, interspersed with occasional comedies. Though his material was often banal, Sjöström's early work is said to have been distinguished by a gift for characterization and "his way of using sets and landscapes with an absolute stylistic economy." Unlike most of his contemporaries, he filmed on location whenever he could—for example in *Halvblod* (*Halfbreed*, 1913), a "Western" shot in the forest near Stockholm, and in *Miraklet* (*The Miracle*, 1913), a medieval drama based on Zola's *Lourdes* and filmed at the ruins of Visby in Gotland.

In 1916 Charles Magnusson asked Sjöström to make a film based on Ibsen's epic poem *Terje Vigen*. The director at first refused this assignment, arguing that there was no place for a serious work of literature in the show-business atmosphere of the contemporary film industry. He was in fact at a low point in his career, demoralized by the vulgar rubbish that occupied his days at Svenska Bio and bruised by the failure of his second marriage. That summer he went on a bicycle tour of his birthplace near the

Norwegian border, searching for his roots in that inhospitable landscape. An old nurse's memories of his mother awoke his regard and admiration for her and renewed his sense of himself. Continuing his journey down the southern Norwegian coast, he came to Grimstad and Terje Vigen's rocky islands. Sjöström experienced a kind of epiphany there, from which developed the almost pantheistic feeling for landscape and nature that infuses his mature work. He cabled Magnusson that he would film *Terje Vigen* and shooting began in August 1916.

The poem was adapted by Gustaf Molander (verses from it being retained as titles) and photographed by Julius Jaenzon—not at Grimstad but more economically on the rocky coast near Stockholm. The Norwegian actor cast as Vigen accepted another assignment and Sjöström decided to play the part himself. The film is set during the Napoleonic Wars. Terje Vigen is a Norwegian fisherman who runs the British blockade to secure food for his family until he is captured by a British frigate and imprisoned. Released after the war, he finds that his wife and baby have died of starvation. With nothing left but hatred, he retires to a lonely island. One day he rouses himself from his dreams of revenge to rescue the crew of a small boat that is foundering in a storm. In the boat is the English captain who had captured him years before. Terje Vigen is tempted to let him drown, but the sight of the officer's wife with a baby in her arms reawakens his humanity. He relents, and his obsession with revenge ebbs away.

Einar Lauritzen wrote that in *Terje Vigen* "that peculiar juxtaposition of man and nature that was to be the hallmark of the 'Swedish school'" was for the first time fully evident. Peter Cowie agrees, saying that here, "for the first time in the cinema, the natural background reflects the struggles between the characters and within themselves. . . . The film is swept along by the feeling for landscape and atmosphere, by the almost prehensile attacks of the sea, and by that brilliantly syncopated editing which is at its most impressive in the scene where Terje rows desperately away from the frigate's boat. Sjöström alternates close-ups of Terje's tired arms heaving the oars back and forth with shots of the well-drilled English crew slipping easily through the breakers. The sea is Terje's real foe and there is a magnificent back view of Sjöström shaking his fist at the boiling waves. This defiance in the face of nature runs through the best Swedish films."

Released in 1917, *Terje Vigen* became a major international success, screened and admired in the United States, Latin America, India, Japan,

China, and all over Europe. And Sjöström's next picture confirmed that the Swedish cinema had matured into a serious threat to Hollywood's domination of world screens. This was *Berg-Evjind och hans hustru* (*The Outlaw and His Wife*, 1918), based on a play by Johan Sigurjönsson in which Sjöström had scored one of his greatest successes as a stage actor. He recreated the part for the screen and himself wrote the adaptation, in collaboration with Sam Ask. The heroine was played by Edith Arastoff, who had appeared as the British officer's wife in *Terje Vigen* and who became Sjöström's third wife in 1922, beginning a happy marriage that lasted until his death. The film was shot partly in the studio and partly in the mountains of northern Sweden, with further exterior camerawork by Julius Jaenzon in Iceland.

Like Terje Vigen, Berg-Evjind is a man of iron integrity who does what he believes is right and is punished for it by an unjust society: in nineteenth-century Iceland, he steals a sheep to feed his family and is imprisoned. Escaping, he finds work on a farm belonging to Halla (Arastoff), a rich young widow. They fall deeply and passionately in love, and when Berg-Evjind is forced to flee to the mountains, she joins him there, abandoning her estates. In that magnificent landscape they share a few years of ecstatic happiness, and a child is born. Then they are betrayed. Driven higher into the mountains, with time and hope running out, they kill their little daughter—casting her from a precipice almost as a propitiary sacrifice to the gods of nature (or perhaps to conventional morality). In the end, exhausted and starving, they die together in the snow: nature gives, and nature takes away.

The Outlaw has two central themes: Halla's belief that "love is the one and only law"; and Berg-Evjind's stoic recognition that "no man can escape his fate, though he run faster than the wind." The second theme in particular is deeply embedded in Scandinavian literature, all the way back to the sagas, with their stories of men and women who intransigently offend the old gods of nature and pay the penalty. This fatalism pervades Sjöström's most deeply felt work, along with his belief that "human love . . . is the only answer to fling in the face of a cruel . . . nature." Both themes recur in the products of the "Swedish school" of cinema that Sjöström fathered, as they still do in the work of Ingmar Bergman.

The film's success exceeded even that of *Terje Vigen*. It was praised for its acting and above all for its photography. One critic wrote that "particularly in the scene at the sheepfold with its snow and subtle night-lighting, its sense of silence and desperation, Sjöström created effects not found outside the work of Griffith, yet more sophisticated and complex than anything even he had done." Maurice Bardèche and Robert Brassilach called it "an important event in the history of cinema art, perhaps the most important since 1895, because here for the first time a film consciously invaded the domain of art." And for Louis Delluc it was simply "the most beautiful film in the world . . . , directed with a dignity that is beyond words. . . . It is the first love duet heard in the cinema. A duet that comprises all life."

Tösen från Stormyrtorpet (*The Girl From Stormy Croft*), Sjöström's next picture, was released in September 1917, a few months before *The Outlaw*. This rustic drama was the first of his adaptations from the novels of Selma Lagerlöf, who had assigned the screen rights to her books to Svenska Bio partly on account of her admiration for Sjöström. Later to become the first woman writer to receive the Nobel Prize, Lagerlöf was, like Sjöström, a native of Värmland. Many of her voluminous novels were inspired by the legends and folktales of the province and by her conception of nature as an active force in the destiny of her characters, torn as they are between good and evil.

The girl from Stormy Croft is Helga (Greta Almroth), who lives in poverty in a wretchedly overcrowded mountain hut. Scorned as the mother of an illegitimate child, she is taken in as a servant by Gudmund (Lars Hanson), a landowner's son in the rich valley below. This angers Gudmund's fiancée (Karin Molander) and her magistrate father. After a brawl in the local tavern, Gudmund finds himself facing a murder charge and the elaborate wedding preparations are called off. It is Helga who, with selfless devotion, proves his innocence and wins his love and the respect of the community.

Once again, landscape is used with a subtlety and symbolic weight unequalled by Sjöström's contemporaries, and the film also provides a convincing and detailed study of an unfamiliar society. Regarded by contemporary reviewers as a minor piece, this was more recently described by Tom Milne as "a deceptively simple, low-key film infused by a quiet lyricism. . . . [It] has its melodramatic flaws . . . but still manages to astonish by its psychological accuracy and emotional subtlety . . . full of delicate nuances and exquisitely underplayed." Writing in Richard Roud's *Cinema: A Critical Dictionary* (1980), Milne in fact states an extremely unconventional and interesting view of Sjöström's work as a whole. The received opinion, as he says, is more or less that voiced (in French) by René Jeanne

and Charles Ford in their 1963 monograph on Sjöström: "After painting a depressing view of Sjöström and his work as slow, sombre and impeccably sincere, they define his dominant theme as 'redemption by Nature, the purification of souls by vast natural phenomena,'" dismissing as minor or misguided films that do not fit these preconceptions. Milne, on the contrary, tends to reserve his warmest praise for precisely those works that escaped the adulation of the director's contemporaries, and to denigrate the established masterpieces. Thus, for him, *The Outlaw and His Wife* is not "the most beautiful film in the world," but "a tempestuous melodrama . . . in which all the attention is lavished on the majestic, inimical landscapes"—a movie as "monumental but hollow" as the three Lagerlöf adaptations that followed between 1919 and 1921.

The first of these was *Ingmarsönerna* (*The Sons of Ingmar*), released in two parts in 1919. This massive and ponderous family saga, shot partly on location in Jerusalem and largely an exercise in social realism, also reflects something of Lagerlöf's fondness for the supernatural—notably in the famous scene in which Ingmar climbs an enormous ladder to Heaven to seek the advice of his ancestors. Though modern critics find the film lacking in the emotional intensity of *Terje Vigen* or *The Outlaw*, it was an immense commercial success in 1919, enabling Charles Magnusson to build new studios and to amalgamate Svenska Bio with its principal rival to form Svensk Filmindustri, still the largest Swedish production company.

The Ingmar saga continued in *Karin Ingmarsdotter* (*Karin, Daughter of Ingmar*, 1920), Sjöström's first film for the new company. This was followed by the most famous of his Lagerlöf adaptations, *Körkarlen* (*The Phantom Carriage/Thy Soul Shall Bear Witness/Clay*), made in 1920 and released in 1921. It begins on New Year's Eve, with a dying Salvation Army nurse sending for the alcoholic David Holm (Sjöström) so that she can make one last attempt to return him to his penniless wife and children. David is at this time drinking with his cronies in a cemetery, where in a drunken squabble he is knocked out, apparently dead. According to legend, a man who dies at midnight on New Year's Eve must drive the phantom carriage for a year, collecting the souls of the dead. A long flashback shows us how David had fallen from grace, tempted by his boon companion Georg (Tore Svennberg), now himself deceased. It is Georg who has been driving the phantom carriage, and he now delivers it to David. But the latter is only unconscious and, recovering, hurries home in time to save his family from communal suicide.

"Sjöström plays David Holm with dazzling ease and without any make-up," writes Peter Cowie; here he retains the control that he sometimes lost as an actor, ranging "from cynicism and wry humour to moments of agony and bewilderment. . . . But *The Phantom Carriage* derives its originality from the luminous, double exposure photography of Julius Jaenzon. The construction of flashbacks is highly complex, and in fact about four-fifths of the film takes place in the cemetery itself. Occasionally, as many as four images are superimposed in one frame. . . . The images of the carriage moving over the waves, or silhouetted . . . against a twilight sky, carry a highly charged appeal to the imagination. . . . The phantasmic scenes are even more credible because they are placed at intervals between the often brutally realistic incidents . . . [of] daily life."

It seemed to Léon Moussinac that Sjöström had "attained an encompassing lyricism, unknown until now on the screen: tragic stillness, noble and potent serenity of some scenes. Though he tries to hypnotize us with the tragic dream of his *Phantom Carriage* . . . he never fails to draw out the gentle, pervasive force of familial intimacy and of the nuances of feelings externalized through a gesture or an illuminating expression. His films are for the most part freely elaborated etchings." Greeted as a masterpiece in 1920, the film, as Cowie says, has not endured as well as some of Sjöström's earlier work—perhaps "because its advances were technical rather than psychological." There have been two inferior remakes of *The Phantom Carriage*—by Julien Duvivier in 1938 and by Arne Mattsson in 1958.

But while Sjöström was trudging through his massive series of Lagerlöf adaptations, he was also producing other works of a quite different nature. *Hans nåds testamente* (*His Lordship's Last Will,* 1919), scripted by Hjalmar Bergman from his own play, is an eccentric comedy about an old aristocrat (Karl Mantzius) who, having discovered the vanity of all human endeavor, desires to pass what remains of his life in absolute indolence, undisturbed by any kind of activity whatever, anywhere on his domain. He nevertheless manages to settle his inheritance to the benefit of two young lovers "without actually doing anything about it."

The conventional view is that, of the two masters of the Swedish silent cinema, Stiller was the exponent of comedy, Sjöström the somber intellectual (who, as an actor, achieved some memorable comic performances, thanks mainly to Stiller's direction). Tom Milne allows that Sjöström may well have been profoundly serious

by temperament, but maintains that he could match Stiller as a director of comedy when he chose to try. Milne writes that "few films of the period could rival the airy grace with which *His Lordship's Last Will* opens. A shot of a stately mansion. Pan down to a shabby tramp sleeping in the sunshine outside the gates. Cut to a farm-labourer and a bevy of pigs happily blending their snores in the courtyard. Cut inside to a kitchen where the butler and his staff doze with their heads on the table while a cuckoo clock vainly chimes the hour."

Milne goes on: "With a lazy wit oddly reminiscent of the Renoir of *Boudu sauvé des eaux,* Sjöström uses this opening sequence not only to establish an unusually precise picture of the geographical layout of the house, but to adumbrate his theme. . . . Aided by a performance of marvellous fantasy by Karl Mantzius . . . Sjöström scarcely puts a foot wrong in elaborating an exquisitely funny and touching comic fable out of this story of a sleeping beauty who stubbornly resists the world's efforts to free him from a self-imposed spell."

Mästerman (*Master Samuel,* 1920), also scripted by Sjöström's friend Hjalmar Bergman, is another comedy—a "wonderfully funny and touching" original story about a fearsome old moneylender (played by the director) whose hard heart is melted by a young woman (Concordia Selander) whom he rashly accepts as a debtor's pledge. At the same time, Sjöström was exploring a Gothic vein in *Klostret i Sendomir* (*The Monastery of Sendomir,* 1920), adapted by himself from a novel by Franz Grillparzer. A "lurid tale of marital deceit and revenge," full of chiaroscuro lighting effects, flickering candles, and deceitful mirrors, it impressed Carl Dreyer above all because of the skill with which Sjöström had given visual expression to mental suffering.

Vem Dömer (*Love's Crucible*), made in 1920 but not released until 1922, is another story of marital infidelity, set this time in Renaissance Florence, and photographed by Julius Jaenzon with a "glowing opulence" inspired by the paintings of the period. It ends with a spectacular scene in which the wife, accused of poisoning her husband, undergoes a terrifying trial by fire amid "a crowd of black shadows" and drifting smoke. By this time, indeed, Sjöström—influenced perhaps by the example of Mauritz Stiller—was showing a greater willingness to entertain his audiences with exciting set-pieces, and to spare them tedium by accelerating the pace of his editing.

All the same, Hans Pensel describes *Love's Crucible* as "an unusually beautiful but otherwise fairly empty picture," and there is a general feeling that Sjöström's last Swedish pictures showed a decline in vitality and confidence that reflected the condition of the industry as a whole. "During World War I," Pensel says, "neutral Sweden experienced a boom in its film production, supplying paralyzed Europe with pictures. After the war, both the USA and the Continent were increasing their production . . . and the market for artistic Swedish film fell off badly. . . . Svensk Filmindustri made desperate efforts to produce pictures with 'international appeal.' Sjöström's last silent Swedish films . . . are all examples of this effort."

Beginning with *Love's Crucible*, Pensel goes on, "these films were all set in a foreign milieu and many parts were played by foreign actors. It is also significant that all were studio films and not made on outdoor locations." *Det omringade huset* (*The Surrounded House*, 1922) is a routine story about a party of British soldiers in the African desert, featuring the English actor Matheson Lang. *Eld ombord* (*The Tragic Ship*, 1923) is an equally conventional drama, combining a shipwreck story and a love triangle, in which Sjöström "loses the heroine to Matheson Lang in order to please the English audience."

In 1931, in an article called "Sweden and Sjöström," C. A. Lejeune wrote that "ten years ago Sweden was to the screen what Russia is today. It was first in intelligence, first in force, first in imaginative zeal. . . . Watching those old Swedish pictures, we used to feel almost under our fingers the texture of the velvets, the satins, the lace. . . . The candlelight too, the pale sunlight, the shadows, were rich in an almost tangible quality; we felt the light as a physical experience. . . . The old personification of the elements has never quite left the Scandinavian mind, and wind, wood, water is still alive; light and darkness are still elementals." For her, Sjöström would "always stand as the classic representative of Sweden in the cinema," and the decline in that cinema began when first Sjöström and then Stiller left for Hollywood.

Ironically enough, it was in 1922, when Svensk Filmindustri was fighting for its life and Sjöström's own work had begun to falter, that he was "discovered" in the United States. It was then that *The Phantom Carriage* reached America and that *The Girl From Stormy Croft* (then five years old) was voted the best foreign film of the year. In December 1922 Sjöström signed a contract with Goldwyn Pictures in which, among other things, he agreed to sign himself Victor Seastrom. In return, he was granted quite exceptional privileges, including the right to choose his own scripts.

Sjöström arrived in Hollywood with his wife and two daughters in February 1923. He had hoped to interest Goldwyn in an Ibsen adaptation; instead he was offered novels by Elinor Glyn. Finally, in desperation, he chose as his first script a melodramatic novel by Hall Caine, adapted by Paul Bern as *Name the Man* (1924). It is a courtroom drama involving an unmarried mother (Mae Busch) who happens to be the mistress of a judge (Conrad Nagel). In the United States, *Name the Man* was a success, both critically and financially; perhaps predictably, it was less warmly received by the Swedish reviewers, one of whom found it "badly composed and unartistic to a high degree, revealing that Sjöström had worked without joy or interest."

In the spring of 1924, when Goldwyn Pictures became Metro-Goldwyn-Mayer, the new company's first picture was assigned to Victor Sjöström. This time, thanks to MGM's brilliant young production chief Irving Thalberg, the director was given a far more sympathetic project than his first—an adaptation of Leonid Andreyev's nihilistic play *He Who Gets Slapped*. Sjöström wrote the adaptation himself, in collaboration with Carey Wilson and, with Thalberg as his producer, worked quite without studio interference. The only difficulty he reported was in persuading the MGM technicians not to drench every scene with brilliant and unmodified light. Filming was completed within a month, at the low cost of $140,000.

As adapted, the movie tells the story of a dedicated scientist (Lon Chaney) whose false friend steals not only his wife but the fruit of a lifetime's research. In a moment of absolute disillusionment, it comes to him that his only possible future is as a clown—the personification of humiliation and ridicule. "The moment, brilliantly enacted by Lon Chaney, is also brilliantly realised by Sjöström," wrote Tom Milne; "as the scientist sinks down in despair at his cluttered desk, he accidentally knocks over a globe of the world that rolls away to become a ball spinning on the fingertip of a grimy, white-faced clown, which in turn becomes a huge globe with a horde of tiny clowns clambering down invisible ropes to perch on its horizontal band, which, in a final metamorphosis, becomes a circus ring with a troupe of clowns watching a rehearsal." In the circus, the sad hero falls in love with a beautiful bareback rider (Norma Shearer). Renouncing any hope of claiming her for himself, he rescues her from the attentions of an evil aristocrat, facilitates her happy marriage (to John Gilbert), and is murdered for his pains—though not before he has set the lions on the disgusting baron.

He Who Gets Slapped opened in November 1924 at the Capitol Theatre in New York, accompanied by a big stage show and much bally-hoo. It was an enormous financial success, breaking a whole series of box-office records. The critical reception was equally positive, and not only in the United States, where the New York *Times* reviewer found in it "the genius of a Chaplin or a Lubitsch," and called it "the most flawless picture we have ever seen." The Swedish critic Bengt Idestam-Almquist concluded that it and *The Phantom Chariot* were Sjöström's best films to date. The director's use of light and shade was universally admired, and so was the acting. The movie launched Norma Shearer's career and confirmed Chaney's status as a major star.

In spite of its melodramatic plot, *He Who Gets Slapped* has stood up remarkably well to the test of time. It is said to show a greater concern for narrative and characterization than Sjöström's Swedish films, and a "new grace." Tom Milne regards it as "one of Sjöström's most daringly inventive films. . . . In its acute masochism, expressionism blending neatly into the horror film ethos, *He Who Gets Slapped* is *sui generis* in Sjöström's work. A blood brother here to the Tod Browning of *The Unknown*, Sjöström visualizes the clown's searing pain as a series of stark black-and-white contrasts radiating from the astonishing moment when, as he broods alone in the ring, the spotlight is switched out on him, leaving his chalk-white face as a tiny balloon suspended in a sea of darkness where it gradually vanishes, leaving emptiness."

After this piece of "expressionistic sophistication" came *Confessions of a Queen* (1925), an opulent costume romance ruined by a weak script, and then *The Tower of Lies* (1925), which reunited Lon Chaney and Norma Shearer. Adapted from one of Selma Lagerlöf's best-known novels, the latter is a film very much in the manner of Sjöström's Swedish pictures. Chaney plays a peasant driven to madness by the discovery that his beloved daughter has become a prostitute in the evil city. Filmed on location in California, this was in its day one of the most admired of Sjöström's American movies, praised above all for its psychological penetration.

And the director had an even greater success with a radically truncated adaptation of Nathaniel Hawthorne's novel about adultery and intolerance in seventeenth-century Massachusetts, *The Scarlet Letter*. It was Lillian Gish, then one of MGM's greatest stars, who sold this production to the studio, calming Mayer's anxieties about her daring project by canvassing the support of the Federal Council of Churches of Christ. Thalberg selected Sjöström as director, and Gish was delighted by his Scandinavian

thoroughness and the restrained acting style he demanded, calling him the finest director she had ever worked with. Sjöström devoted a year and a half to this film, some of which was shot on location in New England. Released in August 1926, it earned critical superlatives for its authenticity of detail and atmosphere, and for the excellence of Gish's performance as Hester Prynne.

The Puritan pastor Dimmesdale in *The Scarlet Letter* was played by the Swedish actor Lars Hanson, who in Sjöström's next film was cast opposite the most famous of Hollywood's Swedish immigrants, Greta Garbo—it is said that all three "felt as if they were working back in Stockholm again." *The Divine Woman* (1928) was very loosely based on a play about incidents in the early career of Sarah Bernhardt. Rather coolly received by contemporary reviewers, it was nevertheless another box-office success and is now (as Richard Roud says) among the more interesting of Hollywood's "lost" films.

Lillian Gish's second picture for Sjöström is generally regarded as the greatest of his American films, *The Wind* (1928). Adapted from a novel by Dorothy Scarborough, it centers on a repressed and fastidious young Southern belle who goes to live with her cousin and his wife in Texas. The coarseness, dirt, and ugliness of pioneer life reduce her to a state of almost unbearable revulsion, and the endless wind drives her to the edge of insanity. And there is worse to come. Forced into a marriage of convenience with a clumsy but goodhearted cowboy (Lars Hanson) whom she despises, she welcomes during his absence an ingratiating stranger in whom she sees hope of deliverance. The man is a rapist, and in defending herself she kills him.

The exterior shooting was done in the Mojave Desert under such dreadful conditions that Gish found it easy "to enter into the state of the character I play." But the result justified the sufferings of cast and crew. "Illusions are literally swept away by the eternally raging wind, buried under the choking drifts of sand that creep into every crevice of the soul," wrote Tom Milne. "And in the final magnificent sequence where Letty watches in terror as the wind gradually erodes the grave to expose the dead hand of the stranger she accidentally killed and tried to bury, her hallucinated terror materializes in the form of a white stallion . . . who rides the duststorm like a beautiful, haunting omen of doom. Here Sjöström blends fact and fantasy so completely that the West itself . . . becomes a towering poetic image."

The Wind reminded Peter Cowie of the Westerns of John Huston and of Stroheim's *Greed*, but he also found "an undeniably Scandinavian character" in this "masterpiece of the Twenties," with its characters drifting at the mercy of their environment. It was reportedly the studio that insisted on the happy ending, in which the trauma of the rape and killing exorcises Letty's fear of the elements, allowing her to adjust to her new environment and to recognize her husband's simple goodness. Some but not all critics thought the film weakened by this conclusion; most agreed that Lillian Gish's performance was the most powerfully dramatic of her career.

After filming *Masks of the Devil* (1928), an unexceptional variation on the Dorian Gray theme, Sjöström returned to Sweden to be at the deathbed of his great friend Mauritz Stiller. Back in Hollywood, he made his first talkie, *A Lady to Love* (1930), based on Sidney Howard's play *They Knew What They Wanted,* a routine comedy about a mail-order bride. After that Sjöström made another visit to Sweden. He intended a temporary stay but, once there, decided to remain.

It is not entirely clear why Sjöström abandoned his Hollywood career, which had been so much more successful than Stiller's. Some critics maintain that he had been unhappy at MGM, and that his grapplings with commercial texts like *Name the Man* and *Confessions of a Queen* had damaged him as an artist. C. A. Lejeune thought that "Sjöström, on leaving Sweden, has ceased to be Sjöström," and Andrew Sarris wrote much later that it was "as if when Seastrom left Sweden, his artistic soul couldn't breathe. There was not enough air on the Hollywood sound-stages." But in a letter to Lillian Gish the director himself referred to his Hollywood experience as "perhaps the happiest days of my life," and recent criticism has tended to the view expressed by Tom Milne—that the handful of Sjöström's Hollywood films that survive "suggest that these may have been *anni mirabili* for him."

Back in Sweden, Sjöström planned a film based on Strindberg's *Miss Julie,* a project later triumphantly realized by Alf Sjöberg. Instead Sjöström made and starred in *Markurells i Wadköping* (*The Markurells of Wadköping*), a revenge drama reminiscent of *Terje Vigen,* adapted from a novel by Hjalmar Bergman and photographed by his old colleague Julius Jaenzon. Peter Cowie called this study of small-town life "the last significant work directed by Sjöström, and arguably the last Swedish film of quality for a decade." It is generally assumed that Sjöström ended his career as a director partly because he was uncomfortable with sound, partly because he had no interest in the frivolity that dominated the Swedish cinema during the

1930s. The only other picture he directed, *Under the Red Robe,* was a historical romance made in 1937 for Alexander Korda in Britain.

During the last part of his long life, Sjöström returned to his first career as an actor. Between his return to Sweden in 1931 and his death in 1960 at the age of eighty, he appeared in a total of nineteen films, most of them for Gustaf Molander or Arne Mattsson. From 1942 to 1949 Sjöström also served as an "artistic advisor" to Svensk Filmindustri, where Ingmar Bergman was among his protegés. A profound admirer of Sjöström, Bergman has said that he works always with an image of the older director and his Swedish films before him as a model. Sjöström was cast as the old orchestral conductor in Bergman's *Till gladje* (*To Joy,* 1950), and gave his last and greatest performance in *Smultronstället* (*Wild Strawberries,* 1957). Already ill and in pain, he played the lead role as Professor Isak Borg, brought through dreams and human contacts to a recognition of his failures in humanity.

At a Swedish Film Academy tribute to Sjöström in February 1960, shortly after his death, Ingmar Bergman said that what he had observed in Sjöström's performance in *Wild Strawberries* was "a colossal fight of will against the forces of destruction which raged continuously." And Bergman quoted from his diary of the film's making: "I never tire of studying, with unabashed curiosity, this mighty face. Occasionally there passes over it a muffled shriek of pain. Sometimes it is disfigured by suspicion and mistrust, by senile distemper. . . . All of a sudden he can turn around with a smile of spontaneous tenderness, and speak with a shrewd wisdom." Finally, of the close-ups of Isak Borg arriving at understanding and reconciliation, Bergman wrote: "For these close-ups Sjöström's face shone with a mystic brightness, as though it reflected the light of another world; his manner became mild, almost meek. . . . It was marvelous—the clarity and tranquillity of a soul at rest. Never before had I contemplated a face so noble and free of care."

Peter Cowie writes that "Victor Sjöström is one of that small band of directors. . . . who have led the cinema into altogether fresh channels. No filmmaker before Sjöström integrated landscape so fundamentally into his work or conceived of nature as a mystical as well as a physical force in terms of film language." Hans Pensel calls him "the first important intellectual of the screen," who "showed that an exciting film can be created by revealing what goes on in the human mind and heart." And Andrew Sarris thinks it possible that he "was the world's first great director, even before Chaplin and Griffith."

FILMS: Trädgårdsmästaren (The Gardener), 1912; Ett hemligt giftermål (A Secret Marriage), 1912; Lady Marions sommarflirt (Lady Marion's Summer Flirtation), 1912; En sommersaga (A Summer Tale), 1912 (not released); Äktenskapsbryån (The Marriage Agency), 1912; Löjen och tårar (Smiles and Tears/Ridicule and Tears), 1913; Blodets röst (Voice of the Blood), 1913; Ingeborg Holm, 1913; Prästen (The Priest), 1913; Halvblod (Halfbreed), 1913; Miraklet (The Miracle), 1913; Pa livets ödesvägar (On the Roads of Fate), 1913; Det var i Maj (It Was in May), 1914; Kärlek starkare än hat (Love Stronger Than Hate), 1914; Dömen icke (Do Not Judge), 1914; Bra flicka reder sig själv (A Clever Girl Takes Care of Herself), 1914; Gatans barn (Children of the Street), 1914; Högfjällets dotter (Daughter of the Mountain), 1914; Hjärtan som mötas (Meeting Hearts), 1914; Strejken (The Strike), 1915; En av de många (One of the Many), 1915; Sonad oskuld (Expiated Guilt), 1915; Skomakare bliv vid din läst (Cobbler Stick to Your Last), 1915; Judaspengar (Judas Money/Traitor's Reward), 1915; Landshövdingens dottar (The Governor's Daughters), 1916; Rösen pa tistelön/Havsgammar (The Rose of Thistle Island/Sea Eagle/Sea Vulture), 1916; I prövningens stund (Hour of Trial), 1916; Skepp som mötas (Ships That Meet), 1916; Hon segrade (She Conquered), 1916; Thérèse, 1916; Dödskyssen (The Kiss of Death), 1917; Terje Vigen (A Man There Was), 1917; Tösen från Stormyrtorpet (The Girl From Stormy Croft/The Girl From the Marsh Croft/The Woman He Chose), 1917; Berg-Evjind och hans hustru (The Outlaw and His Wife), 1918; Ingmarsönerna (The Sons of Ingmar/The Ingmarssons), in two parts (1919); Hans nåds testamente (His Lordship's Last Will/His Grace's Will), 1919; Klostret i Sendomir (The Monastery of Sendomir/The Secret of the Monastery), 1920; Karin Ingmarsdotter (Karin, Daughter of Ingmar/God's Way), 1920; Mästerman (Master Samuel), 1920; Körkarlen (The Phantom Chariot/The Phantom Carriage/Thy Soul Shall Bear Witness/Clay/The Stroke of Midnight), 1921; Vem dömer? (Love's Crucible), 1922; Det omringade huset (The Surrounded House), 1922; Eld ombord (The Tragic Ship/The Hell Ship/Fire on Board), 1923; Name the Man, 1924; He Who Gets Slapped, 1924; Confessions of a Queen, 1925; The Tower of Lies, 1925; The Scarlet Letter, 1927; The Divine Woman, 1928; The Wind, 1928; Masks of the Devil, 1928; A Lady to Love, 1930; Markurells i Wadköping (The Markurells of Wadköping), 1931; Under the Red Robe, 1937.

ABOUT: Béranger, J. La grande aventure du cinéma suédois, 1960; Idestam-Almquist, B. Sjöström, 1965 (in Swedish); Jeanne, R. and Ford, C. Victor Sjöström, 1963 (in French); Pensel, H. Seastrom and Stiller in Hollywood, 1969; Petrie, G. Hollywood Destinies: European Directors in America 1922–1931, 1986; Roud, R. (ed.) Cinema: A Critical Dictionary, 1980. Periodicals—American Classic Screen Fall 1979; Chaplin (25th anniversary issue) 1984; Cinema (Switzerland) October 1970; Cinéma (France) April 1960; Close Up January 1929; Écran September 1978; Filmograph 1 1976; Films in Review May and June–July 1960; National Film Theatre Booklet (Britain) April–May 1975, October 1977; Sight and Sound Spring 1960, Summer 1974, Autumn 1975; Thousand Eyes Magazine March 1977.

SOLDATI, MARIO (November 17, 1906–   ), Italian director, scenarist, actor, novelist, short story writer, and journalist, was born into an aristocratic family in Turin and educated there in a Jesuit college, subsequently studying literature at the University of Turin. As a student he wrote art criticism for local reviews and frequented the circle of the antifascist writer and critic Piero Gobetti. Graduating in 1927, Soldati for a time studied history of art in Rome. His first volume of short stories appeared in 1929, and the same year he went on a fellowship to Columbia University in New York. Soldati spent two years in the United States, studying and lecturing at Columbia, traveling widely, and eking out his fellowship by working as a correspondent for the Genoese newspaper *Il Lavoro*.

Returning to Italy in 1931, Soldati entered the film industry at the beginning of the sound era as a scriptwriter. He made his mark almost immediately as coscenarist of Mario Camerini's wry, romantic comedy *Gli uomini, che mascalzoni (What Rogues Men Are, 1932)* and then collaborated on a series of films by Camerini, including the memorable *Il cappello a tre punte (The Three-Cornered Hat, 1934)*. In 1935 he published *America, primo amore*, a collection of impressions and vignettes of American life that was extremely successful and established him as a writer of great charm and perception. More screenplays followed, most of them for Camerini or Alessandro Blasetti.

In 1937 Soldati made his directorial debut with *La principessa Tarakanova*, the Italian version of a French film made by Fedor Ozep. He performed a similar chore on A. Berthomieu's *La signora di Montecarlo* (1938), and then codirected with Carlo Borghesio a comedy called *Due milioni per un sorriso* (1939). His first solo feature, *Dora Nelson* (1939), starred Assia Noris in a tangled story about a woman, twice married, who becomes involved in an elaborate subterfuge in an attempt to save her step-daughter's marriage. It was followed by a routine comedy, and then by the film that made Soldati's name as a director of international standing, *Piccolo mondo antico (Little Old-Fashioned World, 1941)*. Based on the novel by Antonio Fogazzaro, its "little world" is that of Turin and the Italian lake district in the mid-nineteenth century, when that region was still under Austrian domination. The social constraints and political upheavals of the period provide a backdrop to the painful love story of Franco (Massimo Serato)

MARIO SOLDATI

and his wife Luisa (Alida Valli in her first important role).

Piccolo mondo antico made an enormous impact and was universally admired for its telling use of natural settings, its scrupulous sense of place and period, and the elegance of Gastone Madin's design. The deep-toned photography gave one critic the impression of a documentary reconstruction. Giuseppe De Santis, a critic notoriously hard to please, wrote: "For the first time in our cinema we have seen a landscape where the air is no longer rarified, which is no longer greedily intent on the picturesque, but one which responds finally to the humanity of the characters."

Ironically, however, this movie has been recognized in retrospect as the prototype of a whole genre of escapist and generally much less distinguished films that flourished in Italy in the early 1940s, and which De Santis contemptuously labeled "calligraphist." Unwilling to churn out propaganda films for the Fascist regime and prevented by the censors from showing the increasingly ugly realities of life in wartime Italy, directors like Soldati, Poggioli, Lattuada, and Castellani addressed themselves to style rather than content, turning out elegant, refined, and often highly mannered adaptations of romantic literary classics. Though they were scornfully dismissed after the emergence of neorealism, the calligraphist films have their historical importance, as Pierre Leprohon has pointed out: "They are as far from the decadent films of the 'golden age' with their glittering sets and gesticulating *dive* as they are from the first neorealist films. They form the bridge between these two

styles in every respect, be it in their use of location shooting or the restraint shown in their sets and acting."

After the peasant drama *Tragica notte* (1942), Soldati made a second calligraphist film, *Malombra* (1942), that was notably lacking in the restraint Leprohon ascribes to the genre. Also based on a Fogazzaro novel, it has a performance of "Garbo-like intensity" by Isa Miranda as a spoiled young heiress who develops an obsession with the tragic fate of an ancestor and is driven to murder and suicide. "The stress in *Malombra* has shifted to the irrational and the decorative," wrote Roy Armes, "and the film culminates in a finale of splendidly grand-guignolesque absurdity. On a windswept terrace overlooking the lake a group of black-garbed figures assemble by candlelight to participate in a formal dinner that ends abruptly when Maria shoots her hapless lover."

This strange film has gathered a growing band of admirers nonetheless—Ted Perry relished the way "the visual style of late nineteenth-century painting and psychological obsessiveness are fused into a brooding, almost crazed romanticism." And an Italian critic, in *The Fabulous Thirties*, called this "gothic . . . often delirious" movie the best of all the calligraphist films: "The remote past that returns to upset the life of an apparently peaceful house, the crumbling of all conventional values, the explosion of the passions that leads to death, all that makes me think of an Italy that is disappearing, sumptuously and baroquely, with a final grand funeral banquet. *Malombra* is the last, brilliant burst of fireworks before the final tragedy."

The "final tragedy" was indeed imminent. In 1943 Soldati began work on *Quartieri alti (High Places)* but was forced into hiding by the German occupation and could not complete the film until after the liberation of Rome the following year. Another stylish literary adaptation (from a novel by Ercole Patti and a play by Jean Anouilh), it is a satirical piece about a young Roman con artist's attempt to seduce a rich girl by providing himself with an imaginary *haut bourgeois* family.

Like *Piccolo mondo antico,* Soldati's next film was set in nineteenth-century Turin. *Le miserie del signor Travet (His Young Wife,* 1946) is based on a novel published in 1862 by Vittorio Bersezio about a downtrodden government clerk. According to Vernon Jarratt, Soldati gives life to the story "not only by the human and understanding way in which he built his characters up into the round . . . but also by the extraordinarily convincing way in which he places his characters right *in* the Turin of the sixties of last century. His ability to do this is indeed one of Soldati's great virtues as a director. . . . Travet, his wife, and the bullying *commèndatóre* who is Travet's boss, played respectively by Carlo Campanini, Vera Carmi, and Gino Cervi, are by no means the usual theatrical players gesticulating in front of unconvincing sets; you feel that they really live . . . in the Turin of eighty years ago."

An expensive adaptation of Balzac's *Eugènie Grandet* followed in 1947; the Grandet mansion was constructed whole for this movie on Scalera's biggest stage—every room with four walls and a ceiling. *Daniele Cortis* (1947) is another Fogazzaro adaptation, a nineteenth-century cameo of misery and eventual acceptance starring Sarah Churchill, Vittorio Gassman, and Gino Cervi. Feeling perhaps that it was time to break out of this bookish rut, Soldati then made *Fuga in Francia (Flight Into France*, 1948), a war film about a collaborationist and his attempt to escape retribution.

After this movie, marred by a rather weak performance by Folco Lulli in the lead, came a string of strictly commercial projects, until in 1953 Soldati once more attracted serious attention with *La provinciale (The Wayward Wife)*, from a story by Alberto Moravia. Gina Lollobrigida plays Gemma, eager to be rescued from provincial penury by a rich husband. Foiled at the first attempt by the discovery that her intended is also her stepbrother, she settles for a dull but worthy professor and almost loses him too when she is blackmailed on account of a brief indiscretion by a wicked Romanian countess. Lollobrigida's greatest contributions seem to have been "her historic *embonpoint*" and "her superb wardrobe of black lingerie," but the film was admired all the same for "its convincing 'lived-in' sets" by Flavio Mongherini and the "impressively atmospheric exterior photography" by the late G. R. Aldo; Leprohon rather surprisingly called it Soldati's best film.

Soldati worked as second unit director on King Vidor's *War and Peace* (1956) and William Wyler's *Ben Hur* (1959). In 1956 he directed a remake of Blasetti's small masterpiece *Four Steps in the Clouds* called *Era di venerdì 17* and in 1959 took the comedy award at Cannes with *Policarpo De Tappetti, ufficiale di scrittura (Policarpo, Master Writer)*, starring Renato Rascel and Peppino De Filippo. None of Soldati's other late films was of any great interest and since the late 1950s he has largely abandoned the cinema to concentrate on writing, though he has made a few films for television. He said once that only a handful of his pictures were worth taking seriously, the rest having been made strictly for the money.

In fact, Soldati has always regarded himself primarily as a writer. The three novellas in *A cena col commèndatóre* (1950) and the long short story *Il vero Silvestri* (1959) established him as a contemporary master of the form. His novels include *Lettere da Capri* (1954), winner of the Strega Prize; *Le due città* (1964); *La busta arancione* (1966); and *L'attore* (1970), which satirizes the Italian film and television industries and received the Campiello Prize. Soldati is an accomplished linguist, a popular radio and television commentator, and a critic of art and literature. According to Vernon Jarratt, the English language in his hands is "a very vigorous if slightly uncertain weapon which he wields with enormous gusto and occasionally devastating effect." He has occasionally appeared in films by other directors, and gave a notable performance in Castellani's *Mio figlio professore* (1946). He has been married twice, the first time to an American.

FILMS: La principessa Tarakanova, 1937 (Italian version of a film by Fedor Ozep); La signora di Montecarlo, 1938 (Italian version of a film by A. Berthomieu); (with Carlo Borghesio) Due milioni per un sorriso, 1939; Dora Nelson, 1939; Tutto per la donna. 1940; Piccolo mondo antico (Little Old-Fashioned World/ Little Old World), 1941; Tragica notte, 1942; Malombra, 1942; Quartieri alti (High Places), 1945; Le miserie del signor Travet (His Young Wife), 1946; Eugenia Grandet, 1947; Daniele Cortis, 1947; Fuga in Francia (Flight Into France), 1948; Chi è Dio?, 1948 (short); Quel bandito sono io, 1950; Botta e risposta, 1950; Donne e briganti (Of Love and Bandits), 1951; O.K. Nerone, 1951; Il sogno di Zorro, 1952; Le avventure di Mandrin, 1952; I tre corsari (The Three Pirates), 1952; Jolanda la figlia del corsaro nero (Yolanda, the Daughter of the Black Pirate). 1953; La provinciale (The Wayward Wife), 1953; La mano dello straniero (The Stranger's Hand), 1954; Il ventaglio (The Fan) *in* Questa è la vita (Of Life and Love), 1954; La donna del fiume (Woman of the River), 1955; Era di venerdì 17 (The Virtuous Bigamist), 1956; Italia piccola, 1957; Policarpo De Tappetti, ufficiale di scrittura (Policarpo, Master Writer), 1959.

ABOUT: Apra, A. and Pistagnesi, P. (eds.) The Fabulous Thirties, 1979; Armes, R. Patterns of Realism, 1971; Bondanella, P. Italian Cinema, 1983; Caldiron, O. Letteratura al cinema, 1979; Current Biography, 1958; International Who's Who, 1980–81; Jarratt, V. The Italian Cinema, 1951; Katz, E. The Film Encyclopedia, 1979; Liehm, M. Passion and Defiance: Film in Italy From 1942 to the Present, 1984; Leprohon, P. The Italian Cinema, 1972; Soldati, M. Da spettore, 1973; World Authors: 1950–1970, 1975. *Periodicals*—Bianco e Nero May 1959; Image et son May 1980; Sight and Sound Summer 1948.

STAHL, JOHN M. (January 21, 1886–
January 12, 1950), American director and producer, was born in New York City, the son of a
prosperous businessman, and attended public
schools until he was fourteen. At that time, according to a Universal press release, he attempted to finance the staging of a play at a
neighborhood theatre, but failed. Humiliated,
he ran away from home and joined a theatre
company that was leaving to tour the Midwest,
thereafter working with touring and stock companies for fourteen years as an actor and,
increasingly, as a director, winding up on Broadway. This account is reasonably well attested,
though Andrew Sarris has it that Stahl did not
make his "acting debut on the legitimate stage"
until 1909, "appearing in movie bit parts as early
as 1913."

At any rate, there is general agreement that
in 1914 Stahl joined an independent film production company in New York as a director,
though there is very little published information
about this first stage of his movie career apart
from a few titles: *The Boy and the Law,* apparently an early seven-reeler; *The Lincoln Cycle*;
and *Scandal Mongers.* A little more is known
about two films he directed in 1917—*Today,*
adapted from a play by Channing Pollock, and
The Call of Hearts, scripted by Basil Dickey.

Both of these 1917 films starred Florence
Reed and Frank Mills, and so did *Wives of Men*
(1918), a seven-reel Pioneer production scripted
by Stahl himself. He next directed three or four
movies for Tiffany Pictures, including *The
Serpent* (1918), another Stahl script (from a novel by Winifred May), with Mollie King in the
lead.

According to a program note for the Stahl retrospective at Britain's National Film Theatre in
1981, it is not possible to screen most of his silents
on account of print problems. The earliest example of his work shown at the NFT was *Her Code
of Honor* (UK, *Call of the Heart,* 1919), described as "a taut romantic drama about a girl
who believes her lover to be the son of the man
who seduced her mother. Naturally, all is explained at the end, but not before the plot has
taken several devious turns and provided some
startling encounters."

By 1920 Stahl was in Hollywood, where for
seven years he worked almost exclusively for
Louis B. Mayer, initially at First National and
then, beginning in 1926, at MGM. An exception
was *Suspicious Wives,* made for the World Film
Corporation in 1921. A wife (Mollie King) believes her husband to be unfaithful and leaves
him. The husband (H. J. Herbert) is temporarily
blinded in a road accident but nursed back to

JOHN M. STAHL

health by an unknown woman. When he recovers his sight he finds that she is his faithful wife,
and reconciliation follows. The NFT program
note says that "Stahl's treatment hints at several
themes to be developed in later work [most obviously in *Magnificent Obsession*], and the plot
construction and shooting style make the most of
the somewhat intractable material." Stahl also
completed *The Great Divide* (1925) after the
original director, Reginald Barker, was taken off
the picture.

In 1927 Stahl established his own production
company in partnership with Tiffany Pictures,
the independent studio specializing in low-
budget programmers for which he had worked
ten years earlier. As vice president in charge of
production at Tiffany-Stahl, he produced about
forty-five movies between 1927 and 1929, none
of them of much significance, and none of them
directed by himself. He returned to direction in
1930, when he joined Universal. His first four
films there were all scripted by Gladys Lehman
and produced by Carl Laemmle, Jr., with the exception of *Seed,* produced in 1931 by Stahl himself. A drama about a budding writer who leaves
his wife and five children for another woman, it
was a resounding flop.

The movie that followed, *Strictly Dishonorable* (1931), was adapted from a play by Preston
Sturges. Paul Lukas plays a blasé, opera-singing
count, whose determinedly dishonorable intentions turn into something more romantic when
he meets Southern belle Sidney Fox. This comedy-romance is set for the most part in a speakeasy full of larger-than-life characters like the
amiable toper Judge Dempsey (Lewis Stone).

Sturges himself is said to have been delighted by the adaptation, and it was a hit at the box office.

It was Stahl's next picture, *Back Street* (1932), that established him as a master of the "woman's picture." Adapted by Lehman from the novel by Fannie Hurst and photographed by Karl Freund, it stars Irene Dunne as Ray Schmidt, the daughter of German immigrants in Cincinnati. She has a suitably ambitious boyfriend but is not interested in suitability. When she meets Walter Saxel (John Boles), a handsome traveling salesman, she falls in love with him, absolutely and forever. Unfortunately, Walter is just as conventional as her first boyfriend; her failure to turn up on time for a meeting with his mother is enough to make him give her up. In due course he marries a rich woman, but Ray goes on loving him. After a decent interval, Walter resumes the affair, installing Ray in the "back streets" of his life. She goes on loving him until he dies, and perhaps afterwards.

As George Morris writes in his article about Stahl in *Film Comment* (May–June 1977), Irene Dunne in *Back Street* "is a woman who has recognized her destiny, and has followed it with the single-minded obsessiveness common to so many Stahl women. Her devotion to the John Boles character, through generations of suffering and self-denial, is totally unsentimentalized. Stahl understands obsession as few directors do. . . . [His] style has never been sparer than it is in *Back Street* . . . and it is in this film, which is arguably his masterpiece, that one begins to glimpse the power of his style. His customary restraint paradoxically results in an overpowering intensity. Actually, it is . . . Dreyer whom Stahl resembles more than directors such as Sirk and Borzage."

Morris goes on to discuss Stahl's Dreyer-like sensitivity to the relationship between cinematic and real time, saying that in *Back Street* the tension between the two "is reinforced by the use of extremely long takes" which "simultaneously convey the emotional interactions and behavioral patterns of human beings and parallel the natural rhythms one associates with 'real life.' This simulation of the natural rhythms of human behavior is a signature of Stahl's work, and the deliberately slow pacing is perhaps off-putting to one accustomed to more flamboyant treatment of melodrama. At the end of *Back Street,* however, the director pulls off a stylistic conceit whose audacity is beyond even Sirk at his most delirious. As Irene Dunne prepares to follow her lover to a life beyond death, Stahl flashbacks to what might have been, if fate had not intervened. . . . This stunning sequence represents the cumulative missed opportunities of a life-

time, and yet it is totally free of sorrow and self-pity."

Margaret Sullavan, who was to star in Robert Stevenson's 1941 remake of *Back Street,* had her first—and some say her greatest—screen role in Stahl's *Only Yesterday* (1933). The film opens with scenes of the Wall Street crash of 1929. James Emerson (John Boles), ruined, goes into his study to shoot himself. Taking a revolver from his desk, he notices a letter on it. The letter is a revelation of the life of Mary Lane (Sullavan), whom he had seduced one romantic night in Virginia during World War I. Unknown to him, she had borne him a son while he married another woman. By the time they met again, ten years later, he had quite forgotten her, but the affair had been briefly resumed. Ill with heart disease, Mary had written the letter and died. Transfigured, Emerson puts his gun away and sets off to face his son and the future.

Tom Milne, seeing the film in 1981, called it "something of a triumph of Stahl over script. Sometimes compared for obvious reasons to *Letter From an Unknown Woman,* it in fact displays none of the brooding obsession that hangs over Ophuls' film like a cloud. . . . Instead, like *Back Street,* it tries to describe its social and moral problems in a reasoned monotone, gradually imposing the irrefutability of its arguments, but falling short of this aim (unlike the earlier film) because the script keeps straying into areas that are shadowy, tendentious, or quite simply irrelevant. . . . On the other hand, Stahl does wonders with the script's bland habit of disgorging contrivance like an overfed boa constrictor. . . . If the film . . . falls from grace by hurrying indecently towards its death scene, not to mention some horribly lumpish last-minute emoting from John Boles and the tiresomely manly child, it has at least come to a climax which almost prefigures Bresson: silently watching her lover across a crowded restaurant of New York revellers, trying to read some message of recognition in his eyes, Margaret Sullavan's face is an extraordinary *tabula rasa* revealing the cataract of hope and despair tumbling beneath it."

Another Fannie Hurst adaptation followed, *Imitation of Life* (1934). Bea Pullman (Claudette Colbert), white and widowed, with a young daughter, befriends black Delilah Johnson (Louise Beavers), giving her and *her* daughter a home (albeit below stairs). They go into business to exploit Delilah's marvelous pancake recipe and are hugely successful, though Delilah will accept none of the fruits of her talent except the promise of "a nice funeral." Troubles arise when Delilah's daughter Peola rejects her mother, passing as white, and both Bea and her daughter (Rochelle Hudson) fall for the same man (Warren William). All is resolved, though none too ecstatically, when Delilah dies and a conscience-stricken Peola shows up at the famous funeral, and Bea turns away her beloved in order to spare her daughter's feelings.

The movie's approach to the race issue caused a mild controversy in 1934, and seemed to Tim Pulleine in 1981 its "most startling aspect. . . . Whole passages cannot but seem grossly offensive—most obviously, perhaps, when Delilah menially excludes herself from the (all-white) party being thrown to celebrate the company's success." Not so the National Film Theatre program note, which maintains that "Stahl shows the developing relationship between the white woman and her black friend . . . by treating them primarily as human beings and only secondarily as part of a 'racial situation.'" And for Andrew Sarris, the film "survives as a truer testament to that racism of American life more ineradicable than most white Americans have ever cared to acknowledge. Again it is Stahl's extraordinary care and deliberation which is the key to his stylistic sincerity." This was the first of three Stahl movies subsequently remade by Douglas Sirk, in this case with Lana Turner and Juanita Moore in the lead roles.

The second such was *Magnificent Obsession* (1935), adapted from the novel by Lloyd C. Douglas about a feckless young playboy, Bobby Merrick (Robert Taylor), who is indirectly responsible for the death of a much-loved physician, an adherent of a Christian sect or society dedicated to doing good by stealth. Not content with this, Bobby then falls in love with the doctor's young widow Helen (Irene Dunne), whom he unfortunately blinds in an accident. Although he proposes marriage, Helen chooses to disappear. Seized by the late doctor's "magnificent obsession," Bobby takes up medicine and rapidly becomes a Nobel Prize–winning eye surgeon. He finds Helen, cares for her anonymously, and ultimately restores her sight.

Contemporary reviewers tended to dismiss the picture as another of Stahl's "long, sweet chronicles of human suffering," while praising the simplicity and perceptiveness of Irene Dunne's performance. Yann Tobin, writing about Stahl in Jean-Pierre Coursodon's *American Directors* (1983), called *Magnificent Obsession* "a film both richer and easier to ridicule than those that preceded it." Whereas Sirk, in his 1954 remake, "was to emphasize the 'bizarre' mystical aspects of the story, making it one of his most Borzagian works, Stahl's version is "as usual . . . extremely restrained, stylized rather than stylish. . . . The silences and whispers of the soundtrack, with occasional departures into Leo McCarey–type humor, define the unemotional tone he uses: effects are limited, climaxes turned into anticlimaxes. . . . As in *Back Street,* the function of the 'fatal coincidences' in *Magnificent Obsession* is at least as symbolic as it is dramatic. Thus Irene Dunne's accidental blindness is simply the translation, in melodramatic terms, of the falseness of her existence" before love and suffering enable her to "see the light."

Stahl had had a string of hits at Universal, all produced by Carl Laemmle, Jr. After *Magnificent Obsession,* one of his greatest box-office successes, Stahl rejoined Louis B. Mayer at MGM for his biggest flop, *Parnell* (1937). Scripted by John Van Druten and S. N. Behrman and produced by Stahl himself, it miscast Clark Gable as the Irish patriot and politician and Myrna Loy as Kitty O'Shea. "It seems a pity," one contemporary reviewer wrote, "if we have to be given a film which is ineffective as entertainment, that we should not get, by way of recompense, a less wildly inaccurate picture of the events as they happened and the characters of the people concerned."

Back at Universal after this expensive fiasco, Stahl continued as his own producer, making a series of what Yann Tobin calls "imitations of films." *Letter of Introduction* (1938), the first of these, features Adolphe Menjou as a matinee idol who receives a letter informing him that the bearer, a struggling young actress (Andrea Leeds), is his daughter by his first marriage. What follows is a curious amalgam of comedy and melodrama, doubling as a showcase for the ventriloquist Edgar Bergen, who was newly under contract to Universal. Tobin called this "a poor man's *Stage Door*" but Frank Nugent, agreeing that it was "a variant, almost a sequel to *Stage Door,*" found it "a surprisingly fresh, uncommonly diverting, remarkably well-done film. . . . All the while, with deft bits of business—satirical, tragic, comic and sentimental—the tale keeps spinning and never lets you realize how frail it is."

When Tomorrow Comes (1939) has something in common with *Back Street* and again stars Irene Dunne, of whom Andrew Sarris says that "words alone cannot convey the grace and gallantry" of her performances in her three films with Stahl. Here she plays Helen, a waitress and union activist who falls in love with a piano-player who turns out to be a famous concert pianist (Charles Boyer). They spend a chaste night together, marooned in a Long Island church by a tremendous storm, and it emerges that Philippe is miserably married to a suicidal depressive. He invites Helen to accompany him on a European concert tour but, undone by an appeal from the wretched wife, the brokenhearted Helen remains in New York while her lover sails away.

Of the opening sequence in the restaurant, Tom Milne writes: "beautifully designed to simulate the continuity of a *plan-séquence* through its fluid montage of movement, it also yields a sense of ineluctability, a feeling that fate has a hand in this meeting, which emerges more overtly in the clouding sense of despair as the budding love affair begins to fringe the delirium of *amour fou* in the storm-bound church." George Morris has drawn attention to Stahl's use of storms and other natural catastrophes "to reflect the human drama being enacted below. An awareness of a larger metaphysic pervades these films." And Milne concludes that "Stahl has constructed an astonishingly persuasive film, starting in light comedy, ending in perfectly controlled emotionalism . . . , but taking off between times into the unknown."

Leaving Universal after ten very successful years, Stahl went to Columbia on a one-film contract to make *Our Wife* (1941), seen as an attempt to exploit the success of Leo McCarey's *My Favorite Wife*. It was something of a departure for Stahl, a screwball comedy about a trumpet player (Melvyn Douglas) eager to marry socialite Ruth Hussey, but obliged to wait until he can obtain a divorce from his selfish first wife (Ellen Drew). He moves his intended into the house, the wife poses as a cripple in an attempt to recover his affections, and all problems are solved when the house catches fire. Andrew Sarris thought that the result was "relatively strained as a comedy and, indeed, lacks the grace and charm of many of his . . . dramas."

After that, Stahl signed a fat contract with 20th Century–Fox, where he spent the remainder of his career. His first picture there—and the last in his series of "imitations of films"—was *The Immortal Sergeant* (1943), made in the wake of Howard Hawks' *Sergeant York*. Based on John Brophy's novel, and produced and scripted by Lamar Trotti, it deals with a lost patrol of British soldiers fighting in the Libyan desert during World War II. After his tough old sergeant (Thomas Mitchell) is killed, the shy and withdrawn corporal (Henry Fonda) has to face the challenges of command. Andrew Sarris pointed out that this generally rather routine war film has its moments of audacious imagery, as when Fonda, thirsting in the desert, conjures up an image of his girlfriend (Maureen O'Hara) emerging lightly clad and dripping wet from a swimming pool.

Much more notable was *Holy Matrimony* (1943), produced by Nunnally Johnson, who also wrote this adaptation of Arnold Bennett's novel *Buried Alive*. Monty Woolley plays Priam Farll, a famous artist in Edwardian England desperate for anonymity. When his valet Henry Leek dies, Farll has him buried in Westminster Abbey and takes his place, marrying Leek's penfriend Alice Challice (Gracie Fields) in the bargain. Complications ensue when the latter innocently sells some of his new pictures, which are taken to be Farll forgeries, and when it emerges that Leek already had a wife, not to mention two children. Woolley and Fields are splendid, and so is Laird Cregar as a cynical art expert.

Yann Tobin describes this as "a high-class comedy, a perfect blending of social satire and screwball humor, unique in Stahl's career, and perhaps in all Hollywood history. One of the very few comedies ever directed by Stahl, it was praised to the skies by the critics, so delighted were they to see him at last emerge from weepie land. . . . The sparkling dialogue and the outrageousness of the scenario poke uncommonly wicked fun at some sacrosanct British institutions. . . . Everything that was denounced in a pathetic vein by Stahl's dramas is here joyously lampooned. . . . The funeral in *Imitation of Life,* for example, can be reinterpreted in the light of the one in *Holy Matrimony.*" Attending his own burial service, Farll is overcome by so much ceremonial grieving: "he begins to cry, then to shout out his true identity, and, taken for a drunk, is promptly thrown out into the street."

The Eve of St. Mark (1946), from Maxwell Anderson's play, follows a platoon of GIs from prewar training to heroic strife in the Philippines. It centers on Quizz West (William Eythe), a farmboy from upstate New York who, like Fonda in *The Immortal Sergeant,* is forced to relinquish his customary diffidence and assume responsibility for the lives of other men. "It must be admitted," wrote one British reviewer, "that during the course of it an American soldier in the jaws of death carries on by long-range telepathy a philosophical discussion with mother and fiancée, and that this and similar situations have become a somewhat over-publicised aspect of military operations in the Pacific" but "there are first-rate sequences, beautifully scripted and acted, in barracks and in a disreputable café."

Keys of the Kingdom (1944) stars Gregory Peck (in his first major role) as a young priest in China who, at first disillusioned and doubting, gradually establishes a flourishing mission. Based on the novel by A. J. Cronin, it was produced by Joseph L. Mankiewicz, who also scripted in collaboration with Nunnally Johnson, and masterfully lit and photographed by Arthur Miller. *Time* called it "two hours and seventeen minutes of rather pedestrian sincerity," while conceding that it "never grows tedious."

Neither does *Leave Her to Heaven* (1945), in which Stahl returned with a vengeance to the melodrama. Gene Tierney plays Ellen Berent, whose incestuous passion for her dead father is transferred to the novelist Richard Harland (Cornel Wilde). They marry and set up house in an idyllic log cabin, but Ellen's obsessive love will brook no claims on Richard's affections other than her own. When she becomes pregnant, she throws herself downstairs to procure a miscarriage; when Richard's crippled young brother comes to stay, she engineers his death; when Richard turns to her gentle sister (Jeanne Crain), she kills herself.

"Cool, discreet, muted," wrote Yann Tobin, "the direction of *Leave Her to Heaven* is marked by the occasional typically Stahlian lyrical outburst, transcended by the lush Technicolor photography (which won Leon Shamroy a deserved Academy Award). The striking use of background and space, especially in the outdoor locations, assists in the drama's progression. It is clear, for instance, that Ellen the unstable needs a 'moving' decor to act against. She first flirts with Richard on a moving train, completes the seduction while swimming in a pool, and conceives the murder while rowing in a boat, a silent, terrifying scene. It is no coincidence either that the most memorable sequence has Gene Tierney scattering her father's ashes to the winds as she rides her horse; for a moment, the world is hers." The National Film Theatre called this "indisputably one of the great '40s melodramas. . . . Gene Tierney fills out the character to the last, calculated detail, while the narrative encapsulates all of Stahl's stylistic methods, from groupings within rooms to precise camera distances."

Leave Her to Heaven had been based on a rubbishy bestseller by Ben Ames Williams, and *The Foxes of Harrow* (1947) derived from another by Frank Yerby. The story is set in Louisiana and, as succinctly described by one contemporary reviewer, "tells how a nineteenth-century Irish emigrant (Rex Harrison) to America made a fortune, won a wife (Maureen O'Hara), had a son, lost the son, lost the fortune and nearly lost the wife." The same critic added that "the picture is immeasurably long and unspeakably dreary," and most of his colleagues agreed, though the public flocked to it.

Thirty years later, George Morris was more complimentary: "The plethora of natural catastrophes in *The Foxes of Harrow* lends an operat-

ic sweep to a movie whose epic structure is perhaps more formally realized than any other of the director's films. . . . O'Hara refuses to let Harrison mold *their* son in his image. The child, who in a further twist of fate has been born with one deformed foot, thus becomes the source of a power struggle between mother and father. . . . The thunderstorms that accompany the boy's death and, later, O'Hara's futile efforts to save Harrow [their house], conversely evoke rupture and reconciliation. While the first storm represents an external manifestation of the internal conflicts within the characters, the second gains even more power in contrast, the fury of the storm giving way to the emerging harmony which unites O'Hara and Harrison at their son's tombstone."

This was the last of Stahl's films of any real interest. *The Walls of Jericho* (1948), produced and scripted by Lamar Trotti from a novel by Paul Wellman, is solidly and observantly set in a small Kansas town early in this century, but goes on to tell the long and not very persuasive story of a county attorney (Cornel Wilde) whose political career is almost wrecked by a jealous admirer (Linda Darnell). *Father Was a Fullback* (1949), a tedious college comedy with Fred MacMurray and Maureen O'Hara, was followed by Stahl's only musical, *Oh, You Beautiful Doll* (1949), a dismal conclusion to his career. He died early the following year, survived by his wife of a late marriage, the former Mrs. Roxana Wray.

As George Morris says, "the woman's film has been generally neglected in the outpouring of theorizing on generic signs and structures that has characterized a great deal of recent film criticism. . . . Yet it can seriously be argued that the romantic melodrama is one of the richest sources of aesthetic expression in the cinema. . . . Stahl's approach to the woman's film is as unique as it is personal. In lieu of Borzage's transcendent romanticism and Sirk's subversive irony, Stahl confronts his unlikely narratives with quiet directness. . . . The implicit faith in his material is at once Stahl's major virtue and weakness. . . . His failures are often as endearing as his successes, simply because he maintained the integrity to resist embellishing his more hopeless properties with gimmicks. . . . Stahl's movies contain some of the most remarkable, forward-thinking female characters in American films. . . . Independent, determined, and free of self-pity, these women choose their destinies, and having chosen, shape their lives accordingly, with no recriminations or regrets."

John Gillett and Jane Clarke, in their introduction to the NFT retrospective, maintain that "to understand the secret of Stahl's allusive style, we must first examine his shooting methods: a predilection for the tight two-shot with the characters face to face, a distancing effect obtained by shooting flat-on to the set, and a remarkable flair for fluid character groupings in order to reveal looks, gestures, postures and, in some of the most beautifully judged close-ups in cinema, love. Apparently a meticulous worker and stern disciplinarian on the set, he moulded his performers into the very fabric of his films, enabling players like Margaret Sullavan, Irene Dunne, Claudette Colbert and Gene Tierney to produce their most rounded portraits of women caught up in a world of conflicting emotions and double standards . . . , matters which take on an even greater relevance today. On moving from the rich, personalised romances of the Universal period to the more solid, well-carpentered Fox dramas of the '40s, Stahl maintained his discreet passion and innate feeling for the *right* distance of camera from object which (to paraphrase Dreyer) is always the director's main task."

Stahl himself circa 1935 spoke of "dialogue pictures," in which "the story is carried forward by the speech of the characters, rather than by swift exciting action. Thus the basic structure of the entire screenplay is changed and the story must be treated differently by the camera. . . . To maintain smoothness of action, then, and to give the dialogue a chance to carry the story forward sweepingly, I strive to keep the camera in flowing motion, following various characters adroitly from one point to another without, in effect, interrupting their conversation. . . . In a motion picture of this type, emotion takes the place of action."

FILMS: *complete from 1918*—Wives of Men, 1918; Suspicion, 1918; The Serpent, 1918; Her Code of Honor (UK, Call of the Heart), 1919; A Woman Under Oath, 1919; Greater Than Love, 1919; Women Men Forget, 1920; The Woman in His House, 1920; Sowing the Wind, 1921; The Child Thou Gavest Me, 1921; Suspicious Wives, 1921; The Song of Life, 1921; One Clear Call, 1922; The Dangerous Age, 1922; The Wanters, 1923; Why Men Leave Home, 1924; Husbands and Lovers, 1924; Fine Clothes, 1925; Memory Lane, 1926; The Gay Deceiver, 1926; Lovers?, 1927; In Old Kentucky, 1927; A Lady Surrenders, 1930; Seed, 1931; Strictly Dishonorable, 1931; Back Street, 1932; Only Yesterday, 1933; Imitation of Life, 1934; Magnificent Obsession, 1935; Parnell, 1937; Letter of Introduction, 1938; When Tomorrow Comes, 1939; Our Wife, 1941; The Immortal Sergeant, 1943; Holy Matrimony, 1943; The Eve of St. Mark, 1944; Keys of the Kingdom, 1944; Leave Her to Heaven, 1945; The Foxes of Harrow, 1947; The Walls of Jericho, 1948; Father Was a Fullback, 1949; Oh, You Beautiful Doll, 1949.

ABOUT: Canham, K. John M. Stahl: The Romantic Im-

age, 1981 (annotated filmography); Coursodon, J.-P. American Directors Vol. 1, 1983; Roud, R. (ed.) Cinema: A Critical Dictionary, 1980; Thomson, D. A Biographical Dictionary of the Cinema, 1980. *Periodicals*—Film Comment May–June 1977; Monthly Film Bulletin November 1981; National Film Theatre (Britain) Booklet August 1981; Positif July–August 1979; Village Voice April 29, 1986.

*STAUDTE, WOLFGANG (October 9, 1906–January 19, 1984), German director, scenarist, and actor, was born in Saarbrücken, the son of Fritz Staudte and the former Matilde Firmans. Both parents were actors and their careers took them in 1912 to Berlin, where Wolfgang Staudte grew up. His first interest was not show business but engineering, and he began studies in that subject at Oldenburg. He disliked the theoretical work, however, and after two years took up an apprenticeship, first with Mercedes in Berlin, then with Hansa-Werken in Varel.

Staudte's mother had died when he was fifteen, but Fritz Staudte had become well known as an actor at Berlin's left-wing "people's theatre," the Volksbühne. Having made up his mind to resume his engineering studies, Wolfgang Staudte first visited his father at the Volksbühne—then under the direction of Erwin Piscator—and was immediately fascinated by what he saw. Instead of returning to Oldenburg he went off to a theatrical agency and was soon hired by a manager who apparently mistook him for his father. Staudte survived his debut at a theatre in Schneidemühl, but flopped in a second play and was fired.

In 1926, returning to Berlin, Staudte joined his father at the Volksbühne, appearing during the next few years in productions directed by Piscator and Max Reinhardt, among others. Beginning in 1931, he also secured his first small movie roles. During this period his father, a committed socialist, founded his own politically oriented theatre company. Staudte appeared in two of his father's productions and through him had contact with radical circles in Berlin. Though sympathetic to his father's views, Staudte did not really regard himself as a radical artist. Nevertheless, these contacts, and his involvement with the Volksbühne, were enough to cost him his actor's permit when Hitler came to power in 1933.

For the next two years, Staudte earned his living dubbing foreign films for the Rythmoton Company. By 1935 the situation had eased a little; he was able to get a radio job reading children's stories and commercials, and the same year he entered the film business, making advertisements to be shown in movie theatres. Staudte

°shtaud´ tə

WOLFGANG STAUDTE

is said to have directed and edited (and often scripted as well) about a hundred of these commercials, each between 80 and 130 seconds long, in this way mastering the rudiments of his craft and in particular learning how to present the essentials of what he had to say with maximum economy and clarity. He was also able to resume his work as a bit-player in films by other directors, including Veit Harlan's *Jud Süss* (1940). (It should be said that, according to Harlan himself, "virtually every actor" in this disgusting work of anti-Semitic propaganda was "performing under duress.")

Staudte's experience as a director of commercials finally brought him an invitation from the Tobis production company to make his first fiction film. This was a satirical short called *Ins Grab kann nichts mitnehmen (You Can't Take It With You,* 1941). Other shorts followed, and in 1942, when Tobis hired the circus clown Charlie Rivel and needed a vehicle for him, Staudte submitted a synopsis and was assigned to direct his first feature, *Akrobat schö-ö-ö-n (Lo-o-o-vely Acrobat,* 1943). A circus story based on Rivel's own rise to stardom, it has been described as a "leaden" and "misguided" comedy.

Staudte nevertheless went on to make four more films for Tobis, which by that time was wholly under government control. A romance called *Ich hab' von Dir geträumt (I Dreamed of You,* 1944) was followed in 1944–1945 by *Der Mann, dem Man den Namen stahl (The Man Whose Name Was Stolen).* A satire on bureaucracy, it was banned by Goebbels' propaganda ministry, which reportedly wanted Staudte sent to the front by way of punishment. Thanks to the

intervention of the actor Heinrich George, Staudte was given another chance and made *Frau über Bord (Woman Overboard),* also known as *Kabine 27.* He finished shooting this film before the end of the war, but apparently never completed the editing.

After the war, film production in Germany resumed in various forms in the various zones. In the zones occupied by the United States, Britain, and France, licenses were issued to individual production units, while in the East the Soviet Union established DEFA, a state-owned monopoly based on the old UFA studios. Though Staudte lived in the West, he at first worked for DEFA, writing and directing its first postwar feature, *Die Mörder sind unter Uns (Murderers Among Us,* 1946).

Like a number of subsequent East German films, it is a study in war guilt. A former army doctor (Ernst Fischer) is wracked by agonizing memories of a civilian massacre in Poland. He has become a self-pitying alcoholic, haunting the ruins of Berlin obsessed by the desire to murder the officer who had ordered the massacre, now a prosperous businessman with a devoted family. The doctor's sanity and self-respect is restored by Susanne, who has survived years in a concentration camp determined to make sense of her life and the lives around her, and who is still capable of love.

Manvell and Fraenkel write in *The German Cinema* that the film "was remarkable not only for its subject, a significant one for the period, but also for its use of the ruins of Berlin, its sparse music score by Ernst Roters, and perhaps above all for the performance of a young actress new to the screen, Hildegard Knef, who played Susanne. The film is full of imaginatively visualized moments, created out of a deep experience which the filmmaker shares with his characters. At the opening, a piano plays light jazz as the camera covers the ruins of Berlin, the crowded dance-halls, the overladen trains, the derelict railway station. Gradually the girl is singled out of the crowd until she is in close-shot; she is absorbing the pure pleasure of her freedom, her eyes full of tears. The doctor, finally seen in a haze of tobacco smoke poring in a drunken trance over a chessboard, has also been first glimpsed in the crowded streets. Suddenly the words 'mass grave' are followed by a spinning shot of the legs of ballet dancers and then a scene of rain-drenched streets. The ruins themselves are the recurrent motif of the film; in some shots the rubble seems like a landscape from the moon."

The success of *Murderers Among Us* encouraged others to produce what became known as

Trümmerfilme ("rubble films"). These portrayals of the physical and psychological wreckage of postwar Germany, resigned and often self-pitying in tone, were shot on location rather than in the studio and seemed to some critics to promise a German realist movement comparable to Italian neorealism, though without the latter's use of nonprofessional actors. No such development in fact occurred, and Staudte's own next DEFA film was *Die seltsamen Abenteuer des Herrn Fridolin B.* (1948), a much-revised version of *Der Mann, dem Man den Namen stahl*, the satire on bureaucracy banned by the Nazis.

In 1948 Staudte directed the German episode in the international coproduction released four years later as *Geschichte von fünf Städten (A Tale of Five Women/A Tale of Five Cities)*. Staudte wrote or coauthored most of his films, and in the case of his next film, *Rotation* (1949), conceived the original idea as well. It tells the story of an ordinary German worker from the late 1920s to 1945. Hans Behnke (Paul Esser) reluctantly joins the Nazi party during the depression because he will lose his job if he does not. It seems an understandable decision, but the rest of the film illustrates the appalling costs of such a compromise, and makes it clear that Behnke's son—and all of us—face equally crucial choices.

Rotation was generally admired as "a powerful technical and artistic performance," and there was higher praise for *Der Untertan (The Underdog*, 1951). Based on a novel by Heinrich Mann, and set in Germany at the turn of the century, it shows how a timid and obsequious boy, through blind loyalty to the social hierarchy, rises to a position of great power and authority. Some critics found it turgid and clumsy in its didacticism, but many others did not. The French director Chris Marker wrote that "one is presented, with a power and cruelty which recall von Stroheim, with German society as it was at the end of the Empire. . . . But the most interesting part of the story is the furore which the film has caused in West Germany; because old, pre-1914 Germany had disconcerting similarities, on essential points, with that which is reviving under Adenauer."

Another notable film of the period, also made for DEFA, was *Die Geschichte des kleinen Muck (Little Mook*, 1953), a children's film in Agfacolor about an unloved hunchback boy who achieves influence at the Sultan's decadent court and uses it for the good of the people. *Ciske de Rat* (1955), dealing with the rehabilitation of a boy who accidentally kills his mother, was based on a Dutch bestseller and made in the Netherlands. It won the Silver Lion at Venice. Work then began on a DEFA adaptation of Brecht's

Mutter Courage, but this project fell through and the film was later completed by Peter Palitzsch and Manfred Wekwerth.

By this time, according to Manvell and Fraenkel, "Staudte was becoming restive under the increasing controls in East Germany and, without actually breaking with DEFA, began to direct films in West Germany." The first of these was *Rose Bernd (The Sins of Rose Bernd*, 1956), starring Maria Schell and derived from Hauptmann's grimly naturalistic drama about an unmarried mother driven by a heartless society to murder her baby. *Madeleine und der Legionär* (1957), with Hildegard Knef having to choose between love and patriotism, was followed by *Kanonen-Serenade (Always Victorious/Il Capitano*, 1958), a West German–Italian coproduction in which Vittorio De Sica plays the captain of a banana boat who is dragged reluctantly into wartime heroics.

After *Der Maulkorb* (1958), another literary adaptation—this time from a novel by Heinrich Spoerl—came one of the most notable of Staudte's West German films, *Rosen für den Staatsanwalt (Roses for the Prosecutor*, 1959). In the chaos of Hitler's last days, an SS prosecutor (Martin Held) condemns a feckless soldier to death for a trivial crime. The soldier escapes to become an equally feckless peddler. Some years after the war, he runs afoul of the laws of a theoretically very different regime, but is confronted in court by the same Himmler-like prosecutor (who finds the encounter considerably more embarrassing than he does). Dilys Powell called it a "satire with . . . political teeth" that is "directed and played with a kind of wry grace. . . . Suddenly one thinks hopefully of the prospect of a reviving German cinema." This ironic and intelligent film took the first prize at Karlovy Vary as well as a West German award.

The return of former Nazis to positions of power in West Germany is also the theme of *Kirmes (Fairground*, 1960). The erection of a carousel in a small town involves excavations which reveal the body of a wartime deserter. It emerges that he had been hounded to his death by an SS official—a man who has since become the town's mayor. *Der letzte Zeuge (The Last Witness*, 1960) stars Martin Held and Ellen Schwiers in an effective drama about a woman wrongly accused of murdering her own child and the lawyer who sets out to find the real killer.

In 1963 Staudte made a new version of *Die Dreigroschenoper (The Threepenny Opera*, 1963), starring Curt Jürgens, Hildegard Knef, and Gert Fröbe. It had a moderately good press, though some critics found it an excessively lavish adaptation of a play about "the poorest of the poor." None of Staudte's later movies had added much to his reputation and, beginning in the late 1960s, he concentrated mainly on television, directing numerous episodes of *Der Kommisar, Der Seewolf,* and other series, as well as individual television films, until his death in 1984. He was survived by his wife, the former Rita Heidelbach.

Staudte was not a particularly innovative or influential filmmaker (except as the originator of the short-lived *Trümmerfilme*) but he was an extremely civilized, humane, and intelligent one, a craftsman of great professional accomplishment and resource, and a splendid director of actors. In the 1950s and early 1960s, before the advent of the New German Cinema, he and Helmut Käutner were almost the only West German directors who continued to make movies of quality. Staudte was awarded the German National Prize in 1951, the German Film Prize in 1975, and the Federal Cross of Merit in 1979.

FILMS: Akrobat schö-ö-ö-n, 1943; Ich hab' von Dir geträumt, 1944; Der Mann, dem Man den Namen stahl, 1945 (banned, remade as Die seltsamen Abenteuer des Herrn Fridolin B., 1948); Frau über Bord/Kabine 27, 1945 (not released); Die Mörder sind unter Uns (Murderers Among Us/The Murderers Are Amongst Us), 1946; Rotation, 1949; Schicksal aus zweiter Hand, 1949; Der Untertan (The Underdog/The Kaiser's Lackey), 1951; (with others) Geschichte von fünf Städten/Fünf Mädchen und ein Mann (A Tale of Five Women/A Tale of Five Cities), 1952; Die Geschichte des kleinen Muck (Little Mook), 1953; Leuchtfeuer, 1954; Ciske de Rat/Ciske—Ein Kind braucht Liebe, 1955; Rose Bernd (The Sins of Rose Bernd), 1956; Madeleine und der Legionär, 1957; Kanonen-Serenade (Always Victorious/Il Capitano), 1958; Der Maulkorb, 1958; Rosen für den Staatsanwalt (Roses for the Prosecutor), 1959; Kirmes (Fairground), 1960; Der letzte Zeuge (The Last Witness), 1960; Die Rebellion, 1962; (with John Olden) Die glücklichen Jahre der Thorwalds, 1962; Die Dreigroschenoper (The Threepenny Opera), 1963; Herrenpartie (Stag Party), 1964; Das Lamm, 1964; Der Fall Kapitan Behrens, 1965 (for TV); Ganovenehre (Crooks' Honor), 1966; Die Klasse, 1968 (for TV); Heimlichkeiten (Secrets), 1968; Die Herren mit der weissen Weste (The Robbers), 1970; Die Kriminalerzählung, 1970 (for TV); Die Gartenlaube, 1970 (for TV); Die Person, 1970 (for TV); Fluchtweg St. Pauli—Grossalarm für die Davidswache, 1971; Uhrwerk Orange (German-language version of Kubrick's A Clockwork Orange), 1972; Verrat ist klein Gesellschaftsspiel, 1972 (for TV); Marya Sklodowska-Curie, 1972 (for TV); Nerze nachts am Strassenrand, 1972 (for TV); Ein Herrliches Dasein, 1974 (for TV). *Published scripts*—Herrenpartie, 1964; Die Mörder sind unter Uns *and* Rotation *in* Vier Filmerzählungen nach den bekannten DEFA-Filmen, 1969.

ABOUT: Gregor, U. Wie sie filmen, 1966; Hull, D. Film in the Third Reich, 1969; Manvell, R. and Fraenkel, H. The German Cinema, 1971; Orbanz, E. (ed.) Wolfgang Staudte, 1974 (in German); Welch, D. Propaganda and the German Cinema 1933–1945, 1983; Who's Who in Germany, 1980. *Periodicals*—Celluloide January 1961; Film Summer 1963; Film und Fernsehen May 1979; Filmstudio January 1966.

STERNBERG, "JOSEF VON" (**Jonas Sternberg**) (May 29, 1894–December 22, 1969), American director, was born in Vienna, eldest child of a poor, Orthodox Jewish family. His father, Moses Sternberg, "was an enormously strong man, who often used his strength on me. . . . After each beating, the punishing hand was extended to be kissed, this in a noble tradition then prevalent." Moses' wife Serafin (born Singer), whom her son described as "gentle, with no experience in taming a lion," could do little to protect the children. When Sternberg was three, his father, unable to find work in Vienna, left for America to seek his fortune, planning to send for his wife and children later. Meanwhile the boy was left largely to his own devices, happy to explore the "children's paradise" of Vienna, and especially the nearby Prater amusement park, until he was sent to school at the age of six. Here he was taught compulsory Hebrew by "a frightening monster with beard and piercing eyes" whose favorite diversion—according to Sternberg—was to terrify his young pupils until they messed their pants, and then beat them for doing so.

In 1901 Moses Sternberg sent for his family to join him in New York, though without providing any money for their fares. Somehow Serafin Sternberg transported herself and her three children to Hamburg, and from there across the Atlantic. In New York Sternberg picked up basic English and attended the local public school. "The three years spent there are an absolute blank. Not one single day can I recall, nor one teacher." At the end of those three years Moses Sternberg, who had managed to find only menial, dead-end jobs, returned with his family to Vienna. "But not long after, like a squirrel that keeps turning a cage, he once more left us to try his fortune, went again to the same country, and again in vain." In 1908 his family once more followed him, this time for good. Sternberg attended high school on Long Island, but dropped out after a year spent "doing nothing but struggling with the English language."

An aunt who owned a millinery store offered him work as an apprentice; from there he moved to the stockroom of a large lace house on Fifth Avenue. At seventeen he changed his first name

JOSEF VON STERNBERG

to Josef and left home. He lived anywhere, took any work he could find, and in his spare time read all he could and studied art, determinedly making up for his scanty and haphazard education. A chance encounter during a rainstorm led to Sternberg's first contact with films: he became apprentice to a man who coated, patched, and repaired film stock, a job that also involved occasional stints as a projectionist. Rapidly gaining skill and expertise, in 1914 he joined a more prestigious organization, the impressively named World Film Corporation of Fort Lee, New Jersey, becoming chief assistant to the director general, William A. Brady. Sternberg's instincts for the visual image and for effective editing were by now well developed. His main task was to cut, patch, retitle, and generally doctor the crude products of Brady's company.

When the United States entered the war in 1917, Sternberg joined the Signal Corps, where he helped make training films; Victor Fleming, Wesley Ruggles, and Lewis Milestone were among his fellow workers. After being discharged he returned briefly to the World Film Corporation, before leaving to gain wider experience on a number of independent productions in America and Britain. His first credit as assistant director was on *The Mystery of the Yellow Room* (1919), directed at the Fort Lee studios by the émigré Frenchman Emile Chautard. In 1921 he traveled to Europe, staying for two months in Vienna, where he met the Viennese author Karl Adolph and undertook the translation of Adolph's novel *Töchter (Daughters of Vienna,* 1923). In London Sternberg worked as assistant director on several films for Sir Charles

Higham's Alliance Productions, including *The Bohemian Girl* (1922), before returning to the United States. In 1923 he arrived in Hollywood.

With the exception of Chautard, for whom he retained both professional and personal respect, Sternberg had been distinctly unimpressed by the directors he had worked with (although they were, he commented dryly, "not altogether without value, for they showed that no special skill was needed to be a director"). His opinion of the Hollywood output he had seen was scarcely any higher. Most of it he dismissed as worthless, although he appreciated D. W. Griffith's skill with the camera, and commended Chaplin for his "pictorial sobriety" and ability to portray "the most primitive emotions." One of the few directors who earned Sternberg's unqualified approval was Erich von Stroheim, "who invested his films . . . with an intensity that bristled." Sternberg's admiration for Stroheim (also, by coincidence, the product of a poor Jewish Viennese family) was manifested less in his work—though traces of Stroheim's visual influence are evident in Sternberg's early output—than in the public persona he chose to adopt: arrogant, tyrannical, and intolerant of all who contradicted him, or whose abilities he considered inferior to his own. The last category included virtually everybody—especially actors—with whom Sternberg came in contact.

In Hollywood, he soon found work as assistant director on *By Divine Right* (1923), an independent production directed by Roy William Neill. Thanks to the film's star and coproducer, Elliott Dexter, Sternberg acquired a further attribute in common with Stroheim: the aristocratic particle "von," which Dexter thought would look better on the credits. The addition, according to Sternberg, was made without his knowledge, but he seems to have made no objection, then or later.

After working on some half-dozen independent productions, in which he was allowed to direct an occasional scene, Sternberg got his chance to direct a picture of his own. He was approached by a young British comic actor, George K. Arthur, whose Hollywood career was flagging. Arthur had a script he had written, entitled "Just Plain Bugs," and a few thousand dollars of savings. He was prepared to finance the movie and to pay Sternberg $500 to direct him in it. Sternberg read Arthur's script and returned it with the advice that he burn it before anyone else could see it. In its place, said Sternberg, he would provide a script of his own, at no extra cost—an offer which Arthur accepted "with tears in his eyes." Sternberg, for his part, was attracted by the idea of directing a film without interference and with no restrictions apart from those imposed by the minuscule budget.

The Salvation Hunters (1925) was filmed in three-and-a-half weeks and cost $4,900. The story concerned three young derelicts (expressionistically designated The Boy, The Girl, and The Child) living on a huge dredge in San Pedro harbor, the vicissitudes they undergo, and their eventual—and somewhat unconvincing—triumph over their muddy circumstances. "There are important fragments of life that have been ignored by the motion picture," proclaimed Sternberg's opening title portentously, "because Body is more important than Thought. Our aim has been to photograph a Thought." This aspiration was scarcely fulfilled by the movie that followed, for all its pictorial originality. Kevin Brownlow found it "pretentious . . . a flat and largely unimaginative exercise in filmcraft," although he allowed it "a certain austere dignity."

Certainly the acting in *The Salvation Hunters* was, by the standards of the day, unusually restrained—Sternberg's legendary control over his actors seems to have been exercised from the very start—and the squalid locations were effectively exploited. Already the director's preoccupation with pictorial composition—especially the play of light and shadow—and his relative indifference to story line were clearly in evidence. "Instead of the Elinor Glyn plots of the day, I had in mind a visual poem. Instead of flat lighting, shadows. In the place of pasty masks, faces in relief, plastic and deep-eyed. Instead of scenery which meant nothing, an emotionalized background that would transfer itself into my foreground. Instead of saccharine characters, sober figures moving in rhythm. . . . And . . . the hero of the film was to be a dredge."

The premiere of *The Salvation Hunters,* in a small theatre on Sunset Boulevard, was a disaster. "The members of the cast were in the audience, which greeted my work with laughter and jeers and finally rioted. Many walked out, and so did I." However, George K. Arthur had contrived to show the film privately to Charlie Chaplin and Douglas Fairbanks, both of whom responded with enthusiasm. (Chaplin is said to have claimed, later, that he only praised it by way of a joke.) United Artists bought the picture for release, and Sternberg, now suddenly famous, was invited by Mary Pickford to direct her next film, to a scenario of his own choosing.

Sternberg duly came up with an outline of the proposed movie. It was to be called *Backwash,* and Pickford would play a blind girl living in a Pittsburgh slum. Most of the action would take place in her own mind, using subjective camera. Pickford, who had commended Sternberg for his "freshness and originality," decided that such qualities might be taken too far, and the contract

was terminated. Sternberg, now much in demand, accepted instead an eight-picture contract with MGM. His first assignment was *The Exquisite Sinner* (1925), a romantic drama set in Brittany.

Both studio and stars were bewildered by Sternberg's idiosyncratic—and autocratic—working methods. Robert Florey, assistant director on the film, described the final product as being exquisitely photographed, "full of interest, and the direction showed the humor of which Sternberg was a master." The studio, however, found the film incomprehensible and had it completely reshot by Phil Rosen (as *Heaven on Earth*). "The result," said Sternberg, "was two ineffective films instead of one." Nonetheless, he let himself be persuaded by Louis B. Mayer to undertake another assignment: *The Masked Bride* (1925), with Mae Murray. This was an even greater fiasco. After two weeks of shooting, Sternberg pointed his camera upwards at the studio roof, finding there "more interest than was apparent in the perfect material that clung to the polished floor," walked off the set, and took his leave of MGM. (The picture was completed by Christy Cabanne, who took directorial credit.)

Charlie Chaplin now asked Sternberg to direct a film for him. Entitled *The Sea Gull* (no connection with Chekhov's play) or alternatively *A Woman of the Sea* (1926), it was intended as a comeback vehicle for Chaplin's former costar, Edna Purviance. Sternberg's screenplay, based on an idea by Chaplin, was a love story set in a fishing community on the California coast. When the film was completed, it received one private screening, after which Chaplin withdrew it, allowing no further showings. The only print was eventually burned by the US tax authorities, this being the only condition under which they would allow Chaplin to list the film as a tax loss. John Grierson, one of the few people to see the picture, described it as "a strangely beautiful and empty affair—possibly the most beautiful I have ever seen—of net patterns, sea patterns and hair in the wind." Sternberg took the episode philosophically: "[Chaplin] charged off its cost against his formidable income tax, and I charged it off to experience."

The possibility of working with the theatre director Max Reinhardt now took Sternberg to Germany, but the project came to nothing. Returning via England, he met and married a minor actress named Riza Royce, and together they traveled back to Hollywood. With four failed assignments behind him, Sternberg's reputation had slipped badly, and he was glad to accept an offer from B. P. Schulberg of work as an assistant director at Paramount. He was to remain at the studio for eight years and to make fourteen films for it—the bulk of his output, including all those now reckoned to be his finest work.

His first major assignment was to direct retakes on Frank Lloyd's *Children of Divorce* (1927), a task that involved reshooting half the film within three days. Sternberg accomplished this so successfully that the studio decided to entrust him with a picture of his own—"a little one," Sternberg later explained, "a film no one might notice if it were left unfinished." The script was adapted from a story by Ben Hecht, based on his experiences as a crime reporter in gangster-era Chicago, and the title, which Sternberg thought a good one, was *Underworld* (1927). George Bancroft starred as the mobster Bull Weed, with Clive Brook as his melancholy protégé—an alcoholic lawyer who has fallen for Weed's mistress Feathers (Evelyn Brent).

Underworld, wrote Kevin Brownlow, "was the film that began the gangster cycle, and it remains the masterpiece of the genre, containing all the elements which became clichés in later pictures." Similar assessments of the film have often been made, though not all critics would agree. Andrew Sarris thought it "less of a proto-gangster film than a pre-gangster film," and John Baxter wrote that its "reputation as 'the first gangster film' is unearned. . . . After four decades of gangster films, its histrionic and decorative style are unconvincing, and the plot fatally episodic." But though any claims of realism now seem hard to sustain, the film remains effective through the power of its emotionally charged images, notably in the central sequence of the gangland ball.

Hecht's initial reaction to *Underworld* was to demand that his name be removed from the credits. The studio, with misgivings about the film's commercial potential, premiered it surreptitiously in a minor New York theatre, without a press showing. Against all expectations, and apparently through word-of-mouth alone, it became a smash hit, and all-night screenings had to be arranged to meet the demand. Hecht, having presumably overcome his aversion, was awarded an Oscar for best original screenplay, and Paramount gave Sternberg a $10,000 bonus. Possibly as a further token of their regard, the studio also asked him to cut Stroheim's *The Wedding March* (1928) to an acceptable length. Sternberg claimed that he had Stroheim's approval for this operation, but whether he did or not, Stroheim apparently never spoke to him again.

In 1927 Paramount had borrowed Emil Jannings, then widely regarded as the world's greatest actor, from the UFA studios in Berlin and were searching for suitable properties to display their prestigious acquisition. Sternberg provided the story for *Street of Sin* (1928), assigned to Mauritz Stiller, which cast Jannings in the improbable role of a Soho burglar named Basher Bill; and also directed him in a far more suitable vehicle, *The Last Command* (1928).

Andrew Sarris described *The Last Command* as "Sternberg's most Pirandellian film." Undoubtedly its plot—suggested by Lubitsch—is more dominant, and more closely structured, than usual. Jannings plays a Hollywood extra, a frail old recluse who is cast as a Russian general in a war picture. A long flashback shows that the old man *is* a Russian general, who once jailed as a revolutionary the man who is now directing the Hollywood movie. In the film's final sequences the old general imagines he is leading a real charge against the enemy and dies on the set. The story allowed Sternberg to alternate biting satire on the Hollywood studio system, shown as both obsequious and callous, with bravura visual episodes in the revolutionary sequences. His aim, he wrote, "was to extract the essence of the Hollywood film factory and to flash the essentials of a revolution, without being realistic with either. I was an unquestioned authority on Hollywood, and that made it difficult to be unrealistic in picturing it. I felt more at home with the Russian Revolution, for there I was free to use my imagination alone."

Both aspects of the film worried the studio executives, who maintained that Sternberg's view of the Russian Revolution was "distorted," and that his "untruthful" presentation of Hollywood would alienate the public. *The Last Command* would have been shelved, had not a major company shareholder seen it and insisted on its release. The film was a considerable critical success, gaining Academy Award nominations for best picture and best story and an Oscar for Jannings' performance, though returns at the box office were disappointing.

By now Sternberg had acquired his permanent reputation as a cinematic tyrant, an arrogant perfectionist demanding total and unquestioning obedience from everybody on the set, actors in particular. "The only way to succeed," he is supposed to have remarked, "is to make people hate you. That way they remember you." Anecdotes abound concerning his outrageous behavior. Among the actors with whom he most notoriously clashed were Jannings, Sam Jaffe, Grace Moore, Wallace Beery, and William Powell; the latter demanded a clause in his contract exempting him from ever working with Sternberg again. John Wayne confessed that

Sternberg "scared him stiff," and Janet Leigh recalled that the director "had the most quietly infuriating way of saying something," though she conceded the effectiveness of his methods. In his role of tyrannical genius, Sternberg costumed himself appropriately, generally favoring jodhpurs and riding boots. He invariably carried a cane on set, and for *I, Claudius* he added an ornate Javanese turban.

Sternberg's own attitude was simple and—granted his premise—eminently logical. He believed that "anything that aspires to be a work of art can have but one creator"—who, in the case of a film, was the director. Actors, therefore, were merely one element—albeit a highly important one—of the material with which the creative artist worked. "An actor is turned on and off like a spigot, and like the spigot, is not the source of the liquid that flows through him. . . . How can the sculptor be honest with the piece of clay that considers itself more important than the hands that mold it?" Such views could hardly fail to arouse resentment among the majority of actors. For Sternberg, the ideal player was one who—like Dietrich—would place herself unquestioningly and unreservedly in his hands.

Of Sternberg's three remaining silent pictures, two may no longer exist; no prints are available in any archive. The first of the missing films, *The Drag Net* (1928), returned to the gangster milieu of *Underworld,* with George Bancroft playing a police detective, and William Powell a smooth gangland boss. It was poorly received at the box office, as was *The Docks of New York* (1928)—of which prints have, fortunately, survived. This was a waterfront drama about a ship's stoker (Bancroft) who rescues a prostitute (Betty Compson) from drowning and goes through a fake marriage ceremony with her. He plans to leave her the next morning but at the last moment changes his mind. Sternberg made superb use of his grimy settings, with dark figures silhouetted against gleaming nets or looming through iridescent fogs. But he also depicted his protagonists with uncharacteristic affection. "He achieves," wrote Kevin Brownlow, "a feeling of warmth and humanity—he seems to care about his characters, instead of using them . . . merely to form patterns of light and shade." And Andrew Sarris thought that here, "more than in any previous film, Sternberg has integrated spectacle and psychology."

Accounts of the other "lost" film, *The Case of Lena Smith* (1929), suggest that this may have been an even more personal work, and perhaps the finest of his silent movies. Set in the Vienna of Sternberg's childhood, it recounted the mis-

fortunes of a peasant girl who has a child by a dissolute young officer, and is said to have been an exceptionally beautiful film, suffused with nostalgia. *Thunderbolt* (1929) was Sternberg's first talkie, shot initially as a silent and hurriedly remade with sound. The splices show, most obviously in the sequence where the gangster hero (George Bancroft yet again) is serenaded in the death cell by a full prison orchestra rendering negro spirituals. Elsewhere, though, the film displays some interestingly experimental use of the soundtrack. Peter Baxter singled out "an almost frenetic nightclub scene" that "exploits the dramatic possibilities of multiple sources of sound."

But once more Sternberg's career seemed to be in decline. *Underworld* apart, none of his Paramount films had done well in commercial terms. He badly needed a hit—and got one, from a rather unexpected source. In the temperamental, self-indulgent Emil Jannings, Sternberg the great manipulator of actors had almost met his match. After completing *The Last Command,* he had informed Jannings that he never wanted to work with him again. The actor had returned the compliment. Yet word now came from Germany that, to guide him through his first sound movie, Jannings would accept no other director than Sternberg. The film would be a Paramount/UFA coproduction. Sternberg arrived in Berlin with his wife late in 1929.

Rejecting UFA's first suggestion of a film about Rasputin, Sternberg chose a subject adapted from a novel by Heinrich Mann, *Professor Unrath.* It provided a vehicle for the archetypal Jannings role: a figure of self-satisfied dignity brought low. In this case, the protagonist is a provincial schoolteacher who becomes hopelessly infatuated with Lola-Lola, a singer in a sleazy café, and is utterly humiliated and degraded, ending as a stage clown. When Lola leaves him for another man, he returns old and broken to his school and dies at his desk. Lola was yet to be cast; against everyone's advice, Sternberg chose a little-known revue artiste, Marlene Dietrich, who had given little previous evidence of acting talent. "Her appearance was ideal; what she did with it was something else again. That would be my concern."

The Blue Angel (1930), wrote Andrew Sarris, "is the one Sternberg film the director's severest detractors will concede is beyond reproach and ridicule." Much of it, though—especially considered beside his Hollywood films with Dietrich—looks crude and clumsy, particularly in the English version. (The film was shot in English and German versions; most critics prefer the latter.) Jannings' style of acting has not worn well, and many sequences seem static and overarranged.

But despite its weaknesses, the film retains remarkable psychological and emotional power, thanks to the cold, ironic intensity with which Sternberg observes his characters and to the casual sexuality of Dietrich's performance, which created one of the cinema's most enduring erotic icons.

Siegfried Kracauer saw in *The Blue Angel* a prefiguration of coming political events, asserting that it "poses anew the problem of German immaturity and moreover elaborates its consequences. . . . These screen figures anticipate what will happen in real life a few years later. The boys are born Hitler Youths." Sternberg denied any such intentions, stating that he knew at the time little about Germany and nothing at all about Nazism. Andrew Sarris concurred: "It is not specifically Germany or the German character with which Sternberg is concerned here, but rather the spectacle of a prudent, prudish man blocked off from all means of displaying his manhood except the most animalistic," although Sternberg many have "felt the conflict between order and nature would be more violent in a German setting than in any other." Certainly this conflict, between the forces of reason and emotion—or, in Joyce Rheuban's terms (*Sight and Sound,* Winter 1972–1973), "the scientist and the vamp"—was to furnish the theme for all Sternberg's pictures with Dietrich and for several of his other films.

Response to *The Blue Angel,* in Germany and all over Europe, was immediate and spectacular. Even before the film opened Dietrich had accepted a contract from Paramount (offered on Sternberg's recommendation), and she sailed for New York on the night of the Berlin premiere. She was greeted on arrival by a lawsuit from Riza Royce von Sternberg, alleging alienation of affection. The Sternberg marriage had never been a great success (the couple had already divorced in 1927, but were subsequently reunited), and it now collapsed in a mess of accusations, legal claims, and emotional scenes. Paramount tried to hush the affair up, to little effect, and Mrs. von Sternberg was granted a divorce—on grounds of cruelty—in June 1930. Sternberg himself never admitted that his relationship with Dietrich was anything but professional, and claimed that even in that regard he lost interest in her after *Morocco.* Against this stands the evidence of the films, which would appear to trace an ever more obsessive fascination, though tempered by ironic self-awareness, as he transformed a "modest little German *Hausfrau*" into "a celluloid monument," a mythic figure of ambiguous sexuality.

Morocco (1930) contains, if only in embryo, all the key elements of the Sternberg-Dietrich Hollywood cycle. The plot, taken from a novel by Benno Vigny, is novelettish and trivial, with little concern for plausibility. Nor do the settings aim at any degree of authenticity. This is a Morocco of the mind, an impressionistic sketch of wind and sand and palm trees. What interests Sternberg is the play of emotions, the masquerade of the senses, mirrored in the play of light and shadow, illusion and reality. Dietrich, as the cabaret singer Amy Jolly, "materializes in top hat, white tie and tails," wrote Andrew Sarris, "and is thereafter immortalized as the purveyor of pansexuality"—an impression confirmed when she publicly kisses a woman on the lips. The object of her affections is Gary Cooper, as unlikely a legionnaire as ever stuck a rose behind his ear; and Adolphe Menjou, courteous and self-denying, plays the third in the triangle, closely resembling Sternberg himself in his pained elegance.

"It is in the ability to suggest inner emotional experience merely with a control of light and shadow that Sternberg excels," wrote Curtis Harrington, and *Morocco* is full of the patterns of light and shade in constant movement—light intersected through slatted shades, fluttered by fans, deflected by hangings and veils. The cameraman on this and on Sternberg's next three pictures was Lee Garmes, who later claimed that he, rather than the director, created "the Dietrich face." At any rate, Garmes was nominated for an Oscar for *Morocco,* as were also Sternberg, Dietrich, and Hans Dreier (art director on nearly all Sternberg's Paramount films). The picture was an outstanding commercial success and, released in the USA before *The Blue Angel,* immediately established Dietrich as a major new star. She and her Svengali—as Sternberg was generally portrayed—were promptly signed to a new three-picture contract.

A spy story Sternberg had written, *X-27,* provided the basis for *Dishonored* (1931)—a title that he always disliked. Set in his native city, it concerns a prostitute who is recruited as a spy, falls in love with her Russian opposite number, allows him to escape, and is executed by firing squad. The film lacks the emotional intensity of its two predecessors—partly because it would be difficult to accept Victor McLaglen, playing the Russian spy, as the cause of anyone's *Liebestod*—but deploys in its place an engagingly mocking humor, not least in the episode where Dietrich disguises herself as a simple peasant girl in order to trap a lecherous officer. "One of Sternberg's most assured though lightest works," wrote John Baxter, citing the visual and aural virtuosity of a labyrinthine, streamer-clogged masked ball and of the final execution sequence in a vast, echoing hangar.

While Dietrich took a prolonged vacation in Germany, Sternberg was asked by Adolph Zukor to direct an adaptation of Theodore Dreiser's *An American Tragedy*. This had been assigned to Eisenstein, but Paramount took fright at his proposed treatment, finding it too political. Sternberg, on his own admission, was not interested in the novel's political dimension: his version of Dreiser's story of a young man impelled to murder by his social ambitions concentrates on the personal angle, emphasizing the self-destructive nature of the hero's sexual drive. He regarded the assignment, though, as no more than "a little finger exercise," and his lack of involvement shows in the film, which is flat and cold. Dreiser subsequently sued Paramount for distorting his novel, much to Sternberg's amusement.

Sternberg's concept of film as "a visual poem" reached its apotheosis in *Shanghai Express* (1932), perhaps his finest picture. The *plot* of the film concerns a train journey from Peking to Shanghai, interrupted by a bandit attack. But the *subject* of the film is Dietrich's face, on which it plays an endless series of variations: veiled, shadowed, wreathed with smoke, nestling in furs or feathers, framed in patterns of black on white. Even more than in Sternberg's previous films, the action is claustrophobically confined, thus concentrating yet further the emotional charge of the *mise-en-scène*. "The exiguous areas to which Sternberg confines himself," wrote Claude Ollier, "arise not from any need for confinement, but rather from a desire to use these areas as laboratories where he is allowed to provoke, and study at leisure, such reactions as interest him. . . . His universe is not so much restricted as *reduced*."

The reduced universe in which the "notorious China coaster," Shanghai Lily (Dietrich), meets her former lover (Clive Brook as an emotionally repressed British captain) is a superbly conceived and totally fictitious China, most memorably embodied in the opening sequence in which the dazzlingly white train steams out of the station in the middle of a narrow street seething with coolies, stallholders, children, and animals, all apparently living within a few inches of the tracks. "His settings," David Thomson commented, "are the Shanghai, Morocco, Imperial Russia and Spain only possible on the sound stages and backlots of California, and the plots are as melodramatically separate from ordinary patterns of life as his images are from a Chinese or Spanish reality." When, some years later, Sternberg first visited China, he was gratified to find that the reality differed so greatly from his imagined version.

Both critically and at the box office, *Shanghai Express* did extremely well. Lee Garmes won an Oscar for best camerawork, and the film and director were both nominated. Meanwhile Sternberg had produced an original story for his next picture. The studio found it immoral and demanded changes; Sternberg refused and was suspended; another director, Richard Wallace, was assigned to the film; Dietrich refused to work with him, and she too was suspended. Eventually all parties climbed down from their high horses, and with both Sternberg and Dietrich (and a slightly revised script) work began on *Blonde Venus* (1932).

In this film, Sternberg took his indifference to plot and plausibility to the extreme of total absurdity. Dietrich plays a devoted wife and mother who, in order to finance her husband's vital medical treatment, becomes a nightclub singer, kept woman, and prostitute. She sinks into destitution, is deprived of her son, soars to international success, and is finally reconciled with husband, child, grubby apartment, and maternal virtue. Sternberg uses this nonsensical farrago as the excuse for an amazing series of visual arabesques, of which the most famous is probably the "Hot Voodoo" number, in which Dietrich in a blonde fright-wig erupts from a gorilla suit. The sequence in which the heroine flees with her child, wandering through sleazy cafés, flophouses, and cheap hotels to end in a heat-shimmering, paint-peeling Deep South, shows that Sternberg could create a dream fantasy version of America as readily as of more exotic lands.

For all its incoherence, writes John Baxter, "*Blonde Venus* has a visual and intellectual lightness that enchants." Many contemporary critics responded less kindly, however. Dwight Macdonald, for example, wrote that all of Sternberg's great gifts had "degenerated into the hollowest, most patent kind of technical trickery" in a movie that is "perhaps the worst ever made. . . . The photography is definitely 'arty'—a nauseating blend of hazy light, soft focus, over-blacks and over-whites, with each shot so obviously 'composed' as to be painful."

B. P. Schulberg now cautiously suggested that Dietrich might make a film with another director. To his surprise, Sternberg agreed and departed on a trip to Europe, while Dietrich prepared for *Song of Songs* (1933) with Rouben Mamoulian directing. Abruptly, she refused to make the film; the studio, suspecting her and Sternberg of planning to set up independent production in Germany, sued her for $180,000 and sought an injunction to prevent her from leaving the United States. The court found for Paramount, and Dietrich reluctantly began shooting with Mamoulian. Sternberg, meanwhile, was finding that his plans for production in Berlin were making little progress—hardly surprising, since his arrival had coincided with Hitler's accession to power. He returned to Hollywood in April 1933 and signed a new two-picture contract with Paramount.

In his last two films with Dietrich, Sternberg claimed to have "completely subjugated my bird of paradise to my peculiar tendency to prove that a film might well be an art medium." The first of these films, *The Scarlet Empress* (1934), he described as "a relentless excursion into style, which, taken for granted in any work of art, is considered to be unpardonable in this medium." The film traces the metamorphosis of the innocent young German princess, Sophia Frederica, into the tyrannical and sexually rapacious Russian empress, Catherine the Great. Curtis Harrington called it "one of the most completely unique experiences in the cinema repertoire, achieving an extraordinary visual impact." It is also extremely funny; the excesses of style and subject matter allow Sternberg to indulge his sardonic humor to the full, constantly undercutting his own grandiosity. "This caustic detachment of Sternberg's from his films' own qualities," Raymond Durgnat observed (*Movie*, Summer 1965), "keeps them on their superb knife-edge of arrogance and fetishism"—a view most fully exemplified by *Scarlet Empress*. "In its final, delirious vindication of Dietrich's open-mouthed depravity," asserted David Thomson, "it is American cinema's triumph of *l'amour fou* and a surrealist masterpiece."

The Imperial Russia that Sternberg created for this film is the most overwhelming of all his fantasy countries: an unsettling blend of the luxurious and the barbarically primitive, constructed on an inhuman scale. Decorating the gigantic sets were hundreds of grotesque statues, commissioned from the Swiss sculptor Peter Ballbusch, depicting gaunt, tormented figures bearing candles or crucifixes. Against this background Sternberg staged some magnificent set pieces, most notably the ceremony at which Catherine is married to the idiot Prince Peter (Sam Jaffe in a Harpo Marx wig) in a bravura display of stylized ritual, all veils, candles, icons, and incense. The whole film reflects Sternberg's obsessive control; he even composed, and conducted, some of the music. "With one exception, every detail, scenery, paintings, sculptures, costumes, story, photography, every gesture by a player was dominated by me."

The one exception was a brief crowd scene which Ernst Lubitsch, soon to be appointed the studio's production chief, singled out as an example of willful extravagance. Sternberg was too proud or too amused to explain that the scene was a piece of footage lifted from *The Patriot* (1928), directed by Lubitsch himself. The joke was ill-timed. B. P. Schulberg, who had always supported Sternberg despite their differences, was soon to be ousted, and Lubitsch was in the ascendant. *The Scarlet Empress* failed badly at the box office and was condemned by the critics as self-indulgent rubbish, irrelevant to Depression-torn America. Sternberg's position was precarious, and Lubitsch—no doubt with intention—left him free to do as he liked with his next picture.

In *The Devil Is a Woman* (1935), Sternberg "paid a final tribute to the lady I had seen lean against the wings of a Berlin stage," and it is hard not to see the film as a valedictory summing-up of his relationship with the star he had created. Set in a fantasy Seville at carnival time, the story recounts—mainly in flashback—the doomed, one-sided love affair between Concha Perez (Dietrich) and Don Antonio Galvan (Lionel Atwill). Of all the masochistic, abused surrogates for himself that Sternberg inserted into his films—from Menjou in *Morocco* to the husband in *Anatahan*—Atwill comes closest to an exact physical replica of the director.

No Sternberg film is more densely, elaborately decorated than this. Lee Russell's description (in *New Left Review*, March–April 1966) of "the typical Sternberg film" best fits *The Devil Is a Woman*: "festooned with streamers, ribbons, nets, fronds, tendrils, lattices, veils, gauze, interposed between the camera and the subject, bringing the background into the foreground, casting a web of light and shadow. . . . All sharp edges and corners are veiled and obscured, and everything, as far as possible, made awash with swirls of moving light." Andrew Sarris thought it, "despite the sumptuousness of its surface, Sternberg's coldest film"; it is certainly his clearest, most dispassionate presentation of Dietrich as predatory and destructive temptress. Sternberg disliked the title, chosen by Lubitsch; he had wanted to call the film *Capriccio Espagnol*. But whatever its name, the picture flopped. It also ran into trouble from the Spanish government, which claimed that it "insulted the Spanish armed forces." The studio agreed to suppress the film, and Sternberg's contract was not renewed. His "period of servitude," as he termed it, at Paramount—and with Marlene Dietrich—was at an end.

The seven films with Dietrich are generally agreed, by both his admirers and his detractors, to form the central achievement of Sternberg's oeuvre. Many critics, especially those writing at the period, disliked them intensely. "Made up of ravishing pictorial effects, peppered with lewdness and suggestive symbols, set in a macabre, unreal world created solely for the senses, these films trace the gradual withering of a talent who has withdrawn into a cinematic ivory tower," wrote Lewis Jacobs. "They are tonal tapestries, two-dimensional fabrications valuable only for their details." John Grierson saw Sternberg as "a simple romanticist" corrupted by the fleshpots of Hollywood into "a sophisticated purveyor of the meretricious Dietrich . . . devoted to making the hokum as good-looking as possible." Similarly, Rudolph Arnheim, while acknowledging the skill and sensitivity of Sternberg's talent, suggested that it had been wasted on trivial material: "The art of the perfect craftsman Sternberg exhausts itself in overnourishing the eye, while the spirit languishes. . . . One sees in the work an intelligence in command of the maximum richness of means for the realization of its capacities, and which lacks only one thing: an object worth the trouble."

More recent criticism, though, has treated the seeming inanity of much of Sternberg's subject matter as an integral element in his achievement. "His world," according to David Thomson, "is pessimistic because it mocks the idea of meaning. . . . The human willfulness and stupidity that attempt to control it are true gestures of vanity in the face of destiny." Commenting on the charge of social irrelevance, Andrew Sarris asserted that "paradoxically, Sternberg and Dietrich today look deeper and more dazzling than ever, while most of the cinema of the breadlines looks excessively mannered," adding that "the subtle humor of the Sternberg *oeuvre* as a whole has been overlooked by critics intent on confusing seriousness with solemnity." Sternberg's films, in John Baxter's view, "have a psychological power that transcends simple plot. Under his scrutiny a reality emerges that is at once obvious and infinitely complex in its implications, the world of human emotion, of love and its dark concomitant, the desire to destroy."

Sternberg was forty when he broke with Dietrich. He was to live another thirty-four years, and make seven more films (plus the unfinished *I, Claudius*), but in none of them did he regain the same intensity, the "marvellous, scathing langour" (in David Thomson's phrase) of the Dietrich movies; although twice—in *The Shanghai Gesture* and *Anatahan*—he came close to it. Little of his flair, however, was evident in the two films he made for Columbia after leaving Paramount. B. P. Schulberg, who had moved there, offered him a two-picture contract. It was a well-meaning gesture, but Sternberg was hopelessly out of place at Harry Cohn's cut-rate studio. *Crime and Punishment* (1935) proved a drab and lifeless version of Dostoevski's novel, with Peter Lorre clearly uneasy as Raskolnikov. *The King Steps Out* (1936) was even worse, an adaptation of a schmaltzy Viennese operetta by Fritz Kreisler. Sternberg clashed constantly with the star, soprano Grace Moore, and quit Columbia as soon as shooting was completed. The two films he had made there "carried my name and little else."

Weary of Hollywood, Sternberg left on a long trip to the Far East, visiting China, Japan, Thailand, and Indonesia. In Java he contracted a bowel infection that obliged him to cut short his trip and undergo surgery in a London hospital. While convalescing, he was visited by Alexander Korda, head of London Films, who was planning a major production based on Robert Graves' *Claudius* novels. Korda had cast Charles Laughton in the role of the stuttering cripple who becomes Emperor of Rome, and had planned to direct the film himself; but now (possibly recalling his own earlier problems with the temperamental Laughton) he offered the job to Sternberg.

"I should have known how topsy-turvy it was to chart a project by selecting a story to fit an actor and then selecting a director to fit them both," Sternberg said afterwards. He accepted the assignment, however, and shooting began at Denham early in 1937. The footage that remains of *I, Claudius*—some of it was assembled into a BBC-TV program, *The Epic That Never Was*, in 1966—suggests that, had the film been completed, it would have been at the least a fascinating failure, and at best Sternberg's masterpiece. Laughton, however, proved even more difficult to direct than Jannings (though for rather different reasons), and this, together with Sternberg's exacting methods of directing, caused the production to run dangerously over schedule and budget. When Merle Oberon (playing Claudius' wife Messalina) was injured in an auto accident after six weeks' shooting, Korda seized his chance to shelve the film and claim the insurance.

A plan to film Zola's *Germinal*, along with other projects, was delayed by a recurrence of Sternberg's illness and then abandoned in the face of approaching war. Returning to Hollywood, Sternberg accepted a short-term contract with MGM. His second stint with the studio was scarcely more successful than his first, fourteen years earlier. After shooting some extra scenes for Duvivier's *The Great Waltz* (1938), he was assigned to a contrived Hedy Lamarr vehicle, *New York Cinderella*, and resigned after a week's shooting. (He was replaced by Frank Borzage, who in turn was replaced by W. S. Van

Dyke, whose version was finally released in 1940 as *I Take This Woman*—or, as studio wags called it, "I Retake This Woman." It flopped.) To fullfil his contract, Sternberg directed *Sergeant Madden* (1939), a routine crime melodrama with Wallace Beery in the title role.

An old friend, the German producer Arnold Pressburger, invited Sternberg to direct an independent production of *The Shanghai Gesture* (1941). The original play, a 1920s shocker by John Colton, had already been adapted into scenario form thirty-two times, and each time turned down by the Hays Office. Sternberg, to whom conveying depravity by implication was second nature, had little trouble in making version No. 33 acceptable. The oriental madam, Mother Goddam, became "Mother Gin Sling," her brothel was transmuted into a gambling den, and her half-caste daughter Poppy was never openly stated to be a drug addict, but the message was clear enough. Gene Tierney, as Poppy, had all the right languid beauty, though was by nature too bland to carry the erotic charge of a Dietrich; but the rest of the cast were excellent, especially Ona Munson, coldly venomous as Gin Sling, and Victor Mature, giving the performance of his life as the epicene voluptuary Doctor Omar. Sternberg, whose health was still poor, directed much of the film lying on a cot.

"What is most felicitous in *The Shanghai Gesture*," wrote Andrew Sarris, "is the sheer beauty and meaningful grace of physical gestures and movements." Raymond Durgnat described the film as "a labyrinth of doors, each opening on to nothing, or on to one another, leading back and forth between eroticism, fatalism, banality, pride, dread, fascination, pain, but never to a way out." A line spoken by Poppy sums up the picture and could almost sum up Sternberg's world: "It has a ghastly familiarity, like a half-forgotten dream. Anything could happen here." In John Baxter's estimation, *The Shanghai Gesture* is "the last classic Sternberg film."

For nearly ten years, Sternberg directed no films apart from a propaganda short, *The Town*, made for the United States Office of War Information in 1943. That same year he married his twenty-one-year-old secretary, Jeanne Annette MacBride. The couple had two children, a son and a daughter. In 1946, at the invitation of David Selznick, Sternberg acted as assistant director to King Vidor on *Duel in the Sun*.

Jules Furthman, who had scripted several of Sternberg's Paramount films, was now a producer at RKO, owned by the eccentric and elusive Howard Hughes, and in 1950 called in Sternberg to direct *Jet Pilot*. This ambitious flying epic was intended by Hughes as the *Hell's Angels* of the jet era, as well as a contribution to the anticommunist cycle then in vogue. Sternberg did what he could with this "right-wing camp on a comicstrip level" (Andrew Sarris), his only film in color; but Hughes then held on to the film for years, obsessively reshooting and tinkering with it, until it was finally released, looking hopelessly dated, in 1957. In the meantime Sternberg had directed a second film for RKO, a thriller. Although he disowned the final result, irritated that Nicholas Ray had been called in to reshoot some footage, *Macao* (1952) is a recognizably Sternbergian work, at least in decor and ambiance—most clearly in a scene where the hero (Robert Mitchum) is pursued by Oriental hoods through a nocturnal harbor full of junks and hanging nets.

Sternberg described his last film, "made under almost ideal conditions," as "my best film— and my most unsuccessful one." *The Saga of Anatahan* (1953) was made in Japan at the invitation of Nagamasa Kawakita, a producer whom Sternberg had met there before the war. The subject, chosen by the director, was taken from a memoir by Michiro Maruyama, recounting his experiences as one of a group of shipwrecked sailors who held out on a tiny Pacific island for six years after the war ended. On the island they found two inhabitants, a man and a woman. By the time they were rescued, five men had died, killed in the struggle for dominance and sexual possession. The story furnished Sternberg with an almost clinically pure demonstration of his perennial thesis: the destructive power of sexuality and uncontrolled emotion.

The "island" was constructed in an aircraft hangar on the outskirts of Kyoto, which Sternberg converted into a tortuous artificial jungle of cellophane strips, foliage, and upended swamp trees. Backed by admiring and deferential producers, Sternberg had complete control of every aspect of the film; for the only time in his career, he took sole cinematographic credit. His cast of unknowns spoke unsubtitled Japanese dialogue, leaving the narration to a spoken English commentary, written and delivered by Sternberg himself; the director's authorial role could hardly be more explicit. Such absolute control creates a hypnotic reality within the closed, artificial world of the island. When a montage of newsreel shots, showing the end of the war, briefly intrudes, it is the outer world which seems unreal. On its release, *Anatahan* was received with incomprehension and hostility in Japan and elsewhere. Its reputation has since grown, and some critics now regard it as Sternberg's final masterpiece—in John Baxter's words, "at once summary and anthology."

The last sixteen years of Sternberg's life were devoted largely to his family at their home in Hollywood, and to much international travel, often to film festivals where retrospectives of his work were shown and tributes paid to it. From 1959 to 1963 he taught a course on the aesthetics of film at the University of California. In 1965 he published a waspish, rambling, and highly idiosyncratic autobiography, *Fun in a Chinese Laundry*. In his final years he suffered from increasingly poor health; he died of a heart attack in a Hollywood hospital at the age of seventy-five.

As Andrew Sarris says, "the limitations of Sternberg's aesthetic are self-evident. An insufficient grasp of one's time and place is hardly a positive virtue even for the most lyrical poet," and it lost him the respect of his socially conscious contemporaries. But, Sarris goes on, "it is only when we look around at the allegedly significant cinema of Sternberg's contemporaries that we recognize the relative stature of a director who chose to write with a camera in the first person long before Alexandre Astruc's '*camera-stylo*' made such impious subjectivity fashionable and such personal poetry comprehensible." For David Thomson, as for many others, "Sternberg now stands clear as one of the greatest directors and the first poet of underground cinema."

—*P.K.*

FILMS: The Salvation Hunters, 1925; The Exquisite Sinner, 1925; A Woman of the Sea/The Sea Gull, 1926; Underworld, 1927; The Last Command, 1928; The Drag Net, 1928; The Docks of New York, 1928; The Case of Lena Smith, 1929; Thunderbolt, 1929; The Blue Angel/Der Blaue Engel, 1930; Morocco, 1930; Dishonored, 1931; An American Tragedy, 1931; Shanghai Express, 1932; Blonde Venus, 1932; The Scarlet Empress, 1934; The Devil Is a Woman, 1935; Crime and Punishment, 1935; The King Steps Out, 1936; I, Claudius (unfinished), 1937; Sergeant Madden, 1939; The Shanghai Gesture, 1941; The Town, 1943 (documentary); Macao, 1952; The Saga of Anatahan/Ana-Ta-Han, 1953; Jet Pilot, 1957 (completed 1950). *Published scripts*—The Blue Angel (English translation of the German version), 1968 (Lorrimer); The Last Command *in* Motion Picture Continuities, edited by F. T. Patterson, 1929; Morocco *and* Shanghai Express, 1973 (Lorrimer); The Saga of Anatahan (voice-over commentary only) *in* Josef von Sternberg by H. G. Weinberg, 1966.

ABOUT: Baxter, J. The Cinema of Josef von Sternberg, 1971; Baxter, P. (ed.) Sternberg, 1980; Braudy, L. and Dickstein, M. (eds.) Great Film Directors: A Critical Anthology, 1978; Brownlow, K. The Parade's Gone By, 1968; Buttafava, G. Josef von Sternberg, 1976 (in Italian); Cameron, I. (ed.) Movie Reader, 1972; Fontenla, C. S. Josef von Sternberg, 1969 (in Spanish); Goetz, A.

and Bantz, H. W. Josef von Sternberg: eine Darstellung, 1966; Grierson, J. Grierson on Documentary, 1966; Harrington, C. An Index to the Films of Josef von Sternberg, 1949; Jacobs, L. The Rise of the American Film, 1939; Kracauer, S. From Caligari to Hitler, 1947; Oms, M. Josef von Sternberg, 1970 (in French); Sarris, A. The Films of Josef von Sternberg, 1966; Sternberg, J. von Fun in a Chinese Laundry, 1965; Thomson, D. Movie Man, 1967; Thomson, D. A Biographical Dictionary of the Cinema, 1975; Weinberg, H. G. Josef von Sternberg, 1966. *Periodicals* —Cahiers du Cinéma October–November 1951, July 1965; Chaplin December 1966, February 1967; Cinéma (France) December 1982; Cinema (Switzerland) Summer 1967; Experimental Cinema 1:5 1934; Film (Germany) 1 1965; Film Culture Winter 1955; Film Heritage Winter 1965–1966; Film Ideal April 1965, 5 1969; Film Journal December 1965; Filmkritik February 1969; Films and Filming June 1974; Films in Review January 1981; Filmstudio January 1967; Image et Son April 1970; Movie Summer 1965; New Left Review March–April 1966; New York Times December 23, 1969; Positif 37–38 1961, 75 1966; Sight and Sound Autumn 1962, Autumn 1965, Winter 1972–1973, Spring 1978; Theatre Arts November 1950.

STEVENS, GEORGE (December 18, 1904– March 8, 1975), American director and producer, was born in Oakland, California. He was the son of Landers Stevens and Georgia Cooper-Stevens, the stars and proprietors of a West Coast touring stock company. His uncle, Ashton Stevens, was a well-known Chicago drama critic, and his maternal grandmother, Georgia Woodthorpe, had been the toast of San Francisco during the gold rush.

Following this family tradition, Stevens made his acting debut at the age of five, when he appeared with the tragedienne Nance O'Neill in *Sappho,* at the Alcazar Theatre in San Francisco. Stevens attended various grade schools in northern California, had one year of high school in Sonoma, then abandoned formal education to join his parents' touring company as an actor and stage manager.

In 1921 the family settled in Los Angeles, where Landers Stevens began a new career as a film actor. George Stevens was equally interested in the movies and entered the industry the same year as a camera assistant. By 1924 he was a full-fledged first cameraman with the Hal Roach studios, shooting mostly short comedies featuring Laurel and Hardy, Our Gang, Harry Langdon, and other Roach stars. Starting in 1928 he also worked as a gag writer, and in 1930, when he was twenty-six, he began to direct Laurel and Hardy comedies, shorts in the "Boy Friends" series, and other Roach two- and three-reelers.

GEORGE STEVENS

In 1932 Stevens moved to Universal, where he directed more shorts and also his first feature, *The Cohens and the Kellys in Trouble* (1933). Starring the then-popular comedy team of George Sidney and Charlie Murray, supported by the likes of Andy Devine and Maureen O'Sullivan, it was the last in Universal's Cohen and Kelly series and received little attention. Stevens moved on again in 1933 to RKO, where he remained for seven years, directing half a dozen shorts and twelve features.

Herbert G. Luft, in his article about Stevens in *Films in Review* (November 1958), says that even in his early RKO programmers the director showed the detailed and sometimes laborious perfectionism that was to become his trademark. His first RKO feature was *Bachelor Bait* (1934), a farce starring Rochelle Hudson, Stuart Erwin, and Skeets Gallagher. Interviewed by Luft, Rochelle Hudson recalled that Stevens "carefully rehearsed his actors and waited patiently until they played a scene his way, regardless of how many takes were required." He also "worked out a complete cutting continuity . . . , knew what editing problems he would have to surmount and tried to solve them before completion of principal photography."

Two more low-budget comedies followed, *Kentucky Kernels* (1934) and *The Nitwits* (1935), both starring the vaudeville team of Wheeler and Woolsey, and then *Laddie* (1935), a children's fantasy based on a novel by Gene Stratton Porter. It was Stevens' next picture that first attracted attention to his work. RKO had decided that Booth Tarkington's Pulitzer-winning novel *Alice Adams*, previously filmed

as a silent with Florence Vidor, would make a suitable vehicle for Katharine Hepburn. That arrogant young star objected first to the property, then to the choice of Stevens as director, but fortunately for him (and for herself) finally gave way.

Alice Adams (1935) is a Cinderella story about a prickly, idealistic girl (Hepburn) who happens to live on the wrong side of the tracks in her class-bound small town. She can't afford the extravagant social whirl enjoyed by her contemporaries and therefore pretends to despise parties and smart clothes. But the town's most eligible bachelor (Fred MacMurray) recognizes Alice's worth. A fairytale romance begins that is wrecked by the social ineptness of her grotesque family (though the script imposes a happy ending not sanctioned by the novel or by probability).

The film was a great financial and critical success, and a personal triumph for Hepburn. *Time*'s reviewer wrote that "the direction of George Stevens, who at thirty is the youngest important director in Hollywood, is almost flawless." This was the majority view, though Otis Ferguson complained that the movie was "designed not so much as a show as for purposes of elevation." Moreover, it seemed to Ferguson that at the famous dinner party where the full awfulness of Alice's family is revealed to her Prince Charming, "everything goes wrong in the most stock manner, until the audience is all set for the shot where the old man's galluses drop his dress trousers down clear to the floor, revealing a pair of bright polka-dot drawers. The actual treatment, that is, seems a cross between harrowing tragedy and the honeymoon breakfast routine in a Charley Chase [slapstick comedy]."

Later criticism has been much kinder than this, praising Stevens for his "sense of detail and milieu," and Hepburn for making Alice "one of the few authentic American movie heroines." Donald Ritchie, in his 1970 monograph on Stevens, wrote that it was in *Alice Adams* that the director discovered "the great romantic theme of the individual and his society . . . the needs of the individual whose society has no place for him." It is this theme, Ritchie maintains, that Stevens made "particularly his own, by following its assumptions to their conclusion, by exposing their roots."

Rescued from a treadmill of low-budget farces by the success of *Alice Adams*, Stevens had Barbara Stanwyck and Melvyn Douglas as his stars in the amiable circus Western *Annie Oakley* (1935), and Fred Astaire and Ginger Rogers in his first musical, *Swing Time* (1936), which incidentally featured the director's father, Landers Stevens. Astaire plays a dancer and gambler who, needing money to finance his marriage to a society girl, forms a cabaret act with a dance teacher (Rogers) and falls for her instead. One of the most likable of the Astaire-Rogers movies, it introduced such Jerome Kern classics as "A Fine Romance" and the Oscar-winning "The Way You Look Tonight," as well as "Pick Yourself Up," the theme of a memorable and mercurial dance routine.

A too-stiff and painstaking version of J. M. Barrie's *Quality Street* (1937), with Katharine Hepburn and Franchot Tone, was followed by a second Fred Astaire musical, *A Damsel in Distress* (1937). Based on a P. G. Wodehouse novel, it casts the then unknown Joan Fontaine as an English aristocrat, Astaire as the visiting American who teaches her to enjoy the plebeian pleasures of the masses. In spite of a Gershwin score and a supporting cast that included George Burns, Gracie Allen, Reginald Gardiner, and Constance Collier, this "slow and careful" film flopped. In Donald Ritchie's opinion, "the fact that Stevens could never not care is why he was unable to make light, spontaneous-appearing films."

Ritchie sees George Stevens as an "American romantic"—an heir to the idealism and optimism of the pioneers who, "as he turned from movie craftsman into film artist," learned to question his original assumptions. "The romantic," Ritchie says, "knows that reality is . . . different from his subjective feelings of what it should be. Stevens came to this realization early in his career, and sought a number of ways to circumvent the difficulty." Quite often in his early films, "the difficulty" is presented as a social schism between two individuals that is miraculously bridged by true love. In this way, Alice Adams moves "up" in society to join her Prince Charming while Lady Alyce in *A Damsel in Distress* moves "down" to join Fred Astaire—partly for love, partly because she recognizes that his plebeian way of life is more "real"—and more fun—than her own. This is a distinctly populist notion of the sort found also in the contemporary films of Frank Capra and Preston Sturges, and it recurs in Stevens' films of the late 1930s and early 1940s. In *Vivacious Lady* (1938), it is upper-crust college professor James Stewart who learns to relish "normal healthy vulgarity" when he marries chorus girl Ginger Rogers.

The reviewers were not sure what to make of the gangling James Stewart, still an unfamiliar figure, but the public liked him and *Vivacious Lady* was a box-office success. Stevens followed it with *Gunga Din* (1939), a smash hit that consolidated his reputation as a bankable director.

Victor McLaglen, Douglas Fairbanks, Jr., and Cary Grant play three army sergeants in British India—respectively the old-timer MacChesney, the quick-witted intellectual Ballantine, and the irrepressible Cockney joker Cutter. This brawling, boozing, wenching threesome is wrecked when Ballantine resigns to marry Joan Fontaine—an aberrant notion that is quickly abandoned when Cutter is captured by rebellious Afghans. His buddies set out to rescue him, are captured in their turn, and saved at the last moment by the selfless heroism of the despised Indian water carrier Gunga Din (Sam Jaffe in brown-face).

Gunga Din's only ambition had been to become a real British soldier, and his wish is granted posthumously, at a grand military funeral. In the film's own terms, he thus moves up the racial scale as surely as Alice Adams moves up the social scale. Outrageous as this seems by modern standards, it was perfectly acceptable in 1939, and in other respects the movie is irresistibly exciting and entertaining. Pauline Kael called it "a model of the action genre . . . so exuberant and high-spirited that it both exalted and mocked a schoolboy's version of heroism."

Vigil in the Night (1940), Stevens' last RKO picture for several years, was an A. J. Cronin melodrama about a heroic nurse (Carole Lombard), her less heroic sister (Anne Shirley), and a doctor (Brian Aherne). A financial and critical failure, it was followed by the equally sentimental *Penny Serenade* (1941), which was a success. Cary Grant and Irene Dunne play a young couple who, unable to have a baby, adopt one. She dies at the age of six, and the distraught parents almost divorce, but in the end decide to adopt another child.

Otis Ferguson called *Penny Serenade* "frankly a weeper, but . . . not quite like any other picture I can think of. . . . For all the lack of action in the strictest sense, you will notice whole sections here where narration has been devised purely for the camera." It seemed to Ferguson that "the fact of its unassuming humanity, and its direct appeal without other aids," was evidence that the movies were "growing up after all." Discussing "those contrasts, seemingly fortuitous, which account for much of the best in Stevens' films," Donald Ritchie quotes an example early in *Penny Serenade* when newspaperman Cary Grant asks Irene Dunne "if she won't marry him and eventually go off to Tokyo. They kiss. At that instant it is suddenly the new year. Bells, snow, whistles, shouts—and a private celebration is suddenly public, magically augmented."

After this came three notable comedies, beginning with *Woman of the Year* (1942). Made for MGM and produced by Joseph L. Mankiewicz, it had an Oscar-winning script by Ring Lardner Jr. and Michael Kanin, and began the long and fruitful partnership of Katharine Hepburn and Spencer Tracy. Tracy is a sportswriter, Sam Craig, whose journalistic feud with Tess Harding, an intellectual world affairs columnist on the same paper, ends when they actually meet. He introduces her to baseball, she loves it and him, and they marry. But Sam finds that he is expected to make his own breakfast while Tess writes her column, and when she adopts an orphaned Greek refugee whom she is ill-equipped to look after—and is voted "Outstanding Woman of the Year" to boot—Sam walks out. Realizing what she has lost, Tess trims her liberated principles to get him back.

Like *Gunga Din,* the film embodies social attitudes that seem pernicious by modern standards, but were perfectly conventional when it was made. Indeed, Tess Harding is only one of a whole gallery of Stevens heroines who learn where a woman's place is. But (like *Gunga Din* again), *Woman of the Year* is hard to dismiss as a mere anachronism—it remains "a polished and astringent comedy" with some "sensuously charming, witty and tender episodes of lovemaking." It never loses "the charge of feeling" between Hepburn and Tracy, and was widely regarded as one of the best comedies of the year.

Sidney Buchman and Irwin Shaw scripted *The Talk of the Town* (1942), which shows a more acceptable side of Stevens' social optimism. Cary Grant plays Leopold Dilg, a union militant in a corrupt mill town who is framed for murder and arson. Jailed, he breaks out and takes refuge under an assumed identity in the home of Michael Lightcap (Ronald Colman), who happens to be a professor of law. Jean Arthur provides the "romantic interest" and some scatterbrained wit.

Stuffed-shirt Lightcap learns to value Dilg's innate folk wisdom and instinctive sense of justice above academic legalism—yet another piece of Stevens populism. As Donald Ritchie says, Lightcap is "softened up by that great spiritual tonic, a real American baseball game." He "shaves off his beard, symbol of difference and distinction," and goes into action on Dilg's behalf. It seemed to Penelope Houston that "a fair amount of lecturing on corruption and civic duty was adroitly camouflaged by the smooth and civilised surface of the comedy, beautifully played by Jean Arthur, Cary Grant, and Ronald Colman." John T. McManus found it "a totally unexpected and therefore particularly reward-

ing experience, something like, say, finding a pearl in a clam."

The More the Merrier (1943) is a flimsier comedy about the housing shortage in wartime Washington, with Jean Arthur and Charles Coburn as incongruous roommates who in due course are joined by a third, Joel McCrea. Coburn got an Oscar as best supporting actor and Stevens, who was nominated for another as best director, was chosen as such by the New York Film Critics Circle. James Agee, however, called the movie "a tired soufflé, for unfortunately Stevens doesn't know where to stop. Farce, like melodrama, offers very special chances for accurate observation, but here accuracy is avoided ten times to one in favor of easy burlesque or the easier idealization which drops the bottom out of farce."

In the summer of 1943, Stevens joined the Army Signal Corps, serving with the unit that recorded the campaigns of the Sixth Army in North Africa and Europe for the National Archives. He accompanied the army from Normandy to Berlin, filming among other things the liberation of Paris, the V-2 rocket factory at Nordhausen and its slave workers, and the opening of the concentration camp at Dachau. Some of the latter footage was used at the Nuremberg war crimes trials. Released in 1945 with the rank of lieutenant colonel, he returned to Hollywood much affected by his experiences.

The immediate result was that Stevens, with William Wyler, Frank Capra, and the producer Samuel J. Briskin, formed Liberty Films Inc. to produce movies that would, they hoped, make for a better world. Each of the three directors chose a different theme, Stevens opting for a comedy about the problems of the returning GI. But after he had invested $100,000 of his own money in the movie, he abandoned the project—he decided that it was a delusion to suppose that audiences, in the immediate aftermath of the war, would share his social concerns. Liberty Films wound up with only one film to its credit, Capra's *It's a Wonderful Life* (1946).

As it turned out, Stevens' first postwar film was *I Remember Mama,* made for RKO in 1948. It was adapted by DeWitt Bodeen from John Van Druten's play, itself based on a novel by Kathryn Forbes. Barbara Bel Geddes plays the young novelist Katrin, fondly recalling her girlhood in San Francisco as a member of a large Norwegian immigrant family whose "fire, force, inspiration and comfort" was Katrin's shrewd, tired, indomitable mother (Irene Dunne). There is a splendid performance from Oscar Homolka as the fierce but kindly Uncle Chris.

Douglas McVay wrote that "the sustainedly

calculated *mise-en-scène*, with its turn-of-the-century texture of townscape, chiaroscuro and decor, its emphasis on panning, tracking, slow fades and grouping . . . , its occasional vivid cutting . . . , is utterly typical of Stevens." Penelope Houston thought that Stevens "played up the character sketches for all that they were worth, and sometimes for rather more; taking the film at a slow, reflective pace, he constantly emphasized its reminiscent quality, so that it seemed less like something actual and present than like something affectionately remembered."

It is widely held that Stevens' postwar films differ from his earlier work. "To read his filmography," wrote Donald Ritchie, "is like reading a history of popular movie taste during the thirties and forties: sentimental romances, followed by screwball comedies, followed by social-interest melodramas. . . . George Stevens, a sentimental romantic, made films for a nation of sentimental romantics." But the director's war experiences were "so harrowing that optimistic sentimentality was largely banished from his thoughts and his works."

Some critics dislike Stevens' late films, accusing them of "stylistic inflation," but Ritchie values them above the early movies, claiming that in them a "facile optimist" had become an artist who recognized that "he inhabits a howling wilderness" yet still "chose to believe in the innate goodness of man. . . . Stevens' slowness, his carefulness, his ability to watch, his extraordinary craftsmanship, the fact that he—the least cynical of all motion-picture directors—has always been able to care: these qualities fused to created a series of motion pictures which are much more meaningful to us and our times than is generally admitted."

Ritchie sees some evidence of this change even in *I Remember Mama*, sentimental as it often is—the narrator-heroine Katrin is a novelist, ordering and analyzing her own memories. For Ritchie, at least, this is the beginning of objectivity, "the attitude of the mature artist." The objective artist inevitably comes to recognize the essential tragedy of the human condition, and Stevens addressed himself directly to this theme in *A Place in the Sun* (1951), adapted by Michael Wilson and Harry Brown from a stage version of Theodore Dreiser's novel, *An American Tragedy*, previously filmed twenty years earlier by Sternberg.

The subject of Dreiser's novel is the emptiness of the American Dream. Pursuing that chimera, and in love with the beautiful heiress who he believes can deliver it to him, the ambitious young hero murders the pregnant factory girl he ought to marry, and dies for it. In Stevens' version, updated to 1951, George Eastman (Montgomery Clift) takes Alice Tripp (Shelley Winters) for a boat ride, meaning to kill her, but loses his nerve. She drowns anyway, by accident, and George goes to the chair for a murder he did not quite commit, obsessed to the last by swooningly beautiful close-ups of Angela Vickers (Elizabeth Taylor).

Dreiser portrays his hero as the victim of a corrupt and greedy society; Sternberg portrays him as the victim of self-destructive passion; Stevens divides the blame between society and George Eastman's own psychological make-up. His method, as Pauline Kael wrote, is "studied, slow, and accumulative. . . . It is full of meaning-charged details, murky psychological overtones, darkening landscapes, the eerie sounds of a loon, and overlapping dissovles designed to affect you emotionally without your conscious awareness." Kael found the result impressive but overly portentous, as did many European and British reviewers, but in America the majority of the critics greeted the film with ecstatic enthusiasm: one promised that it would "bankrupt the emotions" of the viewer. Stevens received an Oscar as best director, and there were Academy Awards also for the screenplay, the cinematography (William Mellor), the score (Franz Waxman), and the costumes (Edith Head).

A Place in the Sun established Stevens as the preeminent stylist of the American cinema in the postwar years. Doubts raised by the failure of *Something to Live For* (1952), which put Ray Milland back on the alcoholic skids of *The Lost Weekend*, were swept away by Stevens' next film, *Shane* (1953). Scripted by A. B. Guthrie, Jr., from a novel by Jack Schaefer, it is regarded by many (if not by genre buffs) as one of the greatest of all Westerns.

Shane is set in an isolated pioneer community in Wyoming—a one-street town and a handful of homesteads scattered beneath the towering peaks of the Grand Tetons. A taciturn former gunfighter, Shane (Alan Ladd), rides out of nowhere and accepts a job and a bed from Starrett (Van Heflin), one of the homesteaders. Slowly he becomes involved in Starrett's battle against Ryker (Emile Meyer), the cattleman who is trying to drive the sodbusters out. When Ryker tips the scales by hiring Wilson (Jack Palance), a professional killer, Shane buckles on his gun again. Afterwards, aware that he has become a dangerously glamorous figure in the eyes of Starrett's hero-worshipping young son (Brandon de Wilde)—and to some extent those of Starrett's wife (Jean Arthur)—he rides away towards the mountains: there is no place for his sort on a frontier that he has helped to tame.

Writing in *Films and Filming* (April and May 1965), Douglas McVay described *Shane* as a nearly perfect blending of naturalism (in the scenes that build up an almost documentary picture of frontier life) and poetic formalism (in the key episodes). McVay quotes several examples, including "the Fordesque spontaneity of the Fourth of July celebrations . . . set against the rigorously planned sequence of the murder of Torrey. Stevens shapes the murder scene unerringly, with thunder rumbling ominously above, the pathetically pugnacious little Southerner (Elisha Cook, Jr.) slipping towards the smiling killer . . . on the muddy ground. Wilson whispers his taunts, Torrey goes for his gun, but the assassin's weapon is already drawn . . . : the action freezes into a ghastly tableau, then the shot blasts shudderingly forth."

McVay is equally impressed by the staging of Torrey's funeral on the hill: "The villains watch, half contemptuous, half uneasy, from the store; the horses shift and whinny, a dog snuffles at the descending coffin, a man intones 'Dixie' softly on a harmonica; and the Lord's Prayer is murmured in ragged chorus, the mourning figures outlined on a silent sky. . . . Alan Ladd's Shane, created only in externals, is exactly right: the definitive Western hero, the personification of legend. . . . The piece is a *poetic* quintessence, a symbolic distillation of the whole Western myth, legend, ethos, magic." And Penelope Houston echoed Donald Ritchie's assertion that Stevens had matured and "taken command of his material; he has acquired the grand manner, the note of unmistakeable authority. There is a magisterial quality about *Shane*."

Shane was nominated for six Oscars but received only one, for Loyal Grigg's color photography, though the film brought Stevens an Irving Thalberg Memorial Award. It was his next picture that earned him his second Academy Award as best director. *Giant* (1956), based on Edna Ferber's novel, has Rock Hudson as Bick Benedict, the young feudal master of a gigantic Texas ranch, and Elizabeth Taylor as the Southern belle he marries and brings home to the family's American Gothic mansion on the flat Texas plains. James Dean plays Jett Rink, the poor ranch hand, ignorant, jealous, and ambitious, who strikes oil on the meager patch of land he inherits and becomes another martyr to the American Dream, boundlessly rich and boundlessly lonely.

Giant was James Dean's last film before his death in a car crash. His performance, at least in the first half of the picture, and his legendary status as a "tragic ideal" for the disaffected young, monopolized many of the reviews. "Yet," wrote *Time*'s critic, "despite the blazing up of this lost light, the picture belongs to the director. Scene after scene—a cultivated dinner party, a brawl in a diner, a quarrel between a conventional father and a free-thinking son—is worked over with a care for the meanings beneath the meanings on the surface: something that Hollywood almost never takes time for." At three and a quarter hours, however, many reviewers thought that Stevens had taken altogether too much time, losing the edge of the story in endless gossip about the vicissitudes of the Benedict clan.

Anne Frank was a mercurial teenager who hid in an Amsterdam attic with seven other Jews for twenty-six months before the Nazis found her and killed her. She left behind in the attic an intimate diary that records the pangs of first love as heartbreakingly as the fear of death, and still achieves humor and an unshaken faith in human goodness. The diary formed the basis of a play by Frances Goodrich and Albert Hackett, who adapted it as the screenplay of Stevens' next film, *The Diary of Anne Frank* (1959).

For Douglas McVay, the film was "not quite a masterpiece," but close to one in its "superlatively thorough" craftsmanship and its imaginative translation into the stuff of art of "the hideout's hermetic world, with the hourly, daily, monthly, yearly pattern of . . . [displaced] domestic routine, spasmodically interspersed with tension, danger, hysteria and horror." McVay thought that "the nearest thing to genius in the production is the screech of the police car's brakes, scarring our nerves like a razor, at the instant when Anne and Peter kiss." Many considered Millie Perkins miscast in the title role, but there were superlative performances from Shelley Winters as the blowsy, goodhearted Mrs. Van Daan, from Joseph Schildkraut as Anne's father, and from Diane Baker as her timid older sister. Shelley Winters and the photographer William Mellor both received Oscars.

Stevens, who worked for two years on *A Place in the Sun* and for even longer on *Giant,* spent no less than five years on *The Greatest Story Ever Told,* a biopic nearly four hours long, with Max Von Sydow as Jesus Christ and half of Hollywood in cameo roles. Philip T. Hartung thought *Story* the best cinematic attempt to date at its impossible subject, but most reviewers found it dull, plodding, and unconvincing, and it flopped at the box office. Stevens made only one more film, *The Only Game in Town* (1970), a slight but moderately entertaining piece about the romance that develops between a Las Vegas floorshow dancer (Elizabeth Taylor) and a bar pianist addicted to gambling (Warren Beatty).

Stanley Kauffmann has called George Stevens "the most overrated craftsman in American film history," and David Thomson says that his later films were "borne down by preparation, solemnity and a shooting method that reportedly involved filming from every possible angle before assembling the film in the cutting room." But Thomson allows the director a "story instinct and . . . [a] sympathetic treatment of actors," and Willard Van Dyke noted his "great sensitivity for the relationship between music and the visual flow of his images."

There is no doubt that, at the end of his career, Stevens became too self-conscious a guardian of his reputation as a stylist, but his achievements in *Shane, Giant,* and the comedies of the 1930s and early 1940s cannot for long be dismissed as casually as they were a few years after his death. As Donald Ritchie says, "quite beyond the excellences of many of his films," George Stevens was "very much a part of something larger than himself. Standing almost as the epitome of his place and time, he also reveals in his artistic evolution possibilities concerning his country and his future."

Stevens' son George Jr., who worked with him as associate producer on *Anne Frank* and *The Greatest Story Ever Told,* served as chief of the USIA's motion picture service in 1962–1967, then as director of the American Film Institute.

FILMS: *Short films* (partial list)—Ladies Past, 1930; Call a Cop!, 1931; High Gear, 1931; The Kick-off, 1931; Mama Loves Papa, 1931; The Finishing Touch, 1932; Boys Will Be Boys, 1932; Family Troubles, 1932; Should Crooners Marry?, 1933; Hunting Trouble, 1933; Rock-a-Bye Cowboy, 1933; Room Mates, 1933; A Divorce Courtship, 1933; Flirting in the Park, 1933; Quiet Please, 1933; Grin and Bear It, 1933; Bridal Bail, 1934; Ocean Swells, 1934. *Features*—The Cohens and the Kellys in Trouble, 1933; Bachelor Bait, 1934; Kentucky Kernels, 1934; Laddie, 1935; The Nitwits, 1935; Alice Adams, 1935; Annie Oakley, 1935; Swing Time, 1936; Quality Street, 1937; A Damsel in Distress, 1937; Vivacious Lady, 1938; Gunga Din, 1939; Vigil in the Night, 1940; Penny Serenade, 1941; Woman of the Year, 1942; The Talk of the Town, 1942; The More the Merrier, 1943; I Remember Mama, 1948; A Place in the Sun, 1951; Something to Live For, 1952; Shane, 1953; Giant, 1956; The Diary of Anne Frank, 1959; The Greatest Story Ever Told, 1965; The Only Game in Town, 1970.

ABOUT: Ritchie, D. George Stevens: An American Romantic, 1970; Roud, R. (ed.) Cinema: A Critical Dictionary,1980; Thomson, D. A Biographical Dictionary of the Cinema, 1980. *Periodicals*—Action May–June 1975; Bright Lights 8 1979; Dialogue on Film May–June 1975 (Stevens issue); Film Comment July–August 1975; Film Culture 1 1957; Films and Filming July 1959, April and May 1965; Films in Review November 1958; Sight and Sound October–December 1953. *Films about*—George Stevens: A Filmmaker's Journey (compiled by George Stevens Jr.), 1985.

STEVENSON, ROBERT (1905–   ), American director, scenarist, and producer, was born in England, at Buxton in Derbyshire, the son of a prominent local businessman. He was educated at Shrewsbury School and went on with a scholarship to St. John's College, Cambridge University. A brilliant student, he graduated in 1926 with a first-class honors degree in mechanical sciences, the same year winning the John Bernard Seely Prize for independent work in aerodynamics.

Stevenson's interests were not limited to science and technology, however. In 1927, as a graduate student of psychology, he became editor of the Cambridge University literary magazine, *Granta,* and the following year was president of the Union, the university's famous debating society. What did *not* interest him was the cinema, until he decided to write a thesis (never completed) on the psychology of this popular art form. According to Patrick McGilligan in his article about Stevenson in *American Film* (March 1978), this project took him to see Joan Crawford in *Sarah, Irene, and Mary,* and he "promptly fell in love with both Joan Crawford and the 'ki-ne-ma.'"

In 1929 Stevenson went to work for a newsreel agency, soon moving on to Michael Balcon's Gainsborough and Gaumont-British studios, where he wrote story synopses, supplementing his income by reviewing films. Gaumont-British then sent him to Germany to supervise some ventures in cooperation with UFA. According to McGilligan, "he found himself instead dispatched all over the continent. First he was loaned to a studio in France as dialogue director of *The Battle,* a Charles Boyer picture, and then he was sent to the Libyan desert to supervise *The Camels Are Coming.* In the cast was actress Anna Lee, who was to become his first wife and frequent star."

When he got back to England, Balcon put him to work as codirector with Jack Hulbert of *Falling for You* (1933), a vehicle for that popular musical comedy star and his wife Cicely Courtneidge. They play rival journalists on the track of a runaway princess (Tamari Desni) in Switzerland. The setting allows the two comedians generous scope for pratfalls while skating or skiing, and in the end Hulbert rescues the princess from her obnoxious royal suitor (Garry Marsh) and claims her himself. There are some pleasant songs by Vivian Ellis, and a haunted house is

ROBERT STEVENSON

thrown in for good measure. The reviewers complained that the sight of Hulbert falling down eventually palled, but found the movie on the whole "agreeable and amusing."

Hulbert also starred in and codirected *Jack of All Trades* (1936; called *The Two of Us* in America). Loosely based on a stage play, *Youth at the Helm,* it has Hulbert, down and out in London, bluffing his way to success in a bank. "Mr. Hulbert talks very loud and very often," wrote one disenchanted critic, "and he sings a few songs, and taps a bit, and saves a lady from a burning shoe factory."

Stevenson's first solo feature was much more considerable. *Tudor Rose* (1936; called *Nine Days a Queen* in America) was scripted by the director in collaboration with the actor-writer Miles Malleson (who also appears in the picture). Set during the period of ruthless political intrigue following the death of Henry VIII, it tells the tragic story of Lady Jane Grey (Nova Pilbeam). A reluctant pawn in the power struggle between the Seymours and the Earl of Warwick (Cedric Hardwicke), she was thrust onto the British throne in 1554 at the age of seventeen, and beheaded by Mary Tudor nine days later "for the good of the country." The excellent cast included John Mills, Felix Aylmer, Sybil Thorndike, and Gwen Ffrangcon-Davies.

Tudor Rose carried Stevenson at once into the front rank of English directors, and was received as enthusiastically in the United States as at home—a rare achievement then for a British film. It was widely and favorably compared to Korda's blockbusting *Private Life of Henry VIII,* and was enormously successful at the box office.

Mark Van Doren wrote that it was "serious and convincing and intelligently respectful of its material: one of the best historical films, indeed, among the many now to be seen." Howard Barnes, who found it "absorbing and hauntingly beautiful," praised Nova Pilbeam's "inspired performance," but reserved his greatest admiration for the young director's "triumph" in guiding his cast "in a tremendously exciting human pattern that makes his screen work one of the greatest genuflections that the cinema has made to the past."

The Man Who Changed His Mind (1936; called *The Man Who Lived Again* in America) was, by contrast, a thriller, with Boris Karloff as a mad scientist experimenting with personality transference. Anna Lee is his frightened assistant, and John Loder her gallant admirer. Howard Barnes was again impressed, reporting that "the camera-minded Robert Stevenson has directed the work with properly tricky effects. Boris Karloff bares his fangs and rumples up his hair in a more credible impersonation than he usually offers; the dialogue has some concise and authentic speech to offset the medical nonsense, and the supporting players are excellent." William Boehnel agreed that it was "first-rate weird entertainment."

Stevenson's next assignment was an adaptation of *King Solomon's Mines,* Rider Haggard's famous adventure story about a search for legendary diamond mines in darkest Africa. The movie was made in the studio, with background material shot on location by Geoffrey Barkas. Cedric Hardwicke plays the expedition's leader, Allan Quatermain, and Paul Robeson is a heroic Umbopo, with Anna Lee and John Loder again supplying romantic interest. The latter was absent from the original novel, and Basil Wright objected to this and other liberties with the text.

All the same, Wright went on, "Robert Stevenson has created some intelligently directed sequences, notably the crossing of the waterless desert, when similar shots of the footsore, thirsty travelers dissolve one into another and the distant mountains are never nearer. In the mountain caverns also studio ingenuity provides plenty of excitement as the lava spurts and huge rocks crash down on every side. But best of all is the scene where Gagool smells out the evildoers, the Zulus snarl forward with their terrifying chant, and the screams of the victims punctuate the suspense as the little party of whites wait anxiously for the eclipse of the sun." Modern critics agree that Stevenson's version of the story was "vastly superior" to MGM's 1951 remake.

After this ambitious production, Balcon assigned Stevenson to a second feature, *Non-Stop New York* (1937), again pairing John Loder and Anna Lee in a comedy-thriller presumably aimed at the American market. One British critic noted that it "works up to a lively climax on the plane, but is let down by some of the dialogue and a rather weak attempt to achieve an American atmosphere, though the good-humoured chaffing between hero and heroine is obviously based on American models."

Owd Bob (1938; called *To the Victor* in America) was based on Alfred Ollivant's novel about the rivalry between the owners of two champion sheepdogs in the Yorkshire Dales. Will Fyffe hammed endearingly as an old Scottish misanthrope, Margaret Lockwood was miscast as his daughter, and John Loder was acted off the screen by the dogs, a collie and an Alsatian, who compete in the climactic trials, "a long brilliantly sustained sequence."

Stevenson produced as well as directed *The Ware Case* (1939), adapted from a once-popular play about a philandering man-about-town who is charged with murder and acquitted, only to commit suicide when he discovers that his wife loves another man. Clive Brook has the role created on stage by Sir Gerald Du Maurier and, wrote Basil Wright, he and a talented cast "involve themselves in all the postures of inconceivable refinement with a confident ease which only collapses before the blunt question—is all this necessary?"

Remaining in the uppper reaches of society, Stevenson next directed *A Young Man's Fancy* (1939), in which a duke's son (Griffith Jones), escaping from an arranged marriage, falls in love with an Irish girl (Anna Lee) who is fired from a cannon into his lap. Stevenson himself was responsible for this story and, according to a National Film Theatre program note, "finds precisely the right tone . . . and the cast to play it, notably Martita Hunt as a *grande dame* who has all the best lines and relishes them all." The director also coscripted *Return to Yesterday* (1939), a pleasantly nostalgic piece about a star, tired of fame, who returns incognito to the little seaside stock company and boardinghouse where his career began. Clive Brook again had the lead, opposite Anna Lee.

Ever since *Tudor Rose,* David O. Selznick had been inviting Stevenson to Hollywood and in the end he succumbed, first taking a year off to write a novel, *Darkness in the Land.* He joined Selznick in 1939 but the producer found little for him to do, instead loaning him out to other studios. Stevenson thus made his first American film for RKO, a lavish adaptation of *Tom Brown's Schooldays* (1940), Thomas Hughes'

novel about schoolboy brutality and stiff upper lips at Victorian Rugby. Cedric Hardwicke played the stern but just headmaster Dr. Arnold, and Jimmy Lydon gave an attractive performance as Tom Brown, but British reviewers in particular objected to some of the other casting—particularly of Dead End Kid Billy Halop as Flashman, the school bully. More recently the National Film Theatre called the film "a lively entertainment, superbly shot by Nicholas Musuraca, and infinitely better than the 1951 remake."

This was followed by a well-staged remake for Universal of John M. Stahl's *Back Street* (1941), based on Fannie Hurst's bestselling weepie about a woman (Margaret Sullavan) in love with a selfish married financier (Charles Boyer) and content to spend her life in the background of his. The movie was well received and repeated the great financial success of the earlier version starring Irene Dunne and John Boles.

There was another self-sacrificing woman in *Joan of Paris* (1942), this time a French barmaid (Michèle Morgan) who helps a Free French flyer (Paul Henreid) escape from occupied France. She winds up in front of a firing squad, murmuring "Tally-ho, Paul," as the Robert Mitchell Choir bursts into celestial song. The director agreed that "that was a stinker."

Stevenson was next involved in *Forever and a Day* (1943), to which Hollywood's British colony and others donated their services in gratitude for America's contributions to the British war effort. Twenty-one writers, seven directors and producers, and seventy-eight actors took part in a series of "breathless episodes" following the history of a great London house from its building in 1804 to its destruction by a German bomb. The *Guardian* called it "patchy and inconsequent."

One of Stevenson's best films followed from 20th Century–Fox, an adaptation of Charlotte Brontë's *Jane Eyre* with a taut, vivid, and literate script by Aldous Huxley, John Houseman, and the director. Joan Fontaine played the governess heroine with a proper mixture of modesty and determination, and Orson Welles was magnificent as her tormented employer Edward Rochester. Welles so dominates the screen that, William Whitebait suggested, he "leaves to Joan Fontaine little more than the role of spectator; her Jane Eyre is affecting though rather subdued. Indeed, the childhood scenes (excellently done) seem to set the stage for a biography which hardly materializes. Rochester comes instead, and thunder and lightning with him" (the latter photographed to great effect by George Barnes). The *Guardian*'s reviewer agreed that the film "has a speed, a unity, which suggests the nervous force of the original."

An American citizen since 1940, Stevenson went to the U.S. War Department in 1942 as a producer, the following year joining the Signal Corps under Colonel Frank Capra. He served until 1946 with the rank of captain, including overseas duty on the Italian front.

Stevenson's first postwar picture was *Dishonored Lady* (1947), with Hedy Lamarr as the helplessly promiscuous art editor of a slick magazine who, advised by a psychiatrist, abandons this empty life, changes her name, and goes off to "grow a new soul." She does this in Greenwich Village, where she paints in a garret, falls in love with a penniless young pathologist (Dennis O'Keefe), and settles into a fulfilling life as his helpmeet, though not before she has been cleared of murdering a former lover (John Loder) who "becomes shot." Reviewers found all this lush, absurd, and enjoyable.

To the Ends of the Earth (1948) is a crime drama in the pseudo-documentary style then fashionable, with something of the travelogue mixed in. Dick Powell stars as a narcotics agent whose battle against an international opium ring takes him to Japan, Shanghai, Egypt, and Havana. Signe Hasso plays a lovely suspect. C. A. Lejeune, who enjoyed the movie, was impressed by the ingenious methods of the dope smugglers and thought the film "should prove invaluable to anyone proposing to elude the customs officials in a somewhat exotic way."

It was at that point that Howard Hughes took over at RKO, where Stevenson was then under contract. The director told Patrick McGilligan that he enjoyed working with Hughes: "He was not the monster people made him out to be. I learned a tremendous amount from him, particularly from a technical point of view. I thought he knew more technically than anybody, except for Walt [Disney]. Walt knew more. Both of them hated not to know."

Perhaps Stevenson's admiration for Hughes explains his willingness to take on *The Woman on Pier 13* (also known as *I Married a Communist*), which had been turned down by every reputable director on the lot, from Losey to Nicholas Ray. It was a noirish Cold War movie of a type common enough during the witchhunting years of the House Un-American Activities Committee. Robert Ryan, dissatisfied with social conditions during the Depression, joins the Communist Party. Years later, now a successful shipping executive married to Laraine Day, he realizes the error of his former ways and wants out, but wicked commie Thomas Gomez tries to blackmail him into paralyzing San Francisco shipping. There are four deaths before this political contretemps is resolved.

John Gillett called this "a standard political-chase thriller with a good deal of sinister, low-key lighting . . . and the feeling of being made to a set formula. . . . Like other films in the cycle, this is not concerned with serious analysis, only with crude melodrama. The casting also raised some points of interest: Robert Ryan and Thomas Gomez were known as actors with a declared liberal background and it is curious to find them in this cheap farrago. . . . Perhaps the explanation lies in the fact that people were being asked to 'prove' their loyalty at this time."

Walk Softly Stranger (1950) has Joseph Cotten as a professional card-sharp trying to go straight. He changes his name and moves to a small town, where he takes a job in a factory and sets out to marry the boss's crippled daughter (Alida Valli). This project is well on the way to fruition—and Cotten to redemption through love—when his sins and the law catch up with him. The idea of starting over in life evidently appeals to Stevenson, who had already treated the subject in *Return to Yesterday, Dishonored Lady* and, arguably, *The Man Who Lived Again. Walk Softly Stranger* had a mixed reception, some reviewers finding it tedious, others liking its contrast between big-city corruption and small-town complacency. Several were reminded of Hitchcock's *Shadow of a Doubt,* and Patrick McGilligan called it a "neglected gem of *film noir.*"

There was very little enthusiasm for *My Forbidden Past,* completed in 1949 but not released until 1951. Set in New Orleans in 1900, it stars Ava Gardner as a smoldering Southern beauty who bribes her dastardly cousin (Melvyn Douglas) to seduce the wife of the Yankee doctor (Robert Mitchum) she loves, precipitating a situation in which both men wind up in a fine mess, charged with murder. "Stale oysters and flat champagne," one critic said. *The Las Vegas Story* (1952) was a mildly entertaining B thriller, chiefly notable, according to the reviews, for Jane Russell's décolletage and an early example of the helicopter chase.

Stevenson's loyalty to the increasingly eccentric Hughes was, he says, not "very good for my reputation in the industry." In 1952 he turned to television, over the next four years scripting fifteen shows and directing over a hundred for Ford Theatre, The Playhouse of the Stars, General Electric Theatre, Alfred Hitchcock Presents, Fireside Theatre, Cavalcade of America, and Gunsmoke, among other programs. In 1956 he "started over" yet again when he joined Walt Disney, "the best executive I ever met in my life."

His first film for Disney was *Johnny Tremain* (1957). The British-born Stevenson was an odd choice for this assignment, an account of the American War of Independence from the viewpoint of a young apprentice silversmith (Hal Stalmaster) in Boston. The London *Times* thought the film showed "a pleasant determination to be fair" and commended it as "a boy's-book version of the Boston Tea Party and its aftermath, a book full of bright illustrations drawn with clear, simple lines."

Old Yeller (1957), set in pioneer days in Texas, features Dorothy McGuire and Fess Parker as the lovable parents of manly young sons (Tommy Kirk and Kevin Corcoran). The real star, however, is Old Yeller, a flop-eared hound (unrelated to Owd Bob) who passes his time defending various members of the family from bears, wild hogs, and maddened wolves, and dies a martyr to canine loyalty. The picture was found generally likable, "friendly," and finally moving.

A pre-Bond Sean Connery starred (opposite Janet Munro) in *Darby O'Gill and the Little People* (1959), in which a romantic old drunk of an Irish gamekeeper (Albert Sharpe) not only insists that leprechauns exist but captures their ferocious little king (Jimmy O'Dea). The film had "a lot of charm," reviewers thought, as well as some alarmingly convincing touches of the macabre.

Stevenson, who says that he is distantly related to the author of *Kidnapped,* went to Scotland to film his version of the story. Young David Balfour is diddled out of his inheritance by his wicked uncle, shipwrecked, and then hunted for murder through the Scottish Highlands before laying his uncle by the heels and collecting the bawbees. Hollis Alpert wrote that "the Robert Louis Stevenson classic has been given a fine, handsome, virile production, with suitably gloomy Scottish castles, eye-filling glimpses of the islands and highlands, and spirited action on land and sea. The expert British cast is headed by Peter Finch as bold, romantic Alan Breck Stewart; and young James MacArthur, the only American on hand, makes a credibly sturdy and resourceful David."

One of Stevenson's biggest hits followed, *The Absent-Minded Professor* (1961). Fred MacMurray plays a college chemistry instructor known to his students as Neddie the Nut who nevertheless invents Flubber, an anti-gravity fluid that enables him, among other things, to fly his Model-T to the White House and to give the basketball squad the lift it needs. Keenan Wynn is the villain, out to steal the formula but satisfactorily bounced.

Time praised Bill Walsh's script and Stevenson's direction, calling this "a very funny piece of hyperbolic humor in the grand American tradition of Paul Bunyan." Dilys Powell thought it made excellent use "of the tricks and technical effects in which Disney delights" and that its jokes "have a good-humoured fantasy which is all too rarely found in the cinema; their extravangance, one feels, has been enjoyed in the making. And they are film jokes: they couldn't be produced with the same effect in another medium; Méliès, one feels, would have liked the make them." The public liked the movie, too. It grossed over $8 million—only a little less than the year's box-office champion, *The Guns of Navarone,* which had cost a great deal more to make.

In Search of the Castaways (1962), loosely adapted from Jules Verne's *Captain Grant's Children,* has Wilfrid Hyde-White as a wacky English nobleman, Maurice Chevalier as a know-all French scientist, and Wilfrid Brambell as a crazy castaway. George Sanders plays the villain, an oily gunrunner, and the result was called (paradoxically) "robust and unreal." After that came *Son of Flubber* (1963), an enjoyable sequel to *The Absent-Minded Professor,* and then the most successful film Stevenson or Disney ever made, *Mary Poppins* (1964).

This was a musical version of the books by P. L. Travers about a literally magical English nanny. The film moved the story back from the 1930s to Edwardian London, and committed the sacrilege (as some thought it) of implying a romantic attachment between the prim Mary (Julie Andrews) and Bert (Dick Van Dyke), the Cockney sweep and sidewalk artist. These liberties distressed purists, as did the Disneyesque "sugaring, softening, and prettifying" of the story. Others, like *Newsweek*'s reviewer, found it "sheer delight—to the eye, the ear, the senses." No one questioned "the breathtaking ingenuity" of the special effects or the excellence of a cast that included Glynis Johns, Elsa Lanchester, Hermione Baddeley, Arthur Treacher, and Ed Wynn. By 1978, the movie had grossed $42 million.

Continuing the tradition of the Flubber films, *The Monkey's Uncle* (1965) deals with another eccentric college genius (Tommy Kirk) who uses sleep-teaching techniques on his pet chimpanzee and invents a man-powered flying machine. *That Darn Cat* (1965) was another hit, with Hayley Mills gumshoeing around Southern California after a Siamese cat which shows up wearing a watch that might belong to a kidnapped bank teller. Eccentric comedy bits are supplied by Roddy MacDowall, Ed Wynn, Elsa Lanchester, and Iris Adrian.

Poor Walter Brennan had two roles in *The*

Gnome-Mobile (1967)—as D. J. Mulrooney, a California lumber tycoon, and as a 900-year-old gnome named Knobby. In this unlikely adaptation of an unlikely book by Upton Sinclair, it emerges that the redwood forests have been depopulated of their gnomes by Mulrooney's depredations. The old man and his grandchildren set out to put matters right, aided by the "gnome-mobile" (a 1930 Rolls Royce) and opposed by Horatio Quaxton (Sean McClory), who would like a gnome or two for his Academy of Fantastic Freaks.

Considerably better was *Blackbeard's Ghost* (1968), starring Peter Ustinov as the ghost of a riotous and rum-soaked pirate who returns to save his genteel descendant Elsa Lanchester from eviction by gangsters from the family inn. Romantic relief is provided by Suzanne Pleshette and Dean Jones from the local college (which also benefits from the mostly invisible revenant's interventions on the athletics field). Reviewers enjoyed Stevenson's "jaunty" direction and Ustinov's "infectious delight in his own clowning."

The Love Bug (1969) introduced Herbie, a small Volkswagen car with a heart of gold and a mind of its own. Looking for a good home, it foists itself on racing driver Dean Jones, plays Cupid in a romance between Jones and Michele Lee, and helps its lucky owner win the big race against egregious David Tomlinson. When its efforts go unappreciated, Herbie considers suicide but is dissuaded, to the dismay of such hard-eyed, weak-stomached critics as Richard Roud, who called the movie "absolutely sick-making." Those who held this view were evidently in a minority, however, since it was the year's top-grossing picture ($17 million) and spawned such sequels as Stevenson's own *Herbie Rides Again* (1974).

In between, Stevenson made *Bedknobs and Broomsticks* (1971), adapted from Mary Norton's *The Magic Bedknob* and featuring Angela Lansbury as a well-intentioned and patriotic witch who is unfortunately only halfway through her correspondence course. David Robinson commended this picture as a "glossy, spirited, old-fashioned farcical entertainment . . . a close variation on the *Poppins* formula with energetic numbers (by Richard and Robert Sherman) and nice grotesque animated characters added to the human ones."

After the adventure epic *Island at the Top of the World* (1974) came *One of Our Dinosaurs Is Missing* (1975), which pleased all but the sourest reviewers. Set in London in the 1920s, it has another wonderfully outsize performance by Peter Ustinov, this time as a fiendish Oriental criminal who masterminds the transport through aston-

ished streets of a gigantic dinosaur skeleton, stolen from the Natural History Museum because it is supposed to contain a secret formula. The picture "is all much nearer to Ealing comedy than Disney," wrote Kenneth Robinson, and "if you don't enjoy the film, there is something seriously wrong with you." *The Shaggy D.A.* (1976) has Dean Jones running for district attorney, considerably handicapped by the fact that he turns into an Old English sheepdog every time wicked Keenan Wynn reads out the inscription on his magic ring. Most thought it "a joke that really cannot be spun out for 92 minutes."

This undistinguished movie, made when he was over seventy, was Stevenson's last, though it is doubtful whether anyone outside Walt Disney Productions noticed. Stevenson has never courted fame and has never had much, though he worked as a director for over forty years and made his share of good films. In spite of *Tudor Rose, King Solomon's Mines, Tom Brown's Schooldays, Back Street, Jane Eyre, The Absent-Minded Professor,* and *Mary Poppins,* he does not appear in Andrew Sarris' *The American Cinema,* David Thomson's *Biographical Dictionary of the Cinema,* or *The Oxford Companion to Film.*

Part of the reason for Stevenson's obscurity is his disappearance in the mid-1950s into what Patrick McGilligan rightly calls the "hermetically sealed" world of the Disney Studios at Burbank, "from which insiders tell no tales." And yet, McGilligan suggests, the British-born Stevenson "has perhaps exerted a more profound cultural influence on his adopted country than any other director. . . . His movies for Disney are the movies a generation has grown up with."

What is less conjectural and more surprising is that, according to *Variety,* Stevenson is "the most commerically successful director in the history of films." *Variety* estimates his US and Canadian rentals alone at $178 million—probably $250 million in world rentals. Sixteen of Stevenson's Disney films have appeared on *Variety's* list of all-time top box-office successes—more than any other director's.

McGilligan says that Stevenson is "a genial, reticent, and occasionally witty man with a scholarly intelligence" and a scarcely modified British accent. He has been married since 1963 to the former Ursula Henderson, who teaches or taught medicine at UCLA. On set, Stevenson is said to be calm and polite. He likes to adhere to the script and does not welcome improvisation, but is hospitable to an actor's view of how a part should be played. In 1977 the BBC made an admiring and affectionate documentary about the director, *Hollywood Dream-Maker.*

FILMS: (with Jack Hulbert) Falling for You, 1933; (with Jack Hulbert) Jack of All Trades (U.S., The Two of Us), 1936; Tudor Rose (U.S., Nine Days a Queen), 1936; The Man Who Changed His Mind (U.S., The Man Who Lived Again), 1936; King Solomon's Mines, 1937; Non-Stop New York, 1937; Owd Bob (U.S., To the Victor), 1938; The Ware Case, 1939; A Young Man's Fancy, 1939; Return to Yesterday, 1939; Tom Brown's Schooldays, 1940; Back Street, 1941; Joan of Paris, 1942; (with others) Forever and a Day, 1943; Jane Eyre, 1944; Dishonored Lady, 1947; To the Ends of the Earth, 1948; The Woman on Pier 13/I Married a Communist, 1949; Walk Softly Stranger, 1950; My Forbidden Past, 1951; The Las Vegas Story, 1952; Johnny Tremain, 1957; Old Yeller, 1957; Darby O'Gill and the Little People, 1959; Kidnapped, 1960; The Absent-Minded Professor, 1961; In Search of the Castaways, 1962; Son of Flubber, 1963; The Misadventures of Merlin Jones, 1964; Mary Poppins, 1964; The Monkey's Uncle, 1965; That Darn Cat, 1965; The Gnome-Mobile, 1967; Blackbeard's Ghost, 1968; The Love Bug, 1969; Bedknobs and Broomsticks, 1971; Herbie Rides Again, 1974; The Island at the Top of the World, 1974; One of Our Dinosaurs Is Missing, 1975; The Shaggy D.A., 1976.

ABOUT: Who's Who, 1985. *Periodicals*—American Film March 1978; Film Ideal 220–221 1970; Film Weekly August 6, 1938; National Film Theatre (Britain) Booklet January 1979.

MAURITZ STILLER

STILLER, MAURITZ (July 17, 1883– November 8, 1928), Swedish director and scenarist, was born Mosche Stiller in Helsinki, Finland, of Russian-Jewish parents. His mother committed suicide when he was three years old and his father, an army musician, died a few years later. Four of the six Stiller children eventually emigrated to the United States. Poverty and emotional deprivation made a "double character" of Mauritz Stiller: he became a hustler and a huckster, both ruthless and flamboyant; but he was also a capable violinist and a lover of music, and "a man who lived through his eyes"—his friend Victor Sjöström said that "he'd get physically sick when he saw anything ugly."

Stiller saw much that was ugly in his youth. After a minimal education, he worked in a cap factory and elsewhere in Helsinki, finding his first acting jobs at the age of sixteen as a film extra and bit player. Technically a Russian citizen, he was drafted into the Imperial Army in 1904 but fled to Sweden instead, arriving in Stockholm penniless. He "starved and inhabited park benches" until he established himself as a stage actor with various touring companies. In 1907 he

returned to Finland to join the Swedish Theatre in Helsinki. He was not a particularly good actor, but he was tall and handsome, with a good singing voice, and he had some success in musicals, both in Finland and on tour in Sweden.

In 1910, back in Stockholm, Stiller joined the Lilla Teatern (Little Theatre), an avant-garde actors' cooperative that had been the first to stage the revolutionary works of August Strindberg. Stiller became manager of the company and then its director. It was his acclaimed production of a Tolstoy play that brought him to the attention of Charles Magnusson, the shrewd production manager of the Svenska Biograf film studios in Stockholm, later to become Svensk Filmindustri. A dandy and bon vivant who always tended to live beyond his means, Stiller was then in dire financial straits. He accepted Magnusson's offer with alacrity, joining Svenska Bio in 1912—the same year as the actor and director Victor Sjöström.

Stiller's first movie was *Mor och dotter* (*Mother and Daughter*, 1912), a melodrama that he wrote himself—as he did the majority of his films—and in which he played the central role as a vile seducer. He gave Sjöström the lead in his second picture, *De svarta maskerna* (*The Black Masks*, 1912). This benefited from Stiller's study of the D. W. Griffith shorts then being screened in Sweden. It reportedly contained over a hundred scenes, and surprised the reviewers with its technical sophistication, including parallel action and trick perspectives. It culminated in a spectacular scene in which the hero and heroine escape from a tall building by climbing down a rope.

More than thirty short features followed between 1912 and 1916, most of them comedies or melodramas based on pulp fiction or folksy peasant dramas. According to one authority, Stiller also drew on Russian fiction that he could assume would be unfamiliar to Swedish audiences. A born showman, he is said to have had little real regard for literature, which he simply ransacked for exciting incidents that could be worked into his pictures. This philistinism displeased some critics (and authors), but it reflected an instinctive understanding of the essentially visual nature of film, and played an important part in rescuing European cinema from slavish dependence on literary texts.

However trivial his material, Stiller devoted great and ever-increasing attention to sets, props, and costumes. There are signs of exceptional ability even in an early melodrama like *Gränsfolken* (*Frontier People*, 1914), in which scenes from a Zola novel set in France are translated into a story about a Cossack attack on a Russian settlement. The film was destroyed by fire, but existing stills make it clear that the battle sequences were poetically conceived and beautifully composed, "with smoke drifting over wheels and barrows and fallen fighters."

Stiller also excelled in the handling of comedy, in this as in other respects differing from his gloomily intellectual friend Sjöström. The only early film by Stiller that has survived complete is *Kärlek och journalistik* (*Love and Journalism*, 1916), a sparkling romantic comedy written by Harriet Bloch. Karin Molander, then the wife of the future director Gustaf Molander, plays a young journalist who, in pursuit of a scoop, goes to work as a maid in the home of a famous explorer, winding up with a husband instead.

By this time, most of the characteristics of Stiller's comedy style were already evident—the rapid, imaginative editing; the sharp eye for revealing detail; the spirited and intelligent heroine. "What is most striking about this brisk little farce," wrote Richard Combs, "is how its adventurer-hero is so often left at a disadvantage. Where the gloomy, haunted heroes of his dramas clearly preempt the stage, Stiller's comedies are largely ruled by the reckless *joie de vivre* and scheming intelligence of his heroines."

All of these elements are present in the most likable of Stiller's comedies, *Thomas Graals bästa film* (*Thomas Graal's Best Film*, 1917), scripted by Gustaf Molander and "Harald B. Harald" (Stiller). Thomas Graal is a famous scriptwriter who is being hounded by the philistine studio manager to come up with a new story. Temporarily "blocked," he is further distracted by his infatuation with his new typist Bessie (Karin Molander). When she walks out on him after a tiff, Thomas is inspired to write a scenario based on Bessie's account of the poverty and hardship of her home life (touching scenes from which are visualized for us). In fact, she had told Thomas a pack of lies—she is really the reckless and imaginative daughter of a rich family. Bessie and Thomas are reunited when she bravely intervenes in what turns out to be a movie fight, and she is cast as the heroine of Thomas' new film.

Thomas Graal has been described as "one of the liveliest figures of the silent cinema, and one knows him intimately because the very structure of the film reflects his approach to life, his devious fancies, and his disarming jokes." There is some amiable satire on the early movie industry, and an extremely complex structure of fantasies and flashbacks, very deftly handled. Stiller had molded Sjöström and Molander into a perfectly balanced team that has reminded many of William Powell and Myrna Loy in the "Thin Man" series—wonderfully free of the exaggerated gestures and expressions that marred most contemporary performances. There was an equally successful though rather over-extended sequel, *Thomas Graals bästa barn* (*Thomas Graal's Best Child*, 1918), which opens with Thomas having to undress at the wedding in order to find the ring and continues with a violent dispute between him and Bessie about their first child—still unconceived—and what sex it should be.

However, the first of Stiller's pictures to bring him international recognition was in a very different vein—a pastoral morality that in mood and manner resembles the work of Victor Sjöström. The increasingly serious content of Stiller's later films has been widely attributed to Sjöström's influence—just as the growing attention to visual qualities in Sjöström's films has been credited to Stiller. But Sjöström denied that he and his friend ever cooperated directly, or even read each other's scripts. When a picture was completed, "we might . . . make a criticism or two about some editing. But I do not think either of us followed the advice. We were both rather stubborn men . . . , but otherwise we were of entirely different disposition. We were great, very great friends." This being so, it seems likely that the transition in Stiller's work was inspired partly by his honest admiration for Sjöström's films, partly by the recognition that "trivial" comedies, however brilliant, would never bring him the kind of artistic fame and influence Sjöström had already won.

Sången om den eldröda blomman (*Song of the Scarlet Flower*, 1919) was based on a serious work of literature, adapted by Gustaf Molander from a novel by the Finnish author Johannes Linnakoski. The young hero Olof (Lars Hanson) is banished from his father's house because of his affair with a servant girl and becomes a wanderer, working as a sailor on a freighter and then as a logger. After various emotional adventures he shyly begins to court a girl of his own class (Edith Erastoff). Olof is scorned as a vagabond by the girl's stern old father, who tells his daughter that, if she goes, she must leave his house with no more than she had when she entered it. She promptly begins to strip, calling the patriarch's bluff and ensuring a happy ending.

Shot on location in the wilderness of northern Sweden, the film was shown all over the world. In Britain (where it was called *The Flame of Life*) it was screened at court for Queen Alexandra and acclaimed for "a devotion and artistry that one seldom sees on the screen." A scene where Olof shoots the rapids poised on a log was called "the strongest 'attraction' that the movie world . . . has seen." Writing sixty years later, Richard Combs said that the film's narrative was "strong enough to withstand its division into chapters, complete with lessons pointed in the headings; what drives the film are its scenes of family strife and acrimonious confrontation. . . . The wilfulness of such scenes . . . startles into life these stolid figures in a country landscape, and hints at the perversity and tortured sensitivity that wreak havoc in the later dramas."

After *Fiskebyn* (*The Fishing Village/The Vengeance of Jakob Vindas*), made in 1919 but not released until 1920, came *Herr Arnes Pengar* (*Sir Arne's Treasure*, 1919), regarded by many as Stiller's masterpiece. Originally assigned to Victor Sjöström, who turned it over to his friend, it was the first of Stiller's adaptations of the novels of Selma Lagerlöf, scripted by himself with Molander. The film is set in sixteenth-century Sweden and begins with the defeat of the king's rebellious Scottish Guard. Three of the Scottish captains escape and set out for the fishing village of Marstrand, where they hope to find a ship. On the way they come to Solberga, the house of Sir Arne (Hjalmar Selander). Half-mad with hunger, they steal its famous treasure, burn the house, and murder all the occupants except one young girl, Elsalill (Mary Johnson), who is in hiding.

Neighbors find Elsalill and she is taken to Marstrand, where she falls in love with the youngest of the mercenaries, Sir Archie (Richard Lund)—unrecognizable in the sumptuous clothes the stolen treasure has bought him. Their tenuous and oddly touching romance is doomed from the outset. Elsalill is increasingly troubled

by nightmares and fainting spells, and a visitation from her dead sister shows her that her beloved is the butcher of Solberga. She denounces him and then, in an agony of remorse, warns him. Sir Archie has no such qualms and, renouncing love in favor of survival, flees towards the ship on which he has booked passage, using Elsalill's body as a shield. She is killed by a spearthrust meant for him, but the three Scotsmen are captured. The gray-robed women of Marstrand move in solemn procession over the frozen sea to recover Elsalill's corpse (a scene echoed twenty-five years later at the end of Eisenstein's *Ivan the Terrible*).

In his usual cavalier fashion, Stiller had lifted from Lagerlöf's atmospheric novel only what he wanted, having first secured her approval of a much more faithful scenario. This naturally led to conflicts between director and author that grew increasingly bitter in subsequent "collaborations." In one early, restrained, and perceptive complaint, Lagerlöf wrote: "Now, when I see that you consider that the book should only be a source of inspiration and that the contents should be changed to something quite new, exclusively meant for the film, then I must honestly say that I can no longer agree with you. . . . I understand that you, with your great ability, are trying to raise the film to . . . a new branch of art, like music of the eye, if I may say so, but in order to do this it certainly is necessary that the story be meant for the film from the beginning."

In purely cinematic terms, nevertheless, Stiller's unscrupulousness was fully justified. He and Molander reorganized the narrative into a readily comprehensible chronological form and visualized in exciting detail events only implied in the novel. Thus we see the mercenaries being driven to the border like cattle through the snow, the escape from prison of the three captains, and their journey to Marstrand through trackless forests, enduring hardships that turn them into "ravening wolves." One of the captains leaps to freedom from a very tall tower. This feat was rigged by filming him as he jumped first into an unseen net fifty feet below, then from a low platform to the ground. The two shots were then cut together to give the effect of an uninterrupted leap—and this *before* Stiller could have seen the identical (and much acclaimed) scene in Griffith's *Intolerance*. The prison buildings and the streets of Marstrand—all highly convincing— were actually studio sets, fortuitously covered by a heavy snowfall that disguised their artificiality.

But some disturbing scenes were not faked, and demonstrate Stiller's absolute ruthlessness in realizing his intentions. There is, for example, no reason to believe that the sequence in which a sled and struggling horse disappear through a hole in the ice was anything but authentic. And the final, powerfully symbolic shots of the sea ice breaking up and the waves returning were filmed by Julius Jaenzon, the finest Swedish cameraman of his day, at the risk of his life.

According to Bengt Idestam-Almquist, *Sir Arne's Treasure* has about eight hundred scenes and a hundred rather long titles (most of them quoted directly from the novel). The same critic notes that "the change of scenes is not as fast as that of Soviet films seven or eight years later, but it is still rather lively. Each scene lasts an average of about seven seconds. . . . Stiller cut into the middle of action: the movement in one scene continues into the next. The scenes melt together into an organic whole of a sort different from the montages produced later in the Soviet." This technique is most brilliantly used in the sequence where guests at a banquet see the smoke from Arne's burning house: "The guests rush to their sled, a hectic scramble of angle shots with people and horses, like gray shadows, streaking past the lens. . . . They gallop to Solberga, throw up ladders and start fighting the fire, while the madmen force the horse onto the weak ice in order to hinder possible pursuit."

Stiller had an approach to casting much like that later developed by Eisenstein as his "typage" theory, choosing actors not for their ability but for the suitability of their appearance and personality for a particular role. The cast of *Sir Arne's Treasure* included film actors, stage actors, revue artists, a fur dealer, and an office manager. "Stiller drove them impartially," wrote Idestam-Almquist, "bawled them out, frightened the life out of them, flattered them until he had broken through their inhibitions and clichés of expression and had reduced them to putty. . . . As a director Stiller was a Svengali, a torturing devil beyond compare, but he was loved by his sacrificial victims because he produced results."

Peter Cowie describes the film as "not merely a spectacular adventure, but a study of the human condition that works on several levels. The landscape and the background are bound up inextricably with the fate of every character. *Sir Arne's Treasure* is a tragedy in the fatalistic tradition of the Swedish cinema, but it also hints at psychological motives and effects in a far more mature way than does most of Sjöström's work. . . . [Elsalill's] blighted romance is one of the most touching in Swedish cinema. . . . For the first time Stiller reveals a grasp of *mise-en-scène* that can attain epic proportions.

The weakness and folly of the characters in *Sir Arne's Treasure* appear black against the endless expanse of white snow. . . . This visual beauty is aided by the matchless photography of Julius Jaenzon. The original tinted copy must have been unimaginably splendid."

From this "epic masterpiece," Stiller turned back to his earlier mode to make *Erotikon* (1920, in Britain called *Bonds That Chafe*). Based by Stiller and Molander on a play by Franz Herzeg, it is an elaborate comedy of sexual manners involving a bumbling old entomologist, his elegant and faithless wife (Tora Teje), the niece who wants to take her place (Karin Molander), and the wife's two lovers—a celebrated roué and a fashionable sculptor (Lars Hanson). Their maneuvers are implicitly compared (in a boring lecture given by the old professor) to the "communal life of the striver beetle," and indeed the film offers an almost entomological view of human folly.

Erotikon's risqué wit and cheerful amorality made it a sensation in its time and it was a huge success, critically and financially. Chaplin admired it, and Lubitsch later acknowledged its influence on his own comedies. Eisenstein, who at one time conceived the cinema as a "montage of attractions," said that Stiller's films were "amusement parks of attractions." *Erotikon's* elaborate trappings included eight hundred extras, private airplanes, luxurious apartments and splendid restaurants, and a specially composed ballet presented by the Stockholm Royal Opera. However, the effect of these embellishments was to divert Stiller's attention from characterization and pace, and the result now seems curiously static, lacking the lightness of touch of his earlier comedies.

Johan (1920), from the novel by Juhani Aho, marks Stiller's final transition to the fatalistic mood associated with Sjöström and the Swedish tradition, in which landscape and weather play major roles in shaping human destiny. Johan (Mathias Taube) lives on a remote farm with his tyrannical mother and Marit (Jenny Hasselqvist), a young orphan they have rescued from the snow. Johan and Marit fall in love and, against the mother's wishes, are married. When the ingratiating stranger Vallavan arrives (Urho Sommersalmi), he seems to offer Marit something more attractive than a loving but inarticulate husband and a bullying mother-in-law, and she runs off with him down the river. Johan catches up with them and beats Vallavan, but Marit insists that she left of her own free will. Seeing each other with new eyes after this trauma and recognizing their mutual dependence, the young couple row home together.

This movie has been generally rather overlooked or dismissed as "conventional," but Peter Cowie values it highly. The stylized acting in the flirtation scenes between Marit and Vallavan seem to him a deliberate parody of "the heavy, louring acting style of the Sjöström school," demonstrating Stiller's "astonishing perception and ironic vision," while the sequences illustrating the special excitement that attaches to a stranger in the somber lives of Scandinavian country people reveal the director's "profound grasp of the Nordic character and temperament." When Marit and Vallavan set out together downriver, "Marit's emotional confusion and remorse . . . are brilliantly suggested by the waves lashing the tiny boat. The editing is so mature that the trip down the river appears as a continuous movement, a whirling descent into chaos and misadventure. The daily round of pastoral life and physical labour is well sketched, and the scenery is integrated into the story in a sophisticated, unostentatious way. . . . The themes that are adumbrated in the film dominate not only much of Bergman's oeuvre, but also the films of Mattsson and Sjöberg."

De Landsflyktige (The Exiles, 1921), adapted from a novel by Runar Schildt, is a comparatively minor work, but Stiller's next picture had been called his "last film of genius." *Gunnar Hedes Saga,* released in January 1923, and variously translated as *The Old Manor* and *The Judgment,* was the director's second Lagerlöf adaptation, scripted by himself from her novel *En Herrgardssägen.* The "old manor" of the story is Monkhyttan, the palatial home of Gunnar Hede (Einar Hanson). His grandfather had established the family fortune by driving Lappland reindeer down from the Arctic Circle and selling at a large profit, but Gunnar himself is more interested in playing the violin. When his domineering mother tries to end his romance with Ingrid (Mary Johnson), a gypsy musician whose family he has housed on his estate, he becomes another of Stiller's homeless wanderers.

Gunnar goes to northern Sweden as a concert violinist, but once there is possessed by his grandfather's adventurous spirit. He buys a reindeer herd and begins the long trek south. Julius Jaenzon's high-angle shots of the vast herd moving slowly over snow captures the epic quality of the great Westerns. Then there is a tremendous stampede in which—in a "series of dazzing tracking shots"—we see Gunnar dragged by a stag over ice and through woodland until he is unconscious. We see him next at home at Monkhyttan, but in a trance-like state of total amnesia. He wanders through beautiful woods, possessed by delusions and struggling to unlock his memory. In the end it is the sound of a violin, played by the devoted Ingrid, that lifts the darkness from his mind. The stones he had collected in his madness turn out to contain valuable minerals that will save the now impoverished Monkhyttan.

The depth of Stiller's feeling for music comes through strongly in this film, which conveys a fervent spirituality remote from his ironic comedies and owes much to Mary Johnson's ethereal beauty and the poise and delicacy of her portrayal of Ingrid. Richard Combs, who finds *Sir Arne's Treasure* somewhat marred by "an overabundance of character and incident," maintains that *Gunnar Hedes Saga* "has a fair claim to being the most personal of all . . . [Stiller's] films and his one incontestable masterpiece."

According to Bengt Idestam-Almquist, "Stiller was not normally attracted to women, in spite of which he dreamed . . . of his own home and a calm family life. His ideal woman was supersensual, spiritual and mystic. He tried to mold Mary Johnson into that ideal, but he did not succeed with her as well as he did with other more malleable material: Greta Garbo." Stiller has been called a Svengali, and it seems that he did indeed dream of creating a great international star who would assure his own fame. He found her when Greta Gustafsson, a young student at the Royal Dramatic Theatre's school in Stockholm, auditioned for a major role in his last Lagerlöf adaptation (and last Swedish film), *Gösta Berlings Saga (The Atonement of Gösta Berling).* Indirectly, she caused his downfall.

Gösta Berling (Lars Handon) is a dissolute young pastor in nineteenth-century Sweden. Expelled from his church, he works for a time as tutor to a young girl, and then takes up residence at Ekeby Manor, along with other wild young men who have been given refuge by the owner's unfaithful wife. It is she who saves Gösta's life when he comes close to suicide. He acquires a mistress, Marianne Sinclair (Jenny Hasselqvist), and brings her to Ekeby, but her beauty is destroyed by smallpox. Then the outraged populace set fire to Ekeby Manor. Gösta rescues Marianne and returns her to her home, and is then redeemed by his love for a beautiful Italian girl, Elisabeth (Greta Garbo). They become the owners of Ekeby Manor, and Gösta sets about rebuilding the house, whose dark past has been purged by fire.

The film was first released in 1924 in two parts totaling nearly 14,000 feet and running three and a half hours. In 1933, when sound had arrived, the two parts were edited down into a single film of two and three-quarter hours, and music was added. The editor was Ragnar Hylten-Cavellius, who had been Stiller's coscenarist.

Many long sequences were radically shortened, and some important connecting scenes were removed altogether and replaced with explanatory titles. Above all, the rhythm of Stiller's editing was lost in the shortened version—the only one that has survived.

The damage would have been even greater if Stiller had not already reduced the sprawling novel to what one critic called "a series of loosely connected visual 'attractions,'" of which the most famous are the burning of Ekeby Manor and the scene in which a horse-drawn sleigh is pursued by wolves over a frozen lake. The studio scenes are said to clash embarrasingly with those shot on location, though "some of the interiors do have a plastic beauty as though based on the paintings of Vermeer." The acting was called "conspicuously broad," except in the case of the novice Greta Garbo, whose "warm and sparkling performance" relied far less on "histrionic poses and gestures" than the others.

Stiller is said to have "tyrannized" Garbo into losing some twenty pounds for the film, and Peter Cowie writes that it was his achievement "to isolate—and then magnify—the innate control and coolness of her expression." But, though Stiller is universally regarded as the principal begetter of the Garbo legend, *Gösta Berling's Saga* was the only one of his films in which she appeared. After it, they went to Turkey for location shooting on a film whose working title was "The Odalisque From Smolna." When financing for that collapsed, Stiller secured an important role for Garbo in Pabst's *Street Without Joy.* Then Louis B. Mayer saw *Gösta Berling* in Berlin and, encouraged by Sjöström, invited Stiller and his protégée to join MGM.

The couple arrived in Hollywood in September 1925. Garbo was soon cast in Monta Bell's *The Torrent,* but Stiller was given nothing to do until the spring of 1926, when Mayer accepted his adaptation of an Ibáñez novel for filming as *The Temptress* (1926), with Garbo in the lead as a devastatingly destructive Argentinian vamp. The filming was turbulent. Stiller was outraged by what the MGM script department had done to his script and disliked his leading man, Antonio Moreno. An absolute dictator in his Swedish productions, he was now expected to tolerate "supervision" by studio "busybodies." He was, moreover, suffering from acute rheumatism. His rages became the talk of Hollywood, and in the end he was removed, most of his scenes being reshot and the film completed by Fred Niblo. When Stiller saw the preview he tried to stop the movie's release, convinced that it would ruin Garbo's career. In fact it was a great success, and Garbo was called "magnificent."

By the late summer of 1926, Stiller was out of work again, and it was clear that he could expect no more assignments from MGM, in spite of his three-year contract. His health declining, he was rescued by an old friend, Erich Pommer, by then production chief at Paramount. Stiller's first film for that studio—and his last of any merit—was *Hotel Imperial* (1927). Adapted by Jules Furthman from a play by Lajos Biro, it is a story of love and espionage in World War I, set in a run-down Polish hotel, and starring Pola Negri as a chambermaid who hides an Austrian officer from the Russians and falls in love with him.

Seeing his opportunity, Stiller threw all his energy into the project. For the hotel, he built an enormous set of eight connecting rooms, all with solid walls, and with rails above on which the camera could move in virtually any direction. "The story is told swiftly and economically," wrote one reviewer, "with the camera industriously searching for significant details and making the most of them." Iris Barry found the opening scenes "unparalleled anywhere. Stragglers from the Austro-Hungarian Army are riding, dog-tired, in the bleak misty darkness. Challenged, pursued, one of them escapes by dropping into a courtyard and creeps into the quiet house beyond it. . . . He is nearly dead with weariness, and knowing that he must not linger a moment he humors his tired body with sitting down for a moment. His brain plays him a trick; he thinks he is on horseback again, swaying. He is dead asleep in an instant, while the Russian Army draws nearer and nearer. That whole scene was conceived, directed, and photographed without a flaw."

The movie was a commercial as well as a critical success, bringing Stiller a new Paramount contract at $2,500 a week and a second Pola Negri vehicle to direct, *The Woman on Trial* (1927). A love-triangle story that ends with the heroine on trial for murder, it was, as Stiller acknowledged to his friend Lars Hanson, "genuine garbage," though again it did well at the box office. A third collaboration with Pola Negri followed in *Barbed Wire* (1927), based on Hall Caine's pacifist novel *The Woman of Knockaloe,* but Stiller's health broke down during filming and he had to abandon the picture to Rowland W. Lee. He tried again with *Street of Sin,* starring Emil Jannings as a London gangster who falls in love with a Salvation Army girl, but he had shot only a few scenes when he became too ill to continue and was obliged to cede the project to Ludvig Berger. His career was over, while Greto Garbo, after her triumph in *Flesh and the Devil* (1927), was on her way to glory as the cinema's greatest star.

In December 1927, sick and disappointed, Stiller returned to Stockholm. He subsequently directed a stage musical, *Broadway,* but there were no more films, though several were discussed. Stiller became seriously ill in the fall of 1928 and died in November, attended by his friend Sjöström.

In 1931, mourning the decline of the Swedish cinema, C. A. Lejeune wrote that it had "had only a short season of maturity. For three or four years, at a time when Russia was unknown in the cinema, when Germany was still cut off from a foreign market and France was developing a timid *avant-garde,* Sweden created and sent out into the world a mass of strongly nationalised and richly considered productions that embodied new ideas of cinema material, and presented new combinations of cinema technique."

The heroes of that brief golden age were Sjöström and Stiller, in that order. At least to their contemporaries, Sjöström was "the classic representative of Sweden in the cinema," Stiller a brilliant showman who, after wasting years on commercial entertainments, finally saw the light and made a handful of major films as a disciple of Sjöström. It is still generally agreed that Stiller's last Swedish films were his greatest, but some later critics go so far as to suggest (as Richard Combs had done) that his "most innovative work was probably done in the comedies, which allowed his natural flamboyance free rein without resulting in the over-elaborate bravura of the costume epics." And there are some who find it easier to relish Stiller's irony than Sjöström's sometimes ponderous fatalism. Richard Roud calls Stiller "one of the truly great directors," who "has still to be rediscovered."

FILMS: Mor och dotter (Mother and Daughter), 1912; De svarta maskerna (The Black Masks), 1912; Den tyraniske fästmannen (The Despotic Fiancé), 1913; Vampyren (The Vampire), 1913; Barnet (The Child), 1913; När kärleken dödar (When Love Kills), 1913; När larmlockan ljuder (When the Tocsin Calls), 1913; När svärmor regerar (When Mother-in-Law Dictates), 1914; Livets konflikter (Life's Conflicts), 1913; Moderna suffragetten (The Modern Suffragette), 1913; Den okända (The Unknown Woman), 1913; Mannekängen (The Fashion Model), 1913; Bröderna (The Brothers), 1914; Gränsfolken (Frontier People), 1914; För sin kärleks skull (Because of Love), 1914; Kammarjunkaren (The Chamberlain), 1914; Stormfågeln (Stormy Petrel/Storm Bird), 1914; Skottet (The Shot), 1914; Det röda tornet (The Red Tower), 1914; När konstnärer älska (When Artists Love), 1915; Lekkamraterna (Playmates), 1915; Hans hustrus förflutna (His Wife's Past), 1915; Dolken (The Dagger), 1915 (banned); Mästertjuven (The Master Thief), 1915; Madame de Thebes, 1915; Hämneren (The Revenger), 1916; Minlotsen (The Mine-Pilot), 1916; Hans bröllopsnatt/Äventyret (His Wedding Night/The Ad-venture), 1916; Lyckonålen (The Lucky Pin/The Lucky Brooch), 1916; Kärlek och journalistik (Love and Journalism), 1916; Vingarna (Wings), 1916; Kampen om hans hjärta (The Fight for His Heart), 1916; Balettprimadonnan/Wolo (The Ballerina/Wolo, Wolo), 1916; Thomas Graals bästa film (Thomas Graal's Best Film/Wanted: A Film Actress), 1917; Alexander den store (Alexander the Great), 1917; Thomas Graals bästa barn (Thomas Graal's Best Child/Thomas Graal's First Child), 1918; Sången om den eldröda blomman (Song of the Scarlet Flower/The Flame of Life), 1919; Herr Arnes Pengar (Sir Arne's Treasure/The Treasure of Arne/Three Who Were Doomed/Snows of Destiny), 1919; Fiskebyn (The Fishing Village/The Vengeance of Jakob Vindas), 1920; Erotikon (Bonds That Chafe), 1920; Johan, 1920; De Landsflyktige (The Exiles/The Emigrants), 1921; Gunnar Hedes Saga (The Old Mansion/The Judgment), 1923; Gösta Berlings Saga (The Atonement of Gösta Berling/The Story of Gösta Berling/The Saga of Gösta Berling), 1924; Hotel Imperial, 1927; The Woman on Trial, 1927.

ABOUT: Béranger, J. La Grande aventure du cinéma suédois, 1960, (in French); Cowie, P. Sweden (Screen Series) vols. 1 and 2, 1970; Idestam-Almquist, B. Mauritz Stiller; 1884–1928, 1967 (in French); Pensel, H. Seastrom and Stiller in Hollywood, 1969; Petrie, G. Hollywood Destinies, 1986; Roud, R. (ed.) Cinema: A Critical Dictionary, 1980; Waldekranz, R. Swedish Cinema, 1959; Werner, G. Mauritz Stiller och hans filmer, 1969 (in Swedish). *Periodicals*—Cinema Journal Winter 1974–1975; Écran September 1978; Monthly Film Bulletin December 1977; National Film Theatre Booklet (Britain) April–May 1975, October 1977; Sight and Sound Summer 1974; Thousand Eyes Magazine March 1977.

STROHEIM, ERICH VON (September 22, 1885–May 12, 1957), American director, scenarist, and actor. On November 25, 1909, the German liner *Prince Friedrich Wilhelm* arrived at the port of New York. Among the many new immigrants interviewed by the examiners at Ellis Island was one Erich Oswald Hans Carl Maria von Stroheim. He described himself as a Hungarian clerk headed for employment at the Max Grab Fashion Company, an import house located at 38 East 21st Street in Manhattan. But he was no clerk, and no Hungarian. His Uncle Max Grab might have served as a reference, but until the new immigrant developed a reasonable command of English (nearly two years later) his employment opportunities would consist of an assortment of odd jobs—wrapping packages, waiting on tables, even a brief stint handling horses for the New York National Guard. Most significantly, he was no "von."

The facts, hidden throughout his lifetime, are these. Erich Oswald Stroheim was born in Vien-

ERICH VON STROHEIM

na on September 22, 1885. His parents, Benno Stroheim and Johanna Bondy, were practicing Jews who registered the birth of their son Erich (and later his younger brother, Bruno) in the archives of Vienna's Jewish community. The elder Stroheim was a dealer in felt, straw, and feathers, and later became a hat manufacturer. Erich's upbringing was comfortably middle-class, but he was restless and unhappy with the opportunities available to him. He had no taste for the business world, and a brief military career was completely undistinguished—indeed, he seems to have deserted from the Austrian ranks rather abruptly before his trip to America.

All of this would be unremarkable but for the myth regarding his origins constructed by Erich von Stroheim when he arrived triumphantly on the Hollywood scene in 1919 as the director of one of that season's most acclaimed films, *Blind Husbands.*

A Universal studio press release for that period announced him as "the son of a German Baroness and Austrian Count," the graduate of a prestigious military academy, and a much-honored veteran of the war of the Bosnia-Herzegovina annexation. All of that was a fabrication designed to separate von Stroheim (we will use his adopted name here) from the reality of his workaday origins, and provide as well an aura of authenticity for that vision of Hapsburg culture which figures so prominently in his films.

It is important to note that von Stroheim was working on this myth long before he entered films. He had ennobled himself for the benefit of the Ellis Island examiners, and when he married for the first time, on February 19, 1913, he swore in the marriage contract that his father was Benno "von" Stroheim, and his mother was the Baroness Bondy. The need to lose himself in a constructed world of Austrian nobility was deeply ingrained, and hardly an idea spawned by Hollywood publicists years later. Instead, von Stroheim would take advantage of Hollywood's mythmaking apparatus to rebuild the Hapsburg empire across the back lots of Paramount, MGM, and Universal, casting himself as the handsome prince whenever possible.

His first marriage, to Margaret Knox of Oakland, California, was the result of a whirlwind romance, and ultimately dissolved under the pressures of von Stroheim's inability to make a career for himself in the Bay area. He claimed to have been sent there by the Max Grab Company while representing their line of imported fashions, but the job disappeared and he was again reduced to waiting on tables when Margaret first saw him. She was six years older than Erich, and a member of Oakland's social set. They lived together at her cabin in Mill Valley for over half a year before the wedding (an unusual and unexplained breach of convention for that period), and it was here that Margaret Knox encouraged von Stroheim to try his hand at writing. His first play script, "In the Morning" (1912), is a sketch for the great films to follow, a tale of Prince Nikki, hounded by moneylenders, and his true love Mitzi, a loving and understanding *susse madel.* But the play did not sell (von Stroheim once claimed to have submitted it to Broncho Billy Anderson's Essanay Film company as a possible movie script), and when von Stroheim eventually grew bitter and even violent, Margaret left him and sued for divorce.

He fled San Francisco for Lake Tahoe, already a popular resort region far in the mountains of northern California. Again his occupations were menial—serving as a tourist guide and handling horses. In the summer of 1914 von Stroheim had to accompany a shipment of horses to Los Angeles, arriving in the city for the first time just as D. W. Griffith was beginning production on his masterpiece, *The Birth of a Nation.*

Von Stroheim claimed to have worked in the film as an extra, appearing at one point as the man shot from the roof during the guerrilla raid on Piedmont. There is no documentary proof of this, but there is evidence of his interest in theatre and film as early as 1912, and beginning in the spring of 1915 his face can been seen among the extras in various short films produced at Griffith's Mutual studio. In the summer of that year he received his first screen credit as the villain in Mutual's *Farewell to Thee,* a one-reel melodrama focused on the Hawaiian activities of a pair of con artists played by von Stroheim (already sporting a monocle) and Lucille Young.

At this point von Stroheim began a two-year association with John Emerson, a Broadway director hired by Mutual to act and direct at their Hollywood studio. Von Stroheim served variously as assistant director, technical advisor, bit player, and production manager on such Emerson-directed films as *Old Heidelberg*, *The Flying Torpedo*, *Macbeth* (starring Sir Herbert Beerbohm Tree), and the early Douglas Fairbanks films *In Again, Out Again* and *Wild and Woolly*. Here he was given his first opportunity to observe the day-to-day routine of film production, and he appears to have been allowed certain creative decisions by Emerson, who respected his initiative and apparent knowledge.

Like everyone else on the Mutual lot, von Stroheim was drafted into service on *Intolerance* (1916), functioning as an assistant director and taking a bit part in the Biblical sequence (although exactly which part is open to question). He married Mae Jones, a New York seamstress who made clothes for the Griffith company. Their son, Erich von Stroheim, Jr., was born on August 25, 1916, but this marriage also failed to prosper and the couple soon separated.

When America entered the World War in 1917 von Stroheim was dropped from the Fairbanks production unit, purportedly on account of the Germanic sound of his name (a few others in the film industry with similarly Teutonic surnames changed them for the duration). The war, however, opened up new opportunities, and von Stroheim began to specialize in "horrible Hun" roles. He was in Griffith's *Hearts of the World* (1918), on which he also served as technical advisor, and appeared in such lesser efforts as *For France*, *The Unbeliever* (where he leads his troops in executing an old woman hostage and her infant grandchild), *The Hun Within*, and the notorious *The Heart of Humanity*, in which he tosses a crying infant out of a window when the noise distracts him from his rape of a Red Cross nurse. Promoted as "The Man You Love to Hate," Von Stroheim was apparently given considerable leeway in handling these episodes, writing, and possibly even directing, many of his own scenes.

The close of the war brought an end to such roles, but von Stroheim had gained an entrée at Universal during the production of *The Heart of Humanity*, and managed to convince studio head Carl Laemmle to let him star in and direct his own script, *The Pinnacle*. Carl Laemmle was known in the business as an inveterate gambler, as well as a man with a weakness for hiring his relatives and other recent arrivals from the old country. Von Stroheim may have appealed to him on this level, and the cost-conscious Laemmle no doubt saw a bargain in the terms von Stroheim was offering. He would give Universal the script for nothing, and take only $200 per week for playing the leading role. With a budget of only $25,000 the project was irresistible, and von Stroheim began shooting on April 3, 1919.

The Pinnacle is a triangle romance set in the Italian Dolomites. The period is unclear, for while the script claims the action is set "three years after the close of the present war" (that is, two years in the future), the ambience is distinctly pre-war. American tourists Dr. Robert Armstrong (Sam de Grasse) and his wife Margaret (Francellia Billington) are vacationing in Cortina when they encouter an unscrupulous Austrian womanizer, Lieutenant Eric von Steuben. Von Steuben is able to tempt Margaret, whose husband is affectionate but neglectful, unschooled in the niceties of continental gallantry. The doctor ultimately becomes suspicious and challenges the lieutenant to accompany him on an ascent of the local pinnacle. Von Stueben proves a coward whose boasts of climbing prowess are hollow. With the lieutenant dangling beneath him on a rope, the doctor demands to know the truth: has Margaret been unfaithful? Thinking he knows what the doctor wants to hear, von Steuben lies and says that she has. But the doctor abandons him on the peak, from which he falls while attempting the descent. Armstrong, meanwhile, has found a note that proves Margaret's innocence. The couple leave Cortina the wiser for their holiday.

The story contains allusions to von Stroheim's adventures in the Austrian military and the time he spent in the Tyrol, as well as episodes from his days at Lake Tahoe and his marriage to Margaret Knox. Casting himself in the leading role (and giving that character a name so close to the one he had already given himself) completes the film's autobiographical subtext. Critics at the time were unaware of these details, and supposed that he was merely recreating an environment familiar to him during his European career. Nonetheless, they were astonished by the film's sense of realism and its sophisticated handling of the prospective extramarital affair. As Kevin Brownlow says, von Stroheim "includes sexual symbols and references which were instantly recognisable to the sophisticated but which totally eluded the censors." *The Pinnacle* was widely acclaimed as one of the finest films of the year (along with *Broken Blossoms* and *The Miracle Man*) and, although its actual production cost was in excess of $112,000, the returns of $327,000 marked it as highly profitable. The only fly in the ointment was that Universal had changed the title at the last moment (after some of the initial reviews appeared) to *Blind Husbands*. Von Stroheim though this "the absolute essence of commercialism" and complained bitterly in the trade press, but the disagreement would presage greater problems to come.

Von Stroheim began work on his second film, *The Devil's Pass Key*, even before the successful release of *Blind Husbands*. He did not play a part here, but adapted and directed a story by Baroness de Meyer set in postwar Paris, with a background of the fashion world and the Comédie Française. Warren Goodwright (Sam de Grasse) is an American living in Paris on a small inheritance, trying to write plays and support his spendthrift wife, Grace (Una Trevelyan). As Warren's plays are rejected for their "lack of realism," his wife is ensnared by Madame Malot (Maude George), an unscrupulous modiste to whom she owes thousands of francs, and who arranges an assignation for her with a handsome American officer, Captain Rex Strong (Clyde Fillmore). But the Captain realizes that Grace is a good woman and refuses to take advantage of her. Instead he helps Grace turn the tables on Madame, catching her in a blackmail scheme. Warren knows nothing of this, and when the story anonymously is leaked to the press he seizes on it as the basis of a new play. This work is successfully presented at the Comédie Française, but only Warren fails to realize that the foolish wife is actually his own. When he finally learns this he confronts Grace and Rex and offers to "forgive" them, but they insist that he must believe in her innocence. The drama is resolved with the husband and wife reunited, but the question of "belief" and "innocence" is unsettled.

The film was a great popular success in the summer of 1920, its view of the collision of cultures produced by Americans in postwar Paris prefiguring much of the work of Fitzgerald and Hemingway. This is the only von Stroheim film dealing with artistic creation, and it is significant that it is autobiographical art that is the focus here, along with a strong dose of that sexual humiliation which would become a von Stroheim obsession. Unfortunately, no prints of *The Devil's Pass Key* are known to exist today.

In New York for the launching of *The Devil's Pass Key*, von Stroheim won a new contract from Universal, increasing his salary from $200 to $800 per week, with escalator clauses bringing that to $1,750 per week in three years. There would also be an additional fee for any films in which he would act. On the strength of his new success he was married for the third time, to Valerie Germonprez, an actress he had met during the filming of *The Heart of Humanity*. She would act as a sounding-board while he was developing his scripts and accompany him to the set each day, calming the rages that periodically threatened to disrupt production. Their son Josef was born on September 18, 1922.

Now one of the industry's major directors, von Stroheim began production on his first epic work, *Foolish Wives*, on July 12, 1920. By June 15 of the following year he had shot 326,000 feet of negative, and production costs had soared to over $1 million, quadrupling the original projections. *Foolish Wives* is the story of "Count" Wladyslaw Sergius Karamzin, a bogus Russian aristocrat passing counterfeit money and swindling wealthy women on the Riviera. He lives with two female "cousins" in the Villa Amorosa, a monastery-like building that also contains the private casino where he passes his money. Karamzin involves himself with Helen Hughes, "Miss Dupont," the wife of the American ambassador, compromising her and wheedling 30,000 francs from her into the bargain. All the while he is carrying on active sexual liaisons with the "cousins," his maid (who is pregnant by him), and the mentally retarded daughter of the old counterfeiter who prints his bills.

Karamzin is caught with Helen Hughes when the wronged maid sets fire to the villa. The ambassador realizes Karamzin's duplicity, knocks him down, and challenges him to a duel, but the Russian fails to appear. Visiting the counterfeiter's daughter, he had been caught by the old man, murdered, and stuffed down a sewer. The final images show the American couple not only reunited but the parents of a new baby (whose coming had been kept secret by the wife!). Karamzin's body is last seen floating out to sea along with Monte Carlo's refuse and old champagne bottles.

There were several good reasons for the production overruns on *Foolish Wives*, including the destruction by storms of vast sets including a life-sized replica of Monte Carlo's central plaza, built on the Monterey coast, and the death of the actor playing the ambassador midway through production. But von Stroheim's own intransigence, his insistence on shooting multiple takes of the simplest scene, and his demands for absolute realism in the decor and props were also major factors—he was arrested by Treasury agents for printing counterfeit French currency for use in the casino episodes. The young Irving Thalberg, newly appointed as general manager of the Universal Studio, threatened to remove von Stroheim from the picture, but since he was also the film's star and could not be replaced, the threat carried no weight.

Von Stroheim spent months cutting the film to around thirty reels, but finally the print was taken away from him and cut by the studio to fourteen reels for its premiere early in 1922. Critics still found it overlong, and attacked such scenes as the birth of the baby, which had suffered greatly in the recutting. Von Stroheim, in New York for the opening, was reported to have run from the theatre during the final scenes. The strongest reactions, however, were from critics who resented the film's picture of Americans, and especially the ambassador and his wife, as "fools." *Photoplay* magazine labeled the film "an insult to every American," a jingoistic reaction that reflected the continuing anti-German hysteria of the postwar period. (Although not a German, von Stroheim was generally perceived as such by the public, largely on the strength of his "horrible Hun" film appearances and the clipped, monocled persona he affected.) *Foolish Wives* was cut again to around ten reels for general release, and the longest prints existing today approximate this version.

The film completed a trilogy of variations on a single theme—that of the sexual awakening of a neglected American wife in Europe. In Karamzin, von Stroheim had created another character around which he could drape his filmic autobiography. A bogus nobleman who uses his wiles on naive Americans, Karamzin creates little scenarios, dramatic situations intended to help him fleece or seduce his prey. He "directs" these situations much as his creator directs films. Maude George and Mae Busch, who played the "cousins," Cesare Gravina (the counterfeiter), and Dale Fuller, excellent as the maid, all became regular members of von Stroheim's "stock company."

Foolish Wives grossed only $869,000, a considerable sum, but far below the costs of production and advertising. Severe tensions were in the air at Universal as von Stroheim negotiated with Irving Thalberg over his next picture, *Merry-Go-Round*, and it was decided that in this film he would *not* act. Von Stroheim's script dealt with the tragic realities of life in postwar Vienna, illustrating the destruction of the city's moral and social fabric through the tale of a dissipated young count redeemed by his love for Mitzi, a young girl working in The Prater, Vienna's amusement park. Von Stroheim discovered and cast Mary Philbin for this part, and signed Norman Kerry as the count, a role he would have liked to play himself.

Production began on August 25, 1922, amid terrific strain on all sides. Von Stroheim was dissatisfied with the sets and would roam about them screaming that the grass was the wrong shade of green. Kerry would appear on the set drunk. Night shooting was beset by persistent power failures. Wild rumors abounded about von Stroheim's perfectionism and extravagance—including the claim that all the military extras had been supplied with underwear embroidered with the imperial coat of arms. Thalberg sent spies to the set, a tactic that infuriated von Stroheim. Finally, on October 6, Thalberg ordered von Stroheim off the picture.

The move was unprecedented, asserting the primacy of the producer (previously concerned only with administrative matters) over the director. It signaled a new era in the Hollywood studio system, and the end of the days when strong-willed directors like Griffith or von Stroheim held absolute sway on the studios lots. The picture was finished by Rupert Julian, who in general followed von Stroheim's script but jettisoned some of his more telling dramatic effects and considerably lightened the ending. When released *Merry-Go-Round* was a major commercial success, but von Stroheim's name was not attached to it and he had in fact disowned it.

By then von Stroheim was already under contract to the Goldwyn Company, directing his first picture with an American location, an adaptation of Frank Norris' novel *McTeague* that he called *Greed*. It was set in San Francisco, a city von Stroheim knew and loved almost as well as Vienna. In order to achieve the realism he felt the story required, he returned to that city with his crews and began shooting on March 13, 1923. A leading American exponent of the literary school of naturalism, Norris was concerned with the effects of heredity, environment and fate on the lives of his characters. They are prisoners of these forces, unable to alter their predetermined destinies.

The novel dealt with the effect of a $5,000 lottery prize on three members of San Francisco's working class: McTeague, a huge slow-witted dentist (Gibson Gowland); Marcus Schouler (Jean Hersholt), his socialistic friend, who works in the local dog hospital; and Marcus' cousin Trina, the girl they both covet, but who marries McTeague. Schouler informs the authorities that the so-called dentist has no license, and the McTeagues sink into poverty. McTeague takes to drink and torments Trina but she will not spend a penny of the lottery winnings. In the end McTeague murders her and flees into the desert with the gold. When Schouler tracks him down in Death Valley, McTeague kills him, but not before Schouler has handcuffed them together. McTeague waits for death beside the corpse of his former friend and the gold that has destroyed three lives. To play Trina, von Stroheim hired ZaSu Pitts, a light-comedy actress whom he would later describe as "the greatest psycho-pathological actress in the American cinema."

Von Stroheim felt that studio settings, which he had been happy to use previously, would be out of place for this production. He wanted to create a world so vividly defined that it would not be a mere backdrop but a major character in the tragedy. And in order to seem real, he was convinced that it all had to *be* real. He acquired a building at the corner of Hayes and Laguna, had the actors live in it, and proceeded to film his story with as much "documentary" detail as current technical limitations allowed. "It is possible to tell a great story in motion pictures in such a way that the spectator forgets he is looking at beauteous Gertie Gefelta, the producer's pet, and discovers himself intensely interested, just as if he were looking out of a window at life itself," he told a reporter for the New York *Times*. "He will come to believe that what he is gazing at is real—a cameraman was present in the household and nobody knew it. They went on in their daily life with their joys, fun, and tragedies, and the camera stole it all, holding it up afterward for all to see."

In order to achieve this illusion von Stroheim drove his actors and technicians to achieve effects of unmatched intensity. To film scenes inside the rooms while observing the real world across the street through the windows, the interior lighting had to be boosted to unprecedented levels. His regular camera crew, William Daniels and Ben Reynolds, were able to deliver an increased depth of field that allowed von Stroheim to keep foreground and background objects clearly in focus at the same time. Never was the "world" of these characters allowed to disappear into the blurred, soft-focus backdrop fashionable at the time.

But von Stroheim was not shooting a newsreel, nor was he slavishly transposing Norris' text in a page-by-page fashion, as some have asserted. Dream sequences of surreal terror appear at intervals throughout the screenplay, in vivid contrast to the realism of the main drama. And to amplify the sketchy background Norris supplied for his main character, von Stroheim created reels of material showing his life as a young goldminer, which he filmed at the actual Big Dipper Mine described in the novel.

The climax of the film, when McTeague is hunted down by Marcus in Death Valley, was not shot in the Oxnard dunes north of Los Angeles, as the studio hoped. Instead von Stroheim took his crew to the most inhospitable corner of Death Valley at the worst time of the year—midsummer. Fourteen men fell ill of the heat, including costar Jean Hersholt, whose skin was a mass of heat blisters. Von Stroheim followed his usual habit of filming take after take of each scene, regardless of the immediate consequences. As his actors struggled in the film's climactic fight scene, he screamed at them, "Fight! Fight! Try to hate each other as you both hate me!"

Shooting stopped on October 6, 1923, with von Stroheim having exposed 446,000 feet of negative. By January he had begun screening a version of nine or nine-and-a-half hours to selected critics in an effort to gather support for the picture before the studio (inevitably) would try cutting it to a more marketable length. Although the few who saw this rough-cut were astonished, von Stroheim continued to shorten it himself, bringing it down to twenty-two reels (about four hours) by March 1924. But the following month the Goldwyn Company merged with Marcus Loew's Metro Pictures, and the fate of the film passed into the hands of Louis B. Mayer and his production head, Irving Thalberg. Once more Thalberg removed von Stroheim, and that December he released a version of some ten-and-a-half reels.

Critics and audiences were aghast at the intensity of von Stroheim's vision, and his criticism of the corrupting power of money in American society. "The filthiest, vilest, most putrid picture in the history of the motion picture business," wrote one trade paper. The film had cost $550,000 to produce (plus prints and advertising) and earned less than half that on the international market. MGM had not only destroyed the integrity of von Stroheim's masterpiece, but lost a fortune in the bargain. The "uncut *Greed*" soon became a holy grail for film archivists, not only for its artistic quality but because it came to epitomize the most crass machinations of the Hollywood studio system at a time when that system was increasingly under attack from artists and intellectuals. Von Stroheim's career and reputation were soon tied to this will-o'-the-wisp, which began to overshadow the considerable achievements he *was* able to accomplish.

Von Stroheim's contract with Goldwyn had been a multi-picture deal, with *The Merry Widow* to be the second production. Despite the *Greed* situation, Mayer and Thalberg allowed von Stroheim to go ahead with that project, assigning him the studio's most difficult star, Mae Murray. Murray had previously operated her own production company under the Metro banner and was accustomed to giving orders, not taking them. Production began on December 1, 1924, and immediately a series of battles between Murray and von Stroheim broke out. The atmosphere surrounding the von Stroheim unit was extremely tense, with *Greed* being cut by unknown hands elsewhere at the studio during pre-production, and its disastrous New York premiere occuring only a few weeks into shooting. Von Stroheim had already been involved in one fistfight with Louis B. Mayer over the director's interpretation of the leading role ("Sonya is a whore," he insisted), and Mae Murray had her own ideas as well.

The Merry Widow was very loosely adapted by von Stroheim and Benjamin Glazer from the Franz Lehár operetta, a charmingly lightweight fantasy which was transformed into another revelation of aristocratic decadence, sadism, and moral squalor. Mae Murray plays Sally O' Hara, an American dancer on tour in the Balkans who attracts the attentions of both the conscienceless Crown Prince Mirko (Roy d' Aray) and his nobler cousin Prince Danilo (John Gilbert). Danilo wants to marry her but is prevented by the queen, and Sally instead marries Baron Sadoja (Tully Marshall), a loathsome old pervert who is the richest man in the kingdom. Sadoja drops dead on the wedding night and Sally goes off to enjoy her riches in Paris. The royal family, alarmed to see so much of the kingdom's wealth in foreign hands, now dispatch Mirko to woo the "merry widow," but fate ultimately helps the deserving Danilo get Sally and the throne.

At one time a Follies dancer, Murray was affronted when von Stroheim attempted to direct her dancing during the crucial waltz scene at the Paris embassy. "You dirty Hun, you think you know everything!" she screamed. Von Stroheim and his wife left the set and refused to return. Mayer assigned another director, Monta Bell, to complete the picture, but the extras refused to work for him. The problem was ultimately patched up and von Stroheim completed the film on March 9, 1925. Characteristically lavish in its sets and costumes, it was on the studio's books at a cost of $608,000, although von Stroheim claimed the true cost was only $275,000. The discrepancy was significant, because when the film began earning huge amounts of money $4.5—$5 million according to some accounts—von Stroheim demanded the 25 percent of the profits specified in his contract. MGM paid him nothing, insisting that the losses on *Greed* outweighed all the profits on this picture. (According to von Stoheim's contract, the two films were to be considered as one when the time came to assess profitability.)

Von Stroheim tended to disown *The Merry Widow* as a piece of assigned work, but in fact the project appears to have been his own idea, and the glorious "happy ending" which he always disparaged appears in even more exuber-

ant form in his own script. Perhaps von Stroheim was responding to the unpleasant working conditions associated with the picture, but the film as released is closer to his original conception than most surviving von Stroheim pictures.

The box-office success of this film enabled von Stroheim to sign a very advantageous contract with the independent producer Pat Powers. He would star in and direct his own script *The Wedding March*, a nostalgic evocation of prewar Vienna and the world of the Hapsburgs, a more mature version of themes he had explored earlier in *Merry-Go-Round* and his play "In the Morning."

Von Stroheim plays Prince Nicki, last of the decayed line of Wildeliebe-Rauffenburgs. In order to sponsor his eternal round of "parties and girlies" he agrees to marry Cecelia, the lame heiress to a corn-plaster fortune (ZaSu Pitts). Normally this would be bearable, but only weeks before the wedding he meets and fall in love with Mitzi, a poor harpist in a beer garden. (Von Stroiheim cast Fay Wray in this role, an actress who previously had appeared mainly in cheap Westerns.) Schani (Matthew Betz), a brutish butcher who considers himself Mitzi's fiancé, complicates matters. The centerpiece of von Stroheim's story was the lavish marriage of Nicki and Cecelia, with rain falling in torrents and Mitzi and Schani waiting in the crowd. The honeymoon at Nicki's mountain lodge proves unbearable, for the Prince cannot forget Mitzi. In a highly melodramatic climax Schani travels to the lodge to shoot Nicki, but Mitzi arrives in time to cry out a warning, and it is Cecelia who takes the bullet. Nicki returns to Vienna a wealthy widower, but Mitzi has disappeared. The World War begins, and Nicki's unit is assigned to patrol the borders. Mitzi has run off to a convent which is attacked by a band of brigands led by Schani. Nicki's unit arrives in time to save the nuns and the Prince kills Schani in single combat. Mitzi and Nicki promise to face the future together as the noise of battle calls his troops to the front.

Although exceedingly novelettish when synopsized in this manner, *The Wedding March* is actually a richly symbolic yet painfully personal evocation of a lost romantic world. The film, however, was never able to correspond to this treatment.

Shooting began on June 2, 1926, and was stopped on January 30, 1927, after some $1,125,000 had been spent. Powers had run out of money midway, and he transferred the project to Paramount, which had little interest in subsidizing so costly a personal statement. The convent scenes remained unfilmed, and von Stroheim attempted to edit the picture using material already shot. Months went by as he tinkered with the film, and ultimately it was taken out of his hands and a host of cutters went to work on it, among them Josef von Sternberg. Not until October 1928 was the film released, in a version that ended with the wedding scene (a so-called sequel, consisting mainly of the hunting lodge episodes, was released briefly overseas under the title *The Honeymoon*).

By this time the film was playing in competition with talking pictures and had difficulty attracting an audience. In addition, those who did see it were dismayed by von Stroheim's deliberate pacing, and the intensity of his *mise en scéne*, which featured a heavy use of close-ups frowned on by many of the more thoughtful reviewers of the period. Condemned as long and slow, *The Wedding March* quickly sank from sight.

This was doubly unfortunate, not only because it seriously damaged von Stroheim's career at a crucial moment but because the film was perhaps his most accomplished work. Following the tradition of Griffith, von Stroheim had managed to humanize a great historical moment by focusing on the lives of a handful of characters. That the relationship between the personal story and the collapse of empire works so well is largely the result of von Stroheim's having worked out their interrelationships many times over the preceding decade. With Powers' money he was finally able to realize his dream image of Vienna, and even though the film as released was truncated at the midpoint, what did reach the screen followed the outlines of von Stroheim's original quite closely, successfully capturing its mood and imagery.

While *The Wedding March* was being cut by Paramount, von Stroheim was able to set himself up with another independent producer, one of Hollywood's most important stars, Gloria Swanson. Apparently at the behest of her lover and business partner, Joseph P. Kennedy, Swanson allowed von Stroheim to develop for her a script based on his story "The Swamp," about a Ruritanian convent girl who inherits a brothel in German East Africa. The theme was daring, but Swanson had just scored a great success under Raoul Walsh's direction in *Sadie Thompson* and apparently was looking for more of the same. The title was changed to *Queen Kelly*, and filming began on November 1, 1928. The film was divided into two segments: a European episode and a contrasting African episode. These halves were to reflect and reinforce one another, carrying a complex inverse symbolism (white vs black, lust vs love, order vs chaos, etc.). Von Stroheim began shooting in sequence, starting with an episode in which young Kitty

Kelly (Swanson) encounters Prince Wolfram (Walter Byron) and his troop on a country lane, and enraptures him when her underpants fall down. The Prince later kidnaps her and takes her to the palace, but their courtship is stopped by the appearance of the perverse and insanely jealous Queen Regina (Seena Owen), the Prince's fiancée. The Queen whips Kelly from the palace, and the girl attempts suicide by leaping from a bridge but is saved by a convenient gendarme. Returning to the convent she is greeted by a letter calling her to the home in Dar-es-Salaam of the aunt who has supported her schooling. This turns out to be a seedy brothel where the dying aunt has arranged Kelly's marriage to her syphilitic backer (played by Tully Marshall). Kelly goes through with the marriage but keeps her distance from Marshall, and when he dies becomes the new brothel madame, adopting the name "Queen Kelly." Ultimately the Prince arrives on a German cruiser, and after a series of wild adventures rescues Kelly (who has kept herself pure for him) and marries her.

On November 1, 1928, von Stroheim began shooting the film in his usual fashion, working eighteen hours a day, demanding numerous retakes, and generally acting as if budgetary limitations did not exist. In addition, Swanson began to worry about the censorable elements of the script, which she had apparently ignored earlier. On January 21, 1929, during the filming of the marriage scene, Tully Marshall grabbed Swanson's hand and drooled tobacco juice on it. When informed that von Stroheim had called for this business, Swanson walked off the set and telephoned her partner. "Joseph, you'd better get out here fast. Our director is a madman!" Kennedy never arrived. He simply telephoned von Stroheim and fired him.

There had been plans to add sound to the film in some fashion (as was the case with numerous other films that season), but despite three years of effort by Swanson and a host of collaborators to salvage the picture, it was never completed, a dead loss of $800,000. In 1932 Swanson briefly released overseas a version formed out of the European episodes, ending it with Kelly's suicide leap—now shown as successful. Never given a wide theatical release, the film was finally issued in a restored version (including extant reels of the African episode) in 1985.

The collapse of the film effectively ended von Stroheim's career as a major figure in Hollywood. He had not had a commercial success since 1925, and three of his last four pictures were costly disasters. The coming of sound threw all Hollywood directors off balance, and only those with stable reputations were able to survive. Von Stroheim developed projects at MGM and Universal but they failed to go into production. He decided to try acting once more and appeared in a low budget film directed by his friend James Cruze, *The Great Gabbo* (1929). He played an insane ventriloquist, an artist driven mad, in effect a parody of his own outsized persona.

One small project that did reach production was *Walking Down Broadway*, a moderately budgeted Fox programmer. Since this was his first chance to direct a talking picture, von Stroheim did his best to behave, but to no avail. Based on a rather daring unproduced play by Dawn Powell, *Walking Down Broadway* was the story of two girls and two boys in Depression-era New York. The idyllic romance of "two nice kids," Jimmy (James Dunn) and Peggy (Boots Mallory) is almost destroyed by the jealousies and machinations of their roommates. The situation has urgency due to Peggy's pregnancy, but a melodramatic conclusion provides a happy ending for the young lovers.

Von Stroheim developed the script with Leonard Spiegelgass, a young contract writer on the Fox lot. Spiegelgass was worn out by the director's all-night bouts of writing and drinking, dismayed at the fact that von Stroheim, nominally a Catholic, had apparently converted from Judaism (he discovered this when he heard von Stroheim cursing under his breath in Yiddish), and appalled at the script's obsessions with sewers, tampons, douche bags, and similar unmentionables. According to Spiegelgass the script was "pornography," but offset somehow by von Stroheim's incisive dissections of the characters. Von Stroheim shot it in forty-eight days between August and October, 1932, bringing it in for close to the $300,000 budget. But preview screenings were disastrous ("fit only to be shown to a convention of psychoanalysts," one executive reported) and the studio turned the film over to Edwin Burke and Alfred Werker for "considerable retakes." This pair kept parts of von Stroheim's footage, cut more, and reshot others. As *Hello, Sister!* the film opened to poor notices in May, 1933. It bore no directorial credit. No prints of von Stroheim's version exist today, although an intriguing amount of his footage can be found in *Hello, Sister!*.

Von Stroheim was never again given the opportunity to direct almost until his death in 1957. He continued to find work as an actor, appearing in a few worthwhile pictures, including *As You Desire Me* (1932) with Garbo, and *The Lost Squadron* (1932), in which he parodied his own situation as a film director driven mad by a passion for realism. More often his appearances

were in disgraceful poverty-row films like *Crimson Romance* (1934) and *The Crime of Dr. Crespi* (1935). His wife Valerie had heavy medical bills due to burns received in a 1933 beauty parlor explosion, and von Stroheim took any sort of work in order to raise cash. He wrote a torrid novel of gypsy life, *Paprika* (published in 1935), but a hoped-for screen sale never materialized. Faced with mounting bills and no hope of real work von Storheim attempted suicide at Christmas 1934, but was dissuaded by friends. Then in March of 1935 he began work as a contract writer for MGM. For $150 a week he doctored the scripts of other writers, adding spice and characterization. He hoped to direct a script of his own, "General Hospital," inspired by Valerie's convalescence, but it was given to George B. Seitz instead. Released in 1937 as *Between Two Women*, the finished film followed von Stroheim's script very closely, with the exception of an added happy ending.

In November, 1936, von Stroheim quit his MGM job and went to France to appear in Raymond Bernard's film *Marthe Richard* (1937). What began as a single assignment turned into an extended exile when Jean Renoir invited him to appear in *La Grande Illusion* (1937). Von Stroheim was offered his choice of two roles: the pilot who shoots down Fresnay and Gabin at the start, or the commandant of the prison camp. He suggested combining the two parts, and hit upon the neck brace as a means of indicating the reason for the change in this character's fortunes. Not unlike von Stroheim, the character he plays finds this demeaning prison camp duty the only way he can continue in the vocation to which he has devoted his life.

Von Stroheim was able to establish himself as an actor in the prewar French film industry, but his attempts to direct proved fruitless. While in Paris he met Denise Vernac, a young actress who became his constant companion for the rest of his life. Although von Stroheim was separated from his wife Valerie, they never divorced. At the start of World War II von Stroheim attempted to enlist in the French forces, but was persuaded by Jean Renoir to take an opportunity offered by Darryl F. Zanuck, and set off for Hollywood for an appearance in the film *I Was an Adventuress*. On November 19, 1939, he left with Denise on the Lisbon clipper. Although they had round-trip tickets, the fall of France made it impossible for them to return until after the war.

In America von Stroheim worked in a variety of films, some good (Billy Wilder's *Five Graves to Cairo*, in which he played Rommel), and some not so good (*The Mask of Dijon*, a low-grade thriller from PRC). He replaced Boris Karloff in the road company of *Arsenic and Old Lace* and later took over the part on Broadway, but steady work like this was hard to find.

With Denise he went back to France on the first postwar freighter, but the European film industry was slow to recover. A film of Strindberg's *Dödsdansen* (*La Danse de Mort* 1947) in which both appeared proved disappointing, and finally he agreed to accept the part of Max von Mayerling in Billy Wilder's *Sunset Boulevard* (1950). At first von Stroheim had resisted playing this role, that of a great silent film director reduced to working as butler for his former star. That she was played by Gloria Swanson must have opened additional psychic wounds, but von Stroheim was artist enough to recognize the quality of the film and returned to Hollywood to appear in it. It would be his last trip there, and for his efforts he came away with his only Academy Award nomination, as best supporting actor.

Between then and his death on May 12, 1957, von Stroheim continued to appear occasionally on European screens. He published a two-volume novel, *Les Feux de la St. Jean* in 1951 and 1954, and another novel, *Poto-Poto* (an adaptation of his *Queen Kelly* script) in 1956, meanwhile working on his memoirs at Maurepas, the chateau outside Paris he shared with Denise Vernac. In March 1957 the French government awarded him the Legion of Honor, but he was already confined to bed with cancer that would take his life a few weeks later.

Many have cited the twenty-five years in which von Stroheim was kept from directing as a tragic loss for the cinema. But unlike his great contemporaries, D. W. Griffith or Rex Ingram, von Stroheim never allowed himself to be shunted into inactivity. Unable to work as a director, this indefatigable artist diverted his energies elsewhere—to his scripts and novels, to his acting appearances, and above all else to the life of Erich von Stroheim, his most complex and intriguing creation.

—*R.K.*

Editorial Note: Von Stroheim carefully cultivated his reputation as "the man you love to hate." Asked once if he was as brutal and sadistic in real life as on the screen, he replied: "Much more so." In fact, according to his friend and biographer Thomas Quinn Curtiss, "beneath the arrogant surface there was a very different inner man, kind and generous to his colleagues and associates. . . . He had in a high degree what the French call 'politeness of the heart.' He did not make friends quickly, being by nature distrustful, and he was not a good mixer. To conceal his acute embarrassment among strangers, he resorted to an iron reserve. He had a morbid fear of being mocked." Discussing his endless problems with producers, Kevin Brownlow suggested that he "required intolerable pressures in order to wring from himself the last ounce of creative energy. It could be argued that it was his own paranoia which created such conditions in the first place. The more he was given, the more he demanded."

Andrew Sarris spoke of the "technical chastity" of von Stroheim's style. Another writer, in the *Oxford Companion to Film*, noted that the director "depended little on conventional editing, achieving a singular density of dramatic effect by piling up detail within extended shots in a way which was profoundly to influence Renoir and others." Jonathan Rosenbaum, in Richard Roud's *Cinema*, maintains that while von Stroheim "tended to move his camera less often than Murnau and was less of a montage director than Griffith, it is misleading to conclude from this that he was 'technically chaste.' . . . Stroheim could make expressive use of montage when he wanted to without any technical handicap. Camera movement plays a significant role in all his work, even if he usually resorts to it so few times in a single film as to make each occurrence a privileged one. . . . Nor does this constitute anything approaching the whole of his technical arsenal: blurred focus (generally to suggest tears in point-of-view shots assigned to heroines), superimpositions, various uses of colour (missing in contemporary prints), slow lap dissolves as carefully calculated as Sternberg's, and above all, a masterful use of the iris and fade, are only a few of the techniques in his vocabulary. . . . Eyes have an unusual authority in Stroheim's films, and what is frequently meant by his 'control of detail' is his uncanny gift for conveying information through an actor's eye movements."

Rosenbaum nevertheless quotes with approval André Bazin's dictum on von Stroheim's films, in which "reality lays itself bare like a suspect confessing under the relentless examination of the commissioner of police. He has one simple rule for direction. Take a close look at the world, keep on doing so, and in the end it will lay bare for you all its cruelty and its ugliness. One could easily imagine as a matter of fact a film by Stroheim composed of a single shot as long-lasting and as close up as you like."

FILMS: Blind Husbands, 1919; The Devil's Pass Key, 1920; Foolish Wives, 1922; Merry-Go-Round (completed by Rupert Julian), 1923; Greed, 1924; The Merry Widow, 1925; The Wedding March, 1928; Queen Kelly, 1928–1929 (not completed or released domestically; reconstructed version issued 1985); Walking Down Broadway, 1932 (unreleased; substantially remade by Alfred Werker as Hello, Sister!, released in 1933). *Published scripts*—Greed, Simon & Schuster, 1972; The Complete "Greed" of Erich von Stroheim, edited by Herman G. Weinberg, Arno Press, 1972; The Complete "Wedding March" of Erich von Stroheim, edited by Herman G. Weinberg, Little Brown, 1974.

ABOUT: Barna, J. Erich von Stroheim, 1966 (in German); Bergut, B. Erich von Stroheim, 1960 (in French); Buache, F. Erich von Stroheim, 1972 (in French); Casiraghi, U. Umanita di Stroheim ed Altri Saggi, 1945; Castello, G. C. Von Stroheim, 1959 (in Italian); Castello, G. C. and Buache, F. Erich von Stroheim, (in French 1963); Ciment, M. Erich von Stroheim *in* Anthologie du Cinéma, Vol. III, 1968; Curtiss, T. Q. Von Stroheim, 1971; Fink, G. Erich von Stroheim, 1963 (in Italian); Finler, J. Stroheim, 1968; Fronval, G. Erich von Stroheim: Sa Vie, Ses Films, 1939; Gobeil, C. (ed.) Hommage à von Stroheim (Canada Film Institute), 1966; Koszarski, R. The Man You Loved to Hate: Erich von Stroheim and Hollywood, 1983; Lennig, A. (ed.) Von Stroheim, 1973; Marion, D. and Amengual, B. Erich von Stroheim, 1966 (in French); Mitry, J. Erich von Stroheim, 1963 (in French); Noble, P. Hollywood Scapegoat: The Biography of Erich von Stroheim, 1950; Rosenbaum, J. Erich von Stroheim *in* Roud, R. (ed.) Cinema: A Critical Dictionary, 1980; Stegelmann, J. Erich von Stroheim, 1963 (in Danish); Stroheim, E. von *in* Hughes, L. (ed.) The Truth About the Movies, 1924; Weinberg, H. G. Saint Cinema, 1970; Weinberg, H. G. Stroheim: A Pictorial Record of His Nine Films, 1975. *Periodicals*—American Film March 1985; L'Avant Scène du Cinéma July–September 1968; Bianco e Nero February–March 1950, February–March 1959; Cahiers du Cinéma January 1957; Cinéma (Paris) February 1957; Cinema (Rome) June 15, 1950; Cinema (Zurich) December 1973; Decision March 1941; Film Comment May–June 1975; Film Culture January 1955, April 1958; Film Survey Spring 1947; Film Weekly (London) April–May 1935; Filmkritik (Munich) February 1976; New York Times September 22, 1985; Sight and Sound April–June 1953, Winter 1961–1962; Theatre November 1927. Documentary film—Montgomery, P. (dir.) The Man You Loved to Hate, 1979 (Film Profiles).

JOHN STURGES

Monica, California, where he attended grade school. His father died there in 1918.

During the 1920s, when Sturges' elder brother was studying architecture at the University of California and his sister was working for Assistant DA Earl Warren in Alameda County, their mother moved the family home to Berkeley, where he completed high school. "In the beginning," he says in an *Action* interview (November–December 1969), "money was no particular problem because Mother was fairly well off. But then the Depression hit. It seemed that every savings and loan that failed had Mother as an investor."

Hard up, but intent on a college education, Sturges followed a friend's example and applied for a football scholarship at Marin Junior College. He claims that he had never played the game, but he was six foot two and weighed 185 pounds. Marin not only accepted him but played him as a center in games in which he was "knocked down by some of the finest football players on the West Coast." It did not help that his mother required her children to cultivate self-reliance; Sturges had to eat and train on his $14-a-week scholarship.

His majors at Marin were mathematics and physics. After the football season he earned a little extra by tutoring and then worked as stage manager of the San Rafael Players, where he eventually got his first experience directing actors. "It didn't pay very much," he says, "but I liked the work. . . . It wasn't terribly good, I suppose, but we did a lot of plays."

Sturges graduated from Marin in the depths of the Depression. Thanks to his brother, by then

STURGES, JOHN (January 3, 1911–), American director and producer, was born in Oak Park, Illinois. He is the son of Reginald Sturges, a real estate lawyer, and the former Grace Delafield. His maternal grandfather had been president of the Chicago bar and his family on both sides had produced distinguished lawyers and architects. The Sturgeses moved to Chicago soon after he was born, and then out to Santa

an art director with RKO-Radio Pictures, he landed a job in the studio's blueprint department. According to his own account, he made himself indispensable by operating a filing system that no one else could understand and in due course was promoted to office assistant.

RKO was eager to employ the new three-strip Technicolor process and brought the New York stage designer Robert Edmond Jones out to Hollywood to work with it. Sturges was assigned to Jones as his personal assistant but, he says, "nobody knew too much about color in those days. They just went around dying pieces of cloth and talking mysteriously. Jones soon got fed up and went back to New York." Nevertheless, on the strength of this association, according to Sturges, "Dave Selznick hired me as color consultant for . . . Richard Boleslawski's *Garden of Allah.* This was about 1934–1935, remember, so when he told me my salary would be $300 a week and that my name would be on the picture, I couldn't believe it." His skepticism seems to have been justified, since his name does not appear on the credits of that "sumptuously beautiful" picture.

In any case, Sturges by this time wanted to direct. Deciding that editing was the best first step towards that goal, he took a massive salary cut and returned to RKO as a film carrier, from there working his way up through the cutting-room ranks alongside the future directors Robert Wise and Mark Robson.

A full-fledged editor by the time America entered World War II, Sturges enlisted in the Signal Corps and then transferred to the Air Force, rising from private to captain as editor and/or director of thirty-seven training films and five documentaries. He served in Africa, Italy, Corsica, and Britain, earning the Bronze Star and four battle stars. The most notable of his wartime films was *Thunderbolt* (1945), a documentary about a fighter-bomber that he co-directed with Lieutenant Colonel William Wyler, and which later achieved commercial release through Allied Artists.

Back in Hollywood in 1945, Sturges was married to Dorothy Lynn Brooks, a former publicity secretary at Warner Brothers. About the same time he joined Columbia as a director of "twelve-day wonders"—cut-rate programmers made on a murderous twelve-day schedule. Directors who survived this regimen learned a great deal very quickly, and Sturges made ten such movies between 1945 and 1950.

Discussing the director's career in a two-part article in *Films and Filming* (January and February 1974), DuPre Jones reports that no one seems to have "detected early promise" in Stur-

ges' first six Columbia pictures, from *The Man Who Dared* (released in 1946, with Leslie Brooks and George Macready) through *Best Man Wins* (1948). This last sounds interesting, in synopsis at least, being an adaptation by Edward Huebsch of Mark Twain's story "The Celebrated Jumping Frog of Calaveras County," set in 1853 and featuring Edgar Buchanan as a gambler with itchy feet who goes home to Dawson's Landing, Missouri, after an absence of many years to find that his long-suffering wife (Anna Lee) is about to divorce him for desertion.

This promising little property seems to have been pretty much ignored, but *The Sign of the Ram* (1948), a murky melodrama ostensibly set in Cornwall, boasted one star name—Susan Peters, attempting a comeback after a crippling accident—and did attract some reviews. Unfortunately they were almost unanimously unsympathetic; Bosley Crowther called the picture a "flat and fatuous fable." Sturges' first Western followed, *The Walking Hills* (1949), scripted by Alan Lemay and with an excellent cast that included Randolph Scott, Ella Raines, John Ireland, Edgar Buchanan, Arthur Kennedy, and the singer Josh White. This "lust-for-gold" desert drama was found convoluted and somber, but featured an impressive sandstorm and seemed to C. A. Lejeune "in its modest way . . . a good and exciting picture."

There was an equally encouraging response to *The Capture* (1950). Another modern Western, it has Lew Ayres as an American oilman in Mexico who mistakenly kills an innocent man, taking him to be a payroll robber. Driven first by conscience and then by love, he marries his victim's widow (Teresa Wright) and sets out to clear the dead man's name. It is said that Niven Busch considers this his finest script. Not everyone agrees to that—there were complaints about a shortage of action and a redundant flashback structure—but there was a good deal of praise for the stark photography, for "a fine feeling for place and incident," and for some of the performances, especially that of Jimmy Hunt as the heroine's small son.

At that point Sturges left Columbia and moved over to MGM for more B movies, beginning with an excellent thriller, *Mystery Street* (1950). It shows in absorbing detail how a Harvard medical specialist (Bruce Bennett) identifies a skeleton found on a Cape Cod beach, allowing a local police detective (Ricardo Montalban) to solve the murder. *Time*'s reviewer wrote that "director John Sturges and scripters Sydney Boehm and Richard Brooks have treated the picture with such taste and craftsmanship that it is just about perfect. All the performers seem to be working on the theory that there should be no difference in quality between a B picture and its budgetary betters. Montalban is natural and likable as an eager small-town detective on his first case . . . and Elsa Lanchester is a delight as a snooping, gin-drinking landlady with genteel airs." Montalban also stars in the less interesting *Right Cross* (1950), playing a Mexican-American boxer warped by his hatred of gringos but redeemed by the love of June Allyson.

After these low-budget genre pictures MGM gave Sturges a more respectable assignment, *The Magnificent Yankee* (1951), a biopic of Oliver Wendell Holmes featuring Louis Calhern, and then *Kind Lady* (1951), an adaptation of a Broadway melodrama in which, for the first time, Sturges directed a starry cast. The setting is London at the turn of the century. Ethel Barrymore plays a rich collector of art treasures, and Maurice Evans an oily con man who wheedles his way into her house, installs his wife (Betsy Blair), his baby, and two confederates (Keenan Wynn and Angela Lansbury), and sets about driving the old lady insane. Although some thought that the movie failed to drum up any real sense of menace, it was elsewhere praised for its "splendid performances, outstanding direction."

Kind Lady lifted Sturges out of MGM's ranks of B directors. His next film was a vehicle for Spencer Tracy, *The People Against O'Hara* (1951). Tracy plays a once-famous criminal lawyer who makes a comeback to rescue a penniless young murder suspect (James Arness) from the overzealous DA (John Hodiak). Convinced of the boy's innocence, he rashly tries to bribe a hostile witness, is disgraced, and takes to drink, in the end sacrificing his own life while nailing the real killer. "Principally as the result of first-class character studies by minor actors," wrote Felix Barker, "the film sustains interest for three-quarters of its length but then dissipates it in an over-dramatic and largely incomprehensible climax."

It's a Big Country (1951) was an omnibus film of eight episodes, each exploring a different aspect of American life. Unrelievedly superficial and sentimental, its only justification seemed to be the employment it provided for half-a-dozen MGM directors and as many stars. As bad or worse was *The Girl in White* (1952), with June Allyson battling male chauvinism and other diseases as New York's first woman doctor.

Things picked up for Sturges with *Jeopardy* (1953), a tense little thriller set in the Mexican wilderness, where a vacationing Barbara Stanwyck has to cope with a psychotic fugitive

(Ralph Meeker) as well as the problem of rescuing her trapped husband (Barry Sullivan) from the incoming tide. This mostly dismal phase of Sturges' career ended dismally with *Fast Company* (1953), a fatuous musical comedy about a dancing racehorse.

Sturges returned to the Western with the film that established him as a minor master of the genre, *Escape From Fort Bravo* (1953). Intelligently scripted by Frank Fenton and shot in Death Valley by Robert L. Surtees, it has William Holden as the tough commander of a Yankee prison camp in Arizona during the Civil War, John Forsythe as the gentlemanly leader of the Confederate prisoners, and Eleanor Parker as the Texas belle they both love. The climax of the film is a terrifying attack by well-drilled Mescalero bowmen which, DuPre Jones suggests, may have been modeled on the Agincourt sequence in Olivier's *Henry V*.

Time's reviewer called this "one of the most imaginative Indian attacks ever filmed," and the movie itself "in some ways the best Western since 1943's memorable *Ox-Bow Incident*. . . . The implacable, carefully photographed beauty of the Badlands stands behind the film's every moment. . . . Fenton's dialogue is always clear and quick, and occasionally it reaches down to pluck some nerve of real human sensibility." For DuPre Jones this picture—though a "watershed" for Sturges—"is not the classic Western which some critics . . . canonised it as at the time," but "a very good one," which "adroitly and economically maximises" the script's various tensions and gives "the first convincing demonstration of what was to become . . . Sturges' greatest knack as a director: the staging of violent action."

Fort Bravo was a commercial success as well as a critical one, and Sturges followed it with his first real box-office hit, *Bad Day at Black Rock* (1955), produced by Dore Schary, written by Millard Kaufman from a story by Howard Breslin, and photographed in CinemaScope and Technicolor by William C. Mellor. "One-Shot" Sturges filmed the picture in three weeks, wrapping up all but twelve of its 455 shots in a single take. "I believe in Take One for spontaneity," the director says. "If I feel it doesn't come off I move the camera to another viewpoint. Freshness is paramount."

Black Rock is a dusty whistle-stop in the California desert. Its bad day begins when John J. McReedy (Spencer Tracy), a one-armed war veteran in a business suit, trudges into town and starts asking questions about the mysterious disappearance of a Japanese tenant farmer. The citizens of Black Rock close ranks against the inquisitive stranger and ugly ranks they are: racists, sadists, drunks, and assorted psychopaths represented by Robert Ryan, Ernest Borgnine, Lee Marvin, and Dean Jagger, among others. Walter Brennan as a philosophical undertaker and Anne Francis fill out the cast. McReedy is advised to leave, threatened, and attacked, but stays until he has the answers he came for.

DuPre Jones wrote that "few communities portrayed by the movies have ever been so heavy with menace" as Black Rock in "this now classic suspense film . . . suffused with the threat and the memory, with the *atmosphere* of violence." Jean-Pierre Coursodon has drawn attention to the way the CinemaScope frame "was brilliantly, if a bit self-consciously, filled by Sturges' strategic positioning of his actors in relation to the huge empty spaces around them." Most reviewers mentioned the cathartic moment when the crippled McReedy, who has patiently borne every kind of insult and threat, is finally attacked by a brutish Borgnine, and reveals himself to be a karate expert of serene mastery.

"The story is modern in style," wrote Dilys Powell, "the plot, the mystery . . . edging its way into the superficial action, the narrative taking shape in fragments of dialogue, in hints and looks. But it has a classical economy of form. . . . There is unity of time—the action is confined within twenty-four hours. The scene, except for two brief passages of savage incident in the surrounding desert, may be called enclosed—for though the characters move from shanty to garage, from bar to sheriff's office, they cannot go far in the scatter of buildings which is Black Rock. . . . Little by little the questions are answered. We are told enough about the people in the story to account for their actions and make us accept them as characters. But we know them only by their behaviour within the story. For an hour and twenty minutes they have moved into a rectangle of bright light. When at the end of the film they move out of it we go on wondering about them."

After that, Sturges went free-lance, working over the next few years for most of the big studios. He began with a three-million-dollar belly flop called *Underwater* (1955), made for RKO and featuring Jane Russell in an aqualung, and the same year directed *The Scarlet Coat* for MGM. An account of Benedict Arnold's treachery in the War of Independence, it was well acted by Cornell Wilde, George Sanders, and especially the British actor Michael Wilding, and directed with considerable pace and imagination. It deserved more attention than it got. The same is true of *Backlash* (1956), a "psychological" Western scripted by Borden

Chase. Richard Widmark, pursuing the man who is supposed to have robbed his father (John McIntire) and left him to die, encounters hostile Indians, Donna Reed, and a whole series of the gunfights that Sturges stages so expertly.

The director's longest and most famous shoot-out climaxes *Gunfight at the OK Corral* (1957), produced by Hal Wallis for Paramount. This was the first of Sturges' two versions of the oft-told story of Marshall Wyatt Earp and the consumptive gambler and gunfighter Doc Holliday, and their 1881 battle in Tombstone, Arizona, against the Clanton gang. *Gunfight* stars Burt Lancaster as Earp, Kirk Douglas as Holliday. Written by Leon Uris, it is historically the least acccurate of all the many movie accounts of the fight (which actually lasted about half a minute), and further marred by unconvincing motivations and clichéd dialogue, though it has some excellent performances and moments of high excitement, including the final shoot-out itself.

A less ambitious Western followed, *The Law and Jake Wade* (1958). It pits a reformed bank robber turned lawman (Robert Taylor) against his demonic former sidekick (Richard Widmark) in a search for buried loot through Indian territory. The film had a mixed reception. Derek Prouse found it "virile, entertaining and the purest stuff of the cinema," with an intelligent script by William Bowers and "unobtrusive but informed direction," but Brian Garfield, while praising the exciting action scenes, thought the script disappointing and the characterizations ludicrous.

There was even greater critical dissension over Warner Brothers' four-million-dollar attempt at a screen adaptation of Hemingway's novella *The Old Man and the Sea*, directed by Sturges after Fred Zinnemann withdrew. The book is a parable about the indestructability of the human spirit. An old Cuban fisherman (Spencer Tracy) hooks the biggest marlin he has ever seen, fights it for days and wins, only to see the great fish stripped to its skeleton by sharks before he can get it back to Havana. Peter Viertel's adaptation reverently preserves the highly mannered Hemingway prose, dividing it between what the old man says and what he thinks—his voice-over musings and memories. Photographed by James Wong Howe, the film is virtually a monologue for Spencer Tracy.

The Old Man and the Sea (1958) seemed to Arthur Knight to "set a new high for Hollywood," deserving "to become an American screen classic." By no means everyone agreed; Isabel Quigly, for example, found that "the visual equivalent of purple passages" kept intruding—"striking but extraneous and obtrusive bits of seascape and colour. . . . The whole thing is contrived almost, at times, to the point of absurdity, as indeed the book is, that monument of the Hemingway code and manner, stylised and often glorious, but basically sentimental, soft-centred."

Back on dry land, Sturges made *Last Train From Gun Hill* (1959), starring Kirk Douglas as a marshall whose wife has been raped and murdered by the son of his old friend (Anthony Quinn), now a powerful rancher. When Douglas captures the killer (Earl Holliman) and holes up in a hotel to wait for the train out, he is beseiged by Quinn and his hirelings in a situation all too similar to that in Delmer Daves' *3:10 to Yuma* (1957). The result was nevertheless praised for its "slow growth of tension . . . , the timing of the jagged spurts of action, the sweating tick-off of the minutes." *Never So Few* (1959) is best forgotten, a World War II vehicle for Frank Sinatra at his most arrogant, slaughtering Japanese and seducing women with equal ease and satisfaction.

At that point Sturges established his own independent production company, releasing through United Artists. He launched it with the most profitable of all his films, *The Magnificent Seven* (1960), produced like many of his subsequent movies by himself. Scripted by William Roberts, it takes Akira Kurosawa's *chambara* epic, *Seven Samurai* (1954), and translates it into a Western set in Mexico. An impoverished village is regularly pillaged by bandits (led by Eli Wallach at his most splendidly hammy). The desperate peasants enlist the protection of a professional gunfighter (Yul Brynner). With half-a-dozen hand-picked and variously qualified fighting men, he trains the peasants to defend themselves. In the climactic battle, the bandits are utterly defeated, though four of the Seven die in defense of the village.

Sturges possesses to an extraordinary degree the mysterious ability to detect the mysterious quality that turns actors into stars. *The Magnificent Seven* elevated no less than four little-known performers into the big time—Steve McQueen, James Coburn, Charles Bronson, and Robert Vaughn. Brian Garfield found the picture "faultlessly directed, tunefully scored (Elmer Bernstein; it became a standard), heroically photographed (Charles Lang, Jr.). . . . *The Magnificent Seven,* to many buffs, has become a minor classic—and perhaps it would have been a major one if it weren't for the obvious obligation to compare it with the Kurosawa film on which it was based; that one was rich with artistry, while the American version is simply a damned engaging diversion, keyed by a taut lit-

erate script that invests each character with a strongly individual and empathetic personality. . . . The action is filmed with edge-of-the-seat excitement and we really *care* about the characters. It's a compelling movie, masterful entertainment." The film spawned three inferior sequels, none of them directed by Sturges.

After that triumph, the director unaccountably turned to James Gould Cozzen's novel about heavy-breathing Republicans, *By Love Possessed.* Crassly adapted by John Dennis, it has Lana Turner as "a human being with human wants and needs," Jason Robards as the lawyer husband who cannot meet these needs since his accident, and Efram Zimbalist as Robards' partner, who does. This movie was universally excoriated, and there was only limited enthusiasm for *Sergeants Three* (1962), a remake as a broadly comic Western of *Gunga Din,* with Frank Sinatra and his "Rat Pack" making poor substitutes for Cary Grant, Douglas Fairbanks Jr., and Victor McLaglen. There followed *A Girl Named Tamiko* (1963), a dreary soaper set in Tokyo, where France Nuyen and Martha Hyer vie for the debatable charms of Laurence Harvey.

Pulling himself together after this string of duds, Sturges produced and directed a splendid and very successful piece of entertainment in *The Great Escape* (1963). As DuPre Jones wrote, the film "details the planning and carrying out of a massive breakout of POWs from a German camp, and the fate of the escapees on the outside. . . . It is a very simple story, told with terrific momentum and suspense. . . . Sturges is not a director with a notable talent for deep or penetrating character studies. But he is marvellously adept at establishing the identity and individuality of his characters, even minor ones, with a few telling, economical touches. . . . Here, as in all his best films, we come to be involved with and concerned for the escapees, and in this instance to root for them. Their capture and execution—which we don't expect—is quite shattering and moving, while we are genuinely heartened and uplifted by the success of those who do make it." The fine script was by James Clavell and W. R. Burnett, and the cast includes Steve McQueen, James Garner, James Coburn, Richard Attenborough, and Charles Bronson.

Clavell also coauthored *The Satan Bug* (1965), along with Edward Anhalt, but this was an altogether weaker script—a verbose and plodding story about a mad scientist on the run with a flask of genocidal virus. Sturges next attempted a comic Western, *The Hallelujah Trail* (1965), which has cavalry colonel Burt Lancaster escorting a wagon train of whiskey through hordes of thirsty Indians to Denver, and Lee Remick as temperance crusader. Good performances (and an excellent one from Brian Keith as a drunken braggart) were not enough to save this turgid and overblown film.

In *Hour of the Gun* (1967), another Edward Anhalt script, Sturges returned to the story of Wyatt Earp and Doc Holliday. This version opens with the OK Corral shoot-out and then follows Earp's merciless pursuit of the surviving Clantons—a manhunt that is shown to be inspired not by a regard for justice but by an obsessive greed for vengeance. James Garner gave one of his best, least facile, performances as Earp, and Robards is equally memorable as the self-destructive Holliday, a complex figure who is not only Earp's loyal lieutenant but his conscience. A number of critics regard this as Sturges' best Western, and a film that has been shamefully neglected.

Ice Station Zebra (1968), an efficient adaptation of Alastair McLean's bestseller about Cold War skulduggery aboard a nuclear submarine, was followed by *Marooned* (1969). The latter, much less entertaining, is a solemn space epic in which Gregory Peck masterminds the rescue of three stranded astronauts. Pauline Kael found it "straight Dullsville."

After these routine exercises there was an unexplained gap of three years in Sturges' filmography. *Joe Kidd* (1972) seemed to Michael McKegney a welcome comeback—a moderately exciting Western with Clint Eastwood as a once-renowned gunfighter who joins ruthless land baron Robert Duvall in his battle against a socially conscious Mexican outlaw (John Saxon), then experiences a change of heart and allegiance. Sturges made his next picture for Dino de Laurentiis in Spain, a spaghetti Western called *Valdez il Mezzosangue* (*Chino/The Wild Horses,* 1973), in which Charles Bronson and Jill Ireland head a mostly Italian cast. *McQ* (1974) features an old and tired John Wayne in a routine cops-and-pushers thriller set in Seattle.

Two years later Sturges made a better movie, *The Eagle Has Landed,* which remains his last to date. Adapted from the best-selling novel by Jack Higgins, it tells the story of an imaginary incident late in World War II—an attempt by a German task force to kidnap Winston Churchill while the great man is weekending near the pretty Norfolk village where the film is set. Robert Duvall plays the plot's mastermind, Michael Caine the gallant anti-Nazi commander of the assault team. Donald Sutherland appears also as an Irish nationalist who makes a temporary alliance with the Germans, and Jenny Agutter is his tormented mistress. Richard Schickel called the

result "modest and well-crafted"—"an action film of a rather traditional sort—meaning that however improbable it is in detail, it retains some sense of scale and traditional human values," and has "a satisfying surprise ending that serves as a neat moral reckoning as well."

Always at the mercy of his scripts, John Sturges has made too many bad films to be regarded as a major director, but too many good ones to be ignored. His best pictures can be unusually rich and likable, not least because of his ability to people them with believable, three-dimensional minor characters. A writer in the *Oxford Companion to Film* notes that his "cool, unemotional style, which makes use of pans and long shots to relate characters to their environment, is particularly well-suited to the Western, traditionally concerned with the isolation of the individual in a vast landscape . . . and his best Westerns reveal a personal quality not always felt in his other work."

Sturges has a son and a daughter by his marriage to Dorothy Lynn Brooks, from whom he is separated. He lives alone in a house overlooking the Pacific, owns a racing yacht, and enjoys deep-sea fishing, skiing, and Spanish music. For a Hollywood veteran, Sturges is unusually articulate about cinema, drama, and art in general, but refuses to claim that he himself is anything more than a craftsman.

FILMS: (with William Wyler) Thunderbolt, 1945 (documentary); The Man Who Dared, 1946; Shadowed, 1946; Alias Mr. Twilight, 1947; For the Love of Rusty, 1947; Keeper of the Bees, 1947; Best Man Wins, 1948; The Sign of the Ram, 1948; The Walking Hills, 1949; The Capture, 1950; Mystery Street, 1950; Right Cross, 1950; The Magnificent Yankee, 1951; Kind Lady, 1951; The People Against O'Hara, 1951; (with others) It's a Big Country, 1951; The Girl in White, 1952; Jeopardy, 1953; Fast Company, 1953; Escape From Fort Bravo, 1953; Bad Day at Black Rock, 1955; Underwater, 1955; The Scarlet Coat, 1955; Backlash, 1956; Gunfight at the OK Corral, 1957; The Law and Jake Wade, 1958; The Old Man and the Sea, 1958; Last Train From Gun Hill, 1959; Never So Few, 1959; The Magnificent Seven, 1960; By Love Possessed, 1961; Sergeants Three, 1962; A Girl Named Tamiko, 1963; The Great Escape, 1963; The Satan Bug, 1965; The Hallelujah Trail, 1965; Hour of the Gun, 1967; Ice Station Zebra, 1968; Marooned, 1969; Joe Kidd, 1972; Valdez il Mezzosangue (Chino/Wild Horses), 1973; McQ, 1974; The Eagle Has Landed, 1976.

ABOUT: Coursodon, J.-P. American Directors Vol. II, 1983; Garfield, B. Western Films, 1982; Warman, E. and Vallance, T. (eds.) Westerns: A Preview Special, 1964. *Periodicals*—Action (USA) November–December 1969; American Film June 1979; Film Ideal 210 1969; Films and Filming December 1962, January and February 1974; Films Illustrated July 1976; Focus

on Film Autumn 1972; Photoplay
August 1976; Screen International May 22, 1976.

STURGES, (EDMUND) PRESTON (August 29, 1898–August 6, 1959), American film
director, scenarist, and dramatist, was born in
Chicago, the son of Edmund Biden, a traveling
salesman, and his wife, Mary Desti. After a year
of marriage Desti left her husband and went off
with her infant son to study music in Paris.
There she met and began her long friendship
with the dancer Isadora Duncan. Short of money, she returned to Chicago, divorced Biden, and
married Solomon Sturges, a wealthy broker who
adopted her son in 1902.

Preston Sturges idolized his stepfather, a
champion cyclist, amateur baseball player, and
self-made man who gave the boy what little stability and security his extraordinary childhood
provided. Mary Desti, on the other hand, found
her husband almost intolerably vulgar. For six
months of every year, like some cosmopolitan
Persephone, she escaped from him and Chicago
to Isadora and *la vie bohème* in Paris. She took
her son with her, dressing him in Greek tunics,
enrolling him in experimental schools, and immersing him in Shakespeare, Molière, Greek
drama, opera, music, and museums. "They did
everything they could to make me an artist,"
Sturges said, "but I didn't want to be an artist.
I wanted to be a good businessman like my
father."

When Preston Sturges was eleven this hopeless
marriage came to an end. The boy was now installed all year round in French schools while his
mother and Isadora toured Europe. In due
course Mary Desti married Vely Bey, son of a
Turkish court physician whose preparations for
the beautification of the harem they began to
market through a cosmetics company, Maison
Desti, with branches in France and New York.
With the outbreak of World War I in 1914, Preston Sturges was shipped back to the United
States (by this time speaking English with a
French accent). His mother, traveling again
with Isadora, had turned Maison Desti over to
Vely, in whose hands it was foundering. Seeing
a chance to prove himself a businessman, Sturges, still in his teens, took charge. Living in great
poverty in New York, he worked day and night
to solicit famous customers and to market the
new products he himself developed (including a
"kiss-proof" lipstick), soon putting the business
on its feet again. But the stock market was the
arena in which he really wanted to succeed, and
while continuing to direct Maison Desti he took
a job as a runner with a New York brokerage
house at seven dollars a week.

PRESTON STURGES

His plans were thwarted in 1917 by America's
entry into the war. Sturges, then nineteen, tried
to enlist in the air service but was turned down
because of a minor sight defect. His mother, aggrieved by this rejection, returned from Europe
and pulled strings until he was accepted. Having
served out stateside what remained of the war,
Sturges returned to Maison Desti. The business
was once more in trouble, however, and this
time not even Sturges' energy and ingenuity
could save it. At this point he made the first of
his four marriages, to an heiress named Estelle
de Wolfe Mudge. For a time he settled down in
the country and devoted himself to developing
a variety of inventions, including a ticker tape
machine and a small automobile with the engine
in the rear. Sturges remained an amateur inventor all his life, but none of the devices he designed in the postwar years found a market and
he seems for a while to have lost all his energy
and ambition. His marriage broke up and in December 1927 he became desperately ill with
acute appendicitis.

Sturges survived, but this encounter with
death changed him—seems, indeed, to have
been a "rebirth" like those experienced by characters in several of his films. For the moment he
put aside his hopes of a business career and
turned to the world that his mother had tried so
hard to prepare him for, the theatre. His first
play, *The Guinea Pig* (1929), made no great stir.
He followed it with another comedy, written in
two weeks, called *Strictly Dishonorable* (1929).
It was immediately accepted and produced on
Broadway by Antoinette Perry with immense
success. It concerns a naive American girl choos-

ing between her stuffy fiancé and a sophisticated European (and preferring the latter). This hit, which brought Sturges instant celebrity, was followed by two failures: the marital drama *Recapture* (1930) and the operetta *The Well of Romance* (1930), for which he wrote the lyrics as well as the dialogue. Sturges, who often invested in his own productions, lost a good deal of money on these and, to recoup, wrote his first screenplays.

The Big Pond and *Fast and Loose*, both filmed by Paramount in 1930, were play adaptations, and both credited Sturges only as author of the dialogue. In fact, the contributions of the so-called scenarists seem to have been slight, and both films follow Sturges' original scripts very closely. *The Big Pond*, for example, seems in retrospect a highly characteristic work in its love-triangle theme, its shameless reliance on the intervention of fate, its introduction of a tycoon character, and its delight in puns and verbal misunderstandings. Sturges' own play, *Strictly Dishonorable*, was filmed by Universal in 1931 (the adaptation being written by Gladys Lehmann) and Sturges then sold his 1932 play, *Child of Manhattan*, to Columbia for $40,000. After that, to quote his biographer James Ursini, he "moved to where the money and the creative opportunities lay—Hollywood."

Sturges' first big success as a scenarist was *The Power and the Glory* (Fox, 1933), an original story about a railroad tycoon, Tom Garner, who wins power and wealth at the cost of emotional tragedy. The film employs an original and interesting technique that the studio dubbed "narratage," the story being told in a complex, nonchronological series of flashbacks purporting to be the recollections of a narrator whose voice, on occasion, is synchronized to the characters we see speaking on the screen. Directed by William K. Howard and moodily photographed by James Wong Howe, it provided a meaty part for Spencer Tracy and has been seen as a precursor, in some respects, of *Citizen Kane*.

After working on several scripts that were subsequently much revised by others, or abandoned, Sturges wrote *The Good Fairy* (Universal, 1935), adapted from Molnar's cynical comedy (and considerably sentimentalized in the process). Sturges was already recognized as one of Hollywood's more civilized and cosmopolitan writers, and on that account was often assigned to adapt foreign classics. His next script, however, was an original one and very much in the American grain, *Diamond Jim* (Universal, 1935). Another study of the rise and fall of a tycoon, it gave Edward Arnold one of his richest and most sympathetic roles. There is a good deal

of Solomon Sturges in his stepson's portrait of Diamond Jim Brady, as there is in all the self-made captains of industry he drew.

Sturges contributed to several other movies during the mid-1930s, though how much is not clear. He also wrote the Mitchell Leisen comedy *Easy Living* (Paramount, 1937), adapted Marcel Pagnol's "Marseilles Trilogy" as *Port of Seven Seas* (MGM, 1938), and followed it with another adaptation called *If I Were King* (Paramount, 1938) derived from a play about François Villon. After *Never Say Die* (Paramount, 1939), a Bob Hope vehicle somewhat mauled by Hope's regular gag writers, came another Leisen comedy, *Remember the Night* (Paramount, 1940), a celebration of small-town America.

Ambitious as he was, Sturges had long been eager to direct the films he wrote, and had learned all he could by watching others. In 1940 he offered Paramount a promising script for ten dollars on condition that he directed it himself. The studio agreed and the same year Sturges went to work on *The Great McGinty*. He had a three-week shooting schedule and a budget of about $350,000. The movie opens in a seedy Latin American bar, where the bartender McGinty (Brian Donlevy) begins the story of how he got there. In 1920 he had been a bum in Chicago. Offered two dollars for his vote, he had ingeniously sold it thirty-seven times, thus earning the admiration of the local political boss (Akim Tamiroff). Muscle and a talent for graft had taken McGinty rapidly up through the political ranks. He had become mayor and then governor, meanwhile acquiring a wife and a fortune. Unfortunately his wife had been chronically honest and eventually she had infected McGinty with the same disease. Bucking the system, he had wound up alongside the boss in jail, whence they had escaped into exile.

As James Ursini writes, the film shows Sturges' "budding visual sense" in scenes like one in which a suicide attempt is reflected in a dirty mirror that is shattered when the attempt is foiled, and in visual gags reminiscent of the silents. Sturges' screenplay won an Oscar and the picture was a hit. In spite of its savage cynicism about American politics and the American Dream, it established him at once as a comedy director of the first rank. In *McGinty* Sturges used a number of character actors for whom he had written parts in earlier movies—men like William Demarest, Harry Rosenthal, Frank C. Moran, Jimmy Conlin, and Robert Warwick. Together with Eric Blore, Franklin Pangborn, Edgar Kennedy, and one or two others, they became permanent members of Sturges' "stock company," appearing in film after film in the cameo parts he loved to write for them. Far more than employees, some of them were among Sturges' closest friends and favorite companions.

Half a dozen of these old pros feature in *Christmas in July* (Paramount, 1940), which stars Dick Powell as an obsessive contest competitor who is tricked into believing that he has won a fortune with a terrible coffee slogan. The unpredictable working of destiny is a recurrent theme in Sturges' movies, and this film makes effective use of relevant images (a turning wheel, a black cat). The huge office where the hero works before his "ludey break," with row upon row of identical desks, is almost as overwhelming a symbol of the automation of human beings as the similar set in Billy Wilder's *The Apartment* (1960). Sturges' penchant for slapstick emerges in the scene where the hero and his wife (Ellen Drew) arrive home with a convoy of taxis loaded with gifts for their neighbors. As they are distributing them, the trick is discovered and the storeowners arrive to reclaim their goods in a scene that rapidly escalates into a frenetic comedy riot. In general, however, this film is gentler in its humor than its predecessor, and respectful of the "little people" of America. Full of warnings about the fickleness of fortune, it nevertheless has a happy ending: having been tricked into thinking that he did win $25,000, the hero becomes the sort of person who does.

Sturges was given his first chance at a big-budget production with *The Lady Eve* (Paramount, 1941), in which Charles, a naive millionaire snakecollector (Henry Fonda), returns from an Amazonian Garden of Eden to the perils of civilization. He is hooked by Barbara Stanwyck who, exposed as a hustler, disguises herself as an English aristocrat to try again and eventually gets her sadder but wiser Adam: it is another example of the notion of character rebirth which Sturges had used for the first time in *The Great McGinty*.

One of the most accomplished and enjoyable of all Sturges' movies, *The Lady Eve,* as Ursini says, showed that the director had mastered "the complex, contrapuntal harmonies of image and sound." Ursini has drawn particular attention to the sequence in which Eve assaults Charles with an endless list of her earlier love affairs: as the train they are on speeds through Freudian tunnels, Charles' mounting jealousy is echoed in the storm that grows outside, the screaming train whistle, and the background use of Von Suppé's "Poet and Peasant" overture. The film gave Fonda one of his first important comedy roles and Stanwyck is perfectly cast as the typical Sturges heroine—cool, witty, sexy, and dominant. There

are memorable performances also from Charles Coburn (as an old con artist), Eugene Pallette (as Charles' tycoon father), William Demarest (as his faithful bodyguard), and many members of Sturges' "stock company" (playing bartenders, stewards, piano tuners, etc.).

Sullivan's Travels (1941) is Sturges' most personal film, a comedy with dark undertones about movie-making, about America, and about Preston Sturges. John L. Sullivan (Joel McCrea) is a successful Hollywood comedy director who, inspired by conscience (and the example of filmmakers like Frank Capra) sells his reluctant bosses on the idea of a socially "meaningful" movie—"a commentary on modern conditions . . . something that would realize the potentialities of Film as the sociological and artistic medium that it is . . . with a little sex in it."

Determined to experience poverty first-hand, Sullivan disguises himself as a hobo and sets out on his travels. In the company of a disenchanted starlet (Veronica Lake) he hops trains, sleeps in flophouses, raids garbage cans, and attends a revival meeting, but gets more than he bargained for when a fracas with a yard boss lands him on a prison farm where he is flogged, chained, and worked half to death. The prisoners' only treat is an outing to a black church for a movie show, and in that assorted congregation, watching a Pluto cartoon, Sullivan learns that the wretched of the earth don't want to see serious studies of their condition—they want to escape from their pain into laughter, which for an hour or two can join together black and white, warden and prisoner. At the end Sullivan, free and reunited with his girl, announces that "There's a lot to be said for making people laugh. Did you know that's all some people have? It isn't much but it's better than nothing in this cockeyed caravan." His bosses had been right.

It is a complacently sentimental conclusion to a film that nevertheless presents a remarkably honest and sometimes harrowing picture of poverty and injustice in America, lightened though it is by witty lines, eccentric characterizations, and slapstick visual humor. Music (the so-called Hobo Symphony) is effectively used in the otherwise silent sequence where the principals experience the routine degradations of poverty. Andrew Sarris called the picture "a Swiftian glimpse of Hollywood and its occasional flirtations with social consciousness."

There are none of these uneasy undertones in the "almost perfect comic masterpiece" that followed in 1942, *The Palm Beach Story.* An unremitting but lighthearted satire on ambition and greed, it has Claudette Colbert reluctantly leaving her husband, an innocent and penniless inventor (Joel McCrea), and heading for Florida in search of a man with money. She scrounges the train fare from a gang of exuberant millionaires (the Sturges circus of eccentrics in full cry) and picks up a melancholy billionaire (wonderfully played by Rudy Vallee) who wants to marry her. Her husband, who follows her to Palm Beach, is similarly pursued by Vallee's voracious sister (Mary Astor). Further complications ensue when husband and wife pose as brother and sister, but true love wins out in the end (and Colbert and McCrea each bring on an identical twin to appease the disappointed suitors). "The rhythmic beat in *The Palm Beach Story* remains pretty constant," wrote Jay Leyda, "but the key switches madly from bar to bar, with a Molièresque alternation of comedy and farce."

Sturges was an inventor and he put several examples of the breed into his movies—impractical ones like the husband in *The Palm Beach Story,* or tragic like W. T. G. Morton, the real-life inventor of anesthesia, whose life is the subject of *The Great Moment.* The director was fascinated by the story of this Boston dentist who, to spare a young servant girl pain, gave away the secret of his discovery and died in povery and ignominy. Sturges did all he could to infuse his somber theme with "entertainment value," introducing humor and satire, daring shifts of mood, and a characteristically complex flashback structure. On the other hand he marred the film by loyally casting his comic regulars in serious roles (and period costume), and some of his effects are grossly vulgar (like the blare of trumpets when Morton gives away his secret). The picture was completed in 1942 but not released until 1944, after Paramount had edited it into hopeless confusion.

Sturges followed this depressing excursion with two comedies about small-town America during World War II. *The Miracle of Morgan's Creek* centers on Trudy Kockenlocker (Betty Hutton), daughter of the local constable (William Demarest). One night she meets and is impregnated by a soldier who then disappears. The solution seems to be marriage to the town dummy, Norval Jones (Eddie Bracken), but a misunderstanding lands him in jail. However, Trudy's union is blessed by not one but six babies, and Morgan's Creek becomes worldwide front-page news. Precisely where the town is located is not made clear, but it is in the state governed by Dan McGinty (Brian Donlevy again). He finds it expedient to bend the law a little and "legalize" Trudy's nonexistent marriage to Norval, who is transformed from schnook to hero in the process. The film's astonishingly iconoclastic satire on marriage, motherhood, the Nativity, the nuclear family, patriotism, and American politics led it

into a series of censorship battles from which it emerged, apparently, almost unscathed. When it was released in 1944, almost a year after its completion, James Agee concluded that the Hays Office must have been "raped in its sleep." Not surprisingly, perhaps, it was Sturges' greatest financial success, grossing over ten million dollars.

Having built Morgan's Creek in the studio and populated it with his gallery of character actors, Sturges used the same resources again in *Hail the Conquering Hero* (1944), a much less extreme satire on small-town values. Eddie Bracken stars again as the bumbling hero, now named Woodrow Truesmith. Like Norval he is rejected for military service on medical grounds (he has hay fever) but this time the rejection is critical, since he is the son of a Marine hero, weaned on the glories of the Corps. Woodrow takes a job in a shipyard and pretends to be overseas, then enters into a conspiracy with some sympathetic leathernecks to masquerade as a hero like his father. Returning home in spurious triumph, he is feted by the whole town, rediscovered by his old girlfriend, and nominated to replace the venal mayor. Discovered, Woodrow confesses all to the assembled populace with such touching frankness that he is renominated.

The frantic pace that builds throughout the last half of *Morgan's Creek* is redoubled in this movie. As James Ursini writes, "each medium shot is filled to the brim with characters naturalistically overlapping their lines and generally exuding the excitement of the moment. One cannot help but be amazed at the perfect timing Sturges' stock company demonstrates in these bits of ensemble acting." Ursini, who elsewhere points out how frugal Sturges is with close-ups throughout his work, goes on to explain that "the cinematic device which ties *Miracle* irrevocably to *Hail* is the long tracking shot. In this film as in its predecessor, there is an abundance of camera movements which follow the characters through entire blocks of the town, thereby giving us a feel for the people and their daily surroundings." However, what James Agee wrote of *Morgan's Creek* is even more applicable to this picture: "In the stylization of actions as well as language it seems to me clear that Sturges holds his characters, and the people they comically represent, and their predicament, and his audience, and the best potentialities of his own work, essentially in contempt."

Hail the Conquering Hero, completed in 1943, was Sturges' last film for Paramount. He wanted independence, and Paramount, for its part, was increasingly bothered by his soaring budgets, his arrogance, and his habit of writing most of the night so that shooting could not begin until the afternoon. When *Morgan's Creek* and *Conquering Hero* were released in 1944, their enormous profits gave Paramount second thoughts, but by that time Sturges had gone into partnership with Howard Hughes to form California Pictures Corporation, releasing through United Artists. CPC was launched with a film that was intended as the comeback of the silent movie comedian Harold Lloyd, *The Sin of Harold Diddlebock* (1947).

The picture opens with the last reel of *The Freshman* (1925), in which Lloyd saves the day in a college football game. Sturges added sound to dovetail this silent footage into the next sequence, in which Lloyd is offered a job by an admiring local businessman. Twenty years pass and the former hero, no longer young, is still trapped in the same menial job. He does even that badly, and is fired. At this low ebb, encouraged by a little hustler named Wormy (Jimmy Conlin), he squanders his life savings on an enormous bender in the course of which he buys a run-down circus. Reborn like other Sturges heroes before him, he recovers his old drive and optimism, makes his fortune, and gets the girl of his dreams. The result is an act of homage to the great silent comedies that Sturges loved, full of sight gags and slapstick, including a ledge-hanging scene that outdoes the famous one in Lloyd's *Safety Last* by adding Wormy and a circus lion to the act.

Before this picture was released, Hughes and Sturges went to work on *Vendetta*, an adaptation of a Corsican revenge story by Prosper Mérimée. Max Ophuls was hired to direct, but Hughes soon fired him and Sturges took over. He also displeased Hughes and CPC was dissolved, *Vendetta* eventually being completed by a string of other directors. Hughes released *Diddlebock* briefly in 1947, withdrew it, and distributed a revised version in 1950 as *Mad Wednesday*; it struck one critic as "almost a slapstick equivalent of *Death of a Salesman*."

With the dissolution of CPC, Sturges went looking for a new backer with a script written fifteen years earlier, and landed Darryl F. Zanuck. He gave Sturges a suite of offices at 20th Century–Fox, a spectacularly generous contract, a two million dollar budget, and complete autonomy. *Unfaithfully Yours* concerns a famous conductor (Rex Harrison) who suspects that his wife (Linda Darnell) is having an affair with a younger man. In the course of a single concert he imagines himself killing her, forgiving her, and challenging her lover to Russian roulette, the nature of his fantasy reflecting the nature of the music he is conducting. Leaving the concert

hall, he attempts to put his fantasies into effect, but all his plans mingle and collapse into absurdity. In the end his wife offers an explanation of the suspicious events that he gratefully accepts, though the audience may not.

Sturges had once offered the script to Ernst Lubitsch, who had turned it down on the grounds that the public wanted "corned beef and hash," not caviar. *Unfaithfully Yours* is nevertheless a film very much in the Lubitsch tradition, albeit laced with Sturgesian slapstick. Lubitsch seems to have been right, however—it had mixed reviews and, perhaps because of the blackness of its humor, was not successful at the box office. Seeking to redeem himself at Fox, Sturges then embarked on a spoof Western called *The Beautiful Blonde From Bashful Bend* (1949), a rickety vehicle for Betty Grable. She plays a pistol-packing singer who falls in love with a card sharp, is jailed for shooting a judge, escapes, impersonates a schoolmarm, and takes on the local baddies in a final shoot-out. Sturges' only film in color, it is one of the weakest and least imaginative of all his works.

This second failure ended the director's brief career at Fox and branded him throughout the industry as a bad risk. He stoically returned to his beginnings as a writer for other directors. Over the next few years he wrote half-a-dozen screenplays, of which some were optioned but none filmed. He also turned his attention to his other interests. These included a factory, Sturges Engineering Company, which had helped to make him a millionaire during the war years, turning out diesel engines among other items, and a Hollywood restaurant, The Players. In 1951 he added a theatre and a dance hall to the restaurant, offering diners one-act plays and other entertainments which he produced, directed, designed, and sometimes wrote himself, turning his troupe of old actors into a repertory company. This venture was ahead of its time and failed, leaving Sturges near bankruptcy, hounded for debts, taxes, and alimony. After a brief interlude in New York he went even further back into his past, settling in Paris, where he had spent his childhood.

Sturges' last years, full of aborted plans and projects, produced one more completed film, *Les Carnets du Major Thompson (The French They Are a Funny Race*, 1956). Adapted from Pierre Daninos' best-seller, it became in Sturges' hands a "conjugal comedy" about a stuffy Englishman (Jack Buchanan) in France, clumsily satirizing French and British stereotypes. It had some success in Europe, none in America. For three more years Sturges shuttled between Europe and the United States in search of backers for his manifold schemes, but without success. In 1959 he died of a heart attack.

"No one made better dialogue comedies than Sturges," wrote Gerald Mast, "primarily because no one wrote better dialogue. . . . The Sturges emphasis on dialogue determines his film technique, which relies on the conventional American two-shot to capture the faces and features while the characters talk, talk, talk. But it is such good talk—incredibly rapid, crackling, brittle—that the film has plenty of life. Like Hawks, Sturges was a master of the lightning pace. When Sturges uses special cinematic devices, he inevitably turns them into self-conscious bits of trickery and gimmickry that harmonize well with the parodic spirit of the film." James Ursini has discussed Sturges' debt to Molière, Shakespeare, Congreve, and Feydeau, saying that he united "the sophistication of the stage with the visual slapstick that was so much a part of the silent film."

James Agee, who analyzed Sturges almost obsessively in his *Nation* articles, said of his films: "They seem to me wonderfully, uncontrollably, almost proudly corrupt, vengeful, fearful of intactness and self-commitment. . . . Their mastering object, aside from success, seems to be to sail as steep into the wind as possible without for an instant incurring the disaster of becoming seriously, wholly acceptable as art. They seem . . . the elaborately counterpointed image of a neurosis." Penelope Houston, rather similarly, wrote: "His defences were built up in depth, and his favourite approach was the oblique and glancing one, with all the retreats into burlesque left open. The world of his comedy is self-contained and self-protected, and he becomes ill at ease when confronted with an idea to be followed straight through, or a situation that can't be resolved in an explosion of nervous energy." This energy, which carries his plots over "chasms of improbability," and his crowded canvases, persuaded Andrew Sarris that he was "the Brueghel of American comedy directors."

Sturges' fondness for pratfalls, slapstick, and his "seamy old character actors" no doubt reflects his lifelong struggle to cast off his mother's influence—the "stubborn pretense to philistinism" that his films conclusively refute. According to Alistair Cooke, he was "an accomplished linguist, a canny art critic . . . an epicure of extravagant tastes." Hollywood he once described as "a comic opera in which fat businessmen, good fathers, are condemned to a conjugal existence with a heap of drunkards, madmen, divorcees, sloths, epileptics, and morphinomaniacs who are—in the considered opinion of the management—artists." Another wit,

Alexander King, said of Sturges himself that he was "actuated by a genuine affection for people, which rises naturally from a well of deep sympathy for anyone who must go through life without being Preston Sturges." He was married four times—to Estelle Mudge, Eleanor Post Hutton, Louise Sargent Tervis, and Anne Margaret Nagle—and had three sons. Courtly in manner, he had friends at every level of society.

FILMS: The Great McGinty (UK, Down Went McGinty), 1940; Christmas in July, 1940; The Lady Eve, 1941; Sullivan's Travels, 1941; The Palm Beach Story, 1942; The Miracle of Morgan's Creek, 1944; Hail the Conquering Hero, 1944; The Great Moment, 1944; The Sin of Harold Diddlebock, 1947 (rereleased in shortened version as Mad Wednesday, 1950); Unfaithfully Yours, 1948; The Beautiful Blonde from Bashful Bend, 1949; The French They Are a Funny Race (France: Les Carnets du Major Thompson; UK, The Diary of Major Thompson), 1956. *Published scripts*—The Miracle of Morgan's Creek *and* Hail the Conquering Hero *in* Gassner, J. and Nichols, D. (eds) Best Film Plays of 1943–1944.

ABOUT: Agee, J. Agee on Film 1, 1960; Bazin A. Le cinéma de la cruauté, 1975 (in French); Corliss, R. (ed.) The Hollywood Screenwriters, 1972; Curtis, J. Between Flops, 1982; Durgnat, R. The Crazy Mirror, 1969; Farber, M. Negative Space, 1971; Mast, G. The Comic Mind, 1973; Montgomery, J. Comedy Films, 1954; Roud, R. (ed.) Cinema: A Critical Dictionary, 1980; Sarris, A. (ed.) Interviews with Film Directors, 1967; Ursini, J. The Fabulous Life and Times of Preston Sturges: An American Dreamer, 1973. *Periodicals*—Cinema (USA) Spring 1972; Film Comment Winter 1970–1971; Film Culture Winter 1962; Film Society Review January 1968; Films in Review February 1950; Life August 28, 1944; New Republic December 21, 1942; New York Times November 10, 1946, July 11, 1948; Positif December 1977–January 1978; Reader's Digest March 1945; Saturday Evening Post March 8 and 15, 1941; Sequence Summer 1948; Sight and Sound Summer 1965; Times (London) August 7, 1959; Vogue August 15, 1944.

*SUCKSDORFF, ARNE (February 3, 1917–), Swedish documentarist, director, cinematographer, scenarist, editor, and producer, was born in Stockholm, the son of a wealthy wholesale dealer, and grew up partly in the beautiful country around Södertälje. "When he was a boy," according to C. A. Lejeune, "he longed to draw; forests and spiderwebs and patterns in the snow; most of all animals. But he was never satisfied with the results. The grace, the line, the quick eluded him."

Sucksdorff studied zoology and genetics in high school and then painting with Otte Sköld. In 1937 he went to Berlin and explored the possi-

° $\overline{\text{sooks}}$´ dorf

ARNE SUCKSDORFF

bilities of theatre at the Reimannschule under Rudolf Klein-Rogge, the actor who had appeared in so many of the great silent films of Fritz Lang—some sources suggest that Sucksdorff actually worked for a time in some junior capacity at the UFA film studios. What is more certain is that he witnessed and was deeply disturbed by the excesses of the Nazi regime.

The same year—1937—Sucksdorff visited Sicily with some friends from the Reimann-schule, recording what he saw with a newly bought Rolleiflex. These still photographs subsequently won a number of prizes, and encouraged by this success, Sucksdorff decided to see what he could do with a movie camera. His first film was *En Augustirapsodi* (*An August Rhapsody*, 1939), a seven-minute "hymn to the Swedish summer." Impressed by this, a company called Folkfilm invited him to make another, similar documentary in collaboration with the poet Harry Martinson: *Din tillvaros land* (*Your Own Land*, 1940).

Forsyth Hardy says that these first films "were very clearly the work of a man who could compose beautifully within the frame but had very little idea about how to make a film move." This problem had been overcome by the time Sucksdorff made his next picture, *En sommersaga* (*A Summer's Tale*, 1941), which was the first of his works to attract international attention. Distributed by Svensk Filmindustri, the largest Swedish production company, it was—like virtually all of Sucksdorff's films—written, photographed, and edited by him alone.

A work of great visual beauty, this thirteen-minute film is yet another "hymn" to the brief Swedish summer, made up of "astonishingly intimate shots of flowers and insects and birds," and starring an engaging pair of fox cubs. But along with the lyricism goes a tough-minded recognition that the natural world is one of relentless hunger and violence, in which a caterpillar's pathetic struggle to survive is doomed the moment it chances to catch the sharp eye of a playful cub.

During the 1940s, Sucksdorff made a dozen more short nature films at an average rate of one a year, all of them for Svensk Filmindustri. *Vinden från väster* (*The Wind From the West*, 1943) was said to communicate "by almost entirely visual means the stunning impact of the arrival of spring in the far north"—an event that in Lapland precipitates an annual migration northward. It seemed to Forsyth Hardy that "the most revealing shot in the film is of a wrinkled old Lapp with longing in his eyes gazing at the younger and fitter men setting out on the journey he is now too old to make." *Sarvtid* (*Reindeer Time*, 1943) is a companion piece dealing with the annual roundup of the Lapland reindeer. This film was supervised by Gunnar Skoglund, who also wrote and spoke the "somewhat strident" commentary. The result, though beautifully photographed, was found less reflective than Sucksdorff's other films, and the experience confirmed him in his determination to preserve complete artistic independence and control.

Sucksdorff spent three months on the Baltic island of Stora Karlsö shooting *Trut!* (*The Gull*, 1944), in which we see a predatory seagull terrorizing a colony of guillemots, swooping on their nests and devouring their eggs at will. It is obvious that the guillemots could easily drive off the aggressor if they joined forces against him, but they lack the will or the intelligence to do this. It is not surprising that some contemporary critics saw in this film an allegory about the depredations of Nazi Germany, though Sucksdorff has rejected the parallel. Forsyth Hardy saw another theme in Sucksdorff's constant references to the island's ancient cliffs, "with their cross sections from a bygone world," and concluded that this was "a strange, complex film whose full meaning is yielded only after several viewings."

Vernon Young has said that "the brief nature films made by Sucksdorff in the forties were wrested from a background of anxiety as unrestful as any expressed by Bergman. But in Sucksdorff's work, controlled by the documentary intention, there is no trace of the assailed ego to despoil the poetry." Elsewhere, Young calls these films "parables, evoked from a mind that has been moved by moral contradictions, most effective when least didactic." Something of the complexity these statements imply is evident in two very short films—eight and eleven minutes long, respectively—that can be seen as variations on a single theme.

The first of these is *Gryning* (*Dawn,* 1944), in which woodland birds exhibit the same sort of aggression and rivalry as the seabirds in *Trut!* Then a man enters the forest with a gun and the birds and small animals forget their rivalry and flee from the common enemy. The hunter sights a pair of deer drinking at the edge of a small lake. He takes aim and then draws back because (as Peter Cowie puts it) he has become "suddenly and spontaneously aware of the order he will be disturbing." This conscious moral choice is implicitly contrasted with the behavior of the beautiful creatures who are a part of that order, wholly subject to its laws.

The same contrast is drawn in different terms in *Skuggor över snön* (*Shadows Over the Snow,* 1945). The man who stalks a bear through the moonlit forest at first seems no different in kind from the lesser predators around him, each seeking its own survival untroubled by moral considerations. The hunter fires at the bear but misses. And then, wrote Forsyth Hardy, "he becomes conscious of the menace of the forest, with the trees throwing dark shadows across his path and eerie sounds issuing from their black depths. It is extraordinary how vivid Sucksdorff makes this struggle between the man and the unseen forces he senses around him." Catherine de la Roche was equally moved by Sucksdorff's "incomparable photography," in which "light and shade assume symbolical meaning."

Människor i stad (*People of the City,* 1947) is a seventeen-minute study of what is ostensibly a totally different world—that of contemporary Stockholm on a summer's day of drowsy heat and sudden thunderstorms. The film has no commentary and needs none. When people turn to watch a speeding ambulance, we can see the momentary anxiety in their faces. When a small boy drops his marbles on the hard floor of a church, the shattering noise reflects his terror, and we share his relief when an old verger smiles indulgently.

It seemed to Forsyth Hardy that "there is no deliberate search for significant incident, no determination to pursue a consciously social-critical line. There is still a sense of innocence, of wonderment, in Sucksdorff's camera eye. It is contemplative rather than analytical." But for Peter Cowie, who believes that "each of Sucksdorff's films is founded on the struggle for existence," *People of the City* shows Stockholm "to be a place where the fittest survive best," just

as they do in the forest: "At the end there is the spectacle of a blind man fumbling for his violin bow on the cobbles." This film was shown in the United States shorn of all credit to Sucksdorff; the Oscar it won was presented to Edmund C. Reek, who "edited" it for its American distributor, 20th Century–Fox.

Den Drömda dalen (*The Dream Valley,* 1947), which explores the mountains and waterfalls of the Soria-Moria fjord through the eyes of a little girl, was followed by *Uppbrott* (*The Open Road,* 1948), recording the traditional all-night celebrations at a gypsy camp in Stockholm before the nomads move on. In *En kluven värld* (*A Divided World,* 1948), Sucksdorff returns to the theme of the incessant struggle for survival in the Swedish forest, this time on a moonlit night in deepest winter. A fox cub kills a hare, only to have the carcass snatched from it by an owl. And this brutal drama is played out against a musical background evoking the highest cultural traditions of Western society—a Bach *Fantasia* performed in a little church. The film was seriously marred for many critics by the intrusion of some clumsily faked shots (including a church that was obviously only a table-top model), but Catherine de la Roche thought it the "nearest to a parable on modern times" of all Sucksdorff's animal films.

But it was obvious that by now Sucksdorff's interests were turning increasingly to the direct investigation of human societies. *Strandhugg* (*Summer Interlude,* 1950), set in a seaside village on Sweden's west coast, ironically contrasts the lives of the natives with those of the well-heeled sun worshippers who visit the place every summer. And *Ett hörn i norr* (*The Living Stream,* 1950) is a relatively lengthy essay (twenty-six minutes) on the interdependence of the Scandinavian countries and their economic relationship with other parts of the world.

Early in 1950 Sucksdorff went to India, rented a houseboat on the Jelum River in Kashmir, and settled down to absorb the spirit and tempo of this unfamiliar world. Characteristically, he did not expose a single frame until he felt attuned to life on the river, and when he did start work on a film, he began by recording the folk music of the region, later cutting his images to that rhythm. Sucksdorff was appalled by what he saw: "thousands of years of religious inheritance of a code of life-long self-denial, of subjection during life in the hope and belief of reincarnation."

The result was *Indisk by* (*Indian Village,* 1951), about a village dying of drought. The elders squat in the dust, stubbornly insisting that the only hope lies in divine intervention, until visiting engineers persuade the villagers to drill for water. Then the land is fruitful again, the knowing vultures put to flight. But the inbred attitude of passivity and submission remains, and the film implies that the village will eventually perish unless its people elect to take their part in the struggle with nature. *Vinden och floden* (*The Wind and the River,* 1951), made at the same time, is an attractive but less purposeful film, described as "no more than a charming reminder that in India the river is the serene and vital source of life."

Back in Sweden, Sucksdorff worked for nearly three years on his first full-length feature, *Det stora äventyret* (*The Great Adventure,* 1953), shooting over 24,000 feet of film, of which only 790 were eventually used. Rune Waldekranz writes that in all of Sucksdorff's films, "life is experienced as a dramatic harmony, a unity, which paradoxically combines two opposing worlds, the unconscious realm of nature, the conscious one of mankind. Of all living creatures, man alone is responsible for his deeds, hence man must break the laws of nature and create his own." In Sucksdorff's view, Waldekranz suggests, these "two opposing worlds" touch at "the moment in childhood when the human does not realize the price that must be paid for mastering nature." This is the theme of *The Great Adventure,* which like its briefer predecessors was written, photographed, and edited by the director. Sucksdorff also has a small role in the movie as the father of the two boys, the younger of whom is played by his own son Kjell.

The film opens at dawn on a spring morning in a forest in central Sweden and follows the changing seasons through a year. In the winter, when the lakes are frozen, an otter is driven to poaching a fisherman's catch and is trapped by the fisherman. Two boys from a nearby farm, Anders (Anders Nohrborg) and his younger brother Kjell, free the otter and tame him as a pet, hiding him from their parents. At the same time, as Peter Cowie says, "the life of the neighbouring forests is shown: a vixen is smoked out of her burrow by one of the farmhands after she has stolen some chickens as food for her cubs; male woodgrouse fight viciously in the marshes during the mating season; a lynx watches menacingly from the slopes at night, ready to pounce whenever a lesser animal allows its guard to drop."

When spring returns, the lakes and rivers thaw, and the "tame" otter returns to the wild. Anders realizes that, as the commentary says, "no one can encage a dream alive for long." As the weather improves, the cranes fly back to the marshes. A new seasonal cycle has begun, but Anders' innocent sense of harmony with nature has gone forever. Instead he is reconciled with Kjell, who had committed the crime of divulging to their parents the secret of their "great adventure." In this film, Sucksdorff said, "I try to show an acceptance of life and . . . of other human beings."

The Great Adventure was awarded the Grand Prix at Cannes and has been described by Peter Cowie as "the most felicitous blend of fiction and documentary that Sucksdorff has achieved. . . . Unlike nearly all his fellow Swedes, Sucksdorff is an incorrigible optimist." Another critic, suggesting that the picture might invite comparisons with the Disney nature films, said that any such comparison would be like "attempting to discuss the poetry of Edgar Guest with that of Rainer Maria Rilke." In fact, this "extraordinary film poem" evoked more references to Flaherty than to Disney, Vernon Young making this distinction: "In Flaherty's films, man is the sum of the work he does; in Sucksdorff's, he is the mystery of the web he inhabits."

In February 1955 Sucksdorff returned to India with his wife Astrid to make his second feature—and his first in color and 'scope—*En djungelsaga* (*The Flute and the Arrow,* 1957). It is set in the Bastar district of central India, the home of the aboriginal Muria tribe, who have retained their faith in nature gods. When their hard-working agricultural community is disrupted by the arrival of a leopard, their fears for themselves and their beasts are compounded by the suspicion that the predator is possessed by demons. The hunt for the leopard and the rituals that precede it are seen through the eyes of a boy just coming to manhood.

"Sucksdorff is at his best when describing the ceaseless physical work of the villagers as they struggle to cultivate the broad plains," wrote Peter Cowie. "Against this he sets the sinister, lightning movements of the leopard as he catches a buffalo by the stream. . . . The editing is necessarily false, and one never sees the leopard in relation to the hunters in the same image. Thus the final sacrifice of one of the tribe does not contain such an emotional impact as it is clearly meant to do." Most critics agreed, and Arthur Knight wrote that Sucksdorff "demonstrates again his uncanny ability to get right on top of the wildest of animals with his camera. Unfortunately, he also demonstrates his strange inability to get at all close to people."

The accuracy of this last statement was even more painfully obvious in *Pojken i trädet* (*The Boy in the Tree,* 1961), an entirely fictional feature shot not by Sucksdorff but by Gunnar Fischer. The story centers on three bored and alienated youths from differing social backgrounds who, partly for gain and partly for excitement, spend their evenings poaching roebuck in the forest near their homes in southwest Sweden. Like the gangsters in the thrillers they read, they escape with their booty in a high-powered car with false license plates. Eventually one of the boys is caught by a local farmer (Anders Henrikson) and, in his panic, shoots himself. Visually, the film is magnificent, but the characterization is unconvincing and the dialogue embarrassingly banal.

During the early 1960s, Sucksdorff went to Brazil as director of a film school in Rio de Janeiro, and there made *Mitt hem är Copacabana* (*My Home Is Copacabana*, 1965), set in the notorious slums that overlook the city and the sea. Sucksdorff photographed and edited the film himself and also collaborated on the script, which draws on recorded interviews with the many orphaned or runaway children who live by their wits in the urban jungle of Copacabana. "These children live happily and freely for a while," Sucksdorff said, "and it is only when they grow up and become aware of their situation that they become really unhappy."

It is this process that the movie describes. When we first encounter its four young heroes, they still have a sense of humor and a defiant kind of animal cunning. One of them has a "killer" kite, its string coated with powdered glass. They take this down to the affluent beaches and use it to cut down more elegant kites that can then be sold. Their precarious economy is wrecked when the wretched shanty they share is occupied by bandits. Homeless as well as destitute, they resort to begging—inventing hardluck stories even more appalling than the reality—and then to stealing. But hunger and cold are wearing them down, and when one of the boys develops a toothache he bows to the inevitable and surrenders his hard-won freedom, returning to the reform school from which he had escaped.

Sucksdorff drew splendidly unself-conscious performances from his child actors. The film is often funny and sometimes moving, and the kites provide a beautiful and touching symbol of youthful hopefulness (as they do in the films of Bo Widerberg). But there is, finally, something tendentious and even presumptuous about Sucksdorff's attempt to demonstrate in his half-starved and rejected children the innocence and freedom of young animals; the cost of such deprivation must, we feel, be uglier than anything we are shown—something closer, perhaps, to what Buñuel shows us in *Los Olvidados*. Robert Robinson wrote that Sucksdorff offers the viewer "a chance to experience the wrong sort of pity, the sort where the audience goes home more consoled than the victim"—the bright-eyed children "seem to be *advertising* poverty."

Sucksdorff has remained in Brazil, where he has taken an active role in the international effort to save tribal peoples from extinction. He has made no more films, although he did shoot footage of Antarctic animals for *Forbush and the Penguins* (1971). His reputation must stand on *The Great Adventure* and the short nature films that preceded it. He always understood animals better than people—better, perhaps, than any other filmmaker. As Forsyth Hardy said, he handled the camera "as freely and fluently as if it were a brush in his hand." Filming for months at a time in the woods and marshes he had known as a child, he would become completely immersed in the savage world he was recording, forgetting to eat properly and sleeping wherever he found himself. Georges Sadoul considered him "one of the greatest modern documentarists."

FILMS: *Shorts*—En Augustirapsodi (An August Rhapsody), 1939; Din tillvaros land (Your Own Land), 1940; En sommersaga (A Summer's Tale), 1941; Vinden från väster (The Wind From the West/The West Wind), 1943; Sarvtid (Reindeer Time), 1943; Trut! (The Gull/Cliff Face), 1944; Gryning (Dawn), 1944; Skuggor över snön (Shadows Over the Snow/Shadows on the Snow), 1945; Människor i stad (People of the City/Symphony of a City/Rhythm of a City), 1947; Den Drömda dalen (Dream Valley), 1947; Uppbrott (The Open Road/Moving On), 1948; En kluven värld (A Divided World), 1948; Strandhugg (Summer Interlude/Going Ashore), 1950; Ett hörn i norr (The Living Stream),1950; Indisk by (Indian Village), 1951; Vinden och floden (The Wind and the River), 1951. *Features*—Det stora äventyret (The Great Adventure), 1953; En djungelsaga (The Flute and the Arrow), 1957; Pojken i trädet (The Boy in the Tree), 1961; Mitt hem är Copacabana (My Home Is Copacabana), 1965.

ABOUT: Béranger, J. La grande aventure du cinéma suédois, 1960; Cowie, P. Sweden (Screen Series), vols. 1 and 2, 1970; Edström, M. Sucksdorff, 1968 (in Swedish); Osten, G. Det förlorade paradiset, 1947 (in Swedish); Widerberg, B. Visionen i svensk film, 1962. *Periodicals*—Chaplin (Sweden) 19 1961; Film Forum November 1959; Films and Filming November 1954; Sight and Sound Summer 1948.

TAUROG, NORMAN (February 23, 1899–April 7, 1981), American director, was born in Chicago, the son of Arthur Taurog and the former Anita Goldsmith. He made his stage debut in 1912 in the David Belasco hit *The Good Little Devil*, with Mary Pickford. Continuing as a child

NORMAN TAUROG

actor, he worked with various stock companies around the country and then returned to Broadway for a fifteen-month engagement in *Potash and Perlmutter.*

According to Ephraim Katz, Taurog entered the movie industry as early as 1913, appearing as a boy actor with the Ince studios. He was in Hollywood by about 1916. "After an aborted career as a leading man," wrote a *Variety* reporter, "he turned to behind-the-scenes work, starting as a property man and cutter and gradually becoming a director of two-reel comedies." Taurog directed Larry Semon shorts for Vitagraph, and Lloyd Hamilton and Lupino Lane comedies at Educational Pictures. It is estimated that he made a total of 275 two-reel silents between about 1919 and 1928, when he graduated to full-length talkies.

Taurog's first three features were apparently all codirected by more experienced hands, though *Lucky Boy* (1929), a surviving Tiffany production that filmographies attribute to Taurog and Charles C. Wilson, excludes the latter's name from the credits. An obvious attempt to capitalize on the huge success of *The Jazz Singer* (1927), it stars George Jessel as a poor Jewish boy ambitious for success in vaudeville who goes west and makes his name with the sentimental ballad "My Mother's Eyes," which is ruthlessly reprised throughout the movie. *Bioscope* thought it had "strong attraction for a popular audience," something that could be said for the great majority of Taurog's seventy-six features.

Moving to Paramount, he had his first hit in 1931 with *Skippy,* featuring the six-year-old Jac-

kie Cooper, nephew of Taurog's first wife. Cooper was a seasoned performer who had appeared from the age of three in Bobby Clark and Lloyd Hamilton two-reelers (some of them directed by Taurog), and he handled the title role with immense naturalness and charm. *Skippy* is set in a small town where the young hero's father, the Medical Health Officer, is proposing to demolish an unsanitary shantytown and evict its occupants. After a fight, Skippy makes friends with ragged shantytowner Sooky (played by Jackie Coogan's brother Robert). Together they mount a "grand entertainment" to raise the price of a $3 license for Sooky's dog Penny but fall short of their goal by 30¢. Penny is shot in accordance with an order signed by Skippy's father, but the latter repents in the face of his son's grief, buying a new dog for Sooky and ordaining that Shantytown will survive.

"Judiciously mixing pathos and comedy," *Skippy* brought Taurog his first and only Oscar as best director and established his reputation as a director especially gifted at working with child actors. In the same year Taurog also directed a sequel, *Sooky,* as well as a version of *Huckleberry Finn,* with Junior Durkin as Huck and Jackie Coogan as Tom Sawyer.

A string of successful comedies and musicals followed, made for Paramount during the first half of the 1930s. Taurog directed W. C. Fields in one episode of *If I Had a Million* (1932) and again in *Mrs. Wiggs of the Cabbage Patch* (1934), with Pauline Lord as Mrs. Wiggs, dealing philosophically with poverty, an absent husband, and a superfluity of children. ZaSu Pitts almost stole the picture as Miss Hazy, enamored of Fields and intent on matrimony.

The same year, 1934, Taurog made a very different kind of comedy, *We're Not Dressing,* vaguely based on J. M. Barrie's *The Admirable Crichton.* When drunken millionaire Leon Errol and his yacht party are shipwrecked on a desert island, it is humble seaman Bing Crosby who, when not busy crooning, shows a talent for command, thus winning the hand of Errol's spoiled niece Carole Lombard. As one reviewer commented, Taurog was "quite right not to have attempted to make any sense out of the story," while "the superb inanities of Miss Gracie Allen and Mr. George Burns [as two wacky scientists] are in perfect harmony with the general pattern." Another critic remarked on how deftly the humor "is kept on one plane, instead of being allowed . . . to run up and down the scale from drama to broadcast farce."

Taurog directed Crosby again in *Rhythm on the Range* (1936) and in *The Big Broadcast of 1936* (1935), the latter also featuring Burns and

Allen (this time as the inventors of a televisual device called the Radio Eye), not to mention Jack Oakie, Ethel Merman, Richard Tauber, the Vienna Boys' Choir, and twenty-four dancing elephants. Taurog left Paramount after that enjoyable romp and for the next few years worked as a freelance.

Among the pictures he made at that time was *Strike Me Pink* (1936) for Samuel Goldwyn, an entertaining slapstick comedy with Eddie Cantor as a meek campus tailor who learns courage by correspondence and takes over the management of an amusement park that is threatened by racketeer Brian Donlevy. Ethel Merman is "a vague sort of villainess." It seemed to Richard Watts that, in the movie's climax, "the glorious tradition of the chase, which is the finest flower of cinema farce, is celebrated with admirable pictorial abandon." *Reunion* (1936), primarily an excuse for exhibiting the Dionne quintuplets at the age of two, was less kindly received.

Because of his reputation as a director of child actors, Taurog was then hired by David Selznick to direct a lavish Technicolor remake of *The Adventures of Tom Sawyer*. John V. A. Weaver was assigned to write a faithful adaptation of Mark Twain's novel, and a nationwide talent hunt unearthed two gifted juveniles (Tommy Kelly and Ann Gillis) to play Tom and his sweetheart, Becky Thatcher. Ronald Haver makes the interesting claim—unsubstantiated elsewhere—that "Taurog was an ex-cartoonist whose method of working included sketching out all his shots in a sort of story-board technique, which included lighting, sets, angles and camera movement. Selznick immediately appropriated this device. He asked [the art director] William Cameron Menzies . . . to utilize this technique for the cave sequence" in which Tom and Becky are pursued by the murderous Injun Joe. This terrifying passage was filmed by James Wong Howe in the darkness of a real cavern by equipping Tommy Kelly with a harness supporting a lamp that threw light up through an imitation candle.

"Mark Twain's unabashed sentimentality is accepted without reservations," wrote one British critic, "and there is no attempt to alter for the modern taste his childlike and peculiarly Victorian habit of mixing the fantasy and daydream of a boys' adventure story with a direct assault on the most serious emotions. The treatment of the more harrowing episodes is masterly. . . . Though the coloured landscapes may be too florid the colour in the interiors and in the dresses is often very attractive." According to Ronald Haver, this expensive picture was initially "not the success hoped for, but over the years,

through careful reissue and foreign sales marketing, it finally returned a profit."

Mad About Music (1938), a mediocre Deanna Durbin vehicle for Universal, was followed by one of Taurog's greatest successes, *Boys' Town,* made the same year for MGM. It is a highly fictionalized and sentimentalized account of the founding and growth of Boys' Town, the self-governing community for homeless boys near Omaha, Nebraska. Spencer Tracy plays Father Flanagan, who established the community in the belief that "there is no such thing as a bad boy." Mickey Rooney is the tough kid who almost proves him wrong but comes through in the end to save the town from disaster. Tracy received an Oscar for his performance, and both Taurog and the film itself were nominated. Leslie Halliwell says it "set the Hollywood fashion in boys and priests for years." Taurog made a sequel in 1941, *Men of Boys' Town.*

Settling down at MGM, he worked there almost exclusively for thirteen years. *Young Tom Edison* (1940), showing the future inventor growing up in Port Huron, Michigan, was praised for the skill with which Taurog evoked the atmosphere of small-town America in the nineteenth century. He had another hit with *Broadway Melody of 1940,* a backstage musical starring Fred Astaire and Eleanor Powell, with music by Cole Porter.

Taurog directed Judy Garland in *Little Nellie Kelly* in 1940 and twice in 1943—in *Presenting Lily Mars,* another backstage musical in which Garland plays a small-town girl who makes good and marries the producer (Van Heflin), and again in Gershwin's *Girl Crazy.* The latter has Mickey Rooney as the concupiscent heir to millions, consigned for the good of his soul to a midwestern school of agriculture. He finds true love with Garland, granddaughter of the dean, and stages a rodeo that does wonders for the college's enrollment. *Kinematograph Weekly* called the film an "excellent light booking . . . for the masses, family and the troops," adding dryly that "there is very little story to the picture, but luckily the majority of the gags have stood the test of time."

After that Taurog prepared three pictures in a row that had to be axed or postponed because their stars were inducted into the armed services. When he finally got back behind the camera, it was to see William Powell weeping on his knees before an altar in *The Hoodlum Saint* (1946), a project that he and MGM might have been better advised to pass up. Presumably an attempt to emulate the success of *Going My Way,* it inflicts on Powell the role of a cynical journalist who sets out to exploit the cult of Saint

Ditmas, the penitent thief of the Crucifixion, and winds up believing. James Gleason, Slim Summerville, and Frank McHugh play Powell's gambling companions, Esther Williams his girlfriend, and Angela Lansbury a moll. One reviewer called it "the most nauseating example I remember . . . of complete contempt for the mentality of the audience."

Taurog's next project for MGM, *The Beginning or the End* (1947), was greeted with no less hostility in some quarters. According to *Time*, this account of the development of the atomic bomb and of its first deployment had to satisfy "the official and personal tastes of numerous politicians, brasshats and scientists. . . . Far from straining at the seams of security, it tells the average citizen little he doesn't already know about atomic fission. Of the peculiar terror and agony of the bomb in human terms, it tells incomparably less in two hours than certain newsreel shots of Hiroshima's survivors told in as many minutes. The treatment of the moral problems exacerbated by the bomb is once-over-lightly. Problems of atomic control . . . are shunned like the plague." Others reacted more strongly against the movie—its insertion of "love interest" into the apocalypse and its "fatuous and impious" conclusion that "atomic energy is a hand God has extended."

A series of routine comedies followed, and one good musical, *Words and Music* (1948). A biopic of Richard Rodgers (Tom Drake) and Lorenz Hart (Mickey Rooney), it is stuffed with good songs splendidly performed by stars like Lena Horne, Judy Garland, and Perry Como and incorporates one of the first original screen ballets, danced by Gene Kelly and Vera-Ellen to a version of "Slaughter on Tenth Avenue." Taurog's subsequent work at MGM included two Mario Lanza movies, *That Midnight Kiss* (1949) and *The Toast of New Orleans* (1950), before he wound up his contract with the Jane Powell–Vic Damone musical *Rich, Young and Pretty* (1951).

When he left MGM, Taurog told Eileen Creelman that he intended in future to make no more than two pictures a year and to undertake only projects that he wanted to make. There is statistical evidence that he failed in the first endeavor, and it seems unlikely that he really wanted to devote the remainder of his career to churning out drive-in fodder for Hal Wallis. That is what he did, however, beginning with *Jumping Jacks* (1952), in which Dean Martin enlists the catastrophic services of Jerry Lewis in organizing camp shows for a tough paratroop outfit.

Taurog said that Lewis and Martin were "just like children; just as much fun. With all that craziness though, such good minds behind it all." He worked with them on five more movies over the next four years—*The Stooge, The Caddy, Living It Up, You're Never Too Young,* and *Pardners*—and after the team split up directed two of Lewis's solo efforts, *Don't Give Up the Ship* (1959) and *Visit to a Small Planet* (1960). Many of these movies were extremely profitable, though it is generally agreed that Taurog's Lewis and Martin pictures never matched the surreal lunacy of Frank Tashlin's.

Lewis went on to direct and produce his own films, and Hal Wallis turned Taurog's attention to another American phenomenon, Elvis Presley. Along with other unremarkable entertainments, Taurog directed nine Presley movies between 1960 and 1968. These were *GI Blues,* a "sniggery little dogface farce" capitalizing on Presley's well-publicized hitch in the army; *Girls! Girls! Girls!,* " a period piece belonging to the dark ages of Hollywood"; *It Happened at the World's Fair* ("nothing much happened"); *Tickle Me; Spinout; Double Trouble* ("how can such a film have emerged from a major Hollywood company?"); *Speedway;* and *Live a Little, Love a Little,* "one of Presley's dimmest vehicles."

After *Live a Little,* Taurog understandably retired. He died thirteen years later at the age of eighty-two and was survived by his wife, the former Susan Ream, and a son and two daughters. He was "an amiable, portly man" of whom it was said that, long after his heyday as a director of child actors, his pockets still bulged "with chocolate bars which he . . . [would pass out] to cast members upon completion of a particularly outstanding scene."

Ephraim Katz describes Taurog as "the ideal studio director, an excellent craftsman capable of turning almost any assignment into an attractive box-office package." Not even the French have claimed *auteur* status for Norman Taurog. He did what he was told, but did it well enough to create—amid all the dross—ten or a dozen splendid entertainments. Many more prestigious figures achieved less.

FILMS: (Features only)—(with Arthur Rosson?) The Farmer's Daughter, 1928; (with Charles C. Wilson?) Lucky Boy, 1929; (with Reaves Eason) Troopers Three, 1930; Sunny Skies, 1930; Hot Curves, 1930; Follow the Leader, 1930; (with Norman Z. McLeod) Finn and Hattie, 1931; Skippy, 1931; Newly Rich, 1931; Huckleberry Finn, 1931; Sooky, 1931; Hold 'Em Jail!, 1932; The Phantom President, 1932; (with others) If I Had a Million, 1932; A Bedtime Story, 1933; The Way to Love, 1933; We're Not Dressing, 1934; Mrs. Wiggs of the Cabbage Patch,1934; College Rhythm, 1934; The Big Broadcast of 1936, 1935; Strike Me Pink, 1936; Rhythm on the Range, 1936; Reunion, 1936; Fifty

Roads to Town, 1937; You Can't Have Everything, 1937; The Adventures of Tom Sawyer, 1938; Mad About Music, 1938; Boys' Town, 1938; The Girl Downstairs, 1938; Lucky Night, 1939; Young Tom Edison, 1940; Broadway Melody of 1940, 1940; Little Nellie Kelly, 1940; Men of Boys' Town, 1941; Design for Scandal, 1941; Are Husbands Necessary?, 1942; A Yank at Eton, 1942; Presenting Lily Mars, 1943; Girl Crazy, 1943; The Hoodlum Saint, 1946; The Beginning or the End, 1947; Big City, 1948; The Bride Goes Wild, 1948; Words and Music, 1948; That Midnight Kiss, 1949; Please Believe Me, 1950; The Toast of New Orleans, 1950; Mrs. O'Malley and Mr. Malone, 1950; Rich, Young and Pretty, 1951; Room for One More, 1952; Jumping Jacks, 1952; The Stooge, 1953; The Stars Are Singing, 1953; The Caddy, 1953; Living It Up, 1954; You're Never Too Young, 1955; The Birds and the Bees, 1956; Pardners, 1956; Bundle of Joy, 1956; The Fuzzy Pink Nightgown, 1957; Onionhead, 1958; Don't Give Up the Ship, 1959; Visit to a Small Planet, 1960; G.I. Blues, 1960; All Hands on Deck, 1961; Blue Hawaii, 1961; Girls! Girls! Girls!, 1962; It Happened at the World's Fair, 1963; Palm Springs Weekend, 1963; Tickle Me, 1965; Sergeant Deadhead, 1965; Dr. Goldfoot and the Bikini Machine, 1965; Spinout, 1966; Double Trouble, 1967; Speedway, 1968; Live a Little, Love a Little, 1968.

ABOUT: *Periodicals*—Action (USA) November–December 1973; Film Daily January 27, 1953; Image et Son June 1981; Variety April 15, 1981.

*TOURNEUR, JACQUES (November 12, 1904–December 19, 1977), American director, was born in Paris, the son of Maurice Thomas, better known as Maurice Tourneur. Originally an artist, the elder Tourneur adopted his pseudonym when he became a stage actor and director, and retained it when he joined the film production company Éclair. His wife, and Jacques Tourneur's mother, was Fernande Petit, herself an actress who worked as Fernande Van Doren.

With characteristic understatement, Tourneur described his childhood as "rather tough." His father was an aesthete and a solitary, cynical and sarcastic. Jacques Tourneur's "first confrontation with fear" came in his father's studio on Christmas Eve when he was four. His parents had put his gifts in a "huge, mysterious room" and told him that he must go alone to see them: "There was a long corridor, pitch dark, and in the distance I could see the white shapes of my presents. I went all on my own, torn between my desire for the toys and a fear which nearly paralyzed me."

On other occasions, if he misbehaved, his parents "would put the maid in the cupboard and she used to jiggle a bowler hat while my parents would tell me: 'That's the terrible

JACQUES TOURNEUR

Thunderman.'" Tourneur believed that this grotesque punishment was the root of one of his cinematic obsessions: "to suddenly introduce something inexplicable into the shot, such as, for instance, the hand on the balustrade . . . in *Curse of the Demon*; in the reverse shot the hand isn't there any more."

In 1914 Maurice Tourneur went to Fort Lee, New Jersey, to take charge of the small studio Éclair had built there. He sent his son "to a school which happened to be in the poorer section of town. The other kids were very violent and, as I was a foreigner who couldn't speak their language, I got into some sticky situations. But I learned very quickly. . . . I was the only kid who wore suspenders. My father insisted on that, and the other kids were always pulling on them, very hard, and then they would let them slap against my back. After a while . . . I had to walk holding up my trousers myself. I think this is what prompted me to introduce comic touches into the dramatic moments of my films. . . . Mixing fear and the ridiculous can be very exciting."

According to Jacques Tourneur, his father "was passionately interested in scientific, medical, and philosophic research. He had an incredible library and followed all the discoveries in psychoanalysis very closely. It is through him that I discovered Freud, Jung, Adler, Havelock Ellis. I never read novels, only essays, scientific works. They are much more exciting. I was already fascinated by the cinema and my father bought story ideas from me for ten dollars apiece. At that time he was a very important filmmaker in America."

°toor nûr´

Indeed, by the end of World War I, Maurice Tourneur was head of his own production company and generally regarded as the great aesthetician of the American cinema. In 1918 he moved his company to Hollywood, where the following year Jacques Tourneur became an American citizen. In 1922 Jacques appeared as an extra in Rex Ingram's *Scaramouche,* and in 1924, finishing high school, he went to MGM as a script clerk. He worked in the same capacity for his father in 1925–1926, but in the latter year Maurice Tourneur, whose Hollywood career was in decline, returned to Europe. He left his son a hundred dollar bill and the suggestion that he try and make it to Europe himself.

Jacques Tourneur did not at first take advantage of this offer, instead finding odd jobs in Hollywood as an actor and usher. But in 1927 his father invited him to Germany to work on *Das Schiff der verlorene Menschen (Ship of Lost Men),* and this time he went. He served as his father's editor and assistant on this film and then on a series of talkies made in Paris for Pathé-Nathan in 1929–1934. It was during this period that Jacques Tourneur directed his own first movies for the same company, beginning in 1931 with *Tout ça ne vaut pas l'amour (None of That's Worth Love).*

In an interview with Bertrand Tavernier in *Positif* (November 1971), translated in Johnston and Willemen's *Jacques Tourneur* (1975), the director said that in his own opinion the best of his four French films was *Les Filles de la concierge (The Concierge's Daughters,* 1934)—"a little . . . comedy [inspired by Unanimism], it was realistic, giving a fairly accurate portrait of a social milieu. It had many comic elements, especially for that time. The other films weren't very good, at least not as far as I can remember."

In 1934 Tourneur broke away from his father and returned to Hollywood. He directed sequences in Charles Riesner's *The Winning Ticket* and Jack Conway's *A Tale of Two Cities,* and in 1936–1938 made a whole series of one-reelers for MGM. The following year he directed his first American feature, *They All Came Out,* and there were three more B-pictures in 1939–1941, two of them starring Walter Pidgeon as the "master detective" Nick Carter.

Tourneur had worked with Val Lewton on the crowd scenes in *A Tale of Two Cities,* and in 1942 he began his seven-year association with RKO, where Lewton was then working as a producer. Their first movie grew out of a party conversation—a suggestion that "Cat People" was an oddly suggestive title from which an interesting thriller could be derived. A script was developed by DeWitt Bodeen (with the uncredited participation of Lewton and Tourneur), and the movie was made on a budget of $130,000.

Val Lewton was an eccentric workaholic of exceptional ability, and there are those who credit him rather than Tourneur with the quality of the three low-budget pictures they made together. One argument against this view is that what David Thomson calls the same "sense of unrevealed horror within the everyday" is evident in a film that Tourneur made years after Lewton's early death, *Curse of the Demon.* Robin Wood concludes that Tourneur's personality was the decisive influence on the films, though "much of their taste, intelligence and discretion is attributable to . . . [Lewton's] planning and supervision." Tourneur himself said that "with Val Lewton, we really worked together as a team. Everyone participated in the preparation of the script, and yet he never set foot on the set. He left you completely free."

Cat People (1942) tells the story of Irena Dubrovna (Simone Simon), a feline young woman obsessed by cats, which arch their backs and spit when they encounter her. She half-believes the legend that her Serbian ancestors became cats when aroused and dares not make love to her husband Oliver (Kent Smith) for fear that she will sprout claws and destroy him. She discusses these fears with a psychiatrist (Tom Conway), who scoffs, while Oliver finds a more sympathetic confidante in Alice at the office (Jane Randolph). One night, in the park, Alice hears ominous snarls and more frightening encounters follow on a dark street and in a swimming pool with something like a great cat. Then the lustful psychiatrist makes a pass at Irena. His torn body is found in her apartment. Hunted and desperate, Irena frees a black panther at the zoo and is killed by it.

According to Tourneur, the Serbian legend was Lewton's idea, but he himself "was the one who proposed that we should suggest the presence of the panther rather than show it. I was so afraid that the studio people would come along and add a superimposition of the panther in the swimming pool scene I decided to combine a pan with a long traveling shot while making the shadow of the panther by moving my fist in front of the camera in the middle of the movement. Then, no matter what happened, they couldn't spoil the scene afterwards."

Cat People has been called "the first monster film to refrain from showing us the monster." Tourneur said that RKO were "furious" when they discovered this and wanted to sell the movie off. In fact, it did immensely well at the box office. Together with Lewton's other low-budget thrillers and Hitchcock's *Suspicion,* it saved the studio, which at that time was in great financial difficulty. One morning, Tourneur found in his mailbox "a check for a quite vast amount, signed by the head of the studio, to thank me for having made such a film. That kind of thing doesn't happen anymore."

Robin Wood, writing in *Film Comment* (Summer 1972), carefully analyzes the "accumulation of suggestive detail" that accounts for the extraordinary power of this movie, saying that its "packed, complex and suggestive" dream sequence "concisely embodies the film's sense of life itself as a shadow-world in which nothing is certain, no issue is clear-cut, nothing is what it seems." Wood calls *Cat People* "a small masterpiece—perhaps the most delicate poetic fantasy in the American cinema." It was remade in 1982 by Paul Schrader.

"To show that, unconsciously, we all live in fear—that is genuine horror," Tourneur wrote. "Many people today are constantly prey to a kind of fear they don't wish to analyze. When the audience, sitting in a darkened room, recognizes its own insecurity in that of the characters of the film, then you can show unbelievable situations in the certain knowledge that the audience will follow you." It seemed to Michael Henry that "with these words Tourneur doesn't just give a definition of the horror film, he outlines an aesthetic of disquiet undoubtedly far more in tune with contemporary anxieties than the costumed fantasies of the Gothic tradition."

Tourneur's second venture into "disquiet" was one of the few films he himself initiated: "One day I said to Val Lewton 'I have an idea. We are going to take *Jane Eyre* and we're going to do a remake of it without telling anyone, simply by radically changing the setting.'" The result was *I Walked With a Zombie* (1943) which, in spite of its crass title, some place even above *Cat People*.

Betsy Connell (Frances Dee), a nurse, is engaged to attend the wife of sugar planter Paul Holland (Tom Conway) on an island in the West Indies. Her patient, Jessica Holland (Christine Gordon), is a beautiful woman reduced— apparently by a fever—to a mindless somnambulism. Betsy learns that the enmity between Paul Holland and his half brother Wesley Rand (James Ellison) results from Rand's love for Jessica Holland. Before long, Betsy finds that she herself is in love with Paul Holland.

Anxious for his sake to restore Jessica to mental health, Betsy seeks the help of the island's voodoo priests. Their rituals are interrupted by Mrs. Rand (Edith Barrett), mother of both Paul and Wesley. The priests send the giant zombie Carrefour (Darby Jones) to bring Jessica back to their temple. Mrs. Rand confesses that she has turned Jessica into a zombie to prevent her from breaking up the family. Deranged by this discovery, Wesley kills Jessica and, pursued by Carrefour, carries her body into the ocean. Betsy is left to start a new life with Paul. At intervals throughout this packed sixty-nine-minute movie, Tourneur uses the calypso singer Sir Lancelot "as a sort of Ancient Greek chorus commenting on the action."

As Robin Wood wrote, this film "hints at an equation between the zombie state . . . and emotional death" (just as *Cat People* can be read as an investigation in symbolic terms of sexual repression). In *Zombie*, Wood says, "all our moral preconceptions are subtly undermined, all motivations prove ambiguous or suspect, and even the apparently immaculate heroine is not exempt from doubt. The shadowy nocturnal world of the film is more than 'atmosphere': it becomes the visual expression of Tourneur's sense of the mystery and ambiguity underlying all human action and interaction." In the zombie Carrefour, Wood found "one of Tourneur's most haunting characters, guardian of the crossroads, speechless intermediary between the shadowy otherworld and the world of consciousness, at once knowing and unknowing; the enigma at the heart of Tourneur's universe." The director himself thought this picture "more profound than *Cat People*" and "less childish."

After these two masterly films, Tourneur's third and last collaboration with Lewton was sadly disappointing. *The Leopard Man* (1943) was adapted from a Cornell Woolrich thriller about a series of murders committed in a Mexican town by a man dressed as a leopard. It has some interesting touches but, as Tourneur said, it is no more than "a series of vignettes, and it didn't hold together." He was even more scathing about his next assignment, *Days of Glory* (1944), which marked Gregory Peck's screen debut as an American officer working with Russian partisans during World War II. Tourneur called it "atrocious."

The unevenness of his output resulted from his practice of accepting "all scripts that were offered to me, always, regardless of what the script was about." It was a policy urged upon him by his friend William K. Howard who, just before his death, spoke with regret of his own misguided fastidiousness. And indeed, Tourneur said, "How is one to know what can be done with a script? . . . Do you really know your own sensibilities so accurately that you can positively say: my kind of sensibility will make me do a good job with this scene rather than that one? You have to be a bit more modest and try to handle whatever you are given as best you can and allow your unconscious to go to work."

In fact, Tourneur was relatively well served by his next script, *Experiment Perilous* (1944), an atmospheric melodrama set in the early years of the century, and even better by *Canyon Passage* (1946), his first Western. Made not for RKO but for Universal, it stars Dana Andrews in one of his best roles as Logan Stewart, intent on building a mule freight line in mid–nineteenth-century Oregon but constantly distracted by his compassion for variously afflicted buddies. Susan Hayward is the spirited heroine, Onslow Stevens contributes a memorable cameo as a charmingly cynical gambler dying of tuberculosis, and the cast also includes Brian Donlevy, Andy Devine, and Ward Bond, with Hoagy Carmichael (who wrote "Ole Buttermilk Sky" for this film) as the wandering minstrel Hi Bennett.

In *Canyon Passage,* wrote Brian Garfield, "a richly assorted cast of characters inhabits a complicated and romantically realistic plot," while "Edward Cronjager's understated location color photography is magnificently suited to the story." Garfield regards this as "the only movie to have rendered on the screen a reasonably true reflection of the spirit and feeling of Ernest Haycox's storytelling, right down to his poetic and fascinating dialogue." The film was warmly received on release for its pace, gusto, and almost documentary evocation of frontier life, and its reputation has continued to rise.

Back at RKO, Tourneur made another film which—underrated at the time—has achieved the status of "a classic B-picture," *Out of the Past* (1947). It was adapted by "Geoffrey Homes" (Daniel Mainwaring) from his own highly complicated thriller *Build My Gallows High* (the film's title in Britain). Jane Greer plays the treacherous Kathie Moffat, who shoots her rich gambler boyfriend (Kirk Douglas) and lights out for Mexico with 40,000 of his dollars. Recovering, he hires a private eye (Robert Mitchum) to bring her back. Mitchum tracks her down, believes her protestations of innocence, and falls in love with her himself. She spoils their idyll by shooting his partner dead and returning to Douglas. Thereafter the double- and triple-crosses multiply past the comprehension of most reviewers, who tended to dismiss the movie as a disagreeably violent farrago of nonsense.

Since then, *Out of the Past* has come to be recognized as one of the best *films noirs* of the immediate postwar years, beautifully played by Mitchum and Greer, and lit and photographed to marvelous atmospheric effect by Nicholas Musuraca, who had been Tourneur's camera-

man on all three of his films with Lewton. It has been called "one of Tourneur's [visually] most elaborate works," telling its story "through a camera which never merely records but draws us implacably into a dark spider's web of conflicting emotions."

Out of the Past shares the cynicism and downbeat sophistication of such contemporary thrillers as Howard Hawks' *The Big Sleep* (and is almost as well written as that film). Feminist critics have condemned its portrayal of Kathie Moffat as "a personification of the bitch goddess archetype," and Stephen Farber has made the interesting suggestion that the frequency with which such anti-heroines appeared in the movies of the period "reflected the fantasies and fears of a wartime society, in which women had taken control of many of the positions customarily held by men."

In *Berlin Express* (1948), an American agricultural expert (Robert Ryan), en route from Paris to Berlin just after the war, defeats a neo-Nazi organization and rescues an enlightened German statesman (Paul Lukas) with the aid of an English teacher and a Russian officer. Lucien Ballard contributed some powerful images of the bombed-out ruins of Frankfurt to this often exciting film, but Tourneur was seriously handicapped by Merle Oberon's wooden performance as the great man's secretary and by the inflated democratic pieties of Harold Medford's script.

This "train film" was followed by a football movie, *Easy Living* (1949)—Tourneur's last as an RKO contract director—and then by *Stars in My Crown,* made in 1950 for MGM. Adapted by Margaret Fitts from Joe David Brown's novel, it is set in a small southern town just after the Civil War. It follows the gun-toting new parson (Joel McCrea) through his marriage to a local girl (Ellen Drew), a typhoid epidemic, a friendly dispute with the town skeptic (Alan Hale), a feud with a novice doctor (James Mitchell), and a brush with the Ku Klux Klan in defense of a black parishioner (Juano Hernandez).

Presented as the recollections of the parson's ward (Dean Stockwell), this gentle, sentimental movie, as one reviewer wrote, "breathes that magic sunlit air with which one likes to remember the best of one's childhood." Tourneur himself thought that his best films were *I Walked With a Zombie, Out of the Past* and, first and foremost, *Stars in My Crown,* a "truly American film" which "nobody has ever seen" and which, he said, "almost ruined my career."

Thereafter, Tourneur worked for one studio after another, making *The Flame and the Arrow* (1950) for Warner Brothers. An excellent swashbuckler set in medieval Lombardy, it has Burt

Lancaster performing marvels of acrobatics and bowmanship as an Italian Robin Hood, Nick Cravat as his equally accomplished mute henchman, and Virginia Mayo as a persecuted princess. After the mediocre British-made thriller *Circle of Danger* (1951) came two films for 20th Century–Fox—*Anne of the Indies* (1951), with Jean Peters turning pirate (and masquerading as a man) to avenge her brother's death, and *Way of a Gaucho* (1952). The latter starred Rory Calhoun as an Argentinian cowboy whose love of freedom leads him to murder, desertion from the militia, and the arms of Gene Tierney. Richard Boone is impressive as his inexorable pursuer Major Salinas, and Harry Jackson's Technicolor location photography is magnificent.

The five films Tourneur made over the next four years included three Westerns. *Stranger on Horseback* (1955) and *Wichita* (1955) both starred Joel McCrea as a lawman cleaning up terrorized communities, in the first as a gunslinging judge and in the second as Wyatt Earp. Both movies contain memorable sequences, and *Great Day in the Morning* (1956), set in Civil War Colorado, was admired by some for its "unusual attention to atmosphere," though Tourneur himself thought it spoiled by a badly constructed script.

His last important picture was *Curse of the Demon*, made for a minor British company in 1957. A return to the concerns of Tourneur's first successes, it has Dana Andrews as John Holden, an American psychologist (and representative of rational modern man). Holden goes to England to visit a colleague and finds that he has died while investigating a diabolist cult led by Dr. Karswell (Niall MacGinnis). Holden joins forces with the dead man's daughter (Peggy Cummins) to unmask Karswell as a fraud and a murderer, but soon finds frightening evidence that the man's claims to supernatural powers are only too well-founded.

As Michael Henry writes, in *Curse of the Demon*, as in *Cat People* and *I Walked With a Zombie*, the protagonist is invited "to explore an occult reality which, although reason can indeed throw light upon it, nevertheless remains beyond the imagination of the investigator. The unbelievable situation receives an irrefutable explanation, but not before it has put into question all the certainties of the person experiencing it. . . . The hero abandons his attempt to pronounce on the nature of the phenomenon registered by his senses, while the medium of the forces of darkness dies without relinquishing his secret. The signs retain their ambivalence right up to the end."

"I hate the expression 'horror film,'" Jacques Tourneur said. "For me, I make films about the supernatural because I believe in it. I believe in the power of the dead, witches. I even met a few when I was preparing *Curse of the Demon*. I had a long conversation with the oldest witch in England about the spirit world, the power of cats. . . . I happen to possess some powers myself." He was appalled by the crude process shots of an avenging demon inserted into the film against his wishes, though as Robin Wood says these "emphasize by contrast the restraint and delicacy of his treatment elsewhere."

None of Tourneur's subsequent films were of anything like the same quality, being ruined by poor scripts or interfering producers. He recognized this himself and made his last "very bad" picture in 1965. Before and after that he worked in television, a medium he despised. His *Positif* interview with Bertrand Tavernier gives some useful insights into his working methods—his concern for realism in the way his actors spoke, moved, entered a room with which they were supposed to be familiar or unfamiliar; above all, the importance he attached to light.

Tourneur said he had one basic principle he always imposed on his cameramen: "Only use natural, logical sources of light (a window, a lamp) and you must be able to see this source in every single shot. The presence of the light must be very concrete, you should be able to feel it. Cameramen hate that kind of thing because they have to rack their brains trying to find new solutions every time" but "in this way I also obtain very heavy contrasts which often lend dignity and truth to the human relationships. . . . It also changes the acting. . . . For instance, a young woman in order to be able to read a letter, will go to the oil lamp or to the window. . . . Another actor will unconsciously lower his voice. . . . I look for a very strong visual unity by using a type of framing and camera movement that is very simple. Everything must come from inside. It mustn't be superficial. I hate weird camera angles and distorting lenses."

For Robin Wood, Tourneur's camera style, "which is the most distinctive feature of his heterogeneous *oeuvre*, has two chief characteristics, movement and distance. The fluid long takes that keep the characters in long shot within the shadowy environments, branches and foliage obtruding darkly in the foreground, greatly enhance the haunting, sinister atmosphere of the suspense sequences; they also help to preserve the objectivity with which Tourneur customarily views his characters, and on which the ambiguities of the horror movies depend."

In Higham and Greenberg's *The Celluloid Muse*, Tourneur is described as an "extremely amiable, comfortable-looking, plump man" who "speaks slowly, diffidently, modestly, and carefully, anxious at all times to make every point absolutely clear." He and his wife lived in a Hollywood duplex, furnished with "quiet but exquisite taste," that once belonged to F. Scott Fitzgerald.

FILMS: Tout ça ne vaut pas l'amour (None of That's Worth Love), 1931; Toto, 1933; Pour être aimer (To Be Loved), 1933; Les Filles de la concierge (The Concierge's Daughters), 1934; They All Came Out, 1939; Nick Carter, Master Detective, 1939; Phantom Raiders, 1940; Doctors Don't Tell, 1941; Cat People, 1942; I Walked With a Zombie, 1943; The Leopard Man, 1943; Days of Glory, 1944; Experiment Perilous, 1944; Canyon Passage, 1946; Out of the Past (UK, Build My Gallows High), 1947; Berlin Express, 1948; Easy Living, 1949; Stars in My Crown, 1950; The Flame and the Arrow, 1950; Circle of Danger, 1951; Anne of the Indies, 1951; Way of a Gaucho, 1952; Appointment in Honduras, 1953; Stranger on Horseback, 1955; Wichita, 1955; Great Day in the Morning, 1956; Nightfall, 1956; Curse of the Demon (UK, Night of the Demon), 1957; The Fearmakers, 1958; Timbuktu, 1958; Forest Rangers, 1959; La Battaglia di Maratone (The Battle of Marathon/The Giant of Marathon), 1959; The Comedy of Terrors, 1963; City Under the Sea/War Gods of the Deep, 1965.

ABOUT: Garfield, B. Western Films, 1982; Higham, C. and Greenberg, J. The Celluloid Muse, 1969; Johnston, C. and Willemen, P. (eds.) Jacques Tourneur, 1975; Présence du Cinéma; Dwan, A. Jacques Tourneur, 1966 (in French); Roud, R. (ed.) Cinema: A Critical Dictionary, 1980; Siegel, J. Val Lewton, 1972; Thomson, D. A Biographical Dictionary of the Cinema, 1980; Wood, R. Personal Views, 1976. Periodicals—Cahiers du Cinéma May 1964, August 1966; Cinefantastique Summer 1973; Cinéma (France) February 1978; Cinématographe February 1978; Film Comment Summer 1972; Filmkritik March 1977; Monthly Film Bulletin (Britain) July 1971; Positif November 1971, April 1973; Présence du Cinéma Autumn 1966.

*"TOURNEUR," MAURICE (Maurice Thomas) (February 2, 1876–August 4, 1961), French director, scenarist, and producer, was born at Belleville, on the outskirts of Paris, where his father was a jeweler and manufacturer of imitation pearls. Maurice Tourneur had a younger sister who became a stage actress and a younger brother who managed a Paris theatre.

Tourneur's own artistic talents were already evident during his student years at the Lycée Condorcet in Paris. There he made friends with François Jourdain, a young painter through whom he met the poet Léon-Paul Fargue and other Parisian artists and writers. These contacts

MAURICE TOURNEUR

led to commissions that made it possible for Tourneur to begin his career as an artist and designer as soon as he graduated from the Lycée at the age of eighteen. He was soon established as a book and magazine illustrator, a designer of posters and fabrics, and an interior decorator.

After completing his obligatory military service (as an artillery officer in Africa), Tourneur worked in the studios of the sculptor Auguste Rodin and the muralist Puvis de Chavannes, assisting the latter on his sketches for the decoration of the great staircase of the Boston Public Library. According to George Geltzer, "such work, and such associations, fixed in Tourneur's psyche the conviction that the esthetical should be a part of whatever one does. And it was this mental attitude which later led Tourneur to try to make the esthetical a part of the motion picture."

Meanwhile, various assignments as a set designer had aroused Tourneur's interest in the theatre, and in 1900 he embarked on a new career as a stage actor (at that time adopting his pseudonym). The following year he joined Réjane's company and toured with her in England, Portugal, Spain, Italy, Algeria, and the United States. He subsequently worked with the actor-manager André Antoine as an actor and director at the Théâtre Antoine and the Odéon. He was married in 1904 to Fernande Petit, who acted with Antoine as Fernande Van Doren. Leaving Antoine after a dispute in 1909, Tourneur became an actor and designer at the Théâtre de la Renaissance in Paris.

In 1910 the actor Émile Chautard, a colleague of Tourneur's at the Renaissance, joined the film

°toor nûr´

production company Éclair as a director. He convinced Tourneur that the future belonged to the cinema rather than the stage, and in 1911 Tourneur went to Éclair as Chautard's assistant, working on a score of routine melodramas in 1911–1912 and acting in several of them. There has been some confusion between the films Tourneur made as an assistant to Chautard and his own first attempts as a director in 1912, but the latter probably include *Le Friquet*, adapted by Tourneur from a contemporary novel; a Grand Guignol piece called *Le Système du Docteur Goudron et du Professeur Plume (The Lunatics)*; and *Figures de cire (Waxworks)*, based on a book by André de Lorde. All of them starred Henri Roussel, as did the eight films Tourneur directed for Éclair in 1913.

A number of Tourneur's French pictures were successfully distributed in the United States, and by May 1914 he was sufficiently well established at Éclair to be sent to Fort Lee, New Jersey, as head of the small studio Éclair had built there. The job had been offered first to Émile Chautard, but he had declined it because he knew no English, whereas Tourneur's acting tours had made him fluent. Tourneur made two successful films for Éclair before the end of 1914, *Mother* and *The Man of the Hour,* both adaptations of William A. Brady stage hits and produced in association with that impresario's small movie company, Brady Motion Pictures. A series of complicated financial deals followed, typical of the period, which left the Fort Lee studios in the hands of the World Film Corporation (involving Brady and Lewis J. Selznick, among others) and Peerless Pictures (involving Selznick and Jules Brulatour). It was therefore these two companies that produced Tourneur's next two movies, *The Wishing Ring* (1914) and *The Pit* (1914).

The Wishing Ring was adapted by Tourneur from a romantic fantasy by Owen Davis about a poor clergyman's daughter whose passion for roses leads her into the strong arms of an earl's son. The director's first film of real merit and importance, it made a star of Vivian Martin, used naturalistic sets by Ben Carré, and showed Tourneur's determination to master all the newest techniques of the medium—close-ups, cutaways, time-cutting, parallel action, and a long tracking shot—introduced into a *mise en scène* that placed beauty of composition even above such technical flourishes.

As Kevin Brownlow has said, most films at that time "were photographed as from the front stalls of a cheap theatre," and this profoundly innovative movie was a revelation of the cinema's possibilities. Brownlow writes that *The Wishing Ring* "has pace, imagination, charm, two excel-

lent performances (from Alec B. Francis and Vivian Martin)—and, despite one or two awkward moments, a genuine quality."

Thanks to further wheeling and dealing, the seven pictures Tourneur made during 1915 were produced at Fort Lee under the auspices of Equitable-World. By this time, however, he had assembled a creative team that remained with him from film to film, giving his work a stylistic consistency and polish that were unaffected by the shifting fortunes of the moguls. Ben Carré became his regular art director, John van den Broek his cameraman, and the youthful Clarence Brown his editor; scripts not written by Tourneur himself (as most of the early ones were) were generally the work of Charles E. Whittaker or Charles Maigne.

The most notable of Tourneur's films for Equitable-World was *Trilby* (1915), adapted from George du Maurier's novel about the artist's model transformed into a great singer by the evil hypnotist Svengali. The film was a major critical and commerical success in the United States but was welcomed more grudgingly by the French critic Louis Delluc. He conceded that Clara Kimball Young's nude poses were "academically correct and beautifully done" and that Tourneur's *mise en scène* had given the story "a new look," but concluded that "many happy details do not compensate for others that are somewhat vulgar in taste."

At this time (June 1915), Tourneur gave an interview in the New York *Dramatic Mirror* in which he called for scenarists who would write exclusively or primarily for the screen, developing "a new sort of creative literary brain." He said that a director's first concern must be for his audience; his second, to achieve the new and unexpected. He insisted that it is the director who must be held responsible for a picture's faults and expressed his admiration for D. W. Griffith, who "stands alone. The secret of his success is good taste."

In 1916–1917 Tourneur worked at Fort Lee for Paragon-World, turning out half-a-dozen competent $25,000 movies with great efficiency. The most interesting of these was probably *The Hand of Peril* (1916), adapted by Tourneur from an Arthur Stringer story. The plot called for much movement from one room to another, and Ben Carré devised a set that showed a cross section of an entire house—an extremely unfamiliar notion—so that the action could be followed without loss of continuity.

Moving on to Lasky-Paramount (1917), Tourneur made three films with Olga Petrova, then (for Artcraft-Paramount) directed two Mary Pickford vehicles, *The Pride of the Clan* (1917), a "Scottish" drama shot on the Massachusetts coast, and *The Poor Little Rich Girl* (1917), a box-office hit adapted from an Eleanor Gates fantasy and notable for Carré's ingenious sets. Before he left Artcraft, Tourneur also directed a version of Ibsen's *A Doll's House* starring Elsie Ferguson, Holmes Herbert, and Alex Shannon, though this suffered by comparison with another screen version of the play, made the same year by Joseph de Grasse.

In 1918, working with Famous Players-Lasky-Paramount, Tourneur made two films that some critics regard as his best. *The Blue Bird* (1918) was adapted by Charles Maigne from Maeterlinck's symbolist drama in which two children set out to look for the blue bird of happiness, discover it in their own turtle dove, and lose it again, learning that the search must be endlessly renewed. The real stars of the movie were the sets designed by Carré in collaboration with the French painter André Ibels to create the fantastic world through which the children search.

Tourneur acknowledged the influence on *The Blue Bird* of the stage designer and theorist Gordon Craig and the artists associated with Diaghilev's Ballets Russes. He said that Craig's impressionism had released the stage from slavery to realistic detail and that he himself had similarly "brought stylization to the screen," trying in *The Blue Bird* "to sound the note of fragile fantasy. . . . We are not mere photographers. We are artists. At least I hope so. We must put on the screen, not literal reality, but an effect which will stimulate a mental and emotional reaction in the audience."

The Blue Bird caused a sensation, at least in intellectual circles, establishing Tourneur as the great aesthetician of the American cinema. Released a year before Robert Wiene's *The Cabinet of Dr. Caligari*, it preceded the German expressionists in its use of painted sets and its eschewal of naturalism in favor of a subjective notion of "essential" reality. *Prunella* (1918), based on another symbolist play by Harley Granville-Barker and Lawrence Houseman, and also designed by Carré and Ibels, was less innovative than its predessor, being virtually a transposition to the screen of Winthrop Ames's Broadway production, but it was nevertheless much admired by the reviewers.

The same year, Tourneur established his own production company with backing from Jules Brulatour and launched it with *Woman* (1918), inspired by Griffith's *Intolerance* and written by Charles E. Whittaker. It set out to capture the essence of womanhood in five scenes, beginning in the Garden of Eden and moving on to ancient Rome, Héloise and Abelard, a fantasy about a Breton fisherman and a mermaid, and the American Civil War. A prologue and epilogue shows the transformation of a social butterfly into a dedicated nurse. Unlike *Intolerance,* *Woman* made money; it also confirmed Tourneur's standing and popularity in the forefront of contemporary American filmmakers. A *Photoplay* poll in 1918 placed him fourth among the greatest living directors, preceded only by Griffith, Ince, and Cecil B. De Mille. *Woman* was nevertheless a costly achievement; while filming the Breton scene on the Maine coast, Tourneur's cinematographer John van den Broek was swept out to sea and drowned.

In 1918–1919 Tourneur's production company made five films, and during this period moved from Fort Lee to Hollywood, where Jules Brulatour rented space in the Goldwyn studios at Culver City. *Sporting Life* (1918), an adaptation of a witless British stage success, was notable for its atmospheric use of shadow and fog, preceding by a year Griffith's similar experiments in *Broken Blossoms.* Otherwise, none of these movies was of much merit; even Tourneur's ambitious version of Conrad's *Victory* (with a cast including Jack Holt, Lon Chaney, and Wallace Beery) failed to catch anything resembling a Conradian flavor. During 1919, moreover, Ben Carré left Tourneur to join Marshall Neilan, so that in the space of a year Tourneur had lost the two central members of his brilliant production team.

Tourneur's young editor and assistant Clarence Brown was also anxious to try his wings as a director, and in 1920 Tourneur supervised Brown's first movie, a highly successful piece called *The Great Redeemer*. Brown has always been generous in his praise of Tourneur, whom he regards as "the greatest of them all"—"my god." Tourneur's own next film of importance was his remarkable version, now lost, of *Treasure Island* (Tourneur-Paramount, 1920), with Lon Chaney and Charles Ogle, and a girl (Shirley Mason) in the Jim Hawkins role. Tourneur's masterly use of light, shadow, and silhouette brilliantly captured the sinister atmosphere of the story, making the picture, according to Jean Mitry, "the most advanced film so far shot in the United States, comparable to the best German films of the same period."

At the end of 1920 Tourneur left Jules Brulatour's financial shelter and joined Associated Producers, an independent company whose members included Thomas Ince, Mack Sennett, and Marshall Neilan, among others. Tourneur's first film for the new company was *The Last of the Mohicans* (1921), which many critics prefer to *The Blue Bird* and regard as his masterpiece.

The picture was scripted by Robert F. Dillon and shot by Charles Van Enger and Philip DuBois—much of it on location at Big Bear Lake. During the filming, Tourneur became ill from ptomaine poisoning and pleurisy, and the greater part of the location work was directed by Clarence Brown, working to Tourneur's instruction. It is for this reason hard to know who deserves most credit for the result. According to Jean Mitry, it is unlike Tourneur's earlier movies in that "the composition was that of a *cinéaste* rather than a designer—of photography and not of painting. Instead of fabricating an artificial world [like that in *The Blue Bird*], it was composed *with* the world."

However, a National Board of Review critic gives an almost opposite view, saying that its "superb" composition" "ranges in almost exact impression from that of the color sketches of Remington to that of the drawings of Doré. Here are color, tone, line, sky, cliff, forest and human figures at their most impressive in motion-photography. It is the forerunner of that impressionism which the future of the motion picture holds perhaps beyond that of all other arts. . . . Mr. Tourneur's shots with the camera are dramatic in themselves, his lights and shadows strike back on the nerves and make pictures beyond the picture on the screen, create moods and bring the onlooker into understanding with the feeling of the actors in the given situation of which the composition of the picture is an analysis in terms of line, light and shadow."

After *Foolish Matrons* (1921), a polished adaptation (codirected with Clarence Brown) of Don Byrne's "problem" novel about marriage, came *Lorna Doone* (1922). Scrupulously researched by Tourneur (always a stickler for accuracy), photographed by Henry Sharp, and designed by Milton Menasco, it was a notable spectacle. Associated Producers had by this time failed, and in 1922 Samuel Goldwyn hired Tourneur as director of his remake with Richard Dix and Mae Bush of *The Christian*, based on Hall Caine's melodramatic story of spiritual redemption. Tourneur took Van Enger and Menasco to England and the Isle of Man for the exterior shooting, filling Trafalgar Square with thousands of extras for the climactic scenes of mob violence. He greatly enjoyed this experience, which finally convinced him of the advantages of location shooting. *The Christian* was a hit, and so was *The Isle of Lost Ships* (1923), one of the series of movies he then made for M. C. Levee–First National. *The Brass Bottle* (1923) is also of some interest—a fantasy derived from a Frederick Anstey story, it is a tour de force of special effects.

By then Tourneur seems to have grown somewhat disillusioned with his situation in America. In 1924 he issued an odd, sour statement insisting that the cinema was an industry, not an art, and remarking (perversely, from the industry's point of view) that "today we have, I believe, too much beauty on the screen." None of his subsequent American films was of much interest, apart perhaps from the exotic *Aloma of the South Seas* (Paramount, 1926). In 1926 Tourneur prepared a version of Jules Verne's *The Mysterious Island* for MGM; a few days after shooting began, finding that he was expected to work under a supervisor, he quit and returned to Europe.

Tourneur's first film there was made in Germany—*Das Schiff der verlorene Menschen* (*Ship of Lost Men,* 1927), chiefly remarkable for giving Marlene Dietrich one of her first important roles. Back home in France, he made *L'Équipage* (*Last Flight,* 1928), an excellent war film based on a novel by Joseph Kessel. It was followed by Tourneur's first talkie, a well-carpentered thriller called *Accusée, levez-vous* (*Will the Accused Please Rise,* 1930), starring Gaby Morlay and Charles Vanel, that was immensely successful in France.

In 1931 Tourneur directed *Les Gaîtés de l'escadron* (*The Escapades of the Squadron*), based on Courteline's play about two young soldiers doing their military service in the cavalry in 1900. It was a fine remake of Tourneur's 1913 silent movie, with a cast that included Raimu, Henri Roussel, and the young Jean Gabin (taking the part that Roussel had played in the original). Notable among Tourneur's later talkies were *Avec le sourire* (*With a Smile,* 1936), a comedy of Lubitschean cynicism starring Maurice Chevalier; the sumptuous costume drama *Katia* (1938), with Danièle Darrieux and John Loder; and an impressive version of *Volpone* (1940), adapted by Jules Romains and Stefan Zweig, and starring Harry Bauer, Louis Jouvet, Charles Dullin, and Fernand Ledoux. Most of Tourneur's subsequent movies were thrillers, but excellent examples of the genre. The last of them, *Impasse des deux anges* (*Deadlock for Two Angels,* 1948), was photographed by Claude Renoir and starred Simone Signoret, Paul Meurisse, and Danièle Delorme.

In 1949 Tourneur lost a leg in a car accident. He made no more films, spending his retirement translating detective novels from English into French. A rather solitary and introspective man, pessimistic, cynical, and sarcastic, he separated from his wife in 1927. Their son Jacques Tourneur, who worked as assistant on a number of his father's later films, became a respected Hollywood filmmaker in his own right, director of *Cat People* (1942) and other notable horror movies.

Lewis Jacobs thought that "Tourneur's scenes of visual beauty . . . while often compensating for structural weakness, failed to cover the vast stretches of mere grandiosity and emptiness in his work. Vivid in light, shadow, composition, his films were devoid both of inner integrity and significant content. When his imagery was not overwrought, however, Tourneur did bring to the camera a splendor that affected later pictorial techniques. . . . Much of the atmosphere, design, and pictorial beauty of pictures today are due indirectly to Tourneur's influence." Louis Delluc called him "a sincere and thoughtful craftsman who fashions for himself that kind of atmosphere that gives form, style, and superior quality to a work. He does not transform a given theme. He rises above it. Its merits only shine the more."

George Geltzer called Tourneur "the first director to insist that each individual shot should be so composed as to produce a beautiful as well as a dramatic effect," and Kevin Brownlow said he was "one of the men who introduced visual beauty to the American screen." It is commonly said that Tourneur's "aestheticism"—the product of his early experience as an artist and designer in fin-de-siècle Paris—accounts for both the strengths and the weaknesses of his films. He himself often expressed ideas that were strikingly at variance with (and in advance of) his own practice. In a 1923 interview he insisted that filmmakers should abandon "the old-fashioned idea that everything should be beautiful, as in the old stage productions. . . . Instead we should be snapping . . . like an amateur in the street with his Kodak. Then we could get real life." The screen itself, he said, "is a beautiful thing—that rectangular white sheet. . . . We could show anything in the world up there. We have the money to do it. There is no limit to the possibilities. We'll do it someday. Some new generation of writers will come up—men who think in pictures instead of words."

FILMS: Le Friquet, 1912; Jean la Poudre, 1912; Le Système du Docteur Goudron et du Professeur Plume (The Lunatics), 1912; Figures de cire, 1912; Le Dernier pardon, 1913; Le Puits mitoyen, 1913; Soeurette (The Sparrow), 1913; Le Corso rouge, 1913; Mademoiselle 100 millions, 1913; Les Gaîtés de l'escadron, 1913; La Dame de Montsoreau, 1913; Monsieur Lecocq, 1914; Le Mystère'de la chambre jaune (Rouletabille I), 1914; La Dernière Incarnation de Larsan (Rouletabille II), 1914; Mother, 1914; The Man of the Hour, 1914; The Wishing Ring, 1914; The Pit, 1914; Alias Jimmy Valentine, 1915; The Cub, 1915; Trilby, 1915; The Ivory Snuff Box, 1915; A Butterfly on the Wheel, 1915; (with Émile Chautard) Human Driftwood, 1915; The Pawn of Fate, 1916; The Hand of Peril, 1916; The Closed Road, 1916; The Rail Rider, 1916; The Velvet Paw, 1916; A Girl's Folly, 1917; The Whip, 1917; The Undying Flame, 1917; The Exile, 1917; The Law of the Land, 1917; The Pride of the Clan, 1917; The Poor Little Rich Girl, 1917; Barbary Sheep, 1917; The Rise of Jenny Cushing, 1917; Rose of the World, 1918; A Doll's House, 1918; The Blue Bird, 1918; Prunella, 1918; Woman, 1918; Sporting Life (Lady Love), 1918; My Lady's Garter, 1919; The White Heather, 1919; The Life Line, 1919; Victory, 1919; The Broken Butterfly, 1919; (with Edward J. Mortimer) The County Fair, 1920; Treasure Island, 1920; The White Circle, 1920; Deep Waters, 1920; (with Jack Gilbert) The Bait, 1920; (with Clarence Brown) The Last of the Mohicans, 1921; (with Clarence Brown) Foolish Matrons, 1921; (with Robert Thornby) Lorna Doone, 1922; The Christian, 1923; The Isle of Lost Ships, 1923; The Brass Bottle, 1923; Jealous Husbands, 1923; While Paris Sleeps, 1923 (completed 1920); Torment, 1924; The White Moth, 1924; Never the Twain Shall Meet, 1925; Sporting Life, 1925 (remake); Clothes Make the Pirate, 1925; Aloma of the South Seas, 1926; Old Loves and New, 1926; Das Schiff der verlorene Menschen (Ship of Lost Men), 1927; L'Équipage (Last Flight), 1928; Accusée, levez-vous, 1930; Maison de danses, 1931; Partir!, 1931; Au nom de la loi, 1932; Les Gaîtés de l'escadron, 1932 (remake); Lidoire, 1933 (short); Les Deux orphelines, 1933; Le Voleur, 1933; L'Homme mystérieux (Obsession), 1934; Justin de Marseille, 1935; Koenigsmark (Crimson Dynasty), 1935; Samson, 1936; Avec le sourire, 1936; Le Patriote (The Mad Emperor), 1938; Katia, 1938; Volpone, 1940; Péchés de jeunesse, 1941; Mam'zelle Bonoparte, 1942; La Main du diable (Carnival of Sinners), 1943; Le Val d'enfer, 1943; Cécile est morte, 1944; Après l'amour, 1948; Impasse des deux anges, 1948. *Published scripts*—Volpone *in* L'Avant-Scène du Cinéma June 1977.

ABOUT: Brownlow, K. The Parade's Gone By, 1968; Mitry, J. Maurice Tourneur: 1876–1961, 1968 (in French); Spears, J. Hollywood: The Golden Era, 1971. *Periodicals*—L'Avant-Scène du Cinéma June 1977; Cahiers du Cinéma January 1962; Film Comment March–April 1973; Films in Review April 1961; Lumière du Cinéma July–August 1977; Motion Picture Magazine September 1918.

ULMER, EDGAR G(EORG) (September 17, 1900 or 1904–September 30, 1972), American director, producer, scenarist, and set designer, was born in Vienna of Jewish parentage. Little is known about his background or childhood, and even the year of his birth is uncertain. (Ulmer himself gave different dates in different interviews.) He studied architecture at the Viennese Academy of Arts, and philosophy at the University of Vienna, simultaneously finding time to work as an actor and assistant set designer at the Burg Theatre. In 1919 he found a job in Berlin as set designer with Decla-Bioscop, an offshoot of the UFA studios; his first assignment was to cut silhouettes for Paul Wegener's

EDGAR G. ULMER

second version of *The Golem* (1920). "Two
weeks later," he said, "I was building sets, because Pelitzer [the set designer] didn't care."
Around this time Ulmer also became assistant to
Max Reinhardt, then the dominant figure in
German theatre, and worked with him for three
years, accompanying him to the United States in
1923 with his production of *The Miracle.*

While in the States, Ulmer worked briefly for
Universal as a set designer before returning in
1924 to Germany. There he became production
assistant to F. W. Murnau (whom he had met
through Reinhardt). Ulmer stayed with Murnau
for the next six years, working on all his major
films from *Der Letzte Mann* (*The Last Laugh,*
1924) to *Tabu* (1931) but receiving only one
credit—as assistant art director of *Sunrise*
(1927). Murnau earned Ulmer's wholehearted
respect: "Murnau was the greatest . . . a man
who had the camera up there, a man who saw
pictures and built pictures in his head." In between assignments for Murnau, Ulmer also
worked on other UFA productions, notably Fritz
Lang's *Die Niebelungen* (1924) and *Metropolis*
(1927). When Murnau was invited to Hollywood
in 1927, Ulmer went with him, only returning
to Germany for a short stay in 1929, during
which he directed his first film.

Ulmer later claimed, in an interview with Peter Bogdanovich, that around 1925 he was working as a director for Universal, churning out two-
reel production-line Westerns at the rate of
twenty-four a year. "There were two Western
streets—on the uppper part of one, Willy
[Wyler] worked; on the lower part of the street
I worked. When Willy used the horses and the

cowboys, I had to do close-ups in my pictures.
Then when I ran out of close-ups, I'd get the
horses." According to Wyler's memoirs, Ulmer
was indeed working with him at this period,
though only as a junior assistant. Quite how he
managed both this and his work at UFA remains
something of a mystery.

The first film for which Ulmer can undoubtedly claim directorial credit is *Menschen am
Sonntag* (*People on Sunday,* 1929). This was a
semi-documentary, clearly influenced by contemporary social realism and by the Soviet
school of Dziga Vertov, following five supposedly typical Berliners through their day off. Ulmer's collaborators on the film read like a roll-
call of future Hollywood emigré talent: his codirector was Robert Siodmak, and both of them
shared script credit with Billy Wilder and Fred
Zinneman; the cinematographer was Eugen
Schüfftan. The picture has dated rather less than
most of its realist contemporaries, thanks partly
to the cheerful exuberance of the treatment, and
partly because Ulmer and his colleagues wisely
avoided preaching, letting the political implications of the subject speak for themselves. In
Kings of the Bs, Myron Meisel found in the film
"an innovative impulse for freedom and fresh air
not unlike the contemporaneous work of Jean
Vigo in France."

Back in America, after Murnau's death, Ulmer worked as a set designer for the Philadelphia Grand Opera Company and as an art
director at MGM, before directing his first
American film, *Mr. Broadway* (1933), an Ed Sullivan vehicle filmed largely on location in New
York. "Didn't like it at all, because Sullivan
forced it into one of these moonlight and pretzel
things. It was a nightmare, a mixture of all kinds
of styles." His next film was also independently
financed, this time by the American Social Hygiene Society. *Damaged Lives* (1933) attempted
a serious dramatic treatment of venereal disease
and predictably ran into trouble with the censors, who banned it from public showing. The
film's sponsors appealed against the ban and
won their case; the resultant publicity did neither the box-office takings nor Ulmer's reputation any harm at all. On the strength of it, Ulmer
was invited by Carl Laemmle to Universal,
where he made his finest prewar film, *The Black
Cat* (1934).

Universal had struck a lucrative vein of Gothic horror with the double success, in 1931, of Tod
Browning's *Dracula* and James Whale's
Frankenstein, starring, respectively, Bela Lugosi
and Boris Karloff. *The Black Cat* was the first
film to feature both actors. John Baxter (in
Hollywood in the Thirties) reckoned it "one of

the most interesting yet least typical horror films of the Thirties . . . another excursion into the Ulmer mystique, its people moved by motivations rooted in abstract attitudes of mind, concepts of duty and revenge so complex as to defy analysis." The plot bears not the least relation to the Poe story on which it claims to be based: Lugosi plays an Austrian doctor, newly released from captivity, who comes to take revenge on his daughter's seducer, a Satanist engineer (Karloff) who has built a futuristic castle on the ruins of the fort he betrayed to the enemy during the war. Into this situation blunder the mandatory pair of innocent young newlyweds; in the film's final, apocalyptic sequence they flee in horror, while Lugosi flays Karloff alive and the castle is blown sky-high by vast quantities of dynamite that have been buried—for no discernible reason—in its foundations. Scripted by Peter Ruric and atmospherically photographed by John Mescal, *The Black Cat* follows its own doomed, hermetic logic, throwing off haunting images en route—as when Karloff, having mysteriously resurrected his cat, paces solemnly through a subterranean gallery lined with the corpses of women enclosed in glass cases.

After *The Black Cat* Ulmer made no more films for Universal, nor indeed ever again directed for a major Hollywood studio. For the remainder of his career he worked in the precarious, hand-to-mouth world of the small, independent production companies, generally within miniscule budgets and hectic schedules. This seems not to have been a matter of necessity but largely through his own choice: "I did not want," he explained, "to be ground up in the Hollywood hash machine." For all their financial constraints, ramshackle sets, variable scripts, and frequently incompetent acting, these productions offered him the freedom to make the kinds of films that he wanted, free from outside interference. (Producers on Poverty Row were disinclined to interfere, since this could cost both time and money.) Many of Ulmer's films, not surprisingly under such conditions, were ludicrously bad, but the best of them, despite glaring lapses in production standards, display a consistent vision and an unmistakably individual style. "That a personal style could emerge from the lowest depths of Poverty Row," commented Andrew Sarris, "is a tribute to a director without alibis."

In the mid-thirties Ulmer directed a handful of low-budget independent Westerns, at least some of them under the pseudonym of John Warner, since he was apparently still under contract to Universal. The first of these, *Thunder Over Texas* (1934), was based on a story by Shirley Castle, who became Ulmer's wife. (Their

daughter, Arianne, acted in several of her father's postwar films.) In 1937 he was invited to New York to direct a film in Ukrainian for the immigrant community, *Natalka Poltavka* (1937). This independently financed musical comedy was warmly received, and Ulmer stayed on the East Coast to direct several more films in Ukrainian and Yiddish (and reportedly also in Spanish and Armenian). Of these the best-known was *Greene Felde* (*Green Fields*, 1937), a pastoral romance made on an $8,000 budget that proved a great box-office success and was named in Paris as Best Foreign Film of 1938. (Since Ulmer spoke no Yiddish, he codirected with Jacob Ben-Ami.) The film concerns a young Talmudic student finding love and happiness in the countryside, and it has remained a popular classic with Yiddish audiences; in *Film Comment* (January–February 1976), Patricia Erent observed that "*Greene Felde* is as fresh and airy as . . . *The Black Cat* was dark and haunted; its *mise-en-scène* is incomparably better than that of other Yiddish films." Ulmer himself thought it "one of the nicest comedies I ever made."

Besides these foreign-language movies, Ulmer also directed a musical for the black community, *Moon Over Harlem* (1939). "The singers . . . were paid 25¢ a day. . . . It was one of the most pitiful things I ever did. It was done on nothing. . . . But we made quite a good picture." From 1940 to 1942 Ulmer made a number of documentary shorts, including three commissioned by the National Tuberculosis and Health Association, aimed mainly at ethnic groups. During this period he also worked for the Ford Motor Corporation's motion picture department, and directed some teaching films for the US Army.

In 1942, through a connection at Pathé Laboratories, Ulmer met Leon Fromkess, newly appointed production supervisor of Producers Releasing Corporation. Financially backed by Pathé and an association of local state distributors, PRC was one of the most prolific of the Hollywood independents, turning out copious B movies, plus the occasional, more ambitious production that aspired to A-feature status. Over the next four years Ulmer directed eleven films for PRC, scripted several more, and helped plan the studio's entire output—though "plan" might be too grand a term. "At the beginning of the season, Fromkess would sit down with me and Neufeld [Sigmund Neufeld, head of PRC], and we would invent forty-eight titles. We didn't have stories yet; they had to be written to fit the cockeyed titles." Ulmer evidently enjoyed working at PRC: "I could use my crew, and I was nearly running the studio from a technical end. . . . At that time I was called 'the Capra of PRC.' It was a nice family feeling, not too much interference—if there was interference, it was only that we had no money, that was all."

The majority of Ulmer's films at PRC were shot on six-day schedules, which could involve, he later recalled, up to eighty camera setups a day. As might be expected, many of these films were sheer dross—little can be said, for example, to justify *Girls in Chains* (1943) or *Jive Junction* (1943)—but they also include some that are now numbered among Ulmer's most accomplished work: notably *Bluebeard, Strange Illusion,* and above all *Detour. Bluebeard* (1944), although apparently shot within the regulation six days, displays considerably higher production values than most of PRC's output, perhaps because it was one of Ulmer's pet projects. "On the one hand, I was absolutely concerned with box office and on the other I was trying to create art and decency, with a style." The film, evocatively photographed by Eugen Schüfftan, is set in late nineteenth-century Paris. John Carradine, at his most gauntly sinister, plays an artist who strangles his models after he has painted them—driven, like many of Ulmer's protagonists, by irrational, destructive (and ultimately self-destructive) impulses. "Ulmer's decor," suggested John Belton, "echoes the dark, abstract forces that motivate the character: after one murder, we follow him down into the Parisian sewers into which he dumps his victims. The underground setting works as a visual metaphor for the character's psychological interment in a horrible past he continues to re-enact."

The atmosphere of nightmare that pervades so many of Ulmer's films becomes explicit in *Strange Illusion* (1945), opening with a nightmare sequence, dreamt by the hero, which subsequently starts to come true in his waking life. The plot reworks *Hamlet*: a young man, dominated by the spirit of his dead father, discovers that the man about to marry his mother is his father's murderer. Despite some jarringly inadequate performances, the film creates a powerfully unsettling mood of helpless fatalism.

The bleakest and most complete expression, though, of the doomed world through which Ulmer's characters move, deprived of any semblance of free will, is *Detour* (1946), now generally agreed to be his masterpiece. Described by Don Miller (*Films in Review,* October 1961) as "sixty-five compact minutes of straight-forward cinema—lean, taut and no irrelevance," *Detour* can rarely have been equaled for its masterly use of scant materials. Using unknown actors and filming with no more than three minimal sets, a sole exterior (a used-car lot) to represent Los Angeles, a few stock shots, and some shaky back-projection, Ulmer conjures up a black, paranoid vision, totally untainted by glamour, of shabby characters trapped in a spiral of irrational guilt. The plot is coolly perfunctory. A New York piano player, Al Roberts, hitching to Los Angeles to see his girl, accepts a lift from a man who dies in accidental circumstances. Panicking, Roberts takes the dead man's car and is at once fastened upon by a shrill, predatory woman, Vera, who blackmails him into staying with her and urges him to further crime. He unintentionally kills her and proceeds gloomily along the highway, waiting for retribution to catch up with him.

"*Detour,*" wrote David Rodowick in a program note for the University of Texas Film Department (November 22, 1978), "may be one of the great unrecognized works in the absurdist style, rivaling even Kafka in its determination to strip life of logic and stability." Similarly, John Belton saw Ulmer's universe as "an irrational one governed by crazy nightmare more than by any coldly mechanical sense of fate," and his characters as "powerless prisoners of an irrational series of experiences which they can neither understand nor control." The film's structure takes the form of a flashback, as Al Roberts slumps dejectedly on the counter of a Nevada roadside diner, recalling the incomprehensible events that have robbed him of everything, including his identity. These events as we watch them are accompanied by his dulled, fatalistic narration, heightening the sense of subjective nightmare—as do Ulmer's characteristically allusive camera movements, "the most outstanding and unsettling element" (according to David Rodowick) "of his visual style." After Roberts has killed Vera, the camera begins a slow, unbroken pan around the dingy hotel room, starting on his stunned face and sliding in and out of focus on the various objects that link him inescapably with the dead woman. As Vera, Ann Savage gives a portrayal of a femme fatale that is breathtaking in its sheer repellence.

PRC's rickety finances finally collapsed in 1946. Ulmer tried to found a company of his own, Mid Century, but it survived only a few months, and he returned to working for a variety of small independent outfits. His first film after leaving PRC, *The Strange Woman* (1946), deployed a more than usually distinguished cast—Hedy Lamarr, George Sanders, Louis Hayward—in the tale of a woman who obsessively destroys the men that she loves. *Ruthless* (1948), described by Myron Meisel as "a *Citizen Kane* in miniature," also benefited from strong casting, with Zachary Scott as the unscrupulously acquisitive Horace Woodruff Vendig and Sydney

Greenstreet as his ruined enemy, Buck Mansfield. Although nominally motivated by financial greed, Vendig's compulsive treachery, clearly in excess of its ostensible aim, marks him as yet another of Ulmer's self-destructive obsessives. At the climax of the film Vendig and Mansfield drown, locked together, each grimly throttling the other as they sink beneath the nocturnal waters that lap Vendig's grandiose mansion.

During the last fifteen years of his active career, Ulmer increasingly filmed abroad, in Italy, Germany, or Spain, and turned his hand to a wide variety of genres, moving with ready facility from period swashbuckler (*The Pirates of Capri*, 1949), to Runyonesque comedy (*St. Benny the Dip*, 1951), to science fiction (*The Man From Planet X*, 1951), to horror movie (*The Daughter of Dr. Jekyll*, 1957), to historical epic (*Hannibal*, 1960). Few of these films display much of Ulmer's characteristic preoccupations or give the impression of being more than routine assignments. Exceptions were *Murder Is My Beat* (1955), a disturbingly fragmented thriller; and the finest of his later films, *The Naked Dawn* (1955).

David Thomson has described *The Naked Dawn* as "a wretched Western plot . . . transformed by Ulmer's masterly camera style. His sense of movement, of changing composition in elaborately long takes and his ability to record confined action with utter clarity, all show a debt to Murnau." The "wretched" plot, in fact, also owes something to Murnau's *Sunrise*: a naive peasant farmer and his wife are seduced by the romantic exoticism represented by a sympathetic outlaw. Ulmer derives a bleak lyricism from his Mexican locations, and as the outlaw, Santiago, Arthur Kennedy gives a fine performance of appealing ambiguity. François Truffaut cited *The Naked Dawn*, with its shifting loyalties and three-way central relationship, as his inspiration for *Jules et Jim*.

In 1961, after a pair of offbeat science fiction movies—*The Amazing Transparent Man* (1960) and *Beyond the Time Barrier* (1960), shot back-to-back in eleven days—Ulmer took over from the ailing Frank Borzage on *L'Atlantide* (1961), rewriting and completing the film. This mediocre version of the much-used story, though, scarcely bore comparison with earlier versions by Feyder (1921) and Pabst (1932). Ulmer's last film, which he also produced, was *The Cavern* (1965), filmed in Yugoslavia but set in Italy during World War II. The story of seven people from both sides of the conflict trapped together for several weeks in an underground cave, it formed, wrote Jean-Loup Bourget (*Monogram*,

October 1975), "the fitting, enigmatic epilogue to a highly individual, largely confidential career."

Like many American directors of his generation, Ulmer was little regarded—indeed, hardly heard of—until he was discovered by the French critics during the 1950s. In an article in *Cahiers du Cinéma* of April 1956, Luc Moullet hailed Ulmer as a neglected *auteur*, "le plus maudit des cinéastes," and detected in his films "the great solitude of man without God, the spiritual progression leading from yielding to sin to the salvation of the soul, from the emptiness of existence to happiness." Moullet adduced no examples for this analysis, and it would seem less than totally apt as a summary of, for example, *The Black Cat*—let alone *Detour* or *Ruthless*. But this and subsequent articles served to bring Ulmer to general attention; his films, hitherto rarely shown and largely considered beneath critical notice, began to be sought out and, at least by a minority, taken seriously.

Those critics who have written about Ulmer have generally concurred that his intensely distinctive personal vision, together with his technical mastery, succeeds in his finest films in overcoming the tawdriness of his material. "Far more than any other director," Myron Meisel asserted, "Ulmer represents the primacy of the visual over the narrative, the ineffable ability of the camera to transcend the most trivial foolishness and make images that defy the lame literary content of the dramatic material. . . . For Ulmer, a few sticks of wood in primary shapes, dressed with a modicum of essential props, when photographed in shadows that respect no natural light, can create a world cognizant of the legitimacy of nightmare." John Belton's view is similar: "[Ulmer's] set design, lighting, editing and camera technique frequently transcend the banality of his scripts and the weakness of his actors' performances."

Some writers, though, have maintained that to speak of Ulmer "transcending" his material may be misleading. In *Monthly Film Bulletin* (July 1982), Steve Jenkins pointed out that "the singular power of *Detour* seems largely due to the impossibility of separating its 'effect' or 'meaning' from the way it reflects-exemplifies the meagre conditions and speed of its own production. The style doesn't 'emerge from' these conditions, it *is* them"; and the same could be said of several of Ulmer's other movies. Myron Meisel commented that "Ulmer made no excuses and his work stands as it is—intransigent in its disregard for the normal niceties of conventional aesthetics." Given increasing critical notice, it may be that Ulmer is emerging from minority cult status and becoming recognized, in John Belton's words, as "one of his era's bleakest artists and one of *film noir*'s blackest visionaries." Certainly Ulmer's vision, despite his evident—and readily acknowledged—debt to Murnau, is uniquely personal, imbued with an idiosyncratic morality, more Old Testament than Christian, filled with a sense of doom and self-imposed retribution. "The road I have followed," he once remarked, "veers between Kafka and Camus. . . . I want to show that good and evil are always two sides of the same coin." In an interview towards the end of his life he observed ironically: "I really am looking for absolution for all the things I had to do for money's sake."

Altogether, Ulmer reckoned that he had directed one hundred and twenty-eight pictures, although most filmographies list only forty or so. After *The Cavern,* ill health prevented him from making any more films, and in 1969 he suffered the first of a series of strokes that left him increasingly disabled. During the last few months of his life Ulmer was almost totally paralyzed and could no longer speak, or move more than a single forefinger. He died of a final stroke in September 1972, at the Motion Picture Country Home in Woodland Hills, California.

—*P.K.*

FILMS: (with Robert Siodmak) Menschen am Sonntag (People on Sunday), 1929; Mr. Broadway, 1933; Damaged Lives, 1933; The Black Cat (House of Doom), 1934; (as John Warner) Thunder Over Texas, 1934; (as John Warner) From Nine to Nine, 1935; Natalka Poltavka, 1937; (with Jacob Ben-Ami) Greene Felde (Green Fields), 1937; Yankel der Schmidt (The Singing Blacksmith), 1938; Zaporozh za Dunayem (Cossacks in Exile/Cossacks Across the Danube), 1939; Die Klatsche (Fischke der Drume/The Light Ahead), 1939; Moon Over Harlem, 1939; Americaner Schadchen (American Matchmaker/The Marriage Broker), 1940; Cloud in the Sky, 1940 (short); Another to Conquer, 1941 (short); Let My People Live, 1942 (short); Tomorrow We Live, 1942; My Son, the Hero, 1943; Girls in Chains, 1943; Isle of Forgotten Sins/Monsoon, 1943; Jive Junction, 1943; Bluebeard, 1944; Strange Illusion/ Out of the Night, 1945; Club Havana, 1945; Detour, 1946; The Wife of Monte Cristo, 1946; Her Sister's Secret, 1946; The Strange Woman, 1946; Carnegie Hall, 1947; Ruthless, 1948; I Pirati di Capri (The Pirates of Capri/Captain Sirocco), 1949; St. Benny the Dip, 1951; The Man From Planet X, 1951; Babes in Bagdad, 1952; The Naked Dawn, 1955; Murder Is My Beat/ Dynamite Anchorage, 1955; The Daughter of Dr. Jekyll, 1957; The Perjurer, 1957; (with Carlo Ludovico Bragaglia) Annibale (Hannibal), 1960; The Amazing Transparent Man, 1960; Beyond the Time Barrier, 1960; L'Atlantide (Queen of Atlantis/Journey Beneath the Desert/Antinea l'Amante della Citta Sepolta), 1961; Sette Contro la Morte (The Cavern), 1965. *Published scripts*—Menschen am Sonntag (*as* Les Hommes le Dimanche) *in* Le Cinéma réaliste allemande (edited by R. Borde and others), 1965.

ABOUT: Belton, J. The Hollywood Professionals, vol. 3: Hawks, Borzage, Ulmer, 1974; Belton J. Cinema Stylists, 1983; McCarthy, T. and Flynn, C. Kings of the Bs, 1975; Sarris, A. The American Cinema, 1968; Thomson, D. A Biographical Dictionary of the Cinema, 1980. *Periodicals*—Cahiers du Cinéma April 1956, August 1961; Écran December 1972; Film Comment January–February 1976, August 1983; Film Culture 58–60 1974; Films in Review October 1961; Focus Spring–Summer 1973; Midi-Minuit Fantastique November 13, 1965; Monogram October 1975; Monthly Film Bulletin July 1982; Screen Education Autumn 1979–Winter 1980; Velvet Light Trap Summer 1972.

VAN DYKE, W(OODBRIDGE) S(TRONG) (II) (March 21, 1889–February 5, 1943), American director, was born in San Diego, California, the son of Superior Court Judge W. S. Van Dyke and the former Laura Winston, an actress before her marriage. Both sides of the family had distinguished origins, the Winstons descended from Virginia colonists and Western pioneers, the Van Dykes from Dutch settlers in New Amsterdam (New York). "Woody" Van Dyke's cousins included the clergyman and author Henry Van Dyke and the art historian John C. Van Dyke.

Judge Van Dyke died only nine days before his son's birth. To provide for him and herself, Laura Winston returned to the theatre, joining the Morosco Players, a traveling stock company based in San Francisco. Woody Van Dyke grew up in the theatre, making his stage debut at the age of three as Damon's child in *Damon and Pythias.* For the title role in *Ruth the Blind Girl* he was dressed in pinafore and curls, and proved so popular with audiences that he and his mother were offered the lead roles in *Little Lord Fauntleroy* with the touring Frank Redich Company, then in *The Prince and the Pauper* with the Howe Company.

As a child actor, Van Dyke traveled from coast to coast during the 1890s. He got what schooling he could in the towns where he performed, usually for runs of one to four weeks, but was educated and tutored primarily by his mother. On the road he developed into a fine athlete, horseman, and boxer, and also began to write stories and poems, specializing in Wild West themes. When his mother formed her own company, the Laura Winston Players, he began to take a hand in production as well as acting.

In 1903, when he was fourteen, Van Dyke went to live with his grandmother in Seattle while working his way through business school as a grocery clerk, janitor, waiter, door-to-door salesman, railroad attendant, and express wagon driver. He graduated, but finding that he had little taste for business, took off in search of ad-

W. S. VAN DYKE

venture, working as a miner, an electrician, a sailor, a singer in vaudeville, a mercenary in Mexico, an explorer and gold prospector in Alaska. Working as a lumberjack in Washington State, he met and married Zina Ashford and returned with her to the Laura Winston Players. Van Dyke and Zina thereafter divided their time between country life in Ashford, Washington, and touring with the Vin Moore Company, the Del Lawrence Company, and Alexander Pantages.

The Pantages tour took them in 1915 to Los Angeles, where Van Dyke was introduced to the film industry by the actor Walter Long, formerly of the Laura Winston Players. His first job was as an assistant director to Charles Brabin on *The Raven* (1915). After that he turned to screenwriting for the directors Lawrence Windom and Arthur Berthelet. For Windom he wrote *A Daughter of the City* (1915), *The Little Girl Next Door* (1916), and *The Discard* (1916); for Berthelet he scripted *The Little Shepherd of Bargain Row, Orphan Joyce, The Chaperon, The Return of Eve,* and *The Primitive Strain,* all 1916.

Walter Long had played Gus in *The Birth of a Nation* (1915), and he introduced Van Dyke to D. W. Griffith, who was impressed by his theatrical experience. Van Dyke ingratiated himself with Griffith by helping with character makeup for a Babylonian prince in *Intolerance* (1916) and found himself acting a number of roles in the picture, including a high priest, a groom, a Christian soldier, and a charioteer. Then Griffith took him onto his massive production team as a "captain," rehearsing hundreds of extras, before

promoting him to second assistant director and finally to first assistant under George Siegmann.

In this capacity, Van Dyke joined such talents as Allan Dwan, Erich von Stroheim, Tod Browning, Victor Fleming, and Jack Conway. He told Frank Nugent in a 1935 interview that he "was really just one of Griffith's 10,000 messenger boys. My salary was $3 a day, some days. But I was working under Griffith and that meant everything." And in 1937, in an article in the Buffalo *Evening News,* he said of his stint with Griffith, "It was a case of hero-worship, pure and simple, on my part. I took advantage of every opportunity to watch his technique. I'm still trying to do the things I learned from him."

After the commercial failure of *Intolerance,* Griffith was forced to trim his staff and Van Dyke was let go. He "just about starved to death" and was down to his last 35¢ when Fox bought a script from him for a thousand dollars. It was filmed as *Sins of the Parents* (1916), with Gladys Brockwell in her first starring role. Soon after, Van Dyke was hired by Famous Players–Lasky as assistant to James Young on *Oliver Twist* (1916), on which he also served as set dresser and negative cutter, and even directed one scene with Marie Doro. When James Young moved to the Essanay Studios in Chicago, owned by George K. Spoor and the Western star Broncho Billy Anderson, Van Dyke joined him there. In *Van Dyke and the Mythical City Hollywood,* his biography of the director, Robert Cannom says that he got his chance when Young was called off a picture to go to New York. Van Dyke (uncredited) finished the job, so impressing Spoor that he gave him a contract as writer-director and sent him to open a new Essanay studio in Culver City, California.

Immensely prolific from the beginning, Van Dyke directed ten five-reelers for Essanay in the course of 1917, scripting most of them himself. There were Westerns, melodramas, and action thrillers, several of them starring Jack Gardner and/or Edward Arnold and the last of them (*Sadie Goes to Heaven*) featuring his mother, Laura Winston, who appeared in several of his early pictures. They taught Van Dyke how to shoot economically and fast, and he began in his first year as a director to establish the reputation that later earned him the nickname "One-Take Woody."

Essanay suffered drastically when Charlie Chaplin left the company in 1916, and turned increasingly to the manufacture of cameras. Out of work again, Van Dyke was taken on as director and co-scenarist of a remarkable Western called *Lady of the Dugout* (1918). The film starred and was produced by Al Jennings, a former Western outlaw (pardoned by President Roosevelt) who turned to politics and then to filmmaking. According to Kevin Brownlow in *The War, the West, and the Wilderness*, Jennings had a passion for authenticity, shooting his films in old western towns with real westerners in rigorously unglamorous clothes, stained with dust and sweat.

Jennings claimed that *Lady of the Dugout* was based on a factual incident—a chance meeting between him and a woman (Corene Grant) abandoned by her husband and living close to starvation with her small son in a shelter dug out of the soil of the prairie. When she told him that she had been cheated out of her property by a Texas bank, he assembled his gang and set out to square accounts by robbing the bank. The movie was shot on location in Tehachapi, California. Brownlow writes that "although the story has been romanticized for the benefit of entertainment, *Lady of the Dugout* remains an outstanding Western. From the point of view of authenticity, it is one of the best surviving from that period."

Van Dyke served in the Marines in 1918–1919, but to his chagrin the war was over before he had completed his training. He returned to Hollywood and in 1920 was divorced from his first wife. In 1920–1922 Van Dyke coscripted and directed five fifteen-episode serials, beginning with *Daredevil Jack* (1920), which starred the boxer Jack Dempsey. Van Dyke received a $500 weekly bonus from Pathé for undertaking to complete the fifteen episodes in twelve weeks. *The Hawk's Trail* followed the same year, with King Baggott and Rhea Mitchell, then *Double Adventure* (1921), with Charles Hutchinson and Josie Sedgwick. Van Dyke's other two serials starred Ruth Roland: *The Avenging Arrow* (1921), codirected by William Bowman, and *White Eagle* (1922), codirected by Fred Jackman; Van Dyke, uncredited, also handled the action sequences for another Ruth Roland serial, *Ruth of the Range* (1922), directed by Ernest C. Warde.

All but one of Van Dyke's serials were made for Pathé, the exception being *The Hawk's Trail*, coscripted and produced by an independent, Louis Burston. In 1922, leaving the serials behind, Van Dyke directed two features for Burston, *The Milky Way* and the society melodrama *Forget Me Not*, and one—*According to Hoyle*—for another independent producer, David Butler, who also starred in this comedy. The same year Van Dyke went to Fox for a Buck Jones Western, *Boss of Camp Four*.

After a difficult year working for various Poverty Row studios, he returned to Fox and in 1924–1926 made six more Buck Jones Westerns, a series to which both John Ford and William Wellman had contributed. These movies included *Hearts and Spurs* (1925) with the young Carole Lombard (who had to be tied onto her horse) and *The Gentle Cyclone* (1926) with Oliver Hardy playing a sheriff. Van Dyke took a break from Buck Jones in 1925 to direct *Barriers Burned Away*, based on a novel by Edward Payson Roe and featuring an impressive recreation of the Chicago fire of 1871.

The Buck Jones movies were very profitable, and when MGM decided to follow the trend with a series of Westerns starring Colonel Tim McCoy, they hired Van Dyke to direct them. Lesley Selander, his assistant at Fox, joined him at Metro, where Van Dyke began to assemble the team that worked with him for many years: Selander, the cinematographer Clyde De Vinna, stuntman Bob Rose, key grip "Pop" Arnold, and property master Harry Albiez.

Tim McCoy, a former Wyoming Indian Agent, was an authority on Indian customs and dialects. He and Van Dyke shared a concern for historical accuracy and authenticity and (for the period) an unusually enlightened attitude towards the Indians. In these respects, and in their superior production values, the McCoy Westerns were far more rewarding than the Buck Jones pictures, as was evident with the first of them, *War Paint* (1926). This was a cavalry-versus-Indians saga set in the 1880s, from a Peter Kyne story. De Vinna shot the film on location at the Wind River Reservation in the Grand Tetons. Van Dyke used Cossack horsemen for riding stunts but also cast genuine Shoshones and Arapahoes both as extras and in featured roles.

Winners of the Wilderness (1927) costarred McCoy and Joan Crawford in a story of the French and Indian Wars of the 1750s and included several scenes in Technicolor. *Motion Picture News* praised the period costumes and "the interesting sequences . . . in which are seen such historical figures as Washington and Braddock. The latter's disastrous defeat is the film's highlight and is carried out with realism."

California (1927), another Peter Kyne story, dealt with the Mexican War of 1848 and was followed by a McCoy "Eastern," *Foreign Devils* (1927), set in China during the Boxer Rebellion of 1900. Van Dyke and McCoy returned to the old West with two films scripted by Madeleine Ruthven and Ross B. Willis, *Spoilers of the West* (1927) and *Wyoming* (1928), produced for MGM by the young David O. Selznick. He and Van Dyke impressed the front office by going out to rugged Colorado locations and shooting the two pictures back-to-back for $120,000, instead of one for $90,000.

William K. Everson wrote in *American Silent Film* that "the McCoy westerns were unique but also problematical. They contained too much history and romance and not quite enough continuous action to be juvenile-oriented, yet at the same time they were too short, snappy, and simplistic to have major adult appeal." But Everson concluded that it was "a thoughtful, well-made, . . . and still most impressive series."

In November 1927, MGM's young production chief Irving Thalberg sent the great documentarist Robert Flaherty to Tahiti to film *White Shadows in the South Seas*, from Frederick O'Brien's novel about a drunken white doctor (Monte Blue) and an island girl (the unknown Raquel Torres). Van Dyke was sent along as associate director to make some linking footage and to serve in effect as a line producer; according to Kevin Brownlow his selection "was entirely due to his superb generalship on location." The arrangement never worked. Forced to follow a set scenario, Flaherty, as Brownlow says, "suffered a creative block." In the end he resigned and Van Dyke finished the picture, returning home in April 1928. Equipped by Douglas Shearer with synchronized sound effects (including the roar of MGM's trademark Leo the Lion) and musical score, it was premiered in July 1928 as MGM's first sound film.

Van Dyke's mentor D. W. Griffith said at the premiere that "*White Shadows in the South Seas* is a work of art and Woody Van Dyke is the artist who brought it into being." Contemporary reviewers mostly agreed, but more academic critics have tended to dismiss it as a mere travesty of the masterpiece Flaherty would have made of it, complaining also that it skirted the central theme of O'Brien's book, the destructive effects of white exploitation in the islands. Brownlow disputes this, calling the film "as sharp an attack on the exploitation by the white man as had been made up to that time. . . . The film is as romantic as anything Flaherty might have made, and its documentary detail is as rich," although "one does not know the islanders" as one would in a Flaherty film; they merely provide "a picturesque background." Luis Buñuel regarded the picture as one of the ten best ever made.

The exoticism of *White Shadows* (and its barebreasted Tahitian women) made it a huge box-office success, and De Vinna collected an Oscar for his photography. Though he had suffered dreadfully from the heat in Tahiti, Van Dyke returned to the South Pacific in the fall of 1928 to film *The Pagan* (1929) in the Tuamotu Archipelago. Starring Ramon Novarro and Renée Adorée, it was a nine-reeler like *White Shadows*, shot silent but with music and sound effects added. Another box-office smash, it launched Ar-

thur Freed and Nacio Herb Brown's hit, "Pagan Love Song." MGM renewed Van Dyke's contract and he became one of the mainstays of the studio's directorial staff along with King Vidor and Victor Fleming, remaining with MGM for the remainder of his career.

The director had only just returned from the South Pacific when, as he said, "*Trader Horn* burst forth as the literary sensation of the day. 'Why not send Van Dyke to Africa to make it?' said the boys at MGM. And so we were off again." "Trader Horn's" real name was Alfred Aloysius Smith. He was a penniless but courtly old adventurer whose improbable reminiscences of younger days on the Ivory Coast were edited by the South African novelist Ethelreda Lewis and became a best seller. Van Dyke's expedition left for Africa early in 1929, landed in Mombasa, and over the next six months traversed Tanganyika, Uganda, Kenya, and the Congo. There were thirty-five whites and nearly two hundred Africans traveling in twenty-five trucks—the largest safari on record. MGM's decision to shoot the film with sound added two seven-ton sound trucks and a nine-ton generator truck to the procession.

Van Dyke shot 450,000 feet of film in Africa and, as Kevin Brownlow says, the picture's documentary material, with (mostly) on-the-spot recordings, is "of priceless value . . . covering four African colonies, thirty-five varieties of big game, and fifteen tribes." The cast and crew were often in mortal danger from disease, the lethal tse-tse fly, and assorted predators, and Van Dyke staged "buffalo stampedes, rhino charges, and general zoological mayhem." By way of plot, he used one of the book's wilder anecdotes, about an English missionary's daughter abducted by bloodthirsty Isorga tribesmen to serve as their reluctant goddess. She is rescued by Trader Horn (Harry Carey) and his young friend Peru (Duncan Renaldo), son of the Peruvian president, and marries Peru.

The heroine was portrayed by a stunning blonde "discovered" in a ballyhooed "talent" contest and dubbed "Edwina Booth." Brownlow says that "her scanty costume and her sado-masochistic behavior with a whip would never have survived the censors in a less educational picture." In spite of these attractions and Harry Carey's assured and relaxed performance, the film's acting honors were stolen by Mutia Oomooloo, a giant Wagomba farmer of enormous serenity and presence who played Horn's faithful gunbearer Renchero.

Unfortunately, the fascinating material that Van Dyke brought back from Africa included nothing resembling a coherent story line, and

Trader Horn was almost abandoned. In the end, additional dialogue scenes were shot secretly on the MGM back lot and skillfully integrated. For additional excitement, Van Dyke went to Mexico (out of reach of the Society for the Prevention of Cruelty to Animals) and set half-starved predators loose on deer and monkeys. Two years after the film's release, the wretched Edwina Booth (who had been paid only $100 a week for working half-naked in the bush) sued MGM for a million dollars, claiming that her health had been ruined and her marriage wrecked, while Renaldo's wife sued her for alienation of affection; Booth got $37,000. Rumors that she died three years later of a mysterious tropical disease are apparently untrue.

These squalid facts, needless to say, do not figure in Van Dyke's own account, *Horning Into Africa* (1931). And in spite of them, *Trader Horn* is a magnificent portrait of a partly imaginary Dark Continent, savage and beautiful. Ernest Hemingway said that it was when he saw *Trader Horn* that he fell in love with Africa, and he was by no means alone. The picture was nominated for an Oscar, received rave reviews, and made a profit of almost a million on its $1.3 million investment.

Guilty Hands (1931), a play adaptation starring Lionel Barrymore and Kay Francis, was followed the same year by a remake of Maurice Tourneur's silent *Never the Twain Shall Meet,* from Peter Kyne's best seller about a rich young American (Leslie Howard) and his doomed love for Tamea, an untamed Polynesian beauty (Conchita Montenegro). She can no more adapt to servants and store-bought shoes in San Francisco than he can to the languid life of her coral atoll, and he ends in alcoholic despair. Shot by Merritt Gerstad partly on location in Hawaii, it was generally well received.

The Cuban Love Song (1931) was another cross-cultural love story, lifted from *Madame Butterfly.* The opera star Lawrence Tibbet plays an American marine who falls for a Creole peanut vendor (Lupe Velez) in 1917 Havana. They are separated by the war and years later the marine, now married to a society woman back home in San Francisco, returns to Cuba. He finds that his mistress has died of a broken heart, but is able to claim their son. Jimmy Durante and Ernest Torrence provided light relief, and the Dorothy Fields–Jimmy McHugh hits included "Tramps at Sea" and "The Cuban Love Song," as well as the authentic Cuban song "The Peanut Vendor."

Miles Kreuger, in his notes for the Museum of Modern Art series "The Roots of the American Musical Film," wrote that this movie, "photographed with a soft, dreamy delicacy by Harold Rosson and directed with warmth and affection by W. S. Van Dyke . . . , transforms a familiar, hackneyed love triangle into a work of astonishing beauty." Kreuger added that *The Cuban Love Song* is "one of the few talkies in which . . . [Lupe] Velez has the chance to reveal her exquisite sensitivity as a serious actress, in addition to her beauty and flair for fiery comedy."

MGM still had in its vaults hundreds of thousands of feet of material shot for *Trader Horn* and never used. Irving Thalberg was approached by a representative of Edgar Rice Burroughs Inc. with the suggestion that this material could be put to work in the first sound version of the Tarzan stories. Seeing the possibilities, MGM established a budget of $1 million for *Tarzan, The Ape Man* (1932), shot over five months near Lake Sherwood. Van Dyke, the obvious choice as director, demanded and got an artificial jungle of twelve acres, with a river and a native village, as well as a whole zoo of animals. He also had his two favorite cinematographers, Clyde De Vinna and Harold Rosson. Cyril Hume wrote the script, and the dialogue, improbably enough, was written by Ivor Novello, better known as the creator of marshmallow musicals.

Elmo Lincoln and other early screen Tarzans had all been jungle aristocrats, courteous and pure. Van Dyke overturned this convention, conceiving of a wilder ape-man, more at ease with animals than people, more physical than verbal. Charles Bickford, Joel McCrea, Douglas Fairbanks Jr., and Clark Gable were all tested but found "too civilized." It was the scenarist Cyril Hume who suggested the Olympic swimming champion Johnny Weissmuller. With his magnificent physique, feline grace and speed of movement, and gaucheness of manner, Weissmuller was everything Van Dyke had imagined. Teamed with Maureen O'Sullivan as Jane, he became the definitive Tarzan. He appeared in eleven films up to 1948, many of them using and re-using *Trader Horn* process shots.

David Robinson, discussing a revival twenty-five years later, wrote that *Tarzan, the Ape Man* "shows an astonishingly clear and unmixed romantic spirit," especially in the sequences involving Tarzan and Jane: "Some of their scenes together—one in which they bathe, with a good deal of impolite horseplay from Tarzan; another in which she tries to teach him some basic words; and the final fade-out, ridiculous but touching, as the two stand silhouetted against the sky, a chimpanzee nursed between them—are completely genuine and consistent in feeling."

After this blockbuster, MGM handed Van Dyke a low-budget drama, *Night Court* (1932), about political corruption in the courts, and then two lightweight entertainments starring Myrna Loy. *Penthouse* (1933), co-starring Warner Baxter, is a neglected and witty little thriller scripted by Frances Goodrich and Albert Hackett. *The Prizefighter and the Lady* (1933) cast Loy opposite the future heavyweight champion Max Baer, throwing in Jack Dempsey and Primo Carnera for good measure. Harvé Dumont, in his monograph (in French) on Van Dyke, wrote that "this joyous farce . . . compares favorably with the best comedies of Hawks" (who in fact had begun shooting the picture before Van Dyke took over). Frances Marion's original script was nominated for an Oscar.

After so many journeys to the tropics, Van Dyke went north for his last great filmmaking expedition. *Eskimo* (1933) was produced (like many of Van Dyke's films) by Hunt Stromberg and adapted by John Lee Mahin from books by the Danish explorer Peter Freuchen, who had lived among Eskimos for twenty-seven years. Freuchen accompanied Van Dyke to Alaska in June 1932 on the schooner *Nanuk* (later used in Victor Fleming's *Treasure Island* and Frank Lloyd's *Mutiny on the Bounty*). Van Dyke set up camp at Teller, in a region where he had prospected for gold in his youth. He recruited his cast mostly from among local Eskimos (who speak their own language in the film, with subtitles), casting Freuchen and himself as the white villains of the story.

Problems began when the Eskimo lead actor quit after a technician had made advances to his wife. He was replaced by Ray Wise, an assistant cameraman of Eskimo origins, and Van Dyke started again. Meanwhile, the temperature had fallen to 65° below, and the expedition spent the winter of 1932 on the *Nanuk* in Grantley Harbor. They went back to work as soon as it was humanly possible, afflicted by snowstorms, frostbite, frozen equipment, hunger, and illness, and threatened by walruses and polar bears. Van Dyke returned to Culver City in August 1933 and spent the rest of the year on retakes and editing.

Eskimo (called *Mala the Magnificent* in Britain) tells the story of the hunter Mala (Ray Wise). His life is hard but happy until the day a white man's ship arrives. Eager to buy a gun, Mala seeks out the captain (Freuchen), who asks him to kill a whale for the crew. During the hunt (one of the film's most exciting sequences) the captain rapes Mala's wife. Mad with rage, Mala harpoons the captain to death. He saves the life of Mounties sent to arrest him but is nevertheless imprisoned by their officer (Van Dyke). He escapes, retrieves his wife, and heads north. The Mounties are about to recapture the couple when the ice pack begins to break up. Mala and his wife drift away from their pursuers on an ice floe, and the Mounties, in an access of belated humanity, lower their guns and let them go.

"As in *Trader Horn*," wrote Hervé Dumont, "Van Dyke sustains for two hours an unflagging rhythm, swept along by his delight at filming in the complete freedom that he loved, scorning the most elementary rules of dramatic construction. His crazy virtuosity in combining exteriors, transparencies, documentary, and fiction prefigures the most modern research into the connections between reality and fiction." Released at the end of 1933, *Eskimo* had great success in Europe but less in the United States, though it received one Oscar, for Conrad Nervig's editing.

Oliver LaFarge's novel *Laughing Boy* won a Pulitzer and caused a furor with its story of a young Navajo who accidentally kills his wife in a fight with the white man who has prostituted her. William Wyler tried to film it at Universal, but Carl Laemmle Jr. lost his nerve and sold the rights to MGM. Van Dyke shot the film under very difficult conditions in Arizona, but his desire for ethnic authenticity was frustrated by Mayer's insistence on casting Ramon Novarro and Lupe Velez in the leading roles, and the picture was dreadfully mutilated to appease the newly constituted Legion of Decency.

Van Dyke next proposed to film Melville's *Typee,* but withdrew when he found that this script also had been bowdlerized. Hervé Dumont suggests that, after that, "Van Dyke resigned himself progressively to filming whatever his masters at MGM handed him. Only some intimate friends, in fact, divined the secret bitterness that possessed him until his death, for want of having fully satisfied his hunger for adventure and his creative spirit. . . . *Eskimo* and *Laughing Boy* were among the last works that he took really to heart. . . . Disillusioned, he was henceforth exactly what the MGM publicity proclaimed: 'Hollywood's most amazing man in captivity.'"

It is very difficult to judge the truth of this claim. Van Dyke liked to say that he hated going to remote and uncomfortable places on location, but against this must be set his youthful journeys in search of adventure and his lifelong membership in various travelers' clubs. If he became embittered at MGM, however, there is no sign of it in the string of excellent and highly successful studio pictures he made there during the middle 1930s.

Van Dyke began this phase of his career with

Manhattan Melodrama (1934), produced by Selznick, photographed by James Wong Howe, and with dialogue by Joseph L. Mankiewicz. Clark Gable and William Powell star as East Side orphans who remain buddies even when Gable becomes a reckless gambler and eventually a killer, and Powell the D.A. who regretfully sends him to the chair. Myrna Loy, in her third film with Van Dyke, is the woman who deserts the former for the latter. Most reviewers recognized it as "formula stuff saved by the highly efficient acting and direction," though the fatuous original story of Arthur Caesar for some reason won an Oscar. Its box-office success was fortuitously enhanced when John Dillinger, Public Enemy No. 1, went to see it at the Chicago Biograph on July 22, 1934 and emerged blinking into a hail of FBI bullets.

Myrna Loy had until then been cast mostly as a slinky adventuress. Van Dyke recognized her gift for comedy and her rapport in *Manhattan Melodrama* with William Powell. Against studio advice he cast them in his screen version of Dashiell Hammett's *The Thin Man* in 1934, instituting a new phase in the history of the detective movie and contributing also, it has been suggested, to the development of another genre, the screwball comedy. To avoid front-office intervention, Van Dyke (working again with James Wong Howe, and improvising frenetically) shot the film in sixteen days, presenting MGM with a marvelous *fait accompli.*

Powell played Nick Charles, an amateur detective who relies a good deal on inductive reasoning and booze; Loy was his wife Nora, rich, charming, and as witty as her husband, though sometimes dangerously short on common sense: "two slender sophisticates," David Thomson called them," "smiling haughtily at one another through a mist of wisecracks." The couple are childless but possess a fox terrier of considerable character named Asta.

The Thin Man's plot concerns the mysterious disappearance of an inventor and the murder of his mistress, solved at a dinner party to which all the suspects have been invited. The movie works extremely well both as a thriller and as a witty comedy, but what gave it its unique character was the relationship between Nick and Nora Charles—the fact that this husband and wife are quite evidently and unsentimentally in love. As a contemporary reviewer wrote in the London *Times,* "the two of them suggest in a peculiarly personal and intimate way, assisted by an apt and economic dialogue, an affection which has its counterpart in many homes but seldom finds its reflection on the screen."

This film, which it has been said revitalized the institution of marriage for thousands of depressed Depression moviegoers, won Oscar nominations for best picture, best direction, best actor, and best adaptation (by Frances Goodrich and Albert Hacker). One of MGM's greatest successes of the 1930s, it earned over $2 million. Van Dyke himself made three more "Thin Man" movies, and the characters (though not Loy and Powell) were featured in a television series.

Goodrich and Hacker also collaborated on the script of *Hide Out* (1934). Robert Montgomery stars as a gangster on the run who finds refuge with a sweet-natured Connecticut farm girl (Maureen O'Sullivan) and snatches an idyllic respite before the police catch up with him. This bittersweet story reminded Hervé Dumont of both Frank Borzage and Tay Garnett, though he thought its "delicacy and humor . . . left no doubt of its paternity." C. A. Lejeune wrote: "A few more pictures like this and *The Thin Man,* and we shall be putting W. S. Van Dyke near the top of the American directors; he has grown immeasurably in authority during the last year, shows no longer any signs of being story-bound, and still gives the impression that his work is increasing in power and resource."

Van Dyke had another hit the same year with *Forsaking All Others,* a triangular comedy-romance in which Joan Crawford is forsaken by Robert Montgomery but not by Clark Gable. Joseph L. Mankiewicz scripted and Gregg Toland shot the film, partly on location in the Sierra Nevadas (here doubling for the Adirondacks). "It has enough first-rate lines, smart cutting, and nimble action to make the specialist realize that he is watching a Van Dyke picture," wrote one reviewer.

The director was married in 1935 to Ruth Mannix, niece of the MGM vice president Eddie Mannix. He worked uncredited on several movies around this time, among them Richard Boleslawski's *The Painted Veil* (1934) and Jack Conway's *A Tale of Two Cities* (1935). Van Dyke boasted that he never turned down an assignment. It is, all the same, startling to consider that the creator of *Trader Horn* and *Tarzan, the Ape Man* could then turn with equal success to the operetta, a genre ignored since the early days of the talkies.

The project was Victor Herbert's *Naughty Marietta,* about a French princess in eighteenth-century Louisiana who is rescued from pirates by a handsome officer and renounces wealth and position to marry him. Characteristically, Van Dyke shot this soufflé on location in the Everglades (photographer William Daniels) and included genuine Natchez Indians in his cast. For his leads he had the MGM singing star Jeanette

MacDonald and a newcomer from the Philadelphia Civic Opera, the baritone Nelson Eddy. Warbling such hits as "Ah, Sweet Mystery of Life" in exotic locales and costumes, the couple perfectly fulfilled the Depression audiences' hunger for escapism and were established forthwith as an American institution—though known in some circles as "the iron butterfly and the singing capon." (They are spoofed by Madeline Kahn and Peter Boyle in Mel Brooks' *Young Frankenstein,* 1974.)

Naughty Marietta (1935) won an Oscar for Douglas Shearer's sound recording and a nomination as best picture. It was one of MGM's alltime moneymakers, and Van Dyke's second MacDonald-Eddy vehicle, the Oscar Hammerstein operetta *Rose Marie* (1936), was even more profitable. This time MacDonald is a Montreal prima donna searching for her criminal brother (James Stewart) in the Canadian wilderness, where she encounters a Mountie (Eddy) grimly engaged in the same pursuit. Love eventually triumphs over family loyalty, allowing the couple to sing the title song and "The Indian Love Call," among other delights. The genteel MacDonald is pleasantly discomfited in a scene in which she trills prettily for her supper in a backwoods bar and is totally ignored, while a riproaring hip-wriggling number belted out by Gilda Gray brings the audience cheering to its feet.

Rose Marie was released in 1936 and inaugurated an *annus mirabilis* for Van Dyke. It was followed by the film some regard as his masterpiece, *San Francisco.* MGM gave Van Dyke a budget of $4 million, a screenplay by Anita Loos (with dialogue by Erich von Stroheim), and a cast headed by Clark Gable, Jeanette MacDonald, and Spencer Tracy. The story opens on New Year's Eve 1905. Gable plays Blackie Norton, a godless Barbary Coast saloon owner who provides penniless opera singer Mary Blake (MacDonald) with a job and a chance to sing "San Francisco" and "Would You?" Blackie falls for Mary but so does businessman Jack Holt, who puts Blackie out of business. Tracy, as the rambunctious priest Father Mullin, pretty much steals the picture and has the additional satisfaction of seeing Blackie converted to the faith when he finds Mary alive after the earthquake of April 1906.

Photographed by Oliver T. Marsh, and with dazzling montages by Slavko Vorkapich, the film's climax is its twenty-minute recreation of the earthquake, done in collaboration with James Basevi, who rebuilt whole sections of the old city on movable platforms. "Everything stops with the earthquake," wrote John Baxter in *Hollywood in the Thirties,* "a magnificently

staged cataclysm to which Van Dyke's direction builds up with fast-tempo editing of trembling ceilings and clashing chandeliers. The final sequence, where a battered but unbroken population strides back, to the tune of "The Battle Hymn of the Republic," into the ruined city, is sentimental, but few can resist its triumphant chauvinism."

San Francisco grossed over $6 million and remained MGM's greatest box-office success until *Gone With the Wind* (1939). Douglas Shearer won an Oscar for sound, and there were nominations for best picture, director, actor (Tracy), original story (Robert Hopkins), and assistant director (Joseph Newman). Continuing his majestic progress through the genres, Van Dyke next made *His Brother's Wife,* a slick sub-Maugham tropical drama starring Barbara Stanwyck and Robert Taylor, decribed by one reviewer as "a triumph of machine-made art."

Yet another hit followed in *The Devil Is a Sissy,* scripted by John Lee Mahin and Richard Schayer. It shows how a posh English boy (Freddie Bartholomew), translated to the New York slums, earns his place in a tough gang headed by Jackie Cooper and Mickey Rooney. Baxter thought that Van Dyke's "observation of behaviour among slum kids and the mechanics of social acceptance in this complex environment is remarkably apt. Occasionally the script takes flight, as where Rooney struggles through the days after his father is electrocuted for murder, refusing to break down. . . . The picture of slum life is accurate without criticism, funny without sentiment, and Van Dyke's direction is, as always, assured."

Screwball comedy came next in *Love on the Run,* with Clark Gable and Franchot Tone as New York newspapermen in London. Tone is assigned to cover the high-altitude flight of rascally Baron Reginald Owen, while Gable is supposed to handle the marriage of reporter-hating Joan Crawford to impoverished aristocrat Ivan Lebedeff: neither event takes place, Gable instead eloping with Crawford in the Baron's plane. The Hollywood *Spectator* called this "unbelievable but joyous. . . . The combination of Cedric Gibbons sets, Adrian gowns, and Oliver Marsh photography is enough to make any picture worth looking at, and the story and acting in this one make it well worth listening to." Even reviewers who found the plot hackneyed thought that "the sheer momentum" of Van Dyke's direction compensated for this, and there were comparisons with both Frank Capra and René Clair. Van Dyke's last film of 1936 was *After the Thin Man.* A Hackett and Goodrich script, like *The Thin Man,* it seemed to Leonard

Maltin "genuinely first-rate, in many ways better than the original."

Van Dyke turned down *The Good Earth* because it was "a story of futility" and was reluctant to accept *Personal Property* (1937), a remake of Sam Wood's *The Man in Possession* (1931), itself based on a play by H. M. Harwood. He finally agreed to make this pleasant romantic comedy on condition that he be given Jean Harlow and Robert Taylor as his stars, and the result was called "just as flip and amusing as was its predecessor."

They Gave Him a Gun (1937) was a film more likely to have come from Warner Brothers than from MGM—a crime drama with a pacifist message. Spencer Tracy stars as a circus barker who during World War I tries to "make a man" of frightened bookkeeper Franchot Tone. The latter emerges as a hero and gets the girl (Gladys George) Tracy loves. Trained to kill, Tone becomes a murderous racketeer, but he eventually chooses to die in a shoot-out with the FBI, freeing his wife to marry Tracy. "Constructed like a classic *film noir*," wrote Hervé Dumont, "*They Gave Him a Gun* stands essentially on the performances of the actors, a very spared montage, and expressionistic lighting; in its tone, it prefigures the postwar films of Wyler, Dmytryk, and Zinnemann." The same year, David Selznick borrowed Van Dyke to direct the memorable fencing scene between Ronald Colman and Douglas Fairbanks Jr. in John Cromwell's *Prisoner of Zenda*.

By this time, Van Dyke was the most prolific and highest paid director in Hollywood's richest studio. But things were changing at MGM. Irving Thalberg had died in 1936, leaving the studio at the mercy of the ignorant tyrant Louis B. Mayer. Little by little, MGM's directors became mere servants of the studio's star system, their every move supervised by front-office hatchet men. At the same time, Thalberg's fondness for lavish literary adaptations began to give way to wholesome "family" films, inoffensive comedies, and low-budget, high-profit series like "Andy Hardy," "Dr. Kildare," and "Tarzan."

The decline was gradual, however, and after *Rosalie* (1937), a screen version of Cole Porter's musical starring Nelson Eddy and Eleanor Powell, Van Dyke took over from the ailing Sidney Franklin as director of the $1.8 million 160-minute *Marie Antoinette* (1938), a project initiated by Thalberg and starring his wife Norma Shearer. Adapted from the novel by Stefan Zweig and photographed by William Daniels, this glittering production was sumptuously designed by Cedric Gibbons and had Tyrone Power as Count Axel de Fersen, John Barrymore as

Louis XV, and Robert Morley as Louis XVI. "One-Take Woody" completed the film in sixty days, doing a good deal of violence to history but producing "a giddy ballet of luxury, love, and death."

During the generally dismal last phase of his career, Van Dyke made three more MacDonald-Eddy musicals, Victor Herbert's *Sweethearts* (1938), Noel Coward's *Bittersweet* (1948), and Rodgers and Hart's *I Married an Angel* (1942). His contributions to Metro series included *Andy Hardy Gets Spring Fever* (1939), *Dr. Kildare's Victory* (1942), *Another Thin Man* (1939) and *Shadow of the Thin Man* (1941). He also directed Powell, Loy, and Rosalind Russell in *I Love You Again* (1940), an entertaining comedy in which Powell plays a womanizing vagabond temporarily converted by a bang on the head into a solid citizen. *I Take This Woman* (1940), a soap opera starring Spencer Tracy and Hedy Lamarr, was begun by Josef von Sternberg and continued by Frank Borzage before Van Dyke completed the film, dubbed by the columnists "I Retake This Woman."

The best of Van Dyke's last films were *It's a Wonderful World* (1939), *Rage in Heaven* (1941), and *Journey for Margaret* (1942). The first, scripted by Ben Hecht and starring Claudette Colbert and James Stewart, was a screwball comedy-thriller in the Thin Man tradition; William K. Everson has called it "one of the most underrated films of the late Thirties." And François Truffaut said that *Rage in Heaven* was the first film to excite his imagination. Adapted from a James Hilton novel, it is a full-blooded psychological thriller, with paranoid Robert Montgomery scheming to murder his wife Ingrid Bergman and best friend George Sanders, and then cunningly killing himself so as to get Sanders hanged. *Journey for Margaret*, made for Dore Schary's unit at MGM, was a sensitive adaptation of William L. White's autobiographical account of the adoption by an American war correspondent of an orphan of the London Blitz. It provided the first important role for Margaret O'Brien, arguably the most likable of all child stars.

Van Dyke was a major in the Marine Corps Reserve when the United States entered World War II and was responsible for activating the 22nd Battalion of the Tenth Marines. His health was failing, however, and he was no more successful in achieving combat than he had been in World War I. Mustered out, he went back to work on a Western, *Gentle Annie,* but was soon forced by illness to give this up as well. (Tay Garnett took over as director, but the picture was shelved for a year and then reshot by Andrew

Marton.) Six months later, Van Dyke died at his home in Brentwood, California, aged only fifty-three. He was survived by his wife Ruth and their three children, Barbara, Woodbridge Strong III, and Winston.

The adventurous director Carl Denham in *King Kong* was modeled on Van Dyke. Like his friend "Wild Bill" Wellman, he was of the "man's man" school of Hollywood directors, fond of riding, hunting, and boxing, boozing and brawling; he was once blackjacked by the riot squad at the Coconut Grove. However, "the exuberance of his behavior," according to Hervé Dumont, "masked a vulnerable nature, generous, and profoundly conscious of his responsibilities." He was no respecter of persons, greeting Louis B. Mayer with the words "Hi, kid," but capable of seeking out has-been actors and giving them work, as he did King Baggott and Rhea Mitchell in *San Francisco*. He always insisted that "a film is not a matter of life or death," and people had fun on his sets.

Directing, Van Dyke told Frank Nugent, is "just a technical job. You have to possess some power of visualization, imagination, but that's not genius." And he told another interviewer, "I haven't an artistic bone in my body. . . . I direct to make money." Modern critics have tended to agree. William K. Everson, in his book on Claudette Colbert, wrote that Van Dyke "made films fast, under budget, without pretensions, and usually with big box-office results. . . . Other MGM directors were scornful of his methods, yet envious of the results he achieved." John Baxter called his films "intellectually disreputable," though conceding that "Van Dyke had no equal as a studio technician and as an estimator of public taste." And Andrew Sarris concluded that "Woody Van Dyke made more good movies than his reputation for carelessness and haste would indicate."

Van Dyke believed that what he lost in polish by shooting fast, he made up for in vitality and spontaneity. "The first shot is always the best," he said; "it may be imperfect, but the general effect is superior." At the time of his death, Van Dyke was cited by the *Motion Picture Herald* as "the leading all-time director." Perhaps, as Hervé Dumont suggests, a Van Dyke retrospective would "confirm beyond doubt the importance of a poetic and exotic romantic."

—J.A.G.

FILMS: Her Good Name, 1917; Clouds, 1917; Mother's Ordeal, 1917; The Land of Long Shadows, 1917; The Range Boss, 1917; The Open Places, 1917; The Men of the Desert, 1917; Our Little Nell, 1917; The Gift o' Gab, 1917; Sadie Goes to Heaven, 1917; The Lady of the Dugout, 1918; Daredevil Jack, 1920 (serial: 15 epi-sodes); The Hawk's Trail, (serial: 15 episodes); Double Adventure, 1921 (serial: 15 episodes); (with William Bowman) The Avenging Arrow, 1921 (serial: 15 episodes); (with Fred Jackman) White Eagle, (serial: 15 episodes) 1922 The Milky Way, 1922; According to Hoyle, 1922; Forget Me Not, 1922; The Boss of Camp Four, 1922; The Girl Next Door (You Are In Danger), 1923; The Destroying Angel, 1923; The Miracle Makers, 1923; Half-a-Dollar Bill, 1923; Loving Lies, 1924; The Battling Fool, 1924; The Beautiful Sinner, 1924; Winner Takes All, 1924; Gold Heels, 1924; Barriers Burned Away (The Chicago Fire), 1925; Ranger of the Big Pines, 1925; The Trail Rider, 1925; Hearts and Spurs, 1925; The Timber Wolf, 1925; The Desert's Price, 1925; The Gentle Cyclone, 1925; War Paint (U.K., Rider of the Plains), 1926; Winners of the Wilderness, 1927; California, 1927; The Heart of the Yukon, 1927; Eyes of the Totem, 1927; Spoilers of the West, 1927; Foreign Devils, 1927; Wyoming, 1928; Under the Black Eagle, 1928; White Shadows in the South Seas, 1928; The Pagan, 1929; Trader Horn, 1931; Guilty Hands, 1931; Never the Twain Shall Meet, 1931; The Cuban Love Song, 1931; Tarzan, the Ape Man, 1931; Night Court (U.K., Justice for Sale), 1932; Penthouse, 1933; The Prizefighter and the Lady (U.K., Every Woman's Man), 1933; Eskimo (U.K., Mala the Magnificent), 1933; Laughing Boy, 1934; Manhattan Melodrama, 1934; The Thin Man, 1934; Hide Out, 1934; Forsaking All Others, 1934; Naughty Marietta, 1935; I Live My Life, 1935; Rose Marie, 1936; San Francisco, 1936; His Brother's Wife (U.K., Lady of the Tropics), 1936; The Devil Is a Sissy (U.K., The Devil Takes the Count), 1936; Love on the Run, 1936; After the Thin Man, 1936; Personal Property (U.K., Man in Possession), 1937; They Gave Him a Gun, 1937; Rosalie, 1937; Marie Antoinette, 1938; Sweethearts, 1938; Stand Up and Fight, 1938; It's a Wonderful World, 1939; Andy Hardy Gets Spring Fever, 1939; Another Thin Man, 1939; I Take This Woman, 1940; I Love You Again, 1940; Bittersweet, 1940; Rage in Heaven, 1941; Shadow of the Thin Man, 1941; The Feminine Touch, 1941; Dr. Kildare's Victory (U.K., The Doctor and the Debutante), 1941; I Married An Angel, 1941; Cairo, 1942, Journey for Margaret, 1942. *Published scripts*—San Francisco, 1979.

ABOUT: Baxter, J. Hollywood in the Thirties, 1968; Brownlow, K. The War, the West, and the Wilderness, 1979; Cannom, R. Van Dyke and the Mythical City Hollywood, 1948; Crowther, B. The Lion's Share, 1957; Dumont, H. W. W. Van Dyke, 1975 (in French); Eames, J. The MGM Story, 1975; Everson, W. American Silent Film, 1978; Koszarski, R. Hollywood Directors 1914–1960, 1976; Parish, J. and Mank, G. The Best of MGM, 1981; Thomson, D. A Biographical Dictionary of the Cinema, 1980; Van Dyke, W. S. Horning Into Africa, 1931. *Periodicals*—Action January–February 1971; American Heritage June 1968; Collier's May 18, 1935; Cue March 16, 1935; Kaleidoscope Summer 1971; New Yorker September 28, 1935; Photophy December 1936; Stage April 13, 1936; Travelling (Switzerland) Summer 1973 (Van Dyke issue); views and Reviews Summer 1971.

"VERTOV, DZIGA" (Denis Arkadievich **Kaufman)** (January 2, 1896–February 12, 1954), Soviet documentarist and prophet of *cinéma-vérité,* was born in Bialystok, Poland, the son of a librarian. Vertov's younger brothers both became well-known film cameramen, Mikhail Kaufman being Vertov's principal cameraman on virtually all of his films, while Boris, after working for Jean Vigo in France, went to Hollywood to film for such directors as Elia Kazan and Sidney Lumet.

In 1906, as a schoolboy in Bialystok, Vertov wrote his first poems, and in 1912–1915 he studied music at the Bialystok conservatory. The family fled eastwards when Germany invaded Poland in 1915, settling in Moscow, where Denis and Mikhail remained when their parents returned to Poland. Between 1914 and 1916 Denis Kaufman wrote poems, verse satires, essays, and science-fiction novels, and it was apparently at this time that he took the pseudonym Dziga Vertov. The name signifies something like "spinning top" and has connotations of perpetual motion—appropriate enough for a vigorous, stocky young man who proclaimed himself a futurist—an adherent of a movement that sought to give artistic expression to the dynamic energy of machinery.

In 1916–1917 Vertov studied medicine in St. Petersburg (and/or, according to some accounts, at the Psycho-Neurological Institute in Moscow). He continued to write, his experimental verse reflecting an increasing interest (shared with other futurists) in the aesthetic and psychological effects of sound and noise. This led him to the experiments with recorded sound, conducted in St. Petersburg on an old phonograph, which he dignified as his "laboratory of hearing." He recorded and juxtaposed in various combinations the sounds of machines, wind, rushing water, human speech, and music. He also struggled to find a way to transcribe nonverbal sounds (for example, of a sawmill and a waterfall) using words and letters "in musical-thematic creations of word-montage." These experiments, as David Bordwell points out, reflect a "characteristic Vertov duality of scientific control and artistic impulse, two preoccupations which fused in a concern with the idea of montage." It should be said that the techniques of montage and collage—the fragmentation and recombinations of often diverse materials—were much in the air at that time, as is evident in contemporary avant-garde art of all kinds.

In the spring of 1918 Vertov met Mikhail Koltzov, who offered him a chance to work in the cinema, and thus to extend his montage experiments to visual material. Vertov accepted and became an editor (soon senior editor) of the Moscow Film Committee's first regular news-

DZIGA VERTOV

reel. *Kino-nedelya* (Cinema Week) used material filmed by Soviet cameramen who covered the civil war from agit-trains, along with all kinds of other documentary material. The intention was always as much propagandist as documentary, and the newsreels were intended to show that despite invasions and civil war, the new Soviet government was spreading its authority throughout the vast territories of the USSR. Vertov put together twenty-nine issues of *Kino-nedelya* between June 1918 and the end of the year, and ten more in the first half of 1919. It was invaluable experience for a young filmmaker, and some issues of the newsreel show him beginning to develop touches of originality in his handling of the material, especially in his use of rapid cutting.

Vertov ceased to work on *Kino-nedelya* in July 1919, but used the newsreel material already accumulated to assemble a long historical (and propagandist) document, *Godoushchine revolyutsii* (*Anniversary of the Revolution,* 1919). By the end of 1919 Vertov, guided by the cameraman Pyotr Yermolov, was himself filming the battle between the Red Army and the Whites for possession of Tsaritsyn, soon afterwards working this footage into a short film. In January 1920 he accompanied the Soviet president Kalinin on a propaganda tour of the southwestern front, showing *Anniversary of the Revolution* and filming the journey for use in subsequent short documentaries. Further such expeditions (and short films) followed, and in 1921–1922 Vertov made another long (thirteen-reel) compilation film, *Istoriya grazhdanskoy voyny* (*History of the Civil War*).

In 1922 Vertov became director of *Kino-Pravda,* a new series of newsreel magazines of which there were twenty-three issues between 1922 and 1925. The series was called *Kino-Pravda* because it was conceived as a kind of cinematic adjunct of the newspaper *Pravda,* but the name literally means "cinema-truth," and it is nowadays widely recognized that Vertov developed the concept and principles of *cinéma-vérité* some forty years before that movement came into its own. In fact, Vertov's importance as an innovatory filmmaker was matched almost from the beginning of his career by his influence as a theorist. His first essays and manifestos on cinema appeared as early as 1919, written in the stridently iconoclastic style favored by the futurists.

In 1922 Vertov established the Council of Three, whose other two members were his wife and assistant Yelizaveta Svilova and his brother Mikhail. The Council's manifesto was issued in December 1922 and published as "Kinoki-Perevorot" (Kinoks-Revolution) in the June 1923 issue of *LEF* (Left Arts Front), the futurist-constructivist magazine founded by the poet Vladimir Mayakovsky. The Kinoki (as they were thereafter called) demanded an end to film drama—to actors, sets, studios, scripts, and other manifestations of the "bourgeois imagination." They insisted that the proper concern of the cinema was "the ordinary people, filmed in everyday life and at work." And they called for a revolutionary cinema—one that would look at the real world with the *kino-glaz* (cinema-eye) and see the beauty of the new technology and the people who controlled it: "I am the cinema-eye, I am the mechanical eye, I am the machine revealing the world to you as only I can see it."

However, as David Bordwell points out, Vertov was always torn between the attractions of reality and imagination, science and art. We find him praising the camera's ability to record reality more fully and objectively than the human eye, and *also* the cinema's ability, through montage, to impose its own order on "the chaos of visual phenomena filling the universe": "The cinema-eye is a means of making the invisible visible, the obscure clear, the hidden obvious, the disguised exposed, and acting not acting. But it is not enough to show bits of truth on the screen, separate frames of truth. These frames must be thematically organized so that the whole is also truth."

The same dichotomy is evident in Vertov's pioneering *Kino-Pravda* newsreels. The raw material for the newsreels was gathered by a team of cameramen stationed throughout the USSR and loosely supervised by Vertov. The film was processed and edited by Vertov and Svilova in a Moscow basement: "It was dark and damp, with an earthen floor and holes that you stumbled into at every turn. Large hungry rats scuttled over our feet. . . . You had to take care that your film never touched anything but the table, or it would get wet. This dampness prevented our reels of lovingly-edited film from sticking together properly, rusted our scissors and our splicers. Don't lean back on that chair—film is hanging there, as it was all over the room. Before dawn—damp—cold—teeth chattering, I wrap Comrade Svilova in a *third* jacket."

Vertov said that each issue of *Kino-Pravda* was different from its predecessor: "Slowly but surely the alphabet of film-language was built up in this unusual laboratory. . . . Every day one had to invent something new." In pursuit of unique images of reality, the Kinoki fixed their cameras to motorcycles or the fenders of trains, climbed houses and swung from cranes. And in pursuit of "cinema-truth" (which, as Jean Rouch points out, can mean not "the truth" but "the truth of the cinema") Vertov delightedly explored all of the cinema's devices for the manipulation of space and time: "Cinema-eye avails itself of all the current means of recording: ultra-high speed, microcinematography, reverse motion, multiple exposure, foreshortening, etc., and does not consider these as tricks, but as normal techniques of which wide use must be made. Cinema-eye makes use of all the resources of montage, drawing together and linking the various points of the universe in a chronological or anachronistic order as one wills."

The part of Vertov's nature that made him the prophet of *cinéma-vérité* is nowhere more evident than in a film he made in 1924, and called *Kinoglaz.* Using "candid camera" techniques, Vertov and his brother Mikhail took concealed cameras to Moscow markets and beer-parlors, rode with ambulances to accidents, and spied on criminals from behind windows. But at the same time that he was pursuing so rigorously the *cinéma-vérité* ideal of "life caught unawares," he was experimenting with the creative artificialities of animated film (including *Segodnia—Today,* 1924, the first animated film made in the Soviet Union).

Vertov's experiments did not please everyone, and his rambunctious manifestos and articles made him many enemies. The critic I. Sokolov complained that "montage deforms facts. The rearrangement of fragments changes their sense." And the distinguished screenwriter and novelist Viktor Shklovsky argued that newsreels should provide exact information, not montage and visual trickery: "A newsreel needs titles and dates. . . . Mussolini talking interests me. But a straightforward plump and bald-headed man who talks can go and talk behind the screen. The whole sense of a newsreel is in the date, time and place. A newsreel without this is like a card catalogue in the gutter." But Vertov and the Kinoki had their ardent supporters, too—some critics, Mayakovsky and *LEF, Pravda* and other newspapers, and the movie audiences themselves, who would complain to the film trusts if *Kino-Pravda* did not arrive on schedule.

In 1924 Vertov joined a new studio, Kultkine, which took over the production of *Kino-Pravda* and another film magazine produced by the Kinoki in 1923–1925 (*Kino-Kalendar,* later called *Goskino-Kalendar*). It was at Kultkine that Vertov made the first of several ambitious feature-length documentaries, *Shagai, Soviet* (*Stride, Soviet,* 1926). Its famous "heart of the machines" sequence, celebrating the power and beauty of the new technology, marked a new level of virtuosity in Vertov's mastery of montage, and there was much praise also for the way in which the film's commentary, on titles, is integrated with the images. Indeed, Vertov's artistic instincts were plainly overcoming his concern for "life caught unawares." His next film, *Shestaya chast mira* (*A Sixth of the World,* 1926) was subtitled "a lyrical film poem," and used montage techniques to impose an impression of unity on material shot all over the Soviet Union. Similarly, in *Odinnadtsatyi* (*The Eleventh Year,* 1928), superimposition, repetition of images, and rhythmic cutting turn the story of the building of the Dneiper Dam into a metaphor for Soviet solidarity.

Vertov's last silent film was technically the most dazzling of all, *Chelovek s kinoapparatom* (*The Man With a Movie Camera,* 1929). Working as usual with his brother Mikhail as his cameraman and Svilova as editor, Vertov turned this Moscow travelogue into a demonstration of all the resources of the movie camera and the cutting room, employing among other devices variable speeds, dissolves, split-screen effects, prismatic lenses, and multiple superimposition. It is perhaps the first film that clearly establishes the camera as a participant in what it records. We see people in a movie theatre watching the film that *we* are watching, and then we see a cameraman shooting that film. A man points a camera at us and in its lens we see reflected the camera that is filming that camera. In Russia the film was condemned for its preoccupation with form, and even Eisenstein attacked its "purposeless camera hooliganism," but foreign critics were stunned by its brilliance. A more recent critic, David Bordwell, calls it "a continuous autocritique of filmmaking" which "explores film as art, artifice, and artifact."

Vertov, who had begun with experiments in sound montage, believed that the "cinema-eye" should be allied to the "radio-ear," and showed what he meant by this in his first sound film, *Entuziasm* (*Enthusiasm,* 1931). A documentary about the achievements of the miners of the Don coal basin, it astonished audiences with the novelty and vividness of its soundtrack and the inventiveness with which Vertov used it— orchestrating sound in synchronization, in parallelism, in counterpoint, with all the flexibility that distinguished his manipulation of visual images. Again, however, there was much criticism from Russian reviewers, and it may be that, as Jay Leyda says, "Vertov's intoxication with his new instrument often got the better of him and obstructed a normal perception of his new film by even its most sympathetic audiences."

In 1931, nevertheless, Vertov was allowed to tour Europe with *Entuziasm* and *Chelovek s kinoapparatom.* His behavior in London left Thorold Dickinson with the impression that "Vertov was probably the most obstinate film personality of all time." Dickinson says that when the director attended a showing of *Entuziasm* at the Film Society of London, "he insisted on controlling the sound projection. During the rehearsal he kept it at a normal level, but at the performance, flanked on either side by the sound manager of the Tivoli Theatre and an officer of the Society, he raised the volume at the climaxes to an earsplitting level. Begged to desist, he refused, and finished the performance fighting for the instrument of control, while the building seemed to tremble with the flood of noise coming from behind the screen." His personal eccentricities notwithstanding, Vertov's ideas by this time had reached and influenced many foreign directors of the greatest significance, among them Ruttmann, Vigo, Carné, Ivens, and Grierson, and his work was received with fervent admiration all over Europe. After seeing *Entuziasm* Chaplin wrote to Vertov: "I would never have imagined that industrial noises could be ordered in such a way and become so beautiful. I consider *Enthusiasm* to be a staggering symphony." Returning to Russia, and increasingly embattled, Vertov assembled all such compliments in an article defending himself against his Soviet critics.

It was three years before Vertov showed his second sound film, *Tri pesni o Lenine* (*Three Songs of Lenin,* 1934), which is generally regarded as his masterpiece. Made to commemorate the tenth anniversary of Lenin's death, this is a free collage of documentary and archive material built around ballads sung in Lenin's praise by peasant women from the Central Asian republic of Uzbekistan. The strange, exotic blending of old and new in the film is particularly compelling in the first song, "My face was in a dark prison," about women being freed from the veil. For Vertov's original idea for a straightforward documentary had developed into a lyrical meditation on Lenin's work and influence, and there were few whose lives had been more completely transformed than the women of Soviet Central Asia. David Bordwell has noted how "images recur like leitmotifs from song to song," and "sound and image sometimes converge, sometimes separate" in a way that successfully reconciles documentary reportage with formal control. Jay Leyda refers to a passage during the second song "where newsreel material of Lenin's funeral is juxtaposed to a series of faces, of many times and places, flooded with sorrow, creating a passage of genuine tragic beauty. . . . [Vertov] knew how far the pure document can be useful, because he had advanced beyond it."

Like its predecessors, however, *Three Songs of Lenin* was less successful at home (where it was soon withdrawn from circulation) than abroad. Noting that it received a prize at the 1935 Venice Film Festival, Richard Taylor wrote: "It is rather surprising that a Soviet film praising Lenin and his achievements should have received such an accolade in Fascist Italy and this is perhaps a tribute to the power of the film. At home, despite the obvious adulation of Lenin in the film, Vertov's work never quite escaped the suspicion that surrounds all innovatory and experimental works of art, and the accusation that haunted Eisenstein in the 1920s—that his films were incomprehensible to the masses."

The attacks on Vertov's formalism mounted, and *Kolibelnaya* (*Lullaby*, 1937), a film about the women of the Soviet Union and Spain, seems to have been his last fully independent work. He codirected with Svilova and J. Bliokh a montage film, *Serge Ordjonikidze* in 1937, and seems to have directed *Tri geroini* (*Three Heroines*, 1938), a seven-reel tribute to the women of the Soviet armed forces. Threreafter there were a few short documentaries and a number of unrealized projects. Between 1947 and his death from cancer in 1954, he made many unexceptional newsreels. Vertov's career ended in frustration, and throughout the 1940s and 1950s his work and ideas seemed almost forgotten. Both were rediscovered by a new generation of filmmakers in the 1960s, when the development of the lightweight camera made his ideal of "life caught unawares" into an achievable reality. As Georges Sadoul has said, his "significance in the history of the cinema has only increased with the years."

FILMS: Kino-nedelya (Cinema Week) 1918–1919 (43 numbers); Godouschchine revolyutsii (Anniversary of the Revolution), 1919; Istoriya grazhdanskoy voyny (History of the Civil War), 1922; Kino-Pravda (Cinema-Truth), 1922–1925 (23 numbers); Kino-Glaz (Cinema-Eye), 1924; Shagai, Soviet (Stride, Soviet), 1926; Shestaya chast mira (A Sixth of the World), 1926; Odinnadtsatyi (The Eleventh Year), 1928; Chelovek s kinoapparatom (The Man with a Movie Camera), 1929; Entuziasm: Simfoniya Donbasa (Enthusiasm: Donbass Symphony), 1931; Tri pesni o Lenine (Three Songs of Lenin), 1934; Kolibelnaya (Lullaby), 1937; (with Y. Svilova and J. Bliokh) Serge Ordjonikidze, 1937; Tri geroini (Three Heroines), 1938; Novostni Dnia (News of the Day), 1944–1954.

ABOUT: Abramov, N. Dziga Vertov, 1963 (Russia); Bryher, W. Film Problems of Soviet Russia, 1929; Dickinson, T. and De la Roche, C. Soviet Cinema, 1948; Le Grice, M. Abstract Film and Beyond, 1977; Leyda, J. Kino, 1960; Manvell, R. (ed.) Experiment in the Film, 1949; Montani, P. Dziga Vertov, 1975 (Italy); Sadoul, G. Dziga Vertov, 1971 (France); Schnitzer, L. and J. Dziga Vertov, 1968 (originally published as supplement to L'Avant-Scène du Cinéma April 1968); Schnitzer, J. and L. (eds.) Cinema in Revolution, translated by David Robinson, 1976; Taylor, R. Film Propaganda: Soviet Russia and Nazi Germany, 1979; Thomson, D. A Biographical Dictionary of the Cinema, 1975; Vertov, D. Articles, journaux, projets, translated into French by Sylviane Mossé and Andrée Robel, 1972. Periodicals—Afterimage April 1970; Artforum March 1972; Cahiers du cinéma May–June 1970; Cinema Journal Autumn 1978; Film Comment Spring 1972; Film Culture Summer 1962; Framework Autumn 1979; Image et Son April 1965; Iskusstvo Kino 12 1965; Screen Winter 1972–1973; Sight and Sound Winter 1973–1974; Young Cinema Winter 1974.

*VIDOR, CHARLES (July 27, 1900–June 5, 1959), American director, was born in Budapest, Hungary. According to an article in *Films and Filming* (June 1956), Vidor was educated at the universities of Budapest and Berlin, studying civil engineering and "indulging his interest in music, writing, and sculpture via a general arts course on the side." An infantry lieutenant during World War I, he was reportedly wounded three times and received four decorations. After the war, "he tried first to use his engineering knowledge to earn a livelihood, then his singing voice. The first landed him only a chance to dig ditches, the second to sing in beer halls."

Turning to the film industry, Vidor joined the great new UFA studios in Berlin as an odd job man, over the next few years graduating to assistant cutter, editor, and then assistant director. After assisting in the making of *Frederick the Great,* he decided in 1924 to try his luck in the United States. He went first to New York where, unable to find work in the movie industry, he be-

°vē´ dor

CHARLES VIDOR

came a singer again, joining a Wagnerian opera company and singing lead roles as a bass-baritone.

Vidor still wanted to make films, and in 1927 he left the opera company and went to Hollywood. For the next three years he worked for various studios as an editor, writer, and assistant director. Impatient to direct, he finally made a short film, *The Bridge* (1931), financed out of his own savings. Much praised for its freshness and vitality, it brought him a contract as a feature director with MGM.

His first film there, credited to Charles Brabin but codirected by Vidor, was *The Mask of Fu Manchu* (1932), from the novels of Sax Rohmer. William K. Everson called it "handsome, erotic, wildly melodramatic, easily the best of the handful of Fu Manchu movies, and the most faithful to its source material. The epitome of the 'Yellow Peril' movies, with Fu promising his followers that he will wipe the whole accursed white race from the face of the earth, after permitting mating with their women! Lewis Stone, as Nayland Smith, imperturbably calls every Oriental a yellow monster or a heathen, and for his pains is justifiably subjected to several colorful tortures, including a see-saw in a crocodile pit. With Boris Karloff as Fu Manchu, and Myrna Loy as his astonishing masochistic-nymphomaniac daughter. It's still hard to believe that this unrestrained piece of serial-hoke emerged from MGM."

Sensation Hunters (1933), Vidor's first solo feature, was little reviewed, but *Double Door* (1934) attracted a certain amount of attention, apparently showing traces in its chiaroscuro camerawork of Vidor's years with UFA. Adapted from a Guignolesque stage play, *Double Door* featured Mary Morris as a psychotically snobbish New Yorker who, when her younger brother (Kent Taylor) marries "beneath" him, locks his hapless bride (Evelyn Venable) in a soundproof secret room and leaves her to die. A reviewer in the London *Times* found Mary Morris insufficiently maniacal, so that "what was macabre on the stage becomes merely silly," but added that there are compensations: "Some of the photography is quite beautiful. . . . The gloom of the Van Brett mansion on Fifth Avenue gives the camera plenty of chances for subtlety in its grouping of light and shade."

Moving to RKO, Vidor made his first Western, *The Arizonian* (1935), with Richard Dix cleaning up a town polluted by the activities of a crooked sheriff. The excellent supporting cast included Preston Foster, Louis Calhern, James Busch, and the English actress Margot Grahame, playing a cabaret singer "with a British accent you could cut with a knife." Shot mostly on the RKO ranch in the San Fernando Valley, the movie was well received, and praised especially for the well-staged and exciting climactic gunfight.

A comedy-drama followed, *His Family Tree* (1935), about a shabby old Irishman (James Barton) who come to the United States, embarrassing his politically ambitious son (William Harrigan). The old man is not as naive as he looks, however, and is able to teach his son a thing or two about political shenanigans, finally landing him the mayoralty he craves. A Boston reviewer wrote that "James Barton may be credited with making a skillful and moving film out of a slight political drama."

There was an interestingly mixed response to *Muss 'Em Up* (1936), produced for RKO by Pandro Berman and based on a thriller by James Edward Grant. The title refers to a contemporary New York police commissioner's famous advice to his men about the proper treatment of criminals. Preston Foster plays a hardboiled wisecracking detective, coping with kidnap, murder, and a corrupt and brutal police department. Some reviewers found the picture both confusing and unpleasant, but others were impressed, comparing it with *The Maltese Falcon.* "Where *Muss 'Em Up* rises notably above the level of most mystery films," wrote William Boehnel, "is in its characterization. . . . Indeed, these types . . . are more than just melodramatic—they are authentic portraits of certain peculiar elements in American life and the slight exaggerations in their characterization for dramatic purposes have been accomplished so dexterously that one can barely detect them."

Muss 'Em Up, one of the first films to show Vidor's potential, was followed by a generally unrewarding stint at Paramount, where his three B movies all featured the forgettable and forgotten John Trent. *A Doctor's Diary* (1937), produced by B. P. Schulberg and set in a fashionable private hospital, casts Trent as a brilliant young physician wrestling with medical ethics and torn between science and Nurse Helen Burgess. *The Great Gambini* (1937) benefited from Akim Tamiroff's performance as a nightclub "mind reader" who uses his talents to revenge himself on the man who destroyed his wife, to run rings around the police, and to foster the romance between Trent and Marian Marsh. *She's No Lady* was a complicated comedy-thriller with detective Trent passing as a drunk; and insurance investigator Ann Dvorak masquerading as a jewel thief to capture two real criminals, uncover an insurance swindle, and live happily ever after.

Vidor's career began to take off when he moved to Columbia in 1939, though he was at first still confined to B-pictures. After *Romance of the Redwoods* (1939), a Jack London logging story with Charles Bickford and Jean Parker, came the interesting *Blind Alley* (1939), from a play by James Warwick. Chester Morris plays Hal Wilson, an escaped killer who takes over a country cottage where one of his prisoners, a psychology professor (Ralph Bellamy), analyzes Wilson's recurrent nightmare and uncovers the sources of his murderous impulses. "In addition to its originality," wrote one enthusiastic reviewer, "*Blind Alley* gives us periods of suspense rarely equaled on the screen for intensity and power . . . and presents a clear exposition of Freudian principles. The action is circumscribed practically to one set, which has obviously been the subject of much care and attention. . . . Few more crudely truthful depictions of the gangster mind and outlook have been conceived, and director Charles Vidor has seen to it that none of its brutality or bitterness escape the camera."

The director's third picture of 1939, *Those High Grey Walls,* was scripted by Lewis Meltzer and Gladys Lehman from an original story by William U. Ullman Jr. Walter Connolly gave one of his best performances as a country doctor, jailed for a misdemeanor, who sets out to improve the lot of his fellow convicts. The reviewers were almost unanimous in their pleasure at finding so much freshness and originality in the treatment of such routine material. "All studios—major and independent—make their complement of prison pictures for theatres everywhere," wrote Robert Joseph in the Hollwood *Spectator.* "As a result . . . , few of them reach the screen that show any imagination or

color. An exception to this rule, however, is Columbia's *Those High Grey Walls,* for in every department, from writing through acting and direction, the picture shows an unusual excellence." John Mosher, writing thirty years before *M.A.S.H.,* drew attention to "the odd element of humor injected in an operating scene. An operation in the intestinal region would seem dubious material to stimulate giggles."

After *My Son! My Son!* (1940), a mawkish adaptation of the novel by Phyllis Bottome, came *The Lady in Question* (1940), based on a play by Marcel Achard. Parisian shopkeeper Brian Aherne serves as a juror in a murder trial. Rita Hayworth is the accused, and Aherne's son was played by the little-known Glenn Ford, whose screen infatuation with Hayworth began in this movie. The cast also included Irene Rich, George Coulouris, and Evelyn Keyes, and the film was photographed by Lucien Andriot.

The Lady in Question was well received, and so was *Ladies in Retirement* (1941), a thriller set in Victorian England. The young Ida Lupino, playing a middle-aged housekeeper who commits murder for the sake of her insane sisters, achieved a convincing interpretation of a role created on the stage by Flora Robson. "Elsa Lanchester and Edith Barrett, as the sisters, are as mad as you could wish," wrote C. A. Lejeune, "and the general air of wildness is intensified by glimpses of the dark marsh and low-key interior lighting."

Vidor moved up another notch at Columbia when he directed Fred MacMurray in *New York Town* (1941), a pleasant romantic comedy about the assorted inhabitants of a Manhattan tenement. MacMurray plays a good-hearted sidewalk photographer who tries to equip small-town girl Mary Martin with a rich husband (Robert Preston) but finally realizes that she prefers a good-hearted sidewalk photographer. *The Tuttles of Tahiti* (1942) has Charles Laughton as the patriarch of a marvelously feckless family living in an island paradise and supporting themselves, after a fashion, by cock-fighting. Noting that the fight scenes are "bloodless and devoted wholly to evasive action," Dilys Powell called the movie "a trifle, but a tolerable trifle." Glenn Ford starred in Vidor's second Western, *The Desperadoes* (1943), set in Red Valley, Utah. The story was an entirely conventional one, but the movie was generally enjoyed for its action and excellent Technicolor photography.

In 1944, after twelve years as a director, Vidor had his first major hit with his first musical, *Cover Girl,* with music by Jerome Kern and lyrics by Ira Gershwin. It opens in a small Brooklyn nightclub whose attractions include Gene Kelly, who owns the joint, Phil Silvers, and a contingent of lightly clad chorines. One of these is Rita Hayworth, whom Kelly loves but seems likely to lose when her appearance on the cover of a national magazine rockets her to stardom and a rich suitor. At the last moment, this being a musical, true love vanquishes ambition and Hayworth heads back to Brooklyn.

Along with Minnelli's *Meet Me in St. Louis, Cover Girl* has been recognized as an important transitional work in the development of the musical from its prewar form—typically a backstage story stringing together a series of stage turns—to the modern style in which songs and dances are integrated with the story, being used to express character and mood and to further the plot. Many of the numbers in *Cover Girl* are of this sort and take place outdoors, in spite of the backstage story. Hayworth and Kelly's "amatory ups-&-downs, " wrote *Time*'s reviewer, "have a warmth and poignancy which is unprecedented in a musical. When they cue into a song—especially the sentimental bull's-eye 'Long Ago'—they do not step out of character for the number. Their dance duets are the best since Astaire and Rogers split." For this reviewer, *Cover Girl* was "the best cinemusical the year has produced, and one of the best in years."

Firmly established now as a front-rank director at Columbia, Vidor next directed Irene Dunne and Charles Boyer in *Together Again* (1944), reuniting these stars six years after *Love Affair*. Dunne plays the mayor of a New England town who goes to New York to commission a new head for her late husband's statue, decapitated by lightning. Boyer is the sculptor she hires, and though she struggles to remember her duty to the community and her revered husband, it is immediately clear that Brookhaven will soon need a new mayor. Charles Coburn, as Dunne's father-in-law, cheerfully abets Eros. Coscripted and produced by Virginia Van Upp, this was found to be a "neat, ingenious" comedy about "really pleasant people in really funny situations."

There were many who thought *A Song to Remember* even funnier than *Together Again*, but unfortunately this effect was unintentional—the product of a crass script and Columbia's ill-founded belief that Cornel Wilde could pass himself off as Frederic Chopin and that Merle Oberon could convincingly impersonate the passionate and eccentric George Sand. Richard Winnington found the result "painfully serious and appallingly silly," misusing "a great romantic story, the finest piano recording on the screen, and some of the best Technicolor." *Over 21* (1945), from the play by Ruth Gordon, was good or goodish comedy, with Irene Dunne this time playing the novelist wife of editorial writer Alexander Knox, successfully ghosting for him while he struggles to make the grade as an army officer.

Vidor's masterpiece followed in 1946, "the evergreen of screen erotica," *Gilda,* scripted by Marion Parsonnet and produced by Virginia Van Upp. The film is set in Buenos Aires, where Hitlerian tycoon Ballan Mundsen (George Macready) runs his vast and lavish gambling casino. Mundsen's protegé Johnny Farrell (Glenn Ford) becomes his rival for the love of the infinitely desirable Gilda (Rita Hayworth), once Farrell's mistress and now Mundsen's wife.

"This is a film with the intense surrealist quality of a dream," wrote Higham and Greenberg in *Hollywood in the Forties*. "Its Buenos Aires is a creation totally of the imagination, with its winding dark streets, its gambling hell, Mundsen's white glittering house. The ambience is one of heat, decadence, sexual ferocity barely concealed behind civilized gestures and phrases. [Rudolph] Maté's photography has a lacquered finish: the husband smoking a cigarette in silhouette, the first glimpse of Gilda, like every GI's dream, sitting on a bed and throwing back her head in ecstasy, the wedding scene glimpsed through windows streaming with rain. George Macready gives a marvelous performance as Mundsen. . . . Against this basilisk, Rita Hayworth plays with an extraordinary animal abandon: a healthy exuberant beauty haunted by suspicion and terror."

Radley Metzer called *Gilda* "the sexiest picture I've seen." Rita Hayworth said: "Every man I've known has fallen in love with Gilda and awakened with me." The atomic bomb used in the first test detonation on Bikini was named Gilda. In her Cinema-Texas program note on the film (November 15, 1977), Marjorie Baumgarten offers a feminist reading of this movie, suggesting that "the entire film is a showcase for the belief in the [sexual] rapaciousness of the American woman. . . . Although the final sequence of *Gilda* presents the transcendence of true love over all obstacles, this culmination belies all the suspicion and sexual hatred which precede it. Women are agents of man's destruction and, if there's any doubt, just listen to the lyrics of 'Put the Blame on Mame.'"

In 1946 Vidor became involved in rather ludicrous litigation with Harry Cohn, head of Columbia, over Cohn's foul language. Vidor lost the case and had to return, humiliated, to work at Columbia. He made only one more film there—a dispirited attempt to resurrect the magic sexuality of *Gilda,* with the same stars.

This was *The Loves of Carmen,* in which Rita Hayworth, though "she spits and plays the castenets a little," was altogether too high-heeled and Hollywood to persuade reviewers that she was Mérimée's passionate and unwashed gypsy. Glenn Ford was found "glum and passive" as Don José, and only the fights and the Seville street scenes were admired. Vidor bought out his Columbia contract for $75,000 and therafter worked, on one- or two-film contracts, for other major studios.

He began this itinerant phase of his career with *Hans Christian Andersen* (1952), produced by Sam Goldwyn. Danny Kaye gave a performance of "muted whimsicality" in a "fairy tale" biopic of the great teller of fairy tales. There were songs by Frank Loesser, including "Wonderful, Wonderful, Copenhagen," and a Roland Petit ballet with Renée Jeanmarie dancing the Little Mermaid. This "charming entertainment" disarmed many. Not Hollis Alpert, though: he wrote that the picture "avoids coming to grips with the facts of Andersen's life or the nature of his work. It is sterile and thoroughly saccharine, and a fine opportunity to provide something both genuine and popular has been lost."

For Paramount, Vidor made "a flabby, farfetched thriller" set in India and called *Thunder in the East* (1952), with Alan Ladd, Deborah Kerr, and Charles Boyer, then directed Elizabeth Taylor in an equally fatuous romance for MGM, *Rhapsody* (1954). *Love Me or Leave Me* (1955) was not much better, a song-filled catalog of woes vaguely based on the miserable life and times of the 1920s singer Ruth Etting (Doris Day), with James Cagney as her hoodlum Svengali.

Grace Kelly's last film before she married the Prince of Monaco was, by a Hollywood coincidence, a story about a young woman who marries a prince—*The Swan* (1956), adapted by John Dighton from a play by Vidor's fellow-countryman Ferenc Molnar. Kelly was at her most ice-maidenly regal, Alec Guinness authoritatively moustached as her princely suitor, and Louis Jourdan irresistible as the young tutor who briefly diverts her from the path to the throne. There were excellent supporting performances from Brian Aherne, Jessie Royce Landis, Estelle Winwood, and Agnes Moorehead, among others. The result was called "the most pleasant, bittersweet of whimsies," and Isabel Quigly found Vidor's direction "light-footed and at times even elegant."

From the upper reaches of Ruritanian society, Vidor turned back in *The Joker Is Wild* to Ruth Etting country, the Chicago nightclub circuit, for another painful showbiz biopic. Frank Sinatra stars as the comedian Joe E. Lewis who, in his youth, was said to be one of the few who could make Al Capone laugh. Capone's colleague Machine Gun Jack McGurn was not amused, however, and caused Lewis to be beaten and sliced almost to death. Lewis turned for consolation to drink but came back, nevertheless, to construct a reputation as "the comic's comic" and a brilliant ad-libbing nemesis to hecklers. A reviewer in *Time* thought that Sinatra served up Lewis's material "in showmanly style," but that the movie in the end "produces an unpleasant sensation known to both medicine and show business as 'the gag reflex.'"

Vidor next replaced John Huston as director of David O. Selznick's *A Farewell to Arms* (1958), adapted by Ben Hecht from Hemingway's novel of World War I. Frank Borzage's 1932 version had starred Gary Cooper and Helen Hayes; Vidor had Rock Hudson and Jennifer Jones. With the help of a massive advertising campaign, this lavish picture eventually made a small profit, but the reviewers were cool to scathing, complaining that Hemingway's tragic love story had been inflated into a pseudo-epic, overproduced and miscast.

This failure was a great blow to Selznick, who never produced another film. Vidor began one more, *Song Without End* (1960), which did for or to Franz Liszt what *A Song to Remember* had done to Chopin. Shooting was two-thirds completed when Vidor, on location in Vienna, died suddenly of a heart attack in his room at the Hotel Imperial. The film was completed by George Cukor.

Vidor had a son by his first marriage, to the actress Karen Morley; two sons and a daughter by his second wife, the former Doris Warner. The director was a short man, quiet, congenial, and respected for the craftsmanship and flair that he brought to the most mundane studio assignments.

FILMS: The Bridge, 1931 (short); (with Charles Brabin; uncredited) The Mask of Fu Manchu, 1932; Sensation Hunters, 1933; Double Door, 1934; Strangers All, 1935; The Arizonian, 1935; His Family Tree, 1935; Muss 'em Up, 1936; A Doctor's Diary, 1937; The Great Gambini, 1937; She's No Lady, 1937; Romance of the Redwoods, 1939; Blind Alley, 1939; Those High Grey Walls, 1939; My Son! My Son!, 1940; The Lady in Question, 1940; Ladies in Retirement, 1941; New York Town, 1941; The Tuttles of Tahiti, 1942; The Desperadoes, 1943; Cover Girl, 1944; Together Again, 1944; A Song to Remember, 1945; Over 21, 1945; Gilda, 1946; The Loves of Carmen, 1948; (with others) It's a Big Country, 1951; Han Christian Andersen, 1952; Thunder in the East, 1952; Rhapsody, 1954; Love Me or Leave Me, 1955; The Swan, 1956; The Joker Is Wild,

1957; A Farewell to Arms, 1958; Song Without End, 1960 (completed by George Cukor).

ABOUT: Thomson, D. A Biographical Dictionary of the Cinema, 1980. *Periodicals*—Films and Filming June 1956.

*VIDOR, KING (WALLIS) (February 8, 1894–November 1, 1982), American director, scenarist, and producer, was born in Galveston, Texas, an offshore island port which he remembered as "a very cosmopolitan place." He was the son of Charles Vidor, then a dealer in South American lumber, and the former Kate Wallis. King Vidor's paternal grandfather had emigrated to Texas from Hungary in 1865; the boy was named King after his mother's favorite brother. As a small child he became very ill with a nervous affliction that was never satisfactorily diagnosed; this led him to share his mother's interest in Christian Science. As John Baxter says, "the blend of pragmatic self-help and religious mysticism in Mary Baker Eddy's teaching often appeared in Vidor's films." Another formative experience was the Galveston flood of 1900, when a great storm overwhelmed the island and left the streets piled with dead. "It was an indelible experience," Vidor said. "You can't fear extinction so closely without lasting effect." One effect, visible in very many of his pictures, was his sense of nature itself (and especially water) as an expression of divine power—beautiful, but to be feared as much as loved.

King Vidor was educated at Galveston High School and later at Peacock Military Academy in San Antonio (which he hated and escaped from after a few months). His interests as a boy included writing, acting, and photography, and he bought his first Brownie with cash earned by singing in the church choir and selling the *Saturday Evening Post* from door to door. In his teens he became ticket-taker and relief projectionist at a Galveston movie theatre, and then began making movies of his own with a friend named Roy Clough "who had built a camera out of part of a projection machine and cigar boxes."

Clough used this contraption to film a hurricane striking Galveston, with Vidor (aged fifteen) "holding the tripod down" in sixty-mile-an-hour winds.

Three years later Vidor offered his services as Texas representative to the Mutual Film Corporation's newsreel division, and was immediately assigned to film some major troop movements in the Houston area. Vidor had not expected this and had no camera, but at the last possible moment managed to borrow one from a Houston

KING VIDOR

chauffeur who gave him these instructions: "If the sun is shining, *f* 11—if it's cloudy, *f* 8—two turns per second—good luck."

Though the camera jammed and nearly ruined everything, Vidor got his film and sold it to Mutual. It was shown all over the world and inspired a Houston newspaperman to set up a local newsreel company, with Vidor as chief cameraman. He borrowed the company's equipment to make his first feature, *In Tow* (1914), a two-reel comedy about the Galveston auto races. It featured a local actress named Florence Arno, who also appeared in Vidor's 1914 documentary about the sugar industry and who soon became his wife. At about the same time Vidor worked on two one-reelers made by a comedian named Edward Sedgwick.

For Florence and King Vidor and for Sedgwick, as for screen-struck young hopefuls all over the United States, Hollywood beckoned with irresistible urgency. In 1915 the three pooled their resources, made a down payment on a Model T, and set out for California—Vidor with the stated intention of becoming "a second D. W. Griffith." Along the way he shot scenic footage that he hoped to sell to Ford's advertising department, but by the time the trio reached California they were broke, subsisting at one point on free food samples at the Panama-Pacific International Exposition.

In Hollywood, however, an acquaintance secured a screen test for Florence which brought her an immediate contract with Thomas Ince. King Vidor at first had to settle for occasional stints as an extra and an office job with Universal, but he was soon selling freelance scripts to that studio. Living near the vast Babylon set for Griffith's *Intolerance,* he studied the tactics of the master at first hand. In 1918 he directed a series of two-reelers featuring (and financed by) Judge Willis Brown, whose unorthodox approach to the rehabilitation of young delinquents these miniature dramas were intended to illustrate.

Vidor's first true feature was *The Turn in the Road* (1919), a Christian Scientist tract rather surprisingly financed by a group of doctors and dentists who formed themselves into the Brentwood Film Corporation. Brentwood also backed the three movies that followed. *Better Times* (1919), a comedy about a wallflower who wins the love of a famous ballplayer, starred an unknown comedienne named ZaSu Pitts (whom Vidor had spotted on a streetcar). She was also featured in *The Other Half* (1919) and *Poor Relations* (1919), but the star of both was Florence Vidor. In the first the heroine launches a radical newspaper when her fiancé loses his social idealism, and in *Poor Relations* she is an equally independent career woman—a grocer's daughter who becomes an architect. Vidor scripted all four of his Brentwood movies, adapting the last from a play of his own.

In 1920, when he was twenty-five, Vidor landed a contract with the new distribution company First National, receiving an advance of $75,000. He spent $15,000 of this building his own studio, Vidor Village, on Santa Monica Boulevard, committing himself to make movies that would carry "a message to humanity" and be "founded upon principles of right." These intentions, which underlie all his work, are demonstrated in *The Jack-Knife Man* (1920), about an old shanty boat bum on the Mississippi redeemed by his love for an orphaned boy. Like its predecessors, it was much influenced by Griffith, and it was warmly praised for its "humor, pathos, and . . . convincingness." Vidor brought the picture in $11,000 under budget, but First National were not impressed either by this economy or by the film's passages of bleak realism, and Vidor was obliged to modify his puritanism in order to maintain Vidor Village.

A string of romances and comedies followed, many of them starring Florence Vidor and some partly backed by Vidor's own company, King W. Vidor Productions, or his wife's (Florence Vidor Productions). *Woman, Wake Up* (1922) and *The Real Adventure* (1922) resemble *The Other Half* and *Poor Relations* in that they center on women who achieve success in a male-dominated society: all four have been seen as early examples of feminist cinema (in spite of their heroines' tendency to abandon ambition in favor of romance). It should be said that the directorship of *Woman, Wake Up* is disputed; it is copyrighted in Vidor's name, but Marcus Harrison is credited as director.

The last film Vidor made with his first wife was *Dusk to Dawn* (1922), in which she plays both a modern city girl and an Indian beggar. As Vidor says, Florence "had gone forward so steadily that she was beginning to be known as 'the first lady of the screen'. . . . Somewhere along the roads of our divergent professional interests could be found the cause of our estranged personal relationship and subsequent divorce." The same year, the director was forced to abandon the hopeless struggle to keep Vidor Village alive. He returned to freelancing, making nine more or less routine entertainments between 1922 and 1925 for Louis B. Mayer's Metro, for Sam Goldwyn, and finally, after the merger, for Metro-Goldwyn-Mayer, where he then remained for twenty years.

These contract jobs included *Peg o' My Heart* (1922) and *Happiness* (1924)—both sentimental comedies starring the aging ingenue Laurette Taylor; Vidor found them demanding assignments, but they were highly successful. Several of these pictures starred Eleanor Boardman, a rising young actress who became Vidor's second wife in 1926. The best of the movies he made during this period was *Wild Oranges* (1924), adapted by Vidor from a novel by Joseph Hergesheimer and set on an island off the Georgia coast, where four people are trapped by an escaped killer. There is a strong and characteristic sense that nature itself—wind, swamps, alligators—is as great a menace as the dim-witted murderer.

By 1925 Vidor was bored and hungry for a less ephemeral project. He asked Irving Thalberg, MGM's prodution chief, for a picture on some such universal theme as wheat, steel, or war. Thalberg gave him the five-page synopsis of a World War I story by Laurence Stallings. *The Big Parade* tells the story of a young Southerner, Jim Apperson ("a person"), who enlists in the Army, is sent to France, learns to wisecrack with his tough buddies, and falls in love with a French girl (Renée Adorée). He loses a leg in battle and goes home to marry his fiancée. She, however, has transferred her affections to his brother, and he is able to return to France and his Melisande.

Many of the extras Vidor used in the battle scenes were veterans, which partly accounts for the authenticity of the massed troop movements. But if he had to choose between authenticity and aesthetic or dramatic effect, Vidor readily surrendered authenticity. (For one scene he wanted to show a long, straight road choked with Army trucks as in the march he had filmed as a boy in Texas; he had to borrow the trucks from the Army and has described the struggle he had to persuade the responsible officer to countenance so suicidal a deployment.) Elsewhere there was a good deal of improvisation on the part of the actors, as in the famous scene where the wounded hero (John Gilbert) shares a cigarette in a shell hole with the dying German he has shot. The night battle that follows this powerful scene was directed by George W. Hill.

The Big Parade was released in 1925, ballyhooed as a savage indictment of the horrors of war. Some British reviewers complained that it gave the impression that America had won the war singlehandedly, but elsewhere the critics outdid each other in their encomiums for a film that "renews faith in the cinematic form." Made at a cost of $382,000, it earned profits for the studio of $3,485,000. Greater war pictures followed, however, and *The Big Parade* has been attacked in some quarters as an escapist film that actually glamorizes war; Vidor himself said in 1974 that he had seen it again and "I don't like it much." For most contemporary critics it survives less as a war film (in spite of some memorable sequences) than as an account of a young man's sentimental education. However, in 1925 the movie's impact was enormous. It brought stardom to John Gilbert and turned Vidor from a contract drudge into a director of prestige and influence.

Gilbert starred again in Vidor's *La Bohème* (1926), a frequently witty version of Murger's novel which nevertheless supports a performance of disturbing intensity by Lillian Gish. After a Sabatini swashbuckler, *Bardelys the Magnificent* (1926), again with Gilbert, Vidor went to work on "the *Big Parade* of peace," *The Crowd* (1928). John Sims (James Murray), born on July 4, 1900, seems to his father "a little man the world is going to hear from." But when the go-getting John tries his luck in New York, the big city soon cuts him down to size. His situation is pinpointed in the remarkable sequence in which the camera travels up the face of a skyscraper and into a vast office where John is finally located, one of scores of Johns at scores of identical desks (a scene borrowed by Billy Wilder, with acknowledgement, for *The Apartment*). There is another, equally expressionist, sequence when John is waiting for his blind date and future wife Mary (Eleanor Boardman) outside an office building where a stream of similar girls pair off with a stream of similar young men en route to the febrile delights of Coney Island. John, who aims for glory as an ad man, loses his job after his small daughter is killed and winds up carrying a sandwich-board. Along the way he learns that if you can't "beat the crowd" you can join it, and that this has its own rewards. Several endings were filmed but the one most commonly used has the young couple visiting a vaudeville show. They are laughing uproariously at the antics of a clown as the camera pulls back and back through the audience until they are lost in the laughing crowd.

Cinematic essays on the impersonality and man-killing loneliness of city life were in vogue at the time, and it was an appealing theme for Vidor. Nevertheless, *The Crowd* is an ambivalent film, celebrating the excitement and challenge of New York while dramatizing its capacity for disillusionment and despair. It was respectfully received in the United States, and in France Jean George Auriol, though he complained of "many useless, ugly, and heavy repetitions," concluded that the film's direction was "full of breathtaking surprises; it is neither discreet nor elegant; often it attacks and overwhelms you." Too bleakly disturbing to enjoy anything like the financial success of *The Big Parade*, it is now widely regarded as Vidor's masterpiece.

His next assignment was on a very different level. *The Patsy* (1928) was a comedy vehicle for Marion Davies, mistress of William Randolph Hearst, who had influence at MGM. Though she had little talent as an actress, Davies had vivacity and humor and a gift for mimicry, and the movie did well enough to be followed by two others, *Show People* (1928) and *Not So Dumb* (1930)—the former with "guest appearances" by Chaplin, John Gilbert, Douglas Fairbanks, Mae Murray, and Elinor Glyn, among others.

Vidor had begun as a documentarist, and then during his early days as a contract director he had been confined mostly to the studio. By the late 1920s, however, he thought that he was "developing a style that could integrate . . . the dramatic, entertaining story line with the realism and credibility of a Flaherty-style documentary." Something of what he meant can be seen in his first sound film, *Hallelujah* (1929), a musical drama with an all-black cast. John Baxter says that "so convincing are the scenes of black life in the South, shot around Memphis, Tennessee, that footage of cotton-picking and the loading of a riverboat from lines of bale-laden wagons have been mistaken for newsreel and used in compilation films. The mass baptism in the river and many scenes set in the black shanty town are equally realistic, with little attempt at fantasy. They contrast markedly with the film's dramatic plot."

Hallelujah centers on a cotton-growing family whose eldest son, Zeke (Daniel Haynes), is bedazzled by a "fast" city girl, Chick (Nina Mae McKinney). This leads to a fight in which Zeke accidentally kills his younger brother. Overcome with guilt, he becomes an itinerant preacher. When Chick betrays him, he pursues her and her lover to their death in the swamp. After a spell on the chain gang, Zeke goes home, purged of evil. Baxter objects to Vidor's paternalistic "vision of the black as a mindless hedonist" but concedes that "it is of its time" and goes on: "Vidor's contribution to the film is a freshness of technique, a delight in the use of natural sound and a sense of animal vitality in his people. Above all, he celebrates the landscape as one people use, live in and, at moments of tension, are subject to. The pursuit of the fleeing lovers through the swamp amid bird cries and the predatory sucking of the mud is one of the most impressive sequences in all his work." Others drew attention to Vidor's "exhilarating" staging of the film's many musical set pieces, while for Richard Combs it is "the strongest of all Vidor's pastoral idylls" in its "exploration of the roots of home and community." In 1929, however, exhibitors were nervous about its theme and it failed to make money (but in France, as Pierre Bost reported, it became an underground classic—something you saw "at two in the morning in a cellar" so that you could one-up your friends).

In the earliest days of the talkies Vidor saw the advantage of a laconic style of dialogue, modeled on the work of Ernest Hemingway (whom he had met in 1928). He employed such a style with telling effect in *Billy the Kid* (1930). This brutal Western places Billy (Johnny Mack Brown) and Pat Garrett (Wallace Beery) in a vast barren landscape which seems to mock their puny concerns. Shot partly on location in New Mexico, this film could scarcely have been more remote from its successor, *Street Scene* (1931), for which Goldwyn insisted on building an entire city block in the studio. The result was a stagey and politically emasculated adaptation of Elmer Rice's play, itself a relentless indictment of social injustice.

The Champ (1931) stars Wallace Beery as a washed-up boxer and Jackie Cooper as his son, scraping a living in Tijuana. The boy is torn between a raffish but colorful life with his father and domestic security with his mother, who has remarried. Harry Alan Potamkin thought that only "Vidor's innocence and goodwill—and Beery's acting" saved the film from shoddy sentimentality, but this is another Vidor picture whose stock has risen in recent years. It was followed by *Bird of Paradise* (1932), a mildly erotic film made on location in Hawaii. Elizabeth Hill, script girl on this movie, became Vidor's third

wife after his 1932 divorce from Eleanor Boardman. *Cynara* (1932) has an excellent performance by Ronald Colman as a respectable British lawyer ruined by a tragic love affair. *The Stranger's Return* (1933) stars Miriam Hopkins and Lionel Barrymore in a story about a city girl who goes home to her grandfather's farm in Iowa and learns to share his respect for the soil.

Having dealt with war in *The Big Parade*, Vidor was still eager to confront his other great themes, and tackled wheat in *Our Daily Bread* (1934), which he financed independently and released through United Artists. In it, John and Mary Sims are translated from *The Crowd* to the country when an uncle leaves them a farm. John turns it into an agricultural cooperative for victims of the Depression. Emotionally and politically simplistic, the film nevertheless has some striking sequences, like the famous one at the end in which John and his band of brothers race against time to dig a vital irrigation ditch. In *The Big Parade*, Vidor had used a metronome to control the advance through woods, with a drum marking the rhythm; he used the same "silent music" technique in this scene. As Vidor describes it: "The picks came down on the counts of one and three, the shovels scooped dirt on count two and tossed it on count four. Each scene was enacted in strict 4/4 time with the metronome's speed gradually increasing on each cut," driving the diggers to a "feverish pitch." According to Eileen Bowser, "skillful and varied camera placements make important contributions to the total effect. The workers appear in long shot over the horizon; they approach the camera; their backs retreat from it; they disappear in clouds of dust. There is no music under the sequence: instead the track bears the clink of the picks and shovels in an insistent beat, up to the point where the water breaks through. Here the music swells with the triumph of the workers. The shots become shorter, the action more frenzied, the spectator is deluged with images."

In *The Wedding Night* (1935) Gary Cooper rather uneasily plays a big-city writer in a Polish immigrant community, where he loves and loses Anna Sten. After *So Red the Rose* (1935), a clichéd and (by present-day standards) even racist drama of the feudal Old South, and the equally banal *The Texas Rangers* (1936), came an undistinguished remake of *Stella Dallas* (1937), with Barbara Stanwyck as the self-sacrificing mother. Vidor then went to Britain and made his memorable screen version of A. J. Cronin's novel *The Citadel*. Robert Donat plays the doctor who goes from a Welsh mining village to a fashionable practice in London, then relinquishes success to work with an eccentric medical pioneer. The Anglo-American cast includes Ralph Richardson, Rosalind Russell, Rex Harrison, Emlyn Williams, Francis L. Sullivan, Cecil Parker, and Felix Aylmer, among many others. Robert Stebbins welcomed it as a film in which Vidor "has found himself after the almost self-imposed trivialities of straight commercial production," making "a simple, direct use of sound, image and cutting that achieves genuine impact in a manner stricly and classically filmic."

Northwest Passage (1940), based on Kenneth Roberts' sprawling novel about pre-Revolutionary America, was to have been made in two parts; in fact only the first was completed, subtitled "Rogers' Rangers." Vidor's first film in color, it deals with the long march through the wilderness of a party of irregulars led by the unorthodox officer Robert Rogers (splendidly played by Spencer Tracy). They accomplish their mission—the massacre of a tribe of "bad" Indians—but are themselves decimated by starvation and the implacable swamps and rivers of the French Canadian borderlands (the picture was actually shot around Lake Payette, Idaho). John Baxter notes that "Vidor trained for his excursion into color by taking up painting, and if the film has a fault it is its 'painterly' look. . . . But Vidor commendably neutralizes the sweetness of the color with documentary realism; in cutting for tension, in evoking the special character of a location and, notably, in a scene of portaging boats over a mountain. . . . In sheer manipulation of the medium, *Northwest Passage* is unmistakably a masterwork." Clive Denton agrees, and draws attention to the fact that the film relies surprisingly little on camera movements: "The forward movement, the pulse of the adventure, is maintained instead by keeping the group of Rangers massed together and either advancing towards the camera or departing from it. It is characteristic of Vidor that most of the important action is arranged to happen before the camera, which *records* more than takes part in [it]."

Vidor had to contend with Hedy Lamarr's limited talent in *Comrade X* (1940), a poor man's *Ninotchka* in which she plays a Moscow tram conductor, and again in *H. M. Pulham Esq.* (1941), opposite Robert Young. *An American Romance* (1944) was a film much closer to Vidor's heart—his attempt at the third of his great American themes: steel. He had wanted Spencer Tracy for the lead, but had to be content with Brian Donlevy to portray the rise of a young immigrant from steelworker to magnate. Savagely cut by the studio, the movie was a failure and Vidor left MGM in disgust, making no more pictures for two years.

When he went back to work it was for David O. Selznick on *Duel in the Sun* (1947). How much of this monumental Western is Vidor's is far from clear: Selznick, still trying to top *Gone With the Wind,* had written the scenario himself and retained ultimate control over *mise-en-scène* and lighting, while his obsession with his protégée Jennifer Jones is said to have been so extreme as to make his frequent visits to the set embarrassing. Vidor had many battles with the producer during shooting and quit before the end; several other directors worked on the movie, before and after Vidor. However, the film is credited to Vidor and Richard Combs finds in the result "a delirious consummation of some recognizable Vidor moods and themes."

Texas land-baron Senator McCanles (Lionel Barrymore) fiercely defends his empire against homesteaders and the encroaching railroad. His ne'er-do-well son Lewt (Gregory Peck) helps out by derailing one of the offending locomotives, while his decent son Jess (Joseph Cotten) joins the forces of progress (i.e., the enemy). The plot is considerably thickened by the presence of the half-breed beauty Pearl Chavez (Jennifer Jones), courted by Jess but fiercely attracted to Lewt. Eventually, as Combs says, "the clash of these demon lovers seems to draw all the energies of the film, is nourished on the hot sultry style of the colour and imagery and, by its very intensity, casts a spell which transfixes all the epic forces of this most 'barbarous' vision of the 'civilizing' of the West. The whole pageant then dissolves—into the timeless world of the Indian legend, invoked at the beginning and ending of the film, which tells of 'Squaw's Head Rock' and the 'lovers who found heaven and hell in its shadow.'"

Some film historians see *Duel in the Sun* as a watershed in Vidor's career: before it, socially conscious movies with a message; after it, intense and often erotic melodramas. This is much too simple—there are violent and erotic films in the first phase (*Hallelujah, Billy the Kid, Bird of Paradise*) and idealistic ones among the later work. But there is an element of truth in the theory, and the change has been attributed to Vidor's disillusionment over the failure of *An American Romance* and the great financial success of the lurid, violent, and erotic *Duel in the Sun.* At any rate, the latter was followed by another period of inactivity for Vidor, apart from his codirection of a star-studded anthology of short stories called *A Miracle Can Happen* (1948).

Vidor's next three films were produced by Henry Blanke for Warner Brothers. *The Fountainhead,* based on Ayn Rand's controversial anti-egalitarian novel, deals with a visionary architect (Gary Cooper) who will destroy his work rather than see it spoiled by lesser men, and who finds his soulmate in a rich woman whose marriage is loveless and empty (Patricia Neal). The intense relationship that developed between the two stars communicates itself in the film but, Baxter writes, "for all its sexual tension, *The Fountainhead*'s most remarkable quality is the stylization at which Vidor so accurately aimed. Partly because of a low budget, most of the buildings are reduced to simple, elegant abstractions, rooms to harmonious geometrical arrangements of objects. Some rooms do not exist at all, but are merely suggested; one of his favorite effects, learned, Vidor acknowledged, from his studies of German painting, is to create with perspective and lighting an effect of space where none exists. . . . In [the film's] stark invention and the flamboyant finale in which Roark stands atop a phallic skyscraper while Dominique races to meet him, one sees Vidor at his paradoxical best."

A similar theme is explored with less conviction in *Beyond the Forest* (1949), a Midwestern *Madame Bovary* in which Bette Davis was forced to don off-the-shoulder blouses and youthful wig as the wife of a decent but stodgy Wisconsin doctor (Joseph Cotten). She ought to be happy but in fact she is bored; she yearns to escape to the arms of her industrialist lover in the wicked city, and does so at the cost of her life: God is seldom mocked with impunity in Vidor's world. Another melodrama, *Lightning Strikes Twice* (1951), miscasting the British actor Richard Todd as a rancher accused of his wife's murder, has little to recommend it.

Japanese War Bride (1952) is about a GI who marries his Japanese nurse and takes her home to a seaside community in California where they have to struggle to gain acceptance and to succeed as truck farmers. Vidor himself had an unaccountably low opinion of this return to social idealism; in its unpretentious way it is both absorbing and satisfying, with an almost documentary realism in the farming scenes, and some notable seascapes.

It was followed by one of the most admired of Vidor's late films, *Ruby Gentry* (1952), which he produced himself with Joseph Bernhard under the auspices of Selznick. It is set in a small town in the Carolina marshes, where a stormy, half-outcast girl (Jennifer Jones) becomes involved with the local crown prince (Charlton Heston). Long after he has put her out of his life, she remains bound to him by a passionate hatred; in time she destroys him, and floods the land he has struggled to reclaim from the swamp. Vidor, this time with no interference from Selznick, succeeded, as he said, "in getting something out of Jennifer, something quite profound and subtle." And the swamp in which she and her lover seek each other out is, as one critic remarked, "an apt model of the bog of human subconscious." There has also been a great deal of praise for *Man Without a Star* (1955), a frequently violent range-war Western with a very engaging performance by Kirk Douglas as a rootless cowboy—a more feckless Shane.

Vidor's last two films were both spectaculars. *War and Peace* (Ponti–De Laurentiis–Paramount, 1956) was shot on location in Italy with a cast that includes Audrey Hepburn, Henry Fonda, and Mel Ferrer, and with Herbert Lom as Napoleon. Vidor reduced the massive novel to four hours of film, which his producers cut to less than three. Philip Hartung found it "a cold and handsomely made epic that one watches from a comfortable distance without projecting oneself into the story." All the same, the battle scenes are magnificently done, as is the duel between Pierre and Kuragin, and Audrey Hepburn is touching as Natasha. Raymond Durgnat, in his very long and thorough study of Vidor's work in *Film Comment,* points out that the work has certain parallels with *The Big Parade,* which also presents war less for its own sake than for what it reveals about individual characters. *Solomon and Sheba* (1959) is a routine Biblical epic featuring Gina Lollobrigida and Yul Brynner.

Andrew Sarris wrote of Vidor that "he has created more great moments and fewer great films than any director of his rank," but John Baxter, in his excellent monograph on the director, places him "among the greatest filmmakers of modern times." Richard Combs considers that for Vidor "the family and the group experience are just as central, and as much a model for the growth of America itself, as they are for Ford. More thoroughly, perhaps, than anyone else, Vidor has worked through the fluctuating fortunes of the family—from optimistic affimation and expansion to neurotic withdrawal and disintegration—as a way of measuring shifting versions of the American Dream." Baxter prefers to center his analysis on Vidor's ambiguous attitude to the land—he loves it and is grateful for its beauty and its fruitfulness, but fears the destructive power of its swamps and waters and deserts. In Vidor's films, it is natural for man to struggle to tame nature, and industry is shown again and again "as man's most potent attempt to subdue the earth." The city, in which nature is totally subdued, is seen with equal ambivalence, however—perhaps because Vidor believed that man was meant for struggle, not victory. Baxter concludes that Vidor's "development from the rural school of Griffith through the new American realism to the revealing personal statement of *Ruby Gentry* concentrates in one career the growth of the American cinema."

Vidor made uncredited contributions to several films in the course of his career, among them Victor Fleming's *The Wizard of Oz*, for which Vidor directed a number of scenes, including the one in which Judy Garland sings "Somewhere Over the Rainbow." In 1957 he received the Christopher Award and the D. W. Griffith Award. During the sixties, after his retirement, he taught at UCLA and in the film department at the University of Southern California. For a time he considered making a film about a famous Hollywood scandal: the murder in 1922 of director William Desmond Taylor. Vidor spent most of 1967 quietly investigating the case himself and believed that he had solved the mystery of the killer's identity, but since some of the principals were still alive, he shelved the film project. (Sorting through Vidor's papers after his death, the scholar Sidney Kirkpatrick found these researches, and the Los Angeles police were able to close the case.) In 1974 Vidor made a 16mm short called *Truth and Illusion: An Introduction to Metaphysics*, said to be a "rather mawkish" Christian Scientist essay. He was awarded an honorary Oscar in 1979, and in 1980, at the age of eighty-four, he was reported to have accepted an acting role in a film called *Love and Money*. Until his death in 1982, he still traveled a good deal in Europe, alone or in the company of his friend Colleen Moore (who starred in one of Vidor's first movies, *The Sky Pilot*, in 1921). A quiet and "courtly" man, Vidor had three daughters by his marriage to Eleanor Boardman.

FILMS: The Turn in the Road, 1919; Better Times, 1919; The Other Half, 1919; Poor Relations, 1919; The Jack-Knife Man, 1920; The Family Honor, 1920; The Sky Pilot, 1921; Love Never Dies, 1921; Conquering the Woman, 1922; Woman, Wake Up, 1922 (directorship disputed); The Real Adventure, 1922; Dusk to Dawn, 1922; Peg o' My Heart, 1922; The Woman of Bronze, 1923; Three Wise Fools, 1923; Wild Oranges, 1924; Happiness, 1924; Wine of Youth, 1924; His Hour, 1924; Wife of the Centaur, 1924; Proud Flesh, 1925; The Big Parade, 1925; La Bohème, 1926; Bardelys the Magnificent, 1926; The Crowd, 1928; The Patsy (UK, The Politic Flapper), 1928; Show People, 1928; Hallelujah, 1929; Not So Dumb, 1930; Billy the Kid, 1930; Street Scene, 1931; The Champ, 1931; Bird of Paradise, 1932; Cynara, 1932; The Stranger's Return, 1933; Our Daily Bread (UK, The Miracle of Life), 1934; The Wedding Night, 1935; So Red the Rose, 1935; The Texas Rangers, 1936; Stella Dallas, 1937; The Citadel, 1938; Northwest Passage (Book One: Rogers' Rangers), 1940; Comrade X, 1940; H. M. Pulham, Esq., 1941; An American Romance, 1944; Duel in the Sun, 1947;

(with Leslie Fenton) A Miracle Can Happen/On Our Merry Way, 1948; The Fountainhead, 1949; Beyond the Forest, 1949; Lightning Strikes Twice, 1951; Japanese War Bride, 1952; Ruby Gentry, 1952; Man Without a Star, 1955; War and Peace, 1956; Solomon and Sheba, 1959.

ABOUT: Baxter, J. King Vidor, 1976; Brownlow, K. The War, the West, and the Wilderness, 1979; Denton, C. King Vidor *in* The Hollywood Professionals 5 1976; Higham, C. and Greenberg, J. The Celluloid Muse, 1979; Jacobs, L. The Rise of the American Film, 1939; Kirkpatrick, S. A Cast of Killers, 1986; Roud, R. (ed.) Cinema: A Critical Dictionary, 1980; Schickel, R. The Men Who Made the Movies, 1975; Vidor, K. On Film Making, 1972; Vidor, K. A Tree Is a Tree, 1953 (autobiography); Who's Who in America, 1978–1979. *Periodicals*—Cahiers du Cinéma 104 1960, 136 1952; Cinestudio July and August–September 1972; Experimental Cinema Fall 1931; Film (London) Winter 1962; Film Comment July–August and September–October 1973; Film Ideal 212 1969; Film Journal Summer 1971; Films in Review March 1964; Interview October 1972; New York Times September 3, 1972; Positif October 1966, September 1974 (Vidor issue), November 1974; Sight and Sound April–June 1953, Autumn 1968.

*VIGO, JEAN (BONAVENTURE DE) (April 26, 1905–October 5, 1934), French director and scenarist, was born in Paris, as his biographer says, "the son of undernourished parents, in a dirty little attic room full of scrawny cats." The parents were Eugène Bonaventure de Vigo, who became much better known as the militant anarchist Miguel Almereyda, and his companion and comrade Emily Cléro. Almereyda was of Spanish descent, but his nom de guerre was indirectly French, an anagram of *"y a la merde"*—"there is shit"—that reflected his belief in the revolutionary virtues of street talk.

This passionately dedicated libertarian was repeatedly jailed from adolescence onwards for his antimilitarist and revolutionary activities, but his changing political allegiances and alliances led him in time to a more moderate socialism. In 1913 he became editor of the satirical daily *Le Bonnet Rouge.* The paper grew increasingly respectable and Almereyda the starving revolutionary became an elegant devotee of the high life, with automobiles, mistresses, and several residences. Various scandals and the machinations of political opponents led to the suppression of *Le Bonnet Rouge* in 1917. In August of the same year Almereyda was arrested, accused of treasonous dealing with the Germans, and a week later he was strangled to death with his own bootlaces in Fresnes prison. A violent debate followed, but the truth of the charges

° vē gō

JEAN VIGO

against Almereyda and the real reason for the assassination were never established.

Except during his infancy, Jean Vigo had seen little of his busy parents. He had spent the later part of his childhood mostly at a villa in Saint-Cloud, cared for by servants. During the summer he often stayed at Montpellier in the south with Gabriel Aubès, a photographer who had married his grandmother after his grandfather died of tuberculosis. Vigo was twelve when his own father died: a pale, delicate, and taciturn child, precocious in his libertarian political views and his anticlericalism. Aubès, who was fond of the boy, adopted him. It was necessary to conceal the identity of this "son of the traitor," and as soon as his precarious health allowed, Vigo was enrolled pseudonymously at a school in Nîmes, not far from Montpellier.

In 1918, for the sake of his health, Vigo was moved to another boarding school at Millau, in the mountains. He hated the regimentation he encountered there, and his authoritarian teachers, but grew stronger. He learned to fight to defend himself, earned a reputation as a troublemaker, and made some equally rebellious friends, including Georges Caussat and Jacques Bruel, who, like him, often received "zero for conduct." His vacations he spent at Montpellier with Gabriel Aubès, who taught him photography (as he had taught Vigo's father). Aubès was impressed by the soundness of Vigo's eye and, having a poor opinion of photography as a career, suggested that the boy might consider cinematography.

Vigo's mother was living in Paris, and in 1922, at her request, Aubès moved Vigo to a boarding school at Chartres so that he could be nearer to her. Their relationship was never a close one and deteriorated rather than improved. At Chartres, however, Vigo became a conscientious student. He showed talent in philosophy and French composition and distinguished himself as an athlete. By the time he left school in 1925, he had committed himself to work for the rehabilitation of his father's reputation as a revolutionary hero, and had decided on a career in the cinema.

About this time Vigo became ill, and in 1926 it was discovered that he had tuberculosis. He was sent to a sanatorium at Font-Romeu, near the Spanish border, and made a partial recovery but had to return there the following year. It was at the sanatorium that he met Elisabeth Lozinska—"Lydou"—daughter of a Polish industrialist, who became his fiancée. The left Font-Romeu together in 1928, apparently cured but weak and penniless.

With help from his father's old friends and others (including Claude Autant-Lara and Germain Dulac), Vigo found a job with the prodcution company Franco-Film and went to its new studio at Nice. He and Lydou were married in 1929. Vigo had his first assignment that year as assistant cameraman on a movie called *Vénus,* but no further work (or income) followed. Then a gift of 100,000 francs from Lydou's father enabled him to buy a second-hand Debrie camera and to consider making a film of his own. He decided on a documentary about Nice, the gambling and resort town where he lived, largely because he could tackle such a film without expensive studio work.

Vigo was planning this film in the fall of 1929 when he met the cinematographer Boris Kaufman, younger brother of Mikhail and Denis Kaufman (the famous pioneer of the "cinema-eye" who called himself Dziga Vertov). They became friends, and Kaufman joined Vigo in Nice to work as his cameraman on *À Propos de Nice.* By March 1929 they had shot 13,000 feet of film, though some of it was of very poor quality. This was edited down to about 2,600 feet, and Vigo's first movie had its premiere at the Vieux-Colombier in Paris in May 1930.

À Propos de Nice open with fireworks and superimposed aerial views of the city, dissolving to a roulette wheel. We see dolls arriving on a toy train (a sequence substituted for the original actuality footage, which was too poor to use). The doll "tourists" are promptly raked in by a croupier. After more aerial shots we move on to the preparations for the carnival and views of the Promenade des Anglais, peopled with old and ugly rich women. A younger woman at a terrace café repeatedly changes her clothes, appearing finally naked except for her shoes. These opulent scenes are contrasted with the patient misery and hard work of the old city—washerwomen, sewers, garbage, a fingerless child. The carnival follows: giant masks and puppets, military pomp, women frenziedly dancing, intercut with shots of trampled flowers and cemetery effigies. The dancers move more slowly; a phallic factory chimney becomes a revolutionary cannon.

Introducing *À Propos de Nice* at its second screening before the Groupement des Spectateurs d'Avant-Garde, Vigo said that "in this film, by showing certain basic aspects of a city, a way of life is put on trial. In fact, as soon as the atmosphere of Nice and the kind of life lived there—and not only there, unfortunately—has been suggested, the film develops into a generalized view of the vulgar pleasures that come under the sign of the grotesque, and the flesh, and of death. These pleasures are the last gasps of a society so lost in its escapism that it sickens you and makes you sympathetic to a revolutionary solution."

Vigo had subtitled his film "*point de vue documenté*"—"a documented point of view" —and in his speech he made it clear that he had in mind something close to Dziga Vertov's "cinema-eye." He said: "I don't know whether the result will be a work of art, but I am sure it will be cinema. Cinema in the sense that no other art, no science, can take its place. . . . Social documentary is distinct from the ordinary short film and the weekly newsreel, in that its creator will establish his own point of view. . . . It will dot its own i's. If it doesn't involve an artist it involves at least a man. Conscious acting cannot be tolerated; the character must be surprised by the camera. . . . We shall achieve our aim if we can reveal the hidden reason for a gesture, if we can extract from an ordinary person, quite by chance, his interior beauty—or a caricature of him—if we can reveal his complete inner spirit through his purely external manifestations."

In the same speech Vigo praised Buñuel and Dali's *Un Chien Andalou* as an example of the proper approach, and this may account partly for the tendency to place him with the surrealists, where he does not really belong. There is evidence in the film itself that he had also learned from Von Stroheim, René Clair, and perhaps the German avant-gardists Richter and Ruttmann, as well as from Boris Kaufman and his famous brother. However, Vigo's biographer, P. E. Salles Gomes, suggests that in his case "one senses a sort of joyous personal rediscovery of the cinema's means, rather than any influence from his predecessors."

In fact, *À Propos de Nice* has few of the slick and gratuitous effects favored by the contemporary avant-garde, and is indeed often rough and naive. As Gomes says, "when Vigo tries to use facile techniques . . . he fails. When the beauty or ugliness of a palm tree or of a woman dazzles us, it springs from the discovery-creation of Vigo's eye (later to become almost infallible)." Carl Vincent agreed, writing that the film "mingles a romantic evocation . . . with ferocious social caricature. Sarcasm exists side by side with poetry, and human absurdity with a tender love of light. His sharp, brutal vision reveals an acute sense of cinema." Such encomiums came later, however; in 1930 the picture's two Paris showings produced only a handful of reviews which, though favorable and encouraging, did nothing to arouse the interest of the commercial distributors.

A large part of Vigo's capital had sunk with *À Propos de Nice,* and he had been counting on a sale to finance a planned documentary about Lourdes. He put this project aside and turned to another long-considered idea—the establishment of a film club in Nice that would specialize in works banned or mutilated by the censors. His plans were delayed by a decline in his health, but Les Amis du Cinéma opened in September 1930 with Lydou as treasurer and Vigo's old school friend Georges Caussat as secretary and errand boy. The first program was screened in a disused chapel, with an inaugural speech by Germaine Dulac. Later shows were given in suburban movie theatres on Sunday evenings, and the club slowly built up a loyal following, though at first it broke even at best.

Meanwhile, Vigo was trying to find a job as assistant to an established director. His reputation within the industry was enhanced when the famous Ursulines theatre in Paris programmed *À Propos de Nice* in October 1930, and at the end of the year he was called to Paris to direct a short film for Gaumont. The company was initiating a series of documentaries about sport, and Vigo was assigned to make a film about swimming, centering on the French champion Jean Taris. Much of the picture was shot at the Automobile Club de France, where the swimming pool had glass portholes through which underwater shots could be taken. *Taris* is devoted mainly to the champion's demonstration and explanation of the Australian crawl, but there are many whimsically inventive touches, as when we see Taris apparently walking on the water, or the sequence in which a woman practices swimming strokes in her own house, lying across a stool— with a lifeguard in attendance. Vigo himself thought very little of the movie, except for some of the underwater shots—a resource he remembered when he came to make *L'Atalante.*

Though many admired *Taris* far more than Vigo did, the assignment brought in very little money. Vigo was soon penniless and in debt, but unable to accept offers of work that involved leaving Lydou. She was by now pregnant and very weak and ill. He decided to sell his old Debrie camera—an appalling sacrifice for him—but was cheated, receiving only enough to pay off his most urgent debts. After their daughter was born in June 1931 they were in desperate straits until a little more money arived from Lydou's father. Even then they were sunk in a depressive lethargy that made it difficult for Vigo to concentrate. After a rest at a sanatorium, Vigo began work on a second sports documentary for Gaumont, this time about tennis. It was to have been a much more poetic piece than its predecessor, but in the end the script was rejected. The Vigos were saved once more by Lydou's father, who visited them in Nice, and to some extent by the slowly growing success of the Les Amis du Cinéma.

Ignoring the advice of their doctors, Vigo and Lydou went to Paris. Lydou's health failed again, however, and she had to be sent to the mountains for another 'cure.' Vigo explored a whole series of film projects, but all of them fell through. His spirits were at their lowest when in July he met Jacques-Louis Nounez, a rich and enlightened businessman who had developed an interest in the movie industry. Nounez liked Vigo and they discussed a variety of possibilities, eventually deciding that Vigo would make a medium-length film based on his own bitter experience of boarding-school life.

Zéro de conduite (Zero for Conduct) was filmed in December 1932 and January 1933 on a modest budget of 200,000 francs and with a cast made up almost entirely of nonprofessionals—friends, friends of friends, boys spotted on the streets of Paris. Vigo served as scenarist, director, editor, and producer. He had Boris Kaufman as his cinematographer, Maurice Jaubert as composer, and his friend Henri Storck as production manager and general assistant. The four principal child characters are Caussat and Bruel, named for and based on Vigo's real-life friends at Millau; Colin, based on someone he had known at Chartres; and the frail Tabard, who more or less represents Vigo himself.

The film's adult characters are savage caricatures of the teachers he had hated at school. Vigo imbues these petty tyrants with some of the mannerisms of the guards at La Petite Roquette, the children's prison where his father had once been incarcerated, and Gomes says that "he had come to identify one childhood completely with the other. This resulted in Vigo's extreme sensitivity to anything concerning a child's vulnerability in the adult world." Elsewhere, Gomes writes that "respect for children and for their freedom" was very close to Vigo's heart and that "to him . . . children are symbolic of mankind, and especially the weak and the wretched."

The movie opens in the train taking Caussat and Bruel back to school after the summer vacation—an inventive and charming scene in which the boys show off the (often reprehensible) skills they have acquired during the holidays. They alight at a small provincial station and we meet the new boy, Tabard, and supervisor Parrain, known as Dry-Fart. Later, in Dry-Fart's dormitory after lights-out, the supervisor punishes Caussat, Bruel, and Colin—inveterate troublemakers—by ordering them to stand for two hours by his bed while he sleeps. Colin develops a stomachache, and all three beg Dry-Fart to let him go to the lavatory. They repeat the information about Colin's stomachache in a strange kind of litany—a form of dialogue that is used a good deal in this film and also by Père Jules in *L'Atalante*. Vigo apparently devised the technique to make his dialogue understood in spite of the poor diction of his actors and the inadequacy of his sound equipment, but it has an oddly haunting, poetic quality of its own that is very much a part of the unique flavor of both films.

In the dormitory scene, at any rate, the boys' variations on the theme of Colin's sufferings have the desired effect—Colin departs to the lavatory and the sleepy Dry-Fart abandons the punishment. "These scenes in the dormitory," Gomes wrote, "show Vigo in a moment of complete control over the cinema, which bends obediently to his desire to recreate the sense of delicious intimacy he had dredged out of his childhood memories. Here, the editing, the camera movements, the composition and inner rhythm of the images, the dialogue, the lighting, all is fused into a harmonious whole which was probably one of Vigo's most ambitious dreams."

Next day, Caussat, Bruel, and Colin are plotting something with a map. When one of the supervisors approaches, the new young teacher Huguet covers their retreat, and later delights the children by imitating Charlie Chaplin in a scene which becomes a "respectful parody" of one in *Easy Street*. The supervisor known as Gas-Snout, by contrast, searches the boys' desks, hoping for pornography. Caussat responds by pouring glue where Gas-Snout might be expected to encounter it. Later, in the study hall, Huguet further demonstrates his goodwill by standing on his hands and drawing a caricature of Gas-Snout.

Huguet then leads the boys on an excursion into the town, dreamily wandering on without them but picking up the whole party again later without ever realizing that they had gone, and then leading them all in pursuit of a young woman who has taken his fancy. This scene is intercut with a meeting between Gas-Snout and the school principal—a heavily bearded dwarf—which establishes their (misplaced) anxiety about the growing friendship between Bruel and Tabard. We also learn that there is to be a school fête, at which no bad behavior can be tolerated, before proceeding to a scene in which the dwarf principal gives Tabard an incoherent and humiliating lecture on the supposed dangers of his relationship with Bruel.

In the scenes that follow, the dreadfulness of the school is further emphasized. The cook complains that she has to dish out yet another meal of beans, but unaware of her concern, the boys blame her for their miserable diet (to the bitter shame of Colin, who is her son). Then Tabard becomes the object of the tentative sexual advances of the most revolting of all the teachers, and responds by saying "shit on you"—directly quoting a famous headline once addressed by Miguel Almereyda to the governments of the world. Brought before the entire staff and "given another chance," Tabard repeats the phrase, this time addressing it to the principal himself.

The battle lines are drawn, and Tabard, returning to his companions in misery, calls for revolution. A scene of fantastic and anarchic poetry develops as beds are overturned, pillows and quilts are burst open, and a snowstorm of feathers falls over everything. The day of the school fête follows, with the four rebels locked in the attic. Three distinguished guests arrive, representing Vigo's principal enemies—the state, the clergy, and the military. They are watching a notably uninspired athletic demonstration by uniformed firemen when they come under a barrage of books, stones, and shoes hurled from the rooftop by the four mutineers. Encouraged by Huguet, all the boys join in. They take over the school, lower the tricolor, and raise their own revolutionary flag. Caussat, Bruel, Colin, and Tabard scramble singing up the roof into the freedom of the sky.

As Gomes says "in addition to being a real school, with its source in Vigo's childhood memories, the school in Zéro de conduite is also society as seen by the adult Vigo. The division into children and adults inside the school corresponds to the division of society into classes outside: a strong minority imposing its will on a weak majority." Vigo was still a novice working with a small budget, and he became seriously ill during the making of the film. The sound quality is bad and there are a number of loose ends and bewildering inconsistencies in the narrative, as well as clumsy transitions and much poor acting. In his best scenes, nevertheless, Vigo's instinctive mastery of camera movements, his willingness to sacrifice clarity to style, and Jaubert's splendid score combine to achieve effects of miraculous freshness and beauty.

Zéro de conduite was first shown at a Paris movie theatre in April 1933. Many members of the audience were shocked, and there was much hissing, drowned out by the applause of Jacques Prévert and his friends. The critics were equally divided, some dismissing the film as "simply ridiculous" or "lavatory-flushings," others praising it as the "fiery, daring" work of "a Céline of the cinema." A Catholic journal described it as a scatalogical work by "an obsessed maniac," and soon afterwards the film was banned. It is widely believed that the banning was ordered by the Ministry of the Interior—not on moral grounds but for fear that it might "create disturbances and hinder the maintenance of order." Apart from film club showings, it was not until 1945 that Zéro de conduite was seen again in France. At that time some reviewers were disappointed, tending to attribute the movie's inadequacies to (nonexistent) cuts by the censors. Others, however, recognized it as an imperfect but "magnificent poem of childhood," and its reputation has continued to grow. Truffaut refers to this film in Les Quatre Cent Coups (1959), and it was the acknowledged inspiration of Lindsay Anderson's If (1968).

Even before this film was finished, Vigo and Nounez were discussing a full-length feature about prison life, to be based on the unjust imprisonment of the anarchist Eugène Dieudonné, whom Almereyda had defended. The banning of Zéro de conduite alarmed Nounez, but he wanted to give Vigo another chance, and looked for a thoroughly innocuous script. He found it in an original scenario by Jean Guinée (R. de Guichen). As adapted by Vigo, it tells the story of Jean, the young captain of a motorized barge called L'Atalante, which plies the inland waterways of France. Passing through Normandy, Jean marries a country girl named Juliette and brings her aboard. They live on the barge with the mate, an old mariner named Père Jules, a cabin boy, and Jules' army of stray cats. A charming young peddler tempts Juliette away from the montony of barge life to visit the wonders of Paris. In a fit of rage, Jean sails without her; Juliette is robbed and has to take a job; both are miserable. When the barge returns to the area, Père Jules goes in search of Juliette, finds her by a miracle, and reunites her and Jean.

The production plan for *L'Atalante* was the same as for *Zéro de conduite*. Nounez was to serve as producer, while Gaumont supplied studio facilities and arranged distribution. Boris Kaufman was cinematographer and Jaubert wrote the music and songs. In addition, Almereyda's old friend Francis Jourdain was taken on as art director. This time, with a budget of almost a million francs, Vigo could afford some well-known actors: Michel Simon was cast as Père Jules, Dita Parlo as Juliette. Jean Dasté, who had played Haguet, was Jean. The film was shot partly at the Gaumont studios, where a replica of the interior of the barge had been built, partly on location.

"As in *Zéro de conduite*," writes Gavin Millar, "Vigo's acute sense of movement is what chiefly fills in the banal outlines of the story, as much as the richness of invention he brings to the characters. The boat moves all the time upon the water, and on the boat's deck the people move too, back and forth, with or against the current, with or against the direction in which they are travelling. The sense that Juliette is exchanging a fixed landlocked life for hazardous movement is announced in one extraordinary shot from the wedding scene. Taken from low down on the bank, it frames only empty sky when suddenly Juliette sweeps across it, clinging to the end of a boom which has swung her from the shore to the deck. The sexual symbolism is overt but not coarse, and it is deepened by what follows."

Others have written with equal enthusiasm of the scene in which Père Jules boasts to Juliette about his colorful and somewhat shady past as a sailor, shows his skill with her sewing machine, models the dress she is making, and demonstrates an international medley of dances. According to Gomes, "it seems that Vigo's direction of Michel Simon was as amazing as the scene itself. Explaining all his intentions to Simon, acting out all the movements himself, and speaking all the lines, the director made the actor run through the scene several times until it was perfect. Then the sequence was broken down into several shots and filmed. The result was sensational. It is perhaps the high spot of their careers for both Vigo as a director and Michel Simon as an actor. Or rather, it is the most spectucular *tour de force* in their respective careers, and the sequence in *L'Atalante* where the continuity and rhythm achieve perfection."

Most critics agree that *L'Atalante* lacks overall unity, being rather an assemblage of brilliant scenes. Two of these occur during the unhappy period when the two lovers are parted. Juliette has told Jean that if you dunk your head in a bowl of water and open your eyes, you will see your beloved. Delighted by this game, Jean plays it repeatedly. When he believes that he has lost her, he plays it more seriously, diving into the canal and swimming (like Taris) underwater, his face distorted by despair, until he is magically rewarded by a vision of Juliette in her wedding dress.

"There is magic on board too," writes Gavin Millar. "Père Jules has miraculously succeeded in getting an old phonograph to work again and it plays a haunting waltz. There then occurs a moment of inexplicable beauty which is one of the cinema's great triumphs. Père Jules and the [cabin] boy decide that playing the phonograph to *le patron* might cheer him up. He has just climbed from the water where he has been searching for the image of Juliette. Proudly the boy, bearing the phonograph and its huge horn, like some precious gift, leads Jean and Père Jules along the whole length of the boat to the prow, where the camera awaits them. The waltz continues to sing out across the water. A long vista down the shining canal shows trees reflected on the surface and, in the distance, a factory chimney silently smoking. Jean stares, rapt, at the rebirth of the phonograph. As the waltz plays on, a remote and secret smile begins to steal across his face. There seems no question that he will find Juliette again."

Filming for four months in bitterly cold weather, Vigo became ill again. Exhausted and feverish, he went on working until the actual shooting was virtually completed and a first rough cut had been made. At that point he took a vacation, but his condition did not improve and he was confined to bed. The final cut was made by the editor, Louis Chavance, and the film was previewed in April 1934. The distributors in the audience were not impressed and the Gaumont officials demanded changes.

A few reviews appeared at that point. Jean Pascal said the film was "a confused, incoherent, wilfully absurd, long, dull, commercially worthless film," in spite of its "undeniable qualities." The art historian Elie Faure was much more appreciative—he was reminded of the painter Corot as he watched "these landscapes of water, trees, little houses on peaceful banks, and boats slowly threading their way ahead of a silver wake: the same impeccable composition, the same power invisibly present because so much a master of itself, the same balance of all the elements of a visual drama in the tender embrace of complete acceptance, the same pearly, golden veil translucently masking the sharpness of composition and the firmness of line. And perhaps it was this simplicity of composition, entirely devoid of flourishes or decoration—classical, in a word—that made me appreciate all the more the pleasure of savoring the very spirit of Vigo's work, almost violent, certainly tormented, feverish, brimming with ideas and truculent fantasy, with virulent, even demonic, and yet constantly human romanticism."

Pascal's review apparently carried more weight than Faure's or the other favorable notices, and by now Vigo was to ill to defend his film. Gaumont took over. They cut the picture mercilessly and retitled it *Le Chaland qui passe (The Passing Barge)*. This was the title of an extremely popular song of the time by C. A. Bixio. Part of Jaubert's magnificent score was lopped out and replaced by Bixio's song. The result was a commercial failure, the film being so mutilated as to be incoherent. Most of the critics were as hostile as the general public. The movie was called amateurish, self-indulgent, and morbid, though even in this version a few recognized its mastery. Shortly after *Le Chaland qui passe* ended its first Paris run, on October 5, 1934, Jean Vigo died. He was twenty-nine and had been making films for five years.

Throughout the seven months of his final illness, Vigo's spirits never wavered—he joked, spoke of the future, described the streptococcus that afflicted him as "a little fat man in a top hat." Lydou nursed him and was holding him in her arms when he died. Outside, a street musician was playing "Le Chaland qui passe." When Lydou understood what had happened, she had to be restrained from jumping out of the window. Vigo was buried in Paris at the Bagneux cemetery, in a grave next to that of Miguel Almereyda. Lydou joined him there in April 1939.

Various attempts have been made by film clubs and historians (including Gomes) to reconstitute the original version of *L'Atalante* and, though Gomes will go no further than to say that "some progress has been made, and more is always possible," the film is almost universally recognized to be Vigo's masterpiece. During the late 1930s, Vigo was almost forgotten, though an at least partly restored version of *L'Atalante* was shown in Paris in 1940 and attracted some attention. A revival of interest began in France in 1945 and rapidly spread. In Britain, Roger Manvell wrote that Vigo was "perhaps the most original and promising of the greater French directors." In the United States, James Agee called him "one of the very few real originals who have ever worked in film." The Italian director Luigi Comencinci showed *L'Atalante* to his friends, and the opinion was that they were confronted with a masterpiece capable of shaking up any notions about cinema the average spectator might have." And Glauco Viazzi said

that "the handful of films he had made at the time of his death placed him in a position of eminence not only in the French cinema along with René Clair and Jean Renoir, but in all contemporary art. . . . The discovery of a poet is not something that happens every day."

FILMS: À Propos de Nice, 1930; Taris/Jean Taris, Chapion de natation/Taris: Roi de l'eau, 1931; Zéro de conduite, 1933; L'Atalante (originally released in a mutilated version as Le Chaland qui passe), 1934.

ABOUT: Brunius, J. B. En marge du cinéma français, 1954; Buache, F. (ed.) Hommage à Jean Vigo, 1962; Chardère, B. (and others) Jean Vigo, 1961 (in French); Estève, M. (ed.) Jean Vigo, 1966 (in French); Gomes, P. E. Salles Jean Vigo, 1957 (in French; English version 1971) Lherminier, P. Jean Vigo, 1967 (in French); Martin, M. Jean Vigo, 1966 (in French); Rhode, E. Jean Vigo, 1966 (in English); Roud, R. (ed.) Cinema: A Critical Dictionary, 1980; Sitney, P. A. (ed.) The Essential Cinema, 1975; Smith, J. M. Jean Vigo, 1972 (in English); Weinberg, H. G. (ed.) Jean Vigo, 1951 (in English). *Periodicals*—Film Heritage Fall 1973; Hollywood Quarterly April 1947, Winter 1947–1948; Nation July 12, 1947.

*VISCONTI, LUCHINO (Count don Luchino Visconti di Modrone) (November 2, 1906–March 17, 1976), was born in Milan, Italy, the third son of Giuseppe Visconti and the former Carla Erba. His mother was the daughter of a millionaire industrialist and his father was the son of the Duke of Modrone. His father's family, wealthy landowners, had received their dukedom from Napoleon. They trace their ancestry to the Visconti who ruled Milan from 1277 to 1447, and on back to Desiderius, father-in-law of Charlemagne.

With his six brothers and sisters, Luchino Visconti grew up in his father's *palazzo* in Milan. His education was supervised by his mother. She was a talented musician and he at first envisaged a musical career also, studying the cello for ten years in childhood and adolescence. His delight in the theatre and opera also developed in childhood, inspired by the plays and entertainments his father liked to arrange in the *palazzo*'s private theatre. From the age of seven, he attended performances at La Scala opera house in Milan, which his grandfather and then his uncle had helped to support. Although Visconti usually described his childhood as idyllic, there was discord between his parents. In 1921 they separated for good, and a bitter court battle over Carla Visconti's share of the Erba fortune ensued. She eventually regained her property but lived thereafter in retirement, the children staying sometimes with her, sometimes with their father.

°vēs kōn´ tē

LUCHINO VISCONTI

As a youth Visconti was restless and discontented. He ran away repeatedly from home, and once from a college in Geneva. Hoping that military discipline might bring him under control, his father sent him to the cavalry school at Pinerolo, where he conceived a passion for horses.

For some ten years after that the breeding of racehorses was Visconti's principal interest—he often remarked on the similarity between the problems involved in schooling horses and directing actors (and said that horses were on the whole preferable because they didn't talk). During this period Visconti dabbled in the arts but remained uncertain of his direction. He painted, designed sets for one or two plays, and tried his hand as a film scenarist. He was nearly thirty when in 1936 he left Italy with the intention of working in the cinema in England or France. The same year, having been introduced by Coco Chanel to Jean Renoir at a racetrack, he found himself on the great French director's production team.

At first in charge of costumes, Visconti then served as Renoir's third assistant director on *Une Partie de campagne* (1936) and *Les Bas Fonds* (1937). Escaping in this way from the claustrophobia of Italy, home, and Fascism, and finding himself accepted by a group of dedicated and talented artists in the heady atmosphere of the Popular Front, permanently changed Visconti's life. Of Renoir himself he said: "His was a human influence, not a professional one. To be with Renoir, to listen to him, that opened my mind."

After a brief, disillusioning visit to Hollywood

in 1937, Visconti went home. In 1940 he was able to work once more with Renoir, who had gone to Italy to film an adaptation of *La Tosca*. Renoir had to abandon the movie when Italy declared war on France and it was completed by Charles Koch. Visconti himself remained in Italy, where he joined the editorial staff of the magazine *Cinema*. The young critics and filmmakers associated with *Cinema* were in vigorous revolt against the insipidity and conformism of the contemporary Italian film industry. Their aim was to make cinema an extension of the literary realism that had developed in Italy at the end of the nineteenth century, notably in the work of the Sicilian novelist Giovanni Verga.

Visconti's first film was *Ossessione* (*Obsession*, 1942), based on James M. Cain's starkly naturalistic thriller *The Postman Always Rings Twice*, with the action translated from America to the Romagna region of Italy. Visconti had been looking for a subject that would not invite the hostility of the Fascist censors, and the Cain novel had been suggested to him by Renoir (whose stylistic influence can be detected in this but in none of Visconti's later films). *Ossessione* is about the destructive passion that develops between Giovanna, wife of an aging innkeeper, and Gino, a young wanderer who takes a casual job at the inn. At Giovanna's instigation, the husband is disposed of in a contrived accident, and his murderers take over the inn. Gino begins to suspect that he has been used and goes to another woman, a young dancer with whom his relationship is purely physical, uncomplicated by financial greed or sexual politics. But the police are closing in, and Gino and Giovanna, reconciled, die together as they try to escape arrest.

Several members of the *Cinema* group had a hand in the script of *Ossessione*, which thus became a kind of manifesto. At its first showing in Rome in 1942 it had an effect that was described as "explosive." Appearing at a time when the Italian cinema was devoted to optimistic trivia, *Ossessione*'s social and psychological authenticity and sexual frankness outraged the Church and the Fascist censors, and terrified the commercial distributors. When the censors tried to ban it, Visconti and his friends appealed to Mussolini himself, who passed it with only a few cuts. In the confusion following the Allied invasion, the film was destroyed. Visconti managed to preserve a duplicate, however, and a somewhat mutilated version of *Ossessione* was finally released some years after the war. It was almost universally hailed as the first masterpiece of Italian neorealism. Pierre Leprohon has called it "a great film, the portrait of a miserable, greedy, sensual, obstinate race at grips with the daily struggle for existence and with instincts that they are unable to master. For, over and above the neorealism, this film has the ingredient indispensable for its lasting greatness: poetry."

For a time during the war, Visconti was imprisoned by the Fascist authorities, charged with aiding the Resistance. Moved from jail to jail and threatened with shooting, he was only reprieved by the Allied invasion. After the liberation of Rome, he filmed the trial and execution of several Fascist officials, including his jailer, and the death of another at the hands of an angry mob; these sequences appear in *Giorni di gloria (Days of Glory*, 1945), a documentary produced by the Allies.

In 1945 Visconti began another and immensely successful and influential career as a theatre director. No one did more to free the Italian stage from outworn conventions, techniques, and attitudes or to modernize its repertoire, to which he added the works of such contemporary French and American writers as Sartre, Cocteau, Anouilh, Arthur Miller, Tennessee Williams, Hemingway, and Erskine Caldwell. Visconti built up a repertory company which later provided acting and technical talent for his films, and whose best-known products are the actor Marcello Mastroianni and the director Franco Zeffirelli.

There were no professional actors at all in Visconti's next film, however. Visconti was a Marxist, though an unorthodox one, much influenced by the Italian socialist leader and theorist Antonio Gramsci. In 1947 he went to Sicily with some funds advanced by the Communist Party, intending to make a short documentary. What he saw there inspired a far more ambitious project—a vast fresco of the life of the Sicilian poor, in three parts dealing respectively with the fishermen, the peasants, and the sulfur miners. In the event, only one part was completed—*La terra trema: Episodio del mare*.

The film is loosely based on Verga's novel *I malavoglia*, but in Visconti's Marxist adaptation the great enemy of the poor Sicilian fishermen is not the sea but the local wholesalers, who own the boats and pay the fishermen derisory prices for what they catch. One family, the Valastro, try to free themselves from this pernicious system. They mortgage their house and buy their own boat, but are ruined when it is destroyed in a storm. The film centers around two key episodes in the development of the political consciousness of the young 'Ntoni Valastro—when he leads a spontaneous if short-lived revolt against the wholesalers, and when, at the end, he recognizes the need for concerted rather than individual action against exploitation.

La terra trema is performed entirely by the people of the village of Aci-Trezza, who contributed in important ways to Visconti's scenario and who say what they have to say in their own dialect (which is so obscure that it was necessary to overlay the dialogue with a commentary in standard Italian). There is an elemental quality in the film that has reminded critics of Flaherty and Eisenstein. It has occasional longueurs, and purists have complained of certain hauntingly beautiful shots whose only function is aesthetic. Nevertheless, as Geoffrey Nowell-Smith has said, "the chiselled beauty of its images, the simplicity and rigour of its narrative, and its unbending concern with social realities have all caused *La terra trema* to be hailed as a masterpiece of the propaganda film." It received first prize at the Venice Film Festival in 1948. It was nevertheless not popular with audiences used to lighter fare, was not widely distributed, and is said to have cost Visconti almost $200,000 of his own money.

For some years after that Visconti restricted his activities to the theatre, presenting among other things a number of innovatory interpretations of the classics like his celebrated 1948 production of *As You Like It* (with additional scenery and costumes by Salvador Dali), and an equally famous version of John Ford's *'Tis Pity She's a Whore*, produced in Paris in 1951. The excessive visual effects and self-indulgent *coups de théâtre* that had marred some of his earlier productions gave way to a more purposive and disciplined use of all the resources of the theatre, but he never lost his love of spectacle or his meticulous concern for realistic detail (luxuries that he was prepared to pay for himself if necessary).

The same qualities distinguished his operatic productions, which were often lavishly staged, but in which his singers were required to curb the traditional extravagance of operatic gesture and to "act like people." Many considered Visconti the greatest operatic director of his day, especially in a triumphant series of productions with Maria Callas. "The real reason I have done opera," he once asserted, "is the particular opportunity of working with Mme. Callas, who is such a great artist." His operas were produced not only at La Scala and elsewhere in Italy but at Covent Garden in London (where he staged an unforgettable production of Verdi's *Don Carlos* in 1958) and in other foreign countries. In 1958 he helped Gian-Carlo Menotti to launch the Spoleto Festival of Two Worlds, for which he directed a number of operas over the years.

Meanwhile Visconti had made his third film, *Bellissima* (The Most Beautiful, 1951), starring Anna Magnani as a working-class woman befuddled by the movies. She enters her small daughter in a competition to find "the prettiest child in Rome," who will star in a new film. The child eventually wins the competition, but by that time her mother has seen something of the ruthless commercialism of the movie industry; she rejects the proffered contract and is restored to her long-suffering husband. The director himself collaborated on the script, as he always did, along with Suso Cecchi d'Amico, who was thereafter his principal writer, and Francesco Rosi, himself now an important director. *Bellissima*, the first of Visconti's films to be released in the United States, is an amiable satire on the petty greeds and snobberies of Italian society and on the parasitic nature of the cinema. It is all the same a minor work in the Visconti canon, and an atypical one.

It was followed by *Senso* (*Feeling*, 1954), widely regarded as one of his greatest films. Set in the *risorgimento* of the mid-1860s, it opens with a brilliant scene in a Venetian theatre where a performance of Verdi's *Il Trovatore* disintegrates into an Italian nationalist demonstration against the occupying Austrian forces. The story (from a novella by Camillo Boito) turns on the love affair that develops between an Italian countess—a nationalist, played by Alida Valli—and a young Austrian officer (Farley Granger) for whom she betrays her husband, her brother, and her political allegiance. This personal drama resembles that of *Obsessione*, not least in the way that emotional responses and moral standards are shown to be influenced by class and historical factors—notably in the complex characterization of the Austrian officer Franz. As Geoffrey Nowell-Smith points out there is, moreover, "an implicit parallel between the events of 1866 and those of 1943–1945. In each case, one élite replaced another, and the new élite came to look suspiciously similar to the old."

It has often been pointed out that Visconti brought to the theatre the skills of a film director, and to the cinema those of a stage (and especially operatic) director. From the beginning his films were in some respects operatic in form, made up of scenes involving two or at most three people, with occasional interventions by larger groups having the function of a chorus. This is particularly true of *Senso*, which actually begins with an operatic performance, and whose plot would look perfectly at home in a romantic opera (though in fact it escapes melodrama because of the subtlety of the characterization). *Senso* is operatic also in the opulence of its technique. It was the first of Visconti's films in color, which he used with absolute mastery, making *Senso*, as Pierre Leprohon says, "a landmark as important in its day as Renoir's *Carrosse d'or*."

Visconti used three different cameramen to achieve the effects he sought at different points in the film—effects that were often derived from various styles of nineteenth-century Venetian painting. Admired as it was and is by the critics, *Senso* was nevertheless a failure commercially. A dubbed and shortened version was shown in Britain as *The Wanton Countess*, with English dialogue by Tennessee Williams and Paul Bowles.

With a growing reputation for extravagance in production and failure at the box office, Visconti was unable to find producers. In an effort to vindicate himself, he shot his next film in seven weeks, with a relatively small budget provided by himself and some wealthy friends. This was *Le notti bianche* (*White Nights*, 1957), adapted from Dostoevsky's short story. Natalia (played by Maria Schell) lives with her blind grandmother. Their mysterious lodger, whom she loves, has left them, promising to return. Every evening she awaits his return on a bridge over the canal that separates her dreamy private world from the vital, noisy, transient life of the big city. On this bridge—which is also a bridge between memory and actuality, illusion and reality—she meets one evening a man (Marcello Mastroianni) who is as lonely as herself, an exile in the city. He falls in love with her, but loses her when her half-imaginary lover quite unexpectedly returns.

For the first time Visconti filmed entirely in the studio with constructed sets, deliberately achieving a stylized and theatrical atmosphere that is intensified by grainy photography in soft definition, reminiscent of the "poetic realism" of Marcel Carné. The result was admired at the Venice Film Festival, but at the time of its release received generally tepid reviews. The adherents of neorealism indeed greeted it with considerable hostility, as a further step away from the naturalism of Visconti's early films—a kind of betrayal. Most critics now regard it as a work of great charm but no particular significance, though it has been claimed as an influence on the films of Jacques Demy and Resnais.

Visconti's retreat from naturalism was reversed in his next film, *Rocco e i suoi fratelli* (*Rocco and His Brothers*, 1960). It may be seen almost as a continuation of *La terra trema*, examining the fate of the widowed Rosaria Pafundi and her five sons, a peasant family from the impoverished south trying to make a new life in the northern industrial city of Milan. Each brother in effect illustrates a different approach to the problems they all face: one opts for unobtrusive integration, another (the saintlike Rocco) clings loyally but hopelessly to the traditional peasant values, and one decisively rejects them. Widely regarded as a requiem for these virtues, the film was actually intended to convey something very different—a recognition that the old values, and the traditional Italian family in which they are embodied, must be modified if society is ever to become less confining and unjust. When Ciro denounces his brother Simone to the police—for a murder committed in the name of "honor"—he is freeing himself from the bonds of the past. If the film confused its critics it is because of something ambivalent in Visconti's own view of the world—its persistent opposition of what Geoffrey Nowell-Smith calls "two conflicting ideals, one rooted emotionally in the past, and the other projected intellectually into the future."

Like most of Visconti's movies, *Rocco and His Brothers* changed considerably in the course of its filming. Although the nucleus of the story was original, the script incorporates material from the Milanese stories of Giovanni Testori, and from Dostoevsky, Thomas Mann, and Verga; a number of scriptwriters were called in at different stages. The distinguished international cast included Katina Paxinou, Alain Delon, Claudia Cardinale, and Annie Girardot. *Rocco and His Brothers* was the first of Visconti's films to gain worldwide distribution and not to lose money. It won a special jury prize at the 1961 Venice Film Festival and several other international awards. Though the version seen in the United States was damaged by extensive cuts, it was warmly received by most American critics. One in *Newsweek* found it "a moving humanitarian report" comparable to John Ford's *The Grapes of Wrath*, with a "persistent reality that finally drowns out the movie's faults."

This success made possible Visconti's ambitious screen version of Giuseppe di Lampedusa's novel *Il gattopardo* (*The Leopard*, 1963). A return to the *risorgimento*, it is a study of an ancient family of Sicilian aristocrats at a time of rapid social change. This theme, and the fact that Visconti undertook it with a multi-million dollar budget provided by 20th Century–Fox, using a wide screen and Technicolor, greatly disquieted the nostalgics of neorealism. In fact, Visconti recreates the story in his own way. Where the Prince of Lampedusa accounts for the survival of the House of Salina in almost mystical terms, the "Red Duke" Visconti attributes it to political and economic cunning—as another example of the way the old order perpetuates itself in the face of revolutionary ferment. He shows the old Prince (played by Burt Lancaster) coming to terms with a changing social order. Over the timid objections of the family priest, the Prince gives his blessing and a bag of gold to his nephew Tancredi (Alain Delon), off to join Garibaldi's forces, and upon Tancredi's return, arranges a marriage between this fiery young opportunist and the beautiful Angela (Claudia Cardinale), daughter of a rich bourgeois. In the brilliant and immensely long ball scene at the end, the alliance between aristocrats and parvenus is sealed, amid rumors of reprisals against Garibaldi's peasant followers and intimations of the old Prince's mortality. Politically the film is highly ambiguous. The stratagems by which the privileged class will survive are set forth with unsparing realism, but as we see through the Prince's eyes what endures and what is lost of the past, the dominant note is unmistakably one of nostalgia.

The film won the Golden Palm at the Cannes Film Festival and had a splendid reception in Italy and elsewhere in Europe. The version shown in Britain and the United States, however, was shorn of several important scenes, badly printed on inferior color stock, and insensitively dubbed. Visconti, denying paternity of this version, remarked: "It is our destiny to be always in the hands of assassins. . . . We work for months and months to create material that is then torn to shreds by ravening dogs." Even thus mutilated, the film seemed to David Robinson "a beautiful and fascinating spectacle. . . . The *mise-en-scène* is superb. Each scene is staged with the rhythm of a choreographer and the composition of a painter" and "it is a film of enormous virtuosity and brio." Robinson's most serious complaint was that he would have expected deeper social and psychological perception from Visconti, who "apart from anything else, reflects the central historical situation of *Il gattopardo* in his own life." In 1983, a new print of *The Leopard*, dubbed in Italian with English subtitles and longer by twenty-five minutes, was released in the United States and Britain to general acclaim. "The reappearance of this enchanting work," Vincent Canby wrote, "proves that . . . two decades make no difference whatsoever, but twenty-five minutes can transform a very good film into a possibly great one. . . . The replaced footage now reveals the shapeliness and elegance of the movie Visconti conceived, which is more about the inevitability of change than about the specific nature of those changes."

Vaghe stelle dell'orsa (1965), shown in the United States as *Sandra* and in Britain as *Of a Thousand Delights*, is one of the most complex and difficult of Visconti's films. Sandra and her American husband drive from Geneva to the ancient Italian hill-town of Volterra—a journey into the past. They are to attend a ceremony in which the garden of Sandra's family home is to be opened as a public park in memory of her Jewish father, who died in Auschwitz. Enigmatic incidents begin to hint at two dark possibilities—that an incestuous relationship had existed between Sandra and her brother Gianni, and that their mother (now insane) had betrayed their father to the Nazis, At the end of the film Gianni is dead by suicide, and Sandra, her ghosts exorcized, has achieved a dubious liberation. Inspired partly by the *Oresteia* of Aeschylus, the theme of the transmission across the generations of a family curse becomes in Visconti's hands a historical and existential phenomenon. The film won the major award, the Golden Lion, at the Venice Film Festival in 1965, and seemed to at least one critic Visconti's greatest single work. But many reviewers, struck as they were by the film's brooding atmosphere, its striking visual contrasts of light and shade, remained more puzzled than impressed.

Lo straniero (*The Stranger*, 1967), Visconti's rather flat-footed attempt to film Camus' *L'Étranger*, was followed by *La caduta degli Dei* (*The Damned*, 1969), a baroque and intricately plotted study, through the microcosm of a family of German steel barons, of the conditions that gave rise to Nazism in Germany. John Coleman thought it "surely the worst Visconti yet, a great wallow in decor and decadence," while Geoffrey Nowell-Smith called it "a confident, if not entirely successful, return to the operatic-melodramatic mode" of *Senso*. It seemed to the latter critic that Visconti was becoming less and less a critic of society as his interest shifted from history to culture, and Nowell-Smith dealt dismissively with *Morte a Venezia* (*Death in Venice*), which followed in 1971.

In the novella by Thomas Mann on which the film is based, Gustav von Aschenbach is a great writer whose work and life alike have celebrated the classical virtues of order, restraint, and discipline. On a vacation in Venice he encounters a Polish youth, Tadzio. They never so much as speak to one another but the boy's beauty—itself the embodiment of a Platonic ideal—unlocks the ecstatic and Dionysian part of Aschenbach's nature, so long denied. The moral certainties of a lifetime are swept away in an anguished discovery of the terrible powers of chaos and unreason. Mann based Aschenbach on Gustav Mahler; in Visconti's film he is presented as a composer rather than a writer, and Mahler's music fills the soundtrack. Visconti said: "I think of *Death in Venice* as essentially the search by an artist for perfection in art and the impossibility of achieving it. When he achieves it, that's death. There is a second theme: the dualism between bourgeois respectability and the corruption within the artist—the seeds of genius and self-

destruction. . . . The boy [is] a sort of angel of destiny, a fatal presence; he knows, instinctively, that he will lead Aschenbach to his death."

Visconti's perfectionism is legendary, and his attention to authenticity of detail was carried to extreme lengths in this film. At one point Aschenbach carries a newspaper and some letters: the newspaper is one actually published on June 11, 1911, and the stamps on the letters are equally authentic and correctly franked for that time and place. Dirk Bogarde, who plays Aschenbach, said of Visconti: "He concentrates every second, oh, Christ, every split second. You're supposed to do your job perfectly, because he does his perfectly." Whether in this instance Visconti had done his job perfectly is a matter of opinion. No one denied that it was a film of great visual beauty and power, brilliantly capturing the diseased beauty of the ancient city in which it is set. Jan Dawson noted that "the social nuances and sartorial niceties of life in an expensive hotel are lovingly observed, the self-conscious nonchalance of the guests minutely choreographed." Georges Sadoul called it "unquestionably [Visconti's] most perfect film . . . a richly textured, obsessional study of passion and social putrefaction," and at the Cannes Film Festival it received the Twenty-Fifth Anniversary Prize and the Golden Globe. For many critics, however, it was a vulgarization of Mann's story: Jan Dawson thought it "only the pathetic self-discovery of an elderly closet queen," and David Thomson called it "a disguised weepie, its surface a sticky crust, covering nothing."

Soon after completing *Death in Venice* Visconti collapsed with "nicotine poisoning." He never fully recovered his health, but continued to work, making three more films. *Ludwig* (1973), about the mad king of nineteenth-century Bavaria, seemed to Stanley Kauffman "as mad as its subject—in every way but one. It is gorgeous." *Gruppo di famiglia in un interno* (*Conversation Piece*, 1974) stars Burt Lancaster as an old professor whose home is invaded by a rich, vulgar, and imperious countess and her retinue; it was warmly received in Paris but hissed at the New York Film Festival in 1975. *L'innocente* (*The Innocent*, 1976) has Giancarlo Giannini as a heroic D'Annunzian hedonist who murders his wife's illegitimate baby in the interests of uxorious delight and, finding this existential gesture unappreciated, kills himself. Directed from a wheelchair, this "ravishingly elegant movie" was Visconti's last. He was editing it when he died in his sumptuous Roman villa of influenza and heart disease.

Luchino Visconti was a stocky, elegant man,

deep-voiced, dark-eyed, with heavy eyebrows and the prominent nose of his great ancestors. He was said to be liable to "sky-rending rages" on set but in conversation was a person of "totally disarming courtesy and sly, laconic wit." Often accused of "voting Left and living Right," he remained a communist all his life, though he would not join the party. He was also a Christian, though often anticlerical. As a young man, he said: "I was impelled toward the cinema by, above all, the need to tell stories of people who were alive, of people living amid things and not of the things themselves. The cinema that interests me is an anthropomorphic cinema. The most humble gestures of man, his bearing, his feelings and instincts, are enough to make the things that surround him poetic and alive. . . . And [his] momentary absence from the luminous rectangle gives to everything an appearance of still life [*natura morta*]."

Geoffrey Nowell-Smith, to whose study of Visconti this note is much indebted, says that "the commonly held stereotypes about Visconti are that he is totally humourless and incapable of self-irony, that his imagination is sensual rather than intellectual, and that he is a crude social realist with a taste for 'positive heroes,' and an antifeminist who neither likes nor understands his women characters." And elsewhere Nowell-Smith writes: "Aristocratic, temperamentally aloof, conscious of the advantages and anomalies of his privileged position, he remained unaffected by the general atmosphere of passionate outgoing concern for immediate questions in which so many of his contemporaries were caught up. . . . His Marxist commitment was different in kind from the diffuse leftism of many of his colleagues. It had its source in a sense of history, and of his personal situation in the historical process, rather than in sentiment, and it expressed itself in historical reflection mediated by a sense of artistic form."

Long recognized as one of the three masters (with Fellini and Antonioni) of contemporary Italian cinema, he has recently been denigrated and called "trivial, ornate, and unconvinced," a director who made his name by his "flamboyant treatment of a few prestigious ventures." Even those who continue to admire Visconti's work reserve their praise for his early films. An artist's reputation often slumps after his death, however, and the visual brilliance of his late films may yet receive its due.

FILMS: Ossessione (Obsession), 1942; Giorni di gloria (Days of Glory; documentary), directed by Mario Serandrei in collaboration with Visconti and others, 1945; La terra trema: Episodio del mare (The Earth Trembles), 1947; Bellissima (The Most Beautiful), 1951;

Episode in Siamo donne (We, The Women), 1953; Senso (Feeling), 1954; Le notti bianche (White Nights), 1957; Rocco e i suoi fratelli (Rocco and His Brothers), 1960; "Il lavoro" ("The Job"), *episode in* Boccaccio '70, 1962; Il gattopardo (The Leopard), 1963; Vaghe stelle dell'orsa (US: Sandra/UK: Of a Thousand Delights), 1965; Le streghe, episode in Le strega bruciata viva, 1966; Lo straniero (The Stranger), 1967; La caduti degli Dei (The Damned), 1969; Morte a Venezia (Death in Venice), 1971; Ludwig, 1973; Gruppo di famiglia in un interno (Conversation Piece), 1974; L'innocente (the Innocent), 1976. Published screenplays: Luchino Visconti: Two Screenplays (contains La terra trema, Senso), translated by Judith Green, 1970; Luchino Visconti: Three Screenplays (contains White Nights, Rocco and His Brothers, Il lavoro), translated by Judith Green, 1970.

ABOUT: Baldelli, P. I film di Luchino Visconti, 1965; Bawden, L. The Oxford Companion to Film, 1976; Castello, G. C. Visconti, 1962; Constantini, C. L'ultimo Visconti, 1976; Covi, A. Diabattiti di film, 1971; Current Biography, 1965; Estève, M. Luchino Visconti, 1963; Elizondo, S. Luchino Visconti, 1963; Ferrara, G. Luchino Visconti, 1963; Guillaume, Y. Luchino Visconti, 1966; Hovald, P. G. Le néo-realisme italien, 1959; Leprohon, P. The Italian Cinema (translated from the French by Roger Greaves and Oliver Stallybrass), 1966; Micciche, L. (ed.) Morte a Venezia di Luchino Visconti, 1971; Nowell-Smith, G. Luchino Visconti (second edition), 1973; Sadoul, G. Dictionary of Film Makers, 1972; Schlappner, M. and others, Luchino Visconti, 1975; Servadio, G. Luchino Visconti: A Biography, 1983; Sperenzi, M. (ed.) L'opera di Luchino Visconti, 1969; Thomson, D. A Biographical Dictionary of the Cinema, 1975. Periodicals—Cue December 20, 1969; June 27, 1970; Film March–April 1957; Winter 1961; Film Comment May 1976; Film Quarterly Spring 1960; Films and Filming July 1956, October 1962, April 1963; Guardian April 4, 1970; March 4, 1971; Hi Fi October 1968; Musical America November 1961; New York Times March 18, 1976; September 11, 1983; New Yorker July 20, 1968; September 19, 1983; Opera News September 28, 1963; Saturday Review December 29, 1962; August 8, 1970; December 19, 1970; Show March 1970, June 1971; Sight and Sound Spring 1956, Summer–Autumn 1959, Summer 1976; Theatre Arts March 1959; Time March 29, 1976; Times (London) March 3, 1971.

WALSH, "RAOUL" (ALBERT EDWARD)

(March 11, 1887–December 31, 1980), American director, scenarist, producer, and actor, was born in Manhattan, the second of four children. His father, Thomas Walsh, was one of four brothers who had emigrated from Ireland via Spain, having—at least according to his son's account—helped *their* rebel father break out of Dublin jail. Once he had arrived in New York, Thomas Walsh resumed his profession as a men's clothing designer and married Elizabeth Brough, a strikingly attractive woman of mixed

RAOUL WALSH

Irish-Spanish descent. The family was prosperous and sociable; Walsh grew up in a large brownstone on East 48th Street and later in a palatial mansion on Riverside Drive, both of which were constantly filled with visitors. Among those whom he recalled meeting during his boyhood were Edwin Booth, Buffalo Bill Cody, Enrico Caruso, Mark Twain, the artist Frederic Remington, and the heavyweight boxing champion Gentleman Jim Corbett.

After graduating from Public School 93 on Amsterdam Avenue, Walsh enrolled at the Jesuit-run Seton College. About this time, though, his mother died of cancer, aged only forty-two. Deeply affected by her death and finding his home unbearable, he decided to interrupt his education and leave New York for a while. Accounts of the next few years in Walsh's life differ considerably. His own version, as given in his autobiography, is the most colorful and provided him in later life with a rich store of anecdotes that he retailed with gusto.

Invited by his uncle Matthew, owner of a cargo schooner, to sail with him for Havana, Walsh readily accepted, so enjoying the outward trip that he resolved to become a sailor. On the way home, however, the ship was hit by a hurricane in the Caribbean and drifted for three days before being towed into Veracruz. Disenchanted with seafaring, Walsh learned to ride and rope steers and joined a trail herd heading north for Texas: "Looking back on that drive, I still wonder why more cow men did not lose their reason." After a torrid entanglement with the mistress of a Mexican general, he crossed the Rio Grande two jumps ahead of both the lady and

the *rurales* and surfaced at a ranch in southern Texas. From there, in 1905, he was sent up to Butte, Montana, with a trainload of horses.

In Butte, having lost all his cash in a poker game, Walsh took a job as undertaker's assistant. Since the undertaker never paid him any wages, he soon quit and went to work instead for the local doctor, René Echinelle, who claimed that his father had been personal physician to Napoleon. Acting as operating assistant and chief anesthetist, Walsh succeeded in killing at least one patient. ("He had no chance anyhow," observed Echinelle.) When the doctor himself expired of a lung hemorrhage, Walsh quit Butte and made his way back to Texas, where he found work in San Antonio breaking horses for the US Cavalry. Recuperating after a horse had fallen on him and injured his knee, he was noticed by the manager of an itinerant theatrical troupe who needed someone to ride a horse on stage. The play was *The Clansman,* later to be adapted by D. W. Griffith as *The Birth of a Nation;* Walsh's role required him to dress up in Ku Klux Klan gear and ride across the stage on a treadmill, waving a fiery cross. His pay was $30 a week: "I said, 'Oh gee, this is great. . . . No more cowboys for me.'"

The tour wound up in Saint Louis. Along with a fellow actor, Walsh decided to try his luck with the New York theatrical agencies. Back in his home town in 1909, he discovered that stage work was harder to come by than jobs in the newfangled movies, scorned by most self-respecting thespians. Walsh had no such prejudices and soon found himself playing juvenile leads for the Pathé brothers in New Jersey. Tall, fearless, and ruggedly handsome, he was physically well-equipped for the work, though he later always insisted that he had been hopelessly untalented. For a while he alternated stage and film acting, and also studied playwrighting with Paul Armstrong, a family friend and author of several successful plays. It was apparently at Armstrong's suggestion that Walsh adopted the more exotic "Raoul" in place of his own given names, though he later claimed that Raoul was his baptismal name.

The Pathé films in which Walsh appeared were mostly, as he put it, "dreadful clunkers." One of them, *Paul Revere's Ride,* involved his galloping hell-for-leather down a street furnished with trolley tracks. He pointed out the anachronism to the director, Émile Couteau (*sic?*—this may have been the émigré Frenchman, Émile Chautard, later Sternberg's mentor). "I said, 'Say, they didn't have any trolley tracks in—.' He said, 'Who the hell is directing this picture, you or me?' That's about when I decided I'd have to become a director."

Meanwhile Walsh's riding skill had been noticed by the director Christy Cabanne, who was working with D. W. Griffith at Biograph. Walsh, who had seen some Biograph pictures ("Not as god-awful as the stuff Pathé was making"), accepted the offer of a job and appeared in a number of one- and two-reelers with such actors as Mary Pickford, the Gish sisters, Blanche Sweet, and Lionel Barrymore. When, in 1913, Griffith left Biograph to join Mutual in California, he invited Walsh along with him. "Griffith said: 'Someday I'll make you a director.' I don't know why he said that, maybe because I was a lousy actor."

At Griffith's new Fine Art studios in Hollywood, Walsh was soon working as assistant director as well as actor, taking every opportunity to watch the boss at work. "I admired everything he did. . . . He really was a master to me." His first independent assignment came when, on the strength of his knowledge of Mexico, he was sent to El Paso to shoot scenes for a film about Pancho Villa with—it was hoped—the General himself playing the lead. Through a shrewd combination of bribery and flattery, Walsh secured Villa's cooperation, even persuading him to restage the battle of Durango for the camera's benefit, and took part in the triumphal entry into Mexico City. To Walsh's footage were added some highly romanticized episodes (directed by Cabanne) from the life of the young Villa (played by Walsh) to complete *The Life of General Villa* (1914).

Walsh returned from Mexico with a suitcaseful of pesos given him by the grateful Villa (they turned out to be worthless) in time to act as assistant director on Griffith's Civil War epic, *The Birth of a Nation* (1915), handling most of the battle sequences. "Mr. Walsh," observed Griffith, "if you had been a Confederate general, the South would never have lost the war." Walsh was now judged ready to direct films of his own and was assigned to a string of two-reelers. These were the usual cheerfully eclectic mixture of the period—mainly Westerns, comedies, and melodramas. He attacked them all with lively enthusiasm, often also playing lead roles and, most likely, scripting as well. Other lead players often included his younger brother George, then just starting out on his acting career, and Miriam Cooper, a dark, soulfully pretty actress whom Walsh married in 1916.

Just how many of these quickies Walsh directed under the banner of Reliance-Majestic, Mutual's associate company, would be hard to determine—a dozen or so for certain, though he himself reckoned more like forty. His last work for the company was his first full-length feature, *Pillars of Society* (1916), an adaptation of Ibsen's play that he took over and completed, under Griffith's supervision, after the original director, "poor devil, had hit the laughing water." (Griffith made a few minor changes to the completed film and released it some months after Walsh had moved on.)

Walsh's direction had already attracted some favorable reviews, as well as the attention of other film companies. In June 1915 he was offered a job by Winfield Sheehan of the newly founded Fox studio in New York, at the then munificent salary of $400 a week. Walsh would work for Fox, on and off, for the next twenty years; his first picture for the company was *The Regeneration* (1915), which may well be also the first feature-length gangster film ever made. One scene called for a crowded riverboat on the Hudson to catch fire: Walsh shot it with such realism that three fireboats and a police launch showed up, and the rising young director was hauled off to the station house. The studio was delighted by the free publicity and equally pleased by the laudatory notices, which suggest that Walsh's sentimentally robust style of filmmaking was evident from the outset. "There is a grim sort of humor in many of the scenes," wrote Lynde Denig in *Motion Picture Weekly*; "there is an abundance of excitement in others, and throughout the picture carries a genuine heart interest."

Learning that Cecil B. DeMille was planning a film of *Carmen* with Geraldine Farrar, Walsh swiftly came up with his own Theda Bara version. DeMille got the better reviews, but Walsh's film took more at the box office, and Fox raised his salary to $1,000 a week. He followed with *The Serpent* (1916), a Russian melodrama (originally planned as *The Siren of Seville*, but it snowed in New Jersey) before returning to the West Coast, where Fox was just installing itself. Walsh's first picture there was an energetic Western, *Blue Blood and Red* (1916), which launched his brother George as an athletic star in the Fairbanks style.

Opinions of Walsh's early films have to be taken on trust, since few of them have survived. Among those missing is *The Honor System* (1917), which John Ford once named as one of the ten best movies he had ever seen. Set—and largely filmed—in the Arizona State Penitentiary, it hinged on a system of penal reform espoused by the state governor, whereby selected felons were released to visit their families, on their word to return at a set time. To enhance the authenticity of his script, Walsh even spent a few nights in the jail as an ordinary prisoner. For the New York premiere, the gratified governor volunteered to send along a genuine convict to ad-

dress the audience, on honor release. The con
duly arrived and made a heartfelt speech affirming his contrition and lively sense of honor,
after which he lit out for the Canadian border
and was never seen again.

A hit with both reviewers and public, *The
Honor System* established Walsh as a major director. That same year he released six more
films, including *The Conqueror,* an ambitious
biography of General Sam Houston starring William Farnum, and said to have cost $300,000;
This Is the Life, a surreal comedy in which a
movie-mad young man (George Walsh) has various bizarre experiences while under gas at the
dentist's; two vehicles for the director's wife,
Miriam Cooper, *Betrayed* and *The Innocent
Sinner;* and *The Silent Lie,* a rough-and-tumble
adventure set in the far Northwest. This last led
Edward Weitzel to protest in *Motion Picture
World* that "spitting tobacco juice over the
shoulders of a woman of even doubtful reputation is carrying the realism of a Northwestern
dance hall a step too far."

In November 1917 Walsh was offered a long-
term deal by Sam Goldwyn. However, Fox had
cannily included an option clause in *its* contract
and, to Walsh's annoyance, refused to release
him. As his contribution to the war effort he directed *The Pride of New York* (1917), in which
an ex-construction worker becomes a hero on the
battlefield, and *The Prussian Cur* (1918), a propaganda piece that overshot its mark. A scene
reminiscent of *Birth of a Nation,* in which the
Ku Klux Klan exercise lynch law against a group
of pro-German "traitors," was widely condemned, even at the time.

Evangeline (1919), based on Longfellow's
narrative poem, marks a rare foray by Walsh
into art movies. Miriam Cooper played the title
role of a French Canadian girl finally reunited
with her lost lover, only to have him expire of the
plague. Much praised for its pictorial beauty, the
film—Walsh later recalled—"got the most
wonderful write-ups of any picture I ever
made. . . . But it didn't make a quarter. So I decided then to play to Main Street and to hell with
art."

In 1920, having finally worked out his Fox
contract, Walsh set up his own production company, the Mayflower Photoplay Corporation.
His first production, *The Deep Purple* (1920),
starred his wife as an innocent country girl adrift
in the wicked city, and was based on a story by
his old friend and mentor, Paul Armstrong.
Miriam Cooper also featured in *The Oath*
(1921), as a Jew who marries a Gentile in defiance of her father; in *Serenade* (1921), as an aristocratic Castilian heiress in New Mexico; and in

Kindred of the Dust (1922), as a poor squatter's
daughter in love with a rich boy. None of these
melodramas much impressed the critics, and
box-office response was equally lukewarm.

Walsh always preferred to shoot on location
whenever possible—partly for the sake of realism but also to indulge his lifelong passion for
travel. He now accepted a commission from
Goldwyn to make a South Sea pirate movie
and—according to his own account—spent an
orgiastic six months on Tahiti, at one point having his nose pierced while drunk. The resultant
film, *Lost and Found on a South Sea Island*
(1923), he always considered one of his best, but
few reviewers agreed. *Photoplay* dismissed it as
"the same old melodramatic hokum . . . before
a Tahiti backdrop."

The slump in Walsh's critical fortunes was decisively reversed by his next picture, perhaps the
finest of his silent period and, in the opinion of
some critics, the best film he ever directed. *The
Thief of Bagdad* (1924), made for Douglas Fairbanks Pictures, remains (wrote Julian Fox in
Films and Filming, June 1973) "probably the
most truly magical entertainment of the silent
era." Fairbanks took the title role and (as "Elton
John") wrote the story, loosely derived from *The
Thousand and One Nights.* The film deployed a
dazzling battery of special effects, several of
them purloined from Fritz Lang's *Der Müde
Tod,* to which Fairbanks held the US rights, and
whose release he delayed until after his own film
had appeared. *The Thief* conveys an infectious
sense of delight in its own visual wizardry. Fairbanks, at the height of his athletic prowess,
gracefully swashbuckles his way through a fairy-
tale plot full of monsters, marvels, exotic villains,
flying carpets,winged horses, mermaids, and
dragons before finally rescuing the beautiful
princess whom he loves. William Cameron Menzies' sets, luminously photographed by Arthur
Edeson, created a fantastical world whose structures, as a studio handout put it, seemed to be
"hanging from the clouds rather than . . . set
firmly upon earth."

Walsh enjoyed switching "from the rough
stuff I'd been doing to this dreamy kind of epic,"
and he got on well with Fairbanks, whose dynamic acting style accorded perfectly with his
own energetic approach to filmmaking. *The
Thief of Bagdad,* which cost a million dollars,
was shot in only thirty-five days. Walsh intended
it to be "the best picture I had ever directed" and
was gratified by the reviews, even if inevitably
Fairbanks attracted most of the attention. "Here
is magic, here is beauty," enthused *Photoplay.*
"Here is all the colour and phantasy of the greatest work of imaginative literature." Other re-

views called it "the greatest conjuring trick ever performed" and "a feat of motion picture art which will never be equalled." Sixty years later, at the 1984 London Film Festival, the film was re-released in a fresh print with live musical accompaniment and proved to have lost little of its appeal.

Walsh now signed a five-picture deal with Paramount, but results were disappointing. *East of Suez* (1925) refashioned a Somerset Maugham play as a vehicle for Pola Negri; *The Spaniard* (1925) was lurid sub-Valentino stuff, an English girl succumbing to the macho brutalities of her bullfighting abductor; and *The Wanderer* (1925) found Walsh rather unexpectedly in De-Mille territory, expanding the brief parable of the prodigal son into a moralistic spectacular, complete with wicked temple dances and fiery retribution. Flecker's baroque-oriental play *Hassan,* rehashed with a happy ending, furnished the plot for *The Lady of the Harem* (1926), but the enchantment of *The Thief of Bagdad* was wholly absent.

In 1926 Walsh's marriage to Miriam Cooper ended in divorce, rancor, and financial wrangling. On Walsh's side the bitterness endured. In his autobiography, published nearly fifty years later, his first wife is never mentioned by name, referred to only as "a bitch" and "a mercenary witch." (Cooper, in her own autobiography, showed less resentment, acknowledging Walsh's great charm, though observing drily that "he never bored you with the truth.") A few months later Walsh married Lorraine Walker; this marriage also ended in divorce after about ten years, but goes completely unmentioned in his autobiography.

His contract with Paramount fulfilled, Walsh returned to Fox, after an absence of six years, to make the biggest commercial hit of his career. *What Price Glory?,* by Maxwell Anderson and Laurence Stallings, had enjoyed a huge success on Broadway, where its blend of roughhouse humor and pacifism suited the spirit of the time. Walsh's film version (1926) played down the antiwar elements in favor of the brawling, boozy, love-hate relationship between Captain Flagg of the US Marines (Victor McLaglen) and Sergeant Quirk (Edmund Lowe—the character's name became Quirt in the sequels), to the point where Eileen Bowser called it "the archetypal celebration of war as a game played by roistering comrades." Others, like Peter Hogue (*Movietone News,* November 1975), detected "perhaps a wiser movie than its joyously lowbrow air might make it seem," reading the raucous humor of Flagg and Quirk as a defensive response to the horrors of the trenches, while Manny Farber

found it full of "the sweet-tough-earthy feeling that is a Walsh trademark." Walsh staged the battle scenes with unprecedented realism; visitors to the set were terrified, and at least one man was killed during filming. Nearby residents of Beverly Hills, indignant at the incessant explosions, repeatedly called the police, and Walsh appointed a succession of assistant directors as fall guys: "The sheriff would drive up and say 'Who's in charge here?' And the assistant would say 'I am.' They'd put him in the car and take him away, and I'd start again."

For the film's titles, the play's rough language was considerably toned down; not so the actual exchanges improvised by McLaglen and Lowe, as lip-reading members of the public discovered, to their horror or delight. Word soon got around, and the ensuing scandal did nothing but good to the already booming box-office receipts. *What Price Glory?* had two sequels, both directed by Walsh, was remade in 1952 by John Ford, and may well qualify as the archetypal "buddy movie": though Flagg and Quirk brawl endlessly over women—notably over Dolores Del Rio, in one of her earliest starring roles—their lasting emotional commitment is unmistakably to one another.

The Monkey Talks (1927) also derived from a stage hit, a comedy-drama whose bizarre plot involved an undersized man impersonating a circus monkey. It was "possibly a task . . . beyond the ken of any director," suggested Mordaunt Hall in the New York *Times,* though *Photoplay* found it "one of the best pictures of its kind of the year." In *The Loves of Carmen* (1927) Walsh cheerfully burlesqued his earlier film and reunited Del Rio, as a slapstick Carmen, with McLaglen, an improbable Escamillo. The result was "not for the sensitive and not for the family trade," noted *Photoplay*.

Somerset Maugham's play *Rain,* dramatized from his own short story, had made a great hit on Broadway with Jeanne Eagels in the lead. Gloria Swanson, undeterred by anticipated problems with the censor, bought the movie rights and invited Walsh to direct. As Sadie Thompson, the San Francisco hooker stranded on a South Sea island, she gave one of her finest performances, well supported by Lionel Barrymore as the puritanical bigot who succumbs to the fleshly lures he denounces. At Swanson's urging, Walsh himself took the role of the Marine sergeant, Tim O'Hara—his first screen part for a dozen years and as it turned out, his last.

Sadie Thompson (1928)—the original title was vetoed by the Hays Office—is generally held to be the best film treatment of Maugham's play. (Other versions were *Rain* [1932], directed by Milestone with a miscast Joan Crawford, and *Miss Sadie Thompson* [1953], a dire musical version starring Rita Hayworth.) Julian Fox found it "atmospheric, superbly capturing the air of foetid decay in the tropics" and skirting "a very thin line between the acceptable and the downright inflammatory." In Swanson's view, "I had better luck with *Sadie* than any other movie star because I had the advantage of making a good silent of it. If you have to censor Sadie's language, how can you really portray her?" Once again, the titles were fairly innocuous, but lip-readers received different signals.

Reacting with characteristic insouciance to the coming of sound, Walsh commandeered a Fox Movietone van and set off for Utah to shoot the first Western talkie on location. *In Old Arizona* (1929), based on an O. Henry story, was to have been only two reels, but when the Fox executives saw the rushes they asked for five. In the leading role of the Cisco Kid, Walsh cast himself, complete with Pancho Villa moustache and accent to match. The film was nearly finished when the sound van broke down, and it was decided to go home and shoot the final scenes on the Fox back lot. The company drove back through the desert at night, with Walsh riding in the first car. A startled jackrabbit jumped straight through the windshield, hitting him in the face and cutting him badly. He was rushed to hospital in Salt Lake City, but his right eye was beyond saving. Rejecting the offer of a glass substitute ("No, I'd get drunk and lose it"), Walsh adopted a black eye patch, which he wore thereafter with buccaneering panache.

In Old Arizona was completed by Irving Cummings, with Warner Baxter taking over as the Cisco Kid, and was highly successful. Baxter won an Oscar, the only player in a Walsh film ever to do so, and went on to play the Kid in various sequels. Walsh made a rapid recovery from his accident and that same year, his directorial abilities seemingly unimpaired by monocularism, shot the first of the Flagg and Quirt sequels, *The Cock-Eyed World* (1929), to his own script. Released in silent and sound versions, this offered the knockabout clowning of its predecessor minus the antiwar elements and proved even more popular. Lily Damita provided the main female love interest.

John Ford had originally been assigned to remake an old silent Western, *The Oregon Trail,* but dissatisfied with the script, he passed the project on to Walsh along with his choice for the lead, a young bit player named Marion Morrison. Walsh renamed both film and actor, and John Wayne made his starring debut in *The Big Trail* (1930). Fox had recently developed a 70mm widescreen process known as Grandeur Film and planned to make this the first Grandeur release. As a result, Walsh had to shoot everything twice, once for normal ratio and once for 70mm. *The Big Trail* took five months to shoot and cost two million, little of which was recouped, since the picture flopped. The Grandeur process was junked, and Wayne spent eight years slogging through B-Westerns before John Ford rescued him for *Stagecoach.*

The films Walsh directed in the 1930s, prior to joining Warners at the end of the decade, represent on the whole a low point in his creative output. Andrew Sarris described the bulk of them as "maddeningly routine," and John Baxter, in *Hollywood in the Thirties,* summed them up as "stumbling apprentice efforts"—an odd term for the work of someone who had been making films for twenty years. Kingsley Canham has suggested that at this period Walsh "had trouble finding the right studio to develop his talent. Fox had been a major company in the late silent days, but . . . with the coming of sound, it was overshadowed by Warner Brothers, Metro, and Paramount. . . . [Its] films lacked a uniform style, unlike those of its rivals."

Against his own better judgment, Walsh let Fox talk him into a third Flagg and Quirt picture, *Women of All Nations* (1931). His misgivings were justified; the public had tired of the formula, and the film did poorly. *The Yellow Ticket* (1931), a garish melodrama scripted by Jules Furthman and set in Czarist Russia, might have worked in the hands of Furthman's usual director, von Sternberg; Walsh reduced it to comic strip by bucketing through at a breakneck pace, probably to the relief of an evidently embarrassed Laurence Olivier, playing the clean-cut young hero. The energetic Walsh style worked better in *Me and My Gal* (1932), a lively comedy-drama with Spencer Tracy as a soft-hearted New York cop. In a National Film Theatre booklet (September–November 1974), Peter Lloyd described *Me and My Gal* as "a fine example of dramatic eclecticism justified by narrative pacing which constructs rhythm out of wildly shifting depth and scope in the material."

Some critics have rated *The Bowery* (1933), directed by Walsh on loan to United Artists, as his finest pre-Warner film of the decade. "The film emerges as a beautifully accented 'mood' piece," wrote Julian Fox, "whose polished structure and general high spirits more than compensate for the conventionality of its plot and the rather improbable optimism of its protagonists." Set in the New York underworld of the 1890s, the action centers round the rivalry of two flashy gang leaders. George Raft plays Steve Brodie (of

Brooklyn Bridge fame) and Wallace Beery is Chuck Connors (reteamed with tough kid Jackie Cooper in shameless imitation of *The Champ*). Much of the action recalls the Flagg and Quirt formula; both men love the same woman (Fay Wray) and finally go off to fight side by side in the Spanish-American War.

For all its felicitous period detail and lively brio, parts of *The Bowery* leave an unpleasant taste. Jean-Pierre Coursodon, who considers that "much of [Walsh's] pre-Warners output is marred by a gratingly strident vulgarity," singled out the film as a particularly blatant example of the director's "good-natured, matter-of-fact racism"—common enough at the time, but unusually gross in a shot of screaming Chinese burning to death while rival fire brigades brawl over the privilege of extinguishing the fire. Nonetheless, "to clean up the film's loose ends and nasty lapses," Peter Hogue suggested, "might have been to kill it altogether. Its unique flavor and spirit are inseparable from its rawness."

For MGM Walsh directed his first musical, *Going Hollywood* (1933), bringing good humor if no outstanding aptitude to the genre. The last film in his long association with Fox was *Under Pressure* (1935), a final entry, in all but name, in the Flagg and Quirt series, with McLaglen and Lowe as sandhogs digging a tunnel under the East River. After quitting Fox, Walsh freelanced for four years, directing ten or so routine movies. *Klondike Annie* (1936), a Mae West vehicle, suffered badly from the Hays Office clampdown on the star's inspired bawdiness. It was notable only for the final screen appearance of George Walsh, whose career had been in decline since the mid-1920s (after this he retired to raise horses), and for the gloriously unlikely spectacle of Ms. West leading a prayer meeting. In 1937, Walsh traveled to Europe and made a couple of bad films in Britain.

Back in Hollywood, he turned out a number of indifferent musicals. By 1939, Walsh's career had reached its lowest ebb. Had he followed his brother's example and retired from filmmaking, he would probably now rank among the once-prominent directors whose reputations never survived the coming of sound. Instead, at the age of fifty-two, he signed a contract with Warners Brothers, where he stayed for twelve years and made two dozen pictures—among them, by general consent, most of his finest films. "The atmosphere of disciplined creativity and dynamic professionalism that prevailed there," Coursodon suggested, suited Walsh perfectly and brought out the best of his talent.

With his very first film for Warners, *The*

Roaring Twenties (1939), Walsh recouped his reputation, creating a box-office smash and a key masterpiece of the gangster genre. "It was in this film," Julian Fox maintained, "that he reached maturity as a director of talent, and his later work, brilliant though some of it is, never quite attains the impact and visual flair of *The Roaring Twenties*." A fitting culmination to the great decade of Warner gangster movies, the film also serves as a valedictory summation; in place of the tabloid immediacy of *Public Enemy* or *Little Caesar*, *The Roaring Twenties*, as the title implies, chronicles what had by then become an historic era.

Opening with the Armistice, the film traces the fortunes of three comrades from the trenches: Eddie (James Cagney) starts a taxi business but slides into bootlegging; George (Humphrey Bogart) joins the mob; Lloyd (Jeffrey Lynn) becomes a lawyer. Eddie and George set up in uneasy partnership; Lloyd at first works as their attorney but then goes straight and launches an anticrime crusade. George double-crosses Eddie, who has been ruined by the 1929 crash; to protect Lloyd from George's gunmen, Eddie shoots his ex-partner but is himself fatally wounded. In a classic finale, Cagney staggers along the shadowed sidewalk, crashing into garbage cans, to collapse and die on the steps of a church in the arms of his chanteuse lover, Panama (Gladys George). "What was his business?" asks a cop. Panama looks up, her face wet with tears: "He used to be a big shot." The scene encapsulates a whole era of cinematic mythology.

They Drive by Night (1940) begins in fine gritty Warners style as a downbeat study of the lives of long-distance truck drivers, with Raft and Bogart in the leading roles and Ann Sheridan in good form as a friendly waitress. Midway, however, the film deteriorates into a howling melodrama, bearing scant relation to what had preceded it and requiring Ida Lupino to go stark staring mad in the witness box—a task she accomplished with far more conviction than the script deserved.

Both Walsh and Lupino (who was one of his favorite actresses) were luckier with *High Sierra* (1941), which inaugurated a new style of gangster movie. Where the hoods of the 1930s had been young, dynamic, ambitious, reveling in their sharp suits and newly acquired power, their counterparts in the 1940s were a breed of weary, disillusioned antiheroes, looking to pull "one last good job" before retiring. From the moment Roy Earle gets out of an Illinois jail and heads west, an unmistakable air of existential doom hangs over him—"just rushin' towards death," observes a fellow gangster, quoting Dillinger. *High Sierra*, as David Thomson noted, "is the first clear statement of the inevitable destruction of the self-sufficient outsider."

The role of Earle had been intended for George Raft; when he ill-advisedly turned it down, it went instead to Bogart, who at last achieved star billing. His playing could hardly be bettered—even if the mind boggles at the idea of the quintessentially urban Bogey yearning to settle down on "a little Indiana farm"—and was well matched by Lupino's taut performance as the battered moll who loves him. Apart from a maudlin subplot involving a crippled girl whose operation Earle finances, the film's pace rarely slackens; Walsh drives relentlessly toward the inevitable showdown in the mountains, at one point throwing in an effortless 600-degree pan. (*High Sierra* also gave John Huston, who wrote the script from W. R. Burnett's novel, a lift to the director's chair for *The Maltese Falcon*.)

Nineteen forty-one was an exceptional year for Walsh. Besides *High Sierra* he directed three more pictures, all good in their very different ways. *The Strawberry Blonde*, Walsh's own favorite among his sound pictures ("It brought me back to my childhood"), came as a complete change of pace, a charmingly nostalgic period piece with Cagney cast against type as a small-time Brooklyn dentist. (The film was a remake of a 1933 Gary Cooper movie called *One Sunday Aternoon*, under which title Walsh later directed yet another remake.) *Manpower* featured George Raft and Edward G. Robinson as power linesmen who quarrel when one falls for the other's wife, played by Marlene Dietrich. Jean-Pierre Coursodon found this "a film notable for its high-tension relationships and its brilliant nonstop flow of tension-relieving, wisecracking dialogue."

Walsh's fourth film of 1941 was *They Died With Their Boots On*, the first of seven he would make with Errol Flynn. Having just quarreled finally and irrevocably with Michael Curtiz, Flynn was badly in need of another regular director to lend him some measure of confidence and stability. Walsh established an excellent rapport with him and became known at Warners as one of the few who could handle the increasingly drunken and recalcitrant star. *They Died* was a thoroughly fictionalized biopic of George Armstrong Custer, with the cavalry general portrayed as a flamboyant but compassionate friend of the Indians, finally forced to take the field against them by the evil machinations of rapacious whites. Historical distortions aside, the film exerts an irresistible romantic sweep, whereby the final massacre of the Seventh Cavalry at Lit-

tle Bighorn attains the moral dimensions of a glorious victory. Writing in *Brighton Film Review* (June 1970), Peter Lloyd cited the film as a prime example of the perennial Walshian theme of "ambition . . . transcending life itself. . . . Walsh's heroes are men of courage and daring, strength and determination, characterized by the expansiveness of their gestures, and the breadth of their ambition. . . . Movies such as *High Sierra* and *They Died With Their Boots On* become elegies for characters who aspire to the status of epic heroes."

In the same busy year, Walsh married again, for the third and last time. His bride was Mary Edna Simpson, daughter of a Kentucky horse-breeder, whom Walsh met on a visit to the yearling sales at Lexington. Mary Edna was seventeen to her husband's fifty-four, but by all accounts the marriage was a very happy one, lasting until Walsh's death forty years later.

Of Walsh's next six pictures, five starred Flynn. *Desperate Journey* (1942) was minor wartime fare, with the crew of a crashed RAF bomber (including such staunchly British types as Flynn, Ronald Reagan, and Alan Hale) making their way home through Germany, pursued by Raymond Massey as a glowering Nazi officer. *Gentleman Jim* (1942) was rather better: a biopic of the nineteenth-century boxer, Jim Corbett, whom Walsh had known in his youth. The film displays Walsh's innate skill in capturing evocative period detail and was summed up by Edgardo Cozarinsky (in Richard Roud's *Cinema*) as "the most elegant variation on an idea of gallantry that Walsh embodied in Errol Flynn" (even though some ponderously comic episodes involving Corbett's rowdy Irish family recall Ford at his most tedious).

After *Background to Danger* (1943), a spy melodrama with George Raft that jettisoned all the subtlety of Eric Ambler's novel, there followed three more exhibitions of wartime heroics with Flynn. In *Northern Pursuit* (1943) he was a Mountie foiling Nazi saboteurs in Canada; *Uncertain Glory* (1944)—"probably the most preposterous of all the Walsh-Flynn cycle," according to Julian Fox—had him playing a French criminal turned Resistance fighter. The third was *Objective Burma!* (1945), the notorious film in which Flynn allegedly "took Burma singlehanded," so incensing the British public that the movie was withdrawn after a week and remained banned in Britain for several years, eventually being reissued with a tactful prologue paying due tribute to those non-American forces that took part in the Burma campaign.

With the cries of national outrage long since stilled, *Objective Burma!* now looks like Walsh's best war movie and the last good picture of Flynn's career—if not quite the great antiwar statement and "masterpiece of the genre" hailed by some French critics. For Cozarinsky, it furnished "almost a textbook example of the war action film—factually all false, yet eliciting the fullest suspension of disbelief as it develops on the screen with a logic of physical action, a balance of tension and relaxation that has never been equaled." A paratroop company, sent behind enemy lines to take out a radio station, complete their mission but find their rendezvous airstrip under attack. After trekking through 150 miles of hostile jungle, the survivors reach their new rendezvous, an exposed hilltop, only to realize that Command has used them as a decoy to draw off Japanese forces, while the counterinvasion takes place further south. Filmed entirely on a ranch near Pasadena, the picture's reconstruction of a Burmese jungle seems—at least to a non-Burmese—wholly convincing, while Walsh's grasp of guerrilla tactics was such that the Israeli Haganah are said to have used *Objective Burma!* as a training film.

Walsh's only comedy of the decade (*Strawberry Blonde* perhaps excepted) was *The Horn Blows at Midnight* (1945), with Jack Benny as an incompetent minor angel sent down from an oppressively bureaucratic heaven (suspiciously like the Warner Brothers studio) to blow the last trump. Undemandingly amusing, the film remains as little known in Walsh's output as does *The Man I Love* (1946), a romantic melodrama about the doomed love between a singer (Ida Lupino, superb as ever) and a pianist (Robert Alda), and possibly the closest Walsh ever came to making a *film noir.*

Noir elements also inform *Pursued* (1947), with which Walsh inaugurated the cycle of "psychological Westerns" that became fashionable in the 1950s. Written by Niven Busch, it was described by Peter Lloyd as "a horror story of the great outdoors, an extraordinary tale of family rivalry, atavism, and grotesque vengeance." Robert Mitchum, in a role originally meant for John Garfield, gave one of his finest early performances as a man haunted by a past he can neither escape nor comprehend, well supported by Judith Anderson and Teresa Wright as his adoptive mother and sister. Aided by James Wong Howe's photography, all shadows and ominous angles, Walsh used his landscape to emphasize claustrophobia and confinement, dwarfing his characters and trapping them within their own obsessive terrain.

A more conventional Western, *Silver River* (1948), marked Walsh's last collaboration with Errol Flynn. Cast for once as an unsympathetic

character, Flynn gave one of the best performances of his career, though Walsh retained unhappy memories of both Flynn and his costar, Ann Sheridan: "They were both on the bottle. . . . They wanted to get away from Warner. It was just terrible." After a dull war movie, *Fighter Squadron* (1948), notable only as his first color film, Walsh remade a couple of his earlier successes. *One Sunday Afternoon* (1948) was *The Strawberry Blonde* with songs and Technicolor; pleasant enough, but Dennis Morgan, Janis Paige, and Dorothy Malone made pallid substitutes for Cagney, Hayworth, and de Havilland. However, *Colorado Territory* (1949), which replayed *High Sierra* as a Western, worked well in its own right. William K. Everson considered it "excellent and underrated . . . its tragic ending dovetailing neatly into the fashionable defeatism that marked so many psychological dramas of the forties." This ending, in which both hero and heroine die in a fusillade of bullets (in *High Sierra* only Bogart, not Lupino, died in the end), apparently turned the film into a cult hit in Japan. It pales, though—as do most movie endings—beside the apocalyptic finale of Walsh's next film, the finest of his postwar period, and one of the classic gangster movies.

On initial release, *White Heat* (1949) was widely criticized for excessive brutality, and even today the film can still shock with the unrelenting intensity of its violence, the gleeful blackness of its vision. "There is not a reliable or healthy human relationship in the film," wrote David Thomson; "instead, people are restlessly vicious and untrustworthy; fate impels the hero towards disaster, as the only release from psychopathy and grotesque hopes of success." As gangleader Cody Jarrett, a homicidal paranoiac subject to epileptic fits and a prodigious mother fixation, Cagney gives a performance that is a tour de force of manic energy. At one point, learning in the prison dining room of his mother's death, he erupts into a sustained and terrifying fit—sobbing, raving, staggering, and sliding the length of the table, demolishing dishes, furniture, fellow cons, and every guard that comes at him. No mere bullet, it seems, could stop such a force; it needs an explosion of commensurate violence to finish Cody. Betrayed during a robbery by an undercover cop who has infiltrated the gang, he takes refuge on top of a huge gas storage tank, and as the cops close in, shoots into it screaming "Made it, Ma! Top of the world!"—immolating himself in a titanic burst of flame.

The last three films that Walsh made at Warners were more interesting visually than dramatically. *Along the Great Divide* (1951), a somber revenge Western with Kirk Douglas, made striking use of its austere desert locations, where the pervasive dust clouds became an integral component of the action. *Captain Horatio Hornblower* (1951), for Warners' British studio, featured Gregory Peck as C. S. Forester's Nelsonian naval hero; both his performance and the film were handsomely mounted but flat. Elements of *Objective Burma!* were reworked into a period adventure story for *Distant Drums* (1951), with Gary Cooper leading an 1840 expedition into Seminole territory in the Florida swamps.

After his Warners contract expired, Walsh freelanced for the last twelve years of his career, working for most of the Hollywood majors and directing nineteen more films. Many English-language critics have seen these pictures as marking a deterioration in quality, although in France several of them are ranked among Walsh's finest work. Coursodon suggested that "the easygoing style of his late years makes up in charm what it may lack in power. . . . His last period, while not his most successful, is his most personal and probably his most appealing." Most of Walsh's favorite genres were covered: Westerns, period adventures, war movies, and a swashbuckler or two—including the ineffable *Blackbeard the Pirate* (1952), in which Robert Newton's eye-rolling rendition of the title role made his earlier performance as Long John Silver seem by comparison a model of restraint.

Sea Devils (1953), another nautical drama, was based fairly remotely on *Les Travailleurs de la mer* by Victor Hugo (one of Walsh's three favorite writers, along with Shakespeare and de Maupassant). There followed an intriguing *film maudit*, the last of his four pictures with Cagney. Set in an unnamed southern state, *A Lion Is in the Streets* (1953) traces the rise of an itinerant pedlar to political power through his knack for populist rhetoric. Adapted from a novel by Adria Locke Langley, the plot was clearly based on the career of Huey Long, prewar governor of Louisiana, which had also inspired *All the King's Men*. The parallels were close enough for Columbia, producers of Rossen's film, to take out a plagiarism suit. *Lion* was withdrawn from distribution and has rarely been shown since. Walsh himself called it "an awful picture. . . . the film just didn't work at all." Others have disagreed; Julian Fox found it a "beautifully stylised evocation of a Southern state during the Depression . . . which contained a performance of incredible force and eloquence by James Cagney. . . . The film is as forceful a study of political corruption as any seen up to that time." In keeping with the style of his films, Walsh always preferred working with actors who pro-

jected a tough, masculine image, such as Raft, Bogart, Cagney, and Flynn, all of whom made some of their best films with him. (His dealings with those of a more thoughtful or gentle cast, like Ronald Colman or Gregory Peck, often lacked cordiality.) The last of these fruitful relationships was with the supreme icon of screen masculinity, Clark Gable, who made three films with Walsh in the mid-1950s: *The Tall Men* (1955), a rugged, good-looking widescreen Western with Jane Russell and Robert Ryan, "a neglected masterpiece of the genre" in Peter Lloyd's opinion; another Western, *The King and Four Queens* (1956), a comedy-drama that Jo Van Fleet, as a gun-toting mother-in-law, neatly stole from Gable and the rest of the cast; and *Band of Angels* (1957), which found Gable back in Rhett Butler territory, marrying a half-breed ex-slave in the antebellum South—"a film so bad," according to *Newsweek*, "that it has to be seen to be disbelieved." In between the Gable pictures came *The Revolt of Mamie Stover* (1956), with Jane Russell as a "hostess" on the make in Honolulu around the time of Pearl Harbor. Something of Russell's "uninhibited eroticism" (David Thomson) eluded the censors, along with a fine performance from Agnes Moorehead as a formidable madame, but the film as a whole suffered from the caution of the period.

Throughout his career, Walsh felt hampered and frustrated by the narrow constrictions of Hollywood censorship. "If we could be working today," he remarked after his retirement, "the theaters would catch fire with the scenes we'd put on. I've sometimes had a whole reel thrown out of a picture." Another heavily mutilated work was *The Naked and the Dead* (1958), taken from Norman Mailer's celebrated best-seller of the war in the Pacific. Except in France, where it was highly regarded (Michel Marmin referred to its "marvelous dramatic richness"), most critics saw the film as a sadly bowdlerized and diminished version of the novel. Walsh concurred: "The censors cut out all the naked and left the dead."

Walsh's long career wound down in an assorted handful of minor films, including a couple of thinly plotted service comedies, *A Private's Affair* (1959) and *Marines, Let's Go!* (1961), and two films made abroad: a feeble spoof-Western, *The Sheriff of Fractured Jaw* (1958), in Britain, and in Italy a biblical minispectacular, *Esther and the King* (1960), on which Walsh took his last script credit. His final film was an elegiac cavalry Western, *A Distant Trumpet* (1964), let down by a poor cast: "Those people didn't belong that were in it." Thereafter, apart from an abortive project or two, Walsh withdrew from filmmaking. The sight in his remaining eye was beginning to weaken, and he retired to his ranch in the Simi Valley, north of Los Angeles, to raise horses and cattle and paint pictures.

The traditional assessment of Raoul Walsh casts him as an ultra-professional studio workhorse, a supreme director of tough, fast-paced outdoor action movies filmed with a robust lack of pretension—"one of the great primitives of the screen," in Ephraim Katz's words. As such, he has often been compared with such directors as Ford and Hawks, slightly to his detriment. In Andrew Sarris's formulation: "If the heroes of Ford are sustained by tradition, and the heroes of Hawks by professionalism, the heroes of Walsh are sustained by nothing more than a feeling for adventure. The Fordian hero knows why he is doing something even if he doesn't know how. The Hawksian hero knows how to do what he is doing even if he doesn't know why. The Walshian hero is less interested in the why or the how than in the what. He is always plunging into the unknown, and he is never too sure what he will find there." (Walsh, confronted with this view, responded, "I guess it's so. Everyone has his own impression of things. Maybe the guy was drunk.") Sarris added that Walsh "has always possessed the necessary technical skills and artistic instincts to bring off the most ambitious physical spectacles. His best films are genuinely exciting, though neither profound nor pretentious."

Philip French, like many other critics, noted a sentimental underside to the brash heroics of Walsh's action sagas. "Beneath the tough surface of the Westerns, gangster movies, war pictures and swashbucklers he so vigorously directed, there is a vein of tenderness and sensitivity that not only humanises them, but gives his best films a moral strength and psychological depth." Jean-Pierre Coursodon even questioned whether Walsh's films are as relentlessly fast-paced as most writers assert: "Slack pace—whether a charm or a nuisance—is a recurring trait throughout his work, a result, in part, of his taste for rambling story lines, but also a sign of a basically leisurely approach to filmmaking." The same critic found in Walsh's later work "an unexpected flair for individual psychology, especially in the treatment of female characters."

During most of his career Walsh rarely attracted "serious" critical notice, but toward the end of the 1950s he was discovered and taken up in France as a great neglected master, "one of the greatest living American filmmakers" in Claude Beylie's words. Retrospectives of his work were mounted, accompanied by laudatory articles, though since much of the writing was characterized by what Peter Lloyd called "a mystical but totally unclarified reverence," it was sometimes hard to detect just what qualities Walsh was being valued for. "I would say," wrote Michel Marmin, "that Raoul Walsh's films need no justification, and that the only proper way to speak of them would be rather as a gratified lover offers his homage to a woman's body." More coherently, Claude-Jean Philippe commented that "in the most fertile tradition of American cinema, Walsh's mise-en-scène relies on verbs, not adjectives. A man is reduced to the sum of his actions." The films of Walsh's last years, often dismissed elsewhere, received in France particular appreciation. Beylie singled out The Naked and the Dead and Esther and the King as "two works of accomplished perfection," and Jacques Joly saw the latter film as "the purest example of Walsh's genius."

Following the French lead, albeit in less ecstatic terms, English-language critics also began mining Walsh's output for underlying themes and attitudes. Some found an existential fatalism, often expressed through the relationship between protagonists and landscape. "The landscape," wrote Roger McNiven (Velvet Light Trap, Fall 1975), "always ultimately diminishes the hero's aspirations"; similarly, David Thomson noted that "many of his best films move inexorably towards remote, barren locales, where the people are tiny, hurrying insects." Others have detected a recurrent theme of the compulsive overreacher, the maverick, sustained by the determination of his (or, just occasionally, her) chosen self-image. As Peter Lloyd put it, "the paradox of the great heroes of Walsh lies in their extraordinary assertion of the individual Will in the face of the world." Walsh himself never gave such speculation any encouragement: "I just did my job. I let others make up the theories." His views on directorial technique were equally terse: "Action, action, action. . . . Let the screen be filled ceaselessly with events. Logical things in a logical sequence. That's always been my rule—a rule I've never had to change." Peter Hogue concluded that Walsh was "probably not a great auteur, but one who consistently brought to the movies a feeling for American life that few of his contemporaries in Hollywood could match."

The 1970s saw several major retrospectives of Walsh's work, including one at the 1974 Edinburgh Festival and another the same year at the Museum of Modern Art in New York, the latter lasting three months and comprising sixty-seven movies. Walsh took this new-found critical prestige in his stride, as he had so much else in his career. Visitors to his ranch were welcomed with cordiality and a fine repertoire of colorful anecdotes, but rarely succeeded in prizing out of him any but the most factual comments on his films. "I made some hits, I made some near-hits and I made a lot of turkeys," he once remarked laconically. "You make a lot of pictures. . . . Some go out and make good, and some don't. And you don't want to play any favorite. Let it go, you know."

In 1972 Walsh published his first novel, a Western; it appeared in France, under the title of *La Colère des justes*. (The original English title was *Come Hell or High Water*.) The glaucoma in his left eye steadily worsened, finally leaving him totally blind, but he continued to dictate scripts. He could also, he told a visitor, "sit on my porch and enjoy the bird-calls and the aroma of the flowers and detect the footsteps of the approaching Internal Revenue agents." He died of a heart attack at th age of ninety-three, in the closing hours of 1980.

—*P.K.*

FILMS: *Two-reelers*:—The Double Knot, 1914; The Mystery of the Hindu Image, 1914; The Gunman, 1914; The Final Verdict, 1914; The Death Dice, 1915; His Return, 1915; The Greaser, 1915; The Fencing Master, 1915; A Man for All That, 1915; Eleven-Thirty, 1915; The Buried Hand, 1915; The Celestial Code, 1915; A Ban Man and Others, 1915. *Features*—(with Christy Cabanne) The Life of General Villa, 1914; The Regeneration, 1915; Carmen, 1915; (with D. W. Griffith) Pillars of Society, 1916; The Serpent, 1916; Blue Blood and Red, 1916; The Honor System, 1917; The Conqueror, 1917; Betrayed, 1917; This Is the Life, 1917; The Pride of New York, 1917; The Silent Lie, 1917; The Innocent Sinner, 1917; The Woman and the Law, 1918; The Prussian Cur, 1918; On the Jump, 1918; Every Mother's Son, 1918; I'll Say So, 1918; Evangeline, 1919; The Strongest, 1919; Should a Husband Forgive?, 1919; From Now On, 1920; The Deep Purple, 1920; The Oath, 1921; Serenade, 1921; Kindred of the Dust, 1922; Lost and Found on a South Sea Island (UK, Lost and Found), 1923; The Thief of Bagdad, 1924; East of Suez, 1925; The Spaniard (UK, Spanish Lover), 1925; The Wanderer, 1925; The Lucky Lady, 1926; The Lady of the Harem, 1926; What Price Glory?, 1926; The Monkey Talks, 1927; The Loves of Carmen, 1927; Sadie Thompson, 1928; The Red Dance (UK, The Red Dancer of Moscow), 1928; Me, Gangster, 1928; Hot for Paris, 1929; (with Irving Cummings) In Old Arizona, 1929; The Cock-Eyed World, 1929; The Big Trail, 1930; The Man Who Came Back, 1931; Women of All Nations, 1931; The Yellow Ticket (UK, The Yellow Passport), 1931; Wild Girl (UK, Salome Jane), 1932; Me and My Gal (UK, Pier 13), 1932; Sailor's Luck, 1933; The Bowery, 1933; Going Hollywood, 1933; Under Pressure, 1935; Baby Face Harrington, 1935; Every Night at Eight, 1935; Klondike Annie, 1936; Big Brown Eyes, 1936; Spendthrift, 1936; OHMS (UK, You're in the Army Now), 1937; Jump for Glory (UK, When Thief Meets Thief), 1937; Artists and Models, 1937; Hitting a New High, 1937; College Swing (UK, Swing, Teacher, Swing),

1938; St. Louis Blues, 1939; The Roaring Twenties, 1939; Dark Command, 1940; They Drive by Night (UK, Road to Frisco), 1940; High Sierra, 1941; The Strawberry Blonde, 1941; Manpower, 1941; They Died With Their Boots On, 1941; Desperate Journey, 1942; Gentleman Jim, 1942; Background to Danger, 1943; Northern Pursuit, 1943; Uncertain Glory, 1944; Objective Burma!, 1945; Salty O'Rourke, 1945; The Horn Blows at Midnight, 1945; The Man I Love, 1946; Pursued, 1947; Cheyenne (UK, The Wyoming Kid), 1947; Silver River, 1948; Fighter Squadron, 1948; One Sunday Afternoon, 1948; Colorado Territory, 1949; White Heat, 1949; Along the Great Divide, 1951; Captain Horatio Hornblower, 1951; Distant Drums, 1951; Glory Alley, 1952; The World in His Arms, 1952; The Lawless Breed, 1952; Blackbeard the Pirate, 1952; Sea Devils, 1953; A Lion Is in the Streets, 1953; Gun Fury, 1953; Saskatchewan (UK, O'Rourke of the Royal Mounted), 1954; Battle Cry, 1955; The Tall Men, 1955; The Revolt of Mamie Stover, 1956; The King and Four Queens, 1956; Band of Angels, 1957; The Naked and the Dead, 1958; The Sheriff of Fractured Jaw, 1958; A Private's Affair, 1959; Esther and the King (Esther e il Re), 1960; Marines, Let's Go!, 1961; A Distant Trumpet, 1964. *Published scripts*—High Sierra (University of Wisconsin Press), 1979; White Heat (University of Wisconsin Press), 1984.

ABOUT: Brownlow, K. The War, the West and the Wilderness, 1979; Canham, K. Michael Curtiz, Raoul Walsh, Henry Hathaway (The Hollywood Professionals, Vol. 1), 1973; Cooper, M. (with Herndon, B.) Dark Lady of the Silents, 1973; Coursodon, J.-P. American Directors, (Vol. I), 1983; Hardy, F. (ed.) Raoul Walsh, 1974; Marmin, M. Raoul Walsh, 1970 (in French); Meyer, W. R. Warner Brothers Directors, 1978; Roud, R. (ed.) Cinema: A Critical Dictionary, 1980; Sarris, A. The American Cinema, 1968; Schickel, R. The Men Who Made the Movies, 1977; Thomson, D. A Biographical Dictionary of the Cinema, 1980; Uppsala Studenters Filmstudio Raoul Walsh, 1970 (in Swedish); Veillon, O.-R. Le Cinéma américain—les années 50, 1984; Walsh, R. Each Man in His Time, 1974. *Periodicals*—Artforum November 1971; L'Avant-Scène du Cinéma March–April 1976, October 15, 1976; Brighton Film Review November–December 1969, June 1970; Cahiers de la Cinémathèque Summer 1978; Cahiers du Cinéma April 1964; Cinéma (France) February 1966; Commentary November 1957; Écran May 1976; Film (BFFS) November 1974; Film (FFS) Autumn 1967; Film Comment July–August 1981; Film Fan Monthly May 1974; Film Heritage Spring 1975; Film Ideal June 15, 1965–July 1, 1965; Films and Filming June–August 1973; Films in Review May 1976, April 1982; Framework Spring 1981; Image et Son November 1971; Movietone News November 1975; National Film Theatre Booklet September–November 1974; Observer Magazine (London) December 2, 1979; Photoplay November 1928; Positif February 1973; Présence du Cinéma May 1962; Sight and Sound Winter 1972–3, Winter 1974–5; Silent Picture Winter 1970–1; Téléciné December 1965; Velvet Light Trap Fall 1975.

WALTERS, CHARLES (November 17, 1911–August 13, 1982), American director, choreographer, and dance director, was born in Pasadena, California, and grew up there and in Anaheim. In high school his chief interest was the drama class, and by the time he entered the Universiy of Southern California, he was an accomplished amateur actor and dancer. Leaving the University in 1934, he became a professional dancer, appearing first in the chorus of Fanchon and Marco road shows. His engagements included stints at the Pasadena Playhouse, where a few years earlier he had often sat on the other side of the footlights.

The MGM studios were only twenty miles down the road from Pasadena, but for Walters the path to Hollywood led him first to New York, where he landed a dancing role in the revue *New Faces,* then one in *Fools Rush In.* Partnered by Dorothy Fox, he had a featured part in *Musical Parade* (1935) and the same year acted and danced as the prince in Cole Porter's *Jubilee.* Roles followed in 1936 in *Transatlantic Rhythm* and *The Show Is On,* and in 1937 he played Freddie Hill in *Between the Devil.* He was Peter Mueller in Rodgers and Hart's *I Married an Angel* (1938) and Harry Norton in Cole Porter's *Du Barry Was a Lady,* in which his dancing partner was Betty Grable.

Invited to direct the student show at Princeton, Walters made such an impression that he was hired to choreograph dance numbers for the Fields–Cole Porter show *Let's Face It* (1941), with Danny Kaye, and then for Eddie Cantor's *Banjo Eyes.* His first movie credit was as dance director of Tim Whelan's *Seven Days' Leave* (1942). Signed by MGM, where he spent virtually the whole of his career, Walters went on to direct or choreograph dances in Norman Taurog's *Presenting Lily Mars* (in which he also danced with Judy Garland), the screen version of *Du Barry Was a Lady* (1943), *Girl Crazy* (1943), *Broadway Rhythm* (1944), *Meet Me in St. Louis* (1944), *Ziegfield Follies* (1946), and *Summer Holiday* (1948), among other musicals.

Douglas McVay, in his article about Walters in *Focus on Film* (Spring 1977), says that in Roy Del Ruth's *Broadway Rhythm,* "Walters not only choreographed but directed 'Brazilian Boogie,' which featured Lena Horne as vocalist; right from its initial travelling close-ups of hands beating bongo-drums, this sequence was excitingly staged and shot, benefiting from costumes in green, mauve and yellow (with, at one point, two vertical rows of waving yellow gloves irrupting into the frame at either side, to striking pictorial and dramatic effect.) Throughout 1944, in fact, Walters went from strength to strength as a dance director, mounting Garland's 'A Great

CHARLES WALTERS

Lady Has an Interview' episode in *Ziegfield Follies,* and handling almost all the musical items in Minnelli's classic *Meet Me in St. Louis.*"

Good News (1947), Walters' first film as a full-fledged director, is now regarded as one of his best. Produced by Arthur Freed, it was a remake of a 1930 movie that was itself based on a 1927 Broadway musical about a campus football hero who has to pass his astronomy examination before he can participate in the big game. Walters, who shared choreography credit with Robert Alton, retained the 1920s setting in his Technicolor version, scripted by Betty Comden and Adolph Green (their first Hollywood assignment). June Allyson and Peter Lawford starred, but for many the movie was stolen from them by Joan McCracken, who gave the performance of her brief career as a sexy coed.

As Douglas McVay wrote, the film opens with "a brilliant ensemble song-and-dance to the title number. Walters at once exhibits his mastery of choreography and staging, both in the drilling of the vivacious and athletic chorus, and in the fluently mobile use of tracking and crane shots, panning and cutting. . . . Walters' admirable debut as a full-scale film director is soon proved to extend to the chromatic as well as the choreographic elements of the piece. In this respect, his earlier collaboration (as dance director) with cinematographer Charles Schoenbaum on Mamoulian's *Summer Holiday* was plainly of crucial importance. . . . The two pictures resemble each other in their pictorial, photographic surface and texture; they share the same fondness for sunlight, for brightly attractive hues. . . . Not only the photographic tones but the use of grassy, leafy settings on which song and dance occur (and the employment of college interiors, complete with academic busts and student chants), mingling with the humorously evocative manipulation of period cars . . . , link this pair of musicals unmistakably together."

After that, MGM handed Walters a lavish package of talent in *Easter Parade* (1948)—a cast headed by Fred Astaire, Judy Garland, and Ann Miller, songs by Irving Berlin, and choreography by Robert Alton. The result includes some memorable high spots, including Astaire's solo "Drum Crazy," Miller's exuberant "Shakin' the Blues Away," and Garland and Astaire in "We're a Couple of Swells." The movie was a hit, but for many critics, as for McVay, "it tends to lack real visual style and to be somewhat uninventive in the treatment of many of its routines."

There was also a mixed response to *The Barkleys of Broadway* (1949), which reunited Astaire and Ginger Rogers after a ten-year interval in a story about two Broadway stars who are also husband and wife. Their triumphs in various musicals are interspersed with domestic crises, in one of which Rogers is persuaded to embark on a new career as a tragic actress. C. A. Lejeune wrote: "There are one or two magic moments when their dancing is all that we remembered; when they move together like a shaft of light. . . . The film is worth seeing for these moments, but for very little else. The story has an awful lot of foolish and embarrassing situations." Other reviewers were kinder, however, and Oscar Levant received a good press for his well-polished bit as a cynical but good-hearted composer.

Summer Stock (1950; in Britain called *If You Feel Like Singing*) stars Gene Kelly as a professional trouper who initiates farmer Judy Garland into the ways of show business and wins her away from her multifariously allergic fiancé (Eddie Bracken). Endlessly inventive, it features one of Walker's most magical sequences. This begins with Kelly alone on a bare stage, pensively whistling "You Wonderful You." Kelly steps on a creaky board, considers, tries it again, and slowly begins to dance, using the offending noise to orchestrate his solo, and then adding new effects by dancing on a discarded sheet of rustling newspaper. The paper becomes a matador's cape and is then ripped neatly into eight segments by the dancer's feet. His interest caught by a news item, Kelly picks up one of the fragments and strolls slowly off stage, reading intently and once more whistling quietly.

Walters' first nonmusical followed, a vehicle for the charms of Jane Wyman called *Three Guys Named Mike* (1951). She plays a bright small-town girl whose career as an airline hostess and talent for inventing advertising campaigns lead her into various difficulties involving her three suitors: an adventurous pilot (Howard Keel), a dynamic adman (Barry Sullivan), and a quiet research chemist (Van Johnson). "The thin idea is spread pretty thin," wrote *Time*'s reviewer, but "actress Wyman, well-supported by her leading men and occasional sprightly dialogue, buoys *Three Guys* into good-humored entertainment."

Van Johnson gets the girl in *Three Guys*; it was Howard Keel's turn in the dude ranch musical *Texas Carnival* (1951), featuring Red Skelton. Esther Williams costars as Skelton's sister, and such plot as there is turns on what happens when these two carnival performers are mistaken for the richest siblings in Texas. Williams spends less time than usual in bathing suits but makes up for it (in a superimposition scene fantasized by Keel) by swimming languorously around his hotel room swathed in diaphanous veils. Ann Miller provides one of the film's best sequences in "Dynamite," tap-dancing on the drums in a bandstand and across a series of tables, with chorus boys whisking the tableclothes from under her flying feet. Skelton's greenhorn routines were generally enjoyed, reminding several reviewers of Bob Hope in *The Paleface*.

Walters had Arthur Freed as his producer again in *The Belle of New York* (1952), a much more notable musical, photographed in Technicolor by Robert Planck and choreographed by Alton. Fred Astaire plays Charlie Hill, an idle playboy, and Vera-Ellen the repressed Salvation Army girl Angela Collins, an ardent believer in the work ethic. Inspired by love, Charlie tries honest labor—as a Western Union delivery man (who performs elegant balancing tricks on his bicycle), as a streetsweeper who turns his job into a ballet, and as a trolley driver who puts his vehicle at the sole disposal of his beloved for an exhilarating piece of sustained choreographic invention. It is well known that lovers walk on air, and at the end of this film Charlie and Angela do precisely that, looking down in the midst of an argument to find themselves floating above the buildings.

"In this moment," wrote Martin Sutton, "the dreamer has triumphed over the restrictions of the 'real' world. The couple literally rise above all the social restraints that frustrated their relationship back on the ground (class, career, money and morality). The 'useless' act becomes the couple's ultimate poetic gesture." Others drew attention to "the delightful visionary montage of wedding pictures based on Currier and Ives prints."

The film for which Walters is best known and remembered followed the same year. *Lili*, adapted by Helen Deutsch from the fantasy by Paul Gallico, has Leslie Caron as a drab French waif who gets a job as waitress with a traveling circus, where she falls in love with philandering magician Jean-Pierre Aumont. When she loses him and her job and tries to kill herself, she is dissuaded by the puppets belonging to the morose and crippled Mel Ferrer. Her conversations with the puppets become a feature of Ferrer's act and, though he treats her as surlily as ever, he woos her through the voices of the dolls.

It seemed to C. A. Lejeune that "*Lili* has its faults—sometimes both sentiment and fantasy are over-worked—but . . . I find myself remembering it for its real tenderness and charm." Dilys Powell agreed, noting that "in a medium such as the cinema, where everything can be made only too clearly and closely visible, the dangers of handling an idea of this kind are obvious; merely to escape bathos is difficult enough. That the scenes between the girl and the puppets are touching is a little triumph. This success is due to both playing and direction."

Discussing the same picture in his article about Walters in Jean-Pierre Coursodon's *American Directors, Volume 2*, Alain Masson wrote that its choreography, "rather than advancing the action . . . , changes it into something unreal. The musical numbers do not result from the plot or atmosphere of the film; on the contrary they are an excuse for the general tone of the work. . . . The musical has been used as a pretense to work out a new form. . . . *Lili* and *The Glass Slipper* pretend to be musicals in order to find a clear formal definition but pursue their own purposes beyond that definition. For they are meant to arouse emotions (fear and pity) more easily associated with tragedy than with musical comedy."

Walters made two aquatic musicals with Esther Williams in 1953. In *Dangerous When Wet* she displays her prowess and physique variously in an Arkansas swimming hole and the lavish pool of a French château, before swimming the English Channel, encouraged by a champagne salesman (played by her third husband, Fernando Lamas). There is also an underwater dream sequence in which she capers among the coral with the cartoon characters Tom and Jerry. Jack Carson makes the most of his role as a two-bit Romeo.

This amiable movie, with pleasant songs by Arthur Schwartz and Johnny Mercer, was generally enjoyed. *Easy to Love*, less cosmopolitan and less lively, casts Williams as the overworked star of a Florida water show, pursued by Tony Mar-

tin and fellow-swimmer John Bromfield, but cleaving to her ruthless boss (Van Johnson), even when he seems too busy selling televisions to notice.

In between these innocuous entertainments came a movie of a very different sort, *Torch Song*, adapted from a novel by I.A.R. Wylie, photographed by Robert Planck, and choreographed by Walters himself. Joan Crawford plays a Broadway star who has given her all to her art and has consequently become lonely and embittered. The English actor Michael Wilding is the blind vet who has secretly loved her for years and gets to play the piano at her rehearsals for a new show. A writer in *Saturday Review* said that in this film, Crawford "has everything, success and failure, loneliness and acclaim, tenderness and cruelty . . . all to be crowned by the love of a good blind man. There is never any possible sequel to a Crawford film. . . . We need Miss Crawford always before our eyes, a need which in *Torch Song* she isn't reluctant to satisfy. All the scenes are her scenes, and every moment tends to be magnificent."

Torch Song was so much a one-woman show that Michael Wilding, it was said, "barely gets a chance to act." He fared better as the prince in *The Glass Slipper* (1955), a modern version (by Helen Deutsch) of the Cinderella story, with Leslie Caron as the ill-used but ultimately triumphant heroine. Arthur Knight was one of a number of critics who saw it as an attempt "to repeat the miracle" of *Lili*, and "an extremely good try," even if *The Glass Slipper* is at times "too self-consciously winsome."

For Alain Masson, this picture is one of several in which Walters "tries to explore the borders of the musical. . . . In *The Glass Slipper* the audience would even gladly do without Roland Petit's strained choreography, but, bad as it is, the dancing hardly spoils the film inasmuch as restrained gestures and unaccomplished impulses make up the substance of the story. . . . Scarce, restrained, and sometimes abruptly and beautifully terminated, the musical numbers find a new meaning: instead of expressing a feeling, they suggest the girl's surprise, bewilderment, and fear when discovering the depth of feeling."

The Tender Trap (1955), which most reviewers found moderately entertaining, is not really a musical but, as Masson says, a comedy "embedded . . . in a musical frame." Frank Sinatra stars as a bachelor theatrical agent in New York where, since marriage-minded girls greatly outnumber the available men, he is to his satisfaction endlessly pursued and wooed by beautiful women. The "tender trap" of matrimony begins to close around him when he carelessly falls in love with a rising young musical comedy star (Debbie Reynolds). A subplot concerns Sinatra's friend David Wayne, visiting from the sticks. Long married, and deeply envious of Sinatra's freedom, he is soon involved with one of the latter's discards (Celeste Holm).

Walters' last major musical was *High Society* (1956), adapted from Philip Barry's nonmusical play and George Cukor's film *The Philadelphia Story*. As *Time* said, Sol Siegel "assembled a *Who's Who* cast. He talked Bing Crosby and Frank Sinatra into teaming in a movie for the first time, snagged the services of Grace Kelly for her last screen appearance before embarking for Monaco, paid Cole Porter a reported $250,000 for his first original movie score in eight years, and hired Louis Armstrong to blow and gravel-growl his way through it."

John Patrick's adaptation shifted the story from Philadelphia to Newport, Rhode Island, where imperious beauty Tracy Lord (Kelly) dithers coolly between the three men in her life: her jazz-loving ex-husband (Crosby), her stuffy new fiancé (John Lund), and a brash young journalist (Sinatra). Thawed by the latter, she finally learns to love her first husband. Reviewers who remembered *The Philadelphia Story* thought the remake, as Hollis Alpert put it, "a dispirited rehash . . . ,with practically all of its charm gone and with the cast seemingly aware of the fact." Douglas McVay, writing twenty years later, disagreed. *High Society,* he maintained, "is the closest of Charles Walters' musicals to being an all-singing affair, and it reminds us . . . that he filmed singers with at least as much skill as Minnelli, Kelly or Donen." For McVay, the "long, marvellous central section of the picture" is "virtually a non-stop, effortless, rapturous flow of brilliant numbers brilliantly performed and filmed."

Walters' next four films were all nonmusicals. *Don't Go Near the Water* (1957), from William Brinkley's comic novel of World War II, has Glenn Ford as an incompetent navy PR man on a Pacific Island and Fred Clark as his manic commander, intent on press-releasing Japan into surrender. Mickey Shaughnessy plays Farragut Jones, the foul-mouthed brute Clark selects unseen (on the strength of this impressive name) as "the typical Navyman"; Anne Francis and Gia Scala provide typical romantic interest. Mildly entertaining, the movie has one muchpraised slapstick scene in which—in the interest of morale—Clark puts his officers to work building their own club.

Ask Any Girl (1959) owed its success mainly to the presence of Shirley MacLaine. A bumpkin in New York, she goes to work for a motivational researcher (David Niven) and then employs MR to investigate the sexual preferences of Niven's younger brother (Gig Young), her favorite consumer. MacLaine earned comparisons with Carole Lombard in this film which, as David Robinson wrote, "must stand or fall on its charm . . . ; few other artist could have contributed so much of this quality as Miss MacLaine."

A forgettable screen version of *Please Don't Eat the Daisies,* (1960) a collection of funny autobiographical essays by Jean Kerr, was followed by another Shirley MacLaine vehicle, *Two Loves* (1961; called *Spinster* in Britain). Alain Masson found this "an interesting and significant" drama and quoted Walters as saying (in an interview with Pierre Sauvage) that "he had filmed a dream that was to be used as a prologue but was eventually cut by the producer; it made clear that Anna (Shirley MacLaine) was deeply affected by sexual desire and frustration. But what is clear in a dream may be quite difficult to enact in real life, as another deleted scene was to show: she was going to sleep with her lover (Laurence Harvey), but he refused because she appeared to him as 'a lamb before the sacrifice.' As it stands, the film still retains something of that lost sense in the way it contrasts sensuousness with puritanism or sweetness and reserve with occasional outbursts of passion and disorder."

Walters returned to the musical with *Jumbo* (also known as *Billy Rose's Jumbo*), starring Doris Day and Stephen Boyd. A circus story with some memorable moments, this uneven musical was followed by an outright bad one, *The Unsinkable Molly Brown* (1964), from Meredith Willson's Broadway show. Debbie Reynolds plays the half-wild Rocky Mountain girl who, after her husband strikes it rich, conquers European society and is eventually accepted by the Denver elite on account of her heroism in the aftermath of the *Titanic* disaster. Douglas McVay found it "boringly rowdy, only sporadically endurable."

The director's next film was his last, as it was Cary Grant's. *Walk, Don't Run* (1966), independently produced by Sol Siegel, is set in Tokyo during the Olympics. The city is packed with tourists and Grant, playing an English industrial magnate in need of a bed, is obliged to double up with Samantha Eggar. John Coleman called it "the sort of professional light comedy we all thought Hollywood had thrown away the mould of." Penelope Gilliatt was less impressed, complaining that "most of the comic business in the film is about washing timetables and breakfast making . . . about sexual protocol without any sexual content, and about rules without any comic pressure of longing."

Thereafter Walters worked occasionally and without much enthusiasm in television, directing among other things two episodes of *Here's Lucy* and Two Lucille Ball "specials," mostly as a favor to the star with whom he had worked first in *Du Barry Was a Lady* in 1942. In 1980 he was a guest lecturer in directing at his alma mater, the University of Southern California. He died two years later at the age of seventy and was survived by an adopted son.

"Charles Walters' best films certainly have a charm of their own," wrote Alain Masson. "This nobody denies, but it is quite another matter to understand how it works, so that many critics yielded to the temptation of assigning most of the merit to the studio [MGM] and to the genre [the musical]. . . . His work is not an individual achievement and will not be of any support to the auteur theory, but his films have a special tone and a recognizable mood, fanciful and romantic, tense and genial, melancholy and lively." For Masson, Walters "is a modern film maker insofar as his films . . . involve a play with the genre itself" and also in "his sense of feminine vulnerability" and his willingness to offer "a picture of women's sexual desire. . . . Walters finally appears as an original artist, subtle and sensitive, whose delicacy and charm are not evanescent qualities but are deeply rooted in an unobtrusive yet thoughtful meditation on the musical form itself."

FILMS: Spreadin' the Jam, 1945 (short); Good News, 1947; Easter Parade, 1948; The Barkleys of Broadway, 1949; Summer Stock (UK, If You Feel Like Singing), 1950; Three Guys Named Mike, 1951; Texas Carnival, 1951; The Belle of New York, 1952; Lili, 1953; Dangerous When Wet, 1953; Torch Song, 1953; Easy to Love, 1953; The Glass Slipper, 1955; The Tender Trap, 1955; High Society, 1956; Don't Go Near the Water, 1957; Ask Any Girl, 1959; Please Don't Eat the Daisies, 1960; Two Loves (UK, Spinster), 1961; Jumbo (UK, Billy Rose's Jumbo), 1962; The Unsinkable Molly Brown, 1964; Walk, Don't Run, 1966.

ABOUT: Coursodon, J.-P. American Directors, Vol. 2, 1983. *Periodicals*—Cinéma (France) October 1982; Focus on Film Spring 1977; Monthly Film Bulletin October 1964; Positif November–December 1972.

WATT, (RAYMOND) HARRY (October 10, 1906–), Scottish director and scenarist, was born in Edinburgh, the son of a well-known athlete who became a barrister and a member of the British Parliament—"a confident extrovert" and an ardent antimonarchist who embarrassed his "horribly conventional" son with his loud check suits and buttoned boots. At the age of ten, Harry Watt was sent to a second-rate boarding

HARRY WATT

school, Dollar Academy, where he was intensely unhappy and contracted asthma. Three years in this wretched institution were followed by two years of almost complete freedom when he lived on a farm in the beautiful Moniaive valley with his mother, a strong-willed woman who had walked out on her husband after a fight. He eventually outmaneuvered her and reunited the family by buying the farm "over her head."

Harry Watt completed his secondary education at a snobbish day school, Edinburgh Academy, where he discovered that he was a socialist, and went on to study for a commerce degree at Edinburgh University. There he distinguished himself as a drinker, an athlete, and a militant member of the Labour party, but not as a student, dropping out in 1929 to take his first job as a traveling salesman. Soon tiring of this, he impulsively signed on as a deckhand on a schooner and sailed to Newfoundland, from there making his way to mainland Canada. He worked in an automobile plant in Oshawa, sold musical walking sticks to American Shriners at a Toronto carnival, and got a job as a wine waiter to earn his fare home.

Back in England in the midst of the Depression, Watt invested an inheritance in an ingenious technique for recycling rubber tires. The thousands of beach balls he manufactured in this way unfortunately leaked, and his factory went bankrupt. Watt found occasional casual jobs, but it was during this period, he says, that he experienced and came to understand real poverty. Then one day, in a Soho café, he "heard that a Scotsman was forming a film unit." This was 1931 and the Scotsman was John Grierson, already installed as Films Officer of the Empire Marketing Board (EMB). Watt secured an interview with Grierson and was taken on as a trainee—mostly because the sea-loving Grierson was impressed by his account of his adventurous voyage to Newfoundland.

The EMB was established to promote Britain, its products, and its institutions, but Grierson had other intentions as well, deriving from a socialist (but non-Marxist) belief in the need to awaken the working class to its own social importance, its political responsibilities and rights. Watt says that Grierson was a puritan who "paid us bugger-all . . . about two pounds ten [shillings] a week—but we were learning our job. . . . We adored him, and we knew that he had the basic idea. . . . We were putting the British workingman . . . onto the screen. Before that, the workingman was the comic relief in the ghastly British films of those days."

Most of Grierson's young men (unlike Harry Watt) were products of the British public school system, and under Grierson's leadership they developed an extraordinary team spirit, with everyone contributing his own ideas and enthusiasm to the films of others, without regard for credit or reward. What they lacked was technical skill, and Watt writes with some skepticism about the intellectual and aesthetic pretensions of his colleagues: "No one ever seems to have recorded that we were just a bunch of enthusiastic kids, accepting the basic theme of the dignity of man from our brilliant but erratic boss, learning our job by trial and error, bubbling with ideas but making thousands of mistakes."

Grierson's own notion of film had been shaped mainly by the work of the great Soviet directors of the 1920s. He also had a great though not unmixed admiration for Robert Flaherty, whom he brought to the EMB as guide and mentor to his young disciples. One of Watt's first important assignments was as assistant to Flaherty in the filming of *Man of Aran* (1933), a characteristic story of simple people battling with nature on an island off the Irish coast. Watt was not impressed by the great documentarist's methods. He deplored the waste of time and footage that resulted from Flaherty's refusal to provide himself with a script, and thought the film a "romanticised pictorial record of what may have been the island's way of life about a hundred years back."

In 1933 the government closed down the Empire Marketing Board, and Grierson moved on to the General Post Office (GPO), taking with him most of his EMB staff and all of his ideas. The following year the Brazilian filmmaker Alberto Cavalcanti joined the GPO Film Unit, and it was Cavalcanti rather than Grierson or Flaherty who was Watt's mentor. "Cavalcanti was a professional," Watt says, "and we were all a lot of bloody amateurs then, trying to learn our job. So was Grierson. . . . I would say here and now that anything I know of the film business I learned from Cavalcanti, particularly when sound came in. We didn't know what a piece of sound was, we didn't even know that picture and sound were shot separately. . . . I think documentary became *professional* because of Cavalcanti."

Watt made his own first films for the GPO Film Unit in 1934, codirecting with Edgar Anstey *6.30 Collection* and *BBC: Droitwich*. After an instructive period on loan to the *March of Time,* he made his first important documentary, *Night Mail* (1936, 25 minutes), showing how the mail was carried overnight by train from London to Scotland. It has a splendidly rhythmic verse commentary by W. H. Auden and music by Benjamin Britten (who was paid about £10 for his work). The exteriors were shot on location, sometimes under hazardous conditions, the interiors in the studio, where the impression of movement was achieved by having the mail sorters sway gently as they worked. The sound of the locomotive clacking along the rails—in reality drowned by the noise of the engine—was obtained by the use of a model.

James Beveridge saw *Night Mail* as a student in Vancouver and found in it "an entirely new world. . . . In this new, strange film, there was a sense of the intimate presence of human beings, not actors disturbingly near. . . . They spoke a strange language, that of working-class England. . . . Underlying the terse, straightforward progress of the film was a rhythm, a natural, hypnotic, powerful sound—the train clacking over the rails as it rushed northward toward Scotland. . . . Then the poetry—*poetry* in a film! . . . We were stunned."

Watt is generally credited as codirector of *Night Mail* with Basil Wright, but he himself says that he directed the film in its entirety, though Auden's verse and Britten's music "were the ideas and work of Wright and Cavalcanti," who were also mainly responsible for the editing. It is generally recognized to be one of the finest of all documentary films, and Roy Armes has called it "in many ways . . . the culmination of the GPO period—a collaborative effort which balances Grierson's concern with public information, Watt's naturalistic direction and the more lyrical and experimental approaches of Cavalcanti and Wright."

Britten also provided the score for Watt's next film, *The Saving of Bill Blewett* (1936, 25 minutes). Watt had been instructed to make a film to promote the work of the Post Office Savings Section (although "the whole idea of saving was—and has remained—anathema" to him). Casting around for locations, Watt "came across Bill Blewett, the local postmaster of Mousehole, Cornwall, one of the greatest characters I've ever met. We worked up a little story and played in it all the local people. Everything, including interiors, were shot on location."

The "little story" featured Blewett—a natural actor—not as postmaster but as a feckless fisherman who loses his boat, is trapped into starting a savings account, and winds up with a new boat. Watt says that he learned a great deal during the making of this film from Cavalcanti, who "moved in and helped me when I started to get into a mess." It was Cavalcanti who taught him the difference between an "atmospheric" documentary and a narrative (in which it is necessary to focus on the principals), and about continuity in dialogue scenes. He also introduced him to "the gentle art of faking"—many of the interiors, for example, were shot in a derelict cottage with the roof removed and gauze over the windows to give "a lovely even light."

The Saving of Bill Blewett already hinted at the direction Watt was to take—toward fictionalized documentary—a tendency developed further in his next significant film, *North Sea* (1938). This tells the story of a Scottish trawler that gets into difficulties in a storm but finally makes its way home thanks to the GPO's ship-to-shore radio link. The script was based on fact, but it was acted out by Bill Blewett and a cast recruited from among out-of-work seamen in Aberdeen, and shot partly on an old trawler, partly on an ingenious studio set.

By this time Grierson had left the GPO Film Unit, intent on taking films to people who did not attend movie theatres but might be reached through a "non-theatrical circuit" of schools, village halls, exhibitions, and the like. Watt and Cavalcanti believed, on the contrary, that it was important to gain acceptance for documentaries on the ordinary commercial circuits, where the mass audience could be reached. *North Sea,* was a deliberate and successful attempt to make a documentary that could be sold commercially.

With the outbreak of World War II in 1939, the GPO Film Unit was taken over by the Ministry of Information to make propaganda films, in 1940 becoming the Crown Film Unit. Watt's first war film was *The First Days* (1939, 23 minutes), made in collaboration with Humphrey Jennings and Pat Jackson, and produced by Cavalcanti. A portrait of London as it armed itself for war, it seemed to Erik Barnouw, as to others,

that it "somehow caught the spirit of the moment. Its style was precise, calm, rich in resonance."

Britain at Bay followed in 1940, and then another collaboration with Jennings, *London Can Take It* (1940, 10 minutes), intended primarily for export to America. With a commentary by the American journalist Quentin Reynolds, it shows London carrying on bravely and matter-of-factly under the German blitz, and is an extremely effective mixture of drama and laconic humor. After the publication of Lovell and Hillier's *Studies in Documentary* (1973), which gave most of the credit for this film to Humphrey Jennings, Watt wrote to the authors asserting that the idea was his, that he wrote the original treatment, and that he "directed all the interiors, a good deal of the night exteriors and all the model shots—which most people never recognised as such," as well as securing Reynolds' commentary.

Far less well known, but greatly admired by those who have seen it, is Watt's *Squadron 992* (1940), dealing with the training of a barrage balloon squad and its baptism of fire during a German air raid on the Firth of Forth. Watt's reconstruction of the raid is a small masterpiece, and H. Forsyth Hardy called the film as a whole "brilliantly arranged and exciting . . . with a warm human quality we were beginning to think of as characteristic of Watt's work."

Two minor propaganda films followed, and then Watt's first feature-length picture, *Target for Tonight* (1941, 50 minutes). All of the previous war documentaries had been defensive in attitude—tributes to a "Britain at bay"; Watt's idea was to show the country moving on to the offensive. An account of a British bombing raid on oil storage tanks in Germany, it shows the crews being briefed, the excitement and tension of the takeoff—brilliantly shot and lit—and the long procession of cloudscapes to the target. The film centers on one of the Wellingtons, F for Freddie, which is damaged during the attack, but which eventually limps back to its base.

The actors in *Target for Tonight* were flyers from RAF Bomber Command. The film was shot where possible on location, otherwise in the fuselage of an obsolete aircraft, and Watt showed again his extraordinary talent for drawing convincing performances from nonprofessional actors. Paul Rotha wrote that the impact achieved by the film "was way ahead of any comparable film of the time, due not to the overt dramatics of war in the air but to the people it described." *Target for Tonight* was shown as a first feature in Britain and in twelve thousand movie theatres in the United States, where it was seen by an estimated fifty million people. Its propaganda effects were incalculable, and the film's title passed into the language.

In 1942–1943 Watt served with the Army Kinematograph Service, taking vigorous part in the dangers of the Vaagso commando raid, and in 1943 he followed Cavalcanti to Michael Balcon's Ealing Studios, where he found a team spirit not unlike that of the GPO Film Unit. His first entirely fictional movie followed the same year, *Nine Men*. Scripted by Watt from a story by Gerald Kersh, it deals with a small group of British soldiers in the North African desert who, cut off from their brigade and under attack, turn an old tomb into a fortress.

Nine Men was made for about £20,000. A Welsh beach stood in for the African desert, and the little-known cast included Gordon Jackson, Jack Lambert, and Bill Blewett. The film's style was very much the one that Watt had developed in his fictionalized documentaries, and it seemed to Ernest Lindgren "as near to a native style of British filmmaking as anything which has yet been seen." Extremely popular, it made profits out of all proportions to its miniscule investment.

Ordinary British soldiers are the central characters also in *Fiddlers Three* (1944), but here they are transported back in time to the Rome of Nero in a dire musical comedy starring Tommy Trinder. This was Harry Watt's only attempt at the genre and is best forgotten. In 1944 he went to Australia with the idea of making a film about that country's contribution to the war. He traveled 30,000 miles in three months, searching for a story, and finally, by chance, heard of the "great round-up" of 1942, when 85,000 head of cattle were driven across the "Dead Heart" of the continent to prevent their use by the Japanese should an invasion occur.

Watt wrote a script centering on a single droving outfit and the family of refugees who attach themselves to it. The head drover was played by Chips Rafferty, but most of the rest of the cast were amateurs, including the heroine, Daphne Campbell, herself an experienced cattlewoman. Watt's method was to buy five hundred cattle and re-enact the 1,600 mile trek. "There is no faking in it," he says. "We took the actors to the scenery, instead of faking the scenery from country near . . . cities. . . . We had to build roads and camps, we did everything for ourselves." The result was *The Overlanders* (1946), welcomed as "the first British Western" and generally admired, though there were complaints about the lack of "deliberate momentum" in the episodic narrative and about the naivety of the love story.

Another "Antipodean Western" followed, *Eureka Stockade* (1948), about the conflict between the diggers and the colonial government during the gold rush of 1853. The script was by Watt and Walter Greenwood, and the cast included Chips Rafferty, Jack Lambert, Gordon Jackson, and Peter Finch. Raymond Durgnat found it well-meaning but politically confused and thin in its characterization, though "much that is poignant in wartime documentary is perpetuated in Chips Rafferty's lean grave figure and sadly firm, elegiac voice."

Turning his attention to Africa, Watt again set out on a long research tour and devised a story based on the career of a well-known Kenyan conservationist, Mervyn Cowie. In *Where No Vultures Fly (Ivory Hunter,* 1951), Cowie is translated into Bob Payton (Anthony Steel), a game warden who overcomes bureaucratic and commercial obstacles to end the traffic in ivory. This robust adventure story was one of the most profitable of all Ealing films. Charles Barr, who thought that *The Overlanders* had affinities with Hawks' *Red River,* found this film reminiscent of *Hatari.*

A somewhat inferior sequel appeared in 1954 as *West of Zanzibar,* with Steel this time playing a District Commissioner whose African protégés are lured into ivory smuggling by an unscrupulous Arab. Barr found this film "much less 'open,' technically and thematically," than its predecessor, and "deeply paternalistic" in its attitude to the Africans. The Kenyan government evidently agreed, and banned the picture.

After that, "disillusioned with the big time," Watt approached various documentary units but could not find a job. In 1955 he worked for Granada Television as a producer. Then he was offered the film that became *People Like Maria* (1958)—a tribute to the World Health Organization and its work in various parts of the world. It had to be made in six months on a budget of £40,000. Watt's "main memories of *Maria* are of appallingly hard work, shooting at 14,000 feet in the Andes with a local unit, battling . . . ill health in the stinking heat of Northern Nigeria, and struggling with the charming Buddhist confusion that is modern Burma." The film was completed on time and on budget and took the two principal documentary prizes at Venice in 1958.

Watt then rejoined Ealing and in fact made the studio's last film, *The Siege of Pinchgut* (1959), a thriller set in Sydney, Australia. Aldo Ray plays a convict who escapes from jail, determined to prove his innocence. He and his brother hole up on an island in Sydney harbor, take hostages, and use them to put pressure on the authorities. Disillusioned when the hero resorts to violence, the brother eventually betrays him to the police—a denouement that distressed some socialist critics.

Speaking of his work at the EMB and the GPO, Watt says that "by showing, for the first time, the achievement, the essential and overwhelming contribution of the ordinary man to society, we could give them a pride and a realization of their strength that would encourage them to act on their own behalf." This was Grierson's dream, and no one made a more sincere and effective attempt at realizing it than Harry Watt, though he recognizes that he and his colleagues, in their celebration of the "dignity of labor," fell short of serious social criticism.

Most critics would agree with Watt that he "drew the documentary away from the accepted assemblage of visuals tied together with a commentary, to a dramatized, more human approach," though some believe that he was wrong to have blurred in this way the distinction between documentary and fiction. His feature movies, according to Charles Barr, "are the most robust of Ealing films," and he himself is "the most evident individualist at Ealing, the nearest approach in the British cinema to the great Hollywood 'adventurer,' Howard Hawks."

FILMS: *Documentaries*—(with Edgar Anstey) 6.30 Collection, 1934; (with Edgar Anstey) BBC: Droitwich, 1934; (with Basil Wright) Night Mail, 1936; The Saving of Bill Blewett, 1936; Men of the Alps, 1936; Sorting Office, 1936; (with John Grierson) Four Barriers, 1937; Big Money, 1938; North Sea, 1938; Health in Industry, 1938; (with Humphrey Jennings and Pat Jackson) The First Days, 1939; Britain at Bay, 1940; (with Humphrey Jennings) London Can Take It, 1940; Squadron 992 (shortened version shown in America as Flying Elephants), 1940; Dover: Front Line, 1940; The Story of an Air Communiqué, 1940; Target for Tonight, 1941; Christmas Under Fire, 1941; Dover Revisited, 1942; Twenty-One Miles, 1942; People Like Maria, 1958. *Features*—Nine Men, 1943; Fiddlers Three (While Nero Fiddled), 1944; The Overlanders, 1946; Eureka Stockade, 1948; Where No Vultures Fly (Ivory Hunter), 1951; West of Zanzibar, 1954; The Siege of Pinchgut, 1959.

ABOUT: Armes, R. A Critical History of the British Cinema, 1978; Barr, C. Ealing Studios, 1977; Beveridge, J. John Grierson, 1978; Lovell, A. and Hillier, J. Studies in Documentary, 1972; Manvell, R. (ed.) Experiment in the Film, 1949; Sussex, E. Rise and Fall of the British Documentary, 1975; Watt, H. Don't Look at the Camera, 1974. *Periodicals*—Cinéma d'Aujourd'hui February–March 1977; Film Forum February 1949; Films and Filming June 1959, June 1974; Leader Magazine March 2, 1946.

WELLES, (GEORGE) ORSON (May 6, 1915–October 9, 1985), American director, actor, screenwriter, and producer, was born—to his lasting chagrin—in Kenosha, Wisconsin. (Having been conceived in Paris and named in Rio de Janeiro, he felt that Kenosha lacked, as a birthplace, a certain éclat.) Wisconsin happened to be where his father, Richard Head Welles, who hailed from Virginia, owned two factories. A dilettante engineer and idiosyncratic inventor, sixty-four years old when Orson Welles was born, his preferred occupations were travel and gambling; "a wandering *bon viveur*" was his son's description. Welles' mother, Beatrice Ives Welles, was an accomplished concert pianist whose acquaintances included Ravel and Stravinsky; she was also exceptionally beautiful, a crack rifle shot, and a political radical who had once been imprisoned as a suffragist. Welles adored both his parents. "[My father] was a gentle, sensitive soul. . . . To him I owe the advantage of not having had a formal education until I was ten years old. From him I inherited the love of travel which has become ingrained within me. From my mother I inherited a real and lasting love of music and the spoken word."

Welles was the second and youngest child. (His brother Richard, ten years his senior, is said to have been a quietly eccentric character. At one point he joined a monastery in California, from which he was later ejected.) Orson Welles was treated virtually as an adult from infancy. Tales of his precocity have passed into legend. At two, he spoke "fluent and considered English" and rejected Lamb's *Tales From Shakespeare*, which his mother was reading to him, demanding "the real thing." At three, he was reading Shakespeare for himself, starting with *A Midsummer Night's Dream*. He made his public stage debut the same year in *Madame Butterfly*, as the heroine's infant son. At four, he was writing, designing, and presenting his own stage plays in a miniature theatre given him by Dr. Maurice Bernstein, a Kenosha physician and family friend who was fascinated by his prodigious talents. At eight, Welles said "I was a *Wunderkind* of music. I played the violin, piano, I conducted." He could also draw, paint, and perform conjuring tricks with professional facility, and had written a well-researched paper on "The Universal History of the Drama."

His parents separated when he was six, and he went to live with his mother, mainly in Chicago. Two years later Beatrice Welles died, and the boy passed from a world of international high culture into one that involved (according to John Houseman) "long, wild nights . . . with his father, in the red-light districts of the Mediterranean, Hong Kong and Singapore." Welles seems

ORSON WELLES

to have found both environments equally stimulating. A term at the Washington School in Madison, Wisconsin, when he was nine, was not a success; a year later, at the suggestion of Dr. Bernstein, he was sent to Roger Hill's progressive Todd School for Boys at Woodstock, Illinois. Among the school's assets was a well-equipped theatre, where Welles promptly staged *Androcles and the Lion,* not only directing but playing both title roles. During his five years at Todd he mounted some thirty productions, including a widely acclaimed *Julius Caesar* in which he played Antony, Cassius, *and* the Soothsayer. He also coauthored with Roger Hill a popular textbook entitled *Everybody's Shakespeare,* which sold twenty thousand copies.

During his vacations Welles continued globetrotting with his father. Richard Welles took his son to most of the great cities of Europe and the Far East and made him at ease in a world of actors, circus folk, and conjurors. "My father loved magic; that's what bound us together." In 1928 Richard Welles killed himself in a Chicago hotel, flat broke. His son became the ward of Dr. Bernstein, of whom he later said, "I have never known a person of more real kindness, nor with a greater capacity for love and friendship."

Welles left Todd in 1930 and studied for a time at the Chicago Art Institute. At sixteen he was supposed to enter Harvard. Instead he took off to Ireland, where he bought a donkey and cart and traveled round the country painting. By the time he reached Dublin, his money had run out. "I guess I could have gotten an honest job, as a dishwasher or a gardener, but I became an actor." To do so, he presented himself to Hilton

Edwards, manager of the famous Gate Theatre, as a star of the New York Theater Guild. According to Micheál MacLiammóir, Edwards' partner, they instantly knew Welles for an impostor but were taken by his audacity and by the sheer vehemence of his acting. Welles auditioned for the role of the Duke in Feuchtwanger's *Jew Süss:* "It was an astonishing performance," observed MacLiammóir, "wrong from beginning to end, but with all the qualities of fine acting tearing their way through a chaos of inexperience." After nearly a year at the Gate, Welles moved to London, hoping no doubt to take the West End by storm, but was refused a work permit. He returned briefly to the United States, failed to gate-crash Broadway, and left for Spain, where he learned bullfighting in Seville. After that he went on a solitary sketching tour in the mountains of Morocco, where he was reputedly on excellent terms with the local bandits.

Back in America in 1933, he was hired by Katharine Cornell, on the recommendation of Thornton Wilder and Alexander Woollcott, to join her national repertory company tour of *Candida* and *Romeo and Juliet.* Welles played Marchbanks and Tybalt; John Houseman's first sight of him was in the latter role, his Broadway debut: "Death, in scarlet and black, in the form of a monstrous boy—flat-footed and graceless, yet swift and agile; soft as jelly one moment and uncoiled, the next, in a spring of such furious energy that, once released, it could be checked by no human intervention."

Around this time Welles directed his first film. *The Hearts of Age* (1934) was a four-minute surrealist spoof, satirizing such avant-garde works as Cocteau's *Le Sang d'un poète.* It was made by Welles and his friend William Vance for a drama festival at the Todd School. Along with Welles (who played Death) and Vance was the third member of the cast, Virginia Nicholson, an ethereally beautiful young actress whom Welles married that same year. They had one daughter, Christopher, born in 1937.

Filmmaking, at this stage in Welles' career, was a lighthearted diversion. The theatre was where he planned to make his mark. He first did so in the spring of 1936, when he and John Houseman staged their all-black "Voodoo Macbeth" for the Federal Theatre Project in Harlem. It was the sensation of the season, and Welles went on to stage several more notable productions, including *Horse Eats Hat* (an adaptation of Labiche's *Italian Straw Hat*) and *Doctor Faustus.* In 1937 he and Houseman formed their own company, the Mercury Theatre, which rapidly became one of the most influential companies in the history of Broadway.

Their first production was a modern-dress *Julius Caesar*, with Welles as Brutus, drawing explicit parallels with contemporary fascism. It was spectacularly successful, gaining rave reviews, and would have taken a fortune at the box office had not Welles and Houseman, in accordance with their left-wing principles, insisted on keeping ticket prices to a minimum. (Seats ranged from 50¢ to $2.00.) Other Mercury productions included a socialist opera, *The Cradle Will Rock*, by Marc Blitzstein, mounted in defiance of an Equity ban; Dekker's *The Shoemaker's Holiday*; Shaw's *Heartbreak House*; Büchner's *Danton's Death*; and a creaky old William Gillette farce, *Too Much Johnson* (1938), for which Welles shot some forty minutes of film to be incorporated into the play. (The sole print of this film, described by Welles as "beautiful . . . a sort of dream Cuba in New York," was destroyed in a fire in his Madrid villa in 1970.)

Much of the funding for Mercury productions was provided by Welles' prolific radio work. His rich, commanding baritone voice, once described by Kenneth Tynan as "bottled thunder," suited him ideally for the medium, and while producing and acting on stage he was also providing voices for, among others, The Shadow ("Who knows what evil lurks in the hearts of men? The Shadow knows. . . . "), Emperor Haile Selassie, and a chocolate pudding. Starting in July 1938, he persuaded CBS to employ the Mercury company in a weekly dramatization of a literary classic, initially under the title of *First Person Singular,* and later as *The Mercury Theatre of the Air.* On the evening of October 30, 1938, the chosen work was H. G. Welles' *The War of the Worlds.*

Accounts of mass hysteria, fleeing multitudes, packed congregations weeping in churches, panic calls to police and army, and even suicides were undoubtedly exaggerated by a gloating press. Nonetheless, an astounding number of people, hoodwinked by Welles' narrative method of simulated newsflashes, evidently did believe that Martians had landed at Grovers Mill, New Jersey, intent on annihilating the human race. By the next morning a highbrow radio show had become the most famous program in broadcasting history. Editorials thundered of criminal irresponsibility; writs and lawsuits were threatened; CBS grovelled in apology; and Welles, delighted beyond measure, expressed his heartfelt contrition. *Macbeth* and *Julius Caesar* had made him famous among the intelligentsia, but with *War of the Worlds* he had become, at twenty-three, a household name.

The Mercury Theatre had never repeated its first triumphant success with *Julius Caesar.* The company's shaky finances finally collapsed in 1939 under the weight of *Five Kings,* Welles' ambitious and disaster-prone conflation of eight of Shakespeare's histories. Offers had been coming in from Hollywood for some time; after the *War of the Worlds* scandal, they had increased sharply in frequency and munificence. Welles accepted the most attractive, from RKO, and headed west, stopping off in Chicago to stage a production of William Archer's melodrama *The Green Goddess.* As a prologue, he shot a few minutes of film depicting an air crash in the Himalayas; all prints seem to have vanished.

Of all the major Hollywood studios, RKO had the most trouble in establishing a consistent identity for itself—partly thanks to frequent changes of ownership, invariably followed by management reshuffles. Lacking the long-term leadership—for good or bad—of a Mayer, Zukor, or Cohn, the studio had veered indecisively from prestige ventures to cut-price programmers and back again. The current studio head, George Schaefer, was hoping to establish a reputation for progressive, sophisticated filmmaking, an aim backed by the more highbrow board members such as Nelson Rockefeller and NBC chief David Sarnoff. Hence the offer to Welles.

The terms of the contract were unprecedented. Welles was to make one picture a year for three years, receiving for each $150,000 plus 25 percent of the gross. He could produce, direct, write, and/or star as he wished. He could choose his own subjects, cast whomever he liked, and no studio executive had the right to interfere in any way before or during filming, nor even ask to see what had been shot until the film was complete. Hollywood was full of veterans who had been struggling for years to achieve a fraction of the autonomy that was being handed to the "boy wonder." Even before Welles arrived, resentment against him was widespread and intense. The quip, "There, but for the grace of God, goes God," has been attributed to several local wits, including Herman Mankiewicz; but whoever said it summed up the general feeling in the movie capital at the time.

Initially, it seems, Welles had no intention of making the movies his life's work; they were simply a useful source of funds for future theatrical projects. He arrived at RKO in June 1939 with an entourage of Mercury associates, thus arousing further rancor in Hollywood. One former associate was absent, though: Virginia Nicholson was in Nevada, getting a divorce. (After it was through, Welles pronounced himself "unsuited to marriage.") Virginia Nicholson soon remarried; her second husband was the writer

Charles Lederer, favorite nephew of the actress Marion Davies. The wedding took place at San Simeon, the fabulous residence of Miss Davies and the newspaper tycoon William Randolph Hearst.

For his first Hollywood movie, Welles announced an adaptation of Conrad's *Heart of Darkness,* with himself as Kurtz, and Marlowe, the narrator, to be represented by a subjective camera. But months passed and nothing was filmed except a few tests. Welles spent much of his time watching movies, especially those of Lang, Clair, Capra, Vidor—and Ford, whose *Stagecoach* he screened over forty times. Schaefer, getting nervous, suggested he should choose a less ambitious project. Welles agreed, and switched to *The Smiler With a Knife,* a crime novel by Nicholas Blake. This, too, came to nothing. It was a full year after his arrival in Hollywood that Welles began shooting his first feature film.

More has probably been written about *Citizen Kane* (1941) than about any other film ever made. Acclaimed on release as a work of striking originality, it has since attained an unassailable position as a landmark in American filmmaking and the most influential film in the history of cinema. "Less by imitation than by inspiration," wrote Arthur Knight in *Action* (May–June 1969), "*Citizen Kane* has altered the look not only of American films, but of films the world over." Since it is, as François Truffaut pointed out, "the only first film made by a man who was already famous," Welles therefore "felt constrained to make a movie which would sum up everything that had come before in cinema, and would prefigure everything to come."

Citizen Kane recounts, by means of a complex and ingenious flashback structure, the life of a great American press tycoon. Charles Foster Kane—despite Welles' subsequent disclaimers—is modeled fairly closely on William Randolph Hearst. Kane's mistress Susan Alexander, a talentless singer whom he tries to mold into a diva, is an unjust caricature of Hearst's mistress Marion Davies, whose career as a movie actress was backed by Hearst and his newspaper empire. Kane's mansion Xanadu was obviously inspired by Hearst's San Simeon.

The film starts with Kane's death, then cuts with jarring abruptness to the blare of a fake newsreel—a perfect imitation of the *March of Time* series—recounting the late tycoon's life and exploits. The newsreel editor, though, is dissatisfied, and—rather implausibly—assigns one of his reporters to find out not just what Kane did, but "who he was," and why he died with the word "rosebud" on his lips. The rest of the film

follows the reporter as he sifts the recollections of five people who knew Kane well, trying to arrive at the truth. He fails, but the camera (as well as audience) discovers at least part of the answer. At the very end we watch the casual destruction of Kane's "junk," including the sled he had used as a boy in the Midwest. The sled is thrown into the furnace and the camera catches for a moment the word painted on its side: "Rosebud." There is a dissolve to the exterior of Xanadu— and the sign we had seen at the beginning of the film: "No Trespassing."

"The best way to understand *Citizen Kane,*" David Bordwell asserted in *Film Comment* (Summer 1971), "is to stop worshiping it as a triumph of technique." Bordwell points out, as have other writers, that none of the technical devices deployed by Welles in *Kane* were brandnew. Deep-focus photography, ceilinged sets, chiaroscuro lighting, temporal jump cuts, expressionist distortion—all had been used before, mostly by the great German silent directors whose influence pervaded Hollywood in the 1930s. But never before in America had they all been used together with such exuberance, style, and ferocious narrative intensity. Welles' inexperience worked for him: unaware of the "right way" to make a film, he created from the first a style completely his own, one that David Thomson characterized as "simultaneously baroque and precise, overwhelmingly emotional and deeply founded in reality." Perhaps no other director's work is so immediately recognizable; "his signature," as Ronald Gottesman wrote, "is unmistakably inscribed in virtually every frame."

In a contemporary review (*The Clipper,* May 1941), Cedric Belfrage noted that "of all the delectable flavours that linger on the palate after seeing *Kane,* the use of sound is strongest." Though Welles was a novice—albeit a staggeringly gifted one—at filmmaking, he could bring to bear more knowledge of radio techniques than anyone else in Hollywood. The soundtrack of *Kane*—as of his other American films, *Macbeth* excepted—is of a complexity and subtlety unprecedented at the time. Dialogue overlaps, cuts across spatial and temporal dissolves; sounds are dislocated, distorted, deployed nonnaturalistically to comment on or counterpoint the visuals; voices alter in timbre according to distance, placing, or physical surroundings; music and sounds are used across transitions, to effect narrative ellipses. Phyllis Goldfarb (*Take One,* October 1972) quotes a sequence in illustration: "Susan's singing in the parlor is heard, without a lapse, over the dissolve which moves us to the parlor at a later date. Then Kane's applause [for Susan] turns into light clapping heard behind Leland's campaign speech. Leland's voice, in turn, becomes Kane's heard over the microphone in a large auditorium."

In casting *Kane,* Welles largely ignored the established pool of Hollywood acting talent, preferring for his lead roles stage actors with little or no movie experience. Most of them—Joseph Cotten, Everett Sloane, George Coulouris, Agnes Moorehead—had belonged to his Mercury troupe. He himself, inevitably, played Kane.

Controversy still surrounds the authorship of the script: in *The Citizen Kane Book,* Pauline Kael provocatively alleged that Herman Mankiewicz deserved sole credit but "was blackmailed into sharing credit with Welles." The general consensus is that Mankiewicz had the original idea and created the initial script, which Welles then rewrote and modified considerably in shooting—and that the final credit, coauthorship with Mankiewicz's name first, is about right. No one, at any rate, has ever disputed the enormous contribution made by the superb deep-focus photography of Gregg Toland, in Welles' estimation "the best director of photography that ever existed." *Kane*'s masterly score was the work of another beginner in movies, Bernard Herrmann.

For all Welles' leftist political stance, there is nothing particularly subversive about *Citizen Kane.* Its message, insofar as it carries one, is the sentimental Capraesque thesis that the rich should not be envied their wealth and power, since they have forfeited the simple pleasures (vouchsafed to poorer folk) of happiness and true love—a conservative doctrine at bottom and mightily comforting to the rich and powerful. But to point out that Welles' originality lies not in what he says but in how he says it is hardly to diminish him as an artist—much the same, after all, is true of Shakespeare. *Kane* broaches themes that were to recur throughout Welles' films: the irrecoverable loss of innocence and idealism, the loneliness of power, potential unrealized and talent abused, the fear of death. In Charles Foster Kane, Welles presents the first in his gallery of brooding, unscrupulous predators, who nonetheless retain a small area of human vulnerability that arouses our sympathy. That Kane died in anguished nostalgia for a symbol of his lost Midwest boyhood may be "dollar-book Freud," as Welles later remarked, but it remains a potent and unforgettable image.

One of Hearst's biographers wrote that he was "unrivaled in the magnificence of his failure, the scope of his defeats, the size and scope of his disappointments." It would fit Kane; it would also fit Welles, whose outsized personality—as has often been pointed out—bears comparison with that of Kane and of the other flawed-monster figures in his films. (Kane's flippant line: "It might be fun to run a newspaper" echoes Welles' reported comment on arrival at RKO "This is the greatest train set a boy ever had.") "Every time I bring out a new movie," Welles once protested, "nobody bothers to review it. . . . Instead, they write a long essay on 'the Welles Phenomenon and what has become of it.' They don't review my work; they review me!" True—yet to some extent Welles could be said to have invited such treatment by so often playing blatantly recognizable, if distorted, versions of himself—"ironic, bombastic, pathetic, and, above all, presumptuous" (Andrew Sarris). It should be added, though, that apart from Falstaff all the Welles-personae were far less likable than the man himself.

Even before *Kane* was complete, rumors about its subject matter had spread beyond Hollywood. Louella Parsons, Hearst's leading gossip columnist, squealed in outrage; RKO was threatened with a total boycott by the Hearst press. Louis B. Mayer of MGM, afraid that Hearst reprisals might hit the whole industry, offered to buy the film for its cost plus a sizable margin and suppress it. The RKO board wavered, but Schaefer, to his credit, stood firm and released *Kane* without cuts or changes. (Not for over twenty years would another Welles picture be released the way he left it.) The other studios, though, largely barred it from exhibition in their outlets, thus restricting distribution to the few cinemas controlled by RKO. Even the famous Radio City Music Hall in New York, though part-owned by RKO, refused to premiere the film.

Citizen Kane was received by most reviewers—barring those in the Hearst papers—with enthusiasm, even adulation. In the New York *Times* Bosley Crowther hailed it as "one of the greatest (if not *the* greatest) films in history." Dilys Powell observed that "there is no question here of experiment for experiment's sake; it is a question of a man with a problem of narrative to solve, using lighting, setting, sound, camera angles and movement much as a genuine writer uses words, phrases, cadences, rhythms; using them with the ease and boldness and resource of one who controls and is not controlled by his medium." The film's reputation declined slightly in the late 1940s and 1950s but has since soared. In 1962 the international critics' poll in *Sight and Sound* voted it best film of all time; in 1972, and again in 1982, it maintained its position, increasing its lead over all other contenders. (In 1972 and 1982 *The Magnificent Ambersons* also made the top ten.) "*Citizen Kane,*" David Thomson wrote, "grows with every year as America comes to resemble it."

Kane was nominated for nine Oscars but won only one—for Best Screenplay. At the Academy Awards ceremony booing broke out every time Welles' name came up. Shortly before the film's release, he had further enraged the Hollywood establishment with a snook-cocking article in *Stage* (February 1941) in which he said, among other things, that "the producer is not a necessary evil. He's unnecessary, and he's an evil. . . . In England, a producer is a man who stages a play; on Broadway, he is the man who finances a play; in Hollywood, he is the man who interferes with a movie." When *Kane,* despite the rave reviews, flopped badly at the box office, satisfaction was widespread among the studio regulars.

Kane's failure set the pattern: most of Welles' movies lost money on initial release, and he never had a box-office hit. But for all its lavish appearance, *Kane* was in no way an expensive movie. Its total cost, pre-publicity, was around $600,000—for comparison, *Gone With the Wind,* made two years earlier, had cost $4.25 million. Of all the charges later flung at Welles by the film industry, that of extravagance was the least justified. As Charlton Heston pointed out, "there are directors who have *wasted* more money on one film than Orson has spent on all the pictures he's directed in his career."

From the grandiose public gestures of *Citizen Kane,* Welles turned next to "a film of deliberately subdued, plain photographic character . . . a world as formally nostalgic as a cameo brooch" (Charles Higham). François Truffaut remarked that *The Magnificent Ambersons* (1942) seemed to have "been shot in a fury by a different director who hated [*Kane*] and wanted to give Welles a lesson in modesty." Taken from a novel by Booth Tarkington (who had been a friend of Welles' father), the film traces the gradual, inexorable decline from social eminence of one family in a Midwest town around the turn of the century. The subject is parochial—even trivial—but Welles invests it with an aching nostalgia for an irrecoverable world of charm and graciousness. The romantic vision of a vanished childhood paradise that enclosed the scenes of Kane's snowbound boyhood has expanded in *Ambersons* to suffuse the entire film.

Though his voice speaks the narration, *Ambersons* is the only Welles film to date in which he himself never appears. ("A very happy experience for me. . . . it was a joy not to have to stand in front of a camera.") The main role, of the spoiled, willful George Amberson Minafer, was taken by Tim Holt, who had previously appeared mainly in B Westerns. Around him Welles again cast members of his Mercury troupe—most notably Joseph Cotten as Eugene Morgan, gentlemanly representative of ruthless progress, and Agnes Moorehead giving the performance of a lifetime as the frustrated, hysterical Aunt Fanny. Moorehead's portrayal, wrote Stephen Farber in *Film Comment* (Summer 1971), makes Fanny "one of the first truly *modern* characters in American films."

Welles intended *The Magnificent Ambersons* as an elegy "not so much for an epoch as for the sense of moral values which are destroyed." From the living cameos of the opening scenes, misty-edged like old sepia prints come to life, through the febrile gaiety of "the last of the great, long-remembered dances" and the exhilaration of the sleigh-ride, Welles shows us the shadows of death and dissolution gathering around the family. Nor does he suggest that the Ambersons, narrow-minded and intolerably self-satisfied, did anything other than bring their downfall upon themselves. Yet his characters are portrayed with such evocative affection that the sense of loss is irresistible. "Remove the intimations of destiny," noted Penelope Houston, "and the Ambersons would be merely a snobbish little clan clinging to empty aristocratic illusions. Welles's achievement is in lending them his own romanticism, at the same time keeping a due, dispassionate distance." Charles Higham described the film as "a doomed, beautiful thing. Its darkness, its nostalgia, fill one still, like the knowledge of its partial destruction, with an unbearable sadness."

Like *Kane, Ambersons* is distinguished by the sheer visual richness with which Welles informs every shot—a quality enhanced by the luminous deep-focus photography of Stanley Cortez. (Welles had been unable to get Gregg Toland, who was off working with John Ford's navy unit; but Cortez, whose later credits include Laughton's *Night of the Hunter,* achieved equally fine effects.) This visual opulence, which characterizes all his finest work—and which some critics have found excessive—is something Welles aimed for quite deliberately: "I try to keep the screen as rich as possible, because I never forget that the film itself is a dead thing and, for me at least, the illusion of life fades very quickly when the texture is thin."

Surviving prints of *The Magnificent Ambersons* represent scarcely two-thirds of Welles' conception. "Something had happened," comments the narration at the film's climax. "A thing which years ago had been the eagerest hope of many, many good citizens of the town. . . . George Amberson Minafer had got his comeuppance." Many of the good citizens of Hollywood had been waiting no less eagerly for the comeuppance of George Orson Welles. They were now to be gratified.

While still shooting *Ambersons,* Welles was also taking part in the third film due under his contract. This was *Journey Into Fear* (1943), a thriller based on an Eric Ambler novel, directed by Norman Foster. Welles was billed as producer and coscriptwriter (with Joseph Cotten) and played the role of a Turkish police chief, Colonel Haki. He also apparently directed a good deal of the picture, including all his own scenes—though he has never admitted as much.

In February 1942, two weeks after shooting on *Ambersons* was completed, RKO sent Welles to South America to direct a multi-episode documentary film to be called *It's All True.* This was at the suggestion of Nelson Rockefeller, who was worried by the strength of pro-German feeling in Latin America and hoped Welles might act both as artist and cultural ambassador. The project was presented as a patriotic act, with script and budget to be left flexible; Welles agreed to direct unpaid. With him he took a rough cut of *Ambersons,* which he polished in long-distance communication with his editor, Robert Wise.

After Welles' final cut, *The Magnificent Ambersons* ran 131 minutes. RKO put it into sneak previews, found audience response disappointing, and ordered drastic recutting. Some 50 minutes were taken out, many of the later scenes were rearranged, and a new "happy ending" was shot. The butchered version, lasting 88 minutes, was released on the lower half of a double bill with a Lupe Velez vehicle, *Mexican Spitfire Sees a Ghost.*

Things were changing at RKO. The dominant force on the board was now the Texan millionaire Floyd Odlum, who regarded Welles as a pretentious, irresponsible liability. In June 1942 Odlum sacked Schaefer, replacing him with Charles Koerner, head of the theatre circuit. Welles was recalled from "squandering money" in Rio, his contract terminated; shooting on *It's All True* was stopped; and the Mercury team were told to vacate their offices within twenty-four hours to make room for a *Tarzan* unit. *Journey Into Fear* was edited against Welles' wishes; the released version, though amusing in parts, was dramatically incoherent and utterly lacking in tension.

For the rest of the war years Welles directed no more films. A projected version of *War and Peace,* to be made for Alexander Korda, got nowhere; and Welles' plan to direct Chaplin as a Landru-style murderer was taken over by Chaplin himself in *Monsieur Verdoux.* In 1943 he embarked on his parallel career as an actor in other people's movies with a thunderously melodra-

matic Rochester in Robert Stevenson's *Jane Eyre.* Brooding lighting effects and baroque camera angles lend credibility to rumors that he also helped out with the direction. That same year, after ending a long-term liaison with Dolores del Rio (who had starred in *Journey Into Fear*), Welles married Rita Hayworth, then at the height of her career as Hollywood's "love goddess." The couple had one daughter, Rebecca, born in 1944.

Rejected both by Hollywood and the draft board (in the latter case, for asthma and flat feet), Welles made his contribution to the war effort through lecture tours, political broadcasts, and speechwriting for Roosevelt. He got on well with the President, who suggested at one point that Welles should embark on a political career himself. Welles seriously considered running for the Senate in his native Wisconsin and later greatly regretted his decision not to—the more so since the contest was won by an obscure Republican, Joseph McCarthy. "I'm a disappointed political, no doubt about that. . . . I'd rather sit all night and talk about politics than about movies." His main reason against running, he explained not long after Reagan's election, was that: "I didn't think anybody could get elected President who had been divorced and who had been an actor. I made a hell of a mistake."

He eventually returned to direction with *The Stranger* (1946), made for Sam Spiegel. Most critics have rated it his least interesting work, and André Bazin even called it a parody of a Welles film. Welles himself admitted that "there is nothing of me in that picture. I did it to prove that I could put out a movie as well as anyone else." A war crimes investigator (played by Edward G. Robinson) traces a Nazi war criminal, Franz Kindler, to a quiet New England town, where he is living as a schoolmaster under the name of Charles Rankin. The script, by Anthony Veiller and an uncredited John Huston, is riddled with implausibilities—we're asked to believe, for example, that there would be no extant photographs of a top Nazi leader—and the film is toppled into farce by Welles' manic performance as the supposedly cautious and unobtrusive Rankin-Kindler. "The film demonstrates conclusively," wrote Joseph McBride, "that Welles cannot play a self-effacing character." Spiegel excised two reels set in South America that Welles considered "the best stuff in the picture." For all that, *The Stranger* showed a modest profit, one of the few Welles films to do so.

Any financial gain Welles may have made, though, was promptly swallowed up by his spectacular, highly acclaimed, but ruinously expenive Broadway production of Jules Verne's *Around the World,* with songs by Cole Porter. The producer, Mike Todd, pulled out in alarm as costs mounted, and Welles was left with personal debts of $350,000. He was also left owing Harry Cohn a film, having promised to write and direct one for him in return for an immediate $50,000 to get the costumes out of hock.

The film Cohn got, not entirely to his satisfaction, was *The Lady From Shanghai* (1948). According to Welles, its subject was determined by the choice, at random, of a paperback from a stand by the phone on which he was calling Cohn for the money: *If I Die Before I Wake,* a hard-boiled thriller by Sherwood King. "Later I read the book and it was horrible, so I set myself, top speed, to write a story." What he came up with was the most convoluted of *noir* thrillers, even in a genre notable for tortuous plotting. With the exception of the hero, Michael O'Hara (played by Welles with an air of glazed bemusement and a disarmingly phoney brogue), every character is a ruthless predator, set on double-and triple-crossing all the others. Most evil of all beneath her icy beauty, a *femme* as *fatale* as they come, is the heroine, Elsa—a role in which, with sardonic amusement, Welles cast his then wife, Rita Hayworth.

The plot revolves around a brilliant, crippled lawyer, Bannister (Everett Sloane), his wife (Hayworth), and his partner Grisby (Glenn Anders). Each of them—insofar as motivation can be disentangled—plans to bump off the other two, using the naive O'Hara as fall guy. At one point, during an edgy yacht trip, O'Hara tells how he watched a whole pack of sharks devour each other: "I saw the ocean so darkened with blood it was black. . . . you could smell the death reeking up out of the sea." Later, the marine imagery recurs in a scene set in San Francisco's Steinhart Aquarium where Elsa, still playing the injured innocent, begs O'Hara's help; as she lies with tremulous fluency, conger eels, stingray, and squids drift behind her in lazy menace.

For all its rancid, disenchanted view of humanity, *Lady From Shanghai* is in many ways, as Joseph McBride suggested, Welles' "most purely enjoyable film. There is a new freedom of visual style. . . . In no other film, not even *Citizen Kane,* do we share with Welles such a spontaneous delight in the exercise of his gifts." Some critics have even seen the film as essentially comic; James Naremore described it as "a dark, grotesquely stylized comedy, a film that takes us beyond expressionism toward absurdity. . . . The sinister moments keep verging on farce." Frequently, Welles seems to enjoy heightening the excesses of *noir* convention with the baroque flourishes of his own style. The camera swoops, spirals and planes, careering off at vertiginous angles; scenes are framed and distorted through mirrors, balconies, water tumblers, and windshields; sequences of sun-dazzled whiteness give way to half-glimpsed images amid shifting shadows. The film's climax comes in the famous Hall of Mirrors shoot-out, a conscious tour de force of cinematic technique in which, as the images of Elsa, Bannister, and O'Hara splinter and multiply, Welles slyly taunts us to guess when a reflection of the camera crew will slide fortuitously into shot. (It never does.)

It would be difficult to say whether the film's frequent discrepancies in continuity and editing were a deliberate ploy by Welles to disconcert the audience, leaving us as disoriented as his hero—or whether they resulted from Columbia's frantic attempts to "save" what they regarded as an incomprehensible jumble. Cohn detested the film and was horrified by what Welles had done to the image of the studio's top female star. Though completed in 1946, the picture was not released until eighteen months later, by which time Hayworth ("I just can't stand that man's genius") and Welles were divorced. *The Lady From Shanghai,* despite (or because of) Columbia's revisions, flopped badly, completing the ruin of Welles' Hollywood reputation.

Between the shooting and the release of *Lady From Shanghai,* Welles had made one last Hollywood movie before his by then inevitable exile. This was *Macbeth* (1948), the first of his idiosyncratic adaptations of Shakespeare. Less a considered reading than (in his own description) "a violently sketched charcoal drawing of a great play," the film was shot in twenty-three days at Herbert Yates's Republic Studios, where cheap quickies were a way of life. The budget has been variously quoted from $700,000—which is more than *Kane* cost—to $30,000, which is incredible. From the look of the film, McBride's "less than $200,000" seems most probable.

Welles' deep and lasting love of Shakespeare had never been in the least reverential, and he rarely scrupled to cut and rewrite the plays in any way that suited his purpose. (Back in the Mercury Theatre days, John Houseman was asked when the eagerly awaited production of *Julius Caesar* would be ready. "When Orson's finished writing it," he responded.) In the case of *Macbeth,* Welles dropped large chunks of what was already one of Shakespeare's shortest plays, added lines of his own, and created one entirely new character: a "Holy Father," played by Alan Napier in long plaited braids and look-

ing (in Charles Higham's words) "like a cross between Boris Karloff and Heidi." Shot amid
Republic's papier-mâché crags and caverns,
with costumes deriving from some weird Picto-
Mongol dark age—several of the extras seem to
have wandered in from *Alexander Nevsky*
—Welles' *Macbeth* is by far the least satisfactory
of his Shakespeare movies.

The picture was execrated on its release and
is still thought by many to be Welles' worst film.
Yet despite the obvious faults—a badly garbled
soundtrack, frequently inept acting (especially
from Jeanette Nolan, hopelessly out of her depth
as Lady Macbeth), a near-total loss of the play's
moral complexity—*Macbeth* intermittently attains a degree of sheer emotional power that
more conventional cinematic treatments of
Shakespeare (such as Olivier's) never approach.
"At its best moments," wrote Michael Mullin, the
film "leads us deep into the nightmare realms
where Macbeth lives, where nothing is but what
is not, where fair is foul and foul is fair. Although
a reduction of Shakespeare's great tragedy, it is
a reduction through intensity." Similarly, Jack
Jorgens noted that "what seems important to
Welles is not the moral and social dimensions of
Macbeth's acts . . . but the subjective experience of pushing deeper into the heart of
darkness."

By the time *Macbeth* was released, Welles had
quit Hollywood in disgust, setting out on the
restless, peripatetic career he followed to the end
of his life. Increasingly, acting in other people's
films began to occupy his time, to the exclusion
of directing his own; though he always insisted
that he only acted in order to finance his own
films. With his imposing presence—six foot
three in height and, from the mid-1950s on, no
less impressive in girth—and magnificent voice,
Welles never lacked for film offers and rarely refused any that came his way. Opinions of his acting ability differ widely. The "prodigious actor"
(François Truffaut), "most shamefully
underrated" (Laurence Olivier), was, according
to Dwight Macdonald, "an embarrassingly bad
actor who always hams it up and is even worse
when he underplays." "The only thing that was
ever seriously wrong with Orson Welles," maintained Walter Kerr, "was his unfortunate notion
that he was an actor," and Margaret Hinxman
unkindly summed him up as "a kind of intellectual Boris Karloff." Welles himself supported his
detractors: "I honestly believe I am not a good
movie actor. . . . I have an unfortunate personality. . . . I have only to walk into camera range
and the critics are convinced that I am a
hambone."

Most of the films in which Welles appeared

were utter rubbish, as he readily acknowledged:
"They hire me when they have a really bad mov
ie and they want a cameo that will give it a littl
class." Occasionally, the cameo was set in some
thing worthwhile: a five-minute tour de force a
Father Mapple in Huston's *Moby Dick*; a bloat
ed, red toad of a Wolsey in Zinnemann's *Man fo
All Seasons*; the bedridden patriarch in Harry
Kümel's gothic labyrinth, *Malpertuis*. By gener
al consent, though, his only memorable role out
side his own films was as the charmingly corrup
Harry Lime in Carol Reed's *The Third Ma*
(1949), expounding his solipsist philosophy as th
giant Ferris wheel revolves above the Prater
Graham Greene, who scripted, credits Welle
with the authorship of the famous "cuckoo
clock" speech; other accounts have also attribut
ed part of the direction to him.

Much critical debate has centered around the
question of whether Welles' European films rep
resent a creative decline from his Hollywood
work. (That they represent a *technical* decline i
scarcely in doubt.) James Naremore cogently
summed up the opposing arguments: "In some
ways the European films are more satisfying
than the American ones. They are free not only
of Hollywood formulas but of the aestheticism
and tendentiousness of the worst of the avant-
garde. . . . And yet something is always missing. . . . The deepest problem with these film
as a group . . . is that their director has los
touch with the social and cultural environmen
he knows best. . . . His best work was always
grounded in contemporary American mores,
politics, and popular myth. . . . Hence what
Welles gains in seriousness, he loses in vitality
and the shock of recognition. . . . Splendidly
constructed and mature in outlook as some of
these later pictures may be, they have never
been able to generate the sheer excitement of the
more populist American work."

After Welles left Hollywood, several projects
reached scenario stage but remained unrealized:
Cyrano de Bergerac, for Korda; *Moby Dick*;
Around the World in 80 Days (eventually filmed
by Mike Todd in 1956); *The Odyssey*. Instead,
Welles returned to Shakespeare. But whereas
Macbeth had taken just over three weeks,
Othello (1952) took more than three years.

Though notoriously idiosyncratic, unpredictable, and on occasions autocratic, Welles was always able to command the dedication, and even
devotion, of his actors and crew. Several of them,
such as Akim Tamiroff and Jeanne Moreau,
worked with him repeatedly, often in preference to superficially more attractive assignments. "If he calls you and says 'I need you,'"
Moreau explained, "then you say 'Orson needs

me and it's something important.' . . . He's capable of such beautiful things and it's so hard for him now to make a film that you wouldn't be the little stone that would stop the machine." Also, as many actors and technicians have testified, Welles was an exceptionally stimulating director to work with. "Orson *seduces* you in a marvelous way," Charlton Heston observed. "Orson has the capacity as a director to somehow persuade you that each time is *indeed* the most important day in the picture. . . . I recall performing in [*Touch of Evil*] as being as satisfying creatively as anything I've ever done." In the case of *Othello*, that any kind of film—let alone one of merit—emerged from the chaos attests to Welles' exceptional powers of seduction.

Micheál MacLiammóir, Welles's former employer in Dublin, was cast as Iago and kept a diary (published in *Put Money in Thy Purse*) of this ramshackle, interminable enterprise. Filming was spread over five towns in Italy and three in Morocco; each time the money ran out, Welles would vanish to act in another worthless movie, sometimes returning with purloined costumes and equipment as well as the vital cash; leading roles were cast and recast; and the company, a "chic but highly neurotic lumber camp" in MacLiammóir's words, awaited events with resigned incredulity.

After the dank claustrophobia of *Macbeth*, Welles threw his *Othello* open to the elements. Charles Higham characterized the film as "full of sun-drenched, wind-lashed exteriors, of settings that are extravaganzas of baroque, a chiaroscuro of whipping flags, sky-piercing turrets, bristling spurs, and lashing foam. . . . [His] lucid, dashing, vibrant style has seldom been so perfectly wedded to its subject." Other critics, though, have argued that Welles swamps the play through stylistic excess; William Pechter (*Sight and Sound*, Winter 1963–4) wrote that: "All is sacrificed to the *mise-en-scène*, but it is a *mise-en-scène* now become an orgy of tilted camera angles, intricate composition, and florid chiaroscuro. Concern is now exclusively for effects . . . indulged in only for themselves. Each scene is invested with an impact out of all proportion to its meaning or its relevance to context."

Once again, Welles cut and revised the play considerably. He opens with Othello's funeral procession, a visually stunning sequence of black-cowled silhouettes against the skyline, while a choir intones solemnly and Iago's cringing figure is dragged through the crowd to be hauled aloft in a cage. Throughout the film Welles makes telling use of his locations, staging the jealousy scene on the towering battlements

of a castle, where Iago tempts Othello ever nearer the abyss of insanity; or—an inspired improvisation when costumes were lacking—setting Roderigo's murder in the steamy vaults of a Turkish bath, the actors clad only in towels, Iago's sword plunging viciously down through the shadowed slats.

Though less ragged than in *Macbeth,* the acting was once more the film's main weakness. Perhaps because of the fractured shooting schedule, few of the performances attained much subtlety or depth. Suzanne Cloutier's cool Desdemona suggested innocence but little of the passion underlying it. As Othello, Welles conveyed not much more than injured nobility. Only MacLiammóir's Iago achieved tragic resonance; at Welles' suggestion, all trace of Mephistophelean wit was drained from the role, leaving instead a cold, twisted resentment stemming from (in the actor's own words) "the immemorial hatred of life, the secret isolation of impotence under the soldier's muscles, the flabby solitude gnawing at the groins, the eye's untiring calculation." But despite its uneven acting and technical shortcomings (soundtrack problems again), many writers would support Jack Jorgens's view that *Othello* is "one of the few Shakespeare films in which the images on the screen generate enough beauty, variety and graphic power to stand comparison with Shakespeare's poetic images . . . an authentic flawed masterpiece." At all events, the film was tumultuously acclaimed at the 1952 Cannes Film Festival and took the Grand Prix.

In quitting Hollywood, Welles had not only plunged himself into a virtually permanent state of financial insecurity; he had also cut himself off from the huge infrastructure of technical backup that the studios could offer. Much of the richness, the multilayered complexity of *Kane* and *Ambersons* depended upon the skills of Hollywood's technicians, on whom Welles could rely to execute his most imaginative strokes with professional sureness. In Europe, the best film technicians were no doubt the equals of their Hollywood counterparts; but Welles could no longer afford the best. "In America," wrote Charles Higham, "the interior of Welles' films is as intricate as that of a prize-winning watch; in Europe the springs hang out." Several springs from his next film seem to have been missing altogether.

Mr. Arkadin (UK, *Confidential Report,* 1955), based on a novel Welles had written in French, has often been described as a parody of *Citizen Kane*. Gregory Arkadin, a legendary financial giant, lives in a Disneyesque Spanish castle; his past life is investigated by a crass young American, Van Stratten, who has designs on Arkadin's daughter. Various eccentric characters supply elements of the financier's story and are then mysteriously killed off. It emerges that Arkadin himself had inspired the investigation into his evil past so that he could obliterate all evidence of it. In the end Arkadin is undone, jumping from his private plane in the belief that Van Stratten has revealed to his adored daughter the unsavory source of his wealth—white slavery, an empire of prostitution.

Arkadin, apparently, was badly mutilated by the Spanish producers; but traces of a lost masterpiece are hard to discern in existing prints. Production values are pitiful; continuity scarcely exists; and the soundtrack, on which Welles is said to have dubbed eighteen roles besides his own, makes *Macbeth* and *Othello* seem models of clarity. Furthermore, there is a void at the center of *Arkadin* where Arkadin himself should be. The wretched Van Stratten (inadequately played by Robert Arden) is clearly never meant to engage our interest but the object of his quest ought to. However, neither Arkadin nor his alleged wealth and power convey the least conviction: he remains a pasteboard mogul, left over from some prewar potboiler by Edgar Wallace or E. Phillips Oppenheim. Around this vacuum the perfunctory plot fragments entirely. Joseph McBride compared the film to "one of those fiendishly complicated, ultimately shallow and pointless magic tricks Welles performs on TV talk shows."

Yet even in his most slipshod film, Welles achieves moments and images of memorable intensity—the ominous gyrations of a masked ball, a procession of Spanish penitents, and above all the gallery of sinister little cameos encountered by Van Stratten in his travels: Michael Redgrave as an epicene Amsterdam junk dealer, in dressing gown and hair net; Mischa Auer inspecting his pet fleas through a huge magnifying glass; Akim Tamiroff slumped on a grimy attic bed whining for goose liver. The film's most famous episode, though, is the fable of the scorpion and the frog, related by Welles-Arkadin to his guests. The scorpion asks the frog for a lift across a river. The frog nervously demurs, but the scorpion points out that he would have to be crazy to sting, since they would then both drown. Midway over, the scorpion stings the frog: "'Logic!' cried the dying frog, as he started under, bearing the scorpion down with him. 'There is no logic in this!' 'I know,' said the scorpion, 'but I can't help it—it's my character.' Let's drink to character!"

Several writers, including Andrew Sarris, have pounced on this parable as an allegory of Welles'

own self-destructive career, but the parallels seem hard to sustain. If Welles is seen as the scorpion, the movie industry scarcely fits the role of naive and subservient frog, and in any case packs a fair sting of its own.

In May 1955 the Italian actress Paola Mori, who had played Arkadin's daughter, became Welles' third wife. Their daughter Beatrice was born in 1956. Also in 1955, Welles began work on the most prolonged of all his unfinished projects, *Don Quixote.* Having initially planned it as a half-hour television film, he "fell completely in love" with his subject and continued shooting scenes in Mexico, France, Spain—wherever and whenever he had the money—over the next ten years. In 1965 he told *Cahiers du Cinéma* that it was "really finished; it only needs about three weeks' work." Shooting, according to Peter Cowie, was completed in 1971. Yet the film, in whatever state, remains unseen, and at the time of his death Welles had grown touchy on the subject. Both the principal actors—Akim Tamiroff as Sancho Panza and the Mexican Francisco Reiguera as Quixote—are long since dead.

While directing his Broadway production of *King Lear* in 1956, Welles unexpectedly found himself invited back to Hollywood to direct a film—apparently through a misunderstanding. As Welles told the story, Albert Zugsmith, producer of low-budget thrillers at Universal, had cast him in a supporting role in a forthcoming project and wanted Charlton Heston to star. Who else have you got, inquired Heston. Well, we've got Orson Welles—began the studio executive. Great, said Heston, he's a superb director; I'll act in anything he wants to direct. Zugsmith, trapped, offered Welles the job, which he accepted on one condition—that he could rewrite the "ridiculous" scenario in toto.

Touch of Evil (1958), freely adapted from a pulp novel by Whit Masterson, was Welles' finest film since *The Magnificent Ambersons* —even, in the opinion of some critics, since *Kane.* Set in a squalid, peeling township straddling the US-Mexican border (for which the sleazy California resort town of Venice stood in admirably), it centers around the clash between an upright Mexican narcotics investigator, Mike Vargas (Heston), and a bloated, corrupt American cop, Quinlan (a sweaty and mountainously padded Welles). When a local magnate is killed by a bomb, Quinlan, following his usual practice, plants evidence on the likeliest suspect. To prevent Vargas exposing him, he then arranges to have the Mexican's young American wife framed in compromising circumstances. Vargas manages to convince Quinlan's deputy, Menzies, of his boss' crooked methods, and Menzies helps to trick Quinlan into a taped confession.

Welles was a lifelong sufferer from insomnia, and many of his films suggest an insomniac's vision of the world—shadowed and ominous, shot through with a heightened, unreal clarity. In *Touch of Evil,* wrote Terry Comito (*Film Comment,* Summer 1971), "any place a character may for an instant inhabit is only the edge of the depth that opens dizzily behind him. . . . Menace lurches suddenly forward, and chases disappear down long perspectives. . . . By opening upon the vertiginous ambiguities of space [Welles denies us] the safety of the frame of reference through which we habitually contemplate the world." Frequent use of an anamorphic lens exacerbates this sense of a distorted, nightmare universe where spatial dimensions cannot be trusted. *Touch of Evil* generates a miasma of total instability, both moral and physical—anything may give. Corruption oozes from walls and furniture like a palpable presence; the very buildings become emanations of Quinlan's bulbous, looming person. When, in the film's final moments, his vast cadaver sinks slowly into a canal turgid with oil-slicked garbage, it seems an inevitable symbiosis, a reabsorption into the constituent elements.

Yet, as Truffaut observed, "we are brought somehow to shed real tears over the corpse of the magnificent monster." At one point Quinlan encounters the local madam, Tanya (Marlene Dietrich); she at first fails to recognize him, then comments laconically, "You're a mess, honey. You'd better lay off those candy bars." Quinlan grunts disconsolately, surveying his own decrepit bulk; the moment conveys unexpected pathos. Even this truculent, crooked cop, we realize, has a lost innocence to look back on. Welles always acknowledged, in regard to Quinlan, Kane, Arkadin and the rest of his overreaching villains, a feeling of "human sympathy for these different characters that I have created, though morally I find them detestable." Around his own central performance Welles deploys a vivid range of supporting roles: "Uncle" Joe Grandi, the local gang boss (Akim Tamiroff at his most greasily repellent); Mercedes McCambridge as a butch hoodlum in black leather; Dennis Weaver's twitching, giggling motel clerk, described by Welles as "the complete Shakespearean clown . . . a real Pierrot Lunaire"; and Dietrich's Sternbergian Tanya, left to speak Quinlan's off-hand epitaph, "He was some kind of a man. . . . What does it matter what you say about people?"

The unbroken three-minute take that opens *Touch of Evil* has become deservedly famous. Starting on a close-up of a hand placing a time bomb in a car, the camera pulls back to show a dark figure vanishing round a corner as a couple enter, get in the car, and drive off; then cranes up, over a building, and down to follow the couple as they drive slowly along a busy street alongside another couple on foot (Vargas and his wife), stop at a border post to swap casual banter with the customs officer, and drive on into the desert; finally holds on Vargas and his wife kissing in close-up as, deep-focus in the background, the car explodes in a sheet of flame. Even the producer's inane decision to run the credits over this shot could do little to detract from its masterly buildup of tension.

Universal, who had intended a run-of-the-mill thriller, were bewildered to find an offbeat masterpiece on their hands—not that *Touch of Evil* ("What a silly title," said Welles) was acknowledged as such at the time, except in France. Inevitably, the studio tampered with the film, calling in a hack director (Harry Keller) for additional scenes to "explain" the action. The essence of Welles' conception nevertheless survived intact. His temporary return to Hollywood was received by most American reviewers with contempt or indifference ("Pure Orson Welles and impure balderdash, which may be the same thing," sneered Gerald Weales in the *Reporter*) and flopped at the box office. Europe, as usual, proved rather more receptive; the film was praised at Cannes, won an award at Brussels, and played for months to packed houses in Paris.

In 1958 Welles made a thirty-minute pilot film for ABC, entitled *The Fountain of Youth,* based on a short story by John Collier. It was planned as the first of a series of short story adaptations that Welles would script, direct, and narrate—a television equivalent, in effect, of his prewar radio series. In the end, only *The Fountain of Youth* was made; it was broadcast once and then—despite receiving a Peabody Award for creative achievement—consigned to the vaults. It remains Welles' only fictional work made for television.

The producer Alexander Salkind had cast Welles in a minor role in *Austerlitz,* directed by Abel Gance in a doomed attempt to recapture the glories of his great silent *Napoléon.* During filming, Salkind offered Welles the backing to direct a film and gave him a list of fifteen subjects to choose from. Welles selected Kafka's *Der Prozess* (*The Trial*). Kafka's novel is an existential fable, urban paranoia laced with black humor. In the opening sentence his protagonist, Joseph K, is accused of an unspecified crime; in the final paragraph, still without knowing what he was accused of, K is executed. In between he struggles hopelessly with the impenetrable labyrinth of the law, not only getting no answers, but never so much as discovering to whom he should put his questions. "It has been said," Welles hints in his spoken introduction to the film, "that the logic of this story is the logic of a dream—of a nightmare."

Though most of *The Trial* (1962) was shot on location—in Zagreb, Rome, and Paris—Welles' intent was anything but realistic. In line with his view of the story as a nightmare, settings are juxtaposed in defiance of all logic, less locations than dislocations: an artist's studio opens into a courtroom, a Roman palazzo fronts a dingy Zagreb apartment block. Most effective of all is Welles' use of the dilapidated grandeur of the deserted Gare d'Orsay, whose "monstrous perspectives," in Peter Cowie's words, "the vistas of imprisoned glass, the iron stairways and myriad corridors combine to form a symbolic background to the film that is an equivalent to the labyrinthine ways and mournful buildings of Prague."

In Anthony Perkins's angular, edgy performance, K succeeds in being at once indignant and apologetic. Welles characterized him as "a little bureaucrat. I consider him guilty. . . . Not guilty as accused, but he is guilty all the same. He belongs to a guilty society." Besides dubbing several supporting characters, Welles himself took the crucial role of Hastler, the all-powerful advocate—if not the highest embodiment of the law, at least the highest accessible to K. Enthroned on a vast, gilded bed, lit by innumerable candles, Hastler is a diabolic presence, master of the maze through which K must impotently scuttle. Yet K, in Welles' only major departure from Kafka, never submits, remaining defiant even in death. In the novel he lets himself be stabbed "like a dog"; in the film, he reaches for the dynamite that has been thrown at him, as if to fling it back. There follows a shattering explosion, and in the film's final image a vast mushroom cloud rises over the landscape.

The Trial was Welles' first film since *Kane*, twenty years earlier, to be released in the form he had intended. It was also, he averred in a 1965 interview, "the best film I have ever made." Few critics, then or since, have agreed; the general verdict was that Welles and Kafka were temperamentally unsuited. Parker Tyler saw in the film only "acrid, mannered, at times cutely flattened grandiloquence," and Andrew Sarris reckoned it "the most hateful, the most repellent, and the most perverted film Welles ever made." In Penelope Huston's view "it lacks Wellesian geniality, as it lacks the cool, logical apprehension of Kafka; and stylistically it is in the most literal sense overblown, an expression of weary audacity, a film seemingly dominated by its decors." Some writers accused Welles of distorting Kafka, though William Johnson (*Film Quarterly*, Fall 1967) suggested that "the trouble is not so much that Welles departs from the book but that he does not depart far enough." A strongly dissenting view, though, came from Peter Cowie: "To my mind, *The Trial* remains Welles' finest film since *Kane* and . . . achieves an effect through cinematic means that conveys perfectly [Kafka's] terrifying vision of the modern world. . . . No other film of Welles' bears so clearly the stamp of his personality."

Even since the theatrical debacle of *Five Kings* in 1939, Welles had planned to return to his concept of a great Shakespearian portmanteau, with Falstaff as its center. *Chimes at Midnight* (in America called *Falstaff*) first surfaced as a stage production at the Grand Opera House, Belfast, in 1960; four years later, filming of it began in Spain. As incubator of the project, an opera house was appropriate enough: more than one critic has noted that Welles' three Shakespeare adaptations coincide neatly with those of Verdi—and that both men combined an infinite devotion to the spirit of Shakespeare with an unabashed readiness to modify his texts in any way they saw fit.

Of Welles' three Shakespeare films, the last (1966) is by far the best—both as Shakespeare and as cinema. Drawing on both parts of *Henry IV*, plus bits from *Richard II, Henry V*, and *The Merry Wives of Windsor* (and adding a narrative taken from Holinshed), Welles creates a richly lyrical elegy for "the death of Merrie England." His Falstaff is not the conventional cowardly buffoon, but "the most completely good man in all drama. His faults are so small. . . . But his goodness is like bread, like wine." *Chimes at Midnight*, like *The Magnificent Ambersons*, is a lament for a lost innocence, a golden age that most likely never existed, but is nonetheless to be mourned. "It is more than Falstaff who is dying. It's the old England, dying and betrayed."

In this reading, much of the comedy is necessarily lost, overshadowed as it is by constant intimations of the coming, crushing rejection of Falstaff by his beloved prince and the old man's death. The film's dramatic emphasis, noted Jack Jorgens, is on leave-takings, the breaking up of groups and relationships: "Welles portrays people alienated, people driven apart by death and the forces of history, people betraying each other." For Shakespeare, Falstaff, despite his vitality and gusto, must rightly be sacrificed as an obstacle to the greater cause of responsible kingship; but to Welles, Falstaff *is* the greater cause, standing for an instinctive moral nobility spurned by Hal's cold, Machiavellian new orld. In a last valedictory shot, Falstaff's vast offin is trundled away across a bleak terrain, eneath grey winter skies: the chill spirit of the d king (an incisive performance by John Gielud) has irrevocably triumphed.

As Falstaff, Welles gives his finest screen perormance, "the creation of an actor who has ripned and even softened into the part," as enelope Huston put it. Beside him, Keith Baxr's saturnine Hal, beadily calculating, recalls facLiammóir's Iago—an ideal counterpoint oth to Falstaff and to Norman Rodway's impetous Hotspur. Not all the supporting roles are qually well cast (Jeanne Moreau, in particular, ems ill at ease as Doll Tearsheet); several interiediate scenes look sketchy, as if hastily conructed; and the soundtrack—recurrent roblem of Welles' European movies—is often ritatingly unfocused. Despite these faults, `himes at Midnight` contains some of Welles' reatest work: the scenes in Shallow's orchard, ie old king's death, the rejection scene and bove all the Battle of Shrewsbury, which coneys as no film had ever done before the sheer lind brutality of battle—writhing, agonized gures hacking and clubbing each other in the ud. For Joseph McBride, `Chimes` was unequivcally "Welles' masterpiece, the fullest, most ompletely realised expression of everything he ad been working toward since `Citizen Kane`."

`Chimes at Midnight` was premiered at the `annes Film Festival in 1966. Once again the stival audience gave Welles a rapturous recepon, and the jury added a special Twentieth nniversary Tribute. But the American distribuirs, apparently disheartened by an unfavorable dvance review from Bosley Crowther in the 'ew York Times, furnished scant publicity and tinimal distribution. The film has since recovred from this initial neglect; many critics now ite it the best of Welles' European movies.

"I am frustrated, you understand?" Welles old interviewers in 1965. "And I believe that my 'ork shows that I do not do enough film-ig. . . . I wait too long before I can speak." he struggle for financial backing, he said, had ecome "more bitter than ever." Matters hardly nproved subsequently; in the twenty years folowing `Chimes`, not a single full-length feature irected by Welles was released. One film was tid to be complete but remained unshown. Aner, started in 1970, was apparently left unfinhed. Two Welles pictures *have* been released: ne lasts under an hour, the other is less a film nan a tongue-in-cheek collage, based on somene else's material.

Though commissioned by French television, `he Immortal Story` (1968) was conceived in terms of cinema. Fifty-eight minutes long and Welles' first film in color, it was taken from a short story by the Danish writer Karen Blixen, who wrote in English under the pen name Isak Dinesen and whose work Welles greatly admired. The story tells of an aged, fabulously wealthy Shanghai merchant, Mr. Clay, who believes (like Kane or Arkadin) that his wealth allows him to play God. Hearing that a familiar tale of a rich old man who paid a sailor to impregnate his beautiful young wife is nothing but a legend, Clay resolves to make it truth by hiring two people to enact it for him. But people are not puppets and Clay—as his name suggests—is mortal; as dawn breaks the old monster lies dead on his verandah.

Apart from shifting the action from Shanghai to Macao, Welles sticks closely to Dinesen's story. The film is a chamber piece for four players: Clay, his clerk Levinsky, and the two lovers. Despite the crudity of his makeup—here, as so often, giving the odd impression of having been conceived for the stage, forgetting the camera's intimate scrutiny—Welles as Clay exerts a dessicated authority, cold and remote in his highbacked chair, groping with dying fingers after vicarious life and the last remnants of power. Jeanne Moreau, in her third consecutive Welles film, touchingly suggests the aging beauty recapturing a brief illusion of youthful innocence.

Hermetically contained in the circularity of its own plot, `Immortal Story` achieves, James Naremore observed, "a serenity and simplicity of visual effect unlike any of Welles' previous movies." Already in `Chimes at Midnight` his cinematic style, once luxuriantly baroque, had become quieter, even restrained. Some critics have seen this as evidence of the turbulent young lion mellowing into serenity; in one interview Welles referred to "maturity . . . not technical surprises or shocks, but a more complete unity of forms, of shapes." He gave Joseph McBride a less ascetic explanation, though: "All the great technicians are dead or dying. . . . I have to make do with what I can get."

Between 1967 and 1969, off the Dalmatian coast, Welles directed a film known either as `Dead Reckoning` or `The Deep` (no connection with Peter Yates' subaqueous hokum of 1977). Based on Charles Williams' novel `Dead Calm`, it featured Laurence Harvey, Jeanne Moreau, Michael Bryant, and Welles, who described it as "a thriller taking place on a couple of small boats in the middle of the ocean." Though by all accounts complete, the picture has never been released. Welles at one point claimed that he was unable to find a distributor, though other reports suggest that he thought it "not good enough" to release.

At the 1970 Academy Award ceremony Hollywood made belated—and inadequate—amends to Welles with an Honorary Award for "superlative artistry and versatility in the creation of motion pictures"; not that any of the studios seemed ready to let him exercise that artistry on their premises. However, there have been rumors (*Film Comment,* March–April 1978) that certain studios *did* make offers to Welles, which he ignored. As Jonathan Rosenbaum once wrote, "possibly no other director has been the subject of so many conflicting accounts, in large matters as well as small ones."

"I am an experimenter. I don't believe much in accomplishment." In 1970 Welles began shooting another of his legendary unfinished films, *The Other Side of the Wind,* called by those who have seen extracts "the greatest home movie ever made." John Huston plays a venerated movie director, Jake Hannaford, besieged at his seventieth birthday party by friends, hangers-on, and the media, and troubled by the recognition of his own suppressed homosexuality. Joseph McBride, who plays a small role in the picture as a pretentious movie critic, sums up its theme as "a legendary man being swallowed up in his self-created image and ultimately being destroyed by it." Other characters are said to include recognizable caricatures of those critics who have fallen foul of Welles, such as Pauline Kael and Charles Higham. Welles screened excerpts from *Other Side* when, in 1975, he was presented with the American Film Institute's Life Achievement Award, which he accepted "in the name of all the mavericks"—signing off his speech "not only your obedient servant but also, in this age of supermarkets, your friendly neighborhood grocery store."

Welles' last complete film, with production credited to France, Iran, and West Germany, was premiered in France under the title *Vérités et mensonges* (1973). *F for Fake* is the usual English title, though *Fake?* and simply *?* are sometimes given. "This Quixotic essay in fictional documentary," suggested Richard Combs (*Monthly Film Bulletin,* January 1977), "may be Welles' most concerted, complete and certainly his wittiest attempt to exorcise the ghosts of Kane, Rosebud, and his own 'failed' genius."

Around 1968, François Reichenbach had made a film for ORTF about the notorious art forger, Elmyr de Hory. A major source for the film's material was the author Clifford Irving, who had written a book on de Hory (entitled *Fake*), and who appeared in Reichenbach's documentary. Soon afterward Irving also attained notoriety as the forger of Howard Hughes' purported autobiography. Welles, as a professional conjuror and self-styled "charlatan," was in-

trigued by the labyrinthine potential of forger talking about fakers talking about fakes, and b the further implication that all art—not least h own—could be presented as a gigantic con tric Taking Reichenbach's footage, he proceeded t pull it apart and rearrange it, interspersed wit material of his own, into an ironic disquisition o truth and illusion.

F for Fake opens with Welles performing few conjuring tricks and promising that every thing he will tell us for the next hour, howeve bizarre, will be the absolute truth. There follo chunks of Reichenbach's film, intercut wit Welles ruminating about de Hory, Irving, an Hughes, reminiscing about his own career, an meditating on the splendors of Chartres Cathe dral. From time to time a beautiful mysteriou girl appears (the Hungarian actress Oja Koda whom Welles met while filming *The Trial,* an who became his companion after his marriage t Paola Mori broke up). Eventually Welles tells u how Oja, by agreeing to pose nude for Picass conned him out of twenty-two canvases for th benefit of her grandfather, the world's greates unknown art forger—and finally, having fin ished this story, points out that his promise to tel the truth ran out some time ago, since when " have been lying my head off. . . . " Penelop Houston thought *Fake* "dazzling, invigoratin fun," and John Russell Taylor, writing in *Sigh and Sound* (Autumn 1973), found it "enjoyabl and holding, if somewhat over-extended." Othe critics, while agreeing on the thinness of the ma terial, were less amused: Richard Roud called i "disappointing . . . a scissors and paste job. For these writers, *Fake* confirmed their belie that Welles had declined from a major directo to a facile illusionist, all manner and no matte trading on his own legend.

After *Fake,* various projects were mooted bu fell through: a filmed *King Lear*; a compilatio of Isak Dinesen stories to be called *Th Dreamers*; a political drama, *The Big Bras Ring.* Meanwhile Welles continued, in Ken Ty nan's famous phrase, to "grow fat spreadin; himself thin." He was featured in some forgetta ble movies, appeared on countless talk shows and even lent his impressive presence to televi sion ads—a melancholy fate for the man wh once said that advertisers "are not only drawin; on [the artist], they are sucking the soul out o him. . . . Among the advertisers, you find art ists who have betrayed their kind." More recent ly, Welles had rationalized such trivial activities "I do it for the exposure. If you don't, you ge forgotten."

That the director of *Citizen Kane* should "ge forgotten" seems a safely remote possibility—

though Welles became understandably weary of being known primarily for his first movie. Yet any discussion of Welles' films must inevitably come back to—as well as start from—*Kane*, simply because it remains the only film where Welles was able to do exactly what he wanted to, with the resources his talent deserved. For every subsequent film the viewer is forced to make allowances, to try to reconstruct in the mind's eye the movie that Welles intended—to imagine *Ambersons, Lady From Shanghai, Touch of Evil* without the studios' mangling and botching, or *Othello, The Trial, Chimes at Midnight* filmed under reasonable conditions. Only with *Kane* can we be sure of seeing and hearing what Welles meant.

"I started at the top," Welles was fond of remarking, "and worked down." With a single film, he permanently affected the whole of Western cinema, making available to future filmmakers a resonance and depth of cinematic vocabulary, a dramatic intensity and complexity that have enriched both the way films are constructed and the way we watch them. "I believe in the film as a poetic medium. . . . The danger in the cinema is that you see everything, because it's a camera. So what you have to do is manage to evoke, to incant, to raise up things which are not really there." This poetic necromancy, as James Naremore pointed out, stems from a "multiplication of artistic stimuli, so that he not only expresses psychology through the settings but gives us the feelings of many actions, visual and aural, occurring simultaneously. It is this richness, this seven-layer-cake profusion, that most distinguishes his work in Hollywood." Many critics consider that nothing in Welles' subsequent films (*Ambersons* perhaps excepted) goes beyond his first overwhelming achievement, that the later works, in David Thomson's words, simply consist of "offshoots of *Kane,* variations on its rich theme."

One of the greatest problems in assessing Welles' movies is attempting to disentangle the man from his works—perhaps a harder task in his case than in that of any other director. We can appreciate the films of Hawks, Huston, even of Ford, without knowing anything of their respective directors' biographies. But with Welles—and not only because he appears in all but one of his own films—that compelling, legendary figure constantly comes between us and the screen. "I drag my myth around with me," Welles lamented. The myth, as befits any Wellesian artifact, is at once true and false, a dazzling tapestry of reality interwoven with illusion: the *enfant terrible,* irresistible conqueror of one art after another, iconoclast of all accepted notions of filmmaking—then, hubris incarnate, the fall-

en angel, dragged down by his own overweening ambition—to become finally the tragic exile, dragging the tattered shreds of his former glory from one country to the next, wasting his gifts on unworthy activities to fund his next precarious venture.

The portrait is impressively, histrionically larger than life; and the suspicion persists that Welles, even while deploring this inflated image of himself, nonetheless derived a certain ironic amusement from it and could never resist giving a last tug to the flowing cape, an extra jaunty tilt to the wide-brimmed hat. Many observers—and not only hostile ones—have suggested that Welles' greatest creation may have been himself. As André Bazin put it: "If Welles had not existed, Graham Greene would have had to invent him."

Any such attempt at critical dissociation is in any case probably impossible and also counterproductive. Much of the creative tension of Welles' movies, which makes them even at their weakest so unfailingly watchable, derives from what James Naremore described as "the contradiction between Welles' philosophic stance and the personality which is implicit in his style." If we remember above all the Kanes and the Quinlans, rather than those characters who, like Leland and Vargas, embody Welles' own liberal and humanist philosophy, it may be because, as Naremore intimated, "they have something deeply in common with the personality of the director himself, as it is suggested in the gorgeous excess of his style." Welles himself readily conceded such inconsistencies: "Everything about me is a contradiction, and so is everything about everybody I know. . . . You don't reconcile the poles. You just recognize them."

Opinions differ on the status of his later films, but few critics would now dispute Welles' reputation as "the most striking moviemaker of our time" (Peter Bogdanovich). In France—where he was awarded the Légion d'Honneur in 1982—he ranks virtually as a local deity. Welles himself always claimed to despise success and to be indifferent to posterity. Yet perhaps the most regrettable aspect of his disrupted career is that he became cut off, not only from his roots, but from the greater part of his true audience. Welles should have been, like his hero Shakespeare, one of the great universal artists—able to appeal by his sheer theatrical sweep to sophisticated and unsophisticated alike, uniting emotional and intellectual reactions in one engulfing response. Instead, his films have become elitist texts—the preserve of highbrow critics, film festivals, and art house audiences.

Not that Welles, the genial and convivial, invited condolences. As Leslie Megahey, who directed an extended interview with him for the BBC in 1982, put it: "There's no way you can pity the man when he's obviously enjoying himself up to the hilt." After his years of European wanderings, during which he lived in Madrid or London, Welles began to spend time again in Hollywood. In September 1984, an item in *Screen International* announced that he was about to direct his first American film for a quarter of a century: *The Cradle Will Rock,* an account of the memorable Mercury production of Marc Blitzstein's political opera in 1937. Before much progress was made, Welles was found dead in his home, apparently of a heart attack.

In the summer of 1986, the Venice Film Festival premiered *It's All True: Four Men on a Raft,* a 22-minute short made from footage from Welles's 1942 Brazilian project. The footage—all that remained after RKO and its successor, Paramount, destroyed much of what Welles had shot—had been found in a studio vault before Welles' death. According to the Paramount executive who made the discovery, Welles was not pleased to hear the news. "To my surprise, he told me he didn't want to see it. He told me the film was cursed. He believed it marked the downfall of his career in Hollywood. But if he had seen the footage again, I think he would have changed his mind. It shows a very different Orson Welles from anything we've seen. It was the first film he shot outside the studio, and you can tell that he was freed by the experience."

—*P.K.*

FILMS: Hearts of Age (short), 1934; Citizen Kane, 1941; The Magnificent Ambersons, 1942; (with Norman Foster) Journey Into Fear (uncredited), 1943; The Stranger, 1946; The Lady From Shanghai, 1948; Macbeth, 1948; Othello, 1952; Mr. Arkadin (UK, Confidential Report), 1955; Don Quixote (unreleased), 1955–?; Touch of Evil, 1958; The Trial (Le Procès), 1962; Chimes at Midnight (Campanadas a medianoche/US, Falstaff), 1966; The Deep (Dead Reckoning, unreleased), 1967–69; The Immortal Story (Une Histoire immortelle), 1968; The Other Side of the Wind (unreleased), 1970–?; F for Fake (Vérités et mensonges/Fake?/?), 1973. *Published scripts*—Citizen Kane *in* The Citizen Kane Book, edited by Pauline Kael, Little Brown, 1971; The Trial, edited by Nicholas Fry, Lorrimer 1970, Simon & Schuster, 1971; Hearts of Age, The Immortal Story, and Mr. Arkadin were published in French in L'Avant-Scène du Cinéma July 1982.

ABOUT: Allais, J.–C. Orson Welles, 1961 (in French); Bazin, A. and Cocteau, J. Orson Welles, 1950 (in French; revised ed. 1972); Bazin, A. et al La Politique des auteurs, 1972; Bazin, A. Orson Welles; A Critical View, 1978; Bergala, A. and Narboni, J. (eds.) Orson Welles, 1982 (in French); Bessy, M. Orson Welles, 1963 (in French; revised ed. 1982; English translation,

1971); Bogdanovich, P. The Cinema of Orson Welles, 1961; Buchka, P. et al Orson Welles, 1977 (in German); Ciment, M. Les Conquérants d'un Nouveau Monde, 1981; Comito, T. (ed.) Touch of Evil: Orson Welles, Director, 1985; Contemporary Literary Criticism, 1982; Cowie, P. (ed.) International Film Guide, 1964; Cowie, P. The Cinema of Orson Welles, 1965; Cowie, P. A Ribbon of Dreams: The Cinema of Orson Welles, 1973; Current Biography Yearbook, 1965; Estève, M. (ed.) Orson Welles: l'éthique et l'esthétique, 1963; Fowler, R. A. Orson Welles: A First Biography, 1946; Giannetti, L. Masters of the American Cinema, 1981; Gottesman, R. (ed.) Focus on Citizen Kane, 1971; Gottesman, R. (ed.) Focus on Orson Welles, 1976; Higham, C. The Films of Orson Welles, 1970; Higham, C. Orson Welles: The Rise and Fall of an American Genius, 1985; Houseman, J. Run-through: A Memoir, 1972; Jacob, G. Le Cinéma moderne, 1964; Jorgens, J. L. Shakespeare on Film, 1977; Kael, P. The *Citizen Kane* Book, 1971; Leaming, B. Orson Welles, 1986; McBride, J. Orson Welles, 1972; McBride, J. Orson Welles: Actor and Director, 1977; MacLiammóir, M. Put Money in Thy Purse, 1952; Maland, C. American Visions, 1977; Manvell, R. Shakespeare and the Film, 1971; Naremore, J. The Magic World of Orson Welles, 1978; Nemes, K. Orson Welles, 1977 (in Hungarian); Noble, P. The Fabulous Orson Welles, 1956; Oxford companion to the Theatre, 1983; Roud, R. (ed.) Cinema: A Critical Dictionary, 1980; Sarris, A. (ed.) Interviews With Film Directors, 1967; Sarris, A. The American Cinema, 1968; Thomson, D. America in the Dark, 1977; Thomson, D. A Biographical Dictionary of the Cinema, 1980; Truffaut, F. The Films in My Life, 1978; Tyler, P. Sex, Psyche, Etcetera, in the Film, 1969; Tynan, K. Tynan Right and Left, 1967; Valentinetti, C. M. Orson Welles, 1981 (in Italian); Who's Who in America, 1984; Wollen, P. Orson Welles, 1969. *Periodicals*—Action (USA) May–June 1969; American Cinematographer April 1975; American Film July–August 1976, November 1978, September 1985; Avant-Scène du Cinéma July 1982; Bianco e Nero January 1949; Cahiers du Cinéma May 1952, July 1956, June 1958, July 1958, September 1958, October 1958, March 1961, April 1965, May–June 1965, June 1966, August 1966; Cahiers du Cinéma in English 5 1966, 11 1967; Cahiers de la Cinématheque Summer 1976; Chaplin 33 1962; Cineforum November 1962, December 1963; Cinéma (France) November 1955, January 1960, December 1962, May 1965; Cinema a Cinema April–July 1975; Cinema Journal Fall 1972, Spring 1985, Winter 1985; Cinema Nuovo July–August 1966, July–August 1974; Cinéthique January–February 1970; Ecran February 1975; Ecran français August 1945, July 1946, September 1948; Esquire October 1972; Film (FFS) March–April 1961; Film (Belgium) May 1963; Film Adoba 10, 1965; Film Comment Summer 1971, November–December 1972, March–April 1978, November–December 1978, March–April 1979, January–February 1986; Film Culture January 1955, 2–3 1956, Winter 1962–63, Summer 1963; Film Faust June–September 1982; Film Forum March 1959; Film Heritage Fall 1968, Fall 1974; Film Ideal February 1962, August 1964; Film Library Quarterly 35–4, 1980; Film Notebooks Winter 1977; Film Quarterly all 1967, Fall 1969, Spring 1970, Summer 1982, Fall 985; Film Reader 1, 1975; Filmcritica March–April 964, January 1971; Films and Filming September 959, April 1961, October 1962, December 1963, December 1974; Griffith February–March 1966; Hollywood Reporter November 10, 1978; Image et Son March 1961, August–September 1963, December 964; Inquadrature Autumn 1964; Journal of the University Film Association Summer 1976; Kosmorama ecember 1962, April 1967; Les Lettres françaises November 26, 1959; Literature/Film Quarterly Summer 974; Look November 3, 1970, National Film Theatre ooklet June–July 1972; New Statesman January 21, 956; New York Times October 11, 1985; New York imes Magazine July 14, 1985; Nuovo Spettatore inematografico December 1963; Positif March 1963, une 1963, February 1964, March 1967, March 1975, une 1982, March 1983; Radio Times (Britain) March 1, 1960; Revue du Cinéma December 1946, February 947, Autumn 1947, March 1948, October 1948; creen Spring 1972, May–June 1982; Screen Education May–June 1965; Sight and Sound December 1950, anuary–March 1954, July–September 1954, Spring 960, Winter 1963–4, Autumn 1966, Spring 1970, Autumn 1970, Winter 1970–1, Winter 1971–2, Spring 972, Autumn 1973, Winter 1985; Sunday Times London) February 3, 1963; Take One October 1972; éléciné December 1964; Theater Arts September 951; Time Out February 14, 1982.

WILLIAM A. WELLMAN

WELLMAN, WILLIAM A(UGUSTUS) February 29, 1896–December 9, 1975), American director and producer, was born in Brookne, Massachusetts, one of two sons of Arthur Couverneur Wellman, an insurance broker whose parents were English immigrants, and the former Celia Guinness McCarthy, who was of irish descent. Frank T. Thompson, in his book on Wellman, says that his red-haired and fiery-tempered mother "embodied every cliché of irish girlhood," while his gentle and amiable father "made up in alcoholic thirst what he lacked a business sense." Arthur Wellman's career was erratic, and the family moved frequently round the Boston area, sometimes living in moderate affluence, sometimes reduced to eating "beans every night" on "the other side of the racks."

Wiry and hyperactive, William Wellman was high school star at baseball, football, and especially ice hockey. It was the latter sport that brought him his first show business contact. Douglas Fairbanks, touring with *Hawthorne of he USA* in 1914, saw Wellman play hockey at he Boston Arena and invited him backstage at he Colonial Theatre, beginning a friendship hat became important in Wellman's career.

"Wild Bill" Wellman inherited his mother's temperament. He was reckless and quick-tempered, constantly in fights and sometimes in more serious trouble. According to his own account—and Wellman's colorful recollections should never be swallowed without several grains of salt—he and a friend "used to borrow cars at night. . . . We always brought them back, but we were caught bringing one of them back and I was put on probation for six months and had to report to the probation officer of the city of Newton, who happened to be my own mother." Expelled from Newton High for dropping a stink bomb on the principal's head, Wellman worked briefly and ingloriously in the wool, candy, and lumber trades before a plane flight revealed his true vocation: "I just *had* to fly."

In 1917 Wellman went to war to become a flier. He joined the French Foreign Legion—a necessary (and traumatic) preliminary—and then the Lafayette Flying Corps, an offshoot of the more famous Lafayette Escadrille. As a fighter pilot with the Black Cat squadron, Wellman shot down three German aircraft before his own plane was brought down, leaving him with back injuries that troubled him for the rest of his life.

Wellman left the Lafayette Flying Corps in March 1918 with a Croix de Guerre and several American citations and returned to a hero's welcome in Boston. With the help of a ghostwriter he described his adventures in *Go, Get 'Em,* published in Boston in late 1918. By that time he was serving in the American Air Corps as a flight instructor at Rockwell Field, San Diego, not very far from Hollywood. "There were a lot of strange new people there," he said, "actors and actresses, and they liked me and the uniform and the medals; and I was very humble and my limp was eye-catching." Before the war was over, Wellman was married to a beautiful young starlet, Helene Chadwick. They separated a month later and were subsequently divorced.

Released from the Air Corps at the end of the war, Wellman remembered the telegram he had received from Douglas Fairbanks congratulating him on his war exploits and offering him a job. Donning his uniform and his medals, he went to see Fairbanks, by then a major star, and was promptly given a sizable part in a comedy Western, *The Knickerbocker Buckaroo* (1919). Wellman found himself excited by the movie business but disgusted by the sight of himself on screen at the premiere, mugging in thick makeup: "I just stayed for half the picture and then I went out and vomited for no reason at all."

If he could not stomach so unmanly a profession as acting, Wellman was not ready to give up on Hollywood. Discovering how much Al Parker had been paid for directing *The Knickerbocker Buckaroo,* he decided that he could be happy behind the camera. He started modestly as a messenger at the Goldwyn studios (where he had to deliver fan mail to his estranged wife). Wellman took every chance he could to study the working methods of staff directors like Maurice Tourneur, Frank Lloyd, and Tod Browning. In *A Short Time for Insanity,* his autobiography, he said that he "stole scripts, new ones, old ones, and pored over them, always from a director's point-of-view."

The ambitious messenger caught the attention of Will Rogers, through whose influence he was soon promoted to assistant propman. But Wellman's real break came when General Pershing visited the Goldwyn studios and recognized the ex-aviator (from a wartime encounter in a Paris brothel, according to Wellman). The front office was impressed by this comradely meeting, and Wellman was promoted to assistant director, in this capacity working for Clarence Badger, E. Mason Hopper, and Alfred Green before moving to the Fox studio in late 1921. At Fox, Wellman was assistant to Harry Beaumont, Colin Campbell, Emmett Flynn, and his mentor, Bernard J. Durning. The latter is now almost forgotten, but Wellman told Kevin Brownlow that Durning "gave me two of the greatest years I've ever had and taught me more than anybody in the business. He made all those thrilling melodramas and you learned everything from them—action, pacing, stunts. This was the greatest school a director ever had."

When Durning became ill during the making of *The Eleventh Hour* (1923), Wellman stepped in to finish the picture, pleasing the Fox executives enough to make him a full-fledged direc-

tor. His first feature was a Dustin Farnum vehicle, *The Man Who Won* (1923). A succession of low-budget Buck Jones melodramas followed. When they proved moderately successful, Wellman asked for a raise and was promptly fired. It was the first of his many battles with executives and producers. Thanks to his intransigent nature, "Wild Bill" subsequently worked in every major studio in Hollywood with the exception of Universal.

Out of work for a year, Wellman joined MGM in 1925, taking a demotion to assistant director. Soon afterwards he met a singer and dancer named Margery Chapin and embarked on another short-lived marriage. After "doctoring" Robert Vignola's *The Way of a Girl* and Josef von Sternberg and Phil Rosen's *The Exquisite Sinner,* Wellman was given a project of his own, *The Boob,* one of Joan Crawford's first movies and, the director proudly claims, her worst.

Completed in September 1925, *The Boob* was not released for six months and so was preceded into the theatres by Wellman's next picture, *When Husbands Flirt,* made for Columbia in 1925. Wellman was already building a reputation as a phenomenally rapid worker, and tempted by a bonus, he filmed this Dorothy Arzner script in less than four days. The independent producer B. P. Schulberg was impressed and signed Wellman to a contract with his Preferred Pictures. When Schulberg joined Famous Players–Lasky (soon to become Paramount), he took the young director with him.

Wellman's first film at Paramount was (in his own words) an "atrocious" comedy, *The Cat's Pajamas* (1926)—an ill-advised attempt to make an adult star of the child actress Betty Bronson. Wellman was almost fired, but Paramount gave him one more chance with *You Never Know Women* (1926), adapted by Benjamin Glazer from a story by Ernest Vajda. It was a backstage romance, with Florence Vidor as the star of a Russian theatrical troupe, Lowell Sherman and Clive Brook as the two men who want her.

This has been called the most "European" of Wellman's films, showing the influence of German expressionism in Victor Milner's dramatic lighting, and full of bravura effects. A memorable example occurs in the climactic scene where the heroine, pursued through the darkened theatre by the lustful Sherman, jumps into a magician's rigged cabinet and disappears in a puff of smoke. Notably well acted, the picture was both a critical and a commercial success, rehabilitating Wellman's reputation at Paramount.

When King Vidor's *The Big Parade* and Raoul Walsh's *What Price Glory?* registered at the box office, Paramount wanted its own World War epic. They settled on a flying story suggested by John Monk Saunders, himself a wartime pilot. Although Wellman had only minor credits up to that time, he was the only director in Hollywood with aerial combat experience, and with Schulberg's support, he was handed this choice assignment. John Monk Saunders was sent to Washington to solicit government help, and in the end, according to Kevin Brownlow, Wings "tied up thousands of soldiers, virtually all the pursuit planes the air force had, billions of dollars worth of equipment—and some of the finest military pilots in the country." There were angry speeches in Washington before shooting was completed.

Wings (1927) was the first important picture to deal with the role of the plane in World War I. It also embodied several themes dear to Wellman's heart—the romantic triangle, often squared by the self-abnegation of one of the rivals; male friendship; and the horseplaying but deeply felt comradeship of groups of men engaged in some shared—and usually dangerous—endeavor. Wings follows the wartime fortunes of two young fighter pilots, played by Charles "Buddy" Rogers and Richard Arlen. Rivals for the love of the same woman, they become friends after a bloody fistfight. In the end, through a tragic (or melodramatic) accident, Rogers shoots down and kills Arlen when the latter is escaping from the enemy lines in a German plane. Since both male leads were virtually unknown, the studio cast its biggest box-office draw, Clara Bow, as the heroine.

Wellman, known as a "one take" director, became a perfectionist in the filming of Wings, shooting scenes over and over again until he was satisfied with them. Up to that time, most "aerial" scenes had actually been shot on the ground, but in this film Wellman stipulated that there should be no faking. The cinematographer Harry Perry and his huge team of cameramen shot close-ups of the flyers from the rear cockpits of their planes and followed dogfights from a whole squadron of camera planes.

The movie's climax is a reenactment of the Battle of Saint Mihiel, shot on the plains outside San Antonio, Texas. A huge area was pounded by field guns until it became a convincing replica of the mud and chaos of the western front. A battery of cameras was mounted on a hundred-foot tower, with a further array of twenty-eight hand-held Eyemos in other strategic positions. The battle itself was planned like a real one by army officers in consultation with the filmmakers, and 3,500 troops and sixty pilots were rehearsed for ten days. Previewed in San Antonio as a fourteen-reeler, Wings was cut to 12,300 feet for its New York premiere, when the major scenes were projected in Magnascope on a double-size screen. Then or later (accounts differ), sound effects were added to convey the din of battle.

Wings was a huge success, praised by flyers for its authenticity and by critics for its spectacle. Photoplay's reviewer found the melodramatic plot "weakly built" and lacking in conviction, "with the exception of several touching scenes," but many agreed with Quinn Martin that "there has been no movie . . . which has surpassed it in impressing upon an audience a feeling of personal participation." In its day, the film had an impact on popular culture comparable to that of Star Wars. The aviator became the favorite hero of boys' adventure stories, and the movie's financial success precipitated a 'whole cycle of flying dramas, including Howard Hawks' Dawn Patrol (1930) and Howard Hughes' Hell's Angels (1930). It made stars of both Rogers and Arlen and also boosted the career of Gary Cooper, who made a strong impression in a brief scene in a training camp. Wings received the first Oscar ever awarded for best picture of the year, establishing Wellman as a major director at the age of thirty-one.

Writing in 1978 in The War, the West, and the Wilderness, Kevin Brownlow wrote that "Wings gets better the older it becomes. Values that once seemed overly sentimental now seem so much a part of their time that they no longer irritate. For most of its length, Wings avoids the grimness of war and captures exactly the fierce romanticism that so many veterans feel for it. . . . Wellman hurls his camera around the vast battlefield with exhilarating abandon. Even by today's standards, his setups seem remarkably bold. Although the troops die with rather operatic gestures, his epic handling of the big drive is overwhelming, and the superimposition of thousands of men marching into a horizon where their destruction is pictured in split screen is a moment worthy of Abel Gance's classic J'accuse."

Gary Cooper starred in Wellman's next movie, The Legion of the Condemned (1928), another World War I aviation drama, with Fay Wray as a beautiful spy. Scripted by John Monk Saunders, and using a good deal of material originally shot for Wings, it was generally well received. Not so Ladies of the Mob (1928), Wellman's first crime movie, in which he worked once more with Clara Bow and Richard Arlen. Mordaunt Hall found it "gloomy, artificial and unedifying."

Ladies of the Mob appears to be a lost film, like the majority of Wellman's silents. An excep-

tion—and one of the best of his early films—is
Beggars of Life (1928), featuring Arlen, Louise
Brooks, and Wallace Beery. Brooks gave one of
her best performances as a girl who kills her foster father when he tries to rape her and then goes
on the run with a gentle young hobo. Most of the
picture was shot in Jacumba, California, near the
Mexican border, where Wellman and his crew
are said to have plunged into a riotous two weeks
of drinking, gambling, and brawling. Margaret
Chapin accompanied her husband to Jacumba,
acting as a script girl, but the marriage ended
soon afterward.

Beggars of Life, which offers the first clear indication of Wellman's burgeoning social conscience, includes one sound scene in which
Beery, as the truculent bum Oklahoma Red,
sings a song. Told that Beery would have to stand
motionless in this scene because the microphone
was immovable, Wellman (according to eye-
witness David Selznick) hung it on a broom handle and shot the scene with Beery singing as he
walked. Wellman thus joins the sizable company
of directors credited with the invention of the
boom microphone. Whether or not the claim is
correct, *Beggars of Life*, as Frank T. Thompson
writes, "is a testament of Wellman's exhilaration
with movement"—a film about movement,
about people who are bound to advance constantly. . . . The story and the acting are simply
the catalysts that make the motion occur." On
the basis of this film and *Wings*, Wellman was named by *Film Daily* as one of the
world's best directors for 1928–1929.

He made the transition to sound easily, and as
Thompson says, his first talkies "moved just as
much as his silents," differing from them mostly
in the matter of close-ups. Wellman said, "You
use close-ups . . . to get a point over." With dialogue to do this for him, he seldom moved in
closer than a medium shot, even at moments of
high drama.

Wellman's relationship with Paramount, always shaky, was turning sour. His early sound
films there were strictly routine assignments
—*Chinatown Nights* (1929), made as a silent
then put back into production as a talkie; *The
Man I Love* and *Woman Trap*, both 1929; and
Dangerous Paradise (1930). Disarmingly modest
about his work, Wellman said that "for every
good picture, I made five or six stinkers. But I
always tried to do it a little differently. I don't
know whether I accomplished it, but I tried." In
the opinion of his admirers, he succeeded much
better than he has been given credit for. Frank
Thompson cites by way of example *The Man I
Love*, with Richard Arlen as an arrogant and opportunistic boxer who dumps his wife for a soci-

ety *femme fatale* but hastily retrieves her when
his mistress rejects him.

"Though the plot is moth-eaten and the hero
is something less than sympathetic," Thompson
writes, "the film is engaging on many levels.
Much credit is due Herman Mankiewicz's witty
script. . . . More importantly, *The Man I Love*
is perhaps the first film that is truly representative of Wellman." Thompson goes on to describe
some of the movie's "characteristic touches," including a cut-rate honeymoon trip in a railroad
boxcar. As an amorous scene develops, the camera rises discreetly above the loving couple to focus on the face of the car's other occupant, a
notably impassive horse, and then cuts to the
spinning turntable of a Victrola that no one can
be bothered to turn off. "Dozens of eccentric little touches like this color *The Man I Love*,"
Thompson says, and the film "is filled with interesting camera angles and movement."

Wellman made one more film at Paramount,
another variation on the *Wings* formula called
Young Eagles (1930), then broke his contract to
join Warner Brothers–First National. At about
the same time he married a polo-playing flyer
named Marjorie Crawford—another short-lived
union. Wellman stayed with Warners for three
years, finding a kindred spirit in the tough
young production chief Darryl F. Zanuck. His
first two Warner assignments showed his versatility—the football musical *Maybe It's Love*
(1930), with Joe E. Brown, and the railroad drama *Other Men's Women* (1931), starring Mary
Astor and featuring in minor roles newcomers
Joan Blondell and James Cagney.

Cagney was originally cast as the protagonist's
sidekick in Wellman's next picture, *The Public
Enemy* (1931) but, on the director's recommendation, wound up with the lead role. The movie
traces the rise and fall of a Chicago mobster,
Tom Powers. It was made in twenty-six days at
a cost of $151,000. Economically photographed
by Dev Jennings, it made excellent use of stock
shots of turn-of-the-century Chicago in a scene-
setting prologue. It is said that Wellman shot
only 360 feet of film that was not used in the final cut.

Zanuck had been dubious about the project,
believing that the gangster genre was played
out. Wellman won him over by promising to
make *The Public Enemy* "the toughest goddam
one of them all." He succeeded, especially in the
notorious scene in which Cagney mashes half a
grapefruit into the face of his mistress (Mae
Clarke) and the nightmarish finale, when Tom
Powers' trussed and bullet-ridden corpse is delivered to his mother's house (where she is playing "I'm Forever Blowing Bubbles" on the
Victrola).

The film's tight editing, mobile camerawork, and powerful use of sound, together with Cagney's electric performance, made it, as *Variety*'s reviewer wrote, the "roughest, toughest, and best of the gang films to date. . . . It's lowbrow material given such workmanship as to make it highbrow." Richard Watts Jr. went further, finding in the picture "a quality of grim directness, Zolaesque power, and chilling credibility which makes it far more real and infinitely more impressive than the run of gangster films."

More recently, Garbicz and Klinowski, in *Cinema: The Magic Vehicle* (1983), called *Public Enemy* "the most typical classic of the gangster series, in the sense that its principal value is its registrative, factual, 'journalistic' quality." However, David Thomson gives most of the credit to Cagney, maintaining that it was "the gleeful smartness" in his performance that made the film so influential "and which induced the public's ambivalent feelings about the criminal classes."

Wellman flourished at Warners, where his taut style was ideally suited to the studio's tabloid approach to contemporary issues. The speed and economy of his filmmaking was much appreciated by the thrifty Jack Warner. Having propelled Cagney to stardom in *The Public Enemy*, he set Barbara Stanwyck on the same path in *Night Nurse* (1931), a lurid but fast-paced and highly entertaining thriller. Stanwyck plays an idealistic young nurse who rescues two little girls from the clutches of a murderous doctor and his brutal chauffeur (Clark Gable). Wellman was notoriously more at home with actors than actresses, but the tough and unfazable Stanwyck was an exception, and he made several more movies with her, at Warners and elsewhere.

At this point in his career Wellman was churning out movies at the rate of five or six a year. Few of them are of much artistic interest, though several are remarkable for the candor with which they address America's problems during the Depression. Notable examples are *The Conquerors* (1932), made on loan to RKO and drawing parallels between the Depression and the earlier economic collapse of 1873, and *Heroes for Sale* (1933). The latter has Richard Barthelmess as a wounded war hero who comes home addicted to the morphine administered to him as a painkiller. Cured of his addiction, he reenters society in the midst of the Depression, confused and disillusioned, his job gone, his wife dead. This film offers an astonishingly bleak view of the American dream gone wrong. The upbeat ending, pinning its faith on President Roosevelt's inaugural address, struck many critics as artificial and unconvincing.

In the same year (1933), which saw the release of no less than seven of his pictures, Wellman made one of the best films of his career, *Wild Boys of the Road*. Scripted by Earl Baldwin, it shows how, little by little, a bunch of middle-class young people have their Andy Hardy certainties stripped away from them by the deepening Depression until they are forced to live on the run, stealing and begging to survive. As in *Heroes for Sale,* the film's bleak message is softened at the end. Charged with vagrancy and armed robbery, the central trio are told by a magistrate sympathetic to the New Deal that "things are going to get better now." The largely unknown cast was headed by Frankie Darro, Rochelle Hudson, and Dorothy Coonan, the nineteen-year-old dancer who in March 1934 became Wellman's fourth (and last) wife, and in time the mother of their seven children.

Wild Boys did poorly at the box office and had a mixed reception from contemporary critics. A reviewer in the New York *Times* wrote that "by endowing the film with a happy ending, the producers have robbed it of its value as a social challenge." On the other hand, William Troy thought that "never before does one recall having witnessed an American picture whose climax is made to consist in a pitched battle between a band of ragged outlaws and the police, in which the sympathy is manifestly with the former." The film's reputation has grown since then. It has found its way onto a number of college courses, and Todd McCarthy, in Jean-Pierre Coursodon's *American Directors,* goes so far as to describe it as "Wellman's one film with a claim to greatness."

Wellman had put a great deal of himself into *Wild Boys* and was stung by its apparent failure. His next Warners assignment was a college musical, *College Coach* (1933)—a briskly cynical comedy, featuring a surprisingly vicious fistfight between Dick Powell and Lyle Talbot. After that Wellman went freelance for a time, directing Spencer Tracy in a comedy-drama about wiretapping, *Looking for Trouble* (1934), for Zanuck's newly formed 20th Century Pictures, then *Stingaree* (1934) at RKO—a musical romance based on E. W. Hornung's stories about an Australian Robin Hood. *Looking for Trouble,* appropriately enough, provided ample evidence of Wellman's explosive temper—he and Tracy disliked each other on sight, and the two men twice had to be forcibly extricated from brawls. Before shooting was completed, "Wild Bill" had been involved in another much-publicized fight with his former assistant Mike Lally.

Back with Zanuck, Wellman made *The Call of the Wild* (1935), starring Clark Gable, with

Mt. Baker, Washington, doubling for the Yukon. Gene Fowler and Leonard Praskins' adaptation took considerable liberties with Jack London's novel, most obviously in the addition of romantic interest in the form of Loretta Young, but the film is notable all the same for Charles Rosher's location photography and Wellman's evocation of the Alaskan gold rush.

The success of this movie brought the director an attractive offer from MGM, and he reneged on his contract with Zanuck. As a favor to the director Tay Garnett he did some second unit work on *China Seas* before undertaking *The Robin Hood of El Dorado* (1936), based on a highly romanticized biography of the Mexican bandit Joaquin Murrieta. "Though the film dispensed with the facts," writes Frank Thompson, "Wellman was able to make a hard-hitting film about racial prejudice and the violence that breeds violence. . . . *The Robin Hood of El Dorado* anticipates the 'revisionist' Western of the 1960s in its blurring of 'good guy/bad guy' distinctions, in its violence, and in the questions it raises about the nature of such generic Western themes as 'settling' and 'homesteading.' Specifically . . . [it] prefigures Sam Peckinpah's *The Wild Bunch* (1969) in its mixture of sentimentality and violence and in the strong undercurrent of nostalgia and regret for a way of life that is in the process of vanishing." Both films make similarly elegiac use of the same song, "La Golondrina."

Wellman spent much of his time at MGM feuding with studio head Louis B. Mayer and consequently was relegated to run-of-the-mill material. The last half of 1936 brought him nothing but *Small Town Girl,* a romantic comedy starring Janet Gaynor and Robert Taylor, and some uncredited work on *Tarzan Escapes.* One positive development at MGM was his teaming up with the young writer Robert Carson. Together they scripted *The Last Gangster* (1937), directed by Edward Ludwig, and thereafter Carson worked on all Wellman's films through *The Light That Failed.*

In 1937 Wellman asked to be released from his Metro contract and rejoined David O. Selznick at his new Selznick-International Pictures. Wellman professed a hatred of producers throughout his career, but he and Selznick worked very well together. Their first collaboration at Selznick-International was *A Star Is Born* (1937), scripted by Dorothy Parker, Alan Campbell, and Robert Carson from a story devised by Carson and Wellman. It draws on the real life tragedies of such fallen idols as John Gilbert and John Barrymore, tracing the rise to stardom of Vicki Lester (Janet Gaynor) as her alcoholic husband, Norman Maine (Fredric March), plummets from celebrity to obscurity, finally killing himself to save her career.

This often savage meditation on what lay behind the glamour and glitter of Hollywood was a smash hit. "For about the first time," wrote Otis Ferguson, "the mechanics of the industry are worked in with thorough coverage. . . . And all done with a sense of the actual hardness and fabulous confusion—as for example in the mild burlesque of the screen-test scene, which is a little orchestra of strange hustling sounds and motions in itself." More recently, Henri Agel spoke of the film's "bitter, shimmering poetry." W. Howard Greene received a special Oscar for his Technicolor photography, which avoided the garishness of most pioneer color movies, and Wellman and Carson shared another Academy Award for best original story. The picture has been twice remade, in 1954 brilliantly by George Cukor, with Judy Garland and James Mason, and in 1977 forgettably by Frank Pierson.

Wellman's next Selznick production was the screwball comedy *Nothing Sacred* (1937), also made in Technicolor, and with a blackly acerbic script by Ben Hecht and half a dozen uncredited others. Carole Lombard stars as Hazel Flagg, who is supposedly dying of radium poisoning. An unscrupulous reporter (Fredric March) invites her to New York for a last well-publicized fling, all expenses paid. Hazel accepts, though by then she knows that the diagnosis was mistaken and she is perfectly healthy. The two fall in love and have to find a way out of their predicament while a ghoulish New York public waits avidly to be heartbroken by Hazel's death.

The immense success of *A Star Is Born* and *Nothing Sacred* brought Wellman a contract with Paramount, where for five years he produced as well as directed his films. His first project there was a labor of love, *Men With Wings* (1938), tracing the growth of aviation through the melodramatic story of two pioneering aviators vaguely modeled on the Wright Brothers. Like most of Wellman's flying films, this one is marred by its romantic subplot, which threatens to take over the movie. The best sequences recapture the excitement of the aerial work in *Wings,* with the addition of sound and Technicolor.

A much better film followed, a remake of Herbert Brenon's 1926 adaptation of P. C. Wren's novel of the French Foreign Legion, *Beau Geste.* Wellman assembled an impressive cast, with Gary Cooper, Ray Milland, and Robert Preston as the gallant Geste brothers and Brian Donlevy as the sadistic Sergeant Markoff.

Wellman's *Beau Geste* closely follows Brenon's silent version and was filmed on the same location, in the desert near Yuma, Arizona.

In the opinion of Frank Thompson, the remake "benefited from Wellman's bold composition and fluid camerawork. The battle scenes are so rhythmically exciting, the propulsive tracks along the wall of dead faces so gripping that scene after scene is easily Brenon's better." Most contemporary critics felt very differently—Otis Ferguson said that the new version was "like meeting up with an old schoolmate who has become the town idiot." It was very successful, nevertheless, and has remained so—indeed, thanks to repeated exposure on television, it has become one of the best known of Wellman's films, famous enough to be endlessly parodied.

Another remake followed—the third version of *The Light That Failed,* from Rudyard Kipling's novel. Ronald Colman contributed one of his stronger performances as Dick Heldar, the artist slowly going blind, and Ida Lupino gained her first critical acclaim as the cockney model who destroys his masterpiece. This was Robert Carson's last screenplay for Wellman, who fired the writer after an argument, allegedly jealous over sharing credit for their string of hits.

Wellman made two more films as director-producer at Paramount, both starring Joel McCrea. *Reaching for the Sun* (1941) was a comedy-drama about the automobile industry, based on a novel by Wessel Smitter but eschewing the book's indictment of the motor magnates. The liberal and even left-wing political slant of Wellman's socially conscious films of the 1930s was giving way to a rabid anticommunism. At the same time his extraordinarily rapid output was dwindling as the arthritis induced by his wartime back injury caused him ever-increasing pain.

After *The Great Man's Lady* (1942), an interesting critique of the "pioneer spirit" in which Barbara Stanwyck was required to age from 16 to 108, Wellman left Paramount and rejoined Zanuck at 20th Century–Fox. His first film there was *Roxie Hart* (1942), a fast and raucous comedy in which a gum-chewing Ginger Rogers faces a murder rap in 1920s Chicago, and Adolphe Menjou steals the picture as her "simple, barefoot mouthpiece." Nunnally Johnson wrote the extremely funny script, with uncredited assistance from Ben Hecht.

Walter Van Tilburg Clark's 1940 novel *The Ox-Bow Incident* was a "serious Western," using the genre as a backdrop for a poetic tragedy of intolerance and mob violence. Wellman fell in love with the book and bought the rights himself. He approached several studios, but the down-

beat story—with little action and no romance—was deemed uncommercial. Finally, he made a deal with 20th Century–Fox, which agreed to finance the movie on condition that he direct a picture a year for the studio for five years—two of them to be chosen by Zanuck and directed by Wellman whether he liked them or not.

The Ox-Bow Incident is set in Nevada in 1885. Two cowboys (Henry Fonda and Harry Morgan) ride into a remote cattle town and become witnesses to the hysteria of a lynch mob. Three innocent men are hanged (Dana Andrews, Anthony Quinn, and Francis Ford), and the film, faithfully and intelligently adapted by Lamar Trotti, brings out the various motives that lead the members of the posse to take injustice into their own hands. At the end, Fonda reads aloud to them an intensely moving letter written by one of the murdered men to his wife and then rides out of the silent town.

The movie failed at the box office, as the industry cynics had predicted. Its critical reception, on the other hand, was enthusiastic. There was warm praise for the script, for Arthur Miller's moody chiaroscuro photography, and for the excellent performances Wellman had elicited from his cast. The film was shot on cheap sets of obvious artificiality, but for its admirers this only added to its mood of nightmarish claustrophobia. *The Ox-Bow Incident* was nominated for a best picture Oscar and was soon established as a classic of the genre. However, James Agee wrote that this, "one of the best and most interesting pictures I have seen for a long time," was ultimately disappointing on account of its "stiff over-consciousness." It seemed to him "a mosaic of over-appreciated effects which continually robbed nature of its own warmth and energy." This view has gained ground—like so many of Agee's perceptions—and Frank Thompson maintains that Wellman's most personal films are paradoxically "also among his least characteristic; they are intelligent and well-made—and often quite beautiful—but somehow the Wellman fire and energy are missing."

Thunder Birds (1941), made after *The Ox-Bow Incident* but actually released before it, was by contrast a routine contribution to Hollywood's wartime propaganda effort, glorifying the fighter pilots in training at Thunderbird Field in Arizona. An older American hero was celebrated in equally uncritical terms in *Buffalo Bill* (1944), starring Joel McCrea. Vigorously directed, it featured a bloody and exciting battle sequence that reappeared in at least two other Fox Westerns. The comedy-mystery *Lady of Burlesque,* (1943) Wellman's fifth and last picture with Barbara Stanwyck, was followed by

This Man's Navy (MGM, 1945), a formula drama about the Navy's dirigible service starring Wallace Beery.

Then, for the first time since *The Ox-Bow Incident,* Wellman found a project with which he could involve himself personally and passionately. *The Story of GI Joe* (1945), based on the writings of war correspondent Ernie Pyle, was offered to him by the independent producer Lester Cowan. Wellman at first resisted, saying that he hated "the God-damned infantry," but Cowan won him over, and the film was one of the best of his career.

The Story of GI Joe offers an honest and humanistic view of the common infantryman as seen through the exploits and sufferings of one patrol. Burgess Meredith played Pyle, and Wellman took Robert Mitchum out of B-movies to play the patrol leader Lieutenant Walker—so powerfully that he was nominated for an Oscar as best supporting actor. "Final judgement must wait on time," wrote Richard Griffith, "but I feel that Wellman's film deserves to stand beside *Three Soldiers,* Brady's Civil War photographs, and the pioneer work of Ambrose Bierce and Stephen Crane as one of the greatest documents of warfare." James Agee called it "a tragic and eternal work of art."

Wellman never again reached such heights, but the films he made over the following twelve years included some excellent work. Among his successes were two movies made in 1948 for 20th Century–Fox: the spy thriller *The Iron Curtain* and *Yellow Sky,* a tough and exciting Western based on a story by W. R. Burnett. Gregory Peck plays the leader of a gang of outlaws hiding out in an Arizona ghost town where he begins a passionate and redemptive affair with the half-wild girl who lives there (Anne Baxter).

Wellman went to MGM to direct *Battleground* (1949) for Dore Schary. A realistic and gritty war film set during the Battle of the Bulge, it focused on the travails of one battalion and achieved a little of the power of *The Story of GI Joe.* A commercial success, it won Oscars for best screenplay (Robert Pirosh) and best black-and-white photography (Paul Vogel) and was nominated for best picture and best direction. Settling for a time at MGM, Wellman next made a pleasant turn-of-the-century comedy, *The Happy Years* (1950), based on Owen Johnson's Lawrenceville School stories. An odd little allegory followed, *The Next Voice You Hear* (1950), in which the voice of God speaks out of the radio. Everyone prophesied disaster, but the movie was generally well received and moderately successful. *Across the Wide Missouri* (1951) has Clark Gable as a mountain man of the 1830s

and beautiful color photography by William Mellor. MGM drastically reedited this film and gave poor distribution to Wellman's next two pictures, the interesting *Westward the Women* (1951), in which Robert Taylor leads a caravan of women across the wilderness, and *My Man and I* (1952), a melodramatic story about Mexican Americans.

By then disenchanted with MGM, Wellman was happy to accept the handsome profit participation deal offered to him by John Wayne, who was by then producing his own pictures. Their first project was *Island in the Sky* (1953), adapted by Ernest K. Gann from his own novel about a plane crew lost in the Canadian north woods. Most critics thought that the movie's extended flashbacks detracted from the suspense but warmed to Wayne and Wellman's next effort, *The High and the Mighty* (1954), another Gann adaptation and a forerunner of the *Airport* series with its story of a commercial airliner in jeopardy. Filmed in Cinemascope and Warnercolor, with stereophonic sound, an Oscar-winning score by Dimitri Tiomkin, and a strong cast headed by Wayne, Robert Stack, Claire Trevor, and Robert Newton, it was immensely successful and earned Wellman his third Oscar nomination for best direction.

The Track of the Cat (1954), adapted like *The Ox-Bow Incident* from a novel by Walter Van Tilburg Clark, was another personal film. Visually distinguished by Wellman's attempt to make a color film in which almost the only colors are black and white, it was found otherwise slow, talky, and pretentious. The director made only one other film of real merit, *Goodbye, My Lady* (1956), a beautiful and melancholy story about a boy (Brandon DeWilde) and his basenji dog, set in the Mississippi swampland. Todd McCarthy called it "the surprising grace note of Wellman's late years" and "possibly the most decent of all boy-loves-dog films." Wellman had high hopes for *Lafayette Escadrille* (1958), intended as an autobiographical memoir of his days of flying and fighting. His story had a tragic ending, but Warner Brothers made him change it. "The story was too close to me," he said later, "and it nearly broke my tough old heart when they wouldn't let me make it the way it really happened. . . . The happy ending destroyed the whole thing, and I got out of the business because of it."

Wellman retired in 1962 but continued to write scripts and toy with various projects. He was awarded the D. W. Griffith Award in 1972 and has been honored by major retrospectives in Los Angeles and at the British Film Institute. Wellman died of leukemia at the age of seventy-nine, and as he requested, his ashes were scattered from the skies.

Like his friends John Ford, Victor Fleming, Raoul Walsh, and Howard Hawks, Wellman was a hard-nosed man's man who refused to regard himself as anything so effete as an artist and insisted that his only aim was to entertain. He has often been compared to Hawks because of the similarity of their subject matter and their shared preoccupation with groups of professionals in crisis situations. Unlike Hawks, however, Wellman would direct virtually anything that a studio handed him. "You make all kinds of things," he said, "and that, I think, is what gives you the background to eventually make some very lucky picture."

No one would deny that Wellman made a good many "lucky" pictures, including *Wings, The Public Enemy, Wild Boys of the Road, A Star Is Born, Nothing Sacred, The Ox-Bow Incident,* and *The Story of GI Joe.* For nearly forty years, Wellman was regarded as one of the best directors in Hollywood. His reputation went into decline in the 1950s, and much of his best work was forgotten. *You Never Know Women, Beggars of Life, Heroes for Sale, The President Vanishes,* and *The Robin Hood of El Dorado* went unseen for years, until Wellman was rediscovered and championed by such historians and critics as Kevin Brownlow, Richard Schickel, Gerald Peary, Frank Thompson, and Manny Farber.

Wellman prided himself on working fast, and along the way he made many poor films. At his best, as Richard Combs writes, he "has been compared, on the one hand, to Griffith for the simplicity and lyricism of his treatment of a social order and its outcasts . . . and, on the other, to Stroheim for an inclination toward symbolism, edging close to expressionism in some of the effects by which he attempts to give an entirely subjective cast to the action." The unevenness of his work and its stylistic eclecticism has made it difficult for his admirers to claim *auteur* status for him, but not impossible. Frank Thompson, for one, maintains that "his films' concerns, attitudes, moral perspectives, visual and aural styles are inextricably tied in with Wellman's tastes, moods, and prejudices. There is a wholeness to his work—in style, quality, and point-of-view— that separates it from the run-of-the-mill studio project for which it is often mistaken."

Another of Wellman's champions, Manny Farber, suggests that "in any Bill Wellman operation, there are at least four directors—a sentimentalist, deep thinker, hooey vaudevillian, and an expedient short-cut artist whose special love is for mulish toughs expressing themselves in

drop-kicking heads and somber standing around. Wellman is at his best in stiff, vulgar, low-pulp material. In that setup he has a low-budget ingenuity, which creates flashes of ferocious brassiness, an authentic practical-joke violence, and a brainless hell-raising." As Henri Agel wrote as long ago as 1963, "Wellman's handicap is that he has no doubt made too many films. . . . He will have to be patiently rediscovered."

—J.A.G.

FILMS: The Man Who Won, 1923; Second Hand Love, 1923; Big Dan, 1923; Cupid's Fireman, 1923; Not a Drum Was Heard, 1924; The Vagabond Trail, 1924; The Circus Cowboy, 1924; When Husbands Flirt, 1925; The Boob (UK, The Yokel), 1926; The Cat's Pajamas, 1926; You Never Know Women, 1926; Wings, 1927; Legion of the Condemned, 1928; Ladies of the Mob, 1928; Beggars of Life, 1928; Chinatown Nights, 1929; The Man I Love 1929; Woman Trap, 1929; Dangerous Paradise, 1930; Young Eagles, 1930; Maybe It's Love, 1930; Other Men's Women (Steel Highway), 1931; The Public Enemy (UK, Enemy of the Republic), 1931; Night Nurse, 1931; Star Witness, 1931; Safe in Hell (UK, The Lost Lady), 1931; The Hatchet Man, 1932; So Big, 1932; Love is a Racket, 1932; The Purchase Price, 1932; The Conquerors, 1932; Frisco Jenny, 1933; Central Airport, 1933; Lilly Turner, 1933; Midnight Mary (Lady of the Night), 1933; Heroes for Sale, 1933; Wild Boys of the Road (UK, Dangerous Days), 1933; College Coach, 1933; Looking for Trouble, 1934; Stingaree, 1934; The President Vanishes, 1934; The Call of the Wild, 1935; The Robin Hood of El Dorado, 1936; Small Town Girl, 1936; A Star is Born, 1937; Nothing Sacred, 1937; Men With Wings, 1938; Beau Geste, 1939; The Light That Failed, 1939; Reaching for the Sun, 1941; Roxie Hart, 1942; The Great Man's Lady, 1942; Thunder Birds (UK, Soldiers of the Air), 1942; The Ox-Bow Incident (UK, Strange Incident), 1943; Lady of Burlesque, 1943; Buffalo Bill, 1944; This Man's Navy, 1945; The Story of G.I. Joe, 1945; Gallant Journey, 1946; Magic Town, 1947; The Iron Curtain, 1948; Yellow Sky, 1948; Battleground, 1949; The Happy Years, 1950; The Next Voice You Hear, 1950; Across the Wide Missouri, 1951; Westward the Women, 1951; The Minister in Washington (short) *in* It's a Big Country, 1951; My Man and I, 1952; Island in the Sky, 1953; The High and the Mighty, 1954; The Track of the Cat, 1954; Blood Alley, 1955; Goodbye My Lady, 1956; Darby's Rangers, 1958; Lafayette Escadrille (UK, Hell Bent for Glory), 1958. *Published scripts*—The Public Enemy, University of Wisconsin Press, 1981; The Ox-Bow Incident *in* Best Film Plays 1943–44, Garland, 1977; The Story of G.I. Joe *in* Best Film Plays 1945, Garland, 1977.

ABOUT: Brownlow, K. The Parade's Gone By, 1968; Brownlow, K. The War, the West, and the Wilderness, 1981; Coursodon, J.-P. American Directors, Vol. I, 1983; Farber, M. Negative Space, 1971; Meyer, W. R. Warner Brothers Directors, 1978; Roud, R. (ed.) Cinema: A Critical Dictionary, 1980; Schary, D. and Palmer, C. Case History of a Movie, 1950; Schickel, R.

The Men Who Made the Movies, 1975; Steen, M. Hollywood Speaks, 1974; Thompson, F. William A. Wellman, 1983; Thomson, D. A Biographical Dictionary of the Cinema, 1980; Tuska, J. (ed.) Close-Up, The Hollywood Director 1978; Wellman, W. A. A Short Time for Insanity, 1974. Periodicals—Action March–April 1970; American Classic Screen Summer 1980, Winter 1980; American Film March 1976; Brighton Film Review January 1970; Cinema July 1966; Films and Filming March 1973, April 1973; Films in Review May 1982, June–July 1982; Focus on Film March 1978; Grand Illusions February 1977; The Velvet Light Trap Fall 1975.

"WEST," ROLAND (Roland Van Ziemer)

(1887–March 31, 1951), American director, scenarist, and producer, was born in Cleveland, Ohio. His mother, Margaret Van Tassel, was an actress and his aunt, Cora Van Tassel, a theatrical producer who gave West his first role at the age of twelve in her 1899 Cleveland production *The Volunteers.* At seventeen he landed his first leading part in a road company of *Jockey Jones.* In 1906 he collaborated with W. H. Clifford on a twenty-five-minute vaudeville sketch, *The Criminal* (also known as *The Under World*), a quick-change piece in which the nineteen-year-old West portrayed five different characters. The sketch toured for five years before West relinquished his acting career to write and produce vaudeville sketches—all of them apparently light stories of crime and detection.

In 1915 West formed a partnership with Joseph Schenck, former general manager of bookings for Loew's Theatres and the man who would remain West's mentor and closest friend. With $26,000 they established the Roland West Film Corporation. Later the same year West directed *Lost Souls,* a five-reel melodrama starring Josie Collins as an Italian immigrant pressed into white slavery. It was sold to William Fox—the only distributor, it has been suggested, prepared to market such a film (Fox's own Theda Bara "vamp" pictures were then creating a national furor). Released in 1916 as *A Woman's Honor,* it was dismissed as both tasteless and clumsy.

Schenck set up a production company in 1917 to make films starring his wife, Norma Talmadge. West was appointed general manager. He directed the company's third picture, *De Luxe Annie* (1918), with Talmadge in a Jekyll-and-Hyde role as a genteel woman who, suffering from amnesia, becomes the bait in a badger game. The same year West collaborated with Carlyle Moore on a stage play, *The Unknown Purple,* adapted from one of his old, unsold movie scenarios, *The Vanishing Man.* Its protagonist is an inventor who develops a "purple ray" of in-

visibility and uses it to revenge himself on his faithless wife and her lover, who have stolen his unique patents. Unable to secure backing, West opened the play out of town and then mounted a Broadway production with $50,000 of his own money.

The Unknown Purple was a hit, and shrewd investment of the proceeds assured West's financial security. Thereafter he made films only if and when he wanted to, producing, writing, and directing one carefully prepared feature every year or two. Although they incorporated various genre elements—horror, science fiction, society drama, or romance—all of his films were fundamentally stories of crime or detection, characterized by highly personal moral values, justice frequently being administered in vengeful, vicious, or illegal ways.

West's 1921 release *The Silver Lining,* a vehicle for his wife Jewel Carmen, developed the dual identity theme of *De Luxe Annie* in a story about two orphaned girls, one reared by a decent family, the other by criminals who train her as a pickpocket and confidence trickster. The bad girl is delivered from her life of crime by a sympathetic Secret Service agent, touched by her blossoming love for the young man she had been fleecing. The movie told its story in flashback, and so did *Nobody,* another 1921 release starring Jewel Carmen. As a jury deliberates a murder case, the lone juror holding out for acquittal finally confesses that his own wife had committed the murder after being raped and blackmailed by the dead man. Agreeing never to reveal the reason for their verdict, the jury frees the accused.

The Unknown Purple, West's 1918 Broadway success, was filmed in 1923. In the movie, he perfected the "purple ray" and invisibility effects that had been so costly and difficult to achieve on stage, antedating James Whale's *The Invisible Man* by a decade. Purple tinting was used whenever the inventor (Henry B. Walthall) resorted to the "ray of invisibility"—for example during a midnight robbery, when a purple glow envelops the room as a disembodied hand purloins a necklace. In an even more effective scene, a purple cone of destructive energy strikes the center of the room as the phantom hand writes a threatening note (the vortex was apparently painted into an otherwise black-and-white scene). Truart Corporation, releasing *The Unknown Purple,* announced that West had signed a six-year contract with them as writer-director. In fact, the only other project he completed for them was a scenario based on a *Redbook* story, "Driftwood," filmed by Rowland G. Edwards in 1924 as *Daring Love.*

The following year West directed *The Monster* for MGM release. An adaptation of Crane Wilbur's stage play, it starred Lon Chaney. This is the earliest of West's films that survives and, if it is typical of his silent output, shows that he was at that phase of his career no more than a careful technician who transferred plays to film in a proscenium style, stressing mood and production values rather than opening up the stage with film craft.

Most of the "old house" stage thrillers and their movie adaptations were composed of varying proportions of macabre skulduggery and comic relief; *The Monster* is mostly comedy. Chaney's Dr. Ziska, a madhouse inmate masquerading as the asylum's director, is an entirely tongue-in-cheek conception, his plan to transpose the souls of men and women lacking even the flimsiest of motives. There are echoes of *Caligari* in Wilbur's story but not in West's storytelling. The fondness he demonstrates here for nocturnal atmosphere, action played in long shot, and stage lighting devices like spotlights and dimmers is natural in someone so thoroughly grounded in theatre—just as the sensationalism of West's subjects can be traced to his training in the world of vaudeville road shows.

It was his screen version of Mary Roberts Rinehart's play *The Bat,* made in 1926 for Joe Schenck's United Artists Corporation, that firmly established his reputation as a master of crime and suspense melodramas. The sensation created by the play and by West's silent film is hard to explain today, particularly since the movie has not survived, and frequent remakes of *The Cat and the Canary* have usurped its reputation as the fountainhead of a genre. The Bat is a masked and cloaked master criminal who terrorizes the tenants of an isolated mansion in his quest for a hidden fortune. The New York *Times'* review gave one clue to the film's success, describing how a moth crushed on an automobile headlight is magnified into a fearsome batlike projection on a ceiling and citing this as an example of West's highly cinematic treatment of his material.

The rapid growth of West's film sense must be attributed to his admiration for German expressionism. Films like *Variety, Faust,* and *Metropolis* greatly influenced American filmmakers in the mid-1920s, and few analyzed their effects more carefully than West, who opened his 1928 movie *The Dove* with the camera hurtling over mountains and roadways before coming to rest in the story's locale. He was so taken with German technique that he at one time planned to direct a Norma Talmadge picture at UFA's Berlin studio, in order to study their methods at first hand. *The Dove,* from a play by Willard Mack, was an old-fashioned melodrama pitting a ruthless Mexican brigand against a dance-hall girl and her lover, but West's first sound film, *Alibi* (1929), returned the director to his special milieu, the crime drama.

Alibi, another play adaptation, was scripted by West with C. Gardner Sullivan. Eleanor Griffith plays Joan, a cop's daughter who falls in love with ex-con Chick Williams (Chester Morris). Chick insists that he is an innocent man, framed by the police, and Joan believes him. He is in fact a ruthless criminal, and in the end he is hounded to his death by the young cop (Pat O'Malley) whom he had replaced in the heroine's affections.

"*Alibi* is basically pure corn," wrote Tom Milne in a retrospective review in the (British) *Monthly Film Bulletin* (July 1979); "what matters is the vitality of West's direction, which revels in elliptical action, exhilaratingly febrile camera movements, and highly stylised lighting effects." Much of the film, Milne wrote, is told in "intricate, fluidly dovetailing sequences," and most of the dialogue scenes are superbly handled. Elliott Stein, writing in Richard Roud's *Cinema* (1980), called *Alibi* a "claustrophobic little nightmare" and "one of the most oppressive films ever made."

The film opens, as Milne says, with a "close-up of a twirling truncheon, its shadow looming on the wall behind—of a hand activating an alarm—a truncheon beating time on iron railings—cell doors swinging open in unison—convicts emerging like a well-drilled chorus line . . . one man peeling off diagonally." In ten shots that make powerful use of sound effects but include no dialogue whatever, we see the release of Chick Williams from prison and his arrival at a nightclub to celebrate his first night of freedom.

Milne called this sequence of formalized shots "expressionistic in the purest sense," and the German influence has also been noted in the subjective montage and rhythmic, accelerated dialogue of a police interrogation in which a petty hood is threatened with death; in William Cameron Menzies' stylized sets; and in West's use of shop signs (and the neon nightclub sign) less for the information they convey than for their pictorial value as elements in his composition.

The movie's portrayal of unscrupulous and brutal police methods was not welcomed by the police themselves, and the Chicago police commissioner tried to have the film banned. This did not prevent it from becoming one of the box-office successes of the year, warmly praised by critics as a talkie that did not compromise the visual nature of the medium and (by Lewis Jacobs) as one in which "silence, used to create tension and suspense, proved its strength as a dramatic ally of sound."

Alibi made a star of Chester Morris, whom West kept under personal contract, casting him next as the eponymous master criminal in *The Bat Whispers* (1930), an elaborate sound remake of *The Bat*. West paid out of his own pocket for a 65mm camera and produced the film in both standard and wide-screen versions. His camera movements have a fluidity remarkable in a sound film of that era, achieved partly through the use of a gigantic scaffold 300 feet long and 30 feet high from which the suspended camera could zoom vertiginously through space.

The Bat Whispers remains a frightening film and a technical tour de force. West used miniatures, a specially designed camera dolly, painted shadows, and pinpoint editing to masterful effect: a pullback from a clock tower at night suddenly becomes an elevator shot, plummeting thirty stories to the city streets below to observe a police car racing through the dark streets; airborne, the camera swoops across the expansive grounds of the estate as lightning flashes around the old house, enters by an upper window, and hurtles along the corridor; the Bat, illuminated by a lightning flash, glides from the treetops to claim a victim.

West's timing was wrong: the industry's flirtation with wide-screen lasted all of three months, and the already glutted market for "old house" chillers collapsed a month after West's masterpiece went into general release, superseded by the cycle of supernatural melodramas ushered in by *Dracula*. Ironically, as Morris' business agent, West had vetoed Universal's request to cast Morris as Dracula—"Sorry," he wrote, "but we're looking for romance."

His plans for Morris had included remakes of the sultry Valentino vehicles *The Sheik* and *Son of the Sheik*. However, though he was only forty-three, West was tiring of production and claimed that it was only his sense of responsibility for Morris' career that kept him in the business. Properties he held, such as *Death Takes a Holiday*, were sold. Other originals in development, like a modern-dress version of *The Purple Mask* in which the despotic villain would machine-gun the peasants, were abandoned. West, an avid yachtsman, spoke of retiring and sailing around the world.

He produced and directed one final film with Morris, *Corsair* (1931), a bizarre amalgam of bootlegging, illicit empire-building, and sadistic vengeance loosely based on a novel by Walton Green. The book was a routine thriller, but the movie, according to William K. Everson, "like most of West's films . . . doesn't make it easy on the audience. The plot development is far from straightforward, and the motivations often extremely involved. Many of the strongest plot elements are not present in the original novel at all. . . . At a time when so many talkies were just that, *Corsair* is *all* movie, with a reliance on the same technique that so distinguished *The Bat Whispers*—dramatic lighting and close-ups, superb moving camera shots, an excellent use of shadows, and, in this film, some really lovely night exteriors." There is also West's "casual acceptance of crime, and . . . total lack of any kind of 'moral compensation' for the criminals." For Andrew Sarris, "the misty expressionism and delicate feelings of *Corsair* entitle the director to a place in film history."

Having wrapped up *Corsair,* West set out on his world cruise. His marriage broke up in the course of it. Louella Parsons hinted at the nervous strain the journey had placed on Jewel Carmen, reporting that two and a half years away from civilization "almost proved fatal" to her. When he returned to California, West's attentions were absorbed by Thelma Todd, the "Ice Cream Blonde" who had provided the romantic interest in *Corsair*. They opened an expensive roadhouse—Thelma Todd's Roadside Rest—on the Pacific Coast Highway and moved into a suite of rooms over the nightclub.

Jewel Carmen had vacated West's mansion on the hill overlooking the club, and West and Todd continued to keep their cars in its large garage. It was there, on a windy morning in December 1935, after a midnight shouting match, that Thelma Todd's bruised body was discovered behind the wheel of her roadster. West narrowly escaped a murder charge, but there were also suggestions that Todd's life had been threatened by racketeers because she had refused to let them take over the upper floor of the roadhouse as a gambling casino. In the end, the coroner gave a verdict of accidental death by carbon monoxide poisoning.

West retired into obscurity. In 1940 he married the actress Lola Lane. He did a little writing in the years that followed, but when he died of heart disease in 1951, he was remembered only as an old-time filmmaker and as a figure in the Todd case.

West's reputation has grown in recent years. A writer in the *Monthly Film Bulletin* (July 1979) said that he had the rare gift "of being funny and frightening at the same time. Standing back, tongue in cheek, to observe his own pyrotechnic display of chiaroscuro terrors, he added an extra frisson through the keen intelligence and cynical detachment which may ultimately have been his own undoing in that they put him well ahead of his time." For Elliott Stein, he was "one of America's supremely original visual stylists."

—S.A.MacQ.

FILMS: A Woman's Honor/Lost Souls, 1916; De Luxe Annie, 1918; The Silver Lining, 1921; Nobody, 1921; The Unknown Purple, 1923; The Monster, 1925; The Bat, 1926; The Dove, 1928; Alibi (UK, The Perfect Alibi), 1929; The Bat Whispers, 1930; Corsair, 1931.

ABOUT: Everson, W. K. The Detective in Film, 1972; Higham, C. The Art of the American Film, 1973; Roud, R. (ed.) Cinema: A Critical Dictionary, 1980; Thompson, F. (ed.) Director! Periodicals—Alfred Hitchcock's Mystery Magazine Mid-September 1983; American Classic Screen March–April 1983; Monthly Film Bulletin July 1979.

JAMES WHALE

WHALE, JAMES (July 22, 1889–May 29, 1957), American director, was born in England, at Dudley, Worcestershire, the sixth of seven children. His father, William, was an ironworker who became secretary of the trade union that he had helped to form; his mother, the former Sarah Peters, was a nurse. In later years, Whale took considerable pains to expunge every trace of this working-class background from his dress, accent, and way of life.

Whale's education in Dudley included some art instruction, and as soon as he could he moved to London to pursue these studies, finding work before long as a cartoonist on *The Bystander*. With the outbreak of World War I, Whale obtained a commission as second lieutenant in the 7th Worcestershire Infantry. He served in the trenches on the Western Front, where he was captured in 1917 during a night reconnaissance. Sent to a prisoner-of-war camp at Holzminden, near Hanover, Whale took up acting in camp entertainments, mostly with the aim of staving off boredom. However, he soon developed a taste for the stage and, on his return to England in 1918, joined the Birmingham Repertory Theatre, playing small roles in *The Knight of the Burning Pestle* and Drinkwater's *Abraham Lincoln*.

For the next few years Whale worked with various provincial repertory companies as actor, stage manager, and set designer, before making his London debut in a 1925 production of *A Comedy of Good and Evil* at the Ambassadors Theatre. After that he designed and acted in a number of West End productions (including

The Man With Red Hair, in which he met and began his lifelong friendship with Charles Laughton). In 1928 Whale also took up directing, with tolerable if not spectacular success. The plays he staged were mostly small-scale fringe productions, of which little more than intellectual respectability was expected. This was the case with the play on which Whale founded his career.

Journey's End was the work of an unknown amateur playwright, R. C. Sherriff, based on his own experience as a soldier in the trenches of World War I. It was only at the urging of Bernard Shaw that the play was put on (by the London Stage Society at the Apollo Theatre), since the public was held to have little taste for war dramas. Three directors had turned the job down before Whale accepted it in return for a percentage of the profits—a very shrewd move, as it transpired. *Journey's End* opened in December 1928, with the young Laurence Olivier in the leading role of Captain Stanhope. The play rapidly transferred to the Savoy Theatre, with Colin Clive replacing Olivier, and proved the surprise hit of the West End season. Whale, now famous, was invited to New York to stage the Broadway premiere and then to Hollywood to direct the film version.

His timing was excellent. The coming of sound to the movies had induced a major inferiority complex in Hollywood, and the studios were busily importing talent—actors, directors, drama coaches—from the legitimate theatre of Broadway and London's West End. As the "distinguished British man of the theatre" that he had now become, Whale was received on the

West Coast with honor and deference. While awaiting script approval on *Journey's End,* he gained his first experience of filmmaking as dialogue director for two movies: *The Love Doctor* (1929), and Howard Hughes' ambitious aerial spectacular, *Hell's Angels* (1930).

The film of *Journey's End* (1930), Whale's first directorial credit, has not worn well. Scripted by Sherriff, with Colin Clive recreating his stage role, it now appears static, stagey, and full of strangulated British acting verging on self-parody. But at the time it was warmly received by both public and critics. "It has been transferred to the screen with the greatest possible tact and discretion," wrote James Agate, who compared it favorably with the year's other major war picture, *All Quiet on the Western Front.* It seemed to Marcel Carné that the film had "preserved on the screen those valuable qualities of stark simplicity, sobriety, and concern for objective authenticity that earned the play such a high place in the literature of war." More recently, though, Tom Milne, surveying Whale's work in *Sight and Sound* (Summer 1973), rated *Journey's End* "competent rather than successful. . . . the action is oddly diminished. . . . It is unique among his films in allowing no play for his delight in extravagance."

Journey's End had been made as a coproduction between the small American company Tiffany and the British Gainsborough company. The film's commercial and critical success attracted the attention of Universal Studios, where Carl Laemmle, an enthusiastic nepotist, had just placed his twenty-one-year-old son Carl Jr. in charge of production and announced a policy of "fewer but better pictures." In furtherance of this aim, the studio signed up the prestigious Whale with a long-term contract; almost all of Whale's films, and all those for which he is best remembered, were to be made for Universal.

After directing two more stage plays— Sherriff's *Badger's Green* in London and Molnár's *One, Two, Three* in New York— Whale took on his first assignment for Universal. This was *Waterloo Bridge* (1931), a melodramatic tearjerker taken from a play by Robert E. Sherwood, in which a dancer sinks into prostitution after her soldier fiancé is reported missing in action. Well received at the time, the film was eclipsed by Mervyn LeRoy's equally lachrymose but glossier remake (1940). Whale's next film, though, despite endless remakes, has never been eclipsed.

Universal had just enjoyed a huge success with Tod Browning's *Dracula* (1931), starring Bela Lugosi in the title role. Looking for further subjects in this lucrative vein, the studio hit upon Mary Shelley's gothic novel, *Frankenstein, or the Modern Prometheus,* about a young scientist, Dr. Frankenstein, who raids gallows and graves for corpses from which to construct the creature that he will bring to terrifying life. There had already been two silent film versions and several stage adaptations. Now Robert Florey was assigned to direct, and prepared a treatment based on the 1930 stage version by Peggy Webling, as adapted by John L. Balderston. This was developed into a screenplay by Garrett Fort and Francis E. Faragoh, with additional dialogue by Florey. But Bela Lugosi, cast as the man-made monster, objected to his role, claiming that he would be unrecognizable under so much makeup. While the project hung fire, Whale— according to Florey—snatched it for himself. Florey was given *Murders in the Rue Morgue* (1932) as a consolation prize.

Whale's own explanation of his choice was that, "of thirty available stories, it was the strongest meat and gave me a chance to dabble in the macabre. I thought it would be amusing to try and make what everybody knows is a physical impossibility seem believable for sixty minutes. Also, it offered fine pictorial chances, had two grand characterizations, and had a subject matter that might go anywhere." Whatever his motivation, he produced in *Frankenstein* (1931) a picture generally agreed to be "the most famous of all horror films, and deservedly so" (John Baxter). Strongly influenced by the German cinema of the 1920s—the monster's appearance and behavior owe much to Paul Wegener's *Golem*—Whale's film diverged widely from Mary Shelley's novel but succeeded in creating an effective and potent myth of its own.

Much of the film's power derived from Whale's inspired casting of Boris Karloff as the monster. "Karloff's face," Whale said later, "has always fascinated me, and I made drawings of his head, adding sharp, bony ridges where I imagined the skull might have joined. His physique was weaker than I could wish, but that queer, penetrating personality of his, I felt, was more important than his shape, which could easily be altered." His superb central performance—aided immeasurably by Jack Pierce's makeup—lends the film dignity and emotional depth. "Never was Karloff more impressive," Carlos Clarens has written, "than in this, his first entrance, with Whale cutting breathlessly from medium shot to close shot to extreme close-up, so that the heavy-lidded, cadaverous face comes to fill the screen."

For the role of Dr. Frankenstein, Colin Clive's habitual style of acting through clenched teeth was for once fairly appropriate; the film's main weakness lay in some ludicrous mock-Tyrolean scenes of village jollification. These episodes apart, Whale's direction is smooth, assured, and notably restrained. "In the light of later films," Clarens observes, "there is little gruesomeness in *Frankenstein:* no dismembered hands or gouged eyes and absolutely no blood are to be seen. Its terror is cold, chilling the marrow but never arousing malaise." Even more exceptionally, the film achieved a touching, melancholy poetry, most notably in the famous screen where the escaped monster encounters a child too young to fear him, who teaches him the game of throwing flowers into the water to watch them float. For the first time, the monster smiles, with a grotesque beauty. When there are no more flowers, he reaches innocently for the child, assuming that she, too, will float. . . .

Whale also added some touches of his characteristically quirky humor, as when Frankenstein arrogantly "stages" the awakening of the monster, setting chairs for his audience. "Quite a good scene, isn't it?" he inquires. "One man, crazy; three very sane spectators." But in general the ironic extravagance that pervades Whale's later horror films is absent in *Frankenstein;* it remains the starkest of the series.

The film was an immediate and outstanding success, surpassing even that of *Dracula.* Made at a cost of $250,000, it eventually grossed more than $12 million. And it spawned an endless series of remakes and variations, from Whale's own *Bride of Frankenstein* to *Andy Warhol's Frankenstein* and Mel Brooks's *Young Frankenstein,* via such remote extrapolations as *El infierno del Frankenstein* (Mexico) and *Abbot and Costello Meet Frankenstein.*

Frankenstein effectively fixed the career of Karloff, of the studio—Universal was established as the world's prime source of horror films for the next two decades—and to a large extent of Whale himself. Although he was to make films in many other genres, it was for his four horror films that he became, and has remained, best known. His next film, though, was a romantic comedy, *The Impatient Maiden* (1932), starring Mae Clarke, who had featured in his two previous films. There are some pleasing comic episodes, but the overall impression is slight and unmemorable.

Whale was far more in his element with *The Old Dark House* (1932), adapted by Sherriff from the novel *Benighted* by J. B. Priestley, in which an assortment of travelers seek shelter from a storm in a remote and sinister Welsh mansion. A horror-comedy in the tradition of *The Cat and the Canary,* this was the first film in which Whale's taste for extravagant humor was given full play. It benefited from an outstanding cast: Charles Laughton, Melvyn Douglas, and Raymond Massey, all at the start of their film careers, as three of the benighted guests; Ernest Thesiger and Eva Moore, as two members of the highly eccentric Femm family who inhabit the house; and Karloff again, as a dumb, drunken, and lecherous butler.

"Despite the quality of the players, however," wrote John Pym in *Monthly Film Bulletin* (July 1979), "the honours are ultimately due to Whale himself; the film is shot through in almost every scene by a wholly individual sense of comic timing and bizarre juxtaposition." With conscious theatrical skill, Whale plays on his audience's emotions: building up tension, mockingly deflating it with an anticlimax, and then springing a new shock just as everything seems safe. "But if the methods are those of the stage," commented William K. Everson, "the execution is pure cinema, with a wonderfully mobile camera, Whale's typically effective use of short, sudden close-ups, and beautiful lighting." (The cameraman was Arthur Edeson, who had worked on all Whale's pictures since *Waterloo Bridge.*) John Baxter summarized the film as "a confidence trick worked with cynical humor by a master technician."

The Kiss Before the Mirror (1933), taken from a play by Ladislaus Fodor, was a psychological courtroom thriller, in which a lawyer comes to identify with the wife-murderer whom he is defending. Tom Milne thought it "one of Whale's most stylish films," adding that the direction "is so hypnotic that one completely forgets the basic implausibility of the situation."

The title role of *The Invisible Man* (1933) was originally intended for Boris Karloff. However, Universal—short of cash as usual—had refused him a raise that was due in his contract, and he had quit the studio until better terms were forthcoming. The role went to Claude Rains, making his screen debut with what was virtually a radio performance—not until the last few seconds of the film, when he is dying, does his body appear on screen. Sherriff's script was remarkably faithful to the spirit of H. G. Wells' novel, about a man who discovers the secret of invisibility but then succumbs to megalomania.

Whale made the most of the story's possibilities for sardonic black comedy. Carlos Clarens has remarked that "the private lives of his monsters, the prosaic side of his fiends plainly fascinate Whale"—as instance the scene in which the Invisible Man lists the drawbacks of invisibility: he suffers from the cold, since he can't wear clothes; he has to hide after eating, as the food remains visible until digested; he must avoid rain, since it shows up his silhouette. Such details also serve to make the character sympathetic, for all his fascistic ranting—especially in contrast with the caricatured English villagers, whom the Man deliberately terrorizes. (In one delectable sequence, an empty pair of pants rollicks down the village street, singing "Here We Go Gathering Nuts in May.")

The film's special effects, devised by John P. Fulton, are superbly sustained; one of the most effective moments is the Invisible Man's first "appearance." Writing in *Sight and Sound* (Autumn 1957), Roy Edwards described it thus: "A bandaged head wearing dark glasses appears; gloved hands come up and unwind the first layer of bandages; those underneath fit the face and look like a soft, bleached skull. These, in turn, are unwound from the globe of an invisible head. . . . Nothingness rebandages itself, replaces the dark glasses, puts on a silk dressing-gown and hieratically stalks away."

Wells himself was delighted with the film, which was another critical and popular success, helping to restore Universal's perennially shaky finances. Whale now moved into Lubitsch territory with *By Candlelight* (1933), an elegantly theatrical charade on the old theme of masters and servants changing places. "The whole film," wrote Tom Milne, "fairly glitters with wit." A Galsworthy novel provided the plot for *One More River* (1934), in which a woman married to a brutal husband achieves a divorce by feigning adultery. Effectively scripted by Sherriff, the film, commented Clive Denton, "draws from Whale a more direct and concerned response to everyday human feelings than is usual in his work." Displaying a nice appreciation of the constraints and conventions of polite British society, Whale skillfully conveys the emotional turmoil seething beneath a well-bred surface.

Whale was initially reluctant to provide a sequel to *Frankenstein* but finally let himself be persuaded by Universal, who were anxious to make the most of Karloff, now back on the payroll. The result is considered by most critics Whale's finest and most stylish film. In *The Bride of Frankenstein* (1935), his sardonic humor and delight in extravagance are ideally blended with his mastery of the visually macabre. With virtuoso confidence, he skillfully switches mood from one moment to the next, setting the ambiguous tone in a tongue-in-cheek prologue in which Elsa Lanchester, as Mary Shelley, outlines the Frankenstein story to Shelley and Byron. Much of the film's humor centers on Ernest Thesiger's outrageously idiosyncratic performance as Dr. Pretorius, imperturbably of-

fering the monster a cigar as it lurches menacingly out of the shadows. Virtually all the human participants, in fact, are caricatured; only the monster, as Roy Edwards pointed out, "receives none of the director's gibes. . . . In comparison with his dotty human entourage he remains curiously noble, sad and pathetic."

The climax of the film, in which Elsa Lanchester reappears, fright-wigged and hissing, as the monster's putative bride, provides an irresistible tour de force. "The momentary invitation to laugh," wrote John Baxter, "is stifled by [Lanchester's] magnificent performance as the awakening creature, . . . the white streak in her bush of hair providing a visual exclamation mark to our surprise. Whale the satirist here succumbed to Whale the fantasist, and the result is a striking moment of the cinema." (There may have been something more than purely dramatic inspiration in Whale's doubling of the roles of Mary Shelley and the bride; Ellen Moers, in an article in the *New York Review of Books* (March 21, 1974), describes the deaths and tragedies that littered Mary Shelley's path through life and suggests that "the monstrous agent of destruction" she created embodied her own vision of herself.)

The Bride of Frankenstein broke box-office records, and Whale attained the height of his prestige as the studio's star director—"the Ace of Universal," as Robert Florey called him, with perhaps a hint of malice. His persona in Hollywood so perfectly matched the accepted American image of the English gentleman— impeccably dressed, fastidious, class-conscious, and homosexual—as to arouse the suspicion that it was, to some extent, an ironically cultivated role. Whale's own attitude to Hollywood, and his eminence within it, was one of amused fascination: "That they should pay such fabulous salaries is beyond ordinary reasoning. Who's worth it? But why not take it? And the architecture! And the furnishings! I can have modernistic designs one day—and an antiquated home overnight! All the world's made of plaster of paris!"

Much the same mood, of whimsical make-believe amid lavish surroundings, pervades *Remember Last Night?* (1935), a screwball murder mystery in which a number of party guests awake from their alcoholic stupor to find that the host has somehow been shot during the previous night's revels. With an excellent cast headed by Constance Cummings and Robert Young (whose playing recalls that of Myrna Loy and William Powell in *The Thin Man*), the film keeps up "a non-stop cascade of sparkling visual and verbal gags," wrote Tom Milne, "until this brilliant divertissement eventually takes off into pure surrealism."

Whale was now entrusted by Universal with one of their most treasured properties, the Jerome Kern–Oscar Hammerstein musical *Show Boat,* which they had already filmed in a part-talkie version in 1929. Now they planned a major remake, with Paul Robeson and Helen Morgan repeating their Broadway roles. On his own admission, Whale was somewhat out of his depth with *Show Boat* (1936), especially its more sentimental episodes, and the film is distinctly uneven, although the majority of critics still rate it above MGM's Technicolor version of 1951. (The 1929 version seems not to have survived.) Irene Dunne, as the heroine, was weak; Allan Jones, as the hero, was execrable; and the frequent passages of cornball humor evidently appealed little to Whale's sophisticated tastes. But Robeson's singing was magnificent as ever, and whenever Helen Morgan was on screen the movie visibly came to life. "To see and hear her," wrote Clive Denton rhapsodically, "perched on the piano like a sunshot cloud, pouring out the redeemed emotions of the song 'Bill' is a rare privilege, which the director sensibly left uncluttered in its purity."

Despite its weaknesses, *Show Boat* achieved all the success Universal had hoped for. Unfortunately, the studio's other major production of 1936, James Cruze's *Sutter's Gold,* was a disaster. Universal's long-running financial crisis came to a head; Carl Laemmle retired from the company he had founded in 1912, and Carl Jr. was ousted. The new management announced that close control would henceforth be enforced over the studio's output; directors could make no changes whatsoever to approved scripts while shooting.

Whale seems to have got on well with both Laemmles—he and Carl Jr. even announced that they planned to set up an independent company together, although nothing came of it—and evidently found the new studio bosses far less sympathetic. They in turn rated Whale considerably lower than had their predecessors—especially after his next film, the first flop of his career. *The Road Back* (1937), taken from E. M. Remarque's sequel to *All Quiet on the Western Front,* and shot partly on the same sets as the earlier movie, dealt with the problems of soldiers returning home to the social upheavals of postwar Germany. The film is said to have been extensively reshot by other hands after Whale had completed it, possibly as a result of protests by the German consul in Los Angeles. It was given only a limited release.

After this, Whale's assignments from Universal became conspicuously less attractive, and the best of his later films were made when he was on loan to other studios. The first of these was *The Great Garrick* (1937), made for Warners, an enjoyable theatrical conceit centering around the legend of a visit to Paris by the great actor-manager, and a plot by the company of the Comédie Française to teach the upstart Englishman a lesson. Stylishly staged and acted, the film allowed Whale to indulge in some witty juggling with the paradoxes of truth and illusion. Tom Milne found it "a stunningly elegant exercise in illusionism, featuring some of . . . [Whale's] most entrancing grotesques."

Back at Universal, *Sinners in Paradise* (1938) recycled the tired old formula whereby a bunch of ill-assorted characters are stranded together on a desert island; and *Wives Under Suspicion* (1938) was a remake, with the setting changed from Austria to America, of *A Kiss Before the Mirror.* Whale evidently found little inspiration in either subject and escaped to MGM to make *Port of Seven Seas* (1938), a valiant if ill-advised attempt to cram Marcel Pagnol's Marseilles trilogy (*Marius, Fanny,* and *César*) into a single movie, with an American cast. Preston Sturges made a creditable job of the script, but the local color looked (not surprisingly) painfully synthetic, and Wallace Beery proved a bizarrely inadequate substitute for Raimu. More successful was *The Man in the Iron Mask* (1939), made for United Artists, which Tom Milne considered "the most stylish, spirited and elegantly phrased of all the versions of the Dumas tale. . . . Hollywood swashbuckling at its best." One moment of authentic Whale horror occurs when the wicked twin, trapped in the mask he had designed for his brother, realizes that his hair and beard will grow inexorably—"I can *feel* them growing—they'll strangle me!"

Whale's last film for Universal was *Green Hell* (1940), a jungle melodrama saddled with a script so atrocious as to be almost literally unspeakable. His final feature was made for Columbia: *They Dare Not Love* (1941), an anti-Nazi romantic drama. The opening sequence was vividly atmospheric—an evocative montage depicting the Nazi takeover of Austria—but thereafter the film deteriorated into cardboard heroics, with George Brent improbably cast as the Austrian prince behind whom his people will rally. Whale quit before shooting was finished—the picture was completed by Charles Vidor—and apart from one abortive work in the late 1940s, his cinematic career was over.

Various reasons have been adduced for Whale's retirement from filmmaking. It has been suggested that he wanted to return to the theatre; and there have been dark hints of alcoholism or of some scandal connected with his homosexuality. But the most likely explanation would seem to be that he was no longer getting the assignments he merited and felt disinclined to continue working on third-rate material—especially since, having saved prudently during his years of success, he had no financial need to work.

"The limitation in James Whale's work," Clive Denton has written, "is simply that he is more style than substance, more head than heart. . . . He seemed able to identify more with the outlandish than with the everyday. . . . He could create genuine pathos and yearning when dealing with a man-made monster, whereas he was not invariably so successful with characters born of women." Denton instances a typically elegant camera movement in *The Great Garrick,* adding: "The result is *almost* exquisite but also a trifle precious. In such a context, an unabashedly romantic director of the first rank, a Borzage or an Ophuls, would have sprayed away the slight whiff of canvas and greasepaint, by absolute identification with the lovers, which Whale cannot quite attain."

Technically, though, Whale stands comparison with the most accomplished directors. Writing in *Film Comment* (Spring 1971), Paul Jensen commends Whale's "complicated but smooth editing technique" and sums up his style as "refined, graceful, well-bred; his directorial technique refuses to draw attention to itself, yet is extremely confident and competent. All the mechanical devices of cinema are used—cutting, moving camera, composition—yet with a civilized discretion and an emphasis on subtle character revelation." Even in his best films, though, the level of involvement may fluctuate alarmingly; David Thomson, discussing "the absorbing tension between his wish to keep tongue in cheek and the ability to see unexpected depths in hokum," adds: "It is all too clear that some sequences engrossed him, while on others he didn't give a damn." Tom Milne sums up the complex flavor of Whale's work as "tenderness, mockery, the *frisson* of terror, the touch of alienation: the mixture makes for a peculiarly sophisticated formula, and in his best work Whale is astonishingly contemporary."

After his retirement from the cinema, Whale lived on in Hollywood in relative seclusion. Painting became his main interest, although he returned occasionally to the theatre, directing *Hand in Glove* at the Pasadena Playhouse in 1944 and, in 1951, *Pagan in the Parlor,* which also opened in Pasadena, before transferring to the Royal Theatre, Bath; this was Whale's last visit to England. And he directed one final film, in 1949—a forty-minute version of Saroyan's one-act play *Hello Out There,* produced by Huntington Hartford and intended as part of a portmanteau picture, *Face to Face.* The film was largely a two-character piece for Harry Morgan and Hartford's then wife, Marjorie Steele, and took place on a single, expressionist prison set, designed by Whale himself. It was "premiered" before a private audience that included Saroyan, Jean Renoir, John Huston, and Charles Chaplin, all of whom were apparently favorably impressed. Neither Hartford nor Miss Steele liked her performance, however, and the film was never released, receiving its first public showing only some twenty years later.

In 1957, Whale began designing sets for a science fiction opera, based on stories by Max Beerbohm and Ray Bradbury, which Charles Laughton was planning to stage in New York. On the morning of May 29 Whale was found drowned in his own swimming pool. It now seems almost certain that he had committed suicide, as was rumored at the time, but the official verdict was accidental death, "in mysterious circumstances."

—*P.K.*

FILMS: Journey's End, 1930; Waterloo Bridge, 1931; Frankenstein, 1931; The Impatient Maiden, 1932; The Old Dark House, 1932; The Kiss Before the Mirror, 1933; The Invisible Man, 1933; By Candlelight, 1933; One More River, 1934; The Bride of Frankenstein, 1935; Remember Last Night?, 1935; Show Boat, 1936; The Road Back, 1937; The Great Garrick, 1937; Sinners in Paradise, 1938; Wives Under Suspicion, 1938; Port of Seven Seas, 1938; The Man in the Iron Mask, 1939; Green Hell, 1940; They Dare Not Love, 1941; Hello Out There, 1949.

ABOUT: Baxter, J. Hollywood in the Thirties, 1968; Clarens, C. Horror Movies, an Illustrated Survey, 1968; Curtis, J. James Whale, 1983; Denton, C. James Whale: Ace Director, 1979; Laclos, M. Le Fantastique au Cinéma, 1958; Prawer, S. S. Caligari's Children: The Film as Tale of Terror, 1980; Roud, R. (ed.) Cinema: A Critical Dictionary, 1980; Thomson, D. A Biographical Dictionary of the Cinema, 1980; Whitemore, D. and Cecchettini, P. (eds.) Passport to Hollywood, 1976. *Periodicals*—Bizarre 24–25, 1962; L'Écran Fantastique 10 1979; Film Comment Spring 1971; Films in Review May 1962; Monthly Film Bulletin July 1967; Premiere October 1980; Sight and Sound Autumn 1957, Summer 1973.

*WIENE, ROBERT (1881–July 17, 1938), German director, scenarist, actor, and producer, was born in Sasku, Saxony, the son of a well-known Dresden actor. He studied theatre history at the University of Vienna. In 1914 Wiene went to work as a scriptwriter for Oskar Messter, an

°vē´ nə

ROBERT WIENE

inventor who had established a film production company using equipment he had developed himself. The same year Wiene codirected his first film, *Arme Eva*. Half a dozen routine Messter movies followed during the war, several of them starring the blonde and blue-eyed actress Henny Porten, the darling of the German silent cinema. *Das Cabinett des Dr. Caligari* (*The Cabinet of Dr. Caligari*), the very different film on which Wiene's reputation rests, was made in 1919 and released in 1920.

Caligari's original script was written by two young friends: Carl Mayer, who became one of the greatest of all film scenarists, and the Czech Hans Janowitz. Both drew on their own experiences in devising a story which they set in the fictitious North German town of Holstenwall. A fair comes to town and two young men, Francis and Alan, visit a sideshow where the weird Dr. Caligari presents the somnambulist Cesare, who under hypnosis foretells Alan's imminent death. Alan is murdered that night, and Francis begins to investigate this and other mysterious killings.

Spying on Caligari's wagon, Francis believes he sees Cesare asleep in his coffinlike bed. The audience, however, is shown something different—Cesare in the bedroom of Francis' fiancée Jane, about to murder the sleeping girl. Unable to kill her, the somnambulist carries his screaming victim over the rooftops until he collapses and dies. Meanwhile, Francis and the police have discovered that the "sleeping" Cesare in the wagon is actually a dummy, but Dr. Caligari has vanished. Francis follows his trail to a lunatic asylum and finds out that Caligari is in fact the

director of the place. Searching his office by night, the hero learns that the doctor has modeled himself on an eighteenth-century hypnotist who had used a somnambulist as his tool in a notorious series of murders. Confronted with Cesare's corpse, Caligari descends into raving madness.

According to Siegfried Kracauer, Mayer and Janowitz had intended their script as a metaphoric indictment of the German wartime government and its insane lust for power. The script was accepted by Erich Pommer, the shrewd chief executive of Decla-Bioscop, and at first assigned to Fritz Lang. Finding that the latter had other commitments, Pommer handed it to Robert Wiene, who at Lang's suggestion added an additional twist to the plot—a framing story revealing that Francis is himself an inmate of the asylum, and that the events he describes are the products of his *own* insane delusions. In this version, the asylum director is perfectly rational and well-intentioned. When he has heard Francis' story, he understands the nature of his illness and is able to promise a cure. On this optimistic note, the film ends. Thus, Kracauer says, Mayer and Janowitz's "subversive" script was turned into one that glorified authority and accused its enemies of madness.

If Wiene is guilty of "perverting" the story of *Caligari* into conformism, as Kracauer claims, he must be credited with at least some responsibility for its totally revolutionary form. Janowitz had suggested that the painter Alfred Kubin might design the sets, but Wiene turned instead to three expressionist artists, Hermann Warm, Walter Röhrig, and Walter Reimann. All were members of the Berlin *Sturm* group, which sought to promote expressionism in all the arts, Wiene himself was apparently an enthusiastic supporter of this movement. Although some aspects of expressionism had emerged early in the century, and it had its roots in the German romantic tradition, it only became a major force in literature, the visual arts, and the theatre after World War I. A revolt against naturalism, encouraged by the trauma of the war and Freud's delvings into the subconscious, it sought to probe beneath surface appearances to reveal man's deepest feelings and urges. In the theatre, innovators like Max Reinhardt experimented with deliberately unrealistic lighting and sets, stylized dialogue and stage movements, and every kind of visual distortion that could be used to symbolize the hidden fears and desires of the characters.

It was these theatrical applications of expressionism that Wiene and his designers imported into the cinema in *Caligari*. Their most radical innovation was the use of obviously unreal sets, painted on canvas flats as in the theatre (and welcomed by Pommer on economic grounds). The town of Holstenwall itself was represented in this way as a place of dark, twisting streets, crowded with the "inclined cubes" of dilapidated houses—a semi-abstract dream town created out of sharp-pointed forms calculated to induce "states of anxiety and terror." Shadows painted where no shadows should logically fall added to the sense of unreality and disorientation. Werner Krauss' Caligari and Conrad Veidt's Cesare wore stylized costumes and makeup, and their jerky, zigzag movements "seemed actually to be created by a draftsman's imagination." Even the intertitles were decorated with strange geometry. In strictly cinematic terms the movie is far less inventive. It does use flashbacks, close-ups, pans, and cross-cutting, and transitions are generally effected by the iris-out and the iris-in, but much of the time the camera simply records what is happening in front of it, as in a filmed play.

Released in February 1920, Caligari was not particularly successful at the box office but nevertheless had the effect of a revelation. C. A. Lejeune wrote that "everything about Caligari was pointed to the one purpose, the expression of a world seen through the eyes of a madman; every line, every painted shape, every block of light and shade, every quickening or retarding of pace, was concentrated on the extraction from concrete objects of the sense of the lunatic's own crazy emotion. For the first time in the history of the cinema the full battery of an artistic movement was engaged in the achievement of a film's purpose, all the experience of contemporary painting and literature and theatre-craft put at the director's disposal."

However, Lejeune went on, it was wrong to speak of Caligari "as though it influenced the whole trend of modern production. . . . it founded no school; it effected no revolution in technique," though "filmmaking, after the audacity of Caligari, could never be quite the same smug, comfortable thing again. There were questions to be asked and answered, the place of the camera to be reconsidered, the value of painting to be assessed, the dramatic use of lighting to be determined. . . . and the effect of Caligari was to set production moving rapidly in Europe and America . . . towards a cinema of some individuality, a certain measure of fantasy and design." Kracauer, similarly, said that "apart from giving rise to stray imitations and serving as a yardstick for artistic endeavors, this 'most widely discussed film of the time' never seriously influenced the course of the American or French cinema. It stood out lonely, like a monolith."

In Germany itself, according to Henri Langlois, Caligari had a far greater effect than all this suggests. It rendered obsolete "the productions and the style of the war and pre-war years. . . . It freed the latent powers which the orthodox filmmakers had held in check. It cut the German cinema free from its past, linking its destiny to that of the theatre and the avant-garde arts, thus affirming the audacities of recruits from the world of arts, letters and the theatre. . . . The German cinema after Caligari is thus entirely dominated by its constant intercourse and dialogue with the theatre. It is this that characterises the German cinema and was confused at the time with expressionism."

It may be true that Caligari was the only completely expressionist film apart from a few "stray imitations" and that "it founded no school," but it is hard to agree that "it effected no revolution in technique" or that it "never seriously influenced the course of the American or French cinema." Its chiaroscuro use of lighting was widely emulated in Germany and abroad and was imported by émigré German directors into the Hollywood film noir of the 1940s. The (now discredited) preference for filming in the controlled environment of the studio has also been traced to Caligari.

Kracauer, the most influential critic of the period, admired Caligari but not Wiene, and later critics have followed him in maintaining that the film was not Wiene's personal achievement—that he was simply fortunate in his writers, designers, and actors. In evidence, they point to the fact that Wiene never made another film of comparable merit or importance. This is true, but many artists create only a single masterpiece, and the theme of Caligari was one of peculiar significance to Wiene, whose own father became insane late in life. The film has been recognized as the cinema's first true work of art—"the first significant attempt at the expression of a creative mind in the medium of cinematography." Even Kracauer concedes that Caligari represented a pioneering attempt "to coordinate settings, players, lighting and action"—and that Germany's most admirable contribution to the development of world cinema was precisely "the talent with which, from the time of Caligari, German film directors marshaled the whole visual sphere." Someone was responsible for the coordinating and the marshaling, and there is no evidence that the "creative mind" expressed in the film was anyone but Wiene's.

Wiene made several more films in the expressionist manner, including Genuine (1920). Scripted by Carl Mayer, it is a fantasy about an oriental princess bought in a slave market by a strange old man who confines her in a glass cage like an exotic pet bird. From this crystal prison, Genuine casts her spell over a young barber and, after he has cut her owner's throat for her, goes on to revenge herself on as many members of the unfair sex as come within range. The movie was a failure. According to Lotte Eisner, "the set painted by the otherwise interesting artist Cesar [or Césare] Klein was muddled and overloaded; and the naturalistic actors just vanished into it. The body-wriggling of Fern Andra—a pretty woman but a mediocre actress—would be more appropriate on the stage of a music-hall. Apart from the bald little man with his pale black-ribbed gloves like Caligari's and his old-fashioned clothes emphasizing his satanic aspect, the actors have nothing of the almost Hoffmannesque stylization which Werner Krauss had been able to achieve in Caligari."

Half a dozen more commercial movies followed, including a version of the Salome story, and then Wiene attempted another expressionist film in Raskolnikow (1923), adapted from Dostoevsky's Crime and Punishment. This time he had the benefit of some brilliant three-dimensional sets designed by the architect Andrei Andreiev, strongly reminiscent of Caligari and foreshadowing the same designer's sets for Pabst's Die Dreigroschenoper, including "sharp, splinter-like painted shadows, the spiky, leaning buildings, the impossibly grandiose yet rickety staircases." Wiene drew his cast for this production from Stanislavski's Moscow Art Theatre, with results that have divided the critics.

It seemed to Lotte Eisner that the movie contained "certain shots in which sets and characters really seem to stem from Dostoevsky's universe and act upon each other through a sort of reciprocal hallucination." Karel Reisz, however, found relatively little to admire. He thought that the bizarre effect created by the sets "is not in any way reinforced by the lighting, costume or make-up. The lighting is unimaginative and flat, and the dresses and make-up 'realistic' in the conventional, theatrical manner. . . . Nor is the quality of the playing . . . of a kind that fits easily into the expressionist backgrounds," being "excellent but conventionally theatrical." Reisz thought the film "an uneasy mixture of a number of incompatible elements . . . most successful in the passages where the expressionist technique is employed at its most unadulterated" and especially in "the marvellous image of the Coroner surrounded by a huge spider's web and, most strikingly, the sequences of Raskolnikov's dream, where the distortions produce a few moments of genuine, macabre terror."

INRI, released the same year, is a life of Christ enclosed within a framing story. A man who has assassinated a politician to free the people from oppression meditates on the Passion and sees the error of his ways—an anti-revolutionary message similar in spirit to that of the framing story in Caligari. The picture's impressive cast included Werner Krauss as Pontius Pilate, Asta Nielsen as Mary Magdalen, and Henny Porten as the Virgin Mary, Christ himself being portrayed by the young actor who had played Raskolnikov, Grigori Khmara.

The best known of Wiene's later films was Orlacs Hände (The Hands of Orlac, 1924). Adapted by Ludwig Nerz from the novel by Maurice Renard, it is about a concert pianist who is given new hands after a railroad accident—and comes to believe that these members were formerly the property of a murderer, and have an evil life of their own. Working this time with conventional sets, Wiene nevertheless took the film as close to expressionism as he could, using shadowy, twisting streets, a strange house with long corridors thronged with bizarre characters, a dimly lit inn, and a satanic magician figure. The picture was more successful with the public than with the critics, who found its technique unconvincing and reserved their praise for Conrad Veidt's extraordinary performance in the lead: Eisner describes him "dancing a kind of expressionist ballet, bending and twisting extravagantly, simultaneously drawn and repelled by the murderous dagger held by hands which do not seem to belong to him."

Wiene directed over a dozen more films between 1925 and 1933, but they were mostly routine entertainments, and none of them attracted much attention apart from a "light and delicate" version of Der Rosenkavalier (1926). In 1933 or 1934 Wiene fled from the Nazis to France, but he found it difficult to secure assignments there. His plans for a sound version of Caligari, with sets by Jean Cocteau, never materialized. When he died in 1938 he was working on a drama called Ultimatum starring Erich von Stroheim; the film was completed by Robert Siodmak. Wiene's brother was also a film director.

FILMS: (with A. Berger) Arme Eva, 1914; Die Konservenbraut, 1915; Die Liebesbrief der Königin, 1916; Der Mann im Spiegel, 1916; Die Räuberbraut, 1916; Das wandernde Licht, 1916; Ein gefährliches Spiel, 1919; Das Cabinett (or Kabinett) des Dr. Caligari (The Cabinet of Dr. Caligari), 1920; Die drei Tänze der Mary Wilford, 1920; Genuine, 1920; Die Nacht der Königin Isabeau, 1920; Die Rache einer Frau, 1920; Höllische Nacht, 1921; (with Georg Kroll) Das Spiel mit dem Feuer, 1921; Salome, 1922; Tragikomödie, 1922; Raskolnikow (Raskolnikov/Crime and Punishment), 1923; INRI (Crown of Thorns), 1923; Der Puppenmacher von Kiang-Ning, 1923; Orlacs Hände (The Hands of Orlac), 1925; Pension Groonen, 1925; Der Gardeoffizier (The Guardsman), 1926; Die Königin von Moulin-Rouge, 1926; Der Rosenkavalier, 1926; Die berühmte Frau (The Dancer of Barcelona), 1927; Die Geliebte, 1927; Die Frau auf der Folter (A Scandal in Paris), 1928; Die grosse Abenteurerin, 1928; Leontines Ehemänner, 1928; Unfug der Liebe, 1928; Der Andere, 1930; Panik in Chicago, 1931; Der Liebesexpress/Aus Tag Glück, 1931; Polizeiakte 909, 1934; Ein Nacht in Venedig, 1934; Ultimatum, 1938 (completed by Robert Siodmak).

ABOUT: Arnoux, A. Du muet en parlant, 1946; Eisner, L. The Haunted Screen, 1969; Kracauer, S. From Caligari to Hitler, 1947; Kurtz, R. Expressionismus und Film, 1926; Lejeune, C. A. Cinema, 1931; Manvell, R. and Fraenkel, H. The German Cinema, 1971; Oxford Companion to Film, 1976; Roud, R. (ed.) Cinema: A Critical Dictionary, 1980. *Periodicals*—Avant-Scène du Cinéma July–September 1971; World Film News August 1938.

BILLY WILDER

WILDER, "BILLY" (SAMUEL) (June 22, 1906–), was born in Vienna, Austria, the younger of the two sons of Max Wilder, a hotelier and restaurateur, and the former Eugenie Dittler. Billy Wilder was sent to the Vienna *realgymnasium* and the University of Vienna, which he left after less than a year to work as a copy boy and then as a reporter for *Die Stunde*. In those years after the First World War, young writers working in the ruins of the Austro-Hungarian Empire gravitated naturally to the cultural ferment of Berlin, and Wilder made his way there at the age of twenty. For a time he worked as a crime reporter on *Nachtausgabe* (and/or as a film and drama critic; accounts vary). Many colorful stories are told (mostly by Wilder himself) about this part of his life: it is said that he fell in love with a dancer, neglected his work, lost his job, and became a dancing partner for "lonely ladies," and a gigolo. He spent his spare time on the fringes of Berlin café society, met some young filmmakers, and tried his hand as a scenarist.

The first picture made from a Wilder script was *Menschen am Sonntag* (*People on Sunday*, 1929), directed by another young hopeful, Robert Siodmak. "It was about young people having a good time in Berlin and it was talked about a lot," Wilder says. "It represented a good way to make pictures: no unions, no bureaucracy, no studio, shot silent on cheap stock: we just 'did it.' As a result of its success, we all got jobs at UFA, the huge German studios. . . . I'd write two, three, four pictures a month. I accumulated about a hundred silent picture assignments, and then, in 1929, when sound came in, I did scores

more." They included Gerhard Lamprecht's version of *Emil and the Detectives* and vehicles for many of the German stars of the period.

Wilder had his eye on Hollywood but left Germany faster than he had intended when Hitler came to power in 1933: "It seemed the wise thing for a Jew to do." Stopping over for a time in Paris, Wilder (in collaboration with Alexander Esway) directed his first film, *Mauvaise Graine* (*Bad Blood*, 1933). A fast-paced movie about young auto thieves, it was made on a shoestring and featured Danielle Darrieux, then seventeen. Soon after, Wilder sold a story to Columbia and this paid his way, via Mexico, to California. Wilder arrived in Hollywood speaking almost no English and shared a room and "a can of soup a day" with Peter Lorre.

After two hard years, Wilder became a writer for Paramount. He had no great success, however, until in 1936 the producer Arthur Hornblow asked him to collaborate with Charles Brackett on a script, *Bluebeard's Eighth Wife*, for Ernst Lubitsch. Brackett was a novelist and a *New Yorker* drama critic, an urbane man from an old New England family. In spite of the radical differences between the two men, they formed a highly effective writing team, with Brackett selecting and polishing the most promising of Wilder's "prodigious stream of ideas." Among the excellent entertainments they wrote for Paramount directors in the late 1930s and early 1940s were *Midnight* and *Hold Back the Dawn* for Mitchell Leisen, *Ball of Fire* for Howard Hawks, and Lubitsch's *Ninotchka*.

Wilder was infuriated by directorial misinterpretations of his scripts and frequently bounced onto the set to say so. Eventually Paramount gave him a chance to show how it should be done. His first American film as director was *The Major and the Minor* (1942), about a disenchanted career girl stranded in New York who masquerades as a twelve-year-old because she lacks the adult train fare back to Iowa. Ginger Rogers (then thirty) played the heroine, Ray Milland, the military-school officer she falls in love with, and the result was universally enjoyed as "an enchanting film farce." Wilder followed this very successful debut with *Five Graves to Cairo* (1943), a fairly ludicrous war thriller, which cast Erich von Stroheim as Field Marshal Rommel. Wilder, who was awed by the inventiveness of Stroheim's performance, says "he influenced me greatly as a director: I always think of my style as a curious cross between Lubitsch and Stroheim."

Raymond Chandler, not Brackett, was Wilder's coauthor on *Double Indemnity* (1944), based on the novella by James M. Cain. This brilliant *film noir* starred Barbara Stanwyck and Fred MacMurray as lovers who plan the "accidental" death of Stanwyck's husband, and Edward G. Robinson as the cold-blooded insurance agent who investigates the claim. *Double Indemnity* (which the Hays Office condemned as "a blueprint for murder") is a film of great originality, not least in Wilder's decision to begin the film with MacMurray's Dictaphone confession. Wilder has "always felt that surprise is not as effective as suspense. By identifying the criminals right off the bat—and identifying ourselves with them—we can concentrate on what follows—their efforts to escape, the net closing, closing." Shooting the film on location in Los Angeles, Wilder, and his cameraman John F. Seitz worked for seedy realism rather than Hollywood chic—"I'd go in and kind of dirty up the sets a little bit and make them look worn. I'd take the white out of everything. . . . The whole film was deliberately underplayed, done very quietly; if you have something that's full of violence and drama you can afford to take it easy." Howard Barnes in his review called *Double Indemnity* a thriller that more than once reached "the level of high tragedy," and the film is now widely regarded as a classic of the genre. Neil Sinyard suggests that it is also an indictment of American materialism and a study of the conflict between reason and passion, order and anarchy.

The Lost Weekend (1945) captured four Oscars: one for best picture, one for Ray Milland as best actor, two for Wilder as best director and as coadaptor with Brackett of Charles Jackson's novel. Set (and partly filmed) in New York, it observes an alcoholic writer as he struggles against his craving; then succumbs; then lies, cheats, and steals to buy drink. As in *Double Indemnity,* the audience is forced to share the growing desperation of an individual in a state of moral collapse. We accompany Don Birman through a picaresque nightmare that takes in smart cocktail lounges, cheap bars, the squalor of Third Avenue, and the horrors of Bellevue's alcoholic ward; when he descends into delirium tremens, we go with him. The film has touches of mordant humor and an unconvincing upbeat ending but is otherwise quite uncompromising; it was nevertheless a commercial as well as a critical success, confounding the studio bosses and movie columnists who had prophesied disaster.

The Emperor Waltz (1948) took Wilder from Third Avenue to fin de siècle Vienna, where an American phonograph salesman (Bing Crosby) falls in love with an Austrian countess (Joan Fontaine). This mildly amusing romance was followed by a more acerbic study of the clash between American and European values in *A Foreign Affair* (1948), which has Congresswoman Jean Arthur visiting postwar Berlin to investigate the moral turpitude of occupying GIs. Like many subsequent Wilder films, this one derives excellent comedy from the spectacle of human depravity. Wilder, whose mother, grandmother, and stepfather had all been murdered by the Nazis, had first revisited Berlin in 1945 during a brief tour of duty as a colonel in charge of the film section of the United States Army Psychological Warfare Division. *A Foreign Affair,* in its rigorous eschewal of national stereotypes and its cheerful insistence on the universality of human weakness, is in its ribald way an act of faith. It drew from Marlene Dietrich a wonderfully ironic, coolly defiant performance as a nightclub singer.

A cruel and haunting picture, *Sunset Boulevard* (1950) was a controversial, worldwide success, regarded by many as the best film ever made about Hollywood and by others as a treacherous calumny. The film opens with the body of a young man floating in a Hollywood swimming pool. The corpse (William Holden) begins to explain how he got there. In life, Joe was an unsuccessful screenwriter. In flashbacks we see how he allows himself to be taken on as gigolo by Norma Desmond (Gloria Swanson), once the queen of the silent screen. Joe joins a bizarre household in which the butler (Erich von Stroheim) is Swanson's former husband-director, and her bridge companions are all superannuated stars (Buster Keaton, Anna Q. Nilsson, H. B. Warner). Screening her old movies, the raddled Swanson cries: "They don't make faces like that anymore." She misinterprets a phone call from Cecil B. DeMille and prepares herself for her long-awaited comeback. There follows the inevitable confrontation between illusion and reality; Swanson shoots her young lover and gives way to madness. In the end, seductive in the role of Salome, she descends her staircase into a barrage of newsreel cameras.

Louis B. Mayer wanted Wilder horsewhipped, but it seemed to James Agee that the film allowed Norma Desmond and her contemporaries a barbarous intensity that had a "kind of grandeur" compared to the "small, smart, safe-playing" Hollywood of the 1940s.

Sunset Boulevard, which brought Wilder and Brackett Oscars for best story and best screenplay, was the last film they wrote together—"sometimes match and striking surface wear out," Wilder explained. His next picture was one of the blackest ever to come out of a commercial studio, *Ace in the Hole* (1951), also known as *The Big Carnival*. An Albuquerque newsman down on his luck (Kirk Douglas) finds a man trapped in a mine cave-in and creates a journalistic scoop by postponing a rescue for six days. Vast crowds arrive to enjoy the tragedy, a carnival moves in to exploit the crowds, and in the end the man dies. The film was much admired in Europe, but in the United States it was a disaster, destroying at a stroke Wilder's reputation as an infallible audience-pleaser who could make gold out of trash. *Ace in the Hole* was seen as an insult to the American people in general, and to the Fourth Estate in particular. Its failure was regarded as clear evidence that Wilder had all along owed his success to Charles Brackett. (Since then the picture has been discussed with increasing admiration by critics who praise it as "a harsh allegory of the modern artist" and compare it, in its passion, anger, and courage, to Stroheim's *Greed*.)

Wilder's next three films were all highly profitable adaptations of stage plays—the exuberant prison-camp comedy *Stalag 17* (1953), the romantic satire *Sabrina* (1954; Wilder's last film for Paramount), and *The Seven Year Itch* (1955), in which the dreamy humor is sometimes overwhelmed by the prodigious presence of Marilyn Monroe. *The Spirit of St. Louis* (1957), Wilder's account of Lindbergh's 1927 flight from New York to Paris, was an expensive failure. It was followed by another estimable play adaptation, *Witness for the Prosecution* (1958), with Charles Laughton hamming unforgettably as the barrister defending Tyrone Power against Marlene Dietrich. These five movies were written by Wilder with an assortment of collaborators; the next film, however, marked the beginning of the second great writing partnership of his career, with I. A. L. Diamond. *Love in the Afternoon*

(1957), about the regeneration of an aging American playboy (Gary Cooper) through his love for a Parisian innocent (Audrey Hepburn), has been called "Wilder's most emphatic tribute to Lubitsch," a romantic comedy of the greatest elegance and charm.

In the roaring comedy of errors that followed, two broke speakeasy musicians (Jack Lemmon and Tony Curtis) happen to be in a Chicago garage on February 14, 1929, just in time to witness the St. Valentine's Day Massacre. Choosing between death and dishonor, they dress up as women and join an all-girl band, which is on its way to Florida. Even there, as it turns out, they are not safe. In between narrow escapes from murderous gangsters, Curtis gets out of drag long enough to win the muddled heart of the band's infinitely desirable vocalist (Marilyn Monroe). Lemmon, on the other hand, becomes the plaything of the ancient sugar daddy Joe E. Brown. ("But I'm a man," he confesses, as Brown carries him off into the night. "Well, nobody's perfect," chortles Brown in the movie's stupefying last line.) Completed with great difficulty because of Marilyn Monroe's increasing incapacity for work, *Some Like it Hot* (1959) is widely regarded as one of the cinema's greatest comedies. Gerald Mast, indeed, thinks it Wilder's best film, "a rich multilayered confection of parodies and ironies," calling subtly into question conventional notions of masculinity, femininity, sex, love, and violence.

After the delirious pace of *Some Like It Hot*, Wilder achieved an almost equal success with *The Apartment* (1960), a quiet, sad, often bitter comedy about the perennial conflict between love and money. It centers on the plight of a spineless insurance clerk, hungry for promotion, who lends his apartment to his superiors for their extramarital affairs, then falls in love with the discarded mistress of one of them. There are flawless performances from Jack Lemmon, Shirley MacLaine, and Fred MacMurray, and even the film's minor characters are fully drawn. As Mast points out, Wilder often makes telling dramatic use of physical objects or settings, and the vast insurance office in *The Apartment*, with its "geometric rows of desks . . . the clicking sound of business machines, the visual patterns that reduce people to mechanisms, has become a classic example of the use of composition for the wide screen." (The scene was worked out by the art director Alexander Trauner, who has made important contributions to a number of Wilder movies.) The film brought Wilder Oscars for best film, best director, and—with coauthor Diamond—best story and best screenplay.

None of Wilder's subsequent movies has

equaled the success and prestige of the best of the films he made between 1950 and 1960, though all have had their admirers and defenders. The frenetic *One, Two, Three* (1961) impressed Brendan Gill as a "tour de force of fratricidal subversion." *Irma la Douce* (1963), a comedy about a Parisian prostitute and her pimp, was warmly praised in *Cahiers du Cinéma* for its finesse, intensity, and convincingly Gallic atmosphere. But *Kiss Me, Stupid* (1964), admired abroad for its "glorious" bad taste, its ruthless way of poking fun at American greed and hypocrisy, opened in the United States to a storm of abuse. It was called "sordid" and "slimy" and was condemned by the Catholic Legion of Decency for leaving adultery unpunished. Deeply hurt, Wilder retired for a time to Europe and, according to Maurice Zolotow, actually considered suicide. The improbably positive ending of the otherwise savage satire that followed, *The Fortune Cookie* (1966), was regarded by some critics as evidence that Wilder had lost his nerve.

Reviewers were also divided in their reactions to the films Wilder made in the early 1970s—an affectionate tribute to one of his lifelong heroes in *The Private Life of Sherlock Holmes* (1970); *Avanti!* (1972), another (and relatively mellow) Wilderian study of the conflict between European and American values; and his movie version of Hecht and MacArthur's *The Front Page* (1974). However, even these late films have benefited from the reassessment of his work that accompanied a spate of Wilder retrospectives in the 1970s. *The Private Life of Sherlock Holmes*, for example, which had only a moderately warm reception in 1970, was in 1979 described by Neil Sinyard as "a sublime film"—a "sad and serene" masterpiece.

The most widely discussed of Wilder's late films was *Fedora* (1978), a sadder and wiser variation on the theme of *Sunset Boulevard.* William Holden, who played the young screenwriter in the earlier film, reappears as a fading producer trying to set up one more movie. Dutch Detweiler hopes to attract financial backers by luring out of retirement the ageless star Fedora, with whom he had once had a brief affair. Having thus introduced one of the principal Wilderian themes, the struggle between love and money, the film goes on to explore another of his preoccupations: masquerades, illusions, the nature of identity. For Detweiler learns in the end that the still beautiful actress he has been courting is not the "ageless" Fedora but her daughter Antonia; having impersonated Fedora to preserve the legend, she has *become* Fedora, and as Fedora she dies.

Sunset Boulevard was made when Wilder was at the peak of his success, and it has a confidence and audacity lacking in the later film. Perhaps, as Adrian Turner and Neil Sinyard suggest, *Fedora* is "even richer because of that, the vision of a man who knows the system inside out but who . . . has been increasingly placed in the situation of an outsider looking in. Thus, the tone of the film is extraordinarily ambivalent, constantly pulling between nostalgia and bitterness, between sombreness and romance. . . . this ambivalence is thematically of the utmost relevance and importance. . . . the whole film is about ghosts, mirror images and doubles—about the pull between truth and illusion, youth and age." Some critics, however, found the movie old-fashioned in style and tedious—terms that were applied more strongly to *Buddy Buddy* (1981), a Wilder-Diamond adaptation of a French farce, starring Walter Matthau as a grumpy hit man and Jack Lemmon as the basket case who keeps jittering into the line of fire. The teamwork between the two stars was admired, but not the film as a whole.

Dutch Detweiler in *Fedora* compains that his Hollywood has gone: "The kids with beards have taken over, with their zoom lenses and handheld cameras." Wilder himself, though he has been generous in his praise of some of his juniors, is similarly contemptuous of that which he regards as stylistically pretentious and self-conscious in the contemporary cinema. His own work is for the most part not visually distinctive, relying more on language than on images to convey his misanthropic vision.

Coming of age in Berlin between the wars, it seemed to Wilder that (as one of his characters says) "People will do anything for money. Except some people. They will do *almost* anything for money." That, as he acknowledges, is the theme of all his pictures, and in the best of them he has expressed it dramatically enough or wittily enough to make it palatable to millions. That he has been concerned to sweeten the bitter pills he hands his audiences displeases some of his recent critics: David Thomson, for example, has called him "a heartless exploiter of public taste who manipulates situation in the name of satire." In fact, what has happened, as Neil Sinyard says, is that "a director previously identified with a cinema of acerbity and risk in a climate of tasteful timidity has come to represent a cinema of temperateness and geniality in a climate of sensationalism and shock."

Billy Wilder has a daughter by his 1936 marriage to Judith Coppicus Iribe, which ended in divorce. He lives quietly in Los Angeles with his second wife, the former Audrey Young, in a relatively modest apartment crammed with paintings by such artists as Picasso, Klee, Chagall, Dufy, and Rouault. Wilder is also a collector of canes, riding crops, and clubs, a bridge and chess player, and a baseball fan. He is a chain-smoker and, according to Axel Madsen, his most striking physical trait is restlessness; Walter Reisch similarly says that "speed is absolutely of the essence to him. He cannot do anything slowly." Wilder is a famous wit and sometimes a cruel one; he once remarked that "All that's left on the cutting-room floor when I'm through are cigarette butts, chewing-gum wrappers and tears. A director must be a policeman, a midwife, a psychoanalyst, a sycophant, and a bastard." In March 1986, he received the American Film Institute's Life Achievement Award.

FILMS: (with Alexander Esway) Mauvaise Graine (Bad Blood), 1933; The Major and the Minor, 1942; Five Graves to Cairo, 1943; Double Indemnity, 1944; The Lost Weekend, 1945; The Emperor Waltz, 1948; A Foreign Affair, 1948; Sunset Boulevard, 1950; Ace in the Hole (The Big Carnival), 1951; Stalag 17, 1953; Sabrina (in UK Sabrina Fair), 1954; The Seven Year Itch, 1955; The Spirit of St. Louis, 1957; Love in the Afternoon, 1957; Witness for the Prosecution, 1958; Some Like It Hot, 1959; The Apartment, 1960; One, Two, Three, 1961; Irma la Douce, 1963; Kiss Me, Stupid, 1964; The Fortune Cookie (UK, Meet Whiplash Willie), 1966; The Private Life of Sherlock Holmes, 1970; Avanti!, 1972; The Front Page, 1974; Fedora, 1978; Buddy, Buddy, 1981.

ABOUT: Cappabianca, A. Wilder, 1976 (Italy); Current Biography, 1984; Higham, C. and Greenberg, J. (eds.) The Celluloid Muse, 1969; International Who's Who, 1978–79; Koszarski, R. Hollywood Directors, 1941–1976, 1977; Madsen, A. Billy Wilder, 1968; Mast, G. The Comic Mind, 1973; Seidman, S. The Film Career of Billy Wilder, 1977; Thomson, D. A Biographical Dictionary of the Cinema, 1975; Tuska, J. (ed.) Close-up, 1978; Wood, T. The Bright Side of Billy Wilder, Primarily, 1970; Zolotow, M. Billy Wilder in Hollywood, 1977. Periodicals—American Film July–August 1976; Bianco e Nero November–December 1951 (Wilder issue); Cahiers du Cinéma August 1962, November 1978; Cinema (London) October 1969; Écran April, May 1975; Esquire April 1972; Film Comment July–August 1976, January–February 1979; Film Culture Spring 1963; Film Heritage Summer 1973; Film Quarterly Summer 1970; Films and Filming February 1957, January 1960; Holiday June 1964; Image et Son March 1974; Life December 11, 1964; Listener December 19, 1974; London Magazine June 1968; New Society August 2, 1979; Newsweek June 20, 1960; New York Times December 6, 1981; New York Times Magazine January 24, 1960; Playboy December 1960; Positif May 1971; Saturday Review September 24, 1966; Saturday Evening Post December 17, 1966; Saturday Review December 1980; Sight and Sound Winter 1956–1957, Spring 1963, Winter 1967, Winter 1976, Summer 1979; Sunday Express February 18, 1968; Theatre Arts July 1962; Time June 27, 1960.

WISE, ROBERT (September 10, 1914–), American director and producer, was born in Winchester, Indiana, and grew up in the small town of Connorsville, in the same state. He is the son of Earl Wise, who owned a meat packing business, and his wife Olive. Wise's first ambition was to become a journalist. In a lengthy interview with John Gallagher, which is the source of many of the quotations that follow, Wise explained that he had managed a year at Franklin College in his home state, but "it was mid-Depression, and there just wasn't any money to go back to school for the second year." Instead, in 1933 he went out to California, where his older brother David worked as an accountant with RKO-Radio Pictures in Hollywood.

Robert Wise "had always loved films as a kid, and went to them as often as I could afford," but had never contemplated working in the industry. However, his brother arranged an interview for him with James Wilkinson, head of RKO's editing department. Wilkinson needed "a young eager-beaver boy who could work in the shipping room, carry prints up to the projection room for the executives to run, check prints, store them, patch leader—all those odd jobs around the cutting room."

That was how Wise's career began. After nine months, he was promoted to sound effects apprentice under the supervision of sound editor T. K. Wood, working on John Cromwell's Of Human Bondage (1934), George Stevens' Alice Adams (1935), and John Ford's The Informer (1935). During this period he also served as a music editor on two Fred Astaire–Ginger Rogers musicals, The Gay Divorcee (1934) and Top Hat (1935).

Wise found RKO an invaluable training ground. It was "one of the smaller of the major studios . . . a kind of family studio. They allowed a little bit above average in terms of creativity. Working in that smaller studio atmosphere you had a chance to advance faster and learn more." By 1937 Wise was as assistant film editor, working under William Hamilton on Gregory LaCava's Stage Door among other pictures, and in 1939 he shared editorial credit with Hamilton on LaCava's Fifth Avenue Girl, the Astaire-Rogers musical The Story of Vernon and Irene Castle, and William Dieterle's The Hunchback of Notre Dame.

RKO gave Wise his first solo editorial assignments in 1940 on Garson Kanin's My Favorite Wife and Dorothy Arzner's Dance, Girl, Dance, before assigning him to cut Orson Welles' masterpiece Citizen Kane (1941). Wise recalls that "Orson had been making what were thought to be tests for the picture, but after he had shot sev-

ROBERT WISE

eral sequences, the studio finally realized that he was actually shooting the film. He had an older editor assigned to him for those tests and evidently he was not too happy and asked to have somebody else. I was roughly Orson's age and had several good credits." In the cutting room, Wise and his assistant Mark Robson "could tell certainly that we were getting something very special. It was outstanding film day in and day out."

Citizen Kane brought Wise an Oscar nomination for best editing. He went on to cut Welles' *The Magnificent Ambersons* (1942), a film which also gave him his first experience as a director. After the principal photography, Welles went to Brazil to work on the semi-documentary *It's All True*, never completed. He was therefore, as Wise says, "unavailable to be involved with the final cut of . . . [*The Magnificent Ambersons*] or to attend the sneak previews and see the bad reaction from the audience. We were caught with the task of getting the best film we could out of the material, without altering his concept any more than we had to. I'm sure if Orson had been able to be with us it would have been a better film, but it was a situation where it was just impossible for that to work. We cut about twenty-five minutes out of the film and made several new scenes."

According to Wise himself, his most substantial scene as (uncredited) director was the death of Major Amberson. He also directed Lucy and Eugene's dialogue in the garden, Isabel's voice-over letter to Eugene, and several minor transitional shots. Jean-Pierre Coursodon, in his *American Directors* (Volume 2), concluded that

"no matter who directed what, the non-Wellesian footage is easily identifiable, as no one involved attempted to duplicate Welles's style: the visual flatness of the additions is the obvious clue to their spuriousness."

The same year, 1942, Wise was married to the actress, Patricia Doyle, his partner until her death in 1975. Their son Robert was born in 1943. Wise's editorial credits for that year were Richard Wallace's *Bombardier* and *The Fallen Sparrow*, Tim Whelan's *Seven Days' Leave*, and Ray Enright's *The Iron Major*. Critics bewildered by Wise's versatility as a director tend to forget his intimate involvement as an editor with many of the genres in which he later distinguished himself.

In 1944 Wise was assigned to edit Val Lewton's RKO production *The Curse of the Cat People*, whose director, Gunther von Fritsch, fell seriously behind schedule. Wise, who "had been asking them at the studio for a chance to direct," was told to finish the film and did so in ten days. *The Curse of the Cat People* was intended by the studio as a sequel to Lewton's hugely successful low-budget horror film *Cat People* (1942). The earlier movie, directed for Lewton by Jacques Tourneur, told the story of Irena Dubrovna (Simone Simon), a young woman haunted and eventually destroyed by the fear (or fact) that, if sexually aroused, she is liable to turn into a mankilling great cat.

The same principal characters were reassembled for the sequel which, like *Cat People,* was scripted by DeWitt Bodeen. The result, however, was very different. Oliver Reed (Kent Smith), who had been married to the tragic Irena, now lives with his second wife Alice (Jane Randolph) in Sleepy Hollow, New York State. He is concerned about his dreamy little daughter Amy (Ann Carter) and her strange fantasies, suspecting the posthumous influence of Irena.

The lonely child is befriended by Mrs. Farren, a former actress who lives in an "old dark house" with Barbara, a feline young woman who may or may not be her daughter. Amy wishes on a ring given to her by Mrs. Farren and conjures up a "playmate" whom she later identifies as Irena. Punished by her father for this new fantasy, Amy flees to the Farren house. Mrs. Farren dies suddenly and Amy is menaced by the jealous Barbara but saved by Irena. The film ends when Oliver pretends (or admits) that he also can see Irena, whose fantasized image—or ghost—then fades away.

"Masquerading as a routine case of Grade B horrors," wrote James Agee, "—and it does very well at the job—the picture is in fact a brave, sensitive, and admirable little psychological drama about a lonely six-year-old girl, her inadequate parents, a pair of recluses in a neighboring house, and the child's dead, insane mother, who becomes the friend and playmate of her imagination." Jean-Pierre Coursodon agreed that this debut film was "an altogether exceptional item in Wise's filmography"—insofar as the credit belongs to him and not to Fritsch or Lewton—but not that Irena is a figment of Amy's imagination. Coursodon argues that "the treatment of all their scenes together . . . in effect tells us that the ghost did exist after all." For Martyn Auty, the film sets out "to resolve the contradictions . . . previously explored in *Cat People*. . . . Images of stability . . . predominate as Irena's psychotic fantasy from *Cat People* is recuperated through Amy's harmless fantasy," though "the recuperation is never total."

Val Lewton, with his taste for literate material, psychological drama, and the *film noir* style, became the greatest influence on Wise's career. "He probably influenced me more than Orson," Wise says. "Val was a director's producer in every sense of the word. He not only made a remarkable group of low-budget horror films, but he was committed to giving young talent in the industry a chance to direct, including Mark Robson and Jacques Tourneur." Lewton insisted on Wise for his production of *Mademoiselle Fifi* (1944), and Wise's directing career was fully launched.

Based on Guy de Maupassant's story of the same name, and his "Boule de Suif" (also the basis for John Ford's *Stagecoach*), *Mademoiselle Fifi* is set in German-occupied France during the 1870s and draws a pointed parallel between the Franco-Prussian War and World War II. Simone Simon plays the heroine—not Maupassant's plump prostitute, but a beautiful young laundress. Traveling with a coachload of her social betters, all of them snobs, cowards, sycophants, and collaborators, she gives them a lesson in courage and humanity that earns her nothing but contumely.

According to *Time*, "the picture cost about $200,000; it is by far the least expensive costume picture that has been made since sound added so immensely to production costs. It was shot in twenty-two days. With a little more time and a little more money, it would probably have been a first-rate film. Even as it stands, it makes most of its better-barbered, better-fed competitors look like so many wax dummies in a window." And James Agee, continuing his advocacy of Wise's work, said, "I don't know of any American film which has tried to say as much, as pointedly, about the performance of the middle-class

in war. There is a gallant, fervent quality about the whole picture, faults and all, which gives it a peculiar kind of life and likeableness, and which signifies that there is one group of men working in Hollywood who have neither lost nor taken care to conceal the purity of their hope and intention."

Lewton and Wise returned to psychological horror with *The Body Snatcher* (1945), based on the story by Robert Louis Stevenson. Lewton, credited as coauthor under the pseudonym "Carlos Keith," apparently entirely rewrote Philip MacDonald's script. The film is set in Edinburgh in 1831. Boris Karloff gives one of his best performances as the sinister graverobber John Gray who, if he cannot find a cadaver to exhume for Dr. MacFarlane (Henry Daniell), creates one. But Gray at least acknowledges his wickedness and, to his cost, reminds the soulless MacFarlane of his. In the terrifying climax MacFarlane, driving a runaway coach through a storm, is pursued to his death by visions of John Gray's vengeful corpse.

Lewton's Edinburgh, Tom Milne wrote, "is as usual suggested rather than shown on the tight budgets at his disposal, in a patchwork of bits and pieces . . . but always a dark, sad city of the imagination rather than of reality"—a setting for "a subtle philosophical disquisition on the nature of good and evil. . . . Wise's direction is actually a model of discretion and assurance, making superb use of [Robert] De Grasse's chiaroscuro lighting and bringing off several *morceaux d'anthologie*. Notable are the murder of Karloff watched by a terrified cat, and the bravura of the final hallucination in a jolting carriage illuminated by bolts of lightning." Some critics consider *The Body Snatcher* to be Wise's best picture; others have found it (as James Agee did) "a little dull and bookish" apart from its brilliant set pieces.

Wise says he "had problems putting any sizable creativity" into his next two RKO projects. These were *A Game of Death* (1945), a remake of Schoedsack and Pichel's *The Most Dangerous Game* (1932), and *Criminal Court* (1946), a routine but tautly directed thriller. Wise himself initiated the film that followed, *Born to Kill* (1947), based on James Gunn's thriller *Deadlier Than the Male*, and again photographed by Robert De Grasse. Lawrence Tierney plays a psychopathic killer, Claire Trevor the woman who falls for him and protects him until he kills her. Bob Porfirio in *Film Noir* called this "a grim and complicated melodrama . . . an excellent example of an RKO style, not only for its visuals but also for its offhanded depiction of perturbed sexuality and extreme brutality." Tom Milne re-

gards it as an archetypal *film noir*—"an anthology of characters and situations characteristic of
the *noir* genre as a whole." *Mystery in Mexico*
(1948), a less remarkable crime drama, was
made in Mexico City at the Churubusco Studios,
in which RKO owned an interest.

The studio gave Wise his first "A" film budget
for an ambitious Western, *Blood on the Moon*
(1948). Robert Mitchum stars as a stranger from
Texas who gets caught up in a battle between
cattleman Tom Tully and homesteaders led by
Robert Preston who, it emerges, has fomented
the conflict for his own ends. High spots include
an exciting chase through mountains, an exceptionally prolonged and bloody fistfight between
Mitchum and Preston, and a climactic gun battle. Wise was reputedly closely involved in the
development of Lillie Hayward's screenplay
(from a Luke Short novel), and William K. Everson called this "one of the best-scripted Westerns
of the forties," with "some of the starkness and
austerity of the silent William S. Hart films."

One contemporary reviewer noted that Wise,
"a comparative newcomer to the directorial
ranks . . . has managed to keep the atmosphere
of this leisurely-paced film charged with
impending violence." Richard Combs, writing
thirty years later, found it stylistically "not quite
reconciled between its desire to treat the genre
with unassuming exactness, its outbursts of 'realism' . . . , and its 'expressive' interior lighting
that might be traced back to Wise's work with
Lewton or even with Welles."

Wise says that *The Set-Up* (1949) is "one of
my very favorite pictures. It was a labor of love
for all of us concerned with it. *The Set-Up* was
based on a long blank verse poem by Joseph
Moncure March. It's remarkable that a fight
film should come from that kind of material."
Robert Ryan gives a tremendous performance as
Stoker Thompson, an over-the-hill tank-town
boxer with enough heart left to win a fight he is
supposed to lose; the mob take him afterwards
and smash his hand with a brick. Scripted by the
former sportswriter Art Cohn, *The Set-Up* runs
72 minutes—the "real" duration of the events
that take place during a hot night in an ugly
town. It benefits from Milton Krasner's *noir*-ish
photography and the seedy settings designed by
Maurice Zuberano, who often worked with Wise
thereafter.

The Set-Up was Wise's first major critical success in the United States, won the Critics' Prize
at Cannes, and was nominated for best film by
the British Film Academy. It was much praised
for its uncompromising realism, the virtuoso editing of the fight sequences, and the quasi-
expressionistic reaction shots of the animalistic
ringside crowd. *Cue*'s reviewer wrote: "No film
in years has so effectively stripped the phony
cloak of glamour from the prizefight racket, and
shown it for the brutal, body-and-brain-busting
business it is, as this taut and thrilling ringside
drama. . . . The picture is reminiscent of the
finest of the French and Italian films of realism."
Regarded by many as the best of all fight films,
The Set-Up fared poorly at American box offices—no doubt precisely because it eschewed
the glamour and melodrama of pictures like
Mark Robson's *Champion*.

RKO—by then in the hands of Howard
Hughes—dropped Wise's contract after that and
he departed for a three-year nonexclusive contract with 20th Century–Fox. His first film
there, produced and intelligently scripted by
Casey Robinson from a Frank Nugent story, was
the Civil War Western *Two Flags West* (1950).
The impressive cast was headed by Joseph Cotten, Linda Darnell, Jeff Chandler, and Cornel
Wilde. It tells the story of Confederate prisoners
who, in exchange for freedom, go west to fight
Indians under Union command. The bleak prison camp and the isolated frontier fort were photographed with an authenticity that reminded
one reviewer of Mathew Brady's Civil War
studies, and the climactic Indian attack provided
"some of the most convincing scenes of fighting
Hollywood has produced for a long time"—all
the more remarkable in that the Kiowas win.

On an excursion to Warner Brothers, Wise
next directed *Three Secrets* (1950). Eleanor Parker, Patricia Neal, and Ruth Roman star as three
mothers waiting for news of a little boy lost in
the California mountains, each afraid that the
missing child is hers. Their stories are told in
flashback as they watch for the rescue party's
flares and the tension mounts. This effective
melodrama was widely identified as a variation
on the theme of Joseph L. Mankiewicz's *A Letter
to Three Wives* (1949).

Back at Fox, Wise made *The House on Telegraph Hill* (1951). Valentina Cortese, who nar-
rates the story in flashback, plays a Polish
survivor of Belsen who assumes the identity of
a dead fellow-inmate. She goes to the United
States, claims her rich friend's son as her own,
and marries his guardian. After they move into
the eponymous house in San Francisco, she begins to suspect that her husband is trying to kill
her. The movie was generally well received as an
effective thriller, and particularly admired for
Lucien Ballard's atmospheric photography and
the Lyle Wheeler–John DeCuir art direction,
which received an Oscar nomination.

Wise tried his hand at yet another genre with
the science fiction drama *The Day the Earth*

Stood Still (1951), adapted by Edmund North from a short story by Harry Bates. With its thoughtful script and an innovative electronic score by Bernard Herrmann, the film has been seen as a significant step in the genre's development away from the simpleminded Buck Rogering of the past. A spaceship lands in Washington, DC, bringing Klaatu, an emissary from a highly advanced culture with a message of peace. His friendly overtures are met with chauvinistic mistrust and hysteria. Klaatu becomes a fugitive but is aided by a young woman (Patricia Neal), her son (Billy Gray), and an Einstein-inspired scientist (Sam Jaffe) before leaving the planet with an antinuclear warning for mankind.

As played by the tall and ascetic-looking Michael Rennie, Klaatu (who adopts the name Carpenter) emerges as an extraterrestrial messiah—"put the beard on him," Wise has said, "and you could have the Christ figure. Michael was a new face to American audiences, and I think that contributed quite a lot to it. Also there was the fact that he was supposely dead and then was brought back to life." Overtly opposing the Cold War and the nuclear arms race, the film has also been seen as an antiracist parable. Jean-Pierre Coursodon called it "a small picture done with skill and honesty" which "courageously set out to make a serious statement within a genre without any tradition or respectability."

After that, Wise teamed up with two former editors from his RKO days, the director Mark Robson and the producer Theron Warth, to form Aspen Productions, releasing through United Artists. The short-lived company made only two pictures, Wise's *The Captive City* (1952) and Robson's *Return to Paradise* (1953).

The Captive City was made on a budget of $250,000 and shot entirely on location in Reno, Nevada. It is a documentary-style exposé film, based on fact, with small-town editor John Forsythe fighting corruption. He testifies on Senator Estes Kefauver's Committee to Investigate Organized Crime, and Kefauver himself appears in an epilogue, reminding audiences of their civic duties. "Nothing very novel about the plot," wrote one reviewer, "but neat direction, excellent acting and harshly dramatic photography make it exciting and real." *Something for the Birds* (1952), made for Fox, was Wise's first full-fledged comedy, an innocuous trifle scripted by I.A.L. Diamond. It has Patricia Neal lobbying in Washington on behalf of the endangered California condor, and Victor Mature as a representative of the oil company whose activities threaten the creature.

Wise completed his Fox contract with two excellent World War II movies. *The Desert Rats* (1953) was a sequel to Henry Hathaway's successful *The Desert Fox*, made two years earlier, and recreated the 242-day siege of Tobruk in the Libyan Desert. Richard Burton plays the British commander of Australian troops, while James Mason portrays Field Marshall Rommel (as he had for Hathaway in *The Desert Fox*). Richard Murphy's screenplay was nominated for an Academy Award. *Destination Gobi* (1953), Wise's first color film, was by contrast a tongue-in-cheek adventure story about a Navy weather team stationed in the Gobi desert near the end of the war. After a Japanese air strike, Chief Petty Officer Richard Widmark leads his men eight hundred miles across the desert to the ocean. Captured there, they are rescued by Mongol tribesmen, set sail in a launch, and battle the Japanese at sea before making it to Okinawa. The movie was found "unusual but enjoyable."

So Big, made for Warners in 1953, was based on an Edna Ferber novel already filmed by Charles Brabin in 1924 and William Wellman in 1932. Widowed Jane Wyman, that virtuoso of suffering, cultivates asparagus to send her son So Big to college. After numerous sorrows, she has the satisfaction of seeing him recognize his destiny and renounce affluence as a salesman to become an architect. "Using his own particular strength," wrote François Truffaut, "Wise has made a kind of masterpiece from this long melodrama. His power as a director leads us to overlook the rather simplistic psychology of his characters. . . . *So Big* raises the classic, traditional Hollywood style to its highest degree of effectiveness."

John Houseman, with whom Wise had worked on the Welles films, then brought him into the MGM fold to direct Ernest Lehman's adaptation of Cameron Hawley's bestselling novel *Executive Suite*, a high-powered drama about the struggle for succession that follows the death of a Pennsylvania furniture tycoon. With its glossy Metro production values and starry cast, the film began a new phase in Wise's career. Fredric March dominated the picture as a "night-school CPA" who pits his gutter tactics against designer William Holden's crusade for good craftsmanship and social responsibility. Others involved include Barbara Stanwyck, June Allyson, Louis Calhern, Walter Pidgeon, Shelley Winters, Paul Douglas, Dean Jagger, and Nina Foch.

Arthur Knight said that *Executive Suite*, though it was "not a classic, not a milestone in movie-making . . . , does suggest a standard of production that could bring back to the box office those vast audiences long alienated by trivia." It did so, ending as one of the top-grossing movies of 1954 and collecting several Oscar nominations into the bargain. More recently, Jean-Pierre Coursodon suggested that *Executive Suite* "may be, in terms of pure craftsmanship, [Wise's] masterpiece. . . . Unlike the chair Holden breaks to make his point [against shoddy workmanship], the film has been crafted never to fall to pieces."

After *Executive Suite*'s preview, MGM signed Wise to a handsome three-year contract. First, however, he went to Rome to film *Helen of Troy* for Warners. A CinemaScope epic, centering on the wooden horse episode, it was adapted from Homer by John Twist and Hugh Gray, with Rosanna Podesta in the title role. Raoul Walsh supplied uncredited second-unit direction, and Max Steiner an impressive score. The production was plagued by problems, including a fire that prematurely razed Troy and helped to double the original $3 million budget.

The reviewers were on the whole pleasantly surprised. One in *Saturday Review* concluded that "the ancient story has been told again with more than ordinary attention to the events of the original"; and when the thousand ships are launched "and sailing in full panoply against Troy, when the battles are going full tilt, and in the weirdly impressive scenes of the wooden horse being drawn into the doomed city, this film really hits its stride. Director Robert Wise handles his crowds and spectacle with a firm hand, drawing the audience always into the very heart of every shot, filling the CinemaScope screen with splendid action and yet unmistakably highlighting each significant detail." Wise himself was less enthusiastic, maintaining that "this wasn't historical drama, it was spectacle, a terrible chore" that taught him he was "not cut out to make spectacles."

After *Tribute to a Bad Man* (1956), an unexceptional Western with James Cagney as a tough old rancher, came another Ernest Lehman script, *Somebody Up There Likes Me* (1956), adapted from the autobiography of the middleweight boxing champion Rocky Graziano. The picture traces Graziano's career from youthful thuggery on the Lower East Side through assorted penitentiaries to redemption (via legalized mayhem) in the ring. Paul Newman, in his second screen appearance, was cast in the lead, and Wise says that he and Newman "spent a great deal of time with Rocky in New York. Paul studied him very carefully, his mannerisms, movements, and speech."

Newman's Method-style performance in this film began his rapid rise to stardom, bringing "to awesome life the jungle qualities implicit"

—according to *Time*—"in a slum childhood." There were also excellent performances from Harold Stone as Rocky's brutish father and from Eileen Heckart as his racked mother, and Steve McQueen attracted immediate attention in his debut role as a neighborhood tough. The religious theme embodied in the movie's title embarrassed some critics, but the film was generally admired for its "Gorkian power." It picked up an Oscar for Joseph Ruttenberg's photography and a nomination for its editing. The public, which had turned away from the bleak realism of *The Set-Up*, loved this combination of violence and spiritual uplift and made it Wise's biggest hit of the 1950s.

This Could Be the Night (1957) casts Jean Simmons as a sheltered schoolteacher who gets a part-time job in a nightclub and (much as she had in *Guys and Dolls*) becomes amorously involved with a gangster (Anthony Franciosa). Paul Douglas, Joan Blondell, Zasu Pitts, and J. Carroll Naish also featured in this well-received Runyonesque comedy. *Variety*'s reviewer noted that the film "draws an earthy, aware-of-life sauciness" from "the background bits of business contributed by the [Isobel] Lennart script and Wise's direction."

Jean Simmons also starred in *Until They Sail* (1957), along with Joan Fontaine, Sandra Dee, and Piper Laurie. In this World War II soap opera, adapted by Robert Anderson from a novel by James Michener, they play four New Zealand sisters left to face an invasion by Paul Newman and other American Marines while their own men are away fighting elsewhere. Well enough reviewed in the United States, it was more coolly received by British critics. C. A. Lejeune called it a "nasty little work" in which, "one after another . . . the women of New Zealand fall into the clutches of the Americans, like ripe peaches dropping from a tree."

Although he still owed MGM another picture, Wise now embarked on a series of films made for various independent producers releasing through United Artists. *Run Silent, Run Deep* (1958), made for Hecht-Hill-Lancaster, was set aboard an American submarine operating in Japan's Bungo Strait and racked by conflict between Commander Clark Gable and Lieutenant Burt Lancaster. *Time*'s reviewer thought that the movie "runs noisy, runs shallow" but "gives the moviegoer who is in the market for thrills a fairly good run for his money."

This routine chore was followed by a much more personal film, the controversial *I Want To Live* (1958), made for Walter Wanger's Figaro Productions. It deals with the last few weeks in the life of Barbara Graham, a prostitute and petty criminal who was found guilty of involvement in murder and died in San Quentin's gas chamber in 1955. The script, by Nelson Gidding and Don Mankiewicz, was based on Graham's letters and on newspaper articles by Ed Montgomery, a journalist who campaigned first for indictment, then against her execution. Wise actually witnessed a San Quentin execution because he "wanted to be able to deal with it on screen as honestly and truthfully as I possibly could"—"what we wanted to say is not so much that she is innocent, but that nobody should have to go through the kind of torture that she did."

That mental torment is shown in harrowing detail, as are the inhumanly clinical preparations for the execution. Susan Hayward's "anything-for-a-cry" performance in the lead won her an Academy Award, and there were Oscar nominations for Wise's direction, the script, the editing, the sound, and Lionel Lindon's photography. The picture was another box-office hit, and this did nothing to dispel anxieties in some quarters, not so much about Wise and Wanger's sincerity as about the element of voyeurism that is almost impossible to avoid in tracts of this nature.

Wise was next invited to produce and direct *Odds Against Tomorrow* (1959), the first film made by Harry Belafonte's new Harbel Productions. Adapted by Nelson Gidding and John Killens from the thriller by William McGivern, it stars Belafonte as a nightclub entertainer whose gambling draws him into a plot to rob a bank in upstate New York. His accomplices are a former cop (Ed Begley) and an embittered ex-con (Robert Ryan), and the strong cast also includes Shelley Winters and Gloria Grahame. Much of the film is devoted to the detailed planning of the heist, which ends in disaster on account of the Ryan character's unquenchable racism.

Basically a conventional caper movie, *Odds Against Tomorrow* incorporated a number of new trends, quite apart from the theme of racial prejudice. It was shot mostly on location in the town of Hudson, and in "a frosty winter New York City." Wise eschewed fades and dissolves to give the film a documentary quality and (as he had in *I Want to Live*) used a partly improvised jazz score to increase the sense of tension and danger. The result was praised for its "strength and suspense" and evoked comparisons with John Huston's *The Asphalt Jungle* and Jules Dassin's *Rififi*.

It brought Wise a contract with the Mirisch Company, for whom his first film was the screen version of the hit stage musical *West Side Story*, score by Leonard Bernstein and Stephen Sondheim, book by Arthur Laurents, adapted for the screen by Ernest Lehman. Originally, Wise was to produce the picture and codirect it with Jerome Robbins, who had choreographed the Broadway original. After collaborating on the prologue, Robbins relinquished direction to Wise, who explained that it had been taking too long "to coordinate our thoughts." But Wise adds that Robbins "was involved in all aspects of the film, from the screenplay to the music to the sets and costumes." Even after Robbins left the set, "he had rehearsed the balance of the numbers and his assistant stayed on to help me do it. . . . His contribution was of such stature and such quality that I felt he very definitely deserved codirecting credit with me."

West Side Story (1961) is Romeo and Juliet translated to contemporary New York. The two young lovers, Maria (Natalie Wood) and Tony (Richard Beymer) are separated not by an aristocratic feud but by the conflict between two rival street gangs, the Puerto Rican Sharks and the white ethnic Jets. The stage musical had used stylized sets. Wise took the action out into the slum streets of Manhattan, seen by Daniel Fapp's camera with a freshness that reminded one critic of Ben Shahn.

Arthur Knight called *West Side Story* a "triumphant work of art. . . . From the opening helicopter shots of New York's soaring skyline, gradually closing down to the ominous, snapping fingers of a teenage gang lounging against a mesh fence of a mid-city playground, we know that this production has been recreated in terms of the camera. . . . The effort throughout is toward quality, the same kind of quality that the stage production brought to Broadway. And, at least in my opinion, it has not only succeeded, it has *exceeded* the original." Most critics issued similar paeans, but there were a few dissenting voices. Pauline Kael thought it "a great musical for people who don't like musicals" and John Russell Taylor found it a pretentious film that "never quite makes up its mind whether it is going to be a neorealist musical of social comment or a good old-fashioned Hollywood fantasy star vehicle."

A huge financial success, *West Side Story* won ten Oscars: best direction, best picture, best supporting actor (George Chakiris) and actress (Rita Moreno), best color photography, art direction (Boris Leven), editing (Thomas Sanford), costumes (Irene Sharaff), music scoring, and sound. There was a special Oscar to Jerome Robbins for his contributions to screen choreography. The New York Film Critics voted it the best picture of the year, and Wise also received the Directors Guild Award.

Wise's second film for Mirisch also adapted a Broadway hit—William Gibson's play *Two for *the Seesaw,* a bittersweet love story set in Greenwich Village. Shirley MacLaine gave a virtuoso performance as Gittel Mosca, beatnik refugee from a middle-class Jewish family in the Bronx, but most critics thought that Robert Mitchum was somewhat miscast as the respectable if troubled Nebraska lawyer Jerry Ryan. Richard Roud decided that Wise had, not surprisingly, failed in his attempt to open up this two-character play for the screen: "In spite of some rather ingenious camerawork and an accurately beautiful rendering of the textures of Manhattan's seamier side, he is all too often reduced to falling back on tennis-match cross-cutting." All the same, there were Oscar nominations for Ted McCord's black-and-white photography and the André and Dory Previn song "Second Chance."

The Haunting (1963), also in black and white, completed Wise's commitment to MGM. Adapted by Nelson Gidding from Shirley Jackson's *The Haunting of Hill House,* it was shot for the sake of economy in Britain but purports to take place in an "old dark house" in New England. Investigating reports that the place is haunted, an earnest scientist (Richard Johnson) assembles as his control group a young woman with a talent for ESP (Julie Harris), another with a gift for mind-reading and a tendency toward lesbianism (Claire Bloom), and the skeptical young man who stands to inherit the house (Russ Tamblyn).

For Jean-Pierre Coursodon, *The Haunting* "is arguably the most interesting" of Wise's late films; like *The Curse of the Cat People,* it "emphasized the psychological element, preserving a basic ambiguity as to how much of the supernatural happenings are real and how much created in the heroine's imagination. Considered purely as a haunted-house yarn, the film is among the best of its genre." Coursodon praises "David Boulton's heavily shaded cinematography" and considers that "Wise's use of the sound track . . . makes the film truly exceptional. The supernatural presence is manifested only by means of a variety of noises— poundings, moans, screeches—and violent gusts of wind, which prove more effective than any ghostly apparition." In *Hollywood in the Sixties,* John Baxter suggests that only Polanski's *Rosemary's Baby* "offers competition to *The Haunting* as the sixties' best story of the supernatural" and draws attention to "Wise's intricate cutting to show an interrelationship between the house's sinister architecture and its victims' growing fear."

An adaptation of Richard McKenna's novel *The Sand Pebbles* was announced as Wise's next project. The Mirisch Company were uneasy about the large budget, however, and Wise took the property to 20th Century–Fox. They also were unwilling to commit and instead offered Wise the Richard Rodgers–Oscar Hammerstein musical *The Sound of Music.* William Wyler had originally undertaken this project but had relinquished it when he was sent the script for *The Collector.* When Wise joined the film as producer-director for his newly formed Argyle Productions, Julie Andrews had already been cast and Ernest Lehman had completed his adaptation of the Howard Lindsay–Russel Crouse book. Wise "thought it was a chance to do a different kind of musical, one that would entertain all kinds of people in the best way, and still had something serious to say about the Trapp Family and their escape from the Nazis."

As all the world knows, *The Sound of Music* (1965) tells the slightly true story of Maria (Julie Andrews), a young postulant nun in 1930s Austria who is so full of songful *joie de vivre* that her wise abbess decides she is not meant for the cloister. Instead she is installed as governess to the seven motherless children of Captain von Trapp (Christopher Plummer). The children, who are being raised under naval discipline, greatly resent the intruder, but in due course are won over by her artless charm and the music she brings into their dour household. In spite of competition from a sophisticated Viennese baroness (Eleanor Parker), the Captain finds himself likewise beguiled. Maria turns the children into a prize-winning (and eventually world-famous) choral group and marries the Captain; the Nazis move into Austria; and the whole happy family escape over the mountains, singing as they go.

The three-hour film was shot by Ted McCord on location in Salzburg and the Austrian Alps. The critical response was far from enthusiastic. Patrick Gibbs, in a fairly typical review headed "Mary Poppins in Schmalzburg," complained about "the sickly sweetness of the goings-on" and called the film "a fairy tale after the outmoded style of an Ivor Novello musical." All the same, Gibbs acknowledged the beauty of the settings and "a saving suggestion of simplicity and humour" in Julie Andrews' performance, concluding that the picture might "even be described as stylish in that the style is consistent and appropriate to the material in hand. Easy to see how it could be 'sent-up,' difficult to imagine the popular qualities preserved otherwise."

The Sound of Music has indeed been "sent-up"—ridiculed—as much as any film in history. There is no doubt, however, that the movie's sentimental affirmation of old-fashioned values has warmed numberless simple hearts, some of whose owners have seen it numberless times. Until *The Godfather* topped it in 1972, it was the highest grossing picture ever. Produced at a cost of $8 million, it took ten times that amount in North America alone. It also won five Oscars, including Wise's second as best director, and best film.

Wise grew rich from his profit participations in *West Side Story* and *The Sound of Music*—at one time he was receiving $100,000 a week from the latter alone. He was able to return to the more personal project he had announced a year or two earlier, *The Sand Pebbles,* mounting a $12 million production. Adapted from McKenna's novel by Robert Anderson, the film is set in 1926 in China, where the crew of an American gunboat on the Yangtze are engulfed by the rising tide of Chinese nationalism. Steve McQueen gave one of his finest performances as Jake Holman, the gunboat's engineer and a loner, striving to do his duty both as a sailor and a human being.

The Sand Pebbles (1966) was shot by Joe Mac-Donald on location in Taiwan and Hong Kong. Wise says "it's always been one of my favorite films. I suppose one of the reasons is because it's the most difficult film that I've ever made, from a physical, logistical, and location standpoint. I suppose suffering through bad weather, typhoons, and months of location shooting makes it a more memorable experience."

The reviewers, spared these experiences, nevertheless agreed that the result was memorable. Arthur Knight called it "a vast, wide-ranging adventure tale, panoramic yet also intimate . . . and a far cry indeed from the marshmallowy *Sound of Music.* But just as, within the limitations of that film, director Wise was speaking for human dignity and freedom of the spirit, in the wider dimensions afforded by *The Sand Pebbles* he is able to put forward some provocative ideas about the nature of nationalism [and] American intervention. . . . Robert Anderson's brilliantly succinct script blunts none of this, neither our untenable position in China in 1926 nor its implications for Vietnam in 1966." Nominated for eight Oscars, the film won none of them, but the same year Wise received one of the industry's highest honors, the Irving G. Thalberg Memorial Award, for his consistently high achievement as a producer.

Star!, which followed in 1968, was a $14 million biopic for Fox of the 1930s musical comedy star Gertrude Lawrence. Julie Andrews played the lead, and there were songs by Gershwin, Cole Porter, Kurt Weill, and Noel Coward (splendidly impersonated in the film by Daniel Massey). In spite of all this, the movie was a flop; withdrawn, cut, and re-released a year later as *Those Were the Happy Times,* it flopped again.

Wise says that "we tried to tell a fairly truthful biography of Gertrude Lawrence, but audiences couldn't accept Julie playing that kind of character that she was. It was a different range of emotion and feelings, a lady who can get drunk and get high." Others blamed William Fairchild's script which, in the opinion of Richard Schickel, "deals in types rather than people, romances rather than loves." The movie has its admirers, however, and John Baxter called it "Wise's most satisfying musical," hampered at the box office only "by its imagination and good taste."

Wise next ventured briefly into television as executive producer of a 1968 Mae West special, and then backed two young directors in their first feature films, John Flynn with *The Sergeant* (1968) and James Bridges with *The Baby Maker* (1970). In January 1970 Wise joined with Bridges, Mark Robson, and the former Paramount vice president Bernard Sonnenfeld to form the Filmmakers Group. His first film for the company as producer-director was *The Andromeda Strain* (1971), made under the auspices of Universal.

The Andromeda Strain was adapted by Nelson Gidding from Michael Crichton's novel about a team of scientists working against time to destroy a deadly organism from space. Wise had a budget of $9.6 million, computer animation by Douglas Trumbull, and for the first time in his career the privilege of final cut. His characteristic insistence on scientific accuracy irritated some reviewers—Tom Milne, for example, called the movie "a hopeless compromise between science fiction and science fact, appallingly ponderous on both counts." Like *Star!,* however, the picture has its champions who consider it one of Wise's best and most underrated films.

Wise produced the 1971 Academy Awards show, then planned a low-budget film called *Craig and Joan* from Eliot Asinof's novel about two teenagers who make a suicide pact. That project gave way to an original by Richard De-Roy: *Two People* (1973). Peter Fonda plays a Vietnam deserter who meets a high-fashion model (Lindsay Wagner) in Marrakesh. They move on to Casablanca, Paris, and New York, where Fonda, "tired of running" through these attractive locations, turns himself in. Pauline Kael wrote that "the travelogue material in *Two People* (the great Henri Decaë was the cinematographer) is very handsome . . . but it's shot and edited impersonally, so it is only background, and the hero and heroine seem to be tourists"—"The trouble is, this kind of moviemaking is obsolete. *Two People* isn't offensive; it merely has no interest whatsoever."

The Hindenburg (1975), made at a cost of $15 million, fared no better. It deals with the 1937 zeppelin disaster, attributing it to sabotage by an anti-Nazi crew member. The spectacular special effects won an Oscar, but the movie, hampered by Nelson Gidding's plodding script, failed to recover its investment. "It's not, strictly speaking, a disaster film in the Earthquake vein," wrote Stanley Kauffmann; "the disaster comes only in the last ten minutes. Up to then, it's a shabby Grand Hotel script, with Good and Bad Germans and a cargo of red herrings."

Audrey Rose (1977), based on Frank De Felitta's novel about reincarnation, also failed with audiences accustomed to more graphic horror films. Andrew Sarris thought that it lacked any sense of evil to provide dramatic tension; "hence, all is wailing and hand-wringing without any psychological confrontation." Wise's last feature film to date was Star Trek—The Motion Picture (1979), a $42 million big-screen version of the famous television series created by Gene Roddenberry, who also produced the movie. Most critics thought that, like The Hindenburg, the film was most notable for its special effects (created by Trumbull and John Dykstra). It seemed to Jack Kroll that "the deliberate pace that can be perversely hypnotic on TV expands to a large soporific cloud on the giant screen." Not for the British critic Philip Strick, however; he called Star Trek "one of the screen's finest science fiction achievements, for all its lack of solemnity. The pace, polish and precision with which Alan Dean Foster's story has been fleshed out make the film a sheer pleasure to watch."

David Robinson has described Robert Wise as "peculiarly neat, amiable, elegantly stocky, bespectacled, grey-haired, and quiet-spoken," with "less the air of Hollywood than of an unusually kindly bank-manager." The director is active in many civic and industry affairs. He was one of the founders in 1968 of FAIR (Film Association for Improvement and Reform), which among other things produced a documentary about Martin Luther King. In 1971, along with Robert Aldrich and Ralph Nelson, he visited Russia on a Soviet-US cultural exchange. Wise was president of the Directors Guild of America from 1971 through 1975, and in 1980 chaired their Special Projects Committee. He is a trustee of the American Film Institute, as well as special consultant and chairman of the Institute's Center for Advanced Film Studies.

Wise believes that "the director's job is to entertain the audience and tell a story, so he should be attracted to a story's content. I don't like to burden an audience with a message, but generally I do try to have something to say. Then I work from the story, giving each film a style I think is appropriate for the material." This formula, scrupulously applied by a decent, self-effacing, and immensely able craftsman, won him phenomenal commercial success during the 1950s and 1960s but has now become highly unfashionable.

As Pauline Kael wrote in 1973, Wise's "brand of academic pop, in Hollywood terms 'prestigious' only a few years ago . . . , has less personality than much sleazier work. The impersonality and inexpressiveness of this type of moviemaking is stifling now." At least until the next swing of the critical pendulum, Wise's reputation will rest primarily on the films he directed before his growing budgets made him reluctant to take chances—pictures like the three he made for Val Lewton, and Born to Kill, Blood on the Moon, The Set-Up, Two Flags West, and The Day the Earth Stood Still.

—J.A.G.

FILMS: (with Gunther von Fritsch) The Curse of the Cat People, 1944; Mademoiselle Fifi, 1944; The Body Snatcher, 1945; A Game of Death, 1945; Criminal Court, 1946; Born to Kill (UK, Lady of Deceit), 1947; Mystery in Mexico, 1948; Blood on the Moon, 1948; The Set-Up, 1949; Two Flags West, 1950; Three Secrets, 1950; The House on Telegraph Hill, 1951; The Day the Earth Stood Still, 1951; The Captive City, 1952; Something for the Birds, 1952; The Desert Rats, 1953; Destination Gobi, 1953; So Big, 1953; Executive Suite, 1954; Helen of Troy, 1955; Tribute to a Bad Man, 1956; Somebody Up There Likes Me, 1956; This Could Be the Night, 1957; Until They Sail, 1957; Run Silent, Run Deep, 1958; I Want to Live, 1958; Odds Against Tomorrow, 1959; (with Jerome Robbins) West Side Story, 1961; Two for the Seesaw, 1962; The Haunting, 1963; The Sound of Music, 1965; The Sand Pebbles, 1966; Star!, 1968 (reissued as Those Were the Happy Times); The Andromeda Strain, 1971; Two People, 1973; The Hindenburg, 1975; Audrey Rose, 1977; Star Strek—The Motion Picture, 1979.

ABOUT: Coursodon, J.-P. American Directors, Volume 2, 1983; Higham, C. Celebrity Cinema, 1979; Kantor, B. R. and others, Directors at Work, 1970; Siegel, J. Val Lewton, 1973; Thomson, D. A Biographical Dictionary of the Cinema, 1980. Periodicals— Action March–April 1974, November–December 1975; American Classic Screen September–October 1981; American Film November 1975; L'Avant Scène du Cinéma 13 1962; Cinefantastique Summer 1977; Cinéma (France) January 1978; Dialogue on Film 2 1 1972; Écran February 1972; Film Comment March–April 1977; Filmmakers Newsletter April 1976; Films and Filming July 1971, November 1977; Films in Review January 1963; Focus on Film Winter 1972, Spring 1973, Winter 1973, Autumn 1974; Grand Illusions Winter 1977; Literature-Film Quarterly 4 1978; Millimeter November 1975; Monthly Film Bulletin November 1979.

WYLER, "WILLIAM" (WILLY) (July 1, 1902–July 27, 1981), American director and producer, was born in what was then Mülhausen in the German province of Elsass (Alsace), second of three sons of a prosperous Jewish family. His father, Leopold, was a Swiss citizen who, starting as a traveling salesman, had built up a thriving haberdashery business. His mother, Melanie, came from the culturally distinguished Auerbach family; her uncle Bertold was a well-known novelist. Wyler attended several local schools; something of a hell-raiser, he was more than once expelled for persistent misbehavior. Despite this, his childhood was largely happy. Along with his elder brother Robert, he was taken by his mother to concerts, opera, and the theatre, as well as to the cinema, where he developed a taste for Feuillade's *Fantômas* series. At home, the family and their friends often staged amateur theatricals.

When World War I, broke out, Robert, thanks to the family's Swiss citizenship, could be sent off to a commercial college in Lausanne safe from any risk of conscription. Willy, with his younger brother Gaston, stayed in Mülhausen and watched the city change nationality several times in rapid succession as opposing armies came and went. When the war ended, leaving Mulhouse (as it had become) and the family business relatively unscathed, Wyler was sent to join his brother at the École Supérieure de Commerce in Lausanne. He spent a year there perfecting his French, after which his father arranged an apprenticeship for him at a large clothing store in Paris. Homesick, lonely, and increasingly averse to haberdashery as a career, he stuck it out for some months—consoling himself with occasional violin lessons at the Conservatoire—before quitting and buying a ticket home with his severance pay.

As a last resort, Wyler's mother took him to meet her cousin, Carl Laemmle, who was over on a visit. Head of Universal Studios, which he had built up from a single Chicago nickelodeon in less than ten years, Laemmle was even by Hollywood standards a devout nepotist. ("Uncle Carl Laemmle," ran the current gag, "has a very large faemmle.") He promptly offered Wyler a job in the studio's New York office at $25 a week—less $5 a week to pay off his boat fare. Starting in the shipping department, Wyler was soon elevated to foreign publicity, and in 1921 talked Laemmle into transferring him to Universal City in Hollywood.

Initially his work there was scarcely more glamorous than it had been in New York. As office boy to a casting director, "I did everything: assistant prop man, helping carry film, sweeping steps. I went through the mill." A more interest-

WILLIAM WYLER

ing assignment was helping to marshal the two thousand-odd extras on Universal's current major production, the Lon Chaney *Hunchback of Notre Dame* (1923). During shooting he got himself promoted to assistant to the assistant directors, and by 1924 had risen to assistant director in his own right—albeit only on the production-line two-reel Westerns which, like all the other studios, Universal churned out at a rate of two hundred a year.

Around the end of 1924, Wyler's promising career received a setback: caught in a nearby poolhall when he should have been on set, he was fired. Fortunately, assistant directors were then in demand at MGM, where Fred Niblo was shooting the spectacular chariot-race sequence for *Ben-Hur* with forty-two cameramen and needed all the assistance he could get. Wyler was hired and assigned a section of the massive crowd. "I was given a toga and a set of signals. . . . I got my section of the crowd to stand up and cheer . . . or whatever was called for. There must have been thirty other assistants doing the same job." At one point, it happened that Wyler was summoned by Niblo to receive instructions. "I looked up behind [Niblo] . . . and there was the man who had just fired me at Universal. He was very impressed. . . . The next day, I was hired back."

Thanks, perhaps, to this spurious prestige, Universal soon allowed Wyler to direct his first film—and officially changed his first name to William, in line with the dignity of his new status. Not that *Crook Buster* (1925) was any grand assignment. Like all Universal's two-reel Mustang Westerns, it was made on a $2,000 budget in a week: three days to shoot and two to edit, with Saturday to cast next week's picture. Over the next two years, Wyler directed at least twenty-one of these quickies, learning his trade at $60 a week. (The cameraman got $75.) "It was all routine, but it taught you the business of movement. . . . I did try to make the pictures a little different, to invent a little something that would make them interesting. . . . You had great leeway. If you wanted to change the script, fine. . . . The stories were elementary . . . but they had to have action."

Few of these prentice works have survived intact, but judging from contemporary reviews, Wyler provided all the requisite pace and excitement. (One of the earliest, the 1926 *Ridin' for Love,* gives Wyler story credit—the only writing credit of his career.) The *Motion Picture News* notice for *The Lone Star* (1927) would probably serve for any one of the series: "The usual helping of rough-and-tumble fighting, riders silhouetted against a skyline, the foiling of a plot, a touch of romance . . . numerous narrow escapes. What more could you ask for in two reels?" At all events, the studio was satisfied. Late in 1926, while continuing to shoot two-reelers, Wyler was assigned to Universal's new series of five-reel Blue Streak Westerns, kicking off with *Lazy Lightning* (1926). Budgets were all of $20,000, which allowed for location work.

Wyler directed eight five-reel Westerns before at last escaping from the sagebrush with his first full-length feature. *Anybody Here Seen Kelly?* (1928) was a comedy about a French girl (Bessie Love) arriving in New York in search of her wartime sweetheart. Audaciously, Wyler shot much of the film on location, taking a concealed camera onto the New York streets; the producer was his brother Robert, who had joined him in Hollywood in 1925. No prints of *Kelly* are known to exist, nor of *The Shakedown* (1929), a boxing movie released in two versions: silent and "25% sound." (Universal, like several other studios, was hedging its bets, in case the talkies proved an ephemeral gimmick.) Wyler's earliest surviving feature is *The Love Trap* (1929), also released in two versions. A mildly risqué bedroom comedy, it starred Laura La Plante, then one of the studio's top stars, as a flapper on the make.

As his first all-talking assignment, Wyler was handed a well-thumbed Western property. *Hell's Heroes* (1930) was taken from a novel, *The Three Godfathers,* which had already been filmed twice (once by John Ford), and would be remade twice more (once, again, by Ford). Three hardbitten outlaws on the run come across a woman alone in the desert, about to give birth.

She does so and dies, leaving the three, without horses and almost out of water, to carry the infant to safety. Two of the outlaws die in the process; the third (Charles Bickford) staggers, near dead, into the township of New Jerusalem on Christmas morning, the baby in his arms. Given ample scope for sentimentality, Wyler largely avoided it, aiming instead for a harsh realism in locations and acting that today make the film the least unwatchable of extant versions. *Hell's Heroes* scored a hit at the box office, and Wyler was singled out by the critics as a director to watch.

The Storm (1930), a triangle drama involving two men snowbound in a wilderness cabin with Lupe Velez, did little to enhance his reputation. (Wyler always reckoned it his worst film.) He had better material with *A House Divided* (1931), even if the plot was blatantly lifted from *Desire Under the Elms,* and Walter Huston, as the tough fisherman who sees his young second wife falling for his son, turned in a powerful performance. Even this early in Wyler's career Charles Affron (*International Dictionary of Film and Filmmakers*) detected distinctive preoccupations: "The film's premise holds particular appeal for a director who sees drama in claustrophobic interiors, the actors held in expressive tension by their shifting spatial relationship to each other, the decor, and the camera."

Dialogue credit on *A House Divided* went to Huston's son John; he and Wyler became close friends and, once the film was complete, tried to interest the studio in several hard-hitting socially relevant scenarios. Warners might have bought them, but not Universal. John Huston took off in disgust for Europe, and Wyler was assigned two routine programmers: *Tom Brown of Culver* (young rebel makes good at military academy) and *Her First Mate,* a Slim Summerville–ZaSu Pitts comedy.

Counsellor at Law (1933) is generally held to mark the end of Wyler's apprenticeship. The first of his many adaptations of Broadway hits, it was also his first film to touch (albeit very cautiously) on a "serious" theme—in this case, anti-Semitism, a subject generally taboo within the Jewish-run Hollywood studios. The hero of Elmer Rice's play, a fast-talking lawyer named George Simon, had been played on stage by Paul Muni, making his breakthrough to stardom; but Muni, not wanting to be typecast as a Jewish actor, turned down the film role, which went instead to John Barrymore. Against all expectations, Barrymore gave an impressive if flamboyant performance, seen by many critics as his best in the sound era. Wyler, in line with his later practice, refused to "open up" the play with superfluous outdoor sequences, filming entirely within the tight confines of Simon's law offices. *Counsellor at Law* received enthusiastic reviews, though Barrymore, rather than Wyler, inevitably gained most of the attention.

The film also initiated another Wyler tradition—his reputation as an implacable perfectionist. One scene involving Barrymore was said to have run to fifty-six takes; the legend of "ninety-take Wyler" was in the making.

Counsellor at Law was highly successful, breaking box-office records in its first week's run at Radio City Music Hall. Nonetheless, Wyler was growing increasingly dissatisfied at Universal; he was earning $1,000 a week but getting few of the assignments he wanted. *Glamour* (1934) hardly improved matters—a vapidly romantic weepie, based on a short story by Edna Ferber. If *The Good Fairy* (1935), adapted from a Molnár play, was less inane, it was thanks largely to Preston Sturges, who rewrote the text almost entirely, populating Molnár's flimsy Viennese world with Sturgesian eccentrics named Schlapkohl or Ginglebusher. The lead role, of a naive orphan who innocently disrupts the lives of all around her, was taken by Margaret Sullavan, then at the start of her brief, temperamental career. She and Wyler clashed incessantly. "We were constantly fighting, over the interpretation of her part, over everything. . . . She had a mind of her own and so did I." Midway through shooting, in an attempt to make peace, Wyler invited his star out to dinner. A few days later, on November 24, 1934, they were married.

Sullavan had recently been divorced from her first husband, Henry Fonda, from whom she had separated amicably after two months. Her marriage to Wyler lasted slightly longer. "We had about a year and a half together—lots of fights, lots of good times," Wyler recalled. "It was fighting, making up, and fighting again." They were divorced in March 1936.

In the meantime, Wyler had quit Universal, which was heading rapidly towards bankruptcy. Freelancing, he was offered a picture by Jesse L. Lasky at Fox: *The Gay Deception* (1935), a trivial light comedy. Despite its well-worn Cinderella plot (stenographer posing as grand lady meets prince posing as bellhop), the film was well received, and attracted the attention of the most formidable of the independent producers, Sam Goldwyn, who offered Wyler a contract.

The films which Wyler made during his "Goldwyn years"—not all of them made for Goldwyn—raised him to the summit of his profession. In many ways, the two men were ideally suited. Goldwyn consistently aspired, not always successfully, to produce high-quality prestige pictures; Wyler, with his cultured European background and meticulous technique, could be counted on to make them for him. Not that they always agreed; they often vehemently did not. "To give Sam his due," Wyler later remarked, "let me say that with all his faults, he was no scrawny little fast-buck producer. . . . 'Do it over again,' he'd say, as if money didn't matter. . . . I could practically cast any star in any role, again regardless of cost. Which doesn't mean we didn't fight, but we fought for what we both thought was right."

Wyler's first film for Goldwyn united him with two other significant figures in his career: Gregg Toland, and Lillian Hellman. In Toland, Wyler found a cinematographer who could make his own creative contribution, not simply follow instructions. "You didn't tell Gregg what lens to use, you told him what mood you were after. . . . We would discuss a picture from beginning to end, its overall 'feel' and then the style of each sequence. Toland was an artist." They worked together on six films, during which Toland was developing and perfecting his technique of deep-focus photography; this in turn allowed Wyler to explore the complex pictorial compositions and long, unbroken takes that became his preferred style of filmmaking.

Lillian Hellman, who scripted three of Wyler's most successful pictures, had just had her first Broadway hit, *The Children's Hour*. Since it concerned lesbianism, the play was generally held to be totally unfilmable, and Goldwyn caused great hilarity by paying $50,000 for the rights—the more so since the Hays Office had stipulated that no film version, however expurgated, could use the play's title, or even mention it as a source. Hellman, undeterred, maintained that it could still make an acceptable movie, since her subject was not lesbianism, but the destructive power of a malicious lie. It was her script, under the nonspecific title of *These Three*, that Goldwyn presented to Wyler as his first assignment.

In *The Children's Hour* two women, Martha and Karen, set up a girls' boarding school with the help of Karen's boyfriend Joe. An evil pupil, Mary Tilford, suggests to her grandmother that the two teachers are lovers; the rumor spreads, and the school is forced to close. Martha admits that she does harbor sexual feelings for Karen, and kills herself. For the movie Hellman, with prudent economy, simply switched the triangle around; instead of Martha and Joe both loving Karen, Martha (Miriam Hopkins) and Karen (Merle Oberon) both love Joe (Joel McCrea), and the scandal becomes one of non-marital sex—if not a *ménage à trois*—on the school premises.

These Three (1936) represents the first mature statement of Wyler's central concern: the psychological relationships between characters, expressed through framing, composition, and the considered selection of camera angles. "A recurrent Wyler image," noted Neil Sinyard (*Arts Lab Programme* October 1981), "is that of a frozen confrontation: people . . . separated by ideology or social position daring each other to strike." Or as Wyler put it: "I believe that the emotion and conflict between people in a drawing room can be as exciting as a gun battle, and possibly more exciting."

Despite its compromises and clumsily tacked-on happy ending—which Wyler detested—*These Three* was widely acclaimed. Graham Greene, reviewing it for *The Spectator*, wrote that he had "seldom been so moved by any fictional film," singling out Bonita Granville's chilling portrayal of the malign schoolgirl: "Never before has childhood been represented so convincingly on the screen. . . . This character raises the film from the anecdotal, however ingenious and moving the anecdote; it has enough truth and intensity to stand for the whole of the dark side of childhood." Several aspects of the film—though not Granville's performance—now look dated, but *These Three* remains, in John Baxter's words, "one of Wyler's most integrated and formally perfect films."

Sinclair Lewis's biographer, Mark Schorer, described him as one of the worst important writers in modern American literature—which may be why *Dodsworth* (1936), almost uniquely among films drawn from "classic" novels, is generally reckoned to be an improvement on the original. Sidney Howard scripted the film from his own stage adaptation, making good many of the novel's deficiencies in structure and characterization. From Walter Huston (who had created the role on stage) as the middle-aged American businessman whose marriage disintegrates during a European vacation, and from Mary Astor as the liberated younger woman he meets, Wyler elicited outstanding performances. Ruth Chatterton, as Sam Dodsworth's pretentious wife Fran, proved less tractable; despite all Wyler's efforts, she insisted on "playing Fran like a heavy," caricaturing an already stereotyped role.

Reviews of *Dodsworth* were excellent, and the film was nominated for seven Academy Awards, including one for Wyler's direction, though only the art director, Richard Day, won an Oscar. Box-office response was only respectable; unglamorized accounts of the problems of middle age evidently lacked mass appeal. Still, Goldwyn had hired Wyler for prestige, not profit, and was far from dissatisfied. He was less pleased with

another of his stable, Howard Hawks, who had dared to rewrite part of the film he was shooting: *Come and Get It* (1936), an adaptation of an Edna Ferber novel. Reprimanded, Hawks walked off the picture, and Wyler was summoned to take over. When he refused, Goldwyn furiously threatened him with legal action. "At the end, I had to do it. I don't think it helped much." The film was finally released with joint directorial credit, and flopped. "The trouble with directors," grumbled Goldwyn, "is they bite the hand that lays the golden egg."

Part of Wyler's appeal for Goldwyn, Albert Lavalley suggested (in Peary and Shatzkin's *The Classic American Novel and the Movies*), was that his "famed perfectionism was often spent on small touches, never on the major alteration of a play nor on a strong interpretation that would suggest a personal *auteur* like Lubitsch. . . . The many small touches were fused into a personal style, though of a very detached sort." Similarly, Karel Reisz (*Sequence* 13 1951) commented that by this stage in his career Wyler had "evolved a consistent technical approach, without having established for himself a recognisable creative personality." This detachment, the sense of meticulous craftsmanship overriding any personal attitude, may explain why, though Wyler's films are often revived, none of them has yet become a cult movie—not even those featuring cult actors like Bogart, who stole Wyler's next picture, *Dead End* (1937).

Sidney Kingsley's long-running Broadway hit leaned towards social realism: gangsters, hookers, and juvenile hooligans interacting in a slummy East River cul-de-sac, on to which backs a high-priced apartment building inhabited by the snooty rich. Wyler wanted to shoot the film version on location in New York but was vetoed by Goldwyn, who liked to have his directors on the West Coast where he could keep tabs on them. So Richard Day devised a huge, elaborate set, around which Toland's camera prowled and craned, exploring every angle, peering into sleazy tenements and sidling past carefully grouped garbage cans. (Goldwyn, visiting the set, complained that it looked dirty; Wyler patiently explained that slums usually did.)

Snarling his way towards death as Baby Face Martin, local boy made bad, Bogart gave his best performance so far, with energetic support from the Dead End Kids, starting out on their extensive career of screen delinquency. Inevitably, Lillian Hellman's script toned down the original a good deal—Claire Trevor's streetwalker was no longer admitted to be syphilitic—and the film ended up an uneasy mixture of the grandiose and the grubby, as though a Warners movie had been made over by MGM. At the time, however, both critics and public liked it—though John Grierson recognized that "it lacks gusto"—and *Dead End* was nominated for four Oscars.

Wyler was by now recognized as one of Hollywood's foremost directors, notably skilled in his handling of actors—and as such was specifically requested by Warners to handle one of their major problems. This was Bette Davis, who for some years had been raising hell on the Burbank lot in her demand for better material, and in 1936 had even jumped her contract and fled to London, pursued by Jack Warner frantically waving injunctions. Davis lost the subsequent court case, but the studio, acting generous, not only paid her costs but made serious efforts to provide her with better roles and directors. Hence the loan of Wyler, for whom they paid $3,500 a week—Wyler's regular $2,500, plus $1,000 a week to Goldwyn.

The vehicle chosen for the Davis-Wyler teaming was *Jezebel* (1938), a steamy melodrama set in the antebellum Deep South—partly a consolation prize for Davis having missed out on *Gone With the Wind* and partly a crafty bid to preempt Selznick's much-publicized blockbuster. As Julie Marsden, the spoiled and headstrong Southern belle who comes through during a yellow fever epidemic, Davis was ideally cast, and Wyler succeeded like no director before or since in toning down her mannerisms and drawing from her a performance of concentrated power that transcended the novellettish script. (The film was adapted from a play by Owen Davis; one of the scriptwriters was John Huston, back in harness after his European *Wanderjahre*.) Wyler was eager to film in color, but Warners turned him down. He nonetheless contrived to give a vivid *impression* of color—most notably in the famous ball scene where Julie scandalizes New Orleans society by defiantly wearing a scarlet dress in place of the customary white.

Henry Fonda, playing Julie's fiancé, made a valiant attempt at a Southern acccent, and George Brent was less stolid than usual as a rival admirer. Other actors hardly mattered, though; it was Davis' film, as her Best Actress Oscar confirmed. Despite their later disputes, Davis always gave Wyler full credit for her achievement in *Jezebel*. "It was all Wyler," she wrote in her 1962 autobiography. "I had known all the horrors of no direction and bad direction. I now knew what a great director was and what he could mean to an actress. I will always be grateful to him for his toughness and his genius."

Wyler's notorious toughness was not invariably so appreciated by those actors who experienced it—though most would concede that he got results. "Willy's goading approach, if you can take it, works," Charlton Heston once commented, quoting Anthony Perkins likening a Wyler shoot to a Turkish bath: "You darn near drown but you come out smelling like a rose." Unlike Curtiz or Sternberg, Wyler never abused his actors; but some of them found his relentless pushing towards an often unspecified perfection almost equally intolerable. "For God's sake, man, what do you *want*?" Laurence Olivier exploded, after the twentieth quiet, merciless "Again, please." Wyler smiled sadly and murmured: "I want you to be better."

Wyler's preference for long, complex takes added to the burden on his casts. His own attitude was that "whatever extra trouble was needed to make a scene right, or better, was worth it. . . . I'm not vicious, but I am demanding. I don't give a damn about people's comfort, because I drive myself the same way." The director, he believed, was wholly responsible for performance quality: "There is no such thing as good direction with bad performance. I don't care what you do with the camera. When there is bad performance by anybody, at that moment the direction is not good." Hence the Jekyll-and-Hyde aspects noted by David Niven: "Kind, fun, and cozy at all other times, the moment his bottom touched down in his director's chair he became a fiend." Despite being reduced to "a gibbering wreck," though, Niven added that "any time Wyler wants me to work for him—I'll be there." Many other actors have said the same. Heston observed: "I doubt he likes actors very much. He doesn't empathize with them—they irritate him on the set . . . but invariably, they come off well. The only answer I have is that his taste is impeccable and every actor knows it."

"They may hate me on the set, but they will love me at the premiere," Wyler remarked; his films picked up thirty-two Oscar nominations for acting, and fourteen winners—an unequaled record. Not all actors agreed it was worth it, however. Ruth Chatterton, who at one point slapped his face and locked herself in her dressing-room, described Wyler as "the meanest, worst little man I ever worked with," and Sylvia Sidney claimed he was her main reason for abandoning movies in favor of the stage.

In October 1938 Wyler married for the second time. His bride was Margaret Tallichet, an actress from Texas (though her family, like Wyler's, hailed originally from Switzerland). It was a long and happy marriage, lasting until Wyler's death. They had five children, one of whom died in infancy.

In theory Wyler was legally obliged to direct

any picture Goldwyn assigned him. In practice, he often refused assignments, was duly suspended, and would unconcernedly take off to go skiing or traveling in Europe. Goldwyn could have fired him, but Wyler was far too valuable an asset; besides, "somehow all the scripts I turned down were enormous failures." One film he did want to make, and talked Goldwyn into, was *Wuthering Heights* (1939).

"Out of this strange tale of a tortured romance Mr. Goldwyn and his troupe have fashioned a strong and somber film, poetically written as the novel not always was, sinister and wild as it was meant to be," wrote Frank S. Nugent in the *New York Times*, adding that "it is a faithful adaptation . . . which goes straight to the heart of the book, explores its shadows and draws dramatic fire from the savage flints of scene and character hidden there." Few critics would echo such judgments today. Wyler's respectable, conventionalized translation of Emily Brontë's passionate vision, filmed on studio-built moors planted with four-foot California heather, reduces *Wuthering Heights*, David Thomson felt, to the level of "a novel by Edna Ferber, slow, earnest, and clotted," taming the demonic relationship between Heathcliff and Cathy into a readily comprehensible pattern of class-envy. On its own terms, as a romantic costume drama, the film works well enough; only as a version of *Wuthering Heights* is it inadequate.

Ben Hecht and Charles MacArthur's script simplified the plot considerably, cutting out most of the novel's second half. Olivier's Heathcliff captured something of the role's malevolent power, Flora Robson and Geraldine Fitzgerald stood out among a fine supporting cast, but Merle Oberon's Cathy was a disastrous miscasting—cold-eyed, self-possessed, as unlikely a victim of *amour fou* as could well be imagined. In line with the film's softened, romanticized approach, Toland's lighting was misty and diffused, full of candlelight and warm shadows. To Wyler's annoyance, Goldwyn insisted on adding a sentimental coda, described by Richard Mallet as "that angel-choir business while the shades of Cathy and Heathcliff walk away towards the horizon in the Chaplin manner."

Toland's was the sole Oscar won by *Wuthering Heights*. The film was nominated for six more (including one for Wyler), but that year *Gone With the Wind* scooped most of the awards. However, Wyler's status as one of the industry's top directors was now unquestioned. "His films grow steadily in stature," wrote Lewis Jacobs in *The Rise of the American Film*, published in 1939; "his content becomes deeper, his execution more thoughtful, his problems more

vital and relevant. Purposefulness lifts his films higher and higher out of the ordinary." Later critics have singled out Jacobs' weighty commendation as indicating just where Wyler went wrong. In *Film Comment* (Fall 1970) Gary Carey asserted: "His films are most enjoyable when they aim only at being stylish entertainments. Too many of his later films become pompously inflated as they rise higher and higher in their quest for purposefulness."

For the first time in ten years, Wyler returned for his next film to the genre in which he had learned his trade—not that his quickie Westerns, all slam-bang action and stereotypes, had much in common with *The Westerner* (1940). Virtually an anti-Western, the film was a conversational duel, pitting Gary Cooper's wandering cowhand against Walter Brennan's monomaniac Judge Roy Bean. Underplaying with wit and subtlety, Cooper generously handed his costar most of the best scenes; Brennan's perfectly gauged performance (which gained him an Oscar) contrived to be at once funny and sinister without a hint of self-conscious mugging. Outside their scenes together, the movie sags; the plot, a perfunctory affair of ranchers versus homesteaders, offers little of interest, and the heroine—a sadly uninspired discovery of Goldwyn's named Doris Davenport—still less. Matters pick up during the final showdown in an empty theatre, where Bean has bought every seat in order to watch his adored Lillie Langtry undisturbed: after the shootout, Cooper tenderly helps the dying judge to Langtry's dressing-room for a last glimpse of his idol.

Warners, pleased with Wyler's work on *Jezebel*, invited him back for another Davis picture. *The Letter* (1940), in Gary Carey's opinion, "is Wyler's best film; in it Davis gives her finest performance." Other writers have concurred, often citing the opening sequence. From a view of the full moon the camera pans down to a silent rubber plantation and tracks past huts full of drowsy workers to the porch of a bungalow. A shot rings out; a white cockatoo erupts into flight; and a man stumbles out onto the veranda, followed by a woman who fires five more times into his huddled body. The camera continues to track in, ending on a close-up of the woman's face as she stares up at the moon, her expression fixed and emotionless.

The picture was adapted by Howard Koch from Somerset Maugham's play (already filmed once before, with Jeanne Eagels) about the wife of a British planter in Malaya who murders her lover out of jealousy, then claims he tried to rape her. Thereafter she coolly and contemptuously manipulates the men around her—her husband, her lawyer, the district officer—lying her way towards an inevitable acquittal. Davis superbly conveys the suppressed sensuality beneath a primly respectable facade, her whole performance (as Louis Giannetti noted) "a triumph of nuance and understatement, perhaps the most subtle of her career—a far cry from the bravura effulgence she was noted for."

Wyler filmed in exceptionally long takes, building the tension of the extended conversation scenes where Davis holds center-frame amid deferential men—who could nonetheless, at a single slip, become her jailers and executioners. Michael A. Anderegg, in his monograph on the director, writes that "assisted by Tony Gaudio's low-key photography, Wyler creates a pattern of light and shadow both reminiscent of German Expressionism and anticipatory of the visual style associated with *film noir*." If, as Karel Reisz suggested, "the social life . . . is more Boston than Singapore," it makes little difference; surface realism is not Wyler's aim. The film's only serious blemish is its ludicrous, Production-Code ending—which Wyler deplored—wherein Davis is stabbed by her victim's vengeful Eurasian wife, upon which two policemen materialize from nowhere to ensure that this murder, too, meets with due retribution.

By way of a return match, Davis was now loaned to Goldwyn, to be directed by Wyler in their third and last film together. *The Little Foxes* (1941) was taken from another Hellman play, perhaps her best. Set in the South at the turn of the century, it presented an acid study of a repellent, infinitely rapacious family— illustrating, at least in Hellman's intention, how America's devotion to materialism soured and distorted all other human impulses. That message, in all likelihood, reached few viewers of the film, which comes across rather as a full-blooded melodrama offering Wyler maximum scope for his exploration of personal relationships: in none of his films is the clash of interests, the physical expression of psychological struggle and domination, more vividly presented.

"Wyler always goes into high gear when there are a few steps to whet his imagination," Gary Carey observed. Staircases figure dramatically in several Wyler movies, and never more strikingly than in *The Little Foxes*. From the topmost step Regina Giddens (Davis) disdainfully surveys the other members of her conniving family; in the film's most famous scene, she sits rigidly foregrounded in her chair while her husband, stricken with a fatal heart attack, crawls up the stairs in futile quest for the medicine she has withheld. "The motionless camera on Davis's

whitely determined face and her position of power within the shot are an object lesson in how to achieve the maximum filmic intensity with the minimum of means," wrote Neil Sinyard. With the deep-focus techniques of which Toland, fresh from his work on *Citizen Kane*, was now master, Wyler could employ complex multiplane groupings to express the tensions within each frame, without resorting to constant cutting.

It was over the portrayal of Regina that the rapport between Davis and Wyler broke down, paralleling to some extent—though on a far higher professional level—Wyler's earlier clash with Ruth Chatterton. Davis insisted on playing Regina as a thoroughgoing monster, seething with barely concealed malice. Wyler "wanted her to play it much lighter. This woman was supposed not just to be evil, but to have great charm, humor, and sex." Davis resisted, with Goldwyn's support, and played the role her way. "The filming was torture," she wrote later. Much to her regret, she and Wyler never worked together again. Both *The Letter* and *The Little Foxes* gathered a stack of nominations, but no Oscars. Wyler finally hit the jackpot with his next film, for which—another tribute to his reputation— he had been requested on loan by MGM.

Of all the numerous Hollywood movies made between 1940 and 1945 in support of America's various allies, *Mrs. Miniver* (1942) remains the most famous. Dated, sentimental, hopelessly over-idealized in its depiction of a phony rose-garden England, the film still intermittently exerts surprising emotional impact. As propaganda, it was hugely successful, and much admired by no less an authority than Joseph Goebbels.

Based on a book—less a novel than a series of loosely connected sketches—by Jan Struther, *Mrs. Miniver* presents a supposedly archetypal English middle-class family, prosperous and charming, living in a quaintly idyllic Kent village. In true Metro fashion, any hint of social unrest is smoothed over. Political dissent is voiced only by the Minivers' student son, Vin, shown as a misguided young hothead to whom his pipe-smoking father (Walter Pidgeon) listens with an indulgent smile; class conflict is reduced to rivalry between the lady of the manor and the local stationmaster over the annual rose competition.

Into this cozy world irrupts the war: food rationing, Dunkirk, bombing raids, and death. Vin joins the RAF, Mr. Miniver takes his small boat to Dunkirk, and Mrs. Miniver copes heroically through it all, even at one point disarming a fanatical German airman—an episode that alarmed Louis B. Mayer, still anxious in November 1941 not to offend Nazi susceptibilities. In the face of adversity the village—i.e. Britain—forgetting its differences and revealing the dogged determination hidden beneath its old-world charm, unites against the foe, and at the end of the film the vicar preaches a Churchillian sermon in the bombed-out church. The congregation launches into "Onward, Christian Soldiers," the camera lifts to gaze through the shattered roof—and four flights of Spitfires hurtle overhead, as "Land of Hope and Glory" swells on the soundtrack.

"Wyler treated London of 1940 much as he had treated the New Orleans of 1850 in *Jezebel*," commented Karel Reisz; "from a distance, and with the same prettifying of local customs and sentimentalising of externally imposed hardships." At the time, though, *Mrs. Miniver* was ecstatically received. Roosevelt was so taken with the sermon that he had it reprinted on leaflets to be dropped over German-occupied territory. The film earned Wyler his first director's Oscar—plus five more, including Best Picture. By the time the awards were presented, Wyler was himself in England and in uniform. As soon as *Mrs. Miniver* was finished, he had offered his services to the US armed forces, and was commissioned a major in the Air Force. (He had become an American citizen in 1928.)

Having turned down an invitation from Laurence Olivier to direct his projected film of *Henry V*, Wyler started work on the first of his two wartime documentaries. *Memphis Belle* (1944) concentrates on the twenty-fifth and final bombing mission over Germany of a B-17 Flying Fortress. Filming on grainy 16mm Kodacolor stock, Wyler flew several missions to get the shots he wanted, frequently acting as his own cameraman in an unheated, unpressurized plane at 29,000 feet. The resultant film, furnished with a spare, lyrical commentary by Lester Koenig, is reckoned one of the finest American combat documentaries of the war. Karel Reisz saw in it "a spontaneous, unaffected realism which is to be found nowhere else in . . . [Wyler's] work." Wyler's second combat film, *Thunderbolt*, aimed to do for the P-47 fighter what *Memphis Belle* had done for the B-17 but failed to equal the earlier film's sense of involvement. Completed in 1945, *Thunderbolt* was not released until 1947, and then aroused little interest. While shooting its final scenes over Italy, Wyler sustained damage to his aural nerve and permanently lost the hearing of his right ear.

On his return to Hollywood, Wyler was invited by Frank Capra to join him, together with George Stevens and producer Sam Briskin, in a newly formed independent company, Liberty Films. Wyler was excited by the idea, one of several attempts during the restless postwar years to free filmmakers from the tyranny of the studios. Before he could start work for Liberty, though, he still owed Goldwyn one last movie.

The Best Years of Our Lives (1946), Neil Sinyard wrote, "stands as a monument to . . . [Wyler's] meticulous working methods as well as to the nobility and love he imparts to material to which, with his own war experiences, he felt he could bring a particular authentic knowledge." Three veterans return to their middle-American hometown to face the problems of readjustment; the world they reenter is not the one they left, nor are they the same men who left it. Al Stephenson (Fredric March), an army sergeant, comes back to his middle-class family and banking job and finds himself indefinably dissatisfied with both. Fred Derry (Dana Andrews), an air corps bombardier, confronts a crumbling marriage and a dismal prospect of dead-end jobs. Homer Parrish, a sailor, returns crippled to his fiancée, with both hands blown off; for this role Wyler cast a nonprofessional, a man named Harold Russell who really had lost his hands in the war. Their experiences are interwoven—Fred falls for Al's daughter, and most of the characters attend Homer's wedding—but the film was intended, as Wyler put it, less as "a story of plot" than as "a picture of some people, who were real people, facing real problems."

In *Best Years* the Wyler-Toland style—long takes, intricate composition in depth, subtly formalized naturalism in the acting—reached its apogee. The film's most famous sequence occurs in a bar run by Homer's uncle, Butch (Hoagy Carmichael). In one contained, complex shot we see: right foreground, Butch giving Homer piano instruction, with Al leaning on the piano watching them; a group of customers at the bar, left middle-ground, also watching the piano lessons; and in the far background, framed between the groups, the real object of Al's attention, Fred phoning Al's daughter Peggy to break with her. Everybody in the shot is held in clean, sharp focus, allowing the spectator, as Wyler wished, to "look from one to the other character at his own will, do his own cutting."

Breaking with Hollywood convention, Wyler had his male actors wear no makeup, and the women no more than they would wear in their daily lives—thus rendering even more poignant the moment when Al Stephenson compares his lined, middle-aged reflection with a photograph of his younger self (the handsome young March in matinee idol pose). March gave perhaps his finest performance, perfectly supported by Myrna Loy as his wife. Loy had initially been reluctant to take the role. "I hear Wyler's a sadist," she told Goldwyn. "No, no," responded Goldwyn, leaping to the defense of his star director; "he's just a very mean fellow."

At the Academy Awards, *Best Years* outdid even *Mrs. Miniver*, taking seven Oscars, including Best Picture and Wyler's second as Best Director. The film was praised fulsomely, in America and abroad. Thomas Mann considered it "unsurpassed in its naturalness, profoundly decent in its opinions." In *Theatre Arts* (February 1947) Hermine Isaacs wrote that "the truth of this picture is more than accurate observation . . . it is the truth that compassion tells where the eye cannot follow." James Agee, though disliking the plot's "timidity," commended Wyler for "a style of great purity, directness and warmth, about as cleanly devoid of mannerism, haste, superfluous motion, aesthetic or emotional overreaching as any I know. . . . Wyler has always seemed to me an exceedingly sincere and good director; now he seems one of the great ones."

There were a few dissenting voices. In *Hollywood Quarterly* (April 1947) Abraham Polonsky echoed Agee's misgivings: "The plot forces easy solutions on its creators. . . . As always, the Hollywood fog moved in." Robert Warshow, in *Partisan Review* (May/June 1947), perceived beneath the film's "empty and extremely skillful precision . . . a denial of the reality of politics, if politics means the existence of real incompatibilites of interest and real *social* problems not susceptible of individual solution." He accused Wyler of hoodwinking his liberal audience by simply peddling "the basic Hollywood myths" minus "the cruder dramatic and ideological conventions ordinarily used to express them."

The reputation of *Best Years*, like that of its director, has since declined; more recent critics have tended to side with Polonsky and Warshow. Higham and Greenberg dismissed it as "a banal, occasionally cynical tribute to the American way of life . . . about as radical as a manifesto of the John Birch society. . . . Wyler's handling . . . is mostly so anonymous and pedestrian, so tepid and attenuated, that it reduces the film's visual interest to practically nil." Less pejoratively, Ivan Butler felt that the film was "probably over-praised at its appearance, and has certainly been over-condemned since. Smooth, shining and sure-fire, it nonetheless tells its interwoven stories with skill and sympathy, avoiding bathos narrowly but with confidence. . . . The chief interest of the film today may well lie in its preservation of a mood and an atmosphere long dissipated."

At the time, though, Wyler's critical status was at its peak—especially in France, where Roger Leenhardt headlined an article in *L'Écran français,* "À bas Ford, vive Wyler!" These two, Leenhardt explained, were "the two greatest directors in the world," with Wyler the greater, and "both handle the most diverse subjects without trying to convey a personal vision"—perhaps the most obtuse account of John Ford ever expressed by a serious critic. Leenhardt's view of Wyler was taken up by André Bazin in a long, highly influential article, first published in *Revue du Cinéma,* in which he defined Wyler's filmmaking as "style sans style." Wyler, according to Bazin, "has taken economy of means to the point where it becomes, paradoxically, one of the most personal styles in today's cinema. . . . His great talent lies in achieving clarity through a stripping-down of the formal elements—placing himself at the service both of his subject-matter and of his audience." Bazin contrasted Welles's use of deep focus—"a systematic distension of reality, as if it were drawn on an elastic band which he liked to frighten us by stretching, before letting it snap in our faces"—with that of Wyler, seen as "an act of loyalty towards the spectator . . . liberal and democratic . . . subordinate to the dramatic needs of the *mise-en-scène* and in particular to the dramatic clarity of the plot."

Best Years was Wyler's last film with Toland, who died in 1948, aged only forty-four. It was also the end of his association with Goldwyn. However, Liberty Films was already in financial trouble, and before Wyler could even take up a project the company was forced to sell out to Paramount. Under the terms of the deal, each of the three directors was supposed to make five films for the studio, continuing to act as their own producers; of the three, only Wyler actually completed his quota.

His first film for Paramount, *The Heiress* (1949), was undertaken at the suggestion of its star, Olivia de Havilland. Henry James's novel, *Washington Square,* had been adapted as a play by Ruth and Augustus Goetz, and staged in New York and London. The role de Havilland wanted was that of Catherine Sloper, a plain, awkward young woman, butt of her widowed father's irony, who falls for a handsome and plausible young man. They plan to elope but he, learning that she will be disinherited if she marries against her father's wishes, jilts her.

Inevitably, in the double transition from novel to stage to film, much of the Jamesian subtlety was lost. Jerry Carlson (in Peary and Shatzkin's anthology) wrote that Wyler "sacrifices both moral complexity and dramatic credibility . . . before the mechanical demands of a well-made plot." But purely as a film, *The Heiress* works well, thanks partly to excellent performances from de Havilland and Miriam Hopkins (as her aunt), and a superlative one, probably his finest on screen, from Ralph Richardson as the heroine's father. (Montgomery Clift, as the fortune-hunting Morris Townsend, was less happily cast.)

As Hermione Isaacs wrote in *Films in Review* (February 1950), the action is confined mostly to the house in Washington Square: "Even within these limits there is sufficient potential for movement for the director who knows, as Wyler does, where to look. Shrewdly he pivots his action around the central staircase that leads up two flights to Catherine's room, marking her emotional changes in the way she moves up and down the stairs. The vista of rooms end to end in . . . [the] narrow house provides many variations for the camera, and when their limits are reached there are mirrors to extend the views. In such a setting, with the aid of the long-focus camera the director can deploy his actors for dialogue without appearing to hold the scene in static composition." De Havilland received an Oscar, as did Aaron Copland for his deftly evocative score.

To follow *The Heiress*, Wyler again called in Ruth and Augustus Goetz to adapt a period classic—Theodore Dreiser's *Sister Carrie*. This time the results were far less fortunate—mainly for reasons having little to do with the film itself. Wyler, whose views were staunchly liberal, loathed McCarthyism and was one of the founders and most outspoken members of the anti-HUAC Committee for the First Amendment. His war record and his eminence within the industry protected him from direct attack, but one at least of his films sustained serious damage. *Carrie* (1952)—"Sister" was dropped, lest people think it was about a nun—was shot in 1950 but not released until two years later, heavily cut and restructured.

Dreiser's novel, which caused a scandal when it was published in 1900, recounts the rise of Carrie Meeber from the Chicago factories to fame and fortune on the stage, with the parallel fall into destitution of her lover, the restaurateur George Hurstwood. The Goetzes' adaptation excised most of Dreiser's social criticism, leaving "a romantic story about the doomed love of Carrie and Hurstwood, rather than the description of a society," noted Carolyn Geduld (Peary and Shatzkin). The casting of Jennifer Jones as Carrie further softened the film's impact. Even so, Paramount was still apprehensive— "Someone decided it was un-American to show poverty," Wyler remarked drily—and demanded cuts. As eventually released, *Carrie* not surprisingly

proved incoherent and uncertain in tone; "a film at odds with itself," as Michael Anderegg put it. It did, however, enshrine one outstanding performance: Laurence Olivier's Hurstwood, in Richard Winnington's opinion "the best acting of his career." Many others have concurred.

While *Carrie* was still in dispute, Wyler directed another film in only five weeks—a quickie, by his standards. *Detective Story* (1951) was adapted from a Broadway hit by Sidney Kingsley, author of *Dead End*. This was an altogether harsher, tougher, more downbeat piece, in line with the postwar mood. Set in a New York precinct house, the film traces multiple strands of police activity, centering around the character of an obsessively puritanical detective (Kirk Douglas). Wyler's cinematographer, Lee Garmes, put his camera on a crab dolly, allowing fast intricate movement around the station set on which nearly all the action took place. Something of a link between the Warner crime movies of the 1930s and the "maverick cop" cycle of the 1970s, *Detective Story* comes across like one of its own precinct officers—professional, efficient, and impersonal.

Not since his pre-Goldwyn days, in 1935, had Wyler directed a comedy, and *Roman Holiday* (1953), with its contrived, fairy-tale plot, evokes unmistakable echoes of Capra or Lubitsch. A princess (Audrey Hepburn) on a state visit to Rome escapes briefly from her cage of oppressive ritual and falls in with a hard-bitten American reporter (Gregory Peck). Most of the film was shot on location in Rome, taking in all the standard tourist sites, and cried out for color. Two things saved it from vapidity: Audrey Hepburn, irresistible in her first starring role, and the poignancy of the ending, hinted in the title's cryptic reference to Byron ("Butchered to make a Roman holiday"). Avoiding the temptation of an inanely happy denouement, Wyler shows us the princess back in captivity, irrevocably cut off from the reporter, her youthful beauty and vivacity once more sacrificed to the demands of protocol.

Wyler's last movie for Paramount was again taken from a Broadway play. *The Desperate Hours* (1955) revisits a favorite situation in the films of the paranoid 1950s: a complacent, middle-class household is invaded by a gang of ruthless crooks, who hold the family for ransom. The gang leader was played by Humphrey Bogart, haggard and visibly ill in his penultimate role, and Fredric March brought a neurotic edginess to the part of the father. Thus cast, the two men came to seem oddly akin, making the film, as Neil Sinyard suggested, less the smug hymn to bourgeois values it overtly appeared than a subversive attack on those values, with the gangsters embodying repressed, vital forces in the "innocent" American psyche. Perhaps on account of this ambiguity, *The Desperate Hours* did poorly at the box office.

Having discharged his obligations to Paramount, Wyler spent the rest of his career as an idependent director, moving from one studio to another and often acting as his own producer. For Allied Artists he took up a project mooted by Capra at Liberty Films, *Friendly Persuasion* (1956). Based on a collection of stories by Jessamyn West, the film—Wyler's first feature in color—concerned a family of Quaker settlers in Indiana at the time of the Civil War, with Gary Cooper as the doggedly nonviolent Jess Birdwell. Rather than seriously engaging with the issues involved, Wyler tended to retreat into homespun sentimentality, and at over two and a quarter hours the film's gentle charm often wore thin. It was well received, though, and won the Palme d'Or at Cannes.

Wyler returned to the problem of nonviolence in a violent society for his last and most ambitious Western, *The Big Country* (1958), described by Philip French as a "United Nations hymn to peaceful coexistence." A feud over water rights between two families—the suavely patrician Terrills and the squalid and rampageous Hannasseys—is ironically observed by a quiet-mannered easterner, come west to marry the spoiled Terrill daughter. As the title implied, *The Big Country* was filmed on a grand scale: almost three hours long, in Technicolor and Technirama. Many critics found the film overblown, but Wyler's use of the landscape was deliberately grandiose, showing westerners attempting to match their massive surroundings with equally outsize gestures, and deriding the futility of their efforts. In one sequence the easterner (Gregory Peck) finally accepts the repeated challenge of the Terrill's foreman (Charlton Heston), but only at dead of night, seeing no need to prove his courage in public. As the two men swing wildly and bloodily at each other, Wyler pulls right back to a long-shot, reducing them to a pair of squabbling insects in the vast moonlit silence of the plain.

By this stage in his career, Wyler had slipped from his former critical eminence. His earlier work was still widely esteemed, but some writers detected a lessening of quality in his films of the 1950s. In an article in *Films and Filming* (February 1960), John Howard Reid deplored "the heavy-handedness of *Roman Holiday*, the surefire commonplaces of *The Desperate Hours*, the notable unevenness of *Friendly Persuasion*, and the trite heroics of *The Big Country*. . . . These

last four films reveal a steadily increasing desire to pander to box-office foibles." With his next assignment, Wyler's critical decline was accelerated.

In 1957, for the second time in his career, he was called in by MGM. Things had changed a lot. In 1941 Metro had been the most prestigious and financially successful of the Hollywood studios. Sixteen years later, the studio was asking him to rescue it from imminent bankruptcy with a major hit. In the 1950s, that could only mean a biblical epic. The studio was putting its collective shirt on a remake of *Ben-Hur*—the silent screen's most stupendous epic, on which Wyler had worked thirty years before—this time complete with wide screen, Technicolor, and a budget of $10 million.

Initially reluctant, Wyler let himself be persuaded by the challenge, just to "see if I know how to make a picture like this." Filming at Cinecittà outside Rome took the best part of a year, and the budget rose to $15 million. Of that, a sizeable proportion went on the climactic chariot-race (directed by Andrew Marton and Yakima Canutt) in which the Hebrew prince Ben-Hur (Charlton Heston) finally defeats his enemy, the Roman Messala (Stephen Boyd), who had once consigned him to the galleys. Fortunately for MGM, the gamble paid off. *Ben-Hur* (1959) stacked up an unprecedented eleven Oscars (including Wyler's third) and broke box-office records all round the world. Takings were seemingly unharmed by predominantly lukewarm reviews pointing out that, apart from the two big action set-pieces (the chariot race and an earlier sea battle), most of the film's 219 minutes were insufferably ponderous. For Dwight Macdonald even "the big spectacular moments . . . failed because Wyler doesn't know how to handle crowds nor how to get a culminating rhythm by cutting."

"*Cahiers du Cinéma* never forgave me for directing *Ben-Hur*," Wyler wryly observed. Critical standards were shifting; the Hollywood directors now feted in Paris were the genre specialists, the mavericks and quirky individualists: Ford, Welles, Mann, Nicholas Ray. Wyler's seamless professionalism was hopelessly out of fashion, and even his Goldwyn-period films were being reappraised and downgraded. In *Film Culture* (Spring 1963) Andrew Sarris laid down the *auteurist* line: "Wyler's career is a cipher as far as personal direction is concerned. . . . It would seeem that . . . [his] admirers have long mistaken a lack of feeling for emotional restraint."

The bowdlerization of Hellman's *The Children's Hour* into *These Three* had always irked

Wyler, and in 1961 he took advantage of eased taboos to remake the film, with its lesbian theme restored, under Hellman's original title. As the two teachers he cast Audrey Hepburn and Shirley MacLaine, thus (in Neil Sinyard's view) "letting in wit, perception, subtle shading, and producing performances from them that are not simply accomplished but awe-inspiring." Most reviewers were far less favorable, finding the film dull and dated. Several suggested that most contemporary American parents were too sophisticated to care if their daughters' teachers were lesbian or not. Jean-Pierre Melville disagreed, however: "To anyone who knows the American middle classes of Philadelphia and Boston, the film's a masterpiece."

In 1963, Wyler and his wife visited Russia at the invitation of the Union of Cinema Workers. They were warmly received everywhere, and Wyler was treated with great deference—especially for having directed *Roman Holiday*, a smash hit in the USSR. On his return, 20th Century–Fox offered him his first musical, *The Sound of Music*. Wyler accepted,though without great enthusiasm, and was scouting locations in Austria when a far more interesting—if less lucrative—project came up: a script taken from John Fowles' first novel, *The Collector*. Since *Ben-Hur* had made Wyler financially independent for life, he was able to quit the musical without hesitation; Robert Wise took over.

The Collector (1965) found Wyler back in form. "The direction's unrelentingly obsessive attention to detail and decor, the unobtrusively modern camerawork and the complex performances . . . make *The Collector* his most consistently engrossing picture since *The Letter* and *The Best Years of Our Lives*," wrote Jean-Pierre Coursodon. Andrew Sarris, usually no great fan of Wyler, said it was "the most erotic movie ever to come out past the Production Code, and I urge all my warped friends to rush off and see it." The film is a perverse duet: a repressed, butterfly-collecting clerk (Terence Stamp) becomes obsessed with a lovely art student (Samantha Eggar). Coming unexpectedly into money, he kidnaps her and keeps her in the cellar of a remote mansion. Wyler concentrates on building up the claustrophobic tension between his protagonists, trapping them in tightly framed shots that emphasize both their physical proximity and the hopeless mental gulf dividing them. *The Collector* took no Oscars—losing out, ironically, to *Sound of Music*—but both Stamp and Eggar won Best Acting awards at Cannes.

How To Steal a Million (1966) was a comedy vehicle for Audrey Hepburn and Peter O'Toole—a frothy Parisian caper involving stolen art forgeries, so slight as to make *Roman Holiday* look like neorealism. To follow, Wyler made his delayed debut as a musical director with *Funny Girl* (1968), a movie version of the stage show that had propelled Barbra Streisand to stardom. A brash, highly fictionalized account of the life of the Jewish vaudeville star Fanny Brice, it marked, in John Baxter's opinion, "the nadir of Wyler's creativity." Despite critical disapproval, though, *Funny Girl* triumphed at the box office and won Streisand an Oscar.

By contrast, Wyler's final movie was a complete flop. *The Liberation of L. B. Jones* (1970), the first of a projected five-picture deal with Columbia, tackled the currently fashionable subject of racism with a bitter tale about a black undertaker in a Tennessee town who refuses to condone his wife's affair with a white cop and gets killed for his temerity. The tone of the film is unremittingly pessimistic. Hatred breeds hatred, violence breeds violence, the law is bigoted and corrupt. Wyler refused to end on a facile note of hope or reconciliation, which may explain the film's lack of box-office success. Several critics noted a disturbing unevenness of tone, as though Wyler were uncertain under which conventions he was operating. Ken Doeckel (*Films in Review*, October 1971) found "an unbelievable amalgam of current racial stereotypes and of old-hat melodrama," though more recently Neil Sinyard described the film as "a grim riposte to Hollywood's usual righteousness over the race issue . . . a remarkably uncompromising and uncomfortable summation" of Wyler's career.

A further film for Columbia, *Forty Carats*, a romantic comedy, was in pre-production when Wyler decided that, at seventy, he had had enough, and asked to be released from his contract. "Making a picture is just too goddamn much work. . . . It takes a helluva lot out of me. I did it for over forty years. Now, unless something really excites me. . . . " Nothing did, though he continued to read scripts that were sent him.

William Wyler presents a classic example of the director dethroned by the shifting of cinematic fashion, damned for those very qualities for which he was once praised. His restraint came to be seen as frigidity, good taste as complacency, seriousness as pomposity, technical accomplishment and clarity as bland dullness. Jean-Pierre Coursodon characterized the films from *These Three* to *Wuthering Heights*, which at the time lifted Wyler to the summit of his profession, as "so stiff and lifeless, so devoid of warmth or imagination that one wonders whether it was not the very boredom they induce that awed the critics of the time into their respectful approbation." David Thomson, citing Orson Welles' not wholly complimentary description of Wyler as "a brilliant producer," stated that "Wyler has no cinematic personality, no abiding thematic interests and no proper grasp of camera language. . . . [His] films are put together like budgets: neatness and balance stand in for insight."

His alleged lack of clear thematic preoccupations has often been adduced as the ultimate proof of Wyler's failure to achieve *auteur* status. Against this, Neil Sinyard argued that Wyler's work does "exhibit certain patterns which challenged the idea of impersonality. It was the vision of a man centrally interested in action in character rather than character in action, . . . particularly attentive to social divisions between rich and poor, men and women, the complacent and the envious, divisions which gathered to a characteristic confrontation in which the grievances were dramatically played out. . . . The vision tended to bitterness and tragedy. The scenes one particularly remembers in Wyler . . . are those which dwell painfully on moments of acute social embarrassment or the small cuts of domestic cruelty which gradually destroy a marriage and diminish a person's soul."

Wyler himself readily disclaimed any aspiration to auteurship. "I have been accused of having no style—which is actually true, simply because I have chosen to film so many different types of subject," he remarked, insisting that a director had no business imposing his personality or opinions between the subject and the audience. "A director should not try to attract attention to himself away from the actors and away from the story. He should attract attention to himself by making great films, great performances. . . . I never thought of doing something where people say, 'Oh, that's Wyler.'"

Of recent years, there have been signs that Wyler's reputation may be recovering a little. Andrew Sarris, revising his earlier "harsh judgment," conceded that Wyler had "demonstrated time and again that the movies of a good craftsman are infinitely preferable to those of a bad artist." Within the industry, at any rate, his status was never in doubt. In 1976, to crown his thirty-four Oscars, countless nominations, and numerous other awards, American and foreign, Wyler received the American Film Institute's annual Life Achievement Award. Presenting it, George Stevens Jr. praised him for having "made films of lasting value with a frequency virtually unmatched by his contemporaries. . . . It has been said of Wyler that he shortened the distance between the eye and the mind."

Wyler greatly relished his years of retirement. "I enjoy my grandchildren, I travel, I read. I've been lucky," he told one interviewer. "I don't think about movies that much any more. . . . When I see a movie I think, Jesus, what he did to get that one shot. So much work." He and his wife were now able to indulge their lifelong passion for travel to the full, sometimes taking in tributes and retrospectives of his work. In May 1981, he attended one such season at the National Film Theatre in London. A few weeks later, after his return home to Hollywood, Wyler died suddenly of a heart-attack, aged seventy-nine.
—*P.K.*

FILMS: *Two-reelers*—Crook Buster, 1925; The Gunless Bad Man, 1926; Ridin' for Love, 1926; Fire Barrier, 1926; Don't Shoot, 1926; The Pinnacle Rider, 1926; Martin of the Mounted, 1926; Two Fister, 1927; Kelcy Gets His Man, 1927; Tenderfoot Courage, 1927; The Silent Partner, 1927; Galloping Justice, 1927; The Haunted Homestead, 1927; The Lone Star, 1927; The Ore Raiders, 1927; The Home Trail, 1927; Gun Justice, 1927; Phantom Outlaw, 1927; Square Shooter, 1927; The Horse Trader, 1927; Daze in the West, 1927. *Five-reelers*—Lazy Lightning, 1926; The Stolen Ranch, 1926; Blazing Days, 1927; Hard Fists, 1927; The Border Cavalier, 1927; Straight Shootin', 1927; Desert Dust 1927; Thunder Riders, 1928. *Features*—Anybody Here Seen Kelly?, 1928; The Shakedown, 1929; The Love Trap, 1929; Hell's Heroes, 1930; The Storm, 1930; A House Divided, 1931; Tom Brown of Culver, 1932; Her First Mate, 1933; Counsellor at Law, 1933; Glamour, 1934; The Good Fairy, 1935; The Gay Deception, 1935; These Three, 1936; Dodsworth, 1936; (with Howard Hawks) Come and Get It, 1936; Dead End, 1937; Jezebel, 1938; Wuthering Heights, 1939; The Westerner, 1940; The Letter, 1940; The Little Foxes, 1941; Mrs. Miniver, 1942; Memphis Belle, 1944 (documentary); Thunderbolt, 1945 (released 1947; documentary); The Best Years of Our Lives, 1946; The Heiress, 1949; Detective Story, 1951; Carrie, 1952; Roman Holiday, 1953; The Desperate Hours, 1955; Friendly Persuasion, 1956; The Big Country, 1958; Ben-Hur, 1959; The Children's Hour (The Loudest Whisper), 1961; The Collector, 1965; How to Steal a Million, 1966; Funny Girl, 1968; The Liberation of L. B. Jones, 1970. *Published script*—Wuthering Heights in Twenty Best Film Plays (ed. Gassner, J. and Nichols, D.), 1943.

ABOUT: Affron, C. *in* Lyon, C. (ed.) International Dictionary of Films and Filmmakers, 1984; Anderegg, M. William Wyler, 1979; Baxter, J. Hollywood in the Thirties, 1968; Bazin, A. Qu'est-ce que le cinéma? (vol. 1), 1958; Bluestone, G. Novels Into Film, 1968; Butler, I. The War Film, 1974; Giannetti, L. Masters of the American Cinema, 1981; Green, G. The Pleasure Dome, 1972; Higham, C. and Greenberg, J. Hollywood in the Forties, 1968; Jacobs, L. The Rise of the American Film, 1939; Kantor, B. and others. Directors at Work, 1970; Madsen, A. William Wyler, 1973; Perry, G. and Shatzkin, R. (eds.) The Classic American

Novel and the Movies, 1977; Reisz, K. (ed.) William Wyler: An Index, 1958; Roud, R. (ed.) Cinema: A Critical Dictionary, 1980; Sarris, A. The American Cinema, 1968; Thomson, D. A Biographical Dictionary of the Cinema, 1980; Tuska, J. (ed.) Close-Up: The Hollywood Director, 1978; Wagner, G. The Novel and the Cinema, 1975; Warshow, R. The Immediate Experience, 1962. *Periodicals*—Action January–February 1967; September–October 1973; American Cinematographer February 1975; American Film April 1976; Arts Lab Programme October–December 1981; L'Avant-Scène du Cinéma April 1976; Cahiers du Cinéma June 1966; Cinema (USA) Summer 1967; Cinématographe March–April 1981; Cinemasessanta September–October 1981; Cuadernos de Cine Club April 1963; L'Écran français April 13, 1948; Film (FFS) Autumn 1963; Film Comment Fall 1970; Film Digest January 1967; Film Guide Summer 1957; Film Weekly December 5, 1936; Films and Filming August 1958, February–March 1960, October 1981; Films in Review February 1950–October 1971; Focus on Film Spring 1976; Hollywood Quarterly April 1947; Interview March 1974; National Film Theatre Booklet May 1981; Otro Cine 33 1958; Partisan Review May–June 1947; Picturegoer March 15, 1947; Revue du Cinéma February–March 1948; Séquence 13 1951; Show June 1970; Theatre Arts February 1947.

SERGEI YUTKEVICH

YUTKEVICH, SERGEI (December 28, 1904– April 23, 1985), Soviet film and theatre director, scenarist, designer, and writer, was born in St. Petersburg (later Petrograd, now Leningrad) and educated there and in Kiev, where he studied painting with Alexandra Exter and stage directing with Konstantin Mardjanov. "They were astonishing and wonderful days— the beginnings of a revolutionary art," Yutkevich says in his autobiographical statement in *Cinema in Revolution.* "When we talk about the years when we started artistic work, people are always surprised by the birth-dates of almost all the directors and the major artists of those times. We were incredibly young! It has to be remembered that an entire generation had disappeared. . . . This was a period of tumultuous expansion for Soviet art. It is difficult now to imagine how it was. . . . Leningrad, for instance, in 1919 or 1920 . . . the grass grew on the sidewalks . . . but at the same time the city was experiencing an intense cultural life. There had never been so many theatres . . . never had so many books—particularly volumes of poetry—appeared. Never had there been so much experiment in the theatre and in painting."

Yutkevich goes on to describe some of these experiments, in which the key influences were the futurist poet and dramatist Vladimir Mayakovsky and the avant-garde director Vsevolod Meyerhold. In their search for thoroughly revolutionary means of expression, these young Soviet artists turned toward "the kind of popular art which the aristocracy and bourgeoisie had scorned. To be precise: the music-hall, the circus and the cinema."

It was in Kiev, in this atmosphere of intense intellectual and aesthetic excitement, that Yutkevich, aged fifteen, met another young painter, named Grigori Kozintsev, several months his junior. They were introduced by Mardjanov at the Solvtzovsky Theatre. Kozintsev has recalled how "there appeared in front of me a boy . . . with a pointed nose, lively eyes, dressed in a well-ironed shirt with many pleats, and green trousers. On his head he wore a check cap, and he was twirling a little cane between his fingers." Mardjanov assigned these youngsters to collaborate on decors for an operetta he planned to stage and soon afterwards helped them to launch their first cellar-theatre, the Harlequin, from which they took their clown shows, puppet plays, and melodramas out onto the streets of Kiev.

In August 1921 Yutkevich went to Moscow, hoping to study under Meyerhold. He took the entrance examination in company with Sergei Eisenstein, and both were accepted. They studied directing and acting in Meyerhold's tiny studio and earned their living by working together on designs for some of the innumerable little theatres that were springing up everywhere, and especially for Foregger's Mastfor Theatre. Meanwhile, Kozintsev had gone to Petrograd. Late in 1921 or early in 1922, Yutkevich joined him there and participated with him and Leonid Trauberg in establishing an anarchic little theatre company called the "Factory of the Eccentric Actor" (FEKS). "Eccentricism," Yutkevich wrote years later, "was, it must now be confessed, a strange mixture of mere aberrations and of juvenile passions for the circus burlesque, which for us carried echoes of the tradition of [the great French mime Jean-Baptiste] Deburau. We had just seen the first films of Chaplin and this was at once a revelation and an extension of the line of the music-hall and circus. At the same time the first German expressionist pictures had just appeared on our screens. They had a great influence on us all."

After an interlude in Moscow, Yutkevich returned to Petrograd for the summer of 1922, this time accompanied by Eisenstein, who gave his support and advice to FEKS. While Yutkevich was in Petrograd, he and Kozintsev exhibited in the famous avant-garde "Left Stream" exhibition: "joyous collages, posters representing circus people and eccentric actors, made up of fragments of other posters. Variegated mosaics, strong in color . . . impertinent and eccentric." A distinguished art critic warned them that, if they continued on their downward and antiacademic path, they would "end up in the cinema." A year or two later, FEKS did indeed turn its "impertinent and eccentric" talents to that despised art form, but by then Yutkevich had left the group: "We divided the spheres of influence between us. Kozintsev and Trauberg stayed to conquer Petrograd. Eisenstein and I decided to continue working in Moscow."

It was not long, however, before Eisenstein became disillusioned with the Mastfor Theatre and moved on. Yutkevich stayed for a while as a director and a designer, but early in 1923 he also walked out. A year later he joined Sevzapkino (North-Western Cinema) as assistant director of a short comedy called *Dayoch radio!* (*Give Us Radio,* 1924), a parody of American gangster movies, involving a bunch of Moscow waifs. "The director turned out to be an illiterate imposter," and Yutkevich, then twenty, totally inexperienced, and very frightened, directed the movie himself.

In *Cinema in Revolution,* he says that "the first master who really initiated me into all the mysteries of the profession was the director Abram Room. In 1926 he invited me to be the designer and assistant on his films *The Traitor* and *Bed and Sofa.* . . . As painter, I built the sets; as assistant, I helped the director on the set and in the cutting-room; I prepared the set-ups, dressed the actors, saw to the props. As I refused no work and no problem, but plunged enthusiastically into the most obscure and most menial aspects of the hurly-burly of the business, two films were enough to instill in me a solid professional training."

In 1927, when Yutkevich came to direct his own first feature, he found that his years in the theatre and as a painter had not been wasted: "It is no accident that most of the filmmakers of the 'first contingent' came from painting to films. We were all of us enthralled by the possibilities of the cinema, which permitted us to transform a film into a series of innumerable compositions. . . . In my first film, *Lace,* I remember that I was incapable of working out the form of a scene before seeing it in its pictorial composition. Later the process of the search for essence and for form acquired more and more unity and, thus, the solutions arrived at became more exact."

Kruzheva (*Lace,* 1928) tells in not too earnest a fashion the story of how a factory troublemaker, Petka, is reformed by fellow workers who are Komsomol (young communist) members. Shot on location in a lace factory and using workers as well as professional actors, the picture was said to be an uneven mixture of the metaphorical and the naturalistic. Jay Leyda found it "a lively film, with a tendency that was to characterize Yutkevich's subsequent films: a pleasure in plastic effects that sometimes diluted the dramatic aims of his films."

The same was true of *Chyorni parus* (*The Black Sail,* 1929), about the struggle between a Komsomol fishing cooperative and fishermen anxious to preserve their independence. Designed by Yevgeni Enei, it was praised for its "refined composition, complex montage, and . . . visual associations" and called "the most beautiful Soviet film" of the period. Montage was then regarded as "the philosopher's stone of the cinema," Yutkevich says. "In the beginning this was a healthy and progressive phenomenon, but in subsequent stages of the development of the Soviet cinema the theory of 'the priority of montage' became a dead weight which hampered the forward progress of the cinema." According to one account (in *Who's Who in the Soviet Cinema*), Yutkevich recognized as early as 1929 or 1930 that "the times required a new style for man himself to be given prominence and not to be lost in the complicated visual associations set up by the director. Yutkevich therefore decisively overcame his inclination toward a poetic cinematic style based on montage in favor of establishing concrete human characters. He studied the new reality . . . and brought it to the screen in his film *Mountains of Gold.*"

Zlatye gori (*Mountains of Gold,* 1931), Yutkevich's first sound film, takes place in the war years preceding the 1917 Revolution. Pyotr (Boris Poslavsky) is a poor peasant who loses his horse and gets a factory job in the city in order to buy another. There he gradually becomes aware of the exploitation of the workers and ends up leading a revolt against the bosses. Yutkevich set out to use sound (and a score by Dmitri Shostakovich) as counterpoint to the visual images, in the manner proposed by Eisenstein, Pudovkin, and Alexandrov in their famous *Statement* on the subject. Whether Yutkevich succeeded in giving prominence to "man himself" in this film is arguable—Leyda for one thought its theme "was sometimes obscured by the more immediately interesting execution of each scene, cleverly staged with a touch of stylization (it is one of the few films influenced by Dovzhenko), and photographed by a group of young cameramen whom Yutkevich encouraged to do their best." At any rate, the picture was hotly discussed and highly successful. It was followed by an altogether more naturalistic work, now regarded as one of the key films in the development of Socialist Realism.

Yutkevich involved a number of his friends in the filming of *Vstrechnyi* (*Counterplan*, 1932), made to celebrate the fifteenth anniversary of the October Revolution. Friedrich Ermler, Lev Arnshtam, "D. Dell" (Leonid Lyubashevsky), and Yutkevich all collaborated on the screenplay; Ermler was codirector; Arnshtam was associate director; Shostakovich wrote the score; there were three assistant directors, three cameramen, and three designers. (With the coming of sound, Ermler had lost confidence in his own ability to direct and had decided to abandon filmmaking. Yutkevich involved him in *Counterplan*, to help him regain his self-esteem, and this characteristically kindly ploy succeeded.) The film, set in a Leningrad factory building a great turbine at the time of the first five-year plan, concerns the Komsomols' struggle against older and less committed workers for acceptance of higher production norms and the new plan.

According to Jay Leyda, Ermler and Yutkevich "divided the characters and problems between them, Yutkevich in charge of the young people and Ermler taking on the tougher problems of the older generations: Babchenko, the old foreman, and his cronies of the machine shop, and the traitorous engineer Skvortsov, played by Poslavsky. The actors themselves may have had something to do with maintaining this division, for Gardin, whose performance of Babchenko is always placed among the great Soviet film roles, reports that he could get nothing sympathetic from Yutkevich, and that his only scenes to stay in the finished film were those directed by Ermler. Babchenko and all other roles were constructed from minute observation of their real-life models. Writer-directors and actors drew so much detail from reality that a repeated criticism heard at the time was of excessive 'ornamentation' of the film. The subdued naturalism of its speech and appearance have since raised *Counterplan* to the status of a precursor of 'social realism,' and its success fixed its style as the proper one for the 'improving' function of the Soviet cinema. The music by Shostakovich helped to bind the many separate scene-pieces effectively and his theme-song went far beyond the film's life when it was adopted twelve years later as the United Nations' hymn."

In 1934 Yutkevich established an experimental studio in Leningrad. By this time, however, the freewheeling experimental vitality that distinguished the Soviet cinema of the late 1920s was increasingly under attack, and the great directors of the period were being pilloried for "formalism"—for showing more interest in technical and aesthetic considerations than in suitable political content. The crippling doctrine of Socialist Realism was imposed ever more rigorously by the Party hierarchy, and not even Yutkevich—one of the originators of the style—was beyond censure. After the compilation film *Ankara, Serdze Tourtzyi* (*Ankara—Heart of Turkey*, 1934), Yutkevich began work on *Chakhtiery* (*Miners*, 1936), set in the Donbass and intended to repeat the success of *Counterplan*; the film was in production for three years, constantly being revised to meet changing political requirements.

In 1938 Yutkevich joined the teaching staff of the Moscow Film School (VGIK). The same year he scored a critical triumph with *Chelovek s ruzhyom* (*The Man With a Gun*), adapted by Nikolai Pogodin from his own play. It is a historical drama about the October Revolution as seen through the eyes of a young peasant; at first apolitical, he is inspired by Lenin to become a dedicated revolutionary. The film has a fine score by Shostakovich and a vivid performance by Maxim Strauch, one of the two actors (the other was Boris Shchukin) who were to become identified with the role of Lenin. Yutkevich says that this picture was "nonconformist in that it showed Lenin not in an epic manner but with humor and intimately." Georges Sadoul agreed that in this—and in all his films of the 1928–1941 period—Yutkevich always tried "to show the interiors of his characters rather than use monumental and heroic representations; he reveals his characters through their behavior in apparently ordinary events and not through portentous actions."

From 1939 to 1943 Yutkevich served as head of Soyuzdetfilm, the studio then responsible for children's films. His own next movie was *Yakov Sverdlov* (1940), a biography of the first chairman of the Party's Central Executive Committee (with Strauch again impersonating Lenin). The USSR entered the war in 1941, and Yutkevich contributed two short films to *Fighting Film Album No. 7* (1941). One of these was called "Schweik in the Concentration Camp" and was so well liked that Yutkevich proceeded to make a full-length comedy about the Czech antihero, *Noviye pokhozdeniya Shveika* (*The New Adventures of Schweik*, 1943), in which Schweik is recast as a reluctant Nazi. Yutkevich's documentary about the liberation of his beloved France, highly praised by Eisenstein, was followed by *Zdravstai Moskva* (*Hullo Moscow*, 1945), a musical comedy, and then by another documentary, *Molodost nashei strany* (*The Youth of Our Country*, 1946). The latter, directed in collaboration with I. Posselsky and I. Venger, received a State prize in the USSR and at Cannes was voted the best documentary and the best film serving the cause of world peace.

Busy and successful as he was as a filmmaker and administrator, Yutkevich had never abandoned the theatre. In 1939, for example, he staged a "dramatic-choreographic" work called *Separation* (which he also designed) and a play called *The Keys of Berlin*. There were further stage productions during the war years, including entertainments for soldiers at the front and productions of Čapek's *The Mother* and of J. B. Priestley's *An Inspector Calls*. A collection of four interviews with the director was published in 1947 as *Chelovek na ekrane* (*Man on the Screen*).

Svet nad Rossei (*Light Over Russia*, 1947), Yutkevich's first postwar feature, was based on Nikolai Pogodin's popular play about Lenin's electrification program. For reasons that were never made clear, the film was banned. Yutkevich then collaborated with Vsevolod Pudovkin and Alexander Ptushko on *Tri vstrechi* (*Three Meetings*, 1948), made up of three stories about young men and women returning from the war and throwing themselves joyfully into the peacetime challenges that awaited them. This inspiring effort was evidently not enough to return Yutkevich to favor, and in 1949 he was one of the directors attacked in *Iskusstvo Kino* as an "aesthetician-cosmopolitan." Three years passed before he was able to complete another film—*Przhevalsky* (1951), a "decent" biography of the nineteenth-century explorer. This was followed by another conciliatory exercise, *Veliki voin Albanii, Skanderbeg* (*The Great Warrior Skanderbeg*, 1953), a spectacular Soviet-Albanian epic celebrating the exploits of the fifteenth-century warrior who fought for Albanian freedom against the Turks.

When Yutkevich started work on *Skanderbeg*, he had just learned that Orson Welles was filming *Othello*, a long-cherished project of his own. He sadly "put the idea aside, but in my mind it was still working, and when I came to make *Skanderbeg* I treated it as almost a sketch for my impossible *Othello*. It had something of the same tragic-heroic mood, and the conclusion in particular suggested to me my version of *Othello*, so I borrowed from it." Then, at the Paris Cinémathèque, Yutkevich saw Welles' *Othello* and found it so totally different from his own conception that he felt free to go ahead.

Adapted by the director and based (like Kozintsev's *Hamlet* and *King Lear*) on an excellent free translation by Boris Pasternak, *Othello* has a score by Aram Khachaturian and was photographed by Yevgeni Andrikanis in Sovcolor, which Yutkevich also used in *Skanderbeg*, and which has a special sensitivity to the subtle grays and purples of dawn and dusk. Comparing his version with Welles', Yutkevich told an interviewer that "to begin with, mine is as an adaptation of Shakespeare's play, while Welles' is a series of variations on a theme of Shakespeare. But, more fundamentally, there is the almost symbolic difference between our prologues: I begin with Othello's account of his early life and adventures for Desdemona, while Welles begins with the funeral of Othello and Desdemona (and what a superb sequence that is!). I start from life, Welles from death."

Yutkevich's *Othello* appparently had a mixed press in the USSR, but it was generally very well received abroad and brought Yutkevich the award as best director at Cannes. Some critics were dissatisfied with the dubbed version shown in Britain and the United States, and not everyone was impressed by Sergei Bondarchuk's reading of the title role—it was found lacking in the savage power of Welles' performance (and Emil Jannings' earlier one), at once gentler and more noble. There was an attempt in Britain to present the film as an example of the post-Stalin trend away from propaganda in Soviet cinema, but a critic in the London *Times* found evidence to the contrary in the relationship between Othello and Andrei Popov's unusually extrovert Iago: "This Iago, an outwardly commonplace man, stands for a sophistication directly at odds with, and antagonistic to, the Moor. The two walk on the sands weaving their way in and out of symbolic fishing nets and the tortuous, perverted subtleties of the western mind are shown at work planning the destruction of an instinctive nobility of nature it hated and found alien. . . . The sequence throws an interesting light on the problem of Iago's seeming lack of motive."

The same critic wrote that "the strength of the film is to be found in the colour, in the vivid physical clashes of nature and of temperament, with a cool grey-blue vision, slashed with scarlet cloaks, in Venice, alternating with the grim battlements and flaring torches of Cyprus, while the camera all through rejoices in close-ups which recall Hogarth and Rowlandson."

Yutkevich continued to find time for writing and for the theatre. In 1952 or 1953 he had visited Mao's China, describing his journey in a book called *V teatrakh i kino svobodnoga Kitaya* (*In the Theatres and Cinemas of Free China,* 1953). The following year he designed and codirected a Moscow production of Mayakovsky's 1930 satire on bureaucracy *Banya* (*The Bath House*); it was said to be a revelation to the audience, who found it only too relevant to contemporary realities. A book about the popular arts of Albania appeared in 1958, and during the next few years Yutkevich published two works about the cinema. During this period he assumed the direction of the student theatre at Moscow University, where in 1964, in collaboration with M. Zakharov, he staged Brecht's *The Resistable Rise of Arturo Ui.*

He was equally active in the cinema. A documentary about Yves Montand's tour of the Soviet Union in 1957 was followed by an excellent and intimate biographical film about Lenin, *Rasskazi o Lenin* (*Stories About Lenin,* 1958), with Maxim Strauch again in the title role and Marina Pastukhova as Lenin's wife, Nadezhda Krupskaya. Khrushchev's state visit to France in 1960 was recorded in *Vstrecha s Frantsiey* (*Meeting With France*) and in 1962 came a full-length animated version (using puppets) of *The Bath House,* made in collaboration with Anatoli Karanovich. Yutkevich's Lenin series continued in 1965 with *Lenin v Polshe* (*Lenin in Poland*). Described as "a warm and rather charming film about Lenin's hopes and dreams in the years prior to the 1917 Revolution," it brought Yutkevich another Cannes award as best director. A 1967 film exhibition in Moscow included showings of Yutkevich's still version of *Bezhin lug* (*Bezhin Meadow*), which his old friend Eisenstein had filmed thirty years earlier but had been forbidden to edit.

One of Yutkevich's most remarkable and unexpected films appeared in 1969, when he was sixty-five. *Syuzhet diya nebolshovo rasskaza* (*Theme for a Short Story*) is based on L. Malyugin's play about the period in Chekhov's life when his distress at the disastrous first production of *The Seagull* was compounded by his hopeless love for Lika Mizinova. David Robinson wrote that "Chekhov is beautifully played

by Nikolai Grinko and the mysterious love, Lika, by Marina Vlady. (The film was a coproduction with France.) The elegant formal devices owe nothing to any other film, but span half a century, linking the early mixed media experiments of the Eccentrics with aggressively contemporary graphic styles. It is played as a series of tableaux, against flat sets on which even the furniture is painted, and linked by absurd tricks like toy trains or cardboard stage curtains, with Chekhov quotations interpolated in the style of silent film titles. There is still the willingness of Yutkevich's youth to risk being simply modish, or to chance a mess of disintegrated styles. What matters is the promise that something unexpected and strange may emerge from surprising juxtapositions (the cardboard sets and the intensely naturalistic playing); and the sheer enthusiasm. It is an endearing and singularly *youthful* film."

In 1973 Yutkevich made two films for television, one about *The Girl and the Hooligan,* a movie made by Mayakovsky in 1918, the other an interview with the actor Igor Illynsky, who had appeared in the first production of Mayakovsky's play *Klop* (*The Bedbug*). These were followed in 1975 by *Mayakovsky smeyotsya* (*Mayakovsky Laughs*), a feature-length film, made in collaboration with Karanovich and combining puppet animation and live actors, which draws both on *Klop* and on Mayakovsky's scenario *Pozabud pro kamin* (*Forget About the Fireplace*). Derek Elley called it an "outrageously adventurous exercise in transferring the spirit of Mayakovsky's work to the screen . . . packed to overflowing with allusions, in-jokes and linguistic subtleties," but achieving through "sheer brio" an international appeal.

Yutkevich served as a professor at the Moscow Film School, and also taught in an advanced seminar at Mosfilm for young directors, cinematographers, and art directors. From 1958 on, he was editor of *Iskusstvo Kino.* He continued to write and teach well into his old age. A book about screen adaptations of Shakespeare's plays appeared in 1973, and *Kino—eto pravda 24 kadra v sekundu* (*Film—Truth at 24 Frames per Second*) in 1974. Yutkevich completed a fourth Lenin film, *Lenin v Paridzhe* (*Lenin in Paris*), in 1981, when he was seventy-seven years old. According to David Robinson, Yutkevich was "one of the most attractive personalities in the Soviet cinema; and all his films bear the imprint of his personal charm and urbanity." He shared with some of the other directors of the "heroic age" of Soviet cinema an extraordinary capacity "for constant renewal and rejuvenation."

FILMS: Dayoch radio! (Gives Us Radio/Radio Now),

1924 (short); Kruzheva (Lace), 1928; Chyorni parus (The Black Sail), 1929; Zlatye gori (Mountains of Gold), 1931; (with Friedrich Ermler) Vstrechnyi (Counterplan/The Challenge), 1932; Ankara, serdze Tourtzyi (Ankara, Heart of Turkey), 1934 (documentary); Chakhtiery (Miners), 1936; Kak boudet golossovat izbiratel (How the Elector Will Vote), 1937 (propaganda); Chelovek s ruzhyom (The Man With a Gun/The Man With a Rifle), 1938; Yakov Sverdlov, 1940; Schweik in the Concentration Camp *and* The White Raven *in* Fighting Film Album No. 7, 1941; Noviye pokhozdeniya Shveika (The New Adventures of Schweik), 1943; Osvobozhdennaya Frantsiya (Liberated France), 1944 (documentary); Zdravstai Moskva (Hullo Moscow), 1945; (with I. Posselsky and I. Venger) Molodost nashei strany (The Youth of Our Country), 1946 (documentary); Svet nad Rossei (Light Over Russia/Dawn Over Russia), 1947 (banned); (with Vsevolod Pudovkin and Alexander Ptushko) Tri vstrechi (Three Meetings/Three Encounters), 1948; Przhevalsky, 1951; Veliki voin Albanii, Skanderbeg (The Great Warrior Skanderbeg), 1953; Otello (Othello), 1955; Poyot Yves Montand (Yves Montand Sings), 1957 (documentary); Rasskazi o Lenin (Stories About Lenin), 1958; Vstrecha s Frantsiey (Meeting With France), 1960 (documentary); (with Anatoli Karanovich) Banya (The Bath House), 1962; Lenin v Polshe (Lenin in Poland/Portrait of Lenin), 1965; Bezhin lug (Bezhhin Meadow), 1967 (stills version of Eisenstein's 1937 film); Syuzhet diya nebolshovo rasskaza (Theme for a Short Story/Lika, Chekhov's Love), 1969; Poet na ekrane (Poet on the Screen), 1973 (for television); Illynsky o Mayakovskom (Illynsky on Mayakovski), 1973 (for television); (with Anatoli Karanovich) Mayakovsky smeyotsya (Mayakovski Laughs), 1975; Lenin v Paridzhe (Lenin in Paris), 1981. *Published scripts*—Chelovek s ruzhyom *in* Iskusstvo kino 7 1938; Banya *in* Iskusstvo kino 7 1960.

ABOUT: Birkos, A. S. Soviet Cinema, 1976; Dolmatovskaya, G. and Shilova, I. Who's Who in the Soviet Cinema, 1979; Herlinghaus, H. Sergei Jutkewitsch, 1965 (in German); Leyda, J. Kino, 1960, Schnitzer, L. and J. (eds.) Cinema in Revolution, 1973; Schnitzer, L. and J. Youtkevitch, 1976 (in French); Verdone, M. and Amengual, B. La Feks, 1970. *Periodicals*—Cahiers du Cinéma 124 1961; Films and Filming March 1962, October 1957; Lettres Françaises 618 1956; Soviet Film 7 1969, 12 1974.

ZINNEMANN, FRED (April 29, 1907–   ), American director, was born in Vienna, the older by thirteen years of the two sons of Oskar Zinnemann and the former Anna Feiwel. His father was a prominent physician, and he was encouraged to follow the same profession. At first, however, he set his heart on a musical career. He became a competent violinist but, according to Richard Griffith in a Museum of Modern Art pamphlet about Zinnemann, he recognized "the difference between competence and renown . . . [and] turned to the study of law at

FRED ZINNEMANN

the University of Vienna." He graduated in 1927. Meanwhile, he had seen three films that affected him profoundly: Eisenstein's *Potemkin*, Stroheim's *Greed*, and Vidor's *The Big Parade*. Under their influence, he says, "I made up my mind to forget all about law and in some way break into motion pictures with my sights set upon someday becoming a director."

The Technical School of Cinematography opened in Paris in 1927, and Zinnemann, overcoming his family's determined resistance, immediately enrolled. He studied there for eighteen months, learning the fundamentals of optics, photochemistry, developing, and printing. He got his first job while still a student, contributing a few shots to Eugène Deslaw's avant-garde documentary *La Marche des Machines (The March of the Machines*, 1927).

In 1929, armed with a letter of introduction to the head of Universal, Carl Laemmle, Zinnemann set out for Hollywood. Laemmle gave him a job as an extra in Lewis Milestone's *All Quiet on the Western Front*, doubling as a German soldier and a French ambulance driver. "Even in that very modest way," he says, "I was very happy to be part of it," but after three weeks he was fired for talking back to an assistant director.

Some months without work followed, and then Zinnemann was hired by Fox as assistant to the director Berthold Viertel, a fellow Viennese, on *Man Trouble* (1930) and *The Spy* (1931). Viertel, trained in the German theatre, "had a certain amount of difficulty with camera technique, and, in that sense, I think I helped him," Zinnemann recalls. "I also learned a great deal from him, watching how he handled actors.

That was big news to me; I didn't know anything about them."

At Viertel's home, Zinnemann met the great documentarist Robert Flaherty and asked if he could work with him. Flaherty agreed, and Zinnemann spent six months with him in Berlin planning a documentary about a little-known nomadic tribe in Soviet Central Asia. Nothing came of this because the Russian authorities wanted a propaganda film remote from what Flaherty had envisaged, an elegy for a dying way of life. Nevertheless, Zinnemann has always regarded this brief association with Flaherty as "the most important event of my professional life." In an interview with Michael Buckley in *Films in Review* (January 1983), he said: "Bob taught me more than anyone else—to concentrate on subjects I know and to make a film the way I see it."

Back in Hollywood, Zinnemann rejoined Viertel, who had moved to Paramount, assisting him on two 1932 vehicles for Claudette Colbert, *The Wiser Sex* and *The Man from Yesterday*. This humble phase of Zinnemann's career ended at Goldwyn's, where he assisted Busby Berkeley with the camera setups for his dance numbers in Leo McCarey's *The Kid From Spain* (1932).

Another period of unemployment followed and then a tedious job as a script clerk, from which Zinnemann was rescued by his friend Henwar Rodakiewicz. The photographer Paul Strand had been invited to produce a documentary for the new revolutionary government in Mexico. Rodakiewicz had been assigned to direct as well write the film, but at his suggestion the latter responsiblility was offered to Zinnemann.

The result was *Redes* (*The Wave*, 1935), filmed on location in the Gulf of Vera Cruz. Local fishermen and their families acted out a story, set before the revolution, about a young man who persuades his comrades to form a fisherman's union and is finally murdered by the government. As Zinnemannn says in a *Focus on Film* interview (Spring 1973), "the situation is similar to the one that Visconti used in *La Terra Trema,* but *The Wave* was a much more modest venture. It was a sixty-minute film which was shot silent. But we spent a year in the jungle making it. That was one of the happiest years of my life. In the jungle one was thrown on one's own resources."

Redes was made twelve years before *La Terra Trema* and can be claimed as a forerunner of neorealism in its use of real locations and nonprofessional actors to tell a story of economic exploitation and political oppression. Richard Griffith writes that Zinnemann, like his mentor

Flaherty, "must use the untrained fishermen of the village of Alvarado to play themselves in a drama based on actual happenings in the locality. But, unlike Flaherty, he had a plot to unfold, a conclusion to reach. . . . The solution adopted by Zinnemann and Paul Strand differed from the Flaherty method. . . . They made the players simple units in massive and monumental photographic compositions expressive of grief, pride, anger, despondency—all the emotions which the actors themselves could not portray. This method was not followed consistently—in some scenes the players did awkwardly try to 'act'—and it may be thought more appropriate to still photography than to the moving image, but it gave *Redes* a beauty and power which bought it an international audience."

According to Zinnemann, *Redes* "played in art theatres in the United States and became very well known in Europe, particularly in France; and, as I understand it, the Nazis burned the negative—which was in Paris—so prints are now very hard to come by." In spite of this *succès d'estime,* however, Zinnemann could find no work when he returned to the United States. He and Rodakiewicz filled in the time writing a screenplay, *Bonanza,* set in Mexico. It was sold to MGM but never produced.

Zinnemann was married in 1936 to Renee Bartlett, born in England but raised in Chile, and then working in Paramount's wardrobe department. In 1937 Zinnemann was naturalized as an American citizen, and the following year, having shown part of *Redes* to Jack Chertok, head of MGM's short subject department, he was hired as a director. Between 1938 and 1942 Zinnemann made eighteen one- or two-reel shorts for MGM, including contributions to several regular series—the Pete Smith Specialities, Crime Does Not Pay, John Nesbitt's Passing Parade, and the Carey Wilson Miniatures. One of the latter, *That Mothers May Live,* telling the story of a pioneer in the obstetric use of antiseptics, won an Oscar as best short subject of 1938.

MGM used its short subject department as a training ground for novice directors, and Zinnemann considers this one of the most instructive phases of his career. "We had quite a group of us—Jules Dassin, George Sidney, Jacques Tourneur, Gunther von Fritsch, Roy Rowland—and it was marvelous training." As he told Gene Phillips, "you had a comparatively small amount of time and money to do a short. . . . I remember doing the life of Dr. George Washington Carver from the time he was kidnapped by slave-traders as a baby until he was ninety-five in ten minutes. . . . These shorts had a regular production crew like any feature picture, except that the whole thing had to be shot in six days. You could never use a moving camera because that required too long to light the set. You had to previsualize everything you were going to do in order to make the best possible use of the time. . . . It was a challenge, really."

When MGM promoted Chertok to features, he took Zinnemann with him. The director's first fiction feature film was a grade-B crime story, *Kid Glove Killer* (1942) with Van Heflin in his first lead role. Much of the action takes place in a police laboratory, where forensic scientist Heflin uses his skills to nail the DA's killer (Lee Bowman). It was an auspicious debut, showing what Zinnemann had learned as a director of shorts. The New York *Times* called it "a little crackerjack of a picture, compact and tight as a drum," in which, "out of the routine tests of chemicals and spectographs, Mr. Zinnemann has created a good deal of taut suspense." The review concluded with the suggestion that "it might be a good idea to send some directors of super-colossal specials back to the shorts department to learn a lesson in conciseness."

"Dog Bites Axis" was Cecilia Ager's headline for her review of Zinnemann's second B-movie, *Eyes in the Night* (1942), in which a Nazi spy (Stephen McNally) is exposed by Bayard Kendrick's blind detective Duncan Maclain (Edward Arnold) and his seeing-eye dog. John Howard Reid, in his article about Zinnemann in *Films and Filming* (May 1967) thought his "realistic, documentary" approach inappropriate to this extravagant melodrama, but most reviewers enjoyed the movie. Zinnemann graduated forthwith to his first A movie, *The Seventh Cross*, adapted by Helen Deutsch from the best-selling novel by Anna Seghers.

The film is set in Hitler's Germany in 1936. Seven men escape from a concentration camp, and the Nazis, in their sadistic arrogance, erect seven crosses in the camp to receive them as they are recaptured. Six are brought back and crucified, but George Heisler (Spencer Tracy), a man who believes in nothing and nobody, is succored and aided by a chain of "good Germans." Little by little Heisler learns hope and charity, and the seventh cross waits for him in vain.

The people who help Heisler (and those who do not) form a cross-section of German society under the Third Reich. They include a theatrical costumer (Agnes Moorehead) a rich architect (George Macready), a barmaid (Signe Hasso), and a pro-Hitler workman (Hume Cronyn, who received an Oscar nomination for his performance). "In those days," Cronyn has recalled, "Freddie was insecure. He hadn't made a major picture. And he was stuck with an absolute bas-

tard of a cameraman, Karl Freund, who had done lots of films and didn't make it any easier for him." Cronyn and his wife Jessica Tandy "took a tremendous shine to Freddie" and would go at night to his office "and walk through the next day's shooting—the two of us playing all the parts. In those days, rehearsals were very rare."

The Seventh Cross was generally very well received, praised for its "crackling tension and hard-packed realism." On the other hand, *Time*'s reviewer thought it "two hours of handsome, earnest inadequacy. . . . George Heisler is presented in this cautious film as wholly nonpolitical except for his distaste for Nazism, so are his friends in the underground. With the loss of this political energy the film not only loses its truth as a tribute, it also sacrifices, even as melodrama, its vitality." More recently, in a British National Film Theatre program note, Neil Sinyard pointed out that the picture was "one of the few Hollywood films of the time to offer a compassionate picture of German society," adding that "its precarious affirmation of human decency is characteristic [of Zinnemann] and very moving."

Zinnemann was next assigned to direct Judy Garland in *The Clock* (1945), but was replaced by Vincente Minnelli, whom Garland married the same year. Rather surprisingly, MGM then put Zinnemann back on a B movie, *Little Mr. Jim* (1946), a domestic tearjerker featuring the child star Jackie "Butch" Jenkins. Out of routine material Zinnemann made a picture of some subtlety and charm, but he could do nothing with Morton Thompson's stodgy script for *My Brother Talks to Horses* (1946), another Butch Jenkins vehicle, about a boy who gets racing tips literally from the horse's mouth. After that, Zinnemann turned down three bad scripts in a row. MGM put him on suspension for three weeks, during which, he says, "everybody seemed to treat me as though I'd just got the Purple Heart."

The suspension ended when a Swiss producer, Lazar Wechsler, offered Zinnemann a script that excited him, *The Search*, inspired by Therese Bonney's photographs of displaced children in *Europe's Children*. MGM not only let him go to Europe to make the film but put up most of the money. *The Search* (1948) tells the story of a GI (Montgomery Clift) stationed in occupied Germany who befriends a lost and mute Czech boy (Ivan Jandl), little by little winning his trust and teaching him to speak again. The boy is finally reunited with his mother (played by the singer Jarmila Novotna).

As he always does, Zinnemann began by carefully researching his subject. Influenced by the

Italian neorealists, he wanted to fuse the conventions of fiction with documentary into a form he called a "dramatic document." The fictional story, shot on location in the ruins of postwar Germany, is intercut with harrowing footage of real war orphans in UNRRA camps. Zinnemann used some of these children as extras because " they alone could understand and project the feeling of animal terror." One profoundly disturbing scene reconstructed an incident that actually took place during filming, when the children ran in horror from Red Cross ambulances, mistaking them for the vehicles used by the Nazis in gas chamber roundups.

This was Montgomery Clift's screen debut; *Red River*, shot earlier, was released later. Zinnemann found him "terribly sensitive; difficult, but so exciting that it didn't matter." The director's regard for verisimilitude is reflected in his distrust of the star system; he has always been ready to take chances on unfamiliar faces in major roles and in this way has launched some brilliant careers. Clift's performance in *The Search* earned him an Oscar nomination. There were nominations also for Zinnemann's direction and for the film's story and screenplay credited to Richard Schweizer and the producer's son, David Wechsler (though Clift reportedly wrote all his own dialogue and several scenes). Ivan Jandl (whom Zinnemann chose from a school in Prague) received a special Academy Award for his "outstanding juvenile performance."

Bosley Crowther called *The Search* "a major revelation in our times," and Penelope Houston wrote that it had been "directed with a style, at once natural and exciting, which gives it quality above its emotional appeal. The opening scenes, with the crowds of silent, hopeless faces, and the almost helpless UNRRA officials, are especially impressive." Not everyone was so enthusiastic. Some found the movie excessively sentimental and doubted the happy ending (to which Zinnemann replied: "To show things as they really were would have meant that the American audience would have lost any desire to see it"). And there were complaints about the "intrusive and tiresome commentary" over the early scenes (which Zinnemann did not want and tried to erase, finding that it could not be removed without ruining the remainder of the sound track).

The Search was financially successful and established Zinnemann as an important director. MGM, which had dropped him in an economy drive, promptly rehired him for *Act of Violence* (1948), one of the studio's few attempts at *film noir* and Zinnemann's only work in that genre, though it also continues his pursuit of quasi-documentary realism. Van Heflin stars as an ap-

parently solid citizen of a small California town whose career and marriage are threatened by the arrival of a crippled former sergeant (Robert Ryan), out to get him for betraying an escape plan when both were POWs. Heflin flees to an industrial convention, becomes involved with a prostitute (Mary Astor), and hires a thug to murder Ryan at a lonely railroad depot. Here the themes of moral cowardice and vengeance are played out to a tragic climax.

Not much noticed at the time, this movie has seemed to some later critics Zinnemann's first entirely confident and technically assured picture. John Gillett writes that it "makes expressive use of sets and locations to suggest a continuum of pessimism and entrapment (bars, wire, tunnels predominate). . . . Mary Astor and Janet Leigh are outstanding as the women torn between rational humanity and devotion to their neurotic men."

After that, Zinnemann signed a three-picture contract with the independent producer Stanley Kramer, who shared his interest in social realism. Their first collaboration was *The Men* (1950), which launched the film career of Marlon Brando. He plays a paraplegic veteran, consumed with bitterness, who slowly and painfully comes to terms with his permanent disablement. Brando spent three weeks at the Birmingham Veterans Hospital in California in preparation for the role, often confining himself to bed or traveling by wheelchair with real paraplegics to a nearby bar (where on one occasion he dumbfounded an evangelist by demonstrating the truth of her assertion that, with faith, he could rise from his wheelchair and walk). Most of the film was then shot in the hospital, where Zinnemann was such a constant presence that he came to be regarded as an unofficial member of the staff.

The hospital scenes, with real patients as extras, Jack Webb as their ringleader, and Brando giving a performance of compelling conviction and power, are in the best traditions of Zinnemann's realist (or neorealist) work. Outside the institution, there is a decided loss of momentum. Zinnemann and Carl Foreman, the scriptwriter, had originally planned to balance the veteran's plight with the dilemma of his fiancée (Teresa Wright), who was to be provided with an alternative suitor. But this key role went to an untalented relative of one of the backers, and his performance was so inept that the entire subplot had to be scrapped, leaving Zinnemann (and Wright) with very little to go one. *The Men*, though not financially successful, was respectfully received by the reviewers, and later critics have been particularly impressed by its frankness about the sexual problems of the paraplegics.

Zinnemann returned to MGM for *Teresa* (1951), about the problems of European war brides brought to the United States by returning GIs. Stewart Stern's screenplay, which gained him an Oscar nomination, centers on an Italian girl who has to cope not only with the cultural shock of removal from an impoverished small town to New York, but with an immature husband and his dominating mother. All the typical features of American life are presented as they might appear to a bewildered foreigner.

Teresa provides further examples of Zinnemann's devotion to convincing detail. Having chosen his Italian location in part for its authentic bomb damage, he persuaded the townspeople to delay a long-cherished project—the reconstruction of the local church—until the early scenes of the film had been shot. And again the director found new faces—the eighteen-year-old Pier Angeli played Teresa, and John Ericson, chosen from among three hundred aspirants in an open audition, was cast as her troubled husband. The film also marked the screen debuts, in smaller roles, of Rod Steiger and Ralph Meeker.

The movie had a mixed reception and there was a general feeling that the early scenes in Italy and the later ones in New York looked as if they belonged in two different films. More recently, however, Neil Sinyard has called *Teresa* "a remarkable Lawrentian study" inhabiting "a landscape that reels between violence and serenity, Italian warmth and New World chill. Some scenes are extraordinary—a wedding in a bombed-out church, the claiming of the brides, as in an auction, when they arrive in New York." Stewart Stern also scripted *Benjy* (1951), a fundraising short made for the Orthopedic Hospital of Los Angeles with the cooperation of Paramount; it won an Oscar as best documentary of the year.

Zinnemann's second film for Kramer was the Western *High Noon* (1952), regarded by many as his masterpiece. Another Carl Foreman script, it is set in a frontier town in 1870. Gary Cooper plays Will Kane, an aging lawman. As the film opens, he has just celebrated the end of his successful term as marshal by marrying Grace Kelly, a Quaker opposed to all violence. It is 10:40 a.m. and they are about to leave on their honeymoon. And then they learn that a vicious killer (Lee Van Cleef) whom Kane had once sent to jail will arrive at noon to settle accounts, supported by three other thugs. Noon is the moment the marshal's contract expires; from then on there will be no law in Hadleyville. The townspeople want Kane to run, but being a man of principle and courage, he knows what he must do.

The eighty minutes between 10:40 and high noon are roughly the actual duration of the film, which observes all the classical unities (though time is in fact skillfully manipulated—accelerated and then slowed down—to increase the tension). Kane, his authority visibly evaporating, makes the rounds of the town, trying with growing urgency to find someone who will stand with him against the forces of evil. But no one wants that kind of trouble—not his pacifist wife, nor his fiery ex-mistress (Katy Jurado), nor his jealous deputy (Lloyd Bridges), nor Thomas Mitchell's querulous official, nor Lon Chaney's hopeless former marshal. Certainly not the cynical hotel clerk (Howard Chamberlain) who openly expresses what others conceal—the belief that there is more money to be made in a wide-open town than a law-abiding one.

In the end, having made what preparations he can, Kane has to go out alone to face his enemies. John Howard Reid found the long take as Kane walks out to the depot one of the most memorable in the film: "The camera, tracking with Cooper, begins to draw away from him and rises to show the deserted street, the whole town apparently empty." In the showdown that follows, a crucial shot is fired by Kane's Quaker bride, whose love for her husband overcomes her belief in nonresistance.

Zinnemann had not always been well served in the past by his collaborators, but here he had not only a fine cast but Floyd Crosby as cinematographer, Elmo Williams as editor, and an excellent score by Dimitri Tiomkin (who also wrote the folkish theme tune, "Do Not Forsake Me Oh My Darling"). Zinnemann has said that he wanted the film "to have a conflicting flow of visual concepts," like the numerous shots of dark figures against white skies—visual corollaries of the picture's moral conflicts. He also wanted it to "look like a newsreel would have looked if they had had newsreels in those days." He and Crosby studied the Civil War photographs of Mathew Brady and tried for similar effects: "Crosby used no filters and gave the sky a white, cloudless, burnt-out look. He used flat lighting and that gave the film a grainy quality. From the first day the front office complained about the poor photography. . . . but Floyd went ahead anyway."

High Noon collected Oscars for best actor (revitalizing Cooper's career), best score, best song, and best editing. It was chosen as best film by the New York Film Critics and topped *Film Daily*'s annual poll. Many regard the film as one of the greatest of all Westerns. Others insist that it is not really a Western at all but (as Pauline Kael put it) "a sneak civics lesson," albeit a good one.

André Bazin placed it with *Shane* as "the two films that best illustrate the mutation in the Western genre as an effect of the awareness it has gained of itself and its limits."

Louis Giannetti, in his *Masters of the American Cinema*, says that "*High Noon*, one of the first of the so-called 'psychological' or 'adult' westerns of the early 1950s, began a trend in the demythologizing of genres. . . . Zinnemann treated his Western hero as though he were a real human being, one who feels panic, fear, and even some moments of cowardice. . . . He sweats profusely under the glare of the sun. He gets dirtier, more stooped, and haggard as the urgency of his situation increases. . . . Zinnemann's realistic innovations helped to bring about a new attitude toward the genre, setting the stage for such later 'revisionist' westerns as Peckinpah's *The Wild Bunch*, Penn's *Little Big Man*, and Altman's *McCabe and Mrs. Miller*." Others have seen *High Noon* as a political allegory about the effects of McCarthyism, and the scriptwriter Carl Foreman has confirmed that this was "the only time I consciously wrote a polemic. It was my story of a community corrupted by fear—the end of Hollywood."

Zinnemann's own favorite among his films is said to be *The Member of the Wedding* (1952), adapted by Edward and Edna Anhalt from the novel and play by Carson McCullers. Zinnemann saw the play four times, and was so impressed by its star, Julie Harris, that he decided to do the film largely so that he could work with her, thus introducing another fine actor to the screen. He also cast from the stage production Ethel Waters and Brandon de Wilde.

The twenty-six-year-old Harris gives an astonishing performance as the twelve-year-old Frankie, growing up in a small Southern town. She is on the troubled edge of adolescence and so desperate to belong somewhere that she tries to attach herself to her brother and his fiancée at their marriage and has to be dragged screaming from the honeymoon car. Excluded from the imaginary world she has created, she runs away from home, returning to find her real world shattered as well—her little brother (de Wilde) desperately ill, her surrogate mother Berenice (Waters) distraught at the arrest of her nephew. From this traumatic situation of loss she moves towards a more ordinary attachment to a football player "like a Greek god."

Apart from Frankie's nighttime experiences in town when she runs away, Zinnemann made no attempt to "open up" the play. Most of the action takes place in the run-down kitchen, the domain of Berenice, the black housekeeper whose wisdom and love sustains Frankie through her dark days. This is, as has been pointed out, the first Hollywood "in which the narrative is structured around a black woman," and Ethel Waters contributes a performance of enormous dignity and strength. A critical though not a financial success, *The Member of the Wedding* seemed to Brian Baxter "an almost definitive statement on the agonies of childhood."

This completed Zinnemann's contract with Kramer, and he then joined Columbia for *From Here to Eternity* (1953), Daniel Taradash's adaptation of James Jones' sprawling novel about life, sex, and death on a Honolulu army base on the eve of Pearl Harbor. Zinnemann cast Montgomery Clift as Prewitt, champion boxer, aspiring bugler, and loyal professional soldier. He is the quintessential Zinnemann hero—a principled loner who believes that "a man who don't go his own way is nothing."

An ambitious officer wants Prewitt for the boxing team. When Prewitt declines this honor, the officer orders Sergeant Burt Lancaster to give him "the treatment." During this ordeal, Prewitt's battered spirit is sustained partly by his buddy Maggio (Frank Sinatra in his first non-singing role)—a gallant loser who is eventually beaten to death by a sadistic noncom (Ernest Borgnine). This leads to the moving scene in which Prewitt plays Taps for his dead friend and, it seems, for the end of an era. More famous is the much-parodied sequence in which Burt Lancaster and Deborah Kerr (brilliantly cast against type as a promiscuous army wife) make love on an empty beach, the mounting rhythms of their passion echoed by the surging waves that sweep over them.

From Here to Eternity was a great financial success, and the most honored of Zinnemann's films. It brought him the New York Film Critics Award for the second year in succession, the Directors Guild Award, and his first Oscar as best director (of a feature). In all, the film received thirteen Oscar nominations and won eight of them—best director, best picture, best supporting actor (Sinatra) and supporting actress (Donna Reed, as the prostitute Prewitt loves), best screenplay, best black and white cinematography (Burnett Guffey), best sound recording, and best editing (William Lyon).

This triumph confirmed Zinnemann's position in the forefront of Hollywood directors. However, Karel Reisz was one of a number of critics who thought that the director was not at ease with the film's grimly negative view of life, and had produced a work devoid of "the hopeful, sympathetic mood of his earlier films. . . . everything is hard, disillusioned, boringly blasé in the suggestion that the film's melodramatics present life as it is lived and that one might as well accept it."

In search of light relief, perhaps, Zinnemann then turned to the musical, a genre new to him except for his small involvement twenty years earlier in *The Kid From Spain*. His version of Rodgers and Hammerstein's *Oklahoma!* (1955) was, moreover, the first film made in wide screen Todd-AO. Shirley Jones made her screen debut in the lead, opposite Gordon MacRae, but the film was dominated by Rod Steiger's seething performance as Jud, "the inevitable snake in the American Eden." The movie was successful, but seemed to some critics a rather glum and heavyhanded adaptation, lacking the necessary gusto. David Thomson wrote that Zinnemann "has taken the exclamation mark away from *Oklahoma!*" and the director himself was dissatisfied, saying "I tried to humanize it, and that was my fatal mistake."

A Hatful of Rain, made for Twentieth Century-Fox in 1957, was another adaptation from the stage—this time a murky drama of deceit and betrayal involving a drug-addicted vet (Don Murray), his brother (Anthony Franciosa), and his wife (Eva Marie Saint). One of the first movies to deal with addiction after the lifting of the Production Code ban, this struck most reviewers as a worthy "message" picture heavily flawed both in the writing and the casting.

Zinnemann returned to form with *The Nun's Story* (1958), produced by his own company releasing through Warners. It was adapted by Robert Anderson from a book, based on fact, by Kathryn Hulme. Audrey Hepburn gave the performance of her career as Gabrielle Van Der Mal, daughter of a Belgian surgeon, who entered a religious order in 1927 and left it after a sustained and intense internal struggle, seventeen years later. Photographed by Franz Planer and scored by Franz Waxman, the film also benefited very greatly from the contribution as art director of Alexander Trauner.

The first "movement" of this symphonic film opens with delicate pastel exteriors of the town the heroine leaves behind when she enters the convent. Inside, the colors drain almost to monochromes, recording a way of life as silent and unbending as the grey stones that enclose it. As Gabrielle struggles to detach herself from things, people, and even her memories, the harshness of convent discipline is reflected in natural sounds as much as dialogue, like the clash of scissors as Gabrielle's long hair is cropped.

As Sister Luke, Gabrielle, as she had wished, is sent to the Belgian Congo. Life floods back onto the screen in an explosion of vitality and brilliant color. There is another splendid performance from Peter Finch as the doctor with whom Luke works as a nurse, a wry humanist as dedicated as herself, a "genius and devil" who makes fun of her vocation and teaches her something about her "ferocious will."

The latter is victorious in the film's final "movement," when Gabrielle returns to Belgium as the Nazis advance on the Lowlands. The Church demands neutrality but Gabrielle, her beloved father murdered, elects to join the Resistance and is released from her vows. At the beginning of the film, a great door had opened to let us into the secret world of the convent; at the end another door opens to release Gabrielle, fearful but determined, into a dangerous future.

"The remarkable thing," it seemed to Dilys Powell, "is that the examination of the stresses of mind and will should be so engrossing. Not often does the cinema succeed with a subject of this kind. But then, not often are script and direction so successful in translating the conflict into visual detail. . . . Audrey Hepburn, subduing without effacing her vitality, makes the impression of a radiant and generous nature forcing itself into a mould for which it was never intended." Albert Johnson called the film "the best study of religious life ever made in the American cinema" and "a masterpiece of semidocumentary and character revelation." It was nominated for eight Oscars but recieved none of them. However, the New York Film Critics gave Zinnemann his third award as best director, and voted Audrey Hepburn best actress. Many regard this, rather than *High Noon*, as the director's best picture.

The Sundowners (1960) oddly but successfully casts Robert Mitchum and Deborah Kerr as an itinerant couple in the Australian outback in the mid-1920s. She wants to save some money, buy a farm, and settle down; he is quite happy to take whatever work is offered, gamble his wages away, and move on. Some Australian and British reviewers objected to the film's American casting, but most found the warmth and humanity of the movie irresistible.

Zinnemann himself acknowledges that this adaptation of Jon Cleary's novel was an atypical subject for him, dealing not with an agonizing moral conflict but simply showing "that people can be in love after fifteen years of marriage and can feel secure as long as they are together, even though all they own are the shirts on their backs." Arthur Knight drew attention to the film's minor characters—the farmers, the hard-drinking shearing gangs, the widow who runs a tough pub—saying that "like the principals, they are always credible, always human, and often terribly funny. . . . Similarly, the Australian landscape contributes its own authenticity. . . .

Never does Zinnemann permit such scenes to be merely pictorial; they provide the documentary backing for his characters." Neil Sinyard thought it "Fordian in its local colour, knockabout humour and its sympathy for a woman in a man's world."

Behold a Pale Horse (1964), from a novel by Emeric Pressburger, disappointed the director and most of the reviewers. Anthony Quinn plays a police official in Franco's Spain who lures his old enemy, an exiled hero of the Civil War (Gregory Peck), into a trap. Jean Badal's photography of the Pyrenean Basque country was admired, but Isabel Quigly thought that Zinnemann had directed with "almost offensive tact" (though Franco found it tactless enough to ban it). Some later critics believe that the picture was underrated on first release. For Alan Stanbrook (*Films and Filming* June 1967), "the remarkable opening sequence captures the flavour of 1930s documentaries so well that it comes as a shock to see Gregory Peck slide into frame like some ghostly time-traveller. The rough-hewn, grainy photography of this scene, contrasting so sharply with the smooth, professional gloss of the main story, remind us that Zinnemann's reputation was built on realist foundations."

Having won Oscars for two short films and *From Here to Eternity*, the director won another for *A Man for All Seasons* (1966), adapted by Robert Bolt from his own stage play, and made on a modest budget in England. Paul Scofield repeated his stage performance as Sir Thomas More, friend of Henry VIII and Chancellor of England. More is a man of wit and principle, and his reluctant but absolute inability to sanction the king's divorce and remarriage to Anne Boleyn leads inexorably to his execution—a kind of Tudor *High Noon*. Robert Shaw gave a robust performance as the king, Orson Welles was a clever and mountainous Cardinal Wolsey, and Vanessa Redgrave made a brief but telling appearance as Anne Boleyn.

"By carefully circumscribing his cinematic limits," wrote Hollis Alpert, "Zinnemann has been able to concentrate on fine detail, on performances, and on extracting an existential meaning from More's act of martyrdom. . . . The film symbolically uses the Thames as a highway of history, employs settings that are relatively modest but richly suggestive of authenticity, and rings with words and more intellectual and psychological excitement than are normally common in movies." All in all, as Alpert said, "it would be difficult to imagine a more competent, tasteful, and pleasing adaptation." Most agreed, though Penelope Gilliatt confessed that, for her, it also had a "secret

ingredient . . . it is inoffensively and sweetly boring."

It was seven years before Zinnemann completed another film. Believing that a director "should never compromise on important things" has cost him more assignments in the course of his career than most filmmakers have ever been offered. During the 1950s he had to abandon versions of Irwin Shaw's *The Young Lions*, which he had optioned; of *War and Peace;* and of Hemingway's *Old Man and the Sea*. After *The Sundowners*, he worked for over two years on James Michener's massive novel *Hawaii*, abandoned in the end for lack of a workable script. In the late 1960s and the 1970s Zinnemann tried but failed to film the story of Heloïse and Abelard and an adaptation of Solzhenitsyn's *The First Circle*. Perhaps the worst blow of all was MGM's cancellation in 1970 on economic grounds of *Man's Fate*, a version by Han Suyin of Malraux's novel on which Zinnemann had worked for three years, assembling a "dream" cast, picking his locations, and spending some $3 million on preproduction.

When the director finally completed another film, it featured an unlikely version of the Zinnemann hero, the professional assassin played by Edward Fox in Frederic Forsyth's *The Day of the Jackal*. The seemingly impossible goal towards which he strives is the murder of President de Gaulle. Most reviewers praised the film's air of detailed documentary authenticity and its taut editing, and Neil Sinyard called it "a despairing parable in which torture, treachery and terrorism are seen as the accepted currency of modern politics."

The filming of *Julia* was marred by Zinnemann's conflicts with his producer, Richard Roth, and also with Lillian Hellman, who wrote the autobiographical memoir on which Alvin Sargent's script is based. Jane Fonda plays Hellman, Vanessa Redgrave her friend Julia, a rich intellectual who committed herself to the antifascist cause in the years before World War II, losing first her leg and then her life. The film centers on an incident in 1937 when Julia drew Hellman into her dangerous world, asking her to smuggle $50,000 into Nazi Germany "to bribe out many in prison." Jason Robards impersonates Hellman's lover and literary mentor Dashiell Hammett.

Julia was warmly praised by most critics, especially for Fonda's performance, but by some with reservations. Pauline Kael, for example, wrote that "to say *Julia* is well lighted doesn't do Douglas Slocombe's cinematography exact justice. It's *perfectly* lighted, which is to say, the color is lustrous, the images so completely composed they're almost static. . . . This is conservative—classical humanist—moviemaking, where every detail of meaning is worked out, right down to each flicker of light in the bit player's eyes. The director, Fred Zinnemann, does all the work for you. . . . He does it beautifully— and there are very few directors left who know how to do it at all. . . . *Julia* is romantic in such a studied way that it turns romanticism into a moral lesson."

Another seven years passed before Zinnemann made *Five Days One Summer* (1982). Set in the 1930s in the Swiss Alps, which Zinnemann had loved as a youth, and based loosely on a story by Kay Boyle that the director had long admired, this was a very personal picture. Sean Connery plays a married and middle-aged doctor on an illicit vacation with his young cousin (Betsy Brantley), and Lambert Wilson is the handsome guide. The climax comes when the two men set out on a dangerous climb from which only one of them—but which?—returns. The ending struck many reviewers as contrived and the picture was admired most as an Alpine travelogue of exceptional beauty.

Zinnemann and his wife Renee nowadays spend most of the year in London, though they also have a house in California. Their son Tim is a film producer. All of Zinnemann's Austrian relatives died in the Holocaust and, though he sometimes visits Vienna, he can never bear to stay there for long. He is an opera buff and, nearing eighty, has spoken recently of his interest in filming *Così Fan Tutte*.

According to Louis D. Giannetti in *Masters of the American Cinema*, Zinnemann on set "is polite, tactful, and respectful of the opinions of others. His sets are well organized and efficient, the morale high. . . . A team man, he doesn't hold his judgments infallible, and he accepts suggestions from his collaborators without resentment and with thanks." Zinnemann has said: "I don't like to dictate and I'll be damned if I'll have somebody dictate to me." Even the fearsome Harry Cohn of Columbia failed to bully him out of his ideas for *From Here to Eternity*.

As Giannetti says, Zinnemann's favorite theme is a conflict of conscience, a conflict that may be enacted in the public world or restricted to the private soul (as in *The Nun's Story*): "Generally his protagonists choose solitude over a corrupted solidarity. Hence, many of Zinnemann's movies end in a note of disintegration, loneliness, and shattered hope. . . . His plots are generally constructed like traps, which close in menacingly until the protagonists have no other choice but to flee or confront the inevitable."

"Unlike most realists," Giannetti goes on,

"Zinnemann's techniques emphasize closed forms, with many claustrophobic medium and close shots and tightly framed compositions which permit little freedom of movement. The edges of his frame are often sealed off, and the ceilings are oppressively low, visually reinforcing the sense of confinement. . . . The director's famous lengthy takes, like the alley fight in *Eternity* and the murder of the shy homosexual in *Day of the Jackal*, are unnerving precisely because Zinnemann refuses to dissipate the tension by cutting to a variety of shots. In other words, the unedited shot itself can be a kind of spatial and temporal prison from which there's no escape."

With Elia Kazan, Zinnemann was one of the most admired and honored of Hollywood social realists during the 1950s, but the auteurist critics of the 1960s were dismissive. Andrew Sarris wrote that Zinnemann's career "reflects the rise and fall of the realist aesthetic in Hollywood. . . . his neatness and decorum constitute his gravest artistic defects" and, though his "inclusion in any objective history of the American cinema is mandatory . . . , his true vocation remains the making of antimovies for antimoviegoers." Fifteen years later, in 1982, Sarris said "I still stand by most of what I have written on Zinnemann even now that his undeniable virtues are in short supply. . . . In my moviegoing heart of hearts I may still wish that he were more vulgar, but deeper in my soul I cannot help being moved by his quixotic loyalty to social democracy in cinema."

—D.T.

FILMS: *Shorts*—A Friend Indeed, 1938; The Story of Dr. Carver, 1938; That Mothers Might Live, 1938; Tracing the Sleeping Death, 1938; They Live Again, 1938; Weather Wizards, 1939; While America Sleeps, 1939; Help Wanted, 1939; One Against the World, 1939; The Ash Can Fleet, 1939; Forgotten Victory, 1939; The Old South , 1940; Stuffie, 1940; The Way in the Wilderness, 1940; The Great Meddler, 1940; Forbidden Passage, 1941; Your Last Act, 1941; The Lady or the Tiger?, 1942; Benjy, 1951. *Features*—Redes (The Wave), 1935; The Kid Glove Killer, 1942; Eyes in the Night, 1942; The Seventh Cross, 1944; Little Mr. Jim, 1945; My Brother Talks to Horses, 1946; The Search, 1948; Act of Violence, 1948; The Men (Reissued as Battle Stripe), 1950; Teresa, 1951; High Noon, 1952; The Member of the Wedding, 1952; From Here to Eternity, 1953; Oklahoma!, 1955; A Hatful of Rain, 1957; The Nun's Story, 1958; The Sundowners, 1960; Behold a Pale Horse, 1964; A Man for All Seasons, 1966; The Day of the Jackal, 1973; Julia, 1977; Five Days One Summer 1982. *Published scripts*—High Noon *in* Film Scripts 2, edited by George P. Garrett and others, 1971.

ABOUT: Coursodon, J.-P. American Directors, Vol. II,

1983; Garbicz, A. and Klinowski, J. Cinema: The Magic Vehicle, 1979; Giannetti, L.D. Masters of the American Cinema, 1981; Griffith, R. Fred Zinnemann, 1958 (pamphlet); Rohauer, R. A Tribute to Fred Zinnemann, 1967 (pamphlet). *Periodicals*—Action March-April 1970; Cinema (USA) October-November 1964; Filmmakers Newsletter November 1977; Films and Filming December 1959, May and June 1967, February 1978; Films in Review January 1951, December 1977, January 1983; Focus on Film Spring and Summer 1973; Guardian August 24, 1963; Journal of Popular Film and TV VII/1 1978; National Film Theatre Booklet (Britain) October-December 1982; New York Herald Tribune Magazine October 25, 1953; Quarterly of Film, Radio and TV Fall 1953; Positif March 1983; Show August 1964, May 1970; Sight and Sound Autumn 1948, Autumn 1955; Village Voice November 16, 1982.

Photographic Credits

Academy of Motion Picture Arts and Sciences, Dorothy Arzner, Busby Berkeley, Frank Borzage, Herbert Brenon, Clarence Brown, Tod Browning, Benjamin Christensen, Merian C. Cooper, John Cromwell, James Cruze, George Cukor, Michael Curtiz, Jules Dassin, Delmer Daves, Cecil B. DeMille, William Dieterle, Allan Dwan, Robert J. Flaherty, Richard Fleischer, Victor Fleming, John Ford, Tay Garnett, Edmund Goulding, D. W. Griffith, Henry Hathaway, Alfred Hitchcock, William K. Howard, Rex Ingram, Buster Keaton, Henry King, Henry Koster, Gregory La Cava, Fritz Lang, Mitchell Leisen, Mervyn Leroy, Albert Lewin, Anatole Litvak, Frank Lloyd, Ernst Lubitsch, Leo McCarey, Rouben Mamoulian, Anthony Mann, George Marshall, Lewis Milestone, Jean Negulesco, Robert Rossen, Mack Sennett, Donald Siegel, Robert Siodmak, Victor Sjöström, John M. Stahl, Josef Von Sternberg, George Stevens, Robert Stevenson, Mauritz Stiller, Erich Von Stroheim, Preston Sturges, Norman Taurog, Jacques Tourneur, Maurice Tourneur, W. S. Van Dyke, Charles Vidor, King Vidor, Raoul Walsh, Charles Walters, Orson Welles, James Whale, Robert Wise, William Wyler; *Eve Arnold*, John Huston

Jerry Bauer, Pietro Germi, Marcel Pagnol, Mario Soldati; *Tom Bert*, André De Toth; *Bildarchiv*, Helmut Käutner, Paul Leni, F. W. Murnau, Hans Richter, Leni Riefenstahl, Robert Wiene; *The Bowser Black Film Collection, c/o Chamba Educational Film Services, 71 Joralemon Street, Brooklyn, NY 11201*, Oscar Micheaux; *Cinemateca Brasileira*, Humberto Mauro; *Bundesarchiv*, Walther Ruttmann

Cahiers du cinema, Roger Leenhardt; *CNC AF*, Germaine Dulac, Jean Epstein, Louis Lumière, Georges Méliès; © *1984 Columbia Pictures Industries*, David Lean

Stiftung Deutsche Kinemathek, Slatan Dudow, Henryk Galeen, Max Ophuls, G. W. Pabst, Wolfgang Staudte, Edgar G. Ulmer; *Ph. Doumic*, Marcel Carné

Filmoteca Española, Luis Buñuel
French Cultural Services, Jacques Becker, Robert Bresson, André Cayatte, René Clair, Henri-Georges Clouzot, Jean Cocteau, Julien Duvivier, Jacques Feyder, Abel Gance, Sacha Guitry, Marcel L'Herbier, Max Linder, Jean Renoir

Szovari Gyula, felvetele, Jean Delannoy
Robin Holland, Vincente Minnelli, Douglas Sirk; *William Hubbell*, Pare Lorentz

Instituto Italiano di Cultura, Alessandro Blasetti, Mario Camerini, Giuseppe De Santis, Roberto Rossellini

Japan Society, Kenji Mizoguchi, Yasujiro Ozu
K. Komorowski, Aleksander Ford

Magyar Filmintezet, Paul Fejos; *MOMA*, Anthony Asquith, Boris Vasilievich Barnet, Budd Boetticher, Richard Boleslawski, Roy Boulting, Frank Capra, Charles Chaplin, René Clément, Louis Delluc, Maya Deren, Vittorio De Sica, Alexander Dovzhenko, Carl Theodor Dreyer, Sergei Eisenstein, Friedrich Ermler, Louis Feuillade, Jean Grémillon, Howard Hawks, Joris Ivens, Phil Karlson, William Keighley, Alexander Korda, Laurence Olivier, Edwin S. Porter, Michael Powell, Vsevolod Pudovkin, Irving Rapper, Carol Reed, George Sidney, John Sturges, Dziga Vertov, Jean Vigo, Luchino Visconti, William A. Wellman, Sergei Yutkevich

National Film Archive, London, Mark Donskoi, Sergei Gerasimov, Sidney Gilliat, Alice Guy-Blaché, Robert Hamer, Zoltán Korda, Grigori Kozintsev, Lev Kuleshov, Joseph H. Lewis, Yakov Protazanov, Yuli Raizman, Mikhail Romm, Harry Watt

Portuguese Film Archive, Lisbon, Portugal, Manoel De Oliveira

Foto Schikola, Thorold Dickinson; *Swedish Information Service*, Gustaf Molander, Alf Sjöberg, Arne Sucksdorff; *Andras Szomszed, Mafilm-Budapest*, Edward Dmytryk

James Wentzy, Akira Kurosawa